Sporting News
BOOKS

BASEBALL GUIDE

2003 EDITION

Editors

CRAIG CARTER

TONY NISTLER

DAVE SLOAN

EXPLANATION OF STATISTICAL ABBREVIATIONS

A: assists. **AB:** at-bats. **Avg.:** batting average (hits divided by at-bats). **BB:** bases on balls. **Bk.:** balks. **CG:** complete games. **CS:** caught stealing. **E:** errors. **ER:** earned runs. **ERA:** earned-run average (earned runs times nine divided by innings pitched). **G:** games. **GB:** games behind. **GF:** games finished. **GDP:** grounding into double plays. **GS:** games started. **H:** hits. **HB:** hit batsmen. **HP:** hit by pitches. **HR:** home runs. **IBB:** intentional bases on balls. **IP:** innings pitched. **L:** losses. **LOB:** runners left on base. **OBP:** on-base percentage (hits plus bases on balls plus hit by pitches divided by at-bats plus bases on balls plus hit by pitches plus sacrifice flies). **Pct.:** winning percentage. **PO:** putouts. **Pos.:** position. **R:** runs. **RBI:** runs batted in. **Rel.:** relief appearances. **SB:** stolen bases. **SF:** sacrifice flies (run-scoring flyouts). **SH:** sacrifice hits (bunts that advance one or more runners but result in the batter being retired at first base or reaching first on an error). **ShO:** shutouts. **Slg.:** slugging percentage (total bases divided by at-bats). **SO:** strikeouts. **Sv.:** saves. **Sv. Op.:** save opportunities. **TB:** total bases (hits plus doubles plus two times the number of triples plus three times the number of home runs). **TBF:** total batters faced. **TC:** total chances (putouts plus assists plus errors). **TPA:** total plate appearances (at-bats plus bases on balls plus sacrifice hits plus sacrifice flies plus hit by pitches plus times reaching base on catcher's interference). **W:** wins. **WP:** wild pitches. **2B:** doubles. **3B:** triples.

Major league statistics compiled by STATS, Inc., a News Corporation company, 8130 Lehigh Avenue, Morton Grove, IL 60053. STATS is a trademark of Sports Team Analysis and Tracking Systems, Inc.

Minor league statistics provided by SportsTicker.

ISBN: 0-89204-698-8

10 9 8 7 6 5 4 3 2 1

CONTENTS

2003 SEASON...5
  Major league baseball....................................6
    Commissioner's office.................................6
    Other organizations....................................6
  Individual teams section (schedules, directories,
    rosters, 2002 results and more)....................8
    Anaheim Angels...8
    Baltimore Orioles.....................................13
    Boston Red Sox..18
    Chicago White Sox.....................................23
    Cleveland Indians.....................................28
    Detroit Tigers..33
    Kansas City Royals....................................38
    Minnesota Twins.......................................43
    New York Yankees......................................48
    Oakland Athletics.....................................53
    Seattle Mariners......................................58
    Tampa Bay Devil Rays..................................63
    Texas Rangers...68
    Toronto Blue Jays.....................................73
    Arizona Diamondbacks..................................78
    Atlanta Braves..83
    Chicago Cubs..88
    Cincinnati Reds.......................................93
    Colorado Rockies......................................98
    Florida Marlins......................................103
    Houston Astros.......................................108
    Los Angeles Dodgers..................................113
    Milwaukee Brewers....................................118
    Montreal Expos.......................................123
    New York Mets..128
    Philadelphia Phillies................................133
    Pittsburgh Pirates...................................138
    St. Louis Cardinals..................................143
    San Diego Padres.....................................148
    San Francisco Giants.................................153

2002 REVIEW..**159**
  Year in review...160
    Final standings......................................166
    Interleague records..................................167
  A.L. Division Series...................................168
  N.L. Division Series...................................178
  A.L. Championship Series...............................187
  N.L. Championship Series...............................192
  World Series...197
  All-Star Game..206
  Notable performances...................................208
    No-hit games...208
    Low-hit games..208
    15-strikeout games...................................210
    10-strikeout games...................................210
    1-0 games..211
    Four or more hits in one game........................211
    Five or more hits in one game........................212
    Hitting streaks of 15 or more games..................213
    Multi-homer games....................................213

    Three-homer games....................................214
    Grand slams..214
  Transactions...217
  Award winners..224
    The Sporting News....................................224
    Baseball Writers' Assoc. of America..................224
  Miscellaneous..226
    Attendance...226
    Debuts...226
    Salary arbitration results...........................229
    Free-agent filings...................................230
    Major league Rule 5 draft............................230
  Necrology..231

2002 AMERICAN LEAGUE STATISTICS....**235**
  Batting..236
    Vs. LHP/RHP..242
  Designated hitting.....................................247
  Pinch-hitting..250
  Pitching...254
    Vs. LHB/RHB..258
  Fielding...263
  Miscellaneous..269
    Shutout games..269
    Home record..269
    Road record..269
    Pitching against each club...........................270
    Home runs by parks...................................275
    Park data..277

2002 NATIONAL LEAGUE STATISTICS....**283**
  Batting..284
    Vs. LHP/RHP..292
  Designated hitting.....................................297
  Pinch-hitting..299
  Pitching...304
    Vs. LHB/RHB..309
  Fielding...314
  Miscellaneous..321
    Shutout games..321
    Home record..321
    Road record..321
    Pitching against each club...........................322
    Home runs by parks...................................327
    Park data..330

2002 STATISTICAL LEADERS.................**337**
  American League leaders (even pages).......338
  National League leaders (odd pages)..........339

2002 ACTIVE CAREER LEADERS.............**348**

HISTORY...**353**
  All-time results.......................................354
    American League Champions............................354
    National League Champions............................354
    World Series...355

Division Series	356
Championship Series	356
All-Star Game	357
Award winners	360
The Sporting News	360
Rawlings Gold Glove Teams	375
Hillerich & Bradsby Silver Slugger Teams	379
Baseball Writers' Assoc. of America	381
Early Most Valuable Player awards	384
Hall of Fame	385

MINOR LEAGUES **391**
Farm systems	392
Class AAA	393
International League	393
Mexican League	415
Pacific Coast League	435
Class AA	461

Eastern League	461
Southern League	479
Texas League	495
Class A	508
California League	508
Carolina League	521
Florida State League	532
Midwest League	548
New York-Pennsylvania League	564
Northwest League	579
South Atlantic League	588
Summer Class A	606
Appalachian League	606
Arizona League	616
Gulf Coast League	624
Pioneer League	639
Minor league index	648

ON THE COVER: Angels celebrating World Series victory photo by Dilip Vishwanat/THE SPORTING NEWS; bottom left to right: Pedro Martinez by Mark Bolton for THE SPORTING NEWS; Ichiro Suzuki by Albert Dickson/THE SPORTING NEWS; Sammy Sosa by Dilip Vishwanat/THE SPORTING NEWS.

2003 SEASON

Major League Baseball directories

Team by team

MAJOR LEAGUE BASEBALL

Address
245 Park Avenue
New York, NY 10167
Telephone
212-931-7800
FAX
212-949-5654
Website
www.mlb.com
Commissioner of baseball
Allan H. "Bud" Selig
President and chief operating officer
Robert DuPuy
Executive v.p., baseball operations
Richard "Sandy" Alderson
Executive v.p., business
Timothy J. Brosnan
**Executive v.p., labor relations and
human resources**
Robert D. Manfred
Executive v.p., administration
John McHale
Sr. v.p., int'l business operations
Paul Archey
Sr. v.p., security and facilities
Kevin Hallinan
Sr. v.p., public relations
Rich Levin
Sr. v.p. and chief financial officer
Jonathan Mariner

Sr. v.p., special events
Marla Miller
Sr. v.p. and general counsel
Ethan Orlinsky
Sr. v.p. and general counsel
Tom Ostertag
Sr. v.p., licensing
Howard Smith
Sr. v.p., baseball operations
Jimmie Lee Solomon
Sr. v.p., bus. affairs domestic & int'l
Chris Tully
V.p., domestic licensing
Steve Armus
V.p., community affairs
Tom Brasuell
V.p., baseball operations and admin.
Ed Burns
V.p., management information systems
Julio Carbonell
V.p., accounting and treasurer
Bob Clark
V.p. and gen. counsel, labor relations
Frank Coonelly
V.p., club relations and scheduling
Katy Feeney
V.p., productions
Dave Gavant
V.p., domestic licensing-Cooperstown
Colin Hagen

V.p., publishing and photographs
Don Hintz
V.p., corporate sales
Justin Johnson
V.p., international licensing
Shawn Lawson-Cummings
**V.p., strategic planning, recruiting and
diversity**
Wendy L. Lewis
V.p., broadcast operations
Bernadette McDonald
V.p., international baseball operations
Lou Melendez
V.p., club relations
Phyllis Merhige
V.p., umpiring
Ralph Nelson
V.p., marketing and advertising
Jacqueline Parks
V.p., educational programming
Sharon Robinson
V.p., human resources
Ray Scott
V.p., on-field operations
Bob Watson

OTHER ORGANIZATIONS

LABOR RELATIONS COMMITTEE
Address
245 Park Avenue
New York, NY 10167
Telephone
212-931-7401
212-949-5690 (FAX)
**Exec. vice president, labor relations
and human resources**
Robert D. Manfred Jr.
V.p. & general counsel, labor relations
Francis Coonelly
Associate counsels
Derek Jackson
Paul Mifsud
System administration
John Ricco
Deputy general counsel
Jennifer Gefsky

BASEBALL ASSISTANCE TEAM INC.
Address
245 Park Avenue
New York, NY 10167
Telephone
212-931-7821
Chairman
Bobby Murcer

President
Earl Wilson
Vice presidents
Steve Garvey
Bob Gibson
Lou Gorman
Ed Stack
Executive director
James J. Martin
Secretary
Thomas J. Ostertag
Treasurer
Jonathan Mariner

ASSOCIATION OF PROFESSIONAL
BASEBALL PLAYERS
OF AMERICA
Address
1820 W. Orangewood Ave., Suite 206
Orange, CA 92868
Telephone
714-935-9993
714-935-0431 (FAX)
President
John J. McHale
Vice presidents
Roland Hemond
Robert Kennedy

Secretary/treasurer
Dick Beverage

NATIONAL BASEBALL HALL OF
FAME AND MUSEUM
Address
P.O. Box 590
Cooperstown, NY 13326
Telephone
607-547-7200
607-547-2044 (FAX)
Hall of Fame board of directors chairman
Jane Forbes Clark
President
Dale Petroskey
V.p. of business and administration
Bill Haase
V.p. and chief curator
William T. Spencer Jr.
Curator of collections
Peter P. Clark
Executive director of retail marketing
Barbara Shinn
Controller
Frances L. Althiser
Librarian
James L. Gates
V.p. of communications and education
Jeff Idelson

MAJOR LEAGUE SCOUTING BUREAU

Address
3500 Porsche Way, Suite 100
Ontario, CA 91764
Telephone
909-980-1881
909-980-7794 (FAX)
Director
Frank Marcos

MAJOR LEAGUE BASEBALL PLAYERS ASSOCIATION

Address
12 E. 49th St., 24th Floor
New York, NY 10017
Telephone
212-826-0808
212-752-3649 (FAX)
Executive director and general counsel
Donald M. Fehr
Special assistants
Tony Bernazard
Phil Bradley
Steve Rogers
Associate general counsel
Eugene D. Orza
Assistant general counsel
Jeff Fannell
Doyle R. Pryor
Michael Weiner
Counsel
Robert Leneghan
Director of licensing
Judy Heeter
Director of communications
Greg Bouris

MINOR LEAGUE BASEBALL NATIONAL ASSOCIATION OF PROFESSIONAL BASEBALL LEAGUES

Address
P.O. Box A
St. Petersburg, FL 33731
Telephone
727-822-6937
727-821-5819 (FAX)
President/CEO
Mike Moore
Vice president
Stan Brand

Vice president, administration/COO
Pat O'Connor
General counsel
Scott Poley
Special counsel
George Yund
Exec. director/business operations
Misann Ellmaker
Executive director/Professional Baseball Umpire Corporation
Mike Fitzpatrick
Director/media relations
Jim Ferguson
Director/baseball operations
Tim Brunswick
Director of Professional Baseball Employment Opportunities
Ann Perkins

MAJOR LEAGUE BASEBALL PLAYERS ALUMNI ASSOC.

Address
1631 Mesa Ave., Suite B
Colorado Springs, CO 80906
Telephone
719-477-1870
719-477-1875 (FAX)
President
Brooks Robinson
Vice presidents
Bob Boone
George Brett
Mike Hegan
Chuck Hinton
Al Kaline
Carl Erskine
Rusty Staub
Robin Yount
Vice chairman
Fred Valentine

WORLD UMPIRES ASSOCIATION

Address
P.O. Box 760
Cocoa, FL 32923-0760
Telephone
321-637-3471
321-633-7018 (FAX)
President
John Hirschbeck

Vice president
Joe Brinkman
Secretary/treasurer
Tim Welke
Labor counsel
Joel Smith

BASEBALL WRITERS' ASSOCIATION OF AMERICA

President
Paul Hagen, Philadelphia Daily News
Vice president
Drew Olson, Milwaukee Journal Sentinel
Secretary/treasurer
Jack O'Connell, Hartford Courant

ELIAS SPORTS BUREAU

Address
500 Fifth Ave.
New York, NY 10110
Telephone
212-869-1530
212-354-0980 (FAX)
General manager
Seymour Siwoff

SPORTSTICKER ENTERPRISES, L.P.

Address
Harborside Financial Center
800 Plaza Two
Jersey City, NJ 07311
Boston office
Boston Fish Pier
West Building No. 1
Boston, MA 02210
Telephone
201-309-1200
201-860-9742 (FAX)
Boston office
617-951-1379
617-737-9960 (FAX)
General manager
Jim Morganthaler
Director, minor league operations
Jim Keller
Assistant dir., minor league operations
Michael Walczak

ANAHEIM ANGELS
AMERICAN LEAGUE WEST DIVISION

2003 SEASON

March/April

SUN	MON	TUE	WED	THU	FRI	SAT
30 TEX	31	1 TEX	2 TEX D	3	4 OAK	5 OAK D
6 OAK	7	8 SEA D	9 SEA	10 SEA	11 OAK	12 OAK
13 OAK D	14 TEX	15 TEX	16 TEX	17 TEX D	18 SEA	19 SEA
20 SEA D	21	22 NYY	23 NYY	24 NYY	25 BOS	26 BOS
27 BOS	28	29 CLE	30 CLE			

May

SUN	MON	TUE	WED	THU	FRI	SAT
				1 CLE	2 TOR	3 TOR D
4 TOR D	5	6 CLE	7 CLE	8 CLE	9 TOR	10 TOR
11 TOR D	12	13 NYY	14 NYY	15 NYY	16 BOS	17 BOS D
18 BOS D	19	20 BAL	21 BAL	22 BAL	23 TB	24 TB D
25 TB D	26	27 BAL	28 BAL	29 TB	30 TB	31 TB

June

SUN	MON	TUE	WED	THU	FRI	SAT
1 TB D	2	3 MON †	4 MON †	5 MON †	6 FLA †	7 FLA
8 FLA D	9 PHI	10 PHI	11 PHI	12	13 NYM	14 NYM
15 NYM D	16 SEA	17 SEA	18 SEA	19 SEA D	20 LA	21 LA
22 LA	23	24 SEA	25 SEA	26 SEA	27 LA	28 LA
29 LA D	30 TEX					

July

SUN	MON	TUE	WED	THU	FRI	SAT
		1 TEX	2 TEX	3 TEX D	4 OAK	5 OAK
6 OAK D	7	8 KC	9 KC	10 KC D	11 MIN	12 MIN D
13 MIN D	14	15 *	16	17 BAL	18 BAL	19 BAL
20 BAL D	21 TB	22 TB D	23 TEX	24 TEX	25 OAK	26 OAK D
27 OAK D	28 OAK	29 NYY	30 NYY	31 NYY		

August

SUN	MON	TUE	WED	THU	FRI	SAT
					1 TOR	2 TOR
3 TOR D	4	5 BOS	6 BOS	7 BOS	8 CLE	9 CLE D
10 CLE D	11 CWS	12 CWS	13 CWS	14 CWS	15 DET	16 DET
17 DET	18 CWS	19 CWS	20 CWS	21 DET	22 DET	23 DET D
24 DET D	25	26 MIN	27 MIN	28 MIN D	29 KC	30 KC

September

SUN	MON	TUE	WED	THU	FRI	SAT
31 KC D	1 MIN	2 MIN	3 MIN D	4	5 KC	6 KC
7 KC D	8 OAK	9 OAK	10 OAK	11 OAK D	12 SEA	13 SEA
14 SEA D	15 OAK	16 OAK	17 OAK D	18	19 TEX	20 TEX
21 TEX D	22 SEA	23 SEA	24 SEA D	25	26 TEX	27 TEX D
28 TEX D						

Home games shaded; D—Day game (games starting before 5 p.m.); *—All-Star Game at Comiskey Park, Chicago. †—Game played in Puerto Rico. Subject to change.

CLUB DIRECTORY

Owner
The Walt Disney Company
Chairman and CEO, The Walt Disney Co.
Michael Eisner
Vice president and general manager
Bill Stoneman
Vice president, communications
Tim Mead

Assistant general manager
Ken Forsch
Special assistants to the g.m.
Preston Gomez
Gary Sutherland
Director, scouting
Donny Rowland
Director, player development
Tony Reagins

Manager, baseball operations
Abe Flores
Manager, baseball information
Larry Babcock
Manager, media services
Nancy Mazmanian
Manager, community development
Matt Bennett

MINOR LEAGUE AFFILIATES

Class	Team	League	Manager
AAA	Salt Lake	Pacific Coast	Mike Brumley
AA	Arkansas	Texas	Tyrone Boykin
A	Rancho Cucamonga	California	Bobby Meacham
A	Cedar Rapids	Midwest	Todd Claus
Rookie	Provo	Pioneer	Tom Kotchman
Rookie	Mesa Angels	Arizona	Brian Harper

Follow the Angels all season at: www.sportingnews.com/baseball/teams/angels/

BROADCAST INFORMATION

Radio: ESPN-AM (710).
TV: KCAL-TV (Channel 9).
Cable TV: Fox Sports West.

SPRING TRAINING

Ballpark (city): Tempe Diablo Stadium
(Tempe, Ariz.).
Ticket information: 714-940-2000.

2003 SEASON *Anaheim Angels*

Manager—Mike Scioscia (14).
Coaches—Bud Black (24), Alfredo Griffin (4), Mickey Hatcher (7), Joe Maddon (70), Orlando Mercado (88), Bobby Ramos (13), Ron Roenicke (12).

No.	PITCHERS	B/T	Ht./Wt.	Born	Age*	2002 clubs
27	Appier, Kevin	R/R	6-2/200	12-6-67	35	Anaheim
51	Callaway, Mickey	R/R	6-2/200	5-13-75	27	Salt Lake, Anaheim
53	Donnelly, Brendan	R/R	6-3/205	7-4-71	31	Salt Lake, Anaheim
	Fischer, Rich	R/R	6-3/180	10-21-80	22	Arkansas, Rancho Cucamonga
	Green, Steve	R/R	6-2/195	1-26-78	25	DID NOT PLAY
	Jenks, Bobby	R/R	6-3/240	3-14-81	22	Arkansas, Rancho Cucamonga
41	Lackey, John	R/R	6-6/205	10-23-78	24	Salt Lake, Anaheim
47	Lukasiewicz, Mark	L/L	6-5/240	3-8-73	30	Anaheim, Salt Lake
52	Miadich, Bart	R/R	6-4/205	2-3-76	27	Salt Lake
36	Ortiz, Ramon	R/R	6-0/170	3-23-73	30	Anaheim
40	Percival, Troy	R/R	6-3/235	8-9-69	33	Anaheim
58	Pote, Lou	R/R	6-3/208	8-21-71	31	Anaheim, Salt Lake
57	Rodriguez, Francisco	R/R	6-0/175	1-7-82	21	Arkansas, Salt Lake, Anaheim
60	Schoeneweis, Scott	L/L	6-0/185	10-2-73	29	Anaheim
34	Sele, Aaron	R/R	6-5/220	6-25-70	32	Anaheim
62	Shields, Scot	R/R	6-1/175	7-22-75	27	Salt Lake, Anaheim
54	Turnbow, Derrick	R/R	6-3/200	1-25-78	25	Arizona Angels, Rancho Cucamonga
56	Washburn, Jarrod	L/L	6-1/190	8-13-74	28	Anaheim
77	Weber, Ben	R/R	6-4/210	11-17-69	33	Anaheim
32	Wise, Matt	R/R	6-4/195	11-18-75	27	Salt Lake, Anaheim

No.	CATCHERS	B/T	Ht./Wt.	Born	Age*	2002 clubs
1	Molina, Bengie	R/R	5-11/210	7-20-74	28	Anaheim, Rancho Cucamonga
28	Molina, Jose	R/R	6-1/215	6-3-75	27	Salt Lake, Anaheim
	Nieves, Wil	R/R	5-11/190	9-25-77	25	Portland, San Diego

No.	INFIELDERS	B/T	Ht./Wt.	Born	Age*	2002 clubs
5	Amezaga, Alfredo	B/R	5-10/165	1-16-78	25	Salt Lake, Anaheim
22	Eckstein, David	R/R	5-8/170	1-20-75	28	Anaheim
6	Figgins, Chone	B/R	5-9/155	1-22-78	25	Salt Lake, Anaheim
20	Fullmer, Brad	L/R	6-0/220	1-17-75	28	Anaheim
10	Gil, Benji	R/R	6-2/210	10-6-72	30	Anaheim, Salt Lake
25	Glaus, Troy	R/R	6-5/245	8-3-76	26	Anaheim
2	Kennedy, Adam	L/R	6-1/192	1-10-76	27	Anaheim
	Quinlan, Robb	R/R	6-1/200	3-17-77	26	Salt Lake
23	Spiezio, Scott	B/R	6-2/225	9-21-72	30	Anaheim

No.	OUTFIELDERS	B/T	Ht./Wt.	Born	Age*	2002 clubs
16	Anderson, Garret	L/L	6-3/228	6-30-72	30	Anaheim
33	DaVanon, Jeff	B/R	6-0/185	12-8-73	29	Anaheim, Salt Lake, Arizona Angels
17	Erstad, Darin	L/L	6-2/220	6-4-74	28	Anaheim
38	Haynes, Nathan	L/L	5-9/170	9-7-79	23	Rancho Cucamonga, Salt Lake
16	Owens, Eric	R/R	6-0/208	2-3-71	32	Florida
15	Salmon, Tim	R/R	6-3/225	8-24-68	34	Anaheim
	Wesson, Barry	R/R	6-2/212	4-6-77	25	Houston, New Orleans

*Age as of April 1, 2003.

BALLPARK INFORMATION

Ballpark (capacity, surface)
Edison International Field of Anaheim
(45,050, grass)
Address
2000 Gene Autry Way
Anaheim, CA 92806
Official website
www.angelsbaseball.com
Business phone
714-940-2000
Ticket information
714-634-2000
Field dimensions (from home plate)
To left field at foul line, 330 feet
To center field, 400 feet
To right field at foul line, 330
First game played
April 19, 1966 (White Sox 3, Angels 1)

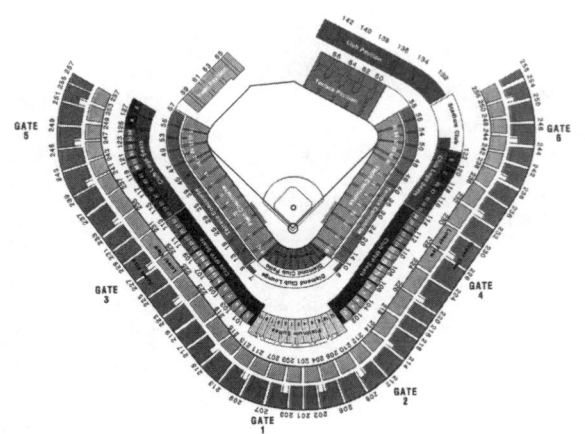

2003 SEASON *Anaheim Angels*

Date	Opp.	Res.	Score	(inn.*)	Hits	Opp. hits	Winning pitcher	Losing pitcher	Save	Record	Pos.	GB
3-31	Cle.	L	0-6		5	11	Colon	Washburn		0-1	4th	0.5
4-2	Cle.	W	7-5		8	6	Weber	Riske	Percival	1-1	T2nd	1.0
4-3	Cle.	L	5-6		11	11	Drese	Sele	Wickman	1-2	3rd	2.0
4-5	At Tex.	W	3-1		6	5	Schoeneweis	Valdes	Levine	2-2	3rd	1.0
4-6	At Tex.	W	6-3		9	5	Ortiz	Irabu	Levine	3-2	T2nd	0.5
4-8	Sea.	L	4-5		7	15	Hasegawa	Weber	Sasaki	3-3	3rd	1.5
4-9	Sea.	L	1-5		4	9	Halama	Appier		3-4	3rd	2.5
4-10	Sea.	L	1-8		5	11	Baldwin	Sele		3-5	3rd	2.5
4-11	Sea.	L	4-8		10	8	Garcia	Schoeneweis		3-6	T3rd	3.5
4-12	Oak.	L	1-5		9	10	Hudson	Ortiz		3-7	T3rd	4.5
4-13	Oak.	L	2-7		4	7	Hiljus	Washburn		3-8	T3rd	5.5
4-14	Oak.	W	4-1		8	4	Appier	Zito	Levine	4-8	3rd	5.5
4-16	Tex.	W	6-5	(10)	10	10	Levine	Rocker		5-8	3rd	6.0
4-17	Tex.	L	1-4		5	12	Valdes	Schoeneweis	Irabu	5-9	3rd	7.0
4-18	At Oak.	L	2-4		7	8	Hiljus	Ortiz	Koch	5-10	3rd	7.5
4-19	At Oak.	W	9-7		12	12	Washburn	Fyhrie	Percival	6-10	3rd	6.5
4-20	At Oak.	L	7-8		10	10	Bradford	Levine	Koch	6-11	3rd	6.5
4-21	At Oak.	L	5-6		12	12	Venafro	Percival		6-12	3rd	7.5
4-22	At Sea.	L	5-16		8	18	Moyer	Schoeneweis		6-13	3rd	8.5
4-23	At Sea.	L	0-1		4	5	Franklin	Ortiz	Sasaki	6-14	3rd	9.5
4-24	At Sea.	W	10-6		16	9	Washburn	Abbott		7-14	3rd	10.5
4-26	Tor.	W	4-0		10	9	Appier	Smith	Percival	7-14	3rd	9.5
4-27	Tor.	W	11-4		10	10	Sele	Borbon		8-14	3rd	8.5
4-28	Tor.	W	8-5	(14)	13	14	Lukasiewicz	Borbon		9-14	3rd	8.5
4-30	At Cle.	W	21-2		22	9	Ortiz	Sabathia		10-14	3rd	7.5
										11-14	3rd	6.5
5-1	At Cle.	W	7-2		11	6	Washburn	Drese		12-14	3rd	5.5
5-2	At Cle.	W	8-0		15	7	Appier	Finley		13-14	3rd	5.5
5-3	At Tor.	W	6-4		9	10	Sele	Lyon	Percival	14-14	3rd	5.5
5-4	At Tor.	L	1-4		5	9	Miller	Schoeneweis	Escobar	14-15	3rd	6.5
5-5	At Tor.	W	8-2		15	5	Ortiz	Prokopec		15-15	3rd	6.5
5-7	Det.	L	0-3		5	5	Greisinger	Weber	Acevedo	15-16	3rd	6.5
5-8	Det.	W	3-2		8	6	Percival	Rodney		16-16	3rd	6.5
5-9	Det.	W	7-6		11	11	Sele	Redman	Percival	17-16	2nd	6.5
5-10	Chi.	W	19-0		24	3	Schoeneweis	Wright		18-16	2nd	6.5
5-11	Chi.	W	6-3		12	7	Ortiz	Garland	Percival	19-16	2nd	6.5
5-12	Chi.	W	5-4		8	11	Percival	Foulke		20-16	2nd	5.5
5-14	At Det.	W	9-2		14	4	Appier	Cornejo		21-16	2nd	4.5
5-15	At Det.	W	10-1		13	6	Sele	Redman		22-16	2nd	4.5
5-17	At Chi.	W	8-4		11	9	Schoeneweis	Garland	Levine	23-16	2nd	5.0
5-18	At Chi.	L	4-10		11	10	Glover	Ortiz		23-17	2nd	5.0
5-19	At Chi.	W	6-1		12	4	Washburn	Buehrle		24-17	2nd	4.0
5-20	K.C.	W	6-3		10	8	Appier	Stein	Percival	25-17	2nd	3.5
5-21	K.C.	W	5-1		5	8	Cook	Reichert		26-17	2nd	2.5
5-22	K.C.	W	7-6		8	9	Weber	May	Percival	27-17	2nd	1.5
5-24	Min.	L	1-5		3	7	Reed	Ortiz		27-18	2nd	3.0
5-25	Min.	W	4-3	(13)	10	7	Levine	Cressend		28-18	2nd	2.0
5-26	Min.	L	2-5		8	14	Milton	Appier	Guardado	28-19	2nd	3.0
5-28	At K.C.	L	4-7		8	13	Byrd	Sele	Hernandez	28-20	2nd	3.0
5-29	At K.C.	W	12-2		17	7	Ortiz	Affeldt		29-20	2nd	3.0
5-30	At Min.	L	6-7	(10)	13	11	Guardado	Pote		29-21	2nd	4.0
5-31	At Min.	W	11-3		16	6	Washburn	Milton		30-21	2nd	3.0
6-1	At Min.	L	2-4		11	10	Lohse	Appier	Guardado	30-22	2nd	3.0
6-2	At Min.	W	5-4		12	5	Sele	Kinney	Percival	31-22	2nd	3.0
6-3	Tex.	W	5-2		7	6	Ortiz	Bell	Percival	32-22	2nd	3.0
6-4	Tex.	W	3-0		7	4	Schoeneweis	Burba	Percival	33-22	2nd	2.0
6-5	Tex.	W	7-5	(10)	11	9	Levine	Irabu		34-22	2nd	2.0
6-6	Tex.	L	8-9		13	15	Rogers	Appier	Telford	34-23	2nd	2.0
6-7	Cin.	W	4-3		8	11	Sele	Reitsma	Percival	35-23	2nd	1.0
6-8	Cin.	L	3-4		8	6	White	Cook	Graves	35-24	2nd	2.0
6-9	Cin.	W	7-4		9	11	Schoeneweis	Hamilton	Percival	36-24	2nd	1.0
6-10	Pit.	W	4-3		10	9	Washburn	Anderson	Percival	37-24	2nd	1.0
6-11	Pit.	L	3-7		7	12	Fogg	Appier		37-25	2nd	1.0
6-12	Pit.	W	8-5		14	12	Weber	Boehringer	Percival	38-25	2nd	1.0
6-14	At L.A.	W	8-4		11	4	Ortiz	Ishii		39-25	2nd	1.0

Date	Opp.	Res.	Score	(inn.*)	Hits	Opp. hits	Winning pitcher	Losing pitcher	Save	Record	Pos.	GB
6-15	At L.A.	L	5-10		10	14	Perez	Schoeneweis		39-26	2nd	1.0
6-16	At L.A.	L	4-5		6	9	Carrara	Levine	Gagne	39-27	2nd	1.0
6-18	At St.L.	L	2-7		7	12	Kile	Appier		39-28	2nd	2.0
6-19	At St.L.	L	2-6		7	9	Morris	Sele		39-29	2nd	3.0
6-20	At St.L.	W	3-2		11	8	Schoeneweis	Smith	Percival	40-29	2nd	3.0
6-21	At Mil.	W	11-4		12	11	Ortiz	Quevedo		41-29	2nd	3.0
6-22	At Mil.	W	8-2		16	10	Washburn	Cabrera		42-29	2nd	2.0
6-23	At Mil.	W	5-2		9	9	Appier	Sheets	Percival	43-29	2nd	2.0
6-24†	At Tex.	L	5-8		7	12	Benoit	Sele		43-30		
6-24‡	At Tex.	L	2-3		11	7	Burba	Lackey	Irabu	43-31	3rd	2.5
6-25	At Tex.	L	5-11		8	7	Valdes	Schoeneweis		43-32	3rd	3.5
6-26	At Tex.	W	7-6		11	8	Weber	Irabu	Percival	44-32	2nd	3.5
6-27	At Tex.	W	6-3		11	7	Washburn	Bell	Percival	45-32	2nd	3.5
6-28	L.A.	L	5-7		9	13	Carrara	Shields	Gagne	45-33	2nd	4.5
6-29	L.A.	W	7-0		14	3	Sele	Ishii		46-33	2nd	4.5
6-30	L.A.	W	5-1		7	5	Lackey	Perez	Weber	47-33	2nd	3.5
7-2	Bal.	L	0-3		4	7	Lopez	Ortiz	Julio	47-34	2nd	4.0
7-3	Bal.	W	1-0		4	4	Washburn	Erickson	Percival	48-34	2nd	4.0
7-4	Bal.	L	2-7		9	10	Driskill	Appier		48-35	2nd	5.0
7-5	T.B.	W	6-5	(10)	15	15	Shields	Yan		49-35	2nd	4.0
7-6	T.B.	W	4-3		4	10	Schoeneweis	Colome	Percival	50-35	2nd	3.0
7-7	T.B.	W	2-1	(10)	10	3	Percival	Harper		51-35	2nd	3.0
7-11	At K.C.	W	1-0		6	4	Washburn	May	Percival	52-35	2nd	3.0
7-12	At K.C.	W	11-3		14	5	Appier	Suppan		53-35	2nd	3.0
7-13	At K.C.	L	0-4		3	8	Byrd	Sele		53-36	2nd	3.0
7-14	At K.C.	L	3-12		12	12	Asencio	Ortiz		53-37	2nd	4.0
7-15	At Min.	L	8-10		6	12	Hawkins	Schoeneweis	Guardado	53-38	2nd	4.0
7-16	At Min.	W	4-2		7	7	Washburn	Milton	Weber	54-38	2nd	3.0
7-17	At Oak.	W	10-4		15	9	Appier	Hudson		55-38	2nd	3.0
7-18	At Oak.	L	0-2		6	8	Zito	Sele	Koch	55-39	2nd	4.0
7-19	Sea.	W	15-3		20	9	Ortiz	Garcia		56-39	2nd	3.0
7-20	Sea.	W	7-6		10	10	Shields	Rhodes	Weber	57-39	2nd	2.0
7-21	Sea.	W	7-5		11	8	Washburn	Nelson	Weber	58-39	2nd	1.0
7-23	Oak.	L	1-2		8	4	Zito	Appier	Koch	58-40	2nd	2.0
7-24	Oak.	W	5-1		9	6	Sele	Hudson		59-40	2nd	1.0
7-25	Oak.	W	5-4		13	9	Shields	Mecir	Weber	60-40	2nd	1.0
7-26	At Sea.	W	8-0		12	7	Lackey	Baldwin		61-40	1st	...
7-27	At Sea.	L	1-3		9	4	Pineiro	Washburn	Sasaki	61-41	2nd	1.0
7-28	At Sea.	W	1-0		6	4	Appier	Sasaki	Percival	62-41	1st	...
7-29	Bos.	W	5-4		8	9	Schoeneweis	Embree	Percival	63-41	1st	...
7-30	Bos.	L	0-6		2	9	Martinez	Ortiz		63-42	2nd	1.0
7-31	Bos.	L	1-2		8	8	Wakefield	Lackey	Urbina	63-43	2nd	2.0
8-1	N.Y.	W	2-1		8	6	Washburn	Weaver	Percival	64-43	2nd	2.0
8-2	N.Y.	L	0-4		4	9	Pettitte	Appier	Mendoza	64-44	2nd	3.0
8-3	N.Y.	W	5-4		11	6	Percival	Mendoza		65-44	2nd	3.0
8-4	N.Y.	L	5-7	(12)	11	13	Stanton	Shields	Mendoza	65-45	2nd	3.0
8-5	At Det.	W	6-3		13	7	Lackey	Powell	Percival	66-45	2nd	2.5
8-6	At Chi.	W	11-2		17	9	Washburn	Wright	Levine	67-45	2nd	1.5
8-7	At Chi.	L	6-7		11	12	Osuna	Donnelly		67-46	2nd	2.5
8-8	At Chi.	L	2-3		7	8	Parque	Sele	Marte	67-47	2nd	3.5
8-9	At Tor.	L	4-5		12	11	Walker	Ortiz	Escobar	67-48	2nd	3.5
8-10	At Tor.	W	11-4		18	7	Lackey	Parris		68-48	2nd	3.5
8-11	At Tor.	W	1-0		9	3	Washburn	Halladay	Percival	69-48	2nd	2.5
8-12	Det.	W	7-0		14	4	Appier	Redman		70-48	2nd	2.0
8-13	Det.	W	7-6	(12)	15	12	Levine	Bernero		71-48	2nd	2.0
8-14	Det.	W	5-4		7	7	Ortiz	Maroth	Percival	72-48	2nd	1.0
8-16	Cle.	W	5-4		10	10	Lackey	Drese	Percival	73-48	2nd	0.5
8-17	Cle.	L	4-9		9	12	Sadler	Washburn		73-49	2nd	0.5
8-18	Cle.	W	4-1		8	2	Appier	Sabathia	Percival	74-49	2nd	0.5
8-20	At N.Y.	L	5-7		12	10	Pettitte	Sele	Stanton	74-50	1st	...
8-21	At N.Y.	W	5-1	(11)	11	7	Weber	Weaver		75-50	1st	...
8-22	At N.Y.	L	2-4		8	11	Wells	Lackey	Karsay	75-51	3rd	1.0
8-23	At Bos.	L	1-4		6	11	Martinez	Washburn	Urbina	75-52	3rd	2.0
8-24	At Bos.	W	2-0		9	5	Appier	Wakefield	Percival	76-52	2nd	2.0
8-25	At Bos.	W	8-3		16	7	Schoeneweis	Lowe		77-52	2nd	2.0
8-26	At Bos.	L	9-10	(10)	17	18	Urbina	Shields		77-53	3rd	3.0
8-27	T.B.	W	7-3		16	12	Lackey	Zambrano	Weber	78-53	2nd	3.0
8-28	T.B.	L	5-8	(10)	10	14	Yan	Levine		78-54	2nd	4.0
8-29	T.B.	W	6-1		11	5	Appier	Sturtze		79-54	2nd	3.5

Date	Opp.	Res.	Score	(inn.*)	Hits	Opp. hits	Winning pitcher	Losing pitcher	Save	Record	Pos.	GB
8-30	Bal.	W	6-2		10	4	Callaway	Johnson	Schoeneweis	80-54	2nd	3.5
8-31	Bal.	W	9-0		16	5	Ortiz	Erickson		81-54	2nd	3.5
9-1	Bal.	W	9-3		9	11	Lackey	Lopez	Percival	82-54	2nd	3.5
9-3	At T.B.	W	10-2		12	10	Washburn	Sosa		83-54	2nd	3.5
9-4	At T.B.	W	4-2		10	7	Appier	Sturtze	Percival	84-54	2nd	3.5
9-5	At T.B.	W	10-1		10	6	Ortiz	Kennedy		85-54	2nd	3.0
9-6	At Bal.	W	6-3		10	6	Lackey	Douglass	Percival	86-54	2nd	2.0
9-7	At Bal.	W	4-2	(10)	5	6	Weber	Julio	Percival	87-54	2nd	2.0
9-8	At Bal.	W	6-2		12	5	Washburn	Hentgen	Weber	88-54	2nd	2.0
9-9	Oak.	L	1-2		6	5	Hudson	Appier	Koch	88-55	2nd	3.0
9-10	Oak.	W	5-2		10	3	Ortiz	Lilly	Percival	89-55	2nd	2.0
9-11	Oak.	W	6-5		14	7	Shields	Tam	Percival	90-55	2nd	1.0
9-12	Oak.	W	7-6		9	8	Donnelly	Koch		91-55	T1st	...
9-13	Tex.	W	3-2		9	5	Washburn	Benoit	Percival	92-55	T1st	...
9-14	Tex.	W	8-6		13	8	Shields	Van Poppel	Percival	93-55	T1st	...
9-15	Tex.	W	13-4		11	6	Ortiz	Rogers		94-55	1st	+1.0
9-16	At Oak.	L	3-4		5	8	Koch	Levine		94-56	T1st	...
9-17	At Oak.	W	1-0	(10)	7	3	Weber	Koch	Percival	95-56	1st	+1.0
9-18	At Oak.	L	4-7		10	7	Zito	Callaway	Koch	95-57	T1st	...
9-19	At Oak.	L	3-5		6	8	Hudson	Appier	Koch	95-58	2nd	1.0
9-20	At Sea.	W	8-1		10	6	Ortiz	Pineiro		96-58	2nd	1.0
9-21	At Sea.	L	4-6		10	7	Garcia	Lackey	Sasaki	96-59	2nd	2.0
9-22	At Sea.	L	2-3		7	8	Franklin	Washburn	Nelson	96-60	2nd	3.0
9-24	At Tex.	L	1-2		6	8	Benoit	Appier	Cordero	96-61	2nd	3.0
9-25	At Tex.	L	3-4		8	6	Seanez	Schoeneweis	Cordero	96-62	2nd	3.0
9-26	At Tex.	W	10-5		8	11	Lackey	Lewis		97-62	2nd	3.0
9-27	Sea.	L	6-7	(12)	14	13	Halama	Pote		97-63	2nd	4.0
9-28	Sea.	W	8-4		14	9	Callaway	Franklin		98-63	2nd	4.0
9-29	Sea.	W	7-6		10	9	Lukasiewicz	Valdes	Donnelly	99-63	2nd	4.0

Monthly records: March (0-1), April (11-13), May (19-7), June (17-12), July (16-10), August (18-11), September (18-9).
*Innings, if other than nine. †First game of a doubleheader. ‡Second game of a doubleheader.

RECORDS

2002 regular-season record: 99-63
Position: 2nd in A.L. West
Home: 54-27 **Road:** 45-36
A.L. East: 28-13 **A.L. Central:** 30-15
A.L. West: 30-28 **N.L.:** 11-7
Vs. LH starters: 30-16
Vs. RH starters: 69-47
Grass: 89-58 **Artificial:** 10-5
Day: 23-12 **Night:** 76-51
1-Run: 31-22 **X-inn.:** 10-5
Doubleheaders: 0-1-0
Team record past five years: 411-399 (.507, ranks 8th in league in that span)

TEAM LEADERS

Batting average: Adam Kennedy (.312).
At-bats: Garret Anderson (638).
Runs: David Eckstein (107).
Hits: Garret Anderson (195).
Total bases: Garret Anderson (344).
Doubles: Garret Anderson (56).
Triples: David Eckstein, Brad Fullmer, Adam Kennedy (6).
Home runs: Troy Glaus (30).
Runs batted in: Garret Anderson (123).
Stolen bases: Darin Erstad (23).

Slugging percentage: Garret Anderson (.539).
On-base percentage: Tim Salmon (.380).
Wins: Jarrod Washburn (18).
Earned-run average: Jarrod Washburn (3.15).
Complete games: Ramon Ortiz (4).
Shutouts: Ramon Ortiz, Aaron Sele (1).
Saves: Troy Percival (40).
Innings pitched: Ramon Ortiz (217.1).
Strikeouts: Ramon Ortiz (162).

GAMES BY POSITION

Catcher: Bengie Molina 121, Jorge Fabregas 32, Jose Molina 29, Sal Fasano 2, Shawn Wooten 2.
First base: Scott Spiezio 143, Brad Fullmer 29, Shawn Wooten 16, Benji Gil 10, Darin Erstad 5, Jose Nieves 3, Clay Bellinger 2.
Second base: Adam Kennedy 139, Benji Gil 26, Jose Nieves 18, Chone Figgins 8, Scott Spiezio 1.
Third base: Troy Glaus 156, Scott Spiezio 20, Jose Nieves 5, Shawn Wooten 1.
Shortstop: David Eckstein 147, Benji Gil 14, Jose Nieves 13, Alfredo Amezaga 5, Troy Glaus 2.

Outfield: Garret Anderson 147, Darin Erstad 143, Tim Salmon 111, Orlando Palmeiro 86, Alex Ochoa 36, Julio Ramirez 23, Jeff DaVanon 10, Scott Spiezio 10, Jose Nieves 2, Adam Kennedy 1.
Designated hitter: Brad Fullmer 94, Shawn Wooten 26, Tim Salmon 25, Garret Anderson 10, Benji Gil 10, Orlando Palmeiro 8, Jeff DaVanon 4, Darin Erstad 4, David Eckstein 3, Jose Nieves 2, Alfredo Amezaga 1, Adam Kennedy 1, Julio Ramirez 1.

TOP DRAFT CHOICES

1. **Joe Saunders,** LHP, Virginia Tech.
2. **Kevin Jepsen,** RHP, Bishop Manogue H.S., Sparks, Nev.
3. **Kyle Pawelczyk,** LHP, Chipola (Fla.) J.C.
4. **Jordan Renz,** OF, Tulsa Union H.S., Broken Arrow, Okla.
5. **Javy Rodriguez,** SS, Miami (Fla.).
6. **Chris Walston,** 1B, El Capitan H.S., Lakeside, Calif.
7. **Jeff Leise,** OF, Nebraska.
8. **James Holcomb,** RHP, Nevada.
9. **Caleb Maher,** OF, Ceres (Calif.) H.S.
10. **Howard Kendrick,** 2B, St. John's River (Fla.) C.C.

BALTIMORE ORIOLES
AMERICAN LEAGUE EAST DIVISION

2003 SEASON

March/April

SUN	MON	TUE	WED	THU	FRI	SAT
30	31 D CLE	1	2 CLE	3 CLE	4 BOS	5 D BOS
6 D BOS	7	8 TB	9 TB	10 TB	11 D BOS	12 BOS
13 D BOS	14	15 CLE	16 CLE	17 CLE	18 TB	19 D TB
20 D TB	21 TB	22 CWS	23 CWS	24 CWS	25 TB	26 TB
27 D TB	28	29 DET	30 DET			

May

SUN	MON	TUE	WED	THU	FRI	SAT
				1 D DET	2 KC	3 D KC
4 D KC	5 DET	6 DET	7 D DET	8 KC	9 KC	10 KC
11 KC	12	13 CWS	14 CWS	15 CWS	16 TB	17 TB
18 D TB	19	20 ANA	21 ANA	22 ANA	23 TEX	24 TEX
25 D TEX	26	27 ANA	28 ANA	29 TEX	30 TEX	31 TEX

June

SUN	MON	TUE	WED	THU	FRI	SAT
1 D TEX	2	3 HOU	4 HOU	5 HOU	6 STL	7 D STL
8 D STL	9	10 CUB	11 CUB	12 CUB	13 MIL	14 MIL
15 D MIL	16	17 TOR	18 TOR	19 D TOR	20 ATL	21 ATL
22 ATL	23 D TOR	24 TOR	25 TOR	26 TOR	27 PHI	28 PHI
29 D PHI	30 NYY					

July

SUN	MON	TUE	WED	THU	FRI	SAT
		1 NYY	2 D NYY	3	4 TOR	5 TOR
6 D TOR	7	8 SEA	9 SEA	10 SEA	11 OAK	12 D OAK
13 D OAK	14	15	* 16	17 ANA	18 ANA	19 ANA
20 D ANA	21 TEX	22 D TEX	23 NYY	24 D NYY	25 TOR	26 D TOR
27 D TOR	28	29 MIN	30 MIN	31 MIN		

August

SUN	MON	TUE	WED	THU	FRI	SAT
					1 BOS	2 BOS
3 D BOS	4 MIN	5 MIN	6 MIN	7 D MIN	8 BOS	9 BOS
10 D BOS	11 TB	12 TB	13 D TB	14	15 NYY	16 NYY
17 D NYY	18	19 TB	20 TB	21 TB	22 NYY	23 D NYY
24 NYY	25 D NYY	26 OAK	27 OAK	28 D OAK	29 SEA	30 D SEA

September

SUN	MON	TUE	WED	THU	FRI	SAT
31 D SEA	1	2 OAK	3 OAK	4 OAK	5 SEA	6 SEA
7 D SEA	8 BOS	9 BOS	10 D BOS	11	12 TOR	13 D TOR
14 TOR	15 NYY	16 NYY	17 NYY	18 NYY	19 TOR	20 TOR
21 D TOR	22 BOS	23 BOS	24 BOS	25 BOS	26 NYY	27 D NYY
28 D NYY						

Home games shaded; D—Day game (games starting before 5 p.m.); *—All-Star Game at Comiskey Park, Chicago. Subject to change.

CLUB DIRECTORY

Chairman of the board/CEO
Peter G. Angelos
Vice chairman/chief operating officer
Joseph E. Foss
Executive vice president
John P. Angelos
Exec. v.p./baseball operations
Jim Beattie
V.p./baseball operations
Mike Flanagan

Special assts. to the v.p., baseball ops.
Ed Kenney Jr., Danny Garcia, Larry Himes, Mel Didier
Director/minor league operations
To be announced
Director/scouting
Tony DeMacio
Executive director/communications
Spiro Alafassos

Director/public relations
Bill Stetka
Manager, baseball information
Kevin Behan
Manager, communications
Monica Pence
Director/community relations
Julie Wagner

MINOR LEAGUE AFFILIATES

Class	Team	League	Manager
AAA	Ottawa	International	To be announced
AA	Bowie	Eastern	To be announced
A	Frederick	Carolina	To be announced
A	Delmarva	South Atlantic	To be announced
A	Aberdeen	New York-Pennsylvania	To be announced
Rookie	Bluefield	Appalachian	To be announced
Rookie	Gulf Coast Orioles	Gulf Coast	To be announced

Follow the Orioles all season at: www.sportingnews.com/baseball/teams/orioles/

BROADCAST INFORMATION

Radio: WBAL-AM (1090).
TV: WJZ (Channel 13), WNUV (Channel 54), WFTY (Channel 50).
Cable TV: Comcast SportsNet.

SPRING TRAINING

Ballpark (city): Ft. Lauderdale Stadium (Ft. Lauderdale, Fla.).
Ticket information: 954-776-1921.

2003 SEASON *Baltimore Orioles*

Manager—Mike Hargrove (30).
Coaches—Terry Crowley (48), Rick Dempsey, Elrod Hendricks (44), Sam Perlozzo (2), Tom Trebelhorn (49), Mark Wiley (34).

No.	PITCHERS	B/T	Ht./Wt.	Born	Age*	2002 clubs
30	Bauer, Rick	R/R	6-6/215	1-10-77	26	Baltimore, Rochester
51	Bechler, Steve	R/R	6-2/240	11-18-79	23	Bowie, Rochester, Baltimore
	Bedard, Erik	L/L	6-1/180	3-6-79	24	Bowie, Baltimore
	Cabrera, Daniel	R/R	6-7/210	5-28-81	21	Bluefield
	Daal, Omar	L/L	6-3/204	3-1-72	31	Los Angeles
47	Douglass, Sean	R/R	6-6/200	4-28-79	23	Rochester, Baltimore
49	Driskill, Travis	R/R	6-0/225	8-1-71	31	Rochester, Baltimore
57	DuBose, Eric	L/L	6-3/231	5-15-76	26	Rochester, Bowie, Baltimore
19	Erickson, Scott	R/R	6-4/230	2-2-68	35	Baltimore
27	Groom, Buddy	L/L	6-2/207	7-10-65	37	Baltimore
41	Hentgen, Pat	R/R	6-2/195	11-13-68	34	Gulf Coast Orioles, Delmarva, Aberdeen, Bowie, Frederick, Baltimore
16	Johnson, Jason	R/R	6-6/235	10-27-73	29	Baltimore, Bowie
50	Julio, Jorge	R/R	6-1/190	3-3-79	24	Baltimore
13	Lopez, Rodrigo	R/R	6-1/180	12-14-75	27	Baltimore
	Paradis, Mike	R/R	6-3/190	5-3-78	24	Bowie
43	Ponson, Sidney	R/R	6-1/225	11-2-76	26	Baltimore
	Riley, Matt	L/L	6-1/201	8-2-79	23	Bowie
37	Roberts, Willis	R/R	6-3/175	6-19-75	27	Baltimore
52	Ryan, B.J.	L/L	6-6/230	12-28-75	27	Baltimore
28	Stephens, John	R/R	6-1/204	11-15-79	23	Rochester, Baltimore

No.	CATCHERS	B/T	Ht./Wt.	Born	Age*	2002 clubs
26	Fordyce, Brook	R/R	6-0/190	5-7-70	32	Baltimore
17	Gil, Geronimo	R/R	6-2/195	8-7-75	27	Baltimore

No.	INFIELDERS	B/T	Ht./Wt.	Born	Age*	2002 clubs
10	Batista, Tony	R/R	6-0/205	12-9-73	29	Baltimore
18	Conine, Jeff	R/R	6-1/220	6-27-66	36	Baltimore
8	Cruz, Deivi	R/R	6-0/184	11-6-72	30	San Diego
15	Hairston, Jerry	R/R	5-10/175	5-29-76	26	Baltimore
31	Leon, Jose	R/R	6-0/175	12-8-76	26	Rochester, Baltimore
1	Roberts, Brian	B/R	5-9/170	10-9-77	25	Rochester, Baltimore
11	Rogers, Eddie	R/R	6-1/172	8-29-78	24	Bowie, Baltimore
23	Segui, David	B/L	6-1/202	7-19-66	36	Baltimore

No.	OUTFIELDERS	B/T	Ht./Wt.	Born	Age*	2002 clubs
3	Bigbie, Larry	L/L	6-4/190	11-4-77	25	Rochester, Baltimore
40	Cordova, Marty	R/R	6-0/206	7-10-69	33	Baltimore
25	Gibbons, Jay	L/L	6-0/200	3-2-77	26	Baltimore
32	Matos, Luis	R/R	6-0/179	10-30-78	24	Frederick, Bowie, Baltimore
36	Matthews, Gary	B/R	6-3/210	8-25-74	28	New York N.L., Baltimore
	McDonald, Darnell	R/R	5-11/201	11-17-78	24	Bowie, Rochester
6	Mora, Melvin	R/R	5-10/180	2-2-72	31	Baltimore
63	Raines, Tim	R/R	5-10/185	8-31-79	23	Bowie
38	Richard, Chris	L/L	6-2/190	6-7-74	28	Gulf Coast Orioles, Bowie, Aberdeen, Rochester, Baltimore

*Age as of April 1, 2003.

BALLPARK INFORMATION

Ballpark (capacity, surface)
Oriole Park at Camden Yards (48,190, grass)
Address
333 W. Camden St.
Baltimore, MD 21201
Official website
www.theorioles.com
Business phone
410-685-9800
Ticket information
410-481-SEAT
Field dimensions (from home plate)
To left field at foul line, 333 feet
To center field, 400 feet
To right field at foul line, 318
First game played
April 6, 1992 (Orioles 2, Indians 0)

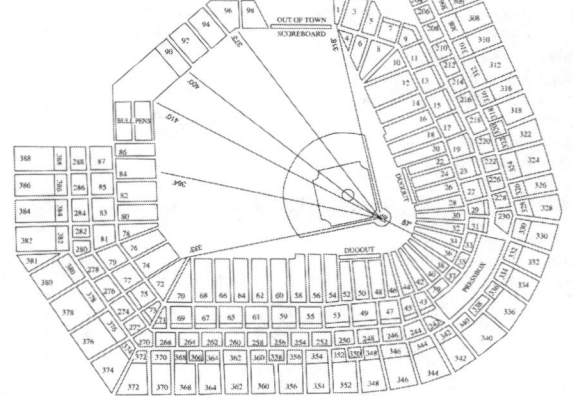

2003 SEASON *Baltimore Orioles*

Date	Opp.	Res.	Score	(inn.*)	Hits	Opp. hits	Winning pitcher	Losing pitcher	Save	Record	Pos.	GB
4-1	N.Y.	W	10-3		9	6	Erickson	Clemens		1-0	T1st	...
4-3	N.Y.	L	0-1		5	6	Wells	Johnson	Rivera	1-1	T3rd	1.0
4-4	N.Y.	L	1-4		5	8	Mussina	Ponson	Rivera	1-2	4th	2.0
4-5	Bos.	L	0-3		2	11	Lowe	Towers	Urbina	1-3	5th	2.0
4-6	Bos.	L	2-4		4	8	Fossum	Erickson	Urbina	1-4	5th	3.0
4-7	Bos.	L	1-4		6	9	Martinez	Maduro	Urbina	1-5	5th	4.0
4-10	T.B.	L	2-3		6	10	Wilson	Johnson	Yan	1-6	5th	5.0
4-11	T.B.	W	15-6		18	6	Lopez	Colome		2-6	5th	4.0
4-12	At Chi.	L	2-5		4	9	Buehrle	Towers	Foulke	2-7	5th	4.0
4-13	At Chi.	L	3-4		4	11	Osuna	Roberts	Foulke	2-8	5th	4.5
4-14	At Chi.	W	9-4		11	12	Maduro	Wright		3-8	5th	4.0
4-15	At Chi.	L	4-13		8	15	Garland	Johnson		3-9	5th	4.5
4-16	At N.Y.	W	5-4		10	9	Bauer	Mendoza	Julio	4-9	5th	4.5
4-17	At N.Y.	L	1-7		7	12	Hernandez	Towers		4-10	5th	5.5
4-18	At N.Y.	L	4-8		7	12	Wells	Erickson		4-11	5th	6.0
4-19	At T.B.	W	6-5	(14)	11	12	Julio	Colome		5-11	5th	6.0
4-20	At T.B.	W	6-3		12	9	Johnson	Wilson	Roberts	6-11	5th	5.5
4-21	At T.B.	L	1-2		4	7	Creek	Ponson	Yan	6-12	5th	7.0
4-23	Bos.	W	7-5		12	8	Erickson	Castillo	Julio	7-12	5th	6.0
4-24	Bos.	W	5-3		10	12	Lopez	Oliver	Julio	8-12	5th	5.0
4-25	Bos.	L	0-7		2	13	Martinez	Maduro		8-13	5th	6.0
4-26	At K.C.	W	10-5	(10)	14	11	Groom	Grimsley		9-13	4th	6.0
4-27	At K.C.	W	9-4		8	8	Ponson	Byrd		10-13	3rd	6.0
4-28	At K.C.	W	13-0		15	4	Erickson	Rekar		11-13	3rd	5.5
4-29	At Bos.	W	5-3		10	8	Lopez	Castillo	Julio	12-13	3rd	4.5
4-30	At Bos.	L	0-4		8	7	Oliver	Maduro		12-14	3rd	5.5
5-1	At Bos.	L	3-15		7	16	Martinez	Douglass		12-15	3rd	6.5
5-2	K.C.	W	6-2		8	8	Ponson	Byrd	Bauer	13-15	3rd	6.0
5-3	K.C.	W	4-3		9	7	Roberts	Bailey	Julio	14-15	3rd	6.0
5-4	K.C.	W	10-0		10	6	Lopez	Suppan		15-15	3rd	6.0
5-5	K.C.	W	3-2		11	9	Maduro	George	Julio	16-15	3rd	6.0
5-6	Cle.	L	4-9		9	15	Drese	Groom		16-16	3rd	7.0
5-7	Cle.	W	4-3	(10)	13	5	Julio	Wohlers		17-16	3rd	7.0
5-8	Cle.	L	2-6		8	6	Baez	Erickson		17-17	3rd	8.0
5-10	At T.B.	W	6-5		7	7	Lopez	Rupe	Julio	18-17	3rd	7.5
5-11	At T.B.	L	4-6		10	10	Yan	Julio		18-18	3rd	7.5
5-12	At T.B.	L	3-6		10	10	Wilson	Ponson	Yan	18-19	3rd	8.5
5-14	At Cle.	L	5-6		9	11	Shuey	Julio		18-20	3rd	9.5
5-15	At Cle.	L	1-3		7	7	Colon	Bauer	Wickman	18-21	3rd	10.5
5-17	T.B.	W	5-3		8	8	Roberts	Zambrano	Julio	19-21	3rd	9.0
5-18	T.B.	L	4-5		11	12	Creek	Bauer	Yan	19-22	3rd	10.0
5-19	T.B.	L	0-4		5	8	Harper	Erickson	Kent	19-23	3rd	11.0
5-21	At Oak.	W	6-4	(14)	11	11	Driskill	Venafro	Julio	20-23	3rd	10.5
5-22	At Oak.	L	6-7		8	13	Fyhrie	Maduro	Koch	20-24	3rd	10.5
5-23	At Oak.	W	11-3		14	8	Ponson	Mulder		21-24	3rd	10.5
5-24	At Sea.	L	2-6		4	10	Garcia	Erickson		21-25	3rd	11.5
5-25	At Sea.	W	3-2		7	6	Driskill	Soriano	Groom	22-25	3rd	10.5
5-26	At Sea.	L	1-8		5	12	Moyer	Lopez		22-26	3rd	10.5
5-28	Oak.	L	2-5		9	10	Mulder	Maduro	Koch	22-27	3rd	12.0
5-29	Oak.	W	10-5		15	10	Bauer	Fyhrie		23-27	3rd	12.0
5-30	Sea.	L	4-5		5	9	Rhodes	Julio	Sasaki	23-28	3rd	12.5
5-31	Sea.	W	8-7	(10)	14	13	Bauer	Halama		24-28	3rd	12.5
6-1	Sea.	W	4-3		6	9	Roberts	Sasaki		25-28	3rd	11.5
6-2	Sea.	L	8-11		12	14	Rhodes	Julio		25-29	3rd	12.5
6-3	At N.Y.	W	4-3		10	5	Julio	Rivera		26-29	3rd	11.5
6-4	At N.Y.	L	5-13		14	15	Mendoza	Erickson		26-30	3rd	12.5
6-5	At N.Y.	W	4-3		8	7	Driskill	Wells	Julio	27-30	3rd	12.5
6-7	L.A.	W	4-2		8	7	Lopez	Ashby	Julio	28-30	3rd	12.0
6-8	L.A.	L	4-8		7	11	Ishii	Johnson		28-31	3rd	12.0
6-9	L.A.	L	1-2		5	5	Perez	Ponson	Gagne	28-32	3rd	12.0
6-10	S.D.	W	8-6		6	10	Groom	Fikac	Julio	29-32	3rd	12.0
6-11	S.D.	W	6-5	(10)	12	11	Julio	Trujillo		30-32	3rd	11.0
6-12	S.D.	L	0-2		6	5	Lawrence	Lopez	Hoffman	30-33	3rd	12.0
6-13	At Cle.	L	1-2	(10)	5	5	Riggan	Roberts		30-34	3rd	12.5
6-14	At Phi.	W	7-3		9	7	Ryan	Bottalico		31-34	3rd	11.5

Date	Opp.	Res.	Score	(inn.*)	Hits	Opp. hits	Winning pitcher	Losing pitcher	Save	Record	Pos.	GB
6-15	At Phi.	L	3-4	(10)	6	9	Cormier	Groom		31-35	3rd	11.5
6-16	At Phi.	W	4-2		5	6	Driskill	Adams	Julio	32-35	3rd	11.5
6-18	At Ari.	L	3-6		11	11	Anderson	Johnson	Kim	32-36	3rd	12.5
6-19	At Ari.	W	6-1		7	4	Brock	Schilling		33-36	3rd	11.5
6-20	At Ari.	L	1-5		6	7	Johnson	Lopez		33-37	3rd	12.5
6-21	At S.F	L	3-4		8	9	Rodriguez	Bauer	Nen	33-38	3rd	12.5
6-22	At S.F	W	4-2		7	8	Driskill	Jensen	Julio	34-38	3rd	11.5
6-23	At S.F	W	3-1		9	6	Johnson	Hernandez	Julio	35-38	3rd	11.0
6-25	N.Y.	W	4-3		12	8	Roberts	Pettitte	Julio	36-38	3rd	10.0
6-26	N.Y.	W	8-7		12	10	Roberts	Stanton		37-38	3rd	9.5
6-27	N.Y.	L	2-3		6	8	Wells	Erickson	Rivera	37-39	3rd	10.0
6-28	Phi.	L	2-6		8	8	Wolf	Driskill		37-40	3rd	11.0
6-29	Phi.	W	11-1		18	6	Johnson	Padilla		38-40	3rd	10.0
6-30	Phi.	L	5-8		9	12	Person	Bauer	Mesa	38-41	3rd	11.0
7-2	At Ana.	W	3-0		7	4	Lopez	Ortiz	Julio	39-41	3rd	11.0
7-3	At Ana.	L	0-1		4	4	Washburn	Erickson	Percival	39-42	3rd	12.0
7-4	At Ana.	W	7-2		10	9	Driskill	Appier		40-42	3rd	12.0
7-5	At Tex.	L	6-7		11	14	Telford	Julio		40-43	3rd	13.0
7-6	At Tex.	W	7-5		8	7	Bauer	Lewis	Perez	41-43	3rd	12.0
7-7	At Tex.	W	10-4		16	4	Lopez	Rogers		42-43	3rd	12.0
7-11	Oak.	L	1-4		6	9	Mulder	Erickson	Koch	42-44	3rd	13.0
7-12	Oak.	L	0-1		8	7	Hudson	Johnson	Koch	42-45	3rd	13.0
7-13	Oak.	L	0-6		3	10	Zito	Driskill		42-46	3rd	14.0
7-14	Oak.	W	6-3		8	7	Lopez	Lidle	Julio	43-46	3rd	13.0
7-15	Sea.	W	6-5		9	8	Ponson	Franklin	Julio	44-46	3rd	12.0
7-16	Sea.	W	6-1		9	6	Erickson	Pineiro		45-46	3rd	12.0
7-17	At Tor.	L	1-7		6	14	Halladay	Johnson		45-47	3rd	13.0
7-18	At Tor.	L	4-5		10	9	Carpenter	Driskill	Escobar	45-48	3rd	14.0
7-19	Chi.	W	10-4		13	8	Lopez	Garland		46-48	3rd	13.0
7-20	Chi.	W	4-3	(14)	17	13	Bauer	Howry		47-48	3rd	13.0
7-21	Chi.	L	7-8		9	10	Howry	Roberts	Osuna	47-49	3rd	14.0
7-22	Tor.	L	3-6		7	10	Halladay	Johnson	Escobar	47-50	3rd	14.5
7-24	Tor.	L	2-5		10	8	Carpenter	Driskill	Politte	47-51	3rd	15.0
7-26	At Bos.	W	9-2		16	4	Lopez	Arrojo		48-51	3rd	15.0
7-27	At Bos.	L	0-4		4	8	Burkett	Ponson		48-52	3rd	15.0
7-28	At Bos.	L	3-12		8	14	Lowe	Erickson		48-53	3rd	16.0
7-29	At T.B.	L	1-6		4	18	Wilson	Driskill		48-54	3rd	17.0
7-30	At T.B.	L	3-10		5	15	Kennedy	Stephens		48-55	3rd	18.0
7-31	At T.B.	W	12-2		18	9	Lopez	de los Santos		49-55	3rd	17.0
8-1	At T.B.	W	4-3		6	9	Ponson	Sosa	Julio	50-55	3rd	16.0
8-2	At Tor.	W	9-8		12	14	Ryan	Escobar	Julio	51-55	3rd	16.0
8-3	At Tor.	W	8-4		16	10	Driskill	Carpenter		52-55	3rd	15.0
8-4	At Tor.	L	4-5		12	10	Heredia	Ryan	Escobar	52-56	3rd	16.0
8-5	At Tor.	L	1-7		6	11	Parris	Lopez		52-57	3rd	16.5
8-6	Min.	W	9-2		7	7	Ponson	Santana		53-57	3rd	15.5
8-7	Min.	W	6-4		12	7	Erickson	Reed	Julio	54-57	3rd	15.5
8-8	Min.	W	4-1		6	9	Driskill	Radke	Julio	55-57	3rd	15.5
8-9	At Det.	L	0-3		6	8	Maroth	Johnson	Acevedo	55-58	3rd	15.5
8-10	At Det.	W	3-2		9	4	Lopez	Santana	Julio	56-58	3rd	14.5
8-11	At Det.	L	1-2		4	7	Sparks	Stephens	Acevedo	56-59	3rd	15.5
8-13	At Min.	L	0-6		5	10	Reed	Erickson		56-60	3rd	16.5
8-14	At Min.	W	6-5	(14)	11	12	Bauer	Fiore		57-60	3rd	16.5
8-15	At Min.	W	3-1		7	7	Johnson	Lohse	Julio	58-60	3rd	16.5
8-16	Det.	L	5-6		12	10	Sparks	Lopez	Acevedo	58-61	3rd	17.5
8-17	Det.	W	7-3		11	7	Stephens	Redman		59-61	3rd	17.5
8-18	Det.	L	4-7		8	18	Bernero	Brock	Acevedo	59-62	3rd	17.5
8-19	T.B.	L	3-7		5	10	Wilson	Driskill		59-63	3rd	18.0
8-20	T.B.	W	7-4		9	12	Groom	Gardner		60-63	3rd	18.0
8-21	T.B.	W	2-1		5	5	Lopez	Zambrano	Groom	61-63	3rd	17.0
8-22	T.B.	W	3-2	(11)	8	6	Julio	Harper		62-63	3rd	17.0
8-23	Tor.	W	11-7		16	13	Brock	Cassidy	Ryan	63-63	3rd	16.0
8-24§	Tor.	L	1-4		6	9	Walker	Driskill	Escobar	63-64		
8-24∞	Tor.	L	3-8		8	13	Loaiza	Bauer		63-65	3rd	17.5
8-25	Tor.	L	2-5		5	11	Miller	Johnson	Escobar	63-66	3rd	17.5
8-27	At Tex.	L	4-9		11	13	Reyes	Lopez		63-67	3rd	19.0
8-28	At Tex.	L	3-5		9	10	Park	Stephens	Cordero	63-68	3rd	20.0
8-29	At Tex.	L	6-9		7	11	Van Poppel	Bauer	Cordero	63-69	3rd	20.0
8-30	At Ana.	L	2-6		4	10	Callaway	Johnson	Schoeneweis	63-70	3rd	21.0
8-31	At Ana.	L	0-9		5	16	Ortiz	Erickson		63-71	3rd	21.0

Date	Opp.	Res.	Score	(inn.*)	Hits	Opp. hits	Winning pitcher	Losing pitcher	Save	Record	Pos.	GB
9-1	At Ana.	L	3-9		11	9	Lackey	Lopez	Percival	63-72	3rd	21.0
9-3	Tex.	L	1-7		1	10	Van Poppel	Stephens	Benoit	63-73	3rd	21.5
9-4	Tex.	W	8-3		10	7	Ponson	Myette		64-73	3rd	21.5
9-5	Tex.	L	2-11		6	14	Rogers	Johnson		64-74	3rd	22.5
9-6	Ana.	L	3-6		6	10	Lackey	Douglass	Percival	64-75	3rd	23.5
9-7	Ana.	L	2-4	(10)	6	5	Weber	Julio	Percival	64-76	3rd	23.5
9-8	Ana.	L	2-6		5	12	Washburn	Hentgen	Weber	64-77	3rd	24.5
9-10§	At N.Y.	L	2-5		7	7	Pettitte	Johnson	Stanton	64-78		
9-10∞	At N.Y.	L	1-3		5	6	Weaver	Ponson	Karsay	64-79	4th	26.5
9-11	At N.Y.	L	4-5	(11)	8	7	Karsay	Bauer		64-80	4th	27.5
9-12	At N.Y.	L	3-7		9	10	Wells	Douglass		64-81	4th	28.5
9-13	At Bos.	W	8-3		12	6	Lopez	Fossum		65-81	4th	27.5
9-14	At Bos.	L	4-6		10	11	Lowe	Hentgen	Urbina	65-82	4th	27.5
9-15	At Bos.	W	8-3		10	10	Johnson	Burkett		66-82	4th	27.5
9-16	Tor.	L	0-2		4	6	Walker	Ponson	Escobar	66-83	4th	28.0
9-17	Tor.	W	10-4		11	8	Stephens	Miller		67-83	4th	27.0
9-18	Tor.	L	1-2		9	5	Halladay	Douglass	Escobar	67-84	4th	28.0
9-19	Tor.	L	3-9		5	16	Hendrickson	Lopez		67-85	4th	28.0
9-20	Bos.	L	2-4		11	5	Lowe	Hentgen	Urbina	67-86	4th	29.0
9-21	Bos.	L	0-3		2	8	Burkett	Johnson	Urbina	67-87	4th	30.0
9-22	Bos.	L	2-13		9	14	Martinez	Ponson		67-88	4th	31.0
9-23	Bos.	L	4-5	(15)	6	11	Embree	Roberts	Gomes	67-89	4th	31.0
9-24	At Tor.	L	1-11		4	12	Halladay	Douglass		67-90	4th	32.0
9-25	At Tor.	L	2-3		7	7	Hendrickson	Lopez	Escobar	67-91	4th	33.0
9-26	At Tor.	L	1-5		5	9	Loaiza	Hentgen		67-92	4th	33.5
9-27	N.Y.	L	2-6		7	10	Pettitte	Ponson		67-93	4th	34.5
9-28	N.Y.	L	2-4		6	9	Wells	Driskill	Stanton	67-94	4th	35.5
9-29	N.Y.	L	1-6		9	6	Mussina	Stephens		67-95	4th	36.5

Monthly records: April (12-14), May (12-14), June (14-13), July (11-14), August (14-16), September (4-24).
*Innings, if other than nine. §Day separate admission. ∞Night separate admission.

RECORDS

2002 regular-season record: 67-95
Position: 4th in A.L. East
Home: 34-47   **Road:** 33-48
A.L. East: 26-50   **A.L. Central:** 18-14
A.L. West: 14-22   **N.L.:** 9-9
Vs. LH starters: 16-28
Vs. RH starters: 51-67
Grass: 56-81   **Artificial:** 11-14
Day: 14-30   **Night:** 53-65
1-Run: 22-25   **X-inn.:** 9-5
Doubleheaders: 0-0-0
Team record past five years: 361-448
(.446, ranks 11th in league in that span)

TEAM LEADERS

Batting average: Gary Matthews Jr.
(.276).
At-bats: Tony Batista (615).
Runs: Tony Batista (90).
Hits: Tony Batista (150).
Total bases: Tony Batista (281).
Doubles: Tony Batista (36).
Triples: Chris Singleton (6).
Home runs: Tony Batista (31).
Runs batted in: Tony Batista (87).
Stolen bases: Jerry Hairston Jr. (21).

Slugging percentage: Jay Gibbons
(.482).
On-base percentage: Gary Matthews Jr.
(.355).
Wins: Rodrigo Lopez (15).
Earned-run average: Rodrigo Lopez
(3.57).
Complete games: Scott Erickson, Sidney
Ponson (3).
Shutouts: Scott Erickson (1).
Saves: Jorge Julio (25).
Innings pitched: Rodrigo Lopez (196.2).
Strikeouts: Rodrigo Lopez (136).

GAMES BY POSITION

Catcher: Geronimo Gil 125, Brook
Fordyce 55, Raul Casanova 2, Fernando
Lunar 2, Izzy Molina 1.
First base: Jeff Conine 103, Jay Gibbons
30, Jose Leon 17, Chris Richard 9, Ryan
McGuire 7, David Segui 7, Howie Clark 1,
Luis Lopez 1.
Second base: Jerry Hairston Jr. 119,
Brian Roberts 25, Luis Lopez 12, Melvin
Mora 12, Mike Moriarty 2.
Third base: Tony Batista 154, Jose Leon
12, Mike Moriarty 1.
Shortstop: Mike Bordick 117, Melvin
Mora 41, Luis Lopez 22, Mike Moriarty

4, Eddie Rogers 4.
Outfield: Chris Singleton 126, Melvin
Mora 104, Gary Matthews Jr. 100, Jay
Gibbons 92, Marty Cordova 72, Luis
Matos 14, Larry Bigbie 12, Jeff Conine 6,
Howie Clark 4, Luis Garcia 2, Jose Leon
2.
Designated hitter: Marty Cordova 56,
Chris Richard 36, David Segui 19, Jay
Gibbons 12, Howie Clark 8, Brian
Roberts 8, Tony Batista 7, Jeff Conine 7,
Melvin Mora 3, Jose Leon 2, Gary
Matthews Jr. 2, Luis Lopez 1, Luis Matos
1, Ryan McGuire 1, Chris Singleton 1.

TOP DRAFT CHOICES

1. **Adam Loewen**, LHP, Fraser Valley
   Christian H.S., Surrey, B.C.
2. **Corey Shafer**, OF, Choctaw (Okla.) H.S.
3. **Val Majewski**, OF, Rutgers.
4. **Tim Gilhooly**, OF, Pacific.
5. **Hayden Penn**, RHP, Santana H.S.,
   Santee, Calif.
6. **John Maine**, RHP, UNC Charlotte.
7. **Paul Henry**, RHP, Ball State.
8. **Ryan Hubele**, C, Texas.
9. **Trevor Caughey**, LHP, Cuesta (Calif.)
   J.C.
10. **Matt Bolander**, RHP, Pendleton
    Heights H.S., Anderson, Ind.

BOSTON RED SOX
AMERICAN LEAGUE EAST DIVISION

2003 SEASON

March/April

SUN	MON	TUE	WED	THU	FRI	SAT
30	31 TB	1 TB	2 TB	3 D TB	4 BAL	5 D BAL
6 D BAL	7	8 TOR	9 TOR	10 TOR	11 D BAL	12 BAL
13 D BAL	14	15 TB	16 TB	17 TB	18 TOR	19 D TOR
20 D TOR	21 D TOR	22 TEX	23 TEX	24 D TEX	25 ANA	26 ANA
27 ANA	28	29 KC	30 KC			

May

SUN	MON	TUE	WED	THU	FRI	SAT
				1 KC	2 MIN	3 D MIN
4 D MIN	5 KC	6 KC	7 D KC	8	9 MIN	10 MIN
11 MIN	12	13 TEX	14 TEX	15 TEX	16 ANA	17 D ANA
18 D ANA	19 NYY	20 NYY	21 NYY	22	23 CLE	24 D CLE
25 CLE	26 D NYY	27 NYY	28 NYY	29	30 TOR	31 D TOR

June

SUN	MON	TUE	WED	THU	FRI	SAT
1 D TOR	2	3 PIT	4 PIT	5 PIT	6 MIL	7 MIL
8 D MIL	9	10 STL	11 STL	12 STL	13 HOU	14 HOU
15 D HOU	16 CWS	17 CWS	18 CWS	19 D CWS	20 PHI	21 D PHI
22 PHI	23 DET	24 DET	25 DET	26 D DET	27 FLA	28 FLA
29 D FLA	30					

July

SUN	MON	TUE	WED	THU	FRI	SAT
		1 TB	2 TB	3 TB	4 D NYY	5 D NYY
6 D NYY	7 NYY	8 TOR	9 TOR	10 TOR	11 DET	12 DET
13 D DET	14	15	16 *	17 TOR	18 TOR	19 TOR
20 D TOR	21 DET	22 DET	23 TB	24 TB	25 D NYY	26 D NYY
27 D NYY	28	29 TEX	30 TEX	31 TEX		

August

SUN	MON	TUE	WED	THU	FRI	SAT
					1 BAL	2 BAL
3 D BAL	4	5 ANA	6 ANA	7 ANA	8 BAL	9 BAL
10 D BAL	11 OAK	12 OAK	13 OAK	14 D OAK	15 SEA	16 D SEA
17 D SEA	18	19 OAK	20 OAK	21 OAK	22 SEA	23 D SEA
24 D SEA	25 D SEA	26 TOR	27 TOR	28	29 NYY	30 D NYY

September

SUN	MON	TUE	WED	THU	FRI	SAT
31 D NYY	1	2 CWS	3 CWS	4	5 NYY	6 D NYY
7 D NYY	8 BAL	9 BAL	10 D BAL	11	12 CWS	13 CWS
14 CWS	15 TB	16 TB	17 TB	18 TB	19 CLE	20 CLE
21 D CLE	22 BAL	23 BAL	24 BAL	25 BAL	26 TB	27 TB
28 D TB						

Home games shaded; D—Day game (games starting before 5 p.m.); *—All-Star Game at Comiskey Park, Chicago. Subject to change.

CLUB DIRECTORY

Principal owner
John W. Henry
President/chief executive officer
Larry Lucchino
General manager
Theo Epstein
Vice president/baseball operations
Michael D. Port
Special assistants to the g.m.
Lee Thomas
Carlton E. Fisk

Director of baseball operations
Kent A. Qualls
Director of player development
David P. Jauss
Director of amateur scouting
David Chadd
Director of international scouting
Louie Eljaua
Vice president, public affairs
Richard L. Bresciani

V.p., assistant g.m. and legal counsel
Elaine W. Steward
Dir. of communications and baseball info.
Kevin J. Shea
Baseball information manager
Glenn Wilburn
Community relations manager
Ronald E. Burton Jr.

MINOR LEAGUE AFFILIATES

Class	Team	League	Manager
AAA	Pawtucket	International	Buddy Bailey
AA	Portland	Eastern	Ron Johnson
A	Sarasota	Florida State	To be announced
A	Augusta	South Atlantic	To be announced
A	Lowell	New York-Pennsylvania	To be announced
Rookie	Gulf Coast Red Sox	Gulf Coast	To be announced

Follow the Red Sox all season at: www.sportingnews.com/baseball/teams/redsox/

BROADCAST INFORMATION

Radio: WEEI-AM (680).
TV: WFXT-TV (Fox 25).
Cable TV: New England Sports Network.

SPRING TRAINING

Ballpark (city): City of Palms Park (Fort Myers, Fla.).
Ticket information: 941-334-4700.

Manager—Grady Little (3).
Coaches—Tony Cloninger (40), Mike Cubbage (39), Dana LaVangie (60), Jerry Narron, Euclides Rojas, Dallas Williams.

No.	PITCHERS	B/T	Ht./Wt.	Born	Age*	2002 clubs
44	Arrojo, Rolando	R/R	6-4/236	7-18-68	34	Boston, Gulf Coast Red Sox, Sarasota
46	Banks, Willie	R/R	6-1/200	2-27-69	34	Boston, Pawtucket
19	Burkett, John	R/R	6-3/215	11-28-64	38	Pawtucket, Boston
	Castillo, Frank	R/R	6-1/198	4-1-69	34	Boston
74	de la Rosa, Jorge	L/L	6-1/190	4-5-81	21	Sarasota, Trenton
43	Embree, Alan	L/L	6-2/190	1-23-70	33	San Diego, Boston
15	Fossum, Casey	B/L	6-1/165	1-6-78	25	Boston, Pawtucket
61	Gomes, Wayne	R/R	6-2/225	1-15-73	30	Nashville, Pawtucket, Boston
46	Howry, Bobby	L/R	6-5/220	8-4-73	29	Chicago A.L., Boston
	Lopez, Javier	L/L	5-10/165	2-22-83	20	El Paso
32	Lowe, Derek	R/R	6-6/214	6-1-73	29	Boston
	Lyon, Brandon	R/R	6-1/185	8-10-79	23	Toronto, Syracuse
73	Martinez, Anastacio	R/R	6-2/180	11-3-80	22	Trenton
45	Martinez, Pedro	R/R	5-11/180	10-25-71	31	Boston
57	Pena, Juan	R/R	6-5/215	6-27-77	25	Pawtucket
24	Rupe, Ryan	R/R	6-5/248	3-31-75	28	Tampa Bay
	Shibilo, Andy	R/R	6-7/220	9-16-76	26	Mobile, Trenton, Pawtucket
50	Timlin, Mike	R/R	6-4/210	3-10-66	37	St. Louis, Philadelphia
49	Wakefield, Tim	R/R	6-2/214	8-2-66	36	Boston
	White, Matt	R/L	6-1/180	8-19-77	25	Akron, Buffalo

No.	CATCHERS	B/T	Ht./Wt.	Born	Age*	2002 clubs
28	Mirabelli, Doug	R/R	6-1/227	10-18-70	32	Boston
33	Varitek, Jason	B/R	6-2/237	4-11-72	30	Boston

No.	INFIELDERS	B/T	Ht./Wt.	Born	Age*	2002 clubs
10	Baerga, Carlos	B/R	5-11/215	11-4-68	34	Boston
2	Crespo, Cesar	B/R	5-11/170	5-23-79	23	Portland, San Diego
5	Garciaparra, Nomar	R/R	6-0/190	7-23-73	29	Boston
7	Giambi, Jeremy	L/L	5-11/216	9-30-74	28	Oakland, Philadelphia
29	Hillenbrand, Shea	R/R	6-1/211	7-27-75	27	Boston
2	Jackson, Damian	R/R	5-11/185	8-16-73	29	Detroit
26	Merloni, Lou	R/R	5-10/201	4-6-71	31	Boston, Pawtucket
	Mueller, Bill	B/R	5-10/180	3-17-71	32	Iowa, Chicago N.L., San Francisco
52	Sanchez, Freddy	R/R	5-11/185	12-21-77	25	Trenton, Pawtucket, Boston
53	Santos, Angel	B/R	5-11/180	8-14-79	23	Pawtucket
12	Walker, Todd	L/R	6-0/190	5-25-73	29	Cincinnati

No.	OUTFIELDERS	B/T	Ht./Wt.	Born	Age*	2002 clubs
50	Agbayani, Benny	R/R	6-0/225	12-28-71	31	Colorado, Colorado Springs, Pawtucket, Boston
13	Brown, Adrian	B/R	6-0/200	2-7-74	29	Pittsburgh, Nashville
18	Damon, Johnny	L/L	6-2/190	11-5-73	29	Boston
35	Henderson, Rickey	R/L	5-10/190	12-25-58	44	Boston
7	Nixon, Trot	L/L	6-2/211	4-11-74	28	Boston
24	Ramirez, Manny	R/R	6-0/213	5-30-72	30	Boston, Pawtucket
67	Stenson, Dernell	L/L	6-1/230	6-17-78	24	Pawtucket

*Age as of April 1, 2003.

Ballpark (capacity, surface)
Fenway Park (33,991; grass)

Address
4 Yawkey Way
Boston, MA 02215-3496

Official website
www.redsox.com

Business phone
617-267-9440

Ticket information
617-267-1700, 617-482-4769

Field dimensions (from home plate)
To left field at foul line, 310 feet
To center field, 390 feet
To right field at foul line, 302 feet

First game played
April 20, 1912
(Red Sox 7, New York Highlanders 6)

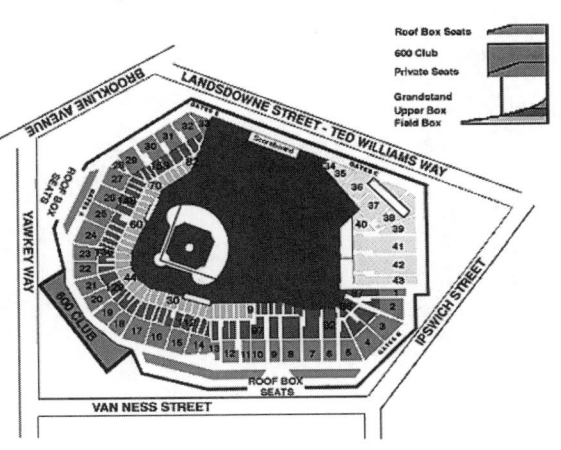

Date	Opp.	Res.	Score	(inn.*)	Hits	Opp. hits	Winning pitcher	Losing pitcher	Save	Record	Pos.	GB
4-1	Tor.	L	11-12		13	14	Escobar	Urbina		0-1	T4th	1.0
4-5	At Bal.	W	3-0		11	2	Lowe	Towers	Urbina	1-1	4th	1.0
4-6	At Bal.	W	4-2		8	4	Fossum	Erickson	Urbina	2-1	2nd	1.0
4-7	At Bal.	W	4-1		9	6	Martinez	Maduro	Urbina	3-1	2nd	1.0
4-9	K.C.	W	8-4		15	5	Wakefield	Reichert		4-1	2nd	1.5
4-10	K.C.	L	2-6		5	12	Byrd	Lowe	Bailey	4-2	2nd	1.5
4-11	K.C.	L	5-8		7	7	Grimsley	Urbina		4-3	2nd	1.5
4-12	N.Y.	W	3-2		11	9	Oliver	Hernandez	Urbina	5-3	2nd	0.5
4-13	N.Y.	W	7-6		9	8	Arrojo	Rivera	Urbina	6-3	1st	+0.5
4-14	N.Y.	L	2-6		6	8	Mussina	Wakefield	Rivera	6-4	2nd	0.5
4-15	N.Y.	W	4-3		11	6	Lowe	Pettitte	Urbina	7-4	1st	+0.5
4-16	At Tor.	W	14-3		14	4	Castillo	Lyon	Arrojo	8-4	1st	+1.5
4-17	At Tor.	W	10-3		13	9	Oliver	Eyre		9-4	1st	+1.5
4-19	At K.C.	W	4-0		7	2	Martinez	George		10-4	1st	+1.0
4-21†	At K.C.	W	12-2		16	7	Burkett	Reichert	Wakefield	11-4		
4-21‡	At K.C.	W	8-7		14	10	Lowe	Rekar	Urbina	12-4	1st	+2.0
4-23	At Bal.	L	5-7		8	12	Erickson	Castillo	Julio	12-5	1st	+1.0
4-24	At Bal.	L	3-5		12	10	Lopez	Oliver	Julio	12-6	1st	...
4-25	At Bal.	W	7-0		13	2	Martinez	Maduro		13-6	1st	+1.0
4-26	T.B.	W	4-2		10	5	Burkett	Wilson	Urbina	14-6	1st	+1.0
4-27	T.B.	W	10-0		13	0	Lowe	James		15-6	1st	+2.0
4-29	Bal.	L	3-5		8	10	Lopez	Castillo	Julio	15-7	1st	+1.0
4-30	Bal.	W	4-0		7	8	Oliver	Maduro		16-7	1st	+1.0
5-1	Bal.	W	15-3		16	7	Martinez	Douglass		17-7	1st	+2.0
5-3	At T.B.	W	3-2		7	7	Fossum	Colome	Urbina	18-7	1st	+2.5
5-4	At T.B.	W	7-5		10	9	Kim	Zambrano	Urbina	19-7	1st	+3.5
5-5	At T.B.	W	2-0		6	4	Castillo	Rupe	Urbina	20-7	1st	+4.5
5-6	At T.B.	W	5-3		14	6	Oliver	Sturtze	Wakefield	21-7	1st	+5.0
5-7	At Oak.	W	9-7		15	12	Arrojo	Mecir	Urbina	22-7	1st	+5.0
5-8	At Oak.	W	12-6		19	9	Burkett	Hiljus		23-7	1st	+5.0
5-9	At Oak.	W	5-1		7	6	Lowe	Hudson		24-7	1st	+5.0
5-10	At Sea.	L	2-7		10	8	Pineiro	Castillo	Soriano	24-8	1st	+4.0
5-11	At Sea.	L	1-3		8	6	Halama	Oliver	Sasaki	24-9	1st	+3.0
5-12	At Sea.	W	10-4		16	6	Martinez	Baldwin		25-9	1st	+3.0
5-14	Oak.	W	6-2		8	11	Burkett	Hudson		26-9	1st	+3.0
5-15	Oak.	W	8-2		12	7	Lowe	Hiljus		27-9	1st	+4.0
5-16	Oak.	L	0-5		7	10	Zito	Castillo		27-10	1st	+3.0
5-17	Sea.	L	3-6		9	9	Franklin	Arrojo	Sasaki	27-11	1st	+2.0
5-18	Sea.	W	4-1		10	6	Martinez	Baldwin	Urbina	28-11	1st	+2.0
5-19	Sea.	W	3-2		9	7	Burkett	Garcia	Urbina	29-11	1st	+2.0
5-20	Chi.	W	9-0		13	3	Lowe	Ritchie		30-11	1st	+2.0
5-21	Chi.	L	3-8		5	15	Wright	Oliver		30-12	1st	+1.0
5-22	Chi.	L	0-2		3	7	Garland	Castillo	Foulke	30-13	1st	+1.0
5-23	N.Y.	W	3-1		8	5	Martinez	Lilly	Urbina	31-13	1st	+2.0
5-24	N.Y.	W	9-8	(11)	16	14	Arrojo	Karsay		32-13	1st	+3.0
5-25	N.Y.	L	2-3		6	8	Mendoza	Lowe	Rivera	32-14	1st	+2.0
5-26	N.Y.	L	5-14		10	15	Mussina	Oliver		32-15	1st	+1.0
5-27	At Tor.	W	8-6		11	11	Castillo	Halladay	Urbina	33-15	1st	+1.0
5-28	At Tor.	W	6-4		12	9	Wakefield	Escobar	Urbina	34-15	1st	+1.0
5-29	At Tor.	W	7-4		6	8	Burkett	Cassidy	Fossum	35-15	1st	+1.0
5-31	At N.Y.	W	5-2		8	6	Lowe	Wells		36-15	1st	+2.0
6-1	At N.Y.	L	2-10		5	13	Mussina	Oliver		36-16	1st	+1.0
6-2	At N.Y.	W	7-1		12	6	Castillo	Lilly		37-16	1st	+2.0
6-3	At Det.	L	6-7	(10)	12	11	Acevedo	Wakefield		37-17	1st	+2.0
6-4	At Det.	W	10-5		13	11	Burkett	Lima		38-17	1st	+2.0
6-5	At Det.	W	11-0		16	5	Lowe	Bernero	Haney	39-17	1st	+3.0
6-6	At Det.	W	4-3		14	6	Arrojo	Redman	Urbina	40-17	1st	+3.5
6-7	Ari.	L	5-7		7	15	Batista	Castillo	Kim	40-18	1st	+2.5
6-8	Ari.	L	2-3		7	7	Schilling	Martinez	Kim	40-19	1st	+2.5
6-9	Ari.	L	3-7		8	12	Helling	Burkett		40-20	1st	+1.5
6-10	Col.	W	7-3		11	10	Lowe	Neagle	Wakefield	41-20	1st	+1.5
6-11	Col.	L	1-3		5	6	Jennings	Fossum	Jimenez	41-21	1st	+0.5
6-12	Col.	W	7-5		11	10	Castillo	Hampton	Urbina	42-21	1st	+1.5
6-14	At Atl.	L	1-2		3	8	Hammond	Martinez	Smoltz	42-22	1st	+0.5
6-15	At Atl.	L	2-4		8	10	Maddux	Burkett	Smoltz	42-23	1st	+0.5

Date	Opp.	Res.	Score	(inn.*)	Hits	Opp. hits	Winning pitcher	Losing pitcher	Save	Record	Pos.	GB
6-16	At Atl.	W	6-1		8	7	Lowe	Glavine		43-23	1st	+1.5
6-18	At S.D.	W	4-2		10	6	Banks	Lawrence	Urbina	44-23	1st	+1.5
6-19	At S.D.	L	2-3		6	5	Tomko	Castillo	Hoffman	44-24	1st	+0.5
6-20	At S.D.	W	5-0		7	2	Martinez	Pickford		45-24	1st	+1.5
6-21	At L.A.	L	2-3		6	8	Nomo	Burkett	Gagne	45-25	1st	+1.5
6-22	At L.A.	L	4-5		7	6	Daal	Lowe	Gagne	45-26	1st	+0.5
6-23	At L.A.	L	6-9		9	13	Ashby	Arrojo		45-27	2nd	0.5
6-25	Cle.	L	2-4		10	9	Baez	Castillo	Wickman	45-28	2nd	0.5
6-26	Cle.	W	7-4		10	7	Martinez	Drese	Urbina	46-28	1st	+0.5
6-28	Atl.	L	2-4		5	11	Remlinger	Wakefield	Smoltz	46-29	2nd	1.0
6-29	Atl.	L	1-2		6	6	Millwood	Lowe	Smoltz	46-30	2nd	1.0
6-30	Atl.	L	3-7	(10)	5	14	Remlinger	Urbina		46-31	2nd	2.0
7-1	Tor.	W	4-0		10	7	Martinez	Parris		47-31	2nd	1.5
7-2§	Tor.	W	2-1		6	6	Banks	Eyre	Embree	48-31		
7-2∞	Tor.	W	6-4		7	9	Kim	Smith	Embree	49-31	2nd	1.0
7-3	Tor.	W	5-2		11	11	Gomes	Politte	Urbina	50-31	2nd	1.0
7-4	Tor.	W	9-5		10	7	Lowe	Heredia		51-31	2nd	1.0
7-5	Det.	L	5-9		11	14	Redman	Castillo		51-32	2nd	2.0
7-6	Det.	W	8-0		10	2	Martinez	Maroth		52-32	2nd	1.0
7-7	Det.	L	8-9		13	14	Farnsworth	Garces	Acevedo	52-33	2nd	2.0
7-11	At Tor.	W	10-3		12	7	Burkett	Walker		53-33	2nd	2.0
7-12	At Tor.	L	0-5		3	9	Halladay	Lowe		53-34	2nd	2.0
7-13	At Tor.	L	1-4		7	12	Carpenter	Castillo		53-35	2nd	3.0
7-14	At Tor.	L	5-6		9	9	Escobar	Urbina		53-36	2nd	3.0
7-15	At Det.	L	3-4	(11)	9	10	Henriquez	Gomes		53-37	2nd	3.0
7-16	At Det.	W	9-4		18	8	Burkett	Farnsworth		54-37	2nd	3.0
7-17	At T.B.	W	6-1		11	2	Lowe	Wilson		55-37	2nd	3.0
7-18	At T.B.	W	4-3		9	5	Wakefield	Yan	Urbina	56-37	2nd	3.0
7-19	At N.Y.	W	4-2		7	5	Martinez	Mussina	Urbina	57-37	2nd	2.0
7-20	At N.Y.	L	8-9	(11)	12	13	Karsay	Gomes		57-38	2nd	3.0
7-21	At N.Y.	L	8-9		11	11	Stanton	Urbina		57-39	2nd	4.0
7-23§	T.B.	W	22-4		19	7	Wakefield	Sturtze	Banks	58-39		
7-23∞	T.B.	L	4-5		11	9	Zambrano	Urbina	Yan	58-40	2nd	3.5
7-24	T.B.	L	5-9		10	14	Colome	Castillo	Zambrano	58-41	2nd	4.5
7-25	T.B.	W	6-0		8	3	Martinez	de los Santos		59-41	2nd	4.0
7-26	Bal.	L	2-9		4	16	Lopez	Arrojo		59-42	2nd	5.0
7-27	Bal.	W	4-0		8	4	Burkett	Ponson		60-42	2nd	4.0
7-28	Bal.	W	12-3		14	8	Lowe	Erickson		61-42	2nd	4.0
7-29	At Ana.	L	4-5		9	8	Schoeneweis	Embree	Percival	61-43	2nd	5.0
7-30	At Ana.	W	6-0		9	2	Martinez	Ortiz		62-43	2nd	5.0
7-31	At Ana.	W	2-1		8	8	Wakefield	Lackey	Urbina	63-43	2nd	4.0
8-1	At Tex.	L	7-19		11	20	Park	Burkett		63-44	2nd	4.0
8-2	At Tex.	W	13-0		15	3	Lowe	Valdes		64-44	2nd	4.0
8-3	At Tex.	L	6-8		12	9	Kolb	Howry		64-45	2nd	4.0
8-4	At Tex.	W	11-3		19	8	Martinez	Myette		65-45	2nd	4.0
8-6	Oak.	L	1-9		7	8	Mulder	Wakefield		65-46	2nd	4.0
8-7	Oak.	L	2-3		7	9	Harang	Burkett	Koch	65-47	2nd	5.0
8-8	Oak.	W	4-2		7	6	Lowe	Zito	Urbina	66-47	2nd	5.0
8-9	Min.	L	4-5		8	12	Romero	Castillo	Guardado	66-48	2nd	5.0
8-10	Min.	W	2-0		9	4	Martinez	Mays	Urbina	67-48	2nd	4.0
8-11	Min.	W	3-1		5	4	Wakefield	Santana	Urbina	68-48	2nd	4.0
8-13	At Sea.	L	3-10		9	16	Pineiro	Burkett		68-49	2nd	5.0
8-14	At Sea.	W	12-5		14	8	Lowe	Moyer		69-49	2nd	5.0
8-15	At Sea.	L	3-4		10	8	Garcia	Fossum	Sasaki	69-50	2nd	6.0
8-16	At Min.	L	0-5		2	8	Mays	Martinez		69-51	2nd	7.0
8-17	At Min.	W	5-2		9	6	Wakefield	Santana		70-51	2nd	7.0
8-18	At Min.	L	2-6		8	10	Reed	Burkett		70-52	2nd	7.0
8-20	Tex.	L	2-3	(10)	7	7	Rodriguez	Banks	Cordero	70-53	2nd	8.0
8-21	Tex.	W	5-3		12	8	Howry	Kolb	Urbina	71-53	2nd	7.0
8-22	Tex.	W	12-3		14	6	Hermanson	Reyes	Castillo	72-53	2nd	7.0
8-23	Ana.	W	4-1		11	6	Martinez	Washburn	Urbina	73-53	2nd	6.0
8-24	Ana.	L	0-2		5	9	Appier	Wakefield	Percival	73-54	2nd	7.0
8-25	Ana.	L	3-8		7	16	Schoeneweis	Lowe		73-55	2nd	7.0
8-26	Ana.	W	10-9	(10)	18	17	Urbina	Shields		74-55	2nd	7.0
8-27	N.Y.	L	0-6		5	13	Wells	Fossum		74-56	2nd	8.0
8-28	N.Y.	L	0-7		3	9	Mussina	Martinez		74-57	2nd	9.0
8-30	At Cle.	W	15-5		16	11	Lowe	Wright		75-57	2nd	8.5
8-31	At Cle.	L	7-8		12	13	Baez	Howry		75-58	2nd	8.5

Date	Opp.	Res.	Score	(inn.*)	Hits	Opp. hits	Winning pitcher	Losing pitcher	Save	Record	Pos.	GB
9-1	At Cle.	W	7-1		10	4	Wakefield	Nagy		76-58	2nd	7.5
9-2	At N.Y.	W	8-4		11	11	Fossum	Mussina		77-58	2nd	6.5
9-3	At N.Y.	L	2-4		5	6	Clemens	Castillo	Stanton	77-59	2nd	7.5
9-4	At N.Y.	L	1-3		8	7	Pettitte	Lowe	Karsay	77-60	2nd	8.5
9-5	Tor.	L	4-5		6	13	Miller	Hermanson	Escobar	77-61	2nd	9.5
9-6	Tor.	W	7-2		15	6	Wakefield	Halladay		78-61	2nd	9.5
9-7	Tor.	W	4-1		7	3	Fossum	Bowles	Urbina	79-61	2nd	8.5
9-8	Tor.	L	4-9		11	13	Loaiza	Castillo		79-62	2nd	9.5
9-9	At T.B.	W	6-3		14	6	Lowe	Sturtze	Urbina	80-62	2nd	9.0
9-10	At T.B.	W	12-1		15	7	Burkett	Kennedy		81-62	2nd	9.5
9-11	At T.B.	W	6-3		12	8	Martinez	Wilson	Urbina	82-62	2nd	9.5
9-12	At T.B.	W	6-3		7	8	Wakefield	Yan	Urbina	83-62	2nd	9.5
9-13	Bal.	L	3-8		6	12	Lopez	Fossum		83-63	2nd	9.5
9-14	Bal.	W	6-4		11	10	Lowe	Hentgen	Urbina	84-63	2nd	8.5
9-15	Bal.	L	3-8		10	10	Johnson	Burkett		84-64	2nd	9.5
9-16§	Cle.	W	6-1		11	4	Martinez	Rodriguez		85-64		
9-16∞	Cle.	L	1-7		6	7	Tallet	Castillo		85-65	2nd	9.5
9-17	Cle.	W	4-2		8	6	Wakefield	Sabathia	Urbina	86-65	2nd	8.5
9-18	Cle.	L	4-6		9	11	Riske	Embree	Baez	86-66	2nd	9.5
9-20	At Bal.	W	4-2		5	11	Lowe	Hentgen	Urbina	87-66	2nd	9.0
9-21	At Bal.	W	3-0		8	2	Burkett	Johnson	Urbina	88-66	2nd	9.0
9-22	At Bal.	W	13-2		14	9	Martinez	Ponson		89-66	2nd	9.0
9-23	At Bal.	W	5-4	(15)	11	6	Embree	Roberts	Gomes	90-66	2nd	8.0
9-24	At Chi.	W	4-2		8	9	Fossum	Garland	Urbina	91-66	2nd	8.0
9-25	At Chi.	L	2-7		6	7	Biddle	Lowe		91-67	2nd	9.0
9-26	At Chi.	L	2-3		4	5	Wright	Hancock	Foulke	91-68	2nd	9.5
9-27	T.B.	W	6-1		9	5	Burkett	Wilson		92-68	2nd	9.5
9-28	T.B.	L	6-9		8	12	Zambrano	Howry	Carter	92-69	2nd	10.5
9-29	T.B.	W	11-8		15	12	Castillo	Alvarez	Urbina	93-69	2nd	10.5

Monthly records: April (16-7), May (20-8), June (10-16), July (17-12), August (12-15), September (18-11).
*Innings, if other than nine. †First game of a doubleheader. ‡Second game of a doubleheader. §Day separate admission. ∞Night separate admission.

RECORDS

2002 regular-season record: 93-69
Position: 2nd in A.L. East
Home: 42-39 **Road:** 51-30
A.L. East: 51-25 **A.L. Central:** 19-17
A.L. West: 18-14 **N.L.:** 5-13
Vs. LH starters: 24-12
Vs. RH starters: 69-57
Grass: 76-64 **Artificial:** 17-5
Day: 30-20 **Night:** 63-49
1-Run: 13-23 **X-inn.:** 3-5
Doubleheaders: 1-0-0
Team record past five years: 446-363 (.551, ranks 4th in league in that span)

TEAM LEADERS

Batting average: Manny Ramirez (.349).
At-bats: Nomar Garciaparra (635).
Runs: Johnny Damon (118).
Hits: Nomar Garciaparra (197).
Total bases: Nomar Garciaparra (335).
Doubles: Nomar Garciaparra (56).
Triples: Johnny Damon (11).
Home runs: Manny Ramirez (33).
Runs batted in: Nomar Garciaparra (120).
Stolen bases: Johnny Damon (31).
Slugging percentage: Manny Ramirez (.647).

On-base percentage: Manny Ramirez (.450).
Wins: Derek Lowe (21).
Earned-run average: Pedro Martinez (2.26).
Complete games: Pedro Martinez (2).
Shutouts: John Burkett, Derek Lowe, Darren Oliver (1).
Saves: Ugueth Urbina (40).
Innings pitched: Derek Lowe (219.2).
Strikeouts: Pedro Martinez (239).

GAMES BY POSITION

Catcher: Jason Varitek 127, Doug Mirabelli 50, Kevin L. Brown 2.
First base: Tony Clark 85, Brian Daubach 60, Jose Offerman 41, Lou Merloni 3, Shane Andrews 2, Juan Diaz 1.
Second base: Rey Sanchez 100, Lou Merloni 66, Carlos Baerga 17, Bry Nelson 11, Freddy Sanchez 5.
Third base: Shea Hillenbrand 156, Lou Merloni 8, Shane Andrews 4, Carlos Baerga 1.
Shortstop: Nomar Garciaparra 154, Rey Sanchez 10, Lou Merloni 5, Freddy Sanchez 5.
Outfield: Trot Nixon 152, Johnny Damon 151, Manny Ramirez 68, Rickey Henderson 54, Brian Daubach 48, Cliff Floyd 26, Benny Agbayani 13, Bry Nelson 11, Lou Merloni 2, Jose Offerman 2, Shane Andrews 1.
Designated hitter: Manny Ramirez 51, Carlos Baerga 32, Brian Daubach 28, Jose Offerman 24, Cliff Floyd 19, Rickey Henderson 5, Doug Mirabelli 4, Tony Clark 2, Shane Andrews 1, Johnny Damon 1, Juan Diaz 1, Bry Nelson 1, Freddy Sanchez 1, Jason Varitek 1.

TOP DRAFT CHOICES

2. **Jon Lester,** LHP, Bellarmine Prep, Puyallup, Wash.
3. **Scott White,** 3B, Walton H.S., Marietta, Ga.
4. **Chris Smith,** RHP, UC Riverside.
5. **Chad Spann,** SS, Southland Academy, Buena Vista, Ga.
6. **Barrett Browning,** LHP, Wayne County H.S., Jesup, Ga.
7. **Jason Neighborgall,** RHP, Riverside H.S., Durham, N.C.
8. **Brandon Moss,** SS, Loganville H.S., Monroe, Ga.
9. **Tyler Pelland,** LHP, Mount Abraham H.S., Bristol, Vt.
10. **Greg Stone,** SS, Bacone (Okla.) J.C.

CHICAGO WHITE SOX
AMERICAN LEAGUE CENTRAL DIVISION

2003 SEASON

March/April

SUN	MON	TUE	WED	THU	FRI	SAT
30	31 D KC	1	2 D KC	3 D KC	4 D DET	5 D DET
6 D DET	7 D CLE	8	9 CLE	10 CLE	11 DET	12 D DET
13 D DET	14	15 KC	16 KC	17 D KC	18 CLE	19 D CLE
20 D CLE	21 D CLE	22 BAL	23 BAL	24 BAL	25 MIN	26 MIN
27 MIN	28	29 OAK	30 OAK			

May

SUN	MON	TUE	WED	THU	FRI	SAT
				1 OAK	2 SEA	3 SEA
4 SEA	5	6 OAK	7 OAK	8 D OAK	9 SEA	10 SEA
11 D SEA	12	13 BAL	14 BAL	15 BAL	16 MIN	17 MIN
18 MIN	19 TOR	20 TOR	21 TOR	22	23 DET	24 DET
25 D DET	26 TOR	27 TOR	28 TOR	29 TOR	30 CLE	31 D CLE

June

SUN	MON	TUE	WED	THU	FRI	SAT
1 CLE	2 D CLE	3 D ARI	4 ARI	5 ARI	6 LA	7 LA
8 D LA	9	10 SF	11 SF	12 SF	13 SD	14 SD
15 D SD	16 D BOS	17 BOS	18 BOS	19 D BOS	20 D CUB	21 D CUB
22 CUB	23	24 MIN	25 MIN	26 D MIN	27 D CUB	28 D CUB
29 CUB	30 D MIN					

July

SUN	MON	TUE	WED	THU	FRI	SAT
		1 MIN	2 MIN	3	4 TB	5 TB
6 D TB	7	8 DET	9 DET	10 DET	11 D CLE	12 CLE
13 D CLE	14	15 *	16	17 DET	18 DET	19 DET
20 D DET	21 CLE	22 D CLE	23 TOR	24 TOR	25 TB	26 TB
27 TB	28	29 KC	30 KC	31 KC		

August

SUN	MON	TUE	WED	THU	FRI	SAT
					1 SEA	2 SEA
3 SEA	4 KC	5 KC	6 D KC	7	8 OAK	9 OAK
10 D OAK	11 ANA	12 ANA	13 ANA	14 ANA	15 TEX	16 TEX
17 TEX	18 ANA	19 ANA	20 ANA	21 TEX	22 TEX	23 TEX
24 D TEX	25	26 NYY	27 NYY	28 D NYY	29 DET	30 DET

September

SUN	MON	TUE	WED	THU	FRI	SAT
31 DET	1 D	2 BOS	3 BOS	4	5 CLE	6 D CLE
7 CLE	8 MIN	9 MIN	10 MIN	11 D MIN	12 BOS	13 BOS
14 BOS	15	16 MIN	17 MIN	18 MIN	19 KC	20 KC
21 KC	22 NYY	23 NYY	24 D NYY	25 KC	26 KC	27 KC
28 D KC						

Home games shaded; D—Day game (games starting before 5 p.m.); *—All-Star Game at Comiskey Park, Chicago. Subject to change.

CLUB DIRECTORY

Chairman
Jerry Reinsdorf
Vice chairman
Eddie Einhorn
Executive vice president
Howard Pizer
Senior vice president, general manager
Ken Williams

Vice president, free agent and major league scouting
Larry Monroe
Executive advisor to Ken Williams
Roland Hemond
Assistant general manager
Rick Hahn
Senior director of scouting
Duane Shaffer

Director of scouting
Doug Laumann
Director of player development
Bob Fontaine Jr.
Director of community relations
Christine O'Reilly
Director of public relations
Scott Reifert

MINOR LEAGUE AFFILIATES

Class	Team	League	Manager
AAA	Charlotte	International	Nick Capra
AA	Birmingham	Southern	Wally Backman
A	Winston-Salem	Carolina	Razor Shines
A	Kannapolis	South Atlantic	John Orton
Rookie	Bristol	Appalachian	Jerry Hairston
Rookie	Great Falls	Pioneer	Chris Cron

BROADCAST INFORMATION

Radio: ESPN-AM (1000).
TV: WGN-TV (Channel 9).
Cable TV: Fox Sports Chicago.

SPRING TRAINING

Ballpark (city): Tucson Electric Park (Tucson, Ariz.).
Ticket information: 520-434-1111.

Follow the White Sox all season at: www.sportingnews.com/baseball/teams/whitesox/

SPRING TRAINING ROSTER

Manager—Jerry Manuel (7).
Coaches—Don Cooper (63), Bruce Kimm, Art Kusnyer (53), Joe Nossek (23), Rafael Santana, Gary Ward (47), Man Soo Lee (59).

No.	PITCHERS	B/T	Ht./Wt.	Born	Age*	2002 clubs
	Adkins, Jon	L/R	6-0/200	8-30-77	25	Modesto, Sacramento, Charlotte
55	Almonte, Edwin	R/R	6-3/200	12-17-76	26	Charlotte
56	Buehrle, Mark	L/L	6-2/200	3-23-79	24	Chicago A.L.
	Colon, Bartolo	R/R	6-0/235	5-24-73	29	Cleveland, Montreal
	Diaz, Felix	R/R	6-1/180	7-27-81	21	Shreveport, Birmingham
52	Garland, Jon	R/R	6-6/205	9-27-79	23	Chicago A.L.
58	Ginter, Matt	R/R	6-1/220	12-24-77	25	Charlotte, Chicago A.L.
38	Glover, Gary	R/R	6-5/205	12-3-76	26	Chicago A.L.
43	Marte, Damaso	L/L	6-2/200	2-14-75	28	Chicago A.L.
41	Porzio, Mike	L/L	6-3/190	8-20-72	30	Chicago A.L., Charlotte
51	Rauch, Jon	R/R	6-10/230	9-27-78	24	Chicago A.L., Charlotte
36	Wright, Dan	R/R	6-5/225	12-14-77	25	Chicago A.L.
65	Wunsch, Kelly	L/L	6-5/225	7-12-72	30	Charlotte, Chicago A.L.
	Wylie, Mitch	R/R	6-3/190	1-14-77	26	Charlotte

No.	CATCHERS	B/T	Ht./Wt.	Born	Age*	2002 clubs
15	Alomar, Sandy	R/R	6-5/235	6-18-66	36	Chicago A.L., Charlotte, Colorado
61	Olivo, Miguel	R/R	6-0/180	7-15-78	24	Birmingham, Chicago A.L.
27	Paul, Josh	R/R	6-1/200	5-19-75	27	Charlotte, Chicago A.L.

No.	INFIELDERS	B/T	Ht./Wt.	Born	Age*	2002 clubs
24	Crede, Joe	R/R	6-2/195	4-26-78	24	Charlotte, Chicago A.L.
17	Graffanino, Tony	R/R	6-1/190	6-6-72	30	Chicago A.L.
12	Harris, Willie	L/R	5-9/175	6-22-78	24	Charlotte, Chicago A.L.
28	Jimenez, D'Angelo	B/R	6-0/194	12-21-77	25	San Diego, Charlotte, Chicago A.L.
14	Konerko, Paul	R/R	6-2/215	3-5-76	27	Chicago A.L.
22	Valentin, Jose	B/R	5-10/185	10-12-69	33	Chicago A.L.

No.	OUTFIELDERS	B/T	Ht./Wt.	Born	Age*	2002 clubs
25	Borchard, Joe	B/R	6-5/220	11-25-78	24	Winston-Salem, Charlotte, Chicago A.L.
45	Lee, Carlos	R/R	6-2/235	6-20-76	26	Chicago A.L.
30	Ordonez, Magglio	R/R	6-0/210	1-28-74	29	Chicago A.L.
	Rios, Armando	L/L	5-9/185	9-13-71	31	Pittsburgh, Altoona, Nashville
44	Rowand, Aaron	R/R	6-1/200	8-29-77	25	Chicago A.L.

*Age as of April 1, 2003.

BALLPARK INFORMATION

Ballpark (capacity, surface)
Comiskey Park (47,098, grass)

Address
333 W. 35th St.
Chicago, IL 60616

Official website
www.whitesox.com

Business phone
312-674-1000

Ticket information
312-674-1000

Field dimensions (from home plate)
To left field at foul line, 330 feet
To center field, 400 feet
To right field at foul line, 335 feet

First game played
April 18, 1991 (Tigers 16, White Sox 0)

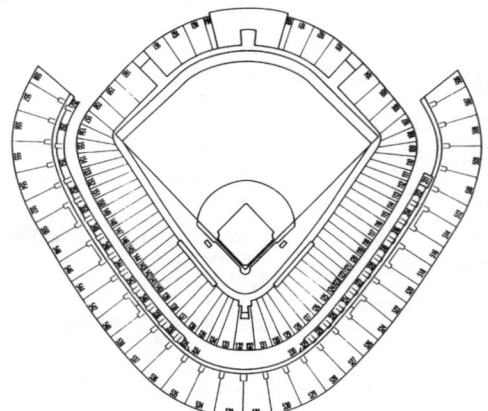

Date	Opp.	Res.	Score	(inn.*)	Hits	Opp. hits	Winning pitcher	Losing pitcher	Save	Record	Pos.	GB
4-1	At Sea.	W	6-5		11	8	Buehrle	Garcia	Foulke	1-0	T1st	...
4-2	At Sea.	L	4-7		10	10	Rhodes	Barcelo	Sasaki	1-1	T2nd	0.5
4-3	At Sea.	L	6-7		5	12	Franklin	Foulke		1-2	3rd	1.5
4-5	At K.C.	L	2-5		10	6	Byrd	Garland	Stein	1-3	4th	2.0
4-6	At K.C.	W	14-0		16	6	Buehrle	Durbin		2-3	3rd	2.0
4-7	At K.C.	L	2-9		7	9	Suppan	Ritchie		2-4	4th	3.0
4-9	At Det.	W	8-2		14	6	Wright	Sparks		3-4	3rd	3.5
4-10	At Det.	W	7-5		9	13	Osuna	Lima	Foulke	4-4	3rd	3.5
4-12	Bal.	W	5-2		9	4	Buehrle	Towers	Foulke	5-4	2nd	4.0
4-13	Bal.	W	4-3		11	4	Osuna	Roberts	Foulke	6-4	2nd	4.0
4-14	Bal.	L	4-9		12	11	Maduro	Wright		6-5	3rd	4.5
4-15	Bal.	W	13-4		15	8	Garland	Johnson		7-5	3rd	4.0
4-16	Cle.	W	10-5		12	7	Marte	Finley		8-5	3rd	3.0
4-17	Cle.	W	7-2		13	7	Buehrle	Baez		9-5	2nd	2.0
4-18	Cle.	W	7-1		8	7	Ritchie	Colon		10-5	2nd	1.0
4-19	Det.	L	2-8		6	14	Sparks	Wright		10-6	3rd	1.0
4-20	Det.	W	12-5		15	8	Garland	Cornejo		11-6	T2nd	0.5
4-21	Det.	W	11-8		11	10	Osuna	Paniagua	Foulke	12-6	2nd	0.5
4-22	At Cle.	L	2-4		6	8	Baez	Buehrle	Wickman	12-7	T2nd	1.0
4-23	At Cle.	W	5-1		13	5	Ritchie	Colon		13-7	T1st	...
4-24	At Cle.	W	9-2		10	8	Wright	Sabathia		14-7	1st	+1.0
4-25	At Cle.	W	6-3		9	6	Garland	Drese	Foulke	15-7	1st	+1.0
4-26	At Oak.	L	4-6		7	9	Lidle	Parque	Koch	15-8	1st	+1.0
4-27	At Oak.	L	1-16		4	19	Fyhrie	Buehrle		15-9	1st	+1.0
4-28	At Oak.	L	0-10		3	11	Hudson	Ritchie		15-10	1st	+1.0
4-30	Sea.	W	8-4		13	9	Wright	Abbott		16-10	1st	+0.5
5-1	Sea.	W	9-2	(8)	12	6	Garland	Franklin	Glover	17-10	1st	+0.5
5-2	Sea.	L	4-15		9	16	Baldwin	Rauch		17-11	2nd	0.5
5-3	Oak.	W	6-1		10	6	Buehrle	Fyhrie		18-11	2nd	0.5
5-4	Oak.	W	10-2		10	11	Ritchie	Hudson		19-11	2nd	0.5
5-5	Oak.	L	2-3		6	5	Zito	Wright	Koch	19-12	2nd	0.5
5-6	At Tex.	L	5-6		12	12	Irabu	Osuna		19-13	2nd	1.5
5-7	At Tex.	W	11-6		14	5	Porzio	Bell	Ginter	20-13	2nd	0.5
5-8	At Tex.	W	5-3		8	7	Buehrle	Davis		21-13	2nd	0.5
5-9	At Tex.	L	1-4		4	9	Benoit	Ritchie	Irabu	21-14	2nd	1.0
5-10	At Ana.	L	0-19		3	24	Schoeneweis	Wright		21-15	2nd	1.0
5-11	At Ana.	L	3-6		7	12	Ortiz	Garland	Percival	21-16	2nd	1.0
5-12	At Ana.	L	4-5		11	8	Percival	Foulke		21-17	2nd	1.0
5-14	Tex.	W	15-4		15	8	Buehrle	Davis		22-17	2nd	0.5
5-15	Tex.	L	2-5		2	11	Valdes	Ritchie	Irabu	22-18	2nd	1.5
5-16	Tex.	W	4-0		8	5	Wright	Rogers		23-18	2nd	1.5
5-17	Ana.	L	4-8		9	11	Schoeneweis	Garland	Levine	23-19	2nd	1.5
5-18	Ana.	W	10-4		10	11	Glover	Ortiz		24-19	2nd	0.5
5-19	Ana.	L	1-6		4	12	Washburn	Buehrle		24-20	2nd	0.5
5-20	At Bos.	L	0-9		3	13	Lowe	Ritchie		24-21	2nd	1.0
5-21	At Bos.	W	8-3		15	5	Wright	Oliver		25-21	2nd	1.0
5-22	At Bos.	W	2-0		7	3	Garland	Castillo	Foulke	26-21	T1st	...
5-24	Det.	W	12-1		14	5	Buehrle	Sparks		27-21	T1st	...
5-25	Det.	W	6-4		9	6	Wunsch	Greisinger	Foulke	28-21	1st	+1.0
5-26	Det.	L	2-9		4	14	Bernero	Ritchie		28-22	T1st	...
5-27	N.Y.	L	6-10		11	12	Thurman	Wright		28-23	2nd	1.0
5-28	N.Y.	L	2-4		4	8	Lilly	Garland	Rivera	28-24	2nd	2.0
5-29	N.Y.	L	3-6		10	12	Karsay	Foulke	Rivera	28-25	2nd	2.0
5-31	At Cle.	L	0-7		8	11	Colon	Glover		28-26	2nd	2.5
6-1	At Cle.	L	4-8		8	6	Baez	Ritchie		28-27	2nd	3.5
6-2	At Cle.	L	3-4		9	8	Finley	Wright	Wickman	28-28	T2nd	3.5
6-3	K.C.	W	4-0		5	6	Garland	Affeldt		29-28	2nd	3.0
6-4	K.C.	L	2-3		8	7	Asencio	Buehrle	Hernandez	29-29	2nd	4.0
6-5	K.C.	W	6-1		9	3	Glover	Suppan		30-29	2nd	3.0
6-6	K.C.	L	3-4		9	10	May	Ritchie	Hernandez	30-30	2nd	4.0
6-7	Mon.	L	3-4		5	8	Armas Jr.	Wright	Tucker	30-31	2nd	5.0
6-8	Mon.	L	1-2		4	5	Stewart	Foulke	Tucker	30-32	2nd	6.0
6-9	Mon.	W	13-2		14	7	Buehrle	Pavano		31-32	2nd	5.0
6-10	N.Y.	L	1-3		6	9	Astacio	Glover	Benitez	31-33	2nd	6.0
6-11	N.Y.	W	10-8		10	16	Ritchie	D'Amico	Osuna	32-33	2nd	5.0

Chicago White Sox

Date	Opp.	Res.	Score	(inn.*)	Hits	Opp. hits	Winning pitcher	Losing pitcher	Save	Record	Pos.	GB
6-12	N.Y.	W	2-1		7	4	Biddle	Leiter	Osuna	33-33	2nd	4.0
6-14	At Chi.	L	4-8		7	11	Clement	Garland		33-34	T2nd	4.0
6-15	At Chi.	L	3-7		8	10	Lieber	Buehrle		33-35	T2nd	5.0
6-16	At Chi.	W	10-7		6	11	Foulke	Wood	Osuna	34-35	T2nd	5.0
6-18	At Phi.	W	6-3	(12)	7	8	Osuna	Coggin	Biddle	35-35	2nd	5.0
6-19	At Phi.	L	3-4		8	7	Plesac	Biddle		35-36	2nd	5.0
6-20	At Phi.	W	6-1		10	6	Buehrle	Person		36-36	2nd	4.0
6-21	At Atl.	L	2-3		9	3	Gryboski	Ritchie	Smoltz	36-37	2nd	4.0
6-22	At Atl.	L	2-15		4	18	Moss	Glover		36-38	2nd	5.0
6-23	At Atl.	L	1-9		5	14	Marquis	Wright		36-39	2nd	6.0
6-24	At Min.	L	4-5		7	12	Hawkins	Howry	Guardado	36-40	2nd	7.0
6-25	At Min.	W	15-7		23	10	Buehrle	Milton		37-40	2nd	6.0
6-26	At Min.	L	5-6		9	10	Lohse	Ritchie	Guardado	37-41	2nd	7.0
6-27	At Min.	W	7-4		16	7	Glover	Reed	Foulke	38-41	2nd	6.0
6-28	Chi.	W	13-9		12	11	Ginter	Borowski		39-41	2nd	6.0
6-29	Chi.	W	5-4		7	8	Garland	Cruz	Osuna	40-41	2nd	5.0
6-30	Chi.	L	2-9		6	12	Clement	Buehrle		40-42	2nd	6.0
7-2	Det.	W	17-9		16	13	Ritchie	Bernero		41-42	2nd	5.5
7-3	Det.	L	4-5		11	11	Moehler	Glover	Paniagua	41-43	2nd	6.5
7-4	Det.	L	5-6		4	8	Sparks	Wunsch	Acevedo	41-44	2nd	6.5
7-5	Cle.	L	2-4		5	6	Baez	Garland	Wickman	41-45	2nd	7.5
7-6	Cle.	W	7-3		8	10	Buehrle	Phillips	Marte	42-45	2nd	7.5
7-7	Cle.	L	3-9		5	10	Drese	Ritchie		42-46	2nd	7.5
7-11	At Det.	W	9-2		15	5	Wright	Sparks		43-46	2nd	7.5
7-12	At Det.	L	1-2		6	5	Redman	Ritchie	Acevedo	43-47	2nd	8.5
7-13§	At Det.	L	3-5		7	9	Rodney	Buehrle	Acevedo	43-48		
7-13∞	At Det.	L	1-3		6	8	Maroth	Biddle	Henriquez	43-49	2nd	9.0
7-14	At Det.	W	6-4		12	8	Garland	Bernero	Osuna	44-49	2nd	9.0
7-15	At Cle.	L	1-7		8	7	Phillips	Glover		44-50	2nd	10.0
7-16	At Cle.	W	5-4		11	9	Osuna	Wickman	Marte	45-50	2nd	9.0
7-17	At K.C.	L	6-8		10	14	Suppan	Ritchie	Hernandez	45-51	2nd	10.0
7-18	At K.C.	L	3-5		10	8	Byrd	Marte		45-52	2nd	11.0
7-19	At Bal.	L	4-10		8	13	Lopez	Garland		45-53	2nd	12.0
7-20	At Bal.	L	3-4	(14)	13	17	Bauer	Howry		45-54	2nd	13.0
7-21	At Bal.	W	8-7		10	9	Howry	Roberts	Osuna	46-54	2nd	13.0
7-22	Min.	L	6-11		12	17	Reed	Ritchie		46-55	2nd	14.0
7-23	Min.	W	8-7		8	11	Buehrle	Santana	Osuna	47-55	2nd	13.0
7-24	Min.	L	1-8		9	13	Lohse	Garland		47-56	2nd	14.0
7-26	K.C.	W	10-2		14	10	Wright	Sedlacek		48-56	2nd	14.0
7-27	K.C.	W	9-1		13	5	Glover	May		49-56	2nd	14.0
7-28	K.C.	W	4-2		9	5	Howry	Suppan	Marte	50-56	2nd	14.0
7-30	At Min.	W	3-0		6	5	Buehrle	Lohse		51-56	2nd	13.0
7-31	At Min.	L	1-2	(10)	5	5	Romero	Osuna		51-57	2nd	14.0
8-1	At Min.	L	0-6		3	9	Milton	Wright		51-58	2nd	15.0
8-2	At T.B.	W	8-5	(12)	16	6	Wunsch	Colome	Osuna	52-58	2nd	15.0
8-3	At T.B.	L	2-6		5	11	Wilson	Ritchie		52-59	2nd	16.0
8-4	At T.B.	L	3-10		9	17	Kennedy	Buehrle		52-60	2nd	17.0
8-5	At T.B.	W	4-3		9	4	Foulke	Yan	Marte	53-60	2nd	16.0
8-6	Ana.	L	2-11		9	17	Washburn	Wright	Levine	53-61	2nd	16.0
8-7	Ana.	W	7-6		12	11	Osuna	Donnelly		54-61	2nd	15.0
8-8	Ana.	W	3-2		8	7	Parque	Sele	Marte	55-61	2nd	14.0
8-9	Sea.	W	10-2		11	7	Buehrle	Garcia		56-61	2nd	14.0
8-10	Sea.	L	3-7		11	8	Nelson	Biddle		56-62	2nd	14.0
8-11	Sea.	W	6-5		9	12	Wright	Baldwin	Osuna	57-62	2nd	13.0
8-13	At Tex.	W	12-3		13	6	Glover	Benoit		58-62	2nd	13.0
8-14	At Tex.	L	6-11		7	13	Valdes	Parque		58-63	2nd	13.0
8-16	At Oak.	L	0-1		6	5	Lidle	Buehrle	Koch	58-64	2nd	13.5
8-17	At Oak.	L	2-9		6	7	Mulder	Garland		58-65	2nd	13.5
8-18	At Oak.	L	4-7		8	12	Zito	Wright		58-66	2nd	14.5
8-19	Min.	L	3-7		10	10	Radke	Glover		58-67	2nd	15.5
8-20	Min.	L	0-5		4	7	Lohse	Parque		58-68	2nd	16.5
8-21	Min.	W	10-1		15	8	Buehrle	Mays		59-68	2nd	15.5
8-23	T.B.	L	2-8		11	12	Sturtze	Garland		59-69	2nd	17.0
8-24	T.B.	W	5-2		7	6	Wright	Wilson	Marte	60-69	2nd	17.0
8-25	T.B.	W	8-3		9	4	Glover	Kennedy		61-69	2nd	16.0
8-26	Tor.	L	4-8		6	10	Thurman	Parque		61-70	2nd	16.5
8-27	Tor.	W	8-4	(10)	9	7	Osuna	Cassidy		62-70	2nd	16.5
8-28	Tor.	W	8-0		10	6	Garland	Parris		63-70	2nd	16.5
8-30	At Det.	W	4-3		11	4	Wright	Maroth	Marte	64-70	2nd	15.0
8-31	At Det.	W	9-4		9	7	Glover	Sparks		65-70	2nd	14.0

Date	Opp.	Res.	Score	(inn.*)	Hits	Opp. hits	Winning pitcher	Losing pitcher	Save	Record	Pos.	GB
9-1	At Det.	W	7-0		16	7	Buehrle	Redman		66-70	2nd	13.0
9-2	At Tor.	W	5-3		8	11	Garland	Thurman	Marte	67-70	2nd	12.0
9-3	At Tor.	W	5-4		8	7	Rauch	Loaiza	Marte	68-70	2nd	11.5
9-4	At Tor.	L	2-6		7	9	Walker	Wright		68-71	2nd	12.5
9-5	Cle.	L	6-11		10	11	Rodriguez	Glover		68-72	2nd	13.0
9-6	Cle.	L	7-9		9	10	Burba	Buehrle	Baez	68-73	2nd	14.0
9-7	Cle.	L	2-4		4	8	Sabathia	Garland	Wohlers	68-74	2nd	14.0
9-8	Cle.	W	7-6		8	8	Osuna	Baez		69-74	2nd	13.0
9-9	At K.C.	W	10-6		11	10	Wright	Byrd		70-74	2nd	13.0
9-10	At K.C.	W	12-4		13	8	Porzio	Hernandez	Osuna	71-74	2nd	13.0
9-11	At K.C.	L	6-9		10	13	May	Buehrle		71-75	2nd	14.0
9-12	At K.C.	W	5-1		11	3	Garland	Asencio		72-75	2nd	13.0
9-13	At N.Y.	W	13-2		13	3	Biddle	Mussina	Osuna	73-75	2nd	12.0
9-14	At N.Y.	W	8-1		11	5	Wright	Clemens		74-75	2nd	12.0
9-15	At N.Y.	L	4-8	(6)	5	8	Pettitte	Porzio		74-76	2nd	13.0
9-17	K.C.	W	6-1		11	7	Buehrle	Asencio		75-76	2nd	13.0
9-18	K.C.	W	3-1		11	4	Garland	Suppan	Marte	76-76	2nd	13.0
9-19	K.C.	L	1-2		8	6	Byrd	Biddle	Hernandez	76-77	2nd	13.5
9-20	Min.	W	10-2		12	6	Wright	Rincon		77-77	2nd	12.5
9-21	Min.	W	14-4		18	8	Rauch	Radke		78-77	2nd	11.5
9-22	Min.	W	8-2		9	12	Buehrle	Mays		79-77	2nd	10.5
9-24	Bos.	L	2-4		9	8	Fossum	Garland	Urbina	79-78	2nd	11.5
9-25	Bos.	W	7-2		7	6	Biddle	Lowe		80-78	2nd	11.5
9-26	Bos.	W	3-2		5	4	Wright	Hancock	Foulke	81-78	2nd	10.5
9-27	At Min.	L	1-3		7	7	Fiore	Glover	Guardado	81-79	2nd	11.5
9-28	At Min.	L	2-3		6	10	Hawkins	Buehrle	Guardado	81-80	2nd	12.5
9-29	At Min.	L	1-3		8	9	Wells	Porzio	Romero	81-81	2nd	13.5

Monthly records: April (16-10), May (12-16), June (12-16), July (11-15), August (14-13), September (16-11).
*Innings, if other than nine. §Day separate admission. ∞Night separate admission.

RECORDS

2002 regular-season record: 81-81
Position: 2nd in A.L. Central
Home: 47-34   **Road:** 34-47
A.L. East: 18-14   **A.L. Central:** 40-36
A.L. West: 15-21   **N.L.:** 8-10
Vs. LH starters: 17-24
Vs. RH starters: 64-57
Grass: 72-70   **Artificial:** 9-11
Day: 30-28   **Night:** 51-53
1-Run: 15-21   **X-inn.:** 3-2
Doubleheaders: 0-0-0
Team record past five years: 414-395
(.512, ranks 6th in league in that span)

TEAM LEADERS

Batting average: Magglio Ordonez (.320).
At-bats: Magglio Ordonez (590).
Runs: Magglio Ordonez (116).
Hits: Magglio Ordonez (189).
Total bases: Magglio Ordonez (352).
Doubles: Magglio Ordonez (47).
Triples: Kenny Lofton (6).
Home runs: Magglio Ordonez (38).

Runs batted in: Magglio Ordonez (135).
Stolen bases: Kenny Lofton (22).
Slugging percentage: Magglio Ordonez (.597).
On-base percentage: Ray Durham (.390).
Wins: Mark Buehrle (19).
Earned-run average: Mark Buehrle (3.58).
Complete games: Mark Buehrle (5).
Shutouts: Mark Buehrle (2).
Saves: Keith Foulke, Antonio Osuna (11).
Innings pitched: Mark Buehrle (239.0).
Strikeouts: Dan Wright (136).

GAMES BY POSITION

Catcher: Mark L. Johnson 85, Sandy Alomar Jr. 50, Josh Paul 32, Miguel Olivo 6.
First base: Paul Konerko 140, Jeff Liefer 31, Frank Thomas 4.
Second base: Ray Durham 92, Willie Harris 38, Tony Graffanino 25, D'Angelo Jimenez 17.
Third base: Jose Valentin 83, Joe Crede 53, Tony Graffanino 35, D'Angelo Jimenez 1.

Shortstop: Royce Clayton 109, Jose Valentin 50, D'Angelo Jimenez 10, Tony Graffanino 8.
Outfield: Magglio Ordonez 150, Carlos Lee 137, Aaron Rowand 120, Kenny Lofton 92, Jeff Liefer 36, Joe Borchard 15, Willie Harris 6, Josh Paul 1.
Designated hitter: Frank Thomas 140, Paul Konerko 7, Jeff Liefer 6, Carlos Lee 2, Magglio Ordonez 1, Jose Valentin 1.

TOP DRAFT CHOICES

1. **Royce Ring,** LHP, San Diego State.
2. **Jeremy Reed,** OF, Long Beach State.
3. **Josh Rupe,** RHP, Louisburg (N.C.) J.C.
4. **Ryan Rodriguez,** LHP, Keller (Texas) H.S.
5. **B.J. LaMura,** RHP, Clemson.
6. **Chris Getz,** SS, Grosse Pointe (Mich.) South H.S.
7. **Micah Schnurstein,** 3B, Basic H.S., Henderson, Nev.
8. **Sean Tracey,** RHP, UC Irvine.
9. **Todd Deininger,** RHP, Texas A&M.
10. **Orionny Lopez,** RHP, Forest Hills H.S., West Palm Beach, Fla.

CLEVELAND INDIANS
AMERICAN LEAGUE CENTRAL DIVISION

2003 SEASON

March/April

SUN	MON	TUE	WED	THU	FRI	SAT
30	31 D BAL	1	2 BAL	3 BAL	4 KC	5 D KC
6 D KC	7 D CWS	8	9 CWS	10 CWS	11 KC	12 D KC
13 D KC	14 KC	15 BAL	16 BAL	17 BAL	18 CWS	19 D CWS
20 D CWS	21 D CWS	22 SEA	23 SEA	24 SEA	25 OAK	26 D OAK
27 OAK	28	29 ANA	30 ANA			

May

SUN	MON	TUE	WED	THU	FRI	SAT
				1 ANA	2 TEX	3 D TEX
4 D TEX	5	6 ANA	7 ANA	8 ANA	9 TEX	10 TEX
11 D TEX	12	13 SEA	14 SEA	15 SEA	16 OAK	17 D OAK
18 D OAK	19 DET	20 DET	21 DET	22 DET	23 BOS	24 D BOS
25 BOS	26 D DET	27 DET	28 DET	29	30 CWS	31 D CWS

June

SUN	MON	TUE	WED	THU	FRI	SAT
1 D CWS	2 D CWS	3 COL	4 COL	5 D COL	6 ARI	7 D ARI
8 D ARI	9	10 SD	11 SD	12 SD	13 LA	14 D LA
15 D LA	16	17 DET	18 DET	19 DET	20 D PIT	21 PIT
22 PIT	23	24 KC	25 KC	26 KC	27 CIN	28 D CIN
29 CIN	30 KC					

July

SUN	MON	TUE	WED	THU	FRI	SAT
		1 KC	2 KC	3 MIN	4 MIN	5 MIN
6 D MIN	7	8 NYY	9 NYY	10 NYY	11 CWS	12 CWS
13 D CWS	14	15 *	16	17 NYY	18 NYY	19 D NYY
20 D NYY	21 CWS	22 CWS	23 D DET	24 DET	25 MIN	26 MIN
27 D MIN	28	29 OAK	30 OAK	31 D OAK		

August

SUN	MON	TUE	WED	THU	FRI	SAT
					1 TEX	2 TEX
3 TEX	4	5 SEA	6 SEA	7 SEA	8 ANA	9 D ANA
10 D ANA	11 MIN	12 MIN	13 MIN	14 D MIN	15 TB	16 TB
17 D TB	18 D TB	19 MIN	20 MIN	21	22 TB	23 TB
24 D TB	25	26 DET	27 DET	28 DET	29 TOR	30 TOR

September

SUN	MON	TUE	WED	THU	FRI	SAT
31 D TOR	1 D DET	2 D DET	3 DET	4 DET	5 D CWS	6 D CWS
7 D CWS	8	9 KC	10 KC	11 D KC	12 MIN	13 MIN
14 D MIN	15 MIN	16 KC	17 KC	18 KC	19 BOS	20 BOS
21 D BOS	22	23 MIN	24 MIN	25	26 TOR	27 D TOR
28 D TOR						

Home games shaded; D—Day game (games starting before 5 p.m.); *—All-Star Game at Comiskey Park, Chicago. Subject to change.

CLUB DIRECTORY

President and chief executive officer
Lawrence J. Dolan
Executive vice president, general manager
Mark Shapiro
Vice president, public relations
Bob DiBiasio

Assistant g.m., scouting operations
John Mirabelli
Assistant general manager
Neal Huntington
Assistant general manager
Chris Antonetti

Director of player development
John Farrell
Director of player personnel
Steve Lubratich
Director of media relations
Bart Swain

MINOR LEAGUE AFFILIATES

Class	Team	League	Manager
AAA	Buffalo	International	Marty Brown
AA	Akron	Eastern	Brad Komminsk
A	Kinston	Carolina	Torey Lovullo
A	Lake County	South Atlantic	Luis Rivera
A	Mahoning Valley	New York-Pennsylvania	Ted Kubiak
Rookie	Burlington	Appalachian	Rouglas Odor

Follow the Indians all season at: www.sportingnews.com/baseball/teams/indians/

BROADCAST INFORMATION

Radio: WTAM-AM (1100).
Cable TV: Fox Sports Net Ohio.

SPRING TRAINING

Ballpark (city): Chain Of Lakes (Winter Haven, Fla.).
Ticket information: 863-293-3900.

Manager—Eric Wedge (22).

Coaches—Buddy Bell (6), Mike Brown (45), Jeff Datz (29), Luis Isaac (4), Dave Keller (87), Eddie Murray (33), Joel Skinner (35), Dan Williams (43).

No.	PITCHERS	B/T	Ht./Wt.	Born	Age*	2002 clubs
34	Anderson, Brian	R/L	6-1/183	4-26-72	30	Arizona
55	Baez, Danys	R/R	6-3/225	9-10-77	25	Cleveland
	Bere, Jason	R/R	6-3/225	5-26-71	31	Chicago N.L., Iowa
	Cressend, Jack	R/R	6-1/185	5-13-75	27	Minnesota, Gulf Coast Twins, Fort Myers
64	Davis, Jason	R/R	6-6/195	5-8-80	22	Kinston, Akron, Cleveland
	Guthrie, Jeremy	R/R	6-1/195	4-8-79	23	DID NOT PLAY
49	Herrera, Alex	L/L	5-11/175	11-5-76	26	Akron, Cleveland, Buffalo
65	Lee, Cliff	L/L	6-3/190	8-30-78	24	Harrisburg, Akron, Buffalo, Cleveland
45	Mulholland, Terry	R/L	6-3/200	3-9-63	41	Los Angeles, Cleveland
	Myette, Aaron	R/R	6-4/210	9-26-77	25	Oklahoma, Texas
16	Paronto, Chad	R/R	6-5/250	7-28-75	27	Buffalo, Cleveland, Akron
51	Riggan, Jerrod	R/R	6-3/197	5-16-74	28	Cleveland, Buffalo
54	Riske, Dave	R/R	6-2/175	10-23-76	26	Cleveland, Akron, Buffalo
46	Rodriguez, Ricardo	R/R	6-3/165	5-21-78	24	Jacksonville, Las Vegas, Buffalo, Cleveland
52	Sabathia, C.C.	L/L	6-7/270	7-21-80	22	Cleveland
53	Sadler, Carl	L/L	6-2/180	10-11-76	26	Akron, Buffalo, Cleveland
60	Tallet, Brian	L/L	6-7/208	9-21-77	25	Akron, Buffalo, Cleveland
37	Westbrook, Jake	R/R	6-3/185	9-29-77	25	Cleveland, Akron, Buffalo
26	Wickman, Bob	R/R	6-1/240	2-6-69	34	Cleveland
39	Wohlers, Mark	R/R	6-4/207	1-23-70	33	Cleveland

No.	CATCHERS	B/T	Ht./Wt.	Born	Age*	2002 clubs
44	Bard, Josh	B/R	6-3/215	3-30-78	25	Buffalo, Cleveland
23	Hinch, A.J.	R/R	6-1/205	5-15-74	28	Kansas City
63	Martinez, Victor	B/R	6-2/170	12-23-78	24	Akron, Cleveland

No.	INFIELDERS	B/T	Ht./Wt.	Born	Age*	2002 clubs
17	Fryman, Travis	R/R	6-1/195	3-25-69	34	Cleveland
	Garcia, Luis	R/R	6-4/185	11-5-78	24	New Haven, Akron
12	Gutierrez, Ricky	R/R	6-1/190	5-23-70	32	Cleveland
	Hafner, Travis	L/R	6-3/240	6-3-77	25	Oklahoma, Texas
8	McDonald, John	R/R	5-11/175	9-24-74	28	Cleveland
61	Phillips, Brandon	R/R	5-11/185	6-28-81	21	Harrisburg, Ottawa, Buffalo, Cleveland
22	Snyder, Earl	R/R	6-0/207	5-6-76	26	Buffalo, Cleveland
13	Vizquel, Omar	B/R	5-9/175	4-24-67	35	Cleveland

No.	OUTFIELDERS	B/T	Ht./Wt.	Born	Age*	2002 clubs
24	Bradley, Milton	B/R	6-0/190	4-15-78	24	Cleveland, Buffalo, Akron
28	Broussard, Ben	L/L	6-2/220	9-24-76	26	Louisville, Buffalo, Cleveland
23	Burks, Ellis	R/R	6-2/205	9-11-64	38	Cleveland
10	Crisp, Coco	B/R	6-0/185	11-1-79	23	New Haven, Akron, Cleveland, Buffalo
46	Escobar, Alex	R/R	6-1/180	9-6-78	24	DID NOT PLAY
20	Garcia, Karim	L/L	6-0/195	10-29-75	27	Columbus, New York A.L., Buffalo, Cleveland
11	Lawton, Matt	L/R	5-10/186	11-3-71	31	Cleveland, Akron
30	Magruder, Chris	B/R	5-11/200	4-26-77	25	Cleveland, Buffalo
	Spencer, Shane	R/R	5-11/225	2-20-72	31	New York A.L.

*Age as of April 1, 2003.

BALLPARK INFORMATION

Ballpark (capacity, surface)
Jacobs Field (43,368, grass)

Address
2401 Ontario St.
Cleveland, OH 44115

Official website
www.indians.com

Business phone
216-420-4200

Ticket information
216-420-4200

Field dimensions (from home plate)
To left field at foul line, 325 feet
To center field, 405 feet
To right field at foul line, 325 feet

First game played
April 4, 1994
(Indians 4, Mariners 3, 11 innings)

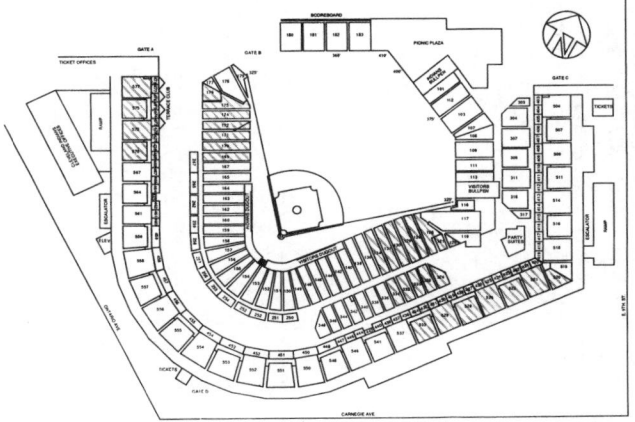

2003 SEASON Cleveland Indians

Date	Opp.	Res.	Score	(inn.*)	Hits	Opp. hits	Winning pitcher	Losing pitcher	Save	Record	Pos.	GB
3-31	At Ana.	W	6-0		11	5	Colon	Washburn		1-0	1st	+0.5
4-2	At Ana.	L	5-7		6	8	Weber	Riske	Percival	1-1	T2nd	0.5
4-3	At Ana.	W	6-5		11	11	Drese	Sele	Wickman	2-1	2nd	0.5
4-5	At Det.	W	10-1		12	6	Baez	Redman		3-1	T1st	...
4-6	At Det.	W	5-3		10	6	Colon	Cornejo	Wickman	4-1	T1st	...
4-7	At Det.	W	5-1		11	4	Sabathia	Weaver	Wickman	5-1	T1st	...
4-8	Min.	W	9-5		8	13	Drese	Milton		6-1	1st	+1.0
4-9	Min.	W	5-4		6	11	Finley	Mays	Wickman	7-1	1st	+2.0
4-10	Min.	W	9-3		9	7	Baez	Reed		8-1	1st	+3.0
4-11	Min.	W	8-4		9	9	Colon	Lohse		9-1	1st	+4.0
4-12	K.C.	W	3-1		5	6	Sabathia	Suppan	Wickman	10-1	1st	+4.0
4-13	K.C.	W	8-7		10	9	Shuey	Bailey		11-1	1st	+4.0
4-16	At Chi.	L	5-10		7	12	Marte	Finley		11-2	1st	+2.5
4-17	At Chi.	L	2-7		7	13	Buehrle	Baez		11-3	1st	+2.0
4-18	At Chi.	L	1-7		7	8	Ritchie	Colon		11-4	1st	+1.0
4-19	At Min.	L	3-12		7	14	Lohse	Sabathia		11-5	1st	+0.5
4-20	At Min.	L	2-6		6	9	Kinney	Drese		11-6	T2nd	0.5
4-21	At Min.	L	2-4		8	13	Reed	Finley	Guardado	11-7	3rd	1.5
4-22	Chi.	W	4-2		8	6	Baez	Buehrle	Wickman	12-7	T2nd	1.0
4-23	Chi.	L	1-5		5	13	Ritchie	Colon		12-8	3rd	1.0
4-24	Chi.	L	2-9		8	10	Wright	Sabathia		12-9	3rd	2.0
4-25	Chi.	L	3-6		6	9	Garland	Drese	Foulke	12-10	3rd	3.0
4-26	At Tex.	W	7-4		11	12	Finley	Davis		13-10	3rd	2.0
4-27	At Tex.	L	2-4		6	8	Bell	Baez	Irabu	13-11	3rd	2.0
4-28	At Tex.	L	1-2		7	5	Valdes	Colon	Irabu	13-12	3rd	2.0
4-30	Ana.	L	2-21		9	22	Ortiz	Sabathia		13-13	3rd	3.0
5-1	Ana.	L	2-7		6	11	Washburn	Drese		13-14	3rd	4.0
5-2	Ana.	L	0-8		7	15	Appier	Finley		13-15	3rd	4.5
5-3	Tex.	L	2-4		8	6	Davis	Baez	Irabu	13-16	3rd	5.5
5-4	Tex.	W	3-0		7	5	Colon	Valdes	Wickman	14-16	3rd	5.5
5-5	Tex.	W	9-2		16	11	Sabathia	Rogers		15-16	3rd	4.5
5-6	At Bal.	W	9-4		15	9	Drese	Groom		16-16	3rd	4.5
5-7	At Bal.	L	3-4	(10)	5	13	Julio	Wohlers		16-17	3rd	4.5
5-8	At Bal.	W	6-2		6	8	Baez	Erickson		17-17	3rd	4.5
5-9	At K.C.	L	3-5		7	8	Suppan	Rincon	Hernandez	17-18	3rd	5.0
5-10	At K.C.	L	0-9		7	11	Reichert	Sabathia		17-19	3rd	5.0
5-12	At K.C.	L	1-4		5	7	Byrd	Finley	Hernandez	17-20	3rd	4.5
5-14	Bal.	W	6-5		11	9	Shuey	Julio		18-20	3rd	4.0
5-15	Bal.	W	3-1		7	7	Colon	Bauer	Wickman	19-20	3rd	4.0
5-17	K.C.	L	2-6		5	6	Byrd	Finley		19-21	3rd	4.5
5-18§	K.C.	L	2-4		7	6	Reichert	Wickman	Hernandez	19-22		
5-18∞	K.C.	W	4-1		4	4	Drese	May	Wickman	20-22	3rd	4.0
5-19	K.C.	L	4-5		5	7	Grimsley	Wickman	Hernandez	20-23	3rd	4.0
5-20	At Det.	L	3-4		10	11	Santana	Rincon	Walker	20-24	3rd	4.5
5-21	At Det.	L	1-5		10	7	Redman	Nagy		20-25	3rd	5.5
5-22	At Det.	L	0-2		1	6	Weaver	Finley		20-26	3rd	5.5
5-24	At Tor.	W	5-2		10	8	Drese	Miller	Wickman	21-26	3rd	5.5
5-25	At Tor.	W	3-0		7	5	Sabathia	Loaiza	Wickman	22-26	3rd	5.5
5-26	At Tor.	W	3-1		6	4	Colon	Prokopec		23-26	3rd	4.5
5-27	Det.	L	1-4		4	10	Redman	Baez		23-27	3rd	5.5
5-28	Det.	W	4-2		8	5	Finley	Weaver	Wickman	24-27	3rd	5.5
5-29	Det.	L	5-9		11	11	Sparks	Riske	Acevedo	24-28	3rd	5.5
5-30	Det.	W	11-7		14	11	Riske	Lima		25-28	3rd	5.5
5-31	Chi.	W	7-0		11	8	Colon	Glover		26-28	3rd	4.5
6-1	Chi.	W	8-4		6	8	Baez	Ritchie		27-28	3rd	4.5
6-2	Chi.	W	4-3		8	9	Finley	Wright	Wickman	28-28	T2nd	3.5
6-4	At Min.	L	2-23		4	25	Reed	Drese		28-29	3rd	4.5
6-5	At Min.	W	6-4		12	11	Sabathia	Milton	Riske	29-29	3rd	3.5
6-6	At Min.	L	3-8		8	11	Lohse	Colon		29-30	3rd	4.5
6-7	N.Y.	L	3-4		5	7	Leiter	Baez	Benitez	29-31	3rd	5.5
6-8	N.Y.	L	6-8		8	11	Trachsel	Finley	Benitez	29-32	3rd	6.5
6-9	N.Y.	W	8-3		9	9	Drese	Estes		30-32	3rd	5.5
6-10	Phi.	L	1-3		6	9	Adams	Sabathia	Mesa	30-33	3rd	6.5
6-11	Phi.	W	5-1		7	6	Colon	Wolf	Wickman	31-33	3rd	5.5

Date	Opp.	Res.	Score	(inn.*)	Hits	Opp. hits	Winning pitcher	Losing pitcher	Save	Record	Pos.	GB
6-12	Phi.	L	3-7		11	11	Padilla	Paronto		31-34	3rd	5.5
6-13	Bal.	W	2-1	(10)	5	5	Riggan	Roberts		32-34	3rd	5.0
6-14	At Col.	W	5-3		11	9	Drese	Thomson	Wickman	33-34	T2nd	4.0
6-15	At Col.	L	4-7		7	11	Jones	Paronto	Jimenez	33-35	T2nd	5.0
6-16	At Col.	W	5-4		9	9	Colon	Neagle	Wickman	34-35	T2nd	5.0
6-18	At Fla.	L	0-4		4	11	Dempster	Finley		34-36	3rd	6.0
6-19	At Fla.	L	1-2		5	5	Tavarez	Riggan	Nunez	34-37	3rd	6.0
6-20	At Fla.	L	0-3	(6)	2	7	Burnett	Drese		34-38	3rd	6.0
6-21	At Mon.	L	1-3		5	6	Vazquez	Sabathia	Stewart	34-39	3rd	6.0
6-22	At Mon.	W	5-4		8	13	Colon	Day	Wickman	35-39	3rd	6.0
6-23	At Mon.	L	2-7		7	11	Armas Jr.	Finley		35-40	3rd	7.0
6-25	At Bos.	W	4-2		9	10	Baez	Castillo	Wickman	36-40	3rd	6.5
6-26	At Bos.	L	4-7		7	10	Martinez	Drese	Urbina	36-41	3rd	7.5
6-28	Ari.	W	8-2		7	4	Sabathia	Batista		37-41	3rd	7.0
6-29	Ari.	L	2-4		6	8	Anderson	Finley	Kim	37-42	3rd	7.0
6-30	Ari.	L	2-5		5	6	Schilling	Baez		37-43	3rd	8.0
7-2	At N.Y.	L	5-10		7	9	Mendoza	Rincon		37-44	3rd	8.5
7-3	At N.Y.	L	8-11		14	12	Wells	Sabathia	Rivera	37-45	3rd	9.5
7-4	At N.Y.	L	1-7		8	11	Mussina	Finley		37-46	3rd	9.5
7-5	At Chi.	W	4-2		6	5	Baez	Garland	Wickman	38-46	3rd	9.5
7-6	At Chi.	L	3-7		10	8	Buehrle	Phillips	Marte	38-47	3rd	10.5
7-7	At Chi.	W	9-3		10	5	Drese	Ritchie		39-47	3rd	9.5
7-11	N.Y.	L	4-7		10	10	Pettitte	Sabathia	Rivera	39-48	3rd	10.5
7-12	N.Y.	W	2-1	(10)	7	5	Wohlers	Karsay		40-48	3rd	10.5
7-13	N.Y.	L	5-14		12	15	Wells	Drese		40-49	3rd	10.5
7-14	N.Y.	W	10-7		13	11	Rincon	Rivera		41-49	3rd	10.5
7-15	Chi.	W	7-1		7	8	Phillips	Glover		42-49	3rd	10.5
7-16	Chi.	L	4-5		9	11	Osuna	Wickman	Marte	42-50	3rd	10.5
7-17	Min.	L	5-8		10	12	Reed	Baez	Guardado	42-51	3rd	11.5
7-18	Min.	L	6-8		10	15	Fiore	Rincon	Guardado	42-52	3rd	12.5
7-19	At K.C.	L	5-8		12	10	Mullen	Murray	Hernandez	42-53	3rd	13.5
7-20†	At K.C.	L	5-7		10	10	Hernandez	Wright	Hernandez	42-54		
7-20‡	At K.C.	W	5-3	(10)	10	7	Shuey	Voyles	Wickman	43-54	3rd	14.0
7-21	At K.C.	L	12-13	(10)	20	13	Mullen	Murray		43-55	T3rd	15.0
7-23	N.Y.	W	9-3		15	6	Baez	Pettitte		44-55	3rd	14.5
7-24	N.Y.	L	7-14		10	18	Wells	Drese		44-56	3rd	15.5
7-26	Det.	L	5-8		8	19	Powell	Nagy	Henriquez	44-57	3rd	16.5
7-27	Det.	L	1-5		7	12	Sparks	Sabathia		44-58	3rd	17.5
7-28	Det.	W	9-6		11	11	DePaula	Acevedo		45-58	3rd	17.5
7-29	At Oak.	W	8-6		16	9	Mulholland	Magnante	Wohlers	46-58	3rd	17.0
7-30	At Oak.	W	5-4		7	14	Drese	Lidle	Wohlers	47-58	3rd	16.0
7-31	At Oak.	L	4-6		6	11	Mulder	Westbrook	Koch	47-59	3rd	17.0
8-1	At Sea.	L	6-10		11	13	Nelson	DePaula		47-60	3rd	18.0
8-2	At Sea.	L	1-3		4	5	Moyer	Baez	Sasaki	47-61	3rd	19.0
8-3	At Sea.	L	4-12		7	14	Garcia	Wright		47-62	3rd	20.0
8-4	At Sea.	W	10-8		15	15	Westbrook	Sasaki	Wohlers	48-62	3rd	20.0
8-6	T.B.	W	4-2		8	8	Nagy	Sosa	Wohlers	49-62	3rd	18.5
8-7	T.B.	W	6-2		7	6	Sabathia	Sturtze		50-62	3rd	17.5
8-8	T.B.	L	2-4		7	8	Wilson	Baez	Yan	50-63	3rd	17.5
8-9	Tex.	L	2-3		2	9	Rogers	Wohlers	Cordero	50-64	3rd	18.5
8-10	Tex.	W	4-3		4	11	Wickman	Kolb		51-64	3rd	17.5
8-11	Tex.	L	5-11		7	15	Myette	Nagy		51-65	3rd	17.5
8-13	At T.B.	W	9-5		9	8	Sabathia	Sturtze	Wohlers	52-65	3rd	17.5
8-14	At T.B.	W	6-4		11	10	Baez	Wilson	Wohlers	53-65	3rd	16.5
8-15	At T.B.	L	3-4		7	9	Harper	Wohlers		53-66	3rd	16.5
8-16	At Ana.	L	4-5		10	10	Lackey	Drese	Percival	53-67	3rd	17.5
8-17	At Ana.	W	9-4		12	9	Sadler	Washburn		54-67	3rd	16.5
8-18	At Ana.	L	1-4		2	8	Appier	Sabathia	Percival	54-68	3rd	17.5
8-19	Oak.	L	1-8		6	12	Hudson	Baez		54-69	3rd	18.5
8-20	Oak.	L	3-6		8	12	Harang	Westbrook	Koch	54-70	3rd	19.5
8-21	Oak.	L	0-6		1	5	Lidle	Rodriguez		54-71	3rd	19.5
8-22	Oak.	L	3-9		5	14	Mulder	Phillips	Bradford	54-72	3rd	20.5
8-23	Sea.	W	4-2		8	6	Wohlers	Baldwin		55-72	3rd	20.5
8-24	Sea.	W	5-3		7	6	Mulholland	Creek		56-72	3rd	20.5
8-25	Sea.	L	4-12		8	16	Garcia	Westbrook		56-73	3rd	20.5
8-26	Det.	W	8-2		13	5	Rodriguez	Sparks		57-73	3rd	20.0
8-27	Det.	L	5-8		7	8	Redman	Phillips	Acevedo	57-74	3rd	21.0
8-28	Det.	W	2-1		8	6	Sabathia	Powell	Baez	58-74	3rd	21.0
8-30	Bos.	L	5-15		11	16	Lowe	Wright		58-75	3rd	20.5
8-31	Bos.	W	8-7		13	12	Baez	Howry		59-75	3rd	19.5

Date	Opp.	Res.	Score	(inn.*)	Hits	Opp. hits	Winning pitcher	Losing pitcher	Save	Record	Pos.	GB
9-1	Bos.	L	1-7		4	10	Wakefield	Nagy		59-76	3rd	19.5
9-2	At Det.	W	11-1		12	6	Sabathia	Powell		60-76	3rd	18.5
9-3	At Det.	L	0-4		8	11	Van Hekken	Mulholland		60-77	3rd	19.0
9-4	At Det.	W	9-3		9	6	Wright	Maroth		61-77	3rd	19.0
9-5	At Chi.	W	11-6		11	10	Rodriguez	Glover		62-77	3rd	18.5
9-6	At Chi.	W	9-7		10	9	Burba	Buehrle	Baez	63-77	3rd	18.5
9-7	At Chi.	W	4-2		8	4	Sabathia	Garland	Wohlers	64-77	3rd	17.5
9-8	At Chi.	L	6-7		8	8	Osuna	Baez		64-78	3rd	17.5
9-9	Tor.	L	9-11		13	15	Bowles	Sadler	Escobar	64-79	3rd	18.5
9-10	Tor.	L	4-5		5	10	Bowles	Wohlers	Escobar	64-80	3rd	19.5
9-11	Tor.	L	5-6	(11)	9	7	Cassidy	Elder	Kershner	64-81	3rd	20.5
9-12	Min.	W	5-4		11	8	Riggan	Mays	Baez	65-81	3rd	19.5
9-13	Min.	W	12-5		16	8	Mulholland	Milton		66-81	3rd	18.5
9-14	Min.	L	2-3		5	10	Reed	Sadler	Guardado	66-82	3rd	19.5
9-15	Min.	L	0-5		3	5	Lohse	Lee		66-83	3rd	20.5
9-16§	At Bos.	L	1-6		4	11	Martinez	Rodriguez		66-84		
9-16∞	At Bos.	W	7-1		7	6	Tallet	Castillo		67-84	3rd	20.5
9-17	At Bos.	L	2-4		6	8	Wakefield	Sabathia	Urbina	67-85	3rd	21.5
9-18	At Bos.	W	6-4		11	9	Riske	Embree	Baez	68-85	3rd	21.5
9-20	At K.C.	W	6-2		12	7	Davis	Obermueller	Baez	69-85	3rd	20.5
9-21	At K.C.	L	2-3		12	8	Grimsley	Mulholland		69-86	3rd	20.5
9-22	At K.C.	W	6-5		9	11	Sabathia	Grimsley	Baez	70-86	3rd	19.5
9-24	At Min.	L	3-4		9	5	Hawkins	Elder		70-87	3rd	20.5
9-25	At Min.	L	5-7	(12)	12	11	Romero	Maurer		70-88	3rd	21.5
9-26	At Min.	W	8-4		11	8	Drese	Jackson		71-88	3rd	20.5
9-27	K.C.	W	8-3		13	7	Sabathia	Obermueller		72-88	3rd	20.5
9-28	K.C.	W	6-5	(10)	11	8	Wohlers	MacDougal		73-88	3rd	20.5
9-29	K.C.	W	7-3		6	9	Wright	Mullen		74-88	3rd	20.5

Monthly records: March (1-0), April (12-13), May (13-15), June (11-15), July (10-16), August (12-16), September (15-13).
*Innings, if other than nine. †First game of a doubleheader. ‡Second game of a doubleheader. §Day separate admission. ∞Night separate admission.

RECORDS

2002 regular-season record: 74-88
Position: 3rd in A.L. Central
Home: 39-42   **Road:** 35-46
A.L. East: 19-17   **A.L. Central:** 37-39
A.L. West: 12-20   **N.L.:** 6-12
Vs. LH starters: 23-23
Vs. RH starters: 51-65
Grass: 66-78   **Artificial:** 8-10
Day: 25-20   **Night:** 49-68
1-Run: 16-17   **X-inn.:** 4-4
Doubleheaders: 0-0-1
Team record past five years: 441-369
(.544, ranks 5th in league in that span)

TEAM LEADERS

Batting average: Jim Thome (.304).
At-bats: Omar Vizquel (582).
Runs: Jim Thome (101).
Hits: Omar Vizquel (160).
Total bases: Jim Thome (325).
Doubles: Omar Vizquel (31).
Triples: Omar Vizquel (5).
Home runs: Jim Thome (52).
Runs batted in: Jim Thome (118).
Stolen bases: Omar Vizquel (18).
Slugging percentage: Jim Thome (.677).
On-base percentage: Jim Thome (.445).
Wins: C.C. Sabathia (13).

Earned-run average: Bartolo Colon (2.55).
Complete games: Bartolo Colon (4).
Shutouts: Bartolo Colon (2).
Saves: Bob Wickman (20).
Innings pitched: C.C. Sabathia (210.0).
Strikeouts: C.C. Sabathia (149).

GAMES BY POSITION

Catcher: Einar Diaz 100, Eddie Perez 42, Josh Bard 24, Victor Martinez 9.
First base: Jim Thome 128, Lee Stevens 25, Earl Snyder 12, Ben Broussard 4, Wil Cordero 1.
Second base: Ricky Gutierrez 93, John McDonald 64, Brandon Phillips 11, Bill Selby 6, Jolbert Cabrera 3, Greg LaRocca 3.
Third base: Travis Fryman 113, Bill Selby 33, Greg LaRocca 15, John McDonald 10, Russell Branyan 8, Earl Snyder 2.
Shortstop: Omar Vizquel 150, John McDonald 21.
Outfield: Matt Lawton 108, Milton Bradley 94, Chris Magruder 83, Karim Garcia 51, Russell Branyan 42, Jolbert Cabrera 34, Ben Broussard 32, Coco Crisp 32, Brady Anderson 29, Bill Selby 18, Lee Stevens 16, Bruce Aven 7, Ellis Burks 6, Chad Allen 4, Wil Cordero 4, Todd Dunwoody 2.
Designated hitter: Ellis Burks 127, Jim Thome 18, Ben Broussard 3, Matt Lawton 3, Lee Stevens 3, Brady Anderson 1, Milton Bradley 1, Russell Branyan 1, Jolbert Cabrera 1, Ricky Gutierrez 1, Greg LaRocca 1, Victor Martinez 1, John McDonald 1, Earl Snyder 1.

TOP DRAFT CHOICES

1a. **Jeremy Guthrie,** RHP, Stanford.
1b. **Matt Whitney,** 3B, Palm Beach Gardens (Fla.) H.S.
1c. **Micah Schilling,** 2B, Silliman Institute (La.).
2a. **Brian Slocum,** RHP, Villanova.
2b. **Pat Osborn,** 3B, Florida.
3a. **Jason Cooper,** OF, Stanford.
3b. **Daniel Cevette,** LHP, Elkland (Pa.) H.S.
4. **Fernando Pacheco,** 1B, Montgomery H.S., San Ysidro, Calif.
5. **Ben Francisco,** OF, UCLA.
6. **Michael Hernandez,** LHP, Fresno State.
7. **Brian Wright,** OF, North Carolina State
8. **Blake Allen,** LHP, Union (Tenn.).
9. **Shaun Larkin,** 2B, Cal State Northridge.
10. **Keith Ramsey,** LHP, Florida.

DETROIT TIGERS
AMERICAN LEAGUE CENTRAL DIVISION

2003 SEASON

March/April

SUN	MON	TUE	WED	THU	FRI	SAT
30	31 D MIN	1	2 MIN	3 MIN	4 D CWS	5 D CWS
6 D CWS	7	8 KC	9 D KC	10 D KC	11 CWS	12 D CWS
13 D CWS	14	15 MIN	16 MIN	17 MIN	18 KC	19 D KC
20 D KC	21	22 OAK	23 OAK	24 D OAK	25 SEA	26 SEA
27 D SEA	28	29 BAL	30 BAL			

May

SUN	MON	TUE	WED	THU	FRI	SAT
				1 D BAL	2 TB	3 D TB
4 D TB	5 BAL	6 BAL	7 D BAL	8	9 TB	10 TB
11 D TB	12	13 OAK	14 OAK	15 OAK	16 SEA	17 D SEA
18 D SEA	19 CLE	20 CLE	21 CLE	22 CLE	23 CWS	24 CWS
25 D CWS	26 D CLE	27 D CLE	28 CLE	29	30 NYY	31 D NYY

June

SUN	MON	TUE	WED	THU	FRI	SAT
1 D NYY	2	3 SD	4 SD	5 D SD	6 SF	7 D SF
8 D SF	9	10 LA	11 LA	12 LA	13 COL	14 COL
15 D COL	16	17 CLE	18 CLE	19 D CLE	20 COL	21 COL
22 D COL	23 BOS	24 BOS	25 BOS	26 BOS	27 ARI	28 ARI
29 D ARI	30 TOR					

July

SUN	MON	TUE	WED	THU	FRI	SAT
		1 TOR	2 TOR	3 KC	4 KC	5 KC
6 D KC	7	8 CWS	9 CWS	10 D CWS	11 BOS	12 BOS
13 D BOS	14	15 *	16	17 CWS	18 CWS	19 CWS
20 D CWS	21 BOS	22 BOS	23 CLE	24 CLE	25 KC	26 KC
27 D KC	28	29 SEA	30 SEA	31 D SEA		

August

SUN	MON	TUE	WED	THU	FRI	SAT
					1 MIN	2 MIN
3 D MIN	4	5 OAK	6 OAK	7 D OAK	8 D MIN	9 MIN
10 D MIN	11 TEX	12 TEX	13 TEX	14 TEX	15 ANA	16 ANA
17 D ANA	18 TEX	19 TEX	20 TEX	21 ANA	22 ANA	23 D ANA
24 D ANA	25	26 CLE	27 CLE	28 CLE	29 CWS	30 CWS

September

SUN	MON	TUE	WED	THU	FRI	SAT
31 D CWS	1 D CLE	2 CLE	3 CLE	4 D CLE	5 D TOR	6 D TOR
7 D TOR	8	9 NYY	10 NYY	11 NYY	12 KC	13 KC
14 D KC	15	16 TOR	17 TOR	18 TOR	19 MIN	20 D MIN
21 D MIN	22 KC	23 KC	24 KC	25 MIN	26 MIN	27 MIN
28 D MIN						

Home games shaded; D—Day game (games starting before 5 p.m.); *—All-Star Game at Comiskey Park, Chicago. Subject to change.

CLUB DIRECTORY

Owner
Michael Ilitch
President, CEO, general manager
David Dombrowski
Special assistants to the president
Al Kaline, Willie Horton
Sr. v.p., marketing and communications
Mike Veeck
Vice president of player personnel
Scott Reid

V.p., assistant general manager
Al Avila
Special assistant to the g.m.
Al Hargesheimer
Director of scouting
Greg Smith
Director of player development
Steve Boros
Director of minor league operations
Ricky Bennett

Senior director of communications
Cliff Russell
Manager, media relations
Jim Anderson
Manager, broadcasting and media relations
Molly Light
Director, community relations
Celia Bobrowsky

MINOR LEAGUE AFFILIATES

Class	Team	League	Manager
AAA	Toledo	International	Larry Parrish
AA	Erie	Eastern	Kevin Bradshaw
A	Lakeland	Florida State	Gary Green
A	West Michigan	Midwest	Phil Regan
A	Oneonta	New York-Pennsylvania	Randy Ready
Rookie	Gulf Coast Tigers	Gulf Coast	Howard Bushong

Follow the Tigers all season at: www.sportingnews.com/baseball/teams/tigers/

BROADCAST INFORMATION

Radio: WXYT-AM (1270).
TV: WKBD (Channel 50).
Cable TV: Fox Sports Net Detroit.

SPRING TRAINING

Ballpark (city): Joker Marchant Stadium (Lakeland, Fla.).
Ticket information: 863-686-8075.

SPRING TRAINING ROSTER

Manager—Alan Trammell (3).
Coaches—Bob Cluck, Bruce Fields, Kirk Gibson, Mick Kelleher, Lance Parrish, Juan Samuel.

No.	PITCHERS	B/T	Ht./Wt.	Born	Age*	2002 clubs
14	Anderson, Matt	R/R	6-4/190	8-17-76	26	Detroit
24	Bernero, Adam	R/R	6-4/205	11-28-76	26	Toledo, Detroit
	Burnside, Adrian	R/L	6-4/190	3-15-77	26	Altoona
	Cordova, Jorge	R/R	6-0/190	1-13-78	25	Stockton, Chattanooga, Louisville
34	Cornejo, Nate	R/R	6-5/240	9-24-79	23	Toledo, Detroit
61	Eckenstahler, Eric	L/L	6-7/220	12-17-76	26	Toledo, Detroit
62	German, Franklyn	R/R	6-4/170	1-20-80	23	Midland, Toledo, Detroit
41	Henriquez, Oscar	R/R	6-6/220	1-28-74	29	Toledo, Detroit
70	Kalita, Tim	R/L	6-2/220	11-21-78	24	Toledo
	Knotts, Gary	R/R	6-3/230	2-12-77	26	Florida, Calgary
	Ledezma, Wil	L/L	6-3/152	1-21-81	22	Augusta, Gulf Coast Red Sox
58	Loux, Shane	R/R	6-2/205	8-31-79	23	Toledo, Detroit
46	Maroth, Mike	L/L	6-0/180	8-17-77	25	Toledo, Detroit
28	Patterson, Danny	R/R	6-0/185	2-17-71	32	Detroit, Toledo
	Robertson, Nate	R/L	6-2/215	9-3-77	25	Portland, Florida
56	Rodney, Fernando	R/R	5-11/170	3-18-77	26	Erie, Detroit, Toledo
	Roney, Matt	R/R	6-4/225	1-10-80	23	Asheville, Carolina
37	Sparks, Steve	R/R	6-0/195	7-2-65	37	Detroit
50	Van Hekken, Andy	R/L	6-3/175	7-31-79	23	Erie, Toledo, Detroit
32	Walker, Jamie	L/L	6-2/190	7-1-71	31	Toledo, Detroit

No.	CATCHERS	B/T	Ht./Wt.	Born	Age*	2002 clubs
15	Inge, Brandon	R/R	5-11/189	5-19-77	25	Toledo, Detroit

No.	INFIELDERS	B/T	Ht./Wt.	Born	Age*	2002 clubs
22	Bocachica, Hiram	R/R	5-11/165	3-4-76	27	Los Angeles, Detroit
	Chapman, Travis	R/R	6-2/185	6-5-78	24	Reading
9	Easley, Damion	R/R	5-11/187	11-11-69	33	Detroit, Toledo
	Espinosa, David	B/R	6-1/170	12-16-81	21	Stockton
17	Halter, Shane	R/R	6-0/180	11-8-69	33	Detroit
20	Infante, Omar	R/R	5-9/150	12-26-81	21	Toledo, Detroit
33	Munson, Eric	L/R	6-3/228	10-3-77	25	Toledo, Detroit
7	Palmer, Dean	R/R	6-1/219	12-27-68	34	Detroit
8	Paquette, Craig	R/R	6-0/190	3-28-69	34	Detroit
43	Pena, Carlos	L/L	6-2/210	5-17-78	24	Oakland, Sacramento, Detroit
39	Santiago, Ramon	B/R	5-11/150	8-31-79	23	Erie, Toledo, Detroit

No.	OUTFIELDERS	B/T	Ht./Wt.	Born	Age*	2002 clubs
4	Higginson, Bobby	L/R	5-11/202	8-18-70	32	Detroit
	Kingsale, Gene	B/R	6-3/190	8-20-76	26	Tacoma, Seattle, San Diego
30	Lombard, George	L/R	6-0/212	9-14-75	27	Greenville, Richmond, Detroit
31	Monroe, Craig	R/R	6-1/195	2-27-77	26	Toledo, Detroit
	Ross, Cody	R/L	5-11/180	12-23-80	22	Erie
20	Torres, Andres	B/R	5-10/175	1-26-78	25	Toledo, Detroit
26	Young, Dmitri	B/R	6-2/235	10-11-73	29	Detroit

*Age as of April 1, 2003.

BALLPARK INFORMATION

Ballpark (capacity, surface)
Comerica Park (40,120, grass)
Address
2100 Woodward
Detroit, MI 48201
Official website
www.detroittigers.com
Business phone
313-471-2000
Ticket information
313-471-2255
Field dimensions (from home plate)
To left field at foul line, 345 feet
To center field, 420 feet
To right field at foul line, 330 feet
First game played
April 11, 2000 (Tigers 5, Mariners 2)

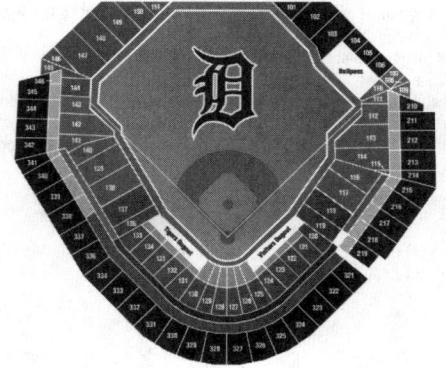

Detroit Tigers

2003 SEASON

Date	Opp.	Res.	Score	(inn.*)	Hits	Opp. hits	Winning pitcher	Losing pitcher	Save	Record	Pos.	GB
4-2	At T.B.	L	5-9		12	12	Zambrano	Acevedo		0-1	T4th	1.0
4-3	At T.B.	L	1-2	(12)	10	10	Colome	Farnsworth		0-2	T4th	2.0
4-4	At T.B.	L	2-9		6	10	Rupe	Lima		0-3	5th	2.0
4-5	Cle.	L	1-10		6	12	Baez	Redman		0-4	5th	3.0
4-6	Cle.	L	3-5		6	10	Colon	Cornejo	Wickman	0-5	5th	4.0
4-7	Cle.	L	1-5		4	11	Sabathia	Weaver	Wickman	0-6	5th	5.0
4-9	Chi.	L	2-8		6	14	Wright	Sparks		0-7	5th	6.5
4-10	Chi.	L	5-7		13	9	Osuna	Lima	Foulke	0-8	5th	7.5
4-12	At Min.	L	2-4		8	8	Radke	Redman	Guardado	0-9	5th	9.0
4-13	At Min.	L	3-7		14	9	Milton	Weaver		0-10	5th	10.0
4-14	At Min.	L	7-13		11	16	Romero	Anderson		0-11	5th	10.5
4-16	T.B.	W	9-3		11	11	Lima	James		1-11	5th	9.5
4-17	T.B.	W	7-6		15	7	Anderson	Zambrano		2-11	5th	8.5
4-18	T.B.	L	4-6		11	14	Rupe	Weaver	Yan	2-12	5th	8.5
4-19	At Chi.	W	8-2		14	6	Sparks	Wright		3-12	5th	7.5
4-20	At Chi.	L	5-12		8	15	Garland	Cornejo		3-13	5th	8.0
4-21	At Chi.	L	8-11		10	11	Osuna	Paniagua	Foulke	3-14	5th	9.0
4-22	At K.C.	L	0-6		6	9	Byrd	Redman		3-15	5th	9.5
4-23	At K.C.	W	3-0		5	5	Weaver	Suppan		4-15	5th	8.5
4-24	At K.C.	L	2-8		7	12	Affeldt	Sparks		4-16	5th	9.5
4-26	Min.	W	3-2	(10)	12	9	Anderson	Wells		5-16	5th	9.0
4-27	Min.	W	5-1		9	9	Cornejo	Kinney		6-16	5th	8.0
4-28	Min.	W	5-4		10	9	Santana	Jackson		7-16	5th	7.0
4-29	K.C.	L	0-4		2	10	Suppan	Weaver		7-17	5th	7.5
4-30	K.C.	W	9-3		13	2	Sparks	George		8-17	5th	7.5
5-1	K.C.	W	7-6		12	9	Walker	Bailey	Acevedo	9-17	4th	7.5
5-3	At Min.	L	4-8		6	13	Radke	Cornejo		9-18	4th	8.5
5-4	At Min.	L	2-3		8	4	Jackson	Rodney		9-19	4th	9.5
5-5	At Min.	W	7-6		10	10	Weaver	Lohse	Acevedo	10-19	4th	8.5
5-6	At Min.	L	1-3		7	11	Reed	Sparks	Guardado	10-20	4th	9.5
5-7	At Ana.	W	3-0		5	5	Greisinger	Weber	Acevedo	11-20	4th	8.5
5-8	At Ana.	L	2-3		6	8	Percival	Rodney		11-21	4th	9.5
5-9	At Ana.	L	6-7		11	11	Sele	Redman	Percival	11-22	4th	10.0
5-10	At Tex.	L	0-2		8	5	Rogers	Weaver	Irabu	11-23	5th	10.0
5-11	At Tex.	L	6-10		11	14	Burba	Sparks		11-24	5th	10.0
5-12	At Tex.	L	1-5		6	10	Park	Greisinger	Van Poppel	11-25	5th	10.0
5-14	Ana.	L	2-9		4	14	Appier	Cornejo		11-26	5th	10.5
5-15	Ana.	L	1-10		6	13	Sele	Redman		11-27	5th	11.5
5-17	Tex.	W	6-3		7	10	Weaver	Burba	Acevedo	12-27	5th	11.0
5-18	Tex.	W	8-7		12	9	Santana	Seanez	Acevedo	13-27	5th	10.0
5-19	Tex.	W	2-1		7	6	Greisinger	Davis	Acevedo	14-27	5th	9.0
5-20	Cle.	W	4-3		11	10	Santana	Rincon	Walker	15-27	5th	8.5
5-21	Cle.	W	5-1		7	10	Redman	Nagy		16-27	4th	8.5
5-22	Cle.	W	2-0		6	1	Weaver	Finley		17-27	4th	7.5
5-24	At Chi.	L	1-12		5	14	Buehrle	Sparks		17-28	4th	8.5
5-25	At Chi.	L	4-6		6	9	Wunsch	Greisinger	Foulke	17-29	T4th	9.5
5-26	At Chi.	W	9-2		14	4	Bernero	Ritchie		18-29	5th	8.5
5-27	At Cle.	W	4-1		10	4	Redman	Baez		19-29	T4th	8.5
5-28	At Cle.	L	2-4		5	8	Finley	Weaver	Wickman	19-30	5th	9.5
5-29	At Cle.	W	9-5		11	11	Sparks	Riske	Acevedo	20-30	T4th	8.5
5-30	At Cle.	L	7-11		11	14	Riske	Lima		20-31	5th	9.5
5-31	Tor.	L	2-4		10	5	Loaiza	Bernero	Escobar	20-32	5th	9.5
6-1	Tor.	L	1-4	(11)	7	10	Politte	Patterson	Escobar	20-33	5th	10.5
6-2	Tor.	L	6-7		12	10	Halladay	Weaver	Escobar	20-34	5th	10.5
6-3	Bos.	W	7-6	(10)	11	12	Acevedo	Wakefield		21-34	5th	10.0
6-4	Bos.	L	5-10		11	13	Burkett	Lima		21-35	5th	11.0
6-5	Bos.	L	0-11		5	16	Lowe	Bernero	Haney	21-36	5th	11.0
6-6	Bos.	L	3-4		6	14	Arrojo	Redman	Urbina	21-37	5th	12.0
6-7	Phi.	L	1-11		8	15	Padilla	Weaver		21-38	5th	13.0
6-8	Phi.	L	1-2		5	10	Person	Patterson	Mesa	21-39	5th	14.0
6-9	Phi.	L	5-7		10	12	Duckworth	Sparks	Mesa	21-40	5th	14.0
6-10	Mon.	W	6-4		13	11	Bernero	Vazquez	Acevedo	22-40	5th	14.0
6-11	Mon.	W	2-1		13	8	Redman	Herges	Acevedo	23-40	5th	13.0
6-12	Mon.	L	1-2	(10)	6	4	Stewart	Acevedo	Lloyd	23-41	5th	13.0
6-14	At Ari.	W	6-3		11	6	Maroth	Schilling	Acevedo	24-41	5th	12.0

Date	Opp.	Res.	Score	(inn.*)	Hits	Opp. hits	Winning pitcher	Losing pitcher	Save	Record	Pos.	GB
6-15	At Ari.	L	1-3		8	8	Johnson	Santana	Kim	24-42	5th	13.0
6-16	At Ari.	L	2-11		9	15	Helling	Redman		24-43	5th	14.0
6-18	At Atl.	W	6-0		8	5	Weaver	Marquis		25-43	5th	14.0
6-19	At Atl.	L	1-4		6	7	Millwood	Maroth	Smoltz	25-44	5th	14.0
6-20	At Atl.	L	2-3		5	7	Ligtenberg	Acevedo		25-45	5th	14.0
6-21	At Fla.	L	1-4		2	13	Tejera	Sparks	Nunez	25-46	5th	14.0
6-22	At Fla.	L	4-5		9	7	Neal	Acevedo		25-47	5th	15.0
6-23	At Fla.	W	3-2		5	7	Farnsworth	Almanza	Acevedo	26-47	5th	15.0
6-25	At K.C.	L	6-8		10	13	Suppan	Santana	Hernandez	26-48	5th	15.5
6-26	At K.C.	L	5-6		11	8	Reichert	Bernero	Hernandez	26-49	5th	16.5
6-27	At K.C.	L	2-5		6	9	Byrd	Sparks	Hernandez	26-50	5th	16.5
6-28	Pit.	L	1-3		2	10	Fogg	Redman	Williams	26-51	5th	17.5
6-29	Pit.	W	2-1		10	9	Weaver	Beimel	Acevedo	27-51	5th	16.5
6-30	Pit.	L	2-6		10	13	Benson	Maroth	Williams	27-52	5th	17.5
7-2	At Chi.	L	9-17		13	16	Ritchie	Bernero		27-53	5th	18.0
7-3	At Chi.	W	5-4		11	11	Moehler	Glover	Paniagua	28-53	5th	18.0
7-4	At Chi.	W	6-5		8	4	Sparks	Wunsch	Acevedo	29-53	5th	17.0
7-5	At Bos.	W	9-5		14	11	Redman	Castillo		30-53	5th	17.0
7-6	At Bos.	L	0-8		2	10	Martinez	Maroth		30-54	5th	18.0
7-7	At Bos.	W	9-8		14	13	Farnsworth	Garces	Acevedo	31-54	5th	17.0
7-11	Chi.	L	2-9		5	15	Wright	Sparks		31-55	5th	18.0
7-12	Chi.	W	2-1		5	6	Redman	Ritchie	Acevedo	32-55	5th	18.0
7-13§	Chi.	W	5-3		9	7	Rodney	Buehrle	Acevedo	33-55		
7-13∞	Chi.	W	3-1		8	6	Maroth	Biddle	Henriquez	34-55	5th	16.5
7-14	Chi.	L	4-6		8	12	Garland	Bernero	Osuna	34-56	5th	17.5
7-15	Bos.	W	4-3	(11)	10	9	Henriquez	Gomes		35-56	5th	17.5
7-16	Bos.	L	4-9		8	18	Burkett	Farnsworth		35-57	5th	17.5
7-17	At N.Y.	L	1-2		11	6	Pettitte	Redman		35-58	5th	18.5
7-18	At N.Y.	L	5-6		10	13	Mendoza	Rodney	Rivera	35-59	5th	19.5
7-19	Min.	L	1-5		8	12	Lohse	Moehler	Santana	35-60	5th	20.5
7-20	Min.	L	4-14		10	17	Mays	Bernero		35-61	5th	21.5
7-21	Min.	L	2-4		7	7	Milton	Sparks	Guardado	35-62	5th	22.5
7-23	K.C.	W	10-1		19	4	Redman	Suppan		36-62	5th	22.0
7-24	K.C.	W	3-0		6	3	Lima	Byrd	Acevedo	37-62	5th	22.0
7-25	K.C.	W	5-2		8	9	Maroth	Asencio	Acevedo	38-62	5th	21.5
7-26	At Cle.	W	8-5		19	8	Powell	Nagy	Henriquez	39-62	5th	21.5
7-27	At Cle.	W	5-1		12	7	Sparks	Sabathia		40-62	5th	21.5
7-28	At Cle.	L	6-9		11	11	DePaula	Acevedo		40-63	5th	22.5
7-29	At Sea.	L	3-4		9	7	Rhodes	Santana	Sasaki	40-64	5th	23.0
7-30	At Sea.	L	4-5	(10)	11	14	Hasegawa	Farnsworth		40-65	5th	23.0
7-31	At Sea.	L	2-5		6	9	Baldwin	Powell	Sasaki	40-66	5th	24.0
8-1	At Oak.	L	3-5		8	7	Bowie	Sparks	Koch	40-67	5th	25.0
8-2	At Oak.	W	3-1		8	7	Redman	Zito	Acevedo	41-67	5th	25.0
8-3	At Oak.	L	4-8		6	11	Hudson	Lima		41-68	5th	26.0
8-4	At Oak.	L	0-4		1	6	Lidle	Maroth		41-69	5th	27.0
8-5	Ana.	L	3-6		7	13	Lackey	Powell	Percival	41-70	5th	27.0
8-6	Tex.	W	8-2		11	7	Sparks	Park		42-70	5th	26.0
8-7	Tex.	L	2-7	(11)	8	14	Cordero	Santana		42-71	5th	26.0
8-8	Tex.	W	2-1		4	11	Lima	Valdes	Acevedo	43-71	5th	25.0
8-9	Bal.	W	3-0		8	6	Maroth	Johnson	Acevedo	44-71	5th	25.0
8-10	Bal.	L	2-3		4	9	Lopez	Santana	Julio	44-72	5th	25.0
8-11	Bal.	W	2-1		7	4	Sparks	Stephens	Acevedo	45-72	5th	24.0
8-12	At Ana.	L	0-7		4	14	Appier	Redman		45-73	5th	24.5
8-13	At Ana.	L	6-7	(12)	12	15	Levine	Bernero		45-74	5th	25.5
8-14	At Ana.	L	4-5		7	7	Ortiz	Maroth	Percival	45-75	5th	25.5
8-16	At Bal.	W	6-5		10	12	Sparks	Lopez	Acevedo	46-75	5th	25.0
8-17	At Bal.	L	3-7		7	11	Stephens	Redman		46-76	5th	25.0
8-18	At Bal.	W	7-4		18	8	Bernero	Brock	Acevedo	47-76	5th	25.0
8-19	Sea.	W	4-3		9	12	Lima	Moyer	Acevedo	48-76	5th	25.0
8-20	Sea.	W	6-3		13	7	Maroth	Garcia	Acevedo	49-76	5th	25.0
8-21	Sea.	L	2-8		6	14	Valdes	Sparks		49-77	5th	25.0
8-22	Sea.	L	2-4		4	13	Franklin	Redman	Sasaki	49-78	5th	26.0
8-23	Oak.	L	1-9		7	14	Zito	Powell		49-79	5th	27.0
8-24	Oak.	L	3-12		8	14	Hudson	Lima		49-80	5th	28.0
8-25	Oak.	L	7-10		11	14	Mecir	Walker	Koch	49-81	5th	28.0
8-26	At Cle.	L	2-8		5	13	Rodriguez	Sparks		49-82	5th	28.5
8-27	At Cle.	W	8-5		8	7	Redman	Phillips	Acevedo	50-82	5th	28.5
8-28	At Cle.	L	1-2		6	8	Sabathia	Powell	Baez	50-83	5th	29.5
8-30	Chi.	L	3-4		4	11	Wright	Maroth	Marte	50-84	5th	29.0
8-31	Chi.	L	4-9		7	9	Glover	Sparks		50-85	5th	29.0

Date	Opp.	Res.	Score	(inn.*)	Hits	Opp. hits	Winning pitcher	Losing pitcher	Save	Record	Pos.	GB
9-1	Chi.	L	0-7		7	16	Buehrle	Redman		50-86	5th	29.0
9-2	Cle.	L	1-11		6	12	Sabathia	Powell		50-87	5th	29.0
9-3	Cle.	W	4-0		11	8	Van Hekken	Mulholland		51-87	5th	28.5
9-4	Cle.	L	3-9		6	9	Wright	Maroth		51-88	5th	29.5
9-5	At N.Y.	L	3-9		7	13	Hernandez	Sparks		51-89	5th	30.0
9-6	At N.Y.	L	1-8		5	11	Wells	Redman		51-90	5th	31.0
9-7	At N.Y.	W	2-1		7	7	German	Mussina	Acevedo	52-90	5th	30.0
9-8	At N.Y.	L	4-6		11	8	Stanton	Henriquez	Karsay	52-91	5th	30.0
9-9	At Min.	L	2-5		7	9	Reed	Maroth	Guardado	52-92	5th	31.0
9-10	At Min.	L	4-11		11	15	Lohse	Loux		52-93	5th	32.0
9-11	At Min.	L	2-8		4	8	Radke	Redman		52-94	5th	33.0
9-13	K.C.	W	4-2	(10)	10	8	Eckenstahler	Mullen		53-94	5th	31.5
9-14	K.C.	L	1-5		4	11	Byrd	Van Hekken		53-95	5th	32.5
9-15	K.C.	L	3-9		7	13	Hernandez	Beverlin		53-96	5th	33.5
9-16	K.C.	W	5-2		8	6	Maroth	May	German	54-96	5th	33.0
9-17	Min.	L	4-7		13	16	Radke	Loux	Guardado	54-97	5th	34.0
9-18	Min.	L	0-2		6	9	Mays	Sparks	Guardado	54-98	5th	35.0
9-20	N.Y.	L	1-5		8	11	Clemens	Van Hekken		54-99	5th	35.0
9-21	N.Y.	L	2-3		5	7	Pettitte	Beverlin	Karsay	54-100	5th	35.0
9-22	N.Y.	L	3-4		7	6	Wells	Maroth	Stanton	54-101	5th	35.0
9-24	At K.C.	L	2-17		6	15	Asencio	Loux		54-102	5th	36.0
9-25	At K.C.	W	7-6	(12)	15	14	Bernero	Hill		55-102	5th	36.0
9-26	At K.C.	L	2-7		5	9	Suppan	Cornejo		55-103	5th	36.0
9-27	At Tor.	L	2-5		6	11	Walker	Van Hekken	Escobar	55-104	5th	37.0
9-28	At Tor.	L	2-10		6	12	Miller	Beverlin		55-105	5th	38.0
9-29	At Tor.	L	0-1		2	7	Halladay	Maroth	Escobar	55-106	5th	39.0

Monthly records: April (8-17), May (12-15), June (7-20), July (13-14), August (10-19), September (5-21).
*Innings, if other than nine. §Day separate admission. ∞Night separate admission.

RECORDS

2002 regular-season record: 55-106
Position: 5th in A.L. Central
Home: 33-47   **Road:** 22-59
A.L. East: 11-25   **A.L. Central:** 29-46
A.L. West: 9-23   **N.L.:** 6-12
Vs. LH starters: 12-22
Vs. RH starters: 43-84
Grass: 54-91   **Artificial:** 1-15
Day: 15-37   **Night:** 40-69
1-Run: 23-23   **X-inn.:** 5-6
Doubleheaders: 0-0-0
Team record past five years: 334-474
(.413, ranks 13th in league in that span)

TEAM LEADERS

Batting average: Randall Simon (.301).
At-bats: Robert Fick (556).
Runs: Robert Fick (66).
Hits: Robert Fick (150).
Total bases: Robert Fick (241).
Doubles: Robert Fick (36).
Triples: Shane Halter (6).
Home runs: Randall Simon (19).
Runs batted in: Randall Simon (82).
Stolen bases: George Lombard (13).
Slugging percentage: Carlos Pena (.462).
On-base percentage: Bobby Higginson (.345).
Wins: Mark Redman, Steve W. Sparks (8).

Earned-run average: Jeff Weaver (3.18).
Complete games: Mark Redman, Steve W. Sparks, Jeff Weaver (3).
Shutouts: Jeff Weaver (3).
Saves: Juan Acevedo (28).
Innings pitched: Mark Redman (203.0).
Strikeouts: Mark Redman (109).

GAMES BY POSITION

Catcher: Brandon Inge 94, Michael Rivera 37, Matt Walbeck 27, Mitch Meluskey 8.
First base: Carlos Pena 73, Randall Simon 59, Dmitri Young 15, Craig Paquette 14, Jacob Cruz 4, Eric Munson 4, Shane Halter 1.
Second base: Damion Easley 84, Damian Jackson 56, Jose Macias 17, Oscar Salazar 6, Shane Halter 4, Hiram Bocachica 2, Omar Infante 2.
Third base: Chris Truby 89, Craig Paquette 49, Shane Halter 30, Jose Macias 8, Damian Jackson 2, Oscar Salazar 1, Dmitri Young 1.
Shortstop: Shane Halter 81, Ramon Santiago 63, Omar Infante 16, Damian Jackson 6, Oscar Salazar 1.
Outfield: Robert Fick 140, Bobby Higginson 117, Wendell Magee 91, George Lombard 69, Hiram Bocachica 32, Andres Torres 19, Jacob Cruz 12, Jose Macias 10, Craig Monroe 9, Shane Halter 8, Craig Paquette 8, Damian Jackson 6, Ryan Jackson 3, Dmitri Young 1.
Designated hitter: Randall Simon 65, Dmitri Young 35, Jacob Cruz 15, Eric Munson 14, Robert Fick 6, Damian Jackson 5, Craig Paquette 5, Wendell Magee 4, Dean Palmer 4, Craig Monroe 3, Shane Halter 2, George Lombard 2, Carlos Pena 2, Hiram Bocachica 1, Damion Easley 1, Bobby Higginson 1, Brandon Inge 1, Michael Rivera 1, Ramon Santiago 1.

TOP DRAFT CHOICES

1. **Scott Moore**, SS, Cypress H.S., Long Beach, Calif.
2. **Brent Clevlen**, OF, Westwood H.S., Cedar Park, Texas.
3a. **Curtis Granderson**, OF, Illinois-Chicago.
3b. **Matt Pender**, RHP, Kennesaw State (Ga.).
4. **Robbie Sovie**, OF, Stratford Academy, Macon, Ga.
5. **Bo Flowers**, OF, Walter Lutheran H.S., Maywood, Ill.
6. **Chris Maples**, RHP, North Carolina.
7. **Wilton Reynolds**, OF, Oral Roberts.
8. **Troy Pickford**, RHP, Oral Roberts.
9. **Marcos Hernandez**, RHP, Juan Ponce de Leon H.S., San Juan, P.R.
10. **Luke Carlin**, C, Northeastern.

KANSAS CITY ROYALS
AMERICAN LEAGUE CENTRAL DIVISION

2003 SEASON

March/April

SUN	MON	TUE	WED	THU	FRI	SAT
	31 CWS D	1 CWS	2 CWS D	3 CWS D	4 CLE	5 CLE D
6 CLE D	7	8 DET	9 DET D	10 DET	11 CLE	12 CLE D
13 CLE	14 CLE	15 CWS	16 CWS	17 CWS	18 DET D	19 DET D
20 DET D	21	22 MIN	23 MIN	24 MIN D	25 TOR	26 TOR D
27 TOR	28	29 BOS	30 BOS			

May

SUN	MON	TUE	WED	THU	FRI	SAT
				1 BOS	2 BAL	3 BAL D
4 BAL D	5 BOS D	6 BOS	7 BOS D	8 BAL	9 BAL	10 BAL
11 BAL D	12 MIN	13 MIN	14 MIN	15 MIN D	16 TOR	17 TOR
18 TOR D	19	20 SEA	21 SEA	22 SEA	23 OAK	24 OAK D
25 OAK D	26	27 SEA	28 SEA D	29 SEA	30 OAK	31 OAK D

June

SUN	MON	TUE	WED	THU	FRI	SAT
1 OAK D	2	3 LA	4 LA	5 LA	6 COL	7 COL
8 COL D	9	10 ARI	11 ARI	12 ARI	13 SF	14 SF
15 SF D	16	17 MIN	18 MIN	19 MIN D	20 STL	21 STL
22 STL D	23	24 CLE	25 CLE	26 CLE	27 STL	28 STL
29 STL D	30 CLE					

July

SUN	MON	TUE	WED	THU	FRI	SAT
		1 CLE	2 CLE	3 DET	4 DET	5 DET
6 DET D	7	8 ANA	9 ANA	10 ANA	11 TEX	12 TEX
13 TEX	14	15 *	16	17 SEA	18 SEA	19 SEA
20 SEA	21 OAK	22 OAK	23 MIN	24 MIN D	25 DET	26 DET
27 DET D	28	29 CWS	30 CWS	31 CWS		

August

SUN	MON	TUE	WED	THU	FRI	SAT
					1 TB	2 TB
3 TB D	4 CWS	5 CWS	6 CWS D	7 TB	8 TB	9 TB
10 TB D	11 NYY	12 NYY	13 NYY	14	15 MIN	16 MIN D
17 MIN D	18 NYY	19 NYY	20 NYY D	21 MIN	22 MIN	23 MIN
24 MIN D	25	26 TEX	27 TEX	28 TEX	29 ANA	30 ANA

September

SUN	MON	TUE	WED	THU	FRI	SAT
31 ANA D	1 TEX D	2 TEX	3 TEX	4	5 ANA	6 ANA
7 ANA D	8	9 CLE	10 CLE	11 CLE D	12 DET	13 DET
14 DET D	15	16 CLE	17 CLE	18 CLE	19 CWS	20 CWS
21 CWS D	22 DET	23 DET	24 DET	25 CWS	26 CWS	27 CWS
28 CWS D						

Home games shaded; D—Day game (games starting before 5 p.m.); *—All-Star Game at Comiskey Park, Chicago. Subject to change.

CLUB DIRECTORY

Chairman/owner
David Glass
President
Dan Glass
Executive v.p. & chief operating officer
Herk Robinson
Sr. v.p. & g.m., baseball operations
Allard Baird
Vice president, baseball operations
George Brett

Assistant g.m., player personnel
Muzzy Jackson
Senior advisor to the general manager
Art Stewart
Assistant to the general manager
Brian Murphy
Special assistants to the g.m.
Pat Jones, Frank White Jr.
Senior director, scouting
Deric Ladnier

Manager, baseball operations
Jim Wong
Director, community relations
Shani Tate
Senior director, broadcasting & p.r.
David Witty
Manager, media relations
Aaron Babcock
Manager, media services
Chris Stathos

MINOR LEAGUE AFFILIATES

Class	Team	League	Manager
AAA	Omaha	Pacific Coast	Mike Jirschele
AA	Wichita	Texas	Keith Bodie
A	Wilmington	Carolina	Bill Gardner Jr.
A	Burlington	Midwest	Joe Szekely
Rookie	Arizona Royals	Arizona	Lloyd Simmons

BROADCAST INFORMATION

Radio: KMBZ-AM (980).
Cable TV: Royals Television Network, LLC.

SPRING TRAINING

Ballpark (city): Surprise Stadium (Surprise, Ariz.).
Ticket information: 623-594-5600.

Follow the Royals all season at: www.sportingnews.com/baseball/teams/royals/

SPRING TRAINING ROSTER

Manager—Tony Pena (6).
Coaches—John Cumberland (47); Tom Gamboa (21), John Mizerock (13), Jeff Pentland, Bob Schaefer (44), Luis Silverio.

No.	PITCHERS	B/T	Ht./Wt.	Born	Age*	2002 clubs
48	Affeldt, Jeremy	L/L	6-4/215	6-6-79	23	Kansas City, Wichita
53	Asencio, Miguel	R/R	6-2/160	9-29-80	22	Kansas City
26	Austin, Jeff	R/R	6-0/185	10-19-76	26	Kansas City, Omaha
35	Bukvich, Ryan	R/R	6-2/250	5-13-78	24	Wichita, Omaha, Kansas City
	Carrasco, Dan	R/R	6-2/191	4-12-77	25	Lynchburg
	Ferguson, Ian	R/R	6-4/220	8-23-79	23	Wilmington, Wichita
32	George, Chris	L/L	6-2/200	9-16-79	23	Omaha, Kansas City
	Gobble, Jimmy	L/L	6-3/175	7-19-81	21	Wichita
38	Grimsley, Jason	R/R	6-3/205	8-7-67	35	Kansas City, Wichita
40	Hernandez, Runelvys	R/R	6-1/205	4-27-78	24	Wilmington, Wichita, Kansas City
52	Hill, Jeremy	R/R	5-10/185	8-8-77	25	Wichita, Kansas City
	Lopez, Albie	R/R	6-2/240	8-18-71	31	Atlanta, Greenville
54	MacDougal, Mike	B/R	6-4/195	3-5-77	26	Omaha, Wichita, Gulf Coast Royals, Wilmington, Kansas City
31	May, Darrell	L/L	6-2/184	6-13-72	30	Omaha, Kansas City, Wichita
45	Moreno, Orber	R/R	6-3/200	4-27-77	25	Gulf Coast Royals
57	Mullen, Scott	R/L	6-2/195	1-17-75	28	Omaha, Kansas City
43	Obermueller, Wes	R/R	6-2/195	12-22-76	26	Wilmington, Wichita, Kansas City
56	Sedlacek, Shawn	R/R	6-4/200	6-29-77	25	Wichita, Kansas City, Omaha
59	Snyder, Kyle	B/R	6-8/220	9-9-77	25	Wilmington, Wichita
46	Voyles, Brad	R/R	6-0/195	12-30-76	26	Omaha, Kansas City
51	Wilson, Kris	R/R	6-4/225	8-6-76	26	Omaha, Wichita, Kansas City

No.	CATCHERS	B/T	Ht./Wt.	Born	Age*	2002 clubs
2	Mayne, Brent	L/R	6-1/190	4-19-68	34	Kansas City, Wichita
	Paulino, Ron	R/R	6-1/194	4-21-81	21	Lynchburg
	Tonis, Mike	R/R	6-3/215	2-9-79	24	Gulf Coast Royals

No.	INFIELDERS	B/T	Ht./Wt.	Born	Age*	2002 clubs
4	Berroa, Angel	R/R	6-0/175	1-27-78	25	Omaha, Kansas City
3	Febles, Carlos	R/R	5-11/185	5-24-76	26	Kansas City, Omaha
28	Harvey, Ken	R/R	6-2/240	3-1-78	25	Omaha
	Machado, Alejandro	R/R	6-0/160	4-26-82	20	Wilmington
16	Randa, Joe	R/R	5-11/190	12-18-69	33	Kansas City
	Relaford, Desi	B/R	5-9/174	9-16-73	29	Seattle
29	Sweeney, Mike	R/R	6-3/225	7-22-73	29	Kansas City, Omaha

No.	OUTFIELDERS	B/T	Ht./Wt.	Born	Age*	2002 clubs
15	Beltran, Carlos	B/R	6-1/190	4-24-77	25	Kansas City
30	Berger, Brandon	R/R	5-11/205	2-21-75	28	Omaha, Kansas City
27	Brown, Dee	L/R	6-0/225	3-27-78	25	Omaha, Kansas City
9	Gomez, Alexis	L/L	6-2/180	8-6-80	22	Wichita, Kansas City
45	Guiel, Aaron	L/R	5-10/200	10-5-72	30	Omaha, Kansas City
18	Ibanez, Raul	L/R	6-2/200	6-2-72	30	Kansas City
14	Quinn, Mark	R/R	6-1/195	5-21-74	28	Omaha, Wichita, Kansas City
24	Tucker, Michael	L/R	6-2/195	6-25-71	31	Kansas City

*Age as of April 1, 2003.

BALLPARK INFORMATION

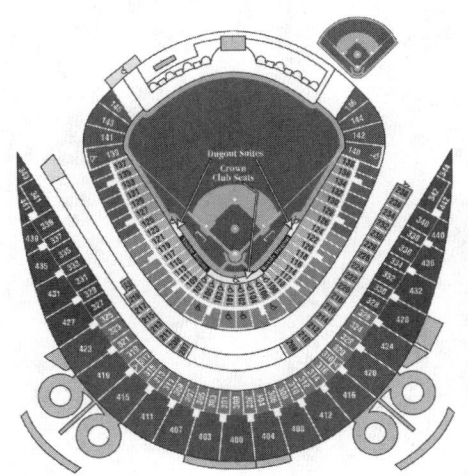

Ballpark (capacity, surface)
Kauffman Stadium (40,793, grass)
Address
P.O. Box 419969
Kansas City, MO 64141-6969
Official website
www.kcroyals.com
Business phone
816-921-8000
Ticket information
816-504-4040, 800-6ROYALS
Field dimensions (from home plate)
To left field at foul line, 330 feet
To center field, 400 feet
To right field at foul line, 330 feet
First game played
April 10, 1973 (Royals 12, Rangers 1)

2002 REVIEW
DAY BY DAY

Date	Opp.	Res.	Score	(inn.*)	Hits	Opp. hits	Winning pitcher	Losing pitcher	Save	Record	Pos.	GB
4-1	Min.	L	6-8		10	12	Romero	Bailey	Guardado	0-1	5th	1.0
4-3	Min.	L	0-1		3	7	Milton	Reichert	Guardado	0-2	T4th	2.0
4-5	Chi.	W	5-2		6	10	Byrd	Garland	Stein	1-2	3rd	1.5
4-6	Chi.	L	0-14		6	16	Buehrle	Durbin		1-3	4th	2.5
4-7	Chi.	W	9-2		9	7	Suppan	Ritchie		2-3	3rd	2.5
4-9	At Bos.	L	4-8		5	15	Wakefield	Reichert		2-4	4th	4.0
4-10	At Bos.	W	6-2		12	5	Byrd	Lowe	Bailey	3-4	4th	4.0
4-11	At Bos.	W	8-5		7	7	Grimsley	Urbina		4-4	T2nd	4.0
4-12	At Cle.	L	1-3		6	5	Sabathia	Suppan	Wickman	4-5	4th	5.0
4-13	At Cle.	L	7-8		9	10	Shuey	Bailey		4-6	4th	6.0
4-16	At Min.	L	5-8		10	13	Fiore	Stein	Guardado	4-7	4th	6.0
4-17	At Min.	W	16-3		16	7	Byrd	Radke		5-7	4th	5.0
4-18	At Min.	L	1-4		4	8	Milton	Suppan	Guardado	5-8	4th	5.0
4-19	Bos.	L	0-4		2	7	Martinez	George		5-9	4th	5.0
4-21†	Bos.	L	2-12		7	16	Burkett	Reichert	Wakefield	5-10		
4-21‡	Bos.	L	7-8		10	14	Lowe	Rekar	Urbina	5-11	4th	6.5
4-22	Det.	W	6-0		9	6	Byrd	Redman		6-11	4th	6.0
4-23	Det.	L	0-3		5	5	Weaver	Suppan		6-12	4th	6.0
4-24	Det.	W	8-2		12	7	Affeldt	Sparks		7-12	4th	6.0
4-26	Bal.	L	5-10	(10)	11	14	Groom	Grimsley		7-13	4th	6.5
4-27	Bal.	L	4-9		8	8	Ponson	Byrd		7-14	4th	6.5
4-28	Bal.	L	0-13		4	15	Erickson	Rekar		7-15	4th	6.5
4-29	At Det.	W	4-0		10	2	Suppan	Weaver		8-15	4th	6.0
4-30	At Det.	L	3-9		2	13	Sparks	George		8-16	4th	7.0
5-1	At Det.	L	6-7		9	12	Walker	Bailey	Acevedo	8-17	5th	8.0
5-2	At Bal.	L	2-6		8	8	Ponson	Byrd	Bauer	8-18	5th	8.5
5-3	At Bal.	L	3-4		7	9	Roberts	Bailey	Julio	8-19	5th	9.5
5-4	At Bal.	L	0-10		6	10	Lopez	Suppan		8-20	5th	10.5
5-5	At Bal.	L	2-3		9	11	Maduro	George	Julio	8-21	5th	10.5
5-7	At Min.	W	4-1		6	5	Byrd	Kinney	Hernandez	9-21	5th	10.0
5-8	At Min.	L	1-3		5	8	Radke	Affeldt		9-22	5th	11.0
5-9	Cle.	W	5-3		8	7	Suppan	Rincon	Hernandez	10-22	5th	10.5
5-10	Cle.	W	9-0		11	7	Reichert	Sabathia		11-22	4th	9.5
5-12	Cle.	W	4-1		7	5	Byrd	Finley	Hernandez	12-22	4th	8.0
5-13	Min.	L	2-3		4	7	Romero	Grimsley	Guardado	12-23	4th	9.0
5-14	Min.	W	8-1		11	9	Suppan	Kinney		13-23	4th	8.0
5-15	Min.	L	6-8		11	10	Milton	Reichert	Guardado	13-24	4th	9.0
5-16	Min.	L	5-14		9	18	Lohse	George		13-25	4th	10.0
5-17	At Cle.	W	6-2		6	5	Byrd	Finley		14-25	4th	9.0
5-18§	At Cle.	W	4-2		6	7	Reichert	Wickman	Hernandez	15-25		
5-18∞	At Cle.	L	1-4		4	4	Drese	May	Wickman	15-26	4th	8.5
5-19	At Cle.	W	5-4		7	5	Grimsley	Wickman	Hernandez	16-26	4th	7.5
5-20	At Ana.	L	3-6		8	10	Appier	Stein	Percival	16-27	4th	8.0
5-21	At Ana.	L	1-5		8	5	Cook	Reichert		16-28	5th	9.0
5-22	At Ana.	L	6-7		9	8	Weber	May	Percival	16-29	5th	9.0
5-25	Tex.	W	6-3		10	6	Suppan	Burba	Hernandez	17-29	T4th	9.5
5-26†	Tex.	W	7-5		9	8	Bailey	Irabu		18-29		
5-26‡	Tex.	W	9-8		18	13	Bailey	Michalak	Hernandez	19-29	4th	8.0
5-28	Ana.	W	7-4		13	8	Byrd	Sele	Hernandez	20-29	4th	8.5
5-29	Ana.	L	2-12		7	17	Ortiz	Affeldt		20-30	T4th	8.5
5-31	At Tex.	W	10-7	(11)	15	17	Bailey	Irabu		21-30	4th	8.0
6-1	At Tex.	L	1-3		5	7	Rogers	May		21-31	4th	9.0
6-2	At Tex.	L	6-8		6	11	Park	Byrd	Irabu	21-32	4th	9.0
6-3	At Chi.	L	0-4		6	5	Garland	Affeldt		21-33	4th	9.5
6-4	At Chi.	W	3-2		7	8	Asencio	Buehrle	Hernandez	22-33	4th	9.5
6-5	At Chi.	L	1-6		3	9	Glover	Suppan		22-34	4th	9.5
6-6	At Chi.	W	4-3		10	9	May	Ritchie	Hernandez	23-34	4th	9.5
6-7	St.L.	L	6-12		11	17	Kile	Byrd		23-35	4th	10.5
6-8	St.L.	L	3-11		6	15	Morris	Affeldt		23-36	4th	11.5
6-9	St.L.	W	3-2		4	6	Hernandez	Timlin		24-36	4th	10.5
6-10	Fla.	L	8-15	(14)	16	17	Almanza	Suzuki		24-37	4th	11.5
6-11	Fla.	W	6-0	(5)	10	4	May	Tejera		25-37	4th	10.5
6-12	Fla.	L	5-13		9	17	Dempster	Byrd		25-38	4th	10.5
6-14	At St.L.	L	0-3		3	7	Morris	Asencio	Kline	25-39	4th	10.5
6-15	At St.L.	L	3-5		7	9	Simontacchi	Suppan	Veres	25-40	4th	11.5

Date	Opp.	Res.	Score	(inn.*)	Hits	Opp. hits	Winning pitcher	Losing pitcher	Save	Record	Pos.	GB
6-16	At St.L.	L	1-5		5	9	Williams	May		25-41	4th	12.5
6-18	At Mon.	L	4-5		8	6	Day	Mullen	Stewart	25-42	4th	13.5
6-19	At Mon.	L	3-6		10	8	Ohka	Suzuki	Stewart	25-43	4th	13.5
6-20	At Mon.	L	4-5	(11)	15	8	Eischen	Mullen		25-44	4th	13.5
6-21	At N.Y.	L	3-4		8	12	Guthrie	Voyles		25-45	4th	13.5
6-22	At N.Y.	W	5-1		7	8	Byrd	Astacio		26-45	4th	13.5
6-23	At N.Y.	L	4-5		8	9	Strickland	Grimsley	Benitez	26-46	4th	14.5
6-25	Det.	W	8-6		13	10	Suppan	Santana	Hernandez	27-46	4th	14.0
6-26	Det.	W	6-5		8	11	Reichert	Bernero	Hernandez	28-46	4th	14.0
6-27	Det.	W	5-2		9	6	Byrd	Sparks	Hernandez	29-46	4th	13.0
6-28	S.D.	W	14-10		18	15	Grimsley	Cyr		30-46	4th	13.0
6-29	S.D.	L	4-8	(10)	7	10	Reed	Grimsley		30-47	4th	13.0
6-30	S.D.	W	13-1		15	5	Suppan	Peavy		31-47	4th	13.0
7-1	At Sea.	L	0-7		5	9	Moyer	May		31-48	4th	14.0
7-2	At Sea.	W	7-5		13	11	Byrd	Sasaki	Hernandez	32-48	4th	13.0
7-3	At Sea.	L	0-3		2	7	Pineiro	Asencio	Sasaki	32-49	4th	14.0
7-4	At Oak.	L	2-3		4	7	Koch	Hernandez		32-50	4th	14.0
7-5	At Oak.	L	3-4		9	7	Mecir	Hernandez		32-51	4th	15.0
7-6	At Oak.	W	4-3	(10)	12	7	Mullen	Koch	Voyles	33-51	4th	15.0
7-7	At Oak.	L	2-3		6	9	Zito	Byrd	Koch	33-52	4th	15.0
7-11	Ana.	L	0-1		4	6	Washburn	May	Percival	33-53	4th	16.0
7-12	Ana.	L	3-11		5	14	Appier	Suppan		33-54	4th	17.0
7-13	Ana.	W	4-0		8	3	Byrd	Sele		34-54	4th	16.0
7-14	Ana.	W	12-3		12	12	Asencio	Ortiz		35-54	4th	16.0
7-15†	Tex.	W	8-6		5	7	Sedlacek	Benoit	Hernandez	36-54		
7-15‡	Tex.	W	6-4		12	11	Wilson	Telford	Hernandez	37-54	4th	15.5
7-16	Tex.	W	6-5	(11)	12	10	Wilson	Alvarez		38-54	4th	14.5
7-17	Chi.	W	8-6		14	10	Suppan	Ritchie	Hernandez	39-54	4th	14.5
7-18	Chi.	W	5-3		8	10	Byrd	Marte		40-54	4th	14.5
7-19	Cle.	W	8-5		10	12	Mullen	Murray	Hernandez	41-54	4th	14.5
7-20†	Cle.	W	7-5		10	10	Hernandez	Wright	Hernandez	42-54		
7-20‡	Cle.	L	3-5	(10)	7	10	Shuey	Voyles	Wickman	42-55	4th	15.0
7-21	Cle.	W	13-12	(10)	13	20	Mullen	Murray		43-55	T3rd	15.0
7-23	At Det.	L	1-10		4	19	Redman	Suppan		43-56	4th	15.5
7-24	At Det.	L	0-3		3	6	Lima	Byrd	Acevedo	43-57	4th	16.5
7-25	At Det.	L	2-5		9	8	Maroth	Asencio	Acevedo	43-58	4th	17.0
7-26	At Chi.	L	2-10		10	14	Wright	Sedlacek		43-59	4th	18.0
7-27	At Chi.	L	1-9		5	13	Glover	May		43-60	4th	19.0
7-28	At Chi.	L	2-4		5	9	Howry	Suppan	Marte	43-61	4th	20.0
7-29	Tor.	W	4-1		7	5	Byrd	Carpenter		44-61	4th	19.5
7-30	Tor.	L	4-13		9	17	Walker	Asencio		44-62	4th	19.5
7-31	Tor.	L	2-9		10	14	Parris	Sedlacek		44-63	4th	20.5
8-1	Tor.	L	2-3		5	9	Halladay	Hernandez	Escobar	44-64	4th	21.5
8-2	At Min.	L	1-2		4	8	Reed	Suppan	Guardado	44-65	4th	22.5
8-3	At Min.	L	3-4	(10)	7	10	Santana	May		44-66	4th	23.5
8-4	At Min.	L	4-5	(10)	10	12	Romero	Mullen		44-67	4th	24.5
8-5	At Min.	W	12-4		17	8	Sedlacek	Mays		45-67	4th	23.5
8-6	At N.Y.	W	6-2		17	4	Hernandez	Mussina		46-67	4th	22.5
8-7	At N.Y.	L	2-6		6	9	Clemens	Suppan		46-68	4th	22.5
8-8	At N.Y.	L	3-6		10	10	Pettitte	Byrd	Rivera	46-69	4th	22.5
8-9	T.B.	W	5-4	(12)	15	12	May	Phelps		47-69	4th	22.5
8-10	T.B.	L	6-13		9	16	Zambrano	Sedlacek	Alvarez	47-70	4th	22.5
8-11	T.B.	W	10-0		14	2	Hernandez	Sosa		48-70	4th	21.5
8-13	N.Y.	L	5-10		11	14	Clemens	Suppan		48-71	4th	22.5
8-14	N.Y.	L	2-3	(14)	11	14	Mendoza	Stein	Rivera	48-72	4th	22.5
8-15	N.Y.	L	5-7		12	18	Stanton	Hernandez	Rivera	48-73	4th	22.5
8-16	At T.B.	W	6-5		9	8	Bukvich	Yan	Hernandez	49-73	4th	22.5
8-17	At T.B.	W	7-3	(12)	12	9	Mullen	Colome	Hernandez	50-73	4th	21.5
8-18	At T.B.	L	6-8		9	12	Sturtze	Suppan		50-74	4th	22.5
8-19	At Tor.	L	0-2		4	4	Walker	Byrd	Escobar	50-75	4th	23.5
8-20	At Tor.	W	6-5	(12)	7	16	Affeldt	Cassidy	Hernandez	51-75	4th	23.5
8-21	At Tor.	W	7-4		12	9	Sedlacek	Halladay	Hernandez	52-75	4th	22.5
8-22	Min.	L	6-8		11	12	Santana	Hernandez	Guardado	52-76	4th	23.5
8-23	Min.	L	2-9		6	11	Reed	Suppan		52-77	4th	24.5
8-24	Min.	L	5-6		16	12	Radke	Byrd	Guardado	52-78	4th	25.5
8-25	Min.	W	4-2		11	6	Asencio	Lohse	Hernandez	53-78	4th	24.5
8-26	Oak.	L	3-6		6	14	Lidle	May	Koch	53-79	4th	25.0
8-27	Oak.	L	4-6		9	12	Mulder	Hernandez	Koch	53-80	4th	26.0
8-28	Oak.	L	1-7		4	11	Zito	Sedlacek		53-81	4th	27.0

Date	Opp.	Res.	Score	(inn.*)	Hits	Opp. hits	Winning pitcher	Losing pitcher	Save	Record	Pos.	GB
8-30	At Sea.	W	5-1		9	10	Byrd	Garcia	Grimsley	54-81	4th	25.5
8-31	At Sea.	W	4-2		10	6	Affeldt	Rhodes	Hernandez	55-81	4th	24.5
9-1	At Sea.	L	4-9		8	10	Valdes	Suppan		55-82	4th	24.5
9-2	At Oak.	L	6-7		14	8	Koch	Grimsley		55-83	4th	24.5
9-4	At Oak.	L	11-12		15	15	Koch	Grimsley		55-84	4th	25.5
9-6	Sea.	L	7-14		17	15	Garcia	Sedlacek		55-85	4th	26.5
9-7	Sea.	L	2-9		8	13	Franklin	Asencio		55-86	4th	26.5
9-8	Sea.	L	9-16	(11)	12	15	Creek	Stein		55-87	4th	26.5
9-9	Chi.	L	6-10		10	11	Wright	Byrd		55-88	4th	27.5
9-10	Chi.	L	4-12		8	13	Porzio	Hernandez	Osuna	55-89	4th	28.5
9-11	Chi.	W	9-6		13	10	May	Buehrle		56-89	4th	28.5
9-12	Chi.	L	1-5		3	11	Garland	Asencio		56-90	4th	28.5
9-13	At Det.	L	2-4	(10)	8	10	Eckenstahler	Mullen		56-91	4th	28.5
9-14	At Det.	W	5-1		11	4	Byrd	Van Hekken		57-91	4th	28.5
9-15	At Det.	W	9-3		13	7	Hernandez	Beverlin		58-91	4th	28.5
9-16	At Det.	L	2-5		6	8	Maroth	May	German	58-92	4th	29.0
9-17	At Chi.	L	1-6		7	11	Buehrle	Asencio	Foulke	58-93	4th	30.0
9-18	At Chi.	L	1-3		4	11	Garland	Suppan	Marte	58-94	4th	31.0
9-19	At Chi.	W	2-1		6	8	Byrd	Biddle	Hernandez	59-94	4th	30.5
9-20	Cle.	L	2-6		7	12	Davis	Obermueller	Baez	59-95	4th	30.5
9-21	Cle.	W	3-2		8	12	Grimsley	Mulholland		60-95	4th	29.5
9-22	Cle.	L	5-6		11	9	Sabathia	Grimsley	Baez	60-96	4th	29.5
9-24	Det.	W	17-2		15	6	Asencio	Loux		61-96	4th	29.5
9-25	Det.	L	6-7	(12)	14	15	Bernero	Hill		61-97	4th	30.5
9-26	Det.	W	7-2		9	5	Suppan	Cornejo		62-97	4th	29.5
9-27	At Cle.	L	3-8		7	13	Sabathia	Obermueller		62-98	4th	30.5
9-28	At Cle.	L	5-6	(10)	8	11	Wohlers	MacDougal		62-99	4th	31.5
9-29	At Cle.	L	3-7		9	6	Wright	Mullen		62-100	4th	32.5

Monthly records: April (8-16), May (13-14), June (10-17), July (13-16), August (11-18), September (7-19).
*Innings, if other than nine. †First game of a doubleheader. ‡Second game of a doubleheader. §Day separate admission. ∞Night separate admission.

RECORDS

2002 regular-season record: 62-100
Position: 4th in A.L. Central
Home: 37-44   **Road:** 25-56
A.L. East: 10-22   **A.L. Central:** 33-43
A.L. West: 14-22   **N.L.:** 5-13
Vs. LH starters: 15-23
Vs. RH starters: 47-77
Grass: 55-89   **Artificial:** 7-11
Day: 21-31   **Night:** 41-69
1-Run: 14-27   **X-inn.:** 7-12
Doubleheaders: 2-1-1
Team record past five years: 340-468
(.421, ranks 12th in league in that span)

TEAM LEADERS

Batting average: Mike Sweeney (.340).
At-bats: Carlos Beltran (637).
Runs: Carlos Beltran (114).
Hits: Carlos Beltran (174).
Total bases: Carlos Beltran (319).
Doubles: Carlos Beltran (44).
Triples: Carlos Beltran (7).
Home runs: Carlos Beltran (29).
Runs batted in: Carlos Beltran (105).
Stolen bases: Carlos Beltran (35).
Slugging percentage: Mike Sweeney (.563).

On-base percentage: Mike Sweeney (.417).
Wins: Paul Byrd (17).
Earned-run average: Paul Byrd (3.90).
Complete games: Paul Byrd (7).
Shutouts: Paul Byrd (2).
Saves: Roberto Hernandez (26).
Innings pitched: Paul Byrd (228.1).
Strikeouts: Paul Byrd (129).

GAMES BY POSITION

Catcher: Brent Mayne 99, A.J. Hinch 68, Juan Brito 9, Dusty Wathan 3.
First base: Mike Sweeney 102, Raul Ibanez 49, Kit Pellow 10, Dave McCarty 9, Chan Perry 5, Michael Tucker 5, Luis Alicea 2, Brandon Berger 1.
Second base: Carlos Febles 116, Luis Alicea 32, Luis Ordaz 28, Neifi Perez 5, Mike Caruso 4, Donnie Sadler 4, Michael Tucker 2.
Third base: Joe Randa 129, Luis Alicea 32, Kit Pellow 12, Donnie Sadler 11, Luis Ordaz 6, Mike Caruso 2.
Shortstop: Neifi Perez 139, Angel Berroa 20, Mike Caruso 3, Donnie Sadler 4, Luis Ordaz 2, Luis Alicea 1, Carlos Febles 1.
Outfield: Carlos Beltran 149, Michael Tucker 108, Chuck Knoblauch 74, Aaron Guiel 61, Raul Ibanez 55, Brandon Berger 36, Mark Quinn 15, Donnie Sadler 15, Dee Brown 8, Donzell McDonald 7, Alexis Gomez 2, Luis Alicea 1.
Designated hitter: Raul Ibanez 36, Mike Sweeney 24, Michael Tucker 23, Joe Randa 19, Luis Alicea 17, Carlos Beltran 12, Brandon Berger 10, Mark Quinn 7, Dee Brown 5, Kit Pellow 5, Donnie Sadler 3, Aaron Guiel 2, Chuck Knoblauch 2, Dave McCarty 2.

TOP DRAFT CHOICES

1. **Zack Greinke,** RHP, Apopka H.S., Orlando.
2. **Adam Donachie,** C, Timber Creek H.S., Orlando.
3. **David Jensen,** 1B, Brigham Young.
4. **Danny Christensen,** LHP, Xavierian H.S., Brooklyn.
5. **Don Murphy,** SS, Orange Coast (Calif.) JC.
6. **Brandon Jones,** SS, Wewahitchka (Fla.) H.S.
7. **Jonah Bayliss,** RHP, Trinity (Conn.) College.
8. **Kenard Springer,** 3B, Nettleton (Miss.) H.S.
9. **Matt Tupman,** C, Massachusetts-Lowell.
10. **Greg Atencio,** RHP, Lamar (Colo.) C.C.

MINNESOTA TWINS
AMERICAN LEAGUE CENTRAL DIVISION

2003 SEASON

March/April

SUN	MON	TUE	WED	THU	FRI	SAT
30	31 D DET	1	2 DET	3 D DET	4 TOR	5 TOR
6 TOR	7 D NYY	8	9 NYY	10 NYY	11 TOR	12 D TOR
13 TOR	14	15 DET	16 DET	17 DET	18 NYY	19 NYY
20 D NYY	21 NYY	22 KC	23 KC	24 KC	25 D CWS	26 CWS
27 CWS	28	29 TB	30 TB			

May

SUN	MON	TUE	WED	THU	FRI	SAT
				1 D TB	2 BOS	3 D BOS
4 D BOS	5	6 TB	7 TB	8 TB	9 BOS	10 BOS
11 BOS	12 KC	13 KC	14 KC	15 D KC	16 CWS	17 CWS
18 D CWS	19	20 OAK	21 OAK	22 OAK	23 D SEA	24 SEA
25 SEA	26	27 OAK	28 D OAK	29 SEA	30 SEA	31 D SEA

June

SUN	MON	TUE	WED	THU	FRI	SAT
1 D SEA	2	3 SF	4 SF	5 SF	6 SD	7 SD
8 D SD	9	10 COL	11 COL	12 COL	13 ARI	14 ARI
15 D ARI	16	17 KC	18 KC	19 D KC	20 MIL	21 MIL
22 MIL	23	24 CWS	25 CWS	26 D CWS	27 MIL	28 MIL
29 MIL	30 CWS					

July

SUN	MON	TUE	WED	THU	FRI	SAT
		1 CWS	2 CWS	3 CLE	4 CLE	5 CLE
6 D CLE	7	8 TEX	9 TEX	10 TEX	11 ANA	12 D ANA
13 D ANA	14	15	16 *	17 OAK	18 OAK	19 D OAK
20 D OAK	21 SEA	22 SEA	23 KC	24 D KC	25 CLE	26 CLE
27 CLE	28	29 BAL	30 BAL	31 BAL		

August

SUN	MON	TUE	WED	THU	FRI	SAT
					1 DET	2 DET
3 DET	4 BAL	5 BAL	6 BAL	7 BAL	8 D DET	9 DET
10 D DET	11 CLE	12 CLE	13 CLE	14 D CLE	15 KC	16 D KC
17 KC	18	19 CLE	20 CLE	21 KC	22 KC	23 KC
24 D KC	25	26 ANA	27 ANA	28 D ANA	29 TEX	30 TEX

September

SUN	MON	TUE	WED	THU	FRI	SAT
31 D TEX	1 D ANA	2 ANA	3 D ANA	4	5 TEX	6 D TEX
7 TEX	8 D CWS	9 CWS	10 CWS	11 D CWS	12 CLE	13 CLE
14 CLE	15 CLE	16 CWS	17 CWS	18 CWS	19 DET	20 D DET
21 D DET	22	23 CLE	24 CLE	25 DET	26 DET	27 DET
28 D DET						

Home games shaded; D—Day game (games starting before 5 p.m.); *—All-Star Game at Comiskey Park, Chicago. Subject to change.

CLUB DIRECTORY

Owner
Carl R. Pohlad
President, Twins Sports Inc.
T. Geron Bell
President, Minnesota Twins
Dave St. Peter
Vice president, general manager
Terry Ryan

Vice president, asst. general manager
Bill Smith
Vice president, operations
Matt Hoy
Assistant general manager
Wayne Krivsky
Director of minor leagues
Jim Rantz

Director of baseball operations
Rob Antony
Director of scouting
Mike Radcliff
Director of communications
Brad Ruiter
Media relations manager
Sean Harlin

MINOR LEAGUE AFFILIATES

Class	Team	League	Manager
AAA	Rochester	International	Phil Roof
AA	New Britain	Eastern	Stan Cliburn
A	Fort Myers	Florida State	Jose Marzan
A	Quad City	Midwest	Jeff Carter
Rookie	Elizabethton	Appalachian	Ray Smith
Rookie	Gulf Coast Twins	Gulf Coast	Rudy Hernandez

Follow the Twins all season at: www.sportingnews.com/baseball/teams/twins/

BROADCAST INFORMATION

Radio: WCCO-AM (830).
TV: KMSP-TV (Channel 9).
Cable TV: Fox Sports Net North.

SPRING TRAINING

Ballpark (city): Lee County Sports Complex (Fort Myers, Fla.).
Ticket information: 800-33-TWINS.

SPRING TRAINING ROSTER

Manager—Ron Gardenhire (35).
Coaches—Rick Anderson (40), Steve Liddle (9), Al Newman (62), Rick Stelmaszek (43), Scott Ullger (45), Jerry White (13).

No.	PITCHERS	B/T	Ht./Wt.	Born	Age*	2002 clubs
19	Balfour, Grant	R/R	6-2/170	12-30-77	25	Edmonton
	Eyre, Willie	R/R	6-1/200	7-21-78	24	Fort Myers, New Britain
52	Fiore, Tony	R/R	6-4/210	10-12-71	31	Edmonton, Minnesota
50	Frederick, Kevin	L/R	6-1/208	11-4-76	26	Edmonton, Minnesota
18	Guardado, Eddie	R/L	6-0/194	10-2-70	32	Minnesota
32	Hawkins, LaTroy	R/R	6-5/204	12-21-72	30	Minnesota
	Hoard, Brent	R/L	6-4/210	11-3-76	26	New Britain
37	Johnson, Adam	R/R	6-2/210	7-12-79	23	Edmonton
	Kemp, Beau	R/R	6-0/182	10-31-80	22	Fort Myers
49	Lohse, Kyle	R/R	6-2/190	10-4-78	24	Minnesota
25	Mays, Joe	B/R	6-1/185	12-10-75	27	Minnesota, Fort Myers, New Britain
21	Milton, Eric	L/L	6-3/220	8-4-75	27	Minnesota
	Pridie, Jon	R/R	6-4/205	12-7-79	23	Fort Myers, New Britain
22	Radke, Brad	R/R	6-2/188	10-27-72	30	Minnesota, Gulf Coast Twins, Fort Myers
31	Reed, Rick	R/R	6-1/195	8-16-65	37	Minnesota
39	Rincon, Juan	R/R	5-11/190	1-23-79	24	Edmonton, Minnesota
33	Romero, J.C.	B/L	5-11/195	6-4-76	26	Minnesota
57	Santana, Johan	L/L	6-0/195	3-13-79	24	Edmonton, Minnesota
56	Thomas, Brad	L/L	6-4/220	10-22-77	25	Edmonton

No.	CATCHERS	B/T	Ht./Wt.	Born	Age*	2002 clubs
	Bowen, Rob	B/R	6-2/206	2-24-81	22	Fort Myers, Quad City
24	LeCroy, Matt	R/R	6-2/225	12-13-75	27	Edmonton, Minnesota
26	Pierzynski, A.J.	L/R	6-3/220	12-30-76	26	Minnesota
12	Prince, Tom	R/R	5-11/206	8-13-64	38	Minnesota

No.	INFIELDERS	B/T	Ht./Wt.	Born	Age*	2002 clubs
5	Cuddyer, Mike	R/R	6-2/215	3-27-79	24	Edmonton, Minnesota
15	Guzman, Cristian	B/R	6-0/195	3-21-78	25	Minnesota
7	Hocking, Denny	B/R	5-10/183	4-2-70	32	Minnesota
47	Koskie, Corey	L/R	6-3/217	6-28-73	29	Minnesota
16	Mientkiewicz, Doug	L/R	6-2/200	6-19-74	28	Minnesota
	Morban, Jose	R/R	6-1/170	12-2-79	23	Charlotte
	Morneau, Justin	L/R	6-4/205	5-15-81	21	New Britain
2	Rivas, Luis	R/R	5-11/175	8-30-79	23	Minnesota, Fort Myers
58	Sears, Todd	L/R	6-5/215	10-23-75	27	Edmonton, Minnesota

No.	OUTFIELDERS	B/T	Ht./Wt.	Born	Age*	2002 clubs
	Ford, Lew	R/R	6-0/190	8-12-76	26	New Britain, Edmonton
	Garbe, B.J.	R/R	6-2/195	2-3-81	22	Fort Myers
48	Hunter, Torii	R/R	6-2/205	7-18-75	27	Minnesota
11	Jones, Jacque	L/L	5-10/176	4-25-75	27	Minnesota
23	Kielty, Bobby	B/R	6-1/215	8-5-76	26	Edmonton, Minnesota
17	Mohr, Dustan	R/R	6-0/210	6-19-76	26	Minnesota
41	Restovich, Michael	R/R	6-4/233	1-3-79	24	Edmonton, Minnesota
54	Ryan, Michael	L/R	6-0/185	7-6-77	25	Edmonton, Minnesota

*Age as of April 1, 2003.

BALLPARK INFORMATION

Ballpark (capacity, surface)
Hubert H. Humphrey Metrodome (48,678, artificial)
Address
34 Kirby Puckett Place
Minneapolis, MN 55415
Official website
www.twinsbaseball.com
Business phone
612-375-1366
Ticket information
1-800-338-9467
Field dimensions (from home plate)
To left field at foul line, 343 feet
To center field, 408 feet
To right field at foul line, 327 feet
First game played
April 6, 1982 (Mariners 11, Twins 7)

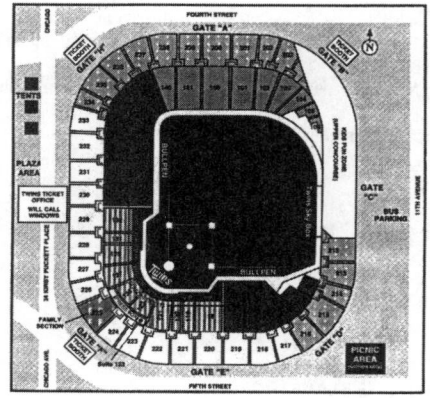

Date	Opp.	Res.	Score	(inn.*)	Hits	Opp. hits	Winning pitcher	Losing pitcher	Save	Record	Pos.	GB
4-1	At K.C.	W	8-6		12	10	Romero	Bailey	Guardado	1-0	T1st	...
4-3	At K.C.	W	1-0		7	3	Milton	Reichert	Guardado	2-0	1st	+0.5
4-4	At Tor.	L	2-7		6	14	Halladay	Mays		2-1	T1st	...
4-5	At Tor.	W	4-3		10	4	Reed	Lyon	Guardado	3-1	T1st	...
4-6	At Tor.	W	7-5		10	13	Hawkins	Eyre	Guardado	4-1	1st	...
4-7	At Tor.	W	10-6		11	8	Radke	Cooper		5-1	T1st	...
4-8	At Cle.	L	5-9		13	8	Drese	Milton		5-2	2nd	1.0
4-9	At Cle.	L	4-5		11	6	Finley	Mays	Wickman	5-3	2nd	2.0
4-10	At Cle.	L	3-9		7	9	Baez	Reed		5-4	2nd	3.0
4-11	At Cle.	L	4-8		9	9	Colon	Lohse		5-5	T2nd	4.0
4-12	Det.	W	4-2		8	8	Radke	Redman	Guardado	6-5	3rd	4.0
4-13	Det.	W	7-3		9	14	Milton	Weaver		7-5	3rd	4.0
4-14	Det.	W	13-7		16	11	Romero	Anderson		8-5	2nd	3.5
4-16	K.C.	W	8-5		13	10	Fiore	Stein	Guardado	9-5	2nd	2.5
4-17	K.C.	L	3-16		7	16	Byrd	Radke		9-6	3rd	2.5
4-18	K.C.	W	4-1		8	4	Milton	Suppan	Guardado	10-6	3rd	1.5
4-19	Cle.	W	12-3		14	7	Lohse	Sabathia		11-6	2nd	0.5
4-20	Cle.	W	6-2		9	6	Kinney	Drese		12-6	1st	+0.5
4-21	Cle.	W	4-2		13	8	Reed	Finley	Guardado	13-6	1st	+0.5
4-23	At T.B.	L	4-6		10	8	Kennedy	Radke	Yan	13-7	T1st	...
4-24	At T.B.	L	1-9		3	10	Rupe	Milton		13-8	2nd	1.0
4-25	At T.B.	W	6-2		12	8	Jackson	Yan		14-8	2nd	1.0
4-26	At Det.	L	2-3	(10)	9	12	Anderson	Wells		14-9	2nd	1.0
4-27	At Det.	L	1-5		9	9	Cornejo	Kinney		14-10	2nd	1.0
4-28	At Det.	L	4-5		9	10	Santana	Jackson		14-11	2nd	1.0
4-29	T.B.	W	3-2		7	6	Milton	Kennedy	Guardado	15-11	2nd	0.5
4-30	T.B.	W	6-3		10	7	Lohse	Rupe	Guardado	16-11	2nd	0.5
5-1	T.B.	W	5-3		13	10	Reed	Sturtze	Guardado	17-11	2nd	0.5
5-2	T.B.	W	7-6	(10)	10	12	Fiore	Kent		18-11	1st	+0.5
5-3	Det.	W	8-4		13	6	Radke	Cornejo		19-11	1st	+0.5
5-4	Det.	W	3-2		4	8	Jackson	Rodney		20-11	1st	+0.5
5-5	Det.	L	6-7		10	10	Weaver	Lohse	Acevedo	20-12	1st	+0.5
5-6	Det.	W	3-1		11	7	Reed	Sparks	Guardado	21-12	1st	+1.5
5-7	K.C.	L	1-4		5	6	Byrd	Kinney	Hernandez	21-13	1st	+0.5
5-8	K.C.	W	3-1		8	5	Radke	Affeldt		22-13	1st	+0.5
5-10	N.Y.	L	3-5		10	10	Wells	Milton	Rivera	22-14	1st	+1.0
5-11	N.Y.	L	2-4		6	8	Stanton	Guardado	Rivera	22-15	1st	+1.0
5-12	N.Y.	L	4-10		10	18	Mussina	Reed		22-16	1st	+1.0
5-13	At K.C.	W	3-2		7	4	Romero	Grimsley	Guardado	23-16	1st	+1.5
5-14	At K.C.	L	1-8		9	11	Suppan	Kinney		23-17	1st	+0.5
5-15	At K.C.	W	8-6		10	11	Milton	Reichert	Guardado	24-17	1st	+1.5
5-16	At K.C.	W	14-5		18	9	Lohse	George		25-17	1st	+1.5
5-17	At N.Y.	L	12-13	(14)	20	20	Hitchcock	Trombley		25-18	1st	+1.5
5-18	At N.Y.	L	2-6		7	12	Lilly	Fiore		25-19	1st	+0.5
5-19	At N.Y.	L	0-3		5	9	Clemens	Kinney	Rivera	25-20	1st	+0.5
5-21	Tex.	W	8-2		15	11	Milton	Valdes		26-20	1st	+1.0
5-22	Tex.	L	5-6		9	9	Rogers	Lohse	Irabu	26-21	T1st	...
5-24	At Ana.	W	5-1		7	3	Reed	Ortiz		27-21	T1st	...
5-25	At Ana.	L	3-4	(13)	7	10	Levine	Cressend		27-22	2nd	1.0
5-26	At Ana.	W	5-2		14	8	Milton	Appier	Guardado	28-22	T1st	...
5-27	At Tex.	W	5-2		9	10	Lohse	Rogers	Guardado	29-22	1st	+1.0
5-28	At Tex.	W	11-4		8	8	Fiore	Park		30-22	1st	+2.0
5-29	At Tex.	L	8-9		12	14	Irabu	Romero		30-23	1st	+2.0
5-30	Ana.	W	7-6	(10)	11	13	Guardado	Pote		31-23	1st	+2.5
5-31	Ana.	L	3-11		6	16	Washburn	Milton		31-24	1st	+2.5
6-1	Ana.	W	4-2		10	11	Lohse	Appier	Guardado	32-24	1st	+3.5
6-2	Ana.	L	4-5		5	12	Sele	Kinney	Percival	32-25	1st	+3.5
6-4	Cle.	W	23-2		25	4	Reed	Drese		33-25	1st	+4.0
6-5	Cle.	L	4-6		11	12	Sabathia	Milton	Riske	33-26	1st	+3.0
6-6	Cle.	W	8-3		11	8	Lohse	Colon		34-26	1st	+4.0
6-7	Fla.	W	12-7		13	11	Santana	Dempster		35-26	1st	+5.0
6-8	Fla.	W	5-3		11	7	Kinney	Olsen	Guardado	36-26	1st	+6.0
6-9	Fla.	L	3-6		9	12	Tavarez	Reed	Nunez	36-27	1st	+5.0
6-10	Atl.	W	6-5	(15)	14	11	Fiore	Ligtenberg		37-27	1st	+6.0
6-11	Atl.	L	0-11		2	14	Glavine	Lohse		37-28	1st	+5.0

Date	Opp.	Res.	Score	(inn.*)	Hits	Opp. hits	Winning pitcher	Losing pitcher	Save	Record	Pos.	GB
6-12	Atl.	L	2-3		5	8	Moss	Santana	Smoltz	37-29	1st	+4.0
6-14	At Mil.	L	5-7		11	13	King	Jackson	DeJean	37-30	1st	+4.0
6-15	At Mil.	W	5-2		9	7	Milton	Wright	Guardado	38-30	1st	+5.0
6-16	At Mil.	W	7-6		10	11	Fiore	Figueroa	Guardado	39-30	1st	+5.0
6-18	At N.Y.	W	6-1		12	4	Santana	D'Amico		40-30	1st	+5.0
6-19	At N.Y.	L	2-4		8	11	Leiter	Kinney	Benitez	40-31	1st	+5.0
6-20	At N.Y.	L	2-3		6	6	Trachsel	Fiore	Benitez	40-32	1st	+4.0
6-21	At Phi.	L	0-3		4	6	Duckworth	Lohse	Mesa	40-33	1st	+4.0
6-22	At Phi.	W	4-1	(11)	8	4	Hawkins	Plesac	Guardado	41-33	1st	+5.0
6-23	At Phi.	W	5-1		9	3	Fiore	Wolf		42-33	1st	+6.0
6-24	Chi.	W	5-4		12	7	Hawkins	Howry	Guardado	43-33	1st	+7.0
6-25	Chi.	L	7-15		10	23	Buehrle	Milton		43-34	1st	+6.0
6-26	Chi.	W	6-5		10	9	Lohse	Ritchie	Guardado	44-34	1st	+7.0
6-27	Chi.	L	4-7		7	16	Glover	Reed	Foulke	44-35	1st	+6.0
6-28	Mil.	W	5-1		9	4	Santana	Sheets		45-35	1st	+6.0
6-29	Mil.	L	2-10		6	17	Cabrera	Kinney		45-36	1st	+5.0
6-30	Mil.	W	4-3		10	5	Milton	Rusch	Guardado	46-36	1st	+6.0
7-1	At Oak.	W	5-4		14	11	Romero	Venafro	Guardado	47-36	1st	+6.5
7-2	At Oak.	L	3-4		8	9	Bradford	Guardado		47-37	1st	+5.5
7-3	At Oak.	W	2-1		6	8	Santana	Mulder	Guardado	48-37	1st	+6.5
7-4	At Sea.	L	1-2		6	6	Rhodes	Rodriguez	Sasaki	48-38	1st	+6.5
7-5	At Sea.	W	8-4		11	7	Milton	Nelson		49-38	1st	+7.5
7-6	At Sea.	W	7-2		16	9	Lohse	Moyer		50-38	1st	+7.5
7-7	At Sea.	L	2-8		6	11	Halama	Reed	Sasaki	50-39	1st	+7.5
7-11	Tex.	W	4-3		4	9	Milton	Park	Guardado	51-39	1st	+7.5
7-12	Tex.	W	4-3	(11)	10	9	Fiore	Irabu		52-39	1st	+8.5
7-13	Tex.	L	1-8		6	12	Rogers	Rincon		52-40	1st	+9.0
7-14	Tex.	W	5-4		11	7	Romero	Lewis	Guardado	53-40	1st	+9.0
7-15	Ana.	W	10-8		12	6	Hawkins	Schoeneweis	Guardado	54-40	1st	+10.0
7-16	Ana.	L	2-4		7	7	Washburn	Milton	Weber	54-41	1st	+9.0
7-17	At Cle.	W	8-5		12	10	Reed	Baez	Guardado	55-41	1st	+10.0
7-18	At Cle.	W	8-6		15	10	Fiore	Rincon	Guardado	56-41	1st	+11.0
7-19	At Det.	W	5-1		12	8	Lohse	Moehler	Santana	57-41	1st	+12.0
7-20	At Det.	W	14-4		17	10	Mays	Bernero		58-41	1st	+13.0
7-21	At Det.	W	4-2		7	7	Milton	Sparks	Guardado	59-41	1st	+13.0
7-22	At Chi.	W	11-6		17	12	Reed	Ritchie		60-41	1st	+14.0
7-23	At Chi.	L	7-8		11	8	Buehrle	Santana	Osuna	60-42	1st	+13.0
7-24	At Chi.	W	8-1		13	9	Lohse	Garland		61-42	1st	+14.0
7-26	Tor.	W	10-5		16	6	Fiore	Prokopec		62-42	1st	+14.0
7-27	Tor.	W	5-4	(10)	10	9	Wells	Escobar		63-42	1st	+14.0
7-28	Tor.	W	4-0		9	3	Santana	Loaiza		64-42	1st	+14.0
7-30	Chi.	L	0-3		5	6	Buehrle	Lohse		64-43	1st	+13.0
7-31	Chi.	W	2-1	(10)	5	5	Romero	Osuna		65-43	1st	+14.0
8-1	Chi.	W	6-0		9	3	Milton	Wright		66-43	1st	+15.0
8-2	K.C.	W	2-1		8	4	Reed	Suppan	Guardado	67-43	1st	+15.0
8-3	K.C.	W	4-3	(10)	10	7	Santana	May		68-43	1st	+16.0
8-4	K.C.	W	5-4	(10)	12	10	Romero	Mullen		69-43	1st	+17.0
8-5	K.C.	L	4-12		8	17	Sedlacek	Mays		69-44	1st	+16.0
8-6	At Bal.	L	2-9		7	7	Ponson	Santana		69-45	1st	+16.0
8-7	At Bal.	L	4-6		7	12	Erickson	Reed	Julio	69-46	1st	+15.0
8-8	At Bal.	L	1-4		9	6	Driskill	Radke	Julio	69-47	1st	+14.0
8-9	At Bos.	W	5-4		12	8	Romero	Castillo	Guardado	70-47	1st	+14.0
8-10	At Bos.	L	0-2		4	9	Martinez	Mays	Urbina	70-48	1st	+14.0
8-11	At Bos.	L	1-3		4	5	Wakefield	Santana	Urbina	70-49	1st	+13.0
8-13	Bal.	W	6-0		10	5	Reed	Erickson		71-49	1st	+13.0
8-14	Bal.	L	5-6	(14)	12	11	Bauer	Fiore		71-50	1st	+13.0
8-15	Bal.	L	1-3		7	7	Johnson	Lohse	Julio	71-51	1st	+12.5
8-16	Bos.	W	5-0		8	2	Mays	Martinez		72-51	1st	+13.5
8-17	Bos.	L	2-5		6	9	Wakefield	Santana		72-52	1st	+13.5
8-18	Bos.	W	6-2		10	8	Reed	Burkett		73-52	1st	+14.5
8-19	At Chi.	W	7-3		10	10	Radke	Glover		74-52	1st	+15.5
8-20	At Chi.	W	5-0		7	4	Lohse	Parque		75-52	1st	+16.5
8-21	At Chi.	L	1-10		8	15	Buehrle	Mays		75-53	1st	+15.5
8-22	At K.C.	W	8-6		12	11	Santana	Hernandez	Guardado	76-53	1st	+16.0
8-23	At K.C.	W	9-2		11	6	Reed	Suppan		77-53	1st	+17.0
8-24	At K.C.	W	6-5		12	16	Radke	Byrd	Guardado	78-53	1st	+17.0
8-25	At K.C.	L	2-4		6	11	Asencio	Lohse	Hernandez	78-54	1st	+16.0
8-27	Sea.	W	5-2		12	9	Mays	Valdes	Guardado	79-54	1st	+16.5
8-28	Sea.	W	2-1		8	8	Santana	Pineiro	Guardado	80-54	1st	+16.5
8-29	Sea.	L	0-2		5	9	Moyer	Reed	Sasaki	80-55	1st	+16.0

Date	Opp.	Res.	Score	(inn.*)	Hits	Opp. hits	Winning pitcher	Losing pitcher	Save	Record	Pos.	GB
8-30	At Oak.	L	2-4		8	10	Hudson	Radke	Koch	80-56	1st	+15.0
8-31	At Oak.	L	3-6		7	7	Mecir	Romero	Koch	80-57	1st	+14.0
9-1	At Oak.	L	5-7		6	12	Koch	Guardado		80-58	1st	+13.0
9-2	At Sea.	L	2-5		7	12	Rhodes	Santana	Sasaki	80-59	1st	+12.0
9-4	At Sea.	W	3-2		13	7	Reed	Moyer	Guardado	81-59	1st	+12.5
9-6	Oak.	W	6-0		10	6	Radke	Lidle		82-59	1st	+14.0
9-7	Oak.	L	0-2		7	6	Mulder	Mays	Koch	82-60	1st	+14.0
9-8	Oak.	L	0-6		3	11	Zito	Milton		82-61	1st	+13.0
9-9	Det.	W	5-2		9	7	Reed	Maroth	Guardado	83-61	1st	+13.0
9-10	Det.	W	11-4		15	11	Lohse	Loux		84-61	1st	+13.0
9-11	Det.	W	8-2		8	4	Radke	Redman		85-61	1st	+14.0
9-12	At Cle.	L	4-5		8	11	Riggan	Mays	Baez	85-62	1st	+13.0
9-13	At Cle.	L	5-12		8	16	Mulholland	Milton		85-63	1st	+12.0
9-14	At Cle.	W	3-2		10	5	Reed	Sadler	Guardado	86-63	1st	+12.0
9-15	At Cle.	W	5-0		5	3	Lohse	Lee		87-63	1st	+13.0
9-17	At Det.	W	7-4		16	13	Radke	Loux	Guardado	88-63	1st	+13.0
9-18	At Det.	W	2-0		9	6	Mays	Sparks	Guardado	89-63	1st	+13.0
9-20	At Chi.	L	2-10		6	12	Wright	Rincon		89-64	1st	+12.5
9-21	At Chi.	L	4-14		8	18	Rauch	Radke		89-65	1st	+11.5
9-22	At Chi.	L	2-8		12	9	Buehrle	Mays		89-66	1st	+10.5
9-24	Cle.	W	4-3		5	9	Hawkins	Elder		90-66	1st	+11.5
9-25	Cle.	W	7-5	(12)	11	12	Romero	Maurer		91-66	1st	+11.5
9-26	Cle.	L	4-8		8	11	Drese	Jackson		91-67	1st	+10.5
9-27	Chi.	W	3-1		7	7	Fiore	Glover	Guardado	92-67	1st	+11.5
9-28	Chi.	W	3-2		10	6	Hawkins	Buehrle	Guardado	93-67	1st	+12.5
9-29	Chi.	W	3-1		9	8	Wells	Porzio	Romero	94-67	1st	+13.5

Monthly records: April (16-11), May (15-13), June (15-12), July (19-7), August (15-14), September (14-10).
*Innings, if other than nine.

RECORDS

2002 regular-season record: 94-67
Position: 1st in A.L. Central
Home: 54-27 **Road:** 40-40
A.L. East: 15-17 **A.L. Central:** 50-25
A.L. West: 19-17 **N.L.:** 10-8
Vs. LH starters: 23-29
Vs. RH starters: 71-38
Grass: 34-36 **Artificial:** 60-31
Day: 25-24 **Night:** 69-43
1-Run: 29-16 **X-inn.:** 10-4
Doubleheaders: 0-0-0
Team record past five years: 381-426
(.472, ranks 10th in league in that span)

TEAM LEADERS

Batting average: A.J. Pierzynski (.300).
At-bats: Cristian Guzman (623).
Runs: Jacque Jones (96).
Hits: Jacque Jones (173).
Total bases: Jacque Jones (295).
Doubles: Torii Hunter, Jacque Jones, Corey Koskie (37).
Triples: Cristian Guzman, A.J. Pierzynski (6).
Home runs: Torii Hunter (29).
Runs batted in: Torii Hunter (94).
Stolen bases: Torii Hunter (23).
Slugging percentage: Torii Hunter (.524).

On-base percentage: Bobby Kielty (.405).
Wins: Rick Reed (15).
Earned-run average: Johan Santana (2.99).
Complete games: Eric Milton, Brad Radke, Rick Reed (2).
Shutouts: Kyle Lohse, Joe Mays, Eric Milton, Brad Radke, Rick Reed (1).
Saves: Eddie Guardado (45).
Innings pitched: Rick Reed (188.0).
Strikeouts: Johan Santana (137).

GAMES BY POSITION

Catcher: A.J. Pierzynski 124, Tom Prince 50, Matthew LeCroy 6, Javier Valentin 4.
First base: Doug Mientkiewicz 143, David Ortiz 15, Matthew LeCroy 8, Michael Cuddyer 6, Denny Hocking 6, Todd Sears 6, Bobby Kielty 5, Casey Blake 3.
Second base: Luis Rivas 93, Denny Hocking 56, Jay Canizaro 30, Warren Morris 4, David Lamb 2.
Third base: Corey Koskie 138, Denny Hocking 16, Michael Cuddyer 10, Jay Canizaro 8, Casey Blake 5, David Lamb 1.
Shortstop: Cristian Guzman 147, Denny Hocking 25, David Lamb 4.
Outfield: Torii Hunter 146, Jacque Jones 143, Dustan Mohr 113, Bobby Kielty 82, Michael Cuddyer 25, Brian Buchanan 24, Denny Hocking 5, Michael Restovich 5, Michael Ryan 5.
Designated hitter: David Ortiz 95, Matthew LeCroy 41, Brian Buchanan 17, Bobby Kielty 11, Michael Cuddyer 3, Jacque Jones 3, Dustan Mohr 3, Michael Restovich 2, Casey Blake 1, Cristian Guzman 1, Torii Hunter 1, Corey Koskie 1, Michael Ryan 1.

TOP DRAFT CHOICES

1. **Denard Span,** OF, Tampa (Fla.) Catholic H.S.
2. **Jesse Crain,** RHP, Houston.
3. **Mark Sauls,** RHP, Bay H.S., Panama City, Fla.
4. **Alex Merricks,** LHP, Oxnard (Calif.) H.S.
5. **Clete Thomas,** OF, Mosley H.S., Lynn Haven, Fla.
6. **Pat Neshek,** RHP, Butler.
7. **Ricky Barrett,** LHP, U. of San Diego.
8. **Adam Lind,** 1B, Highland H.S., Anderson, Ind.
9. **Doug Deeds,** OF, Ohio State.
10. **Kyle Phillips,** C, El Capitan H.S., Lakeside, Calif.

NEW YORK YANKEES
AMERICAN LEAGUE EAST DIVISION

2003 SEASON

March/April

SUN	MON	TUE	WED	THU	FRI	SAT
30	31 TOR	1 D TOR	2 TOR	3	4 TB	5 TB
6 D TB	7 MIN	8	9 MIN	10 D MIN	11 TB	12 D TB
13 D TB	14 TOR	15 TOR	16 TOR	17 D TOR	18 MIN	19 MIN
20 D MIN	21 D MIN	22 ANA	23 ANA	24 ANA	25 TEX	26 TEX
27 TEX	28	29 SEA	30 SEA			

May

SUN	MON	TUE	WED	THU	FRI	SAT
				1 SEA	2 OAK	3 D OAK
4 D OAK	5	6 SEA	7 SEA	8 SEA	9 OAK	10 D OAK
11 D OAK	12	13 ANA	14 ANA	15 ANA	16 TEX	17 D TEX
18 D TEX	19 BOS	20 BOS	21 BOS	22 TOR	23 TOR	24 TOR
25 D TOR	26 D BOS	27 D BOS	28 BOS	29	30 DET	31 DET

June

SUN	MON	TUE	WED	THU	FRI	SAT
1 D DET	2	3 CIN	4 CIN	5 CIN	6 CUB	7 D CUB
8 CUB	9	10 HOU	11 HOU	12 D HOU	13 STL	14 D STL
15 D STL	16	17 TB	18 TB	19 D TB	20 NYM	21 NYM
22 NYM	23 TB	24 TB	25 TB	26 D TB	27 NYM	28 NYM
29 NYM	30 BAL					

July

SUN	MON	TUE	WED	THU	FRI	SAT
		1 BAL	2 D BAL	3	4 D BOS	5 D BOS
6 D BOS	7 BOS	8 CLE	9 CLE	10 CLE	11 TOR	12 D TOR
13 D TOR	14	15 *	16	17 CLE	18 CLE	19 D CLE
20 D CLE	21 TOR	22 TOR	23 BAL	24 D BAL	25 BOS	26 D BOS
27 D BOS	28	29 ANA	30 ANA	31 ANA		

August

SUN	MON	TUE	WED	THU	FRI	SAT
					1 OAK	2 D OAK
3 D OAK	4	5 TEX	6 TEX	7 D TEX	8 SEA	9 D SEA
10 D SEA	11 KC	12 KC	13 KC	14	15 BAL	16 BAL
17 D BAL	18 KC	19 KC	20 D KC	21	22 BAL	23 D BAL
24 D BAL	25 BAL	26 CWS	27 CWS	28 D CWS	29 BOS	30 D BOS

September

SUN	MON	TUE	WED	THU	FRI	SAT
31 D BOS	1 D TOR	2	3 TOR	4 TOR	5 BOS	6 D BOS
7 D BOS	8	9 DET	10 DET	11 DET	12 TB	13 D TB
14 D TB	15 BAL	16 BAL	17 BAL	18 BAL	19 TB	20 TB
21 D TB	22 CWS	23 CWS	24 D CWS	25	26 BAL	27 BAL
28 D BAL						

Home games shaded; D—Day game (games starting before 5 p.m.); *—All-Star Game at Comiskey Park, Chicago. Subject to change.

CLUB DIRECTORY

Principal owner
George M. Steinbrenner III
President
Randy Levine
Special advisors
Yogi Berra, Reggie Jackson, Clyde King, Don Mattingly
Senior vice president, general manager
Brian Cashman
Sr. vice president, baseball operations
Mark Newman

Assistant general manager
Jean Afterman
Vice president, major league scouting
Gene Michael
V.p., int'l and professional scouting
Gordon Blakeley
Vice president, scouting
Lin Garrett
Vice president, player personnel
Billy Connors

V.p., corp. and community relations
Brian Smith
Director of player development
Rob Thomson
Director of player personnel
Damon Oppenheimer
Director of baseball operations
Eric Wicks
Director of media relations & publicity
Rick Cerrone

MINOR LEAGUE AFFILIATES

Class	Team	League	Manager
AAA	Columbus	International	Bucky Dent
AA	Trenton	Eastern	Stump Merrill
A	Tampa	Florida State	To be announced
A	Battle Creek	Midwest	To be announced
A	Staten Island	New York-Pennsylvania	To be announced
Rookie	Gulf Coast Yankees	Gulf Coast	To be announced

Follow the Yankees all season at: www.sportingnews.com/baseball/teams/yankees/

BROADCAST INFORMATION

Radio: WCBS-AM (880).
TV: WCBS-TV (Channel 2).
Cable TV: Yankee Entertainment and Sports Network.

SPRING TRAINING

Ballpark (city): Legends Field (Tampa, Fla.).
Ticket information: 813-879-2244, 813-287-8844.

Manager—Joe Torre (6).
Coaches—Rick Down (56), Lee Mazzilli (53), Rich Monteleone (52), Willie Randolph (30), Mel Stottlemyre (34), Don Zimmer (54).

No.	PITCHERS	B/T	Ht./Wt.	Born	Age*	2002 clubs
38	Choate, Randy	L/L	6-1/180	9-5-75	27	Columbus, New York A.L.
77	Claussen, Brandon	L/L	6-2/175	5-1-79	23	Columbus
22	Clemens, Roger	R/R	6-4/235	8-4-62	40	New York A.L., Tampa, Norwich
	Field, Nate	R/R	6-2/200	12-11-75	27	Omaha, Kansas City, Columbus
76	Graman, Alex	L/L	6-4/200	11-17-77	25	Norwich, Columbus
32	Hammond, Chris	L/L	6-1/195	1-21-66	37	Atlanta
65	Hernandez, Adrian	R/R	6-1/185	3-25-75	28	Columbus, New York A.L.
41	Hitchcock, Sterling	L/L	6-0/205	4-29-71	31	Tampa, Columbus, New York A.L., Gulf Coast Yankees
31	Karsay, Steve	R/R	6-3/215	3-24-72	31	New York A.L.
62	Keisler, Randy	L/L	6-3/190	2-24-76	27	DID NOT PLAY
48	Knight, Brandon	L/R	6-0/170	10-1-75	27	Columbus, New York A.L.
35	Mussina, Mike	L/R	6-2/185	12-8-68	34	New York A.L.
	Osuna, Antonio	R/R	5-11/205	4-12-73	29	Chicago A.L.
46	Pettitte, Andy	L/L	6-5/225	6-15-72	30	New York A.L., Tampa, Norwich
42	Rivera, Mariano	R/R	6-2/185	11-29-69	33	New York A.L., Gulf Coast Yankees
18	Weaver, Jeff	R/R	6-5/200	8-22-76	26	Detroit, New York A.L.
33	Wells, David	L/L	6-4/240	5-20-63	39	New York A.L.

No.	CATCHERS	B/T	Ht./Wt.	Born	Age*	2002 clubs
20	Posada, Jorge	B/R	6-2/205	8-17-71	31	New York A.L.
11	Widger, Chris	R/R	6-2/215	5-21-71	31	Columbus, New York A.L.

No.	INFIELDERS	B/T	Ht./Wt.	Born	Age*	2002 clubs
58	Almonte, Erick	R/R	6-2/180	2-1-78	25	Columbus, Norwich
25	Giambi, Jason	L/R	6-3/235	1-8-71	32	New York A.L.
57	Henson, Drew	R/R	6-5/222	2-13-80	23	Columbus, New York A.L.
2	Jeter, Derek	R/R	6-3/195	6-26-74	28	New York A.L.
36	Johnson, Nick	L/L	6-3/224	9-19-78	24	New York A.L., Columbus
12	Soriano, Alfonso	R/R	6-1/180	1-7-78	25	New York A.L.
19	Ventura, Robin	L/R	6-1/198	7-14-67	35	New York A.L.
14	Wilson, Enrique	B/R	5-11/195	7-27-73	29	New York A.L.
	Zeile, Todd	R/R	6-1/200	9-9-65	37	Colorado

No.	OUTFIELDERS	B/T	Ht./Wt.	Born	Age*	2002 clubs
55	Matsui, Hideki	L/R	6-1/210	12-6-74	28	Yomiuri
43	Mondesi, Raul	R/R	5-11/230	3-12-71	32	Toronto, New York A.L.
59	Rivera, Juan	R/R	6-2/170	7-3-78	24	Columbus, New York A.L., Gulf Coast Yankees
18	Thames, Marcus	R/R	6-2/205	3-6-77	26	Columbus, New York A.L.
27	White, Rondell	R/R	6-1/225	2-23-72	31	New York A.L.
51	Williams, Bernie	B/R	6-2/205	9-13-68	34	New York A.L.

*Age as of April 1, 2003.

BALLPARK INFORMATION

Ballpark (capacity, surface)
Yankee Stadium (57,478, grass)
Address
Yankee Stadium
E. 161 St. and River Ave.
Bronx, NY 10451
Official website
www.yankees.com
Business phone
718-293-4300
Ticket information
212-307-1212, 718-293-6013
Field dimensions (from home plate)
To left field at foul line, 318 feet
To center field, 408 feet
To right field at foul line, 314 feet
First game played
April 18, 1923 (Yankees 4, Red Sox 1)

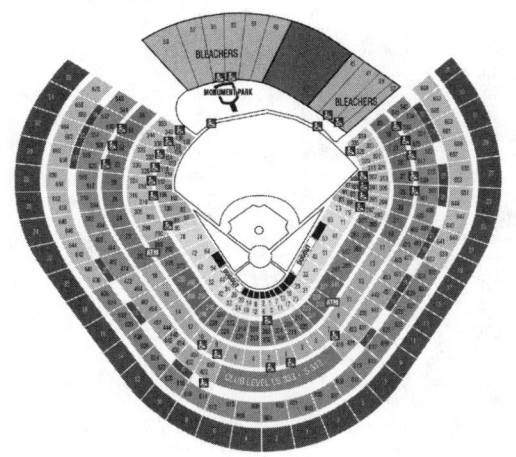

New York Yankees · 2003 SEASON

Date	Opp.	Res.	Score	(inn.*)	Hits	Opp. hits	Winning pitcher	Losing pitcher	Save	Record	Pos.	GB
4-1	At Bal.	L	3-10		6	9	Erickson	Clemens		0-1	T4th	1.0
4-3	At Bal.	W	1-0		6	5	Wells	Johnson	Rivera	1-1	T3rd	1.0
4-4	At Bal.	W	4-1		8	5	Mussina	Ponson	Rivera	2-1	3rd	1.0
4-5	T.B.	W	4-0		9	3	Pettitte	Kennedy		3-1	T1st	...
4-6	T.B.	W	3-0		7	3	Hernandez	Alvarez	Rivera	4-1	1st	+1.0
4-7	T.B.	W	7-2		11	6	Clemens	Sturtze		5-1	1st	+1.0
4-8	At Tor.	W	16-3		22	7	Wells	Prokopec		6-1	1st	+1.5
4-9	At Tor.	W	5-2		10	2	Mussina	Plesac	Rivera	7-1	1st	+1.5
4-10	At Tor.	L	7-9		12	16	Borbon	Lilly	Escobar	7-2	1st	+1.5
4-11	At Tor.	L	3-11		7	12	Eyre	Clemens		7-3	1st	+1.5
4-12	At Bos.	L	2-3		9	11	Oliver	Hernandez	Urbina	7-4	1st	+0.5
4-13	At Bos.	L	6-7		8	9	Arrojo	Rivera	Urbina	7-5	2nd	0.5
4-14	At Bos.	W	6-2		8	6	Mussina	Wakefield	Rivera	8-5	1st	+0.5
4-15	At Bos.	L	3-4		6	11	Lowe	Pettitte	Urbina	8-6	2nd	0.5
4-16	Bal.	L	4-5		9	10	Bauer	Mendoza	Julio	8-7	2nd	1.5
4-17	Bal.	W	7-1		12	7	Hernandez	Towers		9-7	2nd	1.5
4-18	Bal.	W	8-4		12	7	Wells	Erickson		10-7	2nd	1.0
4-19	Tor.	W	6-5		11	8	Rivera	File		11-7	2nd	1.0
4-20	Tor.	L	4-5	(10)	6	9	Plesac	Mendoza		11-8	2nd	1.5
4-21	Tor.	W	9-2		10	4	Clemens	Carpenter		12-8	2nd	2.0
4-23	At Oak.	W	2-1		4	6	Hernandez	Hudson	Rivera	13-8	2nd	1.0
4-24	At Oak.	W	8-5		14	8	Stanton	Magnante	Rivera	14-8	2nd	...
4-25	At Oak.	L	2-6		7	8	Zito	Mussina		14-9	2nd	1.0
4-26	At Sea.	W	7-1		15	6	Clemens	Baldwin		15-9	2nd	1.0
4-27	At Sea.	L	0-1		5	1	Garcia	Lilly	Sasaki	15-10	2nd	2.0
4-28	At Sea.	W	4-3		9	5	Karsay	Rhodes	Rivera	16-10	2nd	1.5
4-30	Oak.	W	8-2		10	7	Wells	Zito		17-10	2nd	1.0
5-1	Oak.	L	1-4		5	5	Hiljus	Mussina	Koch	17-11	2nd	2.0
5-2	Oak.	W	9-2		16	6	Clemens	Lidle		18-11	2nd	1.5
5-3	Sea.	L	2-6		4	8	Garcia	Lilly		18-12	2nd	2.5
5-4	Sea.	L	5-9		9	11	Nelson	Karsay		18-13	2nd	3.5
5-5	Sea.	L	6-10		9	14	Pineiro	Wells		18-14	2nd	4.5
5-7	At T.B.	W	5-2		11	4	Mussina	Wilson	Rivera	19-14	2nd	5.0
5-8	At T.B.	W	7-2		8	8	Clemens	James		20-14	2nd	5.0
5-9	At T.B.	W	3-1		5	3	Hernandez	Kennedy	Rivera	21-14	2nd	5.0
5-10	At Min.	W	5-3		10	10	Wells	Milton	Rivera	22-14	2nd	4.0
5-11	At Min.	W	4-2		8	6	Stanton	Guardado	Rivera	23-14	2nd	3.0
5-12	At Min.	W	10-4		18	10	Mussina	Reed		24-14	2nd	3.0
5-14	T.B.	W	10-3		11	5	Clemens	Harper		25-14	2nd	3.0
5-15	T.B.	L	7-10		8	12	Kennedy	Hernandez	Yan	25-15	2nd	4.0
5-16	T.B.	W	13-0		15	3	Wells	Rupe		26-15	2nd	3.0
5-17	Min.	W	13-12	(14)	20	20	Hitchcock	Trombley		27-15	2nd	2.0
5-18	Min.	W	6-2		12	7	Lilly	Fiore		28-15	2nd	2.0
5-19	Min.	W	3-0		9	5	Clemens	Kinney	Rivera	29-15	2nd	2.0
5-20	Tor.	W	6-3		13	6	Mendoza	Heredia	Rivera	30-15	2nd	2.0
5-21	Tor.	W	4-1		4	4	Mussina	Prokopec	Karsay	31-15	2nd	1.0
5-22	Tor.	L	3-8		11	7	Halladay	Hernandez		31-16	2nd	1.0
5-23	At Bos.	L	1-3		5	8	Martinez	Lilly	Urbina	31-17	2nd	2.0
5-24	At Bos.	L	8-9	(11)	14	16	Arrojo	Karsay		31-18	2nd	3.0
5-25	At Bos.	W	3-2		8	6	Mendoza	Lowe	Rivera	32-18	2nd	2.0
5-26	At Bos.	W	14-5		15	10	Mussina	Oliver		33-18	2nd	1.0
5-27	At Chi.	W	10-6		12	11	Thurman	Wright		34-18	2nd	1.0
5-28	At Chi.	W	4-2		8	4	Lilly	Garland	Rivera	35-18	2nd	1.0
5-29	At Chi.	W	6-3		12	10	Karsay	Foulke	Rivera	36-18	2nd	1.0
5-31	Bos.	L	2-5		6	8	Lowe	Wells		36-19	2nd	2.0
6-1	Bos.	W	10-2		13	5	Mussina	Oliver		37-19	2nd	1.0
6-2	Bos.	L	1-7		6	12	Castillo	Lilly		37-20	2nd	2.0
6-3	Bal.	L	3-4		5	10	Julio	Rivera		37-21	2nd	2.0
6-4	Bal.	W	13-5		15	14	Mendoza	Erickson		38-21	2nd	2.0
6-5	Bal.	L	3-4		7	8	Driskill	Wells	Julio	38-22	2nd	3.0
6-7	S.F	W	2-1		7	8	Mussina	Hernandez	Rivera	39-22	2nd	2.5
6-8	S.F	L	3-4		2	10	Schmidt	Rivera	Nen	39-23	2nd	2.5
6-9	S.F	W	4-2		6	7	Clemens	Rodriguez	Karsay	40-23	2nd	1.5
6-10	Ari.	W	7-5		8	11	Stanton	Johnson		41-23	2nd	1.5
6-11	Ari.	W	6-4		10	6	Wells	Anderson	Mendoza	42-23	2nd	0.5

Date	Opp.	Res.	Score	(inn.*)	Hits	Opp. hits	Winning pitcher	Losing pitcher	Save	Record	Pos.	GB
6-12	Ari.	L	5-9		9	16	Batista	Mussina	Kim	42-24	2nd	1.5
6-14	At N.Y.	W	4-2	(10)	10	8	Karsay	Komiyama		43-24	2nd	0.5
6-15	At N.Y.	L	0-8		5	10	Estes	Clemens		43-25	2nd	0.5
6-16	At N.Y.	L	2-3		7	8	Guthrie	Wells	Benitez	43-26	2nd	1.5
6-18	At Col.	W	10-5		17	12	Mussina	Jennings	Stanton	44-26	2nd	1.5
6-19	At Col.	W	20-10		18	11	Mendoza	White		45-26	2nd	0.5
6-20	At Col.	L	11-14	(10)	19	18	Stark	Karsay		45-27	2nd	1.5
6-21	At S.D.	L	1-9		6	10	Perez	Wells		45-28	2nd	1.5
6-22	At S.D.	W	1-0		3	3	Lilly	Peavy		46-28	2nd	0.5
6-23	At S.D.	W	3-2		10	8	Mendoza	Reed	Karsay	47-28	1st	+0.5
6-25	At Bal.	L	3-4		8	12	Roberts	Pettitte	Julio	47-29	1st	+0.5
6-26	At Bal.	L	7-8		10	12	Roberts	Stanton		47-30	2nd	0.5
6-27	At Bal.	W	3-2		8	6	Wells	Erickson	Rivera	48-30	2nd	...
6-28	N.Y.	W	11-5		12	9	Mussina	D'Amico	Hernandez	49-30	1st	+1.0
6-29	N.Y.	L	2-11		9	16	Leiter	Lilly		49-31	1st	+1.0
6-30	N.Y.	W	8-0		11	3	Pettitte	Trachsel		50-31	1st	+2.0
7-2	Cle.	W	10-5		9	7	Mendoza	Rincon		51-31	1st	+1.0
7-3	Cle.	W	11-8		12	14	Wells	Sabathia	Rivera	52-31	1st	+1.0
7-4	Cle.	W	7-1		11	8	Mussina	Finley		53-31	1st	+1.0
7-5	Tor.	W	6-3		10	8	Hernandez	Loaiza	Rivera	54-31	1st	+2.0
7-6	Tor.	L	3-8		6	13	Parris	Pettitte		54-32	1st	+1.0
7-7	Tor.	W	10-6		15	6	Weaver	Thurman		55-32	1st	+2.0
7-11	At Cle.	W	7-4		10	10	Pettitte	Sabathia	Rivera	56-32	1st	+2.0
7-12	At Cle.	L	1-2	(10)	5	7	Wohlers	Karsay		56-33	1st	+2.0
7-13	At Cle.	W	14-5		15	12	Wells	Drese		57-33	1st	+3.0
7-14	At Cle.	L	7-10		11	13	Rincon	Rivera		57-34	1st	+3.0
7-15	At Tor.	L	5-8		11	13	Parris	Hernandez	Escobar	57-35	1st	+3.0
7-16	At Tor.	W	7-6		7	13	Karsay	Politte	Rivera	58-35	1st	+3.0
7-17	Det.	W	2-1		6	11	Pettitte	Redman		59-35	1st	+3.0
7-18	Det.	W	6-5		13	10	Mendoza	Rodney	Rivera	60-35	1st	+3.0
7-19	Bos.	L	2-4		5	7	Martinez	Mussina	Urbina	60-36	1st	+2.0
7-20	Bos.	W	9-8	(11)	13	12	Karsay	Gomes		61-36	1st	+3.0
7-21	Bos.	W	9-8		11	11	Stanton	Urbina		62-36	1st	+4.0
7-23	At Cle.	L	3-9		6	15	Baez	Pettitte		62-37	1st	+3.5
7-24	At Cle.	W	14-7		18	10	Wells	Drese		63-37	1st	+4.5
7-26	At T.B.	W	12-9		10	17	Mussina	Sosa	Karsay	64-37	1st	+5.0
7-27	At T.B.	L	4-7		7	11	Harper	Weaver	Yan	64-38	1st	+4.0
7-28	At T.B.	W	9-1		12	4	Pettitte	Sturtze		65-38	1st	+4.0
7-29	At Tex.	W	9-2		12	9	Hernandez	Rogers		66-38	1st	+5.0
7-30	At Tex.	W	9-6		11	10	Wells	Myette	Mendoza	67-38	1st	+5.0
7-31	At Tex.	L	6-17		11	21	Bell	Mussina		67-39	1st	+4.0
8-1	At Ana.	L	1-2		6	8	Washburn	Weaver	Percival	67-40	1st	+4.0
8-2	At Ana.	W	4-0		9	4	Pettitte	Appier	Mendoza	68-40	1st	+4.0
8-3	At Ana.	L	4-5		6	11	Percival	Mendoza		68-41	1st	+4.0
8-4	At Ana.	W	7-5	(12)	13	11	Stanton	Shields	Mendoza	69-41	1st	+4.0
8-6	K.C.	L	2-6		4	17	Hernandez	Mussina		69-42	1st	+4.0
8-7	K.C.	W	6-2		9	6	Clemens	Suppan		70-42	1st	+5.0
8-8	K.C.	W	6-3		7	10	Pettitte	Byrd	Rivera	71-42	1st	+5.0
8-9	Oak.	L	2-3	(16)	11	14	Bowie	Hitchcock		71-43	1st	+5.0
8-10	Oak.	L	0-8		10	13	Lidle	Wells		71-44	1st	+4.0
8-11	Oak.	W	8-5		12	14	Mussina	Mulder		72-44	1st	+4.0
8-13	At K.C.	W	10-5		14	11	Clemens	Suppan		73-44	1st	+5.0
8-14	At K.C.	W	3-2	(14)	14	11	Mendoza	Stein	Rivera	74-44	1st	+5.0
8-15	At K.C.	W	7-5		18	12	Stanton	Hernandez	Rivera	75-44	1st	+6.0
8-16	At Sea.	W	9-3		12	10	Wells	Halama	Weaver	76-44	1st	+7.0
8-17	At Sea.	W	8-3		13	6	Mussina	Franklin	Karsay	77-44	1st	+7.0
8-18	At Sea.	L	2-5		6	10	Pineiro	Clemens	Sasaki	77-45	1st	+7.0
8-20	Ana.	W	7-5		10	12	Pettitte	Sele	Stanton	78-45	1st	+8.0
8-21	Ana.	L	1-5	(11)	7	11	Weber	Weaver		78-46	1st	+7.0
8-22	Ana.	W	4-2		11	8	Wells	Lackey	Karsay	79-46	1st	+7.0
8-23	Tex.	L	2-6		7	12	Park	Mussina		79-47	1st	+6.0
8-24	Tex.	W	3-2		5	5	Clemens	Alvarez	Karsay	80-47	1st	+7.0
8-25	Tex.	L	2-6		8	13	Benoit	Pettitte		80-48	1st	+7.0
8-26	Tex.	W	10-3		19	9	Hernandez	Rogers	Weaver	81-48	1st	+7.0
8-27	At Bos.	W	6-0		13	5	Wells	Fossum		82-48	1st	+8.0
8-28	At Bos.	W	7-0		9	3	Mussina	Martinez		83-48	1st	+9.0
8-29	At Tor.	L	4-7		9	14	Loaiza	Clemens		83-49	1st	+8.5
8-30	At Tor.	W	9-7		11	14	Weaver	Walker	Karsay	84-49	1st	+8.5
8-31	At Tor.	L	1-5		3	7	Miller	Hernandez		84-50	1st	+8.5

Date	Opp.	Res.	Score	(inn.*)	Hits	Opp. hits	Winning pitcher	Losing pitcher	Save	Record	Pos.	GB
9-1	At Tor.	L	6-7		12	13	Halladay	Wells	Escobar	84-51	1st	+7.5
9-2	Bos.	L	4-8		11	11	Fossum	Mussina		84-52	1st	+6.5
9-3	Bos.	W	4-2		6	5	Clemens	Castillo	Stanton	85-52	1st	+7.5
9-4	Bos.	W	3-1		7	8	Pettitte	Lowe	Karsay	86-52	1st	+8.5
9-5	Det.	W	9-3		13	7	Hernandez	Sparks		87-52	1st	+9.5
9-6	Det.	W	8-1		11	5	Wells	Redman		88-52	1st	+9.5
9-7	Det.	L	1-2		7	7	German	Mussina	Acevedo	88-53	1st	+8.5
9-8	Det.	W	6-4		8	11	Stanton	Henriquez	Karsay	89-53	1st	+9.5
9-10§	Bal.	W	5-2		7	7	Pettitte	Johnson	Stanton	90-53		
9-10∞	Bal.	W	3-1		6	5	Weaver	Ponson	Karsay	91-53	1st	+9.5
9-11	Bal.	W	5-4	(11)	7	8	Karsay	Bauer		92-53	1st	+9.5
9-12	Bal.	W	7-3		10	9	Wells	Douglass		93-53	1st	+9.5
9-13	Chi.	L	2-13		3	13	Biddle	Mussina	Osuna	93-54	1st	+9.5
9-14	Chi.	L	1-8		5	11	Wright	Clemens		93-55	1st	+8.5
9-15	Chi.	W	8-4	(6)	8	5	Pettitte	Porzio		94-55	1st	+9.5
9-17	At T.B.	L	7-9		12	16	Carter	Mendoza		94-56	1st	+8.5
9-18	At T.B.	W	7-1		13	6	Weaver	Zambrano		95-56	1st	+9.5
9-19	At T.B.	L	2-3	(10)	7	11	Yan	Hitchcock		95-57	1st	+9.0
9-20	At Det.	W	5-1		11	8	Clemens	Van Hekken		96-57	1st	+9.0
9-21	At Det.	W	3-2		7	5	Pettitte	Beverlin	Karsay	97-57	1st	+9.0
9-22	At Det.	W	4-3		6	7	Wells	Maroth	Stanton	98-57	1st	+9.0
9-23	T.B.	L	2-3		6	9	Zambrano	Hernandez	Yan	98-58	1st	+8.0
9-24	T.B.	W	6-0		9	2	Mussina	Harper		99-58	1st	+8.0
9-25	T.B.	W	4-3		10	6	Weaver	Sturtze	Rivera	100-58	1st	+9.0
9-27	At Bal.	W	6-2		10	7	Pettitte	Ponson		101-58	1st	+9.5
9-28	At Bal.	W	4-2		9	6	Wells	Driskill	Stanton	102-58	1st	+10.5
9-29	At Bal.	W	6-1		6	9	Mussina	Stephens		103-58	1st	+10.5

Monthly records: April (17-10), May (19-9), June (14-12), July (17-8), August (17-11), September (19-8).
*Innings, if other than nine. §Day separate admission. ∞Night separate admission.

RECORDS

2002 regular-season record: 103-58
Position: 1st in A.L. East
Home: 52-28   **Road:** 51-30
A.L. East: 46-29   **A.L. Central:** 29-7
A.L. West: 17-15   **N.L.:** 11-7
Vs. LH starters: 25-11
Vs. RH starters: 78-47
Grass: 90-49   **Artificial:** 13-9
Day: 32-26   **Night:** 71-32
1-Run: 21-21   **X-inn.:** 6-7
Doubleheaders: 0-0-0
Team record past five years: 497-309
(.617, ranks 1st in league in that span)

TEAM LEADERS

Batting average: Bernie Williams (.333).
At-bats: Alfonso Soriano (696).
Runs: Alfonso Soriano (128).
Hits: Alfonso Soriano (209).
Total bases: Alfonso Soriano (381).
Doubles: Alfonso Soriano (51).
Triples: Alfonso Soriano, Shane Spencer, Bernie Williams, Enrique Wilson (2).
Home runs: Jason Giambi (41).
Runs batted in: Jason Giambi (122).

Stolen bases: Alfonso Soriano (41).
Slugging percentage: Jason Giambi (.598).
On-base percentage: Jason Giambi (.435).
Wins: David Wells (19).
Earned-run average: Andy Pettitte (3.27).
Complete games: Andy Pettitte (3).
Shutouts: Mike Mussina (2).
Saves: Mariano Rivera (28).
Innings pitched: Mike Mussina (215.2).
Strikeouts: Roger Clemens (192).

GAMES BY POSITION

Catcher: Jorge Posada 138, Chris Widger 21, Alberto Castillo 14.
First base: Jason Giambi 92, Nick Johnson 78, Ron Coomer 11, John Vander Wal 6, Robin Ventura 5.
Second base: Alfonso Soriano 155, Enrique Wilson 7.
Third base: Robin Ventura 137, Ron Coomer 26, Enrique Wilson 26, Alex Arias 4.
Shortstop: Derek Jeter 156, Enrique Wilson 14, Alex Arias 1.

Outfield: Bernie Williams 147, Rondell White 113, Shane Spencer 91, Raul Mondesi 70, John Vander Wal 57, Gerald Williams 30, Juan Rivera 28, Marcus Thames 7, Karim Garcia 2, Nick Johnson 2, Enrique Wilson 1.
Designated hitter: Jason Giambi 63, Nick Johnson 50, John Vander Wal 16, Ron Coomer 15, Rondell White 11, Bernie Williams 7, Jorge Posada 5, Drew Henson 2, Enrique Wilson 2, Derek Jeter 1, Raul Mondesi 1, Alfonso Soriano 1, Shane Spencer 1, Gerald Williams 1.

TOP DRAFT CHOICES

2. **Brandon Weeden,** RHP-SS, Santa Fe H.S., Edmond, Okla.
4. **Alan Bomer,** RHP, Texas.
5. **Matt Carson,** OF, Brigham Young.
6. **Brandon Harmsen,** RHP, Grand Rapids (Mich.) J.C.
7. **Ross Michelsen,** 1B, Lamar (Texas) H.S.
8. **Brad Halsey,** LHP, Texas.
9. **Eric Verbryke,** OF, Cal State Northridge.
10. **Gary Bell,** LHP, South Carolina.

OAKLAND ATHLETICS
AMERICAN LEAGUE WEST DIVISION

2003 SEASON

March/April

SUN	MON	TUE	WED	THU	FRI	SAT
23	24	25 SEA ‡	26 SEA ‡	27	28	29
30	31	1 SEA	2 SEA	3	4 ANA	5 ANA D
6 ANA	7	8 TEX	9 TEX	10 TEX D	11 ANA	12 ANA
13 ANA D	14 SEA	15 SEA	16 SEA	17 SEA	18 TEX D	19 TEX
20 TEX	21	22 DET	23 DET	24 DET	25 CLE D	26 CLE
27 CLE D	28	29 CWS	30 CWS			

May

SUN	MON	TUE	WED	THU	FRI	SAT
				1 CWS	2 NYY	3 NYY D
4 NYY D	5	6 CWS	7 CWS	8 CWS D	9 NYY	10 NYY D
11 NYY D	12	13 DET	14 DET	15 DET	16 CLE	17 CLE D
18 CLE D	19	20 MIN	21 MIN	22 MIN D	23 KC	24 KC D
25 KC D	26	27 MIN	28 MIN D	29 KC	30 KC	31 KC D

June

SUN	MON	TUE	WED	THU	FRI	SAT
1 KC D	2	3 FLA	4 FLA	5 FLA	6 PHI	7 PHI D
8 PHI D	9	10 ATL	11 ATL	12 ATL D	13 MON	14 MON D
15 MON D	16	17 TEX	18 TEX	19 TEX D	20 SF	21 SF
22 SF D	23 TEX	24 TEX	25 TEX	26 SF	27 SF	28 SF D
29 SF D	30					

July

SUN	MON	TUE	WED	THU	FRI	SAT
		1 SEA	2 SEA	3 SEA D	4 ANA	5 ANA
6 ANA D	7	8 TB	9 TB	10 TB D	11 BAL	12 BAL D
13 BAL D	14	15	16 *	17 MIN	18 MIN	19 MIN D
20 MIN D	21 KC	22 KC	23 SEA	24 SEA	25 ANA	26 ANA D
27 ANA	28 ANA	29 CLE	30 CLE	31 CLE D		

August

SUN	MON	TUE	WED	THU	FRI	SAT
					1 NYY	2 NYY D
3 NYY D	4	5 DET	6 DET	7 DET D	8 CWS	9 CWS
10 CWS D	11 BOS	12 BOS	13 BOS	14 BOS D	15 TOR	16 TOR D
17 TOR D	18	19 BOS	20 BOS	21 BOS	22 TOR	23 TOR D
24 TOR D	25 TOR	26 BAL	27 BAL	28 BAL D	29 TB	30 TB

September

SUN	MON	TUE	WED	THU	FRI	SAT
31 TB D	1	2 BAL	3 BAL	4 BAL	5 TB	6 TB
7 TB D	8 ANA	9 ANA	10 ANA	11 ANA D	12 TEX	13 TEX
14 TEX	15 ANA	16 ANA	17 ANA D	18	19 SEA	20 SEA D
21 SEA D	22 TEX	23 TEX	24 TEX D	25	26 SEA	27 SEA
28 SEA D						

Home games shaded; D—Day game (games starting before 5 p.m.); *—All-Star Game at Comiskey Park, Chicago. ‡—Game played in Tokyo, Japan. Subject to change.

CLUB DIRECTORY

Owners
Stephen C. Schott
Ken Hofmann
President
Michael P. Crowley
Vice president and general manager
Billy Beane
Assistant general manager
Paul DePodesta

Special assistants to general manager
Randy Johnson
Matt Keough
Director of player development
Keith Lieppman
Director of scouting
Eric Kubota
Director of minor league operations
Ted Polakowski

V.p., broadcasting and communications
Ken Pries
Director of public relations
Jim Young
Baseball information manager
Mike Selleck

MINOR LEAGUE AFFILIATES

Class	Team	League	Manager
AAA	Sacramento	Pacific Coast	Tony DeFrancesco
AA	Midland	Texas	Greg Sparks
A	Modesto	California	Rich Rodriguez
A	Kane County	Midwest	Webster Garrison
A	Vancouver	Northwest	To be announced
Rookie	Scottsdale A's	Arizona	Ruben Escalera

BROADCAST INFORMATION

Radio: KFRC-AM (610).
TV: KICU-TV (Channel 36).
Cable TV: Fox Sports Bay Area.

SPRING TRAINING

Ballpark (city): Phoenix Stadium (Phoenix, Ariz.).
Ticket information: 602-392-0074.

Follow the Athletics all season at: www.sportingnews.com/baseball/teams/athletics/

SPRING TRAINING ROSTER

Manager—Ken Macha (38).
Coaches—Thad Bosley (41), Brad Fischer (35), Rick Peterson (47), Mike Quade (48), Ron Washington.

No.	PITCHERS	B/T	Ht./Wt.	Born	Age*	2002 clubs
	Bazzell, Shane	L/R	6-2/180	3-22-79	24	Midland
57	Bowie, Micah	L/L	6-4/210	11-10-74	28	Sacramento, Oakland
53	Bradford, Chad	R/R	6-5/203	9-14-74	28	Oakland
	Duchscherer, Justin	R/R	6-3/165	11-19-77	25	Sacramento
	Fikac, Jeremy	R/R	6-2/185	4-8-75	27	San Diego, Mobile
29	Foulke, Keith	R/R	6-0/210	10-19-72	30	Chicago A.L.
56	Harang, Aaron	R/R	6-7/240	5-9-78	24	Midland, Sacramento, Oakland
32	Harville, Chad	R/R	5-9/180	9-16-76	26	Sacramento
	Hernandez, Buddy	R/R	5-9/170	3-3-79	24	Greenville
37	Hiljus, Erik	R/R	6-6/222	12-25-72	30	Oakland, Sacramento
15	Hudson, Tim	R/R	6-1/164	7-14-75	27	Oakland
31	Lilly, Ted	L/L	6-0/185	1-4-76	27	New York A.L., Oakland
45	Mecir, Jim	B/R	6-1/230	5-16-70	32	Oakland
20	Mulder, Mark	L/L	6-6/215	8-5-77	25	Oakland
	Neu, Michael	B/R	5-10/190	3-9-78	25	Chattanooga, Louisville
73	Rincon, Ricky	L/L	5-9/187	4-13-70	32	Cleveland, Oakland
	Smith, Roy	R/R	6-6/235	5-18-76	26	Buffalo, Cleveland
40	Snow, Bert	R/R	6-1/200	3-23-77	26	Visalia, Midland
	Valentine, Joe	R/R	6-2/195	12-24-79	23	Birmingham
75	Zito, Barry	L/L	6-4/215	5-13-78	24	Oakland

No.	CATCHERS	B/T	Ht./Wt.	Born	Age*	2002 clubs
55	Hernandez, Ramon	R/R	6-0/210	5-20-76	26	Oakland
8	Johnson, Mark	L/R	6-0/185	9-12-75	27	Chicago A.L.

No.	INFIELDERS	B/T	Ht./Wt.	Born	Age*	2002 clubs
	Bynum, Freddie	L/R	6-1/180	3-15-80	23	Visalia
3	Chavez, Eric	L/R	6-1/206	12-7-77	25	Oakland
44	Durazo, Erubiel	L/L	6-3/240	1-23-74	29	Tucson, Arizona, El Paso
14	Ellis, Mark	R/R	5-11/180	6-6-77	25	Sacramento, Oakland
40	German, Esteban	R/R	5-9/165	1-26-78	25	Sacramento, Oakland
2	Grabowski, Jason	L/R	6-3/200	5-24-76	26	Sacramento, Oakland
10	Hatteberg, Scott	L/R	6-1/210	12-14-69	33	Oakland
58	Lopez, Luis	R/R	6-0/205	10-5-73	29	Sacramento
11	Menechino, Frank	R/R	5-8/198	1-7-71	32	Oakland, Sacramento
	Morrissey, Adam	R/R	5-11/170	6-8-81	21	Modesto, Midland
4	Tejada, Miguel	R/R	5-9/200	5-25-76	26	Oakland

No.	OUTFIELDERS	B/T	Ht./Wt.	Born	Age*	2002 clubs
22	Byrnes, Eric	R/R	6-2/210	2-16-76	27	Sacramento, Oakland
24	Dye, Jermaine	R/R	6-5/220	1-28-74	29	Sacramento, Modesto, Oakland
	Johnson, Rontrez	R/R	5-10/165	12-8-76	26	Omaha
12	Long, Terrence	L/L	6-1/202	2-29-76	27	Oakland
6	Piatt, Adam	R/R	6-2/205	2-8-76	27	Sacramento, Oakland
29	Singleton, Chris	L/L	6-2/210	8-15-72	30	Baltimore

*Age as of April 1, 2003.

BALLPARK INFORMATION

Ballpark (capacity, surface)
Network Associates Coliseum (43,662, grass)

Address
Oakland Athletics
7000 Coliseum Way
Oakland, CA 94621

Official website
www.oaklandathletics.com

Business phone
510-638-4900

Ticket information
510-638-4627

Field dimensions (from home plate)
To left field at foul line, 330 feet
To center field, 400 feet
To right field at foul line, 330 feet

First game played
April 17, 1968 (Orioles 4, Athletics 1)

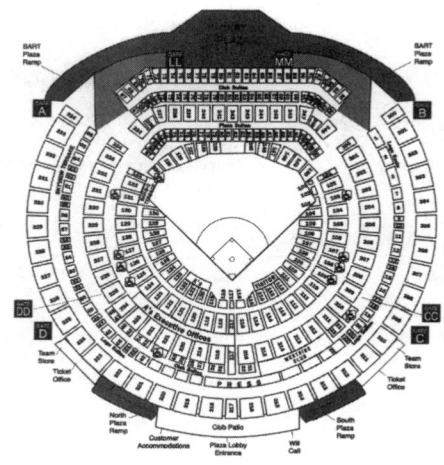

Date	Opp.	Res.	Score	(inn.*)	Hits	Opp. hits	Winning pitcher	Losing pitcher	Save	Record	Pos.	GB
4-1	Tex.	W	8-3		13	7	Mulder	Park		1-0	1st	+1.0
4-2	Tex.	W	3-2		5	6	Koch	Miceli		2-0	1st	+1.0
4-3	Tex.	W	9-6		7	12	Mecir	Rodriguez	Koch	3-0	1st	+1.0
4-4	Tex.	L	5-7		12	10	Davis	Lidle		3-1	1st	+0.5
4-5	At Sea.	L	1-7		6	10	Baldwin	Hiljus		3-2	2nd	0.5
4-6	At Sea.	W	8-3		13	5	Mulder	Garcia		4-2	1st	+0.5
4-7	At Sea.	W	6-5		11	9	Hudson	Moyer	Koch	5-2	1st	+1.0
4-9	At Tex.	W	5-4	(11)	13	7	Koch	Seanez		6-2	1st	+1.0
4-10	At Tex.	L	2-4		6	9	Burba	Lidle	Rocker	6-3	T1st	...
4-11	At Tex.	L	0-7		2	14	Davis	Mulder		6-4	2nd	1.0
4-12	At Ana.	W	5-1		10	9	Hudson	Ortiz		7-4	2nd	1.0
4-13	At Ana.	W	7-2		7	4	Hiljus	Washburn		8-4	2nd	1.0
4-14	At Ana.	L	1-4		4	8	Appier	Zito	Levine	8-5	2nd	2.0
4-16	Sea.	L	2-6	(7)	5	11	Pineiro	Lidle		8-6	2nd	3.5
4-17	Sea.	L	4-7		11	12	Moyer	Hudson	Sasaki	8-7	2nd	4.5
4-18	Ana.	W	4-2		8	7	Hiljus	Ortiz	Koch	9-7	2nd	4.0
4-19	Ana.	L	7-9		12	12	Washburn	Fyhrie	Percival	9-8	2nd	4.0
4-20	Ana.	W	8-7		10	10	Bradford	Levine	Koch	10-8	2nd	4.0
4-21	Ana.	W	6-5		12	12	Venafro	Percival		11-8	2nd	4.0
4-23	N.Y.	L	1-2		6	4	Hernandez	Hudson	Rivera	11-9	2nd	5.5
4-24	N.Y.	L	5-8		8	14	Stanton	Magnante	Rivera	11-10	2nd	5.5
4-25	N.Y.	W	6-2		8	7	Zito	Mussina		12-10	2nd	5.0
4-26	Chi.	W	6-4		9	7	Lidle	Parque	Koch	13-10	2nd	4.0
4-27	Chi.	W	16-1		19	4	Fyhrie	Buehrle		14-10	2nd	4.0
4-28	Chi.	W	10-0		11	3	Hudson	Ritchie		15-10	2nd	3.0
4-30	At N.Y.	L	2-8		7	10	Wells	Zito		15-11	2nd	3.0
5-1	At N.Y.	W	4-1		5	5	Hiljus	Mussina	Koch	16-11	2nd	2.0
5-2	At N.Y.	L	2-9		6	16	Clemens	Lidle		16-12	2nd	3.0
5-3	At Chi.	L	1-6		6	10	Buehrle	Fyhrie		16-13	2nd	4.0
5-4	At Chi.	L	2-10		11	10	Ritchie	Hudson		16-14	2nd	5.0
5-5	At Chi.	W	3-2		5	6	Zito	Wright	Koch	17-14	2nd	5.0
5-7	Bos.	L	7-9		12	15	Arrojo	Mecir	Urbina	17-15	2nd	5.0
5-8	Bos.	L	6-12		9	19	Burkett	Hiljus		17-16	2nd	6.0
5-9	Bos.	L	1-5		6	7	Lowe	Hudson		17-17	3rd	7.0
5-10	Tor.	L	2-6		6	13	Prokopec	Mulder		17-18	3rd	8.0
5-11	Tor.	W	7-4		8	8	Zito	Miller		18-18	3rd	8.0
5-12	Tor.	L	4-11		10	13	Halladay	Lidle	Walker	18-19	T3rd	8.0
5-14	At Bos.	L	2-6		11	8	Burkett	Hudson		18-20	T3rd	8.0
5-15	At Bos.	L	2-8		7	12	Lowe	Hiljus		18-21	4th	9.0
5-16	At Bos.	W	5-0		10	7	Zito	Castillo		19-21	T3rd	9.0
5-17	At Tor.	L	1-7		7	11	Halladay	Mulder		19-22	T3rd	10.0
5-18	At Tor.	L	3-6		7	6	Miller	Fyhrie	Escobar	19-23	T3rd	10.0
5-19	At Tor.	L	0-11		2	10	Loaiza	Hudson		19-24	T3rd	10.0
5-21	Bal.	L	4-6	(14)	11	11	Driskill	Venafro	Julio	19-25	T3rd	10.0
5-22	Bal.	W	7-6		13	8	Fyhrie	Maduro	Koch	20-25	T3rd	9.0
5-23	Bal.	L	3-11		8	14	Ponson	Mulder		20-26	4th	10.0
5-24	T.B.	W	9-8		12	10	Mecir	Zambrano	Koch	21-26	3rd	10.0
5-25	T.B.	W	6-0		8	3	Harang	Harper	Bradford	22-26	3rd	9.0
5-26	T.B.	W	7-0		8	2	Zito	Kennedy		23-26	3rd	9.0
5-28	At Bal.	W	5-2		10	9	Mulder	Maduro	Koch	24-26	3rd	8.0
5-29	At Bal.	L	5-10		10	15	Bauer	Fyhrie		24-27	3rd	9.0
5-30	At T.B.	L	3-4	(13)	7	19	Harper	Bradford		24-28	3rd	10.0
5-31	At T.B.	W	13-9		17	17	Venafro	Yan		25-28	3rd	9.0
6-1	At T.B.	W	8-3		12	9	Zito	Kennedy		26-28	3rd	8.0
6-2	At T.B.	W	4-2		7	10	Mulder	Rupe	Koch	27-28	3rd	8.0
6-3	Sea.	L	1-4		5	11	Garcia	Harang	Sasaki	27-29	3rd	9.0
6-4	Sea.	W	3-2	(10)	5	14	Koch	Hasegawa		28-29	3rd	8.0
6-5	Sea.	L	0-5		4	13	Moyer	Lidle		28-30	3rd	9.0
6-6	Sea.	W	10-4		12	11	Zito	Baldwin		29-30	3rd	8.0
6-7	Hou.	W	5-3		9	6	Mulder	Oswalt	Koch	30-30	3rd	7.0
6-8	Hou.	W	5-1		8	7	Harang	Reynolds		31-30	3rd	7.0
6-9	Hou.	W	7-6		10	11	Koch	Dotel		32-30	3rd	6.0
6-10	Mil.	W	8-6		10	16	Bradford	de los Santos	Koch	33-30	3rd	6.0
6-11	Mil.	W	11-2		14	5	Zito	Figueroa		34-30	3rd	5.0
6-12	Mil.	W	8-0		10	9	Mulder	Sheets		35-30	3rd	5.0

Date	Opp.	Res.	Score	(inn.*)	Hits	Opp. hits	Winning pitcher	Losing pitcher	Save	Record	Pos.	GB
6-14	At S.F	W	3-2		7	11	Hudson	Schmidt	Koch	36-30	3rd	5.0
6-15	At S.F	L	2-6		9	6	Zerbe	Harang		36-31	3rd	5.0
6-16	At S.F	W	2-1		10	5	Zito	Rueter	Koch	37-31	3rd	4.0
6-18	At Pit.	W	4-2		10	8	Mulder	Fogg	Koch	38-31	3rd	4.0
6-19	At Pit.	W	3-2	(10)	5	9	Bradford	Williams	Koch	39-31	3rd	4.0
6-20	At Pit.	W	5-3		10	8	Hudson	Benson	Koch	40-31	3rd	4.0
6-21	At Cin.	W	5-3		8	7	Harang	Williamson	Koch	41-31	3rd	4.0
6-22	At Cin.	W	10-3		10	3	Zito	Chen		42-31	3rd	3.0
6-23	At Cin.	W	5-1		9	7	Mulder	Reitsma		43-31	3rd	3.0
6-24	At Sea.	W	13-2		13	9	Lidle	Garcia		44-31	2nd	2.0
6-25	At Sea.	L	1-7		8	11	Baldwin	Hudson		44-32	2nd	3.0
6-26	At Sea.	L	0-1		2	5	Hasegawa	Bradford	Sasaki	44-33	3rd	4.0
6-27	At Sea.	L	4-7		9	12	Halama	Zito	Rhodes	44-34	3rd	5.0
6-28	S.F	W	10-6		15	9	Mulder	Hernandez		45-34	3rd	5.0
6-29	S.F	L	3-5		7	10	Schmidt	Lidle	Nen	45-35	3rd	6.0
6-30	S.F	W	7-0		11	5	Hudson	Ortiz		46-35	3rd	5.0
7-1	Min.	L	4-5		11	14	Romero	Venafro	Guardado	46-36	3rd	6.0
7-2	Min.	W	4-3		9	8	Bradford	Guardado		47-36	3rd	5.0
7-3	Min.	L	1-2		8	6	Santana	Mulder	Guardado	47-37	3rd	6.0
7-4	K.C.	W	3-2		7	4	Koch	Hernandez		48-37	3rd	5.0
7-5	K.C.	W	4-3		7	9	Mecir	Hernandez		49-37	3rd	5.0
7-6	K.C.	L	3-4	(10)	7	12	Mullen	Koch	Voyles	49-38	3rd	5.0
7-7	K.C.	W	3-2		9	6	Zito	Byrd	Koch	50-38	3rd	5.0
7-11	At Bal.	W	4-1		9	6	Mulder	Erickson	Koch	51-38	3rd	5.0
7-12	At Bal.	W	1-0		7	8	Hudson	Johnson	Koch	52-38	3rd	5.0
7-13	At Bal.	W	6-0		10	3	Zito	Driskill		53-38	3rd	4.0
7-14	At Bal.	L	3-6		7	8	Lopez	Lidle	Julio	53-39	3rd	5.0
7-15	At T.B.	W	4-0		8	4	Lilly	Rupe		54-39	3rd	4.0
7-16	At T.B.	W	2-1		8	9	Mulder	Sosa	Koch	55-39	3rd	3.0
7-17	Ana.	L	4-10		9	15	Appier	Hudson		55-40	3rd	4.0
7-18	Ana.	W	2-0		8	6	Zito	Sele	Koch	56-40	3rd	4.0
7-19	Tex.	W	10-0		10	1	Lidle	Myette		57-40	3rd	3.0
7-20	Tex.	W	6-5		12	8	Koch	Burba		58-40	3rd	2.0
7-21	Tex.	L	3-7	(12)	11	10	Powell	Mecir		58-41	3rd	2.0
7-23	At Ana.	W	2-1		4	8	Zito	Appier	Koch	59-41	3rd	2.0
7-24	At Ana.	L	1-5		6	9	Sele	Hudson		59-42	3rd	2.0
7-25	At Ana.	L	4-5		9	13	Shields	Mecir	Weber	59-43	3rd	3.0
7-26	At Tex.	L	4-12		12	12	Rodriguez	Mulder		59-44	3rd	3.0
7-27	At Tex.	L	6-10	(10)	10	14	Kolb	Koch		59-45	3rd	4.0
7-28	At Tex.	W	12-2		15	6	Zito	Alvarez		60-45	3rd	3.0
7-29	Cle.	L	6-8		9	16	Mulholland	Magnante	Wohlers	60-46	3rd	4.0
7-30	Cle.	L	4-5		14	7	Drese	Lidle	Wohlers	60-47	3rd	5.0
7-31	Cle.	W	6-4		11	6	Mulder	Westbrook	Koch	61-47	3rd	5.0
8-1	Det.	W	5-3		7	8	Bowie	Sparks	Koch	62-47	3rd	5.0
8-2	Det.	L	1-3		7	8	Redman	Zito	Acevedo	62-48	3rd	6.0
8-3	Det.	W	8-4		11	6	Hudson	Lima		63-48	3rd	6.0
8-4	Det.	W	4-0		6	1	Lidle	Maroth		64-48	3rd	5.0
8-6	At Bos.	W	9-1		8	7	Mulder	Wakefield		65-48	3rd	4.0
8-7	At Bos.	W	3-2		9	7	Harang	Burkett	Koch	66-48	3rd	4.0
8-8	At Bos.	L	2-4		6	7	Lowe	Zito	Urbina	66-49	3rd	5.0
8-9	At N.Y.	W	3-2	(16)	14	11	Bowie	Hitchcock		67-49	3rd	4.0
8-10	At N.Y.	W	8-0		13	10	Lidle	Wells		68-49	3rd	4.0
8-11	At N.Y.	L	5-8		14	12	Mussina	Mulder		68-50	3rd	4.0
8-12	Tor.	L	1-2		9	5	Loaiza	Harang	Escobar	68-51	3rd	4.5
8-13	Tor.	W	5-4		7	4	Zito	Carpenter	Koch	69-51	3rd	4.5
8-14	Tor.	W	4-2		4	7	Hudson	Walker	Koch	70-51	3rd	3.5
8-16	Chi.	W	1-0		5	6	Lidle	Buehrle	Koch	71-51	3rd	3.0
8-17	Chi.	W	9-2		7	6	Mulder	Garland		72-51	3rd	2.0
8-18	Chi.	W	7-4		12	8	Zito	Wright		73-51	3rd	2.0
8-19	At Cle.	W	8-1		12	6	Hudson	Baez		74-51	3rd	1.0
8-20	At Cle.	W	6-3		12	8	Harang	Westbrook	Koch	75-51	T2nd	...
8-21	At Cle.	W	6-0		5	1	Lidle	Rodriguez		76-51	T2nd	...
8-22	At Cle.	W	9-3		14	5	Mulder	Phillips	Bradford	77-51	T1st	...
8-23	At Det.	W	9-1		14	7	Zito	Powell		78-51	1st	+1.0
8-24	At Det.	W	12-3		14	8	Hudson	Lima		79-51	1st	+2.0
8-25	At Det.	W	10-7		14	11	Mecir	Walker	Koch	80-51	1st	+2.0
8-26	At K.C.	W	6-3		14	6	Lidle	May	Koch	81-51	1st	+2.5
8-27	At K.C.	W	6-4		12	9	Mulder	Hernandez	Koch	82-51	1st	+3.0
8-28	At K.C.	W	7-1		11	4	Zito	Sedlacek		83-51	1st	+4.0

Date	Opp.	Res.	Score	(inn.*)	Hits	Opp. hits	Winning pitcher	Losing pitcher	Save	Record	Pos.	GB
8-30	Min.	W	4-2		10	8	Hudson	Radke	Koch	84-51	1st	+3.5
8-31	Min.	W	6-3		7	7	Mecir	Romero	Koch	85-51	1st	+3.5
9-1	Min.	W	7-5		12	6	Koch	Guardado		86-51	1st	+3.5
9-2	K.C.	W	7-6		8	14	Koch	Grimsley		87-51	1st	+4.0
9-4	K.C.	W	12-11		15	15	Koch	Grimsley		88-51	1st	+3.5
9-6	At Min.	L	0-6		6	10	Radke	Lidle		88-52	1st	+2.0
9-7	At Min.	W	2-0		6	7	Mulder	Mays	Koch	89-52	1st	+2.0
9-8	At Min.	W	6-0		11	3	Zito	Milton		90-52	1st	+2.0
9-9	At Ana.	W	2-1		5	6	Hudson	Appier	Koch	91-52	1st	+3.0
9-10	At Ana.	L	2-5		3	10	Ortiz	Lilly	Percival	91-53	1st	+2.0
9-11	At Ana.	L	5-6		7	14	Shields	Tam	Percival	91-54	1st	+1.0
9-12	At Ana.	L	6-7		8	9	Donnelly	Koch		91-55	T1st	...
9-13	Sea.	W	5-0		10	2	Zito	Valdes		92-55	T1st	...
9-14	Sea.	W	1-0		3	4	Hudson	Moyer		93-55	T1st	...
9-15	Sea.	L	3-6		6	10	Pineiro	Harang	Sasaki	93-56	2nd	1.0
9-16	Ana.	W	4-3		8	5	Koch	Levine		94-56	T1st	...
9-17	Ana.	L	0-1	(10)	3	7	Weber	Koch	Percival	94-57	2nd	1.0
9-18	Ana.	W	7-4		7	10	Zito	Callaway	Koch	95-57	T1st	...
9-19	Ana.	W	5-3		8	6	Hudson	Appier	Koch	96-57	1st	+1.0
9-20	Tex.	W	4-2		6	5	Mecir	Kolb	Rincon	97-57	1st	+1.0
9-21	Tex.	W	6-3		9	5	Tam	Nitkowski	Koch	98-57	1st	+2.0
9-22	Tex.	W	7-5		9	12	Mulder	Park	Koch	99-57	1st	+3.0
9-24	At Sea.	L	7-8		14	14	Hasegawa	Tam	Rhodes	99-58	1st	+3.0
9-25	At Sea.	L	2-3		7	10	Rhodes	Mecir	Sasaki	99-59	1st	+3.0
9-26	At Sea.	W	5-3	(10)	11	6	Koch	Hasegawa		100-59	1st	+3.0
9-27	At Tex.	W	3-2		8	7	Mulder	Park	Koch	101-59	1st	+4.0
9-28	At Tex.	W	10-8		10	9	Lilly	Kolb	Mecir	102-59	1st	+4.0
9-29	At Tex.	W	8-7		9	10	Zito	Benoit		103-59	1st	+4.0

Monthly records: April (15-11), May (10-17), June (21-7), July (15-12), August (24-4), September (18-8).
*Innings, if other than nine.

RECORDS

2002 regular-season record: 103-59
Position: 1st in A.L. West
Home: 54-27   **Road:** 49-32
A.L. East: 23-22   **A.L. Central:** 32-9
A.L. West: 32-26   **N.L.:** 16-2
Vs. LH starters: 20-14
Vs. RH starters: 83-45
Grass: 96-54   **Artificial:** 7-5
Day: 35-16   **Night:** 68-43
1-Run: 32-14   **X-inn.:** 5-6
Doubleheaders: 0-0-0
Team record past five years: 457-352
(.565, ranks 2nd in league in that span)

TEAM LEADERS

Batting average: Miguel Tejada (.308).
At-bats: Miguel Tejada (662).
Runs: Miguel Tejada (108).
Hits: Miguel Tejada (204).
Total bases: Miguel Tejada (336).
Doubles: Terrence Long (32).
Triples: Ray Durham, Mark Ellis, Scott Hatteberg, Terrence Long (4).
Home runs: Eric Chavez, Miguel Tejada (34).
Runs batted in: Miguel Tejada (131).
Stolen bases: Eric Chavez (8).

Slugging percentage: Eric Chavez (.513).
On-base percentage: David Justice (.376).
Wins: Barry Zito (23).
Earned-run average: Barry Zito (2.75).
Complete games: Tim Hudson (4).
Shutouts: Tim Hudson, Cory Lidle (2).
Saves: Billy Koch (44).
Innings pitched: Tim Hudson (238.1).
Strikeouts: Barry Zito (182).

GAMES BY POSITION

Catcher: Ramon Hernandez 135, Greg Myers 53, Cody McKay 1.
First base: Scott Hatteberg 91, John Mabry 50, Carlos Pena 40, Olmedo Saenz 34, Larry Sutton 6, Randy Velarde 5, Adam Piatt 1.
Second base: Mark Ellis 85, Randy Velarde 38, Frank Menechino 32, Ray Durham 11, Esteban German 8, Jose Flores 2.
Third base: Eric Chavez 143, Olmedo Saenz 15, Mark Ellis 7, Frank Menechino 4, Randy Velarde 1.
Shortstop: Miguel Tejada 162, Mark Ellis 8, Frank Menechino 2, Jose Flores 1.
Outfield: Terrence Long 162, Jermaine Dye 111, Eric Byrnes 79, David Justice

75, John Mabry 53, Adam Piatt 50, Jeremy Giambi 40, Mike Colangelo 19, Jason Grabowski 4, Larry Sutton 3, Eric Chavez 1.
Designated hitter: Ray Durham 43, Scott Hatteberg 42, David Justice 37, Jermaine Dye 19, Eric Chavez 9, Eric Byrnes 7, Olmedo Saenz 7, Randy Velarde 5, Jeremy Giambi 2, Mark Ellis 1, Jose Flores 1, Frank Menechino 1, Greg Myers 1.

TOP DRAFT CHOICES

1a. **Nick Swisher,** 1B-OF, Ohio State.
1b. **Joseph Blanton,** RHP, Kentucky.
1c. **John McCurdy,** SS, Maryland.
1d. **Ben Fritz,** RHP, Fresno State.
1e. **Jeremy Brown,** C, Alabama.
1f. **Steve Obenchain,** RHP, Evansville.
1g. **Mark Teahen,** 3B, St. Mary's (Calif.).
2. **Steve Stanley,** OF, Notre Dame.
3. **Bill Murphy,** LHP, Cal State Northridge.
4. **John Baker,** C, California.
5. **Mark Kiger,** SS, Florida.
6. **Brian Stavisky,** OF, Notre Dame.
7. **Brant Colamarino,** 1B, Pittsburgh.
8. **Jared Burton,** RHP, Western Carolina.
9. **Shane Komine,** RHP, Nebraska.
10. **J.R. Pickens,** RHP, Mississippi.

SEATTLE MARINERS
AMERICAN LEAGUE WEST DIVISION

2003 SEASON

March/April

SUN	MON	TUE	WED	THU	FRI	SAT
23	24	25 ‡ OAK	26 ‡ OAK	27	28	29
30	31	1 OAK	2 OAK	3	4 D TEX	5 TEX
6 D TEX	7	8 D ANA	9 ANA	10 ANA	11 TEX	12 TEX
13 D TEX	14 OAK	15 OAK	16 OAK	17 D OAK	18 ANA	19 ANA
20 D ANA	21	22 CLE	23 CLE	24 CLE	25 DET	26 DET
27 D DET	28	29 NYY	30 NYY			

July

SUN	MON	TUE	WED	THU	FRI	SAT
		1 OAK	2 OAK	3 D OAK	4 TEX	5 TEX
6 TEX	7	8 BAL	9 BAL	10 BAL	11 TB	12 TB
13 D TB	14	15 *	16	17 KC	18 KC	19 KC
20 KC	21 MIN	22 MIN	23 OAK	24 OAK	25 TEX	26 D TEX
27 D TEX	28 TEX	29 DET	30 DET	31 D DET		

May

SUN	MON	TUE	WED	THU	FRI	SAT
				1 NYY	2 CWS	3 CWS
4 CWS	5	6 NYY	7 NYY	8 NYY	9 CWS	10 CWS
11 D CWS	12	13 CLE	14 CLE	15 CLE	16 DET	17 D DET
18 D DET	19	20 KC	21 KC	22 D KC	23 MIN	24 MIN
25 MIN	26	27 KC	28 D KC	29 MIN	30 MIN	31 D MIN

August

SUN	MON	TUE	WED	THU	FRI	SAT
					1 CWS	2 CWS
3 D CWS	4	5 CLE	6 CLE	7 CLE	8 NYY	9 D NYY
10 D NYY	11 TOR	12 TOR	13 TOR	14 TOR	15 BOS	16 D BOS
17 D BOS	18	19 TOR	20 TOR	21 TOR	22 BOS	23 D BOS
24 D BOS	25 D BOS	26 TB	27 TB	28 D TB	29 BAL	30 D BAL

June

SUN	MON	TUE	WED	THU	FRI	SAT
1 D MIN	2	3 PHI	4 PHI	5 PHI	6 NYM	7 NYM
8 D NYM	9	10 MON	11 MON	12 MON	13 ATL	14 D ATL
15 ATL	16 ANA	17 ANA	18 ANA	19 D ANA	20 SD	21 SD
22 SD	23	24 ANA	25 ANA	26 ANA	27 SD	28 SD
29 D SD	30					

September

SUN	MON	TUE	WED	THU	FRI	SAT
31 D BAL	1	2 TB	3 TB	4 TB	5 BAL	6 BAL
7 D BAL	8	9 TEX	10 TEX	11 TEX	12 ANA	13 ANA
14 D ANA	15 TEX	16 TEX	17 TEX	18 D TEX	19 OAK	20 D OAK
21 OAK	22 ANA	23 ANA	24 D ANA	25	26 OAK	27 D OAK
28 D OAK						

Home games shaded; D—Day game (games starting before 5 p.m.); *—All-Star Game at Comiskey Park, Chicago. ‡—Game played in Tokyo, Japan. Subject to change.

CLUB DIRECTORY

Chairman & chief executive officer
Howard Lincoln
President and chief operating officer
Chuck Armstrong
Executive v.p., g.m., baseball operations
Pat Gillick
V.p., scouting and player development
Roger Jongewaard

Vice president, baseball administration
Lee Pelekoudas
Vice president, communications
Randy Adamack
Vice president, player development
Benny Looper
Director, professional scouting
Ken Compton

Director, scouting
Frank Mattox
Director, baseball information
Tim Hevly
Director, public information
Rebecca Hale

MINOR LEAGUE AFFILIATES

Class	Team	League	Manager
AAA	Tacoma	Pacific Coast	Dan Rohn
AA	San Antonio	Texas	Dave Brundage
A	San Bernardino	California	Steve Roadcap
A	Wisconsin	Midwest	Daren Brown
A	Everett	Northwest	To be announced
Rookie	Peoria Mariners	Arizona	Scott Steinmann

BROADCAST INFORMATION

Radio: KOMO-AM (1000).
TV: KSTW (Channel 11).
Cable TV: Fox Sports Net Northwest.

SPRING TRAINING

Ballpark: Peoria Stadium (Peoria, Ariz.).
Ticket information: 480-784-4444.

Follow the Mariners all season at: www.sportingnews.com/baseball/teams/mariners/

Manager—Bob Melvin (3).
Coaches—Orlando Gomez (49), Lamar Johnson (33), Rene Lachemann (9), John Moses, Dave Myers (31), Bryan Price (32).

No.	PITCHERS	B/T	Ht./Wt.	Born	Age*	2002 clubs
56	Anderson, Ryan	L/L	6-10/215	7-12-79	23	DID NOT PLAY
37	Charlton, Norm	B/L	6-3/205	1-6-63	40	DID NOT PLAY
45	Franklin, Ryan	R/R	6-3/165	3-5-73	30	Seattle, Everett
34	Garcia, Freddy	R/R	6-4/235	6-10-76	26	Seattle
17	Hasegawa, Shigetoshi	R/R	5-11/178	8-1-68	34	Seattle
58	Heaverlo, Jeff	R/R	6-1/185	1-13-78	25	DID NOT PLAY
	Johnson, Rett	L/R	6-2/211	7-6-79	23	San Bernardino, San Antonio
	Kent, Steve	B/L	5-11/170	10-3-78	24	Tampa Bay
	Looper, Aaron	R/R	6-2/185	9-7-76	26	San Antonio
	Madritsch, Bobby	L/L	6-2/190	2-28-76	27	Winnipeg
40	Mateo, Julio	R/R	6-0/177	8-2-77	25	San Antonio, Tacoma, Seattle
55	Meche, Gil	R/R	6-3/200	9-8-78	24	San Antonio
50	Moyer, Jamie	L/L	6-0/175	11-18-62	40	Seattle
43	Nelson, Jeff	R/R	6-8/235	11-17-66	36	Seattle, Everett
38	Pineiro, Joel	R/R	6-1/180	9-25-78	24	Seattle
61	Putz, J.J.	R/R	6-5/220	2-22-77	26	San Antonio, Tacoma
53	Rhodes, Arthur	L/L	6-2/205	10-24-69	33	Seattle
22	Sasaki, Kazuhiro	R/R	6-4/220	2-22-68	35	Seattle
60	Simpson, Allan	R/R	6-4/185	8-26-77	25	San Antonio
39	Soriano, Rafael	R/R	6-1/175	12-19-79	23	San Antonio, Seattle
52	Taylor, Aaron	R/R	6-7/230	8-20-77	25	San Antonio, Seattle
65	Thornton, Matt	L/L	6-6/220	9-15-76	26	San Antonio

No.	CATCHERS	B/T	Ht./Wt.	Born	Age*	2002 clubs
	Christianson, Ryan	R/R	6-2/210	4-21-81	21	San Bernardino, San Antonio
13	Davis, Ben	B/R	6-4/214	3-10-77	26	Seattle
6	Wilson, Dan	R/R	6-3/214	3-25-69	34	Seattle

No.	INFIELDERS	B/T	Ht./Wt.	Born	Age*	2002 clubs
29	Boone, Bret	R/R	5-10/190	4-6-69	33	Seattle
9	Cirillo, Jeff	R/R	6-1/190	9-23-69	33	Seattle
	Colbrunn, Greg	R/R	6-0/212	7-26-69	33	Tucson, Arizona
8	Guillen, Carlos	B/R	6-1/202	9-30-75	27	Seattle
11	Martinez, Edgar	R/R	5-11/210	1-2-63	40	Seattle
5	Olerud, John	L/L	6-5/220	8-5-68	34	Seattle
23	Ugueto, Luis	B/R	5-11/170	2-15-79	24	Seattle, Tacoma

No.	OUTFIELDERS	B/T	Ht./Wt.	Born	Age*	2002 clubs
16	Bloomquist, Willie	R/R	5-11/180	11-27-77	25	Tacoma, Seattle
44	Cameron, Mike	R/R	6-2/195	1-8-73	30	Seattle
59	Kelly, Kenny	R/R	6-2/180	1-26-79	24	Tacoma
	Mabry, John	L/R	6-4/210	10-17-70	32	Philadelphia, Oakland
4	McLemore, Mark	B/R	5-11/207	10-4-64	38	Seattle
	Strong, Jamal	R/R	5-10/180	8-5-78	24	San Antonio
51	Suzuki, Ichiro	L/R	5-9/160	10-22-73	29	Seattle
	Winn, Randy	B/R	6-2/197	6-9-74	28	Tampa Bay

*Age as of April 1, 2003.

BALLPARK INFORMATION

Ballpark (capacity, surface)
Safeco Field (47,772, grass).
Address
1250 First Avenue South
Seattle, WA 98104
Official website
www.seattlemariners.com
Business phone
206-346-4000
Ticket information
206-346-4001
Field dimensions (from home plate)
To left field at foul line, 331 feet
To center field, 405 feet
To right field at foul line, 326 feet
First game played
July 15, 1999 (Padres 3, Mariners 2)

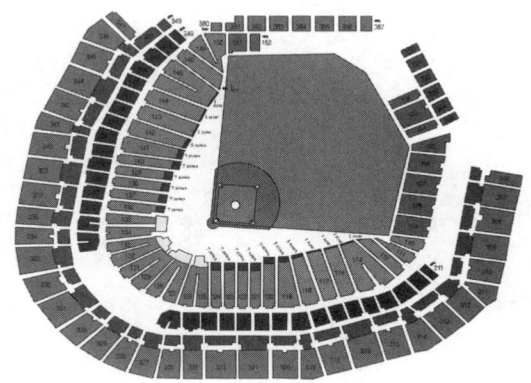

2003 SEASON *Seattle Mariners*

Date	Opp.	Res.	Score	(inn.*)	Hits	Opp. hits	Winning pitcher	Losing pitcher	Save	Record	Pos.	GB
4-1	Chi.	L	5-6		8	11	Buehrle	Garcia	Foulke	0-1	T2nd	1.0
4-2	Chi.	W	7-4		10	10	Rhodes	Barcelo	Sasaki	1-1	T2nd	1.0
4-3	Chi.	W	7-6		12	5	Franklin	Foulke		2-1	2nd	1.0
4-5	Oak.	W	7-1		10	6	Baldwin	Hiljus		3-1	1st	+0.5
4-6	Oak.	L	3-8		5	13	Mulder	Garcia		3-2	T2nd	0.5
4-7	Oak.	L	5-6		9	11	Hudson	Moyer	Koch	3-3	3rd	1.5
4-8	At Ana.	W	5-4		15	7	Hasegawa	Weber	Sasaki	4-3	2nd	1.0
4-9	At Ana.	W	5-1		9	4	Halama	Appier		5-3	2nd	1.0
4-10	At Ana.	W	8-1		11	5	Baldwin	Sele		6-3	T1st	...
4-11	At Ana.	W	8-4		8	10	Garcia	Schoeneweis		7-3	1st	+1.0
4-12	At Tex.	W	7-3		9	9	Moyer	Valdes		8-3	1st	+1.0
4-13	At Tex.	W	9-4		16	9	Abbott	Irabu		9-3	1st	+1.0
4-14	At Tex.	W	9-7		18	10	Hasegawa	Seanez	Sasaki	10-3	1st	+2.0
4-15	At Tex.	W	13-11	(10)	15	16	Sasaki	Miceli	Hasegawa	11-3	1st	+2.5
4-16	At Oak.	W	6-2	(7)	11	5	Pineiro	Lidle		12-3	1st	+3.5
4-17	At Oak.	W	7-4		12	11	Moyer	Hudson	Sasaki	13-3	1st	+4.5
4-19	Tex.	L	0-9		5	10	Rogers	Abbott		13-4	1st	+4.0
4-20	Tex.	W	3-2	(11)	8	8	Hasegawa	Michalak		14-4	1st	+4.0
4-21	Tex.	W	5-3		8	9	Garcia	Davis	Sasaki	15-4	1st	+4.0
4-22	Ana.	W	16-5		18	8	Moyer	Schoeneweis		16-4	1st	+4.5
4-23	Ana.	W	1-0		5	4	Franklin	Ortiz	Sasaki	17-4	1st	+5.5
4-24	Ana.	L	6-10		9	16	Washburn	Abbott		17-5	1st	+5.5
4-26	N.Y.	L	1-7		6	15	Clemens	Baldwin		17-6	1st	+4.0
4-27	N.Y.	W	1-0		1	5	Garcia	Lilly	Sasaki	18-6	1st	+4.0
4-28	N.Y.	L	3-4		5	9	Karsay	Rhodes	Rivera	18-7	1st	+3.0
4-30	At Chi.	L	4-8		9	13	Wright	Abbott		18-8	1st	+3.0
5-1	At Chi.	L	2-9	(8)	6	12	Garland	Franklin	Glover	18-9	1st	+2.0
5-2	At Chi.	W	15-4		16	9	Baldwin	Rauch		19-9	1st	+3.0
5-3	At N.Y.	W	6-2		8	4	Garcia	Lilly		20-9	1st	+4.0
5-4	At N.Y.	W	9-5		11	9	Nelson	Karsay		21-9	1st	+5.0
5-5	At N.Y.	W	10-6		14	9	Pineiro	Wells		22-9	1st	+5.0
5-7	Tor.	L	1-4		4	9	Halladay	Baldwin	Escobar	22-10	1st	+5.0
5-8	Tor.	W	5-4	(10)	10	9	Sasaki	Eyre		23-10	1st	+6.0
5-9	Tor.	W	8-7	(11)	14	9	Franklin	Thurman		24-10	1st	+6.5
5-10	Bos.	W	7-2		8	10	Pineiro	Castillo	Soriano	25-10	1st	+6.5
5-11	Bos.	W	3-1		6	8	Halama	Oliver	Sasaki	26-10	1st	+6.5
5-12	Bos.	L	4-10		6	16	Martinez	Baldwin		26-11	1st	+5.5
5-14	At Tor.	L	3-6		10	7	Loaiza	Garcia	Escobar	26-12	1st	+4.5
5-15	At Tor.	W	8-6		10	9	Rhodes	Escobar	Sasaki	27-12	1st	+4.5
5-16	At Tor.	W	15-2		16	6	Pineiro	Prokopec		28-12	1st	+5.0
5-17	At Bos.	W	6-3		9	9	Franklin	Arrojo	Sasaki	29-12	1st	+5.0
5-18	At Bos.	L	1-4		6	10	Martinez	Baldwin	Urbina	29-13	1st	+5.0
5-19	At Bos.	L	2-3		7	9	Burkett	Garcia	Urbina	29-14	1st	+4.0
5-21	T.B.	L	0-1		4	4	Kennedy	Moyer		29-15	1st	+2.5
5-22	T.B.	L	2-3		8	8	Rupe	Pineiro	Yan	29-16	1st	+1.5
5-23	T.B.	W	7-3		11	4	Baldwin	Sturtze		30-16	1st	+2.0
5-24	Bal.	W	6-2		10	4	Garcia	Erickson		31-16	1st	+3.0
5-25	Bal.	L	2-3		6	7	Driskill	Soriano	Groom	31-17	1st	+2.0
5-26	Bal.	W	8-1		12	5	Moyer	Lopez		32-17	1st	+3.0
5-28	At T.B.	L	1-5		5	7	Rupe	Pineiro		32-18	1st	+3.0
5-29	At T.B.	W	5-2		10	5	Garcia	Sturtze	Sasaki	33-18	1st	+3.0
5-30	At Bal.	W	5-4		9	5	Rhodes	Julio	Sasaki	34-18	1st	+4.0
5-31	At Bal.	L	7-8	(10)	13	14	Bauer	Halama		34-19	1st	+3.0
6-1	At Bal.	L	3-4		9	6	Roberts	Sasaki		34-20	1st	+3.0
6-2	At Bal.	W	11-8		14	12	Rhodes	Julio		35-20	1st	+3.0
6-3	At Oak.	W	4-1		11	5	Garcia	Harang	Sasaki	36-20	1st	+3.0
6-4	At Oak.	L	2-3	(10)	14	5	Koch	Hasegawa		36-21	1st	+2.0
6-5	At Oak.	W	5-0		13	4	Moyer	Lidle		37-21	1st	+2.0
6-6	At Oak.	L	4-10		11	12	Zito	Baldwin		37-22	1st	+2.0
6-7	Chi.	L	0-2		5	7	Prior	Pineiro	Alfonseca	37-23	1st	+1.0
6-8	Chi.	W	4-2		5	6	Garcia	Clement	Sasaki	38-23	1st	+2.0
6-9	Chi.	L	1-5		10	9	Lieber	Soriano		38-24	1st	+1.0
6-10	St.L.	W	10-0		14	5	Moyer	Smith		39-24	1st	+1.0
6-11	St.L.	L	4-7		7	10	Williams	Baldwin		39-25	1st	+1.0
6-12	St.L.	W	5-0		8	5	Pineiro	Kile		40-25	1st	+1.0

Date	Opp.	Res.	Score	(inn.*)	Hits	Opp. hits	Winning pitcher	Losing pitcher	Save	Record	Pos.	GB
6-14	At S.D.	W	6-3		11	5	Garcia	Tomko	Sasaki	41-25	1st	+1.0
6-15	At S.D.	L	1-3		8	9	Jones	Soriano	Hoffman	41-26	1st	+1.0
6-16	At S.D.	L	3-5		6	8	Perez	Moyer	Hoffman	41-27	1st	+1.0
6-18	At Cin.	W	8-1		9	8	Pineiro	Reitsma		42-27	1st	+2.0
6-19	At Cin.	W	2-0		7	5	Garcia	Dessens	Sasaki	43-27	1st	+3.0
6-20	At Cin.	W	3-2		11	6	Baldwin	Hamilton	Sasaki	44-27	1st	+3.0
6-21	At Hou.	W	8-0		11	4	Moyer	Hernandez		45-27	1st	+3.0
6-22	At Hou.	L	2-3	(12)	6	12	Stone	Halama		45-28	1st	+2.0
6-23	At Hou.	W	10-5		15	10	Pineiro	Saarloos		46-28	1st	+2.0
6-24	Oak.	L	2-13		9	13	Lidle	Garcia		46-29	1st	+2.0
6-25	Oak.	W	7-1		11	8	Baldwin	Hudson		47-29	1st	+3.0
6-26	Oak.	W	1-0		5	2	Hasegawa	Bradford	Sasaki	48-29	1st	+3.5
6-27	Oak.	W	7-4		12	9	Halama	Zito	Rhodes	49-29	1st	+3.5
6-28	Col.	W	6-2		9	6	Pineiro	Jennings		50-29	1st	+4.5
6-29	Col.	W	8-1		14	6	Garcia	Hampton		51-29	1st	+4.5
6-30	Col.	L	3-4		6	14	Speier	Sasaki	Jimenez	51-30	1st	+3.5
7-1	K.C.	W	7-0		9	5	Moyer	May		52-30	1st	+4.0
7-2	K.C.	L	5-7		11	13	Byrd	Sasaki	Hernandez	52-31	1st	+4.0
7-3	K.C.	W	3-0		7	2	Pineiro	Asencio	Sasaki	53-31	1st	+4.0
7-4	Min.	W	2-1		6	6	Rhodes	Rodriguez	Sasaki	54-31	1st	+5.0
7-5	Min.	L	4-8		7	11	Milton	Nelson		54-32	1st	+4.0
7-6	Min.	L	2-7		9	16	Lohse	Moyer		54-33	1st	+3.0
7-7	Min.	W	8-2		11	6	Halama	Reed	Sasaki	55-33	1st	+3.0
7-11	At T.B.	W	4-0		8	6	Pineiro	Kennedy		56-33	1st	+3.0
7-12	At T.B.	W	2-1		8	4	Moyer	Harper	Sasaki	57-33	1st	+3.0
7-13	At T.B.	L	3-4	(10)	8	13	Yan	Halama		57-34	1st	+3.0
7-14	At T.B.	W	7-6		10	12	Watson	Phelps	Sasaki	58-34	1st	+4.0
7-15	At Bal.	L	5-6		8	9	Ponson	Franklin	Julio	58-35	1st	+4.0
7-16	At Bal.	L	1-6		6	9	Erickson	Pineiro		58-36	1st	+3.0
7-17	At Tex.	W	6-3		10	5	Moyer	Valdes		59-36	1st	+3.0
7-18	At Tex.	W	5-3		9	6	Hasegawa	Alvarez	Sasaki	60-36	1st	+4.0
7-19	At Ana.	L	3-15		9	20	Ortiz	Garcia		60-37	1st	+3.0
7-20	At Ana.	L	6-7		10	10	Shields	Rhodes	Weber	60-38	1st	+2.0
7-21	At Ana.	L	5-7		8	11	Washburn	Nelson	Weber	60-39	1st	+1.0
7-23	Tex.	W	4-1		10	6	Rhodes	Powell	Sasaki	61-39	1st	+1.0
7-24	Tex.	L	3-4		7	6	Rogers	Garcia	Kolb	61-40	1st	+1.0
7-25	Tex.	W	7-2		13	10	Halama	Myette		62-40	1st	+1.0
7-26	Ana.	L	0-8		7	12	Lackey	Baldwin		62-41	2nd	...
7-27	Ana.	W	3-1		4	9	Pineiro	Washburn	Sasaki	63-41	1st	+1.0
7-28	Ana.	L	0-1		4	6	Appier	Sasaki	Percival	63-42	2nd	...
7-29	Det.	W	4-3		7	9	Rhodes	Santana	Sasaki	64-42	2nd	...
7-30	Det.	W	5-4	(10)	14	11	Hasegawa	Farnsworth		65-42	1st	+1.0
7-31	Det.	W	5-2		9	6	Baldwin	Powell	Sasaki	66-42	1st	+2.0
8-1	Cle.	W	10-6		13	11	Nelson	DePaula		67-42	1st	+2.0
8-2	Cle.	W	3-1		5	4	Moyer	Baez	Sasaki	68-42	1st	+3.0
8-3	Cle.	W	12-4		14	7	Garcia	Wright		69-42	1st	+3.0
8-4	Cle.	L	8-10		15	15	Westbrook	Sasaki	Wohlers	69-43	1st	+3.0
8-6	At Tor.	L	12-14		15	20	Halladay	Baldwin	Escobar	69-44	1st	+1.5
8-7	At Tor.	W	5-4	(10)	16	9	Sasaki	Prokopec		70-44	1st	+2.5
8-8	At Tor.	W	3-1		8	6	Moyer	Carpenter	Nelson	71-44	1st	+3.5
8-9	At Chi.	L	2-10		7	11	Buehrle	Garcia		71-45	1st	+3.5
8-10	At Chi.	W	7-3		8	11	Nelson	Biddle		72-45	1st	+3.5
8-11	At Chi.	L	5-6		12	9	Wright	Baldwin	Osuna	72-46	1st	+2.5
8-13	Bos.	W	10-3		16	9	Pineiro	Burkett		73-46	1st	+2.0
8-14	Bos.	L	5-12		8	14	Lowe	Moyer		73-47	1st	+1.0
8-15	Bos.	W	4-3		8	10	Garcia	Fossum	Sasaki	74-47	1st	+1.5
8-16	N.Y.	L	3-9		10	12	Wells	Halama	Weaver	74-48	1st	+0.5
8-17	N.Y.	L	3-8		6	13	Mussina	Franklin	Karsay	74-49	1st	+0.5
8-18	N.Y.	W	5-2		10	6	Pineiro	Clemens	Sasaki	75-49	1st	+0.5
8-19	At Det.	L	3-4		12	9	Lima	Moyer	Acevedo	75-50	2nd	...
8-20	At Det.	L	3-6		7	13	Maroth	Garcia	Acevedo	75-51	T2nd	...
8-21	At Det.	W	8-2		14	6	Valdes	Sparks		76-51	T2nd	...
8-22	At Det.	W	4-2		8	4	Franklin	Redman	Sasaki	77-51	T1st	...
8-23	At Cle.	L	2-4		6	8	Wohlers	Baldwin		77-52	2nd	1.0
8-24	At Cle.	L	3-5		6	7	Mulholland	Creek		77-53	3rd	2.0
8-25	At Cle.	W	12-4		16	8	Garcia	Westbrook		78-53	3rd	2.0
8-27	At Min.	L	2-5		9	12	Mays	Valdes	Guardado	78-54	3rd	3.5
8-28	At Min.	L	1-2		8	8	Santana	Pineiro	Guardado	78-55	3rd	4.5
8-29	At Min.	W	2-0		9	5	Moyer	Reed	Sasaki	79-55	3rd	4.0
8-30	K.C.	L	1-5		10	9	Byrd	Garcia	Grimsley	79-56	3rd	5.0
8-31	K.C.	L	2-4		6	10	Affeldt	Rhodes	Hernandez	79-57	3rd	6.0

Date	Opp.	Res.	Score	(inn.*)	Hits	Opp. hits	Winning pitcher	Losing pitcher	Save	Record	Pos.	GB
9-1	K.C.	W	9-4		10	8	Valdes	Suppan		80-57	3rd	6.0
9-2	Min.	W	5-2		12	7	Rhodes	Santana	Sasaki	81-57	3rd	6.0
9-4	Min.	L	2-3		7	13	Reed	Moyer	Guardado	81-58	3rd	7.0
9-6	At K.C.	W	14-7		15	17	Garcia	Sedlacek		82-58	3rd	6.0
9-7	At K.C.	W	9-2		13	8	Franklin	Asencio		83-58	3rd	6.0
9-8	At K.C.	W	16-9	(11)	15	12	Creek	Stein		84-58	3rd	6.0
9-9	At Tex.	L	7-12		9	11	Reyes	Halama		84-59	3rd	7.0
9-10	At Tex.	L	2-3		8	5	Rodriguez	Pineiro	Cordero	84-60	3rd	7.0
9-11	At Tex.	L	3-4		10	7	Cordero	Rhodes		84-61	3rd	7.0
9-12	At Tex.	L	3-7		9	11	Park	Franklin		84-62	3rd	7.0
9-13	At Oak.	L	0-5		2	10	Zito	Valdes		84-63	3rd	8.0
9-14	At Oak.	L	0-1		4	3	Hudson	Moyer		84-64	3rd	9.0
9-15	At Oak.	W	6-3		10	6	Pineiro	Harang	Sasaki	85-64	3rd	8.0
9-16	Tex.	W	6-5	(11)	11	13	Hasegawa	Kolb		86-64	3rd	8.0
9-17	Tex.	W	3-2	(10)	7	3	Rhodes	Rodriguez		87-64	3rd	8.0
9-18	Tex.	W	3-2	(10)	14	7	Sasaki	Reyes		88-64	3rd	8.0
9-19	Tex.	L	7-12	(10)	10	12	Powell	Hasegawa		88-65	3rd	8.0
9-20	Ana.	L	1-8		6	10	Ortiz	Pineiro		88-66	3rd	9.0
9-21	Ana.	W	6-4		7	10	Garcia	Lackey	Sasaki	89-66	3rd	9.0
9-22	Ana.	W	3-2		8	7	Franklin	Washburn	Nelson	90-66	3rd	9.0
9-24	Oak.	W	8-7		14	14	Hasegawa	Tam	Rhodes	91-66	3rd	8.0
9-25	Oak.	W	3-2		10	7	Rhodes	Mecir	Sasaki	92-66	3rd	7.0
9-26	Oak.	L	3-5	(10)	6	11	Koch	Hasegawa		92-67	3rd	8.0
9-27	At Ana.	W	7-6	(12)	13	14	Halama	Pote		93-67	3rd	8.0
9-28	At Ana.	L	4-8		9	14	Callaway	Franklin		93-68	3rd	9.0
9-29	At Ana.	L	6-7		9	10	Lukasiewicz	Valdes	Donnelly	93-69	3rd	10.0

Monthly records: April (18-8), May (16-11), June (17-11), July (15-12), August (13-15), September (14-12).
*Innings, if other than nine.

RECORDS

2002 regular-season record: 93-69
Position: 3rd in A.L. West
Home: 48-33   **Road:** 45-36
A.L. East: 25-20   **A.L. Central:** 23-18
A.L. West: 34-24   **N.L.:** 11-7
Vs. LH starters: 27-18
Vs. RH starters: 66-51
Grass: 84-63   **Artificial:** 9-6
Day: 25-20   **Night:** 68-49
1-Run: 24-25   **X-inn.:** 11-6
Doubleheaders: 0-0-0
Team record past five years: 455-354
(.562, ranks 3rd in league in that span)

TEAM LEADERS

Batting average: Ichiro Suzuki (.321).
At-bats: Ichiro Suzuki (647).
Runs: Ichiro Suzuki (111).
Hits: Ichiro Suzuki (208).
Total bases: Bret Boone (281).
Doubles: John Olerud (39).
Triples: Ichiro Suzuki (8).
Home runs: Mike Cameron (25).
Runs batted in: Bret Boone (107).
Stolen bases: Mike Cameron, Ichiro Suzuki (31).
Slugging percentage: John Olerud (.490).

On-base percentage: Edgar Martinez (.403).
Wins: Freddy Garcia (16).
Earned-run average: Joel Pineiro (3.24).
Complete games: Jamie Moyer (4).
Shutouts: Jamie Moyer (2).
Saves: Kazuhiro Sasaki (37).
Innings pitched: Jamie Moyer (230.2).
Strikeouts: Freddy Garcia (181).

GAMES BY POSITION

Catcher: Dan Wilson 113, Ben Davis 77, Pat Borders 2.
First base: John Olerud 152, Jeff Cirillo 11, Jose Offerman 11, Dan Wilson 4, Ben Davis 2.
Second base: Bret Boone 153, Desi Relaford 11, Luis Ugueto 11, Willie Bloomquist 4, Mark McLemore 2, Jose Offerman 1.
Third base: Jeff Cirillo 141, Desi Relaford 38, Mark McLemore 14, Charles Gipson 4, Luis Ugueto 1.
Shortstop: Carlos Guillen 130, Desi Relaford 40, Luis Ugueto 8, Mark McLemore 1.
Outfield: Mike Cameron 155, Ichiro Suzuki 152, Mark McLemore 88, Charles Gipson 73, Ruben Sierra 60, Desi Relaford 35, Scott Podsednik 11, Chris Snelling 8, Willie Bloomquist 7, Jose Offerman 6, Gene Kingsale 2.
Designated hitter: Edgar Martinez 91, Ruben Sierra 52, Luis Ugueto 16, Mark McLemore 4, Jose Offerman 4, Desi Relaford 4, Ichiro Suzuki 4, Charles Gipson 3, Carlos Guillen 3, Willie Bloomquist 2, Pat Borders 2, John Olerud 2, Scott Podsednik 2, Bret Boone 1, Mike Cameron 1, Ron Wright 1.

TOP DRAFT CHOICES

1. **John Mayberry Jr.,** OF, Rockhurst H.S., Kansas City, Mo.
2. **Josh Womack,** OF, Crawford H.S., San Diego.
3. **Eddy Martinez-Esteve,** OF, Westminster Christian H.S., Miami.
4. **Randy Frye,** RHP, Lake Orion (Mich.) H.S.
5. **Kendall Bergdall,** LHP, Cimarron H.S., Layhoma, Okla.
6. **Troy Cate,** LHP, Ricks (Idaho) J.C.
7. **Evel Bastida-Martinez,** 2B, Miami.
8. **Brandon Perry,** LHP, Graham (N.C.) H.S.
9. **Terry Forbes,** RHP, Auburn Drive H.S., Halifax, Nova Scotia.
10. **Brian Stitt,** RHP, Indian River (Fla.) C.C.

![Tampa Bay logo]

TAMPA BAY DEVIL RAYS
AMERICAN LEAGUE EAST DIVISION

2003 SEASON

March/April

SUN	MON	TUE	WED	THU	FRI	SAT
30	31 BOS	1 BOS	2 BOS	3 D BOS	4 NYY	5 NYY
6 D NYY	7	8 BAL	9 BAL	10 BAL	11 NYY	12 D NYY
13 D NYY	14	15 BOS	16 BOS	17 BOS	18 BAL	19 D BAL
20 D BAL	21 BAL	22 TOR	23 TOR	24 TOR	25 BAL	26 BAL
27 D BAL	28	29 MIN	30 MIN			

May

SUN	MON	TUE	WED	THU	FRI	SAT
				1 D MIN	2 DET	3 D DET
4 D DET	5	6 MIN	7 MIN	8 MIN	9 DET	10 DET
11 D DET	12	13 TOR	14 TOR	15 D TOR	16 BAL	17 BAL
18 D BAL	19	20 TEX	21 TEX	22 D TEX	23 ANA	24 D ANA
25 ANA	26	27 TEX	28 TEX	29 ANA	30 ANA	31 ANA

June

SUN	MON	TUE	WED	THU	FRI	SAT
1 D ANA	2	3 CUB	4 CUB	5 D CUB	6 HOU	7 HOU
8 HOU	9	10 CIN	11 CIN	12 CIN	13 PIT	14 PIT
15 D PIT	16	17 NYY	18 NYY	19 D NYY	20 FLA	21 FLA
22 D FLA	23 NYY	24 NYY	25 NYY	26 D NYY	27 ATL	28 ATL
29 D ATL	30					

July

SUN	MON	TUE	WED	THU	FRI	SAT
		1 BOS	2 BOS	3 BOS	4 CWS	5 CWS
6 D CWS	7	8 OAK	9 D OAK	10 D OAK	11 SEA	12 SEA
13 D SEA	14	15 *	16	17 TEX	18 TEX	19 TEX
20 D TEX	21 ANA	22 D ANA	23 BOS	24 D BOS	25 CWS	26 CWS
27 CWS	28	29 TOR	30 TOR	31 D TOR		

August

SUN	MON	TUE	WED	THU	FRI	SAT
					1 KC	2 KC
3 D KC	4 TOR	5 TOR	6 D TOR	7 KC	8 KC	9 KC
10 D KC	11 BAL	12 BAL	13 D BAL	14	15 CLE	16 CLE
17 D CLE	18 CLE	19 BAL	20 BAL	21 BAL	22 CLE	23 CLE
24 D CLE	25	26 SEA	27 SEA	28 D SEA	29 OAK	30 OAK

September

SUN	MON	TUE	WED	THU	FRI	SAT
31 D OAK	1	2 SEA	3 SEA	4 SEA	5 OAK	6 OAK
7 D OAK	8	9 TOR	10 TOR	11 D TOR	12 NYY	13 D NYY
14 D NYY	15 BOS	16 BOS	17 BOS	18 BOS	19 NYY	20 NYY
21 D NYY	22 TOR	23 TOR	24 TOR	25 TOR	26 BOS	27 BOS
28 D BOS						

Home games shaded; D—Day game (games starting before 5 p.m.); *—All-Star Game at Comiskey Park, Chicago. Subject to change.

CLUB DIRECTORY

Managing general partner/CEO
Vincent J. Naimoli
Sr. v.p. baseball operations/g.m.
Chuck LaMar
Vice president of public relations
Rick Vaughn

Assistant general managers
Bart Braun
Scott Proefrock
Special assistants to the g.m.
Eddie Bane
Hal McRae

Director of scouting and player personnel
Cam Bonifay
Director of media relations
Chris Costello
Manager of community relations
Liz-Beth Lauck

MINOR LEAGUE AFFILIATES

Class	Team	League	Manager
AAA	Durham	International	Bill Evers
AA	Orlando	Southern	To be announced
A	Bakersfield	California	To be announced
A	Charleston (S.C.)	South Atlantic	To be announced
A	Hudson Valley	New York-Pennsylvania	To be announced
Rookie	Princeton	Appalachian	To be announced

BROADCAST INFORMATION

Radio: WFLA-AM (970).
Cable TV: Fox Sports Net.

SPRING TRAINING

Ballpark (city): Progress Energy Park
Home of Al Lang Field (St. Petersburg, Fla.).
Ticket information: 727-825-3250.

Follow the Devil Rays all season at: www.sportingnews.com/baseball/teams/devilrays/

SPRING TRAINING ROSTER

Manager—Lou Piniella (14).
Coaches—Chris Bosio (29), Lee Elia (4), Tom Foley (16); Billy Hatcher (22), John McLaren (7), Matt Sinatro (15).

No.	PITCHERS	B/T	Ht./Wt.	Born	Age*	2002 clubs
37	Backe, Brandon	R/R	6-0/182	4-5-78	24	Orlando, Tampa Bay
32	Bierbrodt, Nick	L/L	6-5/185	5-16-78	24	DID NOT PLAY
65	Brazelton, Dewon	R/R	6-4/214	6-16-80	22	Orlando, Durham, Tampa Bay
38	Carter, Lance	R/R	6-1/190	12-18-74	28	Durham, Tampa Bay
46	Colome, Jesus	R/R	6-4/205	12-23-77	25	Tampa Bay, Durham
36	De Los Santos, Luis	R/R	6-2/216	11-1-77	25	Durham, Tampa Bay
	Garcia, Geraldo	R/R	6-0/160	2-13-80	23	Orlando, Durham
58	Harper, Travis	R/R	6-4/192	5-21-76	26	Durham, Tampa Bay
48	James, Delvin	R/R	6-4/240	1-3-78	25	Durham, Tampa Bay, Orlando
17	Kennedy, Joe	R/L	6-4/237	5-24-79	23	Tampa Bay
	McClung, Seth	R/R	6-6/235	2-7-81	22	Bakersfield, Orlando
61	Phelps, Travis	R/R	6-2/166	7-25-77	25	Tampa Bay, Durham
34	Reichert, Dan	R/R	6-3/175	7-12-76	26	Kansas City, Omaha, Wichita
27	Seay, Bobby	L/L	6-2/221	6-20-78	24	Orlando, Durham
	Smith, Hans	L/L	6-9/265	8-3-78	24	Orlando
59	Sosa, Jorge	B/R	6-2/177	4-28-77	25	Tampa Bay, Orlando
53	Standridge, Jason	R/R	6-4/230	11-9-78	24	Durham, Tampa Bay
	Stokes, Brian	R/R	6-1/203	9-7-79	23	Bakersfield
	Waechter, Doug	R/R	6-4/210	1-28-81	22	Charleston, S.C., Bakersfield, Orlando
21	White, Matt	R/R	6-5/230	8-13-78	24	Charleston, S.C., Orlando
60	Zambrano, Victor	R/R	6-0/203	8-6-75	27	Tampa Bay, Durham

No.	CATCHERS	B/T	Ht./Wt.	Born	Age*	2002 clubs
44	Hall, Toby	R/R	6-3/240	10-21-75	27	Tampa Bay, Durham
	LaForest, Pete	L/R	6-2/208	1-27-78	25	Orlando, Durham

No.	INFIELDERS	B/T	Ht./Wt.	Born	Age*	2002 clubs
3	Abernathy, Brent	R/R	6-1/191	9-23-77	25	Tampa Bay
5	Escalona, Felix	R/R	6-0/196	3-12-79	24	Tampa Bay
19	Huff, Aubrey	L/R	6-4/231	12-20-76	26	Durham, Tampa Bay
	Luna, Hector	R/R	6-1/170	2-1-82	21	Kinston
10	Ordonez, Rey	R/R	5-9/159	1-11-71	32	New York N.L.
	Perez, Antonio	R/R	5-11/175	1-26-80	23	San Antonio, Arizona Mariners
33	Rolls, Damian	R/R	6-2/215	9-15-77	25	Orlando, Durham, Tampa Bay
10	Sandberg, Jared	R/R	6-3/226	3-2-78	25	Durham, Tampa Bay

No.	OUTFIELDERS	B/T	Ht./Wt.	Born	Age*	2002 clubs
	Baldelli, Rocco	R/R	6-4/187	9-25-81	21	Bakersfield, Orlando, Durham
4	Conti, Jason	L/R	5-11/175	1-27-75	28	Tampa Bay
6	Crawford, Carl	L/L	6-2/219	8-5-81	21	Durham, Tampa Bay
18	Grieve, Ben	L/R	6-4/216	5-4-76	26	Tampa Bay
31	Hamilton, Josh	L/L	6-4/200	5-21-81	21	Bakersfield
14	Tyner, Jason	L/L	6-1/168	4-23-77	25	Tampa Bay, Durham
23	Vaughn, Greg	R/R	6-0/206	7-3-65	37	Tampa Bay

*Age as of April 1, 2003.

BALLPARK INFORMATION

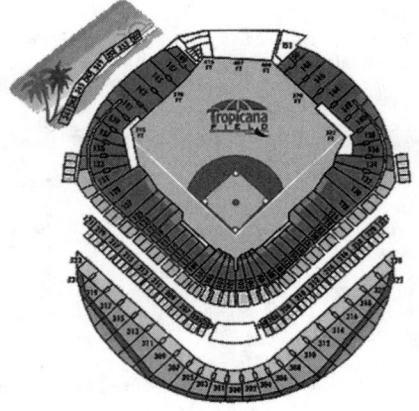

Ballpark (capacity, surface)
Tropicana Field (44,445, artificial)

Address
One Tropicana Drive
St. Petersburg, FL 33705

Official website
www.devilrays.com

Business phone
727-825-3137

Ticket information
727-825-3250

Field dimensions (from home plate)
To left field at foul line, 315 feet
To center field, 404 feet
To right field at foul line, 322 feet

First game played
March 31, 1998 (Tigers 11, Devil Rays 6)

Date	Opp.	Res.	Score	(inn.*)	Hits	Opp. hits	Winning pitcher	Losing pitcher	Save	Record	Pos.	GB
4-2	Det.	W	9-5		12	12	Zambrano	Acevedo		1-0	T1st	...
4-3	Det.	W	2-1	(12)	10	10	Colome	Farnsworth		2-0	1st	+0.5
4-4	Det.	W	9-2		10	6	Rupe	Lima		3-0	1st	+0.5
4-5	At N.Y.	L	0-4		3	9	Pettitte	Kennedy		3-1	T1st	...
4-6	At N.Y.	L	0-3		3	7	Hernandez	Alvarez	Rivera	3-2	3rd	1.0
4-7	At N.Y.	L	2-7		6	11	Clemens	Sturtze		3-3	3rd	2.0
4-10	At Bal.	W	3-2		10	6	Wilson	Johnson	Yan	4-3	3rd	2.0
4-11	At Bal.	L	6-15		6	18	Lopez	Colome		4-4	3rd	2.0
4-12	Tor.	L	7-14		14	16	Miller	Rupe		4-5	4th	2.0
4-13	Tor.	L	4-5		13	8	Prokopec	Sturtze	Escobar	4-6	4th	2.5
4-14	Tor.	W	5-4	(10)	9	5	Yan	Coco		5-6	4th	2.0
4-16	At Det.	L	3-9		11	11	Lima	James		5-7	4th	3.0
4-17	At Det.	L	6-7		7	15	Anderson	Zambrano		5-8	4th	4.0
4-18	At Det.	W	6-4		14	11	Rupe	Weaver	Yan	6-8	T3rd	3.5
4-19	Bal.	L	5-6	(14)	12	11	Julio	Colome		6-9	T3rd	4.5
4-20	Bal.	L	3-6		9	12	Johnson	Wilson	Roberts	6-10	4th	5.0
4-21	Bal.	W	2-1		7	4	Creek	Ponson	Yan	7-10	T3rd	5.5
4-23	Min.	W	6-4		8	10	Kennedy	Radke	Yan	8-10	T3rd	4.5
4-24	Min.	W	9-1		10	3	Rupe	Milton		9-10	3rd	3.5
4-25	Min.	L	2-6		8	12	Jackson	Yan		9-11	3rd	4.5
4-26	At Bos.	L	2-4		5	10	Burkett	Wilson	Urbina	9-12	3rd	5.5
4-27	At Bos.	L	0-10		0	13	Lowe	James		9-13	4th	6.5
4-29	At Min.	L	2-3		6	7	Milton	Kennedy	Guardado	9-14	4th	6.5
4-30	At Min.	L	3-6		7	10	Lohse	Rupe	Guardado	9-15	4th	7.5
5-1	At Min.	L	3-5		10	13	Reed	Sturtze	Guardado	9-16	4th	8.5
5-2	At Min.	L	6-7	(10)	12	10	Fiore	Kent		9-17	4th	9.0
5-3	Bos.	L	2-3		7	7	Fossum	Colome	Urbina	9-18	4th	10.0
5-4	Bos.	L	5-7		9	10	Kim	Zambrano	Urbina	9-19	T4th	11.0
5-5	Bos.	L	0-2		4	6	Castillo	Rupe	Urbina	9-20	T4th	12.0
5-6	Bos.	L	3-5		6	14	Oliver	Sturtze	Wakefield	9-21	5th	13.0
5-7	N.Y.	L	2-5		4	11	Mussina	Wilson	Rivera	9-22	5th	14.0
5-8	N.Y.	L	2-7		8	8	Clemens	James		9-23	5th	15.0
5-9	N.Y.	L	1-3		3	5	Hernandez	Kennedy	Rivera	9-24	5th	16.0
5-10	Bal.	L	5-6		7	7	Lopez	Rupe	Julio	9-25	5th	16.0
5-11	Bal.	W	6-4		10	10	Yan	Julio		10-25	5th	15.0
5-12	Bal.	W	6-3		10	10	Wilson	Ponson	Yan	11-25	5th	15.0
5-14	At N.Y.	L	3-10		5	11	Clemens	Harper		11-26	5th	16.0
5-15	At N.Y.	W	10-7		12	8	Kennedy	Hernandez	Yan	12-26	5th	16.0
5-16	At N.Y.	L	0-13		3	15	Wells	Rupe		12-27	5th	16.0
5-17	At Bal.	L	3-5		8	8	Roberts	Zambrano	Julio	12-28	5th	16.0
5-18	At Bal.	W	5-4		12	11	Creek	Bauer	Yan	13-28	5th	16.0
5-19	At Bal.	W	4-0		8	5	Harper	Erickson	Kent	14-28	5th	16.0
5-21	At Sea.	W	1-0		4	4	Kennedy	Moyer		15-28	5th	15.5
5-22	At Sea.	W	3-2		8	8	Rupe	Pineiro	Yan	16-28	5th	14.5
5-23	At Sea.	L	3-7		4	11	Baldwin	Sturtze		16-29	5th	15.5
5-24	At Oak.	L	8-9		10	12	Mecir	Zambrano	Koch	16-30	5th	16.5
5-25	At Oak.	L	0-6		3	8	Harang	Harper	Bradford	16-31	5th	16.5
5-26	At Oak.	L	0-7		2	8	Zito	Kennedy		16-32	5th	16.5
5-28	Sea.	W	5-1		7	5	Rupe	Pineiro		17-32	T4th	17.0
5-29	Sea.	L	2-5		5	10	Garcia	Sturtze	Sasaki	17-33	T4th	18.0
5-30	Oak.	W	4-3	(13)	19	7	Harper	Bradford		18-33	4th	17.5
5-31	Oak.	L	9-13		17	17	Venafro	Yan		18-34	5th	18.5
6-1	Oak.	L	3-8		9	12	Zito	Kennedy		18-35	5th	18.5
6-2	Oak.	L	2-4		10	7	Mulder	Rupe	Koch	18-36	5th	19.5
6-3	At Tor.	L	1-6		6	9	Walker	Sturtze		18-37	5th	19.5
6-4	At Tor.	L	1-3		4	6	Miller	Wilson	Escobar	18-38	5th	20.5
6-5	At Tor.	W	8-6		16	9	Alvarez	Loaiza		19-38	5th	20.5
6-6	At Tor.	L	4-5		6	6	Escobar	Harper		19-39	5th	21.5
6-7	S.D.	L	4-8		9	8	Lawrence	Rupe		19-40	5th	21.5
6-8	S.D.	W	3-2	(10)	12	7	Zambrano	Embree		20-40	5th	20.5
6-9	S.D.	L	6-9		10	16	Jones	Wilson	Hoffman	20-41	5th	20.5
6-10	L.A.	L	5-10		9	14	Nomo	Alvarez		20-42	5th	21.5
6-11	L.A.	W	11-2		14	6	Kennedy	Daal		21-42	5th	20.5
6-12	L.A.	L	2-4		8	7	Ashby	Rupe	Gagne	21-43	5th	21.5
6-14	At Fla.	W	4-3	(14)	12	6	Yan	Mairena	Harper	22-43	5th	20.5

2003 SEASON *Tampa Bay Devil Rays*

Date	Opp.	Res.	Score	(inn.*)	Hits	Opp. hits	Winning pitcher	Losing pitcher	Save	Record	Pos.	GB
6-15	At Fla.	L	0-3		3	9	Burnett	Wilson		22-44	5th	20.5
6-16	At Fla.	W	4-1		11	6	Zambrano	Almanza	Yan	23-44	5th	20.5
6-18	At S.F	W	8-3		14	8	Kennedy	Hernandez		24-44	5th	20.5
6-19	At S.F	L	0-8		5	11	Schmidt	Rupe		24-45	5th	20.5
6-20	At S.F	L	2-10		6	16	Ortiz	Sturtze		24-46	5th	21.5
6-21	At Col.	L	7-8	(10)	12	17	Speier	Yan		24-47	5th	21.5
6-22	At Col.	L	5-6	(11)	9	15	Jimenez	Kent		24-48	5th	21.5
6-23	At Col.	L	5-6		12	9	White	Kennedy	Jimenez	24-49	5th	22.0
6-25	Tor.	L	11-20		17	19	Walker	Sosa		24-50	5th	22.0
6-26	Tor.	W	4-2		4	7	Sturtze	Parris	Yan	25-50	5th	21.5
6-27	Tor.	W	6-4		10	6	Harper	Politte	Yan	26-50	5th	21.0
6-28	Fla.	W	4-0		9	5	Alvarez	Dempster		27-50	5th	21.0
6-29	Fla.	L	2-3		7	6	Tavarez	Kennedy	Nunez	27-51	5th	21.0
6-30	Fla.	W	6-5	(12)	12	9	Yan	Nunez		28-51	5th	21.0
7-2	At Tex.	L	1-3		3	9	Rogers	Sturtze	Irabu	28-52	5th	22.0
7-3	At Tex.	L	5-6		14	11	Rocker	Colome		28-53	5th	23.0
7-4	At Tex.	L	8-11		12	11	Lewis	Harper	Irabu	28-54	5th	24.0
7-5	At Ana.	L	5-6	(10)	15	15	Shields	Yan		28-55	5th	25.0
7-6	At Ana.	L	3-4		10	4	Schoeneweis	Colome	Percival	28-56	5th	25.0
7-7	At Ana.	L	1-2	(10)	3	10	Percival	Harper		28-57	5th	26.0
7-11	Sea.	L	0-4		6	8	Pineiro	Kennedy		28-58	5th	27.0
7-12	Sea.	L	1-2		4	8	Moyer	Harper	Sasaki	28-59	5th	27.0
7-13	Sea.	W	4-3	(10)	13	8	Yan	Halama		29-59	5th	27.0
7-14	Sea.	L	6-7		12	10	Watson	Phelps	Sasaki	29-60	5th	27.0
7-15	Oak.	L	0-4		4	8	Lilly	Rupe		29-61	5th	27.0
7-16	Oak.	L	1-2		9	8	Mulder	Sosa	Koch	29-62	5th	28.0
7-17	Bos.	L	1-6		2	11	Lowe	Wilson		29-63	5th	29.0
7-18	Bos.	L	3-4		5	9	Wakefield	Yan	Urbina	29-64	5th	30.0
7-19	At Tor.	L	8-11		11	12	Loaiza	Creek	Escobar	29-65	5th	30.0
7-20	At Tor.	L	10-12		9	10	Parris	de los Santos	Escobar	29-66	5th	31.0
7-21	At Tor.	W	7-5		12	9	Sosa	Walker	Yan	30-66	5th	31.0
7-23§	At Bos.	L	4-22		7	19	Wakefield	Sturtze	Banks	30-67		
7-23∞	At Bos.	W	5-4		9	11	Zambrano	Urbina	Yan	31-67	5th	30.5
7-24	At Bos.	W	9-5		14	10	Colome	Castillo	Zambrano	32-67	5th	30.5
7-25	At Bos.	L	0-6		3	8	Martinez	de los Santos		32-68	5th	31.0
7-26	N.Y.	L	9-12		17	10	Mussina	Sosa	Karsay	32-69	5th	32.0
7-27	N.Y.	W	7-4		11	7	Harper	Weaver	Yan	33-69	5th	31.0
7-28	N.Y.	L	1-9		4	12	Pettitte	Sturtze		33-70	5th	32.0
7-29	Bal.	W	6-1		18	4	Wilson	Driskill		34-70	5th	32.0
7-30	Bal.	W	10-3		15	5	Kennedy	Stephens		35-70	5th	32.0
7-31	Bal.	L	2-12		9	18	Lopez	de los Santos		35-71	5th	32.0
8-1	Bal.	L	3-4		9	6	Ponson	Sosa	Julio	35-72	5th	32.0
8-2	Chi.	L	5-8	(12)	6	16	Wunsch	Colome	Osuna	35-73	5th	33.0
8-3	Chi.	W	6-2		11	5	Wilson	Ritchie		36-73	5th	32.0
8-4	Chi.	W	10-3		17	9	Kennedy	Buehrle		37-73	5th	32.0
8-5	Chi.	L	3-4		4	9	Foulke	Yan	Marte	37-74	5th	32.5
8-6	At Cle.	L	2-4		8	8	Nagy	Sosa	Wohlers	37-75	5th	32.5
8-7	At Cle.	L	2-6		6	7	Sabathia	Sturtze		37-76	5th	33.5
8-8	At Cle.	W	4-2		8	7	Wilson	Baez	Yan	38-76	5th	33.5
8-9	At K.C.	L	4-5	(12)	12	15	May	Phelps		38-77	5th	33.5
8-10	At K.C.	W	13-6		16	9	Zambrano	Sedlacek	Alvarez	39-77	5th	32.5
8-11	At K.C.	L	0-10		2	14	Hernandez	Sosa		39-78	5th	33.5
8-13	Cle.	L	5-9		8	9	Sabathia	Sturtze	Wohlers	39-79	5th	34.5
8-14	Cle.	L	4-6		10	11	Baez	Wilson	Wohlers	39-80	5th	35.5
8-15	Cle.	W	4-3		9	4	Harper	Wohlers		40-80	5th	35.5
8-16	K.C.	L	5-6		8	9	Bukvich	Yan	Hernandez	40-81	5th	36.5
8-17	K.C.	L	3-7	(12)	9	12	Mullen	Colome	Hernandez	40-82	5th	37.5
8-18	K.C.	W	8-6		12	9	Sturtze	Suppan		41-82	5th	36.5
8-19	At Bal.	W	7-3		10	5	Wilson	Driskill		42-82	5th	36.0
8-20	At Bal.	L	4-7		12	9	Groom	Gardner		42-83	5th	37.0
8-21	At Bal.	L	1-2		5	5	Lopez	Zambrano	Groom	42-84	5th	37.0
8-22	At Bal.	L	2-3	(11)	6	8	Julio	Harper		42-85	5th	38.0
8-23	At Chi.	W	8-2		12	11	Sturtze	Garland		43-85	5th	37.0
8-24	At Chi.	L	2-5		6	7	Wright	Wilson	Marte	43-86	5th	38.0
8-25	At Chi.	L	3-8		4	9	Glover	Kennedy		43-87	5th	38.0
8-27	At Ana.	L	3-7		12	16	Lackey	Zambrano	Weber	43-88	5th	39.5
8-28	At Ana.	W	8-5	(10)	14	10	Yan	Levine		44-88	5th	39.5
8-29	At Ana.	L	1-6		5	11	Appier	Sturtze		44-89	5th	39.5
8-30	At Tex.	W	9-7		17	13	Phelps	Van Poppel	Yan	45-89	5th	39.5
8-31	At Tex.	W	7-5		12	13	Gardner	Kolb	Yan	46-89	5th	38.5

Date	Opp.	Res.	Score	(inn.*)	Hits	Opp. hits	Winning pitcher	Losing pitcher	Save	Record	Pos.	GB
9-1	At Tex.	W	8-3		8	11	Zambrano	Reyes	Carter	47-89	5th	37.5
9-3	Ana.	L	2-10		10	12	Washburn	Sosa		47-90	5th	38.0
9-4	Ana.	L	2-4		7	10	Appier	Sturtze	Percival	47-91	5th	39.0
9-5	Ana.	L	1-10		6	10	Ortiz	Kennedy		47-92	5th	40.0
9-6	Tex.	L	3-9		6	15	Reyes	Harper	Rodriguez	47-93	5th	41.0
9-7	Tex.	L	2-11		7	13	Park	Zambrano		47-94	5th	41.0
9-8	Tex.	W	6-3		10	7	Sosa	Benoit		48-94	5th	41.0
9-9	Bos.	L	3-6		6	14	Lowe	Sturtze	Urbina	48-95	5th	41.5
9-10	Bos.	L	1-12		7	15	Burkett	Kennedy		48-96	5th	43.0
9-11	Bos.	L	3-6		8	12	Martinez	Wilson	Urbina	48-97	5th	44.0
9-12	Bos.	L	3-6		8	7	Wakefield	Yan	Urbina	48-98	5th	45.0
9-13	At Tor.	L	2-5		9	6	Halladay	Brazelton	Escobar	48-99	5th	45.0
9-14	At Tor.	L	4-8		8	10	Hendrickson	Sturtze	Escobar	48-100	5th	45.0
9-15	At Tor.	W	7-4		14	8	Kennedy	Loaiza	Yan	49-100	5th	45.0
9-17	N.Y.	W	9-7		16	12	Carter	Mendoza		50-100	5th	44.0
9-18	N.Y.	L	1-7		6	13	Weaver	Zambrano		50-101	5th	45.0
9-19	N.Y.	W	3-2	(10)	11	7	Yan	Hitchcock		51-101	5th	44.0
9-20	Tor.	W	11-7		12	7	Sturtze	Loaiza		52-101	5th	44.0
9-21	Tor.	W	4-3		9	6	Carter	Walker		53-101	5th	44.0
9-22	Tor.	L	6-12		10	19	Miller	Wilson		53-102	5th	45.0
9-23	At N.Y.	W	3-2		9	6	Zambrano	Hernandez	Yan	54-102	5th	44.0
9-24	At N.Y.	L	0-6		2	9	Mussina	Harper		54-103	5th	45.0
9-25	At N.Y.	L	3-4		6	10	Weaver	Sturtze	Rivera	54-104	5th	46.0
9-27	At Bos.	L	1-6		5	9	Burkett	Wilson		54-105	5th	47.0
9-28	At Bos.	W	9-6		12	8	Zambrano	Howry	Carter	55-105	5th	47.0
9-29	At Bos.	L	8-11		12	15	Castillo	Alvarez	Urbina	55-106	5th	48.0

Monthly records: April (9-15), May (9-19), June (10-17), July (7-20), August (11-18), September (9-17).
*Innings, if other than nine. §Day separate admission. ∞Night separate admission.

RECORDS

2002 regular-season record: 55-106
Position: 5th in A.L. East
Home: 30-51   **Road:** 25-55
A.L. East: 25-50   **A.L. Central:** 13-19
A.L. West: 10-26   **N.L.:** 7-11
Vs. LH starters: 8-21
Vs. RH starters: 47-85
Grass: 22-44   **Artificial:** 33-62
Day: 14-27   **Night:** 41-79
1-Run: 17-28   **X-inn.:** 9-10
Doubleheaders: 0-0-0
Team record past five years: 318-490
(.394, ranks 14th in league in that span)

TEAM LEADERS

Batting average: Aubrey Huff (.313).
At-bats: Randy Winn (607).
Runs: Randy Winn (87).
Hits: Randy Winn (181).
Total bases: Randy Winn (280).
Doubles: Randy Winn (39).
Triples: Randy Winn (9).
Home runs: Aubrey Huff (23).
Runs batted in: Randy Winn (75).
Stolen bases: Randy Winn (27).

Slugging percentage: Aubrey Huff (.520).
On-base percentage: Aubrey Huff (.364).
Wins: Joe Kennedy, Victor Zambrano (8).
Earned-run average: Joe Kennedy (4.53).
Complete games: Joe Kennedy (5).
Shutouts: Joe Kennedy (1).
Saves: Esteban Yan (19).
Innings pitched: Tanyon Sturtze (224.0).
Strikeouts: Tanyon Sturtze (137).

GAMES BY POSITION

Catcher: Toby Hall 83, John Flaherty 75, Paul Hoover 4.
First base: Steve Cox 110, Aubrey Huff 45, Bobby Smith 6, Jared Sandberg 3.
Second base: Brent Abernathy 116, Andy Sheets 26, Felix Escalona 25, Russ Johnson 1, Jason Smith 1.
Third base: Jared Sandberg 97, Russ Johnson 27, Aubrey Huff 14, Jason Smith 12, Bobby Smith 10, Felix Escalona 4, Andy Sheets 4.
Shortstop: Chris Gomez 130, Felix Escalona 26, Andy Sheets 11, Jason Smith 9, Russ Johnson 2.
Outfield: Randy Winn 146, Ben Grieve 118, Jason Conti 74, Carl Crawford 63, Jason Tyner 42, Greg Vaughn 31, Damian Rolls 21, Dave McCarty 11, Bobby Smith 2.
Designated hitter: Aubrey Huff 53, Greg Vaughn 38, Steve Cox 35, Ben Grieve 16, Russ Johnson 5, Randy Winn 4, Jared Sandberg 2, Brent Abernathy 1, Felix Escalona 1, Bobby Smith 1, Jason Smith 1, Jason Tyner 1.

TOP DRAFT CHOICES

1. **B.J. Upton**, SS, Greenbrier Christian Academy, Chesapeake, Va.
2. **Jason Pridie**, OF, Prescott (Ariz.) H.S.
3. **Elijah Dukes**, OF, Hillsborough H.S., Tampa.
4. **Wes Bankston**, OF, Plano (Texas) East H.S.
5. **Mark Romanczuk**, LHP, St. Mark's H.S., Newark, Del.
6. **Cesar Ramos**, LHP, El Rancho H.S., Pico Rivera, Calif.
7. **Scott Autrey**, RHP, North Carolina.
8. **Joey Gomes**, OF, Santa Clara.
9. **Chris Leroux**, C, St. Joseph's SS, Mississauga, Ontario.
10. **Jason Hammel**, RHP, Treasure Valley (Ore.) J.C.

TEXAS RANGERS
AMERICAN LEAGUE WEST DIVISION

2003 SEASON

March/April

SUN	MON	TUE	WED	THU	FRI	SAT
30 ANA	31	1 ANA	2 D ANA	3	4 D SEA	5 SEA
6 D SEA	7	8 OAK	9 OAK	10 OAK	11 SEA	12 SEA
13 D SEA	14 ANA	15 ANA	16 ANA	17 D ANA	18 OAK	19 D OAK
20 OAK	21	22 BOS	23 BOS	24 D BOS	25 NYY	26 NYY
27 D NYY	28	29 TOR	30 TOR			

May

SUN	MON	TUE	WED	THU	FRI	SAT
				1 TOR	2 CLE	3 D CLE
4 D CLE	5	6 TOR	7 TOR	8 D TOR	9 CLE	10 CLE
11 D CLE	12	13 BOS	14 BOS	15 BOS	16 NYY	17 D NYY
18 D NYY	19	20 TB	21 TB	22 D TB	23 BAL	24 BAL
25 D BAL	26	27 TB	28 TB	29 BAL	30 BAL	31 BAL

June

SUN	MON	TUE	WED	THU	FRI	SAT
1 D BAL	2	3 ATL	4 ATL	5 ATL	6 † MON	7 † MON
8 D† MON	9	10 NYM	11 NYM	12 NYM	13 FLA	14 FLA
15 FLA	16	17 OAK	18 OAK	19 D OAK	20 HOU	21 HOU
22 HOU	23 OAK	24 OAK	25 OAK	26 HOU	27 HOU	28 D HOU
29 D HOU	30 ANA					

July

SUN	MON	TUE	WED	THU	FRI	SAT
		1 ANA	2 ANA	3 ANA	4 SEA	5 SEA
6 D SEA	7	8 MIN	9 MIN	10 MIN	11 KC	12 KC
13 D KC	14	15 *	16	17 TB	18 TB	19 TB
20 D TB	21 BAL	22 D BAL	23 ANA	24 ANA	25 SEA	26 D SEA
27 D SEA	28 SEA	29 BOS	30 BOS	31 BOS		

August

SUN	MON	TUE	WED	THU	FRI	SAT
					1 CLE	2 CLE
3 CLE	4	5 NYY	6 NYY	7 D NYY	8 TOR	9 D TOR
10 D TOR	11 DET	12 DET	13 DET	14 DET	15 CWS	16 CWS
17 CWS	18 DET	19 DET	20 DET	21 CWS	22 CWS	23 CWS
24 D CWS	25	26 KC	27 KC	28 KC	29 MIN	30 MIN

September

SUN	MON	TUE	WED	THU	FRI	SAT
31 D MIN	1 D KC	2 KC	3 KC	4	5 MIN	6 D MIN
7 D MIN	8	9 SEA	10 SEA	11 SEA	12 OAK	13 OAK
14 D OAK	15 SEA	16 SEA	17 SEA	18 D SEA	19 ANA	20 ANA
21 D ANA	22 OAK	23 OAK	24 D OAK	25	26 ANA	27 D ANA
28 D ANA						

Home games shaded; D—Day game (games starting before 5 p.m.); *—All-Star Game at Comiskey Park, Chicago. †—Game played in Puerto Rico. Subject to change.

CLUB DIRECTORY

Chairman of the board and owner
Thomas O. Hicks
CEO, Southwest Sports Group
Michael J. Cramer
President
James R. Lites
Exec. vice president, general manager
John Hart

Senior vice president, communications
John Blake
Asst. g.m., player dev. & scouting
Grady Fuson
Assistant g.m., baseball operations
Dan O'Brien
Director, player development
Trey Hillman

Director, minor league operations
John Lombardo
Director, community relations
Taunee Taylor
Media relations manager
Rich Rice

MINOR LEAGUE AFFILIATES

Class	Team	League	Manager
AAA	Oklahoma	Pacific Coast	Bobby Jones
AA	Frisco	Texas	Tim Ireland
A	Stockton	California	To be announced
A	Clinton	Midwest	To be announced
A	Spokane	Northwest	To be announced
Rookie	Arizona Rangers	Arizona	To be announced

BROADCAST INFORMATION

Radio: KRLD-AM (1080); KESS (1270), Spanish.
TV: KDFW (Channel 4); KDFI (Channel 27).
Cable TV: Fox Sports Southwest.

SPRING TRAINING

Ballpark (city): Surprise Stadium (Surprise, Fla.).
Ticket information: 623-594-5600.

Follow the Rangers all season at: www.sportingnews.com/baseball/teams/rangers/

Manager—Buck Showalter.
Coaches—Mark Conner, DeMarlo Hale (20), Rudy Jaramillo (8), Steve Smith (1), Don Wakamatsu.

No.	PITCHERS	B/T	Ht./Wt.	Born	Age*	2002 clubs
30	Bell, Rob	R/R	6-5/225	1-17-77	26	Oklahoma, Texas, Tulsa
53	Benoit, Joaquin	R/R	6-3/205	7-26-77	25	Oklahoma, Texas, Charlotte
56	Cedeno, Jovanny	R/R	6-0/170	10-25-79	23	Gulf Coast Rangers
31	Cordero, Francisco	R/R	6-2/200	5-11-75	27	Texas, Oklahoma
17	Davis, Doug	R/L	6-4/190	9-21-75	27	Texas, Oklahoma
	Drese, Ryan	R/R	6-3/220	4-5-76	26	Cleveland, Buffalo
38	Fultz, Aaron	L/L	6-0/200	9-4-73	29	San Francisco, Fresno
21	Garcia, Reynaldo	R/R	6-3/170	4-15-74	28	Tulsa, Oklahoma, Texas
73	Hughes, Travis	R/R	6-5/215	5-25-78	24	Tulsa
52	Kolb, Danny	R/R	6-4/215	3-29-75	28	Charlotte, Tulsa, Texas
	Koronka, John	L/L	6-1/180	6-3-80	22	Stockton, Chattanooga
56	Kozlowski, Ben	L/L	6-6/220	8-16-80	22	Myrtle Beach, Charlotte, Tulsa, Texas
48	Lewis, Colby	R/R	6-4/215	8-2-79	23	Texas, Oklahoma
61	Park, Chan Ho	R/R	6-2/204	6-30-73	29	Texas, Oklahoma
39	Powell, Jay	R/R	6-4/225	1-9-72	31	Tulsa, Oklahoma, Texas
	Ramos, Mario	L/L	6-0/180	10-19-77	25	Oklahoma
	Thomson, John	R/R	6-3/190	10-1-73	29	Colorado, New York N.L.
41	Urbina, Ugueth	R/R	6-0/205	2-15-74	29	Boston
	Valdes, Ismael	R/R	6-4/225	8-21-73	29	Texas, Seattle
47	Van Poppel, Todd	R/R	6-5/240	12-9-71	31	Texas
43	Yan, Esteban	R/R	6-4/255	6-22-75	27	Tampa Bay
59	Zimmerman, Jeff	R/R	6-1/200	8-9-72	30	Charlotte, Tulsa

No.	CATCHERS	B/T	Ht./Wt.	Born	Age*	2002 clubs
2	Diaz, Einar	R/R	5-10/190	12-28-72	30	Cleveland
27	Greene, Todd	R/R	5-10/208	5-8-71	31	Las Vegas, Texas, Oklahoma
	Laird, Gerald	R/R	6-2/195	11-13-79	23	Tulsa

No.	INFIELDERS	B/T	Ht./Wt.	Born	Age*	2002 clubs
12	Blalock, Hank	L/R	6-1/192	11-21-80	22	Texas, Oklahoma
16	Hart, Jason	R/R	6-4/240	9-5-77	25	Oklahoma, Texas
13	Lamb, Mike	L/R	6-1/195	8-9-75	27	Oklahoma, Texas
	McDougall, Marshall	R/R	6-1/200	12-19-78	24	Midland, Mahoning Valley, Akron
25	Palmeiro, Rafael	L/L	6-0/190	9-24-64	38	Texas
35	Perry, Herbert	R/R	6-2/225	9-15-69	33	Texas
3	Rodriguez, Alex	R/R	6-3/210	7-27-75	27	Texas
23	Teixeira, Mark	B/R	6-3/225	4-11-80	22	Charlotte, Tulsa
10	Young, Mike	R/R	6-1/190	10-19-76	26	Texas

No.	OUTFIELDERS	B/T	Ht./Wt.	Born	Age*	2002 clubs
2	Everett, Carl	B/R	6-0/215	6-3-71	31	Texas, Charlotte
	Glanville, Doug	R/R	6-2/174	8-25-70	32	Philadelphia
19	Gonzalez, Juan	R/R	6-3/220	10-16-69	33	Texas
29	Greer, Rusty	L/L	6-0/195	1-21-69	34	Texas, Tulsa
15	Ludwick, Ryan	R/L	6-3/203	7-13-78	24	Oklahoma, Texas
28	Mench, Kevin	R/R	6-0/215	1-7-78	25	Oklahoma, Texas
	Nix, Laynce	L/L	6-0/190	10-30-80	22	Charlotte

*Age as of April 1, 2003.

Ballpark (capacity, surface)
The Ballpark in Arlington (49,115, grass)

Address
1000 Ballpark Way
Arlington, TX 76011

Official website
www.texasrangers.com

Business phone
817-273-5222

Ticket information
817-273-5100

Field dimensions (from home plate)
To left field at foul line, 332 feet
To center field, 400 feet
To right field at foul line, 325 feet

First game played
April 11, 1994 (Brewers 4, Rangers 3)

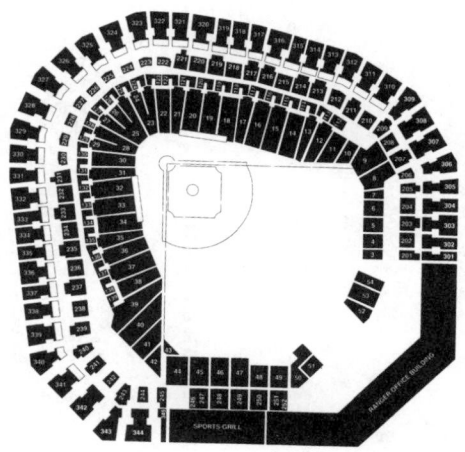

2003 SEASON *Texas Rangers*

Date	Opp.	Res.	Score	(inn.*)	Hits	Opp. hits	Winning pitcher	Losing pitcher	Save	Record	Pos.	GB
4-1	At Oak.	L	3-8		7	13	Mulder	Park		0-1	T2nd	1.0
4-2	At Oak.	L	2-3		6	5	Koch	Miceli		0-2	4th	2.0
4-3	At Oak.	L	6-9		12	7	Mecir	Rodriguez	Koch	0-3	4th	3.0
4-4	At Oak.	W	7-5		10	12	Davis	Lidle		1-3	4th	2.0
4-5	Ana.	L	1-3		5	6	Schoeneweis	Valdes	Levine	1-4	4th	2.5
4-6	Ana.	L	3-6		5	9	Ortiz	Irabu	Levine	1-5	4th	3.0
4-9	Oak.	L	4-5	(11)	7	13	Koch	Seanez		1-6	4th	4.5
4-10	Oak.	W	4-2		9	6	Burba	Lidle	Rocker	2-6	4th	3.5
4-11	Oak.	W	7-0		14	2	Davis	Mulder		3-6	T3rd	3.5
4-12	Sea.	L	3-7		9	9	Moyer	Valdes		3-7	T3rd	4.5
4-13	Sea.	L	4-9		9	16	Abbott	Irabu		3-8	T3rd	5.5
4-14	Sea.	L	7-9		10	18	Hasegawa	Seanez	Sasaki	3-9	4th	6.5
4-15	Sea.	L	11-13	(10)	16	15	Sasaki	Miceli	Hasegawa	3-10	4th	7.5
4-16	At Ana.	L	5-6	(10)	10	10	Levine	Rocker		3-11	4th	8.5
4-17	At Ana.	W	4-1		12	5	Valdes	Schoeneweis	Irabu	4-11	4th	8.5
4-19	At Sea.	W	9-0		10	5	Rogers	Abbott		5-11	4th	7.5
4-20	At Sea.	L	2-3	(11)	8	8	Hasegawa	Michalak		5-12	4th	8.5
4-21	At Sea.	L	3-5		9	8	Garcia	Davis	Sasaki	5-13	4th	9.5
4-23	Tor.	L	1-2		4	6	Lyon	Valdes	Escobar	5-14	4th	11.0
4-24	Tor.	W	3-2		6	5	Rogers	Prokopec	Irabu	6-14	4th	10.0
4-25	Tor.	W	11-9		11	14	Van Poppel	Plesac	Irabu	7-14	T3rd	9.5
4-26	Cle.	L	4-7		12	11	Finley	Davis		7-15	4th	9.5
4-27	Cle.	W	4-2		8	6	Bell	Baez	Irabu	8-15	4th	9.5
4-28	Cle.	W	2-1		5	7	Valdes	Colon	Irabu	9-15	4th	8.5
4-30	At Tor.	W	10-3		13	5	Rogers	Prokopec		10-15	4th	7.5
5-1	At Tor.	W	8-1		12	4	Burba	Halladay		11-15	4th	6.5
5-2	At Tor.	W	5-3		9	7	Bell	Smith	Irabu	12-15	4th	6.5
5-3	At Cle.	W	4-2		6	8	Davis	Baez	Irabu	13-15	4th	6.5
5-4	At Cle.	L	0-3		5	7	Colon	Valdes	Wickman	13-16	4th	7.5
5-5	At Cle.	L	2-9		11	16	Sabathia	Rogers		13-17	4th	8.5
5-6	Chi.	W	6-5		12	12	Irabu	Osuna		14-17	4th	8.0
5-7	Chi.	L	6-11		5	14	Porzio	Bell	Ginter	14-18	4th	8.0
5-8	Chi.	L	3-5		7	8	Buehrle	Davis		14-19	4th	9.0
5-9	Chi.	W	4-1		9	4	Benoit	Ritchie	Irabu	15-19	4th	9.0
5-10	Det.	W	2-0		5	8	Rogers	Weaver	Irabu	16-19	4th	9.0
5-11	Det.	W	10-6		14	11	Burba	Sparks		17-19	4th	9.0
5-12	Det.	W	5-1		10	6	Park	Greisinger	Van Poppel	18-19	T3rd	8.0
5-14	At Chi.	L	4-15		8	15	Buehrle	Davis		18-20	T3rd	8.0
5-15	At Chi.	W	5-2		11	2	Valdes	Ritchie	Irabu	19-20	3rd	8.0
5-16	At Chi.	L	0-4		5	8	Wright	Rogers		19-21	T3rd	9.0
5-17	At Det.	L	3-6		10	7	Weaver	Burba	Acevedo	19-22	T3rd	10.0
5-18	At Det.	L	7-8		9	12	Santana	Seanez	Acevedo	19-23	T3rd	10.0
5-19	At Det.	L	1-2		6	7	Greisinger	Davis	Acevedo	19-24	T3rd	10.0
5-21	At Min.	L	2-8		11	15	Milton	Valdes		19-25	T3rd	10.0
5-22	At Min.	W	6-5		9	9	Rogers	Lohse	Irabu	20-25	T3rd	9.0
5-25	At K.C.	L	3-6		6	10	Suppan	Burba	Hernandez	20-26	4th	10.0
5-26†	At K.C.	L	5-7		8	9	Bailey	Irabu		20-27		
5-26‡	At K.C.	L	8-9		13	18	Bailey	Michalak	Hernandez	20-28	4th	11.5
5-27	Min.	L	2-5		10	9	Lohse	Rogers	Guardado	20-29	4th	12.0
5-28	Min.	L	4-11		8	8	Fiore	Park		20-30	4th	12.0
5-29	Min.	W	9-8		14	12	Irabu	Romero		21-30	4th	12.0
5-31	K.C.	L	7-10	(11)	17	15	Bailey	Irabu		21-31	4th	12.5
6-1	K.C.	W	3-1		7	5	Rogers	May		22-31	4th	11.5
6-2	K.C.	W	8-6		11	6	Park	Byrd	Irabu	23-31	4th	11.5
6-3	At Ana.	L	2-5		6	7	Ortiz	Bell	Percival	23-32	4th	12.5
6-4	At Ana.	L	0-3		4	7	Schoeneweis	Burba	Percival	23-33	4th	12.5
6-5	At Ana.	L	5-7	(10)	9	11	Levine	Irabu		23-34	4th	13.5
6-6	At Ana.	W	9-8		15	13	Rogers	Appier	Telford	24-34	4th	12.5
6-7	Atl.	L	7-13		12	19	Hammond	Park		24-35	4th	12.5
6-8	Atl.	L	3-6	(10)	10	11	Remlinger	Irabu	Smoltz	24-36	4th	13.5
6-9	Atl.	L	3-9		11	10	Marquis	Burba		24-37	4th	13.5
6-10	Cin.	W	8-2		9	11	Valdes	Almanzar		25-37	4th	13.5
6-11	Cin.	L	5-8		9	11	Haynes	Rogers	Graves	25-38	4th	13.5
6-12	Cin.	W	10-4		9	4	Rocker	Sullivan		26-38	4th	13.5
6-14	At Hou.	W	9-6		16	13	Powell	Cruz	Flores	27-38	4th	13.5

Date	Opp.	Res.	Score	(inn.*)	Hits	Opp. hits	Winning pitcher	Losing pitcher	Save	Record	Pos.	GB
6-15	At Hou.	L	0-4		3	11	Miller	Valdes		27-39	4th	13.5
6-16	At Hou.	L	6-7		10	11	Wagner	Rocker		27-40	4th	13.5
6-18	At Chi.	L	3-4		4	6	Alfonseca	Rocker		27-41	4th	14.5
6-19	At Chi.	W	7-4	(10)	12	10	Irabu	Fassero	Cordero	28-41	4th	14.5
6-20	At Chi.	W	7-4		9	5	Telford	Cruz	Cordero	29-41	4th	14.5
6-21	At Pit.	W	2-0		8	5	Rogers	Wells	Cordero	30-41	4th	14.5
6-22	At Pit.	W	3-2		10	5	Bell	Lincoln	Irabu	31-41	4th	13.5
6-23	At Pit.	W	10-4		11	7	Park	Fogg		32-41	4th	13.5
6-24†	Ana.	W	8-5		12	7	Benoit	Sele		33-41		
6-24‡	Ana.	W	3-2		7	11	Burba	Lackey	Irabu	34-41	4th	12.0
6-25	Ana.	W	11-5		7	8	Valdes	Schoeneweis		35-41	4th	12.0
6-26	Ana.	L	6-7		8	11	Weber	Irabu	Percival	35-42	4th	13.0
6-27	Ana.	L	3-6		7	11	Washburn	Bell	Percival	35-43	4th	14.0
6-28	Hou.	L	5-6		10	8	Oswalt	Park	Wagner	35-44	4th	15.0
6-29	Hou.	L	5-8		9	14	Puffer	Powell	Wagner	35-45	4th	16.0
7-2	T.B.	W	3-1		9	3	Rogers	Sturtze	Irabu	36-45	4th	15.0
7-3	T.B.	W	6-5		11	14	Rocker	Colome		37-45	4th	15.0
7-4	T.B.	W	11-8		11	12	Lewis	Harper	Irabu	38-45	4th	15.0
7-5	Bal.	W	7-6		14	11	Telford	Julio		39-45	4th	14.0
7-6	Bal.	L	5-7		7	8	Bauer	Lewis	Perez	39-46	4th	14.0
7-7	Bal.	L	4-10		4	16	Lopez	Rogers		39-47	4th	15.0
7-11	At Min.	L	3-4		9	4	Milton	Park	Guardado	39-48	4th	16.0
7-12	At Min.	L	3-4	(11)	9	10	Fiore	Irabu		39-49	4th	17.0
7-13	At Min.	W	8-1		12	6	Rogers	Rincon		40-49	4th	16.0
7-14	At Min.	L	4-5		7	11	Romero	Lewis	Guardado	40-50	4th	17.0
7-15†	At K.C.	L	6-8		7	5	Sedlacek	Benoit	Hernandez	40-51		
7-15‡	At K.C.	L	4-6		11	12	Wilson	Telford	Hernandez	40-52	4th	17.5
7-16	At K.C.	L	5-6	(11)	10	12	Wilson	Alvarez		40-53	4th	17.5
7-17	Sea.	L	3-6		5	10	Moyer	Valdes		40-54	4th	18.5
7-18	Sea.	L	3-5		6	9	Hasegawa	Alvarez	Sasaki	40-55	4th	19.5
7-19	At Oak.	L	0-10		1	10	Lidle	Myette		40-56	4th	19.5
7-20	At Oak.	L	5-6		8	12	Koch	Burba		40-57	4th	19.5
7-21	At Oak.	W	7-3	(12)	10	11	Powell	Mecir		41-57	4th	18.5
7-23	At Sea.	L	1-4		6	10	Rhodes	Powell	Sasaki	41-58	4th	19.5
7-24	At Sea.	W	4-3		6	7	Rogers	Garcia	Kolb	42-58	4th	18.5
7-25	At Sea.	L	2-7		10	13	Halama	Myette		42-59	4th	19.5
7-26	Oak.	W	12-4		12	12	Rodriguez	Mulder		43-59	4th	18.5
7-27	Oak.	W	10-6	(10)	14	10	Kolb	Koch		44-59	4th	18.5
7-28	Oak.	L	2-12		6	15	Zito	Alvarez		44-60	4th	18.5
7-29	N.Y.	L	2-9		9	12	Hernandez	Rogers		44-61	4th	19.5
7-30	N.Y.	L	6-9		10	11	Wells	Myette	Mendoza	44-62	4th	20.5
7-31	N.Y.	W	17-6		21	11	Bell	Mussina		45-62	4th	20.5
8-1	Bos.	W	19-7		20	11	Park	Burkett		46-62	4th	20.5
8-2	Bos.	L	0-13		3	15	Lowe	Valdes		46-63	4th	21.5
8-3	Bos.	W	8-6		9	12	Kolb	Howry		47-63	4th	21.5
8-4	Bos.	L	3-11		8	19	Martinez	Myette		47-64	4th	21.5
8-6	At Det.	L	2-8		7	11	Sparks	Park		47-65	4th	21.5
8-7	At Det.	W	7-2	(11)	14	8	Cordero	Santana		48-65	4th	21.5
8-8	At Det.	L	1-2		11	4	Lima	Valdes	Acevedo	48-66	4th	22.5
8-9	At Cle.	W	3-2		9	2	Rogers	Wohlers	Cordero	49-66	4th	21.5
8-10	At Cle.	L	3-4		11	4	Wickman	Kolb		49-67	4th	22.5
8-11	At Cle.	W	11-5		15	7	Myette	Nagy		50-67	4th	21.5
8-13	Chi.	L	3-12		6	13	Glover	Benoit		50-68	4th	22.5
8-14	Chi.	W	11-6		13	7	Valdes	Parque		51-68	4th	21.5
8-16	Tor.	W	6-5		10	10	Kolb	Escobar		52-68	4th	21.0
8-17	Tor.	W	9-5		13	10	Reyes	Parris		53-68	4th	20.0
8-18	Tor.	W	10-7		12	9	Myette	Loaiza		54-68	4th	20.0
8-20	At Bos.	W	3-2	(10)	7	7	Rodriguez	Banks	Cordero	55-68	4th	18.5
8-21	At Bos.	L	3-5		8	12	Howry	Kolb	Urbina	55-69	4th	19.5
8-22	At Bos.	L	3-12		6	14	Hermanson	Reyes	Castillo	55-70	4th	20.5
8-23	At N.Y.	W	6-2		12	7	Park	Mussina		56-70	4th	20.5
8-24	At N.Y.	L	2-3		5	5	Clemens	Alvarez	Karsay	56-71	4th	21.5
8-25	At N.Y.	W	6-2		13	8	Benoit	Pettitte		57-71	4th	21.5
8-26	At N.Y.	L	3-10		9	19	Hernandez	Rogers	Weaver	57-72	4th	22.5
8-27	Bal.	W	9-4		13	11	Reyes	Lopez		58-72	4th	22.5
8-28	Bal.	W	5-3		10	9	Park	Stephens	Cordero	59-72	4th	22.5
8-29	Bal.	W	9-6		11	7	Van Poppel	Bauer	Cordero	60-72	4th	22.0
8-30	T.B.	L	7-9		13	17	Phelps	Van Poppel	Yan	60-73	4th	23.0
8-31	T.B.	L	5-7		13	12	Gardner	Kolb	Yan	60-74	4th	24.0

Date	Opp.	Res.	Score	(inn.*)	Hits	Opp. hits	Winning pitcher	Losing pitcher	Save	Record	Pos.	GB
9-1	T.B.	L	3-8		11	8	Zambrano	Reyes	Carter	60-75	4th	25.0
9-2	Hou.	W	7-2		14	9	Park	Robertson		61-75	4th	25.0
9-3	At Bal.	W	7-1		10	1	Van Poppel	Stephens	Benoit	62-75	4th	24.5
9-4	At Bal.	L	3-8		7	10	Ponson	Myette		62-76	4th	25.5
9-5	At Bal.	W	11-2		14	6	Rogers	Johnson		63-76	4th	25.0
9-6	At T.B.	W	9-3		15	6	Reyes	Harper	Rodriguez	64-76	4th	24.0
9-7	At T.B.	W	11-2		13	7	Park	Zambrano		65-76	4th	24.0
9-8	At T.B.	L	3-6		7	10	Sosa	Benoit		65-77	4th	25.0
9-9	Sea.	W	12-7		11	9	Reyes	Halama		66-77	4th	25.0
9-10	Sea.	W	3-2		5	8	Rodriguez	Pineiro	Cordero	67-77	4th	24.0
9-11	Sea.	W	4-3		7	10	Cordero	Rhodes		68-77	4th	23.0
9-12	Sea.	W	7-3		11	9	Park	Franklin		69-77	4th	22.0
9-13	At Ana.	L	2-3		5	9	Washburn	Benoit	Percival	69-78	4th	23.0
9-14	At Ana.	L	6-8		8	13	Shields	Van Poppel	Percival	69-79	4th	24.0
9-15	At Ana.	L	4-13		6	11	Ortiz	Rogers		69-80	4th	25.0
9-16	At Sea.	L	5-6	(11)	13	11	Hasegawa	Kolb		69-81	4th	25.0
9-17	At Sea.	L	2-3	(10)	3	7	Rhodes	Rodriguez		69-82	4th	26.0
9-18	At Sea.	L	2-3	(10)	7	14	Sasaki	Reyes		69-83	4th	26.0
9-19	At Sea.	W	12-7	(10)	12	10	Powell	Hasegawa		70-83	4th	26.0
9-20	At Oak.	L	2-4		5	6	Mecir	Kolb	Rincon	70-84	4th	27.0
9-21	At Oak.	L	3-6		5	9	Tam	Nitkowski	Koch	70-85	4th	28.0
9-22	At Oak.	L	5-7		12	9	Mulder	Park	Koch	70-86	4th	29.0
9-24	Ana.	W	2-1		8	6	Benoit	Appier	Cordero	71-86	4th	28.0
9-25	Ana.	W	4-3		6	8	Seanez	Schoeneweis	Cordero	72-86	4th	27.0
9-26	Ana.	L	5-10		11	6	Lackey	Lewis		72-87	4th	28.0
9-27	Oak.	L	2-3		7	8	Mulder	Park	Koch	72-88	4th	29.0
9-28	Oak.	L	8-10		9	10	Lilly	Kolb	Mecir	72-89	4th	30.0
9-29	Oak.	L	7-8		10	9	Zito	Benoit		72-90	4th	31.0

Monthly records: April (10-15), May (11-16), June (14-14), July (10-17), August (15-12), September (12-16).
*Innings, if other than nine. †First game of a doubleheader. ‡Second game of a doubleheader.

RECORDS

2002 regular-season record: 72-90
Position: 4th in A.L. West
Home: 42-39   **Road:** 30-51
A.L. East: 25-16   **A.L. Central:** 18-27
A.L. West: 20-38   **N.L.:** 9-9
Vs. LH starters: 15-31
Vs. RH starters: 57-59
Grass: 65-85   **Artificial:** 7-5
Day: 15-21   **Night:** 57-69
1-Run: 18-26   **X-inn.:** 6-12
Doubleheaders: 1-2-0
Team record past five years: 399-411
(.493, ranks 9th in league in that span)

TEAM LEADERS

Batting average: Ivan Rodriguez (.314).
At-bats: Alex Rodriguez (624).
Runs: Alex Rodriguez (125).
Hits: Alex Rodriguez (187).
Total bases: Alex Rodriguez (389).
Doubles: Rafael Palmeiro (34).
Triples: Michael Young (8).
Home runs: Alex Rodriguez (57).
Runs batted in: Alex Rodriguez (142).
Stolen bases: Frank Catalanotto, Alex Rodriguez (9).

Slugging percentage: Alex Rodriguez (.623).
On-base percentage: Alex Rodriguez (.392).
Wins: Kenny Rogers (13).
Earned-run average: Kenny Rogers (3.84).
Complete games: Kenny Rogers (2).
Shutouts: Doug Davis, Kenny Rogers (1).
Saves: Hideki Irabu (16).
Innings pitched: Kenny Rogers (210.2).
Strikeouts: Chan Ho Park (121).

GAMES BY POSITION

Catcher: Ivan Rodriguez 100, Bill Haselman 67, Todd Greene 15, Hector Ortiz 7, Mike Lamb 3.
First base: Rafael Palmeiro 97, Mike Lamb 52, Frank Catalanotto 15, Todd Greene 15, Herbert Perry 12, Travis Hafner 3, Jason Hart 2, Rusty Greer 1, Gabe Kapler 1.
Second base: Michael Young 152, Frank Catalanotto 23, Jason Romano 8, Donnie Sadler 2, Mike Lamb 1.
Third base: Herbert Perry 112, Hank Blalock 46, Mike Lamb 14, Donnie Sadler 4, Michael Young 4, Jason Romano 1.

Shortstop: Alex Rodriguez 162, Donnie Sadler 12, Michael Young 11.
Outfield: Kevin Mench 106, Carl Everett 83, Ruben Rivera 67, Gabe Kapler 64, Juan Gonzalez 62, Todd Hollandsworth 38, Calvin Murray 34, Frank Catalanotto 26, Rusty Greer 26, Ryan Ludwick 22, Jason Romano 18, Donnie Sadler 18, Mike Lamb 16, Jason Hart 7, Todd Greene 1, Herbert Perry 1.
Designated hitter: Rafael Palmeiro 55, Rusty Greer 22, Mike Lamb 21, Carl Everett 18, Travis Hafner 13, Frank Catalanotto 8, Juan Gonzalez 8, Herbert Perry 6, Ivan Rodriguez 6, Todd Greene 4, Jason Romano 4, Kevin Mench 3, Bill Haselman 2, Calvin Murray 2, Ruben Rivera 2, Gabe Kapler 1, Donnie Sadler 1, Michael Young 1.

TOP DRAFT CHOICES

1. **Drew Meyer,** SS, South Carolina.
6. **John Barnett,** RHP, Florida Southern College.
7. **Andrew Tisdale,** RHP, Chapman (Calif.).
8. **Chris O'Riordan,** 2B, Stanford.
9. **Steven Herce,** RHP, Rice.
10. **Nate Gold,** 1B, Gonzaga.

TORONTO BLUE JAYS
AMERICAN LEAGUE EAST DIVISION

2003 SEASON

March/April

SUN	MON	TUE	WED	THU	FRI	SAT
30	31 NYY	1 D NYY	2 NYY	3	4 MIN	5 MIN
6 D MIN	7	8 BOS	9 BOS	10 BOS	11 MIN	12 D MIN
13 D MIN	14 NYY	15 NYY	16 NYY	17 D NYY	18 BOS	19 D BOS
20 BOS	21 D BOS	22 TB	23 TB	24 TB	25 KC	26 D KC
27 D KC	28	29 TEX	30 TEX			

May

SUN	MON	TUE	WED	THU	FRI	SAT
				1 TEX	2 ANA	3 D ANA
4 D ANA	5	6 TEX	7 TEX	8 D TEX	9 ANA	10 ANA
11 D ANA	12	13 TB	14 TB	15 TB	16 KC	17 KC
18 D KC	19 CWS	20 CWS	21 CWS	22 NYY	23 NYY	24 D NYY
25 D NYY	26 CWS	27 CWS	28 CWS	29 CWS	30 BOS	31 D BOS

June

SUN	MON	TUE	WED	THU	FRI	SAT
1 D BOS	2	3 STL	4 STL	5 STL	6 CIN	7 CIN
8 D CIN	9	10 PIT	11 PIT	12 PIT	13 CUB	14 D CUB
15 D CUB	16	17 BAL	18 BAL	19 D BAL	20 MON	21 MON
22 D MON	23 BAL	24 BAL	25 BAL	26 BAL	27 MON	28 D MON
29 D MON	30 DET					

July

SUN	MON	TUE	WED	THU	FRI	SAT
		1 DET	2 DET	3	4 BAL	5 BAL
6 D BAL	7	8 BOS	9 BOS	10 BOS	11 NYY	12 D NYY
13 D NYY	14	15 *	16	17 BOS	18 BOS	19 BOS
20 D BOS	21 D NYY	22 NYY	23 CWS	24 CWS	25 BAL	26 D BAL
27 D BAL	28	29 TB	30 TB	31 D TB		

August

SUN	MON	TUE	WED	THU	FRI	SAT
					1 ANA	2 ANA
3 D ANA	4 TB	5 TB	6 D TB	7	8 TEX	9 D TEX
10 D TEX	11 SEA	12 SEA	13 SEA	14 SEA	15 OAK	16 D OAK
17 D OAK	18	19 SEA	20 SEA	21 SEA	22 OAK	23 D OAK
24 D OAK	25 D OAK	26 BOS	27 BOS	28	29 CLE	30 CLE

September

SUN	MON	TUE	WED	THU	FRI	SAT
31 D CLE	1 D NYY	2 NYY	3 NYY	4 NYY	5 DET	6 D DET
7 D DET	8	9 TB	10 TB	11 D TB	12 BAL	13 D BAL
14 D BAL	15	16 DET	17 DET	18 DET	19 BAL	20 BAL
21 D BAL	22 TB	23 TB	24 TB	25 CLE	26 CLE	27 D CLE
28 D CLE						

Home games shaded; D—Day game (games starting before 5 p.m.); *—All-Star Game at Comiskey Park, Chicago. Subject to change.

CLUB DIRECTORY

President & CEO
Paul Godfrey
Senior v.p., baseball & general manager
J.P. Ricciardi
Senior vice president, communications and external affairs
Paul Godfrey
Vice presidents, baseball
Bob Mattick, Tim Wilken
V.p., baseball operations & asst. g.m.
Tim McCleary

Special assistant to general manager
Bill Livesey
Assistant to the general manager
Tony LaCava
Special assistant to president, baseball & g.m./director, international scouting
Wayne Morgan
Vice president, special projects
Howard Starkman
Director, scouting
Chris Buckley

Director, player development
Dick Scott
Director, minor leagues
Bob Nelson
Director, communications
Jay Stenhouse
Dir., comm., player and alumni relations
Laurel Lindsay

MINOR LEAGUE AFFILIATES

Class	Team	League	Manager
AAA	Syracuse	International	Omar Malave
AA	New Haven	Eastern	Marty Pevey
A	Dunedin	Florida State	Mike Basso
A	Charleston (W.Va.)	South Atlantic	Mark Meleski
A	Auburn	New York-Pennsylvania	Dennis Holmberg
Rookie	Pulaski	Appalachian	Paul Elliott

Follow the Blue Jays all season at: www.sportingnews.com/baseball/teams/bluejays/

BROADCAST INFORMATION

Radio: The Fan (590).
Cable TV: Rogers SportsNet (RSN).

SPRING TRAINING

Ballpark (city): Dunedin Stadium at Grant Field (Dunedin, Fla.).
Ticket information: 800-707-8269; 727-733-0429.

SPRING TRAINING ROSTER

Manager—Carlos Tosca (14).
Coaches—Mike Barnett (56), Brian Butterfield (55), John Gibbons (58), Gil Patterson (47), Bruce Walton (52).

No.	PITCHERS	B/T	Ht./Wt.	Born	Age*	2002 clubs
	Baker, Chris	L/R	6-1/195	8-24-77	25	Syracuse
37	Bowles, Brian	R/R	6-5/220	8-18-76	26	Syracuse, Toronto
	Chulk, Vinny	R/R	6-2/185	12-19-78	24	Tennessee, Syracuse
38	Coco, Pasqual	R/R	6-1/180	9-24-77	25	Syracuse, Toronto
	Creek, Doug	L/L	6-0/227	3-1-69	34	Tampa Bay, Seattle
45	Escobar, Kelvim	R/R	6-1/210	4-11-76	26	Toronto
36	File, Bob	R/R	6-4/215	1-28-77	26	Dunedin, Toronto, Syracuse
32	Halladay, Roy	R/R	6-6/230	5-14-77	25	Toronto
43	Hendrickson, Mark	L/L	6-9/230	6-23-74	28	Syracuse, Toronto
27	Lidle, Cory	R/R	5-11/192	3-22-72	31	Oakland, Sacramento
	Lopez, Aquilino	R/R	6-3/165	7-30-80	22	Tacoma
	Majewski, Gary	R/R	6-2/200	2-26-80	23	Birmingham
	Markwell, Diegomar	L/L	6-2/197	8-8-80	22	Tennessee
34	Miller, Justin	R/R	6-2/195	8-27-77	25	Syracuse, Toronto
19	Politte, Cliff	R/R	5-11/185	2-27-74	29	Philadelphia, Toronto
	Rosario, Francisco	R/R	6-0/160	9-28-80	22	Charleston, W.Va., Dunedin
53	Smith, Mike	R/R	5-11/195	9-19-77	25	Syracuse, Toronto
49	Sturtze, Tanyon	R/R	6-5/221	10-12-70	32	Tampa Bay
	Tam, Jeff	R/R	6-1/219	8-19-70	32	Oakland, Sacramento
35	Thurman, Corey	R/R	6-1/215	11-5-78	24	Toronto
41	Walker, Pete	R/R	6-2/195	4-8-69	33	Norfolk, New York N.L., Toronto

No.	CATCHERS	B/T	Ht./Wt.	Born	Age*	2002 clubs
29	Cash, Kevin	R/R	6-0/185	12-6-77	25	Syracuse, Toronto
20	Huckaby, Ken	R/R	6-1/205	1-27-71	32	Syracuse, Toronto
37	Myers, Greg	L/R	6-2/225	4-14-66	36	Oakland
17	Phelps, Josh	R/R	6-3/220	5-12-78	24	Syracuse, Toronto
	Quiroz, Guillermo	R/R	6-1/202	11-29-81	21	Dunedin, Syracuse
15	Wilson, Tom	R/R	6-3/220	12-19-70	32	Toronto

No.	INFIELDERS	B/T	Ht./Wt.	Born	Age*	2002 clubs
2	Berg, David	R/R	5-11/196	9-3-70	32	Toronto
14	Bordick, Mike	R/R	5-11/175	7-21-65	37	Baltimore
25	Delgado, Carlos	L/R	6-3/230	6-25-72	30	Toronto
11	Hinske, Eric	L/R	6-2/225	8-5-77	25	Toronto
3	Hudson, Orlando	B/R	6-0/185	12-12-77	25	Syracuse, Toronto
	Rich, Dominic	L/R	5-10/190	8-22-79	23	Dunedin, Tennessee
5	Woodward, Chris	R/R	6-0/185	6-27-76	26	Dunedin, Toronto

No.	OUTFIELDERS	B/T	Ht./Wt.	Born	Age*	2002 clubs
27	Catalanotto, Frank	L/R	5-11/195	4-27-74	28	Texas, Tulsa
	Dubois, Jason	R/R	6-5/225	3-26-79	24	Daytona
	Johnson, Reed	R/R	5-10/180	12-8-76	26	Dunedin, Syracuse
	Rios, Alexis	R/R	6-5/185	2-18-81	22	Dunedin
24	Stewart, Shannon	R/R	6-1/210	2-25-74	29	Toronto
10	Wells, Vernon	R/R	6-1/225	12-8-78	24	Toronto
54	Werth, Jayson	R/R	6-5/190	5-20-79	23	Syracuse, Toronto
16	Wise, DeWayne	L/L	6-1/180	2-24-78	25	Toronto, Tennessee

*Age as of April 1, 2003.

BALLPARK INFORMATION

Ballpark (capacity, surface)
SkyDome (45,100, artificial)

Address
One Blue Jays Way
Suite 3200
Toronto, Ontario M5V 1J1

Official website
www.bluejays.com

Business phone
416-341-1000

Ticket information
416-341-1234 and 1-888-OK GO JAY

Field dimensions (from home plate)
To left field at foul line, 330 feet
To center field, 400 feet
To right field at foul line, 330 feet

First game played
June 5, 1989 (Brewers 5, Blue Jays 3)

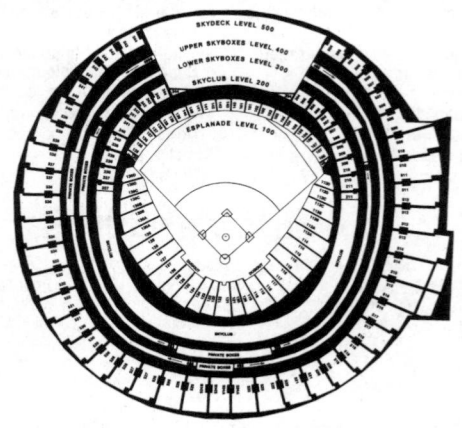

Date	Opp.	Res.	Score	(inn.*)	Hits	Opp. hits	Winning pitcher	Losing pitcher	Save	Record	Pos.	GB
4-1	At Bos.	W	12-11		14	13	Escobar	Urbina		1-0	T1st	...
4-4	Min.	W	7-2		14	6	Halladay	Mays		2-0	2nd	0.5
4-5	Min.	L	3-4		4	10	Reed	Lyon	Guardado	2-1	3rd	0.5
4-6	Min.	L	5-7		13	10	Hawkins	Eyre	Guardado	2-2	4th	1.5
4-7	Min.	L	6-10		8	11	Radke	Cooper		2-3	4th	2.5
4-8	N.Y.	L	3-16		7	22	Wells	Prokopec		2-4	4th	3.5
4-9	N.Y.	L	2-5		2	10	Mussina	Plesac	Rivera	2-5	4th	4.5
4-10	N.Y.	W	9-7		16	12	Borbon	Lilly	Escobar	3-5	4th	3.5
4-11	N.Y.	W	11-3		12	7	Eyre	Clemens		4-5	4th	2.5
4-12	At T.B.	W	14-7		16	14	Miller	Rupe		5-5	3rd	1.5
4-13	At T.B.	W	5-4		8	13	Prokopec	Sturtze	Escobar	6-5	3rd	1.0
4-14	At T.B.	L	4-5	(10)	5	9	Yan	Coco		6-6	3rd	1.5
4-16	Bos.	L	3-14		4	14	Castillo	Lyon	Arrojo	6-7	3rd	2.5
4-17	Bos.	L	3-10		9	13	Oliver	Eyre		6-8	3rd	3.5
4-19	At N.Y.	L	5-6		8	11	Rivera	File		6-9	T3rd	4.5
4-20	At N.Y.	W	5-4	(10)	9	6	Plesac	Mendoza		7-9	3rd	4.0
4-21	At N.Y.	L	2-9		4	10	Clemens	Carpenter		7-10	T3rd	5.5
4-23	At Tex.	W	2-1		6	4	Lyon	Valdes	Escobar	8-10	T3rd	4.5
4-24	At Tex.	L	2-3		5	6	Rogers	Prokopec	Irabu	8-11	4th	4.5
4-25	At Tex.	L	9-11		14	11	Van Poppel	Plesac	Irabu	8-12	4th	5.5
4-26	At Ana.	L	0-4		9	10	Appier	Smith	Percival	8-13	5th	6.5
4-27	At Ana.	L	4-11		10	10	Sele	Borbon		8-14	5th	7.5
4-28	At Ana.	L	5-8	(14)	14	13	Lukasiewicz	Borbon		8-15	5th	8.0
4-30	Tex.	L	3-10		5	13	Rogers	Prokopec		8-16	5th	8.5
5-1	Tex.	L	1-8		4	12	Burba	Halladay		8-17	5th	9.5
5-2	Tex.	L	3-5		7	9	Bell	Smith	Irabu	8-18	5th	10.0
5-3	Ana.	L	4-6		10	9	Sele	Lyon	Percival	8-19	5th	11.0
5-4	Ana.	W	4-1		9	5	Miller	Schoeneweis	Escobar	9-19	T4th	11.0
5-5	Ana.	L	2-8		5	15	Ortiz	Prokopec		9-20	T4th	12.0
5-7	At Sea.	W	4-1		9	4	Halladay	Baldwin	Escobar	10-20	4th	12.5
5-8	At Sea.	L	4-5	(10)	9	10	Sasaki	Eyre		10-21	4th	13.5
5-9	At Sea.	L	7-8	(11)	9	14	Franklin	Thurman		10-22	4th	14.5
5-10	At Oak.	W	6-2		13	6	Prokopec	Mulder		11-22	4th	13.5
5-11	At Oak.	L	4-7		8	8	Zito	Miller		11-23	4th	13.5
5-12	At Oak.	W	11-4		13	10	Halladay	Lidle	Walker	12-23	4th	13.5
5-14	Sea.	W	6-3		7	10	Loaiza	Garcia	Escobar	13-23	4th	13.5
5-15	Sea.	L	6-8		9	10	Rhodes	Escobar	Sasaki	13-24	4th	14.5
5-16	Sea.	L	2-15		6	16	Pineiro	Prokopec		13-25	4th	14.5
5-17	Oak.	W	7-1		11	7	Halladay	Mulder		14-25	4th	13.5
5-18	Oak.	W	6-3		6	7	Miller	Fyhrie	Escobar	15-25	4th	13.5
5-19	Oak.	W	11-0		10	2	Loaiza	Hudson		16-25	4th	13.5
5-20	At N.Y.	L	3-6		6	13	Mendoza	Heredia	Rivera	16-26	4th	14.5
5-21	At N.Y.	L	1-4		4	4	Mussina	Prokopec	Karsay	16-27	4th	14.5
5-22	At N.Y.	W	8-3		7	11	Halladay	Hernandez		17-27	4th	13.5
5-24	Cle.	L	2-5		8	10	Drese	Miller	Wickman	17-28	4th	15.0
5-25	Cle.	L	0-3		5	7	Sabathia	Loaiza	Wickman	17-29	4th	15.0
5-26	Cle.	L	1-3		4	6	Colon	Prokopec		17-30	4th	15.0
5-27	Bos.	L	6-8		11	11	Castillo	Halladay	Urbina	17-31	4th	16.0
5-28	Bos.	L	4-6		9	12	Wakefield	Escobar	Urbina	17-32	T4th	17.0
5-29	Bos.	L	4-7		8	6	Burkett	Cassidy	Fossum	17-33	T4th	18.0
5-31	At Det.	W	4-2		5	10	Loaiza	Bernero	Escobar	18-33	4th	18.0
6-1	At Det.	W	4-1	(11)	10	7	Politte	Patterson	Escobar	19-33	4th	17.0
6-2	At Det.	W	7-6		10	12	Halladay	Weaver	Escobar	20-33	4th	17.0
6-3	T.B.	W	6-1		9	6	Walker	Sturtze		21-33	4th	16.0
6-4	T.B.	W	3-1		6	4	Miller	Wilson	Escobar	22-33	4th	16.0
6-5	T.B.	L	6-8		9	16	Alvarez	Loaiza		22-34	4th	17.0
6-6	T.B.	W	5-4		6	6	Escobar	Harper		23-34	4th	17.0
6-7	Col.	W	8-0		14	2	Halladay	Hampton		24-34	4th	16.0
6-8	Col.	W	3-1		6	4	Walker	Thomson	Escobar	25-34	4th	15.0
6-9	Col.	W	3-2		6	6	Escobar	Jimenez		26-34	4th	14.0
6-10	S.F.	W	6-5		8	10	Thurman	Rueter	Escobar	27-34	4th	14.0
6-11	S.F.	L	2-9		9	12	Jensen	Lyon		27-35	4th	14.0
6-12	S.F.	L	3-6		12	13	Hernandez	Halladay	Nen	27-36	4th	15.0
6-14	At Mon.	L	2-8		7	14	Ohka	Miller		27-37	4th	15.0
6-15	At Mon.	L	3-9		7	11	Day	Loaiza		27-38	4th	15.0

Date	Opp.	Res.	Score	(inn.*)	Hits	Opp. hits	Winning pitcher	Losing pitcher	Save	Record	Pos.	GB
6-16	At Mon.	L	5-6		11	11	Stewart	Escobar		27-39	4th	16.0
6-18	At L.A.	W	2-1		8	4	Halladay	Ashby		28-39	4th	16.0
6-19	At L.A.	L	2-5		5	8	Ishii	Miller	Gagne	28-40	4th	16.0
6-20	At L.A.	L	1-2		6	6	Perez	Loaiza	Gagne	28-41	4th	17.0
6-21	At Ari.	L	3-4		4	10	Kim	Escobar		28-42	4th	17.0
6-22	At Ari.	W	6-3		10	13	Carpenter	Batista		29-42	4th	16.0
6-23	At Ari.	W	9-3		12	9	Halladay	Anderson		30-42	4th	15.5
6-25	At T.B.	W	20-11		19	17	Walker	Sosa		31-42	4th	14.5
6-26	At T.B.	L	2-4		7	4	Sturtze	Parris	Yan	31-43	4th	15.0
6-27	At T.B.	L	4-6		6	10	Harper	Politte	Yan	31-44	4th	15.5
6-28	Mon.	L	1-2		3	5	Armas Jr.	Halladay	Stewart	31-45	4th	16.5
6-29	Mon.	W	5-4	(10)	7	10	Escobar	Herges		32-45	4th	15.5
6-30	Mon.	W	7-5		12	10	Eyre	Lloyd	Escobar	33-45	4th	15.5
7-1	At Bos.	L	0-4		7	10	Martinez	Parris		33-46	4th	16.0
7-2§	At Bos.	L	1-2		6	6	Banks	Eyre	Embree	33-47		
7-2∞	At Bos.	L	4-6		9	7	Kim	Smith	Embree	33-48	4th	17.5
7-3	At Bos.	L	2-5		11	11	Gomes	Politte	Urbina	33-49	4th	18.5
7-4	At Bos.	L	5-9		7	10	Lowe	Heredia		33-50	4th	19.5
7-5	At N.Y.	L	3-6		8	10	Hernandez	Loaiza	Rivera	33-51	4th	20.5
7-6	At N.Y.	W	8-3		13	6	Parris	Pettitte		34-51	4th	19.5
7-7	At N.Y.	L	6-10		6	15	Weaver	Thurman		34-52	4th	20.5
7-11	Bos.	L	3-10		7	12	Burkett	Walker		34-53	4th	21.5
7-12	Bos.	W	5-0		9	3	Halladay	Lowe		35-53	4th	20.5
7-13	Bos.	W	4-1		12	7	Carpenter	Castillo		36-53	4th	20.5
7-14	Bos.	W	6-5		9	9	Escobar	Urbina		37-53	4th	19.5
7-15	N.Y.	W	8-5		13	11	Parris	Hernandez	Escobar	38-53	4th	18.5
7-16	N.Y.	L	6-7		13	7	Karsay	Politte	Rivera	38-54	4th	19.5
7-17	Bal.	W	7-1		14	6	Halladay	Johnson		39-54	4th	19.5
7-18	Bal.	W	5-4		9	10	Carpenter	Driskill	Escobar	40-54	4th	19.5
7-19	T.B.	W	11-8		12	11	Loaiza	Creek	Escobar	41-54	4th	18.5
7-20	T.B.	W	12-10		10	9	Parris	de los Santos	Escobar	42-54	4th	18.5
7-21	T.B.	L	5-7		9	12	Sosa	Walker	Yan	42-55	4th	19.5
7-22	At Bal.	W	6-3		10	7	Halladay	Johnson	Escobar	43-55	4th	19.0
7-24	At Bal.	W	5-2		8	10	Carpenter	Driskill	Politte	44-55	4th	18.5
7-26	At Min.	L	5-10		6	16	Fiore	Prokopec		44-56	4th	19.5
7-27	At Min.	L	4-5	(10)	9	10	Wells	Escobar		44-57	4th	19.5
7-28	At Min.	L	0-4		3	9	Santana	Loaiza		44-58	4th	20.5
7-29	At K.C.	L	1-4		5	7	Byrd	Carpenter		44-59	4th	21.5
7-30	At K.C.	W	13-4		17	9	Walker	Asencio		45-59	4th	21.5
7-31	At K.C.	W	9-2		14	10	Parris	Sedlacek		46-59	4th	20.5
8-1	At K.C.	W	3-2		9	5	Halladay	Hernandez	Escobar	47-59	4th	19.5
8-2	Bal.	L	8-9		14	12	Ryan	Escobar	Julio	47-60	4th	20.5
8-3	Bal.	L	4-8		10	16	Driskill	Carpenter		47-61	4th	20.5
8-4	Bal.	W	5-4		10	12	Heredia	Ryan	Escobar	48-61	4th	20.5
8-5	Bal.	W	7-1		11	6	Parris	Lopez		49-61	4th	20.0
8-6	Sea.	W	14-12		20	15	Halladay	Baldwin	Escobar	50-61	4th	19.0
8-7	Sea.	L	4-5	(10)	9	16	Sasaki	Prokopec		50-62	4th	20.0
8-8	Sea.	L	1-3		6	8	Moyer	Carpenter	Nelson	50-63	4th	21.0
8-9	Ana.	W	5-4		11	12	Walker	Ortiz	Escobar	51-63	4th	20.0
8-10	Ana.	L	4-11		7	18	Lackey	Parris		51-64	4th	20.0
8-11	Ana.	L	0-1		3	9	Washburn	Halladay	Percival	51-65	4th	21.0
8-12	At Oak.	W	2-1		5	9	Loaiza	Harang	Escobar	52-65	4th	20.5
8-13	At Oak.	L	4-5		4	7	Zito	Carpenter	Koch	52-66	4th	21.5
8-14	At Oak.	L	2-4		7	4	Hudson	Walker	Koch	52-67	4th	22.5
8-16	At Tex.	L	5-6		10	10	Kolb	Escobar		52-68	4th	24.0
8-17	At Tex.	L	5-9		10	13	Reyes	Parris		52-69	4th	25.0
8-18	At Tex.	L	7-10		9	12	Myette	Loaiza		52-70	4th	25.0
8-19	K.C.	W	2-0		4	4	Walker	Byrd	Escobar	53-70	4th	24.5
8-20	K.C.	L	5-6	(12)	16	7	Affeldt	Cassidy	Hernandez	53-71	4th	25.5
8-21	K.C.	L	4-7		9	12	Sedlacek	Halladay	Hernandez	53-72	4th	25.5
8-23	At Bal.	L	7-11		13	16	Brock	Cassidy	Ryan	53-73	4th	26.0
8-24§	At Bal.	W	4-1		9	6	Walker	Driskill	Escobar	54-73		
8-24∞	At Bal.	W	8-3		13	8	Loaiza	Bauer		55-73	4th	25.5
8-25	At Bal.	W	5-2		11	5	Miller	Johnson	Escobar	56-73	4th	24.5
8-26	At Chi.	W	8-4		10	6	Thurman	Parque		57-73	4th	24.5
8-27	At Chi.	L	4-8	(10)	7	9	Osuna	Cassidy		57-74	4th	25.5
8-28	At Chi.	L	0-8		6	10	Garland	Parris		57-75	4th	26.5
8-29	N.Y.	W	7-4		14	9	Loaiza	Clemens		58-75	4th	25.5
8-30	N.Y.	L	7-9		14	11	Weaver	Walker	Karsay	58-76	4th	26.5
8-31	N.Y.	W	5-1		7	3	Miller	Hernandez		59-76	4th	25.5

Date	Opp.	Res.	Score	(inn.*)	Hits	Opp. hits	Winning pitcher	Losing pitcher	Save	Record	Pos.	GB
9-1	N.Y.	W	7-6		13	12	Halladay	Wells	Escobar	60-76	4th	24.5
9-2	Chi.	L	3-5		11	8	Garland	Thurman	Marte	60-77	4th	24.5
9-3	Chi.	L	4-5		7	8	Rauch	Loaiza	Marte	60-78	4th	25.5
9-4	Chi.	W	6-2		9	7	Walker	Wright		61-78	4th	25.5
9-5	At Bos.	W	5-4		13	6	Miller	Hermanson	Escobar	62-78	4th	25.5
9-6	At Bos.	L	2-7		6	15	Wakefield	Halladay		62-79	4th	26.5
9-7	At Bos.	L	1-4		3	7	Fossum	Bowles	Urbina	62-80	4th	26.5
9-8	At Bos.	W	9-4		13	11	Loaiza	Castillo		63-80	4th	26.5
9-9	At Cle.	W	11-9		15	13	Bowles	Sadler	Escobar	64-80	4th	26.0
9-10	At Cle.	W	5-4		10	5	Bowles	Wohlers	Escobar	65-80	3rd	26.5
9-11	At Cle.	W	6-5	(11)	7	9	Cassidy	Elder	Kershner	66-80	3rd	26.5
9-13	T.B.	W	5-2		6	9	Halladay	Brazelton	Escobar	67-80	3rd	26.0
9-14	T.B.	W	8-4		10	8	Hendrickson	Sturtze	Escobar	68-80	3rd	25.0
9-15	T.B.	L	4-7		8	14	Kennedy	Loaiza	Yan	68-81	3rd	26.0
9-16	At Bal.	W	2-0		6	4	Walker	Ponson	Escobar	69-81	3rd	25.5
9-17	At Bal.	L	4-10		8	11	Stephens	Miller		69-82	3rd	25.5
9-18	At Bal.	W	2-1		5	9	Halladay	Douglass	Escobar	70-82	3rd	25.5
9-19	At Bal.	W	9-3		16	5	Hendrickson	Lopez		71-82	3rd	24.5
9-20	At T.B.	L	7-11		7	12	Sturtze	Loaiza		71-83	3rd	25.5
9-21	At T.B.	L	3-4		6	9	Carter	Walker		71-84	3rd	26.5
9-22	At T.B.	W	12-6		19	10	Miller	Wilson		72-84	3rd	26.5
9-24	Bal.	W	11-1		12	4	Halladay	Douglass		73-84	3rd	26.0
9-25	Bal.	W	3-2		7	7	Hendrickson	Lopez	Escobar	74-84	3rd	26.0
9-26	Bal.	W	5-1		9	5	Loaiza	Hentgen		75-84	3rd	25.5
9-27	Det.	W	5-2		11	6	Walker	Van Hekken	Escobar	76-84	3rd	25.5
9-28	Det.	W	10-2		12	6	Miller	Beverlin		77-84	3rd	25.5
9-29	Det.	W	1-0		7	2	Halladay	Maroth	Escobar	78-84	3rd	25.5

Monthly records: April (8-16), May (10-17), June (15-12), July (13-14), August (13-17), September (19-8).
*Innings, if other than nine. §Day separate admission. ∞Night separate admission.

RECORDS

2002 regular-season record: 78-84
Position: 3rd in A.L. East
Home: 42-39 **Road:** 36-45
A.L. East: 41-35 **A.L. Central:** 16-16
A.L. West: 12-24 **N.L.:** 9-9
Vs. LH starters: 16-24
Vs. RH starters: 62-60
Grass: 32-34 **Artificial:** 46-50
Day: 33-25 **Night:** 45-59
1-Run: 23-21 **X-inn.:** 4-8
Doubleheaders: 0-0-0
Team record past five years: 413-397
(.510, ranks 7th in league in that span)

TEAM LEADERS

Batting average: Shannon Stewart (.303).
At-bats: Vernon Wells (608).
Runs: Carlos Delgado, Shannon Stewart (103).
Hits: Shannon Stewart (175).
Total bases: Vernon Wells (278).
Doubles: Eric Hinske, Shannon Stewart (38).
Triples: Shannon Stewart (6).
Home runs: Carlos Delgado (33).

Runs batted in: Carlos Delgado (108).
Stolen bases: Shannon Stewart (14).
Slugging percentage: Carlos Delgado (.549).
On-base percentage: Carlos Delgado (.406).
Wins: Roy Halladay (19).
Earned-run average: Roy Halladay (2.93).
Complete games: Esteban Loaiza (3).
Shutouts: Roy Halladay, Esteban Loaiza (1).
Saves: Kelvim Escobar (38).
Innings pitched: Roy Halladay (239.1).
Strikeouts: Roy Halladay (168).

GAMES BY POSITION

Catcher: Ken Huckaby 88, Tom Wilson 65, Darrin Fletcher 36, Kevin Cash 7.
First base: Carlos Delgado 140, Brian Lesher 12, Tom Wilson 11, Dave Berg 10, Chris Woodward 3, Josh Phelps 2.
Second base: Dave Berg 52, Orlando Hudson 52, Joe Lawrence 49, Homer Bush 22, Chris Woodward 6.
Third base: Eric Hinske 148, Dave Berg 20, Felipe Lopez 2, Chris Woodward 2.
Shortstop: Felipe Lopez 79, Chris Woodward 79, Dave Berg 13.
Outfield: Vernon Wells 159, Jose Cruz 119, Shannon Stewart 99, Raul Mondesi 62, Dewayne Wise 33, Jayson Werth 15, Dave Berg 13, Brian Lesher 5, Pedro Swann 1.
Designated hitter: Josh Phelps 71, Shannon Stewart 38, Raul Mondesi 13, Tom Wilson 12, Dave Berg 8, Darrin Fletcher 4, Carlos Delgado 3, Brian Lesher 3, Pedro Swann 3, Dewayne Wise 3, Jose Cruz 2, Chris Woodward 2, Homer Bush 1, Joe Lawrence 1, Felipe Lopez 1.

TOP DRAFT CHOICES

1. **Russ Adams,** SS, North Carolina.
2. **David Bush,** RHP, Wake Forest.
3. **Justin Maureau,** LHP, Wichita State.
4. **Adam Peterson,** RHP, Wichita State.
5. **Chad Pleiness,** RHP, Central Michigan.
6. **Jason Perry,** OF, Georgia Tech.
7. **Brian Grant,** RHP, C.B. Aycock H.S., Goldsboro, N.C.
8. **Chris Leonard,** LHP, Miami of Ohio.
9. **Russell Savickas,** RHP, Johnston (R.I.) H.S.
10. **Eric Arnold,** 2B, Rice.

ARIZONA DIAMONDBACKS
NATIONAL LEAGUE WEST DIVISION

2003 SEASON

March/April

SUN	MON	TUE	WED	THU	FRI	SAT
30	31 D LA	1 LA	2 LA	3	4 COL	5 D COL
6 D COL	7 D LA	8 LA	9 D LA	10	11 MIL	12 MIL
13 D MIL	14 COL	15 COL	16 COL	17 D COL	18 STL	19 D STL
20 D STL	21	22 MON	23 MON	24 MON	25 NYM	26 D NYM
27 D NYM	28 FLA	29 FLA	30 FLA			

May

SUN	MON	TUE	WED	THU	FRI	SAT
				1 FLA	2 ATL	3 ATL
4 D ATL	5 PHI	6 PHI	7 D PHI	8	9 PIT	10 PIT
11 D PIT	12	13 PHI	14 PHI	15 D PHI	16 PIT	17 PIT
18 PIT	19 SF	20 SF	21 SF	22	23 SD	24 SD
25 SD	26 D SD	27 SF	28 SF	29	30 SD	31 SD

June

SUN	MON	TUE	WED	THU	FRI	SAT
1 D SD	2 SD	3 CWS	4 CWS	5 CWS	6 CLE	7 D CLE
8 D CLE	9	10 KC	11 KC	12 KC	13 MIN	14 MIN
15 D MIN	16	17 HOU	18 HOU	19 HOU	20 CIN	21 CIN
22 D CIN	23 HOU	24 HOU	25 D HOU	26	27 DET	28 DET
29 D DET	30 COL					

July

SUN	MON	TUE	WED	THU	FRI	SAT
		1 COL	2 COL	3 COL	4 LA	5 D LA
6 LA	7 COL	8 COL	9 COL	10 D SD	11 SF	12 D SF
13 D SF	14	15 *	16	17 D SD	18 SD	19 SD
20 D SD	21 SF	22 SF	23 SF	24 D SF	25 LA	26 D LA
27 D LA	28 FLA	29 FLA	30 FLA	31		

August

SUN	MON	TUE	WED	THU	FRI	SAT
					1 D CUB	2 D CUB
3 D CUB	4	5 MON	6 MON	7 MON	8 NYM	9 NYM
10 D NYM	11	12 CIN	13 CIN	14 CIN	15 ATL	16 ATL
17 D ATL	18 D ATL	19 CIN	20 CIN	21 CIN	22 CUB	23 D CUB
24 D CUB	25 SD	26 SD	27 SD	28	29 SF	30 SF

September

SUN	MON	TUE	WED	THU	FRI	SAT
31 SF	1 D SF	2 SD	3 SD	4	5 SF	6 SF
7 D SF	8 LA	9 LA	10 LA	11 LA	12 COL	13 COL
14 D COL	15	16 LA	17 LA	18 LA	19 MIL	20 MIL
21 D MIL	22	23 COL	24 COL	25 D COL	26 STL	27 D STL
28 D STL						

Home games shaded; D—Day game (games starting before 5 p.m.); *—All-Star Game at Comiskey Park, Chicago. Subject to change.

CLUB DIRECTORY

Managing general partner
Jerry Colangelo
President
Richard Dozer
Sr. v.p. and general manager
Joe Garagiola Jr.

Assistant general manager
Sandy Johnson
Director of public relations
Mike Swanson
Director of player development
Tommy Jones

Director of scouting
Mike Rizzo
Director of baseball operations
Bob Miller

MINOR LEAGUE AFFILIATES

Class	Team	League	Manager
AAA	Tucson	Pacific Coast	Al Pedrique
AA	El Paso	Texas	Scott Coolbaugh
A	Lancaster	California	Mike Aldrete
A	South Bend	Midwest	Von Hayes
A	Yakima	Northwest	Bill Plummer
Rookie	Missoula	Pioneer	Tony Perezchica

Follow the Diamondbacks all season at:
www.sportingnews.com/baseball/teams/diamondbacks/

BROADCAST INFORMATION

Radio: KTAR-AM (620).
TV: KTVK (Channel 3)
Cable TV: Fox Sports Net Arizona.

SPRING TRAINING

Ballpark (city): Tucson Electric Park (Tucson, Ariz.).
Ticket information: 520-434-1111.

SPRING TRAINING ROSTER

Manager—Bob Brenly (15).
Coaches—Chuck Kniffin (51), Dwayne Murphy (21), Eddie Rodriguez (14), Glenn Sherlock (53), Robin Yount (19).

No.	PITCHERS	B/T	Ht./Wt.	Born	Age*	2002 clubs
43	Batista, Miguel	R/R	6-2/195	2-19-71	32	Arizona
45	Dessens, Elmer	R/R	6-0/187	1-13-72	31	Cincinnati
51	Johnson, Randy	R/L	6-10/232	9-10-63	39	Arizona
49	Kim, Byung-Hyun	R/R	5-11/177	1-19-79	24	Arizona
58	Koplove, Mike	R/R	6-0/170	8-30-76	26	Tucson, Arizona
31	Mantei, Matt	R/R	6-1/200	7-7-73	29	El Paso, Tucson, Arizona
35	Myers, Mike	L/L	6-4/212	6-26-69	33	Arizona
47	Oropesa, Eddie	L/L	6-3/215	11-23-71	31	Arizona, Tucson
24	Patterson, John	R/R	6-5/183	1-30-78	25	Tucson, Arizona
41	Prinz, Bret	R/R	6-3/185	6-15-77	25	Arizona, Tucson, Lancaster
68	Randolph, Steve	L/L	6-3/185	5-1-74	28	Tucson
38	Schilling, Curt	R/R	6-4/231	11-14-66	36	Arizona
30	Stottlemyre, Todd	L/R	6-2/210	5-20-65	37	Tucson, Arizona
22	Swindell, Greg	R/L	6-3/239	1-2-65	38	Tucson, Arizona
45	Valverde, Jose	R/R	6-4/220	7-24-79	23	Tucson
46	Ward, Jeremy	R/R	6-3/220	2-24-78	25	Tucson

No.	CATCHERS	B/T	Ht./Wt.	Born	Age*	2002 clubs
48	Barajas, Rod	R/R	6-2/229	9-5-75	27	Arizona, Tucson
16	Moeller, Chad	R/R	6-3/210	2-18-75	28	Tucson, Arizona

No.	INFIELDERS	B/T	Ht./Wt.	Born	Age*	2002 clubs
10	Cintron, Alex	B/R	6-2/185	12-17-78	24	Tucson, Arizona
4	Counsell, Craig	L/R	6-0/175	8-21-70	32	Arizona
18	Donnels, Chris	L/R	6-0/185	4-21-66	36	Arizona, Tucson
23	Overbay, Lyle	L/L	6-2/215	1-28-77	26	Tucson, Arizona
37	Spivey, Junior	R/R	6-0/185	1-28-75	28	Arizona
9	Williams, Matt	R/R	6-2/219	11-28-65	37	Arizona, Tucson, Lancaster
5	Womack, Tony	L/R	5-9/170	9-25-69	33	Arizona

No.	OUTFIELDERS	B/T	Ht./Wt.	Born	Age*	2002 clubs
29	Bautista, Danny	R/R	5-11/204	5-24-72	30	Arizona
25	Dellucci, David	L/L	5-11/198	10-31-73	29	Arizona, Tucson
62	Devore, Doug	L/L	6-4/200	12-14-77	25	Tucson
12	Finley, Steve	L/L	6-2/195	3-12-65	38	Arizona
20	Gonzalez, Luis	L/R	6-2/195	9-3-67	35	Arizona
8	Jose, Felix	B/R	6-1/220	5-8-65	37	Mexico City Red Devils, Arizona
65	Terrero, Luis	B/R	6-2/185	5-18-80	22	El Paso

*Age as of April 1, 2003.

BALLPARK INFORMATION

Ballpark (capacity, surface)
Bank One Ballpark (49,033, grass)
Address
401 East Jefferson
Phoenix, AZ 85004
Official website
www.azdiamondbacks.com
Business phone
602-462-6500
Ticket information
602-514-8400
Field dimensions (from home plate)
To left field at foul line, 330 feet
To center field, 407 feet
To right field at foul line, 334 feet
First game played
March 31, 1998 (Rockies 9, Diamondbacks 2)

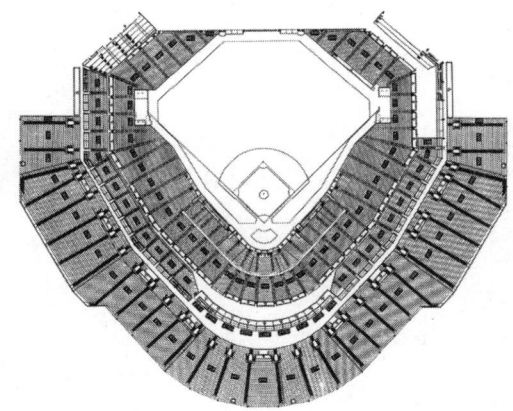

2002 REVIEW
DAY BY DAY

Date	Opp.	Res.	Score	(inn.*)	Hits	Opp. hits	Winning pitcher	Losing pitcher	Save	Record	Pos.	GB
4-1	S.D.	W	2-0		5	6	Johnson	Jarvis		1-0	1st	+0.5
4-2	S.D.	W	9-0		13	9	Schilling	Tollberg		2-0	1st	+0.5
4-3	S.D.	L	7-8		14	11	Fikac	Myers	Hoffman	2-1	1st	0.5
4-5	At Mil.	L	2-6		3	10	Rusch	Helling		2-2	T2nd	2.0
4-6	At Mil.	W	6-3		6	8	Johnson	Neugebauer	Kim	3-2	2nd	2.0
4-7	At Mil.	W	2-0		7	1	Schilling	Sheets		4-2	2nd	2.0
4-8	At S.D.	L	0-8		4	11	Lawrence	Anderson		4-3	2nd	2.5
4-9	At S.D.	L	2-5		9	6	Jones	Stottlemyre	Hoffman	4-4	3rd	2.5
4-10	At S.D.	L	1-2		5	8	Embree	Helling	Hoffman	4-5	T3rd	3.5
4-11	At Col.	W	8-4		15	6	Johnson	Reyes		5-5	3rd	2.5
4-12	At Col.	W	8-3		13	10	Schilling	Hampton		6-5	3rd	2.5
4-13	At Col.	W	7-5	(10)	12	15	Myers	Jimenez		7-5	2nd	2.5
4-14	At Col.	W	6-3		8	10	Batista	Thomson	Kim	8-5	2nd	1.5
4-15	St.L.	W	14-5		11	8	Helling	Benes		9-5	2nd	0.5
4-16	St.L.	W	5-3		11	8	Johnson	Smith	Myers	10-5	2nd	0.5
4-17	St.L.	L	4-8		10	10	Morris	Schilling	Isringhausen	10-6	2nd	0.5
4-19	Col.	L	6-8		8	10	Neagle	Anderson	Jimenez	10-7	T2nd	1.5
4-20	Col.	W	9-8		6	8	Helling	Thomson	Myers	11-7	T2nd	1.5
4-21	Col.	W	7-1		9	2	Johnson	Chacon		12-7	2nd	0.5
4-23	At Atl.	W	5-2		8	5	Schilling	Bong	Kim	13-7	2nd	0.5
4-24	At Atl.	L	3-4		5	9	Foster	Prinz	Smoltz	13-8	T2nd	0.5
4-25	At Atl.	W	11-5		10	11	Helling	Maddux		14-8	1st	+0.5
4-26	At Fla.	W	5-3		12	7	Johnson	Olsen	Kim	15-8	1st	+1.0
4-27	At Fla.	L	3-6		11	10	Penny	Batista	Nunez	15-9	1st	+0.5
4-28	At Fla.	W	5-4		8	8	Schilling	Beckett	Kim	16-9	T1st	...
4-30	N.Y.	L	1-10		3	16	Leiter	Helling		16-10	T1st	...
5-1	N.Y.	L	1-7		3	12	Trachsel	Stottlemyre		16-11	T1st	...
5-2	N.Y.	W	7-3		11	8	Batista	Estes	Kim	17-11	T1st	...
5-3	Mon.	W	6-3		13	5	Schilling	Chen	Kim	18-11	1st	+0.5
5-4	Mon.	W	6-5	(11)	13	8	Oropesa	Lloyd		19-11	1st	+0.5
5-5	Mon.	W	5-2		10	6	Morgan	Vazquez	Kim	20-11	1st	+0.5
5-6	Pit.	L	2-3		7	9	Fogg	Johnson	Williams	20-12	2nd	...
5-7	Pit.	W	7-6		15	10	Myers	Beimel	Kim	21-12	2nd	...
5-8	Pit.	W	4-3		13	6	Schilling	Wells	Kim	22-12	2nd	...
5-10	At Phi.	L	0-4		2	9	Padilla	Helling		22-13	2nd	0.5
5-11	At Phi.	W	6-5	(10)	8	10	Kim	Mesa		23-13	2nd	0.5
5-12	At Phi.	L	1-3		4	10	Adams	Batista	Mesa	23-14	2nd	0.5
5-13	At Pit.	W	11-0		14	6	Schilling	Benson		24-14	2nd	0.5
5-14	At Pit.	L	1-2		6	7	Wells	Anderson	Williams	24-15	2nd	1.5
5-15	At Pit.	W	6-2		11	4	Helling	Anderson		25-15	2nd	0.5
5-16	Phi.	W	4-2		7	8	Johnson	Santiago	Kim	26-15	1st	+0.5
5-17	Phi.	W	12-9		13	17	Oropesa	Cormier	Kim	27-15	1st	+0.5
5-18	Phi.	W	5-4		8	10	Myers	Mesa		28-15	1st	+0.5
5-19	Phi.	L	3-4		8	7	Wolf	Parra	Mesa	28-16	1st	+0.5
5-21	S.F	W	9-4		13	9	Johnson	Fultz		29-16	1st	+1.5
5-22	S.F	L	5-12		11	17	Zerbe	Morgan		29-17	1st	+0.5
5-24	L.A.	W	14-3		15	10	Schilling	Perez		30-17	1st	+1.5
5-25	L.A.	L	5-10		11	10	Ashby	Helling	Gagne	30-18	1st	+1.5
5-26	L.A.	W	10-9	(10)	16	16	Kim	Springer		31-18	1st	+2.5
5-27	At S.F	L	3-7		8	11	Hernandez	Anderson		31-19	1st	+1.5
5-28	At S.F	L	0-1	(10)	3	3	Nen	Myers		31-20	1st	+0.5
5-29	At S.F	W	7-3		14	3	Schilling	Ortiz		32-20	1st	+1.5
5-30	At S.F	W	1-0		5	4	Helling	Rueter	Kim	33-20	1st	+2.0
5-31	At L.A.	W	6-3		10	7	Johnson	Daal	Kim	34-20	1st	+3.0
6-1	At L.A.	L	0-2		5	2	Ashby	Anderson	Gagne	34-21	1st	+2.0
6-2	At L.A.	L	3-6		8	10	Ishii	Batista	Gagne	34-22	1st	+1.0
6-3	Hou.	W	10-4		10	7	Schilling	Redding		35-22	1st	+1.0
6-4	Hou.	L	4-6		9	13	Borbon	Prinz	Wagner	35-23	T1st	...
6-5	Hou.	W	5-4	(13)	13	9	Anderson	Mann		36-23	1st	+1.0
6-7	At Bos.	W	7-5		15	7	Batista	Castillo	Kim	37-23	1st	+2.0
6-8	At Bos.	W	3-2		7	7	Schilling	Martinez	Kim	38-23	1st	+2.0
6-9	At Bos.	W	7-3		12	8	Helling	Burkett		39-23	1st	+2.0
6-10	At N.Y.	L	5-7		11	8	Stanton	Johnson		39-24	1st	+1.0
6-11	At N.Y.	L	4-6		6	10	Wells	Anderson	Mendoza	39-25	1st	+1.0
6-12	At N.Y.	W	9-5		16	9	Batista	Mussina	Kim	40-25	1st	+1.0

Date	Opp.	Res.	Score	(inn.*)	Hits	Opp. hits	Winning pitcher	Losing pitcher	Save	Record	Pos.	GB
6-14	Det.	L	3-6		6	11	Maroth	Schilling	Acevedo	40-26	1st	+1.0
6-15	Det.	W	3-1		8	8	Johnson	Santana	Kim	41-26	1st	+1.0
6-16	Det.	W	11-2		15	9	Helling	Redman		42-26	1st	+1.0
6-18	Bal.	W	6-3		11	11	Anderson	Johnson	Kim	43-26	1st	+2.0
6-19	Bal.	L	1-6		4	7	Brock	Schilling		43-27	1st	+1.0
6-20	Bal.	W	5-1		7	6	Johnson	Lopez		44-27	1st	+1.0
6-21	Tor.	W	4-3		10	4	Kim	Escobar		45-27	1st	+1.0
6-22	Tor.	L	3-6		13	10	Carpenter	Batista		45-28	T1st	...
6-23	Tor.	L	3-9		9	12	Halladay	Anderson		45-29	2nd	1.0
6-25	At Hou.	L	3-7		8	9	Wagner	Myers		45-30	2nd	1.5
6-26	At Hou.	W	9-1		13	5	Johnson	Miller		46-30	2nd	1.5
6-27	At Hou.	L	4-7		11	5	Dotel	Kim		46-31	2nd	2.5
6-28	At Cle.	L	2-8		4	7	Sabathia	Batista		46-32	2nd	3.5
6-29	At Cle.	W	4-2		8	6	Anderson	Finley	Kim	47-32	2nd	2.5
6-30	At Cle.	W	5-2		6	5	Schilling	Baez		48-32	2nd	1.5
7-1	L.A.	L	0-4		6	11	Nomo	Johnson	Gagne	48-33	2nd	2.5
7-2	L.A.	L	0-8		4	7	Daal	Helling		48-34	2nd	3.5
7-3	L.A.	W	5-3		7	7	Mantei	Orosco	Kim	49-34	2nd	2.5
7-4	S.F	W	6-3		10	7	Anderson	Schmidt	Kim	50-34	2nd	1.5
7-5	S.F	W	2-1		6	4	Schilling	Ortiz		51-34	2nd	1.5
7-6	S.F	L	2-3		7	10	Worrell	Mantei	Nen	51-35	2nd	2.5
7-7	S.F	L	2-5		7	10	Jensen	Helling	Nen	51-36	2nd	2.5
7-11	At L.A.	W	4-3		8	7	Koplove	Quantrill	Kim	52-36	2nd	1.5
7-12	At L.A.	W	3-2		9	5	Schilling	Perez	Kim	53-36	2nd	0.5
7-13	At L.A.	W	7-5		11	9	Anderson	Ashby	Kim	54-36	1st	+0.5
7-14	At L.A.	L	1-2		3	5	Ishii	Batista	Gagne	54-37	2nd	0.5
7-15	At S.F	L	3-6		10	10	Jensen	Helling		54-38	2nd	0.5
7-16	At S.F	W	5-3		10	5	Johnson	Rodriguez	Kim	55-38	1st	+0.5
7-17	At Col.	W	12-3		19	10	Schilling	Hampton		56-38	1st	+1.5
7-18	At Col.	L	4-6		7	13	Speier	Swindell	Jimenez	56-39	1st	+1.5
7-19	At S.D.	L	1-6		10	10	Jones	Batista		56-40	1st	+1.0
7-20	At S.D.	W	7-1		10	6	Myers	Holtz		57-40	1st	+1.5
7-21	At S.D.	L	9-11		9	11	Peavy	Johnson	Hoffman	57-41	1st	+1.0
7-22	Col.	W	5-1		8	7	Schilling	Hampton		58-41	1st	+2.0
7-23	Col.	W	8-5		12	9	Kim	Jones		59-41	1st	+2.5
7-24	Col.	W	7-1		11	3	Batista	Chacon		60-41	1st	+3.0
7-25	S.D.	W	10-0		12	6	Patterson	Perez		61-41	1st	+4.0
7-26	S.D.	W	12-0		10	4	Johnson	Peavy		62-41	1st	+4.0
7-27	S.D.	W	4-3		9	10	Schilling	Lawrence		63-41	1st	+4.0
7-28	S.D.	W	5-4	(10)	11	8	Koplove	Hoffman		64-41	1st	+5.0
7-30	At Mon.	L	4-5	(10)	9	9	Tucker	Kim		64-42	1st	+5.0
7-31	At Mon.	W	5-1		7	8	Johnson	Yoshii		65-42	1st	+5.0
8-1	At Mon.	L	1-2		7	7	Eischen	Schilling		65-43	1st	+5.0
8-3†	At N.Y.	W	8-5	(10)	13	10	Kim	Strickland		66-43		
8-3‡	At N.Y.	W	9-2		11	7	Batista	Thomson		67-43	1st	+6.0
8-4	At N.Y.	W	12-7		13	15	Koplove	Guthrie	Kim	68-43	1st	+6.0
8-5	At N.Y.	W	2-0		6	2	Johnson	Estes		69-43	1st	+7.0
8-6	Atl.	L	3-4	(13)	11	10	Ligtenberg	Koplove		69-44	1st	+6.5
8-7	Atl.	W	6-3		8	14	Mantei	Remlinger	Kim	70-44	1st	+6.5
8-8	Atl.	L	1-4		4	11	Glavine	Anderson	Smoltz	70-45	1st	+6.0
8-9	Fla.	W	2-1		5	3	Kim	Looper		71-45	1st	+6.0
8-10	Fla.	W	9-2		15	5	Johnson	Tejera		72-45	1st	+6.0
8-11	Fla.	W	9-2		16	7	Schilling	Beckett		73-45	1st	+7.0
8-13	At Cin.	W	6-1		7	6	Helling	Haynes		74-45	1st	+7.5
8-14	At Cin.	W	7-2		10	6	Anderson	Riedling		75-45	1st	+8.0
8-15	At Cin.	W	7-2		11	4	Johnson	Dempster	Myers	76-45	1st	+8.0
8-16	At Chi.	W	2-1		6	7	Schilling	Smyth	Kim	77-45	1st	+8.0
8-17	At Chi.	W	6-2		11	10	Fetters	Farnsworth		78-45	1st	+8.0
8-18	At Chi.	L	2-3		5	8	Alfonseca	Mantei		78-46	1st	+7.0
8-20	Cin.	W	5-3		7	9	Fetters	Hamilton	Kim	79-46	1st	+8.0
8-21	Cin.	W	11-3		13	6	Schilling	Moehler		80-46	1st	+8.0
8-22	Cin.	W	6-3		7	8	Batista	Reitsma	Kim	81-46	1st	+8.0
8-23	Chi.	W	3-2		3	9	Koplove	Wood	Kim	82-46	1st	+8.0
8-24	Chi.	L	0-4		3	9	Clement	Anderson		82-47	1st	+7.0
8-25	Chi.	W	7-0		7	6	Johnson	Zambrano		83-47	1st	+8.0
8-26	At L.A.	W	6-3	(12)	11	9	Kim	Mota		84-47	1st	+9.0
8-27	At L.A.	L	1-6		7	8	Shuey	Batista		84-48	1st	+8.0
8-28	At L.A.	L	0-1		6	4	Perez	Helling	Gagne	84-49	1st	+7.0
8-30	S.F	L	6-7		8	9	Schmidt	Johnson	Nen	84-50	1st	+7.0
8-31	S.F	L	0-5		5	8	Rueter	Schilling		84-51	1st	+6.0

Date	Opp.	Res.	Score	(inn.*)	Hits	Opp. hits	Winning pitcher	Losing pitcher	Save	Record	Pos.	GB
9-1	S.F	W	7-6		8	10	Kim	Nen		85-51	1st	+6.0
9-2	L.A.	L	1-19		5	24	Perez	Helling		85-52	1st	+5.0
9-3	L.A.	L	2-3		8	6	Ishii	Anderson	Gagne	85-53	1st	+4.0
9-4	L.A.	W	7-1		10	3	Johnson	Ashby		86-53	1st	+5.0
9-5	At S.F	W	8-5		11	9	Schilling	Schmidt		87-53	1st	+5.5
9-6	At S.F	L	0-1		4	6	Rodriguez	Fetters		87-54	1st	+4.5
9-7	At S.F	L	3-4		7	10	Rodriguez	Kim		87-55	1st	+4.5
9-8	At S.F	L	1-3		8	7	Ortiz	Anderson	Nen	87-56	1st	+4.5
9-9	S.D.	W	5-2		12	10	Johnson	Tomko	Kim	88-56	1st	+5.5
9-10	S.D.	W	8-2		13	5	Schilling	Peavy		89-56	1st	+5.5
9-11	S.D.	W	6-5		8	7	Koplove	Walker	Myers	90-56	1st	+6.5
9-13	Mil.	L	4-8		7	9	Rusch	Helling		90-57	1st	+6.0
9-14	Mil.	W	5-0		11	3	Johnson	Neugebauer		91-57	1st	+6.0
9-15	Mil.	W	6-5	(13)	10	10	Koplove	Figueroa		92-57	1st	+7.0
9-17	At S.D.	L	2-3		4	5	Eaton	Batista	Hoffman	92-58	1st	+6.5
9-18	At S.D.	W	10-3		13	10	Helling	Perez		93-58	1st	+6.5
9-19	At S.D.	W	3-1		5	5	Johnson	Condrey	Kim	94-58	1st	+7.5
9-20	At Col.	L	4-9		11	14	Lowe	Schilling		94-59	1st	+6.5
9-21	At Col.	L	8-15		12	20	Fuentes	Fetters		94-60	1st	+5.5
9-22	At Col.	L	7-11		12	18	Fuentes	Swindell		94-61	1st	+4.5
9-23	At St.L.	L	1-13		6	18	Wright	Helling		94-62	1st	+4.0
9-24	At St.L.	L	2-3		8	5	Isringhausen	Fetters		94-63	1st	+3.0
9-25	At St.L.	L	1-6		4	6	Stephenson	Schilling		94-64	1st	+2.0
9-26	Col.	W	4-2		7	6	Johnson	Flores		95-64	1st	+2.5
9-27	Col.	W	8-6		15	8	Batista	Neagle	Kim	96-64	1st	+2.5
9-28	Col.	W	17-8		16	15	Helling	Lowe		97-64	1st	+2.5
9-29	Col.	W	11-8		15	14	Patterson	Stark	Kim	98-64	1st	+2.5

Monthly records: April (16-10), May (18-10), June (14-12), July (17-10), August (19-9), September (14-13).
*Innings, if other than nine. †First game of a doubleheader. ‡Second game of a doubleheader.

RECORDS

2002 regular-season record: 98-64
Position: 1st in N.L. West
Home: 55-26 **Road:** 43-38
N.L. East: 21-11 **N.L. Central:** 23-13
N.L. West: 43-33 **A.L.:** 11-7
Vs. LH starters: 28-22
Vs. RH starters: 70-42
Grass: 96-60 **Artificial:** 2-4
Day: 36-21 **Night:** 62-43
1-Run: 23-20 **X-inn.:** 9-3
Doubleheaders: 1-0-0
Team record past five years: 440-370
(.543, ranks 5th in league in that span)

TEAM LEADERS

Batting average: Quinton McCracken (.309).
At-bats: Tony Womack (590).
Runs: Junior Spivey (103).
Hits: Junior Spivey (162).
Total bases: Luis Gonzalez (260).
Doubles: Junior Spivey (34).
Triples: Quinton McCracken (8).
Home runs: Luis Gonzalez (28).

Runs batted in: Luis Gonzalez (103).
Stolen bases: Tony Womack (29).
Slugging percentage: Steve Finley (.499).
On-base percentage: Luis Gonzalez (.400).
Wins: Randy Johnson (24).
Earned-run average: Randy Johnson (2.32).
Complete games: Randy Johnson (8).
Shutouts: Randy Johnson (4).
Saves: Byung-Hyun Kim (36).
Innings pitched: Randy Johnson (260.0).
Strikeouts: Randy Johnson (334).

GAMES BY POSITION

Catcher: Damian Miller 100, Rod Barajas 69, Chad Moeller 35.
First base: Mark Grace 98, Erubiel Durazo 56, Greg Colbrunn 40, Jay Bell 5, Rod Barajas 1, Chris Donnels 1.
Second base: Junior Spivey 143, Alex Cintron 18, Craig Counsell 13, Jay Bell 2.
Third base: Craig Counsell 94, Matt Williams 56, Chris Donnels 26, Alex Cintron 9, Jay Bell 6, Greg Colbrunn 5,

Danny Klassen 2.
Shortstop: Tony Womack 149, Craig Counsell 22, Alex Cintron 8, Jay Bell 2, Danny Klassen 1.
Outfield: Luis Gonzalez 146, Steve Finley 144, Quinton McCracken 97, David Dellucci 64, Danny Bautista 39, Jose Guillen 37, Mark Little 12, Felix Jose 5, Erubiel Durazo 2, Tony Womack 1.
Designated hitter: Erubiel Durazo 6, Greg Colbrunn 3, David Dellucci 3, Jose Guillen 1.

TOP DRAFT CHOICES

1. **Sergio Santos,** SS, Mater Dei H.S., Hacienda Heights, Calif.
2. **Chris Snyder,** C, Houston.
3. **Jared Doyle,** LHP, James Madison.
4. **Lance Cormier,** RHP, Alabama.
5. **Mark Rosen,** LHP, Salisbury (Conn.) Prep.
6. **Brian Barden,** 3B, Oregon State.
7. **Matt Henrie,** RHP, Clemson.
8. **Ryan Mahoney,** C, Carmel H.S., Patterson, N.Y.
9. **Klent Corley,** RHP, Grand Canyon U.
10. **Mike Pierce,** C, Clovis (Calif.) H.S.

ATLANTA BRAVES
NATIONAL LEAGUE EAST DIVISION

2003 SEASON

March/April

SUN	MON	TUE	WED	THU	FRI	SAT
30	31 MON	1	2 MON	3 MON	4 FLA	5 FLA
6 D FLA	7 D FLA	8 PHI	9 PHI	10 PHI	11 FLA	12 FLA
13 D FLA	14	15 † MON	16 † MON	17 D† MON	18 PHI	19 PHI
20 D PHI	21	22 STL	23 STL	24 STL	25 MIL	26 MIL
27 D MIL	28	29 HOU	30 HOU			

May

SUN	MON	TUE	WED	THU	FRI	SAT
				1 HOU	2 ARI	3 ARI
4 D ARI	5	6 COL	7 COL	8 COL	9 SF	10 SF
11 D SF	12 LA	13 LA	14 LA	15 SD	16 SD	17 SD
18 D SD	19	20 CIN	21 CIN	22 CIN	23 NYM	24 D NYM
25 D NYM	26 D CIN	27 CIN	28 CIN	29	30 NYM	31 D NYM

June

SUN	MON	TUE	WED	THU	FRI	SAT
1 NYM	2	3 TEX	4 TEX	5 D TEX	6 PIT	7 PIT
8 D PIT	9	10 OAK	11 OAK	12 OAK	13 SEA	14 D SEA
15 SEA	16	17 PHI	18 PHI	19 D PHI	20 BAL	21 BAL
22 D BAL	23	24 PHI	25 PHI	26 PHI	27 TB	28 TB
29 D TB	30 FLA					

July

SUN	MON	TUE	WED	THU	FRI	SAT
		1 FLA	2 FLA	3 MON	4 MON	5 MON
6 D MON	7 NYM	8 NYM	9 NYM	10 D CUB	11 D CUB	12 D CUB
13 D CUB	14	15 *	16	17 NYM	18 NYM	19 D NYM
20 NYM	21 CUB	22 CUB	23 FLA	24 FLA	25 D MON	26 MON
27 MON	28 MON	29 HOU	30 HOU	31 HOU		

August

SUN	MON	TUE	WED	THU	FRI	SAT
					1 LA	2 D LA
3 D LA	4	5 MIL	6 MIL	7 D MIL	8 STL	9 D STL
10 D STL	11	12 SD	13 SD	14 SD	15 ARI	16 ARI
17 D ARI	18 D ARI	19 SF	20 SF	21 SF	22 COL	23 COL
24 D COL	25	26 NYM	27 NYM	28 NYM	29 PIT	30 D PIT

September

SUN	MON	TUE	WED	THU	FRI	SAT
31 D PIT	1 D NYM	2 NYM	3 NYM	4	5 PIT	6 PIT
7 D PIT	8 PHI	9 PHI	10 PHI	11 PHI	12 FLA	13 FLA
14 FLA	15 MON	16 MON	17 D MON	18	19 FLA	20 FLA
21 D FLA	22 FLA	23 MON	24 MON	25	26 PHI	27 D PHI
28 D PHI						

Home games shaded; D—Day game (games starting before 5 p.m.); *—All-Star Game at Comiskey Park, Chicago. †—Game played in Puerto Rico. Subject to change.

CLUB DIRECTORY

Chairman of the board of directors
William C. Bartholomay
President
Stanley H. Kasten
Executive v.p. and general manager
John Schuerholz
Senior v.p. and asst. to the president
Henry L. Aaron
Senior vice president, administration
Bob Wolfe

Vice president, assistant g.m.
Frank Wren
Special assistants to general manager
Dick Balderson, Jim Fregosi, Chuck McMichael, Scott Nethery, Paul Snyder
Special asst. to g.m./player dev.
Jose Martinez
Director of scouting
Roy Clark

Dir. of player personnel
Dayton Moore
Director of community relations
Cara Maglione
Director of public relations
Jim Schultz
Media relations manager
Glen Serra

MINOR LEAGUE AFFILIATES

Class	Team	League	Manager
AAA	Richmond	International	Pat Kelly
AA	Greenville	Southern	Brian Snitker
A	Myrtle Beach	Carolina	Randy Ingle
A	Rome	South Atlantic	Rocket Wheeler
Rookie	Danville	Appalachian	Ralph Henriquez
Rookie	Gulf Coast Braves	Gulf Coast	Rick Albert

BROADCAST INFORMATION

Radio: WSB-AM (750).
TV: TBS-TV (Channel 17).
Cable TV: Fox Sports Net South, Turner South.

SPRING TRAINING

Ballpark (city): Disney's Wide World of Sports Baseball Stadium (Kissimmee, Fla.).
Ticket information: 407-839-3900, 407-939-4263.

Follow the Braves all season at: www.sportingnews.com/baseball/teams/braves/

SPRING TRAINING ROSTER

Manager—Bobby Cox (6).
Coaches—Pat Corrales (39), Bobby Dews (52), Frank Fultz (59), Fredi Gonzalez, Glenn Hubbard (16), Leo Mazzone (54), Otis Nixon, Terry Pendleton (9).

No.	PITCHERS	B/T	Ht./Wt.	Born	Age*	2002 clubs
	Belisle, Matt	B/R	6-3/195	6-6-80	22	Greenville
30	Bong, Jung	L/L	6-3/175	7-15-80	22	Greenville, Atlanta
34	Byrd, Paul	R/R	6-1/185	12-3-70	32	Kansas City
33	Dawley, Joey	R/R	6-4/205	9-19-71	31	Richmond, Atlanta
56	Ennis, John	R/R	6-5/220	10-17-79	23	Greenville, Atlanta
	Evert, Brett	L/R	6-6/200	10-23-80	22	Greenville, Myrtle Beach
49	Gryboski, Kevin	R/R	6-5/235	11-15-73	29	Richmond, Atlanta, Macon
32	Hampton, Mike	R/L	5-10/180	9-9-72	30	Colorado
45	Hodges, Trey	R/R	6-3/187	6-29-78	24	Richmond, Atlanta
46	King, Ray	L/L	6-1/242	1-15-74	29	Milwaukee, Indianapolis
31	Maddux, Greg	R/R	6-0/185	4-14-66	36	Atlanta
38	Marquis, Jason	L/R	6-1/210	8-21-78	24	Atlanta
48	Ortiz, Russ	R/R	6-1/208	6-5-74	28	San Francisco
26	Pratt, Andy	L/L	5-11/160	8-27-79	23	Greenville, Richmond, Atlanta
51	Ramirez, Horacio	L/L	6-1/170	11-24-79	23	Macon, Greenville
29	Smoltz, John	R/R	6-3/220	5-15-67	35	Atlanta
50	Spurling, Chris	R/R	6-6/240	6-28-77	25	Altoona
66	Sylvester, Billy	R/R	6-5/220	10-1-76	26	Richmond, Greenville
	Venafro, Mike	L/L	5-10/180	8-2-73	29	Oakland, Sacramento
	Waters, Chris	L/L	6-0/170	8-17-80	22	Myrtle Beach

No.	CATCHERS	B/T	Ht./Wt.	Born	Age*	2002 clubs
20	Blanco, Henry	R/R	5-11/220	8-29-71	31	Atlanta
39	Estrada, Johnny	B/R	5-11/209	6-27-76	26	Scranton/Wilkes-Barre, Philadelphia
8	Lopez, Javy	R/R	6-3/225	11-5-70	32	Atlanta

No.	INFIELDERS	B/T	Ht./Wt.	Born	Age*	2002 clubs
24	Betemit, Wilson	B/R	6-2/155	11-2-81	21	Gulf Coast Braves, Richmond
19	Castilla, Vinny	R/R	6-1/205	7-4-67	35	Atlanta
16	DeRosa, Mark	R/R	6-1/205	2-26-75	28	Atlanta, Richmond, Myrtle Beach
4	Franco, Matt	L/R	6-1/210	8-19-69	33	Richmond, Atlanta
1	Furcal, Rafael	B/R	5-10/165	8-24-77	25	Atlanta
22	Giles, Marcus	R/R	5-8/180	5-18-78	24	Atlanta, Richmond
70	Green, Nick	R/R	6-0/178	9-10-78	24	Greenville
	LaRoche, Adam	L/L	6-3/180	11-6-79	23	Myrtle Beach, Greenville

No.	OUTFIELDERS	B/T	Ht./Wt.	Born	Age*	2002 clubs
28	Aldridge, Cory	L/R	6-0/210	6-13-79	23	Gulf Coast Braves
	Fick, Robert	L/R	6-1/200	3-15-74	29	Detroit
25	Jones, Andruw	R/R	6-1/210	4-23-77	25	Atlanta
10	Jones, Chipper	B/R	6-4/210	4-24-72	30	Atlanta
73	Langerhans, Ryan	L/L	6-3/195	2-20-80	23	Greenville, Atlanta
11	Sheffield, Gary	R/R	6-0/205	11-18-68	34	Atlanta

*Age as of April 1, 2003.

BALLPARK INFORMATION

Ballpark (capacity, surface)
Turner Field (50,091, grass)
Address
P.O. Box 4064
Atlanta, GA 30302
Official website
www.atlantabraves.com
Business phone
404-522-7630
Ticket information
404-249-6400 or 800-326-4000
Field dimensions (from home plate)
To left field at foul line, 335 feet
To center field, 401 feet
To right field at foul line, 330 feet
First game played
April 4, 1997 (Braves 5, Cubs 4)

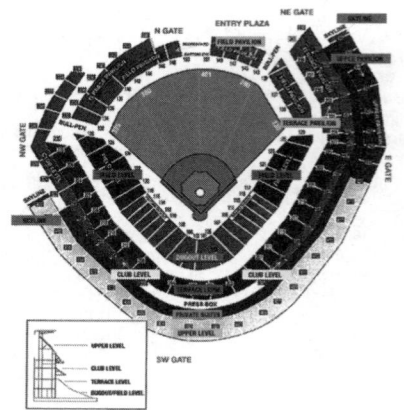

Date	Opp.	Res.	Score	(inn.*)	Hits	Opp. hits	Winning pitcher	Losing pitcher	Save	Record	Pos.	GB
4-1	Phi.	W	7-2		8	5	Glavine	Person		1-0	T1st	...
4-3	Phi.	L	1-3		4	9	Padilla	Millwood	Mesa	1-1	T1st	...
4-4	Phi.	W	11-2		15	5	Marquis	Adams		2-1	T1st	...
4-5	N.Y.	L	3-9		9	13	Astacio	Lopez		2-2	T1st	...
4-6	N.Y.	L	2-11		6	14	Weathers	Smoltz		2-3	T4th	1.0
4-7	N.Y.	W	5-2	(14)	10	8	Lopez	Komiyama		3-3	T1st	...
4-8	At Phi.	W	2-1		6	6	Millwood	Padilla	Smoltz	4-3	T1st	...
4-9	At Phi.	L	4-7		8	11	Santiago	Marquis	Mesa	4-4	T2nd	0.5
4-10	At Phi.	L	5-7	(11)	8	13	Politte	Ligtenberg		4-5	4th	1.5
4-11	At Phi.	W	6-2		8	7	Glavine	Coggin	Holmes	5-5	T3rd	0.5
4-12	At Fla.	W	2-0		8	5	Maddux	Beckett	Smoltz	6-5	2nd	0.5
4-13	At Fla.	L	4-5	(14)	11	8	Knotts	Gryboski		6-6	3rd	0.5
4-14	At Fla.	L	0-7		4	14	Burnett	Marquis		6-7	T4th	1.5
4-15	At N.Y.	L	6-7	(12)	12	13	Strickland	Hammond		6-8	5th	2.5
4-16	At N.Y.	L	1-3		8	9	Astacio	Glavine		6-9	5th	3.5
4-17	At N.Y.	W	2-1		8	5	Millwood	D'Amico	Smoltz	7-9	5th	2.5
4-19	Fla.	W	3-2		7	6	Holmes	Dempster	Smoltz	8-9	4th	2.0
4-20	Fla.	W	3-1		4	7	Maddux	Burnett	Smoltz	9-9	3rd	1.0
4-21	Fla.	W	4-2		15	7	Glavine	Olsen	Smoltz	10-9	T2nd	1.0
4-22	Fla.	L	3-8		8	13	Penny	Millwood		10-10	3rd	1.5
4-23	Ari.	L	2-5		5	8	Schilling	Bong	Kim	10-11	4th	2.5
4-24	Ari.	W	4-3		9	5	Foster	Prinz	Smoltz	11-11	3rd	2.5
4-25	Ari.	L	5-11		11	10	Helling	Maddux		11-12	4th	3.5
4-26	Hou.	W	9-0		16	3	Glavine	Redding		12-12	3rd	2.5
4-27	Hou.	L	3-6		5	10	Mlicki	Millwood	Wagner	12-13	4th	2.5
4-28	Hou.	L	1-7		6	12	Hernandez	Lopez		12-14	4th	3.5
4-30	At Mil.	L	3-4		6	8	Figueroa	Maddux	DeJean	12-15	4th	4.5
5-1	At Mil.	W	3-1		8	3	Glavine	Quevedo	Smoltz	13-15	4th	4.5
5-2	At Mil.	W	3-2	(10)	8	8	Holmes	DeJean	Smoltz	14-15	4th	3.5
5-3	At St.L.	W	2-1	(11)	5	3	Hammond	Stechschulte	Smoltz	15-15	4th	3.5
5-4	At St.L.	L	2-3		6	10	Simontacchi	Lopez	Isringhausen	15-16	4th	3.5
5-5	At St.L.	W	4-2		12	8	Maddux	Kile	Smoltz	16-16	4th	2.5
5-7	L.A.	L	5-6	(16)	12	14	Carrara	Ligtenberg	Orosco	16-17	4th	2.5
5-8	L.A.	L	1-3		5	8	Perez	Millwood	Gagne	16-18	4th	2.5
5-9	L.A.	W	6-2		7	7	Moss	Ashby		17-18	4th	2.5
5-10	S.D.	W	7-3		8	6	Remlinger	Fikac		18-18	4th	2.5
5-11	S.D.	W	6-1		7	4	Marquis	Lawrence		19-18	4th	1.5
5-12	S.D.	L	5-6		11	11	Boyd	Glavine	Hoffman	19-19	4th	2.5
5-13	At S.F	L	6-7	(11)	17	13	Worrell	Hammond		19-20	4th	2.5
5-14	At S.F	L	0-2		5	8	Jensen	Moss	Nen	19-21	4th	3.5
5-15	At S.F	W	6-1		10	6	Maddux	Hernandez		20-21	4th	2.5
5-16	At S.F	W	5-4		5	7	Marquis	Schmidt		21-21	3rd	1.5
5-17	At Col.	W	4-2		9	6	Glavine	Thomson	Smoltz	22-21	3rd	1.5
5-18	At Col.	L	3-7		8	12	Stark	Millwood		22-22	3rd	2.5
5-19	At Col.	W	2-1		4	7	Remlinger	Nichting	Smoltz	23-22	3rd	1.5
5-21	At Mon.	L	4-5	(10)	12	15	Tucker	Holmes		23-23	3rd	1.5
5-22	At Mon.	W	2-0		6	4	Glavine	Armas Jr.		24-23	2nd	0.5
5-24	Cin.	W	11-2		15	10	Millwood	Hamilton		25-23	2nd	1.0
5-25	Cin.	L	4-6		10	10	Haynes	Marquis	Graves	25-24	T2nd	1.0
5-26	Cin.	W	7-5		10	11	Maddux	Reitsma		26-24	2nd	1.0
5-27	Mon.	W	5-1		7	5	Glavine	Armas Jr.		27-24	T1st	...
5-28	Mon.	W	5-2		11	7	Moss	Yoshii	Smoltz	28-24	1st	+1.0
5-29	Mon.	L	3-4		8	9	Tucker	Smoltz	Stewart	28-25	T1st	...
5-30	Mon.	W	5-2		12	7	Marquis	Pavano		29-25	1st	+0.5
5-31	At Cin.	W	7-0		13	4	Maddux	Reitsma		30-25	1st	+0.5
6-1	At Cin.	W	7-1		10	6	Glavine	Rijo		31-25	1st	+1.5
6-2	At Cin.	L	1-5		9	6	Dessens	Moss		31-26	1st	+1.5
6-3	N.Y.	W	5-4		8	8	Hammond	Trachsel	Smoltz	32-26	1st	+2.5
6-5	N.Y.	W	6-4		9	8	Hammond	Strickland	Smoltz	33-26	1st	+3.0
6-6	N.Y.	W	3-2		8	8	Glavine	Weathers	Smoltz	34-26	1st	+3.5
6-7	At Tex.	W	13-7		19	12	Hammond	Park		35-26	1st	+4.5
6-8	At Tex.	W	6-3	(10)	11	10	Remlinger	Irabu	Smoltz	36-26	1st	+4.5
6-9	At Tex.	W	9-3		10	11	Marquis	Burba		37-26	1st	+5.5
6-10	At Min.	L	5-6	(15)	11	14	Fiore	Ligtenberg		37-27	1st	+4.5
6-11	At Min.	W	11-0		14	2	Glavine	Lohse		38-27	1st	+5.5

Date	Opp.	Res.	Score	(inn.*)	Hits	Opp. hits	Winning pitcher	Losing pitcher	Save	Record	Pos.	GB
6-12	At Min.	W	3-2		8	5	Moss	Santana	Smoltz	39-27	1st	+5.5
6-14	Bos.	W	2-1		8	3	Hammond	Martinez	Smoltz	40-27	1st	+6.5
6-15	Bos.	W	4-2		10	8	Maddux	Burkett	Smoltz	41-27	1st	+6.5
6-16	Bos.	L	1-6		7	8	Lowe	Glavine		41-28	1st	+5.5
6-18	Det.	L	0-6		5	8	Weaver	Marquis		41-29	1st	+4.5
6-19	Det.	W	4-1		7	6	Millwood	Maroth	Smoltz	42-29	1st	+4.5
6-20	Det.	W	3-2		7	5	Ligtenberg	Acevedo		43-29	1st	+4.5
6-21	Chi.	W	3-2		3	9	Gryboski	Ritchie	Smoltz	44-29	1st	+4.5
6-22	Chi.	W	15-2		18	4	Moss	Glover		45-29	1st	+5.5
6-23	Chi.	W	9-1		14	5	Marquis	Wright		46-29	1st	+5.5
6-24	At N.Y.	W	3-2		8	6	Gryboski	Strickland	Smoltz	47-29	1st	+6.0
6-25	At N.Y.	L	4-7		9	11	Trachsel	Lopez	Benitez	47-30	1st	+6.0
6-26	At N.Y.	W	6-3		8	7	Hammond	Weathers	Smoltz	48-30	1st	+7.0
6-28	At Bos.	W	4-2		11	6	Remlinger	Wakefield	Smoltz	49-30	1st	+6.5
6-29	At Bos.	W	2-1		6	6	Millwood	Lowe	Smoltz	50-30	1st	+7.5
6-30	At Bos.	W	7-3	(10)	14	5	Remlinger	Urbina		51-30	1st	+8.5
7-1	Mon.	W	7-5		9	13	Ligtenberg	Vazquez	Smoltz	52-30	1st	+9.5
7-2	Mon.	L	2-5		6	8	Colon	Moss	Stewart	52-31	1st	+8.5
7-3	Mon.	W	6-5		10	7	Smoltz	Brower		53-31	1st	+9.5
7-4	Chi.	W	5-1		9	7	Remlinger	Prior	Smoltz	54-31	1st	+9.5
7-5	Chi.	W	4-3		9	5	Millwood	Clement	Smoltz	55-31	1st	+9.5
7-6	Chi.	L	3-7		6	10	Zambrano	Glavine		55-32	1st	+8.5
7-7	Chi.	W	2-0		6	3	Maddux	Lieber	Smoltz	56-32	1st	+9.5
7-11	At Mon.	W	8-5		8	8	Millwood	Armas Jr.	Smoltz	57-32	1st	+10.5
7-12	At Mon.	W	8-3		12	4	Remlinger	Tucker		58-32	1st	+11.5
7-13	At Mon.	L	3-6		9	8	Colon	Glavine		58-33	1st	+10.5
7-14	At Mon.	L	3-10		10	12	Vazquez	Moss		58-34	1st	+9.5
7-15	At Chi.	L	2-3		7	7	Zambrano	Marquis	Alfonseca	58-35	1st	+9.5
7-16	At Chi.	W	2-0		8	2	Millwood	Lieber	Smoltz	59-35	1st	+10.5
7-17	Fla.	W	10-0		16	7	Maddux	Burnett		60-35	1st	+11.5
7-18	Fla.	W	3-1		4	9	Glavine	Tavarez	Smoltz	61-35	1st	+11.5
7-19	At Phi.	W	4-1		8	7	Moss	Duckworth	Smoltz	62-35	1st	+12.5
7-20	At Phi.	W	4-3		8	5	Marquis	Adams	Smoltz	63-35	1st	+12.5
7-21	At Phi.	W	2-1		4	4	Millwood	Wolf	Spooneybarger	64-35	1st	+13.5
7-22	At Fla.	L	1-2		6	7	Burnett	Maddux	Looper	64-36	1st	+12.5
7-23	At Fla.	W	5-3		10	10	Glavine	Tavarez	Smoltz	65-36	1st	+12.5
7-24	At Fla.	W	10-0		12	1	Moss	Tejera		66-36	1st	+13.5
7-26	Phi.	L	2-3		5	9	Wolf	Millwood	Mesa	66-37	1st	+12.5
7-27	Phi.	W	5-3		10	9	Maddux	Roa	Smoltz	67-37	1st	+13.5
7-28	Phi.	L	1-7		6	12	Padilla	Glavine		67-38	1st	+12.5
7-30	Mil.	W	3-2		6	6	Moss	Quevedo	Smoltz	68-38	1st	+13.5
7-31	Mil.	W	9-1		12	6	Millwood	Sheets		69-38	1st	+13.5
8-1	Mil.	W	4-0		9	7	Maddux	Rusch		70-38	1st	+14.5
8-2	St.L.	W	11-5		12	11	Glavine	Simontacchi		71-38	1st	+15.0
8-3	St.L.	W	6-1		7	7	Marquis	Morris		72-38	1st	+16.5
8-4	St.L.	W	2-1		6	1	Smoltz	Veres		73-38	1st	+17.5
8-6	At Ari.	W	4-3	(13)	10	11	Ligtenberg	Koplove		74-38	1st	+18.0
8-7	At Ari.	L	3-6		14	8	Mantei	Remlinger	Kim	74-39	1st	+17.0
8-8	At Ari.	W	4-1		11	4	Glavine	Anderson	Smoltz	75-39	1st	+18.0
8-9	At Hou.	W	6-5	(13)	15	13	Spooneybarger	Cruz	Smoltz	76-39	1st	+18.0
8-10	At Hou.	L	5-8		8	14	Saarloos	Marquis	Wagner	76-40	1st	+18.0
8-11	At Hou.	W	13-3		20	10	Millwood	Mlicki		77-40	1st	+19.0
8-13	S.F	L	2-7		6	12	Ortiz	Maddux		77-41	1st	+18.0
8-14	S.F	W	1-0		8	5	Glavine	Hernandez	Smoltz	78-41	1st	+19.0
8-15	S.F	T	3-3	(10)	5	5				78-41	1st	+19.5
8-16	Col.	W	4-1		5	6	Millwood	Chacon	Smoltz	79-41	1st	+19.5
8-17	Col.	L	3-10		11	11	Stark	Marquis		79-42	1st	+19.5
8-18	Col.	L	3-6		8	15	Jennings	Maddux	Jimenez	79-43	1st	+18.5
8-19	Col.	W	7-6		11	11	Smoltz	Jimenez		80-43	1st	+18.5
8-20	At S.D.	L	2-6		7	9	Tomko	Moss		80-44	1st	+18.5
8-21	At S.D.	W	6-3		10	6	Millwood	Tankersley	Smoltz	81-44	1st	+18.5
8-22	At S.D.	L	2-9		10	12	Bynum	Marquis		81-45	1st	+18.5
8-23	At L.A.	L	3-4		5	9	Gagne	Holmes		81-46	1st	+17.5
8-24	At L.A.	L	3-4		9	7	Shuey	Glavine	Gagne	81-47	1st	+16.5
8-25	At L.A.	W	7-5		10	10	Moss	Ishii	Smoltz	82-47	1st	+17.5
8-27	At Pit.	W	5-4		7	6	Millwood	Fogg	Smoltz	83-47	1st	+18.0
8-28	At Pit.	L	0-1	(10)	6	10	Williams	Remlinger		83-48	1st	+17.5
8-29	At Pit.	L	1-4		8	5	Arroyo	Glavine	Williams	83-49	1st	+17.0
8-30	At Mon.	W	4-2		7	4	Moss	Armas Jr.	Smoltz	84-49	1st	+17.0
8-31	At Mon.	W	5-3		8	12	Hammond	Vazquez	Smoltz	85-49	1st	+17.0

Date	Opp.	Res.	Score	(inn.*)	Hits	Opp. hits	Winning pitcher	Losing pitcher	Save	Record	Pos.	GB
9-1	At Mon.	W	6-4		12	7	Millwood	Yoshii	Smoltz	86-49	1st	+17.0
9-2	Pit.	W	5-1		8	7	Maddux	Meadows		87-49	1st	+18.0
9-3	Pit.	L	0-3		5	8	Torres	Glavine	Williams	87-50	1st	+18.0
9-4	Pit.	W	6-0		9	5	Moss	Wells		88-50	1st	+19.0
9-6	Mon.	W	5-0		12	3	Millwood	Yoshii		89-50	1st	+19.5
9-7	Mon.	W	4-0		7	7	Maddux	Ohka		90-50	1st	+20.5
9-8	Mon.	L	0-7		5	14	Colon	Glavine		90-51	1st	+20.5
9-10	N.Y.	W	12-6		13	14	Hodges	Astacio		91-51	1st	+21.0
9-11§	N.Y.	W	8-5		11	11	Millwood	Trachsel	Smoltz	92-51		
9-11∞	N.Y.	L	0-5		6	16	Leiter	Marquis		92-52	1st	+21.5
9-13	At Fla.	L	3-13		3	16	Pavano	Maddux		92-53	1st	+21.0
9-14	At Fla.	W	10-5		13	14	Glavine	Beckett		93-53	1st	+21.5
9-15	At Fla.	W	6-4		8	8	Moss	Wayne	Smoltz	94-53	1st	+21.5
9-16	At Fla.	L	1-5		4	10	Penny	Millwood		94-54	1st	+21.0
9-17	Phi.	W	2-1		10	5	Maddux	Padilla	Smoltz	95-54	1st	+21.0
9-18	Phi.	L	5-6		11	13	Silva	Ligtenberg	Mesa	95-55	1st	+20.0
9-19	Phi.	W	6-0		11	6	Glavine	Roa		96-55	1st	+20.0
9-20	Fla.	L	2-6		6	8	Wayne	Moss		96-56	1st	+19.0
9-21	Fla.	L	4-6		9	12	Penny	Millwood	Looper	96-57	1st	+19.0
9-22	Fla.	W	4-1		6	4	Maddux	Tavarez	Smoltz	97-57	1st	+19.0
9-24	At Phi.	L	3-5		11	7	Junge	Glavine	Mesa	97-58	1st	+19.0
9-25	At Phi.	W	7-1		11	6	Moss	Myers		98-58	1st	+20.0
9-27†	At N.Y.	W	3-1		8	7	Maddux	Thomson	Smoltz	99-58		
9-27‡	At N.Y.	W	7-4		12	6	Millwood	Astacio		100-58	1st	+20.0
9-28	At N.Y.	W	5-2		13	8	Hodges	Leiter	Smoltz	101-58	1st	+20.0
9-29	At N.Y.	L	1-6		7	10	Trachsel	Remlinger		101-59	1st	+19.0

Monthly records: April (12-15), May (18-10), June (21-5), July (18-8), August (16-11), September (16-10).
*Innings, if other than nine. †First game of a doubleheader. ‡Second game of a doubleheader. §Day separate admission. ∞Night separate admission.

RECORDS

2002 regular-season record: 101-59
Position: 1st in N.L. East
Home: 52-28   **Road:** 49-31
N.L. East: 47-28   **N.L. Central:** 24-12
N.L. West: 15-16   **A.L.:** 15-3
Vs. LH starters: 14-9
Vs. RH starters: 87-50
Grass: 87-52   **Artificial:** 14-7
Day: 33-17   **Night:** 68-42
1-Run: 28-17   **X-inn.:** 7-8
Doubleheaders: 1-0-0
Team record past five years: 493-315 (.610, ranks 1st in league in that span)

TEAM LEADERS

Batting average: Chipper Jones (.327).
At-bats: Rafael Furcal (636).
Runs: Rafael Furcal (95).
Hits: Chipper Jones (179).
Total bases: Chipper Jones (294).
Doubles: Chipper Jones (35).
Triples: Rafael Furcal (8).
Home runs: Andruw Jones (35).
Runs batted in: Chipper Jones (100).
Stolen bases: Rafael Furcal (27).

Slugging percentage: Chipper Jones (.536).
On-base percentage: Chipper Jones (.435).
Wins: Tom Glavine, Kevin Millwood (18).
Earned-run average: Greg Maddux (2.62).
Complete games: Tom Glavine (2).
Shutouts: Tom Glavine, Kevin Millwood (1).
Saves: John Smoltz (55).
Innings pitched: Tom Glavine (224.2).
Strikeouts: Kevin Millwood (178).

GAMES BY POSITION

Catcher: Javy Lopez 103, Henry Blanco 79, Steve Torrealba 12.
First base: Julio Franco 95, Matt Franco 51, Wes Helms 45, B.J. Surhoff 11.
Second base: Keith Lockhart 89, Marcus Giles 52, Mark DeRosa 32, Jesse Garcia 21, Rafael Furcal 4.
Third base: Vinny Castilla 139, Wes Helms 24, Marcus Giles 8, Mark DeRosa 4, Keith Lockhart 1.
Shortstop: Rafael Furcal 150, Mark DeRosa 19, Jesse Garcia 5.

Outfield: Andruw Jones 154, Chipper Jones 152, Gary Sheffield 127, Darren Bragg 63, Wes Helms 9, B.J. Surhoff 9, Mark DeRosa 7, Matt Franco 4, Jesse Garcia 4, Ryan Langerhans 1.
Designated hitter: Gary Sheffield 4, Darren Bragg 3, Julio Franco 2, Andruw Jones 1.

TOP DRAFT CHOICES

1a. **Jeff Francoeur**, OF, Parkview H.S., Lilburn, Ga.
1b. **Dan Meyer**, LHP, James Madison.
2a. **Brian McCann**, C, Duluth (Ga.) H.S.
2b. **Tyler Greene**, SS, St. Thomas Aquinas H.S., Plantation, Fla.
3. **Charlie Morton**, RHP, Joel Barlow H.S., Redding, Conn.
4. **Steve Russell**, RHP, Cimarron Memorial H.S., Las Vegas.
5. **Kris Harvey**, C, Bandys H.S., Catawba, N.C.
6. **James Jurries**, 1B, Tulane.
7. **Patrick Clayton**, RHP, Walton H.S., Marietta, Ga.
8. **Jon Schuerholz**, SS, Auburn.
9. **Nick Starnes**, RHP, Graham H.S., Haw River, N.C.
10. **Yaron Peters**, 1B, South Carolina.

CHICAGO CUBS
NATIONAL LEAGUE CENTRAL DIVISION

2003 SEASON

March/April

SUN	MON	TUE	WED	THU	FRI	SAT
30	31 D NYM	1	2 NYM	3 D NYM	4 CIN	5 D CIN
6 D CIN	7 D MON	8	9 D MON	10 D MON	11 D PIT	12 D PIT
13 D PIT	14 CIN	15 D CIN	16 CIN	17 D CIN	18 PIT	19 PIT
20 D PIT	21	22 SD	23 SD	24 D SD	25 COL	26 D COL
27 D COL	28	29 SF	30 SF			

May

SUN	MON	TUE	WED	THU	FRI	SAT
				1 D SF	2 D COL	3 D COL
4 COL	5 MIL	6 MIL	7 D MIL	8	9 D STL	10 D STL
11 STL	12 MIL	13 MIL	14 MIL	15 MIL	16 STL	17 D STL
18 D STL	19 D STL	20 PIT	21 PIT	22 PIT	23 HOU	24 HOU
25 D HOU	26 D PIT	27 PIT	28 PIT	29	30 D HOU	31 D HOU

June

SUN	MON	TUE	WED	THU	FRI	SAT
1 D HOU	2	3 TB	4 TB	5 D TB	6 D NYY	7 D NYY
8 NYY	9	10 BAL	11 BAL	12 BAL	13 TOR	14 D TOR
15 D TOR	16 CIN	17 CIN	18 CIN	19 CIN	20 D CWS	21 D CWS
22 CWS	23	24 MIL	25 D MIL	26 D MIL	27 D CWS	28 D CWS
29 D CWS	30 PHI					

July

SUN	MON	TUE	WED	THU	FRI	SAT
		1 PHI	2 PHI	3 PHI	4 D STL	5 D STL
6 D STL	7 D FLA	8 D FLA	9 D FLA	10 D ATL	11 D ATL	12 D ATL
13 D ATL	14	15 *	16	17	18 FLA	19 FLA
20 D FLA	21 D ATL	22 ATL	23 PHI	24 D PHI	25 HOU	26 HOU
27 D HOU	28	29 SF	30 D SF	31 D SF		

August

SUN	MON	TUE	WED	THU	FRI	SAT
					1 D ARI	2 ARI
3 D ARI	4	5 SD	6 SD	7 D SD	8 LA	9 LA
10 D LA	11 HOU	12 HOU	13 HOU	14 HOU	15 D LA	16 D LA
17 D LA	18	19 HOU	20 HOU	21 HOU	22 ARI	23 ARI
24 D ARI	25	26 STL	27 STL	28 STL	29 D MIL	30 D MIL

September

SUN	MON	TUE	WED	THU	FRI	SAT
31 D MIL	1 D STL	2 STL	3 STL	4 D STL	5 MIL	6 MIL
7 D MIL	8	9 † MON	10 † MON	11 D† MON	12 D CIN	13 D CIN
14 CIN	15 NYM	16 NYM	17 D NYM	18	19 PIT	20 PIT
21 D PIT	22	23 CIN	24 CIN	25 CIN	26 D PIT	27 PIT
28 D PIT						

Home games shaded; D—Day game (games starting before 5 p.m.); *—All-Star Game at Comiskey Park, Chicago. †—Game played in Puerto Rico. Subject to change.

CLUB DIRECTORY

President and chief executive officer
Andrew B. MacPhail
Vice president, general manager
Jim Hendry
Director, baseball operations
Scott Nelson

Special assistants to the g.m.
Keith Champion, Ken Kravec, Ed Lynch, Billy Williams
Director of scouting
John Stockstill

Dir of player dev./Latin American ops.
Oneri Fleita
Director, media relations
Sharon Pannozzo
Manager, media information
Chuck Wasserstrom

MINOR LEAGUE AFFILIATES

Class	Team	League	Manager
AAA	Iowa	Pacific Coast	Mike Quade
AA	West Tenn	Southern	Bobby Dickerson
A	Daytona	Florida State	Rick Kranitz
A	Lansing	Midwest	Julio Garcia
A	Boise	Northwest	Steve McFarland
Rookie	Mesa Cubs	Arizona	Carmelo Martinez

BROADCAST INFORMATION

Radio: WGN-AM (720).
TV: WGN-TV (Channel 9); WCIU-TV (Channel 26).
Cable TV: Fox Sports Net Chicago.

SPRING TRAINING

Ballpark (city): HoHoKam Park (Mesa, Ariz.).
Ticket information: 800-638-4253.

Follow the Cubs all season at: www.sportingnews.com/baseball/teams/cubs/

Manager—Dusty Baker.
Coaches—Gene Clines, Wendell Kim, Juan Lopez, Gary Matthews, Dick Pole, Larry Rothschild.

No.	PITCHERS	B/T	Ht./Wt.	Born	Age*	2002 clubs
57	Alfonseca, Antonio	R/R	6-5/250	4-16-72	30	Chicago N.L.
53	Beltran, Francis	R/R	6-5/220	11-29-79	23	West Tenn, Chicago N.L.
35	Benes, Alan	R/R	6-5/235	1-21-72	31	Iowa, Chicago N.L.
48	Borowski, Joe	R/R	6-2/240	5-4-71	31	Chicago N.L.
	Bruback, Matt	R/R	6-7/215	1-12-79	24	West Tenn
37	Chiasson, Scott	R/R	6-3/200	8-14-77	25	Iowa, Chicago N.L., West Tenn
30	Clement, Matt	R/R	6-3/213	8-12-74	28	Chicago N.L.
51	Cruz, Juan	R/R	6-2/165	10-15-78	24	Chicago N.L.
55	Estes, Shawn	R/L	6-2/200	2-18-73	30	New York N.L., Cincinnati
44	Farnsworth, Kyle	R/R	6-4/235	4-14-76	26	Chicago N.L., Iowa
	Leicester, Jon	R/R	6-2/220	2-7-79	24	Daytona, West Tenn
91	Ohman, Will	L/L	6-2/195	8-13-77	25	DID NOT PLAY
22	Prior, Mark	R/R	6-5/225	9-7-80	22	West Tenn, Iowa, Chicago N.L.
37	Remlinger, Mike	L/L	6-1/210	3-23-66	37	Atlanta
	Sanchez, Felix	R/L	6-3/180	8-3-81	21	Lansing
33	Sirotka, Mike	L/L	6-1/200	5-13-71	31	DID NOT PLAY
39	Smyth, Steve	L/L	6-1/195	6-3-78	24	West Tenn, Iowa, Chicago N.L.
	Veres, Dave	R/R	6-2/220	10-19-66	36	St. Louis
	Webb, John	R/R	6-3/205	5-23-79	23	Daytona, West Tenn
34	Wood, Kerry	R/R	6-5/230	6-16-77	25	Chicago N.L.
38	Zambrano, Carlos	R/R	6-5/250	6-1-81	21	Iowa, Chicago N.L.

No.	CATCHERS	B/T	Ht./Wt.	Born	Age*	2002 clubs
	Bako, Paul	L/R	6-2/205	6-20-72	30	Milwaukee
	Miller, Damian	R/R	6-2/218	10-13-69	33	Arizona, Tucson

No.	INFIELDERS	B/T	Ht./Wt.	Born	Age*	2002 clubs
28	Bellhorn, Mark	B/R	6-1/205	8-23-74	28	Chicago N.L.
19	Choi, Hee Seop	L/L	6-5/235	3-16-79	24	Iowa, Chicago N.L.
56	Frese, Nate	R/R	6-3/200	7-10-77	25	West Tenn
8	Gonzalez, Alex	R/R	6-0/200	4-8-73	29	Chicago N.L.
	Grudzielanek, Mark	R/R	6-1/185	6-30-70	32	Los Angeles
17	Hill, Bobby	B/R	5-10/190	4-3-78	24	Iowa, Chicago N.L.
	Karros, Eric	R/R	6-4/226	11-4-67	35	Los Angeles
	Kelton, Dave	R/R	6-3/205	12-17-79	23	West Tenn
	Martinez, Ramon	R/R	6-1/183	10-10-72	30	San Francisco
1	Ojeda, Augie	B/R	5-8/170	12-20-74	28	Chicago N.L., Iowa
15	Orie, Kevin	R/R	6-4/215	9-1-72	30	Iowa, Chicago N.L.

No.	OUTFIELDERS	B/T	Ht./Wt.	Born	Age*	2002 clubs
18	Alou, Moises	R/R	6-3/220	7-3-66	36	Daytona, Chicago N.L.
	Jackson, Nic	L/R	6-3/205	9-25-79	23	West Tenn
76	Melian, Jackson	R/R	6-2/190	1-7-80	23	Huntsville, West Tenn
	O'Leary, Troy	L/L	6-0/208	8-4-69	33	Ottawa, Montreal
20	Patterson, Corey	L/R	5-9/175	8-13-79	23	Chicago N.L.
21	Sosa, Sammy	R/R	6-0/220	11-12-68	34	Chicago N.L.

*Age as of April 1, 2003.

BALLPARK INFORMATION

Ballpark (capacity, surface)
Wrigley Field (39,241, grass)

Address
1060 W. Addison St.
Chicago, IL 60613-4397

Official website
www.cubs.com

Business phone
773-404-2827

Ticket information
773-404-2827

Field dimensions (from home plate)
To left field at foul line, 355 feet
To center field, 400 feet
To right field at foul line, 353 feet

First game played
April 20, 1916 (Cubs 7, Reds 6)

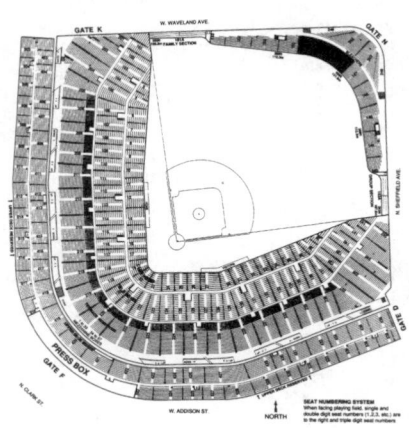

2003 SEASON *Chicago Cubs*

Date	Opp.	Res.	Score	(inn.*)	Hits	Opp. hits	Winning pitcher	Losing pitcher	Save	Record	Pos.	GB
4-1	At Cin.	L	4-5		10	12	Graves	Fassero		0-1	T5th	1.0
4-3	At Cin.	W	10-3		13	6	Wood	Dessens		1-1	T1st	...
4-4	At Cin.	L	1-3		8	3	Acevedo	Cruz	Graves	1-2	T4th	1.0
4-5	Pit.	L	1-2		4	6	Williams	Bere	Williams	1-3	6th	2.0
4-6	Pit.	L	1-6		6	10	Fogg	Clement		1-4	6th	3.0
4-9	N.Y.	W	2-0		8	2	Lieber	Trachsel	Alfonseca	2-4	5th	3.0
4-10	N.Y.	L	2-3		3	6	Weathers	Fassero	Benitez	2-5	5th	3.0
4-11	N.Y.	L	2-3		12	6	Astacio	Cruz	Benitez	2-6	5th	3.5
4-12	At Pit.	W	7-3		10	5	Bere	Williams		3-6	5th	3.5
4-13	At Pit.	L	2-3		6	6	Fogg	Clement	Williams	3-7	5th	4.5
4-14	At Pit.	W	5-1	(8)	12	5	Lieber	Villone	Borowski	4-7	5th	3.5
4-15	At Mon.	W	6-4		12	9	Wood	Pavano	Alfonseca	5-7	T4th	2.5
4-16	At Mon.	L	4-8		12	8	Yoshii	Cruz	Tucker	5-8	5th	3.0
4-17	At Mon.	L	8-15		12	19	Chen	Osborne		5-9	5th	4.0
4-19	Cin.	W	5-2		5	7	Clement	Hamilton	Alfonseca	6-9	5th	4.0
4-20	Cin.	L	1-6		7	9	Dessens	Wood		6-10	5th	5.0
4-21	Cin.	L	3-5		7	5	Rijo	Cruz	Graves	6-11	6th	6.0
4-23	S.F	L	4-12		5	13	Rueter	Bere		6-12	6th	6.0
4-24	S.F	W	10-4		14	9	Borowski	Fultz		7-12	5th	5.0
4-25	S.F	W	2-1		7	7	Lieber	Hernandez	Alfonseca	8-12	5th	5.0
4-26	L.A.	L	0-10		1	11	Perez	Wood		8-13	5th	5.5
4-28†	L.A.	L	4-5		6	12	Ishii	Cruz	Gagne	8-14		
4-28‡	L.A.	L	1-4		3	10	Ashby	Bere		8-15	5th	6.5
4-30	At S.D.	L	1-2		6	5	Fikac	Borowski	Hoffman	8-16	5th	7.5
5-1	At S.D.	L	3-4		7	6	Jones	Lieber	Hoffman	8-17	5th	8.5
5-2	At S.D.	W	6-1		7	4	Wood	Tomko		9-17	5th	7.5
5-3	At L.A.	W	8-3		10	10	Mahay	Orosco		10-17	5th	6.5
5-4	At L.A.	L	2-3		4	11	Ishii	Bere	Gagne	10-18	5th	6.5
5-5	At L.A.	W	3-0		7	4	Mahay	Brown	Alfonseca	11-18	5th	5.5
5-6	St.L.	W	6-5		8	12	Fassero	Timlin		12-18	5th	5.5
5-7	St.L.	W	8-0		9	4	Wood	Smith		13-18	5th	5.5
5-8	St.L.	L	2-3		4	4	Morris	Cruz	Isringhausen	13-19	5th	6.5
5-9	Mil.	L	4-9		9	12	Sheets	Bere		13-20	5th	7.0
5-10	Mil.	L	4-6		10	7	King	Borowski	DeJean	13-21	5th	7.0
5-12	Mil.	L	4-13		10	11	Rusch	Lieber		13-22	5th	7.5
5-13	At St.L.	L	0-3		4	2	Morris	Wood		13-23	5th	8.5
5-14	At St.L.	L	2-11		6	17	Timlin	Cruz		13-24	5th	9.5
5-15	At St.L.	L	1-4		4	9	Stechschulte	Bere	Isringhausen	13-25	5th	10.5
5-17	At Mil.	L	2-6		6	10	Rusch	Clement		13-26	5th	11.0
5-18	At Mil.	L	1-3		8	9	Cabrera	Lieber	DeJean	13-27	5th	12.0
5-19	At Mil.	W	5-4	(11)	8	7	Borowski	de los Santos		14-27	5th	11.0
5-21†	Pit.	L	1-12		3	13	Anderson	Bere		14-28		
5-21‡	Pit.	W	4-3		6	6	Cruz	Fogg	Alfonseca	15-28	5th	11.0
5-22	Pit.	W	7-4		9	7	Prior	Williams	Alfonseca	16-28	5th	11.0
5-23	Pit.	W	11-6		15	10	Clement	Benson		17-28	5th	10.0
5-24	At Hou.	W	5-4	(11)	10	11	Mahomes	Wagner	Borowski	18-28	5th	9.0
5-25	At Hou.	W	5-1		8	4	Wood	Mlicki		19-28	5th	9.0
5-26	At Hou.	L	5-7		14	12	Dotel	Fassero	Wagner	19-29	5th	9.0
5-27	At Pit.	L	2-3	(10)	9	8	Williams	Alfonseca		19-30	5th	9.5
5-28	At Pit.	W	3-0		6	2	Clement	Benson		20-30	5th	9.5
5-29	At Pit.	L	0-5		4	13	Wells	Lieber		20-31	5th	10.5
5-30	At Pit.	W	9-8		8	10	Wood	Anderson	Alfonseca	21-31	5th	10.5
5-31	Hou.	L	1-4		4	7	Hernandez	Bere	Wagner	21-32	5th	10.5
6-1	Hou.	L	3-7		9	11	Oswalt	Prior	Dotel	21-33	5th	10.5
6-2	Hou.	W	4-2		7	6	Clement	Reynolds	Alfonseca	22-33	T1st	10.5
6-3	At Mil.	L	6-7		8	12	de los Santos	Borowski	DeJean	22-34	5th	11.0
6-4	At Mil.	L	5-6	(11)	9	13	Vizcaino	Fassero		22-35	5th	11.0
6-5	At Mil.	W	5-1	(10)	7	7	Farnsworth	DeJean		23-35	5th	10.5
6-7	At Sea.	W	2-0		7	5	Prior	Pineiro	Alfonseca	24-35	5th	10.0
6-8	At Sea.	L	2-4		6	5	Garcia	Clement	Sasaki	24-36	5th	11.0
6-9	At Sea.	W	5-1		9	10	Lieber	Soriano		25-36	5th	10.0
6-10	At Hou.	L	2-4		8	9	Miller	Wood	Wagner	25-37	5th	10.0
6-11	At Hou.	W	9-5		13	9	Farnsworth	Borbon		26-37	5th	10.0
6-12	At Hou.	L	4-5		10	10	Oswalt	Cruz	Wagner	26-38	5th	10.0
6-14	Chi.	W	8-4		11	7	Clement	Garland		27-38	5th	10.0

Date	Opp.	Res.	Score	(inn.*)	Hits	Opp. hits	Winning pitcher	Losing pitcher	Save	Record	Pos.	GB
6-15	Chi.	W	7-3		10	8	Lieber	Buehrle		28-38	5th	10.0
6-16	Chi.	L	7-10		11	6	Foulke	Wood	Osuna	28-39	5th	10.0
6-18	Tex.	W	4-3		6	4	Alfonseca	Rocker		29-39	5th	10.0
6-19	Tex.	L	4-7	(10)	10	12	Irabu	Fassero	Cordero	29-40	5th	11.0
6-20	Tex.	L	4-7		5	9	Telford	Cruz	Cordero	29-41	5th	11.0
6-21	St.L.	W	2-1		3	3	Lieber	Williams		30-41	5th	10.0
6-23	St.L.	W	8-3		10	7	Wood	Simontacchi		31-41	5th	9.0
6-24	Cin.	W	6-4		10	8	Fassero	Williamson	Alfonseca	32-41	3rd	8.5
6-25	Cin.	L	2-5		8	7	Pineda	Clement	Graves	32-42	5th	8.5
6-26	Cin.	L	6-8		14	11	Haynes	Bere	Graves	32-43	5th	9.5
6-27	Cin.	L	4-5	(10)	7	11	Graves	Farnsworth		32-44	5th	9.5
6-28	At Chi.	L	9-13		11	12	Ginter	Borowski		32-45	5th	10.5
6-29	At Chi.	L	4-5		8	7	Garland	Cruz	Osuna	32-46	5th	10.5
6-30	At Chi.	W	9-2		12	6	Clement	Buehrle		33-46	5th	9.5
7-1	At Fla.	L	1-11		5	15	Tejera	Zambrano		33-47	5th	10.5
7-2	At Fla.	L	7-9		11	13	Neal	Lieber		33-48	5th	11.5
7-3	At Fla.	W	6-2		11	4	Wood	Dempster		34-48	5th	11.5
7-4	At Atl.	L	1-5		7	9	Remlinger	Prior	Smoltz	34-49	5th	12.5
7-5	At Atl.	L	3-4		5	9	Millwood	Clement	Smoltz	34-50	5th	12.5
7-6	At Atl.	W	7-3		10	6	Zambrano	Glavine		35-50	5th	11.5
7-7	At Atl.	L	0-2		3	6	Maddux	Lieber	Smoltz	35-51	5th	12.5
7-12	Fla.	W	5-4	(16)	10	13	Fassero	Pavano		36-51	5th	11.5
7-13	Fla.	W	9-2		13	3	Clement	Tavarez		37-51	5th	11.5
7-14	Fla.	W	10-3		13	9	Prior	Tejera	Farnsworth	38-51	5th	11.5
7-15	Atl.	W	3-2		7	7	Zambrano	Marquis	Alfonseca	39-51	5th	11.5
7-16	Atl.	L	0-2		2	8	Millwood	Lieber	Smoltz	39-52	5th	12.5
7-17	At Phi.	L	3-4	(10)	5	8	Mesa	Fassero		39-53	5th	12.5
7-18	At Phi.	W	6-4		10	9	Clement	Padilla		40-53	5th	12.5
7-19	Hou.	W	5-0		5	3	Prior	Cruz		41-53	5th	11.5
7-20	Hou.	L	2-3		6	4	Saarloos	Zambrano	Wagner	41-54	5th	11.5
7-21	Hou.	W	3-2		6	7	Fassero	Redding	Alfonseca	42-54	5th	11.5
7-22	Phi.	W	7-6		10	11	Farnsworth	Mesa		43-54	5th	11.5
7-23	Phi.	L	4-7		10	7	Coggin	Clement	Mesa	43-55	5th	12.5
7-24	Phi.	L	2-4		5	6	Myers	Prior	Mesa	43-56	5th	12.5
7-25	Phi.	L	2-6		6	9	Silva	Farnsworth		43-57	5th	13.5
7-26	At St.L.	L	4-8		7	13	Finley	Lieber		43-58	5th	14.5
7-27	At St.L.	W	7-3		8	7	Wood	Simontacchi		44-58	5th	13.5
7-28	At St.L.	L	9-10		9	14	Veres	Alfonseca		44-59	5th	14.5
7-30	S.D.	L	5-6		10	11	Holtz	Gordon	Hoffman	44-60	5th	15.5
7-31	S.D.	L	6-8	(11)	8	14	Villafuerte	Farnsworth	Hoffman	44-61	5th	15.5
8-1	S.D.	W	8-7		13	11	Gordon	Hoffman		45-61	5th	14.5
8-2	Col.	W	6-4	(12)	11	10	Borowski	Santos		46-61	5th	13.5
8-3	Col.	L	1-2		3	9	Neagle	Clement	Jimenez	46-62	5th	13.5
8-4	Col.	W	4-1		7	5	Prior	Chacon		47-62	5th	12.5
8-6	At S.F	L	10-11		14	12	Worrell	Farnsworth	Nen	47-63	5th	12.5
8-7	At S.F	L	3-4	(10)	7	10	Nen	Alfonseca		47-64	5th	12.5
8-8	At S.F	W	9-3		10	5	Clement	Hernandez		48-64	5th	12.5
8-9	At Col.	L	0-2		5	5	Neagle	Zambrano	Jimenez	48-65	5th	12.5
8-10	At Col.	W	15-1		20	6	Prior	Chacon		49-65	5th	12.5
8-11	At Col.	W	12-9		13	12	Smyth	Stark		50-65	5th	12.5
8-12	Hou.	L	6-9		7	13	Oswalt	Wood	Wagner	50-66	5th	13.5
8-13	Hou.	L	4-5		10	8	Munro	Clement	Wagner	50-67	5th	14.5
8-14	Hou.	L	3-4		7	4	Miller	Zambrano	Stone	50-68	5th	15.5
8-15	Hou.	W	6-4		10	7	Fassero	Saarloos	Alfonseca	51-68	5th	15.5
8-16	Ari.	L	1-2		7	6	Schilling	Smyth	Kim	51-69	5th	15.5
8-17	Ari.	L	2-6		10	11	Fetters	Farnsworth		51-70	5th	16.5
8-18	Ari.	W	3-2		8	5	Alfonseca	Mantei		52-70	5th	16.5
8-20	At Hou.	W	14-12		24	16	Cunnane	Puffer	Alfonseca	53-70	5th	16.0
8-21	At Hou.	L	0-4		7	12	Hernandez	Prior	Dotel	53-71	5th	17.0
8-22	At Hou.	L	1-9		7	13	Oswalt	Smyth		53-72	5th	18.0
8-23	At Ari.	L	2-3		9	3	Koplove	Wood	Kim	53-73	5th	18.0
8-24	At Ari.	W	4-0		9	3	Clement	Anderson		54-73	5th	17.0
8-25	At Ari.	L	0-7		6	7	Johnson	Zambrano		54-74	5th	17.0
8-26	At Mil.	L	1-2		6	3	Sheets	Prior	DeJean	54-75	5th	17.5
8-27	At Mil.	W	6-2		10	10	Benes	Osting		55-75	5th	17.0
8-28	At Mil.	L	1-5		7	9	Rusch	Wood	Vizcaino	55-76	5th	18.0
8-29	At Mil.	W	13-10		14	9	Clement	Lorraine		56-76	5th	17.0
8-30	St.L.	L	3-6		8	6	Wright	Zambrano	Veres	56-77	5th	18.0
8-31§	St.L.	L	1-8		9	11	Hackman	Prior		56-78		
8-31∞	St.L.	L	4-10		9	11	Benes	Bere		56-79	5th	20.0

Date	Opp.	Res.	Score	(inn.*)	Hits	Opp. hits	Winning pitcher	Losing pitcher	Save	Record	Pos.	GB
9-1	St.L.	W	5-4		6	7	Cruz	Finley	Alfonseca	57-79	5th	19.0
9-2†	Mil.	L	2-4		9	12	Rusch	Smyth	DeJean	57-80		
9-2‡	Mil.	W	17-4		14	8	Wood	Diggins		58-80	5th	18.5
9-3	Mil.	W	10-1		12	6	Clement	Pember		59-80	5th	18.5
9-4	Mil.	W	3-0		8	4	Zambrano	Figueroa	Alfonseca	60-80	5th	18.5
9-6	At St.L.	L	2-11		9	12	Benes	Benes		60-81	5th	19.5
9-7	At St.L.	L	5-6	(13)	10	12	Fassero	Alfonseca		60-82	5th	20.5
9-8	At St.L.	L	1-3		6	9	Simontacchi	Wood	Kline	60-83	5th	21.5
9-9	Mon.	W	3-2		7	7	Borowski	Brower		61-83	5th	21.5
9-10	Mon.	L	2-6		6	9	Vazquez	Zambrano		61-84	5th	22.5
9-11	Mon.	W	6-3		7	9	Benes	Yoshii	Alfonseca	62-84	5th	22.5
9-12	At Cin.	L	12-15		22	17	Riedling	Farnsworth	Williamson	62-85	5th	22.5
9-13	At Cin.	W	7-6		11	8	Wood	Reitsma	Alfonseca	63-85	5th	22.5
9-14	At Cin.	L	1-3		4	8	Dempster	Clement	Williamson	63-86	5th	23.5
9-15	At Cin.	W	6-0		9	7	Zambrano	Sullivan		64-86	5th	22.5
9-17	At N.Y.	L	1-3		4	7	Weathers	Cruz		64-87	5th	23.5
9-18	At N.Y.	L	1-2		5	6	Trachsel	Wood	Benitez	64-88	5th	24.5
9-19	At N.Y.	L	2-3	(12)	9	10	Roberts	Cunnane		64-89	5th	25.5
9-20	At Pit.	L	4-5		10	8	Sauerbeck	Alfonseca		64-90	5th	26.5
9-21	At Pit.	W	4-2		9	10	Farnsworth	Sauerbeck	Cruz	65-90	5th	25.5
9-22	At Pit.	L	4-5		9	10	Benson	Benes	Williams	65-91	5th	26.5
9-24	Cin.	L	0-1		4	6	Haynes	Wood	Williamson	65-92	5th	28.0
9-25	Cin.	L	2-8		6	12	Dempster	Clement		65-93	5th	29.0
9-26	Cin.	L	0-1		5	6	Graves	Zambrano	Williamson	65-94	5th	30.0
9-27	Pit.	L	3-13		11	19	Torres	Mahomes		65-95	5th	30.0
9-28	Pit.	W	5-4		7	8	Cruz	Boehringer		66-95	5th	30.0
9-29	Pit.	W	7-3		8	11	Wood	Fogg		67-95	5th	30.0

Monthly records: April (8-16), May (13-16), June (12-14), July (11-15), August (12-18), September (11-16).
*Innings, if other than nine. †First game of a doubleheader. ‡Second game of a doubleheader. §Day separate admission. ∞Night separate admission.

RECORDS

2002 regular-season record: 67-95
Position: 5th in N.L. Central
Home: 36-45   **Road:** 31-50
N.L. East: 12-18   **N.L. Central:** 36-54
N.L. West: 13-17   **A.L.:** 6-6
Vs. LH starters: 15-24
Vs. RH starters: 52-71
Grass: 65-92   **Artificial:** 2-3
Day: 38-49   **Night:** 29-46
1-Run: 18-36   **X-inn.:** 5-9
Doubleheaders: 0-1-2
Team record past five years: 377-434 (.465, ranks 12th in league in that span)

TEAM LEADERS

Batting average: Sammy Sosa (.288).
At-bats: Corey Patterson (592).
Runs: Sammy Sosa (122).
Hits: Sammy Sosa (160).
Total bases: Sammy Sosa (330).
Doubles: Corey Patterson (30).
Triples: Alex S. Gonzalez, Corey Patterson (5).
Home runs: Sammy Sosa (49).
Runs batted in: Sammy Sosa (108).
Stolen bases: Corey Patterson (18).
Slugging percentage: Sammy Sosa (.594).
On-base percentage: Sammy Sosa (.399).
Wins: Matt Clement, Kerry Wood (12).
Earned-run average: Mark Prior (3.32).
Complete games: Kerry Wood (4).
Shutouts: Matt Clement (2).
Saves: Antonio Alfonseca (19).
Innings pitched: Kerry Wood (213.2).
Strikeouts: Kerry Wood (217).

GAMES BY POSITION

Catcher: Joe Girardi 88, Todd Hundley 79, Robert Machado 21, Mike Mahoney 16.
First base: Fred McGriff 137, Mark Bellhorn 22, Hee Seop Choi 22, Angel Echevarria 13, Robert Machado 1.
Second base: Mark Bellhorn 77, Bobby Hill 55, Delino DeShields 41, Chris Stynes 20, Augie Ojeda 10.
Third base: Bill Mueller 101, Chris Stynes 40, Mark Bellhorn 36, Kevin Orie 12, Augie Ojeda 5.
Shortstop: Alex S. Gonzalez 142, Augie Ojeda 16, Mark Bellhorn 12, Bobby Hill 1.
Outfield: Sammy Sosa 150, Corey Patterson 147, Moises Alou 124, Roosevelt Brown 64, Darren Lewis 47, Chad Hermansen 21, Angel Echevarria 19, Mario Encarnacion 2, Mark Bellhorn 1, Delino DeShields 1.
Designated hitter: Moises Alou 2, Fred McGriff 2, Roosevelt Brown 1, Todd Hundley 1.

TOP DRAFT CHOICES

1a. **Bobby Brownlie**, RHP, Rutgers.
1b. **Luke Hagerty**, LHP, Ball State.
1c. **Chadd Blasko**, RHP, Purdue.
1d. **Matt Clanton**, RHP, Orange Coast (Calif.) J.C.
2a. **Brian Dopirak**, 1B, Dunedin (Fla.) H.S.
2b. **Justin Jones**, LHP, Kellam H.S., Virginia Beach.
3a. **Billy Petrick**, RHP, Morris (Ill.) H.S.
3b. **Matt Craig**, SS, Richmond.
4a. **Rich Hill**, LHP, Michigan.
4b. **Alan Rick**, C, Palatka (Fla.) H.S.
5. **Sean Scobee**, OF, Rio Linda (Calif.) H.S.
6. **Chris Walker**, OF, Georgia Southern.
7. **Joey Monahan**, SS, Liberty.
8. **Jason Fransz**, OF, Oklahoma.
9. **Adam Greenberg**, OF, North Carolina.
10. **Keith Butler**, OF, Liberty.

CINCINNATI REDS
NATIONAL LEAGUE CENTRAL DIVISION

2003 SEASON

March/April

SUN	MON	TUE	WED	THU	FRI	SAT
30	31 D PIT	1 PIT	2 PIT	3 D PIT	4 CUB	5 D CUB
6 D CUB	7	8 HOU	9 HOU	10 HOU	11 PHI	12 D PHI
13 D PHI	14 CUB	15 D CUB	16 D CUB	17 CUB	18 † MON	19 † MON
20 D† MON	21	22 LA	23 LA	24 LA	25 SD	26 D SD
27 D SD	28	29 COL	30 COL			

May

SUN	MON	TUE	WED	THU	FRI	SAT
				1 D COL	2 SF	3 D SF
4 D SF	5 STL	6 STL	7 STL	8 D STL	9 MIL	10 MIL
11 D MIL	12	13 STL	14 STL	15 D STL	16 MIL	17 D MIL
18 D MIL	19	20 ATL	21 ATL	22 ATL	23 FLA	24 FLA
25 D FLA	26 ATL	27 D ATL	28 ATL	29	30 FLA	31 FLA

June

SUN	MON	TUE	WED	THU	FRI	SAT
1 D FLA	2	3 NYY	4 NYY	5 NYY	6 TOR	7 TOR
8 D TOR	9	10 TB	11 TB	12 TB	13 PHI	14 PHI
15 D PHI	16 CUB	17 CUB	18 CUB	19 D CUB	20 ARI	21 ARI
22 D ARI	23	24 STL	25 STL	26 STL	27 CLE	28 D CLE
29 D CLE	30					

July

SUN	MON	TUE	WED	THU	FRI	SAT
		1 PIT	2 PIT	3 PIT	4 D NYM	5 NYM
6 D NYM	7 HOU	8 HOU	9 HOU	10 HOU	11 MIL	12 MIL
13 D MIL	14	15 *	16	17 HOU	18 HOU	19 D HOU
20 D HOU	21 MIL	22 MIL	23 PIT	24 D PIT	25 NYM	26 NYM
27 D NYM	28	29 COL	30 COL	31 COL		

August

SUN	MON	TUE	WED	THU	FRI	SAT
					1 SF	2 D SF
3 D SF	4	5 LA	6 LA	7 LA	8 SD	9 SD
10 D SD	11	12 ARI	13 ARI	14 ARI	15 HOU	16 D HOU
17 D HOU	18	19 ARI	20 ARI	21 ARI	22 HOU	23 HOU
24 D HOU	25 MIL	26 MIL	27 MIL	28 D MIL	29 STL	30 STL

September

SUN	MON	TUE	WED	THU	FRI	SAT
31 D STL	1 D MIL	2 MIL	3 MIL	4	5 STL	6 STL
7 D STL	8 PIT	9 PIT	10 PIT	11 PIT	12 D CUB	13 D CUB
14 D CUB	15 PIT	16 PIT	17 PIT	18 PIT	19 PHI	20 PHI
21 D PHI	22	23 CUB	24 CUB	25 CUB	26 MON	27 D MON
28 D MON						

Home games shaded; D—Day game (games starting before 5 p.m.); *—All-Star Game at Comiskey Park, Chicago. †—Game played in Puerto Rico. Subject to change.

CLUB DIRECTORY

General manager
Jim Bowden
Assistant general manager
Brad Kullman
Assistant g.m./director of scouting
Leland Maddox
Spec. asst. to the g.m. and sr. advisor/player development
Johnny Almaraz

Sr. special asst. to the g.m. & advance scout
Gene Bennett
Special assistants to the g.m.
Larry Barton Jr., Al Goldis, Darrell "Doc" Rodgers
Special consultants to the g.m.
Johnny Bench, Ken Griffey Sr.

Director of player development
Tim Naehring
Director of media relations
Rob Butcher
Dir. of communications and community relations
Michael Ringering

MINOR LEAGUE AFFILIATES

Class	Team	League	Manager
AAA	Louisville	International	Dave Miley
AA	Chattanooga	Southern	Phil Wellman
A	Potomac	Carolina	Jayhawk Owens
A	Dayton	Midwest	Donnie Scott
Rookie	Billings	Pioneer	Rick Burleson
Rookie	Gulf Coast Reds	Gulf Coast	Edgar Caceres

Follow the Reds all season at: www.sportingnews.com/baseball/teams/reds/

BROADCAST INFORMATION

Radio: WLW-AM (700).
Cable TV: Fox Sports Net.

SPRING TRAINING

Ballpark (city): Ed Smith Stadium (Sarasota, Fla.).
Ticket information: 941-954-4101.

SPRING TRAINING ROSTER

Manager—Bob Boone (9).
Coaches—Mark Berry (55), Jose Cardenal (33), Tim Foli (10), Don Gullett (35), Tom Hume (47), Ray Knight (25), Jim Lefebvre (4).

No.	PITCHERS	B/T	Ht./Wt.	Born	Age*	2002 clubs
29	Acevedo, Jose	R/R	6-0/185	12-18-77	25	Cincinnati, Louisville
87	Aramboles, Ricardo	R/R	6-4/220	12-4-81	21	Chattanooga
58	Booker, Chris	R/R	6-3/230	12-9-76	26	DID NOT PLAY
52	Chen, Bruce	L/L	6-2/210	6-19-77	25	New York N.L., Montreal, Cincinnati
40	Dempster, Ryan	R/R	6-3/215	5-3-77	25	Florida, Cincinnati
	Etherton, Seth	R/R	6-1/200	10-17-76	26	Dayton, Chattanooga, Louisville, Norwich
	Gamble, Jerome	R/R	6-2/202	4-5-80	22	Augusta
32	Graves, Danny	R/R	6-0/185	8-7-73	29	Cincinnati
	Hall, Josh	R/R	6-2/175	12-16-80	22	Stockton, Chattanooga
43	Haynes, Jimmy	R/R	6-4/219	9-5-72	30	Cincinnati
54	Hudson, Luke	R/R	6-3/195	5-2-77	25	Louisville, Cincinnati
	Prokopec, Luke	L/R	5-11/175	2-23-78	25	Toronto, Syracuse
	Reith, Brian	R/R	6-5/220	2-28-78	25	Scranton/Wilkes-Barre, Louisville
41	Reitsma, Chris	R/R	6-5/215	12-31-77	25	Cincinnati, Louisville
46	Riedling, John	R/R	5-11/190	8-29-75	27	Chattanooga, Louisville, Cincinnati
56	Sullivan, Scott	R/R	6-3/210	3-13-71	32	Cincinnati
36	White, Gabe	L/L	6-2/204	11-20-71	31	Cincinnati
	Williams, Blake	R/R	6-5/210	2-22-79	24	New Jersey
48	Williamson, Scott	R/R	6-0/185	2-17-76	27	Cincinnati
	Wilson, Paul	R/R	6-5/214	3-28-73	30	Tampa Bay

No.	CATCHERS	B/T	Ht./Wt.	Born	Age*	2002 clubs
23	LaRue, Jason	R/R	5-11/200	3-19-74	29	Cincinnati
37	Miller, Corky	R/R	6-1/225	3-18-76	27	Louisville, Cincinnati
70	Sardinha, Dane	R/R	5-11/205	4-8-79	23	Chattanooga
31	Stinnett, Kelly	R/R	5-11/225	2-4-70	33	Cincinnati, Louisville

No.	INFIELDERS	B/T	Ht./Wt.	Born	Age*	2002 clubs
17	Boone, Aaron	R/R	6-2/200	3-9-73	30	Cincinnati
33	Branyan, Russell	L/R	6-3/195	12-19-75	27	Cleveland, Cincinnati
21	Casey, Sean	L/R	6-4/225	7-2-74	28	Cincinnati, Louisville
7	Castro, Juan	R/R	5-11/195	6-20-72	30	Louisville, Cincinnati
3	Dawkins, Gookie	R/R	6-1/180	5-12-79	23	Cincinnati, Chattanooga, Louisville
11	Larkin, Barry	R/R	6-0/185	4-28-64	38	Cincinnati
16	Larson, Brandon	R/R	6-0/210	5-24-76	26	Louisville, Cincinnati
	Lopez, Felipe	B/R	6-0/185	5-12-80	22	Toronto, Syracuse
	Olmedo, Ranier	R/R	5-11/155	5-31-81	21	Chattanooga

No.	OUTFIELDERS	B/T	Ht./Wt.	Born	Age*	2002 clubs
44	Dunn, Adam	L/R	6-6/240	11-9-79	23	Cincinnati
30	Griffey, Ken	L/L	6-3/205	11-21-69	33	Cincinnati
6	Guillen, Jose	R/R	5-11/195	5-17-76	26	Arizona, Colorado Springs, Louisville, Cincinnati
28	Kearns, Austin	R/R	6-3/220	5-20-80	22	Chattanooga, Cincinnati, Louisville
15	Mateo, Ruben	R/R	6-0/185	2-10-78	25	Louisville, Cincinnati
26	Pena, Wily	R/R	6-3/215	1-23-82	21	Chattanooga, Cincinnati
	Smitherman, Steve	R/R	6-4/230	9-1-78	24	Stockton
19	Taylor, Reggie	L/R	6-1/178	1-12-77	26	Cincinnati

*Age as of April 1, 2003.

BALLPARK INFORMATION

Ballpark (capacity, surface)
Great American Ball Park (42,000, grass)
Address
100 Main St.
Cincinnati, OH 45202
Official website
www.cincinnatireds.com
Business phone
513-765-7000
Ticket information
513-765-7400
Field dimensions (from home plate)
To left field at foul line, 328 feet
To center field, 404 feet
To right field at foul line, 325 feet
First game played
Scheduled for March 31, 2003 vs. Pittsburgh

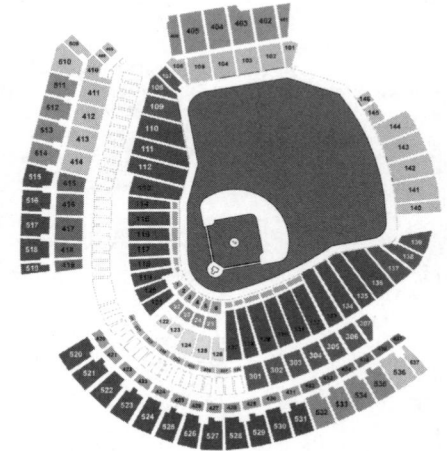

Cincinnati Reds

2003 SEASON

Date	Opp.	Res.	Score	(inn.*)	Hits	Opp. hits	Winning pitcher	Losing pitcher	Save	Record	Pos.	GB
4-1	Chi.	W	5-4		12	10	Graves	Fassero		1-0	T1st	...
4-3	Chi.	L	3-10		6	13	Wood	Dessens		1-1	T1st	...
4-4	Chi.	W	3-1		3	8	Acevedo	Cruz	Graves	2-1	T1st	...
4-5	Mon.	L	7-8		13	12	Yoshii	Haynes	Lloyd	2-2	T2nd	1.0
4-6	Mon.	L	2-5		5	7	Ohka	Pineda	Lloyd	2-3	T3rd	2.0
4-7	Mon.	W	6-5	(10)	15	11	Sullivan	Lloyd		3-3	T2nd	1.5
4-8	At Pit.	L	0-1		4	4	Villone	Dessens	Williams	3-4	4th	2.5
4-10	At Pit.	W	8-5		13	6	Acevedo	Wells	Graves	4-4	3rd	1.5
4-11	At Pit.	W	3-2		8	7	Haynes	Anderson	Graves	5-4	3rd	1.0
4-12	At Phi.	W	8-5		12	11	Brower	Cormier	Graves	6-4	2nd	1.0
4-13	At Phi.	W	5-2		10	9	Hamilton	Person	Graves	7-4	2nd	1.0
4-14	At Phi.	L	1-3		6	8	Padilla	Dessens	Mesa	7-5	2nd	1.0
4-16	Hou.	L	3-8		7	11	Mlicki	Acevedo		7-6	3rd	1.0
4-17	Hou.	L	2-7		4	8	Hernandez	Haynes		7-7	T3rd	2.0
4-18	Hou.	W	5-4	(10)	14	11	White	Cruz		8-7	3rd	1.5
4-19	At Chi.	L	2-5		7	5	Clement	Hamilton	Alfonseca	8-8	3rd	2.5
4-20	At Chi.	W	6-1		9	7	Dessens	Wood		9-8	2nd	2.5
4-21	At Chi.	W	5-3		5	7	Rijo	Cruz	Graves	10-8	2nd	2.5
4-23	Col.	W	3-2		7	6	Haynes	Jennings	Graves	11-8	2nd	1.5
4-24	Col.	W	4-3		10	8	Williamson	Jimenez		12-8	2nd	0.5
4-25	Col.	W	4-3		7	9	Sullivan	White	Graves	13-8	2nd	0.5
4-26	S.F	W	4-3		9	8	Sullivan	Rodriguez	Graves	14-8	1st	+0.5
4-27	S.F	W	8-4	(8)	9	8	Rijo	Jensen		15-8	1st	+1.0
4-28	S.F	L	4-5		6	10	Rueter	Haynes	Nen	15-9	1st	+0.5
4-30	At L.A.	W	3-1		7	8	Reitsma	Brown	Graves	16-9	1st	+1.5
5-1	At L.A.	W	4-0		5	8	Hamilton	Nomo		17-9	1st	+2.5
5-2	At L.A.	L	2-3	(14)	5	12	Carrara	Pineda		17-10	1st	+2.5
5-3	At S.F	L	1-6		10	9	Rueter	Rijo		17-11	1st	+1.5
5-4	At S.F	L	0-3		2	6	Jensen	Haynes	Nen	17-12	1st	+1.5
5-5	At S.F	L	5-6	(10)	10	11	Nen	Pineda		17-13	1st	+1.5
5-6	Mil.	W	8-5		10	12	Brower	Quevedo	Graves	18-13	1st	+1.5
5-7	Mil.	W	8-2		15	5	Dessens	Rusch		19-13	1st	+2.5
5-8	Mil.	W	14-5		13	10	Acevedo	Neugebauer		20-13	1st	+3.5
5-10	St.L.	L	2-4		7	11	Stechschulte	White	Isringhausen	20-14	1st	+2.5
5-11	St.L.	W	8-1		10	5	Reitsma	Kile		21-14	1st	+2.5
5-12	St.L.	L	8-10		9	14	Stechschulte	Graves	Isringhausen	21-15	1st	+2.5
5-13	At Mil.	W	5-0		9	5	Rijo	Cabrera		22-15	1st	+3.5
5-14	At Mil.	W	4-3		5	5	Acevedo	Quevedo	Graves	23-15	1st	+3.5
5-15	At Mil.	W	7-4		15	8	Haynes	Stull	Graves	24-15	1st	+4.5
5-16	At Mil.	W	2-1	(11)	5	6	White	DeJean	Graves	25-15	1st	+5.0
5-17	At St.L.	L	1-3		2	8	Kile	Sullivan	Isringhausen	25-16	1st	+4.0
5-18	At St.L.	W	7-3		11	5	Rijo	Morris		26-16	1st	+5.0
5-19	At St.L.	L	1-10		7	10	Stephenson	Acevedo		26-17	1st	+4.0
5-20	At St.L.	L	3-7		10	6	Williams	Haynes		26-18	1st	+3.0
5-21	Fla.	W	6-1		6	7	Reitsma	Burnett	Graves	27-18	1st	+3.0
5-22	Fla.	W	6-2		8	7	Dessens	Dempster		28-18	1st	+3.0
5-23	Fla.	L	4-8		12	9	Tavarez	Rijo	Nunez	28-19	1st	+2.0
5-24	At Atl.	L	2-11		10	15	Millwood	Hamilton		28-20	1st	+2.0
5-25	At Atl.	W	6-4		10	10	Haynes	Marquis	Graves	29-20	1st	+2.0
5-26	At Atl.	L	5-7		11	10	Maddux	Reitsma		29-21	1st	+1.0
5-28	At Fla.	W	6-5	(11)	10	14	Graves	Nunez		30-21	1st	+0.5
5-29	At Fla.	W	8-2		14	11	Hamilton	Beckett		31-21	1st	+1.5
5-30	At Fla.	W	4-1		7	7	Haynes	Olsen	Graves	32-21	1st	+2.0
5-31	Atl.	L	0-7		4	13	Maddux	Reitsma		32-22	1st	+2.0
6-1	Atl.	L	1-7		6	10	Glavine	Rijo		32-23	1st	+1.0
6-2	Atl.	W	5-1		6	9	Dessens	Moss		33-23	1st	+2.0
6-4	St.L.	L	5-8		11	9	Simontacchi	Hamilton		33-24	1st	+1.0
6-6	St.L.	W	3-2		7	9	Haynes	Williams	Graves	34-24	1st	+2.0
6-7	At Ana.	L	3-4		11	8	Sele	Reitsma	Percival	34-25	1st	+1.0
6-8	At Ana.	W	4-3		6	8	White	Cook	Graves	35-25	1st	+1.0
6-9	At Ana.	L	4-7		11	9	Schoeneweis	Hamilton	Percival	35-26	1st	+1.0
6-10	At Tex.	L	2-8		11	9	Valdes	Almanzar		35-27	1st	+1.0
6-11	At Tex.	W	8-5		11	9	Haynes	Rogers	Graves	36-27	1st	+1.0
6-12	At Tex.	L	4-10		4	9	Rocker	Sullivan		36-28	1st	+1.0
6-14	Pit.	W	4-3	(11)	9	12	Williamson	Williams		37-28	1st	+1.0

Date	Opp.	Res.	Score	(inn.*)	Hits	Opp. hits	Winning pitcher	Losing pitcher	Save	Record	Pos.	GB
6-15	Pit.	W	4-3		9	9	Sullivan	Lincoln	Graves	38-28	1st	+1.0
6-16	Pit.	L	1-5		5	10	Anderson	Haynes		38-29	T1st	...
6-18	Sea.	L	1-8		8	9	Pineiro	Reitsma		38-30	2nd	1.0
6-19	Sea.	L	0-2		5	7	Garcia	Dessens	Sasaki	38-31	2nd	2.0
6-20	Sea.	L	2-3		6	11	Baldwin	Hamilton	Sasaki	38-32	2nd	2.0
6-21	Oak.	L	3-5		7	8	Harang	Williamson	Koch	38-33	2nd	2.0
6-22	Oak.	L	3-10		3	10	Zito	Chen		38-34	2nd	2.5
6-23	Oak.	L	1-5		7	9	Mulder	Reitsma		38-35	2nd	2.5
6-24	At Chi.	L	4-6		8	10	Fassero	Williamson	Alfonseca	38-36	2nd	3.0
6-25	At Chi.	W	5-2		7	8	Pineda	Clement	Graves	39-36	2nd	2.0
6-26	At Chi.	W	8-6		11	14	Haynes	Bere	Graves	40-36	2nd	2.0
6-27	At Chi.	W	5-4	(10)	11	7	Graves	Farnsworth		41-36	2nd	1.0
6-28	At St.L.	L	2-3		10	8	Simontacchi	Reitsma	Isringhausen	41-37	2nd	2.0
6-29	At St.L.	W	4-2		11	9	Dessens	Hackman	Graves	42-37	2nd	1.0
6-30	At St.L.	W	12-8		16	13	Sullivan	Isringhausen		43-37	2nd	...
7-1	Hou.	W	7-5		9	9	Haynes	Hernandez	Graves	44-37	2nd	...
7-2	Hou.	L	5-6	(10)	15	10	Dotel	Graves	Wagner	44-38	2nd	1.0
7-3	Hou.	L	4-11		9	13	Oswalt	Reitsma		44-39	2nd	2.0
7-4	Mil.	L	4-5		7	9	Durocher	Graves	DeJean	44-40	2nd	3.0
7-5	Mil.	W	8-6		9	12	White	Rusch	Graves	45-40	2nd	2.0
7-6	Mil.	W	6-4		9	12	Haynes	Wright	Sullivan	46-40	2nd	1.0
7-7	Mil.	L	4-7		9	14	de los Santos	Hamilton		46-41	2nd	2.0
7-11	At Hou.	L	3-4		8	6	Oswalt	Dessens	Wagner	46-42	2nd	2.5
7-12	At Hou.	L	3-6		11	7	Miller	Dempster	Wagner	46-43	2nd	2.5
7-13	At Hou.	L	1-2		6	10	Munro	Sullivan	Dotel	46-44	2nd	3.5
7-14	At Hou.	W	8-3		15	10	Fernandez	Redding	Graves	47-44	2nd	3.5
7-15	At Mil.	W	2-0		10	5	Reitsma	Cabrera		48-44	2nd	3.5
7-16	At Mil.	W	6-1		9	4	Dessens	Sheets		49-44	2nd	3.5
7-17	At Pit.	L	3-6		7	7	Anderson	Dempster	Williams	49-45	2nd	3.5
7-18	At Pit.	W	7-5		12	9	Sullivan	Boehringer	Graves	50-45	2nd	3.5
7-19	N.Y.	L	2-4		7	10	Astacio	Fernandez	Benitez	50-46	2nd	3.5
7-20	N.Y.	L	7-8		12	11	Weathers	Reitsma	Benitez	50-47	2nd	3.5
7-21	N.Y.	W	9-1		11	7	Dessens	Leiter		51-47	2nd	3.5
7-22	Pit.	L	5-6		14	12	Anderson	Dempster	Williams	51-48	2nd	4.5
7-23	Pit.	W	7-2		12	7	Haynes	Wells		52-48	2nd	4.5
7-24	Pit.	W	10-5		9	11	Moehler	Beimel		53-48	2nd	3.5
7-26	At N.Y.	L	2-3		6	8	Guthrie	Riedling		53-49	2nd	5.0
7-27	At N.Y.	W	2-1	(11)	9	5	Graves	Corey		54-49	2nd	4.0
7-28	At N.Y.	L	5-6		8	12	Trachsel	Williamson	Benitez	54-50	2nd	5.0
7-30	L.A.	W	12-4		10	10	Dempster	Ishii		55-50	2nd	5.0
7-31	L.A.	L	5-11		12	15	Nomo	Moehler		55-51	2nd	5.0
8-1	L.A.	W	6-4	(13)	7	13	Williamson	Daal		56-51	2nd	4.0
8-2	At S.D.	L	2-5		5	12	Lawrence	Fernandez	Hoffman	56-52	2nd	4.0
8-3	At S.D.	W	4-3		6	11	Haynes	Tomko	Graves	57-52	2nd	3.0
8-4	At S.D.	W	15-10		17	13	White	Hoffman		58-52	2nd	2.0
8-6	At Col.	L	6-7		5	15	Stark	Moehler	Jimenez	58-53	T2nd	2.0
8-7	At Col.	L	2-7		5	7	Jennings	Hamilton		58-54	3rd	2.0
8-8	At Col.	L	3-10		5	17	Hampton	Haynes		58-55	3rd	3.0
8-9	S.D.	W	12-10		14	14	Riedling	Tomko		59-55	T2nd	2.0
8-10	S.D.	W	9-0		16	5	Dempster	Jones		60-55	T2nd	2.0
8-11	S.D.	W	9-7	(12)	11	10	Rijo	Villafuerte		61-55	2nd	2.0
8-13	Ari.	L	1-6		6	7	Helling	Haynes		61-56	3rd	3.5
8-14	Ari.	L	2-7		6	10	Anderson	Riedling		61-57	3rd	4.5
8-15	Ari.	L	2-7		4	11	Johnson	Dempster	Myers	61-58	3rd	5.5
8-16	Hou.	W	9-3		13	8	Moehler	Mlicki		62-58	3rd	4.5
8-17	Hou.	L	1-6		6	15	Oswalt	Hamilton		62-59	T3rd	5.5
8-18	Hou.	W	2-1	(10)	4	3	White	Stone		63-59	3rd	5.5
8-19	Hou.	L	5-7		8	9	Miller	Fernandez	Wagner	63-60	3rd	6.5
8-20	At Ari.	L	3-5		9	7	Fetters	Hamilton	Kim	63-61	3rd	6.5
8-21	At Ari.	L	3-11		6	13	Schilling	Moehler		63-62	3rd	7.5
8-22	At Ari.	L	3-6		8	7	Batista	Reitsma	Kim	63-63	3rd	8.5
8-23	At Hou.	L	4-6		10	10	Munro	Estes	Wagner	63-64	3rd	8.5
8-24	At Hou.	W	5-3	(11)	6	9	Graves	Gordon		64-64	3rd	7.5
8-25	At Hou.	L	0-1		5	3	Saarloos	Dempster	Borbon	64-65	3rd	7.5
8-27†	St.L.	W	5-4		9	14	Reitsma	Simontacchi	Graves	65-65		
8-27‡	St.L.	L	0-5		2	9	Finley	Dessens		65-66	3rd	7.5
8-28	St.L.	L	2-9		6	12	Kline	Estes		65-67	3rd	8.5
8-29	St.L.	W	7-0		11	7	Haynes	Williams		66-67	3rd	7.5
8-30	Mil.	L	4-9		11	11	King	Sullivan		66-68	3rd	8.5
8-31	Mil.	L	2-11		8	17	Sheets	Reitsma		66-69	3rd	10.0

Date	Opp.	Res.	Score	(inn.*)	Hits	Opp. hits	Winning pitcher	Losing pitcher	Save	Record	Pos.	GB
9-1	Mil.	L	2-4		8	6	Cabrera	Dessens	DeJean	66-70	3rd	10.0
9-2	At St.L.	W	5-3		12	6	Estes	Stephenson	Graves	67-70	3rd	9.0
9-3	At St.L.	L	1-3		5	8	Williams	Haynes	Veres	67-71	3rd	10.0
9-4	At St.L.	L	5-10		11	12	Hackman	Chen		67-72	3rd	11.0
9-6	At Mil.	W	5-3	(12)	11	7	Graves	DeJean	Hamilton	68-72	3rd	11.0
9-7	At Mil.	L	6-9		8	13	Rusch	Estes	DeJean	68-73	3rd	12.0
9-8	At Mil.	W	5-4		9	12	Haynes	Neugebauer	Graves	69-73	3rd	12.0
9-9	Pit.	W	9-8		10	12	Dempster	Torres	Williamson	70-73	3rd	12.0
9-10	Pit.	W	3-0		8	6	Reitsma	Wells	Williamson	71-73	3rd	12.0
9-11	Pit.	L	1-4		4	4	Villone	Dessens	Williams	71-74	3rd	13.0
9-12	Chi.	W	15-12		17	22	Riedling	Farnsworth	Williamson	72-74	3rd	12.0
9-13	Chi.	L	6-7		8	11	Wood	Reitsma	Alfonseca	72-75	3rd	13.0
9-14	Chi.	W	3-1		8	4	Dempster	Clement	Williamson	73-75	3rd	13.0
9-15	Chi.	L	0-6		7	9	Zambrano	Sullivan		73-76	3rd	13.0
9-16	At Pit.	W	4-3		12	7	Silva	Lincoln	Williamson	74-76	3rd	12.5
9-17	At Pit.	L	3-11		7	9	Benson	Reitsma		74-77	3rd	13.5
9-18	At Pit.	L	2-3		4	7	Lincoln	Riedling	Williams	74-78	3rd	14.5
9-19	At Pit.	W	5-4		9	14	Hamilton	Williams	Williamson	75-78	3rd	14.5
9-21§	Phi.	L	3-5	(10)	6	14	Adams	Williamson	Mesa	75-79		
9-21∞	Phi.	L	4-5	(11)	10	12	Adams	Hamilton	Mesa	75-80	3rd	15.5
9-22	Phi.	L	3-4		8	9	Duckworth	Rijo	Mesa	75-81	3rd	16.5
9-24	At Chi.	W	1-0		6	4	Haynes	Wood	Williamson	76-81	3rd	17.0
9-25	At Chi.	W	8-2		12	6	Dempster	Clement		77-81	3rd	17.0
9-26	At Chi.	W	1-0		6	5	Graves	Zambrano	Williamson	78-81	3rd	17.0
9-27	At Mon.	L	3-4	(11)	8	10	Eischen	Riedling		78-82	3rd	17.0
9-28	At Mon.	L	0-6		6	8	Kim	Moehler		78-83	3rd	18.0
9-29	At Mon.	L	2-7		5	7	Drew	Haynes		78-84	3rd	19.0

Monthly records: April (16-9), May (16-13), June (11-15), July (12-14), August (11-18), September (12-15).

*Innings, if other than nine. †First game of a doubleheader. ‡Second game of a doubleheader. §Day separate admission. ∞Night separate admission.

RECORDS

2002 regular-season record: 78-84
Position: 3rd in N.L. Central
Home: 38-43   **Road:** 40-41
N.L. East: 12-18   **N.L. Central:** 50-40
N.L. West: 14-16   **A.L.:** 2-10
Vs. LH starters: 17-21
Vs. RH starters: 61-63
Grass: 76-80   **Artificial:** 2-4
Day: 30-28   **Night:** 48-56
1-Run: 26-23   **X-inn.:** 12-6
Doubleheaders: 0-0-1
Team record past five years: 402-409
(.496, ranks 8th in league in that span)

TEAM LEADERS

Batting average: Austin Kearns (.315).
At-bats: Todd Walker (612).
Runs: Adam Dunn (84).
Hits: Todd Walker (183).
Total bases: Aaron Boone (266).
Doubles: Todd Walker (42).
Triples: Reggie Taylor (4).
Home runs: Aaron Boone, Adam Dunn (26).
Runs batted in: Aaron Boone (87).
Stolen bases: Aaron Boone (32).

Slugging percentage: Austin Kearns (.500).
On-base percentage: Austin Kearns (.407).
Wins: Jimmy Haynes (15).
Earned-run average: Elmer Dessens (3.03).
Complete games: Ryan Dempster, Chris Reitsma (1).
Shutouts: Chris Reitsma (1).
Saves: Danny Graves (32).
Innings pitched: Jimmy Haynes (196.2).
Strikeouts: Jimmy Haynes (126).

GAMES BY POSITION

Catcher: Jason LaRue 110, Corky Miller 38, Kelly Stinnett 30.
First base: Sean Casey 108, Adam Dunn 44, Russell Branyan 18, Brandon Larson 2, Juan Castro 1.
Second base: Todd Walker 154, Juan Castro 17, Wilton Guerrero 10, Gookie Dawkins 3.
Third base: Aaron Boone 154, Russell Branyan 16, Brandon Larson 5, Wilton Guerrero 3, Juan Castro 1.
Shortstop: Barry Larkin 135, Juan Castro 25, Gookie Dawkins 21, Aaron Boone 16, Wilton Guerrero 7.

Outfield: Adam Dunn 119, Austin Kearns 103, Reggie Taylor 103, Juan Encarnacion 82, Ken Griffey Jr. 55, Jose Guillen 27, Russell Branyan 25, Ruben Mateo 24, Brady Clark 22, Brandon Larson 9, Raul Gonzalez 6, Wily Mo Pena 4.
Designated hitter: Russell Branyan 4, Sean Casey 1, Adam Dunn 1.

TOP DRAFT CHOICES

1a. **Chris Gruler,** RHP, Liberty Union H.S., Brentwood, Calif.
1b. **Mark Schramek,** 3B, Texas-San Antonio.
2. **Joey Votto,** C, Richview Collegiate Institute, Toronto.
3. **Kyle Edens,** RHP, Baylor.
4. **Camilio Vazquez,** LHP, Hialeah (Fla.) H.S.
5. **Kevin Howard,** 3B, Miami (Fla.).
6. **Walter Olmstead,** 1B, Texas Christian.
7. **Corey Wachman,** RHP, Valdosta State (Ga.).
8. **O.J. King,** RHP, Northwestern State (La.).
9. **Steve Booth,** C, San Francisco.
10. **Frankie Keller,** LHP, Abilene Christian (Tex.).

COLORADO ROCKIES
NATIONAL LEAGUE WEST DIVISION

2003 SEASON

March/April

SUN	MON	TUE	WED	THU	FRI	SAT
30	31	1 HOU	2 HOU	3 D HOU	4 ARI	5 D ARI
6 D ARI	7	8 STL	9 STL	10 STL	11 SD	12 SD
13 D SD	14 ARI	15 ARI	16 ARI	17 ARI	18 SD	19 D SD
20 D SD	21	22 PHI	23 PHI	24 D PHI	25 CUB	26 D CUB
27 D CUB	28	29 CIN	30 CIN			

July

SUN	MON	TUE	WED	THU	FRI	SAT
		1 ARI	2 ARI	3 ARI	4 D MIL	5 MIL
6 D MIL	7 ARI	8 ARI	9 SF	10 SF	11 LA	12 LA
13 D LA	14	15 *	16	17 SF	18 SF	19 D SF
20 D SF	21 LA	22 LA	23 LA	24 D LA	25 MIL	26 MIL
27 D MIL	28	29 CIN	30 CIN	31 CIN		

May

SUN	MON	TUE	WED	THU	FRI	SAT
				1 D CIN	2 D CUB	3 D CUB
4 D CUB	5	6 ATL	7 ATL	8 ATL	9 FLA	10 FLA
11 D FLA	12 NYM	13 NYM	14 D NYM	15 MON	16 MON	17 D MON
18 MON	19	20 LA	21 LA	22 D LA	23 SF	24 D SF
25 D SF	26 D SF	27 LA	28 LA	29 D LA	30 SF	31 D SF

August

SUN	MON	TUE	WED	THU	FRI	SAT
					1 PIT	2 PIT
3 D PIT	4	5 PHI	6 PHI	7 D PHI	8 PIT	9 PIT
10 D PIT	11 MON	12 MON	13 MON	14	15 NYM	16 NYM
17 NYM	18 D NYM	19 FLA	20 FLA	21 FLA	22 ATL	23 ATL
24 D ATL	25	26 SF	27 SF	28 D SF	29 LA	30 LA

June

SUN	MON	TUE	WED	THU	FRI	SAT
1 D SF	2 SF	3 CLE	4 CLE	5 D CLE	6 D KC	7 KC
8 D KC	9	10 MIN	11 MIN	12 MIN	13 DET	14 DET
15 D DET	16 SD	17 SD	18 SD	19 SD	20 DET	21 DET
22 D DET	23 SD	24 SD	25 SD	26	27 PIT	28 PIT
29 D PIT	30 ARI					

September

SUN	MON	TUE	WED	THU	FRI	SAT
31 LA	1	2 SF	3 D SF	4	5 LA	6 D LA
7 D LA	8	9 STL	10 STL	11 D STL	12 ARI	13 ARI
14 D ARI	15	16 HOU	17 HOU	18 D HOU	19 SD	20 D SD
21 D SD	22	23 ARI	24 ARI	25 ARI	26 SD	27 SD
28 D SD						

Home games shaded; D—Day game (games starting before 5 p.m.); *—All-Star Game at Comiskey Park, Chicago. Subject to change.

CLUB DIRECTORY

Chairman and chief executive officer
Jerry D. McMorris
Vice chairmen
Charles K. Monfort, Richard L. Monfort
President
Keli S. McGregor

Executive vice president, g.m.
Daniel J. O'Dowd
Sr. director, communications/p.r.
Jay Alves
Sr. director, community & retail ops.
Jim Kellogg

Director, player personnel
Bill Geivett
Director, major league operations
Paul Egins
Director, scouting
Bill Schmidt

MINOR LEAGUE AFFILIATES

Class	Team	League	Manager
AAA	Colorado Springs	Pacific Coast	Rick Sofield
AA	Tulsa	Texas	Marv Foley
A	Visalia	California	Stu Cole
A	Asheville	South Atlantic	Joe Mikulik
A	Tri-City	Northwest	Ron Gideon
Rookie	Casper	Pioneer	P.J. Carey

BROADCAST INFORMATION

Radio: KOA-AM (850), KCUV-AM (1150).
TV: KWGN-TV (Channel 2).
Cable TV: Fox Sports Rocky Mountain.

SPRING TRAINING

Ballpark (city): Hi Corbett Field (Tucson, Ariz.).
Ticket information: 1-800-388-ROCK.

Follow the Rockies all season at: www.sportingnews.com/baseball/teams/rockies/

Manager—Clint Hurdle (13).
Coaches—Sandy Alomar Sr., Brad Andress (00), Bob Apodaca, Dave Collins, Duane Espy, Rick Mathews, Jamie Quirk, Mark Strittmatter.

No.	PITCHERS	B/T	Ht./Wt.	Born	Age*	2002 clubs
34	Chacon, Shawn	R/R	6-3/212	12-23-77	25	Colorado, Colorado Springs
35	Cook, Aaron	R/R	6-3/175	2-8-79	24	Carolina, Colorado Springs, Colorado
41	Cruz, Nelson	R/R	6-1/185	9-13-72	30	Houston, New Orleans
50	Elarton, Scott	R/R	6-7/240	2-23-76	27	DID NOT PLAY
57	Esslinger, Cam	R/R	6-0/180	12-28-76	26	Colorado Springs, Carolina
51	Flores, Randy	L/L	6-0/180	7-31-75	27	Oklahoma, Texas, Colorado Springs, Colorado
39	Fuentes, Brian	L/L	6-4/220	8-9-75	27	Colorado Springs, Colorado
32	Jennings, Jason	L/R	6-2/242	7-17-78	24	Colorado
16	Jimenez, Jose	R/R	6-3/228	7-7-73	29	Colorado
59	Jones, Todd	B/R	6-3/230	4-24-68	34	Colorado
15	Neagle, Denny	L/L	6-3/225	9-13-68	34	Colorado
30	Speier, Justin	R/R	6-4/205	11-6-73	29	Colorado Springs, Colorado
41	Stark, Dennis	R/R	6-2/210	10-27-74	28	Colorado Springs, Colorado
53	Vance, Cory	L/L	6-1/195	6-20-79	23	Carolina, Colorado
62	Young, Colin	L/L	6-0/185	8-1-77	25	Carolina

No.	CATCHERS	B/T	Ht./Wt.	Born	Age*	2002 clubs
8	Estalella, Bobby	R/R	6-1/213	8-23-74	28	Colorado Springs, Colorado
	Johnson, Charles	R/R	6-3/250	7-20-71	31	Florida

No.	INFIELDERS	B/T	Ht./Wt.	Born	Age*	2002 clubs
5	Butler, Brent	R/R	6-0/180	2-11-78	25	Colorado, Colorado Springs
	Eberwein, Kevin	R/R	6-4/200	3-30-77	26	Lake Elsinore, Portland
23	Gload, Ross	L/L	6-0/185	4-5-76	26	Colorado Springs, Colorado
17	Helton, Todd	L/L	6-2/204	8-20-73	29	Colorado
28	Holliday, Matt	R/R	6-4/235	1-1-80	23	Carolina
14	Norton, Greg	B/R	6-1/200	7-6-72	30	Colorado, Colorado Springs
	Ozuna, Pablo	R/R	6-0/160	8-25-74	28	Calgary, Florida
3	Romano, Jason	R/R	6-0/185	6-24-79	23	Oklahoma, Texas, Colorado Springs, Colorado
	Stynes, Chris	R/R	5-10/205	1-19-73	30	Chicago N.L.
4	Uribe, Juan	R/R	5-11/173	7-22-79	23	Colorado

No.	OUTFIELDERS	B/T	Ht./Wt.	Born	Age*	2002 clubs
21	Cust, Jack	L/R	6-1/205	1-16-79	24	Colorado Springs, Colorado
27	Payton, Jay	R/R	5-10/185	11-22-72	30	New York N.L., Colorado
6	Petrick, Ben	R/R	6-0/200	4-7-77	25	Colorado, Colorado Springs
	Reyes, Rene	B/R	5-11/215	2-21-78	25	Carolina
33	Walker, Larry	L/R	6-3/233	12-1-66	36	Colorado
44	Wilson, Preston	R/R	6-2/213	7-19-74	28	Florida

*Age as of April 1, 2003.

2003 SEASON *Colorado Rockies*

BALLPARK INFORMATION

Ballpark (capacity, surface)
Coors Field (50,449, grass)
Address
2001 Blake St.
Denver, CO 80205-2000
Official website
www.coloradorockies.com
Business phone
303-292-0200
Ticket information
800-388-7625
Field dimensions (from home plate)
To left field at foul line, 347 feet
To center field, 415 feet
To right field at foul line, 350
First game played
April 26, 1995 (Rockies 11, Mets 9, 14 innings)

2003 SEASON *Colorado Rockies*

Date	Opp.	Res.	Score	(inn.*)	Hits	Opp. hits	Winning pitcher	Losing pitcher	Save	Record	Pos.	GB
4-1	At St.L.	L	2-10		8	14	Morris	Hampton		0-1	T4th	1.0
4-3	At St.L.	W	6-3		7	9	Neagle	Stephenson	Jimenez	1-1	3rd	1.0
4-4	At St.L.	W	6-1		5	8	Thomson	Benes		2-1	T2nd	1.0
4-5	At L.A.	L	0-9		1	11	Ashby	Chacon		2-2	T2nd	2.0
4-6	At L.A.	L	2-9		7	9	Ishii	Jennings		2-3	T3rd	3.0
4-7	At L.A.	L	4-6		10	13	Brown	Hampton	Gagne	2-4	4th	4.0
4-8	Hou.	L	4-8		13	10	Oswalt	Neagle		2-5	T4th	4.5
4-9	Hou.	W	10-5		13	8	Thomson	Reynolds		3-5	T4th	3.5
4-10	Hou.	W	4-1		10	7	Chacon	Mlicki	Jimenez	4-5	T3rd	3.5
4-11	Ari.	L	4-8		6	15	Johnson	Reyes		4-6	5th	3.5
4-12	Ari.	L	3-8		10	13	Schilling	Hampton		4-7	5th	4.5
4-13	Ari.	L	5-7	(10)	15	12	Myers	Jimenez		4-8	5th	5.5
4-14	Ari.	L	3-6		10	8	Batista	Thomson	Kim	4-9	5th	5.5
4-15	L.A.	L	2-5		5	9	Perez	Chacon		4-10	5th	5.5
4-16	L.A.	W	6-4		10	11	Jennings	Ashby	Jimenez	5-10	5th	5.5
4-17	L.A.	L	3-6		9	10	Ishii	White	Gagne	5-11	5th	5.5
4-19	At Ari.	W	8-6		10	8	Neagle	Anderson	Jimenez	6-11	5th	5.5
4-20	At Ari.	L	8-9		8	6	Helling	Thomson	Myers	6-12	5th	6.5
4-21	At Ari.	L	1-7		2	9	Johnson	Chacon		6-13	5th	6.5
4-23	At Cin.	L	2-3		6	7	Haynes	Jennings	Graves	6-14	5th	7.5
4-24	At Cin.	L	3-4		8	10	Williamson	Jimenez		6-15	5th	7.5
4-25	At Cin.	L	3-4		9	7	Sullivan	White	Graves	6-16	5th	8.0
4-26	Phi.	W	4-1		10	7	Thomson	Adams	Jimenez	7-16	5th	8.0
4-27	Phi.	W	8-6		9	12	Chacon	Duckworth	Jimenez	8-16	5th	7.0
4-28	Phi.	W	4-2		9	9	Jennings	Wolf	Jimenez	9-16	5th	7.0
4-30	Pit.	W	10-0		13	3	Hampton	Williams		10-16	5th	6.0
5-1	Pit.	W	6-0		11	3	Neagle	Fogg		11-16	5th	5.0
5-2	Pit.	W	7-2		9	2	Thomson	Villone		12-16	5th	5.0
5-3	At Phi.	L	2-3		7	5	Duckworth	Chacon	Mesa	12-17	5th	6.0
5-4	At Phi.	L	5-6		10	11	Mercado	White	Mesa	12-18	5th	7.0
5-5	At Phi.	L	4-7		8	11	Padilla	Hampton	Mesa	12-19	5th	8.0
5-7	At Mon.	W	5-3		9	11	Thomson	Armas Jr.	Jimenez	13-19	5th	7.5
5-8	At Mon.	W	5-0		7	6	Chacon	Pavano		14-19	5th	7.5
5-9	At Mon.	L	5-6	(12)	15	8	Lloyd	White		14-20	5th	8.5
5-10	At N.Y.	W	9-5		15	9	Jennings	D'Amico		15-20	5th	7.5
5-11	At N.Y.	L	3-4		4	6	Leiter	Hampton	Strickland	15-21	5th	8.5
5-12	At N.Y.	W	4-3	(13)	10	10	White	Davis	Jimenez	16-21	5th	7.5
5-13	Fla.	W	7-3		8	8	Stark	Penny		17-21	5th	7.5
5-14	Fla.	L	2-6		8	11	Beckett	Neagle	Nunez	17-22	5th	8.5
5-15	Fla.	W	7-2		10	8	Jennings	Burnett		18-22	5th	7.5
5-16	Fla.	W	10-3		12	4	Hampton	Tavarez		19-22	5th	7.0
5-17	Atl.	L	2-4		6	9	Glavine	Thomson	Smoltz	19-23	5th	8.0
5-18	Atl.	W	7-3		12	8	Stark	Millwood		20-23	5th	8.0
5-19	Atl.	L	1-2		7	4	Remlinger	Nichting	Smoltz	20-24	5th	8.0
5-21	S.D.	W	7-6		10	8	Speier	Embree	Jimenez	21-24	5th	8.0
5-22	S.D.	W	5-3		14	8	Mercker	Fikac	Jimenez	22-24	T4th	7.0
5-23	S.D.	W	16-3		18	5	Thomson	Tomko		23-24	4th	6.5
5-24	S.F	W	8-5		12	11	Stark	Ortiz	Jimenez	24-24	4th	6.5
5-25	S.F	W	6-3		10	8	Nichting	Rueter	Jimenez	25-24	4th	5.5
5-26	S.F	W	10-6		13	9	Jennings	Jensen		26-24	4th	5.5
5-27	At S.D.	L	5-8		7	13	Lawrence	Hampton	Hoffman	26-25	4th	5.5
5-28	At S.D.	W	3-2	(12)	6	12	Jimenez	Fikac	Speier	27-25	4th	4.5
5-29	At S.D.	L	3-11		9	10	Middlebrook	Stark		27-26	4th	5.5
5-30	At S.D.	W	4-2		7	6	Neagle	Jones	Jimenez	28-26	4th	5.5
5-31	At S.F	W	6-2		12	5	Jennings	Jensen	Jones	29-26	4th	5.5
6-1	At S.F	W	5-4		12	12	Hampton	Hernandez	Jimenez	30-26	4th	4.5
6-2	At S.F	L	2-9		7	11	Schmidt	Thomson		30-27	4th	4.5
6-3	L.A.	L	5-11		10	12	Mota	Jimenez		30-28	4th	5.5
6-4	L.A.	L	4-10		13	13	Orosco	Jones		30-29	4th	5.5
6-5	L.A.	W	8-6		9	14	Jennings	Daal	Jimenez	31-29	4th	5.5
6-7	At Tor.	L	0-8		2	14	Halladay	Hampton		31-30	4th	6.5
6-8	At Tor.	L	1-3		4	6	Walker	Thomson	Escobar	31-31	4th	7.5
6-9	At Tor.	L	2-3		6	6	Escobar	Jimenez		31-32	4th	8.5
6-10	At Bos.	L	3-7		10	1?	Lowe	Neagle	Wakefield	31-33	4th	8.5
6-11	At Bos.	W	3-1		6	5	Jennings	Fossum	Jimenez	32-33	4th	7.5

Date	Opp.	Res.	Score	(inn.*)	Hits	Opp. hits	Winning pitcher	Losing pitcher	Save	Record	Pos.	GB
6-12	At Bos.	L	5-7		10	11	Castillo	Hampton	Urbina	32-34	4th	8.5
6-14	Cle.	L	3-5		9	11	Drese	Thomson	Wickman	32-35	4th	8.5
6-15	Cle.	W	7-4		11	7	Jones	Paronto	Jimenez	33-35	4th	8.5
6-16	Cle.	L	4-5		9	9	Colon	Neagle	Wickman	33-36	4th	9.5
6-18	N.Y.	L	5-10		12	17	Mussina	Jennings	Stanton	33-37	4th	10.5
6-19	N.Y.	L	10-20		11	18	Mendoza	White		33-38	4th	10.5
6-20	N.Y.	W	14-11	(10)	18	19	Stark	Karsay		34-38	4th	10.5
6-21	T.B.	W	8-7	(10)	17	12	Speier	Yan		35-38	4th	10.5
6-22	T.B.	W	6-5	(11)	15	9	Jimenez	Kent		36-38	4th	9.5
6-23	T.B.	W	6-5		9	12	White	Kennedy	Jimenez	37-38	4th	9.5
6-24	At L.A.	W	4-1		9	5	Hampton	Ishii	Jimenez	38-38	4th	8.5
6-25	At L.A.	L	0-4		1	5	Perez	Thomson		38-39	4th	9.5
6-26	At L.A.	L	3-5		4	9	Nomo	Chacon	Gagne	38-40	4th	10.5
6-27	At L.A.	L	1-7		6	13	Daal	Neagle		38-41	4th	11.5
6-28	At Sea.	L	2-6		6	9	Pineiro	Jennings		38-42	4th	12.5
6-29	At Sea.	L	1-8		6	14	Garcia	Hampton		38-43	4th	12.5
6-30	At Sea.	W	4-3		14	6	Speier	Sasaki	Jimenez	39-43	4th	11.5
7-1	S.F	L	6-8		8	11	Rodriguez	Jimenez	Nen	39-44	4th	12.5
7-2	S.F	L	5-18		11	23	Jensen	Neagle		39-45	4th	13.5
7-3	S.F	W	14-4		17	11	Jennings	Hernandez		40-45	4th	12.5
7-5	S.D.	W	9-6		13	11	Hampton	Tomko	Jimenez	41-45	4th	12.0
7-6	S.D.	W	3-2		11	7	Thomson	Peavy	Jimenez	42-45	4th	12.0
7-7	S.D.	L	1-7		2	14	Perez	Chacon		42-46	4th	12.0
7-11	At S.F	L	2-3		6	11	Worrell	Jimenez		42-47	4th	12.0
7-12	At S.F	L	0-9		4	12	Hernandez	Hampton		42-48	4th	12.0
7-13	At S.F	L	1-6		5	9	Schmidt	Thomson		42-49	4th	12.5
7-14	At S.F	L	5-3		8	7	Chacon	Rueter		43-49	4th	12.0
7-15	At S.D.	W	5-0		7	3	Stark	Perez		44-49	4th	11.0
7-16	At S.D.	L	1-5		8	7	Peavy	Jennings	Reed	44-50	4th	11.5
7-17	Ari.	L	3-12		10	19	Schilling	Hampton		44-51	4th	12.5
7-18	Ari.	W	6-4		13	7	Speier	Swindell	Jimenez	45-51	4th	11.5
7-19	Mil.	W	9-5		11	6	Chacon	Quevedo		46-51	4th	10.5
7-20	Mil.	W	6-5		12	8	Stark	Cabrera	Jimenez	47-51	4th	10.5
7-21	Mil.	W	6-4		12	11	Jennings	Sheets	Jimenez	48-51	4th	9.5
7-22	At Ari.	L	1-5		7	8	Schilling	Hampton		48-52	4th	10.5
7-23	At Ari.	L	5-8		9	12	Kim	Jones		48-53	4th	11.5
7-24	At Ari.	L	1-7		3	11	Batista	Chacon		48-54	4th	12.5
7-26	At Mil.	L	3-10		8	13	Sheets	Stark	Vizcaino	48-55	4th	14.0
7-27	At Mil.	L	5-6	(10)	8	13	DeJean	Jimenez		48-56	4th	15.0
7-28	At Mil.	L	3-5		12	11	Wright	Hampton	DeJean	48-57	4th	16.0
7-30	At Pit.	L	1-4		4	6	Benson	Neagle	Williams	48-58	4th	16.0
7-31	At Pit.	L	6-7		10	12	Boehringer	White	Williams	48-59	4th	17.0
8-1	At Pit.	W	3-0		13	2	Jennings	Meadows	Jimenez	49-59	4th	16.0
8-2	At Chi.	L	4-6	(12)	10	11	Borowski	Santos		49-60	4th	16.5
8-3	At Chi.	W	2-1		9	3	Neagle	Clement	Jimenez	50-60	4th	17.0
8-4	At Chi.	L	1-4		5	7	Prior	Chacon		50-61	4th	18.0
8-6	Cin.	W	7-6		15	5	Stark	Moehler	Jimenez	51-61	4th	17.5
8-7	Cin.	W	7-2		7	5	Jennings	Hamilton		52-61	4th	16.5
8-8	Cin.	W	10-3		17	5	Hampton	Haynes		53-61	4th	16.5
8-9	Chi.	W	2-0		5	5	Neagle	Zambrano	Jimenez	54-61	4th	16.5
8-10	Chi.	L	1-15		6	20	Prior	Chacon		54-62	4th	17.5
8-11	Chi.	L	9-12		12	13	Smyth	Stark		54-63	4th	18.5
8-12	At Fla.	W	1-0		4	5	Jennings	Burnett	Jimenez	55-63	4th	18.0
8-13	At Fla.	W	5-4		14	8	Hampton	Nunez	Jimenez	56-63	4th	18.0
8-14	At Fla.	L	0-1		2	3	Lloyd	Santos		56-64	4th	19.0
8-16	At Atl.	L	1-4		6	5	Millwood	Chacon	Smoltz	56-65	4th	20.5
8-17	At Atl.	W	10-3		11	11	Stark	Marquis		57-65	4th	20.5
8-18	At Atl.	W	6-3		15	8	Jennings	Maddux	Jimenez	58-65	4th	19.5
8-19	At Atl.	L	6-7		11	11	Smoltz	Jimenez		58-66	4th	20.0
8-20	Mon.	W	8-6		12	10	Neagle	Vazquez	Jimenez	59-66	4th	20.0
8-21	Mon.	L	5-13		6	14	Yoshii	Chacon		59-67	4th	21.0
8-22	Mon.	W	14-6		16	7	Stark	Armas Jr.		60-67	4th	21.0
8-23	N.Y.	W	10-4		14	7	Jennings	Astacio		61-67	4th	21.0
8-24	N.Y.	L	2-5		8	11	Weathers	Jimenez	Benitez	61-68	4th	21.0
8-25	N.Y.	L	4-7		8	7	Leiter	Neagle	Benitez	61-69	4th	22.0
8-26	S.F	L	3-4		10	11	Rodriguez	Jones	Nen	61-70	4th	23.0
8-27	S.F	L	4-7		10	14	Rodriguez	Jones	Nen	61-71	4th	23.0
8-28	S.F	L	1-9		6	12	Ortiz	Jennings		61-72	4th	23.0
8-29	S.F	L	6-10		5	10	Hernandez	Hampton		61-73	4th	23.5
8-30	At S.D.	L	0-2		4	7	Tomko	Neagle	Hoffman	61-74	4th	23.5
8-31	At S.D.	L	0-3		5	10	Condrey	Cook	Hoffman	61-75	4th	23.5

Date	Opp.	Res.	Score	(inn.*)	Hits	Opp. hits	Winning pitcher	Losing pitcher	Save	Record	Pos.	GB
9-1	At S.D.	L	5-9		11	13	Nickle	Santos	Hoffman	61-76	4th	24.5
9-2	At S.D.	W	5-2		10	7	Jennings	Jones	Jimenez	62-76	4th	23.5
9-3	At S.F	L	2-4		9	8	Ortiz	Hampton	Nen	62-77	4th	23.5
9-4	At S.F	W	2-1		7	4	Neagle	Hernandez	Jimenez	63-77	4th	23.5
9-6	S.D.	W	7-3		7	8	Cook	Eaton		64-77	4th	23.0
9-7	S.D.	W	5-3		5	5	Mercker	Holtz	Jimenez	65-77	4th	22.0
9-8	S.D.	L	4-9		11	13	Lawrence	Jennings	Hoffman	65-78	4th	22.0
9-9	At Hou.	L	5-6	(10)	9	8	Lidge	Flores		65-79	4th	23.0
9-10	At Hou.	L	4-11		12	14	Miller	Neagle		65-80	4th	24.0
9-11	At Hou.	W	8-6		11	13	Cook	Saarloos	Jimenez	66-80	4th	24.0
9-12	L.A.	W	7-1		11	3	Stark	Daal		67-80	4th	23.5
9-13	L.A.	W	5-4		11	10	Mercker	Mota	Jimenez	68-80	4th	22.5
9-14	L.A.	L	3-16		13	20	Perez	Santos		68-81	4th	23.5
9-15	L.A.	W	5-4		7	9	Speier	Ashby	Jimenez	69-81	4th	23.5
9-17	St.L.	L	4-11		7	17	Fassero	Mercker		69-82	4th	23.5
9-18	St.L.	L	5-8		11	8	White	Speier	Kline	69-83	4th	24.5
9-19	St.L.	L	6-12		10	18	Simontacchi	Jennings		69-84	4th	25.5
9-20	Ari.	W	9-4		14	11	Lowe	Schilling		70-84	4th	24.5
9-21	Ari.	W	15-8		20	12	Fuentes	Fetters		71-84	4th	23.5
9-22	Ari.	W	11-7		18	12	Fuentes	Swindell		72-84	4th	22.5
9-24	At L.A.	W	1-0		5	3	Stark	Perez	Jimenez	73-84	4th	21.0
9-25	At L.A.	L	2-3		6	11	Gagne	Jimenez		73-85	4th	21.0
9-26	At Ari.	L	2-4		6	7	Johnson	Flores		73-86	4th	22.0
9-27	At Ari.	L	6-8		8	15	Batista	Neagle	Kim	73-87	4th	23.0
9-28	At Ari.	L	8-17		15	16	Helling	Lowe		73-88	4th	24.0
9-29	At Ari.	L	8-11		14	15	Patterson	Stark	Kim	73-89	4th	25.0

Monthly records: April (10-16), May (19-10), June (10-17), July (9-16), August (13-16), September (12-14).
*Innings, if other than nine.

RECORDS

2002 regular-season record: 73-89
Position: 4th in N.L. West
Home: 47-34   **Road:** 26-55
N.L. East: 18-14   **N.L. Central:** 17-19
N.L. West: 31-45   **A.L.:** 7-11
Vs. LH starters: 16-26
Vs. RH starters: 57-63
Grass: 71-82   **Artificial:** 2-7
Day: 28-28   **Night:** 45-61
1-Run: 18-19   **X-inn.:** 5-5
Doubleheaders: 0-0-0
Team record past five years: 377-433
(.465, ranks 11th in league in that span)

TEAM LEADERS

Batting average: Larry Walker (.338).
At-bats: Juan Pierre (592).
Runs: Todd Helton (107).
Hits: Todd Helton (182).
Total bases: Todd Helton (319).
Doubles: Larry Walker (40).
Triples: Juan Uribe (7).
Home runs: Todd Helton (30).

Runs batted in: Todd Helton (109).
Stolen bases: Juan Pierre (47).
Slugging percentage: Larry Walker (.602).
On-base percentage: Todd Helton (.429).
Wins: Jason Jennings (16).
Earned-run average: Denny Stark (4.00).
Complete games: Denny Neagle (1).
Shutouts: None.
Saves: Jose Jimenez (41).
Innings pitched: Jason Jennings (185.1).
Strikeouts: Jason Jennings (127).

GAMES BY POSITION

Catcher: Gary Bennett 90, Sandy Alomar Jr. 38, Bobby Estalella 38, Ben Petrick 14, Walt McKeel 5.
First base: Todd Helton 156, Greg Norton 15, Ross Gload 4.
Second base: Brent Butler 72, Terry Shumpert 60, Jose Ortiz 53, Jason Romano 12.
Third base: Todd Zeile 139, Brent Butler 33, Greg Norton 22, Jose Ortiz 1, Jason Romano 1, Terry Shumpert 1.
Shortstop: Juan Uribe 155, Brent Butler 13, Jason Romano 5, Terry Shumpert 3.
Outfield: Juan Pierre 149, Larry Walker 123, Todd Hollandsworth 90, Jay Payton 44, Gabe Kapler 38, Benny Agbayani 37, Mark Little 36, Jack Cust 18, Ben Petrick 16, Terry Shumpert 8, Jason Romano 3, Ross Gload 2, Greg Norton 2.
Designated hitter: Larry Walker 7, Benny Agbayani 1, Greg Norton 1.

TOP DRAFT CHOICES

1. **Jeff Francis,** LHP, U. of British Columbia.
2. **Micah Owings,** RHP, Gainesville (Ga.) H.S.
3. **Ben Crockett,** RHP, Harvard.
4. **Jeff Baker,** 3B, Clemson.
5a. **Neil Wilson,** C, Vero Beach (Fla.) H.S.
5b. **Doug Johnson,** RHP, Bryant (R.I.) College.
6. **Sean Barker,** OF, Louisiana State.
7. **Ryan Spilborghs,** OF, UC Santa Barbara.
8. **Jeff Salazar,** OF, Oklahoma State.
9. **John Tetuan,** RHP, Wichita State.
10. **Isaac Pavlik,** LHP, Seton Hall.

FLORIDA MARLINS
NATIONAL LEAGUE EAST DIVISION

2003 SEASON

March/April

SUN	MON	TUE	WED	THU	FRI	SAT
30	31 D PHI	1	2 PHI	3 D PHI	4 ATL	5 ATL
6 D ATL	7 D ATL	8 NYM	9 NYM	10 NYM	11 ATL	12 ATL
13 ATL	14 PHI	15 PHI	16 PHI	17 D PHI	18 NYM	19 D NYM
20 D NYM	21	22 MIL	23 MIL	24 MIL	25 STL	26 STL
27 D STL	28 ARI	29 ARI	30 ARI			

May

SUN	MON	TUE	WED	THU	FRI	SAT
				1 ARI	2 HOU	3 HOU
4 D HOU	5	6 SF	7 SF	8 SF	9 COL	10 COL
11 D COL	12 SD	13 SD	14 SD	15	16 LA	17 LA
18 D LA	19	20 MON	21 MON	22 MON	23 CIN	24 CIN
25 D CIN	26 D MON	27 MON	28 MON	29 CIN	30 CIN	31 CIN

June

SUN	MON	TUE	WED	THU	FRI	SAT
1 D CIN	2	3 OAK	4 OAK	5 OAK	6 ANA	7 ANA
8 D ANA	9	10 MIL	11 MIL	12 D MIL	13 TEX	14 TEX
15 TEX	16 NYM	17 NYM	18 NYM	19 NYM	20 TB	21 TB
22 D TB	23	24 NYM	25 NYM	26 NYM	27 BOS	28 BOS
29 D BOS	30 ATL					

July

SUN	MON	TUE	WED	THU	FRI	SAT
		1 ATL	2 ATL	3	4 D PHI	5 PHI
6 D PHI	7 CUB	8 D CUB	9 D CUB	10	11 MON	12 MON
13 D MON	14	15 *	16	17	18 CUB	19 CUB
20 D CUB	21 MON	22 MON	23 ATL	24 D ATL	25 PHI	26 PHI
27 D PHI	28 ARI	29 ARI	30 ARI	31		

August

SUN	MON	TUE	WED	THU	FRI	SAT
					1 HOU	2 HOU
3 D HOU	4	5 STL	6 STL	7 STL	8 MIL	9 MIL
10 D MIL	11 LA	12 LA	13 LA	14 D LA	15 SD	16 SD
17 SD	18	19 COL	20 COL	21 COL	22 SF	23 D SF
24 D SF	25	26 PIT	27 PIT	28 PIT	29 MON	30 MON

September

SUN	MON	TUE	WED	THU	FRI	SAT
31 D MON	1 D MON	2 PIT	3 PIT	4 D PIT	5 † MON	6 † MON
7 D† MON	8 NYM	9 NYM	10 D NYM	11	12 ATL	13 ATL
14 D ATL	15	16 PHI	17 PHI	18 PHI	19 ATL	20 ATL
21 D ATL	22 ATL	23 PHI	24 PHI	25 PHI	26 NYM	27 NYM
28 D NYM						

Home games shaded; D—Day game (games starting before 5 p.m.); *—All-Star Game at Comiskey Park, Chicago. †—Game played in Puerto Rico. Subject to change.

CLUB DIRECTORY

Chairman, CEO and managing gen. partner
Jeffrey H. Loria
President
David P. Samson
Vice chairman
Joel A. Mael
Special assistants to president
Andre Dawson, Tony Perez
Senior v.p. and general manager
Larry Beinfest
Vice president/assistant g.m.
Michael Hill

Vice president, player personnel
Dan Jennings
Special assistant to the g.m./pro scout
Orrin Freeman
Sr. v.p./dir. of international operations
Fred Ferreira
V.p., player development and scouting
Jim Fleming
Director of player development
Marc DelPiano
Director of minor league operations
Cheryl Evans

V.p., communications & broadcasting
P.J. Loyello
Director, media relations
Steve Copses
Manager, media relations
Andrew Fierstein
Manager, community affairs
Angela Smith

MINOR LEAGUE AFFILIATES

Class	Team	League	Manager
AAA	Albuquerque	Pacific Coast	Dean Treanor
AA	Carolina	Southern	Tracy Woodson
A	Jupiter	Florida State	Luis Dorante
A	Greensboro	South Atlantic	Steve Phillips
A	Jamestown	New York-Pennsylvania	Benny Castillo
Rookie	Gulf Coast Marlins	Gulf Coast	Timothy Cossins

Follow the Marlins all season at: www.sportingnews.com/baseball/teams/marlins/

BROADCAST INFORMATION

Radio: WQAM-AM (560); WQBA-AM (1140, Spanish language).
TV: PAX-TV
Cable TV: Fox Sports Net.

SPRING TRAINING

Ballpark (city): Roger Dean Stadium (Jupiter, Fla.).
Ticket information: 561-775-1818.

2003 SEASON *Florida Marlins*

Manager—Jeff Torborg.

Coaches—Brad Arnsberg, Pierre Arsenault, Jeff Cox, Ozzie Guillen, Perry Hill, Bill Robinson.

No.	PITCHERS	B/T	Ht./Wt.	Born	Age*	2002 clubs
55	Almanza, Armando	L/L	6-3/240	10-26-72	30	Jupiter, Florida
64	Anderson, Wes	R/R	6-4/175	9-10-79	23	Gulf Coast Marlins
61	Beckett, Josh	R/R	6-5/216	5-15-80	22	Florida, Gulf Coast Marlins, Jupiter
	Bump, Nate	R/R	6-2/185	7-24-76	26	Portland
43	Burnett, A.J.	R/R	6-4/229	1-3-77	26	Florida
	Cueto, Jose	R/R	6-2/175	9-13-76	26	Portland
59	Goetz, Geoff	L/L	5-11/165	4-3-79	23	Portland
41	Looper, Braden	R/R	6-3/220	10-28-74	28	Florida
46	Mairena, Oswaldo	L/L	5-11/165	6-30-74	28	Calgary, Florida, Gulf Coast Marlins
54	Neal, Blaine	L/R	6-5/240	4-6-78	24	Calgary, Florida
36	Nunez, Vladimir	R/R	6-4/240	3-15-75	28	Florida
56	Olsen, Kevin	R/R	6-2/196	7-26-76	26	Florida, Calgary
45	Pavano, Carl	R/R	6-5/230	1-8-76	27	Montreal, Ottawa, Florida
31	Penny, Brad	R/R	6-4/247	5-24-78	24	Florida, Jupiter
	Redman, Mark	L/L	6-5/245	1-5-74	29	Detroit
	Snare, Ryan	L/L	6-0/190	2-8-79	24	Stockton, Chattanooga, Portland
	Spooneybarger, Tim	R/R	6-3/190	10-21-79	23	Atlanta, Richmond
58	Tejera, Michael	L/L	5-9/175	10-18-76	26	Florida
48	Wayne, Justin	R/R	6-3/200	4-16-79	23	Harrisburg, Florida, Portland, Calgary

No.	CATCHERS	B/T	Ht./Wt.	Born	Age*	2002 clubs
17	Castro, Ramon	R/R	6-3/235	3-1-76	27	Florida
52	Redmond, Mike	R/R	5-11/208	5-5-71	31	Florida

No.	INFIELDERS	B/T	Ht./Wt.	Born	Age*	2002 clubs
1	Castillo, Luis	B/R	5-11/190	9-12-75	27	Florida
6	Fox, Andy	L/R	6-4/202	1-12-71	32	Florida
11	Gonzalez, Alex	R/R	6-0/200	2-15-77	26	Florida, Gulf Coast Marlins
	Hooper, Kevin	R/R	5-10/160	12-7-76	26	Calgary
25	Lee, Derrek	R/R	6-5/248	9-6-75	27	Florida
19	Lowell, Mike	R/R	6-3/217	2-24-74	29	Florida
	Medrano, Jesus	R/R	6-0/185	9-11-78	24	Portland
12	Mordecai, Mike	R/R	5-10/185	12-13-67	35	Montreal, Florida
	Valdez, Wilson	R/R	5-11/160	5-20-80	22	Portland
	Willingham, Josh	R/R	6-1/200	2-17-79	24	Jupiter
	Wilson, Josh	R/R	6-1/165	3-26-81	22	Jupiter, Portland

No.	OUTFIELDERS	B/T	Ht./Wt.	Born	Age*	2002 clubs
62	Ambres, Chip	R/R	6-1/190	12-19-79	23	Jupiter
4	Banks, Brian	B/R	6-3/210	9-28-70	32	Calgary, Florida
43	Encarnacion, Juan	R/R	6-3/215	3-8-76	27	Cincinnati, Florida
	Hollandsworth, Todd	L/L	6-2/207	4-20-73	29	Colorado, Texas
27	Nunez, Abraham	B/R	6-2/186	2-5-77	26	Calgary, Florida
	Pierre, Juan	L/L	6-0/180	8-14-77	25	Colorado
	Williams, Gerald	R/R	6-2/187	8-10-66	36	New York A.L., Memphis, Louisville

*Age as of April 1, 2003.

BALLPARK INFORMATION

Ballpark (capacity, surface)
Pro Player Stadium (36,331, grass)

Address
2267 Dan Marino Blvd.
Miami, Fla. 33056

Official website
www.floridamarlins.com

Business phone
305-626-7400

Ticket information
877-MARLINS

Field dimensions (from home plate)
To left field at foul line, 330 feet
To center field, 434 feet
To right field at foul line, 345 feet

First game played
April 5, 1993 (Marlins 6, Dodgers 3)

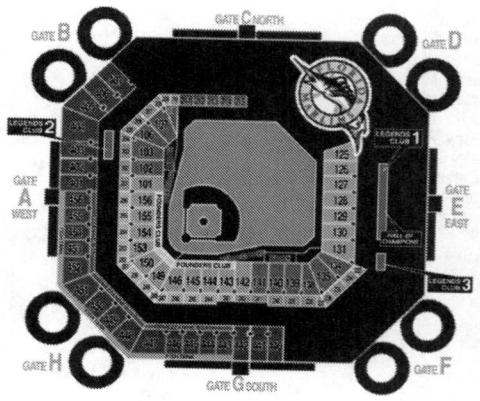

2003 SEASON *Florida Marlins*

Date	Opp.	Res.	Score	(inn.*)	Hits	Opp. hits	Winning pitcher	Losing pitcher	Save	Record	Pos.	GB
4-2	At Mon.	L	6-7		8	11	Herges	Looper		0-1	T4th	1.0
4-3	At Mon.	W	6-5		10	9	Burnett	Armas Jr.	Tejera	1-1	T1st	...
4-4	At Mon.	W	1-0		9	4	Penny	Pavano		2-1	T1st	...
4-5	At Phi.	L	2-6		8	9	Duckworth	Tavarez	Mesa	2-2	T1st	...
4-6	At Phi.	W	7-3		10	9	Nunez	Santiago		3-2	T1st	...
4-7	At Phi.	L	2-3	(11)	7	9	Politte	Looper		3-3	T1st	...
4-8	Mon.	L	2-10		4	15	Armas Jr.	Burnett		3-4	T4th	1.0
4-10	Mon.	L	7-9		15	12	Pavano	Penny		3-5	5th	2.0
4-11	Mon.	W	7-5		11	8	Tavarez	Yoshii	Nunez	4-5	5th	1.0
4-12	Atl.	L	0-2		5	8	Maddux	Beckett	Smoltz	4-6	5th	2.0
4-13	Atl.	W	5-4	(14)	8	11	Knotts	Gryboski		5-6	4th	1.0
4-14	Atl.	W	7-0		14	4	Burnett	Marquis		6-6	T2nd	1.0
4-16	Phi.	W	7-6		11	7	Knotts	Mesa		7-6	2nd	1.5
4-17	Phi.	L	5-7		5	14	Cormier	Looper	Mesa	7-7	3rd	1.5
4-18	Phi.	W	8-7		9	9	Nunez	Bottalico		8-7	2nd	1.5
4-19	At Atl.	L	2-3		6	7	Holmes	Dempster	Smoltz	8-8	3rd	1.5
4-20	At Atl.	L	1-3		7	4	Maddux	Burnett	Smoltz	8-9	4th	1.5
4-21	At Atl.	L	2-4		7	15	Glavine	Olsen	Smoltz	8-10	4th	2.5
4-22	At Atl.	W	8-3		13	8	Penny	Millwood		9-10	4th	2.0
4-23	Hou.	W	4-3	(12)	12	5	Nunez	Puffer		10-10	3rd	2.0
4-24	Hou.	L	4-7		8	12	Oswalt	Dempster	Wagner	10-11	4th	3.0
4-25	Hou.	W	5-4		6	6	Burnett	Reynolds	Nunez	11-11	3rd	3.0
4-26	Ari.	L	3-5		7	12	Johnson	Olsen	Kim	11-12	4th	3.0
4-27	Ari.	W	6-3		10	11	Penny	Batista	Nunez	12-12	3rd	2.0
4-28	Ari.	L	4-5		8	8	Schilling	Beckett	Kim	12-13	4th	3.0
4-30	At St.L.	W	7-2		11	3	Burnett	Kile		13-13	3rd	3.0
5-1	At St.L.	L	4-6		8	13	Smith	Dempster	Isringhausen	13-14	3rd	4.0
5-2	At St.L.	W	9-6		17	10	Tejera	Veres	Nunez	14-14	3rd	3.0
5-3	At Mil.	W	8-4		12	7	Darensbourg	Buddie		15-14	3rd	3.0
5-4	At Mil.	L	4-6		4	10	Sheets	Teut	DeJean	15-15	3rd	3.0
5-5	At Mil.	W	7-4		11	7	Burnett	Figueroa	Nunez	16-15	3rd	2.0
5-7	S.D.	W	12-4		12	9	Dempster	Jones		17-15	T2nd	1.0
5-8	S.D.	W	7-4		9	8	Mairena	Fikac	Nunez	18-15	T1st	...
5-9	S.D.	W	1-0		8	5	Izquierdo	Tollberg	Nunez	19-15	1st	+1.0
5-10	L.A.	W	4-3		9	6	Nunez	Carrara		20-15	1st	+1.0
5-11	L.A.	L	0-3		6	6	Brown	Tavarez	Gagne	20-16	1st	+1.0
5-12	L.A.	W	11-3		13	9	Dempster	Nomo		21-16	1st	+1.0
5-13	At Col.	L	3-7		8	8	Stark	Penny		21-17	1st	+1.0
5-14	At Col.	W	6-2		11	8	Beckett	Neagle	Nunez	22-17	1st	+2.0
5-15	At Col.	L	2-7		8	10	Jennings	Burnett		22-18	1st	+1.0
5-16	At Col.	L	3-10		4	12	Hampton	Tavarez		22-19	T1st	...
5-17	At S.F	L	3-9		10	10	Ortiz	Dempster	Nen	22-20	2nd	1.0
5-18	At S.F	L	5-10		10	14	Rueter	Penny	Nen	22-21	2nd	2.0
5-19	At S.F	W	4-2		7	2	Beckett	Jensen	Nunez	23-21	2nd	1.0
5-21	At Cin.	L	1-6		7	6	Reitsma	Burnett	Graves	23-22	2nd	1.0
5-22	At Cin.	L	2-6		7	8	Dessens	Dempster		23-23	3rd	1.0
5-23	At Cin.	W	8-4		9	12	Tavarez	Rijo	Nunez	24-23	T2nd	1.0
5-24	At N.Y.	L	4-5	(10)	9	6	Strickland	Darensbourg		24-24	3rd	2.0
5-25	At N.Y.	W	6-5		14	9	Almanza	Weathers	Nunez	25-24	T2nd	1.0
5-26	At N.Y.	L	0-3		5	6	D'Amico	Burnett	Strickland	25-25	4th	2.0
5-27	At N.Y.	W	5-3		10	9	Dempster	Leiter	Nunez	26-25	3rd	1.0
5-28	Cin.	L	5-6	(11)	14	10	Graves	Nunez		26-26	3rd	2.0
5-29	Cin.	L	2-8		11	14	Hamilton	Beckett		26-27	4th	2.0
5-30	Cin.	L	1-4		7	7	Haynes	Olsen	Graves	26-28	4th	3.0
5-31	N.Y.	L	5-6	(10)	7	8	Roberts	Nunez	Benitez	26-29	4th	4.0
6-1	N.Y.	W	9-7		11	11	Mairena	Komiyama	Nunez	27-29	4th	4.0
6-2	N.Y.	W	7-3		12	9	Tavarez	Leiter	Nunez	28-29	3rd	3.0
6-4	At Phi.	W	5-0		7	4	Izquierdo	Adams		29-29	3rd	3.0
6-5	At Phi.	W	2-1		10	6	Burnett	Wolf		30-29	2nd	3.0
6-7	At Min.	L	7-12		11	13	Santana	Dempster		30-30	T2nd	4.5
6-8	At Min.	L	3-5		7	11	Kinney	Olsen	Guardado	30-31	4th	5.5
6-9	At Min.	W	6-3		12	9	Tavarez	Reed	Nunez	31-31	T2nd	5.5
6-10	At K.C.	W	15-8	(14)	17	16	Almanza	Suzuki		32-31	T2nd	4.5
6-11	At K.C.	L	0-6	(5)	4	10	May	Tejera		32-32	T2nd	5.5
6-12	At K.C.	W	13-5		17	9	Dempster	Byrd		33-32	2nd	5.5

Date	Opp.	Res.	Score	(inn.*)	Hits	Opp. hits	Winning pitcher	Losing pitcher	Save	Record	Pos.	GB
6-14	T.B.	L	3-4	(14)	6	12	Yan	Mairena	Harper	33-33	T2nd	6.5
6-15	T.B.	W	3-0		9	3	Burnett	Wilson		34-33	T2nd	6.5
6-16	T.B.	L	1-4		6	11	Zambrano	Almanza	Yan	34-34	T3rd	6.5
6-18	Cle.	W	4-0		11	4	Dempster	Finley		35-34	3rd	5.5
6-19	Cle.	W	2-1		5	5	Tavarez	Riggan	Nunez	36-34	3rd	5.5
6-20	Cle.	W	3-0	(6)	7	2	Burnett	Drese		37-34	3rd	5.5
6-21	Det.	W	4-1		13	2	Tejera	Sparks	Nunez	38-34	3rd	5.5
6-22	Det.	W	5-4		7	9	Neal	Acevedo		39-34	T2nd	5.5
6-23	Det.	L	2-3		7	5	Farnsworth	Almanza	Acevedo	39-35	3rd	6.5
6-24	Phi.	L	4-15		8	17	Padilla	Tavarez		39-36	3rd	7.5
6-25	Phi.	L	6-7	(11)	11	13	Mesa	Darensbourg	Plesac	39-37	T3rd	7.5
6-26	Phi.	W	6-2		10	6	Tejera	Duckworth		40-37	3rd	7.5
6-27	Phi.	L	3-7		8	10	Adams	Olsen		40-38	3rd	8.0
6-28	At T.B.	L	0-4		5	9	Alvarez	Dempster		40-39	3rd	9.0
6-29	At T.B.	W	3-2		6	7	Tavarez	Kennedy	Nunez	41-39	3rd	9.0
6-30	At T.B.	L	5-6	(12)	9	12	Yan	Nunez		41-40	3rd	10.0
7-1	Chi.	W	11-1		15	5	Tejera	Zambrano		42-40	3rd	10.0
7-2	Chi.	W	9-7		13	11	Neal	Lieber		43-40	3rd	9.0
7-3	Chi.	L	2-6		4	11	Wood	Dempster		43-41	3rd	10.0
7-4	N.Y.	W	9-7		12	14	Tavarez	Leiter		44-41	3rd	10.0
7-5	N.Y.	L	3-5		11	7	Bacsik	Burnett	Benitez	44-42	3rd	11.0
7-6	N.Y.	W	5-2		7	5	Tejera	Estes	Almanza	45-42	3rd	10.0
7-7	N.Y.	L	3-9		6	13	Roberts	Mairena		45-43	3rd	11.0
7-12	At Chi.	L	4-5	(16)	13	10	Fassero	Pavano		45-44	3rd	12.5
7-13	At Chi.	L	2-9		3	13	Clement	Tavarez		45-45	3rd	12.5
7-14	At Chi.	L	3-10		9	13	Prior	Tejera	Farnsworth	45-46	T3rd	12.5
7-15	At N.Y.	L	3-8		7	11	Bacsik	Penny		45-47	4th	12.5
7-16	At N.Y.	L	5-10		9	9	Leiter	Beckett		45-48	4th	13.5
7-17	At Atl.	L	0-10		7	16	Maddux	Burnett		45-49	4th	14.5
7-18	At Atl.	L	1-3		9	4	Glavine	Tavarez	Smoltz	45-50	4th	15.5
7-19	Mon.	W	4-2		5	9	Tejera	Vazquez	Nunez	46-50	4th	15.5
7-20	Mon.	W	3-0		8	4	Penny	Yoshii	Looper	47-50	4th	15.5
7-21	Mon.	W	4-0		7	3	Beckett	Armas Jr.	Nunez	48-50	4th	15.5
7-22	Atl.	W	2-1		7	6	Burnett	Maddux	Looper	49-50	T3rd	14.5
7-23	Atl.	L	3-5		10	10	Glavine	Tavarez	Smoltz	49-51	T3rd	15.5
7-24	Atl.	L	0-10		1	12	Moss	Tejera		49-52	4th	16.5
7-25	At Mon.	W	3-2		11	5	Nunez	Tucker		50-52	T3rd	16.0
7-26	At Mon.	L	5-6	(10)	15	8	Tucker	Nunez		50-53	4th	16.0
7-27	At Mon.	W	7-2		10	6	Burnett	Ohka		51-53	T3rd	16.0
7-28	At Mon.	L	1-4		2	6	Colon	Tavarez		51-54	4th	16.0
7-30	St.L.	L	0-5		4	12	Benes	Tejera		51-55	4th	17.0
7-31	St.L.	W	8-5		10	9	Beckett	Smith	Looper	52-55	4th	17.0
8-1	St.L.	W	4-0		9	4	Burnett	Finley		53-55	4th	17.0
8-2	Mil.	L	0-1		3	10	Wright	Tavarez	DeJean	53-56	4th	18.0
8-3	Mil.	W	11-7		12	13	Penny	Cabrera	Looper	54-56	4th	18.0
8-4	Mil.	W	7-2		12	9	Tejera	Quevedo		55-56	T3rd	18.0
8-6	At Hou.	L	0-2		8	5	Mlicki	Beckett	Wagner	55-57	4th	19.0
8-7	At Hou.	L	2-7		3	9	Oswalt	Burnett		55-58	4th	19.0
8-8	At Hou.	W	4-3		11	9	Tavarez	Munro	Looper	56-58	4th	19.0
8-9	At Ari.	L	1-2		3	5	Kim	Looper		56-59	4th	20.0
8-10	At Ari.	L	2-9		5	15	Johnson	Tejera		56-60	4th	20.0
8-11	At Ari.	L	2-9		7	16	Schilling	Beckett		56-61	4th	21.0
8-12	Col.	L	0-1		5	4	Jennings	Burnett	Jimenez	56-62	4th	21.5
8-13	Col.	L	4-5		8	14	Hampton	Nunez	Jimenez	56-63	5th	21.5
8-14	Col.	W	1-0		3	2	Lloyd	Santos		57-63	5th	21.5
8-16	S.F	W	4-2		9	7	Tejera	Rueter	Looper	58-63	T4th	21.5
8-17	S.F	W	7-3		7	9	Beckett	Jensen		59-63	T3rd	20.5
8-18	S.F	W	3-0		9	3	Burnett	Ortiz		60-63	3rd	19.5
8-19	S.F	L	0-3		5	5	Hernandez	Tavarez		60-64	3rd	20.5
8-20	At L.A.	W	6-3		11	7	Penny	Ishii		61-64	3rd	19.5
8-21	At L.A.	L	3-4	(10)	12	8	Shuey	Looper		61-65	3rd	20.5
8-22	At L.A.	L	2-6		5	10	Nomo	Lloyd	Shuey	61-66	4th	20.5
8-23	At S.D.	L	2-18		8	18	Peavy	Pavano		61-67	4th	20.5
8-24	At S.D.	W	8-4		12	11	Tavarez	Lawrence		62-67	4th	19.5
8-25	At S.D.	W	7-6		13	15	Borland	Villafuerte	Looper	63-67	4th	19.5
8-27	N.Y.	L	5-10		11	13	Thomson	Tejera		63-68	4th	20.5
8-28	N.Y.	W	7-3		10	9	Almanza	Strickland		64-68	4th	19.5
8-30	Pit.	W	4-3		5	10	Tavarez	Wells	Looper	65-68	4th	19.0
8-31	Pit.	W	3-2		6	9	Nunez	Sauerbeck	Looper	66-68	3rd	19.0

Date	Opp.	Res.	Score	(inn.*)	Hits	Opp. hits	Winning pitcher	Losing pitcher	Save	Record	Pos.	GB
9-1	Pit.	W	8-4		11	9	Neal	Fogg		67-68	3rd	19.0
9-3†	At N.Y.	W	3-2	(12)	11	8	Looper	Strickland		68-68		
9-3‡	At N.Y.	L	5-11		11	14	Bacsik	Wayne		68-69	3rd	19.0
9-4	At N.Y.	L	3-11		6	13	Astacio	Tavarez		68-70	4th	20.0
9-5	At N.Y.	L	1-4		7	6	Trachsel	Penny	Benitez	68-71	4th	20.5
9-6	At Pit.	L	0-11		9	14	Benson	Tejera		68-72	4th	21.5
9-7	At Pit.	L	1-4		7	8	Fogg	Robertson	Williams	68-73	4th	22.5
9-8	At Pit.	W	11-1		14	8	Pavano	Meadows		69-73	4th	21.5
9-10†	At Phi.	W	6-4		8	9	Lloyd	Wolf	Almanza	70-73		
9-10‡	At Phi.	W	2-1		8	4	Wayne	Padilla	Looper	71-73	2nd	21.0
9-11	At Phi.	L	2-9		9	10	Myers	Penny		71-74	2nd	21.5
9-12	At Phi.	L	1-6		8	10	Roa	Tejera		71-75	3rd	22.0
9-13	Atl.	W	13-3		16	3	Pavano	Maddux		72-75	2nd	21.0
9-14	Atl.	L	5-10		14	13	Glavine	Beckett		72-76	4th	22.0
9-15	Atl.	L	4-6		8	8	Moss	Wayne	Smoltz	72-77	4th	23.0
9-16	Atl.	W	5-1		10	4	Penny	Millwood		73-77	4th	22.0
9-17	Mon.	L	5-8	(14)	11	16	Stewart	Lloyd		73-78	4th	23.0
9-18	Mon.	L	2-4	(11)	10	8	Eischen	Mairena	Drew	73-79	4th	23.0
9-19	Mon.	L	5-6		12	12	Colon	Knotts	Drew	73-80	5th	24.0
9-20	At Atl.	W	6-2		8	6	Wayne	Moss		74-80	4th	23.0
9-21	At Atl.	W	6-4		12	9	Penny	Millwood	Looper	75-80	4th	22.0
9-22	At Atl.	L	1-4		4	6	Maddux	Tavarez	Smoltz	75-81	4th	23.0
9-24	At Mon.	W	9-6		11	14	Pavano	Reames	Looper	76-81	4th	22.0
9-25	At Mon.	W	10-2		10	11	Beckett	Colon		77-81	4th	22.0
9-26	At Mon.	L	3-4		7	12	Armas Jr.	Penny	Day	77-82	4th	22.5
9-27	Phi.	W	5-2		12	6	Knotts	Wolf	Looper	78-82	4th	23.0
9-28	Phi.	L	3-9		8	11	Duckworth	Wayne		78-83	4th	24.0
9-29	Phi.	W	4-3	(10)	12	12	Looper	Mercado		79-83	4th	23.0

Monthly records: April (13-13), May (13-16), June (15-11), July (11-15), August (14-13), September (13-15).
*Innings, if other than nine. †First game of a doubleheader. ‡Second game of a doubleheader.

RECORDS

2002 regular-season record: 79-83
Position: 4th in N.L. East
Home: 46-35 **Road:** 33-48
N.L. East: 36-40 **N.L. Central:** 18-18
N.L. West: 15-17 **A.L.:** 10-8
Vs. LH starters: 19-23
Vs. RH starters: 60-60
Grass: 66-71 **Artificial:** 13-12
Day: 21-25 **Night:** 58-58
1-Run: 24-20 **X-inn.:** 5-12
Doubleheaders: 1-0-1
Team record past five years: 352-457
(.435, ranks 13th in league in that span)

TEAM LEADERS

Batting average: Kevin Millar (.306).
At-bats: Luis Castillo (606).
Runs: Derrek Lee (95).
Hits: Luis Castillo (185).
Total bases: Derrek Lee (287).
Doubles: Mike Lowell (44).
Triples: Derrek Lee (7).
Home runs: Derrek Lee (27).

Runs batted in: Mike Lowell (92).
Stolen bases: Luis Castillo (48).
Slugging percentage: Cliff Floyd (.537).
On-base percentage: Cliff Floyd (.414).
Wins: A.J. Burnett (12).
Earned-run average: A.J. Burnett (3.30).
Complete games: A.J. Burnett (7).
Shutouts: A.J. Burnett (5).
Saves: Vladimir Nunez (20).
Innings pitched: A.J. Burnett (204.1).
Strikeouts: A.J. Burnett (203).

GAMES BY POSITION

Catcher: Charles Johnson 82, Mike Redmond 80, Ramon Castro 37.
First base: Derrek Lee 162, Kevin Millar 2, Mike Redmond 2, Brian Banks 1, Mike Mordecai 1.
Second base: Luis Castillo 144, Homer Bush 12, Pablo Ozuna 10, Andy Fox 7, Marty Malloy 3.
Third base: Mike Lowell 159, Mike Mordecai 7, Andy Fox 4, Marty Malloy 2, Kevin Millar 2, Brian Banks 1.
Shortstop: Andy Fox 112, Alex Gonzalez 42, Mike Mordecai 24, Homer Bush 4.
Outfield: Preston Wilson 138, Eric Owens 121, Kevin Millar 108, Cliff Floyd 80, Juan Encarnacion 67, Abraham Nunez 15, Tim Raines Sr. 14, Brian Banks 8, Andy Fox 1, Pablo Ozuna 1.
Designated hitter: Kevin Millar 6, Ramon Castro 1, Cliff Floyd 1, Tim Raines Sr. 1.

TOP DRAFT CHOICES

1. **Jeremy Hermida**, OF, Wheeler H.S., Marietta, Ga.
2. **Robert Andino**, SS, Southridge H.S., Miami.
3. **Trevor Hutchinson**, RHP, California.
4. **Josh Johnson**, RHP, Jenks H.S., Tulsa, Okla.
5. **Nick Hundley**, C, Lake Washington H.S., Redmond, Wash.
6. **Scott Olson**, LHP, Crystal Lake (Ill.) South H.S.
7. **Xavier Arroyo**, OF, Antilles H.S., Fort Buchanan, P.R.
8. **Ryan Warpinski**, RHP, Texas A&M.
9. **Eric Reed**, OF, Texas A&M.
10. **Robert Word**, 1B, Virginia.

HOUSTON ASTROS
NATIONAL LEAGUE CENTRAL DIVISION

2003 SEASON

March/April

SUN	MON	TUE	WED	THU	FRI	SAT
30	31	1 COL	2 COL	3 D COL	4 STL	5 D STL
6 D STL	7	8 CIN	9 CIN	10 CIN	11 STL	12 STL
13 D STL	14 SF	15 SF	16 SF	17 MIL	18 MIL	19 D MIL
20 D MIL	21	22 NYM	23 NYM	24 NYM	25 MON	26 D MON
27 D MON	28	29 ATL	30 ATL			

May

SUN	MON	TUE	WED	THU	FRI	SAT
				1 ATL	2 FLA	3 FLA
4 D FLA	5 PIT	6 PIT	7 PIT	8 D PIT	9 PHI	10 PHI
11 D PHI	12 PIT	13 PIT	14 PIT	15 D PIT	16 PHI	17 D PHI
18 PHI	19	20 STL	21 STL	22 STL	23 CUB	24 CUB
25 D CUB	26 D STL	27 STL	28 STL	29	30 D CUB	31 D CUB

June

SUN	MON	TUE	WED	THU	FRI	SAT
1 D CUB	2	3 BAL	4 BAL	5 BAL	6 TB	7 TB
8 D TB	9	10 NYY	11 NYY	12 D NYY	13 BOS	14 BOS
15 D BOS	16	17 ARI	18 ARI	19 ARI	20 TEX	21 TEX
22 TEX	23 ARI	24 ARI	25 D ARI	26	27 TEX	28 D TEX
29 D TEX	30					

July

SUN	MON	TUE	WED	THU	FRI	SAT
		1 MIL	2 MIL	3 MIL	4 D PIT	5 PIT
6 D PIT	7	8 CIN	9 CIN	10 CIN	11 PIT	12 PIT
13 D PIT	14	15 *	16	17 CIN	18 CIN	19 D CIN
20 D CIN	21 PIT	22 PIT	23 MIL	24 MIL	25 CUB	26 D CUB
27 D CUB	28	29 ATL	30 ATL	31 ATL		

August

SUN	MON	TUE	WED	THU	FRI	SAT
					1 FLA	2 FLA
3 D FLA	4	5 NYM	6 NYM	7 NYM	8 MON	9 MON
10 D MON	11 CUB	12 CUB	13 D CUB	14 D CUB	15 CIN	16 D CIN
17 D CIN	18	19 CUB	20 CUB	21 CUB	22 CIN	23 CIN
24 D CIN	25	26 LA	27 LA	28 LA	29 SD	30 SD

September

SUN	MON	TUE	WED	THU	FRI	SAT
31 D SD	1 LA	2 LA	3 LA	4	5 SD	6 SD
7 D SD	8 MIL	9 MIL	10 MIL	11 D MIL	12 STL	13 STL
14 D STL	15	16 COL	17 COL	18 D COL	19 STL	20 D STL
21 D STL	22 SF	23 SF	24 D SF	25 MIL	26 MIL	27 MIL
28 D MIL						

Home games shaded; D—Day game (games starting before 5 p.m.); *—All-Star Game at Comiskey Park, Chicago. Subject to change.

CLUB DIRECTORY

Chairman and chief executive officer
Drayton McLane Jr.
President, baseball operations
Tal Smith
General manager
Gerry Hunsicker

Assistant general manager
Tim Purpura
Director of scouting
David Lakey
Special asst. to the g.m. for international scouting and development
Andres Reiner

Sr. v.p., ops. and communications
Rob Matwick
V.p., community development
Marian Harper
Director of media relations
Warren Miller

MINOR LEAGUE AFFILIATES

Class	Team	League	Manager
AAA	New Orleans	Pacific Coast	Chris Maloney
AA	Round Rock	Texas	Jackie Moore
A	Salem	Carolina	John Massarelli
A	Lexington	South Atlantic	Russ Nixon
A	Tri-City	New York-Pennsylvania	Ivan DeJesus
Rookie	Martinsville	Appalachian	Jorge Orta

BROADCAST INFORMATION

Radio: KTRH-AM (740); To be announced (Spanish language).
TV: To be announced.
Cable TV: Fox Sports Southwest.

SPRING TRAINING

Ballpark (city): Osceola County Stadium (Kissimmee, Fla.).
Ticket information: 407-839-3900.

Follow the Astros all season at: www.sportingnews.com/baseball/teams/astros/

SPRING TRAINING ROSTER

Manager—Jimy Williams (22).
Coaches—Mark Bailey (6), Jose Cruz (25), Burt Hooton (48), Gene Lamont (38), John Tamargo (30), Harry Spilman (12).

No.	PITCHERS	B/T	Ht./Wt.	Born	Age*	2002 clubs
	Barrett, Jimmy	R/R	6-2/190	6-7-81	21	Lexington
29	Dotel, Octavio	R/R	6-0/200	11-25-73	29	Houston
55	Hernandez, Carlos	B/L	5-10/185	4-22-80	22	Houston, New Orleans, Round Rock
54	Lidge, Brad	R/R	6-5/200	12-23-76	26	Round Rock, Houston, New Orleans
65	Miller, Greg	L/L	6-5/215	9-30-79	23	Round Rock
52	Miller, Wade	R/R	6-2/210	9-13-76	26	Houston, New Orleans
53	Munro, Peter	R/R	6-3/210	6-14-75	27	New Orleans, Houston
44	Oswalt, Roy	R/R	6-0/175	8-29-77	25	Houston
59	Puffer, Brandon	R/R	6-3/190	10-5-75	27	New Orleans, Houston
	Ramirez, Santiago	R/R	5-11/189	8-15-78	24	Round Rock, New Orleans
51	Redding, Tim	R/R	6-0/195	2-12-78	25	New Orleans, Houston
37	Reynolds, Shane	R/R	6-3/215	3-26-68	35	Houston
60	Robertson, Jeriome	L/L	6-1/190	3-30-77	26	New Orleans, Houston
68	Rosario, Rodrigo	R/R	6-2/165	12-14-79	23	Round Rock
50	Saarloos, Kirk	R/R	6-0/185	5-23-79	23	Round Rock, New Orleans, Houston
	Saladin, Miguel	R/R	5-11/165	5-22-75	27	Round Rock, New Orleans
20	Stone, Ricky	R/R	6-1/190	2-28-75	28	Houston
13	Wagner, Billy	L/L	5-11/195	7-25-71	31	Houston

No.	CATCHERS	B/T	Ht./Wt.	Born	Age*	2002 clubs
11	Ausmus, Brad	R/R	5-11/200	4-14-69	33	Houston
67	Buck, John	R/R	6-3/210	7-7-80	22	Round Rock
46	Chavez, Raul	R/R	5-11/210	3-18-73	30	New Orleans, Houston
2	Zaun, Gregg	B/R	5-10/190	4-14-71	31	Houston

No.	INFIELDERS	B/T	Ht./Wt.	Born	Age*	2002 clubs
5	Bagwell, Jeff	R/R	6-0/215	5-27-68	34	Houston
7	Biggio, Craig	R/R	5-11/185	12-14-65	37	Houston
27	Blum, Geoff	B/R	6-3/200	4-26-73	29	Houston
14	Ensberg, Morgan	R/R	6-2/210	8-26-75	27	Houston, New Orleans
28	Everett, Adam	R/R	6-0/160	2-2-77	26	Houston, New Orleans
	Kent, Jeff	R/R	6-1/220	3-7-68	35	San Francisco
4	Lugo, Julio	R/R	6-1/170	11-16-75	27	Houston
10	Vizcaino, Jose	B/R	6-1/185	3-26-68	35	Houston
	Whiteman, Tommy	R/R	6-3/175	7-14-79	23	Round Rock, Lexington

No.	OUTFIELDERS	B/T	Ht./Wt.	Born	Age*	2002 clubs
17	Berkman, Lance	B/L	6-1/220	2-10-76	27	Houston
	Hall, Victor	L/L	6-0/170	9-16-80	22	Lancaster, El Paso
15	Hidalgo, Richard	R/R	6-3/220	7-2-75	27	Houston
21	Hunter, Brian	R/R	6-3/180	3-25-71	32	Houston, New Orleans
24	Lane, Jason	R/L	6-2/215	12-22-76	26	New Orleans, Houston
16	Merced, Orlando	L/R	6-1/195	11-2-66	36	Houston
	Stanley, Henri	L/L	5-10/190	12-15-77	25	Round Rock
31	Ward, Daryle	L/L	6-2/240	6-27-75	27	Houston

*Age as of April 1, 2003.

BALLPARK INFORMATION

Ballpark (capacity, surface)
Minute Maid Park (40,950, grass)
Address
P.O. Box 288
Houston, TX 77001-0288
Official website
www.astros.com
Business phone
713-259-8000
Ticket information
713-259-8500; 1-877-9-ASTROS
Field dimensions (from home plate)
To left field at foul line, 315 feet
To center field, 435 feet
To right field at foul line, 326 feet
First game played
April 7, 2000 (Phillies 4, Astros 1)

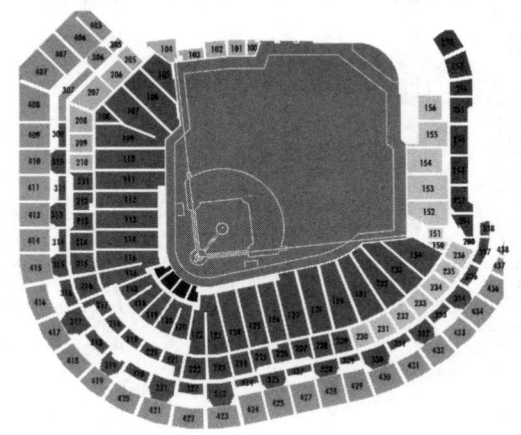

2003 SEASON *Houston Astros*

Date	Opp.	Res.	Score	(inn.*)	Hits	Opp. hits	Winning pitcher	Losing pitcher	Save	Record	Pos.	GB
4-2	Mil.	L	3-9		12	12	Sheets	Miller		0-1	T4th	1.0
4-3	Mil.	W	15-2		15	7	Oswalt	Quevedo		1-1	T1st	...
4-4	Mil.	W	6-3		10	10	Reynolds	Wright		2-1	T1st	...
4-5	St.L.	L	1-5		8	11	Stechschulte	Mlicki		2-2	T2nd	1.0
4-6	St.L.	L	4-8		9	15	Morris	Cruz		2-3	T3rd	2.0
4-7	St.L.	W	7-6	(12)	15	11	Stone	Hackman		3-3	T2nd	1.5
4-8	At Col.	W	8-4		10	13	Oswalt	Neagle		4-3	2nd	1.5
4-9	At Col.	L	5-10		8	13	Thomson	Reynolds		4-4	3rd	2.0
4-10	At Col.	L	1-4		7	10	Chacon	Mlicki	Jimenez	4-5	4th	2.0
4-12	At St.L.	L	3-7		9	11	Morris	Miller		4-6	4th	3.0
4-13	At St.L.	L	1-2		2	11	Isringhausen	Stone		4-7	4th	4.0
4-14	At St.L.	W	5-4		9	10	Reynolds	Stephenson	Wagner	5-7	4th	3.0
4-16	At Cin.	W	8-3		11	7	Mlicki	Acevedo		6-7	4th	2.0
4-17	At Cin.	W	7-2		8	4	Hernandez	Haynes		7-7	T3rd	2.0
4-18	At Cin.	L	4-5	(10)	11	14	White	Cruz		7-8	4th	2.5
4-19	S.F	L	2-3		6	9	Hernandez	Reynolds	Nen	7-9	4th	3.5
4-20	S.F	L	9-13		10	19	Ortiz	Redding	Nen	7-10	4th	4.5
4-21	S.F	W	4-0		11	2	Mlicki	Jensen		8-10	4th	4.5
4-23	At Fla.	L	3-4	(12)	5	12	Nunez	Puffer		8-11	4th	4.5
4-24	At Fla.	W	7-4		12	8	Oswalt	Dempster	Wagner	9-11	4th	3.5
4-25	At Fla.	L	4-5		6	6	Burnett	Reynolds	Nunez	9-12	4th	4.5
4-26	At Atl.	L	0-9		3	16	Glavine	Redding		9-13	4th	5.0
4-27	At Atl.	W	6-3		10	5	Mlicki	Millwood	Wagner	10-13	4th	5.0
4-28	At Atl.	W	7-1		12	6	Hernandez	Lopez		11-13	4th	4.0
4-30	Mon.	L	1-5		5	8	Vazquez	Oswalt		11-14	4th	5.0
5-1	Mon.	L	4-5		8	9	Armas Jr.	Dotel	Herges	11-15	4th	6.0
5-2	Mon.	W	8-2		15	4	Redding	Pavano		12-15	4th	5.0
5-3	N.Y.	L	3-11		9	15	Astacio	Mlicki		12-16	4th	5.0
5-4	N.Y.	W	3-1		6	5	Hernandez	D'Amico	Wagner	13-16	4th	4.0
5-5	N.Y.	W	12-1		15	4	Oswalt	Leiter		14-16	3rd	3.0
5-7	At Phi.	L	4-7		4	11	Silva	Pichardo	Mesa	14-17	3rd	4.5
5-8	At Phi.	L	3-5		8	5	Mesa	Cruz		14-18	4th	5.5
5-9	At Phi.	L	1-3		5	6	Wolf	Mlicki	Mesa	14-19	4th	6.0
5-10	At Pit.	L	1-5		4	8	Anderson	Hernandez		14-20	4th	6.0
5-11	At Pit.	L	2-4		5	5	Fogg	Oswalt	Williams	14-21	4th	7.0
5-12	At Pit.	W	5-1		8	4	Reynolds	Williams		15-21	4th	6.0
5-13	Phi.	W	17-3		20	8	Redding	Duckworth		16-21	4th	6.0
5-14	Phi.	W	5-1		7	5	Dotel	Wolf	Wagner	17-21	4th	6.0
5-15	Phi.	W	6-2		12	5	Hernandez	Padilla		18-21	4th	6.0
5-16	Pit.	W	3-1		5	9	Oswalt	Boehringer	Wagner	19-21	4th	6.0
5-17	Pit.	W	7-4		7	6	Stone	Villone	Dotel	20-21	3rd	5.0
5-18	Pit.	W	2-1		8	4	Dotel	Lowe		21-21	T2nd	5.0
5-19	Pit.	L	3-5		10	9	Wells	Mlicki	Williams	21-22	3rd	5.0
5-21	At St.L.	L	1-3		6	6	Simontacchi	Hernandez	Isringhausen	21-23	T3rd	5.5
5-22	At St.L.	L	2-3		7	8	Veres	Stone		21-24	T3rd	6.5
5-23	At St.L.	L	4-5		10	11	Hackman	Dotel	Isringhausen	21-25	T3rd	6.5
5-24	Chi.	L	4-5	(11)	11	10	Mahomes	Wagner	Borowski	21-26	4th	6.5
5-25	Chi.	L	1-5		4	8	Wood	Mlicki		21-27	4th	7.5
5-26	Chi.	W	7-5		12	14	Dotel	Fassero	Wagner	22-27	T3rd	6.5
5-27	St.L.	L	3-4		10	9	Stechschulte	Oswalt	Isringhausen	22-28	4th	7.0
5-28	St.L.	L	1-4		10	6	Morris	Reynolds	Isringhausen	22-29	4th	8.0
5-29	St.L.	W	10-5		13	8	Redding	Stephenson		23-29	4th	8.0
5-31	At Chi.	W	4-1		7	4	Hernandez	Bere	Wagner	24-29	4th	7.5
6-1	At Chi.	W	7-3		11	9	Oswalt	Prior	Dotel	25-29	3rd	6.5
6-2	At Chi.	L	2-4		6	7	Clement	Reynolds	Alfonseca	25-30	4th	7.5
6-3	At Ari.	L	4-10		7	10	Schilling	Redding		25-31	4th	8.0
6-4	At Ari.	W	6-4		13	9	Borbon	Prinz	Wagner	26-31	4th	7.0
6-5	At Ari.	L	4-5	(13)	9	13	Anderson	Mann		26-32	4th	7.5
6-7	At Oak.	L	3-5		6	9	Mulder	Oswalt	Koch	26-33	4th	8.0
6-8	At Oak.	L	1-5		7	8	Harang	Reynolds		26-34	4th	9.0
6-9	At Oak.	L	6-7		11	10	Koch	Dotel		26-35	4th	9.0
6-10	Chi.	W	4-2		9	8	Miller	Wood	Wagner	27-35	4th	8.0
6-11	Chi.	L	5-9		9	13	Farnsworth	Borbon		27-36	4th	9.0
6-12	Chi.	W	5-4		10	10	Oswalt	Cruz	Wagner	28-36	4th	8.0
6-14	Tex.	L	6-9		13	16	Powell	Cruz	Flores	28-37	4th	9.0

Date	Opp.	Res.	Score	(inn.*)	Hits	Opp. hits	Winning pitcher	Losing pitcher	Save	Record	Pos.	GB
6-15	Tex.	W	4-0		11	3	Miller	Valdes		29-37	4th	9.0
6-16	Tex.	W	7-6		11	10	Wagner	Rocker		30-37	4th	8.0
6-17	At Mil.	L	2-5		5	10	Cabrera	Oswalt	DeJean	30-38	4th	8.5
6-18	At Mil.	L	1-7		7	8	Sheets	Saarloos		30-39	4th	9.5
6-19	At Mil.	L	1-8		5	11	Rusch	Redding		30-40	4th	10.5
6-20	At Mil.	W	9-3		9	10	Miller	Wright		31-40	4th	9.5
6-21	Sea.	L	0-8		4	11	Moyer	Hernandez		31-41	4th	9.5
6-22	Sea.	W	3-2	(12)	12	6	Stone	Halama		32-41	T3rd	9.0
6-23	Sea.	L	5-10		10	15	Pineiro	Saarloos		32-42	T3rd	9.0
6-25	Ari.	W	7-3		9	8	Wagner	Myers		33-42	T3rd	8.0
6-26	Ari.	L	1-9		5	13	Johnson	Miller		33-43	4th	9.0
6-27	Ari.	W	7-4		5	11	Dotel	Kim		34-43	T3rd	8.0
6-28	At Tex.	W	6-5		8	10	Oswalt	Park	Wagner	35-43	T3rd	8.0
6-29	At Tex.	W	8-5		14	9	Puffer	Powell	Wagner	36-43	3rd	7.0
7-1	At Cin.	L	5-7		9	9	Haynes	Hernandez	Graves	36-44	3rd	7.5
7-2	At Cin.	W	6-5	(10)	10	15	Dotel	Graves	Wagner	37-44	3rd	7.5
7-3	At Cin.	W	11-4		13	9	Oswalt	Reitsma		38-44	3rd	7.5
7-4	At Pit.	W	8-6		11	12	Borbon	Beimel		39-44	3rd	7.5
7-5	At Pit.	L	3-4		6	10	Fetters	Borbon	Williams	39-45	3rd	7.5
7-6	At Pit.	W	10-2		11	7	Cruz	Wells		40-45	3rd	6.5
7-7	At Pit.	W	6-1		8	4	Miller	Anderson		41-45	3rd	6.5
7-11	Cin.	W	4-3		6	8	Oswalt	Dessens	Wagner	42-45	3rd	6.0
7-12	Cin.	W	6-3		7	11	Miller	Dempster	Wagner	43-45	3rd	5.0
7-13	Cin.	W	2-1		10	6	Munro	Sullivan	Dotel	44-45	3rd	5.0
7-14	Cin.	L	3-8		10	15	Fernandez	Redding	Graves	44-46	3rd	6.0
7-15	Pit.	L	4-5		9	7	Lowe	Wagner	Williams	44-47	3rd	7.0
7-16	Pit.	L	3-7		7	11	Fogg	Oswalt	Boehringer	44-48	3rd	8.0
7-17	At Mil.	W	7-3		10	5	Miller	Rusch		45-48	3rd	7.0
7-18	At Mil.	W	4-2		6	8	Borbon	Wright	Wagner	46-48	3rd	7.0
7-19	At Chi.	L	0-5		3	5	Prior	Cruz		46-49	3rd	7.0
7-20	At Chi.	W	3-2		4	6	Saarloos	Zambrano	Wagner	47-49	3rd	6.0
7-21	At Chi.	L	2-3		7	6	Fassero	Redding	Alfonseca	47-50	3rd	7.0
7-22	Mil.	W	3-1		13	7	Miller	Rusch	Wagner	48-50	3rd	7.0
7-23	Mil.	W	7-4		10	4	Munro	Wright	Dotel	49-50	3rd	7.0
7-24	Mil.	L	8-12		12	14	Quevedo	Puffer	Vizcaino	49-51	3rd	7.0
7-25	Pit.	W	8-0		9	6	Saarloos	Benson		50-51	3rd	7.0
7-26	Pit.	W	4-3		5	5	Wagner	Sauerbeck		51-51	3rd	7.0
7-27	Pit.	W	3-0		12	4	Oswalt	Anderson	Wagner	52-51	3rd	6.0
7-28	Pit.	W	4-0		8	5	Miller	Wells		53-51	3rd	6.0
7-30	At N.Y.	W	16-3		20	8	Saarloos	D'Amico		54-51	3rd	6.0
7-31	At N.Y.	L	0-10		2	13	Estes	Mlicki		54-52	3rd	6.0
8-1	At N.Y.	W	3-1		11	7	Oswalt	Astacio	Wagner	55-52	3rd	5.0
8-2	At Mon.	L	1-3		4	8	Reames	Munro	Stewart	55-53	3rd	5.0
8-3	At Mon.	W	5-3		8	4	Miller	Tucker	Wagner	56-53	3rd	4.0
8-4	At Mon.	W	5-4		11	12	Saarloos	Vazquez	Wagner	57-53	3rd	3.0
8-6	Fla.	W	2-0		5	8	Mlicki	Beckett	Wagner	58-53	T2nd	2.0
8-7	Fla.	W	7-2		9	3	Oswalt	Burnett		59-53	2nd	1.0
8-8	Fla.	L	3-4		9	11	Tavarez	Munro	Looper	59-54	2nd	2.0
8-9	Atl.	L	5-6	(13)	13	15	Spooneybarger	Cruz	Smoltz	59-55	T2nd	2.0
8-10	Atl.	W	8-5		14	8	Saarloos	Marquis	Wagner	60-55	T2nd	2.0
8-11	Atl.	L	3-13		10	20	Millwood	Mlicki		60-56	3rd	3.0
8-12	At Chi.	W	9-6		13	7	Oswalt	Wood	Wagner	61-56	3rd	3.0
8-13	At Chi.	W	5-4		8	10	Munro	Clement	Wagner	62-56	2nd	3.0
8-14	At Chi.	W	4-3		4	7	Miller	Zambrano	Stone	63-56	2nd	3.0
8-15	At Chi.	L	4-6		7	10	Fassero	Saarloos	Alfonseca	63-57	2nd	4.0
8-16	At Cin.	L	3-9		8	13	Moehler	Mlicki		63-58	2nd	4.0
8-17	At Cin.	W	6-1		15	6	Oswalt	Hamilton		64-58	2nd	4.0
8-18	At Cin.	L	1-2	(10)	3	4	White	Stone		64-59	2nd	5.0
8-19	At Cin.	W	7-5		9	8	Miller	Fernandez	Wagner	65-59	2nd	5.0
8-20	Chi.	L	12-14		16	24	Cunnane	Puffer	Alfonseca	65-60	2nd	5.0
8-21	Chi.	W	4-0		12	7	Hernandez	Prior	Dotel	66-60	2nd	5.0
8-22	Chi.	W	9-1		13	7	Oswalt	Smyth		67-60	2nd	5.0
8-23	Cin.	W	6-4		10	10	Munro	Estes	Wagner	68-60	2nd	4.0
8-24	Cin.	L	3-5	(11)	9	6	Graves	Gordon		68-61	2nd	4.0
8-25	Cin.	W	1-0		3	5	Saarloos	Dempster	Borbon	69-61	2nd	3.0
8-27	S.D.	L	6-11		9	16	Fikac	Mlicki		69-62	2nd	3.5
8-28	S.D.	W	2-1		8	4	Oswalt	Peavy	Wagner	70-62	2nd	3.5
8-29	S.D.	W	5-0		13	4	Munro	Lawrence	Dotel	71-62	2nd	2.5
8-30	L.A.	W	8-4		9	5	Miller	Ashby		72-62	2nd	2.5
8-31	L.A.	L	0-4		3	6	Daal	Saarloos		72-63	2nd	4.0

Date	Opp.	Res.	Score	(inn.*)	Hits	Opp. hits	Winning pitcher	Losing pitcher	Save	Record	Pos.	GB
9-1	L.A.	L	1-2		7	9	Nomo	Hernandez	Gagne	72-64	2nd	4.0
9-2	At Tex.	L	2-7		9	14	Park	Robertson		72-65	2nd	4.0
9-3	At S.D.	W	6-2		12	12	Oswalt	Lawrence	Wagner	73-65	2nd	4.0
9-4	At S.D.	L	1-5		6	10	Tomko	Munro		73-66	2nd	5.0
9-5	At S.D.	W	5-0	(11)	11	7	Wagner	Johnson		74-66	2nd	4.5
9-6	At L.A.	L	2-3		6	7	Quantrill	Dotel	Gagne	74-67	2nd	5.5
9-7	At L.A.	W	6-1		14	6	Hernandez	Daal		75-67	2nd	5.5
9-8	At L.A.	W	6-2		10	4	Oswalt	Ishii		76-67	2nd	5.5
9-9	Col.	W	6-5	(10)	8	9	Lidge	Flores		77-67	2nd	5.5
9-10	Col.	W	11-4		14	12	Miller	Neagle		78-67	2nd	5.5
9-11	Col.	L	6-8		13	11	Cook	Saarloos	Jimenez	78-68	2nd	6.5
9-12	St.L.	W	6-3		9	12	Dotel	Veres	Wagner	79-68	2nd	5.5
9-13	St.L.	L	2-3	(10)	9	11	White	Gordon	Isringhausen	79-69	2nd	6.5
9-14	St.L.	L	1-2		7	5	Williams	Munro	Isringhausen	79-70	2nd	7.5
9-15	St.L.	W	8-0		16	3	Miller	Morris		80-70	2nd	6.5
9-17	At Mil.	L	4-5		9	7	Sheets	Saarloos	Vizcaino	80-71	2nd	7.5
9-18	At Mil.	W	3-1		6	6	Puffer	Rusch	Wagner	81-71	2nd	7.5
9-19	At Mil.	L	4-5		10	5	Franklin	Oswalt	DeJean	81-72	2nd	8.5
9-20	At St.L.	L	3-9		7	14	White	Munro		81-73	2nd	9.5
9-21	At St.L.	W	6-3		11	7	Miller	Morris		82-73	2nd	8.5
9-22	At St.L.	L	3-7		7	10	Finley	Saarloos		82-74	2nd	9.5
9-23	Mil.	W	8-6		8	10	Puffer	Rusch	Wagner	83-74	2nd	9.5
9-24	Mil.	L	1-3		5	7	Franklin	Oswalt	DeJean	83-75	2nd	10.5
9-25	Mil.	W	7-5		8	9	Cruz	de los Santos	Wagner	84-75	2nd	10.5
9-27	At S.F	L	1-2		5	9	Schmidt	Miller	Nen	84-76	2nd	11.0
9-28	At S.F	L	2-5		9	7	Rueter	Robertson	Nen	84-77	2nd	12.0
9-29	At S.F	L	0-7		5	12	Jensen	Oswalt		84-78	2nd	13.0

Monthly records: April (11-14), May (13-15), June (12-14), July (18-9), August (18-11), September (12-15).
*Innings, if other than nine.

RECORDS

2002 regular-season record: 84-78
Position: 2nd in N.L. Central
Home: 47-34   **Road:** 37-44
N.L. East: 16-14   **N.L. Central:** 49-41
N.L. West: 14-16   **A.L.:** 5-7
Vs. LH starters: 21-16
Vs. RH starters: 63-62
Grass: 82-74   **Artificial:** 2-4
Day: 35-26   **Night:** 49-52
1-Run: 18-25   **X-inn.:** 5-8
Doubleheaders: 0-0-0
Team record past five years: 448-362
(.553, ranks 3rd in league in that span)

TEAM LEADERS

Batting average: Jose Vizcaino (.303).
At-bats: Lance Berkman (578).
Runs: Lance Berkman (106).
Hits: Lance Berkman (169).
Total bases: Lance Berkman (334).
Doubles: Craig Biggio (36).
Triples: Geoff Blum, Richard Hidalgo (4).
Home runs: Lance Berkman (42).
Runs batted in: Lance Berkman (128).

Stolen bases: Craig Biggio (16).
Slugging percentage: Lance Berkman (.578).
On-base percentage: Lance Berkman (.405).
Wins: Roy Oswalt (19).
Earned-run average: Octavio Dotel (1.85).
Complete games: Wade Miller, Kirk Saarloos (1).
Shutouts: Wade Miller, Kirk Saarloos (1).
Saves: Billy Wagner (35).
Innings pitched: Roy Oswalt (233.0).
Strikeouts: Roy Oswalt (208).

GAMES BY POSITION

Catcher: Brad Ausmus 129, Gregg Zaun 44, Raul Chavez 2, Alan Zinter 1.
First base: Jeff Bagwell 153, Alan Zinter 8, Orlando Merced 7, Jose Vizcaino 5, Geoff Blum 1.
Second base: Craig Biggio 142, Jose Vizcaino 25, Mark Loretta 3, Geoff Blum 1.
Third base: Geoff Blum 104, Morgan Ensberg 43, Jose Vizcaino 30, Mark Loretta 10, Keith Ginter 4, Orlando Merced 1.
Shortstop: Julio Lugo 84, Jose Vizcaino 58, Adam Everett 34, Mark Loretta 6, Geoff Blum 2, Keith Ginter 1.
Outfield: Lance Berkman 156, Daryle Ward 122, Richard Hidalgo 110, Brian L. Hunter 88, Orlando Merced 56, Jason Lane 38, Barry Wesson 15, Geoff Blum 10, Craig Biggio 1.
Designated hitter: Jeff Bagwell 4, Orlando Merced 1, Daryle Ward 1.

TOP DRAFT CHOICES

1. **Derick Grisby,** RHP, Northeast Texas C.C.
2. **Mitch Talbot,** RHP, Canyon View H.S., Cedar City, Utah.
3. **Rory Shortell,** RHP, San Diego State.
4. **Mark McLemore,** LHP, Oregon State.
5. **Pat Misch,** LHP, Western Michigan.
6. **J.P. Duran,** RHP, St. Mary's (Texas) U.
7. **Scott Robinson,** 1B-OF, Rancho Bernardo H.S., San Diego.
8. **Bill Westhoff,** RHP, U of Dallas.
9. **Drew Topham,** SS, Stanford.
10. **Brad Chedister,** RHP, Panola (Texas) J.C.

LOS ANGELES DODGERS
NATIONAL LEAGUE WEST DIVISION

2003 SEASON

March/April

SUN	MON	TUE	WED	THU	FRI	SAT
30	31 ARI D	1 ARI	2 ARI	3 SD D	4 SD	5 SD
6 SD D	7 ARI D	8 ARI	9 ARI D	10 SF	11 SF	12 SF D
13 SF	14	15 SD	16 SD	17 SD	18 SF	19 SF
20 SF	21	22 CIN	23 CIN	24 CIN	25 PIT	26 PIT
27 PIT D	28 PHI	29 PHI	30 PHI			

May

SUN	MON	TUE	WED	THU	FRI	SAT
				1 PHI	2 PIT	3 PIT
4 PIT D	5	6 NYM	7 NYM	8 NYM	9 MON	10 MON D
11 MON D	12 ATL	13 ATL	14 ATL	15	16 FLA	17 FLA
18 FLA D	19	20 COL	21 COL	22 COL D	23 MIL	24 MIL
25 MIL D	26	27 COL	28 COL	29 COL D	30 MIL	31 MIL

June

SUN	MON	TUE	WED	THU	FRI	SAT
1 MIL D	2	3 KC	4 KC	5 KC	6 CWS	7 CWS
8 CWS D	9	10 DET	11 DET	12 DET	13 CLE	14 CLE D
15 CLE D	16	17 SF	18 SF	19 SF	20 ANA	21 ANA D
22 ANA	23 SF	24 SF	25 SF	26	27 ANA	28 ANA
29 ANA D	30					

July

SUN	MON	TUE	WED	THU	FRI	SAT
		1 SD	2 SD	3 SD	4 ARI	5 ARI D
6 ARI	7 SD	8 SD	9 STL	10 STL	11 COL	12 COL
13 COL D	14	15 *	16	17 STL	18 STL	19 STL D
20 STL	21 COL	22 COL	23 COL	24 COL D	25 ARI	26 ARI D
27 ARI D	28	29 PHI	30 PHI	31 PHI		

August

SUN	MON	TUE	WED	THU	FRI	SAT
					1 ATL	2 ATL D
3 ATL D	4	5 CIN	6 CIN	7 CIN	8 CUB	9 CUB
10 CUB D	11 FLA	12 FLA	13 FLA	14 FLA D	15 CUB D	16 CUB D
17 CUB D	18	19 MON	20 MON	21 MON	22 NYM	23 NYM
24 NYM	25	26 HOU	27 HOU	28 HOU	29 COL	30 COL

September

SUN	MON	TUE	WED	THU	FRI	SAT
31 COL	1 HOU	2 HOU	3 HOU	4	5 COL	6 COL D
7 COL D	8 ARI	9 ARI	10 ARI	11 ARI	12 SD	13 SD
14 SD D	15	16 ARI	17 ARI	18 ARI	19 SF	20 SF
21 SF D	22 SD	23 SD	24 SD	25 SD	26 SF	27 SF D
28 SF D						

Home games shaded; D—Day game (games starting before 5 p.m.); *—All-Star Game at Comiskey Park, Chicago. Subject to change.

CLUB DIRECTORY

Managing partner, chairman
Robert Daly
President and chief operating officer
Bob Graziano
Executive vice president and g.m.
Dan Evans
Vice president, assistant g.m.
Kim Ng
Senior vice president, communications
Derrick Hall
Senior v.p., baseball operations
Dave Wallace
Senior vice president
Tommy Lasorda

Director of player development
Bill Bavasi
Director, chief information officer
Mike Mularky
Director, public relations
John Olguin
Director, community affairs
Erikk Aldridge
Director, community relations
Don Newcombe
Director, professional scouting
Matt Slater
Director, amateur scouting
Logan White

Director, international scouting
Rene Francisco
Senior advisor, baseball operations
John Boles
Senior advisor, baseball operations
Joe Amalfitano
Special asst. to the general manager, director, international scouting
Jeff Schugal

MINOR LEAGUE AFFILIATES

Class	Team	League	Manager
AAA	Las Vegas	Pacific Coast	John Shoemaker
AA	Jacksonville	Southern	Dino Ebel
A	Vero Beach	Florida State	Scott Little
A	South Georgia	South Atlantic	Dann Bilardello
Rookie	Ogden	Pioneer	Travis Barbary
Rookie	Gulf Coast Dodgers	Gulf Coast	Luis Salazar

Follow the Dodgers all season at: www.sportingnews.com/baseball/teams/dodgers/

BROADCAST INFORMATION

Radio: XTRA-AM (1150); KWKW-AM (1330, Spanish language).
TV: KCOP-TV (Channel 13)
Cable TV: Fox Sports Net 2.

SPRING TRAINING

Ballpark (city): Holman Stadium (Vero Beach, Fla.).
Ticket information: 772-569-4900.
General number: 772-569-4900.

SPRING TRAINING ROSTER

Manager—Jim Tracy (12).
Coaches—Jack Clark (44), Jim Colburn (45), Glenn Hoffman (35), Jim Lett (17), Manny Mota (11), Jim Riggleman (5), John Shelby (31).

No.	PITCHERS	B/T	Ht./Wt.	Born	Age*	2002 clubs
57	Alvarez, Victor	L/L	5-10/150	11-8-76	26	Las Vegas, Los Angeles
43	Ashby, Andy	R/R	6-1/202	7-11-67	35	Los Angeles
	Brown, Andrew	R/R	6-6/230	2-17-81	22	Vero Beach
27	Brown, Kevin	R/R	6-4/200	3-14-65	38	Los Angeles, Las Vegas
55	Carrara, Giovanni	R/R	6-2/235	3-4-68	35	Los Angeles
	Colyer, Steve	L/L	6-4/205	2-22-79	24	Jacksonville
	Diaz, Jose	R/R	6-4/230	2-27-84	19	South Georgia
37	Dreifort, Darren	R/R	6-2/211	5-3-72	30	DID NOT PLAY
38	Gagne, Eric	R/R	6-2/195	1-7-76	27	Los Angeles
	Gonzalez, Alfredo	R/R	6-2/181	9-17-79	23	Vero Beach, Jacksonville, Las Vegas
17	Ishii, Kaz	L/L	6-0/190	9-9-73	29	Los Angeles
	Kuo, Hong-Chih	L/L	6-0/200	7-23-81	21	Gulf Coast Dodgers, Vero Beach
	Mallette, Brian	R/R	6-0/185	1-19-75	28	Indianapolis, Milwaukee
58	Mota, Guillermo	R/R	6-4/205	7-25-73	29	Las Vegas, Los Angeles
10	Nomo, Hideo	R/R	6-2/210	8-31-68	34	Los Angeles
45	Perez, Odalis	L/L	6-0/150	6-11-77	25	Los Angeles
46	Quantrill, Paul	L/R	6-1/195	11-3-68	34	Los Angeles
	Roberts, Rick	L/L	6-1/200	5-20-79	23	Jacksonville
44	Shuey, Paul	R/R	6-3/215	9-16-70	32	Cleveland, Akron, Los Angeles
	Thompson, Derek	L/L	6-2/180	1-8-81	22	Columbia, Kinston

No.	CATCHERS	B/T	Ht./Wt.	Born	Age*	2002 clubs
	Hill, Koyie	B/R	6-0/190	3-9-79	24	Jacksonville
9	Hundley, Todd	B/R	5-11/200	5-27-69	33	Chicago N.L., Iowa
16	LoDuca, Paul	R/R	5-10/185	4-12-72	30	Los Angeles
40	Ross, Dave	R/R	6-2/205	3-19-77	26	Las Vegas, Los Angeles

No.	INFIELDERS	B/T	Ht./Wt.	Born	Age*	2002 clubs
29	Beltre, Adrian	R/R	5-11/170	4-7-79	23	Los Angeles
50	Cabrera, Jolbert	R/R	6-1/190	12-8-72	30	Buffalo, Cleveland, Las Vegas, Los Angeles
13	Cora, Alex	L/R	6-0/180	10-18-75	27	Los Angeles
3	Izturis, Cesar	B/R	5-9/175	2-10-80	23	Los Angeles
7	Kinkade, Mike	R/R	6-1/210	5-6-73	29	Las Vegas, Los Angeles
29	McGriff, Fred	L/L	6-3/225	10-31-63	39	Chicago N.L.
41	Thurston, Joe	L/R	5-11/175	9-29-79	23	Las Vegas, Los Angeles

No.	OUTFIELDERS	B/T	Ht./Wt.	Born	Age*	2002 clubs
49	Allen, Luke	L/R	6-2/208	8-4-78	24	Las Vegas, Los Angeles
52	Chen, Chin-Feng	R/R	6-1/189	10-28-77	25	Las Vegas, Los Angeles
15	Green, Shawn	L/L	6-4/200	11-10-72	30	Los Angeles
	Hermansen, Chad	R/R	6-2/192	9-10-77	25	Nashville, Pittsburgh, Chicago N.L.
33	Jordan, Brian	R/R	6-1/205	3-29-67	36	Los Angeles
30	Roberts, Dave	L/L	5-10/180	5-31-72	30	Los Angeles
26	Ruan, Wilkin	R/R	6-0/170	9-18-78	24	Jacksonville, Las Vegas, Los Angeles

*Age as of April 1, 2003.

BALLPARK INFORMATION

Ballpark (capacity, surface)
Dodger Stadium (56,000, grass)

Address
1000 Elysian Park Ave.
Los Angeles, CA 90012

Official website
www.dodgers.com

Business phone
323-224-1500

Ticket information
323-224-1448

Field dimensions (from home plate)
To left field at foul line, 330 feet
To center field, 395 feet
To right field at foul line, 330 feet

First game played
April 10, 1962 (Reds 6, Dodgers 3)

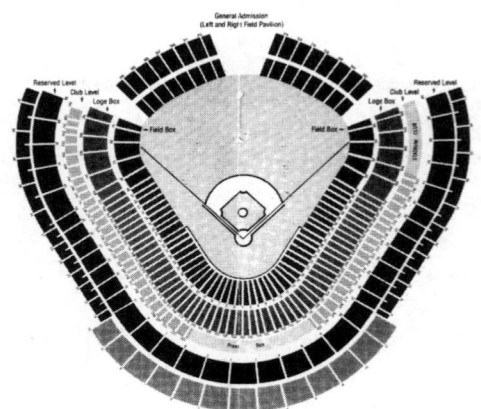

Date	Opp.	Res.	Score	(inn.*)	Hits	Opp. hits	Winning pitcher	Losing pitcher	Save	Record	Pos.	GB
4-2	S.F	L	2-9		5	12	Hernandez	Brown		0-1	T3rd	1.5
4-3	S.F	L	0-12		4	15	Ortiz	Nomo		0-2	5th	2.0
4-4	S.F	L	0-3		3	5	Jensen	Perez	Nen	0-3	5th	3.0
4-5	Col.	W	9-0		11	1	Ashby	Chacon		1-3	T4th	3.0
4-6	Col.	W	9-2		9	7	Ishii	Jennings		2-3	T3rd	3.0
4-7	Col.	W	6-4		13	10	Brown	Hampton	Gagne	3-3	3rd	3.0
4-9	At S.F	W	3-0		10	5	Nomo	Ortiz	Gagne	4-3	2nd	2.0
4-10	At S.F	L	1-2		8	7	Nen	Quantrill		4-4	2nd	3.0
4-11	At S.F	W	4-3		10	8	Daal	Rueter	Gagne	5-4	2nd	2.0
4-12	At S.D.	W	3-0		9	2	Ishii	Jarvis	Gagne	6-4	2nd	2.0
4-13	At S.D.	L	4-6		9	9	Fikac	Quantrill	Hoffman	6-5	3rd	3.0
4-14	At S.D.	L	0-1		5	5	Lawrence	Nomo	Hoffman	6-6	T3rd	3.0
4-15	At Col.	W	5-2		9	5	Perez	Chacon		7-6	T3rd	2.0
4-16	At Col.	L	4-6		11	10	Jennings	Ashby	Jimenez	7-7	T3rd	3.0
4-17	At Col.	W	6-3		10	9	Ishii	White	Gagne	8-7	T3rd	2.0
4-18	S.D.	W	5-2		9	5	Daal	Tollberg	Gagne	9-7	3rd	1.5
4-19	S.D.	W	5-2		7	5	Nomo	Lawrence	Gagne	10-7	T2nd	1.5
4-20	S.D.	W	4-1		9	6	Perez	Jones	Carrara	11-7	T2nd	1.5
4-21	S.D.	L	0-5		3	9	Tomko	Ashby		11-8	3rd	1.5
4-23	At Pit.	W	9-6		14	9	Ishii	Anderson	Gagne	12-8	3rd	1.5
4-24	At Pit.	W	5-1		10	8	Daal	Williams		13-8	T2nd	0.5
4-25	At Pit.	L	2-3		9	5	Fogg	Nomo	Williams	13-9	3rd	1.0
4-26	At Chi.	W	10-0		11	1	Perez	Wood		14-9	2nd	1.0
4-28†	At Chi.	W	5-4		12	6	Ishii	Cruz	Gagne	15-9		
4-28‡	At Chi.	W	4-1		10	3	Ashby	Bere		16-9	T1st	...
4-30	Cin.	L	1-3		8	7	Reitsma	Brown	Graves	16-10	T1st	...
5-1	Cin.	L	0-4		8	5	Hamilton	Nomo		16-11	T1st	...
5-2	Cin.	W	3-2	(14)	12	5	Carrara	Pineda		17-11	T1st	...
5-3	Chi.	L	3-8		10	10	Mahay	Orosco		17-12	3rd	1.0
5-4	Chi.	W	3-2		11	4	Ishii	Bere	Gagne	18-12	3rd	1.0
5-5	Chi.	L	0-3		4	7	Mahay	Brown	Alfonseca	18-13	3rd	2.0
5-7	At Atl.	W	6-5	(16)	14	12	Carrara	Ligtenberg	Orosco	19-13	3rd	1.5
5-8	At Atl.	W	3-1		8	5	Perez	Millwood	Gagne	20-13	3rd	1.5
5-9	At Atl.	L	2-6		7	7	Moss	Ashby		20-14	3rd	2.5
5-10	At Fla.	L	3-4		6	9	Nunez	Carrara		20-15	3rd	2.5
5-11	At Fla.	W	3-0		6	6	Brown	Tavarez	Gagne	21-15	3rd	2.5
5-12	At Fla.	L	3-11		9	13	Dempster	Nomo		21-16	3rd	2.5
5-13	N.Y.	W	3-2	(13)	13	10	Carrara	Corey		22-16	3rd	2.5
5-14	N.Y.	L	0-3		2	9	Astacio	Ashby		22-17	3rd	3.5
5-15	N.Y.	L	0-2		2	6	D'Amico	Ishii		22-18	3rd	3.5
5-16	Mon.	W	4-3		12	7	Daal	Ohka	Gagne	23-18	3rd	3.0
5-17	Mon.	W	8-5		10	11	Nomo	Armas Jr.	Gagne	24-18	3rd	3.0
5-18	Mon.	L	1-3		7	10	Pavano	Perez	Tucker	24-19	3rd	4.0
5-19	Mon.	W	10-1		15	4	Ashby	Chen		25-19	3rd	3.0
5-21	At Mil.	L	6-8		11	10	Buddie	Carrara	DeJean	25-20	3rd	4.0
5-22	At Mil.	W	1-0		7	6	Nomo	Sheets	Gagne	26-20	3rd	3.0
5-23	At Mil.	W	16-3		19	10	Ishii	Rusch		27-20	3rd	2.5
5-24	At Ari.	L	3-14		10	15	Schilling	Perez		27-21	3rd	3.5
5-25	At Ari.	W	10-5		10	11	Ashby	Helling	Gagne	28-21	3rd	2.5
5-26	At Ari.	L	9-10	(10)	16	16	Kim	Springer		28-22	3rd	3.5
5-27	Mil.	W	5-3		14	11	Nomo	Sheets	Gagne	29-22	3rd	2.5
5-28	Mil.	W	8-4		13	6	Ishii	Rusch		30-22	3rd	1.5
5-29	Mil.	W	4-3		4	13	Perez	Wright	Gagne	31-22	3rd	1.5
5-31	Ari.	L	3-6		7	10	Johnson	Daal	Kim	31-23	2nd	3.0
6-1	Ari.	W	2-0		2	5	Ashby	Anderson	Gagne	32-23	2nd	2.0
6-2	Ari.	W	6-3		10	8	Ishii	Batista	Gagne	33-23	2nd	1.0
6-3	At Col.	W	11-5		12	10	Mota	Jimenez		34-23	2nd	1.0
6-4	At Col.	W	10-4		13	13	Orosco	Jones		35-23	T1st	...
6-5	At Col.	L	6-8		14	9	Jennings	Daal	Jimenez	35-24	2nd	1.0
6-7	At Bal.	L	2-4		7	8	Lopez	Ashby	Julio	35-25	2nd	2.0
6-8	At Bal.	W	8-4		11	7	Ishii	Johnson		36-25	2nd	2.0
6-9	At Bal.	W	2-1		5	5	Perez	Ponson	Gagne	37-25	2nd	2.0
6-10	At T.B.	W	10-5		14	9	Nomo	Alvarez		38-25	2nd	1.0
6-11	At T.B.	L	2-11		6	14	Kennedy	Daal		38-26	2nd	1.0
6-12	At T.B.	W	4-2		7	8	Ashby	Rupe	Gagne	39-26	2nd	1.0

Date	Opp.	Res.	Score	(inn.*)	Hits	Opp. hits	Winning pitcher	Losing pitcher	Save	Record	Pos.	GB
6-14	Ana.	L	4-8		4	11	Ortiz	Ishii		39-27	2nd	1.0
6-15	Ana.	W	10-5		14	10	Perez	Schoeneweis		40-27	2nd	1.0
6-16	Ana.	W	5-4		9	6	Carrara	Levine	Gagne	41-27	2nd	1.0
6-18	Tor.	L	1-2		4	8	Halladay	Ashby		41-28	2nd	2.0
6-19	Tor.	W	5-2		8	5	Ishii	Miller	Gagne	42-28	2nd	1.0
6-20	Tor.	W	2-1		6	6	Perez	Loaiza	Gagne	43-28	2nd	1.0
6-21	Bos.	W	3-2		8	6	Nomo	Burkett	Gagne	44-28	2nd	1.0
6-22	Bos.	W	5-4		6	7	Daal	Lowe	Gagne	45-28	T1st	...
6-23	Bos.	W	9-6		13	9	Ashby	Arrojo		46-28	1st	+1.0
6-24	Col.	L	1-4		5	9	Hampton	Ishii	Jimenez	46-29	1st	+0.5
6-25	Col.	W	4-0		5	1	Perez	Thomson		47-29	1st	+1.5
6-26	Col.	W	5-3		9	4	Nomo	Chacon	Gagne	48-29	1st	+1.5
6-27	Col.	W	7-1		13	6	Daal	Neagle		49-29	1st	+2.5
6-28	At Ana.	W	7-5		13	9	Carrara	Shields	Gagne	50-29	1st	+3.5
6-29	At Ana.	L	0-7		3	14	Sele	Ishii		50-30	1st	+2.5
6-30	At Ana.	L	1-5		5	7	Lackey	Perez	Weber	50-31	1st	+1.5
7-1	At Ari.	W	4-0		11	6	Nomo	Johnson	Gagne	51-31	1st	+2.5
7-2	At Ari.	W	8-0		7	4	Daal	Helling		52-31	1st	+3.5
7-3	At Ari.	L	3-5		7	7	Mantei	Orosco	Kim	52-32	1st	+2.5
7-4	At St.L.	L	2-3		11	5	Smith	Ishii	Isringhausen	52-33	1st	+1.5
7-5	At St.L.	W	6-5		10	11	Perez	Morris	Gagne	53-33	1st	+1.5
7-6	At St.L.	W	4-2	(11)	7	4	Quantrill	Kline	Gagne	54-33	1st	+2.5
7-7	At St.L.	L	6-12		13	17	Matthews	Daal		54-34	1st	+2.5
7-11	Ari.	L	3-4		7	8	Koplove	Quantrill	Kim	54-35	1st	+1.5
7-12	Ari.	L	2-3		5	9	Schilling	Perez	Kim	54-36	1st	+0.5
7-13	Ari.	L	5-7		9	11	Anderson	Ashby	Kim	54-37	2nd	0.5
7-14	Ari.	W	2-1		5	3	Ishii	Batista	Gagne	55-37	1st	+0.5
7-15	St.L.	L	2-4		11	6	Smith	Daal	Isringhausen	55-38	1st	+0.5
7-16	St.L.	L	2-9		5	11	Hackman	Nomo		55-39	2nd	0.5
7-17	S.D.	L	0-7		4	11	Lawrence	Perez		55-40	2nd	1.5
7-18	S.D.	L	1-4		5	12	Tomko	Ashby	Hoffman	55-41	2nd	1.5
7-19	S.F	L	2-3	(12)	9	5	Nen	Mota		55-42	3rd	1.5
7-20	S.F	W	4-2		11	7	Quantrill	Rodriguez	Gagne	56-42	2nd	1.5
7-21	S.F	L	4-6		11	10	Ortiz	Carrara	Nen	56-43	3rd	1.5
7-22	At S.D.	L	2-5		13	10	Lawrence	Perez	Hoffman	56-44	3rd	2.5
7-23	At S.D.	W	8-6		11	14	Carrara	Fikac	Gagne	57-44	2nd	2.5
7-24	At S.D.	L	0-8		5	11	Jones	Ishii		57-45	3rd	3.5
7-26	At S.F	W	11-6		18	11	Nomo	Ortiz		58-45	2nd	4.0
7-27	At S.F	W	5-1		11	4	Daal	Hernandez		59-45	2nd	4.0
7-28	At S.F	L	1-3		4	9	Schmidt	Ashby	Nen	59-46	2nd	5.0
7-30	At Cin.	L	4-12		10	10	Dempster	Ishii		59-47	T2nd	5.0
7-31	At Cin.	W	11-5		15	12	Nomo	Moehler		60-47	2nd	5.0
8-1	At Cin.	L	4-6	(13)	13	7	Williamson	Daal		60-48	2nd	5.0
8-2	At Phi.	L	1-3		5	6	Silva	Quantrill	Mesa	60-49	2nd	5.5
8-3	At Phi.	W	8-6	(12)	14	9	Gagne	Coggin	Quantrill	61-49	2nd	6.0
8-4	At Phi.	W	4-3		9	9	Daal	Myers	Gagne	62-49	2nd	6.0
8-5	At Phi.	L	5-7		9	7	Timlin	Shuey	Mesa	62-50	2nd	7.0
8-6	Pit.	L	1-3		8	8	Fogg	Perez	Williams	62-51	3rd	7.0
8-7	Pit.	W	4-0		7	6	Ashby	Meadows	Gagne	63-51	3rd	7.0
8-8	Pit.	W	10-5		13	9	Beirne	Anderson		64-51	2nd	6.0
8-9	Phi.	W	7-6		10	9	Shuey	Timlin	Gagne	65-51	2nd	6.0
8-10	Phi.	W	10-8		15	14	Quantrill	Cormier	Gagne	66-51	2nd	6.0
8-11	Phi.	L	3-6		7	13	Timlin	Shuey	Mesa	66-52	2nd	7.0
8-13	At Mon.	L	3-4		7	9	Smith	Gagne	Stewart	66-53	3rd	8.0
8-14	At Mon.	W	5-2		14	4	Ishii	Colon	Gagne	67-53	2nd	8.0
8-15	At Mon.	W	1-0		7	7	Daal	Vazquez	Gagne	68-53	2nd	8.0
8-16	At N.Y.	W	3-2		7	5	Brown	Guthrie	Gagne	69-53	2nd	8.0
8-17	At N.Y.	W	10-4		17	4	Perez	Astacio		70-53	2nd	8.0
8-18	At N.Y.	W	2-1		9	4	Ashby	Trachsel	Gagne	71-53	2nd	7.0
8-20	Fla.	L	3-6		7	11	Penny	Ishii		71-54	2nd	8.0
8-21	Fla.	W	4-3	(10)	8	12	Shuey	Looper		72-54	2nd	8.0
8-22	Fla.	W	6-2		10	5	Nomo	Lloyd	Shuey	73-54	2nd	8.0
8-23	Atl.	W	4-3		9	5	Gagne	Holmes		74-54	2nd	8.0
8-24	Atl.	W	4-3		7	9	Shuey	Glavine	Gagne	75-54	2nd	7.0
8-25	Atl.	L	5-7		10	10	Moss	Ishii	Smoltz	75-55	2nd	8.0
8-26	Ari.	L	3-6	(12)	9	11	Kim	Mota		75-56	2nd	9.0
8-27	Ari.	W	6-1		8	7	Shuey	Batista		76-56	2nd	8.0
8-28	Ari.	W	1-0		4	6	Perez	Helling	Gagne	77-56	2nd	7.0
8-30	At Hou.	L	4-8		5	9	Miller	Ashby		77-57	2nd	7.0
8-31	At Hou.	W	4-0		6	3	Daal	Saarloos		78-57	2nd	6.0

Date	Opp.	Res.	Score	(inn.*)	Hits	Opp. hits	Winning pitcher	Losing pitcher	Save	Record	Pos.	GB
9-1	At Hou.	W	2-1		9	7	Nomo	Hernandez	Gagne	79-57	2nd	6.0
9-2	At Ari.	W	19-1		24	5	Perez	Helling		80-57	2nd	5.0
9-3	At Ari.	W	3-2		6	8	Ishii	Anderson	Gagne	81-57	2nd	4.0
9-4	At Ari.	L	1-7		3	10	Johnson	Ashby		81-58	2nd	5.0
9-6	Hou.	W	3-2		7	6	Quantrill	Dotel	Gagne	82-58	2nd	4.5
9-7	Hou.	L	1-6		6	14	Hernandez	Daal		82-59	2nd	4.5
9-8	Hou.	L	2-6		4	10	Oswalt	Ishii		82-60	2nd	4.5
9-9	At S.F	L	5-6		9	9	Hernandez	Perez	Nen	82-61	T2nd	5.5
9-10	At S.F	L	2-5		6	7	Schmidt	Brown	Nen	82-62	3rd	6.5
9-11	At S.F	W	7-3		14	8	Nomo	Rueter		83-62	T2nd	6.5
9-12	At Col.	L	1-7		3	11	Stark	Daal		83-63	T2nd	7.0
9-13	At Col.	L	4-5		10	11	Mercker	Mota	Jimenez	83-64	3rd	7.0
9-14	At Col.	W	16-3		20	13	Perez	Santos		84-64	3rd	7.0
9-15	At Col.	L	4-5		9	7	Speier	Ashby	Jimenez	84-65	3rd	8.0
9-16	S.F	W	7-6		12	8	Nomo	Schmidt	Gagne	85-65	T2nd	7.5
9-17	S.F	L	4-6		10	11	Rueter	Daal	Nen	85-66	3rd	7.5
9-18	S.F	L	4-7		8	13	Ortiz	Ellis		85-67	3rd	8.5
9-19	S.F	W	6-3		8	7	Perez	Hernandez		86-67	3rd	8.5
9-20	At S.D.	L	4-8		10	14	Tomko	Ashby		86-68	3rd	8.5
9-21	At S.D.	W	5-3		9	6	Nomo	Hoffman	Gagne	87-68	3rd	7.5
9-22	At S.D.	W	4-3		9	10	Quantrill	Johnson	Gagne	88-68	3rd	6.5
9-24	Col.	L	0-1		3	5	Stark	Perez	Jimenez	88-69	3rd	6.0
9-25	Col.	W	3-2		11	6	Gagne	Jimenez		89-69	3rd	5.0
9-26	S.D.	W	6-5		13	8	Shuey	Lawrence	Gagne	90-69	3rd	5.0
9-27	S.D.	W	1-0	(10)	5	3	Gagne	Fikac		91-69	3rd	5.0
9-28	S.D.	W	14-2		18	8	Beirne	Tankersley		92-69	3rd	5.0
9-29	S.D.	L	0-2		8	4	Perez	Alvarez	Villafuerte	92-70	3rd	6.0

Monthly records: April (16-10), May (15-13), June (19-8), July (10-16), August (18-10), September (14-13).
*Innings, if other than nine. †First game of a doubleheader. ‡Second game of a doubleheader.

RECORDS

2002 regular-season record: 92-70
Position: 3rd in N.L. West
Home: 46-35   **Road:** 46-35
N.L. East: 20-12   **N.L. Central:** 20-16
N.L. West: 40-36   **A.L.:** 12-6
Vs. LH starters: 24-15
Vs. RH starters: 68-55
Grass: 86-66   **Artificial:** 6-4
Day: 29-18   **Night:** 63-52
1-Run: 33-15   **X-inn.:** 7-4
Doubleheaders: 1-0-0
Team record past five years: 424-386
(.523, ranks 7th in league in that span)

TEAM LEADERS

Batting average: Shawn Green (.285).
At-bats: Adrian Beltre (587).
Runs: Shawn Green (110).
Hits: Shawn Green (166).
Total bases: Shawn Green (325).
Doubles: Paul Lo Duca (38).
Triples: Dave Roberts (7).
Home runs: Shawn Green (42).
Runs batted in: Shawn Green (114).
Stolen bases: Dave Roberts (45).
Slugging percentage: Shawn Green (.558).

On-base percentage: Shawn Green (.385).
Wins: Hideo Nomo (16).
Earned-run average: Odalis Perez (3.00).
Complete games: Odalis Perez (4).
Shutouts: Odalis Perez (2).
Saves: Eric Gagne (52).
Innings pitched: Odalis Perez (222.1).
Strikeouts: Hideo Nomo (193).

GAMES BY POSITION

Catcher: Paul Lo Duca 137, Chad Kreuter 41, Dave Ross 6.
First base: Eric Karros 142, Dave Hansen 27, Paul Lo Duca 18, Tyler Houston 12, Mike Kinkade 11.
Second base: Mark Grudzielanek 147, Alex Cora 40, Jeff Reboulet 11, Joe Thurston 4, Jolbert Cabrera 1, Cesar Izturis 1.
Third base: Adrian Beltre 157, Dave Hansen 11, Jolbert Cabrera 3, Jeff Reboulet 3, Tyler Houston 2.
Shortstop: Cesar Izturis 128, Alex Cora 61, Jeff Reboulet 5.
Outfield: Shawn Green 156, Brian Jordan 125, Dave Roberts 117, Marquis Grissom 102, Hiram Bocachica 22, Paul Lo Duca 9, Mike Kinkade 8, Wilkin Ruan 5, Jolbert Cabrera 4, Luke Allen 3, Chin-Feng Chen 1.
Designated hitter: Dave Hansen 4, Brian Jordan 3, Hiram Bocachica 1, Shawn Green 1, Mark Grudzielanek 1, Cesar Izturis 1, Jeff Reboulet 1.

TOP DRAFT CHOICES

1a. **James Loney,** 1B, Elkins H.S., Missouri City, Texas.
1b. **Greg Miller,** LHP, Esperanza H.S., Yorba Linda, Calif.
2a. **Zach Hammes,** RHP, Iowa City (Iowa) H.S.
2b. **Jonathan Broxton,** RHP, Burke County H.S., Waynesboro, Ga.
3. **Mike Nixon,** C, Sunnyslope H.S., Phoenix.
4. **Delwyn Young,** 2B, Santa Barbara (Calif.) C.C.
5. **Mike Megrew,** LHP, Chariho Regional H.S., Hope Valley, R.I.
6. **Marshall Looney,** LHP, La Pine (Ore.) H.S.
7. **David Bagley,** 3B, U. of San Diego.
8. **Jamaal Hamilton,** LHP, Monterey H.S., Lubbock, Texas.
9. **Denver Kitch,** SS, Oklahoma.
10. **Ryan Williams,** RHP, Old Dominion.

MILWAUKEE BREWERS
NATIONAL LEAGUE CENTRAL DIVISION

2003 SEASON

March/April

SUN	MON	TUE	WED	THU	FRI	SAT
30	31 D STL	1	2 STL	3 D STL	4 D SF	5 D SF
6 D SF	7 D PIT	8	9 PIT	10 D PIT	11 ARI	12 ARI
13 D ARI	14 STL	15 STL	16 D STL	17 HOU	18 HOU	19 D HOU
20 HOU	21	22 FLA	23 FLA	24 FLA	25 ATL	26 ATL
27 D ATL	28	29 MON	30 MON			

May

SUN	MON	TUE	WED	THU	FRI	SAT
				1 D MON	2 NYM	3 NYM
4 D NYM	5 CUB	6 CUB	7 D CUB	8	9 CIN	10 CIN
11 CIN	12 CUB	13 CUB	14 CUB	15 CUB	16 CIN	17 D CIN
18 CIN	19 SD	20 SD	21 D SD	22	23 LA	24 LA
25 D LA	26	27 SD	28 SD	29 SD	30 LA	31 LA

June

SUN	MON	TUE	WED	THU	FRI	SAT
1 D LA	2	3 NYM	4 NYM	5 NYM	6 BOS	7 BOS
8 D BOS	9	10 FLA	11 FLA	12 FLA	13 BAL	14 BAL
15 BAL	16 STL	17 STL	18 STL	19 D STL	20 MIN	21 MIN
22 D MIN	23	24 CUB	25 D CUB	26 D CUB	27 MIN	28 MIN
29 D MIN	30					

July

SUN	MON	TUE	WED	THU	FRI	SAT
		1 HOU	2 HOU	3 HOU	4 D COL	5 COL
6 D COL	7 PIT	8 PIT	9 PIT	10 PIT	11 CIN	12 CIN
13 D CIN	14	15 *	16	17 PIT	18 PIT	19 PIT
20 D PIT	21 CIN	22 CIN	23 HOU	24 HOU	25 COL	26 COL
27 D COL	28	29 NYM	30 NYM	31 D NYM		

August

SUN	MON	TUE	WED	THU	FRI	SAT
				1 MON	2 MON
3 D MON	4	5 ATL	6 ATL	7 D ATL	8 FLA	9 FLA
10 D FLA	11	12 PHI	13 PHI	14 PHI	15 PIT	16 D PIT
17 D PIT	18	19 PHI	20 PHI	21 D PHI	22 PIT	23 PIT
24 D PIT	25 CIN	26 CIN	27 CIN	28 CIN	29 D CUB	30 D CUB

September

SUN	MON	TUE	WED	THU	FRI	SAT
31 D CUB	1 D CIN	2 CIN	3 CIN	4	5 CUB	6 CUB
7 D CUB	8 HOU	9 HOU	10 HOU	11 D HOU	12 SF	13 D SF
14 D SF	15 STL	16 STL	17 STL	18 STL	19 ARI	20 ARI
21 D ARI	22	23 STL	24 STL	25 HOU	26 HOU	27 HOU
28 D HOU						

Home games shaded; D—Day game (games starting before 5 p.m.); *—All-Star Game at Comiskey Park, Chicago. Subject to change.

CLUB DIRECTORY

President and chief executive officer
Ulyce Payne Jr.
Sr. vice president and general manager
Doug Melvin
Vice president and general counsel
Tom Gausden

Assistant general manager
Gord Ash
Director, community relations
Leonard Peace
Director, media relations
Jon Greenberg

Director, scouting
Jack Zduriencik
Special asst. to the g.m./player dev.
Reid Nichols
Special assistant to the g.m./scouting
Dick Groch

MINOR LEAGUE AFFILIATES

Class	Team	League	Manager
AAA	Indianapolis	International	Cecil Cooper
AA	Huntsville	Southern	Frank Kremblas
A	High Desert	California	Tim Blackwell
A	Beloit	Midwest	Don Money
Rookie	Helena	Pioneer	Ed Sedar
Rookie	Maryvale	Arizona	Hector Torres

Follow the Brewers all season at: www.sportingnews.com/baseball/teams/brewers/

BROADCAST INFORMATION

Radio: WTMJ-AM (620).
TV: WCGV-TV (Channel 24).
Cable TV: Fox Sports North.

SPRING TRAINING

Ballpark (city): Maryvale Baseball Park (Phoenix, Ariz.).
Ticket information: 623-245-5500.

Manager—Ned Yost.
Coaches—Bill Castro, Rich Dauer, Rich Donnelly, Mike Maddux, Dave Nelson, Butch Wynegar.

No.	PITCHERS	B/T	Ht./Wt.	Born	Age*	2002 clubs
31	Campos, Francisco	R/R	6-0/165	8-12-72	30	Campeche, Indianapolis
43	Childers, Matt	R/R	6-5/195	12-3-78	24	Huntsville, Milwaukee, Indianapolis
28	De Los Santos, Valerio	L/L	6-2/206	10-6-72	30	Indianapolis, Milwaukee
48	DeJean, Mike	R/R	6-4/219	9-28-70	32	Milwaukee
53	Diggins, Ben	R/R	6-7/230	6-13-79	23	Vero Beach, Huntsville, Milwaukee
56	Durocher, Jayson	R/R	6-3/195	8-18-74	28	Indianapolis, Milwaukee
	Ford, Matthew	B/L	6-1/175	4-8-81	21	Dunedin
48	Foster, John	L/L	6-0/200	5-17-78	24	Richmond, Atlanta
26	Franklin, Wayne	L/L	6-2/205	3-9-74	29	New Orleans, Milwaukee
55	Gold, J.M.	R/R	6-5/220	4-18-80	22	High Desert
50	Kinney, Matt	R/R	6-5/220	12-16-76	26	Edmonton, Minnesota, Gulf Coast Twins, Fort Myers, New Britain
33	Leskanic, Curtis	R/R	6-0/196	4-2-68	34	Indianapolis, Huntsville
64	Liriano, Pedro	R/R	6-2/160	10-23-80	22	Rancho Cucamonga
59	Martinez, Luis	L/L	6-7/225	1-20-80	23	Huntsville
30	Matthews, Mike	L/L	6-2/175	10-24-73	29	St. Louis, Milwaukee
	Mlicki, Dave	R/R	6-4/200	6-8-68	34	Houston, New Orleans, Round Rock
47	Nance, Shane	L/L	5-8/180	9-7-77	25	Las Vegas, Indianapolis, Milwaukee
32	Neugebauer, Nick	R/R	6-3/235	7-15-80	22	Milwaukee, Indianapolis
13	Pember, Dave	R/R	6-5/225	5-24-78	24	Huntsville, Milwaukee
37	Quevedo, Ruben	R/R	6-1/245	1-5-79	24	Milwaukee, Indianapolis
31	Rigdon, Paul	R/R	6-5/242	11-2-75	27	Indianapolis
	Ritchie, Todd	R/R	6-3/210	11-7-71	31	Chicago A.L.
39	Rusch, Glendon	L/L	6-1/200	11-7-74	28	Milwaukee
15	Sheets, Ben	R/R	6-1/203	7-18-78	24	Milwaukee
51	Vizcaino, Luis	R/R	5-11/174	8-6-74	28	Milwaukee

No.	CATCHERS	B/T	Ht./Wt.	Born	Age*	2002 clubs
72	Machado, Robert	R/R	6-1/210	6-3-73	29	Chicago N.L., Milwaukee
58	McKay, Cody	L/R	6-0/208	1-11-74	29	Sacramento, Oakland
8	Valentin, Javier	B/R	5-10/192	9-19-75	27	Edmonton, Minnesota

No.	INFIELDERS	B/T	Ht./Wt.	Born	Age*	2002 clubs
	Clayton, Royce	R/R	6-0/185	1-2-70	33	Chicago A.L.
	Cruz, Enrique	R/R	6-1/175	11-21-81	21	St. Lucie
1	Ginter, Keith	R/R	5-10/190	5-5-76	26	New Orleans, Houston, Milwaukee
2	Hall, Bill	R/R	6-0/175	12-28-79	23	Indianapolis, Milwaukee
18	Helms, Wes	R/R	6-4/230	5-12-76	26	Atlanta
11	Sexson, Richie	R/R	6-8/227	12-29-74	28	Milwaukee
7	Young, Eric	R/R	5-8/180	5-18-67	35	Milwaukee

No.	OUTFIELDERS	B/T	Ht./Wt.	Born	Age*	2002 clubs
57	Guerrero, Cristian	R/R	6-5/200	4-12-80	22	Huntsville
41	Hammonds, Jeffrey	R/R	6-0/200	3-5-71	32	Milwaukee
5	Jenkins, Geoff	L/R	6-1/213	7-21-74	28	Milwaukee
20	Podsednik, Scott	L/L	6-0/170	3-18-76	27	Tacoma, Seattle
22	Sanchez, Alex	L/L	5-10/159	8-26-76	26	Milwaukee

*Age as of April 1, 2003.

2003 SEASON *Milwaukee Brewers*

BALLPARK INFORMATION

Ballpark (capacity, surface)
Miller Park (41,900, grass)

Address
One Brewers Way
Milwaukee, WI 53214-3652

Official website
www.milwaukeebrewers.com

Business phone
414-902-4400

Ticket information
414-902-4000, 800-933-7890

Field dimensions (from home plate)
To left field at foul line, 342 feet
To center field, 400 feet
To right field at foul line, 345 feet

First game played
April 6, 2001 (Brewers 5, Reds 4)

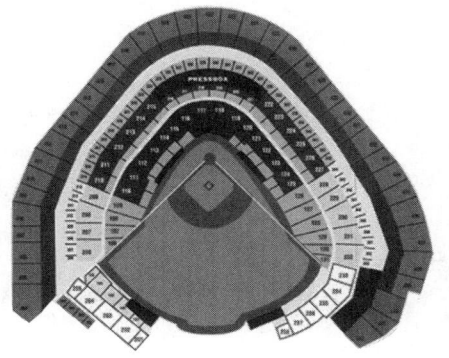

2003 SEASON *Milwaukee Brewers*

Date	Opp.	Res.	Score	(inn.*)	Hits	Opp. hits	Winning pitcher	Losing pitcher	Save	Record	Pos.	GB
4-2	At Hou.	W	9-3		12	12	Sheets	Miller		1-0	T1st	...
4-3	At Hou.	L	2-15		7	15	Oswalt	Quevedo		1-1	T1st	...
4-4	At Hou.	L	3-6		10	10	Reynolds	Wright		1-2	T4th	1.0
4-5	Ari.	W	6-2		10	3	Rusch	Helling		2-2	T2nd	1.0
4-6	Ari.	L	3-6		8	6	Johnson	Neugebauer	Kim	2-3	T3rd	2.0
4-7	Ari.	L	0-2		1	7	Schilling	Sheets		2-4	5th	2.5
4-9	At St.L.	L	5-6		9	6	Veres	Cabrera	Isringhausen	2-5	6th	3.5
4-10	At St.L.	L	5-6	(11)	10	10	Isringhausen	Vizcaino		2-6	6th	3.5
4-11	At St.L.	L	5-6		7	11	Veres	Cabrera	Kline	2-7	6th	4.0
4-12	At S.F	L	1-5		5	5	Ainsworth	Sheets		2-8	6th	5.0
4-13	At S.F	L	2-3		9	5	Hernandez	Figueroa	Nen	2-9	6th	6.0
4-14	At S.F	W	4-3		8	10	Vizcaino	Rodriguez	DeJean	3-9	6th	5.0
4-15	Pit.	L	1-6		7	12	Wells	Rusch		3-10	6th	5.0
4-16	Pit.	L	1-5		4	7	Anderson	Neugebauer		3-11	6th	5.5
4-17	Pit.	L	2-3		5	8	Williams	Buddie	Williams	3-12	6th	6.5
4-18	St.L.	W	7-5		10	7	Cabrera	Hackman	DeJean	4-12	6th	6.0
4-19	St.L.	W	6-1		10	8	Quevedo	Timlin	Vizcaino	5-12	6th	6.0
4-20	St.L.	W	5-3		9	7	Vizcaino	Veres	DeJean	6-12	6th	6.0
4-21	St.L.	W	5-3		10	6	Neugebauer	Smith	DeJean	7-12	5th	6.0
4-23	At Mon.	L	4-5		8	8	Ohka	Sheets	Herges	7-13	5th	6.0
4-24	At Mon.	L	4-5	(15)	12	13	Tucker	Cabrera		7-14	6th	6.0
4-25	At Mon.	L	1-5		4	10	Armas Jr.	Quevedo	Lloyd	7-15	6th	7.0
4-26	At N.Y.	L	0-1		1	3	Estes	Rusch		7-16	6th	7.5
4-27	At N.Y.	L	1-2		3	7	Astacio	Neugebauer	Benitez	7-17	6th	8.5
4-28	At N.Y.	L	6-9		12	15	Davis	King		7-18	6th	8.5
4-30	Atl.	W	4-3		8	6	Figueroa	Maddux	DeJean	8-18	6th	8.5
5-1	Atl.	L	1-3		3	8	Glavine	Quevedo	Smoltz	8-19	6th	9.5
5-2	Atl.	L	2-3	(10)	8	8	Holmes	DeJean	Smoltz	8-20	6th	9.5
5-3	Fla.	L	4-8		7	12	Darensbourg	Buddie		8-21	6th	9.5
5-4	Fla.	W	6-4		10	4	Sheets	Teut	DeJean	9-21	6th	8.5
5-5	Fla.	L	4-7		7	11	Burnett	Figueroa	Nunez	9-22	6th	8.5
5-6	At Cin.	L	5-8		12	10	Brower	Quevedo	Graves	9-23	6th	9.5
5-7	At Cin.	L	2-8		5	15	Dessens	Rusch		9-24	6th	10.5
5-8	At Cin.	L	5-14		10	13	Acevedo	Neugebauer		9-25	6th	11.5
5-9	At Chi.	W	9-4		12	9	Sheets	Bere		10-25	6th	11.0
5-10	At Chi.	W	6-4		7	10	King	Borowski	DeJean	11-25	6th	10.0
5-12	At Chi.	W	13-4		11	10	Rusch	Lieber		12-25	6th	9.5
5-13	Cin.	L	0-5		5	9	Rijo	Cabrera		12-26	6th	10.5
5-14	Cin.	L	3-4		5	5	Acevedo	Quevedo	Graves	12-27	6th	11.5
5-15	Cin.	L	4-7		8	15	Haynes	Stull	Graves	12-28	6th	12.5
5-16	Cin.	L	1-2	(11)	6	5	White	DeJean	Graves	12-29	6th	13.5
5-17	Chi.	W	6-2		10	6	Rusch	Clement		13-29	6th	12.5
5-18	Chi.	W	3-1		9	8	Cabrera	Lieber	DeJean	14-29	6th	12.5
5-19	Chi.	L	4-5	(11)	7	8	Borowski	de los Santos		14-30	6th	12.5
5-21	L.A.	W	8-6		10	11	Buddie	Carrara	DeJean	15-30	6th	12.0
5-22	L.A.	L	0-1		6	7	Nomo	Sheets	Gagne	15-31	6th	13.0
5-23	L.A.	L	3-16		10	19	Ishii	Rusch		15-32	6th	13.0
5-24	S.D.	W	6-2		9	8	Wright	Tollberg		16-32	6th	12.0
5-25	S.D.	W	2-0		5	3	Quevedo	Pickford		17-32	6th	12.0
5-26	S.D.	L	7-8		11	13	Tankersley	Figueroa	Hoffman	17-33	6th	12.0
5-27	At L.A.	L	3-5		11	14	Nomo	Sheets	Gagne	17-34	6th	12.5
5-28	At L.A.	L	4-8		6	13	Ishii	Rusch		17-35	6th	13.5
5-29	At L.A.	L	3-4		13	4	Perez	Wright	Gagne	17-36	6th	14.5
5-31	At S.D.	W	12-1		19	8	Quevedo	Tankersley		18-36	6th	14.0
6-1	At S.D.	W	4-3		10	9	Vizcaino	Embree	DeJean	19-36	6th	13.0
6-2	At S.D.	W	4-3		11	8	Fox	Reed	DeJean	20-36	6th	13.0
6-3	Chi.	W	7-6		12	8	de los Santos	Borowski	DeJean	21-36	6th	12.5
6-4	Chi.	W	6-5	(11)	13	9	Vizcaino	Fassero		22-36	6th	11.5
6-5	Chi.	L	1-5	(10)	7	7	Farnsworth	DeJean		22-37	6th	12.0
6-7	At Pit.	L	1-6		5	12	Beimel	Sheets		22-38	6th	12.5
6-8	At Pit.	L	8-9	(11)	13	15	Boehringer	King		22-39	6th	13.5
6-9	At Pit.	L	4-5		10	7	Sauerbeck	Wright	Williams	22-40	6th	13.5
6-10	At Oak.	L	6-8		16	10	Bradford	de los Santos	Koch	22-41	6th	13.5
6-11	At Oak.	L	2-11		5	14	Zito	Figueroa		22-42	6th	14.5
6-12	At Oak.	L	0-8		9	10	Mulder	Sheets		22-43	6th	14.5

Date	Opp.	Res.	Score	(inn.*)	Hits	Opp. hits	Winning pitcher	Losing pitcher	Save	Record	Pos.	GB
6-14	Min.	W	7-5		13	11	King	Jackson	DeJean	23-43	6th	14.5
6-15	Min.	L	2-5		7	9	Milton	Wright	Guardado	23-44	6th	15.5
6-16	Min.	L	6-7		11	10	Fiore	Figueroa	Guardado	23-45	6th	15.5
6-17	Hou.	W	5-2		10	5	Cabrera	Oswalt	DeJean	24-45	6th	15.0
6-18	Hou.	W	7-1		8	7	Sheets	Saarloos		25-45	6th	15.0
6-19	Hou.	W	8-1		11	5	Rusch	Redding		26-45	6th	15.0
6-20	Hou.	L	3-9		10	9	Miller	Wright		26-46	6th	15.0
6-21	Ana.	L	4-11		11	12	Ortiz	Quevedo		26-47	6th	15.0
6-22	Ana.	L	2-8		10	16	Washburn	Cabrera		26-48	6th	15.5
6-23	Ana.	L	2-5		9	9	Appier	Sheets	Percival	26-49	6th	15.5
6-25	At St.L.	W	2-0		7	4	Rusch	Morris		27-49	6th	14.5
6-26	At St.L.	L	2-5		7	9	Williams	Wright	Isringhausen	27-50	6th	15.5
6-27	At St.L.	W	7-2	(11)	12	8	Vizcaino	Stechschulte		28-50	6th	14.5
6-28	At Min.	L	1-5		4	9	Santana	Sheets		28-51	6th	15.5
6-29	At Min.	W	10-2		17	6	Cabrera	Kinney		29-51	6th	14.5
6-30	At Min.	L	3-4		5	10	Milton	Rusch	Guardado	29-52	6th	14.5
7-1	At Pit.	W	2-0		3	3	Wright	Wells		30-52	6th	14.5
7-2	At Pit.	W	12-6		18	9	Quevedo	Anderson		31-52	6th	14.5
7-3	At Pit.	L	1-3		7	8	Fogg	Sheets	Williams	31-53	6th	15.5
7-4	At Cin.	W	5-4		9	7	Durocher	Graves	DeJean	32-53	6th	15.5
7-5	At Cin.	L	6-8		12	9	White	Rusch	Graves	32-54	6th	15.5
7-6	At Cin.	L	4-6		12	9	Haynes	Wright	Sullivan	32-55	6th	15.5
7-7	At Cin.	W	7-4		14	9	de los Santos	Hamilton		33-55	6th	15.5
7-11	Pit.	L	2-3	(10)	7	9	Boehringer	DeJean	Williams	33-56	6th	16.0
7-12	Pit.	L	2-9		12	9	Lowe	Rusch		33-57	6th	16.0
7-13	Pit.	L	3-5		8	8	Wells	Wright	Williams	33-58	6th	17.0
7-14	Pit.	W	5-3		6	7	Quevedo	Beimel	DeJean	34-58	6th	17.0
7-15	Cin.	L	0-2		5	10	Reitsma	Cabrera		34-59	6th	18.0
7-16	Cin.	L	1-6		4	9	Dessens	Sheets		34-60	6th	19.0
7-17	Hou.	L	3-7		5	10	Miller	Rusch		34-61	6th	19.0
7-18	Hou.	L	2-4		8	6	Borbon	Wright	Wagner	34-62	6th	20.0
7-19	At Col.	L	5-9		6	11	Chacon	Quevedo		34-63	6th	20.0
7-20	At Col.	L	5-6		8	12	Stark	Cabrera	Jimenez	34-64	6th	20.0
7-21	At Col.	L	4-6		11	12	Jennings	Sheets	Jimenez	34-65	6th	21.0
7-22	At Hou.	L	1-3		7	13	Miller	Rusch	Wagner	34-66	6th	22.0
7-23	At Hou.	L	4-7		4	10	Munro	Wright	Dotel	34-67	6th	23.0
7-24	At Hou.	W	12-8		14	12	Quevedo	Puffer	Vizcaino	35-67	6th	22.0
7-26	Col.	W	10-3		13	8	Sheets	Stark	Vizcaino	36-67	6th	22.5
7-27	Col.	W	6-5	(10)	13	8	DeJean	Jimenez		37-67	6th	21.5
7-28	Col.	W	5-3		11	12	Wright	Hampton	DeJean	38-67	6th	21.5
7-30	At Atl.	L	2-3		6	6	Moss	Quevedo	Smoltz	38-68	6th	22.5
7-31	At Atl.	L	1-9		6	12	Millwood	Sheets		38-69	6th	22.5
8-1	At Atl.	L	0-4		7	9	Maddux	Rusch		38-70	6th	22.5
8-2	At Fla.	W	1-0		10	3	Wright	Tavarez	DeJean	39-70	6th	21.5
8-3	At Fla.	L	7-11		13	12	Penny	Cabrera	Looper	39-71	6th	21.5
8-4	At Fla.	L	2-7		9	12	Tejera	Quevedo		39-72	6th	21.5
8-6	N.Y.	L	1-5		3	13	Astacio	Sheets		39-73	6th	21.5
8-7	N.Y.	W	6-2		9	9	Rusch	D'Amico		40-73	6th	20.5
8-8	N.Y.	L	0-9		5	14	Trachsel	Wright		40-74	6th	21.5
8-9	Mon.	L	4-11		10	16	Colon	Quevedo		40-75	6th	21.5
8-10	Mon.	W	5-2		12	10	Cabrera	Vazquez	DeJean	41-75	6th	21.5
8-11	Mon.	W	6-2		10	7	Sheets	Yoshii		42-75	6th	21.5
8-13	At Phi.	L	1-3		5	7	Padilla	Rusch	Mesa	42-76	6th	23.0
8-14	At Phi.	L	1-4		4	6	Myers	Wright		42-77	6th	24.0
8-15	At Phi.	L	0-5		5	9	Roa	Quevedo		42-78	6th	25.0
8-16	At Pit.	W	10-3		15	8	Sheets	Fogg		43-78	6th	24.0
8-17	At Pit.	L	0-5		6	6	Meadows	Cabrera		43-79	6th	25.0
8-18	At Pit.	L	2-3		9	8	Arroyo	Rusch	Williams	43-80	6th	26.0
8-20	Phi.	W	2-1		9	6	Wright	Myers	DeJean	44-80	6th	25.5
8-21	Phi.	L	3-13		6	17	Roa	Sheets		44-81	6th	26.5
8-22	Phi.	L	0-7		4	10	Wolf	Osting		44-82	6th	27.5
8-23	Pit.	L	3-6		6	8	Lincoln	Durocher	Williams	44-83	6th	27.5
8-24	Pit.	L	10-17		20	16	Wells	Cabrera		44-84	6th	27.5
8-25	Pit.	L	2-3		9	9	Benson	Wright	Williams	44-85	6th	27.5
8-26	Chi.	W	2-1		3	6	Sheets	Prior	DeJean	45-85	6th	27.0
8-27	Chi.	L	2-6		10	10	Benes	Osting		45-86	6th	27.5
8-28	Chi.	W	5-1		9	7	Rusch	Wood	Vizcaino	46-86	6th	27.5
8-29	Chi.	L	10-13		9	14	Clement	Lorraine		46-87	6th	27.5
8-30	At Cin.	W	9-4		11	11	King	Sullivan		47-87	6th	27.5
8-31	At Cin.	W	11-2		17	8	Sheets	Reitsma		48-87	6th	28.0

Date	Opp.	Res.	Score	(inn.*)	Hits	Opp. hits	Winning pitcher	Losing pitcher	Save	Record	Pos.	GB
9-1	At Cin.	W	4-2		6	8	Cabrera	Dessens	DeJean	49-87	6th	27.0
9-2†	At Chi.	W	4-2		12	9	Rusch	Smyth	DeJean	50-87		
9-2‡	At Chi.	L	4-17		8	14	Wood	Diggins		50-88	6th	26.5
9-3	At Chi.	L	1-10		6	12	Clement	Pember		50-89	6th	27.5
9-4	At Chi.	L	0-3		4	8	Zambrano	Figueroa	Alfonseca	50-90	6th	28.5
9-6	Cin.	L	3-5	(12)	7	11	Graves	DeJean	Hamilton	50-91	6th	29.5
9-7	Cin.	W	9-6		13	8	Rusch	Estes	DeJean	51-91	6th	29.5
9-8	Cin.	L	4-5		12	9	Haynes	Neugebauer	Graves	51-92	6th	30.5
9-9	St.L.	L	0-3		6	6	Williams	Diggins	Kline	51-93	6th	31.5
9-10	St.L.	L	3-8		9	11	Morris	Franklin		51-94	6th	32.5
9-11	St.L.	L	3-4		9	10	Fassero	Sheets	Isringhausen	51-95	6th	33.5
9-13	At Ari.	W	8-4		9	7	Rusch	Helling		52-95	6th	33.0
9-14	At Ari.	L	0-5		3	11	Johnson	Neugebauer		52-96	6th	34.0
9-15	At Ari.	L	5-6	(13)	10	10	Koplove	Figueroa		52-97	6th	34.0
9-17	Hou.	W	5-4		7	9	Sheets	Saarloos	Vizcaino	53-97	6th	34.0
9-18	Hou.	L	1-3		6	6	Puffer	Rusch	Wagner	53-98	6th	35.0
9-19	Hou.	W	5-4		5	10	Franklin	Oswalt	DeJean	54-98	6th	35.0
9-20	S.F	L	1-5		6	9	Jensen	Neugebauer		54-99	6th	36.0
9-21	S.F	L	1-3		3	9	Schmidt	Diggins	Nen	54-100	6th	36.0
9-22	S.F	L	1-3		5	5	Rodriguez	Vizcaino	Nen	54-101	6th	37.0
9-23	At Hou.	L	6-8		10	8	Puffer	Rusch	Wagner	54-102	6th	38.0
9-24	At Hou.	W	3-1		7	5	Franklin	Oswalt	DeJean	55-102	6th	38.0
9-25	At Hou.	L	5-7		9	8	Cruz	de los Santos	Wagner	55-103	6th	39.0
9-26	At St.L.	L	1-9		7	12	Morris	Diggins		55-104	6th	40.0
9-27	At St.L.	W	2-1		5	4	Sheets	White	DeJean	56-104	6th	39.0
9-28	At St.L.	L	1-3		3	4	Finley	Rusch	Isringhausen	56-105	6th	40.0
9-29	At St.L.	L	0-4		4	5	Crudale	Vizcaino		56-106	6th	41.0

Monthly records: April (8-18), May (10-18), June (11-16), July (9-17), August (10-18), September (8-19).
*Innings, if other than nine. †First game of a doubleheader. ‡Second game of a doubleheader.

RECORDS

2002 regular-season record: 56-106
Position: 6th in N.L. Central
Home: 31-50   **Road:** 25-56
N.L. East: 7-23   **N.L. Central:** 35-55
N.L. West: 12-18   **A.L.:** 2-10
Vs. LH starters: 9-23
Vs. RH starters: 47-83
Grass: 55-98   **Artificial:** 1-8
Day: 17-37   **Night:** 39-69
1-Run: 14-28   **X-inn.:** 3-10
Doubleheaders: 0-0-1
Team record past five years: 345-464
(.426, ranks 16th in league in that span)

TEAM LEADERS

Batting average: Alex Sanchez (.289).
At-bats: Richie Sexson (570).
Runs: Richie Sexson (86).
Hits: Richie Sexson (159).
Total bases: Richie Sexson (287).
Doubles: Richie Sexson (37).
Triples: Alex Sanchez (7).
Home runs: Richie Sexson (29).
Runs batted in: Richie Sexson (102).

Stolen bases: Alex Sanchez (37).
Slugging percentage: Richie Sexson (.504).
On-base percentage: Richie Sexson (.363).
Wins: Ben Sheets (11).
Earned-run average: Ben Sheets (4.15).
Complete games: Glendon Rusch (4).
Shutouts: Ruben Quevedo, Glendon Rusch, Jamey Wright (1).
Saves: Mike DeJean (27).
Innings pitched: Ben Sheets (216.2).
Strikeouts: Ben Sheets (170).

GAMES BY POSITION

Catcher: Paul Bako 76, Robert Machado 48, Raul Casanova 28, Jorge Fabregas 20, Marcus Jensen 15.
First base: Richie Sexson 154, Lenny Harris 12, Mark Loretta 5, Izzy Alcantara 2, Robert Machado 2, Tyler Houston 1.
Second base: Eric Young 123, Ronnie Belliard 49, Mark Loretta 3.
Third base: Tyler Houston 72, Mark Loretta 47, Ronnie Belliard 42, Keith Ginter 21, Lenny Harris 14, Bill Hall 2.

Shortstop: Jose Hernandez 149, Bill Hall 13, Mark Loretta 12, Luis Lopez 4.
Outfield: Jeffrey Hammonds 125, Alex Sanchez 100, Matt Stairs 84, Alex Ochoa 72, Geoff Jenkins 66, Ryan Thompson 51, Jim Rushford 22, Ryan Christenson 21, Lenny Harris 16, Izzy Alcantara 7, Eric Young 2.
Designated hitter: Lenny Harris 2, Eric Young 2, Mark Loretta 1, Richie Sexson 1.

TOP DRAFT CHOICES

1. **Prince Fielder,** 1B, Eau Gallie H.S., Melbourne, Fla.
2. **Josh Murray,** SS, Jesuit H.S., Tampa.
3. **Eric Thomas,** RHP, South Alabama.
4. **Nic Carter,** OF, Campbell.
5. **Jarrad Page,** SS, San Leandro (Calif.) H.S.
6. **Khalid Ballouli,** RHP, Texas A&M.
7. **Tom Wilhelmsen,** RHP, Tucson (Ariz.) Magnet H.S.
8. **Steve Kahn,** RHP, Servite H.S., Anaheim, Calif.
9. **Edwin Walker,** LHP, Highland H.S., San Antonio.
10. **Jeremy Frost,** C, Central Florida.

MONTREAL EXPOS
NATIONAL LEAGUE EAST DIVISION

2003 SEASON

March/April

SUN	MON	TUE	WED	THU	FRI	SAT
30	31 ATL	1	2 ATL	3 ATL	4 NYM	5 D NYM
6 NYM	7 D CUB	8	9 D CUB	10 D CUB	11 † NYM	12 † NYM
13 D† NYM	14 D† NYM	15 † ATL	16 † ATL	17 D† ATL	18 † CIN	19 † CIN
20 D† CIN	21	22 ARI	23 ARI	24 ARI	25 HOU	26 D HOU
27 D HOU	28	29 MIL	30 MIL			

May

SUN	MON	TUE	WED	THU	FRI	SAT
				1 D MIL	2 STL	3 D STL
4 D STL	5	6 SD	7 SD	8 SD	9 LA	10 D LA
11 D LA	12 SF	13 SF	14 D SF	15 COL	16 COL	17 D COL
18 D COL	19	20 FLA	21 FLA	22 FLA	23 PHI	24 PHI
25 D PHI	26 D FLA	27 FLA	28 FLA	29 FLA	30 PHI	31 PHI

June

SUN	MON	TUE	WED	THU	FRI	SAT
1 D PHI	2	3 † ANA	4 † ANA	5 † ANA	6 † TEX	7 † TEX
8 D† TEX	9	10 SEA	11 SEA	12 SEA	13 OAK	14 D OAK
15 D OAK	16	17 PIT	18 PIT	19 PIT	20 TOR	21 TOR
22 D TOR	23 PIT	24 D PIT	25 D PIT	26	27 TOR	28 D TOR
29 D TOR	30 NYM					

July

SUN	MON	TUE	WED	THU	FRI	SAT
		1 NYM	2 NYM	3 ATL	4 ATL	5 ATL
6 D ATL	7 PHI	8 PHI	9 PHI	10	11 FLA	12 FLA
13 D FLA	14	15 *	16	17 PHI	18 PHI	19 PHI
20 D PHI	21 FLA	22 FLA	23 NYM	24 NYM	25 ATL	26 ATL
27 D ATL	28 ATL	29 STL	30 STL	31 STL		

August

SUN	MON	TUE	WED	THU	FRI	SAT
					1 MIL	2 MIL
3 D MIL	4	5 ARI	6 ARI	7 ARI	8 HOU	9 HOU
10 D HOU	11 COL	12 COL	13 COL	14	15 SF	16 SF
17 D SF	18 D SF	19 LA	20 LA	21 D LA	22 SD	23 SD
24 D SD	25 PHI	26 PHI	27 PHI	28 D PHI	29 FLA	30 FLA

September

SUN	MON	TUE	WED	THU	FRI	SAT
31 FLA	1 D FLA	2 D PHI	3 D PHI	4	5 † FLA	6 † FLA
7 D† FLA	8	9 † CUB	10 † CUB	11 D† CUB	12 NYM	13 NYM
14 D NYM	15 ATL	16 ATL	17 D ATL	18 NYM	19 NYM	20 D NYM
21 D NYM	22	23 ATL	24 ATL	25	26 CIN	27 D CIN
28 D CIN						

Home games shaded; D—Day game (games starting before 5 p.m.); *—All-Star Game at Comiskey Park, Chicago. †—Game played in Puerto Rico. Subject to change.

CLUB DIRECTORY

President
Tony Tavares

Vice president & general manager
Omar Minaya

Assistant general manager
Tony Siegle

Special assistant to the general manager
Dan Lunetta

Director, player development
Adam Wogan

Director, pro scouting
Lee MacPhail

Director, amateur scouting
Dana Brown

Director, media services
Monique Giroux

Manager, media relations
Matt Charbonneau

MINOR LEAGUE AFFILIATES

Class	Team	League	Manager
AAA	Edmonton	Pacific Coast	Dave Huppert
AA	Harrisburg	Eastern	Dave Machemer
A	Brevard County	Florida State	Doug Sisson
A	Savannah	South Atlantic	Joey Cora
A	Vermont	New York-Pennsylvania	To be announced
Rookie	Gulf Coast Expos	Gulf Coast	To be announced

BROADCAST INFORMATION

Radio: To be announced.
TV: To be announced.

SPRING TRAINING

Ballpark (city): Space Coast Stadium (Melbourne, Fla.).
Ticket information: 321-633-8119.

Follow the Expos all season at: www.sportingnews.com/baseball/teams/expos/

2003 SEASON *Montreal Expos*

Manager—Frank Robinson (20).
Coaches—Manny Acta (14), Tom McCraw (17), Jerry Morales (28), Bob Natal (13), Claude Raymond (16).

No.	PITCHERS	B/T	Ht./Wt.	Born	Age*	2002 clubs
36	Armas, Tony	R/R	6-4/215	4-29-78	24	Montreal
	Ayala, Luis	R/R	6-2/175	1-12-78	25	Saltillo, Ottawa
	Biddle, Rocky	R/R	6-3/230	5-21-76	26	Charlotte, Chicago A.L.
32	Brower, Jim	R/R	6-3/215	12-29-72	30	Cincinnati, Montreal
57	Chiaviacci, Ron	R/R	6-2/220	9-5-77	25	Harrisburg
54	Day, Zach	R/R	6-4/185	6-15-78	24	Ottawa, Montreal
37	Downs, Scott	L/L	6-2/190	3-17-76	27	Brevard County, Ottawa
47	Drew, Tim	R/R	6-1/195	8-31-78	24	Buffalo, Ottawa, Montreal
58	Eischen, Joey	L/L	6-0/210	5-25-70	32	Ottawa, Montreal
	Gonzalez, Dicky	R/R	5-11/170	12-21-78	24	Norfolk, Ottawa
	Hernandez, Orlando	R/R	6-2/220	10-11-69	33	New York A.L., Columbus
31	Kim, Sun-Woo	R/R	6-2/188	9-4-77	25	Pawtucket, Boston, Ottawa, Montreal
44	Manon, Julio	L/R	6-0/200	6-10-73	29	Ottawa, Harrisburg
24	Ohka, Tomo	R/R	6-1/180	3-18-76	27	Montreal
34	Reames, Britt	R/R	5-11/175	8-19-73	29	Montreal, Ottawa
43	Smith, Dan	R/R	6-3/210	9-15-75	27	Montreal, Ottawa
	Song, Seung	R/R	6-1/192	6-29-80	22	Trenton, Harrisburg
51	Stewart, Scott	R/L	6-2/225	8-14-75	27	Montreal
52	Tucker, T.J.	R/R	6-3/245	8-20-78	24	Montreal
	Vargas, Claudio	R/R	6-3/210	5-19-79	23	Calgary, Harrisburg
23	Vazquez, Javier	R/R	6-2/195	7-25-76	26	Montreal

No.	CATCHERS	B/T	Ht./Wt.	Born	Age*	2002 clubs
5	Barrett, Michael	R/R	6-2/200	10-22-76	26	Montreal
39	Schneider, Brian	L/R	6-1/200	11-26-76	26	Montreal

No.	INFIELDERS	B/T	Ht./Wt.	Born	Age*	2002 clubs
18	Cabrera, Orlando	R/R	5-10/185	11-2-74	28	Montreal
2	Carroll, Jamey	R/R	5-10/175	2-18-74	29	Harrisburg, Ottawa, Montreal
58	Hodges, Scott	L/R	6-0/185	12-26-78	24	Harrisburg
	Liefer, Jeff	L/R	6-3/210	8-17-74	28	Chicago A.L.
12	Mateo, Henry	B/R	5-11/180	10-14-76	26	Ottawa, Montreal
21	Tatis, Fernando	R/R	5-10/180	1-1-75	28	Brevard County, Montreal
3	Vidro, Jose	B/R	5-11/195	8-27-74	28	Montreal

No.	OUTFIELDERS	B/T	Ht./Wt.	Born	Age*	2002 clubs
11	Bergeron, Peter	L/R	6-0/190	11-9-77	25	Montreal, Ottawa
53	Calloway, Ron	L/L	6-0/190	9-4-76	26	Ottawa
29	Cepicky, Matt	L/R	6-2/215	11-10-77	25	Harrisburg, Montreal
19	Chavez, Endy	L/L	6-0/165	2-7-78	25	Ottawa, Montreal
26	Cordero, Wil	R/R	6-2/200	10-3-71	31	Cleveland, Montreal
27	Guerrero, Vladimir	R/R	6-3/210	2-9-76	27	Montreal
1	Macias, Jose	B/R	5-10/189	1-25-72	31	Detroit, Montreal
33	Mouton, Lyle	R/R	6-4/230	5-13-69	33	DID NOT PLAY
66	Pascucci, Val	R/R	6-6/235	11-17-78	24	Harrisburg
	Sledge, Terrmel	L/L	6-0/185	3-18-77	26	Harrisburg, Ottawa
6	Wilkerson, Brad	L/L	6-0/200	6-1-77	25	Montreal

*Age as of April 1, 2003.

Ballpark (capacity, surface)
Olympic Stadium (46,620, artificial)

Address
P.O. Box 500, Station M
Montreal, Que. H1V 3P2

Official website
www.montrealexpos.com

Business phone
514-253-3434

Ticket information
800-GO-EXPOS

Field dimensions (from home plate)
To left field at foul line, 325 feet
To center field, 404 feet
To right field at foul line, 325 feet

First game played
April 15, 1977 (Phillies 7, Expos 2)

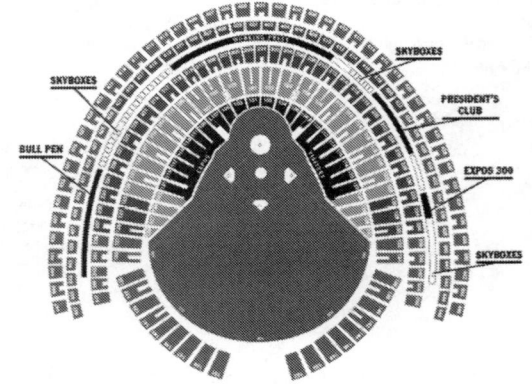

Date	Opp.	Res.	Score	(inn.*)	Hits	Opp. hits	Winning pitcher	Losing pitcher	Save	Record	Pos.	GB
4-2	Fla.	W	7-6		11	8	Herges	Looper		1-0	T1st	...
4-3	Fla.	L	5-6		9	10	Burnett	Armas Jr.	Tejera	1-1	T1st	...
4-4	Fla.	L	0-1		4	9	Penny	Pavano		1-2	T3rd	1.0
4-5	At Cin.	W	8-7		12	13	Yoshii	Haynes	Lloyd	2-2	T1st	...
4-6	At Cin.	W	5-2		7	5	Ohka	Pineda	Lloyd	3-2	T1st	...
4-7	At Cin.	L	5-6	(10)	11	15	Sullivan	Lloyd		3-3	T1st	...
4-8	At Fla.	W	10-2		15	4	Armas Jr.	Burnett		4-3	T1st	...
4-10	At Fla.	W	9-7		12	15	Pavano	Penny		5-3	1st	+0.5
4-11	At Fla.	L	5-7		8	11	Tavarez	Yoshii	Nunez	5-4	T1st	...
4-12	At N.Y.	L	1-2		4	8	D'Amico	Ohka	Benitez	5-5	3rd	1.0
4-13	At N.Y.	W	9-8	(11)	12	9	Herges	Strickland		6-5	T1st	...
4-14	At N.Y.	L	4-6		6	6	Trachsel	Armas Jr.	Benitez	6-6	T2nd	1.0
4-15	Chi.	L	4-6		9	12	Wood	Pavano	Alfonseca	6-7	T3rd	2.0
4-16	Chi.	W	8-4		8	12	Yoshii	Cruz	Tucker	7-7	3rd	2.0
4-17	Chi.	W	15-8		19	12	Chen	Osborne		8-7	2nd	1.0
4-18	N.Y.	L	0-1		2	7	Leiter	Vazquez		8-8	3rd	2.0
4-19	N.Y.	W	5-3		10	9	Armas Jr.	Trachsel	Herges	9-8	2nd	1.0
4-20	N.Y.	W	7-5		12	10	Pavano	Estes	Herges	10-8	T1st	...
4-21	N.Y.	W	6-3		12	10	Chen	Astacio	Lloyd	11-8	1st	+1.0
4-23	Mil.	W	5-4		8	8	Ohka	Sheets	Herges	12-8	1st	+1.0
4-24	Mil.	W	5-4	(15)	13	12	Tucker	Cabrera		13-8	1st	+2.0
4-25	Mil.	W	5-1		10	4	Armas Jr.	Quevedo	Lloyd	14-8	1st	+2.0
4-26	St.L.	L	6-7	(11)	11	17	Stechschulte	Ohka	Veres	14-9	1st	+1.0
4-27	St.L.	L	0-5		5	8	Matthews	Chen		14-10	T1st	...
4-28	St.L.	W	5-2		10	10	Ohka	Morris	Herges	15-10	T1st	...
4-30	At Hou.	W	5-1		8	5	Vazquez	Oswalt		16-10	T1st	...
5-1	At Hou.	W	5-4		9	8	Armas Jr.	Dotel	Herges	17-10	T1st	...
5-2	At Hou.	L	2-8		4	15	Redding	Pavano		17-11	T1st	...
5-3	At Ari.	L	3-6		5	13	Schilling	Chen	Kim	17-12	2nd	1.0
5-4	At Ari.	L	5-6	(11)	8	13	Oropesa	Lloyd		17-13	2nd	1.0
5-5	At Ari.	L	2-5		6	10	Morgan	Vazquez	Kim	17-14	2nd	1.0
5-7	Col.	L	3-5		11	9	Thomson	Armas Jr.	Jimenez	17-15	T2nd	1.0
5-8	Col.	L	0-5		6	7	Chacon	Pavano		17-16	3rd	1.0
5-9	Col.	W	6-5	(12)	8	15	Lloyd	White		18-16	T2nd	1.0
5-10	S.F	W	6-3		11	8	Vazquez	Hernandez		19-16	2nd	1.0
5-11	S.F	L	2-3		9	7	Fultz	Reames	Nen	19-17	T2nd	1.0
5-12	S.F	W	4-2		9	5	Armas Jr.	Ortiz	Herges	20-17	2nd	1.0
5-13	At S.D.	L	3-7		9	12	Tomko	Pavano		20-18	2nd	1.0
5-14	At S.D.	L	4-5		8	13	Hoffman	Stewart		20-19	T2nd	2.0
5-15	At S.D.	L	1-2	(14)	8	10	Embree	Eischen		20-20	3rd	2.0
5-16	At L.A.	L	3-4		7	12	Daal	Ohka	Gagne	20-21	4th	2.0
5-17	At L.A.	L	5-8		11	10	Nomo	Armas Jr.	Gagne	20-22	4th	3.0
5-18	At L.A.	W	3-1		10	7	Pavano	Perez	Tucker	21-22	4th	3.0
5-19	At L.A.	L	1-10		4	15	Ashby	Chen		21-23	4th	3.0
5-21	Atl.	W	5-4	(10)	15	12	Tucker	Holmes		22-23	4th	2.0
5-22	Atl.	L	0-2		4	6	Glavine	Armas Jr.		22-24	4th	2.0
5-24	Phi.	W	4-1		10	5	Ohka	Wolf	Stewart	23-24	4th	2.5
5-25	Phi.	W	13-9	(10)	14	10	Tucker	Mercado		24-24	4th	1.5
5-26	Phi.	W	6-5		12	10	Lloyd	Padilla	Stewart	25-24	3rd	1.5
5-27	At Atl.	L	1-5		5	7	Glavine	Armas Jr.		25-25	4th	1.5
5-28	At Atl.	L	2-5		7	11	Moss	Yoshii	Smoltz	25-26	4th	2.5
5-29	At Atl.	W	4-3		9	8	Tucker	Smoltz	Stewart	26-26	4th	1.5
5-30	At Atl.	L	2-5		7	12	Marquis	Pavano		26-27	3rd	2.5
5-31	At Phi.	W	8-7		8	11	Vazquez	Duckworth	Stewart	27-27	3rd	2.5
6-1	At Phi.	L	4-8		10	10	Padilla	Armas Jr.		27-28	3rd	3.5
6-2	At Phi.	L	3-18		8	16	Person	Reames		27-29	4th	3.5
6-3	Pit.	W	7-5		7	12	Ohka	Wells	Stewart	28-29	T3rd	3.5
6-4	Pit.	L	2-5		9	6	Anderson	Pavano	Williams	28-30	4th	4.0
6-5	Pit.	W	3-1		9	3	Vazquez	Fogg		29-30	4th	4.0
6-7	At Chi.	W	4-3		8	5	Armas Jr.	Wright	Tucker	30-30	T2nd	4.5
6-8	At Chi.	W	2-1		5	4	Stewart	Foulke	Tucker	31-30	T2nd	4.5
6-9	At Chi.	L	2-13		7	14	Buehrle	Pavano		31-31	4th	5.5
6-10	At Det.	L	4-6		11	13	Bernero	Vazquez	Acevedo	31-32	4th	5.5
6-11	At Det.	L	1-2		8	13	Redman	Herges	Acevedo	31-33	4th	6.5
6-12	At Det.	W	2-1	(10)	4	6	Stewart	Acevedo	Lloyd	32-33	T3rd	6.5

Date	Opp.	Res.	Score	(inn.*)	Hits	Opp. hits	Winning pitcher	Losing pitcher	Save	Record	Pos.	GB
6-14	Tor.	W	8-2		14	7	Ohka	Miller		33-33	T2nd	6.5
6-15	Tor.	W	9-3		11	7	Day	Loaiza		34-33	T2nd	6.5
6-16	Tor.	W	6-5		11	11	Stewart	Escobar		35-33	2nd	5.5
6-18	K.C.	W	5-4		6	8	Day	Mullen	Stewart	36-33	2nd	4.5
6-19	K.C.	W	6-3		8	10	Ohka	Suzuki	Stewart	37-33	2nd	4.5
6-20	K.C.	W	5-4	(11)	8	15	Eischen	Mullen		38-33	2nd	4.5
6-21	Cle.	W	3-1		6	5	Vazquez	Sabathia	Stewart	39-33	2nd	4.5
6-22	Cle.	L	4-5		13	8	Colon	Day	Wickman	39-34	T2nd	5.5
6-23	Cle.	W	7-2		11	7	Armas Jr.	Finley		40-34	2nd	5.5
6-25	At Pit.	L	1-4		9	10	Benson	Ohka	Williams	40-35	2nd	6.0
6-26	At Pit.	L	4-7		8	10	Wells	Vazquez	Williams	40-36	2nd	7.0
6-27	At Pit.	W	7-2	(7)	13	5	Brower	Villone		41-36	2nd	6.5
6-28	At Tor.	W	2-1		5	3	Armas Jr.	Halladay	Stewart	42-36	2nd	6.5
6-29	At Tor.	L	4-5	(10)	10	7	Escobar	Herges		42-37	2nd	7.5
6-30	At Tor.	L	5-7		10	12	Eyre	Lloyd	Escobar	42-38	2nd	8.5
7-1	At Atl.	L	5-7		13	9	Ligtenberg	Vazquez	Smoltz	42-39	2nd	9.5
7-2	At Atl.	W	5-2		8	6	Colon	Moss	Stewart	43-39	2nd	8.5
7-3	At Atl.	L	5-6		7	10	Smoltz	Brower		43-40	2nd	9.5
7-4	At Phi.	W	2-1		6	5	Eischen	Mesa	Stewart	44-40	2nd	9.5
7-5	At Phi.	W	8-3		8	5	Ohka	Person		45-40	2nd	9.5
7-6	At Phi.	W	5-3		12	8	Vazquez	Duckworth	Stewart	46-40	2nd	8.5
7-7	At Phi.	L	8-10		11	8	Cormier	Herges	Mesa	46-41	2nd	9.5
7-11	Atl.	L	5-8		8	8	Millwood	Armas Jr.	Smoltz	46-42	2nd	10.5
7-12	Atl.	L	3-8		4	12	Remlinger	Tucker		46-43	2nd	11.5
7-13	Atl.	W	6-3		8	9	Colon	Glavine		47-43	2nd	10.5
7-14	Atl.	W	10-3		12	10	Vazquez	Moss		48-43	2nd	9.5
7-15	Phi.	L	8-11		9	13	Coggin	Herges	Mesa	48-44	2nd	9.5
7-16	Phi.	L	3-6		9	8	Wolf	Armas Jr.	Mesa	48-45	2nd	10.5
7-17	N.Y.	L	6-9		13	15	Guthrie	Stewart		48-46	T2nd	11.5
7-18	N.Y.	W	2-1		8	13	Colon	Corey		49-46	2nd	11.5
7-19	At Fla.	L	2-4		9	5	Tejera	Vazquez	Nunez	49-47	T2nd	12.5
7-20	At Fla.	L	0-3		4	8	Penny	Yoshii	Looper	49-48	3rd	13.5
7-21	At Fla.	L	0-4		3	7	Beckett	Armas Jr.	Nunez	49-49	3rd	14.5
7-22	At N.Y.	L	2-5		5	12	Weathers	Ohka	Benitez	49-50	3rd	14.5
7-23	At N.Y.	L	3-4		5	5	D'Amico	Colon	Benitez	49-51	3rd	15.5
7-24	At N.Y.	W	2-1		8	7	Vazquez	Estes	Stewart	50-51	3rd	15.5
7-25	Fla.	L	2-3		5	11	Nunez	Tucker		50-52	T3rd	16.0
7-26	Fla.	W	6-5	(10)	8	15	Tucker	Nunez		51-52	3rd	15.0
7-27	Fla.	L	2-7		6	10	Burnett	Ohka		51-53	T3rd	16.0
7-28	Fla.	W	4-1		6	2	Colon	Tavarez		52-53	3rd	15.0
7-30	Ari.	W	5-4	(10)	9	9	Tucker	Kim		53-53	3rd	15.0
7-31	Ari.	L	1-5		8	7	Johnson	Yoshii		53-54	3rd	16.0
8-1	Ari.	W	2-1		7	7	Eischen	Schilling		54-54	3rd	16.0
8-2	Hou.	W	3-1		8	4	Reames	Munro	Stewart	55-54	3rd	16.0
8-3	Hou.	L	3-5		4	8	Miller	Tucker	Wagner	55-55	3rd	17.0
8-4	Hou.	L	4-5		12	11	Saarloos	Vazquez	Wagner	55-56	T3rd	18.0
8-6	At St.L.	W	10-1		13	7	Yoshii	Finley		56-56	T2nd	18.0
8-7	At St.L.	W	4-1		10	6	Ohka	Simontacchi	Stewart	57-56	2nd	17.0
8-8	At St.L.	L	3-5		7	10	Morris	Reames	Isringhausen	57-57	T2nd	18.0
8-9	At Mil.	W	11-4		16	10	Colon	Quevedo		58-57	T2nd	18.0
8-10	At Mil.	L	2-5		10	12	Cabrera	Vazquez	DeJean	58-58	T2nd	18.0
8-11	At Mil.	L	2-6		7	10	Sheets	Yoshii		58-59	T2nd	19.0
8-13	L.A.	W	4-3		9	7	Smith	Gagne	Stewart	59-59	2nd	18.0
8-14	L.A.	L	2-5		4	14	Ishii	Colon	Gagne	59-60	2nd	19.0
8-15	L.A.	L	0-1		7	7	Daal	Vazquez	Gagne	59-61	2nd	19.5
8-16	S.D.	W	11-6		14	10	Day	Kershner		60-61	2nd	19.5
8-17	S.D.	L	5-6		7	9	Johnson	Herges	Hoffman	60-62	2nd	19.5
8-18	S.D.	W	9-2		11	11	Ohka	Peavy		61-62	2nd	18.5
8-19	S.D.	W	4-0		6	2	Colon	Lawrence		62-62	2nd	18.5
8-20	At Col.	L	6-8		10	12	Neagle	Vazquez	Jimenez	62-63	2nd	18.5
8-21	At Col.	W	13-5		14	6	Yoshii	Chacon		63-63	2nd	18.5
8-22	At Col.	L	6-14		7	16	Stark	Armas Jr.		63-64	2nd	18.5
8-23	At S.F	W	7-2		8	6	Ohka	Ortiz	Eischen	64-64	2nd	17.5
8-24	At S.F	W	7-2		11	6	Colon	Hernandez	Stewart	65-64	2nd	16.5
8-25	At S.F	L	4-8		8	12	Schmidt	Vazquez		65-65	2nd	17.5
8-27	At Phi.	L	2-4		8	11	Roa	Yoshii	Mesa	65-66	3rd	18.5
8-28	At Phi.	W	6-3		10	5	Ohka	Coggin		66-66	2nd	17.5
8-29	At Phi.	L	1-2		3	6	Duckworth	Colon	Mesa	66-67	3rd	17.5
8-30	Atl.	L	2-4		4	7	Moss	Armas Jr.	Smoltz	66-68	3rd	18.5
8-31	Atl.	L	3-5		12	8	Hammond	Vazquez	Smoltz	66-69	4th	19.5

Date	Opp.	Res.	Score	(inn.*)	Hits	Opp. hits	Winning pitcher	Losing pitcher	Save	Record	Pos.	GB
9-1	Atl.	L	4-6		7	12	Millwood	Yoshii	Smoltz	66-70	4th	20.5
9-2	Phi.	W	5-1		10	6	Ohka	Roa		67-70	4th	20.5
9-3	Phi.	W	7-6	(10)	10	11	Eischen	Adams		68-70	4th	19.5
9-4	Phi.	W	8-5		13	8	Armas Jr.	Padilla	Eischen	69-70	3rd	19.5
9-5	Phi.	L	1-4		5	10	Wolf	Vazquez		69-71	3rd	20.0
9-6	At Atl.	L	0-5		3	12	Millwood	Yoshii		69-72	3rd	21.0
9-7	At Atl.	L	0-4		7	7	Maddux	Ohka		69-73	3rd	22.0
9-8	At Atl.	W	7-0		14	5	Colon	Glavine		70-73	3rd	21.0
9-9	At Chi.	L	2-3		7	7	Borowski	Brower		70-74	3rd	21.5
9-10	At Chi.	W	6-2		9	6	Vazquez	Zambrano		71-74	3rd	21.5
9-11	At Chi.	L	3-6		9	7	Benes	Yoshii	Alfonseca	71-75	T3rd	22.0
9-12	N.Y.	L	2-8		6	10	Middlebrook	Ohka		71-76	4th	22.5
9-13	N.Y.	W	11-8		16	16	Colon	Thomson	Smith	72-76	T3rd	21.5
9-14	N.Y.	W	5-4		7	9	Armas Jr.	Bacsik	Smith	73-76	T2nd	21.5
9-15	N.Y.	W	10-1		8	7	Vazquez	Astacio		74-76	T2nd	21.5
9-17	At Fla.	W	8-5	(14)	16	11	Stewart	Lloyd		75-76	2nd	21.0
9-18	At Fla.	W	4-2	(11)	8	10	Eischen	Mairena	Drew	76-76	2nd	20.0
9-19	At Fla.	W	6-5		12	12	Colon	Knotts	Drew	77-76	2nd	20.0
9-20	At N.Y.	W	6-1		12	9	Armas Jr.	Thomson		78-76	2nd	19.0
9-21	At N.Y.	L	3-6	(11)	7	12	Benitez	Smith		78-77	2nd	19.0
9-22	At N.Y.	W	5-1		10	7	Day	Leiter		79-77	2nd	19.0
9-24	Fla.	L	6-9		14	11	Pavano	Reames	Looper	79-78	T2nd	19.0
9-25	Fla.	L	2-10		11	10	Beckett	Colon		79-79	T2nd	20.0
9-26	Fla.	W	4-3		12	7	Armas Jr.	Penny	Day	80-79	2nd	19.5
9-27	Cin.	W	4-3	(11)	10	8	Eischen	Riedling		81-79	2nd	20.0
9-28	Cin.	W	6-0		8	6	Kim	Moehler		82-79	2nd	20.0
9-29	Cin.	W	7-2		7	5	Drew	Haynes		83-79	2nd	19.0

Monthly records: April (16-10), May (11-17), June (15-11), July (11-16), August (13-15), September (17-10).
*Innings, if other than nine.

RECORDS

2002 regular-season record: 83-79
Position: 2nd in N.L. East
Home: 49-32   **Road:** 34-47
N.L. East: 37-39   **N.L. Central:** 21-15
N.L. West: 13-19   **A.L.:** 12-6
Vs. LH starters: 18-18
Vs. RH starters: 65-61
Grass: 28-40   **Artificial:** 55-39
Day: 22-21   **Night:** 61-58
1-Run: 30-22   **X-inn.:** 13-6
Doubleheaders: 0-0-0
Team record past five years: 351-459 (.433, ranks 14th in league in that span)

TEAM LEADERS

Batting average: Vladimir Guerrero (.336).
At-bats: Vladimir Guerrero (614).
Runs: Vladimir Guerrero (106).
Hits: Vladimir Guerrero (206).
Total bases: Vladimir Guerrero (364).
Doubles: Orlando Cabrera, Jose Vidro (43).
Triples: Brad Wilkerson (8).
Home runs: Vladimir Guerrero (39).
Runs batted in: Vladimir Guerrero (111).

Stolen bases: Vladimir Guerrero (40).
Slugging percentage: Vladimir Guerrero (.593).
On-base percentage: Vladimir Guerrero (.417).
Wins: Tomokazu Ohka (13).
Earned-run average: Tomokazu Ohka (3.18).
Complete games: Bartolo Colon (4).
Shutouts: Bartolo Colon (1).
Saves: Scott Stewart (17).
Innings pitched: Javier Vazquez (230.1).
Strikeouts: Javier Vazquez (179).

GAMES BY POSITION

Catcher: Michael Barrett 110, Brian Schneider 65.
First base: Andres Galarraga 89, Lee Stevens 58, Brad Wilkerson 23, Wil Cordero 10, Michael Barrett 6, Mike Mordecai 3, Chris Truby 2.
Second base: Jose Vidro 152, Wilton Guerrero 7, Jose Macias 6, Mike Mordecai 4, Henry Mateo 3, Lou Collier 2, Jamey Carroll 1.
Third base: Fernando Tatis 99, Chris Truby 31, Mike Mordecai 28, Jose Macias 22, Jamey Carroll 13, Wilton Guerrero 2, Lou Collier 1.

Shortstop: Orlando Cabrera 153, Jose Macias 4, Jamey Carroll 3, Mike Mordecai 3, Henry Mateo 2.
Outfield: Vladimir Guerrero 161, Brad Wilkerson 129, Troy O'Leary 70, Jose Macias 49, Endy Chavez 35, Peter Bergeron 31, Wil Cordero 28, Matt Cepicky 17, Cliff Floyd 13, Wilton Guerrero 12, Lou Collier 7, Henry Rodriguez 5, Brian Schneider 2, Mike Mordecai 1, Chris Truby 1.
Designated hitter: Fernando Tatis 4, Troy O'Leary 3, Wil Cordero 2.

TOP DRAFT CHOICES

1. **Clint Everts,** RHP, Cypress Falls H.S., Houston.
2. **Darrell Rasner,** RHP, Nevada.
3. **Larry Broadway,** 1B, Duke.
4. **Jon Felfoldi,** LHP, Glendale (Calif.) C.C.
5. **Anthony Pearson,** RHP, Jackson State.
6. **Chad Chop,** 1B, Vanguard (Calif.).
7. **Mike O'Conner,** LHP, George Washington.
8. **Friedel Pinkston,** RHP, Hart County H.S., Hartwell, Ga.
9. **Chris Barlow,** RHP, LeMoyne College.
10. **Justin Azze,** LHP, Orange Coast (Calif.) J.C.

NEW YORK METS
NATIONAL LEAGUE EAST DIVISION

2003 SEASON

March/April

SUN	MON	TUE	WED	THU	FRI	SAT
30	31 D CUB	1	2 CUB	3 D CUB	4 MON	5 D MON
6 D MON	7	8 FLA	9 FLA	10 FLA	11 † MON	12 † MON
13 D† MON	14 D† MON	15 PIT	16 PIT	17 PIT	18 FLA	19 D FLA
20 D FLA	21	22 HOU	23 HOU	24 HOU	25 ARI	26 ARI
27 D ARI	28	29 STL	30 STL			

May

SUN	MON	TUE	WED	THU	FRI	SAT
				1 D STL	2 MIL	3 MIL
4 D MIL	5	6 LA	7 LA	8 LA	9 SD	10 D SD
11 D SD	12 COL	13 COL	14 COL	15 D SF	16 SF	17 D SF
18 D SF	19	20 PHI	21 PHI	22 D PHI	23 ATL	24 ATL
25 D ATL	26	27 PHI	28 PHI	29 PHI	30 ATL	31 D ATL

June

SUN	MON	TUE	WED	THU	FRI	SAT
1 ATL	2	3 MIL	4 MIL	5 MIL	6 SEA	7 SEA
8 D SEA	9	10 TEX	11 TEX	12 TEX	13 ANA	14 ANA
15 D ANA	16 FLA	17 FLA	18 FLA	19 FLA	20 NYY	21 NYY
22 NYY	23	24 FLA	25 FLA	26 FLA	27 NYY	28 D NYY
29 NYY	30 MON					

July

SUN	MON	TUE	WED	THU	FRI	SAT
		1 MON	2 MON	3	4 D CIN	5 CIN
6 D CIN	7 ATL	8 ATL	9 D ATL	10 PHI	11 PHI	12 D PHI
13 D PHI	14	15 *	16	17 ATL	18 ATL	19 D ATL
20 D ATL	21 PHI	22 D PHI	23 MON	24 MON	25 CIN	26 CIN
27 D CIN	28	29 MIL	30 MIL	31 D MIL		

August

SUN	MON	TUE	WED	THU	FRI	SAT
					1 STL	2 D STL
3 D STL	4	5 HOU	6 HOU	7 HOU	8 ARI	9 ARI
10 D ARI	11	12 SF	13 SF	14 SF	15 COL	16 COL
17 D COL	18 D COL	19 SD	20 SD	21 D SD	22 LA	23 LA
24 LA	25	26 ATL	27 ATL	28 ATL	29 PHI	30 PHI

September

SUN	MON	TUE	WED	THU	FRI	SAT
31 D PHI	1 D ATL	2 D ATL	3 ATL	4 D PHI	5 PHI	6 PHI
7 D PHI	8 FLA	9 FLA	10 D FLA	11	12 MON	13 MON
14 D MON	15 CUB	16 CUB	17 D CUB	18 MON	19 MON	20 D MON
21 D MON	22	23 PIT	24 PIT	25 PIT	26 FLA	27 FLA
28 D FLA						

Home games shaded; D—Day game (games starting before 5 p.m.); *—All-Star Game at Comiskey Park, Chicago. †—Game played in Puerto Rico. Subject to change.

CLUB DIRECTORY

Chairman and chief executive officer
Fred Wilpon
President
Saul B. Katz
Senior v.p. and general manager
Stephen F. Phillips
Special assistant to the g.m.
Fred Wright

Sr. assistant g.m./player personnel
Jim Duquette
Assistant g.m./dir. of scouting operations
Gary LaRocque
Assistant g.m./scouting development
Carmen Fusco
Director, amateur scouting
Jack Bowen

Vice president, media relations
Jay Horwitz
Director of minor league operations
Kevin Morgan

MINOR LEAGUE AFFILIATES

Class	Team	League	Manager
AAA	Norfolk	International	Bobby Floyd
AA	Binghamton	Eastern	John Stearns
A	St. Lucie	Florida State	Ken Oberkfell
A	Capital City	South Atlantic	Tony Tijerina
A	Brooklyn	New York-Pennsylvania	Tim Teufel
Rookie	Kingsport	Appalachian	Dave Howard

Follow the Mets all season at: www.sportingnews.com/baseball/teams/mets/

BROADCAST INFORMATION

Radio: WFAN-AM (660).
TV: WPIX-TV (Channel 11).
Cable TV: Fox Sports New York, MSG Network.

SPRING TRAINING

Ballpark (city): Thomas J. White Stadium (Port St. Lucie, Fla.).
Ticket information: 772-871-2115.

SPRING TRAINING ROSTER

Manager—Art Howe (18).
Coaches—Chris Chambliss (51), Matt Galante (8), Randy Niemann (52), Mookie Wilson (1).

No.	PITCHERS	B/T	Ht./Wt.	Born	Age*	2002 clubs
34	Astacio, Pedro	R/R	6-2/210	11-28-69	33	New York N.L.
33	Bacsik, Mike	L/L	6-3/190	11-11-77	25	Norfolk, New York N.L.
49	Benitez, Armando	R/R	6-4/229	11-3-72	30	New York N.L.
	Bevis, P. J.	R/R	6-3/180	7-28-80	22	El Paso, Binghamton
43	Cerda, Jaime	L/L	6-0/175	10-26-78	24	Binghamton, Norfolk, New York N.L.
45	Franco, John	L/L	5-10/185	9-17-60	42	DID NOT PLAY
47	Glavine, Tom	L/L	6-0/185	3-25-66	37	Atlanta
22	Leiter, Al	L/L	6-3/220	10-23-65	37	New York N.L.
27	Middlebrook, Jason	R/R	6-3/215	6-26-75	27	Portland, San Diego, Norfolk, New York N.L.
	Nunez, Franklin	R/R	6-0/175	1-18-77	26	Scranton/Wilkes-Barre, Gulf Coast Phillies
	Orloski, Joe	R/R	6-3/180	5-17-79	23	Tennessee
36	Roberts, Grant	R/R	6-3/205	9-13-77	25	New York N.L., Binghamton
	Seo, Jae	R/R	6-1/215	5-24-77	25	Binghamton, Norfolk, New York N.L.
29	Stanton, Mike	L/L	6-1/215	6-2-67	35	New York A.L.
38	Strange, Pat	R/R	6-5/243	8-23-80	22	Norfolk, New York N.L.
25	Strickland, Scott	R/R	5-11/180	4-26-76	26	Montreal, New York N.L.
29	Trachsel, Steve	R/R	6-4/205	10-31-70	32	New York N.L., Binghamton
46	Walker, Tyler	R/R	6-3/255	5-15-76	26	Norfolk, New York N.L.
35	Weathers, Dave	R/R	6-3/230	9-25-69	33	New York N.L.
32	Yates, Tyler	R/R	6-4/220	8-7-77	25	Norfolk
	Zamora, Pete	L/L	6-3/185	8-13-75	27	Scranton/Wilkes-Barre

No.	CATCHERS	B/T	Ht./Wt.	Born	Age*	2002 clubs
7	Phillips, Jason	R/R	6-1/177	9-27-76	26	Norfolk, New York N.L.
31	Piazza, Mike	R/R	6-3/215	9-4-68	34	New York N.L.
3	Wilson, Vance	R/R	5-11/190	3-17-73	30	New York N.L.

No.	INFIELDERS	B/T	Ht./Wt.	Born	Age*	2002 clubs
12	Alomar, Roberto	B/R	6-0/185	2-5-68	35	New York N.L.
	Reyes, Jose	B/R	6-0/160	6-11-83	19	St. Lucie, Binghamton
13	Sanchez, Rey	R/R	5-9/175	10-5-67	35	Boston
26	Scutaro, Marcos	R/R	5-10/170	10-30-75	27	Norfolk, New York N.L.
42	Vaughn, Mo	L/R	6-1/275	12-15-67	35	New York N.L.
9	Wigginton, Ty	R/R	6-0/200	10-11-77	25	Norfolk, New York N.L.

No.	OUTFIELDERS	B/T	Ht./Wt.	Born	Age*	2002 clubs
20	Burnitz, Jeromy	L/R	6-0/213	4-15-69	33	New York N.L.
19	Cedeno, Roger	B/R	6-1/205	8-16-74	28	New York N.L.
15	Clark, Brady	R/R	6-2/195	4-18-73	29	Cincinnati, Louisville, New York N.L.
30	Floyd, Cliff	L/R	6-4/260	12-5-72	30	Florida, Montreal, Boston
21	Gonzalez, Raul	R/R	5-9/190	12-27-73	29	Louisville, Cincinnati, New York N.L.
47	McEwing, Joe	R/R	5-11/170	10-19-72	30	New York N.L., Brooklyn, Binghamton
6	Perez, Timo	L/L	5-9/167	4-8-75	27	Norfolk, New York N.L.
	Shinjo, Tsuyoshi	R/R	6-1/185	1-28-72	31	San Francisco, Fresno
23	Snead, Esix	B/R	5-10/175	6-7-76	26	Binghamton, New York N.L.
43	Tarasco, Tony	L/R	6-0/205	12-9-70	32	Norfolk, New York N.L.

*Age as of April 1, 2003.

BALLPARK INFORMATION

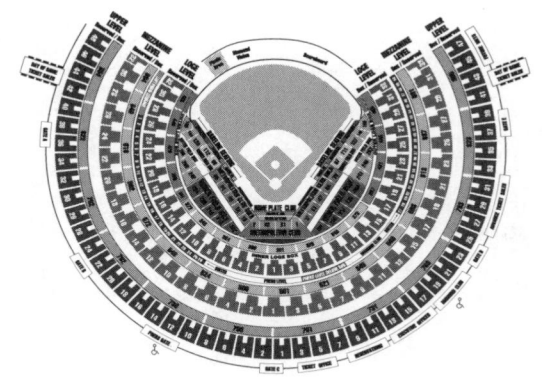

Ballpark (capacity, surface)
Shea Stadium (56,749, grass)

Address
123-01 Roosevelt Ave.
Flushing, NY 11368

Official website
www.mets.com

Business phone
718-507-METS

Ticket information
718-507-TIXX

Field dimensions (from home plate)
To left field at foul line, 338 feet
To center field, 410 feet
To right field at foul line, 338 feet

First game played
April 17, 1964 (Pirates 4, Mets 3)

2003 SEASON *New York Mets*

Date	Opp.	Res.	Score	(inn.*)	Hits	Opp. hits	Winning pitcher	Losing pitcher	Save	Record	Pos.	GB
4-1	Pit.	W	6-2		9	4	Leiter	Villone		1-0	T1st	...
4-3	Pit.	L	3-5		7	11	Wells	Trachsel	Williams	1-1	T1st	...
4-4	Pit.	L	2-3		5	8	Anderson	Estes	Williams	1-2	T3rd	1.0
4-5	At Atl.	W	9-3		13	9	Astacio	Lopez		2-2	T1st	...
4-6	At Atl.	W	11-2		14	6	Weathers	Smoltz		3-2	T1st	...
4-7	At Atl.	L	2-5	(14)	8	10	Lopez	Komiyama		3-3	T1st	...
4-9	At Chi.	L	0-2		2	8	Lieber	Trachsel	Alfonseca	3-4	T4th	1.0
4-10	At Chi.	W	3-2		6	3	Weathers	Fassero	Benitez	4-4	3rd	1.0
4-11	At Chi.	W	3-2		6	12	Astacio	Cruz	Benitez	5-4	T1st	...
4-12	Mon.	W	2-1		8	4	D'Amico	Ohka	Benitez	6-4	1st	+0.5
4-13	Mon.	L	8-9	(11)	9	12	Herges	Strickland		6-5	T1st	...
4-14	Mon.	W	6-4		6	6	Trachsel	Armas Jr.	Benitez	7-5	1st	+1.0
4-15	Atl.	W	7-6	(12)	13	12	Strickland	Hammond		8-5	1st	+1.5
4-16	Atl.	W	3-1		9	8	Astacio	Glavine		9-5	1st	+1.5
4-17	Atl.	L	1-2		5	8	Millwood	D'Amico	Smoltz	9-6	1st	+1.0
4-18	At Mon.	W	1-0		7	2	Leiter	Vazquez		10-6	1st	+1.5
4-19	At Mon.	L	3-5		9	10	Armas Jr.	Trachsel	Herges	10-7	1st	+1.0
4-20	At Mon.	L	5-7		10	12	Pavano	Estes	Herges	10-8	T1st	...
4-21	At Mon.	L	3-6		10	12	Chen	Astacio	Lloyd	10-9	T2nd	1.0
4-23	St.L.	W	4-3		9	8	D'Amico	Morris	Benitez	11-9	2nd	1.0
4-24	St.L.	L	2-4		6	6	Kile	Leiter	Isringhausen	11-10	2nd	2.0
4-25	St.L.	W	7-6		8	10	Strickland	Veres	Benitez	12-10	2nd	2.0
4-26	Mil.	W	1-0		3	1	Estes	Rusch		13-10	2nd	1.0
4-27	Mil.	W	2-1		7	3	Astacio	Neugebauer	Benitez	14-10	T1st	...
4-28	Mil.	W	9-6		15	12	Davis	King		15-10	T1st	...
4-30	At Ari.	W	10-1		16	3	Leiter	Helling		16-10	T1st	...
5-1	At Ari.	W	7-1		12	3	Trachsel	Stottlemyre		17-10	T1st	...
5-2	At Ari.	L	3-7		8	11	Batista	Estes	Kim	17-11	T1st	...
5-3	At Hou.	W	11-3		15	9	Astacio	Mlicki		18-11	1st	+1.0
5-4	At Hou.	L	1-3		5	6	Hernandez	D'Amico	Wagner	18-12	1st	+1.0
5-5	At Hou.	L	1-12		4	15	Oswalt	Leiter		18-13	1st	+1.0
5-7	S.F	L	1-5		5	10	Ortiz	Trachsel		18-14	1st	+1.0
5-8	S.F	L	2-8		6	10	Rueter	Estes		18-15	T1st	...
5-9	S.F	L	3-4		4	7	Jensen	Astacio	Nen	18-16	T2nd	1.0
5-10	Col.	L	5-9		9	15	Jennings	D'Amico		18-17	3rd	2.0
5-11	Col.	W	4-3		6	4	Leiter	Hampton	Strickland	19-17	T2nd	1.0
5-12	Col.	L	3-4	(13)	10	10	White	Davis	Jimenez	19-18	3rd	2.0
5-13	At L.A.	L	2-3	(13)	10	13	Carrara	Corey		19-19	3rd	2.0
5-14	At L.A.	W	3-0		9	2	Astacio	Ashby		20-19	T2nd	2.0
5-15	At L.A.	W	2-0		6	2	D'Amico	Ishii		21-19	2nd	1.0
5-16	At S.D.	W	3-1		11	8	Leiter	Lawrence	Guthrie	22-19	T1st	...
5-17	At S.D.	W	13-4		11	9	Trachsel	Middlebrook		23-19	1st	+1.0
5-18	At S.D.	W	5-2		8	8	Estes	Tomko	Benitez	24-19	1st	+2.0
5-19	At S.D.	L	3-4		7	10	Reed	Strickland		24-20	1st	+1.0
5-21	At Phi.	L	0-4		3	7	Padilla	D'Amico		24-21	1st	+1.0
5-22	At Phi.	L	2-5		13	7	Adams	Leiter	Mesa	24-22	1st	+0.5
5-23	At Phi.	W	1-0		7	5	Strickland	Mesa	Benitez	25-22	1st	+1.0
5-24	Fla.	W	5-4	(10)	6	9	Strickland	Darensbourg		26-22	1st	+1.0
5-25	Fla.	L	5-6		9	14	Almanza	Weathers	Nunez	26-23	1st	+1.0
5-26	Fla.	W	3-0		6	5	D'Amico	Burnett	Strickland	27-23	1st	+1.0
5-27	Fla.	L	3-5		9	10	Dempster	Leiter	Nunez	27-24	T1st	...
5-28	Phi.	L	3-5		11	12	Cormier	Trachsel	Mesa	27-25	2nd	1.0
5-29	Phi.	W	4-3		8	10	Strickland	Santiago	Benitez	28-25	T1st	...
5-31	At Fla.	W	6-5	(10)	8	7	Roberts	Nunez	Benitez	29-25	2nd	0.5
6-1	At Fla.	L	7-9		11	11	Mairena	Komiyama	Nunez	29-26	2nd	1.5
6-2	At Fla.	L	3-7		9	12	Tavarez	Leiter	Nunez	29-27	2nd	1.5
6-3	At Atl.	L	4-5		8	8	Hammond	Trachsel	Smoltz	29-28	2nd	2.5
6-5	At Atl.	L	4-6		8	9	Hammond	Strickland	Smoltz	29-29	3rd	3.5
6-6	At Atl.	L	2-3		8	8	Glavine	Weathers	Smoltz	29-30	T3rd	4.5
6-7	At Cle.	W	4-3		7	5	Leiter	Baez	Benitez	30-30	T2nd	4.5
6-8	At Cle.	W	8-6		11	8	Trachsel	Finley	Benitez	31-30	T2nd	4.5
6-9	At Cle.	L	3-8		9	9	Drese	Estes		31-31	2nd	5.5
6-10	At Chi.	W	3-1		9	6	Astacio	Glover	Benitez	32-31	T2nd	4.5
6-11	At Chi.	L	8-10		16	10	Ritchie	D'Amico	Osuna	32-32	T2nd	5.5
6-12	At Chi.	L	1-2		4	7	Biddle	Leiter	Osuna	32-33	T3rd	6.5

Date	Opp.	Res.	Score	(inn.*)	Hits	Opp. hits	Winning pitcher	Losing pitcher	Save	Record	Pos.	GB
6-14	N.Y.	L	2-4	(10)	8	10	Karsay	Komiyama		32-34	4th	7.5
6-15	N.Y.	W	8-0		10	5	Estes	Clemens		33-34	4th	7.5
6-16	N.Y.	W	3-2		8	7	Guthrie	Wells	Benitez	34-34	T3rd	6.5
6-18	Min.	L	1-6		4	12	Santana	D'Amico		34-35	4th	6.5
6-19	Min.	W	4-2		11	8	Leiter	Kinney	Benitez	35-35	4th	6.5
6-20	Min.	W	3-2		6	6	Trachsel	Fiore	Benitez	36-35	4th	6.5
6-21	K.C.	W	4-3		12	8	Guthrie	Voyles		37-35	4th	6.5
6-22	K.C.	L	1-5		8	7	Byrd	Astacio		37-36	4th	7.5
6-23	K.C.	W	5-4		9	8	Strickland	Grimsley	Benitez	38-36	4th	7.5
6-24	Atl.	L	2-3		6	8	Gryboski	Strickland	Smoltz	38-37	4th	8.5
6-25	Atl.	W	7-4		11	9	Trachsel	Lopez	Benitez	39-37	T3rd	7.5
6-26	Atl.	L	3-6		7	8	Hammond	Weathers	Smoltz	39-38	4th	8.5
6-28	At N.Y.	L	5-11		9	12	Mussina	D'Amico	Hernandez	39-39	4th	9.5
6-29	At N.Y.	W	11-2		16	9	Leiter	Lilly		40-39	4th	9.5
6-30	At N.Y.	L	0-8		3	11	Pettitte	Trachsel		40-40	4th	10.5
7-1	At Phi.	L	3-6		7	8	Duckworth	Estes	Mesa	40-41	4th	11.5
7-2	At Phi.	W	12-6		15	11	Astacio	Adams		41-41	4th	10.5
7-3	At Phi.	L	7-8		8	14	Plesac	Strickland	Mesa	41-42	4th	11.5
7-4	At Fla.	L	7-9		14	12	Tavarez	Leiter		41-43	4th	12.5
7-5	At Fla.	W	5-3		7	11	Bacsik	Burnett	Benitez	42-43	4th	12.5
7-6	At Fla.	L	2-5		5	7	Tejera	Estes	Almanza	42-44	4th	12.5
7-7	At Fla.	W	9-3		13	6	Roberts	Mairena		43-44	4th	12.5
7-11	Phi.	W	9-1		11	9	Guthrie	Cormier		44-44	4th	12.5
7-12	Phi.	L	8-9		14	14	Person	D'Amico		44-45	4th	13.5
7-13	Phi.	L	6-7	(12)	15	11	Mercado	Strickland	Silva	44-46	4th	13.5
7-14	Phi.	W	4-2		4	7	Astacio	Duckworth	Benitez	45-46	T3rd	12.5
7-15	Fla.	W	8-3		11	7	Bacsik	Penny		46-46	3rd	11.5
7-16	Fla.	W	10-5		9	9	Leiter	Beckett		47-46	3rd	11.5
7-17	At Mon.	W	9-6		15	13	Guthrie	Stewart		48-46	T2nd	11.5
7-18	At Mon.	L	1-2		13	8	Colon	Corey		48-47	3rd	12.5
7-19	At Cin.	W	4-2		10	7	Astacio	Fernandez	Benitez	49-47	T2nd	12.5
7-20	At Cin.	W	8-7		11	12	Weathers	Reitsma	Benitez	50-47	2nd	12.5
7-21	At Cin.	L	1-9		7	11	Dessens	Leiter		50-48	2nd	13.5
7-22	Mon.	W	5-2		12	5	Weathers	Ohka	Benitez	51-48	2nd	12.5
7-23	Mon.	W	4-3		5	9	D'Amico	Colon	Benitez	52-48	2nd	12.5
7-24	Mon.	L	1-2		7	8	Vazquez	Estes	Stewart	52-49	2nd	13.5
7-26	Cin.	W	3-2		8	6	Guthrie	Riedling		53-49	2nd	12.5
7-27	Cin.	L	1-2	(11)	5	9	Graves	Corey		53-50	2nd	13.5
7-28	Cin.	W	6-5		12	8	Trachsel	Williamson	Benitez	54-50	2nd	12.5
7-30	Hou.	L	3-16		8	20	Saarloos	D'Amico		54-51	2nd	13.5
7-31	Hou.	W	10-0		13	2	Estes	Mlicki		55-51	2nd	13.5
8-1	Hou.	L	1-3		7	11	Oswalt	Astacio	Wagner	55-52	2nd	14.5
8-3†	Ari.	L	5-8	(10)	10	13	Kim	Strickland		55-53		
8-3‡	Ari.	L	2-9		7	11	Batista	Thomson		55-54	2nd	16.5
8-4	Ari.	L	7-12		15	13	Koplove	Guthrie	Kim	55-55	2nd	17.5
8-5	Ari.	L	0-2		2	6	Johnson	Estes		55-56	T2nd	18.0
8-6	At Mil.	W	5-1		13	3	Astacio	Sheets		56-56	T2nd	18.0
8-7	At Mil.	L	2-6		9	9	Rusch	D'Amico		56-57	3rd	18.0
8-8	At Mil.	W	9-0		14	5	Trachsel	Wright		57-57	T2nd	18.0
8-9	At St.L.	W	2-1		5	5	Leiter	Matthews	Benitez	58-57	T2nd	18.0
8-10	At St.L.	L	4-5		13	5	Veres	Reed	Isringhausen	58-58	T2nd	18.0
8-11	At St.L.	L	0-9		7	13	Finley	Astacio		58-59	T2nd	19.0
8-13	S.D.	L	2-7		5	12	Peavy	Trachsel	Hoffman	58-60	3rd	19.0
8-14	S.D.	L	2-6		8	8	Lawrence	Leiter	Hoffman	58-61	3rd	20.0
8-15	S.D.	L	3-5		8	11	Tomko	Thomson	Hoffman	58-62	T3rd	20.5
8-16	L.A.	L	2-3		5	7	Brown	Guthrie	Gagne	58-63	T4th	21.5
8-17	L.A.	L	4-10		4	17	Perez	Astacio		58-64	5th	21.5
8-18	L.A.	L	1-2		4	9	Ashby	Trachsel	Gagne	58-65	5th	21.5
8-20	At S.F	L	0-1		5	7	Schmidt	Leiter		58-66	5th	22.0
8-21	At S.F	L	1-3		7	5	Rueter	Thomson	Nen	58-67	5th	23.0
8-22	At S.F	L	1-3		6	9	Jensen	Bacsik	Nen	58-68	5th	23.0
8-23	At Col.	L	4-10		7	14	Jennings	Astacio		58-69	5th	23.0
8-24	At Col.	W	5-2		11	8	Weathers	Jimenez	Benitez	59-69	5th	22.0
8-25	At Col.	W	7-4		7	8	Leiter	Neagle	Benitez	60-69	5th	22.0
8-27	At Fla.	W	10-5		13	11	Thomson	Tejera		61-69	5th	22.0
8-28	At Fla.	L	3-7		9	10	Almanza	Strickland		61-70	5th	22.0
8-30	Phi.	L	5-7		6	8	Padilla	Astacio	Mesa	61-71	5th	22.5
8-31	Phi.	L	0-1		4	7	Wolf	Trachsel		61-72	5th	23.5

Date	Opp.	Res.	Score	(inn.*)	Hits	Opp. hits	Winning pitcher	Losing pitcher	Save	Record	Pos.	GB
9-1	Phi.	L	5-9		9	15	Myers	Leiter		61-73	5th	24.5
9-3†	Fla.	L	2-3	(12)	8	11	Looper	Strickland		61-74		
9-3‡	Fla.	W	11-5		14	11	Bacsik	Wayne		62-74	5th	24.5
9-4	Fla.	W	11-3		13	6	Astacio	Tavarez		63-74	5th	24.5
9-5	Fla.	W	4-1		6	7	Trachsel	Penny	Benitez	64-74	5th	24.0
9-6	At Phi.	W	7-2		9	9	Leiter	Myers		65-74	5th	24.0
9-7	At Phi.	W	5-4		6	9	Walker	Roa	Benitez	66-74	5th	24.0
9-8	At Phi.	W	11-3		15	9	Thomson	Duckworth		67-74	5th	23.0
9-9	At Phi.	W	6-4		6	12	D'Amico	Timlin	Benitez	68-74	5th	22.5
9-10	At Atl.	L	6-12		14	13	Hodges	Astacio		68-75	5th	23.5
9-11§	At Atl.	L	5-8		11	11	Millwood	Trachsel	Smoltz	68-76		
9-11∞	At Atl.	W	5-0		16	6	Leiter	Marquis		69-76	5th	23.5
9-12	At Mon.	W	8-2		10	6	Middlebrook	Ohka		70-76	5th	23.0
9-13	At Mon.	L	8-11		16	16	Colon	Thomson	Smith	70-77	5th	23.0
9-14	At Mon.	L	4-5		9	7	Armas Jr.	Bacsik	Smith	70-78	5th	24.0
9-15	At Mon.	L	1-10		7	8	Vazquez	Astacio		70-79	5th	25.0
9-17	Chi.	W	3-1		7	4	Weathers	Cruz		71-79	5th	24.5
9-18	Chi.	W	2-1		6	5	Trachsel	Wood	Benitez	72-79	5th	23.5
9-19	Chi.	W	3-2	(12)	10	9	Roberts	Cunnane		73-79	4th	23.5
9-20	Mon.	L	1-6		9	12	Armas Jr.	Thomson		73-80	5th	23.5
9-21	Mon.	W	6-3	(11)	12	7	Benitez	Smith		74-80	5th	22.5
9-22	Mon.	L	1-5		7	10	Day	Leiter		74-81	5th	23.5
9-24	At Pit.	L	3-6		4	12	Sauerbeck	Guthrie	Williams	74-82	5th	23.5
9-25	At Pit.	L	3-4		10	5	Villone	Roberts	Williams	74-83	5th	24.5
9-27†	Atl.	L	1-3		7	8	Maddux	Thomson	Smoltz	74-84		
9-27‡	Atl.	L	4-7		6	12	Millwood	Astacio		74-85	5th	26.5
9-28	Atl.	L	2-5		8	13	Hodges	Leiter	Smoltz	74-86	5th	27.5
9-29	Atl.	W	6-1		10	7	Trachsel	Remlinger		75-86	5th	26.5

Monthly records: April (16-10), May (13-15), June (11-15), July (15-11), August (6-21), September (14-14).
*Innings, if other than nine. †First game of a doubleheader. ‡Second game of a doubleheader. §Day separate admission. ∞Night separate admission.

RECORDS

2002 regular-season record: 75-86
Position: 5th in N.L. East
Home: 38-43 **Road:** 37-43
N.L. East: 35-41 **N.L. Central:** 20-15
N.L. West: 10-22 **A.L.:** 10-8
Vs. LH starters: 18-21
Vs. RH starters: 57-65
Grass: 66-75 **Artificial:** 9-11
Day: 21-33 **Night:** 54-53
1-Run: 27-26 **X-inn.:** 5-9
Doubleheaders: 0-2-1
Team record past five years: 436-374
(.538, ranks 6th in league in that span)

TEAM LEADERS

Batting average: Edgardo Alfonzo (.308).
At-bats: Roberto Alomar (590).
Runs: Edgardo Alfonzo (78).
Hits: Roberto Alomar (157).
Total bases: Mike Piazza (260).
Doubles: Timo Perez (27).
Triples: Timo Perez (6).
Home runs: Mike Piazza (33).
Runs batted in: Mike Piazza (98).

Stolen bases: Roger Cedeno (25).
Slugging percentage: Mike Piazza (.544).
On-base percentage: Edgardo Alfonzo (.391).
Wins: Al Leiter (13).
Earned-run average: Steve Trachsel (3.37).
Complete games: Pedro Astacio (3).
Shutouts: Al Leiter (2).
Saves: Armando Benitez (33).
Innings pitched: Al Leiter (204.1).
Strikeouts: Al Leiter (172).

GAMES BY POSITION

Catcher: Mike Piazza 121, Vance Wilson 66, Jason Phillips 7.
First base: Mo Vaughn 134, John Valentin 22, Joe McEwing 20, Mark P. Johnson 15, Ty Wigginton 13, Tony Tarasco 7, Vance Wilson 1.
Second base: Roberto Alomar 147, Joe McEwing 13, Marco Scutaro 12, Ty Wigginton 12, John Valentin 3.
Third base: Edgardo Alfonzo 134, John Valentin 18, Ty Wigginton 14, Joe McEwing 10, Marco Scutaro 3.

Shortstop: Rey Ordonez 142, John Valentin 24, Joe McEwing 21, Marco Scutaro 6.
Outfield: Jeromy Burnitz 140, Roger Cedeno 132, Timo Perez 122, Jay Payton 82, Joe McEwing 35, Tony Tarasco 29, Raul Gonzalez 24, Brady Clark 6, Esix Snead 6, McKay Christensen 3, Ty Wigginton 2, Mark P. Johnson 1, Mark Little 1, Marco Scutaro 1.
Designated hitter: Mike Piazza 6, Tony Tarasco 2, John Valentin 2, Jeromy Burnitz 1.

TOP DRAFT CHOICES

1. **Scott Kazmir**, LHP, Cypress Falls H.S., Houston.
4. **Bob Malek**, OF, Michigan State.
5. **Jon Slack**, OF, Texas Tech.
6. **Adam Elliott**, RHP, Clayton Valley H.S., Concord, Calif.
7. **Jim Anderson**, C, UC Riverside.
8. **Tyler Davidson**, OF, Washington.
9. **Christian Colonel**, SS, Southern Idaho J.C.
10. **Matt Lindstrom**, RHP, Ricks (Idaho) J.C.

PHILADELPHIA PHILLIES
NATIONAL LEAGUE EAST DIVISION

2003 SEASON

March/April

SUN	MON	TUE	WED	THU	FRI	SAT
30	31 D FLA	1	2 FLA	3 D FLA	4 D PIT	5 D PIT
6 D PIT	7	8 ATL	9 ATL	10 ATL	11 CIN	12 D CIN
13 D CIN	14 FLA	15 FLA	16 FLA	17 D FLA	18 ATL	19 ATL
20 D ATL	21	22 COL	23 COL	24 D COL	25 D SF	26 SF
27 D SF	28 LA	29 LA	30 LA			

May

SUN	MON	TUE	WED	THU	FRI	SAT
				1 LA	2 SD	3 SD
4 D SD	5 ARI	6 ARI	7 D ARI	8	9 HOU	10 HOU
11 D HOU	12	13 ARI	14 ARI	15 D ARI	16 HOU	17 D HOU
18 HOU	19	20 NYM	21 NYM	22 D NYM	23 MON	24 MON
25 D MON	26	27 NYM	28 NYM	29 NYM	30 MON	31 MON

June

SUN	MON	TUE	WED	THU	FRI	SAT
1 D MON	2	3 SEA	4 SEA	5 SEA	6 OAK	7 D OAK
8 D OAK	9 ANA	10 ANA	11 ANA	12	13 CIN	14 CIN
15 D CIN	16	17 ATL	18 ATL	19 D ATL	20 BOS	21 D BOS
22 D BOS	23	24 ATL	25 ATL	26 ATL	27 BAL	28 BAL
29 D BAL	30 CUB					

July

SUN	MON	TUE	WED	THU	FRI	SAT
		1 CUB	2 CUB	3 CUB	4 D FLA	5 FLA
6 D FLA	7 MON	8 MON	9 MON	10 NYM	11 NYM	12 D NYM
13 D NYM	14	15 *	16	17 MON	18 MON	19 MON
20 D MON	21 NYM	22 D NYM	23 CUB	24 D CUB	25 FLA	26 FLA
27 D FLA	28	29 LA	30 LA	31 LA		

August

SUN	MON	TUE	WED	THU	FRI	SAT
					1 SD	2 SD
3 D SD	4 D SD	5 COL	6 COL	7 D COL	8 SF	9 D SF
10 D SF	11	12 MIL	13 MIL	14 MIL	15 STL	16 STL
17 D STL	18	19 MIL	20 MIL	21 D MIL	22 STL	23 D STL
24 D STL	25 MON	26 MON	27 MON	28 D MON	29 NYM	30 NYM

September

SUN	MON	TUE	WED	THU	FRI	SAT
31 D NYM	1	2 MON	3 MON	4 D NYM	5 NYM	6 NYM
7 D NYM	8 ATL	9 ATL	10 ATL	11 ATL	12 PIT	13 PIT
14 D PIT	15	16 FLA	17 FLA	18 FLA	19 CIN	20 CIN
21 D CIN	22	23 FLA	24 FLA	25 FLA	26 ATL	27 D ATL
28 D ATL						

Home games shaded; D—Day game (games starting before 5 p.m.); *—All-Star Game at Comiskey Park, Chicago. Subject to change.

CLUB DIRECTORY

General partner, president and CEO
David Montgomery
Chairman
Bill Giles
Vice president & general manager
Ed Wade

Vice president, public relations
Larry Shenk
Assistant general manager
Ruben Amaro Jr.
Asst. g.m., scouting & player dev.
Mike Arbuckle

Director, minor league operations
Steve Noworyta
Director, media relations
Leigh Tobin
Director, community relations
Gene Dias

MINOR LEAGUE AFFILIATES

Class	Team	League	Manager
AAA	Scranton/Wilkes-Barre	International	Marc Bombard
AA	Reading	Eastern	Greg Legg
A	Clearwater	Florida State	Roly de Armas
A	Lakewood	South Atlantic	Buddy Biancalana
A	Batavia	New York-Pennsylvania	To be announced
Rookie	Gulf Coast Phillies	Gulf Coast	Ruben Amaro Sr.

BROADCAST INFORMATION

Radio: WPEN-AM (950).
TV: UPN 57.
Cable TV: Comcast SportsNet.

SPRING TRAINING

Ballpark (city): Jack Russell Stadium (Clearwater, Fla.).
Ticket information: 215-463-1000, 727-442-8496.

Follow the Phillies all season at: www.sportingnews.com/baseball/teams/phillies/

SPRING TRAINING ROSTER

Manager—Larry Bowa (10).
Coaches—Greg Gross (21), Ramon Henderson (59), Joe Kerrigan, Tony Scott (30), Gary Varsho (25), John Vukovich (18).

No.	PITCHERS	B/T	Ht./Wt.	Born	Age*	2002 clubs
62	Baisley, Brad	R/R	6-9/205	8-24-79	23	Reading
48	Coggin, Dave	R/R	6-4/205	10-30-76	26	Philadelphia
37	Cormier, Rheal	L/L	5-10/187	4-23-67	35	Philadelphia
56	Duckworth, Brandon	R/R	6-2/185	1-23-76	27	Philadelphia
	Hancock, Josh	R/R	6-3/217	4-11-78	24	Trenton, Pawtucket, Boston
28	Junge, Eric	R/R	6-5/215	1-5-77	26	Scranton/Wilkes-Barre, Philadelphia
	Madson, Ryan	L/R	6-6/180	8-28-80	22	Reading
54	Mercado, Hector	L/L	6-3/235	4-29-74	28	Scranton/Wilkes-Barre, Philadelphia
49	Mesa, Jose	R/R	6-3/225	5-22-66	36	Philadelphia
34	Millwood, Kevin	R/R	6-4/220	12-24-74	28	Atlanta
41	Myers, Brett	R/R	6-4/215	8-17-80	22	Scranton/Wilkes-Barre, Philadelphia
44	Padilla, Vicente	R/R	6-2/200	9-27-77	25	Philadelphia
	Perez, Franklin	R/R	6-2/175	6-10-81	21	Reading
19	Plesac, Dan	L/L	6-5/217	2-4-62	41	Toronto, Philadelphia
35	Roa, Joe	R/R	6-1/194	10-11-71	31	Scranton/Wilkes-Barre, Philadelphia
67	Serrano, Elio	R/R	6-3/215	12-4-78	24	Scranton/Wilkes-Barre
52	Silva, Carlos	R/R	6-4/225	4-23-79	23	Philadelphia, Reading
	Smith, Bud	L/L	6-0/170	10-23-79	23	Memphis, St. Louis, Scranton/Wilkes-Barre
	Wedel, Jeremy	R/R	6-0/195	11-27-76	26	Scranton/Wilkes-Barre
99	Wendell, Turk	L/R	6-2/205	5-19-67	35	DID NOT PLAY
43	Wolf, Randy	L/L	6-0/194	8-22-76	26	Clearwater, Philadelphia

No.	CATCHERS	B/T	Ht./Wt.	Born	Age*	2002 clubs
24	Lieberthal, Mike	R/R	6-0/190	1-18-72	31	Philadelphia
7	Pratt, Todd	R/R	6-3/230	2-9-67	36	Philadelphia

No.	INFIELDERS	B/T	Ht./Wt.	Born	Age*	2002 clubs
28	Bell, David	R/R	5-10/195	9-14-72	30	San Francisco
	Houston, Tyler	L/R	6-1/218	1-17-71	32	Milwaukee, Los Angeles
65	Machado, Anderson	B/R	5-11/165	1-25-81	22	Reading
9	Perez, Tomas	B/R	5-11/177	12-29-73	29	Reading, Philadelphia
23	Polanco, Placido	R/R	5-10/168	10-10-75	27	St. Louis, Philadelphia
34	Punto, Nick	B/R	5-9/170	11-8-77	25	Philadelphia, Scranton/Wilkes-Barre
	Richardson, Juan	R/R	6-1/175	1-10-81	22	Clearwater
11	Rollins, Jimmy	B/R	5-8/165	11-27-78	24	Philadelphia
25	Thome, Jim	L/R	6-4/220	8-27-70	32	Cleveland
	Utley, Chase	L/R	6-1/185	12-17-78	24	Scranton/Wilkes-Barre

No.	OUTFIELDERS	B/T	Ht./Wt.	Born	Age*	2002 clubs
53	Abreu, Bobby	L/R	6-0/195	3-11-74	29	Philadelphia
5	Burrell, Pat	R/R	6-4/222	10-10-76	26	Philadelphia
29	Byrd, Marlon	R/R	6-0/225	8-30-77	25	Scranton/Wilkes-Barre, Philadelphia
33	Ledee, Ricky	L/L	6-1/190	11-22-73	29	Philadelphia
22	Michaels, Jason	R/R	6-0/204	5-4-76	26	Scranton/Wilkes-Barre, Philadelphia
66	Padilla, Jorge	R/R	6-2/200	8-11-79	23	Reading
12	Valent, Eric	L/L	6-0/191	4-4-77	25	Scranton/Wilkes-Barre, Philadelphia

*Age as of April 1, 2003.

BALLPARK INFORMATION

Ballpark (capacity, surface)
Veterans Stadium (62,418, artificial)

Address
P.O. Box 7575
Philadelphia, PA 19101

Official website
www.phillies.com

Business phone
215-463-6000

Ticket information
215-463-1000

Field dimensions (from home plate)
To left field at foul line, 330 feet
To center field, 408 feet
To right field at foul line, 330 feet

First game played
April 10, 1971 (Phillies 4, Expos 1)

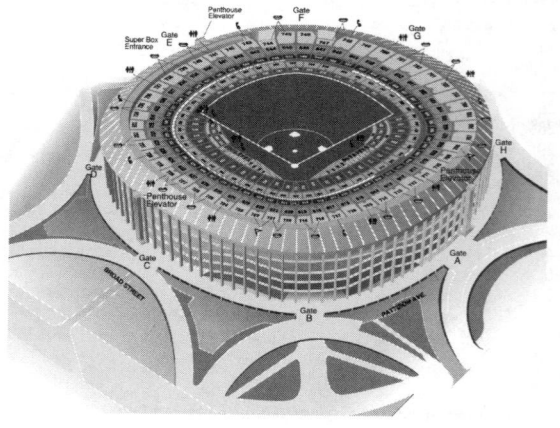

2003 SEASON *Philadelphia Phillies*

Date	Opp.	Res.	Score	(inn.*)	Hits	Opp. hits	Winning pitcher	Losing pitcher	Save	Record	Pos.	GB
4-1	At Atl.	L	2-7		5	8	Glavine	Person		0-1	5th	1.0
4-3	At Atl.	W	3-1		9	4	Padilla	Millwood	Mesa	1-1	T1st	...
4-4	At Atl.	L	2-11		5	15	Marquis	Adams		1-2	T3rd	1.0
4-5	Fla.	W	6-2		9	8	Duckworth	Tavarez	Mesa	2-2	T1st	...
4-6	Fla.	L	3-7		9	10	Nunez	Santiago		2-3	T4th	1.0
4-7	Fla.	W	3-2	(11)	9	7	Politte	Looper		3-3	T1st	...
4-8	Atl.	L	1-2		6	6	Millwood	Padilla	Smoltz	3-4	T4th	1.0
4-9	Atl.	W	7-4		11	8	Santiago	Marquis	Mesa	4-4	T2nd	0.5
4-10	Atl.	W	7-5	(11)	13	8	Politte	Ligtenberg		5-4	2nd	0.5
4-11	Atl.	L	2-6		7	8	Glavine	Coggin	Holmes	5-5	T3rd	0.5
4-12	Cin.	L	5-8		11	12	Brower	Cormier	Graves	5-6	4th	1.5
4-13	Cin.	L	2-5		9	10	Hamilton	Person	Graves	5-7	4th	1.5
4-14	Cin.	W	3-1		8	6	Padilla	Dessens	Mesa	6-7	T4th	1.5
4-16	At Fla.	L	6-7		7	11	Knotts	Mesa		6-8	4th	3.0
4-17	At Fla.	W	7-5		14	5	Cormier	Looper	Mesa	7-8	4th	2.0
4-18	At Fla.	L	7-8		9	9	Nunez	Bottalico		7-9	T4th	3.0
4-19	At Pit.	L	4-7		7	7	Lowe	Padilla	Williams	7-10	5th	3.0
4-20	At Pit.	L	5-6		6	11	Villone	Adams	Williams	7-11	5th	3.0
4-21	At Pit.	L	3-9		6	15	Wells	Duckworth		7-12	5th	4.0
4-23	S.D.	W	8-5		13	5	Wolf	DeWitt	Mesa	8-12	5th	4.0
4-24	S.D.	L	2-7		7	13	Lawrence	Person		8-13	5th	5.0
4-25	S.D.	L	4-6		10	11	Jones	Cormier	Hoffman	8-14	5th	6.0
4-26	At Col.	L	1-4		7	10	Thomson	Adams	Jimenez	8-15	5th	6.0
4-27	At Col.	L	6-8		12	9	Chacon	Duckworth	Jimenez	8-16	5th	6.0
4-28	At Col.	L	2-4		9	9	Jennings	Wolf	Jimenez	8-17	5th	7.0
4-29	At S.F	L	5-8		7	8	Worrell	Cormier	Nen	8-18	5th	7.5
4-30	At S.F	W	8-2		14	5	Padilla	Hernandez		9-18	5th	7.5
5-1	At S.F	L	1-2		7	4	Rodriguez	Bottalico	Nen	9-19	5th	8.5
5-3	Col.	W	3-2		5	7	Duckworth	Chacon	Mesa	10-19	5th	8.0
5-4	Col.	W	6-5		11	10	Mercado	White	Mesa	11-19	5th	7.0
5-5	Col.	W	7-4		11	8	Padilla	Hampton	Mesa	12-19	5th	6.0
5-7	Hou.	W	7-4		11	4	Silva	Pichardo	Mesa	13-19	5th	5.0
5-8	Hou.	W	5-3		5	8	Mesa	Cruz		14-19	5th	4.0
5-9	Hou.	W	3-1		6	5	Wolf	Mlicki	Mesa	15-19	5th	4.0
5-10	Ari.	W	4-0		9	2	Padilla	Helling		16-19	5th	4.0
5-11	Ari.	L	5-6	(10)	10	8	Kim	Mesa		16-20	5th	4.0
5-12	Ari.	W	3-1		10	4	Adams	Batista	Mesa	17-20	5th	4.0
5-13	At Hou.	L	3-17		8	20	Redding	Duckworth		17-21	5th	4.0
5-14	At Hou.	L	1-5		5	7	Dotel	Wolf	Wagner	17-22	5th	5.0
5-15	At Hou.	L	2-6		5	12	Hernandez	Padilla		17-23	5th	5.0
5-16	At Ari.	L	2-4		8	7	Johnson	Santiago	Kim	17-24	5th	5.0
5-17	At Ari.	L	9-12		17	13	Oropesa	Cormier	Kim	17-25	5th	6.0
5-18	At Ari.	L	4-5		10	8	Myers	Mesa		17-26	5th	7.0
5-19	At Ari.	W	4-3		7	8	Wolf	Parra	Mesa	18-26	5th	6.0
5-21	N.Y.	W	4-0		7	3	Padilla	D'Amico		19-26	5th	5.0
5-22	N.Y.	W	5-2		7	13	Adams	Leiter	Mesa	20-26	5th	4.0
5-23	N.Y.	L	0-1		5	7	Strickland	Mesa	Benitez	20-27	5th	5.0
5-24	At Mon.	L	1-4		5	10	Ohka	Wolf	Stewart	20-28	5th	6.0
5-25	At Mon.	L	9-13	(10)	10	14	Tucker	Mercado		20-29	5th	6.0
5-26	At Mon.	L	5-6		10	12	Lloyd	Padilla	Stewart	20-30	5th	7.0
5-28	At N.Y.	W	5-3		12	11	Cormier	Trachsel	Mesa	21-30	5th	6.5
5-29	At N.Y.	L	3-4		10	8	Strickland	Santiago	Benitez	21-31	5th	6.5
5-31	Mon.	L	7-8		11	8	Vazquez	Duckworth	Stewart	21-32	5th	8.0
6-1	Mon.	W	8-4		10	10	Padilla	Armas Jr.		22-32	5th	8.0
6-2	Mon.	W	18-3		16	8	Person	Reames		23-32	5th	7.0
6-4	Fla.	L	0-5		4	7	Izquierdo	Adams		23-33	5th	8.0
6-5	Fla.	L	1-2		6	10	Burnett	Wolf		23-34	5th	9.0
6-7	At Det.	W	11-1		15	8	Padilla	Weaver		24-34	5th	9.5
6-8	At Det.	W	2-1		10	5	Person	Patterson	Mesa	25-34	5th	9.5
6-9	At Det.	W	7-5		12	10	Duckworth	Sparks	Mesa	26-34	5th	9.5
6-10	At Cle.	W	3-1		9	6	Adams	Sabathia	Mesa	27-34	5th	8.5
6-11	At Cle.	L	1-5		6	7	Colon	Wolf	Wickman	27-35	5th	9.5
6-12	At Cle.	W	7-3		11	11	Padilla	Paronto		28-35	5th	9.5
6-14	Bal.	L	3-7		7	9	Ryan	Bottalico		28-36	5th	10.5
6-15	Bal.	W	4-3	(10)	9	6	Cormier	Groom		29-36	5th	10.5

Date	Opp.	Res.	Score	(inn.*)	Hits	Opp. hits	Winning pitcher	Losing pitcher	Save	Record	Pos.	GB
6-16	Bal.	L	2-4		6	5	Driskill	Adams	Julio	29-37	5th	10.5
6-18	Chi.	L	3-6	(12)	8	7	Osuna	Coggin	Biddle	29-38	5th	10.5
6-19	Chi.	W	4-3		7	8	Plesac	Biddle		30-38	5th	10.5
6-20	Chi.	L	1-6		6	10	Buehrle	Person		30-39	5th	11.5
6-21	Min.	W	3-0		6	4	Duckworth	Lohse	Mesa	31-39	5th	11.5
6-22	Min.	L	1-4	(11)	4	8	Hawkins	Plesac	Guardado	31-40	5th	12.5
6-23	Min.	L	1-5		3	9	Fiore	Wolf		31-41	5th	13.5
6-24	At Fla.	W	15-4		17	8	Padilla	Tavarez		32-41	5th	13.5
6-25	At Fla.	W	7-6	(11)	13	11	Mesa	Darensbourg	Plesac	33-41	5th	12.5
6-26	At Fla.	L	2-6		6	10	Tejera	Duckworth		33-42	5th	13.5
6-27	At Fla.	W	7-3		10	8	Adams	Olsen		34-42	5th	13.0
6-28	At Bal.	W	6-2		8	8	Wolf	Driskill		35-42	5th	13.0
6-29	At Bal.	L	1-11		6	18	Johnson	Padilla		35-43	5th	14.0
6-30	At Bal.	W	8-5		12	9	Person	Bauer	Mesa	36-43	5th	14.0
7-1	N.Y.	W	6-3		8	7	Duckworth	Estes	Mesa	37-43	5th	14.0
7-2	N.Y.	L	6-12		11	15	Astacio	Adams		37-44	5th	14.0
7-3	N.Y.	W	8-7		14	8	Plesac	Strickland	Mesa	38-44	5th	14.0
7-4	Mon.	L	1-2		5	6	Eischen	Mesa	Stewart	38-45	5th	15.0
7-5	Mon.	L	3-8		5	8	Ohka	Person		38-46	5th	16.0
7-6	Mon.	L	3-5		8	12	Vazquez	Duckworth	Stewart	38-47	5th	16.0
7-7	Mon.	W	10-8		8	11	Cormier	Herges	Mesa	39-47	5th	16.0
7-11	At N.Y.	L	1-9		9	11	Guthrie	Cormier		39-48	5th	17.0
7-12	At N.Y.	W	9-8		14	14	Person	D'Amico		40-48	5th	17.0
7-13	At N.Y.	W	7-6	(12)	11	15	Mercado	Strickland	Silva	41-48	5th	16.0
7-14	At N.Y.	L	2-4		7	4	Astacio	Duckworth	Benitez	41-49	5th	16.0
7-15	At Mon.	W	11-8		13	9	Coggin	Herges	Mesa	42-49	5th	15.0
7-16	At Mon.	W	6-3		8	9	Wolf	Armas Jr.	Mesa	43-49	5th	15.0
7-17	Chi.	W	4-3	(10)	8	5	Mesa	Fassero		44-49	5th	15.0
7-18	Chi.	L	4-6		9	10	Clement	Padilla		44-50	5th	16.0
7-19	Atl.	L	1-4		7	8	Moss	Duckworth	Smoltz	44-51	5th	17.0
7-20	Atl.	L	3-4		5	8	Marquis	Adams	Smoltz	44-52	5th	18.0
7-21	Atl.	L	1-2		4	4	Millwood	Wolf	Spooneybarger	44-53	5th	19.0
7-22	At Chi.	L	6-7		11	10	Farnsworth	Mesa		44-54	5th	19.0
7-23	At Chi.	W	7-4		7	10	Coggin	Clement	Mesa	45-54	5th	19.0
7-24	At Chi.	W	4-2		6	5	Myers	Prior	Mesa	46-54	5th	19.0
7-25	At Chi.	W	6-2		9	6	Silva	Farnsworth		47-54	5th	18.5
7-26	At Atl.	W	3-2		9	5	Wolf	Millwood	Mesa	48-54	5th	17.5
7-27	At Atl.	L	3-5		9	10	Maddux	Roa	Smoltz	48-55	5th	18.5
7-28	At Atl.	W	7-1		12	6	Padilla	Glavine		49-55	5th	17.5
7-30	S.F	L	3-10		10	10	Rueter	Myers		49-56	5th	18.5
7-31	S.F	W	8-6		8	12	Timlin	Brohawn	Mesa	50-56	5th	18.5
8-1	S.F	W	2-1		6	6	Wolf	Ortiz	Mesa	51-56	5th	18.5
8-2	L.A.	W	3-1		6	5	Silva	Quantrill	Mesa	52-56	5th	18.5
8-3	L.A.	L	6-8	(12)	9	14	Gagne	Coggin	Quantrill	52-57	5th	19.5
8-4	L.A.	L	3-4		9	9	Daal	Myers	Gagne	52-58	5th	20.5
8-5	L.A.	W	7-5		7	9	Timlin	Shuey	Mesa	53-58	5th	20.0
8-6	At S.D.	W	5-4	(16)	14	14	Cormier	Jones		54-58	5th	20.0
8-7	At S.D.	L	2-5		7	10	Peavy	Padilla	Hoffman	54-59	5th	20.0
8-8	At S.D.	L	4-7		10	14	Davey	Adams		54-60	5th	21.0
8-9	At L.A.	L	6-7		9	10	Shuey	Timlin	Gagne	54-61	5th	22.0
8-10	At L.A.	L	8-10		14	15	Quantrill	Cormier	Gagne	54-62	5th	22.0
8-11	At L.A.	W	6-3		13	7	Timlin	Shuey	Mesa	55-62	5th	22.0
8-13	Mil.	W	3-1		7	5	Padilla	Rusch	Mesa	56-62	4th	21.0
8-14	Mil.	W	4-1		6	4	Myers	Wright		57-62	4th	21.0
8-15	Mil.	W	5-0		9	5	Roa	Quevedo		58-62	T3rd	20.5
8-16	St.L.	W	4-0		8	4	Wolf	Finley		59-62	3rd	20.5
8-17	St.L.	L	1-5		4	9	Simontacchi	Coggin		59-63	T3rd	20.5
8-18	St.L.	L	1-5		8	8	Morris	Padilla		59-64	4th	20.5
8-20	At Mil.	L	1-2		6	9	Wright	Myers	DeJean	59-65	4th	21.0
8-21	At Mil.	W	13-3		17	6	Roa	Sheets		60-65	4th	21.0
8-22	At Mil.	W	7-0		10	4	Wolf	Osting		61-65	3rd	20.0
8-23	At St.L.	W	5-4	(14)	18	13	Adams	Joseph		62-65	3rd	19.0
8-24	At St.L.	W	4-0		10	5	Padilla	Benes	Mesa	63-65	3rd	18.0
8-25	At St.L.	W	5-3		12	10	Silva	Isringhausen	Mesa	64-65	3rd	18.0
8-27	Mon.	W	4-2		11	8	Roa	Yoshii	Mesa	65-65	2nd	18.0
8-28	Mon.	L	3-6		5	10	Ohka	Coggin		65-66	3rd	18.0
8-29	Mon.	W	2-1		6	3	Duckworth	Colon	Mesa	66-66	2nd	17.0
8-30	At N.Y.	W	7-5		8	6	Padilla	Astacio	Mesa	67-66	2nd	17.0
8-31	At N.Y.	W	1-0		7	4	Wolf	Trachsel		68-66	2nd	17.0

Date	Opp.	Res.	Score	(inn.*)	Hits	Opp. hits	Winning pitcher	Losing pitcher	Save	Record	Pos.	GB
9-1	At N.Y.	W	9-5		15	9	Myers	Leiter		69-66	2nd	17.0
9-2	At Mon.	L	1-5		6	10	Ohka	Roa		69-67	2nd	18.0
9-3	At Mon.	L	6-7	(10)	11	10	Eischen	Adams		69-68	2nd	18.0
9-4	At Mon.	L	5-8		8	13	Armas Jr.	Padilla	Eischen	69-69	2nd	19.0
9-5	At Mon.	W	4-1		10	5	Wolf	Vazquez		70-69	2nd	18.5
9-6	N.Y.	L	2-7		9	9	Leiter	Myers		70-70	2nd	19.5
9-7	N.Y.	L	4-5		9	6	Walker	Roa	Benitez	70-71	2nd	20.5
9-8	N.Y.	L	3-11		9	15	Thomson	Duckworth		70-72	2nd	20.5
9-9	N.Y.	L	4-6		12	6	D'Amico	Timlin	Benitez	70-73	2nd	21.0
9-10†	Fla.	L	4-6		9	8	Lloyd	Wolf	Almanza	70-74		
9-10‡	Fla.	L	1-2		4	8	Wayne	Padilla	Looper	70-75	4th	22.5
9-11	Fla.	W	9-2		10	9	Myers	Penny		71-75	T3rd	22.0
9-12	Fla.	W	6-1		10	8	Roa	Tejera		72-75	2nd	21.5
9-13	Pit.	L	3-5		9	5	Beimel	Timlin	Williams	72-76	T3rd	21.5
9-14	Pit.	W	4-1		8	5	Junge	Meadows	Mesa	73-76	T2nd	21.5
9-15	Pit.	W	1-0	(10)	9	2	Mesa	Sauerbeck		74-76	T2nd	21.5
9-17	At Atl.	L	1-2		5	10	Maddux	Padilla	Smoltz	74-77	3rd	22.0
9-18	At Atl.	W	6-5		13	11	Silva	Ligtenberg	Mesa	75-77	3rd	21.0
9-19	At Atl.	L	0-6		6	11	Glavine	Roa		75-78	3rd	22.0
9-21§	At Cin.	W	5-3	(10)	14	6	Adams	Williamson	Mesa	76-78		
9-21∞	At Cin.	W	5-4	(11)	12	10	Adams	Hamilton	Mesa	77-78	3rd	20.0
9-22	At Cin.	W	4-3		9	8	Duckworth	Rijo	Mesa	78-78	3rd	20.0
9-24	Atl.	W	5-3		7	11	Junge	Glavine	Mesa	79-78	T2nd	19.0
9-25	Atl.	L	1-7		6	11	Moss	Myers		79-79	T2nd	20.0
9-27	At Fla.	L	2-5		6	12	Knotts	Wolf	Looper	79-80	3rd	21.5
9-28	At Fla.	W	9-3		11	8	Duckworth	Wayne		80-80	3rd	21.5
9-29	At Fla.	L	3-4	(10)	12	12	Looper	Mercado		80-81	3rd	21.5

Monthly records: April (9-18), May (12-14), June (15-11), July (14-13), August (18-10), September (12-15).
*Innings, if other than nine. †First game of a doubleheader. ‡Second game of a doubleheader. §Day separate admission. ∞Night separate admission.

RECORDS

2002 regular-season record: 80-81
Position: 3rd in N.L. East
Home: 40-40 **Road:** 40-41
N.L. East: 34-41 **N.L. Central:** 22-14
N.L. West: 14-18 **A.L.:** 10-8
Vs. LH starters: 16-20
Vs. RH starters: 64-61
Grass: 37-35 **Artificial:** 43-46
Day: 24-29 **Night:** 56-52
1-Run: 22-24 **X-inn.:** 11-7
Doubleheaders: 0-1-0
Team record past five years: 383-426
(.473, ranks 10th in league in that span)

TEAM LEADERS

Batting average: Bobby Abreu (.308).
At-bats: Jimmy Rollins (637).
Runs: Bobby Abreu (102).
Hits: Bobby Abreu (176).
Total bases: Pat Burrell (319).
Doubles: Bobby Abreu (50).
Triples: Jimmy Rollins (10).
Home runs: Pat Burrell (37).

Runs batted in: Pat Burrell (116).
Stolen bases: Bobby Abreu, Jimmy Rollins (31).
Slugging percentage: Pat Burrell (.544).
On-base percentage: Bobby Abreu (.413).
Wins: Vicente Padilla (14).
Earned-run average: Randy Wolf (3.20).
Complete games: Randy Wolf (3).
Shutouts: Randy Wolf (2).
Saves: Jose Mesa (45).
Innings pitched: Randy Wolf (210.2).
Strikeouts: Randy Wolf (172).

GAMES BY POSITION

Catcher: Mike Lieberthal 129, Todd Pratt 34, Johnny Estrada 10.
First base: Travis Lee 148, Jeremy Giambi 21, Dave Hollins 5, Tomas Perez 3, Todd Pratt 2, John Mabry 1, Eric Valent 1.
Second base: Marlon Anderson 143, Tomas Perez 50, Nick Punto 1, Jimmy Rollins 1.
Third base: Scott Rolen 100, Placido Polanco 53, Tomas Perez 14, Jason Michaels 1.
Shortstop: Jimmy Rollins 152, Tomas Perez 13, Nick Punto 1.
Outfield: Pat Burrell 157, Bobby Abreu 154, Doug Glanville 117, Ricky Ledee 51, Jason Michaels 26, Jeremy Giambi 20, Marlon Byrd 10, Eric Valent 2, John Mabry 1.
Designated hitter: Jeremy Giambi 8, Jason Michaels 2.

TOP DRAFT CHOICES

1. **Cole Hamels**, LHP, Rancho Bernardo H.S., San Diego.
2. **Zach Segovia**, RHP, Forney (Texas) H.S.
3. **Kiel Fisher**, 3B-OF, Riverside Poly (Calif.) H.S.
4. **Nick Bourgeois**, LHP, Tulane.
5. **Jake Blalock**, 3B, Rancho Bernardo H.S., San Diego.
6. **Lee Gwaltney**, RHP, Louisiana Tech.
7. **Robby Read**, RHP, Florida State.
8. **Steven Doetsch**, OF, Dunedin (Fla.) H.S.
9. **Rob Harrand**, RHP, San Diego State.
10. **Ryan Barthelemy**, 1B, Florida State.

PITTSBURGH PIRATES
NATIONAL LEAGUE CENTRAL DIVISION

2003 SEASON

March/April

SUN	MON	TUE	WED	THU	FRI	SAT
30	31 CIN D	1	2 CIN	3 CIN D	4 PHI D	5 PHI D
6 PHI D	7 MIL D	8	9 MIL	10 MIL D	11 CUB D	12 CUB D
13 CUB D	14	15 NYM	16 NYM	17 NYM	18 CUB	19 CUB
20 CUB D	21	22 SF	23 SF	24 SF D	25 LA	26 LA
27 LA D	28	29 SD	30 SD			

May

SUN	MON	TUE	WED	THU	FRI	SAT
				1 SD D	2 LA	3 LA
4 LA D	5 HOU	6 HOU	7 HOU	8 HOU D	9 ARI	10 ARI
11 ARI D	12 HOU	13 HOU	14 HOU	15 HOU D	16 ARI	17 ARI
18 ARI D	19	20 CUB	21 CUB	22 CUB	23 STL	24 STL
25 STL D	26 CUB D	27 CUB	28 CUB D	29	30 STL	31 STL D

June

SUN	MON	TUE	WED	THU	FRI	SAT
1 STL D	2	3 BOS	4 BOS	5 BOS	6 ATL	7 ATL
8 ATL D	9	10 TOR	11 TOR	12 TOR	13 TB	14 TB
15 TB D	16	17 MON	18 MON	19 MON D	20 CLE	21 CLE
22 CLE D	23 MON	24 MON D	25 MON D	26	27 COL	28 COL
29 COL D	30					

July

SUN	MON	TUE	WED	THU	FRI	SAT
		1 CIN	2 CIN	3 CIN	4 HOU D	5 HOU
6 HOU D	7 MIL	8 MIL	9 MIL	10 MIL D	11 HOU	12 HOU
13 HOU D	14	15 *	16	17 MIL	18 MIL	19 MIL
20 MIL D	21 HOU	22 HOU	23 CIN	24 CIN D	25 STL	26 STL D
27 STL D	28 STL D	29 SD	30 SD	31 SD D		

August

SUN	MON	TUE	WED	THU	FRI	SAT
					1 COL	2 COL
3 COL D	4	5 SF	6 SF	7 SF D	8 COL	9 COL
10 COL D	11 STL	12 STL	13 STL	14 STL D	15 MIL	16 MIL D
17 MIL D	18	19 STL	20 STL	21 STL	22 MIL	23 MIL
24 MIL D	25	26 FLA	27 FLA	28 FLA	29 ATL	30 ATL D

September

SUN	MON	TUE	WED	THU	FRI	SAT
31 ATL D	1	2 FLA	3 FLA	4 FLA D	5 ATL	6 ATL
7 ATL D	8 CIN	9 CIN	10 CIN	11 CIN D	12 PHI	13 PHI
14 PHI D	15 CIN	16 CIN	17 CIN	18 CIN	19 CUB	20 CUB
21 CUB D	22	23 NYM	24 NYM	25 NYM	26 CUB D	27 CUB D
28 CUB D						

Home games shaded; D—Day game (games starting before 5 p.m.); *—All-Star Game at Comiskey Park, Chicago. Subject to change.

CLUB DIRECTORY

General partner
Kevin S. McClatchy
Chief operating officer
Dick Freeman
Sr. v.p. and general manager
Dave Littlefield

Assistant g.m./player personnel
Roy Smith
Special assistants to the g.m.
John Flores, Jax Robertson, Bill Singer, Pete Vuckovich
V.p, communications & ballpark dev.
Patty Paytas

Director of media relations
Jim Trdinich
Director of player development
Brian Graham
Dir. of community & player relations
Kathy Guy

MINOR LEAGUE AFFILIATES

Class	Team	League	Manager
AAA	Nashville	Pacific Coast	Trent Jewett
AA	Altoona	Eastern	Dale Sveum
A	Lynchburg	Carolina	Dave Clark
A	Hickory	South Atlantic	Tony Beasley
A	Williamsport	New York-Pennsylvania	Andy Stewart
Rookie	Gulf Coast Pirates	Gulf Coast	Woody Huyke

BROADCAST INFORMATION

Radio: KDKA-AM (1020).
Cable TV: Fox Sports Pittsburgh.

SPRING TRAINING

Ballpark (city): McKechnie Field (Bradenton, Fla.).
Ticket information: 941-748-4610.

Follow the Pirates all season at: www.sportingnews.com/baseball/teams/pirates/

SPRING TRAINING ROSTER

Manager— Lloyd McClendon (23).
Coaches—Alvaro Espinoza, Rusty Kuntz, Pete Mackanin, Gerald Perry, John Russell, Bruce Tanner (52), Spin Williams (54).

No.	PITCHERS	B/T	Ht./Wt.	Born	Age*	2002 clubs
69	Arroyo, Bronson	R/R	6-5/194	2-24-77	26	Nashville, Pittsburgh
53	Beimel, Joe	L/L	6-3/215	4-19-77	25	Pittsburgh
34	Benson, Kris	R/R	6-4/200	11-7-74	28	Nashville, Altoona, Pittsburgh
71	Boehringer, Brian	B/R	6-2/190	1-8-70	33	Pittsburgh
	Bradley, Bobby	R/R	6-1/164	12-15-80	22	DID NOT PLAY
27	Fogg, Josh	R/R	6-0/202	12-13-76	26	Pittsburgh
51	Gonzalez, Mike	R/L	6-2/215	5-23-78	24	Gulf Coast Pirates, Altoona
0	Guerrier, Matt	R/R	6-3/185	8-2-78	24	Nashville
49	Herges, Matt	L/R	6-0/200	4-1-70	33	Montreal
57	Lincoln, Mike	R/R	6-2/203	4-10-75	27	Pittsburgh, Nashville
	Mann, Jim	R/R	6-3/225	11-17-74	28	New Orleans, Houston, Round Rock
46	Meadows, Brian	R/R	6-4/220	11-21-75	27	Nashville, Pittsburgh
39	Reyes, Al	R/R	6-1/206	4-10-71	31	Nashville, Pittsburgh
45	Sanchez, Duaner	R/R	6-0/190	10-14-79	23	El Paso, Arizona, Tucson, Nashville, Pittsburgh
47	Sauerbeck, Scott	R/L	6-3/197	11-9-71	31	Pittsburgh
31	Torres, Salomon	R/R	5-11/165	3-11-72	31	Nashville, Pittsburgh
22	Vogelsong, Ryan	R/R	6-3/195	7-22-77	25	Lynchburg, Altoona
32	Wells, Kip	R/R	6-3/205	4-21-77	25	Pittsburgh
58	Williams, David	L/L	6-2/213	3-12-79	24	Pittsburgh
43	Williams, Mike	R/R	6-2/200	7-29-68	34	Pittsburgh

No.	CATCHERS	B/T	Ht./Wt.	Born	Age*	2002 clubs
11	Cota, Humberto	R/R	6-0/205	2-7-79	24	Nashville, Pittsburgh
	Doumit, Ryan	B/R	6-0/180	4-3-81	21	Hickory
25	House, J.R.	R/R	6-1/202	11-11-79	23	Altoona, Gulf Coast Pirates
18	Kendall, Jason	R/R	6-0/195	6-26-74	28	Pittsburgh

No.	INFIELDERS	B/T	Ht./Wt.	Born	Age*	2002 clubs
	Castillo, Jose	R/R	5-11/185	3-19-81	22	Lynchburg
59	Mackowiak, Rob	L/R	5-10/190	6-20-76	26	Pittsburgh
2	Meares, Pat	R/R	6-0/187	9-6-68	34	DID NOT PLAY
10	Nunez, Abraham	B/R	5-11/190	3-16-76	27	Pittsburgh, Nashville
16	Ramirez, Aramis	R/R	6-1/211	6-25-78	24	Pittsburgh
3	Reese, Pokey	R/R	5-11/188	6-10-73	29	Pittsburgh
	Rivera, Carlos	L/L	5-11/230	6-10-78	24	Altoona
	Simon, Randall	L/L	6-0/230	5-26-75	27	Detroit
12	Wilson, Jack	R/R	6-0/195	12-29-77	25	Pittsburgh
29	Young, Kevin	R/R	6-3/225	6-16-69	33	Pittsburgh
	Young, Walter	L/R	6-5/295	2-18-80	23	Hickory

No.	OUTFIELDERS	B/T	Ht./Wt.	Born	Age*	2002 clubs
56	Alvarez, Tony	R/R	6-1/200	5-10-79	23	Altoona, Pittsburgh
26	Davis, J.J.	R/R	6-5/250	10-25-78	24	Altoona, Pittsburgh
24	Giles, Brian	L/L	5-10/202	1-20-71	32	Pittsburgh
38	Hyzdu, Adam	R/R	6-2/220	12-6-71	31	Nashville, Pittsburgh
36	Wilson, Craig	R/R	6-2/225	11-30-76	26	Pittsburgh

*Age as of April 1, 2003.

BALLPARK INFORMATION

Ballpark (capacity, surface)
PNC Park (37,898, grass)

Address
PNC Park at North Shore
115 Federal Street
Pittsburgh, PA 15212

Official website
www.pittsburghpirates.com

Business phone
412-323-5000

Ticket information
800-BUY-BUCS

Field dimensions (from home plate)
To left field at foul line, 325 feet
To center field, 399 feet
To right field at foul line, 320 feet

First game played
April 9, 2001 (Reds 8, Pirates 2)

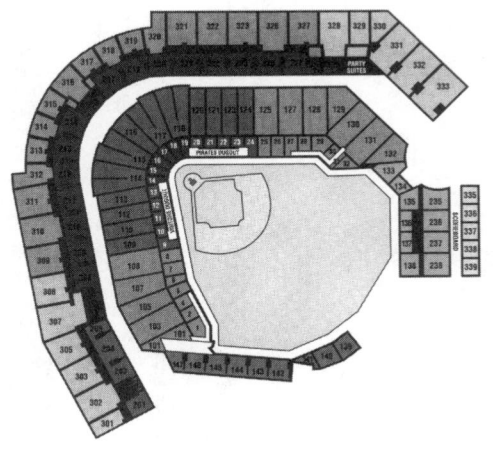

2003 SEASON *Pittsburgh Pirates*

Date	Opp.	Res.	Score	(inn.*)	Hits	Opp. hits	Winning pitcher	Losing pitcher	Save	Record	Pos.	GB
4-1	At N.Y.	L	2-6		4	9	Leiter	Villone		0-1	T5th	1.0
4-3	At N.Y.	W	5-3		11	7	Wells	Trachsel	Williams	1-1	T1st	...
4-4	At N.Y.	W	3-2		8	5	Anderson	Estes	Williams	2-1	T1st	...
4-5	At Chi.	W	2-1		6	4	Williams	Bere	Williams	3-1	1st	+1.0
4-6	At Chi.	W	6-1		10	6	Fogg	Clement		4-1	1st	+1.0
4-8	Cin.	W	1-0		4	4	Villone	Dessens	Williams	5-1	1st	+1.5
4-10	Cin.	L	5-8		6	13	Acevedo	Wells	Graves	5-2	1st	+0.5
4-11	Cin.	L	2-3		7	8	Haynes	Anderson	Graves	5-3	2nd	0.5
4-12	Chi.	L	3-7		5	10	Bere	Williams		5-4	3rd	1.5
4-13	Chi.	W	3-2		6	6	Fogg	Clement	Williams	6-4	3rd	1.5
4-14	Chi.	L	1-5	(8)	5	12	Lieber	Villone	Borowski	6-5	3rd	1.5
4-15	At Mil.	W	6-1		12	7	Wells	Rusch		7-5	T2nd	0.5
4-16	At Mil.	W	5-1		7	4	Anderson	Neugebauer		8-5	1st	+0.5
4-17	At Mil.	W	3-2		8	5	Williams	Buddie	Williams	9-5	1st	+0.5
4-19	Phi.	W	7-4		7	7	Lowe	Padilla	Williams	10-5	1st	+2.0
4-20	Phi.	W	6-5		11	6	Villone	Adams	Williams	11-5	1st	+2.5
4-21	Phi.	W	9-3		15	6	Wells	Duckworth		12-5	1st	+2.5
4-23	L.A.	L	6-9		9	14	Ishii	Anderson	Gagne	12-6	1st	+1.5
4-24	L.A.	L	1-5		8	10	Daal	Williams		12-7	1st	+0.5
4-25	L.A.	W	3-2		5	9	Fogg	Nomo	Williams	13-7	1st	+0.5
4-26	S.D.	L	1-10		6	13	Tomko	Villone		13-8	2nd	0.5
4-28†	S.D.	W	3-2		9	6	Sauerbeck	Embree	Williams	14-8		
4-28‡	S.D.	L	2-7		8	9	Tollberg	Anderson		14-9	2nd	0.5
4-30	At Col.	L	0-10		3	13	Hampton	Williams		14-10	2nd	1.5
5-1	At Col.	L	0-6		3	11	Neagle	Fogg		14-11	2nd	2.5
5-2	At Col.	L	2-7		2	9	Thomson	Villone		14-12	2nd	2.5
5-3	At S.D.	W	6-4		11	8	Wells	Howard	Williams	15-12	2nd	1.5
5-4	At S.D.	L	0-3		7	9	Jarvis	Anderson	Hoffman	15-13	2nd	1.5
5-5	At S.D.	L	5-6		9	12	Lawrence	Lowe	Hoffman	15-14	2nd	1.5
5-6	At Ari.	W	3-2		9	7	Fogg	Johnson	Williams	16-14	2nd	1.5
5-7	At Ari.	L	6-7		10	15	Myers	Beimel	Kim	16-15	2nd	2.5
5-8	At Ari.	L	3-4		6	13	Schilling	Wells	Kim	16-16	2nd	3.5
5-10	Hou.	W	5-1		8	4	Anderson	Hernandez		17-16	2nd	2.5
5-11	Hou.	W	4-2		5	5	Fogg	Oswalt	Williams	18-16	2nd	2.5
5-12	Hou.	L	1-5		4	8	Reynolds	Williams		18-17	2nd	2.5
5-13	Ari.	L	0-11		6	14	Schilling	Benson		18-18	2nd	3.5
5-14	Ari.	W	2-1		7	6	Wells	Anderson	Williams	19-18	2nd	3.5
5-15	Ari.	L	2-6		4	11	Helling	Anderson		19-19	T2nd	4.5
5-16	At Hou.	L	1-3		9	5	Oswalt	Boehringer	Wagner	19-20	3rd	5.5
5-17	At Hou.	L	4-7		6	7	Stone	Villone	Dotel	19-21	4th	5.5
5-18	At Hou.	L	1-2		4	8	Dotel	Lowe		19-22	4th	6.5
5-19	At Hou.	W	5-3		9	10	Wells	Mlicki	Williams	20-22	4th	5.5
5-21†	At Chi.	W	12-1		13	3	Anderson	Bere		21-22		
5-21‡	At Chi.	L	3-4		6	6	Cruz	Fogg	Alfonseca	21-23	T3rd	5.5
5-22	At Chi.	L	4-7		7	9	Prior	Williams	Alfonseca	21-24	T3rd	6.5
5-23	At Chi.	L	6-11		10	15	Clement	Benson		21-25	T3rd	6.5
5-24	St.L.	W	5-2		9	6	Wells	Stephenson		22-25	3rd	5.5
5-25	St.L.	L	3-6		3	11	Williams	Anderson	Isringhausen	22-26	3rd	6.5
5-26	St.L.	L	3-7		9	11	Simontacchi	Fogg		22-27	T3rd	6.5
5-27	Chi.	W	3-2	(10)	8	9	Williams	Alfonseca		23-27	3rd	6.0
5-28	Chi.	L	0-3		2	6	Clement	Benson		23-28	3rd	7.0
5-29	Chi.	W	5-0		13	4	Wells	Lieber		24-28	3rd	7.0
5-30	Chi.	L	8-9		10	8	Wood	Anderson	Alfonseca	24-29	3rd	8.0
5-31	At St.L.	W	3-1		11	4	Fogg	Williams	Williams	25-29	3rd	7.0
6-1	At St.L.	L	4-9		8	13	Kile	Arroyo		25-30	4th	7.0
6-2	At St.L.	W	5-2		9	8	Lowe	Morris	Williams	26-30	3rd	7.0
6-3	At Mon.	L	5-7		12	7	Ohka	Wells	Stewart	26-31	3rd	7.5
6-4	At Mon.	W	5-2		6	9	Anderson	Pavano	Williams	27-31	3rd	6.5
6-5	At Mon.	L	1-3		3	9	Vazquez	Fogg		27-32	3rd	7.0
6-7	Mil.	W	6-1		12	5	Beimel	Sheets		28-32	3rd	6.5
6-8	Mil.	W	9-8	(11)	15	13	Boehringer	King		29-32	3rd	6.5
6-9	Mil.	W	5-4		7	10	Sauerbeck	Wright	Williams	30-32	3rd	5.5
6-10	At Ana.	L	3-4		9	10	Washburn	Anderson	Percival	30-33	3rd	5.5
6-11	At Ana.	W	7-3		12	7	Fogg	Appier		31-33	3rd	5.5
6-12	At Ana.	L	5-8		12	14	Weber	Boehringer	Percival	31-34	3rd	5.5

Date	Opp.	Res.	Score	(inn.*)	Hits	Opp. hits	Winning pitcher	Losing pitcher	Save	Record	Pos.	GB
6-14	At Cin.	L	3-4	(11)	12	9	Williamson	Williams		31-35	3rd	6.5
6-15	At Cin.	L	3-4		9	9	Sullivan	Lincoln	Graves	31-36	3rd	7.5
6-16	At Cin.	W	5-1		10	5	Anderson	Haynes		32-36	3rd	6.5
6-18	Oak.	L	2-4		8	10	Mulder	Fogg	Koch	32-37	3rd	7.5
6-19	Oak.	L	2-3	(10)	9	5	Bradford	Williams	Koch	32-38	3rd	8.5
6-20	Oak.	L	3-5		8	10	Hudson	Benson	Koch	32-39	3rd	8.5
6-21	Tex.	L	0-2		5	8	Rogers	Wells	Cordero	32-40	3rd	8.5
6-22	Tex.	L	2-3		5	10	Bell	Lincoln	Irabu	32-41	T3rd	9.0
6-23	Tex.	L	4-10		7	11	Park	Fogg		32-42	T3rd	9.0
6-25	Mon.	W	4-1		10	9	Benson	Ohka	Williams	33-42	T3rd	8.0
6-26	Mon.	W	7-4		10	8	Wells	Vazquez	Williams	34-42	3rd	8.0
6-27	Mon.	L	2-7	(7)	5	13	Brower	Villone		34-43	T3rd	8.0
6-28	At Det.	W	3-1		10	2	Fogg	Redman	Williams	35-43	T3rd	8.0
6-29	At Det.	L	1-2		9	10	Weaver	Beimel	Acevedo	35-44	4th	8.0
6-30	At Det.	W	6-2		13	10	Benson	Maroth	Williams	36-44	4th	7.0
7-1	Mil.	L	0-2		3	3	Wright	Wells		36-45	4th	8.0
7-2	Mil.	L	6-12		9	18	Quevedo	Anderson		36-46	4th	9.0
7-3	Mil.	W	3-1		8	7	Fogg	Sheets	Williams	37-46	4th	9.0
7-4	Hou.	L	6-8		12	11	Borbon	Beimel		37-47	4th	10.0
7-5	Hou.	W	4-3		10	6	Fetters	Borbon	Williams	38-47	4th	9.0
7-6	Hou.	L	2-10		7	11	Cruz	Wells		38-48	4th	9.0
7-7	Hou.	L	1-6		4	8	Miller	Anderson		38-49	4th	10.0
7-11	At Mil.	W	3-2	(10)	9	7	Boehringer	DeJean	Williams	39-49	4th	9.5
7-12	At Mil.	W	9-2		9	12	Lowe	Rusch		40-49	4th	8.5
7-13	At Mil.	W	5-3		8	8	Wells	Wright	Williams	41-49	4th	8.5
7-14	At Mil.	L	3-5		7	6	Quevedo	Beimel	DeJean	41-50	4th	9.5
7-15	At Hou.	W	5-4		7	9	Lowe	Wagner	Williams	42-50	4th	9.5
7-16	At Hou.	W	7-3		11	7	Fogg	Oswalt	Boehringer	43-50	4th	9.5
7-17	Cin.	W	6-3		7	7	Anderson	Dempster	Williams	44-50	4th	8.5
7-18	Cin.	L	5-7		9	12	Sullivan	Boehringer	Graves	44-51	4th	9.5
7-19	St.L.	W	12-9		15	13	Sauerbeck	Veres		45-51	4th	8.5
7-20	St.L.	W	15-6		14	14	Benson	Smith		46-51	4th	7.5
7-21	St.L.	L	4-8		10	14	Finley	Fogg	Kline	46-52	4th	8.5
7-22	At Cin.	W	6-5		12	14	Anderson	Dempster	Williams	47-52	4th	8.5
7-23	At Cin.	L	2-7		7	12	Haynes	Wells		47-53	4th	9.5
7-24	At Cin.	L	5-10		11	9	Moehler	Beimel		47-54	4th	9.5
7-25	At Hou.	L	0-8		6	9	Saarloos	Benson		47-55	4th	10.5
7-26	At Hou.	L	3-4		5	5	Wagner	Sauerbeck		47-56	4th	11.5
7-27	At Hou.	L	0-3		4	12	Oswalt	Anderson	Wagner	47-57	4th	11.5
7-28	At Hou.	L	0-4		5	8	Miller	Wells		47-58	4th	12.5
7-30	Col.	W	4-1		6	4	Benson	Neagle	Williams	48-58	4th	12.5
7-31	Col.	W	7-6		12	10	Boehringer	White	Williams	49-58	4th	11.5
8-1	Col.	L	0-3		2	13	Jennings	Meadows	Jimenez	49-59	4th	11.5
8-2	S.F	W	6-5		11	11	Boehringer	Nen		50-59	4th	10.5
8-3	S.F	L	6-11		9	16	Schmidt	Wells		50-60	4th	10.5
8-4	S.F	L	5-10		6	16	Rueter	Benson		50-61	4th	10.5
8-6	At L.A.	W	3-1		8	8	Fogg	Perez	Williams	51-61	4th	9.5
8-7	At L.A.	L	0-4		6	7	Ashby	Meadows	Gagne	51-62	4th	9.5
8-8	At L.A.	L	5-10		9	13	Beirne	Anderson		51-63	4th	10.5
8-9	At S.F	W	4-3		6	7	Wells	Schmidt	Williams	52-63	4th	9.5
8-10	At S.F	L	3-8		7	6	Aybar	Lincoln		52-64	4th	10.5
8-11	At S.F	L	4-5	(11)	9	17	Nen	Williams		52-65	4th	11.5
8-12	St.L.	L	6-10		12	16	Simontacchi	Meadows		52-66	4th	12.5
8-13	St.L.	L	5-9		9	18	Morris	Anderson	Isringhausen	52-67	4th	13.5
8-14	St.L.	L	3-7		4	11	Benes	Wells		52-68	4th	14.5
8-15	St.L.	L	5-11		6	13	Kline	Williams		52-69	4th	15.5
8-16	Mil.	L	3-10		8	15	Sheets	Fogg		52-70	4th	15.5
8-17	Mil.	W	5-0		6	6	Meadows	Cabrera		53-70	4th	15.5
8-18	Mil.	W	3-2		8	9	Arroyo	Rusch	Williams	54-70	4th	15.5
8-19	At St.L.	L	2-7		5	11	Benes	Wells		54-71	4th	16.5
8-20	At St.L.	W	8-0		11	1	Benson	Hackman		55-71	4th	15.5
8-21	At St.L.	L	1-4		3	8	Finley	Fogg	Isringhausen	55-72	4th	16.5
8-22	At St.L.	L	4-5		7	10	Molina	Williams		55-73	4th	17.5
8-23	At Mil.	W	6-3		8	6	Lincoln	Durocher	Williams	56-73	4th	16.5
8-24	At Mil.	W	17-10		16	20	Wells	Cabrera		57-73	4th	15.5
8-25	At Mil.	W	3-2		9	9	Benson	Wright	Williams	58-73	4th	14.5
8-27	Atl.	L	4-5		6	7	Millwood	Fogg	Smoltz	58-74	4th	15.0
8-28	Atl.	W	1-0	(10)	10	6	Williams	Remlinger		59-74	4th	15.0
8-29	Atl.	W	4-1		5	8	Arroyo	Glavine	Williams	60-74	4th	14.0
8-30	At Fla.	L	3-4		10	5	Tavarez	Wells	Looper	60-75	4th	15.0
8-31	At Fla.	L	2-3		9	6	Nunez	Sauerbeck	Looper	60-76	4th	16.5

Date	Opp.	Res.	Score	(inn.*)	Hits	Opp. hits	Winning pitcher	Losing pitcher	Save	Record	Pos.	GB
9-1	At Fla.	L	4-8		9	11	Neal	Fogg		60-77	4th	16.5
9-2	At Atl.	L	1-5		7	8	Maddux	Meadows		60-78	4th	16.5
9-3	At Atl.	W	3-0		8	5	Torres	Glavine	Williams	61-78	4th	16.5
9-4	At Atl.	L	0-6		5	9	Moss	Wells		61-79	4th	17.5
9-6	Fla.	W	11-0		14	9	Benson	Tejera		62-79	4th	17.5
9-7	Fla.	W	4-1		8	7	Fogg	Robertson	Williams	63-79	4th	17.5
9-8	Fla.	L	1-11		8	14	Pavano	Meadows		63-80	4th	18.5
9-9	At Cin.	L	8-9		12	10	Dempster	Torres	Williamson	63-81	4th	19.5
9-10	At Cin.	L	0-3		6	8	Reitsma	Wells	Williamson	63-82	4th	20.5
9-11	At Cin.	W	4-1		4	4	Villone	Dessens	Williams	64-82	4th	20.5
9-13	At Phi.	W	5-3		5	9	Beimel	Timlin	Williams	65-82	4th	20.0
9-14	At Phi.	L	1-4		5	8	Junge	Meadows	Mesa	65-83	4th	21.0
9-15	At Phi.	L	0-1	(10)	2	9	Mesa	Sauerbeck		65-84	4th	21.0
9-16	Cin.	L	3-4		7	12	Silva	Lincoln	Williamson	65-85	4th	21.5
9-17	Cin.	W	11-3		9	7	Benson	Reitsma		66-85	4th	21.5
9-18	Cin.	W	3-2		7	4	Lincoln	Riedling	Williams	67-85	4th	21.5
9-19	Cin.	L	4-5		14	9	Hamilton	Williams	Williamson	67-86	4th	22.5
9-20	Chi.	W	5-4		8	10	Sauerbeck	Alfonseca		68-86	4th	22.5
9-21	Chi.	L	2-4		10	9	Farnsworth	Sauerbeck	Cruz	68-87	4th	22.5
9-22	Chi.	W	5-4		10	9	Benson	Benes	Williams	69-87	4th	22.5
9-24	N.Y.	W	6-3		12	4	Sauerbeck	Guthrie	Williams	70-87	4th	23.0
9-25	N.Y.	W	4-3		5	10	Villone	Roberts	Williams	71-87	4th	23.0
9-27	At Chi.	W	13-3		19	11	Torres	Mahomes		72-87	4th	22.5
9-28	At Chi.	L	4-5		8	7	Cruz	Boehringer		72-88	4th	23.5
9-29	At Chi.	L	3-7		11	8	Wood	Fogg		72-89	4th	24.5

Monthly records: April (14-10), May (11-19), June (11-15), July (13-14), August (11-18), September (12-13).
*Innings, if other than nine. †First game of a doubleheader. ‡Second game of a doubleheader.

RECORDS

2002 regular-season record: 72-89
Position: 4th in N.L. Central
Home: 38-42   **Road:** 34-47
N.L. East: 16-13   **N.L. Central:** 43-47
N.L. West: 10-20   **A.L.:** 3-9
Vs. LH starters: 19-16
Vs. RH starters: 53-73
Grass: 70-85   **Artificial:** 2-4
Day: 22-27   **Night:** 50-62
1-Run: 27-24   **X-inn.:** 4-4
Doubleheaders: 0-0-2
Team record past five years: 350-458
(.433, ranks 15th in league in that span)

TEAM LEADERS

Batting average: Brian Giles (.298).
At-bats: Jason Kendall (545).
Runs: Brian Giles (95).
Hits: Jason Kendall (154).
Total bases: Brian Giles (309).
Doubles: Brian Giles (37).
Triples: Brian Giles (5).
Home runs: Brian Giles (38).
Runs batted in: Brian Giles (103).

Stolen bases: Brian Giles, Jason Kendall (15).
Slugging percentage: Brian Giles (.622).
On-base percentage: Brian Giles (.450).
Wins: Josh Fogg, Kip Wells (12).
Earned-run average: Kip Wells (3.58).
Complete games: Jimmy Anderson, Kip Wells (1).
Shutouts: Kip Wells (1).
Saves: Mike Williams (46).
Innings pitched: Kip Wells (198.1).
Strikeouts: Kip Wells (134).

GAMES BY POSITION

Catcher: Jason Kendall 143, Keith Osik 27, Humberto Cota 7, Craig A. Wilson 5.
First base: Kevin Young 144, Craig A. Wilson 42, Keith Osik 3, Mike Benjamin 1, Adam Hyzdu 1.
Second base: Pokey Reese 117, Abraham O. Nunez 46, Mike Benjamin 11, Rob Mackowiak 3, Keith Osik 1.
Third base: Aramis Ramirez 131, Mike Benjamin 62, Rob Mackowiak 26, Keith Osik 4.
Shortstop: Jack Wilson 143, Abraham O. Nunez 24, Mike Benjamin 15.

Outfield: Brian Giles 151, Rob Mackowiak 106, Craig A. Wilson 75, Adrian Brown 71, Chad Hermansen 60, Armando Rios 56, Adam Hyzdu 50, Tony Alvarez 8, J.J. Davis 4, Mike Benjamin 1, Keith Osik 1.
Designated hitter: Aramis Ramirez 3, Craig A. Wilson 3, Mike Benjamin 1, Abraham O. Nunez 1.

TOP DRAFT CHOICES

1. **Bryan Bullington,** RHP, Ball State.
2. **Blair Johnson,** RHP, Washburn H.S., Topeka, Kan.
3. **Taber Lee,** SS, San Diego State.
4. **Wardell Starling,** RHP, Elkins H.S., Missouri City, Texas.
5. **Alex Hart,** RHP, Florida.
6. **Brad Eldred,** 1B, Florida International.
7. **Matt Capps,** RHP, Alexander H.S., Douglasville, Ga.
8. **Bobby Kingsbury,** OF, Fordham.
9. **Joseph Hicks,** OF, Forest Brook H.S., Houston.
10. **David Davidson,** LHP, Dennis Morris H.S., Thorold, Ontario.

ST. LOUIS CARDINALS
NATIONAL LEAGUE CENTRAL DIVISION

2003 SEASON

March/April

SUN	MON	TUE	WED	THU	FRI	SAT
30	31 D MIL	1	2 MIL	3 D MIL	4 D HOU	5 D HOU
6 D HOU	7	8 COL	9 COL	10 D COL	11 HOU	12 HOU
13 D HOU	14 MIL	15 MIL	16 D MIL	17	18 ARI	19 D ARI
20 D ARI	21	22 ATL	23 ATL	24 ATL	25 FLA	26 FLA
27 D FLA	28	29 NYM	30 NYM			

May

SUN	MON	TUE	WED	THU	FRI	SAT
				1 D NYM	2 MON	3 D MON
4 D MON	5 CIN	6 CIN	7 CIN	8 D CIN	9 D CUB	10 D CUB
11 D CUB	12	13 CIN	14 CIN	15 D CIN	16 CUB	17 CUB
18 D CUB	19 D CUB	20 HOU	21 HOU	22 HOU	23 PIT	24 PIT
25 D PIT	26 D HOU	27 HOU	28 HOU	29	30 PIT	31 D PIT

June

SUN	MON	TUE	WED	THU	FRI	SAT
1 D PIT	2	3 TOR	4 TOR	5 TOR	6 BAL	7 D BAL
8 D BAL	9	10 BOS	11 BOS	12 BOS	13 NYY	14 D NYY
15 NYY	16 MIL	17 MIL	18 MIL	19 D MIL	20 KC	21 KC
22 D KC	23	24 CIN	25 CIN	26 CIN	27 KC	28 KC
29 D KC	30 SF					

July

SUN	MON	TUE	WED	THU	FRI	SAT
		1 SF	2 SF	3 D SF	4 D CUB	5 D CUB
6 D CUB	7 SF	8 D SF	9 LA	10 LA	11 SD	12 SD
13 D SD	14	15 *	16	17 LA	18 LA	19 D LA
20 LA	21 SD	22 SD	23 D SD	24	25 PIT	26 D PIT
27 D PIT	28 D PIT	29 MON	30 MON	31 MON		

August

SUN	MON	TUE	WED	THU	FRI	SAT
					1 NYM	2 D NYM
3 D NYM	4	5 FLA	6 FLA	7 FLA	8 ATL	9 D ATL
10 D ATL	11 PIT	12 PIT	13 PIT	14 D PIT	15 PHI	16 PHI
17 D PHI	18	19 PIT	20 PIT	21 PIT	22 PHI	23 PHI
24 D PHI	25	26 CUB	27 CUB	28 CUB	29 CIN	30 CIN

September

SUN	MON	TUE	WED	THU	FRI	SAT
31 D CIN	1 D CUB	2 D CUB	3 CUB	4 D CUB	5 D CIN	6 CIN
7 D CIN	8	9 COL	10 COL	11 D COL	12 HOU	13 HOU
14 D HOU	15 MIL	16 MIL	17 MIL	18 MIL	19 HOU	20 D HOU
21 D HOU	22	23 MIL	24 MIL	25	26 ARI	27 D ARI
28 D ARI						

Home games shaded; D—Day game (games starting before 5 p.m.); *—All-Star Game at Comiskey Park, Chicago. Subject to change.

CLUB DIRECTORY

Chairman of the board/general partner
William O. DeWitt Jr.
Vice chairman
Frederick O. Hanser
President
Mark C. Lamping
Vice president, general manager
Walt Jocketty
Vice president/player personnel
Jerry Walker

V.p., special asst. to the g.m.
Bob Gebhard
Special assistant to the general manager
Mike Jorgensen
Vice president, community relations
Marty Hendin
Director, media relations
Brian Bartow
Director, player development
Bruce Manno

Director, baseball operations
John Mozeliak
Director, professional scouting
Marteese Robinson
Director, amateur scouting
Marty Maier
Director, minor league operations
Scott Smulczenski

MINOR LEAGUE AFFILIATES

Class	Team	League	Manager
AAA	Memphis	Pacific Coast	Tom Spencer
AA	Tennessee	Southern	Mark DeJohn
A	Palm Beach	Florida State	Tom Nieto
A	Peoria	Midwest	Joe Cunningham
A	New Jersey	New York-Pennsylvania	Tommy Shields
Rookie	Johnson City	Appalachian	Danny Sheaffer

Follow the Cardinals all season at: www.sportingnews.com/baseball/teams/cardinals/

BROADCAST INFORMATION

Radio: KMOX-AM (1120).
TV: KPLR-TV (Channel 11).
Cable TV: Fox Sports Midwest.

SPRING TRAINING

Ballpark (city): Roger Dean Stadium (Jupiter, Fla.).
Ticket information: 561-966-3309.

SPRING TRAINING ROSTER

Manager—Tony La Russa (10).
Coaches—Dave Duncan (18), Marty Mason (38), Dave McKay (39), Jose Oquendo (11), Mitchell Page (12), Joe Pettini (24).

No.	PITCHERS	B/T	Ht./Wt.	Born	Age*	2002 clubs
66	Ankiel, Rick	L/L	6-1/210	7-19-79	23	DID NOT PLAY
70	Caple, Chance	R/R	6-6/215	8-9-78	24	Peoria
	Carpenter, Chris	R/R	6-6/215	4-27-75	27	Toronto, Tennessee, Syracuse
54	Crudale, Mike	R/R	6-0/205	1-3-77	26	Memphis, St. Louis
52	Duff, Matt	R/R	6-1/192	10-6-74	28	Potomac, New Haven, St. Louis, Memphis
13	Fassero, Jeff	L/L	6-1/200	1-5-63	40	Chicago N.L., St. Louis
	Hamilton, Joey	R/R	6-4/240	9-9-70	32	Cincinnati, Louisville
44	Isringhausen, Jason	R/R	6-3/230	9-7-72	30	St. Louis
73	Journell, Jimmy	R/R	6-4/205	12-29-77	25	New Haven, Memphis
49	Kline, Steve	B/L	6-1/215	8-22-72	30	St. Louis, Peoria, New Haven
71	Lambert, Jeremy	R/R	6-1/195	1-10-79	24	New Haven
79	Layfield, Scotty	R/R	6-2/205	9-13-76	26	New Haven
	Levine, Al	L/R	6-3/190	5-22-68	34	Anaheim, Salt Lake
56	Molina, Gabe	R/R	6-1/220	5-3-75	27	Memphis, St. Louis
35	Morris, Matt	R/R	6-5/210	8-9-74	28	St. Louis
60	Pearce, Josh	R/R	6-3/215	8-20-77	25	Memphis, St. Louis
46	Simontacchi, Jason	R/R	6-2/185	11-13-73	29	Memphis, St. Louis
36	Stechschulte, Gene	R/R	6-5/210	8-12-73	29	St. Louis, Memphis
55	Stephenson, Garrett	R/R	6-5/208	1-2-72	31	St. Louis, Peoria, Memphis
40	Tomko, Brett	R/R	6-4/215	4-7-73	29	San Diego
64	Walrond, Les	L/L	6-0/195	11-7-76	26	New Haven, Memphis
19	Williams, Woody	R/R	6-0/195	8-19-66	36	St. Louis, Memphis

No.	CATCHERS	B/T	Ht./Wt.	Born	Age*	2002 clubs
22	Matheny, Mike	R/R	6-3/205	9-22-70	32	St. Louis
	Torrealba, Steve	R/R	6-0/175	2-24-78	25	Richmond, Atlanta

No.	INFIELDERS	B/T	Ht./Wt.	Born	Age*	2002 clubs
41	Cairo, Miguel	R/R	6-1/200	5-4-74	28	St. Louis
30	Delgado, Wilson	B/R	5-11/165	7-15-72	30	Memphis, St. Louis
21	Martinez, Tino	L/R	6-2/210	12-7-67	35	St. Louis
33	Perez, Eduardo	R/R	6-4/215	9-11-69	33	St. Louis
5	Pujols, Albert	R/R	6-3/210	1-16-80	23	St. Louis
3	Renteria, Edgar	R/R	6-1/180	8-7-75	27	St. Louis
27	Rolen, Scott	R/R	6-4/226	4-4-75	27	Philadelphia, St. Louis
4	Vina, Fernando	L/R	5-9/174	4-16-69	33	St. Louis

No.	OUTFIELDERS	B/T	Ht./Wt.	Born	Age*	2002 clubs
7	Drew, J.D.	L/R	6-1/195	11-20-75	27	St. Louis
15	Edmonds, Jim	L/L	6-1/212	6-27-70	32	St. Louis
26	Marrero, Eli	R/R	6-1/180	11-17-73	29	St. Louis
0	Robinson, Kerry	L/L	6-0/175	10-3-73	29	St. Louis
99	Taguchi, So	R/R	5-10/163	7-2-69	33	Memphis, St. Louis, New Haven

*Age as of April 1, 2003.

BALLPARK INFORMATION

Ballpark (capacity, surface)
Busch Stadium (50,354, grass)
Address
250 Stadium Plaza
St. Louis, MO 63102
Official website
www.stlcardinals.com
Business phone
314-421-3060
Ticket information
314-421-2400
Field dimensions (from home plate)
To left field at foul line, 330 feet
To center field, 402 feet
To right field at foul line, 330 feet
First game played
May 12, 1966 (Cardinals 4, Braves 3)

St. Louis Cardinals

2003 SEASON

Date	Opp.	Res.	Score	(inn.*)	Hits	Opp. hits	Winning pitcher	Losing pitcher	Save	Record	Pos.	GB
4-1	Col.	W	10-2		14	8	Morris	Hampton		1-0	T1st	...
4-3	Col.	L	3-6		9	7	Neagle	Stephenson	Jimenez	1-1	T1st	...
4-4	Col.	L	1-6		8	5	Thomson	Benes		1-2	T4th	1.0
4-5	At Hou.	W	5-1		11	8	Stechschulte	Mlicki		2-2	T2nd	1.0
4-6	At Hou.	W	8-4		15	9	Morris	Cruz		3-2	2nd	1.0
4-7	At Hou.	L	6-7	(12)	11	15	Stone	Hackman		3-3	T2nd	1.5
4-9	Mil.	W	6-5		6	9	Veres	Cabrera	Isringhausen	4-3	2nd	1.5
4-10	Mil.	W	6-5	(11)	10	10	Isringhausen	Vizcaino		5-3	2nd	0.5
4-11	Mil.	W	6-5		11	7	Veres	Cabrera	Kline	6-3	1st	+0.5
4-12	Hou.	W	7-3		11	9	Morris	Miller		7-3	1st	+1.0
4-13	Hou.	W	2-1		11	2	Isringhausen	Stone		8-3	1st	+1.0
4-14	Hou.	L	4-5		10	9	Reynolds	Stephenson	Wagner	8-4	1st	+1.0
4-15	At Ari.	L	5-14		8	11	Helling	Benes		8-5	1st	+0.5
4-16	At Ari.	L	3-5		8	11	Johnson	Smith	Myers	8-6	2nd	0.5
4-17	At Ari.	W	8-4		10	10	Morris	Schilling	Isringhausen	9-6	2nd	0.5
4-18	At Mil.	L	5-7		7	10	Cabrera	Hackman	DeJean	9-7	2nd	1.0
4-19	At Mil.	L	1-6		8	10	Quevedo	Timlin	Vizcaino	9-8	2nd	2.0
4-20	At Mil.	L	3-5		7	9	Vizcaino	Veres	DeJean	9-9	3rd	3.0
4-21	At Mil.	L	3-5		6	10	Neugebauer	Smith	DeJean	9-10	3rd	4.0
4-23	At N.Y.	L	3-4		8	9	D'Amico	Morris	Benitez	9-11	3rd	4.0
4-24	At N.Y.	W	4-2		6	6	Kile	Leiter	Isringhausen	10-11	3rd	3.0
4-25	At N.Y.	L	6-7		10	8	Strickland	Veres	Benitez	10-12	3rd	4.0
4-26	At Mon.	W	7-6	(11)	17	11	Stechschulte	Ohka	Veres	11-12	3rd	3.5
4-27	At Mon.	W	5-0		8	5	Matthews	Chen		12-12	3rd	3.5
4-28	At Mon.	L	2-5		10	10	Ohka	Morris	Herges	12-13	3rd	3.5
4-30	Fla.	L	2-7		3	11	Burnett	Kile		12-14	3rd	4.5
5-1	Fla.	W	6-4		13	8	Smith	Dempster	Isringhausen	13-14	3rd	4.5
5-2	Fla.	L	6-9		10	17	Tejera	Veres	Nunez	13-15	3rd	4.5
5-3	Atl.	L	1-2	(11)	3	5	Hammond	Stechschulte	Smoltz	13-16	3rd	4.5
5-4	Atl.	W	3-2		10	6	Simontacchi	Lopez	Isringhausen	14-16	3rd	3.5
5-5	Atl.	L	2-4		8	12	Maddux	Kile	Smoltz	14-17	4th	3.5
5-6	At Chi.	L	5-6		12	8	Fassero	Timlin		14-18	4th	4.5
5-7	At Chi.	L	0-8		4	9	Wood	Smith		14-19	4th	5.5
5-8	At Chi.	W	3-2		4	4	Morris	Cruz	Isringhausen	15-19	3rd	5.5
5-10	At Cin.	W	4-2		11	7	Stechschulte	White	Isringhausen	16-19	3rd	4.5
5-11	At Cin.	L	1-8		5	10	Reitsma	Kile		16-20	3rd	5.5
5-12	At Cin.	W	10-8		14	9	Stechschulte	Graves	Isringhausen	17-20	3rd	4.5
5-13	Chi.	W	3-0		2	4	Morris	Wood		18-20	3rd	4.5
5-14	Chi.	W	11-2		17	6	Timlin	Cruz		19-20	3rd	4.5
5-15	Chi.	W	4-1		9	4	Stechschulte	Bere	Isringhausen	20-20	T2nd	4.5
5-17	Cin.	W	3-1		8	2	Kile	Sullivan	Isringhausen	21-20	T2nd	4.0
5-18	Cin.	L	3-7		5	11	Rijo	Morris		21-21	T2nd	5.0
5-19	Cin.	W	10-1		10	7	Stephenson	Acevedo		22-21	2nd	4.0
5-20	Cin.	W	7-3		6	10	Williams	Haynes		23-21	2nd	3.0
5-21	Hou.	W	3-1		6	6	Simontacchi	Hernandez	Isringhausen	24-21	2nd	3.0
5-22	Hou.	W	3-2		8	7	Veres	Stone		25-21	2nd	3.0
5-23	Hou.	W	5-4		11	10	Hackman	Dotel	Isringhausen	26-21	2nd	2.0
5-24	At Pit.	L	2-5		6	9	Wells	Stephenson		26-22	2nd	2.0
5-25	At Pit.	W	6-3		11	3	Williams	Anderson	Isringhausen	27-22	2nd	2.0
5-26	At Pit.	W	7-3		11	9	Simontacchi	Fogg		28-22	2nd	1.0
5-27	At Hou.	W	4-3		9	10	Stechschulte	Oswalt	Isringhausen	29-22	2nd	0.5
5-28	At Hou.	W	4-1		6	10	Morris	Reynolds	Isringhausen	30-22	2nd	0.5
5-29	At Hou.	L	5-10		8	13	Redding	Stephenson		30-23	2nd	1.5
5-31	Pit.	L	1-3		4	11	Fogg	Williams	Williams	30-24	2nd	2.0
6-1	Pit.	W	9-4		13	8	Kile	Arroyo		31-24	2nd	1.0
6-2	Pit.	L	2-5		8	9	Lowe	Morris	Williams	31-25	2nd	2.0
6-4	At Cin.	W	8-5		9	11	Simontacchi	Hamilton		32-25	2nd	1.0
6-6	At Cin.	L	2-3		9	7	Haynes	Williams	Graves	32-26	2nd	2.0
6-7	At K.C.	W	12-6		17	11	Kile	Byrd		33-26	2nd	1.0
6-8	At K.C.	W	11-3		15	6	Morris	Affeldt		34-26	2nd	1.0
6-9	At K.C.	L	2-3		6	4	Hernandez	Timlin		34-27	2nd	1.0
6-10	At Sea.	L	0-10		5	14	Moyer	Smith		34-28	2nd	1.0
6-11	At Sea.	W	7-4		10	7	Williams	Baldwin		35-28	2nd	1.0
6-12	At Sea.	L	0-5		5	8	Pineiro	Kile		35-29	2nd	1.0
6-14	K.C.	W	3-0		7	3	Morris	Asencio	Kline	36-29	2nd	1.0

Date	Opp.	Res.	Score	(inn.*)	Hits	Opp. hits	Winning pitcher	Losing pitcher	Save	Record	Pos.	GB
6-15	K.C.	W	5-3		9	7	Simontacchi	Suppan	Veres	37-29	2nd	1.0
6-16	K.C.	W	5-1		9	5	Williams	May		38-29	T1st	...
6-18	Ana.	W	7-2		12	7	Kile	Appier		39-29	1st	+1.0
6-19	Ana.	W	6-2		9	7	Morris	Sele		40-29	1st	+2.0
6-20	Ana.	L	2-3		8	11	Schoeneweis	Smith	Percival	40-30	1st	+2.0
6-21	At Chi.	L	1-2		3	3	Lieber	Williams		40-31	1st	+2.0
6-23	At Chi.	L	3-8		7	10	Wood	Simontacchi		40-32	1st	+2.5
6-25	Mil.	L	0-2		4	7	Rusch	Morris		40-33	1st	+2.0
6-26	Mil.	W	5-2		9	7	Williams	Wright	Isringhausen	41-33	1st	+2.0
6-27	Mil.	L	2-7	(11)	8	12	Vizcaino	Stechschulte		41-34	1st	+1.0
6-28	Cin.	W	3-2		8	10	Simontacchi	Reitsma	Isringhausen	42-34	1st	+2.0
6-29	Cin.	L	2-4		9	11	Dessens	Hackman	Graves	42-35	1st	+1.0
6-30	Cin.	L	8-12		13	16	Sullivan	Isringhausen		42-36	1st	...
7-1	S.D.	W	7-3		10	6	Williams	Perez		43-36	1st	...
7-2	S.D.	W	11-5		12	11	Crudale	Jarvis		44-36	1st	+1.0
7-3	S.D.	W	4-1		5	5	Simontacchi	Lawrence	Isringhausen	45-36	1st	+2.0
7-4	L.A.	W	3-2		5	11	Smith	Ishii	Isringhausen	46-36	1st	+3.0
7-5	L.A.	L	5-6		11	10	Perez	Morris	Gagne	46-37	1st	+2.0
7-6	L.A.	L	2-4	(11)	4	7	Quantrill	Kline	Gagne	46-38	1st	+1.0
7-7	L.A.	W	12-6		17	13	Matthews	Daal		47-38	1st	+2.0
7-12	At S.D.	L	3-4		6	7	Holtz	Veres	Hoffman	47-39	1st	+2.5
7-13	At S.D.	W	2-1	(10)	7	5	Crudale	Reed	Isringhausen	48-39	1st	+3.5
7-14	At S.D.	W	4-1		13	6	Smith	Jones	Isringhausen	49-39	1st	+3.5
7-15	At L.A.	W	4-2		6	11	Smith	Daal	Isringhausen	50-39	1st	+3.5
7-16	At L.A.	W	9-2		11	5	Hackman	Nomo		51-39	1st	+3.5
7-17	S.F	L	4-5		12	7	Worrell	Veres	Nen	51-40	1st	+3.5
7-18	S.F	W	5-1		8	9	Morris	Schmidt		52-40	1st	+3.5
7-19	At Pit.	L	9-12		13	15	Sauerbeck	Veres		52-41	1st	+3.5
7-20	At Pit.	L	6-15		14	14	Benson	Smith		52-42	1st	+3.5
7-21	At Pit.	W	8-4		14	10	Finley	Fogg	Kline	53-42	1st	+3.5
7-22	At S.F	W	5-3		12	10	Hackman	Worrell	Isringhausen	54-42	1st	+4.5
7-23	At S.F	W	4-0		10	7	Morris	Schmidt		55-42	1st	+4.5
7-24	At S.F	L	4-6		9	9	Rueter	Benes	Nen	55-43	1st	+3.5
7-25	At S.F	W	4-3		7	8	Smith	Jensen	Isringhausen	56-43	1st	+4.0
7-26	Chi.	W	8-4		13	7	Finley	Lieber		57-43	1st	+5.0
7-27	Chi.	L	3-7		7	8	Wood	Simontacchi		57-44	1st	+4.0
7-28	Chi.	W	10-9		14	9	Veres	Alfonseca		58-44	1st	+5.0
7-30	At Fla.	W	5-0		12	4	Benes	Tejera		59-44	1st	+5.0
7-31	At Fla.	L	5-8		9	10	Beckett	Smith	Looper	59-45	1st	+5.0
8-1	At Fla.	L	0-4		4	9	Burnett	Finley		59-46	1st	+4.0
8-2	At Atl.	L	5-11		11	12	Glavine	Simontacchi		59-47	1st	+4.0
8-3	At Atl.	L	1-6		7	7	Marquis	Morris		59-48	1st	+3.0
8-4	At Atl.	L	1-2		1	6	Smoltz	Veres		59-49	1st	+2.0
8-6	Mon.	L	1-10		7	13	Yoshii	Finley		59-50	1st	+2.0
8-7	Mon.	L	1-4		6	10	Ohka	Simontacchi	Stewart	59-51	1st	+1.0
8-8	Mon.	W	5-3		10	7	Morris	Reames	Isringhausen	60-51	1st	+2.0
8-9	N.Y.	L	1-2		5	5	Leiter	Matthews	Benitez	60-52	1st	+2.0
8-10	N.Y.	W	5-4		5	13	Veres	Reed	Isringhausen	61-52	1st	+2.0
8-11	N.Y.	W	9-0		13	7	Finley	Astacio		62-52	1st	+2.0
8-12	At Pit.	W	10-6		16	12	Simontacchi	Meadows		63-52	1st	+2.5
8-13	At Pit.	W	9-5		18	9	Morris	Anderson	Isringhausen	64-52	1st	+3.0
8-14	At Pit.	W	7-3		11	4	Benes	Wells		65-52	1st	+3.0
8-15	At Pit.	W	11-5		13	6	Kline	Williams		66-52	1st	+4.0
8-16	At Phi.	L	0-4		4	8	Wolf	Finley		66-53	1st	+4.0
8-17	At Phi.	W	5-1		9	4	Simontacchi	Coggin		67-53	1st	+4.0
8-18	At Phi.	W	5-1		8	8	Morris	Padilla		68-53	T1st	+5.0
8-19	Pit.	W	7-2		11	5	Benes	Wells		69-53	1st	+5.0
8-20	Pit.	L	0-8		1	11	Benson	Hackman		69-54	1st	+5.0
8-21	Pit.	W	4-1		8	3	Finley	Fogg	Isringhausen	70-54	1st	+5.0
8-22	Pit.	W	5-4		10	7	Molina	Williams		71-54	1st	+5.0
8-23	Phi.	L	4-5	(14)	13	18	Adams	Joseph		71-55	1st	+4.0
8-24	Phi.	L	0-4		5	10	Padilla	Benes	Mesa	71-56	1st	+4.0
8-25	Phi.	L	3-5		10	12	Silva	Isringhausen	Mesa	71-57	1st	+3.0
8-27†	At Cin.	L	4-5		14	9	Reitsma	Simontacchi	Graves	71-58		
8-27‡	At Cin.	W	5-0		9	2	Finley	Dessens		72-58	1st	+3.5
8-28	At Cin.	W	9-2		12	6	Kline	Estes		73-58	1st	+3.5
8-29	At Cin.	L	0-7		7	11	Haynes	Williams		73-59	1st	+2.5
8-30	At Chi.	W	6-3		6	8	Wright	Zambrano	Veres	74-59	1st	+2.5
8-31§	At Chi.	W	8-1		11	9	Hackman	Prior		75-59		
8-31∞	At Chi.	W	10-4		11	9	Benes	Bere		76-59	1st	+4.0

Date	Opp.	Res.	Score	(inn.*)	Hits	Opp. hits	Winning pitcher	Losing pitcher	Save	Record	Pos.	GB
9-1	At Chi.	L	4-5		7	6	Cruz	Finley	Alfonseca	76-60	1st	+4.0
9-2	Cin.	L	3-5		6	12	Estes	Stephenson	Graves	76-61	1st	+4.0
9-3	Cin.	W	3-1		8	5	Williams	Haynes	Veres	77-61	1st	+4.0
9-4	Cin.	W	10-5		12	11	Hackman	Chen		78-61	1st	+5.0
9-6	Chi.	W	11-2		12	9	Benes	Benes		79-61	1st	+5.5
9-7	Chi.	W	6-5	(13)	12	10	Fassero	Alfonseca		80-61	1st	+5.5
9-8	Chi.	W	3-1		9	6	Simontacchi	Wood	Kline	81-61	1st	+5.5
9-9	At Mil.	W	3-0		6	6	Williams	Diggins	Kline	82-61	1st	+5.5
9-10	At Mil.	W	8-3		11	9	Morris	Franklin		83-61	1st	+5.5
9-11	At Mil.	W	4-3		10	9	Fassero	Sheets	Isringhausen	84-61	1st	+6.5
9-12	At Hou.	L	3-6		12	9	Dotel	Veres	Wagner	84-62	1st	+5.5
9-13	At Hou.	W	3-2	(10)	11	9	White	Gordon	Isringhausen	85-62	1st	+6.5
9-14	At Hou.	W	2-1		5	7	Williams	Munro	Isringhausen	86-62	1st	+7.5
9-15	At Hou.	L	0-8		3	16	Miller	Morris		86-63	1st	+6.5
9-17	At Col.	W	11-4		17	7	Fassero	Mercker		87-63	1st	+7.5
9-18	At Col.	W	8-5		8	11	White	Speier	Kline	88-63	1st	+7.5
9-19	At Col.	W	12-6		18	10	Simontacchi	Jennings		89-63	1st	+8.5
9-20	Hou.	W	9-3		14	7	White	Munro		90-63	1st	+9.5
9-21	Hou.	L	3-6		7	11	Miller	Morris		90-64	1st	+8.5
9-22	Hou.	W	7-3		10	7	Finley	Saarloos		91-64	1st	+9.5
9-23	Ari.	W	13-1		18	6	Wright	Helling		92-64	1st	+9.5
9-24	Ari.	W	3-2		5	8	Isringhausen	Fetters		93-64	1st	+10.5
9-25	Ari.	W	6-1		6	4	Stephenson	Schilling		94-64	1st	+10.5
9-26	Mil.	W	9-1		12	7	Morris	Diggins		95-64	1st	+11.0
9-27	Mil.	L	1-2		4	5	Sheets	White	DeJean	95-65	1st	+11.0
9-28	Mil.	W	3-1		4	3	Finley	Rusch	Isringhausen	96-65	1st	+12.0
9-29	Mil.	W	4-0		5	4	Crudale	Vizcaino		97-65	1st	+13.0

Monthly records: April (12-14), May (18-10), June (12-12), July (17-9), August (17-14), September (21-6).
*Innings, if other than nine. †First game of a doubleheader. ‡Second game of a doubleheader. §Day separate admission. ∞Night separate admission.

RECORDS

2002 regular-season record: 97-65
Position: 1st in N.L. Central
Home: 52-29   **Road:** 45-36
N.L. East: 11-19   **N.L. Central:** 57-33
N.L. West: 21-9   **A.L.:** 8-4
Vs. LH starters: 21-16
Vs. RH starters: 76-49
Grass: 93-63   **Artificial:** 4-2
Day: 33-26   **Night:** 64-39
1-Run: 22-19   **X-inn.:** 5-5
Doubleheaders: 0-0-1
Team record past five years: 443-366
(.548, ranks 4th in league in that span)

TEAM LEADERS

Batting average: Albert Pujols (.314).
At-bats: Fernando Vina (622).
Runs: Albert Pujols (118).
Hits: Albert Pujols (185).
Total bases: Albert Pujols (331).
Doubles: Albert Pujols (40).
Triples: Fernando Vina (5).
Home runs: Albert Pujols (34).

Runs batted in: Albert Pujols (127).
Stolen bases: Edgar Renteria (22).
Slugging percentage: Albert Pujols (.561).
On-base percentage: Jim Edmonds (.420).
Wins: Matt Morris (17).
Earned-run average: Woody Williams (2.53).
Complete games: Andy Benes, Chuck Finley, Matt Morris, Woody Williams (1).
Shutouts: Chuck Finley, Matt Morris (1).
Saves: Jason Isringhausen (32).
Innings pitched: Matt Morris (210.1).
Strikeouts: Matt Morris (171).

GAMES BY POSITION

Catcher: Mike Matheny 106, Mike DiFelice 61, Eli Marrero 44.
First base: Tino Martinez 149, Albert Pujols 21, Eduardo Perez 10, Ivan Cruz 7, Miguel Cairo 4, Eli Marrero 4, Mike Matheny 1.
Second base: Fernando Vina 150, Miguel Cairo 18, Placido Polanco 6.
Third base: Placido Polanco 78, Scott Rolen 55, Albert Pujols 41, Miguel Cairo 7, Eduardo Perez 6, Mike Coolbaugh 4.
Shortstop: Edgar Renteria 149, Placido Polanco 13, Wilson Delgado 8, Miguel Cairo 6, Albert Pujols 1.
Outfield: Jim Edmonds 139, J.D. Drew 120, Albert Pujols 118, Eli Marrero 106, Kerry Robinson 76, Eduardo Perez 35, Miguel Cairo 24, So Taguchi 14.
Designated hitter: Miguel Cairo 3, Albert Pujols 2, Eduardo Perez 1, Kerry Robinson 1.

TOP DRAFT CHOICES

3. **Calvin Hayes,** SS, East Rowan H.S., Salisbury, N.C.
4. **Kyle Boyer,** SS, Dixie (Utah) J.C.
5. **Josh Bell,** C, North Side H.S., Jackson, Tenn.
6. **Cody Haerther,** 3B, Chaminade Prep, Chatsworth, Calif.
7. **David Williamson,** LHP, Massachusetts-Lowell.
8. **Tyler Parker,** C, Georgia Tech.
9. **Travis Hanson,** SS, Portland.
10. **Matt Lemanczyk,** OF, Sacred Heart (Conn.).

SAN DIEGO PADRES
NATIONAL LEAGUE WEST DIVISION

2003 SEASON

March/April

SUN	MON	TUE	WED	THU	FRI	SAT
30	31 D SF	1 SF	2 SF	3 D LA	4 LA	5 LA
6 LA	7 D SF	8 SF	9 D SF	10	11 COL	12 COL
13 D COL	14	15 LA	16 LA	17 LA	18 COL	19 D COL
20 D COL	21	22 CUB	23 CUB	24 D CUB	25 CIN	26 D CIN
27 D CIN	28	29 PIT	30 PIT			

May

SUN	MON	TUE	WED	THU	FRI	SAT
				1 D PIT	2 D PHI	3 PHI
4 D PHI	5	6 MON	7 MON	8 MON	9 NYM	10 D NYM
11 D NYM	12 FLA	13 FLA	14 FLA	15 D ATL	16 ATL	17 ATL
18 D ATL	19 MIL	20 MIL	21 D MIL	22	23 ARI	24 ARI
25 D ARI	26 D ARI	27 MIL	28 MIL	29 D MIL	30 ARI	31 ARI

June

SUN	MON	TUE	WED	THU	FRI	SAT
1 D ARI	2 ARI	3 DET	4 DET	5 DET	6 MIN	7 MIN
8 D MIN	9	10 CLE	11 CLE	12 CLE	13 CWS	14 CWS
15 CWS	16 COL	17 COL	18 COL	19 COL	20 SEA	21 SEA
22 D SEA	23 COL	24 COL	25 COL	26	27 SEA	28 SEA
29 SEA	30					

July

SUN	MON	TUE	WED	THU	FRI	SAT
		1 LA	2 LA	3 LA	4 SF	5 SF
6 D SF	7 LA	8 LA	9 ARI	10 D ARI	11 STL	12 STL
13 D STL	14	15 *	16	17 D ARI	18 D ARI	19 ARI
20 D ARI	21 STL	22 STL	23 D STL	24	25 SF	26 D SF
27 D SF	28	29 PIT	30 PIT	31 D PIT		

August

SUN	MON	TUE	WED	THU	FRI	SAT
					1 PHI	2 PHI
3 D PHI	4 D PHI	5 CUB	6 CUB	7 CUB	8 D CIN	9 CIN
10 D CIN	11	12 ATL	13 ATL	14 ATL	15 FLA	16 FLA
17 D FLA	18	19 NYM	20 NYM	21 NYM	22 D MON	23 MON
24 D MON	25 ARI	26 ARI	27 ARI	28	29 HOU	30 HOU

September

SUN	MON	TUE	WED	THU	FRI	SAT
31 HOU	1	2 ARI	3 ARI	4	5 HOU	6 HOU
7 D HOU	8	9 SF	10 SF	11 SF	12 LA	13 LA
14 D LA	15 SF	16 SF	17 SF	18 D SF	19 COL	20 D COL
21 D COL	22 LA	23 LA	24 LA	25 LA	26 COL	27 COL
28 D COL						

Home games shaded; D—Day game (games starting before 5 p.m.); *—All-Star Game at Comiskey Park, Chicago. Subject to change.

CLUB DIRECTORY

Chairman
John Moores
Vice chairman
Bob Vizas
President and chief operating officer
Dick Freeman
Exec. v.p., baseball operations and g.m.
Kevin Towers

Vice president, community relations
Michele Anderson
Assistant general manager
Fred Uhlman Jr.
Director, scouting
Bill "Chief" Gayton
Director, minor league operations
Priscilla Oppenheimer

Director, player development
Tye Waller
Manager, baseball information
John Dever

MINOR LEAGUE AFFILIATES

Class	Team	League	Manager
AAA	Portland	Pacific Coast	Rick Sweet
AA	Mobile	Southern	Craig Colbert
A	Lake Elsinore	California	Jeff Gardner
A	Fort Wayne	Midwest	George Hendrick
A	Eugene	Northwest	Roy Howell
Rookie	Idaho Falls	Pioneer	Carlos Lezcano

BROADCAST INFORMATION

Radio: KOGO-AM (600), KURS-AM (1040, Spanish)
TV: KUSI (Channel 9/51).
Cable TV: Channel 4 Padres.

SPRING TRAINING

Ballpark (city): Peoria Stadium (Peoria, Ariz.).
Ticket information: 623-878-4337, 800-409-1511.

Follow the Padres all season at: www.sportingnews.com/baseball/teams/padres/

Manager—Bruce Bochy (15).
Coaches—Darrell Akerfelds (48), Greg Booker (38), Davey Lopes, Mark Merila (71), Tony Muser, Rob Picciolo (5).

No.	PITCHERS	B/T	Ht./Wt.	Born	Age*	2002 clubs
65	Bartosh, Cliff	L/L	6-2/175	9-5-79	23	Mobile
54	Bynum, Mike	L/L	6-4/200	3-20-78	25	Mobile, Portland, San Diego
41	Condrey, Clay	R/R	6-3/195	11-19-75	27	Portland, San Diego
32	Cordova, Francisco	R/R	6-1/204	4-26-72	30	DID NOT PLAY
49	Cyr, Eric	R/L	6-4/200	2-11-79	24	Mobile, San Diego, Portland
53	Eaton, Adam	R/R	6-2/190	11-23-77	25	Lake Elsinore, Portland, San Diego
	Garcia, Carlos	R/R	6-3/232	9-23-78	24	Gulf Coast Dodgers, South Georgia, Fort Wayne
	Hackman, Luther	R/R	6-4/195	10-10-74	28	St. Louis
51	Hoffman, Trevor	R/R	6-0/205	10-13-67	35	San Diego
36	Howard, Ben	R/R	6-2/190	1-15-79	24	Mobile, San Diego, Portland
32	Jarvis, Kevin	L/R	6-2/200	8-1-69	33	San Diego, Mobile, Lake Elsinore
50	Lawrence, Brian	R/R	6-0/195	5-14-76	26	San Diego
	Orosco, Jesse	R/L	6-2/205	4-21-57	45	Los Angeles
44	Peavy, Jake	R/R	6-1/180	5-31-81	21	Mobile, San Diego
59	Perez, Oliver	L/L	6-3/160	8-15-81	21	Lake Elsinore, Mobile, San Diego
45	Tankersley, Dennis	R/R	6-2/185	2-24-79	24	Mobile, San Diego, Portland
55	Tollberg, Brian	R/R	6-3/195	9-16-72	30	San Diego
47	Villafuerte, Brandon	R/R	5-11/165	12-17-75	27	Portland, San Diego
56	Walker, Kevin	L/L	6-4/190	9-20-76	26	Lake Elsinore, Portland, San Diego
27	Wright, Jaret	R/R	6-2/230	12-29-75	27	Buffalo, Cleveland

No.	CATCHERS	B/T	Ht./Wt.	Born	Age*	2002 clubs
29	Bennett, Gary	R/R	6-0/208	4-17-72	30	Colorado
7	Gonzalez, Wiki	R/R	5-11/203	5-17-74	28	San Diego, Lake Elsinore
	Rivera, Mike	R/R	6-0/210	9-8-76	26	Detroit, Toledo

No.	INFIELDERS	B/T	Ht./Wt.	Born	Age*	2002 clubs
21	Burroughs, Sean	L/R	6-2/200	9-12-80	22	San Diego, Portland
	Bush, Homer	R/R	5-10/185	11-12-72	30	Toronto, Florida
30	Flores, Jose	R/R	5-11/180	6-28-73	29	Sacramento, Oakland
	Hansen, Dave	L/R	6-0/195	11-24-68	34	Los Angeles
30	Klesko, Ryan	L/L	6-3/220	6-12-71	31	San Diego
8	Loretta, Mark	R/R	6-0/186	8-14-71	31	Milwaukee, Houston
17	Mendez, Donaldo	R/R	6-1/155	6-7-78	24	Mobile, Portland
22	Nady, Xavier	R/R	6-2/205	11-14-78	24	Lake Elsinore, Portland
23	Nevin, Phil	R/R	6-2/231	1-19-71	32	San Diego, Lake Elsinore
1	Vazquez, Ramon	L/R	5-11/170	8-21-76	26	San Diego

No.	OUTFIELDERS	B/T	Ht./Wt.	Born	Age*	2002 clubs
	Anderson, Brady	L/L	6-1/202	1-18-64	39	Cleveland
34	Buchanan, Brian	R/R	6-4/230	7-21-73	29	Minnesota, Edmonton, San Diego
60	Donovan, Todd	R/R	6-1/175	8-12-78	24	Mobile, Lake Elsinore
14	Kotsay, Mark	L/L	6-0/201	12-2-75	27	San Diego
27	Trammell, Bubba	R/R	6-2/220	11-6-71	31	San Diego
	Victorino, Shane	R/R	5-9/160	11-30-80	22	Jacksonville

*Age as of April 1, 2003.

2003 SEASON San Diego Padres

BALLPARK INFORMATION

Ballpark (capacity, surface)
Qualcomm Stadium (63,890, grass)

Address
P.O. Box 2000
San Diego, CA 92112-2000

Official website
www.padres.com

Business phone
619-881-6500

Ticket information
888-697-2373

Field dimensions (from home plate)
To left field at foul line, 327 feet
To center field, 405 feet
To right field at foul line, 330 feet

First game played
April 8, 1969 (Padres 2, Astros 1)

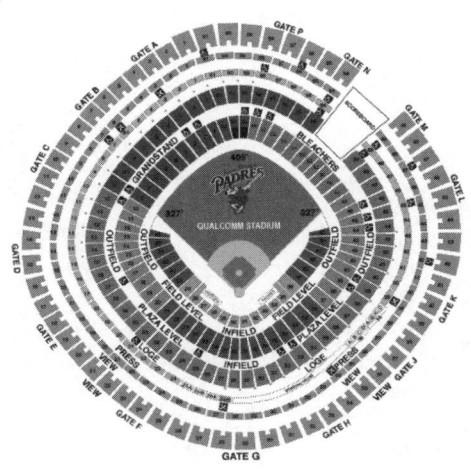

2003 SEASON *San Diego Padres*

Date	Opp.	Res.	Score	(inn.*)	Hits	Opp. hits	Winning pitcher	Losing pitcher	Save	Record	Pos.	GB
4-1	At Ari.	L	0-2		6	5	Johnson	Jarvis		0-1	T4th	1.0
4-2	At Ari.	L	0-9		9	13	Schilling	Tollberg		0-2	5th	2.0
4-3	At Ari.	W	8-7		11	14	Fikac	Myers	Hoffman	1-2	4th	1.5
4-5	At S.F	L	1-3	(10)	7	7	Worrell	Reed		1-3	T4th	3.0
4-6	At S.F	L	1-4		8	7	Fultz	Jarvis	Nen	1-4	5th	4.0
4-7	At S.F	L	1-10		4	12	Hernandez	Tollberg		1-5	5th	4.0
4-8	Ari.	W	8-0		11	4	Lawrence	Anderson		2-5	T4th	4.5
4-9	Ari.	W	5-2		6	9	Jones	Stottlemyre	Hoffman	3-5	T4th	3.5
4-10	Ari.	W	2-1		8	5	Embree	Helling	Hoffman	4-5	T3rd	3.5
4-12	L.A.	L	0-3		2	9	Ishii	Jarvis	Gagne	4-6	4th	4.0
4-13	L.A.	W	6-4		9	9	Fikac	Quantrill	Hoffman	5-6	4th	4.0
4-14	L.A.	W	1-0		5	5	Lawrence	Nomo	Hoffman	6-6	T3rd	3.0
4-15	S.F	W	4-3		10	8	Embree	Christiansen		7-6	T3rd	2.0
4-16	S.F	L	1-5		6	11	Rueter	Tomko		7-7	T3rd	3.0
4-17	S.F	W	5-3		11	8	Jarvis	Ainsworth	Hoffman	8-7	T3rd	2.0
4-18	At L.A.	L	2-5		5	9	Daal	Tollberg	Gagne	8-8	4th	2.5
4-19	At L.A.	L	2-5		5	7	Nomo	Lawrence	Gagne	8-9	4th	3.5
4-20	At L.A.	L	1-4		6	9	Perez	Jones	Carrara	8-10	4th	4.5
4-21	At L.A.	W	5-0		9	3	Tomko	Ashby		9-10	4th	3.5
4-23	At Phi.	L	5-8		5	13	Wolf	DeWitt	Mesa	9-11	4th	4.5
4-24	At Phi.	W	7-2		13	7	Lawrence	Person		10-11	4th	3.5
4-25	At Phi.	W	6-4		11	10	Jones	Cormier	Hoffman	11-11	4th	3.0
4-26	At Pit.	W	10-1		13	6	Tomko	Villone		12-11	4th	3.0
4-28†	At Pit.	L	2-3		6	9	Sauerbeck	Embree	Williams	12-12		
4-28‡	At Pit.	W	7-2		9	8	Tollberg	Anderson		13-12	4th	3.0
4-30	Chi.	W	2-1		5	6	Fikac	Borowski	Hoffman	14-12	4th	2.0
5-1	Chi.	W	4-3		6	7	Jones	Lieber	Hoffman	15-12	4th	1.0
5-2	Chi.	L	1-6		4	7	Wood	Tomko		15-13	4th	2.0
5-3	Pit.	L	4-6		8	11	Wells	Howard	Williams	15-14	4th	3.0
5-4	Pit.	W	3-0		9	7	Jarvis	Anderson	Hoffman	16-14	4th	3.0
5-5	Pit.	W	6-5		12	9	Lawrence	Lowe	Hoffman	17-14	4th	3.0
5-7	At Fla.	L	4-12		9	12	Dempster	Jones		17-15	4th	3.5
5-8	At Fla.	L	4-7		8	9	Mairena	Fikac	Nunez	17-16	4th	4.5
5-9	At Fla.	L	0-1		5	8	Izquierdo	Tollberg	Nunez	17-17	4th	5.5
5-10	At Atl.	L	3-7		6	8	Remlinger	Fikac		17-18	4th	5.5
5-11	At Atl.	L	1-6		4	7	Marquis	Lawrence		17-19	4th	6.5
5-12	At Atl.	W	6-5		11	11	Boyd	Glavine	Hoffman	18-19	4th	5.5
5-13	Mon.	W	7-3		12	9	Tomko	Pavano		19-19	4th	5.5
5-14	Mon.	W	5-4		13	8	Hoffman	Stewart		20-19	4th	5.5
5-15	Mon.	W	2-1	(14)	10	8	Embree	Eischen		21-19	4th	4.5
5-16	N.Y.	L	1-3		8	11	Leiter	Lawrence	Guthrie	21-20	4th	5.0
5-17	N.Y.	L	4-13		9	11	Trachsel	Middlebrook		21-21	4th	6.0
5-18	N.Y.	L	2-5		8	8	Estes	Tomko	Benitez	21-22	4th	7.0
5-19	N.Y.	W	4-3		10	7	Reed	Strickland		22-22	4th	6.0
5-21	At Col.	L	6-7		8	10	Speier	Embree	Jimenez	22-23	4th	7.0
5-22	At Col.	L	3-5		8	14	Mercker	Fikac	Jimenez	22-24	T4th	7.0
5-23	At Col.	L	3-16		5	18	Thomson	Tomko		22-25	5th	7.5
5-24	At Mil.	L	2-6		8	9	Wright	Tollberg		22-26	5th	8.5
5-25	At Mil.	L	0-2		3	5	Quevedo	Pickford		22-27	5th	8.5
5-26	At Mil.	W	8-7		13	11	Tankersley	Figueroa	Hoffman	23-27	5th	8.5
5-27	Col.	W	8-5		13	7	Lawrence	Hampton	Hoffman	24-27	5th	7.5
5-28	Col.	L	2-3	(12)	12	6	Jimenez	Fikac	Speier	24-28	5th	7.5
5-29	Col.	W	11-3		10	9	Middlebrook	Stark		25-28	5th	7.5
5-30	Col.	L	2-4		6	7	Neagle	Jones	Jimenez	25-29	5th	8.5
5-31	Mil.	L	1-12		8	19	Quevedo	Tankersley		25-30	5th	9.5
6-1	Mil.	L	3-4		9	10	Vizcaino	Embree	DeJean	25-31	5th	9.5
6-2	Mil.	L	3-4		8	11	Fox	Reed	DeJean	25-32	5th	9.5
6-3	S.F.	L	3-11		6	20	Ortiz	Middlebrook		25-33	5th	10.5
6-4	S.F.	L	1-3		9	6	Rueter	Jones	Nen	25-34	5th	10.5
6-5	S.F.	L	2-12		8	13	Jensen	Tankersley		25-35	5th	11.5
6-7	At T.B.	W	8-4		8	9	Lawrence	Rupe		26-35	5th	11.5
6-8	At T.B.	L	2-3	(10)	7	12	Zambrano	Embree		26-36	5th	12.5
6-9	At T.B.	W	9-6		16	10	Jones	Wilson	Hoffman	27-36	5th	12.5
6-10	At Bal.	L	6-8		10	6	Groom	Fikac	Julio	27-37	5th	12.5
6-11	At Bal.	L	5-6	(10)	11	12	Julio	Trujillo		27-38	5th	12.5

Date	Opp.	Res.	Score	(inn.*)	Hits	Opp. hits	Winning pitcher	Losing pitcher	Save	Record	Pos.	GB
6-12	At Bal.	W	2-0		5	6	Lawrence	Lopez	Hoffman	28-38	5th	12.5
6-14	Sea.	L	3-6		5	11	Garcia	Tomko	Sasaki	28-39	5th	12.5
6-15	Sea.	W	3-1		9	8	Jones	Soriano	Hoffman	29-39	5th	12.5
6-16	Sea.	W	5-3		8	6	Perez	Moyer	Hoffman	30-39	5th	12.5
6-18	Bos.	L	2-4		6	10	Banks	Lawrence	Urbina	30-40	5th	13.5
6-19	Bos.	W	3-2		5	6	Tomko	Castillo	Hoffman	31-40	5th	12.5
6-20	Bos.	L	0-5		2	7	Martinez	Pickford		31-41	5th	13.5
6-21	N.Y.	W	9-1		10	6	Perez	Wells		32-41	5th	13.5
6-22	N.Y.	L	0-1		3	3	Lilly	Peavy		32-42	5th	13.5
6-23	N.Y.	L	2-3		8	10	Mendoza	Reed	Karsay	32-43	5th	14.5
6-24	S.F	L	6-7		8	12	Worrell	Hoffman	Nen	32-44	5th	14.5
6-25	S.F	W	10-7		11	12	Myers	Rodriguez	Hoffman	33-44	5th	14.5
6-26	At S.F	L	5-6	(12)	11	12	Witasick	Myers		33-45	5th	15.5
6-27	At S.F	L	6-11		9	12	Jensen	Middlebrook	Nen	33-46	5th	16.5
6-28	At K.C.	L	10-14		15	18	Grimsley	Cyr		33-47	5th	17.5
6-29	At K.C.	W	8-4	(10)	10	7	Reed	Grimsley		34-47	5th	16.5
6-30	At K.C.	L	1-13		5	15	Suppan	Peavy		34-48	5th	16.5
7-1	At St.L.	L	3-7		6	10	Williams	Perez		34-49	5th	17.5
7-2	At St.L.	L	5-11		11	12	Crudale	Jarvis		34-50	5th	18.5
7-3	At St.L.	L	1-4		5	5	Simontacchi	Lawrence	Isringhausen	34-51	5th	18.5
7-5	At Col.	L	6-9		11	13	Hampton	Tomko	Jimenez	34-52	5th	19.0
7-6	At Col.	L	2-3		7	11	Thomson	Peavy	Jimenez	34-53	5th	20.0
7-7	At Col.	W	7-1		14	2	Perez	Chacon		35-53	5th	19.0
7-12	St.L.	W	4-3		7	6	Holtz	Veres	Hoffman	36-53	5th	17.5
7-13	St.L.	L	1-2	(10)	5	7	Crudale	Reed	Isringhausen	36-54	5th	18.0
7-14	St.L.	L	1-4		6	13	Smith	Jones	Isringhausen	36-55	5th	18.5
7-15	Col.	L	0-5		3	7	Stark	Perez		36-56	5th	18.5
7-16	Col.	W	5-1		7	8	Peavy	Jennings	Reed	37-56	5th	18.0
7-17	At L.A.	W	7-0		11	4	Lawrence	Perez		38-56	5th	18.0
7-18	At L.A.	W	4-1		12	5	Tomko	Ashby	Hoffman	39-56	5th	17.0
7-19	Ari.	W	6-1		10	10	Jones	Batista		40-56	5th	16.0
7-20	Ari.	L	1-7		6	10	Myers	Holtz		40-57	5th	17.0
7-21	Ari.	W	11-9		11	9	Peavy	Johnson	Hoffman	41-57	5th	16.0
7-22	L.A.	W	5-2		10	13	Lawrence	Perez	Hoffman	42-57	5th	16.0
7-23	L.A.	L	6-8		14	11	Carrara	Fikac	Gagne	42-58	5th	17.0
7-24	L.A.	W	8-0		11	5	Jones	Ishii		43-58	5th	17.0
7-25	At Ari.	L	0-10		6	12	Patterson	Perez		43-59	5th	18.0
7-26	At Ari.	L	0-12		4	10	Johnson	Peavy		43-60	5th	19.0
7-27	At Ari.	L	3-4		10	9	Schilling	Lawrence		43-61	5th	20.0
7-28	At Ari.	L	4-5	(10)	8	11	Koplove	Hoffman		43-62	5th	21.0
7-30	At Chi.	W	6-5		11	10	Holtz	Gordon	Hoffman	44-62	5th	20.0
7-31	At Chi.	W	8-6	(11)	14	8	Villafuerte	Farnsworth	Hoffman	45-62	5th	20.0
8-1	At Chi.	L	7-8		11	13	Gordon	Hoffman		45-63	5th	20.0
8-2	Cin.	W	5-2		12	5	Lawrence	Fernandez	Hoffman	46-63	5th	19.5
8-3	Cin.	L	3-4		11	6	Haynes	Tomko	Graves	46-64	5th	21.0
8-4	Cin.	L	10-15		13	17	White	Hoffman		46-65	5th	22.0
8-6	Phi.	L	4-5	(16)	14	14	Cormier	Jones		46-66	5th	22.5
8-7	Phi.	W	5-2		10	7	Peavy	Padilla	Hoffman	47-66	5th	22.5
8-8	Phi.	W	7-4		14	10	Davey	Adams		48-66	5th	21.5
8-9	At Cin.	L	10-12		14	14	Riedling	Tomko		48-67	5th	22.5
8-10	At Cin.	L	0-9		5	16	Dempster	Jones		48-68	5th	23.5
8-11	At Cin.	L	7-9	(12)	10	11	Rijo	Villafuerte		48-69	5th	24.5
8-13	At N.Y.	W	7-2		12	5	Peavy	Trachsel	Hoffman	49-69	5th	24.5
8-14	At N.Y.	W	6-2		8	8	Lawrence	Leiter	Hoffman	50-69	5th	24.5
8-15	At N.Y.	W	5-3		11	8	Tomko	Thomson	Hoffman	51-69	5th	24.5
8-16	At Mon.	L	6-11		10	14	Day	Kershner		51-70	5th	25.5
8-17	At Mon.	W	6-5		9	7	Johnson	Herges	Hoffman	52-70	5th	25.5
8-18	At Mon.	L	2-9		11	11	Ohka	Peavy		52-71	5th	25.5
8-19	At Mon.	L	0-4		2	6	Colon	Lawrence		52-72	5th	26.0
8-20	Atl.	W	6-2		9	7	Tomko	Moss		53-72	5th	26.0
8-21	Atl.	L	3-6		6	10	Millwood	Tankersley	Smoltz	53-73	5th	27.0
8-22	Atl.	W	9-2		12	10	Bynum	Marquis		54-73	5th	27.0
8-23	Fla.	W	18-2		18	8	Peavy	Pavano		55-73	5th	27.0
8-24	Fla.	L	4-8		11	12	Tavarez	Lawrence		55-74	5th	27.0
8-25	Fla.	L	6-7		15	13	Borland	Villafuerte	Looper	55-75	5th	28.0
8-27	At Hou.	W	11-6		16	9	Fikac	Mlicki		56-75	5th	27.5
8-28	At Hou.	L	1-2		4	8	Oswalt	Peavy	Wagner	56-76	5th	27.5
8-29	At Hou.	L	0-5		4	13	Munro	Lawrence	Dotel	56-77	5th	28.0
8-30	Col.	W	2-0		7	4	Tomko	Neagle	Hoffman	57-77	5th	27.0
8-31	Col.	W	3-0		10	5	Condrey	Cook	Hoffman	58-77	5th	26.0

Date	Opp.	Res.	Score	(inn.*)	Hits	Opp. hits	Winning pitcher	Losing pitcher	Save	Record	Pos.	GB
9-1	Col.	W	9-5		13	11	Nickle	Santos	Hoffman	59-77	5th	26.0
9-2	Col.	L	2-5		7	10	Jennings	Jones	Jimenez	59-78	5th	26.0
9-3	Hou.	L	2-6		12	12	Oswalt	Lawrence	Wagner	59-79	5th	26.0
9-4	Hou.	W	5-1		10	6	Tomko	Munro		60-79	5th	26.0
9-5	Hou.	L	0-5	(11)	7	11	Wagner	Johnson		60-80	5th	27.0
9-6	At Col.	L	3-7		8	7	Cook	Eaton		60-81	5th	27.0
9-7	At Col.	L	3-5		5	5	Mercker	Holtz	Jimenez	60-82	5th	27.0
9-8	At Col.	W	9-4		13	11	Lawrence	Jennings	Hoffman	61-82	5th	26.0
9-9	At Ari.	L	2-5		10	12	Johnson	Tomko	Kim	61-83	5th	27.0
9-10	At Ari.	L	2-8		5	13	Schilling	Peavy		61-84	5th	28.0
9-11	At Ari.	L	5-6		7	8	Koplove	Walker	Myers	61-85	5th	29.0
9-12	S.F	W	3-2	(10)	10	8	Hoffman	Worrell		62-85	5th	28.5
9-13	S.F	L	3-10		7	17	Ortiz	Lawrence		62-86	5th	28.5
9-14	At S.F	L	4-12		13	15	Hernandez	Tomko		62-87	5th	29.5
9-15	At S.F	W	4-1		5	11	Peavy	Ainsworth	Hoffman	63-87	5th	29.5
9-17	Ari.	W	3-2		5	4	Eaton	Batista	Hoffman	64-87	5th	28.5
9-18	Ari.	L	3-10		10	13	Helling	Perez		64-88	5th	29.5
9-19	Ari.	L	1-3		5	5	Johnson	Condrey	Kim	64-89	5th	30.5
9-20	L.A.	W	8-4		14	10	Tomko	Ashby		65-89	5th	29.5
9-21	L.A.	L	3-5		6	9	Nomo	Hoffman	Gagne	65-90	5th	29.5
9-22	L.A.	L	3-4		10	9	Quantrill	Johnson	Gagne	65-91	5th	29.5
9-24	At S.F	L	3-12		9	15	Ortiz	Perez		65-92	5th	29.0
9-25	At S.F	L	0-6		2	8	Hernandez	Condrey		65-93	5th	29.0
9-26	At L.A.	L	5-6		8	13	Shuey	Lawrence	Gagne	65-94	5th	30.0
9-27	At L.A.	L	0-1	(10)	3	5	Gagne	Fikac		65-95	5th	31.0
9-28	At L.A.	L	2-14		8	18	Beirne	Tankersley		65-96	5th	32.0
9-29	At L.A.	W	2-0		4	8	Perez	Alvarez	Villafuerte	66-96	5th	32.0

Monthly records: April (14-12), May (11-18), June (9-18), July (11-14), August (13-15), September (8-19).
*Innings, if other than nine. †First game of a doubleheader. ‡Second game of a doubleheader.

RECORDS

2002 regular-season record: 66-96
Position: 5th in N.L. West
Home: 41-40   **Road:** 25-56
N.L. East: 16-16   **N.L. Central:** 13-23
N.L. West: 29-47   **A.L.:** 8-10
Vs. LH starters: 19-25
Vs. RH starters: 47-71
Grass: 61-91   **Artificial:** 5-5
Day: 22-31   **Night:** 44-65
1-Run: 18-25   **X-inn.:** 4-11
Doubleheaders: 0-0-1
Team record past five years: 393-417
(.485, ranks 9th in league in that span)

TEAM LEADERS

Batting average: Ryan Klesko (.300).
At-bats: Mark Kotsay (578).
Runs: Ryan Klesko (90).
Hits: Mark Kotsay (169).
Total bases: Ryan Klesko (290).
Doubles: Ryan Klesko (39).
Triples: Mark Kotsay (7).
Home runs: Ryan Klesko (29).
Runs batted in: Ryan Klesko (95).
Stolen bases: Mark Kotsay (11).

Slugging percentage: Ryan Klesko (.537).
On-base percentage: Ryan Klesko (.388).
Wins: Brian Lawrence (12).
Earned-run average: Brian Lawrence (3.69).
Complete games: Brett Tomko (3).
Shutouts: Brian Lawrence (2).
Saves: Trevor Hoffman (38).
Innings pitched: Brian Lawrence (210.0).
Strikeouts: Brian Lawrence (149).

GAMES BY POSITION

Catcher: Tom Lampkin 94, Wiki Gonzalez 54, Wil Nieves 27, Javier Cardona 14.
First base: Ryan Klesko 112, Phil Nevin 36, Brian Buchanan 15, Mark Sweeney 11, Kevin Barker 6, Julius Matos 2, Deivi Cruz 1, Alex Pelaez 1.
Second base: Ramon Vazquez 81, D'Angelo Jimenez 54, Julius Matos 49, Sean Burroughs 13, Cesar Crespo 4, Trenidad Hubbard 4, Alex Pelaez 1.
Third base: Phil Nevin 71, Sean Burroughs 48, D'Angelo Jimenez 32, Ramon Vazquez 20, Julius Matos 17, Trenidad Hubbard 6, Cesar Crespo 4,

Alex Pelaez 1.
Shortstop: Deivi Cruz 147, Ramon Vazquez 41, Julius Matos 4, Cesar Crespo 1.
Outfield: Mark Kotsay 147, Bubba Trammell 122, Gene Kingsale 82, Ron Gant 80, Ray Lankford 59, Trenidad Hubbard 57, Ryan Klesko 31, Brian Buchanan 14, Kory DeHaan 9, Cesar Crespo 7, Mark Sweeney 5, Julius Matos 3.
Designated hitter: Ron Gant 4, Bubba Trammell 2, Trenidad Hubbard 1, Ryan Klesko 1, Ray Lankford 1, Julius Matos 1, Mark Sweeney 1.

TOP DRAFT CHOICES

1. **Khalil Greene,** SS, Clemson.
2. **Michael Johnson,** 1B, Clemson.
3. **Kennard Jones,** OF, Indiana.
4. **Aaron Coonrod,** RHP, John A. Logan (Ill.) J.C.
5. **Sean Thompson,** LHP, Thunder Ridge H.S., Denver.
6. **Adam Shorsher,** C, San Jose State.
7. **Matt Lynch,** LHP, Florida State.
8. **Luke Steidlmayer,** RHP, UC Davis.
9. **Brian Burgamy,** 2B, Wichita State.
10. **L.J. Biernbaum,** OF, Florida Atlantic.

SAN FRANCISCO GIANTS
NATIONAL LEAGUE WEST DIVISION

2003 SEASON

March/April

SUN	MON	TUE	WED	THU	FRI	SAT
30	31 D SD	1 SD	2 SD	3	4 D MIL	5 D MIL
6 D MIL	7 D SD	8 SD	9 D SD	10 LA	11 LA	12 D LA
13 LA	14 HOU	15 HOU	16 HOU	17	18 LA	19 LA
20 LA	21	22 PIT	23 PIT	24 D PIT	25 PHI	26 PHI
27 D PHI	28	29 CUB	30 CUB			

May

SUN	MON	TUE	WED	THU	FRI	SAT
				1 D CUB	2 D CIN	3 D CIN
4 D CIN	5	6 FLA	7 FLA	8 FLA	9 ATL	10 ATL
11 D ATL	12 MON	13 D MON	14 D MON	15 D NYM	16 NYM	17 D NYM
18 D NYM	19 ARI	20 ARI	21 ARI	22	23 COL	24 D COL
25 D COL	26 D COL	27 D ARI	28 ARI	29	30 COL	31 D COL

June

SUN	MON	TUE	WED	THU	FRI	SAT
1 D COL	2 COL	3 MIN	4 MIN	5 MIN	6 DET	7 D DET
8 D DET	9	10 CWS	11 CWS	12 CWS	13 KC	14 KC
15 D KC	16	17 LA	18 LA	19 LA	20 OAK	21 D OAK
22 OAK	23 LA	24 LA	25 LA	26	27 OAK	28 D OAK
29 D OAK	30 STL					

July

SUN	MON	TUE	WED	THU	FRI	SAT
		1 STL	2 STL	3 D STL	4 SD	5 SD
6 D SD	7 STL	8 D STL	9 COL	10 COL	11 ARI	12 D ARI
13 D ARI	14	15 *	16	17 COL	18 COL	19 D COL
20 D COL	21 ARI	22 ARI	23 ARI	24 ARI	25 SD	26 D SD
27 D SD	28	29 CUB	30 D CUB	31 D CUB		

August

SUN	MON	TUE	WED	THU	FRI	SAT
					1 CIN	2 D CIN
3 D CIN	4	5 PIT	6 PIT	7 PIT	8 D PHI	9 D PHI
10 D PHI	11	12 NYM	13 NYM	14 NYM	15 MON	16 MON
17 D MON	18 D MON	19 D ATL	20 ATL	21 ATL	22 FLA	23 D FLA
24 D FLA	25	26 COL	27 COL	28 D COL	29 ARI	30 D ARI

September

SUN	MON	TUE	WED	THU	FRI	SAT
31 ARI	1 D ARI	2 COL	3 D COL	4	5 ARI	6 ARI
7 D ARI	8	9 SD	10 SD	11 SD	12 MIL	13 D MIL
14 D MIL	15 SD	16 SD	17 SD	18 SD	19 LA	20 LA
21 LA	22 HOU	23 HOU	24 D HOU	25	26 LA	27 D LA
28 LA						

Home games shaded; D—Day game (games starting before 5 p.m.); *—All-Star Game at Comiskey Park, Chicago. Subject to change.

CLUB DIRECTORY

President and managing general partner
Peter A. Magowan
Executive vice president/COO
Larry Baer
Senior v.p. and general manager
Brian Sabean
Vice president and assistant g.m.
Ned Colletti

Vice president of player personnel
Dick Tidrow
Special assistant to the general manager
Ron Perranoski
Director of player development
Jack Hiatt
Media relations manager
Jim Moorehead

Baseball information manager
Blake Rhodes
Manager, media services & broadcasting
Maria Jacinto

MINOR LEAGUE AFFILIATES

Class	Team	League	Manager
AAA	Fresno	Pacific Coast	Fred Stanley
AA	Norwich	Eastern	Shane Turner
A	San Jose	California	Bill Hayes
A	Hagerstown	South Atlantic	Mike Ramsey
A	Salem-Keizer	Northwest	Jack Lind
Rookie	Arizona Giants	Arizona	Bert Hunter

BROADCAST INFORMATION

Radio: KNBR-AM (680).
TV: KTVU-TV (Channel 2).
Cable TV: Fox Sports Net.

SPRING TRAINING

Ballpark (city): Scottsdale Stadium (Scottsdale, Ariz.).
Ticket information: 602-990-7972.

Follow the Giants all season at: www.sportingnews.com/baseball/teams/giants/

2003 SEASON *San Francisco Giants*

Manager—Felipe Alou (23).
Coaches—Mark Gardner, Gene Glynn, Joe Lefebvre (18), Luis Pujols, Dave Righetti (19), Ron Wotus (10).

No.	PITCHERS	B/T	Ht./Wt.	Born	Age*	2002 clubs
22	Ainsworth, Kurt	R/R	6-3/192	9-9-78	24	Fresno, San Francisco
	Bonser, Boof	R/R	6-4/230	10-14-81	21	Shreveport, San Jose
40	Christiansen, Jason	R/L	6-5/241	9-21-69	33	San Francisco
49	Eyre, Scott	L/L	6-1/210	5-30-72	30	Toronto, San Francisco
	Foppert, Jesse	R/R	6-6/210	7-10-80	22	Shreveport, Fresno
61	Hernandez, Livan	R/R	6-2/240	2-20-75	28	San Francisco
43	Jensen, Ryan	R/R	6-0/205	9-17-75	27	San Francisco
27	Moss, Damian	R/L	6-0/187	11-24-76	26	Atlanta
36	Nathan, Joe	R/R	6-4/195	11-22-74	28	Fresno, San Francisco
31	Nen, Robb	R/R	6-5/222	11-28-69	33	San Francisco
47	Rodriguez, Felix	R/R	6-1/198	9-9-72	30	San Francisco
46	Rueter, Kirk	L/L	6-3/212	12-1-70	32	San Francisco
29	Schmidt, Jason	R/R	6-5/205	1-29-73	30	Fresno, San Francisco
52	Urban, Jeff	R/L	6-8/215	1-25-77	26	Fresno
	Williams, Jerome	R/R	6-3/190	12-4-81	21	Fresno
45	Worrell, Tim	R/R	6-4/230	7-5-67	35	San Francisco
41	Zerbe, Chad	L/L	6-0/200	4-27-72	30	Fresno, San Francisco

No.	CATCHERS	B/T	Ht./Wt.	Born	Age*	2002 clubs
52	Lunsford, Trey	R/R	6-1/195	5-25-79	23	San Jose, Shreveport, Fresno, San Francisco
33	Santiago, Benito	R/R	6-1/200	3-9-65	38	San Francisco
9	Torrealba, Yorvit	R/R	5-11/180	7-19-78	24	San Francisco

No.	INFIELDERS	B/T	Ht./Wt.	Born	Age*	2002 clubs
	Alfonzo, Edgardo	R/R	5-11/187	11-8-73	29	New York N.L.
35	Aurilia, Rich	R/R	6-1/185	9-2-71	31	San Francisco
	Durham, Ray	B/R	5-8/180	11-30-71	31	Chicago A.L., Oakland
39	Feliz, Pedro	R/R	6-1/205	4-27-77	25	San Francisco
13	Guzman, Edwards	L/R	5-11/205	9-11-76	26	Fresno
37	Minor, Damon	L/L	6-7/230	1-5-74	29	San Francisco, Fresno
	Niekro, Lance	R/R	6-3/210	1-29-79	24	Shreveport
	Perez, Neifi	B/R	6-0/175	6-2-73	29	Kansas City
2	Ransom, Cody	R/R	6-2/196	2-17-76	27	Fresno, San Francisco
50	Santos, Deivis	L/L	6-1/175	2-9-80	23	Shreveport, Fresno
6	Snow, J.T.	L/L	6-2/209	2-26-68	35	San Francisco

No.	OUTFIELDERS	B/T	Ht./Wt.	Born	Age*	2002 clubs
7	Benard, Marvin	L/L	5-9/191	1-20-70	33	San Francisco
25	Bonds, Barry	L/L	6-2/228	7-24-64	38	San Francisco
	Ellison, Jason	R/R	5-10/180	4-4-78	24	San Jose, Fresno
24	Goodwin, Tom	L/R	6-1/175	7-27-68	34	Fresno, San Francisco
	Grissom, Marquis	R/R	5-11/188	4-17-67	35	Los Angeles
14	Torcato, Tony	L/R	6-1/195	10-25-79	23	Fresno, San Francisco
54	Valderrama, Carlos	R/R	5-11/175	11-30-77	25	Shreveport, San Jose

*Age as of April 1, 2003.

BALLPARK INFORMATION

Ballpark (capacity, surface)
Pacific Bell Park (41,341, grass)

Address
24 Willie Mays Plaza
San Francisco, CA 94107

Official website
www.sfgiants.com

Business phone
415-972-2000

Ticket information
415-972-2000

Field dimensions (from home plate)
To left field at foul line, 339 feet
To center field, 399 feet
To right field at foul line, 309 feet

First game played
April 11, 2000 (Dodgers 6, Giants 5)

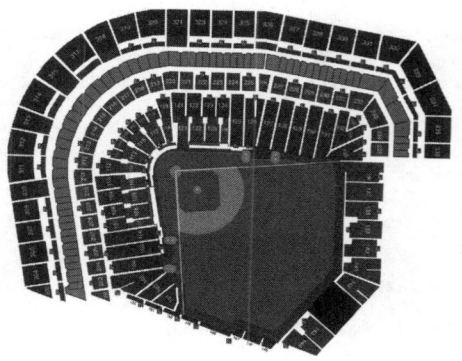

2003 SEASON *San Francisco Giants*

Date	Opp.	Res.	Score	(inn.*)	Hits	Opp. hits	Winning pitcher	Losing pitcher	Save	Record	Pos.	GB
4-2	At L.A.	W	9-2		12	5	Hernandez	Brown		1-0	2nd	0.5
4-3	At L.A.	W	12-0		15	4	Ortiz	Nomo		2-0	1st	+0.5
4-4	At L.A.	W	3-0		5	3	Jensen	Perez	Nen	3-0	1st	+1.0
4-5	S.D.	W	3-1	(10)	7	7	Worrell	Reed		4-0	1st	+2.0
4-6	S.D.	W	4-1		7	8	Fultz	Jarvis	Nen	5-0	1st	+2.0
4-7	S.D.	W	10-1		12	4	Hernandez	Tollberg		6-0	1st	+2.0
4-9	L.A.	L	0-3		5	10	Nomo	Ortiz	Gagne	6-1	1st	+2.0
4-10	L.A.	W	2-1		7	8	Nen	Quantrill		7-1	1st	+3.0
4-11	L.A.	L	3-4		8	10	Daal	Rueter	Gagne	7-2	1st	+2.0
4-12	Mil.	W	5-1		5	5	Ainsworth	Sheets		8-2	1st	+2.0
4-13	Mil.	W	3-2		5	9	Hernandez	Figueroa	Nen	9-2	1st	+2.5
4-14	Mil.	L	3-4		10	8	Vizcaino	Rodriguez	DeJean	9-3	1st	+1.5
4-15	At S.D.	L	3-4		8	10	Embree	Christiansen		9-4	1st	+0.5
4-16	At S.D.	W	5-1		11	6	Rueter	Tomko		10-4	1st	+0.5
4-17	At S.D.	L	3-5		8	11	Jarvis	Ainsworth	Hoffman	10-5	1st	+0.5
4-19	At Hou.	W	3-2		9	6	Hernandez	Reynolds	Nen	11-5	1st	+1.5
4-20	At Hou.	W	13-9		19	10	Ortiz	Redding	Nen	12-5	1st	+1.5
4-21	At Hou.	L	0-4		2	11	Mlicki	Jensen		12-6	1st	+0.5
4-23	At Chi.	W	12-4		13	5	Rueter	Bere		13-6	1st	+0.5
4-24	At Chi.	L	4-10		9	14	Borowski	Fultz		13-7	1st	+0.5
4-25	At Chi.	L	1-2		7	7	Lieber	Hernandez	Alfonseca	13-8	2nd	0.5
4-26	At Cin.	L	3-4		8	9	Sullivan	Rodriguez	Graves	13-9	3rd	1.5
4-27	At Cin.	L	4-8	(8)	8	9	Rijo	Jensen		13-10	3rd	1.5
4-28	At Cin.	W	5-4		10	6	Rueter	Haynes	Nen	14-10	3rd	1.5
4-29	Phi.	W	8-5		8	7	Worrell	Cormier	Nen	15-10	3rd	1.0
4-30	Phi.	L	2-8		5	14	Padilla	Hernandez		15-11	3rd	1.0
5-1	Phi.	W	2-1		4	7	Rodriguez	Bottalico	Nen	16-11	T1st	...
5-3	Cin.	W	6-1		9	10	Rueter	Rijo		17-11	2nd	0.5
5-4	Cin.	W	3-0		6	2	Jensen	Haynes	Nen	18-11	2nd	0.5
5-5	Cin.	W	6-5	(10)	11	10	Nen	Pineda		19-11	2nd	0.5
5-7	At N.Y.	W	5-1		10	5	Ortiz	Trachsel		20-11	1st	...
5-8	At N.Y.	W	8-2		10	6	Rueter	Estes		21-11	1st	...
5-9	At N.Y.	W	4-3		7	4	Jensen	Astacio	Nen	22-11	1st	+0.5
5-10	At Mon.	L	3-6		8	11	Vazquez	Hernandez		22-12	1st	+0.5
5-11	At Mon.	W	3-2		7	9	Fultz	Reames	Nen	23-12	1st	+0.5
5-12	At Mon.	L	2-4		5	9	Armas Jr.	Ortiz	Herges	23-13	1st	+0.5
5-13	Atl.	W	7-6	(11)	13	17	Worrell	Hammond		24-13	1st	+0.5
5-14	Atl.	W	2-0		8	5	Jensen	Moss	Nen	25-13	1st	+1.5
5-15	Atl.	L	1-6		6	10	Maddux	Hernandez		25-14	1st	+0.5
5-16	Atl.	L	4-5		7	5	Marquis	Schmidt		25-15	2nd	0.5
5-17	Fla.	W	9-3		10	10	Ortiz	Dempster	Nen	26-15	2nd	0.5
5-18	Fla.	W	10-5		14	10	Rueter	Penny	Nen	27-15	2nd	0.5
5-19	Fla.	L	2-4		2	7	Beckett	Jensen	Nunez	27-16	2nd	0.5
5-21	At Ari.	L	4-9		9	13	Johnson	Fultz		27-17	2nd	1.5
5-22	At Ari.	W	12-5		17	11	Zerbe	Morgan		28-17	2nd	0.5
5-24	At Col.	L	5-8		11	12	Stark	Ortiz	Jimenez	28-18	2nd	1.5
5-25	At Col.	L	3-6		8	10	Nichting	Rueter	Jimenez	28-19	2nd	1.5
5-26	At Col.	L	6-10		9	13	Jennings	Jensen		28-20	2nd	2.5
5-27	Ari.	W	7-3		11	8	Hernandez	Anderson		29-20	2nd	1.5
5-28	Ari.	W	1-0	(10)	3	3	Nen	Myers		30-20	2nd	0.5
5-29	Ari.	L	3-7		3	14	Schilling	Ortiz		30-21	2nd	1.5
5-30	Ari.	L	0-1		4	5	Helling	Rueter	Kim	30-22	3rd	2.5
5-31	Col.	L	2-6		5	12	Jennings	Jensen	Jones	30-23	3rd	3.5
6-1	Col.	L	4-5		12	12	Hampton	Hernandez	Jimenez	30-24	3rd	3.5
6-2	Col.	W	9-2		11	7	Schmidt	Thomson		31-24	3rd	2.5
6-3	At S.D.	W	11-3		20	6	Ortiz	Middlebrook		32-24	3rd	2.5
6-4	At S.D.	W	3-1		6	9	Rueter	Jones	Nen	33-24	3rd	1.5
6-5	At S.D.	W	12-2		13	8	Jensen	Tankersley		34-24	3rd	1.5
6-7	At N.Y.	L	1-2		8	7	Mussina	Hernandez	Rivera	34-25	3rd	2.5
6-8	At N.Y.	W	4-3		10	2	Schmidt	Rivera	Nen	35-25	3rd	2.5
6-9	At N.Y.	L	2-4		7	6	Clemens	Rodriguez	Karsay	35-26	3rd	3.5
6-10	At Tor.	L	5-6		10	8	Thurman	Rueter	Escobar	35-27	3rd	3.5
6-11	At Tor.	W	9-2		12	9	Jensen	Lyon		36-27	3rd	2.5
6-12	At Tor.	W	6-3		13	12	Hernandez	Halladay	Nen	37-27	3rd	2.5
6-14	Oak.	L	2-3		11	7	Hudson	Schmidt	Koch	37-28	3rd	2.5

Date	Opp.	Res.	Score	(inn.*)	Hits	Opp. hits	Winning pitcher	Losing pitcher	Save	Record	Pos.	GB
6-15	Oak.	W	6-2		6	9	Zerbe	Harang		38-28	3rd	2.5
6-16	Oak.	L	1-2		5	10	Zito	Rueter	Koch	38-29	3rd	3.5
6-18	T.B.	L	3-8		8	14	Kennedy	Hernandez		38-30	3rd	4.5
6-19	T.B.	W	8-0		11	5	Schmidt	Rupe		39-30	3rd	3.5
6-20	T.B.	W	10-2		16	6	Ortiz	Sturtze		40-30	3rd	3.5
6-21	Bal.	W	4-3		9	8	Rodriguez	Bauer	Nen	41-30	3rd	3.5
6-22	Bal.	L	2-4		8	7	Driskill	Jensen	Julio	41-31	3rd	3.5
6-23	Bal.	L	1-3		6	9	Johnson	Hernandez	Julio	41-32	3rd	4.5
6-24	At S.D.	W	7-6		12	8	Worrell	Hoffman	Nen	42-32	3rd	3.5
6-25	At S.D.	L	7-10		12	11	Myers	Rodriguez	Hoffman	42-33	3rd	4.5
6-26	S.D.	W	6-5	(12)	12	11	Witasick	Myers		43-33	3rd	4.5
6-27	S.D.	W	11-6		12	9	Jensen	Middlebrook	Nen	44-33	3rd	4.5
6-28	At Oak.	L	6-10		9	15	Mulder	Hernandez		44-34	3rd	5.5
6-29	At Oak.	W	5-3		10	7	Schmidt	Lidle	Nen	45-34	3rd	4.5
6-30	At Oak.	L	0-7		5	11	Hudson	Ortiz		45-35	3rd	4.5
7-1	At Col.	W	8-6		11	8	Rodriguez	Jimenez	Nen	46-35	3rd	4.5
7-2	At Col.	W	18-5		23	11	Jensen	Neagle		47-35	3rd	4.5
7-3	At Col.	L	4-14		11	17	Jennings	Hernandez		47-36	3rd	4.5
7-4	At Ari.	L	3-6		7	10	Anderson	Schmidt	Kim	47-37	3rd	4.5
7-5	At Ari.	L	1-2		4	6	Schilling	Ortiz		47-38	3rd	5.5
7-6	At Ari.	W	3-2		10	7	Worrell	Mantei	Nen	48-38	3rd	5.5
7-7	At Ari.	W	5-2		10	7	Jensen	Helling	Nen	49-38	3rd	4.5
7-11	Col.	W	3-2		11	6	Worrell	Jimenez		50-38	3rd	3.5
7-12	Col.	W	9-0		12	4	Hernandez	Hampton		51-38	3rd	2.5
7-13	Col.	W	6-1		9	5	Schmidt	Thomson		52-38	3rd	2.0
7-14	Col.	L	3-5		7	8	Chacon	Rueter		52-39	3rd	2.5
7-15	Ari.	W	6-3		10	10	Jensen	Helling		53-39	3rd	1.5
7-16	Ari.	L	3-5		5	10	Johnson	Rodriguez	Kim	53-40	3rd	2.0
7-17	At St.L.	W	5-4		7	12	Worrell	Veres	Nen	54-40	3rd	2.0
7-18	At St.L.	L	1-5		9	8	Morris	Schmidt		54-41	3rd	2.0
7-19	At L.A.	W	3-2	(12)	5	9	Nen	Mota		55-41	2nd	1.0
7-20	At L.A.	L	2-4		7	11	Quantrill	Rodriguez	Gagne	55-42	3rd	2.0
7-21	At L.A.	W	6-4		10	11	Ortiz	Carrara	Nen	56-42	2nd	1.0
7-22	St.L.	L	3-5		10	12	Hackman	Worrell	Isringhausen	56-43	2nd	2.0
7-23	St.L.	L	0-4		7	10	Morris	Schmidt		56-44	3rd	3.0
7-24	St.L.	W	6-4		9	9	Rueter	Benes	Nen	57-44	2nd	3.0
7-25	St.L.	L	3-4		8	7	Smith	Jensen	Isringhausen	57-45	T2nd	4.0
7-26	L.A.	L	6-11		11	18	Nomo	Ortiz		57-46	3rd	5.0
7-27	L.A.	L	1-5		4	11	Daal	Hernandez		57-47	3rd	6.0
7-28	L.A.	W	3-1		9	4	Schmidt	Ashby	Nen	58-47	3rd	6.0
7-30	At Phi.	W	10-3		10	10	Rueter	Myers		59-47	T2nd	5.0
7-31	At Phi.	L	6-8		12	8	Timlin	Brohawn	Mesa	59-48	3rd	6.0
8-1	At Phi.	L	1-2		6	6	Wolf	Ortiz	Mesa	59-49	3rd	6.0
8-2	At Pit.	L	5-6		11	11	Boehringer	Nen		59-50	3rd	6.5
8-3	At Pit.	W	11-6		16	9	Schmidt	Wells		60-50	3rd	7.0
8-4	At Pit.	W	10-5		16	6	Rueter	Benson		61-50	3rd	7.0
8-6	Chi.	W	11-10		12	14	Worrell	Farnsworth	Nen	62-50	2nd	6.5
8-7	Chi.	W	4-3	(10)	10	7	Nen	Alfonseca		63-50	2nd	6.5
8-8	Chi.	L	3-9		5	10	Clement	Hernandez		63-51	3rd	6.5
8-9	Pit.	L	3-4		7	6	Wells	Schmidt	Williams	63-52	3rd	7.5
8-10	Pit.	W	8-3		6	7	Aybar	Lincoln		64-52	3rd	7.5
8-11	Pit.	W	5-4	(11)	17	9	Nen	Williams		65-52	3rd	7.5
8-13	At Atl.	W	7-2		12	6	Ortiz	Maddux		66-52	2nd	7.5
8-14	At Atl.	L	0-1		5	8	Glavine	Hernandez	Smoltz	66-53	3rd	8.5
8-15	At Atl.	T	3-3	(10)	5	5				66-53	3rd	9.0
8-16	At Fla.	L	2-4		7	9	Tejera	Rueter	Looper	66-54	3rd	10.0
8-17	At Fla.	L	3-7		9	7	Beckett	Jensen		66-55	3rd	11.0
8-18	At Fla.	L	0-3		3	9	Burnett	Ortiz		66-56	3rd	11.0
8-19	At Fla.	W	3-0		5	5	Hernandez	Tavarez		67-56	3rd	10.5
8-20	N.Y.	W	1-0		7	5	Schmidt	Leiter		68-56	3rd	10.5
8-21	N.Y.	W	3-1		5	7	Rueter	Thomson	Nen	69-56	3rd	10.5
8-22	N.Y.	W	3-1		9	6	Jensen	Bacsik	Nen	70-56	3rd	10.5
8-23	Mon.	L	2-7		6	8	Ohka	Ortiz	Eischen	70-57	3rd	11.5
8-24	Mon.	L	2-7		6	11	Colon	Hernandez	Stewart	70-58	3rd	11.5
8-25	Mon.	W	8-4		12	8	Schmidt	Vazquez		71-58	3rd	11.5
8-26	At Col.	W	4-3		11	10	Rodriguez	Jones	Nen	72-58	3rd	11.5
8-27	At Col.	W	7-4		14	10	Rodriguez	Jones	Nen	73-58	3rd	10.5
8-28	At Col.	W	9-1		12	6	Ortiz	Jennings		74-58	3rd	9.5
8-29	At Col.	W	10-6		10	5	Hernandez	Hampton		75-58	3rd	9.0
8-30	At Ari.	W	7-6		9	8	Schmidt	Johnson	Nen	76-58	3rd	8.0
8-31	At Ari.	W	5-0		8	5	Rueter	Schilling		77-58	3rd	7.0

Date	Opp.	Res.	Score	(inn.*)	Hits	Opp. hits	Winning pitcher	Losing pitcher	Save	Record	Pos.	GB
9-1	At Ari.	L	6-7		10	8	Kim	Nen		77-59	3rd	8.0
9-3	Col.	W	4-2		8	9	Ortiz	Hampton	Nen	78-59	3rd	6.5
9-4	Col.	L	1-2		4	7	Neagle	Hernandez	Jimenez	78-60	3rd	7.5
9-5	Ari.	L	5-8		9	11	Schilling	Schmidt		78-61	3rd	8.5
9-6	Ari.	W	1-0		6	4	Rodriguez	Fetters		79-61	3rd	7.5
9-7	Ari.	W	4-3		10	7	Rodriguez	Kim		80-61	3rd	6.5
9-8	Ari.	W	3-1		7	8	Ortiz	Anderson	Nen	81-61	3rd	5.5
9-9	L.A.	W	6-5		9	9	Hernandez	Perez	Nen	82-61	T2nd	5.5
9-10	L.A.	W	5-2		7	6	Schmidt	Brown	Nen	83-61	T2nd	5.5
9-11	L.A.	L	3-7		8	14	Nomo	Rueter		83-62	T2nd	6.5
9-12	At S.D.	L	2-3	(10)	8	10	Hoffman	Worrell		83-63	T2nd	7.0
9-13	At S.D.	W	10-3		17	7	Ortiz	Lawrence		84-63	2nd	6.0
9-14	S.D.	W	12-4		15	13	Hernandez	Tomko		85-63	2nd	6.0
9-15	S.D.	L	1-4		11	5	Peavy	Ainsworth	Hoffman	85-64	2nd	7.0
9-16	At L.A.	L	6-7		8	12	Nomo	Schmidt	Gagne	85-65	T2nd	7.5
9-17	At L.A.	W	6-4		11	10	Rueter	Daal	Nen	86-65	2nd	6.5
9-18	At L.A.	W	7-4		13	8	Ortiz	Ellis		87-65	2nd	6.5
9-19	At L.A.	L	3-6		7	8	Perez	Hernandez		87-66	2nd	7.5
9-20	At Mil.	W	5-1		9	6	Jensen	Neugebauer		88-66	2nd	6.5
9-21	At Mil.	W	3-1		9	3	Schmidt	Diggins	Nen	89-66	2nd	5.5
9-22	At Mil.	W	3-1		5	5	Rodriguez	Vizcaino	Nen	90-66	2nd	4.5
9-24	S.D.	W	12-3		15	9	Ortiz	Perez		91-66	2nd	3.0
9-25	S.D.	W	6-0		8	2	Hernandez	Condrey		92-66	2nd	2.0
9-27	Hou.	W	2-1		9	5	Schmidt	Miller	Nen	93-66	2nd	2.5
9-28	Hou.	W	5-2		7	9	Rueter	Robertson	Nen	94-66	2nd	2.5
9-29	Hou.	W	7-0		12	5	Jensen	Oswalt		95-66	2nd	2.5

Monthly records: April (15-11), May (15-12), June (15-12), July (14-13), August (18-10), September (18-8).
*Innings, if other than nine.

RECORDS

2002 regular-season record: 95-66
Position: 2nd in N.L. West
Home: 50-31   **Road:** 45-35
N.L. East: 17-14   **N.L. Central:** 23-13
N.L. West: 47-29   **A.L.:** 8-10
Vs. LH starters: 21-18
Vs. RH starters: 74-48
Grass: 91-61   **Artificial:** 4-5
Day: 35-30   **Night:** 60-36
1-Run: 28-22   **X-inn.:** 8-1
Doubleheaders: 0-0-0
Team record past five years: 457-353
(.564, ranks 2nd in league in that span)

TEAM LEADERS

Batting average: Barry Bonds (.370).
At-bats: Jeff Kent (623).
Runs: Barry Bonds (117).
Hits: Jeff Kent (195).
Total bases: Jeff Kent (352).
Doubles: Jeff Kent (42).
Triples: Reggie Sanders (6).
Home runs: Barry Bonds (46).

Runs batted in: Barry Bonds (110).
Stolen bases: Reggie Sanders (18).
Slugging percentage: Barry Bonds (.799).
On-base percentage: Barry Bonds (.582).
Wins: Russ Ortiz, Kirk Rueter (14).
Earned-run average: Kirk Rueter (3.23).
Complete games: Livan Hernandez (5).
Shutouts: Livan Hernandez (3).
Saves: Robb Nen (43).
Innings pitched: Livan Hernandez (216.0).
Strikeouts: Jason Schmidt (196).

GAMES BY POSITION

Catcher: Benito Santiago 125, Yorvit Torrealba 53, Trey Lunsford 3.
First base: J.T. Snow 135, Damon Minor 44, Jeff Kent 9, Ramon E. Martinez 4, David Bell 2, Shawon Dunston 1.
Second base: Jeff Kent 149, Ramon E. Martinez 17, David Bell 12.
Third base: David Bell 139, Pedro Feliz 44, Bill Mueller 3, Ramon E. Martinez 2.

Shortstop: Rich Aurilia 131, Ramon E. Martinez 40, David Bell 3, Cody Ransom 3, Shawon Dunston 1, Pedro Feliz 1.
Outfield: Reggie Sanders 137, Barry Bonds 135, Tsuyoshi Shinjo 117, Tom Goodwin 53, Shawon Dunston 49, Kenny Lofton 44, Marvin Benard 38, Calvin Murray 10, Ramon E. Martinez 3, Tony Torcato 1, Pedro Feliz 1.
Designated hitter: Barry Bonds 5, Shawon Dunston 3, Damon Minor 3.

TOP DRAFT CHOICES

1. **Matt Cain,** RHP, Houston H.S., Germantown, Tenn.
2. **Freddie Lewis,** OF, Southern U.
3. **Dan Ortmeier,** OF, Texas-Arlington.
4. **Kevin Correia,** RHP, Cal Poly.
5. **Kevin Kelly,** SS, Duke.
6. **Jesse English,** LHP, Rancho Buena Vista, Calif..
7. **Michael Musgrave,** RHP, Forest H.S., Ocala, Fla.
8. **Clay Hensley,** RHP, Lamar.
9. **Randy Walter,** OF, Wichita State.
10. **Glenn Woolard,** RHP, Kutztown (Pa.).

2002 REVIEW

Year in review

American League Division Series

National League Division Series

American League Championship Series

National League Championship Series

World Series

All-Star Game

Notable Performances

Transactions

Award Winners

Miscellaneous

Necrology

By STEVE GIETSCHIER
TSN Senior Managing Editor

To many observers, what was most remarkable about the 2002 baseball season was the simple fact that it got played to a conclusion. Since the collective bargaining agreement between owners and players had expired in November 2001, those following the game closely spent the better part of the season watching pennant races unfold with one eye and labor-management negotiations seemingly go nowhere with the other. Given the track record that Major League Baseball and the Major League Baseball Players Association had established over the past quarter-century, few were willing to opine that the season would not at some point be interrupted by a work stoppage, and the more pessimistic needed little convincing that the end of the season might well be truncated, as had been the case in 1994. When the two sides reached an agreement without a stoppage on August 30, fans were simultaneously stunned and relieved, and some were even critical that a deal had not been consummated weeks or even months before.

Whatever anguish accompanied the uncertainties inherent in the collective bargaining process, fans who could concentrate on the game played on the field were entertained by a rollicking good regular season and an exciting postseason. Barry Bonds' encore to his stunning 2001 season included becoming the oldest first-time league batting champion at age 38, surpassing the 600-home run plateau and moving into fourth place on the career home run list, just 47 behind his godfather, Willie Mays. Overall offensive production declined a bit from the previous year, perhaps reflecting baseball's continued emphasis on expanding the strike zone to conform to its definition in the rule book. Runs per game dropped from 9.55 to 9.24, and home runs per game declined from 2.25 to 2.09. The number of players hitting 30 or more home runs fell from 41 to 28, and the number driving in 100 or more runs dropped from 46 to 36. Overall batting average declined .003 on .261, and total earned-run average fell as well, from 4.41 to 4.27. Yet, strikeouts per game also declined (13.34 to 12.94), and walks per game rose a bit, from 6.51 to 6.70.

Perhaps more encouraging was a lessening of the relationship between team payrolls and postseason success. When Anaheim Angels center fielder Darin Erstad caught Kenny Lofton's fly ball to end the seventh game of the World Series, baseball's championship passed to a team that stood 13th in team payroll (the losing San Francisco Giants stood ninth). In fact, the top dozen teams in payroll included but five of the eight teams that made the postseason, and two A.L. division winners—the Oakland A's and the Minnesota Twins—stood 21st and 26th, respectively, in payroll. Three of the teams with the five highest payrolls did not qualify for the postseason, and the two that did— the New York Yankees and the Arizona Diamondbacks— both lost in the Division Series.

THREE CLUBS CHANGE HANDS

As the year began, MLB officials were trying to put the finishing touches on a tangled transfer of franchises between ownership groups. In December 2001, owners of the Boston Red Sox, including the Jean R. Yawkey Trust, holders of a majority stake, had announced the sale of the team to a group headed by Florida Marlins owner John Henry and former San Diego Padres owner Tom Werner for $660 million plus $40 million in assumed debt.

Massachusetts Attorney General Thomas Reilly intervened, claiming that the Red Sox had rejected a larger offer said to be $750 million from a group headed by Miles Prentice. Reilly's responsibility in this matter was to see that the charities and charitable trusts standing to gain from liquidation of the Yawkey Trust's interests would receive maximum benefit from the sale. The Red Sox countered that the Henry proposal, despite the lower price tag, was designed to give the Yawkey Trust more money than it would receive under the Prentice bid. A late offer of about $750 million from Cablevision's Charles Dolan further complicated matters. After a couple of weeks of negotiations, Reilly announced that the Henry group had agreed to donate more than $20 million additional over 10 years to youth and educational organizations and that the Red Sox limited partners would add $10 million to the Yawkey Trust's share. Under these terms, MLB owners approved the sale of the team, with Reilly's blessing, on January 16.

Henry still owned the Marlins and a small piece of the Yankees. Commissioner Allan H. (Bud) Selig ordered him to divest himself of his share in the Yankees, and on February 12, the owners approved the sale of the Marlins from Henry to Montreal Expos owner Jeffrey Loria for $158.5 million. Simultaneously, the owners approved the sale of the Expos to MLB itself for $120 million and lent Loria $38.5 million, the difference between the two sale prices.

BASEBALL OWNS EXPOS

MLB thus found itself in the unprecedented position of owning one of its franchises, a unique situation save for a short time in the 1940s when baseball controlled the Philadelphia Phillies. MLB used its central fund, said to contain more than $500 million, and credit lines of credit to underwrite the purchase. Teams were not assessed fees to pay for the franchise. The commissioner and Sandy Alderson, MLB's executive vice president for baseball operations, insisted that the Expos would be run as an independent operation with a budget comparable to the team's 2001 budget. MLB installed Tony Tavares, former president of the Angels, as president and hired Omar Minaya, senior assistant general manager of the New York Mets, as general manager. Frank Robinson left his post as MLB's vice president for discipline to become field manager. Minaya proved to be a creative and aggressive executive. The Expos' average salary rose from $926,333 in 2001 to $1,497,309, and the team finished second in the N.L. East.

CONTRACTION POSTPONED

On December 27, 2001, attorneys for MLB and the Twins had argued before the Minnesota Court of Appeals that Hennepin County District Judge Harry S. Crump had erred when he issued a temporary injunction ordering the team to play its 2002 season in the Hubert H. Humphrey Metrodome. Baseball's appeal was assumed to be part of its plan to eliminate two teams, rumored to be the Twins and the Expos. But the Metropolitan Sports Facilities Commission, owners of the Metrodome, the state's attorney general's office and season ticket holder Charles Spevacek had sued the Twins to hold them to their lease. The Players Association filed a grievance before arbitrator Shyam Das, claiming that contraction violated the expired collective bargaining agreement. Representative John

Conyers of Michigan, co-sponsor of legislation to make the elimination or relocation of teams subject to antitrust challenges from injured parties, called upon Selig to resign.

On January 22, the three-judge Court of Appeals unanimously upheld the injunction, reasoning that "money could not compensate the (Sports Facilities) commission for the intangible losses that would result if the Twins breached their promise to play." MLB appealed this ruling to the Minnesota Supreme Court, but the court refused to take the case on February 5. Selig then announced that baseball would put off contraction until 2003, but MLB continued to press to have the commission's lawsuit dismissed. Further negotiations, following passage of a bill in the Minnesota legislature providing a financial framework for construction of a new ball park, led to a settlement. The sports commission dropped its lawsuit, and MLB agreed to keep the Twins in Minnesota through the 2003 season, thereby fulfilling the final year of the current lease.

PLAYERS ASSOCIATION'S GRIEVANCE

Hearings before Das on the Players Association's grievance began in December 2001, and continued sporadically thereafter. The union held that discussion of the possible contraction of teams should be part of the negotiations for a new collective bargaining agreement, while MLB argued that contraction could occur without union approval with only the details subject to negotiation. The union later said it would seek damages since talk of contraction had adversely affected the market for free agents. Das announced that he hoped to rule on the grievance by July 15, but he then asked for a delay until August 1 and then a further delay. Eventually, settlement of the grievance was rolled into the labor talks.

COLLECTIVE BARGAINING NEGOTIATIONS

The road to a new labor agreement became rockier in early January upon disclosure that the Milwaukee Brewers had borrowed $3 million in 1995 from an investment company owned by Carl Pohlad, owner of the Twins. Critics of the loan called it a violation of Major League Rule 20(c), prohibiting an owner, stockholder, manager or player from lending money to another club's owner or employee unless all clubs in the league gave their approval. Conyers, noting that Pohlad would receive more money under Selig's contraction plan than he would if he sold his club, called the loan a conflict of interest. Two other loans, one from Pohlad to Jerry McMorris of the Colorado Rockies and one to the St. Louis Cardinals from a bank controlled by Carl Lindner, owner of the Cincinnati Reds, also came under scrutiny, but owners dismissed concerns about them as without merit. Referring to Selig and Pohlad, Fred Wilpon, president and CEO of the Mets, told the Associated Press, "You're talking about two men of the highest, highest integrity. I'm offended by making it a cause celebre. It pains me."

Selig opened the year's collective bargaining negotiations on January 9 with a four-hour presentation explaining MLB's central economic proposals. He asked for a luxury tax of 50 percent on all payroll amounts above $98 million and an increase in the percentage of shared locally-generated revenue from 20 to 50 percent, after expenses. He also told the union's representatives that MLB wanted a worldwide amateur draft, thereby eliminating the ability of players from beyond the United States, Puerto Rico and Canada to become high-priced free agents. The Association responded to management's proposal on March 13, declining to support any luxury tax and proposing that revenue sharing be limited to 22.5 percent. Moreover, the union advocated continuation of the split-pool approach to revenue sharing instead of MLB's straight pool offer. Whereas a straight pool would divide the shared revenue equally among all the clubs, the split pool in the agreement that expired in 2001 had divided 75 percent of the revenue equally and divided the remaining 25 percent among the clubs whose net local revenue was below the average revenue total. "We don't want a split pool because you end up with certain clubs being treated differently than everyone else," said Robert D. Manfred, Jr., MLB's executive vice president for labor relations and human resources, to The New York Times.

Before the opening of the season, Selig pledged not to lock the players out through the World Series. He also continued to argue that baseball's economic house needed massive restructuring. He called a report in the April 15 issue of Forbes Magazine that 20 clubs had made money in 2001 "pure fiction," and he warned in May that 6-8 clubs could go out of business if the system were not changed. Then, on July 10, he suggested that one team might have trouble meeting its next payroll. Further complicating this situation were published allegations from former players Ken Caminiti and Jose Canseco that at least half of all major leaguers were using steroids. The union did not respond with a no-strike pledge, but at a meeting on July 8, its executive board refused to set a strike date. Moreover, on August 7, the union dropped its opposition to mandatory drug testing. The following day, both sides showed that progress was being made by agreeing to settle several minor issues, including raising the minimum salary from $200,000 to $300,000.

Still, negotiations on the major issues separating the two sides seemed to be stalled despite a plea from 40 members of the Hall of Fame to submit the dispute to mediation. The union's executive board again declined to set a strike date on August 12, but during a conference call four days later, the board voted to strike on August 30 if no agreement had been reached. With this threat hanging over the game's head, progress came quicker than it had before. Both sides presented new ideas on the basic issues: the payroll threshold at which a luxury tax might take effect, the tax rate on the portion of payrolls above that threshold, the percentage of local revenues to be shared and the way these revenues would be split. By late August, published reports, trying to measure how close the sides had come by figuring the total amount of money to be transferred, suggested that the parties were quite close to an agreement. In addition, both sides agreed to a drug-testing plan.

THE NEW AGREEMENT

Settlement came on the morning of August 30, just a few hours before a game between the Cardinals and the Chicago Cubs that would have been the first one cancelled by a strike. The agreement, retroactive to the start of the 2002 season and expiring on December 19, 2006, included the following major provisions:

• no luxury tax in 2002; a tax threshold of $117 million in 2003, $120.5 million in 2004, $128 million in 2005 and $136.5 million in 2006;

• luxury tax rates of 17.5 percent in 2003, 22.5 percent in 2004 for first-time violators and 30 percent for second-time violators; 22.5 percent for first-time violators in 2005, 30 percent for second-time violators and 40 percent for third-time violators; no tax for first-time violators in 2006, 30 percent for second-time violators and 40 percent for third- and fourth-time violators;

• sharing of local revenues at 34 percent using the straight pool approach;

• random testing of all players for illegal steroids during the 2003 season, but not the offseason, with random testing to continue during the next two seasons if five percent of the players test positive.

In addition, the sides agreed to set a $300,000 minimum salary for 2003 and 2004 with cost-of-living raises in 2005 and 2006; to establish a joint committee for the proposed worldwide draft; to retain the existing system of salary arbitration; and to maintain the existing number of clubs through the 2006 season.

The owners ratified this deal on September 5 by a vote of 29-1, with the Yankees voting no. The parties signed a memorandum of understanding outlining terms of the deal on October 1, at which time the players ratified the agreement.

UMPIRES AT ODDS WITH MLB

In January, both MLB and the umpires' union appealed U.S. District Court Judge Harvey Bartle III's ruling from December 2001, upholding the decision of arbitrator Alan Symonette ordering the rehiring of nine of the 22 umpires dismissed in 1999 following their failed mass resignation orchestrated by the Major League Umpires Association. MLB argued against rehiring any of the nine while the union wanted all 22 reinstated. A month later, baseball agreed to rehire five of the 22 (Gary Darling, Bill Hohn, Larry Poncino, Larry Vanover and Joe West) and to allow four to retire (Drew Coble, Greg Kosc, Frank Pulli and Terry Tata). Bartle's ruling upheld the termination of 10 umpires (Bob Davidson, Tom Hallion, Jim Evans, Dale Ford, Richie Garcia, Eric Gregg, Ed Hickox, Mark Johnson, Ken Kaiser and Larry McCoy), and ordered new arbitration hearings for Bruce Dreckman, Sam Holbrook and Paul Nauert. In August, these three were also rehired. Lawyers for the dismissed 10 appealed their case before the 3rd U.S. Circuit Court of Appeals in December.

The Associated Press reported that baseball officials had sent umpire John Hirschbeck a warning letter on May 10, accusing him of misconduct in a game played on April 28. The letter alleged that Hirschbeck had told the plate umpire that day to refrain from issuing warnings to pitchers who might throw brushback pitches and also accused him of a poor performance behind the plate during a game on May 4. The World Umpires Association, successor union to the MLUA, attempted to file a grievance over this matter on May 29, but baseball sued the union, arguing that the matter was a disciplinary procedure not subject to arbitration.

The WUA also continued to oppose MLB's use of Questec, Inc.'s Umpire Information System, a computer system designed to analyze the accuracy of umpires' calls of balls and strikes. Upset that baseball had not provided sufficient information on how the Questec system works, the union filed a grievance asking that the American Arbitration Association resolve the dispute, and in September, the union filed unfair labor practice charges with the National Labor Relations Board.

CINERGY FIELD CLOSES; ENRON RENAMED

The Reds played their final game at Cinergy Field on September 22, losing to the Phillies, 4-3, before a crowd of 40,964. Known as Riverfront Stadium when it opened in 1970, Cinergy Field will be replaced in 2003 by the Great American Ball Park. Enron Field, home to the Houston Astros, became Astros Field, pursuant to the bankruptcy of Enron Corporation, and then Minute Maid Park.

SIXTH YEAR OF INTERLEAGUE PLAY

Regular-season games between A.L. and N.L. clubs continued for the sixth consecutive season, but with a difference. For the first time, teams did not play most interleague games against teams in the corresponding division of the other league. Rather, teams in the A.L. East played most of their games against the N.L. West, A.L. Central teams played the N.L. East, and A.L. West teams played the

N.L. Central. There was one period of interleague play, June 7-23, followed by a short break and then a final weekend of interleague series. The schedule had all teams playing 18 interleague games, except for N.L. Central teams, which each played 12.

Overall, N.L. teams won 129 games and lost 123, increasing their slim lead, 726-718, in total interleague play. Oakland compiled the best interleague mark among A.L. teams (16-2) while the Red Sox and Kansas City Royals won only five games each. In the N.L., the Atlanta Braves finished with the best record (15-3), and the Reds and Brewers finished worst (2-10). Attendance during the interleague period averaged 31,962, down from 2001's 33,703, but was 19.7 percent higher than the average for intraleague games played to that point in the season.

TED WILLIAMS DIES

Ted Williams, generally regarded as one of the greatest hitters the game has ever seen and the last man to hit .400 in a season, died at Citrus Memorial Hospital in Inverness, Florida, on July 5. He was 83. Following the Hall of Famer's death a dispute about the disposition of his body arose among his three children. Williams' 1996 will had expressed a desire for cremation, and Bobby-Jo Williams Ferrell fought to have this intention fulfilled. Claudia and John Henry Williams alleged that at a later date, Williams had chosen to have his body cryonically frozen and that they had agreed to have their bodies frozen, too. A court fight ensued, during which a document apparently bearing Williams' handwritten preference for cryonics proved to be decisive. In December, Ferrell dropped her objections to her siblings' preference after a judge ruled that a trust controlling part of Williams' estate be divided equally among the three children.

ATLANTA WINS DIVISION AGAIN

The Braves won the N.L. East title for the eighth year in a row. Leaving aside the incomplete 1994 season, Atlanta has now won an unprecedented 11 straight division crowns. The Braves had an easy time of it as none of their opponents mounted a sustained challenge. Atlanta led the Expos by 8.5 games at the end of June, the Mets by 13.5 games at the end of July and the Phillies by 17 games at the end of August. The Braves clinched the title on September 9, even though idle, when New York beat Philadelphia. Bobby Cox was named TSN's N.L. Manager of the Year.

The Braves' offense was again led by Chipper Jones, who hit .327 (fifth in the N.L.) with 26 home runs and 100 runs batted in, and Andruw Jones, who added 35 homers and 94 RBIs despite batting only .264. Gary Sheffield, acquired in an offseason trade with the Los Angeles Dodgers, hit .307 with 25 homers and 84 RBIs.

Atlanta's pitching staff led the league in ERA again (3.13) and batting-average-against (.240). Tom Glavine and Kevin Millwood each won 18 games (tied for fourth in the league), and Glavine finished third in ERA (2.96). Greg Maddux won 16 games, joining Cy Young as the only pitchers to win 15 or more games in 15 consecutive seasons, and was second in ERA (2.62). John Smoltz, TSN's N.L. Relief Pitcher of the Year, set a league record with 55 saves.

CARDINALS TAKE N.L. CENTRAL TITLE

Overcoming the trauma associated with the deaths of longtime announcer Jack Buck on June 18 and pitcher Darryl Kile on June 22, St. Louis won the division title outright after tying for first place in 2001 and settling for the wild-card spot in the playoffs. The Cardinals did not take over first place by themselves until June 18 (in a game won by Kile), but after that, they were never headed. They led the division by five games at the end of July and by four at the end of August. A record of 21-6 in September enabled them to clinch the title on September 20 and finish with a margin of 13 games over the Astros.

The St. Louis offense was again led by Albert Pujols, who batted .314 with 34 home runs and 127 runs batted in (second in the league). Jim Edmonds hit .311 with 28 homers and 83 RBIs, and Edgar Renteria batted .305 with 83 RBIs. Tino Martinez hit 21 homers, and Scott Rolen added 14 after arriving via trade from Philadelphia on July 29.

The Cardinals used 14 starting pitchers with only one, Matt Morris, starting more than 30 games. Twenty-one pitchers earned victories, but only two reached double digits in wins. Morris won 17, and rookie Jason Simontacchi won 11. Jason Isringhausen had 32 saves.

ARIZONA RETAINS N.L. WEST FLAG

The defending World Series champions won their second consecutive division title in a close battle with the Dodgers and the hard-charging Giants. The Diamondbacks led the division by five games at the end of July and six at the end of August, but they did not clinch the flag until September 28 when they beat the Rockies.

Arizona led the league in runs scored despite having no player with outstanding offensive numbers. Junior Spivey batted .301, Luis Gonzalez hit 28 home runs and drove in 103 runs, and Steve Finley added 25 homers and 89 RBIs.

Randy Johnson and Curt Schilling again headed the Diamondbacks' pitching staff. Johnson led the league in wins (24), ERA (2.32), strikeouts (334), innings pitched (260), winning percentage (.828) and batting-average-against (.208), and he was second in shutouts with four. Schilling had 23 wins, a 3.23 ERA, 316 strikeouts, 259.1 innings pitched, a .767 winning percentage and an opponents' batting average of .224. He was named TSN's N.L. Pitcher of the Year. Byung-Hyun Kim had 36 saves.

GIANTS GRAB WILD CARD

After losing the race for the wild card in 2001 by three games, San Francisco captured it in 2002, edging out the Dodgers by 3.5 games. The Giants spent most of the season's opening month in first place, but fell into third place for an extended stretch and did not reach second place (and the lead in the wild-card chase) until September 9. Finishing the season with an eight-game winning streak, they clinched the wild card on September 28 by defeating Houston, 5-2. Bonds led the San Francisco offense. He hit .370 with 46 home runs (second in the league) and 110 runs batted in. Jeff Kent (.313, 37, 108), Reggie Sanders (23 HRs and 85 RBIs) and David Bell (20 HRs and 73 RBIs) supplemented the attack. Kirk Rueter and Russ Ortiz each won 14 games, and Ryan Jensen and Jason Schmidt each won 13. The Giants finished second in the N.L. in ERA. Robb Nen saved 43 games, fifth best in the league.

YANKEES WIN FIFTH STRAIGHT

The Yankees won their fifth consecutive A.L. East title and their sixth in seven seasons. Like the previous year, they trailed the Red Sox for most of the first half, moving into first place for good on June 28. They led Boston by four games at the end of July, 8.5 games at the end of August and 10.5 games when the season was over. New York clinched the division on September 21, beating the Detroit Tigers, 3-2.

The Yankees' offense was led by free-agent acquisition Jason Giambi, who hit .314 with 41 home runs and 122 runs batted in. Alfonso Soriano complemented Giambi, batting .300 with 39 homers and 102 RBIs. Bernie Williams hit .333 (third in the league) and drove in 102 runs, Robin Ventura hit 27 homers and drove in 93 runs and Jorge Posada hit 20 homers with 99 RBIs. Soriano led the league with 128 runs scored and 41 stolen bases.

David Wells led the New York pitching staff with 19 wins. Mike Mussina added 18, and Andy Pettitte and Roger Clemens each had 13. Mariano Rivera, on the 15-day disabled list three times, recorded a career-low 28 saves.

TWINS NAB A.L. CENTRAL CROWN

Despite the uncertainties surrounding baseball's plan to contract two clubs, Minnesota won its first division title since 1991 with surprising ease. The Twins led the Chicago White Sox by 2.5 games at the end of May, six games at the end of June, 14 games at the end of July and 14 games at the end of August. They clinched the division title on September 15 when they beat the Cleveland Indians and New York defeated Chicago.

Minnesota's offensive leaders were outfielders Jacque Jones and Torii Hunter, both also superb defensive players. Jones batted .300 with 27 home runs and 85 runs batted in. Hunter hit .289 with 29 home runs and 94 RBIs. Rick Reed led the pitching staff with 15 wins. Kyle Lohse and Eric Milton each added 13. Eddie Guardado led the A.L. in saves with 45.

OAKLAND WINS A.L. WEST TITLE

Oakland won 103 games, tying the Yankees for most wins in either league, and took the division crown by four games over the Angels. The A's were in fourth place, 10 games behind the Seattle Mariners, as late as May 23. They went 83-33 thereafter, the best record in baseball over that span, and reached first place on August 22. Battling Anaheim down to the wire, Oakland won three out of four games from the Angels in mid-September and clinched the division on September 26 by beating Seattle in 10 innings, 5-3.

The As' offense was led by shortstop Miguel Tejada, who batted .308 with 34 home runs and 131 runs batted in, third in the league. Eric Chavez added 34 homers and 109 RBIs, and Jermaine Dye hit 24 home runs with 86 runs batted in.

Barry Zito led the A.L. in wins with 23 and was third in ERA (2.75). He was named TSN's A.L. Pitcher of the Year. Mark Mulder won 19 games, and Tim Hudson added 15. The A's led the league in ERA (3.68) and shutouts (19) and were third lowest in opponents' batting average (.252). Billy Koch saved 44 games, second best in the league, and was named TSN's A.L. Reliever of the Year.

ANGELS TAKE WILD CARD

Led by Mike Scioscia, TSN's A.L. Manager of the Year, Anaheim won the wild card spot in the playoffs, clinching it on September 26 by beating the Texas Rangers, 10-5. The Angels won 99 games, 24 more than in 2001 when they finished 41 games behind the Mariners. A dozen wins came when the team trailed after six innings. The Angels stood alone in first place as late as September 17, but settled for the wild card ahead of the Mariners and the Red Sox. Anaheim led the league in batting (.282) and was fourth in runs scored. Adam Kennedy batted .312, Troy Glaus hit 30 home runs, and Garret Anderson drove in 123 runs. Tim Salmon hit .286 with 22 homers and 88 RBIs and was named TSN's A.L. Comeback Player of the Year. Jarrod Washburn won 18 games with a 3.15 ERA. Ramon Ortiz had 15 wins, and Kevin Appier added 14. Troy Percival saved 40 games, tied for third in the league.

DIVISION SERIES WINNERS

All four best-of-five division series were won by the teams opening on the road. In the N.L., the Cardinals swept the Diamondbacks, and the Giants overcame a 2-1 deficit to defeat the Braves. In the A.L., the Angels dropped the first game to the Yankees and then won three straight, and the Twins ousted the A's after being down two games to one.

GIANTS DEFEAT CARDS IN FIVE

In the N.L. Championship Series, the Giants won the first two games in St. Louis. Rueter beat Morris in Game 1, 9-6, thanks to home runs from Lofton, Bell and Benito Santiago. In Game 2, Schmidt pitched shutout ball into the eighth, and Rich Aurilia homered twice in a 4-1 victory.

When the series shifted to Pac Bell Park, the Cardinals overcame Bonds' fourth postseason homer in Game 3 with three of their own, including the game winner in the sixth inning by Eli Marrero, to win, 5-4. The Giants won Game 4, 4-3, as Bonds scored twice after being walked, once intentionally. With two out in the sixth, J.T. Snow doubled Kent and Bonds home to tie the score, 2-2. In the eighth, Santiago hit a two-out, two-run homer with Bonds aboard to give San Francisco a 4-2 lead. Rueter faced Morris again in Game 5 and beat him again, 2-1. St. Louis took a 1-0 lead in the seventh when Fernando Vina drove in Mike Matheny on a sacrifice fly. The Giants tied the game in the eighth when Bonds' sacrifice fly scored Lofton and won it with two out in the ninth when Lofton singled home Bell. San Francisco thus advanced to the World Series for the first time since 1989.

ANGELS BEAT TWINS IN FIVE

Minnesota and Anaheim split the first two games of the A.L. Championship Series. The Twins won Game 1 at home, 2-1, with Joe Mays besting Appier. Anaheim managed only four hits and one unearned run. The Twins scored the winning run in the fifth when Corey Koskie doubled home Luis Rivas. The Angels jumped on Reed in Game 2, with home runs from Erstad and Brad Fullmer, to win, 6-3.

When the series moved to Anaheim, the Angels eked out a 2-1 win in Game 3 on homers by Anderson in the second and Glaus in the eighth. Washburn struck out seven and yielded only one run in seven innings. Game 4, matching Anaheim rookie John Lackey against Brad Radke, was scoreless until the Angels scored a pair of runs in the seventh and five in the eighth to win, 7-1. Minnesota took a 2-0 lead in Game 5 behind Mays and had a 5-3 lead, but crumbled when Anaheim scored 10 runs in the seventh. Kennedy hit three home runs and drove in five runs as the Angels triumphed, 13-5. Anaheim thus advanced to the World Series for the first time in its 42-year history.

ANAHEIM WINS FIRST SERIES

The Series opened in Anaheim with Washburn opposing Schmidt in a game that featured five home runs. Bonds and Sanders connected for San Francisco in the top of the second inning, and Glaus answered them in the same inning. Snow homered with one on in the sixth, and Glaus answered again. Kennedy drove in another run with a single, but the Giants' bullpen preserved the 4-3 lead. Game 2 was a slugfest that Anaheim won, 11-10, as Salmon hit a pair of two-run homers. The Angels opened the scoring with five runs in the first, but in the second, Sanders' three-run homer and Bell's with none on cut the lead to 5-4. Salmon hit his first home run in the second, but Kent answered for the Giants in the third. San Francisco added four more runs in the fifth to take the lead, but Anaheim tied the score with single runs in the fifth and sixth. Salmon's homer in the eighth gave the Angels a two-run margin that Bonds' solo homer in the ninth did not overcome. The 11 homers hit by the two teams in the first two games caused pitchers to complain that the balls being used in the Series were "juiced," with the interior yarn wound tighter and the cowhide exterior stretched a bit more than balls used during the regular season.

Anaheim pounded the ball again in Game 3, getting 16 hits, as the Series shifted to San Francisco. After yielding a run in the first, the Angels tallied four in the third on a walk, a double, an error, a single and a triple by Scott Spiezio. They added four more in the fourth on a single, a walk, a double steal, a groundout, a walk and three singles. The Giants rebounded in the fifth as Aurilia homered and Bonds homered with Kent on, but Anaheim scored single runs in the sixth and eighth to salt away a 10-4 win. Rueter battled Lackey in Game 4, as the pitchers regained the upper hand, and the Giants tied the Series at two games each. Anaheim jumped to a 3-0 lead with two runs scoring on Glaus' homer in the third, but Rueter and three relievers shut the Angels down after that. San Francisco tied the score in the fifth on three singles, a sacrifice fly, an error, a walk and another single and won the game, 4-3, in the eighth when Snow singled, went to second on a passed ball and scored on a single by Bell. The Giants won Game 5, 16-4, as well. They scored three runs in the first and three more in the second, two in the sixth and four each in the seventh and eighth. Lofton, Kent and Bonds had three hits apiece with Kent driving in four runs on a double and two homers while Santiago and Aurilia drove in three each. Schmidt pitched only into the fifth, but four relievers yielded only three Angels hits. A near-accident involving 3-year-old Darren Baker, son of manager Dusty Baker and one of the Giants' batboys, caused general managers in December to ask the commissioner to set a minimum age for batboys consistent with existing child labor laws.

Back in Anaheim for Game 6, the Giants came within six outs of winning their first World Series since 1954. Powered by a two-run homer by Shawon Dunston and another homer by Bonds, San Francisco took a 5-0 lead into the seventh. But Spiezio greeted reliever Felix Rodriguez with a three-run home run, and the Angels scored three more times in the eighth to win, 6-5. Erstad hit a home run, and Glaus doubled in the tying and winning runs. The following night, Lackey became the second rookie to start and win a seventh game as Anaheim defeated the Giants, 4-1. San Francisco opened the scoring in the second on Sanders' sacrifice fly, but the Angels tied the score in the same inning when Bengie Molina doubled home Spiezio. In the third, Anderson doubled home three runs, giving his team all the runs it would need. Lackey pitched five innings, and the bullpen surrendered only two hits as the Angels won the first Series in their history, which dates from 1961.

The size of a World Series share paid to players on the winning team fell for the fourth year in a row. The Angels voted 42 full World Series shares, each worth $272,147.47, 14 partial shares and eight cash awards. The Giants voted 40 full shares, each worth $186,185.62, 15 partial shares and 14 cash awards. Television ratings for the Series hit an all-time low, finishing four percent worse than the 2000 Mets-Yankees Series, the previous low.

OTHER FEATS AND EVENTS

Picking up where he left off in 2001, Bonds hit two home runs in the Giants' first game of the season, the 568th and 569th of his career. He then hit two more in the second game of the season, and later passed Harmon Killebrew (573), Mark McGwire (583) and Frank Robinson (586) to reach fourth place on the all-time list. He hit number 600 on August 9 off Kip Wells of the Pittsburgh Pirates and finished the year with 613. In addition, Bonds set another slew of major league records, including highest on-base percentage (.582), most walks (198), most intentional walks (68), and several N.L. records, including highest career slugging percentage (.595), most consecutive seasons with 30 or more home runs (11) and most consecutive games with one or more walks (18). Seattle's Mike Cameron and the Dodgers' Shawn Green became the first pair of players to hit four home runs in a game in the same season. Cameron hit his against the White Sox on May 2, and Green hit his on May 23 against the Brewers. Cameron was the fifth batter to achieve this feat in four consecutive at-bats. Atlanta's Andruw Jones also hit four consecutive home runs, but his were spread over two games, September 7 and 10.

Derek Lowe of the Red Sox won 21 games and pitched a no-hitter on April 27 against the Tampa Bay Devil Rays, winning 10-0. He allowed only one base runner, a walk to Brent Abernathy in the third inning, and struck out six. Rickey Henderson, also with the Red Sox, added to his major league records for most career stolen bases (1,403), most career caught stealing (335), most career walks (2,179) and most career runs (2,288).

Sammy Sosa of the Cubs led the N.L. in home runs with 49, and Houston's Lance Berkman led with N.L. with 128 RBIs. Luis Castillo of the Marlins had a 35-game hitting streak and led the N.L. in stolen bases with 48. Mark Bellhorn of the Cubs became the first player in N.L. history to hit home runs from both sides of the plate in the same inning, doing so in the fourth inning on August 29 against the Brewers. Boston's Manny Ramirez led the A.L. in batting (.349), and Alex Rodriguez of the Rangers won his second straight home run title (57) and led the league in RBIs with 142.

The All-Star Game, played in Milwaukee on July 9, was called after 11 innings with the score tied, 7-7. Commissioner Selig, in consultation with the managers and other officials, made the unpopular decision after the teams, committed to getting every player into the game, had run out of pitchers and catchers.

Early in the year, Bob Watson, MLB's vice president of on-field operations, announced seven policy changes designed to quicken the pace of the game. Among the adjustments: managers to signal pitching changes from the top step of the dugout before they step onto the field; pitchers to deliver each pitch within 12 seconds after stepping on the rubber; batters not to get an automatic timeout by stepping out of the batter's box to disrupt the pitcher; theme music for batters to be limited to 5-8 seconds; batters to take two bats with them to the on-deck circle in case one is broken; games to resume within seconds after the end of a commercial break; and pregame ceremonies to conclude five minutes before game time. The average length of a nine-inning game fell two minutes to 2:52.

ATTENDANCE DROPS

According to figures released in November, major league baseball games drew 67,859,176 fans, down more than six percent from 2001. Average attendance, 28,134, dropped below the 30,000-mark for the first time in three years. N.L. teams drew 36,948,707 to their home games while A.L. teams attracted 30,910,469 to theirs.

Six teams drew more than three million fans: Seattle (which led both leagues with 3,540,482) and New York in the A.L., and San Francisco, Arizona, Los Angeles and St. Louis in the N.L. Twelve other teams exceeded the two-million mark, including Colorado, which fell below three million for the first time, and all other clubs except Florida (813,111) and Montreal (732,901) drew at least one million.

Ten teams saw attendance rise, led by the Angels (up 304,648). The Brewers, in their second season at Miller Park, declined the most, down 841,348 to 1,969,693.

MANAGERIAL CHANGES

The Twins began an unusual year on the managerial merry-go-round by hiring Ron Gardenhire on January 4 to replace the retired Tom Kelly. Thereafter, 16 other teams changed managers, beginning with those whose ownership changed at the start of the year. On February 12, Jeff Torborg moved from the Expos to the Marlins when

Robinson became manager of the Expos. Boston's new owners fired Joe Kerrigan on March 5, replacing him temporarily with third base coach Mike Cubbage and then hiring Cleveland bench coach Grady Little on March 11. He guided Boston to second place in the A.L. East with a 93-69 record. Just a week into the season, the Tigers (0-6) fired Phil Garner and named bench coach Luis Pujols to replace him. After the team finished last in the A.L. Central (55-106), Pujols was fired on September 30 and replaced by San Diego coach and former Tigers star Alan Trammell on October 9. Milwaukee fired Davey Lopes on April 18 with the team last in the N.L. Central (3-12) and replaced him with bench coach Jerry Royster, who was fired on October 2 after the team finished last (56-106); Royster was replaced by Atlanta third base coach Ned Yost on October 29. The Rockies, last in the N.L. West, fired Buddy Bell on April 26 and replaced him with hitting coach Clint Hurdle. He led the team to a fourth-place finish (73-89). The Royals fired Tony Muser on April 29 with the team in fourth place in the A.L. Central (8-15). John Mizerock was named interim manager, and Houston bench coach Tony Pena was named manager on May 15. He guided the team to a fourth-place finish (62-100).

The Toronto Blue Jays, fourth in the A.L. East (20-33), fired Buck Martinez on June 3. They named third base coach Carlos Tosca as his replacement and finished third at 78-84. The Cubs fired Don Baylor on July 5 with the team fifth in the N.L. Central (34-49) and replaced him with Bruce Kimm, manager of their Class AAA club. Kimm was fired on the morning of the last day of the season, but he chose to manage the team during its final game. The Cubs finished fifth at 67-95. The Indians fired Charlie Manuel on July 11 with the team in third place in the A.L. Central (39-47) and replaced him with third base coach Joel Skinner on an interim basis. He led the team to a third-place finish (74-88) and was replaced on October 29 by Eric Wedge, manager of Cleveland's Class AAA club.

Three other teams discharged their managers at the close of the season. The Rangers fired Jerry Narron after they finished last in the A.L. West (72-90), the Mets fired Bobby Valentine after they finished last in the N.L. East (75-86) and the Devil Rays fired Hal McRae after they finished last in the A.L. East (55-106). Texas hired former Yankees and Diamondbacks manager Buck Showalter on October 11, and the Mets hired Oakland manager Art Howe on October 28. The next day, Oakland promoted bench coach Ken Macha as its manager, and Tampa Bay hired Seattle manager Lou Piniella after securing the right to negotiate with him by trading outfielder Randy Winn to the Mariners.

The Giants allowed Baker's contract to expire on November 6, marking the first time that a World Series manager left his team since Dick Williams resigned from Oakland in 1973. The Giants replaced Baker with former Expos manager Felipe Alou on November 13. The Mariners hired Arizona bench coach Bob Melvin to replace Piniella on November 15, and Baker agreed to manage the Cubs on the same day.

FIVE ARBITRATION CASES

Ninety-three players filed for salary arbitration, but only five cases proceeded through the hearing and decision stage. Teams exchanged figures with 42 players. The Yankees' Posada was the year's big winner. He asked for a salary of $7.75 million versus New York's offer of $6.7 million and then avoided a hearing by signing a five-year, $51 million contract. The Phillies and Rolen signed a one-year contract for $8.6 million, the largest single-season deal for a position player eligible for arbitration.

Pitcher Dennys Reyes of the Rockies was the only player to win his case. He asked for and won a salary of

$900,000 against Colorado's $700,000 offer. Rolando Arrojo, Orlando Cabrera, Neifi Perez and Esteban Yan lost their cases. These decisions gave the owners a cumulative record of 254-192 since salary arbitration began in 1974.

The players who filed earned an average increase of 130 percent, down from 144 percent in 2001. The 93 received an average salary of $2,717,661, breaking the previous mark of $2,646,444 set in 2001. Minnesota's Mays got the largest increase. He made $260,000 in 2001 and signed a four-year, $20 million contract, a 19-fold raise. The Reds' Scott Williamson, who signed for $400,000, was the only player not to get any increase.

SALARIES RISE

According to figures compiled by the Players Association and released by the Associated Press in December, the average major league salary rose 7.3 percent to $2,295,694, the smallest increase since 1998.

FINAL STANDINGS

AMERICAN LEAGUE

EAST DIVISION

Team	N.Y.	Bos.	Tor.	Bal.	T.B.	Min.	Chi.	Cle.	K.C.	Det.	Oak.	Ana.	Sea.	Tex.	N.L.	W	L	Pct.	GB	LD1st	DIF	Lead
New York	....	10	10	13	13	6	4	6	5	8	5	4	4	4	11-7	103	58	.640	....	9/29	107	10.5
Boston	9	....	13	13	16	3	2	5	4	5	6	4	4	4	5-13	93	69	.574	10.5	6/27	72	5.0
Toronto	9	6	....	15	11	1	2	3	4	6	6	2	3	1	9-9	78	84	.481	25.5	4/2	2	0.0
Baltimore	6	6	4	....	10	5	3	1	7	2	4	2	5	3	9-9	67	95	.414	36.5	4/2	2	0.0
Tampa Bay	5	3	8	9	....	2	3	2	2	4	1	1	4	4	7-11	55	106	.342	48.0	4/5	4	0.5

CENTRAL DIVISION

Team	Min.	Chi.	Cle.	K.C.	Det.	N.Y.	Bos.	Tor.	Bal.	T.B.	Oak.	Ana.	Sea.	Tex.	N.L.	W	L	Pct.	GB	LD1st	DIF	Lead
Minnesota	....	11	14	14	14	0	3	6	1	5	3	5	5	6	10-8	94	67	.584	....	9/29	162	17.0
Chicago	8	....	9	11	12	2	4	4	4	4	2	3	5	5	8-10	81	81	.500	13.5	5/26	15	1.0
Cleveland	8	10	....	9	10	3	4	3	5	4	2	3	3	4	6-12	74	88	.457	20.5	4/19	18	4.0
Kansas City	5	8	10	....	10	1	2	3	0	4	1	3	3	7	5-13	62	100	.383	32.5	....	....	....
Detroit	4	7	9	9	....	1	4	0	4	2	1	1	2	5	6-12	55	106	.342	39.0	....	....	....

WEST DIVISION

Team	Oak.	Ana.	Sea.	Tex.	N.Y.	Bos.	Tor.	Bal.	T.B.	Min.	Chi.	Cle.	K.C.	Det.	N.L.	W	L	Pct.	GB	LD1st	DIF	Lead
Oakland	....	11	8	13	4	3	3	5	8	6	7	5	8	6	16-2	103	59	.636	....	9/29	48	4.0
Anaheim	9	....	9	12	3	3	7	7	8	4	6	6	6	8	11-7	99	63	.611	4.0	9/18	13	1.0
Seattle	11	10	....	13	5	5	6	4	4	4	4	6	5		11-7	93	69	.574	10.0	8/22	131	6.5
Texas	6	7	7	....	3	3	8	6	5	3	4	5	2	4	9-9	72	90	.444	31.0	3/31	1	0.0

NOTE: Read across for wins, down for losses; final standings are shaded.

Abbreviations: LD1st denotes last date in 1st place; DIF denotes days in first place; Lead denotes largest lead.

Clinching dates: New York (East)—September 21; Minnesota (Central)—September 15; Oakland (West)—September 26; Anaheim (wild card)—September 26.

NATIONAL LEAGUE

EAST DIVISION

Team	Atl.	Mon.	Phi.	Fla.	N.Y.	St.L.	Hou.	Cin.	Pit.	Chi.	Mil.	Ari.	S.F.	L.A.	Col.	S.D.	A.L.	W	L	Pct.	GB	LD1st	DIF	Lead
Atlanta	....	13	11	11	12	5	3	4	3	4	5	3	3	2	4	3	15-3	101	59	.631	....	9/29	134	21.5
Montreal	6	....	11	9	11	3	3	5	3	4	2	4	2	2	3		12-6	83	79	.512	19.0	5/2	23	2.0
Philadelphia	7	8	....	9	10	3	4	3	4	2	4	5	3	3	3	2	10-8	80	81	.497	21.5	4/7	3	0.0
Florida	8	10	10	....	8	4	3	1	4	2	4	1	4	3	2	5	10-8	79	83	.488	23.0	5/16	14	2.0
New York	7	8	9	11	....	3	2	4	1	5	5	2	0	2	3	3	10-8	75	86	.466	26.5	5/29	41	2.0

CENTRAL DIVISION

Team	St.L.	Hou.	Cin.	Pit.	Chi.	Mil.	Atl.	Mon.	Phi.	Fla.	N.Y.	Ari.	S.F.	L.A.	Col.	S.D.	A.L.	W	L	Pct.	GB	LD1st	DIF	Lead
St. Louis	....	13	11	11	12	10	1	3	2	2	3	4	4	4	4	5	8-4	97	65	.599	....	9/29	115	13.0
Houston	6	....	11	11	11	10	3	3	3	4	3	1	3	3	4	5	5-7	84	78	.519	13.0	4/4	2	0.0
Cincinnati	8	6	....	11	12	13	2	1	2	5	2	0	2	4	3	5	2-10	78	84	.481	19.0	6/17	57	5.0
Pittsburgh	6	6	7	....	9	15	3	3	8	2	4	2	2	2	2	2	3-9	72	89	.447	24.5	4/25	18	2.5
Chicago	6	8	5	10	....	7	2	3	2	4	1	2	3	2	4	2	6-6	67	95	.414	30.0	4/3	1	0.0
Milwaukee	7	8	6	4	10	....	1	2	1	2	1	2	1	1	1	3	2-10	56	106	.346	41.0	4/3	2	0.0

WEST DIVISION

Team	Ari.	S.F.	L.A.	Col.	S.D.	Atl.	Mon.	Phi.	Fla.	N.Y.	St.L.	Hou.	Cin.	Pit.	Chi.	Mil.	A.L.	W	L	Pct.	GB	LD1st	DIF	Lead
Arizona	....	8	9	14	12	3	4	4	5	5	2	3	6	4	4	4	11-7	98	64	.605	....	9/29	129	9.0
San Fran.	11	....	11	11	14	3	2	3	3	6	2	5	4	4	3	5	8-10	95	66	.590	2.5	5/15	33	3.0
Los Angeles	10	8	....	12	10	4	5	4	3	4	2	3	2	4		5	12-6	92	70	.568	6.0	7/15	29	3.5
Colorado	5	8	7	....	11	3	4	3	3	2	4	2	3				7-11	73	89	.451	25.0	....	....	....
San Diego	7	5	9	8	....	3	4	4	1	4	1	2	1	4	4	1	8-10	66	96	.407	32.0	....	....	....

NOTE: Read across for wins, down for losses; final standings are shaded.

Tie game—San Francisco at Atlanta (3-3), August 15 (10 innings).

Abbreviations: LD1st denotes last date in 1st place; DIF denotes days in first place; Lead denotes largest lead.

Clinching dates: Atlanta (East)—September 9; St. Louis (Central)—September 20; Arizona (West)—September 28; San Francisco (wild card)—September 28.

(Salary figure calculations, it should be noted, can differ, depending on what factors are included.) The Yankees had the highest average salary for the fourth consecutive year, $4,902,777, and the Devil Rays had the lowest, $1,131,474.

RETIREMENTS

After a 23-year major league career that began with the Expos in 1979 and later took him to five other teams, Tim Raines announced his retirement on September 29. Raines, who played in four league championship series, two World Series and seven All-Star Games, leaves as the fifth most prolific base stealer (808) in baseball history.

After a major league broadcasting career spanning 55 years, 42 of them with the Tigers, Ernie Harwell retired following the season. Winner of the 1981 Ford C. Frick Award, Harwell, 84, got his first major league job with the Brooklyn Dodgers in 1948. When Red Barber fell ill, Dodgers general manager Branch Rickey secured Harwell's services from the minor league Atlanta Crackers. In exchange, Rickey sent the Crackers catcher Cliff Dapper. Harwell later worked for the New York Giants, where he was the television announcer for Bobby Thomson's famed home run in the 1951 N.L. playoff, and the Baltimore Orioles.

CONCLUSION

When Donald M. Fehr, executive director and general counsel of the Players Association, commented on the agreement between the owners and the union, he said, "Hopefully, what we're going to going to end up with is a lot of focus back on the game."

INTERLEAGUE RECORDS

AMERICAN LEAGUE

EAST DIVISION

A.L. team vs.	Ari.	Atl.	Chi.	Cin.	Col.	Fla.	Hou.	L.A.	Mil.	Mon.	N.Y.	Phi.	Pit.	St.L.	S.D.	S.F.	W	L	Pct.
New York	2-1				2-1						3-3				2-1	2-1	11	7	.611
Boston	0-3	1-5			2-1			0-3							2-1		5	13	.278
Toronto	2-1			3-0				1-2	2-4							1-2	9	9	.500
Baltimore	1-2							1-2				3-3			2-1	1-2	9	9	.500
Tampa Bay					0-3	4-2		1-2							1-2	1-2	7	11	.389

CENTRAL DIVISION

A.L. team vs.	Ari.	Atl.	Chi.	Cin.	Col.	Fla.	Hou.	L.A.	Mil.	Mon.	N.Y.	Phi.	Pit.	St.L.	S.D.	S.F.	W	L	Pct.
Minnesota		1-2			2-1		4-2			1-2	2-1						10	8	.556
Chicago		0-3	3-3						1-2	2-1	2-1						8	10	.444
Cleveland	1-2			2-1	0-3				1-2	2-1	1-2						6	12	.333
Kansas City					1-2				0-3	1-2				1-5	2-1		5	13	.278
Detroit	1-2	1-2			1-2					2-1			0-3	1-2			6	12	.333

WEST DIVISION

A.L. team vs.	Ari.	Atl.	Chi.	Cin.	Col.	Fla.	Hou.	L.A.	Mil.	Mon.	N.Y.	Phi.	Pit.	St.L.	S.D.	S.F.	W	L	Pct.
Oakland			3-0				3-0		3-0			3-0				4-2	16	2	.889
Anaheim			2-1					3-3	3-0			2-1	1-2				11	7	.611
Seattle			1-2	3-0	2-1		2-1							2-1	1-2		11	7	.611
Texas		0-3	2-1	2-1			2-4						3-0				9	9	.500

NOTE: Teams are listed in order of their final standings, not by their interleague records.

NATIONAL LEAGUE

EAST DIVISION

N.L. team vs.	Ana.	Bal.	Bos.	Chi.	Cle.	Det.	K.C.	Min.	N.Y.	Oak.	Sea.	T.B.	Tex.	Tor.	W	L	Pct.
Atlanta			5-1	3-0		2-1		2-1					3-0		15	3	.833
Montreal				2-1	2-1	1-2	3-0							4-2	12	6	.667
Philadelphia		3-3		1-2	2-1	3-0		1-2							10	8	.556
Florida					3-0	2-1	2-1	1-2				2-4			10	8	.556
New York				1-2	2-1			2-1	2-1	3-3					10	8	.556

CENTRAL DIVISION

N.L. team vs.	Ana.	Bal.	Bos.	Chi.	Cle.	Det.	K.C.	Min.	N.Y.	Oak.	Sea.	T.B.	Tex.	Tor.	W	L	Pct.
St. Louis	2-1					5-1				1-2					8	4	.667
Houston							0-3	1-2				4-2			5	7	.417
Cincinnati	1-2						0-3			0-3	0-3		1-2		2	10	.167
Pittsburgh	1-2				2-1					0-3			0-3		3	9	.250
Chicago				3-3							2-1		1-2		6	6	.500
Milwaukee	0-3							2-4		0-3					2	10	.167

WEST DIVISION

N.L. team vs.	Ana.	Bal.	Bos.	Chi.	Cle.	Det.	K.C.	Min.	N.Y.	Oak.	Sea.	T.B.	Tex.	Tor.	W	L	Pct.
Arizona		2-1	3-0		2-1	2-1		1-2						1-2	11	7	.611
San Francisco		1-2						1-2	2-4		2-1		2-1		8	10	.444
Los Angeles	3-3	2-1	3-0								2-1		2-1		12	6	.667
Colorado			1-2	1-2				1-2	1-2		3-0		0-3		7	11	.389
San Diego		1-2	1-2			1-2			2-1		2-1				8	10	.444

NOTE: Teams are listed in order of their final standings, not by their interleague records.

A.L. DIVISION SERIES
MINNESOTA VS. OAKLAND

RESULTS

Day	Date	Place	Score
Tue.	Oct. 1	Oakland	Minnesota 7, Oakland 5
Wed.	Oct. 2	Oakland	Oakland 9, Minnesota 1
Fri.	Oct. 4	Minnesota	Oakland 6, Minnesota 3
Sat.	Oct. 5	Minnesota	Minnesota 11, Oakland 2
Sun.	Oct. 6	Oakland	Minnesota 5, Oakland 4

BOX SCORES
GAME 1

MINNESOTA 7, OAKLAND 5

TUESDAY, OCTOBER 1, AT OAKLAND

Minnesota	AB	R	H	RBI	BB	SO	PO	A
Jones, lf	5	0	1	1	0	2	5	0
Guzman, ss	4	1	2	0	1	0	2	0
Koskie, 3b	5	1	1	3	0	1	0	2
Ortiz, dh	5	0	0	0	0	3	0	0
Hunter, cf	4	1	1	0	1	0	2	0
Mientkiewicz, 1b	5	1	1	1	0	1	8	0
Cuddyer, rf	3	1	2	1	1	0	2	0
Mohr, rf	0	0	0	0	0	0	0	0
Pierzynski, c	4	1	4	1	0	0	7	0
Rivas, 2b	3	1	1	0	0	0	1	1
Radke, p	0	0	0	0	0	0	0	1
Santana, p	0	0	0	0	0	0	0	1
Romero, p	0	0	0	0	0	0	0	2
Guardado, p	0	0	0	0	0	0	0	0
Totals	38	7	13	7	3	7	27	7
Oakland	AB	R	H	RBI	BB	SO	PO	A
Durham, dh	5	1	2	0	0	1	0	0
Hatteberg, 1b	2	2	1	1	1	0	7	0
Saenz, ph-1b	0	0	0	0	1	0	3	0
Velarde, ph-1b	1	0	1	0	0	0	1	0
Tejada, ss	5	1	1	0	0	2	0	2
Chavez, 3b	5	1	2	2	0	0	1	3
Dye, rf	5	0	2	0	0	1	2	0
Justice, lf	5	0	2	1	0	1	0	0
Ellis, 2b	4	0	1	0	1	1	3	4
Long, cf	4	0	0	0	0	0	3	0
Piatt, ph	1	0	0	0	0	0	0	0
Hernandez, c	4	0	0	0	0	1	7	0
Hudson, p	0	0	0	0	0	0	0	1
Lilly, p	0	0	0	0	0	0	0	0
Lidle, p	0	0	0	0	0	0	0	0
Rincon, p	0	0	0	0	0	0	0	0
Mecir, p	0	0	0	0	0	0	0	0
Totals	41	5	12	4	3	7	27	10

Minnesota	0	1	2		0	0	3		1	0	0—7
Oakland	3	2	0		0	0	0		0	0	0—5

Minnesota	IP	H	R	ER	HR	BB	SO
Radke (W)	5.0	8	5	1	0	1	3
Santana	1.2	2	0	0	0	1	2
Romero	1.1	1	0	0	0	0	1
Guardado (S)	1.0	1	0	0	0	1	1
Oakland	IP	H	R	ER	HR	BB	SO
Hudson	5.1	8	4	4	2	2	4
Lilly (L)	0.2	3	2	2	0	1	1
Lidle	1.0	2	1	1	0	0	0
Rincon	1.0	0	0	0	0	0	0
Mecir	1.0	0	0	0	0	0	2

E—Pierzynski, Koskie, C.Guzman. DP—Oakland 1. LOB—Minnesota 8, Oakland 12. Hitting with runners in scoring position—Minnesota 3 for 10, Oakland 4 for 11. 2B—Jones, Hunter, Cuddyer, Durham 2, Ellis. 3B—Pierzynski. HR—Koskie (3rd inning, 1 out, 1 on) off Hudson, Mientkiewicz (6th inning, 0 out, 0 on) off Hudson. SH—Rivas. T—3:44. A—34,853. U—Davis, plate; Meriwether, first; Marquez, second; Cousins, third; West, left field; Diaz, right field.

HOW THEY SCORED

FIRST INNING

Athletics—Durham struck out and was tagged out by Pierzynski after a dropped third strike. Hatteberg walked. Tejada reached first on a fielder's choice and Hatteberg reached second on Guzman's throwing error. Chavez singled to right, scoring Hatteberg. Tejada also scored and Chavez advanced to second on the play when Pierzynski dropped a throw to the plate. Dye grounded out, Koskie to Mientkiewicz. Justice singled to center, scoring Chavez. Ellis struck out. Three runs. Athletics 3, Twins 0.

SECOND INNING

Twins—Hunter doubled to right-center. Mientkiewicz flied to Long as Hunter advanced to third. Cuddyer doubled to left, scoring Hunter. Pierzynski singled to left as Cuddyer advanced to third. Rivas grounded into a double play, Chavez to Ellis to Hatteberg. One run. Athletics 3, Twins 1.
Athletics—Long flied to Cuddyer. Hernandez struck out. Durham doubled to left. Hatteberg singled to the mound, scoring Durham. Tejada reached first on a throwing error by Koskie as Hatteberg advanced to third. Chavez singled to right-center, scoring Hatteberg as Tejada advanced to third. Dye popped to Mientkiewicz. Two runs. Athletics 5, Twins 1.

THIRD INNING

Twins—Jones struck out. Guzman singled to center. Koskie homered to right, scoring Guzman. Ortiz lined to Dye. Hunter walked. Mientkiewicz grounded out, Ellis to Hatteberg. Two runs. Athletics 5, Twins 3.

SIXTH INNING

Twins—Mientkiewicz homered to right. Cuddyer grounded out, Chavez to Hatteberg. Lilly now pitching. Pierzynski singled to left. Rivas singled to left as Pierzynski advanced to second. Jones doubled to left, scoring Pierzynski as Rivas advanced to third. Guzman walked. Koskie grounded out to Hatteberg, scoring Rivas as Jones advanced to third and Guzman to second. Ortiz struck out. Three runs. Twins 6, Athletics 5.

SEVENTH INNING

Twins—Saenz now at first and Lidle pitching. Hunter grounded out, Chavez to Saenz. Mientkiewicz grounded out to Saenz. Cuddyer singled to third. Pierzynski tripled to right-center, scoring Cuddyer. Rivas flied to Long. One run. Twins 7, Athletics 5.

GAME 2

OAKLAND 9, MINNESOTA 1

WEDNESDAY, OCTOBER 2, AT OAKLAND

Minnesota	AB	R	H	RBI	BB	SO	PO	A
Jones, lf	3	0	1	0	0	1	4	0
Mohr, lf	1	0	1	0	0	0	0	0
Guzman, ss	3	1	1	1	0	0	1	2
Koskie, 3b	3	0	0	0	0	1	2	2
LeCroy, dh	4	0	2	0	0	0	0	0
Hunter, cf	3	0	0	0	0	1	1	0
Hocking, rf	1	0	1	0	0	0	0	0
Mientkiewicz, 1b	4	0	0	0	0	0	8	1
Cuddyer, rf	1	0	0	0	1	0	2	0
Kielty, ph-rf-cf	2	0	0	0	0	0	0	0
Pierzynski, c	2	0	0	0	0	1	0	0
Prince, c	2	0	0	0	0	2	4	0
Rivas, 2b	2	0	1	0	1	0	1	2
Mays, p	0	0	0	0	0	0	1	0
Fiore, p	0	0	0	0	0	0	0	1
Lohse, p	0	0	0	0	0	0	0	0
Hawkins, p	0	0	0	0	0	0	0	0
Totals	31	1	7	1	2	5	24	8

Oakland	AB	R	H	RBI	BB	SO	PO	A
Durham, dh	3	3	1	0	1	1	0	0
Hatteberg, 1b	4	1	2	1	0	0	10	0
Mabry, ph-1b	1	0	0	0	0	1	2	0
Tejada, ss	4	1	1	1	1	0	2	1
Chavez, 3b	4	2	2	3	1	1	0	1
Dye, rf	4	1	1	0	1	1	0	0
Justice, lf	5	1	2	3	0	0	1	0
Byrnes, lf	0	0	0	0	0	0	1	0
Ellis, 2b	4	0	3	1	0	0	2	6
Long, cf	4	0	2	0	0	0	4	0
Hernandez, c	4	0	0	0	0	1	5	0
Mulder, p	0	0	0	0	0	0	0	4
Bradford, p	0	0	0	0	0	0	0	1
Koch, p	0	0	0	0	0	0	0	0
Totals	37	9	14	9	4	5	27	13

Minnesota	0	0	0	0	0	1	0	0	0—1
Oakland	3	0	0	5	1	0	0	x—	9

Minnesota	IP	H	R	ER	HR	BB	SO
Mays (L)	3.2	9	6	6	1	2	1
Fiore	1.1	4	3	3	0	2	0
Lohse	2.0	1	0	0	0	0	2
Hawkins	1.0	0	0	0	0	0	2

Oakland	IP	H	R	ER	HR	BB	SO
Mulder (W)	6.0	5	1	1	1	2	3
Bradford	2.0	1	0	0	0	0	1
Koch	1.0	1	0	0	0	0	1

E—Jones. DP—Minnesota 1, Oakland 2. LOB—Minnesota 7, Oakland 9. Hitting with runners in scoring position—Minnesota 0 for 4, Oakland 6 for 15. 2B—Mohr, Durham, Hatteberg, Tejada, Dye, Ellis. 3B—Justice. HR—Chavez (1st inning, 1 out, on 2) off Mays, Guzman (6th inning, 0 out, 0 on) off Mulder. SH—Guzman. WP—Fiore. HBP—Durham by Mays, Koskie by Bradford. T—3:04. A—31,953. U—Meriwether, plate; Marquez, first; Cousins, second; West, third; Diaz, left field; Davis, right field.

HOW THEY SCORED

FIRST INNING
Athletics—Durham walked. Hatteberg doubled to right as Durham advanced to third. Tejada grounded out, Koskie to Mientkiewicz. Chavez homered to right, scoring Durham and Hatteberg. Dye doubled to left. Justice lined into a double play, Mays to Mientkiewicz to Koskie. Three runs. Athletics 3, Twins 0.

FOURTH INNING
Athletics—Hernandez grounded out, Rivas to Mientkiewicz. Durham was hit by a pitch. Hatteberg flied to Hunter. Tejada doubled to left-center, scoring Durham. Chavez was walked intentionally. Fiore now pitching. Dye walked. Justice tripled to right, scoring Tejada, Chavez and Dye. Ellis doubled to right, scoring Justice. Long grounded out, Guzman to Mientkiewicz. Five runs. Athletics 8, Twins 0.

FIFTH INNING
Athletics—Hernandez grounded out, Koskie to Mientkiewicz. Durham doubled to right-center. Durham advanced to third on a wild pitch. Hatteberg singled to first, scoring Durham. Tejada walked. Chavez fouled to Jones. Dye popped to Rivas. One run. Athletics 9, Twins 0.

SIXTH INNING
Twins—Guzman homered to left. Koskie grounded out, Mulder to Hatteberg. LeCroy singled to right. Hunter struck out. Mientkiewicz grounded out to Hatteberg. One run. Athletics 9, Twins 1.

GAME 3

OAKLAND 6, MINNESOTA 3

FRIDAY, OCTOBER 4, AT MINNESOTA

Oakland	AB	R	H	RBI	BB	SO	PO	A
Durham, dh	4	2	1	1	1	1	0	0
Hatteberg, 1b	2	1	2	1	1	0	3	0
Velarde, ph-1b	2	1	1	1	0	1	5	0
Tejada, ss	4	0	0	1	0	2	0	2
Chavez, 3b	4	0	1	0	1	0	4	3
Dye, rf	4	1	1	1	0	2	0	0
Justice, lf	4	0	0	0	0	2	1	0
Ellis, 2b	4	0	1	0	0	0	0	2
Long, cf	3	1	1	1	1	1	2	0
Hernandez, c	4	0	1	0	0	1	10	0
Zito, p	0	0	0	0	0	0	2	0
Rincon, p	0	0	0	0	0	0	0	0
Koch, p	0	0	0	0	0	0	0	0
Totals	35	6	9	6	4	10	27	7

Minnesota	AB	R	H	RBI	BB	SO	PO	A
Jones, lf	4	1	2	0	1	1	5	0
Guzman, ss	4	0	0	0	1	2	0	2
Koskie, 3b	5	1	1	1	0	2	0	1
Ortiz, dh	3	0	0	0	0	1	0	0
Kielty, ph-dh	1	0	0	0	0	0	0	0
Hunter, cf	4	1	2	1	0	0	2	0
Mientkiewicz, 1b	3	0	1	0	1	0	9	0
Cuddyer, rf	4	0	1	0	0	2	0	0
Pierzynski, c	3	0	1	1	1	1	10	0
Rivas, 2b	3	0	0	0	0	1	1	4
Hocking, ph	1	0	0	0	0	0	0	0
Reed, p	0	0	0	0	0	0	0	0
Santana, p	0	0	0	0	0	0	0	0
Jackson, p	0	0	0	0	0	0	0	0
Romero, p	0	0	0	0	0	0	0	0
Hawkins, p	0	0	0	0	0	0	0	0
Totals	35	3	8	3	4	10	27	7

Oakland	2	0	0	1	0	1	2	0	0—6
Minnesota	0	0	0	1	2	0	0	0	0—3

Oakland	IP	H	R	ER	HR	BB	SO
Zito (W)	6.0	5	3	3	0	4	8
Rincon	2.0	2	0	0	0	0	2
Koch (S)	1.0	1	0	0	0	0	0

Minnesota	IP	H	R	ER	HR	BB	SO
Reed (L)	*5.0	6	4	4	4	2	8
Santana	1.1	1	2	2	0	1	0
Jackson	0.2	0	0	0	0	0	0
Romero	1.0	1	0	0	0	1	0
Hawkins	1.0	0	0	0	0	0	2

*Pitched to one batter in sixth.
E—Ellis. DP—Oakland 1. LOB—Oakland 7, Minnesota 9. Hitting with runners in scoring position—Oakland 0 for 2, Minnesota 3 for 11. 2B—Velarde, Jones, Hunter. 3B—Koskie. HR—Durham (1st inning, 0 out, 0 on) off Reed, Hatteberg (1st inning, 0 out, 0 on) off Reed, Long (4th inning, 2 out, 0 on) off Reed, Dye (6th inning, 0 out, 0 on) off Reed. SB—Guzman. S—Tejada. WP—Zito. T—3:26. A—55,932. U—Joyce, plate; Winters, first; McClelland, second; Culbreth, third; Crawford, left field; Eddings, right field.

HOW THEY SCORED

FIRST INNING
Athletics—Durham hit an inside-the-park home run. Hatteberg homered to right-center. Tejada struck out. Chavez flied to Jones. Dye struck out. Two runs. Athletics 2, Twins 0.

FOURTH INNING
Athletics—Justice struck out. Ellis grounded out, Guzman to Mientkiewicz. Long homered to right. Hernandez struck out. One run. Athletics 3, Twins 0.
Twins—Hunter doubled to left. Mientkiewicz singled to left as Hunter advanced to third. Cuddyer struck out. Pierzynski singled to center, scoring Hunter as Mientkiewicz advanced to second. Rivas grounded into a double play, Chavez to Hatteberg. One run. Athletics 3, Twins 1.

FIFTH INNING
Twins—Jones walked. Guzman struck out. Koskie tripled to left, scoring Jones. Ortiz popped to Chavez. Hunter singled to center, scoring Koskie. Mientkiewicz popped to Chavez. Two runs. Athletics 3, Twins 3.

SIXTH INNING
Athletics—Dye homered to left. Santana now pitching. Justice grounded out, Rivas to Mientkiewicz. Ellis popped to Rivas. Long flied to Jones. One run. Athletics 4, Twins 3.

SEVENTH INNING

Athletics—Hernandez grounded out, Rivas to Mientkiewicz. Durham walked. Velarde, pinch-hitting for Hatteberg, doubled to left-center, scoring Durham, and Velarde advanced to third on the throw to the plate. Jackson now pitching. Tejada scored Velarde on a sacrifice fly to Hunter. Chavez singled to left. Dye fouled to Mientkiewicz. Two runs. Athletics 6, Twins 3.

GAME 4

MINNESOTA 11, OAKLAND 2

SATURDAY, OCTOBER 5, AT MINNESOTA

Oakland	AB	R	H	RBI	BB	SO	PO	A
Durham, dh	4	0	0	0	0	1	0	0
Hatteberg, 1b	3	1	1	0	0	0	6	1
Tejada, ss	4	1	1	2	0	1	2	3
Chavez, 3b	4	0	1	0	0	0	0	1
Dye, rf	3	0	3	0	0	0	0	0
Mabry, rf	1	0	0	0	0	0	0	0
Justice, lf	3	0	0	0	0	0	2	1
Piatt, lf	1	0	1	0	0	0	0	0
Ellis, 2b	3	0	0	0	0	1	1	1
Myers, c	1	0	0	0	0	1	2	0
Long, cf	3	0	0	0	0	1	3	0
Byrnes, ph	1	0	0	0	0	1	0	0
Hernandez, c	3	0	0	0	0	0	8	0
Velarde, 2b	0	0	0	0	0	0	0	0
Hudson, p	0	0	0	0	0	0	0	0
Lilly, p	0	0	0	0	0	0	0	0
Bowie, p	0	0	0	0	0	0	0	0
Totals	34	2	7	2	1	6	24	7

Minnesota	AB	R	H	RBI	BB	SO	PO	A
Jones, lf	3	2	1	0	0	1	4	0
Kielty, ph-rf	1	0	0	0	0	1	1	0
Guzman, ss	5	1	0	1	0	1	1	1
Koskie, 3b	4	1	1	1	1	0	0	2
Ortiz, dh	3	0	2	1	0	1	0	0
LeCroy, ph-dh	2	0	0	0	0	2	0	0
Hunter, cf	4	2	2	1	0	1	5	0
Mientkiewicz, 1b	4	2	3	3	0	0	5	1
Cuddyer, rf	3	0	0	0	0	1	1	0
Mohr, rf-lf	1	0	1	0	0	0	1	0
Pierzynski, c	3	2	1	0	1	0	6	0
Rivas, 2b	4	1	1	0	0	1	1	0
Milton, p	0	0	0	0	0	0	2	0
Lohse, p	0	0	0	0	0	0	0	0
Totals	37	11	12	7	2	9	27	4

Oakland	0	0 2	0 0 0	0 0 0—	2
Minnesota	0	0 2	7 0 0	2 0 x—11

Oakland	IP	H	R	ER	HR	BB	SO
Hudson (L)	3.1	5	7	2	0	2	4
Lilly	3.1	7	4	4	1	0	2
Bowie	1.1	0	0	0	0	0	3

Minnesota	IP	H	R	ER	HR	BB	SO
Milton (W)	7.0	6	2	2	1	1	3
Lohse	2.0	1	0	0	0	0	3

E—Hatteberg, Tejada. LOB—Oakland 6, Minnesota 5. Hitting with runners in scoring position—Oakland 0 for 9, Minnesota 4 for 10. 2B—Hatteberg, Dye, Piatt, Jones, Ortiz, Hunter, Rivas. HR—Tejada (3rd inning, 2 out, 1 on) off Milton, Mientkiewicz (7th inning, 0 out, 1 on) off Lilly. WP—Hudson, Lilly. HBP—Jones by Hudson. T—3:20. A—55,960. U—Winters, plate; McClelland, first; Culbreth, second; Crawford, third; Eddings, left field; Joyce, right field.

HOW THEY SCORED

THIRD INNING

Athletics—Hernandez grounded out, Koskie to Mientkiewicz. Durham flied to Hunter. Hatteberg walked. Tejada homered to left, scoring Hatteberg. Chavez flied to Jones. Two runs. Athletics 2, Twins 0.

Twins—Pierzynski singled to left. Rivas struck out. Jones doubled to right as Pierzynski advanced to third. Guzman grounded

out, Tejada to Hatteberg, scoring Pierzynski. Koskie walked. Ortiz doubled to left, scoring Jones as Koskie advanced to third. Hunter grounded out, Chavez to Hatteberg. Two runs. Athletics 2, Twins 2.

FOURTH INNING

Twins—Mientkiewicz singled to center. Cuddyer struck out. Pierzynski walked. Rivas reached first on a fielder's choice and advanced to second on a wild throw by Tejada, attempting to force Mientkiewicz at third. Mientkiewicz scored and Pierzynski advanced to third on the play. Pierzynski scored and Rivas advanced to third on a wild pitch. Jones was hit by a pitch. Guzman reached first on a fielder's choice and Rivas scored on a throwing error by Hatteberg. Jones advanced to second on the play. Lilly now pitching. Koskie singled to center, scoring Jones as Guzman advanced to third. Ortiz struck out. Guzman scored and Koskie advanced to second on a wild pitch. Hunter doubled to left-center, scoring Koskie. Mientkiewicz singled to center, scoring Hunter. Cuddyer flied to Justice. Seven runs. Twins 9, Athletics 2.

SEVENTH INNING

Twins—Hunter singled to center. Mientkiewicz homered to right, scoring Hunter. Mohr singled to right. Pierzynski flied to Long. Rivas doubled to left, but Mohr was thrown out at the plate, Justice to Tejada to Hernandez as Rivas advanced to third. Bowie now pitching. Kielty, pinch-hitting for Jones, struck out. Two runs. Twins 11, Athletics 2.

GAME 5

MINNESOTA 5, OAKLAND 4

SUNDAY, OCTOBER 6, AT OAKLAND

Minnesota	AB	R	H	RBI	BB	SO	PO	A
Jones, lf	5	0	0	0	0	3	2	0
Guzman, ss	5	2	3	0	0	1	1	2
Koskie, 3b	4	0	1	0	1	2	0	3
LeCroy, dh	3	1	2	1	0	1	0	0
Ortiz, ph-dh	2	0	1	1	0	0	0	0
Hunter, cf	5	0	1	0	0	2	2	0
Mientkiewicz, 1b	4	0	0	0	0	0	5	1
Cuddyer, rf	2	0	2	0	1	0	2	0
Mohr, rf	0	0	0	1	1	0	0	0
Pierzynski, c	4	1	1	2	0	1	7	0
Hocking, 2b	4	0	2	1	0	1	7	2
Radke, p	0	0	0	0	0	0	1	1
Romero, p	0	0	0	0	0	0	0	1
Hawkins, p	0	0	0	0	0	0	0	0
Guardado, p	0	0	0	0	0	0	0	0
Totals	38	5	12	5	3	11	27	10

Oakland	AB	R	H	RBI	BB	SO	PO	A
Durham, dh	5	1	3	1	0	0	0	0
Hatteberg, 1b	3	0	1	0	0	0	8	1
Piatt, ph	1	0	0	0	0	1	0	0
Myers, c	0	0	0	0	0	0	2	0
Tejada, ss	4	0	0	0	0	2	3	3
Chavez, 3b	4	0	2	0	0	0	2	1
Dye, rf	4	1	1	0	0	1	2	1
Justice, lf	4	1	1	0	0	1	0	0
Ellis, 2b	4	1	2	3	0	0	1	4
Long, cf	4	0	0	0	0	0	0	0
Hernandez, c	2	0	0	0	0	1	8	1
Velarde, ph-1b	2	0	1	0	0	0	1	0
Mulder, p	0	0	0	0	0	0	0	0
Bradford, p	0	0	0	0	0	0	0	0
Koch, p	0	0	0	0	0	0	0	0
Totals	37	4	11	4	0	6	27	11

Minnesota	0	1 1	0 0 0	0 0 3—	5
Oakland	0	0 1	0 0 0	0 0 3—	4

Minnesota	IP	H	R	ER	HR	BB	SO
Radke (W)	6.2	6	1	1	1	0	4
Romero	1.0	1	0	0	0	0	0
Hawkins	0.1	0	0	0	0	0	1
Guardado	1.0	4	3	3	1	0	0

Oakland	IP	H	R	ER	HR	BB	SO
Mulder (L)	7.0	9	2	2	0	1	9
Bradford	1.0	0	0	0	0	0	0
Koch	1.0	3	3	3	1	2	2

DP—Minnesota 1. LOB—Minnesota 9, Oakland 6. Hitting with runners in scoring position—Minnesota 3 for 11, Oakland 1 for 2. 2B—Guzman 2, Hunter, Hocking, Ortiz, Justice. HR—Durham (3rd inning, 2 out, 0 on) off Radke, Pierzynski (9th inning, 0 out, 1 on) off Koch, Ellis (9th inning, 1 out, 2 on) off Guardado. SB—Guzman, Durham. WP—Mulder. T—3:23. A—32,146. U—West, plate; Diaz, first; Davis, second; Meriwether, third; Marquez, left field; Cousins, right field.

HOW THEY SCORED

SECOND INNING

Twins—LeCroy singled to short. Hunter doubled to left as LeCroy advanced to third. Mientkiewicz lined to Tejada. Cuddyer was walked intentionally. Pierzynski popped to Tejada. Hocking singled to center, scoring LeCroy as Hunter advanced to third and Cuddyer to second. Jones struck out. One run. Twins 1, Athletics 0.

THIRD INNING

Twins—Guzman doubled to left-center. Koskie struck out. LeCroy singled to center, scoring Guzman. Hunter forced LeCroy

at second, Tejada to Ellis. Mientkiewicz grounded out to Hatteberg. One run. Twins 2, Athletics 0.

Athletics—Long grounded out, Guzman to Mientkiewicz. Hernandez struck out. Durham homered to center. Hatteberg grounded out, Mientkiewicz to Radke. One run. Twins 2, Athletics 1.

NINTH INNING

Twins—Myers now catching, Velarde at first and Koch pitching. Mohr walked. Pierzynski homered to right, scoring Mohr. Hocking grounded out, Chavez to Velarde. Jones struck out. Guzman singled to second. Guzman stole second. Koskie walked. Ortiz doubled to right-center, scoring Guzman as Koskie advanced to third. Hunter struck out. Three runs. Twins 5, Athletics 1.

Athletics—Guardado now pitching. Chavez singled to second. Dye forced Chavez at second, Koskie to Hocking. Justice doubled to right-center as Dye advanced to third. Ellis homered to left, scoring Dye and Justice. Long flied to Hunter. Velarde singled to right. Durham fouled to Hocking. Three runs. Twins 5, Athletics 4.

STATISTICS

MINNESOTA TWINS' BATTING AND FIELDING AVERAGES

Player, position	G	AB	R	H	TB	2B	3B	HR	RBI	BB	IBB	SO	Avg.	OBP	Slg.	PO	A	E	Avg.
Mohr, lf-rf	4	2	1	2	3	1	0	0	0	1	0	0	1.000	1.000	1.500	1	0	0	1.000
Hocking, 2b-rf-ph	3	6	0	3	4	1	0	0	1	0	0	1	.500	.500	.667	7	2	0	1.000
LeCroy, dh	3	9	1	4	4	0	0	0	1	0	0	3	.444	.444	.444	0	0	0	.000
Pierzynski, c	5	16	4	7	12	0	1	1	4	2	0	2	.438	.500	.750	31	4	1	.969
Cuddyer, rf	5	13	1	5	6	1	0	0	1	3	1	3	.385	.500	.462	7	0	0	1.000
Hunter, cf	5	20	4	6	10	4	0	0	2	1	0	4	.300	.333	.500	12	0	0	1.000
Guzman, ss	5	21	5	6	11	2	0	1	2	2	0	4	.286	.348	.524	5	7	1	.923
Jones, lf	5	20	3	5	8	3	0	0	1	1	0	8	.250	.318	.400	20	0	1	.952
Mientkiewicz, 1b	5	20	3	5	11	0	0	2	4	1	0	1	.250	.286	.550	35	3	0	1.000
Rivas, 2b	4	12	2	3	4	1	0	0	0	1	0	2	.250	.308	.333	4	7	0	1.000
Ortiz, dh	4	13	0	3	5	2	0	0	2	0	0	5	.231	.231	.385	0	0	0	.000
Koskie, 3b	5	21	3	3	8	0	1	1	5	2	0	6	.143	.250	.381	2	10	1	.923
Fiore, p	1	0	0	0	0	0	0	0	0	0	0	0	.000	.000	.000	0	0	0	.000
Guardado, p	2	0	0	0	0	0	0	0	0	0	0	0	.000	.000	.000	0	0	0	.000
Hawkins, p	3	0	0	0	0	0	0	0	0	0	0	0	.000	.000	.000	0	0	0	.000
Jackson, p	1	0	0	0	0	0	0	0	0	0	0	0	.000	.000	.000	0	0	0	.000
Lohse, p	2	0	0	0	0	0	0	0	0	0	0	0	.000	.000	.000	0	0	0	.000
Mays, p	1	0	0	0	0	0	0	0	0	0	0	0	.000	.000	.000	0	1	0	1.000
Milton, p	1	0	0	0	0	0	0	0	0	0	0	0	.000	.000	.000	2	0	0	1.000
Radke, p	2	0	0	0	0	0	0	0	0	0	0	0	.000	.000	.000	1	2	0	1.000
Reed, p	1	0	0	0	0	0	0	0	0	0	0	0	.000	.000	.000	0	3	0	1.000
Romero, p	3	0	0	0	0	0	0	0	0	0	0	0	.000	.000	.000	0	0	0	.000
Santana, p	2	0	0	0	0	0	0	0	0	0	0	0	.000	.000	.000	0	1	0	1.000
Prince, c	1	2	0	0	0	0	0	0	0	0	0	0	.000	.000	.000	4	0	0	1.000
Kielty, cf-rf-dh-ph	3	4	0	0	0	0	0	0	0	0	0	1	.000	.000	.000	1	0	0	1.000
Totals	5	179	27	52	86	15	2	5	23	14	1	42	.291	.349	.480	132	36	4	.977

OAKLAND ATHLETICS' BATTING AND FIELDING AVERAGES

Player, position	G	AB	R	H	TB	2B	3B	HR	RBI	BB	IBB	SO	Avg.	OBP	Slg.	PO	A	E	Avg.
Velarde, 1b-2b-ph	4	5	1	3	4	1	0	0	1	0	0	1	.600	.600	.800	7	0	0	1.000
Hatteberg, 1b	5	14	5	7	12	2	0	1	3	3	0	0	.500	.588	.857	34	2	1	.973
Dye, rf	5	20	3	8	13	2	0	1	1	1	0	5	.400	.429	.650	4	1	0	1.000
Chavez, 3b	5	21	3	8	11	0	0	1	5	2	1	1	.381	.435	.524	7	9	0	1.000
Ellis, 2b	5	19	1	7	12	2	0	1	4	1	0	2	.368	.400	.632	7	17	1	.960
Durham, dh	5	21	7	7	16	3	0	2	2	2	0	4	.333	.417	.762	0	0	0	.000
Piatt, lf-ph	3	3	0	1	2	1	0	0	0	0	0	1	.333	.333	.667	0	0	0	.000
Justice, lf	5	21	2	5	8	1	1	0	4	0	0	4	.238	.238	.381	4	1	0	1.000
Long, cf	5	18	1	3	6	0	0	1	1	1	0	2	.167	.211	.333	12	0	0	1.000
Tejada, ss	5	21	3	3	7	1	0	0	4	1	0	7	.143	.174	.333	7	11	1	.947
Hernandez, c	5	17	0	1	1	0	0	0	0	0	0	4	.059	.059	.059	38	1	0	1.000
Bowie, p	1	0	0	0	0	0	0	0	0	0	0	0	.000	.000	.000	0	0	0	.000
Bradford, p	2	0	0	0	0	0	0	0	0	0	0	0	.000	.000	.000	0	1	0	1.000
Hudson, p	2	0	0	0	0	0	0	0	0	0	0	0	.000	.000	.000	0	1	0	1.000
Koch, p	3	0	0	0	0	0	0	0	0	0	0	0	.000	.000	.000	0	0	0	.000
Lidle, p	1	0	0	0	0	0	0	0	0	0	0	0	.000	.000	.000	0	0	0	.000
Lilly, p	2	0	0	0	0	0	0	0	0	0	0	0	.000	.000	.000	0	0	0	.000

Player, position	G	AB	R	H	TB	2B	3B	HR	RBI	BB	IBB	SO	Avg.	OBP	Slg.	PO	A	E	Avg.
								BATTING									**FIELDING**		
Mecir, p	1	0	0	0	0	0	0	0	0	0	0	0	.000	.000	.000	0	0	0	.000
Mulder, p	2	0	0	0	0	0	0	0	0	0	0	0	.000	.000	.000	0	4	0	1.000
Rincon, p	2	0	0	0	0	0	0	0	0	0	0	0	.000	.000	.000	0	0	0	.000
Saenz, 1b-ph	1	0	0	0	0	0	0	0	0	1	0	0	.000	1.000	.000	3	0	0	1.000
Zito, p	1	0	0	0	0	0	0	0	0	0	0	0	.000	.000	.000	2	0	0	1.000
Byrnes, lf-ph	2	1	0	0	0	0	0	0	0	0	0	1	.000	.000	.000	1	0	0	1.000
Myers, c	2	1	0	0	0	0	0	0	0	0	0	1	.000	.000	.000	4	0	0	1.000
Mabry, 1b-rf-ph	2	2	0	0	0	0	0	0	0	0	0	1	.000	.000	.000	2	0	0	1.000
Totals	5	184	26	53	92	13	1	8	25	12	1	34	.288	.333	.500	132	48	3	.984

MINNESOTA TWINS' PITCHING RECORDS

Pitcher	G	GS	CG	IP	H	R	ER	HR	BB	IBB	SO	HB	WP	W	L	Pct.	ERA
Lohse	2	0	0	4.0	2	0	0	0	0	0	5	0	0	0	0	.000	0.00
Romero	3	0	0	3.1	3	0	0	0	1	0	2	0	0	0	0	.000	0.00
Hawkins	3	0	0	2.1	0	0	0	0	0	0	5	0	0	0	0	.000	0.00
Jackson	1	0	0	0.2	1	0	0	0	0	0	0	0	0	0	0	.000	0.00
Radke	2	2	0	11.2	14	6	2	1	1	0	7	0	0	2	0	1.000	1.54
Milton	1	1	0	7.0	6	2	2	1	1	0	3	0	0	1	0	1.000	2.57
Santana	2	0	0	3.0	3	2	2	0	2	0	2	0	0	0	0	.000	6.00
Reed	1	1	0	5.0	6	4	4	4	2	0	8	0	0	0	1	.000	7.20
Guardado	2	0	0	2.0	5	3	3	1	1	0	1	0	0	0	0	.000	13.50
Mays	1	1	0	3.2	9	6	6	1	2	1	1	1	0	0	1	.000	14.73
Fiore	1	0	0	1.1	4	3	3	0	2	0	0	0	1	0	0	.000	20.25
Totals	5	5	0	44.0	53	26	22	8	12	1	34	1	1	3	2	.600	4.50

No shutouts. Save—Guardado.

OAKLAND ATHLETICS' PITCHING RECORDS

Pitcher	G	GS	CG	IP	H	R	ER	HR	BB	IBB	SO	HB	WP	W	L	Pct.	ERA
Bradford	2	0	0	3.0	1	0	0	0	0	0	1	1	0	0	0	.000	0.00
Rincon	2	0	0	3.0	2	0	0	0	0	0	2	0	0	0	0	.000	0.00
Bowie	1	0	0	1.1	0	0	0	0	0	0	3	0	0	0	0	.000	0.00
Mecir	1	0	0	1.0	0	0	0	0	0	0	2	0	0	0	0	.000	0.00
Mulder	2	2	0	13.0	14	3	3	1	3	1	12	0	1	1	1	.500	2.08
Zito	1	1	0	6.0	5	3	3	0	4	0	8	0	1	1	0	1.000	4.50
Hudson	2	2	0	8.2	13	11	6	2	4	0	8	1	1	0	1	.000	6.23
Koch	3	0	0	3.0	5	3	3	1	2	0	3	0	0	0	0	.000	9.00
Lidle	1	0	0	1.0	2	1	1	0	0	0	0	0	0	0	0	.000	9.00
Lilly	2	0	0	4.0	10	6	6	1	1	0	3	0	1	0	1	.000	13.50
Totals	5	5	0	44.0	52	27	22	5	14	1	42	2	4	2	3	.400	4.50

No shutouts. Save—Koch.

SCORE BY INNINGS

Minnesota	0	2	5	8	2	4	3	0	3—27
Oakland	8	2	3	6	1	1	2	0	3—26

MISCELLANEOUS STATISTICS

Sacrifice hits—Guzman, Rivas.

Sacrifice fly—Tejada.

Stolen bases—Guzman 2, Durham.

Caught stealing—None.

Double plays—Chavez and Hatteberg; Chavez, Ellis and Hatteberg; Ellis and Mabry; Koskie, Hocking and Mientkiewicz; Mays, Mientkiewicz and Koskie; Tejada and Hatteberg.

Left on bases—Minnesota 8, 7, 9, 5, 9—38; Oakland 12, 9, 7, 6, 6—40.

Hitting with runners in scoring position—Minnesota 3 for 10, 0 for 4, 3 for 11, 4 for 10, 3 for 11—13 for 46; Oakland 4 for 11, 6 for 15, 0 for 2, 0 for 9, 1 for 2—11 for 39.

Hit by pitcher—By Bradford (Koskie), by Mays (Durham), by Hudson (Jones).

Passed balls—None.

Balks—None.

Time of games—3:44, 3:04, 3:26, 3:20, 3:23—Avg.: 3:23.

Attendance—34,853, 31,953, 55,932, 55,960, 32,146—210,844.

Umpires—Gerry Davis, Chuck Meriwether, Alfonso Marquez, Derryl Cousins, Joe West, Laz Diaz, Jim Joyce, Mike Winters, Tim McClelland, Fieldin Culbreth, Jerry Crawford, Doug Eddings.

Official scorers—Chuck Dybdal, Tom Mee.

2002 REVIEW *A.L. Division Series*

ANAHEIM VS. NEW YORK

RESULTS

Day	Date	Place	Score
Tue.	Oct. 1	New York	New York 8, Anaheim 5
Wed.	Oct. 2	New York	Anaheim 8, New York 6
Fri.	Oct. 4	Anaheim	Anaheim 9, New York 6
Sat.	Oct. 5	Anaheim	Anaheim 9, New York 5

BOX SCORES

GAME 1

NEW YORK 8, ANAHEIM 5

TUESDAY, OCTOBER 1, AT NEW YORK

Anaheim	AB	R	H	RBI	BB	SO	PO	A
Eckstein, ss	5	1	2	0	0	0	3	2
Erstad, cf	4	1	3	0	0	1	4	0
Salmon, rf	4	0	1	1	1	1	1	0
Anderson, lf	5	0	2	2	0	0	2	0
Fullmer, dh	4	0	0	0	0	0	0	0
Glaus, 3b	4	2	2	2	0	1	1	4
Spiezio, 1b	3	0	0	0	1	1	6	1
B. Molina, c	4	0	1	0	0	1	3	0
Kennedy, 2b	3	1	1	0	1	1	4	3
Washburn, p	0	0	0	0	0	0	0	0
Weber, p	0	0	0	0	0	0	0	0
Schoeneweis, p	0	0	0	0	0	0	0	0
Donnelly, p	0	0	0	0	0	0	0	0
Totals	36	5	12	5	3	6	24	10

New York	AB	R	H	RBI	BB	SO	PO	A
Soriano, 2b	3	1	0	0	1	0	3	4
Jeter, ss	2	3	2	1	2	0	1	3
Giambi, 1b	4	2	3	3	0	0	12	0
Williams, cf	4	1	2	3	0	0	4	0
Posada, c	4	0	0	0	0	1	5	1
Mondesi, rf	3	0	0	0	0	1	0	0
Ventura, 3b	3	0	0	0	0	0	1	1
White, lf	3	1	1	1	0	0	0	0
J. Rivera, lf	1	0	0	0	1	0	1	0
Vander Wal, ph	1	0	0	0	0	0	0	0
Spencer, lf	0	0	0	0	0	0	0	0
Clemens, p	0	0	0	0	0	0	0	3
Mendoza, p	0	0	0	0	0	0	0	0
Karsay, p	0	0	0	0	0	0	0	0
M. Rivera, p	0	0	0	0	0	0	0	0
Totals	28	8	8	8	4	2	27	12

Anaheim	0 0 1	0 2 1	0 1 0—5
New York	1 0 0	2 1 0	0 4 x—8

Anaheim	IP	H	R	ER	HR	BB	SO
Washburn	7.0	6	4	4	3	2	2
Weber (L)	0.2	0	2	2	0	2	0
Schoeneweis	*0.0	1	1	1	0	0	0
Donnelly	0.1	1	1	1	1	0	0

New York	IP	H	R	ER	HR	BB	SO
Clemens	5.2	8	4	4	1	3	5
Mendoza	*1.1	3	1	1	1	0	0
Karsay (W)	1.0	0	0	0	0	0	1
M. Rivera (S)	1.0	1	0	0	0	0	0

*Pitched to one batter in eighth.

E—Posada. DP—Anaheim 4, New York 2. LOB—Anaheim 8. Hitting with runners in scoring position—Anaheim 2 for 9, New York 2 for 2. 2B—Anderson, B. Molina. HR—Jeter (1st inning, 1 out, 0 on) off Washburn; Giambi (4th inning, 0 out, 1 on) off Washburn, White (5th inning, 1 out, 0 on) off Washburn, Glaus (6th inning, 0 out, 0 on) off Clemens, Glaus (8th inning, 0 out, 0 on) off Mendoza, Williams (8th inning, 2 out, 2 on) off Donnelly. SB—Eckstein, Erstad, Soriano. SH—Erstad. T—3:27. A—56,710. U—Crawford, plate; Eddings, first; Joyce, second; Winters, third; McClelland, left field; Culbreth, right field.

HOW THEY SCORED

FIRST INNING
Yankees—Soriano popped to Kennedy. Jeter homered to left-center. Giambi singled to right. Williams grounded into a double play, Glaus to Kennedy to Spiezio. One run. Yankees 1, Angels 0.

THIRD INNING
Angels—Eckstein grounded out, Ventura to Giambi. Erstad singled to right. Erstad stole second and reached third on a throwing error by Posada. Salmon singled to center, scoring Erstad. Anderson grounded into a double play, Soriano to Jeter to Giambi. One run. Yankees 1, Angels 1.

FOURTH INNING
Yankees—Jeter walked. Giambi homered to right-center, scoring Jeter. Williams singled to left. Posada grounded into a double play, Eckstein to Kennedy to Spiezio. Mondesi popped to Eckstein. Two runs. Yankees 3, Angels 1.

FIFTH INNING
Angels—B. Molina flied to Williams. Kennedy walked. Eckstein singled to left as Kennedy advanced to third. Erstad struck out. Eckstein stole second. Salmon walked. Anderson doubled to left, scoring Kennedy and Eckstein as Salmon advanced to third. Fullmer grounded out to Giambi. Two runs. Yankees 3, Angels 3.
Yankees—Ventura popped to Eckstein. White homered to right-center. J. Rivera flied to Erstad. Soriano grounded out, Glaus to Spiezio. One run. Yankees 4, Angels 3.

SIXTH INNING
Angels—Glaus homered to left. Spiezio struck out. B. Molina struck out and was retired at first after a dropped third strike, Posada to Giambi. Kennedy singled to right. Mendoza now pitching. Eckstein popped to Soriano. One run. Yankees 4, Angels 4.

EIGHTH INNING
Angels—Glaus homered to left. Karsay now pitching. Spiezio popped to Soriano. B. Molina grounded out, Soriano to Giambi. Kennedy struck out. One run. Angels 5, Yankees 4.
Yankees—Weber now pitching. White grounded out, Glaus to Spiezio. Vander Wal, pinch-hitting for J. Rivera, lined to Anderson. Soriano walked. Soriano stole second. Jeter walked. Schoeneweis now pitching. Giambi singled to first, scoring Soriano as Jeter advanced to third. Donnelly now pitching. Williams homered to right, scoring Jeter and Giambi. Posada flied to Anderson. Four runs. Yankees 8, Angels 5.

GAME 2

ANAHEIM 8, NEW YORK 6

WEDNESDAY, OCTOBER 2, AT NEW YORK

Anaheim	AB	R	H	RBI	BB	SO	PO	A
Eckstein, ss	5	0	1	0	0	0	1	2
Erstad, cf	5	0	1	0	0	0	2	0
Salmon, rf	5	1	1	1	0	1	3	0
Ochoa, rf	0	0	0	0	0	0	0	0
Anderson, lf	5	3	3	1	0	1	0	0
Glaus, 3b	5	1	2	1	0	1	0	0
Spiezio, 1b	5	1	3	3	0	0	11	0
Wooten, dh	4	1	3	0	0	1	0	0
Figgins, pr-dh	0	1	0	0	0	0	0	0
Fullmer, ph-dh	0	0	0	0	1	0	0	0
B. Molina, c	5	0	2	0	0	0	8	0
Gil, 2b	2	0	1	1	0	0	2	2
Kennedy, ph-2b	1	0	0	1	0	1	0	1
Appier, p	0	0	0	0	0	0	0	1
Rodriguez, p	0	0	0	0	0	0	0	0
Weber, p	0	0	0	0	0	0	0	0
Donnelly, p	0	0	0	0	0	0	0	0
Percival, p	0	0	0	0	0	0	0	0
Totals	42	8	17	8	1	5	27	6

New York	AB	R	H	RBI	BB	SO	PO	A
Soriano, 2b	4	1	1	2	0	1	2	3
Jeter, ss	5	1	3	1	0	1	0	8

A.L. Division Series

2002 REVIEW

New York	AB	R	H	RBI	BB	SO	PO	A
Giambi, dh	3	1	1	0	2	0	0	0
Williams, cf	5	0	0	0	0	1	3	0
Ventura, 3b	5	1	2	0	0	1	0	1
Posada, c	5	0	1	1	0	1	6	0
Wilson, pr	0	0	0	0	0	0	0	0
Johnson, 1b	4	1	1	0	1	2	10	0
Mondesi, rf	4	0	2	0	0	0	3	0
J. Rivera, lf	3	1	1	2	0	0	3	0
Vander Wal, ph-lf	1	0	0	0	0	1	0	0
Pettitte, p	0	0	0	0	0	0	0	1
Hernandez, p	0	0	0	0	0	0	0	1
Karsay, p	0	0	0	0	0	0	0	0
Stanton, p	0	0	0	0	0	0	0	0
Weaver, p	0	0	0	0	0	0	0	0
Totals	39	6	12	6	3	8	27	14

Anaheim	1	2	1	0	0	0	0	3	1—8
New York	0	0	1	2	0	2	0	0	1—6

Anaheim	IP	H	R	ER	HR	BB	SO
Appier	5.0	5	3	3	1	3	3
Rodriguez (W)	2.0	2	2	2	1	0	1
Weber	0.1	2	0	0	0	0	0
Donnelly	0.1	0	0	0	0	0	1
Percival (S)	1.1	3	1	1	0	0	3

New York	IP	H	R	ER	HR	BB	SO
Pettitte	3.0	8	4	4	2	0	1
Hernandez (L)	*4.0	3	2	2	2	0	4
Karsay	0.1	2	1	1	0	0	0
Stanton	0.2	1	0	0	0	0	0
Weaver	1.0	3	1	1	0	1	0

*Pitched to two batters in eighth.

E—Gil, Jeter. DP—New York 1. LOB—Anaheim 9, New York 11. Hitting with runners in scoring position—Anaheim 4 for 10, New York 3 for 14. 2B—Spiezio. HR—Salmon (1st inning, 2 out, 0 on) off Pettitte, Spiezio (2nd inning, 1 out, 0 on) off Pettitte, Jeter (3rd inning, 1 out, 0 on) off Appier, Soriano (6th inning, 2 out, 1 on) off Rodriguez, Anderson (8th inning, 0 out, 0 on) off Hernandez, Glaus (8th inning, 0 out, 0 on) off Hernandez. SB—Figgins. S—Kennedy. HBP—Mondesi by Appier, Soriano by Percival. T—4:11. A—56,695. U—Eddings, plate; Joyce, first; Winters, second; McClelland, third; Culbreth, left field; Crawford, right field.

HOW THEY SCORED

FIRST INNING

Angels—Eckstein flied to J. Rivera. Erstad grounded out, Jeter to Johnson. Salmon homered to left. Anderson struck out. One run. Angels 1, Yankees 0.

SECOND INNING

Angels—Glaus flied to Mondesi. Spiezio homered to left. Wooten singled to right. B. Molina singled to center as Wooten advanced to third. Gil singled to center, scoring Wooten as B. Molina advanced to second. Eckstein flied to Williams. Erstad fouled to Posada. Two runs. Angels 3, Yankees 0.

THIRD INNING

Angels—Salmon grounded out, Pettitte to Jeter to Johnson. Anderson singled to left. Glaus flied to J. Rivera as Anderson advanced to second. Spiezio singled to center, scoring Anderson. Wooten singled to right as Spiezio advanced to second. B. Molina forced Wooten at second, Jeter to Soriano. One run. Angels 4, Yankees 0.

Yankees—Soriano struck out. Jeter homered to left. Giambi lined to Spiezio. Williams grounded out, Gil to Spiezio. One run. Angels 4, Yankees 1.

FOURTH INNING

Yankees—Ventura singled to center. Posada flied to Salmon. Johnson walked. Mondesi popped to Spiezio. J. Rivera singled to center and advanced to second on the throw home as Ventura and Johnson scored. Soriano grounded out, Eckstein to Spiezio. Two runs. Angels 4, Yankees 3.

SIXTH INNING

Yankees—Rodriguez now pitching. Johnson struck out. Mondesi singled to left-center. J. Rivera forced Mondesi at second, Eckstein to Gil, but on the play, J. Rivera advanced to second when Gil threw wildly to first for an error. Soriano homered to left, scoring J. Rivera. Jeter fouled to Salmon. Two runs. Yankees 5, Angels 4.

EIGHTH INNING

Angels—Anderson homered to right. Glaus homered to center. Karsay now pitching. Spiezio grounded out, Jeter to Johnson. Wooten singled to center. Figgins now running for Wooten. Figgins stole second. B. Molina singled to center as Figgins advanced to third. Stanton now pitching. Kennedy scored Figgins on a sacrifice fly to Mondesi. Eckstein singled to center as B. Molina advanced to second. Erstad flied to Mondesi. Three runs. Angels 7, Yankees 5.

NINTH INNING

Angels—Vander Wal now in left field and Weaver pitching. Salmon grounded out, Soriano to Johnson. Anderson singled to right. Glaus singled to center as Anderson advanced to third. Spiezio doubled to right, scoring Anderson as Glaus advanced to third. Fullmer, pinch-hitting for Figgins, was walked intentionally. B. Molina grounded into a double play, Jeter to Soriano to Johnson. One run. Angels 8, Yankees 5.

Yankees—Ochoa now in right field. Giambi singled to left. Williams struck out. Ventura singled to right as Giambi advanced to third. Posada singled to left, scoring Giambi as Ventura advanced to second. Wilson now running for Posada. Johnson struck out. Mondesi popped to Eckstein. One run. Angels 8, Yankees 6.

GAME 3

ANAHEIM 9, NEW YORK 6

FRIDAY, OCTOBER 4, AT ANAHEIM

New York	AB	R	H	RBI	BB	SO	PO	A
Soriano, 2b	5	0	0	0	0	1	2	4
Jeter, ss	5	1	1	0	0	1	0	1
Giambi, 1b	3	2	0	0	2	0	8	0
Williams, cf	2	2	1	0	2	1	3	0
Ventura, 3b	3	0	1	3	0	1	0	1
Posada, c	3	0	0	1	0	0	5	0
Mondesi, rf	2	1	0	0	1	0	3	0
Johnson, dh	4	0	1	1	0	2	0	0
J. Rivera, lf	4	0	2	1	0	2	3	0
Mussina, p	0	0	0	0	0	0	0	0
Weaver, p	0	0	0	0	0	0	0	0
Stanton, p	0	0	0	0	0	0	0	0
Karsay, p	0	0	0	0	0	0	0	0
Totals	31	6	6	6	5	8	24	6

Anaheim	AB	R	H	RBI	BB	SO	PO	A
Eckstein, ss	3	0	0	0	0	0	0	2
Erstad, cf	5	2	2	1	0	0	2	0
Salmon, rf	5	1	2	4	0	2	2	0
Ochoa, rf	0	0	0	0	0	0	0	0
Anderson, lf	4	1	1	0	1	1	4	0
Glaus, 3b	3	1	1	0	1	0	0	3
Fullmer, dh	3	1	2	0	0	1	0	0
Wooten, ph-dh	1	0	0	0	0	0	0	0
Spiezio, 1b	3	0	1	2	1	0	8	1
B. Molina, c	3	0	0	0	0	0	8	0
Kennedy, 2b	3	3	3	2	0	0	2	3
Ortiz, p	0	0	0	0	0	0	0	0
Lackey, p	0	0	0	0	0	0	1	0
Schoeneweis, p	0	0	0	0	0	0	0	0
Rodriguez, p	0	0	0	0	0	0	0	0
Percival, p	0	0	0	0	0	0	0	0
Totals	33	9	12	9	3	4	27	9

New York	3	0	3	0	0	0	0	0	0—6
Anaheim	0	1	2	1	0	1	1	3	x—9

New York	IP	H	R	ER	HR	BB	SO
Mussina	4.0	6	4	4	1	0	2
Weaver	1.2	1	1	1	0	2	1
Stanton (L)	1.2	4	3	3	0	1	1
Karsay	0.2	1	1	1	1	0	0

Anaheim	IP	H	R	ER	HR	BB	SO
Ra.Ortiz	2.2	3	6	6	0	4	1
Lackey	3.0	3	0	0	0	1	3
Schoeneweis	0.1	0	0	0	0	0	0
Rodriguez (W)	2.0	0	0	0	0	0	4
Percival (S)	1.0	0	0	0	0	0	0

LOB—New York 6, Anaheim 8. Hitting with runners in scoring position—New York 3 for 8, Anaheim 5 for 13. 2B—Williams, Ventura, Erstad, Salmon, Anderson, Fullmer, Kennedy. HR—Kennedy (4th inning, 2 out, 0 on) off Mussina, Salmon (8th inning, 1 out, 1 on) off Karsay. SB—Kennedy. S—Ventura, Posada, Kennedy. SH—Eckstein, B. Molina. WP—Ortiz. HBP—Mondesi by Ortiz, Glaus by Mussina, Eckstein by Weaver. T—3:52. A—45,072. U—Marquez, plate; Cousins, first; West, second; Diaz, third; Davis, left field; Meriwether, right field.

HOW THEY SCORED

FIRST INNING

Yankees—Soriano flied to Salmon. Jeter singled to center. Giambi walked. Jeter advanced to third on a fielder's choice. Williams walked. Ventura doubled to right-center, scoring Jeter and Giambi as Williams advanced to third. Posada scored Williams on a sacrifice fly to Salmon as Ventura advanced to third. Mondesi was hit by a pitch. Johnson fouled to Anderson. Three runs. Yankees 3, Angels 0.

SECOND INNING

Angels—Anderson struck out. Glaus singled to left. Fullmer doubled to right as Glaus advanced to third. Spiezio grounded to Giambi, scoring Glaus as Fullmer advanced to third. B. Molina grounded out, Soriano to Giambi. One run. Yankees 3, Angels 1.

THIRD INNING

Yankees—Giambi walked. Williams doubled to left as Giambi advanced to third. Ventura scored Giambi on a sacrifice fly to Erstad. Williams advanced to third on a wild pitch. Posada grounded out, Glaus to Spiezio. Lackey now pitching. Johnson singled to center, scoring Williams as Mondesi advanced to second. J. Rivera singled to left, scoring Mondesi as Johnson advanced to second. Soriano struck out. Three runs. Yankees 6, Angels 1.

Angels—Kennedy singled to center. Kennedy stole second. Eckstein lined to Giambi. Erstad singled to right as Kennedy advanced to third. Salmon doubled to left, scoring Kennedy and Erstad. Anderson grounded out, Soriano to Giambi, as Salmon advanced to third. Glaus was hit by a pitch. Fullmer struck out. Two runs. Yankees 6, Angels 3.

FOURTH INNING

Angels—Spiezio fouled to Mondesi. B. Molina flied to Mondesi. Kennedy homered to right. Eckstein grounded out, Soriano to Giambi. One run. Yankees 6, Angels 4.

SIXTH INNING

Angels—Fullmer singled to left. Spiezio walked. B. Molina sacrificed Fullmer to third and Spiezio to second, Giambi, unassisted. Kennedy scored Fullmer on a sacrifice fly to J. Rivera. Eckstein was hit by a pitch. Stanton now pitching. Erstad flied to Williams. One run. Yankees 6, Angels 5.

SEVENTH INNING

Angels—Salmon struck out. Anderson doubled to right. Glaus was walked intentionally. Wooten, pinch-hitting for Fullmer, popped to Soriano. Spiezio singled to center, scoring Anderson as Glaus advanced to third. B. Molina flied to Williams. One run. Yankees 6, Angels 6.

EIGHTH INNING

Angels—Kennedy doubled to right. Eckstein sacrificed Kennedy to third, Ventura to Soriano. Erstad doubled to right, scoring Kennedy. Karsay now pitching. Salmon homered to left, scoring Erstad. Anderson grounded out, Soriano to Giambi. Glaus flied to Mondesi. Three runs. Angels 9, Yankees 6.

GAME 4

ANAHEIM 9, NEW YORK 5

SATURDAY, OCTOBER 5, AT ANAHEIM

New York	AB	R	H	RBI	BB	SO	PO	A
Soriano, 2b	5	0	1	0	0	2	3	2
Jeter, ss	4	1	2	1	0	1	2	2
Giambi, 1b	4	0	1	0	0	1	6	1
Williams, cf	4	1	2	0	1	0	5	0
Posada, c	5	2	3	1	0	1	3	1
Mondesi, rf	3	0	1	1	2	0	4	0

New York	AB	R	H	RBI	BB	SO	PO	A
Coomer, dh	2	0	1	0	0	0	0	0
Johnson, ph-dh	3	0	0	0	0	1	0	0
Ventura, 3b	3	0	1	1	1	0	0	1
J. Rivera, lf	4	1	0	0	0	1	1	0
Wells, p	0	0	0	0	0	0	0	0
Mendoza, p	0	0	0	0	0	0	0	0
Hernandez, p	0	0	0	0	0	0	0	0
Karsay, p	0	0	0	0	0	0	0	0
Stanton, p	0	0	0	0	0	0	0	0
Totals	37	5	12	4	4	7	24	7

Anaheim	AB	R	H	RBI	BB	SO	PO	A
Eckstein, ss	5	1	2	1	0	0	2	1
Erstad, cf	5	1	2	1	0	0	3	0
Salmon, rf	5	1	1	1	0	1	2	0
Ochoa, rf	0	0	0	0	0	0	0	0
Anderson, lf	4	1	1	1	0	1	3	0
Glaus, 3b	4	0	0	0	0	1	1	4
Spiezio, 1b	4	1	2	1	0	0	7	1
Wooten, dh	4	3	3	2	0	0	0	0
B. Molina, c	3	0	1	2	0	0	7	0
Gil, 2b	3	1	3	0	0	0	2	1
Kennedy, ph-2b	1	0	0	0	0	0	0	0
Washburn, p	0	0	0	0	0	0	0	0
Donnelly, p	0	0	0	0	0	0	0	0
Schoeneweis, p	0	0	0	0	0	0	0	0
Rodriguez, p	0	0	0	0	0	0	0	1
Percival, p	0	0	0	0	0	0	0	0
Totals	38	9	15	9	0	3	27	8

New York	0	1	0		0	1	1		1	0	1—5
Anaheim	0	0	1		0	8	0		x—9

New York	IP	H	R	ER	HR	BB	SO
Wells (L)	4.2	10	8	8	1	0	0
Mendoza	*0.0	2	1	1	0	0	0
Hernandez	2.1	2	0	0	0	0	3
Karsay	0.2	0	0	0	0	0	0
Stanton	0.1	1	0	0	0	0	0

Anaheim	IP	H	R	ER	HR	BB	SO
Washburn (W)	5.0	6	2	1	0	1	2
Donnelly	1.1	2	2	2	1	1	1
Schoeneweis	†0.0	1	0	0	0	0	0
Rodriguez	1.2	0	0	0	0	2	3
Percival	1.0	3	1	1	0	0	1

*Pitched to two batters in fifth.
†Pitched to one batter in seventh.

E—Wells, Soriano, Glaus. DP—New York 2, Anaheim 2. LOB—New York 11, Anaheim 6. Hitting with runners in scoring position—New York 3 for 11, Anaheim 8 for 16. 2B—Soriano, Ventura, Erstad, B. Molina. HR—Wooten (5th inning, 0 out, 0 on) off Wells, Posada (6th inning, 0 out, 0 on) off Donnelly. S—Jeter. SH—B. Molina. WP—F. Rodriguez. HBP—Giambi by Washburn. T—3:37. A—45,067. U—Cousins, plate; West, first; Diaz, second; Davis, third; Meriwether, left field; Marquez, right field.

HOW THEY SCORED

SECOND INNING

Yankees—Posada singled to right. Mondesi flied to Erstad. Coomer singled to left as Posada advanced to third. Ventura doubled to center, scoring Posada as Coomer advanced to third. J. Rivera grounded out, Glaus to Spiezio. Soriano flied to Salmon. One run. Yankees 1, Angels 0.

THIRD INNING

Angels—Wooten singled to center. B. Molina sacrificed Wooten to second, Posada to Soriano. Gil singled to left as Wooten advanced to third. Eckstein reached first on a fielding error by Soriano as Wooten scored and Gil advanced to third. Erstad grounded into a double play, Soriano to Jeter to Giambi. One run. Yankees 1, Angels 1.

FIFTH INNING

Yankees—J. Rivera reached first on a throwing error by Glaus. Soriano doubled to left as J. Rivera advanced to third. Jeter scored J. Rivera on a sacrifice fly to Anderson. Giambi flied to Anderson. Williams lined to Glaus. One run. Yankees 2, Angels 1.

Angels—Wooten homered to left-center. B. Molina flied to Mondesi. Gil singled to center. Eckstein singled to right as Gil advanced to third. Erstad singled to center, scoring Gil as Eckstein advanced to second. Salmon singled to left-center, scoring Eckstein as Erstad advanced to third. Anderson singled to right, scoring Erstad as Salmon advanced to third. Glaus flied to Mondesi. Spiezio singled to left, scoring Salmon as Anderson advanced to second. Mendoza now pitching. Wooten singled to center, scoring Anderson as Spiezio advanced to third. B. Molina doubled to left, scoring Spiezio and Wooten. Hernandez now pitching. Gil singled to center as B. Molina advanced to third. Eckstein flied to Williams. Eight runs. Angels 9, Yankees 2.

SIXTH INNING

Yankees—Donnelly now pitching. Posada homered to center. Mondesi flied to Erstad. Johnson, pinch-hitting for Coomer, struck out. Ventura walked. J. Rivera grounded out, Glaus to Spiezio. One run. Angels 9, Yankees 3.

SEVENTH INNING

Yankees—Soriano popped to Gil. Jeter singled to left. Schoeneweis now pitching. Giambi singled to right as Jeter advanced to second. Rodriguez now pitching. Williams walked. Jeter scored on a wild pitch as Giambi advanced to third and Williams to second. Posada struck out. Mondesi walked. Johnson grounded out, Rodriguez to Spiezio. One run. Angels 9, Yankees 4.

NINTH INNING

Yankees—Kennedy now at second, Ochoa in right field and Percival pitching. Jeter struck out. Giambi flied to Erstad. Williams singled to center. Williams advanced to second on defensive indifference. Posada singled to right as Williams advanced to third. Mondesi singled to second, scoring Williams as Posada advanced to second. Johnson popped to Eckstein. One run. Angels 9, Yankees 5.

STATISTICS

ANAHEIM ANGELS' BATTING AND FIELDING AVERAGES

Player, position	G	AB	R	H	TB	2B	3B	HR	RBI	BB	IBB	SO	Avg.	OBP	Slg.	PO	A	E	Avg.
Gil, 2b	2	5	1	4	4	0	0	0	1	0	0	0	.800	.800	.800	4	3	1	.875
Wooten, dh	3	9	4	6	9	0	0	1	2	0	0	1	.667	.667	1.000	0	0	0	.000
Kennedy, 2b-ph	4	8	4	4	8	1	0	1	3	1	0	2	.500	.455	1.000	6	7	0	1.000
Erstad, cf	4	19	4	8	10	2	0	0	2	0	0	1	.421	.421	.526	11	0	0	1.000
Spiezio, 1b	4	15	2	6	10	1	0	1	6	2	0	1	.400	.471	.667	32	3	0	1.000
Anderson, lf	4	18	5	7	12	2	0	1	4	1	0	3	.389	.421	.667	9	0	0	1.000
Glaus, 3b	4	16	4	5	14	0	0	3	3	1	1	3	.313	.389	.875	2	11	1	.929
Fullmer, dh	3	7	1	2	3	1	0	0	0	1	1	1	.286	.375	.429	0	0	0	.000
Eckstein, ss	4	18	2	5	5	0	0	0	1	0	0	0	.278	.316	.278	6	7	0	1.000
B. Molina, c	4	15	0	4	6	2	0	0	2	0	0	1	.267	.267	.400	26	0	0	1.000
Salmon, rf	4	19	3	5	12	1	0	2	7	1	0	5	.263	.300	.632	8	0	0	1.000
Appier, p	1	0	0	0	0	0	0	0	0	0	0	0	.000	.000	.000	0	1	0	1.000
Donnelly, p	1	0	1	0	0	0	0	0	0	0	0	0	.000	.000	.000	0	0	0	.000
Lackey, p	1	0	0	0	0	0	0	0	0	0	0	0	.000	.000	.000	1	0	0	1.000
Ochoa, rf	3	0	0	0	0	0	0	0	0	0	0	0	.000	.000	.000	0	0	0	.000
Ortiz, p	1	0	0	0	0	0	0	0	0	0	0	0	.000	.000	.000	0	0	0	.000
Percival, p	3	0	0	0	0	0	0	0	0	0	0	0	.000	.000	.000	0	0	0	.000
Rodriguez, p	3	0	0	0	0	0	0	0	0	0	0	0	.000	.000	.000	0	1	0	1.000
Schoeneweis, p	3	0	0	0	0	0	0	0	0	0	0	0	.000	.000	.000	0	0	0	.000
Washburn, p	2	0	0	0	0	0	0	0	0	0	0	0	.000	.000	.000	0	0	0	.000
Weber, p	2	0	0	0	0	0	0	0	0	0	0	0	.000	.000	.000	0	0	0	.000
Totals	4	149	31	56	93	10	0	9	31	7	2	18	.376	.406	.624	105	33	2	.986

NEW YORK YANKEES' BATTING AND FIELDING AVERAGES

Player, position	G	AB	R	H	TB	2B	3B	HR	RBI	BB	IBB	SO	Avg.	OBP	Slg.	PO	A	E	Avg.
Jeter, ss	4	16	6	8	14	0	0	2	3	2	0	3	.500	.526	.875	3	14	1	.944
Coomer, dh	1	2	0	1	1	0	0	0	0	0	0	0	.500	.500	.500	0	0	0	.000
Giambi, 1b-dh	4	14	5	5	8	0	0	1	3	4	0	1	.357	.526	.571	26	1	0	1.000
Williams, cf	4	15	4	5	9	1	0	1	3	3	0	2	.333	.444	.600	15	0	0	1.000
White, dh	1	3	1	1	4	0	0	1	1	0	0	0	.333	.333	1.333	0	0	0	.000
Ventura, 3b	4	14	1	4	6	2	0	0	4	1	0	2	.286	.313	.429	1	4	0	1.000
Mondesi, rf	4	12	1	3	3	0	0	0	1	3	0	1	.250	.471	.250	10	0	0	1.000
J. Rivera, lf	4	12	2	3	3	0	0	0	3	1	0	3	.250	.308	.250	8	0	0	1.000
Posada, c	4	17	2	4	7	0	0	1	3	0	0	3	.235	.222	.412	19	2	1	.955
Johnson, 1b-dh	3	11	1	2	2	0	0	0	1	1	0	5	.182	.250	.182	10	0	0	1.000
Soriano, 2b	4	17	2	2	6	1	0	1	2	1	0	4	.118	.211	.353	10	13	1	.958
Clemens, p	1	0	0	0	0	0	0	0	0	0	0	0	.000	.000	.000	0	3	0	1.000
Hernandez, p	2	0	0	0	0	0	0	0	0	0	0	0	.000	.000	.000	0	1	0	1.000
Karsay, p	4	0	0	0	0	0	0	0	0	0	0	0	.000	.000	.000	0	0	0	.000
Mendoza, p	2	0	0	0	0	0	0	0	0	0	0	0	.000	.000	.000	0	0	0	.000
Mussina, p	1	0	0	0	0	0	0	0	0	0	0	0	.000	.000	.000	0	0	0	.000
Pettitte, p	1	0	0	0	0	0	0	0	0	0	0	0	.000	.000	.000	0	1	0	1.000
M. Rivera, p	1	0	0	0	0	0	0	0	0	0	0	0	.000	.000	.000	0	0	0	.000
Spencer, lf	1	0	0	0	0	0	0	0	0	0	0	0	.000	.000	.000	0	0	0	.000
Stanton, p	3	0	0	0	0	0	0	0	0	0	0	0	.000	.000	.000	0	0	0	.000
Weaver, p	2	0	0	0	0	0	0	0	0	0	0	0	.000	.000	.000	0	0	0	.000
Wells, p	1	0	0	0	0	0	0	0	0	0	0	0	.000	.000	.000	0	0	1	.000
Wilson, pr	1	0	0	0	0	0	0	0	0	0	0	0	.000	.000	.000	0	0	0	.000
Vander Wal, lf-ph	2	2	0	0	0	0	0	0	0	0	0	1	.000	.000	.000	0	0	0	.000
Totals	4	135	25	38	63	4	0	7	24	16	0	25	.281	.367	.467	102	39	4	.972

ANAHEIM ANGELS' PITCHING RECORDS

Pitcher	G	GS	CG	IP	H	R	ER	HR	BB	IBB	SO	HB	WP	W	L	Pct.	ERA
Lackey	1	0	0	3.0	3	0	0	0	1	0	3	0	0	0	0	.000	0.00
Rodriguez	3	0	0	5.2	2	2	2	1	2	0	8	0	1	2	0	1.000	3.18
Washburn	2	2	0	12.0	12	6	5	3	3	0	4	1	0	1	0	1.000	3.75
Appier	1	1	0	5.0	5	3	3	1	3	0	3	1	0	0	0	.000	5.40
Percival	3	0	0	3.1	6	2	2	0	0	0	4	1	0	0	0	.000	5.40
Donnelly	3	0	0	2.0	3	3	3	2	1	0	2	0	0	0	0	.000	13.50
Weber	2	0	0	1.0	2	2	2	0	2	0	0	0	0	0	1	.000	18.00
Ortiz	1	1	0	2.2	3	6	6	0	4	0	1	1	1	0	0	.000	20.25
Schoeneweis	3	0	0	0.1	2	1	1	0	0	0	0	0	0	0	0	.000	27.00
Totals	4	4	0	35.0	38	25	24	7	16	0	25	4	2	3	1	.750	6.17

No shutouts. Saves—Percival 2.

NEW YORK YANKEES' PITCHING RECORDS

Pitcher	G	GS	CG	IP	H	R	ER	HR	BB	IBB	SO	HB	WP	W	L	Pct.	ERA
M. Rivera	1	0	0	1.0	1	0	0	0	0	0	0	0	0	0	0	.000	0.00
Hernandez	2	0	0	6.1	5	2	2	2	0	0	7	0	0	0	1	.000	2.84
Clemens	1	1	0	5.2	8	4	4	1	3	0	5	0	0	0	0	.000	6.35
Karsay	4	0	0	2.2	3	2	2	1	0	0	1	0	0	1	0	1.000	6.75
Weaver	2	0	0	2.2	4	2	2	0	3	1	1	1	0	0	0	.000	6.75
Mussina	1	1	0	4.0	6	4	4	1	0	0	2	1	0	0	0	.000	9.00
Stanton	3	0	0	2.2	6	3	3	0	1	1	1	0	0	0	1	.000	10.13
Pettitte	1	1	0	3.0	8	4	4	2	0	0	1	0	0	0	0	.000	12.00
Mendoza	2	0	0	1.1	5	2	2	1	0	0	0	0	0	0	0	.000	13.50
Wells	1	1	0	4.2	10	8	8	1	0	0	0	0	0	0	1	.000	15.43
Totals	4	4	0	34.0	56	31	31	9	7	2	18	2	0	1	3	.250	8.21

No shutouts. Save—Rivera.

SCORE BY INNINGS

Anaheim	1	3	5	1	10	2	1	7	1—31
New York	4	1	4	4	2	3	1	4	2—25

MISCELLANEOUS STATISTICS

Sacrifice hits—B. Molina 2, Eckstein, Erstad.
Sacrifice flies—Kennedy 2, Jeter, Posada, Ventura.
Stolen bases—Eckstein, Erstad, Figgins, Kennedy, Soriano.
Caught stealing—None.
Double plays—Eckstein, Kennedy and Spiezio 2; Soriano, Jeter and Giambi 2; Giambi and Jeter; Gil and Spiezio; Glaus, Kennedy and Spiezio; Jeter, Soriano and Giambi; Jeter, Soriano and Johnson; Spiezio, Eckstein and Spiezio; Spiezio, Glaus and Spiezio.
Left on bases—Anaheim 8, 9, 8, 6—31; New York 0, 11, 6, 11—28.
Hitting with runners in scoring position—Anaheim 2 for 9, 4 for 10, 5 for 13, 8 for 16—19 for 48; New York 2 for 2, 3 for 14, 3 for 8, 3 for 11—11 for 35.
Hit by pitcher—By Appier (Mondesi), by Mussina (Glaus), by Percival (Soriano), by Washburn (Giambi), by Weaver (Eckstein), by Ortiz (Mondesi).
Passed balls—None.
Balks—None.
Time of games—3:27, 4:11, 3:52, 3:37—Avg.: 3:46.
Attendance—56,710, 56,695, 45,072, 45,067—203,544.
Umpires—Jerry Crawford, Doug Eddings, Jim Joyce, Mike Winters, Tim McClelland, Fieldin Culbreth, Alfonso Marquez, Derryl Cousins, Joe West, Laz Diaz, Gerry Davis, Chuck Meriwether.
Official scorers—Joe Donnelly, Ed Munson, Bill Shannon.

N.L. DIVISION SERIES
ST. LOUIS VS. ARIZONA

RESULTS

Day	Date	Place	Score
Tue.	Oct. 1	Arizona	St. Louis 12, Arizona 2
Thur.	Oct. 3	Arizona	St. Louis 2, Arizona 1
Sat.	Oct. 5	St. Louis	St. Louis 6, Arizona 3

BOX SCORES

GAME 1

ST. LOUIS 12, ARIZONA 2

TUESDAY, OCTOBER 1, AT ARIZONA

St. Louis	AB	R	H	RBI	BB	SO	PO	A
Vina, 2b	6	2	3	0	0	0	2	2
Marrero, rf	5	0	0	1	0	1	2	0
Edmonds, cf	4	1	3	2	1	0	3	0
Pujols, lf	4	2	2	2	1	0	1	1
Rolen, 3b	5	1	1	2	0	2	1	2
Renteria, ss	4	2	2	0	1	0	3	3
Martinez, 1b	4	1	0	0	1	0	8	1
Matheny, c	3	2	2	2	1	0	6	0
M.Morris, p	4	1	1	2	0	2	1	1
Fassero, p	0	0	0	0	0	0	0	0
Robinson, ph	1	0	0	0	0	0	0	0
Crudale, p	0	0	0	0	0	0	0	0
Totals	40	12	14	11	5	5	27	10

Arizona	AB	R	H	RBI	BB	SO	PO	A
Womack, ss	5	1	1	0	0	0	0	3
Spivey, 2b	5	0	1	0	0	1	2	7
S. Finley, cf	2	1	0	1	1	0	3	0
Grace, 1b	3	0	1	0	1	0	13	0
Williams, 3b	4	0	1	0	0	0	0	1
Cintron, 3b	0	0	0	0	0	0	0	0
McCracken, rf	4	0	2	1	0	0	1	0
Dellucci, lf	3	0	1	0	0	0	4	0
Little, ph-lf	1	0	0	0	0	0	0	0
Moeller, c	3	0	1	0	0	1	4	1
Barajas, c	1	0	0	0	0	1	0	1
Johnson, p	2	0	0	0	0	2	0	0
Mantei, p	0	0	0	0	0	0	0	0
Swindell, p	0	0	0	0	0	0	0	0
Fetters, p	0	0	0	0	0	0	0	0
Donnels, ph	1	0	0	0	0	0	0	0
Helling, p	0	0	0	0	0	0	0	1
Durazo, ph	0	0	0	0	1	0	0	0
Totals	34	2	8	2	3	5	27	14

St. Louis	2	0	0	3	0	1	6	0 0—12
Arizona	1	0	1	0	0	0	0	0 0—2

St. Louis	IP	H	R	ER	HR	BB	SO
Morris (W)	7.0	7	2	1	0	2	3
Fassero	1.0	1	0	0	0	0	0
Crudale	1.0	0	0	0	0	1	2

Arizona	IP	H	R	ER	HR	BB	SO
Johnson (L)	6.0	10	6	5	2	2	4
Mantei	0.1	1	2	2	0	1	0
Swindell	*0.0	2	4	1	0	1	0
Fetters	0.2	1	0	0	0	1	1
Helling	2.0	0	0	0	0	0	0

*Pitched to four batters in seventh.

E—Renteria, Swindell, Womack. LOB—St. Louis 8, Arizona 9. Hitting with runners in scoring position—St. Louis 6 for 13, Arizona 2 for 6. 2B—Matheny. 3B—Pujols. HR—Edmonds (1st inning, 1 out, 1 on) off Johnson, Rolen (4th inning, 0 out, 1 on) off Johnson. SB—Renteria, S. Finley. CS—Edmonds. S—Marrero, S. Finley. SH—Matheny. T—2:55. A—49,154. U—Froemming, plate; Miller, first; Kulpa, second; Darling, third; Rippley, left field; M. Hirschbeck, right field.

HOW THEY SCORED

FIRST INNING

Cardinals—Vina reached first on a throwing error by Womack. Marrero flied to Dellucci as Vina advanced to second. Edmonds homered to right, scoring Vina. Pujols flied to Dellucci. Rolen struck out. Two runs. Cardinals 2, Diamondbacks 0.

Diamondbacks—Womack reached first on a fielding error by Renteria. Spivey singled to left as Womack advanced to third. S. Finley scored Womack on a sacrifice fly to Edmonds. Grace singled to center as Spivey advanced to second. Williams singled to left as Spivey advanced to third and Grace to second, but Spivey was thrown out trying to score, Pujols to Matheny. McCracken flied to Pujols. One run. Cardinals 2, Diamondbacks 1.

THIRD INNING

Diamondbacks—Spivey grounded out, Rolen to Martinez. S. Finley walked. Finley stole second. Grace walked. Williams fouled to Martinez. McCracken singled to left, scoring S. Finley as Grace advanced to second. Dellucci fouled to Rolen. One run. Cardinals 2, Diamondbacks 2.

FOURTH INNING

Cardinals—Pujols tripled to right-center. Rolen homered to left-center, scoring Pujols. Renteria singled to center. Renteria stole second. Martinez grounded out, Spivey to Grace, as Renteria advanced to third. Matheny singled to left, scoring Renteria. Morris struck out. Vina singled to center as Matheny advanced to second. Marrero struck out. Three runs. Cardinals 5, Diamondbacks 2.

SIXTH INNING

Cardinals—Matheny doubled to left. Morris struck out. Vina singled to center as Matheny advanced to third. Marrero scored Matheny on a sacrifice fly to S. Finley. Edmonds grounded out, Spivey to Grace. One run. Cardinals 6, Diamondbacks 2.

SEVENTH INNING

Cardinals—Mantei now pitching and Barajas catching. Pujols walked. Rolen fouled to Grace. Renteria singled to center as Pujols advanced to second. Swindell now pitching. Martinez walked. Matheny bunted and was safe at first on a throwing error by Swindell. Pujols and Renteria scored on the play and Martinez advanced to third and Matheny to second. Morris singled to left, scoring Martinez and Matheny. Vina singled to left as Morris advanced to second. Fetters now pitching. Marrero flied to Dellucci. Edmonds walked. Pujols singled to left, scoring Morris and Vina, as Edmonds advanced to second. Rolen struck out and was retired at first after a dropped third strike, Barajas to Grace. Six runs. Cardinals 12, Diamondbacks 2.

GAME 2

ST. LOUIS 2, ARIZONA 1

THURSDAY, OCTOBER 3, AT ARIZONA

St. Louis	AB	R	H	RBI	BB	SO	PO	A
Vina, 2b	5	0	4	1	0	0	2	3
Drew, rf	4	1	1	1	1	1	2	0
Edmonds, cf	4	0	0	0	0	2	4	0
Pujols, lf-3b-1b	4	0	0	0	0	1	1	0
Rolen, 3b	2	0	2	0	0	0	1	2
Marrero, ph-lf	1	0	0	0	0	0	0	0
Martinez, 1b	4	0	0	0	0	1	7	0
Fassero, p	0	0	0	0	0	0	0	0
Isringhausen, p	0	0	0	0	0	0	0	0
Renteria, ss	4	1	1	0	0	0	2	1
Matheny, c	3	0	1	0	0	1	8	2
C. Finley, p	3	0	0	0	0	2	0	1
Kline, p	0	0	0	0	0	0	0	0
White, p	0	0	0	0	0	0	0	0
Cairo, 3b	1	0	1	1	0	0	0	0
Totals	35	2	10	2	1	8	27	9

Arizona	AB	R	H	RBI	BB	SO	PO	A
Womack, ss	4	0	1	0	1	0	3	3
Spivey, 2b	5	0	1	0	0	1	4	2
Colbrunn, 1b	3	1	0	0	1	1	4	1
Dellucci, lf	0	0	0	0	0	0	0	0
Williams, 3b	4	0	0	0	0	2	1	1
S. Finley, cf	4	0	1	0	0	1	4	0
McCracken, rf	4	0	1	1	0	1	0	0
Miller, c	2	0	1	0	2	0	8	0
Little, lf	3	0	0	0	0	2	1	0
Grace, ph-1b	1	0	0	0	0	0	1	1
Schilling, p	2	0	0	0	0	0	0	0
Moeller, ph	1	0	1	0	0	0	0	0
Cintron, pr	0	0	0	0	0	0	0	0
Koplove, p	0	0	0	0	0	0	1	0
Myers, p	0	0	0	0	0	0	0	1
Donnels, ph	1	0	0	0	0	0	0	0
Totals	34	1	6	1	4	8	27	9

St. Louis	0 0 1		0 0 0		0 0 1—2			
Arizona	0 0 0		0 0 0		0 1 0—1			

St. Louis	IP	H	R	ER	HR	BB	SO
C. Finley	6.1	4	0	0	0	2	7
Kline	0.1	1	0	0	0	1	0
White	1.0	1	1	0	0	1	0
Fassero (W)	0.1	0	0	0	0	0	0
Isringhausen (S)	1.0	0	0	0	0	0	1

Arizona	IP	H	R	ER	HR	BB	SO
Schilling	7.0	7	1	1	1	1	7
Koplove (L)	1.1	1	1	1	0	0	1
Myers	0.2	1	0	0	0	0	0

E—Pujols. LOB—St. Louis 9, Arizona 10. Hitting with runners in scoring position—St. Louis 1 for 3, Arizona 0 for 7. 2B—McCracken, Miller. HR—Drew (3rd inning, 2 out, 0 on) off Schilling. SB—Renteria. CS—Cairo. SH—Matheny. HBP—Rolen by Schilling. T—3:20. A—48,856. U—Miller, plate; Kulpa, first; Darling, second; Rippley, third; M. Hirschbeck, left field; Froemming, right field

HOW THEY SCORED

THIRD INNING

Cardinals—C. Finley struck out. Vina flied to S. Finley. Drew homered to left. Edmonds flied to Little. One run. Cardinals 1, Diamondbacks 0.

EIGHTH INNING

Diamondbacks—Marrero now in left field and Pujols moves to third. Colbrunn reached first on a fielding error by Pujols. Williams fouled to Martinez. S. Finley popped to Renteria. McCracken doubled to right, scoring Colbrunn. Miller walked. Grace now pinch-hitting for Little. Cairo now at third, Fassero pitching and Pujols moves to first. Grace flied to Drew. One run. Cardinals 1, Diamondbacks 1.

NINTH INNING

Cardinals—Grace now at first and Dellucci in left field. Renteria singled to left. Matheny sacrificed Renteria to second, Grace to Spivey. Cairo singled to center, scoring Renteria, and Cairo advanced to second on the play. Myers now pitching. Cairo was caught trying to steal third, Myers to Williams to Womack. Vina singled to center. Drew popped to Grace. One run. Cardinals 2, Diamondbacks 1.

GAME 3

ST. LOUIS 6, ARIZONA 3

SATURDAY, OCTOBER 5, AT ST. LOUIS

Arizona	AB	R	H	RBI	BB	SO	PO	A
Womack, ss	4	0	0	0	0	1	4	3
Spivey, 2b	3	0	0	1	1	1	2	3
S. Finley, cf	3	0	1	0	1	1	5	0
Williams, 3b	4	0	0	0	0	1	2	0
Durazo, 1b	4	0	0	0	0	1	6	2
McCracken, rf	3	1	1	0	1	1	0	0
Dellucci, lf	4	1	1	2	0	1	0	0
Barajas, c	3	1	1	1	0	0	4	1

Arizona	AB	R	H	RBI	BB	SO	PO	A
Batista, p	1	0	0	0	0	1	0	0
Swindell, p	0	0	0	0	0	0	0	1
Donnels, ph	0	0	0	1	0	0	0	0
Helling, p	0	0	0	0	0	0	0	0
Moeller, ph	1	0	0	0	0	0	0	0
Myers, p	0	0	0	0	0	0	1	0
Kim, p	0	0	0	0	0	0	0	1
Totals	30	3	4	3	4	8	24	11

St. Louis	AB	R	H	RBI	BB	SO	PO	A
Vina, 2b	4	1	2	1	1	0	1	3
Drew, rf	5	0	1	0	0	1	3	0
Edmonds, cf	3	0	0	0	1	2	4	0
Pujols, lf	2	1	1	1	2	0	1	1
Martinez, 1b	3	1	0	0	1	0	7	0
Renteria, ss	4	0	0	0	0	1	1	0
Cairo, 3b	3	2	3	2	0	0	0	2
Matheny, c	3	1	1	0	1	0	10	1
Benes, p	1	0	0	1	0	0	0	0
Fassero, p	0	0	0	0	0	0	0	0
White, p	0	0	0	0	0	0	0	0
Perez, ph	1	0	0	0	0	0	0	0
Kline, p	0	0	0	0	0	0	0	0
Robinson, ph	1	0	1	1	0	0	0	0
Isringhausen, p	0	0	0	0	0	0	0	0
Totals	30	6	9	6	6	4	27	7

Arizona	0 2 0		0 1 0		0 0 0—3			
St. Louis	0 1 1		2 0 0		0 2 x—6			

Arizona	IP	H	R	ER	HR	BB	SO
Batista (L)	3.2	5	4	4	0	3	1
Swindell	0.1	0	0	0	0	0	0
Helling	2.0	1	0	0	0	0	2
Myers	1.0	1	0	0	0	0	1
Kim	1.0	2	2	2	0	3	0

St. Louis	IP	H	R	ER	HR	BB	SO
Benes	4.2	2	3	3	2	4	5
Fassero (W)	1.1	2	0	0	0	0	2
White	1.0	0	0	0	0	0	1
Kline	1.0	0	0	0	0	0	0
Isringhausen (S)	1.0	0	0	0	0	0	0

DP—Arizona 1. LOB—Arizona 4, St. Louis 8. Hitting with runners in scoring position—Arizona 1 for 2, St. Louis 4 for 7. 2B—Cairo. HR—Dellucci (2nd inning, 1 out, 1 on) off Benes, Barajas (5th inning, 1 out, 0 on) off Benes. CS—Vina. SH—Benes. BK—Benes. HBP—Cairo by Batista. T—3:14. A—52,189. U—Hernandez, plate; Layne, first; Tschida, second; Barrett, third; Reilly, left field; Emmel, right field.

HOW THEY SCORED

SECOND INNING

Diamondbacks—Durazo flied to Drew. McCracken walked. Dellucci homered to right-center, scoring McCracken. Barajas flied to Edmonds. Batista struck out. Two runs. Diamondbacks 2, Cardinals 0.

Cardinals—Pujols and Martinez walked. Renteria grounded into a double play, Spivey to Womack to Durazo, as Pujols advanced to third. Cairo singled to left, scoring Pujols. Matheny grounded out, Womack to Durazo. One run. Diamondbacks 2, Cardinals 1.

THIRD INNING

Cardinals—Benes grounded out, Womack to Durazo. Vina singled to left. Drew struck out. Edmonds walked. Pujols singled to right, scoring Vina as Edmonds advanced to third. Martinez lined to Williams. One run. Diamondbacks 2, Cardinals 2.

FOURTH INNING

Cardinals—Renteria grounded out, Spivey to Durazo. Cairo was hit by a pitch. Matheny singled to right-center as Cairo advanced to third. Benes scored Cairo and advanced Matheny to second with a sacrifice bunt, Barajas to Spivey. Vina singled to right, scoring Matheny. Swindell now pitching. Vina was caught trying to steal second, Swindell to Durazo to Womack. Two runs. Cardinals 4, Diamondbacks 2.

FIFTH INNING

Diamondbacks—Dellucci grounded out, Vina to Martinez. Barajas homered to left. Donnels, pinch-hitting for Swindell, walked. Womack fouled to Renteria. Spivey walked. Fassero now pitching. S. Finley singled to left and advanced to second as Donnels advanced to third, but was out trying to score, Pujols to Matheny. One run. Cardinals 4, Diamondbacks 3.

EIGHTH INNING

Cardinals—Kim now pitching. Pujols walked. Martinez forced Pujols at second, Kim to Womack. Renteria popped to Spivey. Cairo doubled to left-center, scoring Martinez. Matheny was walked intentionally. Robinson, pinch-hitting for Kline, singled to left, scoring Cairo as Matheny advanced to second. Vina walked. Drew flied to S. Finley. Two runs. Cardinals 6, Diamondbacks 3.

STATISTICS

ST. LOUIS CARDINALS' BATTING AND FIELDING AVERAGES

Player, position	G	AB	R	H	TB	2B	3B	HR	RBI	BB	IBB	SO	Avg.	OBP	Slg.	PO	A	E	Avg.
Cairo, 3b	2	4	2	4	5	1	0	0	3	0	0	0	1.000	1.000	1.250	0	2	0	1.000
Vina, 2b	3	15	3	9	9	0	0	0	1	1	0	0	.600	.625	.600	5	8	0	1.000
Robinson, ph	2	2	0	1	1	0	0	0	1	0	0	0	.500	.500	.500	0	0	0	.000
Matheny, c	3	9	3	4	5	1	0	0	2	2	1	1	.444	.545	.556	24	3	0	1.000
Rolen, 3b	2	7	1	3	6	0	0	1	2	0	0	2	.429	.500	.857	2	4	0	1.000
Pujols, 1b-3b-lf	3	10	3	3	5	0	1	0	3	3	0	1	.300	.462	.500	3	2	1	.833
Edmonds, cf	3	11	1	3	6	0	0	1	2	2	0	4	.273	.385	.545	11	0	0	1.000
Renteria, ss	3	12	3	3	3	0	0	0	0	1	1	1	.250	.308	.250	6	4	1	.909
Morris, p	1	4	1	1	1	0	0	0	2	0	0	0	.250	.250	.250	1	1	0	1.000
Drew, rf	2	9	1	2	5	0	0	1	1	1	0	2	.222	.300	.556	5	0	0	1.000
Crudale, p	1	0	0	0	0	0	0	0	0	0	0	0	.000	.000	.000	0	0	0	.000
Fassero, p	3	0	0	0	0	0	0	0	0	0	0	0	.000	.000	.000	0	0	0	.000
Isringhausen, p	2	0	0	0	0	0	0	0	0	0	0	0	.000	.000	.000	0	0	0	.000
Kline, p	2	0	0	0	0	0	0	0	0	0	0	0	.000	.000	.000	0	0	0	.000
White, p	2	0	0	0	0	0	0	0	0	0	0	0	.000	.000	.000	0	0	0	.000
Benes, p	1	1	0	0	0	0	0	0	1	0	0	0	.000	.000	.000	0	0	0	.000
Perez, ph	1	1	0	0	0	0	0	0	0	0	0	0	.000	.000	.000	0	0	0	.000
C. Finley, p	1	3	0	0	0	0	0	0	0	0	0	2	.000	.000	.000	0	1	0	1.000
Marrero, lf-rf-ph	2	6	0	0	0	0	0	0	1	0	0	1	.000	.000	.000	2	0	0	1.000
Martinez, 1b	3	11	2	0	0	0	0	0	0	2	0	1	.000	.154	.000	22	1	0	1.000
Totals	3	105	20	33	46	2	1	3	19	12	2	17	.314	.392	.438	81	26	2	.982

ARIZONA DIAMONDBACKS' BATTING AND FIELDING AVERAGES

Player, position	G	AB	R	H	TB	2B	3B	HR	RBI	BB	IBB	SO	Avg.	OBP	Slg.	PO	A	E	Avg.
Miller, c	1	2	0	1	2	1	0	0	0	2	0	0	.500	.750	1.000	8	0	0	1.000
Moeller, c-ph	3	5	0	2	2	0	0	0	0	0	0	1	.400	.400	.400	4	1	0	1.000
McCracken, rf	3	11	1	4	5	1	0	0	2	1	0	2	.364	.417	.455	1	0	0	1.000
Dellucci, lf	3	7	1	2	5	0	0	1	2	0	0	1	.286	.286	.714	4	0	0	1.000
Barajas, c	2	4	1	1	4	0	0	1	1	0	0	1	.250	.250	1.000	4	2	0	1.000
Grace, 1b-ph	2	4	0	1	1	0	0	0	0	1	0	0	.250	.400	.250	14	1	0	1.000
S. Finley, cf	3	9	1	2	2	0	0	0	1	2	0	0	.222	.333	.222	12	0	0	1.000
Spivey, 2b	3	13	0	2	2	0	0	0	0	1	0	2	.154	.214	.154	8	12	0	1.000
Womack, ss	3	13	1	2	2	0	0	0	0	1	0	1	.154	.214	.154	7	9	1	.941
Williams, 3b	3	12	0	1	1	0	0	0	0	0	0	3	.083	.083	.083	3	2	0	1.000
Cintron, 3b-pr	2	0	0	0	0	0	0	0	0	0	0	0	.000	.000	.000	0	0	0	.000
Fetters, p	1	0	0	0	0	0	0	0	0	0	0	0	.000	.000	.000	0	0	0	.000
Helling, p	2	0	0	0	0	0	0	0	0	0	0	0	.000	.000	.000	0	1	0	1.000
Kim, p	1	0	0	0	0	0	0	0	0	0	0	0	.000	.000	.000	0	1	0	1.000
Koplove, p	1	0	0	0	0	0	0	0	0	0	0	0	.000	.000	.000	1	0	0	1.000
Mantei, p	1	0	0	0	0	0	0	0	0	0	0	0	.000	.000	.000	0	0	0	.000
Myers, p	2	0	0	0	0	0	0	0	0	0	0	0	.000	.000	.000	1	1	0	1.000
Swindell, p	2	0	0	0	0	0	0	0	0	0	0	0	.000	.000	.000	0	1	1	.500
Batista, p	1	1	0	0	0	0	0	0	0	0	0	1	.000	.000	.000	0	1	0	1.000
Donnels, ph	3	2	0	0	0	0	0	0	0	1	0	0	.000	.333	.000	0	0	0	.000
Johnson, p	1	2	0	0	0	0	0	0	0	0	0	2	.000	.000	.000	0	0	0	.000
Schilling, p	1	2	0	0	0	0	0	0	0	0	0	0	.000	.000	.000	0	0	0	.000
Colbrunn, 1b	1	3	1	0	0	0	0	0	0	1	0	1	.000	.250	.000	4	1	0	1.000
Durazo, 1b-ph	2	4	0	0	0	0	0	0	0	1	0	1	.000	.200	.000	6	2	0	1.000
Little, lf-ph	2	4	0	0	0	0	0	0	0	0	0	2	.000	.000	.000	1	0	0	1.000
Totals	3	98	6	18	26	2	0	2	6	11	0	21	.184	.264	.265	78	34	2	.982

ST. LOUIS CARDINALS' PITCHING RECORDS

Pitcher	G	GS	CG	IP	H	R	ER	HR	BB	IBB	SO	HB	WP	W	L	Pct.	ERA
C. Finley	1	1	0	6.1	4	0	0	0	2	0	7	0	0	0	0	.000	0.00
Fassero	3	0	0	2.2	3	0	0	0	0	0	2	0	0	0	0	.000	0.00
Isringhausen	2	0	0	2.0	0	0	0	0	0	0	1	0	0	2	0	1.000	0.00
White	2	0	0	2.0	1	1	0	0	1	0	1	0	0	0	0	.000	0.00

Pitcher	G	GS	CG	IP	H	R	ER	HR	BB	IBB	SO	HB	WP	W	L	Pct.	ERA
Kline	2	0	0	1.1	1	0	0	0	1	0	0	0	0	0	0	.000	0.00
Crudale	1	0	0	1.0	0	0	0	0	1	0	2	0	0	0	0	.000	0.00
Morris	1	1	0	7.0	7	2	1	0	2	0	3	0	0	1	0	1.000	1.29
Benes	1	1	0	4.2	2	3	3	2	4	0	5	0	0	0	0	.000	5.79
Totals	3	3	0	27.0	18	6	4	2	11	0	21	0	0	3	0	1.000	1.33

No shutouts. Saves—Isringhausen 2.

ARIZONA DIAMONDBACKS' PITCHING RECORDS

Pitcher	G	GS	CG	IP	H	R	ER	HR	BB	IBB	SO	HB	WP	W	L	Pct.	ERA
Helling	2	0	0	4.0	1	0	0	0	0	0	2	0	0	0	0	.000	0.00
Myers	2	0	0	1.2	2	0	0	0	0	0	1	0	0	0	0	.000	0.00
Fetters	1	0	0	0.2	1	0	0	0	1	0	1	0	0	0	0	.000	0.00
Schilling	1	1	0	7.0	7	1	1	1	1	0	7	1	0	0	0	.000	1.29
Koplove	1	0	0	1.1	2	1	1	0	0	0	1	0	0	0	1	.000	6.75
Johnson	1	1	0	6.0	10	6	5	2	2	1	4	0	0	0	1	.000	7.50
Batista	1	1	0	3.2	5	4	4	0	3	0	1	1	0	0	1	.000	9.82
Kim	1	0	0	1.0	2	2	2	0	3	1	0	0	0	0	0	.000	18.00
Swindell	2	0	0	0.1	2	4	1	0	1	0	0	0	0	0	0	.000	27.00
Mantei	1	0	0	0.1	1	2	2	0	1	0	0	0	0	0	0	.000	54.00
Totals	3	3	0	26.0	33	20	16	3	12	2	17	2	0	0	3	.000	5.54

No shutouts or saves.

SCORE BY INNINGS

St. Louis	2	1	2	5	0	1	6	2	1—20
Arizona	1	2	1	0	1	0	0	1	0— 6

MISCELLANEOUS STATISTICS

Sacrifice hits—Matheny 2, Benes.
Sacrifice flies—S. Finley, Marrero.
Stolen bases—Renteria 2, S. Finley.
Caught stealing—Cairo, Edmonds, Vina.
Double plays—Spivey, Womack and Durazo.
Left on bases—St. Louis 8, 9, 8—25; Arizona 9, 10, 4—23.
Hitting with runners in scoring position—St. Louis 6 for 13, 1 for 3, 4 for 7—11 for 23; Arizona 2 for 6, 0 for 7, 1 for 2—3 for 15.
Hit by pitcher—By Schilling (Rolen), by Batista (Cairo).
Passed balls—None.
Balk—Benes.
Time of games—2:55, 3:20, 3:14—Avg.: 3:09.
Attendance—49,154, 48,856, 52,189—150,199.
Umpires—Bruce Froemming, Bill Miller, Ron Kulpa, Gary Darling, Steve Rippley, Mark Hirschbeck, Angel Hernandez, Jerry Layne, Tim Tschida, Ted Barrett, Mike Reilly, Paul Emmel.
Official scorers—Rodney Johnson, Gary Mueller.

SAN FRANCISCO VS. ATLANTA

RESULTS

Day	Date	Place	Score
Wed.	Oct. 2	Atlanta	San Francisco 8, Atlanta 5
Thur.	Oct. 3	Atlanta	Atlanta 7, San Francisco 3
Sat.	Oct. 5	San Fran.	Atlanta 10, San Francisco 2
Sun.	Oct. 6	San Fran.	San Francisco 8, Atlanta 3
Mon.	Oct. 7	Atlanta	San Francisco 3, Atlanta 1

BOX SCORES

GAME 1

SAN FRANCISCO 8, ATLANTA 5

WEDNESDAY, OCTOBER 2, AT ATLANTA

San Francisco	AB	R	H	RBI	BB	SO	PO	A
Lofton, cf	4	1	1	1	1	1	4	0
Aurilia, ss	5	0	1	2	0	1	0	4
Kent, 2b	4	1	1	0	1	1	6	5
Bonds, lf	4	1	1	0	1	0	2	0
Santiago, c	5	1	3	2	0	1	4	0
Sanders, rf	4	1	1	0	1	1	1	0
Snow, 1b	5	1	1	2	0	1	8	0
Bell, 3b	4	1	2	1	1	0	2	3
Ortiz, p	4	1	1	0	0	3	0	0
Worrell, p	0	0	0	0	0	0	0	0
Eyre, p	0	0	0	0	0	0	0	0
Nen, p	0	0	0	0	0	0	0	0
Totals	39	8	12	8	5	9	27	12

Atlanta	AB	R	H	RBI	BB	SO	PO	A
Furcal, ss	5	0	2	0	0	0	1	1
J. Franco, 1b	5	0	1	0	0	0	8	0
Sheffield, rf	4	1	1	1	1	1	1	0
C. Jones, lf	3	0	1	0	1	0	2	0
A. Jones, cf	4	2	1	0	0	0	3	0
Lopez, c	4	1	1	2	0	0	9	0
Castilla, 3b	4	1	2	0	0	0	0	2
Lockhart, 2b	1	0	0	0	2	1	3	3
Moss, p	0	0	0	0	0	0	0	0
M. Franco, ph	0	0	0	0	0	0	0	0
Giles, ph	1	0	0	0	0	0	0	0
Holmes, p	0	0	0	0	0	0	0	0
Glavine, p	1	0	1	2	0	0	0	1
Bragg, ph	1	0	0	0	0	0	0	0
Hammond, p	0	0	0	0	0	0	0	1
Gryboski, p	0	0	0	0	0	0	0	0
DeRosa, ph-2b	1	0	0	0	1	1	0	1
Totals	34	5	10	5	5	3	27	9

San Francisco	0 3 0		3 0 2		0 0 0—8			
Atlanta	0 2 0		0 0 0		0 3 0—5			

San Francisco	IP	H	R	ER	HR	BB	SO
Ortiz (W)	7.0	5	2	2	0	4	3
Worrell	0.2	4	3	1	2	0	0
Eyre	0.1	0	0	0	0	0	0
Nen (S)	1.0	1	0	0	0	1	0

Atlanta	IP	H	R	ER	HR	BB	SO
Glavine (L)	5.0	10	6	6	0	2	3
Hammond	0.2	2	2	2	0	2	0
Gryboski	1.1	0	0	0	0	1	2
Moss	1.0	0	0	0	0	0	2
Holmes	1.0	0	0	0	0	0	2

E—Santiago, Bonds. DP—San Francisco 3. LOB—San Francisco 9, Atlanta 7. Hitting with runners in scoring position—San Francisco 5 for 8, Atlanta 1 for 5. 2B—Aurilia, Kent, Santiago, Snow. HR—Sheffield (8th inning, 1 out, 0 on) off Worrell, Lopez (8th inning, 2 out, 1 on) off Worrell. WP—Ortiz. T—3:24. A—41,903. U—Reilly, plate; Emmel, first; Hernandez, second; Layne, third; Tschida, left field; Barrett, right field.

HOW THEY SCORED

SECOND INNING

Giants—Bonds grounded out, Lockhart to J. Franco. Santiago singled to right. Sanders singled to center as Santiago advanced to second. Snow doubled to right, scoring Santiago and Sanders. Bell singled to left-center, scoring Snow. Ortiz and Lofton struck out. Three runs. Giants 3, Braves 0.

Braves—C. Jones grounded out, Kent to Snow. A. Jones singled to left. Lopez popped to Bell. Castilla singled to center as A. Jones advanced to second. A. Jones advanced to third and Castilla to second on a wild pitch. Glavine singled to left, scoring A. Jones and Castilla. A throwing error by Bonds on the play allowed Lockhart to reach third and Glavine second. Furcal flied to Lofton. Two runs. Giants 3, Braves 2.

FOURTH INNING

Giants—Sanders grounded out, Castilla to J. Franco. Snow grounded out, Lockhart to J. Franco. Bell singled to center. Ortiz singled to left-center as Bell advanced to third. Lofton singled to center, scoring Bell as Ortiz advanced to second. Aurilia doubled to right-center, scoring Ortiz and Lofton. Kent walked. Bonds flied to A. Jones. Three runs. Giants 6, Braves 2.

SIXTH INNING

Giants—Hammond now pitching. Lofton grounded out, Lockhart to J. Franco. Aurilia grounded out, Hammond to J. Franco. Kent doubled to left. Bonds was walked intentionally. Santiago doubled to right-center, scoring Kent and Bonds. Sanders walked. Gryboski now pitching. Snow flied to C. Jones. Two runs. Giants 8, Braves 2.

EIGHTH INNING

Braves—Worrell now pitching. J. Franco grounded out, Bell to Snow. Sheffield homered to left-center. C. Jones singled to center. A. Jones forced C. Jones at second, Aurilia to Kent. After his at-bat was prolonged by an error by Santiago, Lopez homered to left, scoring A. Jones. Castilla singled to left. M. Franco now pinch-hitting for Moss. Eyre now pitching. Giles, pinch-hitting for M. Franco, fouled to Santiago. Three runs. Giants 8, Braves 5.

GAME 2

ATLANTA 7, SAN FRANCISCO 3

THURSDAY, OCTOBER 3, AT ATLANTA

San Francisco	AB	R	H	RBI	BB	SO	PO	A
Lofton, cf	4	0	1	0	0	1	1	0
Aurilia, ss	4	1	1	1	0	1	1	3
Kent, 2b	4	0	0	0	0	2	3	3
Bonds, lf	4	1	1	1	0	1	2	0
Santiago, c	4	0	1	0	0	2	4	2
Snow, 1b	4	1	2	1	0	2	12	2
Sanders, rf	4	0	1	0	0	1	0	0
Bell, 3b	3	0	0	0	0	1	0	7
Rueter, p	1	0	0	0	0	1	1	0
Aybar, p	0	0	0	0	0	0	0	0
Feliz, p	1	0	0	0	0	1	0	0
Witasick, p	0	0	0	0	0	0	0	0
Goodwin, ph	1	0	0	0	0	1	0	0
Rodriguez, p	0	0	0	0	0	0	0	0
Totals	34	3	7	3	0	14	24	17

Atlanta	AB	R	H	RBI	BB	SO	PO	A
Furcal, ss	4	0	1	1	0	2	1	2
J. Franco, 1b	3	1	0	0	1	1	5	1
Smoltz, p	0	0	0	0	0	0	0	0
Sheffield, rf	4	0	0	0	0	0	2	0
C. Jones, lf	3	0	1	1	1	0	2	0
A. Jones, cf	4	0	1	0	0	1	1	0
Lopez, c	4	2	2	1	0	0	14	0
Castilla, 3b	2	2	1	1	1	0	1	2
DeRosa, 2b	3	2	2	2	1	0	0	0
Remlinger, p	0	0	0	0	0	0	0	0

Atlanta	AB	R	H	RBI	BB	SO	PO	A
Holmes, p	0	0	0	0	0	0	0	0
Helms, 1b	0	0	0	0	0	0	0	0
Millwood, p	1	0	0	0	0	0	1	0
Lockhart, ph-2b	1	0	0	0	0	0	0	0
Totals	29	7	8	6	3	4	27	5

San Francisco	0	1	0	0	0	1	0	0 1—3
Atlanta	1	3	0	3	0	0	0	0 x—7

San Francisco	IP	H	R	ER	HR	BB	SO
Rueter (L)	*3.0	7	7	6	2	2	1
Aybar	2.0	0	0	0	0	1	2
Witasick	2.0	0	0	0	0	0	1
Rodriguez	1.0	1	0	0	0	0	0

Atlanta	IP	H	R	ER	HR	BB	SO
Millwood (W)	6.0	3	2	2	2	0	7
Remlinger	1.0	2	0	0	0	0	2
Holmes	0.2	1	0	0	0	0	1
Smoltz	1.1	1	1	1	1	0	4

*Pitched to three batters in fourth.
DP—San Francisco 1. LOB—San Francisco 4, Atlanta 2. Hitting with runners in scoring position—San Francisco 0 for 1, Atlanta 3 for 5. 2B—DeRosa. 3B—DeRosa. HR—Snow (2nd inning, 2 out, 0 on) off Millwood, Lopez (2nd inning, 0 out, 0 on) off Rueter, Castilla (2nd inning, 0 out, 0 on) off Rueter, Aurilia (6th inning, 2 out, 0 on) off Millwood, Bonds (9th inning, 0 out, 0 on) off Smoltz. CS—Furcal. SH—Millwood. PB—Santiago. T—2:58. A—47,167. U—Emmel, plate; Hernandez, first; Layne, second; Tschida, third; Barrett, left field; Reilly, right field.

HOW THEY SCORED

FIRST INNING
Braves—Furcal grounded out, Snow to Rueter. Franco walked. Sheffield grounded out, Bell to Snow, as Franco advanced to second. C. Jones singled to left, scoring Franco. A. Jones struck out. One run. Braves 1, Giants 0.

SECOND INNING
Giants—Bonds struck out. Santiago lined to Sheffield. Snow homered to left. Sanders fouled to Sheffield. One run. Braves 1, Giants 1.
Braves—Lopez homered to left-center. Castilla homered to center. DeRosa doubled to right. Millwood sacrificed DeRosa to third, Santiago to Kent. Furcal singled to center, scoring DeRosa. Furcal caught trying to steal second, Santiago to Aurilia to Snow to Kent. Franco grounded out, Bell to Snow. Three runs. Braves 4, Giants 1.

FOURTH INNING
Braves—Lopez singled to center. Castilla walked. DeRosa tripled to right, scoring Lopez and Castilla. Aybar now pitching. Millwood grounded out, Bell to Snow. Furcal struck out. DeRosa scored on a passed ball by Santiago. Franco struck out. Three runs. Braves 7, Giants 1.

SIXTH INNING
Giants—Feliz, pinch-hitting for Aybar, struck out. Lofton grounded out, Franco to Millwood. Aurilia homered to left-center. Kent grounded out, Furcal to Franco. One run. Braves 7, Giants 2.

NINTH INNING
Giants—Bonds homered to right. Santiago, Snow and Sanders struck out. One run. Braves 7, Giants 3.

GAME 3

ATLANTA 10, SAN FRANCISCO 2
SATURDAY, OCTOBER 5, AT SAN FRANCISCO

Atlanta	AB	R	H	RBI	BB	SO	PO	A
Furcal, ss	5	2	2	0	0	2	3	4
J. Franco, 1b	5	1	2	1	0	1	10	0
Sheffield, rf	2	2	0	0	3	0	2	0
C. Jones, lf	3	2	1	1	2	1	2	0
Gryboski, p	0	0	0	0	0	0	0	0
A. Jones, cf	3	1	1	2	2	0	3	0
Castilla, 3b	5	1	1	2	0	1	1	3
Lockhart, 2b	5	1	2	4	0	1	0	3

Atlanta	AB	R	H	RBI	BB	SO	PO	A
Blanco, c	5	0	1	0	0	1	6	0
Maddux, p	3	0	0	0	0	1	0	0
Hammond, p	0	0	0	0	0	0	0	0
Remlinger, p	0	0	0	0	0	0	0	0
M. Franco, ph	1	0	0	0	0	0	0	0
Bragg, lf	0	0	0	0	0	0	0	0
Totals	37	10	10	10	7	8	27	10

San Francisco	AB	R	H	RBI	BB	SO	PO	A
Lofton, cf	4	1	2	0	0	0	2	0
Aurilia, ss	4	0	0	0	0	0	0	5
Kent, 2b	3	0	1	1	0	1	1	1
Bonds, lf	3	1	1	1	1	0	3	0
Santiago, c	4	0	0	0	0	0	9	0
Snow, 1b	3	0	1	0	0	0	7	1
Sanders, rf	3	0	0	0	0	1	3	0
Bell, 3b	3	0	0	0	0	2	0	1
Schmidt, p	2	0	0	0	0	1	1	0
Aybar, p	0	0	0	0	0	0	0	0
Rodriguez, p	0	0	0	0	0	0	0	0
Eyre, p	0	0	0	0	0	0	1	0
Dunston, ph	1	0	0	0	0	1	0	0
Worrell, p	0	0	0	0	0	0	0	0
Fultz, p	0	0	0	0	0	0	0	0
Nen, p	0	0	0	0	0	0	0	0
Witasick, p	0	0	0	0	0	0	0	0
Totals	30	2	5	2	1	6	27	8

Atlanta	0	0	1	0	0	5	0	0 4—10
San Francisco	1	0	0	0	0	1	0	0 0—2

Atlanta	IP	H	R	ER	HR	BB	SO
Maddux (W)	6.0	5	2	2	1	1	3
Hammond	1.0	0	0	0	0	0	1
Remlinger	1.0	0	0	0	0	0	1
Gryboski	1.0	0	0	0	0	0	1

San Francisco	IP	H	R	ER	HR	BB	SO
Schmidt (L)	5.1	3	4	4	0	4	5
Aybar	0.2	2	2	2	1	0	1
Rodriguez	1.1	0	0	0	0	2	2
Eyre	0.2	0	0	0	0	0	0
Worrell	0.1	2	3	3	0	1	0
Fultz	*0.0	1	1	1	0	0	0
Nen	0.1	2	0	0	0	0	0
Witasick	0.1	0	0	0	0	0	0

*Pitched to one batter in ninth.
DP—Atlanta 2. LOB—Atlanta 7, San Francisco 3. Hitting with runners in scoring position—Atlanta 5 for 9, San Francisco 1 for 4. 2B—Kent. 3B—Furcal. HR—Lockhart (6th inning, 1 out, 2 on) off Aybar, Bonds (6th inning, 2 out, 0 on) off Maddux. SB—J. Franco, Lofton. HBP—Kent by Maddux. T—3:23. A—43,043. U—Kulpa, plate; Darling, first; Rippley, second; M. Hirschbeck, third; Froemming, left field; Miller, right field.

HOW THEY SCORED

FIRST INNING
Giants—Lofton bunted safely to third. Aurilia grounded out, Furcal to Franco, as Lofton advanced to second. Kent doubled to left, scoring Lofton. Bonds was walked intentionally. Santiago grounded into a double play, Castilla to Franco. One run. Giants 1, Braves 0.

THIRD INNING
Braves—Furcal tripled to left. Franco scored Furcal on a groundout, Aurilia to Snow. Sheffield flied to Sanders. C. Jones grounded out to Snow. One run. Giants 1, Braves 1.

SIXTH INNING
Braves—Franco struck out. Sheffield, C. Jones and A. Jones walked. Aybar now pitching. Castilla singled to left, scoring Sheffield and C. Jones, as A. Jones advanced to second. Lockhart homered to right, scoring A. Jones and Castilla. Blanco struck out. Maddux grounded out, Aurilia to Snow. Five runs. Braves 6, Giants 1.
Giants—Aurilia grounded out, Furcal to Franco. Kent lined to Furcal. Bonds homered to left. Santiago grounded out, Castilla to Franco. One run. Braves 6, Giants 2.

NINTH INNING

Braves—Worrell now pitching. M. Franco, pinch-hitting for Remlinger, flied to Lofton. Furcal bunted safely to the mound. J. Franco singled to center as Furcal advanced to second. Sheffield walked. Fultz now pitching. C. Jones singled to third, scoring Furcal, as J. Franco advanced to third and Sheffield to second. Nen now pitching. A. Jones singled to center, scoring J. Franco and Sheffield, as C. Jones advanced to second. Castilla flied to Bonds. Lockhart singled to center, scoring C. Jones, as A. Jones advanced to second. Witasick now pitching. Blanco flied to Bonds. Four runs. Braves 10, Giants 2.

GAME 4

SAN FRANCISCO 8, ATLANTA 3

SUNDAY, OCTOBER 6, AT SAN FRANCISCO

Atlanta	AB	R	H	RBI	BB	SO	PO	A
Furcal, ss	5	0	1	1	0	0	1	2
J. Franco, 1b	5	0	0	0	0	1	8	0
Sheffield, rf	4	0	0	0	0	1	1	0
C. Jones, lf	4	1	1	0	0	1	5	0
A. Jones, cf	4	0	1	0	0	1	1	0
Lopez, c	3	1	1	1	1	1	3	1
Castilla, 3b	3	1	2	1	1	0	0	4
Lockhart, 2b	3	0	2	0	0	0	5	1
Glavine, p	1	0	0	0	0	1	0	1
Gryboski, p	0	0	0	0	0	0	0	0
Bragg, ph	1	0	0	0	0	0	0	0
Moss, p	0	0	0	0	0	0	0	1
DeRosa, ph	1	0	0	0	0	0	0	0
Ligtenberg, p	0	0	0	0	0	0	0	0
M. Franco, ph	0	0	0	0	0	0	0	0
Giles, ph	1	0	1	0	0	0	0	0
Totals	35	3	9	3	2	6	24	10

San Francisco	AB	R	H	RBI	BB	SO	PO	A
Lofton, cf	4	3	2	0	1	0	0	0
Aurilia, ss	5	3	3	4	0	1	1	6
Kent, 2b	4	0	3	0	1	0	1	2
Bonds, lf	3	0	0	1	1	0	2	0
Santiago, c	4	0	1	3	1	1	6	0
Sanders, rf	4	1	1	0	1	0	4	0
Snow, 1b	3	0	0	0	1	1	11	2
Bell, 3b	3	2	1	0	0	0	0	2
Hernandez, p	2	0	0	0	0	0	2	1
Eyre, p	0	0	0	0	0	0	0	1
Nen, p	0	0	0	0	0	0	0	0
Totals	32	8	11	8	7	3	27	14

Atlanta	0	0	0	0	1	2	0	0	0—3
San Francisco	2	2	3	0	1	0	0	0	x—8

Atlanta	IP	H	R	ER	HR	BB	SO
Glavine (L)	2.2	7	7	7	1	5	1
Gryboski	1.1	2	0	0	0	1	0
Moss	2.0	2	1	1	0	1	1
Ligtenberg	2.0	0	0	0	0	0	1

San Francisco	IP	H	R	ER	HR	BB	SO
Hernandez (W)	8.1	8	3	3	0	2	6
Eyre	0.1	1	0	0	0	0	0
Nen	0.1	0	0	0	0	0	0

DP—San Francisco 1. LOB—Atlanta 8, San Francisco 10. Hitting with runners in scoring position—Atlanta 2 for 8, San Francisco 4 for 12. 2B—Furcal, A. Jones, Lopez, Santiago, Sanders. HR—Aurilia (3rd inning, 2 out, 2 on) off Glavine. S—Bonds. SH—Hernandez 2. HBP—Lockhart by Hernandez. T—3:03. A—43,070. U—Darling, plate; Rippley, first; M. Hirschbeck, second; Froemming, third; Miller, left field; Kulpa, right field.

HOW THEY SCORED

FIRST INNING

Giants—Lofton singled to left. Aurilia singled to center as Lofton advanced to second. Kent walked. Bonds scored Lofton on a sacrifice fly to Sheffield as Aurilia advanced to third. Santiago scored Aurilia on a groundout, Castilla to Franco, as Kent advanced to second. Sanders was walked intentionally. Snow struck out. Two runs. Giants 2, Braves 0.

SECOND INNING

Giants—Bell singled to center. Hernandez sacrificed Bell to second, Lopez to Lockhart. Lofton flied to C. Jones. Aurilia singled to left, scoring Bell. Kent singled to left-center as Aurilia advanced to third. Bonds was walked intentionally. Santiago walked, scoring Aurilia. Sanders popped to Lockhart. Two runs. Giants 4, Braves 0.

THIRD INNING

Giants—Snow grounded out, Furcal to Franco. Bell walked. Hernandez sacrificed Bell to second, Glavine to Lockhart. Lofton singled to center as Bell advanced to third. Aurilia homered to left, scoring Bell and Lofton. Gryboski now pitching. Kent singled to short. Bonds flied to C. Jones. Three runs. Giants 7, Braves 0.

FIFTH INNING

Braves—Castilla singled to third. Lockhart singled to center as Castilla advanced to second. Bragg, pinch-hitting for Gryboski, grounded into a double play, Snow to Aurilia to Hernandez, as Castilla advanced to third. Furcal doubled to right, scoring Castilla. Franco struck out. One run. Giants 7, Braves 1.

Giants—Moss now pitching. Lofton walked. Aurilia struck out. Kent singled to left as Lofton advanced to second. Bonds flied to C. Jones as Lofton advanced to third. Santiago doubled to left, scoring Lofton as Kent advanced to third. Sanders popped to Franco. One run. Giants 8, Braves 1.

SIXTH INNING

Braves—Sheffield struck out. C. Jones singled to right. A. Jones flied to Sanders. Lopez doubled to center, scoring C. Jones. Castilla singled to left-center, scoring Lopez. Lockhart grounded out, Aurilia to Snow. Two runs. Giants 8, Braves 3.

GAME 5

SAN FRANCISCO 3, ATLANTA 1

MONDAY, OCTOBER 7, AT ATLANTA

San Francisco	AB	R	H	RBI	BB	SO	PO	A
Lofton, cf	4	0	1	1	0	1	4	0
Aurilia, ss	3	0	0	0	1	2	3	0
Kent, 2b	4	0	0	0	0	3	2	0
Bonds, lf	3	2	2	1	1	0	1	0
Santiago, c	4	0	0	0	0	1	9	0
Snow, 1b	4	1	2	0	0	1	4	2
Sanders, rf	3	0	1	1	2	3	0	0
Bell, 3b	3	0	0	0	1	1	1	1
Ortiz, p	2	0	0	0	0	1	0	1
Fultz, p	0	0	0	0	0	0	0	0
Rodriguez, p	0	0	0	0	0	0	0	0
Dunston, ph	1	0	0	0	0	0	0	0
Goodwin, ph	1	0	0	0	0	1	0	0
Worrell, p	0	0	0	0	0	0	0	1
Martinez, ph	0	0	0	0	1	0	0	0
Nen, p	0	0	0	0	0	0	0	0
Totals	31	3	6	3	5	13	27	5

Atlanta	AB	R	H	RBI	BB	SO	PO	A
Furcal, ss	5	0	0	0	0	1	0	3
J. Franco, 1b	4	0	1	0	1	0	6	0
Sheffield, rf	2	0	0	0	3	1	1	0
C. Jones, lf	4	0	1	0	1	0	1	0
A. Jones, cf	4	1	2	0	0	1	5	0
Lopez, c	4	0	1	0	0	2	10	0
Smoltz, p	0	0	0	0	0	0	0	0
Castilla, 3b	4	0	1	0	0	1	0	1
Lockhart, 2b	2	0	0	0	0	2	0	0
DeRosa, ph-2b	2	0	1	1	0	0	2	0
Millwood, p	1	0	0	0	0	0	0	0
Bragg, ph	1	0	0	0	0	0	0	0
Hammond, p	0	0	0	0	0	0	0	0
Giles, ph	0	0	0	0	0	0	0	0
M. Franco, ph	1	0	0	0	0	1	0	0
Remlinger, p	0	0	0	0	0	0	0	0
Holmes, p	0	0	0	0	0	0	0	0
Blanco, c	1	0	0	0	0	1	2	2
Totals	35	1	7	1	5	9	27	6

San Francisco	0	1	0	0	1	0	0	1	0	0—3
Atlanta	0	0	0	0	0	1	0	0	0—1

San Francisco	IP	H	R	ER	HR	BB	SO
Ortiz (W)	5.1	4	1	1	0	4	5
Fultz	*0.0	1	0	0	0	0	0
Rodriguez	0.2	0	0	0	0	0	0
Worrell	2.0	1	0	0	0	1	3
Nen (S)	1.0	1	0	0	0	0	1

Atlanta	IP	H	R	ER	HR	BB	SO
Millwood (L)	5.0	4	2	2	1	0	7
Hammond	1.0	0	0	0	0	1	1
Remlinger	†0.0	1	1	1	0	2	0
Holmes	1.0	0	0	0	0	0	2
Smoltz	2.0	1	0	0	0	2	3

*Pitched to one batter in sixth.
†Pitched to three batters in seventh.

E—Kent, Bell. DP—San Francisco 1. LOB—San Francisco 7, Atlanta 12. Hitting with runners in scoring position—San Francisco 1 for 8, Atlanta 2 for 10. 2B—Lofton, Snow. HR—Bonds (4th inning, 0 out, 0 on) off Millwood. SB—Furcal. CS—Bonds. S—Lofton. WP—Ortiz, Millwood. T—3:47. A—45,203. U—Layne, plate; Tschida, first; Barrett, second; Reilly, third; Emmel, left field; Hernandez, right field.

HOW THEY SCORED

SECOND INNING

Giants—Bonds singled to left-center. Santiago grounded out, Castilla to J. Franco as Bonds advanced to second. Snow struck out. Sanders singled to center, scoring Bonds. Sanders advanced to second on a wild pitch. Bell flied to A. Jones. One run. Giants 1, Braves 0.

FOURTH INNING

Giants—Bonds homered to left-center. Santiago grounded out, Furcal to J. Franco. Snow grounded out to J. Franco. Sanders struck out. One run. Giants 2, Braves 0.

SIXTH INNING

Braves—A. Jones singled to left-center. Lopez struck out. Castilla singled to center as A. Jones advanced to second. Fultz now pitching. DeRosa, pinch-hitting for Lockhart, singled to center, scoring A. Jones as Castilla advanced to second. Giles now pinch-hitting for Hammond. Rodriguez now pitching. M. Franco, pinch-hitting for Giles, popped to Lofton. Furcal lined to Lofton. One run. Giants 2, Braves 1.

SEVENTH INNING

Giants—DeRosa now at second and Remlinger pitching. Snow doubled to right. Sanders and Bell walked. Dunston now pinch-hitting for Rodriguez. Holmes now pitching. Goodwin, pinch-hitting for Dunston, struck out. Lofton scored Snow on a sacrifice fly to A. Jones as Sanders advanced to third. Aurilia struck out. One run. Giants 3, Braves 1.

STATISTICS

SAN FRANCISCO GIANTS' BATTING AND FIELDING AVERAGES

Player, position	G	AB	R	H	TB	2B	3B	HR	RBI	BB	IBB	SO	Avg.	OBP	Slg.	PO	A	E	Avg.
Lofton, cf	5	20	5	7	8	1	0	0	2	2	0	3	.350	.391	.400	11	0	0	1.000
Snow, 1b	5	19	3	6	11	2	0	1	3	1	1	5	.316	.350	.579	42	7	0	1.000
Bonds, lf	5	17	5	5	14	0	0	3	4	4	3	1	.294	.409	.824	10	0	1	.909
Kent, 2b	5	19	1	5	7	2	0	0	1	2	0	7	.263	.364	.368	13	11	1	.960
Aurilia, ss	5	21	4	5	12	1	0	2	7	1	0	5	.238	.273	.571	5	18	0	1.000
Santiago, c	5	21	1	5	7	2	0	0	5	1	0	5	.238	.273	.333	32	2	1	.971
Sanders, rf	5	18	1	4	5	1	0	0	1	3	1	5	.222	.333	.278	11	0	0	1.000
Bell, 3b	5	16	3	3	3	0	0	0	1	3	1	4	.188	.316	.188	3	14	1	.944
Ortiz, p	2	6	1	1	1	0	0	0	0	0	0	4	.167	.167	.167	0	1	0	1.000
Aybar, p	2	0	0	0	0	0	0	0	0	0	0	0	.000	.000	.000	0	0	0	.000
Eyre, p	3	0	0	0	0	0	0	0	0	0	0	0	.000	.000	.000	1	1	0	1.000
Fultz, p	2	0	0	0	0	0	0	0	0	0	0	0	.000	.000	.000	0	0	0	.000
Martinez, ph	1	0	0	0	0	0	0	0	0	1	0	0	.000	1.000	.000	0	0	0	.000
Nen, p	4	0	0	0	0	0	0	0	0	0	0	0	.000	.000	.000	0	0	0	.000
Rodriguez, p	3	0	0	0	0	0	0	0	0	0	0	0	.000	.000	.000	0	0	0	.000
Witasick, p	2	0	0	0	0	0	0	0	0	0	0	0	.000	.000	.000	0	1	0	1.000
Worrell, p	3	0	0	0	0	0	0	0	0	0	0	0	.000	.000	.000	0	0	0	.000
Dunston, ph	2	1	0	0	0	0	0	0	0	0	0	1	.000	.000	.000	0	0	0	.000
Feliz, ph	1	1	0	0	0	0	0	0	0	0	0	1	.000	.000	.000	0	0	0	.000
Rueter, p	1	1	0	0	0	0	0	0	0	0	0	1	.000	.000	.000	1	0	0	1.000
Goodwin, ph	2	2	0	0	0	0	0	0	0	0	0	2	.000	.000	.000	2	1	0	1.000
Hernandez, p	1	2	0	0	0	0	0	0	0	0	0	0	.000	.000	.000	1	0	0	1.000
Schmidt, p	1	2	0	0	0	0	0	0	0	0	0	1	.000	.000	.000	1	0	0	1.000
Totals	5	166	24	41	68	9	0	6	24	18	6	45	.247	.321	.410	132	56	4	.979

ATLANTA BRAVES' BATTING AND FIELDING AVERAGES

Player, position	G	AB	R	H	TB	2B	3B	HR	RBI	BB	IBB	SO	Avg.	OBP	Slg.	PO	A	E	Avg.
Giles, ph	3	2	0	1	1	0	0	0	0	0	0	0	.500	.500	.500	0	0	0	.000
Glavine, p	2	2	0	1	1	0	0	0	2	0	0	1	.500	.500	.500	0	2	0	1.000
DeRosa, 2b-ph	4	7	2	3	6	1	1	0	3	1	0	1	.429	.500	.857	2	1	0	1.000
Castilla, 3b	5	18	5	7	10	0	0	1	4	2	0	2	.389	.450	.556	2	12	0	1.000
Lopez, c	4	15	4	5	12	1	0	2	4	1	0	3	.333	.375	.800	36	1	0	1.000
Lockhart, 2b-ph	5	12	1	4	7	0	0	1	4	2	1	4	.333	.467	.583	8	7	0	1.000
A. Jones, cf	5	19	4	6	7	1	0	0	2	2	0	3	.316	.381	.368	13	0	0	1.000
C. Jones, lf	5	17	3	5	5	0	0	0	2	5	1	2	.294	.455	.294	12	0	0	1.000
Furcal, ss	5	24	2	6	9	1	1	0	2	0	0	5	.250	.250	.375	6	12	0	1.000
J. Franco, 1b	5	22	2	4	4	0	0	0	1	2	0	0	.182	.250	.182	37	1	0	1.000

Player, position	G	AB	R	H	TB	2B	3B	HR	RBI	BB	IBB	SO	Avg.	OBP	Slg.	PO	A	E	Avg.
Blanco, c	2	6	0	1	1	0	0	0	0	0	0	2	.167	.167	.167	8	2	0	1.000
Sheffield, rf	5	16	3	1	4	0	0	1	1	7	0	3	.063	.348	.250	7	0	0	1.000
Gryboski, p	3	0	0	0	0	0	0	0	0	0	0	0	.000	.000	.000	0	0	0	.000
Hammond, p	3	0	0	0	0	0	0	0	0	0	0	0	.000	.000	.000	0	1	0	1.000
Helms, 1b	1	0	0	0	0	0	0	0	0	0	0	0	.000	.000	.000	0	0	0	.000
Holmes, p	3	0	0	0	0	0	0	0	0	0	0	0	.000	.000	.000	0	0	0	.000
Ligtenberg, p	1	0	0	0	0	0	0	0	0	0	0	0	.000	.000	.000	0	0	0	.000
Moss, p	2	0	0	0	0	0	0	0	0	0	0	0	.000	.000	.000	0	1	0	1.000
Remlinger, p	3	0	0	0	0	0	0	0	0	0	0	0	.000	.000	.000	0	0	0	.000
Smoltz, p	2	0	0	0	0	0	0	0	0	0	0	0	.000	.000	.000	0	0	0	.000
M. Franco, ph	4	2	0	0	0	0	0	0	0	0	0	0	.000	.000	.000	0	0	0	.000
Millwood, p	2	2	0	0	0	0	0	0	0	0	0	0	.000	.000	.000	1	0	0	1.000
Bragg, lf-ph	4	3	0	0	0	0	0	0	0	0	0	0	.000	.000	.000	0	0	0	.000
Maddux, p	1	3	0	0	0	0	0	0	0	0	0	1	.000	.000	.000	0	0	0	.000
Totals	5	170	26	44	67	4	2	5	25	22	2	30	.259	.347	.394	132	40	0	1.000

SAN FRANCISCO GIANTS' PITCHING RECORDS

Pitcher	G	GS	CG	IP	H	R	ER	HR	BB	IBB	SO	HB	WP	W	L	Pct.	ERA
Rodriguez	3	0	0	3.0	1	0	0	0	2	0	2	0	0	0	0	.000	0.00
Nen	4	0	0	2.2	4	0	0	0	1	0	1	0	0	0	0	.000	0.00
Witasick	2	0	0	2.1	0	0	0	0	0	0	1	0	0	0	0	.000	0.00
Eyre	3	0	0	1.1	1	0	0	0	0	0	0	0	0	0	0	.000	0.00
Ortiz	2	2	0	12.1	9	3	3	0	8	1	8	0	2	2	0	1.000	2.19
Hernandez	1	1	0	8.1	8	3	3	0	2	0	6	1	0	1	0	1.000	3.24
Schmidt	1	1	0	5.1	3	4	4	0	4	1	5	0	0	0	1	.000	6.75
Aybar	2	0	0	2.2	2	2	2	1	1	0	3	0	0	0	0	.000	6.75
Worrell	3	0	0	3.0	7	6	4	2	2	0	3	0	0	0	0	.000	12.00
Rueter	1	1	0	3.0	7	7	6	2	2	0	1	0	0	0	1	.000	18.00
Fultz	2	0	0	0.0	2	1	1	0	0	0	0	0	0	0	0	.000	-
Totals	5	5	0	44.0	44	26	23	5	22	2	30	1	2	3	2	.600	4.70

No shutouts. Saves—Nen 2.

ATLANTA BRAVES' PITCHING RECORDS

Pitcher	G	GS	CG	IP	H	R	ER	HR	BB	IBB	SO	HB	WP	W	L	Pct.	ERA
Gryboski	3	0	0	3.2	2	0	0	0	2	1	3	0	0	0	0	.000	0.00
Holmes	3	0	0	2.2	1	0	0	0	0	0	5	0	0	0	0	.000	0.00
Ligtenberg	1	0	0	2.0	0	0	0	0	0	0	1	0	0	0	0	.000	0.00
Smoltz	2	0	0	3.1	2	1	1	1	2	0	7	0	0	0	0	.000	2.70
Maddux	1	1	0	6.0	5	2	2	1	1	1	3	1	0	1	0	1.000	3.00
Moss	2	0	0	3.0	2	1	1	0	1	0	3	0	0	0	0	.000	3.00
Millwood	2	2	0	11.0	7	4	4	3	0	0	14	0	1	1	1	.500	3.27
Remlinger	3	0	0	2.0	3	1	1	0	2	0	3	0	0	0	0	.000	4.50
Hammond	3	0	0	2.2	2	2	2	0	3	1	2	0	0	0	0	.000	6.75
Glavine	2	2	0	7.2	17	13	13	1	7	3	4	0	0	0	2	.000	15.26
Totals	5	5	0	44.0	41	24	24	6	18	6	45	1	1	2	3	.400	4.91

No shutouts or saves.

SCORE BY INNINGS

San Francisco	3	7	3	4	1	4	1	0	1—24
Atlanta	1	5	1	3	1	8	0	3	4—26

MISCELLANEOUS STATISTICS

Sacrifice hits—Hernandez 2, Millwood.
Sacrifice flies—Bonds, Lofton.
Stolen bases—Franco, Furcal, Lofton.
Caught stealing—Bonds, Furcal.
Double plays—Aurilia, Kent and Snow 3; Castilla and Franco; Kent and Snow; Lockhart, Furcal and Franco; Snow and Aurilia; Snow, Aurilia and Hernandez.
Left on bases—San Francisco 9, 4, 3, 10, 7—33; Atlanta 7, 2, 7, 8, 12—36.
Hitting with runners in scoring position—San Francisco 5 for 8, 0 for 1, 1 for 4, 4 for 12, 1 for 8—11 for 33; Atlanta 1 for 5, 3 for 5, 5 for 9, 2 for 8, 2 for 10—13 for 37.
Hit by pitcher—By Maddux (Kent), by Hernandez (Lockhart).
Passed ball—Santiago.
Balks—None.
Time of games—3:24, 2:58, 3:23, 3:03, 3:47—Avg.: 3:19.
Attendance—41,903, 47,167, 43,043, 43,070, 45,203—220,386.
Umpires—Mike Reilly, Paul Emmel, Angel Hernandez, Jerry Layne, Tim Tschida, Ted Barrett, Ron Kulpa, Gary Darling, Steve Rippley, Mark Hirschbeck, Bruce Froemming, Bill Miller.
Official scorers—Dick O'Connor, Mike Stamus.

A.L. CHAMPIONSHIP SERIES
ANAHEIM VS. MINNESOTA

RESULTS

Day	Date	Place	Score
Tue.	Oct. 8	Minnesota	Minnesota 2, Anaheim 1
Wed.	Oct. 9	Minnesota	Anaheim 6, Minnesota 3
Fri.	Oct. 11	Anaheim	Anaheim 2, Minnesota 1
Sat.	Oct. 12	Anaheim	Anaheim 7, Minnesota 1
Sun.	Oct. 13	Anaheim	Anaheim 13, Minnesota 5

BOX SCORES
GAME 1

MINNESOTA 2, ANAHEIM 1

TUESDAY, OCTOBER 8, AT MINNESOTA

Anaheim	AB	R	H	RBI	BB	SO	PO	A
Eckstein, ss	4	0	1	0	0	0	1	1
Erstad, cf	4	0	1	0	0	1	2	0
Salmon, rf	3	0	0	0	1	1	5	0
Figgins, pr	0	0	0	0	0	0	0	0
Anderson, lf	4	0	0	0	0	0	3	0
Glaus, 3b	4	0	0	0	0	2	2	1
Fullmer, dh	3	0	1	0	0	0	0	0
Spiezio, 1b	3	0	0	0	0	0	7	0
B. Molina, c	2	0	0	0	0	0	2	3
Palmeiro, ph	1	0	0	0	0	1	0	0
J. Molina, c	0	0	0	0	0	0	2	0
Kennedy, 2b	3	1	1	0	0	0	0	0
Appier, p	0	0	0	0	0	0	0	0
Donnelly, p	0	0	0	0	0	0	0	0
Schoeneweis, p	0	0	0	0	0	0	0	0
Weber, p	0	0	0	0	0	0	0	0
Totals	31	1	4	0	1	5	24	5

Minnesota	AB	R	H	RBI	BB	SO	PO	A
Jones, lf	4	0	0	0	0	1	3	0
Guzman, ss	3	0	1	0	0	0	0	6
Koskie, 3b	4	0	2	1	0	0	0	2
D. Ortiz, dh	3	0	1	0	0	0	0	0
Kielty, ph-dh	1	0	0	0	0	0	0	0
Hunter, cf	3	1	1	0	0	2	2	0
Mientkiewicz, 1b	3	0	0	0	1	1	13	0
Cuddyer, rf	2	0	0	0	1	0	1	0
Mohr, rf	0	0	0	0	0	0	1	0
Pierzynski, c	2	0	0	1	0	1	6	0
Rivas, 2b	2	1	0	0	1	1	1	3
Mays, p	0	0	0	0	0	0	0	1
Guardado, p	0	0	0	0	0	0	0	0
Totals	27	2	5	2	3	6	27	12

Anaheim								
Anaheim	0	0	1	0	0	0	0	0	0—1
Minnesota	0	1	0	0	1	0	0	0	x—2

Anaheim	IP	H	R	ER	HR	BB	SO
Appier (L)	5.0	5	2	2	0	3	2
Donnelly	1.2	0	0	0	0	0	2
Schoeneweis	0.2	0	0	0	0	0	0
Weber	0.2	0	0	0	0	0	2

Minnesota	IP	H	R	ER	HR	BB	SO
Mays (W)	8.0	4	1	0	0	0	3
Guardado (S)	1.0	0	0	0	0	1	2

E—Guzman. DP—Minnesota 1. LOB—Anaheim 4, Minnesota 7. Hitting with runners in scoring position—Anaheim 0 for 2, Minnesota 1 for 6. 2B—Koskie, Hunter. S—Pierzynski. SH—Hunter. WP—Appier. HBP—Guzman by Donnelly. T—2:58. A—55,562. U—Montague, plate; Everitt, first; Gorman, second; Young, third; DeMuth, left field; Rapuano, right field

HOW THEY SCORED

SECOND INNING
Twins—Hunter doubled to right-center. Hunter advanced to third on a wild pitch. Mientkiewicz fouled to Glaus. Cuddyer walked. Pierzynski scored Hunter on a sacrifice fly to Erstad. Rivas struck out. One run. Twins 1, Angels 0.

THIRD INNING
Angels—Spiezio fouled to Pierzynski. B. Molina flied to Cuddyer. Kennedy singled to left. Eckstein singled to right as Kennedy advanced to second. Erstad reached first on Guzman's fielding error, scoring Kennedy as Eckstein advanced to third. Salmon flied to Hunter. One run. Twins 1, Angels 1.

FIFTH INNING
Twins—Rivas walked. Jones flied to Anderson. Guzman singled to center as Rivas advanced to second. Koskie doubled to right, scoring Rivas as Guzman advanced to third. Ortiz fouled to Spiezio. Hunter struck out and was retired at first after a dropped third strike, B. Molina to Spiezio. One run. Twins 2, Angels 1.

GAME 2

ANAHEIM 6, MINNESOTA 3

WEDNESDAY, OCTOBER 9, AT MINNESOTA

Anaheim	AB	R	H	RBI	BB	SO	PO	A
Eckstein, ss	5	2	1	0	1	1	0	3
Erstad, cf	5	1	2	1	0	0	1	0
Salmon, rf	2	0	0	0	0	0	2	0
Palmeiro, rf	1	0	0	0	0	0	0	0
Ochoa, ph-rf	2	0	0	0	0	2	0	0
Anderson, lf	4	0	0	0	0	0	1	0
Glaus, 3b	3	2	2	0	1	0	0	0
Fullmer, dh	3	1	2	2	0	0	0	0
Wooten, ph-dh	1	0	0	0	0	1	0	0
Spiezio, 1b	4	1	2	1	0	0	10	0
B. Molina, c	4	0	0	0	0	1	10	0
Kennedy, 2b	4	1	0	0	0	1	3	3
R. Ortiz, p	0	0	0	0	0	0	0	1
Donnelly, p	0	0	0	0	0	0	0	0
Rodriguez, p	0	0	0	0	0	0	0	0
Percival, p	0	0	0	0	0	0	0	0
Totals	38	6	10	5	1	6	27	7

Minnesota	AB	R	H	RBI	BB	SO	PO	A
Jones, lf	5	0	0	0	0	2	3	0
Guzman, ss	4	1	2	0	0	1	0	2
Koskie, 3b	3	1	1	1	1	0	0	0
D. Ortiz, dh	4	0	1	0	0	1	0	0
Hunter, cf	3	1	1	0	1	0	4	0
Mientkiewicz, 1b	4	0	3	2	0	0	9	0
Cuddyer, rf	3	0	1	0	0	1	5	0
Kielty, ph-rf	1	0	0	0	0	1	0	0
Pierzynski, c	4	0	1	0	0	1	6	0
Rivas, 2b	3	0	1	0	0	1	0	3
Mohr, ph	1	0	0	0	0	1	0	0
Reed, p	0	0	0	0	0	0	0	2
Santana, p	0	0	0	0	0	0	0	1
Romero, p	0	0	0	0	0	0	0	0
Hawkins, p	0	0	0	0	0	0	0	0
Jackson, p	0	0	0	0	0	0	0	0
Totals	35	3	11	3	2	10	27	8

Anaheim								
Anaheim	1	3	0	0	0	2	0	0	0—6
Minnesota	0	0	0	0	3	0	0	0	0—3

Anaheim	IP	H	R	ER	HR	BB	SO
R. Ortiz (W)	5.1	10	3	3	0	1	3
Donnelly	0.2	0	0	0	0	0	1
Rodriguez	1.2	1	0	0	0	1	3
Percival (S)	1.1	0	0	0	0	0	3

Minnesota	IP	H	R	ER	HR	BB	SO
Reed (L)	5.1	8	6	6	2	0	0
Santana	1.2	0	0	0	0	0	3
Romero	0.1	0	0	0	0	1	0
Hawkins	0.2	0	0	0	0	0	1
Jackson	1.0	2	0	0	0	0	2

E—Pierzynski. DP—Anaheim 2. LOB—Anaheim 6, Minnesota 7. Hitting with runners in scoring position—Anaheim 3 for 7, Minnesota 2 for 3. 2B—Fullmer, Spiezio, Guzman, Hunter. 3B—Glaus. HR—Erstad (1st inning, 1 out, 0 on) off Reed, Fullmer (6th inning, 1 out, 1 on) off Reed. SB—Spiezio, Kennedy. WP—Santana. T—3:13. A—55,990. U—Everitt, plate; Gorman, first; Young, second; DeMuth, third; Rapuano, left field; Montague, right field.

HOW THEY SCORED

FIRST INNING
Angels—Eckstein grounded out, Reed to Mientkiewicz. Erstad homered to right-center. Salmon flied to Hunter. Anderson grounded out, Rivas to Mientkiewicz. One run. Angels 1, Twins 0.

SECOND INNING
Angels—Glaus singled to right. Fullmer doubled to right as Glaus advanced to third. Spiezio doubled to right, scoring Glaus as Fullmer advanced to third. B. Molina flied to Cuddyer. Kennedy reached first on a fielder's choice and Spiezio advanced to third as Fullmer was thrown out at the plate, Reed to Pierzynski. Spiezio was caught trying to steal home, but scored on an error by Pierzynski (Reed and Mientkiewicz assisted). Kennedy advanced to third on the play. Eckstein singled to right, scoring Kennedy. Erstad flied to Jones. Three runs. Angels 4, Twins 0.

SIXTH INNING
Angels—Anderson grounded out, Rivas to Mientkiewicz. Glaus tripled to right. Fullmer homered to center, scoring Glaus. Santana now pitching. Spiezio flied to Cuddyer. B. Molina struck out, but was safe at first on a wild pitch. Kennedy grounded out to Mientkiewicz. Two runs. Angels 6, Twins 0.

Twins—Guzman doubled to right-center. Koskie singled to right, scoring Guzman. Ortiz struck out. Hunter doubled to left as Koskie advanced to third. Mientkiewicz singled to center, scoring Koskie and Hunter. Donnelly now pitching. Cuddyer struck out. Pierzynski popped to Kennedy. Three runs. Angels 6, Twins 3.

GAME 3

ANAHEIM 2, MINNESOTA 1

FRIDAY, OCTOBER 11, AT ANAHEIM

Minnesota	AB	R	H	RBI	BB	SO	PO	A
Jones, lf	4	0	1	1	0	0	4	0
Guzman, ss	4	0	0	0	0	1	2	0
Koskie, 3b	4	0	0	0	0	4	0	0
LeCroy, dh	3	0	1	0	0	1	0	0
D. Ortiz, ph-dh	1	0	0	0	0	1	0	0
Hunter, cf	4	0	1	0	0	0	3	0
Mientkiewicz, 1b	4	0	0	0	0	1	4	0
Mohr, rf	4	1	2	0	0	1	4	0
Pierzynski, c	4	0	0	0	0	0	7	0
Rivas, 2b	3	0	1	0	0	0	0	1
Milton, p	0	0	0	0	0	0	0	0
Hawkins, p	0	0	0	0	0	0	0	0
Santana, p	0	0	0	0	0	0	0	0
Jackson, p	0	0	0	0	0	0	0	0
Romero, p	0	0	0	0	0	0	0	0
Totals	35	1	6	1	0	9	24	1

Anaheim	AB	R	H	RBI	BB	SO	PO	A
Eckstein, ss	4	0	1	0	0	0	0	3
Erstad, cf	4	0	1	0	0	1	2	0
Salmon, rf	3	0	0	0	1	0	2	0
Ochoa, rf	0	0	0	0	0	0	2	0
Anderson, lf	4	1	2	0	0	0	5	0
Glaus, 3b	3	1	2	1	1	1	0	1
Spiezio, 1b	3	0	0	0	1	1	5	0
Wooten, dh	4	0	1	0	0	1	0	0
B. Molina, c	2	0	0	0	1	1	7	0
Figgins, pr	0	0	0	0	0	0	0	0
J. Molina, c	1	0	0	0	0	0	2	0

Anaheim	AB	R	H	RBI	BB	SO	PO	A
Gil, 2b	2	0	0	0	0	1	2	1
Washburn, p	0	0	0	0	0	0	0	0
Rodriguez, p	0	0	0	0	0	0	0	0
Percival, p	0	0	0	0	0	0	0	0
Totals	30	2	7	2	4	6	27	5

Minnesota	0 0 0	0 0 0	1 0 0	— 1
Anaheim	0 1 0	0 0 0	0 1 x	— 2

Minnesota	IP	H	R	ER	HR	BB	SO
Milton	6.0	5	1	1	1	2	4
Hawkins	0.1	1	0	0	0	1	0
Santana	0.1	0	0	0	0	0	0
Jackson	*0.0	0	0	0	0	1	0
Romero (L)	1.1	1	1	1	1	0	2

Anaheim	IP	H	R	ER	HR	BB	SO
Washburn	7.0	6	1	1	0	0	7
Rodriguez (W)	1.0	0	0	0	0	0	2
Percival (S)	1.0	0	0	0	0	0	0

*Pitched to one batter in seventh.
E—Gil, Eckstein. LOB—Minnesota 7, Anaheim 9. Hitting with runners in scoring position—Minnesota 0 for 5, Anaheim 1 for 7. 2B—Jones, Anderson. HR—Anderson (2nd inning, 0 out, 0 on) off Milton, Glaus (8th inning, 0 out, 0 on) off Romero. SB—Mohr. SH—Gil. WP—Santana. T—3:13. A—44,234. U—Gorman, plate; Young, first; DeMuth, second; Rapuano, third; Montague, left field; Everitt, right field.

HOW THEY SCORED

SECOND INNING
Angels—Anderson homered to right. Glaus struck out. Spiezio walked. Wooten singled to right as Spiezio advanced to third. B. Molina popped to Mientkiewicz. Gil struck out. One run. Angels 1, Twins 0.

SEVENTH INNING
Twins—Mohr singled to left. Pierzynski flied to Anderson. Rivas flied to Salmon. Jones doubled to left, scoring Mohr. Guzman popped to Gil. One run. Angels 1, Twins 1.

EIGHTH INNING
Angels—Glaus homered to right. Spiezio and Wooten struck out. J. Molina popped to Mientkiewicz. One run. Angels 2, Twins 1.

GAME 4

ANAHEIM 7, MINNESOTA 1

SATURDAY, OCTOBER 12, AT ANAHEIM

Minnesota	AB	R	H	RBI	BB	SO	PO	A
Jones, lf	4	0	0	0	0	1	1	0
Guzman, ss	4	0	0	0	0	1	2	4
Koskie, 3b	4	1	1	0	0	2	1	2
D. Ortiz, dh	4	0	2	1	0	2	0	0
Hunter, cf	4	0	0	0	0	1	1	0
Mientkiewicz, 1b	3	0	1	0	0	0	9	0
Mohr, rf	3	0	1	0	0	2	1	0
Pierzynski, c	3	0	0	0	0	0	5	0
Rivas, 2b	2	0	1	0	0	0	4	1
Kielty, ph	1	0	0	0	0	1	0	0
Lamb, 2b	0	0	0	0	0	0	0	0
Radke, p	0	0	0	0	0	0	0	1
Santana, p	0	0	0	0	0	0	0	0
Hawkins, p	0	0	0	0	0	0	0	0
Romero, p	0	0	0	0	0	0	0	0
Jackson, p	0	0	0	0	0	0	0	0
Wells, p	0	0	0	0	0	0	0	0
Totals	32	1	6	1	0	10	24	8

Anaheim	AB	R	H	RBI	BB	SO	PO	A
Eckstein, ss	4	0	1	0	0	1	3	3
Erstad, cf	4	2	2	0	0	1	0	0
Salmon, rf	2	0	0	0	1	0	1	0
Ochoa, pr-rf	1	1	0	0	0	0	0	0
Anderson, lf	4	1	1	1	0	0	0	0
Glaus, 3b	4	1	2	1	0	0	0	0
Fullmer, dh	4	1	1	2	0	2	0	0
Spiezio, 1b	3	1	1	1	1	0	9	1

Anaheim	AB	R	H	RBI	BB	SO	PO	A
B. Molina, c	3	0	2	2	0	0	10	1
Kennedy, 2b	3	0	0	0	0	1	2	7
Lackey, p	0	0	0	0	0	0	2	0
Rodriguez, p	0	0	0	0	0	0	0	0
Weber, p	0	0	0	0	0	0	0	0
Totals	32	7	10	7	2	5	27	12

Minnesota	0 0 0		0 0 0			0 0 1—1		
Anaheim	0 0 0		0 0 0			2 5 x—7		

Minnesota	IP	H	R	ER	HR	BB	SO
Radke (L)	6.2	5	2	2	0	1	4
Santana	0.2	1	1	1	0	0	0
Hawkins	0.1	0	0	0	0	0	0
Romero	*0.0	1	1	1	0	0	0
Jackson	†0.0	3	3	3	0	1	0
Wells	0.1	0	0	0	0	0	1

Anaheim	IP	H	R	ER	HR	BB	SO
Lackey (W)	7.0	3	0	0	0	0	7
Rodriguez	1.0	0	0	0	0	0	2
Weber	1.0	2	1	1	0	0	1

*Pitched to one batter in eighth.
†Pitched to four batters in eighth.

E—Santana, Pierzynski. DP—Minnesota 1. LOB—Minnesota 4, Anaheim 5. Hitting with runners in scoring position—Minnesota 1 for 4, Anaheim 5 for 11. 2B—Koskie, Mientkiewicz, Fullmer, Spiezio. 3B—B. Molina. SB—Erstad. CS—Pierzynski. SH—Kennedy. HBP—B. Molina by Radke. T—2:49. A—44,830. U—Young, plate; DeMuth, first; Rapuano, second; Montague, third; Everitt, left field; Gorman, right field.

HOW THEY SCORED

SEVENTH INNING

Angels—Erstad singled to center. Erstad stole second and advanced to third on a throwing error by Pierzynski. Salmon walked. Anderson popped to Koskie. Glaus singled to left, scoring Erstad as Salmon advanced to second. Ochoa now running for Salmon. Fullmer struck out. Spiezio doubled to right, scoring Ochoa as Glaus advanced to third. B. Molina was hit by a pitch. Santana now pitching. Kennedy grounded out to Mientkiewicz. Two runs. Angels 2, Twins 0.

EIGHTH INNING

Angels—Lamb now at second. Eckstein popped to Mientkiewicz. Erstad singled to left. Erstad advanced to second on a wild pickoff throw by Santana. Hawkins now pitching. Ochoa grounded out, Guzman to Mientkiewicz, as Erstad advanced to third. Romero now pitching. Anderson singled to right, scoring Erstad. Jackson now pitching. Glaus singled to left as Anderson advanced to second. Fullmer doubled to right-center, scoring Anderson and Glaus. Spiezio was walked intentionally. B. Molina tripled to center, scoring Fullmer and Spiezio. Wells now pitching. Kennedy struck out. Five runs. Angels 7, Twins 0.

NINTH INNING

Twins—Weber now pitching. Jones lined to Eckstein. Guzman grounded out, Kennedy to Spiezio. Koskie doubled to right-center. Ortiz singled to right, scoring Koskie. Hunter struck out. One run. Angels 7, Twins 1.

GAME 5

ANAHEIM 13, MINNESOTA 5

SUNDAY, OCTOBER 13, AT ANAHEIM

Minnesota	AB	R	H	RBI	BB	SO	PO	A
Jones, lf	3	0	1	1	0	0	0	0
Guzman, ss	3	0	0	0	0	0	3	6
Koskie, 3b	3	1	1	0	1	1	1	3
D. Ortiz, dh	4	0	1	1	0	1	0	0
Hunter, cf	4	0	0	0	0	1	1	0
Cuddyer, rf	0	0	0	0	0	0	0	0
Mientkiewicz, 1b	4	1	1	0	0	0	13	0
Mohr, rf-cf	4	2	2	0	0	0	0	0
Pierzynski, c	3	1	3	1	0	0	5	1
Prince, c	1	0	0	0	0	1	0	0
Rivas, 2b	2	0	0	0	0	1	0	4

Minnesota	AB	R	H	RBI	BB	SO	PO	A
Kielty, ph	0	0	0	1	1	0	0	0
Lamb, 2b	0	0	0	0	0	0	0	0
Mays, p	0	0	0	0	0	0	0	0
Santana, p	0	0	0	0	0	0	0	0
Hawkins, p	0	0	0	0	0	0	0	0
Romero, p	0	0	0	0	0	0	0	0
Wells, p	0	0	0	0	0	0	0	0
Lohse, p	0	0	0	0	0	0	0	0
Totals	31	5	9	4	2	3	24	14

Anaheim	AB	R	H	RBI	BB	SO	PO	A
Eckstein, ss	4	1	1	1	0	0	1	2
Erstad, cf	5	1	2	1	0	0	9	0
Salmon, rf	4	0	3	0	0	0	3	0
Ochoa, pr-rf	1	1	0	0	0	1	1	0
Anderson, lf	4	1	2	1	1	0	1	1
Glaus, 3b	5	0	0	0	0	2	0	1
Fullmer, dh	2	0	0	0	0	0	0	0
Wooten, ph-dh	3	1	1	1	0	1	0	0
Spiezio, 1b	4	3	3	3	0	0	5	1
B. Molina, c	3	0	1	0	0	0	3	0
Figgins, pr	1	2	1	0	0	0	0	0
J. Molina, c	0	0	0	0	0	0	0	0
Kennedy, 2b	4	3	4	5	0	0	4	3
Appier, p	0	0	0	0	0	0	0	0
Donnelly, p	0	0	0	0	0	0	0	0
Rodriguez, p	0	0	0	0	0	0	0	1
Weber, p	0	0	0	0	0	0	0	0
Percival, p	0	0	0	0	0	0	0	0
Totals	40	13	18	12	1	4	27	9

Minnesota	1 1 0		0 0 0		3 0 0— 5			
Anaheim	0 0 1		0 2 0		10 0 x—13			

Minnesota	IP	H	R	ER	HR	BB	SO
Mays	5.1	8	3	3	3	0	0
Santana (L)	*0.2	3	3	3	1	0	1
Hawkins	*0.0	3	3	3	0	0	0
Romero	0.1	2	3	3	0	1	1
Wells	0.2	2	1	1	0	0	1
Lohse	1.0	0	0	0	0	0	1

Anaheim	IP	H	R	ER	HR	BB	SO
Appier	5.1	5	2	2	0	1	1
Donnelly	1.0	3	3	3	0	0	2
Rodriguez (W)	0.2	0	0	0	0	1	0
Weber	1.0	1	0	0	0	0	0
Percival	1.0	0	0	0	0	0	0

*Pitched to three batters in seventh.

DP—Minnesota 2, Anaheim 2. LOB—Minnesota 3, Anaheim 5. Hitting with runners in scoring position—Minnesota 3 for 7, Anaheim 5 for 12. 2B—Ortiz, Mohr. HR—Kennedy (3rd inning, 0 out, 0 on) off Mays, Spiezio (5th inning, 0 out, 0 on) off Mays, Kennedy (5th inning, 1 out, 0 on) off Mays, Kennedy (7th inning, 0 out, 2 on) off Santana. CS—Anderson. S—Jones. SH—Guzman. WP—Romero, Appier, Donnelly, F. Rodriguez. HBP—Eckstein by Wells. T—3:30. A—44,835. U—DeMuth, plate; Rapuano, first; Montague, second; Everitt, third; Gorman, left field; Young, right field.

HOW THEY SCORED

FIRST INNING

Twins—Jones flied to Salmon. Guzman flied to Erstad. Koskie walked. Koskie advanced to second on a wild pitch. Ortiz doubled to right, scoring Koskie. Hunter popped to Spiezio. One run. Twins 1, Angels 0.

SECOND INNING

Twins—Mientkiewicz flied to Anderson. Mohr doubled to left-center. Pierzynski singled to left, but was out trying for second, Anderson to Glaus to Kennedy. Mohr scored on the play. Rivas struck out. One run. Twins 2, Angels 0.

THIRD INNING

Angels—Kennedy homered to right. Eckstein grounded out, Rivas to Mientkiewicz. Erstad grounded out, Guzman to Mientkiewicz. Salmon popped to Guzman. One run. Twins 2, Angels 1.

FIFTH INNING

Angels—Spiezio homered to right. B. Molina grounded out, Koskie to Mientkiewicz. Kennedy homered to right-center.

Eckstein grounded out, Rivas to Mientkiewicz. Erstad grounded out, Guzman to Mientkiewicz. Two runs. Angels 3, Twins 2.

SEVENTH INNING

Twins—Hunter flied to Salmon. Mientkiewicz singled to center. Mohr singled to center as Mientkiewicz advanced to second. Pierzynski singled to right as Mientkiewicz advanced to third and Mohr to second. Rodriguez now pitching. Kielty, pinch-hitting for Rivas, walked, scoring Mientkiewicz. Mohr scored on a wild pitch as Pierzynski advanced to third and Kielty to second. Jones scored Pierzynski on a sacrifice fly to Erstad. Guzman grounded out, Kennedy to Spiezio. Three runs. Twins 5, Angels 3.

Angels—Lamb now at second. Spiezio singled to right. B. Molina singled to left as Spiezio advanced to second. Figgins now running for B. Molina. Kennedy homered to right-center, scoring

Spiezio and Figgins. Hawkins now pitching. Eckstein singled to third. Erstad singled to left as Eckstein advanced to second. Salmon singled to left as Eckstein advanced to third and Erstad to second. Ochoa now running for Salmon. Romero now pitching. Anderson walked, scoring Eckstein. Glaus struck out. Wooten singled to right, scoring Erstad as Ochoa advanced to third and Anderson to second. Ochoa scored on a wild pitch as Anderson advanced to third and Wooten to second. Spiezio singled to left, scoring Anderson and Wooten. Wells now pitching. Figgins singled to left as Spiezio advanced to second. Kennedy singled to left as Spiezio advanced to third and Figgins to second. Eckstein was hit by a pitch, scoring Spiezio. Erstad grounded out to Mientkiewicz, scoring Figgins as Kennedy advanced to third and Eckstein to second. Ochoa struck out. Ten runs. Angels 13, Twins 5.

STATISTICS

ANAHEIM ANGELS' BATTING AND FIELDING AVERAGES

Player, position	G	AB	R	H	TB	2B	3B	HR	RBI	BB	IBB	SO	Avg.	OBP	Slg.	PO	A	E	Avg.
Figgins, pr	3	1	2	1	1	0	0	0	0	0	0	0	1.000	1.000	1.000	0	0	0	.000
Erstad, cf	5	22	4	8	11	0	0	1	2	0	0	3	.364	.364	.500	14	0	0	1.000
Kennedy, 2b	4	14	5	5	14	0	0	3	5	0	0	2	.357	.357	1.000	9	13	0	1.000
Spiezio, 1b	5	17	5	6	11	2	0	1	5	2	1	1	.353	.421	.647	36	2	0	1.000
Fullmer, dh	4	12	2	4	9	2	0	1	4	0	0	2	.333	.333	.750	0	0	0	.000
Glaus, 3b	5	19	4	6	11	0	1	1	2	2	0	5	.316	.381	.579	2	3	0	1.000
Eckstein, ss	5	21	1	6	6	0	0	0	2	0	0	2	.286	.318	.286	5	12	1	.944
Anderson, lf	5	20	3	5	9	1	0	1	3	1	0	2	.250	.286	.450	10	1	0	1.000
Wooten, dh	3	8	1	2	2	0	0	0	1	0	0	3	.250	.250	.250	0	0	0	.000
B. Molina, c	5	14	0	3	5	0	1	0	2	1	0	2	.214	.313	.357	32	4	0	1.000
Salmon, rf	5	14	0	3	3	0	0	0	0	3	0	1	.214	.353	.214	13	0	0	1.000
Appier, p	2	0	0	0	0	0	0	0	0	0	0	0	.000	.000	.000	0	0	0	.000
Donnelly, p	3	0	0	0	0	0	0	0	0	0	0	0	.000	.000	.000	0	0	0	.000
Lackey, p	1	0	0	0	0	0	0	0	0	0	0	0	.000	.000	.000	2	0	0	1.000
Ortiz, p	1	0	0	0	0	0	0	0	0	0	0	0	.000	.000	.000	0	1	0	1.000
Percival, p	3	0	0	0	0	0	0	0	0	0	0	0	.000	.000	.000	0	0	0	.000
Rodriguez, p	4	0	0	0	0	0	0	0	0	0	0	0	.000	.000	.000	0	0	0	.000
Schoeneweis, p	1	0	0	0	0	0	0	0	0	0	0	0	.000	.000	.000	0	0	0	.000
Washburn, p	1	0	0	0	0	0	0	0	0	0	0	0	.000	.000	.000	0	0	0	.000
Weber, p	3	0	0	0	0	0	0	0	0	0	0	0	.000	.000	.000	0	1	0	1.000
J. Molina, c	3	1	0	0	0	0	0	0	0	0	0	0	.000	.000	.000	4	0	0	1.000
Gil, 2b	1	2	0	0	0	0	0	0	0	0	0	1	.000	.000	.000	2	1	1	.750
Palmeiro, ph-rf	2	2	0	0	0	0	0	0	0	0	0	1	.000	.000	.000	0	0	0	.000
Ochoa, rf-ph-pr	4	4	2	0	0	0	0	0	0	0	0	3	.000	.000	.000	3	0	0	1.000
Totals	5	171	29	49	82	5	2	8	26	9	1	26	.287	.330	.480	132	38	2	.988

MINNESOTA TWINS' BATTING AND FIELDING AVERAGES

Player, position	G	AB	R	H	TB	2B	3B	HR	RBI	BB	IBB	SO	Avg.	OBP	Slg.	PO	A	E	Avg.
Mohr, rf-ph-cf	5	12	3	5	6	1	0	0	0	0	0	4	.417	.417	.500	6	0	0	1.000
LeCroy, dh	1	3	0	1	1	0	0	0	0	0	0	1	.333	.333	.333	0	0	0	.000
Ortiz, dh	5	16	0	5	6	1	0	0	2	0	0	5	.313	.313	.375	0	0	0	.000
Koskie, 3b	5	18	3	5	7	2	0	0	2	2	0	8	.278	.350	.389	2	7	0	1.000
Mientkiewicz, 1b	5	18	1	5	6	1	0	0	2	1	0	2	.278	.316	.333	48	0	0	1.000
Pierzynski, c	5	16	1	4	4	0	0	0	2	0	0	2	.250	.235	.250	29	1	2	.938
Rivas, 2b	5	12	1	3	3	0	0	0	0	1	0	3	.250	.308	.250	5	12	0	1.000
Cuddyer, rf	3	5	0	1	1	0	0	0	0	1	0	1	.200	.333	.200	6	0	0	1.000
Guzman, ss	5	18	1	3	4	1	0	0	0	0	0	3	.167	.211	.222	7	18	1	.962
Hunter, cf	5	18	2	3	5	2	0	0	0	1	0	3	.167	.211	.278	11	0	0	1.000
Jones, lf	5	20	0	2	3	1	0	0	2	0	0	4	.100	.095	.150	11	0	0	1.000
Guardado, p	1	0	0	0	0	0	0	0	0	0	0	0	.000	.000	.000	0	0	0	.000
Hawkins, p	4	0	0	0	0	0	0	0	0	0	0	0	.000	.000	.000	0	0	0	.000
Jackson, p	3	0	0	0	0	0	0	0	0	0	0	0	.000	.000	.000	0	0	0	.000
Lamb, 2b	2	0	0	0	0	0	0	0	0	0	0	0	.000	.000	.000	0	0	0	.000
Lohse, p	1	0	0	0	0	0	0	0	0	0	0	0	.000	.000	.000	0	0	0	.000
Mays, p	2	0	0	0	0	0	0	0	0	0	0	0	.000	.000	.000	0	1	0	1.000
Milton, p	1	0	0	0	0	0	0	0	0	0	0	0	.000	.000	.000	0	0	0	.000
Radke, p	1	0	0	0	0	0	0	0	0	0	0	0	.000	.000	.000	0	1	0	1.000
Reed, p	1	0	0	0	0	0	0	0	0	0	0	0	.000	.000	.000	0	2	0	1.000
Romero, p	4	0	0	0	0	0	0	0	0	0	0	0	.000	.000	.000	0	0	0	.000

Player, position	G	AB	R	H	TB	2B	3B	HR	RBI	BB	IBB	SO	Avg.	OBP	Slg.	PO	A	E	Avg.
									BATTING							**FIELDING**			
Santana, p	4	0	0	0	0	0	0	0	0	0	0	0	.000	.000	.000	0	1	1	.500
Wells, p	2	0	0	0	0	0	0	0	0	0	0	0	.000	.000	.000	0	0	0	.000
Prince, c	1	1	0	0	0	0	0	0	0	0	0	0	.000	.000	.000	1	0	0	1.000
Kielty, dh-rf-ph	4	3	0	0	0	0	0	0	1	1	0	2	.000	.250	.000	0	0	0	.000
Totals	5	160	12	37	46	9	0	0	11	7	0	38	.231	.265	.288	126	43	4	.977

ANAHEIM ANGELS' PITCHING RECORDS

Pitcher	G	GS	CG	IP	H	R	ER	HR	BB	IBB	SO	HB	WP	W	L	Pct.	ERA
Lackey	1	1	0	7.0	3	0	0	0	0	0	7	0	0	1	0	1.000	0.00
Rodriguez	4	0	0	4.1	2	0	0	0	2	0	7	0	1	2	0	1.000	0.00
Percival	3	0	0	3.1	0	0	0	0	0	0	3	0	0	0	0	.000	0.00
Schoeneweis	1	0	0	0.2	0	0	0	0	0	0	0	0	0	0	0	.000	0.00
Washburn	1	1	0	7.0	6	1	1	0	0	0	7	0	0	0	0	.000	1.29
Weber	3	0	0	2.2	3	1	1	0	0	0	3	0	0	0	0	.000	3.38
Appier	2	2	0	10.1	10	4	4	0	4	0	3	0	2	0	1	.000	3.48
Ortiz	1	1	0	5.1	10	3	3	0	1	0	3	0	0	1	0	1.000	5.06
Donnelly	3	0	0	3.1	3	3	3	0	0	0	5	1	1	0	0	.000	8.10
Totals	5	5	0	44.0	37	12	12	0	7	0	38	1	4	4	1	.800	2.45

No shutouts. Saves—Percival 2.

MINNESOTA TWINS' PITCHING RECORDS

Pitcher	G	GS	CG	IP	H	R	ER	HR	BB	IBB	SO	HB	WP	W	L	Pct.	ERA
Guardado	1	0	0	1.0	0	0	0	0	1	0	2	0	0	0	0	.000	0.00
Lohse	1	0	0	1.0	0	0	0	0	0	0	1	0	0	0	0	.000	0.00
Milton	1	1	0	6.0	5	1	1	1	2	0	4	0	0	0	0	.000	1.50
Mays	2	2	0	13.1	12	4	3	3	0	0	3	0	0	1	0	1.000	2.03
Radke	1	1	0	6.2	5	2	2	0	1	1	4	1	0	0	1	.000	2.70
Wells	2	0	0	1.0	2	1	1	0	0	0	2	1	0	0	0	.000	9.00
Reed	1	1	0	5.1	8	6	6	2	0	0	0	0	0	0	1	.000	10.13
Santana	4	0	0	3.1	4	4	4	1	0	0	4	0	2	0	1	.000	10.80
Hawkins	4	0	0	1.1	4	3	3	0	1	0	1	0	0	0	0	.000	20.25
Romero	4	0	0	2.0	4	5	5	1	2	0	3	0	1	0	1	.000	22.50
Jackson	3	0	0	1.0	5	3	3	0	2	1	2	0	0	0	0	.000	27.00
Totals	5	5	0	42.0	49	29	28	8	9	1	26	2	3	1	4	.200	6.00

No shutouts. Save—Guardado.

SCORE BY INNINGS

Anaheim	1	4	2	0	2	2	12	6	0	—29
Minnesota	1	2	0	0	1	3	4	0	1	—12

MISCELLANEOUS STATISTICS

Sacrifice hits—Gil, Guzman, Hunter, Kennedy.
Sacrifice flies—Jones, Pierzynski.
Stolen bases—Erstad, Kennedy, Mohr, Spiezio.
Caught stealing—Anderson, Pierzynski.
Double plays—Eckstein, Kennedy and Spiezio 3; Guzman, Rivas and Mientkiewicz; Rivas and Guzman; Rivas, Guzman and Mientkiewicz; Weber, Kennedy and Spiezio.
Left on bases—Anaheim 4, 6, 9, 5, 5—29; Minnesota 7, 7, 7, 4, 3—28.
Hitting with runners in scoring position—Anaheim 0 for 2, 3 for 7, 1 for 7, 5 for 11, 5 for 12—14 for 39; Minnesota 1 for 6, 2 for 3, 0 for 5, 1 for 4, 3 for 7—7 for 25.
Hit by pitcher—By Wells (Eckstein), by Radke (Molina), by Donnelly (Guzman).
Passed balls—None.
Balks—None.
Time of games—2:58, 3:13, 2:49, 3:30, 3:13—Avg.: 3:08.
Attendance—55,562, 44,234, 44,830, 44,835, 55,990—245,451.
Umpires—Ed Montague, Mike Everitt, Brian Gorman, Larry Young, Dana DeMuth, Ed Rapuano.
Official scorers—Tom Mee, Ed Munson.

2002 REVIEW A.L. Championship Series

N.L. CHAMPIONSHIP SERIES
SAN FRANCISCO VS. ST. LOUIS

RESULTS

Day	Date	Place	Score
Wed.	Oct. 9	St. Louis	San Francisco 9, St. Louis 6
Thur.	Oct. 10	St. Louis	San Francisco 4, St. Louis 1
Sat.	Oct. 12	San Francisco	St. Louis 5, San Francisco 4
Sun.	Oct. 13	San Francisco	San Francisco 4, St. Louis 3
Mon.	Oct. 14	San Francisco	San Francisco 2, St. Louis 1

BOX SCORES
GAME 1

SAN FRANCISCO 9, ST. LOUIS 6

WEDNESDAY, OCTOBER 9, AT ST. LOUIS

San Francisco	AB	R	H	RBI	BB	SO	PO	A
Lofton, cf	4	3	2	1	1	0	3	0
Aurilia, ss	4	1	1	1	0	0	4	2
Kent, 2b	5	1	2	0	0	1	2	3
Bonds, lf	2	2	1	2	3	0	1	0
Santiago, c	5	1	3	4	0	0	4	1
Snow, 1b	4	0	1	0	1	2	8	1
Sanders, rf	4	0	0	0	0	1	4	0
Bell, 3b	4	1	1	1	0	1	0	4
Rueter, p	3	0	0	0	0	1	1	1
Rodriguez, p	1	0	0	0	0	1	0	0
Worrell, p	0	0	0	0	0	0	0	0
Nen, p	0	0	0	0	0	0	0	1
Totals	36	9	11	9	5	7	27	13

St. Louis	AB	R	H	RBI	BB	SO	PO	A
Vina, 2b	5	0	0	1	0	0	2	3
Marrero, rf	4	0	1	0	1	0	5	0
Edmonds, cf	4	1	2	0	1	1	1	0
Pujols, lf	4	1	1	2	1	1	0	0
Renteria, ss	4	0	1	0	0	0	1	0
T. Martinez, 1b	4	1	1	0	0	0	10	0
Cairo, 3b	4	2	3	2	0	1	1	2
Matheny, c	4	0	1	0	0	1	7	0
Morris, p	1	0	0	0	0	0	1	0
Crudale, p	0	0	0	0	0	0	0	1
Robinson, ph	0	0	0	0	1	0	0	0
Veres, p	0	0	0	0	0	0	0	1
Drew, ph	1	1	1	1	0	0	0	0
Kline, p	0	0	0	0	0	0	0	1
Totals	35	6	11	6	4	4	27	8

San Francisco	1	4	1	0	1	2	0 0 0—9
St. Louis	0	1	0	0	2	2	0 1 0—6

San Francisco	IP	H	R	ER	HR	BB	SO
Rueter (W)	*5.0	9	5	5	2	1	1
Rodriguez	2.0	1	0	0	0	2	1
Worrell	1.0	1	1	1	1	0	1
Nen (S)	1.0	0	0	0	0	1	1

St. Louis	IP	H	R	ER	HR	BB	SO
Morris (L)	4.1	10	7	7	2	4	2
Crudale	1.2	1	2	2	1	1	2
Veres	2.0	0	0	0	0	0	2
Kline	1.0	0	0	0	0	0	1

*Pitched to two batters in sixth.

DP—San Francisco 1, St. Louis 1. LOB—San Francisco 6, St. Louis 8. Hitting with runners in scoring position—San Francisco 4 for 9, St. Louis 1 for 6. 2B—Marrero, Edmonds. 3B—Bonds. HR—Lofton (3rd inning, 2 out, 0 on) off Morris, D.Bell (5th inning, 1 out, 0 on) off Morris, Pujols (5th

inning, 2 out, 1 on) off Rueter, Santiago (6th inning, 2 out, 1 on) off Crudale, Cairo (6th inning, 0 out, 1 on) off Rueter, Drew (8th inning, 2 out, 0 on) off Worrell. SB—Lofton. CS—Robinson. SH—Aurilia, Morris. HBP—Renteria by Rueter. T—3:31. A—52,175. U—Marsh, plate; Nelson, first; Scott, second; Kellogg, third; Welke, left field; Reliford, right field.

HOW THEY SCORED

FIRST INNING

Giants—Lofton walked. Aurilia sacrificed Lofton to second, T. Martinez, unassisted. Kent grounded out, Vina to T. Martinez, as Lofton advanced to third. Bonds walked. Santiago singled to third, scoring Lofton as Bonds advanced to second. Snow walked. Sanders grounded out, Vina to T. Martinez. One run. Giants 1, Cardinals 0.

SECOND INNING

Giants—Bell and Rueter struck out. Lofton singled to center. Lofton stole second. Aurilia singled to right, scoring Lofton. Kent singled to center as Aurilia advanced to second. Bonds tripled to right-center, scoring Aurilia and Kent. Santiago singled to right, scoring Bonds. Snow singled to right as Santiago advanced to third. Sanders flied to Marrero. Four runs. Giants 5, Cardinals 0.

Cardinals—Cairo singled to right. Matheny singled to center as Cairo advanced to second. Morris sacrificed Cairo to third and Matheny to second, Bell to Kent. Vina grounded out, Kent to Snow, scoring Cairo as Matheny advanced to third. Marrero flied out to Sanders. One run. Giants 5, Cardinals 1.

THIRD INNING

Giants—Bell flied to Marrero. Rueter grounded out, Cairo to T. Martinez. Lofton homered to right. Aurilia flied to Marrero. One run. Giants 6, Cardinals 1.

FIFTH INNING

Giants—Sanders lined to Morris. Bell homered to left-center. Crudale now pitching. Rueter grounded out, Crudale to T. Martinez. Lofton flied to Edmonds. One run. Giants 7, Cardinals 1.

Cardinals—Vina grounded out, Kent to Snow. Marrero flied to Sanders. Edmonds doubled to right. Pujols homered to center, scoring Edmonds. Renteria grounded out, Kent to Snow. Two runs. Giants 7, Cardinals 3.

SIXTH INNING

Giants—Aurilia flied to Marrero. Kent struck out. Bonds walked. Santiago homered to left-center, scoring Bonds. Snow struck out. Two runs. Giants 9, Cardinals 3.

Cardinals—T. Martinez singled to left. Cairo homered to left, scoring T. Martinez. Rodriguez now pitching. Matheny lined to Aurilia. Robinson, pinch-hitting for Crudale, walked. Vina flied to Bonds. Robinson caught trying to steal second, Santiago to Aurilia. Two runs. Giants 9, Cardinals 5.

EIGHTH INNING

Cardinals—Worrell now pitching. Cairo struck out. Matheny lined to Aurilia. Drew, pinch-hitting for Veres, homered to right-center. Vina grounded out, Bell to Snow. One run. Giants 9, Cardinals 6.

GAME 2

SAN FRANCISCO 4, ST. LOUIS 1

THURSDAY, OCTOBER 10, AT ST. LOUIS

San Francisco	AB	R	H	RBI	BB	SO	PO	A
Lofton, cf	4	0	0	0	1	2	2	1
Aurilia, ss	3	2	2	3	1	0	2	3
Nen, p	1	0	0	0	0	1	0	0
Kent, 2b	4	0	1	0	0	1	1	1
Bonds, lf	3	0	0	0	1	2	2	0
Santiago, c	4	0	0	0	0	1	9	0

San Francisco	AB	R	H	RBI	BB	SO	PO	A
Snow, 1b	4	1	2	0	0	1	6	0
Sanders, rf	4	0	0	0	0	1	4	0
Bell, 3b	3	1	2	0	1	0	0	1
Schmidt, p	2	0	0	0	0	2	0	1
Eyre, p	0	0	0	0	0	0	0	0
R. Martinez, ss	0	0	0	1	0	0	1	1
Totals	32	4	7	4	4	11	27	8

St. Louis	AB	R	H	RBI	BB	SO	PO	A
Vina, 2b	4	0	1	0	0	0	3	0
Cairo, 3b	4	0	0	0	0	0	0	1
Edmonds, cf	4	0	1	0	0	2	2	0
Pujols, lf	4	0	1	0	0	2	0	0
T. Martinez, 1b	3	0	0	0	1	1	4	1
Renteria, ss	4	0	0	0	0	1	1	0
Drew, rf	3	0	1	0	0	1	5	0
Matheny, c	3	0	1	0	0	1	12	0
Williams, p	0	0	0	0	0	0	0	0
Robinson, ph	1	0	0	0	0	0	0	0
White, p	0	0	0	0	0	0	0	0
Fassero, p	0	0	0	0	0	0	0	0
Perez, ph	1	1	1	1	0	0	0	0
Isringhausen, p	0	0	0	0	0	0	0	1
Totals	31	1	6	1	1	8	27	3

San Francisco	1	0	0		0	2	0		0	0	1—4
St. Louis	0	0	0		0	0	0		0	1	0—1

San Francisco	IP	H	R	ER	HR	BB	SO
Schmidt (W)	7.2	4	1	1	1	1	8
Eyre	*0.0	1	0	0	0	0	0
Nen (S)	1.1	1	0	0	0	0	0

St. Louis	IP	H	R	ER	HR	BB	SO
Williams (L)	6.0	6	3	3	2	1	7
White	1.1	0	0	0	0	1	2
Fassero	0.2	0	0	0	0	0	1
Isringhausen	1.0	1	1	1	0	2	1

*Pitched to one batter in eighth.
DP—San Francisco 1. LOB—San Francisco 7, St. Louis 5. Hitting with runners in scoring position—San Francisco 1 for 5, St. Louis 0 for 5. 2B—Edmonds. 3B—Snow. HR—Aurilia (1st inning, 1 out, 0 on) off Williams, Aurilia (5th inning, 2 out, 1 on) off Williams, Perez (8th inning, 2 out, 0 on) off Schmidt. SH—Schmidt, R. Martinez, Williams. T—3:17. A—52,195. U—Nelson, plate; Scott, first; Kellogg, second; Welke, third; Reliford, left field; Marsh, right field.

HOW THEY SCORED

FIRST INNING
Giants—Lofton flied to Drew. Aurilia homered to left-center. Kent popped to Renteria. Bonds flied to Drew. One run. Giants 1, Cardinals 0.

FIFTH INNING
Giants—Bell singled to left. Schmidt sacrificed Bell to second, T. Martinez to Vina. Lofton struck out. Aurilia homered to left-center, scoring Bell. Kent fouled to T. Martinez. Two runs. Giants 3, Cardinals 0.

EIGHTH INNING
Cardinals—Drew and Matheny struck out. Perez, pinch-hitting for Fassero, homered to left. Eyre now pitching. Vina singled to left. R. Martinez now at shortstop and Nen pitching. Cairo forced Vina at second, R. Martinez, unassisted. One run. Giants 3, Cardinals 1.

NINTH INNING
Giants—Isringhausen now pitching. Snow tripled. Sanders popped to Vina. Bell was walked intentionally. R. Martinez sacrificed Bell to second and scored Snow, Isringhausen to T. Martinez. Lofton was walked intentionally. Nen struck out. One run. Giants 4, Cardinals 1.

ST. LOUIS 5, SAN FRANCISCO 4
SATURDAY, OCTOBER 12, AT SAN FRANCISCO

St. Louis	AB	R	H	RBI	BB	SO	PO	A
Vina, 2b	5	1	1	0	0	0	2	1
Renteria, ss	3	0	0	1	0	1	2	2
Edmonds, cf	3	1	1	2	1	1	4	0
Pujols, 3b	3	0	1	0	1	0	1	1
Drew, rf	3	0	1	0	1	0	2	0
T. Martinez, 1b	4	0	0	0	0	0	8	5
Marrero, lf	4	1	1	1	0	0	1	0
Matheny, c	4	1	1	1	0	0	7	3
Finley, p	2	1	0	0	0	1	1	0
DiFelice, ph	1	0	0	0	0	0	0	0
Veres, p	0	0	0	0	0	0	0	0
Kline, p	0	0	0	0	0	0	0	1
White, p	0	0	0	0	0	0	0	0
Perez, ph	1	0	0	0	0	0	0	0
Isringhausen, p	0	0	0	0	0	0	0	0
Totals	33	5	6	5	3	4	27	13

San Francisco	AB	R	H	RBI	BB	SO	PO	A
Lofton, cf	5	0	0	0	0	0	4	0
Aurilia, ss	2	1	1	1	1	0	0	3
Kent, 2b	5	1	2	0	0	2	1	1
Bonds, lf	2	1	1	3	3	0	2	0
Santiago, c	5	0	2	0	0	2	3	1
Sanders, rf	5	0	0	0	0	1	4	0
Snow, 1b	4	0	1	0	0	0	11	0
Bell, 3b	3	1	2	0	1	1	2	2
Ortiz, p	1	0	1	0	0	0	0	0
Fultz, p	0	0	0	0	0	0	0	0
Witasick, p	0	0	0	0	0	0	0	0
Feliz, ph	1	0	0	0	0	0	0	0
Rodriguez, p	0	0	0	0	0	0	0	0
Eyre, p	0	0	0	0	0	0	0	0
Dunston, ph	0	0	0	0	0	0	0	0
Worrell, p	0	0	0	0	0	0	0	0
Totals	33	4	10	4	5	6	27	7

St. Louis	0	0	2		1	1	1		0	0	0—5
San Francisco	0	1	0		0	3	0		0	0	0—4

St. Louis	IP	H	R	ER	HR	BB	SO
Finley (W)	5.0	7	4	4	1	3	1
Veres	1.2	2	0	0	0	1	3
Kline	1.0	1	0	0	0	0	0
White	0.1	0	0	0	0	0	0
Isringhausen (S)	1.0	0	0	0	0	1	2

San Francisco	IP	H	R	ER	HR	BB	SO
Ortiz	4.2	5	4	4	2	3	3
Fultz	0.1	0	0	0	0	0	0
Witasick (L)	1.0	1	1	1	1	0	0
Rodriguez	1.0	0	0	0	0	0	1
Eyre	1.0	0	0	0	0	0	0
Worrell	1.0	0	0	0	0	0	0

E—Renteria. DP—St. Louis 2. LOB—St. Louis 5, San Francisco 11. Hitting with runners in scoring position—St. Louis 0 for 3, San Francisco 4 for 15. 2B—Vina, Pujols, Aurilia. HR—Matheny (4th inning, 1 out, 0 on) off Ortiz, Edmonds (5th inning, 1 out, 0 on) off Ortiz, Bonds (5th inning, 2 out, 2 on) off Finley, Marrero (6th inning, 0 out, 0 on) off Witasick. S—Renteria, Aurilia. SH—Aurilia, Ortiz, Dunston. WP—Ortiz. T—3:32. A—42,177. U—Scott, plate; Kellogg, first; Welke, second; Reliford, third; Marsh, left field; Nelson, right field.

HOW THEY SCORED

SECOND INNING
Giants—Snow singled to right. Bell singled to right as Snow advanced to second. Ortiz singled to third as Snow advanced to third and Bell to second. Lofton forced Snow at the plate, T. Martinez to Matheny, as Bell advanced to third and Ortiz to second. Aurilia scored Bell on a sacrifice fly to Edmonds. Kent singled to center as Ortiz advanced to third and Lofton to second. Bonds flied to Drew. One run. Giants 1, Cardinals 0.

THIRD INNING

Cardinals—Finley struck out, but was safe at first on a wild pitch. Vina doubled to center as Finley advanced to third. Renteria scored Finley on a sacrifice fly to Sanders as Vina advanced to third. Edmonds grounded out, Aurilia to Snow, scoring Vina. Pujols and Drew walked. T. Martinez grounded out, Santiago to Snow. Two runs. Cardinals 2, Giants 1.

FOURTH INNING

Cardinals—Marrero struck out. Matheny homered to left. Finley flied to Lofton. Vina grounded out, Kent to Snow. One run. Cardinals 3, Giants 1.

FIFTH INNING

Cardinals—Renteria flied to Sanders. Edmonds homered to left. Pujols flied to Sanders. Drew singled to right. Fultz now pitching. T. Martinez fouled to Bell. One run. Cardinals 4, Giants 1.

Giants—Aurilia walked. Kent singled to left as Aurilia advanced to second. Bonds homered to right, scoring Aurilia and Kent. Santiago singled to left. Sanders fouled to Pujols. Snow grounded into a double play, T. Martinez to Renteria to T. Martinez. Three runs. Cardinals 4, Giants 4.

SIXTH INNING

Cardinals—Witasick now pitching. Marrero homered to left. Matheny grounded out, Aurilia to Snow. DiFelice, pinch-hitting for Finley, grounded out, Bell to Snow. Vina fouled to Bell. One run. Cardinals 5, Giants 4.

GAME 4

SAN FRANCISCO 4, ST. LOUIS 3

SUNDAY, OCTOBER 13, AT SAN FRANCISCO

St. Louis	AB	R	H	RBI	BB	SO	PO	A
Vina, 2b	5	1	3	0	0	0	0	2
Renteria, ss	4	0	0	0	0	1	2	1
Edmonds, cf	5	0	2	2	0	0	3	0
Pujols, 3b	4	1	1	0	0	1	1	1
Drew, rf	5	0	2	0	0	1	0	0
T. Martinez, 1b	3	0	1	1	1	0	10	0
Marrero, lf	4	0	1	0	0	0	2	0
Kline, p	0	0	0	0	0	0	0	0
Matheny, c	4	0	2	0	0	0	7	1
Benes, p	2	0	0	0	0	0	0	0
White, p	0	0	0	0	0	0	0	0
Robinson, lf	1	1	0	0	0	1	0	0
Totals	37	3	12	3	1	3	24	6
San Francisco	**AB**	**R**	**H**	**RBI**	**BB**	**SO**	**PO**	**A**
Lofton, cf	4	0	0	0	0	2	2	0
Worrell, p	0	0	0	0	0	0	0	0
Nen, p	0	0	0	0	0	0	0	0
Aurilia, ss	4	0	0	0	0	1	3	4
Kent, 2b	2	1	0	0	2	0	2	4
Bonds, lf	2	2	1	0	2	0	1	0
Santiago, c	3	1	1	2	1	1	3	0
Snow, 1b	4	0	1	0	0	1	12	1
Sanders, rf	3	0	1	0	0	1	3	0
Rodriguez, p	0	0	0	0	0	0	0	0
Eyre, p	0	0	0	0	0	0	0	0
Goodwin, rf	0	0	0	0	0	0	0	0
Bell, 3b	3	0	0	0	0	1	0	2
Hernandez, p	1	0	0	0	0	1	0	2
Shinjo, rf-cf	1	0	0	0	0	0	1	0
Totals	27	4	4	4	5	8	27	13

St. Louis	2	0	0		0	0	0		0	0	1—3
San Francisco	0	0	0		0	0	2		0	2	x—4

St. Louis	IP	H	R	ER	HR	BB	SO
Benes	5.1	2	2	2	0	4	5
White (L)	2.1	2	2	2	1	1	3
Kline	0.1	0	0	0	0	0	0
San Francisco	**IP**	**H**	**R**	**ER**	**HR**	**BB**	**SO**
Hernandez	6.1	9	2	2	0	1	0
Rodriguez	0.2	0	0	0	0	0	0
Eyre	0.1	0	0	0	0	0	0

San Francisco	IP	H	R	ER	HR	BB	SO
Worrell (W)	0.2	0	0	0	0	0	0
Nen (S)	1.0	2	1	1	0	0	3

E—Aurilia. DP—San Francisco 2. LOB—St. Louis 11, San Francisco 5. Hitting with runners in scoring position—St. Louis 2 for 17, San Francisco 1 for 5. 2B—Vina, Matheny, Snow. HR—Santiago (8th inning, 2 out, 1 on) off White. SB—T. Martinez. SH—Renteria, Benes, Hernandez. WP—Nen. HBP—Pujols by Hernandez. T—3:26. A—42,676. U—Kellogg, plate; Welke, first; Reliford, second; Marsh, third; Nelson, left field; Scott, right field.

HOW THEY SCORED

FIRST INNING

Cardinals—Vina doubled to right-center. Renteria flied to Sanders as Vina advanced to third. Edmonds grounded out, Kent to Snow, scoring Vina. Pujols was hit by a pitch. Drew singled to center as Pujols advanced to second. T. Martinez singled to left, scoring Pujols as Drew advanced to third. Marrero grounded out, Bell to Snow. Two runs. Cardinals 2, Giants 0.

SIXTH INNING

Giants—Aurilia struck out. Kent and Bonds walked. White now pitching. Santiago struck out. Snow doubled to left-center, scoring Kent and Bonds. Sanders struck out. Two runs. Cardinals 2, Giants 2.

EIGHTH INNING

Giants—Aurilia flied to Edmonds. Kent grounded out to T. Martinez. Bonds was walked intentionally. Santiago homered to left, scoring Bonds. Robinson now in left field and Kline pitching. Snow grounded out, Renteria to T. Martinez. Two runs. Giants 4, Cardinals 2.

NINTH INNING

Cardinals—Nen now pitching. Robinson struck out, but was safe at first on a wild pitch. Vina singled to right as Robinson advanced to second. Renteria grounded out, Aurilia to Snow, as Robinson advanced to third and Vina to second. Edmonds singled to right, scoring Robinson as Vina advanced to third. Pujols and Drew struck out. One run. Giants 4, Cardinals 3.

GAME 5

SAN FRANCISCO 2, ST. LOUIS 1

MONDAY, OCTOBER 14, AT SAN FRANCISCO

St. Louis	AB	R	H	RBI	BB	SO	PO	A
Vina, 2b	4	0	1	1	0	0	3	3
Cairo, 3b	5	0	2	0	0	1	2	3
Edmonds, cf	4	0	2	0	0	1	1	0
Pujols, 1b	4	0	1	0	0	1	9	1
Perez, rf	2	0	0	0	1	0	1	0
Drew, rf	1	0	0	0	0	0	0	0
Renteria, ss	4	0	2	0	0	0	0	1
Marrero, lf	4	0	0	0	0	0	5	0
Matheny, c	4	1	1	0	0	0	5	0
Morris, p	3	0	0	0	0	1	0	2
Kline, p	0	0	0	0	0	0	0	0
Totals	35	1	9	1	1	4	26	10
San Francisco	**AB**	**R**	**H**	**RBI**	**BB**	**SO**	**PO**	**A**
Lofton, cf	4	1	3	1	0	0	3	0
Aurilia, ss	2	0	1	0	0	1	0	0
Kent, 2b	3	0	0	0	0	0	5	0
Bonds, lf	2	0	0	1	1	0	5	0
Santiago, c	3	0	1	0	0	1	5	0
Goodwin, rf	3	0	0	0	0	2	2	0
Eyre, p	0	0	0	0	0	0	0	0
Worrell, p	0	0	0	0	0	0	0	0
R. Martinez, ph	1	0	0	0	0	0	0	0
Snow, 1b	4	0	0	0	0	0	11	0
Bell, 3b	4	1	2	0	0	0	0	1
Rueter, p	2	0	0	0	0	0	1	2
Rodriguez, p	0	0	0	0	0	0	0	0
Dunston, rf	2	0	1	0	0	1	0	0
Totals	30	2	7	2	2	4	27	8

St. Louis......................	0 0 0	0 0 0	1 0 0—1
San Francisco	0 0 0	0 0 0	0 1 1—2

St. Louis	IP	H	R	ER	HR	BB	SO
Morris (L)	8.2	6	2	2	0	2	4
Kline.................................	*0.0	1	0	0	0	0	0

San Francisco	IP	H	R	ER	HR	BB	SO
Rueter	6.0	6	0	0	0	1	2
Rodriguez	1.0	2	1	1	0	0	0
Eyre	0.1	0	0	0	0	0	0
Worrell (W).......................	1.2	1	0	0	0	0	2

*Pitched to one batter in ninth.

DP—St. Louis 1. LOB—St. Louis 10, San Francisco 9. Hitting with runners in scoring position—St. Louis 0 for 8, San Francisco 1 for 7. 2B—Matheny, Bell. S—Vina, Bonds. SH—Morris, Aurilia. HBP—Lofton by Morris, Kent by Morris, Aurilia by Morris. T—3:01. A—42,673. U—Welke, plate; Reliford, first; Marsh, second; Nelson, third; Scott, left field; Kellogg, right field.

HOW THEY SCORED

SEVENTH INNING

Cardinals—Rodriguez now pitching. Matheny doubled to right-center. Morris sacrificed Matheny to third, but Morris was also safe on a fielder's choice. Vina scored Matheny on a sacrifice fly to Bonds. Cairo singled to center as Morris advanced to second. Edmonds and Pujols flied to Bonds. One run. Cardinals 1, Giants 0.

EIGHTH INNING

Giants—Dunston struck out. Lofton singled to center. Aurilia singled to left as Lofton advanced to second. Kent was hit by a pitch. Bonds scored Lofton on a sacrifice fly to Marrero as Aurilia advanced to third. Santiago grounded out, Vina to Pujols. One run. Cardinals 1, Giants 1.

NINTH INNING

Giants—R. Martinez, pinch-hitting for Worrell, fouled to Matheny. Snow flied to Marrero. Bell singled to left-center. Dunston singled to center as Bell advanced to second. Kline now pitching. Lofton singled to right-center, scoring Bell as Dunston advanced to second. One run. Giants 2, Cardinals 1.

STATISTICS

SAN FRANCISCO GIANTS' BATTING AND FIELDING AVERAGES

Player, position	G	AB	R	H	TB	2B	3B	HR	RBI	BB	IBB	SO	Avg.	OBP	Slg.	PO	A	E	Avg.
Ortiz, p	1	1	0	1	1	0	0	0	0	0	0	0	1.000	1.000	1.000	0	0	0	.000
Dunston, ph-rf	2	2	0	1	1	0	0	0	0	0	0	1	.500	.500	.500	0	0	0	.000
Bell, 3b	5	17	4	7	11	1	0	1	1	2	1	3	.412	.474	.647	2	10	0	1.000
Aurilia, ss	5	15	4	5	12	1	0	2	5	2	0	2	.333	.421	.800	9	12	1	.955
Santiago, c	5	20	2	6	12	0	0	2	6	2	0	4	.300	.364	.600	24	2	0	1.000
Bonds, lf	5	11	5	3	8	0	1	1	6	10	3	2	.273	.591	.727	11	0	0	1.000
Kent, 2b	5	19	3	5	5	0	0	0	0	2	0	4	.263	.364	.263	6	14	0	1.000
Snow, 1b	5	20	1	5	8	1	1	0	2	1	0	4	.250	.286	.400	48	2	0	1.000
Lofton, cf	5	21	4	5	8	0	0	1	2	2	1	4	.238	.333	.381	14	1	0	1.000
Sanders, rf	4	16	0	1	1	0	0	0	0	0	0	4	.063	.063	.063	15	0	0	1.000
Eyre, p.........................	4	0	0	0	0	0	0	0	0	0	0	0	.000	.000	.000	0	0	0	.000
Fultz, p........................	1	0	0	0	0	0	0	0	0	0	0	0	.000	.000	.000	0	0	0	.000
Witasick, p	1	0	0	0	0	0	0	0	0	0	0	0	.000	.000	.000	0	0	0	.000
Worrell, p	4	0	0	0	0	0	0	0	0	0	0	0	.000	.000	.000	0	0	0	.000
Feliz, ph.......................	1	1	0	0	0	0	0	0	0	0	0	0	.000	.000	.000	0	0	0	.000
Hernandez, p.................	1	1	0	0	0	0	0	0	0	0	0	1	.000	.000	.000	0	2	0	1.000
R. Martinez, ss-ph	2	1	0	0	0	0	0	0	1	0	0	1	.000	.000	.000	1	1	0	1.000
Nen, p	3	1	0	0	0	0	0	0	0	0	0	1	.000	.000	.000	0	1	0	1.000
Rodriguez, p	4	1	0	0	0	0	0	0	0	0	0	0	.000	.000	.000	0	0	0	.000
Shinjo, cf-rf	1	1	0	0	0	0	0	0	0	0	0	0	.000	.000	.000	1	0	0	1.000
Schmidt, p	1	2	0	0	0	0	0	0	0	0	0	2	.000	.000	.000	0	1	0	1.000
Goodwin, rf...................	2	3	0	0	0	0	0	0	0	0	0	2	.000	.000	.000	2	0	0	1.000
Rueter, p	2	5	0	0	0	0	0	0	0	0	0	1	.000	.000	.000	2	3	0	1.000
Totals	5	158	23	39	67	3	2	7	23	21	5	36	.247	.342	.424	135	49	1	.995

ST. LOUIS CARDINALS' BATTING AND FIELDING AVERAGES

Player, position	G	AB	R	H	TB	2B	3B	HR	RBI	BB	IBB	SO	Avg.	OBP	Slg.	PO	A	E	Avg.
Edmonds, cf.................	5	20	2	8	13	2	0	1	4	2	0	5	.400	.455	.650	11	0	0	1.000
Cairo, 3b	3	13	2	5	8	0	0	1	2	0	0	2	.385	.385	.615	3	6	0	1.000
Drew, ph-rf	5	13	1	5	8	0	0	1	1	1	0	2	.385	.429	.615	7	0	0	1.000
Matheny, c	5	19	2	6	11	2	0	1	1	0	0	2	.316	.316	.579	38	4	0	1.000
Pujols, lf-3b-1b.............	5	19	2	5	9	1	0	1	2	2	0	5	.263	.364	.474	11	3	0	1.000
Vina, 2b	5	23	2	6	8	2	0	0	2	0	0	0	.261	.250	.348	10	9	0	1.000
Perez, ph-rf..................	3	4	1	1	4	0	0	1	1	1	0	0	.250	.400	1.000	1	0	0	1.000
Marrero, rf-lf................	4	16	1	3	7	1	0	1	1	1	0	1	.188	.235	.438	12	0	0	1.000
Renteria, ss.................	5	19	0	3	3	0	0	0	1	0	0	2	.158	.190	.158	4	5	1	.900
T. Martinez, 1b	4	14	1	2	2	0	0	0	1	2	0	1	.143	.250	.143	32	6	0	1.000
Crudale, p	1	0	0	0	0	0	0	0	0	0	0	0	.000	.000	.000	0	1	0	1.000
Fassero, p	1	0	0	0	0	0	0	0	0	0	0	0	.000	.000	.000	0	0	0	.000
Isringhausen, p.............	2	0	0	0	0	0	0	0	0	0	0	0	.000	.000	.000	0	1	0	1.000

Player, position	G	AB	R	H	TB	2B	3B	HR	RBI	BB	IBB	SO	Avg.	OBP	Slg.	PO	A	E	Avg.
Kline, p	4	0	0	0	0	0	0	0	0	0	0	0	.000	.000	.000	0	2	0	1.000
Veres, p	2	0	0	0	0	0	0	0	0	0	0	0	.000	.000	.000	0	1	0	1.000
White, p	3	0	0	0	0	0	0	0	0	0	0	0	.000	.000	.000	0	0	0	.000
Williams, p	1	0	0	0	0	0	0	0	0	0	0	0	.000	.000	.000	0	0	0	.000
DiFelice, ph	1	1	0	0	0	0	0	0	0	0	0	0	.000	.000	.000	0	0	0	.000
Benes, p	1	2	0	0	0	0	0	0	0	0	0	0	.000	.000	.000	0	0	0	.000
Finley, p	1	2	1	0	0	0	0	0	0	0	0	1	.000	.000	.000	1	0	0	1.000
Robinson, ph-lf	3	2	1	0	0	0	0	0	0	1	0	1	.000	.333	.000	0	0	0	.000
Morris, p	2	4	0	0	0	0	0	0	0	0	0	1	.000	.000	.000	1	2	0	1.000
Totals	5	171	16	44	73	8	0	7	16	10	0	23	.257	.303	.427	131	40	1	.994

SAN FRANCISCO GIANTS' PITCHING RECORDS

Pitcher	G	GS	CG	IP	H	R	ER	HR	BB	IBB	SO	HB	WP	W	L	Pct.	ERA
Eyre	4	0	0	1.2	2	0	0	0	0	0	0	0	0	0	0	.000	0.00
Fultz	1	0	0	0.1	0	0	0	0	0	0	0	0	0	0	0	.000	0.00
Schmidt	1	1	0	7.2	4	1	1	1	1	0	8	0	0	1	0	1.000	1.17
Rodriguez	4	0	0	4.2	3	1	1	0	2	0	2	0	0	0	0	.000	1.93
Worrell	4	0	0	4.1	2	1	1	1	0	0	3	0	0	2	0	1.000	2.08
Nen	3	0	0	3.1	3	1	1	0	1	0	4	0	1	0	0	.000	2.70
Hernandez	1	1	0	6.1	9	2	2	0	1	0	0	1	0	0	0	.000	2.84
Rueter	2	2	0	11.0	15	5	5	2	2	0	3	1	0	1	0	1.000	4.09
Ortiz	1	1	0	4.2	5	4	4	2	3	0	3	0	1	0	0	.000	7.71
Witasick	1	0	0	1.0	1	1	1	1	0	0	0	0	0	0	1	.000	9.00
Totals	5	5	0	45.0	44	16	16	7	10	0	23	2	2	4	1	.800	3.20

No shutouts. Saves—Nen 3.

ST. LOUIS CARDINALS' PITCHING RECORDS

Pitcher	G	GS	CG	IP	H	R	ER	HR	BB	IBB	SO	HB	WP	W	L	Pct.	ERA
Veres	2	0	0	3.2	2	0	0	0	1	1	5	0	0	0	0	.000	0.00
Kline	4	0	0	2.1	2	0	0	0	0	0	1	0	0	0	0	.000	0.00
Fassero	1	0	0	0.2	0	0	0	0	0	0	1	0	0	0	0	.000	0.00
Benes	1	1	0	5.1	2	2	2	0	4	0	5	0	0	0	0	.000	3.38
Williams	1	1	0	6.0	6	3	3	2	1	0	7	0	0	0	1	.000	4.50
White	3	0	0	4.0	2	2	2	1	2	1	5	0	0	0	1	.000	4.50
Isringhausen	2	0	0	2.0	1	1	1	0	3	2	3	0	0	0	0	.000	4.50
Morris	2	2	0	13.0	16	9	9	2	6	1	6	3	0	0	2	.000	6.23
Finley	1	1	0	5.0	7	4	4	1	3	0	1	0	0	1	0	1.000	7.20
Crudale	1	0	0	1.2	1	2	2	1	1	0	2	0	0	0	0	.000	10.80
Totals	5	5	0	43.2	39	23	23	7	21	5	36	3	0	1	4	.200	4.74

No shutouts. Save—Isringhausen.

SCORE BY INNINGS

San Francisco	2	5	1	0	6	4	0	3	2—	23
St. Louis	2	1	2	1	3	3	1	2	1—	16

MISCELLANEOUS STATISTICS

Sacrifice hits—Aurilia 3, Morris 2, Benes, Dunston, Hernandez, R. Martinez, Ortiz, Renteria, Schmidt, Williams.

Sacrifice flies—Aurilia, Bonds, Renteria, Vina.

Stolen bases—Lofton, T. Martinez.

Caught stealing—Robinson.

Double plays—Cairo and T. Martinez; Cairo and Pujols; Kent, Aurilia and Snow; T. Martinez and Renteria; T. Martinez, Renteria and T. Martinez; Rueter, Aurilia and Snow; Snow and Aurilia.

Left on bases—San Francisco 6, 7, 11, 5, 9—38; St. Louis 8, 5, 5, 11, 10—39.

Hitting with runners in scoring position—San Francisco 4 for 9, 1 for 5, 4 for 15, 1 for 5, 1 for 7—11 for 41; St. Louis 1 for 6, 0 for 5, 0 for 3, 2 for 17, 0 for 8—3 for 39.

Hit by pitcher—By Morris 3 (Aurilia, Kent, Lofton), by Rueter (Renteria), by Hernandez (Pujols).

Passed balls—None.

Balks—None.

Time of games—3:31, 3:17, 3:32, 3:26, 3:01—Avg.: 3:21.

Attendance—52,175, 52,195, 42,177, 42,676, 42,673—231,896.

Umpires—Randy Marsh, Jeff Nelson, Dale Scott, Jeff Kellogg, Tim Welke, Charlie Reliford.

Official scorers—Jeff Durbin, Art Santo Domingo.

WORLD SERIES
ANAHEIM VS. SAN FRANCISCO

RESULTS

Day	Date	Place	Score
Sat.	Oct. 19	Anaheim	San Francisco 4, Anaheim 3
Sun.	Oct. 20	Anaheim	Anaheim 11, San Francisco 10
Tue.	Oct. 22	San Francisco	Anaheim 10, San Francisco 4
Wed.	Oct. 23	San Francisco	San Francisco 4, Anaheim 3
Thur.	Oct. 24	San Francisco	San Francisco 16, Anaheim 4
Sat.	Oct. 26	Anaheim	Anaheim 6, San Francisco 5
Sun.	Oct. 27	Anaheim	Anaheim 4, San Francisco 1

*Piitched to one batter in eighth.

†Pinch-ran for Spiezio in eighth. ‡Fouled out for B. Molina in eighth. §Grounded out for Shinjo in ninth.

LOB—San Francisco 5, Anaheim 8. Hitting with runners in scoring position—San Francisco 0 for 4, Anaheim 1 for 8. 2B—Spiezio, Kennedy. HR—Bonds (2nd inning, 0 out, 0 on) off Washburn, Sanders (2nd inning, 1 out, 0 on) off Washburn, Glaus (2nd inning, 1 out, 0 on) off Schmidt, Snow (6th inning, 2 out, 1 on) off Washburn, Glaus (6th inning, 0 out, 0 on) off Schmidt. SB—Fullmer. SH—Lofton. T—3:44. A—44,603. U—Crawford, plate; Hernandez, first; Tschida, second; Winters, third; Reilly, left field; McClelland, right field.

BOX SCORES
GAME 1

SAN FRANCISCO 4, ANAHEIM 3

SATURDAY, OCTOBER 19, AT ANAHEIM

San Francisco	AB	R	H	RBI	BB	SO	PO	A
Lofton, cf	3	0	0	0	0	1	3	0
Aurilia, ss	4	0	0	0	0	0	1	0
Kent, 2b	4	0	0	0	0	1	1	3
Bonds, lf	3	1	1	1	1	1	3	0
Santiago, c	4	0	1	0	0	1	9	0
Sanders, rf	3	2	2	1	1	1	3	0
Snow, 1b	3	1	1	2	1	0	6	0
Bell, 3b	4	0	0	0	0	1	1	2
Shinjo, dh	3	0	1	0	0	1	0	0
§Goodwin, ph-dh	1	0	0	0	0	0	0	0
Schmidt, p	0	0	0	0	0	0	0	0
Fe. Rodriguez, p	0	0	0	0	0	0	0	0
Worrell, p	0	0	0	0	0	0	0	0
Nen, p	0	0	0	0	0	0	0	0
Totals	32	4	6	4	3	7	27	5

Anaheim	AB	R	H	RBI	BB	SO	PO	A
Eckstein, ss	5	0	1	0	0	1	0	6
Erstad, cf	5	0	1	0	0	2	1	0
Salmon, rf	4	0	0	0	0	1	1	0
Anderson, lf	4	0	1	0	0	2	4	0
Glaus, 3b	4	2	2	2	0	1	1	4
Fullmer, dh	3	1	1	0	1	1	0	0
Spiezio, 1b	3	0	1	0	1	0	11	1
†Figgins, pr	0	0	0	0	0	0	0	0
Wooten, 1b	0	0	0	0	0	0	1	0
B. Molina, c	3	0	0	0	0	0	6	0
‡Palmeiro, ph	1	0	0	0	0	0	0	0
J. Molina, c	0	0	0	0	0	0	1	0
Kennedy, 2b	4	0	2	1	0	1	0	1
Washburn, p	0	0	0	0	0	0	1	1
Donnelly, p	0	0	0	0	0	0	0	0
Schoeneweis, p	0	0	0	0	0	0	0	0
Weber, p	0	0	0	0	0	0	0	0
Totals	36	3	9	3	2	9	27	13

San Francisco	0 2 0	0 0 2	0 0 0	0—4
Anaheim	0 1 0	0 0 2	0 0 0	0—3

San Francisco	IP	H	R	ER	HR	BB	SO
Schmidt (W)	5.2	9	3	3	2	1	6
Fe. Rodriguez	1.1	0	0	0	0	0	1
Worrell	1.0	0	0	0	0	1	1
Nen (S)	1.0	0	0	0	0	0	1

Anaheim	IP	H	R	ER	HR	BB	SO
Washburn (L)	5.2	6	4	4	3	2	5
Donnelly	1.2	0	0	0	0	0	0
Schoeneweis	*0.0	0	0	0	0	1	0
Weber	1.2	0	0	0	0	0	2

PLAY BY PLAY

FIRST INNING
Giants—Lofton struck out. Aurilia fouled to Glaus. Kent struck out.

Angels—Eckstein and Erstad flied to Bonds. Salmon struck out.

SECOND INNING
Giants—Bonds homered to right. Santiago grounded out, Glaus to Spiezio. Sanders homered to right. Snow grounded out, Kennedy to Spiezio. Bell grounded out, Glaus to Spiezio. Two runs. Giants 2, Angels 0.

Angels—Anderson struck out. Glaus homered to left. Fullmer singled to right. Spiezio flied to Lofton. Fullmer stole second. B. Molina flied to Bonds. One run. Giants 2, Angels 1.

THIRD INNING
Giants—Shinjo struck out. Lofton flied to Erstad. Aurilia grounded out, Eckstein to Spiezio.

Angels—Kennedy doubled to right. Eckstein grounded out, Kent to Snow. Erstad struck out. Salmon flied to Lofton.

FOURTH INNING
Giants—Kent grounded out, Eckstein to Spiezio. Bonds struck out. Santiago singled to center. Sanders and Snow walked. Bell flied to Salmon.

Angels—Anderson singled to right. Glaus popped to Kent. Fullmer struck out. Spiezio doubled to right as Anderson advanced to third. B. Molina grounded out, Bell to Snow.

FIFTH INNING
Giants—Shinjo singled to center. Lofton sacrificed Shinjo to second, Washburn to Spiezio. Aurilia flied to Anderson. Kent grounded out, Eckstein to Spiezio.

Angels—Kennedy struck out. Eckstein singled to second. Erstad singled to center as Eckstein advanced to third. Salmon fouled to Snow. Anderson struck out.

SIXTH INNING
Giants—Bonds grounded out, Spiezio to Washburn. Santiago struck out. Sanders singled to left. Snow homered to left, scoring Sanders. Donnelly now pitching. Bell fouled to Anderson. Two runs. Giants 4, Angels 1.

Angels—Glaus homered to left. Fullmer walked. Spiezio flied to Sanders. B. Molina grounded out, Bell to Snow, as Fullmer advanced to second. Kennedy singled to right as Fullmer scored. Fe. Rodriguez now pitching. Eckstein lined to Aurilia. Two runs. Giants 4, Angels 3.

SEVENTH INNING
Giants—Shinjo grounded out, Glaus to Spiezio. Lofton flied to Anderson. Aurilia grounded out, Glaus to Spiezio.

Angels—Erstad struck out. Salmon flied to Sanders. Anderson grounded out, Kent to Snow.

EIGHTH INNING

Giants—Kent grounded out, Eckstein to Spiezio. Schoeneweis now pitching. Bonds walked. Weber now pitching. Santiago grounded out, Eckstein to Spiezio, as Bonds advanced to second. Sanders struck out.

Angels—Worrell now pitching. Glaus struck out. Fullmer grounded out, Kent to Snow. Spiezio walked. Figgins now running for Spiezio. Palmeiro, pinch-hitting for B. Molina, fouled to Bell.

NINTH INNING

Giants—Wooten now at first and J. Molina catching. Snow flied to Anderson. Bell grounded out, Eckstein to Wooten. Goodwin, pinch-hitting for Shinjo, grounded out, Eckstein to Wooten.

Angels—Nen now pitching. Kennedy flied to Sanders. Eckstein struck out. Erstad flied to Lofton. Final score: Giants 4, Angels 3.

GAME 2

ANAHEIM 11, SAN FRANCISCO 10

SUNDAY, OCTOBER 20, AT ANAHEIM

San Francisco	AB	R	H	RBI	BB	SO	PO	A
Lofton, cf	5	0	1	0	0	1	5	0
Aurilia, ss	5	1	1	0	0	2	2	2
Kent, 2b	5	1	1	1	0	2	2	3
Bonds, lf	2	3	1	1	3	0	1	0
Santiago, c	5	1	1	0	0	1	0	0
Snow, 1b	4	2	2	2	0	0	11	2
Sanders, rf	4	1	2	3	0	2	2	1
Bell, 3b	4	1	2	2	0	0	0	4
Dunston, dh	4	0	1	1	0	0	0	0
Ru. Ortiz, p	0	0	0	0	0	0	0	1
Zerbe, p	0	0	0	0	0	0	1	1
Witasick, p	0	0	0	0	0	0	0	0
Fultz, p	0	0	0	0	0	0	0	0
Fe. Rodriguez, p	0	0	0	0	0	0	0	0
Worrell, p	0	0	0	0	0	0	0	0
Totals	38	10	12	10	3	8	24	14

Anaheim	AB	R	H	RBI	BB	SO	PO	A
Eckstein, ss	5	3	3	0	0	0	1	3
Erstad, cf	5	2	2	1	0	0	4	0
Salmon, rf	4	3	4	4	1	0	0	0
Ochoa, rf	0	0	0	0	0	0	0	0
Anderson, lf	5	1	2	2	0	0	2	0
Glaus, 3b	4	1	2	0	0	0	1	0
Fullmer, dh	3	1	2	1	1	0	0	0
Spiezio, 1b	3	0	1	2	0	0	10	0
B. Molina, c	4	0	0	0	0	0	8	0
Kennedy, 2b	4	0	0	0	0	0	1	3
Appier, p	0	0	0	0	0	0	0	1
Lackey, p	0	0	0	0	0	0	0	1
Weber, p	0	0	0	0	0	0	0	0
Fr. Rodriguez, p	0	0	0	0	0	0	0	1
Percival, p	0	0	0	0	0	0	0	0
Totals	37	11	16	10	2	0	27	9

San Francisco	0 4 1	0 4 0	0 0 1	—10
Anaheim	5 2 0	0 1 1	0 2 x	—11

San Francisco	IP	H	R	ER	HR	BB	SO
Ru. Ortiz	1.2	9	7	7	1	0	0
Zerbe	4.0	4	2	1	0	0	0
Witasick	†0.0	0	0	0	0	1	0
Fultz	0.1	1	0	0	0	0	0
Fe. Rodriguez (L)	1.2	2	2	2	1	1	0
Worrell	0.1	0	0	0	0	0	0

Anaheim	IP	H	R	ER	HR	BB	SO
Appier	*2.0	5	5	5	3	2	2
Lackey	2.1	2	2	2	0	1	1
Weber	0.2	4	2	2	0	0	1
Fr. Rodriguez (W)	3.0	0	0	0	0	0	4
Percival (S)	1.0	1	1	1	1	0	0

*Pitched to two batters in third.
†Pitched to one batter in sixth.

E—Lofton, Anderson. DP—San Francisco 1, Anaheim 1. LOB—San Francisco 4, Anaheim 5. Hitting with runners in scoring position—San Francisco 5 for 10, Anaheim 5 for 9. 2B—Aurilia, Erstad 2, Glaus. HR—Sanders (2nd inning, 1 out, 2 on) off Appier, Bell (2nd inning, 1 out, 0 on) off Appier, Salmon (2nd inning, 1 out, 1 on) off Ru. Ortiz, Kent (3rd inning, 0 out, 0 on) off Appier, Salmon (8th inning, 2 out, 1 on) off Fe. Rodriguez, Bonds (9th inning, 2 out, 0 on) off Percival. SB—Sanders, Fullmer, Spiezio. S—Spiezio. PB—Santiago. T—3:57. A—44,584. U—Hernandez, plate; Tschida, first; Winters, second; Reilly, third; McClelland, left field; Crawford, right field.

PLAY BY PLAY

FIRST INNING

Giants—Lofton struck out. Aurilia grounded out, Eckstein to Spiezio. Kent grounded out, Appier to Spiezio.

Angels—Eckstein singled to right. Erstad doubled to right, scoring Eckstein. Salmon singled to right as Erstad advanced to third. Anderson singled to right, scoring Erstad as Salmon advanced to second. Glaus flied to Lofton as Salmon advanced to third. Fullmer singled to center, scoring Salmon as Anderson advanced to third. Spiezio singled to right, scoring Anderson as Fullmer advanced to third. Fullmer stole home as Spiezio stole second. B. Molina flied to Sanders as Spiezio advanced to third. Kennedy grounded out, Ortiz to Snow. Five runs. Angels 5, Giants 0.

SECOND INNING

Giants—Bonds walked. Santiago flied to Erstad. Snow singled to right as Bonds advanced to third. Sanders homered to left, scoring Bonds and Snow. Bell homered to center. Dunston grounded out, Kennedy to Spiezio. Lofton singled to center. Aurilia struck out. Four runs. Angels 5, Giants 4.

Angels—Eckstein bunted safely to the pitcher. Erstad flied to Lofton. Salmon homered to left, scoring Eckstein. Anderson popped to Snow. Glaus doubled to center. Zerbe now pitching. Glaus advanced to third on a passed ball by Santiago. Fullmer grounded out, Snow to Zerbe. Two runs. Angels 7, Giants 4.

THIRD INNING

Giants—Kent homered to left. Bonds walked. Lackey now pitching. Santiago lined into a double play, Eckstein to Spiezio. Snow flied to Erstad. One run. Angels 7, Giants 5.

Angels—Spiezio grounded out, Kent to Snow. B. Molina grounded out, Aurilia to Snow. Kennedy grounded out, Zerbe to Snow.

FOURTH INNING

Giants—Sanders singled to left. Sanders stole second. Bell grounded out, Lackey to Spiezio. Dunston reached first on a fielder's choice as Sanders was retired, Eckstein to Kennedy to Glaus. Lofton flied to Erstad.

Angels—Eckstein grounded out, Bell to Snow. Erstad grounded out, Bell to Snow. Salmon singled to left. Anderson grounded out, Kent to Snow.

FIFTH INNING

Giants—Aurilia doubled to center. Kent struck out. Bonds was walked intentionally. Weber now pitching. Santiago singled to left as Aurilia advanced to third and Bonds to second. Snow singled to right, scoring Aurilia and Bonds as Santiago advanced to third. Sanders struck out. Bell singled to second, scoring Santiago as Snow advanced to second. Dunston singled to left and advanced to second on a throwing error by Anderson as Snow scored and Bell advanced to third. Lofton grounded out, Kennedy to Spiezio. Four runs. Giants 9, Angels 7.

Angels—Glaus singled to center. Fullmer singled to center and Glaus advanced to third when Lofton bobbled the ball. Spiezio hit a sacrifice fly to Lofton, scoring Glaus. B. Molina grounded into a double play, Bell to Kent to Snow. One run. Giants 9, Angels 8.

SIXTH INNING

Giants—Fr. Rodriguez now pitching. Aurilia and Kent struck out. Bonds grounded to Spiezio.

Angels—Kennedy grounded to Snow. Eckstein grounded out, Aurilia to Snow. Erstad doubled to right. Witasick now pitching. Salmon walked. Fultz now pitching. Anderson singled to right, scoring Erstad, but Salmon was thrown out, Sanders to Snow to Bell to Aurilia. One run. Giants 9, Angels 9.

SEVENTH INNING

Giants—Santiago struck out. Snow grounded to Spiezio. Sanders struck out.

Angels—Fe. Rodriguez now pitching. Glaus popped to Kent. Fullmer walked. Spiezio flied to Lofton. B. Molina flied to Sanders.

EIGHTH INNING

Giants—Bell flied to Erstad. Dunston fouled to Spiezio. Lofton grounded out, Fr. Rodriguez to Spiezio.

Angels—Kennedy flied to Lofton. Eckstein singled to right. Erstad flied to Bonds. Salmon homered to left, scoring Eckstein. Worrell now pitching. Anderson popped to Aurilia. Two runs. Angels 11, Giants 9.

NINTH INNING

Giants—Percival now pitching and Ochoa in right field. Aurilia and Kent flied to Anderson. Bonds homered to right. Santiago popped to Kennedy. One run. Final score: Angels 11, Giants 10.

GAME 3

ANAHEIM 10, SAN FRANCISCO 4

TUESDAY, OCTOBER 22, AT SAN FRANCISCO

Anaheim	AB	R	H	RBI	BB	SO	PO	A
Eckstein, ss	5	1	2	1	1	0	2	2
Erstad, cf	6	2	3	0	0	0	3	0
Salmon, rf	4	2	1	1	2	1	2	0
Schoeneweis, p	0	0	0	0	0	0	0	0
Anderson, lf	6	0	1	1	0	0	3	0
Glaus, 3b	5	2	2	1	1	0	0	1
Spiezio, 1b	5	1	2	3	1	0	10	0
Kennedy, 2b	5	1	2	1	0	2	2	2
B. Molina, c	2	1	2	1	3	0	5	0
Ra. Ortiz, p	3	0	0	0	0	2	0	1
‡Wooten, ph	1	0	0	0	0	0	0	0
Donnelly, p	0	0	0	0	0	0	0	0
∞Gil, ph	1	0	1	0	0	0	0	0
Ochoa, rf	0	0	0	0	0	0	0	0
Totals	43	10	16	9	8	5	27	6

San Francisco	AB	R	H	RBI	BB	SO	PO	A
Lofton, cf	4	1	0	0	1	0	5	0
Aurilia, ss	5	1	2	1	0	2	1	4
Kent, 2b	4	1	2	0	0	0	1	1
Bonds, lf	2	1	1	2	2	1	3	0
Santiago, c	4	0	0	1	0	0	6	1
Snow, 1b	4	0	1	0	0	0	8	1
Sanders, rf	4	0	0	0	0	1	1	0
Bell, 3b	1	0	0	0	3	0	0	2
Hernandez, p	0	0	0	0	0	0	2	1
Witasick, p	0	0	0	0	0	0	0	0
†Feliz, ph	1	0	0	0	0	0	0	0
Fultz, p	0	0	0	0	0	0	0	0
§Dunston, ph	1	0	0	0	0	0	0	0
Fe. Rodriguez, p	0	0	0	0	0	0	0	0
Eyre, p	0	0	0	0	0	0	0	1
▲Martinez, ph	1	0	0	0	0	1	0	0
Totals	31	4	6	4	6	5	27	11

Anaheim	0	0 4		4 0 1		0 1 0—10
San Francisco	1	0 0		0 3 0		0 0 0— 4

Anaheim	IP	H	R	ER	HR	BB	SO
Ra. Ortiz (W)	5.0	5	4	4	2	4	3
Donnelly	2.0	0	0	0	0	2	0
Schoeneweis	2.0	1	0	0	0	0	2

San Francisco	IP	H	R	ER	HR	BB	SO
Hernandez (L)	3.2	5	6	5	0	5	3
Witasick	0.1	3	2	2	0	1	1
Fultz	2.0	3	1	1	0	1	0
Fe. Rodriguez	1.0	1	0	0	0	0	0
Eyre	2.0	4	1	0	0	1	1

†Flied out for Witasick in fourth. ‡Fouled out for Ra. Ortiz in sixth. §Flied out for Fultz in sixth. ∞Singled for Donnelly in eighth. ▲Struck out for Eyre in ninth.

E—Santiago, Bell. DP—Anaheim 1, San Francisco 1. LOB—Anaheim 15, San Francisco 7. Hitting with runners in scoring position—Anaheim 7 for 22, San Francisco 1 for 4. 2B—Erstad, Salmon, Kennedy. 3B—Spiezio. HR—Aurilia (5th inning, 1 out, 0 on) off Ra. Ortiz, Bonds (5th inning, 1 on) off Ra. Ortiz. SB—Erstad, Salmon, Lofton. SH—Hernandez. HBP—Kennedy by Fultz. T—3:37. A—42,707. U—Tschida, plate; Winters, first; Reilly, second; McClelland, third; Crawford, left field; Hernandez, right field.

PLAY BY PLAY

FIRST INNING

Angels—Eckstein lined to Hernandez. Erstad grounded out, Bell to Snow. Salmon struck out.

Giants—Lofton walked. Aurilia struck out. Lofton stole second. Kent singled to the pitcher as Lofton advanced to third. Bonds was walked intentionally. Santiago grounded out, Kennedy to Spiezio, as Lofton scored, Kent advanced to third and Bonds to second. Snow grounded out, Ra. Ortiz to Spiezio. One run. Giants 1, Angels 0.

SECOND INNING

Angels—Anderson grounded out, Snow to Hernandez. Glaus flied to Lofton. Spiezio walked. Kennedy doubled to left as Spiezio advanced to third. B. Molina was walked intentionally. Ra. Ortiz struck out.

Giants—Sanders struck out. Bell walked. Hernandez sacrificed Bell to second, Spiezio, unassisted. Lofton grounded to Spiezio.

THIRD INNING

Angels—Eckstein walked. Erstad doubled to right as Eckstein advanced to third. Salmon reached base on a fielding error by Bell, scoring Eckstein. Anderson flied to Bonds. Glaus singled to left-center, scoring Erstad as Salmon advanced to third. Spiezio tripled to right-center, scoring Salmon and Glaus. Kennedy struck out. B. Molina was walked intentionally. Ra. Ortiz grounded out, Hernandez to Snow. Four runs. Angels 4, Giants 1.

Giants—Aurilia singled to left. Kent fouled to Spiezio. Bonds struck out. Santiago grounded out, Glaus to Spiezio.

FOURTH INNING

Angels—Eckstein grounded out, Aurilia to Snow. Erstad singled to center. Salmon walked. Erstad stole third and Salmon stole second. Anderson grounded to Snow, scoring Erstad as Salmon advanced to third. Witasick now pitching. Glaus walked. Spiezio singled to right, scoring Salmon as Glaus advanced to second. Kennedy singled to center, scoring Glaus as Spiezio advanced to second. B. Molina singled to right-center, scoring Spiezio as Kennedy advanced to third. Ra. Ortiz struck out. Four runs. Angels 8, Giants 1.

Giants—Snow grounded to Spiezio. Sanders fouled to Spiezio. Bell walked. Feliz, pinch-hitting for Witasick, flied to Anderson.

FIFTH INNING

Angels—Fultz now pitching. Eckstein grounded out, Aurilia to Snow. Erstad singled to left-center. Salmon flied to Bonds. Anderson singled to right as Erstad advanced to third. Glaus flied to Sanders.

Giants—Lofton flied to Salmon. Aurilia homered to left. Kent singled to left. Bonds homered to center, scoring Kent. Santiago grounded out, Eckstein to Spiezio. Snow flied to Anderson. Three runs. Angels 8, Giants 4.

SIXTH INNING

Angels—Spiezio grounded out, Aurilia to Snow. Kennedy was hit by a pitch. B. Molina walked. Wooten, pinch-hitting for Ra. Ortiz, fouled to Snow. Eckstein singled to center, scoring Kennedy as B. Molina advanced to second. Erstad popped to Aurilia. One run. Angels 9, Giants 4.

Giants—Donnelly now pitching. Sanders flied to Salmon. Bell walked. Dunston, pinch-hitting for Fultz, flied to Anderson. Lofton popped to Eckstein.

SEVENTH INNING

Angels—Fe. Rodriguez now pitching. Salmon doubled to left. Anderson, Glaus and Spiezio flied to Lofton.

Giants—Aurilia and Kent flied to Erstad. Bonds walked. Santiago popped to Eckstein.

EIGHTH INNING

Angels—Eyre now pitching. Kennedy flied to Bonds. B. Molina singled to center. Gil, pinch-hitting for Donnelly, singled to left as B. Molina advanced to second. Eckstein singled to first as B. Molina advanced to third and Gil to second. Erstad reached first on a fielder's choice and advanced to second on a throwing error by Santiago as B. Molina scored. On the play, Gil advanced to third, but was out trying to score, Santiago to Bell to Santiago, as Eckstein advanced to third. Salmon was walked intentionally. Anderson flied to Lofton. One run. Angels 10, Giants 4.

Giants—Schoeneweis now pitching and Ochoa in right field. Snow singled to left. Sanders popped to Kennedy. Bell grounded into a double play, Eckstein to Kennedy to Spiezio.

NINTH INNING

Angels—Glaus singled to right-center. Spiezio grounded into a double play, Aurilia to Kent to Snow. Kennedy struck out.

Giants—Martinez, pinch-hitting for Eyre, struck out. Lofton flied to Erstad. Aurilia struck out. Final score: Angels 10, Giants 4.

GAME 4

SAN FRANCISCO 4, ANAHEIM 3

WEDNESDAY, OCTOBER 23, AT SAN FRANCISCO

Anaheim	AB	R	H	RBI	BB	SO	PO	A
Eckstein, ss	3	0	0	1	0	0	1	3
Erstad, cf	4	0	0	0	0	0	1	0
Salmon, rf	4	0	1	0	0	1	3	0
Anderson, lf	4	1	2	0	0	0	2	1
Glaus, 3b	4	1	1	2	0	0	1	0
Spiezio, 1b	4	0	1	0	0	1	7	1
Gil, 2b	3	1	2	0	0	1	3	3
∞Kennedy, ph	1	0	1	0	0	0	0	0
B. Molina, c	3	0	1	0	0	0	4	1
▲Fullmer, ph	1	0	0	0	0	0	0	0
Lackey, p	2	0	1	0	0	0	2	0
Weber, p	0	0	0	0	0	0	0	0
‡Palmeiro, ph	1	0	0	0	0	1	0	0
Fr. Rodriguez, p	0	0	0	0	0	0	0	0
Totals	34	3	10	3	0	3	24	9

San Francisco	AB	R	H	RBI	BB	SO	PO	A
Lofton, cf	4	1	3	0	0	0	3	0
Aurilia, ss	4	1	3	1	0	0	4	5
Kent, 2b	3	0	0	1	0	2	2	5
Bonds, lf	1	0	0	0	3	0	1	0
Santiago, c	4	0	1	1	0	0	3	0
Snow, 1b	4	1	1	0	0	0	10	2
Sanders, rf	4	0	1	0	0	1	1	0
Bell, 3b	4	0	2	1	0	0	1	1
Rueter, p	2	1	1	0	0	0	1	2
†Goodwin, ph	0	0	0	0	1	0	0	0
Fe. Rodriguez, p	0	0	0	0	0	0	1	0
Worrell, p	0	0	0	0	0	0	0	0
§Martinez, ph	1	0	0	0	0	1	0	0
Nen, p	0	0	0	0	0	0	0	0
Totals	31	4	12	4	4	4	27	15

	1 2 3	4 5 6	7 8 9	R
Anaheim	0 1 2	0 0 0	0 0 0	—3
San Francisco	0 0 0	0 3 0	0 1 x	—4

Anaheim	IP	H	R	ER	HR	BB	SO
Lackey	5.0	9	3	3	0	3	2
Weber	1.0	1	0	0	0	1	0
Fr. Rodriguez (L)	2.0	2	1	0	0	0	2

San Francisco	IP	H	R	ER	HR	BB	SO
Rueter	6.0	9	3	3	1	0	2
Fe. Rodriguez	1.0	0	0	0	0	0	1
Worrell (W)	1.0	0	0	0	0	0	0
Nen (S)	1.0	1	0	0	0	0	0

†Walked for Rueter in sixth. ‡Struck out for Weber in seventh. §Struck out into a double play for Worrell in eighth. ∞Singled for Gil in ninth. ▲Grounded into double play for B. Molina in ninth.

E—Salmon, Bell. DP—Anaheim 3, San Francisco 2. LOB—Anaheim 5, San Francisco 8. Hitting with runners in scoring position—Anaheim 1 for 3, San Francisco 3 for 13. 2B—Aurilia. HR—Glaus (3rd inning, 1 out, 1 on) off Rueter. SB—Goodwin. CS—Bell. S—Eckstein, Kent. PB—B. Molina. T—3:02. A—42,703. U—Winters, plate; Reilly, first; McClelland, second; Crawford, third; Hernandez, left field; Tschida, right field.

PLAY BY PLAY

FIRST INNING

Angels—Eckstein grounded out, Aurilia to Snow. Erstad grounded out, Kent to Snow. Salmon reached first on Bell's throwing error. Anderson singled to center as Salmon advanced to third. Glaus forced Anderson at second, Kent to Aurilia.

Giants—Lofton singled to center. Aurilia singled to right as Lofton advanced to third. Kent struck out. Bonds was walked intentionally. Santiago grounded into a double play, Eckstein to Spiezio.

SECOND INNING

Angels—Spiezio grounded out, Aurilia to Snow. Gil singled to right. B. Molina singled to center as Gil advanced to second. Lackey singled to right as Gil advanced to third and B. Molina to second. Eckstein scored Gil on a sacrifice fly to Lofton. Erstad grounded out, Kent to Snow. One run. Angels 1, Giants 0.

Giants—Snow grounded out, Spiezio to Lackey. Sanders singled to center. Bell grounded out, Eckstein to Spiezio as Sanders advanced to second. Rueter grounded out, Gil to Spiezio.

THIRD INNING

Angels—Salmon singled to center. Anderson forced Salmon at second, Aurilia to Kent. Glaus homered to center, scoring Anderson. Spiezio lined to Lofton. Gil singled to center. B. Molina flied to Sanders. Two runs. Angels 3, Giants 0.

Giants—Lofton singled to right. Aurilia doubled to center as Lofton advanced to third. Kent lined to Lackey. Bonds was walked intentionally. Santiago grounded into a double play, Eckstein to Gil to Spiezio.

FOURTH INNING

Angels—Lackey grounded out, Rueter to Snow. Eckstein grounded out, Bell to Snow. Erstad grounded out, Kent to Snow.

Giants—Snow grounded out, Gil to Spiezio. Sanders flied to Salmon. Bell flied to Anderson.

FIFTH INNING

Angels—Salmon struck out. Anderson singled to left. Glaus grounded into a double play, Aurilia to Kent to Snow.

Giants—Rueter singled to the pitcher. Lofton hit a bunt single to third as Rueter advanced to second. Aurilia singled to right, scoring Rueter as Lofton advanced to third. Kent scored Lofton on a sacrifice fly to Salmon and Aurilia advanced to second on Salmon's throwing error. Bonds was walked intentionally. Santiago singled to center, scoring Aurilia as Bonds advanced to second. Snow flied to Salmon. Sanders struck out. Three runs. Angels 3, Giants 3.

SIXTH INNING

Angels—Spiezio singled to center. Gil struck out. B. Molina grounded into a double play, Snow to Aurilia to Rueter.

Giants—Weber now pitching. Bell singled to left, but was out trying for second, Anderson to Gil. Goodwin, pinch-hitting for Rueter, walked. Goodwin stole second. Lofton flied to Erstad as Goodwin advanced to third. Aurilia lined to Glaus.

SEVENTH INNING

Angels—Fe. Rodriguez now pitching. Palmeiro, pinch-hitting for Weber, struck out. Eckstein popped to Kent. Erstad grounded out, Snow to Fe. Rodriguez.

Giants—Fr. Rodriguez now pitching. Kent struck out. Bonds grounded to Spiezio. Santiago flied to Anderson.

EIGHTH INNING

Angels—Worrell now pitching. Salmon flied to Lofton. Anderson grounded to Snow. Glaus flied to Bonds.

Giants—Snow singled to right. Snow advanced to second on B. Molina's passed ball. Sanders fouled to Spiezio. Bell singled to center, scoring Snow. Martinez, pinch-hitting for Worrell, struck out as Bell was caught trying to steal second, B. Molina to Gil, for a double play. One run. Giants 4, Angels 3.

NINTH INNING

Angels—Nen now pitching. Spiezio fouled to Bell. Kennedy, pinch-hitting for Gil, singled to right. Fullmer, pinch-hitting for B. Molina, grounded into a double play, Aurilia to Snow. Final score: Giants 4, Angels 3.

GAME 5

SAN FRANCISCO 16, ANAHEIM 4

THURSDAY, OCTOBER 24, AT SAN FRANCISCO

Anaheim	AB	R	H	RBI	BB	SO	PO	A
Eckstein, ss	4	1	2	1	1	1	0	1
Erstad, cf	4	0	1	1	0	1	5	0
Salmon, rf	4	1	1	0	0	2	1	0
Ochoa, rf	1	0	0	0	0	0	1	0
Anderson, lf	5	0	1	0	0	1	3	0
Glaus, 3b	4	0	1	1	0	3	0	1
Spiezio, 1b	2	0	0	0	2	1	4	0
Shields, p	0	0	0	0	0	0	0	0
Kennedy, 2b	4	0	0	0	0	1	2	3
B. Molina, c	4	1	1	0	0	1	6	0
J. Molina, c	0	0	0	0	0	0	0	0
Washburn, p	1	0	0	0	0	0	0	1
†Palmeiro, ph	1	1	1	0	0	0	0	0
‡Gil, ph	1	0	1	0	0	0	0	0
Donnelly, p	0	0	0	0	0	0	0	0
Weber, p	0	0	0	0	0	0	0	1
Wooten, 1b	1	0	1	0	0	0	2	0
Totals	36	4	10	3	3	11	24	7

San Francisco	AB	R	H	RBI	BB	SO	PO	A
Lofton, cf	6	3	3	2	0	0	1	0
Eyre, p	0	0	0	0	0	0	0	0
Aurilia, ss	6	2	2	3	0	1	1	2
Kent, 2b	5	4	3	4	1	0	1	2
Bonds, lf	4	2	3	1	1	0	0	0
Santiago, c	3	0	1	3	1	0	11	0
Sanders, rf	1	0	0	1	1	1	2	0
Fe. Rodriguez, p	0	0	0	0	0	0	0	0
§Dunston, ph	1	0	0	0	0	1	0	0
Worrell, p	0	0	0	0	0	0	0	0
∞Feliz, ph	1	0	0	0	0	0	0	0
Goodwin, rf	0	0	0	0	0	0	1	0
Snow, 1b	4	2	2	0	1	1	7	0
Bell, 3b	3	2	2	1	1	0	1	1
Schmidt, p	1	0	0	0	0	1	0	0
Zerbe, p	0	0	0	0	0	0	1	0
Shinjo, rf-cf	2	1	0	0	0	1	1	0
Totals	37	16	16	15	6	6	27	5

Anaheim			0	0	0		0	3	1		0	0	0—	4
San Francisco			3	3	0		0	0	2		4	4	x—	16

Anaheim	IP	H	R	ER	HR	BB	SO
Washburn (L)	4.0	6	6	6	0	5	1
Donnelly	1.0	0	0	0	0	0	2
Weber	1.1	5	5	5	1	1	2
Shields	1.2	5	5	1	2	0	1

San Francisco	IP	H	R	ER	HR	BB	SO
Schmidt	4.2	7	3	3	0	3	8
Zerbe (W)	1.0	2	1	1	0	0	0
Fe. Rodriguez	0.1	0	0	0	0	0	0
Worrell	2.0	1	0	0	0	0	2
Eyre	1.0	0	0	0	0	0	1

†Doubled for Washburn in fifth. ‡Doubled for Donnelly in sixth. §Struck out for Fe. Rodriguez in sixth. ∞Flied out for Worrell in eighth.

E—Glaus, Erstad. LOB—Anaheim 9, San Francisco 6. Hitting with runners in scoring position—Anaheim 3 for 11, San Francisco 5 for 13. 2B—Glaus, Palmeiro, Gil, Kent, Bonds 2. 3B—Lofton. HR—Kent (6th inning, 2 out, 1 on) off Weber, Kent (7th inning, 2 out, 1 on) off Shields, Aurilia (8th inning, 2 out, 2 on) off Shields. SB—Eckstein, Goodwin. S—Erstad, Santiago, Sanders. SH—Schmidt, Shinjo. WP—Schmidt. HBP—D. Bell by Weber. T—3:53. A—42,713. U—Reilly, plate; McClelland, first; Crawford, second; Hernandez, third; Tschida, left field; Winters, right field.

PLAY BY PLAY

FIRST INNING

Angels—Eckstein singled to center. Erstad forced Eckstein at second, Kent to Aurilia. Salmon struck out. Anderson singled to left as Erstad advanced to second. Glaus struck out.

Giants—Lofton singled to left. Aurilia flied to Erstad. Kent walked. Bonds doubled to right, scoring Lofton as Kent advanced to third. Santiago scored Kent on a sacrifice fly to Anderson. Sanders was walked intentionally. Snow walked. Bell walked, scoring Bonds. Schmidt struck out. Three runs. Giants 3, Angels 0.

SECOND INNING

Angels—Spiezio struck out. Kennedy grounded to Snow. B. Molina struck out.

Giants—Lofton singled to center. Aurilia lined to Erstad. Kent doubled to right as Lofton advanced to third. Bonds was walked intentionally. Santiago singled to center and advanced to second on Erstad's throwing error as Lofton and Kent scored and Bonds advanced to third. Sanders scored Bonds on a sacrifice fly to Erstad as Santiago advanced to third. Snow flied to Erstad. Three runs. Giants 6, Angels 0.

THIRD INNING

Angels—Washburn grounded out, Aurilia to Snow. Eckstein walked. Eckstein stole second. Erstad singled to left as Eckstein advanced to third. Salmon struck out. Anderson lined to Sanders.

Giants—Bell singled to short. Schmidt sacrificed Bell to second, Washburn to Kennedy. Lofton grounded out, Kennedy to Spiezio as Bell advanced to third. Aurilia flied to Erstad.

FOURTH INNING

Angels—Glaus struck out. Spiezio walked. Kennedy struck out. B. Molina popped to Kent.

Giants—Kent flied to Salmon. Bonds flied to Anderson. Santiago grounded out, Glaus to Spiezio.

FIFTH INNING

Angels—Palmeiro, pinch-hitting for Washburn, doubled to right. Eckstein singled to left as Palmeiro advanced to third. Erstad scored Palmeiro on a sacrifice fly to Sanders. Salmon singled to center as Eckstein advanced to third. Eckstein scored and Salmon advanced to second on a wild pitch by Schmidt. Anderson struck out. Glaus doubled to left, scoring Salmon. Spiezio walked. Zerbe now pitching. Kennedy flied to Lofton. Three runs. Giants 6, Angels 3.

World Series

2002 REVIEW

Giants—Donnelly now pitching. Sanders and Snow struck out. Bell fouled to Spiezio.

SIXTH INNING

Angels—B. Molina singled to center, Gil, pinch-hitting for Donnelly, doubled to center as B. Molina advanced to third. Eckstein grounded out, Aurilia to Snow, scoring B. Molina as Gil advanced to third. Erstad grounded to Zerbe. Fe. Rodriguez now pitching and Shinjo in right field. Salmon grounded out, Bell to Snow. One run. Giants 6, Angels 4.

Giants—Weber now pitching. Shinjo struck out. Lofton grounded out, Kennedy to Spiezio. Aurilia singled to left. Kent homered to left, scoring Aurilia. Bonds doubled to left. Santiago was walked intentionally. Dunston, pinch-hitting for Fe. Rodriguez, struck out. Two runs. Giants 8, Angels 4.

SEVENTH INNING

Angels—Worrell now pitching. Anderson fouled to Bell. Glaus struck out. Spiezio grounded to Snow.

Giants—Snow singled to center. Bell was hit by a pitch. Shinjo sacrificed Snow to third and Bell to second, Weber to Kennedy. Lofton tripled to right, scoring Snow and Bell. Shields now pitching and Wooten at first base. Aurilia struck out. Kent homered to left, scoring Lofton. Bonds singled to center. Santiago grounded out, Eckstein to Wooten. Four runs. Giants 12, Angels 4.

EIGHTH INNING

Angels—Kennedy grounded to Snow. B. Molina flied to Shinjo. Wooten singled to center. Eckstein struck out.

Giants—J. Molina now catching and Ochoa in right field. Feliz, pinch-hitting for Worrell, flied to Ochoa. Snow singled to right. Bell singled to center as Snow advanced to second. Shinjo reached first on a fielding error by Glaus as Snow scored and Bell advanced to second. Lofton grounded out, Kennedy to Wooten as Bell advanced to third and Shinjo to second. Aurilia homered to left, scoring Bell and Shinjo. Kent flied to Anderson. Four runs. Giants 16, Angels 4.

NINTH INNING

Angels—Eyre now pitching and Goodwin in right field as Shinjo moves to left field. Erstad struck out. Ochoa flied to Goodwin. Anderson grounded out, Kent to Snow. Final score: Giants 16, Angels 4.

GAME 6

ANAHEIM 6, SAN FRANCISCO 5

SATURDAY, OCTOBER 26, AT ANAHEIM

San Francisco	AB	R	H	RBI	BB	SO	PO	A
Lofton, cf	5	2	2	0	0	0	3	0
Aurilia, ss	4	0	0	0	1	2	2	3
Kent, 2b	4	0	2	1	0	0	0	4
Bonds, lf	2	1	1	1	2	1	1	0
Santiago, c	3	0	0	0	1	1	5	0
Snow, 1b	4	0	1	0	0	0	8	1
Sanders, rf	4	0	0	0	0	3	4	0
Bell, 3b	4	1	1	0	0	2	0	1
Dunston, dh	3	1	1	2	0	0	0	0
∞Goodwin, ph	1	0	0	0	0	1	0	0
Ru. Ortiz, p	0	0	0	0	0	0	1	0
Fe. Rodriguez, p	0	0	0	0	0	0	0	0
Eyre, p	0	0	0	0	0	0	0	0
Worrell, p	0	0	0	0	0	0	0	0
Nen, p	0	0	0	0	0	0	0	1
Totals	34	5	8	4	4	10	24	10

Anaheim	AB	R	H	RBI	BB	SO	PO	A
Eckstein, ss	4	0	0	0	0	0	4	1
Erstad, cf	3	1	1	1	1	0	3	0
Salmon, rf	4	0	2	0	0	1	1	0
§Figgins, pr	0	1	0	0	0	0	0	0
Ochoa, rf	0	0	0	0	0	0	0	0

Anaheim	AB	R	H	RBI	BB	SO	PO	A
Anderson, lf	4	1	1	0	0	0	0	0
Glaus, 3b	3	1	2	2	1	0	1	3
Fullmer, dh	4	1	1	0	0	1	0	0
Spiezio, 1b	3	1	1	3	1	0	7	0
B. Molina, c	2	0	0	0	0	0	6	0
‡Palmeiro, ph	1	0	0	0	0	1	0	0
J. Molina, c	0	0	0	0	0	0	4	0
Kennedy, 2b	4	0	2	0	0	2	1	2
Appier, p	0	0	0	0	0	0	0	0
Fr. Rodriguez, p	0	0	0	0	0	0	0	0
Donnelly, p	0	0	0	0	0	0	0	0
Percival, p	0	0	0	0	0	0	0	0
Totals	32	6	10	6	3	5	27	6

San Francisco	0	0	0	0	3	1	1	0	0—5
Anaheim	0	0	0	0	0	0	3	3	x—6

San Francisco	IP	H	R	ER	HR	BB	SO
Ru. Ortiz	6.1	4	2	2	0	2	2
Fe. Rodriguez	0.1	1	1	1	1	0	1
Eyre	*0.0	1	0	0	0	0	0
Worrell (L)	†0.1	3	3	2	1	0	0
Nen	1.0	1	0	0	0	1	2

Anaheim	IP	H	R	ER	HR	BB	SO
Appier	4.1	4	3	3	1	3	2
Fr. Rodriguez	2.2	4	2	2	1	0	4
Donnelly (W)	1.0	0	0	0	0	1	2
Percival (S)	1.0	0	0	0	0	0	2

*Pitched to one batter in the seventh.
†Pitched to three batters in eighth.
‡Struck out for B. Molina in seventh. §Pinch-ran for Salmon in eighth.
∞Struck out for Dunston in ninth.

E—Bonds, B. Molina. DP—San Francisco 1, Anaheim 1. LOB—San Francisco 6, Anaheim 6. Hitting with runners in scoring position—San Francisco 1 for 4, Anaheim 2 for 5. 2B—Lofton, Glaus. HR—Dunston (5th inning, 1 out, 1 on) off Appier, Bonds (6th inning, 0 out, 0 on) off Fr. Rodriguez, Spiezio (7th inning, 1 out, 2 on) off Fe. Rodriguez, Erstad (8th inning, 0 out, 0 on) off Worrell. SB—Lofton 2. SH—J. Molina. WP—Fr. Rodriguez. T—3:48. A—44,506. U—McClelland, plate; Crawford, first; Hernandez, second; Tschida, third; Winters, left field; Reilly, right field.

PLAY BY PLAY

FIRST INNING

Giants—Lofton popped to Eckstein. Aurilia flied to Erstad. Kent singled to center. Bonds was walked intentionally. Santiago fouled to Spiezio.

Angels—Eckstein flied to Bonds. Erstad grounded out, Kent to Snow. Salmon grounded out, Bell to Snow.

SECOND INNING

Giants—Snow flied to Erstad. Sanders and Bell struck out.

Angels—Anderson flied to Lofton. Glaus walked. Fullmer popped to Aurilia. Spiezio flied to Lofton.

THIRD INNING

Giants—Dunston flied to Salmon. Lofton grounded out, Glaus to Spiezio. Aurilia walked. Kent popped to Eckstein.

Angels—B. Molina flied to Sanders. Kennedy struck out. Eckstein grounded out, Aurilia to Snow.

FOURTH INNING

Giants—Bonds walked. Santiago grounded into a double play, Glaus to Kennedy to Spiezio. Snow grounded out, Kennedy to Spiezio.

Angels—Erstad grounded out, Kent to Snow. Salmon singled to short. Anderson grounded into a double play, Kent to Aurilia to Snow.

FIFTH INNING

Giants—Sanders popped to Eckstein. Bell singled to short. Dunston homered to left, scoring Bell. Lofton doubled to right-center. Fr. Rodriguez now pitching. Lofton stole third. Aurilia grounded out, Eckstein to Spiezio. Lofton scored on Fr. Rodriguez's wild pitch. Kent grounded out, Glaus to Spiezio. Three runs. Giants 3, Angels 0.

Angels—Glaus flied to Lofton. Fullmer flied to Sanders. Spiezio grounded out, Snow to Ru. Ortiz.

SIXTH INNING

Giants—Bonds homered to right. Santiago struck out. Snow singled to left. Sanders struck out. Bell fouled to Spiezio. One run. Giants 4, Angels 0.

Angels—B. Molina flied to Sanders. Kennedy singled to center. Eckstein grounded out, Aurilia to Snow, as Kennedy advanced to second. Erstad walked. Salmon struck out.

SEVENTH INNING

Giants—Dunston popped to Eckstein. Lofton singled to right. Lofton stole second and advanced to third on B. Molina's throwing error. Aurilia struck out. Kent singled to center, scoring Lofton. Bonds struck out. One run. Giants 5, Angels 0.

Angels—Anderson grounded out, Kent to Snow. Glaus singled to left. Fullmer singled to right as Glaus advanced to second. Fe. Rodriguez now pitching. Spiezio homered to right, scoring Glaus and Fullmer. Palmeiro, pinch-hitting for B. Molina, struck out. Eyre now pitching. Kennedy singled to left. Worrell now pitching. Eckstein flied to Sanders. Three runs. Giants 5, Angels 3.

EIGHTH INNING

Giants—Donnelly now pitching and J. Molina catching. Santiago walked. Snow flied to Erstad. Sanders and Bell struck out.

Angels—Erstad homered to right. Salmon singled to center. Figgins now running for Salmon. Anderson singled to left and reached second on Bonds' bobble as Figgins advanced to third. Nen now pitching. Glaus doubled to left-center, scoring Figgins and Anderson. Fullmer struck out. Spiezio was walked intentionally. J. Molina sacrificed Glaus to third and Spiezio to second, Nen to Snow. Kennedy struck out. Three runs. Angels 6, Giants 5.

NINTH INNING

Giants—Percival now pitching and Ochoa in right field. Goodwin, pinch-hitting for Dunston, struck out. Lofton fouled to Glaus. Aurilia struck out. Final score: Angels 6, Giants 5.

GAME 7

ANAHEIM 4, SAN FRANCISCO 1

SUNDAY, OCTOBER 27, AT ANAHEIM

San Francisco	AB	R	H	RBI	BB	SO	PO	A
Lofton, cf	4	0	0	0	1	0	4	1
Aurilia, ss	4	0	0	0	0	2	0	2
Kent, 2b	4	0	0	0	0	2	3	3
Bonds, lf	3	0	1	0	1	0	1	0
Santiago, c	3	1	2	0	1	1	6	0
Snow, 1b	4	0	3	0	0	0	7	1
Sanders, rf	1	0	0	1	0	0	0	0
†Goodwin, ph-rf	2	0	0	0	0	1	1	0
Bell, 3b	3	0	0	0	1	1	1	1
Feliz, dh	3	0	0	0	0	2	0	0
‡Shinjo, ph	1	0	0	0	0	1	0	0
Hernandez, p	0	0	0	0	0	0	0	1
Zerbe, p	0	0	0	0	0	0	0	0
Rueter, p	0	0	0	0	0	0	0	1
Worrell, p	0	0	0	0	0	0	1	0
Totals	32	1	6	1	4	10	24	10

Anaheim	AB	R	H	RBI	BB	SO	PO	A
Eckstein, ss	3	1	1	0	1	0	3	0
Erstad, cf	3	1	1	0	0	1	4	0
Salmon, rf	2	1	0	0	1	1	3	0
Ochoa, rf	0	0	0	0	0	0	0	0

Anaheim	AB	R	H	RBI	BB	SO	PO	A
Anderson, lf	4	0	1	3	0	0	3	0
Glaus, 3b	2	0	0	0	2	2	0	2
Fullmer, dh	4	0	0	0	0	0	0	0
Spiezio, 1b	3	1	0	0	1	0	5	0
B. Molina, c	3	0	2	1	0	0	9	1
Kennedy, 2b	3	0	0	0	0	1	0	2
Lackey, p	0	0	0	0	0	0	0	1
Donnelly, p	0	0	0	0	0	0	0	0
Fr. Rodriguez, p	0	0	0	0	0	0	0	0
Percival, p	0	0	0	0	0	0	0	0
Totals	27	4	5	4	5	5	27	6

San Francisco	0	1	0		0	0		0	0	0—1
Anaheim	0	1	3		0	0		0	0	x—4

San Francisco	IP	H	R	ER	HR	BB	SO
Hernandez (L)	*2.0	4	4	4	0	4	1
Zerbe	1.0	0	0	0	0	0	0
Rueter	4.0	1	0	0	0	1	3
Worrell	1.0	0	0	0	0	0	1

Anaheim	IP	H	R	ER	HR	BB	SO
Lackey (W)	5.0	4	1	1	0	1	4
Donnelly	2.0	1	0	0	0	1	2
Fr. Rodriguez	1.0	0	0	0	0	1	3
Percival (S)	1.0	1	0	0	0	1	1

*Pitched to five batters in third.

†Struck out for Sanders in sixth. ‡Struck out for Feliz in ninth.

DP—San Francisco 1. LOB—San Francisco 9, Anaheim 6. Hitting with runners in scoring position—San Francisco 0 for 5, Anaheim 1 for 8. 2B—Snow, Anderson, B. Molina 2. S—Sanders. SH—Erstad. HBP—Salmon by Hernandez. T—3:16. A—44,598. U—Crawford, plate; Hernandez, first; Tschida, second; Winters, third; Reilly, left field; McClelland, right field.

PLAY BY PLAY

FIRST INNING

Giants—Lofton grounded out, Lackey to Kennedy to Spiezio. Aurilia struck out and was thrown out on the dropped third strike, B. Molina to Spiezio. Kent flied to Salmon.

Angels—Eckstein walked. Erstad sacrificed Eckstein to second, Hernandez to Snow. Salmon walked. Anderson flied to Lofton, who threw to Kent to double Eckstein off second.

SECOND INNING

Giants—Bonds lined to Eckstein. Santiago singled to center. Snow singled to right-center as Santiago advanced to third. Sanders scored Santiago on a sacrifice fly to Anderson. Bell struck out. One run. Giants 1, Angels 0.

Angels—Glaus struck out. Fullmer flied to Lofton. Spiezio walked. B. Molina doubled to left-center, scoring Spiezio. Kennedy flied to Lofton. One run. Giants 1, Angels 1.

THIRD INNING

Giants—Feliz grounded out, Glaus to Spiezio. Lofton grounded to Spiezio. Aurilia flied to Anderson.

Angels—Eckstein singled to left. Erstad singled to left as Eckstein advanced to second. Salmon was hit by a pitch. Anderson doubled to right, scoring Eckstein, Erstad and Salmon. Glaus was walked intentionally. Zerbe now pitching. Fullmer forced Glaus at second, Aurilia to Kent, as Anderson advanced to third. Spiezio reached first on a fielder's choice as Anderson was thrown out at home, Bell to Santiago. Fullmer advanced to second on the play. B. Molina grounded out, Kent to Snow. Three runs. Angels 4, Giants 1.

FOURTH INNING

Giants—Kent struck out. Bonds singled to short. Santiago singled to center as Bonds advanced to second. Snow flied to Erstad. Sanders flied to Salmon.

Angels—Rueter now pitching. Kennedy struck out. Eckstein flied to Bonds. Erstad struck out.

FIFTH INNING

Giants—Bell lined to Erstad. Feliz struck out. Lofton walked. Aurilia flied to Salmon.

Angels—Salmon grounded out, Aurilia to Snow. Anderson grounded to Snow. Glaus walked. Fullmer grounded out, Rueter to Snow.

SIXTH INNING

Giants—Donnelly now pitching. Kent grounded out, Glaus to Spiezio. Bonds popped to Eckstein. Santiago walked. Snow doubled to right as Santiago advanced to third. Goodwin, pinch-hitting for Sanders, struck out.

Angels—Goodwin now in right field. Spiezio flied to Goodwin. B. Molina doubled to right-center. Kennedy grounded out, Kent to Snow, as B. Molina advanced to third. Eckstein lined to Kent.

SEVENTH INNING

Giants—Bell flied to Anderson. Feliz struck out. Lofton flied to Erstad.

Angels—Erstad grounded out, Kent to Snow. Salmon struck out. Anderson flied to Lofton.

EIGHTH INNING

Giants—Fr. Rodriguez now pitching and Ochoa in right field. Aurilia and Kent struck out. Bonds walked. Santiago struck out.

Angels—Worrell now pitching. Glaus struck out. Fullmer grounded out, Snow to Worrell. Spiezio popped to Bell.

NINTH INNING

Giants—Percival now pitching. Snow singled to right. Goodwin forced Snow at second, Kennedy to Eckstein. Goodwin advanced to second on defensive indifference. Bell walked. Shinjo, pinch-hitting for Feliz, struck out. Lofton flied to Erstad. Final score: Angels 4, Giants 1.

STATISTICS

ANAHEIM ANGELS' BATTING AND FIELDING AVERAGES

Player, position	G	AB	R	H	TB	2B	3B	HR	RBI	BB	IBB	SO	Avg.	OBP	Slg.	PO	A	E	Avg.
Gil, ph-2b	3	5	1	4	5	1	0	0	0	0	0	1	.800	.800	1.000	3	3	0	1.000
Lackey, p	3	2	0	1	1	0	0	0	0	0	0	0	.500	.500	.500	2	2	0	1.000
Wooten, 1b-ph	3	2	0	1	1	0	0	0	0	0	0	0	.500	.500	.500	3	0	0	1.000
Glaus, 3b	7	26	7	10	22	3	0	3	8	4	1	6	.385	.467	.846	4	11	1	.938
Salmon, rf	7	26	7	9	16	1	0	2	5	4	1	7	.346	.452	.615	11	0	1	.917
Eckstein, ss	7	29	6	9	9	0	0	0	3	3	0	2	.310	.364	.310	11	16	0	1.000
Erstad, cf	7	30	6	9	15	3	0	1	3	1	0	4	.300	.313	.500	21	0	1	.955
B. Molina, c	7	21	2	6	8	2	0	0	2	3	2	1	.286	.375	.381	44	2	1	.979
Anderson, lf	7	32	3	9	10	1	0	0	6	0	0	3	.281	.281	.313	17	1	1	.947
Kennedy, 2b-ph	7	25	1	7	9	2	0	0	2	0	0	7	.280	.308	.360	6	13	0	1.000
Fullmer, dh-ph	5	15	3	4	4	0	0	0	1	2	0	2	.267	.353	.267	0	0	0	.000
Spiezio, 1b	7	23	3	6	12	1	1	1	8	6	1	1	.261	.400	.522	54	2	0	1.000
Palmeiro, ph	4	4	1	1	2	1	0	0	0	0	0	2	.250	.250	.500	0	0	0	.000
Appier, p	2	0	0	0	0	0	0	0	0	0	0	0	.000	.000	.000	0	1	0	1.000
Donnelly, p	5	0	0	0	0	0	0	0	0	0	0	0	.000	.000	.000	0	0	0	.000
Figgins, pr	2	0	1	0	0	0	0	0	0	0	0	0	.000	.000	.000	0	0	0	.000
J. Molina, c	3	0	0	0	0	0	0	0	0	0	0	0	.000	.000	.000	5	0	0	1.000
Percival, p	3	0	0	0	0	0	0	0	0	0	0	0	.000	.000	.000	0	0	0	.000
Fr. Rodriguez, p	4	0	0	0	0	0	0	0	0	0	0	0	.000	.000	.000	0	1	0	1.000
Schoeneweis, p	2	0	0	0	0	0	0	0	0	0	0	0	.000	.000	.000	0	0	0	.000
Shields, p	1	0	0	0	0	0	0	0	0	0	0	0	.000	.000	.000	0	0	0	.000
Weber, p	4	0	0	0	0	0	0	0	0	0	0	0	.000	.000	.000	0	1	0	1.000
Ochoa, rf	5	1	0	0	0	0	0	0	0	0	0	0	.000	.000	.000	1	0	0	1.000
Washburn, p	2	1	0	0	0	0	0	0	0	0	0	0	.000	.000	.000	1	2	0	1.000
Ortiz, p	1	3	0	0	0	0	0	0	0	0	0	2	.000	.000	.000	0	1	0	1.000
Totals	7	245	41	76	114	15	1	7	38	23	5	38	.310	.370	.465	183	56	5	.980

SAN FRANCISCO GIANTS' BATTING AND FIELDING AVERAGES

Player, position	G	AB	R	H	TB	2B	3B	HR	RBI	BB	IBB	SO	Avg.	OBP	Slg.	PO	A	E	Avg.
Rueter, p	2	2	1	1	1	0	0	0	0	0	0	0	.500	.500	.500	1	3	0	1.000
Bonds, lf	7	17	8	8	22	2	0	4	6	13	7	3	.471	.700	1.294	10	0	1	.909
Snow, 1b	7	27	6	11	15	1	0	1	4	2	0	1	.407	.448	.556	57	7	0	1.000
Bell, 3b	7	23	4	7	10	0	0	1	4	5	0	4	.304	.448	.435	4	12	2	.889
Lofton, cf	7	31	7	9	12	1	1	0	2	2	0	2	.290	.333	.387	24	1	1	.962
Kent, 2b	7	29	6	8	18	1	0	3	7	1	0	7	.276	.290	.621	10	21	0	1.000
Aurilia, ss	7	32	5	8	16	2	0	2	5	1	0	9	.250	.273	.500	11	18	0	1.000
Sanders, rf	7	21	3	5	11	0	0	2	6	2	1	9	.238	.280	.524	13	1	0	1.000
Santiago, c	7	26	2	6	6	0	0	0	5	3	1	4	.231	.300	.231	40	1	1	.976
Dunston, dh-ph	4	9	1	2	5	0	0	1	3	0	0	1	.222	.222	.556	0	0	0	.000
Shinjo, dh-cf-rf	3	6	1	1	1	0	0	0	0	0	0	3	.167	.167	.167	1	0	0	1.000
Eyre, p	3	0	0	0	0	0	0	0	0	0	0	0	.000	.000	.000	0	1	0	1.000
Fultz, p	2	0	0	0	0	0	0	0	0	0	0	0	.000	.000	.000	0	0	0	.000

Player, position	G	AB	R	H	TB	2B	3B	HR	RBI	BB	IBB	SO	Avg.	OBP	Slg.	PO	A	E	Avg.
Hernandez, p	2	0	0	0	0	0	0	0	0	0	0	0	.000	.000	.000	2	2	0	1.000
Nen, p	3	0	0	0	0	0	0	0	0	0	0	0	.000	.000	.000	0	1	0	1.000
Ortiz, p	2	0	0	0	0	0	0	0	0	0	0	0	.000	.000	.000	1	1	0	1.000
Fe. Rodriguez, p	6	0	0	0	0	0	0	0	0	0	0	0	.000	.000	.000	1	0	0	1.000
Witasick, p	2	0	0	0	0	0	0	0	0	0	0	0	.000	.000	.000	0	0	0	.000
Worrell, p	6	0	0	0	0	0	0	0	0	0	0	0	.000	.000	.000	1	0	0	1.000
Zerbe, p	3	0	0	0	0	0	0	0	0	0	0	0	.000	.000	.000	2	1	0	1.000
Schmidt, p	2	1	0	0	0	0	0	0	0	0	0	1	.000	.000	.000	0	0	0	.000
Martinez, ph	2	2	0	0	0	0	0	0	0	0	0	2	.000	.000	.000	0	0	0	.000
Goodwin, dh-ph-rf	5	4	0	0	0	0	0	0	0	1	0	2	.000	.200	.000	2	0	0	1.000
Feliz, ph-dh	3	5	0	0	0	0	0	0	0	0	0	2	.000	.000	.000	0	0	0	.000
Totals	7	235	44	66	117	7	1	14	42	30	9	50	.281	.359	.498	180	70	5	.980

ANAHEIM ANGELS' PITCHING RECORDS

Pitcher	G	GS	CG	IP	H	R	ER	HR	BB	IBB	SO	HB	WP	W	L	Pct.	ERA
Donnelly	5	0	0	7.2	1	0	0	0	4	0	6	0	0	1	0	1.000	0.00
Schoeneweis	2	0	0	2.0	1	0	0	0	1	0	2	0	0	0	0	.000	0.00
Fr. Rodriguez	4	0	0	8.2	6	3	2	1	1	0	13	0	1	1	1	.500	2.08
Percival	3	0	0	3.0	2	1	1	1	1	0	3	0	0	0	0	.000	3.00
Lackey	3	2	0	12.1	15	6	6	0	5	4	7	0	0	1	0	1.000	4.38
Shields	1	0	0	1.2	5	5	1	2	0	0	1	0	0	0	0	.000	5.40
Ortiz	1	1	0	5.0	5	4	4	2	4	1	3	0	0	1	0	1.000	7.20
Washburn	2	2	0	9.2	12	10	10	3	7	2	6	0	0	0	2	.000	9.31
Appier	2	2	0	6.1	9	8	8	4	5	1	4	0	0	0	0	.000	11.37
Weber	4	0	0	4.2	10	7	7	1	2	1	5	1	0	0	0	.000	13.50
Totals	7	7	0	61.0	66	44	39	14	30	9	50	1	1	4	3	.571	5.75

No shutouts. Saves—Percival 3.

SAN FRANCISCO GIANTS' PITCHING RECORDS

Pitcher	G	GS	CG	IP	H	R	ER	HR	BB	IBB	SO	HB	WP	W	L	Pct.	ERA
Eyre	3	0	0	3.0	5	1	0	0	1	1	2	0	0	0	0	.000	0.00
Nen	3	0	0	3.0	2	0	0	0	1	1	3	0	0	0	0	.000	0.00
Rueter	2	1	0	10.0	10	3	3	1	1	0	5	0	0	0	0	.000	2.70
Zerbe	3	0	0	6.0	6	3	2	0	0	0	0	0	0	1	0	1.000	3.00
Worrell	6	0	0	5.2	4	3	2	1	1	0	4	0	0	1	1	.500	3.18
Fultz	2	0	0	2.1	4	1	1	0	1	0	0	1	0	0	0	.000	3.86
Fe. Rodriguez	6	0	0	5.2	4	3	3	2	1	0	3	0	0	0	1	.000	4.76
Schmidt	2	2	0	10.1	16	6	6	2	4	0	14	0	1	1	0	1.000	5.23
Ortiz	2	2	0	8.0	13	9	9	1	2	0	2	0	0	0	0	.000	10.13
Hernandez	2	2	0	5.2	9	10	9	0	9	3	4	1	0	0	2	.000	14.29
Witasick	2	0	0	0.1	3	2	2	0	2	0	1	0	0	0	0	.000	54.00
Totals	7	7	0	60.0	76	41	37	7	23	5	38	2	1	3	4	.429	5.55

No shutouts. Saves—Nen 2.

SCORE BY INNINGS

Anaheim	5	5	9	4	4	5	3	6	0—41
San Francisco	4	10	1	0	13	5	5	5	1—44

MISCELLANEOUS STATISTICS

Sacrifice hits—Erstad, Hernandez, Lofton, Molina, Schmidt, Shinjo.
Sacrifice flies—Sanders 2, Eckstein, Erstad, Kent, Santiago, Spiezio.
Stolen bases—Lofton 3, Fullmer 2, Eckstein, Erstad, Goodwin, Salmon, Sanders, Spiezio.
Caught stealing—Bell.
Double plays—Aurilia, Kent and Snow 2; Eckstein and Spiezio 2; Aurilia and Snow; Bell, Kent and Snow; Eckstein, Gil and Spiezio; Eckstein, Kennedy and Spiezio; Glaus, Kennedy and Spiezio; Kent, Aurilia and Snow; Lofton and Kent; Snow, Aurilia and Rueter.
Left on bases—Anaheim 8, 5, 15, 5, 9, 6—54; San Francisco 5, 4, 7, 8, 8, 6, 9—47.
Hitting with runners in scoring position—Anaheim 1 for 8, 5 for 9, 7 for 22, 1 for 3, 3 for 11, 2 for 5, 1 for 8—20 for 66; San Francisco 0 for 4, 5 for 10, 1 for 4, 3 for 13, 5 for 13, 1 for 4, 0 for 5—15 for 53.
Hit by pitcher—By Hernandez (Salmon), by Weber (Bell), by Fultz (Kennedy).
Passed balls—Molina, Santiago.
Balks—None.
Time of games—3:44, 3:57, 3:37, 3:02, 3:53, 3:48, 3:16—Avg.: 3:37
Attendance—44,603, 44,584, 42,707, 42,703, 42,713, 44,506, 44,598—306,414.
Umpires—Jerry Crawford, Angel Hernandez, Tim Tschida, Mike Winters, Mike Reilly, Tim McClelland.
Official scorers—Bill Center, Mike DiGiovanna, Ed Munson, Dick O'Connor, Henry Schulman.

2002 REVIEW World Series

ALL-STAR GAME

BOX SCORE

AMERICAN LEAGUE 7, NATIONAL LEAGUE 7

TUESDAY, JULY 9, AT MILLER PARK, MILWAUKEE

American League	AB	R	H	RBI	BB	SO	PO	A
Suzuki, rf (Mariners)	2	0	0	0	0	0	0	0
Winn, rf (Devil Rays)	2	1	1	0	1	1	1	0
Urbina, p (Red Sox)	0	0	0	0	0	0	0	0
Rivera, p (Yankees)	0	0	0	0	0	0	0	0
Garcia, p (Mariners)	1	0	0	0	0	0	0	0
Hillenbrand, 3b (Red Sox)	2	0	0	0	0	1	1	0
Ventura, 3b (Yankees)	1	0	0	0	0	1	0	1
∞Batista, ph-3b (Orioles)	3	1	1	1	0	1	0	4
Rodriguez, ss (Rangers)	2	0	0	0	0	2	0	2
Tejada, ss (Athletics)	2	1	1	0	0	0	0	1
■Garciaparra, ph-ss (R. Sox)	1	0	0	0	0	0	0	0
Giambi, 1b (Yankees)	2	1	1	0	0	1	4	0
Konerko, 1b (White Sox)	2	0	2	2	0	0	5	0
Sweeney, 1b (Royals)	1	0	0	0	0	0	3	0
Ramirez, lf (Red Sox)	2	0	2	1	0	0	1	1
Buehrle, p (White Sox)	0	0	0	0	0	0	0	0
‡Pierzynski, ph-c (Twins)	3	0	0	0	0	0	7	1
Posada, c (Yankees)	3	0	0	0	0	2	3	0
Zito, p (Athletics)	0	0	0	0	0	0	0	0
Guardado, p (Twins)	0	0	0	0	0	0	0	0
Sasaki, p (Mariners)	0	0	0	0	0	0	0	0
◆Fick, ph-rf (Tigers)	2	1	1	0	0	0	1	0
Hunter, cf (Twins)	2	0	0	0	0	0	2	0
Damon, cf (Red Sox)	3	1	1	0	0	1	3	0
Soriano, 2b (Yankees)	2	1	1	1	0	1	1	1
Vizquel, 2b (Indians)	2	0	1	1	1	0	1	1
Lowe, p (Red Sox)	0	0	0	0	0	0	0	0
*Jeter, ph (Yankees)	1	0	0	0	0	1	0	0
Halladay, p (Blue Jays)	0	0	0	0	0	0	0	0
Anderson, lf (Angels)	4	0	0	0	0	0	0	0
Totals	**45**	**7**	**12**	**7**	**2**	**12**	**33**	**12**

National League	AB	R	H	RBI	BB	SO	PO	A
Vidro, 2b (Expos)	2	0	0	0	0	0	0	2
Spivey, 2b (D'backs)	2	0	0	0	0	1	0	2
Nen, p (Giants)	0	0	0	0	0	0	0	0
Smoltz, p (Braves)	0	0	0	0	0	0	0	0
▼Santiago, ph-c (Giants)	2	0	1	0	0	1	0	0
Helton, 1b (Rockies)	2	1	1	1	0	0	4	0
Berkman, lf-1b (Astros)	3	0	1	2	0	0	8	1
Bonds, lf (Giants)	2	1	1	2	0	0	0	0
Sexson, 1b (Brewers)	1	0	0	0	0	0	2	0
Dunn, lf (Reds)	1	0	0	0	1	0	0	0
Sosa, rf (Cubs)	2	0	1	0	0	1	0	0
Green, rf (Dodgers)	3	0	1	0	0	1	4	0
Guerrero, cf (Expos)	2	1	1	0	0	1	0	0
§A. Jones, ph-cf (Braves)	3	0	0	0	0	2	1	0
Piazza, c (Mets)	2	0	0	0	0	0	7	0
Gagne, p (Dodgers)	0	0	0	0	0	0	0	0
Hernandez, ss (Brewers)	3	0	0	0	0	2	0	2
Rolen, 3b (Phillies)	3	0	0	0	0	1	0	0
Castillo, 2b (Marlins)	2	0	0	0	0	0	0	3
Rollins, ss (Phillies)	2	2	2	0	0	0	1	0
Hoffman, p (Padres)	0	0	0	0	0	0	0	0
Remlinger, p (Braves)	0	0	0	0	0	0	0	0
Kim, p (D'backs)	0	0	0	0	0	0	0	0
▲Lowell, ph-3b (Marlins)	3	1	2	0	0	0	0	0
Schilling, p (D'backs)	0	0	0	0	0	0	0	0
Williams, p (Pirates)	0	0	0	0	0	0	0	0
†Gonzalez, ph (D'backs)	1	0	0	0	0	0	0	0
Perez, p (Dodgers)	0	0	0	0	0	0	0	0
Miller, c (D'backs)	3	1	2	1	0	0	5	0
Padilla, p (Phillies)	1	0	0	0	0	1	1	0
Totals	**45**	**7**	**13**	**7**	**1**	**11**	**33**	**10**

American League..	0	0	0	1	1	0	4	1	0	0 0—7
National League....	0	1	3	0	1	0	2	0	0	0 0—7

American League	IP	H	R	ER	HR	BB	SO
Lowe (Red Sox)	2.0	2	1	1	0	0	0
Halladay (Blue Jays)	1.0	3	3	3	1	0	1
Buehrle (White Sox)	2.0	2	1	1	0	0	2
Zito (Athletics)	0.1	0	0	0	0	0	0
Guardado (Twins)	0.2	0	0	0	0	0	2
Sasaki (Mariners)	1.0	3	2	2	0	1	2
Urbina (Red Sox)	1.0	0	0	0	0	0	1
Rivera (Yankees)	1.0	1	0	0	0	0	0
Garcia (Mariners)	2.0	2	0	0	0	0	3

National League	IP	H	R	ER	HR	BB	SO
Schilling (Diamondbacks)	2.0	1	0	0	0	0	3
Williams (Pirates)	1.0	2	0	0	0	0	2
Perez (Dodgers)	1.0	2	1	0	0	0	2
Gagne (Dodgers)	1.0	2	1	1	1	0	1
Hoffman (Padres)	1.0	1	0	0	0	0	1
Remlinger (Braves)	0.2	1	2	2	0	1	0
Kim (Diamondbacks)	0.1	3	2	2	0	0	0
Nen (Giants)	1.0	2	1	1	0	0	2
Smoltz (Braves)	1.0	0	0	0	0	0	1
Padilla (Phillies)	2.0	0	0	0	0	1	0

*Struck out for Lowe in third. †Grounded out for Williams in third. ‡Grounded out for Buehrle in sixth. §Struck out for Guerrero in sixth. ∞Singled for Ventura in seventh. ▲Singled for Kim in seventh. ◆Singled for Sasaki in eighth. ■Grounded out for Tejada in ninth. ▼Singled for Smoltz in ninth.

LOB—A.L. 7, N.L. 6. Hitting with runners in scoring position—A.L. 4 for 15, N.L. 2 for 12. 2B—Winn, Konerko 2, Miller 2. 3B—Vizquel. HR—Bonds (3rd inning, off Halladay, 1 on, 2 out), Soriano (5th inning, off Gagne, 0 on, 1 out). SB—Damon, Winn, Fick, Berkman, Green. PB—Piazza. WP—Garcia. Balk—Lowe. T—3:29. A—41,871. U—Davis, plate; Tschida, first; Meriwether, second; Meals, third; Foster, left field; Emmel, right field. Official scorers—Tim O'Driscoll, Bill Center and Drew Olson.

Players listed on rosters but not used: None.

PLAY BY PLAY

FIRST INNING

A.L.—Suzuki grounded to Helton. Hillenbrand and Rodriguez struck out.

N.L.—Vidro and Helton grounded out, Rodriguez to Giambi. Bonds flied to Hunter.

SECOND INNING

A.L.—Giambi struck out. Ramirez singled to center. Posada grounded to Helton as Ramirez advanced to second. Hunter grounded out, Vidro to Helton.

N.L.—Sosa singled to center. Guerrero singled to left, but Ramirez threw to Hillebrand to retire Sosa trying for third as Guerrero advanced to second on the play. Guerrero advanced to third on a balk by Lowe. Piazza grounded out, Soriano to Giambi, as Guerrero scored. Rolen flied to Hunter. One run. N.L. 1, A.L. 0.

THIRD INNING

A.L.—Williams now pitching. Soriano struck out. Jeter, pinch-hitting for Lowe, struck out. Suzuki grounded out, Vidro to Helton.

N.L.—Halladay now pitching. Rollins singled to center. Gonzalez, pinch-hitting for Williams, grounded to Giambi as Rollins advanced to second. Vidro flied to Ramirez. Helton singled to center, scoring Rollins. Bonds homered to right, scoring Helton. Sosa struck out. Three runs. N.L. 4, A.L. 0.

FOURTH INNING

A.L.—Sexson now at first, Spivey at second, Berkman in left, Green in right and Perez pitching. Hillenbrand flied to Berkman.

Rodriguez struck out. Giambi singled to center. Giambi advanced to second on a passed ball. Ramirez singled to right, scoring Giambi. Posada struck out. One run. N.L. 4, A.L. 1.

N.L.—Konerko now at first, Ventura at third, Anderson in left, Winn in right and Buehrle pitching. Guerrero struck out. Piazza flied to Winn. Rolen popped to Soriano.

FIFTH INNING

A.L.—Miller now catching and Gagne pitching. Hunter popped to Rollins. Soriano homered to left-center. Anderson grounded to Sexson. Winn doubled to left. Ventura struck out. One run. N.L. 4, A.L. 2.

N.L.—Vizquel now at second, Tejada at shortstop and Damon in center. Rollins singled to center. Miller doubled to center, scoring Rollins. Spivey struck out. Berkman grounded out, Vizquel to Konerko, as Miller advanced to third. Sexson grounded out, Ventura to Konerko. One run. N.L. 5, A.L. 2.

SIXTH INNING

A.L.—Hernandez now at shortstop and Hoffman pitching. Tejada flied to Green. Konerko doubled to right-center. Pierzynski, pinch-hitting for Buehrle, grounded to Sexson as Konerko advanced to third. Posada struck out.

N.L.—Pierzynski now catching and Zito pitching. Green grounded out, Tejada to Konerko. Jones now pinch-hitting for Guerrero. Guardado now pitching. Jones struck out. Hernandez struck out and was thrown out at first, Pierzynski to Konerko, on the dropped third strike.

SEVENTH INNING

A.L.—Berkman now at first, Dunn in left, Jones in center and Remlinger pitching. Damon singled to first. Damon stole second. Vizquel flied to Green as Damon advanced to third. Anderson grounded out, Spivey to Berkman, as Damon scored. Winn walked. Batista now pinch-hitting for Ventura. Kim now pitching. Winn stole second. Batista singled to left, scoring Winn. Tejada singled to center as Batista advanced to second. Konerko doubled to left-center, scoring Batista and Tejada. Pierzynski grounded out, Spivey to Berkman. Four runs. A.L. 6, N.L. 5.

N.L.—Batista now at third and Sasaki pitching. Rolen struck out. Lowell, pinch-hitting for Kim, singled to left. Miller doubled to left

as Lowell advanced to third. Spivey grounded out, Batista to Konerko. Berkman singled to center, scoring Lowell and Miller. Berkman stole second. Dunn walked. Green struck out. Two runs. N.L. 7, A.L. 6.

EIGHTH INNING

A.L.—Castillo now at second, Lowell at third and Nen pitching. Fick, pinch-hitting for Sasaki, singled to right-center. Damon struck out as Fick stole second. Vizquel tripled to right, scoring Fick. Anderson grounded out, Castillo to Berkman. Winn struck out. One run. N.L. 7, A.L. 7.

N.L.—Sweeney now at first, Fick in right and Urbina pitching. Jones grounded out, Batista to Sweeney. Hernandez struck out. Castillo flied to Damon.

NINTH INNING

A.L.—Smoltz now pitching. Batista struck out. Garciaparra, pinch-hitting for Tejada, grounded out, Hernandez to Berkman. Sweeney flied to Green.

N.L.—Garciaparra now at shortstop and Rivera pitching. Lowell flied to Fick. Miller grounded out, Batista to Sweeney. Santiago, pinch-hitting for Smoltz, singled to center. Berkman popped to Vizquel.

10TH INNING

A.L.—Santiago now catching and Padilla pitching. Pierzynski flied to Jones. Fick grounded out, Castillo to Berkman. Damon grounded out, Berkman to Padilla.

N.L.—Garcia now pitching. Dunn flied to Damon. Green singled to center. Jones struck out as Green stole second. Hernandez grounded out, Batista to Sweeney.

11TH INNING

A.L.—Vizquel walked. Anderson grounded out, Castillo to Berkman, as Vizquel advanced to second. Garcia grounded out, Hernandez to Berkman, as Vizquel advanced to third. Batista flied to Green.

N.L.—Castillo flied to Damon. Lowell singled to left. Lowell advanced to second on a wild pitch. Padilla and Santiago struck out. **Game called due to league decision.** Final score: A.L. 7, N.L. 7.

NOTABLE PERFORMANCES

BOX SCORE OF NO-HIT GAME

DEREK LOWE

BOSTON 10, TAMPA BAY 0
SATURDAY, APRIL 27, AT BOSTON

TAMPA BAY	AB	R	H	RBI	BOSTON	AB	R	H	RBI
Tyner, lf	4	0	0	0	Henderson, cf	4	3	2	1
Winn, cf	3	0	0	0	Offerman, 1b	3	3	2	0
Cox, 1b	3	0	0	0	Garciaparra, ss	5	0	2	2
Hall, c	3	0	0	0	Ramirez, lf	3	1	1	1
Grieve, rf	2	0	0	0	Daubach, dh	4	1	1	0
Conti, rf	1	0	0	0	Hillenbrand, 3b	4	1	1	2
Vaughn, dh	3	0	0	0	Varitek, c	5	1	1	2
Abernathy, 2b	2	0	0	0	Nixon, rf	5	0	2	0
Johnson, 3b	3	0	0	0	Sanchez, 2b	4	0	1	2
Escalona, ss	3	0	0	0					
Totals	27	0	0	0	**Totals**	37	10	13	10

Tampa Bay .... 0 0 0   0 0 0   0 0 0— 0
Boston .... 1 0 6   1 0 0   0 2 x—10

TAMPA BAY	IP	H	R	ER	HR	BB	SO
James (L, 0-2)	2.1	5	6	6	1	2	1
Sosa	1.2	4	2	2	0	1	1
Harper	2.0	1	0	0	0	0	4
Zambrano	1.0	2	0	0	0	0	1
Creek	1.0	1	2	2	0	3	3
BOSTON	**IP**	**H**	**R**	**ER**	**HR**	**BB**	**SO**
Lowe (W, 4-1)	9.0	0	0	0	0	1	6

E—Cox, Abernathy. DP—Tampa Bay 1. LOB—Tampa Bay 1, Boston 10. Scoring position—Tampa Bay 0 for 1, Boston 5 for 19. 2B—Offerman, Garciaparra, Varitek, Nixon. HR—Henderson (1st inning, off James, 0 on, 0 out). HBP—By Creek (Hillenbrand). Balk—James. T—2:28. A—32,837. U—Rippley, plate; Darling, first; Emmel, second; Timmons, third.

LOW-HIT GAMES

AMERICAN LEAGUE

ONE-HIT GAMES

Date   **Pitcher(s), Team, Opponent, Result—Player with hit**
4-27   Ted Lilly, New York at Seattle, L 0-1—Desi Relaford (single in eighth)
5-22   Jeff Weaver, Detroit vs. Cleveland, W 2-0—Chris Magruder (double in eighth)
7-19   Cory Lidle, Oakland vs. Texas, W 10-0—Juan Gonzalez (double in eighth)
8-4   Cory Lidle (7 innings), Ricardo Rincon (0.2 inn.), Chad Bradford (0.1 inn.) and Billy Koch (1 inn.), Oakland vs. Detroit, W 4-0—Wendell Magee (single in sixth)
8-21   Cory Lidle, Oakland at Cleveland, W 6-0—Ellis Burks (single in first)
9-3   Aaron Myette (0 inn.), Todd Van Poppel (2 inn.) and Joaquin Benoit (7 inn.), Texas at Baltimore, W 7-1—Jerry Hairston Jr. (triple in ninth)

TWO-HIT GAMES

Date   **Pitcher(s), Team, Opponent, Result—Player(s) with hit(s)**
4-5   Derek Lowe (7 inn.), Rich Garces (1 inn.) and Ugueth Urbina (1 inn.), Boston at Baltimore, W 3-0—Tony Batista (single in eighth), Chris Singleton (double in ninth)
4-9   Mike Mussina (8 inn.) and Mariano Rivera (1 inn.), New York at Toronto, W 5-2—Felipe Lopez (home run in third), Raul Mondesi (home run in sixth)
4-11   Doug Davis, Texas vs. Oakland, W 7-0—Miguel Tejada (single in second), Carlos Pena (double in third)
4-19   Pedro Martinez (8 inn.) and Rich Garces (1 inn.), Boston at Kansas City, W 4-0—Mike Sweeney (single in fourth), Neifi Perez (single in ninth)
4-25   Pedro Martinez (7 inn.), Sun-Woo Kim (1 inn.) and Willie Banks (1 inn.), Boston at Baltimore, W 7-0—Gary Matthews Jr. (single in sixth), Brook Fordyce (single in eighth)
4-29   Jeff Suppan, Kansas City at Detroit, W 4-0—Shane Halter (single in second), Randall Simon (single in seventh)
4-30   Steve W. Sparks, Detroit vs. Kansas City, W 9-3—A.J. Hinch (triple in fifth), Carlos Beltran (home run in ninth)
5-15   Ismael Valdes (6 inn.), John Rocker (2 inn.) and Hideki Irabu (1 inn.), Texas at Chicago, W 5-2—Frank Thomas (home run in second), Paul Konerko (single in fourth)
5-19   Esteban Loaiza, Toronto vs. Oakland, W 11-0—Jermaine Dye (singles in fifth and eighth)
5-26   Barry Zito (7 inn.), Jim Mecir (1 inn.) and Billy Koch (1 inn.), Oakland vs. Tampa Bay, W 7-0—Chris Gomez (double in second), Jason Conti (double in third)
6-7   Roy Halladay, Toronto vs. Colorado N.L., W 8-0—Benny Agbayani (double in sixth), Todd Helton (single in seventh)

Date	Pitcher(s), Team, Opponent, Result—Player(s) with hit(s)
6-20	Pedro Martinez (8 inn.) and Chris Haney (1 inn.), Boston at San Diego N.L., W 5-0—D'Angelo Jimenez (single in second), Mark Kotsay (single in third)
6-26	Jamie Moyer (7 inn.), Shigetoshi Hasegawa (1 inn.) and Kazuhiro Sasaki (1 inn.), Seattle vs. Oakland, W 1-0—Olmedo Saenz (single in fifth), Miguel Tejada (single in sixth)
7-3	Joel Pineiro (8 inn.) and Kazuhiro Sasaki (1 inn.), Seattle vs. Kansas City, W 3-0—Joe Randa (double in second), Raul Ibanez (single in second)
7-6	Pedro Martinez (5 inn.), Wayne Gomes (2 inn.), Chris Haney (1 inn.) and Willie Banks (1 inn.), Boston vs. Detroit, W 8-0—Ramon Santiago (single in third), Shane Halter (single in sixth)
7-17	Derek Lowe (8 inn.) and Rich Garces (1 inn.), Boston at Tampa Bay, W 6-1—Randy Winn (double in fourth), Aubrey Huff (double in fourth)
7-30	Pedro Martinez (8 inn.) and Ugueth Urbina (1 inn.), Boston at Anaheim, W 6-0—Brad Fullmer (single in second), Darin Erstad (single in fourth)
8-9	Kenny Rogers (8 inn.) and Francisco Cordero (1 inn.), Texas at Cleveland, W 3-2—Milton Bradley (double in eighth), Ricky Gutierrez (double in eighth)
8-11	Runelvys Hernandez (5 inn.), Ryan Bukvich (1 inn.), Jason Grimsley (2 inn.) and Roberto Hernandez (1 inn.), Kansas City vs. Tampa Bay, W 10-0—Brent Abernathy (single in first), Chris Gomez (double in sixth)
8-16	Joe Mays, Minnesota vs. Boston, W 5-0—Johnny Damon (double in sixth), Carlos Baerga (single in ninth)
8-18	Kevin Appier (6 inn.), Brendan Donnelly (1 inn.), Ben Weber (1 inn.) and Troy Percival (1 inn.), Anaheim vs. Cleveland, W 4-1—Ellis Burks (single in first), Jim Thome (double in ninth)
9-13	Barry Zito (8 inn.) and Ricardo Rincon (1 inn.), Oakland vs. Seattle, W 5-0—John Olerud (single in eighth), Ruben Sierra (single in eighth)
9-21	John Burkett (8 inn.) and Ugueth Urbina (1 inn.), Boston at Baltimore, W 3-0—Jay Gibbons (single in second), Luis Lopez (double in eighth)
9-24	Mike Mussina, New York vs. Tampa Bay, W 6-0—Aubrey Huff (single in second), Toby Hall (single in fifth)
9-29	Roy Halladay (8 inn.) and Kelvim Escobar (1 inn.), Toronto vs. Detroit, W 1-0—Chris Truby (single in third), Craig Monroe (double in eighth)

NATIONAL LEAGUE

ONE-HIT GAMES

Date	Pitcher(s), Team, Opponent, Result—Player with hit
4-5	Andy Ashby (7 inn.) and Omar Daal (2 inn.), Los Angeles vs. Colorado, W 9-0—Todd Zeile (single in fifth)
4-7	Curt Schilling, Arizona at Milwaukee, W 2-0—Raul Casanova (single in third)
4-26	Odalis Perez, Los Angeles at Chicago, W 10-0—Corey Patterson (single in seventh)
4-26	Shawn Estes, New York vs. Milwaukee, W 1-0—Eric Young (single in seventh)
6-25	Odalis Perez, Los Angeles vs. Colorado, W 4-0—Bobby Estalella (single in sixth)
7-24	Damian Moss (7 inn.) and Albie Lopez (2 inn.), Atlanta at Florida, W 10-0—Derrek Lee (single in fifth)
8-4	Damian Moss (8 inn.) and John Smoltz (1 inn.), Atlanta vs. St. Louis, W 2-1—Mike Matheny (single in third)
8-20	Kris Benson (7 inn.), Brian Boehringer (1 inn.) and Al Reyes (1 inn.), Pittsburgh at St. Louis, W 8-0—Kerry Robinson (single in first)

TWO-HIT GAMES

Date	Pitcher(s), Team, Opponent, Result—Player(s) with hit(s)
4-9	Jon Lieber (8 inn.) and Antonio Alfonseca (1 inn.), Chicago vs. New York, W 2-0—Jay Payton (single in second), Roberto Alomar (single in third)
4-12	Kazuhisa Ishii (6 inn.), Giovanni Carrara (2 inn.) and Eric Gagne (1 inn.), Los Angeles at San Diego, W 3-0—Deivi Cruz (double in second), Phil Nevin (single in sixth)
4-13	Darryl Kile (6 inn.), Luther Hackman (2 inn.) and Jason Isringhausen (1 inn.), St. Louis vs. Houston, W 2-1—Brad Ausmus (single in first), Daryle Ward (single in seventh)
4-18	Al Leiter, New York at Montreal, W 1-0—Michael Barrett (double in fifth), Jose Vidro (double in sixth)
4-21	Dave Mlicki (8 inn.) and Billy Wagner (1 inn.), Houston vs. San Francisco, W 4-0—J.T. Snow (single in second), David Bell (double in ninth)
4-21	Randy Johnson, Arizona vs. Colorado, W 7-1—Juan Pierre (single in first), Juan Uribe (triple in sixth)
5-2	John Thomson (7 inn.), Kent Mercker (1 inn.) and Dennys Reyes (1 inn.), Colorado vs. Pittsburgh, W 7-2—Armando Rios (single in seventh), Jason Kendall (single in seventh)
5-4	Jason Schmidt (0.2 inn.), Ryan Jensen (6.1 inn.), Felix Rodriguez (1 inn.) and Robb Nen (1 inn.), San Francisco vs. Cincinnati, W 3-0—Jason LaRue (single in eighth), Todd Walker (single in eighth)
5-10	Vicente Padilla, Philadelphia vs. Arizona, W 4-0—Chris Donnels (double in eighth), Danny Bautista (single in ninth)
5-13	Kerry Wood (6 inn.), Joe Borowski (1 inn.) and Jeff Fassero (1 inn.), Chicago at St. Louis, L 0-3—Albert Pujols (single in fourth), Tino Martinez (home run in sixth)
5-14	Pedro Astacio, New York at Los Angeles, W 3-0—Hiram Bocachica (double in fourth), Cesar Izturis (single in sixth)
5-15	Jeff D'Amico, New York at Los Angeles, W 2-0—Paul Lo Duca (single in second), Mark Grudzielanek (single in second)
5-17	Darryl Kile (7 inn.), Gene Stechschulte (1 inn.) and Jason Isringhausen (1 inn.), St. Louis vs. Cincinnati, W 3-1—Jason LaRue (single in ninth), Austin Kearns (double in seventh)
5-19	Josh Beckett (7 inn.), Braden Looper (1 inn.) and Vladimir Nunez (1 inn.), Florida at San Francisco, W 4-2—Tom Goodwin (single in sixth), Reggie Sanders (home run in ninth)
5-28	Matt Clement, Chicago at Pittsburgh, W 3-0—Brian Giles (single in seventh), Adrian Brown (single in eighth)
6-1	Brian Anderson (7 inn.) and Bret Prinz (1 inn.), Arizona at Los Angeles, L 0-2—Cesar Izturis (single in fourth), Brian Jordan (home run in fourth)
6-8	Jason Schmidt (8 inn.) and Robb Nen (1 inn.), San Francisco at New York A.L., W 4-3—Robin Ventura (single in second), Nick Johnson (home run in ninth)
6-11	Tom Glavine (7 inn.), Darren Holmes (1 inn.) and Albie Lopez (1 inning), Atlanta at Minnesota A.L., W 11-0—Matthew LeCroy (double in second), Bobby Kielty (single in fifth)

Date	Pitcher(s), Team, Opponent, Result—Player(s) with hit(s)
6-20	A.J. Burnett, Florida vs. Cleveland A.L., W 3-0—Milton Bradley (single in second), Ellis Burks (double in sixth)
6-21	Michael Tejera (7 inn.), Braden Looper (1 inn.) and Vladimir Nunez (1 inn.), Florida vs. Detroit A.L., W 4-1—Brandon Inge (home run in second), Chris Truby (double in fifth)
6-28	Josh Fogg (7 inn.), Brian Boehringer (1 inn.) and Mike Williams (1 inn.), Pittsburgh at Detroit A.L., W 3-1—Randall Simon (single in fourth), Brandon Inge (home run in seventh)
7-7	Oliver Perez (6.2 inn.), Brian Lawrence (0.2 inn.), Mike Holtz (0 inn.), Steve Reed (0.2 inn.) and Trevor Hoffman (1 inn.), San Diego at Colorado, W 7-1—Larry Walker (double in third), Ross Gload (single in ninth)
7-16	Kevin Millwood (7 inn.), Mike Remlinger (1 inn.) and John Smoltz (1 inn.), Atlanta at Chicago, W 2-0—Fred McGriff (single in second), Bill Mueller (single in fifth)
7-28	Bartolo Colon, Montreal vs. Florida, W 4-1—Eric Owens (double in first), Andy Fox (triple in eighth)
7-31	Shawn Estes (7 inn.) and Mike Bacsik (2 inn.), New York vs. Houston, W 10-0—Lance Berkman (double in fourth), Jose Vizcaino (double in seventh)
8-1	Jason Jennings (7 inn.), Justin Speier (1 inn.) and Jose Jimenez (1 inn.), Colorado at Pittsburgh, W 3-0—Rob Mackowiak (single in seventh), Craig A. Wilson (single in eighth)
8-5	Randy Johnson, Arizona at New York, W 2-0—Roger Cedeno (single in sixth), Mo Vaughn (single in seventh)
8-14	Brad Penny (8 inn.) and Graeme Lloyd (1 inn.), Florida vs. Colorado, W 1-0—Denny Neagle (single in third), Brent Butler (single in seventh)
8-19	Bartolo Colon, Montreal vs. San Diego, W 4-0—Deivi Cruz (single in third), Bubba Trammell (single in eighth)
8-27	Chuck Finley, St. Louis at Cincinnati, W 5-0—Juan Castro (singles in sixth and ninth)
9-15	Randy Wolf (8 inn.) and Jose Mesa (2 inn.), Philadelphia vs. Pittsburgh, W 1-0—Tony Alvarez (single in third), Jack Wilson (single in ninth)
9-25	Livan Hernandez, San Francisco vs. San Diego, W 6-0—Phil Nevin (single in second), Ryan Klesko (single in seventh)

15-STRIKEOUT GAMES

AMERICAN LEAGUE

No occurrences

NATIONAL LEAGUE

Date	Pitcher, Team, Opponent	IP	H	R	ER	BB	SO	Result
4-7	Curt Schilling, Arizona at Milwaukee	9	1	0	0	2	17	W 2-0
4-21	Randy Johnson, Arizona vs. Colorado	9	2	1	0	1	17	W 7-1
7-31	Randy Johnson, Arizona at Montreal	9	8	1	1	3	15	W 5-1
8-25	Randy Johnson, Arizona vs. Chicago	9	6	0	0	2	16	W 7-0
9-14	Randy Johnson, Arizona vs. Milwaukee	9	3	0	0	2	17	W 5-0

10-STRIKEOUT GAMES

AMERICAN LEAGUE

Team	No.	Pitchers
Boston	11	Pedro Martinez 9, Derek Lowe 1, Casey Fossum 1.
New York	10	Roger Clemens 4, Mike Mussina 3, Andy Pettitte 1, Orlando Hernandez 1, Ted Lilly 1.
Oakland	6	Mark Mulder 3, Barry Zito 2, Aaron Harang 1.
Minnesota	3	Eric Milton 2, Johan Santana 1.
Anaheim	2	Jarrod Washburn 1, Ramon Ortiz 1.
Cleveland	2	Chuck Finley 1, Ryan Drese 1.
Seattle	2	Jamie Moyer 1, Freddy Garcia 1.
Baltimore	1	Scott Erickson 1.
Detroit	1	Jeff Weaver 1.
Tampa Bay	1	Joe Kennedy 1.
Chicago	0	None.
Kansas City	0	None.
Texas	0	None.
Toronto	0	None.

NATIONAL LEAGUE

Team	No.	Pitchers
Arizona	30	Randy Johnson 15, Curt Schilling 14, Brian Anderson 1.
Chicago	20	Kerry Wood 7, Matt Clement 6, Mark Prior 6, Carlos Zambrano 1.
Philadelphia	8	Randy Wolf 4, Brandon Duckworth 3, Vicente Padilla 1.
Florida	8	A.J. Burnett 4, Josh Beckett 2, Ryan Dempster 1, Brad Penny 1.
Los Angeles	6	Hideo Nomo 3, Kevin Brown 1, Odalis Perez 1, Kazuhisa Ishii 1.
San Diego	5	Brian Lawrence 2, Oliver Perez 2, Brett Tomko 1.
San Francisco	5	Jason Schmidt 5.
St. Louis	4	Chuck Finley 2, Matt Morris 2.
Houston	3	Roy Oswalt 2, Wade Miller 1.
Montreal	3	Javier Vazquez 2, Tomokazu Ohka 1.
Atlanta	2	Kevin Millwood 2.
New York	2	Pedro Astacio 1, Shawn Estes 1.
Milwaukee	1	Ruben Quevedo 1.
Cincinnati	1	Ryan Dempster 1.
Pittsburgh	1	Josh Fogg 1.
Colorado	0	None.

1-0 GAMES
AMERICAN LEAGUE

Date	Winner	Loser	Inn.*	Site
4-3	†David Wells, New York	†Jason Johnson, Baltimore	7	Baltimore
4-3	†Eric Milton, Minnesota	†Dan Reichert, Kansas City	3	Kansas City
4-23	†Ryan Franklin, Seattle	Ramon Ortiz, Anaheim	5	Seattle
4-27	†Freddy Garcia, Seattle	Ted Lilly, New York	8	Seattle
5-21	Joe Kennedy, Tampa Bay	Jamie Moyer, Seattle	8	Seattle
6-22	Ted Lilly, New York	†Jake Peavy, San Diego N.L.	1	San Diego
6-26	†Shigetoshi Hasegawa, Seattle	†Chad Bradford, Oakland	8	Seattle
7-3	†Jarrod Washburn, Anaheim	Scott Erickson, Baltimore	8	Anaheim
7-11	†Jarrod Washburn, Anaheim	Darrell May, Kansas City	6	Kansas City
7-12	†Tim Hudson, Oakland	†Jason Johnson, Baltimore	1	Baltimore
7-28	†Kevin Appier, Anaheim	†Kazuhiro Sasaki, Seattle	9	Seattle
8-11	†Jarrod Washburn, Anaheim	†Roy Halladay, Toronto	4	Toronto
8-16	†Cory Lidle, Oakland	Mark Buehrle, Chicago	2	Oakland
9-14	Tim Hudson, Oakland	Jamie Moyer, Seattle	2	Oakland
9-17	†Ben Weber, Anaheim	†Billy Koch, Oakland	10	Oakland
9-29	†Roy Halladay, Toronto	†Mike Maroth, Detroit	8	Toronto

PLAYERS HITTING HOME RUNS IN 1-0 GAMES: 4-3—Robin Ventura, New York; 7-11—Shawn Wooten, Anaheim; 8-11—David Eckstein, Anaheim; 8-16—Jermaine Dye, Oakland; 9-17—Tim Salmon, Anaheim.

*Inning in which run scored. †Did not pitch complete game. Note: Interleague 1-0 games are listed in the winning club's league.

NATIONAL LEAGUE

Date	Winner	Loser	Inn.*	Site
4-4	Brad Penny, Florida	†Carl Pavano, Montreal	4	Montreal
4-8	†Ron Villone, Pittsburgh	†Elmer Dessens, Cincinnati	6	Pittsburgh
4-14	†Brian Lawrence, San Diego	†Hideo Nomo, Los Angeles	7	San Diego
4-18	Al Leiter, New York	†Javier Vazquez, Montreal	4	Montreal
4-26	Shawn Estes, New York	Glendon Rusch, Milwaukee	2	New York
5-9	†Hansel Izquierdo, Florida	†Brian Tollberg, San Diego	2	Florida
5-22	†Hideo Nomo, Los Angeles	†Ben Sheets, Milwaukee	3	Milwaukee
5-23	†Scott Strickland, New York	†Jose Mesa, Philadelphia	9	Philadelphia
5-28	†Robb Nen, San Francisco	†Mike Myers, Arizona	10	San Francisco
5-30	†Rick Helling, Arizona	†Kirk Rueter, San Francisco	4	San Francisco
8-2	†Jamey Wright, Milwaukee	†Julian Tavarez, Florida	4	Florida
8-12	†Jason Jennings, Colorado	A.J. Burnett, Florida	4	Florida
8-14	†Tom Glavine, Atlanta	†Livan Hernandez, San Francisco	1	Atlanta
8-14	†Graeme Lloyd, Florida	†Victor Santos, Colorado	9	Florida
8-15	†Omar Daal, Los Angeles	†Javier Vazquez, Montreal	3	Montreal
8-20	Jason Schmidt, San Francisco	†Al Leiter, New York	6	San Francisco
8-25	†Kirk Saarloos, Houston	†Ryan Dempster, Cincinnati	1	Houston
8-28	†Odalis Perez, Los Angeles	†Rick Helling, Arizona	5	Los Angeles
8-28	†Mike Williams, Pittsburgh	†Mike Remlinger, Atlanta	10	Pittsburgh
8-31	Randy Wolf, Philadelphia	†Steve Trachsel, New York	8	New York
9-6	†Felix Rodriguez, San Francisco	†Mike Fetters, Arizona	9	San Francisco
9-15	†Jose Mesa, Philadelphia	†Scott Sauerbeck, Pittsburgh	10	Philadelphia
9-24	†Jimmy Haynes, Cincinnati	†Kerry Wood, Chicago	1	Chicago
9-24	†Denny Stark, Colorado	†Odalis Perez, Los Angeles	1	Los Angeles
9-26	†Danny Graves, Cincinnati	†Carlos Zambrano, Chicago	4	Chicago
9-27	†Eric Gagne, Los Angeles	†Jeremy Fikac, San Diego	10	Los Angeles

PLAYERS HITTING HOME RUNS IN 1-0 GAMES: 4-4—Derrek Lee, Florida; 4-26—Jay Payton, New York; 5-30—Luis Gonzalez, Arizona; 8-25—Lance Berkman, Houston; 8-28—Odalis Perez, Los Angeles; 9-24—Aaron Boone, Cincinnati; 9-27—Paul Lo Duca, Los Angeles.

*Inning in which run scored. †Did not pitch complete game. Note: Interleague 1-0 games are listed in the winning club's league.

FOUR OR MORE HITS IN ONE GAME
AMERICAN LEAGUE

Team	No.	Hitters
Boston	20	Manny Ramirez 4, Nomar Garciaparra 4, Shea Hillenbrand 4, Johnny Damon 3, Jose Offerman 1, Cliff Floyd 1, Trot Nixon 1, Jason Varitek 1, Brian Daubach 1.
Anaheim	19	Tim Salmon 3, Darin Erstad 3, David Eckstein 3, Garret Anderson 2, Bengie Molina 2, Adam Kennedy 2, Orlando Palmeiro 1, Troy Glaus 1, Shawn Wooten 1, Alfredo Amezaga 1.
Toronto	15	Shannon Stewart 4, Eric Hinske 3, Vernon Wells 2, Orlando Hudson 2, Raul Mondesi 1, Carlos Delgado 1, Ken Huckaby 1, Jose Cruz 1.
Minnesota	13	Jacque Jones 4, Luis Rivas 2, Bobby Kielty 2, Torii Hunter 1, David Ortiz 1, A.J. Pierzynski 1, Brian Buchanan 1, Dustan Mohr 1.

Team	No.	Hitters
Seattle	13	John Olerud 3, Bret Boone 2, Mike Cameron 2, Mark McLemore 1, Ruben Sierra 1, Dan Wilson 1, Desi Relaford 1, Ichiro Suzuki 1, Willie Bloomquist 1.
Chicago	12	Magglio Ordonez 3, Paul Konerko 3, Sandy Alomar Jr. 1, Frank Thomas 1, Ray Durham 1, Tony Graffanino 1, Carlos Lee 1, Aaron Rowand 1.
New York	11	Jason Giambi 4, Alfonso Soriano 3, Bernie Williams 2, Derek Jeter 1, Jorge Posada 1.
Tampa Bay	11	Randy Winn 5, Aubrey Huff 2, Steve Cox 1, Jason Conti 1, Toby Hall 1, Brent Abernathy 1.
Baltimore	10	Gary Matthews Jr. 3, Jeff Conine 2, Chris Singleton 2, David Segui 1, Marty Cordova 1, Tony Batista 1.
Detroit	9	Randall Simon 4, Robert Fick 3, Craig Paquette 1, Bobby Higginson 1.
Kansas City	9	Mike Sweeney 2, Raul Ibanez 2, Luis Alicea 1, Brent Mayne 1, Chuck Knoblauch 1, Neifi Perez 1, Carlos Febles 1.
Texas	9	Ivan Rodriguez 1, Carl Everett 1, Rusty Greer 1, Alex Rodriguez 1, Gabe Kapler 1, Mike Lamb 1, Michael Young 1, Kevin Mench 1, Travis Hafner 1.
Oakland	6	Ray Durham 2, Miguel Tejada 2, John Mabry 1, Scott Hatteberg 1.
Cleveland	5	Ricky Gutierrez 2, Ellis Burks 1, Omar Vizquel 1, Milton Bradley 1.

NATIONAL LEAGUE

Team	No.	Hitters
Colorado	19	Larry Walker 4, Juan Pierre 4, Jay Payton 3, Todd Helton 2, Jose Ortiz 2, Sandy Alomar Jr. 1, Gary Bennett 1, Gabe Kapler 1, Juan Uribe 1.
Houston	14	Jose Vizcaino 3, Lance Berkman 3, Craig Biggio 2, Brad Ausmus 1, Mark Loretta 1, Richard Hidalgo 1, Daryle Ward 1, Geoff Blum 1, Julio Lugo 1.
Los Angeles	13	Brian Jordan 2, Shawn Green 2, Adrian Beltre 2, Marquis Grissom 1, Mark Grudzielanek 1, Tyler Houston 1, Paul Lo Duca 1, Dave Roberts 1, Cesar Izturis 1, Joe Thurston 1.
Philadelphia	12	Bobby Abreu 2, Travis Lee 2, Marlon Anderson 2, Jimmy Rollins 2, Todd Pratt 1, Mike Lieberthal 1, Scott Rolen 1, Ricky Ledee 1.
Arizona	12	Craig Counsell 2, Matt Williams 1, Mark Grace 1, Luis Gonzalez 1, Greg Colbrunn 1, Danny Bautista 1, Tony Womack 1, Erubiel Durazo 1, Rod Barajas 1, Junior Spivey 1, Chad Moeller 1.
Cincinnati	11	Todd Walker 4, Ken Griffey Jr. 2, Aaron Boone 2, Sean Casey 2, Austin Kearns 1.
Montreal	11	Vladimir Guerrero 2, Orlando Cabrera 2, Jose Macias 2, Wil Cordero 1, Mike Mordecai 1, Jose Vidro 1, Brian Schneider 1, Endy Chavez 1.
San Diego	11	Ryan Klesko 2, Phil Nevin 2, Bubba Trammell 2, Mark Kotsay 2, Ramon Vazquez 2, D'Angelo Jimenez 1.
Atlanta	10	Chipper Jones 2, Rafael Furcal 2, Gary Sheffield 2, Vinny Castilla 1, Darren Bragg 1, Matt Franco 1, Wes Helms 1, Mark DeRosa 1.
St. Louis	10	Eli Marrero 2, Tino Martinez 1, Fernando Vina 1, Jim Edmonds 1, Edgar Renteria 1, Scott Rolen 1, Placido Polanco 1, J.D. Drew 1, Albert Pujols 1.
San Francisco	10	Barry Bonds 2, Damon Minor 2, Tsuyoshi Shinjo 2, Jeff Kent 1, J.T. Snow 1, Rich Aurilia 1, Marvin Benard 1.
Milwaukee	9	Alex Sanchez 4, Jose Hernandez 2, Lenny Harris 1, Eric Young 1, Richie Sexson 1.
Florida	8	Luis Castillo 2, Juan Encarnacion 2, Mike Lowell 2, Eric Owens 1, Kevin Millar 1.
Chicago	7	Moises Alou 4, Joe Girardi 1, Corey Patterson 1, Bobby Hill 1.
New York	5	Roberto Alomar 1, Mo Vaughn 1, Rey Ordonez 1, Timo Perez 1, Ty Wigginton 1.
Pittsburgh	5	Kevin Young 1, Pokey Reese 1, Adam Hyzdu 1, Craig A. Wilson 1, Jack Wilson 1.

FIVE OR MORE HITS IN ONE GAME
AMERICAN LEAGUE

Date	Player, Team, Opponent	AB	R	H	2B	3B	HR	RBI	Result
4-8	Alfonso Soriano, New York at Toronto	7	3	5	1	0	1	3	W 16- 3
4-14	Ruben Sierra, Seattle at Texas	5	1	5	1	0	0	1	W 9- 7
5-5	Omar Vizquel, Cleveland vs. Texas	5	2	5	3	0	0	2	W 9- 2
5-16	Mark McLemore, Seattle at Toronto	5	2	5	1	0	1	3	W 15- 2
6-14	Michael Young, Texas at Houston N.L.	5	3	5	0	0	2	2	W 9- 6
6-29	Gary Matthews Jr., Baltimore vs. Philadelphia N.L.	5	2	5	1	0	1	2	W 11- 1
7-16	Manny Ramirez, Boston at Detroit	6	3	5	1	0	1	3	W 9- 4
7-19	Tim Salmon, Anaheim vs. Seattle	5	3	5	0	0	1	5	W 15- 3
7-21	Milton Bradley, Cleveland at Kansas City (10 inn.)	6	2	5	3	0	1	5	L 12- 13
7-22	Jacque Jones, Minnesota at Chicago	6	2	5	2	0	1	2	W 11- 6
8-15	Bernie Williams, New York at Kansas City	5	1	5	1	0	0	0	W 7- 5
8-26	Manny Ramirez, Boston vs. Anaheim (10 inn.)	5	3	5	0	0	2	4	W 10- 9
8-27	Darin Erstad, Anaheim vs. Tampa Bay	5	1	5	2	0	0	0	W 7- 3
9-17	Alfonso Soriano, New York at Tampa Bay	5	2	5	1	0	1	1	L 7- 9
9-19	Shannon Stewart, Toronto at Baltimore	5	2	5	1	0	1	2	W 9- 3

NATIONAL LEAGUE

Date	Player, Team, Opponent	AB	R	H	2B	3B	HR	RBI	Result
5-17	Marlon Anderson, Philadelphia at Arizona	6	2	5	1	0	0	1	L 9- 12
5-23	Shawn Green, Los Angeles at Milwaukee	6	6	6	1	0	4	7	W 16- 3
5-26	Craig Counsell, Arizona vs. Los Angeles (10 inn.)	6	2	5	1	0	0	2	W 10- 9
7-2	Tsuyoshi Shinjo, San Francisco at Colorado	6	2	5	1	0	2	5	W 18- 5
7-7	Placido Polanco, St. Louis vs. Los Angeles	5	3	5	0	0	0	1	W 12- 6
8-11	Chipper Jones, Atlanta at Houston	5	3	5	2	0	0	0	W 13- 3
8-11	Jimmy Rollins, Philadelphia at Los Angeles	5	1	5	0	0	0	1	W 6- 3
8-17	Jose Vizcaino, Houston at Cincinnati	5	2	5	0	0	1	2	W 6- 1
9-18	Greg Colbrunn, Arizona at San Diego	6	4	5	1	1	2	4	W 10- 3
9-21	Juan Pierre, Colorado vs. Arizona	6	3	5	0	0	0	2	W 15- 8

HITTING STREAKS OF 15 OR MORE GAMES

AMERICAN LEAGUE

G	Player, Team	Span of streak
24	Miguel Tejada, Oakland	July 11-Aug. 4
23	Cristian Guzman, Minnesota	Aug. 1-Aug. 25
19	David Ortiz, Minnesota	July 17-Aug. 6
	Bernie Williams, New York	Aug. 7-Aug. 28
18	Paul Konerko, Chicago	Apr. 13-May 1
	Johnny Damon, Boston	Apr. 15-May 8
	Dmitri Young, Detroit	May 17-June 5
	Robert Fick, Detroit	May 29-June 16
	Omar Vizquel, Cleveland	July 14-Aug. 1
17	Magglio Ordonez, Chicago	Aug. 2-Aug. 21
	Aubrey Huff, Tampa Bay	Aug. 23-Sept. 10
16	Derek Jeter, New York	May 9-May 25
	A.J. Pierzynski, Minnesota	May 26-June 14
	John Olerud, Seattle	May 30-June 15
	Jason Varitek, Boston	July 14-July 30
	Trot Nixon, Boston	July 16-July 31
15	Nomar Garciaparra, Boston	Apr. 13-May 1
	Miguel Tejada, Oakland	Apr. 17-May 3
	Chris Singleton, Baltimore	May 6-May 26
	Ichiro Suzuki, Seattle	May 22-June 6
	Garret Anderson, Anaheim	July 14-July 29
	David Eckstein, Anaheim	Aug. 24-Sept. 8

NATIONAL LEAGUE

G	Player, Team	Span of streak
35	Luis Castillo, Florida	May 8-June 21
26	Vladimir Guerrero, Montreal	June 3-July 3
25	Kevin Millar, Florida	Aug. 24-Sept. 19
21	Jose Vidro, Montreal	May 4-May 27
18	Kevin Millar, Florida	Apr. 20-June 7
	Junior Spivey, Arizona	May 31-July 4
17	Juan Uribe, Colorado	Apr. 16-May 5
	Larry Walker, Colorado	July 15-Aug. 3
	Bobby Abreu, Philadelphia	Sep. 5-Sept. 24
16	Ryan Klesko, San Diego	Apr. 9-Apr. 28
	Mark Kotsay, San Diego	May 24-June 9
	Mike Lowell, Florida	Sep. 3-Sept. 18
	Endy Chavez, Montreal	Sep. 10-Sept. 27
15	Daryle Ward, Houston	Apr. 13-Apr. 30
	Deivi Cruz, San Diego	May 17-June 2
	Rafael Furcal, Atlanta	June 21-July 6
	Alex S. Gonzalez, Chicago	Aug. 6-Aug. 21
	Jeff Bagwell, Houston	Aug. 10-Aug. 24

2002 REVIEW *Notable performances*

MULTI-HOMER GAMES
AMERICAN LEAGUE

Team	No.	Hitters
Chicago	20	Magglio Ordonez 5, Paul Konerko 4, Jose Valentin 3, Carlos Lee 3, Joe Crede 2, Sandy Alomar Jr. 1, Frank Thomas 1, Tony Graffanino 1.
Texas	18	Alex Rodriguez 10, Ivan Rodriguez 2, Carl Everett 2, Rafael Palmeiro 1, Herbert Perry 1, Michael Young 1, Kevin Mench 1.
Boston	16	Manny Ramirez 7, Nomar Garciaparra 3, Trot Nixon 2, Shea Hillenbrand 2, Johnny Damon 1, Brian Daubach 1.
Oakland	14	Eric Chavez 4, Miguel Tejada 2, Terrence Long 2, John Mabry 1, Scott Hatteberg 1, Jermaine Dye 1, Jeremy Giambi 1, Ramon Hernandez 1, Adam Piatt 1.
Cleveland	12	Jim Thome 5, Ellis Burks 2, Omar Vizquel 1, Lee Stevens 1, Karim Garcia 1, Bill Selby 1, Russell Branyan 1.
Toronto	12	Carlos Delgado 4, Josh Phelps 2, Eric Hinske 2, Jose Cruz 1, Tom Wilson 1, Chris Woodward 1, Vernon Wells 1.
Minnesota	11	Jacque Jones 4, Corey Koskie 2, Tom Prince 1, Torii Hunter 1, David Ortiz 1, Doug Mientkiewicz 1, Matthew LeCroy 1.
New York	11	Jason Giambi 4, Alfonso Soriano 4, Bernie Williams 2, Jorge Posada 1.
Baltimore	10	Jay Gibbons 4, Jeff Conine 1, Marty Cordova 1, Tony Batista 1, Chris Singleton 1, Melvin Mora 1, Geronimo Gil 1.
Anaheim	7	Troy Glaus 3, Garret Anderson 2, Darin Erstad 1, Adam Kennedy 1.
Seattle	7	Mike Cameron 2, John Olerud 1, Bret Boone 1, Jeff Cirillo 1, Ben Davis 1, Ichiro Suzuki 1.
Tampa Bay	7	Greg Vaughn 2, Jared Sandberg 2, Ben Grieve 1, Steve Cox 1, Aubrey Huff 1.
Kansas City	6	Raul Ibanez 2, Carlos Beltran 2, Mike Sweeney 1, Brandon Berger 1.
Detroit	5	Robert Fick 2, Craig Paquette 1, Dmitri Young 1, Ramon Santiago 1.

Team	No.	Hitters
San Francisco	16	Barry Bonds 5, Reggie Sanders 4, Jeff Kent 3, David Bell 2, Damon Minor 1, Tsuyoshi Shinjo 1.
Chicago	14	Sammy Sosa 4, Fred McGriff 3, Moises Alou 3, Mark Bellhorn 2, Todd Hundley 1, Corey Patterson 1.
Florida	12	Preston Wilson 3, Cliff Floyd 2, Derrek Lee 2, Mike Lowell 2, Juan Encarnacion 1, Kevin Millar 1, Ramon Castro 1.
Atlanta	11	Andruw Jones 5, Chipper Jones 3, Gary Sheffield 2, Marcus Giles 1.
Houston	11	Lance Berkman 4, Jeff Bagwell 3, Orlando Merced 1, Richard Hidalgo 1, Daryle Ward 1, Julio Lugo 1.
Los Angeles	10	Shawn Green 6, Marquis Grissom 2, Brian Jordan 1, Adrian Beltre 1.
New York	10	Mike Piazza 4, Mo Vaughn 2, Roberto Alomar 1, Jeromy Burnitz 1, Jay Payton 1, Raul Gonzalez 1.
Arizona	10	Erubiel Durazo 3, Steve Finley 2, Matt Williams 1, Greg Colbrunn 1, Tony Womack 1, Damian Miller 1, Chad Moeller 1.
Cincinnati	9	Aaron Boone 3, Russell Branyan 2, Adam Dunn 2, Todd Walker 1, Jason LaRue 1.
San Diego	9	Ryan Klesko 3, Bubba Trammell 2, Ron Gant 1, Ray Lankford 1, Phil Nevin 1, Mark Kotsay 1.
Milwaukee	8	Jose Hernandez 2, Richie Sexson 2, Matt Stairs 1, Ryan Thompson 1, Jorge Fabregas 1, Ronnie Belliard 1.
Montreal	7	Vladimir Guerrero 5, Jose Vidro 1, Brad Wilkerson 1.
Philadelphia	7	Mike Lieberthal 2, Robert Person 1, Scott Rolen 1, Bobby Abreu 1, Jeremy Giambi 1, Pat Burrell 1.
Pittsburgh	5	Brian Giles 2, Adam Hyzdu 1, Craig A. Wilson 1, Rob Mackowiak 1.
St. Louis	5	Tino Martinez 1, Jim Edmonds 1, Edgar Renteria 1, Scott Rolen 1, Placido Polanco 1.
Colorado	5	Larry Walker 1, Bobby Estalella 1, Todd Helton 1, Ben Petrick 1, Brent Butler 1.

THREE-HOMER GAMES

AMERICAN LEAGUE

Date	Player, Team, Opponent	AB	R	H	2B	3B	HR	RBI	Result
5-2	Mike Cameron, Seattle at Chicago	5	4	4	0	0	4	4	W 15- 4
7-23†	Nomar Garciaparra, Boston vs. Tampa Bay	5	3	3	0	0	3	8	W 22- 4
8-7	Chris Woodward, Toronto vs. Seattle (10 inn.)	4	3	3	0	0	3	3	L 4- 5
8-17	Alex Rodriguez, Texas vs. Toronto	4	3	3	0	0	3	4	W 9- 5
9-15	Troy Glaus, Anaheim vs. Texas	5	4	3	0	0	3	6	W 13- 4

†a.m. game.

NATIONAL LEAGUE

Date	Player, Team, Opponent	AB	R	H	2B	3B	HR	RBI	Result
4-16	Lance Berkman, Houston at Cincinnati	5	3	3	0	0	3	5	W 8- 3
5-17	Erubiel Durazo, Arizona vs. Philadelphia	5	3	4	1	0	3	9	W 12- 9
5-23	Shawn Green, Los Angeles at Milwaukee	6	6	6	1	0	4	7	W 16- 3
8-4	Russell Branyan, Cincinnati at San Diego	4	4	3	0	0	3	5	W 15- 10
8-9	Aaron Boone, Cincinnati vs. San Diego	5	3	4	0	0	3	5	W 12- 10
8-10	Mike Lieberthal, Philadelphia at Los Angeles	5	3	4	0	0	3	4	L 8- 10
8-10	Sammy Sosa, Chicago at Colorado	4	3	3	0	0	3	9	W 15- 1
8-27	Barry Bonds, San Francisco at Colorado	4	4	4	1	0	3	3	W 7- 4
9-25	Andruw Jones, Atlanta at Philadelphia	4	3	3	0	0	3	4	W 7- 1

GRAND SLAMS

AMERICAN LEAGUE

Date	Batter, Team	Pitcher, Team	Inn.*	Site
4-1	Tony Batista, Baltimore	Roger Clemens, New York	4	Baltimore
4-4	Randy Winn, Tampa Bay	Matt Miller, Detroit	5	Tampa Bay
4-8	Travis Fryman, Cleveland	Eric Milton, Minnesota	3	Cleveland
4-9	Chuck Knoblauch, Kansas City	Tim Wakefield, Boston	5	Boston
4-10	Jim Thome, Cleveland	Rick Reed, Minnesota	2	Cleveland
4-12	Ruben Sierra, Seattle	Ismael Valdes, Texas	1	Texas
4-16	Magglio Ordonez, Chicago	Chuck Finley, Cleveland	2	Chicago
4-20	Paul Konerko, Chicago	Nate Cornejo, Detroit	3	Chicago
4-21‡	Johnny Damon, Boston	Bryan Rekar, Kansas City	3	Kansas City
4-22	Mark McLemore, Seattle	Scott Schoeneweis, Anaheim	3	Seattle
4-27	David Eckstein, Anaheim	Scott Cassidy, Toronto	5	Anaheim
4-28	David Eckstein, Anaheim	Pedro Borbon, Toronto	14	Anaheim
5-4	Shea Hillenbrand, Boston	Victor Zambrano, Tampa Bay	9	Tampa Bay
5-11	Eric Chavez, Oakland	Justin Miller, Toronto	2	Oakland
5-16	Mike Cameron, Seattle	Pete Walker, Toronto	7	Toronto
5-17	Jason Giambi, New York	Mike Trombley, Minnesota	14	New York
5-19	Travis Fryman, Cleveland	Jeff Suppan, Kansas City	6	Cleveland
5-28	Jacque Jones, Minnesota	Chan Ho Park, Texas	2	Texas

Date	Batter, Team	Pitcher, Team	Inn.*	Site
5-28	John Flaherty, Tampa Bay	Joel Pineiro, Seattle	3	Tampa Bay
5-31	Carlos Beltran, Kansas City	Francisco Cordero, Texas	7	Texas
6-1	Enrique Wilson, New York	Rich Garces, Boston	6	New York
6-2	Bret Boone, Seattle	Buddy Groom, Baltimore	8	Baltimore
6-9	David Eckstein, Anaheim	Joey Hamilton, Cincinnati	2	Anaheim
6-10	Shane Spencer, New York	Bret Prinz, Arizona	8	New York
6-16	Carlos Lee, Chicago	Kerry Wood, Chicago	3	Chicago
6-21	Ruben Sierra, Seattle	Carlos Hernandez, Houston	2	Houston
7-2	Magglio Ordonez, Chicago	Jose Paniagua, Detroit	8	Chicago
7-2	Jorge Posada, New York	Jerrod Riggan, Cleveland	7	New York
7-5	Torii Hunter, Minnesota	Jeff Nelson, Seattle	7	Seattle
7-7	Milton Bradley, Cleveland	Todd Ritchie, Chicago	3	Chicago
7-13	Jorge Posada, New York	Jake Westbrook, Cleveland	3	Cleveland
7-14	Bill Selby, Cleveland	Mariano Rivera, New York	9	Cleveland
7-14	Raul Ibanez, Kansas City	Ramon Ortiz, Anaheim	1	Kansas City
7-16	Trot Nixon, Boston	Jose Paniagua, Detroit	8	Detroit
7-18	Milton Bradley, Cleveland	Juan Rincon, Minnesota	3	Cleveland
7-21	Carlos Beltran, Kansas City	Sean DePaula, Cleveland	6	Kansas City
7-23†	Nomar Garciaparra, Boston	Brandon Backe, Tampa Bay	4	Boston
7-27	Alex Rodriguez, Texas	Billy Koch, Oakland	10	Texas
7-28	Jim Thome, Cleveland	Juan Acevedo, Detroit	9	Cleveland
7-28	Robin Ventura, New York	Tanyon Sturtze, Tampa Bay	3	Tampa Bay
7-30	Jared Sandberg, Tampa Bay	John Stephens, Baltimore	1	Tampa Bay
8-1	Michael Cuddyer, Minnesota	Dan Wright, Chicago	3	Minnesota
8-1	Carl Everett, Texas	Frank Castillo, Boston	2	Texas
8-6	Luis Lopez, Baltimore	LaTroy Hawkins, Minnesota	7	Baltimore
8-6	Tim Salmon, Anaheim	Matt Ginter, Chicago	4	Chicago
8-13	Jose Valentin, Chicago	Dennys Reyes, Texas	4	Texas
8-13	Karim Garcia, Cleveland	Tanyon Sturtze, Tampa Bay	5	Tampa Bay
8-25	Ben Davis, Seattle	Jake Westbrook, Cleveland	3	Cleveland
8-25	Randall Simon, Detroit	Micah Bowie, Oakland	4	Detroit
8-27	Joe Crede, Chicago	Felix Heredia, Toronto	10	Chicago
8-29	Ivan Rodriguez, Texas	Rick Bauer, Baltimore	6	Texas
9-5	Karim Garcia, Cleveland	Mike Porzio, Chicago	5	Chicago
9-8	Ben Davis, Seattle	Kris Wilson, Kansas City	11	Kansas City
9-10	Jeff Liefer, Chicago	Jeremy Affeldt, Kansas City	9	Kansas City
9-11	Manny Ramirez, Boston	Paul Wilson, Tampa Bay	5	Tampa Bay
9-19	Rafael Palmeiro, Texas	Jamie Moyer, Seattle	3	Seattle
9-21	Carlos Lee, Chicago	Bob Wells, Minnesota	7	Chicago
9-22	Trot Nixon, Boston	Steve Bechler, Baltimore	9	Baltimore
9-29	Troy Glaus, Anaheim	Ismael Valdes, Seattle	1	Anaheim
9-29	Jermaine Dye, Oakland	Joaquin Benoit, Texas	4	Texas

*Inning in which grand slam was hit. †First game of doubleheader. ‡Night separate admission.

NATIONAL LEAGUE

Date	Batter, Team	Pitcher, Team	Inn.*	Site
4-2	Preston Wilson, Florida	Britt Reames, Montreal	7	Montreal
4-2	Damian Miller, Arizona	Brian Tollberg, San Diego	2	Arizona
4-3	Derrek Lee, Florida	Tony Armas Jr., Montreal	1	Montreal
4-6	Brian Jordan, Los Angeles	Todd Jones, Colorado	7	Los Angeles
4-17	Jim Edmonds, St. Louis	Curt Schilling, Arizona	5	Arizona
4-23	Deivi Cruz, San Diego	Randy Wolf, Philadelphia	1	Philadelphia
5-6	Adam Dunn, Cincinnati	Ruben Quevedo, Milwaukee	1	Cincinnati
5-11	Javy Lopez, Atlanta	Brian Lawrence, San Diego	4	Atlanta
5-12	Richie Sexson, Milwaukee	Ron Mahay, Chicago	8	Chicago
5-12	Raul Casanova, Milwaukee	Scott Chiasson, Chicago	7	Chicago
5-12	Reggie Taylor, Cincinnati	Travis Smith, St. Louis	1	Cincinnati
5-13	Greg Norton, Colorado	Gary Knotts, Florida	6	Colorado
5-17	Mike Piazza, New York	Jason Boyd, San Diego	7	San Diego
5-17	Tsuyoshi Shinjo, San Francisco	Braden Looper, Florida	8	San Francisco
5-21	Austin Kearns, Cincinnati	A.J. Burnett, Florida	5	Cincinnati
5-22	Todd Walker, Cincinnati	Ryan Dempster, Florida	5	Cincinnati
5-25	Jose Vidro, Montreal	Hector Mercado, Philadelphia	10	Montreal
5-25	Dave Roberts, Los Angeles	Rick Helling, Arizona	2	Arizona
5-26	Fernando Vina, St. Louis	Josh Fogg, Pittsburgh	2	Pittsburgh
5-30	Mark Bellhorn, Chicago	Jimmy Anderson, Pittsburgh	3	Pittsburgh
5-30	Greg Norton, Colorado	Bobby J. Jones, San Diego	1	San Diego
5-31	Geoff Jenkins, Milwaukee	Dennis Tankersley, San Diego	4	San Diego
6-2	Robert Person, Philadelphia	Bruce Chen, Montreal	1	Philadelphia
6-3	Vinny Castilla, Atlanta	Steve Trachsel, New York	1	Atlanta

Date	Batter, Team	Pitcher, Team	Inn.*	Site
6-5	Barry Bonds, San Francisco	Dennis Tankersley, San Diego	3	San Diego
6-5	Benny Agbayani, Colorado	Omar Daal, Los Angeles	4	Colorado
6-7	Ramon Vazquez, San Diego	Ryan Rupe, Tampa Bay	2	Tampa Bay
6-11	Albert Pujols, St. Louis	James Baldwin, Seattle	6	Seattle
6-15	Reggie Sanders, San Francisco	Aaron Harang, Oakland	4	San Francisco
6-20	Lance Berkman, Houston	Jamey Wright, Milwaukee	4	Milwaukee
6-20	Todd Hollandsworth, Colorado	Mike Thurman, New York	6	Colorado
6-26	Gary Sheffield, Atlanta	Scott Strickland, New York	8	New York
6-27	Gregg Zaun, Houston	Byung-Hyun Kim, Arizona	9	Houston
6-29	Ron Gant, San Diego	Dan Reichert, Kansas City	10	Kansas City
7-1	Matt Franco, Atlanta	Javier Vazquez, Montreal	5	Atlanta
7-2	Fernando Tatis, Montreal	Damian Moss, Atlanta	6	Atlanta
7-2	Tsuyoshi Shinjo, San Francisco	Denny Neagle, Colorado	1	Colorado
7-6	Daryle Ward, Houston	Kip Wells, Pittsburgh	5	Pittsburgh
7-14	Wil Cordero, Montreal	Damian Moss, Atlanta	3	Montreal
7-18	Jason LaRue, Cincinnati	Brian Boehringer, Pittsburgh	8	Pittsburgh
7-19	Adam Hyzdu, Pittsburgh	Bud Smith, St. Louis	5	Pittsburgh
7-24	Todd Walker, Cincinnati	Joe Beimel, Pittsburgh	3	Cincinnati
7-26	Mark Loretta, Milwaukee	Denny Stark, Colorado	3	Milwaukee
8-2	Wes Helms, Atlanta	Jason Simontacchi, St. Louis	1	Atlanta
8-4	Mark Kotsay, San Diego	Ryan Dempster, Cincinnati	2	San Diego
8-7	Todd Helton, Colorado	Joey Hamilton, Cincinnati	5	Colorado
8-9	Pat Burrell, Philadelphia	Paul Shuey, Los Angeles	8	Los Angeles
8-10	Albert Pujols, St. Louis	Shawn Estes, New York	1	St. Louis
8-10	Benito Santiago, San Francisco	Mike Lincoln, Pittsburgh	7	San Francisco
8-11	Sammy Sosa, Chicago	Justin Speier, Colorado	7	Colorado
8-17	Erubiel Durazo, Arizona	Kyle Farnsworth, Chicago	9	Chicago
8-18	Edgar Renteria, St. Louis	Vicente Padilla, Philadelphia	6	Philadelphia
8-23	Adam Hyzdu, Pittsburgh	Jayson Durocher, Milwaukee	7	Milwaukee
8-27	Ryan Klesko, San Diego	Nelson Cruz, Houston	7	Houston
8-29	Richie Sexson, Milwaukee	Kyle Farnsworth, Chicago	9	Milwaukee
8-31‡	Eli Marrero, St. Louis	Jason Bere, Chicago	3	Chicago
9-4	Jason LaRue, Cincinnati	Jamey Wright, St. Louis	2	St. Louis
9-4	Edgar Renteria, St. Louis	Ryan Dempster, Cincinnati	3	St. Louis
9-9	Jose Guillen, Cincinnati	Al Reyes, Pittsburgh	6	Cincinnati
9-9	Mike Piazza, New York	Jose Santiago, Philadelphia	7	Philadelphia
9-15	Matt Cepicky, Montreal	Pedro Astacio, New York	1	Montreal
9-15	Javy Lopez, Atlanta	Graeme Lloyd, Florida	6	Florida
9-16	Brian Jordan, Los Angeles	Jason Schmidt, San Francisco	3	Los Angeles
9-17	Tino Martinez, St. Louis	Sean Lowe, Colorado	8	Colorado
9-19	Kelly Stinnett, Cincinnati	Mike Williams, Pittsburgh	9	Pittsburgh

*Inning in which grand slam was hit. ‡Night separate admission.

TRANSACTIONS

JANUARY 1, 2002-DECEMBER 31, 2002

JANUARY 2

Athletics signed LHP Mike Holtz.
Blue Jays acquired C Tom Wilson from **Athletics** for C Mike Kremblas.
Cubs signed INF Chris Stynes.
Pirates signed RHP Mike Williams.
Padres organization signed C Matt Walbeck.

JANUARY 4

Yankees claimed RHP Brett Jodie off waivers from **Padres**.
Brewers claimed RHP George Perez off waivers from **Blue Jays**.

JANUARY 5

Giants signed OF Reggie Sanders.

JANUARY 11

Athletics signed INF Randy Velarde.
Mariners signed RHP Shigetoshi Hasegawa.
Diamondbacks organization signed INF-OF Chris Donnels.
Reds organization signed RHP Jimmy Haynes and LHP Brian Bohanon.
Rockies signed RHP Todd Jones.
Expos organization signed RHP Dan Smith.
Giants signed INF Desi Relaford.

JANUARY 12

Blue Jays organization signed INF Dave Berg.

JANUARY 14

Twins organization signed INF Kurt Abbott.
Athletics acquired 1B Carlos Pena and LHP Mike Venafro from **Rangers** for 1B Jason Hart, LHP Mario Ramos, C Gerald Laird and OF Ryan Ludwick.
Rangers organization signed RHP Steve Woodard.
Cubs signed OF Darren Lewis.
Phillies organization signed LHP Pete Schourek.

JANUARY 15

Twins organization signed RHP Brian Meadows.
Braves acquired OF Gary Sheffield from **Dodgers** for OF Brian Jordan, LHP Odalis Perez and RHP Andrew Brown.
Rockies organization signed C Carlos Hernandez, RHP Chris Holt and OF Cliff Brumbaugh.
Mets organization signed OF Darren Bragg.
Phillies signed RHP Terry Adams.

JANUARY 16

Red Sox signed C Doug Mirabelli.
Cubs organization signed RHP Alan Benes.
Brewers signed 2B Eric Young.
Pirates organization signed RHP Scott Service, SS Luis Garcia, LHP Sean Fesh, 1B Dave Post, 2B Randy Meadows and 2B Victor Rodriguez.
Giants organization signed C Scott Servais.

JANUARY 17

White Sox claimed LHP Thomas Jacquez off waivers from **Phillies**.
Yankees signed INF Enrique Wilson. Released INF-OF Clay Bellinger.
Rangers organization signed OF Patrick Boyd.
Blue Jays acquired RHP Brian Cooper from **Angels** for 1B-DH Brad Fullmer.
Astros organization signed RHP Jamie Arnold, RHP Mark Guerra, RHP Peter Munro, LHP Jason Jacome, C Frank Charles, C Chris Tremie, C Alan Zinter, INF Tripp Cromer, OF Chris Prieto and OF Scott Pose.

JANUARY 18

Braves acquired RHP Kevin Gryboski from **Mariners** for RHP Elvis Perez.
Padres organization signed OF Ron Gant.
Giants signed RHP Jay Witasick.

JANUARY 20

Diamondbacks organization signed RHP Rick Helling.

JANUARY 21

Mets acquired RHP Jeff D'Amico, OF Jeromy Burnitz, INF Lou Collier, INF Mark Sweeney and cash from **Brewers**, and INF-OF Ross Gload and RHP Craig House from **Rockies**. Sent LHP Glendon Rusch to **Brewers**, and INF Todd Zeile, OF Benny Agbayani, INF Lenny Harris and cash to **Rockies**. **Brewers** also received OF Alex Ochoa from **Rockies**. **Mets** organization signed OF Tony Tarasco.

JANUARY 23

Twins organization signed RHP Mike Jackson.
Padres organization signed RHP Steve Reed.

JANUARY 24

Tigers claimed INF Oscar Salazar off waivers from **Athletics**.
Devil Rays organization signed LHP Stevenson Agosto, RHP Carlos Chantres, RHP Luis De Los Santos, RHP Jason Dickson, C Kevin Brown, INF Kevin Sefcik and OF Ryan Freel.

JANUARY 25

Yankees organization signed INF Ron Coomer.
Mariners traded 3B David Bell to **Giants** for INF Desi Relaford and cash.
Brewers signed OF Matt Stairs.

JANUARY 26

Mets traded OF-1B Ross Gload to **Rockies** for cash.

JANUARY 28

Tigers organization signed RHP Bill Simas.
Devil Rays organization signed LHP Tom Martin, RHP Randy Galvez, C Sal Fasano, C Yamid Haad, INF Andy Sheets and OF Emil Brown.
Rangers signed RHP Ismael Valdes and RHP Rudy Seanez.
Braves organization signed RHP Darren Holmes.
Phillies organization signed OF John Mabry.

JANUARY 29

White Sox acquired 2B-OF Willie Harris from **Orioles** for OF Chris Singleton.
Twins organization signed RHP Dave Lee.
Yankees organization signed RHP Mike Thurman.
Devil Rays organization signed OF Troy O'Leary.
Rangers organization signed RHP Dan Miceli.
Brewers signed LHP Takaki Nomura.
Phillies signed OF Ricky Ledee.

JANUARY 30

Mariners signed RHP James Baldwin.
Cubs organization signed RHP Pat Mahomes.
Reds signed RHP Ricardo Aramboles.
Rockies organization signed RHP Mike James.
Dodgers organization signed OF Dante Bichette.
Mets organization signed INF John Valentin.
Pirates signed 2B Pokey Reese.
Padres signed INF Deivi Cruz.

JANUARY 31

Angels organization signed INF-OF Clay Bellinger and RHP Donne Wall.
Indians organization signed INF Mike Lansing.
Rockies organization signed LHP Kent Mercker and RHP Bobby Chouinard.

FEBRUARY 1

White Sox signed OF Kenny Lofton.
Indians organization signed OF Bruce Aven and OF Brooks Kieschnick.
Tigers claimed OF Craig Monroe off waivers from **Rangers**.
Yankees organization signed C Chris Widger.
Athletics claimed RHP Allen Levrault off waivers from **Brewers**.
Braves organization signed LHP Rich Rodriguez.
Mets claimed OF Endy Chavez off waivers from **Tigers**.

FEBRUARY 2

Rangers organization signed C Pat Borders.

FEBRUARY 4

Orioles organization signed INF Howie Clark, RHP Travis Driskill, LHP Eric DuBose, OF Luis Garcia, C Mike Hubbard, RHP Rodrigo Lopez, RHP Lee Marshall, 1B Domingo Martinez, OF-1B Ryan McGuire, C Izzy Molina, INF Mike Moriarty and LHP Sean Runyan.
Red Sox organization signed INF Quilvio Veras, OF Jeff Abbott and C Henry Mercedes.
Devil Rays signed LHP Doug Creek.

FEBRUARY 5

Indians organization signed RHP Omar Olivares.
Rangers signed OF Juan Gonzalez.
Cubs organization signed LHP Donovan Osborne.
Dodgers claimed RHP Craig House off waivers from **Mets**.
Padres organization signed RHP Brad Clontz.
Giants signed RHP Manny Aybar.

FEBRUARY 6

Astros organization signed LHP Chuck McElroy.

FEBRUARY 8

Mariners released LHP Norm Charlton.
Brewers organization signed OF Midre Cummings and INF Izzy Alcantara.
Pirates organization signed RHP Pat Rapp.
Cardinals organization signed OF Al Martin and OF Eduardo Perez.

FEBRUARY 10

Indians organization signed RHP Jose Mercedes.

FEBRUARY 11

Rangers organization signed INF Ed Sprague.
Astros signed RHP Hipolito Pichardo.

FEBRUARY 12

Rockies signed RHP Pete Harnisch.
Dodgers signed RHP Tim Crabtree.
Pirates organization signed LHP Ron Villone.

FEBRUARY 13

Red Sox organization signed OF Rickey Henderson.
Rangers released RHP Mark Petkovsek.
Giants announced retirement of RHP Mark Gardner.

FEBRUARY 14

Yankees signed OF Ruben Rivera.
Brewers signed RHP J.M. Gold.

FEBRUARY 15

Red Sox organization signed SS Gary DiSarcina.
Dodgers organization signed P Shigeki Sano.

FEBRUARY 18

Marlins organization signed OF Tim Raines Sr. and OF Mark Smith.

FEBRUARY 19

Yankees organization signed C Jim Leyritz.
Brewers organization signed RHP Francisco Campos.
Expos organization signed OF Jose Canseco and LHP Ed Vosberg.

FEBRUARY 20

Red Sox organization signed 3B Andy Morales.

FEBRUARY 21

Yankees organization signed LHP Allen Watson.
Mets traded RHP Corey Brittan to **Rockies** for RHP Kane Davis.

FEBRUARY 22

Expos organization signed OF Lance Johnson and RHP Osvaldo Fernandez to minor league contracts. **Expos** claimed OF Endy Chavez off waivers from **Mets**.

FEBRUARY 23

Padres organization signed OF Trenidad Hubbard.

FEBRUARY 27

Red Sox organization signed INF Rey Sanchez.
Pirates organization signed RHP Josias Manzanillo.

MARCH 5

Indians released C Tim Laker and signed him to a minor league contract.
Reds released RHP Arnie Gooch.

MARCH 7

Expos organization signed RHP Alan Mills. Agreed to terms with 1B Andres Galarraga.

MARCH 9

Royals released LHP Jose Rosado.

MARCH 11

White Sox released OF Julio Ramirez.
Yankees released OF Ruben Rivera.

MARCH 12

Astros released LHP Chuck McElroy. Acquired INF Geoff Blum from **Expos** for 3B Chris Truby.

MARCH 13

Yankees released INF Manny Alexander and LHP Eric Gunderson.
Mets released OF Mark Sweeney and OF Danny Peoples.
Pirates released RHP Gregg Olson and 2B Warren Morris.

MARCH 15

Twins organization signed 2B Warren Morris.
Yankees released LHP Allen Watson.

MARCH 17

Yankees released C Jim Leyritz.
Dodgers released OF Roberto Kelly.
Padres organization signed INF-OF Mark Sweeney.

MARCH 18

Athletics traded RHP Luis Vizcaino to **Rangers** for RHP Justin Duchscherer.
Devil Rays claimed RHP Jorge Sosa off waivers from **Brewers**.

MARCH 19

Yankees released SS Kevin Elster.

MARCH 20

Braves acquired C Henry Blanco from **Brewers** for C Paul Bako and RHP Jose Cabrera.

MARCH 21

Indians acquired C Eddie Perez from **Braves** for a player to be named.

MARCH 23

Tigers traded C Javier Cardona and OF Rich Gomez to **Padres** for INF Damian Jackson and C Matt Walbeck.
Athletics announced INF-OF Jason Grabowski refused outright assignment to Sacremento and elected free agency.
Rangers traded RHP Luis Vizcaino to **Brewers** for LHP Jesus Pena.
Rockies released C Tony Eusebio.
Dodgers announced retirement of OF Dante Bichette.
Expos traded RHP Guillermo Mota and OF Wilkin Ruan to **Dodgers** for RHP Matt Herges and INF Jorge Nunez.
Phillies sold contract of OF Felipe Crespo to Yomiuri of Japanese Central League.

MARCH 25

White Sox waived OF Brian Simmons.
Devil Rays released OF Troy O'Leary.
Rangers acquired LHP Rich Rodriguez from **Braves** for a player to be named.
Rockies traded RHP Jose Paniagua to **Tigers** for RHP Victor Santos and INF Ronnie Merrill. Acquired RHP Chuck Smith from **Marlins** for a player to be named.
Astros released LHP C.J. Nitkowski.
Padres returned RHP Ryan Baerlocher to **Royals** per major league Rule 5 guidelines.

MARCH 26

Indians waived LHP Scott Radinsky.
Yankees released C Todd Greene.
Devil Rays released INF Felix Martinez.
Mets traded INF Lou Collier to **Expos** for RHP Jimmy Serrano and OF Jason Bay.

MARCH 27

Orioles organization signed LHP Yorkis Perez.
White Sox acquired LHP Damaso Marte and INF Edwin Yan from **Pirates** for RHP Matt Guerrier.
Indians waived OF Karim Garcia.
Royals organization signed LHP Jose Rosado.
Devil Rays claimed INF Felix Escalona off waivers from **Giants**.
Diamondbacks released LHP Troy Brohawn and LHP Yorkis Perez.
Cubs acquired RHP Antonio Alfonseca and RHP Matt Clement from **Marlins** for RHP Julian Tavarez, RHP Jose Cueto, LHP Dontrelle Willis and C Ryan Jorgensen.
Rockies released C Carlos Hernandez.
Expos released OF Jose Canseco.
Mets claimed OF Chris Latham off waivers from **Blue Jays** and 1B Andy Tracy off waivers from **Expos**.
Phillies released LHP Pete Schourek.

MARCH 28

Indians traded OF Donzell McDonald to **Royals** for a player to be named. Released RHP J.D. Brammer.
Astros organization signed LHP C.J. Nitkowski.
Expos organization signed OF Troy O'Leary and OF Henry Rodriguez to minor league contracts. **Expos** released OF Lance Johnson.
Phillies traded OF Reggie Taylor to **Reds** for a player to be named.

MARCH 29

Royals released RHP Doug Henry.
Phillies released INF Kevin Jordan.

MARCH 30

Rangers organization signed OF Ruben Rivera.
Marlins claimed SS Wilson Valdez off waivers from **Expos**.
Phillies acquired LHP Hector Mercado from **Reds** to complete an earlier trade.
Pirates released OF Derek Bell.

APRIL 2

Dodgers organization signed C Todd Greene, INF Felix Martinez and OF Scott Pose.

APRIL 3

Reds released OF Jermaine Allensworth. Organization signed INF Kevin Jordan.
Brewers claimed RHP Nelson Figueroa off waivers from **Phillies**.
Mets traded OF Gary Matthews Jr. to **Orioles** for LHP John Bale. Claimed OF McKay Christensen off waivers from **Dodgers**.
Padres acquired LHP Juan Moreno from **Rangers** for SS Jason Moore.

APRIL 4

Indians acquired OF Chris Magruder from **Rangers** for OF Rashad Eldridge. Traded RHP Jeff D'Amico to **Phillies** for a player to be named.
Cubs claimed OF Mario Encarnacion off waivers from **Rockies**.

APRIL 5

Mets acquired RHP Scott Strickland, OF Matt Watson and LHP Philip Seibel from **Expos** for LHP Bruce Chen, RHP Dicky Gonzalez, INF Luis Figueroa and a player to be named. Claimed INF Marcos Scutaro off waivers from **Brewers**.

APRIL 8

Mariners organization signed C Pat Borders.
Dodgers waived OF Tom Goodwin and RHP Mike Trombley.

APRIL 13

Indians released RHP Omar Olivares.
Cubs organization signed OF Bernard Gilkey. **Cubs** acquired RHP Marc Deschenes from **Pirates** for future considerations.

APRIL 15

Twins organization signed RHP Mike Trombley.
Pirates claimed INF Tomas De La Rosa off waivers from **Expos**.

APRIL 16

Pirates organization signed INF Kevin Sefcik.

APRIL 17

Yankees organization signed LHP Bill Pulsipher.

APRIL 18

White Sox organization signed OF Jose Canseco.

APRIL 22

Rangers acquired OF Calvin Murray from **Giants** for cash.

APRIL 23

Padres acquired LHP Andrew Hazlett from **Red Sox** for LHP Juan Moreno.

APRIL 26

Rangers purchased contract of C Hector Ortiz from **Royals**.

APRIL 29

Indians released OF-1B Wil Cordero.

MAY 3

Blue Jays claimed RHP Pete Walker off waivers from **Mets**.

MAY 6

Rangers released RHP Dan Miceli.

MAY 7

Diamondbacks organization signed INF Hanley Frias.

MAY 8

Devil Rays released INF Bobby Smith.

MAY 10

Blue Jays released 2B Homer Bush.

MAY 12

Expos signed OF Wil Cordero.

MAY 13

White Sox announced retirement of OF Jose Canseco.

MAY 15

Blue Jays traded LHP Pedro Borbon to **Astros** for a player to be named.

MAY 16

White Sox organization signed OF Damon Buford and OF Brooks Kieschnick.
Tigers acquired 3B Chris Truby from **Expos** for INF-OF Jose Macias.

MAY 17

Rockies traded RHP Eduardo Villacis to **Royals** for RHP Bryan Rekar.

MAY 21

Indians released OF Brady Anderson.

MAY 22

Athletics traded OF Jeremy Giambi to **Phillies** for INF-OF John Mabry.

MAY 23

Mariners claimed INF-OF Nate Rolison off waivers from **Marlins**. Released RHP Greg Wooten.

MAY 26

Blue Jays traded LHP Dan Plesac to **Phillies** for RHP Cliff Politte.

JUNE 3

Rangers released RHP Steve Woodard.

JUNE 4

Phillies organization signed RHP Steve Woodard.

JUNE 6

Cardinals organization signed LHP C.J. Nitkowski and C Alex Andreopoulos.

JUNE 7

Indians traded INF Russell Branyan to **Reds** for 1B Ben Broussard.

JUNE 9

Cubs traded C Robert Machado to **Brewers** for OF Jackson Melian.

JUNE 10
Giants claimed LHP Jason Pearson off waivers from **Padres**.

JUNE 11
Twins traded 2B Warren Morris to **Cardinals** for a player to be named.

JUNE 12
Yankees claimed RHP Nate Field off waivers from **Royals**.
Cardinals organization signed OF Gerald Williams.

JUNE 14
Angels released RHP Donne Wall.
Expos organization signed RHP Mike Buddie.
Padres claimed OF Eugene Kingsale off waivers from **Mariners**.

JUNE 19
Braves traded OF George Lombard to **Tigers** for RHP Kris Keller.

JUNE 20
Twins acquired SS Seth Davidson from **Cardinals** to complete an earlier trade.

JUNE 21
Rockies organization signed RHP Donne Wall.

JUNE 25
Indians traded OF Bruce Aven to **Phillies** for RHP Jeff D'Amico.
Marlins traded OF Brett Roneberg to **Expos** for RHP Donnie Bridges.

JUNE 26
Twins released LHP Travis Miller unconditionally.

JUNE 27
Indians traded RHP Bartolo Colon and future considerations to **Expos** for 1B Lee Stevens, SS Brandon Phillips, LHP Cliff Lee and OF Grady Sizemore. Released RHP Martin Vargas.

JUNE 28
Indians sent RHP Tim Drew to **Expos** to complete a previous trade.

JUNE 30
Cubs organization signed LHP Travis Miller.

JULY 1
Yankees acquired OF Raul Mondesi from **Blue Jays** for LHP Scott Wiggins.

JULY 2
Red Sox waived LHP Darren Oliver.

JULY 4
Royals organization signed RHP Edwin Hurtado.

JULY 5
Yankees acquired RHP Jeff Weaver from **Tigers**. Sent LHP Ted Lilly, OF John-Ford Griffin and RHP Jason Arnold to **Athletics**.
Athletics sent 1B Carlos Pena, RHP Franklyn German and a player to be named to **Tigers**.

JULY 8
Rangers claimed INF Donnie Sadler off waivers from **Royals**.

JULY 11
Marlins traded OF Cliff Floyd and RHP Claudio Vargas to **Expos** for RHP Carl Pavano, LHP Graeme Lloyd and two minor league players. Traded RHP Ryan Dempster to **Reds** for OF Juan Encarnacion.

JULY 12
White Sox acquired INF D'Angelo Jimenez from **Padres** for OF Alex Fernandez and C Humberto Quintero.
Indians traded INF Anthony Medrano to **Expos** for 1B Nick Dempsey and traded RHP Jeff D'Amico to **Reds** for a player to be named. Organization signed RHP Jason Rakers.
Twins traded RF Brian Buchanan to **Padres** for SS Jason Bartlett.
Reds acquired OF Gerald Williams from **Cardinals**.

JULY 13
Padres released OF Mark Sweeney and RHP Dave Lundquist.

JULY 18
Yankees organization signed RHP Jason Rakers and RHP Ryan Bradley.
Rockies claimed LHP Randy Flores on waivers from **Rangers** and released RHP Chuck Smith.
Mets claimed RHP Ryan Jamison off waivers from **Astros**.

JULY 19
Cardinals acquired LHP Chuck Finley from **Indians** for 1B Luis Garcia and a player to be named.

JULY 22
Dodgers acquired INF-OF Jolbert Cabrera from **Indians** for LHP Lance Caraccioli.

JULY 23
Reds acquired RHP Brian Moehler and INF Matt Boone from **Tigers** for INF David Espinosa and two players to be named.
Brewers traded INF Tyler Houston and a player to be named to **Dodgers** for RHP Ben Diggins and LHP Shane Nance.

JULY 24
Mariners acquired LHP Doug Creek from **Devil Rays** for cash.

JULY 25
Tigers acquired INF Hiram Bocachica from **Dodgers** for RHP Tom Farmer and a player to be named.
Athletics acquired 2B Ray Durham from **White Sox** for RHP Jon Adkins.

JULY 26
Blue Jays announced retirement of C Darrin Fletcher.

JULY 28
Indians traded RHP Paul Shuey to **Dodgers** for LHP Terry Mulholland, RHP Ricardo Rodriguez and RHP Francisco Cruceta.
Astros released RHP T.J. Mathews.
Giants traded RHP Felix Diaz and LHP Ryan Meaux to **White Sox** for OF Kenny Lofton.

JULY 29
White Sox traded C Sandy Alomar Jr. to **Rockies** for RHP Enemencio Pacheco.
Rangers released RHP Dave Burba and organization signed LHP C.J. Nitkowski.
Phillies traded 3B Scott Rolen, RHP Doug Nickle and cash to **Cardinals** for INF Placido Polanco, LHP Bud Smith and RHP Mike Timlin.

JULY 30
Red Sox acquired OF Cliff Floyd from **Expos** for RHP Seung Jun Song, RHP Sun Woo Kim and a player to be named.
Athletics acquired LHP Ricardo Rincon from **Indians** for INF Marshall McDougall.

JULY 31
White Sox traded RHP Bob Howry and cash to **Red Sox** for RHP Franklin Francisco and LHP Byeong An.
Rockies traded OF Todd Hollandsworth and LHP Dennys Reyes to **Rangers** for OF Gabe Kapler and 2B-OF Jason Romano.
Brewers traded OF Alex Ochoa and C Sal Fasano to **Angels** for C Jorge Fabregas and two players to be named.
Mets traded OF Jay Payton, RHP Mark Corey and OF Robert Stratton to **Rockies** for RHP John Thomson and OF Mark Little. Claimed INF Oscar Salazar off waivers from **Tigers**.
Pirates traded OF Chad Hermansen to **Cubs** for OF Darren Lewis.
Padres traded RHP Steve Reed and RHP Jason Middlebrook to **Mets** for LHP Bobby Jones, RHP Josh Reynolds and OF Jay Bay.

AUGUST 2
Athletics released LHP Mike Magnante.
Cubs acquired OF Aron Weston from **Pirates** for LHP Ricardo Palma, LHP Tim Lavery and cash.

AUGUST 5
Marlins acquired RHP Don Levinski from **Expos** to complete an earler trade.

AUGUST 6

Indians acquired OF Covelli Crisp from **Cardinals** to complete July 19 trade for LHP Chuck Finley.

AUGUST 7

Indians organization signed RHP Dave Burba and LHP Travis Miller.

AUGUST 8

Mariners acquired INF Jose Offerman from **Red Sox** for cash.
Giants claimed LHP Scott Eyre off waivers from **Blue Jays**.

AUGUST 9

Cubs waived INF Delino DeShields.

AUGUST 12

Rockies claimed LHP Brian Fitzgerald off waivers from **Mariners**.

AUGUST 14

Angels sent INF Johnny Raburn to **Brewers** to complete July 31 trade for OF Alex Ochoa.
Pirates released RHP Josias Manzanillo.

AUGUST 15

Reds acquired LHP Shawn Estes and cash from **Mets** for LHP Pedro Feliciano, OF Elvin Andujar and two players to be named.

AUGUST 16

Tigers claimed RHP Jason Beverlin off waivers from **Indians** and optioned him to Toledo (IL).
Diamondbacks acquired OF Mark Little from **Mets** for a player to be named.
Dodgers organization signed LHP Mike Magnante.

AUGUST 18

Mariners acquired RHP Ismael Valdes from **Rangers** for INF Jermaine Clark and LHP Derrick Van Dusen.
Cardinals signed RHP Rick White.

AUGUST 20

Reds traded OF Raul Gonzalez to the **Mets** to complete an earlier trade. Organization signed OF Jose Guillen.
Mets acquired RHP P.J. Bevis from **Diamondbacks** to complete an earlier trade.

AUGUST 22

Athletics sent RHP Jeremy Bonderman to **Tigers** to complete an earlier trade.
Cubs traded RHP Tom Gordon to **Astros** for LHP Russ Rohlicek and two players to be named.

AUGUST 23

Padres claimed RHP Carlos Garcia off waivers from **Dodgers**.

AUGUST 25

Cardinals acquired LHP Jeff Fassero from **Cubs** for two minor leaguers to be named and cash.

AUGUST 28

Indians announced retirement of 3B Travis Fryman at the end of the season.
Padres claimed RHP Doug Nickle off waivers from **Cardinals**.

AUGUST 29

Brewers traded RHP Jamey Wright and cash to **Cardinals** for OF Chris Morris and a player to be named.

AUGUST 30

Tigers acquired OF Gary Varner from **Reds** to partially complete an earlier trade.
Blue Jays claimed LHP Jason Kershner off waivers from **Padres**.

SEPTEMBER 1

Marlins released INF Homer Bush.
Brewers traded INF Mark Loretta and cash to **Astros** for two players to be named.
Padres released LHP Bobby M. Jones.

SEPTEMBER 3

Astros sent LHP Wayne Franklin to **Brewers** as one of two players to be named in the trade for INF Mark Loretta.
Giants acquired INF Bill Mueller and cash considerations from **Cubs** for RHP Jeff Verplancke.

SEPTEMBER 4

Diamondbacks acquired contract of OF Felix Jose from Mexico City Reds of the Mexican League.

SEPTEMBER 5

Astros sent INF Keith Ginter to **Brewers** to complete an earlier trade.

SEPTEMBER 7

White Sox released SS Royce Clayton.
Tigers released RHP Jose Lima and RHP Jose Paniagua.
Pirates released RHP Sean Lowe.

SEPTEMBER 9

Mets acquired OF Brady Clark from **Reds** to complete an earlier trade.

SEPTEMBER 11

Cubs acquired RHP Travis Anderson and RHP Mike Nannini from **Astros** to complete an earlier trade.

SEPTEMBER 18

Tigers sent RHP Jason Frasor to **Dodgers** to complete an earlier trade.

SEPTEMBER 19

Indians traded OF Jason Fitzgerald to **Braves** to complete an earlier trade.

SEPTEMBER 20

Angels sent RHP Pedro Liriano to **Brewers** to complete an earlier trade.

SEPTEMBER 21

Devil Rays released OF Toe Nash.

SEPTEMBER 24

Tigers claimed LHP Jason Jimenez off waivers from **Devil Rays**.
Cardinals sent RHP Jason Karnuth and RHP Jared Blasdell to **Cubs** to complete an earlier trade.
Reds sent RHP Jorge Cordova to **Tigers** to complete an earlier trade.

SEPTEMBER 29

Marlins announced retirement of OF Tim Raines Sr.

SEPTEMBER 30

Devil Rays released LHP Wilson Alvarez, SS Chris Gomez and LHP Tom Martin.
Rangers granted free agency to OF Ruben Rivera, INF Donnie Sadler and LHP C.J. Nitkowski after they refused outright assignments to Oklahoma (PCL).

OCTOBER 1

Orioles released RHP Chris Brock, LHP Yorkis Perez, INF Luis Lopez and C Raul Casanova.
Cubs released LHP Jesus Sanchez.

OCTOBER 2

Red Sox claimed RHP Jason Shiell off waivers from **Padres**.
Indians released LHP Heath Murray.
Reds released RHP Jose Silva.
Mets claimed RHP Doug Nickle off waivers from **Padres**.
Padres released LHP Mike Holtz and RHP Matt DeWitt.

OCTOBER 3

Rangers released LHP John Rocker.
Marlins released RHP Hansel Izquierdo and LHP Benito Baez.

OCTOBER 7

Orioles released RHP Calvin Maduro.

OCTOBER 9

Red Sox claimed RHP Brandon Lyon off waivers from **Blue Jays**.

OCTOBER 10

Expos released INF-OF Wilton Guerrero.
Mets claimed RHP Joe Orloski off waivers from **Blue Jays** and RHP Franklin Nunez from **Phillies**.
Pirates released OF Adrian Brown. Claimed RHP Jim Mann off waivers from **Astros**.

OCTOBER 11

Tigers claimed LHP Pedro Feliciano off waivers from **Mets**.

OCTOBER 13

Brewers claimed OF Scott Podsednik off waivers from **Mariners**.

OCTOBER 16

Dodgers acquired RHP Brian Mallette from **Brewers** to complete an earlier trade.

OCTOBER 17

Red Sox organization signed RHP Hansel Izquierdo.
Indians claimed RHP Jack Cressend off waivers from **Twins**.

OCTOBER 28

Mariners acquired OF Randy Winn from **Devil Rays** for INF Antonio Perez as compensation for losing Lou Piniella as manager.

OCTOBER 29

Blue Jays signed LHP Doug Creek.

OCTOBER 30

Blue Jays organization signed RHP Doug Linton and LHP Trever Miller.
Cubs organization signed LHP Mike Sirotka.

NOVEMBER 1

Twins released INF David Lamb.
Blue Jays signed RHP Jeff Tam. Organization signed RHP Evan Thomas, LHP Tim Young and INF Mike Moriarty.
Astros organization signed RHP Chris Gissell, RHP Jonathan Johnson, RHP Miguel Saladin and LHP Ken Vining.

NOVEMBER 3

Indians signed RHP Jose Santiago.

NOVEMBER 4

Dodgers organization signed RHP Luke Prokopec.

NOVEMBER 5

Angels released C Sal Fasano.
Red Sox signed LHP Alan Embree.
Blue Jays organization signed INF Howie Clark and OF Rob Ryan.

NOVEMBER 6

Angels released OF Julio Ramirez.
Devil Rays organization signed OF Adrian Brown, OF Chad Mottola, INF Jay Canizaro, RHP Mike James and LHP Matt Perisho.

NOVEMBER 8

Blue Jays organization signed OF Bruce Aven and RHP Josh Towers.

NOVEMBER 13

Athletics acquired RHP Roy Smith from **Indians** for cash.
Rangers waived RHP Hideki Irabu. Organization signed RHP Robert Ellis, RHP Rosman Garcia, RHP Victor Santos, LHP Ron Mahay, LHP Brian Shouse, C Danny Ardoin, C Fernando Lunar, INF Donnie Sadler and OF Rontrez Johnson.
Cubs acquired C Damian Miller from **Diamondbacks** for LHP David Noyce and OF Gary Johnson.
Phillies organization signed INF Mike Coolbaugh.

NOVEMBER 15

Twins traded RHP Matt Kinney and C Javier Valentin to **Brewers** for RHP Matt Yeatman and RHP Gerard Oakes.
Rangers organization signed LHP C.J. Nitkowski and LHP Ray Beasley.
Padres traded OF Gene Kingsale to **Tigers** for C Michael Rivera.
Giants waived OF Tsuyoshi Shinjo.

NOVEMBER 17

Athletics traded RHP Cory Lidle to **Blue Jays** for INF Michael Rouse and RHP Christopher Mowday.

NOVEMBER 18

Tigers organization signed C Matt Walbeck.
Royals waived SS Neifi Perez.
Athletics organization signed RHP Jose Silva, C Mitch Meluskey, 1B David McCarty and OF Billy McMillon.
Rangers released LHP Juan Alvarez.
Rockies traded LHP Mike Hampton, OF Juan Pierre and $6.5 million to **Marlins** for C Charles Johnson, OF Preston Wilson, LHP Vic Darensbourg and 2B Pablo Ozuna.
Marlins traded LHP Mike Hampton and $30 million to **Braves** for RHP Tim Spooneybarger and RHP Ryan Baker.

NOVEMBER 19

Mariners released RHP Paul Abbott.
Reds organization signed INF Ryan Freel, RHP Sean DePaula, LHP Mark Watson, INF Kelly Dransfeldt, C Reed Secrist, OF Emil Brown, IF Felipe Crespo, LHP Lance Davis, OF Robin Jennings, INF Jason Maxwell, RHP Carlos Almanzar, RHP Shane Hearns, OF Mike Curry, OF Bobby Darula, RHP Kyle Stanton, RHP Scott MacRae and C Creighton Gubanich.
Padres signed LHP Jesse Orosco and RHP Francisco Cordova.

NOVEMBER 20

Tigers released INF Damian Jackson unconditionally.
Devil Rays released RHP Ryan Rupe.
Giants claimed INF Neifi Perez off waivers from **Royals**.

NOVEMBER 21

Red Sox organization signed RHP Paul Stewart, RHP Justin Kaye, C-INF Chris Coste, C Jeff Smith, INF James Lofton and INF Nelson Castro.
Devil Rays organization signed INF Justin Baughman, C Charlie Greene, C Sandy Martinez, C Angel Pena, OF Ryan Jackson, RHP Leslie Brea, RHP Jeremi Gonzalez and LHP Cedrick Bowers.

NOVEMBER 22

Red Sox organization signed RHP Steve Woodard, RHP Tom Davey, LHP Kevin Tolar, 1B-OF Larry Sutton and INF Julio Zuleta.

NOVEMBER 23

Phillies signed 3B David Bell.

NOVEMBER 25

Marlins organization signed OF Chad Allen, RHP Toby Borland, RHP Rick Croushore, C Paul Hoover, RHP Allen Levrault, OF Robert Stratton, C Matt Treanor and OF Chris Wakeland.
Brewers signed INF Wilton Veras, INF Jed Hansen and OF Mark Budzinski.
Pirates acquired 1B Randall Simon from **Tigers** for LHP Adrian Burnside and two minor league players to be named.

NOVEMBER 26

Brewers traded C Paul Bako to **Cubs** for a player to be named.

NOVEMBER 27

Red Sox claimed RHP Ryan Rupe off waivers from **Devil Rays**.
Mariners claimed LHP Steve Kent off waivers from **Devil Rays**.

DECEMBER 2

Orioles organization signed LHP Bill Pulsipher.

DECEMBER 3

Athletics traded RHP Billy Koch and two minor league players to **White Sox** for RHP Keith Foulke, C Mark Johnson and RHP Joe Valentine and cash.
Cubs signed LHP Mike Remlinger.
Expos waived RHP Masato Yoshii.
Phillies signed 1B Jim Thome.
Cardinals signed C Steve Torrealba.

DECEMBER 4

Yankees signed OF Chris Latham.
Cubs traded C Todd Hundley and OF Chad Hermansen to **Dodgers** for 1B Eric Karros, 2B Mark Grudzielanek and $2 million.
Cubs released INF Chris Stynes.
Padres signed INF-OF Chris Sexton.

DECEMBER 5

Red Sox signed RHP Willie Banks and RHP Ryan Rupe.
Mets signed LHP Tom Glavine.

DECEMBER 6

Indians acquired 1B Travis Hafner and RHP Aaron Myette from **Rangers** for C Einar Diaz and RHP Ryan Drese.
Dodgers sold contract of RHP Kevin Beirne to Osaka of Japanese Pacific League and LHP Jeff Williams to Hanshin of Japanese Central League.
Padres organization signed OF Brady Anderson.

DECEMBER 8

Yankees signed C Chris Widger.
Giants signed 2B Ray Durham and OF Marquis Grissom.

DECEMBER 10

Devil Rays reached agreement with Yokohama of Japan Central League that allows Yokohama to purchase services of 1B Steve Cox.
Astros organization signed LHP Jesus Sanchez.
Padres signed INF Dave Hansen and RHP Jaret Wright.

DECEMBER 11

Blue Jays signed C Greg Myers.
Cubs signed C Damian Miller.
Brewers signed SS Royce Clayton and organization signed C Joe Lawrence.

DECEMBER 12

Reds traded 2B Todd Walker to **Red Sox** for two players to be named.
Padres organization signed INF Homer Bush.

DECEMBER 13

Devil Rays sold rights to INF Andy Sheets to Hiroshima of Japanese Central League.
Cardinals signed RHP Chris Carpenter.

DECEMBER 14

Orioles signed SS Deivi Cruz.
Red Sox acquired OF Jeremy Giambi from **Phillies** for RHP Josh Hancock.
Diamondbacks traded 1B Erubiel Durazo to **Athletics**. Received RHP Elmer Dessens and cash from **Reds**. **Reds** acquired SS Felipe Lopez from **Blue Jays**. **Blue Jays** received a player to be named from **Athletics**.
Reds released RHP Jared Fernandez.
Mets traded SS Rey Ordonez to **Devil Rays** for two players to be named.
Padres traded RHP Brett Tomko to **Cardinals** for RHP Luther Hackman and a player to be named.
Giants signed 3B Edgardo Alfonzo.

DECEMBER 16

Red Sox acquired INF Cesar Crespo from **Padres** for INF Luis Cruz.
White Sox acquired LHP Neal Cotts and OF Daylan Holt from **Athletics** to complete an earlier trade.
Tigers acquired RHP Matt Roney from **Pirates**, and 3B Travis Chapman from **Indians** for cash. Released LHP Pedro Feliciano. Acquired RHP Roberto Novoa from **Pirates** as part of their Nov. 25 trade.
Twins released DH David Ortiz.
Athletics released RHP Mike Fyhrie.
Blue Jays acquired RHP Jason Arnold from **Athletics** to complete an earlier trade.
Reds acquired RHP Josh Thigpen and 3B Tony Blanco from **Red Sox** to complete an earlier trade.
Astros acquired OF Victor Hall from **Rockies** in exchange for a player to be named or cash. Traded RHP Nelson Cruz to **Rockies** to complete the earlier trade.
Dodgers acquired LHP Derek Thompson from **Cubs** for cash.
Brewers acquired 3B Wes Helms and LHP John Foster from **Braves** for LHP Ray King.
Mets signed LHP Mike Stanton. Claimed LHP Peter Zamora off waivers from **Phillies**.
Pirates released LHP Jimmy Anderson.
Padres signed 2B Mark Loretta. Acquired INF-OF Jose Flores from **Athletics** for RHP Buddy Hernandez, and RHP Mike Wodnicki from **Cardinals** to complete an earlier trade.

DECEMBER 17

Braves signed RHP Paul Byrd and organization signed LHP Chris Haney.
Cubs signed OF Troy O'Leary.
Cardinals signed C Joe Girardi.
Giants acquired LHP Damian Moss and RHP Manuel Mateo from **Braves** for RHP Russ Ortiz.

DECEMBER 18

Angels claimed C Wilbert Nieves off waivers from **Padres**.
Red Sox signed RHP Mike Timlin and INF Damian Jackson.
Indians organization signed INF Casey Blake and RHP Mike Thurman.
Yankees signed 3B Todd Zeile.
Rangers signed OF Doug Glanville.
Astros signed 2B Jeff Kent.
Cardinals organization signed RHP Cal Eldred and LHP Lance Painter.

DECEMBER 19

Indians signed RHP Jason Bere and organization signed C Dusty Wathan.
Tigers organization signed 2B Warren Morris, OF Ernie Young, RHP Carlos Alvarado, RHP Fernando De La Cruz, RHP Tim McClaskey, RHP Chris Mears, RHP Brian Schmack, LHP Rafael Roque, LHP Mike Spiegel, C Robinson Cancel, C Luis Taveras and C Bill Haselman.
Yankees signed OF Hideki Matsui.
Devil Rays organization signed LHP Brian Fitzgerald, RHP John Frascatore, RHP Mel Rojas, RHP Eric Sabel, RHP Blake Stein, OF Brian Lesher, SS Gabby Martinez and C Hector Ortiz.

DECEMBER 20

White Sox signed C Sandy Alomar Jr.
Blue Jays signed INF Mike Bordick.
Braves traded RHP Kevin Millwood to **Phillies** for C Johnny Estrada.
Cubs signed LHP Shawn Estes.
Astros organization signed RHP Jared Fernandez.
Dodgers signed 1B Fred McGriff.
Expos traded RHP Matt Herges to **Pirates** for RHP Chris Young and RHP Jon Searles.
Mets signed OF Cliff Floyd.
Padres organization signed RHP Charles Nagy.

DECEMBER 21

Rangers signed RHP Ugueth Urbina.
Blue Jays signed RHP Tanyon Sturtze.

DECEMBER 23

Indians signed LHP Brian Anderson and organization signed C A.J. Hinch.
Athletics signed OF Chris Singleton.
Padres signed C Gary Bennett.

DECEMBER 26

Rangers signed RHP Esteban Yan.

DECEMBER 27

Mets signed INF Rey Sanchez.

DECEMBER 30

Angels signed OF Eric Owens.
Yankees re-signed RHP Roger Clemens.
Blue Jays signed OF Frank Catalanotto.

DECEMBER 31

Rangers signed LHP Aaron Fultz.

AWARD WINNERS

THE SPORTING NEWS

AMERICAN LEAGUE

Pitcher of the Year: Barry Zito, Oakland
Rookie Player of the Year: Eric Hinske, Toronto, 3B
Rookie Pitcher of the Year: Rodrigo Lopez, Baltimore
Fireman of the Year: Billy Koch, Oakland
Comeback Player of the Year: Tim Salmon, Anaheim
Manager of the Year: Mike Scioscia, Anaheim

MAJOR LEAGUE

Player of the Year: Alex Rodriguez, Texas
Executive of the Year: Terry Ryan, Minnesota

NATIONAL LEAGUE

Pitcher of the Year: Curt Schilling, Arizona
Rookie Player of the Year: Brad Wilkerson, Montreal, OF-1B
Rookie Pitcher of the Year: Jason Jennings, Colorado
Fireman of the Year: John Smoltz, Atlanta
Comeback Player of the Year: Mike Lieberthal, Philadelphia
Manager of the Year: Bobby Cox, Atlanta

MINOR LEAGUE

Player of the Year: Jason Stokes, Kane County, Midwest
Manager of the Year: Eric Wedge, Buffalo, International
Executive of the Year: Gary Arthur, Sacramento, Pacific Coast

BASEBALL WRITERS' ASSOCIATION OF AMERICA
AMERICAN LEAGUE

MOST VALUABLE PLAYER

Player, Team	1	2	3	4	5	6	7	8	9	10	Pts.
Miguel Tejada, Oakland	21	6	1	-	-	-	-	-	-	-	356
Alex Rodriguez, Texas	5	7	11	4	-	1	-	-	-	-	254
Alfonso Soriano, New York	2	11	9	4	1	-	-	-	-	1	234
Garret Anderson, Anaheim	-	4	5	7	7	1	2	-	2	-	184
Jason Giambi, New York	-	-	2	8	10	4	1	1	1	1	162
Torii Hunter, Minnesota	-	-	-	5	5	8	1	5	4	-	132
Jim Thome, Cleveland	-	-	-	-	2	3	3	8	1	4	69
Magglio Ordonez, Chicago	-	-	-	-	1	4	5	3	-	4	59
Manny Ramirez, Boston	-	-	-	-	-	2	5	1	2	2	39
Bernie Williams, New York	-	-	-	-	1	-	3	2	3	2	32
David Eckstein, Anaheim	-	-	-	-	1	1	-	1	4	2	24
Nomar Garciaparra, Boston	-	-	-	-	-	2	1	1	2	3	24
Barry Zito, Oakland	-	-	-	-	-	1	2	1	2	2	22
Eric Chavez, Oakland	-	-	-	-	-	-	-	2	3	2	14
Troy Percival, Anaheim	-	-	-	-	-	1	1	1	-	-	12
Eddie Guardado, Minnesota	-	-	-	-	-	-	2	1	-	1	12
Ichiro Suzuki, Seattle	-	-	-	-	-	-	-	1	3	1	10
Billy Koch, Oakland	-	-	-	-	-	-	2	-	-	-	8
Derek Lowe, Boston	-	-	-	-	-	-	-	-	1	1	3
Pedro Martinez, Boston	-	-	-	-	-	-	-	-	1	-	1
Mike Sweeney, Kansas City	-	-	-	-	-	-	-	-	-	1	1

Fourteen points awarded for a first-place vote, nine for second and down to one for 10th.

CY YOUNG AWARD

Pitcher, Team	1	2	3	Pts.
Barry Zito, Oakland	17	9	2	114
Pedro Martinez, Boston	11	12	5	96
Derek Lowe, Boston	-	7	20	41
Jarrod Washburn, Anaheim	-	-	1	1

Five points awarded for a first-place vote, three for second and one for third.

MANAGER OF THE YEAR

Manager, Team	1	2	3	Pts.
Mike Scioscia, Anaheim	17	10	1	116
Art Howe, Oakland	9	5	14	74
Ron Gardenhire, Minnesota	2	13	10	59
Joe Torre, New York	-	-	3	3

Five points awarded for a first-place vote, three for second and one for third.

ROOKIE OF THE YEAR

Player, Team	1	2	3	Pts.
Eric Hinske, Toronto	19	9	-	122
Rodrigo Lopez, Baltimore	9	17	1	97
Jorge Julio, Baltimore	-	1	11	14
Bobby Kielty, Minnesota	-	1	2	5
John Lackey, Anaheim	-	-	5	5
Josh Phelps, Toronto	-	-	3	3
Kevin Mench, Texas	-	-	2	2
Mark Ellis, Oakland	-	-	1	1
Tony Fiore, Minnesota	-	-	1	1
Dustan Mohr, Minnesota	-	-	1	1
Carlos Pena, Detroit	-	-	1	1

Five points awarded for a first-place vote, three for second and one for third.

MOST VALUABLE PLAYER

Player, Team	1	2	3	4	5	6	7	8	9	10	Pts.
Barry Bonds, San Francisco	32	-	-	-	-	-	-	-	-	-	448
Albert Pujols, St. Louis	-	26	4	-	1	-	1	-	-	-	276
Lance Berkman, Houston	-	1	7	5	6	5	2	3	1	1	181
Vladimir Guerrero, Montreal	-	4	5	3	3	5	2	3	5	1	168
Shawn Green, Los Angeles	-	-	3	8	4	3	2	3	3	4	146
Jeff Kent, San Francisco	-	-	3	2	4	8	5	2	3	1	135
Randy Johnson, Arizona	-	-	5	3	4	4	2	4	1	-	127
John Smoltz, Atlanta	-	1	3	5	2	1	6	2	3	3	124
Sammy Sosa, Chicago	-	-	-	2	3	1	1	4	4	2	63
Curt Schilling, Arizona	-	-	-	1	2	3	2	1	3	2	53
Chipper Jones, Atlanta	-	-	2	2	-	-	4	-	1	2	50
Eric Gagne, Los Angeles	-	-	-	1	2	1	1	4	1	2	44
Brian Giles, Pittsburgh	-	-	-	-	-	-	2	4	2	3	27
Junior Spivey, Arizona	-	-	-	-	-	-	2	-	-	-	8
Pat Burrell, Philadelphia	-	-	-	-	-	-	-	1	2	1	8
Andruw Jones, Atlanta	-	-	-	-	-	1	-	-	1	-	7
Gary Sheffield, Atlanta	-	-	-	-	1	-	-	-	-	-	6
Jim Edmonds, St. Louis	-	-	-	-	-	-	-	1	1	1	6
Todd Helton, Colorado	-	-	-	-	-	-	-	-	-	3	3
Benito Santiago, San Francisco	-	-	-	-	-	-	-	-	1	-	2
Edgar Renteria, St. Louis	-	-	-	-	-	-	-	-	-	2	2
Larry Walker, Colorado	-	-	-	-	-	-	-	-	-	2	2
Roy Oswalt, Houston	-	-	-	-	-	-	-	-	-	1	1
Jose Vidro, Montreal	-	-	-	-	-	-	-	-	-	1	1

Fourteen points awarded for a first-place vote, nine for second and down to one for 10th.

CY YOUNG AWARD

Pitcher, Team	1	2	3	Pts.
Randy Johnson, Arizona	32	-	-	160
Curt Schilling, Arizona	-	29	3	90
John Smoltz, Atlanta	-	1	18	21
Eric Gagne, Los Angeles	-	2	2	8
Roy Oswalt, Houston	-	-	8	8
Bartolo Colon, Montreal	-	-	1	1

Five points awarded for a first-place vote, three for second and one for third.

MANAGER OF THE YEAR

Manager, Team	1	2	3	Pts.
Tony La Russa, St. Louis	22	6	1	129
Bobby Cox, Atlanta	9	14	6	93
Frank Robinson, Montreal	-	6	5	23
Jim Tracy, Los Angeles	-	4	10	22
Dusty Baker, San Francisco	1	2	7	18
Bob Brenly, Arizona	-	-	2	2
Bob Boone, Cincinnati	-	-	1	1

Five points awarded for a first-place vote, three for second and one for third.

ROOKIE OF THE YEAR

Player, Team	1	2	3	Pts.
Jason Jennings, Colorado	27	5	-	150
Brad Wilkerson, Montreal	2	14	5	57
Austin Kearns, Cincinnati	2	8	6	40
Kazuhisa Ishii, Los Angeles	1	2	5	16
Damian Moss, Atlanta	-	2	6	12
Ryan Jensen, San Francisco	-	-	4	4
Mark Prior, Chicago	-	1	-	3
Josh Fogg, Pittsburgh	-	-	3	3
Alex Sanchez, Milwaukee	-	-	1	1
Jason Simontacchi, St. Louis	-	-	1	1
Dennis Stark, Colorado	-	-	1	1

Five points awarded for a first-place vote, three for second and one for third.

2002 REVIEW Award winners

MISCELLANEOUS

ATTENDANCE

AMERICAN LEAGUE

	2002				2001			*Pct.
	Home	Road	Dates	Home Avg.	Home	Dates	Average	Change
Seattle	3,540,482	2,233,145	81	43,710	3,507,975	81	43,308	+0.9
New York	3,461,644	2,940,048	80	43,271	3,264,777	80	40,810	+6.0
Baltimore	2,682,917	2,019,608	81	33,122	3,094,841	80	38,686	-14.4
Boston	2,650,063	2,474,060	81	32,717	2,625,333	81	32,412	+0.9
Cleveland	2,616,940	1,924,931	81	32,308	3,175,523	80	39,694	-18.6
Texas	2,352,447	2,251,033	80	29,406	2,806,399	81	34,647	-15.1
Anaheim	2,305,565	2,144,024	81	28,464	2,000,917	81	24,703	+15.2
Oakland	2,169,811	2,416,196	81	26,788	2,133,277	81	26,337	+1.7
Minnesota	1,924,473	2,144,110	81	23,759	1,782,926	80	22,287	+6.6
Chicago	1,676,804	2,075,811	81	20,701	1,766,172	80	22,077	-6.2
Toronto	1,636,904	2,086,535	81	20,209	1,915,438	81	23,647	-14.5
Detroit	1,503,623	2,033,697	80	18,795	1,921,305	80	24,016	-21.7
Kansas City	1,323,034	2,166,489	77	17,182	1,486,597	81	18,353	-6.4
Tampa Bay	1,065,762	2,122,092	81	13,158	1,227,673	81	15,156	-13.2
Totals	30,910,469	31,031,779	1127	27,427	32,709,153	1128	28,997	-5.4

*Percentage change refers to the change in average home attendance between 2002 and 2001.

NATIONAL LEAGUE

	2002				2001			*Pct.
	Home	Road	Dates	Home Avg.	Home	Dates	Average	Change
San Francisco	3,253,205	2,671,331	81	40,163	3,277,244	81	40,460	-0.7
Arizona	3,200,725	2,689,308	81	39,515	2,740,554	81	33,834	+16.8
Los Angeles	3,131,077	2,442,648	81	38,655	3,017,502	81	37,253	+3.8
St. Louis	3,011,756	2,311,490	81	37,182	3,113,091	81	38,433	-3.3
New York	2,804,838	2,141,748	78	35,959	2,617,433	81	32,314	+11.3
Colorado	2,737,918	2,372,413	81	33,801	3,159,385	81	39,005	-13.3
Chicago	2,693,071	2,621,840	78	34,527	2,744,387	79	34,739	-0.6
Atlanta	2,603,482	2,121,286	81	32,142	2,823,494	81	34,858	-7.8
Houston	2,517,407	2,237,917	81	31,079	2,904,280	81	35,855	-13.3
San Diego	2,220,416	2,414,675	81	27,413	2,377,969	80	29,725	-7.8
Milwaukee	1,969,693	2,111,690	81	24,317	2,811,041	81	34,704	-29.9
Cincinnati	1,855,973	2,319,051	80	23,200	1,882,732	79	23,832	-2.7
Pittsburgh	1,784,993	2,146,882	79	22,595	2,436,126	79	30,887	-26.7
Philadelphia	1,618,141	2,214,598	79	20,483	1,782,460	78	22,852	-10.4
Florida	813,111	2,028,570	81	10,038	1,261,220	80	15,765	-36.3
Montreal	732,901	1,981,950	81	9,048	609,473	81	7,524	+20.3
Totals	36,948,707	36,827,397	1285	28,754	39,558,391	1285	30,785	-6.6
Major League totals	67,859,176	67,859,176	2412	28,134	72,267,544	2413	29,949	-6.1

*Percentage change refers to the change in average home attendance between 2002 and 2001.

DEBUTS

Player	Pos.	Team	Birth date	Birthplace	Debut	*Age
Affeldt, Jeremy David	P	Kansas City	6- 6-79	Phoenix, Arizona	4-6	22
Allen, Lucas G.	PH	Los Angeles	8- 4-78	Covington, Georgia	9-10	24
Alvarez, Antonio Enrique	PH	Pittsburgh	5-10-79	Caracas, Venezuela	9-4	23
Alvarez, Victor	P	Los Angeles	11- 8-76	Culiacan, Mexico	7-30	25
Amezaga, Alfredo	SS	Anaheim	1-16-78	Obregon, Mexico	5-24	24
Asencio, Miguel DePaula	P	Kansas City	9-29-80	Villa Mella, Dominican Republic	4-6	21
Backe, Brandon Allen	P	Tampa Bay	4- 5-78	Galveston, Texas	7-19	24
Bard, Joshua David	C	Cleveland	3-30-78	Ithaca, New York	8-23	24
Bechler, Steven Scott	P	Baltimore	11-18-79	Medford, Oregon	9-6	22
Bedard, Erik Joseph	P	Baltimore	3- 6-79	Navan, Canada	4-17	23
Beltran, Francis	P	Chicago N.L.	11-29-79	Santo Domingo, Dominican Republic	6-28	22
Beverlin, Jason Robert	P	Cleveland	11-27-73	Ashtabula, Ohio	7-29	28
Blalock, Hank Joe	3B	Texas	11-21-80	San Diego, California	4-1	21
Bloomquist, William Paul	PR	Seattle	11-27-77	Bremerton, Washington	9-1	24
Bong, Jung Kuen	P	Atlanta	7-15-80	Seoul, South Korea	4-23	21
Borchard, Joseph Edward	RF	Chicago A.L.	11-25-78	Panorama City, California	9-2	23
Brazelton, Dewon Cortez	P	Tampa Bay	6-16-80	Tullahoma, Tennessee	9-13	22
Brito, Juan Ramon	C	Kansas City	11- 7-79	Santiago Rodriguez, Dominican Republic	5-3	22

Player	Pos.	Team	Birth date	Birthplace	Debut	*Age
Broussard, Benjamin Isaac	PH	Cleveland	9-24-76	Beaumont, Texas	6-22	25
Bukvich, Ryan Adrien	P	Kansas City	5-13-78	Naperville, Illinois	7-12	24
Burroughs, Sean Patrick	3B	San Diego	9-12-80	Atlanta, Georgia	4-2	21
Bynum, Michael Alan	P	San Diego	3-20-78	Tampa, Florida	8-17	24
Byrd, Marlon Jerrard	CF	Philadelphia	8-30-77	Boynton Beach, Florida	9-8	25
Carroll, Jamey Blake	3B	Montreal	2-18-74	Evansville, Indiana	9-11	28
Cash, Kevin Forrest	C	Toronto	12- 6-77	Tampa, Florida	9-6	24
Cassidy, Scott Robert	P	Toronto	10- 3-75	Syracuse, New York	4-1	26
Cepicky, Matthew William	RF	Montreal	11-10-77	St. Louis, Missouri	7-31	24
Cerda, Jaime M.	P	New York N.L.	10-26-78	Fresno, California	6-28	23
Chen, Chin-Feng	PH	Los Angeles	10-28-77	Tainan City, Taiwan	9-14	24
Childers, Matthew Wilkie	P	Milwaukee	12- 3-78	Douglas, Georgia	8-3	23
Choi, Hee Seop	1B	Chicago N.L.	3-16-79	Chun-Nam, South Korea	9-3	23
Clark, Howard Roddy	DH	Baltimore	2-13-74	San Diego, California	7-16	28
Condrey, Clayton Lee	P	San Diego	11-19-75	Beaumont, Texas	8-28	26
Cook, Aaron Lane	P	Colorado	2- 8-79	Ft. Campbell, Kentucky	8-10	23
Crawford, Carl Demonte	LF	Tampa Bay	8- 5-81	Houston, Texas	7-20	20
Crisp, Covelli Loyce	CF	Cleveland	11- 1-79	Los Angeles, California	8-15	22
Crudale, Michael Christopher	P	St. Louis	1- 3-77	San Diego, California	4-10	25
Cyr, Eric	P	San Diego	2-11-79	Montreal, Canada	6-23	23
Davis, Jason T.	P	Cleveland	5- 8-80	Chattanooga, Tennessee	9-9	22
Davis, Jerry C.	PH	Pittsburgh	10-25-78	Glendora, California	9-4	23
Dawley, Joseph Thomas	P	Atlanta	9-19-71	Riverside, California	9-29	31
Day, Stephen Zachary	P	Montreal	6-15-78	Cincinnati, Ohio	6-15	24
de los Santos, Luis	P	Tampa Bay	11- 1-77	Santo Domingo, Dominican Republic	7-20	24
Diaz, Juan Carlos	DH	Boston	2-19-74	San Jose de las Lajas, Cuba	6-12	28
Diggins, Benjamin H.	P	Milwaukee	6-13-79	Leota, Kansas	9-2	23
Donnelly, Brendan Kevin	P	Anaheim	7- 4-71	Washington, District of Columbia	4-9	30
Driskill, Travis Corey	P	Baltimore	8- 1-71	Omaha, Nebraska	4-26	30
DuBose, Eric Ladell	P	Baltimore	5-15-76	Bradenton, Florida	9-19	26
Duff, Matthew Clark	P	St. Louis	10- 6-74	Clarksdale, Mississippi	7-30	27
Durocher, Jayson Paul	P	Milwaukee	8-18-74	Hartford, Connecticut	6-11	27
Eckenstahler, Eric R.	P	Detroit	12-17-76	Waukegan, Illinois	9-9	25
Elder, David Matthew	P	Cleveland	9-23-75	Atlanta, Georgia	7-24	26
Ellis, Mark William	PR	Oakland	6- 6-77	Rapid City, South Dakota	4-9	24
Ennis, John Wayne	P	Atlanta	10-17-79	Montrose, Colorado	4-10	22
Escalona, Felix Eduardo	SS	Tampa Bay	3-12-79	Puerto Cabello, Venezuela	4-4	23
Farnsworth, Jeffrey Ellis	P	Detroit	10- 6-75	Wichita, Kansas	4-3	26
Feliciano, Pedro Juan	P	New York N.L.	8-25-76	Rio Piedras, Puerto Rico	9-4	26
Field, Nathan Patrick	P	Kansas City	12-11-75	Denver, Colorado	4-12	26
Figgins, Desmond DeChone	PR	Anaheim	1-22-78	Leary, Georgia	8-25	24
Fitzgerald, Brian Michael	P	Seattle	12-26-74	Woodbridge, Virginia	4-17	27
Flores, Jose Carlos	PR	Oakland	6-28-73	New York, New York	9-7	29
Flores, Randy Alan	P	Texas	7-31-75	Bellflower, California	4-23	26
Foster, John Norman	P	Atlanta	5-17-78	Stockton, California	4-24	23
Frederick, Kevin Albert Francis	P	Minnesota	11- 4-76	Evanston, Illinois	7-15	25
Garcia, Luis Carlos	PR	Baltimore	9-22-75	Hermosillo, Mexico	4-10	26
Garcia, Reynaldo	P	Texas	4-15-74	Nayua, Dominican Republic	7-19	28
Gardner, Terrence Lee	P	Tampa Bay	1-16-75	Hartland, Michigan	5-24	27
German, Esteban	2B	Oakland	1-26-78	Santo Domingo, Dominican Republic	5-21	24
German, Franklyn Miguel	P	Detroit	1-20-80	San Cristobal, Dominican Republic	9-7	22
Gomez, Alexis De Jesus	RF	Kansas City	8- 6-80	Loma de Cabrera, Dominican Republic	6-16	21
Grabowski, Jason William	LF	Oakland	5-24-76	New Haven, Connecticut	9-22	26
Gryboski, Kevin John	P	Atlanta	11-15-73	Wilkes-Barre, Pennsylvania	4-13	28
Guiel, Aaron Colin	PH	Kansas City	10- 5-72	Vancouver, Canada	6-22	29
Hafner, Travis Lee	PH	Texas	6- 3-77	Jamestown, North Dakota	8-6	25
Hall, William	3B	Milwaukee	12-28-79	Nettleton, Mississippi	9-1	22
Hancock, Joshua Morgan	P	Boston	4-11-78	Cleveland, Mississippi	9-10	24
Harang, Aaron Michael	P	Oakland	5- 9-78	San Diego, California	5-25	24
Hart, Jason Wyatt	PH	Texas	9- 5-77	Walnut Creek, California	8-18	24
Hendrickson, Mark A.	P	Toronto	6-23-74	Mount Vernon, Washington	8-6	28
Henson, Drew Daniel	PR	New York A.L.	2-13-80	San Diego, California	9-5	22
Hernandez, Runelvys Antonio	P	Kansas City	4-27-78	Santo Domingo, Dominican Republic	7-15	24
Herrera, Alexander J.	P	Cleveland	11- 5-76	Maracaibo, Venezuela	9-13	25
Hill, Jeremy Dee	P	Kansas City	8- 8-77	Dallas, Texas	9-7	25
Hill, William Robert	2B	Chicago N.L.	4- 3-78	San Jose, California	5-10	24
Hinske, Eric Scott	3B	Toronto	8- 5-77	Menasha, Wisconsin	4-1	24
Hodges, Trey Alan	P	Atlanta	6-29-78	Houston, Texas	9-10	24
Howard, Benjamin Richard	P	San Diego	1-15-79	Danville, Illinois	4-28	23
Hudson, Luke Stephen	P	Cincinnati	5- 2-77	Fountain Valley, California	7-1	25
Hudson, Orlando Thill	2B	Toronto	12-12-77	Darlington, South Carolina	7-24	24
Infante, Omar	SS	Detroit	12-26-81	Puerto la Cruz, Venezuela	9-7	20

Player	Pos.	Team	Birth date	Birthplace	Debut	*Age
Ishii, Kazuhisa	P	Los Angeles	9- 9-73	Chiba, Japan	4-6	28
Izquierdo, Hansel	P	Florida	1- 2-77	Havana, Cuba	4-21	25
James, Delvin Dewayne	P	Tampa Bay	1- 3-78	Nacogdoches, Texas	4-16	24
Jimenez, Jason Jon	P	Tampa Bay	1-10-76	Modesto, California	6-3	26
Joseph, Kevin John	P	St. Louis	8- 1-76	Camp Hill, Pennsylvania	8-1	25
Junge, Eric Debari	P	Philadelphia	1- 5-77	Manhasset, New York	9-11	25
Kaye, Justin Malcolm	P	Seattle	6- 9-76	Fort Lauderdale, Florida	5-9	25
Kearns, Austin Ryan	LF	Cincinnati	5-20-80	Lexington, Kentucky	4-17	21
Keller, Kristopher Shane	P	Detroit	3- 1-78	Williamsport, Pennsylvania	5-24	24
Kent, Steven Patrick	P	Tampa Bay	10- 3-78	Frankfurt, Germany	4-4	23
Kershner, Jason Ashley	P	San Diego	12-19-76	Scottsdale, Arizona	7-25	25
Komiyama, Satoru	P	New York N.L.	9-15-65	Chiba, Japan	4-4	36
Kozlowski, Benjamin Anthony	P	Texas	8-16-80	St. Petersburg, Florida	9-19	22
Lackey, John Derran	P	Anaheim	10-23-78	Abilene, Texas	6-24	23
Lane, Jason Dean	PH	Houston	12-22-76	Santa Rosa, California	5-10	25
Langerhans, Ryan David	LF	Atlanta	2-20-80	San Antonio, Texas	4-28	22
Lawrence, Joseph Dudley	2B	Toronto	2-13-77	Lake Charles, Louisiana	4-8	25
Lee, Clifton Phifer	P	Cleveland	8-30-78	Benton, Alaska	9-15	24
Leon, Jose Geraldo	1B	Baltimore	12- 8-76	Caguas, Puerto Rico	6-16	25
Lewis, Colby Preston	P	Texas	8- 2-79	Bakersfield, California	4-1	22
Lidge, Bradley Thomas	P	Houston	12-23-76	Sacramento, California	4-26	25
Loux, Shane A.	P	Detroit	8-31-79	Rapid City, South Dakota	9-10	23
Ludwick, Ryan Andrew	RF	Texas	7-13-78	Satellite Beach, Florida	6-5	23
Lunsford, James L.	C	San Francisco	5-25-79	Odessa, Texas	9-12	23
Mallette, Brian Mallette	P	Milwaukee	1-19-75	Dublin, Georgia	4-12	27
Maroth, Michael Warren	P	Detroit	8-17-77	Orlando, Florida	6-8	24
Martinez, Victor Jesus	C	Cleveland	12-23-78	Ciudad Bolivar, Venezuela	9-10	23
Mateo, Julio Cesar	P	Seattle	8- 2-77	Bani, Dominican Republic	5-7	24
Matos, Julius	RF	San Diego	12-12-74	New York, New York	5-31	27
McKay, Cody Dean	PH	Oakland	1-11-74	Vancouver, Canada	9-22	28
Mench, Kevin Ford	LF	Texas	1- 7-78	Wilmington, Delaware	4-9	24
Miller, Justin Mark	P	Toronto	8-27-77	Torrance, California	4-12	24
Moriarty, Michael Thomas	PH	Baltimore	3- 8-74	Camden, New Jersey	4-11	28
Myers, Brett Allen	P	Philadelphia	8-17-80	Jacksonville, Florida	7-24	21
Nance, Joseph Shane	P	Milwaukee	9- 7-77	Pasadena, Texas	8-24	24
Nelson, Bryant Lawrence	RF	Boston	1-27-74	Crossett, Arkansas	5-14	28
Nieves, Wilbert	C	San Diego	9-25-77	San Juan, Puerto Rico	7-21	24
Nomura, Takahito	P	Milwaukee	1-10-69	Kouchi, Japan	4-3	33
Nunez, Abraham	PR	Florida	2- 5-77	Haina, Dominican Republic	9-3	25
Obermueller, Wesley Mitchell	P	Kansas City	12-22-76	Cedar Rapids, Iowa	9-20	25
Olivo, Miguel Eduardo	C	Chicago A.L.	7-15-78	Monte Cristi, Dominican Republic	9-15	24
Patterson, John Hollis	P	Arizona	1-30-78	Orange, Texas	7-20	24
Pearce, Joshua Ray	P	St. Louis	8-20-77	Yakima, Washington	4-20	24
Pearson, Jason John	P	San Diego	12-29-75	Freeport, Illinois	6-4	26
Pearson, Terry G.	P	Detroit	11-10-71	Tuscaloosa, Alabama	4-4	30
Peavy, Jacob Edward	P	San Diego	5-31-81	Mobile, Alabama	6-22	21
Pelaez, Alejandro	1B	San Diego	4- 6-76	San Diego, California	5-16	26
Pellow, Kit Donovan	1B	Kansas City	8-28-73	Kansas City, Missouri	8-14	28
Pember, David J.	P	Milwaukee	5-24-78	Cincinnati, Ohio	9-3	24
Pena, Wily Modesto	PH	Cincinnati	1-23-82	Laguna Salada, Dominican Republic	9-10	20
Perez, Oliver	P	San Diego	8-15-81	Culiacan, Mexico	6-16	20
Phillips, Brandon Emil	2B	Cleveland	6-28-81	Raleigh, North Carolina	9-13	21
Pickford, Kevin Patrick	P	San Diego	3-12-75	Fresno, California	5-16	27
Pratt, Andrew Elias	P	Atlanta	8-27-79	Mesa, Arizona	9-28	23
Prior, Mark William	P	Chicago N.L.	9- 7-80	San Diego, California	5-22	21
Puffer, Brandon Duane	P	Houston	10- 5-75	Downey, California	4-17	26
Rauch, Jon Erich	P	Chicago A.L.	9-27-78	Louisville, Kentucky	4-2	23
Restovich, Michael Jerome	RF	Minnesota	1- 3-79	Rochester, Minnesota	9-18	23
Robertson, Jeriome Paul	P	Houston	3-30-77	San Jose, California	9-2	25
Robertson, Nathan D.	P	Florida	9- 3-77	Wichita, Kansas	9-7	25
Rodney, Fernando	P	Detroit	3-18-77	Samana, Dominican Republic	5-4	25
Rodriguez, Francisco Jose	P	Anaheim	1- 7-82	Caracas, Venezuela	9-18	20
Rodriguez, Ricardo Antonio	P	Cleveland	5-21-78	Manga, Dominican Republic	8-21	24
Rogers, Edward Antonio	SS	Baltimore	8-29-78	San Pedro de Macoris, Dominican Republic	9-5	24
Romano, Jason Anthony	LF	Texas	6-24-79	Tampa, Florida	4-17	22
Ross, David Wade	PH	Los Angeles	3-19-77	Bainbridge, Georgia	6-29	25
Ruan, Wilkin Chal	PR	Los Angeles	9-18-78	Ramon Santana, Dominican Republic	9-1	23
Rushford, James Thomas	LF	Milwaukee	3-24-74	Chicago, Illinois	9-3	28
Ryan, Michael Sean	LF	Minnesota	7- 6-77	Indiana, Pennsylvania	9-20	25
Saarloos, Kirk Craig	P	Houston	5-23-79	Long Beach, California	6-18	23
Sadler, William Carl	P	Cleveland	10-11-76	Gainesville, Florida	7-31	25
Salazar, Oscar Enrique	PR	Detroit	6-27-78	Maracay, Venezuela	4-10	23

Player	Pos.	Team	Birth date	Birthplace	Debut	*Age
Sanchez, Duaner	P	Arizona	10-14-79	Cotui, Dominican Republic	6-14	22
Sanchez, Frederick P.	PH	Boston	12-21-77	Hollywood, California	9-10	24
Santiago, Ramon D.	SS	Detroit	8-31-79	Las Matas de Farfan, Dominican Republic	5-17	22
Scutaro, Marcos	2B	New York N.L.	10-30-75	Yaracuy, Venezuela	7-21	26
Sears, Todd Andrew	1B	Minnesota	10-23-75	Des Moines, Iowa	9-17	26
Sedlacek, Shawn Patrick	P	Kansas City	6-29-77	Cedar Rapids, Iowa	6-18	24
Seo, Jae Weong	P	New York N.L.	5-24-77	Kwanju, South Korea	7-21	25
Shiell, Jason Alexander	P	San Diego	10-19-76	Savannah, Georgia	9-8	25
Silva, Carlos	P	Philadelphia	4-23-79	Bolivar, Venezuela	4-1	22
Simontacchi, Jason William	P	St. Louis	11-13-73	Mountain View, California	5-4	28
Smith, Michael Anthony	P	Toronto	9-19-77	Norwood, Massachusetts	4-26	24
Smyth, Steven Delton	P	Chicago N.L.	6- 3-78	Brawley, California	8-6	24
Snead, Esix	PR	New York N.L.	6- 7-76	Fort Myers, Florida	9-3	26
Snelling, Christopher Doyle	LF	Seattle	12- 3-81	North Miami, Florida	5-25	20
Snyder, Earl Clifford	PH	Cleveland	5- 6-76	New Britain, Connecticut	4-28	25
Soriano, Rafael	P	Seattle	12-19-79	San Jose, Dominican Republic	5-10	22
Sosa, Jorge Bolivar	P	Tampa Bay	4-28-77	Santo Domingo, Dominican Republic	4-4	24
Stephens, John M.	P	Baltimore	11-15-79	Sydney, Australia	7-30	22
Strange, Patrick Martin	P	New York N.L.	8-23-80	Springfield, Massachusetts	9-13	22
Taguchi, So	CF	St. Louis	7- 2-69	Hyogo Prefecture, Japan	6-10	32
Tallet, Brian Curtis	P	Cleveland	9-21-77	Midwest City, Oklahoma	9-16	24
Tankersley, Dennis Lee	P	San Diego	2-24-79	Troy, Missouri	5-10	23
Taylor, Aaron Wade	P	Seattle	8-20-77	Valdosta, Georgia	9-9	25
Teut, Nathan Mark	P	Florida	3-11-76	Newton, Iowa	5-4	26
Thames, Marcus Markey	RF	New York A.L.	3- 6-77	Louisville, Mississippi	6-10	25
Thurman, Corey Lamar	P	Toronto	11- 5-78	Augusta, Georgia	4-5	23
Thurston, Joseph William	2B	Los Angeles	9-29-79	Fairfield, California	9-2	22
Torcato, Anthony Dale	RF	San Francisco	10-25-79	Woodland, California	7-26	22
Torres, Andres	CF	Detroit	1-26-78	Aguada, Puerto Rico	4-7	24
Trujillo, John	P	San Diego	10- 9-75	Corpus Christi, Texas	6-11	26
Ugueto, Luis Enrique	PR	Seattle	2-15-79	Caracas, Venezuela	4-3	23
Van Hekken, Andrew William	P	Detroit	7-31-79	Holland, Michigan	9-3	23
Vance, Cory	P	Colorado	6-20-79	Dayton, Ohio	9-21	23
Walker, Tyler Lanier	P	New York N.L.	5-15-76	San Francisco, California	7-2	26
Wathan, Dustin James	C	Kansas City	8-22-73	Jacksonville, Florida	9-24	29
Wayne, Justin Morgan	P	Florida	4-16-79	Honolulu, Hawaii	9-3	23
Werth, Jayson Richard	RF	Toronto	5-20-79	Springfield, Illinois	9-1	23
Wesson, Barry Jarvis	CF	Houston	4- 6-77	Tupelo, Mississippi	7-15	25
Wiggins, Scott Joseph	P	Toronto	3-24-76	Fort Thomas, Kentucky	9-11	26
Wigginton, Ty Allen	PH	New York N.L.	10-11-77	San Diego, California	5-16	24
Wright, Ronald Wade	DH	Seattle	1-21-76	Delta, Utah	4-14	26
Zinter, Alan Michael	PH	Houston	5-19-68	El Paso, Texas	6-18	34

*Denotes age on date of debut.

SALARY ARBITRATION RESULTS

WINNER

Player, Team	Salary awarded	Team's offer
Dennys Reyes, Colorado	$900,000	$700,000

LOSERS

Player, Team	Salary awarded	Player's request
Neifi Perez, Kansas City	$4,100,000	$5,000,000
Orlando Cabrera, Montreal	$2,400,000	$3,100,000
Rolando Arrojo, Boston	$1,900,000	$2,800,000
Esteban Yan, Tampa Bay	$1,500,000	$2,400,000

AMERICAN LEAGUE

Anaheim: Dennis Cook, Alex Ochoa, Orlando Palmeiro.
Baltimore: Mike Bordick.
Boston: Shane Andrews, Carlos Baerga, Willie Banks, Frank Castillo, Tony Clark, Cliff Floyd, Rickey Henderson, Dustin Hermanson, Rey Sanchez, Ugueth Urbina.
Chicago: Frank Thomas.
Cleveland: Dave Burba, Terry Mulholland, Charles Nagy, Eduardo Perez, Lee Stevens, Jim Thome.
Detroit: Juan Acevedo, Matt Walbeck.
Kansas City: Luis Alicea, Paul Byrd, Roberto Hernandez, Chuck Knoblauch.
Minnesota: Mike Jackson, Bob Wells.
New York: Alex Arias, Roger Clemens, Ron Coomer, Ramiro Mendoza, Mike Stanton, John Vander Wal, Robin Ventura, Chris Widger.
Oakland: Ray Durham, David Justice, John Mabry, Greg Myers, Randy Velarde.
Seattle: James Baldwin, Pat Borders, Norm Charlton, Jamie Moyer, Jose Offerman, John Olerud, Ruben Sierra, Ismael Valdes.
Tampa Bay: John Flaherty.
Texas: Bill Haselman, Todd Hollandsworth, Ivan Rodriguez, Rich Rodriguez, Kenny Rogers, Rudy Seanez.
Toronto: Felix Heredia, Esteban Loaiza, Steve Parris.

NATIONAL LEAGUE

Arizona: Brian Anderson, Jay Bell, Jeff Colbrunn, Chris Donnels, Mike Fetters, Steve Finley, Mark Grace, Rick Helling, Mike Morgan, Armando Reynoso.
Atlanta: Darren Bragg, Julio Franco, Tom Glavine, Chris Hammond, Darren Holmes, Keith Lockhart, Albie Lopez, Greg Maddux, Dave Martinez, Mike Remlinger, B.J. Surhoff.
Chicago: Jason Bere, Joe Girardi, Jon Lieber, Pat Mahomes, Fred McGriff.
Cincinnati: Shawn Estes, Joey Hamilton, Jimmy Haynes, Brian Moehler, Jose Rijo.
Colorado: Sandy Alomar Jr., Pete Harnisch, Kent Mercker, Terry Shumpert, Todd Zeile.
Florida: Graeme Lloyd, Tim Raines Sr., Julian Tavarez.
Houston: Pedro Borbon, Doug Brocail, Tom Gordon, Chad Kreuter, Mark Loretta, Dave Mlicki, Shane Reynolds.
Los Angeles: Omar Daal, Marquis Grissom, Dave Hansen, Tyler Houston, Jesse Orosco, Jeff Reboulet.
Milwaukee: Jorge Fabregas, Lenny Harris, Jose A. Hernandez, Matt Stairs.
Montreal: Wil Cordero, Andres Galarraga, Troy O'Leary.
New York: Edgardo Alfonso, Jeff C. D'Amico, Mark Guthrie, Steve Reed, Steve Trachsel, John Valentin.
Philadelphia: Terry Adams, Ricky Bottalico, Doug Glanville, Dave Hollins, Robert Person, Dan Plesac, Todd Pratt, Mike Timlin.
Pittsburgh: Mike Benjamin, Brian Boehringer, Darren Lewis, Keith Osik, Ron Villone.
St. Louis: Andy Benes, Mike DiFelice, Jeff Fassero, Chuck Finley, Dave Veres, Rick White, Woody Williams, Jamey Wright.
San Diego: Deivi Cruz, Ron Gant, Tom Lampkin, Ray Lankford.
San Francisco: David Bell, Shawon Dunston, Tom Goodwin, Jeff Kent, Kenny Lofton, Bill Mueller, Reggie Sanders.

(Listed in order of selection)

Player	Pos.	Drafted by	Drafted from (major league organization)
Enrique Cruz	SS	Milwaukee	Norfolk, International League (Mets)
Hector Luna	SS	Tampa Bay	Buffalo, International League (Indians)
Carl Hernandez III	RHP	San Diego	Richmond, International League (Braves)
Wilfredo Ledezma	LHP	Detroit	Pawtucket, International League (Red Sox)
Derek Thompson	LHP	Chicago Cubs	Buffalo, International League (Indians)
Daniel Carrasco	RHP	Kansas City	Nashville, Pacific Coast League (Pirates)
Matthew Roney	RHP	Pittsburgh	Colorado Springs, Pacific Coast League (Rockies)
Victor Hall	CF	Colorado	Tucson, Pacific Coast League (Diamondbacks)
Marshall McDougall	3B	Texas	Buffalo, International League (Indians)
Travis Chapman	3B	Cleveland	Scranton/Wilkes-Barre, International League (Phillies)
Kenneth Prokopec	RHP	Cincinnati	Las Vegas, Pacific Coast League (Dodgers)
Aquilino Lopez	RHP	Toronto	Tacoma, Pacific Coast League (Mariners)
Javier Lopez	LHP	Boston	Tucson, Pacific Coast League (Diamondbacks)
Luis Ayala	RHP	Montreal	Tucson, Pacific Coast League (Diamondbacks)
Jose Morban	SS	Minnesota	Oklahoma, Pacific Coast League (Rangers)
Michael Neu	RHP	Oakland	Louisville, International League (Reds)
Christopher Spurling	RHP	Atlanta	Nashville, Pacific Coast League (Pirates)
Matthew Ford	LHP	Milwaukee	Syracuse, International League (Blue Jays)
Shane Victorino	CF	San Diego	Las Vegas, Pacific Coast League (Dodgers)
Ronny Paulino	C	Kansas City	Nashville, Pacific Coast League (Pirates)
John Koronka	LHP	Texas	Louisville, International League (Reds)
Blake Williams	RHP	Cincinnati	Memphis, Pacific Coast League (Cardinals)
Gary Majewski	RHP	Toronto	Charlotte, International League (White Sox)
Matthew White	LHP	Boston	Buffalo, International League (Indians)
Rontrez Johnson	OF	Oakland	Oklahoma, Pacific Coast League (Rangers)
Jerome Gamble	RHP	Cincinnati	Pawtucket, International League (Red Sox)
Jason Dubois	OF	Toronto	Iowa, Pacific Coast League (Cubs)
Adrian Brown	CF	Boston	Durham, International League (Devil Rays)

Fritz Ackley, 65, at Duluth, Minn., on May 22. Ackley, a right-hander, pitched in a total of five games for the White Sox in 1963 and 1964.

Bill Adair, 86, at Bay Minette, Ala., on June 17. A minor league manager for more than two decades, he was a coach for the Milwaukee Braves in 1962, the Atlanta Braves in 1967, the White Sox in 1970 and the Expos in 1976. He also was briefly interim manager of the White Sox in '70.

Hank Arft, 80, at Chesterfield, Mo., on December 14. First base-man Arft saw action with the St. Louis Browns from 1948 through 1952. His most extensive duty came in 1951 when he appeared in 112 games.

Bob Barr, 94, at Dover, N.H., on August 1. Barr made two relief appearances for Brooklyn in 1935.

Nelson Barrera, 44, electrocuted in an accident at home in Campeche, Mexico, on July 14. Barrera was the Mexican League's all-time leader in home runs with 455.

Lefty Bertrand, 93, at The Dalles, Ore., on March 17. He pitched in one game for the 1936 Phillies.

Joe Black, 78, at Scottsdale, Ariz., on May 17. Righthander Black was the National League's Rookie of the Year in 1952, a season in which he posted a 15-4 record and a 2.15 ERA for the Dodgers. Black made 54 relief appearances in '52, winning 14 times in that role and saving 15 games. He started three World Series games that year, beating the Yankees in Game 1 before los-ing Games 4 and 7. He was the first black pitcher to win a Series game. Later bothered by arm trouble, he was traded to the Reds in 1955 and wound up his career with Washington in 1957.

Jimmy Bloodworth, 85, at Apalachicola, Fla., on August 17. Playing his next-to-last season in an 11-year major league career, Bloodworth was a reserve infielder for the 1950 pennant-winning Phillies. His career included regular duty at second base for the Washington Senators, Detroit, Pittsburgh and Cincinnati. He bat-ted .248 in 1,002 big-league games.

Hank Boney, 98, at Lake Worth, Fla., on June 12. Boney, a right-hander, made three relief appearances for the 1927 New York Giants.

Mace Brown, 92, at Greensboro, N.C., on March 24. Primarily a relief pitcher, he compiled a 76-57 record over 10 major league seasons. Brown went 15-9 for the Pirates in 1938 and 9-3 for the Red Sox in 1942. Late in the '38 season, the righthander yielded Gabby Hartnett's "Homer in the Gloamin'" at Wrigley Field—a ninth-inning, game-winning home run with darkness descending that enabled the pennant-bound Cubs to wrest the league lead from Pittsburgh.

Jack Buck, 77, at St. Louis on June 18. Buck broadcast Cardinals games for nearly a half-century, beginning in 1954 when he joined Harry Caray in the Cards' booth. When Caray left St. Louis after the 1969 season, Buck soon emerged as one of the best and most popular announcers in the game. In 1987, he was enshrined in the broadcasters' wing of the Baseball Hall of Fame.

Don Carlsen, 75, at Denver on September 22. Righthander Carlsen made one appearance for the Cubs in 1948 and a total of 12 for the Pirates in 1951 and 1952.

Joe Cascarella, 94, at Baltimore on May 22. The righthander broke into the majors in 1934, posting a 12-15 record for the Phila-delphia Athletics. He was 15-33 in his other four big-league seasons.

Harry Chiti, 69, at Haines City, Fla., on January 31. Chiti saw catching duty for the Cubs, Kansas City Athletics, Tigers and orig-inal (1962) Mets in a 10-season major league career. He played extensively for the Cubs in 1955 and the A's in 1958.

Chet Clemens, 84, at San Clemente, Calif., on February 10. Outfielder Clemens played a total of 28 games for the Boston Bees/Braves in 1939 and 1944.

Pete Coscarart, 89, at Escondido, Calif., on July 24. Coscarart, a light-hitting infielder, appeared in 115 or more games in six major league seasons and played sparingly in three other years. Coscarart was Brooklyn's No. 1 second baseman in 1939 and 1940, but he lost his job to Billy Herman early in the 1941 season when the Dodgers obtained Herman from the Cubs. Coscarart started the final two games of the '41 World Series when Herman was sidelined because of an injury.

Al Cowens, 50, at Downey, Calif., on March 11. Cowens was the regular right fielder for the Royals' 1976, 1977 and 1978 A.L. West Division championship teams. In '77, he hit 23 homers, drove in 112 runs and batted .312. He hit .270 over 13 big-league seasons.

Jack Creel, 86, at Houston on August 13. Despite being born with slightly deformed hands, righthander Creel made it to the majors with the Cardinals in 1945, his only big-league season.

Frank Crosetti, 91, at Stockton, Calif., on February 11. As a player and then a coach, he wore a Yankees uniform for 37 con-secutive seasons. Crosetti, the Yanks' shortstop during the club's four consecutive World Series titles in the late 1930s, was a solid defender and light hitter who played in seven Series for New York and coached in 15 other Fall Classics for the Yankees. In 1938, he led the A.L. in stolen bases with 27. He was a coach for the Yankees from 1947 through 1968.

Mike Darr, 25, in a highway accident near Phoenix on February 15. Padres outfielder Darr appeared in 105 games in 2001 and batted .277. In 188 major league games over three seasons, he hit .273 for San Diego.

Bob Davids, 75, at Washington, D.C., on February 10. Davids founded the Society for American Baseball Research in 1971.

John "Red" Davis, 86, at Laurel, Miss., on April 26. Davis, who was a minor league manager for 27 seasons, played 21 games with the New York Giants in 1941.

Sam Dente, 79, at Montclair, N.J., on April 21. Dente, primarily a shortstop, played for the Red Sox, St. Louis Browns, Washington Senators, White Sox and Indians in a nine-season major league career that began in 1947. His best season was 1949, when he played in 153 games for the Senators and batted .273.

Paul Erickson, 86, at Fond du Lac, Wis., on April 5. Erickson compiled a 37-48 record while pitching in the majors from 1941 through 1948. The righthander made 201 of his 207 career appearances for the Cubs, for whom he relieved in four games in the 1945 World Series.

Ralph Erickson, 100, at Chandler, Ariz., on June 27. Lefthander Erickson made a total of eight relief appearances for the Pirates in 1929 and 1930.

Bill Faul, 61, at Cincinnati on February 21. Faul, a righthander, was a starter/reliever over six seasons in the majors. His best year was 1965, when he went 6-6 for the Cubs and tossed three shutouts.

Earl Francis, 65, at Pittsburgh on July 3. Righthander Francis, who spent most of his six-year big-league career with the Pirates, compiled a 9-8 record and a 3.07 ERA for Pittsburgh in 1962, his best season in the majors.

Jim Gallagher, 97, at Harrisonburg, Va., on April 9. Gallagher was a key member of the Cubs' front office from 1941 through 1956, serving first as general manager and later as business manager. Gallagher was G.M. when the Cubs won their last pen-nant, in 1945.

Paul Giel, 69, at Minneapolis on May 22. Giel, a baseball and football star at the University of Minnesota, signed a bonus con-tract with the New York Giants in 1954 and went on to pitch in 102 major league games over six seasons. Used mostly in relief, the righthander pitched for the Giants, Pirates, Twins and Athletics and compiled an 11-9 record.

Pete Gray, 87, at Sheatown, Pa., on June 30. Gray, who lost his right arm in a childhood accident, was given a wartime shot at major league ball at age 30 and hit .218 in 234 at-bats for the 1945 St. Louis Browns.

Steve Gromek, 82, at Clinton, Mich., on March 12. Gromek won 19 games for the 1945 Indians and posted 18 victories for the 1954 Tigers. Over 17 big-league seasons (12-plus with Cleveland, the remainder with Detroit), the righthander compiled a 123-108 record. Pitching for Cleveland, he threw a seven-hitter in Game 4 of the 1948 World Series and beat the Boston Braves, 2-1.

Warren Hacker, 77, at Lenzburg, Ill., on May 22. Hacker pitched for the Cubs from 1948 through 1956 and posted double-digit victory totals three times. The righthander's best season was 1952, when he went 15-9, fashioned a 2.58 ERA, tossed five shutouts and allowed only 144 hits in 185 innings. Hacker later pitched for the Reds, Phillies and White Sox, finishing his career with a 62-89 record.

Andy Hansen, 77, at Lake Worth, Fla., on February 2. Hansen pitched in 270 big-league games, 231 of them in relief, over nine years in the majors. The righthander was 15-21 in six seasons with the Giants and 8-9 in three years with the Phillies.

Mel Harder, 93, at Chardon, Ohio, on October 20. He pitched all 20 of his major league seasons for the Indians, winning 223 games (second on Cleveland's all-time list, behind Bob Feller's 266). The righthander was a double-figure winner 13 times, notching 20 victories in 1934 (a year in which he hurled six shutouts) and 22 in 1935. He pitched in four All-Star Games and did not allow a run in 13 innings. Harder later served five teams (including the Indians) as a pitching coach.

Mickey Haslin, 91, at Wilkes-Barre, Pa., on March 7. Infielder Haslin played in 318 big-league games. His most extensive duty came in 1935, when he appeared in 110 games with the Phillies and batted .265. Haslin, who played from 1933 through 1938, also saw duty with the Braves and Giants.

Ray Hayworth, 98, at Salisbury, N.C., on September 25. Hayworth was the backup catcher for the Tigers' 1934 A.L. champions and Detroit's 1935 World Series titlists. A major leaguer for 15 seasons, he saw his most extensive duty in 1933, when he appeared in 134 games for Detroit and batted .245. An excellent defensive catcher, Hayworth played in 699 major league games and hit .265 overall.

Willis Hudlin, 96, at Little Rock, Ark., on August 5. Righthander Hudlin was a double-figure winner for Cleveland nine times in an 11-year stretch and racked up 157 victories for the Indians in 13 full years with the club and brief duty in two other seasons. After breaking into the majors with eight appearances for the Indians in 1926, Hudlin compiled an 18-12 record in 1927. His best overall season was 1929, when he won 17 games and fashioned a career-low 3.34 ERA. Also in '29, he allowed the 500th home run of Babe Ruth's career.

Jack Jenkins, 59, at Tampa on June 18. Righthander Jenkins appeared in three games for Washington in 1962, four games for the Senators in 1963 and one game for the Dodgers in 1969. He was 0-3 overall.

Lou Kahn, 85, at Albany, Ga., on March 13. A catcher, coach and manager in a longtime minor league career, he was a Cardinals coach for part of the 1955 season.

Irv Kaze, 75, at Glendale, Calif., on June 29. Kaze was the first public relations director for the Angels, an expansion franchise that made its debut in 1961, and he later was head of media relations for the Yankees. Kaze also worked in other professional sports and was a Los Angeles radio talk-show host at the time of his death.

Darryl Kile, 33, at Chicago on June 22. Cardinals righthander Kile, pitching in his 12th big-league season, was found dead in his room in a Chicago hotel; his death was attributed to blockage of the coronary arteries. Originally a member of the Astros organization, Kile compiled a 133-119 record in the majors. He won 20 games for St. Louis in 2000, went 19-7 with a 2.57 ERA for the Astros in 1997 and finished 15-8 for Houston in 1993 (a year

in which he threw a no-hitter against the Mets). Kile spent seven seasons with Houston, two with Colorado after signing a free-agent contract with the Rockies in December 1997 and was in his third year with St. Louis.

Ron Kline, 70, at Callery, Pa., on June 22. The righthander was a key member of the Pirates' rotation from 1955 through 1959. He compiled a 14-18 record (3.38 ERA) in 1956 and a 13-16 mark (3.53 ERA) in 1958. Kline was traded to the Cardinals after the '59 season, and he moved on to the American League in 1961 (a year he split between the new Los Angeles Angels and the Tigers). By 1962, he was pitching almost exclusively out of the bullpen for Detroit. He was 114-144 over 17 major league seasons.

John Lazor, 90, at Renton, Wash., on December 9. Outfielder Lazor was primarily a wartime player for Red Sox. He saw his most extensive duty in 1945, when he had 335 at-bats and hit .310. He appeared in a total of 99 games in 1943 and 1944 and wound up his career with a 23-game stint for the Sox in 1946.

Izzy Leon, 91, at Miami on July 25. Righthander Leon appeared in 14 games for the 1945 Phillies and was 0-4.

Hal Marnie, 83, at Philadelphia on January 7. Infielder Marnie played a total of 96 games for the Phillies from 1940 through 1942.

Ned Martin, 78, at Raleigh, N.C., on July 23. Martin called Red Sox games on radio and television from 1961 through 1992.

Lee Maye, 67, at Riverside, Calif., on July 17. Outfielder Maye, who played for the Milwaukee Braves, Astros, Indians, Senators and White Sox, batted .274 over 13 major league seasons. His best year was 1964, when he played 153 games for Milwaukee and hit a league-leading 44 doubles.

Ed McGah, 81, at Oakland, Calif., on September 30. McGah, a catcher, appeared in 15 games for the pennant-winning Red Sox of 1946 and in nine games for the A.L. club in 1947. He later was a longtime limited partner in the ownership of pro football's Raiders franchise.

Mel McGaha, 75, at Tulsa, Okla., on February 3. Having reached only Class AAA as a player, McGaha went on to become a major league manager. He guided the Indians to an 80-82 record in 1962 and compiled a 45-91 mark while managing the Kansas City A's over parts of the 1964 and 1965 seasons.

Jim McKee, 55, near Columbus, Ohio, in an automobile accident on September 14. McKee posted a 1-1 record while making a total of 17 appearances for the Pirates in 1972 and 1973.

Dave McNally, 60, at Billings, Mont., on December 1. Left-hander McNally built a .607 winning percentage (184-119) over 14 major league seasons. McNally, who came up with the Baltimore in 1962 and pitched for the Orioles through 1974, won 20 or more games in four consecutive years (1968 through 1971) and tossed 33 career shutouts. In 1968, he won 22 games and fashioned a 1.95 ERA; in 1968-69, he won 17 consecutive decisions, equaling a since-broken A.L. record; and in 1970, he tied for the league lead in victories with 24. McNally capped the Orioles' sweep of the Dodgers in the 1966 World Series with a four-hit shutout; four years later, when Baltimore defeated Cincinnati in the Fall Classic, he became the only pitcher in Series history to hit a grand slam. Dealt to the Expos in late 1974, McNally finished his career with 12 starts for Montreal in 1975, a year in which he and Dodgers pitcher Andy Messersmith played without contracts and challenged baseball's reserve clause. McNally and Messersmith were declared free agents, a landmark ruling that ushered in the era of free agency.

Roy Nichols, 81, at Hot Springs, Ark., on April 3. Infielder Nichols appeared in 11 games for the 1944 Giants.

Dick O'Connell, 87, at Lexington, Mass., on August 18. O'Connell became general manager of the Red Sox in September 1965 and served through 1977. He oversaw two pennant-winning seasons in Boston—the Red Sox's Impossible Dream feat of 1967 and their A.L. title year of 1975.

Sam Page, 86, at Greenville, S.C., on May 29. A righthander who appeared in four games with the 1939 Philadelphia Athletics, Page lost all three of his decisions as a major leaguer.

Mike Payne, 40, at Dunnellon, Fla., on August 4. Payne made one start and two relief appearances for the 1984 Braves. He was 0-1.

Les Peden, 78, at Jacksonville on February 11. Peden's major league career consisted of 28 at-bats for the 1953 Senators. The catcher collected seven hits—one of them a home run.

Darrell Porter, 50, at Sugar Creek, Mo., on August 5. Porter, a catcher, played 17 years in the major leagues. Playing for Kansas City in '79, he achieved career highs in home runs (20), RBIs (112) and batting average (.291). Three years later, as a member of the Cardinals, Porter won MVP honors in both the N.L. Championship Series (.556 average) and the World Series (.286, eight hits, five RBIs). He spent six seasons with the Brewers, four with the Royals, five with the Cards and two with the Rangers, batting .247 overall with 188 home runs.

Bob Poser, 92, at Columbus, Wis., on May 21. Poser pitched in one game for the 1932 White Sox and in four games for the 1935 St. Louis Browns.

Dykes Potter, 91, at Greenup, Ky., on February 27. Potter made two relief appearances for Brooklyn in 1938.

Steve Rachunok, 85, at Corona, Calif., on May 11. Rachunok pitched in two games for Brooklyn in 1940.

Kenny Raffensberger, 85, at York, Pa., on November 10. Lefthander Raffensberger, who pitched for the Cardinals, Cubs, Phillies and Reds, went 119-154 over 15 big-league seasons. A 20-game loser for the Phils in 1944, he posted victory totals of 18, 14, 16 and 17 for the Reds from 1949 through 1952 and twice shared the National League lead in shutouts over that time. He was the winning pitcher in the '44 All-Star Game.

Minnie Rojas, 63, at Los Angeles on March 24. Rojas, who made 45 relief appearances and two starts for the Angels in his rookie year of 1966 and compiled a 2.88 ERA that season, was The Sporting News' A.L. Fireman of the Year in 1967 when he saved 27 games and won 12 others for the Angels. Two years later, righthander Rojas, beset by arm problems, was back in the minors. In the spring of 1970, he was paralyzed as the result of injuries suffered in an automobile accident in Florida.

Johnny Roseboro, 69, at Los Angeles on August 16. Roseboro was the Dodgers' No. 1 catcher in their first 10 seasons in Los Angeles, 1958 through 1967, years in which the Dodgers won four pennants and three World Series titles. He batted a personal-best .287 in 1964 and hit a career-high 18 home runs in 1961. Known for his toughness, Roseboro was a great handler of pitchers—and he worked with such standouts as Don Drysdale and Sandy Koufax. In one of the ugliest incidents in baseball history, he was struck on the head by bat-wielding Giants pitcher Juan Marichal at home plate in a 1965 game at Candlestick Park. Roseboro wound up batting .249 over 14 major league seasons.

Steve Roser, 84, at Utica, N.Y., on February 8. Roser pitched for the Yankees and the Boston Braves in a three-season major league career during which he compiled a 6-5 record. The righthander was 4-3 for the 1944 Yanks.

Ed Runge, 84, at San Diego on July 26. Runge was an American League umpire from 1954 through 1970. Son Paul and grandson Brian also became major league umpires.

Ted Sepkowski, 78, at Severna Park, Md., on March 8. An outfielder/infielder, Sepkowski played in 19 major league games over three seasons—a total of 17 for the Indians in 1942, 1946 and 1947 and two for the Yankees in '47.

Frank "Spec" Shea, 81, at New Haven, Conn., on July 19. Righthander Shea, who pitched eight seasons in the big leagues, had an outstanding rookie year in 1947, finishing 14-5 with a 3.07 ERA for the Yankees, going 2-0 in the World Series and getting the win for the American League in the All-Star Game. He was 42-41 the rest of his career, reaching double-figure victory totals with Washington in 1952 and '53.

Al Silvera, 66, at Los Angeles on July 24. Outfielder Silvera, a mid-1950s Reds bonus baby, appeared in 13 games for Cincinnati in '55 and in one game for the Reds in '56.

Enos Slaughter, 86, at Durham, N.C., on August 12. Slaughter, known for his all-out style of play, hit exactly .300 over his 19-year major league career. He batted .300 or higher for the Cardinals seven times in one eight-season span, capping the stretch with a career-best .336 average in 1949. Slaughter amassed 2,383 career hits despite missing three years because of military duty. Slaughter, who joined the Cardinals in 1938, was a member of the Cards' 1942 and '46 World Series championship teams, forever winning a place in baseball lore with his 1946 Series-deciding "Mad Dash" from first base to home plate on Harry Walker's medium-range hit to left-center field. Also in '46, he led the National League in RBIs with 130. Traded to the Yankees before the 1954 season, the future Hall of Famer played in three World Series with the Yanks and twice came away a winner.

Al Smith, 73, at Hammond, Ind., on January 3. Outfielder/third baseman Smith was a regular on two pennant-winning clubs, the 1954 Indians and the 1959 White Sox. He scored an A.L.-leading 123 runs for Cleveland in 1955, a year in which he batted .306 with 22 home runs. In 1961, he hit 28 homers for the White Sox. Over 12 big-league seasons, he batted .272 with 164 homers.

Clay Smith, 87, at Cambridge, Kan., on March 5. Righthander Smith broke into the majors with four relief appearances for the 1938 Indians, then appeared in 14 games and went 1-1 for Detroit in 1940 (his only other big-league season).

Steve Souchock, 83, at Westland, Mich., on July 28. Primarily an outfielder/first baseman, Souchock played in 473 major league games over eight seasons and batted .255. In 278 at-bats for the 1953 Tigers, he hit .302 with 11 home runs. He also played for the Yankees (with whom he made his big-league debut in 1946) and the White Sox.

Jim Spencer, 55, at Fort Lauderdale, Fla., on February 10. Spencer, a first baseman and designated hitter, spent 15 years in the majors and batted .250 overall with 146 homers. He played for the Angels, Rangers, White Sox, Yankees and A's. A part-time player for the 1978 World Series champion Yankees, he started three games in the Series that fall against the Dodgers.

Bob Stevens, 85, at San Bruno, Calif., on January 2. Stevens, a member of the writers' wing of the Baseball Hall of Fame, was a reporter and baseball beat man for the San Francisco Chronicle for more than 40 years. He covered the San Francisco Seals of the Pacific Coast League and then the major league Giants.

Dick Stuart, 70, at Redwood City, Calif., on December 15. Stuart walloped 228 home runs in his 10 years in the majors. The first baseman had three standout seasons, hitting 35 homers and driving in 117 runs for the 1961 Pirates and posting big power numbers (42 homers/118 RBIs and 33 homers/114 RBIs) for the Red Sox in 1963 and 1964. A notoriously poor fielder, Stuart also was an offensive force for Pittsburgh's 1960 World Series championship team (23 homers, 83 RBIs). He had won minor league fame in 1956 by smashing 66 homers for Lincoln of the Western League.

Tom Sunkel, 89, at Paris, Ill., on April 6. The lefthander went 9-15 while pitching for the Cardinals in 1937 and 1939, the Giants in 1941, 1942 and 1943 and the Dodgers in 1944.

Karl Swanson, 101, at Rock Island, Ill., on April 3. Second baseman Swanson appeared in 22 games for the White Sox in 1928 and two in '29.

Fred Taylor, 77, at Hilliard, Ohio, on January 6. Taylor achieved his greatest athletic fame as a basketball coach, directing Ohio State to the 1960 NCAA championship. As a baseball player, he was a first baseman who appeared in a total of 22 games for the Washington Senators in 1950, 1951 and 1952.

Jack Tighe, 88, at Pompano Beach, Fla., on August 1. A long-time minor league manager and a Tigers coach in 1942, 1955 and 1956, Tighe managed Detroit in 1957 and part of 1958. In '57, he led the Tigers to a fourth-place finish (78-76 record); in '58, he was dismissed after the club got off to a 21-28 start. Tighe spent most of his 5 ½ decades in pro ball in the Tigers' organization.

Jim Toomey, 84, at Town and Country, Mo., on March 24. Toomey was a Cardinals fixture for nearly four decades, serving as the club's longtime public relations director and then as assistant general manager. He retired in 1987 but stayed on as a consultant.

Ben Wade, 80, at Los Angeles on December 2. Wade, a righthander, went 11-9 for Brooklyn in 1952 while making 24 starts and 13 relief appearances. Exclusively a reliever in 1953, he compiled a 7-5 record for the Dodgers in 32 games and appeared in two World Series games against the Yankees that fall. He later became a scout and scouting director for the Los Angeles Dodgers.

Jim Warfield, 60, at Cleveland on July 16. Warfield, who was serving as an assistant trainer for Cleveland at the time of his death, was the Indians' head trainer from 1971 through 1996.

Wes Westrum, 79, at Clearbrook, Minn., on May 28. Westrum was a gifted defensive catcher who played for the Giants in the club's last 11 seasons in New York (1947 through 1957). He was a member of the Giants' 1954 World Series champions and the 1951 pennant-winning team. Only a .217 career hitter, he later managed the Mets and San Francisco Giants.

Barney White, 78, at Tyler, Texas, on July 24. Shortstop White appeared in four games for Brooklyn in 1945.

Whitey Wietelmann, 83, at San Diego on March 26. A light-hitting middle infielder, Wietelmann saw extensive duty for the Boston Braves from 1943 through 1945. He played in all 153 of the club's games in '43 and batted .215. He finished his nine-year career with the Pirates in 1947.

Del Wilber, 83, at St. Petersburg, Fla., on July 18. Wilber was a reserve catcher in the majors for eight seasons and later served as a big-league coach and minor league manager. He hit .278 in 245 at-bats for the Phillies in 1951, a year in which he accounted for all the runs in a game against Cincinnati with three bases-empty home runs.

Hoyt Wilhelm, 79, at Sarasota, Fla., on August 23. Possessing what was considered the best knuckleball in the game's history, Wilhelm was the first player to win election to the Hall of Fame based on his success as a relief pitcher. The righthander, who relieved in 1,018 big-league games and made only 52 starts, reached the majors at age 28 in 1952 and compiled a 15-3 record out of the bullpen for the New York Giants. He led the National League in winning percentage (.833), ERA (2.43) and appearances (71). Wilhelm, with the knuckler putting minimal stress on his arm, managed to pitch into the 1972 season, finishing with a 143-122 record and a 2.52 ERA in 1,070 games (a major league mark since broken). Besides the Giants, he pitched for the Cardinals, Indians, Orioles (for whom he threw a no-hitter in 1958), White Sox, Angels, Braves, Cubs and Dodgers.

Ted Williams, 83, at Inverness, Fla., on July 5. Hall of Famer Williams was a career .344 hitter, a six-time American League batting champion, a two-time Triple Crown winner, a two-time A.L. MVP and the last major leaguer to hit .400. He spent all 19 of his big-league seasons with the Red Sox, finishing with 521 home runs and 2,654 hits despite missing nearly five years overall because of military service. Williams set a major league rookie record with 145 RBIs in 1939, batted .406 in 1941, won Triple Crowns in 1942 (36 homers, 137 RBIs, .356 average) and 1947 (32-114-.343) and had career highs in homers (43) and RBIs (159) in 1949. In 1958, at age 40, he won his last batting championship with a .328 average. Williams smashed a game-winning, three-run homer in the ninth inning of the 1941 All-Star Game in Detroit and hit two home runs in the 1946 All-Star Game at Fenway Park. He managed the Washington Senators from 1969 through 1971 and the Texas Rangers (the transplanted Senators) in 1972.

Jerry Witte, 86, at Houston on April 27. First baseman Witte, who hit 308 home runs as a minor leaguer (including 50 in the Texas League in 1949), had four homers in 172 at-bats while playing for the St. Louis Browns in 1946 and 1947.

Ray Yochim, 79, at New Orleans on January 26. Yochim pitched in one game for the Cardinals in 1948 and in three games for the Cards in 1949.

Adrian Zabala, 85, at Jacksonville, Fla., on January 4. Lefthander Zabala pitched for the New York Giants in 1945 and 1949, posting records of 2-4 and 2-3.

2002 A.L. STATISTICS

Batting

Designated hitting

Pinch-hitting

Pitching

Fielding

Miscellaneous

BATTING

TEAM

Team	G	TPA	AB	R	H	TB	2B	3B	HR	RBI	SH	SF	HP	BB	IBB	SO	SB	CS	GDP	LOB	ShO	Avg.	OBP	Slg.
Anaheim	162	6327	5678	851	1603	2456	333	32	152	811	49	64	74	462	42	805	117	51	105	1165	8	.282	.341	.433
Boston	162	6332	5640	859	1560	2505	348	33	177	810	22	53	72	545	39	944	80	28	139	1175	7	.277	.345	.444
New York	161	6377	5601	897	1540	2547	314	12	223	857	23	41	72	640	48	1171	100	38	150	1191	3	.275	.354	.455
Seattle	162	6362	5569	814	1531	2334	285	31	152	771	41	72	51	629	62	1003	137	58	123	1239	7	.275	.350	.419
Minnesota	161	6196	5582	768	1538	2439	348	36	167	731	34	52	56	472	30	1089	79	62	121	1124	8	.272	.332	.437
Texas	162	6332	5618	843	1510	2558	304	27	230	806	48	50	62	554	45	1055	62	34	129	1155	6	.269	.338	.455
Chicago	162	6207	5502	856	1475	2473	289	29	217	819	48	53	49	555	17	952	75	31	111	1085	7	.268	.338	.449
Toronto	162	6230	5581	813	1457	2399	305	38	187	771	17	57	53	522	30	1142	71	18	130	1104	6	.261	.327	.430
Oakland	162	6291	5558	800	1450	2400	279	28	205	772	20	36	68	609	37	1008	46	20	128	1197	6	.261	.339	.432
Kansas City	162	6206	5535	737	1415	2204	285	42	140	695	44	51	52	524	27	921	140	65	106	1092	13	.256	.323	.398
Tampa Bay	161	6198	5604	673	1418	2184	297	35	133	640	44	36	58	456	29	1115	102	45	116	1132	14	.253	.314	.390
Cleveland	162	6099	5423	739	1349	2232	255	26	192	706	39	39	56	542	35	1000	52	37	149	1066	8	.249	.321	.412
Detroit	161	5920	5406	575	1340	2051	265	37	124	546	30	57	64	363	22	1035	65	44	125	1029	10	.248	.300	.379
Baltimore	162	6096	5491	667	1353	2213	311	27	165	636	40	49	64	452	25	993	110	48	128	1037	15	.246	.309	.403
Totals	1132	87173	77788	10892	20519	32995	4218	433	2464	10371	499	710	851	7325	488	14233	1236	579	1760	15791	118	.264	.331	.424

INDIVIDUAL

TOP QUALIFIERS FOR BATTING CHAMPIONSHIP

Minimum 502 plate appearances. *Lefthanded batter. †Switch-hitter.

Player, Team	G	TPA	AB	R	H	TB	2B	3B	HR	RBI	SH	SF	HP	BB	IBB	SO	SB	CS	GDP	Avg.	OBP	Slg.
Ramirez, Manny, Bos.	120	518	436	84	152	282	31	0	33	107	0	1	8	73	14	85	0	0	13	.349	.450	.647
Sweeney, Mike, K.C.	126	545	471	81	160	265	31	1	24	86	0	7	6	61	10	46	9	7	9	.340	.417	.563
Williams, Bernie, N.Y.†	154	699	612	102	204	302	37	2	19	102	0	1	3	83	7	97	8	4	19	.333	.415	.493
Suzuki, Ichiro, Sea.*	157	728	647	111	208	275	27	8	8	51	3	5	5	68	27	62	31	15	8	.321	.388	.425
Ordonez, Magglio, Chi.	153	654	590	116	189	352	47	1	38	135	0	3	7	53	2	77	7	5	21	.320	.381	.597
Giambi, Jason, N.Y.*	155	689	560	120	176	335	34	1	41	122	0	5	15	109	4	112	2	2	18	.314	.435	.598
Kennedy, Adam, Ana.*	144	509	474	65	148	213	32	6	7	52	5	4	7	19	1	80	17	4	5	.312	.345	.449
Garciaparra, Nomar, Bos.	156	693	635	101	197	335	56	5	24	120	0	11	6	41	4	63	5	2	17	.310	.352	.528
Tejada, Miguel, Oak.	162	715	662	108	204	336	30	0	34	131	0	4	11	38	3	84	7	2	21	.308	.354	.508
Anderson, Garret, Ana.*	158	678	638	93	195	344	56	3	29	123	0	10	0	30	11	80	6	4	11	.306	.332	.539
Thome, Jim, Cle.*	147	613	480	101	146	325	19	2	52	118	0	6	5	122	18	139	1	2	5	.304	.445	.677
Konerko, Paul, Chi.	151	630	570	81	173	284	30	0	27	104	0	7	9	44	2	72	0	0	17	.304	.359	.498
Stewart, Shannon, Tor.	141	641	577	103	175	255	38	6	10	45	0	1	9	54	2	60	14	2	17	.303	.371	.442
Burks, Ellis, Cle.	138	570	518	92	156	280	28	0	32	91	1	1	6	44	3	108	2	3	13	.301	.362	.541
Simon, Randall, Det.*	130	506	482	51	145	221	17	1	19	82	0	7	4	13	5	30	0	1	13	.301	.320	.459

DEPARTMENTAL LEADERS: G—Beltran, K.C., Long, Oak., A. Rodriguez, Tex., Tejada, Oak., 162; AB—Soriano, N.Y., 696; R—Soriano, N.Y., 128; H—Soriano, N.Y., 209; TB—A. Rodriguez, Tex., 389; 1B—Suzuki, Sea., 165; 2B—Anderson, Ana., Garciaparra, Bos., 56; 3B—Damon, Bos., 11; HR—A. Rodriguez, Tex., 57; RBI—A. Rodriguez, Tex., 142; SH—Eckstein, Ana., 14; SF—Olerud, Sea., 12; HP—Eckstein, Ana., 27; BB—Thome, Cle., 122; IBB—Suzuki, Sea., 27; SO—Cameron, Sea., 176; SB—Soriano, N.Y., 41; CS—Suzuki, Sea., 15; GDP—Posada, N.Y., 23; Slg.—Thome, Cle., .677; OBP—Ramirez, Bos., .450.

ALL PLAYERS

*Lefthanded batter. †Switch-hitter.

Player, Team	G	TPA	AB	R	H	TB	2B	3B	HR	RBI	SH	SF	HP	BB	IBB	SO	SB	CS	GDP	Avg.	OBP	Slg.
Abernathy, Brent, T.B.	117	504	463	46	112	144	18	4	2	40	8	2	6	25	0	46	10	4	8	.242	.288	.311
Agbayani, Benny, Bos.	13	43	37	5	11	12	1	0	0	8	0	0	0	6	1	5	0	0	1	.297	.395	.324
Alicea, Luis, K.C.†	94	273	237	28	54	69	8	2	1	23	3	0	1	32	1	34	2	3	5	.228	.322	.291
Allen, Chad, Cle.	5	11	10	0	1	2	1	0	0	0	1	0	0	0	0	2	0	0	1	.100	.100	.200
Alomar Jr., Sandy, Chi.	51	176	167	21	48	81	10	1	7	25	1	2	1	5	0	14	0	0	5	.287	.309	.485
Alvarez, Wilson, T.B.*	23	4	4	0	0	0	0	0	0	0	0	0	0	0	0	1	0	0	0	.000	.000	.000
Amezaga, Alfredo, Ana.†	12	13	13	3	7	9	2	0	0	2	0	0	0	0	0	1	1	0	1	.538	.538	.692
Anderson, Brady, Cle.*	34	101	80	4	13	20	4	0	1	5	0	1	2	18	2	23	4	0	5	.163	.327	.250
Anderson, Garret, Ana.*	158	678	638	93	195	344	56	3	29	123	0	10	0	30	11	80	6	4	11	.306	.332	.539
Andrews, Shane, Bos.	7	15	13	2	1	2	1	0	0	2	0	0	0	1	0	3	0	0	0	.077	.200	.154
Appier, Kevin, Ana.	32	4	2	0	0	0	0	0	0	0	0	0	2	0	0	2	0	0	0	.000	.000	.000
Arias, Alex, N.Y.	6	8	7	0	0	0	0	0	0	0	0	0	0	1	0	2	0	0	0	.000	.125	.000
Arrojo, Rolando, Bos.	29	3	2	0	0	0	0	0	0	0	0	0	0	0	0	1	0	0	0	.000	.000	.000
Asencio, Miguel, K.C.	31	2	2	0	0	0	0	0	0	0	0	0	0	0	0	1	0	0	0	.000	.000	.000
Aven, Bruce, Cle.	7	21	17	1	2	2	0	0	0	0	0	0	0	4	0	4	1	0	2	.118	.286	.118
Baerga, Carlos, Bos.†	73	194	182	17	52	69	11	0	2	19	1	2	2	7	1	20	6	0	6	.286	.316	.379
Baez, Danys, Cle.	39	2	2	0	0	0	0	0	0	0	0	0	0	0	0	2	0	0	0	.000	.000	.000
Baldwin, James, Sea.	30	2	2	0	1	1	0	0	0	0	0	0	0	0	0	0	0	0	0	.500	.500	.500
Bard, Josh, Cle.†	24	95	90	9	20	34	5	0	3	12	1	0	0	4	0	13	0	0	6	.222	.255	.378
Batista, Tony, Bal.	161	682	615	90	150	281	36	1	31	87	0	6	11	50	9	107	5	4	13	.244	.309	.457
Bell, Rob, Tex.	17	2	1	0	0	0	0	0	0	0	0	0	1	0	0	0	0	0	0	.000	.500	.000
Bellinger, Clay, Ana.	2	1	1	0	0	0	0	0	0	0	0	0	0	0	0	1	0	0	0	.000	.000	.000
Beltran, Carlos, K.C.†	162	722	637	114	174	319	44	7	29	105	3	7	4	71	1	135	35	7	12	.273	.346	.501
Berg, Dave, Tor.	109	414	374	42	101	143	26	2	4	39	4	5	5	26	1	57	0	2	6	.270	.322	.382
Berger, Brandon, K.C.	51	145	134	16	27	52	5	1	6	17	0	1	2	8	2	32	1	0	2	.201	.255	.388
Bernero, Adam, Det.	28	5	4	0	0	0	0	0	0	0	0	1	0	0	0	4	0	0	0	.000	.000	.000
Berroa, Angel, K.C.	20	83	75	8	17	26	7	1	0	5	0	1	1	7	1	10	3	0	1	.227	.301	.347
Bigbie, Larry, Bal.*	16	36	34	1	6	7	1	0	0	3	0	1	0	1	0	11	1	0	1	.176	.194	.206

Player, Team	G	TPA	AB	R	H	TB	2B	3B	HR	RBI	SH	SF	HP	BB	IBB	SO	SB	CS	GDP	Avg.	OBP	Slg.
Blake, Casey, Min.	9	22	20	2	4	5	1	0	0	1	0	0	0	2	0	7	0	0	0	.200	.273	.250
Blalock, Hank, Tex.*	49	172	147	16	31	48	8	0	3	17	2	2	1	20	1	43	0	0	2	.211	.306	.327
Bloomquist, Willie, Sea.	12	38	33	11	15	19	4	0	0	7	0	0	0	5	0	2	3	1	0	.455	.526	.576
Bocachica, Hiram, Det.	34	109	103	14	23	39	4	0	4	8	1	0	0	5	0	22	2	2	2	.223	.259	.379
Boone, Bret, Sea.	155	675	608	88	169	281	34	3	24	107	2	6	6	53	4	102	12	5	11	.278	.339	.462
Borchard, Joe, Chi.†	16	37	36	5	8	14	0	0	2	5	0	0	0	1	0	14	0	0	0	.222	.243	.389
Borders, Pat, Sea.	4	4	4	0	2	3	1	0	0	1	0	0	0	0	0	1	0	0	0	.500	.500	.750
Bordick, Mike, Bal.	117	413	367	37	85	134	19	3	8	36	6	2	3	35	0	63	7	4	9	.232	.302	.365
Bradley, Milton, Cle.†	98	358	325	48	81	132	18	3	9	38	1	0	0	32	2	58	6	3	12	.249	.317	.406
Branyan, Russell, Cle.*	50	180	161	16	33	61	4	0	8	17	0	2	0	17	0	65	1	2	3	.205	.278	.379
Brito, Juan, K.C.	9	23	23	1	7	9	2	0	0	1	0	0	0	0	0	3	0	0	2	.304	.304	.391
Brock, Chris, Bal.	22	2	2	0	0	0	0	0	0	0	0	0	0	0	0	1	0	0	0	.000	.000	.000
Broussard, Ben, Cle.*	39	120	112	10	27	43	4	0	4	9	0	0	1	7	1	25	0	0	3	.241	.292	.384
Brown, Dee, K.C.*	16	55	51	5	12	20	3	1	1	7	0	0	0	4	0	20	0	0	0	.235	.291	.392
Brown, Kevin L., Bos.	2	1	1	0	0	0	0	0	0	0	0	0	0	0	0	0	0	0	0	.000	.000	.000
Buchanan, Brian, Min.	44	143	135	19	34	56	5	1	5	15	0	0	2	6	0	33	2	1	4	.252	.294	.415
Buehrle, Mark, Chi.*	34	6	6	1	1	1	0	0	0	0	0	0	0	0	0	4	0	0	0	.167	.167	.167
Burba, Dave, Tex.-Cle.	35	5	5	0	1	1	0	0	0	0	0	0	0	0	0	3	0	0	0	.200	.200	.200
Burkett, John, Bos.	29	4	3	0	0	0	0	0	0	0	1	0	0	0	0	1	0	0	0	.000	.000	.000
Burks, Ellis, Cle.	138	570	518	92	156	280	28	0	32	91	1	1	6	44	3	108	2	3	13	.301	.362	.541
Bush, Homer, Tor.	23	83	78	9	18	23	2	0	1	2	1	0	2	2	0	12	2	0	2	.231	.268	.295
Byrd, Paul, K.C.	33	2	2	0	0	0	0	0	0	0	0	0	0	0	0	2	0	0	0	.000	.000	.000
Byrnes, Eric, Oak.	90	104	94	24	23	40	4	2	3	11	1	2	3	4	0	17	3	0	3	.245	.291	.426
Cabrera, Jolbert, Cle.	38	79	72	5	8	9	1	0	0	7	0	1	1	5	0	13	1	1	3	.111	.177	.125
Cameron, Mike, Sea.	158	640	545	84	130	241	26	5	25	80	4	5	7	79	3	176	31	8	8	.239	.340	.442
Canizaro, Jay, Min.	38	126	112	14	24	34	8	1	0	11	1	2	1	10	0	22	0	1	1	.214	.280	.304
Carpenter, Chris, Tor.	13	2	1	1	1	1	0	0	0	0	1	0	0	0	0	0	0	0	0	1.000	1.000	1.000
Caruso, Mike, K.C.*	12	21	20	3	2	2	0	0	0	0	0	0	0	1	0	2	0	0	0	.100	.143	.100
Casanova, Raul, Bal.†	2	1	1	0	0	0	0	0	0	0	0	0	0	0	0	1	0	0	0	.000	.000	.000
Cash, Kevin, Tor.	7	15	14	1	2	2	0	0	0	0	0	0	0	1	0	4	0	0	1	.143	.200	.143
Castillo, Alberto, N.Y.	15	41	37	3	5	8	1	1	0	4	3	0	0	1	0	12	0	0	2	.135	.158	.216
Castillo, Frank, Bos.	36	2	1	0	0	0	0	0	0	0	0	0	0	0	0	1	0	0	0	.000	.000	.000
Catalanotto, Frank, Tex.*	68	250	212	42	57	94	16	6	3	23	3	2	8	25	0	27	9	5	3	.269	.364	.443
Chavez, Eric, Oak.*	153	653	585	87	161	300	31	3	34	109	0	2	1	65	13	119	8	3	8	.275	.348	.513
Choate, Randy, N.Y.*	18	1	1	0	0	0	0	0	0	0	0	0	0	0	0	0	0	0	0	.000	.000	.000
Cirillo, Jeff, Sea.	146	547	485	51	121	159	20	0	6	54	13	9	9	31	0	67	8	4	12	.249	.301	.328
Clark, Howie, Bal.*	14	58	53	3	16	21	5	0	0	4	0	0	2	3	0	6	0	0	5	.302	.362	.396
Clark, Tony, Bos.†	90	298	259	25	57	80	12	1	3	29	0	1	1	21	0	57	0	0	11	.207	.265	.291
Clayton, Royce, Chi.	112	376	342	51	86	125	14	2	7	35	7	4	3	20	0	67	5	1	7	.251	.295	.365
Clemens, Roger, N.Y.	29	4	3	1	2	3	1	0	0	1	0	1	0	0	0	1	0	0	0	.667	.500	1.000
Colangelo, Mike, Oak.	20	26	23	2	4	5	1	0	0	0	0	1	1	1	0	2	0	0	0	.174	.240	.217
Colon, Bartolo, Cle.	16	6	6	0	1	1	0	0	0	0	0	0	0	0	0	3	0	0	0	.167	.167	.167
Conine, Jeff, Bal.	116	488	451	44	123	202	26	4	15	63	0	10	2	25	6	66	8	0	10	.273	.307	.448
Conti, Jason, T.B.*	78	245	222	26	57	85	15	2	3	21	4	0	1	18	1	55	4	2	5	.257	.315	.383
Coomer, Ron, N.Y.	55	156	148	14	39	55	7	0	3	17	1	1	0	6	1	23	0	0	8	.264	.290	.372
Cordero, Francisco, Tex.	39	1	1	0	0	0	0	0	0	0	0	0	0	0	0	1	0	0	0	.000	.000	.000
Cordero, Wil, Cle.	6	18	18	1	4	4	0	0	0	1	0	0	0	0	0	3	0	0	1	.222	.222	.222
Cordova, Marty, Bal.	131	513	458	55	116	199	25	2	18	64	2	3	3	47	3	111	1	6	17	.253	.325	.434
Cox, Steve, T.B.*	148	633	560	65	142	222	30	1	16	72	0	6	7	60	5	116	5	0	15	.254	.330	.396
Crawford, Carl, T.B.*	63	278	259	23	67	96	11	6	2	30	6	1	3	9	0	41	9	5	0	.259	.290	.371
Crede, Joe, Chi.	53	209	200	28	57	103	10	0	12	35	0	1	0	8	0	40	0	2	1	.285	.311	.515
Creek, Doug, T.B.-Sea.*	52	1	1	0	0	0	0	0	0	0	0	0	0	0	0	1	0	0	0	.000	.000	.000
Crisp, Coco, Cle.†	32	143	127	16	33	49	9	2	1	9	3	2	0	11	0	19	4	1	0	.260	.314	.386
Cruz, Jacob, Det.*	35	107	88	12	24	35	3	1	2	6	1	2	3	13	0	20	3	1	2	.273	.377	.398
Cruz, Jose, Tor.†	124	522	466	64	114	204	26	5	18	70	1	4	0	51	1	106	7	1	8	.245	.317	.438
Cuddyer, Michael, Min.	41	123	112	12	29	48	7	0	4	13	1	1	1	8	0	30	2	0	3	.259	.311	.429
Damon, Johnny, Bos.*	154	702	623	118	178	276	34	11	14	63	3	5	6	65	5	70	31	6	4	.286	.356	.443
Daubach, Brian, Bos.*	137	506	444	62	118	206	24	2	20	78	0	4	7	51	4	126	2	1	10	.266	.348	.464
DaVanon, Jeff, Ana.†	16	33	30	3	5	11	3	0	1	4	1	0	0	2	0	6	1	0	0	.167	.219	.367
Davis, Ben, Sea.†	80	253	228	24	59	92	10	1	7	43	1	4	2	18	1	58	1	1	6	.259	.313	.404
Delgado, Carlos, Tor.*	143	628	505	103	140	277	34	2	33	108	0	8	13	102	18	126	1	0	8	.277	.406	.549
Diaz, Einar, Cle.	102	351	320	34	66	91	19	0	2	16	6	2	6	17	1	27	0	1	13	.206	.258	.284
Diaz, Juan, Bos.	4	8	7	2	2	6	1	0	1	2	0	0	1	0	0	2	0	0	0	.286	.375	.857
Drese, Ryan, Cle.	26	5	3	0	0	0	0	0	0	0	1	0	0	1	0	3	0	0	0	.000	.250	.000
Driskill, Travis, Bal.	29	4	3	1	0	0	0	0	0	0	0	0	0	1	0	3	0	0	0	.000	.250	.000
Dunwoody, Todd, Cle.*	2	7	6	0	0	0	0	0	0	0	0	1	0	0	0	3	0	0	0	.000	.000	.000
Durham, Ray, Chi.-Oak.†	150	659	564	114	163	254	34	6	15	70	10	5	7	73	1	93	26	7	15	.289	.374	.450
Dye, Jermaine, Oak.	131	555	488	74	123	224	27	1	24	86	0	5	10	52	2	108	2	0	15	.252	.333	.459
Easley, Damion, Det.	85	346	304	29	68	108	14	1	8	30	1	3	11	27	3	43	1	3	4	.224	.307	.355
Eckstein, David, Ana.	152	702	608	107	178	236	22	6	8	63	14	8	27	45	0	44	21	13	7	.293	.363	.388
Ellis, Mark, Oak.	98	404	345	58	94	136	16	4	6	35	8	3	4	44	1	54	4	2	3	.272	.359	.394
Erickson, Scott, Bal.	29	4	4	0	0	0	0	0	0	0	0	0	0	0	0	2	0	0	0	.000	.000	.000
Erstad, Darin, Ana.*	150	663	625	99	177	243	28	4	10	73	5	4	2	27	4	67	23	3	9	.283	.313	.389
Escalona, Felix, T.B.	59	171	157	17	34	46	8	2	0	9	3	1	7	3	0	44	7	2	2	.217	.262	.293
Everett, Carl, Tex.†	105	418	374	47	100	164	16	0	16	62	1	4	6	33	4	77	2	3	7	.267	.333	.439
Fabregas, Jorge, Ana.*	35	96	88	8	17	18	1	0	0	8	2	0	6	1	1	6	0	0	5	.193	.245	.205
Fasano, Sal, Ana.	2	1	1	0	0	0	0	0	0	0	0	0	0	0	0	0	0	0	0	.000	.000	.000
Febles, Carlos, K.C.	119	404	351	44	86	122	16	4	4	26	5	0	7	41	0	63	16	5	8	.245	.336	.348
Fick, Robert, Det.*	148	614	556	66	150	241	36	2	17	63	0	5	7	46	4	90	0	1	17	.270	.331	.433
Figgins, Chone, Ana.†	15	12	12	6	2	3	1	0	0	1	0	0	0	0	0	5	2	1	1	.167	.167	.250
Finley, Chuck, Cle.*	18	4	4	0	0	0	0	0	0	0	0	0	0	0	0	2	0	0	1	.000	.000	.000
Fiore, Tony, Min.	48	3	3	0	0	0	0	0	0	0	0	0	0	0	0	1	0	0	0	.000	.000	.000

Player, Team	G	TPA	AB	R	H	TB	2B	3B	HR	RBI	SH	SF	HP	BB	IBB	SO	SB	CS	GDP	Avg.	OBP	Slg.
Flaherty, John, T.B.	76	303	281	27	73	105	20	0	4	33	2	4	1	15	0	50	2	2	6	.260	.296	.374
Fletcher, Darrin, Tor.*	45	135	127	8	28	43	6	0	3	22	1	3	0	4	0	13	0	0	4	.220	.239	.339
Flores, Jose, Oak.	7	5	3	2	0	0	0	0	0	0	0	0	1	1	0	0	1	1	0	.000	.400	.000
Floyd, Cliff, Bos.*	47	190	171	30	54	96	21	0	7	18	0	2	2	15	0	28	4	0	6	.316	.374	.561
Fordyce, Brook, Bal.	56	146	130	7	30	41	8	0	1	8	3	0	4	9	0	19	1	0	5	.231	.301	.315
Foulke, Keith, Chi.	65	1	1	0	0	0	0	0	0	0	0	0	0	0	0	0	0	0	0	.000	.000	.000
Fryman, Travis, Cle.	118	439	397	42	86	139	14	3	11	55	0	0	2	40	1	82	0	0	12	.217	.292	.350
Fullmer, Brad, Ana.*	130	479	429	75	124	228	35	6	19	59	0	3	15	32	6	44	10	3	7	.289	.357	.531
Garcia, Freddy, Sea.	34	7	6	0	2	3	1	0	0	0	1	0	0	0	0	1	0	0	0	.333	.333	.500
Garcia, Karim, N.Y.-Cle.*	53	210	202	30	60	116	8	0	16	52	0	2	0	6	0	41	0	3	6	.297	.314	.574
Garcia, Luis, Bal.	6	3	3	0	1	1	0	0	0	0	0	0	0	0	0	1	0	0	0	.333	.333	.333
Garciaparra, Nomar, Bos.	156	693	635	101	197	335	56	5	24	120	0	11	6	41	4	63	5	2	17	.310	.352	.528
Garland, Jon, Chi.	33	3	2	0	0	0	0	0	0	0	1	0	0	0	0	0	0	0	0	.000	.000	.000
German, Esteban, Oak.	9	40	35	4	7	7	0	0	0	0	0	0	1	4	0	11	1	0	0	.200	.300	.200
Giambi, Jason, N.Y.*	155	689	560	120	176	335	34	1	41	122	0	5	15	109	4	112	2	2	18	.314	.435	.598
Giambi, Jeremy, Oak.*	42	187	157	26	43	74	7	0	8	17	0	0	3	27	0	40	0	0	4	.274	.390	.471
Gibbons, Jay, Bal.*	136	541	490	71	121	236	29	1	28	69	0	4	2	45	3	66	1	3	9	.247	.311	.482
Gil, Benji, Ana.	61	139	130	11	37	56	8	1	3	20	2	2	0	5	0	33	2	1	0	.285	.307	.431
Gil, Geronimo, Bal.	125	450	422	38	98	153	19	0	12	45	5	1	1	21	1	88	2	2	17	.232	.270	.363
Gipson, Charles, Sea.	79	84	72	22	17	26	5	2	0	8	2	0	1	9	0	14	4	0	3	.236	.329	.361
Glaus, Troy, Ana.	156	671	569	99	142	258	24	1	30	111	0	8	6	88	4	144	10	3	12	.250	.352	.453
Glover, Gary, Chi.	41	1	1	0	0	0	0	0	0	0	0	0	0	0	0	1	0	0	0	.000	.000	.000
Gomez, Alexis, K.C.*	5	10	10	0	2	2	0	0	0	0	0	0	0	0	0	2	0	0	0	.200	.200	.200
Gomez, Chris, T.B.	130	498	461	51	122	189	31	3	10	46	6	3	7	21	0	58	1	3	8	.265	.305	.410
Gonzalez, Juan, Tex.	70	296	277	38	78	125	21	1	8	35	0	1	1	17	1	56	2	0	11	.282	.324	.451
Grabowski, Jason, Oak.*	4	11	8	3	3	6	1	1	0	1	0	0	0	3	0	1	0	0	0	.375	.545	.750
Graffanino, Tony, Chi.	70	259	229	35	60	98	12	4	6	31	4	2	2	22	1	38	2	1	2	.262	.329	.428
Greene, Todd, Tex.	42	118	112	15	30	65	5	0	10	19	1	2	1	2	0	23	0	0	4	.268	.282	.580
Greer, Rusty, Tex.*	51	219	199	24	59	75	9	2	1	17	0	1	0	19	0	17	1	0	5	.296	.356	.377
Grieve, Ben, T.B.*	136	561	482	62	121	208	30	0	19	64	0	2	8	69	5	121	8	2	15	.251	.353	.432
Guiel, Aaron, K.C.*	70	269	240	30	56	81	13	0	4	38	2	4	4	19	1	61	1	5	3	.233	.296	.338
Guillen, Carlos, Sea.†	134	528	475	73	124	187	24	6	9	56	3	3	1	46	4	91	4	5	8	.261	.326	.394
Gutierrez, Ricky, Cle.	94	384	353	38	97	122	13	0	4	38	3	1	7	20	0	48	0	1	14	.275	.325	.346
Guzman, Cristian, Min.†	148	656	623	80	170	240	31	6	9	59	8	6	2	17	2	79	12	13	12	.273	.292	.385
Hafner, Travis, Tex.*	23	70	62	6	15	24	4	1	1	6	0	0	0	8	1	15	0	1	0	.242	.329	.387
Hairston Jr., Jerry, Bal.	122	479	426	55	114	160	25	3	5	32	8	4	7	34	0	55	21	6	5	.268	.329	.376
Hall, Toby, T.B.	85	353	330	37	85	124	19	1	6	42	2	3	1	17	3	27	0	1	14	.258	.293	.376
Halladay, Roy, Tor.	34	6	6	0	0	0	0	0	0	0	0	0	0	0	0	0	0	0	1	.000	.000	.000
Halter, Shane, Det.	122	458	410	46	98	162	22	6	10	39	1	4	4	39	1	92	0	4	12	.239	.309	.395
Harang, Aaron, Oak.	16	3	3	0	0	0	0	0	0	0	0	0	0	0	0	3	0	0	0	.000	.000	.000
Harris, Willie, Chi.*	49	177	163	14	38	48	4	0	2	12	3	2	0	9	0	21	8	0	3	.233	.270	.294
Hart, Jason, Tex.	10	17	15	2	4	7	3	0	0	0	0	0	0	2	0	7	0	0	0	.267	.353	.467
Haselman, Bill, Tex.	69	193	179	16	44	60	7	0	3	18	1	0	2	11	1	25	0	0	6	.246	.297	.335
Hatteberg, Scott, Oak.*	136	568	492	58	138	213	22	4	15	61	1	1	6	68	1	56	0	0	8	.280	.374	.433
Henderson, Rickey, Bos.	72	222	179	40	40	63	6	1	5	16	0	1	4	38	0	47	8	2	3	.223	.369	.352
Henson, Drew, N.Y.	3	1	1	1	0	0	0	0	0	0	0	0	0	0	0	1	0	0	0	.000	.000	.000
Hernandez, Ramon, Oak.	136	457	403	51	94	135	20	0	7	42	3	3	5	43	1	64	0	0	11	.233	.313	.335
Higginson, Bobby, Det.*	119	499	444	50	125	185	24	3	10	63	1	7	6	41	3	45	12	5	8	.282	.345	.417
Hillenbrand, Shea, Bos.	156	676	634	94	186	291	43	4	18	83	0	5	12	25	4	95	4	2	18	.293	.330	.459
Hinch, A.J., K.C.	72	220	197	25	49	79	7	1	7	27	2	0	3	18	0	35	3	3	2	.249	.321	.401
Hinske, Eric, Tor.*	151	650	566	99	158	272	38	2	24	84	0	5	2	77	5	138	13	1	12	.279	.365	.481
Hocking, Denny, Min.†	102	294	260	28	65	84	13	0	2	25	4	5	1	24	0	44	0	2	3	.250	.310	.323
Hollandsworth, Todd, Tex.*	39	149	132	16	34	55	6	0	5	19	2	1	0	14	0	27	1	1	0	.258	.327	.417
Hoover, Paul, T.B.	5	17	17	1	3	3	0	0	0	2	0	0	0	0	0	5	0	0	0	.176	.176	.176
Huckaby, Ken, Tor.	88	283	273	29	67	84	6	1	3	22	1	0	0	9	1	44	0	0	10	.245	.270	.308
Hudson, Orlando, Tor.†	54	207	192	20	53	85	10	5	4	23	0	2	2	11	0	27	0	1	6	.276	.319	.443
Hudson, Tim, Oak.	34	6	5	1	1	2	1	0	0	0	0	0	0	1	0	1	0	0	0	.200	.333	.400
Huff, Aubrey, T.B.*	113	494	454	67	142	236	25	0	23	59	0	2	1	37	7	55	4	1	17	.313	.364	.520
Hunter, Torii, Min.	148	604	561	89	162	294	37	4	29	94	0	3	5	35	3	118	23	8	17	.289	.334	.524
Ibanez, Raul, K.C.*	137	544	497	70	146	267	37	6	24	103	1	4	2	40	5	76	5	3	11	.294	.346	.537
Infante, Omar, Det.	18	75	72	4	24	30	3	0	1	6	0	0	0	3	0	10	0	1	0	.333	.360	.417
Inge, Brandon, Det.	95	351	321	27	65	107	15	3	7	24	1	1	4	24	0	101	1	3	7	.202	.266	.333
Jackson, Damian, Det.	81	274	245	31	63	88	20	1	1	25	2	3	3	21	0	36	12	3	3	.257	.320	.359
Jackson, Ryan, Det.*	4	7	6	0	2	5	1	1	0	0	0	0	0	1	0	2	0	0	0	.333	.429	.833
Jeter, Derek, N.Y.	157	730	644	124	191	271	26	0	18	75	3	4	7	73	2	114	32	3	14	.297	.373	.421
Jimenez, D'Angelo, Chi.†	27	125	108	22	31	44	4	3	1	11	0	0	1	16	0	10	2	3	1	.287	.384	.407
Johnson, Jason, Bal.	22	3	3	0	0	0	0	0	0	0	0	0	0	0	0	2	0	0	0	.000	.000	.000
Johnson, Mark L., Chi.*	86	302	263	31	55	77	8	1	4	18	6	0	3	30	1	52	0	0	4	.209	.297	.293
Johnson, Nick, N.Y.*	129	441	378	56	92	152	15	0	15	58	3	0	12	48	5	98	1	3	11	.243	.347	.402
Johnson, Russ, T.B.	45	130	111	15	24	32	5	0	1	12	2	0	1	16	1	22	5	2	2	.216	.320	.288
Jones, Jacque, Min.*	149	626	577	96	173	295	37	2	27	85	4	6	2	37	2	129	6	7	8	.300	.341	.511
Justice, David, Oak.*	118	471	398	54	106	163	18	3	11	49	0	2	1	70	3	66	4	1	12	.266	.376	.410
Kapler, Gabe, Tex.	72	214	196	25	51	65	12	1	0	17	7	3	0	8	0	30	5	2	3	.260	.285	.332
Karsay, Steve, N.Y.	78	1	1	0	0	0	0	0	0	0	0	0	0	0	0	0	0	0	0	.000	.000	.000
Kennedy, Adam, Ana.*	144	509	474	65	148	213	32	6	7	52	5	4	7	19	1	80	17	4	5	.312	.345	.449
Kennedy, Joe, T.B.	30	7	7	1	3	3	0	0	0	1	0	0	0	0	0	5	0	0	1	.429	.429	.429
Kielty, Bobby, Min.†	112	348	289	49	84	140	14	3	12	46	0	2	5	52	4	66	4	1	6	.291	.405	.484
Kingsale, Gene, Sea.†	2	3	3	0	2	2	0	0	0	0	0	0	0	0	0	0	0	0	0	.667	.667	.667
Kinney, Matt, Min.	14	2	2	0	0	0	0	0	0	0	0	0	0	0	0	1	0	0	0	.000	.000	.000
Knoblauch, Chuck, K.C.	80	336	300	41	63	90	9	0	6	22	2	2	4	28	1	32	19	3	5	.210	.284	.300
Konerko, Paul, Chi.	151	630	570	81	173	284	30	0	27	104	0	7	9	44	2	72	0	0	17	.304	.359	.498
Koskie, Corey, Min.*	140	576	490	71	131	219	37	3	15	69	0	5	9	72	4	127	10	11	14	.267	.368	.447

Player, Team	G	TPA	AB	R	H	TB	2B	3B	HR	RBI	SH	SF	HP	BB	IBB	SO	SB	CS	GDP	Avg.	OBP	Slg.
Lamb, David, Min.†	7	10	10	0	1	1	0	0	0	0	0	0	0	0	0	2	0	0	1	.100	.100	.100
Lamb, Mike, Tex.*	115	355	314	54	89	129	13	0	9	33	2	3	3	33	5	48	0	0	7	.283	.354	.411
LaRocca, Greg, Cle.	21	60	52	12	14	19	3	1	0	4	0	0	2	6	0	6	1	0	1	.269	.367	.365
Lawrence, Joe, Tor.	55	174	150	16	27	37	4	0	2	15	2	4	2	16	0	38	2	1	1	.180	.262	.247
Lawton, Matt, Cle.*	114	484	416	71	98	166	19	2	15	57	1	0	8	59	0	34	8	9	13	.236	.342	.399
LeCroy, Matthew, Min.	63	196	181	19	47	81	11	1	7	27	0	2	0	13	1	38	0	2	5	.260	.306	.448
Lee, Carlos, Chi.	140	576	492	82	130	238	26	2	26	80	0	7	2	75	4	73	1	4	5	.264	.359	.484
Leon, Jose, Bal.	36	93	89	8	22	33	2	0	3	10	0	0	1	3	0	20	1	0	2	.247	.280	.371
Lesher, Brian, Tor.	24	43	38	2	5	6	1	0	0	2	0	1	0	4	0	15	0	0	2	.132	.209	.158
Lidle, Cory, Oak.	31	2	1	0	0	0	0	0	0	0	1	0	0	0	0	0	0	0	0	.000	.000	.000
Liefer, Jeff, Chi.*	76	224	204	28	47	76	8	0	7	26	0	1	0	19	2	60	0	0	3	.230	.295	.373
Lilly, Ted, N.Y.-Oak.*	22	3	3	0	0	0	0	0	0	0	0	0	0	0	0	2	0	0	0	.000	.000	.000
Loaiza, Esteban, Tor.	25	6	6	0	1	1	0	0	0	0	0	0	0	0	0	1	0	0	0	.167	.167	.167
Lofton, Kenny, Chi.*	93	406	352	68	91	147	20	6	8	42	4	1	0	49	0	51	22	8	0	.259	.348	.418
Lohse, Kyle, Min.	32	4	4	0	1	1	0	0	0	0	0	0	0	0	0	1	0	0	0	.250	.250	.250
Lombard, George, Det.*	72	270	241	34	58	90	11	3	5	13	7	1	1	20	1	78	13	2	0	.241	.300	.373
Long, Terrence, Oak.*	162	640	587	71	141	229	32	4	16	67	0	3	2	48	6	96	3	6	17	.240	.298	.390
Lopez, Felipe, Tor.†	85	309	282	35	64	109	15	3	8	34	2	1	1	23	1	90	5	4	4	.227	.287	.387
Lopez, Luis, Bal.†	52	112	109	10	23	35	6	0	2	9	0	0	0	3	0	20	1	0	3	.211	.232	.321
Lopez, Rodrigo, Bal.	33	3	3	0	0	0	0	0	0	0	0	0	0	0	0	2	0	0	1	.000	.000	.000
Lowe, Derek, Bos.	32	5	3	0	1	1	0	0	0	0	1	0	0	1	0	0	0	0	1	.333	.500	.333
Ludwick, Ryan, Tex.	23	88	81	10	19	28	6	0	1	9	0	0	0	7	0	24	2	1	4	.235	.295	.346
Mabry, John, Oak.*	89	211	193	27	53	101	13	1	11	40	0	3	1	14	1	37	1	1	7	.275	.322	.523
Macias, Jose, Det.†	33	121	107	10	25	29	4	0	0	6	4	1	1	8	0	13	3	2	4	.234	.291	.271
Magee, Wendell, Det.	97	364	347	34	94	133	19	1	6	35	1	5	1	10	0	64	2	4	9	.271	.289	.383
Magruder, Chris, Cle.†	87	278	258	34	56	91	15	1	6	29	2	2	1	15	2	55	2	0	7	.217	.261	.353
Maroth, Mike, Det.*	21	6	6	1	1	1	0	0	0	0	0	0	0	0	0	5	0	0	1	.167	.167	.167
Marte, Damaso, Chi.*	68	1	1	0	0	0	0	0	0	0	0	0	0	0	0	1	0	0	0	.000	.000	.000
Martinez, Edgar, Sea.	97	407	328	42	91	159	23	0	15	59	0	6	6	67	8	69	1	1	6	.277	.403	.485
Martinez, Pedro, Bos.	30	7	5	1	0	0	0	0	0	0	1	0	0	1	0	3	0	0	0	.000	.167	.000
Martinez, Victor, Cle.†	12	36	32	2	9	13	1	0	1	5	0	1	0	3	0	2	0	1	1	.281	.333	.406
Matos, Luis, Bal.	17	33	31	0	4	5	1	0	0	1	1	0	0	1	0	6	1	0	1	.129	.156	.161
Matthews Jr., Gary, Bal.†	109	397	344	54	95	147	25	3	7	38	5	4	1	43	1	69	15	5	4	.276	.355	.427
May, Darrell, K.C.*	30	5	4	0	0	0	0	0	0	0	0	0	0	1	0	2	0	0	0	.000	.200	.000
Mayne, Brent, K.C.*	101	370	326	35	77	101	8	2	4	30	4	4	2	34	1	54	4	4	8	.236	.309	.310
McCarty, Dave, K.C.-TB.	25	74	66	5	9	16	1	0	2	4	0	0	2	6	0	19	0	0	1	.136	.230	.242
McDonald, Donzell, K.C.†	10	27	22	3	4	6	2	0	0	1	0	1	0	4	0	5	1	0	0	.182	.296	.273
McDonald, John, Cle.	93	288	264	35	66	86	11	3	1	12	7	2	5	10	0	50	3	0	4	.250	.288	.326
McGuire, Ryan, Min.*	17	28	26	0	2	3	1	0	0	2	0	0	0	2	0	7	0	0	2	.077	.143	.115
McKay, Cody, Oak.*	2	4	3	0	2	2	0	0	0	2	0	1	0	0	0	1	0	0	0	.667	.500	.667
McLemore, Mark, Sea.†	104	407	337	54	91	133	17	2	7	41	4	4	1	61	1	63	18	10	3	.270	.380	.395
Meluskey, Mitch, Det.†	8	34	27	3	6	6	0	0	0	1	0	1	1	5	0	3	0	0	2	.222	.353	.222
Mench, Kevin, Tex.	110	412	366	52	95	164	20	2	15	60	2	5	8	31	0	83	1	1	4	.260	.327	.448
Mendoza, Ramiro, N.Y.	62	1	1	0	0	0	0	0	0	0	0	0	0	0	0	1	0	0	0	.000	.000	.000
Menechino, Frank, Oak.	38	154	132	22	27	43	7	0	3	15	0	1	1	20	0	32	0	0	4	.205	.312	.326
Merloni, Lou, Bos.	84	222	194	28	48	76	12	2	4	18	2	1	5	20	0	35	1	2	4	.247	.332	.392
Mientkiewicz, Doug, Min.*	143	554	467	60	122	183	29	1	10	64	0	7	6	74	8	69	1	2	7	.261	.365	.392
Miller, Justin, Tor.	25	2	2	0	0	0	0	0	0	0	0	0	0	0	0	1	0	0	0	.000	.000	.000
Milton, Eric, Min.*	30	5	5	0	2	2	0	0	0	1	0	0	0	0	0	1	0	0	0	.400	.400	.400
Mirabelli, Doug, Bos.	57	173	151	17	34	62	7	0	7	25	0	2	3	17	0	33	0	0	6	.225	.312	.411
Mohr, Dustan, Min.	120	417	383	55	103	166	23	2	12	45	2	0	1	31	3	86	6	3	5	.269	.325	.433
Molina, Bengie, Ana.	122	459	428	34	105	138	18	0	5	47	6	6	4	15	3	34	0	0	15	.245	.274	.322
Molina, Izzy, Bal.	1	3	3	1	1	1	0	0	0	0	0	0	0	0	0	0	0	0	0	.333	.333	.333
Molina, Jose, Ana.	29	81	70	5	19	22	3	0	0	5	4	2	0	5	0	15	0	2	2	.271	.312	.314
Mondesi, Raul, Tor.-N.Y.	146	637	569	90	132	246	34	1	26	88	0	4	5	59	3	103	15	6	11	.232	.308	.432
Monroe, Craig, Det.	13	26	25	3	3	7	1	0	1	4	0	1	0	0	0	5	0	2	1	.120	.154	.280
Mora, Melvin, Bal.	149	652	557	86	130	225	30	4	19	64	1	4	20	70	2	108	16	10	7	.233	.338	.404
Moriarty, Mike, Bal.	8	16	16	0	3	4	1	0	0	3	0	0	0	0	0	2	0	1	3	.188	.188	.250
Morris, Warren, Min.*	4	7	7	0	0	0	0	0	0	0	0	0	0	0	0	1	0	0	0	.000	.000	.000
Moyer, Jamie, Sea.*	34	5	5	0	1	1	0	0	0	0	0	0	0	0	0	0	0	0	0	.200	.200	.200
Mulder, Mark, Oak.*	30	5	5	0	0	0	0	0	0	0	0	0	0	0	0	1	0	0	0	.000	.000	.000
Munson, Eric, Det.*	18	67	59	3	11	17	0	0	2	5	0	1	1	6	0	11	0	0	1	.186	.269	.288
Murray, Calvin, Tex.	37	86	77	16	13	20	5	1	0	1	2	0	1	6	0	15	4	0	0	.169	.238	.260
Mussina, Mike, N.Y.*	33	6	5	2	3	3	0	0	0	0	1	0	0	0	0	0	0	0	0	.600	.600	.600
Myers, Greg, Oak.*	65	170	144	15	32	55	5	0	6	21	0	0	0	26	3	36	0	0	4	.222	.341	.382
Nagy, Charles, Cle.*	20	0	0	1	0	0	0	0	0	0	0	0	0	0	0	0	0	0	0	.000	.000	.000
Nelson, Bry, Bos.†	25	39	34	6	9	12	3	0	0	2	1	0	0	4	0	1	1	1	1	.265	.342	.353
Nieves, Jose, Ana.	45	100	97	17	28	30	2	0	0	6	1	0	0	2	0	14	1	1	3	.289	.303	.309
Nixon, Trot, Bos.*	152	612	532	81	136	250	36	3	24	94	3	7	5	65	2	109	4	2	7	.256	.338	.470
Ochoa, Alex, Ana.	37	75	65	8	18	31	7	0	2	10	0	0	0	10	0	5	2	2	2	.277	.373	.477
Offerman, Jose, Bos.-Sea.†	101	326	284	48	66	95	12	1	5	31	1	3	1	37	0	38	9	6	12	.232	.320	.335
Olerud, John, Sea.*	154	668	553	85	166	271	39	0	22	102	0	12	5	98	6	66	0	0	19	.300	.403	.490
Oliver, Darren, Bos.	14	1	1	0	0	0	0	0	0	0	0	0	0	0	0	0	0	0	0	.000	.000	.000
Olivo, Miguel, Chi.	6	21	19	2	4	8	1	0	1	5	0	0	0	2	0	5	0	0	1	.211	.286	.421
Ordaz, Luis, K.C.	33	111	94	11	21	23	2	0	0	4	4	1	0	12	0	13	2	3	2	.223	.308	.245
Ordonez, Magglio, Chi.	153	654	590	116	189	352	47	1	38	135	0	3	7	53	2	77	7	5	21	.320	.381	.597
Ortiz, David, Min.*	125	466	412	52	112	206	32	1	20	75	0	8	3	43	0	87	1	2	5	.272	.339	.500
Ortiz, Hector, Tex.	7	15	14	1	3	7	1	0	1	2	0	0	0	1	0	1	0	0	1	.214	.267	.500
Ortiz, Ramon, Ana.	32	7	7	0	0	0	0	0	0	0	0	0	0	0	0	3	0	0	1	.000	.000	.000
Palmeiro, Orlando, Ana.*	110	300	263	35	79	93	12	1	0	31	4	3	0	30	1	22	7	2	7	.300	.368	.354
Palmeiro, Rafael, Tex.*	155	663	546	99	149	312	34	1	43	105	0	7	6	104	16	94	2	0	10	.273	.391	.571
Palmer, Dean, Det.	4	13	12	0	0	0	0	0	0	0	0	0	0	1	0	5	0	0	1	.000	.077	.000

Player, Team	G	TPA	AB	R	H	TB	2B	3B	HR	RBI	SH	SF	HP	BB	IBB	SO	SB	CS	GDP	Avg.	OBP	Slg.
Paquette, Craig, Det.	72	266	252	20	49	77	14	1	4	20	1	3	0	10	0	53	1	0	7	.194	.223	.306
Park, Chan Ho, Tex.	25	4	4	0	0	0	0	0	0	0	0	0	0	0	0	0	0	0	1	.000	.000	.000
Parris, Steve, Tor.	14	4	4	0	0	0	0	0	0	0	0	0	0	0	0	2	0	0	0	.000	.000	.000
Paul, Josh, Chi.	33	118	104	11	25	29	4	0	0	11	2	2	1	9	0	22	2	0	1	.240	.302	.279
Pellow, Kit, K.C.	29	73	63	6	15	19	1	0	1	5	0	0	1	9	0	21	1	1	2	.238	.342	.302
Pena, Carlos, Oak.-Det.*	115	443	397	43	96	178	17	4	19	52	0	2	3	41	0	111	2	2	7	.242	.316	.448
Perez, Eddie, Cle.	42	125	117	6	25	34	9	0	0	4	2	0	1	5	0	25	0	0	6	.214	.252	.291
Perez, Neifi, K.C.†	145	585	554	65	131	168	20	4	3	37	5	6	0	20	2	53	8	9	11	.236	.260	.303
Perry, Chan, K.C.	5	11	11	0	1	1	0	0	0	3	0	0	0	0	0	1	0	0	1	.091	.091	.091
Perry, Herbert, Tex.	132	496	450	64	124	216	24	1	22	77	4	2	6	34	1	66	4	2	17	.276	.333	.480
Pettitte, Andy, N.Y.*	22	3	3	0	1	2	1	0	0	1	0	0	0	0	0	1	0	0	0	.333	.333	.667
Phelps, Josh, Tor.	74	287	265	41	82	149	20	1	15	58	0	0	3	19	0	82	0	0	7	.309	.362	.562
Phillips, Brandon, Cle.	11	36	31	5	8	13	3	1	0	4	1	0	1	3	0	6	0	0	0	.258	.343	.419
Piatt, Adam, Oak.	55	152	137	18	32	55	8	0	5	18	0	1	2	12	0	33	2	1	1	.234	.303	.401
Pierzynski, A.J., Min.*	130	469	440	54	132	193	31	6	6	49	2	3	11	13	1	61	1	2	14	.300	.334	.439
Pineiro, Joel, Sea.	37	7	7	0	1	1	0	0	0	2	0	0	0	0	0	2	0	0	0	.143	.143	.143
Podsednik, Scott, Sea.*	14	25	20	2	4	7	0	0	1	5	0	1	0	4	0	6	0	0	1	.200	.320	.350
Ponson, Sidney, Bal.	28	3	3	1	1	2	1	0	0	0	0	0	0	0	0	1	0	0	0	.333	.333	.667
Posada, Jorge, N.Y.†	143	598	511	79	137	239	40	1	20	99	0	3	3	81	9	143	1	0	23	.268	.370	.468
Prince, Tom, Min.	51	148	125	14	28	49	7	1	4	16	3	2	4	14	0	26	1	3	4	.224	.317	.392
Quinn, Mark, K.C.	23	84	76	9	18	28	4	0	2	11	1	0	2	5	0	15	2	1	3	.237	.301	.368
Ramirez, Julio, Ana.	29	35	32	6	9	14	0	1	1	7	0	0	1	2	0	14	0	2	0	.281	.343	.438
Ramirez, Manny, Bos.	120	518	436	84	152	282	31	0	33	107	0	1	8	73	14	85	0	0	13	.349	.450	.647
Randa, Joe, K.C.	151	617	549	63	155	234	36	5	11	80	2	11	9	46	1	69	2	1	13	.282	.341	.426
Redman, Mark, Det.*	30	5	5	1	1	1	0	0	0	0	0	0	0	0	0	0	0	0	1	.200	.200	.200
Reed, Rick, Min.	33	6	4	0	1	1	0	0	0	0	1	0	0	1	0	2	0	0	0	.250	.400	.250
Relaford, Desi, Sea.†	112	376	329	55	88	123	13	2	6	43	1	7	6	33	2	51	10	3	6	.267	.339	.374
Restovich, Michael, Min.	8	14	13	3	4	7	0	0	1	1	0	0	0	1	0	4	1	0	2	.308	.357	.538
Richard, Chris, Bal.*	50	171	155	15	36	59	11	0	4	21	0	2	2	12	0	30	0	3	2	.232	.292	.381
Rincon, Ricardo, Cle.-Oak.*	71	1	1	0	0	0	0	0	0	0	0	0	0	0	0	0	0	0	0	.000	.000	.000
Ritchie, Todd, Chi.	27	5	4	1	1	1	0	0	0	0	0	0	0	1	0	1	0	0	0	.250	.400	.250
Rivas, Luis, Min.	93	346	316	46	81	124	23	4	4	35	8	0	3	19	2	51	9	4	12	.256	.305	.392
Rivera, Juan, N.Y.	28	91	83	9	22	30	5	0	1	6	1	1	0	6	0	10	1	1	4	.265	.311	.361
Rivera, Michael, Det.	39	138	132	11	30	43	8	1	1	11	0	1	1	4	0	35	0	0	5	.227	.254	.326
Rivera, Ruben, Tex.	69	186	158	17	33	49	4	0	4	14	4	2	5	17	0	45	4	2	2	.209	.302	.310
Roberts, Brian, Bal.†	38	149	128	18	29	38	6	0	1	11	3	2	1	15	0	21	9	2	3	.227	.308	.297
Rodriguez, Alex, Tex.	162	725	624	125	187	389	27	2	57	142	0	4	10	87	12	122	9	4	14	.300	.392	.623
Rodriguez, Ivan, Tex.	108	440	408	67	128	221	32	2	19	60	1	4	2	25	2	71	5	4	13	.314	.353	.542
Rogers, Eddie, Bal.	5	3	3	0	0	0	0	0	0	0	0	0	0	0	0	0	0	1	0	.000	.000	.000
Rogers, Kenny, Tex.*	34	4	3	0	2	2	0	0	0	1	0	0	0	1	0	1	0	0	0	.667	.750	.667
Rolls, Damian, T.B.	21	95	89	15	26	34	6	1	0	6	1	0	2	3	0	16	2	5	1	.292	.330	.382
Romano, Jason, Tex.	29	60	54	8	11	15	4	0	0	4	1	1	0	4	0	13	2	0	0	.204	.254	.278
Rowand, Aaron, Chi.	126	331	302	41	78	119	16	2	7	29	9	2	6	12	1	54	0	1	8	.258	.298	.394
Rupe, Ryan, T.B.	15	1	1	0	0	0	0	0	0	0	0	0	0	0	0	1	0	0	0	.000	.000	.000
Ryan, B.J., Bal.*	67	1	1	0	0	0	0	0	0	0	0	0	0	0	0	0	0	0	0	.000	.000	.000
Ryan, Michael, Min.*	7	11	11	3	1	1	0	0	0	0	0	0	0	0	0	2	0	0	0	.091	.091	.091
Sabathia, C.C., Cle.*	33	6	5	0	1	1	0	0	0	0	1	0	0	0	0	1	0	0	0	.200	.333	.200
Sadler, Donnie, K.C.-Tex.	73	109	98	16	16	20	2	1	0	7	1	1	2	7	0	19	5	3	1	.163	.231	.204
Saenz, Olmedo, Oak.	68	178	156	15	43	73	10	1	6	18	0	2	7	13	1	31	1	1	2	.276	.354	.468
Salazar, Oscar, Det.	8	23	21	2	4	8	1	0	1	3	1	0	0	1	0	2	0	0	0	.190	.227	.381
Salmon, Tim, Ana.	138	568	483	84	138	243	37	1	22	88	0	7	7	71	3	102	6	3	6	.286	.380	.503
Sanchez, Freddy, Bos.	12	18	16	3	3	3	0	0	0	2	0	0	0	2	0	3	0	0	1	.188	.278	.188
Sanchez, Rey, Bos.	107	386	357	46	102	123	12	3	1	38	5	5	2	17	1	31	2	2	9	.286	.318	.345
Sandberg, Jared, T.B.	102	401	358	55	82	159	21	1	18	54	1	2	1	39	3	139	3	2	7	.229	.305	.444
Santana, Johan, Min.*	27	4	4	0	1	1	0	0	0	0	0	0	0	0	0	0	0	0	0	.250	.250	.250
Santiago, Ramon, Det.†	65	249	222	33	54	81	5	5	4	20	4	2	8	13	0	48	8	5	2	.243	.306	.365
Schoeneweis, Scott, Ana.*.	54	2	2	0	0	0	0	0	0	0	0	0	0	2	0	0	0	0	0	.000	.000	.000
Sears, Todd, Min.*	7	12	12	2	4	6	2	0	0	0	0	0	0	0	0	1	0	0	0	.333	.333	.500
Sedlacek, Shawn, K.C.	16	6	6	0	0	0	0	0	0	0	0	0	0	0	0	4	0	0	0	.000	.000	.000
Segui, David, Bal.†	26	107	95	10	25	35	4	0	2	16	0	1	0	11	0	22	0	0	5	.263	.336	.368
Selby, Bill, Cle.*	65	176	159	15	34	63	7	2	6	21	0	2	0	15	2	27	0	1	4	.214	.278	.396
Sele, Aaron, Ana.	26	2	2	0	1	1	0	0	0	0	0	0	0	0	0	1	0	0	0	.500	.500	.500
Sheets, Andy, T.B.	41	164	149	18	37	53	4	0	4	22	1	2	0	12	0	41	2	3	1	.248	.301	.356
Sierra, Ruben, Sea.†	122	452	419	47	113	175	23	0	13	60	0	2	0	31	5	66	4	0	17	.270	.319	.418
Simon, Randall, Det.*	130	506	482	51	145	221	17	1	19	82	0	7	4	13	5	30	0	1	13	.301	.320	.459
Singleton, Chris, Bal.*	136	502	466	67	122	191	30	6	9	50	6	5	4	21	0	83	20	2	8	.262	.296	.410
Smith, Bobby, T.B.	18	66	63	4	11	16	2	0	1	6	0	0	0	3	0	25	0	0	0	.175	.212	.254
Smith, Jason, T.B.*	26	69	65	9	13	21	1	2	1	6	2	0	0	2	0	24	3	0	0	.200	.224	.323
Snelling, Chris, Sea.*	8	29	27	2	4	7	0	0	1	3	0	0	0	2	0	4	0	0	2	.148	.207	.259
Snyder, Earl, Cle.	18	62	55	5	11	16	2	0	1	4	1	0	0	6	0	21	0	0	1	.200	.279	.291
Soriano, Alfonso, N.Y.	156	741	696	128	209	381	51	2	39	102	1	7	14	23	1	157	41	13	6	.300	.332	.547
Soriano, Rafael, Sea.	11	4	4	0	0	0	0	0	0	0	0	0	0	0	0	1	0	0	0	.000	.000	.000
Sparks, Steve W., Det.	32	2	2	0	0	0	0	0	0	0	0	0	0	0	0	1	0	0	0	.000	.000	.000
Spencer, Shane, N.Y.	94	329	288	32	71	108	15	2	6	34	2	4	4	31	4	62	0	3	5	.247	.324	.375
Spiezio, Scott, Ana.†	153	571	491	80	140	214	34	2	12	82	3	6	4	67	7	52	6	7	12	.285	.371	.436
Stanton, Mike, N.Y.*	79	2	2	0	0	0	0	0	0	0	0	0	0	0	0	0	0	0	0	.000	.000	.000
Stevens, Lee, Cle.*	53	172	153	22	34	58	7	1	5	26	0	4	0	15	0	32	0	0	5	.222	.285	.379
Stewart, Shannon, Tor.	141	641	577	103	175	255	38	6	10	45	0	1	9	54	2	60	14	2	17	.303	.371	.442
Sturtze, Tanyon, T.B.	33	5	4	0	0	0	0	0	0	0	1	0	0	0	0	1	0	0	0	.000	.000	.000
Suppan, Jeff, K.C.	33	5	1	0	0	0	0	0	0	0	3	0	0	1	0	1	0	0	0	.000	.500	.000
Sutton, Larry, Oak.*	7	20	19	3	2	5	0	0	1	3	0	0	0	1	0	8	0	0	1	.105	.150	.263
Suzuki, Ichiro, Sea.*	157	728	647	111	208	275	27	8	8	51	3	5	5	68	27	62	31	15	8	.321	.388	.425

Player, Team	G	TPA	AB	R	H	TB	2B	3B	HR	RBI	SH	SF	HP	BB	IBB	SO	SB	CS	GDP	Avg.	OBP	Slg.
Suzuki, Mac, K.C.	7	2	2	0	1	1	0	0	0	0	0	0	0	0	0	1	0	0	0	.500	.500	.500
Swann, Pedro, Tor.*	13	13	12	3	1	1	0	0	0	1	0	0	0	1	0	6	0	0	0	.083	.154	.083
Sweeney, Mike, K.C.	126	545	471	81	160	265	31	1	24	86	0	7	6	61	10	46	9	7	9	.340	.417	.563
Tejada, Miguel, Oak.	162	715	662	108	204	336	30	0	34	131	0	4	11	38	3	84	7	2	21	.308	.354	.508
Thames, Marcus, N.Y.	7	13	13	2	3	7	1	0	1	2	0	0	0	0	0	4	0	0	0	.231	.231	.538
Thomas, Frank, Chi.	148	628	523	77	132	247	29	1	28	92	0	10	7	88	2	115	3	0	10	.252	.361	.472
Thome, Jim, Cle.*	147	613	480	101	146	325	19	2	52	118	0	6	5	122	18	139	1	2	5	.304	.445	.677
Thurman, Corey, Tor.	43	2	1	0	0	0	0	0	0	0	0	1	0	0	0	0	0	0	0	.000	.000	.000
Torres, Andres, Det.†	19	79	70	7	14	17	1	1	0	3	0	2	1	6	0	16	2	2	2	.200	.266	.243
Truby, Chris, Det.	89	292	277	23	55	78	13	2	2	15	3	5	2	5	0	71	1	1	5	.199	.215	.282
Tucker, Michael, K.C.*	144	543	475	65	118	193	27	6	12	56	7	2	3	56	1	105	23	9	5	.248	.330	.406
Tyner, Jason, T.B.*	44	180	168	17	36	40	2	1	0	9	3	1	1	7	0	19	7	1	1	.214	.249	.238
Ugueto, Luis, Sea.†	62	25	23	19	5	8	0	0	1	1	0	0	0	2	0	8	8	4	0	.217	.280	.348
Valdes, Ismael, Tex.-Sea.	31	4	3	0	0	0	0	0	0	1	1	0	0	0	0	2	0	0	0	.000	.000	.000
Valentin, Javier, Min.†	4	4	4	0	2	2	0	0	0	0	0	0	0	0	0	0	0	0	0	.500	.500	.500
Valentin, Jose, Chi.†	135	527	474	70	118	227	26	4	25	75	3	5	2	43	2	99	3	3	9	.249	.311	.479
Van Poppel, Todd, Tex.	50	1	1	0	0	0	0	0	0	0	0	0	0	0	0	1	0	0	0	.000	.000	.000
Vander Wal, John, N.Y.*	84	245	219	30	57	94	17	1	6	20	0	3	0	23	3	58	1	1	7	.260	.327	.429
Varitek, Jason, Bos.†	132	519	467	58	124	183	27	1	10	61	1	3	7	41	3	95	4	3	13	.266	.332	.392
Vaughn, Greg, T.B.	69	297	251	28	41	79	10	2	8	29	0	2	3	41	1	82	3	2	5	.163	.286	.315
Velarde, Randy, Oak.	56	155	133	22	30	44	8	0	2	8	1	1	5	15	1	32	3	0	4	.226	.325	.331
Ventura, Robin, N.Y.*	141	562	465	68	115	213	17	0	27	93	0	5	2	90	9	101	3	1	14	.247	.368	.458
Vizquel, Omar, Cle.†	151	663	582	85	160	243	31	5	14	72	7	10	8	56	3	64	18	10	7	.275	.341	.418
Walbeck, Matt, Det.†	27	89	85	4	20	22	2	0	0	3	0	1	0	3	0	14	0	0	2	.235	.258	.259
Washburn, Jarrod, Ana.*	32	5	5	0	1	1	0	0	0	0	0	0	0	0	0	3	0	0	0	.200	.200	.200
Wathan, Dusty, K.C.	3	6	5	1	3	4	1	0	0	1	0	0	1	0	0	1	0	0	0	.600	.667	.800
Weaver, Jeff, Det.-N.Y.	32	7	7	0	2	2	0	0	0	1	0	0	0	0	0	4	0	0	0	.286	.286	.286
Wells, David, N.Y.*	31	5	4	0	0	0	0	0	0	0	1	0	0	0	0	3	0	0	0	.000	.000	.000
Wells, Vernon, Tor.	159	648	608	87	167	278	34	4	23	100	2	8	3	27	0	85	9	4	15	.275	.305	.457
Werth, Jayson, Tor.	15	53	46	4	12	16	2	1	0	6	0	1	0	6	0	11	1	0	4	.261	.340	.348
White, Rondell, N.Y.	126	494	455	59	109	172	21	0	14	62	1	5	8	25	1	86	1	2	11	.240	.288	.378
Widger, Chris, N.Y.	21	68	64	4	19	24	5	0	0	5	0	0	2	2	0	9	0	0	0	.297	.338	.375
Williams, Bernie, N.Y.†	154	699	612	102	204	302	37	2	19	102	0	1	3	83	7	97	8	4	19	.333	.415	.493
Williams, Gerald, N.Y.	33	19	17	6	0	0	0	0	0	0	0	0	0	2	0	4	2	0	1	.000	.105	.000
Wilson, Dan, Sea.	115	394	359	35	106	142	16	1	6	44	7	8	2	18	1	81	1	0	8	.295	.326	.396
Wilson, Enrique, N.Y.†	60	119	105	17	19	31	2	2	2	11	6	0	0	8	0	22	1	1	2	.181	.239	.295
Wilson, Paul, T.B.	30	6	5	0	0	0	0	0	0	0	1	0	0	0	0	5	0	0	0	.000	.000	.000
Wilson, Tom, Tor.	96	302	265	33	68	102	10	0	8	37	0	4	5	28	0	79	0	0	6	.257	.334	.385
Winn, Randy, T.B.†	152	674	607	87	181	280	39	9	14	75	1	5	6	55	3	109	27	8	9	.298	.360	.461
Wise, Dewayne, Tor.*	42	116	112	14	20	35	4	1	3	13	0	0	0	4	0	15	5	0	0	.179	.207	.313
Woodward, Chris, Tor.	90	350	312	48	86	146	13	4	13	45	1	8	3	26	0	72	3	0	8	.276	.330	.468
Wooten, Shawn, Ana.	49	121	113	13	33	50	8	0	3	19	0	1	1	6	1	24	2	0	3	.292	.331	.442
Wright, Dan, Chi.	33	4	4	0	0	0	0	0	0	0	0	0	0	0	0	2	0	0	0	.000	.000	.000
Wright, Ron, Sea.	1	3	3	0	0	0	0	0	0	0	0	0	0	0	0	1	0	0	1	.000	.000	.000
Young, Dmitri, Det.†	54	216	201	25	57	92	14	0	7	27	0	1	2	12	5	39	2	0	12	.284	.329	.458
Young, Michael, Tex.	156	633	573	77	150	219	26	8	9	62	13	6	0	41	1	112	6	7	14	.262	.308	.382
Zambrano, Victor, T.B.	42	1	0	0	0	0	0	0	0	0	0	0	0	0	0	0	0	0	0	.000	.000	.000
Zito, Barry, Oak.*	35	6	4	0	0	0	0	0	0	0	2	0	0	0	0	3	0	0	0	.000	.000	.000

PLAYERS WITH TWO OR MORE TEAMS

Player, Team	G	TPA	AB	R	H	TB	2B	3B	HR	RBI	SH	SF	HP	BB	IBB	SO	SB	CS	GDP	Avg.	OBP	Slg.
Burba, Dave, Tex.	23	5	5	0	1	1	0	0	0	0	0	0	0	0	0	3	0	0	0	.200	.200	.200
Burba, Dave, Cle.	12	0	0	0	0	0	0	0	0	0	0	0	0	0	0	0	0	0	0	.000	.000	.000
Creek, Doug, T.B.*	29	1	1	0	0	0	0	0	0	0	0	0	0	0	0	1	0	0	0	.000	.000	.000
Creek, Doug, Sea.*	23	0	0	0	0	0	0	0	0	0	0	0	0	0	0	0	0	0	0	.000	.000	.000
Durham, Ray, Chi.†	96	411	345	71	103	154	20	2	9	48	8	4	5	49	0	59	20	5	13	.299	.390	.446
Durham, Ray, Oak.†	54	248	219	43	60	100	14	4	6	22	2	1	2	24	1	34	6	2	2	.274	.350	.457
Garcia, Karim, N.Y.*	2	5	5	1	1	1	0	0	0	0	0	0	0	0	0	1	0	0	0	.200	.200	.200
Garcia, Karim, Cle.*	51	205	197	29	59	115	8	0	16	52	0	2	0	6	0	40	0	3	6	.299	.317	.584
Lilly, Ted, N.Y.*	16	3	3	0	0	0	0	0	0	0	0	0	0	0	0	2	0	0	0	.000	.000	.000
Lilly, Ted, Oak.*	6	0	0	0	0	0	0	0	0	0	0	0	0	0	0	0	0	0	0	.000	.000	.000
McCarty, Dave, K.C.	13	34	32	3	3	7	1	0	1	2	0	0	0	2	0	10	0	0	1	.094	.147	.219
McCarty, Dave, T.B.	12	40	34	2	6	9	0	0	1	2	0	2	0	4	0	9	0	0	0	.176	.300	.265
Mondesi, Raul, Tor.	75	335	299	51	67	130	16	1	15	45	0	2	3	31	1	57	9	2	8	.224	.301	.435
Mondesi, Raul, N.Y.	71	302	270	39	65	116	18	0	11	43	0	2	2	28	2	46	6	4	3	.241	.315	.430
Offerman, Jose, Bos.†	72	275	237	39	55	77	10	0	4	27	1	3	1	33	0	29	8	5	9	.232	.325	.325
Offerman, Jose, Sea.†	29	51	47	9	11	18	2	1	1	4	0	0	0	4	0	9	1	1	3	.234	.294	.383
Pena, Carlos, Oak.*	40	141	124	12	27	52	4	0	7	16	0	1	1	15	0	38	0	0	2	.218	.305	.419
Pena, Carlos, Det.*	75	302	273	31	69	126	13	4	12	36	0	1	2	26	0	73	2	2	5	.253	.321	.462
Rincon, Ricardo, Cle.*	46	1	1	0	0	0	0	0	0	0	0	0	0	0	0	0	0	0	0	.000	.000	.000
Rincon, Ricardo, Oak.*	25	0	0	0	0	0	0	0	0	0	0	0	0	0	0	0	0	0	0	.000	.000	.000
Sadler, Donnie, K.C.	35	73	68	10	13	16	1	1	0	5	0	1	0	4	0	12	3	1	0	.191	.233	.235
Sadler, Donnie, Tex.	38	36	30	6	3	4	1	0	0	2	1	0	2	3	0	7	2	2	1	.100	.229	.133
Valdes, Ismael, Tex.	23	4	3	0	0	0	0	0	0	1	1	0	0	0	0	2	0	0	0	.000	.000	.000
Valdes, Ismael, Sea.	8	0	0	0	0	0	0	0	0	0	0	0	0	0	0	0	0	0	0	.000	.000	.000
Weaver, Jeff, Det.	17	7	7	0	2	2	0	0	0	1	0	0	0	0	0	4	0	0	0	.286	.286	.286
Weaver, Jeff, N.Y.	15	0	0	0	0	0	0	0	0	0	0	0	0	0	0	0	0	0	0	.000	.000	.000

AWARDED FIRST BASE ON OBSTRUCTION OR CATCHER'S INTERFERENCE—Ordonez, Chicago (Ortiz).

Player	vs.	Avg.	AB	H	2B	3B	HR	RBI	BB	SO	OBP	Slg.
Abernathy, Brent	L	.203	79	16	6	0	1	8	5	11	.259	.316
Bats Right	R	.250	384	96	12	4	1	32	20	35	.294	.310
Agbayani, Benny	L	.385	13	5	0	0	0	2	1	1	.429	.385
Bats Right	R	.250	24	6	1	0	0	6	5	4	.379	.292
Alicea, Luis	L	.205	44	9	1	0	0	2	4	3	.271	.227
Bats Both	R	.233	193	45	7	2	1	21	28	31	.333	.306
Allen, Chad	L	.125	8	1	1	0	0	0	0	2	.125	.250
Bats Right	R	.000	2	0	0	0	0	0	0	0	.000	.000
Alomar Jr., Sandy	L	.226	53	12	3	1	1	7	3	6	.263	.377
Bats Right	R	.316	114	36	7	0	6	18	2	8	.331	.535
Amezaga, Alfredo	L	.800	5	4	1	0	0	1	0	0	.800	1.000
Bats Both	R	.375	8	3	1	0	0	1	0	1	.375	.500
Anderson, Brady	L	.111	9	1	1	0	0	0	1	5	.333	.222
Bats Right	R	.169	71	12	3	0	1	5	17	18	.326	.254
Anderson, Garret	L	.284	208	59	15	0	11	41	7	37	.301	.514
Bats Left	R	.316	430	136	41	3	18	82	23	43	.346	.551
Andrews, Shane	L	.000	4	0	0	0	0	0	1	0	.333	.000
Bats Right	R	.111	9	1	1	0	0	0	0	3	.111	.222
Arias, Alex	L	.000	0	0	0	0	0	0	1	0	.000	.000
Bats Right	R	.000	5	0	0	0	0	0	1	1	.167	.000
Aven, Bruce	L	.182	11	2	0	0	0	0	2	2	.308	.182
Bats Right	R	.000	6	0	0	0	0	0	0	2	.250	.000
Baerga, Carlos	L	.224	49	11	3	0	0	3	1	6	.235	.286
Bats Both	R	.308	133	41	8	0	2	16	6	14	.345	.414
Bard, Josh	L	.229	35	8	3	0	2	5	1	5	.250	.486
Bats Both	R	.218	55	12	2	0	1	7	3	8	.259	.309
Batista, Tony	L	.234	158	37	10	0	3	11	13	30	.295	.354
Bats Right	R	.247	457	113	26	1	28	76	37	77	.314	.492
Bellinger, Clay	L	.000	0	0	0	0	0	0	0	0	.000	.000
Bats Right	R	.000	1	0	0	0	0	0	0	0	.000	.000
Beltran, Carlos	L	.245	163	40	12	1	8	24	15	31	.307	.479
Bats Both	R	.283	474	134	32	6	21	81	56	104	.359	.508
Berg, Dave	L	.264	106	28	5	0	2	10	8	14	.310	.368
Bats Right	R	.272	268	73	21	2	2	29	18	43	.327	.388
Berger, Brandon	L	.214	56	12	3	0	3	5	4	16	.267	.429
Bats Right	R	.192	78	15	2	1	3	12	4	16	.247	.359
Berroa, Angel	L	.261	23	6	2	0	0	1	2	4	.320	.348
Bats Right	R	.212	52	11	5	1	0	4	5	6	.293	.346
Bigbie, Larry	L	.000	2	0	0	0	0	0	0	1	.000	.000
Bats Left	R	.188	32	6	1	0	0	3	1	10	.206	.219
Blake, Casey	L	.143	7	1	0	0	0	0	2	2	.333	.143
Bats Right	R	.231	13	3	1	0	0	1	0	5	.231	.308
Blalock, Hank	L	.067	30	2	0	0	0	3	3	11	.176	.067
Bats Left	R	.248	117	29	8	0	3	14	17	32	.338	.393
Bloomquist, Willie	L	.571	14	8	3	0	0	5	2	0	.625	.786
Bats Right	R	.368	19	7	1	0	0	2	3	2	.455	.421
Bocachica, Hiram	L	.277	47	13	3	0	1	4	3	8	.320	.404
Bats Right	R	.179	56	10	1	0	3	4	2	14	.207	.357
Boone, Bret	L	.295	149	44	10	1	8	26	17	23	.363	.537
Bats Right	R	.272	459	125	24	2	16	81	36	79	.331	.438
Borchard, Joe	L	.250	8	2	0	0	0	0	0	4	.250	.250
Bats Both	R	.214	28	6	0	0	2	5	1	10	.241	.429
Borders, Pat	L	.500	2	1	0	0	0	0	0	1	.500	.500
Bats Right	R	.500	2	1	0	0	0	0	0	1	.500	1.000
Bordick, Mike	L	.236	110	26	6	0	3	6	11	14	.306	.373
Bats Right	R	.230	257	59	13	3	5	30	24	49	.301	.362
Bradley, Milton	L	.293	99	29	6	1	1	11	13	16	.375	.404
Bats Both	R	.230	226	52	12	2	8	27	19	42	.290	.407
Branyan, Russell	L	.296	27	8	0	0	4	8	0	13	.296	.741
Bats Left	R	.187	134	25	4	0	4	9	17	52	.275	.306
Brito, Juan	L	.000	1	0	0	0	0	0	0	0	.000	.000
Bats Right	R	.318	22	7	2	0	0	1	0	3	.318	.409
Broussard, Ben	L	.167	18	3	1	0	1	3	0	4	.167	.389
Bats Left	R	.255	94	24	3	0	3	6	7	21	.314	.383
Brown, Dee	L	.091	11	1	0	0	0	0	0	6	.091	.091
Bats Left	R	.275	40	11	3	1	1	7	4	14	.341	.475
Brown, Kevin L.	L	.000	0	0	0	0	0	0	0	0	.000	.000
Bats Right	R	.000	1	0	0	0	0	0	0	0	.000	.000
Buchanan, Brian	L	.242	62	15	4	1	3	9	3	10	.277	.484
Bats Right	R	.260	73	19	1	0	2	6	3	23	.308	.356
Burks, Ellis	L	.316	136	43	9	0	9	19	19	22	.400	.581
Bats Right	R	.296	382	113	19	0	23	72	25	86	.348	.526
Bush, Homer	L	.240	25	6	1	0	0	0	1	4	.296	.280
Bats Right	R	.226	53	12	1	0	1	2	1	8	.255	.302
Byrnes, Eric	L	.279	43	12	2	0	1	5	0	8	.273	.395
Bats Right	R	.216	51	11	2	2	2	6	4	9	.305	.451
Cabrera, Jolbert	L	.226	31	7	1	0	0	4	3	4	.294	.258
Bats Right	R	.024	41	1	0	0	0	3	2	9	.089	.024
Cameron, Mike	L	.239	142	34	10	1	10	29	20	40	.343	.535
Bats Right	R	.238	403	96	16	4	15	51	59	136	.338	.409
Canizaro, Jay	L	.205	39	8	2	1	0	7	7	5	.313	.308
Bats Right	R	.219	73	16	6	0	0	4	3	17	.260	.301
Caruso, Mike	L	.000	0	0	0	0	0	0	0	0	.000	.000
Bats Left	R	.100	20	2	0	0	0	0	1	2	.143	.100
Casanova, Raul	L	.000	0	0	0	0	0	0	0	0	.000	.000
Bats Right	R	.000	1	0	0	0	0	0	0	1	.000	.000
Cash, Kevin	L	.000	6	0	0	0	0	0	0	2	.000	.000
Bats Right	R	.250	8	2	0	0	0	0	1	2	.333	.250
Castillo, Alberto	L	.000	10	0	0	0	0	0	1	1	.091	.000
Bats Right	R	.185	27	5	1	1	0	4	0	11	.185	.296
Catalanotto, Frank	L	.231	26	6	1	1	0	4	3	5	.364	.346
Bats Left	R	.274	186	51	15	5	3	19	22	22	.364	.457
Chavez, Eric	L	.209	163	34	7	0	6	27	11	37	.261	.362
Bats Right	R	.301	422	127	24	3	28	82	54	82	.379	.571
Cirillo, Jeff	L	.304	148	45	6	0	4	20	10	17	.362	.426
Bats Right	R	.226	337	76	14	0	2	34	21	50	.275	.285
Clark, Howie	L	.000	3	0	0	0	0	0	0	1	.000	.000
Bats Left	R	.320	50	16	5	0	0	4	3	5	.382	.420
Clark, Tony	L	.159	82	13	3	1	1	6	3	24	.188	.256
Bats Both	R	.228	193	44	9	0	2	23	18	33	.296	.306
Clayton, Royce	L	.238	101	24	2	0	3	10	3	20	.257	.347
Bats Right	R	.257	241	62	12	2	4	25	17	47	.311	.373
Colangelo, M	L	.143	14	2	1	0	0	0	1	2	.200	.214
Bats Right	R	.222	9	2	0	0	0	0	1	0	.300	.222
Conine, Jeff	L	.292	113	33	4	1	6	20	10	21	.336	.504
Bats Right	R	.266	338	90	22	3	9	43	15	45	.297	.429
Conti, Jason	L	.367	30	11	3	2	1	3	1	7	.387	.700
Bats Left	R	.240	192	46	12	0	2	18	17	48	.305	.333
Coomer, Ron	L	.288	80	23	4	0	2	10	3	13	.313	.413
Bats Right	R	.235	68	16	3	0	1	7	3	10	.264	.324
Cordero, Wil	L	.214	14	3	0	0	0	0	0	2	.214	.214
Bats Right	R	.250	4	1	0	0	0	0	1	1	.250	.250
Cordova, Marty	L	.274	135	37	6	1	7	19	13	27	.340	.489
Bats Right	R	.245	323	79	19	1	11	45	34	84	.319	.412
Cox, Steve	L	.197	152	30	8	0	4	22	12	39	.260	.329
Bats Left	R	.275	408	112	22	1	12	50	48	77	.356	.422
Crawford, Carl	L	.200	60	12	2	2	0	7	3	10	.250	.300
Bats Left	R	.276	199	55	9	4	2	23	6	31	.303	.392
Crede, Joe	L	.259	54	14	6	0	3	9	2	15	.286	.537
Bats Right	R	.295	146	43	4	0	9	26	6	25	.320	.507
Crisp, Coco	L	.270	37	10	3	0	1	3	2	4	.308	.432
Bats Both	R	.256	90	23	6	2	0	6	9	15	.317	.367
Cruz, Jacob	L	.400	10	4	1	0	0	1	3	4	.500	.500
Bats Left	R	.256	78	20	2	1	2	5	10	16	.359	.385
Cruz, Jose	L	.225	142	32	8	0	3	15	10	24	.275	.345
Bats Both	R	.253	324	82	18	5	15	55	41	82	.334	.478
Cuddyer, Michael	L	.256	43	11	3	0	1	3	3	13	.304	.395
Bats Right	R	.261	69	18	4	0	3	10	5	17	.316	.449
Damon, Johnny	L	.306	157	48	12	4	3	14	10	14	.357	.490
Bats Left	R	.279	466	130	22	7	11	49	55	56	.356	.427
Daubach, Brian	L	.242	62	15	2	0	3	16	6	20	.314	.419
Bats Left	R	.270	382	103	22	2	17	62	45	106	.353	.471
DaVanon, Jeff	L	.091	11	1	1	0	0	1	0	4	.167	.182
Bats Both	R	.211	19	4	2	0	1	4	1	2	.250	.474
Davis, Ben	L	.235	51	12	2	0	0	6	2	13	.278	.275
Bats Both	R	.266	177	47	8	1	7	37	16	45	.323	.441

Player	vs.	Avg.	AB	H	2B	3B	HR	RBI	BB	SO	OBP	Slg.
Delgado, Carlos	L	.238	172	41	9	0	4	29	20	50	.325	.360
Bats Left	R	.297	333	99	25	2	29	79	82	76	.444	.646
Diaz, Einar	L	.225	71	16	5	0	1	4	6	4	.286	.338
Bats Right	R	.201	249	50	14	0	1	12	11	23	.250	.269
Diaz, Juan	L	.200	5	1	1	0	0	0	0	2	.200	.400
Bats Right	R	.500	2	1	0	0	1	2	1	0	.667	2.000
Dunwoody, Todd	L	.000	0	0	0	0	0	0	0	0	.000	.000
Bats Left	R	.000	6	0	0	0	0	0	0	3	.000	.000
Durham, Ray	L	.255	145	37	7	0	3	16	14	22	.327	.366
Bats Both	R	.301	419	126	27	6	12	54	59	71	.390	.480
Dye, Jermaine	L	.212	99	21	5	0	1	5	12	28	.304	.293
Bats Right	R	.262	389	102	22	1	23	81	40	80	.341	.501
Easley, Damion	L	.313	67	21	2	0	4	9	4	8	.370	.522
Bats Right	R	.198	237	47	12	1	4	21	23	35	.290	.308
Eckstein, David	L	.302	172	52	9	2	4	23	16	5	.387	.448
Bats Right	R	.289	436	126	13	4	4	40	29	39	.354	.365
Ellis, Mark	L	.296	54	16	2	1	2	9	10	9	.415	.481
Bats Right	R	.268	291	78	14	3	4	26	34	45	.347	.378
Erstad, Darin	L	.280	193	54	7	1	2	26	6	28	.305	.358
Bats Left	R	.285	432	123	21	3	8	47	21	39	.316	.403
Escalona, Felix	L	.172	29	5	2	0	0	2	0	11	.219	.241
Bats Right	R	.227	128	29	6	2	0	7	3	33	.272	.305
Everett, Carl	L	.220	91	20	2	0	4	11	6	20	.280	.374
Bats Both	R	.283	283	80	14	0	12	51	27	57	.350	.459
Fabregas, Jorge	L	.167	12	2	0	0	0	0	1	3	.231	.167
Bats Left	R	.197	76	15	1	0	0	8	5	3	.247	.211
Fasano, Sal	L	.000	1	0	0	0	0	0	0	1	.000	.000
Bats Right	R	.000	0	0	0	0	0	0	0	0	.000	.000
Febles, Carlos	L	.229	83	19	2	0	1	4	16	21	.354	.289
Bats Right	R	.250	268	67	14	4	3	22	25	42	.330	.366
Fick, Robert	L	.281	171	48	8	1	5	14	13	31	.342	.427
Bats Left	R	.265	385	102	28	1	12	49	33	59	.325	.436
Figgins, Chone	L	.125	8	1	1	0	0	0	0	4	.125	.250
Bats Both	R	.250	4	1	0	0	0	1	0	1	.250	.250
Flaherty, John	L	.250	56	14	4	0	1	4	1	10	.254	.375
Bats Right	R	.262	225	59	16	0	3	29	14	40	.306	.373
Fletcher, Darrin	L	.375	16	6	0	0	2	8	2	2	.421	.750
Bats Left	R	.198	111	22	6	0	1	14	2	11	.209	.279
Flores, Jose	L	.000	1	0	0	0	0	0	2	0	.667	.000
Bats Right	R	.000	2	0	0	0	0	0	0	0	.000	.000
Floyd, Cliff	L	.302	53	16	6	0	3	7	2	11	.321	.585
Bats Left	R	.322	118	38	15	0	4	11	13	17	.396	.551
Fordyce, Brook	L	.103	29	3	1	0	0	1	2	6	.188	.138
Bats Right	R	.267	101	27	7	0	1	7	7	13	.333	.366
Fryman, Travis	L	.281	128	36	4	1	5	20	8	26	.328	.445
Bats Right	R	.186	269	50	10	2	6	35	32	56	.275	.305
Fullmer, Brad	L	.222	63	14	3	0	2	7	1	12	.231	.365
Bats Left	R	.301	366	110	32	6	17	52	31	32	.377	.560
Garcia, Karim	L	.278	72	20	5	0	5	21	5	20	.325	.556
Bats Left	R	.308	130	40	3	0	11	31	1	21	.308	.585
Garcia, Luis	L	1.000	1	1	0	0	0	0	0	0	1.000	1.000
Bats Right	R	.000	2	0	0	0	0	0	0	1	.000	.000
Garciaparra, Nomar	L	.305	118	36	14	2	3	21	10	15	.364	.534
Bats Right	R	.311	517	161	42	3	21	99	31	48	.349	.526
German, Esteban	L	.000	5	0	0	0	0	0	1	1	.286	.000
Bats Right	R	.233	30	7	0	0	0	0	3	10	.303	.233
Giambi, Jason	L	.299	154	46	8	0	9	32	39	39	.400	.526
Bats Left	R	.320	406	130	26	1	32	90	86	73	.448	.626
Giambi, Jeremy	L	.327	52	17	4	0	1	6	10	11	.462	.462
Bats Left	R	.248	105	26	3	0	7	11	17	29	.352	.476
Gibbons, Jay	L	.235	98	23	8	0	2	10	5	11	.272	.378
Bats Left	R	.250	392	98	21	1	26	59	40	55	.320	.508
Gil, Benji	L	.310	87	27	7	0	3	13	5	25	.344	.494
Bats Right	R	.233	43	10	1	1	0	7	0	8	.227	.302
Gil, Geronimo	L	.239	109	26	6	0	4	10	6	15	.276	.404
Bats Right	R	.230	313	72	13	0	8	35	15	73	.267	.348
Gipson, Charles	L	.175	40	7	2	2	0	4	7	4	.313	.325
Bats Right	R	.313	32	10	3	0	0	4	2	10	.353	.406
Glaus, Troy	L	.298	161	48	8	0	10	41	24	39	.389	.534
Bats Right	R	.230	408	94	16	1	20	70	64	105	.337	.422
Gomez, Alexis	L	.000	1	0	0	0	0	0	0	0	.000	.000
Bats Left	R	.222	9	2	0	0	0	0	0	2	.222	.222
Gomez, Chris	L	.172	87	15	2	1	1	8	3	14	.200	.253
Bats Right	R	.286	374	107	29	2	9	38	18	44	.328	.447
Gonzalez, Juan	L	.358	81	29	9	0	3	10	4	13	.384	.580
Bats Right	R	.250	196	49	12	1	5	25	13	43	.300	.398
Grabowski, Jason	L	.667	3	2	0	1	0	1	0	0	.667	1.333
Bats Left	R	.200	5	1	1	0	0	0	3	1	.500	.400
Graffanino, Tony	L	.261	92	24	5	0	4	10	15	13	.361	.446
Bats Right	R	.263	137	36	7	4	2	21	7	25	.306	.416
Greene, Todd	L	.271	48	13	3	0	4	9	1	10	.286	.583
Bats Right	R	.266	64	17	2	0	6	10	1	13	.279	.578
Greer, Rusty	L	.293	58	17	1	1	0	5	3	4	.328	.345
Bats Left	R	.298	141	42	8	1	1	12	16	13	.367	.390
Grieve, Ben	L	.221	131	29	6	0	2	14	15	45	.320	.313
Bats Left	R	.262	351	92	24	0	17	50	54	76	.365	.476
Guiel, Aaron	L	.169	59	10	2	0	2	14	3	17	.219	.305
Bats Left	R	.254	181	46	11	0	2	24	16	44	.320	.348
Guillen, Carlos	L	.221	122	27	4	0	3	16	10	21	.280	.328
Bats Both	R	.275	353	97	20	6	6	40	36	70	.341	.416
Gutierrez, Ricky	L	.371	89	33	3	0	1	14	7	6	.417	.438
Bats Right	R	.242	264	64	10	0	3	24	13	42	.295	.314
Guzman, Cristian	L	.257	214	55	12	3	5	25	6	29	.279	.411
Bats Both	R	.281	409	115	19	3	4	34	11	50	.298	.372
Hafner, Travis	L	.333	6	2	0	1	0	1	1	1	.429	.667
Bats Left	R	.232	56	13	4	0	1	5	7	14	.317	.357
Hairston Jr., Jerry	L	.263	118	31	7	0	1	4	6	16	.290	.347
Bats Right	R	.269	308	83	18	3	4	28	29	39	.343	.386
Hall, Toby	L	.200	65	13	4	0	1	4	6	2	.264	.308
Bats Right	R	.272	265	72	15	1	5	38	11	25	.301	.392
Halter, Shane	L	.243	107	26	8	1	2	7	5	24	.281	.393
Bats Right	R	.238	303	72	14	5	8	32	34	68	.318	.396
Harris, Willie	L	.237	38	9	0	0	0	2	3	6	.293	.237
Bats Left	R	.232	125	29	4	0	2	10	6	15	.263	.312
Hart, Jason	L	.200	10	2	2	0	0	0	1	4	.273	.400
Bats Right	R	.400	5	2	1	0	0	0	1	3	.500	.600
Haselman, Bill	L	.362	47	17	2	0	1	8	4	5	.434	.468
Bats Right	R	.205	132	27	5	0	2	10	7	20	.245	.288
Hatteberg, Scott	L	.233	86	20	2	0	4	12	11	12	.333	.395
Bats Left	R	.291	406	118	20	4	11	49	57	44	.382	.441
Henderson, Rickey	L	.200	85	17	4	0	2	6	20	24	.364	.318
Bats Right	R	.245	94	23	2	1	3	10	18	23	.374	.383
Henson, Drew	L	.000	1	0	0	0	0	0	0	1	.000	.000
Bats Right	R	.000	0	0	0	0	0	0	0	0	.000	.000
Hernandez, Ramon	L	.257	109	28	10	0	3	11	12	11	.325	.431
Bats Right	R	.224	294	66	10	0	4	31	31	53	.308	.299
Higginson, Bobby	L	.241	133	32	3	0	1	15	9	19	.293	.353
Bats Left	R	.299	311	93	21	3	9	48	32	26	.368	.473
Hillenbrand, Shea	L	.269	119	32	10	0	1	12	6	16	.323	.378
Bats Right	R	.299	515	154	33	4	17	71	19	79	.332	.478
Hinch, A.J.	L	.276	76	21	3	0	2	6	6	13	.345	.395
Bats Right	R	.231	121	28	4	1	5	21	12	22	.306	.405
Hinske, Eric	L	.202	124	25	5	0	4	17	15	38	.293	.339
Bats Left	R	.301	442	133	33	2	20	67	62	100	.384	.520
Hocking, Denny	L	.342	76	26	7	0	0	12	10	16	.404	.434
Bats Both	R	.212	184	39	6	0	2	13	14	28	.269	.277
Hollandsworth, T.	L	.313	16	5	0	0	0	0	1	4	.353	.313
Bats Left	R	.250	116	29	6	0	5	19	13	23	.323	.431
Hoover, Paul	L	.500	4	2	0	0	0	2	0	1	.500	.500
Bats Right	R	.077	13	1	0	0	0	0	0	6	.077	.077
Huckaby, Ken	L	.274	62	17	1	0	0	3	4	9	.318	.290
Bats Right	R	.237	211	50	5	1	3	19	5	35	.255	.313
Hudson, Orlando	L	.184	49	9	3	1	0	4	0	8	.184	.286
Bats Both	R	.308	143	44	7	4	4	19	11	19	.361	.497
Huff, Aubrey	L	.307	127	39	13	0	4	15	12	20	.362	.504
Bats Left	R	.315	327	103	12	0	19	44	25	35	.365	.526
Hunter, Torii	L	.296	169	50	16	1	6	23	12	38	.346	.509
Bats Right	R	.286	392	112	21	3	23	71	23	80	.329	.531
Ibanez, Raul	L	.274	124	34	9	2	1	23	2	28	.291	.403
Bats Left	R	.300	373	112	28	4	23	80	38	48	.363	.582

2002 A.L. STATISTICS *Batting*

Player	vs.	Avg.	AB	H	2B	3B	HR	RBI	BB	SO	OBP	Slg.
Infante, Omar	L	.417	12	5	1	0	0	1	0	2	.417	.500
Bats Right	R	.317	60	19	2	0	1	5	3	8	.349	.400
Inge, Brandon	L	.229	70	16	4	0	3	6	4	23	.270	.414
Bats Right	R	.195	251	49	11	3	4	18	20	78	.264	.311
Jackson, Damian	L	.217	60	13	4	0	0	7	8	7	.309	.283
Bats Right	R	.270	185	50	16	1	1	18	13	29	.324	.384
Jackson, Ryan	L	.000	0	0	0	0	0	0	0	0	.000	.000
Bats Left	R	.333	6	2	1	1	0	0	1	2	.429	.833
Jeter, Derek	L	.315	124	39	4	0	5	13	18	23	.410	.468
Bats Right	R	.292	520	152	22	0	13	62	55	91	.364	.410
Jimenez, D'Angelo	L	.300	30	9	2	0	0	1	4	3	.382	.367
Bats Both	R	.282	78	22	2	3	1	10	12	7	.385	.423
Johnson, Mark L.	L	.095	21	2	1	0	0	0	1	6	.136	.143
Bats Left	R	.219	242	53	7	1	4	18	29	46	.310	.306
Johnson, Nick	L	.175	63	11	2	0	2	13	9	23	.316	.302
Bats Left	R	.257	315	81	13	0	13	45	39	75	.354	.422
Johnson, Russ	L	.208	24	5	2	0	1	3	5	1	.345	.417
Bats Right	R	.218	87	19	3	0	0	9	11	21	.313	.253
Jones, Jacque	L	.213	160	34	8	1	3	17	10	50	.259	.331
Bats Left	R	.333	417	139	29	1	24	68	27	79	.372	.580
Justice, David	L	.257	105	27	6	1	1	8	10	21	.328	.362
Bats Left	R	.270	293	79	12	2	10	41	60	45	.392	.427
Kapler, Gabe	L	.229	70	16	6	0	0	3	4	12	.267	.314
Bats Right	R	.278	126	35	6	1	0	14	4	18	.295	.341
Kennedy, Adam	L	.275	69	19	3	0	3	9	2	16	.320	.449
Bats Left	R	.319	405	129	29	6	4	43	17	64	.350	.449
Kielty, Bobby	L	.264	91	24	6	0	4	14	16	18	.380	.462
Bats Both	R	.303	198	60	8	3	8	32	36	48	.417	.495
Kingsale, Gene	L	.000	0	0	0	0	0	0	0	0	.000	.000
Bats Both	R	.667	3	2	0	0	0	0	0	0	.667	.667
Knoblauch, Chuck	L	.231	78	18	1	0	1	2	10	8	.315	.282
Bats Right	R	.203	222	45	8	0	5	20	18	24	.273	.306
Konerko, Paul	L	.279	122	34	3	0	5	19	9	10	.328	.426
Bats Right	R	.310	448	139	27	0	22	85	35	62	.367	.518
Koskie, Corey	L	.253	162	41	11	1	5	15	24	55	.361	.426
Bats Left	R	.274	328	90	26	2	10	54	48	72	.371	.457
Lamb, David	L	.000	2	0	0	0	0	0	0	1	.000	.000
Bats Both	R	.125	8	1	0	0	0	0	0	1	.125	.125
Lamb, Mike	L	.211	38	8	2	0	0	4	6	4	.326	.263
Bats Left	R	.293	276	81	11	0	9	29	27	44	.358	.431
LaRocca, Greg	L	.333	18	6	1	0	0	2	3	2	.455	.389
Bats Right	R	.235	34	8	2	1	0	2	3	4	.316	.353
Lawrence, Joe	L	.171	41	7	1	0	2	5	5	10	.271	.341
Bats Right	R	.183	109	20	3	0	0	10	11	28	.258	.211
Lawton, Matt	L	.178	118	21	2	1	5	16	19	13	.297	.339
Bats Left	R	.258	298	77	17	1	10	41	40	21	.359	.423
LeCroy, Matthew	L	.289	90	26	6	0	5	16	8	12	.347	.522
Bats Right	R	.231	91	21	5	1	2	11	5	26	.265	.374
Lee, Carlos	L	.295	112	33	6	1	3	13	20	11	.400	.446
Bats Right	R	.255	380	97	20	1	23	67	55	62	.347	.495
Leon, Jose	L	.290	62	18	1	0	3	8	1	16	.302	.452
Bats Right	R	.148	27	4	1	0	0	2	2	4	.233	.185
Lesher, Brian	L	.200	20	4	1	0	0	0	3	10	.304	.250
Bats Right	R	.056	18	1	0	0	0	2	1	5	.100	.056
Liefer, Jeff	L	.300	10	3	0	0	1	4	2	6	.417	.600
Bats Left	R	.227	194	44	8	0	6	22	17	54	.288	.361
Lofton, Kenny	L	.217	69	15	3	0	0	7	7	7	.289	.261
Bats Left	R	.269	283	76	17	6	8	35	42	44	.362	.456
Lombard, George	L	.152	33	5	1	0	0	2	1	13	.200	.182
Bats Left	R	.255	208	53	10	3	5	11	19	65	.316	.404
Long, Terrence	L	.250	156	39	1	3	3	15	9	29	.295	.378
Bats Left	R	.237	431	102	23	3	13	52	39	67	.300	.394
Lopez, Felipe	L	.303	66	20	5	0	3	14	3	17	.338	.515
Bats Both	R	.204	216	44	10	3	5	20	20	73	.271	.347
Lopez, Luis	L	.227	22	5	1	0	0	0	0	1	.227	.273
Bats Both	R	.207	87	18	5	0	2	9	3	19	.233	.333
Ludwick, Ryan	L	.167	18	3	0	0	1	3	1	5	.211	.333
Bats Right	R	.254	63	16	6	0	0	6	6	19	.319	.349
Mabry, John	L	.217	23	5	1	0	1	2	0	6	.208	.391
Bats Left	R	.282	170	48	12	1	10	38	14	31	.337	.541

Player	vs.	Avg.	AB	H	2B	3B	HR	RBI	BB	SO	OBP	Slg.
Macias, Jose	L	.320	25	8	2	0	0	3	1	4	.333	.400
Bats Both	R	.207	82	17	2	0	0	3	7	9	.278	.232
Magee, Wendell	L	.236	89	21	6	0	1	6	1	16	.242	.337
Bats Right	R	.283	258	73	13	1	5	29	9	48	.305	.399
Magruder, Chris	L	.275	91	25	5	0	3	11	1	16	.283	.429
Bats Both	R	.186	167	31	10	1	3	18	14	39	.250	.311
Martinez, Edgar	L	.306	85	26	8	0	6	14	26	14	.469	.612
Bats Right	R	.267	243	65	15	0	9	45	41	55	.378	.440
Martinez, Victor	L	.444	9	4	0	0	1	3	1	0	.455	.778
Bats Both	R	.217	23	5	1	0	0	2	2	2	.280	.261
Matos, Luis	L	.160	25	4	1	0	0	1	1	4	.192	.200
Bats Right	R	.000	6	0	0	0	0	0	0	0	.000	.000
Matthews Jr., Gary	L	.239	109	26	7	1	1	10	10	23	.303	.349
Bats Both	R	.294	235	69	18	2	6	28	33	46	.377	.464
Mayne, Brent	L	.162	68	11	0	0	1	2	2	20	.208	.206
Bats Left	R	.256	258	66	8	2	3	28	32	34	.333	.337
McCarty, Dave	L	.188	32	6	1	0	2	4	2	8	.257	.406
Bats Right	R	.088	34	3	0	0	0	0	4	11	.205	.088
McDonald, Donzell	L	.286	7	2	1	0	0	0	0	2	.286	.429
Bats Both	R	.133	15	2	1	0	0	1	4	3	.300	.200
McDonald, John	L	.232	69	16	2	2	1	8	4	11	.280	.362
Bats Right	R	.256	195	50	9	1	0	4	6	39	.291	.313
McGuire, Ryan	L	.000	0	0	0	0	0	0	0	0	.000	.000
Bats Left	R	.077	26	2	1	0	0	2	2	7	.143	.115
McKay, Cody	L	.500	2	1	0	0	0	0	0	1	.500	.500
Bats Left	R	1.000	1	1	0	0	0	0	2	0	.500	1.000
McLemore, Mark	L	.152	33	5	1	0	1	10	11	8	.348	.273
Bats Both	R	.283	304	86	16	2	6	31	50	55	.384	.408
Meluskey, Mitch	L	.143	7	1	0	0	0	0	0	1	.143	.143
Bats Both	R	.250	20	5	0	0	0	1	5	2	.407	.250
Mench, Kevin	L	.269	108	29	2	0	8	21	7	16	.316	.509
Bats Right	R	.256	258	66	18	2	7	39	24	67	.331	.422
Menechino, Frank	L	.185	54	10	3	0	1	6	8	9	.290	.296
Bats Right	R	.218	78	17	4	0	2	9	12	23	.326	.346
Merloni, Lou	L	.321	56	18	6	1	1	8	7	8	.406	.518
Bats Right	R	.217	138	30	6	1	3	10	13	27	.301	.341
Mientkiewicz, Doug	L	.257	152	39	11	0	4	22	21	24	.361	.408
Bats Left	R	.263	315	83	18	1	6	42	53	45	.366	.384
Mirabelli, Doug	L	.364	44	16	2	0	5	12	5	9	.440	.750
Bats Right	R	.168	107	18	5	0	2	13	12	24	.260	.271
Mohr, Dustan	L	.203	133	27	9	0	3	11	17	34	.293	.338
Bats Right	R	.304	250	76	14	2	9	34	14	52	.343	.484
Molina, Bengie	L	.248	125	31	7	0	1	12	5	4	.278	.328
Bats Right	R	.244	303	74	11	0	4	35	10	30	.272	.320
Molina, Izzy	L	.000	0	0	0	0	0	0	0	0	.000	.000
Bats Right	R	.333	3	1	0	0	0	0	0	0	.333	.333
Molina, Jose	L	.100	20	2	0	0	0	0	2	4	.182	.100
Bats Right	R	.340	50	17	3	0	0	5	3	10	.364	.400
Mondesi, Raul	L	.244	135	33	8	1	8	20	22	21	.346	.496
Bats Right	R	.228	434	99	26	0	18	68	37	82	.295	.412
Monroe, Craig	L	.000	6	0	0	0	0	0	0	1	.000	.000
Bats Right	R	.158	19	3	1	0	1	1	0	4	.200	.368
Mora, Melvin	L	.240	146	35	8	0	4	12	18	24	.329	.377
Bats Right	R	.231	411	95	22	4	15	52	52	84	.341	.414
Moriarty, Mike	L	.333	3	1	1	0	0	2	0	0	.333	.667
Bats Right	R	.154	13	2	0	0	0	1	0	2	.154	.154
Morris, Warren	L	.000	0	0	0	0	0	0	0	0	.000	.000
Bats Left	R	.000	7	0	0	0	0	0	0	0	.000	.000
Munson, Eric	L	.200	15	3	0	0	0	0	1	5	.250	.200
Bats Left	R	.182	44	8	0	0	2	5	5	6	.275	.318
Murray, Calvin	L	.190	21	4	2	0	0	1	1	5	.227	.286
Bats Right	R	.161	56	9	3	1	0	0	5	10	.242	.250
Myers, Greg	L	.200	25	5	1	0	0	2	2	8	.259	.240
Bats Left	R	.227	119	27	4	0	6	19	24	28	.357	.412
Nelson, Bry	L	.500	2	1	0	0	0	0	0	0	.500	.667
Bats Both	R	.136	22	3	1	0	0	2	4	1	.269	.182
Nieves, Jose	L	.353	51	18	2	0	1	3	2	6	.377	.392
Bats Right	R	.217	46	10	0	0	0	3	0	8	.217	.217
Nixon, Trot	L	.233	116	27	5	0	3	15	11	39	.303	.353
Bats Left	R	.262	416	109	31	3	21	79	54	70	.348	.502

Player	vs.	Avg.	AB	H	2B	3B	HR	RBI	BB	SO	OBP	Slg.
Ochoa, Alex	L	.294	34	10	4	0	2	6	6	3	.400	.588
Bats Right	R	.258	31	8	3	0	0	4	4	2	.343	.355
Offerman, Jose	L	.216	74	16	3	0	0	1	11	10	.322	.257
Bats Both	R	.238	210	50	9	1	5	26	25	28	.319	.362
Olerud, John	L	.287	164	47	14	0	3	33	25	20	.376	.427
Bats Left	R	.306	389	119	25	0	19	69	73	46	.414	.517
Olivo, Miguel	L	.143	7	1	0	0	1	3	1	2	.250	.571
Bats Right	R	.250	12	3	1	0	0	2	1	3	.308	.333
Ordaz, Luis	L	.200	25	5	1	0	0	1	2	3	.250	.240
Bats Right	R	.232	69	16	1	0	0	3	10	10	.329	.246
Ordonez, Magglio	L	.288	125	36	13	1	9	28	13	23	.357	.624
Bats Right	R	.329	465	153	34	0	29	107	40	54	.388	.589
Ortiz, David	L	.203	118	24	6	0	5	18	6	30	.256	.381
Bats Left	R	.299	294	88	26	1	15	57	37	57	.371	.548
Ortiz, Hector	L	.000	0	0	0	0	0	0	0	0	.000	.000
Bats Right	R	.214	14	3	1	0	1	2	1	1	.267	.500
Palmeiro, Orlando	L	.412	34	14	1	0	0	2	6	3	.500	.441
Bats Left	R	.284	229	65	11	1	0	29	24	19	.348	.341
Palmeiro, Rafael	L	.220	159	35	9	0	10	33	22	29	.315	.465
Bats Left	R	.295	387	114	25	0	33	72	82	65	.420	.615
Palmer, Dean	L	.000	7	0	0	0	0	0	0	3	.000	.000
Bats Right	R	.000	5	0	0	0	0	0	1	2	.167	.000
Paquette, Craig	L	.271	59	16	4	0	0	3	3	10	.306	.339
Bats Right	R	.171	193	33	10	1	4	17	7	43	.197	.295
Paul, Josh	L	.250	44	11	2	0	0	6	5	8	.327	.295
Bats Right	R	.233	60	14	2	0	0	5	4	14	.284	.267
Pellow, Kit	L	.225	40	9	0	0	0	2	3	14	.295	.225
Bats Right	R	.261	23	6	1	0	1	3	6	7	.414	.435
Pena, Carlos	L	.265	132	35	8	2	8	23	12	41	.333	.538
Bats Left	R	.230	265	61	9	2	11	29	29	70	.307	.404
Perez, Eddie	L	.222	45	10	4	0	0	3	1	9	.239	.311
Bats Right	R	.208	72	15	5	0	0	1	4	16	.260	.278
Perez, Neifi	L	.227	154	35	7	0	2	10	5	15	.250	.312
Bats Both	R	.240	400	96	13	4	1	27	15	38	.264	.300
Perry, Chan	L	.000	4	0	0	0	0	1	0	1	.000	.000
Bats Right	R	.143	7	1	0	0	0	2	0	0	.143	.143
Perry, Herbert	L	.260	127	33	8	0	6	22	10	21	.324	.465
Bats Right	R	.282	323	91	16	1	16	55	24	45	.337	.486
Phelps, Josh	L	.286	49	14	4	0	1	10	6	18	.364	.429
Bats Right	R	.315	216	68	16	1	14	48	13	64	.362	.593
Phillips, Brandon	L	.444	9	4	1	0	0	0	2	1	.545	.556
Bats Right	R	.182	22	4	2	1	0	4	1	5	.250	.364
Piatt, Adam	L	.233	43	10	3	0	2	6	4	12	.298	.442
Bats Right	R	.234	94	22	5	0	3	12	8	21	.305	.383
Pierzynski, A.J.	L	.270	89	24	3	1	2	13	1	15	.280	.393
Bats Left	R	.308	351	108	28	5	4	36	12	46	.348	.450
Podsednik, Scott	L	.000	2	0	0	0	0	1	0	0	.000	.000
Bats Left	R	.222	18	4	0	0	1	4	4	6	.348	.389
Posada, Jorge	L	.326	135	44	16	0	5	25	22	33	.420	.556
Bats Both	R	.247	376	93	24	1	15	74	59	110	.351	.436
Prince, Tom	L	.224	76	17	5	1	0	6	8	15	.326	.316
Bats Right	R	.224	49	11	2	0	4	10	6	11	.304	.510
Quinn, Mark	L	.348	23	8	1	0	1	6	2	2	.423	.522
Bats Right	R	.189	53	10	3	0	1	5	3	13	.246	.302
Ramirez, Julio	L	.304	23	7	0	1	1	5	1	9	.360	.522
Bats Right	R	.222	9	2	0	0	0	2	1	5	.300	.222
Ramirez, Manny	L	.438	32	14	1	0	6	21	15	9	.534	.822
Bats Right	R	.331	363	120	21	0	27	86	58	76	.433	.612
Randa, Joe	L	.321	131	42	10	1	2	19	14	14	.378	.458
Bats Right	R	.270	418	113	26	4	9	61	32	55	.330	.416
Relaford, Desi	L	.202	89	18	1	0	1	7	12	13	.301	.247
Bats Both	R	.292	240	70	12	2	5	36	21	38	.353	.421
Restovich, Michael	L	.667	6	4	0	0	1	1	0	2	.667	1.167
Bats Right	R	.000	7	0	0	0	0	0	1	2	.125	.000
Richard, Chris	L	.250	16	4	0	0	0	1	1	3	.278	.250
Bats Left	R	.230	139	32	11	0	4	20	11	27	.294	.396
Rivas, Luis	L	.234	107	25	7	2	3	10	7	24	.287	.421
Bats Right	R	.268	209	56	16	2	1	25	12	27	.314	.378
Rivera, Juan	L	.200	10	2	0	0	0	0	2	1	.333	.200
Bats Right	R	.274	73	20	5	0	1	6	4	9	.308	.384
Rivera, Michael	L	.273	33	9	3	1	0	3	0	13	.273	.424
Bats Right	R	.212	99	21	5	0	1	8	4	22	.248	.293
Rivera, Ruben	L	.200	55	11	1	0	2	5	11	16	.338	.327
Bats Both	R	.214	103	22	3	0	2	9	6	29	.281	.301
Roberts, Brian	L	.146	41	6	1	0	0	3	1	8	.163	.171
Bats Both	R	.264	87	23	5	0	1	8	14	13	.369	.356
Rodriguez, Alex	L	.239	159	38	8	1	8	24	22	34	.331	.453
Bats Right	R	.320	465	149	19	1	49	118	65	88	.412	.682
Rodriguez, Ivan	L	.306	108	33	9	0	4	15	11	15	.372	.500
Bats Right	R	.317	300	95	23	2	15	45	14	56	.346	.557
Rogers, Eddie	L	.000	0	0	0	0	0	0	0	0	.000	.000
Bats Right	R	.000	3	0	0	0	0	0	0	0	.000	.000
Rolls, Damian	L	.500	12	6	3	0	0	1	1	2	.538	.750
Bats Right	R	.260	77	20	3	1	0	5	2	14	.296	.325
Romano, Jason	L	.154	13	2	2	0	0	1	2	2	.267	.308
Bats Right	R	.220	41	9	2	0	0	3	2	11	.250	.268
Rowand, Aaron	L	.265	98	26	4	1	5	13	8	15	.327	.480
Bats Right	R	.255	204	52	12	1	2	16	4	39	.284	.353
Ryan, Michael	L	.000	1	0	0	0	0	0	0	0	.000	.000
Bats Left	R	.100	10	1	0	0	0	0	0	2	.100	.100
Sadler, Donnie	L	.071	28	2	0	0	0	2	0	5	.069	.071
Bats Right	R	.200	70	14	2	1	0	5	7	14	.291	.257
Saenz, Olmedo	L	.317	63	20	2	1	4	10	5	15	.366	.571
Bats Right	R	.247	93	23	8	0	2	8	8	16	.346	.398
Salazar, Oscar	L	.200	10	2	1	0	0	1	0	1	.200	.300
Bats Right	R	.182	11	2	0	0	1	2	1	1	.250	.455
Salmon, Tim	L	.299	137	41	11	1	5	23	27	29	.411	.504
Bats Right	R	.280	346	97	26	0	17	65	44	73	.368	.503
Sanchez, Freddy	L	.333	3	1	0	0	0	2	1	0	.500	.333
Bats Right	R	.154	13	2	0	0	0	0	1	3	.214	.154
Sanchez, Rey	L	.273	77	21	3	3	0	7	3	4	.296	.390
Bats Right	R	.289	280	81	9	0	1	31	14	27	.323	.332
Sandberg, Jared	L	.209	86	18	4	1	4	6	10	30	.299	.419
Bats Right	R	.235	272	64	17	0	14	48	29	109	.307	.452
Santiago, Ramon	L	.222	54	12	2	0	0	2	3	17	.276	.259
Bats Both	R	.250	168	42	3	5	4	18	10	31	.316	.399
Sears, Todd	L	1.000	2	2	1	0	0	0	0	0	1.000	1.500
Bats Left	R	.200	10	2	1	0	0	0	0	1	.200	.300
Segui, David	L	.192	26	5	0	0	0	3	4	6	.300	.192
Bats Both	R	.290	69	20	4	0	2	13	7	16	.351	.435
Selby, Bill	L	.160	25	4	0	0	0	1	1	6	.192	.160
Bats Left	R	.224	134	30	7	2	6	20	14	21	.293	.440
Sheets, Andy	L	.268	41	11	1	0	0	3	3	7	.311	.293
Bats Right	R	.241	108	26	3	0	4	19	9	34	.297	.380
Sierra, Ruben	L	.266	143	38	10	0	1	14	10	24	.312	.357
Bats Both	R	.272	276	75	13	0	12	46	21	42	.322	.449
Simon, Randall	L	.255	141	36	2	0	3	14	2	7	.266	.333
Bats Left	R	.320	341	109	15	1	16	68	11	23	.342	.510
Singleton, Chris	L	.208	72	15	2	1	2	13	2	22	.250	.347
Bats Left	R	.272	394	107	28	5	7	38	18	61	.305	.421
Smith, Bobby	L	.154	13	2	0	0	0	2	0	3	.154	.154
Bats Right	R	.180	50	9	2	0	1	4	3	22	.226	.280
Smith, Jason	L	.000	5	0	0	0	0	0	0	0	.000	.000
Bats Left	R	.217	60	13	1	2	1	6	2	22	.242	.350
Snelling, Chris	L	.000	3	0	0	0	0	0	0	0	.000	.000
Bats Left	R	.167	24	4	0	0	1	3	2	4	.231	.292
Snyder, Earl	L	.192	26	5	1	0	1	3	1	11	.222	.346
Bats Right	R	.207	29	6	1	0	0	1	5	10	.324	.241
Soriano, Alfonso	L	.316	133	42	10	0	8	19	7	32	.359	.571
Bats Right	R	.297	563	167	41	2	31	83	16	125	.326	.542
Spencer, Shane	L	.267	75	20	6	0	1	8	13	16	.361	.467
Bats Right	R	.239	213	51	9	2	5	26	18	47	.309	.371
Spiezio, Scott	L	.368	152	56	8	0	6	35	24	16	.448	.539
Bats Both	R	.248	339	84	26	2	6	47	43	36	.336	.389
Stevens, Lee	L	.200	35	7	0	0	2	5	3	15	.263	.457
Bats Left	R	.229	118	27	7	1	2	18	12	23	.291	.356
Stewart, Shannon	L	.302	129	39	7	1	3	10	16	16	.392	.442
Bats Right	R	.304	448	136	31	5	7	35	38	44	.365	.442
Sutton, Larry	L	.000	0	0	0	0	0	0	0	0	.000	.000
Bats Left	R	.105	19	2	0	0	1	3	1	8	.150	.263

2002 A.L. STATISTICS Batting

Player	vs.	Avg.	AB	H	2B	3B	HR	RBI	BB	SO	OBP	Slg.
Suzuki, Ichiro	L	.356	180	64	8	3	3	19	19	11	.416	.483
Bats Left	R	.308	467	144	19	5	5	32	49	51	.377	.403
Swann, Pedro	L	.000	1	0	0	0	0	0	0	1	.000	.000
Bats Left	R	.091	11	1	0	0	0	1	1	5	.167	.091
Sweeney, Mike	L	.357	112	40	6	0	6	19	11	10	.411	.571
Bats Right	R	.334	359	120	25	1	18	67	50	36	.418	.560
Tejada, Miguel	L	.285	137	39	5	0	9	26	11	15	.342	.518
Bats Right	R	.314	525	165	25	0	25	105	27	69	.357	.505
Thames, Marcus	L	.200	5	1	0	0	1	2	0	2	.200	.800
Bats Right	R	.250	8	2	1	0	0	0	0	2	.250	.375
Thomas, Frank	L	.214	117	25	5	0	6	19	25	22	.352	.410
Bats Right	R	.264	406	107	24	1	22	73	63	93	.364	.490
Thome, Jim	L	.245	159	39	4	0	12	32	27	55	.358	.497
Bats Left	R	.333	321	107	15	2	40	86	95	84	.485	.766
Torres, Andres	L	.235	17	4	0	1	0	1	1	2	.278	.353
Bats Both	R	.189	53	10	1	0	0	2	5	14	.262	.208
Truby, Chris	L	.196	56	11	4	0	1	3	2	15	.224	.321
Bats Right	R	.199	221	44	9	2	1	12	3	56	.212	.271
Tucker, Michael	L	.208	77	16	5	0	3	10	10	21	.299	.390
Bats Left	R	.256	398	102	22	6	9	46	46	84	.336	.410
Tyner, Jason	L	.189	37	7	0	0	0	2	6	6	.231	.189
Bats Left	R	.221	131	29	2	1	0	9	5	13	.254	.252
Ugueto, Luis	L	.250	4	1	0	0	0	0	0	1	.250	.250
Bats Both	R	.211	19	4	0	0	1	1	2	7	.286	.368
Valentin, Javier	L	.333	3	1	0	0	0	0	0	0	.333	.333
Bats Both	R	1.000	1	1	0	0	0	0	0	0	1.000	1.000
Valentin, Jose	L	.152	46	7	2	0	1	4	3	11	.204	.261
Bats Both	R	.259	428	111	24	4	24	71	40	88	.322	.502
Vander Wal, John	L	.238	21	5	2	0	0	1	0	8	.238	.333
Bats Left	R	.263	198	52	15	1	6	19	23	50	.335	.439
Varitek, Jason	L	.263	118	31	7	0	2	21	7	19	.318	.373
Bats Both	R	.266	349	93	20	1	8	40	34	76	.337	.398
Vaughn, Greg	L	.080	50	4	0	0	1	1	13	14	.281	.140
Bats Right	R	.184	201	37	10	2	7	28	28	68	.288	.358
Velarde, Randy	L	.162	37	6	2	0	1	2	8	7	.311	.297
Bats Right	R	.250	96	24	6	0	1	6	7	25	.330	.344
Ventura, Robin	L	.218	101	22	2	0	8	23	14	33	.310	.475
Bats Left	R	.255	364	93	15	0	19	70	76	68	.383	.453
Vizquel, Omar	L	.281	171	48	12	1	3	22	10	16	.319	.415
Bats Both	R	.273	411	112	19	4	11	50	46	48	.350	.418

Player	vs.	Avg.	AB	H	2B	3B	HR	RBI	BB	SO	OBP	Slg.
Walbeck, Matt	L	.286	21	6	0	0	0	2	0	4	.273	.286
Bats Both	R	.219	64	14	2	0	0	1	3	10	.254	.250
Wathan, Dusty	L	.000	0	0	0	0	0	0	0	0	.000	.000
Bats Right	R	.600	5	3	1	0	0	1	0	1	.667	.800
Wells, Vernon	L	.260	154	40	10	0	4	29	9	18	.297	.403
Bats Right	R	.280	454	127	24	4	19	71	18	67	.308	.476
Werth, Jayson	L	.167	12	2	0	0	0	0	1	1	.231	.167
Bats Right	R	.294	34	10	2	1	0	6	5	10	.375	.412
White, Rondell	L	.286	105	30	9	0	3	14	8	23	.347	.457
Bats Right	R	.226	350	79	12	0	11	48	17	63	.269	.354
Widger, Chris	L	.294	17	5	2	0	0	2	1	1	.368	.412
Bats Right	R	.298	47	14	3	0	0	3	1	8	.327	.362
Williams, Bernie	L	.354	164	58	10	0	4	22	21	25	.430	.488
Bats Both	R	.326	448	146	27	2	15	80	62	72	.409	.496
Williams, Gerald	L	.000	5	0	0	0	0	0	0	3	.000	.000
Bats Both	R	.000	12	0	0	0	0	0	2	1	.143	.000
Wilson, Dan	L	.288	104	30	5	0	3	14	9	26	.336	.423
Bats Right	R	.298	255	76	11	1	3	30	9	55	.321	.384
Wilson, Enrique	L	.105	38	4	1	1	0	2	1	10	.128	.184
Bats Both	R	.224	67	15	1	1	2	9	7	12	.297	.358
Wilson, Tom	L	.337	83	28	5	0	3	17	12	23	.412	.506
Bats Right	R	.220	182	40	5	0	5	20	16	56	.298	.330
Winn, Randy	L	.347	144	50	9	4	4	16	10	19	.387	.549
Bats Both	R	.283	463	131	30	5	10	59	45	90	.351	.434
Wise, Dewayne	L	.136	22	3	0	0	0	3	0	4	.136	.136
Bats Left	R	.189	90	17	4	1	3	10	4	11	.223	.356
Woodward, Chris	L	.149	74	11	2	1	0	3	10	19	.247	.203
Bats Right	R	.315	238	75	11	3	13	42	16	53	.356	.550
Wooten, Shawn	L	.282	71	20	3	0	3	14	5	16	.329	.451
Bats Right	R	.310	42	13	5	0	0	5	1	8	.333	.429
Wright, Ron	L	.000	3	0	0	0	0	0	0	1	.000	.000
Bats Right	R	.000	0	0	0	0	0	0	0	0	.000	.000
Young, Dmitri	L	.296	54	16	3	0	1	7	4	12	.345	.407
Bats Both	R	.279	147	41	11	0	6	20	8	27	.323	.476
Young, Michael	L	.290	155	45	7	2	2	11	9	21	.327	.400
Bats Right	R	.251	418	105	19	6	7	51	32	91	.301	.376
American League	**L**	**.258**									**.323**	**.409**
	R	**.266**									**.334**	**.430**

DESIGNATED HITTING

TEAM

Team	G	TPA	AB	R	H	TB	2B	3B	HR	RBI	SH	SF	HP	BB	IBB	SO	SB	CS	GDP	Avg.	OBP	Slg.
Boston	153	676	591	87	176	288	37	0	25	98	2	7	10	66	7	113	7	3	12	.298	.374	.487
Cleveland	153	665	595	109	175	315	30	1	36	104	1	4	7	58	8	126	3	3	15	.294	.361	.529
Anaheim	153	657	590	93	165	294	43	7	24	86	3	4	14	46	3	79	12	3	9	.280	.344	.498
Seattle	153	685	582	77	160	264	35	0	23	99	0	8	6	89	10	111	4	5	18	.275	.372	.454
Detroit	152	632	590	68	160	250	22	1	22	73	0	6	6	30	5	93	4	2	19	.271	.310	.424
Toronto	153	661	595	93	158	262	42	1	20	84	1	3	7	55	4	140	2	1	15	.266	.333	.440
Oakland	153	689	592	80	155	251	28	7	18	63	1	2	8	86	4	88	6	3	13	.262	.362	.424
Kansas City	153	650	582	73	151	229	35	5	11	72	2	7	4	55	5	126	10	6	12	.259	.324	.393
Chicago	153	671	565	85	145	270	33	1	30	101	0	10	7	89	3	122	3	0	10	.257	.359	.478
Texas	153	669	581	91	148	258	35	3	23	79	3	4	5	76	8	101	2	1	16	.255	.344	.444
New York	152	655	555	94	139	241	27	0	25	87	2	1	14	83	9	138	5	3	23	.250	.361	.434
Baltimore	153	640	572	59	143	222	34	3	13	77	0	7	5	56	1	124	5	7	14	.250	.319	.388
Minnesota	152	657	597	75	146	263	41	2	24	89	1	7	2	50	1	138	4	4	12	.245	.302	.441
Tampa Bay	152	655	571	81	133	232	31	1	22	69	0	7	7	70	7	131	6	3	12	.233	.321	.406
Totals	2402	9262	8158	1165	2154	3639	473	32	316	1181	16	77	102	909	75	1630	73	44	200	.264	.342	.446

TOP DESIGNATED HITTERS

Minimum 100 at-bats. *Lefthanded batter. †Switch-hitter.

Player, Team	G	TPA	AB	R	H	TB	2B	3B	HR	RBI	SH	SF	HP	BB	IBB	SO	SB	CS	GDP	Avg.	OBP	Slg.
Ramirez, Manny, Bos.	51	223	188	37	67	111	11	0	11	40	0	0	6	29	6	40	0	0	3	.356	.457	.590
Simon, Randall, Det.*	65	265	253	30	81	130	8	1	13	44	0	3	1	8	2	19	0	1	8	.320	.340	.514
Huff, Aubrey, T.B.*	53	232	216	32	67	116	10	0	13	25	0	2	1	13	3	29	3	0	8	.310	.349	.537
Phelps, Josh, Tor.	71	282	260	40	80	144	20	1	14	54	0	0	3	19	0	81	0	0	7	.308	.362	.554
Burks, Ellis, Cle.	127	542	495	90	150	271	25	0	32	89	1	1	6	39	3	103	2	3	13	.303	.360	.547
Hatteberg, Scott, Oak.*	42	174	152	14	45	76	4	3	7	20	0	0	3	19	0	12	0	0	4	.296	.385	.500
Young, Dmitri, Det.†	35	145	136	18	39	66	9	0	6	21	0	1	1	7	3	27	1	0	6	.287	.324	.485
Fullmer, Brad, Ana.*	94	368	332	56	93	171	27	6	13	49	0	3	11	22	2	34	7	2	6	.280	.342	.515
Martinez, Edgar, Sea.	91	401	323	42	90	158	23	0	15	59	0	6	6	66	8	67	1	1	6	.279	.404	.489
Johnson, Nick, N.Y.*	50	197	166	29	46	75	5	0	8	29	2	0	6	23	4	53	1	1	7	.277	.385	.452
Durham, Ray, Oak.†	43	198	174	36	48	78	10	4	4	19	1	1	2	20	1	27	6	2	2	.276	.355	.448
Palmeiro, Rafael, Tex.*	55	237	193	32	53	102	13	0	12	32	0	3	1	40	6	39	0	0	5	.275	.397	.528
Giambi, Jason, N.Y.*	63	277	229	40	62	112	14	0	12	37	0	0	7	41	2	52	2	2	5	.271	.397	.489
Richard, Chris, Bal.*	36	139	124	14	33	54	9	0	4	20	0	2	2	11	0	23	0	3	2	.266	.331	.435
Ortiz, David, Min.*	95	394	354	47	93	177	28	1	18	62	0	5	2	33	0	75	1	2	5	.263	.325	.500

ALL DESIGNATED HITTERS

*Lefthanded batter. †Switch-hitter.

Player, Team	G	TPA	AB	R	H	TB	2B	3B	HR	RBI	SH	SF	HP	BB	IBB	SO	SB	CS	GDP	Avg.	OBP	Slg.
Abernathy, Brent, T.B.	1	1	1	0	1	1	0	0	0	1	0	0	0	0	0	0	0	0	0	1.000	1.000	1.000
Alicea, Luis, K.C.†	17	59	51	6	11	15	4	0	0	4	0	0	1	7	0	8	0	1	3	.216	.322	.294
Anderson, Brady, Cle.*	1	4	4	1	2	3	1	0	0	0	0	0	0	0	0	1	0	0	2	.500	.500	.750
Anderson, Garret, Ana.*	10	43	41	2	13	19	3	0	1	6	0	0	0	2	0	1	0	0	0	.317	.349	.463
Andrews, Shane, Bos.	1	1	1	0	0	0	0	0	0	0	0	0	0	0	0	0	0	0	0	.000	.000	.000
Baerga, Carlos, Bos.†	32	122	115	9	28	36	5	0	1	13	1	1	2	3	0	13	2	0	4	.243	.273	.313
Batista, Tony, Bal.	7	28	26	2	4	8	1	0	1	1	0	0	0	2	0	6	0	0	0	.154	.214	.308
Beltran, Carlos, K.C.†	12	56	50	10	12	27	3	0	4	11	0	1	0	5	0	12	1	0	1	.240	.304	.540
Berg, Dave, Tor.	8	34	31	2	8	11	3	0	0	2	1	1	0	1	0	7	0	0	1	.258	.273	.355
Berger, Brandon, K.C.	10	35	32	5	8	11	1	1	0	0	0	0	0	3	1	10	0	0	0	.250	.314	.344
Bocachica, Hiram, Det.	1	5	5	2	2	5	0	0	1	1	0	0	0	0	0	1	0	0	1	.400	.400	1.000
Boone, Bret, Sea.	1	4	4	0	0	0	0	0	0	0	0	0	0	0	0	0	0	0	0	.000	.000	.000
Borders, Pat, Sea.	2	2	2	0	1	2	1	0	0	1	0	0	0	0	0	1	0	0	0	.500	.500	1.000
Bradley, Milton, Cle.†	1	0	0	1	0	0	0	0	0	0	0	0	0	0	0	0	0	0	0	.000	.000	.000
Branyan, Russell, Cle.*	1	4	4	0	0	0	0	0	0	0	0	0	0	0	0	2	0	0	0	.000	.000	.000
Broussard, Ben, Cle.*	3	3	3	0	0	0	0	0	0	0	0	0	0	0	0	1	0	0	0	.000	.000	.000
Brown, Dee, K.C.*	5	21	18	4	4	6	0	1	0	3	0	0	0	3	0	8	0	0	0	.222	.333	.333
Buchanan, Brian, Min.	17	64	60	10	16	23	4	0	1	6	0	0	0	2	0	18	2	0	2	.258	.281	.371
Burks, Ellis, Cle.	127	542	495	90	150	271	25	0	32	89	1	1	6	39	3	103	2	3	13	.303	.360	.547
Bush, Homer, Tor.	1	1	1	0	0	0	0	0	0	0	0	0	0	0	0	0	0	0	0	.000	.000	.000
Byrnes, Eric, Oak.	7	5	5	4	0	0	0	0	0	0	0	0	0	0	0	1	0	0	0	.000	.000	.000
Cabrera, Jolbert, Cle.	1	1	1	0	0	0	0	0	0	0	0	0	0	0	0	0	0	0	0	.000	.000	.000
Catalanotto, Frank, Tex.*	8	36	34	4	7	11	2	1	0	2	0	0	2	0	0	8	0	0	2	.206	.250	.324
Chavez, Eric, Oak.*	9	36	31	8	7	24	2	0	5	8	0	0	0	5	1	6	0	0	1	.226	.333	.774
Clark, Howie, Bal.*	8	37	34	3	11	16	5	0	0	4	0	0	1	2	0	4	0	0	3	.324	.378	.471
Clark, Tony, Bos.†	2	4	3	0	1	1	0	0	0	0	0	0	0	1	0	0	0	0	0	.333	.500	.333
Conine, Jeff, Bal.	7	28	27	1	9	11	0	1	0	3	0	1	0	0	0	5	1	0	0	.333	.321	.407
Coomer, Ron, N.Y.	15	39	37	3	6	12	3	0	1	5	0	0	0	2	1	7	0	0	2	.162	.205	.324
Cordova, Marty, Bal.	56	225	199	26	51	84	11	2	6	29	0	2	1	23	0	51	0	1	8	.256	.333	.422
Cox, Steve, T.B.*	35	152	127	18	26	41	6	0	3	17	0	2	2	21	2	29	0	0	2	.205	.322	.323
Cruz, Jacob, Det.*	15	54	43	4	10	12	2	0	0	2	0	1	3	7	0	12	2	1	0	.233	.370	.279
Cruz, Jose, Tor.†	2	11	7	4	1	1	0	0	0	0	0	0	0	4	0	1	0	0	0	.143	.455	.143
Cuddyer, Michael, Min.	3	3	2	0	0	0	0	0	0	0	0	1	0	0	0	1	0	0	0	.000	.000	.000
Damon, Johnny, Bos.*	1	5	2	1	2	2	0	0	0	0	0	0	0	3	0	2	0	0	0	1.000	1.000	1.000

Player, Team	G	TPA	AB	R	H	TB	2B	3B	HR	RBI	SH	SF	HP	BB	IBB	SO	SB	CS	GDP	Avg.	OBP	Slg.
Daubach, Brian, Bos.*	28	119	104	14	26	47	6	0	5	18	0	2	1	12	1	28	0	0	2	.250	.328	.452
DaVanon, Jeff, Ana.†	4	5	4	1	1	2	1	0	0	0	1	0	0	0	0	1	0	0	0	.250	.250	.500
Delgado, Carlos, Tor.*	3	14	10	2	4	6	2	0	0	1	0	0	1	3	2	1	0	0	0	.400	.571	.600
Diaz, Juan, Bos.	1	4	4	1	1	2	1	0	0	0	0	0	0	0	0	1	0	0	0	.250	.250	.500
Durham, Ray, Oak.†	43	198	174	36	48	78	10	4	4	19	1	1	2	20	1	27	6	2	2	.276	.355	.448
Dye, Jermaine, Oak.	19	81	71	4	16	24	5	0	1	5	0	1	2	7	0	12	0	0	3	.225	.309	.338
Eckstein, David, Ana.	3	14	13	3	4	5	1	0	0	2	0	0	0	1	0	1	1	0	0	.308	.357	.385
Ellis, Mark, Oak.	1	1	1	0	0	0	0	0	0	0	0	0	0	0	0	0	0	0	0	.000	.000	.000
Erstad, Darin, Ana.*	4	18	16	0	3	4	1	0	0	1	1	0	0	1	0	2	1	0	0	.188	.235	.250
Escalona, Felix, T.B.	1	0	0	1	0	0	0	0	0	0	0	0	0	0	0	0	0	0	0	.000	.000	.000
Everett, Carl, Tex.†	18	74	64	12	17	33	1	0	5	16	1	1	2	6	0	17	1	1	0	.266	.342	.516
Fick, Robert, Det.*	6	26	26	3	8	13	2	0	1	1	0	0	0	0	0	2	0	0	1	.308	.308	.500
Fletcher, Darrin, Tor.*	4	11	11	0	1	1	0	0	0	0	0	0	0	0	0	2	0	0	0	.091	.091	.091
Floyd, Cliff, Bos.*	19	81	76	12	27	47	8	0	4	10	0	1	1	3	0	14	0	0	3	.355	.383	.618
Fullmer, Brad, Ana.*	94	368	332	56	93	171	27	6	13	49	0	3	11	22	2	34	7	2	6	.280	.342	.515
Giambi, Jason, N.Y.*	63	277	229	40	62	112	14	0	12	37	0	0	7	41	2	52	2	2	5	.271	.397	.489
Giambi, Jeremy, Oak.*	2	9	9	2	3	4	1	0	0	0	0	0	0	0	0	2	0	0	0	.333	.333	.444
Gibbons, Jay, Bal.*	12	49	42	2	10	13	3	0	0	4	0	0	0	7	1	7	0	0	0	.238	.347	.310
Gil, Benji, Ana.	10	17	16	3	7	16	1	1	2	6	0	0	0	1	0	4	0	0	0	.438	.471	1.000
Gonzalez, Juan, Tex.	8	36	35	4	6	14	2	0	2	4	0	0	0	1	0	6	0	0	3	.171	.194	.400
Greene, Todd, Tex.	4	10	8	1	2	6	1	0	1	1	1	0	0	1	0	2	0	0	0	.250	.333	.750
Greer, Rusty, Tex.*	22	96	85	9	21	28	5	1	0	6	0	0	0	11	0	5	0	0	3	.247	.333	.329
Grieve, Ben, T.B.*	16	65	52	9	14	28	8	0	2	10	0	1	2	10	1	10	1	0	1	.269	.400	.538
Guiel, Aaron, K.C.*	2	10	6	3	4	6	2	0	0	3	1	0	1	2	0	1	0	0	0	.667	.778	1.000
Guillen, Carlos, Sea.†	3	8	8	1	0	0	0	0	0	0	0	0	0	0	0	3	0	0	1	.000	.000	.000
Gutierrez, Ricky, Cle.	1	4	4	1	1	2	1	0	0	2	0	0	0	0	0	1	0	0	0	.250	.250	.500
Guzman, Cristian, Min.†	1	1	1	0	0	0	0	0	0	0	0	0	0	0	0	0	0	0	0	.000	.000	.000
Hafner, Travis, Tex.*	13	52	47	4	12	20	3	1	1	5	0	0	0	5	1	9	0	0	0	.255	.327	.426
Halter, Shane, Det.	2	8	8	1	1	1	0	0	0	0	0	0	0	0	0	1	0	0	0	.125	.125	.125
Haselman, Bill, Tex.	2	4	4	1	3	4	1	0	0	1	0	0	0	0	0	0	0	0	0	.750	.750	1.000
Hatteberg, Scott, Oak.*	42	174	152	14	45	76	4	3	7	20	0	0	3	19	0	12	0	0	4	.296	.385	.500
Henderson, Rickey, Bos.	5	5	5	3	1	1	0	0	0	0	0	0	0	0	0	3	0	0	0	.200	.200	.200
Henson, Drew, N.Y.	2	0	0	1	0	0	0	0	0	0	0	0	0	0	0	0	0	0	0	.000	.000	.000
Higginson, Bobby, Det.*	1	4	4	0	0	0	0	0	0	0	0	0	0	0	0	0	0	0	0	.000	.000	.000
Huff, Aubrey, T.B.*	53	232	216	32	67	116	10	0	13	25	0	2	1	13	3	29	3	0	8	.310	.349	.537
Hunter, Torii, Min.	1	4	4	0	0	0	0	0	0	0	0	0	0	0	0	1	0	0	1	.000	.000	.000
Ibanez, Raul, K.C.*	36	138	125	13	30	51	12	0	3	16	1	3	0	9	1	22	1	0	2	.240	.285	.408
Inge, Brandon, Det.	1	5	5	2	3	3	0	0	0	1	0	0	0	0	0	0	0	0	0	.600	.600	.600
Jackson, Damian, Det.	5	7	6	1	1	1	0	0	0	0	0	0	1	0	0	2	0	0	0	.167	.286	.167
Jeter, Derek, N.Y.	1	5	4	2	1	4	0	0	1	3	0	0	0	1	0	0	0	0	0	.250	.400	1.000
Johnson, Nick, N.Y.*	50	197	166	29	46	75	5	0	8	29	2	0	6	23	4	53	1	1	7	.277	.385	.452
Johnson, Russ, T.B.	5	13	9	1	3	5	2	0	0	2	0	0	1	3	0	3	0	0	0	.333	.538	.556
Jones, Jacque, Min.*	3	4	3	0	0	0	0	0	0	1	0	1	0	0	0	2	0	0	0	.000	.000	.000
Justice, David, Oak.*	37	157	125	12	31	38	4	0	1	9	0	0	0	32	2	24	0	1	2	.248	.401	.304
Kapler, Gabe, Tex.	1	0	0	1	0	0	0	0	0	0	0	0	0	0	0	0	0	0	0	.000	.000	.000
Kennedy, Adam, Ana.*	1	5	5	1	1	1	0	0	0	0	0	0	0	0	0	0	0	0	1	.200	.200	.200
Kielty, Bobby, Min.†	11	27	23	2	3	4	1	0	0	0	0	0	0	4	0	7	0	0	0	.130	.259	.174
Knoblauch, Chuck, K.C.	2	9	8	0	1	1	0	0	0	0	0	0	0	1	0	0	0	0	0	.125	.222	.125
Konerko, Paul, Chi.	7	33	31	4	8	11	3	0	0	4	0	0	0	2	0	5	0	0	0	.258	.303	.355
Koskie, Corey, Min.*	1	1	1	0	0	0	0	0	0	1	0	0	0	0	0	0	0	0	0	.000	.000	.000
Lamb, Mike, Tex.*	21	81	71	17	22	32	4	0	2	7	0	0	0	10	1	9	0	0	2	.310	.395	.451
LaRocca, Greg, Cle.	1	1	0	0	0	0	0	0	0	0	0	0	1	0	0	0	0	0	0	.000	1.000	.000
Lawrence, Joe, Tor.	1	1	1	1	0	0	0	0	0	0	0	0	0	0	0	0	0	0	0	.000	.000	.000
Lawton, Matt, Cle.*	3	12	11	2	3	4	1	0	0	1	0	0	0	1	0	1	0	0	0	.273	.333	.364
LeCroy, Matthew, Min.	41	150	138	14	33	58	8	1	5	19	0	1	0	11	1	31	0	2	4	.239	.293	.420
Lee, Carlos, Chi.	2	10	8	2	4	8	1	0	1	1	0	0	0	2	0	0	0	0	0	.500	.600	1.000
Leon, Jose, Bal.	2	4	3	0	0	0	0	0	0	0	0	0	1	0	0	1	1	0	0	.000	.250	.000
Lesher, Brian, Tor.	3	8	6	0	0	0	0	0	0	1	0	1	1	0	1	5	0	0	0	.000	.125	.000
Liefer, Jeff, Chi.*	6	17	16	4	5	12	1	0	2	6	0	0	0	1	1	5	0	0	0	.313	.353	.750
Lombard, George, Det.*	2	1	1	0	0	0	0	0	0	0	0	0	0	0	0	1	1	0	0	.000	.000	.000
Lopez, Felipe, Tor.†	1	0	0	1	0	0	0	0	0	0	0	0	0	0	0	0	0	0	0	.000	.000	.000
Lopez, Luis, Bal.†	1	4	4	0	1	1	0	0	0	0	0	0	0	0	0	0	0	0	0	.250	.250	.250
Magee, Wendell, Det.	4	11	11	0	3	4	1	0	0	0	0	0	0	0	0	4	0	0	0	.273	.273	.364
Martinez, Edgar, Sea.	91	401	323	42	90	158	23	0	15	59	0	6	6	66	8	67	1	1	6	.279	.404	.489
Martinez, Victor, Cle.†	1	1	1	0	0	0	0	0	0	0	0	0	0	0	0	0	0	0	0	.000	.000	.000
Matos, Luis, Bal.	1	1	1	0	1	1	0	0	0	0	0	0	0	0	0	0	0	0	0	1.000	1.000	1.000
Matthews Jr., Gary, Bal.†	2	1	0	0	0	0	0	0	0	0	0	0	0	1	0	0	1	1	0	.000	1.000	.000
McCarty, Dave, K.C.	2	2	2	0	0	0	0	0	0	0	0	0	0	0	0	2	0	0	0	.000	.000	.000
McDonald, John, Cle.	1	1	1	0	0	0	0	0	0	0	0	0	0	0	0	0	0	0	0	.000	.000	.000
McGuire, Ryan, Bal.*	1	3	3	0	0	0	0	0	0	0	0	0	0	0	0	0	0	0	1	.000	.000	.000
McLemore, Mark, Sea.†	4	16	15	0	5	5	0	0	0	0	0	0	0	1	0	4	0	1	0	.333	.375	.333
Mench, Kevin, Tex.	3	1	1	1	0	0	0	0	0	0	0	0	0	0	0	0	0	0	0	.000	.000	.000
Menechino, Frank, Oak.	1	1	0	0	0	0	0	0	0	0	0	0	0	1	0	0	0	0	0	.000	1.000	.000
Mirabelli, Doug, Bos.	4	9	7	2	3	9	0	0	2	5	0	0	0	2	0	2	0	0	0	.429	.556	1.286
Mohr, Dustan, Min.	3	7	7	0	0	0	0	0	0	0	0	0	0	0	0	0	0	0	0	.000	.000	.000
Mondesi, Raul, Tor.-N.Y.	14	67	59	14	14	30	4	0	4	11	0	1	0	7	0	10	1	1	1	.237	.313	.508
Monroe, Craig, Det.	3	4	4	1	0	0	0	0	0	0	0	0	0	0	0	2	0	1	1	.000	.000	.000
Mora, Melvin, Bal.	3	15	14	3	5	9	1	0	1	5	0	0	0	1	0	1	0	0	0	.357	.400	.643
Munson, Eric, Det.*	14	52	45	2	7	10	0	0	1	3	0	1	1	5	0	8	0	0	0	.156	.250	.222
Murray, Calvin, Tex.	2	0	0	1	0	0	0	0	0	0	0	0	0	0	0	0	0	0	0	.000	.000	.000
Myers, Greg, Oak.*	1	1	1	0	0	0	0	0	0	0	0	0	0	0	0	0	0	0	1	.000	.000	.000
Nelson, Bry, Bos.†	1	1	0	0	0	0	0	0	0	0	0	1	0	0	0	0	0	0	0	.000	.000	.000

Player, Team	G	TPA	AB	R	H	TB	2B	3B	HR	RBI	SH	SF	HP	BB	IBB	SO	SB	CS	GDP	Avg.	OBP	Slg.
Offerman, Jose, Bos.-Sea.† ...	28	98	82	10	18	30	6	0	2	11	0	3	0	13	0	11	3	3	0	.220	.316	.366
Olerud, John, Sea.*	2	8	5	0	3	4	1	0	0	0	0	0	0	3	0	0	0	0	1	.600	.750	.800
Ordonez, Magglio, Chi.	1	4	3	0	0	0	0	0	0	1	0	1	0	0	0	2	0	0	0	.000	.000	.000
Ortiz, David, Min.*	95	394	354	47	93	177	28	1	18	62	0	5	2	33	0	75	1	2	5	.263	.325	.500
Palmeiro, Orlando, Ana.*	8	11	9	1	5	5	0	0	0	2	1	0	0	1	0	2	0	0	0	.556	.600	.556
Palmeiro, Rafael, Tex.*	55	237	193	32	53	102	13	0	12	32	0	3	1	40	6	39	0	0	5	.275	.397	.528
Palmer, Dean, Det.	4	13	12	0	0	0	0	0	0	0	0	0	0	1	0	5	0	0	1	.000	.077	.000
Paquette, Craig, Det.	5	20	20	2	4	4	0	0	0	0	0	0	0	0	0	3	0	0	1	.200	.200	.200
Pellow, Kit, K.C.	5	17	15	0	1	1	0	0	0	1	0	0	1	1	0	6	0	0	0	.067	.176	.067
Pena, Carlos, Det.*	2	8	7	1	1	1	0	0	0	0	0	0	0	1	0	2	0	0	0	.143	.250	.143
Perry, Herbert, Tex.	6	14	11	0	1	1	0	0	0	2	1	0	0	2	0	4	0	0	0	.091	.231	.091
Phelps, Josh, Tor.	71	282	260	40	80	144	20	1	14	54	0	0	3	19	0	81	0	0	7	.308	.362	.554
Podsednik, Scott, Sea.*	2	1	1	0	1	1	0	0	0	1	0	0	0	0	0	0	0	0	0	1.000	1.000	1.000
Posada, Jorge, N.Y.†	5	18	16	1	1	1	0	0	0	0	0	0	0	2	0	5	0	0	4	.063	.167	.063
Quinn, Mark, K.C.	7	28	27	5	7	10	3	0	0	3	0	0	1	0	0	9	0	0	0	.259	.286	.370
Ramirez, Manny, Bos.	51	223	188	37	67	111	11	0	11	40	0	0	6	29	6	40	0	0	3	.356	.457	.590
Randa, Joe, K.C.	19	80	76	4	22	29	2	1	1	10	0	1	0	3	0	12	1	0	3	.289	.313	.382
Relaford, Desi, Sea.†	4	1	1	1	0	0	0	0	0	0	0	0	0	0	0	0	0	0	0	.000	.000	.000
Restovich, Michael, Min.	2	2	2	1	1	1	0	0	0	0	0	0	0	0	0	1	0	0	0	.500	.500	.500
Richard, Chris, Bal.*	36	139	124	14	33	54	9	0	4	20	0	2	2	11	0	23	0	3	2	.266	.331	.435
Rivera, Michael, Det.	1	4	4	0	0	0	0	0	0	0	0	0	0	0	0	3	0	0	0	.000	.000	.000
Rivera, Ruben, Tex.	2	1	1	0	0	0	0	0	0	0	0	0	0	0	0	1	0	0	0	.000	.000	.000
Roberts, Brian, Bal.†	8	28	23	3	5	6	1	0	0	2	0	1	1	3	0	7	2	2	0	.217	.321	.261
Rodriguez, Ivan, Tex.	6	26	26	3	4	7	3	0	0	3	0	0	0	0	0	2	0	0	1	.154	.154	.269
Romano, Jason, Tex.	4	1	1	1	0	0	0	0	0	0	0	0	0	0	0	0	0	0	0	.000	.000	.000
Ryan, Michael, Min.*	1	0	0	1	0	0	0	0	0	0	0	0	0	0	0	0	0	0	0	.000	.000	.000
Sadler, Donnie, K.C.	3	1	1	1	0	0	0	0	0	0	0	0	0	0	0	1	0	0	0	.000	.000	.000
Saenz, Olmedo, Oak.	7	20	18	0	4	6	2	0	0	2	0	0	1	1	0	4	0	0	0	.222	.300	.333
Salmon, Tim, Ana.	25	98	82	18	21	43	7	0	5	11	0	0	2	14	0	20	1	1	0	.256	.378	.524
Sandberg, Jared, T.B.	2	9	9	1	1	2	1	0	0	1	0	0	0	0	0	5	0	0	1	.111	.111	.222
Santiago, Ramon, Det.†	1	0	0	1	0	0	0	0	0	0	0	0	0	0	0	0	0	0	0	.000	.000	.000
Segui, David, Bal.†	19	76	70	4	11	17	3	0	1	8	0	1	0	5	0	19	0	0	1	.157	.211	.243
Sierra, Ruben, Sea.†	52	220	202	23	50	81	10	0	7	35	0	1	0	17	2	34	2	0	9	.248	.305	.401
Simon, Randall, Det.*	65	265	253	30	81	130	8	1	13	44	0	3	1	8	2	19	0	0	8	.320	.340	.514
Singleton, Chris, Bal.*	1	2	2	1	2	2	0	0	0	1	0	0	0	0	0	0	0	0	0	1.000	1.000	1.000
Smith, Bobby, T.B.	1	3	3	0	0	0	0	0	0	0	0	0	0	0	0	2	0	0	0	.000	.000	.000
Snyder, Earl, Cle.	1	5	4	0	0	0	0	0	0	0	0	0	0	1	0	2	0	0	0	.000	.200	.000
Soriano, Alfonso, N.Y.	1	2	2	0	2	2	0	0	0	1	0	0	0	0	0	1	1	0	0	1.000	1.000	1.000
Spencer, Shane, N.Y.	1	4	4	0	0	0	0	0	0	0	0	0	0	0	0	0	0	0	0	.000	.000	.000
Stevens, Lee, Cle.*	3	9	7	1	3	3	0	0	0	3	0	2	0	0	0	0	0	0	0	.429	.333	.429
Stewart, Shannon, Tor.	38	178	163	23	39	57	12	0	2	9	0	0	1	14	2	16	1	0	6	.239	.303	.350
Suzuki, Ichiro, Sea.*	4	19	16	5	9	12	0	0	1	3	0	1	0	2	0	0	0	1	0	.563	.579	.750
Swann, Pedro, Tor.*	3	5	5	1	1	1	0	0	0	0	0	0	0	0	0	2	0	0	0	.200	.200	.200
Sweeney, Mike, K.C.	24	107	91	11	28	34	3	0	1	10	0	2	0	14	3	12	2	2	2	.308	.393	.374
Thomas, Frank, Chi.	140	606	506	75	128	239	28	1	27	89	0	9	7	84	2	110	3	0	10	.253	.361	.472
Thome, Jim, Cle.*	18	78	60	13	16	32	2	1	4	9	0	1	0	17	5	16	0	0	0	.267	.423	.533
Tucker, Michael, K.C.*	23	87	80	11	23	38	5	2	2	11	0	0	0	7	0	24	4	3	1	.288	.345	.475
Tyner, Jason, T.B.*	1	1	1	0	0	0	0	0	0	0	0	0	0	0	0	0	0	0	0	.000	.000	.000
Ugueto, Luis, Sea.†	16	2	2	3	1	1	0	0	0	0	0	0	0	0	0	1	1	2	0	.500	.500	.500
Valentin, Jose, Chi.†	1	1	1	0	0	0	0	0	0	0	0	0	0	0	0	0	0	0	0	.000	.000	.000
Vander Wal, John, N.Y.*	16	40	32	5	6	10	1	0	1	2	0	0	0	8	2	8	0	0	1	.188	.350	.313
Varitek, Jason, Bos.†	1	4	4	0	2	2	0	0	0	1	0	0	0	0	0	1	0	0	0	.500	.500	.500
Vaughn, Greg, T.B.	38	161	140	15	18	36	4	1	4	12	0	1	1	19	1	51	1	2	0	.129	.236	.257
Velarde, Randy, Oak.	5	6	5	0	1	1	0	0	0	0	0	0	0	1	0	0	0	0	0	.200	.333	.200
White, Rondell, N.Y.	11	41	36	7	6	13	1	0	2	6	0	1	1	3	0	9	1	0	2	.167	.244	.361
Williams, Bernie, N.Y.†	7	27	25	3	7	9	2	0	0	2	0	0	0	2	0	4	0	0	2	.280	.333	.360
Wilson, Enrique, N.Y.†	2	0	0	1	0	0	0	0	0	0	0	0	0	0	0	0	0	0	0	.000	.000	.000
Wilson, Tom, Tor.	12	48	40	6	12	14	2	0	0	7	0	0	2	6	0	15	0	0	0	.300	.417	.350
Winn, Randy, T.B.†	4	18	13	4	3	3	0	0	0	1	0	1	0	4	0	2	1	1	0	.231	.389	.231
Wise, Dewayne, Tor.*	3	1	1	0	0	0	0	0	0	0	0	0	0	0	0	0	0	0	0	.000	.000	.000
Woodward, Chris, Tor.	2	5	4	1	0	0	0	0	0	0	0	0	0	1	0	0	0	0	0	.000	.200	.000
Wooten, Shawn, Ana.	26	78	72	8	17	28	2	0	3	9	0	1	1	4	1	15	1	0	2	.236	.282	.389
Wright, Ron, Sea.	1	3	3	0	0	0	0	0	0	0	0	0	0	0	0	1	0	0	1	.000	.000	.000
Young, Dmitri, Det.†	35	145	136	18	39	66	9	0	6	21	0	1	1	7	3	27	1	0	6	.287	.324	.485

DESIGNATED HITTERS WITH TWO OR MORE TEAMS

Player, Team	G	TPA	AB	R	H	TB	2B	3B	HR	RBI	SH	SF	HP	BB	IBB	SO	SB	CS	GDP	Avg.	OBP	Slg.
Mondesi, Raul, Tor.	13	62	55	12	12	27	3	0	4	9	0	1	0	6	0	10	1	1	1	.218	.290	.491
Mondesi, Raul, N.Y.	1	5	4	2	2	3	1	0	0	2	0	0	1	0	0	0	0	0	0	.500	.600	.750
Offerman, Jose, Bos.†	24	98	82	8	18	30	6	0	2	11	0	3	0	13	0	11	3	3	0	.220	.316	.366
Offerman, Jose, Sea.†	4	0	0	2	0	0	0	0	0	0	0	0	0	0	0	0	0	0	0	.000	.000	.000

The following designated hitters, each of whom appeared in at least one game, had no plate appearances, runs scored or stolen base attempts: Gipson, Charles, Seattle (3); Bloomquist, Willie, Seattle (2); Nieves, Jose, Anaheim (2); Amezaga, Alfredo, Anaheim; Blake, Casey, Minnesota; Cameron, Mike, Seattle; Easley, Damion, Detroit; Flores, Jose, Oakland; Ramirez, Julio, Anaheim; Sadler, Donnie, Texas; Sanchez, Freddy, Boston; Smith, Jason, Tampa Bay; Williams, Gerald, New York; Young, Michael, Texas.

PINCH-HITTING

TEAM

Team	G	TPA	AB	R	H	TB	2B	3B	HR	RBI	SH	SF	HP	BB	IBB	SO	SB	CS	GDP	Avg.	OBP	Slg.
Anaheim	85	131	118	12	34	48	6	1	2	20	2	0	4	7	2	27	5	0	2	.288	.349	.407
Tampa Bay	39	49	43	5	12	18	0	0	2	10	0	0	2	4	1	11	0	0	0	.279	.367	.419
Minnesota	79	121	108	16	28	48	7	2	3	18	0	2	0	11	1	29	2	0	4	.259	.322	.444
Oakland	82	121	102	9	24	44	5	0	5	18	0	0	4	15	4	29	0	1	4	.235	.355	.431
Boston	75	113	99	10	23	38	6	0	3	16	0	1	3	10	0	27	1	0	4	.232	.319	.384
Cleveland	67	95	82	6	18	22	4	0	0	7	1	1	1	10	1	20	1	0	3	.220	.309	.268
Seattle	62	84	77	5	16	20	1	0	1	15	0	2	0	5	1	20	2	0	3	.208	.250	.260
Detroit	39	47	39	2	8	14	4	1	0	6	0	0	0	8	0	17	1	1	0	.205	.340	.359
Toronto	59	81	75	10	15	28	1	0	4	11	0	0	0	6	0	29	1	1	0	.200	.259	.373
Texas	84	128	109	10	21	24	3	0	0	14	1	3	2	13	1	28	0	0	3	.193	.283	.220
Kansas City	69	108	99	6	19	27	2	0	2	9	0	0	1	9	1	32	2	1	0	.192	.259	.273
Baltimore	65	102	96	8	16	21	5	0	0	2	1	0	0	5	0	28	1	0	3	.167	.208	.219
Chicago	52	77	66	8	11	20	3	0	2	6	1	0	0	10	1	28	3	1	3	.167	.208	.303
New York	57	79	62	7	9	14	2	0	1	12	0	3	0	14	5	17	0	0	0	.145	.291	.226
Totals	914	1336	1175	114	254	386	49	4	25	164	6	12	16	127	17	335	16	4	25	.216	.298	.329

TOP PINCH-HITTERS

Minimum 20 at-bats. *Lefthanded batter. †Switch-hitter.

Player, Team	G	TPA	AB	R	H	TB	2B	3B	HR	RBI	SH	SF	HP	BB	IBB	SO	SB	CS	GDP	Avg.	OBP	Slg.
Kielty, Bobby, Min.†	24	24	23	5	8	15	2	1	1	2	0	0	0	1	0	8	0	0	2	.348	.375	.652
Baerga, Carlos, Bos.†	32	32	29	2	10	12	2	0	0	3	0	1	1	1	0	3	1	0	2	.345	.375	.414
Palmeiro, Orlando, Ana.*	32	30	28	3	8	10	2	0	0	2	1	0	1	1	0	5	1	0	0	.286	.310	.357
Lamb, Mike, Tex.*	29	27	21	3	6	6	0	0	0	5	0	2	4	1	5	0	0	1		.286	.370	.286
Lopez, Luis, Bal.†	24	24	24	4	6	8	2	0	0	0	0	0	0	0	0	7	0	0	1	.250	.250	.333
Saenz, Olmedo, Oak.	26	25	20	2	5	11	0	0	2	3	0	0	2	3	1	3	0	0	1	.250	.400	.550

ALL PINCH-HITTERS

*Lefthanded batter. †Switch-hitter.

Player, Team	G	TPA	AB	R	H	TB	2B	3B	HR	RBI	SH	SF	HP	BB	IBB	SO	SB	CS	GDP	Avg.	OBP	Slg.
Alicea, Luis, K.C.†	25	25	18	3	2	2	0	0	0	1	0	0	0	7	1	5	1	1	0	.111	.360	.111
Allen, Chad, Cle.	1	1	1	0	0	0	0	0	0	0	0	0	0	0	0	0	0	0	0	.000	.000	.000
Alomar Jr., Sandy, Chi.	2	2	2	0	1	2	1	0	0	0	0	0	0	0	0	0	0	0	0	.500	.500	1.000
Anderson, Brady, Cle.*	8	6	2	0	0	0	0	0	0	0	0	0	0	4	1	0	0	0	0	.000	.667	.000
Anderson, Garret, Ana.*	1	1	1	0	0	0	0	0	0	0	0	0	0	0	0	0	0	0	0	.000	.000	.000
Andrews, Shane, Bos.	1	1	1	0	0	0	0	0	0	0	0	0	0	0	0	1	0	0	0	.000	.000	.000
Arias, Alex, N.Y.	1	1	1	0	0	0	0	0	0	0	0	0	0	0	0	1	0	0	0	.000	.000	.000
Aven, Bruce, Cle.	1	1	1	0	0	0	0	0	0	0	0	0	0	0	0	0	0	0	0	.000	.000	.000
Baerga, Carlos, Bos.†	32	32	29	2	10	12	2	0	0	3	0	1	1	1	0	3	1	0	0	.345	.375	.414
Beltran, Carlos, K.C.†	1	1	1	0	0	0	0	0	0	0	0	0	0	0	0	0	0	0	0	.000	.000	.000
Berg, Dave, Tor.	7	7	6	1	2	5	0	0	1	1	0	0	0	1	0	1	0	0	0	.333	.429	.833
Berger, Brandon, K.C.	6	6	6	0	0	0	0	0	0	0	0	0	0	0	0	1	0	0	3	.000	.000	.000
Bigbie, Larry, Bal.*	8	8	8	0	0	0	0	0	0	0	0	0	0	0	0	4	0	0	0	.000	.000	.000
Blalock, Hank, Tex.*	3	3	3	0	0	0	0	0	0	0	0	0	0	0	0	3	0	0	0	.000	.000	.000
Bloomquist, Willie, Sea.	1	1	1	0	0	0	0	0	0	0	0	0	0	0	0	2	0	0	0	.000	.000	.000
Bocachica, Hiram, Det.	7	7	6	1	2	3	1	0	0	2	0	0	0	1	0	2	1	0	0	.333	.429	.500
Boone, Bret, Sea.	2	2	2	0	1	1	0	0	0	0	0	0	0	0	0	0	0	0	0	.500	.500	.500
Borchard, Joe, Chi.†	1	1	1	0	0	0	0	0	0	0	0	0	0	0	0	1	0	0	0	.000	.000	.000
Borders, Pat, Sea.	2	2	2	0	1	2	1	0	0	1	0	0	0	0	0	1	0	0	0	.500	.500	1.000
Bradley, Milton, Cle.†	2	2	1	0	0	0	0	0	0	0	0	0	0	1	0	0	0	0	0	.000	.500	.000
Broussard, Ben, Cle.*	5	5	5	0	1	1	0	0	0	0	0	0	0	0	0	1	0	0	0	.200	.200	.200
Brown, Dee, K.C.*	3	3	3	0	2	3	1	0	0	0	0	0	0	0	0	1	0	0	0	.667	.667	1.000
Brown, Kevin L., Bos.	1	1	1	0	0	0	0	0	0	0	0	0	0	0	0	1	0	0	0	.000	.000	.000
Buchanan, Brian, Min.	6	6	6	1	2	3	1	0	0	0	0	0	0	0	0	1	0	0	0	.333	.333	.500
Burks, Ellis, Cle.	5	5	5	0	1	2	1	0	0	1	0	0	0	0	0	1	0	0	0	.200	.200	.400
Bush, Homer, Tor.	2	2	2	0	0	0	0	0	0	1	0	0	0	0	0	0	0	0	0	.000	.000	.000
Byrnes, Eric, Oak.	11	11	11	1	2	4	2	0	0	0	0	0	0	0	0	5	0	0	0	.182	.182	.364
Cabrera, Jolbert, Cle.	5	5	5	0	0	0	0	0	0	0	0	0	0	0	0	0	0	0	0	.000	.000	.000
Cameron, Mike, Sea.	3	3	2	0	0	0	0	0	0	0	0	0	1	0	0	1	0	0	1	.000	.333	.000
Canizaro, Jay, Min.	2	2	2	0	0	0	0	0	0	1	0	0	0	0	0	1	0	0	0	.000	.000	.000
Castillo, Alberto, N.Y.	1	1	1	0	0	0	0	0	0	0	0	0	0	0	0	0	0	0	0	.000	.000	.000
Catalanotto, Frank, Tex.*	9	9	9	1	2	2	0	0	0	0	0	0	0	0	0	1	0	0	0	.222	.222	.222
Chavez, Eric, Oak.*	2	2	2	0	0	0	0	0	0	1	0	0	0	0	0	1	0	0	1	.000	.000	.000
Cirillo, Jeff, Sea.	4	4	3	0	0	0	0	0	0	0	1	0	0	0	0	1	0	0	0	.000	.000	.000
Clark, Howie, Bal.*	1	1	1	0	0	0	0	0	0	0	0	0	0	0	0	0	0	0	0	.667	.750	.667
Clark, Tony, Bos.†	7	7	7	0	0	0	0	0	0	1	0	0	0	0	0	3	0	0	0	.000	.000	.000
Clayton, Royce, Chi.	2	2	1	0	0	0	0	0	0	0	0	0	0	1	0	0	0	0	0	.000	.500	.000
Colangelo, Mike, Oak.	2	2	1	0	0	0	0	0	0	0	0	0	0	1	0	1	0	0	0	.000	.500	.000
Conine, Jeff, Bal.	1	1	1	0	0	0	0	0	0	0	0	0	0	1	0	1	0	0	0	.000	.500	.000
Conti, Jason, T.B.*	4	4	4	1	2	5	0	0	1	1	0	0	0	0	0	1	0	0	0	.500	.500	1.250
Coomer, Ron, N.Y.	10	10	9	0	1	1	0	0	0	2	0	1	0	0	0	1	0	0	0	.111	.100	.111
Cordero, Wil, Cle.	2	2	2	0	0	0	0	0	0	0	0	0	0	0	0	1	0	0	0	.000	.000	.000
Cordova, Marty, Bal.	7	7	6	0	1	1	0	0	0	0	0	0	0	1	0	2	0	0	0	.167	.286	.167

Player, Team	G	TPA	AB	R	H	TB	2B	3B	HR	RBI	SH	SF	HP	BB	IBB	SO	SB	CS	GDP	Avg.	OBP	Slg.
Cox, Steve, T.B.*	3	3	3	0	1	1	0	0	0	0	0	0	0	0	0	1	0	0	0	.333	.333	.333
Cruz, Jacob, Det.*	4	4	3	1	0	0	0	0	0	0	0	0	0	1	0	2	0	0	0	.000	.250	.000
Cruz, Jose, Tor.†	3	3	3	1	1	4	0	0	1	1	0	0	0	0	0	0	0	0	0	.333	.333	1.333
Cuddyer, Michael, Min.	4	4	4	1	1	2	1	0	0	0	0	0	0	0	0	0	0	0	0	.250	.250	.500
Damon, Johnny, Bos.*	2	2	2	0	0	0	0	0	0	0	0	0	0	0	0	0	0	0	0	.000	.000	.000
Daubach, Brian, Bos.*	15	15	14	2	2	3	1	0	0	0	0	0	0	1	0	7	0	0	2	.143	.200	.214
DaVanon, Jeff, Ana.†	6	6	5	1	1	4	0	0	1	3	1	0	0	0	0	0	0	0	0	.200	.200	.800
Davis, Ben, Sea.†	8	8	8	1	1	4	0	0	1	3	0	0	0	0	0	3	0	0	0	.125	.125	.500
Diaz, Einar, Cle.	1	1	1	0	0	0	0	0	0	0	0	0	0	0	0	0	0	0	0	.000	.000	.000
Diaz, Juan, Bos.	2	2	1	1	1	4	0	0	1	2	0	0	0	1	0	0	0	0	0	1.000	1.000	4.000
Durham, Ray, Chi.†	4	4	4	0	1	1	0	0	0	2	0	0	0	0	0	0	0	0	0	.250	.250	.250
Dye, Jermaine, Oak.	3	3	2	0	1	1	0	0	0	1	0	0	1	0	0	1	0	0	0	.500	.667	.500
Eckstein, David, Ana.	2	2	2	0	1	1	0	0	0	0	0	0	0	0	0	0	0	0	0	.500	.500	.500
Ellis, Mark, Oak.	1	1	1	0	0	0	0	0	0	0	0	0	0	0	0	0	0	0	0	.000	.000	.000
Erstad, Darin, Ana.*	3	3	3	1	3	5	2	0	0	2	0	0	0	0	0	0	1	0	0	1.000	1.000	1.667
Escalona, Felix, T.B.	3	3	3	0	1	1	0	0	0	0	0	0	0	0	0	1	0	0	0	.333	.333	.333
Everett, Carl, Tex.†	7	7	5	0	0	0	0	0	0	0	0	0	0	2	0	2	0	0	0	.000	.286	.000
Fabregas, Jorge, Ana.*	5	5	5	0	1	1	0	0	0	1	0	0	0	0	0	0	0	1	0	.200	.200	.200
Febles, Carlos, K.C.	1	1	1	0	0	0	0	0	0	0	0	0	0	0	0	0	0	0	0	.000	.000	.000
Fick, Robert, Det.*	3	3	2	0	0	0	0	0	0	0	0	0	0	1	0	2	0	0	0	.000	.333	.000
Figgins, Chone, Ana.†	3	3	3	0	0	0	0	0	0	0	0	0	0	0	0	0	0	0	0	.000	.000	.000
Fletcher, Darrin, Tor.*	11	10	10	2	4	8	1	0	1	4	0	0	0	0	0	1	0	0	0	.400	.400	.800
Flores, Jose, Oak.	1	1	1	0	0	0	0	0	0	0	0	0	0	0	0	0	0	0	0	.000	.000	.000
Floyd, Cliff, Bos.*	3	3	2	1	0	0	0	0	0	0	0	0	0	1	0	1	0	0	0	.000	.333	.000
Fordyce, Brook, Bal.	1	1	1	0	0	0	0	0	0	0	0	0	0	0	0	1	0	0	0	.000	.000	.000
Fryman, Travis, Cle.	8	8	8	0	0	0	0	0	0	0	0	0	0	0	0	4	0	0	0	.000	.000	.000
Fullmer, Brad, Ana.*	11	10	7	0	1	1	0	0	0	1	0	0	2	1	1	0	0	0	0	.143	.400	.143
Garcia, Karim, N.Y.-Cle.*	2	2	2	0	0	0	0	0	0	0	0	0	0	0	0	1	0	0	0	.000	.000	.000
Garcia, Luis, Bal.	3	3	3	0	1	1	0	0	0	0	0	0	0	0	0	1	0	0	0	.333	.333	.333
Garciaparra, Nomar, Bos.	3	3	3	0	0	0	0	0	0	0	0	0	0	0	0	0	0	0	0	.000	.000	.000
Gibbons, Jay, Bal.*	5	4	4	0	1	2	1	0	0	1	0	0	0	0	0	1	0	0	0	.250	.250	.500
Gil, Benji, Ana.	11	7	7	1	4	7	1	1	0	2	0	0	0	0	0	2	1	0	0	.571	.571	1.000
Gipson, Charles, Sea.	2	2	2	0	0	0	0	0	0	0	0	0	0	0	0	1	0	0	0	.000	.000	.000
Glaus, Troy, Ana.	1	1	1	0	0	0	0	0	0	0	0	0	0	0	0	1	0	0	0	.000	.000	.000
Gomez, Alexis, K.C.*	2	2	2	0	1	1	0	0	0	0	0	0	0	0	0	0	0	0	0	.500	.500	.500
Gomez, Chris, T.B.	1	1	1	0	0	0	0	0	0	0	0	0	0	0	0	0	0	0	0	.000	.000	.000
Gonzalez, Juan, Tex.	1	1	1	0	0	0	0	0	0	0	0	0	0	0	0	0	0	0	0	.000	.000	.000
Graffanino, Tony, Chi.	8	8	6	0	1	1	0	0	0	1	0	0	0	2	1	0	0	0	0	.167	.375	.167
Greene, Todd, Tex.	11	10	9	0	0	0	0	0	0	1	0	0	0	1	0	5	0	0	0	.000	.100	.000
Greer, Rusty, Tex.*	2	2	2	0	2	3	1	0	0	1	0	0	0	0	0	0	0	0	0	1.000	1.000	1.500
Grieve, Ben, T.B.*	3	3	2	0	0	0	0	0	0	0	0	0	0	1	0	0	0	0	0	.000	.333	.000
Guiel, Aaron, K.C.*	10	10	10	1	1	4	0	0	1	3	0	0	0	0	0	6	0	0	0	.100	.100	.400
Guillen, Carlos, Sea.†	2	2	0	0	0	0	0	0	0	1	0	0	0	2	0	0	0	0	0	.000	1.000	.000
Gutierrez, Ricky, Cle.	1	1	1	0	0	0	0	0	0	0	0	0	0	0	0	0	0	0	0	.000	.000	.000
Guzman, Cristian, Min.†	3	3	3	0	0	0	0	0	0	0	0	0	0	0	0	1	0	0	0	.000	.000	.000
Hafner, Travis, Tex.*	7	7	6	1	1	2	1	0	0	0	0	0	0	1	0	1	0	0	0	.167	.286	.333
Hairston Jr., Jerry, Bal.	2	2	2	0	0	0	0	0	0	0	0	0	0	0	0	1	0	0	0	.000	.000	.000
Hall, Toby, T.B.	2	2	2	0	0	0	0	0	0	0	0	0	0	0	0	0	0	0	0	.000	.000	.000
Halter, Shane, Det.	2	2	1	0	0	0	0	0	0	0	0	0	0	1	0	1	0	0	0	.000	.500	.000
Harris, Willie, Chi.*	3	3	3	0	0	0	0	0	0	0	0	0	0	0	0	0	0	0	0	.000	.000	.000
Hart, Jason, Tex.	2	2	1	0	0	0	0	0	0	0	0	0	0	1	0	1	0	0	0	.000	.500	.000
Haselman, Bill, Tex.	2	2	1	0	1	1	0	0	0	0	0	0	1	0	0	0	0	0	0	1.000	1.000	1.000
Hatteberg, Scott, Oak.*	7	7	7	1	2	5	0	0	1	1	0	0	0	0	0	2	0	0	0	.286	.286	.714
Henderson, Rickey, Bos.	8	8	6	0	0	0	0	0	0	0	0	0	0	2	0	5	0	0	0	.000	.250	.000
Henson, Drew, N.Y.	1	1	1	0	0	0	0	0	0	0	0	0	0	0	0	1	0	0	0	.000	.000	.000
Hernandez, Ramon, Oak.	2	2	2	0	0	0	0	0	0	0	0	0	0	0	0	1	0	0	0	.000	.000	.000
Higginson, Bobby, Det.*	1	1	0	0	0	0	0	0	0	0	1	0	0	1	0	0	0	0	0	.000	1.000	.000
Hillenbrand, Shea, Bos.	1	1	1	1	1	4	0	0	1	4	0	0	0	0	0	0	0	0	0	1.000	1.000	4.000
Hinch, A.J., K.C.	4	4	4	0	0	0	0	0	0	0	0	0	0	0	0	2	0	0	0	.000	.000	.000
Hinske, Eric, Tor.*	10	10	9	1	2	2	0	0	0	1	0	0	0	1	0	4	0	0	0	.222	.300	.222
Hocking, Denny, Min.†	6	6	5	1	1	1	0	0	0	0	0	0	0	1	0	1	0	0	0	.200	.333	.200
Hollandsworth, Todd, Tex.*....	6	6	5	0	0	0	0	0	0	0	0	0	0	1	0	3	0	0	0	.000	.167	.000
Hoover, Paul, T.B.	1	1	1	1	1	1	0	0	0	0	0	0	0	0	0	0	0	0	0	1.000	1.000	1.000
Huckaby, Ken, Tor.	1	1	1	0	0	0	0	0	0	0	0	0	0	0	0	1	0	0	0	.000	.000	.000
Hudson, Orlando, Tor.†	1	1	1	0	0	0	0	0	0	0	0	0	0	0	0	1	0	0	0	.000	.000	.000
Huff, Aubrey, T.B.*	1	1	1	0	0	0	0	0	0	0	0	0	0	0	0	1	0	0	0	.000	.000	.000
Hunter, Torii, Min.	1	1	1	0	0	0	0	0	0	0	0	0	0	0	0	0	0	0	0	.000	.000	.000
Ibanez, Raul, K.C.*	7	7	6	1	1	1	0	0	0	1	0	0	0	1	0	1	0	0	0	.167	.286	.167
Jackson, Damian, Det.	4	4	2	0	0	0	0	0	0	0	0	0	0	2	0	1	0	0	0	.000	.500	.000
Jackson, Ryan, Det.*	2	2	2	0	2	5	1	1	0	0	0	0	0	0	0	0	0	0	0	1.000	1.000	2.500
Johnson, Mark L., Chi.*	4	4	4	0	1	1	0	0	0	0	0	0	0	0	0	1	0	0	1	.250	.250	.250
Johnson, Nick, N.Y.*	3	3	3	0	0	0	0	0	0	0	0	0	0	0	0	0	0	0	0	.000	.000	.000
Johnson, Russ, T.B.	15	14	11	2	2	2	0	0	0	0	0	0	1	2	1	5	0	0	0	.182	.357	.182
Jones, Jacque, Min.*	10	10	9	2	2	2	0	0	0	1	0	1	0	0	0	2	0	0	0	.222	.200	.222
Justice, David, Oak.*	10	10	6	0	2	2	0	0	0	0	0	0	0	4	1	1	0	0	0	.333	.600	.333
Kapler, Gabe, Tex.	10	10	10	3	4	5	1	0	0	0	0	0	0	0	0	3	0	0	0	.400	.400	.500
Kennedy, Adam, Ana.*	12	12	11	0	4	4	0	0	0	1	0	0	0	1	0	4	1	0	0	.364	.417	.364
Kielty, Bobby, Min.†	24	24	23	5	8	15	2	1	1	2	0	0	0	1	0	8	0	0	2	.348	.375	.652
Knoblauch, Chuck, K.C.	2	2	2	0	2	2	0	0	0	0	0	0	0	0	0	0	0	0	0	1.000	1.000	1.000
Konerko, Paul, Chi.	4	4	3	0	0	0	0	0	0	0	0	0	0	1	0	1	0	0	0	.000	.250	.000
Koskie, Corey, Min.*	3	3	1	0	0	0	0	0	0	1	0	0	0	2	0	0	1	0	0	.000	.667	.000
Lamb, David, Min.†	2	2	2	0	0	0	0	0	0	0	0	0	0	0	0	0	0	0	0	.000	.000	.000

Player, Team	G	TPA	AB	R	H	TB	2B	3B	HR	RBI	SH	SF	HP	BB	IBB	SO	SB	CS	GDP	Avg.	OBP	Slg.
Lamb, Mike, Tex.*	29	27	21	3	6	6	0	0	0	5	0	2	0	4	1	5	0	0	1	.286	.370	.286
LaRocca, Greg, Cle.	4	4	2	0	0	0	0	0	0	0	0	0	1	1	0	1	0	0	0	.000	.500	.000
Lawrence, Joe, Tor.	3	3	2	1	0	0	0	0	0	1	0	0	0	1	0	0	0	0	0	.000	.333	.000
Lawton, Matt, Cle.*	4	4	3	0	0	0	0	0	0	0	0	0	0	1	0	1	0	0	0	.000	.250	.000
LeCroy, Matthew, Min.	17	17	16	0	2	3	1	0	0	1	0	0	0	1	0	8	0	0	1	.125	.176	.188
Lee, Carlos, Chi.	3	3	2	1	1	2	1	0	0	1	0	0	0	1	0	1	0	0	0	.500	.667	1.000
Leon, Jose, Bal.	5	4	3	1	1	1	0	0	0	0	0	0	0	1	0	1	1	0	0	.333	.500	.333
Lesher, Brian, Tor.	6	6	5	1	1	1	0	0	0	0	0	0	0	1	0	4	0	0	0	.200	.333	.200
Liefer, Jeff, Chi.*	12	12	11	2	1	1	0	0	0	0	0	0	0	1	0	4	0	0	1	.091	.167	.091
Lofton, Kenny, Chi.*	4	4	4	0	0	0	0	0	0	0	0	0	0	0	0	3	0	0	0	.000	.000	.000
Lombard, George, Det.*	3	3	3	0	0	0	0	0	0	0	0	0	0	0	0	2	0	0	0	.000	.000	.000
Long, Terrence, Oak.*	1	1	1	0	1	1	0	0	0	1	0	0	0	0	0	0	0	1	0	1.000	1.000	1.000
Lopez, Felipe, Tor.†	5	5	5	0	0	0	0	0	0	0	0	0	0	0	0	3	0	0	0	.000	.000	.000
Lopez, Luis, Bal.†	24	24	24	4	6	8	2	0	0	0	0	0	0	0	0	7	0	0	1	.250	.250	.333
Ludwick, Ryan, Tex.	1	1	1	0	1	1	0	0	0	2	0	0	0	0	0	0	0	0	0	1.000	1.000	1.000
Mabry, John, Oak.*	14	14	14	1	5	8	3	0	0	4	0	0	0	0	0	4	0	0	1	.357	.357	.571
Magee, Wendell, Det.	5	5	5	0	1	1	0	0	0	0	0	0	0	0	0	2	0	0	0	.200	.200	.200
Magruder, Chris, Cle.†	4	4	4	0	1	2	1	0	0	0	0	0	0	0	0	1	0	0	0	.250	.250	.500
Martinez, Edgar, Sea.	6	6	5	0	1	1	0	0	0	0	0	0	0	1	0	2	0	0	0	.200	.333	.200
Martinez, Victor, Cle.†	5	5	4	0	2	2	0	0	0	1	0	0	0	1	0	0	0	0	0	.500	.600	.500
Matos, Luis, Bal.	4	4	4	0	2	2	0	0	0	0	0	0	0	0	0	1	0	0	0	.500	.500	.500
Matthews Jr., Gary, Bal.†	10	10	8	0	1	2	1	0	0	0	1	0	0	1	0	1	1	1	0	.125	.222	.250
Mayne, Brent, K.C.	7	7	7	1	2	5	0	0	1	2	0	0	0	0	0	1	0	0	0	.286	.286	.714
McCarty, Dave, K.C.-TB.	6	6	6	0	2	2	0	0	0	1	0	0	0	0	0	3	0	0	0	.333	.333	.333
McDonald, Donzell, K.C.†	3	3	2	0	0	0	0	0	0	0	0	0	0	1	0	1	0	0	0	.000	.333	.000
McDonald, John, Cle.	3	3	2	0	0	0	0	0	0	0	1	0	0	0	0	1	0	0	0	.000	.000	.000
McGuire, Ryan, Bal.*	10	9	9	0	0	0	0	0	0	0	0	0	0	0	0	5	0	0	1	.000	.000	.000
McLemore, Mark, Sea.†	8	8	8	0	2	2	0	0	0	1	0	0	0	0	0	4	1	0	0	.250	.250	.250
Mench, Kevin, Tex.	6	6	5	0	0	0	0	0	0	0	0	0	1	0	0	1	0	0	0	.000	.167	.000
Menechino, Frank, Oak.	2	1	0	0	0	0	0	0	0	0	0	0	0	1	0	0	0	0	0	.000	1.000	.000
Merloni, Lou, Bos.	4	4	3	0	1	2	1	0	0	0	0	0	0	1	0	2	0	0	0	.333	.500	.667
Mientkiewicz, Doug, Min.*	1	1	1	1	1	2	1	0	0	2	0	0	0	0	0	0	0	0	0	1.000	1.000	2.000
Mirabelli, Doug, Bos.	7	7	6	1	2	5	0	0	1	2	0	0	0	1	0	1	0	0	0	.333	.429	.833
Mohr, Dustan, Min.	9	9	7	2	3	6	0	0	1	3	0	0	0	2	0	3	1	0	0	.429	.556	.857
Molina, Bengie, Ana.	7	7	6	0	1	1	0	0	0	1	0	0	1	0	0	1	0	0	0	.167	.286	.167
Mora, Melvin, Bal.	3	3	2	0	0	0	0	0	0	0	0	0	0	1	0	0	0	0	0	.000	.333	.000
Moriarty, Mike, Bal.	2	2	2	0	0	0	0	0	0	0	0	0	0	0	0	0	0	0	0	.000	.000	.000
Morris, Warren, Min.*	1	1	1	0	0	0	0	0	0	0	0	0	0	0	0	0	0	0	0	.000	.000	.000
Munson, Eric, Det.*	1	1	1	0	0	0	0	0	0	0	0	0	0	0	0	1	0	0	0	.000	.000	.000
Myers, Greg, Oak.*	21	21	16	3	5	11	0	0	2	7	0	0	0	5	2	5	0	0	2	.313	.476	.688
Nelson, Bry, Bos.†	4	4	4	1	1	2	1	0	0	0	0	0	0	0	0	0	0	0	0	.250	.250	.500
Nieves, Jose, Ana.	7	5	5	1	2	2	0	0	0	0	0	0	0	0	0	0	0	0	0	.400	.400	.400
Nixon, Trot, Bos.*	2	2	1	1	0	0	0	0	0	0	0	0	0	1	0	0	0	0	0	.000	.500	.000
Ochoa, Alex, Ana.	7	7	6	1	1	1	0	0	0	2	0	0	0	1	0	1	0	0	0	.167	.286	.167
Offerman, Jose, Bos.-Sea.†	17	17	16	2	3	3	0	0	0	2	0	0	1	0	0	5	1	0	1	.188	.235	.188
Olerud, John, Sea.*	1	1	1	0	0	0	0	0	0	0	0	0	0	0	0	0	0	0	0	.000	.000	.000
Ordaz, Luis, K.C.	1	1	1	0	0	0	0	0	0	0	0	0	0	0	0	0	0	0	0	.000	.000	.000
Ordonez, Magglio, Chi.	3	3	2	1	1	4	0	0	1	1	0	0	0	1	0	1	0	0	0	.500	.667	2.000
Ortiz, David, Min.*	17	17	13	2	3	5	0	1	0	5	0	1	0	3	0	3	0	0	0	.231	.353	.385
Ortiz, Hector, Tex.	1	1	1	0	0	0	0	0	0	0	0	0	0	0	0	0	0	0	1	.000	.000	.000
Palmeiro, Orlando, Ana.*	32	30	28	3	8	10	2	0	0	2	1	0	0	1	0	5	1	0	0	.286	.310	.357
Palmeiro, Rafael, Tex.*	5	5	5	0	0	0	0	0	0	0	0	0	0	0	0	0	0	0	0	.000	.000	.000
Palmer, Dean, Det.	1	1	1	0	0	0	0	0	0	0	0	0	0	0	0	0	0	0	0	.000	.000	.000
Paquette, Craig, Det.	3	3	3	0	0	0	0	0	0	0	0	0	0	0	0	1	0	0	0	.000	.000	.000
Pellow, Kit, K.C.	5	3	3	0	1	1	0	0	0	0	0	0	0	0	0	1	0	0	0	.333	.333	.333
Pena, Carlos, Det.*	1	1	0	0	0	0	0	0	0	0	0	0	1	0	0	0	0	1	0	.000	1.000	.000
Perez, Eddie, Cle.	1	1	1	0	0	0	0	0	0	0	0	0	0	0	0	0	0	0	1	.000	.000	.000
Perez, Neifi, K.C.†	1	1	1	0	0	0	0	0	0	0	0	0	0	0	0	0	0	0	0	.000	.000	.000
Perry, Herbert, Tex.	14	14	12	0	3	3	0	0	0	3	0	0	0	2	0	3	0	0	0	.250	.357	.250
Phelps, Josh, Tor.	2	2	2	0	1	1	0	0	0	2	0	0	0	0	0	0	0	0	0	.500	.500	.500
Piatt, Adam, Oak.	11	9	8	1	0	0	0	0	0	1	0	0	0	1	0	3	0	0	0	.000	.111	.000
Pierzynski, A.J., Min.*	11	11	10	0	4	5	1	0	0	2	0	0	0	1	1	1	0	0	1	.400	.455	.500
Podsednik, Scott, Sea.*	3	3	3	0	1	1	0	0	0	0	0	0	0	0	0	0	0	0	0	.333	.333	.333
Posada, Jorge, N.Y.†	7	7	7	0	1	1	0	0	0	0	0	0	0	0	0	1	0	0	0	.143	.143	.143
Prince, Tom, Min.	1	1	1	0	0	0	0	0	0	0	0	0	0	0	0	0	0	0	0	.000	.000	.000
Quinn, Mark, K.C.	1	1	1	0	0	0	0	0	0	0	0	0	0	0	0	0	0	0	0	.000	.000	.000
Ramirez, Julio, Ana.	4	3	3	1	1	4	0	0	1	2	0	0	0	0	0	2	0	0	0	.333	.333	1.333
Ramirez, Manny, Bos.	2	2	1	0	0	0	0	0	0	1	0	0	0	1	0	0	0	0	0	.000	.500	.000
Randa, Joe, K.C.	6	6	6	0	2	2	0	0	0	1	0	0	0	0	0	3	0	0	0	.333	.333	.333
Relaford, Desi, Sea.†	11	11	9	1	1	1	0	0	0	2	0	2	0	0	0	2	0	0	0	.111	.091	.111
Restovich, Michael, Min.	2	2	2	1	1	4	0	0	1	1	0	0	0	0	0	1	0	0	0	.500	.500	2.000
Richard, Chris, Bal.*	5	5	5	1	0	0	0	0	0	0	0	0	0	0	0	2	0	0	0	.000	.000	.000
Ritchie, Todd, Chi.	1	1	1	0	0	0	0	0	0	0	0	0	0	0	0	0	0	0	0	.000	.000	.000
Rivera, Michael, Det.	1	1	1	0	0	0	0	0	0	0	0	0	0	0	0	1	0	0	0	.000	.000	.000
Rivera, Ruben, Tex.	2	2	1	0	0	0	0	0	0	0	0	1	0	0	0	0	0	0	0	.000	.000	.000
Roberts, Brian, Bal.†	4	4	4	0	1	1	0	0	0	0	0	0	0	0	0	0	1	0	0	.250	.250	.250
Rodriguez, Alex, Tex.	2	2	2	1	0	0	0	0	0	0	0	0	0	0	0	0	0	0	0	.000	.000	.000
Rodriguez, Ivan, Tex.	3	3	2	0	0	0	0	0	0	1	0	1	0	0	0	0	0	0	0	.000	.000	.000
Rogers, Eddie, Bal.	1	1	1	0	0	0	0	0	0	0	0	0	0	0	0	0	0	0	1	.000	.000	.000
Romano, Jason, Tex.	2	2	1	0	0	0	0	0	0	0	0	0	1	0	0	1	0	0	0	.000	.500	.000
Rowand, Aaron, Chi.	9	9	9	1	2	3	1	0	0	0	0	0	0	0	0	4	0	0	0	.222	.222	.333
Sadler, Donnie, K.C.-Tex.	7	7	7	0	1	1	0	0	0	0	0	0	0	0	0	1	0	0	0	.143	.143	.143

Player, Team	G	TPA	AB	R	H	TB	2B	3B	HR	RBI	SH	SF	HP	BB	IBB	SO	SB	CS	GDP	Avg.	OBP	Slg.
Saenz, Olmedo, Oak.	26	25	20	2	5	11	0	0	2	3	0	0	2	3	1	3	0	0	1	.250	.400	.550
Salazar, Oscar, Det.	1	1	1	0	1	2	1	0	0	1	0	0	0	0	0	0	0	0	0	1.000	1.000	2.000
Salmon, Tim, Ana.	6	6	6	1	1	1	0	0	0	0	0	0	0	0	0	2	0	0	0	.167	.167	.167
Sanchez, Freddy, Bos.	2	2	1	0	1	1	0	0	0	2	0	0	0	1	0	0	0	0	0	1.000	1.000	1.000
Sanchez, Rey, Bos.	2	2	2	0	1	1	0	0	0	1	0	0	0	0	0	0	0	0	0	.500	.500	.500
Sandberg, Jared, T.B.	1	1	1	0	0	0	0	0	0	0	0	0	0	0	0	0	0	0	0	.000	.000	.000
Sears, Todd, Min.*	1	1	1	0	0	0	0	0	0	0	0	0	0	0	0	0	0	0	0	.000	.000	.000
Selby, Bill, Cle.*	21	20	18	2	6	7	1	0	0	3	0	0	0	2	0	4	0	0	0	.333	.400	.389
Sierra, Ruben, Sea.†	17	17	17	0	3	3	0	0	0	3	0	0	0	0	0	2	0	0	1	.176	.176	.176
Simon, Randall, Det.*	6	6	6	0	2	3	1	0	0	2	0	0	0	0	0	0	0	0	0	.333	.333	.500
Singleton, Chris, Bal.*	9	9	8	2	2	3	1	0	0	1	0	0	0	1	0	1	0	0	0	.250	.333	.375
Smith, Jason, T.B.*	5	5	4	0	0	0	0	0	0	1	0	0	0	1	0	2	0	0	0	.000	.200	.000
Snyder, Earl, Cle.	3	3	3	1	1	1	0	0	0	0	0	0	0	0	0	1	0	0	0	.333	.333	.333
Spencer, Shane, N.Y.	10	10	5	1	1	1	0	0	0	2	0	1	0	4	2	2	0	0	0	.200	.500	.200
Spiezio, Scott, Ana.†	8	8	8	0	1	2	1	0	0	0	0	0	0	0	0	3	0	0	0	.125	.125	.250
Stevens, Lee, Cle.*	13	11	10	3	5	6	1	0	0	2	0	1	0	0	0	2	0	0	1	.500	.455	.600
Stewart, Shannon, Tor.	2	2	2	0	0	0	0	0	0	0	0	0	0	0	0	2	0	0	0	.000	.000	.000
Suzuki, Ichiro, Sea.*	3	3	3	1	0	0	0	0	0	0	0	0	0	0	0	1	0	0	0	.000	.000	.000
Swann, Pedro, Tor.*	9	9	8	1	1	1	0	0	0	0	0	0	0	1	0	4	0	0	0	.125	.222	.125
Sweeney, Mike, K.C.	1	1	1	0	0	0	0	0	0	0	0	0	0	0	0	0	0	0	0	.000	.000	.000
Tejada, Miguel, Oak.	1	1	1	0	0	0	0	0	0	0	0	0	0	0	0	0	0	0	0	.000	.000	.000
Thames, Marcus, N.Y.	1	1	1	0	0	0	0	0	0	0	0	0	0	0	0	0	0	0	0	.000	.000	.000
Thomas, Frank, Chi.	5	5	4	0	0	0	0	0	0	0	0	0	0	1	0	4	0	0	0	.000	.200	.000
Thome, Jim, Cle.*	1	1	1	0	0	0	0	0	0	0	0	0	0	0	0	0	0	0	0	.000	.000	.000
Tucker, Michael, K.C.*	15	15	15	0	4	5	1	0	0	1	0	0	0	0	0	4	0	0	0	.267	.267	.333
Tyner, Jason, T.B.*	2	2	2	0	1	1	0	0	0	0	0	0	0	0	0	0	0	0	0	.500	.500	.500
Ugueto, Luis, Sea.†	2	2	2	0	0	0	0	0	0	0	0	0	0	0	0	2	0	0	0	.000	.000	.000
Valentin, Jose, Chi.†	12	12	9	3	2	5	0	0	1	1	0	0	0	3	0	0	0	0	0	.222	.417	.556
Vander Wal, John, N.Y.*	17	17	13	0	2	3	1	0	0	2	0	1	0	3	1	4	0	0	0	.154	.294	.231
Varitek, Jason, Bos.†	6	6	6	0	2	3	1	0	0	0	0	0	0	0	0	3	0	0	0	.333	.333	.500
Vaughn, Greg, T.B.	1	1	0	0	0	0	0	0	0	0	0	0	1	0	0	0	0	0	0	.000	1.000	.000
Velarde, Randy, Oak.	10	10	9	0	1	1	0	0	0	0	0	0	0	1	0	4	0	0	0	.111	.200	.111
Ventura, Robin, N.Y.*	10	10	8	2	2	5	0	0	1	4	0	0	0	2	2	2	0	0	0	.250	.400	.625
Vizquel, Omar, Cle.†	1	1	1	0	0	0	0	0	0	0	0	0	0	0	0	0	0	0	0	.000	.000	.000
White, Rondell, N.Y.	8	7	5	2	2	3	1	0	0	2	0	0	0	2	0	1	0	0	0	.400	.571	.600
Williams, Bernie, N.Y.†	1	1	1	0	0	0	0	0	0	0	0	0	0	0	0	0	0	0	0	.000	.000	.000
Wilson, Dan, Sea.	1	1	1	0	1	1	0	0	0	0	0	0	0	0	0	0	0	0	0	1.000	1.000	1.000
Wilson, Enrique, N.Y.†	9	9	6	2	0	0	0	0	0	0	0	0	0	3	0	3	0	0	0	.000	.333	.000
Wilson, Tom, Tor.	16	16	15	2	3	6	0	0	1	1	0	0	0	1	0	5	0	0	0	.200	.250	.400
Winn, Randy, T.B.†	6	6	6	1	2	5	0	0	1	7	0	0	0	0	0	0	0	0	0	.333	.333	.833
Wise, Dewayne, Tor.*	3	3	3	0	0	0	0	0	0	0	0	0	0	0	0	2	0	0	0	.000	.000	.000
Woodward, Chris, Tor.	1	1	1	0	0	0	0	0	0	0	0	0	0	0	0	1	0	0	0	.000	.000	.000
Wooten, Shawn, Ana.	15	15	11	2	4	4	0	0	0	3	0	0	1	3	1	2	0	0	1	.364	.533	.364
Young, Dmitri, Det.†	2	2	2	0	0	0	0	0	0	0	0	0	0	0	0	2	0	0	0	.000	.000	.000
Young, Michael, Tex.	4	4	4	1	1	1	0	0	0	0	0	0	0	0	0	0	0	0	0	.250	.250	.250

PINCH-HITTERS WITH TWO OR MORE TEAMS

Player, Team	G	TPA	AB	R	H	TB	2B	3B	HR	RBI	SH	SF	HP	BB	IBB	SO	SB	CS	GDP	Avg.	OBP	Slg.
Garcia, Karim, N.Y.*	1	1	1	0	0	0	0	0	0	0	0	0	0	0	0	0	0	0	0	.000	.000	.000
Garcia, Karim, Cle.*	1	1	1	0	0	0	0	0	0	0	0	0	0	0	0	1	0	0	0	.000	.000	.000
McCarty, Dave, K.C.	4	4	4	0	0	0	0	0	0	0	0	0	0	0	0	3	0	0	0	.000	.000	.000
McCarty, Dave, T.B.	2	2	2	0	2	2	0	0	0	1	0	0	0	0	0	0	0	0	0	1.000	1.000	1.000
Offerman, Jose, Bos.†	9	9	8	0	1	1	0	0	0	0	0	0	1	0	0	2	0	0	1	.125	.222	.125
Offerman, Jose, Sea.†	8	8	8	2	2	2	0	0	0	2	0	0	0	0	0	3	1	0	0	.250	.250	.250
Sadler, Donnie, K.C.	5	5	5	0	1	1	0	0	0	0	0	0	0	0	0	1	0	0	0	.200	.200	.200
Sadler, Donnie, Tex.	2	2	2	0	0	0	0	0	0	0	0	0	0	0	0	0	0	0	0	.000	.000	.000

PITCHING

TEAM

Team	W	L	Pct.	ERA	G	CG	ShO	Rel.	Sv.-Op.	IP	H	TBF	R	ER	HR	SH	SF	HB	BB	IBB	SO	WP	Bk.
Oakland	103	59	.636	3.68	162	9	19	408	48-69	1452.0	1391	6158	654	593	135	50	42	62	474	45	1021	40	9
Anaheim	99	63	.611	3.69	162	7	14	400	54-71	1452.1	1345	6097	644	595	169	27	59	49	509	24	999	52	7
Boston	93	69	.574	3.75	162	5	17	338	51-68	1446.0	1339	6049	665	603	146	30	52	84	430	29	1157	31	6
New York	103	58	.640	3.87	161	9	11	334	53-69	1452.0	1441	6159	697	625	144	38	41	48	403	44	1135	59	2
Seattle	93	69	.574	4.07	162	8	12	343	43-64	1445.1	1422	6117	699	654	178	39	48	49	441	34	1063	42	3
Minnesota	94	67	.584	4.12	161	8	9	435	47-65	1444.2	1454	6133	712	662	184	30	41	45	439	24	1026	62	3
Baltimore	67	95	.414	4.46	162	8	3	407	31-46	1450.2	1491	6258	773	719	208	20	38	54	549	34	967	54	1
Chicago	81	81	.500	4.53	162	7	7	423	35-46	1423.0	1422	6131	798	716	190	41	43	60	528	31	945	54	6
Toronto	78	84	.481	4.80	162	6	6	461	41-70	1438.1	1504	6338	828	767	177	42	52	71	590	56	991	57	4
Cleveland	74	88	.457	4.91	162	9	4	421	34-53	1424.2	1508	6271	837	777	142	39	66	57	603	38	1058	52	8
Detroit	55	106	.342	4.93	161	11	7	372	33-54	1414.0	1593	6215	864	774	163	44	53	62	463	34	794	59	8
Texas	72	90	.444	5.15	162	4	4	487	33-66	1439.2	1528	6446	882	824	194	38	40	76	669	32	1030	84	11
Kansas City	62	100	.383	5.21	162	12	6	421	30-54	1441.0	1587	6386	891	834	212	47	69	52	572	48	909	68	6
Tampa Bay	55	106	.342	5.29	161	12	3	306	25-46	1440.1	1567	6424	918	846	215	35	57	94	620	24	925	62	10
Totals	1129	1135	.499	4.46	1132	115	122	5556	558-841	20164.0	20592	87182	10862	9989	2457	520	701	863	7290	497	14020	776	84

NOTE—Totals for earned runs for several clubs do not agree with composite total for all pitchers of each respective club due to instances in which provisions of Section 10.18(i) of the Scoring Rules were applied. The following differences are to be noted: Oakland pitchers add to 595; New York pitchers add to 627; Chicago pitchers add to 723; Toronto pitchers add to 768; Detroit pitchers add to 776; Texas pitchers add to 826; Kansas City pitchers add to 835; Tampa Bay pitchers add to 847.

INDIVIDUAL
TOP QUALIFIERS FOR EARNED-RUN AVERAGE TITLE

Minimum 162 innings. *Throws lefthanded.

Pitcher, Team	W	L	Pct.	ERA	G	GS	CG	ShO	GF	Sv.-Op.	IP	H	TBF	R	ER	HR	SH	SF	HB	BB	IBB	SO	WP	Bk.
Martinez, Pedro, Bos.	20	4	.833	2.26	30	30	2	0	0	0-0	199.1	144	787	62	50	13	2	4	15	40	1	239	3	0
Lowe, Derek, Bos.	21	8	.724	2.58	32	32	1	1	0	0-0	219.2	166	854	65	63	12	5	2	12	48	0	127	5	0
Zito, Barry, Oak.*	23	5	.821	2.75	35	35	1	0	0	0-0	229.1	182	939	79	70	24	9	7	9	78	2	182	2	1
Wakefield, Tim, Bos.	11	5	.688	2.81	45	15	0	0	10	3-5	163.1	121	657	57	51	15	1	4	9	51	2	134	5	2
Halladay, Roy, Tor.	19	7	.731	2.93	34	34	2	1	0	0-0	239.1	223	993	93	78	10	9	2	7	62	6	168	4	1
Hudson, Tim, Oak.	15	9	.625	2.98	34	34	4	2	0	0-0	238.1	237	983	87	79	19	6	5	8	62	9	152	7	1
Washburn, Jarrod, Ana.*	18	6	.750	3.15	32	32	1	0	0	0-0	206.0	183	852	75	72	19	4	7	3	59	1	139	5	1
Pineiro, Joel, Sea.	14	7	.667	3.24	37	28	2	1	4	0-0	194.1	189	812	75	70	24	5	7	7	54	1	136	8	0
Moyer, Jamie, Sea.*	13	8	.619	3.32	34	34	4	2	0	0-0	230.2	198	931	89	85	28	5	7	9	50	4	147	3	0
Mulder, Mark, Oak.*	19	7	.731	3.47	30	30	2	1	0	0-0	207.1	182	862	88	80	21	6	4	11	55	3	159	7	1
Weaver, Jeff, Det.-N.Y.	11	11	.500	3.52	32	25	3	3	3	2-0	199.2	193	840	88	78	16	6	3	11	48	4	132	6	0
Lopez, Rodrigo, Bal.	15	9	.625	3.57	33	28	1	0	0	0-0	196.2	172	809	83	78	23	2	4	5	62	4	136	2	1
Buehrle, Mark, Chi.*	19	12	.613	3.58	34	34	5	2	0	0-0	239.0	236	984	102	95	25	9	3	3	61	7	134	6	1
Wells, David, N.Y.*	19	7	.731	3.75	31	31	2	1	0	0-0	206.1	210	873	100	86	21	6	5	5	45	2	137	4	0
Ortiz, Ramon, Ana.	15	9	.625	3.77	32	32	4	1	0	0-0	217.1	188	896	97	91	40	2	5	5	68	0	162	7	3

DEPARTMENTAL LEADERS: W—Zito, Oak., 23; L—Sturtze, T.B., 18; G—Koch, Oak., 84; GS—Zito, Oak., 35; CG—Byrd, K.C., 7; ShO—Weaver, Det.-N.Y., 3; GF—Koch, Oak., 79; Sv.—Guardado, Min., 45; Sv. Op.—Guardado, Min., 51; IP—Halladay, Tor., 239.1; H—Sturtze, T.B., 271; TBF—Sturtze, T.B., 1008; R—Sturtze, T.B., 141; ER—Sturtze, T.B., 129; HR—Ortiz, Ana., 40; SH—Buehrle, Chi., Halladay, Tor., Zito, Oak., 9; SF—Byrd, K.C., 13; HB—Park, Tex., 17; TBB—Sturtze, T.B., 89; IBB—Karsay, N.Y., 14; SO—Martinez, Bos., 239; WP—Santana, Min., 15; Bk.—Kent, T.B., Ortiz, Ana., Sabathia, Cle., 3.

ALL PITCHERS

*Throws lefthanded.

Pitcher, Team	W	L	Pct.	ERA	G	GS	CG	ShO	GF	Sv.-Op.	IP	H	TBF	R	ER	HR	SH	SF	HB	BB	IBB	SO	WP	Bk.
Abbott, Paul, Sea.	1	3	.250	11.96	7	5	0	0	1	0-0	26.1	40	137	36	35	5	1	1	1	20	0	22	2	0
Acevedo, Juan, Det.	1	5	.167	2.65	65	0	0	0	48	28-35	74.2	68	314	33	22	4	5	5	5	23	3	43	2	0
Affeldt, Jeremy, K.C.*	3	4	.429	4.64	34	7	0	0	4	0-1	77.2	85	353	41	40	8	2	1	3	37	4	67	5	2
Alvarez, Juan, Tex.*	0	4	.000	4.76	52	0	0	0	12	0-3	39.2	35	173	22	21	7	2	2	3	21	0	30	0	1
Alvarez, Wilson, T.B.*	2	3	.400	5.28	23	10	0	0	3	1-1	75.0	80	339	47	44	13	2	3	4	36	3	56	2	0
Anderson, Matt, Det.	2	1	.667	9.00	12	0	0	0	8	0-2	11.0	17	58	13	11	1	1	2	2	8	1	8	1	0
Appier, Kevin, Ana.	14	12	.538	3.92	32	32	0	0	0	0-0	188.1	191	795	89	82	23	1	8	7	64	2	132	7	0
Arrojo, Rolando, Bos.	4	3	.571	4.98	29	6	0	0	4	1-4	81.1	83	348	47	45	7	4	3	6	27	1	51	2	0
Asencio, Miguel, K.C.	4	7	.364	5.11	31	21	0	0	7	0-0	123.1	136	557	73	70	17	2	6	3	64	2	58	7	0
Austin, Jeff, K.C.	0	0	.000	4.91	10	0	0	0	5	0-0	11.0	14	52	6	6	0	0	2	0	6	1	6	1	0
Backe, Brandon, T.B.	0	0	.000	6.92	9	0	0	0	4	0-0	13.0	15	61	10	10	3	0	0	2	7	0	6	0	0
Baez, Danys, Cle.	10	11	.476	4.41	39	26	1	0	9	0-0	165.1	160	726	84	81	14	2	8	9	82	5	130	6	1
Bailey, Cory, K.C.	3	4	.429	4.11	37	0	0	0	14	1-7	46.0	53	211	24	21	5	3	2	2	31	7	24	1	1
Baldwin, James, Sea.	7	10	.412	5.28	30	23	0	0	0	0-0	150.0	179	662	95	88	26	4	2	7	49	2	88	1	0
Banks, Willie, Bos.	2	1	.667	3.23	29	0	0	0	18	1-1	39.0	32	162	15	14	5	0	1	3	14	0	26	1	0
Barcelo, Lorenzo, Chi.	0	1	.000	9.00	4	0	0	0	0	0-0	6.0	9	28	6	6	1	0	0	0	1	0	1	0	0
Bauer, Rick, Bal.	6	7	.462	3.98	56	1	0	0	15	1-5	83.2	84	358	41	37	12	2	2	4	36	4	45	4	0
Bechler, Steve, Bal.	0	0	.000	13.50	3	0	0	0	2	0-0	4.2	6	25	7	7	3	0	0	1	4	0	3	0	0
Bedard, Erik, Bal.*	0	0	.000	13.50	2	0	0	0	0	0-0	0.2	2	4	1	1	0	0	0	0	1	0	1	0	0
Bell, Rob, Tex.	4	3	.571	6.22	17	15	0	0	0	0-0	94.0	113	425	69	65	16	1	6	1	35	0	70	7	0
Benoit, Danys, Tex.	4	5	.444	5.31	17	13	0	0	2	1-1	84.2	91	405	51	50	6	4	3	5	58	2	59	7	0
Bernero, Adam, Det.	4	7	.364	6.20	28	11	0	0	5	0-0	101.2	128	459	74	70	17	3	5	6	31	1	69	5	1
Beverlin, Jason, Cle.-Det.	0	3	.000	8.69	7	3	0	0	1	0-0	19.2	27	95	22	19	3	0	0	0	9	0	16	2	0
Biddle, Rocky, Chi.	3	4	.429	4.06	44	7	0	0	9	1-3	77.2	72	339	42	35	13	0	1	5	39	4	64	5	0
Borbon, Pedro, Tor.*	1	2	.333	4.97	16	0	0	0	4	0-0	12.2	12	60	8	7	3	0	1	1	6	3	11	1	0

Pitcher, Team	W	L	Pct.	ERA	G	GS	CG	ShO	GF	Sv.-Op.	IP	H	TBF	R	ER	HR	SH	SF	HB	BB	IBB	SO	WP	Bk.
Bowie, Micah, Oak.*	2	0	1.000	1.50	13	0	0	0	4	0-0	12.0	12	55	2	2	1	0	0	1	8	1	8	0	0
Bowles, Brian, Tor.	2	1	.667	4.05	17	0	0	0	7	0-1	20.0	13	89	11	9	0	0	1	3	14	1	19	5	1
Bradford, Chad, Oak.	4	2	.667	3.11	75	0	0	0	14	2-5	75.1	73	311	29	26	2	2	5	14	5	56	0	1
Brazelton, Dewon, T.B.	0	1	.000	4.85	2	2	0	0	0	0-0	13.0	12	51	7	7	3	0	0	2	6	0	5	0	0
Brock, Chris, Bal.	2	1	.667	4.70	22	0	0	0	3	0-0	44.0	52	192	24	23	6	0	2	1	14	1	21	0	0
Buehrle, Mark, Chi.*	19	12	.613	3.58	34	34	5	2	0	0-0	239.0	236	984	102	95	25	9	3	3	61	7	134	6	1
Bukvich, Ryan, K.C.	1	0	1.000	6.12	26	0	0	0	2	0-1	25.0	26	121	19	17	2	4	3	1	19	3	20	1	0
Burba, Dave, Tex.-Cle.	5	5	.500	5.20	35	21	1	0	2	0-0	145.1	155	646	91	84	16	2	3	9	57	3	95	9	1
Burkett, John, Bos.	13	8	.619	4.53	29	29	1	1	0	0-0	173.0	199	760	93	87	25	5	4	8	50	5	124	2	1
Byrd, Paul, K.C.	17	11	.607	3.90	33	33	7	2	0	0-0	228.1	224	935	111	99	36	2	13	7	38	1	129	3	1
Callaway, Mickey, Ana.	2	1	.667	4.19	6	6	0	0	0	0-0	34.1	31	147	20	16	4	1	0	3	11	0	23	2	0
Carpenter, Chris, Tor.	4	5	.444	5.28	13	13	1	0	0	0-0	73.1	89	327	45	43	11	1	4	4	27	0	45	3	0
Carter, Lance, T.B.	2	0	1.000	1.33	8	0	0	0	7	2-2	20.1	15	79	3	3	2	0	0	0	5	1	14	0	0
Cassidy, Scott, Tor.	1	4	.200	5.74	58	0	0	0	17	0-7	66.0	52	282	42	42	12	4	5	7	32	3	48	2	0
Castillo, Frank, Bos.	6	15	.286	5.07	36	23	0	0	2	1-2	163.1	174	711	101	92	19	1	11	7	58	6	112	1	2
Choate, Randy, N.Y.*	0	0	.000	6.04	18	0	0	0	11	0-0	22.1	18	101	18	15	1	0	3	0	15	0	17	3	0
Clemens, Roger, N.Y.	13	6	.684	4.35	29	29	0	0	0	0-0	180.0	172	768	94	87	18	5	5	7	63	6	192	14	0
Coco, Pasqual, Tor.	0	1	.000	18.00	2	0	0	0	1	0-0	1.0	4	10	2	2	0	0	0	0	3	1	0	0	0
Colome, Jesus, T.B.	2	7	.222	8.27	32	0	0	0	15	0-5	41.1	56	204	41	38	6	4	1	2	33	5	33	5	0
Colon, Bartolo, Cle.	10	4	.714	2.55	16	16	4	2	0	0-0	116.1	104	467	37	33	11	6	3	2	31	1	75	3	0
Cook, Dennis, Ana.*	1	1	.500	3.38	37	0	0	0	5	0-1	24.0	21	100	9	9	2	0	2	1	10	0	13	0	0
Cooper, Brian, Tor.	0	1	.000	14.04	2	2	0	0	0	0-0	8.1	14	41	13	13	5	1	1	0	4	0	3	1	0
Cordero, Francisco, Tex.	2	0	1.000	1.79	39	0	0	0	25	10-12	45.1	33	177	12	9	2	0	0	2	13	1	41	1	0
Cornejo, Nate, Det.	1	5	.167	5.04	9	9	1	0	0	0-0	50.0	63	230	33	28	6	1	1	2	18	0	23	2	0
Creek, Doug, T.B.-Sea.*	3	2	.600	5.82	52	0	0	0	17	0-0	55.2	57	262	37	36	10	1	1	7	35	2	56	4	0
Cressend, Jack, Min.	0	1	.000	5.91	23	0	0	0	4	0-0	32.0	40	154	25	21	6	1	2	1	19	4	22	1	0
Davis, Doug, Tex.*	3	5	.375	4.98	10	10	1	1	0	0-0	59.2	67	262	36	33	7	3	3	3	22	0	28	2	2
Davis, Jason, Cle.	1	0	1.000	1.84	3	2	0	0	0	0-0	14.2	12	60	3	3	1	1	0	0	4	0	11	0	1
de los Santos, Luis, T.B.	0	3	.000	11.57	3	3	0	0	0	0-0	14.0	24	71	19	18	5	0	2	3	4	0	7	0	0
DePaula, Sean, Cle.	1	1	.500	12.79	5	0	0	0	1	0-2	6.1	11	33	9	9	3	0	0	3	0	8	0	0	0
Donnelly, Brendan, Ana.	1	1	.500	2.17	46	0	0	0	11	1-3	49.2	32	199	13	12	2	3	1	2	19	3	54	1	0
Douglass, Sean, Bal.	0	5	.000	6.08	15	8	0	0	2	0-0	53.1	58	245	41	36	10	2	1	2	35	2	44	3	0
Drese, Ryan, Cle.	10	9	.526	6.55	26	26	1	0	0	0-0	137.1	176	635	104	100	15	3	9	6	62	1	102	11	0
Driskill, Travis, Bal.	8	8	.500	4.95	29	19	0	0	6	0-0	132.2	150	589	78	73	21	2	2	8	48	1	78	6	0
DuBose, Eric, Bal.*	0	0	.000	3.00	4	0	0	0	2	0-0	6.0	7	25	2	2	1	0	0	1	1	0	4	0	0
Durbin, Chad, K.C.	0	1	.000	11.88	2	2	0	0	0	0-0	8.1	13	43	11	11	3	0	0	1	4	0	5	0	0
Eckenstahler, Eric, Det.*	1	0	1.000	5.63	7	0	0	0	2	0-0	8.0	14	39	5	5	1	0	0	2	0	13	0	0	
Elder, Dave, Cle.	0	2	.000	3.13	15	0	0	0	3	0-0	23.0	18	100	10	8	1	1	2	1	14	3	23	0	0
Embree, Alan, Bos.*	1	2	.333	2.97	32	0	0	0	7	2-5	33.1	24	133	12	11	4	1	2	1	11	1	43	0	0
Erickson, Scott, Bal.	5	12	.294	5.55	29	28	3	1	0	0-0	160.2	192	719	109	99	20	3	7	8	68	2	74	5	0
Escobar, Kelvim, Tor.	5	7	.417	4.27	76	0	0	0	68	38-46	78.0	75	355	39	37	10	1	0	5	44	6	85	4	0
Eyre, Scott, Tor.*	2	4	.333	4.97	49	3	0	0	3	0-1	63.1	69	283	37	35	4	2	4	0	29	7	51	4	0
Farnsworth, Jeff, Det.	2	3	.400	5.79	44	0	0	0	15	0-1	70.0	100	331	47	45	6	3	1	2	29	8	28	6	1
Field, Nate, K.C.	0	0	.000	9.00	5	0	0	0	0	0-0	5.0	8	26	5	5	2	1	0	0	3	1	3	2	0
File, Bob, Tor.	0	1	.000	18.90	5	0	0	0	1	0-0	3.1	8	20	7	7	0	1	0	0	2	0	2	0	0
Finley, Chuck, Cle.*	4	11	.267	4.44	18	18	1	0	0	0-0	105.1	114	454	56	52	6	3	5	4	48	3	91	1	0
Fiore, Tony, Min.	10	3	.769	3.16	48	2	0	0	11	0-0	91.0	74	385	32	32	10	4	2	5	43	4	55	2	0
Fitzgerald, Brian, Sea.*	0	0	.000	8.53	6	0	0	0	0	0-0	6.1	11	36	8	6	2	0	1	1	2	0	3	0	0
Flores, Randy, Tex.*	0	0	.000	4.50	20	0	0	0	5	1-2	12.0	11	52	7	6	2	1	0	2	8	2	7	3	0
Fossum, Casey, Bos.*	5	4	.556	3.46	43	12	0	0	1	1-1	106.2	113	461	56	41	12	2	4	4	30	0	101	3	0
Foulke, Keith, Chi.	2	4	.333	2.90	65	0	0	0	35	11-14	77.2	65	306	26	25	7	2	0	2	13	2	58	1	0
Franklin, Ryan, Sea.	7	5	.583	4.02	41	12	0	0	10	0-1	118.2	117	495	62	53	14	5	5	5	22	1	65	0	0
Frederick, Kevin, Min.	0	0	.000	10.03	4	0	0	0	3	0-0	11.2	13	56	13	13	3	0	0	0	10	0	5	2	0
Fyhrie, Mike, Oak.	2	4	.333	4.44	16	4	0	0	2	0-0	48.2	46	212	25	24	3	1	0	4	20	1	29	1	1
Garces, Rich, Bos.	0	1	.000	7.59	26	0	0	0	7	0-0	21.1	21	97	20	18	4	2	3	3	12	2	16	0	0
Garcia, Freddy, Sea.	16	10	.615	4.39	34	34	1	0	0	0-0	223.2	227	955	110	109	30	4	8	6	63	3	181	7	1
Garcia, Reynaldo, Tex.	0	0	.000	31.50	3	0	0	0	1	0-0	2.0	7	14	7	7	3	0	0	0	1	0	2	1	0
Gardner, Lee, T.B.	1	1	.500	4.05	12	0	0	0	3	0-2	13.1	12	65	11	6	3	1	2	3	8	0	8	0	0
Garland, Jon, Chi.	12	12	.500	4.58	33	33	1	1	0	0-0	192.2	188	827	109	98	23	3	4	9	83	1	112	5	0
George, Chris, K.C.*	0	4	.000	5.60	6	6	0	0	0	0-0	27.1	37	124	17	17	2	0	1	1	8	0	13	1	0
German, Franklyn, Det.	1	0	1.000	0.00	7	0	0	0	1	1-1	6.2	3	25	0	0	0	2	0	1	2	1	6	0	0
Ginter, Matt, Chi.	1	0	1.000	4.47	33	0	0	0	15	1-1	54.1	59	236	34	27	6	0	2	1	21	0	37	2	0
Glover, Gary, Chi.	7	8	.467	5.20	41	22	0	0	10	1-1	138.1	136	604	86	80	21	6	2	7	52	1	70	6	0
Gomes, Wayne, Bos.	1	2	.333	4.64	20	0	0	0	8	1-1	21.1	20	99	11	11	2	1	0	3	12	2	15	0	0
Greisinger, Seth, Det.	2	2	.500	6.21	8	8	0	0	0	0-0	37.2	46	168	26	26	4	1	1	1	13	2	14	0	0
Grimsley, Jason, K.C.	4	7	.364	3.91	70	0	0	0	26	1-3	71.1	64	310	32	31	4	1	0	1	37	8	59	8	0
Groom, Buddy, Bal.*	3	2	.600	1.60	70	0	0	0	17	2-4	62.0	44	239	11	11	4	0	1	2	12	3	48	0	0
Guardado, Eddie, Min.*	1	3	.250	2.93	68	0	0	0	62	45-51	67.2	53	270	22	22	9	2	2	1	18	2	70	0	0
Halama, John, Sea.*	6	5	.545	3.56	31	10	0	0	12	0-0	101.0	112	438	45	40	9	3	2	1	33	5	70	2	1
Halladay, Roy, Tor.	19	7	.731	2.93	34	34	2	1	0	0-0	239.1	223	993	93	78	10	9	2	7	62	6	168	4	1
Hancock, Josh, Bos.	0	1	.000	3.68	3	1	0	0	2	0-0	7.1	5	28	3	3	1	1	0	0	2	0	6	0	0
Haney, Chris, Bos.*	0	0	.000	4.20	24	0	0	0	11	1-1	30.0	32	134	14	14	2	0	3	4	10	2	15	0	0
Harang, Aaron, Oak.	5	4	.556	4.83	16	15	0	0	0	0-0	78.1	78	354	44	42	7	3	4	3	45	2	64	1	0
Harper, Travis, T.B.	5	9	.357	5.46	37	7	0	0	16	1-2	85.2	101	394	54	52	14	5	4	9	27	3	60	2	0
Hasegawa, Shigetoshi, Sea.	8	3	.727	3.20	53	0	0	0	20	1-5	70.1	60	288	26	25	4	3	1	2	30	8	39	0	1
Hawkins, LaTroy, Min.	6	0	1.000	2.13	65	0	0	0	15	0-3	80.1	63	310	23	19	5	2	3	0	15	1	63	5	0
Hendrickson, Mark, Tor.*	3	0	1.000	2.45	16	4	0	0	0	0-1	36.2	25	142	11	10	1	2	2	3	13	0	21	0	0
Henriquez, Oscar, Det.	1	1	.500	4.50	30	0	0	0	12	2-2	28.0	19	115	14	14	5	1	1	15	4	23	3	0	
Hentgen, Pat, Bal.	0	4	.000	7.77	4	4	0	0	0	0-0	22.0	31	103	20	19	6	0	1	0	10	0	11	1	0
Heredia, Felix, Tor.*	1	2	.333	3.61	53	0	0	0	15	0-2	52.1	51	232	29	21	5	3	2	2	26	3	31	5	0
Hermanson, Dustin, Bos.*	1	1	.500	7.77	12	1	0	0	4	0-1	22.0	35	107	19	19	3	0	1	0	6	0	13	2	0
Hernandez, Adrian, N.Y.	0	1	.000	12.00	2	1	0	0	0	0-0	6.0	10	34	8	8	2	0	0	0	6	0	9	1	0

Pitcher, Team	W	L	Pct.	ERA	G	GS	CG	ShO	GF	Sv.-Op.	IP	H	TBF	R	ER	HR	SH	SF	HB	BB	IBB	SO	WP	Bk.
Hernandez, Orlando, N.Y.	8	5	.615	3.64	24	22	0	0	1	1-1	146.0	131	606	63	59	17	1	5	8	36	2	113	8	0
Hernandez, Roberto, K.C.	1	3	.250	4.33	53	0	0	0	42	26-33	52.0	62	227	29	25	6	4	1	3	12	2	39	3	0
Hernandez, Runelvys, K.C.	4	4	.500	4.36	12	12	0	0	0	0-0	74.1	79	316	36	36	8	1	3	1	22	0	45	2	0
Herrera, Alex, Cle.*	0	0	.000	0.00	5	0	0	0	1	0-0	5.1	3	20	0	0	0	0	0	0	1	0	5	0	0
Hiljus, Erik, Oak.	3	3	.500	6.50	9	9	0	0	0	0-0	45.2	52	206	36	33	11	1	1	0	21	1	29	1	0
Hill, Jeremy, K.C.	0	1	.000	3.86	10	0	0	0	6	0-0	9.1	8	43	4	4	1	0	1	0	8	1	7	1	0
Hitchcock, Sterling, N.Y.*	1	2	.333	5.49	20	2	0	0	11	0-0	39.1	57	193	29	24	4	1	1	1	15	3	31	1	0
Holtz, Mike, Oak.*	0	0	.000	6.43	16	0	0	0	7	0-1	14.0	24	77	11	10	3	0	0	1	9	0	7	0	0
Howry, Bob, Chi.-Bos.	3	5	.375	4.19	67	0	0	0	26	0-0	68.2	67	292	37	32	9	4	6	5	21	4	45	2	0
Hudson, Tim, Oak.	15	9	.625	2.98	34	34	4	2	0	0-0	238.1	237	983	87	79	19	6	5	8	62	9	152	7	1
Irabu, Hideki, Tex.	3	8	.273	5.74	38	2	0	0	26	16-20	47.0	51	204	30	30	11	2	2	1	16	2	30	3	0
Jackson, Mike, Min.	2	3	.400	3.27	58	0	0	0	17	0-2	55.0	59	232	20	20	5	4	3	4	13	3	29	2	0
James, Delvin, T.B.	0	3	.000	6.55	8	6	0	0	2	0-0	34.1	40	150	25	25	5	0	1	1	15	1	17	2	1
Jimenez, Jason, T.B.-Det.*	0	0	.000	7.36	6	0	0	0	4	0-0	7.1	12	36	8	6	2	0	1	0	2	0	5	0	0
Johnson, Jason, Bal.	5	14	.263	4.59	22	22	1	0	0	0-0	131.1	141	561	68	67	19	0	3	6	41	2	97	4	0
Julio, Jorge, Bal.	5	6	.455	1.99	67	0	0	0	61	25-31	68.0	55	289	22	15	5	1	1	2	27	3	55	8	0
Karsay, Steve, N.Y.	6	4	.600	3.26	78	0	0	0	38	12-16	88.1	87	379	33	32	7	7	3	2	30	14	65	4	0
Kaye, Justin, Sea.	0	0	.000	12.00	3	0	0	0	2	0-0	3.0	6	15	4	4	0	0	0	0	1	0	3	0	0
Keller, Kris, Det.	0	0	.000	27.00	1	0	0	0	1	0-0	1.0	2	8	3	3	1	0	0	0	3	0	1	0	0
Kennedy, Joe, T.B.*	8	11	.421	4.53	30	30	5	1	0	0-0	196.2	204	840	114	99	23	2	9	16	55	0	109	4	0
Kent, Steve, T.B.*	0	2	.000	5.65	34	0	0	0	10	1-2	57.1	67	272	41	36	6	1	2	3	38	0	41	2	3
Kershner, Jason, Tor.*	0	0	.000	1.69	10	0	0	0	2	1-2	5.1	5	26	2	1	1	0	0	0	4	1	7	3	0
Kim, Sun-Woo, Bos.	2	0	1.000	7.45	15	2	0	0	7	0-0	29.0	34	128	24	24	5	0	2	1	7	0	18	2	0
Kinney, Matt, Min.	2	7	.222	4.64	14	12	0	0	1	0-0	66.0	78	305	39	34	13	3	4	1	33	0	45	5	0
Knight, Brandon, N.Y.	0	0	.000	11.42	7	0	0	0	5	0-0	8.2	11	41	12	11	2	0	0	0	5	0	7	1	0
Koch, Billy, Oak.	11	4	.733	3.27	84	0	0	0	79	44-50	93.2	73	398	38	34	7	6	1	4	46	6	93	5	0
Kolb, Danny, Tex.	3	6	.333	4.22	34	0	0	0	14	1-4	32.0	27	145	17	15	1	1	2	1	22	2	20	6	0
Kozlowski, Ben, Tex.*	0	0	.000	6.30	2	2	0	0	0	0-0	10.0	11	50	7	7	3	0	0	1	11	0	6	0	0
Lackey, John, Ana.	9	4	.692	3.66	18	18	1	0	0	0-0	108.1	113	465	52	44	10	0	4	4	33	0	69	7	2
Lee, Cliff, Cle.*	0	1	.000	1.74	2	2	0	0	0	0-0	10.1	6	44	2	2	0	1	0	0	8	1	6	0	1
Levine, Al, Ana.	4	4	.500	4.24	52	0	0	0	21	5-7	63.2	61	286	35	30	8	2	7	2	34	3	40	2	0
Lewis, Colby, Tex.	1	3	.250	6.29	15	4	0	0	4	0-2	34.1	42	168	26	24	4	2	0	2	26	2	28	3	1
Lidle, Cory, Oak.	8	10	.444	3.89	31	30	2	2	0	0-0	192.0	191	796	90	83	17	5	6	6	39	3	111	6	1
Lilly, Ted, N.Y.-Oak.*	5	7	.417	3.69	22	16	2	1	1	0-0	100.0	80	413	43	41	15	0	3	6	31	3	77	6	1
Lima, Jose, Det.	4	6	.400	7.77	20	12	0	0	3	0-0	68.1	86	304	60	59	12	1	6	2	21	0	33	2	0
Loaiza, Esteban, Tor.	9	10	.474	5.71	25	25	3	1	0	0-0	151.1	192	670	102	96	18	1	6	4	38	3	87	1	0
Lohse, Kyle, Min.	13	8	.619	4.23	32	31	1	1	0	0-1	180.2	181	783	92	85	26	3	3	9	70	2	124	8	0
Lopez, Rodrigo, Bal.	15	9	.625	3.57	33	28	1	0	0	0-0	196.2	172	809	83	78	23	2	4	5	62	4	136	2	1
Loux, Shane, Det.	0	3	.000	9.00	3	3	0	0	0	0-0	14.0	19	64	16	14	4	0	0	1	3	0	7	1	0
Lowe, Derek, Bos.	21	8	.724	2.58	32	32	1	1	0	0-0	219.2	166	854	65	63	12	5	2	12	48	0	127	5	0
Lukasiewicz, Mark, Ana.*	2	0	1.000	3.86	17	0	0	0	4	0-0	14.0	17	67	6	6	0	0	1	0	9	0	15	0	0
Lyon, Brandon, Tor.	1	4	.200	6.53	15	10	0	0	0	0-1	62.0	78	279	47	45	14	3	2	2	19	2	30	2	0
MacDougal, Mike, K.C.	0	1	.000	5.00	6	0	0	0	1	0-0	9.0	5	38	5	5	0	0	0	0	7	1	10	1	0
Maduro, Calvin, Bal.	2	5	.286	5.56	12	10	0	0	2	0-0	56.2	64	253	37	35	12	0	1	1	22	1	29	1	0
Magnante, Mike, Oak.*	0	2	.000	5.97	32	0	0	0	12	0-1	28.2	38	134	22	19	2	0	2	1	11	1	11	2	1
Maroth, Mike, Det.*	6	10	.375	4.48	21	21	0	0	0	0-0	128.2	136	538	68	64	7	5	3	2	36	1	58	4	0
Marte, Damaso, Chi.*	1	1	.500	2.83	68	0	0	0	22	10-12	60.1	44	240	19	19	5	1	1	4	18	2	72	3	1
Martin, Tom, T.B.*	0	0	.000	16.20	2	0	0	0	2	0-0	1.2	5	11	3	3	0	0	0	0	1	0	1	0	0
Martinez, Pedro, Bos.	20	4	.833	2.26	30	30	2	0	0	0-0	199.1	144	787	62	50	13	2	4	15	40	1	239	3	0
Mateo, Julio, Sea.	0	0	.000	4.29	12	0	0	0	7	0-0	21.0	20	94	10	10	2	0	0	1	12	0	15	1	0
Maurer, Dave, Cle.*	0	1	.000	13.50	2	0	0	0	2	0-0	1.1	3	7	2	2	1	0	0	0	0	0	0	0	0
May, Darrell, K.C.*	4	10	.286	5.35	30	21	2	1	3	0-1	131.1	144	579	83	78	28	3	5	1	50	3	95	2	0
Mays, Joe, Min.	4	8	.333	5.38	17	17	1	1	0	0-0	95.1	113	418	60	57	14	2	2	2	25	0	38	6	0
Mecir, Jim, Oak.	6	4	.600	4.26	61	0	0	0	10	1-6	67.2	68	304	36	32	5	4	4	4	29	4	53	4	1
Mendoza, Ramiro, N.Y.	8	4	.667	3.44	62	0	0	0	14	4-8	91.2	102	394	43	35	8	1	4	2	16	2	61	1	0
Miceli, Dan, Tex.	0	2	.000	8.64	9	0	0	0	5	0-1	8.1	13	42	8	8	1	0	0	0	3	0	5	0	1
Michalak, Chris, Tex.*	0	2	.000	4.40	13	0	0	0	4	0-0	14.1	20	71	7	7	1	0	1	1	10	2	5	1	0
Miller, Justin, Tor.	9	5	.643	5.54	25	18	0	0	2	0-0	102.1	103	469	70	63	12	1	6	11	66	2	68	6	0
Miller, Matt, Det.*	0	0	.000	13.50	2	0	0	0	0	0-1	0.2	4	8	2	1	1	0	0	0	1	0	1	0	0
Miller, Travis, Min.*	0	0	.000	4.50	5	0	0	0	3	0-0	4.0	5	19	2	2	0	0	0	0	2	2	3	0	0
Milton, Eric, Min.*	13	9	.591	4.84	29	29	2	1	0	0-0	171.0	173	707	96	92	24	0	4	3	30	0	121	4	0
Moehler, Brian, Det.	1	1	.500	2.29	3	3	0	0	0	0-0	19.2	17	77	5	5	3	1	1	0	2	0	13	0	0
Moyer, Jamie, Sea.*	13	8	.619	3.32	34	34	4	2	0	0-0	230.2	198	931	89	85	28	5	7	9	50	4	147	3	0
Mulder, Mark, Oak.*	19	7	.731	3.47	30	30	2	1	0	0-0	207.1	182	862	88	80	21	6	4	11	55	3	159	7	1
Mulholland, Terry, Cle.*	3	2	.600	4.60	16	3	0	0	5	0-0	47.0	56	210	27	24	5	2	4	4	14	3	21	0	0
Mullen, Scott, K.C.*	4	5	.444	3.15	44	0	0	0	10	0-2	40.0	40	171	16	14	5	4	2	2	13	2	21	1	0
Murray, Heath, Cle.*	0	2	.000	7.50	9	0	0	0	2	0-0	12.0	12	55	10	10	3	1	0	2	7	0	11	1	0
Mussina, Mike, N.Y.	18	10	.643	4.05	33	33	2	2	0	0-0	215.2	208	886	103	97	27	5	5	5	48	1	182	7	0
Myette, Aaron, Tex.	2	5	.286	10.06	15	12	0	0	2	0-0	48.1	64	249	57	54	11	1	4	6	41	0	48	5	0
Nagy, Charles, Cle.	1	4	.200	8.88	19	7	0	0	7	0-0	48.2	76	230	51	48	10	2	2	2	13	1	22	1	0
Nelson, Jeff, Sea.	3	2	.600	3.94	41	0	0	0	12	2-4	45.2	36	199	20	20	4	2	4	3	27	3	55	5	0
Nitkowski, C.J., Tex.*	0	1	.000	2.63	12	0	0	0	2	0-0	13.2	11	63	4	4	0	1	0	0	13	0	14	0	0
Obermueller, Wes, K.C.	0	2	.000	11.74	2	2	0	0	0	0-0	7.2	14	39	10	10	3	0	0	0	2	0	5	0	0
Oliver, Darren, Bos.*	4	5	.444	4.66	14	9	1	1	0	0-0	58.0	70	258	30	30	7	1	3	6	27	0	32	1	0
Ortiz, Ramon, Ana.	15	9	.625	3.77	32	32	4	1	0	0-0	217.1	188	896	97	91	40	2	5	5	68	0	162	7	3
Osuna, Antonio, Chi.	8	2	.800	3.86	59	0	0	0	28	11-14	67.2	64	296	32	29	1	5	3	4	28	4	66	0	1
Paniagua, Jose, Det.	0	1	.000	5.83	41	0	0	0	15	1-2	41.2	50	191	30	27	10	0	3	3	15	1	34	2	0
Park, Chan Ho, Tex.	9	8	.529	5.75	25	25	0	0	0	0-0	145.2	154	666	95	93	20	4	3	17	78	2	121	9	0
Paronto, Chad, Cle.	0	2	.000	4.04	29	0	0	0	11	0-0	35.2	34	154	19	16	3	0	4	2	11	1	23	2	0
Parque, Jim, Chi.*	1	4	.200	9.95	8	4	0	0	0	0-0	25.1	34	126	29	28	11	0	2	1	16	0	13	0	0
Parris, Steve, Tor.	5	5	.500	5.97	14	14	0	0	0	0-0	75.1	96	348	50	50	13	2	2	3	35	5	48	3	0
Patterson, Danny, Det.	0	2	.000	15.00	6	0	0	0	1	0-1	3.0	5	17	5	5	0	0	0	1	2	0	1	0	0

Pitcher, Team	W	L	Pct.	ERA	G	GS	CG	ShO	GF	Sv.-Op.	IP	H	TBF	R	ER	HR	SH	SF	HB	BB	IBB	SO	WP	Bk.
Pearson, Terry, Det.	0	0	.000	10.50	4	0	0	0	3	0-0	6.0	8	27	7	7	2	0	0	0	2	1	4	0	0
Percival, Troy, Ana.	4	1	.800	1.92	58	0	0	0	50	40-44	56.1	38	228	12	12	5	0	1	0	25	1	68	5	0
Perez, Yorkis, Bal.*	0	0	.000	3.29	23	0	0	0	8	1-1	27.1	21	120	12	10	4	0	0	0	14	1	25	3	0
Perisho, Matt, Det.*	0	0	.000	8.71	5	0	0	0	1	0-0	10.1	16	50	11	10	2	0	1	0	6	0	3	0	0
Pettitte, Andy, N.Y.*	13	5	.722	3.27	22	22	3	1	0	0-0	134.2	144	570	58	49	6	3	2	4	32	2	97	2	1
Phelps, Travis, T.B.	1	2	.333	4.78	26	0	0	0	9	0-0	37.2	30	169	20	20	7	0	2	5	27	0	36	6	2
Phillips, Jason C., Cle.	1	3	.250	4.97	8	6	0	0	0	0-0	41.2	41	185	24	23	7	1	2	4	20	0	23	0	1
Pineiro, Joel, Sea.	14	7	.667	3.24	37	28	2	1	4	0-0	194.1	189	812	75	70	24	5	7	7	54	1	136	8	0
Plesac, Dan, Tor.*	1	2	.333	3.38	19	0	0	0	3	0-1	13.1	11	58	5	5	1	0	1	0	6	0	14	0	0
Politte, Cliff, Tor.	1	3	.250	3.61	55	0	0	0	13	1-3	57.1	38	227	23	23	5	2	1	1	19	1	57	1	0
Ponson, Sidney, Bal.	7	9	.438	4.09	28	28	3	0	0	0-0	176.0	172	736	84	80	26	2	3	2	63	1	120	3	0
Porzio, Mike, Chi.*	2	2	.500	4.81	32	0	0	0	8	0-0	43.0	40	190	25	23	10	0	3	3	23	2	33	3	1
Pote, Lou, Ana.	0	2	.000	3.23	31	0	0	0	13	0-1	50.1	33	206	20	18	7	2	5	3	26	2	32	3	0
Powell, Brian, Det.	1	5	.167	4.84	13	9	0	0	1	0-0	57.2	64	254	34	31	11	0	2	1	21	0	30	2	0
Powell, Jay, Tex.	3	2	.600	3.44	51	0	0	0	5	0-4	49.2	50	224	28	19	5	1	0	1	24	4	35	2	0
Prokopec, Luke, Tor.	2	9	.182	6.78	22	12	0	0	4	0-0	71.2	90	336	57	54	19	1	5	7	25	2	41	3	1
Radke, Brad, Min.	9	5	.643	4.72	21	21	2	1	0	0-0	118.1	124	490	64	62	12	2	5	7	20	0	62	0	0
Rauch, Jon, Chi.	2	1	.667	6.59	8	6	0	0	1	0-0	28.2	28	130	26	21	7	0	1	2	14	2	19	1	1
Redman, Mark, Det.*	8	15	.348	4.21	30	30	3	0	0	0-0	203.0	211	858	107	95	15	5	8	6	51	2	109	11	1
Reed, Rick, Min.	15	7	.682	3.78	33	32	2	1	0	0-0	188.0	192	778	89	79	32	1	5	6	26	0	121	1	1
Reichert, Dan, K.C.	3	5	.375	5.32	30	6	0	0	3	0-0	66.0	77	290	48	39	10	6	3	4	25	2	36	3	0
Rekar, Bryan, K.C.	0	2	.000	15.43	2	2	0	0	0	0-0	7.0	12	38	12	12	1	0	1	0	6	0	2	1	0
Reyes, Dennys, Tex.*	4	3	.571	6.38	15	5	0	0	2	0-0	42.1	55	196	33	30	9	1	0	0	21	1	29	6	1
Rhodes, Arthur, Sea.*	10	4	.714	2.33	66	0	0	0	9	2-7	69.2	45	257	18	18	4	2	1	0	13	1	81	2	0
Riggan, Jerrod, Cle.	2	1	.667	7.64	29	0	0	0	9	0-0	33.0	53	165	28	28	3	1	4	0	18	4	22	4	1
Rincon, Juan, Min.	0	2	.000	6.28	10	3	0	0	0	0-1	28.2	44	135	23	20	5	0	1	0	9	0	21	2	0
Rincon, Ricardo, Cle.-Oak.*	1	4	.200	4.18	71	0	0	0	9	1-0	56.0	47	222	28	26	4	2	4	1	11	1	49	0	0
Riske, David, Cle.	2	2	.500	5.26	51	0	0	0	17	1-1	51.1	49	237	32	30	8	4	3	4	35	4	65	1	0
Ritchie, Todd, Chi.	5	15	.250	6.06	26	23	0	0	1	0-0	133.2	176	623	104	90	18	6	7	5	52	2	77	10	0
Rivera, Mariano, N.Y.	1	4	.200	2.74	45	0	0	0	37	28-32	46.0	35	187	16	14	3	2	0	2	11	2	41	1	1
Roberts, Willis, Bal.	5	4	.556	3.36	66	0	0	0	24	1-3	75.0	79	334	34	28	5	1	4	4	32	3	51	7	0
Rocker, John, Tex.*	2	3	.400	6.66	30	0	0	0	10	1-4	24.1	29	114	19	18	5	1	3	0	13	1	30	0	0
Rodney, Fernando, Det.	3	1	.250	6.00	20	0	0	0	10	0-4	18.0	25	89	15	12	2	2	1	0	10	2	10	0	1
Rodriguez, Francisco, Ana.	0	0	.000	0.00	5	0	0	0	4	0-0	5.2	3	21	0	0	0	0	1	2	1	0	13	0	0
Rodriguez, Jose, Min.*	0	1	.000	14.73	4	0	0	0	1	0-0	3.2	8	23	6	6	0	0	0	0	4	1	1	0	0
Rodriguez, Nerio, Cle.	0	0	.000	0.00	1	0	0	0	1	0-0	0.1	0	1	0	0	0	0	0	0	0	0	0	0	0
Rodriguez, Ricardo, Cle.	2	2	.500	5.66	7	7	0	0	0	0-0	41.1	40	183	27	26	5	0	0	8	18	3	24	1	0
Rodriguez, Rich, Tex.*	3	2	.600	5.40	36	0	0	0	6	1-3	16.2	14	72	10	10	1	1	0	1	11	1	12	0	0
Rogers, Kenny, Tex.*	13	8	.619	3.84	33	33	2	1	0	0-0	210.2	212	892	101	90	21	3	1	6	70	1	107	5	1
Romero, J.C., Min.*	9	2	.818	1.89	81	0	0	0	15	1-5	81.0	62	332	17	17	3	1	0	4	36	4	76	9	0
Rupe, Ryan, T.B.	5	10	.333	5.60	15	15	2	0	0	0-0	90.0	83	382	60	56	11	2	4	10	25	0	67	6	0
Ryan, B.J., Bal.*	2	1	.667	4.68	67	0	0	0	13	1-2	57.2	51	252	31	30	7	3	0	4	33	4	56	4	0
Sabathia, C.C., Cle.*	13	11	.542	4.37	33	33	2	0	0	0-0	210.0	198	891	109	102	17	5	10	1	88	2	149	6	3
Sabel, Erik, Det.	0	0	.000	0.00	1	0	0	0	0	0-0	2	2	2	2	1	0	0	0	0	0	0	0	0	0
Sadler, Carl, Cle.*	1	2	.333	4.43	24	0	0	0	5	0-1	20.1	15	82	10	10	2	0	0	0	11	0	23	3	0
Santana, Johan, Min.*	8	6	.571	2.99	27	14	0	0	2	1-1	108.1	84	452	41	36	7	3	3	1	49	0	137	15	2
Santana, Julio, Det.	3	5	.375	2.84	38	0	0	0	8	0-1	57.0	49	239	19	18	8	3	0	2	28	2	38	3	1
Sasaki, Kazuhiro, Sea.	4	5	.444	2.52	61	0	0	0	55	37-45	60.2	44	249	24	17	6	3	5	2	20	4	73	6	0
Schoeneweis, Scott, Ana.*	9	8	.529	4.88	54	15	0	0	4	1-4	118.0	119	510	68	64	17	1	5	5	49	4	65	1	1
Seanez, Rudy, Tex.	1	3	.250	5.73	33	0	0	0	4	0-4	33.0	28	150	25	21	5	3	1	0	24	1	40	6	0
Sedlacek, Shawn, K.C.	3	5	.375	6.72	16	14	0	0	1	0-0	84.1	99	381	64	63	16	5	7	6	36	2	52	5	0
Sele, Aaron, Ana.	8	9	.471	4.89	26	26	1	1	0	0-0	160.0	190	706	92	87	21	5	10	7	49	2	82	5	0
Shields, Scot, Ana.	5	3	.625	2.20	29	1	0	0	13	0-0	49.0	31	188	13	12	4	1	0	1	21	1	30	3	0
Shouse, Brian, K.C.*	0	0	.000	6.14	23	0	0	0	7	0-0	14.2	15	71	10	10	3	1	1	2	9	1	11	2	0
Shuey, Paul, Cle.	3	0	1.000	2.41	39	0	0	0	12	0-2	37.1	31	150	11	10	1	1	1	0	10	1	39	2	0
Smith, Mike, Tor.	0	5	.000	6.62	14	6	0	0	3	0-0	35.1	43	174	28	26	3	3	1	7	20	0	16	2	0
Smith, Roy, Cle.	0	0	.000	3.00	4	1	0	0	1	0-0	6.0	9	35	4	2	1	0	0	1	5	0	2	0	0
Soriano, Rafael, Sea.	0	3	.000	4.56	10	8	0	0	1	1-1	47.1	45	202	25	24	8	1	0	0	16	1	32	2	0
Sosa, Jorge, T.B.	2	7	.222	5.53	31	14	0	0	10	0-0	99.1	88	434	63	61	16	0	5	2	54	0	48	5	0
Sparks, Steve W., Det.	8	16	.333	5.52	32	30	3	0	0	0-0	189.0	238	868	134	116	23	3	8	12	67	3	98	8	2
Standridge, Jason, T.B.	0	0	.000	9.00	1	0	0	0	0	0-0	3.0	7	18	3	3	1	0	0	0	4	0	1	0	0
Stanton, Mike, N.Y.*	7	1	.875	3.00	79	0	0	0	25	6-9	78.0	73	324	29	26	4	4	7	0	28	3	44	4	0
Stein, Blake, K.C.	0	4	.000	7.91	27	2	0	0	7	1-2	46.2	59	227	41	41	6	1	3	3	27	1	42	1	0
Stephens, John, Bal.	2	5	.286	6.09	12	11	0	0	0	0-0	65.0	68	281	44	44	13	1	4	3	22	2	56	2	0
Sturtze, Tanyon, T.B.	4	18	.182	5.18	33	33	4	0	0	0-0	224.0	271	1008	141	129	33	7	6	9	89	2	137	7	2
Suppan, Jeff, K.C.	9	16	.360	5.32	33	33	3	1	0	0-0	208.0	229	912	134	123	32	4	11	7	68	3	109	10	1
Suzuki, Mac, K.C.	0	2	.000	9.00	7	1	0	0	1	0-0	21.0	24	100	21	21	2	1	1	7	12	1	15	6	1
Tallet, Brian, Cle.*	1	0	1.000	1.50	2	2	0	0	0	0-0	12.0	9	47	3	2	0	0	0	1	4	0	5	0	0
Tam, Jeff, Oak.	1	2	.333	5.13	40	0	0	0	14	0-4	40.1	56	188	26	23	2	3	2	2	13	5	14	3	0
Taylor, Aaron, Sea.	0	0	.000	9.00	5	0	0	0	2	0-1	5.0	8	23	5	5	2	0	0	0	1	0	3	0	0
Telford, Anthony, Tex.	2	1	.667	6.46	20	0	0	0	4	1-2	23.2	30	117	18	17	3	1	2	4	15	2	19	0	0
Tessmer, Jay, N.Y.	0	0	.000	6.75	2	0	0	0	0	0-0	1.1	0	6	1	1	0	0	0	0	2	0	0	0	0
Thurman, Corey, Tor.	2	3	.400	4.37	43	1	0	0	5	0-2	68.0	65	310	34	33	11	1	0	2	45	2	56	4	0
Thurman, Mike, N.Y.	1	0	1.000	5.18	12	2	0	0	6	0-0	33.0	45	152	20	19	2	2	0	1	12	1	23	0	0
Towers, Josh, Bal.	0	0	.000	7.90	5	3	0	0	1	0-0	27.1	42	124	24	24	11	1	2	0	5	0	13	1	0
Trombley, Mike, Min.	0	1	.000	15.75	5	0	0	0	3	0-1	4.0	10	23	7	7	2	0	0	1	0	3	0	0
Urbina, Ugueth, Bos.	1	6	.143	3.00	61	0	0	0	55	40-46	60.0	44	242	20	20	8	1	3	0	20	5	71	3	1
Valdes, Ismael, Tex.-Sea.	8	12	.400	4.18	31	31	1	0	0	0-0	196.0	194	818	94	91	26	2	4	9	47	1	102	0	2
Van Hekken, Andy, Det.*	1	3	.250	3.00	5	5	1	1	0	0-0	30.0	38	131	13	10	2	2	1	0	6	0	5	1	0
Van Poppel, Todd, Tex.	3	2	.600	5.45	50	0	0	0	19	1-2	72.2	80	325	44	44	14	1	1	3	29	1	85	8	0
Venafro, Mike, Oak.*	2	2	.500	4.62	47	0	0	0	8	0-0	37.0	45	168	22	19	5	4	2	2	14	2	16	1	0
Voyles, Brad, K.C.	0	2	.000	6.51	22	0	0	0	5	1-2	27.2	31	131	21	20	5	2	0	2	18	1	26	1	0

Pitcher, Team	W	L	Pct.	ERA	G	GS	CG	ShO	GF	Sv.-Op.	IP	H	TBF	R	ER	HR	SH	SF	HB	BB	IBB	SO	WP	Bk.
Wakefield, Tim, Bos.	11	5	.688	2.81	45	15	0	0	10	3-5	163.1	121	657	57	51	15	1	4	9	51	2	134	5	2
Walker, Jamie, Det.*	1	1	.500	3.71	57	0	0	0	16	1-4	43.2	32	175	19	18	9	0	1	4	9	1	40	1	1
Walker, Pete, Tor.	10	5	.667	4.33	37	20	0	0	4	1-1	139.1	143	594	72	67	18	4	6	3	51	5	80	2	1
Wall, Donne, Ana.	0	0	.000	6.43	17	0	0	0	8	0-0	21.0	17	86	15	15	3	0	1	1	7	1	13	2	0
Washburn, Jarrod, Ana.*	18	6	.750	3.15	32	32	1	0	0	0-0	206.0	183	852	75	72	19	4	7	3	59	1	139	5	1
Watson, Mark, Sea.*	1	0	1.000	18.00	3	0	0	0	1	0-0	4.0	8	24	8	8	1	0	1	0	4	0	1	1	0
Weaver, Jeff, Det.-N.Y.	11	11	.500	3.52	32	25	3	3	3	2-0	199.2	193	840	88	78	16	6	3	11	48	4	132	6	0
Weber, Ben, Ana.	7	2	.778	2.54	63	0	0	0	16	7-11	78.0	70	312	25	22	4	4	2	3	22	3	43	2	0
Wells, Bob, Min.	2	1	.667	5.90	48	0	0	0	16	0-0	58.0	78	261	41	38	8	2	2	1	16	1	30	0	0
Wells, David, N.Y.*	19	7	.731	3.75	31	31	2	1	0	0-0	206.1	210	873	100	86	21	6	5	5	45	2	137	4	0
Westbrook, Jake, Cle.	1	3	.250	5.83	11	4	0	0	1	0-2	41.2	50	185	30	27	6	2	1	1	12	1	20	1	0
Wickman, Bob, Cle.	1	3	.250	4.46	36	0	0	0	30	20-22	34.1	42	159	22	17	3	0	0	1	10	0	36	0	0
Wiggins, Scott, Tor.*	0	0	.000	3.38	3	0	0	0	0	0-0	2.2	5	13	1	1	1	0	0	0	3	1	0	0	0
Wilson, Kris, K.C.	2	5	.286	8.20	12	0	0	0	0	0-0	18.2	29	91	18	17	7	0	2	2	5	0	10	0	0
Wilson, Paul, T.B.	6	12	.333	4.83	30	30	1	0	0	0-0	193.2	219	851	113	104	29	2	6	13	67	2	111	4	1
Wise, Matt, Ana.	0	0	.000	3.24	7	0	0	0	6	0-0	8.1	7	33	3	3	0	1	0	1	6	0	6	0	0
Wohlers, Mark, Cle.	3	4	.429	4.79	64	0	0	0	28	7-11	71.1	71	304	41	38	6	1	2	3	26	3	46	7	0
Woodard, Steve, Tex.	0	0	.000	6.62	14	0	0	0	4	0-1	17.2	20	83	13	13	4	0	0	2	8	1	14	0	1
Wright, Dan, Chi.	14	12	.538	5.18	33	33	1	1	0	0-0	196.1	200	855	124	113	32	7	10	6	71	1	136	10	1
Wright, Jaret, Cle.	2	3	.400	15.71	8	6	0	0	1	0-0	18.1	40	116	34	32	3	0	3	2	19	0	12	1	0
Wunsch, Kelly, Chi.*	2	1	.667	3.41	50	0	0	0	9	0-1	31.2	26	138	12	12	3	1	0	5	19	1	21	1	0
Yan, Esteban, T.B.	7	8	.467	4.30	55	0	0	0	47	19-27	69.0	72	305	35	33	10	2	3	1	29	1	53	5	1
Zambrano, Victor, T.B.	8	8	.500	5.53	42	11	0	0	11	1-3	114.0	120	519	77	70	15	7	8	4	68	5	73	10	0
Zito, Barry, Oak.*	23	5	.821	2.75	35	35	1	0	0	0-0	229.1	182	939	79	70	24	9	7	9	78	2	182	2	1

PITCHERS WITH TWO OR MORE TEAMS

Pitcher, Team	W	L	Pct.	ERA	G	GS	CG	ShO	GF	Sv.-Op.	IP	H	TBF	R	ER	HR	SH	SF	HB	BB	IBB	SO	WP	Bk.
Beverlin, Jason, Cle.	0	0	.000	7.36	4	0	0	0	0	0-0	7.1	9	35	7	6	1	0	0	0	4	0	9	1	0
Beverlin, Jason, Det.	0	3	.000	9.49	3	3	0	0	0	0-0	12.1	18	60	15	13	2	0	0	0	5	0	1	1	0
Burba, Dave, Tex.	4	5	.444	5.42	23	18	1	0	2	0-1	111.1	125	499	71	67	13	2	2	7	40	3	70	9	1
Burba, Dave, Cle.	1	0	1.000	4.50	12	3	0	0	0	0-0	34.0	30	147	20	17	3	0	2	1	17	0	25	0	0
Creek, Doug, T.B.*	2	1	.667	6.27	29	0	0	0	6	0-2	37.1	39	172	27	26	8	0	0	3	21	1	37	2	0
Creek, Doug, Sea.*	1	1	.500	4.91	23	0	0	0	11	0-0	18.1	18	90	10	10	2	1	1	4	14	1	19	2	0
Howry, Bob, Chi.	2	2	.500	3.91	47	0	0	0	17	0-0	50.2	45	209	22	22	7	1	4	3	17	2	31	1	0
Howry, Bob, Bos.	1	3	.250	5.00	20	0	0	0	9	0-1	18.0	22	83	15	10	2	3	2	2	4	2	14	1	0
Jimenez, Jason, T.B.*	0	0	.000	5.40	5	0	0	0	4	0-0	6.2	9	29	4	4	2	0	1	0	6	0	5	1	0
Jimenez, Jason, Det.*	0	0	.000	27.00	1	0	0	0	0	0-0	0.2	3	7	4	2	0	0	0	1	0	0	1	0	0
Lilly, Ted, N.Y.*	3	6	.333	3.40	16	11	2	1	0	0-0	76.2	57	314	31	29	10	0	3	5	24	3	59	6	0
Lilly, Ted, Oak.*	2	1	.667	4.63	6	5	0	0	0	0-0	23.1	23	99	12	12	5	0	1	1	7	0	18	0	1
Rincon, Ricardo, Cle.*	1	4	.200	4.79	46	0	0	0	6	0-3	35.2	36	150	21	19	3	2	1	1	7	0	30	0	1
Rincon, Ricardo, Oak.*	0	0	.000	3.10	25	0	0	0	5	1-2	20.1	11	72	7	7	1	0	2	0	4	0	19	0	0
Valdes, Ismael, Tex.	6	9	.400	3.93	23	23	0	0	0	0-0	146.2	135	608	65	64	19	2	2	9	36	1	75	0	0
Valdes, Ismael, Sea.	3	3	.400	4.93	8	8	1	0	0	0-0	49.1	59	210	29	27	7	0	2	0	11	0	27	0	0
Weaver, Jeff, Det.	6	8	.429	3.18	17	17	3	3	0	0-0	121.2	112	509	50	43	4	5	2	8	33	3	84	3	0
Weaver, Jeff, N.Y.	5	3	.625	4.04	15	8	0	0	0	2-2	78.0	81	331	38	35	12	1	1	3	15	1	57	2	0

NOTE—The following pitchers combined to pitch shutout games: **Anaheim (12)**—Appier, Cook, Levine and Percival; Appier, Weber, Cook and Pote; Schoeneweis and Wise; Schoeneweis and Percival; Washburn and Percival; Washburn, Weber, Schoeneweis and Percival; Lackey and Percival; Washburn and Percival; Appier, Levine and Shields; Appier, Donnelly, Schoeneweis and Percival; Washburn, Weber and Percival. **Baltimore (2)**—Lopez, Driskill and Groom; Lopez, Groom, Roberts and Julio; **Boston (14)**—Lowe, Garces and Urbina; Martinez and Garces; Martinez, Kim and Banks; Castillo and Urbina; Lowe and Garces; Lowe and Haney; Martinez and Haney; Martinez and Embree; Martinez, Gomes, Haney and Banks; Martinez and Haney; Martinez and Urbina; Martinez and Urbina; Burkett and Urbina; **Chicago (3)**—Buehrle, Howry and Foulke; Garland and Foulke; Garland, Osuna, Marte, Howry, Wunsch and Foulke; **Cleveland (2)**—Colon and Wickman; Sabathia, Shuey and Wickman; **Detroit (3)**—Greisinger, Paniagua and Acevedo; Lima, Henriquez and Acevedo; Maroth and Acevedo; **Kansas City (2)**—George, Reichert, Bailey and Grimsley; R. Hernandez, Bukvich, Grimsley and R. Hernandez; **Minnesota (4)**—Milton, Romero, Wells and Guardado; Santana and Guardado; Mays, Santana, Jackson and Guardado; Lohse, Santana and Guardado; **New York (6)**—Wells, Karsay, Stanton and Rivera; Pettitte, Karsay and Choate; O. Hernandez and Rivera; Clemens and Rivera; Pettitte and Mendoza; Wells and Karsay; **Oakland (14)**—Hudson and Koch; Zito and Koch; Harang and Bradford; Zito, Mecir and Koch; Hudson, Venafro, Bradford and Koch; Zito, Mecir and Bradford; Lilly, Bradford, Venafro and Koch; Zito, Bradford and Koch; Lidle and Tam; Lidle, Rincon, Bradford and Koch; Mulder and Koch; Zito, Mecir and Rincon; Zito and Rincon; **Seattle (9)**—Franklin, Pineiro, Rhodes and Sasaki; Garcia and Sasaki; Moyer and Rhodes; Garcia and Sasaki; Moyer and Halama; Moyer, Hasegawa and Sasaki; Pineiro and Sasaki; Pineiro and Hasegawa; Moyer, Rhodes and Sasaki; **Tampa Bay (2)**—Harper and Kent; Alvarez, Phelps and Yan; **Texas (2)**—Rogers and Irabu; Rogers, Powell, Rocker, Irabu and Cordero; **Toronto (4)**—Halladay and Escobar; Walker, Politte and Escobar; Walker, Politte and Escobar; Halladay and Escobar.

PITCHERS VS. LEFTHANDED AND RIGHTHANDED BATTERS

Pitcher	vs.	Avg.	AB	H	2B	3B	HR	RBI	BB	SO	OBP	Slg.
Abbott, Paul	L	.383	60	23	2	0	3	14	13	10	.486	.567
Throws Right	R	.315	54	17	8	0	2	18	7	12	.403	.574
Acevedo, Juan	L	.264	140	37	5	2	3	20	16	23	.333	.393
Throws Right	R	.228	136	31	7	3	1	13	7	20	.287	.346
Affeldt, Jeremy	L	.283	92	26	7	0	3	15	12	29	.365	.457
Throws Left	R	.271	218	59	13	0	5	25	25	38	.352	.399
Alvarez, Juan	L	.233	73	17	5	2	4	18	11	22	.356	.521
Throws Left	R	.250	72	18	3	2	3	17	10	8	.333	.472
Alvarez, Wilson	L	.299	77	23	5	1	4	17	11	18	.396	.545
Throws Left	R	.263	217	57	12	2	9	25	25	38	.341	.461
Anderson, Matt	L	.435	23	10	0	1	1	9	6	4	.548	.652
Throws Right	R	.318	22	7	0	0	0	3	2	4	.385	.318
Appier, Kevin	L	.250	376	94	14	1	11	30	38	68	.321	.380
Throws Right	R	.286	339	97	23	0	12	50	26	64	.341	.460
Arrojo, Rolando	L	.313	163	51	10	1	3	22	18	22	.380	.442
Throws Right	R	.221	145	32	4	2	4	25	9	29	.288	.359
Asencio, Miguel	L	.264	250	66	17	4	7	25	39	33	.366	.448
Throws Right	R	.302	232	70	9	1	10	35	25	25	.365	.478
Austin, Jeff	L	.278	18	5	1	0	0	2	3	1	.364	.333
Throws Right	R	.346	26	9	2	0	4	3	0	4	.400	.423
Backe, Brandon	L	.292	24	7	2	0	0	1	3	4	.370	.375
Throws Right	R	.286	28	8	0	0	3	9	4	2	.412	.607
Baez, Danys	L	.278	324	90	23	3	5	37	48	58	.373	.414
Throws Right	R	.233	301	70	14	1	9	40	34	72	.318	.375
Bailey, Cory	L	.282	71	20	5	0	2	12	21	7	.452	.437
Throws Right	R	.324	102	33	3	0	3	20	10	17	.383	.441
Baldwin, James	L	.323	297	96	21	1	11	36	29	45	.382	.512
Throws Right	R	.274	303	83	22	1	15	51	20	43	.332	.502

Pitcher	vs.	Avg.	AB	H	2B	3B	HR	RBI	BB	SO	OBP	Slg.
Banks, Willie	L	.246	69	17	3	0	3	10	4	17	.303	.420
Throws Right	R	.200	75	15	4	0	2	7	10	9	.302	.333
Barcelo, Lorenzo	L	.600	10	6	0	0	1	4	0	0	.600	.900
Throws Right	R	.176	17	3	0	0	0	1	1	1	.222	.176
Bauer, Rick	L	.288	132	38	5	1	5	12	15	14	.360	.455
Throws Right	R	.253	182	46	2	0	7	23	21	31	.340	.379
Bechler, Steve	L	.200	10	2	0	0	2	5	2	2	.385	.800
Throws Right	R	.400	10	4	1	0	1	1	2	1	.500	.800
Bedard, Erik	L	.667	3	2	0	0	0	1	0	1	.667	.667
Throws Left	R	.000	1	0	0	0	0	0	0	0	.000	.000
Bell, Rob	L	.307	205	63	19	2	8	30	22	41	.372	.537
Throws Right	R	.282	177	50	13	2	8	30	13	29	.326	.514
Benoit, Joaquin	L	.275	171	47	8	2	5	29	32	30	.391	.433
Throws Right	R	.268	164	44	10	2	1	17	26	29	.376	.372
Bernero, Adam	L	.321	224	72	16	4	10	42	19	39	.375	.563
Throws Right	R	.295	190	56	10	0	7	28	12	30	.346	.458
Beverlin, Jason	L	.348	46	16	5	0	3	13	4	9	.400	.652
Throws Right	R	.275	40	11	2	1	0	3	5	7	.356	.375
Biddle, Rocky	L	.287	143	41	9	1	9	25	21	31	.393	.552
Throws Right	R	.205	151	31	9	1	4	20	18	33	.292	.358
Borbon, Pedro	L	.207	29	6	2	0	2	5	3	7	.281	.483
Throws Left	R	.261	23	6	3	0	1	8	3	4	.357	.522
Bowie, Micah	L	.273	22	6	2	0	1	5	3	3	.385	.500
Throws Left	R	.250	24	6	5	0	0	2	5	5	.379	.458
Bowles, Brian	L	.222	27	6	2	0	0	8	7	5	.389	.296
Throws Right	R	.159	44	7	3	0	0	3	7	14	.302	.227
Bradford, Chad	L	.267	90	24	4	1	0	11	9	14	.346	.333
Throws Right	R	.247	198	49	9	0	2	25	5	42	.273	.323
Brazelton, Dewon	L	.267	15	4	0	0	2	5	2	1	.389	.667
Throws Right	R	.286	28	8	2	0	1	2	4	4	.394	.464
Brock, Chris	L	.253	83	21	4	1	4	13	8	15	.315	.470
Throws Right	R	.337	92	31	8	1	2	14	6	6	.380	.511
Buehrle, Mark	L	.228	241	55	11	0	10	37	14	43	.275	.398
Throws Left	R	.271	667	181	42	2	15	55	47	91	.319	.408
Bukvich, Ryan	L	.171	41	7	1	0	0	6	11	12	.327	.195
Throws Right	R	.358	53	19	7	0	2	16	8	3	.452	.604
Burba, Dave	L	.247	295	73	18	4	7	31	33	45	.333	.407
Throws Right	R	.293	280	82	30	1	9	51	24	50	.354	.504
Burkett, John	L	.278	352	98	15	1	15	53	28	66	.332	.455
Throws Right	R	.296	341	101	20	3	10	31	22	58	.349	.460
Byrd, Paul	L	.269	472	127	28	6	17	48	18	59	.294	.462
Throws Right	R	.241	403	97	18	1	19	54	20	70	.281	.432
Callaway, Mickey	L	.215	65	14	0	0	1	6	7	13	.292	.262
Throws Right	R	.254	67	17	3	0	3	10	4	10	.324	.433
Carpenter, Chris	L	.329	164	54	7	1	8	24	15	21	.379	.530
Throws Right	R	.276	127	35	8	0	3	16	12	24	.354	.409
Carter, Lance	L	.212	33	7	1	0	1	1	2	4	.257	.333
Throws Right	R	.195	41	8	3	0	1	2	3	5	.250	.341
Cassidy, Scott	L	.242	95	23	9	0	5	17	21	21	.380	.495
Throws Right	R	.209	139	29	3	1	7	27	11	27	.287	.396
Castillo, Frank	L	.281	288	81	16	0	9	49	41	62	.372	.431
Throws Right	R	.269	346	93	15	1	10	44	17	50	.305	.405
Choate, Randy	L	.107	28	3	0	0	0	3	6	12	.265	.107
Throws Left	R	.273	55	15	6	0	1	12	9	5	.403	.436
Clemens, Roger	L	.220	363	80	15	2	9	31	47	104	.313	.347
Throws Right	R	.283	325	92	28	0	9	47	16	88	.322	.432
Coco, Pasqual	L	.500	4	2	1	0	0	1	1	0	.600	.750
Throws Right	R	.667	3	2	0	0	0	1	2	0	.800	.667
Colome, Jesus	L	.414	70	29	3	0	4	21	14	12	.506	.629
Throws Right	R	.287	94	27	5	2	2	17	19	21	.417	.447
Colon, Bartolo	L	.242	223	54	6	2	5	15	21	41	.312	.354
Throws Right	R	.248	202	50	12	1	6	18	10	34	.280	.406
Cook, Dennis	L	.264	53	14	4	1	1	9	7	6	.349	.434
Throws Left	R	.206	34	7	0	0	1	5	3	7	.270	.294
Cooper, Brian	L	.391	23	9	1	0	3	7	3	2	.462	.826
Throws Right	R	.417	12	5	1	0	2	5	1	1	.429	1.000
Cordero, Francisco	L	.189	74	14	2	0	1	9	8	22	.277	.257
Throws Right	R	.216	88	19	5	0	5	6	5	19	.266	.307
Cornejo, Nate	L	.273	110	30	6	1	2	11	11	12	.336	.400
Throws Right	R	.337	98	33	8	0	4	18	7	11	.393	.541
Creek, Doug	L	.239	88	21	2	0	5	18	10	25	.333	.432
Throws Left	R	.277	130	36	13	0	5	23	25	31	.409	.492
Cressend, Jack	L	.355	62	22	7	1	1	15	12	11	.453	.548
Throws Right	R	.261	69	18	1	0	5	12	7	11	.333	.493
Davis, Doug	L	.243	74	18	4	2	2	11	5	10	.296	.432
Throws Left	R	.312	157	49	11	1	5	23	17	18	.382	.490
Davis, Jason	L	.231	39	9	4	0	1	3	2	9	.268	.410
Throws Right	R	.188	16	3	0	0	0	0	2	2	.278	.188
de los Santos, Luis	L	.414	29	12	3	0	3	8	3	3	.441	.828
Throws Right	R	.364	33	12	3	0	2	8	1	4	.432	.636
DePaula, Sean	L	.563	16	9	0	0	3	8	0	4	.563	1.125
Throws Right	R	.143	14	2	1	0	0	1	3	4	.294	.214
Donnelly, Brendan	L	.242	66	16	3	0	2	10	7	9	.320	.379
Throws Right	R	.148	108	16	2	0	0	5	12	45	.240	.167
Douglass, Sean	L	.269	104	28	5	0	8	22	20	28	.392	.548
Throws Right	R	.297	101	30	6	1	2	13	15	16	.390	.436
Drese, Ryan	L	.333	309	103	24	7	7	53	39	55	.410	.524
Throws Right	R	.297	246	73	13	1	8	35	23	47	.355	.455
Driskill, Travis	L	.289	280	81	16	0	11	32	27	33	.362	.464
Throws Right	R	.277	249	69	14	2	10	32	21	45	.338	.470
DuBose, Eric	L	.333	6	2	1	0	1	1	0	2	.429	1.000
Throws Left	R	.294	17	5	1	0	0	1	1	2	.333	.353
Durbin, Chad	L	.250	16	4	1	0	0	1	2	2	.368	.313
Throws Right	R	.409	22	9	2	0	3	9	3	3	.458	.909
Eckenstahler, Eric	L	.400	15	6	1	0	0	4	1	5	.438	.467
Throws Left	R	.364	22	8	3	1	1	5	1	8	.391	.727
Elder, Dave	L	.243	37	9	2	1	0	5	6	8	.341	.351
Throws Right	R	.200	45	9	3	1	1	5	8	15	.327	.378
Embree, Alan	L	.171	41	7	1	0	1	5	4	22	.234	.268
Throws Left	R	.221	77	17	1	1	3	11	7	21	.294	.377
Erickson, Scott	L	.304	342	104	21	1	13	54	45	32	.386	.485
Throws Right	R	.302	291	88	15	1	7	45	23	42	.360	.433
Escobar, Kelvim	L	.245	163	40	6	1	5	20	34	48	.382	.387
Throws Right	R	.246	142	35	5	0	5	21	10	37	.310	.387
Eyre, Scott	L	.218	119	26	5	0	2	17	11	27	.280	.311
Throws Left	R	.333	129	43	8	2	2	22	18	24	.409	.473
Farnsworth, Jeff	L	.364	129	47	9	2	4	24	15	12	.435	.558
Throws Right	R	.317	167	53	13	0	2	21	14	16	.370	.461
Field, Nate	L	.455	11	5	2	0	0	0	1	0	.455	.636
Throws Right	R	.273	11	3	0	0	2	4	3	2	.429	.818
File, Bob	L	.500	8	4	1	0	0	3	0	0	.500	.625
Throws Right	R	.444	9	4	1	0	0	4	2	2	.545	.556
Finley, Chuck	L	.230	74	17	2	0	0	8	8	18	.298	.257
Throws Left	R	.296	328	97	19	2	6	43	40	73	.369	.421
Fiore, Tony	L	.247	154	38	7	2	3	17	26	21	.354	.377
Throws Right	R	.203	177	36	4	0	7	16	17	34	.290	.345
Fitzgerald, Brian	L	.231	13	3	1	0	0	1	0	2	.286	.308
Throws Left	R	.421	19	8	1	0	2	5	2	1	.455	.789
Flores, Randy	L	.368	19	7	1	0	2	12	0	3	.333	.737
Throws Left	R	.182	22	4	0	0	0	2	8	4	.400	.182
Fossum, Casey	L	.277	112	31	7	1	1	18	6	27	.311	.384
Throws Left	R	.265	309	82	18	1	11	33	24	74	.324	.437
Foulke, Keith	L	.266	143	38	4	1	3	12	10	31	.314	.371
Throws Right	R	.185	146	27	3	0	4	12	3	27	.212	.288
Franklin, Ryan	L	.265	219	58	9	2	6	27	10	33	.299	.406
Throws Right	R	.247	239	59	12	1	8	33	12	32	.290	.406
Frederick, Kevin	L	.250	24	6	1	0	2	4	4	3	.357	.542
Throws Right	R	.318	22	7	3	0	1	9	6	2	.464	.591
Fyhrie, Mike	L	.203	79	16	2	0	1	13	9	13	.308	.266
Throws Right	R	.278	108	30	10	0	2	13	11	16	.350	.426
Garces, Rich	L	.364	33	12	1	0	2	11	7	8	.442	.576
Throws Right	R	.205	44	9	3	0	2	9	5	8	.327	.409
Garcia, Freddy	L	.255	482	123	27	1	17	58	37	85	.313	.421
Throws Right	R	.265	392	104	18	1	13	43	26	96	.310	.416
Garcia, Reynaldo	L	.600	5	3	0	0	1	3	0	1	.600	1.200
Throws Right	R	.500	8	4	2	0	2	5	1	1	.556	1.500
Gardner, Lee	L	.286	21	6	0	0	2	4	3	1	.375	.571
Throws Right	R	.200	30	6	0	0	1	5	5	7	.350	.300
Garland, Jon	L	.288	413	119	30	0	14	53	54	53	.374	.462
Throws Right	R	.219	315	69	12	1	9	38	29	59	.293	.349
George, Chris	L	.138	29	4	1	0	0	1	3	8	.242	.172
Throws Left	R	.388	85	33	9	0	2	14	5	5	.418	.565
German, Franklyn	L	.100	10	1	0	0	0	0	2	5	.308	.100
Throws Right	R	.200	10	2	1	0	0	0	1	1	.200	.300

Pitcher	vs.	Avg.	AB	H	2B	3B	HR	RBI	BB	SO	OBP	Slg.
Ginter, Matt	L	.342	111	38	9	0	2	23	8	16	.388	.477
Throws Right	R	.208	101	21	1	0	4	21	13	21	.296	.337
Glover, Gary	L	.280	304	85	19	0	17	45	35	39	.359	.510
Throws Right	R	.219	233	51	11	1	4	33	17	31	.281	.326
Gomes, Wayne	L	.103	39	4	1	0	1	7	6	6	.222	.205
Throws Right	R	.364	44	16	6	0	1	6	6	9	.472	.568
Greisinger, Seth	L	.333	72	24	8	0	3	11	8	7	.407	.569
Throws Right	R	.275	80	22	5	0	1	11	5	7	.314	.375
Grimsley, Jason	L	.248	129	32	2	2	3	15	21	23	.353	.364
Throws Right	R	.225	142	32	10	0	1	25	16	36	.308	.317
Groom, Buddy	L	.181	94	17	2	0	2	7	6	25	.238	.266
Throws Left	R	.208	130	27	3	1	2	13	6	23	.246	.292
Guardado, Eddie	L	.263	57	15	2	0	1	6	2	18	.288	.351
Throws Left	R	.200	190	38	9	0	8	17	16	52	.263	.374
Halama, John	L	.246	134	33	7	0	5	13	5	24	.279	.410
Throws Left	R	.298	265	79	9	0	4	25	28	46	.363	.377
Halladay, Roy	L	.259	475	123	20	2	6	51	36	79	.313	.347
Throws Right	R	.228	438	100	23	2	4	35	26	89	.279	.317
Hancock, Josh	L	.083	12	1	0	0	0	0	1	2	.154	.083
Throws Right	R	.308	13	4	1	0	1	3	1	4	.357	.615
Haney, Chris	L	.286	49	14	6	1	0	7	4	7	.368	.449
Throws Left	R	.265	68	18	3	0	2	10	6	8	.325	.397
Harang, Aaron	L	.237	156	37	9	0	1	19	28	30	.349	.314
Throws Right	R	.287	143	41	8	0	6	17	17	34	.370	.469
Harper, Travis	L	.301	163	49	11	0	10	33	15	32	.370	.552
Throws Right	R	.280	186	52	7	0	4	24	12	28	.337	.382
Hasegawa, S.	L	.284	116	33	9	1	1	19	15	19	.366	.405
Throws Right	R	.199	136	27	7	0	3	11	15	20	.286	.316
Hawkins, LaTroy	L	.225	129	29	7	0	3	16	9	35	.273	.349
Throws Right	R	.211	161	34	4	0	2	15	6	28	.237	.273
Hendrickson, Mark	L	.194	31	6	1	0	0	5	1	5	.242	.226
Throws Left	R	.204	93	19	5	0	1	8	11	16	.290	.290
Henriquez, Oscar	L	.164	55	9	1	0	3	5	10	15	.292	.345
Throws Right	R	.238	42	10	2	0	2	8	5	8	.327	.429
Hentgen, Pat	L	.333	48	16	5	2	2	7	8	7	.429	.646
Throws Right	R	.341	44	15	2	0	4	11	2	4	.362	.659
Heredia, Felix	L	.224	85	19	5	0	3	14	11	14	.309	.388
Throws Left	R	.281	114	32	9	0	2	19	15	17	.371	.412
Hermanson, Dustin	L	.325	40	13	5	0	0	4	4	4	.378	.450
Throws Right	R	.373	59	22	7	0	3	13	3	9	.403	.644
Hernandez, Adrian	L	.364	11	4	1	0	1	5	4	4	.533	.727
Throws Right	R	.353	17	6	2	0	1	3	2	5	.421	.647
Hernandez, Orlando	L	.224	286	64	14	0	12	37	18	57	.282	.399
Throws Right	R	.248	270	67	10	2	5	20	18	56	.297	.356
Hernandez, Ro.	L	.282	103	29	6	1	2	16	8	21	.333	.417
Throws Right	R	.317	104	33	5	0	4	12	4	18	.357	.481
Hernandez, Run.	L	.302	162	49	10	1	6	19	18	23	.368	.488
Throws Right	R	.236	127	30	5	0	2	13	4	22	.263	.323
Herrera, Alex	L	.000	9	0	0	0	0	0	0	4	.000	.000
Throws Left	R	.300	10	3	2	0	0	0	1	1	.364	.500
Hiljus, Erik	L	.274	106	29	6	0	5	20	15	17	.361	.472
Throws Right	R	.299	77	23	7	0	6	13	6	12	.349	.623
Hill, Jeremy	L	.263	19	5	1	0	1	3	4	6	.391	.474
Throws Right	R	.200	15	3	0	1	0	4	4	1	.350	.333
Hitchcock, Sterling	L	.316	57	18	4	0	1	8	3	10	.355	.439
Throws Left	R	.331	118	39	7	0	3	18	12	21	.392	.466
Holtz, Mike	L	.316	19	6	2	1	1	8	3	1	.409	.684
Throws Left	R	.375	48	18	4	0	2	7	6	6	.455	.583
Howry, Bob	L	.239	113	27	11	0	6	22	14	18	.326	.496
Throws Right	R	.280	143	40	8	1	3	25	7	27	.321	.413
Hudson, Tim	L	.283	484	137	27	4	15	53	38	76	.337	.448
Throws Right	R	.239	418	100	16	3	4	23	24	76	.288	.321
Irabu, Hideki	L	.269	93	25	8	1	3	12	7	11	.317	.473
Throws Right	R	.289	90	26	3	0	8	16	9	19	.356	.589
Jackson, Mike	L	.275	69	19	4	0	2	9	8	10	.342	.420
Throws Right	R	.288	139	40	8	1	3	13	5	19	.329	.424
James, Delvin	L	.299	67	20	8	0	2	9	10	6	.397	.507
Throws Right	R	.303	66	20	6	1	3	11	5	11	.347	.561
Jimenez, Jason	L	.250	8	2	0	1	0	1	2	2	.400	.500
Throws Left	R	.400	25	10	0	1	2	6	0	3	.385	.720
Johnson, Jason	L	.261	249	65	8	2	7	30	16	48	.319	.394
Throws Right	R	.290	262	76	15	1	12	32	25	49	.351	.492

Pitcher	vs.	Avg.	AB	H	2B	3B	HR	RBI	BB	SO	OBP	Slg.
Julio, Jorge	L	.213	127	27	8	0	2	12	15	23	.299	.323
Throws Right	R	.214	131	28	9	0	3	11	12	32	.285	.351
Karsay, Steve	L	.243	136	33	4	3	6	20	15	39	.316	.449
Throws Right	R	.269	201	54	8	0	1	20	15	26	.323	.323
Kaye, Justin	L	.429	7	3	2	0	0	3	0	3	.429	.714
Throws Right	R	.429	7	3	1	0	0	1	1	0	.500	.571
Keller, Kris	L	.500	2	1	0	0	0	1	1	1	.667	.500
Throws Right	R	.333	3	1	0	0	1	3	2	0	.600	1.333
Kennedy, Joe	L	.273	172	47	14	1	7	28	6	25	.309	.488
Throws Left	R	.268	586	157	33	1	16	75	49	84	.333	.410
Kent, Steve	L	.316	76	24	3	0	3	19	9	15	.395	.474
Throws Left	R	.283	152	43	8	0	3	26	29	26	.400	.395
Kershner, Jason	L	.333	12	4	0	0	1	2	3	5	.467	.583
Throws Left	R	.100	10	1	0	0	0	1	1	2	.182	.100
Kim, Sun-Woo	L	.250	56	14	3	0	4	12	3	13	.283	.518
Throws Right	R	.323	62	20	4	2	1	10	4	5	.368	.500
Kinney, Matt	L	.336	146	49	7	3	9	23	16	18	.402	.610
Throws Right	R	.246	118	29	3	0	4	15	17	27	.333	.373
Knight, Brandon	L	.357	14	5	1	0	0	2	3	2	.471	.429
Throws Right	R	.273	22	6	2	0	2	9	2	5	.333	.636
Koch, Billy	L	.237	152	36	5	1	3	14	22	38	.337	.342
Throws Right	R	.196	189	37	4	0	4	24	24	55	.295	.280
Kolb, Danny	L	.291	55	16	2	1	1	8	13	8	.420	.418
Throws Right	R	.172	64	11	2	0	0	9	9	12	.280	.203
Kozlowski, Ben	L	.444	9	4	0	0	0	2	1	2	.500	.444
Throws Right	R	.241	29	7	2	0	3	5	10	4	.450	.621
Lackey, John	L	.208	197	41	1	1	1	18	15	22	.265	.239
Throws Right	R	.317	227	72	18	0	9	25	18	47	.372	.515
Lee, Cliff	L	.000	9	0	0	0	0	2	4	2	.182	.000
Throws Left	R	.231	26	6	1	0	1	6	2	9	.375	.269
Levine, Al	L	.240	104	25	5	0	4	15	21	11	.362	.404
Throws Right	R	.263	137	36	6	2	4	20	13	29	.325	.423
Lewis, Colby	L	.320	75	24	4	0	3	12	13	12	.427	.493
Throws Right	R	.286	63	18	2	1	1	11	13	16	.416	.397
Lidle, Cory	L	.248	391	97	26	0	11	36	22	66	.288	.399
Throws Right	R	.269	349	94	17	1	6	36	17	45	.310	.375
Lilly, Ted	L	.154	78	12	5	0	2	6	7	20	.221	.295
Throws Left	R	.231	295	68	17	3	13	33	24	57	.300	.441
Lima, Jose	L	.319	144	46	8	3	7	31	13	16	.377	.563
Throws Right	R	.308	130	40	14	2	5	24	8	17	.340	.562
Loaiza, Esteban	L	.308	325	100	24	1	8	44	26	41	.361	.462
Throws Right	R	.311	296	92	15	5	10	46	12	46	.338	.497
Lohse, Kyle	L	.308	341	105	24	4	13	44	45	51	.394	.516
Throws Right	R	.213	357	76	14	0	13	38	25	72	.272	.361
Lopez, Rodrigo	L	.228	386	88	19	1	10	38	31	74	.291	.360
Throws Right	R	.241	349	84	11	4	13	37	31	62	.303	.407
Loux, Shane	L	.361	36	13	3	1	2	7	2	6	.395	.667
Throws Right	R	.250	24	6	1	0	2	6	1	1	.308	.542
Lowe, Derek	L	.209	407	85	17	3	6	31	33	63	.275	.310
Throws Right	R	.213	380	81	13	0	6	27	15	64	.256	.295
Lukasiewicz, Mark	L	.300	30	9	1	0	0	3	5	7	.389	.333
Throws Left	R	.296	27	8	0	0	2	4	8	8	.387	.296
Lyon, Brandon	L	.321	156	50	9	3	9	22	8	18	.354	.590
Throws Right	R	.289	97	28	7	0	5	14	11	12	.366	.515
MacDougal, Mike	L	.176	17	3	0	0	0	0	4	6	.333	.176
Throws Right	R	.143	14	2	0	0	0	2	3	4	.294	.143
Maduro, Calvin	L	.243	103	25	4	1	4	10	7	18	.295	.417
Throws Right	R	.310	126	39	11	1	8	25	15	11	.383	.603
Magnante, Mike	L	.263	38	10	1	1	1	8	5	5	.356	.421
Throws Left	R	.341	82	28	6	3	1	14	6	6	.382	.524
Maroth, Mike	L	.252	115	29	9	1	1	12	8	15	.301	.374
Throws Left	R	.284	377	107	32	3	6	42	28	43	.334	.432
Marte, Damaso	L	.149	101	15	1	0	2	11	9	35	.237	.218
Throws Left	R	.252	115	29	4	0	3	14	9	37	.312	.365
Martin, Tom	L	.000	2	0	0	0	0	0	0	0	.000	.000
Throws Left	R	.625	8	5	5	0	0	4	1	1	.667	1.250
Martinez, Pedro	L	.203	428	87	20	3	7	32	20	136	.253	.313
Throws Right	R	.191	298	57	15	0	6	23	20	103	.255	.302
Mateo, Julio	L	.333	39	13	5	0	2	8	10	6	.469	.615
Throws Right	R	.167	42	7	1	0	0	3	2	9	.222	.190
Maurer, Dave	L	.500	4	2	1	0	1	2	0	0	.500	1.500
Throws Left	R	.333	3	1	0	0	0	0	0	0	.333	.333

Pitcher	vs.	Avg.	AB	H	2B	3B	HR	RBI	BB	SO	OBP	Slg.
May, Darrell	L	.288	139	40	13	0	6	24	12	32	.340	.511
Throws Left	R	.273	381	104	27	1	22	53	38	63	.338	.522
Mays, Joe	L	.275	222	61	12	0	10	33	14	23	.322	.464
Throws Right	R	.315	165	52	7	0	4	19	11	15	.356	.430
Mecir, Jim	L	.204	108	22	5	1	3	14	15	21	.305	.352
Throws Right	R	.297	155	46	6	2	2	21	14	32	.360	.400
Mendoza, Ramiro	L	.261	165	43	9	2	4	18	6	24	.283	.412
Throws Right	R	.286	206	59	9	0	4	31	10	37	.323	.388
Miceli, Dan	L	.409	22	9	1	0	1	6	2	1	.458	.591
Throws Right	R	.235	17	4	0	0	0	3	1	4	.278	.235
Michalak, Chris	L	.217	23	5	0	0	0	0	5	1	.357	.217
Throws Left	R	.417	36	15	2	0	1	6	5	4	.488	.556
Miller, Justin	L	.296	189	56	9	3	7	41	34	25	.405	.487
Throws Right	R	.240	196	47	9	0	5	24	32	43	.364	.362
Miller, Matt	L	.750	4	3	1	0	0	2	0	1	.750	1.000
Throws Left	R	.333	3	1	0	0	1	4	1	0	.500	1.333
Miller, Travis	L	.000	0	0	0	0	0	0	0	0	.000	.000
Throws Left	R	.357	14	5	1	0	0	0	2	3	.438	.429
Milton, Eric	L	.306	111	34	4	2	9	27	7	19	.345	.622
Throws Left	R	.249	559	139	29	4	15	63	23	102	.281	.395
Moehler, Brian	L	.293	41	12	0	0	3	4	2	7	.318	.512
Throws Right	R	.156	32	5	2	0	0	1	0	6	.156	.219
Moyer, Jamie	L	.276	293	81	8	0	12	38	20	34	.335	.427
Throws Left	R	.206	567	117	25	0	16	45	30	113	.247	.335
Mulder, Mark	L	.244	172	42	8	1	5	18	9	46	.301	.390
Throws Left	R	.228	614	140	31	1	16	61	46	113	.287	.360
Mulholland, Terry	L	.303	76	23	4	2	2	12	2	10	.321	.487
Throws Left	R	.300	110	33	10	0	3	14	12	11	.378	.473
Mullen, Scott	L	.263	76	20	3	0	4	13	4	12	.309	.461
Throws Left	R	.270	74	20	3	0	1	11	9	9	.349	.351
Murray, Heath	L	.125	24	3	0	0	0	2	4	7	.300	.125
Throws Left	R	.429	21	9	0	0	0	3	3	4	.320	.857
Mussina, Mike	L	.257	444	114	20	3	16	53	34	109	.310	.423
Throws Right	R	.248	379	94	19	3	11	40	14	73	.280	.401
Myette, Aaron	L	.396	96	38	11	1	6	26	26	20	.520	.719
Throws Right	R	.257	101	26	5	3	5	23	15	28	.376	.515
Nagy, Charles	L	.415	118	49	10	1	6	24	5	12	.439	.669
Throws Right	R	.290	93	27	6	1	4	22	8	10	.352	.505
Nelson, Jeff	L	.224	76	17	6	0	1	6	15	22	.351	.342
Throws Right	R	.218	87	19	1	0	3	12	12	33	.320	.333
Nitkowski, C.J.	L	.190	21	4	0	0	0	1	2	8	.261	.190
Throws Left	R	.250	28	7	1	0	0	1	11	6	.462	.286
Obermueller, Wes	L	.409	22	9	2	1	2	4	2	2	.458	.864
Throws Right	R	.333	15	5	1	0	1	5	0	3	.333	.600
Oliver, Darren	L	.462	52	24	4	0	1	8	9	8	.563	.596
Throws Left	R	.272	169	46	6	0	6	18	18	24	.347	.414
Ortiz, Ramon	L	.218	404	88	12	6	22	46	39	67	.291	.441
Throws Right	R	.243	412	100	17	1	18	42	29	95	.293	.420
Osuna, Antonio	L	.250	120	30	7	1	0	17	21	28	.366	.325
Throws Right	R	.250	136	34	9	0	1	16	7	38	.295	.338
Paniagua, Jose	L	.276	76	21	1	4	4	19	10	14	.360	.553
Throws Right	R	.309	94	29	3	2	6	19	5	20	.353	.574
Park, Chan Ho	L	.287	328	94	28	4	12	55	53	61	.395	.506
Throws Right	R	.254	236	60	12	1	8	33	25	60	.349	.415
Paronto, Chad	L	.226	53	12	4	1	2	11	7	7	.317	.453
Throws Right	R	.262	84	22	2	1	1	13	4	16	.297	.345
Parque, Jim	L	.394	33	13	1	0	3	8	4	5	.462	.697
Throws Left	R	.284	74	21	2	0	8	18	12	8	.379	.635
Parris, Steve	L	.341	164	56	9	0	6	21	23	21	.421	.506
Throws Right	R	.282	142	40	8	2	7	23	12	27	.346	.514
Patterson, Danny	L	.333	6	2	0	1	0	1	2	0	.500	.667
Throws Right	R	.375	8	3	1	0	0	3	0	1	.444	.500
Pearson, Terry	L	.308	13	4	1	1	0	2	1	0	.357	.538
Throws Right	R	.333	12	4	1	0	2	3	1	4	.385	.917
Percival, Troy	L	.247	93	23	3	0	5	15	18	30	.366	.441
Throws Right	R	.138	109	15	2	1	0	6	7	38	.190	.174
Perez, Yorkis	L	.204	49	10	2	0	1	4	5	8	.278	.306
Throws Left	R	.193	57	11	4	0	3	6	9	17	.303	.421
Perisho, Matt	L	.444	9	4	0	0	0	3	3	2	.583	.444
Throws Left	R	.353	34	12	1	1	2	8	3	1	.395	.618

Pitcher	vs.	Avg.	AB	H	2B	3B	HR	RBI	BB	SO	OBP	Slg.
Phelps, Travis	L	.267	60	16	4	0	4	11	13	12	.429	.533
Throws Right	R	.187	75	14	2	0	3	11	14	24	.315	.333
Phillips, Jason	L	.247	93	23	4	0	5	14	13	16	.340	.452
Throws Right	R	.277	65	18	1	0	2	8	7	7	.372	.385
Pineiro, Joel	L	.270	397	107	22	1	14	41	35	79	.327	.436
Throws Right	R	.240	342	82	15	2	10	30	19	57	.289	.383
Plesac, Dan	L	.111	27	3	1	0	1	5	1	10	.138	.259
Throws Left	R	.333	24	8	4	0	0	4	5	4	.448	.500
Politte, Cliff	L	.220	100	22	2	0	4	9	11	23	.295	.360
Throws Right	R	.154	104	16	3	0	1	10	8	34	.221	.212
Ponson, Sidney	L	.243	325	79	11	1	12	28	42	74	.330	.394
Throws Right	R	.273	341	93	18	1	14	47	21	46	.316	.455
Porzio, Mike	L	.269	78	21	3	0	4	13	8	16	.337	.462
Throws Left	R	.229	83	19	4	1	6	19	15	17	.356	.518
Pote, Lou	L	.221	77	17	1	0	4	10	9	16	.315	.390
Throws Right	R	.172	93	16	2	0	3	11	17	16	.295	.290
Powell, Brian	L	.293	123	36	8	1	8	15	11	18	.353	.569
Throws Right	R	.262	107	28	4	0	3	13	10	12	.322	.383
Powell, Jay	L	.222	72	16	3	0	2	12	10	14	.317	.347
Throws Right	R	.270	126	34	5	0	3	20	14	21	.348	.381
Prokopec, Luke	L	.346	162	56	12	1	12	33	19	22	.426	.654
Throws Right	R	.250	136	34	9	1	7	19	6	19	.283	.485
Radke, Brad	L	.247	239	59	13	3	7	32	14	35	.290	.414
Throws Right	R	.300	217	65	17	2	5	30	6	27	.332	.465
Rauch, Jon	L	.258	66	17	4	0	4	11	10	10	.372	.500
Throws Right	R	.234	47	11	2	0	3	10	4	9	.288	.468
Redman, Mark	L	.289	190	55	11	4	4	26	11	32	.329	.453
Throws Left	R	.261	598	156	33	4	11	66	40	77	.310	.385
Reed, Rick	L	.262	405	106	16	4	25	56	15	85	.290	.506
Throws Right	R	.257	335	86	17	4	7	26	11	36	.286	.394
Reichert, Dan	L	.295	112	33	5	2	3	17	16	10	.377	.455
Throws Right	R	.314	140	44	7	0	7	25	9	26	.370	.514
Rekar, Bryan	L	.400	15	6	2	0	1	4	0	1	.400	.733
Throws Right	R	.375	16	6	0	0	0	3	6	1	.522	.375
Reyes, Dennys	L	.279	61	17	5	0	2	3	7	14	.353	.459
Throws Left	R	.336	113	38	6	0	7	24	14	15	.409	.575
Rhodes, Arthur	L	.158	120	19	5	1	1	20	3	41	.177	.242
Throws Left	R	.215	121	26	2	0	3	10	10	40	.275	.306
Riggan, Jerrod	L	.371	70	26	2	0	2	19	9	7	.443	.486
Throws Right	R	.375	72	27	3	0	1	17	9	15	.424	.458
Rincon, Juan	L	.283	60	17	4	1	2	13	6	9	.343	.483
Throws Right	R	.415	65	27	4	0	3	7	3	12	.441	.615
Rincon, Ricardo	L	.203	118	24	6	0	2	12	5	34	.240	.305
Throws Left	R	.267	86	23	6	0	2	16	6	15	.305	.407
Riske, David	L	.253	75	19	4	0	4	19	16	22	.394	.467
Throws Right	R	.259	116	30	5	1	4	20	19	43	.367	.422
Ritchie, Todd	L	.349	301	105	19	4	13	72	26	44	.398	.568
Throws Right	R	.282	252	71	14	1	5	25	26	33	.353	.405
Rivera, Mariano	L	.181	83	15	1	0	1	13	5	19	.244	.229
Throws Right	R	.225	89	20	4	0	2	10	6	22	.274	.337
Roberts, Willis	L	.276	116	32	3	1	1	18	14	15	.358	.345
Throws Right	R	.266	177	47	7	0	4	23	18	36	.337	.373
Rocker, John	L	.364	33	12	2	1	3	15	9	8	.488	.758
Throws Left	R	.266	64	17	2	0	2	7	4	22	.300	.391
Rodney, Fernando	L	.241	29	7	1	1	1	10	6	5	.361	.448
Throws Right	R	.383	47	18	3	0	1	7	4	5	.431	.511
Rodriguez, F.	L	.286	7	2	0	0	0	0	1	4	.375	.286
Throws Right	R	.091	11	1	0	0	0	1	1	9	.231	.091
Rodriguez, Jose	L	.400	10	4	3	0	0	3	0	1	.400	.700
Throws Left	R	.444	9	4	3	0	0	4	4	0	.615	.778
Rodriguez, Nerio	L	.000	0	0	0	0	0	0	0	0	.000	.000
Throws Right	R	.000	1	0	0	0	0	0	0	0	.000	.000
Rodriguez, Ricardo	L	.278	72	20	3	2	3	13	11	9	.395	.500
Throws Right	R	.235	85	20	5	0	2	10	7	15	.330	.365
Rodriguez, Rich	L	.214	42	9	2	0	1	5	9	8	.365	.333
Throws Left	R	.294	17	5	3	0	0	1	2	4	.368	.471
Rogers, Kenny	L	.193	176	34	7	2	6	17	25	40	.297	.358
Throws Left	R	.280	636	178	39	3	15	69	45	67	.332	.421
Romero, J.C.	L	.216	125	27	1	0	0	8	11	44	.300	.224
Throws Left	R	.211	166	35	12	0	3	16	25	32	.314	.337
Rupe, Ryan	L	.246	183	45	14	0	7	32	14	25	.300	.437
Throws Right	R	.241	158	38	13	1	4	23	11	42	.322	.411

2002 A.L. STATISTICS *Pitching*

Pitcher	vs.	Avg.	AB	H	2B	3B	HR	RBI	BB	SO	OBP	Slg.
Ryan, B.J.	L	.192	99	19	3	0	5	15	16	35	.322	.374
Throws Left	R	.283	113	32	6	1	2	15	17	21	.382	.407
Sabathia, C.C.	L	.240	196	47	8	2	3	16	19	30	.307	.347
Throws Left	R	.255	591	151	34	6	14	81	69	119	.329	.404
Sabel, Erik	L	1.000	1	1	0	0	1	1	0	0	1.000	4.000
Throws Right	R	1.000	1	1	0	0	0	0	0	0	1.000	2.000
Sadler, Carl	L	.205	39	8	2	0	0	4		15	.279	.256
Throws Left	R	.219	32	7	1	0	2	6	7	8	.359	.438
Santana, Johan	L	.195	77	15	5	0	0	7	7	18	.256	.260
Throws Left	R	.216	319	69	11	1	7	25	42	119	.309	.323
Santana, Julio	L	.261	92	24	3	2	3	12	15	16	.376	.435
Throws Right	R	.219	114	25	2	0	5	12	13	22	.299	.368
Sasaki, Kazuhiro	L	.207	116	24	5	0	2	13	10	40	.266	.302
Throws Right	R	.194	103	20	2	1	4	9	10	33	.271	.350
Schoeneweis, Scott	L	.202	129	26	3	0	5	13	10	25	.270	.341
Throws Left	R	.290	321	93	19	1	12	53	39	40	.367	.467
Seanez, Rudy	L	.220	59	13	0	0	2	9	17	19	.390	.322
Throws Right	R	.238	63	15	5	0	3	10	7	21	.314	.460
Sedlacek, Shawn	L	.324	173	56	11	0	10	31	22	21	.393	.561
Throws Right	R	.279	154	43	10	0	6	26	14	31	.354	.461
Sele, Aaron	L	.315	317	100	20	1	7	40	30	44	.374	.451
Throws Right	R	.283	318	90	14	1	14	41	19	38	.328	.465
Shields, Scot	L	.184	76	14	1	0	3	3	10	16	.279	.316
Throws Right	R	.191	89	17	2	0	1	8	11	14	.287	.247
Shouse, Brian	L	.276	29	8	1	0	2	10	3	10	.364	.517
Throws Left	R	.241	29	7	3	0	1	6	6	1	.378	.448
Shuey, Paul	L	.194	67	13	1	1	0	7	6	19	.257	.239
Throws Right	R	.254	71	18	5	0	1	9	4	20	.293	.366
Smith, Mike	L	.378	74	28	2	2	1	18	9	4	.447	.500
Throws Right	R	.217	69	15	4	0	2	8	11	12	.372	.362
Smith, Roy	L	.375	16	6	0	0	1	3	1	1	.412	.563
Throws Right	R	.231	13	3	1	0	0	0	4	1	.444	.308
Soriano, Rafael	L	.297	101	30	6	1	5	14	8	14	.349	.525
Throws Right	R	.179	84	15	5	0	3	10	8	18	.250	.345
Sosa, Jorge	L	.289	187	54	10	1	6	30	32	20	.390	.449
Throws Right	R	.183	186	34	7	0	10	29	22	28	.270	.382
Sparks, Steve W.	L	.299	371	111	17	4	10	61	25	50	.348	.447
Throws Right	R	.312	407	127	38	4	13	69	42	48	.383	.521
Standridge, Jason	L	.444	9	4	1	0	1	3	3	1	.583	.889
Throws Right	R	.600	5	3	0	0	0	0	1	0	.667	.600
Stanton, Mike	L	.268	123	33	6	0	2	19	11	27	.317	.366
Throws Left	R	.247	162	40	8	2	2	15	17	17	.315	.358
Stein, Blake	L	.319	94	30	3	1	3	20	15	19	.409	.468
Throws Right	R	.293	99	29	7	3	3	17	12	23	.379	.515
Stephens, John	L	.268	123	33	7	0	6	20	12	32	.328	.472
Throws Right	R	.273	128	35	3	1	7	24	10	24	.336	.477
Sturtze, Tanyon	L	.323	443	143	28	1	22	68	60	64	.404	.540
Throws Right	R	.282	454	128	29	1	11	64	29	73	.333	.423
Suppan, Jeff	L	.276	424	117	21	3	12	54	40	49	.335	.425
Throws Right	R	.281	398	112	21	2	20	58	28	60	.334	.495
Suzuki, Mac	L	.371	35	13	4	0	0	8	10	4	.511	.486
Throws Right	R	.239	46	11	3	0	2	15	7	11	.333	.435
Tallet, Brian	L	.222	9	2	1	0	0	1	1	2	.364	.333
Throws Left	R	.212	33	7	5	0	0	1	3	3	.278	.364
Tam, Jeff	L	.300	60	18	2	0	0	6	9	3	.386	.333
Throws Right	R	.352	108	38	8	3	2	30	4	11	.383	.537
Taylor, Aaron	L	.444	9	4	0	0	1	2	0	1	.444	.778
Throws Right	R	.286	14	4	1	0	1	4	0	5	.286	.571
Telford, Anthony	L	.273	44	12	3	0	2	9	9	9	.396	.477
Throws Right	R	.353	51	18	3	2	1	13	6	10	.444	.549
Tessmer, Jay	L	.000	0	0	0	0	0	0	1	0	1.000	.000
Throws Right	R	.000	4	0	0	0	0	0	1	0	.200	.000
Thurman, Corey	L	.236	123	29	10	0	5	17	23	32	.305	.439
Throws Right	R	.259	139	36	6	1	6	16	22	24	.360	.446
Thurman, Mike	L	.361	61	22	5	0	1	9	7	9	.426	.492
Throws Right	R	.303	76	23	5	1	1	14	5	14	.354	.434

Pitcher	vs.	Avg.	AB	H	2B	3B	HR	RBI	BB	SO	OBP	Slg.
Towers, Josh	L	.404	57	23	3	0	7	14	5	7	.444	.825
Throws Right	R	.322	59	19	2	0	4	10	0	6	.317	.559
Trombley, Mike	L	.444	9	4	2	0	1	4	1	1	.500	1.000
Throws Right	R	.462	13	6	3	0	1	3	0	2	.462	.923
Urbina, Ugueth	L	.257	113	29	6	0	6	15	14	26	.333	.469
Throws Right	R	.143	105	15	4	2	2	8	6	45	.188	.276
Valdes, Ismael	L	.255	411	105	20	1	15	44	32	52	.315	.418
Throws Right	R	.259	344	89	20	2	11	41	15	50	.297	.424
Van Hekken, Andy	L	.364	11	4	0	0	1	2	5	0	.563	.636
Throws Left	R	.306	111	34	10	0	1	10	1	5	.310	.423
Van Poppel, Todd	L	.291	127	37	8	0	6	16	17	37	.375	.496
Throws Right	R	.262	164	43	13	0	8	36	12	48	.322	.488
Venafro, Mike	L	.270	63	17	2	1	1	7	8	9	.361	.381
Throws Left	R	.337	83	28	3	1	4	20	6	7	.380	.542
Voyles, Brad	L	.318	44	14	2	1	2	9	10	11	.444	.545
Throws Right	R	.262	65	17	5	1	3	11	8	15	.360	.508
Wakefield, Tim	L	.195	272	53	18	1	6	25	33	58	.282	.335
Throws Right	R	.213	320	68	11	0	9	33	18	76	.270	.331
Walker, Jamie	L	.202	89	18	1	0	7	18	3	26	.245	.449
Throws Left	R	.194	72	14	1	1	2	8	6	14	.272	.319
Walker, Pete	L	.284	268	76	19	1	11	40	35	36	.368	.485
Throws Right	R	.256	262	67	20	0	7	35	16	44	.297	.412
Wall, Donne	L	.139	36	5	0	1	0	4	4	9	.220	.194
Throws Right	R	.293	41	12	3	0	3	12	3	4	.356	.585
Washburn, Jarrod	L	.199	181	36	13	0	5	15	15	35	.264	.354
Throws Left	R	.246	598	147	37	1	14	50	44	104	.297	.381
Watson, Mark	L	.222	9	2	0	0	0	1	1	1	.273	.222
Throws Left	R	.600	10	6	1	0	1	6	3	0	.692	1.000
Weaver, Jeff	L	.233	387	90	26	3	6	29	28	71	.296	.362
Throws Right	R	.268	385	103	21	1	10	47	20	61	.308	.405
Weber, Ben	L	.243	103	25	8	1	1	13	15	13	.333	.369
Throws Right	R	.253	178	45	10	0	3	15	7	30	.293	.360
Wells, Bob	L	.355	110	39	7	0	3	16	11	20	.413	.500
Throws Right	R	.300	130	39	4	0	5	26	5	10	.326	.446
Wells, David	L	.213	202	43	12	0	5	19	14	35	.271	.347
Throws Left	R	.274	610	167	39	3	16	68	31	102	.310	.426
Westbrook, Jake	L	.292	89	26	6	1	4	22	10	11	.364	.517
Throws Right	R	.300	80	24	4	1	2	15	2	9	.321	.450
Wickman, Bob	L	.275	80	22	5	0	2	12	6	18	.326	.413
Throws Right	R	.294	68	20	4	0	1	6	4	18	.342	.397
Wiggins, Scott	L	.250	8	2	0	0	0	1	0	3	.250	.250
Throws Left	R	.750	4	3	1	0	1	1	1	0	.800	1.750
Wilson, Kris	L	.378	37	14	4	0	4	11	1	6	.385	.811
Throws Right	R	.333	45	15	5	1	3	12	4	4	.404	.689
Wilson, Paul	L	.309	359	111	28	5	13	50	40	46	.379	.524
Throws Right	R	.267	404	108	19	1	16	56	27	65	.327	.438
Wise, Matt	L	.375	8	3	0	0	0	2	0	2	.375	.375
Throws Right	R	.182	22	4	1	0	0	1	1	4	.250	.227
Wohlers, Mark	L	.256	117	30	5	0	5	21	13	26	.331	.427
Throws Right	R	.265	155	41	8	0	1	20	13	20	.329	.335
Woodard, Steve	L	.323	31	10	2	1	2	7	2	5	.364	.645
Throws Right	R	.238	42	10	2	0	2	8	6	9	.360	.429
Wright, Dan	L	.257	413	106	23	0	18	58	42	83	.327	.443
Throws Right	R	.270	348	94	20	2	14	47	29	53	.326	.460
Wright, Jaret	L	.458	48	22	7	0	1	15	13	4	.578	.667
Throws Right	R	.409	44	18	4	0	2	17	6	8	.462	.636
Wunsch, Kelly	L	.208	72	15	2	0	1	13	8	15	.313	.278
Throws Left	R	.268	41	11	2	0	2	9	11	7	.444	.463
Yan, Esteban	L	.273	128	35	7	2	8	27	20	23	.369	.547
Throws Right	R	.246	142	35	5	0	2	8	9	30	.305	.324
Zambrano, Victor	L	.292	195	57	13	1	6	28	41	31	.416	.462
Throws Right	R	.266	237	63	14	2	9	48	27	42	.339	.456
Zito, Barry	L	.275	171	47	5	1	7	14	20	34	.352	.439
Throws Left	R	.203	665	135	19	2	17	54	58	148	.273	.314
American League	L	.269									.342	.437
	R	.261									.323	.413

FIELDING

TEAM

Team	G	PO	A	E	TC	DP	TP	PB	Pct.
Minnesota	161	4334	1422	74	5830	124	0	5	.987
Anaheim	162	4357	1575	87	6019	151	0	7	.986
Baltimore	162	4352	1720	91	6163	173	0	22	.985
Seattle	162	4336	1515	88	5939	134	0	7	.985
Texas	162	4319	1683	99	6101	152	1	11	.984
Chicago	162	4269	1595	97	5961	148	0	9	.984
Oakland	162	4356	1798	102	6256	144	0	9	.984
Boston	162	4338	1645	104	6087	140	0	20	.983
Toronto	162	4315	1613	107	6035	159	0	18	.982
Cleveland	162	4274	1662	113	6049	161	0	15	.981
Tampa Bay	161	4321	1567	126	6014	168	1	13	.979
Kansas City	162	4323	1702	130	6155	153	0	8	.979
New York	161	4356	1524	127	6007	117	0	10	.979
Detroit	161	4242	1719	142	6103	148	0	23	.977
Totals	1132	60492	22740	1487	84719	2081	2	177	.982

INDIVIDUAL

FIRST BASEMEN

NOTE: All caps denotes fielding-percentage leader based on 81 games for catchers, 108 for all other non-pitchers and 162 innings for pitchers. *Throws lefthanded.

Player, Team	G	GS	PO	A	E	TC	DP	Pct.
Alicea, Luis, K.C.	2	0	8	0	0	8	0	1.000
Andrews, Shane, Bos.	2	1	6	1	0	7	1	1.000
Bellinger, Clay, Ana.	2	0	2	0	0	2	0	1.000
Berg, Dave, Tor.	10	7	61	2	1	64	5	.984
Berger, Brandon, K.C.	1	0	1	0	0	1	0	1.000
Blake, Casey, Min.	3	0	12	0	0	12	0	1.000
Broussard, Ben, Cle.*	4	3	27	1	0	28	2	1.000
Catalanotto, Frank, Tex.	15	9	87	5	0	92	6	1.000
Cirillo, Jeff, Sea.	11	4	32	7	0	39	2	1.000
Clark, Howie, Bal.	1	1	7	0	0	7	2	1.000
Clark, Tony, Bos.	85	70	653	58	6	717	54	.992
Conine, Jeff, Bal.	103	102	947	58	10	1015	99	.990
Coomer, Ron, N.Y.	11	6	60	6	1	67	5	.985
Cordero, Wil, Cle.	1	0	1	0	0	1	0	1.000
Cox, Steve, T.B.*	110	110	852	85	7	944	101	.993
Cruz, Jacob, Det.*	4	2	26	2	0	28	1	1.000
Cuddyer, Michael, Min.	6	5	28	5	0	33	0	1.000
Daubach, Brian, Bos.	60	54	443	30	5	478	37	.990
Davis, Ben, Sea.	2	0	8	0	0	8	0	1.000
Delgado, Carlos, Tor.	140	140	1232	95	12	1339	121	.991
Diaz, Juan, Bos.	1	1	8	0	0	8	0	1.000
Erstad, Darin, Ana.*	5	0	9	0	0	9	2	1.000
Fullmer, Brad, Ana.	29	27	176	8	1	185	22	.995
Giambi, Jason, N.Y.	92	92	761	35	4	800	53	.995
Gibbons, Jay, Bal.*	30	28	208	17	1	226	26	.996
Gil, Benji, Ana.	10	5	33	3	1	37	6	.973
Greene, Todd, Tex.	15	10	92	13	2	107	11	.981
Greer, Rusty, Tex.*	1	1	8	0	0	8	0	1.000
Hafner, Travis, Tex.	3	3	7	3	1	11	0	.909
Halter, Shane, Det.	1	0	8	1	0	9	0	1.000
Hart, Jason, Tex.	2	0	2	0	0	2	0	1.000
Hatteberg, Scott, Oak.	91	88	768	74	5	847	77	.994
Hocking, Denny, Min.	6	0	9	0	0	9	0	1.000
Huff, Aubrey, T.B.	45	45	354	21	5	380	41	.987
Ibanez, Raul, K.C.	49	45	362	30	2	394	36	.995
Johnson, Nick, N.Y.*	78	59	519	44	7	570	46	.988
Kapler, Gabe, Tex.	1	0	1	0	0	1	0	1.000
Kielty, Bobby, Min.	5	4	27	2	0	29	4	1.000
Konerko, Paul, Chi.	140	140	1146	75	8	1229	113	.993
Lamb, Mike, Tex.	52	38	358	28	5	391	36	.987
LeCroy, Matthew, Min.	8	5	39	1	1	41	8	.976
Leon, Jose, Bal.	17	13	135	9	0	144	15	1.000
Lesher, Brian, Tor.*	12	4	34	4	0	38	1	1.000
Liefer, Jeff, Chi.	31	18	187	10	2	199	23	.990
Lopez, Luis, Bal.	1	0	5	0	0	5	0	1.000
Mabry, John, Oak.	50	7	136	14	0	150	10	1.000
McCarty, Dave, K.C.*	9	8	66	5	0	71	5	1.000
McGuire, Ryan, Bal.*	7	4	36	3	0	39	4	1.000
Merloni, Lou, Bos.	3	0	1	0	0	1	0	1.000
Mientkiewicz, Doug, Min.	143	132	1073	69	5	1147	92	.996
Munson, Eric, Det.	4	4	29	3	1	33	3	.970
Nieves, Jose, Ana.	3	0	16	1	0	17	1	1.000
Offerman, Jose, Bos.-Sea.	52	43	365	37	2	404	38	.995
Olerud, John, Sea.*	152	150	1169	101	5	1275	122	.996
Ortiz, David, Min.*	15	13	90	6	1	97	8	.990
Palmeiro, Rafael, Tex.*	97	95	739	84	5	828	83	.994
Paquette, Craig, Det.	14	11	96	9	1	106	5	.991
Pellow, Kit, K.C.	10	3	36	3	0	39	5	1.000

Player, Team	G	GS	PO	A	E	TC	DP	Pct.
Pena, Carlos, Oak.-Det.*	113	111	1010	71	4	1085	96	.996
Perry, Chan, K.C.	5	3	35	2	0	37	2	1.000
Perry, Herbert, Tex.	12	6	55	7	0	62	6	1.000
Phelps, Josh, Tor.	2	1	9	0	0	9	1	1.000
Piatt, Adam, Oak.	1	0	4	0	0	4	1	1.000
Richard, Chris, Bal.*	9	7	63	3	0	66	0	1.000
Saenz, Olmedo, Oak.	34	23	190	12	0	202	17	1.000
Sandberg, Jared, T.B.	3	3	23	2	1	26	4	.962
Sears, Todd, Min.	6	2	26	2	0	28	3	1.000
Segui, David, Bal.*	7	7	61	5	0	66	12	1.000
Simon, Randall, Det.*	59	57	541	27	7	575	48	.988
Smith, Bobby, T.B.	6	3	47	6	1	54	4	.981
Snyder, Earl, Cle.	12	10	98	8	2	108	3	.981
SPIEZIO, Scott, Ana.	143	125	1078	59	3	1140	101	.997
Stevens, Lee, Cle.*	25	21	216	8	3	227	19	.987
Sutton, Larry, Oak.*	6	2	29	0	0	29	0	1.000
Sweeney, Mike, K.C.	102	101	838	105	9	952	94	.991
Thomas, Frank, Chi.	4	4	38	4	2	44	5	.955
Thome, Jim, Cle.	128	128	1063	75	10	1148	118	.991
Tucker, Michael, K.C.	5	2	22	3	1	26	2	.962
Vander Wal, John, N.Y.*	6	4	32	0	0	32	3	1.000
Velarde, Randy, Oak.	5	3	25	0	1	26	2	.962
Ventura, Robin, N.Y.	5	0	19	2	0	21	1	1.000
Wilson, Dan, Sea.	4	1	17	1	0	18	0	1.000
Wilson, Tom, Tor.	11	9	79	2	0	81	12	1.000
Woodward, Chris, Tor.	3	1	9	0	0	9	1	1.000
Wooten, Shawn, Ana.	16	5	62	4	0	66	3	1.000
Young, Dmitri, Det.	15	15	117	16	4	137	5	.971

TRIPLE PLAY: Huff, T.B.

FIRST BASEMEN WITH TWO OR MORE TEAMS

Player, Team	G	GS	PO	A	E	TC	DP	Pct.
Offerman, Jose, Bos.	41	36	309	29	2	340	35	.994
Offerman, Jose, Sea.	11	7	56	8	0	64	3	1.000
Pena, Carlos, Oak.*	40	39	351	42	1	394	25	.997
Pena, Carlos, Det.*	73	72	659	29	3	691	71	.996

SECOND BASEMEN

Player, Team	G	GS	PO	A	E	TC	DP	Pct.
Abernathy, Brent, T.B.	116	115	253	316	12	581	85	.979
Alicea, Luis, K.C.	32	23	56	90	2	148	21	.986
Baerga, Carlos, Bos.	17	10	25	32	1	58	4	.983
Berg, Dave, Tor.	52	43	71	126	7	204	34	.966
Bloomquist, Willie, Sea.	4	2	5	10	0	15	1	1.000
Bocachica, Hiram, Det.	2	1	1	4	0	5	0	1.000
BOONE, Bret, Sea.	153	152	251	387	7	645	84	.989
Bush, Homer, Tor.	22	21	38	58	1	97	12	.990
Cabrera, Jolbert, Cle.	3	2	3	7	0	10	2	1.000
Canizaro, Jay, Min.	30	25	39	62	1	102	13	.990
Caruso, Mike, K.C.	4	2	10	4	1	15	1	.933
Catalanotto, Frank, Tex.	23	15	24	47	1	72	8	.986
Durham, Ray, Chi.-Oak.	103	103	209	298	17	524	73	.968
Easley, Damion, Det.	84	84	181	253	9	443	54	.980
Ellis, Mark, Oak.	85	83	170	232	9	411	48	.978
Escalona, Felix, T.B.	25	20	46	61	4	111	12	.964
Febles, Carlos, K.C.	116	103	193	312	15	520	76	.971
Figgins, Chone, Ana.	8	1	7	9	1	17	2	.941
Flores, Jose, Oak.	2	1	0	0	0	0	0	.000
German, Esteban, Oak.	8	8	22	23	1	46	6	.978
Gil, Benji, Ana.	26	22	41	58	1	100	11	.990
Graffanino, Tony, Chi.	25	17	33	58	5	96	17	.948

Player, Team	G	GS	PO	A	E	TC	DP	Pct.
Gutierrez, Ricky, Cle.	93	92	167	277	11	455	66	.976
Hairston Jr., Jerry, Bal.	119	118	232	365	11	608	75	.982
Halter, Shane, Det.	4	2	6	8	2	16	2	.875
Harris, Willie, Chi.	38	37	87	104	3	194	21	.985
Hocking, Denny, Min.	56	42	69	115	7	191	22	.963
Hudson, Orlando, Tor.	52	51	117	157	4	278	49	.986
Infante, Omar, Det.	2	2	5	9	0	14	4	1.000
Jackson, Damian, Det.	56	53	110	146	5	261	37	.981
Jimenez, D'Angelo, Chi.	17	17	31	53	1	85	16	.988
Johnson, Russ, T.B.	1	0	0	0	0	0	0	.000
Kennedy, Adam, Ana.	139	123	273	367	11	651	90	.983
Lamb, David, Min.	2	1	6	2	0	8	1	1.000
Lamb, Mike, Tex.	1	0	0	2	0	2	0	1.000
LaRocca, Greg, Cle.	3	1	3	4	0	7	1	1.000
Lawrence, Joe, Tor.	49	44	73	131	7	211	20	.967
Lopez, Luis, Bal.	12	8	12	19	1	32	3	.969
Macias, Jose, Det.	17	15	26	54	3	83	5	.964
McDonald, John, Cle.	64	56	94	184	4	282	42	.986
McLemore, Mark, Sea.	2	1	2	2	0	4	0	1.000
Menechino, Frank, Oak.	32	31	37	90	1	128	10	.992
Merloni, Lou, Bos.	66	47	99	142	3	244	28	.988
Mora, Melvin, Bal.	12	9	22	41	2	65	10	.969
Moriarty, Mike, Bal.	2	2	4	10	0	14	4	1.000
Morris, Warren, Min.	4	2	2	6	0	8	1	1.000
Nelson, Bry, Bos.	11	5	11	16	1	28	2	.964
Nieves, Jose, Ana.	18	16	30	31	4	65	8	.938
Offerman, Jose, Sea.	1	0	1	2	0	3	0	1.000
Ordaz, Luis, K.C.	28	26	43	68	2	113	14	.982
Perez, Neifi, K.C.	5	5	14	13	1	28	2	.964
Phillips, Brandon, Cle.	11	8	16	28	2	46	4	.957
Relaford, Desi, Sea.	11	5	14	21	0	35	6	1.000
Rivas, Luis, Min.	93	91	147	205	5	357	51	.986
Roberts, Brian, Bal.	25	25	43	80	3	126	19	.976
Romano, Jason, Tex.	8	2	10	8	1	19	2	.947
Sadler, Donnie, K.C.-Tex.	6	3	11	9	0	20	1	1.000
Salazar, Oscar, Det.	6	4	7	8	1	16	3	.938
Sanchez, Freddy, Bos.	5	3	4	9	0	13	1	1.000
Sanchez, Rey, Bos.	100	97	151	272	4	427	61	.991
Selby, Bill, Cle.	6	3	5	10	0	15	3	1.000
Sheets, Andy, T.B.	26	26	55	72	1	128	26	.992
Smith, Jason, T.B.	1	0	0	0	0	0	0	.000
Soriano, Alfonso, N.Y.	155	154	300	402	23	725	86	.968
Spiezio, Scott, Ana.	1	0	0	0	0	0	0	.000
Tucker, Michael, K.C.	2	1	2	3	1	6	1	.833
Ugueto, Luis, Sea.	11	2	10	14	1	25	3	.960
Velarde, Randy, Oak.	38	28	70	88	3	161	22	.981
Wilson, Enrique, N.Y.	7	7	15	18	0	33	5	1.000
Woodward, Chris, Tor.	6	3	8	14	2	24	4	.917
Young, Michael, Tex.	152	144	298	420	9	727	97	.988

TRIPLE PLAYS: Sheets, T.B.; Young, Tex.

SECOND BASEMEN WITH TWO OR MORE TEAMS

Player, Team	G	GS	PO	A	E	TC	DP	Pct.
Durham, Ray, Chi.	92	92	188	261	15	464	61	.968
Durham, Ray, Oak.	11	11	21	37	2	60	12	.967
Sadler, Donnie, K.C.	4	2	9	5	0	14	0	1.000
Sadler, Donnie, Tex.	2	1	2	4	0	6	1	1.000

THIRD BASEMEN

Player, Team	G	GS	PO	A	E	TC	DP	Pct.
Alicea, Luis, K.C.	32	20	8	39	6	53	1	.887
Andrews, Shane, Bos.	4	2	3	6	0	9	1	1.000
Arias, Alex, N.Y.	4	1	0	3	1	4	1	.750
Baerga, Carlos, Bos.	1	0	0	0	0	0	0	.000
Batista, Tony, Bal.	154	154	111	290	16	417	35	.962
Berg, Dave, Tor.	20	18	10	35	0	45	2	1.000
Blake, Casey, Min.	5	5	5	6	2	13	1	.846
Blalock, Hank, Tex.	46	42	28	72	6	106	7	.943
Branyan, Russell, Cle.	8	6	3	10	1	14	1	.929
Canizaro, Jay, Min.	8	7	3	16	2	21	3	.905
Caruso, Mike, K.C.	2	0	1	0	0	1	0	1.000
Chavez, Eric, Oak.	143	143	120	301	17	438	24	.961
CIRILLO, Jeff, Sea.	141	126	112	217	9	338	23	.973
Coomer, Ron, N.Y.	26	22	12	33	6	51	2	.882
Crede, Joe, Chi.	53	53	33	87	8	128	12	.938
Cuddyer, Michael, Min.	10	4	5	10	0	15	2	1.000
Ellis, Mark, Oak.	7	7	7	18	2	27	0	.926
Escalona, Felix, T.B.	4	4	1	8	2	11	1	.818
Fryman, Travis, Cle.	113	107	53	185	10	248	27	.960
Gipson, Charles, Sea.	4	1	1	1	0	2	0	1.000

Player, Team	G	GS	PO	A	E	TC	DP	Pct.
Glaus, Troy, Ana.	156	153	101	281	20	402	30	.950
Graffanino, Tony, Chi.	35	32	19	61	4	84	5	.952
Halter, Shane, Det.	30	24	21	45	4	70	9	.943
Hillenbrand, Shea, Bos.	156	154	100	283	23	406	27	.943
Hinske, Eric, Tor.	148	141	103	245	20	368	14	.946
Hocking, Denny, Min.	16	9	10	20	0	30	2	1.000
Huff, Aubrey, T.B.	14	13	14	25	3	42	1	.929
Jackson, Damian, Det.	2	0	0	3	0	3	0	1.000
Jimenez, D'Angelo, Chi.	1	1	0	2	0	2	0	1.000
Johnson, Russ, T.B.	27	27	23	38	1	62	5	.984
Koskie, Corey, Min.	138	136	117	254	12	383	16	.969
Lamb, David, Min.	1	0	0	0	0	0	0	.000
Lamb, Mike, Tex.	14	13	12	20	3	35	0	.914
LaRocca, Greg, Cle.	15	13	9	15	6	30	1	.800
Leon, Jose, Bal.	12	8	7	16	0	23	2	1.000
Lopez, Felipe, Tor.	2	2	2	1	0	3	0	1.000
Macias, Jose, Det.	8	7	4	8	2	14	0	.857
McDonald, John, Cle.	10	6	4	11	2	17	0	.882
McLemore, Mark, Sea.	14	10	7	13	2	22	1	.909
Menechino, Frank, Oak.	4	1	1	5	1	7	1	.857
Merloni, Lou, Bos.	8	6	5	24	1	30	1	.967
Moriarty, Mike, Bal.	1	0	0	1	0	1	0	1.000
Nieves, Jose, Ana.	5	1	0	5	0	5	0	1.000
Ordaz, Luis, K.C.	6	0	0	2	0	2	0	1.000
Paquette, Craig, Det.	49	45	35	82	8	125	5	.936
Pellow, Kit, K.C.	12	10	5	22	5	32	3	.844
Perry, Herbert, Tex.	112	105	83	190	14	287	17	.951
Randa, Joe, K.C.	129	128	108	234	10	352	12	.972
Relaford, Desi, Sea.	38	25	25	41	3	69	2	.957
Romano, Jason, Tex.	1	0	0	1	0	1	0	1.000
Sadler, Donnie, K.C.-Tex.	15	6	6	11	1	18	0	.944
Saenz, Olmedo, Oak.	15	10	14	28	5	47	1	.894
Salazar, Oscar, Det.	1	1	0	3	0	3	0	1.000
Sandberg, Jared, T.B.	97	94	83	174	14	271	19	.948
Selby, Bill, Cle.	33	28	20	50	5	75	3	.933
Sheets, Andy, T.B.	4	4	3	10	0	13	0	1.000
Smith, Bobby, T.B.	10	10	7	19	3	29	3	.897
Smith, Jason, T.B.	12	9	7	18	1	26	3	.962
Snyder, Earl, Cle.	2	2	1	4	0	5	0	1.000
Spiezio, Scott, Ana.	20	8	14	19	2	35	2	.943
Truby, Chris, Det.	89	83	71	181	11	263	22	.958
Ugueto, Luis, Sea.	1	0	0	1	0	1	0	1.000
Valentin, Jose, Chi.	83	76	65	152	11	228	14	.952
Velarde, Randy, Oak.	1	1	0	1	0	1	0	1.000
Ventura, Robin, N.Y.	137	130	109	261	23	393	22	.941
Wilson, Enrique, N.Y.	26	8	15	26	3	44	1	.932
Woodward, Chris, Tor.	2	1	2	3	0	5	0	1.000
Wooten, Shawn, Ana.	1	0	0	0	0	0	0	.000
Young, Dmitri, Det.	1	1	2	0	1	3	0	1.000
Young, Michael, Tex.	4	0	0	3	0	3	0	1.000

TRIPLE PLAY: Blalock, Tex.

THIRD BASEMEN WITH TWO OR MORE TEAMS

Player, Team	G	GS	PO	A	E	TC	DP	Pct.
Sadler, Donnie, K.C.	11	4	4	6	1	11	0	.909
Sadler, Donnie, Tex.	4	2	2	5	0	7	0	1.000

SHORTSTOPS

Player, Team	G	GS	PO	A	E	TC	DP	Pct.
Alicea, Luis, K.C.	1	0	0	0	0	0	0	.000
Amezaga, Alfredo, Ana.	5	3	7	11	0	18	1	1.000
Arias, Alex, N.Y.	1	1	0	3	0	3	0	1.000
Berg, Dave, Tor.	13	11	23	25	2	50	8	.960
Berroa, Angel, K.C.	20	20	41	67	4	112	13	.964
BORDICK, Mike, Bal.	117	115	197	372	1	570	92	.998
Caruso, Mike, K.C.	5	2	4	10	0	14	0	1.000
Clayton, Royce, Chi.	109	100	166	292	5	463	72	.989
Eckstein, David, Ana.	147	146	205	397	14	616	91	.977
Ellis, Mark, Oak.	8	1	3	13	0	16	4	1.000
Escalona, Felix, T.B.	26	16	28	58	5	91	16	.945
Febles, Carlos, K.C.	1	0	0	0	0	0	0	.000
Flores, Jose, Oak.	1	0	1	1	0	2	0	1.000
Garciaparra, Nomar, Bos.	154	153	220	467	25	712	92	.965
Gil, Benji, Ana.	14	7	16	32	2	50	5	.960
Glaus, Troy, Ana.	2	0	1	1	0	2	1	1.000
Gomez, Chris, T.B.	130	128	229	356	12	597	94	.980
Graffanino, Tony, Chi.	8	6	13	19	1	33	1	.970
Guillen, Carlos, Sea.	130	127	200	304	18	522	68	.966
Guzman, Cristian, Min.	147	143	247	360	12	619	84	.981
Halter, Shane, Det.	81	78	122	253	15	390	37	.962

Player, Team	G	GS	PO	A	E	TC	DP	Pct.
Hocking, Denny, Min.	25	18	32	43	3	78	8	.962
Infante, Omar, Det.	16	16	18	54	5	77	10	.935
Jackson, Damian, Det.	6	4	4	11	2	17	0	.882
Jeter, Derek, N.Y.	156	156	219	367	14	600	69	.977
Jimenez, D'Angelo, Chi.	10	9	13	31	1	45	8	.978
Johnson, Russ, TB.	2	0	0	0	0	0	0	.000
Lamb, David, Min.	4	0	4	1	0	5	1	1.000
Lopez, Felipe, Tor.	79	74	112	200	8	320	51	.975
Lopez, Luis, Bal.	22	10	18	41	2	61	5	.967
McDonald, John, Cle.	21	14	31	42	2	75	10	.973
McLemore, Mark, Sea.	1	0	0	1	0	1	0	1.000
Menechino, Frank, Oak.	2	0	2	1	0	3	1	1.000
Merloni, Lou, Bos.	5	1	2	4	1	7	1	.857
Mora, Melvin, Bal.	41	36	57	108	7	172	17	.959
Moriarty, Mike, Bal.	4	1	2	6	0	8	0	1.000
Nieves, Jose, Ana.	13	6	11	20	2	33	4	.939
Ordaz, Luis, K.C.	2	2	4	5	0	9	2	1.000
Perez, Neifi, K.C.	139	137	251	400	19	670	107	.972
Relaford, Desi, Sea.	40	34	46	87	5	138	24	.964
Rodriguez, Alex, Tex.	162	160	259	472	10	741	108	.987
Rogers, Eddie, Bal.	4	0	2	5	0	7	1	1.000
Sadler, Donnie, K.C.-Tex.	16	2	5	7	1	13	1	.923
Salazar, Oscar, Det.	1	0	1	1	0	2	0	1.000
Sanchez, Freddy, Bos.	5	1	5	3	0	8	1	1.000
Sanchez, Rey, Bos.	10	7	9	26	1	36	3	.972
Santiago, Ramon, Det.	63	63	97	205	7	309	41	.977
Sheets, Andy, TB.	11	10	19	34	0	53	9	1.000
Smith, Jason, TB.	9	7	15	17	5	37	4	.865
Tejada, Miguel, Oak.	162	161	229	504	19	752	106	.975
Ugueto, Luis, Sea.	8	1	1	10	2	13	4	.846
Valentin, Jose, Chi.	50	47	81	124	8	213	38	.962
Vizquel, Omar, Cle.	150	148	239	431	7	677	98	.990
Wilson, Enrique, N.Y.	14	4	11	21	2	34	5	.941
Woodward, Chris, Tor.	79	77	131	231	13	375	63	.965
Young, Michael, Tex.	11	1	2	10	0	12	2	1.000

TRIPLE PLAYS: Gomez, T.B.; Rodriguez, Tex.

SHORTSTOPS WITH TWO OR MORE TEAMS

Player, Team	G	GS	PO	A	E	TC	DP	Pct.
Sadler, Donnie, K.C.	4	1	2	2	1	5	0	.800
Sadler, Donnie, Tex.	12	1	3	5	0	8	1	1.000

OUTFIELDERS

Player, Team	G	GS	PO	A	E	TC	DP	Pct.
Agbayani, Benny, Bos.	13	9	24	1	1	26	0	.962
Alicea, Luis, K.C.	1	0	0	0	0	0	0	.000
Allen, Chad, Cle.	4	3	4	0	0	4	0	1.000
Anderson, Brady, Cle.*	29	21	52	0	1	53	0	.981
Anderson, Garret, Ana.*	147	147	302	7	2	311	3	.994
Andrews, Shane, Bos.	1	0	0	0	0	0	0	.000
Aven, Bruce, Cle.	7	6	12	0	0	12	0	1.000
Beltran, Carlos, K.C.	149	149	398	12	7	417	0	.983
Berg, Dave, Tor.	13	10	20	0	0	20	0	1.000
Berger, Brandon, K.C.	36	27	60	4	0	64	1	1.000
Bigbie, Larry, Bal.*	12	7	19	0	0	19	0	1.000
Bloomquist, Willie, Sea.	7	6	12	0	0	12	0	1.000
Bocachica, Hiram, Det.	32	19	54	3	2	59	0	.966
Borchard, Joe, Chi.	15	9	21	0	0	21	0	1.000
Bradley, Milton, Cle.	94	86	214	9	4	227	2	.982
Branyan, Russell, Cle.	42	39	66	4	1	71	1	.986
Broussard, Ben, Cle.*	32	29	47	1	2	50	0	.960
Brown, Dee, K.C.	8	8	12	0	1	13	0	.923
Buchanan, Brian, Min.	24	20	48	0	0	48	0	1.000
Burks, Ellis, Cle.	6	6	6	0	0	6	0	1.000
Byrnes, Eric, Oak.	79	19	53	1	1	55	0	.982
Cabrera, Jolbert, Cle.	34	17	42	0	0	42	0	1.000
Cameron, Mike, Sea.	155	146	415	6	5	426	0	.988
Catalanotto, Frank, Tex.	26	19	34	0	1	35	0	.971
Chavez, Eric, Oak.	1	0	0	0	0	0	0	.000
Clark, Howie, Bal.	4	4	10	0	0	10	0	1.000
Colangelo, Mike, Oak.	19	5	17	0	0	17	0	1.000
Conine, Jeff, Bal.	6	6	8	0	0	8	0	1.000
Conti, Jason, TB.	74	59	163	8	6	177	1	.966
Cordero, Wil, Cle.	4	4	8	2	0	10	1	1.000
Cordova, Marty, Bal.	72	72	132	2	4	138	1	.971
Crawford, Carl, TB.*	63	63	160	5	1	166	1	.994
Crisp, Coco, Cle.	32	31	82	1	1	84	1	.988
Cruz, Jacob, Det.*	12	10	13	0	1	14	0	.929
Cruz, Jose, Tor.	119	118	255	9	2	266	2	.992
Cuddyer, Michael, Min.	25	20	47	1	1	49	0	.980
Damon, Johnny, Bos.*	151	150	352	7	1	360	2	.997
Daubach, Brian, Bos.	48	39	64	3	0	67	0	1.000
DaVanon, Jeff, Ana.	10	4	13	0	0	13	0	1.000
Dunwoody, Todd, Cle.*	2	2	1	0	0	1	0	1.000
Dye, Jermaine, Oak.	111	109	171	2	5	178	1	.972
Erstad, Darin, Ana.*	143	142	452	11	1	464	3	.998
Everett, Carl, Tex.	83	80	157	0	5	162	0	.969
Fick, Robert, Det.	140	139	288	21	12	321	5	.963
Floyd, Cliff, Bos.	26	25	41	1	1	43	1	.977
Garcia, Karim, N.Y.-Cle.*	53	50	99	2	1	102	0	.990
Garcia, Luis, Bal.	2	0	1	0	0	1	0	1.000
Giambi, Jeremy, Oak.*	40	40	63	0	1	64	0	.984
Gibbons, Jay, Bal.*	92	91	174	6	1	181	2	.994
Gipson, Charles, Sea.	73	17	65	2	2	69	1	.971
Gomez, Alexis, K.C.*	2	2	4	1	0	5	1	1.000
Gonzalez, Juan, Tex.	62	61	117	9	1	127	1	.992
Grabowski, Jason, Oak.	4	3	6	0	0	6	0	1.000
Greene, Todd, Tex.	1	1	0	0	0	0	0	.000
Greer, Rusty, Tex.*	26	24	36	0	2	38	0	.947
Grieve, Ben, TB.	118	117	249	6	3	258	2	.988
Guiel, Aaron, K.C.	61	53	114	5	6	125	1	.952
Halter, Shane, Det.	8	6	15	2	0	17	1	1.000
Harris, Willie, Chi.	6	4	19	1	0	20	0	1.000
Hart, Jason, Tex.	7	4	9	0	0	9	0	1.000
Henderson, Rickey, Bos.*	54	45	83	4	5	92	0	.946
Higginson, Bobby, Det.	117	116	241	15	7	263	3	.973
Hocking, Denny, Min.	5	0	4	0	0	4	0	1.000
Hollandsworth, Todd, Tex.* ..	38	33	64	0	0	64	0	1.000
Hunter, Torii, Min.	146	144	365	7	3	375	0	.992
Ibanez, Raul, K.C.	55	47	88	3	1	92	0	.989
Jackson, Damian, Det.	6	4	8	0	1	9	0	.889
Jackson, Ryan, Det.*	3	1	2	0	0	2	0	1.000
Johnson, Nick, N.Y.*	2	1	2	0	0	2	0	1.000
Jones, Jacque, Min.*	143	134	330	11	5	346	1	.986
Justice, David, Oak.*	75	72	125	3	2	130	0	.985
Kapler, Gabe, Tex.	64	48	119	7	3	129	0	.977
Kennedy, Adam, Ana.	1	0	0	0	0	0	0	.000
Kielty, Bobby, Min.	82	63	159	4	0	163	0	1.000
Kingsale, Gene, Sea.	2	1	4	0	0	4	0	1.000
Knoblauch, Chuck, K.C.	74	73	145	5	3	153	0	.980
Lamb, Mike, Tex.	16	5	11	0	1	12	0	.917
Lawton, Matt, Cle.	108	107	229	6	6	241	2	.975
Lee, Carlos, Chi.	137	134	249	8	1	258	1	.996
Leon, Jose, Bal.	2	2	4	0	1	5	0	.800
Lesher, Brian, Tor.*	5	3	11	0	0	11	0	1.000
Liefer, Jeff, Chi.	36	31	54	1	0	55	0	1.000
Lofton, Kenny, Chi.*	92	86	229	3	0	232	0	1.000
Lombard, George, Det.	69	65	158	2	3	163	0	.982
Long, Terrence, Oak.*	162	158	382	5	8	395	1	.980
Ludwick, Ryan, Tex.*	22	21	41	0	0	41	0	1.000
Mabry, John, Oak.	53	43	87	1	2	90	0	.978
Macias, Jose, Det.	10	8	24	0	0	24	0	1.000
Magee, Wendell, Det.	91	84	262	6	5	273	1	.982
Magruder, Chris, Cle.	83	63	146	2	2	150	0	.987
Matos, Luis, Bal.	14	8	17	0	0	17	0	1.000
Matthews Jr., Gary, Bal.	100	88	179	6	6	191	1	.969
McCarty, Dave, TB.*	11	9	20	1	0	21	0	1.000
McDonald, Donzell, K.C.	7	6	3	0	0	3	0	1.000
McLemore, Mark, Sea.	88	79	172	2	5	179	0	.972
Mench, Kevin, Tex.	106	96	193	7	2	202	0	.990
Merloni, Lou, Bos.	2	0	0	0	0	0	0	.000
Mohr, Dustan, Min.	113	98	239	4	2	245	2	.992
Mondesi, Raul, Tor.-N.Y.	132	132	240	7	6	253	1	.976
Monroe, Craig, Det.	9	6	18	1	1	20	0	.950
Mora, Melvin, Bal.	104	97	251	9	3	263	5	.989
Murray, Calvin, Tex.	34	24	69	2	0	71	1	1.000
Nelson, Bry, Bos.	11	3	14	1	0	15	0	1.000
Nieves, Jose, Ana.	2	0	1	0	1	2	0	.500
Nixon, Trot, Bos.*	152	145	293	7	5	305	3	.984
Ochoa, Alex, Ana.	36	15	37	2	1	40	1	.975
Offerman, Jose, Bos.-Sea. ...	8	6	10	0	1	11	0	.909
Ordonez, Magglio, Chi.	150	149	282	8	4	294	0	.986
Palmeiro, Orlando, Ana.*	86	62	146	3	1	150	1	.993
Paquette, Craig, Det.	8	6	15	0	0	15	0	1.000
Paul, Josh, Chi.	1	1	3	0	0	3	0	1.000
Perry, Herbert, Tex.	1	0	0	0	0	0	0	.000
Piatt, Adam, Oak.	50	35	66	1	0	67	0	1.000
Podsednik, Scott, Sea.*	11	3	15	0	1	16	0	.938
Quinn, Mark, K.C.	15	15	25	0	0	25	0	1.000
Ramirez, Julio, Ana.	23	7	26	1	0	27	0	1.000
Ramirez, Manny, Bos.	68	68	110	6	5	121	1	.959
Relaford, Desi, Sea.	35	18	41	3	2	46	0	.957

Player, Team	G	GS	PO	A	E	TC	DP	Pct.
Restovich, Michael, Min.	5	2	7	0	0	7	0	1.000
Rivera, Juan, N.Y.	28	25	54	2	2	58	1	.966
Rivera, Ruben, Tex.	67	56	167	2	3	172	1	.983
Rolls, Damian, TB.	21	21	53	1	3	57	1	.947
Romano, Jason, Tex.	18	10	32	0	0	32	0	1.000
Rowand, Aaron, Chi.	120	72	224	5	4	233	3	.983
Ryan, Michael, Min.	5	2	3	0	0	3	0	1.000
Sadler, Donnie, K.C.-Tex.	33	13	40	1	1	42	0	.976
Salmon, Tim, Ana.	111	109	201	4	3	208	0	.986
Selby, Bill, Cle.	18	7	15	0	0	15	0	1.000
Sierra, Ruben, Sea.	60	54	91	1	2	94	0	.979
Singleton, Chris, Bal.*	126	111	274	3	4	281	0	.986
Smith, Bobby, TB.	2	2	3	1	0	4	0	1.000
Snelling, Chris, Sea.*	8	8	16	0	0	16	0	1.000
Spencer, Shane, N.Y.	91	76	152	5	4	161	1	.975
Spiezio, Scott, Ana.	10	0	3	0	0	3	0	1.000
Stevens, Lee, Cle.*	16	15	32	1	0	33	0	1.000
Stewart, Shannon, Tor.	99	99	190	3	2	195	1	.990
Sutton, Larry, Oak.*	3	2	5	1	0	6	0	1.000
Suzuki, Ichiro, Sea.	152	149	333	8	3	344	0	.991
Swann, Pedro, Tor.	1	0	0	0	0	0	0	.000
Thames, Marcus, N.Y.	7	2	7	0	0	7	0	1.000
Torres, Andres, Det.	19	18	51	0	1	52	0	.981
Tucker, Michael, K.C.	108	97	224	9	2	235	1	.991
Tyner, Jason, TB.*	42	40	98	2	1	101	0	.990
Vander Wal, John, N.Y.*	57	52	87	0	2	89	0	.978
Vaughn, Greg, TB.	31	30	75	2	1	78	0	.987
Wells, Vernon, Tor.	159	152	381	10	3	394	1	.992
Werth, Jayson, Tor.	15	13	33	1	0	34	0	1.000
WHITE, Rondell, N.Y.	113	106	246	3	0	249	0	1.000
Williams, Bernie, N.Y.	147	147	350	2	5	357	1	.986
Williams, Gerald, N.Y.	30	2	12	1	0	13	1	1.000
Wilson, Enrique, N.Y.	1	1	0	0	0	0	0	.000
Winn, Randy, TB.	146	142	394	13	3	410	3	.993
Wise, Dewayne, Tor.*	33	28	79	5	0	84	3	1.000
Young, Dmitri, Det.	1	1	1	0	0	1	0	1.000

OUTFIELDERS WITH TWO OR MORE TEAMS

Player, Team	G	GS	PO	A	E	TC	DP	Pct.
Garcia, Karim, N.Y.*	2	1	1	0	0	1	0	1.000
Garcia, Karim, Cle.*	51	49	98	2	1	101	0	.990
Mondesi, Raul, Tor.	62	62	119	3	2	124	1	.984
Mondesi, Raul, N.Y.	70	70	121	4	4	129	0	.969
Offerman, Jose, Bos.	2	2	2	0	1	3	0	.667
Offerman, Jose, Sea.	6	4	8	0	0	8	0	1.000
Sadler, Donnie, K.C.	15	9	22	0	1	23	0	.957
Sadler, Donnie, Tex.	18	4	18	1	0	19	0	1.000

CATCHERS

Player, Team	G	GS	PO	A	E	TC	DP	PB	Pct.
Alomar Jr., Sandy, Chi.	50	46	293	14	2	309	3	2	.994
Bard, Josh, Cle.	24	24	153	13	2	168	4	2	.988
Borders, Pat, Sea.	2	0	2	0	0	2	0	0	1.000
Brito, Juan, K.C.	9	8	42	3	1	46	1	1	.978
Brown, Kevin L., Bos.	2	0	1	0	0	1	0	0	1.000
Casanova, Raul, Bal.	2	0	3	0	0	3	0	0	1.000
Cash, Kevin, Tor.	7	4	26	4	1	31	1	2	.968
Castillo, Alberto, N.Y.	14	12	93	9	1	103	0	2	.990
Davis, Ben, Sea.	77	55	416	23	1	440	5	5	.998
Diaz, Einar, Cle.	100	97	640	75	8	723	4	8	.989
Fabregas, Jorge, Ana.	32	23	156	8	1	165	1	1	.994
Fasano, Sal, Ana.	2	0	10	2	0	12	0	0	1.000
Flaherty, John, TB.	75	74	450	33	4	487	8	7	.992
Fletcher, Darrin, Tor.	36	29	181	12	1	194	1	0	.995
Fordyce, Brook, Bal.	55	39	267	8	4	279	1	3	.986
Gil, Geronimo, Bal.	125	122	740	60	4	804	14	19	.995
Greene, Todd, Tex.	15	11	87	7	1	95	2	2	.989
Hall, Toby, TB.	83	83	506	34	6	546	5	4	.989
Haselman, Bill, Tex.	67	49	310	19	3	332	0	2	.991
Hernandez, Ramon, Oak.	135	125	788	58	7	853	12	6	.992
Hinch, A.J., K.C.	68	60	349	23	4	376	2	2	.989
Hoover, Paul, TB.	4	4	16	2	0	18	0	2	1.000
Huckaby, Ken, Tor.	88	77	494	31	6	531	10	13	.989
Inge, Brandon, Det.	94	94	484	46	1	531	3	10	.998
Johnson, Mark, Chi.	85	80	484	27	3	514	3	3	.994
Lamb, Mike, Tex.	3	1	10	1	0	11	0	1	1.000
LeCroy, Matthew, Min.	6	3	20	1	0	21	0	2	1.000
Lunar, Fernando, Bal.	2	0	2	0	0	2	0	0	1.000
Martinez, Victor, Cle.	9	7	55	2	1	58	0	1	.983
Mayne, Brent, K.C.	99	94	552	39	4	595	4	5	.993
McKay, Cody, Oak.	1	1	6	0	0	6	0	0	1.000
Meluskey, Mitch, Det.	8	8	34	3	0	37	0	1	1.000
Mirabelli, Doug, Bos.	50	41	285	30	0	315	3	10	1.000
MOLINA, Bengie, Ana.	121	114	707	60	1	768	6	5	.999
Molina, Izzy, Bal.	1	1	7	1	0	8	0	0	1.000
Molina, Jose, Ana.	29	24	154	16	3	173	3	1	.983
Myers, Greg, Oak.	53	36	264	21	1	286	0	3	.997
Olivo, Miguel, Chi.	6	6	31	1	0	32	0	2	1.000
Ortiz, Hector, Tex.	7	4	22	0	1	23	0	0	.957
Paul, Josh, Chi.	32	30	200	6	2	208	1	2	.990
Perez, Eddie, Cle.	42	34	235	19	3	257	7	4	.988
Pierzynski, A.J., Min.	124	118	757	41	3	801	3	2	.996
Posada, Jorge, N.Y.	138	131	965	66	12	1043	5	7	.988
Prince, Tom, Min.	50	40	272	14	1	287	2	1	.997
Rivera, Michael, Det.	37	35	189	19	2	210	1	10	.990
Rodriguez, Ivan, Tex.	100	97	632	45	7	684	6	6	.990
Valentin, Javier, Min.	4	0	14	1	0	15	0	0	1.000
Varitek, Jason, Bos.	127	121	912	54	4	970	8	10	.996
Walbeck, Matt, Det.	27	24	127	8	1	136	2	2	.993
Wathan, Dusty, K.C.	3	1	14	0	0	14	0	0	1.000
Widger, Chris, N.Y.	21	18	111	6	2	119	1	1	.983
Wilson, Dan, Sea.	113	107	692	27	2	721	4	2	.997
Wilson, Tom, Tor.	65	52	318	20	4	342	4	3	.988
Wooten, Shawn, Ana.	2	1	2	1	0	3	0	0	1.000

TRIPLE PLAY: Haselman, Tex.

CATCHERS—SPECIAL STATS*

Player, Team	G	Inn.	SBA	CCS	PCS	CS%	ER	CERA
Alomar Jr., Sandy, Chi.	50	404.0	46	9	1	.20	197	4.39
Bard, Josh, Cle.	24	209.1	16	7	0	.44	117	5.03
Borders, Pat, Sea.	2	4.0	0	0	0	0	2	4.50
Brito, Juan, K.C.	9	63.0	11	1	3	.13	34	4.86
Brown, Kevin L., Bos.	2	3.0	0	0	0	0	0	0.00
Casanova, Raul, Bal.	2	2.0	0	0	0	0	4	18.00
Cash, Kevin, Tor.	7	38.0	4	1	0	.25	24	5.68
Castillo, Alberto, N.Y.	14	104.0	13	4	1	.33	45	3.89
Davis, Ben, Sea.	77	538.2	41	12	6	.34	239	3.99
Diaz, Einar, Cle.	100	833.1	118	31	5	.27	479	5.17
Fabregas, Jorge, Ana.	32	214.0	23	5	0	.22	113	4.75
Fasano, Sal, Ana.	2	7.0	3	2	0	.67	5	6.43
Flaherty, John, T.B.	75	669.0	74	20	6	.29	338	4.55
Fletcher, Darrin, Tor.	36	253.2	30	5	2	.18	157	5.57
Fordyce, Brook, Bal.	55	369.0	49	6	2	.13	199	4.85
Gil, Geronimo, Bal.	125	1068.2	96	32	3	.34	507	4.27
Greene, Todd, Tex.	15	104.2	15	2	1	.14	71	6.11
Hall, Toby, T.B.	83	737.1	64	18	6	.31	484	5.91
Haselman, Bill, Tex.	67	453.2	43	8	2	.20	255	5.06
Hernandez, Ramon, Oak.	135	1100.2	75	21	9	.32	429	3.51
Hinch, A.J., K.C.	68	527.1	48	7	2	.15	311	5.31
Hoover, Paul, T.B.	4	34.0	7	2	1	.33	24	6.35
Huckaby, Ken, Tor.	88	683.0	57	18	2	.33	325	4.28
Inge, Brandon, Det.	94	820.1	61	13	4	.23	432	4.74
Johnson, Mark L., Chi.	85	707.1	66	16	8	.28	344	4.38
Lamb, Mike, Tex.	3	7.0	3	0	0	0	7	9.00
LeCroy, Matthew, Min.	6	27.0	0	0	0	0	18	6.00
Lunar, Fernando, Bal.	2	2.0	0	0	0	0	0	0.00
Martinez, Victor, Cle.	9	69.0	13	2	0	.15	28	3.65
Mayne, Brent, K.C.	99	836.2	66	21	2	.33	483	5.20
McKay, Cody, Oak.	1	8.0	0	0	0	0	8	9.00
Meluskey, Mitch, Det.	8	71.1	5	2	1	.50	52	6.56
Mirabelli, Doug, Bos.	50	378.1	56	18	1	.33	159	3.78
Molina, Bengie, Ana.	121	1014.1	78	32	3	.43	404	3.58
Molina, Izzy, Bal.	1	9.0	2	0	1	0	9	9.00
Molina, Jose, Ana.	29	210.0	24	9	0	.38	70	3.00
Myers, Greg, Oak.	53	343.1	39	10	6	.30	156	4.09
Olivo, Miguel, Chi.	6	48.1	2	1	0	.50	22	4.10
Ortiz, Hector, Tex.	7	38.0	0	0	0	0	8	1.89
Paul, Josh, Chi.	32	263.1	23	2	1	.09	153	5.23
Perez, Eddie, Cle.	42	313.0	38	14	0	.37	153	4.40
Pierzynski, A.J., Min.	124	1035.2	64	15	4	.25	472	4.10
Posada, Jorge, N.Y.	138	1190.2	107	23	8	.23	499	3.77
Prince, Tom, Min.	50	371.0	20	8	0	.40	166	4.03
Rivera, Michael, Det.	37	303.0	32	10	2	.33	185	5.50
Rodriguez, Ivan, Tex.	100	836.1	41	13	2	.33	483	5.20
Valentin, Javier, Min.	4	11.0	0	0	0	0	6	4.91
Varitek, Jason, Bos.	127	1064.2	112	29	2	.26	444	3.75
Walbeck, Matt, Det.	27	219.1	8	2	0	.25	105	4.31
Wathan, Dusty, K.C.	3	14.0	1	0	0	0	6	3.86
Widger, Chris, N.Y.	21	157.1	11	3	0	.27	81	4.63
Wilson, Dan, Sea.	113	902.2	60	14	3	.25	413	4.12
Wilson, Tom, Tor.	65	463.2	57	11	2	.20	261	5.07
Wooten, Shawn, Ana.	2	7.0	1	0	0	0	3	3.86

*Inn. denotes the number of innings the catcher was behind the plate. SBA denotes stolen bases attempted. CCS denotes number of runners caught stealing by the catcher. PCS denotes number of runners caught stealing by the pitcher. CS% denotes the catcher's caught stealing percentage, figured by subtracting PCS from SBA and dividing this number into CCS. ER denotes number of earned runs scored when catcher was behind plate. CERA denotes catcher's ERA when he was behind the plate, figured the same way a pitcher's ERA is computed (ER*9/IP).

PITCHERS

Player, Team	G	GS	PO	A	E	TC	DP	Pct.
Abbott, Paul, Sea.	7	5	2	6	0	8	0	1.000
Acevedo, Juan, Det.	65	0	4	11	1	16	0	.938
Affeldt, Jeremy, K.C.*	34	7	4	14	2	20	1	.900
Alvarez, Juan, Tex.*	52	0	5	4	0	9	1	1.000
Alvarez, Wilson, TB.*	23	10	2	6	0	8	0	1.000
Anderson, Matt, Det.	12	0	1	1	0	2	1	1.000
Appier, Kevin, Ana.	32	32	18	14	0	32	0	1.000
Arrojo, Rolando, Bos.	29	8	13	6	2	21	2	.905
Asencio, Miguel, K.C.	31	21	14	11	1	26	1	.962
Austin, Jeff, K.C.	10	0	0	0	0	0	0	.000
Backe, Brandon, TB.	9	0	0	0	0	0	0	.000
Baez, Danys, Cle.	39	26	12	17	2	31	1	.935
Bailey, Cory, K.C.	37	0	7	7	0	14	0	1.000
Baldwin, James, Sea.	30	23	9	25	0	34	2	1.000
Banks, Willie, Bos.	29	0	3	8	1	12	0	.917
Barcelo, Lorenzo, Chi.	4	0	0	3	0	3	1	1.000
Bauer, Rick, Bal.	56	1	1	15	0	16	2	1.000
Bechler, Steve, Bal.	3	0	1	0	0	1	0	1.000
Bedard, Erik, Bal.*	2	0	0	0	0	0	0	.000
Bell, Rob, Tex.	17	15	18	13	1	32	0	.969
Benoit, Joaquin, Tex..	17	13	4	4	0	8	1	1.000
Bernero, Adam, Det.	28	11	4	10	1	15	1	.933
Beverlin, Jason, Cle.-Det.	7	3	0	0	0	0	0	.000
Biddle, Rocky, Chi.	44	7	8	8	0	16	0	1.000
Borbon, Pedro, Tor.*	16	0	3	2	0	5	0	1.000
Bowie, Micah, Oak.*	13	0	1	2	0	3	0	1.000
Bowles, Brian, Tor.	17	0	1	3	0	4	0	1.000
Bradford, Chad, Oak.	75	0	10	10	1	21	1	.952
Brazelton, Dewon, TB.	2	2	1	1	0	2	0	1.000
Brock, Chris, Bal.	22	0	2	6	1	9	2	.889
Buehrle, Mark, Chi.*	34	34	6	46	2	54	2	.963
Bukvich, Ryan, K.C.	26	0	2	4	3	9	0	.667
Burba, Dave, Tex.-Cle.	35	21	10	10	1	21	2	.952
Burkett, John, Bos.	29	29	8	11	1	20	0	.950
Byrd, Paul, K.C.	33	33	18	15	1	34	1	.971
Callaway, Mickey, Ana.	6	6	4	4	2	10	1	.800
Carpenter, Chris, Tor.	13	13	7	3	0	10	0	1.000
Carter, Lance, TB.	8	0	1	3	0	4	1	1.000
Cassidy, Scott, Tor.	58	0	0	8	1	9	0	.889
Castillo, Frank, Bos.	36	23	10	18	0	28	0	1.000
Choate, Randy, N.Y.*	18	0	1	2	0	3	0	1.000
Clemens, Roger, N.Y.	29	29	12	17	0	29	0	1.000
Coco, Pasqual, Tor.	2	0	0	0	0	0	0	.000
Colome, Jesus, TB.	32	0	4	8	0	12	0	1.000
Colon, Bartolo, Cle.	16	16	7	17	2	26	3	.923
Cook, Dennis, Ana.*	37	0	2	0	1	3	0	.667
Cooper, Brian, Tor.	2	2	2	0	0	2	0	1.000
Cordero, Francisco, Tex.	39	0	5	5	0	10	0	1.000
Cornejo, Nate, Det.	9	9	1	8	0	9	0	1.000
Creek, Doug, TB.-Sea.*	52	0	3	5	0	8	0	1.000
Cressend, Jack, Min.	23	0	2	3	0	5	0	1.000
Davis, Doug, Tex.*	10	10	3	6	1	10	0	.900
Davis, Jason, Cle.	3	2	2	4	0	6	0	1.000
de los Santos, Luis, TB.	3	3	2	2	1	5	0	.800
DePaula, Sean, Cle.	5	0	2	0	0	2	0	1.000
Donnelly, Brendan, Ana.	46	0	3	8	0	6	0	1.000
Douglass, Sean, Bal.	15	8	3	8	0	11	2	1.000
Drese, Ryan, Cle.	26	26	11	25	2	38	2	.947
Driskill, Travis, Bal.	29	19	7	13	0	20	1	1.000
DuBose, Eric, Bal.*	4	0	0	1	0	1	0	1.000
Durbin, Chad, K.C.	2	2	1	1	1	3	0	.667
Eckenstahler, Eric, Det.*	7	0	1	0	0	1	0	1.000
Elder, Dave, Cle.	15	0	3	1	0	4	0	1.000
Embree, Alan, Bos.*	32	0	1	5	0	6	0	1.000
Erickson, Scott, Bal.	29	28	14	22	3	39	2	.923
Eyre, Scott, Tor.*	49	3	3	9	0	12	0	1.000
Farnsworth, Jeff, Det.	44	0	6	8	2	16	0	.875
Field, Nate, K.C.	5	0	1	0	0	1	0	1.000
File, Bob, Tor.	5	0	0	0	0	0	0	.000
Finley, Chuck, Cle.*	18	18	3	16	3	22	2	.864
Fiore, Tony, Min.	48	2	4	14	0	18	1	1.000
Fitzgerald, Brian, Sea.*	6	0	0	1	1	2	0	.500
Flores, Randy, Tex.*	20	0	0	4	0	4	1	1.000
Fossum, Casey, Bos.*	43	12	8	5	0	13	2	1.000
Foulke, Keith, Chi.	65	0	6	6	0	12	1	1.000
Franklin, Ryan, Sea.	41	12	9	13	1	23	0	.957
Frederick, Kevin, Min.	8	0	3	0	0	3	0	1.000
Fyhrie, Mike, Oak.	16	4	4	6	0	10	1	1.000
Garces, Rich, Bos.	26	0	0	5	0	5	0	1.000
Garcia, Freddy, Sea.	34	34	12	30	3	45	2	.933
Garcia, Reynaldo, Tex.	3	0	0	0	0	0	0	.000
Gardner, Lee, TB.	12	0	0	3	1	4	0	.750
Garland, Jon, Chi.	33	33	10	21	0	31	3	1.000
George, Chris, K.C.*	6	6	2	8	0	10	1	1.000
German, Franklyn, Det.	7	0	1	1	0	2	0	1.000
Ginter, Matt, Chi.	33	0	4	2	0	6	1	1.000
Glover, Gary, Chi.	41	22	10	19	0	29	0	1.000
Gomes, Wayne, Bos.	20	0	0	0	1	1	0	.000
Greisinger, Seth, Det.	8	8	2	6	0	8	0	1.000
Grimsley, Jason, K.C.	70	0	6	10	1	17	1	.941
Groom, Buddy, Bal.*	70	0	3	4	0	7	0	1.000
Guardado, Eddie, Min.*	68	0	2	8	0	10	0	1.000
Halama, John, Sea.*	31	10	8	20	2	30	1	.933
Halladay, Roy, Tor.	34	34	22	41	2	65	1	.969
Hancock, Josh, Bos.	3	1	0	0	0	0	0	.000
Haney, Chris, Bos.*	24	0	3	3	0	6	0	1.000
Harang, Aaron, Oak.	16	15	6	7	1	14	0	.929
Harper, Travis, TB.	37	7	1	5	1	7	0	.857
Hasegawa, Shigetoshi, Sea..	53	0	5	10	0	15	3	1.000
Hawkins, LaTroy, Min.	65	0	4	12	0	16	1	1.000
Hendrickson, Mark, Tor.*	16	4	0	5	0	5	0	1.000
Henriquez, Oscar, Det.	30	0	0	2	0	2	0	1.000
Hentgen, Pat, Bal.	4	4	4	2	0	6	0	1.000
Heredia, Felix, Tor.*	53	0	3	9	0	12	2	1.000
Hermanson, Dustin, Bos.	12	1	4	0	0	4	0	1.000
Hernandez, Adrian, N.Y.	2	1	0	0	0	0	0	.000
Hernandez, Orlando, N.Y.	24	22	8	22	0	30	0	1.000
Hernandez, Roberto, N.Y.	53	0	6	4	1	11	1	.909
Hernandez, Runelvys, K.C.	12	12	9	12	0	21	1	1.000
Herrera, Alex, Cle.*	5	0	0	0	0	0	0	.000
Hiljus, Erik, Oak.	9	9	3	5	1	9	0	.889
Hill, Jeremy, K.C.	10	0	1	1	0	2	0	1.000
Hitchcock, Sterling, N.Y.*	20	2	1	5	0	6	0	1.000
Holtz, Mike, Oak.*	16	0	1	2	0	3	0	1.000
Howry, Bob, Chi.-Bos.	67	0	3	9	1	13	1	.923
HUDSON, Tim, Oak.	34	34	26	27	0	53	2	1.000
Irabu, Hideki, Tex.	38	2	2	9	0	11	1	1.000
Jackson, Mike, Min.	58	0	2	10	0	12	1	1.000
James, Delvin, TB.	8	6	1	2	0	3	0	1.000
Jimenez, Jason, TB.-Det.*	6	0	0	0	0	0	0	.000
Johnson, Jason, Bal.	22	22	8	12	0	20	4	1.000
Julio, Jorge, Bal.	67	0	5	5	0	10	0	1.000
Karsay, Steve, N.Y.	78	0	6	15	0	21	1	1.000
Kaye, Justin, Sea.	3	0	1	0	0	1	0	1.000
Keller, Kris, Det.	1	0	0	0	0	0	0	.000
Kennedy, Joe, TB.*	30	30	10	21	10	41	2	.756
Kent, Steve, TB.*	34	0	2	7	2	11	2	.818
Kershner, Jason, Tor.*	10	0	0	1	0	1	0	1.000
Kim, Sun-Woo, Bos.	15	2	1	2	0	3	0	1.000
Kinney, Matt, Min.	14	12	5	6	0	11	1	1.000
Knight, Brandon, N.Y.	7	0	1	0	0	1	0	1.000
Koch, Billy, Oak.	84	0	14	12	0	26	2	1.000
Kolb, Danny, Tex.	34	0	2	6	0	8	0	1.000
Kozlowski, Ben, Tex.*	2	2	0	2	0	2	0	1.000
Lackey, John, Ana.	18	18	4	16	0	20	2	1.000
Lee, Cliff, Cle.*	2	2	1	2	0	3	0	1.000
Levine, Al, Ana.	52	0	2	12	0	14	0	1.000
Lewis, Colby, Tex.	15	4	5	7	0	12	2	1.000
Lidle, Cory, Oak.	31	30	15	42	2	59	5	.966
Lilly, Ted, N.Y.-Oak.*	22	16	4	12	0	16	0	1.000
Lima, Jose, Det.	20	12	4	5	0	9	0	1.000
Loaiza, Esteban, Tor.	25	25	12	22	1	35	1	.971
Lohse, Kyle, Min.	32	31	10	18	0	28	0	1.000
Lopez, Rodrigo, Bal.	33	28	6	25	1	32	2	.969
Loux, Shane, Det.	3	3	1	3	0	4	0	1.000
Lowe, Derek, Bos.	32	32	18	31	0	49	2	1.000
Lukasiewicz, Mark, Ana.*	17	0	1	0	1	2	0	.500
Lyon, Brandon, Tor.	15	10	5	12	1	18	1	.944
MacDougal, Mike, K.C.	6	0	1	0	0	1	0	1.000
Maduro, Calvin, Bal.	12	10	7	4	0	11	0	1.000
Magnante, Mike, Oak.*	32	0	3	4	0	7	0	1.000
Maroth, Mike, Det.*	21	21	5	13	0	18	1	1.000

2002 A.L. STATISTICS Fielding

Player, Team	G	GS	PO	A	E	TC	DP	Pct.
Marte, Damaso, Chi.*	68	0	0	10	0	10	1	1.000
Martin, Tom, TB.*	2	0	0	0	0	0	0	.000
Martinez, Pedro, Bos.	30	30	16	16	2	34	1	.941
Mateo, Julio, Sea.	12	0	0	1	0	1	0	1.000
Maurer, Dave, Cle.*	2	0	0	0	0	0	0	.000
May, Darrell, K.C.*	30	21	13	14	2	29	1	.931
Mays, Joe, Min.	17	17	8	13	2	23	4	.913
Mecir, Jim, Oak.	61	0	7	15	0	22	0	1.000
Mendoza, Ramiro, N.Y.	62	0	7	22	1	30	0	.967
Miceli, Dan, Tex.	9	0	0	1	0	1	0	1.000
Michalak, Chris, Tex.*	13	0	0	4	0	4	0	1.000
Miller, Justin, Tor.	25	18	8	10	0	18	0	1.000
Miller, Matt, Det.*	2	0	0	0	0	0	0	.000
Miller, Travis, Min.*	5	0	0	0	0	0	0	.000
Milton, Eric, Min.*	29	29	5	12	1	18	1	.944
Moehler, Brian, Det.	3	3	0	1	0	1	0	1.000
Moyer, Jamie, Sea.*	34	34	22	34	1	57	5	.982
Mulder, Mark, Oak.*	30	30	10	36	0	46	3	1.000
Mulholland, Terry, Cle.*	16	3	8	4	1	13	1	.923
Mullen, Scott, K.C.*	44	0	1	3	2	6	1	.667
Murray, Heath, Cle.*	9	0	0	3	0	3	0	1.000
Mussina, Mike, N.Y.	33	33	16	32	1	49	3	.980
Myette, Aaron, Tex.	15	12	3	2	1	6	0	.833
Nagy, Charles, Cle.	19	7	2	4	0	6	0	1.000
Nelson, Jeff, Sea.	41	0	2	4	0	6	0	1.000
Nitkowski, C.J., Tex.*	12	0	0	2	0	2	0	1.000
Obermueller, Wes, K.C.	2	2	0	0	0	0	0	.000
Oliver, Darren, Bos.*	14	9	2	6	0	8	0	1.000
Ortiz, Ramon, Ana.	32	32	8	19	4	31	1	.871
Osuna, Antonio, Chi.	59	0	7	10	0	17	2	1.000
Paniagua, Jose, Det.	41	0	1	5	0	6	0	1.000
Park, Chan Ho, Tex.	25	25	12	15	1	28	3	.964
Paronto, Chad, Cle.	29	0	2	5	0	7	1	1.000
Parque, Jim, Chi.*	8	4	0	2	0	2	0	1.000
Parris, Steve, Tor.	14	14	6	7	0	13	0	1.000
Patterson, Danny, Det.	6	0	0	1	0	1	0	1.000
Pearson, Terry, Det.	4	0	0	0	0	0	0	.000
Percival, Troy, Ana.	58	0	1	3	0	4	0	1.000
Perez, Yorkis, Bal.*	23	0	2	3	2	7	0	.714
Perisho, Matt, Det.*	5	0	0	1	0	1	0	1.000
Pettitte, Andy, N.Y.*	22	22	8	27	2	37	0	.946
Phelps, Travis, TB.	26	0	0	6	0	6	0	1.000
Phillips, Jason C., Cle.	8	6	2	7	0	9	0	1.000
Pineiro, Joel, Sea.	37	28	14	34	2	50	4	.960
Plesac, Dan, Tor.*	19	0	0	0	0	0	0	.000
Politte, Cliff, Tor.	55	0	1	5	0	6	0	1.000
Ponson, Sidney, Bal.	28	28	20	21	0	41	3	1.000
Porzio, Mike, Chi.*	32	0	3	3	0	6	1	1.000
Pote, Lou, Ana.	31	0	4	11	1	16	0	.938
Powell, Brian, Det.	13	9	6	3	0	9	0	1.000
Powell, Jay, Tex.	51	0	4	9	0	13	0	1.000
Prokopec, Luke, Tor.	22	12	4	6	1	11	0	.909
Radke, Brad, Min.	21	21	10	9	0	19	0	1.000
Rauch, Jon, Chi.	8	6	0	3	1	4	0	.750
Redman, Mark, Det.*	30	30	7	23	6	36	1	.833
Reed, Rick, Min.	33	32	8	20	2	30	1	.933
Reichert, Dan, K.C.	30	6	17	13	1	31	0	.968
Rekar, Bryan, K.C.	2	2	2	1	0	3	0	1.000
Reyes, Dennys, Tex.*	15	5	1	5	1	7	0	.857
Rhodes, Arthur, Sea.*	66	0	6	5	0	11	1	1.000
Riggan, Jerrod, Cle.	29	0	3	3	0	6	1	1.000
Rincon, Juan, Min.	10	3	2	5	1	8	1	.875
Rincon, Ricardo, Cle.-Oak.*	71	0	1	7	0	8	1	1.000
Riske, David, Cle.	51	0	0	8	0	8	1	1.000
Ritchie, Todd, Chi.	26	23	12	18	3	33	1	.909
Rivera, Mariano, N.Y.	45	0	3	6	2	11	1	.818
Roberts, Willis, Bal.	66	0	4	10	2	16	0	.875
Rocker, John, Tex.*	30	0	1	2	1	4	1	.750
Rodney, Fernando, Det.	20	0	1	1	0	2	0	1.000
Rodriguez, Francisco, Ana.	5	0	0	1	0	1	0	1.000
Rodriguez, Jose, Min.*	4	0	0	0	0	0	0	.000
Rodriguez, Nerio, Cle.	1	0	0	0	0	0	0	.000
Rodriguez, Ricardo, Cle.	7	7	5	2	0	7	0	1.000
Rodriguez, Rich, Tex.*	36	0	1	4	1	6	0	.833
Rogers, Kenny, Tex.*	33	33	22	40	3	65	5	.954
Romero, J.C., Min.*	81	0	5	9	0	14	2	1.000
Rupe, Ryan, TB.	15	15	3	7	0	10	0	1.000
Ryan, B.J., Bal.*	67	0	1	8	0	9	1	1.000
Sabathia, C.C., Cle.*	33	33	2	19	1	22	2	.955
Sabel, Erik, Det.	1	0	0	0	0	0	0	.000
Sadler, Carl, Cle.*	24	0	0	2	0	2	0	1.000
Santana, Johan, Min.*	27	14	4	9	2	15	0	.867

Player, Team	G	GS	PO	A	E	TC	DP	Pct.
Santana, Julio, Det.	38	0	0	3	2	5	0	.600
Sasaki, Kazuhiro, Sea.	61	0	1	13	2	16	0	.875
Schoeneweis, Scott, Ana.*	54	15	3	17	1	21	2	.952
Seanez, Rudy, Tex.	33	0	5	2	0	7	0	1.000
Sedlacek, Shawn, K.C.	16	14	11	7	0	18	1	1.000
Sele, Aaron, Ana.	26	26	3	12	0	15	1	1.000
Shields, Scot, Ana.	29	1	2	6	0	8	0	1.000
Shouse, Brian, K.C.*	23	0	1	5	0	6	1	1.000
Shuey, Paul, Cle.	39	0	3	9	0	12	0	1.000
Smith, Mike, Tor.	14	6	2	5	1	8	1	.875
Smith, Roy, Cle.	4	1	1	3	0	4	0	1.000
Soriano, Rafael, Sea.	10	8	2	4	1	7	0	.857
Sosa, Jorge, TB.	31	14	7	4	0	11	0	1.000
Sparks, Steve W., Det.	32	30	15	41	2	58	3	.966
Standridge, Jason, TB.	1	0	1	0	0	1	0	1.000
Stanton, Mike, N.Y.*	79	0	4	9	2	15	1	.867
Stein, Blake, K.C.	27	2	2	1	0	3	0	1.000
Stephens, John, Bal.	12	11	2	10	1	13	1	.923
Sturtze, Tanyon, TB.	33	33	11	23	2	36	4	.944
Suppan, Jeff, K.C.	33	33	23	31	3	57	0	.947
Suzuki, Mac, K.C.	7	1	2	2	1	5	0	.800
Tallet, Brian, Cle.*	2	2	1	0	1	2	0	.500
Tam, Jeff, Oak.	40	0	9	8	0	17	1	1.000
Taylor, Aaron, Sea.	5	0	0	0	0	0	0	.000
Telford, Anthony, Tex.	20	0	4	3	1	8	1	.875
Tessmer, Jay, N.Y.	2	0	0	0	0	0	0	.000
Thurman, Corey, Tor.	43	1	3	6	0	9	0	1.000
Thurman, Mike, N.Y.	12	2	3	3	0	6	0	1.000
Towers, Josh, Bal.	5	3	5	7	0	12	1	1.000
Trombley, Mike, Min.	5	0	0	0	0	0	0	.000
Urbina, Ugueth, Bos.	61	0	7	1	0	8	1	1.000
Valdes, Ismael, Tex.-Sea.	31	31	12	32	1	45	2	.978
Van Hekken, Andy, Det.*	5	5	2	4	0	6	1	1.000
Van Poppel, Todd, Tex.	50	0	4	4	0	8	0	1.000
Venafro, Mike, Oak.*	47	0	1	11	0	12	1	1.000
Voyles, Brad, K.C.	22	0	3	3	0	6	0	1.000
Wakefield, Tim, Bos.	45	15	9	9	1	19	4	.947
Walker, Jamie, Det.*	57	0	0	3	0	3	0	1.000
Walker, Pete, Tor.	37	20	11	22	2	35	3	.943
Wall, Donne, Ana.	17	0	0	6	0	6	0	1.000
Washburn, Jarrod, Ana.*	32	32	6	15	1	22	1	.955
Watson, Mark, Sea.*	3	0	0	1	0	1	0	1.000
Weaver, Jeff, Det.-N.Y.	32	25	13	32	3	48	3	.938
Weber, Ben, Ana.	63	0	4	15	0	19	1	1.000
Wells, Bob, Min.	48	0	5	5	0	10	1	1.000
Wells, David, N.Y.*	31	31	6	24	1	31	2	.968
Westbrook, Jake, Cle.	11	4	4	6	0	10	0	1.000
Wickman, Bob, Cle.	36	0	1	3	1	5	0	.800
Wiggins, Scott, Tor.*	3	0	0	1	0	1	0	1.000
Wilson, Kris, K.C.	12	0	1	1	1	3	0	.667
Wilson, Paul, TB.	30	30	16	21	2	39	4	.949
Wise, Matt, Ana.	7	0	0	0	0	0	0	.000
Wohlers, Mark, Cle.	64	0	7	7	2	16	0	.875
Woodard, Steve, Tex.	14	0	0	3	0	3	0	1.000
Wright, Dan, Chi.	33	33	10	28	0	38	1	1.000
Wright, Jaret, Cle.	8	6	0	2	0	2	0	1.000
Wunsch, Kelly, Chi.*	50	0	1	3	0	4	1	1.000
Yan, Esteban, TB.	55	0	3	7	0	10	1	1.000
Zambrano, Victor, TB.	42	11	9	9	2	20	1	.900
Zito, Barry, Oak.*	35	35	11	31	3	45	3	.933

TRIPLE PLAY: Rogers, Tex.

PITCHERS WITH TWO OR MORE TEAMS

Player, Team	G	GS	PO	A	E	TC	DP	Pct.
Beverlin, Jason, Cle.	4	0	0	0	0	0	0	.000
Beverlin, Jason, Det.	3	3	0	0	0	0	0	.000
Burba, Dave, Tex.	23	18	8	9	0	17	1	1.000
Burba, Dave, Cle.	12	3	2	1	1	4	1	.750
Creek, Doug, TB.*	29	0	1	4	0	5	0	1.000
Creek, Doug, Sea.*	23	0	2	1	0	3	0	1.000
Howry, Bob, Chi.	47	0	3	6	1	10	1	.900
Howry, Bob, Bos.	20	0	0	3	0	3	0	1.000
Jimenez, Jason, TB.*	5	0	0	0	0	0	0	.000
Jimenez, Jason, Bal.	1	0	0	0	0	0	0	.000
Lilly, Ted, N.Y.*	16	11	3	11	0	14	0	1.000
Lilly, Ted, Oak.*	6	5	1	1	0	2	0	1.000
Rincon, Ricardo, Cle.*	46	0	0	5	0	5	1	1.000
Rincon, Ricardo, Oak.*	25	0	1	2	0	3	0	1.000
Valdes, Ismael, Tex.	23	23	10	19	1	30	1	.967
Valdes, Ismael, Sea.	8	8	2	13	0	15	1	1.000
Weaver, Jeff, Det.	17	17	9	22	1	32	1	.969
Weaver, Jeff, N.Y.	15	8	4	10	2	16	2	.875

MISCELLANEOUS

SHUTOUT GAMES

Read across for wins, down for losses.

Team	N.Y.	Oak.	Bos.	Ana.	Sea.	Min.	Chi.	Tor.	Det.	Tex.	Cle.	K.C.	T.B.	Bal.	N.L.	W	L	Pct.
New York	..	0	2	1	0	1	0	0	0	0	0	0	4	1	2	11	3	.786
Oakland	1	..	1	1	2	2	2	0	1	1	1	0	3	2	2	19	6	.760
Boston	0	0	..	1	0	1	1	1	2	1	0	1	3	5	1	17	7	.708
Anaheim	0	1	1	..	2	0	1	2	1	1	1	1	0	2	1	14	8	.636
Seattle	1	2	0	1	..	1	0	0	0	0	0	2	1	0	4	12	7	.632
Minnesota	0	1	1	0	0	..	2	1	1	0	1	1	0	1	0	9	8	.529
Chicago	0	0	1	0	0	1	..	1	1	1	0	2	0	0	0	7	7	.500
Toronto	0	1	1	0	0	0	0	..	1	0	0	1	0	1	1	6	6	.500
Detroit	0	0	0	1	0	0	0	0	..	0	2	2	0	1	1	7	10	.412
Texas	0	1	0	0	1	0	0	0	1	..	0	0	0	0	1	4	6	.400
Cleveland	0	0	0	1	0	0	1	1	0	1	..	0	0	0	0	4	8	.333
Kansas City	0	0	0	1	0	0	0	0	2	0	1	..	1	0	1	6	13	.316
Tampa Bay	0	0	0	0	1	0	0	0	0	0	0	0	..	1	1	3	14	.176
Baltimore	0	0	0	1	0	0	0	0	0	0	0	2	0	..	0	3	15	.167
N.L. Clubs	1	0	0	0	1	2	0	0	0	1	2	1	2	1	..	..	..	..
Lost	3	6	7	8	7	8	7	6	10	6	8	13	14	15	..	122	118	.508

A.L. shutouts vs. N.L. clubs (15): Seattle vs. St. Louis 2, Seattle vs. Cincinnati, Seattle vs. Houston, New York vs. New York, New York vs. San Diego, Oakland vs. Milwaukee, Oakland vs. San Francisco, Anaheim vs. Los Angeles, Boston vs. San Diego, Detroit vs. Atlanta, Kansas City vs. Florida, Tampa Bay vs. Florida, Texas vs. Pittsburgh, Toronto vs. Colorado.

HOME RECORD

Read across for home wins, down for road losses.

Team	Ana.	Min.	Oak.	N.Y.	Sea.	Chi.	Bos.	Tex.	Tor.	Cle.	K.C.	Bal.	Det.	T.B.	N.L.	W	L	Pct.
Anaheim	..	1	6	2	5	3	1	7	3	3	3	4	5	5	6	54	27	.667
Minnesota	3	..	1	0	2	7	2	4	3	7	6	1	9	4	5	54	27	.667
Oakland	7	4	..	1	4	6	0	8	3	1	5	1	3	3	8	54	27	.667
New York	2	3	3	..	0	1	5	2	6	3	2	7	5	7	6	52	28	.650
Seattle	5	3	6	2	..	2	4	7	2	3	3	2	3	1	5	48	33	.593
Chicago	3	5	2	0	4	..	2	2	2	5	7	3	5	2	5	47	34	.580
Boston	2	2	3	5	2	1	..	2	7	3	1	5	1	6	2	42	39	.519
Texas	5	1	4	1	4	3	2	..	5	2	2	4	3	3	4	42	39	.519
Toronto	2	1	3	6	2	1	3	0	..	0	1	7	3	7	6	42	39	.519
Cleveland	0	6	0	3	2	5	1	3	0	..	6	3	5	2	3	39	42	.481
Kansas City	3	2	0	0	0	5	0	6	1	7	..	0	7	2	4	37	44	.457
Baltimore	0	3	2	3	4	2	2	1	2	1	4	..	1	5	4	34	47	.420
Detroit	0	3	0	0	2	3	2	5	0	4	7	2	..	2	3	33	47	.413
Tampa Bay	0	2	1	3	2	2	0	1	5	1	5	3		..	4	30	51	.370
N.L. Clubs	4	4	1	4	3	6	6	3	6	6	8	4	6	6	..	..	..	..
Lost on Road	36	40	32	30	36	47	30	51	45	46	56	48	59	55	..	608	524	.537

HOME RECORDS IN INTERLEAGUE GAMES

Team				Total	Team				Total
Anaheim	2-1 vs. Cin.	2-1 vs. L.A.	2-1 vs. Pit.	6-3	Minnesota	1-2 vs. Atl.	2-1 vs. Fla.	2-1 vs. Mil.	5-4
Baltimore	1-2 vs. L.A.	1-2 vs. Phi.	2-1 vs. S.D.	4-5	New York	2-1 vs. Ari.	2-1 vs. N.Y.	2-1 vs. S.F.	6-3
Boston	0-3 vs. Ari.	0-3 vs. Atl.	2-1 vs. Col.	2-7	Oakland	3-0 vs. Hou.	3-0 vs. Mil.	2-1 vs. S.F.	8-1
Chicago	2-1 vs. Chi.	1-2 vs. Mon.	2-1 vs. N.Y.	5-4	Seattle	1-2 vs. Chi.	2-1 vs. Col.	2-1 vs. St.L.	5-4
Cleveland	1-2 vs. Ari.	1-2 vs. N.Y.	1-2 vs. Phi.	3-6	Tampa Bay	2-1 vs. Fla.	1-2 vs. L.A.	1-2 vs. S.D.	4-5
Detroit	2-1 vs. Mon.	0-3 vs. Phi.	1-2 vs. Pit.	3-6	Texas	0-3 vs. Atl.	2-1 vs. Cin.	1-2 vs. Hou.	3-6
Kansas City	1-2 vs. Fla.	1-2 vs. St.L.	2-1 vs. S.D.	4-5	Toronto	3-0 vs. Col.	2-1 vs. Mon.	1-2 vs. S.F.	6-3

ROAD RECORD

Read across for road wins, down for home losses.

Team	Bos.	N.Y.	Oak.	Ana.	Sea.	Min.	Tor.	Cle.	Chi.	Bal.	Tex.	T.B.	K.C.	Det.	N.L.	W	L	Pct.
Boston	..	4	3	2	2	1	6	2	1	8	2	10	3	4	3	51	30	.630
New York	5	..	2	2	4	3	4	3	3	6	2	6	3	3	5	51	30	.630
Oakland	3	3	..	4	4	2	0	4	1	4	5	5	3	3	8	49	32	.605
Anaheim	2	1	3	..	4	3	4	3	3	3	5	3	3	5	5	45	36	.556
Seattle	1	3	5	5	..	1	4	1	2	2	6	4	3	2	6	45	36	.556
Minnesota	1	0	2	2	3	..	3	4	4	0	2	1	8	5	5	40	40	.500
Toronto	3	3	3	0	1	0	..	3	1	8	1	4	3	3	3	36	45	.444
Cleveland	3	0	2	3	1	2	3	..	5	2	1	2	3	5	3	35	46	.432
Chicago	2	2	0	0	1	3	2	4	..	1	3	2	4	7	3	34	47	.420
Baltimore	4	3	2	2	1	2	2	0	1	..	2	5	3	1	5	33	48	.407
Texas	1	2	2	2	3	2	3	3	1	2	..	2	0	1	6	30	51	.370
Tampa Bay	3	2	0	1	2	0	3	1	1	4	3	..	1	1	3	25	55	.313
Kansas City	2	1	1	2	3	3	2	3	5	1	1	2	..	3	1	25	56	.309

2002 A.L. STATISTICS — Miscellaneous

Team	Bos.	N.Y.	Oak.	Ana.	Sea.	Min.	Tor.	Cle.	Chi.	Bal.	Tex.	T.B.	K.C.	Det.	N.L.	W	L	Pct.
Detroit	2	1	1	1	0	1	0	5	4	2	0	0	2	..	3	22	59	.272
N.L. Clubs	7	3	1	3	4	4	3	6	4	5	6	5	5	6	..	..	..	..
Lost at home	39	28	27	27	33	27	39	42	34	47	39	51	44	47	..	521	611	.460

PITCHING AGAINST EACH CLUB

ANAHEIM—99-63

Pitcher	Bal. W-L	Bos. W-L	Chi. W-L	Cle. W-L	Det. W-L	K.C. W-L	Min. W-L	N.Y. W-L	Oak. W-L	Sea. W-L	T.B. W-L	Tex. W-L	Tor. W-L	N.L. W-L	Total W-L
Appier, Kevin	0-1	1-0	0-0	2-0	2-0	2-0	0-2	0-1	2-3	1-1	2-0	0-2	1-0	1-2	14-12
Callaway, Mickey	1-0	0-0	0-0	0-0	0-0	0-0	0-0	0-0	0-1	1-0	0-0	0-0	0-0	0-0	2-1
Cook, Dennis	0-0	0-0	0-0	0-0	0-0	1-0	0-0	0-0	0-0	0-0	0-0	0-0	0-0	0-1	1-1
Donnelly, Brendan	0-0	0-0	0-1	0-0	0-0	0-0	0-0	0-0	1-0	0-0	0-0	0-0	0-0	0-0	1-1
Lackey, John	2-0	0-1	0-0	1-0	1-0	0-0	0-0	0-1	0-0	1-1	1-0	1-1	1-0	1-0	9-4
Levine, Al	0-0	0-0	0-0	0-0	1-0	0-0	1-0	0-0	0-2	0-0	0-1	2-0	0-0	0-1	4-4
Lukasiewicz, Mark	0-0	0-0	0-0	0-0	0-0	0-0	0-0	0-0	0-0	1-0	0-0	0-0	0-0	0-0	2-0
Ortiz, Ramon	1-1	0-1	1-1	1-0	1-0	1-1	0-1	0-0	1-2	2-1	1-0	3-0	1-1	2-0	15-9
Percival, Troy	0-0	0-0	1-0	0-0	1-0	0-0	0-0	1-0	0-1	0-0	1-0	0-0	0-0	0-0	4-1
Pote, Lou	0-0	0-0	0-0	0-0	0-0	0-0	0-1	0-0	0-0	0-1	0-0	0-0	0-0	0-0	0-2
Schoeneweis, Scott	0-0	2-0	2-0	0-0	0-0	0-0	0-1	0-0	0-0	0-2	1-0	2-3	0-1	2-1	9-8
Sele, Aaron	0-0	0-0	0-1	0-1	2-0	0-0	0-1	1-1	0-1	0-0	0-1	2-0	2-0	2-1	8-9
Shields, Scot	0-0	0-1	0-0	0-0	0-0	0-0	0-0	0-1	2-0	1-0	1-0	0-0	0-0	0-0	5-3
Washburn, Jarrod	2-0	0-0	2-0	1-2	0-0	1-0	2-0	1-0	1-1	1-1	2-2	1-0	2-0	1-0	18-6
Weber, Ben	1-0	0-0	0-0	1-0	0-1	1-0	0-0	1-0	0-0	0-0	0-0	0-0	1-0	0-0	7-2
Totals	7-2	3-4	6-3	6-3	8-1	6-3	4-5	3-4	9-11	9-10	8-1	12-7	7-2	11-7	99-63

NO-DECISIONS: Francisco Rodriguez, Donne Wall, Matt Wise.
INTERLEAGUE: Aaron Sele 1-0, Dennis Cook 0-1, Scott Schoeneweis 1-0 vs. Reds; Ramon Ortiz 1-0, Scott Schoeneweis 0-1, Scot Shields 0-1, Al Levine 0-1, Aaron Sele 1-0, John Lackey 1-0 vs. Dodgers; Ramon Ortiz 1-0, Jarrod Washburn 1-0, Kevin Appier 1-0 vs. Brewers; Jarrod Washburn 1-0, Ben Weber 1-0, Kevin Appier 0-1 vs. Pirates; Kevin Appier 0-1, Aaron Sele 0-1, Scott Schoeneweis 1-0 vs. Cardinals. Total: 11-7.

BALTIMORE—67-95

Pitcher	Ana. W-L	Bos. W-L	Chi. W-L	Cle. W-L	Det. W-L	K.C. W-L	Min. W-L	N.Y. W-L	Oak. W-L	Sea. W-L	T.B. W-L	Tex. W-L	Tor. W-L	N.L. W-L	Total W-L
Bauer, Rick	0-0	0-0	1-0	0-1	0-0	0-0	1-0	1-1	1-0	1-0	0-1	1-1	0-1	0-2	6-7
Brock, Chris	0-0	0-0	0-0	0-0	0-1	0-0	0-0	0-0	0-0	0-0	0-0	0-0	1-0	1-0	2-1
Douglass, Sean	0-1	0-0	0-0	0-0	0-0	0-0	0-0	0-1	0-0	0-0	0-0	0-0	0-2	0-0	0-5
Driskill, Travis	1-0	0-0	0-0	0-0	0-0	0-0	1-0	1-1	1-1	1-0	0-2	0-0	1-3	2-1	8-8
Erickson, Scott	0-2	1-2	0-0	0-1	0-0	1-0	1-1	1-3	0-1	1-1	0-1	0-0	0-0	0-0	5-12
Groom, Buddy	0-0	0-0	0-0	0-1	0-0	0-0	0-0	0-0	0-0	0-0	1-0	0-0	0-0	1-1	3-2
Hentgen, Pat	0-1	0-2	0-0	0-0	0-0	0-0	0-0	0-0	0-0	0-0	0-0	0-0	0-1	0-0	0-4
Johnson, Jason	0-1	1-1	0-1	0-0	0-1	0-0	1-0	0-2	0-1	0-0	0-0	1-1	0-1	2-2	5-14
Julio, Jorge	0-1	0-0	0-0	1-1	0-0	0-0	0-0	1-0	0-0	0-2	2-1	0-1	0-0	1-0	5-6
Lopez, Rodrigo	1-1	4-0	1-0	1-0	0-0	1-1	0-0	0-0	1-0	0-1	4-0	1-1	0-3	1-2	15-9
Maduro, Calvin	0-0	0-3	1-0	0-0	0-0	0-0	0-0	0-2	0-0	0-2	0-0	0-0	0-0	0-0	2-5
Ponson, Sidney	0-0	0-2	0-0	0-0	0-0	1-0	0-3	1-0	0-0	1-0	1-2	1-0	0-1	0-1	7-9
Roberts, Willis	0-0	0-1	0-2	0-1	0-0	0-0	0-0	0-0	0-0	1-0	1-0	1-0	0-0	1-0	5-4
Ryan, B.J.	0-0	0-0	0-0	0-0	0-0	0-0	0-0	0-0	0-0	0-0	0-0	0-0	1-1	1-0	2-1
Stephens, John	0-0	0-0	0-0	0-0	1-1	0-0	0-0	0-1	0-0	0-0	0-1	0-0	1-0	0-0	2-5
Towers, Josh	0-0	0-1	0-1	0-0	0-0	0-0	0-0	0-0	0-0	0-0	0-0	0-0	0-0	0-0	0-3
Totals	2-7	6-13	3-4	1-5	2-4	7-0	5-1	6-13	4-5	5-4	10-9	3-6	4-15	9-9	67-95

NO-DECISIONS: Steve Bechler, Erik Bedard, Eric DuBose, Yorkis Perez.
INTERLEAGUE: Jason Johnson 0-1, Chris Brock 1-0, Rodrigo Lopez 0-1 vs. Diamondbacks; Rodrigo Lopez 1-0, Jason Johnson 0-1, Sidney Ponson 0-1 vs. Dodgers; Rick Bauer 0-1, B.J. Ryan 1-0, Buddy Groom 0-1, Travis Driskill 1-1, Jason Johnson 1-0 vs. Phillies; Buddy Groom 1-0, Jorge Julio 1-0, Rodrigo Lopez 0-1 vs. Padres; Rick Bauer 0-1, Travis Driskill 1-0, Jason Johnson 1-0 vs. Giants. Total: 9-9.

BOSTON—93-69

Pitcher	Ana. W-L	Bal. W-L	Chi. W-L	Cle. W-L	Det. W-L	K.C. W-L	Min. W-L	N.Y. W-L	Oak. W-L	Sea. W-L	T.B. W-L	Tex. W-L	Tor. W-L	N.L. W-L	Total W-L
Arrojo, Rolando	0-0	0-1	0-0	0-0	1-0	0-0	0-0	2-0	1-0	0-0	0-0	0-0	0-0	0-1	4-3
Banks, Willie	0-0	0-0	0-0	0-0	0-0	0-0	0-0	0-0	0-0	0-0	0-0	0-1	1-0	1-0	2-1
Burkett, John	0-0	2-1	0-0	0-0	2-0	1-0	0-1	0-0	2-1	1-1	3-0	0-1	2-0	0-3	13-8
Castillo, Frank	0-0	0-2	0-1	0-2	0-1	0-0	0-1	1-1	0-1	0-1	2-1	0-0	2-2	1-2	6-15
Embree, Alan	0-1	1-0	0-0	0-1	0-0	0-0	0-0	0-0	0-0	0-0	0-0	0-0	0-0	0-0	1-2
Fossum, Casey	0-0	1-1	1-0	0-0	0-0	0-0	0-0	1-1	0-1	0-0	1-0	0-0	1-0	0-1	5-4
Garces, Rich	0-0	0-0	0-0	0-1	0-0	0-0	0-0	0-0	0-0	0-0	0-0	0-0	0-0	0-0	0-1
Gomes, Wayne	0-0	0-0	0-1	0-0	0-0	0-0	0-0	0-0	0-0	0-0	0-0	0-0	1-0	0-0	1-2
Hancock, Josh	0-0	0-0	0-1	0-0	0-0	0-0	0-0	0-0	0-0	0-0	0-0	0-0	0-0	0-0	0-1
Hermanson, Dustin	0-0	0-0	0-0	0-1	0-0	0-0	0-0	0-0	0-0	0-0	1-0	0-1	0-0	0-0	1-3
Howry, Bob	0-0	0-0	0-0	0-1	0-0	0-0	0-0	0-0	0-0	0-0	0-1	1-1	0-0	0-0	1-3
Kim, Sun-Woo	0-0	0-0	0-0	0-0	0-0	0-0	0-0	0-0	0-0	0-0	0-0	0-0	1-0	1-0	2-0
Lowe, Derek	0-1	4-0	1-1	1-0	1-0	1-1	0-0	2-2	3-0	1-0	3-0	1-0	1-1	2-2	21-8
Martinez, Pedro	2-0	4-0	0-0	2-0	1-0	1-0	1-1	2-1	0-1	2-0	2-0	1-0	1-0	1-2	20-4
Oliver, Darren	0-0	1-1	0-0	0-0	0-0	0-0	0-1	0-0	0-1	0-0	1-0	0-0	1-0	0-0	4-5
Urbina, Ugueth	1-0	0-0	0-0	0-0	0-0	0-0	0-0	0-1	0-0	0-0	0-1	0-0	0-2	0-1	1-6
Wakefield, Tim	1-1	0-0	0-0	2-0	0-1	1-0	2-0	0-1	0-0	0-1	3-0	0-0	2-0	0-1	11-5
Totals	4-3	13-6	2-4	5-4	5-4	4-2	3-3	9-10	6-3	4-5	16-3	4-3	13-6	5-13	93-69

NO-DECISIONS: Chris Haney.
INTERLEAGUE: Frank Castillo 0-1, Pedro Martinez 0-1, John Burkett 0-1 vs. Diamondbacks; Pedro Martinez 0-1, John Burkett 0-1, Tim Wakefield 0-1, Derek Lowe 1-1, Ugueth Urbina 0-1 vs. Braves; Derek Lowe 1-0, Casey Fossum 0-1, Frank Castillo 1-0 vs. Rockies; John Burkett 0-1, Derek Lowe 0-1, Rolando Arrojo 0-1 vs. Dodgers; Willie Banks 1-0, Frank Castillo 0-1, Pedro Martinez 1-0 vs. Padres. Total: 5-13.

2002 A.L. STATISTICS Miscellaneous

CHICAGO—81-81

Pitcher	Ana. W-L	Bal. W-L	Bos. W-L	Cle. W-L	Det. W-L	K.C. W-L	Min. W-L	N.Y. W-L	Oak. W-L	Sea. W-L	T.B. W-L	Tex. W-L	Tor. W-L	N.L. W-L	Total W-L
Barcelo, Lorenzo	0-0	0-0	0-0	0-0	0-0	0-0	0-0	0-0	0-0	0-1	0-0	0-0	0-0	0-0	0-1
Biddle, Rocky	0-0	0-0	1-0	0-0	0-1	0-1	0-0	1-0	0-0	0-1	0-0	0-0	0-0	1-1	3-4
Buehrle, Mark	0-1	1-0	0-0	2-2	2-1	2-2	5-1	0-0	1-2	2-0	0-1	2-0	0-0	2-2	19-12
Foulke, Keith	0-1	0-0	0-0	0-0	0-0	0-0	0-0	0-1	0-0	0-1	1-0	0-0	0-0	1-1	2-4
Garland, Jon	0-2	1-1	1-1	1-2	2-0	3-1	0-1	0-1	0-1	1-0	0-1	0-0	2-0	1-1	12-12
Ginter, Matt	0-0	0-0	0-0	0-0	0-0	0-0	0-0	0-0	0-0	0-0	0-0	0-0	0-0	1-0	1-0
Glover, Gary	1-0	0-0	0-0	0-3	1-1	2-0	1-2	0-0	0-0	0-0	1-0	1-0	0-0	0-2	7-8
Howry, Bob	0-0	1-1	0-0	0-0	0-0	1-0	0-1	0-0	0-0	0-0	0-0	0-0	0-0	0-0	2-2
Marte, Damaso	0-0	0-0	0-0	1-0	0-0	0-1	0-0	0-0	0-0	0-0	0-0	0-0	0-0	0-0	1-1
Osuna, Antonio	1-0	1-0	0-0	2-0	2-0	0-0	0-1	0-0	0-0	0-0	0-0	0-1	1-0	1-0	8-2
Parque, Jim	1-0	0-0	0-0	0-0	0-0	0-1	0-0	0-1	0-0	0-0	0-0	0-1	0-1	0-0	1-4
Porzio, Mike	0-0	0-0	0-0	0-0	0-0	1-0	0-1	0-1	0-0	0-0	0-0	1-0	0-0	0-0	2-2
Rauch, Jon	0-0	0-0	0-0	0-0	0-0	0-0	1-0	0-0	0-0	0-1	0-0	0-0	1-0	0-0	2-1
Ritchie, Todd	0-0	0-0	0-1	2-2	1-2	0-3	0-2	0-0	1-1	0-0	0-1	0-2	0-0	1-1	5-15
Wright, Dan	0-2	0-1	2-0	1-1	3-1	2-0	1-1	1-1	0-2	2-0	1-0	1-0	0-1	0-2	14-12
Wunsch, Kelly	0-0	0-0	0-0	0-0	1-1	0-0	0-0	0-0	0-0	0-0	1-0	0-0	0-0	0-0	2-1
Totals	3-6	4-3	4-2	9-10	12-7	11-8	8-11	2-4	2-7	5-4	4-3	5-4	4-2	8-10	81-81

INTERLEAGUE: Todd Ritchie 0-1, Gary Glover 0-1, Dan Wright 0-1 vs. Braves; Jon Garland 1-1, Keith Foulke 1-0, Mark Buehrle 0-2, Matt Ginter 1-0 vs. Cubs; Dan Wright 0-1, Keith Foulke 0-1, Mark Buehrle 1-0 vs. Expos; Gary Glover 0-1, Rocky Biddle 1-0, Todd Ritchie 0-1 vs. Mets; Antonio Osuna 1-0, Rocky Biddle 0-1, Mark Buehrle 1-0 vs. Phillies. Total: 8-10.

CLEVELAND—74-88

Pitcher	Ana. W-L	Bal. W-L	Bos. W-L	Chi. W-L	Det. W-L	K.C. W-L	Min. W-L	N.Y. W-L	Oak. W-L	Sea. W-L	T.B. W-L	Tex. W-L	Tor. W-L	N.L. W-L	Total W-L
Baez, Danys	0-0	1-0	2-0	3-2	1-1	0-0	1-1	1-0	0-1	0-1	1-1	0-2	0-0	0-2	10-11
Burba, Dave	0-0	0-0	0-0	1-0	0-0	0-0	0-0	0-0	0-0	0-0	0-0	0-0	0-0	0-0	1-0
Colon, Bartolo	1-0	1-0	0-0	1-2	1-0	0-0	1-1	0-0	0-0	0-0	0-0	1-1	1-0	3-0	10-4
Davis, Jason	0-0	0-0	0-0	0-0	0-0	1-0	0-0	0-0	0-0	0-0	0-0	0-0	0-0	0-0	1-0
DePaula, Sean	0-0	0-0	0-0	0-0	0-0	0-0	0-0	0-0	0-1	0-0	0-0	0-0	0-0	0-0	1-1
Drese, Ryan	1-2	1-0	0-1	1-1	0-0	1-0	2-2	0-2	1-0	0-0	0-0	0-0	1-0	2-1	10-9
Elder, Dave	0-0	0-0	0-0	0-0	0-0	0-0	0-1	0-0	0-0	0-0	0-0	0-0	0-1	0-0	0-2
Finley, Chuck	0-1	0-0	0-0	1-1	1-1	0-2	1-1	0-1	0-0	0-0	0-0	1-0	0-0	0-4	4-11
Lee, Cliff	0-0	0-0	0-0	0-0	0-0	0-0	0-1	0-0	0-0	0-0	0-0	0-0	0-0	0-0	0-1
Maurer, Dave	0-0	0-0	0-0	0-0	0-0	0-0	0-1	0-0	0-0	0-0	0-0	0-0	0-0	0-0	0-1
Mulholland, Terry	0-0	0-0	0-0	0-0	0-1	0-1	1-0	0-0	1-0	1-0	0-0	0-0	0-0	0-0	3-2
Murray, Heath	0-0	0-0	0-0	0-0	0-0	0-2	0-0	0-0	0-0	0-0	0-0	0-0	0-0	0-0	0-2
Nagy, Charles	0-0	0-0	0-1	0-0	0-2	0-0	0-0	0-0	0-0	0-0	1-0	0-1	0-0	0-0	1-4
Paronto, Chad	0-0	0-0	0-0	0-0	0-0	0-0	0-0	0-0	0-0	0-0	0-0	0-0	0-0	0-2	0-2
Phillips, Jason C.	0-0	0-0	1-1	0-0	0-1	0-0	0-0	0-0	0-1	0-0	0-0	0-0	0-0	0-0	1-3
Riggan, Jerrod	0-0	1-0	0-0	0-0	0-0	0-0	1-0	0-0	0-0	0-0	0-0	0-0	0-0	0-1	2-1
Rincon, Ricardo	0-0	0-0	0-0	0-0	0-1	0-1	0-1	1-1	0-0	0-0	0-0	0-0	0-0	0-0	1-4
Riske, David	0-1	0-0	1-0	0-0	1-1	0-0	0-0	0-0	0-0	0-0	0-0	0-0	0-0	0-0	2-2
Rodriguez, Ricardo	0-0	0-0	0-1	1-0	1-0	0-0	0-0	0-0	0-1	0-0	0-0	0-0	0-0	0-0	2-2
Sabathia, C.C.	0-2	0-0	0-1	1-1	3-1	3-1	1-1	0-2	0-0	0-0	2-0	1-0	1-0	1-2	13-11
Sadler, Carl	1-0	0-0	0-0	0-0	0-0	0-0	0-1	0-0	0-0	0-0	0-0	0-1	0-0	0-0	1-2
Shuey, Paul	0-0	1-0	0-0	0-0	0-0	0-0	0-0	0-0	0-0	0-0	0-0	0-0	0-0	0-0	3-0
Tallet, Brian	0-0	1-0	0-0	0-0	0-0	0-0	0-0	0-0	0-0	0-0	0-0	0-0	0-0	0-0	1-0
Westbrook, Jake	0-0	0-0	0-0	0-0	0-0	0-0	0-0	0-0	0-2	1-1	0-0	0-0	0-0	0-0	1-3
Wickman, Bob	0-0	0-0	0-0	0-1	0-0	0-2	0-0	0-0	0-0	0-0	0-0	1-0	0-0	0-0	1-3
Wohlers, Mark	0-0	0-1	0-0	0-0	0-0	1-0	0-0	1-0	0-0	1-0	0-1	0-1	0-1	0-0	3-4
Wright, Jaret	0-0	0-0	0-1	0-0	1-0	1-1	0-0	0-0	0-0	0-1	0-0	0-0	0-0	0-0	2-3
Totals	3-6	5-1	4-5	10-9	10-9	9-10	8-11	3-6	2-5	3-4	4-2	4-5	3-3	6-12	74-88

NO-DECISIONS: Jason Beverlin, Alex Herrera, Nerio Rodriguez, Roy Smith.

INTERLEAGUE: C.C. Sabathia 1-0, Chuck Finley 0-1, Danys Baez 0-1 vs. Diamondbacks; Ryan Drese 1-0, Chad Paronto 0-1, Bartolo Colon 1-0 vs. Rockies; Chuck Finley 0-1, Jerrod Riggan 0-1, Ryan Drese 0-1 vs. Marlins; C.C. Sabathia 0-1, Bartolo Colon 1-0, Chuck Finley 0-1 vs. Expos; Danys Baez 0-1, Chuck Finley 0-1, Ryan Drese 1-0 vs. Mets; C.C. Sabathia 0-1, Chad Paronto 0-1, Bartolo Colon 1-0 vs. Phillies. Total: 6-12.

DETROIT—55-106

Pitcher	Ana. W-L	Bal. W-L	Bos. W-L	Chi. W-L	Cle. W-L	K.C. W-L	Min. W-L	N.Y. W-L	Oak. W-L	Sea. W-L	T.B. W-L	Tex. W-L	Tor. W-L	N.L. W-L	Total W-L
Acevedo, Juan	0-0	0-0	1-0	0-0	0-1	0-0	0-0	0-0	0-0	0-0	0-1	0-0	0-0	0-3	1-5
Anderson, Matt	0-0	0-0	0-0	0-0	0-0	0-0	1-1	0-0	0-0	0-0	1-0	0-0	0-0	0-0	2-1
Bernero, Adam	0-1	1-0	0-1	1-2	0-0	1-1	0-1	0-0	0-0	0-0	0-0	0-0	0-1	1-0	4-7
Beverlin, Jason	0-0	0-0	0-0	0-0	0-0	0-1	0-0	0-1	0-0	0-0	0-0	0-1	0-0	0-0	0-3
Cornejo, Nate	0-1	0-0	0-0	0-1	0-1	0-1	1-1	0-0	0-0	0-0	0-0	0-0	0-0	0-0	1-5
Eckenstahler, Eric	0-0	0-0	0-0	0-0	0-0	1-0	0-0	0-0	0-0	0-0	0-0	0-0	0-0	0-0	1-0
Farnsworth, Jeff	0-0	0-0	1-1	0-0	0-0	0-0	0-0	0-0	0-0	0-1	0-1	0-0	0-0	1-0	2-3
German, Franklyn	0-0	0-0	0-0	0-0	0-0	0-0	0-0	1-0	0-0	0-0	0-0	0-0	0-0	0-0	1-0
Greisinger, Seth	1-0	0-0	0-0	0-1	0-0	0-0	0-0	0-0	0-0	0-0	0-0	1-1	0-0	0-0	2-2
Henriquez, Oscar	0-0	0-0	1-0	0-0	0-0	0-0	0-1	0-0	0-0	0-0	0-0	0-0	0-0	0-0	1-1
Lima, Jose	0-0	0-0	0-1	0-1	0-1	0-0	0-0	0-0	0-0	1-0	1-1	1-0	0-0	0-0	4-6
Loux, Shane	0-0	0-0	0-0	0-0	0-0	0-1	0-2	0-0	0-0	0-0	0-0	0-0	0-0	0-0	0-3
Maroth, Mike	0-1	1-0	0-1	1-1	0-0	0-1	0-1	0-1	1-0	0-0	0-0	0-1	0-1	1-2	6-10
Moehler, Brian	0-0	0-0	0-0	1-0	0-0	0-0	0-1	0-0	0-0	0-0	0-0	0-0	0-0	0-0	1-1
Paniagua, Jose	0-0	0-0	0-0	0-1	0-0	0-0	0-0	0-0	0-0	0-0	0-0	0-0	0-0	0-0	0-1
Patterson, Danny	0-0	0-0	0-0	0-0	0-0	0-0	0-0	0-0	0-0	0-0	0-0	0-0	0-1	0-1	0-2
Powell, Brian	0-1	0-0	0-0	0-0	1-2	0-0	0-0	0-0	0-1	0-0	0-0	0-0	0-0	0-0	1-5
Redman, Mark	0-3	0-1	1-1	1-1	3-1	0-0	0-2	0-2	1-0	0-0	0-0	0-0	0-1	1-2	8-15

Pitcher	Ana. W-L	Bal. W-L	Bos. W-L	Chi. W-L	Cle. W-L	K.C. W-L	Min. W-L	N.Y. W-L	Oak. W-L	Sea. W-L	T.B. W-L	Tex. W-L	Tor. W-L	N.L. W-L	Total W-L
Rodney, Fernando	0-1	0-0	0-0	1-0	0-0	0-0	0-1	0-1	0-0	0-0	0-0	0-0	0-0	0-0	1-3
Santana, Julio	0-0	0-1	0-0	0-0	1-0	0-1	1-0	0-0	0-0	0-1	0-0	0-0	1-1	0-0	3-5
Sparks, Steve W.	0-0	2-0	0-0	2-4	2-1	1-2	0-3	0-1	0-1	0-1	0-0	0-0	1-1	0-0	8-16
Van Hekken, Andy	0-0	0-0	0-0	0-0	1-0	0-1	0-0	0-1	0-0	0-0	0-0	0-0	0-0	0-1	1-3
Walker, Jamie	0-0	0-0	0-0	0-0	0-0	1-0	0-0	0-0	0-1	0-0	0-0	0-0	0-0	0-0	1-1
Weaver, Jeff	0-0	0-0	0-0	0-0	1-2	1-1	1-1	0-0	0-0	0-0	0-0	0-1	1-1	2-1	6-8
Totals	1-8	4-2	4-5	7-12	9-10	9-10	4-14	1-8	1-6	2-5	2-4	5-4	0-6	6-12	55-106

NO-DECISIONS: Jason Jimenez, Kris Keller, Matt Miller, Terry Pearson, Matt Perisho, Erik Sabel.

INTERLEAGUE: Mike Maroth 1-0, Julio Santana 0-1, Mark Redman 0-1 vs. Diamondbacks; Jeff Weaver 1-0, Mike Maroth 0-1, Juan Acevedo 0-1 vs. Braves; Steve W. Sparks 0-1, Juan Acevedo 0-1, Jeff Farnsworth 1-0 vs. Marlins; Adam Bernero 1-0, Juan Acevedo 0-1, Mark Redman 1-0 vs. Expos; Jeff Weaver 0-1, Danny Patterson 0-1, Steve W. Sparks 0-1 vs. Phillies; Mark Redman 0-1, Jeff Weaver 0-1, Mike Maroth 0-1 vs. Pirates. Total: 6-12.

KANSAS CITY—62-100

Pitcher	Ana. W-L	Bal. W-L	Bos. W-L	Chi. W-L	Cle. W-L	Det. W-L	Min. W-L	N.Y. W-L	Oak. W-L	Sea. W-L	T.B. W-L	Tex. W-L	Tor. W-L	N.L. W-L	Total W-L
Affeldt, Jeremy	0-1	0-0	0-0	0-1	0-0	1-0	0-1	0-0	0-0	1-0	0-0	0-0	1-0	0-1	3-4
Asencio, Miguel	1-0	0-0	0-0	1-2	0-0	1-1	1-0	0-0	0-0	0-2	0-0	0-0	0-1	0-1	4-7
Bailey, Cory	0-0	0-1	0-0	0-0	0-1	0-1	0-1	0-0	0-0	0-0	0-0	3-0	0-0	0-0	3-4
Bukvich, Ryan	0-0	0-0	0-0	0-0	0-0	0-0	0-0	0-0	0-0	0-0	1-0	0-0	0-0	0-0	1-0
Byrd, Paul	2-0	0-2	1-0	3-1	2-0	3-1	2-1	0-1	0-1	2-0	0-0	0-1	1-1	1-2	17-11
Durbin, Chad	0-0	0-0	0-0	0-0	0-0	0-0	0-1	0-0	0-0	0-0	0-0	0-0	0-0	0-0	0-1
George, Chris	0-0	0-1	0-0	0-1	0-0	0-1	0-0	0-0	0-0	0-0	0-0	0-0	0-0	0-0	0-4
Grimsley, Jason	0-0	0-1	1-0	0-0	2-1	0-0	0-1	0-0	0-2	0-0	0-0	0-0	1-2	0-0	4-7
Hernandez, Roberto	0-0	0-0	0-0	0-0	0-0	0-0	0-0	0-1	0-2	0-0	0-0	0-0	1-0	0-0	1-3
Hernandez, Runelvys	0-0	0-0	0-0	0-1	1-0	1-0	0-1	1-0	0-1	0-1	0-0	0-1	0-0	0-0	4-4
Hill, Jeremy	0-0	0-0	0-0	0-0	0-1	0-0	0-0	0-0	0-0	0-0	0-0	0-0	0-0	0-0	0-1
MacDougal, Mike	0-0	0-0	0-0	0-1	0-0	0-0	0-0	0-0	0-0	0-0	0-0	0-0	0-0	0-0	0-1
May, Darrell	0-2	0-0	0-0	2-1	0-1	0-1	0-1	0-0	0-1	0-1	0-1	0-1	0-0	1-1	4-10
Mullen, Scott	0-0	0-0	0-0	2-1	0-1	0-1	0-1	0-0	1-0	0-0	1-0	0-0	0-2	0-0	4-5
Obermueller, Wes	0-0	0-0	0-0	0-0	0-2	0-0	0-0	0-0	0-0	0-0	0-0	0-0	0-0	0-0	0-2
Reichert, Dan	0-1	0-0	0-2	0-0	2-0	1-0	0-2	0-0	0-0	0-0	0-0	0-0	0-0	0-0	3-5
Rekar, Bryan	0-0	0-1	0-1	0-0	0-0	0-0	0-0	0-0	0-0	0-0	0-0	0-0	0-0	0-0	0-2
Sedlacek, Shawn	0-0	0-0	0-0	0-1	0-0	0-0	1-0	0-0	0-1	0-1	0-1	1-0	1-1	0-0	3-5
Stein, Blake	0-1	0-0	0-0	0-0	0-0	0-1	0-1	0-1	0-0	0-0	0-0	0-0	0-0	0-0	0-4
Suppan, Jeff	0-1	0-1	0-0	2-3	1-1	3-2	1-3	0-2	0-0	0-1	0-1	1-0	0-0	1-1	9-16
Suzuki, Mac	0-0	0-0	0-0	0-0	0-0	0-0	0-0	0-0	0-0	0-0	0-0	0-0	0-2	0-2	0-2
Voyles, Brad	0-0	0-0	0-0	0-0	0-0	0-0	0-0	0-0	0-0	0-0	0-0	0-0	0-1	0-1	0-2
Wilson, Kris	0-0	0-0	0-0	0-0	0-0	0-0	0-0	0-0	0-0	0-0	0-0	2-0	0-0	0-0	2-0
Totals	3-6	0-7	2-4	8-11	10-9	10-9	5-14	1-5	1-8	3-6	4-2	7-2	3-4	5-13	62-100

NO-DECISIONS: Jeff Austin, Nate Field, Brian Shouse.

INTERLEAGUE: Mac Suzuki 0-1, Darrell May 1-0, Paul Byrd 0-1 vs. Marlins; Scott Mullen 0-2, Mac Suzuki 0-1 vs. Expos; Brad Voyles 0-1, Paul Byrd 1-0, Jason Grimsley 0-1 vs. Mets; Jason Grimsley 1-1, Jeff Suppan 1-0 vs. Padres; Paul Byrd 0-1, Jeremy Affeldt 0-1, Miguel Asencio 0-1, Roberto Hernandez 1-0, Jeff Suppan 0-1, Darrell May 0-1 vs. Cardinals. Total: 5-13.

MINNESOTA—94-67

Pitcher	Ana. W-L	Bal. W-L	Bos. W-L	Chi. W-L	Cle. W-L	Det. W-L	K.C. W-L	N.Y. W-L	Oak. W-L	Sea. W-L	T.B. W-L	Tex. W-L	Tor. W-L	N.L. W-L	Total W-L
Cressend, Jack	0-1	0-0	0-0	0-0	0-0	0-0	0-0	0-0	0-0	0-0	0-0	0-0	0-0	0-0	0-1
Fiore, Tony	0-0	0-1	0-0	1-0	1-0	0-0	1-0	0-1	0-0	0-0	1-0	2-0	1-0	3-1	10-3
Guardado, Eddie	1-0	0-0	0-0	0-0	0-0	0-0	0-0	0-1	0-2	0-0	0-0	0-0	0-0	0-0	1-3
Hawkins, LaTroy	1-0	0-0	0-0	2-0	1-0	0-0	0-0	0-0	0-0	0-0	0-0	0-0	1-0	1-0	6-0
Jackson, Mike	0-0	0-0	0-0	0-0	0-1	1-1	0-0	0-0	0-0	0-0	1-0	0-0	0-0	0-1	2-3
Kinney, Matt	0-1	0-0	0-0	0-0	1-0	0-1	0-2	0-1	0-0	0-0	0-0	0-0	0-0	1-2	2-7
Lohse, Kyle	1-0	0-1	0-0	3-1	3-1	2-1	1-1	0-0	0-0	1-0	1-0	1-1	0-0	0-2	13-8
Mays, Joe	0-0	0-0	1-1	0-2	0-2	2-0	0-1	0-0	0-1	1-0	0-0	0-0	0-1	0-0	4-8
Milton, Eric	1-2	0-0	0-0	1-1	0-3	2-0	3-0	0-1	0-1	1-0	1-1	2-0	0-0	2-0	13-9
Radke, Brad	0-0	0-1	0-0	1-1	0-0	4-0	2-1	0-0	1-1	0-0	0-0	1-0	0-0	0-1	9-5
Reed, Rick	1-0	1-1	0-0	1-1	4-1	0-0	2-0	0-1	0-0	1-2	1-0	0-0	0-0	1-0	15-7
Rincon, Juan	0-0	0-0	0-0	0-1	0-0	0-0	0-0	0-0	0-0	0-0	0-0	0-1	0-0	0-0	0-2
Rodriguez, Jose	0-0	0-0	0-0	0-0	0-0	0-0	0-0	0-0	0-1	0-0	0-0	0-0	0-0	0-0	0-1
Romero, J.C.	0-0	0-0	1-0	1-0	1-0	1-0	3-0	0-0	1-1	0-0	0-0	1-1	0-0	0-0	9-2
Santana, Johan	0-0	0-1	0-2	0-1	0-0	0-0	2-0	0-0	1-1	1-1	0-0	0-0	1-0	3-1	8-6
Trombley, Mike	0-0	0-0	0-0	0-0	0-0	0-0	0-0	0-1	0-0	0-0	0-0	0-0	1-0	0-0	0-1
Wells, Bob	0-0	0-0	0-0	1-0	0-0	0-1	0-0	0-0	0-0	0-0	0-0	0-0	1-0	0-0	2-1
Totals	5-4	1-5	3-3	11-8	11-8	14-4	14-5	0-6	3-6	5-4	5-2	6-3	6-1	10-8	94-67

NO-DECISIONS: Kevin Frederick, Travis Miller.

INTERLEAGUE: Tony Fiore 1-0, Kyle Lohse 0-1, Johan Santana 0-1 vs. Braves; Johan Santana 1-0, Matt Kinney 1-0, Rick Reed 0-1 vs. Marlins; Mike Jackson 0-1, Eric Milton 2-0, Tony Fiore 1-0, Johan Santana 1-0, Matt Kinney 0-1 vs. Brewers; Johan Santana 1-0, Matt Kinney 0-1, Tony Fiore 0-1 vs. Mets; Kyle Lohse 0-1, LaTroy Hawkins 1-0, Tony Fiore 1-0 vs. Phillies. Total: 10-8.

NEW YORK—103-58

Pitcher	Ana. W-L	Bal. W-L	Bos. W-L	Chi. W-L	Cle. W-L	Det. W-L	K.C. W-L	Min. W-L	Oak. W-L	Sea. W-L	T.B. W-L	Tex. W-L	Tor. W-L	N.L. W-L	Total W-L
Clemens, Roger	0-0	0-1	1-0	0-1	0-0	1-0	2-0	1-0	1-0	1-1	3-0	1-0	1-2	1-1	13-6
Hernandez, Adrian	0-0	0-0	0-0	0-0	0-0	0-0	0-0	0-0	0-0	0-0	0-0	0-0	0-1	0-0	0-1
Hernandez, Orlando	0-0	1-0	0-1	0-0	0-0	1-0	0-0	0-0	1-0	0-0	2-2	2-0	1-2	0-0	8-5
Hitchcock, Sterling	0-0	0-0	0-0	0-0	0-0	0-0	0-0	0-0	0-1	0-0	0-1	0-0	0-0	0-0	1-2
Karsay, Steve	0-0	1-0	1-1	1-0	0-1	0-0	0-0	0-0	0-0	1-1	0-0	0-0	1-0	1-1	6-4
Lilly, Ted	0-0	0-0	0-2	1-0	0-0	0-0	0-0	1-0	0-0	0-2	0-0	0-0	0-1	1-1	3-6

Pitcher	Ana. W-L	Bal. W-L	Bos. W-L	Chi. W-L	Cle. W-L	Det. W-L	K.C. W-L	Min. W-L	Oak. W-L	Sea. W-L	T.B. W-L	Tex. W-L	Tor. W-L	N.L. W-L	Total W-L
Mendoza, Ramiro	0-1	1-1	1-0	0-0	1-0	1-0	1-0	0-0	0-0	0-0	0-1	0-0	1-1	2-0	8-4
Mussina, Mike	0-0	2-0	4-2	0-1	1-0	0-1	0-1	1-0	1-2	1-0	3-0	0-2	2-0	3-1	18-10
Pettitte, Andy	2-0	2-1	1-1	1-0	1-1	2-0	1-0	0-0	0-0	0-0	2-0	0-1	0-1	1-0	13-5
Rivera, Mariano	0-0	0-1	0-1	0-0	0-1	0-0	0-0	0-0	0-0	0-0	0-0	0-0	1-0	0-1	1-4
Stanton, Mike	1-0	0-1	1-0	0-0	0-0	1-0	1-0	1-0	1-0	0-0	0-0	0-0	0-0	1-0	7-1
Thurman, Mike	0-0	0-0	0-0	1-0	0-0	0-0	0-0	0-0	0-0	0-0	0-0	0-0	0-0	0-0	1-0
Weaver, Jeff	0-2	1-0	0-0	0-0	0-0	0-0	0-0	0-0	0-0	0-0	2-1	0-0	2-0	0-0	5-3
Wells, David	1-0	5-1	1-1	1-0	3-0	2-0	0-0	1-0	1-1	1-1	1-0	1-0	1-1	1-2	19-7
Totals	4-3	13-6	10-9	4-2	6-3	8-1	5-1	6-0	5-4	4-5	13-5	4-3	10-9	11-7	103-58

NO-DECISIONS: Randy Choate, Brandon Knight, Jay Tessmer.

INTERLEAGUE: Mike Stanton 1-0, David Wells 1-0, Mike Mussina 0-1 vs. Diamondbacks; Mike Mussina 1-0, Ramiro Mendoza 1-0, Steve Karsay 0-1 vs. Rockies; Andy Pettitte 1-0, Steve Karsay 1-0, Roger Clemens 0-1, Ted Lilly 0-1, David Wells 0-1, Mike Mussina 1-0 vs. Mets; David Wells 0-1, Ramiro Mendoza 1-0, Ted Lilly 1-0 vs. Padres; Mike Mussina 1-0, Mariano Rivera 0-1, Roger Clemens 1-0 vs. Giants. Total: 11-7.

OAKLAND—103-59

Pitcher	Ana. W-L	Bal. W-L	Bos. W-L	Chi. W-L	Cle. W-L	Det. W-L	K.C. W-L	Min. W-L	N.Y. W-L	Sea. W-L	T.B. W-L	Tex. W-L	Tor. W-L	N.L. W-L	Total W-L
Bowie, Micah	0-0	0-0	0-0	0-0	0-0	1-0	0-0	0-0	1-0	0-0	0-0	0-0	0-0	0-0	2-0
Bradford, Chad	1-0	0-0	0-0	0-0	0-0	0-0	0-0	1-0	0-0	0-1	0-1	0-0	0-0	2-0	4-2
Fyhrie, Mike	0-1	1-1	0-0	1-1	0-0	0-0	0-0	0-0	0-0	0-0	0-0	0-1	0-0	0-0	2-4
Harang, Aaron	0-0	0-0	1-0	0-0	1-0	0-0	0-0	0-0	0-0	0-2	1-0	0-0	0-1	2-1	5-4
Hiljus, Erik	2-0	0-0	0-2	0-0	0-0	0-0	0-0	0-0	1-0	0-1	0-0	0-0	0-0	0-0	3-3
Hudson, Tim	3-2	1-0	0-2	1-1	1-0	2-0	0-0	1-0	0-1	2-2	0-0	0-0	1-1	3-0	15-9
Koch, Billy	1-2	0-0	0-0	0-0	0-0	0-0	3-1	1-0	0-0	2-0	0-0	3-1	0-0	1-0	11-4
Lidle, Cory	0-0	0-1	0-0	2-0	1-1	1-0	1-0	0-1	1-1	1-2	0-0	1-2	0-1	0-1	8-10
Lilly, Ted	0-1	0-0	0-0	0-0	0-0	0-0	0-0	0-0	0-0	1-0	1-0	0-0	0-0	0-0	2-1
Magnante, Mike	0-0	0-0	0-0	0-0	0-1	0-0	0-0	0-0	0-1	0-0	0-0	0-0	0-0	0-0	0-2
Mecir, Jim	0-1	0-0	0-1	0-0	0-0	1-0	0-0	0-0	0-1	1-0	2-1	0-0	0-0	0-0	6-4
Mulder, Mark	0-0	2-1	1-0	1-0	2-0	0-0	1-0	1-1	1-1	1-0	2-0	3-2	0-2	5-0	19-7
Tam, Jeff	0-1	0-0	0-0	0-0	0-0	0-0	0-0	0-0	0-0	0-1	0-0	1-0	0-0	0-0	1-2
Venafro, Mike	1-0	0-1	0-0	0-0	0-0	0-0	0-0	0-0	0-0	0-0	0-0	1-0	0-0	0-0	2-2
Zito, Barry	3-1	1-0	1-1	2-0	0-0	1-1	2-0	1-0	1-1	2-1	2-0	2-0	2-0	3-0	23-5
Totals	11-9	5-4	3-6	7-2	5-2	6-1	8-1	6-3	4-5	8-11	8-1	13-6	3-6	16-2	103-59

NO-DECISIONS: Mike Holtz, Ricardo Rincon.

INTERLEAGUE: Aaron Harang 1-0, Barry Zito 1-0, Mark Mulder 1-0 vs. Reds; Mark Mulder 1-0, Billy Koch 1-0, Aaron Harang 1-0 vs. Astros; Chad Bradford 1-0, Barry Zito 1-0, Mark Mulder 1-0 vs. Brewers; Mark Mulder 1-0, Chad Bradford 1-0, Tim Hudson 1-0 vs. Pirates; Tim Hudson 2-0, Aaron Harang 0-1, Cory Lidle 0-1, Barry Zito 1-0, Mark Mulder 1-0 vs. Giants. Total: 16-2.

SEATTLE—93-69

Pitcher	Ana. W-L	Bal. W-L	Bos. W-L	Chi. W-L	Cle. W-L	Det. W-L	K.C. W-L	Min. W-L	N.Y. W-L	Oak. W-L	T.B. W-L	Tex. W-L	Tor. W-L	N.L. W-L	Total W-L
Abbott, Paul	0-1	0-0	0-0	0-1	0-0	0-0	0-0	0-0	0-0	0-0	0-0	1-1	0-0	0-0	1-3
Baldwin, James	1-1	0-0	0-2	1-1	0-1	1-0	0-0	0-0	0-1	2-1	1-0	0-0	0-2	1-1	7-10
Creek, Doug	0-0	0-0	0-0	0-0	0-1	0-0	1-0	0-0	0-0	0-0	0-0	0-0	0-0	0-0	1-1
Franklin, Ryan	2-1	0-1	1-0	1-1	0-0	1-0	1-0	0-0	0-1	0-0	0-0	1-0	0-0	0-0	7-5
Garcia, Freddy	2-1	1-0	1-1	0-2	2-0	0-1	1-1	0-0	2-0	1-2	1-0	1-1	0-1	4-0	16-10
Halama, John	2-0	0-1	1-0	0-0	0-0	1-0	0-0	1-0	0-1	0-0	0-1	1-0	0-1	0-0	6-5
Hasegawa, Shigetoshi	1-0	0-0	0-0	0-0	0-0	0-0	1-0	0-0	0-0	2-2	0-0	4-1	0-0	0-0	8-3
Moyer, Jamie	1-0	1-0	0-1	0-1	1-0	0-0	1-0	1-2	0-0	2-2	1-1	2-0	1-0	2-1	13-8
Nelson, Jeff	0-1	0-0	0-0	1-0	0-0	0-0	0-1	1-0	0-0	0-0	0-0	0-0	0-0	0-0	3-2
Pineiro, Joel	1-1	0-1	2-0	0-0	0-0	0-0	1-0	0-1	2-0	2-0	1-2	0-1	1-0	4-1	14-7
Rhodes, Arthur	0-1	2-0	0-0	1-0	0-0	0-0	0-1	2-0	0-1	1-0	0-0	2-1	1-0	0-0	10-4
Sasaki, Kazuhiro	0-1	0-1	0-0	0-0	0-1	0-0	0-0	0-0	0-0	0-0	0-0	2-0	0-0	0-0	4-5
Soriano, Rafael	0-0	0-1	0-0	0-0	0-0	0-0	0-0	0-0	0-0	0-0	0-0	0-0	0-2	0-0	0-3
Valdes, Ismael	0-1	0-0	0-0	0-0	1-0	0-0	0-1	0-0	0-1	0-0	0-0	0-0	0-0	2-0	2-3
Watson, Mark	0-0	0-0	0-0	0-0	0-0	0-0	0-0	0-0	0-0	0-0	0-0	1-0	0-0	0-0	1-0
Totals	10-9	4-5	5-4	4-5	4-3	5-2	6-3	4-5	5-4	11-8	5-4	13-7	6-3	11-7	93-69

NO-DECISIONS: Brian Fitzgerald, Justin Kaye, Julio Mateo, Aaron Taylor.

INTERLEAGUE: Joel Pineiro 0-1, Freddy Garcia 1-0, Rafael Soriano 0-1 vs. Cubs; Joel Pineiro 1-0, Freddy Garcia 1-0, James Baldwin 1-0 vs. Reds; Joel Pineiro 1-0, Freddy Garcia 1-0, Kazuhiro Sasaki 0-1 vs. Rockies; Jamie Moyer 1-0, John Halama 0-1, Joel Pineiro 1-0 vs. Astros; Freddy Garcia 1-0, Rafael Soriano 0-1, Jamie Moyer 0-1 vs. Padres; Jamie Moyer 1-0, James Baldwin 1-0, Joel Pineiro 1-0 vs. Cardinals. Total: 11-7.

TAMPA BAY—55-106

Pitcher	Ana. W-L	Bal. W-L	Bos. W-L	Chi. W-L	Cle. W-L	Det. W-L	K.C. W-L	Min. W-L	N.Y. W-L	Oak. W-L	Sea. W-L	Tex. W-L	Tor. W-L	N.L. W-L	Total W-L
Alvarez, Wilson	0-0	0-0	0-1	0-0	0-0	0-0	0-0	0-0	0-1	0-0	0-0	0-0	1-0	1-1	2-3
Brazelton, Dewon	0-0	0-0	0-0	0-0	0-0	0-0	0-0	0-0	0-0	0-0	0-0	0-0	0-1	0-0	0-1
Carter, Lance	0-0	0-0	0-0	0-0	0-0	0-0	0-0	1-0	0-0	0-0	0-0	0-0	1-0	0-0	2-0
Colome, Jesus	0-1	0-2	1-1	0-1	0-0	1-0	0-1	0-0	0-0	0-0	0-0	0-1	0-0	0-0	2-7
Creek, Doug	0-0	2-0	0-0	0-0	0-0	0-0	0-0	0-0	0-0	0-0	0-0	0-0	0-0	0-0	2-1
de los Santos, Luis	0-0	0-1	0-1	0-0	0-0	0-0	0-0	0-0	0-0	0-0	0-0	0-0	0-0	0-0	0-3
Gardner, Lee	0-0	0-1	0-0	0-0	0-0	0-0	0-0	0-0	0-0	0-0	0-0	1-0	0-0	0-0	1-1
Harper, Travis	0-1	1-1	0-0	0-0	0-0	0-0	0-0	0-0	1-2	1-1	0-0	0-2	1-1	0-0	5-9
James, Delvin	0-0	0-0	0-1	0-0	0-0	0-0	0-0	0-0	0-1	0-0	0-0	0-0	0-0	0-0	0-3
Kennedy, Joe	0-1	1-0	0-1	1-1	0-0	0-0	0-0	1-2	0-2	1-1	0-1	1-0	1-0	2-0	8-11
Kent, Steve	0-0	0-0	0-0	0-0	0-0	0-0	0-1	0-0	0-0	0-0	0-0	0-0	0-1	0-0	0-2
Phelps, Travis	0-0	0-0	0-0	0-0	0-0	0-0	0-0	0-1	0-0	0-0	0-1	1-0	0-0	0-0	1-2
Rupe, Ryan	0-0	0-1	0-1	0-0	2-0	0-0	1-1	0-1	0-2	2-0	0-0	0-1	1-0	0-3	5-10
Sosa, Jorge	0-1	0-1	0-0	0-0	0-0	0-0	0-0	0-1	0-1	0-0	0-0	1-0	0-0	1-1	2-7

Pitcher	Ana. W-L	Bal. W-L	Bos. W-L	Chi. W-L	Cle. W-L	Det. W-L	K.C. W-L	Min. W-L	N.Y. W-L	Oak. W-L	Sea. W-L	Tex. W-L	Tor. W-L	N.L. W-L	Total W-L
Sturtze, Tanyon	0-2	0-0	0-3	1-0	0-2	0-0	1-0	0-1	0-3	0-0	0-2	0-1	2-3	0-1	4-18
Wilson, Paul	0-0	4-1	0-4	1-1	1-1	0-0	0-0	0-0	0-1	0-0	0-0	0-0	0-2	0-2	6-12
Yan, Esteban	1-1	1-0	0-2	0-1	0-0	0-0	0-1	0-1	1-0	0-1	1-0	0-0	1-0	2-1	7-8
Zambrano, Victor	0-1	0-2	2-1	0-0	0-0	1-1	1-0	0-0	1-1	0-1	0-0	1-1	0-0	2-0	8-8
Totals	1-8	9-10	3-16	3-4	2-4	4-2	2-4	2-5	5-13	1-8	4-5	4-5	8-11	7-11	55-106

NO-DECISIONS: Brandon Backe, Jason Jimenez, Tom Martin, Jason Standridge.

INTERLEAGUE: Esteban Yan 0-1, Steve Kent 0-1, Joe Kennedy 0-1 vs. Rockies; Victor Zambrano 1-0, Esteban Yan 2-0, Paul Wilson 0-1, Wilson Alvarez 1-0, Joe Kennedy 0-1 vs. Marlins; Wilson Alvarez 0-1, Joe Kennedy 1-0, Ryan Rupe 0-1 vs. Dodgers; Ryan Rupe 0-1, Victor Zambrano 1-0, Paul Wilson 0-1 vs. Padres; Joe Kennedy 1-0, Ryan Rupe 0-1, Tanyon Sturtze 0-1 vs. Giants. Total: 7-11.

TEXAS—72-90

Pitcher	Ana. W-L	Bal. W-L	Bos. W-L	Chi. W-L	Cle. W-L	Det. W-L	K.C. W-L	Min. W-L	N.Y. W-L	Oak. W-L	Sea. W-L	T.B. W-L	Tor. W-L	N.L. W-L	Total W-L
Alvarez, Juan	0-0	0-0	0-0	0-0	0-0	0-0	0-1	0-0	0-1	0-1	0-1	0-0	0-0	0-0	0-4
Bell, Rob	0-2	0-0	0-0	0-1	1-0	0-0	0-0	0-0	1-0	0-0	0-0	0-0	1-0	1-0	4-3
Benoit, Joaquin	2-1	0-0	0-0	1-1	0-0	0-0	0-1	0-0	1-0	0-0	0-1	0-0	0-0	0-0	4-5
Burba, Dave	1-1	0-0	0-0	0-0	0-0	1-1	0-1	0-0	0-0	1-1	0-0	0-0	0-0	0-1	4-5
Cordero, Francisco	0-0	0-0	0-0	0-0	0-0	1-0	0-0	0-0	0-0	0-0	1-0	0-0	0-0	0-0	2-0
Davis, Doug	0-0	0-0	0-0	0-2	1-1	0-1	0-1	0-0	0-0	2-0	0-1	0-0	0-0	0-0	3-5
Irabu, Hideki	0-3	0-0	0-0	1-0	0-0	0-0	0-2	1-1	0-0	0-0	0-1	0-0	0-0	1-1	3-8
Kolb, Danny	0-0	0-0	1-0	0-0	0-1	0-0	0-0	0-0	1-2	0-1	0-1	1-0	0-0	0-0	3-6
Lewis, Colby	0-1	0-1	0-0	0-0	0-0	0-0	0-1	0-0	0-0	0-0	1-0	0-0	0-0	0-0	1-3
Miceli, Dan	0-0	0-0	0-0	0-0	0-0	0-0	0-0	0-0	0-1	0-1	0-1	0-0	0-0	0-0	0-2
Michalak, Chris	0-0	0-0	0-0	0-0	0-0	0-0	0-1	0-0	0-0	0-0	0-1	0-0	0-0	0-0	0-2
Myette, Aaron	0-0	0-1	0-1	0-0	1-0	0-0	0-0	0-0	0-1	0-0	0-1	0-0	1-0	0-0	2-5
Nitkowski, C.J.	0-0	0-0	0-0	0-0	0-0	0-0	0-0	0-0	0-1	0-0	0-0	0-0	0-0	0-0	0-1
Park, Chan Ho	0-0	1-0	1-0	0-0	0-0	1-1	1-0	0-2	1-0	0-3	1-0	1-0	0-0	2-2	9-8
Powell, Jay	0-0	0-0	0-0	0-0	0-0	0-0	0-0	0-0	0-0	1-0	1-1	0-0	0-0	1-1	3-2
Reyes, Dennys	0-0	1-0	0-1	0-0	0-0	0-0	0-0	0-0	0-0	0-0	1-1	1-1	0-0	0-0	4-3
Rocker, John	0-1	0-0	0-0	0-0	0-0	0-0	0-0	0-0	0-0	0-0	1-0	0-0	1-2	2-3
Rodriguez, Rich	0-0	0-0	1-0	0-0	0-0	0-0	0-0	0-0	0-0	1-1	1-1	0-0	0-0	3-2
Rogers, Kenny	1-1	1-1	0-0	0-1	1-1	1-0	1-0	2-1	0-2	0-0	2-0	1-0	2-0	1-1	13-8
Seanez, Rudy	1-0	0-0	0-0	0-0	0-0	0-1	0-0	0-0	0-1	0-1	0-0	0-0	0-0	1-3
Telford, Anthony	0-0	1-0	0-0	0-0	0-0	0-0	0-1	0-0	0-0	0-1	0-0	0-0	1-0	2-1
Valdes, Ismael	2-1	0-0	0-1	2-0	1-1	0-1	0-1	0-0	0-1	0-0	0-2	0-0	0-1	1-1	6-9
Van Poppel, Todd	0-1	2-0	0-0	0-0	0-0	0-0	0-0	0-0	0-0	0-0	0-1	1-0	0-0	3-2
Totals	7-12	6-3	3-4	4-5	5-4	4-5	2-7	3-6	3-4	6-13	7-13	5-4	8-1	9-9	72-90

NO-DECISIONS: Randy Flores, Reynaldo Garcia, Ben Kozlowski, Steve Woodard.

INTERLEAGUE: Chan Ho Park 0-1, Hideki Irabu 0-1, Dave Burba 0-1 vs. Braves; Anthony Telford 1-0, John Rocker 0-1, Hideki Irabu 1-0 vs. Cubs; Ismael Valdes 1-0, John Rocker 1-0, Kenny Rogers 0-1 vs. Reds; Jay Powell 1-1, John Rocker 0-1, Ismael Valdes 0-1, Chan Ho Park 1-1 vs. Astros; Kenny Rogers 1-0, Rob Bell 1-0, Chan Ho Park 1-0 vs. Pirates. Total: 9-9.

TORONTO—78-84

Pitcher	Ana. W-L	Bal. W-L	Bos. W-L	Chi. W-L	Cle. W-L	Det. W-L	K.C. W-L	Min. W-L	N.Y. W-L	Oak. W-L	Sea. W-L	T.B. W-L	Tex. W-L	N.L. W-L	Total W-L
Borbon, Pedro	0-2	0-0	0-0	0-0	0-0	0-0	0-0	0-0	1-0	0-0	0-0	0-0	0-0	0-0	1-2
Bowles, Brian	0-0	0-0	0-1	0-0	2-0	0-0	0-0	0-0	0-0	0-0	0-0	0-0	0-0	0-0	2-1
Carpenter, Chris	0-0	2-1	1-0	0-0	0-0	0-0	0-1	0-0	0-1	0-1	0-0	0-0	1-0	4-5
Cassidy, Scott	0-0	0-1	0-1	0-1	1-0	0-0	0-1	0-0	0-0	0-0	0-0	0-0	0-0	1-4
Coco, Pasqual	0-0	0-0	0-0	0-0	0-0	0-0	0-0	0-0	0-0	0-0	0-1	0-0	0-0	0-1
Cooper, Brian	0-0	0-0	0-0	0-0	0-0	0-0	0-0	0-1	0-0	0-0	0-0	0-0	0-0	0-1
Escobar, Kelvim	0-0	0-1	2-1	0-0	0-0	0-0	0-1	0-0	0-0	0-1	1-0	0-1	2-2	5-7
Eyre, Scott	0-0	0-0	0-2	0-0	0-0	0-0	0-0	1-0	0-0	0-1	0-0	0-0	1-0	2-4
File, Bob	0-0	0-0	0-0	0-0	0-0	0-0	0-0	0-1	0-0	0-0	0-0	0-0	0-0	0-1
Halladay, Roy	0-1	4-0	1-2	0-0	0-0	2-0	1-1	1-0	2-0	2-0	2-0	1-0	0-1	3-2	19-7
Hendrickson, Mark	0-0	2-0	0-0	0-0	0-0	0-0	0-0	0-0	0-0	0-0	1-0	0-0	0-0	3-0
Heredia, Felix	0-0	1-0	0-1	0-0	0-0	0-0	0-0	0-1	0-0	0-0	0-0	0-0	0-0	1-2
Loaiza, Esteban	0-0	2-0	1-0	0-1	0-1	1-0	0-0	0-1	1-1	2-0	1-0	1-3	0-1	0-2	9-10
Lyon, Brandon	0-1	0-0	0-1	0-0	0-0	0-0	0-0	0-0	0-0	0-0	0-0	1-0	0-1	1-4
Miller, Justin	1-0	1-1	1-0	0-0	0-0	0-0	1-0	0-0	1-0	1-1	0-0	3-0	0-0	0-2	9-5
Parris, Steve	0-1	1-0	0-1	0-1	0-0	0-0	1-0	0-0	2-0	0-0	0-0	1-1	0-0	5-5
Plesac, Dan	0-0	0-0	0-0	0-0	0-0	0-0	0-0	1-1	0-0	0-0	0-0	0-1	0-0	1-2
Politte, Cliff	0-0	0-0	0-1	0-0	0-1	1-0	0-0	0-1	0-0	0-0	0-0	0-0	0-0	1-3
Prokopec, Luke	0-1	0-0	0-0	0-0	0-1	0-0	0-0	0-2	1-0	0-2	1-0	0-2	0-0	2-9
Smith, Mike	0-1	0-0	0-1	0-0	0-0	0-0	0-0	0-0	0-0	0-1	0-0	0-1	0-0	0-3
Thurman, Corey	0-0	0-0	0-0	1-1	0-0	0-0	0-1	0-0	0-1	0-0	0-1	0-0	1-0	2-3
Walker, Pete	1-0	0-0	0-1	1-0	0-0	1-0	2-0	0-0	0-1	0-1	0-0	2-2	0-0	1-0	10-5
Totals	2-7	15-4	6-13	2-4	3-3	6-0	4-3	1-6	9-10	6-3	3-6	11-8	1-8	9-9	78-84

NO-DECISIONS: Jason Kershner, Scott Wiggins.

INTERLEAGUE: Kelvim Escobar 0-1, Chris Carpenter 1-0, Roy Halladay 1-0 vs. Diamondbacks; Roy Halladay 1-0, Pete Walker 1-0, Kelvim Escobar 1-0 vs. Rockies; Roy Halladay 0-1, Justin Miller 0-1, Esteban Loaiza 0-1 vs. Dodgers; Justin Miller 0-1, Esteban Loaiza 0-1, Scott Eyre 1-0, Kelvim Escobar 1-1, Roy Halladay 0-1 vs. Expos; Corey Thurman 1-0, Brandon Lyon 0-1, Roy Halladay 0-1 vs. Giants. Total: 9-9.

HOME RUNS BY PARKS

	At Ana.	At Bal.	At Bos.	At Chi.	At Cle.	At Det.	At K.C.	At Min.	At N.Y.	At Oak.	At Sea.	At T.B.	At Tex.	At Tor.	At N.L. Parks	Totals 2002	Totals 2001	HR Allow.
Anaheim	71	7	1	8	4	6	7	3	3	6	8	2	12	6	8	152	158	169
Baltimore	4	92	8	5	2	0	5	3	10	5	3	10	5	6	7	165	136	208
Boston	4	13	77	0	7	4	6	2	9	4	6	15	12	9	9	177	198	146
Chicago	4	6	0	132	8	10	14	8	3	3	2	2	9	5	11	217	214	190
Cleveland	6	7	7	16	95	7	18	12	4	1	5	4	4	2	4	192	212	142
Detroit	4	3	2	9	10	61	6	11	2	3	1	3	1	1	7	124	139	163
Kansas City	1	1	2	2	5	2	88	6	0	7	6	5	7	3	5	140	152	212
Minnesota	3	1	0	17	13	11	18	68	0	7	8	2	2	7	10	167	164	184
New York	2	13	14	4	6	0	6	7	108	2	8	13	9	20	11	223	203	144
Oakland	11	9	5	3	5	7	3	2	5	116	12	6	11	0	10	205	199	135
Seattle	12	5	1	9	3	2	5	2	8	4	64	6	12	9	10	152	169	178
Tampa Bay	4	13	9	3	1	3	7	1	4	2	2	63	9	5	7	133	121	215
Texas	12	8	4	2	3	0	12	7	8	8	9	5	132	5	15	230	246	194
Toronto	0	15	5	1	4	3	2	2	10	9	3	15	6	102	10	187	195	177
N.L. clubs	3	11	10	11	5	6	12	16	12	5	9	12	14	11	....	137	131	....
2002 Totals	141	204	145	222	171	122	209	150	186	182	146	163	245	191	124	2464	....	2457
2001 Totals	172	152	174	220	200	129	187	165	198	176	147	158	233	*178	....	....	2506	....

*There were actually 176 home runs hit at Toronto in 2001. The total includes two home runs hit by the Blue Jays when they were the "home" team in a game against Texas at San Juan, Puerto Rico, April 1.

AT ANAHEIM (141):

Anaheim (71)—Anderson 13, Glaus 13, Salmon 10, Fullmer 9, Spiezio 7, Kennedy 6, Eckstein 3, Gil 2, Erstad 2, B. Molina 2, Wooten 2, Ochoa 1, Ramirez 1. **Baltimore (4)**—Gibbons 2, Bordick 1, Hairston 1. **Boston (4)**—Hillenbrand 2, Varitek 1, Daubach 1. **Chicago (4)**—Graffanino 1, Ordonez 1, Konerko 1, Lee 1. **Cincinnati (1)**—Branyan 1. **Cleveland (6)**—Fryman 2, Burks 1, Thome 1, Gutierrez 1, Branyan 1. **Detroit (4)**—Higginson 1, Halter 1, Bocachica 1, Inge 1. **Kansas City (1)**—Sweeney 1. **Minnesota (3)**—Hunter 1, Pierzynski 1, Jones 1. **New York (2)**—B. Williams 1, Mondesi 1. **Oakland (11)**—Tejada 3, Chavez 3, Dye 2, Long 2, Hatteberg 1. **Pittsburgh (2)**—Young 1, C. Wilson 1. **Seattle (12)**—Olerud 3, Boone 2, McLemore 1, Martinez 1, Cameron 1, Relaford 1, Davis 1, Podsednik 1, Ugueto 1. **Tampa Bay (4)**—Grieve 2, Gomez 1, Winn 1. **Texas (12)**—A. Rodriguez 4, Gonzalez 2, Everett 2, Palmeiro 1, I. Rodriguez 1, Greene 1, Lamb 1.

AT BALTIMORE (204):

Anaheim (7)—Glaus 2, Anderson 1, Fullmer 1, B. Molina 1, Kennedy 1, Eckstein 1. **Baltimore (92)**—Gibbons 17, Batista 14, Conine 12, Cordova 11, Mora 8, Bordick 6, Matthews 6, Gil 5, Singleton 4, Hairston 2, Richard 2, Segui 1, L. Lopez 1, Fordyce 1, Leon 1, B. Roberts 1. **Boston (13)**—Damon 3, Garciaparra 3, Hillenbrand 3, Floyd 2, Nixon 2. **Chicago (6)**—Durham 2, Lofton 1, Valentin 1, Graffanino 1, Ordonez 1. **Cleveland (7)**—Branyan 3, Thome 2, Gutierrez 1, Lawton 1. **Detroit (3)**—Halter 1, Simon 1, Pena 1. **Kansas City (1)**—Tucker 1. **Los Angeles (2)**—Green 1, Grudzielanek 1. **Minnesota (1)**—Ortiz 1. **New York (13)**—Giambi 3, Jeter 3, Ventura 2, White 2, Posada 1, Soriano 1, Johnson 1. **Oakland (9)**—Tejada 3, Chavez 2, Saenz 1, Hatteberg 1, Dye 1, Piatt 1. **Philadelphia (5)**—Rolen 1, Abreu 1, Giambi 1, Burrell 1, Rollins 1. **San Diego (4)**—Gant 1, Lankford 1, Klesko 1, Trammell 1. **Seattle (5)**—McLemore 1, Martinez 1, Olerud 1, Boone 1, Cameron 1. **Tampa Bay (13)**—Vaughn 4, Gomez 3, Grieve 3, Cox 1, Huff 1, Hall 1. **Texas (8)**—A. Rodriguez 2, I. Rodriguez 1, Everett 1, Perry 1, Hollandsworth 1, Greene 1, Young 1. **Toronto (15)**—Wells 3, Phelps 3, Delgado 2, Stewart 2, Woodward 2, Cruz 1, Wise 1, Hinske 1.

AT BOSTON (145):

Anaheim (1)—Glaus 1. **Arizona (6)**—Gonzalez 2, Guillen 1, Miller 1, Durazo 1, Spivey 1. **Atlanta (2)**—Sheffield 1, J. Lopez 1. **Baltimore (8)**—Batista 3, Mora 2, Gil 2, L. Lopez 1. **Boston (77)**—Ramirez 18, Daubach 11, Garciaparra 10, Nixon 8, Varitek 6, Damon 5, Mirabelli 5, Hillenbrand 5, Floyd 3, Henderson 1, Baerga 1, Offerman 1, R. Sanchez 1, Clark 1, Merloni 1. **Cleveland (7)**—Thome 3, Burks 1, Fryman 1, Garcia 1, Broussard 1. **Colorado (2)**—Zeile 1, Estalella 1. **Detroit (2)**—Halter 1, Lombard 1. **Kansas City (2)**—Knoblauch 1, Ibanez 1. **New York (14)**—Soriano 4, Ventura 2, Giambi 2, B. Williams 1, White 1, Coomer 1, Jeter 1, Posada 1, Johnson 1. **Oakland (5)**—Justice 1, Saenz 1, Dye 1, Tejada 1, Hernandez 1. **Seattle (1)**—Sierra 1. **Tampa Bay (9)**—Winn 2, Cox 2, Sandberg 2, Sheets 1, Grieve 1, Hall 1. **Texas (4)**—I. Rodriguez 1, Perry 1, Hollandsworth 1, Mench 1. **Toronto (5)**—Phelps 2, Cruz 1, Wilson 1, Wells 1.

AT CHICAGO (222):

Anaheim (8)—Fullmer 2, Glaus 2, Salmon 2, Gil 1, Spiezio 1, Eckstein 1. **Baltimore (8)**—Gibbons 2, Cordova 1, Batista 1, Mora 1. **Chicago (6)**—Alou 2, Bellhorn 2, Gonzalez 1, Patterson 1. **Chicago (132)**—Thomas 24, Ordonez 24, Valentin 15, Lee 14, Konerko 13, Crede 7, Durham 6, Alomar 5, Rowand 5, Clayton 4, Graffanino 4, Liefer 4, Lofton 3, Harris 2, Johnson 1, Jimenez 1. **Cleveland (16)**—Garcia 3, Burks 2, Stevens 2, Lawton 2, Selby 2, Thome 1, Branyan 1, McDonald 1, Bradley 1, Bard 1. **Detroit (9)**—Young 2, Easley 1, Higginson 1, Magee 1, Lombard 1, Fick 1, Truby 1, Salazar 1. **Kansas City (2)**—Sweeney 1, Beltran 1. **Minnesota (17)**—Jones 4, Ortiz 3, Koskie 3, Mientkiewicz 3, Guzman 1, Restovich 1, Kielty 1, Mohr 1. **Montreal (2)**—O'Leary 1, V. Guerrero 1. **New York (3)**—Alomar 1, Piazza 1, Perez 1. **New York (4)**—Giambi 2, B. Williams 1, Johnson 1. **Oakland (3)**—Velarde 1, Justice 1, Giambi 1. **Seattle (9)**—Cameron 4, Boone 3, Olerud 1, Cirillo 1. **Tampa Bay (3)**—Grieve 1, Hall 1, Sandberg 1. **Texas (2)**—Perry 1, Young 1. **Toronto (1)**—Stewart 1.

AT CLEVELAND (171):

Anaheim (4)—Salmon 1, Erstad 1, Glaus 1, DaVanon 1. **Arizona (1)**—Spivey 1. **Baltimore (2)**—Batista 1, Singleton 1. **Boston (7)**—Nixon 2, Daubach 2, Ramirez 1, Garciaparra 1, Merloni 1. **Chicago (8)**—Ordonez 3, Alomar 1, Lofton 1, Clayton 1, Valentin 1, Konerko 1. **Cleveland (95)**—Thome 30, Burks 16, Vizquel 9, Lawton 8, Garcia 7, Fryman 4, Bradley 4, Magruder 3, Gutierrez 2, Selby 2, Broussard 2, Bard 2, Stevens 1, Diaz 1, Branyan 1, Martinez 1, Snyder 1, Crisp 1. **Detroit (10)**—Pena 3, Easley 1, Higginson 1, Cruz 1, D. Jackson 1, Simon 1, Truby 1, Bocachica 1. **Kansas City (5)**—Randa 2, Knoblauch 1, Sweeney 1, Beltran 1. **Minnesota (13)**—Jones 3, Hunter 2, Ortiz 2, LeCroy 2, Mohr 2, Rivas 1, Kielty 1. **New York (3)**—Piazza 1, Alfonzo 1, Perez 1. **New York (6)**—Soriano 2, White 1, Giambi 1, Posada 1, Johnson 1. **Oakland (5)**—Chavez 3, Dye 1, Long 1. **Philadelphia (1)**—Giambi 1. **Seattle (3)**—Davis 1, Cameron 1. **Tampa Bay (1)**—Cox 1. **Texas (3)**—Palmeiro 1, A. Rodriguez 1, Hafner 1. **Toronto (4)**—Delgado 1, Wells 1, Phelps 1, Hinske 1.

AT DETROIT (122):

Anaheim (6)—Fullmer 2, Glaus 2, Salmon 1, Eckstein 1. **Boston (4)**—Nixon 2, Ramirez 1, Damon 1. **Chicago (10)**—Thomas 2, Konerko 2, Lee 2, Crede 2, Lofton 1, Johnson 1. **Cleveland (7)**—Garcia 2, Burks 1, Anderson 1, Stevens 1, Lawton 1, Diaz 1. **Detroit (61)**—Simon 13, Fick 12, Higginson 6, Young 5, Pena 5, Easley 4, Halter 4, Magee 1, Inge 3, Santiago 3, Lombard 3, Bocachica 1. **Kansas City (2)**—Brown 1, Beltran 1. **Minnesota (11)**—Ortiz 4, Koskie 2, Hunter 1, Mientkiewicz 1, Jones 1, Kielty 1, Cuddyer 1. **Montreal (2)**—V. Guerrero 1, Vidro 1. **Oakland (7)**—Mabry 2, Myers 1, Justice 1, Dye 1, Chavez 1, Long 1. **Philadelphia (3)**—Rolen 1, Burrell 1, Rollins 1. **Pittsburgh (1)**—Giles 1. **Seattle (2)**—Cameron 1, Davis 1. **Tampa Bay (3)**—Gomez 1, Johnson 1, Grieve 1. **Toronto (3)**—Fletcher 1, Delgado 1, Hinske 1.

2002 A.L. STATISTICS Miscellaneous

AT KANSAS CITY (209):

Anaheim (7)—Anderson 2, Glaus 2, Salmon 1, Erstad 1, Wooten 1. **Baltimore (5)**—Batista 3, Mora 1, Gil 1. **Boston (6)**—Ramirez 2, Damon 2, Offerman 1, Daubach 1. **Chicago (14)**—Ordonez 2, Crede 2, Rowand 2, Alomar 1, Thomas 1, Lofton 1, Valentin 1, Konerko 1, Lee 1, Liefer 1, Borchard 1. **Cleveland (18)**—Burks 5, Magruder 3, Vizquel 2, Thome 2, Selby 2, Bradley 2, Garcia 1, Broussard 1. **Detroit (6)**—Simon 2, Easley 1, Halter 1, Fick 1, Inge 1. **Florida (5)**—Lee 2, Wilson 2, Owens 1. **Kansas City (88)**—Beltran 19, Sweeney 14, Ibanez 14, Tucker 10, Randa 6, Hinch 6, Berger 5, Guiel 4, Knoblauch 3, Mayne 2, Febles 2, Quinn 2, Perez 1. **Minnesota (18)**—Jones 6, Hunter 3, Buchanan 2, Guzman 2, Prince 1, Ortiz 1, Rivas 1, Kielty 1, Mohr 1. **New York (6)**—Vander Wal 2, Ventura 1, B. Williams 1, Mondesi 1, Giambi 1. **Oakland (3)**—Justice 1, Durham 1, Tejada 1. **St. Louis (4)**—Martinez 1, Cairo 1, Marrero 1, Pujols 1. **San Diego (3)**—Gant 1, Klesko 1, Matos 1. **Seattle (5)**—Martinez 1, Olerud 1, Cameron 1, Davis 1. **Tampa Bay (7)**—Sheets 2, Sandberg 2, Cox 1, Huff 1, Crawford 1. **Texas (12)**—Perry 4, Palmeiro 3, A. Rodriguez 2, Gonzalez 1, Greene 1, Mench 1. **Toronto (2)**—Phelps 1, Hinske 1.

AT MINNESOTA (150):

Anaheim (3)—Salmon 1, Anderson 1, Erstad 1. **Atlanta (7)**—Sheffield 1, Castilla 1, J. Lopez 1, C. Jones 1, Lockhart 1, M. Franco 1, A. Jones 1. **Baltimore (3)**—Singleton 1, Mora 1, Gil 1. **Boston (2)**—Henderson 1, Floyd 1. **Chicago (8)**—Ordonez 2, Konerko 2, Lee 2, Valentin 1, Durham 1. **Cleveland (12)**—Thome 7, Burks 4, Bradley 1. **Detroit (11)**—Paquette 3, Magee 1, Halter 1, Simon 1, Lombard 1, Fick 1, Munson 1, Pena 1, Infante 1. **Florida (5)**—Lee 3, Floyd 1, Lowell 1. **Kansas City (6)**—Beltran 2, Alicea 1, Mayne 1, McCarty 1, Ibanez 1. **Milwaukee (4)**—Stairs 2, Thompson 1, Bako 1. **Minnesota (68)**—Hunter 13, Kielty 8, Koskie 6, Mientkiewicz 6, Guzman 6, Jones 6, Ortiz 5, Prince 3, Buchanan 3, Mohr 3, Pierzynski 2, LeCroy 2, Rivas 2, Cuddyer 2, Hocking 1. **New York (7)**—Ventura 2, Jeter 2, Giambi 1, Posada 1, Johnson 1. **Oakland (2)**—Tejada 1, Piatt 1. **Seattle (2)**—Boone 1, Relaford 1. **Tampa Bay (1)**—Grieve 1. **Texas (7)**—A. Rodriguez 4, Palmeiro 1, Lamb 1, Mench 1. **Toronto (2)**—Delgado 1, Wells 1.

AT NEW YORK (186):

Anaheim (3)—Anderson 1, Ochoa 1, Spiezio 1. **Arizona (5)**—Finley 2, Gonzalez 1, Donnels 1, Barajas 1. **Baltimore (10)**—Batista 3, Conine 2, Gibbons 2, Segui 1, Leon 1, Mora 1. **Boston (9)**—Garciaparra 3, Ramirez 2, Clark 2, Henderson 1, Mirabelli 1. **Chicago (3)**—Liefer 1, Crede 1, Olivo 1. **Cleveland (4)**—Thome 2, Fryman 1, Lawton 1. **Detroit (2)**—Simon 1, Munson 1. **New York (6)**—Vaughn 2, Piazza 1, Cedeno 1, Wilson 1, Perez 1. **New York (108)**—Giambi 19, Soriano 17, B. Williams 13, Posada 12, Ventura 9, Jeter 8, Johnson 7, Mondesi 6, White 5, Spencer 5, Vander Wal 2, Coomer 2, Wilson 2, Thames 1. **Oakland (5)**—Chavez 2, Dye 1, Tejada 1, Long 1. **San Francisco (1)**—Bonds 1. **Seattle (8)**—Cirillo 2, Guillen 2, Sierra 1, Olerud 1, Relaford 1, Davis 1. **Tampa Bay (4)**—Cox 3, Gomez 1. **Texas (8)**—Palmeiro 3, Perry 2, A. Rodriguez 2, Everett 1. **Toronto (10)**—Delgado 2, Hinske 2, Mondesi 1, Huckaby 1, Cruz 1, Wilson 1, Wells 1, Lopez 1.

AT OAKLAND (182):

Anaheim (6)—Glaus 2, Salmon 1, Anderson 1, Spiezio 1, Eckstein 1. **Baltimore (5)**—Gil 2, Cordova 1, Hairston 1, Singleton 1. **Boston (4)**—Offerman 1, Nixon 1, Varitek 1, Hillenbrand 1. **Chicago (3)**—Clayton 1, Ordonez 1, Johnson 1. **Cleveland (1)**—Stevens 1. **Detroit (3)**—Pena 2, Bocachica 1. **Houston (1)**—Merced 1. **Kansas City (7)**—Ibanez 2, Sweeney 1, Perez 1, Hinch 1, Febles 1, Berger 1. **Milwaukee (2)**—Jenkins 2. **Minnesota (7)**—LeCroy 2, Hunter 1, Koskie 1, Jones 1, Cuddyer 1, Mohr 1. **New York (2)**—Jeter 1, Posada 1. **Oakland (116)**—Tejada 17, Chavez 17, Dye 13, Long 9, Mabry 8, Hatteberg 8, Justice 6, Giambi 6, Ellis 6, Durham 5, Pena 5, Saenz 3, Hernandez 3, Piatt 3, Myers 2, Menechino 2, Byrnes 2, Sutton 1. **San Francisco (2)**—Kent 2. **Seattle (4)**—Martinez 1, Olerud 1, Cameron 1, Suzuki 1. **Tampa Bay (2)**—Vaughn 1, Cox 1. **Texas (8)**—Palmeiro 2, Rivera 2, Gonzalez 1, Haselman 1, Everett 1, A. Rodriguez 1. **Toronto (9)**—Delgado 2, Mondesi 1, Stewart 1, Cruz 1, Berg 1, Lopez 1, Phelps 1, Hinske 1.

AT SEATTLE (146):

Anaheim (8)—Salmon 3, Anderson 2, Erstad 1, Fullmer 1, B. Molina 1. **Baltimore (3)**—Conine 1, Batista 1, Mora 1. **Boston (6)**—Ramirez 2, Nixon 2, Floyd 1, Hillenbrand 1. **Chicago (5)**—McGriff 2, Sosa 2, Hundley 1. **Chicago (2)**—Clayton 1, Lee 1. **Cleveland (5)**—Lawton 2, Burks 1, Thome 1, Bradley 1. **Colorado (2)**—Walker 1, Agbayani 1. **Detroit (1)**—Halter 1. **Kansas City (6)**—Sweeney 2, Ibanez 2, Knoblauch 1, Tucker 1. **Minnesota (8)**—Hunter 2, Ortiz 2, Jones 2, Pierzynski 1, LeCroy 1. **New York (8)**—Ventura 2, Soriano 2, Vander Wal 1, Giambi 1, Jeter 1, Posada 1. **Oakland (12)**—Myers 2, Tejada 2, Chavez 2, Pena 2, Hatteberg 1, Giambi 1, Hernandez 1, Menechino 1. **St. Louis (2)**—Martinez 1, Pujols 1. **Seattle (64)**—Boone 13, Martinez 9, Olerud 9, Cameron 7, Sierra 6, McLemore 4, Guillen 4, Suzuki 4, Wilson 3, Cirillo 2, Offerman 1, Relaford 1, Davis 1. **Tampa Bay (2)**—J. Smith 1, Sandberg 1. **Texas (9)**—Palmeiro 4, A. Rodriguez 3, Catalanotto 1, Young 1. **Toronto (2)**—Delgado 2, Hinske 1.

AT TAMPA BAY (163):

Anaheim (2)—Anderson 2. **Baltimore (10)**—Gibbons 4, Cordova 2, Richard 2, Hairston 1, Mora 1. **Boston (15)**—Ramirez 4, Garciaparra 2, Nixon 2, Daubach 2, Henderson 1, Mirabelli 1, Varitek 1, Merloni 1, Hillenbrand 1. **Chicago (2)**—Ordonez 1, Lee 1. **Cleveland (4)**—Thome 2, Garcia 2. **Detroit (3)**—Cruz 1, Fick 1, Rivera 1. **Florida (3)**—Floyd 1, Wilson 1, Lowell 1. **Kansas City (5)**—Sweeney 2, Ibanez 2, Mayne 1. **Los Angeles (3)**—Green 2, Grissom 1. **Minnesota (2)**—Hunter 1, Jones 1. **New York (13)**—Ventura 3, Soriano 3, Giambi 2, Vander Wal 1, Mondesi 1, Jeter 1, Posada 1, J. Rivera 1. **Oakland (6)**—Hatteberg 3, Myers 1, Dye 1, Long 1. **San Diego (6)**—Gant 2, Klesko 2, Trammell 1, Vazquez 1, Matos 1. **Seattle (6)**—Suzuki 2, Sierra 1, Olerud 1, Boone 1, Snelling 1. **Tampa Bay (63)**—Huff 17, Sandberg 10, Winn 9, Grieve 7, Flaherty 4, Cox 4, Gomez 2, Conti 2, Hall 2, Abernathy 2, Vaughn 1, Sheets 1, B. Smith 1, Crawford 1. **Texas (5)**—Perry 2, Palmeiro 1, A. Rodriguez 1, Hollandsworth 1. **Toronto (15)**—Delgado 4, Cruz 3, Mondesi 2, Wells 2, Huckaby 1, Lopez 1, Lawrence 1, Hudson 1.

AT TEXAS (245):

Anaheim (12)—Glaus 4, Anderson 3, Erstad 2, Salmon 1, Spiezio 1, B. Molina 1. **Atlanta (5)**—A. Jones 2, Sheffield 1, J. Lopez 1, M. Franco 1. **Baltimore (5)**—Batista 3, Bordick 1, Leon 1. **Boston (12)**—Damon 3, Garciaparra 3, Nixon 3, Daubach 2, Hillenbrand 1. **Chicago (9)**—Valentin 3, Ordonez 2, Thomas 1, Lofton 1, Konerko 1, Lee 1. **Cincinnati (1)**—Dunn 2, Branyan 1, Taylor 1. **Cleveland (4)**—Branyan 2, Burks 1, Vizquel 1. **Detroit (1)**—Higginson 1. **Houston (5)**—Berkman 2, Merced 1, Blum 1, Zinter 1. **Kansas City (7)**—Randa 2, Beltran 2, Sweeney 1, Perez 1, Febles 1. **Minnesota (2)**—Hunter 1, Jones 1. **New York (9)**—Giambi 2, Soriano 2, B. Williams 1, Mondesi 1, White 1, Posada 1, Johnson 1. **Oakland (11)**—Tejada 3, Dye 2, Chavez 2, Justice 1, Long 1, Hernandez 1, Byrnes 1. **Seattle (12)**—Cameron 5, Sierra 2, Relaford 2, Olerud 1, Boone 1, Suzuki 1. **Tampa Bay (9)**—Cox 2, McCarty 1, Gomez 1, Grieve 1, Winn 1, Huff 1, Hall 1, Sandberg 1. **Texas (132)**—A. Rodriguez 34, Palmeiro 23, I. Rodriguez 15, Everett 11, Perry 9, Mench 8, Lamb 7, Greene 6, Gonzalez 4, Young 3, Hollandsworth 2, Rivera 2, Catalanotto 2, Blalock 2, Haselman 1, Greer 1, Ortiz 1, Ludwick 1. **Toronto (6)**—Mondesi 1, Delgado 1, Stewart 1, Wells 1, Phelps 1, Hudson 1.

AT TORONTO (191):

Anaheim (6)—Anderson 2, Erstad 2, Fullmer 1, Eckstein 1. **Baltimore (6)**—Singleton 2, Mora 2, Batista 1, Matthews 1. **Boston (9)**—Ramirez 3, Offerman 1, Garciaparra 1, Nixon 1, Merloni 1, Daubach 1, Hillenbrand 1. **Chicago (5)**—Valentin 3, Konerko 1, Borchard 1. **Cleveland (2)**—Fryman 1, Thome 1. **Detroit (1)**—Monroe 1. **Kansas City (3)**—Ibanez 1, Beltran 1, Pellow 1. **Minnesota (7)**—Hunter 2, Ortiz 2, Koskie 1, Jones 1, Mohr 1. **Montreal (4)**—V. Guerrero 1, Tatis 1, Barrett 1, Macias 1. **New York (20)**—Soriano 6, Giambi 5, White 3, Ventura 2, Johnson 2, B. Williams 1, Mondesi 1. **San Francisco (3)**—Minor 3, Bonds 1, Snow 1, Aurilia 1, Torrealba 1. **Seattle (9)**—Olerud 2, Guillen 2, McLemore 1, Martinez 1, Boone 1, Wilson 1, Cameron 1. **Tampa Bay (5)**—Huff 2, Winn 1, Conti 1, Sandberg 1. **Texas (5)**—A. Rodriguez 2, Palmeiro 1, Haselman 1, Blalock 1. **Toronto (102)**—Delgado 17, Hinske 15, Cruz 11, Mondesi 10, Wells 10, Woodward 9, Wilson 6, Phelps 6, Lopez 5, Stewart 4, Berg 3, Wise 2, Hudson 2, Huckaby 1, Bush 1.

If you've ever wondered whether a given stadium is a good hitters' park, a haven for home runs or more conducive for triples, this section is for you. This section contains selected batting statistics for all American League parks for 2002. A key component of this section is an index number for each category which is used to determine how a given park influences a particular statistic. For instance, Minnesota's Metrodome has been referred to in past years as the "Homerdome." However, if you look at last year's chart under home runs, you'll find that its park index number of 70 tends to dispel that notion. On the other hand, the Metrodome's index numbers for doubles (118) and triples (177) suggest the park contributes to other extra-base hits besides home runs.

The numbers on all of the major league parks for 2002 are here. For each park, we show how the home team and its opponents performed, both at home and on the road, with the exception being that we do not include data from interleague games. The differences in interleague opponents and ballparks would skew the data.

By comparing the per-game averages at the home park and on the road, we can evaluate the park's impact. This is done by simply dividing the home average by the road average and multiplying the result by 100, generating a park index. If the home and road per-game averages are equal, the index equals 100, and it can be concluded that the park had no impact. An index above 100 means that the park favors that particular statistic. The indexes for at-bats, runs, hits, errors and infield errors are determined on a per-game basis; all other stats are calculated on a per-at-bat basis. "E-infield" denotes infield *fielding* errors. "Alt." is the approximate elevation of the ballpark.

For most parks, data is presented both for 2002 and for the last three years overall. If the park's dimensions have changed over that time, however, the data from the old and new configurations will not be combined. Following all the teams' charts is a ranking section that shows which parks most inflate runs, home runs and batting average.

ANAHEIM

Home park: Edison International Field of Anaheim **Alt.:** 160 feet **Surface:** Grass

| | 2002 Season | | | | | | | 2000-02 Seasons | | | | | | |
| | Home Games | | | Road Games | | | | Home Games | | | Road Games | | | |
Category	Ana.	Opp.	Total	Ana.	Opp.	Total	Index	Ana.	Opp.	Total	Ana.	Opp.	Total	Index
G	72	72	144	72	72	144		216	216	432	216	216	432	
Avg.	.277	.242	.259	.286	.244	.266	97	.274	.263	.268	.271	.259	.265	101
AB	2467	2489	4956	2603	2353	4956	100	7316	7595	14911	7660	7159	14819	101
R	358	284	642	399	284	683	94	1055	1019	2074	1066	992	2058	101
H	683	603	1286	745	574	1319	97	2003	1997	4000	2075	1855	3930	102
2B	142	114	256	156	98	254	101	373	391	764	438	325	763	100
3B	17	4	21	9	12	21	100	38	16	54	43	34	77	70
HR	62	67	129	73	81	154	84	255	241	496	223	256	479	103
BB	198	234	432	210	229	439	98	698	749	1447	691	771	1462	98
SO	352	459	811	364	434	798	102	1189	1271	2460	1303	1205	2508	97
E	40	46	86	43	62	105	82	157	137	294	142	152	294	100
E-Infield	33	37	70	41	48	89	79	139	108	247	127	121	248	100
LHB-Avg.	.280	.241	.261	.295	.234	.269	97	.281	.256	.269	.269	.258	.264	102
LHB-HR	28	30	58	35	34	69	83	114	96	210	113	110	223	93
RHB-Avg.	.274	.244	.258	.277	.251	.264	98	.266	.268	.267	.273	.260	.266	100
RHB-HR	34	37	71	38	47	85	84	141	145	286	110	146	256	111

BALTIMORE

Home park: Oriole Park at Camden Yards **Alt.:** 20 feet **Surface:** Grass

| | 2002 Season | | | | | | | 2001 Season | | | | | | |
| | Home Games | | | Road Games | | | | Home Games | | | Road Games | | | |
Category	Bal.	Opp.	Total	Bal.	Opp.	Total	Index	Bal.	Opp.	Total	Bal.	Opp.	Total	Index
G	72	72	144	72	72	144		71	71	142	73	73	146	
Avg.	.246	.260	.253	.247	.280	.263	96	.242	.262	.252	.257	.272	.265	95
AB	2406	2543	4949	2483	2461	4944	100	2306	2505	4811	2567	2464	5031	98
R	292	331	623	300	374	674	92	267	351	618	349	373	722	88
H	592	661	1253	614	688	1302	96	558	652	1210	661	671	1332	93
2B	111	109	220	160	129	289	76	104	128	232	139	152	291	83
3B	10	5	15	12	19	31	48	11	10	21	10	17	27	81
HR	81	101	182	66	91	157	116	50	87	137	63	83	146	98
BB	207	241	448	195	242	437	102	217	221	438	239	233	472	97
SO	425	426	851	432	448	880	97	421	432	853	451	409	860	104
E	42	54	96	36	38	74	130	47	48	95	56	52	108	90
E-Infield	33	46	79	29	32	61	130	45	42	87	50	43	93	96
LHB-Avg.	.253	.248	.250	.261	.281	.273	92	.213	.259	.239	.256	.283	.271	88
LHB-HR	30	47	77	20	49	69	109	24	40	64	23	46	69	96
RHB-Avg.	.243	.272	.256	.241	.279	.257	99	.259	.262	.260	.259	.263	.260	100
RHB-HR	51	54	105	46	42	88	121	26	47	73	40	37	77	100

2002 A.L. STATISTICS *Miscellaneous*

BOSTON

Home park: Fenway Park **Alt.:** 21 feet **Surface:** Grass

Category	2002 Season Home Games			Road Games			Index	2000-02 Seasons Home Games			Road Games			Index
	Bos.	Opp.	Total	Bos.	Opp.	Total		Bos.	Opp.	Total	Bos.	Opp.	Total	
G	72	72	144	72	72	144		216	216	432	215	215	430	
Avg.	.280	.251	.265	.287	.236	.263	101	.277	.259	.268	.270	.245	.258	104
AB	2415	2478	4893	2634	2379	5013	98	7344	7593	14937	7737	7174	14911	100
R	365	312	677	431	283	714	95	1080	1003	2083	1144	928	2072	100
H	676	621	1297	755	562	1317	98	2034	1965	3999	2091	1758	3849	103
2B	159	145	304	163	97	260	120	461	410	871	433	330	763	114
3B	14	6	20	14	16	30	68	49	31	80	34	42	76	105
HR	71	58	129	91	76	167	79	217	190	407	279	223	502	81
BB	248	173	421	249	202	451	96	762	611	1373	746	684	1430	96
SO	400	544	944	420	488	908	107	1334	1666	3000	1382	1514	2896	103
E	53	54	107	38	47	85	126	160	147	307	130	125	255	120
E-Infield	43	44	87	32	41	73	119	137	121	258	106	107	213	121
LHB-Avg.	.276	.230	.252	.273	.244	.259	97	.275	.253	.264	.262	.242	.252	104
LHB-HR	29	21	50	44	42	86	63	107	75	182	147	110	257	74
RHB-Avg.	.283	.268	.276	.300	.229	.266	104	.279	.264	.271	.278	.248	.263	103
RHB-HR	42	37	79	47	34	81	95	110	115	225	132	113	245	88

CHICAGO

Home park: Comiskey Park **Alt.:** 595 feet **Surface:** Grass

Category	2002 Season Home Games			Road Games			Index	2001-02 Seasons Home Games			Road Games			Index
	Chi.	Opp.	Total	Chi.	Opp.	Total		Chi.	Opp.	Total	Chi.	Opp.	Total	
G	72	72	144	72	72	144		144	144	288	144	144	288	
Avg.	.284	.255	.269	.262	.264	.263	102	.276	.262	.269	.267	.266	.267	101
AB	2392	2447	4839	2519	2393	4912	99	4795	4981	9776	4991	4765	9756	100
R	427	331	758	342	368	710	107	793	708	1501	689	713	1402	107
H	679	623	1302	661	631	1292	101	1324	1304	2628	1332	1269	2601	101
2B	120	127	247	140	124	264	95	249	261	510	285	251	536	95
3B	10	7	17	15	9	24	72	22	17	39	28	26	54	72
HR	120	79	199	74	85	159	127	218	180	398	162	147	309	129
BB	237	241	478	233	229	462	105	498	473	971	438	447	885	109
SO	387	415	802	435	416	851	96	820	838	1658	881	794	1675	99
E	32	49	81	53	49	102	79	84	101	185	101	93	194	95
E-Infield	32	44	76	46	34	80	95	78	86	164	84	74	158	104
LHB-Avg.	.293	.267	.277	.232	.286	.265	105	.282	.265	.272	.249	.281	.268	101
LHB-HR	30	46	76	22	43	65	123	61	94	155	54	70	124	128
RHB-Avg.	.279	.244	.264	.276	.241	.262	101	.273	.259	.267	.275	.252	.266	100
RHB-HR	90	33	123	52	42	94	130	157	86	243	108	77	185	129

CLEVELAND

Home park: Jacobs Field **Alt.:** 660 feet **Surface:** Grass

Category	2002 Season Home Games			Road Games			Index	2000-02 Seasons Home Games			Road Games			Index
	Cle.	Opp.	Total	Cle.	Opp.	Total		Cle.	Opp.	Total	Cle.	Opp.	Total	
G	72	72	144	72	72	144		215	215	430	217	217	434	
Avg.	.248	.274	.261	.257	.276	.266	98	.275	.273	.274	.274	.273	.273	100
AB	2372	2533	4905	2490	2397	4887	100	7265	7623	14888	7643	7256	14899	101
R	337	388	725	341	375	716	101	1166	1125	2291	1168	1113	2281	101
H	588	694	1282	639	661	1300	99	2001	2078	4079	2092	1981	4073	101
2B	120	151	271	114	135	249	108	382	445	827	394	400	794	104
3B	8	13	21	14	25	39	54	33	39	72	50	52	102	71
HR	85	71	156	93	60	153	102	292	217	509	263	198	461	110
BB	209	287	496	264	256	520	95	768	832	1600	813	817	1630	98
SO	435	533	968	453	398	851	113	1348	1635	2983	1414	1458	2872	104
E	43	65	108	55	32	87	124	125	165	290	133	146	279	105
E-Infield	38	58	96	47	30	77	125	109	141	250	106	122	228	111
LHB-Avg.	.251	.288	.268	.252	.277	.264	102	.278	.274	.276	.266	.285	.275	100
LHB-HR	58	35	93	63	25	88	103	170	100	270	143	83	226	115
RHB-Avg.	.245	.263	.255	.261	.275	.268	95	.273	.272	.272	.280	.265	.272	100
RHB-HR	27	36	63	30	35	65	99	122	117	239	120	115	235	105

DETROIT

Home park: Comerica Park **Alt.:** 585 feet **Surface:** Grass

| | 2002 Season | | | | | | | 2001-02 Seasons | | | | | | |
| | Home Games | | | Road Games | | | | Home Games | | | Road Games | | | |
Category	Det.	Opp.	Total	Det.	Opp.	Total	Index	Det.	Opp.	Total	Det.	Opp.	Total	Index
G	71	71	142	72	72	144		143	143	286	144	144	288	
Avg.	.247	.280	.264	.252	.293	.272	97	.255	.278	.267	.252	.295	.273	98
AB	2347	2550	4897	2465	2436	4901	101	4741	5053	9794	4985	4943	9928	99
R	249	356	605	279	436	715	86	558	713	1271	603	850	1453	88
H	579	713	1292	621	713	1334	98	1208	1405	2613	1258	1456	2714	97
2B	92	144	236	153	162	315	75	210	277	487	294	326	620	80
3B	26	31	57	6	21	27	211	66	58	124	21	39	60	209
HR	57	55	112	56	97	153	73	107	115	222	125	191	316	71
BB	162	192	354	167	223	390	91	372	447	819	368	457	825	101
SO	396	363	759	503	352	855	89	771	722	1493	980	740	1720	88
E	63	33	96	71	35	106	92	129	90	219	128	94	222	99
E-Infield	50	24	74	54	31	85	88	104	76	180	94	82	176	103
LHB-Avg.	.266	.282	.273	.268	.298	.282	97	.272	.289	.280	.264	.290	.277	101
LHB-HR	43	34	77	30	43	73	104	70	77	147	60	87	147	100
RHB-Avg.	.225	.278	.255	.236	.289	.263	97	.238	.270	.255	.242	.298	.270	94
RHB-HR	14	21	35	26	54	80	44	37	38	75	65	104	169	45

KANSAS CITY

Home park: Ewing M. Kauffman Stadium **Alt.:** 750 feet **Surface:** Grass

| | 2002 Season | | | | | | | 2000-02 Seasons | | | | | | |
| | Home Games | | | Road Games | | | | Home Games | | | Road Games | | | |
Category	K.C.	Opp.	Total	K.C.	Opp.	Total	Index	K.C.	Opp.	Total	K.C.	Opp.	Total	Index
G	72	72	144	72	72	144		216	216	432	216	216	432	
Avg.	.272	.291	.282	.236	.266	.251	112	.283	.291	.287	.258	.267	.262	109
AB	2466	2637	5103	2444	2397	4841	105	7442	7827	15269	7550	7140	14690	104
R	372	433	805	276	347	623	129	1120	1296	2416	970	1086	2056	118
H	671	767	1438	577	638	1215	118	2104	2279	4383	1946	1905	3851	114
2B	132	159	291	114	130	244	113	373	438	811	368	361	729	107
3B	23	14	37	16	16	32	110	60	50	110	41	42	83	128
HR	75	109	184	47	84	131	133	217	313	530	170	282	452	113
BB	236	243	479	229	244	473	96	628	791	1419	637	840	1477	92
SO	339	399	738	475	437	912	77	1039	1248	2287	1306	1191	2497	88
E	52	55	107	62	42	104	103	155	173	328	151	173	324	101
E-Infield	43	49	92	51	37	88	105	126	144	270	121	155	276	98
LHB-Avg.	.272	.296	.284	.230	.267	.248	114	.280	.291	.287	.247	.268	.259	111
LHB-HR	36	49	85	24	36	60	134	64	151	215	65	132	197	104
RHB-Avg.	.272	.286	.280	.241	.265	.253	110	.284	.291	.287	.264	.265	.265	109
RHB-HR	39	60	99	23	48	71	133	153	162	315	105	150	255	119

MINNESOTA

Home park: Hubert H. Humphrey Metrodome **Alt.:** 815 feet **Surface:** Turf

| | 2002 Season | | | | | | | 2000-02 Seasons | | | | | | |
| | Home Games | | | Road Games | | | | Home Games | | | Road Games | | | |
Category	Min.	Opp.	Total	Min.	Opp.	Total	Index	Min.	Opp.	Total	Min.	Opp.	Total	Index
G	72	72	144	71	71	142		216	216	432	215	215	430	
Avg.	.279	.251	.265	.271	.274	.272	97	.276	.272	.274	.269	.273	.271	101
AB	2432	2521	4953	2523	2435	4958	99	7317	7708	15025	7612	7303	14915	100
R	357	287	644	336	348	684	93	1073	1050	2123	988	1062	2050	103
H	678	634	1312	684	666	1350	96	2019	2098	4117	2048	1993	4041	101
2B	174	132	306	137	122	259	118	481	435	916	420	377	797	114
3B	22	17	39	9	13	22	177	66	52	118	43	38	81	145
HR	63	66	129	89	96	185	70	176	240	416	218	275	493	84
BB	217	195	412	204	197	401	103	701	595	1296	666	659	1325	97
SO	452	472	924	505	417	922	100	1355	1476	2831	1479	1183	2662	106
E	30	51	81	39	53	92	87	116	163	279	150	157	307	90
E-Infield	25	43	68	34	47	81	83	94	138	232	131	138	269	86
LHB-Avg.	.287	.254	.273	.274	.295	.283	96	.288	.281	.285	.274	.282	.277	103
LHB-HR	30	34	64	54	49	103	64	98	110	208	133	115	248	85
RHB-Avg.	.268	.249	.257	.266	.257	.261	99	.259	.267	.264	.262	.266	.265	100
RHB-HR	33	32	65	35	47	82	77	78	130	208	85	160	245	82

NEW YORK — Home park: Yankee Stadium — Alt.: 55 feet — Surface: Grass

| | 2002 Season | | | | | | | 2000-02 Seasons | | | | | | |
| Category | Home Games | | | Road Games | | | Index | Home Games | | | Road Games | | | Index |
	N.Y.	Opp.	Total	N.Y.	Opp.	Total		N.Y.	Opp.	Total	N.Y.	Opp.	Total	
G	71	71	142	72	72	144		214	214	428	216	216	432	
Avg.	.274	.245	.259	.276	.262	.269	96	.277	.251	.264	.271	.266	.269	98
AB	2407	2506	4913	2579	2488	5067	98	7211	7500	14711	7680	7366	15046	99
R	386	298	684	411	305	716	97	1164	954	2118	1129	1006	2135	100
H	660	614	1274	711	653	1364	95	1994	1886	3880	2082	1960	4042	97
2B	125	133	258	149	141	290	92	391	373	764	414	404	818	96
3B	6	9	15	4	13	17	91	23	24	47	26	44	70	69
HR	95	66	161	104	57	161	103	303	217	520	264	198	462	115
BB	281	154	435	288	190	478	94	801	608	1409	766	677	1443	100
SO	494	550	1044	537	473	1010	107	1321	1620	2941	1509	1474	2983	101
E	50	55	105	60	38	98	109	147	160	307	158	140	298	104
E-Infield	43	42	85	50	30	80	108	127	117	244	138	120	258	95
LHB-Avg.	.275	.234	.255	.276	.239	.259	98	.278	.248	.264	.271	.255	.263	100
LHB-HR	52	32	84	57	22	79	107	172	99	271	135	86	221	125
RHB-Avg.	.274	.253	.263	.275	.278	.277	95	.275	.254	.264	.271	.274	.273	97
RHB-HR	43	34	77	47	35	82	99	131	118	249	129	112	241	106

OAKLAND — Home park: Network Associates Coliseum — Alt.: 25 feet — Surface: Grass

| | 2002 Season | | | | | | | 2000-02 Seasons | | | | | | |
| Category | Home Games | | | Road Games | | | Index | Home Games | | | Road Games | | | Index |
	Oak.	Opp.	Total	Oak.	Opp.	Total		Oak.	Opp.	Total	Oak.	Opp.	Total	
G	72	72	144	72	72	144		216	216	432	215	215	430	
Avg.	.263	.248	.255	.254	.260	.257	99	.261	.249	.255	.269	.272	.270	94
AB	2401	2476	4877	2547	2442	4989	98	7183	7530	14713	7675	7308	14983	98
R	363	302	665	334	300	634	105	1156	910	2066	1205	994	2199	94
H	631	613	1244	647	636	1283	97	1877	1876	3753	2062	1987	4049	92
2B	123	123	246	117	123	240	105	356	359	715	432	361	793	92
3B	15	9	24	11	17	28	88	33	30	63	34	39	73	88
HR	104	61	165	79	62	141	120	301	186	487	270	210	480	103
BB	287	196	483	252	232	484	102	926	636	1562	868	735	1603	99
SO	434	483	917	447	427	874	107	1378	1441	2819	1435	1308	2743	105
E	43	49	92	45	39	84	110	157	135	292	157	131	288	101
E-Infield	35	39	74	38	32	70	106	123	105	228	129	109	238	95
LHB-Avg.	.277	.254	.267	.243	.257	.248	107	.274	.251	.264	.274	.271	.273	97
LHB-HR	59	25	84	44	25	69	125	172	71	243	162	91	253	97
RHB-Avg.	.247	.243	.245	.267	.263	.265	93	.247	.248	.247	.262	.272	.268	92
RHB-HR	45	36	81	35	37	72	115	129	115	244	108	119	227	110

SEATTLE — Home park: Safeco Field — Alt.: 2 feet — Surface: Grass

| | 2002 Season | | | | | | | 2001-02 Seasons | | | | | | |
| Category | Home Games | | | Road Games | | | Index | Home Games | | | Road Games | | | Index |
	Sea.	Opp.	Total	Sea.	Opp.	Total		Sea.	Opp.	Total	Sea.	Opp.	Total	
G	72	72	144	72	72	144		144	144	288	144	144	288	
Avg.	.265	.255	.260	.288	.265	.277	94	.275	.240	.257	.290	.257	.274	94
AB	2391	2511	4902	2554	2435	4989	98	4805	4962	9767	5193	4872	10065	97
R	327	306	633	403	348	751	84	722	559	1281	824	659	1483	86
H	633	641	1274	736	646	1382	92	1323	1191	2514	1506	1253	2759	91
2B	105	126	231	145	135	280	84	243	238	481	291	266	557	89
3B	17	3	20	10	11	21	97	30	9	39	29	27	56	72
HR	55	73	128	78	91	169	77	121	133	254	151	173	324	81
BB	308	217	525	257	190	447	120	585	409	994	534	413	947	108
SO	442	506	948	446	434	880	110	857	969	1826	906	908	1814	104
E	37	56	93	40	52	92	101	67	117	184	80	116	196	94
E-Infield	30	49	79	30	47	77	103	56	99	155	63	104	167	93
LHB-Avg.	.274	.264	.269	.308	.276	.292	92	.286	.249	.267	.302	.270	.287	93
LHB-HR	21	41	62	40	37	77	81	43	72	115	56	74	130	91
RHB-Avg.	.256	.247	.252	.271	.255	.263	96	.266	.232	.249	.279	.246	.263	95
RHB-HR	34	32	66	38	54	92	74	78	61	139	95	99	194	74

TAMPA BAY

Home park: Tropicana Field **Alt.:** 15 feet **Surface:** Turf

| | 2002 Season | | | | | | | 2000-02 Seasons | | | | | | |
| | Home Games | | | Road Games | | | | Home Games | | | Road Games | | | |
Category	T.B.	Opp.	Total	T.B.	Opp.	Total	Index	T.B.	Opp.	Total	T.B.	Opp.	Total	Index
G	72	72	144	71	71	142		215	215	430	215	215	430	
Avg.	.264	.268	.266	.239	.293	.266	100	.260	.272	.266	.250	.283	.266	100
AB	2492	2585	5077	2445	2383	4828	104	7297	7708	15005	7436	7173	14609	103
R	308	406	714	287	421	708	99	920	1179	2099	904	1197	2101	100
H	659	694	1353	585	698	1283	104	1900	2097	3997	1861	2030	3891	103
2B	125	148	273	126	150	276	94	397	440	837	346	416	762	107
3B	16	14	30	13	8	21	136	37	46	83	24	33	57	142
HR	54	88	142	63	105	168	80	172	274	446	194	282	476	91
BB	206	288	494	201	270	471	100	673	750	1423	618	801	1419	98
SO	488	455	943	503	364	867	103	1389	1401	2790	1484	1166	2650	103
E	49	39	88	61	45	106	82	157	126	283	174	130	304	93
E-Infield	43	35	78	50	37	87	88	139	113	252	144	111	255	99
LHB-Avg.	.274	.291	.282	.253	.309	.279	101	.267	.278	.273	.263	.299	.281	97
LHB-HR	35	50	85	32	50	82	98	75	128	203	78	124	202	97
RHB-Avg.	.256	.251	.253	.227	.281	.255	99	.256	.267	.261	.241	.270	.255	102
RHB-HR	19	38	57	31	55	86	63	97	146	243	116	158	274	87

TEXAS

Home park: The Ballpark in Arlington **Alt.:** 551 feet **Surface:** Grass

| | 2002 Season | | | | | | | 2000-02 Seasons | | | | | | |
| | Home Games | | | Road Games | | | | Home Games | | | Road Games | | | |
Category	Tex.	Opp.	Total	Tex.	Opp.	Total	Index	Tex.	Opp.	Total	Tex.	Opp.	Total	Index
G	72	72	144	72	72	144		217	217	434	214	214	428	
Avg.	.282	.278	.280	.253	.265	.259	108	.287	.287	.287	.265	.285	.274	105
AB	2440	2579	5019	2549	2417	4966	101	7426	7893	15319	7593	7250	14843	102
R	421	425	846	322	364	686	123	1247	1308	2555	1049	1211	2260	111
H	689	718	1407	645	640	1285	109	2133	2266	4399	2009	2064	4073	107
2B	141	167	308	132	145	277	110	429	530	959	426	448	874	106
3B	13	20	33	12	19	31	105	42	56	98	30	51	81	117
HR	123	99	222	83	72	155	142	326	298	624	255	253	508	119
BB	258	286	544	231	308	539	100	800	841	1641	703	866	1569	101
SO	429	486	915	482	431	913	99	1259	1319	2578	1402	1215	2617	95
E	39	44	83	48	47	95	87	166	155	321	145	149	294	108
E-Infield	29	35	64	40	39	79	81	135	129	264	118	130	248	105
LHB-Avg.	.285	.268	.275	.255	.268	.262	105	.286	.288	.287	.272	.288	.280	102
LHB-HR	43	43	86	28	37	65	126	136	135	271	107	108	215	117
RHB-Avg.	.281	.287	.284	.252	.262	.256	111	.289	.287	.288	.259	.282	.271	106
RHB-HR	80	56	136	55	35	90	154	190	163	353	148	145	293	120

TORONTO

Home park: SkyDome **Alt.:** 300 feet **Surface:** Turf

| | 2002 Season | | | | | | | 2000-02 Seasons | | | | | | |
| | Home Games | | | Road Games | | | | Home Games | | | Road Games | | | |
Category	Tor.	Opp.	Total	Tor.	Opp.	Total	Index	Tor.	Opp.	Total	Tor.	Opp.	Total	Index
G	72	72	144	72	72	144		216	216	432	215	215	430	
Avg.	.270	.267	.269	.256	.274	.265	102	.272	.273	.272	.261	.279	.270	101
AB	2432	2533	4965	2553	2444	4997	99	7346	7667	15013	7676	7350	15026	99
R	370	374	744	372	379	751	99	1100	1141	2241	1062	1084	2146	104
H	657	677	1334	653	669	1322	101	1995	2093	4088	2003	2051	4054	100
2B	151	154	305	126	129	255	120	426	483	909	374	404	778	117
3B	19	9	28	16	17	33	85	37	32	69	46	36	82	84
HR	92	78	170	75	80	155	110	293	234	527	267	248	515	102
BB	226	263	489	230	268	498	99	659	726	1385	657	721	1378	101
SO	483	455	938	544	437	981	96	1377	1394	2771	1542	1282	2824	98
E	47	51	98	50	41	91	108	137	144	281	142	132	274	102
E-Infield	43	42	85	45	35	80	106	125	118	243	115	111	226	107
LHB-Avg.	.260	.279	.271	.261	.287	.276	98	.273	.281	.277	.272	.291	.282	98
LHB-HR	42	43	85	37	44	81	110	142	115	257	137	125	262	100
RHB-Avg.	.276	.256	.267	.253	.259	.255	104	.271	.266	.269	.254	.268	.260	103
RHB-HR	50	35	85	38	36	74	112	151	119	270	130	123	253	105

2002 A.L. STATISTICS *Miscellaneous*

RUNS PER GAME

Team	Games	Home Games Team	Opp.	Total	Games	Road Games Team	Opp.	Total	Index
Kansas City ..	216	1120	1296	2416	216	970	1086	2056	118
Texas	217	1247	1308	2555	214	1049	1211	2260	111
Chicago*	144	793	708	1501	144	689	713	1402	107
Toronto	216	1100	1141	2241	215	1062	1084	2146	104
Minnesota	216	1073	1050	2123	215	988	1062	2050	103
Anaheim........	216	1055	1019	2074	216	1066	992	2058	101
Cleveland	215	1166	1125	2291	217	1168	1113	2281	101
Boston	216	1080	1003	2083	215	1144	928	2072	100
New York	214	1164	954	2118	216	1129	1006	2135	100
Tampa Bay	215	920	1179	2099	215	904	1197	2101	100
Oakland	216	1156	910	2066	215	1205	994	2199	94
Baltimore†	72	292	331	623	72	300	374	674	92
Detroit*	143	558	713	1271	144	603	850	1453	88
Seattle*	144	722	559	1281	144	824	659	1483	86

*Current dimensions began in 2001; †Current dimensions began in 2002.

HOME RUNS PER AT-BAT

Team	Games	Home Games Team	Opp.	Total	Games	Road Games Team	Opp.	Total	Index
Chicago*	144	218	180	398	144	162	147	309	129
Texas	217	326	298	624	214	255	253	508	119
Baltimore†	72	81	101	182	72	66	91	157	116
New York	214	303	217	520	216	264	198	462	115
Kansas City ..	216	217	313	530	216	170	282	452	113
Cleveland	215	292	217	509	217	263	198	461	110
Oakland	216	301	186	487	215	270	210	480	103
Anaheim........	216	255	241	496	216	223	256	479	103
Toronto	216	293	234	527	215	267	248	515	102
Tampa Bay	215	172	274	446	215	194	282	476	91
Minnesota	216	176	240	416	215	218	275	493	84
Boston	216	217	190	407	215	279	223	502	81
Seattle*	144	121	133	254	144	151	173	324	81
Detroit*	143	107	115	222	144	125	191	316	71

*Current dimensions began in 2001; †Current dimensions began in 2002.

BATTING AVERAGE

Team	Games	Home Games Team	Opp.	Total	Games	Road Games Team	Opp.	Total	Index
Kansas City ..	216	.283	.291	.287	216	.258	.267	.262	109
Texas	217	.287	.287	.287	214	.265	.285	.274	105
Boston	216	.277	.259	.268	215	.270	.245	.258	104
Anaheim........	216	.274	.263	.268	216	.271	.259	.265	101
Minnesota	216	.276	.272	.274	215	.269	.273	.271	101
Toronto	216	.272	.273	.272	215	.261	.279	.270	101
Chicago*	144	.276	.262	.269	144	.267	.266	.267	101
Cleveland	215	.275	.273	.274	217	.274	.273	.273	100
Tampa Bay	215	.260	.272	.266	215	.250	.283	.266	100
New York	214	.277	.251	.264	216	.271	.266	.269	98
Detroit*	143	.255	.278	.267	144	.252	.295	.273	98
Baltimore†	72	.246	.260	.253	72	.247	.280	.263	96
Oakland	216	.261	.249	.255	215	.269	.272	.270	94
Seattle*	144	.275	.240	.257	144	.290	.257	.274	94

*Current dimensions began in 2001; †Current dimensions began in 2002.

2002 A.L. STATISTICS Miscellaneous

2002 N.L. STATISTICS

Batting

Designated hitting

Pinch-hitting

Pitching

Fielding

Miscellaneous

BATTING

TEAM

Team	G	TPA	AB	R	H	TB	2B	3B	HR	RBI	SH	SF	HP	BB	IBB	SO	SB	CS	GDP	LOB	ShO	Avg.	OBP	Slg.
Colorado	162	6164	5512	778	1508	2329	283	41	152	726	49	50	56	497	40	1043	103	53	133	1094	7	.274	.337	.423
St. Louis	162	6246	5505	787	1475	2337	285	26	175	758	83	49	67	542	77	927	86	42	123	1160	10	.268	.338	.425
Arizona	162	6316	5508	819	1471	2331	283	40	165	783	62	53	50	643	58	1016	92	46	130	1211	10	.267	.346	.423
San Fran.	162	6298	5497	783	1465	2429	300	35	198	751	68	52	65	616	103	961	74	21	136	1241	7	.267	.344	.442
Los Angeles	162	6146	5554	713	1464	2273	286	29	155	693	67	44	53	428	50	940	96	37	140	1087	13	.264	.320	.409
Houston	162	6252	5503	749	1441	2297	291	32	167	719	64	37	59	589	57	1120	71	27	144	1177	6	.262	.338	.417
Montreal	162	6250	5479	735	1432	2290	300	36	162	695	108	42	46	575	85	1104	118	64	123	1158	10	.261	.334	.418
Florida	162	6260	5496	699	1433	2215	280	32	146	653	59	49	61	595	69	1130	177	73	129	1190	13	.261	.337	.403
Atlanta	161	6223	5495	708	1428	2250	280	25	164	669	67	49	54	558	68	1028	76	39	147	1185	7	.260	.331	.409
Philadelphia	161	6322	5523	710	1428	2330	325	41	165	676	67	39	53	640	70	1095	104	43	129	1260	3	.259	.339	.422
New York	161	6150	5496	690	1409	2171	238	22	160	650	75	30	63	486	46	1044	87	42	142	1111	7	.256	.322	.395
Cincinnati	162	6254	5470	709	1386	2232	297	21	169	678	95	40	66	583	66	1188	116	52	119	1169	8	.253	.330	.408
Milwaukee	162	6083	5415	627	1369	2113	269	29	139	597	79	34	55	500	37	1125	94	50	144	1086	15	.253	.320	.390
San Diego	162	6178	5515	662	1393	2102	243	29	136	627	45	41	30	547	42	1062	71	44	132	1158	16	.253	.321	.381
Chicago	162	6242	5496	706	1351	2268	259	29	200	676	78	39	44	585	52	1269	63	21	117	1173	10	.246	.321	.413
Pittsburgh	161	6049	5330	641	1300	2029	263	20	142	610	68	41	73	537	44	1109	86	49	97	1149	15	.244	.319	.381
Totals	1294	99433	87794	11516	22753	35996	4482	488	2595	10961	1134	689	895	8921	964	17161	1514	703	2085	18609	157	.259	.331	.410

INDIVIDUAL
TOP QUALIFIERS FOR BATTING CHAMPIONSHIP

Minimum 502 plate appearances. *Lefthanded batter. †Switch-hitter.

Player, Team	G	TPA	AB	R	H	TB	2B	3B	HR	RBI	SH	SF	HP	BB	IBB	SO	SB	CS	GDP	Avg.	OBP	Slg.
Bonds, Barry, S.F.*	143	612	403	117	149	322	31	2	46	110	0	2	9	198	68	47	9	2	4	.370	.582	.799
Walker, Larry, Col.*	136	553	477	95	161	287	40	4	26	104	0	4	7	65	6	73	6	5	8	.338	.421	.602
Guerrero, Vladimir, Mon.	161	709	614	106	206	364	37	2	39	111	0	5	6	84	32	70	40	20	20	.336	.417	.593
Helton, Todd, Col.*	156	668	553	107	182	319	39	4	30	109	0	10	5	99	21	91	5	1	10	.329	.429	.577
Jones, Chipper, Atl.†	158	662	548	90	179	294	35	1	26	100	0	5	2	107	23	89	8	2	18	.327	.435	.536
Vidro, Jose, Mon.†	152	681	604	103	190	296	43	3	19	96	11	3	6	60	1	70	2	1	12	.315	.378	.490
Pujols, Albert, St.L.	157	675	590	118	185	331	40	2	34	127	0	4	9	72	13	69	2	4	20	.314	.394	.561
Kent, Jeff, S.F.	152	682	623	102	195	352	42	2	37	108	0	3	4	53	2	101	5	1	20	.313	.368	.565
Edmonds, Jim, St.L.*	144	576	476	96	148	267	31	2	28	83	0	6	8	86	14	134	4	3	9	.311	.420	.561
Alfonzo, Edgardo, N.Y.	135	562	490	78	151	225	26	0	16	56	0	3	7	62	8	55	6	0	5	.308	.391	.459
Abreu, Bobby, Phi.*	157	685	572	102	176	298	50	6	20	85	0	6	3	104	9	117	31	12	11	.308	.413	.521
Sheffield, Gary, Atl.	135	579	492	82	151	252	26	0	25	84	0	4	11	72	2	53	12	2	16	.307	.404	.512
Castillo, Luis, Fla.†	146	668	606	86	185	219	18	5	2	39	4	1	2	55	4	76	48	15	7	.305	.364	.361
Renteria, Edgar, St.L.	152	609	544	77	166	239	36	2	11	83	7	5	4	49	7	57	22	7	17	.305	.364	.439
Spivey, Junior, Ari.	143	626	538	103	162	256	34	6	16	78	1	6	16	65	5	100	11	6	10	.301	.389	.476

DEPARTMENTAL LEADERS: G—Boone, Cin., Lee, Fla., 162; AB—Rollins, Phi. 637; R—Sosa, Chi., 122; H—V. Guerrero, Mon., 206; TB—V. Guerrero, Mon., 364; 1B—Castillo, Fla., 160; 2B—Abreu, Phi., 50; 3B—Rollins, Phi., 10; HR—Sosa, Chi., 49; RBI—Berkman, Hou., 128; SH—J. Wilson, Pit., 17; SF—Lowell, Fla., Ramirez, Pit., 11; HP—C. Wilson, Pit., 21; BB—Bonds, S.F., 198; IBB—Bonds, S.F., 68; SO—Hernandez, Mil., 188; SB—Castillo, Fla., 48; CS—V. Guerrero, Mon., 20; GDP—Ausmus, Hou., 30; Slg.—Bonds, S.F., .799; OBP—Bonds, S.F., .582

ALL PLAYERS

*Lefthanded batter. †Switch-hitter.

Player, Team	G	TPA	AB	R	H	TB	2B	3B	HR	RBI	SH	SF	HP	BB	IBB	SO	SB	CS	GDP	Avg.	OBP	Slg.
Abreu, Bobby, Phi.*	157	685	572	102	176	298	50	6	20	85	0	6	3	104	9	117	31	12	11	.308	.413	.521
Acevedo, Jose, Cin.	6	10	7	1	1	2	1	0	0	2	2	0	0	1	0	6	0	0	0	.143	.250	.286
Adams, Terry, Phi.	46	34	25	0	2	2	0	0	0	1	6	0	0	3	0	13	0	0	1	.080	.179	.080
Agbayani, Benny, Col.	48	128	117	10	24	41	5	0	4	19	0	1	0	10	0	35	1	0	4	.205	.266	.350
Ainsworth, Kurt, S.F.	6	7	6	1	1	2	1	0	0	0	1	0	0	0	0	1	0	0	0	.167	.167	.333
Alcantara, Izzy, Mil.	16	32	32	3	8	15	1	0	2	5	0	0	0	0	0	6	0	1	0	.250	.250	.469
Alfonseca, Antonio, Chi.	66	3	3	0	2	2	0	0	0	2	0	0	0	0	0	0	0	0	0	.667	.667	.667
Alfonzo, Edgardo, N.Y.	135	562	490	78	151	225	26	0	16	56	0	3	7	62	8	55	6	0	5	.308	.391	.459
Allen, Luke, L.A.*	6	9	7	2	1	2	1	0	0	0	0	0	0	2	0	3	0	0	0	.143	.333	.286
Alomar Jr., Sandy, Col.	38	120	116	8	31	35	4	0	0	12	0	0	0	4	0	19	0	0	6	.267	.292	.302
Alomar, Roberto, N.Y.†	149	655	590	73	157	222	24	4	11	53	6	1	1	57	4	83	16	4	12	.266	.331	.376
Alou, Moises, Chi.	132	534	484	50	133	203	23	1	15	61	0	3	0	47	4	61	8	0	15	.275	.337	.419
Alvarez, Tony, Pit.	14	30	26	6	8	13	2	0	1	2	1	0	0	3	0	5	1	0	0	.308	.379	.500
Alvarez, Victor, L.A.*	4	2	2	0	0	0	0	0	0	0	0	0	0	0	0	2	0	0	0	.000	.000	.000
Anderson, Brian, Ari.	38	49	43	0	5	8	1	1	0	2	5	0	1	0	0	9	0	0	0	.116	.136	.186
Anderson, Jimmy, Pit.*	28	47	42	1	5	5	0	0	0	1	3	0	0	2	0	12	0	0	0	.119	.159	.119
Anderson, Marlon, Phi.*	145	592	539	64	139	205	30	6	8	48	2	4	5	42	14	71	5	1	16	.258	.315	.380
Armas Jr., Tony, Mon.	29	56	50	1	5	7	0	1	0	2	5	0	0	1	0	16	0	0	0	.100	.118	.140
Arroyo, Bronson, Pit.	9	6	6	0	0	0	0	0	0	0	0	0	0	0	0	1	0	0	0	.000	.000	.000
Ashby, Andy, L.A.	30	56	48	5	6	9	0	0	1	4	6	0	0	2	0	23	0	0	0	.125	.160	.188
Astacio, Pedro, N.Y.	31	69	62	3	10	12	2	0	0	1	6	0	1	0	0	31	0	0	0	.161	.175	.194
Aurilia, Rich, S.F.	133	589	538	76	138	222	35	2	15	61	3	7	4	37	0	90	1	2	15	.257	.305	.413
Ausmus, Brad, Hou.	130	496	447	57	115	158	19	3	6	50	2	6	3	38	3	71	2	3	30	.257	.322	.353
Aybar, Manny, S.F.	15	1	1	0	0	0	0	0	0	0	0	0	0	0	0	0	0	0	0	.000	.000	.000
Bacsik, Mike, N.Y.*	11	21	18	0	2	3	1	0	0	2	3	0	0	0	0	3	0	0	0	.111	.111	.167
Bagwell, Jeff, Hou.	158	691	571	94	166	296	33	2	31	98	0	9	10	101	8	130	7	3	16	.291	.401	.518
Bako, Paul, Mil.*	87	257	234	24	55	77	8	1	4	20	3	0	0	20	3	46	0	2	4	.235	.295	.329

Player, Team	G	TPA	AB	R	H	TB	2B	3B	HR	RBI	SH	SF	HP	BB	IBB	SO	SB	CS	GDP	Avg.	OBP	Slg.
Banks, Brian, Fla.†	20	29	28	3	9	13	1	0	1	4	0	0	0	1	0	6	0	0	0	.321	.345	.464
Barajas, Rod, Ari.	70	172	154	12	36	55	10	0	3	23	2	3	3	10	4	25	1	0	4	.234	.288	.357
Barker, Kevin, S.D.*	7	20	19	0	3	3	0	0	0	0	0	0	0	1	0	6	1	0	1	.158	.200	.158
Barrett, Michael, Mon.	117	428	376	41	99	157	20	1	12	49	6	5	1	40	7	65	6	3	14	.263	.332	.418
Batista, Miguel, Ari.	36	56	51	5	8	13	2	0	1	2	2	0	0	3	0	28	0	0	2	.157	.204	.255
Bautista, Danny, Ari.	40	166	154	22	50	77	5	2	6	23	0	1	0	11	2	21	4	2	4	.325	.367	.500
Beckett, Josh, Fla.	23	36	31	0	1	2	1	0	0	0	5	0	0	0	0	21	0	0	0	.032	.032	.065
Beimel, Joe, Pit.*	53	13	10	0	3	4	1	0	0	1	2	0	0	1	0	3	0	0	0	.300	.364	.400
Beirne, Kevin, L.A.*	12	6	5	1	2	2	0	0	0	0	1	0	0	0	0	0	0	0	0	.400	.400	.400
Bell, David, S.F.	154	628	552	82	144	237	29	2	20	73	6	7	9	54	2	80	1	2	18	.261	.333	.429
Bell, Jay, Ari.	32	56	49	3	8	15	1	0	2	11	0	1	1	5	0	9	0	0	2	.163	.250	.306
Bellhorn, Mark, Chi.†	146	529	445	86	115	228	24	4	27	56	2	0	6	76	3	144	7	5	6	.258	.374	.512
Belliard, Ronnie, Mil.	104	317	289	30	61	83	13	0	3	26	6	3	1	18	0	46	2	3	9	.211	.257	.287
Beltran, Francis, Chi.	11	1	1	0	0	0	0	0	0	0	0	0	0	0	0	1	0	0	0	.000	.000	.000
Beltre, Adrian, L.A.	159	635	587	70	151	250	26	5	21	75	1	6	4	37	4	96	7	5	17	.257	.303	.426
Benard, Marvin, S.F.*	65	131	123	16	34	50	9	2	1	13	0	0	1	7	0	26	5	1	3	.276	.321	.407
Benes, Alan, Chi.	7	14	13	0	1	1	0	0	0	0	0	0	0	1	0	8	0	0	0	.077	.143	.077
Benes, Andy, St.L.	19	37	34	3	7	11	1	0	1	2	2	0	0	1	0	9	0	0	1	.206	.229	.324
Benjamin, Mike, Pit.	108	130	120	7	18	22	2	1	0	3	1	1	1	7	0	31	0	4	5	.150	.202	.183
Bennett, Gary, Col.	90	314	291	26	77	103	10	2	4	26	2	0	6	15	2	45	1	3	10	.265	.314	.354
Benson, Kris, Pit.	27	44	40	3	7	8	1	0	0	1	4	0	0	0	0	11	0	0	0	.175	.175	.200
Bere, Jason, Chi.	16	31	24	1	3	5	2	0	0	0	7	0	0	0	0	11	0	0	0	.125	.125	.208
Bergeron, Peter, Mon.*	31	148	123	24	23	30	3	2	0	7	3	0	0	22	0	44	10	3	0	.187	.310	.244
Berkman, Lance, Hou.†	158	692	578	106	169	334	35	2	42	128	0	3	4	107	20	118	8	4	10	.292	.405	.578
Biggio, Craig, Hou.	145	655	577	96	146	233	36	3	15	58	9	2	17	50	2	111	16	2	15	.253	.330	.404
Blanco, Henry, Atl.	81	249	221	17	45	74	9	1	6	22	2	5	1	20	5	51	0	2	5	.204	.267	.335
Blum, Geoff, Hou.†	130	421	368	45	104	162	20	4	10	52	1	2	1	49	5	70	2	0	8	.283	.367	.440
Bocachica, Hiram, L.A.	49	70	65	12	14	29	3	0	4	9	0	0	0	5	0	19	1	1	1	.215	.271	.446
Bonds, Barry, S.F.*	143	612	403	117	149	322	31	2	46	110	0	2	9	198	68	47	9	2	4	.370	.582	.799
Bong, Jung, Atl.*	2	2	2	0	0	0	0	0	0	0	0	0	0	0	0	1	0	0	0	.000	.000	.000
Boone, Aaron, Cin.	162	685	606	83	146	266	38	2	26	87	9	4	10	56	4	111	32	8	9	.241	.314	.439
Borbon, Pedro, Hou.*	56	3	3	0	0	0	0	0	0	0	0	0	0	0	0	3	0	0	0	.000	.000	.000
Borowski, Joe, Chi.	73	7	7	1	2	2	0	0	0	0	0	0	0	0	0	5	0	0	0	.286	.286	.286
Bragg, Darren, Atl.*	109	240	212	34	57	85	15	2	3	15	1	1	2	24	0	52	5	2	4	.269	.347	.401
Branyan, Russell, Cin.*	84	255	217	34	53	112	9	1	16	39	0	2	2	34	3	86	3	1	2	.244	.349	.516
Brower, Jim, Cin.-Mon.	52	10	9	0	0	0	0	0	0	0	1	0	0	0	0	3	0	0	0	.000	.000	.000
Brown, Adrian, Pit.†	91	232	208	20	45	62	10	2	1	21	3	1	1	19	0	34	10	6	5	.216	.284	.298
Brown, Kevin, L.A.	17	22	20	2	5	9	1	0	1	2	2	0	0	0	0	11	0	0	2	.250	.250	.450
Brown, Roosevelt, Chi.*	111	231	204	14	43	64	12	0	3	23	0	1	3	23	0	50	2	2	4	.211	.299	.314
Buchanan, Brian, S.D.	48	102	92	12	27	50	5	0	6	13	0	0	1	9	0	26	0	1	2	.293	.363	.543
Buddie, Mike, Mil.	25	2	2	0	0	0	0	0	0	0	0	0	0	0	0	1	0	0	0	.000	.000	.000
Burnett, A.J., Fla.	31	69	57	1	6	11	2	0	1	3	7	0	0	5	0	28	0	0	1	.105	.177	.193
Burnitz, Jeromy, N.Y.*	154	550	479	65	103	175	15	0	19	54	1	2	10	58	5	135	10	7	11	.215	.311	.365
Burrell, Pat, Phi.	157	684	586	96	165	319	39	2	37	116	0	6	3	89	9	153	1	0	16	.282	.376	.544
Burroughs, Sean, S.D.*	63	206	192	18	52	62	5	1	1	11	1	0	1	12	1	30	2	0	6	.271	.317	.323
Bush, Homer, Fla.	40	58	54	7	12	12	0	0	0	5	1	0	0	3	0	13	2	1	0	.222	.263	.222
Butler, Brent, Col.	113	367	344	55	89	142	18	4	9	42	4	4	5	10	3	40	2	6	6	.259	.287	.413
Bynum, Mike, S.D.*	14	8	8	0	0	0	0	0	0	0	0	0	0	0	0	3	0	0	0	.000	.000	.000
Byrd, Marlon, Phi.	10	36	35	2	8	13	2	0	1	1	0	0	0	1	0	8	0	2	0	.229	.250	.371
Cabrera, Jolbert, L.A.	10	15	12	3	4	5	1	0	0	1	1	0	0	2	0	2	0	0	0	.333	.429	.417
Cabrera, Jose, Mil.	50	20	19	1	2	2	0	0	0	0	1	0	0	0	0	10	0	0	0	.105	.105	.105
Cabrera, Orlando, Mon.	153	626	563	64	148	214	43	1	7	56	9	4	2	48	4	53	25	7	16	.263	.321	.380
Cairo, Miguel, St.L.	108	208	184	28	46	65	9	2	2	23	6	2	3	13	2	36	1	1	5	.250	.307	.353
Cardona, Javier, S.D.	15	42	39	2	4	5	1	0	0	2	0	1	0	2	0	10	0	0	1	.103	.143	.128
Carrara, Giovanni, L.A.	63	8	6	0	0	0	0	0	0	0	1	0	0	1	0	3	0	0	0	.000	.143	.000
Carroll, Jamey, Mon.	16	79	71	16	22	36	5	3	1	6	4	0	0	4	0	12	1	0	1	.310	.347	.507
Casanova, Raul, Mil.†	31	99	87	3	16	20	1	0	1	8	0	1	1	10	4	18	0	0	3	.184	.273	.230
Casey, Sean, Cin.*	120	476	425	56	111	154	25	0	6	42	0	3	5	43	6	47	2	1	11	.261	.334	.362
Castilla, Vinny, Atl.	143	578	543	56	126	189	23	2	12	61	0	6	7	22	4	69	4	1	22	.232	.268	.348
Castillo, Luis, Fla.†	146	668	606	86	185	219	18	5	2	39	4	1	2	55	4	76	48	15	7	.305	.364	.361
Castro, Juan, Cin.	54	91	82	5	18	27	3	0	2	11	1	1	0	7	0	18	0	0	0	.220	.278	.329
Castro, Ramon, Fla.	54	119	101	11	24	46	4	0	6	18	1	3	0	14	3	24	0	0	4	.238	.322	.455
Cedeno, Roger, N.Y.†	149	562	511	65	133	177	19	2	7	41	5	2	2	42	1	92	25	4	10	.260	.318	.346
Cepicky, Matt, Mon.*	32	78	74	7	16	28	3	0	3	15	0	0	0	4	1	21	0	0	0	.216	.256	.378
Cerda, Jaime, N.Y.*	32	1	1	0	0	0	0	0	0	0	0	0	0	0	0	0	0	0	0	.000	.000	.000
Chacon, Shawn, Col.	21	37	35	3	9	10	1	0	0	2	2	0	0	0	0	14	0	0	1	.257	.257	.286
Chavez, Endy, Mon.*	36	138	125	20	37	58	8	5	1	9	7	1	0	5	0	16	3	5	0	.296	.321	.464
Chavez, Raul, Hou.	2	6	4	1	1	2	1	0	0	1	0	0	1	1	0	0	0	0	0	.250	.500	.500
Chen, Bruce, N.Y.-Mon.-Cin.*	55	17	15	3	5	6	1	0	0	1	2	0	0	0	0	4	0	0	0	.333	.333	.400
Chen, Chin-Feng, L.A.*	3	6	5	1	0	0	0	0	0	0	0	0	0	1	0	3	0	0	0	.000	.167	.000
Childers, Matt, Mil.	8	1	1	0	0	0	0	0	0	0	0	0	0	0	0	0	0	0	0	.000	.000	.000
Choi, Hee Seop, Chi.*	24	57	50	6	9	16	1	0	2	4	0	0	0	7	0	15	0	0	2	.180	.281	.320
Christensen, McKay, N.Y.*	4	4	3	1	1	1	0	0	0	0	0	0	0	1	0	1	0	0	0	.333	.500	.333
Christensen, Ryan, Mil.	22	66	58	5	9	16	4	0	1	3	3	0	0	5	0	13	0	0	1	.155	.222	.276
Cintron, Alex, Ari.†	38	90	75	11	16	22	6	0	0	4	3	0	0	12	2	13	0	0	2	.213	.322	.293
Clark, Brady, Cin.-N.Y.	61	87	78	9	15	19	4	0	0	10	1	0	1	7	2	11	1	2	2	.192	.267	.244
Clement, Matt, Chi.	32	75	61	4	3	5	2	0	0	4	10	0	3	1	0	34	0	0	1	.049	.108	.082
Coggin, Dave, Phi.	38	11	8	0	0	0	0	0	0	0	2	0	0	1	0	6	0	0	0	.000	.111	.000
Colbrunn, Greg, Ari.	72	185	171	30	57	107	16	2	10	27	0	1	0	13	1	19	0	0	5	.333	.378	.626
Collier, Lou, Mon.	13	14	11	3	1	2	1	0	0	0	1	0	1	1	1	3	0	0	0	.091	.231	.182
Colon, Bartolo, Mon.	17	43	39	1	5	5	0	0	0	3	2	1	1	0	0	20	0	0	0	.128	.146	.128
Condrey, Clay, S.D.	9	6	6	0	0	0	0	0	0	0	0	0	0	0	0	3	0	0	0	.000	.000	.000
Cook, Aaron, Col.	9	12	11	0	1	1	0	0	0	1	0	0	0	0	0	5	0	0	0	.091	.091	.091
Coolbaugh, Mike, St.L.	5	14	12	0	1	1	0	0	0	0	1	0	1	0	0	3	0	0	1	.083	.154	.083
Cora, Alex, L.A.*	115	293	258	37	75	112	14	4	5	28	2	0	7	26	4	38	7	2	3	.291	.371	.434

Player, Team	G	TPA	AB	R	H	TB	2B	3B	HR	RBI	SH	SF	HP	BB	IBB	SO	SB	CS	GDP	Avg.	OBP	Slg.
Cordero, Wil, Mon.	66	166	143	21	39	66	9	0	6	29	0	4	2	17	0	26	2	0	3	.273	.349	.462
Corey, Mark, N.Y.-Col.	27	2	2	0	0	0	0	0	0	0	0	0	0	0	0	2	0	0	0	.000	.000	.000
Cormier, Rheal, Phi.*	54	4	3	0	1	1	0	0	0	0	0	0	0	1	0	0	0	0	0	.333	.500	.333
Cota, Humberto, Pit.	7	18	17	2	5	6	1	0	0	0	0	0	0	1	1	4	0	0	0	.294	.333	.353
Counsell, Craig, Ari.*	112	491	436	63	123	153	22	1	2	51	4	3	1	45	3	52	7	5	10	.282	.348	.351
Crespo, Cesar, S.D.†	25	33	29	5	5	7	2	0	0	0	1	0	0	3	0	6	3	2	0	.172	.250	.241
Crudale, Mike, St.L.	49	2	2	0	0	0	0	0	0	0	0	0	0	0	0	1	0	0	0	.000	.000	.000
Cruz, Deivi, S.D.	151	547	514	49	135	188	28	2	7	47	3	5	3	22	2	58	2	3	20	.263	.294	.366
Cruz, Ivan, St.L.*	17	15	14	2	5	8	0	0	1	3	0	0	0	1	0	3	0	0	0	.357	.400	.571
Cruz, Juan, Chi.	45	16	14	0	2	2	0	0	0	0	2	0	0	0	0	4	0	0	0	.143	.143	.143
Cruz, Nelson, Hou.	43	16	13	0	0	0	0	0	0	1	2	0	0	1	0	8	0	0	0	.000	.071	.000
Cunnane, Will, Chi.	16	5	4	2	1	1	0	0	0	0	0	0	0	1	0	0	0	0	0	.250	.400	.250
Cust, Jack, Col.*	35	78	65	8	11	16	2	0	1	8	0	1	0	12	0	32	0	1	3	.169	.295	.246
Cyr, Eric, S.D.	5	1	1	0	0	0	0	0	0	0	0	0	0	0	0	1	0	0	0	.000	.000	.000
D'Amico, Jeff, N.Y.	29	44	37	2	4	4	0	0	0	0	5	0	0	2	0	22	0	0	1	.108	.154	.108
Daal, Omar, L.A.*	39	48	39	2	6	11	2	0	1	4	8	0	0	1	0	11	0	0	0	.154	.175	.282
Darensbourg, Vic, Fla.*	43	2	1	0	0	0	0	0	0	0	1	0	0	0	0	0	0	0	0	.000	.000	.000
Davis, J.J., Pit.	9	11	10	1	1	1	0	0	0	0	0	0	1	0	0	4	0	0	1	.100	.182	.100
Dawkins, Gookie, Cin.	31	55	48	2	6	8	2	0	0	1	0	0	0	6	0	21	2	1	1	.125	.222	.167
Day, Zach, Mon.	19	9	6	1	1	1	0	0	0	0	2	0	0	1	0	4	0	0	0	.167	.286	.167
de los Santos, Valerio, Mil.*	51	5	2	0	0	0	0	0	0	0	2	0	0	1	0	1	0	0	0	.000	.333	.000
DeHaan, Kory, S.D.*	12	11	11	1	1	1	0	0	0	0	0	0	0	0	0	6	0	0	0	.091	.091	.091
DeJean, Mike, Mil.	68	1	1	0	0	0	0	0	0	0	0	0	0	0	0	0	0	0	0	.000	.000	.000
Delgado, Wilson, St.L.†	12	21	20	2	4	12	2	0	2	5	1	0	0	0	0	6	0	0	0	.200	.200	.600
Dellucci, David, Ari.*	97	261	229	34	56	92	11	2	7	29	0	3	1	28	5	55	2	4	7	.245	.326	.402
Dempster, Ryan, Fla.-Cin.	35	75	63	2	8	11	1	1	0	3	9	0	0	2	0	20	0	0	0	.127	.154	.175
DeRosa, Mark, Atl.	72	232	212	24	63	91	9	2	5	23	2	3	3	12	3	24	2	3	5	.297	.339	.429
DeShields, Delino, Chi.*	67	174	146	20	28	45	6	1	3	10	6	1	0	21	2	38	10	1	0	.192	.292	.308
Dessens, Elmer, Cin.	31	57	45	1	9	9	0	0	0	5	9	0	0	3	0	11	0	0	0	.200	.250	.200
DiFelice, Mike, St.L.	70	197	174	17	40	63	11	0	4	19	2	3	1	17	3	42	0	0	4	.230	.297	.362
Diggins, Ben, Mil.	5	8	7	0	1	1	0	0	0	1	0	0	0	1	0	1	0	0	0	.143	.143	.143
Donnels, Chris, Ari.*	74	93	80	5	19	34	4	1	3	16	0	3	0	10	1	14	0	0	2	.238	.312	.425
Dotel, Octavio, Hou.	83	1	1	0	0	0	0	0	0	0	0	0	0	0	0	0	0	0	0	.000	.000	.000
Drew, J.D., St.L.*	135	496	424	61	107	182	19	1	18	56	3	4	8	57	4	104	8	2	4	.252	.349	.429
Drew, Tim, Mon.	7	4	4	0	0	0	0	0	0	0	0	0	0	0	0	4	0	0	0	.000	.000	.000
Duckworth, Brandon, Phi.	30	59	48	3	9	10	1	0	0	4	6	0	0	5	0	11	0	0	3	.188	.264	.208
Dunn, Adam, Cin.*	158	676	535	84	133	243	28	2	26	71	1	3	9	128	13	170	19	9	8	.249	.400	.454
Dunston, Shawon, S.F.	72	153	147	7	34	42	5	0	1	9	1	1	1	3	0	33	1	0	0	.231	.250	.286
Durazo, Erubiel, Ari.*	76	276	222	46	58	122	12	2	16	48	0	3	2	49	2	60	0	1	1	.261	.395	.550
Durocher, Jayson, Mil.	39	2	2	0	0	0	0	0	0	0	0	0	0	0	0	1	0	0	0	.000	.000	.000
Eaton, Adam, S.D.	6	10	9	0	1	1	0	0	0	0	0	0	0	1	0	4	0	0	1	.111	.200	.111
Echevarria, Angel, Chi.	50	111	98	14	30	46	7	0	3	21	0	4	1	8	0	17	0	0	4	.306	.351	.469
Edmonds, Jim, St.L.*	144	576	476	96	148	267	31	2	28	83	0	6	8	86	14	134	4	3	9	.311	.420	.561
Eischen, Joey, Mon.*	59	9	8	1	1	2	1	0	0	0	1	0	0	1	0	3	0	0	0	.125	.222	.250
Encarnacion, Juan, Cin.-Fla.	152	644	584	77	158	262	22	5	24	85	3	7	4	46	0	113	21	9	18	.271	.324	.449
Encarnacion, Mario, Chi.	3	9	7	0	0	0	0	0	0	0	0	0	0	2	0	3	0	0	0	.000	.222	.000
Ennis, John, Atl.	1	1	1	0	0	0	0	0	0	0	0	0	0	0	0	1	0	0	0	.000	.000	.000
Ensberg, Morgan, Hou.	49	153	132	14	32	52	7	2	3	19	0	3	0	18	0	25	2	0	8	.242	.346	.394
Estalella, Bobby, Col.	38	130	112	17	23	55	8	0	8	25	0	4	0	14	0	33	0	1	1	.205	.285	.491
Estes, Shawn, N.Y.-Cin.	30	50	43	1	3	7	1	0	1	3	7	0	0	0	0	17	0	0	1	.070	.070	.163
Estrada, Johnny, Phi.†	10	19	17	0	2	3	1	0	0	2	0	0	0	2	1	2	0	0	0	.118	.211	.176
Everett, Adam, Hou.	40	103	88	11	17	20	3	0	0	4	2	0	1	12	1	19	3	0	1	.193	.297	.227
Fabregas, Jorge, Mil.*	30	73	67	5	11	23	3	0	3	14	0	4	0	2	0	7	0	0	2	.164	.178	.343
Farnsworth, Kyle, Chi.	45	2	1	0	0	0	0	0	0	0	1	0	1	0	0	0	0	0	0	.000	.000	.000
Fassero, Jeff, Chi.-St.L.*	73	3	3	0	1	1	0	0	0	0	0	0	0	0	0	2	0	0	0	.333	.333	.333
Feliz, Pedro, S.F.	67	153	146	14	37	49	4	1	2	13	0	1	0	6	1	27	0	0	2	.253	.281	.336
Fernandez, Jared, Cin.	14	13	10	2	2	2	0	0	0	1	2	0	0	1	0	7	0	0	0	.200	.273	.200
Figueroa, Nelson, Mil.	30	20	15	0	2	2	0	0	0	3	4	0	0	1	0	6	0	0	0	.133	.188	.133
Fikac, Jeremy, S.D.	65	2	2	0	0	0	0	0	0	0	0	0	0	0	0	1	0	0	0	.000	.000	.000
Finley, Chuck, St.L.*	14	33	28	2	3	4	1	0	0	1	5	0	0	0	0	12	0	0	0	.107	.107	.143
Finley, Steve, Ari.*	150	577	505	82	145	252	24	4	25	89	1	3	3	65	7	73	16	4	10	.287	.370	.499
Flores, Randy, Col.*	8	4	4	0	0	0	0	0	0	0	0	0	0	0	0	3	0	0	0	.000	.000	.000
Floyd, Cliff, Fla.-Mon.*	99	419	349	56	96	181	22	0	21	61	0	1	8	61	19	78	11	5	0	.275	.394	.519
Fogg, Josh, Pit.	34	62	58	2	7	7	0	0	0	1	2	0	0	2	0	22	0	0	1	.121	.150	.121
Fox, Andy, Fla.*	133	502	435	55	109	145	14	5	4	41	5	3	10	49	6	94	31	7	9	.251	.338	.333
Franco, Julio, Atl.	125	383	338	51	96	129	13	1	6	30	2	3	1	39	3	75	5	1	13	.284	.357	.382
Franco, Matt, Atl.*	81	233	205	25	65	106	15	4	6	30	0	1	0	27	2	31	1	0	5	.317	.395	.517
Franklin, Wayne, Mil.*	4	8	6	0	0	0	0	0	0	0	2	0	0	0	0	3	0	0	0	.000	.250	.000
Fultz, Aaron, S.F.*	44	1	1	0	0	0	0	0	0	0	0	0	0	0	0	1	0	0	0	.000	.000	.000
Furcal, Rafael, Atl.†	154	693	636	95	175	246	31	8	8	47	9	2	3	43	0	114	27	15	8	.275	.323	.387
Gagne, Eric, L.A.	77	1	1	0	0	0	0	0	0	0	0	0	0	0	0	1	0	0	0	.000	.000	.000
Galarraga, Andres, Mon.	104	334	292	30	76	115	12	0	9	40	0	3	9	30	6	81	2	2	8	.260	.344	.394
Gant, Ron, S.D.	102	353	309	58	81	151	14	1	18	59	1	5	2	36	1	59	4	6	8	.262	.338	.489
Garcia, Jesse, Atl.	39	61	61	6	12	13	1	0	0	4	0	0	0	0	0	14	0	1	1	.197	.197	.213
Giambi, Jeremy, Phi.*	82	211	156	32	38	84	10	0	12	28	1	0	1	52	2	54	0	1	1	.244	.435	.538
Giles, Brian, Pit.*	153	644	497	95	148	309	37	5	38	103	0	5	7	135	24	74	15	6	10	.298	.450	.622
Giles, Marcus, Atl.	68	242	213	27	49	85	10	1	8	23	1	1	2	25	3	41	1	1	5	.230	.315	.399
Ginter, Keith, Hou.-Mil.	28	99	81	7	19	31	9	0	1	8	0	1	0	17	0	15	0	0	0	.235	.374	.383
Girardi, Joe, Chi.	90	256	234	19	53	68	10	1	1	13	5	1	0	16	3	35	1	0	10	.226	.275	.291
Glanville, Doug, Phi.	138	460	422	49	105	145	16	3	6	29	8	3	2	25	4	57	19	2	5	.249	.292	.344
Glavine, Tom, Atl.*	37	84	68	0	7	8	1	0	0	3	13	0	0	3	0	13	0	0	5	.103	.141	.118
Gload, Ross, Col.*	26	34	31	4	8	12	1	0	1	4	0	0	0	3	0	7	0	0	0	.258	.324	.387
Gonzalez, Alex, Fla.	42	172	151	15	34	49	7	1	2	18	3	2	4	12	1	32	3	1	2	.225	.296	.325
Gonzalez, Alex S., Chi.	142	568	513	58	127	218	27	5	18	61	4	2	3	46	7	136	5	3	11	.248	.312	.425
Gonzalez, Luis, Ari.*	148	633	524	90	151	260	19	3	28	103	0	7	5	97	8	76	9	2	12	.288	.400	.496

Player, Team	G	TPA	AB	R	H	TB	2B	3B	HR	RBI	SH	SF	HP	BB	IBB	SO	SB	CS	GDP	Avg.	OBP	Slg.
Gonzalez, Raul, Cin.-N.Y.	40	111	104	13	27	39	3	0	3	12	0	1	0	6	0	22	4	2	3	.260	.297	.375
Gonzalez, Wiki, S.D.	56	194	164	16	36	49	8	1	1	20	0	2	1	27	3	24	0	0	10	.220	.330	.299
Goodwin, Tom, S.F.*	78	171	154	23	40	52	5	2	1	17	3	0	0	14	0	25	16	2	3	.260	.321	.338
Gordon, Tom, Chi.-Hou.	34	1	1	0	0	0	0	0	0	0	0	0	0	0	0	0	0	0	0	.000	.000	.000
Grace, Mark, Ari.*	124	348	298	43	75	115	19	0	7	48	0	3	1	46	6	30	2	0	5	.252	.351	.386
Graves, Danny, Cin.	69	8	6	1	0	0	0	0	0	0	2	0	0	0	0	2	0	0	0	.000	.000	.000
Green, Shawn, L.A.*	158	685	582	110	166	325	31	1	42	114	0	5	5	93	22	112	8	5	26	.285	.385	.558
Griffey Jr., Ken, Cin.*	70	232	197	17	52	84	8	0	8	23	0	4	3	28	6	39	1	2	6	.264	.358	.426
Grissom, Marquis, L.A.	111	371	343	57	95	175	21	4	17	60	0	4	2	22	2	68	5	1	6	.277	.321	.510
Grudzielanek, Mark, L.A.	150	566	536	56	145	195	23	0	9	50	1	4	3	22	4	89	4	1	17	.271	.301	.364
Guerrero, Vladimir, Mon.	161	709	614	106	206	364	37	2	39	111	0	5	6	84	32	70	40	20	20	.336	.417	.593
Guerrero, Wilton, Cin.-Mon.†	103	156	140	12	31	35	2	1	0	5	9	0	0	7	1	32	7	1	2	.221	.259	.250
Guillen, Jose, Ari.-Cin.*	85	259	240	25	57	88	7	0	8	31	1	1	3	14	1	43	4	5	13	.238	.287	.367
Guthrie, Mark, N.Y.	68	2	2	0	0	0	0	0	0	0	0	0	0	0	0	0	0	0	0	.000	.000	.000
Hackman, Luther, St.L.	43	17	16	0	1	1	0	0	0	0	0	0	0	1	0	6	0	0	0	.063	.118	.063
Hall, Bill, Mil.	19	39	36	3	7	13	1	1	1	5	0	0	0	3	0	13	0	1	1	.194	.256	.361
Hamilton, Joey, Cin.	39	33	28	3	7	10	3	0	0	1	4	1	0	0	0	7	0	0	0	.250	.241	.357
Hammond, Chris, Atl.*	63	2	1	0	0	0	0	0	0	0	0	0	0	1	0	1	0	0	0	.000	.500	.000
Hammonds, Jeffrey, Mil.	128	510	448	47	115	178	26	5	9	41	1	7	2	52	0	86	4	5	13	.257	.332	.397
Hampton, Mike, Col.	36	66	64	9	22	33	2	0	3	5	1	0	0	1	0	13	1	1	1	.344	.354	.516
Hansen, Dave, L.A.*	96	135	120	15	35	47	6	0	2	17	0	1	0	14	3	22	1	0	2	.292	.363	.392
Harris, Lenny, Mil.*	122	215	197	23	60	81	8	2	3	17	1	1	2	14	1	17	4	1	4	.305	.355	.411
Haynes, Jimmy, Cin.	36	72	61	5	10	12	2	0	0	6	10	0	0	1	0	12	0	0	1	.164	.177	.197
Helling, Rick, Ari.	30	61	46	3	2	2	0	0	0	1	6	0	1	8	0	16	0	0	1	.043	.200	.043
Helms, Wes, Atl.	85	231	210	20	51	85	16	0	6	22	1	6	3	11	2	57	1	1	5	.243	.283	.405
Helton, Todd, Col.*	156	668	553	107	182	319	39	4	30	109	0	10	5	99	21	91	5	1	10	.329	.429	.577
Herges, Matt, Mon.*	62	2	1	0	0	0	0	0	0	0	0	0	0	1	0	1	0	0	0	.000	.500	.000
Hermansen, Chad, Pit.-Chi. ...	100	265	237	25	49	89	14	1	8	18	4	1	1	22	0	82	7	5	1	.207	.276	.376
Hernandez, Carlos, Hou.†	25	41	35	3	6	6	0	0	0	1	4	0	0	2	0	11	0	0	0	.171	.216	.171
Hernandez, Jose, Mil.	152	582	525	72	151	251	24	2	24	73	0	1	4	52	5	188	3	5	19	.288	.356	.478
Hernandez, Livan, S.F.	36	75	64	6	15	21	4	1	0	6	10	1	0	0	0	9	0	0	3	.234	.231	.328
Hidalgo, Richard, Hou.	114	439	388	54	91	161	17	4	15	48	0	2	6	43	1	85	6	2	13	.235	.319	.415
Hill, Bobby, Chi.†	59	215	190	26	48	71	7	2	4	20	4	0	4	17	4	42	6	1	0	.253	.327	.374
Hodges, Trey, Atl.	4	3	3	0	0	0	0	0	0	0	0	0	0	0	0	2	0	0	0	.000	.000	.000
Hollandsworth, Todd, Col.*...	95	328	298	39	88	144	21	1	11	48	1	2	1	26	4	71	7	8	8	.295	.352	.483
Hollins, Dave, Phi.†	14	18	17	1	2	2	0	0	0	0	0	0	1	0	0	3	0	1	0	.118	.167	.118
Holmes, Darren, Atl.	55	2	2	0	0	0	0	0	0	0	0	0	0	0	0	0	0	0	0	.000	.000	.000
Holtz, Mike, S.D.*	33	2	2	0	0	0	0	0	0	0	0	0	0	0	0	1	0	0	0	.000	.000	.000
Houston, Tyler, Mil.-L.A.*	111	345	320	34	90	137	20	3	7	40	4	1	4	16	3	62	1	0	9	.281	.323	.428
Howard, Ben, S.D.	3	5	4	0	0	0	0	0	0	0	1	0	0	0	0	2	0	0	0	.000	.000	.000
Hubbard, Trenidad, S.D.	89	144	129	16	27	35	5	0	1	7	0	1	0	14	0	28	9	6	3	.209	.285	.271
Hudson, Luke, Cin.	3	1	0	0	0	0	0	0	0	0	0	0	1	0	0	0	0	0	0	.000	.000	.000
Hundley, Todd, Chi.†	92	303	266	32	56	112	8	0	16	35	1	1	3	32	3	80	0	0	6	.211	.301	.421
Hunter, Brian L., Hou.	98	220	201	32	54	85	16	3	3	20	1	0	2	16	0	39	5	0	3	.269	.329	.423
Hyzdu, Adam, Pit.	59	179	155	24	36	75	6	0	11	34	0	2	1	21	0	44	0	0	1	.232	.324	.484
Ishii, Kazuhisa, L.A.*	28	56	50	1	5	5	0	0	0	2	4	0	0	2	0	21	0	0	2	.100	.135	.100
Izquierdo, Hansel, Fla.	20	2	2	0	0	0	0	0	0	0	0	0	0	0	0	1	0	0	0	.000	.000	.000
Izturis, Cesar, L.A.†	135	468	439	43	102	133	24	2	1	31	10	5	0	14	1	39	7	7	12	.232	.253	.303
Jarvis, Kevin, S.D.*	7	12	9	3	3	3	0	0	0	0	1	0	0	2	0	3	0	0	0	.333	.455	.333
Jenkins, Geoff, Mil.*	67	272	243	35	59	108	17	1	10	29	0	1	6	22	1	60	1	2	8	.243	.320	.444
Jennings, Jason, Col.*	32	68	62	6	19	23	4	0	0	11	2	0	1	3	0	13	0	0	0	.306	.348	.371
Jensen, Marcus, Mil.†	16	40	35	2	4	7	0	0	1	4	0	1	0	4	2	11	0	0	2	.114	.200	.200
Jensen, Ryan, S.F.	32	66	56	5	6	8	2	0	0	2	9	0	1	0	0	18	0	0	0	.107	.123	.143
Jimenez, D'Angelo, S.D.†	87	357	321	39	77	105	11	4	3	33	0	2	0	34	1	63	4	2	10	.240	.311	.327
Johnson, Charles, Fla.	83	280	244	18	53	90	19	0	6	36	1	4	0	31	7	61	0	0	10	.217	.301	.369
Johnson, Mark P., N.Y.*	42	61	51	5	7	14	4	0	1	4	1	0	0	9	0	18	0	0	0	.137	.267	.275
Johnson, Randy, Ari.	35	99	89	4	12	15	3	0	0	8	6	1	0	3	0	40	0	0	3	.135	.161	.169
Jones, Andruw, Atl.	154	659	560	91	148	287	34	0	35	94	0	6	10	83	4	135	8	3	14	.264	.366	.513
Jones, Bobby J., S.D.	19	34	33	2	5	5	0	0	0	2	1	0	0	0	0	11	0	0	1	.152	.152	.152
Jones, Bobby M., N.Y.-S.D. ...	17	3	2	0	0	0	0	0	0	0	1	0	0	0	0	1	0	0	0	.000	.000	.000
Jones, Chipper, Atl.†	158	662	548	90	179	294	35	1	26	100	0	5	2	107	23	89	8	2	18	.327	.435	.536
Jones, Todd, Col.†	79	3	3	0	0	0	0	0	0	0	0	0	0	0	0	2	0	0	0	.000	.000	.000
Jordan, Brian, L.A.	128	515	471	65	134	221	27	3	18	80	0	4	6	34	3	86	2	2	10	.285	.338	.469
Jose, Felix, Ari.†	13	25	19	5	5	11	0	0	2	4	0	2	0	4	0	8	0	0	1	.263	.360	.579
Junge, Eric, Phi.	4	3	3	0	0	0	0	0	0	0	0	0	0	0	0	0	0	0	0	.000	.000	.000
Kapler, Gabe, Col.	40	128	119	12	37	53	4	3	2	17	0	0	1	8	0	23	6	2	2	.311	.359	.445
Karros, Eric, L.A.	142	573	524	52	142	209	26	1	13	73	0	6	6	37	1	74	4	0	11	.271	.323	.399
Kearns, Austin, Cin.	107	435	372	66	117	186	24	3	13	56	0	3	6	54	3	81	6	3	11	.315	.407	.500
Kendall, Jason, Pit.	145	605	545	59	154	194	25	3	3	44	0	2	9	49	1	29	15	8	11	.283	.350	.356
Kent, Jeff, S.F.	152	682	623	102	195	352	42	2	37	108	0	3	4	52	3	101	5	1	20	.313	.368	.565
Kershner, Jason, S.D.*	15	1	0	0	0	0	0	0	0	0	1	0	0	0	0	0	0	0	0	.000	.000	.000
Kile, Darryl, St.L.	14	26	22	0	2	2	0	0	0	0	4	0	0	0	0	9	0	0	0	.091	.130	.091
Kim, Byung-Hyun, Ari.	72	2	2	0	1	1	0	0	0	0	0	0	0	0	0	0	0	0	0	.500	.500	.500
Kim, Sun-Woo, Mon.	4	8	8	2	2	2	0	0	0	0	0	0	0	0	0	1	0	0	0	.250	.250	.250
Kingsale, Gene, S.D.†	89	243	216	27	60	82	10	3	2	28	3	1	3	20	0	47	9	2	5	.278	.346	.380
Kinkade, Mike, L.A.	37	60	50	7	19	30	5	0	2	11	0	0	6	4	0	10	1	0	2	.380	.483	.600
Klassen, Danny, Ari.	4	3	3	0	1	1	0	0	0	0	0	0	0	0	0	1	0	0	0	.333	.333	.333
Klesko, Ryan, S.D.*	146	625	540	90	162	290	39	1	29	95	1	4	4	76	11	86	6	2	7	.300	.388	.537
Kline, Steve, St.L.†	66	1	1	0	0	0	0	0	0	0	0	0	0	0	0	0	0	0	0	.000	.000	.000
Knotts, Gary, Fla.	28	1	1	0	0	0	0	0	0	0	0	0	0	0	0	0	0	0	0	.000	.000	.000
Komiyama, Satoru, N.Y.	25	3	1	0	0	0	0	0	0	0	0	0	0	1	0	1	0	0	0	.000	.500	.000
Koplove, Mike, Ari.	55	1	1	0	0	0	0	0	0	0	0	0	0	0	0	0	0	0	0	.000	.000	.000
Kotsay, Mark, S.D.*	153	646	578	82	169	261	27	7	17	61	2	4	3	59	0	89	11	9	10	.292	.359	.452
Kreuter, Chad, L.A.†	41	108	95	8	25	36	5	0	2	12	0	2	1	10	4	31	1	0	3	.263	.333	.379
Lampkin, Tom, S.D.*	104	327	281	32	61	103	10	1	10	37	1	4	3	38	7	59	4	2	4	.217	.313	.367

Player, Team	G	TPA	AB	R	H	TB	2B	3B	HR	RBI	SH	SF	HP	BB	IBB	SO	SB	CS	GDP	Avg.	OBP	Slg.
Lane, Jason, Hou.	44	80	69	12	20	37	3	1	4	10	0	1	0	10	1	12	1	1	0	.290	.375	.536
Langerhans, Ryan, Atl.*	1	1	1	0	0	0	0	0	0	0	0	0	0	0	0	0	0	0	0	.000	.000	.000
Lankford, Ray, S.D.*	81	240	205	20	46	73	7	1	6	26	1	2	2	30	3	61	2	2	3	.224	.326	.356
Larkin, Barry, Cin.	145	567	507	72	124	186	37	2	7	47	6	7	3	44	9	57	13	4	13	.245	.305	.367
Larson, Brandon, Cin.	23	58	51	8	14	28	2	0	4	13	0	0	1	6	1	10	1	0	1	.275	.362	.549
LaRue, Jason, Cin.	113	397	353	42	88	143	17	1	12	52	2	2	13	27	6	117	1	2	13	.249	.324	.405
Lawrence, Brian, S.D.	35	71	63	1	6	8	2	0	0	6	3	0	0	5	0	14	0	0	2	.095	.162	.127
Ledee, Ricky, Phi.*	96	241	203	33	46	85	13	1	8	23	1	1	1	35	0	50	1	2	3	.227	.342	.419
Lee, Derrek, Fla.	162	688	581	95	157	287	35	7	27	86	0	4	5	98	8	164	19	9	14	.270	.378	.494
Lee, Travis, Phi.*	153	592	536	55	142	211	26	2	13	70	0	2	0	54	10	104	5	3	12	.265	.331	.394
Leiter, Al, N.Y.*	33	64	53	3	8	9	1	0	0	2	3	0	0	8	0	28	0	0	2	.151	.262	.170
Lewis, Darren, Chi.	58	91	79	7	19	24	3	1	0	7	2	0	3	7	0	11	1	3	0	.241	.326	.304
Lidge, Brad, Hou.	6	2	2	0	2	3	1	0	0	2	0	0	0	0	0	0	0	0	0	1.000	1.000	1.500
Lieber, Jon, Chi.*	21	48	43	2	7	8	1	0	0	0	4	0	0	1	0	10	0	0	2	.163	.182	.186
Lieberthal, Mike, Phi.	130	530	476	46	133	211	29	2	15	52	0	2	14	38	2	58	0	1	16	.279	.349	.443
Lincoln, Mike, Pit.	55	5	5	0	0	0	0	0	0	0	0	0	0	0	0	5	0	0	0	.000	.000	.000
Little, Mark, Col.-N.Y.-Ari.	79	154	130	28	27	38	5	3	0	7	1	0	8	15	0	34	2	2	1	.208	.327	.292
Lloyd, Graeme, Mon.-Fla.*	66	4	4	0	0	0	0	0	0	0	0	0	0	0	0	2	0	0	0	.000	.000	.000
Lo Duca, Paul, L.A.	149	632	580	74	163	233	38	1	10	64	4	4	10	34	2	31	3	1	20	.281	.330	.402
Lockhart, Keith, Atl.*	128	331	296	34	64	98	13	3	5	32	5	2	1	27	9	50	0	1	4	.216	.282	.331
Lofton, Kenny, S.F.*	46	205	180	30	48	73	10	3	3	9	1	0	1	23	0	22	7	3	1	.267	.353	.406
Looper, Braden, Fla.	78	1	1	0	0	0	0	0	0	0	0	0	0	0	0	0	0	0	0	.000	.000	.000
Lopez, Albie, Atl.	30	9	9	0	1	1	0	0	0	0	0	0	0	0	0	6	0	0	0	.111	.111	.111
Lopez, Javy, Atl.	109	385	347	31	81	129	15	0	11	52	0	4	8	26	8	63	0	1	15	.233	.299	.372
Lopez, Luis, Mil.†	6	10	8	1	0	0	0	0	0	1	0	0	0	2	0	1	0	0	0	.000	.200	.000
Lopez, Mendy, Pit.	3	3	3	0	0	0	0	0	0	0	0	0	0	0	0	3	0	0	0	.000	.000	.000
Loretta, Mark, Mil.-Hou.	107	329	283	33	86	116	18	0	4	27	6	3	5	32	1	37	1	1	7	.304	.381	.410
Lorraine, Andrew, Mil.*	5	2	1	0	0	0	0	0	0	0	1	0	0	0	0	1	0	0	0	.000	.000	.000
Lowe, Sean, Pit.-Col.	51	16	14	0	1	1	0	0	0	0	2	0	0	0	0	6	0	0	0	.071	.071	.071
Lowell, Mike, Fla.	160	678	597	88	165	281	44	0	24	92	0	11	4	65	5	92	4	3	16	.276	.346	.471
Lugo, Julio, Hou.	88	358	322	45	84	125	15	1	8	35	4	2	2	28	3	74	9	3	6	.261	.322	.388
Lunsford, Trey, S.F.	3	3	3	0	2	3	1	0	0	1	0	0	0	0	0	1	0	0	0	.667	.667	1.000
Mabry, John, Phi.*	21	23	21	1	6	6	0	0	0	3	0	1	0	1	1	5	0	0	0	.286	.304	.286
Machado, Robert, Chi.-Mil.	73	233	211	19	55	80	14	1	3	22	2	2	1	17	4	41	0	0	7	.261	.316	.379
Macias, Jose, Mon.†	90	252	231	33	59	99	17	1	7	33	4	3	1	13	0	44	5	6	2	.255	.294	.429
Mackowiak, Rob, Pit.*	136	439	385	57	94	164	22	0	16	48	3	2	7	42	5	120	9	3	0	.244	.328	.426
Maddux, Greg, Atl.	35	68	59	6	11	14	3	0	0	2	9	0	0	0	0	8	1	0	0	.186	.186	.237
Mahomes, Pat, Chi.	18	5	5	1	0	0	0	0	0	0	0	0	0	0	0	3	0	0	0	.000	.000	.000
Mahoney, Mike, Chi.	16	31	29	2	6	9	3	0	0	3	1	0	0	1	1	10	0	0	1	.207	.233	.310
Malloy, Marty, Fla.*	24	28	25	1	3	3	0	0	0	1	1	0	0	2	0	8	0	0	1	.120	.185	.120
Mann, Jim, Hou.	17	1	1	0	0	0	0	0	0	0	0	0	0	0	0	0	0	0	0	.000	.000	.000
Marquis, Jason, Atl.*	30	41	38	6	5	8	0	0	1	1	3	0	0	0	0	16	0	0	1	.132	.132	.211
Marrero, Eli, St.L.	131	446	397	63	104	179	19	1	18	66	5	4	0	40	11	72	14	2	5	.262	.327	.451
Martinez, Ramon E., S.F.	72	200	181	26	49	75	10	2	4	25	0	1	4	14	2	26	2	0	1	.271	.335	.414
Martinez, Tino, St.L.*	150	576	511	63	134	224	25	1	21	75	1	4	2	58	9	71	3	2	12	.262	.337	.438
Mateo, Henry, Mon.†	22	25	23	1	4	6	0	1	0	0	0	0	0	2	1	6	2	0	0	.174	.240	.261
Mateo, Ruben, Cin.	46	94	86	11	22	34	6	0	2	7	0	0	2	6	0	20	0	0	1	.256	.319	.395
Matheny, Mike, St.L.	110	363	315	31	77	100	12	1	3	35	8	6	2	32	6	49	1	3	3	.244	.313	.317
Mathews, T.J., Hou.	12	1	1	0	0	0	0	0	0	0	0	0	0	0	0	0	0	0	0	.000	.000	.000
Matos, Julius, S.D.	76	200	185	19	44	53	3	0	2	19	3	1	2	9	0	33	1	1	5	.238	.279	.286
Matthews Jr., Gary, N.Y.†	2	1	1	0	0	0	0	0	0	0	0	0	0	0	0	0	0	0	0	.000	.000	.000
Matthews, Mike, St.L.-Mil.*	47	7	6	0	1	1	0	0	0	0	1	0	0	0	0	4	0	0	0	.167	.167	.167
McCracken, Quinton, Ari.†	123	400	349	60	108	160	27	8	3	40	13	4	2	32	0	68	5	4	3	.309	.367	.458
McEwing, Joe, N.Y.	105	214	196	22	39	58	8	1	3	26	3	3	3	9	0	50	4	4	0	.199	.242	.296
McGriff, Fred, Chi.*	146	595	523	67	143	264	27	2	30	103	0	5	4	63	6	99	1	2	13	.273	.353	.505
McKeel, Walt, Col.	5	13	13	1	4	4	0	0	0	0	0	0	0	0	0	3	0	0	0	.308	.308	.308
Meadows, Brian, Pit.	11	22	18	0	0	0	0	0	0	0	1	3	1	0	0	10	0	0	0	.000	.000	.000
Mercado, Hector, Phi.*	31	4	4	0	1	1	0	0	0	0	0	0	0	0	0	2	0	0	0	.250	.250	.250
Merced, Orlando, Hou.*	123	281	251	35	72	109	13	3	6	30	1	3	0	26	5	50	4	0	9	.287	.350	.434
Mercker, Kent, Col.*	58	1	1	0	0	0	0	0	0	0	0	0	0	0	0	0	0	0	0	.000	.000	.000
Michaels, Jason, Phi.	81	121	105	16	28	50	10	3	2	11	0	2	1	13	1	33	1	1	1	.267	.347	.476
Middlebrook, Jason, S.D.-N.Y.	15	13	11	2	2	2	0	0	0	0	1	0	0	1	0	3	0	0	0	.182	.250	.182
Millar, Kevin, Fla.	126	489	438	58	134	223	41	0	16	57	0	6	5	40	0	74	0	2	15	.306	.366	.509
Miller, Corky, Cin.	39	129	114	9	29	48	10	0	3	15	1	1	4	9	2	20	0	0	7	.254	.328	.421
Miller, Damian, Ari.	101	340	297	40	74	129	22	0	11	42	2	0	3	38	5	88	0	0	14	.249	.340	.434
Miller, Wade, Hou.	26	69	62	7	11	14	3	0	0	4	6	1	0	0	0	21	0	0	2	.177	.175	.226
Millwood, Kevin, Atl.	35	82	70	5	14	22	5	0	1	11	11	0	0	0	0	27	0	0	0	.200	.200	.314
Minor, Damon, S.F.*	83	201	173	21	41	77	6	0	10	24	0	2	2	24	6	34	0	0	8	.237	.333	.445
Mlicki, Dave, Hou.	22	27	27	2	5	6	1	0	0	1	0	0	0	0	0	6	0	0	0	.185	.185	.222
Moehler, Brian, Cin.	10	16	14	0	0	0	0	0	0	0	1	0	0	1	0	4	0	0	0	.000	.067	.000
Moeller, Chad, Ari.	37	123	105	10	30	49	11	1	2	16	1	0	0	17	3	23	0	1	6	.286	.385	.467
Mordecai, Mike, Mon.-Fla.	93	176	151	19	37	45	8	0	0	11	10	0	2	13	4	27	2	2	3	.245	.313	.298
Morris, Matt, St.L.	32	79	71	4	12	15	3	0	0	3	5	0	0	3	0	23	0	0	0	.169	.203	.211
Moss, Damian, Atl.	33	60	50	2	5	6	1	0	0	2	6	0	0	4	0	24	0	0	0	.100	.167	.120
Mota, Guillermo, L.A.	43	4	4	1	1	1	0	0	0	0	0	0	0	0	0	2	0	0	0	.250	.250	.250
Mueller, Bill, Chi.-S.F.†	111	427	366	51	96	144	19	4	7	38	4	5	0	52	2	42	0	4	9	.262	.350	.393
Mulholland, Terry, L.A.	21	1	1	0	0	0	0	0	0	0	0	0	0	0	0	0	0	0	0	.000	.000	.000
Munro, Peter, Hou.	19	24	22	1	3	3	0	0	0	2	1	0	0	1	0	6	0	0	1	.136	.174	.136
Murray, Calvin, S.F.	11	13	12	0	0	0	0	0	0	0	0	0	0	1	0	4	0	0	0	.000	.077	.000
Myers, Brett, Phi.	12	26	23	0	3	4	1	0	0	1	3	0	0	0	0	9	0	0	2	.130	.130	.174
Myers, Rodney, S.D.	14	1	1	0	0	0	0	0	0	0	0	0	0	0	0	0	0	0	0	.000	.000	.000
Nance, Shane, Mil.*	4	3	3	0	1	1	0	0	0	0	0	0	0	0	0	2	0	0	0	.333	.333	.333
Neagle, Denny, Col.*	35	50	45	5	12	16	4	0	0	1	5	0	0	0	0	11	0	0	2	.267	.267	.356
Nen, Robb, S.F.	68	2	2	0	1	1	0	0	0	0	0	0	0	0	0	1	0	0	0	.500	.500	.500
Neugebauer, Nick, Mil.	12	20	19	0	2	3	1	0	0	1	1	0	0	0	0	4	0	0	0	.105	.105	.158

Player, Team	G	TPA	AB	R	H	TB	2B	3B	HR	RBI	SH	SF	HP	BB	IBB	SO	SB	CS	GDP	Avg.	OBP	Slg.
Nevin, Phil, S.D.	107	450	407	53	116	168	16	0	12	57	0	4	1	38	4	87	4	0	12	.285	.344	.413
Nichting, Chris, Col.	29	3	3	1	1	1	0	0	0	0	0	0	0	0	0	0	0	0	0	.333	.333	.333
Nickle, Doug, Phi.-S.D.	14	1	1	0	0	0	0	0	0	0	0	0	0	0	0	0	0	0	0	.000	.000	.000
Nieves, Wil, S.D.	28	76	72	2	13	18	3	1	0	3	0	0	0	4	4	15	1	0	1	.181	.224	.250
Nomo, Hideo, L.A.	34	74	63	3	4	9	2	0	1	3	6	0	0	5	0	32	0	0	1	.063	.132	.143
Norton, Greg, Col.†	113	195	168	19	37	68	8	1	7	37	1	2	0	24	0	52	2	3	4	.220	.314	.405
Nunez, Abraham, Fla.†	19	17	17	2	2	2	0	0	0	1	0	0	0	0	0	5	0	1	1	.118	.118	.118
Nunez, Abraham O., Pit.†	112	286	253	28	59	81	14	1	2	15	3	1	2	27	1	44	3	4	2	.233	.311	.320
Nunez, Vladimir, Fla.	77	5	5	0	1	1	0	0	0	0	0	0	0	0	0	4	0	0	0	.200	.200	.200
O'Leary, Troy, Mon.*	97	314	273	27	78	103	12	2	3	37	4	0	3	34	5	47	1	2	6	.286	.371	.377
Ochoa, Alex, Mil.	85	250	215	32	55	82	9	0	6	21	1	0	2	32	2	30	8	5	7	.256	.357	.381
Ohka, Tomokazu, Mon.	32	67	55	3	7	8	1	0	0	2	8	0	0	4	0	28	0	0	0	.127	.186	.145
Ojeda, Augie, Chi.†	30	81	70	4	13	17	4	0	0	4	4	1	1	5	0	5	1	0	2	.186	.247	.243
Olsen, Kevin, Fla.	17	12	12	0	1	1	0	0	0	0	0	0	0	0	0	7	0	0	0	.083	.083	.083
Ordonez, Rey, N.Y.	144	499	460	53	117	149	25	2	1	42	9	4	2	24	11	46	2	2	19	.254	.292	.324
Orie, Kevin, Chi.	13	36	32	4	9	12	3	0	0	5	0	2	1	1	0	4	0	0	1	.281	.306	.375
Orosco, Jesse, L.A.	56	1	0	1	0	0	0	0	0	0	0	0	0	1	0	0	0	0	0	.000	1.000	.000
Ortiz, Jose, Col.	65	215	192	22	48	60	7	1	1	12	2	2	3	16	0	30	2	0	3	.250	.315	.313
Ortiz, Russ, S.F.	33	84	69	11	17	28	5	0	2	9	7	2	0	6	0	17	0	0	1	.246	.299	.406
Osborne, Donovan, Chi.*	11	3	3	0	0	0	0	0	0	0	0	0	0	0	0	1	0	0	0	.000	.000	.000
Osik, Keith, Pit.	55	111	100	6	16	25	3	0	2	11	2	2	1	6	0	25	0	0	2	.160	.211	.250
Osting, Jimmy, Mil.	3	4	3	0	0	0	0	0	0	0	1	0	0	0	0	1	0	0	0	.000	.000	.000
Oswalt, Roy, Hou.	35	89	77	5	10	12	2	0	0	4	7	0	1	4	0	26	0	0	0	.130	.183	.156
Overbay, Lyle, Ari.*	10	10	10	0	1	1	0	0	0	1	0	0	0	0	0	5	0	0	0	.100	.100	.100
Owens, Eric, Fla.	131	426	385	44	104	141	15	5	4	37	8	1	0	31	1	33	26	9	11	.270	.324	.366
Ozuna, Pablo, Fla.	34	50	47	4	13	19	2	2	0	3	0	1	1	1	0	3	1	1	2	.277	.300	.404
Padilla, Vicente, Phi.	32	67	58	1	3	4	1	0	0	5	7	1	1	0	0	31	0	0	1	.052	.067	.069
Patterson, Corey, Chi.*	153	628	592	71	150	232	30	5	14	54	4	5	8	19	1	142	18	3	8	.253	.284	.392
Patterson, John, Ari.	7	12	10	1	1	1	0	0	0	0	1	0	0	1	0	4	0	0	0	.100	.182	.100
Pavano, Carl, Mon.-Fla.	37	45	40	2	8	11	1	1	0	2	5	0	0	0	0	12	0	0	0	.200	.200	.275
Payton, Jay, N.Y.-Col.	134	481	445	69	135	217	20	7	16	59	2	1	4	29	0	54	7	4	11	.303	.351	.488
Pearce, Josh, St.L.	3	6	4	0	1	1	0	0	0	1	2	0	0	0	0	0	0	0	0	.250	.250	.250
Peavy, Jake, S.D.	17	35	33	4	7	10	3	0	0	2	2	0	0	0	0	13	0	1	0	.212	.212	.303
Pelaez, Alex, S.D.	3	8	8	0	2	2	0	0	0	0	0	0	0	0	0	0	0	0	2	.250	.250	.250
Pember, Dave, Mil.	4	1	1	0	0	0	0	0	0	0	0	0	0	0	0	1	0	0	0	.000	.000	.000
Pena, Wily Mo, Cin.	13	18	18	1	4	7	0	0	1	1	0	0	0	0	0	11	0	0	0	.222	.222	.389
Penny, Brad, Fla.	24	49	48	1	8	10	2	0	0	1	1	0	0	0	0	14	0	0	0	.167	.167	.208
Perez, Eduardo, St.L.	96	177	154	22	31	70	9	0	10	26	1	2	3	17	0	36	0	0	7	.201	.290	.455
Perez, Odalis, L.A.*	32	75	64	5	10	18	5	0	1	4	10	0	0	1	0	13	0	0	0	.156	.169	.281
Perez, Oliver, S.D.*	16	33	30	1	4	4	0	0	0	0	3	0	0	0	0	11	0	0	0	.133	.133	.133
Perez, Timo, N.Y.*	136	481	444	52	131	194	27	6	8	47	10	2	2	23	2	36	10	6	10	.295	.331	.437
Perez, Tomas, Phi.†	92	237	212	22	53	83	13	1	5	20	2	1	1	21	6	40	1	0	5	.250	.319	.392
Person, Robert, Phi.	17	29	24	3	2	8	0	0	2	7	3	0	0	2	0	17	0	0	0	.083	.154	.333
Petrick, Ben, Col.	38	106	95	10	20	40	3	1	5	11	0	1	1	9	0	33	0	1	1	.211	.283	.421
Phillips, Jason, N.Y.	11	22	19	4	7	10	0	0	1	3	0	1	1	1	0	1	0	0	1	.368	.409	.526
Piazza, Mike, N.Y.	135	541	478	69	134	260	23	2	33	98	0	3	3	57	9	82	0	3	26	.280	.359	.544
Pickford, Kevin, S.D.*	16	5	5	0	0	0	0	0	0	0	0	0	0	0	0	3	0	0	0	.000	.000	.000
Pierre, Juan, Col.*	152	640	592	90	170	203	20	5	1	35	8	0	9	31	0	52	47	12	7	.287	.332	.343
Pineda, Luis, Cin.	26	3	3	0	0	0	0	0	0	0	0	0	0	0	0	2	0	0	0	.000	.000	.000
Polanco, Placido, St.L.-Phi.	147	595	548	75	158	221	32	2	9	49	13	0	8	26	1	41	5	3	15	.288	.330	.403
Politte, Cliff, Phi.	13	1	1	0	0	0	0	0	0	0	0	0	0	0	0	1	0	0	0	.000	.000	.000
Pratt, Todd, Phi.	39	136	106	14	33	53	11	0	3	16	0	2	4	24	6	28	2	0	3	.311	.449	.500
Prior, Mark, Chi.	19	39	35	3	6	10	4	0	0	4	2	0	0	2	0	15	0	0	1	.171	.216	.286
Puffer, Brandon, Hou.	55	8	6	0	0	0	0	0	0	0	1	0	0	1	0	5	0	0	0	.000	.143	.000
Pujols, Albert, St.L.	157	675	590	118	185	331	40	2	34	127	0	4	9	72	13	69	2	4	20	.314	.394	.561
Punto, Nick, Phi.†	9	7	6	0	1	1	0	0	0	0	1	0	0	0	0	3	0	0	0	.167	.167	.167
Quantrill, Paul, L.A.*	86	3	3	0	1	1	0	0	0	0	0	0	0	0	0	2	0	0	0	.333	.333	.333
Quevedo, Ruben, Mil.	26	47	42	2	4	4	0	0	0	3	3	0	0	2	0	21	0	0	3	.095	.136	.095
Raines, Tim, Fla.†	98	114	89	9	17	23	3	0	1	7	0	2	1	22	4	19	0	0	3	.191	.351	.258
Ramirez, Aramis, Pit.	142	570	522	51	122	202	26	0	18	71	0	11	8	29	3	95	2	0	17	.234	.279	.387
Ransom, Cody, S.F.	7	4	3	2	2	2	0	0	0	1	0	0	0	1	1	1	0	0	0	.667	.750	.667
Reames, Britt, Mon.	42	11	9	0	1	1	0	0	0	1	2	0	0	0	0	1	0	0	0	.111	.111	.111
Reboulet, Jeff, L.A.	38	58	48	3	10	13	3	0	0	2	3	1	0	6	0	13	0	0	1	.208	.291	.271
Redding, Tim, Hou.	18	21	20	0	2	2	0	0	0	2	1	0	0	0	0	12	0	0	0	.100	.100	.100
Redmond, Mike, Fla.	89	290	256	19	78	99	15	0	2	28	2	3	8	21	8	34	0	2	4	.305	.372	.387
Reed, Steve, S.D.-N.Y.	65	2	2	0	0	0	0	0	0	0	0	0	0	0	0	2	0	0	0	.000	.000	.000
Reese, Pokey, Pit.	119	475	421	46	111	148	25	0	4	50	5	5	3	41	4	81	12	1	4	.264	.330	.352
Reitsma, Chris, Cin.	32	38	30	0	3	3	0	0	0	2	7	0	0	1	0	12	0	0	1	.100	.129	.100
Remlinger, Mike, Atl.*	73	2	2	0	0	0	0	0	0	0	0	0	0	0	0	1	0	0	0	.000	.000	.000
Renteria, Edgar, St.L.	152	609	544	77	166	239	36	2	11	83	7	5	4	49	7	57	22	7	17	.305	.364	.439
Reynolds, Shane, Hou.	13	30	21	0	1	2	1	0	0	3	9	0	0	0	0	12	0	0	0	.048	.048	.095
Riedling, John, Cin.	33	1	1	0	0	0	0	0	0	0	0	0	0	0	0	1	0	0	0	.000	.000	.000
Rijo, Jose, Cin.	31	19	16	0	2	2	0	0	0	0	3	0	0	0	0	7	0	0	1	.125	.125	.125
Rios, Armando, Pit.*	76	226	208	20	55	69	11	0	1	24	0	1	1	16	1	39	1	1	8	.264	.319	.332
Roa, Joe, Phi.	14	30	25	1	6	7	1	0	0	2	3	1	0	1	0	5	0	0	0	.240	.259	.280
Roberts, Dave, L.A.*	127	479	422	63	117	154	14	7	3	34	6	1	2	48	0	51	45	10	1	.277	.353	.365
Roberts, Grant, N.Y.	34	1	1	1	1	1	0	0	0	0	0	0	0	0	0	0	0	0	0	1.000	1.000	1.000
Robertson, Nate, Fla.	6	2	2	0	0	0	0	0	0	0	0	0	0	0	0	1	0	0	0	.000	.000	.000
Robinson, Kerry, St.L.*	124	195	181	27	47	65	7	4	1	15	2	1	0	11	3	29	7	4	1	.260	.301	.359
Rodriguez, Felix, S.F.	71	1	1	1	1	1	0	0	0	0	0	0	0	0	0	0	0	0	0	1.000	1.000	1.000
Rodriguez, Henry, Mon.*	20	25	20	1	1	1	0	0	0	3	0	1	0	4	0	8	0	0	0	.050	.200	.050
Rodriguez, Nerio, St.L.	2	1	1	0	0	0	0	0	0	0	0	0	0	0	0	1	0	0	0	.000	.000	.000
Rolen, Scott, Phi.-St.L.	155	667	580	89	154	292	29	8	31	110	0	3	12	72	4	102	8	4	22	.266	.357	.503
Rollins, Jimmy, Phi.†	154	705	637	82	156	242	33	10	11	60	6	4	4	54	3	103	31	13	14	.245	.306	.380
Romano, Jason, Col.	18	41	37	9	12	14	0	1	0	1	1	0	0	3	0	11	4	1	0	.324	.375	.378

Player, Team	G	TPA	AB	R	H	TB	2B	3B	HR	RBI	SH	SF	HP	BB	IBB	SO	SB	CS	GDP	Avg.	OBP	Slg.
Ross, Dave, L.A.	8	13	10	2	2	6	1	0	1	2	0	0	1	2	0	4	0	0	0	.200	.385	.600
Ruan, Wilkin, L.A.	12	11	11	2	3	4	1	0	0	3	0	0	0	0	0	2	0	0	0	.273	.273	.364
Rueter, Kirk, S.F.*	35	79	62	3	11	11	0	0	0	3	13	2	0	2	0	11	0	0	0	.177	.197	.177
Rusch, Glendon, Mil.*	37	81	66	6	19	22	0	0	1	8	14	0	0	1	0	24	0	0	1	.288	.299	.333
Rushford, Jim, Mil.*	23	84	77	8	11	16	2	0	1	6	0	0	1	6	0	9	0	0	3	.143	.214	.208
Saarloos, Kirk, Hou.	17	35	30	0	2	3	1	0	0	2	5	0	0	0	0	11	0	0	0	.067	.067	.100
Sanchez, Alex, Mil.*	112	435	394	55	114	141	10	7	1	33	6	2	2	31	0	62	37	14	4	.289	.343	.358
Sanchez, Jesus, Chi.*	8	1	1	0	0	0	0	0	0	0	0	0	0	0	0	0	0	0	0	.000	.000	.000
Sanders, Reggie, S.F.	140	571	505	75	126	230	23	6	23	85	0	7	12	47	3	121	18	6	10	.250	.324	.455
Santiago, Benito, S.F.	126	517	478	56	133	215	24	5	16	74	3	7	2	27	8	73	4	2	19	.278	.315	.450
Santiago, Jose, Phi.	42	3	2	0	0	0	0	0	0	0	0	0	0	1	0	1	0	0	0	.000	.333	.000
Santos, Victor, Col.	24	2	2	0	1	1	0	0	0	0	0	0	0	0	0	0	0	0	0	.500	.500	.500
Sauerbeck, Scott, Pit.	79	2	2	0	0	0	0	0	0	0	0	0	0	0	0	1	0	0	0	.000	.000	.000
Schilling, Curt, Ari.	36	98	86	7	15	15	0	0	0	3	8	0	0	4	0	26	0	0	2	.174	.211	.174
Schmidt, Jason, S.F.	29	62	56	3	7	9	2	0	0	2	4	0	0	2	0	28	0	0	0	.125	.155	.161
Schneider, Brian, Mon.*	73	232	207	21	57	95	19	2	5	29	2	2	0	21	8	41	1	2	7	.275	.339	.459
Scutaro, Marco, N.Y.	27	38	36	2	8	13	0	1	1	6	1	1	0	0	0	11	0	1	1	.222	.216	.361
Sexson, Richie, Mil.	157	652	570	86	159	287	37	2	29	102	0	4	8	70	7	136	0	0	17	.279	.363	.504
Sheets, Ben, Mil.	34	76	68	2	6	7	1	0	0	3	4	0	0	4	0	39	0	0	0	.088	.139	.103
Sheffield, Gary, Atl.	135	579	492	82	151	252	26	0	25	84	0	4	11	72	2	53	12	2	16	.307	.404	.512
Shinjo, Tsuyoshi, S.F.	118	398	362	42	86	134	15	3	9	37	3	3	6	24	2	46	5	0	5	.238	.294	.370
Shuey, Paul, L.A.	28	3	3	0	1	1	0	0	0	0	0	0	0	0	0	2	0	0	0	.333	.333	.333
Shumpert, Terry, Col.	106	268	234	30	55	87	12	1	6	21	5	4	4	21	0	41	4	1	9	.235	.304	.372
Silva, Carlos, Phi.	68	3	2	0	0	0	0	0	0	0	0	0	0	1	0	1	0	0	0	.000	.333	.000
Silva, Jose, Cin.	12	1	0	0	0	0	0	0	0	0	1	0	0	0	0	0	0	0	0	.000	.000	.000
Simontacchi, Jason, St.L.	25	56	50	5	12	12	0	0	0	2	4	0	0	2	0	15	0	0	0	.240	.269	.240
Smith, Bud, St.L.*	11	18	14	0	3	4	1	0	0	1	3	0	0	1	0	4	0	0	1	.214	.267	.286
Smith, Dan, Mon.	33	3	3	0	0	0	0	0	0	0	0	0	0	0	0	3	0	0	0	.000	.000	.000
Smith, Travis, St.L.	12	20	18	0	3	3	0	0	0	2	2	0	0	0	0	6	0	0	0	.167	.167	.167
Smoltz, John, Atl.	75	2	2	0	0	0	0	0	0	0	0	0	0	0	0	1	0	0	0	.000	.000	.000
Smyth, Steve, Chi.*	8	10	9	1	2	2	0	0	0	1	1	0	0	0	0	1	0	0	1	.222	.222	.222
Snead, Esix, N.Y.†	17	14	13	3	4	7	0	0	1	3	0	0	0	1	0	4	4	3	0	.308	.357	.538
Snow, J.T., S.F.*	143	494	422	47	104	152	26	2	6	53	0	6	7	59	5	90	0	0	11	.246	.344	.360
Sosa, Sammy, Chi.	150	666	556	122	160	330	19	2	49	108	0	4	3	103	15	144	2	0	14	.288	.399	.594
Speier, Justin, Col.	63	3	3	0	1	1	0	0	0	0	0	0	0	0	0	2	0	0	0	.333	.333	.333
Spivey, Junior, Ari.	143	626	538	103	162	256	34	6	16	78	1	6	16	65	5	100	11	6	10	.301	.389	.476
Spooneybarger, Tim, Atl.	51	1	1	0	0	0	0	0	0	0	0	0	0	0	0	1	0	0	0	.000	.000	.000
Stairs, Matt, Mil.*	107	315	270	41	66	129	15	0	16	41	0	1	8	36	4	50	2	0	7	.244	.349	.478
Stark, Denny, Col.	33	45	41	4	7	13	3	0	1	4	3	1	0	0	0	19	0	0	0	.171	.167	.317
Stechschulte, Gene, St.L.	29	2	2	0	0	0	0	0	0	0	0	0	0	0	0	2	0	0	0	.000	.000	.000
Stephenson, Garrett, St.L.	12	15	12	0	0	0	0	0	0	0	2	0	0	1	0	8	0	0	0	.000	.077	.000
Stevens, Lee, Mon.*	63	245	205	28	39	77	6	1	10	31	0	1	0	39	5	57	1	0	4	.190	.318	.376
Stewart, Scott, Mon.	67	2	2	0	0	0	0	0	0	0	0	0	0	0	0	2	0	0	0	.000	.000	.000
Stinnett, Kelly, Cin.	34	108	93	10	21	35	5	0	3	13	0	0	0	15	1	25	2	0	1	.226	.333	.376
Stone, Ricky, Hou.	78	5	4	0	0	0	0	0	0	0	1	0	0	0	0	1	0	0	0	.000	.000	.000
Stottlemyre, Todd, Ari.*	5	6	4	0	0	0	0	0	0	0	1	0	0	1	0	2	0	0	0	.000	.200	.000
Stull, Everett, Mil.	2	3	3	0	1	1	0	0	0	0	0	0	0	0	0	1	0	0	0	.333	.333	.333
Stynes, Chris, Chi.	98	225	195	25	47	73	9	1	5	26	5	3	1	21	1	29	1	1	5	.241	.314	.374
Sullivan, Scott, Cin.	71	3	3	0	1	1	0	0	0	0	0	0	0	0	0	1	0	0	0	.333	.333	.333
Surhoff, B.J., Atl.*	25	85	75	5	22	27	5	0	0	9	1	0	0	9	0	5	1	3	1	.293	.369	.360
Sweeney, Mark, S.D.*	48	69	65	3	11	17	3	0	1	4	0	0	0	4	0	19	0	0	1	.169	.217	.262
Taguchi, So, St.L.	19	19	15	4	6	6	0	0	0	2	2	0	0	2	0	1	1	0	0	.400	.471	.400
Tankersley, Dennis, S.D.	17	13	13	2	4	8	1	0	1	1	0	0	0	0	0	2	0	0	1	.308	.308	.615
Tarasco, Tony, N.Y.*	60	105	96	15	24	47	5	0	6	15	0	1	0	8	0	13	2	1	2	.250	.305	.490
Tatis, Fernando, Mon.	114	430	381	43	87	152	18	1	15	55	1	5	8	35	1	90	2	2	15	.228	.303	.399
Tavarez, Julian, Fla.*	29	47	40	3	5	5	0	0	0	5	5	0	0	2	0	17	0	0	0	.125	.167	.125
Taylor, Reggie, Cin.*	135	311	287	41	73	123	15	4	9	38	5	3	2	14	3	79	11	8	6	.254	.291	.429
Tejera, Michael, Fla.*	49	41	37	5	7	10	0	0	1	5	2	0	1	1	0	6	0	0	0	.189	.231	.270
Teut, Nate, Fla.	2	2	2	0	0	0	0	0	0	0	0	0	0	0	0	2	0	0	0	.000	.000	.000
Thompson, Ryan, Mil.	62	146	137	16	34	71	9	2	8	24	0	0	2	7	0	38	1	0	7	.248	.295	.518
Thomson, John, Col.-N.Y.	30	62	52	4	11	11	0	0	0	3	6	1	0	3	0	19	0	0	0	.212	.250	.212
Thurston, Joe, L.A.*	8	15	13	1	6	7	1	0	0	1	1	1	0	0	0	1	0	0	0	.462	.429	.538
Timlin, Mike, St.L.-Phi.	72	6	6	0	0	0	0	0	0	0	0	0	0	0	0	4	0	0	0	.000	.000	.000
Tollberg, Brian, S.D.	12	22	19	0	3	4	1	0	0	0	1	0	0	2	0	5	0	0	2	.158	.238	.211
Tomko, Brett, S.D.	32	74	66	2	12	14	2	0	0	6	7	0	0	1	0	20	0	0	2	.182	.194	.212
Torcato, Tony, S.F.*	5	11	11	0	3	4	1	0	0	0	0	0	0	0	0	2	0	0	0	.273	.273	.364
Torrealba, Steve, Atl.	13	21	17	1	1	1	0	0	0	1	1	0	0	3	0	4	0	0	0	.059	.200	.059
Torrealba, Yorvit, S.F.	53	155	136	17	38	54	10	0	2	14	3	0	2	14	2	20	0	0	11	.279	.355	.397
Torres, Salomon, Pit.	5	13	13	0	2	2	0	0	0	0	0	0	0	0	0	4	0	0	0	.154	.154	.154
Trachsel, Steve, N.Y.	31	56	46	4	5	7	0	1	0	4	9	0	0	1	0	19	0	0	2	.109	.128	.152
Trammell, Bubba, S.D.	133	465	403	54	98	167	16	1	17	56	3	3	3	53	2	71	1	3	6	.243	.333	.414
Truby, Chris, Mon.	35	112	105	12	27	42	5	2	2	7	1	0	1	5	1	27	1	1	2	.257	.297	.400
Tucker, T.J., Mon.	58	4	4	1	3	3	0	0	0	0	0	0	0	0	0	0	0	0	0	.750	.750	.750
Uribe, Juan, Col.	155	618	566	69	136	193	25	7	6	49	7	6	5	34	1	120	9	2	17	.240	.286	.341
Valent, Eric, Phi.*	7	10	10	1	2	2	0	0	0	0	0	0	0	0	0	3	0	0	1	.200	.200	.200
Valentin, John, N.Y.	114	242	208	18	50	74	15	0	3	30	0	2	10	22	0	37	0	0	6	.240	.339	.356
Vance, Cory, Col.*	2	1	1	0	0	0	0	0	0	0	0	0	0	0	0	1	0	0	0	.000	.000	.000
Vaughn, Mo, N.Y.*	139	558	487	67	126	222	18	0	26	72	0	2	10	59	6	145	0	1	15	.259	.349	.456
Vazquez, Javier, Mon.	34	86	73	7	13	13	0	0	0	4	10	0	0	3	0	9	0	1	2	.178	.211	.178
Vazquez, Ramon, S.D.*	128	474	423	50	116	153	21	5	2	32	3	2	1	45	3	79	7	2	6	.274	.344	.362
Veres, Dave, St.L.	71	3	3	0	1	1	0	0	0	0	0	0	0	0	0	1	0	0	0	.333	.333	.333
Vidro, Jose, Mon.†	152	681	604	103	190	296	43	3	19	96	11	3	3	60	1	70	2	1	12	.315	.378	.490
Villone, Ron, Pit.*	45	16	16	1	4	6	0	1	0	1	0	0	0	0	0	3	0	0	0	.250	.250	.375
Vina, Fernando, St.L.*	150	692	622	75	168	210	29	5	1	54	1	7	18	44	2	36	17	11	11	.270	.333	.338
Vizcaino, Jose, Hou.†	125	438	406	53	123	161	19	2	5	37	5	2	1	24	2	40	3	5	5	.303	.342	.397

Player, Team	G	TPA	AB	R	H	TB	2B	3B	HR	RBI	SH	SF	HP	BB	IBB	SO	SB	CS	GDP	Avg.	OBP	Slg.
Vizcaino, Luis, Mil.	76	2	2	0	0	0	0	0	0	0	0	0	0	0	0	2	0	0	0	.000	.000	.000
Wagner, Billy, Hou.*	70	2	2	0	0	0	0	0	0	0	0	0	0	0	0	2	0	0	0	.000	.000	.000
Walker, Larry, Col.*	136	553	477	95	161	287	40	4	26	104	0	4	7	65	6	73	6	5	8	.338	.421	.602
Walker, Todd, Cin.*	155	675	612	79	183	264	42	3	11	64	7	3	3	50	7	81	8	5	9	.299	.353	.431
Walker, Tyler, N.Y.	5	2	2	0	0	0	0	0	0	0	0	0	0	0	0	1	0	0	0	.000	.000	.000
Ward, Daryle, Hou.*	136	491	453	41	125	192	31	0	12	72	0	4	1	33	5	82	1	3	9	.276	.324	.424
Wayne, Justin, Fla.	5	8	7	0	0	0	0	0	0	0	1	0	0	0	0	3	0	0	0	.000	.000	.000
Weathers, Dave, N.Y.	71	1	1	0	0	0	0	0	0	0	0	0	0	0	0	0	0	0	0	.000	.000	.000
Wells, Kip, Pit.	34	76	63	4	12	17	2	0	1	5	13	0	0	0	0	28	0	0	0	.190	.190	.270
Wesson, Barry, Hou.	15	21	20	1	4	6	0	1	0	1	0	0	0	1	0	5	0	0	2	.200	.238	.300
White, Gabe, Cin.*	62	3	2	0	0	0	0	0	0	0	1	0	0	0	0	2	0	0	0	.000	.000	.000
White, Rick, Col.-St.L.	61	1	1	0	0	0	0	0	0	0	0	0	0	0	0	1	0	0	0	.000	.000	.000
Wigginton, Ty, N.Y.	46	127	116	18	35	61	8	0	6	18	0	1	2	8	0	19	2	1	4	.302	.354	.526
Wilkerson, Brad, Mon.*	153	603	507	92	135	238	27	8	20	59	6	4	5	81	7	161	7	8	5	.266	.370	.469
Williams, Dave, Pit.*	10	16	16	1	2	5	0	0	1	3	0	0	0	0	0	12	0	0	0	.125	.125	.313
Williams, Jeff, L.A.	10	2	2	0	1	1	0	0	0	0	0	0	0	0	0	1	0	0	0	.500	.500	.500
Williams, Matt, Ari.	60	238	215	29	56	103	7	2	12	40	0	2	0	21	1	41	3	1	8	.260	.324	.479
Williams, Mike, Pit.	59	2	1	0	0	0	0	0	0	0	0	0	1	0	0	1	0	0	0	.000	.500	.000
Williams, Woody, St.L.	18	36	29	3	6	12	3	0	1	3	5	1	1	0	0	9	0	0	2	.207	.226	.414
Wilson, Craig A., Pit.	131	424	368	48	97	163	16	1	16	57	1	2	21	32	0	116	2	3	10	.264	.355	.443
Wilson, Jack, Pit.	147	586	527	77	133	175	22	4	4	47	17	1	4	37	2	74	5	2	7	.252	.306	.332
Wilson, Preston, Fla.	141	582	510	80	124	219	22	2	23	65	2	3	9	58	3	140	20	11	17	.243	.329	.429
Wilson, Vance, N.Y.	74	178	163	19	40	62	7	0	5	26	2	0	8	5	0	32	0	1	4	.245	.301	.380
Witasick, Jay, S.F.	44	5	5	0	0	0	0	0	0	0	0	0	0	0	0	4	0	0	0	.000	.000	.000
Wolf, Randy, Phi.*	32	75	59	6	8	15	4	0	1	4	12	0	0	4	0	24	0	0	3	.136	.190	.254
Womack, Tony, Ari.*	153	652	590	90	160	208	23	5	5	57	6	6	4	46	2	80	29	12	9	.271	.325	.353
Wood, Kerry, Chi.	33	81	72	5	12	15	0	0	1	5	6	0	0	3	0	28	0	0	0	.167	.200	.208
Worrell, Tim, S.F.	80	3	3	0	0	0	0	0	0	0	0	0	0	0	0	2	0	0	0	.000	.000	.000
Wright, Jamey, Mil.-St.L.	23	45	38	0	5	8	3	0	0	0	7	0	0	0	0	16	0	0	0	.132	.132	.211
Yoshii, Masato, Mon.	31	44	35	2	2	3	1	0	0	5	5	0	1	3	0	13	0	0	2	.057	.154	.086
Young, Eric, Mil.	138	553	496	57	139	183	29	3	3	28	8	4	6	39	0	38	31	11	14	.280	.338	.369
Young, Kevin, Pit.	146	525	468	60	115	191	26	1	16	51	0	3	4	50	2	101	4	6	13	.246	.322	.408
Zambrano, Carlos, Chi.	32	32	30	0	1	2	1	0	0	0	2	0	0	0	0	15	0	0	0	.033	.033	.067
Zaun, Gregg, Hou.†	76	202	185	18	41	59	7	1	3	24	2	1	2	12	1	36	1	0	4	.222	.275	.319
Zeile, Todd, Col.	144	580	506	61	138	215	23	0	18	87	0	7	1	66	3	92	1	1	27	.273	.353	.425
Zerbe, Chad, S.F.*	50	7	6	0	1	1	0	0	0	1	1	0	0	0	0	2	0	0	0	.167	.167	.167
Zinter, Alan, Hou.†	39	44	44	5	6	14	2	0	2	3	0	0	0	0	0	19	0	0	0	.136	.136	.318

PLAYERS WITH TWO OR MORE TEAMS

Player, Team	G	TPA	AB	R	H	TB	2B	3B	HR	RBI	SH	SF	HP	BB	IBB	SO	SB	CS	GDP	Avg.	OBP	Slg.
Brower, Jim, Cin.	22	5	4	0	0	0	0	0	0	0	1	0	0	0	0	1	0	0	0	.000	.000	.000
Brower, Jim, Mon.	30	5	5	0	0	0	0	0	0	0	0	0	0	0	0	2	0	0	0	.000	.000	.000
Chen, Bruce, N.Y.*	1	0	0	0	0	0	0	0	0	0	0	0	0	0	0	0	0	0	0	.000	.000	.000
Chen, Bruce, Mon.*	15	13	12	3	5	6	1	0	0	1	1	0	0	0	0	3	0	0	0	.417	.417	.500
Chen, Bruce, Cin.*	39	4	3	0	0	0	0	0	0	0	1	0	0	0	0	1	0	0	0	.000	.000	.000
Clark, Brady, Cin.	51	74	66	6	10	13	3	0	0	9	1	0	1	6	2	9	1	2	2	.152	.233	.197
Clark, Brady, N.Y.	10	13	12	3	5	6	1	0	0	1	0	0	0	1	0	2	0	0	0	.417	.462	.500
Corey, Mark, N.Y.	13	1	1	0	0	0	0	0	0	0	0	0	0	0	0	1	0	0	0	.000	.000	.000
Corey, Mark, Col.	14	1	1	0	0	0	0	0	0	0	0	0	0	0	0	1	0	0	0	.000	.000	.000
Dempster, Ryan, Fla.	18	40	34	0	2	4	0	1	0	2	4	0	0	1	0	12	0	0	0	.059	.086	.118
Dempster, Ryan, Cin.	17	35	29	2	6	7	1	0	0	1	5	0	0	1	0	8	0	0	0	.207	.233	.241
Encarnacion, Juan, Cin.	83	354	321	43	89	152	11	2	16	51	3	3	1	26	0	63	9	4	7	.277	.330	.474
Encarnacion, Juan, Fla.	69	290	263	34	69	110	11	3	8	34	0	4	3	20	0	50	12	5	11	.262	.317	.418
Estes, Shawn, N.Y.	24	40	35	1	3	7	1	0	1	3	5	0	0	0	0	14	0	0	1	.086	.086	.200
Estes, Shawn, Cin.	6	10	8	0	0	0	0	0	0	0	2	0	0	0	0	5	0	0	0	.000	.000	.000
Fassero, Jeff, Chi.*	57	3	3	0	1	1	0	0	0	0	0	0	0	0	0	2	0	0	0	.333	.333	.333
Fassero, Jeff, St.L.*	16	0	0	0	0	0	0	0	0	0	0	0	0	0	0	0	0	0	0	.000	.000	.000
Floyd, Cliff, Fla.*	84	362	296	49	85	159	20	0	18	57	0	1	7	58	18	68	10	5	0	.287	.414	.537
Floyd, Cliff, Mon.*	15	57	53	7	11	22	2	0	3	4	0	0	1	3	1	10	1	0	0	.208	.263	.415
Ginter, Keith, Hou.	7	8	5	1	1	2	1	0	0	0	0	0	1	2	0	1	0	0	0	.200	.500	.400
Ginter, Keith, Mil.	21	91	76	6	18	29	8	0	1	8	0	0	0	15	0	14	0	0	0	.237	.363	.382
Gonzalez, Raul, Cin.	10	25	23	4	6	7	1	0	0	1	0	0	0	2	0	5	2	0	1	.261	.320	.304
Gonzalez, Raul, N.Y.	30	86	81	9	21	32	2	0	3	11	0	1	0	4	0	17	2	2	2	.259	.291	.395
Gordon, Tom, Chi.	19	0	0	0	0	0	0	0	0	0	0	0	0	0	0	0	0	0	0	.000	.000	.000
Gordon, Tom, Hou.	15	1	1	0	0	0	0	0	0	0	0	0	0	0	0	0	0	0	0	.000	.000	.000
Guerrero, Wilton, Cin.†	59	89	78	9	19	22	1	1	0	4	5	0	0	6	0	13	2	1	1	.244	.298	.282
Guerrero, Wilton, Mon.†	44	67	62	3	12	13	1	0	0	1	4	0	0	1	0	19	5	0	1	.194	.206	.210
Guillen, Jose, Ari.	54	141	131	13	30	46	4	0	4	15	0	1	2	7	1	25	3	4	7	.229	.277	.351
Guillen, Jose, Cin.	31	118	109	12	27	42	3	0	4	16	1	0	1	7	0	18	1	1	6	.248	.299	.385
Hermansen, Chad, Pit.	65	216	194	22	40	74	11	1	7	15	3	1	1	17	0	68	7	5	1	.206	.272	.381
Hermansen, Chad, Chi.	35	49	43	3	9	13	0	1	3	1	0	0	5	0	14	0	0	0	0	.209	.292	.349
Houston, Tyler, Mil.*	76	278	255	25	77	117	15	2	7	33	4	1	4	14	3	41	1	0	4	.302	.347	.459
Houston, Tyler, L.A.*	35	67	65	9	13	20	5	1	0	7	0	0	0	2	0	21	0	0	5	.200	.224	.308
Jones, Bobby M., N.Y.	13	0	0	0	0	0	0	0	0	0	0	0	0	0	0	0	0	0	0	.000	.000	.000
Jones, Bobby M., S.D.	4	3	2	0	0	0	0	0	0	0	1	0	0	0	0	1	0	0	0	.000	.000	.000
Little, Mark, Col.	61	123	105	20	21	30	5	2	0	5	1	0	4	13	0	28	2	1	1	.200	.311	.286
Little, Mark, N.Y.	3	3	3	0	0	0	0	0	0	0	0	0	0	0	0	1	0	0	0	.000	.000	.000
Little, Mark, Ari.	15	28	22	8	6	8	0	1	0	2	0	0	2	3	0	5	0	0	0	.273	.429	.364
Lloyd, Graeme, Mon.*	41	4	4	0	0	0	0	0	0	0	0	0	0	0	0	2	0	0	0	.000	.000	.000
Lloyd, Graeme, Fla.*	25	0	0	0	0	0	0	0	0	0	0	0	0	0	0	0	0	0	0	.000	.000	.000
Loretta, Mark, Mil.	86	252	217	23	58	78	14	0	2	19	6	1	5	23	1	32	0	0	6	.267	.350	.359
Loretta, Mark, Hou.	21	77	66	10	24	38	4	0	2	8	0	2	0	9	0	5	1	1	1	.364	.481	.576
Lowe, Sean, Pit.	43	15	13	0	1	1	0	0	0	0	0	0	2	0	0	5	0	0	0	.077	.077	.077

Player, Team	G	TPA	AB	R	H	TB	2B	3B	HR	RBI	SH	SF	HP	BB	IBB	SO	SB	CS	GDP	Avg.	OBP	Slg.
Lowe, Sean, Col.	8	1	1	0	0	0	0	0	0	0	0	0	0	0	0	1	0	0	0	.000	.000	.000
Machado, Robert, Chi.	22	64	58	5	16	23	4	0	1	5	1	0	0	5	0	11	0	0	2	.276	.333	.397
Machado, Robert, Mil.	51	169	153	14	39	57	10	1	2	17	1	2	1	12	4	30	0	0	5	.255	.310	.373
Matthews, Mike, St.L.*	43	6	6	0	1	1	0	0	0	0	0	0	0	0	0	4	0	0	0	.167	.167	.167
Matthews, Mike, Mil.*	4	1	0	0	0	0	0	0	0	0	0	1	0	0	0	0	0	0	0	.000	.000	.000
Middlebrook, Jason, S.D.	12	7	6	2	2	2	0	0	0	0	1	0	0	0	0	1	0	0	0	.333	.333	.333
Middlebrook, Jason, N.Y.	3	6	5	0	0	0	0	0	0	0	0	0	0	1	0	2	0	0	0	.000	.167	.000
Mordecai, Mike, Mon.	55	90	74	9	15	19	4	0	0	4	7	0	1	8	3	14	1	1	2	.203	.289	.257
Mordecai, Mike, Fla.	38	86	77	10	22	26	4	0	0	7	3	0	1	5	1	13	1	1	1	.286	.337	.338
Mueller, Bill, Chi.†	103	413	353	51	94	142	19	4	7	37	4	5	0	51	2	41	0	0	8	.266	.355	.402
Mueller, Bill, S.F.†	8	14	13	0	2	2	0	0	0	1	0	0	0	1	0	0	0	0	0	.154	.214	.154
Nickle, Doug, Phi.	4	1	1	0	0	0	0	0	0	0	0	0	0	0	0	0	0	0	0	.000	.000	.000
Nickle, Doug, S.D.	10	0	0	0	0	0	0	0	0	0	0	0	0	0	0	0	0	0	0	.000	.000	.000
Pavano, Carl, Mon.	15	27	24	1	5	6	1	0	0	1	3	0	0	0	0	6	0	0	0	.208	.208	.250
Pavano, Carl, Fla.	22	18	16	1	3	5	0	1	0	2	1	0	0	0	0	6	0	0	0	.188	.188	.313
Payton, Jay, N.Y.	87	300	275	33	78	114	6	3	8	31	2	1	1	21	0	34	4	1	8	.284	.336	.415
Payton, Jay, Col.	47	181	170	36	57	103	14	4	8	28	0	3	8	0	20	3	3	3	3	.335	.376	.606
Polanco, Placido, St.L.	94	367	342	47	97	133	19	1	5	27	9	0	4	12	1	27	3	1	12	.284	.316	.389
Polanco, Placido, Phi.	53	228	206	28	61	88	13	1	4	22	4	0	4	14	0	14	2	2	3	.296	.353	.427
Reed, Steve, S.D.	41	1	1	0	0	0	0	0	0	0	0	0	0	0	0	1	0	0	0	.000	.000	.000
Reed, Steve, N.Y.	24	1	1	0	0	0	0	0	0	0	0	0	0	0	0	1	0	0	0	.000	.000	.000
Rolen, Scott, Phi.	100	438	375	52	97	177	21	4	17	66	0	3	8	52	2	68	5	2	12	.259	.358	.472
Rolen, Scott, St.L.	55	229	205	37	57	115	8	4	14	44	0	0	4	20	2	34	3	2	10	.278	.354	.561
Thomson, John, Col.	21	40	34	2	6	6	0	0	0	2	3	1	0	2	0	12	0	0	0	.176	.216	.176
Thomson, John, N.Y.	9	22	18	2	5	5	0	0	0	1	3	0	0	1	0	7	0	0	0	.278	.316	.278
Timlin, Mike, St.L.	42	6	6	0	0	0	0	0	0	0	0	0	0	0	0	4	0	0	0	.000	.000	.000
Timlin, Mike, Phi.	30	0	0	0	0	0	0	0	0	0	0	0	0	0	0	0	0	0	0	.000	.000	.000
White, Rick, Col.	41	0	0	0	0	0	0	0	0	0	0	0	0	0	0	0	0	0	0	.000	.000	.000
White, Rick, St.L.	20	1	1	0	0	0	0	0	0	0	0	0	0	0	0	1	0	0	0	.000	.000	.000
Wright, Jamey, Mil.	19	39	33	0	5	8	3	0	0	0	6	0	0	0	0	13	0	0	0	.152	.152	.242
Wright, Jamey, St.L.	4	6	5	0	0	0	0	0	0	0	1	0	0	0	0	3	0	0	0	.000	.000	.000

AWARDED FIRST BASE ON OBSTRUCTION OR CATCHER'S INTERFERENCE—Counsell, Arizona 2 (Lieberthal, Fordyce); Dempster, Fla.-Cin. (Kreuter); Giambi, Philadelphia (Hundley); Helton, Colorado (Machado); Lowell, Florida (Miller); Millwood, Atlanta (Zaun); Owens, Florida (Barrett).

BATTERS VS. LEFTHANDED AND RIGHTHANDED PITCHERS

Player	vs.	Avg.	AB	H	2B	3B	HR	RBI	BB	SO	OBP	Slg.	Player	vs.	Avg.	AB	H	2B	3B	HR	RBI	BB	SO	OBP	Slg.
Abreu, Bobby	L	.302	162	49	17	0	0	22	29	47	.411	.407	Bell, Jay	L	.130	23	3	1	0	0	2	4	4	.259	.174
Bats Left	R	.310	410	127	33	6	20	63	75	70	.414	.566	Bats Right	R	.192	26	5	0	0	2	9	1	5	.241	.423
Agbayani, Benny	L	.167	54	9	3	0	1	10	6	13	.250	.278	Bellhorn, Mark	L	.303	122	37	11	2	10	24	18	41	.397	.672
Bats Right	R	.238	63	15	2	0	3	9	4	22	.279	.413	Bats Both	R	.241	323	78	13	2	17	32	58	103	.365	.452
Alcantara, Izzy	L	.313	16	5	1	0	2	4	0	4	.313	.750	Belliard, Ronnie	L	.200	100	20	2	0	3	9	5	16	.238	.310
Bats Right	R	.188	16	3	0	0	1	0	2	8	.188	.188	Bats Right	R	.217	189	41	11	0	0	17	13	30	.267	.275
Alfonzo, Edgardo	L	.364	121	44	10	0	4	18	25	13	.477	.545	Beltre, Adrian	L	.302	126	38	4	1	6	18	2	19	.305	.492
Bats Right	R	.290	369	107	16	0	12	38	37	42	.361	.431	Bats Right	R	.245	461	113	22	4	15	57	35	77	.302	.408
Allen, Luke	L	.200	5	1	1	0	0	0	0	3	.200	.400	Benard, Marvin	L	.389	18	7	1	1	0	2	1	2	.421	.556
Bats Left	R	.000	2	0	0	0	0	0	2	0	.500	.000	Bats Left	R	.257	105	27	8	1	1	11	6	24	.304	.381
Alomar, Roberto	L	.204	162	33	4	1	4	14	12	36	.259	.315	Benjamin, Mike	L	.128	39	5	0	0	0	4	8	.209	.128
Bats Both	R	.290	428	124	20	3	7	39	45	47	.358	.400	Bats Right	R	.160	81	13	2	1	0	3	3	23	.198	.210
Alomar Jr., Sandy	L	.286	28	8	1	0	0	3	1	6	.310	.321	Bennett, Gary	L	.365	63	23	2	0	1	7	5	6	.412	.444
Bats Right	R	.261	88	23	3	0	0	9	3	13	.286	.295	Bats Right	R	.237	228	54	8	2	3	19	10	39	.287	.329
Alou, Moises	L	.322	115	37	9	1	2	12	16	13	.402	.470	Bergeron, Peter	L	.200	20	4	0	1	0	1	4	7	.333	.300
Bats Right	R	.260	369	96	14	0	13	49	31	48	.316	.404	Bats Left	R	.184	103	19	3	1	0	6	18	37	.306	.233
Alvarez, Tony	L	.333	3	1	0	0	0	0	2	1	.600	.333	Berkman, Lance	L	.240	129	31	8	1	2	14	22	20	.351	.364
Bats Right	R	.304	23	7	2	0	1	2	1	4	.333	.522	Bats Both	R	.307	449	138	27	1	40	114	85	98	.420	.639
Anderson, Marlon	L	.220	123	27	4	0	0	10	6	20	.267	.252	Biggio, Craig	L	.183	115	21	2	1	2	8	16	19	.291	.270
Bats Left	R	.269	416	112	26	6	8	38	36	51	.330	.418	Bats Right	R	.271	462	125	34	2	13	50	34	92	.340	.437
Aurilia, Rich	L	.241	116	28	5	0	2	16	7	18	.276	.336	Blanco, Henry	L	.211	38	8	0	0	2	4	7	10	.273	.368
Bats Right	R	.261	422	110	30	2	13	45	30	72	.314	.434	Bats Right	R	.202	183	37	9	1	4	15	16	41	.266	.355
Ausmus, Brad	L	.307	88	27	4	0	3	12	9	7	.390	.455	Blum, Geoff	L	.185	65	12	4	0	1	6	6	19	.254	.292
Bats Right	R	.245	359	88	15	3	3	38	29	64	.305	.329	Bats Both	R	.304	303	92	16	4	9	46	43	51	.390	.472
Bagwell, Jeff	L	.333	108	36	6	1	10	24	26	25	.459	.685	Bocachica, Hiram	L	.273	22	6	1	0	2	5	3	5	.360	.591
Bats Right	R	.281	463	130	27	1	21	74	75	105	.387	.479	Bats Right	R	.186	43	8	2	0	2	4	2	14	.222	.372
Bako, Paul	L	.167	30	5	1	0	0	2	1	8	.194	.200	Bonds, Barry	L	.384	125	48	9	1	21	45	45	16	.556	.976
Bats Left	R	.245	204	50	7	1	4	18	19	38	.309	.348	Bats Left	R	.363	278	101	22	1	25	65	153	31	.592	.719
Banks, Brian	L	.500	8	4	0	1	0	3	0	2	.500	.875	Boone, Aaron	L	.233	150	35	13	1	4	24	24	26	.341	.413
Bats Both	R	.250	20	5	1	0	0	1	1	4	.286	.300	Bats Right	R	.243	456	111	25	1	22	63	32	85	.304	.447
Barajas, Rod	L	.196	51	10	1	0	1	5	6	5	.276	.275	Bragg, Darren	L	.308	26	8	0	0	0	5	6	8	.408	.308
Bats Right	R	.252	103	26	9	0	2	18	4	20	.295	.398	Bats Left	R	.263	186	49	15	2	3	15	19	46	.333	.414
Barker, Kevin	L	.000	6	0	0	0	0	0	1	4	.143	.000	Branyan, Russell	L	.182	33	6	0	0	3	5	2	12	.229	.455
Bats Left	R	.231	13	3	0	0	0	0	0	2	.231	.231	Bats Left	R	.255	184	47	9	1	13	34	32	74	.368	.527
Barrett, Michael	L	.261	111	29	9	0	1	6	11	20	.325	.369	Brown, Adrian	L	.154	52	8	1	0	0	4	1	7	.167	.173
Bats Right	R	.264	265	70	11	1	11	43	29	45	.334	.438	Bats Both	R	.237	156	37	9	2	1	17	18	27	.320	.340
Bautista, Danny	L	.362	47	17	0	0	4	11	4	6	.412	.617	Brown, Roosevelt	L	.200	20	4	1	0	0	3	3	7	.292	.250
Bats Right	R	.308	107	33	5	2	2	12	7	15	.348	.449	Bats Left	R	.212	184	39	11	0	3	20	20	43	.300	.321
Bell, David	L	.263	137	36	6	0	5	22	16	20	.333	.416	Buchanan, Brian	L	.200	40	8	2	0	1	3	5	4	.289	.475
Bats Right	R	.260	415	108	23	2	15	51	38	60	.333	.434	Bats Right	R	.365	52	19	0	3	8	5	14	.421	.596

Player	vs.	Avg.	AB	H	2B	3B	HR	RBI	BB	SO	OBP	Slg.
Burnitz, Jeromy	L	.174	121	21	4	0	3	9	8	39	.242	.281
Bats Left	R	.229	358	82	11	0	16	45	50	96	.333	.394
Burrell, Pat	L	.311	122	38	7	0	12	29	37	32	.469	.664
Bats Right	R	.274	464	127	32	2	25	87	52	121	.347	.513
Burroughs, Sean	L	.218	55	12	0	0	0	1	2	11	.246	.218
Bats Left	R	.292	137	40	5	1	1	9	11	19	.345	.365
Bush, Homer	L	.143	21	3	0	0	0	2	0	7	.143	.143
Bats Right	R	.273	33	9	0	0	0	3	3	6	.333	.273
Butler, Brent	L	.237	76	18	7	1	1	7	4	10	.275	.395
Bats Right	R	.265	268	71	11	3	8	35	6	30	.290	.418
Byrd, Marlon	L	.222	9	2	1	0	1	1	0	1	.222	.667
Bats Right	R	.231	26	6	1	0	0	0	1	7	.259	.269
Cabrera, Jolbert	L	.375	8	3	1	0	0	1	2	2	.500	.500
Bats Right	R	.250	4	1	0	0	0	0	0	0	.250	.250
Cabrera, Orlando	L	.264	125	33	6	0	1	14	14	10	.338	.336
Bats Right	R	.263	438	115	37	1	6	42	34	43	.316	.393
Cairo, Miguel	L	.273	66	18	5	0	2	9	5	7	.342	.439
Bats Right	R	.237	118	28	4	2	0	14	8	29	.287	.305
Cardona, Javier	L	.067	30	2	1	0	0	2	1	9	.094	.100
Bats Right	R	.222	9	2	0	0	0	0	1	1	.300	.222
Carroll, Jamey	L	.400	10	4	2	0	0	0	1	0	.400	.600
Bats Right	R	.295	61	18	3	3	1	6	4	11	.338	.492
Casanova, Raul	L	.154	26	4	0	0	0	0	0	6	.154	.154
Bats Both	R	.197	61	12	1	0	1	8	10	12	.315	.262
Casey, Sean	L	.231	130	30	6	0	2	16	12	17	.299	.323
Bats Left	R	.275	295	81	19	0	4	26	31	30	.349	.380
Castilla, Vinny	L	.224	76	17	1	0	2	10	5	7	.268	.316
Bats Right	R	.233	467	109	22	2	10	51	17	62	.268	.353
Castillo, Luis	L	.329	158	52	8	2	1	10	9	20	.369	.424
Bats Both	R	.297	448	133	10	3	1	29	46	56	.363	.339
Castro, Juan	L	.222	36	8	1	0	0	4	3	4	.282	.250
Bats Right	R	.217	46	10	2	0	2	7	4	14	.275	.391
Castro, Ramon	L	.160	25	4	2	0	0	3	2	5	.214	.240
Bats Right	R	.263	76	20	2	0	6	15	12	19	.356	.526
Cedeno, Roger	L	.231	156	36	6	1	3	8	10	45	.275	.340
Bats Both	R	.273	355	97	13	1	4	33	32	47	.336	.349
Cepicky, Matt	L	.182	11	2	0	0	1	2	1	1	.250	.455
Bats Left	R	.222	63	14	3	0	2	13	3	20	.258	.365
Chavez, Endy	L	.316	19	6	1	0	0	0	4	3	.435	.368
Bats Left	R	.292	106	31	7	5	1	9	1	13	.296	.481
Chavez, Raul	L	.500	2	1	1	0	0	0	0	0	.500	1.000
Bats Right	R	.000	2	0	0	0	0	0	0	1	.500	.000
Chen, Chin-Feng	L	.000	3	0	0	0	0	0	1	2	.250	.000
Bats Right	R	.000	2	0	0	0	0	0	0	1	.000	.000
Choi, Hee Seop	L	.000	4	0	0	0	0	0	1	2	.200	.000
Bats Left	R	.196	46	9	1	0	2	4	6	13	.288	.348
Christensen, McKay	L	.000	1	0	0	0	0	0	0	0	.000	.000
Bats Left	R	.500	2	1	0	0	0	0	1	1	.667	.500
Christenson, Ryan	L	.118	17	2	2	0	0	1	2	3	.211	.235
Bats Right	R	.171	41	7	2	0	1	2	3	10	.227	.293
Cintron, Alex	L	.182	22	4	1	0	0	4	4	4	.308	.227
Bats Both	R	.226	53	12	5	0	0	4	8	9	.328	.321
Clark, Brady	L	.143	28	4	0	0	0	2	6	1	.314	.143
Bats Right	R	.220	50	11	4	0	0	8	1	10	.235	.300
Colbrunn, Greg	L	.368	143	43	14	0	7	21	10	8	.414	.667
Bats Right	R	.259	54	14	2	2	3	6	3	11	.298	.537
Collier, Lou	L	.125	8	1	1	0	0	0	1	0	.300	.250
Bats Right	R	.000	3	0	0	0	0	0	0	3	.000	.000
Coolbaugh, Mike	L	.100	10	1	0	0	0	0	0	3	.100	.100
Bats Right	R	.000	2	0	0	0	0	0	0	1	.333	.000
Cora, Alex	L	.318	22	7	1	1	0	2	2	3	.375	.455
Bats Left	R	.288	236	68	13	3	5	26	24	35	.371	.432
Cordero, Wil	L	.266	79	21	6	0	4	15	12	9	.358	.494
Bats Right	R	.281	64	18	3	0	2	14	5	17	.338	.422
Cota, Humberto	L	.000	4	0	0	0	0	0	0	1	.000	.000
Bats Right	R	.385	13	5	1	0	0	0	1	3	.429	.462
Counsell, Craig	L	.269	145	39	9	0	0	20	18	25	.348	.331
Bats Left	R	.289	291	84	13	1	2	31	27	27	.349	.361
Crespo, Cesar	L	.273	11	3	1	0	0	0	1	1	.333	.364
Bats Right	R	.111	18	2	1	0	0	0	2	5	.200	.167
Cruz, Deivi	L	.242	161	39	6	0	3	11	9	20	.285	.335
Bats Right	R	.272	353	96	22	2	4	36	13	38	.298	.380
Cruz, Ivan	L	.000	0	0	0	0	0	0	0	0	.000	.000
Bats Left	R	.357	14	5	0	0	1	3	1	3	.400	.571
Cust, Jack	L	.000	5	0	0	0	0	0	0	3	.000	.000
Bats Left	R	.183	60	11	2	0	1	8	12	29	.315	.267
Davis, J.J.	L	.000	2	0	0	0	0	0	0	2	.000	.000
Bats Right	R	.125	8	1	0	0	0	0	0	2	.222	.125
Dawkins, Gookie	L	.125	8	1	0	0	0	0	2	4	.300	.125
Bats Right	R	.125	40	5	2	0	0	0	4	17	.205	.175
DeHaan, Kory	L	.000	1	0	0	0	0	0	0	0	.000	.000
Bats Left	R	.100	10	1	0	0	0	0	0	6	.100	.100
Delgado, Wilson	L	.500	4	2	1	0	1	3	0	2	.500	1.500
Bats Both	R	.125	16	2	1	0	1	2	0	4	.125	.375
Dellucci, David	L	.111	27	3	1	0	0	3	2	11	.167	.148
Bats Left	R	.262	202	53	10	2	7	26	26	44	.346	.436
DeRosa, Mark	L	.293	58	17	4	1	1	5	6	5	.369	.448
Bats Right	R	.299	154	46	5	1	4	18	6	19	.327	.422
DeShields, Delino	L	.105	19	2	1	0	0	0	5	6	.292	.158
Bats Left	R	.205	127	26	5	1	3	10	16	32	.292	.331
DiFelice, Mike	L	.216	51	11	5	0	1	6	7	14	.310	.373
Bats Right	R	.236	123	29	6	0	3	13	10	28	.292	.358
Donnels, Chris	L	.222	9	2	0	0	2	4	0	2	.200	.889
Bats Left	R	.239	71	17	4	1	1	12	10	12	.325	.366
Drew, J.D.	L	.262	84	22	4	0	3	13	10	23	.351	.417
Bats Left	R	.250	340	85	15	1	15	43	47	81	.348	.432
Dunn, Adam	L	.254	169	43	12	0	11	27	31	55	.385	.521
Bats Left	R	.246	366	90	16	2	15	44	97	115	.406	.423
Dunston, Shawon	L	.229	48	11	3	0	0	1	0	11	.245	.292
Bats Right	R	.232	99	23	2	0	1	8	3	22	.252	.283
Durazo, Erubiel	L	.167	54	9	1	0	2	5	7	14	.274	.296
Bats Left	R	.292	168	49	11	2	14	43	42	46	.430	.631
Echevarria, Angel	L	.408	49	20	4	0	3	10	3	7	.426	.673
Bats Right	R	.204	49	10	3	0	0	11	5	10	.281	.265
Edmonds, Jim	L	.262	130	34	7	0	7	23	16	40	.357	.477
Bats Left	R	.329	346	114	24	2	21	60	70	94	.443	.592
Encarnacion, Juan	L	.233	133	31	3	0	5	15	9	23	.276	.368
Bats Right	R	.282	451	127	19	5	19	70	37	90	.339	.472
Encarnacion, Mario	L	.000	4	0	0	0	0	0	0	2	.333	.000
Bats Right	R	.000	3	0	0	0	0	0	0	0	.000	.000
Ensberg, Morgan	L	.320	25	8	2	0	2	7	6	3	.469	.640
Bats Right	R	.224	107	24	5	2	1	12	12	22	.314	.336
Estalella, Bobby	L	.136	22	3	0	0	1	5	6	7	.300	.273
Bats Right	R	.222	90	20	8	0	7	20	8	26	.280	.544
Estrada, Johnny	L	.250	4	1	0	0	0	1	1	0	.400	.250
Bats Both	R	.077	13	1	1	0	0	1	1	2	.143	.154
Everett, Adam	L	.261	23	6	1	0	0	2	2	4	.320	.304
Bats Right	R	.169	65	11	2	0	0	2	10	15	.289	.200
Fabregas, Jorge	L	.250	4	1	0	0	0	1	0	0	.250	.250
Bats Left	R	.159	63	10	3	0	3	13	2	7	.176	.349
Feliz, Pedro	L	.184	49	9	1	0	0	3	1	7	.200	.204
Bats Right	R	.289	97	28	3	1	2	10	5	20	.320	.402
Finley, Steve	L	.297	158	47	8	2	9	30	16	27	.371	.544
Bats Left	R	.282	347	98	16	2	16	59	49	46	.369	.478
Floyd, Cliff	L	.218	101	22	4	0	7	17	8	30	.295	.465
Bats Right	R	.298	248	74	18	0	14	44	53	48	.430	.540
Fox, Andy	L	.148	88	13	4	0	0	6	7	30	.208	.193
Bats Left	R	.277	347	96	10	5	4	35	42	64	.369	.369
Franco, Julio	L	.382	76	29	2	0	3	14	9	16	.442	.526
Bats Right	R	.256	262	67	11	1	3	16	30	59	.332	.340
Franco, Matt	L	.333	6	2	1	0	0	1	1	1	.429	.667
Bats Left	R	.317	199	63	15	3	6	30	26	30	.394	.513
Furcal, Rafael	L	.288	111	32	6	2	1	12	8	19	.336	.405
Bats Both	R	.272	525	143	25	6	7	35	35	95	.320	.383
Galarraga, Andres	L	.294	85	25	3	0	9	19	9	19	.368	.329
Bats Right	R	.246	207	51	9	0	9	32	21	62	.335	.420
Gant, Ron	L	.294	109	32	9	0	7	25	17	23	.383	.569
Bats Right	R	.245	200	49	5	1	11	34	19	36	.313	.445
Garcia, Jesse	L	.154	26	4	0	0	0	2	0	5	.154	.154
Bats Right	R	.229	35	8	1	0	0	3	0	5	.229	.257
Giambi, Jeremy	L	.167	18	3	1	0	0	2	4	8	.348	.222
Bats Left	R	.254	138	35	9	0	12	26	48	46	.446	.580
Giles, Brian	L	.231	143	33	9	1	8	29	26	26	.355	.476
Bats Left	R	.325	354	115	28	4	30	74	109	48	.485	.681

2002 N.L. STATISTICS Batting

Player	vs.	Avg.	AB	H	2B	3B	HR	RBI	BB	SO	OBP	Slg.
Giles, Marcus	L	.158	38	6	1	0	1	1	3	9	.238	.263
Bats Right	R	.246	175	43	9	1	7	22	22	32	.332	.429
Ginter, Keith	L	.154	13	2	1	0	0	0	4	4	.353	.231
Bats Right	R	.250	68	17	8	0	1	8	13	11	.378	.412
Girardi, Joe	L	.172	64	11	3	0	0	5	6	9	.239	.219
Bats Right	R	.247	170	42	7	1	1	8	10	26	.289	.318
Glanville, Doug	L	.250	128	32	6	1	4	11	8	16	.292	.406
Bats Right	R	.248	294	73	10	2	2	18	17	41	.292	.316
Gload, Ross	L	.143	7	1	0	0	0	0	1	2	.250	.143
Bats Left	R	.292	24	7	1	0	1	4	2	5	.346	.458
Gonzalez, Alex	L	.200	30	6	1	0	1	7	2	5	.242	.333
Bats Right	R	.231	121	28	6	1	1	11	10	27	.309	.322
Gonzalez, Alex S.	L	.237	114	27	5	2	5	16	8	17	.338	.447
Bats Right	R	.251	399	100	22	3	13	45	28	115	.304	.419
Gonzalez, Luis	L	.272	191	52	4	0	10	41	29	32	.377	.450
Bats Left	R	.297	333	99	15	3	18	62	68	44	.412	.523
Gonzalez, Raul	L	.273	33	9	1	0	1	2	4	7	.351	.394
Bats Right	R	.254	71	18	2	0	2	10	2	15	.270	.366
Gonzalez, Wiki	L	.310	42	13	3	0	1	8	11	6	.453	.452
Bats Right	R	.189	122	23	5	1	0	12	16	18	.284	.246
Goodwin, Tom	L	.053	19	1	0	0	0	1	0	8	.053	.053
Bats Left	R	.289	135	39	5	2	1	16	14	17	.356	.378
Grace, Mark	L	.321	81	26	5	0	3	16	7	7	.382	.494
Bats Right	R	.226	217	49	14	0	4	32	39	23	.340	.346
Green, Shawn	L	.270	163	44	13	0	11	35	18	43	.351	.552
Bats Left	R	.291	419	122	18	1	31	79	75	69	.398	.561
Griffey Jr., Ken	L	.217	60	13	2	0	1	7	6	17	.294	.300
Bats Left	R	.285	137	39	6	0	7	16	22	22	.384	.482
Grissom, Marquis	L	.293	133	39	6	2	11	29	11	25	.354	.617
Bats Right	R	.267	210	56	15	2	6	31	11	43	.299	.443
Grudzielanek, Mark	L	.257	109	28	5	0	3	15	9	14	.317	.385
Bats Right	R	.274	427	117	18	0	6	35	13	75	.297	.358
Guerrero, Vladimir	L	.290	124	36	8	0	6	20	34	8	.443	.500
Bats Right	R	.347	490	170	29	2	33	91	50	62	.410	.616
Guerrero, Wilton	L	.136	44	6	1	0	0	3	1	4	.156	.159
Bats Both	R	.260	96	25	1	1	0	2	6	28	.304	.292
Guillen, Jose	L	.252	107	27	3	0	3	9	5	19	.283	.364
Bats Right	R	.226	133	30	4	0	5	22	9	24	.290	.368
Hall, Bill	L	.125	8	1	0	0	0	0	0	2	.125	.125
Bats Right	R	.214	28	6	1	1	1	5	3	11	.290	.429
Hammonds, Jeffrey	L	.298	84	25	5	2	3	10	12	18	.381	.512
Bats Right	R	.247	364	90	21	3	6	31	40	68	.320	.371
Hansen, Dave	L	.125	8	1	0	0	0	0	2	2	.300	.125
Bats Left	R	.304	112	34	6	0	2	17	12	20	.368	.411
Harris, Lenny	L	.467	15	7	1	0	0	3	0	2	.467	.533
Bats Left	R	.291	182	53	7	2	3	14	14	15	.347	.401
Helms, Wes	L	.167	54	9	5	0	1	5	4	17	.217	.315
Bats Right	R	.269	156	42	11	0	5	17	7	43	.306	.436
Helton, Todd	L	.327	199	65	12	2	11	46	36	38	.437	.573
Bats Left	R	.331	354	117	27	2	19	63	63	53	.424	.579
Hermansen, Chad	L	.178	45	8	1	0	1	4	6	17	.275	.267
Bats Right	R	.214	192	41	13	1	7	14	16	65	.276	.401
Hernandez, Jose	L	.253	99	25	4	0	8	16	10	39	.321	.535
Bats Right	R	.296	426	126	20	2	16	57	42	149	.364	.465
Hidalgo, Richard	L	.263	76	20	5	1	3	11	14	16	.378	.474
Bats Right	R	.228	312	71	12	3	12	37	29	69	.304	.401
Hill, Bobby	L	.327	52	17	4	0	0	5	8	9	.426	.404
Bats Both	R	.225	138	31	3	2	4	15	9	33	.287	.362
Hollandsworth, T.	L	.195	41	8	2	0	1	5	1	12	.283	.317
Bats Left	R	.311	257	80	19	1	10	43	21	59	.363	.510
Hollins, Dave	L	.125	16	2	0	0	0	0	0	3	.176	.125
Bats Both	R	.000	1	0	0	0	0	0	0	0	.000	.000
Houston, Tyler	L	.259	27	7	0	1	0	2	0	5	.259	.333
Bats Left	R	.283	293	83	20	2	7	38	16	57	.328	.437
Hubbard, Trenidad	L	.204	54	11	2	0	1	3	8	12	.302	.296
Bats Right	R	.213	75	16	3	0	0	4	6	16	.272	.253
Hundley, Todd	L	.217	46	10	1	0	2	6	8	14	.350	.370
Bats Both	R	.209	220	46	7	0	14	29	24	66	.291	.432
Hunter, Brian L.	L	.241	108	26	7	2	1	12	11	17	.311	.370
Bats Right	R	.301	93	28	9	1	2	8	5	22	.350	.484
Hyzdu, Adam	L	.204	49	10	2	0	4	14	7	16	.298	.490
Bats Right	R	.245	106	26	4	0	7	20	14	28	.336	.481
Izturis, Cesar	L	.306	147	45	9	1	1	13	6	9	.331	.401
Bats Both	R	.195	292	57	15	1	0	18	8	30	.214	.253
Jenkins, Geoff	L	.200	65	13	3	1	2	7	2	23	.232	.369
Bats Left	R	.258	178	46	14	0	8	22	20	37	.350	.472
Jensen, Marcus	L	.133	15	2	0	0	0	0	2	2	.235	.133
Bats Both	R	.100	20	2	0	0	1	4	2	9	.174	.250
Jimenez, D'Angelo	L	.250	108	27	4	1	0	10	11	17	.317	.306
Bats Both	R	.235	213	50	7	3	3	23	23	46	.308	.338
Johnson, Charles	L	.275	51	14	7	0	1	9	5	11	.333	.471
Bats Right	R	.202	193	39	12	0	5	27	26	50	.293	.342
Johnson, Mark	L	.000	6	0	0	0	0	0	0	4	.000	.000
Bats Left	R	.156	45	7	4	0	1	4	9	14	.296	.311
Jones, Andruw	L	.228	79	18	5	0	2	14	19	22	.370	.367
Bats Right	R	.270	481	130	29	0	33	80	64	113	.365	.536
Jones, Chipper	L	.320	100	32	7	0	4	15	14	16	.400	.510
Bats Both	R	.328	448	147	28	1	22	85	93	73	.442	.542
Jordan, Brian	L	.303	109	33	10	0	6	28	7	18	.347	.560
Bats Right	R	.279	362	101	17	3	12	52	27	68	.335	.442
Jose, Felix	L	.143	7	1	0	0	1	1	2	4	.333	.571
Bats Both	R	.333	12	4	0	0	1	3	2	4	.375	.583
Kapler, Gabe	L	.300	30	9	2	2	0	4	3	4	.364	.500
Bats Right	R	.315	89	28	2	1	2	13	5	19	.358	.427
Karros, Eric	L	.317	101	32	8	0	3	17	13	6	.397	.485
Bats Right	R	.260	423	110	18	1	10	56	24	60	.304	.378
Kearns, Austin	L	.330	91	30	4	0	3	9	25	17	.474	.440
Bats Right	R	.310	281	87	20	3	11	47	29	64	.382	.520
Kendall, Jason	L	.275	109	30	4	1	1	9	23	4	.403	.358
Bats Right	R	.284	436	124	21	2	2	35	26	25	.335	.356
Kent, Jeff	L	.366	145	53	11	0	11	24	18	14	.439	.669
Bats Right	R	.297	478	142	31	2	26	84	34	87	.346	.533
Kingsale, Gene	L	.293	41	12	1	0	1	3	3	9	.356	.390
Bats Right	R	.274	175	48	9	3	1	25	17	38	.344	.377
Kinkade, Mike	L	.400	30	12	4	0	2	7	1	7	.486	.733
Bats Right	R	.350	20	7	1	0	0	4	3	3	.480	.400
Klassen, Danny	L	.000	1	0	0	0	0	0	0	0	.000	.000
Bats Right	R	.500	2	1	0	0	0	0	0	0	.500	.500
Klesko, Ryan	L	.287	157	45	8	0	8	32	20	32	.372	.490
Bats Left	R	.305	383	117	31	1	21	63	56	54	.394	.556
Kotsay, Mark	L	.324	188	61	11	3	5	20	14	34	.372	.495
Bats Left	R	.277	390	108	16	4	12	41	45	55	.352	.431
Kreuter, Chad	L	.462	26	12	2	0	2	6	4	7	.533	.769
Bats Both	R	.188	69	13	3	0	0	6	6	24	.256	.232
Lampkin, Tom	L	.167	48	8	1	0	1	3	1	9	.184	.250
Bats Left	R	.227	233	53	9	1	9	34	37	50	.336	.391
Lane, Jason	L	.349	43	15	2	1	4	10	7	5	.431	.721
Bats Right	R	.192	26	5	1	0	0	0	3	7	.276	.231
Langerhans, Ryan	L	.000	0	0	0	0	0	0	0	0	.000	.000
Bats Left	R	.000	1	0	0	0	0	0	0	0	.000	.000
Lankford, Ray	L	.194	31	6	2	0	0	2	6	10	.359	.258
Bats Left	R	.230	174	40	5	1	6	24	24	51	.320	.374
Larkin, Barry	L	.189	122	23	10	1	3	11	20	13	.299	.361
Bats Right	R	.262	385	101	27	1	4	36	24	44	.307	.369
Larson, Brandon	L	.308	26	8	1	0	4	9	4	5	.419	.808
Bats Right	R	.240	25	6	1	0	0	2	0	5	.296	.280
LaRue, Jason	L	.207	92	19	4	0	2	5	6	30	.291	.315
Bats Right	R	.264	261	69	13	1	10	47	21	87	.336	.437
Ledee, Ricky	L	.080	25	2	1	0	0	0	1	9	.115	.120
Bats Left	R	.247	178	44	12	1	8	23	34	41	.369	.461
Lee, Derrek	L	.264	125	33	5	2	6	18	25	35	.391	.480
Bats Right	R	.272	456	124	30	5	21	68	73	129	.374	.498
Lee, Travis	L	.282	142	40	3	2	6	20	12	28	.338	.458
Bats Left	R	.259	394	102	23	0	7	50	42	76	.329	.371
Lewis, Darren	L	.264	53	14	2	1	0	7	3	9	.328	.340
Bats Right	R	.192	26	5	1	0	0	0	4	2	.323	.231
Lieberthal, Mike	L	.346	107	37	9	1	6	12	12	8	.426	.617
Bats Right	R	.260	369	96	20	1	9	40	26	50	.326	.393
Little, Mark	L	.187	75	14	2	0	0	5	8	18	.307	.267
Bats Right	R	.236	55	13	3	1	0	5	2	7	.354	.327
Lockhart, Keith	L	.067	15	1	0	0	1	2	0	7	.125	.267
Bats Left	R	.224	281	63	13	3	4	30	27	43	.290	.335
Lo Duca, Paul	L	.307	137	42	13	1	2	20	9	5	.351	.460
Bats Right	R	.273	443	121	25	0	8	44	25	26	.323	.384

Player	vs.	Avg.	AB	H	2B	3B	HR	RBI	BB	SO	OBP	Slg.
Lofton, Kenny	L	.300	40	12	3	2	0	1	4	5	.378	.475
Bats Left	R	.257	140	36	7	1	3	8	19	17	.346	.386
Lopez, Javy	L	.255	51	13	3	0	2	11	6	11	.333	.431
Bats Right	R	.230	296	68	12	0	9	41	20	52	.293	.361
Lopez, Luis	L	.000	2	0	0	0	0	0	1	0	.333	.000
Bats Both	R	.000	6	0	0	0	0	1	1	1	.143	.000
Lopez, Mendy	L	.000	1	0	0	0	0	0	0	1	.000	.000
Bats Right	R	.000	2	0	0	0	0	0	0	2	.000	.000
Loretta, Mark	L	.309	94	29	7	0	2	8	19	13	.421	.447
Bats Right	R	.302	189	57	11	0	2	19	13	24	.359	.392
Lowell, Mike	L	.255	145	37	9	0	4	13	15	16	.323	.400
Bats Right	R	.283	452	128	35	0	20	79	50	76	.353	.493
Lugo, Julio	L	.270	74	20	1	0	3	10	5	18	.313	.405
Bats Right	R	.258	248	64	14	1	5	25	23	56	.325	.383
Lunsford, Trey	L	.000	0	0	0	0	0	0	0	0	.000	.000
Bats Right	R	.667	3	2	1	0	0	1	0	1	.667	1.000
Mabry, John	L	.000	3	0	0	0	0	0	0	1	.000	.000
Bats Left	R	.333	18	6	0	0		3	1	4	.350	.333
Machado, Robert	L	.226	62	14	2	1	1	7	6	15	.290	.339
Bats Right	R	.275	149	41	12	0	2	15	11	26	.327	.396
Macias, Jose	L	.229	83	19	8	0		5	5	11	.278	.325
Bats Both	R	.270	148	40	9	1	7	28	8	33	.304	.486
Mackowiak, Rob	L	.302	43	13	2	0	4	7	6	8	.400	.628
Bats Left	R	.237	342	81	20	0	12	41	36	112	.319	.401
Mahoney, Mike	L	.300	10	3	2	0	0	3	0	2	.308	.500
Bats Right	R	.158	19	3	1	0	0		1	8	.200	.211
Marrero, Eli	L	.227	97	22	8	1	1	19	14	14	.321	.361
Bats Right	R	.273	300	82	11	0	17	47	26	58	.328	.480
Martinez, Ramon	L	.254	59	15	4	2	1	8	8	7	.348	.441
Bats Right	R	.279	122	34	6	0	3	17	6	19	.328	.402
Martinez, Tino	L	.207	111	23	3	0	4	12	14	21	.294	.342
Bats Left	R	.278	400	111	22	1	17	63	44	50	.350	.465
Mateo, Henry	L	.000	3	0	0	0	0	0		1	.000	.000
Bats Right	R	.200	20	4	0	1	0	0	2	5	.273	.300
Mateo, Ruben	L	.161	31	5	2	0		1	2	10	.257	.226
Bats Right	R	.309	55	17	4	0	2	6	4	10	.356	.491
Matheny, Mike	L	.265	68	18	5	0		6	9	9	.333	.308
Bats Right	R	.239	247	59	7	1	3	29	25	40	.307	.312
Matos, Julius	L	.200	75	15	0	0		4	5	16	.259	.200
Bats Right	R	.264	110	29	3	0	2	15	4	17	.293	.345
Matthews Jr., Gary	L	.000	0	0	0	0	0	0	0	0	.000	.000
Bats Both	R	.000	1	0	0	0	0	0	0	0	.000	.000
McCracken, Q.	L	.306	144	44	10	3	0	11	13	22	.367	.417
Bats Both	R	.312	205	64	17	5	3	29	19	46	.367	.488
McEwing, Joe	L	.204	93	19	4	0	2	12	3	28	.232	.312
Bats Right	R	.194	103	20	4	1	1	14	6	22	.250	.282
McGriff, Fred	L	.213	141	30	8	1	2	22	16	39	.294	.326
Bats Left	R	.296	382	113	19	1	28	81	47	60	.375	.571
McKeel, Walt	L	.000	1	0	0	0	0	0		1	.000	.000
Bats Right	R	.333	12	4	0	0	0	0		2	.333	.333
Merced, Orlando	L	.231	39	9	1	1	2	6	2	10	.262	.462
Bats Left	R	.297	212	63	12	2	4	24	24	40	.366	.429
Michaels, Jason	L	.242	62	15	8	0	1	5	7	17	.314	.419
Bats Right	R	.302	43	13	2	3	1	6	6	16	.392	.558
Millar, Kevin	L	.317	104	33	8	0	3	9	12	12	.390	.481
Bats Right	R	.302	334	101	33	0	13	48	28	62	.358	.518
Miller, Corky	L	.412	17	7	5	0	1	3	1	1	.444	.882
Bats Right	R	.227	97	22	5	0	2	12	8	19	.309	.340
Miller, Damian	L	.275	91	25	10	0	2	11	18	27	.394	.451
Bats Right	R	.238	206	49	12	0	9	31	20	61	.314	.427
Minor, Damon	L	.250	44	11	2	0	3	10	5	10	.327	.500
Bats Left	R	.233	129	30	4	0	7	14	19	24	.336	.426
Moeller, Chad	L	.120	25	3	0	0	1	1	6	7	.290	.240
Bats Right	R	.338	80	27	11	1	1	15	11	16	.418	.538
Mordecai, Mike	L	.282	78	22	5	0	0	5	8	13	.356	.346
Bats Right	R	.205	73	15	3	0	0	6	5	14	.266	.247
Mueller, Bill	L	.221	68	15	3	1	3	11	8	15	.295	.426
Bats Both	R	.272	298	81	16	3	4	27	44	27	.362	.386
Murray, Calvin	L	.000	0	0	0	0	0	0	0	0	.000	.000
Bats Right	R	.000	12	0	0	0	0	0	1	2	.077	.000
Nevin, Phil	L	.337	101	34	5	0	5	22	14	12	.407	.535
Bats Right	R	.268	306	82	11	0	7	35	24	75	.322	.373
Nieves, Wil	L	.188	32	6	3	1	0	3	3	7	.257	.344
Bats Right	R	.175	40	7	0	0	0	0	1	8	.195	.175
Norton, Greg	L	.167	30	5	1	0	0	4	5	8	.278	.200
Bats Both	R	.232	138	32	7	1	7	33	19	44	.323	.449
Nunez, Abraham	L	.143	7	1	0	0	0	1	0	3	.143	.143
Bats Both	R	.100	10	1	0	0	0	0	0	2	.100	.100
Nunez, Abraham	L	.176	34	6	2	0	0	2	4	10	.282	.235
Bats Both	R	.242	219	53	12	1	2	13	23	34	.316	.333
Ochoa, Alex	L	.263	80	21	0	0	1	8	9	10	.344	.300
Bats Right	R	.252	135	34	9	0	5	13	23	20	.365	.430
Ojeda, Augie	L	.130	23	3	1	0	0	1	1	2	.200	.174
Bats Both	R	.213	47	10	3	0	0	3	4	3	.269	.277
O'Leary, Troy	L	.351	37	13	2	0	0	8	8	2	.467	.405
Bats Left	R	.275	236	65	10	2	3	29	26	45	.355	.373
Ordonez, Rey	L	.193	119	23	4	0	0	3	7	9	.236	.227
Bats Right	R	.276	341	94	21	2	1	39	17	37	.311	.358
Orie, Kevin	L	1.000	1	1	0	0	0	1	0	0	1.000	1.000
Bats Right	R	.258	31	8	3	0	0	4	1	4	.286	.355
Ortiz, Jose	L	.233	43	10	2	1	0	1	4	7	.298	.326
Bats Right	R	.255	149	38	5	0	1	11	12	23	.319	.309
Osik, Keith	L	.091	22	2	0	0	1	4	1	7	.125	.227
Bats Right	R	.179	78	14	3	0	1	7	5	18	.235	.256
Overbay, Lyle	L	.000	0	0	0	0	0	0	0	0	.000	.000
Bats Left	R	.100	10	1	0	0	0	1	0	5	.100	.100
Owens, Eric	L	.266	94	25	0	2	1	6	10	7	.337	.340
Bats Right	R	.271	291	79	15	3	3	31	21	26	.319	.375
Ozuna, Pablo	L	.071	14	1	0	0	0	0	0	1	.133	.071
Bats Right	R	.364	33	12	2	2	0	3	1	2	.371	.545
Patterson, Corey	L	.188	149	28	3	1	2	14	2	40	.215	.262
Bats Left	R	.275	443	122	27	4	12	40	17	102	.307	.436
Payton, Jay	L	.252	135	34	5	2	4	13	9	15	.308	.407
Bats Right	R	.326	310	101	15	5	12	46	20	39	.369	.523
Pelaez, Alex	L	.333	6	2	0	0	0	0	0	0	.333	.333
Bats Right	R	.000	2	0	0	0	0	0	0	0	.000	.000
Pena, Wily Mo	L	.143	7	1	0	0	1	1	0	6	.143	.571
Bats Right	R	.273	11	3	0	0	0	0	0	5	.273	.273
Perez, Eduardo	L	.271	70	19	8	0	6	13	9	13	.354	.643
Bats Right	R	.143	84	12	1	0	4	13	8	23	.237	.298
Perez, Timo	L	.156	64	10	2	0		3	4	8	.206	.188
Bats Left	R	.318	380	121	25	6	8	44	19	28	.352	.479
Perez, Tomas	L	.250	92	23	6	0	2	5	6	13	.296	.380
Bats Both	R	.250	120	30	7	1	3	15	15	27	.336	.400
Petrick, Ben	L	.250	52	13	0	0	4	5	5	14	.316	.481
Bats Right	R	.163	43	7	3	1	1	6	4	19	.245	.349
Phillips, Jason	L	.000	2	0	0	0	0	0	1	0	.333	.000
Bats Right	R	.412	17	7	0	0	1	3	0	1	.421	.588
Piazza, Mike	L	.286	126	36	11	0	8	26	22	18	.396	.563
Bats Right	R	.278	352	98	12	2	25	72	35	64	.344	.537
Pierre, Juan	L	.294	126	37	1	0		3	1	7	.326	.302
Bats Left	R	.285	466	133	19	5	1	32	30	45	.334	.354
Polanco, Placido	L	.338	151	51	12	1	3	12	10	7	.390	.490
Bats Right	R	.270	397	107	20	1	6	37	16	34	.306	.370
Pratt, Todd	L	.417	24	10	4	0	1	4	7	3	.563	.708
Bats Right	R	.280	82	23	7	0	2	12	17	25	.413	.439
Pujols, Albert	L	.309	152	47	15	1	8	32	20	17	.391	.579
Bats Right	R	.315	438	138	25	1	26	95	52	52	.395	.555
Punto, Nick	L	.000	2	0	0	0	0	0	0	1	.000	.000
Bats Both	R	.250	4	1	0	0	0	0	0	0	.250	.250
Raines, Tim	L	.333	12	4	1	0	0	2	3	2	.438	.417
Bats Both	R	.169	77	13	2	0	1	5	19	17	.337	.234
Ramirez, Aramis	L	.260	123	32	5	0	9	20	8	24	.303	.520
Bats Right	R	.226	399	90	21	0	9	51	21	71	.272	.346
Ransom, Cody	L	.000	0	0	0	0	0	0	0	0	.000	.000
Bats Right	R	.667	3	2	0	0	0	1	1	1	.750	.667
Reboulet, Jeff	L	.375	24	9	3	0	0	0	3	5	.444	.500
Bats Right	R	.042	24	1	0	0	0	2	3	8	.143	.042
Redmond, Mike	L	.286	70	20	2	0	1	6	4	10	.346	.357
Bats Right	R	.312	186	58	13	0	1	22	17	24	.381	.398
Reese, Pokey	L	.282	85	24	6	0	1	7	8	19	.340	.388
Bats Right	R	.259	336	87	19	0	3	43	33	62	.327	.342

Player	vs.	Avg.	AB	H	2B	3B	HR	RBI	BB	SO	OBP	Slg.
Renteria, Edgar	L	.288	125	36	9	0	3	12	17	19	.378	.432
Bats Right	R	.310	419	130	27	2	8	71	32	38	.359	.442
Rios, Armando	L	.300	30	9	1	0	1	6	2	6	.333	.433
Bats Left	R	.258	178	46	10	0	0	18	14	33	.316	.315
Roberts, Dave	L	.400	25	10	1	2	0	4	7	3	.531	.600
Bats Left	R	.270	397	107	13	5	3	30	41	48	.340	.350
Robinson, Kerry	L	.222	9	2	0	0	0	0	1	0	.300	.222
Bats Left	R	.262	172	45	7	4	1	15	10	29	.301	.366
Rodriguez, Henry	L	.000	3	0	0	0	0	0	1	3	.250	.000
Bats Left	R	.059	17	1	0	0	0	3	3	5	.190	.059
Rolen, Scott	L	.288	118	34	4	1	6	22	25	18	.413	.492
Bats Right	R	.260	462	120	25	7	25	88	47	84	.342	.506
Rollins, Jimmy	L	.243	173	42	6	4	3	15	13	22	.302	.376
Bats Both	R	.246	464	114	27	6	8	45	41	81	.308	.381
Romano, Jason	L	.125	16	2	0	0	0	0	1	4	.176	.125
Bats Right	R	.476	21	10	0	1	0	1	2	7	.522	.571
Ross, Dave	L	.333	6	2	1	0	1	2	0	2	.429	1.000
Bats Right	R	.000	4	0	0	0	0	0	0	2	.333	.000
Ruan, Wilkin	L	.333	9	3	1	0	0	3	0	1	.333	.444
Bats Right	R	.000	2	0	0	0	0	0	0	1	.000	.000
Rushford, Jim	L	.182	11	2	1	0	0	1	0	3	.182	.273
Bats Left	R	.136	66	9	1	0	1	5	6	6	.219	.197
Sanchez, Alex	L	.267	45	12	0	1	0	4	4	6	.327	.311
Bats Left	R	.292	349	102	10	6	1	29	27	56	.345	.364
Sanders, Reggie	L	.289	121	35	4	1	8	19	13	20	.358	.537
Bats Right	R	.237	384	91	19	5	15	66	34	101	.313	.430
Santiago, Benito	L	.276	116	32	9	1	4	20	12	15	.341	.474
Bats Right	R	.279	362	101	15	4	12	54	15	58	.306	.442
Schneider, Brian	L	.280	25	7	1	1	0	2	2	7	.333	.400
Bats Left	R	.275	182	50	18	1	5	27	19	34	.340	.467
Scutaro, Marco	L	.000	7	0	0	0	0	0	0	4	.000	.000
Bats Right	R	.276	29	8	0	1	1	6	0	7	.267	.448
Sexson, Richie	L	.238	101	24	8	0	3	18	14	28	.330	.406
Bats Right	R	.288	469	135	29	2	26	84	56	108	.371	.525
Sheffield, Gary	L	.293	82	24	4	0	2	8	13	4	.408	.415
Bats Right	R	.310	410	127	22	0	23	76	59	49	.403	.532
Shinjo, Tsuyoshi	L	.291	110	32	4	3	4	20	6	11	.328	.491
Bats Right	R	.214	252	54	11	0	5	17	18	35	.279	.317
Shumpert, Terry	L	.294	85	25	6	1	3	11	9	8	.354	.494
Bats Right	R	.201	149	30	6	0	3	10	12	33	.275	.302
Snead, Esix	L	1.000	1	1	0	0	0	0	0	0	1.000	1.000
Bats Both	R	.250	12	3	0	0	1	3	1	4	.308	.500
Snow, J.T.	L	.229	70	16	6	1	2	10	14	22	.382	.429
Bats Left	R	.250	352	88	20	1	4	43	45	68	.336	.347
Sosa, Sammy	L	.366	101	37	2	1	11	19	34	24	.526	.733
Bats Right	R	.270	455	123	17	1	38	89	69	120	.367	.563
Spivey, Junior	L	.324	170	55	10	3	11	29	33	22	.441	.612
Bats Right	R	.291	368	107	24	3	5	49	32	78	.362	.413
Stairs, Matt	L	.154	13	2	0	0	0	1	1	2	.214	.154
Bats Left	R	.249	257	64	15	0	16	40	35	48	.355	.494
Stevens, Lee	L	.079	38	3	1	0	0	1	2	13	.125	.105
Bats Left	R	.216	167	36	5	1	10	30	37	44	.356	.437
Stinnett, Kelly	L	.286	21	6	1	0	1	5	5	7	.423	.476
Bats Right	R	.208	72	15	4	0	2	8	10	18	.305	.347
Stynes, Chris	L	.240	96	23	3	0	3	12	12	17	.321	.365
Bats Right	R	.242	99	24	6	1	2	14	9	12	.306	.384
Surhoff, B.J.	L	1.000	1	1	0	0	0	0	0	0	1.000	1.000
Bats Left	R	.284	74	21	5	0	0	9	9	5	.361	.351
Sweeney, Mark	L	.083	12	1	1	0	0	1	1	3	.154	.167
Bats Left	R	.189	53	10	2	0	1	3	3	16	.232	.283
Taguchi, So	L	.500	10	5	0	0	0	2	1	0	.545	.500
Bats Right	R	.200	5	1	0	0	0	0	1	1	.333	.200
Tarasco, Tony	L	.333	9	3	0	0	0	2	1	1	.400	.333
Bats Left	R	.241	87	21	5	0	6	13	7	12	.295	.506
Tatis, Fernando	L	.230	87	20	5	0	5	15	9	19	.307	.460
Bats Right	R	.228	294	67	13	1	10	40	26	71	.302	.381
Taylor, Reggie	L	.184	38	7	0	1	0	1	1	13	.205	.237
Bats Left	R	.265	249	66	15	3	9	37	13	66	.303	.458
Thompson, Ryan	L	.300	50	15	3	1	2	8	3	8	.352	.520
Bats Right	R	.218	87	19	6	1	6	16	4	30	.261	.517
Thurston, Joe	L	.833	6	5	0	0	0	1	0	1	.714	.833
Bats Left	R	.143	7	1	1	0	0	0	0	0	.143	.286
Torcato, Tony	L	.000	0	0	0	0	0	0	0	0	.000	.000
Bats Left	R	.273	11	3	1	0	0	0	0	2	.273	.364
Torrealba, Steve	L	.000	4	0	0	0	0	0	1	1	.200	.000
Bats Right	R	.077	13	1	0	0	0	0	2	3	.200	.077
Torrealba, Yorvit	L	.385	26	10	3	0	0	2	4	5	.484	.500
Bats Right	R	.255	110	28	7	0	2	12	10	15	.322	.373
Trammell, Bubba	L	.305	131	40	9	0	7	20	18	21	.387	.534
Bats Right	R	.213	272	58	7	1	10	36	35	50	.308	.357
Truby, Chris	L	.250	12	3	0	2	0	2	2	5	.400	.583
Bats Right	R	.258	93	24	5	0	2	5	3	22	.281	.376
Uribe, Juan	L	.241	141	34	5	2	1	18	8	28	.281	.326
Bats Right	R	.240	425	102	20	5	5	31	26	92	.288	.346
Valent, Eric	L	.000	0	0	0	0	0	0	0	0	.000	.000
Bats Left	R	.200	10	2	0	0	0	0	0	3	.200	.200
Valentin, John	L	.178	73	13	3	0	1	5	12	17	.315	.260
Bats Right	R	.274	135	37	12	0	2	25	10	20	.353	.407
Vaughn, Mo	L	.272	136	37	7	0	7	20	20	47	.381	.478
Bats Left	R	.254	351	89	11	0	19	52	39	98	.337	.447
Vazquez, Ramon	L	.157	70	11	2	0	0	4	2	17	.181	.186
Bats Left	R	.297	353	105	19	5	2	28	43	62	.373	.397
Vidro, Jose	L	.297	155	46	12	0	3	18	20	21	.375	.432
Bats Both	R	.321	449	144	31	3	16	78	40	49	.379	.510
Vina, Fernando	L	.238	143	34	4	0	0	13	16	9	.345	.266
Bats Left	R	.280	479	134	25	5	1	41	28	27	.329	.359
Vizcaino, Jose	L	.337	101	34	6	0	1	17	8	10	.378	.426
Bats Both	R	.292	305	89	13	2	4	20	16	30	.329	.387
Walker, Larry	L	.337	166	56	15	1	5	40	12	27	.390	.530
Bats Right	R	.338	311	105	25	3	21	64	53	46	.437	.640
Walker, Todd	L	.278	158	44	7	1	2	17	8	17	.315	.373
Bats Left	R	.306	454	139	35	2	9	47	42	64	.366	.452
Ward, Daryle	L	.204	54	11	0	0	1	7	3	17	.246	.259
Bats Left	R	.286	399	114	31	0	11	65	30	65	.334	.446
Wesson, Barry	L	.214	14	3	0	1	0	3	0	3	.267	.357
Bats Right	R	.167	6	1	0	0	0	1	0	2	.167	.167
Wigginton, Ty	L	.314	35	11	3	0	2	5	2	5	.351	.571
Bats Right	R	.296	81	24	5	0	4	13	6	14	.356	.506
Wilkerson, Brad	L	.230	87	20	5	1	5	18	17	29	.352	.483
Bats Left	R	.274	420	115	22	7	15	41	64	132	.374	.467
Williams, Matt	L	.289	83	24	4	1	8	18	6	17	.337	.651
Bats Right	R	.242	132	32	3	1	4	22	15	24	.315	.371
Wilson, Craig A.	L	.313	112	35	4	0	5	14	10	28	.376	.482
Bats Right	R	.242	256	62	12	1	11	43	22	88	.346	.426
Wilson, Jack	L	.360	114	41	9	2	2	11	8	14	.402	.526
Bats Right	R	.223	413	92	13	2	2	36	29	60	.280	.278
Wilson, Preston	L	.242	120	29	4	1	8	18	15	34	.328	.492
Bats Right	R	.244	390	95	18	1	15	47	43	106	.330	.410
Wilson, Vance	L	.125	32	4	0	0	1	5	0	7	.176	.219
Bats Right	R	.275	131	36	7	0	4	21	5	25	.331	.420
Womack, Tony	L	.214	182	39	7	0	0	10	16	30	.292	.253
Bats Left	R	.297	408	121	16	5	5	47	30	50	.340	.397
Young, Eric	L	.292	89	26	7	0	1	3	10	7	.364	.404
Bats Right	R	.278	407	113	22	3	2	25	29	31	.332	.361
Young, Kevin	L	.283	106	30	4	0	7	17	14	17	.377	.519
Bats Right	R	.235	362	85	22	1	9	34	36	84	.305	.376
Zaun, Gregg	L	.316	38	12	3	0	0	7	3	4	.386	.395
Bats Both	R	.197	147	29	4	1	3	17	9	32	.252	.299
Zeile, Todd	L	.274	146	40	7	0	4	23	24	16	.372	.404
Bats Right	R	.272	360	98	16	0	14	64	42	76	.346	.433
Zinter, Alan	L	.000	11	0	0	0	0	0	0	4	.000	.000
Bats Both	R	.182	33	6	2	0	2	3	0	15	.182	.424
National League	L	.256									.333	.409
	R	.260									.331	.410

DESIGNATED HITTING

TEAM

Team	G	TPA	AB	R	H	TB	2B	3B	HR	RBI	SH	SF	HP	BB	IBB	SO	SB	CS	GDP	Avg.	OBP	Slg.
Colorado	9	37	27	6	10	19	6	0	1	4	0	1	1	8	0	3	0	0	1	.370	.514	.704
San Francisco	9	42	30	5	10	20	1	0	3	6	0	0	1	11	7	7	0	0	0	.333	.524	.667
Chicago	6	26	25	3	8	12	1	0	1	3	0	0	0	1	0	8	0	0	0	.320	.346	.480
Houston	6	26	23	4	7	10	0	0	1	3	0	0	1	2	1	8	0	0	0	.304	.385	.435
Arizona	9	39	36	6	10	14	1	0	1	2	0	0	0	3	0	5	0	2	2	.278	.333	.389
Cincinnati	6	24	23	3	6	13	1	0	2	5	0	1	0	0	0	3	0	0	0	.261	.250	.565
Philadelphia	9	40	31	7	8	17	3	0	2	4	0	0	1	8	0	9	1	1	2	.258	.425	.548
Los Angeles	9	37	34	6	8	12	4	0	0	2	0	0	0	3	0	11	0	0	0	.235	.297	.353
San Diego	9	41	34	7	8	19	2	0	3	5	0	0	0	7	1	7	0	1	1	.235	.366	.559
Atlanta	9	46	40	5	9	14	5	0	0	2	0	0	0	6	0	7	1	1	1	.225	.326	.350
New York	9	38	36	5	8	17	3	0	2	5	0	0	0	2	0	8	0	1	1	.222	.263	.472
St. Louis	6	24	20	4	4	8	1	0	1	4	1	0	1	2	0	6	0	0	3	.200	.304	.400
Florida	9	41	37	3	6	8	2	0	0	1	0	0	0	4	1	14	0	0	0	.162	.244	.216
Pittsburgh	6	26	21	1	3	3	0	0	0	1	0	1	2	2	0	4	0	0	1	.143	.269	.143
Montreal	9	38	35	2	3	5	2	0	0	1	0	0	1	2	2	5	0	1	0	.086	.158	.143
Milwaukee	6	25	21	1	0	0	0	0	0	0	0	0	0	4	1	7	0	0	1	.000	.160	.000
Totals	145	550	473	68	108	191	32	0	17	48	1	3	8	65	13	112	2	7	13	.228	.330	.404

TOP DESIGNATED HITTERS

Minimum 15 at-bats. *Lefthanded batter. †Switch-hitter.

Player, Team	G	TPA	AB	R	H	TB	2B	3B	HR	RBI	SH	SF	HP	BB	IBB	SO	SB	CS	GDP	Avg.	OBP	Slg.
Walker, Larry, Col.*	7	30	22	5	9	17	5	0	1	4	0	1	1	6	0	2	0	0	1	.409	.533	.773
Sheffield, Gary, Atl.	4	22	20	3	7	10	3	0	0	2	0	0	0	2	0	2	1	0	1	.350	.409	.500
Durazo, Erubiel, Ari.*	6	21	20	5	6	9	0	0	1	1	0	0	0	1	0	4	0	1	0	.300	.333	.450
Branyan, Russell, Cin.*	4	16	15	3	4	11	1	0	2	4	0	1	0	0	0	0	0	0	0	.267	.250	.733
Piazza, Mike, N.Y.	6	25	23	4	6	14	2	0	2	4	0	0	0	2	0	5	0	1	1	.261	.320	.609
Bagwell, Jeff, Hou.	4	17	16	2	4	4	0	0	0	1	0	0	1	0	0	7	0	0	0	.250	.294	.250
Gant, Ron, S.D.	4	20	17	4	4	11	1	0	2	3	0	0	0	3	0	4	0	1	1	.235	.350	.647
Millar, Kevin, Fla.	6	24	22	2	5	7	2	0	0	1	0	0	0	2	0	8	0	0	0	.227	.292	.318
Giambi, Jeremy, Phi.*	8	32	24	6	5	13	2	0	2	3	0	0	1	7	0	8	0	1	1	.208	.406	.542
Tatis, Fernando, Mon.	4	16	15	1	2	4	2	0	0	1	0	0	1	0	0	3	0	0	0	.133	.188	.267

ALL DESIGNATED HITTERS

*Lefthanded batter. †Switch-hitter.

Player, Team	G	TPA	AB	R	H	TB	2B	3B	HR	RBI	SH	SF	HP	BB	IBB	SO	SB	CS	GDP	Avg.	OBP	Slg.
Agbayani, Benny, Col.	1	3	3	0	1	2	1	0	0	0	0	0	0	0	0	0	0	0	0	.333	.333	.667
Alou, Moises, Chi.	2	9	9	2	4	5	1	0	0	0	0	0	0	0	0	1	0	0	0	.444	.444	.556
Bagwell, Jeff, Hou.	4	17	16	2	4	4	0	0	0	1	0	0	1	0	0	7	0	0	0	.250	.294	.250
Bonds, Barry, S.F.*	5	24	14	2	3	6	0	0	1	3	0	0	1	9	5	3	0	0	0	.214	.542	.429
Bragg, Darren, Atl.*	3	12	9	2	1	2	1	0	0	0	0	0	0	3	0	0	1	0	0	.111	.333	.222
Branyan, Russell, Cin.*	4	16	15	3	4	11	1	0	2	4	0	1	0	0	0	0	0	0	0	.267	.250	.733
Brown, Roosevelt, Chi.*	1	4	4	0	1	1	0	0	0	0	0	0	0	0	0	2	0	0	0	.250	.250	.250
Burnitz, Jeromy, N.Y.*	1	4	4	0	0	0	0	0	0	0	0	0	0	0	0	0	0	0	0	.000	.000	.000
Cairo, Miguel, St.L.	3	11	10	1	1	4	0	0	1	3	1	0	0	0	0	5	0	0	1	.100	.100	.400
Casey, Sean, Cin.*	1	4	4	0	0	0	0	0	0	0	0	0	0	0	0	2	0	0	0	.000	.000	.000
Castro, Ramon, Fla.	1	4	4	0	0	0	0	0	0	0	0	0	0	0	0	0	0	0	0	.000	.000	.000
Colbrunn, Greg, Ari.	3	10	9	1	2	3	1	0	0	0	0	0	0	1	0	1	0	0	2	.222	.300	.333
Cordero, Wil, Mon.	2	9	9	1	0	0	0	0	0	0	0	0	0	0	0	1	0	0	0	.000	.000	.000
Dellucci, David, Ari.*	3	5	5	0	0	0	0	0	0	0	0	0	0	0	0	0	0	0	0	.000	.000	.000
Dunn, Adam, Cin.*	1	4	4	0	2	2	0	0	0	1	0	0	0	0	0	1	0	0	0	.500	.500	.500
Dunston, Shawon, S.F.	3	7	7	1	1	1	0	0	0	0	0	0	0	0	0	3	0	0	0	.143	.143	.143
Durazo, Erubiel, Ari.*	6	21	20	5	6	9	0	0	1	1	0	0	0	1	0	4	0	1	0	.300	.333	.450
Floyd, Cliff, Fla.*	1	5	5	0	0	0	0	0	0	0	0	0	0	0	0	3	0	0	0	.000	.000	.000
Franco, Julio, Atl.	2	9	9	0	1	2	1	0	0	0	0	0	0	0	0	4	0	0	0	.111	.111	.222
Gant, Ron, S.D.	4	20	17	4	4	11	1	0	2	3	0	0	0	3	0	4	0	1	1	.235	.350	.647
Giambi, Jeremy, Phi.*	8	32	24	6	5	13	2	0	2	3	0	0	1	7	0	8	0	1	1	.208	.406	.542
Green, Shawn, L.A.*	1	4	3	1	1	1	0	0	0	0	0	0	0	1	0	1	0	0	0	.333	.500	.333
Grudzielanek, Mark, L.A.	1	4	4	1	1	2	1	0	0	0	0	0	0	0	0	2	0	0	0	.250	.250	.500
Guillen, Jose, Ari.	1	3	2	0	2	2	0	0	0	0	0	0	0	1	0	0	0	0	1	1.000	1.000	1.000
Hansen, Dave, L.A.*	4	13	13	1	4	6	2	0	0	2	0	0	0	0	0	2	0	0	0	.308	.308	.462
Harris, Lenny, Mil.*	2	9	7	0	0	0	0	0	0	0	0	0	0	2	1	3	0	0	0	.000	.222	.000
Hubbard, Trenidad, S.D.	1	1	1	0	0	0	0	0	0	0	0	0	0	0	0	0	0	0	0	.000	.000	.000
Hundley, Todd, Chi.†	1	4	4	0	0	0	0	0	0	0	0	0	0	0	0	2	0	0	0	.000	.000	.000
Izturis, Cesar, L.A.†	1	0	0	1	0	0	0	0	0	0	0	0	0	0	0	0	0	0	0	.000	.333	.000
Jones, Andruw, Atl.	1	3	2	0	0	0	0	0	0	0	0	0	0	1	0	1	0	0	0	.000	.333	.000
Jordan, Brian, L.A.	3	13	11	2	2	3	1	0	0	0	0	0	0	2	0	4	0	0	0	.182	.308	.273
Klesko, Ryan, S.D.*	1	4	3	0	0	0	0	0	0	0	0	0	0	1	1	0	0	0	0	.000	.250	.000
Lankford, Ray, S.D.*	1	4	4	2	2	3	1	0	0	1	0	0	0	0	0	1	0	0	0	.500	.500	.750
Loretta, Mark, Mil.	1	3	3	0	0	0	0	0	0	0	0	0	0	0	0	0	0	0	0	.000	.000	.000
Matos, Julius, S.D.	1	1	1	0	0	0	0	0	0	0	0	0	0	0	0	0	0	0	0	.000	.000	.000
McGriff, Fred, Chi.*	2	9	8	1	3	6	0	0	1	3	0	0	0	1	0	3	0	0	0	.375	.444	.750
Merced, Orlando, Hou.*	1	4	3	2	2	5	0	0	1	2	0	0	0	1	0	0	0	0	0	.667	.750	1.667

Player, Team	G	TPA	AB	R	H	TB	2B	3B	HR	RBI	SH	SF	HP	BB	IBB	SO	SB	CS	GDP	Avg.	OBP	Slg.
Michaels, Jason, Phi.	2	8	7	1	3	4	1	0	0	1	0	0	0	1	0	1	1	0	1	.429	.500	.571
Millar, Kevin, Fla.	6	24	22	2	5	7	2	0	0	1	0	0	0	2	0	8	0	0	0	.227	.292	.318
Minor, Damon, S.F.*	3	11	9	2	6	13	1	0	2	3	0	0	0	2	2	1	0	0	0	.667	.727	1.444
Norton, Greg, Col.†	1	4	2	1	0	0	0	0	0	0	0	0	0	2	0	1	0	0	0	.000	.500	.000
Nunez, Abraham O., Pit.†	1	1	1	0	0	0	0	0	0	0	0	0	0	0	0	0	0	0	0	.000	.000	.000
O'Leary, Troy, Mon.*	3	13	11	0	1	1	0	0	0	0	0	0	0	2	2	1	0	1	0	.091	.231	.091
Perez, Eduardo, St.L.	1	5	3	1	1	1	0	0	0	1	0	0	1	1	0	1	0	0	0	.333	.600	.333
Piazza, Mike, N.Y.	6	25	23	4	6	14	2	0	2	4	0	0	0	2	0	5	0	1	1	.261	.320	.609
Pujols, Albert, St.L.	2	7	7	1	2	3	1	0	0	0	0	0	0	0	0	0	0	0	2	.286	.286	.429
Raines, Tim, Fla.†	1	8	6	1	1	1	0	0	0	0	0	0	0	2	1	1	0	0	0	.167	.375	.167
Ramirez, Aramis, Pit.	3	13	10	1	0	0	0	0	0	0	0	0	1	2	0	1	0	0	1	.000	.231	.000
Reboulet, Jeff, L.A.	1	3	3	0	0	0	0	0	0	0	0	0	0	0	0	2	0	0	0	.000	.000	.000
Robinson, Kerry, St.L.*	1	1	0	1	0	0	0	0	0	0	0	0	0	1	0	0	0	0	0	.000	1.000	.000
Sexson, Richie, Mil.	1	4	3	1	0	0	0	0	0	0	0	0	0	1	0	1	0	0	0	.000	.250	.000
Sheffield, Gary, Atl.	4	22	20	3	7	10	3	0	0	2	0	0	0	2	0	2	1	0	1	.350	.409	.500
Sweeney, Mark, S.D.*	1	3	3	0	0	0	0	0	0	0	0	0	0	0	0	1	0	0	0	.000	.000	.000
Tarasco, Tony, N.Y.*	2	4	4	1	2	3	1	0	0	1	0	0	0	0	0	0	0	0	0	.500	.500	.750
Tatis, Fernando, Mon.	4	16	15	1	2	4	2	0	0	1	0	0	1	0	0	3	0	0	0	.133	.188	.267
Trammell, Bubba, S.D.	2	8	5	2	2	5	0	0	1	1	0	0	0	3	0	1	0	0	0	.400	.625	1.000
Valentin, John, N.Y.	2	5	5	0	0	0	0	0	0	0	0	0	0	0	0	2	0	0	0	.000	.000	.000
Walker, Larry, Col.*	7	30	22	5	9	17	5	0	1	4	0	1	1	6	0	2	0	0	1	.409	.533	.773
Ward, Daryle, Hou.*	1	5	4	0	1	1	0	0	0	0	0	0	0	1	1	1	0	0	0	.250	.400	.250
Wilson, Craig A., Pit.	3	12	10	0	3	3	0	0	0	1	0	1	1	0	0	3	0	0	0	.300	.333	.300
Young, Eric, Mil.	2	9	8	0	0	0	0	0	0	0	0	0	0	1	0	3	0	0	1	.000	.111	.000

The following designated hitters, each of whom appeared in at least one game, had no plate appearances, runs scored or stolen base attempts: Benjamin, Mike, Pittsburgh; Bocachica, Hiram, Los Angeles; Shinjo, Tsuyoshi, San Francisco.

PINCH-HITTING

TEAM

Team	G	TPA	AB	R	H	TB	2B	3B	HR	RBI	SH	SF	HP	BB	IBB	SO	SB	CS	GDP	Avg.	OBP	Slg.
Los Angeles	133	271	243	25	68	99	19	0	4	25	3	1	4	20	3	57	2	0	4	.280	.343	.407
Colorado	139	285	247	33	65	92	8	2	5	32	3	1	1	33	1	71	4	2	6	.263	.351	.372
St. Louis	143	294	260	27	67	109	15	3	7	42	6	5	2	21	5	55	4	1	5	.258	.313	.419
Milwaukee	139	277	246	27	63	102	15	0	8	33	7	0	0	24	1	41	1	0	5	.256	.322	.415
New York	140	302	263	29	65	100	15	1	6	43	3	4	3	29	1	49	2	5	9	.247	.324	.380
Cincinnati	144	288	249	23	57	80	9	1	4	31	5	3	2	29	2	71	6	4	3	.229	.311	.321
Houston	133	247	215	21	49	67	9	0	3	24	3	2	2	25	4	57	1	0	1	.228	.311	.312
Arizona	138	293	259	27	58	88	10	1	6	31	2	3	1	28	4	76	2	2	6	.224	.299	.340
Chicago	130	243	207	21	46	73	13	1	4	30	4	4	2	26	3	63	2	0	2	.222	.310	.353
Philadelphia	134	251	209	21	46	74	13	0	5	30	5	4	0	33	3	69	0	0	2	.220	.321	.354
Atlanta	137	255	222	22	47	71	10	1	4	27	2	1	4	26	2	56	1	0	7	.212	.304	.320
Florida	136	252	217	19	45	56	4	2	1	16	4	2	3	26	5	52	2	2	8	.207	.298	.258
Pittsburgh	131	238	211	22	42	65	8	0	5	30	1	2	2	22	0	69	4	2	0	.199	.278	.308
Montreal	126	234	203	19	40	75	6	1	9	30	4	3	2	22	3	65	5	0	4	.197	.278	.369
San Francisco	129	202	184	10	36	48	7	1	1	17	1	3	1	13	1	50	1	1	4	.196	.249	.261
San Diego	133	235	210	21	40	65	5	1	6	17	0	1	2	22	1	59	4	4	6	.190	.272	.310
Totals	2165	4167	3645	367	834	1264	166	15	78	458	53	39	31	399	39	960	41	23	72	.229	.307	.347

TOP PINCH-HITTERS

Minimum 20 at-bats. *Lefthanded batter. †Switch-hitter.

Player, Team	G	TPA	AB	R	H	TB	2B	3B	HR	RBI	SH	SF	HP	BB	IBB	SO	SB	CS	GDP	Avg.	OBP	Slg.
Cordero, Wil, Mon.	31	31	26	5	10	21	2	0	3	10	0	0	0	5	0	5	1	0	0	.385	.484	.808
Colbrunn, Greg, Ari.	26	26	22	1	8	12	1	0	1	3	0	0	0	4	1	3	0	0	0	.364	.462	.545
Brown, Adrian, Pit.†	28	27	25	3	9	11	2	0	0	5	0	0	0	2	0	8	2	1	0	.360	.407	.440
Glanville, Doug, Phi.	23	23	20	2	7	8	1	0	0	2	2	0	0	1	0	3	0	0	0	.350	.381	.400
Kinkade, Mike, L.A.	23	23	20	2	7	9	2	0	0	3	0	0	2	1	0	3	1	0	0	.350	.435	.450
Vizcaino, Jose, Hou.†	26	26	23	1	8	9	1	0	0	1	1	0	0	2	0	3	0	0	0	.348	.400	.391
Cora, Alex, L.A.*	38	36	32	5	11	16	2	0	1	3	0	0	1	3	0	4	1	0	0	.344	.417	.500
Mackowiak, Rob, Pit.*	28	28	24	5	8	17	3	0	2	9	0	0	0	4	0	11	0	0	0	.333	.429	.708
Cairo, Miguel, St.L.	69	69	59	8	19	27	4	2	0	10	3	2	1	4	2	9	0	1	0	.322	.364	.458
Stynes, Chris, Chi.	43	43	39	5	12	15	3	0	0	7	0	1	0	3	1	6	0	0	0	.308	.349	.385
Harris, Lenny, Mil.*	84	80	72	8	22	29	4	0	1	4	1	0	0	7	0	4	0	0	2	.306	.367	.403
Shumpert, Terry, Col.	40	40	37	4	11	15	1	0	1	3	1	0	1	1	0	8	0	0	1	.297	.333	.405
Valentin, John, N.Y.	63	63	51	4	15	22	4	0	1	13	0	1	1	10	0	10	0	0	3	.294	.413	.431
Taylor, Reggie, Cin.*	39	38	38	5	11	22	2	0	3	7	0	0	0	0	0	15	3	2	0	.289	.289	.579
Stairs, Matt, Mil.*	28	27	25	3	7	13	3	0	1	4	0	0	0	2	0	8	0	0	0	.280	.333	.520

ALL PINCH-HITTERS

*Lefthanded batter. †Switch-hitter.

Player, Team	G	TPA	AB	R	H	TB	2B	3B	HR	RBI	SH	SF	HP	BB	IBB	SO	SB	CS	GDP	Avg.	OBP	Slg.
Abreu, Bobby, Phi.*	3	3	3	0	0	0	0	0	0	1	0	0	0	0	0	1	0	0	0	.000	.000	.000
Agbayani, Benny, Col.	14	14	12	0	3	3	0	0	0	2	0	0	0	2	0	6	1	0	0	.250	.357	.250
Alcantara, Izzy, Mil.	9	9	9	1	2	5	0	0	1	2	0	0	0	0	0	2	0	0	0	.222	.222	.556
Alfonzo, Edgardo, N.Y.	4	4	3	0	1	1	0	0	0	1	0	0	0	1	0	1	0	0	0	.333	.500	.333
Allen, Luke, L.A.*	4	3	2	1	1	2	1	0	0	0	0	0	0	1	0	0	0	0	0	.500	.667	1.000
Alomar Jr., Sandy, Col.	1	1	1	0	0	0	0	0	0	0	0	0	0	0	0	0	0	0	0	.000	.000	.000
Alomar, Roberto, N.Y.†	3	3	3	0	1	1	0	0	0	1	0	0	0	0	0	1	0	0	0	.333	.333	.333
Alou, Moises, Chi.	6	6	5	0	0	0	0	0	0	0	0	0	0	0	0	1	0	0	0	.000	.167	.000
Alvarez, Tony, Pit.	4	4	1	2	0	0	0	0	0	0	0	0	0	3	0	0	0	0	0	.000	.750	.000
Anderson, Marlon, Phi.*	3	3	3	0	0	0	0	0	0	0	0	0	0	0	0	1	0	0	0	.000	.000	.000
Aurilia, Rich, S.F.	2	2	2	0	1	1	0	0	0	0	0	0	0	0	0	1	0	0	0	.500	.500	.500
Ausmus, Brad, Hou.	3	3	2	0	0	0	0	0	0	0	0	1	0	0	0	0	0	0	0	.000	.000	.000
Bagwell, Jeff, Hou.	1	1	1	0	1	1	0	0	0	0	0	0	0	0	0	0	0	0	0	1.000	1.000	1.000
Bako, Paul, Mil.*	11	11	10	1	1	1	0	0	0	0	0	0	0	1	0	2	0	0	0	.100	.182	.100
Banks, Brian, Fla.†	11	11	10	1	4	4	0	0	0	1	0	0	0	1	0	3	0	0	0	.400	.455	.400
Barajas, Rod, Ari.	5	5	4	1	1	1	0	0	0	0	0	0	1	1	1	0	0	0	0	.250	.400	.250
Barker, Kevin, S.D.*	1	1	0	0	0	0	0	0	0	0	0	0	0	1	0	0	0	0	0	.000	1.000	.000
Barrett, Michael, Mon.	6	6	3	0	0	0	0	0	0	1	0	1	0	2	1	1	0	0	0	.000	.333	.000
Bautista, Danny, Ari.	1	1	1	0	0	0	0	0	0	0	0	0	0	0	0	1	0	0	0	.000	.000	.000
Bell, David, S.F.	7	7	6	0	2	3	1	0	0	0	0	0	0	1	0	1	0	0	0	.333	.429	.500
Bell, Jay, Ari.	20	19	18	2	4	8	1	0	1	4	0	0	0	1	0	3	0	0	0	.222	.263	.444
Bellhorn, Mark, Chi.†	22	22	17	0	2	3	1	0	0	2	0	0	0	5	0	9	1	0	1	.118	.318	.176
Belliard, Ronnie, Mil.	26	26	23	3	6	11	2	0	1	6	1	0	0	2	0	2	0	0	0	.261	.320	.478
Beltre, Adrian, L.A.	2	2	2	0	1	1	0	0	0	0	0	0	0	0	0	0	0	0	0	.500	.500	.500
Benard, Marvin, S.F.*	33	33	32	4	6	10	2	1	0	3	0	0	1	0	0	7	0	0	1	.188	.212	.313
Benes, Andy, St.L.	1	1	0	0	0	0	0	0	0	0	0	1	0	0	0	0	0	0	0	.000	.000	.000
Benjamin, Mike, Pit.	19	19	18	1	4	6	2	0	0	1	0	0	0	1	0	4	0	0	0	.222	.263	.333
Bennett, Gary, Col.	1	1	1	0	1	1	0	0	0	0	0	0	0	0	0	0	0	0	0	1.000	1.000	1.000
Benson, Kris, Pit.	2	2	2	0	0	0	0	0	0	0	0	0	0	0	0	1	0	0	0	.000	.000	.000
Berkman, Lance, Hou.†	2	2	2	0	1	1	0	0	0	0	0	0	0	0	0	1	0	0	0	.500	.500	.500
Biggio, Craig, Hou.	2	2	2	0	0	0	0	0	0	0	0	0	0	0	0	0	0	0	0	.000	.000	.000
Blanco, Henry, Atl.	2	2	2	0	1	1	0	0	0	0	0	0	0	0	0	0	0	0	0	.500	.500	.500

Player, Team	G	TPA	AB	R	H	TB	2B	3B	HR	RBI	SH	SF	HP	BB	IBB	SO	SB	CS	GDP	Avg.	OBP	Slg.
Blum, Geoff, Hou.†	21	21	16	3	5	5	0	0	0	1	0	0	1	4	0	5	0	0	0	.313	.476	.313
Bocachica, Hiram, L.A.	22	22	21	2	5	11	0	0	2	4	0	0	0	1	0	6	0	0	1	.238	.273	.524
Bonds, Barry, S.F.*	4	4	3	0	0	0	0	0	0	0	0	0	0	1	0	2	0	0	0	.000	.250	.000
Bong, Jung, Atl.*	1	1	1	0	0	0	0	0	0	0	0	0	0	0	0	1	0	0	0	.000	.000	.000
Boone, Aaron, Cin.	5	5	4	1	1	1	0	0	0	1	0	0	0	1	0	1	1	0	0	.250	.400	.250
Borowski, Joe, Chi.	1	1	1	0	1	1	0	0	0	0	0	0	0	0	0	0	0	0	0	1.000	1.000	1.000
Bragg, Darren, Atl.*	46	45	42	3	6	8	2	0	0	1	0	0	0	3	0	14	0	0	1	.143	.200	.190
Branyan, Russell, Cin.*	25	22	16	0	1	1	0	0	0	0	0	0	1	5	0	12	0	0	0	.063	.318	.063
Brown, Adrian, Pit.†	28	27	25	3	9	11	2	0	0	5	0	0	0	2	0	8	2	1	0	.360	.407	.440
Brown, Roosevelt, Chi.*	50	49	43	3	11	20	6	0	1	10	0	0	1	5	0	15	1	0	0	.256	.347	.465
Buchanan, Brian, S.D.	25	25	24	3	6	12	0	0	2	2	0	0	0	1	0	10	0	1	1	.250	.280	.500
Burnitz, Jeromy, N.Y.*	18	18	14	2	4	4	0	0	0	1	0	0	0	4	1	3	0	0	0	.286	.444	.286
Burrell, Pat, Phi.	3	3	1	0	0	0	0	0	0	0	0	0	0	2	0	1	0	0	0	.000	.667	.000
Burroughs, Sean, S.D.*	10	9	8	1	2	2	0	0	0	1	0	0	0	1	0	3	0	0	0	.250	.333	.250
Bush, Homer, Fla.	20	20	17	3	2	2	0	0	0	1	0	0	0	3	0	6	0	1	0	.118	.250	.118
Butler, Brent, Col.	12	12	11	1	3	3	0	0	0	0	1	0	0	0	0	1	0	0	1	.273	.273	.273
Cabrera, Jolbert, L.A.	4	3	2	0	1	2	1	0	0	0	0	0	0	1	0	1	0	0	0	.500	.667	1.000
Cairo, Miguel, St.L.	69	69	59	8	19	27	4	2	0	10	3	2	1	4	2	9	0	1	0	.322	.364	.458
Cardona, Javier, S.D.	2	2	2	0	0	0	0	0	0	0	0	0	0	0	0	1	0	0	0	.000	.000	.000
Casanova, Raul, Mil.†	4	4	4	0	1	1	0	0	0	1	0	0	0	0	0	0	0	0	0	.250	.250	.250
Casey, Sean, Cin.*	11	11	10	0	0	0	0	0	0	1	0	1	0	0	0	1	0	0	0	.000	.000	.000
Castilla, Vinny, Atl.	5	5	3	1	1	1	0	0	0	1	0	0	1	1	0	0	0	0	0	.333	.600	.333
Castillo, Luis, Fla.†	3	3	3	0	2	2	0	0	0	0	0	0	0	0	0	1	1	0	0	.667	.667	.667
Castro, Juan, Cin.	19	19	18	1	3	3	0	0	0	0	0	0	0	1	0	3	0	0	0	.167	.211	.167
Castro, Ramon, Fla.	25	25	23	1	2	2	0	0	0	0	0	0	0	2	0	6	0	0	0	.087	.160	.087
Cedeno, Roger, N.Y.†	19	18	17	0	3	4	1	0	0	0	1	0	0	0	0	2	1	0	1	.176	.176	.235
Cepicky, Matt, Mon.*	17	17	17	2	6	14	2	0	2	4	0	0	0	0	0	5	0	0	0	.353	.353	.824
Chavez, Endy, Mon.*	2	2	2	0	1	1	0	0	0	0	0	0	0	0	0	0	0	0	0	.500	.500	.500
Chen, Chin-Feng, L.A.	2	2	1	1	0	0	0	0	0	0	0	0	0	1	0	0	0	0	0	.000	.500	.000
Choi, Hee Seop, Chi.*	3	3	2	0	0	0	0	0	0	0	0	0	0	1	0	1	0	0	0	.000	.333	.000
Christensen, McKay, N.Y.*	1	1	1	1	1	1	0	0	0	0	0	0	0	0	0	0	0	0	0	1.000	1.000	1.000
Cintron, Alex, Ari.†	6	6	5	0	0	0	0	0	0	0	1	0	0	0	0	2	0	0	1	.000	.000	.000
Clark, Brady, Cin.-N.Y.	38	38	35	4	8	12	4	0	0	6	0	0	0	3	0	5	1	2	1	.229	.289	.343
Colbrunn, Greg, Ari.	26	26	22	1	8	12	1	0	1	3	0	0	0	4	1	3	0	0	0	.364	.462	.545
Collier, Lou, Mon.	4	4	3	0	1	2	1	0	0	0	0	1	0	0	0	1	0	0	0	.333	.333	.667
Coolbaugh, Mike, St.L.	1	1	1	0	0	0	0	0	0	0	0	0	0	0	0	0	0	0	0	.000	.000	.000
Cora, Alex, L.A.*	38	36	32	5	11	16	2	0	1	3	0	0	1	3	0	4	1	0	0	.344	.417	.500
Cordero, Wil, Mon.	31	31	26	5	10	21	2	0	3	10	0	0	0	5	0	5	1	0	0	.385	.484	.808
Corey, Mark, N.Y.	1	1	1	0	0	0	0	0	0	0	0	0	0	0	0	1	0	0	0	.000	.000	.000
Cota, Humberto, Pit.	1	1	1	0	0	0	0	0	0	0	0	0	0	0	0	0	0	0	0	.000	.000	.000
Counsell, Craig, Ari.*	1	1	1	1	1	4	0	0	1	1	0	0	0	0	0	0	0	0	0	1.000	1.000	4.000
Crespo, Cesar, S.D.†	5	5	5	1	1	1	0	0	0	0	0	0	0	0	0	2	0	0	0	.200	.200	.200
Cruz, Deivi, S.D.	8	8	8	0	1	1	0	0	0	0	0	0	0	0	0	0	0	0	0	.125	.125	.125
Cruz, Ivan, St.L.*	12	11	10	1	4	7	0	0	1	3	0	0	0	1	0	2	0	0	0	.400	.455	.700
Cust, Jack, Col.*	20	20	16	2	3	3	0	0	0	1	0	0	0	4	0	9	0	0	1	.188	.350	.188
Darensbourg, Vic, Fla.*	1	1	0	0	0	0	0	0	0	0	1	0	0	0	0	0	0	0	0	.000	.000	.000
Davis, J.J., Pit.	5	3	3	0	0	0	0	0	0	0	0	0	0	0	0	3	0	0	0	.000	.000	.000
Dawkins, Gookie, Cin.	8	8	4	1	0	0	0	0	0	0	0	0	0	3	0	2	0	0	0	.000	.429	.000
DeHaan, Kory, S.D.*	2	2	2	0	1	1	0	0	0	0	0	0	0	0	0	0	0	0	0	.500	.500	.500
Delgado, Wilson, St.L.†	4	4	3	1	1	4	0	0	1	1	1	0	0	0	0	1	0	0	0	.333	.333	1.333
Dellucci, David, Ari.*	35	35	29	4	8	13	2	0	1	6	0	1	1	4	2	7	0	1	0	.276	.371	.448
DeRosa, Mark, Atl.	17	17	14	1	5	6	1	0	0	1	1	0	0	2	0	2	0	0	0	.357	.438	.429
DeShields, Delino, Chi.*	22	22	14	1	3	4	1	0	0	1	2	1	0	5	2	6	0	0	0	.214	.400	.286
DiFelice, Mike, St.L.	12	11	9	0	0	0	0	0	0	0	0	0	0	2	0	4	0	0	0	.000	.182	.000
Donnels, Chris, Ari.*	52	49	43	2	10	17	2	1	1	8	0	1	0	5	0	7	0	0	1	.233	.306	.395
Drew, J.D., St.L.*	22	21	20	0	2	2	0	0	0	0	0	0	0	1	0	9	0	0	0	.100	.143	.100
Dunn, Adam, Cin.*	4	4	4	0	1	1	0	0	0	0	0	0	0	0	0	2	0	0	0	.250	.250	.250
Dunston, Shawon, S.F.	26	25	24	2	4	7	0	0	1	3	0	1	0	0	0	7	0	0	0	.167	.160	.292
Durazo, Erubiel, Ari.*	17	17	15	1	2	2	0	0	0	1	0	0	0	2	0	7	0	0	0	.133	.235	.133
Echevarria, Angel, Chi.	22	20	18	3	5	8	0	0	1	4	0	1	1	0	0	5	0	0	0	.278	.300	.444
Edmonds, Jim, St.L.*	9	9	7	0	4	6	2	0	0	3	0	0	0	2	1	2	1	0	0	.571	.667	.857
Eischen, Joey, Mon.*	1	1	1	0	0	0	0	0	0	0	0	0	0	0	0	0	0	0	0	.000	.000	.000
Encarnacion, Juan, Cin.-Fla.	3	3	3	0	0	0	0	0	0	0	0	0	0	0	0	2	0	0	1	.000	.000	.000
Encarnacion, Mario, Chi.	1	1	1	0	0	0	0	0	0	0	0	0	0	0	0	0	0	0	0	.000	.000	.000
Ensberg, Morgan, Hou.	6	6	3	0	2	3	1	0	0	2	0	0	0	3	0	0	0	0	0	.667	.833	1.000
Estrada, Johnny, Phi.†	1	1	1	0	0	0	0	0	0	0	0	0	0	0	0	0	0	0	0	.000	.000	.000
Fabregas, Jorge, Mil.*	11	11	11	2	3	6	0	0	1	2	0	0	0	0	0	1	0	0	0	.273	.273	.545
Feliz, Pedro, S.F.	25	25	25	1	6	7	1	0	0	2	0	0	0	0	0	8	0	0	0	.240	.240	.280
Finley, Steve, Ari.*	10	10	9	1	2	2	0	0	0	0	0	0	1	0	0	3	1	0	1	.222	.300	.222
Floyd, Cliff, Fla.-Mon.*	5	5	5	0	1	1	0	0	0	0	0	0	0	0	0	2	0	0	0	.200	.200	.200
Fox, Andy, Fla.*	14	14	11	2	4	4	0	0	0	1	0	0	1	2	2	2	1	0	0	.364	.500	.364
Franco, Julio, Atl.	45	45	39	3	7	8	1	0	0	2	0	0	0	6	0	12	0	0	2	.179	.289	.205
Franco, Matt, Atl.*	29	27	23	1	5	8	1	1	0	4	0	0	0	4	1	6	0	0	1	.217	.333	.348
Galarraga, Andres, Mon.	24	24	20	3	4	10	0	0	2	3	0	0	1	3	1	10	1	0	1	.200	.333	.500
Gant, Ron, S.D.	24	24	20	4	4	8	1	0	1	1	0	0	0	4	0	6	0	1	1	.200	.333	.400
Garcia, Jesse, Atl.	7	7	7	1	3	3	0	0	0	1	0	0	0	0	0	0	0	0	0	.429	.429	.429
Giambi, Jeremy, Phi.*	34	33	21	4	3	7	1	0	1	5	0	0	0	11	1	10	0	0	0	.143	.438	.333
Giles, Brian, Pit.*	2	2	2	1	1	4	0	0	1	2	0	0	0	0	0	0	0	0	0	.500	.500	2.000
Giles, Marcus, Atl.	9	9	7	3	3	6	0	0	1	1	0	1	0	1	0	1	0	0	0	.429	.556	.857
Ginter, Keith, Hou.	2	2	1	0	0	0	0	0	0	0	0	0	0	1	0	0	0	0	0	.000	.500	.000
Glanville, Doug, Phi.	23	23	20	2	7	8	1	0	0	2	2	0	1	0	0	3	0	0	0	.350	.381	.400
Glavine, Tom, Atl.*	1	1	1	0	0	0	0	0	0	0	0	0	0	0	0	0	0	0	1	.000	.000	.000

Player, Team	G	TPA	AB	R	H	TB	2B	3B	HR	RBI	SH	SF	HP	BB	IBB	SO	SB	CS	GDP	Avg.	OBP	Slg.
Gload, Ross, Col.*	23	23	22	3	5	8	0	0	1	4	0	0	0	1	0	5	0	0	0	.227	.261	.364
Gonzalez, Luis, Ari.*	3	3	2	0	0	0	0	0	0	0	0	0	0	1	0	2	0	0	0	.000	.333	.000
Gonzalez, Raul, Cin.-N.Y.	14	14	12	0	1	1	0	0	0	1	0	1	0	1	0	3	0	0	1	.083	.143	.083
Gonzalez, Wiki, S.D.	2	2	1	0	0	0	0	0	0	0	0	0	0	1	0	0	0	0	0	.000	.500	.000
Goodwin, Tom, S.F.*	21	21	18	2	7	8	1	0	0	4	0	0	0	3	0	2	1	1	0	.389	.476	.444
Grace, Mark, Ari.*	34	33	29	5	7	9	2	0	0	5	0	1	0	3	0	6	0	0	1	.241	.303	.310
Green, Shawn, L.A.*	1	1	1	0	1	1	0	0	0	0	0	0	0	0	0	0	0	0	0	1.000	1.000	1.000
Griffey Jr., Ken, Cin.*	19	19	13	1	5	9	1	0	1	4	0	1	0	5	1	4	0	0	0	.385	.526	.692
Grissom, Marquis, L.A.	25	25	22	1	6	7	1	0	0	4	0	1	0	2	0	5	0	0	1	.273	.320	.318
Grudzielanek, Mark, L.A.	2	2	2	0	0	0	0	0	0	0	0	0	0	1	0	0	0	0	0	.000	.000	.000
Guerrero, Wilton, Cin.-Mon.†	64	64	56	4	11	11	0	0	0	3	4	0	0	4	0	13	2	0	1	.196	.250	.196
Guillen, Jose, Ari.-Cin.	22	22	21	2	5	8	0	0	1	1	0	0	0	1	0	4	0	1	2	.238	.273	.381
Hall, Bill, Mil.	1	1	1	0	0	0	0	0	0	0	0	0	0	0	0	1	0	0	0	.000	.000	.000
Hammonds, Jeffrey, Mil.	2	2	1	0	0	0	0	0	0	0	0	0	0	1	0	1	0	0	0	.000	.500	.000
Hampton, Mike, Col.	4	4	4	1	1	1	0	0	0	0	0	0	0	0	0	2	0	0	0	.250	.250	.250
Hansen, Dave, L.A.*	66	61	54	2	10	15	2	0	1	4	0	0	0	7	3	15	0	0	1	.185	.279	.278
Harris, Lenny, Mil.*	84	80	72	8	22	29	4	0	1	4	1	0	0	7	0	4	0	0	2	.306	.367	.403
Haynes, Jimmy, Cin.	1	1	1	0	0	0	0	0	0	0	0	0	0	0	0	0	0	0	0	.000	.000	.000
Helms, Wes, Atl.	20	19	16	2	5	7	2	0	0	2	0	1	1	1	0	4	1	0	0	.313	.368	.438
Hermansen, Chad, Pit.-Chi.	21	21	19	0	3	3	0	0	0	0	1	0	0	1	0	7	1	0	0	.158	.200	.158
Hernandez, Jose, Mil.	3	3	3	0	0	0	0	0	0	0	0	0	0	0	0	2	0	0	0	.000	.000	.000
Hernandez, Livan, S.F.	3	3	2	0	0	0	0	0	0	0	0	1	0	0	0	0	0	0	0	.000	.000	.000
Hidalgo, Richard, Hou.	7	7	7	0	1	2	1	0	0	1	0	0	0	0	0	3	0	0	0	.143	.143	.286
Hill, Bobby, Chi.†	4	4	3	1	1	1	0	0	0	0	0	0	0	1	0	1	0	0	0	.333	.500	.333
Hollandsworth, Todd, Col.*.	15	15	11	2	1	1	0	0	0	1	0	1	0	3	1	4	1	0	0	.091	.267	.091
Hollins, Dave, Phi.†	6	5	5	0	0	0	0	0	0	0	0	0	0	0	0	2	0	0	0	.000	.000	.000
Houston, Tyler, Mil.-L.A.*	29	28	26	4	7	12	2	0	1	6	1	0	0	1	0	8	0	2	0	.269	.296	.462
Hubbard, Trenidad, S.D.	26	26	22	2	4	7	0	0	1	3	0	1	0	3	0	4	2	2	0	.182	.269	.318
Hundley, Todd, Chi.†	17	17	16	1	2	2	0	0	0	1	0	1	0	0	0	5	0	0	0	.125	.118	.125
Hunter, Brian L., Hou.	18	18	15	1	4	4	0	0	0	3	0	0	0	3	0	3	1	0	0	.267	.389	.267
Hyzdu, Adam, Pit.	10	10	7	1	1	1	0	0	0	2	0	0	0	3	0	4	0	0	0	.143	.400	.143
Izturis, Cesar, L.A.†	7	7	7	1	3	4	1	0	0	0	0	0	0	0	0	0	0	0	0	.429	.429	.571
Jenkins, Geoff, Mil.*	2	2	2	0	2	3	1	0	0	0	0	0	0	0	0	0	0	0	0	1.000	1.000	1.500
Jensen, Marcus, Mil.†	1	1	1	0	0	0	0	0	0	0	0	0	0	0	0	0	0	0	0	.000	.000	.000
Jimenez, D'Angelo, S.D.†	1	1	1	0	0	0	0	0	0	0	0	0	0	0	0	0	0	0	0	.000	.000	.000
Johnson, Charles, Fla.	1	1	1	0	0	0	0	0	0	0	0	0	0	0	0	0	0	0	0	.000	.000	.000
Johnson, Mark P., N.Y.*	26	22	19	3	4	9	2	0	1	2	0	0	0	3	0	7	0	0	0	.211	.318	.474
Jones, Chipper, Atl.†	6	6	6	0	0	0	0	0	0	0	0	0	0	0	0	1	0	0	0	.000	.000	.000
Jordan, Brian, L.A.	2	2	1	0	0	0	0	0	0	0	0	0	0	1	0	0	0	0	0	.000	.500	.000
Jose, Felix, Ari.†	9	8	7	1	1	1	0	0	0	0	0	0	0	1	0	4	0	0	0	.143	.250	.143
Kapler, Gabe, Col.	7	7	6	2	3	5	0	1	0	0	0	0	0	1	0	1	1	0	0	.500	.571	.833
Karros, Eric, L.A.	1	1	1	1	1	1	0	0	0	0	0	0	0	0	0	0	0	0	0	1.000	1.000	1.000
Kearns, Austin, Cin.	8	8	8	1	3	6	1	1	0	4	0	0	0	0	0	2	0	0	0	.375	.375	.750
Kendall, Jason, Pit.	4	4	3	0	1	1	0	0	0	0	0	0	0	1	0	1	0	0	0	.333	.500	.333
Kent, Jeff, S.F.	1	1	1	0	0	0	0	0	0	0	0	0	0	0	0	1	0	0	0	.000	.000	.000
Kingsale, Gene, S.D.†	15	15	11	5	6	12	1	1	1	6	0	0	1	3	0	1	0	0	0	.545	.667	1.091
Kinkade, Mike, L.A.	23	23	20	2	7	9	2	0	0	3	0	0	2	1	0	3	1	0	0	.350	.435	.450
Klassen, Danny, Ari.	2	2	2	0	1	1	0	0	0	0	0	0	0	0	0	0	0	0	0	.500	.500	.500
Klesko, Ryan, S.D.*	3	3	2	0	2	2	0	0	0	0	0	0	1	0	0	0	0	0	0	1.000	1.000	1.000
Kotsay, Mark, S.D.*	7	7	7	1	2	5	0	0	1	3	0	0	0	0	0	2	0	0	0	.286	.286	.714
Kreuter, Chad, L.A.†	7	7	7	0	2	2	0	0	0	1	0	0	0	0	0	1	0	0	0	.286	.286	.286
Lampkin, Tom, S.D.*	15	15	13	1	0	0	0	0	0	0	0	0	0	2	1	3	1	0	0	.000	.133	.000
Lane, Jason, Hou.	8	8	7	1	2	2	0	0	0	0	0	0	0	1	0	1	0	0	0	.286	.375	.286
Lankford, Ray, S.D.*	23	22	21	0	1	1	0	0	0	0	0	0	0	1	0	5	0	0	2	.048	.091	.048
Larkin, Barry, Cin.	12	12	10	0	3	4	1	0	0	1	0	1	0	1	1	2	0	0	0	.300	.333	.400
Larson, Brandon, Cin.	11	11	10	2	4	5	1	0	0	3	0	0	0	1	0	2	0	0	0	.400	.455	.500
LaRue, Jason, Cin.	3	3	3	1	0	0	0	0	0	1	0	0	0	0	0	2	0	0	0	.000	.000	.000
Ledee, Ricky, Phi.*	51	50	44	4	9	20	2	0	3	10	0	1	0	5	0	18	0	0	0	.205	.280	.455
Lee, Travis, Phi.*	13	13	12	0	4	6	2	0	0	2	0	0	0	1	1	3	0	0	1	.333	.385	.500
Lewis, Darren, Chi.	11	11	10	1	2	5	1	1	0	2	0	0	0	1	0	2	0	0	0	.200	.273	.500
Lieberthal, Mike, Phi.	3	3	3	0	0	0	0	0	0	0	0	0	0	0	0	0	0	0	1	.000	.000	.000
Little, Mark, Col.-N.Y.-Ari.	29	29	24	6	5	8	1	1	0	0	0	0	0	5	0	6	0	1	0	.208	.345	.333
Lo Duca, Paul, L.A.	8	8	8	2	3	3	0	0	0	1	0	0	0	0	0	1	0	0	0	.375	.375	.375
Lockhart, Keith, Atl.*	45	44	40	3	7	13	3	0	1	6	0	0	0	4	0	9	0	0	1	.175	.250	.325
Lofton, Kenny, S.F.*	2	2	2	0	0	0	0	0	0	0	0	0	0	0	0	1	0	0	0	.000	.000	.000
Lopez, Javy, Atl.	14	14	12	3	3	9	0	0	2	6	0	0	1	1	1	3	0	0	1	.250	.357	.750
Lopez, Luis, Mil.†	3	3	3	1	0	0	0	0	0	1	0	0	0	0	0	1	0	0	0	.000	.000	.000
Lopez, Mendy, Pit.	3	3	3	0	0	0	0	0	0	0	0	0	0	0	0	3	0	0	0	.000	.000	.000
Loretta, Mark, Mil.-Hou.	29	28	20	1	3	4	1	0	0	4	2	1	0	5	0	6	0	0	1	.150	.308	.200
Lowell, Mike, Fla.	1	1	1	0	0	0	0	0	0	0	0	0	0	0	0	0	0	0	0	.000	.000	.000
Lugo, Julio, Hou.	4	4	4	0	1	1	0	0	0	0	0	0	0	0	0	2	0	0	0	.250	.250	.250
Mabry, John, Phi.*	19	17	16	1	5	5	0	0	0	2	0	1	0	0	0	5	0	0	0	.313	.294	.313
Machado, Robert, Chi.-Mil.	5	5	5	0	0	0	0	0	0	0	0	0	0	0	0	1	0	0	0	.000	.000	.000
Macias, Jose, Mon.†	18	18	16	1	5	9	1	0	1	4	1	1	0	0	0	6	0	0	0	.313	.294	.563
Mackowiak, Rob, Pit.*	28	28	24	5	8	17	3	0	2	9	0	0	0	4	0	11	0	0	0	.333	.429	.708
Maddux, Greg, Atl.	1	1	0	0	0	0	0	0	0	0	0	0	0	0	0	0	0	0	0	.000	.000	.000
Mahoney, Mike, Chi.	1	1	1	0	0	0	0	0	0	0	0	0	0	0	0	0	0	0	0	.000	.000	.000
Malloy, Marty, Fla.*	18	18	16	0	1	1	0	0	0	0	0	0	0	1	0	7	0	0	1	.063	.118	.063
Marquis, Jason, Atl.*	2	2	2	0	0	0	0	0	0	0	0	0	0	0	0	1	0	0	0	.000	.000	.000
Marrero, Eli, St.L.	12	12	12	3	5	6	1	0	0	2	0	0	0	0	0	1	0	0	0	.417	.417	.500
Martinez, Ramon E., S.F.	8	8	6	0	1	1	0	0	0	2	0	1	0	1	0	3	0	0	0	.167	.250	.167
Martinez, Tino, St.L.*	3	3	2	0	1	2	1	0	0	0	0	0	0	1	0	1	0	0	0	.500	.667	1.000

2002 N.L. STATISTICS Pinch-hitting

Player, Team	G	TPA	AB	R	H	TB	2B	3B	HR	RBI	SH	SF	HP	BB	IBB	SO	SB	CS	GDP	Avg.	OBP	Slg.
Mateo, Henry, Mon.†	13	13	13	0	1	1	0	0	0	0	0	0	0	0	0	3	2	0	0	.077	.077	.077
Mateo, Ruben, Cin.	25	25	22	1	2	2	0	0	0	0	0	0	1	2	0	5	0	0	0	.091	.200	.091
Matheny, Mike, St.L.	4	4	3	0	0	0	0	0	0	1	0	1	0	0	0	0	0	0	0	.000	.000	.000
Matos, Julius, S.D.	7	7	7	0	1	1	0	0	0	1	0	0	0	0	0	4	1	0	1	.143	.143	.143
Matthews Jr., Gary, N.Y.†	1	1	1	0	0	0	0	0	0	0	0	0	0	0	0	0	0	0	0	.000	.000	.000
McCracken, Quinton, Ari.†	32	32	29	5	6	7	1	0	0	1	0	0	0	3	0	10	0	0	0	.207	.281	.241
McEwing, Joe, N.Y.	30	30	29	2	7	9	2	0	0	5	0	1	0	0	0	6	0	1	0	.241	.233	.310
McGriff, Fred, Chi.*	8	8	8	0	1	1	0	0	0	0	0	0	0	0	0	2	0	0	0	.125	.125	.125
Merced, Orlando, Hou.*	62	59	48	7	11	13	2	0	0	1	0	0	0	11	4	16	0	0	1	.229	.373	.271
Michaels, Jason, Phi.	59	57	46	8	11	18	4	0	1	6	0	2	0	9	1	17	0	0	0	.239	.351	.391
Millar, Kevin, Fla.	10	10	9	0	2	3	1	0	0	1	0	0	1	0	0	2	0	0	0	.222	.300	.333
Miller, Corky, Cin.	1	1	0	0	0	0	0	0	0	0	0	0	0	1	0	0	0	0	0	.000	1.000	.000
Miller, Damian, Ari.	3	3	2	0	0	0	0	0	0	0	1	0	0	0	0	2	0	0	0	.000	.000	.000
Minor, Damon, S.F.*	39	39	34	0	5	6	1	0	0	2	0	1	0	4	1	8	0	0	1	.147	.231	.176
Moeller, Chad, Ari.	3	3	2	0	1	1	0	0	0	0	0	0	0	1	0	0	0	0	1	.500	.667	.500
Mordecai, Mike, Mon.-Fla.	29	29	22	4	3	3	0	0	0	2	3	0	0	4	1	5	0	0	2	.136	.269	.136
Mueller, Bill, Chi.-S.F.†	14	14	9	2	1	4	0	0	1	2	0	0	0	5	0	1	0	0	0	.111	.429	.444
Murray, Calvin, S.F.	1	1	1	0	0	0	0	0	0	0	0	0	0	0	0	1	0	0	0	.000	.000	.000
Nieves, Wil, S.D.	3	3	3	0	0	0	0	0	0	0	0	0	0	0	0	1	0	0	0	.000	.000	.000
Norton, Greg, Col.†	78	78	66	6	15	24	3	0	2	13	0	0	0	12	0	22	1	2	2	.227	.346	.364
Nunez, Abraham, Fla.†	3	3	3	0	0	0	0	0	0	0	0	0	0	0	0	1	0	0	1	.000	.000	.000
Nunez, Abraham O., Pit.†	50	50	43	4	5	5	0	0	0	4	1	1	1	4	0	9	0	1	0	.116	.204	.116
O'Leary, Troy, Mon.*	25	23	19	3	4	4	0	0	0	2	0	0	1	3	0	5	0	0	0	.211	.348	.211
Ochoa, Alex, Mil.	19	18	15	3	5	9	1	0	1	2	0	0	0	3	1	1	1	0	0	.333	.444	.600
Ojeda, Augie, Chi.†	2	2	1	0	0	0	0	0	0	0	1	0	0	0	0	0	0	0	0	.000	.000	.000
Ordonez, Rey, N.Y.	2	2	2	0	0	0	0	0	0	0	0	0	0	0	0	0	0	0	0	.000	.000	.000
Orie, Kevin, Chi.	1	1	1	0	0	0	0	0	0	0	0	0	0	0	0	0	0	0	0	.000	.000	.000
Ortiz, Jose, Col.	11	11	10	1	3	4	1	0	0	1	0	0	0	1	0	3	0	0	1	.300	.364	.400
Osik, Keith, Pit.	20	20	19	1	2	5	0	0	1	2	0	0	0	1	0	6	0	0	0	.105	.150	.263
Overbay, Lyle, Ari.*	10	10	10	0	1	1	0	0	0	1	0	0	0	0	0	5	0	0	0	.100	.100	.100
Owens, Eric, Fla.	16	16	15	1	4	4	0	0	0	0	0	1	0	0	0	1	0	1	1	.267	.267	.267
Ozuna, Pablo, Fla.	18	18	18	2	7	12	1	2	0	2	0	0	0	0	0	2	0	0	1	.389	.389	.667
Patterson, Corey, Chi.*	10	10	10	4	3	7	1	0	1	1	0	0	0	0	0	5	0	0	0	.300	.300	.700
Payton, Jay, N.Y.-Col.	18	18	16	3	6	9	0	0	1	2	0	0	1	1	0	1	0	0	0	.375	.444	.563
Pelaez, Alex, S.D.	1	1	1	0	0	0	0	0	0	0	0	0	0	0	0	0	0	0	0	.000	.000	.000
Pena, Wily Mo, Cin.	6	6	6	0	1	1	0	0	0	0	0	0	0	0	0	4	0	0	0	.167	.167	.167
Perez, Eduardo, St.L.	59	59	54	4	10	22	3	0	3	10	0	1	1	3	0	14	0	0	3	.185	.237	.407
Perez, Timo, N.Y.*	20	20	17	2	3	4	1	0	0	1	1	1	0	1	0	1	0	1	0	.176	.211	.235
Perez, Tomas, Phi.†	23	23	18	1	4	7	3	0	0	2	2	0	0	3	0	4	0	0	0	.222	.333	.389
Petrick, Ben, Col.	9	9	8	1	2	5	0	0	1	2	0	0	0	1	0	1	0	0	0	.250	.333	.625
Phillips, Jason, N.Y.	6	6	4	0	1	1	0	0	0	0	0	0	1	1	0	0	0	0	0	.250	.500	.250
Piazza, Mike, N.Y.	10	10	9	3	3	7	1	0	1	6	0	0	0	1	0	1	0	0	1	.333	.400	.778
Pierre, Juan, Col.*	9	9	7	2	4	4	0	0	0	1	1	0	0	1	0	1	0	0	0	.571	.625	.571
Polanco, Placido, St.L.	9	9	9	1	3	3	0	0	0	2	0	0	0	0	0	0	0	0	2	.333	.333	.333
Pratt, Todd, Phi.	3	3	3	0	0	0	0	0	0	0	0	0	0	0	0	0	0	0	0	.000	.000	.000
Pujols, Albert, St.L.	1	1	1	0	1	1	0	0	0	0	0	0	0	0	0	0	0	0	0	1.000	1.000	1.000
Punto, Nick, Phi.†	6	6	5	0	1	1	0	0	0	0	1	0	0	0	0	2	0	0	0	.200	.200	.200
Raines, Tim, Fla.†	86	85	65	8	14	19	2	0	1	7	0	2	1	17	3	13	0	0	2	.215	.376	.292
Ramirez, Aramis, Pit.	9	9	8	1	3	6	0	0	1	3	0	1	0	0	0	3	0	0	0	.375	.333	.750
Reboulet, Jeff, L.A.	25	25	23	0	4	6	2	0	0	1	2	0	0	0	0	10	0	0	0	.174	.174	.261
Redmond, Mike, Fla.	7	7	7	0	0	0	0	0	0	0	0	0	0	0	0	0	0	0	0	.000	.000	.000
Reed, Steve, S.D.	1	1	1	0	0	0	0	0	0	0	0	0	0	0	0	1	0	0	0	.000	.000	.000
Reese, Pokey, Pit.	1	1	1	1	1	2	1	0	0	0	0	0	0	0	0	0	0	0	0	1.000	1.000	2.000
Renteria, Edgar, St.L.	3	3	3	0	1	2	1	0	0	1	0	0	0	0	0	1	1	0	0	.333	.333	.667
Rios, Armando, Pit.*	21	20	19	2	4	4	0	0	0	1	0	0	0	1	0	6	0	0	0	.211	.250	.211
Roberts, Dave, L.A.*	9	9	7	2	5	8	3	0	0	0	0	0	0	2	0	0	0	0	0	.714	.778	1.143
Robinson, Kerry, St.L.*	69	66	60	7	13	21	3	1	1	7	0	1	0	5	2	9	2	0	0	.217	.273	.350
Rodriguez, Henry, Mon.*	16	15	11	0	0	0	0	0	0	2	0	1	0	3	0	7	0	0	0	.000	.200	.000
Rolen, Scott, St.L.	1	1	1	1	1	4	0	0	1	1	0	0	0	0	0	0	0	0	0	1.000	1.000	4.000
Rollins, Jimmy, Phi.†	3	3	2	0	0	0	0	0	0	0	0	0	0	1	0	1	0	0	0	.000	.333	.000
Ross, Dave, L.A.	3	3	3	1	1	2	1	0	0	1	0	0	0	0	0	2	0	0	0	.333	.333	.667
Ruan, Wilkin, L.A.	3	3	3	1	1	1	0	0	0	0	0	0	0	0	0	0	0	0	0	.333	.333	.333
Rusch, Glendon, Mil.*	3	3	1	0	0	0	0	0	0	0	2	0	0	0	0	1	0	0	0	.000	.000	.000
Rushford, Jim, Mil.*	2	2	2	0	0	0	0	0	0	0	0	0	0	0	0	0	0	0	0	.000	.000	.000
Sanchez, Alex, Mil.*	10	10	9	1	1	1	0	0	0	0	0	0	0	1	0	3	0	0	0	.111	.200	.111
Sanders, Reggie, S.F.	3	3	3	0	0	0	0	0	0	0	0	0	0	0	0	1	0	0	0	.000	.000	.000
Santiago, Benito, S.F.	3	3	3	0	1	1	0	0	0	0	0	0	0	0	0	0	0	0	0	.333	.333	.333
Schneider, Brian, Mon.*	7	7	7	0	1	1	0	0	0	0	0	0	0	0	0	1	0	0	1	.143	.143	.143
Scutaro, Marco, N.Y.	8	8	7	0	2	4	0	0	1	2	1	0	0	0	0	3	0	1	1	.286	.286	.571
Sexson, Richie, Mil.	2	2	2	0	0	0	0	0	0	0	0	0	0	0	0	0	0	0	0	.000	.000	.000
Sheffield, Gary, Atl.	4	4	2	1	1	1	0	0	0	2	0	0	0	2	0	0	0	0	0	.500	.750	.500
Shinjo, Tsuyoshi, S.F.	3	2	2	0	1	1	0	0	0	0	0	0	0	0	0	1	0	0	0	.500	.500	.500
Shumpert, Terry, Col.	40	40	37	4	11	15	1	0	1	3	1	0	1	1	0	8	0	0	1	.297	.333	.405
Snead, Esix, N.Y.†	4	4	3	0	0	0	0	0	0	0	0	0	0	1	0	1	1	0	0	.000	.250	.000
Snow, J.T., S.F.*	13	13	11	1	2	3	1	0	0	1	0	0	0	2	0	3	0	0	2	.182	.308	.273
Spivey, Junior, Ari.	1	1	1	0	0	0	0	0	0	0	0	0	0	0	0	1	0	0	0	.000	.000	.000
Stairs, Matt, Mil.*	28	27	25	3	7	13	0	0	2	4	0	0	0	2	0	8	0	0	0	.280	.333	.520
Stark, Denny, Col.	1	1	1	0	0	0	0	0	0	0	0	0	0	0	0	1	0	0	0	.000	.000	.000
Stevens, Lee, Mon.*	6	6	5	1	2	5	0	0	1	3	0	0	0	1	0	0	0	0	1	.400	.500	1.000
Stinnett, Kelly, Cin.	4	4	3	0	0	0	0	0	0	0	0	0	0	1	0	2	0	0	0	.000	.250	.000
Stynes, Chris, Chi.	43	43	39	5	12	15	3	0	0	7	0	1	0	3	1	6	0	0	0	.308	.349	.385
Surhoff, B.J., Atl.*	5	5	4	0	0	0	0	0	0	0	0	0	0	1	0	0	0	0	0	.000	.200	.000

Player, Team	G	TPA	AB	R	H	TB	2B	3B	HR	RBI	SH	SF	HP	BB	IBB	SO	SB	CS	GDP	Avg.	OBP	Slg.
Sweeney, Mark, S.D.*	35	34	31	2	6	8	2	0	0	0	0	0	0	3	0	11	0	0	0	.194	.265	.258
Taguchi, So, St.L.	8	8	5	1	2	2	0	0	0	1	1	0	0	2	0	1	0	0	0	.400	.571	.400
Tarasco, Tony, N.Y.*	32	31	27	5	6	10	1	0	1	3	0	0	0	4	0	2	0	1	0	.222	.323	.370
Tatis, Fernando, Mon.	11	11	11	0	1	1	0	0	0	1	0	0	0	0	0	5	0	0	0	.091	.091	.091
Taylor, Reggie, Cin.*	39	38	38	5	11	22	2	0	3	7	0	0	0	0	0	15	3	2	0	.289	.289	.579
Tejera, Michael, Fla.*	2	2	2	0	1	1	0	0	0	1	0	0	0	0	0	1	0	0	0	.500	.500	.500
Thompson, Ryan, Mil.	20	20	18	1	4	8	1	0	1	5	0	0	0	2	0	6	0	0	1	.222	.300	.444
Thurston, Joe, L.A.*	5	5	4	0	1	2	1	0	0	0	0	1	0	0	0	0	0	0	0	.250	.250	.500
Torcato, Tony, S.F.*	3	3	3	0	0	0	0	0	0	0	0	0	0	0	0	1	0	0	0	.000	.000	.000
Torrealba, Steve, Atl.	1	1	1	0	0	0	0	0	0	0	0	0	0	0	0	1	0	0	0	.000	.000	.000
Torrealba, Yorvit, S.F.	1	1	1	0	0	0	0	0	0	0	0	0	0	0	0	0	0	0	0	.000	.000	.000
Trachsel, Steve, N.Y.	1	1	1	0	0	0	0	0	0	0	0	0	0	0	0	0	0	0	0	.000	.000	.000
Trammell, Bubba, S.D.	14	14	13	0	2	3	1	0	0	0	0	0	0	1	0	3	0	0	0	.154	.214	.231
Truby, Chris, Mon.	4	3	3	0	0	0	0	0	0	0	0	0	0	0	0	3	0	0	0	.000	.000	.000
Tucker, T.J., Mon.	1	1	1	0	0	0	0	0	0	0	0	0	0	0	0	0	0	0	0	.000	.000	.000
Uribe, Juan, Col.	1	1	1	0	0	0	0	0	0	0	0	0	0	0	0	1	0	0	0	.000	.000	.000
Valent, Eric, Phi.*	5	5	5	1	2	2	0	0	0	0	0	0	0	0	0	1	0	0	0	.400	.400	.400
Valentin, John, N.Y.	63	63	51	4	15	22	4	0	1	13	0	1	1	10	0	10	0	0	3	.294	.413	.431
Vaughn, Mo, N.Y.*	6	5	3	0	0	0	0	0	0	0	0	0	0	2	0	1	0	0	0	.000	.400	.000
Vazquez, Ramon, S.D.*	9	8	7	1	1	1	0	0	0	0	0	0	0	1	0	2	0	0	1	.143	.250	.143
Vidro, Jose, Mon.†	1	1	1	0	0	0	0	0	0	0	0	0	0	0	0	0	0	0	0	.000	.000	.000
Vizcaino, Jose, Hou.†	26	26	23	1	8	9	1	0	0	1	1	0	0	2	0	3	0	0	0	.348	.400	.391
Walker, Larry, Col.*	7	7	7	2	3	5	2	0	0	3	0	0	0	0	0	1	0	0	0	.429	.429	.714
Walker, Todd, Cin.*	5	5	5	1	4	4	0	0	0	1	0	0	0	0	0	0	0	0	0	.800	.800	.800
Ward, Daryle, Hou.*	16	16	15	1	3	4	1	0	0	2	0	0	0	1	0	1	0	0	0	.200	.250	.267
Wells, Kip, Pit.	1	1	1	0	0	0	0	0	0	0	0	0	0	0	0	1	0	0	0	.000	.000	.000
Wesson, Barry, Hou.	2	2	2	0	1	1	0	0	0	1	0	0	0	0	0	0	0	0	0	.500	.500	.500
Wigginton, Ty, N.Y.	12	12	11	3	4	8	1	0	1	3	0	0	0	1	0	2	0	0	1	.364	.417	.727
Wilkerson, Brad, Mon.*	9	9	8	1	1	3	0	1	0	0	0	0	0	1	0	3	0	0	0	.125	.222	.375
Williams, Dave, Pit.*	1	1	1	0	0	0	0	0	0	0	0	0	0	0	0	1	0	0	0	.000	.000	.000
Williams, Matt, Ari.	6	5	5	0	0	0	0	0	0	0	0	0	0	0	0	5	0	0	0	.000	.000	.000
Williams, Woody, St.L.	1	1	1	0	0	0	0	0	0	0	0	0	0	0	0	1	0	0	0	.000	.000	.000
Wilson, Craig A., Pit.	17	17	16	0	2	2	0	0	0	1	0	0	1	0	0	7	0	0	0	.125	.176	.125
Wilson, Jack, Pit.	3	3	3	0	0	0	0	0	0	0	0	0	0	0	0	0	0	0	0	.000	.000	.000
Wilson, Preston, Fla.	3	3	3	0	0	0	0	0	0	0	0	0	0	0	0	1	0	0	0	.000	.000	.000
Wilson, Vance, N.Y.	10	10	10	0	1	2	1	0	0	1	0	0	0	0	0	3	0	0	1	.100	.100	.200
Wolf, Randy, Phi.*	1	1	1	0	0	0	0	0	0	0	0	0	0	0	0	1	0	0	0	.000	.000	.000
Womack, Tony, Ari.*	5	5	5	2	2	3	1	0	0	0	0	0	0	0	0	0	1	0	0	.400	.400	.600
Young, Eric, Mil.	7	7	7	1	3	5	2	0	0	0	0	0	0	0	0	1	0	0	0	.429	.429	.714
Young, Kevin, Pit.	4	4	3	0	0	0	0	0	0	0	0	0	0	1	0	0	0	0	0	.000	.250	.000
Zaun, Gregg, Hou.†	34	34	32	3	4	11	1	0	2	8	1	1	0	0	0	9	0	0	0	.125	.121	.344
Zeile, Todd, Col.	4	3	3	0	2	2	0	0	0	1	0	0	0	0	0	1	0	0	0	.667	.667	.667
Zinter, Alan, Hou.†	33	33	33	4	5	10	2	0	1	2	0	0	0	0	0	13	0	0	0	.152	.152	.303

PINCH-HITTERS WITH TWO OR MORE TEAMS

Player, Team	G	TPA	AB	R	H	TB	2B	3B	HR	RBI	SH	SF	HP	BB	IBB	SO	SB	CS	GDP	Avg.	OBP	Slg.
Clark, Brady, Cin.	32	32	29	3	6	9	3	0	0	5	0	0	0	3	0	4	1	2	1	.207	.281	.310
Clark, Brady, N.Y.	6	6	6	1	2	3	1	0	0	1	0	0	0	0	0	1	0	0	0	.333	.333	.500
Encarnacion, Juan, Cin.	1	1	1	0	0	0	0	0	0	0	0	0	0	0	0	1	0	0	0	.000	.000	.000
Encarnacion, Juan, Fla.	2	2	2	0	0	0	0	0	0	0	0	0	0	0	0	1	0	0	1	.000	.000	.000
Floyd, Cliff, Fla.*	3	3	3	0	0	0	0	0	0	0	0	0	0	0	0	2	0	0	0	.000	.000	.000
Floyd, Cliff, Mon.*	2	2	2	0	1	1	0	0	0	0	0	0	0	0	0	0	0	0	0	.500	.500	.500
Gonzalez, Raul, Cin.	4	4	3	0	0	0	0	0	0	0	0	0	0	1	0	1	0	0	0	.000	.250	.000
Gonzalez, Raul, N.Y.	10	10	9	0	1	1	0	0	0	1	0	1	0	0	0	2	0	0	1	.111	.100	.111
Guerrero, Wilton, Cin.†	44	44	36	4	10	10	0	0	0	3	4	0	0	4	0	6	1	0	1	.278	.350	.278
Guerrero, Wilton, Mon.†	20	20	20	0	1	1	0	0	0	0	0	0	0	0	0	7	1	0	0	.050	.050	.050
Guillen, Jose, Ari.	17	17	16	1	3	6	0	0	1	1	0	0	0	1	0	4	0	1	1	.188	.235	.375
Guillen, Jose, Cin.	5	5	5	1	2	2	0	0	0	0	0	0	0	0	0	0	0	0	1	.400	.400	.400
Hermansen, Chad, Pit.	9	9	8	0	1	1	0	0	0	0	0	0	0	1	0	2	1	0	0	.125	.222	.125
Hermansen, Chad, Chi.	12	12	11	0	2	2	0	0	0	1	0	0	0	0	0	5	0	0	0	.182	.182	.182
Houston, Tyler, Mil.*	7	7	6	1	3	6	0	0	1	3	1	0	0	0	0	1	0	0	0	.500	.500	1.000
Houston, Tyler, L.A.*	22	21	20	3	4	6	2	0	0	3	0	0	0	1	0	6	0	0	0	.200	.238	.300
Little, Mark, Col.	25	25	20	6	5	8	1	1	0	0	0	0	0	5	0	4	0	0	0	.250	.400	.400
Little, Mark, N.Y.	2	2	2	0	0	0	0	0	0	0	0	0	0	0	0	0	0	1	0	.000	.000	.000
Little, Mark, Ari.	2	2	2	0	0	0	0	0	0	0	0	0	0	0	0	2	0	0	0	.000	.000	.000
Loretta, Mark, Mil.	26	25	18	1	3	4	1	0	0	3	2	0	0	5	0	5	0	0	1	.167	.348	.222
Loretta, Mark, Hou.	3	3	2	0	0	0	0	0	0	1	0	1	0	0	0	1	0	0	0	.000	.000	.000
Machado, Robert, Chi.	2	2	2	0	0	0	0	0	0	0	0	0	0	0	0	1	0	0	0	.000	.000	.000
Machado, Robert, Mil.	3	3	3	0	0	0	0	0	0	0	0	0	0	0	0	0	0	0	0	.000	.000	.000
Mordecai, Mike, Mon.	20	20	14	3	1	1	0	0	0	0	2	0	0	4	1	3	0	0	1	.071	.278	.071
Mordecai, Mike, Fla.	9	9	8	1	2	2	0	0	0	2	1	0	0	0	0	2	0	0	1	.250	.250	.250
Mueller, Bill, Chi.*	8	8	4	2	1	4	0	0	1	2	0	0	0	4	0	0	0	0	0	.250	.625	1.000
Mueller, Bill, S.F.†	6	6	5	0	0	0	0	0	0	0	0	0	0	1	0	1	0	0	0	.000	.167	.000
Payton, Jay, N.Y.	14	14	13	3	6	9	0	0	1	2	0	0	1	0	0	1	0	0	0	.462	.500	.692
Payton, Jay, Col.	4	4	3	0	0	0	0	0	0	0	0	0	0	1	0	0	0	0	0	.000	.250	.000

PITCHING

TEAM

Team	W	L	Pct.	ERA	G	CG	ShO	Rel.	Sv-Op.	IP	H	TBF	R	ER	HR	SH	SF	HB	BB	IBB	SO	WP	Bk.
Atlanta	101	59	.631	3.13	161	3	15	469	57-71	1467.1	1302	6131	565	511	123	74	32	42	554	63	1058	40	4
San Francisco	95	66	.590	3.54	162	10	13	417	43-60	1437.1	1349	6056	616	566	116	72	43	36	523	44	992	36	2
Los Angeles	92	70	.568	3.69	162	4	15	423	56-71	1457.2	1311	6139	643	598	165	71	38	46	555	45	1132	33	3
St. Louis	97	65	.599	3.70	162	4	9	472	42-63	1446.1	1355	6135	648	595	141	70	56	60	547	39	1009	40	2
New York	75	86	.466	3.89	161	9	10	451	36-51	1442.2	1408	6212	703	624	163	74	42	55	543	75	1107	22	7
Arizona	98	64	.605	3.92	162	14	10	422	40-59	1446.2	1361	6067	674	630	170	63	36	54	421	30	1303	48	11
Montreal	83	79	.512	3.97	162	9	3	437	39-59	1453.0	1475	6246	718	641	165	79	39	46	508	80	1088	51	5
Houston	84	78	.519	4.00	162	2	11	480	43-58	1445.0	1423	6205	695	643	151	76	48	55	546	78	1219	38	3
Philadelphia	80	81	.497	4.17	161	5	9	450	47-71	1449.2	1381	6222	724	671	153	66	34	70	570	54	1075	68	5
Pittsburgh	72	89	.447	4.23	161	2	7	458	47-66	1412.2	1447	6131	730	664	163	60	35	55	572	93	920	34	5
Cincinnati	78	84	.481	4.27	162	2	8	462	42-57	1453.2	1502	6296	774	690	173	62	43	56	550	63	980	52	2
Chicago	67	95	.414	4.29	162	11	9	390	23-48	1441.1	1373	6236	759	687	167	85	57	58	606	53	1333	44	2
Florida	79	83	.488	4.36	162	11	12	461	36-55	1456.1	1449	6340	763	706	151	73	45	58	631	46	1104	55	7
San Diego	66	96	.407	4.62	162	5	10	459	40-62	1436.1	1522	6333	815	737	177	64	58	66	582	61	1108	51	4
Milwaukee	56	106	.346	4.73	162	7	4	446	32-42	1432.1	1468	6339	821	752	199	93	45	62	606	82	1026	64	8
Colorado	73	89	.451	5.20	162	1	8	506	43-59	1426.2	1554	6345	898	825	225	49	47	64	582	49	920	42	6
Totals	1296	1290	.501	4.11	1294	99	153	7203	666-952	23105.0	22680	99433	11546	10540	2602	1113	698	883	8956	955	17374	718	76

NOTE—Totals for earned runs for several clubs do not agree with composite total for all pitchers of each respective club due to instances in which provisions of Section 10.18(i) of the Scoring Rules were applied. The following differences are to be noted: San Francisco pitchers add to 567; New York pitchers add to 626; Arizona pitchers add to 631; Montreal pitchers add to 642; Pittsburgh pitchers add to 665; Cincinnati pitchers add to 693; Chicago pitchers add to 690; San Diego pitchers add to 743; Milwaukee pitchers add to 757; Colorado pitchers add to 826.

INDIVIDUAL

TOP QUALIFIERS FOR EARNED-RUN AVERAGE TITLE

Minimum 162 innings. *Throws lefthanded.

Pitcher, Team	W	L	Pct.	ERA	G	GS	CG	ShO	GF	Sv.-Op.	IP	H	TBF	R	ER	HR	SH	SF	HB	BB	IBB	SO	WP	Bk.
Johnson, Randy, Ari.*	24	5	.828	2.32	35	35	8	4	0	0-0	260.0	197	1035	78	67	26	4	2	13	71	1	334	3	2
Maddux, Greg, Atl.	16	6	.727	2.62	34	34	0	0	0	0-0	199.1	194	820	67	58	14	13	4	4	45	7	118	1	0
Glavine, Tom, Atl.*	18	11	.621	2.96	36	36	2	1	0	0-0	224.2	210	936	85	74	21	12	6	8	78	8	127	2	0
Perez, Odalis, L.A.*	15	10	.600	3.00	32	32	4	2	0	0-0	222.1	182	869	76	74	21	13	7	4	38	5	155	2	3
Oswalt, Roy, Hou.	19	9	.679	3.01	35	34	0	0	0	0-0	233.0	215	956	86	78	17	12	7	5	62	4	208	3	0
Dessens, Elmer, Cin.	7	8	.467	3.03	30	30	0	0	0	0-0	178.0	173	737	70	60	24	7	1	7	49	8	93	3	1
Ohka, Tomokazu, Mon.	13	8	.619	3.18	32	31	2	0	1	0-0	192.2	194	806	83	68	19	13	6	7	45	7	118	2	1
Wolf, Randy, Phi.*	11	9	.550	3.20	31	31	3	2	0	0-0	210.2	172	855	77	75	23	7	6	7	63	5	172	4	0
Rueter, Kirk, S.F.*	14	8	.636	3.23	33	33	0	0	0	0-0	203.2	204	846	83	73	22	6	6	1	54	7	76	3	0
Schilling, Curt, Ari.	23	7	.767	3.23	36	35	5	1	0	0-0	259.1	218	1017	95	93	29	5	2	3	33	1	316	6	0
Millwood, Kevin, Atl.	18	8	.692	3.24	35	34	1	1	0	0-0	217.0	186	895	80	78	16	9	4	8	65	7	178	4	0
Padilla, Vicente, Phi.	14	11	.560	3.28	32	32	1	1	0	0-0	206.0	198	862	83	75	16	10	3	15	53	5	128	6	2
Miller, Wade, Hou.	15	4	.789	3.28	26	26	1	1	0	0-0	164.2	151	688	63	60	14	8	5	6	62	9	144	4	0
Burnett, A.J., Fla.	12	9	.571	3.30	31	29	7	5	0	0-1	204.1	153	844	84	75	12	9	4	9	90	5	203	14	0
Trachsel, Steve, N.Y.	11	11	.500	3.37	30	30	1	1	0	0-0	173.2	170	741	80	65	16	9	3	0	69	4	105	4	0

DEPARTMENTAL LEADERS: W—Johnson, Ari., 24; L—Hernandez, S.F., Rusch, Mil., Sheets, Mil., 13; Pct.—Quantrill, L.A., 86; GS—Glavine, Atl., 36; CG—Johnson, Ari., 8; ShO—Burnett, Fla., 5; GF—Jimenez, Col., 69; Sv.—Smoltz, Atl., 55; Sv. Op.—Smoltz, Atl., 59; IP—Johnson, Ari., 260.0; H—Vazquez, Mon., 243; TBF—Johnson, Ari., 1035; R—Hampton, Col., 135; ER—Dempster, Fla.-Cin., 125; HR—Astacio, N.Y., 32; SH—Nomo, L.A., 17; SF—Thomson, Col.-N.Y., 10; HB—Astacio, N.Y., Wood, Chi., 16; TBB—Ishii, L.A., 106; IBB—Armas, Mon., Beimel, Pit., Fogg, Pit., 12; SO—Johnson, Ari., 334; WP—Armas, Mon., Burnett, Fla., 14; Bk.—Anderson, Ari., 5.

ALL PITCHERS

*Throws lefthanded.

Pitcher, Team	W	L	Pct.	ERA	G	GS	CG	ShO	GF	Sv.-Op.	IP	H	TBF	R	ER	HR	SH	SF	HB	BB	IBB	SO	WP	Bk.
Acevedo, Jose, Cin.	4	2	.667	7.23	6	5	0	0	0	0-0	23.2	28	112	21	19	8	2	0	2	12	0	14	1	0
Adams, Terry, Phi.	7	9	.438	4.35	46	19	0	0	10	0-1	136.2	132	590	76	66	9	10	2	3	58	5	96	8	0
Ainsworth, Kurt, S.F.	1	2	.333	2.10	6	4	0	0	0	0-0	25.2	22	108	7	6	1	2	0	1	12	0	15	1	0
Alfonseca, Antonio, Chi.	2	5	.286	4.00	66	0	0	0	55	19-28	74.1	73	330	34	33	5	4	3	3	36	3	61	1	0
Almanza, Armando, Fla.*	3	2	.600	4.34	51	0	0	0	10	2-4	45.2	36	190	22	22	8	3	3	0	23	1	57	2	1
Almanzar, Carlos, Cin.	0	1	.000	2.31	8	1	0	0	4	0-0	11.2	6	45	4	3	0	0	2	0	5	1	7	1	0
Alvarez, Victor, L.A.*	0	1	.000	4.35	4	1	0	0	1	0-0	10.1	9	40	5	5	1	0	0	0	2	0	7	0	0
Anderson, Brian, Ari.*	6	11	.353	4.79	35	24	0	0	1	0-0	156.0	174	659	86	83	23	6	8	1	32	3	81	2	5
Anderson, Jimmy, Pit.*	8	13	.381	5.44	28	25	1	0	1	0-0	140.2	167	636	91	85	20	5	4	5	63	5	47	4	0
Armas Jr., Tony, Mon.	12	12	.500	4.44	29	29	0	0	0	0-0	164.1	149	705	87	81	22	6	2	7	78	12	131	14	2
Arroyo, Bronson, Pit.	2	1	.667	4.00	9	4	0	0	1	0-0	27.0	30	123	14	12	1	1	0	0	15	3	22	0	0
Ashby, Andy, L.A.	9	13	.409	3.91	30	30	0	0	0	0-0	181.2	179	771	85	79	20	7	6	8	65	3	107	2	0
Astacio, Pedro, N.Y.	12	11	.522	4.79	31	31	3	1	0	0-0	191.2	192	828	106	102	32	8	7	16	63	5	152	1	2
Aybar, Manny, S.F.	1	0	1.000	2.51	15	0	0	0	4	0-0	14.1	16	63	6	4	1	0	0	1	3	2	11	0	1
Bacsik, Mike, N.Y.*	3	2	.600	4.37	11	9	1	0	1	0-0	55.2	63	247	29	27	8	5	1	4	19	3	30	0	0
Batista, Miguel, Ari.	8	9	.471	4.29	36	29	1	0	2	0-0	184.2	172	790	99	88	12	5	8	6	70	3	112	9	2
Beckett, Josh, Fla.	6	7	.462	4.10	23	21	0	0	0	0-0	107.2	93	454	56	49	13	5	3	1	44	2	113	5	0
Beimel, Joe, Pit.*	2	5	.286	4.64	53	8	0	0	8	0-1	85.1	88	389	49	44	9	7	3	4	45	12	53	2	0
Beirne, Kevin, L.A.	2	0	1.000	3.41	12	3	0	0	5	0-0	29.0	26	127	11	11	4	1	2	1	17	2	17	4	0
Beltran, Francis, Chi.	0	0	.000	7.50	7	0	0	0	1	0-0	6.0	5	30	6	5	1	0	0	1	6	1	11	1	0
Benes, Alan, Chi.	2	2	.500	4.35	7	7	0	0	0	0-0	39.1	42	167	22	19	6	3	1	2	12	1	32	2	0
Benes, Andy, St.L.	5	4	.556	2.78	18	17	1	0	0	0-0	97.0	80	417	39	30	10	5	5	3	51	3	64	0	0
Benitez, Armando, N.Y.	1	0	1.000	2.27	62	0	0	0	52	33-37	67.1	46	275	20	17	8	3	2	3	25	0	79	1	0
Benson, Kris, Pit.	9	6	.600	4.70	25	25	0	0	0	0-0	130.1	152	576	76	68	18	5	3	5	50	8	79	3	1

Pitcher, Team	W	L	Pct.	ERA	G	GS	CG	ShO	GF	Sv.-Op.	IP	H	TBF	R	ER	HR	SH	SF	HB	BB	IBB	SO	WP	Bk.
Bere, Jason, Chi.	1	10	.091	5.67	16	16	0	0	0	0-0	85.2	98	379	63	54	13	3	7	3	28	1	65	5	0
Boehringer, Brian, Pit.	4	4	.500	3.39	70	0	0	0	20	1-6	79.2	65	328	30	30	5	6	3	2	33	6	65	1	0
Bong, Jung, Atl.*	0	1	.000	7.50	1	1	0	0	0	0-0	6.0	8	27	5	5	0	0	0	0	2	0	4	0	0
Borbon, Pedro, Hou.*	3	2	.600	5.50	56	0	0	0	3	1-3	37.2	41	172	24	23	7	3	5	2	19	5	39	0	0
Borland, Toby, Fla.	1	0	1.000	5.27	15	0	0	0	3	0-0	13.2	14	62	8	8	3	0	2	3	5	0	11	2	0
Borowski, Joe, Chi.	4	4	.500	2.73	73	0	0	0	25	2-6	95.2	84	391	31	29	10	5	3	1	29	6	97	1	0
Bottalico, Ricky, Phi.	0	3	.000	4.61	30	0	0	0	6	0-1	27.1	33	128	16	14	3	2	1	2	13	2	24	2	0
Boyd, Jason, S.D.	1	0	1.000	7.94	23	0	0	0	6	0-3	28.1	33	131	29	25	6	3	3	0	15	1	18	3	0
Brohawn, Troy, S.F.*	0	1	.000	6.35	11	0	0	0	2	0-0	5.2	5	25	4	4	1	0	0	2	1	0	3	0	0
Brower, Jim, Cin.-Mon.	3	2	.600	4.37	52	0	0	0	23	0-0	80.1	77	344	40	39	7	2	1	4	32	2	57	1	0
Brown, Kevin, L.A.	3	4	.429	4.81	17	10	0	0	0	0-0	63.2	68	278	36	34	9	2	0	5	23	1	58	2	0
Buddie, Mike, Mil.	1	2	.333	4.54	25	0	0	0	6	0-2	39.2	46	185	23	20	5	5	1	1	21	7	28	3	0
Burnett, A.J., Fla.	12	9	.571	3.30	31	29	7	5	0	0-1	204.1	153	844	84	75	12	9	4	9	90	5	203	14	0
Bynum, Mike, S.D.*	1	0	1.000	5.27	14	3	0	0	3	0-0	27.1	33	130	16	16	3	3	2	3	15	2	17	2	0
Cabrera, Jose, Mil.	6	10	.375	6.79	50	11	0	0	8	0-1	103.1	131	474	84	78	23	8	4	9	36	9	61	3	0
Carrara, Giovanni, L.A.	6	3	.667	3.28	63	1	0	0	13	1-6	90.2	83	387	34	33	14	6	2	6	32	4	56	1	0
Cerda, Jaime, N.Y.*	0	0	.000	2.45	32	0	0	0	7	0-0	25.2	22	113	7	7	0	0	3	1	14	0	21	0	1
Chacon, Shawn, Col.	5	11	.313	5.73	21	21	0	0	0	0-0	119.1	122	537	84	76	25	5	2	7	60	3	67	0	1
Chen, Bruce, N.Y.-Mon.-Cin.*	2	5	.286	5.56	55	6	0	0	9	0-0	77.2	85	360	53	48	16	2	3	2	43	5	80	4	0
Chiasson, Scott, Chi.	0	0	.000	23.14	4	0	0	0	0	0-0	4.2	11	31	12	12	2	0	0	0	6	1	3	0	0
Childers, Matt, Mil.	0	0	.000	12.00	8	0	0	0	2	0-0	9.0	13	48	12	12	2	1	0	1	8	1	6	0	0
Christiansen, Jason, S.F.*	0	1	.000	5.40	6	0	0	0	2	0-0	5.0	6	21	3	3	1	0	0	0	2	0	1	0	0
Clement, Matt, Chi.	12	11	.522	3.60	32	32	3	2	0	0-0	205.0	162	858	84	82	18	11	4	6	85	7	215	7	0
Coggin, Dave, Phi.	2	5	.286	4.68	38	7	0	0	7	0-0	77.0	65	339	42	40	4	1	2	4	51	3	64	11	0
Colon, Bartolo, Mon.	10	4	.714	3.31	17	17	4	1	0	0-0	117.0	115	499	48	43	9	13	3	0	39	4	74	1	0
Condrey, Clay, S.D.	1	2	.333	1.69	9	3	0	0	2	0-0	26.2	20	106	7	5	1	2	2	2	8	1	16	1	1
Cook, Aaron, Col.	2	1	.667	4.54	9	5	0	0	1	0-0	35.2	41	154	18	18	4	0	0	2	13	0	14	0	0
Corey, Bryan, L.A.	0	0	.000	0.00	1	0	0	0	1	0-0	1.0	0	3	0	0	0	0	0	0	0	0	0	0	0
Corey, Mark, N.Y.-Col.	0	3	.000	8.59	26	0	0	0	8	0-0	22.0	32	115	23	21	9	1	0	3	16	2	21	1	0
Cormier, Rheal, Phi.*	5	6	.455	5.25	54	0	0	0	7	0-3	60.0	61	268	38	35	6	0	2	4	32	6	49	4	0
Crudale, Mike, St.L.	3	0	1.000	1.88	49	1	0	0	14	0-1	52.2	43	213	11	11	3	3	6	1	14	2	47	3	0
Cruz, Juan, Chi.	3	11	.214	3.98	45	9	0	0	14	1-4	97.1	84	431	56	43	11	7	8	8	59	4	81	1	0
Cruz, Nelson, Hou.	2	6	.250	4.48	43	5	0	0	11	0-2	78.1	90	360	44	39	12	5	3	6	29	4	61	4	0
Cunnane, Will, Chi.	1	1	.500	5.47	16	0	0	0	2	0-1	26.1	27	115	16	16	5	1	0	1	13	1	30	1	0
Cyr, Eric, S.D.*	0	1	.000	10.50	5	0	0	0	0	0-0	6.0	6	29	7	7	0	1	1	0	6	1	4	0	0
Daal, Omar, L.A.*	11	9	.550	3.90	39	23	0	0	3	0-0	161.1	142	668	73	70	20	11	4	4	54	3	105	0	0
D'Amico, Jeff, N.Y.	6	10	.375	4.94	29	22	1	1	1	0-0	145.2	152	621	84	80	20	8	4	3	37	8	101	0	0
Darensbourg, Vic, Fla.*	1	2	.333	6.14	42	0	0	0	13	0-0	48.1	61	233	34	33	10	2	3	2	26	4	33	0	0
Davey, Tom, S.D.	1	0	1.000	5.57	19	0	0	0	2	0-1	21.0	23	97	14	13	2	0	3	3	11	1	21	1	0
Davis, Kane, N.Y.	1	1	.500	7.07	16	0	0	0	5	0-0	14.0	15	70	11	11	2	2	1	1	11	2	24	1	0
Dawley, Joey, Atl.	0	0	.000	0.00	1	0	0	0	1	0-0	0.1	0	1	0	0	0	0	0	0	0	0	1	0	0
Day, Zach, Mon.	4	1	.800	3.62	19	2	0	0	5	1-2	37.1	28	153	18	15	3	1	1	1	15	2	25	1	0
de los Santos, Valerio, Mil.*	2	3	.400	3.12	51	0	0	0	12	0-0	57.2	42	237	21	20	4	3	7	2	26	3	38	1	0
DeJean, Mike, Mil.	1	5	.167	3.12	68	0	0	0	60	27-30	75.0	66	326	28	26	7	4	2	2	39	8	65	7	0
Dempster, Ryan, Fla.-Cin.	10	13	.435	5.38	33	33	4	0	0	0-0	209.0	228	915	127	125	28	9	6	10	93	2	153	2	0
Dessens, Elmer, Cin.	7	8	.467	3.03	30	30	0	0	0	0-0	178.0	173	737	70	60	24	7	1	7	49	8	93	3	1
DeWitt, Matt, S.D.	0	1	.000	1.23	5	0	0	0	4	0-0	7.1	6	30	2	1	1	0	1	0	3	0	5	0	0
Diggins, Ben, Mil.	0	4	.000	8.63	5	5	0	0	0	0-0	24.0	28	118	24	23	4	3	2	1	18	1	15	3	1
Dotel, Octavio, Hou.	6	4	.600	1.85	83	0	0	0	22	6-10	97.1	58	376	21	20	7	3	7	4	27	2	118	2	0
Drew, Tim, Mon.	1	0	1.000	2.81	7	1	0	0	3	2-3	16.0	12	64	8	5	1	1	1	0	2	0	10	0	0
Duckworth, Brandon, Phi.	8	9	.471	5.41	30	29	0	0	0	0-0	163.0	167	725	103	98	26	7	3	7	69	5	167	10	0
Duff, Matt, St.L.	0	0	.000	4.76	7	0	0	0	1	0-0	5.2	3	28	3	3	0	0	0	0	8	2	4	0	0
Duncan, Courtney, Chi.	0	0	.000	0.00	2	0	0	0	1	0-0	2.1	2	10	0	0	0	0	0	0	1	0	1	0	0
Durocher, Jayson, Mil.	1	1	.500	1.88	39	0	0	0	10	0-1	48.0	27	189	13	10	3	0	1	2	21	2	44	1	0
Eaton, Adam, S.D.	1	1	.500	5.40	6	6	0	0	0	0-0	33.1	28	142	20	20	5	2	2	2	17	0	25	2	0
Eischen, Joey, Mon.*	6	1	.857	1.34	59	0	0	0	18	2-3	53.2	43	217	11	8	1	3	2	2	18	5	51	6	1
Ellis, Robert, L.A.	0	1	.000	10.13	3	0	0	0	0	0-0	2.2	6	13	3	3	1	0	0	0	0	0	0	0	0
Embree, Alan, S.D.*	3	4	.429	1.26	36	0	0	0	13	0-2	28.2	23	118	7	4	2	0	0	0	9	2	38	1	0
Ennis, John, Atl.	0	0	.000	4.50	1	1	0	0	0	0-0	4.0	5	18	2	2	0	1	1	0	3	0	1	0	0
Estes, Shawn, N.Y.-Cin.*	5	12	.294	5.10	29	29	1	1	0	0-0	160.2	171	713	94	91	13	7	6	9	83	9	109	3	1
Eyre, Scott, S.F.*	0	0	.000	1.59	21	0	0	0	3	0-0	11.1	11	50	4	2	0	0	0	0	7	1	7	1	0
Farnsworth, Kyle, Chi.	4	6	.400	7.33	45	0	0	0	17	1-7	46.2	53	213	47	38	9	2	5	1	24	7	46	1	0
Fassero, Jeff, Chi.-St.L.*	8	6	.571	5.35	73	0	0	0	18	0-0	69.0	81	315	43	41	9	7	1	3	27	5	56	2	1
Feliciano, Pedro, N.Y.*	0	0	.000	7.50	6	0	0	0	3	0-0	6.0	9	26	5	5	0	0	0	0	1	0	4	0	0
Fernandez, Jared, Cin.	1	3	.250	4.44	14	8	0	0	2	0-0	50.2	59	231	31	25	5	1	2	3	24	1	36	3	0
Fetters, Mike, Pit.-Ari.	3	3	.500	4.09	65	0	0	0	22	0-0	55.0	53	252	31	25	4	0	2	3	37	6	53	8	0
Figueroa, Nelson, Mil.	1	7	.125	5.03	30	11	0	0	4	0-0	93.0	96	412	59	52	18	11	5	4	37	6	51	5	0
Fikac, Jeremy, S.D.	4	7	.364	5.48	65	0	0	0	15	0-6	69.0	74	318	50	42	13	2	2	3	34	8	66	6	1
Finley, Chuck, St.L.*	7	4	.636	3.80	14	14	1	1	0	0-0	85.1	69	351	41	36	7	4	1	1	30	3	83	2	0
Flores, Randy, Col.*	0	2	.000	9.53	8	2	0	0	4	0-0	17.0	29	88	19	18	5	1	0	3	8	1	7	1	0
Fogg, Josh, Pit.	12	12	.500	4.35	33	33	0	0	0	0-0	194.1	199	832	102	94	28	6	3	8	69	12	113	2	0
Foster, John, Atl.*	1	0	1.000	10.80	5	0	0	0	0	0-0	5.0	6	28	6	6	3	0	0	1	6	0	6	0	0
Fox, Chad, Mil.	1	0	1.000	5.79	3	0	0	0	0	0-0	4.2	6	25	3	3	0	1	0	0	5	1	3	0	0
Franklin, Wayne, Mil.*	2	1	.667	2.63	4	4	0	0	0	0-0	24.0	16	103	8	7	1	1	0	0	17	1	17	0	0
Fuentes, Brian, Col.*	2	0	1.000	4.73	31	0	0	0	9	0-0	26.2	25	118	14	14	4	0	2	3	13	0	38	1	0
Fultz, Aaron, S.F.*	2	2	.500	4.79	43	0	0	0	12	0-1	41.1	47	185	22	22	4	2	1	3	19	3	31	1	0
Gagne, Eric, L.A.	4	1	.800	1.97	77	0	0	0	68	52-56	82.1	55	314	18	18	6	3	2	2	16	4	114	1	0
Glavine, Tom, Atl.*	18	11	.621	2.96	36	36	2	1	0	0-0	224.2	210	936	85	74	21	12	6	8	78	8	127	2	0
Gordon, Tom, Chi.-Hou.	1	3	.250	3.38	34	0	0	0	10	0-0	42.2	42	181	19	16	3	3	0	1	16	3	48	0	0
Grace, Mark, Ari.*	0	0	.000	9.00	1	0	0	0	1	0-0	1.0	1	4	1	1	1	0	0	0	0	0	0	0	0
Graves, Danny, Cin.	7	3	.700	3.19	68	4	0	0	54	32-39	98.2	99	412	37	35	7	3	6	3	25	9	58	5	0
Gryboski, Kevin, Atl.	2	1	.667	3.48	57	0	0	0	10	0-2	51.2	50	238	20	20	6	1	0	5	37	5	33	2	0
Guthrie, Mark, N.Y.*	5	3	.625	2.44	68	0	0	0	13	1-2	48.0	35	190	13	13	3	0	1	1	19	3	44	4	0
Hackman, Luther, St.L.	5	4	.556	4.11	43	6	0	0	9	0-1	81.0	90	366	42	37	7	3	6	4	39	3	46	7	1
Hamilton, Joey, Cin.	4	10	.286	5.27	39	17	0	0	9	1-2	124.2	136	554	78	73	11	7	3	6	50	2	85	5	0

Pitcher, Team	W	L	Pct.	ERA	G	GS	CG	ShO	GF	Sv.-Op.	IP	H	TBF	R	ER	HR	SH	SF	HB	BB	IBB	SO	WP	Bk.
Hammond, Chris, Atl.*	7	2	.778	0.95	63	0	0	0	6	0-2	76.0	53	311	15	8	1	5	2	1	31	9	63	1	0
Hampton, Mike, Col.*	7	15	.318	6.15	30	30	0	0	0	0-0	178.2	228	838	135	122	24	2	9	7	91	4	74	9	2
Haynes, Jimmy, Cin.	15	10	.600	4.12	34	34	0	0	0	0-0	196.2	210	852	97	90	21	7	6	3	81	4	126	6	0
Helling, Rick, Ari.	10	12	.455	4.51	30	30	0	0	0	0-0	175.2	180	751	94	88	31	10	6	6	48	6	120	7	1
Herges, Matt, Mon.	2	5	.286	4.04	62	0	0	0	25	6-14	64.2	80	298	33	29	10	6	2	2	26	8	50	3	0
Hernandez, Carlos, Hou.*	7	5	.583	4.38	23	21	0	0	0	0-0	111.0	112	495	56	54	11	2	0	3	61	5	93	1	2
Hernandez, Livan, S.F.	12	16	.429	4.38	33	33	5	3	0	0-0	216.0	233	921	113	105	19	14	8	4	71	5	134	1	1
Hodges, Trey, Atl.	2	0	1.000	5.40	4	0	0	0	0	0-0	11.2	16	53	7	7	2	2	2	1	2	0	6	1	0
Hoffman, Trevor, S.D.	2	5	.286	2.73	61	0	0	0	52	38-41	59.1	52	245	20	18	2	2	2	1	18	2	69	3	0
Holmes, Darren, Atl.	2	2	.500	1.81	55	0	0	0	10	1-2	54.2	41	214	12	11	3	4	1	2	12	4	47	0	0
Holtz, Mike, S.D.*	2	2	.500	4.71	33	0	0	0	5	0-3	21.0	18	101	14	11	2	0	3	1	21	3	19	3	0
Howard, Ben, S.D.	0	1	.000	9.28	3	2	0	0	0	0-0	10.2	13	58	11	11	4	0	1	0	14	1	10	0	0
Hudson, Luke, Cin.	0	0	.000	4.50	3	0	0	0	0	0-0	6.0	5	28	5	3	1	0	0	0	6	0	7	2	0
Ishii, Kazuhisa, L.A.*	14	10	.583	4.27	28	28	0	0	0	0-0	154.0	137	692	82	73	20	6	5	4	106	3	143	7	0
Isringhausen, Jason, St.L.	3	2	.600	2.48	60	0	0	0	51	32-37	65.1	46	257	22	18	0	4	3	1	18	1	68	0	0
Izquierdo, Hansel, Fla.	2	0	1.000	4.55	20	2	0	0	5	0-0	29.2	33	144	17	15	2	1	3	5	21	3	20	0	0
James, Mike, Col.	0	0	.000	5.56	13	0	0	0	6	0-0	11.1	12	51	9	7	2	0	0	1	5	0	10	0	0
Jarvis, Kevin, S.D.	2	4	.333	4.37	7	7	0	0	0	0-0	35.0	36	146	19	17	5	0	1	1	10	1	24	2	0
Jennings, Jason, Col.	16	8	.667	4.52	32	32	0	0	0	0-0	185.1	201	808	102	93	26	9	3	8	70	2	127	10	0
Jensen, Ryan, S.F.	13	8	.619	4.51	32	30	1	0	0	0-0	171.2	183	744	93	86	21	7	8	5	66	4	105	3	0
Jimenez, D'Angelo, S.D.	0	0	.000	0.00	1	0	0	0	1	0-0	1.1	0	4	0	0	0	0	0	0	0	0	0	0	0
Jimenez, Jose, Col.	2	10	.167	3.56	74	0	0	0	69	41-47	73.1	76	307	34	29	7	4	2	3	11	4	47	0	0
Johnson, Jonathan, S.D.	1	2	.333	4.11	16	0	0	0	5	0-0	15.1	15	67	8	7	2	1	0	1	5	1	21	0	0
Johnson, Randy, Ari.*	24	5	.828	2.32	35	35	8	4	0	0-0	260.0	197	1035	78	67	26	4	2	13	71	1	334	3	2
Jones, Bobby J., S.D.	7	8	.467	5.50	19	18	0	0	1	0-0	108.0	134	474	68	66	20	3	2	1	21	1	60	1	0
Jones, Bobby M., N.Y.-S.D.*	0	0	.000	5.74	16	2	0	0	1	0-0	26.2	30	126	18	17	4	2	1	1	18	2	18	0	0
Jones, Todd, Col.	1	4	.200	4.70	79	0	0	0	20	1-3	82.1	84	352	43	43	10	6	3	3	28	3	73	1	0
Joseph, Kevin, St.L.	0	1	.000	4.91	11	0	0	0	6	0-0	11.0	16	52	7	6	1	0	0	2	6	0	2	0	0
Junge, Eric, Phi.	2	0	1.000	1.42	4	1	0	0	2	0-0	12.2	14	56	3	2	0	2	0	0	5	0	11	0	0
Kershner, Jason, S.D.*	0	1	.000	5.79	15	0	0	0	2	0-0	18.2	15	81	14	12	2	0	0	2	10	0	11	0	0
Kile, Darryl, St.L.	5	4	.556	3.72	14	14	0	0	0	0-0	84.2	82	364	36	35	9	6	3	8	28	1	50	0	0
Kim, Byung-Hyun, Ari.	8	3	.727	2.04	72	0	0	0	66	36-42	84.0	64	343	20	19	5	1	2	6	26	2	92	2	0
Kim, Sun-Woo, Mon.	1	0	1.000	0.89	4	3	0	0	0	0-0	20.1	18	80	2	2	0	0	0	1	7	2	11	0	0
King, Ray, Mil.*	3	2	.600	3.05	76	0	0	0	15	0-1	65.0	61	273	24	22	5	5	2	3	24	6	50	0	1
Kline, Steve, St.L.*	2	1	.667	3.39	66	0	0	0	17	6-8	58.1	54	241	23	22	3	2	2	1	21	2	41	1	0
Knotts, Gary, Fla.	3	1	.750	4.40	28	0	0	0	7	0-1	30.2	21	127	15	15	6	0	1	1	16	0	21	1	0
Komiyama, Satoru, N.Y.	0	3	.000	5.61	25	0	0	0	13	0-0	43.1	53	194	29	27	7	0	3	3	12	4	33	1	0
Koplove, Mike, Ari.	6	1	.857	3.36	55	0	0	0	15	0-0	61.2	47	249	24	23	2	4	1	0	23	4	46	1	0
Lawrence, Brian, S.D.	12	12	.500	3.69	35	31	2	2	0	0-0	210.0	230	894	97	86	16	8	4	11	52	6	149	2	1
Leiter, Al, N.Y.*	13	13	.500	3.48	33	33	2	2	0	0-0	204.1	194	868	99	79	23	12	2	8	69	5	172	1	1
Lidge, Brad, Hou.	1	0	1.000	6.23	6	1	0	0	2	0-0	8.2	12	48	6	6	0	1	0	2	9	1	12	0	0
Lieber, Jon, Chi.	6	8	.429	3.70	21	21	3	0	0	0-0	141.0	153	582	64	58	15	10	6	1	12	2	87	0	0
Ligtenberg, Kerry, Atl.	3	4	.429	2.97	52	0	0	0	25	0-0	66.2	52	281	23	22	6	3	1	0	33	3	51	1	1
Lincoln, Mike, Pit.	2	4	.333	3.11	55	0	0	0	9	0-3	72.1	80	309	28	25	7	2	4	0	27	8	50	2	0
Linebrink, Scott, Hou.	0	0	.000	7.03	22	0	0	0	4	0-0	24.1	31	120	21	19	2	0	2	1	13	4	24	0	0
Lloyd, Graeme, Mon.-Fla.*	4	5	.444	5.21	66	0	0	0	19	5-0	57.0	67	253	34	33	6	4	3	2	19	4	37	2	0
Looper, Braden, Fla.	2	5	.286	3.14	78	0	0	0	40	13-16	86.0	73	349	31	30	8	3	0	1	28	3	55	1	0
Lopez, Albie, Atl.	1	4	.200	4.37	30	4	0	0	14	0-0	55.2	66	242	29	27	1	1	3	0	18	3	39	5	0
Lorraine, Andrew, Mil.*	0	1	.000	11.25	5	1	0	0	3	0-0	12.0	22	65	18	15	7	1	0	0	6	0	10	0	0
Lowe, Sean, Pit.-Col.	5	3	.625	5.79	51	1	0	0	8	0-0	79.1	101	379	58	51	9	5	3	7	41	6	64	1	1
Lundquist, David, S.D.	0	0	.000	16.88	3	0	0	0	2	0-1	2.2	8	19	5	5	0	0	0	1	5	2	0	0	0
Maddux, Greg, Atl.	16	6	.727	2.62	34	34	0	0	0	0-0	199.1	194	820	67	58	14	13	4	4	45	7	118	1	0
Mahay, Ron, Chi.*	2	0	1.000	8.59	11	0	0	0	1	0-0	14.2	13	65	14	14	6	0	0	0	8	0	14	0	0
Mahomes, Pat, Chi.	1	1	.500	3.86	16	2	0	0	2	0-1	32.2	36	147	15	14	3	3	0	1	17	3	23	1	0
Mairena, Oswaldo, Fla.*	2	3	.400	5.35	31	0	0	0	10	0-0	33.2	38	148	21	20	7	3	1	0	12	0	21	3	1
Mallette, Brian, Mil.	0	0	.000	10.80	5	0	0	0	2	0-0	5.0	7	26	6	6	3	2	0	1	3	1	5	1	0
Mann, Jim, Hou.	0	1	.000	4.09	17	0	0	0	12	0-0	22.0	19	94	10	10	3	1	0	5	7	1	19	0	0
Mantei, Matt, Ari.	2	2	.500	4.73	31	0	0	0	6	0-1	26.2	28	122	15	14	3	0	0	1	12	0	26	1	0
Manzanillo, Josias, Pit.	0	0	.000	7.62	13	0	0	0	5	0-1	13.0	20	61	11	11	5	0	0	1	5	0	4	0	0
Marquis, Jason, Atl.	8	9	.471	5.04	22	22	0	0	0	0-0	114.1	127	507	66	64	19	4	3	3	49	3	84	4	0
Mathews, T.J., Hou.	0	0	.000	3.44	12	0	0	0	4	0-0	18.1	19	76	7	7	2	1	0	0	5	3	13	0	0
Matthews, Mike, St.L.-Mil.*	2	1	.667	3.94	47	0	0	0	10	0-0	45.2	43	205	23	20	5	2	4	2	29	3	34	5	1
Meadows, Brian, Pit.	1	6	.143	3.88	11	11	0	0	0	0-0	62.2	62	259	29	27	7	2	0	1	14	8	31	2	0
Mercado, Hector, Phi.*	2	2	.500	4.62	31	3	0	0	7	0-0	39.0	32	173	21	20	2	1	1	3	25	2	40	3	1
Mercker, Kent, Col.*	3	1	.750	6.14	58	0	0	0	8	0-3	44.0	55	208	33	30	12	0	0	2	22	2	37	1	0
Mesa, Jose, Phi.	4	6	.400	2.97	74	0	0	0	64	45-54	75.2	65	331	26	25	5	6	1	4	39	7	64	9	0
Middlebrook, Jason, S.D.-N.Y.	2	3	.400	4.73	15	5	0	0	5	0-0	51.1	44	216	27	27	2	4	3	1	22	2	42	2	1
Miller, Wade, Hou.	15	4	.789	3.28	26	26	1	1	0	0-0	164.2	151	688	63	60	14	8	5	6	62	9	144	4	0
Millwood, Kevin, Atl.	18	8	.692	3.24	35	34	1	1	0	0-0	217.0	186	895	83	78	16	9	4	8	65	7	178	4	0
Mlicki, Dave, Hou.	4	10	.286	5.34	22	16	0	0	1	0-0	86.0	101	391	57	51	11	3	3	3	34	5	57	3	0
Moehler, Brian, Cin.	2	4	.333	6.02	10	9	0	0	0	0-0	43.1	61	201	34	29	8	3	1	1	11	0	18	0	0
Molina, Gabe, St.L.	1	0	1.000	1.59	12	0	0	0	3	0-0	11.1	6	43	2	2	1	0	0	0	6	0	4	0	0
Moreno, Juan, S.D.*	0	0	.000	7.50	4	0	0	0	1	0-0	6.0	6	34	6	5	1	0	1	0	10	1	3	0	0
Morgan, Mike, Ari.	1	1	.500	5.29	29	0	0	0	9	0-1	34.0	41	156	22	20	7	2	0	3	9	1	13	3	0
Morris, Matt, St.L.	17	9	.654	3.42	32	32	1	1	0	0-0	210.1	210	890	86	80	16	7	8	6	64	3	171	3	0
Moss, Damian, Atl.*	12	6	.667	3.42	33	29	0	0	2	0-0	179.0	140	743	80	68	20	12	3	6	89	5	111	13	2
Mota, Guillermo, L.A.	1	3	.250	4.15	43	0	0	0	11	0-1	60.2	45	256	30	28	4	3	1	2	27	6	49	3	0
Mulholland, Terry, L.A.*	0	0	.000	7.31	21	0	0	0	12	0-0	32.0	45	147	29	26	10	0	2	2	7	0	17	1	0
Munro, Peter, Hou.	5	5	.500	3.57	19	14	0	0	0	0-0	80.2	89	347	37	32	5	7	0	3	23	3	45	2	0
Myers, Brett, Phi.	4	5	.444	4.25	12	12	1	0	0	0-0	72.0	73	307	38	34	11	6	2	6	29	1	34	2	1
Myers, Mike, Ari.*	4	3	.571	4.38	69	0	0	0	15	4-9	37.0	39	171	18	18	2	3	1	8	17	0	31	0	0
Myers, Rodney, S.D.	1	1	.500	5.91	14	0	0	0	4	0-0	21.1	29	101	20	14	1	1	0	3	10	0	11	2	0
Nance, Shane, Mil.*	0	0	.000	4.26	4	0	0	0	0	0-0	6.1	4	27	3	3	1	0	0	0	4	0	5	0	0
Nathan, Joe, S.F.	0	0	.000	0.00	4	0	0	0	3	0-0	3.2	1	12	0	0	0	0	0	0	0	0	2	0	0
Neagle, Denny, Col.*	8	11	.421	5.26	35	28	1	0	0	0-0	164.1	170	724	101	96	26	5	6	10	63	5	111	4	1

Pitcher, Team	W	L	Pct.	ERA	G	GS	CG	ShO	GF	Sv.-Op.	IP	H	TBF	R	ER	HR	SH	SF	HB	BB	IBB	SO	WP	Bk.
Neal, Blaine, Fla.	3	0	1.000	2.73	32	0	0	0	6	0-0	33.0	32	144	12	10	1	1	0	0	14	2	33	4	0
Nen, Robb, S.F.	6	2	.750	2.20	68	0	0	0	66	43-51	73.2	64	301	19	18	2	4	0	1	20	8	81	1	0
Neugebauer, Nick, Mil.	1	7	.125	4.72	12	12	0	0	0	0-0	55.1	56	260	33	29	10	3	1	0	44	3	47	5	2
Nichting, Chris, Col.	1	1	.500	4.46	29	0	0	0	5	0-0	36.1	40	151	18	18	7	1	1	1	5	0	25	1	0
Nickle, Doug, Phi.-S.D.	1	0	1.000	7.88	14	0	0	0	6	0-0	16.0	26	90	16	14	3	0	1	1	13	0	9	0	0
Nomo, Hideo, L.A.	16	6	.727	3.39	34	34	0	0	0	0-0	220.1	189	926	92	83	26	17	4	2	101	5	193	6	0
Nomura, Takahito, Mil.*	0	0	.000	8.56	21	0	0	0	2	0-1	13.2	11	71	14	13	2	0	2	2	18	4	9	2	1
Nunez, Jose Antonio, S.D.*	0	0	.000	0.00	1	0	0	0	1	0-0	1.0	0	4	0	0	0	0	0	0	1	0	0	0	0
Nunez, Vladimir, Fla.	6	5	.545	3.41	77	0	0	0	43	20-28	97.2	80	404	38	37	8	6	4	0	37	1	73	2	0
Ohka, Tomokazu, Mon.	13	8	.619	3.18	32	31	2	0	1	0-0	192.2	194	806	83	68	19	13	6	7	45	7	118	2	1
Olsen, Kevin, Fla.	0	5	.000	4.53	17	8	0	0	3	0-0	55.2	57	250	31	28	5	5	2	1	31	1	38	3	1
Oropesa, Eddie, Ari.*	2	0	1.000	10.30	32	0	0	0	5	0-1	25.1	39	132	30	29	6	2	1	2	15	0	18	1	1
Orosco, Jesse, L.A.*	1	2	.333	3.00	56	0	0	0	8	1-1	27.0	24	119	10	9	4	1	1	0	12	1	22	2	0
Ortiz, Russ, S.F.	14	10	.583	3.61	33	33	2	0	0	0-0	214.1	191	911	89	86	15	15	6	4	94	5	137	5	0
Osborne, Donovan, Chi.*	0	1	.000	6.19	11	0	0	0	1	0-0	16.0	19	77	11	11	1	2	1	0	10	2	13	0	0
Osting, Jimmy, Mil.*	0	2	.000	7.50	3	3	0	0	0	0-0	12.0	18	64	11	10	3	1	0	0	10	0	7	0	0
Oswalt, Roy, Hou.	19	9	.679	3.01	35	34	0	0	0	0-0	233.0	215	956	86	78	17	12	7	5	62	4	208	3	0
Padilla, Vicente, Phi.	14	11	.560	3.28	32	32	1	1	0	0-0	206.0	198	862	83	75	16	10	3	15	53	5	128	6	2
Parra, Jose, Ari.	0	1	.000	3.21	16	0	0	0	3	0-0	14.0	13	63	5	5	0	0	0	1	11	2	8	1	0
Patterson, John, Ari.	2	0	1.000	3.23	7	5	0	0	1	0-0	30.2	27	123	11	11	7	0	0	1	7	0	31	2	0
Pavano, Carl, Mon.-Fla.	6	10	.375	5.16	37	22	0	0	2	0-0	136.0	174	619	88	78	19	4	4	10	45	8	92	3	2
Pearce, Josh, St.L.	0	0	.000	7.62	3	3	0	0	0	0-0	13.0	20	66	13	11	1	3	1	1	8	0	1	0	0
Pearson, Jason, S.D.*	0	0	.000	0.00	2	0	0	0	1	0-0	1.2	1	6	0	0	0	0	0	0	0	0	3	0	0
Peavy, Jake, S.D.	6	7	.462	4.52	17	17	0	0	0	0-0	97.2	106	430	54	49	11	5	2	3	33	4	90	4	1
Pember, Dave, Mil.	0	1	.000	5.19	4	1	0	0	1	0-0	8.2	7	40	6	5	1	1	1	0	6	0	5	1	0
Penny, Brad, Fla.	8	7	.533	4.66	24	24	1	1	0	0-0	129.1	148	574	76	67	18	6	4	1	50	7	93	4	0
Perez, Odalis, L.A.*	15	10	.600	3.00	32	32	4	2	0	0-0	222.1	182	869	76	74	21	13	7	4	38	5	155	2	3
Perez, Oliver, S.D.*	4	5	.444	3.50	16	15	0	0	0	0-0	90.0	71	387	37	35	13	5	3	5	48	1	94	3	0
Perez, Tomas, Phi.	0	0	.000	0.00	1	0	0	0	1	0-0	0.1	0	2	0	0	0	0	0	0	0	0	0	0	0
Person, Robert, Phi.	4	5	.444	5.44	16	16	0	0	0	0-0	87.2	79	388	58	53	13	2	2	5	51	0	61	2	0
Pichardo, Hipolito, Hou.	0	1	.000	81.00	1	0	0	0	0	0-0	0.1	3	6	3	3	0	0	0	0	2	1	0	1	0
Pickford, Kevin, S.D.*	0	2	.000	6.00	16	4	0	0	3	0-0	30.0	37	144	23	20	3	2	1	3	20	1	18	1	0
Pineda, Luis, Cin.	1	3	.250	4.18	26	2	0	0	9	0-0	32.1	25	144	16	15	4	3	2	2	24	1	31	4	0
Plesac, Dan, Phi.*	2	1	.667	4.70	41	0	0	0	5	1-3	23.0	16	96	12	12	5	0	0	0	12	3	27	0	0
Politte, Cliff, Phi.	2	0	1.000	3.86	13	0	0	0	7	0-1	16.1	19	77	10	7	0	1	0	1	9	1	15	1	0
Pratt, Andy, Atl.*	0	0	.000	6.75	1	0	0	0	0	0-0	1.1	1	9	1	1	0	0	0	0	4	0	1	0	0
Prinz, Bret, Ari.	0	2	.000	9.45	20	0	0	0	5	0-2	13.1	23	71	14	14	1	2	1	1	10	1	10	3	0
Prior, Mark, Chi.	6	6	.500	3.32	19	19	1	0	0	0-0	116.2	98	486	45	43	14	3	4	7	38	0	147	1	0
Puffer, Brandon, Hou.	3	3	.500	4.43	55	0	0	0	19	0-0	69.0	67	310	37	34	3	5	2	5	38	8	48	2	0
Quantrill, Paul, L.A.	5	4	.556	2.70	86	0	0	0	22	1-3	76.2	80	330	27	23	1	1	1	3	25	7	53	0	0
Quevedo, Ruben, Mil.	6	11	.353	5.76	26	25	1	1	0	0-0	139.0	159	634	100	89	28	6	3	4	68	3	93	6	0
Reames, Britt, Mon.	1	4	.200	5.03	42	6	0	0	7	0-1	68.0	70	308	42	38	8	3	1	3	38	6	76	2	0
Redding, Tim, Hou.	3	6	.333	5.40	18	14	0	0	1	0-0	73.1	78	325	49	44	10	4	3	0	35	3	63	5	1
Reed, Steve, S.D.-N.Y.	2	5	.286	2.01	64	0	0	0	15	1-0	67.0	56	269	15	15	2	6	0	8	14	3	50	2	0
Reitsma, Chris, Cin.	6	12	.333	3.64	32	21	1	1	6	0-0	138.1	144	598	73	56	17	4	4	5	45	5	84	4	0
Remlinger, Mike, Atl.*	7	3	.700	1.99	73	0	0	0	7	0-5	68.0	48	275	17	15	3	4	0	1	28	3	69	0	0
Reyes, Al, Pit.	0	0	.000	2.65	15	0	0	0	6	0-1	17.0	9	67	5	5	1	1	1	2	7	0	21	1	0
Reyes, Dennys, Col.*	0	1	.000	4.24	43	0	0	0	13	0-0	40.1	43	182	19	19	1	2	2	0	24	3	30	4	0
Reynolds, Shane, Hou.	3	6	.333	4.86	13	13	0	0	0	0-0	74.0	80	322	43	40	13	2	1	1	26	2	47	1	0
Reynoso, Armando, Ari.	0	0	.000	10.80	2	0	0	0	1	0-0	1.2	3	9	2	2	0	0	0	0	1	0	2	1	0
Riedling, John, Cin.	2	4	.333	2.70	33	0	0	0	7	0-0	46.2	39	203	16	14	2	6	1	3	26	6	30	1	0
Rijo, Jose, Cin.	5	4	.556	5.14	31	9	0	0	6	0-0	77.0	89	340	48	44	13	4	0	1	20	1	38	1	0
Roa, Joe, Phi.	4	4	.500	4.04	14	11	0	0	1	0-0	71.1	78	298	33	32	11	1	3	1	13	2	35	0	1
Roberts, Grant, N.Y.	3	1	.750	2.20	34	0	0	0	6	0-0	45.0	43	192	12	11	3	3	2	1	16	7	31	0	0
Robertson, Jeriome, Hou.*	0	2	.000	6.52	11	1	0	0	1	0-0	9.2	13	46	8	7	4	5	3	0	5	3	6	2	0
Robertson, Nate, Fla.*	0	1	.000	11.88	6	1	0	0	1	0-0	8.1	15	46	11	11	3	0	0	2	4	1	3	0	0
Rodriguez, Felix, S.F.	8	6	.571	4.17	71	0	0	0	12	0-6	69.0	53	288	33	32	5	2	3	4	29	1	58	4	0
Rodriguez, Jose, St.L.*	0	0	.000	54.00	2	0	0	0	0	0-0	0.1	4	7	2	2	0	0	0	0	2	0	0	0	0
Rodriguez, Nerio, St.L.	0	0	.000	4.15	2	0	0	0	2	0-0	4.1	4	19	3	2	1	0	0	0	1	0	2	0	0
Rueter, Kirk, S.F.*	14	8	.636	3.23	33	33	0	0	0	0-0	203.2	204	846	83	73	22	6	6	1	54	7	76	3	0
Rusch, Glendon, Mil.*	10	16	.385	4.70	34	34	4	1	0	0-0	210.2	227	913	118	110	30	14	5	5	76	1	140	6	0
Saarloos, Kirk, Hou.	6	7	.462	6.01	17	17	1	1	0	0-0	85.1	100	372	59	57	12	5	2	6	27	5	54	1	0
Sanchez, Duaner, Ari.-Pit.	0	0	.000	9.00	9	0	0	0	5	0-0	6.0	6	31	6	6	2	0	0	0	7	0	6	0	0
Sanchez, Jesus, Chi.*	0	0	.000	12.96	8	0	0	0	2	0-0	8.1	15	51	12	12	4	0	2	1	10	1	6	3	0
Santiago, Jose, Phi.	1	3	.250	6.70	42	0	0	0	7	0-1	47.0	56	214	35	35	7	1	2	3	15	1	30	1	0
Santos, Victor, Col.	0	4	.000	10.38	24	2	0	0	6	0-0	26.0	41	140	30	30	3	3	1	0	22	3	25	2	0
Sauerbeck, Scott, Pit.*	5	4	.556	2.30	78	0	0	0	21	0-0	62.2	50	255	18	16	4	0	0	1	27	4	70	2	1
Schilling, Curt, Ari.	23	7	.767	3.23	36	35	5	1	0	0-0	259.1	218	1017	95	93	29	5	2	3	33	1	316	6	0
Schmidt, Jason, S.F.	13	8	.619	3.45	29	29	2	2	0	0-0	185.1	148	769	78	71	15	11	5	2	73	1	196	12	0
Seo, Jae Weong, N.Y.	0	0	.000	0.00	1	0	0	0	1	0-0	1.0	0	3	0	0	0	0	0	0	0	0	1	0	0
Sheets, Ben, Mil.	11	16	.407	4.15	34	34	1	0	0	0-0	216.2	237	934	105	100	21	10	0	10	70	10	170	9	0
Shiell, Jason, S.D.	0	0	.000	27.00	3	0	0	0	0	0-0	1.1	7	13	4	4	0	0	0	0	3	0	1	0	0
Shuey, Paul, L.A.	5	2	.714	4.40	28	0	0	0	6	1-3	30.2	25	138	18	15	2	0	1	1	21	1	24	1	0
Silva, Carlos, Phi.	5	0	1.000	3.21	68	0	0	0	21	1-5	84.0	88	350	34	30	4	9	3	4	22	6	41	3	0
Silva, Jose, Cin.	1	0	1.000	4.24	12	0	0	0	1	0-0	23.1	25	101	11	11	3	2	1	3	10	3	6	2	0
Simontacchi, Jason, St.L.	11	5	.688	4.02	24	24	0	0	0	0-0	143.1	134	600	68	64	18	6	4	6	54	4	72	1	0
Small, Aaron, Atl.	0	0	.000	27.00	1	0	0	0	1	0-0	0.1	2	5	1	1	0	0	0	0	2	0	1	1	0
Smith, Bud, St.L.*	1	5	.167	6.94	11	10	0	0	1	0-0	48.0	67	229	39	37	4	2	4	3	22	2	22	0	1
Smith, Dan, Mon.	1	1	.500	3.47	33	0	0	0	13	2-2	46.2	34	188	18	18	6	2	2	1	21	0	34	1	0
Smith, Travis, St.L.	4	2	.667	7.17	12	10	0	0	0	0-0	54.0	69	244	44	43	10	7	0	3	20	0	32	2	0
Smoltz, John, Atl.	3	2	.600	3.25	75	0	0	0	68	55-59	80.1	59	314	30	29	4	2	1	0	24	1	85	1	1
Smyth, Steve, Chi.*	1	3	.250	9.35	8	7	0	0	0	0-0	26.0	34	122	28	27	9	1	4	1	10	0	16	2	0
Speier, Justin, Col.	5	1	.833	4.33	63	0	0	0	7	1-4	62.1	51	259	31	30	9	0	1	3	19	4	47	1	2
Spooneybarger, Tim, Atl.	1	0	1.000	2.63	51	0	0	0	14	1-1	51.1	38	214	16	15	4	1	1	2	26	5	33	4	0
Springer, Dennis, L.A.	0	1	.000	6.75	1	0	0	0	1	0-0	1.1	1	7	1	1	0	0	0	0	2	0	1	0	0

Pitcher, Team	W	L	Pct.	ERA	G	GS	CG	ShO	GF	Sv.-Op.	IP	H	TBF	R	ER	HR	SH	SF	HB	BB	IBB	SO	WP	Bk.
Stark, Denny, Col.	11	4	.733	4.00	32	20	0	0	1	0-1	128.1	108	554	69	57	25	2	4	5	64	4	64	2	0
Stechschulte, Gene, St.L.	6	2	.750	4.78	29	0	0	0	5	0-2	32.0	27	138	19	17	4	1	4	1	17	1	21	3	0
Stephenson, Garrett, St.L.	2	5	.286	5.40	12	10	0	0	0	0-0	45.0	48	205	27	27	4	4	1	5	25	0	34	2	0
Stewart, Scott, Mon.*	4	2	.667	3.09	67	0	0	0	28	17-19	64.0	49	264	29	22	4	2	2	1	22	5	67	1	0
Stone, Ricky, Hou.	3	3	.500	3.61	78	0	0	0	16	1-2	77.1	78	335	36	31	9	5	2	1	34	3	63	1	0
Stottlemyre, Todd, Ari.	0	2	.000	7.52	5	4	0	0	1	0-0	20.1	26	92	17	17	4	1	1	0	7	0	12	0	0
Strange, Pat, N.Y.	0	0	.000	1.13	5	0	0	0	4	0-0	8.0	6	30	1	1	0	0	0	0	1	1	4	0	1
Strickland, Scott, Mon.-N.Y.	6	9	.400	3.54	69	0	0	0	21	2-0	68.2	61	299	29	27	7	1	2	2	33	9	69	3	0
Stull, Everett, Mil.	0	1	.000	6.30	2	2	0	0	0	0-0	10.0	15	53	7	7	0	1	0	1	9	2	7	0	0
Sullivan, Scott, Cin.	6	5	.545	6.06	71	0	0	0	16	1-3	78.2	93	357	60	53	15	2	3	5	31	11	78	2	0
Swindell, Greg, Ari.*	0	2	.000	6.27	34	0	0	0	5	0-1	33.0	38	143	23	23	9	0	2	0	5	1	23	0	0
Tankersley, Dennis, S.D.	1	4	.200	8.06	17	9	0	0	3	0-0	51.1	59	245	46	46	10	3	2	6	40	3	39	3	0
Tavarez, Julian, Fla.	10	12	.455	5.39	29	27	0	0	1	0-1	153.2	188	714	100	92	9	13	2	15	74	7	67	7	2
Tejera, Michael, Fla.*	8	8	.500	4.45	47	18	0	0	2	1-3	139.2	144	611	71	69	17	5	4	6	60	3	95	3	0
Teut, Nate, Fla.*	0	1	.000	9.82	2	1	0	0	0	0-0	7.1	13	36	8	8	0	0	0	0	3	1	4	0	0
Thomson, John, Col.-N.Y.	9	14	.391	4.71	30	30	0	0	0	0-0	181.2	201	800	116	95	28	13	10	2	44	9	107	2	0
Timlin, Mike, St.L.-Phi.	4	6	.400	2.98	72	1	0	0	17	0-0	96.2	75	376	35	32	15	2	1	5	14	2	50	3	0
Tollberg, Brian, S.D.	1	5	.167	6.13	12	11	0	0	0	0-0	61.2	88	288	47	42	11	5	6	1	19	2	33	4	0
Tomko, Brett, S.D.	10	10	.500	4.49	32	32	3	0	0	0-0	204.1	212	871	107	102	31	6	8	2	60	9	126	3	0
Torres, Salomon, Pit.	2	1	.667	2.70	5	5	0	0	0	0-0	30.0	28	127	10	9	2	2	0	3	13	1	12	0	0
Trachsel, Steve, N.Y.	11	11	.500	3.37	30	30	1	1	0	0-0	173.2	170	741	80	65	16	9	3	0	69	4	105	4	0
Trujillo, J.J., S.D.	0	1	.000	10.13	4	0	0	0	1	0-0	2.2	4	18	3	3	1	0	0	1	6	0	3	0	0
Tucker, T.J., Mon.	6	3	.667	4.11	57	0	0	0	19	4-7	61.1	69	276	32	28	5	5	5	2	31	9	42	4	0
Vance, Cory, Col.*	0	0	.000	6.75	2	1	0	0	0	0-0	4.0	4	20	3	3	2	0	1	4	0	1	0	0	0
Vazquez, Javier, Mon.	10	13	.435	3.91	34	34	0	0	0	0-0	230.1	243	971	111	100	28	15	7	4	49	6	179	3	0
Veres, Dave, St.L.	5	8	.385	3.48	71	0	0	0	26	4-8	82.2	67	346	34	32	12	3	3	2	39	4	68	7	0
Villafuerte, Brandon, S.D.	1	2	.333	1.41	31	0	0	0	11	1-1	32.0	29	133	5	5	2	1	1	2	12	2	25	0	0
Villone, Ron, Pit.*	4	6	.400	5.81	45	7	0	0	6	0-1	93.0	95	399	63	60	8	5	3	5	34	3	55	1	0
Vizcaino, Luis, Mil.	5	3	.625	2.99	76	0	0	0	30	5-6	81.1	55	326	27	27	6	3	3	3	30	4	79	3	2
Vosberg, Ed, Mon.*	0	0	.000	18.00	4	0	0	0	1	0-0	1.0	3	8	3	2	1	0	0	0	1	0	1	0	0
Wagner, Billy, Hou.*	4	2	.667	2.52	70	0	0	0	61	35-41	75.0	51	289	21	21	7	2	3	2	22	5	88	6	0
Walker, Kevin, S.D.*	0	1	.000	5.63	11	0	0	0	1	0-0	8.0	12	42	6	5	2	1	0	0	5	1	11	1	0
Walker, Pete, N.Y.	0	0	.000	9.00	1	0	0	0	0	0-0	1.0	2	5	1	1	0	0	0	0	0	0	0	0	0
Walker, Tyler, N.Y.	1	0	1.000	5.91	5	1	0	0	3	0-0	10.2	11	49	7	7	3	0	0	0	5	1	7	0	0
Wayne, Justin, Fla.	2	3	.400	5.32	5	5	0	0	0	0-0	23.2	22	105	16	14	3	0	2	0	13	0	16	2	1
Weathers, Dave, N.Y.	6	3	.667	2.91	71	0	0	0	12	0-5	77.1	69	331	30	25	6	6	4	3	36	7	61	2	0
Wells, Kip, Pit.	12	14	.462	3.58	33	33	1	1	0	0-0	198.1	197	845	92	79	21	7	5	7	71	11	134	7	0
White, Gabe, Cin.*	6	1	.857	2.98	62	0	0	0	7	0-1	54.1	49	219	19	18	3	1	0	2	10	2	41	0	0
White, Rick, Col.-St.L.	5	7	.417	4.31	61	0	0	0	10	0-0	62.2	62	264	33	30	4	3	4	1	21	5	41	3	0
Williams, Dave, Pit.*	2	5	.286	4.98	9	9	0	0	0	0-0	43.1	38	195	26	24	9	2	1	4	24	2	33	2	2
Williams, Jeff, L.A.*	0	0	.000	11.70	10	0	0	0	7	0-0	10.0	15	54	13	13	2	1	1	0	11	1	6	1	0
Williams, Mike, Pit.	2	6	.250	2.93	59	0	0	0	59	46-50	61.1	54	258	24	20	6	4	0	1	21	3	43	2	0
Williams, Woody, St.L.	9	4	.692	2.53	17	17	1	0	0	0-0	103.1	84	412	30	29	10	3	1	4	25	2	76	2	0
Williamson, Scott, Cin.	3	4	.429	2.92	63	0	0	0	23	8-12	74.0	46	299	27	24	5	5	2	2	36	5	84	8	1
Witasick, Jay, S.F.	1	0	1.000	2.37	44	0	0	0	9	0-0	68.1	58	276	19	18	3	1	4	1	21	3	54	3	0
Wolf, Randy, Phi.*	11	9	.550	3.20	31	31	3	2	0	0-0	210.2	172	855	77	75	23	7	6	7	63	1	172	4	0
Wood, Kerry, Chi.	12	11	.522	3.66	33	33	4	1	0	0-0	213.2	169	895	92	87	22	13	5	16	97	5	217	8	1
Worrell, Tim, S.F.	8	2	.800	2.25	80	0	0	0	23	0-1	72.0	55	296	21	18	3	4	0	3	30	2	55	0	0
Wright, Jamey, Mil.-St.L.	7	13	.350	5.29	23	22	1	1	0	0-0	129.1	130	585	80	76	17	9	6	11	75	9	77	9	0
Yoshii, Masato, Mon.	4	9	.308	4.11	31	20	1	0	4	0-0	131.1	143	553	66	60	15	4	3	2	32	2	74	5	0
Zambrano, Carlos, Chi.	4	8	.333	3.66	32	16	0	0	3	0-0	108.1	94	477	53	44	9	9	1	4	63	2	93	6	0
Zeile, Todd, Col.	0	0	.000	0.00	1	0	0	0	1	0-0	1.0	1	3	0	0	0	0	0	0	0	0	1	0	0
Zerbe, Chad, S.F.*	2	0	1.000	3.04	50	0	0	0	16	0-1	56.1	52	240	22	19	3	4	1	4	21	2	26	1	0

PITCHERS WITH TWO OR MORE TEAMS

Pitcher, Team	W	L	Pct.	ERA	G	GS	CG	ShO	GF	Sv.-Op.	IP	H	TBF	R	ER	HR	SH	SF	HB	BB	IBB	SO	WP	Bk.
Brower, Jim, Cin.	2	0	1.000	3.89	22	0	0	0	11	0-0	39.1	38	158	18	17	2	1	1	0	10	1	24	0	0
Brower, Jim, Mon.	1	2	.333	4.83	30	0	0	0	12	0-1	41.0	39	186	22	22	5	1	0	4	22	1	33	1	0
Chen, Bruce, N.Y.*	0	0	.000	0.00	1	0	0	0	0	0-0	0.2	1	3	0	0	0	0	0	0	0	0	0	0	0
Chen, Bruce, Mon.*	2	3	.400	6.99	15	5	0	0	4	0-0	37.1	47	179	29	29	9	0	0	1	23	3	43	3	0
Chen, Bruce, Cin.*	0	2	.000	4.31	39	1	0	0	5	0-0	39.2	37	178	24	19	7	2	3	1	20	2	37	1	0
Corey, Mark, N.Y.	0	3	.000	4.50	12	0	0	0	5	0-0	10.0	10	49	7	5	2	0	0	1	8	1	9	1	0
Corey, Mark, Col.	0	0	.000	12.00	14	0	0	0	3	0-0	12.0	22	66	16	16	7	1	0	2	8	1	12	0	0
Dempster, Ryan, Fla.	5	8	.385	4.79	18	18	3	0	0	0-0	120.1	126	521	66	64	12	7	3	7	55	1	87	0	0
Dempster, Ryan, Cin.	5	5	.500	6.19	15	15	1	0	0	0-0	88.2	102	394	61	61	16	2	3	3	38	1	66	2	0
Estes, Shawn, N.Y.*	4	9	.308	4.55	23	23	1	1	0	0-0	132.1	133	580	70	67	12	7	4	5	66	9	92	2	1
Estes, Shawn, Cin.*	1	3	.250	7.71	6	6	0	0	0	0-0	28.0	38	133	24	24	1	0	2	4	17	0	17	1	0
Fassero, Jeff, Chi.*	5	6	.455	6.18	57	0	0	0	17	0-1	51.0	65	240	37	35	5	6	1	3	22	5	44	2	1
Fassero, Jeff, St.L.*	3	0	1.000	3.00	16	0	0	0	1	0-2	18.0	16	75	6	6	4	1	0	0	5	0	12	0	0
Fetters, Mike, Pit.	1	0	1.000	3.26	32	0	0	0	13	0-1	30.1	25	134	13	11	3	0	1	1	18	1	29	2	0
Fetters, Mike, Ari.	2	3	.400	5.11	33	0	0	0	9	0-1	24.2	28	118	18	14	1	0	1	2	19	5	24	6	0
Gordon, Flash, Chi.	1	1	.500	3.42	19	0	0	0	9	0-1	23.2	27	104	12	9	1	1	1	0	11	1	31	0	0
Gordon, Flash, Hou.	0	2	.000	3.32	15	0	0	0	3	0-0	19.0	15	77	7	7	2	2	0	0	6	2	17	0	0
Jones, Bobby M., N.Y.*	0	0	.000	5.29	12	0	0	0	1	0-0	17.0	20	81	11	10	3	2	0	1	11	2	11	0	0
Jones, Bobby M., S.D.*	0	0	.000	6.52	4	2	0	0	0	0-0	9.2	10	45	7	7	1	0	1	0	7	0	7	0	0
Lloyd, Graeme, Mon.*	2	3	.400	5.87	41	0	0	0	14	5-7	30.2	41	138	21	20	5	2	1	1	8	3	17	1	0
Lloyd, Graeme, Fla.*	2	2	.500	4.44	25	0	0	0	6	0-1	26.1	26	115	13	13	1	2	1	1	11	1	20	1	0
Lowe, Sean, Pit.	4	2	.667	5.35	43	1	0	0	8	0-2	69.0	85	326	45	41	8	5	3	7	34	6	57	1	1
Lowe, Sean, Col.	1	1	.500	8.71	8	0	0	0	0	0-0	10.1	16	53	13	10	1	0	0	0	7	0	7	0	0
Matthews, Mike, St.L.*	2	1	.667	3.89	43	0	0	0	10	0-2	41.2	40	184	21	18	5	2	2	2	22	2	32	0	0
Matthews, Mike, Mil.*	0	0	.000	4.50	4	0	0	0	1	0-0	4.0	3	21	2	2	0	0	0	0	7	1	2	0	1
Middlebrook, Jason, S.D.	1	3	.250	5.09	12	2	0	0	5	0-0	35.1	31	149	20	20	1	3	3	1	15	2	28	2	0
Middlebrook, Jason, N.Y.	1	0	1.000	3.94	3	3	0	0	0	0-0	16.0	13	67	7	7	1	1	0	0	7	0	14	0	1

Pitcher, Team	W	L	Pct.	ERA	G	GS	CG	ShO	GF	Sv.-Op.	IP	H	TBF	R	ER	HR	SH	SF	HB	BB	IBB	SO	WP	Bk.
Nickle, Doug, Phi.	0	0	.000	6.23	4	0	0	0	4	0-0	4.1	6	23	3	3	2	0	0	0	4	0	2	0	0
Nickle, Doug, S.D.	1	0	1.000	8.49	10	0	0	0	0	0-0	11.2	20	67	13	11	1	0	1	1	9	0	7	0	0
Pavano, Carl, Mon.	3	8	.273	6.30	15	14	0	0	0	0-0	74.1	98	350	55	52	14	2	2	7	31	5	51	2	1
Pavano, Carl, Fla.	3	2	.600	3.79	22	8	0	0	2	0-0	61.2	76	269	33	26	5	2	2	3	14	3	41	1	1
Reed, Steve, S.D.	2	4	.333	1.98	40	0	0	0	11	1-3	41.0	33	166	9	9	2	5	0	6	10	2	36	1	0
Reed, Steve, N.Y.	0	1	.000	2.08	24	0	0	0	4	0-1	26.0	23	103	6	6	0	1	0	2	4	1	14	1	0
Sanchez, Duaner, Ari.	0	0	.000	4.91	6	0	0	0	3	0-1	3.2	3	19	2	2	1	0	0	0	5	0	4	0	0
Sanchez, Duaner, Pit.	0	0	.000	15.43	3	0	0	0	2	0-0	2.1	3	12	4	4	1	0	0	0	2	0	2	0	0
Strickland, Scott, Mon.	0	0	.000	0.00	1	0	0	0	0	0-0	1.0	0	3	0	0	0	0	0	0	0	0	2	0	0
Strickland, Scott, N.Y.	6	9	.400	3.59	68	0	0	0	21	2-6	67.2	61	296	29	27	7	1	2	2	33	9	67	3	0
Thomson, John, Col.	7	8	.467	4.88	21	21	0	0	0	0-0	127.1	136	550	77	69	21	7	7	2	27	6	76	2	0
Thomson, John, N.Y.	2	6	.250	4.31	9	9	0	0	0	0-0	54.1	65	250	39	26	7	6	3	0	17	3	31	0	0
Timlin, Mike, St.L.	1	3	.250	2.51	42	1	0	0	10	0-2	61.0	48	236	19	17	9	2	0	4	7	2	35	1	0
Timlin, Mike, Phi.	3	3	.500	3.79	30	0	0	0	7	0-2	35.2	27	140	16	15	6	0	1	1	7	0	15	2	0
White, Rick, Col.	2	6	.250	6.20	41	0	0	0	8	0-1	40.2	49	182	30	28	4	1	4	1	18	4	27	3	0
White, Rick, St.L.	3	1	.750	0.82	20	0	0	0	2	0-0	22.0	13	82	3	2	0	0	0	3	1	14	0	0
Wright, Jamey, Mil.	5	13	.278	5.35	19	19	1	1	0	0-0	114.1	115	515	72	68	15	9	6	11	63	8	69	8	0
Wright, Jamey, St.L.	2	0	1.000	4.80	4	3	0	0	0	0-0	15.0	15	70	8	8	2	0	0	0	12	1	8	1	0

NOTE—The following pitchers combined to pitch shutout games: **Arizona (5)**—Schilling, Myers and Kim; Schilling, Morgan and Myers; Helling and Kim; Patterson, Myers and Mantei; Johnson, Swindell and Fetters; **Atlanta (13)**—Maddux, Remlinger, Spooneybarger, Ligtenberg and Smoltz; Glavine, Holmes and Spooneybarger; Maddux, Gryboski, Ligtenberg and Hammond; Glavine, Holmes and Lopez; Maddux, Hammond and Smoltz; Millwood, Remlinger and Smoltz; Maddux, Gryboski and Lopez; Moss and Lopez; Maddux, Hammond, Remlinger and Smoltz; Glavine, Spooneybarger and Smoltz; Moss, Hammond and Remlinger; Maddux, Spooneybarger, Hammond, Holmes, Remlinger and Smoltz; Glavine, Hammond, Gryboski and Remlinger; **Chicago (6)**—Lieber and Alfonseca; Clement, Mahay, Borowski, Fassero and Alfonseca; Prior, Farnsworth and Alfonseca; Prior and Farnsworth; Zambrano and Alfonseca; Zambrano, Mahomes and Alfonseca; **Cincinnati (7)**—Hamilton, White and Sullivan; Rijo, Brower, Sullivan and Pineda; Dempster, Chen and Hamilton; Haynes and Williamson; Graves, Reitsma, Sullivan, Riedling and Williamson; Haynes, Riedling and Williamson; Graves, Hamilton and Williamson; **Colorado (8)**—Hampton, White and James; Neagle and Jimenez; Chacon, Nichting, Mercker, White and Reyes; Stark, Speier and Jones; Jennings, Speier and Jimenez; Neagle, Jones and Jimenez; Jennings, Speier, Jones and Jimenez; Stark, Jones and Jimenez; **Florida (6)**—Izquierdo, Tejera, Looper and Nunez; Beckett, Izquierdo, Tejera, Almanza, Mairena and Nunez; Penny, Pavano, Almanza and Looper; Beckett, Lloyd and Nunez; Penny and Lloyd; Dempster, Looper and Nunez; **Houston (9)**—Mlicki and Wagner; Miller, Dotel and Wagner; Oswalt and Wagner; Miller, Munro, Borbon, Stone and Dotel; Mlicki, Puffer, Borbon, Stone, Dotel and Wagner; Saarloos and Borbon; Hernandez, Stone and Dotel; Munro, Borbon, Gordon and Dotel; Miller, Gordon, Wagner and Dotel; **Los Angeles (13)**—Ashby and Daal; Nomo, Orosco and Gagne; Ishii, Carrara and Gagne; Brown, Quantrill and Gagne; Nomo, Daal, Quantrill and Gagne; Nomo, Quantrill and Gagne; Daal, Carrara and Mota; Ashby, Orosco, Quantrill and Gagne; Daal, Quantrill, Orosco and Gagne; Perez and Gagne; Daal, Shuey, Orosco and Quantrill; Daal and Gagne; **Milwaukee (1)**—Wright, Vizcaino and DeJean; **Montreal (2)**—Colon, Eischen and Smith; Kim and Stewart; **New York (4)**—Trachsel, Strickland and Benitez; D'Amico, Guthrie and Strickland; Estes, Strickland and Guthrie; Estes and Bacsik; **Philadelphia (6)**—Padilla and Mesa; Duckworth, Plesac and Mesa; Roa, Timlin and Silva; Wolf and Silva; Wolf and Mesa; Padilla, Plesac, Timlin and Mesa; **Pittsburgh (6)**—Villone, Fetters and M. Williams; Meadows, Lincoln, Sauerbeck and Boehringer; Benson, Boehringer and Reyes; Meadows, Sauerbeck and M. Williams; Torres and M. Williams; Benson, Lincoln, Sauerbeck, Reyes and Boehringer; **St. Louis (7)**—Crudale, Matthews, Hackman and Stechschulte; Morris, Veres and Kline; Morris and Veres; Benes, Crudale and Duff; Finley, Kline and Joseph; Williams, White, Crudale, Veres and Kline; Benes, Veres, Crudale and White; **San Diego (8)**—Lawrence, Fikac, Embree and Hoffman; Tomko, Fikac, Embree and Reed; Jarvis, Reed, Fikac and Hoffman; Lawrence and Hoffman; B. Jones and Villafuerte; Tomko and Hoffman; Condrey, Villafuerte and Hoffman; Perez, Condrey and Villafuerte; **San Francisco (8)**—Ortiz, Christiansen and Worrell; Jensen, Rodriguez and Nen; Jensen and Nen; Schmidt and Nen; Rueter, Witasick, Eyre and Nen; Rueter, Fultz and Rodriguez; Schmidt, Jensen, Rodriguez and Nen; Jensen, Zerbe, Witasick, Ainsworth, Nathan and Aybar.

PITCHERS VS. LEFTHANDED AND RIGHTHANDED BATTERS

Pitcher	vs.	Avg.	AB	H	2B	3B	HR	RBI	BB	SO	OBP	Slg.
Acevedo, Jose	L	.348	46	16	3	1	4	10	8	7	.455	.717
Throws Right	R	.240	50	12	1	0	4	10	4	7	.309	.500
Adams, Terry	L	.246	232	57	7	1	5	30	35	45	.345	.349
Throws Right	R	.263	285	75	13	2	4	33	23	51	.323	.365
Ainsworth, Kurt	L	.236	55	13	3	0	1	5	10	10	.364	.345
Throws Right	R	.237	38	9	0	1	0	2	2	5	.275	.289
Alfonseca, Antonio	L	.304	125	38	5	2	3	24	13	17	.362	.448
Throws Right	R	.220	159	35	7	0	2	18	23	44	.330	.302
Almanza, Armando	L	.255	55	14	4	1	0	5	15	20	.408	.364
Throws Left	R	.208	106	22	2	1	8	19	8	37	.259	.472
Almanzar, Carlos	L	.154	13	2	0	0	0	1	0	3	.154	.154
Throws Right	R	.160	25	4	1	0	0	2	5	4	.281	.200
Alvarez, Victor	L	.118	17	2	0	0	0	1	0	6	.118	.118
Throws Left	R	.333	21	7	0	0	1	3	2	1	.391	.476
Anderson, Brian	L	.302	159	48	14	0	6	18	11	23	.343	.503
Throws Left	R	.278	453	126	27	1	17	59	21	58	.308	.455
Anderson, Jimmy	L	.273	128	35	3	0	7	15	11	20	.340	.461
Throws Left	R	.306	431	132	31	2	13	70	52	27	.382	.478
Armas Jr., Tony	L	.308	273	84	19	4	10	37	47	42	.412	.516
Throws Right	R	.192	359	69	13	3	12	40	31	89	.269	.354
Arroyo, Bronson	L	.294	34	10	2	0	0	3	6	3	.390	.353
Throws Right	R	.278	72	20	6	0	1	10	9	19	.358	.403
Ashby, Andy	L	.285	372	106	21	3	7	33	45	47	.363	.414
Throws Right	R	.233	313	73	14	0	13	45	20	60	.289	.403
Astacio, Pedro	L	.239	339	81	14	1	15	45	40	85	.324	.419
Throws Right	R	.281	395	111	17	1	17	52	23	67	.336	.458
Aybar, Manny	L	.429	14	6	1	0	0	2	3	2	.529	.500
Throws Right	R	.222	45	10	3	0	1	3	0	9	.239	.356
Bacsik, Mike	L	.216	37	8	3	1	1	4	5	6	.341	.432
Throws Left	R	.304	181	55	11	1	7	19	14	24	.359	.492
Batista, Miguel	L	.269	334	90	18	4	7	43	39	47	.347	.410
Throws Right	R	.223	367	82	18	2	5	41	31	65	.287	.324
Beckett, Josh	L	.246	195	48	7	4	9	27	29	51	.347	.462
Throws Right	R	.218	206	45	7	1	4	25	15	62	.268	.320
Beimel, Joe	L	.262	103	27	5	1	3	22	9	18	.328	.417
Throws Left	R	.269	227	61	17	0	6	32	36	35	.372	.423
Beirne, Kevin	L	.208	48	10	3	0	1	4	10	9	.356	.333
Throws Right	R	.276	58	16	2	1	3	7	7	8	.358	.500
Beltran, Francis	L	.286	14	4	2	0	0	0	9	3	.565	.429
Throws Right	R	.323	31	10	0	0	2	7	7	8	.436	.516
Benes, Alan	L	.239	67	16	4	0	1	7	6	16	.297	.343
Throws Right	R	.306	85	26	3	0	2	10	6	16	.348	.412
Benes, Andy	L	.250	156	39	7	1	3	14	27	27	.360	.365
Throws Right	R	.210	195	41	9	0	7	18	24	37	.305	.364
Benitez, Armando	L	.160	119	19	3	0	6	12	19	41	.277	.336
Throws Right	R	.220	123	27	7	0	2	10	6	38	.267	.325
Benson, Kris	L	.313	230	72	18	2	10	40	31	27	.394	.539
Throws Right	R	.281	285	80	18	1	8	32	19	52	.329	.435
Bere, Jason	L	.326	141	46	9	3	5	22	13	20	.392	.539
Throws Right	R	.264	197	52	14	1	8	33	15	45	.307	.467
Boehringer, Brian	L	.250	96	24	5	0	1	10	15	19	.348	.333
Throws Right	R	.218	188	41	7	1	4	23	18	46	.290	.330
Bong, Jung	L	.182	11	2	1	0	0	2	1	2	.250	.273
Throws Left	R	.429	14	6	4	0	0	3	1	2	.467	.714
Borbon, Pedro	L	.250	92	23	7	0	2	16	7	29	.294	.391
Throws Left	R	.353	51	18	5	0	5	13	12	10	.478	.745
Borland, Toby	L	.304	23	7	1	0	2	5	2	5	.360	.609
Throws Right	R	.241	29	7	1	0	1	6	3	6	.351	.379
Borowski, Joe	L	.209	148	31	7	1	4	11	12	51	.273	.351
Throws Right	R	.260	204	53	10	1	6	31	17	46	.313	.407
Bottalico, Ricky	L	.311	45	14	2	0	1	6	9	8	.429	.422
Throws Right	R	.292	65	19	5	2	2	16	4	16	.343	.523
Boyd, Jason	L	.235	51	12	2	0	3	12	7	11	.317	.451
Throws Right	R	.356	59	21	6	1	3	17	8	7	.426	.644
Brohawn, Troy	L	.250	12	3	1	0	0	0	0	2	.308	.333
Throws Left	R	.200	54	7	2	0	0	1	1	6	.333	.500
Brower, Jim	L	.254	126	32	9	0	2	14	17	21	.347	.373
Throws Right	R	.251	179	45	8	1	5	24	15	36	.318	.391

Pitcher	vs.	Avg.	AB	H	2B	3B	HR	RBI	BB	SO	OBP	Slg.
Brown, Kevin	L	.245	106	26	3	0	4	16	12	23	.322	.387
Throws Right	R	.296	142	42	5	2	5	14	11	35	.367	.465
Buddie, Mike	L	.319	72	23	5	0	4	10	11	9	.410	.556
Throws Right	R	.271	85	23	6	0	1	12	10	19	.351	.376
Burnett, A.J.	L	.242	359	87	19	3	5	34	46	100	.335	.354
Throws Right	R	.177	373	66	12	0	7	44	44	103	.270	.265
Bynum, Mike	L	.375	24	9	0	0	2	8	2	5	.444	.625
Throws Left	R	.289	83	24	4	2	1	19	13	12	.390	.422
Cabrera, Jose	L	.276	181	50	12	2	13	32	22	26	.365	.580
Throws Right	R	.343	236	81	19	2	10	53	14	35	.388	.568
Carrara, Giovanni	L	.248	137	34	10	0	6	23	11	17	.311	.453
Throws Right	R	.240	204	49	9	1	8	26	21	39	.322	.412
Cerda, Jaime	L	.268	41	11	2	1	0	9	9	9	.385	.366
Throws Left	R	.204	54	11	1	0	0	4	5	12	.279	.222
Chacon, Shawn	L	.319	204	65	9	3	14	36	29	29	.409	.598
Throws Right	R	.220	259	57	17	1	11	37	31	38	.313	.421
Chen, Bruce	L	.252	115	29	5	0	2	17	17	35	.343	.348
Throws Left	R	.287	195	56	15	0	14	35	26	45	.375	.579
Chiasson, Scott	L	.500	10	5	2	0	1	6	3	2	.615	1.000
Throws Right	R	.400	15	6	2	0	1	5	3	1	.500	.733
Childers, Matt	L	.533	15	8	3	1	1	11	6	1	.667	1.067
Throws Right	R	.217	23	5	1	0	1	5	2	5	.308	.391
Christiansen, Jason	L	.143	7	1	0	0	0	0	2	1	.333	.143
Throws Left	R	.417	12	5	2	0	1	2	0	0	.417	.833
Clement, Matt	L	.220	341	75	16	2	7	34	53	81	.322	.340
Throws Right	R	.212	411	87	23	0	11	40	32	134	.278	.348
Coggin, Dave	L	.287	122	35	7	4	2	21	23	18	.400	.459
Throws Right	R	.189	159	30	5	0	2	21	28	46	.321	.258
Colon, Bartolo	L	.242	186	45	8	2	6	16	16	36	.302	.403
Throws Right	R	.271	258	70	18	1	3	27	23	38	.327	.384
Condrey, Clay	L	.250	44	11	2	0	0	2	6	4	.333	.295
Throws Right	R	.188	48	9	2	0	1	4	2	12	.245	.292
Cook, Aaron	L	.295	61	18	2	1	0	5	6	2	.368	.361
Throws Right	R	.295	78	23	3	0	4	13	7	12	.360	.487
Corey, Bryan	L	.000	2	0	0	0	0	0	0	0	.000	.000
Throws Right	R	.000	1	0	0	0	0	0	0	0	.000	.000
Corey, Mark	L	.342	38	13	1	0	3	12	4	8	.432	.605
Throws Right	R	.333	57	19	3	0	6	10	12	13	.457	.702
Cormier, Rheal	L	.291	79	23	3	2	1	16	11	20	.387	.418
Throws Left	R	.253	150	38	8	1	5	20	21	29	.351	.420
Crudale, Mike	L	.247	73	18	5	0	1	7	6	15	.304	.356
Throws Right	R	.216	116	25	7	0	2	18	8	32	.260	.328
Cruz, Juan	L	.250	148	37	4	1	3	22	31	37	.388	.351
Throws Right	R	.234	201	47	5	1	8	28	28	44	.331	.388
Cruz, Nelson	L	.299	147	44	11	2	5	29	13	26	.362	.503
Throws Right	R	.272	169	46	14	1	7	31	16	35	.346	.491
Cunnane, Will	L	.395	38	15	1	0	4	7	7	8	.500	.737
Throws Right	R	.194	62	12	3	0	1	9	6	22	.265	.290
Cyr, Eric	L	.273	11	3	1	0	0	2	3	3	.400	.364
Throws Left	R	.300	10	3	0	0	0	2	3	1	.462	.300
Daal, Omar	L	.243	148	36	5	0	6	18	15	33	.315	.399
Throws Left	R	.237	447	106	23	1	14	51	39	72	.301	.387
D'Amico, Jeff	L	.249	269	67	15	3	5	30	28	44	.322	.383
Throws Right	R	.283	300	85	19	3	15	46	9	57	.304	.517
Darensbourg, Vic	L	.254	67	17	3	0	3	11	8	15	.351	.433
Throws Left	R	.331	133	44	5	4	7	26	18	18	.403	.586
Davey, Tom	L	.281	32	9	2	0	2	8	6	10	.410	.531
Throws Right	R	.292	48	14	3	0	0	11	5	11	.362	.354
Davis, Kane	L	.348	23	8	3	0	2	10	6	7	.467	.739
Throws Right	R	.219	32	7	2	0	0	3	5	17	.342	.281
Dawley, Joey	L	.000	1	0	0	0	0	0	0	1	.000	.000
Throws Right	R	.000	0	0	0	0	0	0	0	0	.000	.000
Day, Zach	L	.158	57	9	3	1	0	4	9	7	.284	.246
Throws Right	R	.244	78	19	5	0	3	12	6	18	.294	.423
DeJean, Mike	L	.259	143	37	5	1	2	14	21	39	.352	.350
Throws Right	R	.213	136	29	5	1	5	14	18	26	.312	.375
de los Santos, V.	L	.219	64	14	1	0	1	10	8	14	.316	.281
Throws Left	R	.207	135	28	11	0	3	12	18	24	.291	.356
Dempster, Ryan	L	.332	358	119	24	6	14	56	68	57	.444	.550
Throws Right	R	.248	439	109	18	5	14	59	25	96	.293	.408
Dessens, Elmer	L	.244	315	77	14	1	7	30	19	30	.302	.362
Throws Right	R	.268	358	96	19	0	17	38	30	54	.324	.464
DeWitt, Matt	L	.300	10	3	0	0	1	3	2	0	.385	.600
Throws Right	R	.188	16	3	0	0	0	1	1	5	.235	.188

Pitcher	vs.	Avg.	AB	H	2B	3B	HR	RBI	BB	SO	OBP	Slg.
Diggins, Ben	L	.316	38	12	1	0	2	9	11	4	.451	.500
Throws Right	R	.286	56	16	4	0	2	8	7	11	.375	.464
Dotel, Octavio	L	.190	153	29	7	0	2	10	20	48	.292	.275
Throws Right	R	.159	182	29	4	1	5	18	7	70	.190	.275
Drew, Tim	L	.273	22	6	1	0	0	2	1	4	.304	.318
Throws Right	R	.158	38	6	0	0	1	2	1	6	.175	.237
Duckworth, B.	L	.248	298	74	22	0	10	38	36	80	.334	.423
Throws Right	R	.273	341	93	21	4	16	57	33	87	.342	.499
Duff, Matt	L	.000	5	0	0	0	0	0	5	0	.500	.000
Throws Right	R	.200	15	3	0	0	0	1	3	4	.333	.200
Duncan, Courtney	L	.333	3	1	0	0	0	2	0	0	.333	.333
Throws Right	R	.167	6	1	0	0	0	0	1	1	.286	.167
Durocher, Jayson	L	.187	75	14	3	1	1	2	15	25	.319	.293
Throws Right	R	.144	90	13	3	1	2	12	6	19	.214	.267
Eaton, Adam	L	.333	51	17	3	1	4	11	12	9	.462	.667
Throws Right	R	.162	68	11	4	1	1	7	5	16	.227	.294
Eischen, Joey	L	.173	81	14	3	0	1	8	6	27	.247	.247
Throws Left	R	.261	111	29	5	0	0	12	12	24	.328	.306
Ellis, Robert	L	.333	3	1	0	0	0	1	0	0	.333	.333
Throws Right	R	.500	10	5	0	1	1	2	0	0	.500	1.000
Embree, Alan	L	.145	55	8	1	1	2	9	4	22	.203	.309
Throws Left	R	.278	54	15	4	0	0	2	5	16	.339	.352
Ennis, John	L	.375	8	3	2	0	0	0	1	1	.444	.625
Throws Left	R	.400	5	2	1	0	0	2	2	0	.500	.600
Estes, Shawn	L	.300	130	39	8	1	2	19	15	32	.409	.423
Throws Left	R	.276	478	132	28	4	11	67	68	77	.362	.421
Eyre, Scott	L	.296	27	8	2	0	0	4	6	5	.424	.370
Throws Left	R	.188	16	3	0	0	0	1	1	2	.235	.188
Farnsworth, Kyle	L	.392	79	31	7	3	5	31	11	19	.457	.747
Throws Right	R	.216	102	22	4	2	4	18	13	27	.303	.412
Fassero, Jeff	L	.318	110	35	3	1	1	14	11	22	.390	.391
Throws Left	R	.275	167	46	8	1	8	26	16	34	.341	.479
Feliciano, Pedro	L	.444	9	4	1	0	0	2	0	1	.444	.556
Throws Left	R	.313	16	5	2	0	0	3	1	3	.353	.438
Fernandez, Jared	L	.191	68	13	2	0	1	7	11	16	.309	.265
Throws Right	R	.346	133	46	12	1	4	22	13	20	.409	.541
Fetters, Mike	L	.306	62	19	5	0	1	8	18	10	.451	.435
Throws Right	R	.230	148	34	3	0	3	23	19	43	.329	.311
Figueroa, Nelson	L	.273	154	42	5	1	12	27	21	23	.362	.552
Throws Right	R	.269	201	54	16	0	6	30	16	28	.326	.438
Fikac, Jeremy	L	.274	117	32	10	2	3	19	21	23	.388	.470
Throws Right	R	.263	160	42	9	2	10	33	13	43	.322	.531
Finley, Chuck	L	.104	48	5	2	0	1	6	9	16	.246	.208
Throws Left	R	.240	267	64	14	2	6	27	21	67	.297	.375
Flores, Randy	L	.292	24	7	1	0	1	3	2	1	.346	.458
Throws Left	R	.423	52	22	6	2	4	16	6	6	.508	.846
Fogg, Josh	L	.293	358	105	16	6	16	45	36	42	.361	.506
Throws Right	R	.242	388	94	18	2	12	48	33	71	.309	.392
Foster, John	L	.286	7	2	0	0	1	1	3	4	.500	.714
Throws Left	R	.286	14	4	0	0	2	5	3	2	.444	.714
Fox, Chad	L	.182	11	2	1	0	0	2	1	2	.250	.273
Throws Right	R	.500	8	4	1	0	0	1	4	1	.667	.625
Franklin, Wayne	L	.000	4	0	0	0	0	0	0	0	.000	.000
Throws Left	R	.198	81	16	2	0	1	4	17	17	.337	.259
Fuentes, Brian	L	.381	42	16	3	0	3	10	5	13	.480	.667
Throws Left	R	.155	58	9	1	0	1	7	8	25	.250	.224
Fultz, Aaron	L	.302	86	26	5	2	1	15	8	14	.368	.442
Throws Left	R	.284	74	21	1	1	3	12	11	17	.386	.446
Gagne, Eric	L	.213	150	32	7	2	2	12	11	52	.268	.327
Throws Right	R	.163	141	23	4	0	4	7	5	62	.197	.277
Glavine, Tom	L	.244	164	40	11	0	6	21	17	18	.319	.421
Throws Left	R	.254	668	170	38	2	15	50	61	109	.321	.385
Gordon, Flash	L	.269	67	18	2	2	2	11	11	20	.372	.448
Throws Right	R	.255	94	24	7	0	1	8	5	28	.300	.362
Graves, Danny	L	.272	151	41	7	1	3	22	13	29	.327	.391
Throws Right	R	.259	224	58	6	1	4	34	12	29	.299	.348
Gryboski, Kevin	L	.169	71	12	0	1	1	3	21	9	.359	.239
Throws Right	R	.306	124	38	5	0	5	25	16	24	.407	.468
Guthrie, Mark	L	.187	75	14	0	0	2	6	10	25	.287	.267
Throws Left	R	.223	94	21	4	0	1	6	9	19	.291	.298
Hackman, Luther	L	.298	124	37	8	1	3	21	14	11	.371	.452
Throws Right	R	.279	190	53	13	1	4	24	25	35	.363	.421
Hamilton, Joey	L	.303	228	69	11	3	8	37	21	40	.373	.482
Throws Right	R	.258	260	67	15	2	3	35	29	45	.332	.365

Pitcher	vs.	Avg.	AB	H	2B	3B	HR	RBI	BB	SO	OBP	Slg.
Hammond, Chris	L	.174	92	16	0	1	1	8	6	26	.232	.228
Throws Left	R	.206	180	37	11	1	0	11	25	37	.300	.278
Hampton, Mike	L	.376	170	64	7	0	10	38	19	22	.442	.594
Throws Left	R	.293	559	164	32	2	14	85	72	52	.374	.433
Haynes, Jimmy	L	.280	328	92	14	1	10	46	44	55	.365	.421
Throws Right	R	.276	427	118	21	2	11	36	37	71	.334	.412
Helling, Rick	L	.283	315	89	20	3	14	43	32	63	.348	.498
Throws Right	R	.249	366	91	15	3	17	45	16	57	.288	.445
Herges, Matt	L	.315	92	29	7	0	3	13	13	17	.400	.489
Throws Right	R	.300	170	51	5	1	7	26	13	33	.353	.465
Hernandez, Carlos	L	.262	84	22	5	0	2	10	16	15	.380	.393
Throws Left	R	.261	345	90	24	2	9	33	45	78	.351	.420
Hernandez, Livan	L	.297	370	110	26	4	8	46	37	59	.362	.454
Throws Right	R	.271	454	123	14	3	11	55	34	75	.321	.388
Hodges, Trey	L	.273	11	3	0	0	0	1	2	1	.385	.273
Throws Right	R	.371	35	13	0	0	2	7	0	5	.368	.543
Hoffman, Trevor	L	.186	102	19	4	1	2	7	13	35	.278	.304
Throws Right	R	.275	120	33	4	1	0	12	5	34	.305	.325
Holmes, Darren	L	.230	74	17	3	2	1	6	8	15	.313	.365
Throws Right	R	.198	121	24	2	0	2	6	4	32	.228	.264
Holtz, Mike	L	.302	43	13	4	1	2	11	7	11	.389	.581
Throws Left	R	.152	33	5	1	0	0	1	14	8	.404	.182
Howard, Ben	L	.333	15	5	3	0	2	6	10	4	.577	.933
Throws Right	R	.286	28	8	1	0	2	5	4	6	.375	.536
Hudson, Luke	L	.222	9	2	0	0	0	0	3	3	.417	.222
Throws Right	R	.231	13	3	0	0	1	2	3	4	.375	.462
Ishii, Kazuhisa	L	.223	130	29	2	0	3	12	12	47	.290	.308
Throws Left	R	.245	441	108	20	0	17	61	94	96	.379	.406
Isringhausen, J.	L	.247	97	24	3	0	0	11	12	25	.333	.278
Throws Right	R	.164	134	22	7	0	0	7	6	43	.197	.216
Izquierdo, Hansel	L	.356	45	16	7	1	1	9	14	6	.492	.622
Throws Right	R	.246	69	17	4	0	1	7	7	14	.354	.348
James, Mike	L	.158	19	3	0	0	1	3	1	6	.238	.316
Throws Right	R	.346	26	9	3	1	1	6	4	4	.433	.654
Jarvis, Kevin	L	.218	55	12	3	2	3	6	4	13	.279	.509
Throws Right	R	.304	79	24	8	0	2	11	6	11	.353	.481
Jennings, Jason	L	.299	298	89	19	2	8	40	34	32	.373	.456
Throws Right	R	.267	420	112	14	0	18	52	36	95	.332	.429
Jensen, Ryan	L	.288	306	88	16	2	12	47	43	46	.371	.471
Throws Right	R	.270	352	95	20	3	9	41	23	59	.320	.420
Jimenez, Jose	L	.266	139	37	3	2	4	16	7	18	.299	.403
Throws Right	R	.264	148	39	9	0	3	19	4	29	.295	.385
Johnson, Jonathan	L	.261	23	6	0	0	1	1	0	6	.261	.391
Throws Right	R	.243	37	9	3	1	1	6	5	15	.349	.459
Johnson, Randy	L	.221	140	31	6	2	5	11	11	47	.310	.400
Throws Left	R	.206	805	166	36	3	21	62	60	287	.266	.337
Jones, Bobby J.	L	.276	214	59	6	2	12	29	15	28	.323	.505
Throws Right	R	.322	233	75	20	3	8	35	6	32	.339	.536
Jones, Bobby M.	L	.333	36	12	4	0	0	4	5	7	.415	.444
Throws Left	R	.265	68	18	6	0	4	14	13	11	.386	.529
Jones, Todd	L	.233	146	34	7	0	2	14	12	38	.289	.322
Throws Right	R	.301	166	50	10	2	8	34	16	35	.369	.530
Joseph, Kevin	L	.600	10	6	0	0	1	1	0		.636	.900
Throws Right	R	.294	34	10	1	0	0	6	5	2	.415	.324
Junge, Eric	L	.167	12	2	0	0	0	0	3	4	.333	.167
Throws Right	R	.324	37	12	4	0	0	2	2	7	.359	.432
Kershner, Jason	L	.222	27	6	2	0	1	4	3	6	.344	.407
Throws Left	R	.214	42	9	2	0	1	6	7	5	.327	.333
Kile, Darryl	L	.246	126	31	5	0	4	14	10	19	.301	.381
Throws Right	R	.264	193	51	14	1	5	20	18	31	.347	.425
Kim, Byung-Hyun	L	.220	141	31	3	0	3	12	16	46	.317	.305
Throws Right	R	.198	167	33	3	0	2	14	10	46	.249	.251
Kim, Sun-Woo	L	.242	33	8	3	0	0	0	2	5	.286	.333
Throws Right	R	.256	39	10	2	0	1	5	6	6	.356	.308
King, Ray	L	.219	96	21	2	0	2	10	8	17	.296	.302
Throws Left	R	.280	143	40	6	1	3	16	16	33	.350	.399
Kline, Steve	L	.230	87	20	4	1	1	7	11	20	.313	.333
Throws Left	R	.266	128	34	6	0	2	13	10	21	.321	.359
Knotts, Gary	L	.191	47	9	1	1	4	9	6	6	.283	.511
Throws Right	R	.194	62	12	3	0	2	7	10	15	.311	.339
Komiyama, Satoru	L	.305	82	25	7	0	4	11	6	10	.344	.537
Throws Right	R	.298	94	28	9	3	3	16	6	23	.356	.489
Koplove, Mike	L	.174	69	12	4	1	0	3	21	18	.367	.261
Throws Right	R	.230	152	35	2	0	2	15	2	28	.239	.283
Lawrence, Brian	L	.324	413	134	18	4	7	45	28	61	.371	.438
Throws Right	R	.236	406	96	16	1	9	38	24	88	.289	.347
Leiter, Al	L	.221	154	34	4	0	4	14	11	45	.281	.325
Throws Left	R	.257	623	160	31	1	19	70	58	127	.325	.401
Lidge, Brad	L	.500	14	7	2	0	0	3	3	2	.611	.643
Throws Right	R	.227	22	5	2	0	0	2	6	10	.414	.318
Lieber, Jon	L	.308	273	84	15	0	11	36	8	33	.325	.484
Throws Right	R	.246	280	69	11	2	4	22	4	54	.255	.343
Ligtenberg, Kerry	L	.214	98	21	3	2	3	11	27	23	.384	.378
Throws Right	R	.212	146	31	7	1	3	12	6	28	.242	.336
Lincoln, Mike	L	.276	87	24	3	1	2	9	14	21	.376	.402
Throws Right	R	.296	189	56	11	1	5	25	13	29	.335	.444
Linebrink, Scott	L	.265	49	13	4	0	0	3	5	11	.321	.347
Throws Right	R	.327	55	18	6	1	2	12	8	13	.422	.582
Lloyd, Graeme	L	.326	86	28	6	0	2	14	4	17	.355	.465
Throws Left	R	.281	139	39	7	0	4	25	15	20	.353	.417
Looper, Braden	L	.278	144	40	7	1	4	17	11	21	.329	.424
Throws Right	R	.191	173	33	5	1	4	15	17	34	.267	.301
Lopez, Albie	L	.344	93	32	5	1	1	12	7	18	.382	.452
Throws Right	R	.268	127	34	6	2	0	12	11	21	.324	.346
Lorraine, Andrew	L	.167	12	2	1	0	0	1	1	3	.231	.250
Throws Left	R	.435	46	20	3	0	7	17	5	7	.490	.957
Lowe, Sean	L	.348	112	39	4	2	6	18	18	19	.438	.580
Throws Right	R	.294	211	62	10	0	3	33	23	45	.377	.384
Lundquist, David	L	.429	7	3	1	0	0	2	3	0	.600	.571
Throws Right	R	.833	6	5	1	0	0	5	2	0	.889	1.000
Maddux, Greg	L	.232	327	76	11	1	6	29	26	52	.291	.327
Throws Right	R	.276	427	118	19	1	8	31	19	66	.310	.382
Mahay, Ron	L	.231	26	6	2	0	3	6	1	7	.259	.654
Throws Left	R	.226	31	7	1	0	3	8	7	7	.368	.548
Mahomes, Pat	L	.308	39	12	2	0	0	3	10	7	.460	.359
Throws Right	R	.276	87	24	7	0	3	8	7	16	.330	.460
Mairena, Oswaldo	L	.315	54	17	5	0	3	9	7	9	.393	.574
Throws Left	R	.269	78	21	4	1	4	13	5	12	.310	.500
Mallette, Brian	L	.500	8	4	1	0	3	5	2	1	.600	1.750
Throws Right	R	.250	12	3	0	0	0	1	1	4	.357	.250
Mann, Jim	L	.243	37	9	2	0	2	7	4	7	.317	.459
Throws Right	R	.227	44	10	3	0	1	3	3	12	.346	.364
Mantei, Matt	L	.250	32	8	2	0	2	5	2	7	.314	.500
Throws Right	R	.260	77	20	3	1	1	7	10	19	.345	.364
Manzanillo, Josias	L	.353	17	6	0	0	2	3	4	2	.500	.706
Throws Right	R	.368	38	14	4	0	3	9	1	2	.385	.711
Marquis, Jason	L	.292	209	61	8	4	7	21	29	35	.379	.469
Throws Right	R	.276	239	66	14	1	12	39	20	49	.335	.494
Mathews, T.J.	L	.357	28	10	2	0	0	2	2	5	.400	.429
Throws Right	R	.214	42	9	3	0	2	6	3	8	.267	.429
Matthews, Mike	L	.208	72	15	3	0	2	8	8	23	.286	.333
Throws Left	R	.292	96	28	5	0	3	17	21	11	.420	.438
Meadows, Brian	L	.267	105	28	7	0	3	10	11	17	.336	.419
Throws Right	R	.248	137	34	8	0	4	13	3	14	.270	.394
Mercado, Hector	L	.125	32	4	1	0	0	1	11	11	.349	.156
Throws Left	R	.252	111	28	8	1	2	20	14	29	.349	.396
Mercker, Kent	L	.209	67	14	6	0	3	9	9	19	.303	.433
Throws Left	R	.350	117	41	11	0	9	24	13	18	.424	.675
Mesa, Jose	L	.225	142	32	9	0	3	11	21	29	.337	.352
Throws Right	R	.237	139	33	6	0	2	12	18	35	.327	.324
Middlebrook, J.	L	.235	68	16	2	1	1	11	14	14	.361	.338
Throws Right	R	.237	118	28	6	1	1	18	8	28	.287	.331
Miller, Wade	L	.254	260	66	16	3	8	25	37	56	.349	.431
Throws Right	R	.245	347	85	18	1	6	33	25	88	.301	.354
Millwood, Kevin	L	.248	379	94	15	1	8	35	38	89	.325	.356
Throws Right	R	.214	430	92	18	2	8	40	27	89	.262	.321
Mlicki, Dave	L	.351	148	52	10	2	5	23	13	23	.411	.547
Throws Right	R	.245	200	49	11	1	6	24	21	34	.316	.400
Moehler, Brian	L	.298	84	25	6	1	4	14	4	8	.333	.536
Throws Right	R	.356	101	36	11	1	4	15	7	10	.398	.604
Molina, Gabe	L	.200	15	3	0	0	1	2	3	1	.333	.400
Throws Right	R	.136	22	3	0	0	0	0	3	3	.240	.136
Moreno, Juan	L	.250	4	1	0	0	0	1	6	1	.700	.500
Throws Left	R	.263	19	5	1	1	1	5	4	2	.375	.579
Morgan, Mike	L	.328	58	19	2	0	2	6	4	7	.381	.466
Throws Right	R	.262	84	22	4	0	5	14	5	6	.319	.488
Morris, Matt	L	.267	374	100	16	2	11	49	31	78	.324	.409
Throws Right	R	.255	431	110	20	0	5	37	33	93	.311	.336

Pitcher	vs.	Avg.	AB	H	2B	3B	HR	RBI	BB	SO	OBP	Slg.
Moss, Damian	L	.165	103	17	3	2	2	7	19	27	.298	.291
Throws Left	R	.232	530	123	28	3	18	65	70	84	.326	.398
Mota, Guillermo	L	.188	96	18	5	2	1	12	18	31	.319	.313
Throws Right	R	.213	127	27	9	0	3	17	9	18	.270	.354
Mulholland, Terry	L	.327	49	16	1	0	3	10	3	7	.377	.531
Throws Left	R	.333	87	29	6	0	7	20	4	10	.362	.644
Munro, Peter	L	.328	122	40	9	2	3	15	7	16	.374	.508
Throws Right	R	.255	192	49	10	0	2	16	16	29	.316	.339
Myers, Brett	L	.225	111	25	5	2	5	13	14	14	.320	.441
Throws Right	R	.314	153	48	5	0	6	18	15	20	.387	.464
Myers, Mike	L	.241	79	19	6	0	0	11	10	24	.358	.316
Throws Left	R	.317	63	20	2	0	2	10	7	7	.411	.444
Myers, Rodney	L	.471	34	16	4	0	1	13	4	3	.538	.676
Throws Right	R	.245	53	13	4	0	0	7	6	8	.344	.321
Nance, Shane	L	.200	5	1	0	0	1	1	1	2	.333	.800
Throws Left	R	.167	18	3	1	0	0	3	3	3	.286	.222
Nathan, Joe	L	.000	4	0	0	0	0	0	0	1	.000	.000
Throws Right	R	.125	8	1	1	0	0	0	0	1	.125	.250
Neagle, Denny	L	.315	149	47	10	0	10	29	15	31	.388	.584
Throws Left	R	.251	491	123	26	5	16	66	48	80	.322	.422
Neal, Blaine	L	.266	64	17	3	0	1	11	4	14	.309	.359
Throws Right	R	.231	65	15	4	1	0	10	10	19	.333	.323
Nen, Robb	L	.224	152	34	9	1	1	12	10	42	.272	.316
Throws Right	R	.242	124	30	1	1	1	14	10	39	.304	.290
Neugebauer, Nick	L	.318	88	28	3	3	4	11	26	16	.474	.557
Throws Right	R	.226	124	28	6	0	6	18	18	31	.322	.419
Nichting, Chris	L	.167	60	10	2	0	0	6	4	12	.219	.200
Throws Right	R	.361	83	30	3	2	7	15	1	13	.372	.699
Nickle, Doug	L	.290	31	9	2	0	0	6	6	4	.405	.355
Throws Right	R	.386	44	17	3	0	3	11	7	5	.472	.659
Nomo, Hideo	L	.218	394	86	19	3	8	38	42	90	.294	.343
Throws Right	R	.253	407	103	19	2	18	47	59	94	.348	.442
Nomura, Takahito	L	.185	27	5	2	1	1	8	7	4	.378	.444
Throws Left	R	.273	22	6	1	0	1	4	11	5	.500	.455
Nunez, Jose A.	L	.000	1	0	0	0	0	0	1	0	.500	.000
Throws Left	R	.000	2	0	0	0	0	0	0	0	.000	.000
Nunez, Vladimir	L	.191	162	31	9	0	2	14	23	49	.286	.284
Throws Right	R	.251	195	49	12	1	6	26	14	24	.301	.415
Ohka, Tomokazu	L	.218	316	69	15	1	6	25	19	42	.260	.329
Throws Right	R	.298	419	125	21	6	13	48	26	76	.347	.470
Olsen, Kevin	L	.292	106	31	7	2	2	11	15	17	.385	.453
Throws Right	R	.248	105	26	6	0	3	17	16	21	.341	.390
Oropesa, Eddie	L	.340	53	18	0	1	2	15	5	14	.397	.491
Throws Left	R	.356	59	21	4	0	4	16	10	4	.458	.627
Orosco, Jesse	L	.238	63	15	3	0	3	9	6	13	.300	.429
Throws Left	R	.214	42	9	2	0	1	3	6	9	.313	.333
Ortiz, Russ	L	.247	397	98	14	4	4	39	50	65	.330	.332
Throws Right	R	.235	395	93	21	2	11	39	44	72	.315	.382
Osborne, Donovan	L	.261	23	6	2	0	0	3	4	6	.357	.348
Throws Left	R	.317	41	13	3	1	1	6	6	7	.404	.512
Osting, Jimmy	L	.400	10	4	1	0	1	2	2	1	.500	.800
Throws Left	R	.326	43	14	2	1	2	9	8	6	.431	.558
Oswalt, Roy	L	.251	390	98	16	3	11	37	29	90	.307	.392
Throws Right	R	.244	480	117	23	5	6	42	33	118	.292	.350
Padilla, Vicente	L	.272	379	103	19	0	9	37	35	53	.336	.393
Throws Right	R	.236	402	95	18	2	7	36	18	75	.290	.343
Parra, Jose	L	.214	14	3	0	0	0	1	5	1	.421	.214
Throws Right	R	.270	37	10	4	0	0	4	6	7	.386	.378
Patterson, John	L	.236	55	13	2	0	5	6	3	13	.288	.545
Throws Right	R	.233	60	14	2	0	2	5	4	18	.281	.367
Pavano, Carl	L	.357	252	90	16	1	8	30	24	41	.414	.524
Throws Right	R	.276	304	84	17	0	11	38	21	51	.337	.441
Pearce, Josh	L	.381	21	8	1	0	1	5	3	0	.480	.571
Throws Right	R	.375	32	12	6	0	0	6	5	1	.447	.563
Pearson, Jason	L	.250	4	1	1	0	0	0	0	2	.250	.500
Throws Left	R	.000	2	0	0	0	0	0	0	1	.000	.000
Peavy, Jake	L	.325	194	63	19	1	8	32	24	39	.405	.557
Throws Right	R	.223	193	43	7	0	3	17	9	51	.256	.306
Pember, Dave	L	.286	14	4	0	0	0	1	5	1	.450	.286
Throws Right	R	.167	18	3	2	0	1	5	1	4	.211	.444
Penny, Brad	L	.294	231	68	19	1	9	30	32	42	.379	.502
Throws Right	R	.284	282	80	10	3	9	41	18	51	.326	.436
Perez, Odalis	L	.223	179	40	4	1	4	13	9	25	.276	.324
Throws Left	R	.226	628	142	29	0	17	61	29	130	.258	.354
Perez, Oliver	L	.294	85	25	3	1	1	5	12	29	.390	.388
Throws Left	R	.191	241	46	6	1	12	29	36	65	.301	.373
Person, Robert	L	.243	144	35	12	2	6	20	25	28	.370	.479
Throws Right	R	.239	184	44	14	1	7	33	26	33	.333	.440
Pichardo, Hipolito	L	.667	3	2	1	0	0	2	1	0	.750	1.000
Throws Right	R	1.000	1	1	0	0	0	0	0	1	1.000	1.000
Pickford, Kevin	L	.375	32	12	5	1	1	9	3	4	.432	.688
Throws Left	R	.291	86	25	6	0	2	9	17	14	.419	.430
Pineda, Luis	L	.250	48	12	4	0	1	2	8	14	.379	.396
Throws Right	R	.200	65	13	4	0	3	11	16	17	.349	.400
Plesac, Dan	L	.125	48	6	0	0	3	7	5	18	.208	.313
Throws Left	R	.278	36	10	2	0	2	3	7	9	.395	.500
Politte, Cliff	L	.480	25	12	2	0	0	7	7	1	.594	.560
Throws Right	R	.171	41	7	3	0	0	3	2	14	.227	.244
Pratt, Andy	L	1.000	1	1	0	0	0	0	0	0	1.000	1.000
Throws Left	R	.000	4	0	0	0	0	0	0	4	1	.500	.000
Prinz, Bret	L	.429	14	6	3	0	0	4	3	4	.529	.643
Throws Right	R	.395	43	17	4	0	1	13	7	6	.481	.558
Prior, Mark	L	.204	186	38	9	0	7	19	22	69	.294	.366
Throws Right	R	.242	248	60	15	1	7	23	16	78	.298	.395
Puffer, Brandon	L	.319	72	23	7	1	1	13	27	17	.505	.486
Throws Right	R	.234	188	44	6	1	2	26	11	31	.289	.309
Quantrill, Paul	L	.254	122	31	13	0	1	11	18	25	.357	.385
Throws Right	R	.275	178	49	6	0	0	11	7	28	.306	.309
Quevedo, Ruben	L	.271	247	67	17	3	17	46	24	43	.339	.571
Throws Right	R	.302	305	92	19	2	11	48	44	50	.391	.485
Reames, Britt	L	.342	79	27	4	1	3	13	25	17	.500	.532
Throws Right	R	.234	184	43	10	1	5	37	13	59	.294	.380
Redding, Tim	L	.258	128	33	7	1	2	13	20	30	.358	.375
Throws Right	R	.290	155	45	14	1	8	27	15	33	.347	.548
Reed, Steve	L	.181	83	15	3	0	0	5	8	9	.261	.217
Throws Right	R	.259	158	41	7	0	2	12	6	41	.316	.342
Reitsma, Chris	L	.265	230	61	15	1	10	28	21	32	.323	.470
Throws Right	R	.268	310	83	21	1	7	38	24	52	.329	.410
Remlinger, Mike	L	.235	68	16	2	1	1	8	6	20	.297	.338
Throws Left	R	.184	174	32	4	1	2	11	22	49	.279	.253
Reyes, Al	L	.158	19	3	2	0	0	1	4	10	.304	.263
Throws Right	R	.162	37	6	1	0	1	7	3	11	.256	.270
Reyes, Dennys	L	.326	46	15	4	1	1	12	13	8	.475	.522
Throws Left	R	.259	108	28	9	3	0	12	11	22	.322	.398
Reynolds, Shane	L	.257	109	28	4	2	2	9	16	19	.357	.385
Throws Right	R	.284	183	52	10	1	11	29	10	28	.320	.530
Reynoso, Armando	L	.333	3	1	0	0	0	1	1	1	.500	.333
Throws Right	R	.400	5	2	1	0	0	1	0	1	.400	.600
Riedling, John	L	.320	75	24	6	0	2	9	13	11	.427	.480
Throws Right	R	.163	92	15	1	0	0	1	13	19	.278	.174
Rijo, Jose	L	.284	134	38	7	1	6	26	16	15	.360	.485
Throws Right	R	.282	181	51	8	1	7	23	4	23	.301	.453
Roa, Joe	L	.328	116	38	5	2	7	19	8	16	.371	.586
Throws Right	R	.244	164	40	7	2	4	16	5	19	.266	.384
Roberts, Grant	L	.261	69	18	2	0	1	7	7	10	.329	.333
Throws Right	R	.248	101	25	4	3	2	8	9	21	.310	.406
Robertson, Jeriome	L	.357	14	5	1	0	2	5	0	4	.294	.857
Throws Left	R	.421	19	8	0	0	2	4	5	2	.542	.737
Robertson, Nate	L	.444	9	4	1	0	2	5	1	1	.545	1.222
Throws Left	R	.355	31	11	1	0	1	6	3	2	.429	.484
Rodriguez, Felix	L	.234	107	25	4	0	3	18	14	28	.338	.355
Throws Right	R	.196	143	28	6	0	2	16	15	30	.280	.280
Rodriguez, Jose	L	1.000	1	1	0	0	0	1	1	0	1.000	1.000
Throws Left	R	.750	4	3	0	0	0	1	0	1	.800	.750
Rodriguez, Nerio	L	.091	11	1	0	0	0	1	0	2	.091	.091
Throws Right	R	.429	7	3	0	0	1	3	1	0	.500	.857
Rueter, Kirk	L	.244	176	43	3	0	3	14	15	19	.302	.313
Throws Left	R	.267	603	161	30	1	19	63	39	57	.307	.415
Rusch, Glendon	L	.235	187	44	6	0	10	33	13	30	.289	.428
Throws Left	R	.292	626	183	29	3	20	75	63	110	.358	.444
Saarloos, Kirk	L	.301	143	43	8	0	8	23	14	23	.365	.524
Throws Right	R	.302	189	57	11	1	4	26	13	31	.361	.434
Sanchez, Duaner	L	.200	10	2	0	0	1	3	1	2	.273	.500
Throws Right	R	.286	14	4	2	0	1	4	6	4	.500	.643
Sanchez, Jesus	L	.222	18	4	1	0	1	8	1	3	.263	.444
Throws Left	R	.550	20	11	2	0	3	9	3	5	.656	1.100
Santiago, Jose	L	.304	69	21	6	1	1	16	6	5	.355	.464
Throws Right	R	.282	124	35	4	2	6	21	9	24	.343	.492

Pitcher	vs.	Avg.	AB	H	2B	3B	HR	RBI	BB	SO	OBP	Slg.
Santos, Victor	L	.277	47	13	4	0	0	8	10	12	.397	.362
Throws Right	R	.418	67	28	5	0	3	21	12	13	.506	.627
Sauerbeck, Scott	L	.147	95	14	2	0	2	9	6	32	.198	.232
Throws Left	R	.273	132	36	9	0	2	14	21	38	.377	.386
Schilling, Curt	L	.242	451	109	22	5	14	46	17	141	.269	.406
Throws Right	R	.208	523	109	10	3	15	44	16	175	.236	.325
Schmidt, Jason	L	.259	328	85	12	1	11	43	46	88	.350	.402
Throws Right	R	.180	350	63	16	0	4	30	27	108	.239	.260
Seo, Jae Weong	L	.000	0	0	0	0	0	0	0	0	.000	.000
Throws Right	R	.000	3	0	0	0	0	0	0	1	.000	.000
Sheets, Ben	L	.318	406	129	33	3	13	58	39	61	.382	.510
Throws Right	R	.247	438	108	22	1	8	37	31	109	.307	.356
Shiell, Jason	L	.600	5	3	0	0	0	2	2	1	.714	.600
Throws Right	R	.800	5	4	0	0	0	0	1	0	.833	.800
Shuey, Paul	L	.271	48	13	2	0	1	8	10	8	.397	.375
Throws Right	R	.179	67	12	3	1	1	9	11	16	.300	.299
Silva, Carlos	L	.292	120	35	10	1	0	9	12	15	.361	.392
Throws Right	R	.276	192	53	11	1	4	30	10	26	.317	.406
Silva, Jose	L	.276	29	8	3	0	2	6	3	8	.447	.586
Throws Right	R	.304	56	17	2	0	1	6	2	3	.344	.393
Simontacchi, Jason	L	.248	226	56	15	0	9	22	27	31	.333	.434
Throws Right	R	.257	304	78	20	1	9	37	27	41	.321	.418
Small, Aaron	L	.000	1	0	0	0	0	0	2	1	.667	.000
Throws Right	R	1.000	2	2	2	0	0	4	0	0	1.000	2.000
Smith, Bud	L	.326	46	15	3	0	0	4	1	9	.353	.391
Throws Left	R	.342	152	52	11	1	4	30	21	13	.420	.507
Smith, Dan	L	.151	53	8	2	0	2	6	8	13	.254	.302
Throws Right	R	.239	109	26	4	1	4	10	13	21	.325	.404
Smith, Travis	L	.273	88	24	4	0	3	11	6	14	.319	.420
Throws Right	R	.357	126	45	8	0	7	27	14	18	.434	.587
Smoltz, John	L	.213	141	30	9	1	1	17	10	44	.265	.312
Throws Right	R	.199	146	29	3	1	3	14	14	41	.267	.295
Smyth, Steve	L	.241	29	7	2	1	2	6	3	5	.313	.586
Throws Left	R	.351	77	27	6	1	7	21	7	11	.393	.727
Speier, Justin	L	.240	104	25	5	0	4	11	7	22	.288	.404
Throws Right	R	.197	132	26	6	0	5	19	12	25	.277	.356
Spooneybarger, T.	L	.150	60	9	4	0	0	2	14	16	.316	.217
Throws Right	R	.234	124	29	1	0	4	15	12	17	.307	.339
Springer, Dennis	L	.333	3	1	1	0	0	1	2	0	.600	.667
Throws Right	R	.000	2	0	0	0	0	0	0	1	.000	.000
Stark, Denny	L	.228	184	42	9	0	13	34	39	28	.361	.489
Throws Right	R	.224	295	66	9	2	12	32	25	36	.292	.390
Stechschulte, Gene	L	.263	38	10	0	0	2	10	5	6	.341	.421
Throws Right	R	.221	77	17	4	0	2	10	12	15	.323	.351
Stephenson, Garrett	L	.355	76	27	7	0	2	16	10	11	.444	.526
Throws Right	R	.223	94	21	8	0	2	7	15	23	.342	.372
Stewart, Scott	L	.159	88	14	1	0	1	5	3	32	.196	.205
Throws Left	R	.235	149	35	8	3	3	19	19	35	.318	.389
Stone, Ricky	L	.288	80	23	3	0	5	14	13	13	.387	.513
Throws Right	R	.258	213	55	7	1	4	34	21	50	.325	.357
Stottlemyre, Todd	L	.310	42	13	1	1	3	11	5	5	.375	.595
Throws Right	R	.317	41	13	2	1	1	6	2	7	.349	.488
Strange, Pat	L	.154	13	2	1	0	0	0	0	2	.154	.231
Throws Right	R	.250	16	4	0	1	0	0	1	2	.294	.375
Strickland, Scott	L	.313	96	30	2	4	3	14	17	12	.416	.510
Throws Right	R	.188	165	31	5	2	4	21	16	57	.265	.315
Stull, Everett	L	.417	24	10	2	0	0	4	6	3	.533	.500
Throws Right	R	.278	18	5	2	0	0	3	3	4	.409	.389
Sullivan, Scott	L	.357	126	45	8	2	7	26	12	26	.414	.619
Throws Right	R	.253	190	48	5	0	8	30	19	52	.330	.405
Swindell, Greg	L	.339	59	20	3	0	6	16	0	10	.333	.695
Throws Left	R	.234	77	18	6	1	3	13	5	13	.277	.455
Tankersley, Dennis	L	.363	80	29	5	0	6	21	18	12	.475	.650
Throws Right	R	.263	114	30	10	0	4	21	22	27	.406	.456
Tavarez, Julian	L	.333	300	100	27	2	3	39	55	32	.437	.467
Throws Right	R	.284	310	88	27	2	6	50	19	35	.352	.442
Tejera, Michael	L	.228	114	26	6	0	4	15	20	22	.350	.386
Throws Left	R	.280	422	118	28	3	13	48	40	73	.345	.453
Teut, Nate	L	.286	7	2	0	0	0	0	1	2	.375	.286
Throws Left	R	.423	26	11	4	0	0	7	2	2	.464	.577
Thomson, John	L	.285	368	105	20	1	13	42	26	58	.328	.451
Throws Right	R	.264	363	96	29	4	15	62	18	49	.299	.490
Timlin, Mike	L	.208	125	26	1	1	4	10	10	12	.272	.328
Throws Right	R	.214	229	49	12	0	11	29	4	38	.239	.410

Pitcher	vs.	Avg.	AB	H	2B	3B	HR	RBI	BB	SO	OBP	Slg.
Tollberg, Brian	L	.373	118	44	11	0	5	19	11	12	.414	.593
Throws Right	R	.317	139	44	14	1	6	21	8	21	.353	.561
Tomko, Brett	L	.270	374	101	24	4	9	35	31	56	.327	.428
Throws Right	R	.264	421	111	23	3	22	62	29	70	.308	.489
Torres, Salomon	L	.241	54	13	1	0	0	9	4	4	.349	.259
Throws Right	R	.273	55	15	2	1	2	5	4	8	.355	.455
Trachsel, Steve	L	.233	318	74	11	1	9	34	34	46	.305	.358
Throws Right	R	.281	342	96	17	1	7	33	35	59	.347	.398
Trujillo, J.J.	L	.200	5	1	0	0	0	1	5	2	.600	.200
Throws Right	R	.500	6	3	1	0	1	2	1	1	.625	1.167
Tucker, T.J.	L	.269	78	21	5	1	1	7	15	8	.383	.397
Throws Right	R	.300	160	48	15	1	4	24	16	34	.362	.481
Vance, Cory	L	.333	3	1	0	0	1	1	3	0	.714	1.333
Throws Left	R	.250	12	3	0	0	1	2	1	1	.308	.500
Vazquez, Javier	L	.283	417	118	24	4	19	49	40	84	.346	.496
Throws Right	R	.261	479	125	32	3	9	54	9	95	.276	.397
Veres, Dave	L	.190	116	22	3	0	4	11	24	27	.324	.319
Throws Right	R	.246	183	45	7	2	8	25	15	41	.308	.437
Villafuerte, Brandon	L	.286	56	16	3	0	0	5	7	13	.369	.339
Throws Right	R	.213	61	13	0	0	2	7	5	12	.284	.311
Villone, Ron	L	.233	120	28	6	0	2	15	8	24	.301	.333
Throws Left	R	.289	232	67	17	5	6	40	26	31	.360	.483
Vizcaino, Luis	L	.225	111	25	7	0	1	13	12	32	.302	.315
Throws Right	R	.170	176	30	5	0	5	14	18	47	.254	.284
Vosberg, Ed	L	.600	5	3	1	0	1	4	1	0	.667	1.400
Throws Left	R	.000	2	0	0	0	0	0	0	0	.000	.000
Wagner, Billy	L	.180	61	11	1	0	1	4	4	21	.231	.246
Throws Left	R	.201	199	40	7	0	6	18	18	67	.270	.327
Walker, Kevin	L	.238	21	5	2	0	1	2	2	8	.304	.476
Throws Left	R	.467	15	7	1	1	1	3	3	3	.556	.867
Walker, Pete	L	.667	3	2	0	0	0	1	0	0	.667	.667
Throws Right	R	.000	2	0	0	0	0	0	0	0	.000	.000
Walker, Tyler	L	.235	17	4	2	0	1	3	3	4	.350	.529
Throws Right	R	.259	27	7	0	0	2	5	2	3	.310	.481
Wayne, Justin	L	.214	42	9	3	0	1	5	8	7	.333	.357
Throws Right	R	.271	48	13	4	0	2	7	5	9	.333	.479
Weathers, Dave	L	.267	105	28	4	1	0	16	16	26	.360	.324
Throws Right	R	.232	177	41	5	1	6	20	20	35	.315	.373
Wells, Kip	L	.274	361	99	14	3	11	39	40	45	.347	.421
Throws Right	R	.249	394	98	21	1	10	42	31	89	.310	.383
White, Gabe	L	.202	89	18	4	1	1	8	5	20	.260	.303
Throws Left	R	.267	116	31	8	2	2	12	5	21	.298	.422
White, Rick	L	.299	87	26	6	3	2	6	10	13	.367	.506
Throws Right	R	.243	148	36	7	2	2	21	11	28	.294	.358
Williams, Dave	L	.086	35	3	1	0	0	4	2	11	.200	.114
Throws Left	R	.271	129	35	8	1	9	17	22	22	.379	.558
Williams, Jeff	L	.267	15	4	0	0	0	3	2	5	.353	.267
Throws Left	R	.367	30	11	2	0	2	7	5	6	.459	.633
Williams, Mike	L	.281	121	34	7	0	1	12	14	22	.356	.364
Throws Right	R	.180	111	20	1	1	5	14	7	21	.235	.342
Williams, Woody	L	.182	176	32	3	0	6	10	14	41	.250	.301
Throws Right	R	.256	203	52	9	1	4	17	11	35	.300	.369
Williamson, Scott	L	.198	101	20	5	1	3	12	18	29	.328	.356
Throws Right	R	.170	153	26	4	0	2	14	18	55	.256	.235
Witasick, Jay	L	.228	101	23	5	1	0	5	13	27	.322	.297
Throws Right	R	.238	147	35	7	0	3	11	8	27	.289	.347
Wolf, Randy	L	.258	120	31	8	1	4	12	18	34	.357	.442
Throws Left	R	.216	652	141	24	3	19	60	45	138	.271	.350
Wood, Kerry	L	.223	363	81	19	0	8	34	61	100	.340	.342
Throws Right	R	.219	401	88	20	1	14	47	36	117	.301	.379
Worrell, Tim	L	.204	103	21	4	2	1	17	18	29	.320	.311
Throws Right	R	.218	156	34	9	0	2	9	12	26	.269	.314
Wright, Jamey	L	.271	229	62	12	0	9	31	51	38	.406	.441
Throws Right	R	.267	255	68	14	0	8	44	24	39	.345	.416
Yoshii, Masato	L	.250	224	56	5	0	5	22	22	32	.317	.339
Throws Right	R	.307	283	87	22	1	10	36	10	42	.334	.498
Zambrano, Carlos	L	.209	163	34	8	2	2	19	35	38	.355	.319
Throws Right	R	.253	237	60	7	0	7	28	28	55	.336	.371
Zerbe, Chad	L	.247	85	21	5	0	0	8	9	13	.333	.306
Throws Right	R	.248	125	31	1	2	3	16	12	13	.321	.360
National League	L	.265									.347	.420
	R	.254									.320	.404

FIELDING

TEAM

Team	G	PO	A	E	TC	DP	TP	PB	Pct.
Houston	162	4335	1663	83	6081	149	0	5	.986
Philadelphia	161	4349	1700	88	6137	156	0	12	.986
Los Angeles	162	4373	1686	90	6149	134	0	12	.985
San Francisco	162	4312	1630	90	6032	166	0	7	.985
Arizona	162	4340	1506	89	5935	116	0	13	.985
St. Louis	162	4339	1674	103	6116	168	1	9	.983
Milwaukee	162	4297	1633	103	6033	154	0	12	.983
Florida	162	4369	1636	106	6111	163	1	6	.983
Atlanta	161	4402	1822	114	6338	170	0	12	.982
Colorado	162	4280	1701	112	6093	158	0	12	.982
Pittsburgh	161	4238	1899	115	6252	177	0	12	.982
Cincinnati	162	4361	1773	120	6254	169	0	28	.981
Chicago	162	4324	1500	114	5938	144	0	15	.981
San Diego	162	4309	1681	128	6118	162	0	14	.979
Montreal	162	4359	1799	139	6297	160	1	12	.978
New York	161	4328	1628	144	6100	138	1	11	.976
Totals	1294	69315	26931	1738	97984	2484	4	192	.982

INDIVIDUAL

FIRST BASEMEN

NOTE: All caps denotes fielding-percentage leader based on 81 games for catchers, 108 for all other non-pitchers and 162 innings for pitchers. *Throws lefthanded.

Player, Team	G	GS	PO	A	E	TC	DP	Pct.
Alcantara, Izzy, Mil.	2	1	13	0	1	14	1	.929
Bagwell, Jeff, Hou.	153	153	1254	112	7	1373	119	.995
Banks, Brian, Fla.	1	0	2	0	1	3	1	.667
Barajas, Rod, Ari.	1	0	2	0	0	2	0	1.000
Barker, Kevin, S.D.*	6	5	49	1	0	50	5	1.000
Barrett, Michael, Mon.	6	2	27	1	0	28	4	1.000
Bell, David, S.F.	2	2	13	4	0	17	2	1.000
Bell, Jay, Ari.	5	3	16	0	0	16	0	1.000
Bellhorn, Mark, Chi.	22	7	90	3	1	94	10	.989
Benjamin, Mike, Pit.	1	0	4	0	0	4	1	1.000
Blum, Geoff, Hou.	1	0	1	0	0	1	1	1.000
Branyan, Russell, Cin.	18	18	170	14	1	185	23	.995
Buchanan, Brian, S.D.	15	7	74	6	0	80	6	1.000
Cairo, Miguel, St.L.	4	1	10	0	0	10	0	1.000
Casey, Sean, Cin.	108	106	927	70	7	1004	93	.993
Castro, Juan, Cin.	1	0	0	1	0	1	0	1.000
Choi, Hee Seop, Chi.*	22	12	106	8	2	116	16	.983
Colbrunn, Greg, Ari.	40	36	260	12	2	274	16	.993
Cordero, Wil, Mon.	10	8	66	5	0	71	6	1.000
Cruz, Deivi, S.D.	1	0	4	0	0	4	0	1.000
Cruz, Ivan, St.L.*	7	0	12	1	0	13	0	1.000
Donnels, Chris, Ari.	1	0	1	0	0	1	0	1.000
Dunn, Adam, Cin.	44	37	360	22	6	388	30	.985
Dunston, Shawon, S.F.	1	1	6	0	0	6	0	1.000
Durazo, Erubiel, Ari.*	56	53	409	26	7	442	29	.984
Echevarria, Angel, Chi.	13	7	61	4	1	66	12	.985
Franco, Julio, Atl.	95	70	717	59	8	784	79	.990
Franco, Matt, St.L.	51	49	353	30	4	387	31	.990
Galarraga, Andres, Mon.	89	72	629	59	13	701	55	.981
Giambi, Jeremy, Phi.*	21	21	169	8	2	179	16	.989
Gload, Ross, Col.*	4	2	20	3	0	23	1	1.000
Grace, Mark, Ari.*	98	70	649	34	7	690	58	.990
Hansen, Dave, L.A.	27	7	76	5	0	81	3	1.000
Harris, Lenny, Mil.	12	5	49	7	0	56	1	1.000
Helms, Wes, Atl.	45	31	285	27	4	316	34	.987
Helton, Todd, Col.*	156	155	1357	113	7	1477	138	.995
Hollins, Dave, Phi.	5	5	37	1	0	38	3	1.000
Houston, Tyler, Mil.-L.A.	13	9	102	3	2	107	9	.981
Hyzdu, Adam, Pit.	1	0	3	0	0	3	0	1.000
Johnson, Mark P., N.Y.*	15	10	84	6	1	91	7	.989
KARROS, Eric, L.A.	142	141	1175	106	4	1285	101	.997
Kent, Jeff, S.F.	9	9	55	2	0	57	7	1.000
Kinkade, Mike, L.A.	11	3	39	4	0	43	3	1.000
Klesko, Ryan, S.D.*	112	111	918	73	7	998	92	.993
Larson, Brandon, Cin.	2	0	5	0	0	5	1	1.000
Lee, Derrek, Fla.	162	161	1312	121	12	1445	138	.992
Lee, Travis, Phi.*	148	130	1262	75	6	1343	120	.996
Lo Duca, Paul, L.A.	18	2	45	1	1	47	3	.979
Loretta, Mark, Mil.	5	2	20	1	0	21	2	1.000
Mabry, John, Phi.	1	1	6	1	0	7	0	1.000
Machado, Robert, Chi.-Mil.	3	0	8	1	0	9	1	1.000
Marrero, Eli, St.L.	4	0	13	0	0	13	2	1.000
Martinez, Ramon E., S.F.	4	4	30	3	0	33	3	1.000
Martinez, Tino, St.L.	149	141	1220	86	5	1311	119	.996
Matheny, Mike, St.L.	1	0	1	0	0	1	1	1.000
Matos, Julius, S.D.	2	0	3	0	0	3	0	1.000
McEwing, Joe, N.Y.	20	2	45	4	0	49	5	1.000
McGriff, Fred, Chi.*	137	136	1005	60	7	1072	84	.993
Merced, Orlando, Hou.	7	6	53	3	0	56	8	1.000
Millar, Kevin, Fla.	2	1	6	1	0	7	0	1.000
Minor, Damon, S.F.*	44	35	310	20	1	331	29	.997
Mordecai, Mike, Mon.-Fla.	4	2	21	2	0	23	1	1.000
Nevin, Phil, S.D.	36	36	269	22	4	295	30	.986
Norton, Greg, Col.	15	5	55	3	0	58	5	1.000
Osik, Keith, Pit.	3	0	7	2	0	9	1	1.000
Pelaez, Alex, S.D.	1	1	12	1	0	13	3	1.000
Perez, Eduardo, St.L.	10	4	52	1	0	53	5	1.000
Perez, Tomas, Phi.	3	2	10	0	0	10	1	1.000
Pratt, Todd, Phi.	2	2	19	1	0	20	1	1.000
Pujols, Albert, St.L.	21	16	140	13	1	154	24	.994
Redmond, Mike, Fla.	2	0	4	0	0	4	0	1.000
Sexson, Richie, Mil.	154	153	1224	119	7	1350	134	.995
Snow, J.T., S.F.*	135	111	939	79	7	1025	104	.993
Stevens, Lee, Mon.*	58	56	512	47	4	563	47	.993
Surhoff, B.J., Atl.	11	11	72	7	0	79	12	1.000
Sweeney, Mark, S.D.*	11	2	32	3	2	37	5	.946
Tarasco, Tony, N.Y.	7	0	11	0	0	11	0	1.000
Truby, Chris, Mon.	2	1	10	0	0	10	2	1.000
Valent, Eric, Phi.*	1	0	3	0	1	4	2	.750
Valentin, John, N.Y.	22	11	106	6	3	115	12	.974
Vaughn, Mo, N.Y.	134	131	1085	47	18	1150	95	.984
Vizcaino, Jose, Hou.	5	1	10	1	0	11	2	1.000
Wigginton, Ty, N.Y.	13	7	56	5	0	61	4	1.000
Wilkerson, Brad, Mon.*	23	21	179	15	0	194	25	1.000
Wilson, Craig A., Pit.	42	34	277	21	3	301	35	.990
Wilson, Vance, N.Y.	1	0	2	0	0	2	0	1.000
Young, Kevin, Pit.	144	127	1277	89	13	1379	119	.991
Zinter, Alan, Hou.	8	2	24	2	0	26	3	1.000

TRIPLE PLAYS: Galarraga, Mon.; Lee, Fla.; Martinez, St.L.; Vaughn, N.Y.

FIRST BASEMEN WITH TWO OR MORE TEAMS

Player, Team	G	GS	PO	A	E	TC	DP	Pct.
Houston, Tyler, Mil.	1	0	4	0	0	4	0	1.000
Houston, Tyler, L.A.	12	9	98	3	2	103	9	.981
Machado, Robert, Chi.	1	0	0	0	0	0	0	.000
Machado, Robert, Mil.	2	0	8	1	0	9	1	1.000
Mordecai, Mike, Mon.	3	2	20	2	0	22	1	1.000
Mordecai, Mike, Fla.	1	0	1	0	0	1	0	1.000

SECOND BASEMEN

Player, Team	G	GS	PO	A	E	TC	DP	Pct.
Alomar, Roberto, N.Y.	147	146	273	348	11	632	94	.983
Anderson, Marlon, Phi.	143	140	272	382	20	674	90	.970
Bell, David, S.F.	12	10	21	29	3	53	6	.943
Bell, Jay, Ari.	2	0	1	2	0	3	0	1.000
Bellhorn, Mark, Chi.	77	63	121	175	6	302	42	.980
Belliard, Ronnie, Mil.	49	40	86	106	5	197	27	.975
Benjamin, Mike, Pit.	11	7	23	23	0	46	6	1.000
Biggio, Craig, Hou.	142	140	313	352	8	673	88	.988
Blum, Geoff, Hou.	1	0	2	2	0	4	0	1.000
Burroughs, Sean, S.D.	13	11	26	23	1	50	8	.980
Bush, Homer, Fla.	12	6	11	14	1	26	2	.962
Butler, Brent, Col.	72	67	121	178	8	307	46	.974
Cabrera, Jolbert, L.A.	1	1	2	1	0	3	0	1.000
Cairo, Miguel, St.L.	18	8	25	31	1	57	8	.982
Carroll, Jamey, Mon.	1	0	0	0	0	0	0	.000

Player, Team	G	GS	PO	A	E	TC	DP	Pct.
Castillo, Luis, Fla.	144	143	269	391	13	673	93	.981
Castro, Juan, Cin.	17	8	15	24	0	39	7	1.000
Cintron, Alex, Ari.	18	14	27	31	0	58	9	1.000
Collier, Lou, Mon.	2	0	1	1	0	2	0	1.000
Cora, Alex, L.A.	40	10	30	53	2	85	11	.976
Counsell, Craig, Ari.	13	10	24	23	0	47	5	1.000
Crespo, Cesar, S.D.	4	0	1	2	0	3	0	1.000
Dawkins, Gookie, Cin.	3	0	0	0	1	1	0	.000
DeRosa, Mark, Atl.	32	27	59	89	4	152	23	.974
DeShields, Delino, Chi.	41	34	65	98	5	168	15	.970
Fox, Andy, Fla.	7	7	18	23	1	42	7	.976
Furcal, Rafael, Atl.	4	4	7	12	0	19	5	1.000
Garcia, Jesse, Atl.	21	11	28	42	1	71	10	.986
Giles, Marcus, Atl.	52	47	118	139	6	263	35	.977
Grudzielanek, Mark, L.A.	147	145	253	366	7	626	76	.989
Guerrero, Wilton, Cin.-Mon.	17	9	20	34	0	54	7	1.000
Hill, Bobby, Chi.	55	48	96	117	2	215	31	.991
Hubbard, Trenidad, S.D.	4	1	0	4	0	4	1	1.000
Izturis, Cesar, L.A.	1	0	1	3	0	4	0	1.000
Jimenez, D'Angelo, S.D.	54	52	116	159	7	282	44	.975
Kent, Jeff, S.F.	149	142	293	411	16	720	113	.978
Lockhart, Keith, Atl.	89	72	141	230	8	379	46	.979
Loretta, Mark, Mil.-Hou.	6	5	14	14	0	28	4	1.000
Macias, Jose, Mon.	6	4	13	15	0	28	5	1.000
Mackowiak, Rob, Pit.	3	1	2	3	1	6	1	.833
Malloy, Marty, Fla.	3	0	5	3	0	8	1	1.000
Martinez, Ramon E., S.F.	17	10	17	25	1	43	6	.977
Mateo, Henry, Mon.	3	1	2	8	0	10	1	1.000
Matos, Julius, S.D.	49	32	72	110	7	189	26	.963
McEwing, Joe, N.Y.	13	4	15	14	0	29	2	1.000
Mordecai, Mike, Mon.	4	1	6	6	2	14	2	.857
Nunez, Abraham O., Pit.	46	37	84	133	2	219	35	.991
Ojeda, Augie, Chi.	10	7	18	13	1	32	4	.969
Ortiz, Jose, Col.	53	52	103	133	3	239	24	.987
Osik, Keith, Pit.	1	0	0	0	0	0	0	.000
Ozuna, Pablo, Fla.	10	6	13	16	1	30	3	.967
Pelaez, Alex, S.D.	1	0	0	0	0	0	0	.000
Perez, Tomas, Phi.	50	21	67	90	1	158	22	.994
Polanco, Placido, St.L.	6	5	11	17	1	29	7	.966
Punto, Nick, Phi.	1	0	1	1	0	2	1	1.000
Reboulet, Jeff, L.A.	11	5	6	22	2	30	2	.933
Reese, Pokey, Pit.	117	116	283	363	8	654	84	.988
Rollins, Jimmy, Phi.	1	0	0	0	0	0	0	.000
Romano, Jason, Col.	12	2	6	14	1	21	2	.952
Scutaro, Marco, N.Y.	12	1	4	7	0	11	0	1.000
Shumpert, Terry, Col.	60	40	95	126	6	227	30	.974
Spivey, Junior, Ari.	143	138	288	358	15	661	64	.977
Stynes, Chris, Chi.	20	10	22	33	0	55	12	1.000
Thurston, Joe, L.A.	4	1	4	6	0	10	3	1.000
Valentin, John, N.Y.	3	1	4	3	0	7	2	1.000
Vazquez, Ramon, S.D.	81	66	131	190	5	326	46	.985
Vidro, Jose, Mon.	152	151	314	448	11	773	93	.986
Vina, Fernando, St.L.	150	149	287	401	13	701	104	.981
Vizcaino, Jose, Hou.	25	19	38	57	0	95	15	1.000
WALKER, Todd, Cin.	154	150	314	438	8	760	93	.989
Wigginton, Ty, N.Y.	12	9	22	34	2	58	4	.966
Young, Eric, Mil.	123	120	249	323	12	584	79	.979

TRIPLE PLAY: Alomar, N.Y.

SECOND BASEMEN WITH TWO OR MORE TEAMS

Player, Team	G	GS	PO	A	E	TC	DP	Pct.
Guerrero, Wilton, Cin.	10	4	11	22	0	33	5	1.000
Guerrero, Wilton, Mon.	7	5	9	12	0	21	2	1.000
Loretta, Mark, Mil.	3	2	7	6	0	13	2	1.000
Loretta, Mark, Hou.	3	3	7	8	0	15	2	1.000

THIRD BASEMEN

Player, Team	G	GS	PO	A	E	TC	DP	Pct.
Alfonzo, Edgardo, N.Y.	134	131	95	278	12	385	22	.969
Banks, Brian, Fla.	1	0	1	1	0	2	0	1.000
Bell, David, S.F.	139	128	78	244	9	331	21	.973
Bell, Jay, Ari.	6	5	4	8	0	12	2	1.000
Bellhorn, Mark, Chi.	36	29	16	33	3	52	3	.942
Belliard, Ronnie, Mil.	42	20	22	43	5	70	5	.929
Beltre, Adrian, L.A.	157	154	120	294	20	434	18	.954
Benjamin, Mike, Pit.	62	5	13	33	1	47	3	.979
Blum, Geoff, Hou.	104	91	68	199	8	275	27	.971
Boone, Aaron, Cin.	154	141	89	324	20	433	42	.954
Branyan, Russell, Cin.	16	13	10	21	3	34	1	.912
Burroughs, Sean, S.D.	48	39	33	68	7	108	5	.935
Butler, Brent, Col.	33	3	4	16	0	20	0	1.000
Cabrera, Jolbert, L.A.	3	1	2	4	0	6	1	1.000
Cairo, Miguel, St.L.	7	5	5	2	1	8	1	.875
Carroll, Jamey, Mon.	13	13	7	26	3	36	2	.917
CASTILLA, Vinny, Atl.	139	138	75	256	6	337	23	.982
Castro, Juan, Cin.	1	1	2	4	1	7	1	.857
Cintron, Alex, Ari.	9	1	2	7	0	9	1	1.000
Colbrunn, Greg, Ari.	5	3	1	3	0	4	0	1.000
Collier, Lou, Mon.	1	0	0	0	0	0	0	.000
Coolbaugh, Mike, St.L.	4	3	0	8	0	8	3	1.000
Counsell, Craig, Ari.	94	88	66	194	7	267	13	.974
Crespo, Cesar, S.D.	4	2	1	5	1	7	1	.857
DeRosa, Mark, Atl.	4	3	1	4	0	5	0	1.000
Donnels, Chris, Ari.	26	11	10	16	0	26	0	1.000
Ensberg, Morgan, Hou.	43	37	28	76	8	112	5	.929
Feliz, Pedro, S.F.	44	32	29	57	3	89	9	.966
Fox, Andy, Fla.	4	0	2	1	0	3	0	1.000
Giles, Marcus, Atl.	8	6	6	13	2	21	2	.905
Ginter, Keith, Hou.-Mil.	25	22	21	35	3	59	4	.949
Guerrero, Wilton, Cin.-Mon.	5	4	2	5	2	9	0	.778
Hall, Bill, Mil.	2	0	2	0	0	2	0	1.000
Hansen, Dave, L.A.	11	5	4	13	2	19	0	.895
Harris, Lenny, Mil.	14	10	7	14	0	21	3	1.000
Helms, Wes, Atl.	24	14	8	24	1	33	0	.970
Houston, Tyler, Mil.-L.A.	74	69	43	105	9	157	8	.943
Hubbard, Trenidad, S.D.	6	3	4	5	1	10	1	.900
Jimenez, D'Angelo, S.D.	32	30	19	70	5	94	9	.947
Klassen, Danny, Ari.	2	0	0	1	0	1	0	1.000
Larson, Brandon, Cin.	5	5	2	10	0	12	3	1.000
Lockhart, Keith, Atl.	1	0	1	0	0	1	0	1.000
Loretta, Mark, Mil.-Hou.	57	54	43	84	2	129	7	.984
Lowell, Mike, Fla.	159	159	150	286	14	450	36	.969
Macias, Jose, Mon.	22	15	10	38	3	51	0	.941
Mackowiak, Rob, Pit.	26	22	13	50	3	66	4	.955
Malloy, Marty, Fla.	2	0	0	1	0	1	0	1.000
Martinez, Ramon E., S.F.	2	0	2	0	0	2	0	1.000
Matos, Julius, S.D.	17	6	9	18	2	29	3	.931
McEwing, Joe, N.Y.	10	5	5	13	2	20	2	.900
Merced, Orlando, Hou.	1	0	0	1	0	1	0	1.000
Michaels, Jason, Phi.	1	0	0	0	2	2	0	.000
Millar, Kevin, Fla.	2	1	1	5	1	7	0	.857
Mordecai, Mike, Mon.-Fla.	35	10	11	25	2	38	5	.947
Mueller, Bill, Chi.-S.F.	104	90	62	159	6	227	19	.974
Nevin, Phil, S.D.	71	71	49	131	14	194	17	.928
Norton, Greg, Col.	22	20	16	27	5	48	4	.896
Ojeda, Augie, Chi.	5	0	1	5	0	6	0	1.000
Orie, Kevin, Chi.	12	9	4	13	2	19	1	.895
Ortiz, Jose, Col.	1	1	1	1	0	2	0	1.000
Osik, Keith, Pit.	4	4	2	16	0	18	1	1.000
Pelaez, Alex, S.D.	1	1	1	1	0	2	0	1.000
Perez, Eduardo, St.L.	6	0	0	0	1	1	0	.000
Perez, Tomas, Phi.	14	9	5	25	3	33	0	.909
Polanco, Placido, St.L.-Phi.	131	115	90	272	8	370	33	.978
Pujols, Albert, St.L.	41	37	25	66	6	97	6	.938
Ramirez, Aramis, Pit.	131	130	78	255	19	352	32	.946
Reboulet, Jeff, L.A.	3	0	0	0	0	0	0	.000
Rolen, Scott, Phi.-St.L.	155	154	133	335	16	484	41	.967
Romano, Jason, Col.	1	0	0	0	0	0	0	.000
Scutaro, Marco, N.Y.	3	0	1	2	0	3	0	1.000
Shumpert, Terry, Col.	1	0	0	2	0	2	0	1.000
Stynes, Chris, Chi.	40	36	15	43	5	63	3	.921
Tatis, Fernando, Mon.	99	99	59	180	13	252	17	.948
Truby, Chris, Mon.	31	25	13	48	5	66	4	.924
Valentin, John, N.Y.	18	14	9	27	5	41	3	.878
Vazquez, Ramon, S.D.	20	10	7	27	0	34	5	1.000
Vizcaino, Jose, Hou.	30	23	18	44	0	62	3	1.000
Wigginton, Ty, N.Y.	14	11	7	20	3	30	3	.900
Williams, Matt, Ari.	56	54	29	94	4	127	7	.969
Zeile, Todd, Col.	139	138	87	257	21	365	23	.942

TRIPLE PLAYS: Alfonzo, N.Y.; Lowell, Fla.; Tatis, Mon.

THIRD BASEMEN WITH TWO OR MORE TEAMS

Player, Team	G	GS	PO	A	E	TC	DP	Pct.
Ginter, Keith, Hou.	4	1	3	4	1	8	1	.875
Ginter, Keith, Mil.	21	21	18	31	2	51	3	.961
Guerrero, Wilton, Cin.	3	2	1	2	1	4	0	.750
Guerrero, Wilton, Mon.	2	2	1	3	1	5	0	.800
Houston, Tyler, Mil.	72	67	43	101	8	152	8	.947
Houston, Tyler, L.A.	2	2	0	4	1	5	0	.800
Loretta, Mark, Mil.	47	44	37	73	1	111	6	.991
Loretta, Mark, Hou.	10	10	6	11	1	18	1	.944
Mordecai, Mike, Mon.	28	8	6	21	2	29	3	.931

Player, Team	G	GS	PO	A	E	TC	DP	Pct.
Mordecai, Mike, Fla.	7	2	5	4	0	9	2	1.000
Mueller, Bill, Chi.	101	88	60	156	6	222	19	.973
Mueller, Bill, S.F.	3	2	2	3	0	5	0	1.000
Polanco, Placido, St.L.	78	63	52	139	5	196	18	.974
Polanco, Placido, Phi.	53	52	38	133	3	174	15	.983
Rolen, Scott, Phi.	100	100	81	206	8	295	23	.973
Rolen, Scott, St.L.	55	54	52	129	8	189	18	.958

SHORTSTOPS

Player, Team	G	GS	PO	A	E	TC	DP	Pct.
Aurilia, Rich, S.F.	131	130	213	334	11	558	97	.980
Bell, David, S.F.	3	3	4	7	0	11	1	1.000
Bell, Jay, Ari.	2	1	1	4	0	5	0	1.000
Bellhorn, Mark, Chi.	12	10	15	22	1	38	7	.974
Benjamin, Mike, Pit.	15	11	18	35	1	54	5	.981
Blum, Geoff, Hou.	2	0	0	0	0	0	0	.000
Boone, Aaron, Cin.	16	13	24	35	2	61	6	.967
Bush, Homer, Fla.	4	1	0	0	0	0	0	.000
Butler, Brent, Col.	13	8	15	24	1	40	5	.975
Cabrera, Orlando, Mon.	153	150	237	498	29	764	102	.962
Cairo, Miguel, St.L.	6	2	7	6	0	13	3	1.000
Carroll, Jamey, Mon.	3	3	6	10	1	17	2	.941
Castro, Juan, Cin.	25	7	20	33	2	55	10	.964
Cintron, Alex, Ari.	8	5	7	18	1	26	5	.962
Cora, Alex, L.A.	61	53	67	144	5	216	32	.977
Counsell, Craig, Ari.	22	11	23	37	1	61	8	.984
Crespo, Cesar, S.D.	1	0	0	0	0	0	0	.000
Cruz, Deivi, S.D.	147	133	169	372	15	556	83	.973
Dawkins, Gookie, Cin.	21	9	18	33	3	54	6	.944
Delgado, Wilson, St.L.	8	4	8	9	0	17	1	1.000
DeRosa, Mark, Atl.	19	14	30	52	2	84	17	.976
Dunston, Shawon, S.F.	1	0	0	0	0	0	0	.000
Everett, Adam, Hou.	34	29	34	93	5	132	22	.962
Feliz, Pedro, S.F.	1	0	0	0	0	0	0	.000
Fox, Andy, Fla.	112	103	187	279	17	483	73	.965
Furcal, Rafael, Atl.	150	147	245	466	27	738	111	.963
Garcia, Jesse, Atl.	5	0	4	7	0	11	4	1.000
Ginter, Keith, Hou.	1	0	2	1	0	3	0	1.000
Gonzalez, Alex, Fla.	42	41	72	113	3	188	32	.984
Gonzalez, Alex S., Chi.	142	139	220	360	21	601	84	.965
Guerrero, Wilton, Cin.	7	2	7	7	1	15	3	.933
Hall, Bill, Mil.	13	9	15	22	2	39	5	.949
Hernandez, Jose, Mil.	149	148	244	451	19	714	107	.973
Hill, Bobby, Chi.	1	0	0	0	1	1	0	.000
Izturis, Cesar, L.A.	128	109	155	306	10	471	69	.979
Klassen, Danny, Ari.	1	0	0	0	0	0	0	.000
Larkin, Barry, Cin.	135	131	191	370	12	573	89	.979
Lopez, Luis, Mil.	4	0	3	1	0	4	0	1.000
Loretta, Mark, Mil.-Hou.	18	10	20	26	3	49	5	.939
Lugo, Julio, Hou.	84	81	121	205	8	334	32	.976
Macias, Jose, Mon.	4	4	3	13	1	17	2	.941
Martinez, Ramon E., S.F.	40	28	52	82	7	141	26	.950
Mateo, Henry, Mon.	2	2	2	7	1	10	0	.900
Matos, Julius, S.D.	4	1	3	0	0	6	1	1.000
McEwing, Joe, N.Y.	21	10	18	40	5	63	4	.921
Mordecai, Mike, Mon.-Fla.	27	20	29	62	1	92	12	.989
Nunez, Abraham O., Pit.	24	15	19	57	5	81	15	.938
Ojeda, Augie, Chi.	16	13	15	41	2	58	4	.966
Ordonez, Rey, N.Y.	142	134	208	388	19	615	82	.969
Perez, Tomas, Phi.	13	12	30	33	0	63	11	1.000
Polanco, Placido, St.L.	13	9	19	24	0	43	7	1.000
Pujols, Albert, St.L.	1	0	0	0	0	0	0	.000
Punto, Nick, Phi.	1	0	1	0	1	2	0	.500
Ransom, Cody, S.F.	3	1	3	3	0	6	0	1.000
Reboulet, Jeff, L.A.	5	0	3	2	2	7	0	.714
Renteria, Edgar, St.L.	149	147	202	410	19	631	72	.970
Rollins, Jimmy, Phi.	152	149	226	455	14	695	90	.980
Romano, Jason, Col.	5	3	6	5	3	14	1	.786
Scutaro, Marco, N.Y.	6	4	5	11	1	17	3	.941
Shumpert, Terry, Col.	3	1	2	4	0	6	0	1.000
Uribe, Juan, Col.	155	150	261	504	27	792	118	.966
Valentin, John, N.Y.	24	13	20	48	2	70	9	.971
Vazquez, Ramon, S.D.	41	28	32	97	2	131	16	.985
Vizcaino, Jose, Hou.	58	47	59	135	4	198	35	.980
Wilson, Jack, Pit.	143	135	187	463	15	665	90	.977
Womack, Tony, Ari.	149	145	175	364	20	559	66	.964

TRIPLE PLAYS: Cabrera, Mon.; Renteria, St.L.

SHORTSTOPS WITH TWO OR MORE TEAMS

Player, Team	G	GS	PO	A	E	TC	DP	Pct.
Loretta, Mark, Mil.	12	5	14	10	2	26	3	.923
Loretta, Mark, Hou.	6	5	6	16	1	23	2	.957

Player, Team	G	GS	PO	A	E	TC	DP	Pct.
Mordecai, Mike, Mon.	3	3	3	9	0	12	1	1.000
Mordecai, Mike, Fla.	24	17	26	53	1	80	11	.988

OUTFIELDERS

Player, Team	G	GS	PO	A	E	TC	DP	Pct.
Abreu, Bobby, Phi.	154	153	282	10	5	297	2	.983
Agbayani, Benny, Col.	37	31	53	1	0	54	0	1.000
Alcantara, Izzy, Mil.	7	5	7	0	0	7	0	1.000
Allen, Luke, L.A.	3	1	4	0	0	4	0	1.000
Alou, Moises, Chi.	124	124	203	6	2	211	1	.991
Alvarez, Tony, Pit.	8	6	10	0	0	10	0	1.000
Banks, Brian, Fla.	8	5	8	0	0	8	0	1.000
Bautista, Danny, Ari.	39	39	65	0	1	66	0	.985
Bellhorn, Mark, Chi.	1	0	0	0	0	0	0	.000
Benard, Marvin, S.F.*	38	17	50	3	0	53	0	1.000
Benjamin, Mike, Pit.	1	0	0	0	0	0	0	.000
Bergeron, Peter, Mon.	31	30	76	0	2	78	0	.974
Berkman, Lance, Hou.*	156	155	293	6	7	306	1	.977
Biggio, Craig, Hou.	1	1	1	0	0	1	0	1.000
Blum, Geoff, Hou.	10	4	8	0	0	8	0	1.000
Bocachica, Hiram, L.A.	22	11	24	0	1	25	0	.960
Bonds, Barry, S.F.*	135	133	241	4	8	253	2	.968
Bragg, Darren, Atl.	63	37	98	2	3	103	0	.971
Branyan, Russell, Cin.	25	21	36	3	2	41	0	.951
Brown, Adrian, Pit.	71	44	112	1	3	116	0	.974
Brown, Roosevelt, Cin.	64	41	78	1	2	81	1	.975
Buchanan, Brian, S.D.	14	13	18	1	1	20	0	.950
Burnitz, Jeromy, N.Y.	140	131	249	7	9	265	0	.966
Burrell, Pat, Phi.	157	154	273	8	6	287	1	.979
Byrd, Marlon, Phi.	10	9	17	0	0	17	0	1.000
Cabrera, Jolbert, L.A.	4	0	4	0	0	4	0	1.000
Cairo, Miguel, St.L.	24	10	19	0	2	21	0	.905
Cedeno, Roger, N.Y.	132	125	225	2	8	235	0	.966
Cepicky, Matt, Mon.	17	14	21	0	0	21	0	1.000
Chavez, Endy, Mon.*	35	27	82	7	1	90	2	.989
Chen, Chin-Feng, L.A.	1	1	3	0	0	3	0	1.000
Christensen, McKay, N.Y.*	3	0	3	0	0	3	0	1.000
Christenson, Ryan, Mil.	21	14	38	0	0	38	0	1.000
Clark, Brady, Cin.-N.Y.	28	7	19	0	1	20	0	.950
Collier, Lou, Mon.	7	3	6	0	0	6	0	1.000
Cordero, Wil, Mon.	28	22	45	1	2	48	0	.958
Crespo, Cesar, S.D.	7	0	2	1	0	3	0	1.000
Cust, Jack, Col.	18	15	24	0	1	25	0	.960
Davis, J.J., Pit.	4	2	3	0	0	3	0	1.000
DeHaan, Kory, S.D.	9	2	6	0	0	6	0	1.000
Dellucci, David, Ari.*	64	53	85	2	3	90	2	.967
DeRosa, Mark, Atl.	7	2	4	0	0	4	0	1.000
DeShields, Delino, Chi.	1	0	2	0	0	2	0	1.000
Drew, J.D., St.L.	120	108	223	4	3	230	1	.987
Dunn, Adam, Cin.	118	114	201	10	9	220	2	.959
Dunston, Shawon, S.F.	49	25	47	0	0	47	0	1.000
Durazo, Erubiel, Ari.*	2	2	3	0	0	3	0	1.000
Echevarria, Angel, Chi.	19	12	33	1	1	35	1	.971
Edmonds, Jim, St.L.*	139	132	347	11	5	363	4	.986
Encarnacion, Juan, Cin.-Fla.	149	147	346	9	6	361	6	.983
Encarnacion, Mario, Chi.	2	2	5	0	0	5	0	1.000
Feliz, Pedro, S.F.	1	0	0	0	0	0	0	.000
Finley, Steve, Ari.*	144	131	319	4	2	325	2	.994
Floyd, Cliff, Fla.-Mon.	93	93	187	7	4	198	1	.980
Fox, Andy, Fla.	1	0	0	0	0	0	0	.000
Franco, Matt, Atl.	4	1	3	0	0	3	0	1.000
Gant, Ron, S.F.	80	73	142	6	3	151	0	.980
Garcia, Jesse, Atl.	4	0	6	0	0	6	0	1.000
Giambi, Jeremy, Phi.*	20	19	26	0	2	28	0	.929
Giles, Brian, Pit.*	151	150	244	13	7	264	5	.973
GLANVILLE, Doug, Phi.	117	95	220	7	0	227	4	1.000
Gload, Ross, Col.*	2	0	0	1	0	1	0	1.000
Gonzalez, Luis, Ari.	146	143	252	4	4	260	1	.985
Gonzalez, Raul, Cin.-N.Y.	30	22	54	2	0	56	0	1.000
Goodwin, Tom, S.F.	53	31	98	0	1	99	0	.990
Green, Shawn, L.A.*	156	156	333	7	2	342	3	.994
Griffey Jr., Ken, Cin.*	55	51	96	4	3	103	1	.971
Grissom, Marquis, L.A.	102	74	169	5	4	178	0	.978
Guerrero, Vladimir, Mon.	161	160	298	14	10	322	4	.969
Guerrero, Wilton, Mon.	12	4	11	1	0	12	0	1.000
Guillen, Jose, Ari.-Cin.	64	55	99	5	1	105	0	.990
Hammonds, Jeffrey, Mil.	125	121	247	3	2	252	1	.992
Harris, Lenny, Mil.	16	12	26	0	0	26	0	1.000
Helms, Wes, Atl.	9	3	15	1	0	16	0	1.000
Hermansen, Chad, Pit.-Chi.	81	52	124	5	4	133	1	.970
Hidalgo, Richard, Hou.	110	101	210	6	1	217	3	.995
Hollandsworth, Todd, Col.*	90	73	138	7	4	149	0	.973

Player, Team	G	GS	PO	A	E	TC	DP	Pct.
Hubbard, Trenidad, S.D.	57	16	49	2	1	52	0	.981
Hunter, Brian L., Hou.	88	40	121	4	0	125	1	1.000
Hyzdu, Adam, Pit.	50	39	85	2	0	87	0	1.000
Jenkins, Geoff, Mil.	66	65	124	7	1	132	1	.992
Johnson, Mark P., N.Y.*	1	0	0	0	0	0	0	.000
Jones, Andruw, Atl.	154	152	404	5	3	412	1	.993
Jones, Chipper, Atl.	152	152	268	8	7	283	0	.975
Jordan, Brian, L.A.	125	123	213	10	4	227	4	.982
Jose, Felix, Ari.	5	4	5	0	0	5	0	1.000
Kapler, Gabe, Col.	38	24	62	3	0	65	0	1.000
Kearns, Austin, Cin.	103	99	223	8	4	235	2	.983
Kingsale, Gene, S.D.	82	46	127	4	2	133	0	.985
Kinkade, Mike, L.A.	8	4	4	0	0	4	0	1.000
Klesko, Ryan, S.D.*	31	30	39	0	0	39	0	1.000
Kotsay, Mark, S.D.*	147	143	349	11	4	364	3	.989
Lane, Jason, Hou.*	38	18	47	3	1	51	1	.980
Langerhans, Ryan, Atl.*	1	0	0	0	0	0	0	.000
Lankford, Ray, S.D.*	59	54	98	4	5	107	1	.953
Larson, Brandon, Cin.	9	7	13	0	0	13	0	1.000
Ledee, Ricky, Phi.*	51	42	97	0	0	97	0	1.000
Lewis, Darren, Chi.	47	15	46	2	0	48	1	1.000
Little, Mark, Col.-N.Y.-Ari.	49	27	76	2	2	80	1	.975
Lo Duca, Paul, L.A.	9	3	4	1	0	5	0	1.000
Lofton, Kenny, S.F.*	44	44	116	3	0	119	0	1.000
Mabry, John, Phi.	1	1	1	0	0	1	0	1.000
Macias, Jose, Mon.	49	29	83	4	2	89	1	.978
Mackowiak, Rob, Pit.	106	77	151	7	2	160	3	.988
Marrero, Eli, St.L.	106	86	185	9	3	197	4	.985
Martinez, Ramon E., S.F.	3	2	8	0	0	8	0	1.000
Mateo, Ruben, Cin.	24	18	33	1	0	34	0	1.000
Matos, Julius, S.D.	3	0	1	0	0	1	0	1.000
McCracken, Quinton, Ari.	97	78	182	5	1	188	1	.995
McEwing, Joe, N.Y.	35	20	48	0	0	48	1	1.000
Merced, Orlando, Hou.	56	46	89	7	2	98	1	.980
Michaels, Jason, Phi.	26	10	22	2	0	24	0	1.000
Millar, Kevin, Fla.	108	108	187	6	3	196	1	.985
Mordecai, Mike, Mon.	1	0	0	0	0	0	0	.000
Murray, Calvin, S.F.	10	2	10	1	1	12	0	.917
Norton, Greg, Col.	2	2	4	0	0	4	0	1.000
Nunez, Abraham, Fla.	15	2	12	0	0	12	0	1.000
Ochoa, Alex, Mil.	72	53	135	5	1	141	1	.993
O'Leary, Troy, Mon.*	70	68	126	1	3	130	0	.977
Osik, Keith, Pit.	1	0	0	0	0	0	0	.000
Owens, Eric, Fla.	121	89	223	10	6	239	1	.975
Ozuna, Pablo, Fla.	1	0	0	0	0	0	0	.000
Patterson, Corey, Chi.	147	136	303	5	3	311	1	.990
Payton, Jay, N.Y.-Col.	126	109	252	9	1	262	1	.996
Pena, Wily Mo, Cin.	4	4	4	0	0	4	0	1.000
Perez, Eduardo, St.L.	35	21	50	4	1	55	1	.982
Perez, Timo, N.Y.*	122	107	266	9	6	281	3	.979
Petrick, Ben, Col.	16	13	20	0	1	21	0	.952
Pierre, Juan, Col.*	149	133	363	2	2	367	1	.995
Pujols, Albert, St.L.	118	101	173	4	4	181	0	.978
Raines, Tim, Fla.	14	4	10	1	1	12	0	.917
Rios, Armando, Pit.*	56	53	89	5	0	94	1	1.000
ROBERTS, Dave, L.A.*	117	111	253	4	0	257	1	1.000
Robinson, Kerry, St.L.*	76	26	85	0	2	87	0	.977
Rodriguez, Henry, Mon.*	5	2	0	0	0	0	0	.000
Romano, Jason, Col.	3	3	7	1	0	8	0	1.000
Ruan, Wilkin, L.A.	5	1	5	0	0	5	0	1.000
Rushford, Jim, Mil.*	22	21	43	0	2	45	0	.956
Sanchez, Alex, Mil.*	100	92	271	1	5	277	0	.982
Sanders, Reggie, S.F.	137	133	290	12	5	307	0	.984
Schneider, Brian, Mon.	2	0	0	0	0	0	0	.000
Scutaro, Marco, N.Y.	1	0	0	0	0	0	0	.000
Sheffield, Gary, Atl.	127	127	232	7	4	243	0	.984
Shinjo, Tsuyoshi, S.F.	117	97	286	10	6	302	3	.980
Shumpert, Terry, Col.	8	8	10	0	0	10	0	1.000
Snead, Esix, N.Y.	6	1	5	0	0	5	0	1.000
Sosa, Sammy, Chi.	150	150	284	7	6	297	1	.980
Stairs, Matt, Mil.	84	75	129	6	1	136	1	.993
Surhoff, B.J., Atl.	9	9	27	2	0	29	0	1.000
Sweeney, Mark, S.D.*	5	2	8	0	0	8	0	1.000
Taguchi, So, St.L.	14	2	11	2	1	14	0	.929
Tarasco, Tony, N.Y.	29	13	40	3	1	44	1	.977
Taylor, Reggie, Cin.	103	55	177	2	5	184	0	.973
Thompson, Ryan, Mil.	51	27	62	2	1	65	0	.985
Torcato, Tony, S.F.	3	2	2	0	0	2	0	1.000
Trammell, Bubba, S.D.	122	107	174	4	5	183	1	.973
Truby, Chris, Mon.	1	0	0	0	0	0	0	.000
Valent, Eric, Phi.*	2	0	0	0	0	0	0	.000
Walker, Larry, Col.	123	122	229	14	4	247	5	.984
Ward, Daryle, Hou.*	122	117	146	9	3	158	3	.981
Wesson, Barry, Hou.	15	4	11	0	0	11	0	1.000
Wigginton, Ty, N.Y.	2	0	0	0	0	0	0	.000
Wilkerson, Brad, Mon.*	129	114	226	13	7	246	3	.972
Wilson, Craig A., Pit.	75	65	106	6	2	114	0	.982
Wilson, Preston, Fla.	138	132	301	8	6	315	2	.981
Womack, Tony, Ari.	1	0	0	0	0	0	0	.000
Young, Eric, Mil.	2	1	1	0	0	1	0	1.000

TRIPLE PLAY: Drew, St.L.

OUTFIELDERS WITH TWO OR MORE TEAMS

Player, Team	G	GS	PO	A	E	TC	DP	Pct.
Clark, Brady, Cin.	22	6	15	0	1	16	0	.938
Clark, Brady, N.Y.	6	1	4	0	0	4	0	1.000
Encarnacion, Juan, Cin.	82	81	211	5	5	221	4	.977
Encarnacion, Juan, Fla.	67	66	135	4	1	140	2	.993
Floyd, Cliff, Fla.	80	80	173	5	3	181	1	.983
Floyd, Cliff, Mon.	13	13	14	2	1	17	0	.941
Gonzalez, Raul, Cin.	6	5	11	1	0	12	0	1.000
Gonzalez, Raul, N.Y.	24	17	43	1	0	44	0	1.000
Guillen, Jose, Ari.	37	30	54	2	0	56	0	1.000
Guillen, Jose, Cin.	27	25	45	3	1	49	0	.980
Hermansen, Chad, Pit.	60	46	107	5	2	114	1	.982
Hermansen, Chad, Chi.	21	6	17	0	2	19	0	.895
Little, Mark, Col.	36	21	62	2	2	66	1	.970
Little, Mark, N.Y.	1	0	0	0	0	0	0	.000
Little, Mark, Ari.	12	6	14	0	0	14	0	1.000
Payton, Jay, N.Y.	82	68	164	6	1	171	0	.994
Payton, Jay, Col.	44	41	88	3	0	91	1	1.000

CATCHERS

Player, Team	G	GS	PO	A	E	TC	DP	PB	Pct.
Alomar Jr., Sandy, Col.	38	30	190	8	0	198	1	3	1.000
Ausmus, Brad, Hou.	129	121	942	65	3	1010	9	2	.997
Bako, Paul, Mil.	76	65	420	33	4	457	2	5	.991
Barajas, Rod, Ari.	69	41	293	18	1	312	1	4	.997
Barrett, Michael, Mon.	110	105	751	55	9	815	9	9	.989
Bennett, Gary, Col.	90	85	453	32	4	489	5	6	.992
Blanco, Henry, Atl.	79	64	417	38	3	458	1	6	.993
Cardona, Javier, S.D.	14	11	76	5	2	83	2	0	.976
Casanova, Raul, Mil.	28	25	166	13	1	180	0	2	.994
Castro, Ramon, Fla.	37	17	148	12	0	160	0	0	1.000
Chavez, Raul, Hou.	2	1	10	0	0	10	0	0	1.000
Cota, Humberto, Pit.	7	4	33	1	0	34	1	0	1.000
DiFelice, Mike, St.L.	61	51	313	32	3	348	5	2	.991
Estalella, Bobby, Col.	38	32	203	9	1	213	2	2	.995
Estrada, Johnny, Phi.	10	3	34	2	0	36	0	1	1.000
Fabregas, Jorge, Mil.	20	17	118	9	1	128	0	1	.992
Girardi, Joe, Chi.	88	67	554	43	6	603	6	6	.990
Gonzalez, Wiki, S.D.	54	52	367	27	6	400	4	6	.985
Hundley, Todd, Chi.	79	71	622	40	11	673	8	7	.984
Jensen, Marcus, Mil.	15	10	73	9	2	84	1	2	.976
Johnson, Charles, Fla.	82	77	488	49	3	540	9	5	.994
Kendall, Jason, Pit.	143	140	797	64	9	870	13	8	.990
Kreuter, Chad, L.A.	41	24	197	16	3	216	1	0	.986
Lampkin, Tom, S.D.	94	79	553	42	5	600	7	7	.992
LaRue, Jason, Cin.	110	100	626	56	4	686	5	20	.994
Lieberthal, Mike, Phi.	129	126	840	56	6	902	8	7	.993
Lo Duca, Paul, L.A.	137	136	965	76	8	1049	9	12	.992
Lopez, Javy, Atl.	103	92	635	54	10	699	8	5	.986
Lunsford, Trey, S.F.	3	0	4	0	1	5	0	0	.800
Machado, Robert, Chi.-Mil.	69	60	387	56	6	449	7	3	.987
Mahoney, Mike, Chi.	16	9	76	7	0	83	0	1	1.000
Marrero, Eli, St.L.	44	15	151	9	4	164	2	2	.976
Matheny, Mike, St.L.	106	96	562	64	4	630	6	5	.994
McKeel, Walt, Col.	5	3	22	0	0	22	0	1	1.000
Miller, Corky, Cin.	38	35	220	23	2	245	4	1	.992
MILLER, Damian, Ari.	100	90	716	49	2	767	8	8	.997
Moeller, Chad, Ari.	35	31	310	7	1	318	0	1	.997
Nieves, Wil, S.D.	27	20	160	8	5	173	0	1	.971
Osik, Keith, Pit.	27	17	118	15	1	134	1	2	.993
Petrick, Ben, Col.	14	12	89	3	2	94	0	0	.979
Phillips, Jason, N.Y.	7	2	27	1	0	28	0	0	1.000
Piazza, Mike, N.Y.	121	119	811	46	12	869	3	8	.986
Pratt, Todd, Phi.	34	32	239	10	0	249	3	4	1.000
Redmond, Mike, Fla.	80	68	492	50	4	546	9	1	.993
Ross, Dave, L.A.	6	2	19	2	0	21	0	0	1.000
Santiago, Benito, S.F.	125	122	738	54	4	796	10	7	.995
Schneider, Brian, Mon.	65	57	382	34	3	419	6	3	.993
Stinnett, Kelly, Cin.	30	27	189	14	2	205	3	7	.990
Torrealba, Steve, Atl.	12	5	40	2	0	42	1	1	1.000
Torrealba, Yorvit, S.F.	53	40	269	20	2	291	3	0	.993

Player, Team	G	GS	PO	A	E	TC	DP	PB	Pct.
Wilson, Craig A., Pit.	5	0	10	0	0	10	0	2	1.000
Wilson, Vance, N.Y.	66	40	315	38	6	359	5	3	.983
Zaun, Gregg, Hou.	44	40	307	18	5	330	3	3	.985
Zinter, Alan, Hou.	1	0	2	0	0	2	0	0	1.000

TRIPLE PLAYS: Schneider, Mon.

CATCHERS WITH TWO OR MORE TEAMS

Player, Team	G	GS	PO	A	E	TC	DP	PB	Pct.
Machado, Robert, Chi.	21	15	110	25	2	137	2	1	.985
Machado, Robert, Mil.	48	45	277	31	4	312	5	2	.987

CATCHERS—SPECIAL STATS*

Player, Team	G	Inn.	SBA	CCS	PCS	CS%	ER	CERA
Alomar Jr., Sandy, Col.	38	272.2	18	4	1	.24	171	5.64
Ausmus, Brad, Hou.	129	1079.0	96	30	1	.32	458	3.82
Bako, Paul, Mil.	76	587.2	61	14	2	.24	311	4.76
Barajas, Rod, Ari.	69	406.0	28	7	3	.28	199	4.41
Barrett, Michael, Mon.	110	931.1	83	21	3	.26	388	3.75
Bennett, Gary, Col.	90	726.2	53	11	1	.21	430	5.33
Blanco, Henry, Atl.	79	594.2	58	19	2	.34	194	2.94
Cardona, Javier, S.D.	14	101.0	9	4	0	.44	38	3.39
Casanova, Raul, Mil.	28	218.1	30	7	2	.25	106	4.37
Castro, Ramon, Fla.	37	202.1	23	7	0	.30	105	4.67
Chavez, Raul, Hou.	2	14.0	0	0	0	0	6	3.86
Cota, Humberto, Pit.	7	40.1	2	1	0	.50	21	4.69
DiFelice, Mike, St.L.	61	435.1	32	9	0	.28	194	4.01
Estalella, Bobby, Col.	38	289.1	24	5	0	.21	142	4.42
Estrada, Johnny, Phi.	10	40.2	5	0	0	0	8	1.77
Fabregas, Jorge, Mil.	20	149.0	12	4	1	.36	67	4.05
Girardi, Joe, Chi.	88	615.2	65	20	0	.31	272	3.98
Gonzalez, Wiki, S.D.	54	442.2	37	15	0	.41	215	4.37
Hundley, Todd, Chi.	79	604.1	77	20	0	.26	270	4.02
Jensen, Marcus, Mil.	15	95.1	9	5	0	.56	47	4.44
Johnson, Charles, Fla.	82	638.1	62	21	4	.36	328	4.62
Kendall, Jason, Pit.	143	1191.2	117	26	13	.25	546	4.12
Kreuter, Chad, L.A.	41	247.2	27	6	4	.26	100	3.63
Lampkin, Tom, S.D.	94	710.1	57	18	0	.32	399	5.06
LaRue, Jason, Cin.	110	906.1	62	25	3	.42	467	4.64
Lieberthal, Mike, Phi.	129	1127.1	79	26	2	.34	536	4.28
Lo Duca, Paul, L.A.	137	1184.0	135	30	12	.24	491	3.73
Lopez, Javy, Atl.	103	815.1	87	23	10	.30	302	3.33
Lunsford, Trey, S.F.	3	7.0	1	0	0	0	2	2.57
Machado, Robert, Chi.-Mil.	69	520.0	66	22	2	.34	312	5.40
Mahoney, Mike, Chi.	16	83.1	4	4	0	1.00	54	5.83
Marrero, Eli, St.L.	44	180.2	22	2	0	.09	80	3.99
Matheny, Mike, St.L.	106	830.1	66	22	1	.34	321	3.48
McKeel, Walt, Col.	5	28.1	7	0	0	0	23	7.31
Miller, Corky, Cin.	38	301.0	21	6	1	.30	125	3.74
Miller, Damian, Ari.	100	763.0	66	23	2	.36	349	4.12
Moeller, Chad, Ari.	35	277.2	26	3	5	.14	82	2.66
Nieves, Wil, S.D.	27	182.1	13	3	0	.23	85	4.20
Osik, Keith, Pit.	27	171.2	19	3	1	.17	93	4.88
Petrick, Ben, Col.	14	109.2	8	1	0	.13	59	4.84
Phillips, Jason, N.Y.	7	37.0	1	0	1	0	7	1.70
Piazza, Mike, N.Y.	121	1006.2	152	21	6	.14	430	3.84
Pratt, Todd, Phi.	34	281.2	24	5	1	.22	127	4.06
Redmond, Mike, Fla.	80	615.2	69	26	3	.39	273	3.99
Ross, Dave, L.A.	6	26.0	1	1	0	1.00	7	2.42
Santiago, Benito, S.F.	125	1066.2	83	22	3	.28	413	3.48
Schneider, Brian, Mon.	65	521.2	46	19	1	.42	253	4.36
Stinnett, Kelly, Cin.	30	246.1	26	6	1	.24	98	3.58
Torrealba, Steve, Atl.	12	57.1	6	1	0	.17	15	2.35
Torrealba, Yorvit, S.F.	53	363.2	39	10	1	.26	151	3.74
Wilson, Craig A., Pit.	5	9.0	0	0	0	0	4	4.00
Wilson, Vance, N.Y.	66	399.0	51	22	3	.46	187	4.22
Zaun, Gregg, Hou.	44	351.0	44	5	0	.11	178	4.56
Zinter, Alan, Hou.	1	1.0	0	0	0	0	1	9.00

CATCHERS WITH TWO OR MORE TEAMS

Player, Team	G	Inn.	SBA	CCS	PCS	CS%	ER	CERA
Machado, Robert, Chi.	21	138.0	20	9	1	.47	91	5.93
Machado, Robert, Mil.	48	382.0	46	13	1	.29	221	5.21

*Inn. denotes the number of innings the catcher was behind the plate. SBA denotes stolen bases attempted. CCS denotes number of runners caught stealing by the catcher. PCS denotes number of runners caught stealing by the pitcher. CS% denotes the catcher's caught stealing percentage, figured by subtracting PCS from SBA and dividing this number into CCS. ER denotes number of earned runs scored when catcher was behind plate. CERA denotes catcher's ERA when he was behind the plate, figured the same way a pitcher's ERA is computed (ER*9/IP).

Player, Team	G	GS	PO	A	E	TC	DP	Pct.
Acevedo, Jose, Cin.	6	5	2	1	0	3	0	1.000
Adams, Terry, Phi.	46	19	11	24	4	39	1	.897
Ainsworth, Kurt, S.F.	6	4	1	8	0	9	0	1.000
Alfonseca, Antonio, Chi.	66	0	4	13	1	18	1	.944
Almanza, Armando, Fla.*	51	0	3	5	0	8	0	1.000
Almanzar, Carlos, S.F.	8	1	0	3	0	3	1	1.000
Alvarez, Victor, L.A.*	4	1	0	1	0	1	0	1.000
Anderson, Brian, Ari.*	35	24	5	36	2	43	4	.953
Anderson, Jimmy, Pit.*	28	25	6	34	1	41	4	.976
Armas Jr., Tony, Mon.	29	29	15	22	0	37	4	1.000
Arroyo, Bronson, Pit.	9	4	3	7	0	10	0	1.000
Ashby, Andy, L.A.	30	30	16	18	1	35	2	.971
Astacio, Pedro, N.Y.	31	31	6	28	1	35	0	.971
Aybar, Manny, S.F.	15	0	2	1	0	3	0	1.000
Bacsik, Mike, N.Y.*	11	9	4	15	1	20	0	.950
Batista, Miguel, Ari.	36	29	8	33	1	42	2	.976
Beckett, Josh, Fla.	23	21	11	9	1	21	0	.952
Beimel, Joe, Pit.*	53	8	1	12	3	16	1	.813
Beirne, Kevin, L.A.	12	3	1	3	0	4	0	1.000
Beltran, Francis, Chi.	11	0	0	4	0	4	1	1.000
Benes, Alan, Chi.	7	7	2	4	0	6	2	1.000
Benes, Andy, St.L.	18	17	5	10	1	16	1	.938
Benitez, Armando, N.Y.	62	0	2	8	2	12	0	.833
Benson, Kris, Pit.	25	25	12	11	2	25	2	.920
Bere, Jason, Chi.	16	16	4	11	2	17	1	.882
Boehringer, Brian, Pit.	70	0	2	7	0	9	0	1.000
Bong, Jung, Atl.*	1	1	0	1	0	1	1	1.000
Borbon, Pedro, Hou.*	56	0	3	4	0	7	1	1.000
Borland, Toby, Fla.	15	0	1	1	0	2	0	1.000
Borowski, Joe, Chi.	73	0	5	9	1	15	3	.933
Bottalico, Ricky, Phi.	30	0	2	3	0	5	0	1.000
Boyd, Jason, S.D.	23	0	3	7	0	10	0	1.000
Brohawn, Troy, S.F.*	11	0	1	0	0	1	0	1.000
Brower, Jim, Cin.-Mon.	52	0	9	12	0	21	0	1.000
Brown, Kevin, L.A.	17	10	5	9	1	15	0	.933
Buddie, Mike, Mil.	25	0	5	10	2	17	0	.882
Burnett, A.J., Fla.	31	29	12	19	4	35	3	.886
Bynum, Mike, S.D.*	14	3	0	4	0	4	0	1.000
Cabrera, Jose, Mil.	50	11	8	10	2	20	2	.900
Carrara, Giovanni, L.A.	63	1	8	18	0	26	1	1.000
Cerda, Jaime, N.Y.*	32	0	1	1	1	3	0	.667
Chacon, Shawn, Col.	21	21	18	15	2	35	1	.943
Chen, Bruce, N.Y.-Mon.-Cin.*.	55	6	6	6	0	12	0	1.000
Chiasson, Scott, Chi.	4	0	0	1	0	1	0	1.000
Childers, Matt, Mil.	8	0	0	2	0	2	1	1.000
Christiansen, Jason, S.F.*	6	0	0	0	0	0	0	.000
Clement, Matt, Chi.	32	32	8	23	2	33	1	.939
Coggin, Dave, Phi.	38	7	5	8	0	13	0	1.000
Colon, Bartolo, Mon.	17	17	6	15	1	22	1	.955
Condrey, Clay, S.D.	9	3	3	2	0	5	1	1.000
Cook, Aaron, Col.	9	5	4	9	1	14	3	.929
Corey, Bryan, L.A.	1	0	0	0	0	0	0	.000
Corey, Mark, N.Y.-Col.	26	0	0	1	0	1	0	1.000
Cormier, Rheal, Phi.*	54	0	3	14	0	17	3	1.000
Crudale, Mike, St.L.	49	1	8	2	1	11	0	.909
Cruz, Juan, Chi.	45	9	3	12	3	18	0	.833
Cruz, Nelson, Hou.	43	5	5	12	0	17	0	1.000
Cunnane, Will, Chi.	16	0	1	2	0	3	1	1.000
Cyr, Eric, S.D.*	5	0	0	0	0	0	0	.000
D'Amico, Jeff, N.Y.	29	22	5	18	0	23	0	1.000
Daal, Omar, L.A.*	39	23	10	33	0	43	5	1.000
Darensbourg, Vic, Fla.*	42	0	2	4	1	7	0	.857
Davey, Tom, S.D.	19	0	1	0	1	1	0	1.000
Davis, Kane, N.Y.	16	0	1	1	0	2	0	1.000
Dawley, Joey, Mil.	1	0	0	0	0	0	0	.000
Day, Zach, Mon.	19	2	6	6	0	12	1	1.000
de los Santos, Valerio, Mil.*.	51	0	3	3	0	6	1	1.000
DeJean, Mike, Mil.	68	0	9	8	0	17	0	1.000
Dempster, Ryan, Fla.-Cin.	33	33	19	26	0	45	4	1.000
Dessens, Elmer, Cin.	30	30	12	27	1	40	3	.975
DeWitt, Matt, S.D.	5	0	1	1	0	2	0	1.000
Diggins, Ben, Mil.	5	5	0	2	0	2	0	1.000
Dotel, Octavio, Hou.	83	0	0	8	0	8	0	1.000
Drew, Tim, Mon.	7	1	1	3	0	4	0	1.000
Duckworth, Brandon, Phi.	30	29	4	15	0	19	1	1.000
Duff, Matt, St.L.	7	0	0	1	0	1	0	1.000
Duncan, Courtney, Chi.	2	0	0	0	0	0	0	.000
Durocher, Jayson, Mil.	39	0	1	5	0	6	0	1.000
Eaton, Adam, S.D.	6	6	1	4	0	5	0	1.000
Eischen, Joey, Mon.*	59	0	3	8	1	12	0	.917

Player, Team	G	GS	PO	A	E	TC	DP	Pct.
Ellis, Robert, L.A.	3	0	0	0	0	0	0	.000
Embree, Alan, S.D.*	36	0	3	2	1	6	0	.833
Ennis, John, Atl.	1	1	1	2	0	3	1	1.000
Estes, Shawn, N.Y.-Cin.*	29	29	3	24	3	30	2	.900
Eyre, Scott, S.F.*	21	0	0	0	0	0	0	.000
Farnsworth, Kyle, Chi.	45	0	0	5	0	5	0	1.000
Fassero, Jeff, Chi.-St.L.*	73	0	4	10	0	14	0	1.000
Feliciano, Pedro, N.Y.*	6	0	0	0	0	0	0	.000
Fernandez, Jared, Cin.	14	8	3	12	0	15	0	1.000
Fetters, Mike, Pit.-Ari.	65	0	4	8	2	14	0	.857
Figueroa, Nelson, Mil.	30	11	4	12	2	18	0	.889
Fikac, Jeremy, S.D.	65	0	4	6	0	10	0	1.000
Finley, Chuck, St.L.*	14	14	1	7	0	8	0	1.000
Flores, Randy, Col.*	8	2	2	2	0	4	1	1.000
Fogg, Josh, Pit.	33	33	9	29	1	39	2	.974
Foster, John, Atl.*	5	0	0	0	0	0	0	.000
Fox, Chad, Mil.	3	0	0	0	0	0	0	.000
Franklin, Wayne, Mil.*	4	4	1	4	0	5	0	1.000
Fuentes, Brian, Col.*	31	0	2	2	1	5	0	.800
Fultz, Aaron, S.F.*	43	0	2	6	0	8	0	1.000
Gagne, Eric, L.A.	77	0	4	10	0	14	1	1.000
GLAVINE, Tom, Atl.*	36	36	22	49	0	71	3	1.000
Gordon, Flash, Chi.-Hou.	34	0	1	6	1	8	1	.875
Grace, Mark, Ari.*	1	0	0	0	0	0	0	.000
Graves, Danny, Cin.	68	4	13	20	0	33	0	1.000
Gryboski, Kevin, Atl.	57	0	2	4	0	6	0	1.000
Guthrie, Mark, N.Y.*	68	0	1	6	0	7	0	1.000
Hackman, Luther, St.L.	43	6	1	11	1	13	1	.923
Hamilton, Joey, Cin.	39	17	7	14	3	24	0	.875
Hammond, Chris, Atl.*	63	0	2	17	0	19	2	1.000
Hampton, Mike, Col.*	30	30	12	35	1	48	1	.979
Haynes, Jimmy, Cin.	34	34	10	28	3	41	4	.927
Helling, Rick, Ari.	30	30	4	17	1	22	1	.955
Herges, Matt, Mon.	62	0	5	7	0	12	0	1.000
Hernandez, Carlos, Hou.*	23	21	7	22	0	29	1	1.000
Hernandez, Livan, S.F.	33	33	18	53	3	74	7	.959
Hodges, Trey, Atl.	4	0	0	2	0	2	0	1.000
Hoffman, Trevor, S.D.	61	0	5	2	1	8	0	.875
Holmes, Darren, Atl.	55	0	4	9	3	16	1	.813
Holtz, Mike, S.D.*	33	0	3	1	0	4	0	1.000
Howard, Ben, S.D.	3	2	0	1	0	1	0	1.000
Hudson, Luke, Cin.	3	0	0	0	0	0	0	.000
Ishii, Kazuhisa, L.A.*	28	28	3	21	1	25	1	.960
Isringhausen, Jason, St.L.	60	0	3	6	2	11	0	.818
Izquierdo, Hansel, Fla.	20	2	1	4	1	6	1	.833
James, Mike, Col.	13	0	0	1	0	1	0	1.000
Jarvis, Kevin, S.D.	7	7	1	2	1	4	0	.750
Jennings, Jason, Col.	32	32	14	28	1	43	1	.977
Jensen, Ryan, S.F.	32	30	11	19	0	30	4	1.000
Jimenez, D'Angelo, S.D.	1	0	0	0	0	0	0	.000
Jimenez, Jose, Col.	74	0	11	15	1	27	2	.963
Johnson, Jonathan, S.D.	16	0	0	0	1	1	0	1.000
Johnson, Randy, Ari.*	35	35	5	20	2	27	2	.926
Jones, Bobby J., S.D.	19	18	7	14	0	21	1	1.000
Jones, Bobby M., N.Y.-S.D.*	16	2	0	3	0	3	0	1.000
Jones, Todd, Col.	79	0	11	13	0	24	1	1.000
Joseph, Kevin, St.L.	11	0	0	1	0	1	0	1.000
Junge, Eric, Phi.	4	1	1	2	0	3	0	1.000
Kershner, Jason, S.D.*	15	0	3	1	1	5	1	.800
Kile, Darryl, St.L.	14	14	3	18	1	22	2	.955
Kim, Byung-Hyun, Ari.	72	0	3	12	1	16	2	.938
Kim, Sun-Woo, Mon.	4	3	1	2	0	3	0	1.000
King, Ray, Mil.*	76	0	10	21	2	33	1	.939
Kline, Steve, St.L.*	66	0	4	6	0	10	0	1.000
Knotts, Gary, Fla.	28	0	1	3	0	4	0	1.000
Komiyama, Satoru, N.Y.	25	0	3	1	0	4	0	1.000
Koplove, Mike, Ari.	55	0	2	12	0	14	2	1.000
Lawrence, Brian, S.D.	35	31	22	31	0	53	1	1.000
Leiter, Al, N.Y.*	33	33	1	31	3	35	2	.914
Lidge, Brad, Hou.	6	1	0	2	0	2	0	1.000
Lieber, Jon, Chi.	21	21	5	19	0	24	1	1.000
Ligtenberg, Kerry, Atl.	52	0	1	8	1	10	1	.900
Lincoln, Mike, Pit.	55	0	4	11	0	15	2	1.000
Linebrink, Scott, Hou.	22	0	1	2	0	3	0	1.000
Lloyd, Graeme, Mon.-Fla.*	66	0	3	2	0	5	2	1.000
Looper, Braden, Fla.	78	0	3	14	0	17	2	1.000
Lopez, Albie, Atl.	30	4	4	3	0	7	1	1.000
Lorraine, Andrew, Mil.*	5	1	0	1	1	2	0	.500
Lowe, Sean, Pit.-Col.	51	1	6	15	0	21	2	1.000
Lundquist, David, S.D.	3	0	0	0	0	0	0	.000
Maddux, Greg, Atl.	34	34	21	48	1	70	3	.986
Mahay, Ron, Chi.*	11	0	1	1	1	3	0	.667
Mahomes, Pat, Chi.	16	2	1	6	0	7	0	1.000
Mairena, Oswaldo, Fla.*	31	0	0	5	0	5	0	1.000
Mallette, Brian, Mil.	5	0	0	2	0	2	0	1.000
Mann, Jim, Hou.	17	0	0	2	0	2	0	1.000
Mantei, Matt, Ari.	31	0	0	2	0	2	0	1.000
Manzanillo, Josias, Pit.	13	0	2	1	0	3	0	1.000
Marquis, Jason, Atl.	22	22	18	10	1	29	1	.966
Mathews, T.J., Hou.	12	0	0	4	0	4	1	1.000
Matthews, Mike, St.L.-Mil.*	47	0	0	9	1	10	1	.900
Meadows, Brian, Pit.	11	11	3	12	2	17	1	.882
Mercado, Hector, Phi.*	31	3	1	3	0	4	0	1.000
Mercker, Kent, Col.*	58	0	3	2	1	6	0	.833
Mesa, Jose, Phi.	74	0	4	16	0	20	0	1.000
Middlebrook, Jason, S.D.-N.Y.	15	5	0	4	0	4	0	1.000
Miller, Wade, Hou.	26	26	22	19	2	43	1	.953
Millwood, Kevin, Atl.	35	34	8	25	2	35	2	.943
Mlicki, Dave, Hou.	22	16	4	8	1	13	0	.923
Moehler, Brian, Cin.	10	9	4	12	0	16	0	1.000
Molina, Gabe, St.L.	12	0	0	2	0	2	1	1.000
Moreno, Juan, S.D.*	4	0	0	0	0	0	0	.000
Morgan, Mike, Ari.	29	0	1	3	1	5	0	.800
Morris, Matt, St.L.	32	32	11	22	0	33	0	1.000
Moss, Damian, Atl.*	33	29	5	37	2	44	3	.955
Mota, Guillermo, L.A.	43	0	2	7	0	9	0	1.000
Mulholland, Terry, L.A.*	21	0	2	9	1	12	1	.917
Munro, Peter, Hou.	19	14	14	18	1	33	1	.970
Myers, Brett, Phi.	12	12	6	11	0	17	2	1.000
Myers, Mike, Ari.*	69	0	2	11	0	13	0	1.000
Myers, Rodney, S.D.	14	0	3	2	0	5	1	1.000
Nance, Shane, Mil.*	4	0	1	1	0	2	0	1.000
Nathan, Joe, S.F.	4	0	0	2	0	2	0	1.000
Neagle, Denny, Col.*	35	28	8	25	1	34	1	.971
Neal, Blaine, Fla.	32	0	3	1	0	4	0	1.000
Nen, Robb, S.F.	68	0	7	5	0	12	0	1.000
Neugebauer, Nick, Mil.	12	12	4	4	0	8	0	1.000
Nichting, Chris, Col.	29	0	2	3	0	5	1	1.000
Nickle, Doug, Phi.-S.D.	14	0	1	2	1	4	0	.750
Nomo, Hideo, L.A.	34	34	10	21	4	35	2	.886
Nomura, Takahito, Mil.*	21	0	0	1	0	1	0	1.000
Nunez, Jose Antonio, S.D.*	1	0	0	0	0	0	0	.000
Nunez, Vladimir, Fla.	77	0	4	13	0	17	1	1.000
Ohka, Tomokazu, Mon.	32	31	24	30	0	54	2	1.000
Olsen, Kevin, Fla.	17	8	8	4	1	13	0	.923
Oropesa, Eddie, Ari.*	32	0	1	4	1	6	0	.833
Orosco, Jesse, L.A.*	56	0	2	3	0	5	0	1.000
Ortiz, Russ, S.F.	33	33	15	47	1	63	2	.984
Osborne, Donovan, Chi.*	11	0	0	2	0	2	0	1.000
Osting, Jimmy, Mil.*	3	3	1	3	0	4	0	1.000
Oswalt, Roy, Hou.	35	34	13	38	1	52	3	.981
Padilla, Vicente, Phi.	32	32	10	32	1	43	1	.977
Parra, Jose, Ari.	16	0	1	1	0	2	0	1.000
Patterson, John, Ari.	7	5	1	5	0	6	0	1.000
Pavano, Carl, Mon.-Fla.	37	22	3	19	1	23	4	.957
Pearce, Josh, St.L.	3	3	2	1	0	3	1	1.000
Pearson, Jason, S.D.*	2	0	0	0	0	0	0	.000
Peavy, Jake, S.D.	17	17	9	19	0	28	0	1.000
Pember, Dave, Mil.	4	1	1	0	0	1	0	1.000
Penny, Brad, Fla.	24	24	12	14	0	26	1	1.000
Perez, Odalis, L.A.*	32	32	23	51	2	76	3	.974
Perez, Oliver, S.D.*	16	15	2	9	1	12	1	.917
Perez, Tomas, Phi.	1	0	0	0	0	0	0	.000
Person, Robert, Phi.	16	16	4	9	0	13	0	1.000
Pichardo, Hipolito, Hou.	1	0	0	0	0	0	0	.000
Pickford, Kevin, S.D.*	16	4	3	5	1	9	1	.889
Pineda, Luis, Cin.	26	2	1	1	0	2	1	1.000
Plesac, Dan, Phi.*	41	0	0	3	0	3	0	1.000
Politte, Cliff, Phi.	13	0	0	0	0	0	0	.000
Pratt, Andy, Atl.*	1	0	0	1	0	1	0	1.000
Prinz, Bret, Ari.	20	0	0	2	0	2	0	1.000
Prior, Mark, Chi.	19	19	1	8	0	9	0	1.000
Puffer, Brandon, Hou.	55	0	10	13	0	23	0	1.000
Quantrill, Paul, L.A.	86	0	4	13	0	17	2	1.000
Quevedo, Ruben, Mil.	26	25	2	13	1	16	1	.938
Reames, Britt, Mon.	42	6	2	10	0	12	2	1.000
Redding, Tim, Hou.	18	14	4	15	2	21	1	.905
Reed, Steve, S.D.-N.Y.	64	0	4	13	0	17	1	1.000
Reitsma, Chris, Cin.	32	21	9	19	1	29	1	.966
Remlinger, Mike, Atl.*	73	0	1	10	0	11	1	1.000
Reyes, Al, Phi.	15	0	1	3	0	4	0	1.000
Reyes, Dennys, Col.*	43	0	0	6	0	6	1	1.000
Reynolds, Shane, Hou.	13	13	2	16	1	19	0	.947
Reynoso, Armando, Ari.	2	0	0	0	0	0	0	.000

Player, Team	G	GS	PO	A	E	TC	DP	Pct.
Riedling, John, Cin.	33	0	4	12	2	18	1	.889
Rijo, Jose, Cin.	31	9	4	14	0	18	0	1.000
Roa, Joe, Phi.	14	11	2	4	0	6	1	1.000
Roberts, Grant, N.Y.	34	0	4	5	0	9	0	1.000
Robertson, Jeriome, Hou.*	11	1	1	4	0	5	1	1.000
Robertson, Nate, Fla.*	6	1	0	1	1	2	0	.500
Rodriguez, Felix, S.F.	71	0	1	5	0	6	0	1.000
Rodriguez, Jose, St.L.*	2	0	0	0	0	0	0	.000
Rodriguez, Nerio, St.L.	2	0	0	0	0	0	0	.000
Rueter, Kirk, S.F.*	33	33	15	37	0	52	5	1.000
Rusch, Glendon, Mil.*	34	34	3	35	2	40	1	.950
Saarloos, Kirk, Hou.	17	17	8	14	1	23	3	.957
Sanchez, Duaner, Ari.-Pit.	9	0	1	0	0	1	0	1.000
Sanchez, Jesus, Chi.*	8	0	0	1	2	3	0	.333
Santiago, Jose, Phi.	42	0	3	4	0	7	0	1.000
Santos, Victor, Col.	24	2	1	2	0	3	0	1.000
Sauerbeck, Scott, Pit.*	78	0	2	12	0	14	2	1.000
Schilling, Curt, Ari.	36	35	9	16	0	25	1	1.000
Schmidt, Jason, S.F.	29	29	5	15	0	20	0	1.000
Seo, Jae Weong, N.Y.	1	0	0	0	0	0	0	.000
Sheets, Ben, Mil.	34	34	28	36	1	65	6	.985
Shiell, Jason, S.D.	3	0	0	0	0	0	0	.000
Shuey, Paul, L.A.	28	0	4	8	0	12	0	1.000
Silva, Carlos, Phi.	68	0	4	19	1	24	2	.958
Silva, Jose, Cin.	12	0	3	8	0	11	1	1.000
Simontacchi, Jason, St.L.	24	24	12	25	0	37	4	1.000
Small, Aaron, Atl.	1	0	0	0	0	0	0	.000
Smith, Bud, St.L.*	11	10	0	3	0	3	0	1.000
Smith, Dan, Mon.	33	0	2	2	0	4	0	1.000
Smith, Travis, St.L.	12	10	4	7	0	11	1	1.000
Smoltz, John, Atl.	75	0	11	11	0	22	1	1.000
Smyth, Steve, Chi.*	8	7	1	1	1	3	0	.667
Speier, Justin, Col.	63	0	0	2	0	2	0	1.000
Spooneybarger, Tim, Atl.	51	0	3	9	1	13	0	.923
Springer, Dennis, L.A.	1	0	1	0	0	1	0	1.000
Stark, Denny, Col.	32	20	6	15	0	21	1	1.000
Stechschulte, Gene, St.L.	29	0	2	4	0	6	0	1.000
Stephenson, Garrett, St.L.	12	10	1	9	0	10	0	1.000
Stewart, Scott, Mon.*	67	0	1	9	1	11	0	.909
Stone, Ricky, Hou.	78	0	2	11	0	13	0	1.000
Stottlemyre, Todd, Ari.	5	4	1	3	0	4	0	1.000
Strange, Pat, N.Y.	5	0	0	1	1	2	0	.500
Strickland, Scott, Mon.-N.Y.	69	0	4	8	2	14	1	.857
Stull, Everett, Mil.	2	2	1	4	0	5	0	1.000
Sullivan, Scott, Cin.	71	0	3	5	3	11	0	.727
Swindell, Greg, Ari.*	34	0	1	3	0	4	1	1.000
Tankersley, Dennis, S.D.	17	9	3	5	0	8	0	1.000
Tavarez, Julian, Fla.	29	27	15	30	4	49	2	.918
Tejera, Michael, Fla.*	47	18	9	24	1	34	4	.971
Teut, Nate, Fla.*	2	1	0	0	0	0	0	.000
Thomson, John, Col.-N.Y.	30	30	20	36	1	57	0	.982
Timlin, Mike, St.L.-Phi.	72	1	9	15	1	25	2	.960
Tollberg, Brian, S.D.	12	11	4	6	0	10	1	1.000
Tomko, Brett, S.D.	32	32	19	26	1	46	1	.978
Torres, Salomon, Pit.	5	5	4	2	0	6	0	1.000
Trachsel, Steve, N.Y.	30	30	12	37	2	51	3	.961
Trujillo, J.J., S.D.	4	0	0	0	0	0	0	.000
Tucker, T.J., Mon.	57	0	6	8	5	19	2	.737
Vance, Cory, Col.*	2	1	1	1	0	2	1	1.000
Vazquez, Javier, Mon.	34	34	14	33	1	48	6	.979
Veres, Dave, St.L.	71	0	3	10	2	15	3	.867
Villafuerte, Brandon, S.D.	31	0	2	4	0	6	0	1.000
Villone, Ron, Pit.*	45	7	6	20	2	28	2	.929
Vizcaino, Luis, Mil.	76	0	3	7	0	10	0	1.000
Vosberg, Ed, Mon.*	4	0	0	0	0	0	0	.000
Wagner, Billy, Hou.*	70	0	5	9	0	14	0	1.000
Walker, Kevin, S.D.*	11	0	0	5	0	5	0	1.000
Walker, Pete, N.Y.	1	0	0	0	0	0	0	.000
Walker, Tyler, N.Y.	5	1	1	1	0	2	0	1.000
Wayne, Justin, Fla.	5	5	5	3	0	8	1	1.000
Weathers, Dave, N.Y.	71	0	1	14	0	15	2	1.000
Wells, Kip, Pit.	33	33	12	30	3	45	1	.933
White, Gabe, Cin.*	62	0	3	5	0	8	0	1.000
White, Rick, Col.-St.L.	61	0	2	9	0	11	2	1.000
Williams, Dave, Pit.*	9	9	1	12	2	15	1	.867
Williams, Jeff, L.A.*	10	0	1	3	0	4	0	1.000
Williams, Mike, Pit.	59	0	8	15	1	24	2	.958
Williams, Woody, St.L.	17	17	7	19	0	26	2	1.000
Williamson, Scott, Cin.	63	0	2	7	1	10	1	.900
Witasick, Jay, S.F.	44	0	2	5	0	7	0	1.000
Wolf, Randy, Phi.*	31	31	9	23	2	34	2	.941
Wood, Kerry, Chi.	33	33	14	20	0	34	3	1.000
Worrell, Tim, S.F.	80	0	2	10	0	12	0	1.000
Wright, Jamey, Mil.-St.L.	23	22	12	23	1	36	3	.972
Yoshii, Masato, Mon.	31	20	9	19	0	28	3	1.000
Zambrano, Carlos, Chi.	32	16	8	26	0	34	4	1.000
Zeile, Todd, Col.	1	0	0	0	0	0	0	.000
Zerbe, Chad, S.F.*	50	0	4	7	0	11	0	1.000

PITCHERS WITH TWO OR MORE TEAMS

Player, Team	G	GS	PO	A	E	TC	DP	Pct.
Brower, Jim, Cin.	22	0	4	6	0	10	0	1.000
Brower, Jim, Mon.	30	0	5	6	0	11	0	1.000
Chen, Bruce, N.Y.*	1	0	1	0	0	1	0	1.000
Chen, Bruce, Mon.*	15	5	1	2	0	3	0	1.000
Chen, Bruce, Cin.*	39	1	4	4	0	8	0	1.000
Corey, Mark, N.Y.	12	0	0	0	0	0	0	.000
Corey, Mark, Col.	14	0	0	1	0	1	0	1.000
Dempster, Ryan, Fla.	18	18	13	17	0	30	1	1.000
Dempster, Ryan, Cin.	15	15	6	9	0	15	3	1.000
Estes, Shawn, N.Y.*	23	23	2	18	3	23	2	.870
Estes, Shawn, Cin.*	6	6	1	6	0	7	0	1.000
Fassero, Jeff, Chi.*	57	0	2	7	0	9	0	1.000
Fassero, Jeff, St.L.*	16	0	2	3	0	5	0	1.000
Fetters, Mike, Pit.	32	0	1	5	1	7	0	.857
Fetters, Mike, Ari.	33	0	3	3	1	7	0	.857
Gordon, Flash, Chi.	19	0	1	4	0	5	1	1.000
Gordon, Flash, Hou.	15	0	0	2	1	3	0	.667
Jones, Bobby M., N.Y.*	12	0	0	2	0	2	0	1.000
Jones, Bobby M., S.D.*	4	2	0	1	0	1	0	1.000
Lloyd, Graeme, Mon.*	41	0	2	1	0	3	1	1.000
Lloyd, Graeme, Fla.*	25	0	1	1	0	2	1	1.000
Lowe, Sean, Pit.	43	1	5	14	0	19	1	1.000
Lowe, Sean, St.L.	8	0	1	1	0	2	1	1.000
Matthews, Mike, St.L.*	43	0	0	8	1	9	1	.889
Matthews, Mike, Mil.*	4	0	0	1	0	1	0	1.000
Middlebrook, Jason, S.D.	12	2	0	2	0	2	0	1.000
Middlebrook, Jason, N.Y.	3	3	0	2	0	2	0	1.000
Nickle, Doug, Phi.	4	0	0	0	0	0	0	.000
Nickle, Doug, S.D.	10	0	1	2	1	4	0	.750
Pavano, Carl, Mon.	15	14	0	12	1	13	1	.923
Pavano, Carl, Fla.	22	8	3	7	0	10	3	1.000
Reed, Steve, S.D.	40	0	4	10	0	14	1	1.000
Reed, Steve, N.Y.	24	0	0	3	0	3	0	1.000
Sanchez, Duaner, Ari.	6	0	0	0	0	0	0	.000
Sanchez, Duaner, Pit.	3	0	1	0	0	1	0	1.000
Strickland, Scott, Mon.	1	0	0	0	0	0	0	.000
Strickland, Scott, N.Y.	68	0	4	8	2	14	1	.857
Thomson, John, Col.	21	21	16	22	0	38	0	1.000
Thomson, John, N.Y.	9	9	4	14	1	19	0	.947
Timlin, Mike, St.L.	42	1	7	11	1	19	2	.947
Timlin, Mike, Phi.	30	0	2	4	0	6	0	1.000
White, Rick, Col.	41	0	1	6	0	7	2	1.000
White, Rick, St.L.	20	0	1	3	0	4	0	1.000
Wright, Jamey, Mil.	19	19	10	20	1	31	3	.968
Wright, Jamey, St.L.	4	3	2	3	0	5	0	1.000

MISCELLANEOUS

SHUTOUT GAMES

Read across for wins, down for losses.

Team	Phi.	Atl.	S.F.	Hou.	N.Y.	L.A.	Col.	Cin.	Fla.	Ari.	Chi.	St.L.	S.D.	Pit.	Mon.	Mil.	A.L.	W	L	Pct.
Philadelphia	..	0	0	0	2	0	0	0	0	1	0	2	0	1	0	2	1	9	3	.750
Atlanta	1	..	1	1	0	0	0	1	3	0	2	0	0	1	3	1	1	15	6	.714
San Francisco	0	1	..	1	1	2	1	1	1	3	0	0	1	0	0	0	1	13	7	.650
Houston	0	0	1	..	0	0	0	1	0	1	0	1	2	3	0	0	1	11	6	.647
New York	1	1	0	1	..	2	0	0	1	0	0	0	0	0	1	2	1	10	7	.588
Los Angeles	0	0	1	1	0	..	2	0	1	4	1	0	2	1	1	1	0	15	13	.536
Colorado	0	0	0	0	0	1	..	0	1	0	1	0	1	3	1	0	0	8	7	.533
Cincinnati	0	0	0	0	0	1	0	..	0	0	2	1	1	1	0	2	0	8	8	.500
Florida	1	0	1	0	0	0	1	0	..	1	0	1	1	0	3	0	3	12	13	.480
Arizona	0	0	1	0	1	0	0	0	0	..	1	0	4	1	0	2	0	10	11	.476
Chicago	0	0	0	1	1	1	0	1	0	1	..	1	0	1	0	1	1	9	10	.474
St. Louis	0	0	1	0	1	0	0	1	1	0	1	..	0	0	1	2	1	9	10	.474
San Diego	0	0	0	0	0	5	2	0	1	0	1	0	..	1	0	0	1	10	16	.385
Pittsburgh	0	2	0	0	0	0	0	1	1	0	1	1	0	..	0	1	0	7	15	.318
Montreal	0	1	0	0	0	0	0	1	0	0	0	0	1	0	..	0	0	3	10	.231
Milwaukee	0	0	0	0	0	0	0	0	1	0	0	1	1	1	0	..	0	4	15	.211
A.L. Clubs	0	1	1	1	1	1	1	1	2	0	0	2	2	1	0	1	..	..	..	
Lost	3	6	7	6	7	13	7	8	13	11	10	10	16	15	10	15	..	153	157	.494

N.L. shutouts vs. A.L. clubs (11): Florida vs. Cleveland 2, Florida vs. Tampa Bay, Atlanta vs. Minnesota, Chicago vs. Seattle, Houston vs. Texas, New York vs. New York, Philadelphia vs. Minnesota, St. Louis vs. Kansas City, San Diego vs. Baltimore, San Francisco vs. Tampa Bay.

HOME RECORD

Read across for home wins, down for road losses.

Team	Ari.	Atl.	St.L.	S.F.	Mon.	Hou.	Col.	L.A.	Fla.	S.D.	Phi.	Pit.	Cin.	N.Y.	Chi.	Mil.	A.L.	W	L	Pct.
Arizona	..	1	2	4	3	2	9	4	3	9	3	2	3	1	2	2	5	55	26	.679
Atlanta	1	..	3	1	7	1	2	1	6	2	5	2	2	6	3	3	7	52	28	.650
St. Louis	3	1	..	1	1	7	1	2	1	3	0	4	6	2	8	7	5	52	29	.642
San Francisco	6	2	1	..	1	3	5	4	2	8	2	2	3	3	2	2	4	50	31	.617
Montreal	2	3	1	2	..	1	1	1	4	3	6	2	3	7	2	3	8	49	32	.605
Houston	2	1	4	1	1	..	2	1	2	2	3	7	5	2	5	6	3	47	34	.580
Colorado	4	1	0	4	2	2	..	5	3	7	3	3	3	1	1	3	5	47	34	.580
Los Angeles	5	2	0	3	3	1	7	..	2	6	2	2	1	1	1	3	7	46	35	.568
Florida	1	5	2	3	4	2	1	2	..	3	5	3	0	5	2	2	6	46	35	.568
San Diego	6	2	1	4	3	1	6	5	1	..	2	2	1	1	2	0	4	41	40	.506
Philadelphia	2	3	1	2	5	3	3	2	4	1	..	2	1	4	1	3	3	40	40	.500
Pittsburgh	1	2	3	1	2	3	2	1	2	1	3	..	4	2	5	6	0	38	42	.475
Cincinnati	0	1	4	2	1	4	3	2	2	3	0	6	..	1	4	5	0	38	43	.469
New York	0	4	2	0	5	1	1	0	7	0	3	1	2	..	3	3	6	38	43	.469
Chicago	1	1	5	2	2	4	2	0	3	1	1	5	2	1	..	3	3	36	45	.444
Milwaukee	1	1	4	0	2	5	3	1	1	2	1	1	1	6	1	..	1	31	50	.383
A.L. Clubs	3	1	3	5	4	7	4	5	5	2	3	4	5	3	5		..	..	..	
Lost on Road	38	31	36	35	47	44	55	35	48	56	41	47	41	43	50	56	..	706	587	.546

HOME RECORDS IN INTERLEAGUE GAMES

Team				Total	Team				Total
Arizona	2-1 vs. Bal.	2-1 vs. Det.	1-2 vs. Tor.	5-4	Milwaukee	0-3 vs. Ana.	1-2 vs. Min.		1-5
Atlanta	2-1 vs. Bos.	3-0 vs. Chi.	2-1 vs. Det.	7-2	Montreal	2-1 vs. Cle.	3-0 vs. K.C.	3-0 vs. Tor.	8-1
Chicago	2-1 vs. Chi.	1-2 vs. Tex.		3-3	New York	2-1 vs. K.C.	2-1 vs. Min.	2-1 vs. N.Y.	6-3
Cincinnati	0-3 vs. Oak.	0-3 vs. Sea.		0-6	Philadelphia	1-2 vs. Bal.	1-2 vs. Chi.	1-2 vs. Min.	3-6
Colorado	1-2 vs. Cle.	1-2 vs. N.Y.	0-3 vs. T.B.	2-7	Pittsburgh	0-3 vs. Oak.	0-3 vs. Tex.		0-6
Florida	3-0 vs. Cle.	2-1 vs. Det.	1-2 vs. T.B.	6-3	St. Louis	2-1 vs. Ana.	3-0 vs. K.C.		5-1
Houston	1-2 vs. Sea.	2-1 vs. Tex.		3-3	San Diego	1-2 vs. Bos.	1-2 vs. N.Y.	2-1 vs. Sea.	4-5
Los Angeles	2-1 vs. Ana.	3-0 vs. Bos.	2-1 vs. Tor.	7-2	San Francisco	1-2 vs. Bal.	1-2 vs. Oak.	2-1 vs. T.B.	4-5

ROAD RECORD

Read across for road wins, down for home losses.

Team	Atl.	L.A.	S.F.	St.L.	Ari.	Cin.	Phi.	N.Y.	Hou.	Mon.	Pit.	Fla.	Chi.	Col.	Mil.	S.D.	A.L.	W	L	Pct.
Atlanta	..	1	2	2	2	2	6	6	2	6	1	5	1	2	2	1	8	49	31	.613
Los Angeles	2	..	5	2	5	1	2	3	2	2	1	3	5	2	4	5	6	46	35	.568
San Francisco	1	7	..	1	5	1	1	3	2	1	2	1	1	6	3	6	4	45	35	.563
St. Louis	0	2	3	..	1	5	2	1	6	2	7	1	4	3	3	2	3	45	36	.556
Arizona	2	5	4	0	..	3	1	4	1	1	2	2	2	5	2	3	6	43	38	.531
Cincinnati	1	2	0	4	0	..	2	1	2	0	5	3	8	0	8	2	2	40	41	.494
Philadelphia	4	1	1	3	1	3	..	6	0	3	0	5	3	0	2	1	7	40	41	.494
New York	3	2	0	1	2	2	6	..	1	3	0	4	2	2	3	4	3	37	43	.463
Houston	2	2	0	2	1	6	0	2	..	2	4	1	6	1	4	2	2	37	44	.457
Montreal	3	1	2	2	0	2	5	4	2	..	1	5	1	1	0	4	3	34	47	.420
Pittsburgh	1	1	1	3	1	3	1	2	3	1	..	0	4	0	9	1	3	34	47	.420
Florida	3	1	1	2	0	1	5	3	1	6	1	..	0	1	2	2	4	33	48	.407

Team	Atl.	L.A.	S.F.	St.L.	Ari.	Cin.	Phi.	N.Y.	Hou.	Mon.	Pit.	Fla.	Chi.	Col.	Mil.	S.D.	A.L.	W	L	Pct.
Chicago	1	2	1	1	1	3	1	0	4	1	5	1	..	2	4	1	3	31	50	.383
Colorado	2	2	4	2	1	0	0	2	1	2	1	2	1	..	0	4	2	26	55	.321
Milwaukee	0	0	1	3	1	5	0	0	3	0	3	1	4	0	..	3	1	25	56	.309
San Diego	1	4	1	0	1	0	2	3	1	1	2	0	2	1	4	..	4	25	56	.309
A.L. Clubs	2	2	5	1	4	6	6	3	3	1	1	6	3	3	4	5	..	25	56	.309
Lost at home	28	35	31	29	26	43	40	43	34	32	42	35	45	34	50	40	..	590	703	.456

PITCHING AGAINST EACH CLUB

ARIZONA—98-64

Pitcher	Atl.	Chi.	Cin.	Col.	Fla.	Hou.	L.A.	Mil.	Mon.	N.Y.	Phi.	Pit.	S.D.	S.F.	St.L.	A.L.	Total
Anderson, Brian	0-1	0-1	1-0	0-1	0-0	1-0	1-2	0-0	0-0	0-0	0-0	0-1	0-1	1-2	0-0	2-2	6-11
Batista, Miguel	0-0	0-0	1-0	3-0	0-1	0-0	0-3	0-0	0-0	2-0	0-1	0-0	0-2	0-0	0-0	2-2	8-9
Fetters, Mike	0-0	1-0	0-0	0-1	0-0	0-0	0-0	0-0	0-0	0-0	0-0	0-0	0-1	0-1	0-0	0-0	2-3
Helling, Rick	1-0	0-0	1-0	2-0	0-0	0-0	0-4	0-2	0-0	0-1	0-1	1-0	1-1	1-2	1-0	0-0	10-12
Johnson, Randy	0-0	1-0	1-0	3-0	2-0	1-0	2-1	2-0	1-0	1-0	1-0	0-1	0-1	1-1	1-1	2-0	24-5
Kim, Byung-Hyun	0-0	0-0	0-0	1-0	1-0	0-0	2-0	0-0	1-0	1-0	0-1	4-1	2-1	1-0	0-0	2-1	8-3
Koplove, Mike	0-1	1-0	0-0	0-0	0-0	0-0	1-0	1-0	0-0	1-0	0-0	0-0	2-0	0-0	0-0	1-0	6-1
Mantei, Matt	1-0	0-1	0-0	0-0	0-0	0-0	1-0	0-0	0-0	0-0	0-0	0-0	0-0	0-0	0-0	0-0	1-1
Morgan, Mike	0-0	0-0	0-0	0-0	0-0	0-0	0-0	0-1	0-0	0-0	0-0	0-0	0-1	0-0	0-0	0-0	2-2
Myers, Mike	0-0	0-0	0-0	1-0	0-0	0-0	0-0	0-0	0-0	0-0	1-0	1-0	1-1	0-1	0-0	0-0	1-1
Oropesa, Eddie	0-0	0-0	0-0	0-0	0-0	0-0	0-0	1-0	0-0	1-0	0-0	0-0	0-1	0-0	0-0	0-0	4-3
Parra, Jose	0-0	0-0	0-0	0-0	0-0	0-0	0-0	0-0	1-0	0-0	1-0	0-0	0-0	0-0	0-0	0-0	2-0
Patterson, John	0-0	0-0	0-0	1-0	0-0	0-0	0-0	0-0	0-0	0-0	0-1	0-0	0-0	0-0	0-0	0-0	0-1
Prinz, Bret	0-1	0-0	0-0	0-0	0-0	0-1	0-0	0-0	0-0	0-0	0-0	0-0	1-0	0-0	0-0	0-0	2-0
Schilling, Curt	1-0	1-0	1-0	3-1	2-0	1-0	2-1	1-0	1-1	0-0	0-0	0-0	2-0	3-0	3-1	0-2	23-7
Stottlemyre, Todd	0-0	0-0	0-0	0-0	0-0	0-0	0-0	0-0	0-0	0-0	0-1	0-0	0-0	0-0	0-0	0-0	0-2
Swindell, Greg	0-0	0-0	0-0	0-2	0-0	0-0	0-0	0-0	0-0	0-0	0-0	0-1	0-0	0-0	0-0	0-0	0-2
Totals	3-3	4-2	6-0	14-5	5-1	3-3	9-10	4-2	4-2	5-2	4-3	4-2	12-7	8-11	2-4	11-7	98-64

NO-DECISIONS: Mark Grace, Armando Reynoso, Duaner Sanchez.

INTERLEAGUE: Brian Anderson 1-0, Curt Schilling 0-1, Randy Johnson 1-0 vs. Orioles; Miguel Batista 1-0, Curt Schilling 1-0, Rick Helling 1-0 vs. Red Sox; Miguel Batista 0-1, Brian Anderson 1-0, Curt Schilling 1-0 vs. Indians; Curt Schilling 0-1, Randy Johnson 1-0, Rick Helling 1-0 vs. Tigers; Randy Johnson 0-1, Brian Anderson 0-1, Miguel Batista 1-0 vs. Yankees; Byung-Hyun Kim 1-0, Brian Anderson 0-1 vs. Blue Jays. Total: 11-7.

ATLANTA—101-59

Pitcher	Ari.	Chi.	Cin.	Col.	Fla.	Hou.	L.A.	Mil.	Mon.	N.Y.	Phi.	Pit.	S.D.	S.F.	St.L.	A.L.	Total
Bong, Jung	0-1	0-0	0-0	0-0	0-0	0-0	0-0	0-0	0-0	0-0	0-0	0-0	0-0	0-0	0-0	0-0	0-1
Foster, John	1-0	0-0	0-0	0-0	0-0	0-0	0-0	0-0	0-0	0-0	0-0	0-0	0-0	0-0	0-0	0-0	1-0
Glavine, Tom	1-0	0-0	1-0	1-0	4-0	1-0	0-1	1-0	2-2	1-1	3-2	0-2	0-1	1-0	1-0	1-1	18-11
Gryboski, Kevin	0-0	0-0	0-0	0-0	0-1	0-0	0-0	0-0	1-0	0-0	0-0	0-0	0-0	0-0	1-0	1-0	2-1
Hammond, Chris	0-0	0-0	0-0	0-0	0-0	0-0	0-0	0-0	1-0	3-1	0-0	0-0	0-0	0-1	1-0	2-0	7-2
Hodges, Trey	0-0	0-0	0-0	0-0	0-0	0-0	0-0	0-0	2-0	0-0	0-0	0-0	0-0	0-0	0-0	0-0	2-0
Holmes, Darren	0-0	0-0	0-0	0-0	0-0	0-0	0-1	1-0	0-1	0-0	0-0	0-0	0-0	0-0	0-0	0-0	2-0
Ligtenberg, Kerry	1-0	0-0	0-0	0-0	0-0	0-0	0-1	0-0	1-0	0-0	0-2	0-0	0-0	0-0	0-0	0-0	2-2
Lopez, Albie	0-0	0-0	0-0	0-0	0-0	0-1	0-0	0-0	0-0	1-2	0-0	0-0	0-0	0-0	0-1	1-1	3-4
Maddux, Greg	0-1	1-0	2-0	0-1	4-2	0-0	1-1	0-0	1-0	2-0	0-0	0-0	0-0	0-1	0-0	1-0	16-6
Marquis, Jason	0-0	0-1	0-1	0-1	0-1	0-0	0-0	1-0	0-1	2-0	1-0	0-0	1-1	1-0	1-0	2-1	8-9
Millwood, Kevin	0-0	2-0	1-0	1-1	0-3	1-1	0-0	1-0	3-0	2-2	2-1	1-0	1-1	0-0	1-0	2-1	18-8
Moss, Damian	0-0	0-0	0-1	0-0	2-1	0-0	2-0	1-0	3-0	2-2	1-0	1-0	0-1	0-0	0-0	2-0	12-6
Remlinger, Mike	0-1	0-0	0-0	1-0	0-0	0-0	0-0	1-0	0-1	0-0	0-0	0-0	0-1	0-1	0-0	2-0	7-3
Smoltz, John	0-0	0-0	0-0	0-0	0-0	0-0	0-0	1-1	0-1	0-0	0-1	1-0	0-0	0-0	3-0	0-0	3-2
Spooneybarger, T.	0-0	0-0	0-0	0-0	0-0	0-0	1-0	0-0	0-0	0-0	0-0	0-0	0-0	0-0	1-0	0-0	3-2
Totals	3-3	4-2	4-2	4-3	11-8	3-3	2-4	5-1	13-6	12-7	11-7	3-3	3-3	3-3	5-1	15-3	101-59

NO-DECISIONS: Joey Dawley, John Ennis, Andy Pratt, Aaron Small.

INTERLEAGUE: Kevin Millwood 1-0, Chris Hammond 1-0, Greg Maddux 1-0, Tom Glavine 0-1, Mike Remlinger 2-0 vs. Red Sox; Kevin Gryboski 1-0, Damian Moss 1-0, Jason Marquis 1-0 vs. White Sox; Jason Marquis 0-1, Kerry Ligtenberg 1-0, Kevin Millwood 1-0 vs. Tigers; Kerry Ligtenberg 1-0, Damian Moss 1-0 vs. Twins; Chris Hammond 1-0, Mike Remlinger 1-0, Jason Marquis 1-0 vs. Rangers. Total: 15-3.

CHICAGO—67-95

Pitcher	Ari.	Atl.	Cin.	Col.	Fla.	Hou.	L.A.	Mil.	Mon.	N.Y.	Phi.	Pit.	S.D.	S.F.	St.L.	A.L.	Total
Alfonseca, Antonio	1-0	0-0	0-0	0-0	0-0	0-0	0-0	0-0	0-0	0-0	0-0	0-2	0-0	0-0	0-2	1-0	2-5
Benes, Alan	0-0	0-0	0-0	0-0	0-0	0-0	0-0	1-0	1-0	0-0	0-0	0-1	0-0	0-0	0-1	1-0	2-2
Bere, Jason	0-0	0-0	0-1	0-0	0-0	0-0	0-2	0-1	0-0	0-0	0-0	1-0	0-0	0-0	0-1	0-0	2-2
Borowski, Joe	0-0	0-0	0-0	1-0	0-0	0-0	0-0	1-2	1-0	0-0	0-0	1-2	0-0	0-1	0-2	0-0	1-10
Clement, Matt	1-0	0-1	1-3	0-1	1-0	1-1	0-0	2-1	0-0	0-0	1-1	2-2	0-1	1-0	0-0	2-1	12-11
Cruz, Juan	0-0	0-0	0-2	0-0	0-0	0-1	0-1	0-2	0-1	2-0	0-0	0-0	1-0	0-0	1-2	0-2	3-11
Cunnane, Will	0-0	0-0	0-0	0-0	0-0	1-0	0-0	0-0	0-1	0-0	0-0	2-0	0-0	0-0	1-2	0-2	3-11
Farnsworth, Kyle	0-1	0-0	0-2	0-0	0-0	1-0	0-0	0-0	0-1	0-0	1-0	1-0	0-1	0-1	0-0	0-0	1-1
Fassero, Jeff	0-0	0-0	1-1	0-0	1-0	2-1	0-0	0-1	0-0	0-1	1-0	0-0	0-1	0-1	0-0	0-0	4-6
Gordon, Tom	0-0	0-0	0-0	0-0	0-0	0-0	0-0	1-0	0-1	0-1	0-0	0-0	0-0	1-0	0-1	2-0	5-6
Lieber, Jon	0-0	0-2	0-0	0-0	0-1	0-0	0-2	0-0	0-0	0-0	0-0	0-0	1-1	0-1	0-0	0-0	1-1
Mahay, Ron	0-0	0-0	0-0	0-0	0-0	0-0	0-0	0-0	1-0	0-0	1-1	0-1	1-0	1-1	2-0	6-8
Mahomes, Pat	0-0	0-0	0-0	0-0	1-0	0-0	0-0	0-0	0-0	0-0	0-0	0-1	0-0	0-0	0-0	0-0	2-0
Osborne, Donovan	0-0	0-0	0-0	0-0	1-0	0-0	0-0	0-1	0-0	0-1	0-0	0-1	0-0	0-0	0-0	0-0	1-1
Prior, Mark	0-0	0-1	0-0	2-0	1-0	1-2	0-0	0-1	0-0	0-0	0-1	1-0	0-0	0-1	1-0	0-0	6-6
Smyth, Steve	0-1	0-0	0-0	1-0	0-0	0-1	0-0	0-1	0-0	0-0	0-1	1-0	0-0	0-0	0-1	1-0	1-3

Pitcher	Ari. W-L	Atl. W-L	Cin. W-L	Col. W-L	Fla. W-L	Hou. W-L	L.A. W-L	Mil. W-L	Mon. W-L	N.Y. W-L	Phi. W-L	Pit. W-L	S.D. W-L	S.F. W-L	St.L. W-L	A.L. W-L	Total W-L
Wood, Kerry	0-1	0-0	2-2	0-0	1-0	1-2	0-1	1-1	1-0	0-1	0-0	2-0	1-0	0-0	3-2	0-1	12-11
Zambrano, Carlos..	0-1	2-0	1-1	0-1	0-1	0-2	0-0	1-0	0-1	0-0	0-0	0-0	0-0	0-0	0-1	0-0	4-8
Totals	**2-4**	**2-4**	**5-12**	**4-2**	**4-2**	**8-11**	**2-4**	**7-10**	**3-3**	**1-5**	**2-4**	**10-9**	**2-4**	**3-3**	**6-12**	**6-6**	**67-95**

NO-DECISIONS: Francis Beltran, Scott Chiasson, Courtney Duncan, Jesus Sanchez.
INTERLEAGUE: Matt Clement 2-0, Jon Lieber 1-0, Juan Cruz 0-1, Kerry Wood 0-1, Joe Borowski 0-1 vs. White Sox; Mark Prior 1-0, Matt Clement 0-1, Jon Lieber 1-0 vs. Mariners; Juan Cruz 0-1, Antonio Alfonseca 0-1, Jeff Fassero 0-1 vs. Rangers. Total: 6-6.

CINCINNATI—78-84

Pitcher	Ari. W-L	Atl. W-L	Chi. W-L	Col. W-L	Fla. W-L	Hou. W-L	L.A. W-L	Mil. W-L	Mon. W-L	N.Y. W-L	Phi. W-L	Pit. W-L	S.D. W-L	S.F. W-L	St.L. W-L	A.L. W-L	Total W-L
Acevedo, Jose	0-0	0-0	1-0	0-0	0-0	0-1	0-0	2-0	0-0	0-0	0-0	1-0	0-0	0-0	0-1	0-0	4-2
Almanzar, Carlos....	0-0	0-0	0-0	0-0	0-0	0-0	0-0	0-0	0-0	0-0	0-0	0-0	0-0	0-0	0-0	0-1	0-1
Brower, Jim	0-0	0-0	0-0	0-0	0-0	0-0	0-0	1-0	0-0	0-0	1-0	0-0	0-0	0-0	0-0	0-0	2-0
Chen, Bruce...........	0-0	0-0	0-0	0-0	0-0	0-0	0-0	0-0	0-0	0-0	0-0	0-0	0-0	0-0	0-1	0-1	0-2
Dempster, Ryan	0-1	0-0	2-0	0-0	0-0	0-2	1-0	0-0	0-0	0-0	0-0	1-2	1-0	0-0	0-0	0-0	5-5
Dessens, Elmer	0-0	1-0	1-1	0-0	1-0	0-1	0-0	2-1	0-0	1-0	0-1	0-2	0-0	0-0	1-1	0-1	7-8
Estes, Shawn.........	0-0	0-0	0-0	0-0	0-0	0-0	0-1	0-0	0-0	0-0	0-0	0-1	0-0	0-0	1-1	0-0	1-3
Fernandez, Jared ...	0-0	0-0	0-0	0-0	0-0	1-1	0-0	0-0	0-0	0-1	0-0	0-1	0-0	0-0	0-0	0-0	1-3
Graves, Danny	0-0	0-0	3-0	0-0	1-0	1-1	0-0	1-1	0-0	1-0	0-0	0-0	0-0	0-0	0-1	0-0	7-3
Hamilton, Joey	0-1	0-1	0-1	0-1	1-0	0-1	1-0	0-1	0-0	0-0	1-1	1-0	0-0	0-0	0-1	0-2	4-10
Haynes, Jimmy	0-1	1-0	2-0	1-1	1-0	1-1	0-0	3-0	0-2	0-0	0-0	2-1	1-0	0-2	2-2	1-0	15-10
Moehler, Brian	0-1	0-0	0-0	0-0	0-0	1-0	0-1	0-0	0-0	0-0	1-0	0-0	0-0	0-0	0-0	0-0	2-4
Pineda, Luis...........	0-0	0-0	1-0	0-0	0-0	0-0	0-1	0-0	0-0	0-1	0-0	0-0	0-1	0-0	0-0	0-0	1-3
Reitsma, Chris	0-1	0-2	0-1	0-0	1-0	0-1	0-1	1-1	0-0	0-1	0-0	1-1	0-0	0-0	2-1	0-3	6-12
Riedling, John	0-0	0-0	1-0	0-0	0-0	0-0	0-1	0-1	0-0	0-1	0-0	0-1	1-0	0-0	0-0	0-0	2-4
Rijo, Jose	0-0	0-1	1-0	0-0	0-1	0-0	0-0	1-0	0-0	0-0	0-1	0-0	1-0	1-1	1-0	0-0	5-4
Silva, Jose	0-0	0-0	0-0	0-0	0-0	0-0	0-0	0-0	0-0	0-0	1-0	0-0	0-0	0-0	0-0	0-0	1-0
Sullivan, Scott	0-0	0-0	0-1	1-0	0-0	0-1	1-0	0-0	0-0	1-0	0-0	2-0	0-0	0-0	1-1	0-1	6-5
White, Gabe...........	0-0	0-0	0-0	0-0	0-0	2-0	0-0	2-0	0-0	0-0	0-0	0-0	1-0	0-0	0-1	1-0	6-1
Williamson, Scott ..	0-0	0-0	0-1	1-0	0-0	0-0	1-0	0-0	0-0	0-0	0-1	1-0	0-0	0-0	0-0	0-1	3-4
Totals	**0-6**	**2-4**	**12-5**	**3-3**	**5-1**	**6-11**	**4-2**	**13-6**	**1-5**	**2-4**	**2-4**	**11-7**	**5-1**	**2-4**	**8-11**	**2-10**	**78-84**

NO-DECISIONS: Luke Hudson.
INTERLEAGUE: Chris Reitsma 0-1, Gabe White 1-0, Joey Hamilton 0-1 vs. Angels; Scott Williamson 0-1, Bruce Chen 0-1, Chris Reitsma 0-1 vs. Athletics; Chris Reitsma 0-1, Elmer Dessens 0-1, Joey Hamilton 0-1 vs. Mariners; Carlos Almanzar 0-1, Scott Sullivan 0-1, Jimmy Haynes 1-0 vs. Rangers. Total: 2-10.

COLORADO—73-89

Pitcher	Ari. W-L	Atl. W-L	Chi. W-L	Cin. W-L	Fla. W-L	Hou. W-L	L.A. W-L	Mil. W-L	Mon. W-L	N.Y. W-L	Phi. W-L	Pit. W-L	S.D. W-L	S.F. W-L	St.L. W-L	A.L. W-L	Total W-L
Chacon, Shawn	0-2	0-1	0-2	0-0	0-0	1-0	0-3	1-0	1-1	0-0	1-1	0-0	0-1	1-0	0-0	0-0	5-11
Cook, Aaron...........	0-0	0-0	0-0	0-0	0-0	1-0	0-0	0-0	0-0	0-0	0-0	1-1	0-0	0-0	0-0	0-0	2-1
Flores, Randy	0-1	0-0	0-0	0-0	0-0	0-1	0-0	0-0	0-0	0-0	0-0	0-0	0-0	0-0	0-0	0-0	0-2
Fuentes, Brian	2-0	0-0	0-0	0-0	0-0	0-0	0-0	0-0	0-0	0-0	0-0	0-0	0-0	0-0	0-0	0-0	2-0
Hampton, Mike	0-3	0-0	0-0	1-0	2-0	0-0	1-1	0-1	0-0	0-1	0-1	1-0	1-1	1-3	0-1	0-3	7-15
Jennings, Jason	0-0	1-0	0-0	1-1	2-0	0-0	2-1	1-0	0-0	2-0	1-0	1-2	3-1	0-1	1-2	16-8
Jimenez, Jose........	0-1	0-1	0-0	0-1	0-0	0-1	0-0	0-1	0-0	0-0	1-0	0-2	0-0	1-1	0-0	2-10
Jones, Todd...........	0-1	0-0	0-0	0-0	0-0	0-0	0-0	0-0	0-0	0-0	0-0	0-2	0-0	1-0	1-0	0-0	1-4
Lowe, Sean............	1-1	0-0	0-0	0-0	0-0	0-0	0-0	0-0	0-0	0-0	0-0	0-0	0-0	0-0	0-0	0-0	1-1
Mercker, Kent	0-0	0-0	0-0	0-0	0-0	0-0	1-0	0-0	0-0	0-0	0-0	2-0	0-0	0-0	0-0	0-0	3-1
Neagle, Denny	1-1	0-0	2-0	0-0	0-0	0-1	0-2	0-0	1-0	0-0	1-1	1-1	1-1	1-0	0-2	8-11
Nichting, Chris........	0-0	0-1	0-0	0-0	0-0	0-0	0-0	0-0	0-0	0-0	0-0	1-0	0-0	0-0	0-0	1-1
Reyes, Dennys........	0-1	0-0	0-0	0-0	0-0	0-0	0-0	0-0	0-0	0-0	0-0	0-0	0-0	0-0	0-0	0-1
Santos, Victor........	0-0	0-0	0-1	0-0	0-1	0-0	0-1	0-0	0-0	0-0	0-1	0-0	0-0	0-0	0-0	0-4
Speier, Justin.........	1-0	0-0	0-0	0-0	0-0	0-0	1-0	0-0	0-0	0-0	1-0	0-0	0-1	0-1	2-0	5-1
Stark, Denny..........	0-1	2-0	0-1	1-0	1-0	0-0	2-0	1-1	1-0	0-0	0-0	1-1	1-0	0-0	1-0	11-4
Thomson, John	0-2	0-1	0-0	0-1	0-0	1-0	0-1	0-0	1-0	1-0	2-0	0-2	1-0	0-2	7-8
White, Rick............	0-0	0-0	0-0	0-0	0-0	0-0	0-0	0-0	0-0	0-0	0-1	0-0	0-0	0-0	0-1	1-1	2-6
Totals	**5-14**	**3-4**	**2-4**	**3-3**	**5-2**	**3-3**	**7-12**	**3-3**	**4-2**	**3-3**	**3-3**	**4-2**	**11-8**	**8-11**	**2-4**	**7-11**	**73-89**

NO-DECISIONS: Mark Corey, Mike James, Cory Vance, Todd Zeile.
INTERLEAGUE: Denny Neagle 0-1, Jason Jennings 1-0, Mike Hampton 0-1 vs. Red Sox; John Thomson 0-1, Todd Jones 1-0, Denny Neagle 0-1 vs. Indians; Jason Jennings 0-1, Denny Stark 1-0, Rick White 0-1 vs. Yankees; Jason Jennings 0-1, Mike Hampton 0-1, Justin Speier 1-0 vs. Mariners; Rick White 1-0, Justin Speier 1-0, Jose Jimenez 1-0 vs. Devil Rays; Mike Hampton 0-1, John Thomson 0-1, Jose Jimenez 0-1 vs. Blue Jays. Total: 7-11.

FLORIDA—79-83

Pitcher	Ari. W-L	Atl. W-L	Chi. W-L	Cin. W-L	Col. W-L	Hou. W-L	L.A. W-L	Mil. W-L	Mon. W-L	N.Y. W-L	Phi. W-L	Pit. W-L	S.D. W-L	S.F. W-L	St.L. W-L	A.L. W-L	Total W-L
Almanza, Armando ..	0-0	0-0	0-0	0-0	0-0	0-0	0-0	0-0	2-0	0-0	0-0	0-0	0-0	0-0	1-2	3-2
Beckett, Josh.........	0-2	0-2	0-0	0-1	1-0	0-1	0-0	2-0	0-1	0-0	0-0	0-0	2-0	1-0	0-0	6-7
Borland, Toby	0-0	0-0	0-0	0-0	0-0	0-0	0-0	0-0	0-0	0-0	0-0	1-0	0-0	0-0	0-0	1-0
Burnett, A.J.	0-0	2-2	0-0	0-0	0-1	1-1	0-0	1-0	2-1	0-1	0-0	0-0	1-0	2-0	2-0	12-9
Darensbourg, Vic....	0-0	0-0	0-0	0-0	0-0	0-0	0-0	0-0	0-1	0-1	0-0	0-0	0-0	0-0	1-2
Dempster, Ryan	0-0	0-1	0-1	0-1	0-0	1-0	0-0	0-0	1-0	0-0	1-0	0-1	0-1	2-2	5-8
Izquierdo, Hansel....	0-0	0-0	0-0	0-0	0-0	0-0	0-0	0-0	0-0	0-0	0-0	2-0	0-0	0-0	0-0	2-0
Knotts, Gary	0-0	1-0	0-0	0-0	0-0	0-0	0-0	0-0	0-0	2-0	0-0	0-0	0-0	0-0	0-0	3-1
Lloyd, Graeme	0-0	0-0	0-0	0-0	0-0	0-0	0-1	0-0	0-1	0-0	1-0	0-0	0-0	0-0	1-0	2-2
Looper, Braden	0-1	0-0	0-0	0-0	0-0	0-1	0-0	1-0	1-2	0-0	0-0	0-0	0-1	0-0	2-5
Mairena, Oswaldo..	0-0	0-0	0-0	0-0	0-0	0-0	0-0	1-1	0-0	0-0	0-0	1-0	0-0	0-1	2-3
Neal, Blaine	0-0	0-0	1-0	0-0	0-0	0-0	0-0	0-0	0-0	0-0	0-0	0-0	0-0	0-0	1-0	3-0
Nunez, Vladimir	0-0	0-0	0-0	0-1	0-1	1-0	0-0	1-1	0-1	2-0	1-0	0-0	0-0	0-1	6-5
Olsen, Kevin	0-1	0-0	0-0	0-0	0-0	0-0	0-0	0-0	0-0	0-0	0-1	0-0	0-0	0-0	0-5

Pitcher	Ari. W-L	Atl. W-L	Chi. W-L	Cin. W-L	Col. W-L	Hou. W-L	L.A. W-L	Mil. W-L	Mon. W-L	N.Y. W-L	Phi. W-L	Pit. W-L	S.D. W-L	S.F. W-L	St.L. W-L	A.L. W-L	Total W-L
Pavano, Carl	0-0	1-0	0-1	0-0	0-0	0-0	0-0	0-0	1-0	0-0	0-0	1-0	0-1	0-0	0-0	0-0	3-2
Penny, Brad	1-0	3-0	0-0	0-0	0-1	0-0	1-0	1-0	2-2	0-2	0-1	0-0	0-0	0-1	0-0	0-0	8-7
Robertson, Nate	0-0	0-0	0-0	0-0	0-0	0-0	0-0	0-0	0-0	0-0	0-0	0-1	0-0	0-0	0-0	0-0	0-1
Tavarez, Julian	0-0	0-3	0-1	1-0	0-1	1-0	0-1	0-1	1-1	2-1	0-2	1-0	1-0	0-1	0-0	3-0	10-12
Tejera, Michael	0-1	0-1	1-1	0-0	0-0	0-0	1-0	1-0	1-1	1-1	0-1	0-0	1-0	1-0	1-1	1-1	8-8
Teut, Nate	0-0	0-0	0-0	0-0	0-0	0-0	0-0	0-0	0-0	0-0	0-0	0-0	0-0	0-0	0-0	0-0	0-1
Wayne, Justin	0-0	1-1	0-0	0-0	0-0	0-0	0-0	0-0	0-1	1-1	0-0	0-0	0-0	0-0	0-0	0-0	2-3
Totals	1-5	8-11	2-4	1-5	2-5	3-3	3-3	4-2	10-9	8-11	10-9	4-2	5-1	4-3	4-2	10-8	79-83

INTERLEAGUE: Ryan Dempster 1-0, Julian Tavarez 1-0, A.J. Burnett 1-0 vs. Indians; Michael Tejera 1-0, Blaine Neal 1-0, Armando Almanza 0-1 vs. Tigers; Armando Almanza 1-0, Michael Tejera 0-1, Ryan Dempster 1-0 vs. Royals; Ryan Dempster 0-1, Kevin Olsen 0-1, Julian Tavarez 1-0 vs. Twins; Julian Tavarez 1-0, Vladimir Nunez 0-1, Oswaldo Mairena 0-1, A.J. Burnett 0-1, Armando Almanza 0-1, Ryan Dempster 0-1 vs. Devil Rays. Total: 10-8.

HOUSTON—84-78

Pitcher	Ari. W-L	Atl. W-L	Chi. W-L	Cin. W-L	Col. W-L	Fla. W-L	L.A. W-L	Mil. W-L	Mon. W-L	N.Y. W-L	Phi. W-L	Pit. W-L	S.D. W-L	S.F. W-L	St.L. W-L	A.L. W-L	Total W-L
Borbon, Pedro	1-0	0-0	0-1	0-0	0-0	0-0	0-0	1-0	0-0	0-0	0-0	1-1	0-0	0-0	0-0	0-0	3-2
Cruz, Nelson	0-0	0-1	0-1	0-1	0-0	0-0	0-0	1-0	0-0	0-0	0-0	1-0	0-0	0-0	0-1	0-1	2-6
Dotel, Octavio	1-0	0-0	1-0	1-0	0-0	0-0	0-1	0-0	0-1	0-0	1-0	1-0	0-0	0-0	1-1	0-1	6-4
Gordon, Tom	0-0	0-0	0-1	0-0	0-0	0-0	0-0	0-0	0-0	0-0	0-0	0-0	0-0	0-0	0-0	0-0	0-2
Hernandez, Carlos	0-0	1-0	2-0	1-1	0-0	0-0	1-1	0-0	1-0	1-0	0-1	0-0	0-0	0-0	0-1	0-1	7-5
Lidge, Brad	0-0	0-0	0-0	0-0	1-0	0-0	0-0	0-0	0-0	0-0	0-0	0-0	0-0	0-0	0-0	0-0	1-0
Mann, Jim	0-1	0-0	0-0	0-0	0-0	0-0	0-0	0-0	0-0	0-0	0-0	0-0	0-0	0-0	0-0	0-0	0-1
Miller, Wade	0-1	0-0	2-0	2-0	1-0	0-0	1-0	3-1	1-0	0-0	0-0	2-0	0-0	0-1	2-1	1-0	15-4
Mlicki, Dave	0-0	1-1	0-1	1-1	0-1	1-0	0-0	0-0	0-2	0-1	0-1	0-1	1-0	0-1	0-0	0-0	4-10
Munro, Peter	0-0	0-0	1-0	2-0	0-0	0-1	0-0	1-0	0-1	0-0	0-0	0-0	1-1	0-0	0-2	0-0	5-5
Oswalt, Roy	0-0	0-0	4-0	3-0	1-0	2-0	1-0	1-3	0-1	2-0	0-0	2-2	2-0	0-1	0-1	1-1	19-9
Pichardo, Hipolito	0-0	0-0	0-0	0-0	0-0	0-0	0-0	0-0	0-0	0-1	0-0	0-0	0-0	0-0	0-0	0-0	0-1
Puffer, Brandon	0-0	0-0	0-1	0-0	0-0	0-1	0-0	2-1	0-0	0-0	0-0	0-0	0-0	0-0	1-0	0-0	3-3
Redding, Tim	0-1	0-1	0-1	0-1	0-0	0-0	0-0	0-1	1-0	0-0	1-0	0-0	0-0	0-0	0-0	0-0	3-6
Reynolds, Shane	0-0	0-0	0-1	0-0	0-1	0-0	0-1	0-0	0-0	1-0	0-0	0-0	1-1	0-1	0-1	0-0	3-6
Robertson, J.	0-0	0-0	0-0	0-0	0-0	0-0	0-0	0-0	0-0	0-0	0-0	0-1	0-0	0-1	0-0	0-0	0-2
Saarloos, Kirk	0-0	1-0	1-1	1-0	0-1	0-0	0-1	0-2	1-0	0-0	1-0	0-0	0-0	0-1	0-1	1-0	6-7
Stone, Ricky	0-0	0-0	0-0	0-0	0-0	0-0	0-0	0-0	0-0	0-0	0-0	0-0	0-0	0-0	1-2	1-0	3-3
Wagner, Billy	1-0	0-0	0-1	0-0	0-0	0-0	0-0	0-0	0-0	0-0	0-0	1-1	1-0	0-0	0-0	1-0	4-2
Totals	3-3	3-3	11-8	11-6	3-3	3-3	3-3	10-8	3-3	4-2	3-3	11-6	4-2	1-5	6-13	5-7	84-78

NO-DECISIONS: Scott Linebrink, T.J. Mathews.

INTERLEAGUE: Roy Oswalt 0-1, Octavio Dotel 0-1, Shane Reynolds 0-1 vs. Athletics; Carlos Hernandez 0-1, Ricky Stone 1-0, Kirk Saarloos 0-1 vs. Mariners; Nelson Cruz 0-1, Brandon Puffer 1-0, Wade Miller 1-0, Billy Wagner 1-0, Roy Oswalt 1-0, Jeriome Robertson 0-1 vs. Rangers. Total: 5-7.

LOS ANGELES—92-70

Pitcher	Ari. W-L	Atl. W-L	Chi. W-L	Cin. W-L	Col. W-L	Fla. W-L	Hou. W-L	Mil. W-L	Mon. W-L	N.Y. W-L	Phi. W-L	Pit. W-L	S.D. W-L	S.F. W-L	St.L. W-L	A.L. W-L	Total W-L
Alvarez, Victor	0-0	0-0	0-0	0-0	0-0	0-0	0-0	0-0	0-0	0-0	0-0	0-0	0-1	0-0	0-0	0-0	0-1
Ashby, Andy	2-2	0-1	1-0	0-0	1-2	0-0	0-1	0-0	1-0	1-1	0-0	0-0	0-3	0-1	0-0	2-2	9-13
Beirne, Kevin	0-0	0-0	0-0	0-0	0-0	0-0	0-0	0-0	0-0	0-0	1-0	0-0	0-0	0-0	0-0	0-0	2-0
Brown, Kevin	0-0	0-0	0-1	0-1	1-0	1-0	0-0	0-0	0-1	0-0	0-0	0-0	0-2	0-0	0-0	0-0	3-4
Carrara, Giovanni	0-0	1-0	0-0	1-0	0-0	0-1	0-0	0-0	1-0	0-0	0-0	1-0	0-1	0-0	0-0	2-0	6-3
Daal, Omar	1-1	0-0	0-0	0-0	1-2	0-0	1-1	0-0	2-0	0-0	1-0	1-0	2-1	0-2	0-2	1-1	11-9
Ellis, Robert	0-0	0-0	0-0	0-0	0-0	0-0	0-0	0-0	0-0	0-0	0-0	0-0	0-1	0-0	0-0	0-0	0-1
Gagne, Eric	0-0	1-0	0-0	0-0	1-0	0-0	0-0	0-1	0-0	1-0	0-0	0-0	1-0	0-0	0-0	0-0	4-1
Ishii, Kazuhisa	3-0	0-1	2-0	0-1	2-1	0-1	0-1	2-0	1-0	0-0	1-0	1-1	0-0	0-1	0-0	2-2	14-10
Mota, Guillermo	0-1	0-0	0-0	0-0	1-1	0-0	0-0	0-0	0-0	0-0	0-0	0-0	0-0	0-0	0-0	0-0	1-3
Nomo, Hideo	1-0	0-0	0-0	1-1	0-0	1-1	1-0	2-0	1-0	0-0	0-0	2-1	4-1	0-1	2-0	1-0	16-6
Orosco, Jesse	0-1	0-0	0-1	0-0	1-0	0-0	0-0	0-0	0-0	0-0	0-0	0-0	0-0	0-0	0-0	0-0	1-2
Perez, Odalis	2-2	1-0	1-0	0-0	3-1	0-0	1-0	1-0	0-0	0-1	1-2	1-2	1-0	1-0	3-1	0-1	15-10
Quantrill, Paul	0-1	0-0	0-0	0-0	0-0	0-0	1-0	0-0	0-0	1-1	0-0	1-1	1-1	1-0	0-0	0-0	5-4
Shuey, Paul	1-0	1-0	0-0	0-0	1-0	0-0	1-0	0-0	0-0	0-0	1-2	0-0	1-0	0-0	0-0	0-0	5-2
Springer, Dennis	0-1	0-0	0-0	0-0	0-0	0-0	0-0	0-0	0-0	0-0	0-0	0-0	0-0	0-0	0-0	0-0	0-1
Totals	10-9	4-2	4-2	2-4	12-7	3-3	3-3	5-2	4-2	4-3	4-2	10-9	8-11	2-4	12-6	92-70	

NO-DECISIONS: Bryan Corey, Terry Mulholland, Jeff Williams.

INTERLEAGUE: Kazuhisa Ishii 0-2, Giovanni Carrara 2-0, Odalis Perez 1-1 vs. Angels; Andy Ashby 0-1, Kazuhisa Ishii 1-0, Odalis Perez 1-0 vs. Orioles; Hideo Nomo 1-0, Omar Daal 1-0, Andy Ashby 1-0 vs. Red Sox; Hideo Nomo 1-0, Omar Daal 0-1, Andy Ashby 1-0 vs. Devil Rays; Andy Ashby 0-1, Kazuhisa Ishii 1-0, Odalis Perez 1-0 vs. Blue Jays. Total: 12-6.

MILWAUKEE—56-106

Pitcher	Ari. W-L	Atl. W-L	Chi. W-L	Cin. W-L	Col. W-L	Fla. W-L	Hou. W-L	L.A. W-L	Mon. W-L	N.Y. W-L	Phi. W-L	Pit. W-L	S.D. W-L	S.F. W-L	St.L. W-L	A.L. W-L	Total W-L
Buddie, Mike	0-0	0-0	0-0	0-0	0-0	0-1	0-0	1-0	0-0	0-0	0-0	0-1	0-0	0-0	0-0	0-0	1-2
Cabrera, Jose	0-0	0-0	1-0	1-2	0-1	0-1	1-0	0-0	1-1	0-0	0-0	0-2	0-0	0-0	1-2	1-1	6-10
de los Santos, V.	0-0	0-0	1-1	1-0	0-0	0-0	0-1	0-0	0-0	0-0	0-0	0-0	0-0	0-0	0-0	0-1	2-3
DeJean, Mike	0-0	0-1	0-1	0-2	1-0	0-0	0-0	0-0	0-0	0-0	0-1	0-0	0-0	0-0	0-0	0-0	1-5
Diggins, Ben	0-0	0-0	0-1	0-0	0-0	0-0	0-0	0-0	0-0	0-0	0-0	0-1	0-0	0-2	0-0	0-0	0-4
Durocher, Jayson	0-0	0-0	0-0	1-0	0-0	0-0	0-0	0-0	0-0	0-0	0-0	0-0	0-0	0-0	0-0	0-0	1-1
Figueroa, Nelson	0-1	1-0	0-1	0-0	0-0	0-0	0-0	0-0	0-0	0-0	0-1	0-0	0-1	0-0	0-2	0-1	1-7
Fox, Chad	0-0	0-0	0-0	0-0	0-0	0-0	0-0	0-0	0-0	0-0	0-0	1-0	0-0	0-0	0-0	0-0	1-0
Franklin, Wayne	0-0	0-0	0-0	0-0	0-0	2-0	0-0	0-0	0-0	0-0	0-0	0-0	0-0	0-1	0-0	0-0	2-1
King, Ray	0-0	0-0	1-0	1-0	0-0	0-0	0-0	0-0	0-0	0-1	0-0	0-0	0-0	0-0	0-0	1-0	3-2
Lorraine, Andrew	0-0	0-0	0-1	0-0	0-0	0-0	0-0	0-0	0-0	0-0	0-0	0-0	0-0	0-0	0-0	0-0	0-1
Neugebauer, Nick	0-2	0-0	0-0	0-2	0-0	0-0	0-0	0-0	0-0	0-0	0-1	0-0	0-1	0-0	1-0	0-0	1-7
Osting, Jimmy	0-0	0-0	0-1	0-0	0-0	0-0	0-0	0-0	0-1	0-0	0-0	0-0	0-0	0-0	0-0	0-0	0-2

Pitcher	Ari. W-L	Atl. W-L	Chi. W-L	Cin. W-L	Col. W-L	Fla. W-L	Hou. W-L	L.A. W-L	Mon. W-L	N.Y. W-L	Phi. W-L	Pit. W-L	S.D. W-L	S.F. W-L	St.L. W-L	A.L. W-L	Total W-L
Pember, Dave	0-0	0-0	0-1	0-0	0-0	0-0	0-0	0-0	0-0	0-0	0-0	0-0	0-0	0-0	0-0	0-0	0-1
Quevedo, Ruben	0-0	0-2	0-0	0-2	0-1	0-1	1-1	0-0	0-2	0-0	0-1	2-0	2-0	0-0	1-0	0-1	6-11
Rusch, Glendon	2-0	0-1	4-0	1-2	0-0	0-0	1-4	0-2	0-0	1-1	0-1	0-3	0-0	0-0	1-1	0-1	10-16
Sheets, Ben	0-1	0-1	2-0	1-1	1-1	1-0	3-0	0-2	1-1	0-1	0-1	1-2	0-0	0-0	1-1	0-3	11-16
Stull, Everett	0-0	0-0	0-0	0-1	0-0	0-0	0-0	0-0	0-0	0-0	0-0	0-0	0-0	0-0	0-0	0-0	0-1
Vizcaino, Luis	0-0	0-0	1-0	0-0	0-0	0-0	0-0	0-0	0-0	0-0	0-0	0-0	1-0	1-1	2-2	0-0	5-3
Wright, Jamey	0-0	0-0	0-0	0-1	1-0	1-0	0-4	0-1	0-0	0-1	1-1	1-3	1-0	0-0	0-1	0-1	5-13
Totals	2-4	1-5	10-7	6-13	3-3	2-4	8-10	1-5	2-4	1-5	1-5	4-15	5-1	1-5	7-10	2-10	56-106

NO-DECISIONS: Matt Childers, Brian Mallette, Mike Matthews, Shane Nance, Takahito Nomura.
INTERLEAGUE: Ruben Quevedo 0-1, Jose Cabrera 0-1, Ben Sheets 0-1 vs. Angels; Glendon Rusch 0-1, Ray King 1-0, Jamey Wright 0-1, Nelson Figueroa 0-1, Ben Sheets 0-1, Jose Cabrera 1-0 vs. Twins; Valerio de los Santos 0-1, Nelson Figueroa 0-1, Ben Sheets 0-1 vs. Athletics. Total: 2-10.

MONTREAL—83-79

Pitcher	Ari. W-L	Atl. W-L	Chi. W-L	Cin. W-L	Col. W-L	Fla. W-L	Hou. W-L	L.A. W-L	Mil. W-L	N.Y. W-L	Phi. W-L	Pit. W-L	S.D. W-L	S.F. W-L	St.L. W-L	A.L. W-L	Total W-L
Armas Jr., Tony	0-0	0-4	0-0	0-0	0-2	2-2	1-0	0-1	1-0	3-1	1-2	0-0	0-0	1-0	0-0	3-0	12-12
Brower, Jim	0-0	0-1	0-1	0-0	0-0	0-0	0-0	0-0	0-0	0-0	0-0	1-0	0-0	0-0	0-0	0-0	1-2
Chen, Bruce	0-1	0-0	1-0	0-0	0-0	0-0	0-0	0-1	0-0	1-0	0-0	0-0	0-0	0-1	0-0	0-0	2-3
Colon, Bartolo	0-0	3-0	0-0	0-0	0-0	2-1	0-0	0-1	1-0	2-1	0-1	0-0	1-0	1-0	0-0	0-0	10-4
Day, Zach	0-0	0-0	0-0	0-0	0-0	0-0	0-0	0-0	0-0	1-0	0-0	0-0	1-0	0-0	0-0	2-1	4-1
Drew, Tim	0-0	0-0	0-0	1-0	0-0	0-0	0-0	0-0	0-0	0-0	0-0	0-0	0-0	0-0	0-0	0-0	1-0
Eischen, Joey	1-0	0-0	0-0	1-0	0-0	1-0	0-0	0-0	0-0	2-0	0-0	0-1	0-1	0-0	1-0	0-0	6-1
Herges, Matt	0-0	0-0	0-0	0-0	0-0	0-0	1-0	0-0	0-0	1-0	0-2	0-0	0-1	0-0	0-2	0-0	2-5
Kim, Sun-Woo	0-0	0-0	0-0	1-0	0-0	0-0	0-0	0-0	0-0	0-0	0-0	0-0	0-0	0-0	0-0	0-0	1-0
Lloyd, Graeme	0-1	0-0	0-0	0-1	1-0	0-0	0-0	0-0	0-0	1-0	0-0	0-0	0-0	0-0	0-1	0-0	2-3
Ohka, Tomokazu	0-0	0-1	0-0	1-0	0-0	0-0	0-1	1-0	0-3	4-0	1-1	1-0	1-0	1-0	2-1	2-0	13-8
Pavano, Carl	0-0	0-1	0-1	0-0	0-1	1-1	0-1	1-0	0-0	1-0	0-0	0-1	0-1	0-0	0-1	0-1	3-8
Reames, Britt	0-0	0-0	0-0	0-0	0-0	0-1	1-0	0-0	0-0	0-1	0-0	0-0	0-0	0-1	0-1	0-0	1-4
Smith, Dan	0-0	0-0	0-0	0-0	0-0	0-0	0-0	1-0	0-0	0-1	0-0	0-0	0-0	0-0	0-0	0-0	1-1
Stewart, Scott	0-0	0-0	0-0	0-0	0-0	0-0	1-0	0-0	0-0	0-1	0-0	0-0	0-0	0-0	3-0	0-0	4-2
Tucker, T.J.	1-0	2-1	0-0	0-0	0-0	1-1	0-1	0-0	1-0	0-0	1-0	0-0	0-0	0-0	0-0	0-0	6-3
Vazquez, Javier	0-1	1-2	1-0	0-0	0-1	0-1	1-1	0-1	2-1	2-1	1-1	0-0	1-1	0-0	1-1	1-1	10-13
Yoshii, Masato	0-1	0-3	1-1	1-0	1-0	0-2	0-0	0-1	0-0	0-1	0-0	0-0	0-0	1-0	0-0	0-0	4-9
Totals	2-4	6-13	3-3	5-1	2-4	9-10	3-3	2-5	4-2	11-8	11-8	3-3	3-4	4-2	3-3	12-6	83-79

NO-DECISIONS: Scott Strickland, Ed Vosberg.
INTERLEAGUE: Tony Armas Jr. 1-0, Scott Stewart 1-0, Carl Pavano 0-1 vs. White Sox; Javier Vazquez 1-0, Zach Day 0-1, Tony Armas Jr. 1-0 vs. Indians; Javier Vazquez 0-1, Matt Herges 0-1, Scott Stewart 1-0 vs. Tigers; Joey Eischen 1-0, Zach Day 1-0, Tomokazu Ohka 1-0 vs. Royals; Tomokazu Ohka 1-0, Matt Herges 0-1, Zach Day 1-0, Graeme Lloyd 0-1, Scott Stewart 1-0, Tony Armas Jr. 1-0 vs. Blue Jays. Total: 12-6.

NEW YORK—75-86

Pitcher	Ari. W-L	Atl. W-L	Chi. W-L	Cin. W-L	Col. W-L	Fla. W-L	Hou. W-L	L.A. W-L	Mil. W-L	Mon. W-L	Phi. W-L	Pit. W-L	S.D. W-L	S.F. W-L	St.L. W-L	A.L. W-L	Total W-L
Astacio, Pedro	0-0	2-2	1-0	1-0	0-1	1-0	1-1	1-1	2-0	0-2	2-1	0-0	0-0	0-1	0-1	1-1	12-11
Bacsik, Mike	0-0	0-0	0-0	0-0	0-0	3-0	0-0	0-0	0-0	0-1	0-0	0-0	0-0	0-1	0-0	0-0	3-2
Benitez, Armando	0-0	0-0	0-0	0-0	0-0	0-0	0-0	0-0	0-0	1-0	0-0	0-0	0-0	0-0	0-0	0-0	1-0
Corey, Mark	0-0	0-0	0-0	0-1	0-0	0-0	0-0	0-1	0-0	0-1	0-0	0-0	0-0	0-0	0-0	0-0	0-3
D'Amico, Jeff	0-0	0-1	0-0	0-0	0-1	1-0	0-2	1-0	0-1	2-0	1-2	0-0	0-0	0-0	1-0	0-3	6-10
Davis, Kane	0-0	0-0	0-0	0-0	0-0	0-1	0-0	0-0	1-0	0-0	0-0	0-0	0-0	0-0	0-0	0-0	1-1
Estes, Shawn	0-2	0-0	0-0	1-0	0-0	0-1	1-0	0-0	1-0	0-2	0-1	0-1	1-0	0-1	0-0	1-1	4-9
Guthrie, Mark	0-1	0-0	0-0	1-0	0-0	0-0	0-1	0-0	1-0	0-1	0-0	0-1	0-0	0-0	2-0	0-0	5-3
Komiyama, Satoru	0-0	0-1	0-0	0-0	0-0	0-1	0-0	0-0	0-0	0-0	0-0	0-0	0-0	0-0	0-1	0-0	0-3
Leiter, Al	1-0	1-1	0-0	0-1	2-0	1-3	0-1	0-0	0-0	1-1	1-2	1-0	1-1	0-0	1-1	3-1	13-13
Middlebrook, J.	0-0	0-0	0-0	0-0	0-0	0-0	0-0	0-0	0-0	1-0	0-0	0-0	0-0	0-0	0-0	0-0	1-0
Reed, Steve	0-0	0-0	0-0	0-0	0-0	0-0	0-0	0-0	0-0	0-0	0-0	0-0	0-0	0-1	0-0	0-0	0-1
Roberts, Grant	0-0	0-0	1-0	0-0	0-0	2-0	0-0	0-0	0-0	0-0	0-1	0-0	0-0	0-0	0-0	0-0	3-1
Strickland, Scott	0-1	1-2	0-0	0-0	0-0	1-2	0-0	0-0	0-1	2-2	0-0	0-0	0-1	0-0	1-0	1-0	6-9
Thomson, John	0-1	0-1	0-0	0-0	0-0	0-0	0-0	0-0	0-0	0-2	1-0	0-0	0-1	0-0	0-0	0-0	2-6
Trachsel, Steve	1-0	2-2	1-1	0-0	0-0	1-0	0-0	0-1	1-0	0-2	0-1	1-1	0-1	0-0	2-1	0-0	11-11
Walker, Tyler	0-0	0-0	0-0	0-0	0-0	0-0	0-0	0-0	0-0	0-0	0-0	1-0	0-0	0-0	0-0	0-0	1-0
Weathers, Dave	0-0	1-2	2-0	1-0	1-0	0-0	0-0	0-0	0-0	1-0	0-0	0-0	0-0	0-0	0-0	0-0	6-3
Totals	2-5	7-12	5-1	4-2	3-3	11-8	2-4	2-4	5-1	8-11	9-10	1-4	3-4	0-6	3-3	10-8	75-86

NO-DECISIONS: Jaime Cerda, Bruce Chen, Pedro Feliciano, Bobby M. Jones, Jae Weong Seo, Pat Strange, Pete Walker.
INTERLEAGUE: Pedro Astacio 1-0, Jeff D'Amico 0-1, Al Leiter 1-0 vs. White Sox; Al Leiter 1-0, Steve Trachsel 0-1, Shawn Estes 0-1 vs. Indians; Scott Strickland 1-0, Mark Guthrie 1-0, Pedro Astacio 0-1 vs. Royals; Jeff D'Amico 0-1, Al Leiter 1-0, Steve Trachsel 0-1 vs. Twins; Steve Trachsel 1-0, Satoru Komiyama 0-1, Shawn Estes 1-0, Jeff D'Amico 0-1, Al Leiter 1-0 vs. Yankees. Total: 10-8.

PHILADELPHIA—80-81

Pitcher	Ari. W-L	Atl. W-L	Chi. W-L	Cin. W-L	Col. W-L	Fla. W-L	Hou. W-L	L.A. W-L	Mil. W-L	Mon. W-L	N.Y. W-L	Pit. W-L	S.D. W-L	S.F. W-L	St.L. W-L	A.L. W-L	Total W-L
Adams, Terry	1-0	0-2	0-0	2-0	0-1	1-1	0-0	0-0	0-0	0-1	1-1	0-1	0-1	0-0	1-0	1-1	7-9
Bottalico, Ricky	0-0	0-0	0-0	0-0	0-0	0-1	0-0	0-0	0-0	0-0	0-0	0-0	0-0	0-1	0-0	0-1	0-3
Coggin, Dave	0-0	0-1	1-0	0-0	0-0	0-0	0-0	0-1	0-0	1-1	0-0	0-0	0-0	0-1	0-1	0-1	2-5
Cormier, Rheal	0-1	0-0	0-0	0-1	0-0	1-0	0-0	0-0	1-0	1-1	0-0	1-1	0-1	0-0	1-0	0-0	5-6
Duckworth, B.	0-0	0-1	0-0	1-0	1-1	2-1	0-0	0-0	1-2	1-2	0-1	0-0	0-0	0-0	2-0	0-0	8-9
Junge, Eric	0-0	1-0	0-0	0-0	0-0	0-0	0-0	0-0	0-0	1-0	0-0	0-0	0-0	0-0	0-0	0-0	2-0
Mercado, Hector	0-0	0-0	0-0	0-0	1-0	0-0	0-0	0-0	0-1	1-0	0-0	0-0	0-0	0-0	0-0	0-0	2-2
Mesa, Jose	0-2	0-0	1-1	0-0	0-0	1-1	1-0	0-0	0-1	0-0	0-1	0-0	0-1	0-0	0-0	0-0	4-6
Myers, Brett	0-0	0-1	0-0	0-0	0-0	1-0	0-0	0-1	1-1	0-0	0-0	1-1	0-0	0-1	1-1	0-0	4-5
Padilla, Vicente	1-0	2-2	0-1	1-0	1-0	1-1	1-0	0-1	1-2	0-1	0-1	1-0	0-1	1-0	2-1	2-1	14-11

Pitcher	Ari. W-L	Atl. W-L	Chi. W-L	Cin. W-L	Col. W-L	Fla. W-L	Hou. W-L	L.A. W-L	Mil. W-L	Mon. W-L	N.Y. W-L	Pit. W-L	S.D. W-L	S.F. W-L	St.L. W-L	A.L. W-L	Total W-L
Person, Robert	0-0	0-1	0-0	0-1	0-0	0-0	0-0	0-0	0-0	1-1	1-0	0-0	0-1	0-0	0-0	2-1	4-5
Plesac, Dan	0-0	0-0	0-0	0-0	0-0	0-0	0-0	0-0	0-0	0-0	1-0	0-0	0-0	0-0	0-0	1-1	2-1
Politte, Cliff	0-0	1-0	0-0	0-0	0-0	1-0	0-0	0-0	0-0	0-0	0-0	0-0	0-0	0-0	0-0	0-0	2-0
Roa, Joe	0-0	0-2	0-0	0-0	0-0	1-0	0-0	0-0	2-0	1-1	0-1	0-0	0-0	0-0	0-0	0-0	4-4
Santiago, Jose	0-1	1-0	0-0	0-0	0-0	0-1	0-0	0-0	0-0	0-0	0-1	0-0	0-0	0-0	0-0	0-0	1-3
Silva, Carlos	0-0	1-0	1-0	0-0	0-0	0-0	1-0	1-0	0-0	0-0	0-0	0-0	0-0	0-0	1-0	0-0	5-0
Timlin, Mike	0-0	0-0	0-0	0-0	0-0	0-0	0-0	2-1	0-0	0-0	0-1	0-1	0-0	1-0	0-0	0-0	3-3
Wolf, Randy	1-0	1-1	0-0	0-0	0-1	0-3	1-1	0-0	1-0	2-1	1-0	0-0	1-0	1-0	1-0	1-2	11-9
Totals	3-4	7-11	4-2	4-2	3-3	9-10	3-3	3-4	5-1	8-11	10-9	2-4	2-4	3-3	4-2	10-8	80-81

NO-DECISIONS: Doug Nickle, Tomas Perez.

INTERLEAGUE: Robert Person 1-0, Rheal Cormier 1-0, Ricky Bottalico 0-1, Terry Adams 0-1, Randy Wolf 1-0, Vicente Padilla 0-1 vs. Orioles; Dave Coggin 0-1, Dan Plesac 1-0, Robert Person 0-1 vs. White Sox; Terry Adams 1-0, Randy Wolf 0-1, Vicente Padilla 1-0 vs. Indians; Vicente Padilla 1-0, Robert Person 1-0, Brandon Duckworth 1-0 vs. Tigers; Brandon Duckworth 1-0, Dan Plesac 0-1, Randy Wolf 0-1 vs. Twins. Total: 10-8.

PITTSBURGH—72-89

Pitcher	Ari. W-L	Atl. W-L	Chi. W-L	Cin. W-L	Col. W-L	Fla. W-L	Hou. W-L	L.A. W-L	Mil. W-L	Mon. W-L	N.Y. W-L	Phi. W-L	S.D. W-L	S.F. W-L	St.L. W-L	A.L. W-L	Total W-L
Anderson, Jimmy ..	0-1	0-0	1-1	3-1	0-0	0-0	1-2	0-2	1-1	1-0	1-0	0-0	0-2	0-0	0-2	0-1	8-13
Arroyo, Bronson	0-1	1-0	0-0	0-0	0-0	0-0	0-0	0-0	1-0	0-0	0-0	0-0	0-0	0-1	0-0	0-0	2-1
Beimel, Joe	0-1	0-0	0-0	0-1	0-0	0-0	0-1	0-0	1-1	0-0	1-0	0-0	0-0	0-0	0-0	0-1	2-5
Benson, Kris	0-1	0-0	1-2	1-0	1-0	1-0	0-1	0-0	1-0	1-0	0-0	0-0	0-1	2-0	1-1	0-0	9-6
Boehringer, Brian..	0-0	0-0	0-1	0-1	1-0	0-0	0-1	0-0	2-0	0-0	0-0	0-0	1-0	0-0	0-1	0-0	4-4
Fetters, Mike	0-0	0-0	0-0	0-0	0-0	0-0	1-0	0-0	0-0	0-0	0-0	0-0	0-0	0-0	0-0	0-0	1-0
Fogg, Josh	1-0	0-1	2-2	0-0	0-1	1-1	2-0	2-0	1-1	0-1	0-0	0-0	0-0	0-0	1-3	2-2	12-12
Lincoln, Mike	0-0	0-0	0-0	1-2	0-0	0-0	0-0	1-0	0-0	0-0	0-0	0-0	0-1	0-0	0-1	0-0	2-4
Lowe, Sean	0-0	0-0	0-0	0-0	0-0	0-0	1-1	0-0	1-0	0-0	1-0	0-1	0-0	1-0	0-0	0-0	4-2
Meadows, Brian	0-0	0-1	0-0	0-0	0-1	0-0	0-1	0-0	0-1	1-0	0-0	0-1	0-0	0-0	0-1	0-0	1-6
Sauerbeck, Scott	0-0	0-0	1-1	0-0	0-0	0-0	0-1	0-1	0-0	0-0	0-0	0-0	1-0	0-0	1-0	0-0	5-4
Torres, Salomon	0-0	1-0	1-0	0-1	0-0	0-0	0-0	0-0	0-0	0-0	0-0	0-0	0-0	0-0	0-0	0-0	2-1
Villone, Ron	0-0	0-0	0-1	2-0	0-1	0-0	0-1	0-0	0-0	0-1	1-1	1-0	0-1	0-0	0-0	0-0	4-6
Wells, Kip	1-1	0-1	1-0	0-3	0-0	0-1	1-2	0-0	3-1	1-1	0-0	1-0	1-0	1-1	1-2	1-2	12-14
Williams, Dave	0-0	0-0	1-2	0-0	0-1	0-0	0-1	0-1	1-0	0-0	0-0	0-0	0-0	0-0	0-0	0-0	2-5
Williams, Mike	0-0	1-0	1-0	0-2	0-0	0-0	0-0	0-0	0-0	0-0	0-0	0-0	0-1	0-0	0-2	0-1	2-6
Totals	2-4	3-3	9-10	7-11	2-4	2-4	6-11	2-4	15-4	3-3	4-1	4-2	2-4	2-4	6-11	3-9	72-89

NO-DECISIONS: Josias Manzanillo, Al Reyes, Duaner Sanchez.

INTERLEAGUE: Jimmy Anderson 0-1, Josh Fogg 1-0, Brian Boehringer 0-1 vs. Angels; Josh Fogg 1-0, Joe Beimel 0-1, Kris Benson 1-0 vs. Tigers; Josh Fogg 0-1, Mike Williams 0-1, Kris Benson 0-1 vs. Athletics; Kip Wells 0-1, Mike Lincoln 0-1, Josh Fogg 0-1 vs. Rangers. Total: 3-9.

ST. LOUIS—97-65

Pitcher	Ari. W-L	Atl. W-L	Chi. W-L	Cin. W-L	Col. W-L	Fla. W-L	Hou. W-L	L.A. W-L	Mil. W-L	Mon. W-L	N.Y. W-L	Phi. W-L	Pit. W-L	S.D. W-L	S.F. W-L	A.L. W-L	Total W-L
Benes, Andy	0-1	0-0	2-0	0-0	0-1	1-0	0-0	0-0	0-0	0-0	0-0	0-1	2-0	0-0	0-1	0-0	5-4
Crudale, Mike	0-0	0-0	0-0	0-0	0-0	0-0	0-0	0-0	1-0	0-0	0-0	0-0	2-0	0-0	0-0	0-0	3-0
Fassero, Jeff	0-0	0-0	1-0	0-0	1-0	0-0	0-0	0-0	0-0	0-0	0-0	0-0	0-0	0-0	0-0	0-0	3-0
Finley, Chuck	0-0	0-0	1-1	1-0	0-0	0-1	1-0	0-0	1-0	0-1	1-0	0-1	0-1	0-0	0-0	0-0	7-4
Hackman, Luther ...	0-0	0-0	1-0	1-1	0-0	0-0	1-1	0-0	0-1	0-0	0-0	0-1	0-1	0-0	1-0	0-0	5-4
Isringhausen, J.	1-0	0-0	0-0	0-1	0-0	0-0	0-0	1-0	0-0	0-0	0-0	1-0	0-0	0-0	0-0	0-0	3-2
Joseph, Kevin	0-0	0-0	0-0	0-0	0-0	0-0	0-0	0-0	0-0	0-0	0-1	0-0	0-0	0-0	0-0	0-0	0-1
Kile, Darryl	0-0	0-1	0-0	1-1	0-0	0-1	0-0	0-0	1-0	0-0	1-0	1-0	0-0	0-0	0-0	2-1	5-4
Kline, Steve	0-0	0-0	0-0	1-0	0-0	0-0	0-0	0-1	0-0	0-0	1-0	0-0	1-0	0-0	0-0	0-0	2-1
Matthews, Mike	0-0	0-0	0-0	0-0	0-0	0-0	1-0	0-0	1-0	0-1	0-0	0-0	0-0	0-0	0-0	0-0	2-1
Molina, Gabe	0-0	0-0	0-0	0-0	0-0	0-0	0-0	0-0	0-0	0-0	0-0	0-0	1-0	0-0	0-0	0-0	1-0
Morris, Matt	1-0	0-1	2-0	0-1	1-0	0-0	3-2	0-1	2-1	1-1	0-1	0-0	1-1	0-0	2-0	3-0	17-9
Simontacchi, J.	0-0	1-1	1-2	2-1	1-0	0-0	1-0	0-0	0-0	0-1	0-0	1-0	2-0	1-0	0-0	1-0	11-5
Smith, Bud	0-1	0-0	0-1	0-0	0-0	0-0	0-0	0-0	0-1	0-0	0-0	0-0	0-0	1-0	0-0	0-2	1-5
Smith, Travis	0-0	0-0	0-0	0-0	0-0	1-1	0-0	2-0	0-0	0-0	0-0	0-0	0-0	1-0	0-0	0-0	4-2
Stechschulte, G. ...	0-0	0-1	1-0	2-0	0-0	0-0	2-0	0-0	0-1	1-0	0-0	0-0	0-0	0-0	0-0	0-0	6-2
Stephenson, G.	1-0	0-0	0-0	1-1	0-1	0-0	0-2	0-0	0-0	0-0	0-0	0-0	0-0	0-0	0-0	0-0	2-5
Timlin, Mike	0-0	0-0	1-1	0-0	0-0	0-0	0-0	0-0	0-0	0-0	0-0	0-0	0-0	0-0	0-0	0-1	1-3
Veres, Dave	0-0	0-1	1-0	0-0	0-0	0-1	1-1	0-0	2-1	0-0	1-1	0-0	0-1	0-1	0-1	0-0	5-8
White, Rick	0-0	0-0	0-0	0-0	1-0	0-0	2-0	0-0	0-1	0-0	0-0	0-0	0-0	0-0	0-0	0-0	3-1
Williams, Woody ...	0-0	0-0	0-1	2-2	0-0	0-0	1-0	0-0	2-0	0-0	0-0	0-0	1-1	1-0	0-0	2-0	9-4
Wright, Jamey	1-0	0-0	1-0	0-0	0-0	0-0	0-0	0-0	0-0	0-0	0-0	0-0	0-0	0-0	0-0	0-0	2-0
Totals	4-2	1-5	12-6	11-8	4-2	2-4	13-6	4-2	10-7	3-3	3-3	2-4	11-6	5-1	4-2	8-4	97-65

NO-DECISIONS: Matt Duff, Josh Pearce, Jose Rodriguez, Nerio Rodriguez.

INTERLEAGUE: Darryl Kile 1-0, Matt Morris 1-0, Bud Smith 0-1 vs. Angels; Darryl Kile 1-0, Mike Timlin 0-1, Matt Morris 2-0, Jason Simontacchi 1-0, Woody Williams 1-0 vs. Royals; Bud Smith 0-1, Woody Williams 1-0, Darryl Kile 0-1 vs. Mariners. Total: 8-4.

SAN DIEGO—66-96

Pitcher	Ari. W-L	Atl. W-L	Chi. W-L	Cin. W-L	Col. W-L	Fla. W-L	Hou. W-L	L.A. W-L	Mil. W-L	Mon. W-L	N.Y. W-L	Phi. W-L	Pit. W-L	S.F. W-L	St.L. W-L	A.L. W-L	Total W-L
Boyd, Jason	0-0	1-0	0-0	0-0	0-0	0-0	0-0	0-0	0-0	0-0	0-0	0-0	0-0	0-0	0-0	0-0	1-0
Bynum, Mike	0-0	1-0	0-0	0-0	0-0	0-0	0-0	0-0	0-0	0-0	0-0	0-0	0-0	0-0	0-0	0-0	1-0
Condrey, Clay	0-1	0-0	0-0	0-0	1-0	0-0	0-0	0-0	0-0	0-0	0-0	0-0	0-1	0-0	0-0	0-0	1-2
Cyr, Eric	0-0	0-0	0-0	0-0	0-0	0-0	0-0	0-0	0-0	0-0	0-0	0-0	0-0	0-0	0-1	0-0	0-1
Davey, Tom	0-0	0-0	0-0	0-0	0-0	0-0	0-0	0-0	0-0	0-0	0-0	1-0	0-0	0-0	0-0	0-0	1-0
DeWitt, Matt	0-0	0-0	0-0	0-0	0-0	0-0	0-0	0-0	0-0	0-0	0-1	0-0	0-0	0-0	0-0	0-0	0-1
Eaton, Adam	1-0	0-0	0-0	0-0	0-1	0-0	0-0	0-0	0-0	0-0	0-0	0-0	0-0	0-0	0-0	0-0	1-1
Embree, Alan	1-0	0-0	0-0	0-0	0-1	0-0	0-0	0-0	0-1	1-0	0-0	0-0	0-1	0-0	0-0	0-1	3-4

Pitcher	Ari. W-L	Atl. W-L	Chi. W-L	Cin. W-L	Col. W-L	Fla. W-L	Hou. W-L	L.A. W-L	Mil. W-L	Mon. W-L	N.Y. W-L	Phi. W-L	Pit. W-L	S.F. W-L	St.L. W-L	A.L. W-L	Total W-L
Fikac, Jeremy	1-0	0-1	1-0	0-0	0-2	0-1	1-0	1-2	0-0	0-0	0-0	0-0	0-0	0-0	0-0	0-1	4-7
Hoffman, Trevor	0-1	0-0	0-1	0-1	0-0	0-0	0-0	0-1	0-0	1-0	0-0	0-0	0-0	1-1	0-0	0-0	2-5
Holtz, Mike	0-1	0-0	1-0	0-0	0-1	0-0	0-0	0-0	0-0	0-0	0-0	0-0	0-0	0-0	1-0	0-0	2-2
Howard, Ben	0-0	0-0	0-0	0-0	0-0	0-0	0-0	0-0	0-0	0-0	0-0	0-0	0-1	0-0	0-0	0-0	0-1
Jarvis, Kevin	0-1	0-0	0-0	0-0	0-0	0-0	0-0	0-1	0-0	0-0	0-0	1-0	1-1	0-1	0-0	0-0	2-4
Johnson, Jonathan	0-0	0-0	0-0	0-0	0-0	0-0	0-1	0-0	0-0	1-0	0-0	0-0	0-0	0-0	0-0	0-0	1-2
Jones, Bobby J.	2-0	0-0	1-0	0-1	0-2	0-1	0-0	1-1	0-0	0-0	0-0	1-1	0-0	0-1	0-1	2-0	7-8
Kershner, Jason	0-0	0-0	0-0	0-0	0-0	0-0	0-0	0-0	0-0	0-1	0-0	0-0	0-0	0-0	0-0	0-0	0-1
Lawrence, Brian	1-1	0-1	0-0	1-0	2-0	0-1	0-2	3-2	0-0	0-1	1-1	1-0	0-1	0-1	0-1	2-1	12-12
Middlebrook, J.	0-0	0-0	0-0	0-0	1-0	0-0	0-0	0-0	0-0	0-1	0-0	0-0	0-2	0-0	0-0	0-0	1-3
Myers, Rodney	0-0	0-0	0-0	0-0	0-0	0-0	0-0	0-0	0-0	0-0	0-0	0-0	1-1	0-0	0-0	0-0	1-1
Nickle, Doug	0-0	0-0	0-0	0-0	1-0	0-0	0-0	0-0	0-0	0-0	0-0	0-0	0-0	0-0	0-0	0-0	1-0
Peavy, Jake	1-2	0-0	0-0	0-0	1-1	1-0	0-1	0-0	0-0	0-1	1-0	1-0	0-0	1-0	0-0	0-2	6-7
Perez, Oliver	0-2	0-0	0-0	0-0	1-1	0-0	0-0	1-0	0-0	0-0	0-0	0-0	0-1	0-1	2-0	0-0	4-5
Pickford, Kevin	0-0	0-0	0-0	0-0	0-0	0-0	0-0	0-0	0-0	0-0	0-0	0-0	0-0	0-0	0-0	0-1	0-2
Reed, Steve	0-0	0-0	0-0	0-0	0-0	0-0	0-0	0-0	0-1	0-0	1-0	0-0	0-0	0-1	0-1	1-1	2-4
Tankersley, Dennis	0-0	0-1	0-0	0-0	0-0	0-0	0-0	0-0	0-1	1-1	0-0	0-0	0-1	0-0	0-0	0-0	1-4
Tollberg, Brian	0-1	0-0	0-0	0-0	0-0	0-1	0-0	0-1	0-0	0-0	0-0	0-0	1-0	0-1	0-0	0-0	1-5
Tomko, Brett	0-1	1-0	0-1	0-2	1-2	0-0	0-0	3-0	0-0	1-0	1-1	0-0	1-0	0-2	0-0	1-1	10-10
Trujillo, J.J.	0-0	0-0	0-0	0-0	0-0	0-0	0-0	0-0	0-0	0-0	0-0	0-0	0-0	0-0	0-0	0-1	0-1
Villafuerte, B.	0-0	0-0	1-0	0-1	0-0	0-1	0-0	0-0	0-0	0-0	0-0	0-0	0-0	0-0	0-0	0-0	1-2
Walker, Kevin	0-1	0-0	0-0	0-0	0-0	0-0	0-0	0-0	0-0	0-0	0-0	0-0	0-0	0-0	0-0	0-0	0-1
Totals	7-12	3-3	4-2	1-5	8-11	1-5	2-4	9-10	1-5	4-3	4-3	4-2	4-2	5-14	1-5	8-10	66-96

NO-DECISIONS: D'Angelo Jimenez, Bobby M. Jones, David Lundquist, Juan Moreno, Jose Antonio Nunez, Jason Pearson, Jason Shiell.
INTERLEAGUE: Jeremy Fikac 0-1, J.J. Trujillo 0-1, Brian Lawrence 1-0 vs. Orioles; Brian Lawrence 0-1, Brett Tomko 1-0, Kevin Pickford 0-1 vs. Red Sox; Eric Cyr 0-1, Steve Reed 1-0, Jake Peavy 0-1 vs. Royals; Oliver Perez 1-0, Steve Reed 0-1, Jake Peavy 0-1 vs. Yankees; Brett Tomko 0-1, Bobby J. Jones 1-0, Oliver Perez 1-0 vs. Mariners; Brian Lawrence 1-0, Alan Embree 0-1, Bobby J. Jones 1-0 vs. Devil Rays. Total: 8-10.

SAN FRANCISCO—95-66

Pitcher	Ari. W-L	Atl. W-L	Chi. W-L	Cin. W-L	Col. W-L	Fla. W-L	Hou. W-L	L.A. W-L	Mil. W-L	Mon. W-L	N.Y. W-L	Phi. W-L	Pit. W-L	S.D. W-L	St.L. W-L	A.L. W-L	Total W-L
Ainsworth, Kurt	0-0	0-0	0-0	0-0	0-0	0-0	0-0	0-0	1-0	0-0	0-0	0-0	0-0	0-2	0-0	0-0	1-2
Aybar, Manny	0-0	0-0	0-0	0-0	0-0	0-0	0-0	0-0	0-0	0-0	0-0	0-0	1-0	0-0	0-0	0-0	1-0
Brohawn, Troy	0-0	0-0	0-0	0-0	0-0	0-0	0-0	0-0	0-0	0-0	0-1	0-0	0-0	0-0	0-0	0-0	0-1
Christiansen, J.	0-0	0-0	0-0	0-0	0-0	0-0	0-0	0-0	0-0	0-0	0-0	0-0	0-1	0-0	0-0	0-0	0-1
Fultz, Aaron	0-1	0-0	0-1	0-0	0-0	0-0	0-0	0-0	1-0	0-0	0-0	0-0	0-0	1-0	0-0	0-0	2-2
Hernandez, Livan	1-0	0-2	0-2	0-0	2-3	1-0	1-0	2-2	1-0	0-2	0-1	0-0	3-0	0-1	1-4		12-16
Jensen, Ryan	2-0	1-0	0-0	1-1	1-2	0-2	1-1	1-0	1-0	2-0	0-0	0-0	2-0	0-1	1-1		13-8
Nen, Robb	1-1	0-0	1-0	1-0	0-0	0-0	0-0	2-0	0-0	0-0	0-0	1-1	0-0	0-0	0-0		6-2
Ortiz, Russ	1-2	1-0	0-0	0-0	2-1	1-1	0-0	3-2	0-0	0-2	1-0	1-0	0-0	1-0	1-1		14-10
Rodriguez, Felix	2-1	0-0	0-0	0-1	3-0	0-0	0-0	0-1	1-1	0-0	0-0	1-0	0-0	0-1	0-0	1-1	8-6
Rueter, Kirk	1-1	0-0	1-0	2-0	0-2	1-1	1-0	1-2	0-0	0-0	2-0	1-0	0-0	2-0	1-0	0-2	14-8
Schmidt, Jason	1-2	0-1	0-0	0-0	2-0	0-0	1-0	2-1	1-0	1-0	0-0	1-1	0-0	0-2	3-1		13-8
Witasick, Jay	0-0	0-0	0-0	0-0	0-0	0-0	0-0	0-0	0-0	0-0	0-0	0-0	0-1	0-0	0-0		1-0
Worrell, Tim	1-0	1-0	1-0	0-0	1-0	0-0	0-0	0-0	0-0	0-0	0-0	1-0	2-1	1-1	0-0		8-2
Zerbe, Chad	1-0	0-0	0-0	0-0	0-0	0-0	0-0	0-0	0-0	0-0	1-0	0-0	0-0	1-0	0-0		3-0
Totals	11-8	3-3	3-3	4-2	11-8	3-4	5-1	11-8	5-1	2-4	6-0	3-3	4-2	14-5	2-4	8-10	95-66

NO-DECISIONS: Scott Eyre, Joe Nathan.
INTERLEAGUE: Felix Rodriguez 1-0, Ryan Jensen 0-1, Livan Hernandez 0-1 vs. Orioles; Livan Hernandez 0-1, Felix Rodriguez 0-1, Jason Schmidt 1-0 vs. Yankees; Jason Schmidt 1-1, Russ Ortiz 0-1, Chad Zerbe 1-0, Kirk Rueter 0-1, Livan Hernandez 0-1 vs. Athletics; Livan Hernandez 0-1, Jason Schmidt 1-0, Russ Ortiz 1-0 vs. Devil Rays; Kirk Rueter 0-1, Ryan Jensen 0-1, Livan Hernandez 1-0 vs. Blue Jays. Total: 8-10.

HOME RUNS BY PARKS

	At Ari.	At Atl.	At Chi.	At Cin.	At Col.	At Fla.	At Hou.	At L.A.	At Mil.	At Mon.	At N.Y.	At Phi.	At Pit.	At St.L.	At S.D.	At S.F.	At A.L. Parks	Totals 2002	Totals 2001	HR Allow.
Arizona	83	1	2	8	11	5	1	8	5	2	9	2	4	2	9	1	12	165	208	170
Atlanta	4	82	0	3	3	10	5	3	5	6	11	10	1	3	2	2	14	164	174	123
Chicago	2	4	99	8	11	3	10	5	10	4	3	2	12	7	6	3	11	200	194	167
Cincinnati	2	6	13	85	6	5	5	4	8	2	3	2	8	8	6	1	5	169	176	173
Colorado	8	5	2	1	97	0	3	4	3	4	5	2	1	3	7	3	4	152	213	225
Florida	1	7	2	2	2	66	0	2	4	15	10	7	2	6	3	4	13	146	166	151
Houston	2	0	11	19	5	3	88	5	6	2	3	1	7	5	1	3	6	167	208	151
Los Angeles	18	2	1	5	14	1	1	73	12	1	2	6	1	1	7	5	5	155	206	165
Milwaukee	1	1	15	19	7	1	9	1	62	1	9	2	1	5	4	3	6	139	209	199
Montreal	3	9	2	0	9	5	2	3	5	85	6	13	5	2	3	2	8	162	131	165
New York	4	6	3	6	6	7	4	2	1	11	81	12	2	1	2	0	12	160	147	163
Philadelphia	4	7	4	3	0	10	3	5	5	12	9	79	4	6	3	2	9	165	164	153
Pittsburgh	3	3	13	14	0	0	5	5	17	3	1	1	61	10	2	1	3	142	161	163
St. Louis	3	0	13	7	11	4	9	2	5	2	4	1	15	88	2	3	6	175	199	141
San Diego	6	3	8	5	10	3	1	8	4	3	2	3	3	2	59	3	13	136	161	177
San Francisco	12	4	4	3	25	1	2	18	5	3	4	4	11	3	17	72	10	198	235	116
A.L. clubs	11	6	12	9	15	2	10	11	7	7	7	7	6	3	3	8	....	124	148	....
2002 Totals	167	146	204	197	232	126	158	159	164	163	162	153	148	154	135	114	137	5059	....	2602
2001 Totals	228	164	170	190	268	153	230	183	222	172	156	164	150	195	178	146	....	....	2952	....

AT ARIZONA (167):

Arizona (83)—Finley 14, Gonzalez 11, Durazo 11, Spivey 9, Williams 7, Grace 4, Bautista 4, Womack 4, Miller 4, Colbrunn 3, Guillen 3, Jose 2, Dellucci 2, Moeller 2, Donnels 1, McCracken 1, Barajas 1. **Atlanta (4)**—J. Franco 1, C. Jones 1, A. Jones 1, DeRosa 1. **Baltimore (3)**—Batista 1, Mora 1, Gil 1. **Chicago**

(2)—Hundley 1, Bellhorn 1. **Cincinnati (2)**—Kearns 2. **Colorado (8)**—Helton 2, Zeile 1, Norton 1, Agbayani 1, Kapler 1, Pierre 1, Butler 1. **Detroit (4)**—Paquette 1, Magee 1, Fick 1, Inge 1. **Florida (1)**—Wilson 1. **Houston (2)**—Hidalgo 1, Berkman 1. **Los Angeles (18)**—Green 6, Beltre 3, Grissom 2, Karros 1, Jordan 1, Lo Duca 1, Kinkade 1, Roberts 1, Izturis 1, Ross 1. **Milwaukee (1)**—Rushford 1. **Montreal (3)**—V. Guerrero 1, Tatis 1, Barrett 1. **New York (4)**—Piazza 2, Burnitz 1, McEwing 1. **Philadelphia (4)**—Rollins 3, Burrell 1. **Pittsburgh (3)**—Giles 1, Kendall 1, C. Wilson 1. **St. Louis (3)**—Edmonds 1, Drew 1, Pujols 1. **San Diego (6)**—Gant 2, Klesko 1, Cruz 1, Trammell 1, Buchanan 1. **San Francisco (12)**—Bonds 3, Bell 3, Aurilia 2, Santiago 1, Sanders 1, Lofton 1, Shinjo 1. **Toronto (4)**—Fletcher 2, Wells 1, Hinske 1.

AT ATLANTA (146):

Arizona (1)—Spivey 1. **Atlanta (82)**—A. Jones 18, C. Jones 17, Sheffield 10, Castilla 5, Blanco 4, Helms 4, Furcal 4, Giles 4, J. Franco 3, Lockhart 3, M. Franco 3, DeRosa 3, Bragg 2, J. Lopez 1, Marquis 1. **Boston (2)**—Nixon 1, Varitek 1. **Chicago (4)**—Alou 2, McGriff 1, Bellhorn 1. **Chicago (3)**—Konerko 2, Lee 1. **Cincinnati (6)**—Dunn 2, Boone 1, Encarnacion 1, Miller 1, Kearns 1. **Colorado (5)**—Walker 2, Payton 2, Zeile 1. **Detroit (1)**—Santiago 1. **Florida (7)**—Floyd 3, Lee 1, Encarnacion 1, Wilson 1, Lowell 1. **Los Angeles (2)**—Jordan 2. **Milwaukee (1)**—Hernandez 1. **Montreal (9)**—Tatis 3, V. Guerrero 2, Vidro 2, Cabrera 1, Barrett 1. **New York (6)**—Piazza 2, Burnitz 1, Alfonzo 1, Cedeno 1, Perez 1. **Philadelphia (7)**—Rolen 2, Glanville 1, Lee 1, Giambi 1, Burrell 1, Rollins 1. **Pittsburgh (3)**—Giles 1, Ramirez 1, C. Wilson 1. **San Diego (3)**—Lankford 1, Cruz 1, Trammell 1. **San Francisco (3)**—Kent 3, Santiago 1.

AT CHICAGO (204):

Arizona (2)—Miller 1, Durazo 1. **Chicago (99)**—Sosa 24, Bellhorn 15, Gonzalez 13, McGriff 11, Hundley 8, Alou 7, Patterson 7, Mueller 4, Echevarria 3, Brown 2, DeShields 1, Stynes 1, Wood 1, Choi 1, Hill 1. **Chicago (5)**—Konerko 2, Lee 2, Johnson 1. **Cincinnati (13)**—Walker 2, Boone 2, Casey 2, Branyan 2, Stinnett 1, Castro 1, Encarnacion 1, Dunn 1, Kearns 1. **Colorado (2)**—Cust 1, Uribe 1. **Florida (2)**—Encarnacion 1, Wilson 1. **Houston (11)**—Hidalgo 3, Bagwell 2, Berkman 2, Biggio 1, Ward 1, Blum 1, Lugo 1. **Los Angeles (2)**—Jordan 1. **Milwaukee (15)**—Hernandez 3, Sexson 3, Belliard 2, Young 1, Hammonds 1, Fabregas 1, Houston 1, Casanova 1, Christenson 1, Hall 1. **Montreal (2)**—Barrett 1, Wilkerson 1. **New York (3)**—Piazza 2, Alomar 1. **Philadelphia (4)**—Abreu 2, Rolen 1, Anderson 1. **Pittsburgh (13)**—Giles 6, Ramirez 2, Young 1, Hermansen 1, C. Wilson 1, Mackowiak 1, Alvarez 1. **St. Louis (13)**—Marrero 3, Pujols 3, Edmonds 2, Drew 2, Benes 1, Perez 1, Renteria 1. **San Diego (8)**—Nevin 2, Gant 1, Lampkin 1, Klesko 1, Kingsale 1, Trammell 1, Kotsay 1. **San Francisco (4)**—Bell 2, Sanders 1, Shinjo 1. **Texas (7)**—Palmeiro 3, Mench 2, Greene 1, Young 1.

AT CINCINNATI (197):

Arizona (8)—Finley 3, Bell 1, Williams 1, Colbrunn 1, McCracken 1, Durazo 1. **Atlanta (3)**—Sheffield 2, A. Jones 1. **Chicago (8)**—Sosa 3, McGriff 1, Hundley 1, Alou 1, Brown 1, Hill 1. **Cincinnati (85)**—Boone 14, Dunn 13, Walker 7, Kearns 7, Encarnacion 6, Taylor 6, LaRue 5, Larkin 4, Griffey 4, Branyan 4, Larson 4, Casey 3, Guillen 2, Mateo 2, Miller 2, Stinnett 1, Pena 1. **Colorado (1)**—Bennett 1. **Florida (2)**—Castillo 1, Wilson 1. **Houston (19)**—Berkman 7, Bagwell 5, Hidalgo 3, Biggio 1, Vizcaino 1, Hunter 1, Zinter 1. **Los Angeles (5)**—Beltre 2, Hansen 1, Green 1, Lo Duca 1. **Milwaukee (19)**—Stairs 3, Thompson 3, Hammonds 2, Fabregas 2, Jenkins 2, Harris 1, Hernandez 1, Loretta 1, Belliard 1, Sexson 1, Bako 1, Sanchez 1. **New York (6)**—Piazza 2, Alfonzo 2, Alomar 1, Vaughn 1. **Oakland (5)**—Mabry 1, Saenz 1, Hatteberg 1, Tejada 1, Chavez 1. **Philadelphia (3)**—Perez 1, Abreu 1, Lee 1. **Pittsburgh (14)**—Giles 4, C. Wilson 4, Young 2, Ramirez 2, Hyzdu 1, J. Wilson 1. **St. Louis (7)**—Rolen 2, Drew 2, Pujols 2, Renteria 1. **San Diego (5)**—Trammell 2, Lampkin 1, Klesko 1, Kotsay 1. **San Francisco (3)**—Santiago 1, Sanders 1, Aurilia 1. **Seattle (4)**—Sierra 1, Boone 1, Cameron 1, Guillen 1.

AT COLORADO (232):

Arizona (11)—Gonzalez 3, Miller 3, Grace 2, Donnels 1, McCracken 1, Dellucci 1. **Atlanta (3)**—J. Franco 1, Millwood 1, Helms 1. **Chicago (11)**—Sosa 4, McGriff 2, Alou 2, Patterson 2, Girardi 1. **Cincinnati (6)**—Taylor 2, Dunn 2, Griffey 1, Boone 1. **Cleveland (2)**—Vizquel 1, Fryman 1. **Colorado (97)**—Walker 18, Helton 18, Zeile 11, Hollandsworth 9, Butler 7, Estalella 6, Payton 5, Shumpert 4, Petrick 4, Uribe 4, Norton 3, Bennett 2, Hampton 1, Agbayani 1, Kapler 1, Stark 1, Ortiz 1, Gload 1. **Florida (2)**—Floyd 1, Johnson 1. **Houston (5)**—Hidalgo 2, Biggio 1, Ausmus 1, Berkman 1. **Los Angeles (14)**—Beltre 4, Grissom 2, Karros 2, Jordan 2, Lo Duca 2, Green 1, Bocachica 1. **Milwaukee (7)**—Hammonds 2, Sexson 2, Hernandez 1, Stairs 1, Ochoa 1. **Montreal (9)**—V. Guerrero 2, Vidro 2, Wilkerson 2, Cordero 1, Cabrera 1, Cepicky 1. **New York (6)**—Alomar 2, Gonzalez 2, Alfonzo 1, Perez 1. **New York (9)**—Ventura 3, Giambi 2, Soriano 2, Jeter 1, Spencer 1. **St. Louis (11)**—Rolen 4, Martinez 2, Edmonds 1, Renteria 1, Cruz 1, Marrero 1, Pujols 1. **San Diego (10)**—Klesko 5, Trammell 2, Lampkin 1, Sweeney 1, Jimenez 1. **San Francisco (25)**—Kent 7, Bonds 6, Bell 3, Minor 3, Sanders 2, Shinjo 2, Santiago 1, Torrealba 1. **Tampa Bay (4)**—Vaughn 1, Gomez 1, Grieve 1, Cox 1.

AT FLORIDA (126):

Arizona (5)—Finley 2, Grace 1, Gonzalez 1, Miller 1. **Atlanta (10)**—J. Lopez 3, A. Jones 2, Sheffield 1, Castilla 1, C. Jones 1, Blanco 1, Helms 1. **Chicago (3)**—McGriff 2, Sosa 1. **Cincinnati (5)**—Boone 3, Larkin 1, Dunn 1. **Detroit (2)**—Easley 1, Inge 1. **Florida (66)**—Lowell 13, Millar 11, Lee 9, Wilson 8, Floyd 7, Castro 4, Fox 3, Johnson 2, Owens 2, Encarnacion 2, Banks 1, Redmond 1, Gonzalez 1, Burnett 1, Tejera 1. **Houston (3)**—Biggio 1, Hidalgo 1, Berkman 1. **Los Angeles (1)**—Jordan 1. **Milwaukee (1)**—Alcantara 1. **Montreal (5)**—Barrett 2, Stevens 1, Vidro 1, Truby 1. **New York (7)**—Alomar 1, Vaughn 1, Piazza 1, Tarasco 1, Cedeno 1, Ordonez 1, Payton 1. **Philadelphia (10)**—Lieberthal 2, Burrell 2, Glanville 1, Rolen 1, Abreu 1, Ledee 1, Anderson 1, Michaels 1. **St. Louis (4)**—Renteria 2, Martinez 1, Edmonds 1. **San Diego (3)**—Klesko 1, Nevin 1, Trammell 1. **San Francisco (1)**—Bonds 1.

AT HOUSTON (158):

Arizona (1)—Miller 1. **Atlanta (5)**—Sheffield 2, Furcal 2, A. Jones 1. **Chicago (10)**—Sosa 3, McGriff 2, Bellhorn 2, Hundley 1, Stynes 1, Patterson 1. **Cincinnati (5)**—Boone 2, Griffey 1, Dunn 1, Kearns 1. **Colorado (3)**—Helton 2, Shumpert 1. **Houston (88)**—Berkman 20, Bagwell 16, Ward 9, Biggio 7, Blum 6, Lugo 6, Vizcaino 4, Merced 4, Ausmus 4, Hidalgo 4, Zaun 3, Ensberg 2, Lane 2, Loretta 1. **Los Angeles (1)**—Beltre 1. **Milwaukee (9)**—Sexson 3, Stairs 2, Ochoa 2, Machado 1, Jenkins 1. **Montreal (2)**—V. Guerrero 2. **New York (4)**—Payton 2, Valentin 1, Burnitz 1. **Philadelphia (3)**—Lieberthal 1, Burrell 1, Rollins 1. **Pittsburgh (5)**—Ramirez 3, Giles 2. **St. Louis (9)**—Edmonds 2, Marrero 2, Pujols 2, Martinez 1, DiFelice 1, Robinson 1. **San Diego (1)**—Klesko 1. **San Francisco (2)**—Snow 1, Aurilia 1. **Seattle (5)**—Sierra 1, Olerud 1, Wilson 1, Cirillo 1, Cameron 1. **Texas (5)**—Perry 2, Young 2, Mench 1.

AT LOS ANGELES (159):

Anaheim (4)—Salmon 2, Anderson 1, Fullmer 1. **Arizona (8)**—Colbrunn 3, Williams 1, Batista 1, Dellucci 1, Barajas 1, Spivey 1. **Atlanta (3)**—C. Jones 2, J. Lopez 1. **Boston (6)**—Hillenbrand 2, Henderson 1, Baerga 1, Garciaparra 1, Diaz 1. **Chicago (5)**—McGriff 2, Sosa 1, Gonzalez 1, Bellhorn 1. **Cincinnati (4)**—Dunn 2, Larkin 1, Encarnacion 1. **Colorado (4)**—Zeile 1, Hampton 1, Bennett 1, Norton 1. **Florida (2)**—Lee 1, Encarnacion 1. **Houston (5)**—Berkman 2, Biggio 1, Bagwell 1, Hunter 1. **Los Angeles (73)**—Green 18, Grissom 10, Karros 9, Jordan 7, Beltre 7, Grudzielanek 5, Lo Duca 5, Cora 4, Kreuter 2, Brown 1, Ashby 1, Nomo 1, Perez 1, Kinkade 1, Bocachica 1. **Milwaukee (1)**—Hernandez 1. **Montreal (3)**—V. Guerrero 1, Tatis 1, Cabrera 1. **New York (2)**—Vaughn 1, Cedeno 1. **Philadelphia (5)**—Lieberthal 3, Burrell 2. **Pittsburgh (5)**—Young 1, Kendall 1, Reese 1, Hyzdu 1, C. Wilson 1. **St. Louis (2)**—Perez 1, Edmonds 1. **San Diego (8)**—Nevin 1, Kotsay 1, Hubbard 1, Buchanan 1, Burroughs 1. **San Francisco (18)**—Bonds 5, Sanders 3, Kent 3, Santiago 2, Ortiz 2, Goodwin 1, Bell 1, Aurilia 1. **Toronto (1)**—Lawrence 1.

AT MILWAUKEE (164):

Anaheim (3)—Fullmer 2, Glaus 1. **Arizona (5)**—Finley 1, Gonzalez 1, Bautista 1, Womack 1, Dellucci 1. **Atlanta (5)**—Giles 2, C. Jones 1, Blanco 1, Furcal 1. **Chicago (10)**—McGriff 3, Mueller 2, Bellhorn 2, Sosa 1, Hundley 1, Patterson 1. **Cincinnati (8)**—LaRue 3, Castro 1, Walker 1, Guillen 1, Casey 1, Kearns 1.

Colorado (3)—Helton 2, Walker 1. Florida (4)—Wilson 2, Johnson 1, Lee 1. Houston (6)—Berkman 2, Biggio 1, Bagwell 1, Hidalgo 1, Ward 1. Los Angeles (12)—Green 6, Jordan 2, Hansen 1, Beltre 1, Roberts 1, Bocachica 1. Milwaukee (62)—Hernandez 13, Sexson 13, Stairs 6, Houston 6, Thompson 4, Jenkins 4, Ochoa 3, Harris 2, Young 2, Hammonds 2, Bako 2, Loretta 1, Jensen 1, Machado 1, Rusch 1, Ginter 1. Minnesota (4)—Hocking 1, Pierzynski 1, Koskie 1, Mohr 1. Montreal (5)—V. Guerrero 3, Vidro 1, Macias 1. New York (1)—Piazza 1. Philadelphia (5)—Burrell 2, Abreu 1, Polanco 1, Wolf 1. Pittsburgh (17)—Giles 5, Young 3, C. Wilson 2, Mackowiak 2, Brown 1, Rios 1, Hermansen 1, Hyzdu 1, J. Wilson 1. St. Louis (5)—Martinez 1, Perez 1, Rolen 1, Drew 1, Pujols 1. San Diego (4)—Klesko 2, Kotsay 1, Tankersley 1. San Francisco (5)—Aurilia 2, Santiago 1, Lofton 1, Kent 1.

AT MONTREAL (163):

Arizona (2)—Gonzalez 1, Dellucci 1. Atlanta (6)—Sheffield 2, A. Jones 2, C. Jones 1, DeRosa 1. Chicago (4)—McGriff 1, Sosa 1, DeShields 1, Stynes 1. Cincinnati (2)—Branyan 2. Cleveland (2)—Vizquel 1, Fryman 1. Colorado (4)—Walker 1, Zeile 1, Hollandsworth 1, Helton 1. Florida (15)—Lee 4, Johnson 2, Encarnacion 2, Wilson 2, Lowell 2, Floyd 1, Millar 1, Castro 1. Houston (2)—Biggio 1, Bagwell 1. Los Angeles (1)—Green 1. Milwaukee (1)—Hernandez 1. Montreal (85)—V. Guerrero 20, Wilkerson 12, Vidro 11, Galarraga 7, Stevens 6, Tatis 5, Barrett 4, Macias 4, Floyd 3, Cabrera 3, Schneider 3, Cordero 2, Cepicky 2, O'Leary 1, Truby 1, Carroll 1. New York (11)—Vaughn 3, Piazza 3, Burnitz 3, Phillips 1, Wigginton 1. Philadelphia (12)—Giambi 3, Burrell 3, Abreu 2, Rolen 1, Ledee 1, Lee 1, Anderson 1. Pittsburgh (3)—Mackowiak 2, Hermansen 1. St. Louis (2)—Perez 1, Matheny 1. San Diego (3)—Klesko 1, Nevin 1, Trammell 1. San Francisco (3)—Bonds 1, Bell 1, Minor 1. Toronto (5)—Woodward 2, Wells 2, Stewart 1.

AT NEW YORK (162):

Arizona (9)—Gonzalez 2, Durazo 2, Bell 1, Williams 1, Finley 1, Colbrunn 1, Counsell 1. Atlanta (11)—Castilla 3, J. Lopez 2, J. Franco 1, Sheffield 1, C. Jones 1, Lockhart 1, Bragg 1, A. Jones 1. Chicago (3)—Sosa 1, Hundley 1, Hill 1. Cincinnati (3)—Griffey 1, Branyan 1, Dunn 1. Colorado (5)—Helton 3, Walker 1, Hampton 1. Florida (10)—Millar 3, Lee 2, Wilson 2, Lowell 2, Raines 1. Houston (3)—Biggio 1, Ausmus 1, Blum 1. Kansas City (3)—Sweeney 1, Ibanez 1, Beltran 1. Los Angeles (2)—Grissom 1, Green 1. Milwaukee (2)—Hernandez 1, Hammonds 1. Minnesota (1)—Hunter 1, Pierzynski 1, Mohr 1. Montreal (6)—V. Guerrero 2, Barrett 1, Schneider 1, Wilkerson 1, Chavez 1. New York (81)—Vaughn 16, Piazza 12, Burnitz 12, Alfonzo 8, Alomar 4, Tarasco 4, Payton 4, Wigginton 4, Wilson 3, Perez 3, Valentin 2, Cedeno 2, McEwing 2, Johnson 1, Estes 1, Gonzalez 1, Scutaro 1, Snead 1. New York (1)—Ventura 1. Philadelphia (9)—Ledee 2, Burrell 2, Pratt 1, Perez 1, Rolen 1, Abreu 1, Lee 1. Pittsburgh (1)—Young 1. St. Louis (4)—Pujols 2, Perez 1, Matheny 1. San Diego (2)—Gant 1, Trammell 1. San Francisco (4)—Bonds 1, Kent 1, Snow 1, Feliz 1.

AT PHILADELPHIA (153):

Arizona (2)—Finley 1, Counsell 1. Atlanta (10)—A. Jones 5, Sheffield 1, Castilla 1, J. Lopez 1, Furcal 1, Giles 1. Baltimore (1)—Gibbons 1. Chicago (2)—McGriff 1, Hundley 1. Chicago (3)—Ordonez 1, Konerko 1, Liefer 1. Cincinnati (2)—Encarnacion 1, Dunn 1. Colorado (2)—Zeile 2. Florida (7)—Floyd 1, Fox 1, Castillo 1, Lee 1, Redmond 1, Gonzalez 1, Lowell 1. Houston (1)—Bagwell 1. Los Angeles (6)—Green 2, Beltre 2, Daal 1, Grudzielanek 1. Milwaukee (1)—Sexson 1. Minnesota (3)—Hunter 1, Koskie 1, Mohr 1. Montreal (13)—Wilkerson 4, Tatis 3, Galarraga 2, Cordero 2, Stevens 1, O'Leary 1. New York (12)—Piazza 3, Alfonzo 2, Vaughn 1, Tarasco 1, Burnitz 1, Cedeno 1, Payton 1, Wilson 1, Wigginton 1. Philadelphia (79)—Burrell 18, Rolen 8, Abreu 8, Lee 8, Lieberthal 7, Giambi 6, Ledee 4, Anderson 4, Glanville 3, Polanco 3, Rollins 3, Pratt 2, Perez 2, Person 2, Byrd 1. Pittsburgh (1)—Hyzdu 1. St. Louis (1)—Renteria 1. San Diego (3)—Lampkin 1, Cruz 1, Kotsay 1. San Francisco (4)—Bonds 1, Lofton 1, Kent 1, Aurilia 1.

AT PITTSBURGH (148):

Arizona (4)—Gonzalez 2, Finley 1, Spivey 1. Atlanta (1)—M. Franco 1. Chicago (12)—Sosa 2, Bellhorn 2, McGriff 1, DeShields 1, Gonzalez 1, Stynes 1, Machado 1, Hermansen 1, Patterson 1, Hill 1. Cincinnati (8)—Encarnacion 2, LaRue 2, Griffey 1, Stinnett 1, Guillen 1, Branyan 1. Colorado (1)—Butler 1. Florida (2)—Lee 1, Lowell 1. Houston (7)—Berkman 3, Bagwell 2, Ward 1, Ensberg 1. Los Angeles (1)—Grissom 1. Milwaukee (5)—Hernandez 2, Sexson 2, Alcantara 1. Montreal (5)—Stevens 1, V. Guerrero 1, Vidro 1, Tatis 1, Macias 1. New York (2)—Piazza 1, Alfonzo 1. Oakland (2)—Dye 1, Tejada 1, Hernandez 1. Philadelphia (4)—Lieberthal 1, Rolen 1, Abreu 1, Michaels 1. Pittsburgh (61)—Giles 15, Mackowiak 9, Young 7, Ramirez 7, Hyzdu 6, Hermansen 4, Reese 3, C. Wilson 3, Nunez 2, J. Wilson 2, Kendall 1, Osik 1, D. Williams 1. St. Louis (15)—Pujols 6, Martinez 2, Marrero 2, Vina 1, Edmonds 1, Renteria 1, Rolen 1, Drew 1. San Diego (3)—Lampkin 1, Klesko 1, Cruz 1. San Francisco (11)—Bonds 2, Sanders 2, Kent 2, Snow 2, Bell 2, Aurilia 1. Texas (3)—I. Rodriguez 1, A. Rodriguez 1, Mench 1.

AT ST. LOUIS (154):

Anaheim (1)—Spiezio 1. Arizona (2)—Williams 1, Spivey 1. Atlanta (3)—C. Jones 1, A. Jones 1, Giles 1. Chicago (7)—Hundley 1, Gonzalez 1, Stynes 1, Mueller 1, Bellhorn 1, Patterson 1, Choi 1. Cincinnati (8)—Encarnacion 3, Boone 2, LaRue 2, Larkin 1. Colorado (3)—Walker 1, Agbayani 1, Uribe 1. Florida (6)—Floyd 3, Lowell 2, Castro 1. Houston (5)—Hunter 1, Loretta 1, Berkman 1, Lugo 1, Lane 1. Kansas City (2)—Randa 1, Beltran 1. Los Angeles (1)—Jordan 1. Milwaukee (4)—Stairs 2, Sexson 2. Montreal (2)—V. Guerrero 1, Schneider 1. New York (1)—Vaughn 1. Philadelphia (6)—Abreu 2, Burrell 2, Lieberthal 1, Anderson 1. Pittsburgh (10)—Giles 3, Ramirez 2, C. Wilson 2, Osik 1, Hyzdu 1, Mackowiak 1. St. Louis (88)—Edmonds 17, Pujols 14, Martinez 12, Marrero 9, Drew 9, Rolen 6, Polanco 5, Perez 4, Renteria 4, DiFelice 3, Delgado 2, Williams 1, Matheny 1, Cairo 1, Vina 1. San Diego (2)—Gant 1, Lankford 1. San Francisco (3)—Santiago 1, Sanders 1, Kent 1.

AT SAN DIEGO (135):

Arizona (9)—Gonzalez 3, Colbrunn 2, Williams 1, Bautista 1, Dellucci 1, Spivey 1. Atlanta (2)—Sheffield 2. Boston (1)—Hillenbrand 1. Chicago (6)—Sosa 4, Alou 1, Gonzalez 1. Cincinnati (6)—Branyan 4, Walker 1, Boone 1. Colorado (7)—Norton 2, Walker 1, Hollandsworth 1, Estalella 1, Helton 1, Petrick 1. Florida (3)—Lee 1, Encarnacion 1, Millar 1. Houston (1)—Bagwell 1. Los Angeles (7)—Karros 1, Green 1, Grudzielanek 1, Cora 1, Lo Duca 1, Beltre 1, Roberts 1. Milwaukee (3)—Hammonds 1, Sexson 1, Jenkins 1. Montreal (3)—Stevens 1, V. Guerrero 1, Cabrera 1. New York (2)—Alomar 1, Piazza 1. New York (1)—White 1. Philadelphia (3)—Perez 1, Glanville 1, Burrell 1. Pittsburgh (2)—Wells 1, Mackowiak 1. St. Louis (2)—Perez 1, Drew 1. San Diego (59)—Klesko 11, Kotsay 11, Gant 9, Lampkin 5, Nevin 5, Trammell 5, Buchanan 4, Lankford 3, Cruz 3, Jimenez 2, Gonzalez 1. San Francisco (17)—Bonds 5, Kent 5, Santiago 2, Dunston 1, Bell 1, Aurilia 1, Benard 1, Shinjo 1. Seattle (1)—Wilson 1.

AT SAN FRANCISCO (114):

Arizona (1)—Gonzalez 1. Atlanta (2)—Sheffield 1, Castilla 1. Baltimore (3)—Cordova 3. Chicago (3)—Sosa 2, McGriff 1. Cincinnati (1)—Encarnacion 1. Colorado (3)—Shumpert 1, Payton 1, Helton 1. Florida (4)—Wilson 2, Owens 1, Lee 1. Houston (3)—Bagwell 1, Blum 1, Lane 1. Los Angeles (6)—Green 2, Jordan 1, Grudzielanek 1, Bocachica 1. Milwaukee (1)—Sexson 1. Montreal (2)—Cordero 1, Barrett 1. Oakland (2)—Velarde 1, Chavez 1. Philadelphia (2)—Lee 1, Rollins 1. Pittsburgh (1)—Ramirez 1. St. Louis (3)—Edmonds 2, Drew 1. San Diego (3)—Klesko 1, Kingsale 1, Vazquez 1. San Francisco (72)—Bonds 19, Sanders 12, Kent 11, Bell 7, Santiago 6, Aurilia 4, Martinez 4, Shinjo 4, Minor 3, Snow 1, Feliz 1. Tampa Bay (3)—Vaughn 1, Grieve 1, Huff 1.

If you've ever wondered whether a given stadium is a good hitters' park, a haven for home runs or more conducive for triples, this section is for you. This section contains selected batting statistics for all National League parks for 2002. A key component of this section is an index number for each category which is used to determine how a given park influences a particular statistic. For example, ever since it opened in 1995, Colorado's Coors Field has been known as hitters' paradise. And its park index numbers certainly support the conventional wisdom. Its home-run index of 151 in 2002 clearly indicates that longballs tend to fly out at Coors. Most of the park's other indexes also convey its offensive nature, including its strikeout index of 87, which shows Coors deflates whiffs.

The numbers on all of the major league parks for 2002 are here. For each park, we show how the home team and its opponents performed, both at home and on the road, with the exception being that we do not include data from interleague games. The differences in interleague opponents and ballparks would skew the data.

By comparing the per-game averages at the home park and on the road, we can evaluate the park's impact. This is done by simply dividing the home average by the road average and multiplying the result by 100, generating a park index. If the home and road per-game averages are equal, the index equals 100, and it can be concluded that the park had no impact. An index above 100 means that the park favors that particular statistic. The indexes for at-bats, runs, hits, errors and infield errors are determined on a per-game basis; all other stats are calculated on a per-at-bat basis. "E-infield" denotes infield *fielding* errors. "Alt." is the approximate elevation of the ballpark.

For most parks, data is presented both for 2002 and for the last three years overall. If the park's dimensions have changed over that time, however, the data from the old and new configurations will not be combined. Following all the teams' charts is a ranking section that shows which parks most inflate runs, home runs and batting average.

ARIZONA   Home park: BankOne Ballpark   Alt.: 1,090 feet   Surface: Grass

| | 2002 Season | | | | | | | 2000-02 Seasons | | | | | | |
| | Home Games | | | Road Games | | | | Home Games | | | Road Games | | | |
Category	Ari.	Opp.	Total	Ari.	Opp.	Total	Index	Ari.	Opp.	Total	Ari.	Opp.	Total	Index
G	72	72	144	72	72	144		219	219	438	219	219	438	
Avg.	.284	.248	.266	.248	.247	.248	107	.283	.257	.270	.250	.248	.249	108
AB	2413	2549	4962	2485	2361	4846	102	7357	7644	15001	7639	7214	14853	101
R	415	313	728	319	284	603	121	1193	1003	2196	1025	899	1924	114
H	686	632	1318	617	584	1201	110	2080	1963	4043	1907	1786	3693	109
2B	131	127	258	116	101	217	116	396	359	755	366	315	681	110
3B	25	22	47	14	8	22	209	62	52	114	48	25	73	155
HR	79	73	152	70	71	141	105	256	267	523	249	221	470	110
BB	331	195	526	255	179	434	118	843	624	1467	774	635	1409	103
SO	432	623	1055	486	541	1027	100	1288	1737	3025	1462	1719	3181	94
E	43	45	88	37	59	96	92	128	129	257	127	152	279	92
E-Infield	39	37	76	30	51	81	94	118	104	222	111	125	236	94
LHB-Avg.	.286	.263	.277	.260	.260	.260	107	.293	.257	.279	.258	.260	.259	108
LHB-HR	45	25	70	41	32	73	98	137	98	235	141	84	225	107
RHB-Avg.	.282	.240	.256	.233	.240	.237	108	.270	.257	.262	.239	.241	.240	109
RHB-HR	34	48	82	29	39	68	114	119	169	288	108	137	245	114

ATLANTA   Home park: Turner Field   Alt.: 1,050 feet   Surface: Grass

| | 2002 Season | | | | | | | 2000-02 Seasons | | | | | | |
| | Home Games | | | Road Games | | | | Home Games | | | Road Games | | | |
Category	Atl.	Opp.	Total	Atl.	Opp.	Total	Index	Atl.	Opp.	Total	Atl.	Opp.	Total	Index
G	72	72	144	71	71	142		216	216	432	215	215	430	
Avg.	.261	.243	.252	.252	.244	.248	102	.267	.251	.259	.257	.249	.253	102
AB	2361	2480	4841	2496	2350	4846	99	7107	7459	14566	7506	7139	14645	99
R	321	257	578	286	258	544	105	988	860	1848	972	844	1816	101
H	617	603	1220	628	573	1201	100	1899	1875	3774	1927	1776	3703	101
2B	118	119	237	122	95	217	109	346	322	668	371	310	681	99
3B	13	12	25	9	16	25	100	35	26	61	33	40	73	84
HR	74	58	132	68	55	123	107	228	198	426	228	198	426	101
BB	243	236	479	250	268	518	93	700	676	1376	753	676	1429	97
SO	433	450	883	485	469	954	93	1275	1445	2720	1477	1443	2920	94
E	52	52	104	50	48	98	105	163	188	351	147	159	306	114
E-Infield	46	46	92	42	35	77	118	147	158	305	123	133	256	119
LHB-Avg.	.274	.250	.262	.260	.236	.248	106	.269	.270	.270	.256	.250	.253	106
LHB-HR	24	16	40	12	17	29	138	66	79	145	60	63	123	117
RHB-Avg.	.255	.240	.247	.248	.248	.248	100	.266	.241	.253	.257	.248	.253	100
RHB-HR	50	42	92	56	38	94	98	162	119	281	168	135	303	94

CHICAGO

Home park: Wrigley Field   **Alt.:** 595 feet   **Surface:** Grass

| | 2002 Season | | | | | | | 2000-02 Seasons | | | | | | |
| | Home Games | | | Road Games | | | | Home Games | | | Road Games | | | |
Category	Chi.	Opp.	Total	Chi.	Opp.	Total	Index	Chi.	Opp.	Total	Chi.	Opp.	Total	Index
G	75	75	150	75	75	150		221	221	442	221	221	442	
Avg.	.236	.243	.240	.253	.266	.259	92	.255	.243	.249	.252	.272	.262	95
AB	2467	2568	5035	2618	2473	5091	99	7284	7572	14856	7680	7403	15083	98
R	305	342	647	336	358	694	93	987	994	1981	1037	1169	2206	90
H	583	623	1206	662	659	1321	91	1858	1838	3696	1937	2013	3950	94
2B	107	125	232	129	130	259	91	332	351	683	394	408	802	86
3B	13	10	23	16	19	35	66	37	24	61	42	56	98	63
HR	88	93	181	90	58	148	124	246	257	503	270	253	523	98
BB	286	265	551	255	289	544	102	842	810	1652	782	848	1630	103
SO	580	680	1260	591	549	1140	112	1553	1852	3405	1604	1634	3238	107
E	58	42	100	49	51	100	100	134	148	282	156	145	301	94
E-Infield	48	36	84	43	42	85	99	105	125	230	131	125	256	90
LHB-Avg.	.236	.247	.241	.251	.277	.263	92	.242	.239	.240	.232	.279	.255	94
LHB-HR	38	35	73	43	30	73	101	85	95	180	112	114	226	79
RHB-Avg.	.237	.239	.238	.255	.258	.256	93	.264	.245	.254	.265	.267	.266	96
RHB-HR	50	58	108	47	28	75	146	161	162	323	158	139	297	112

CINCINNATI

Home park: Cinergy Field   **Alt.:** 550 feet   **Surface:** Grass

| | 2002 Season | | | | | | | 2001-02 Seasons | | | | | | |
| | Home Games | | | Road Games | | | | Home Games | | | Road Games | | | |
Category	Cin.	Opp.	Total	Cin.	Opp.	Total	Index	Cin.	Opp.	Total	Cin.	Opp.	Total	Index
G	75	75	150	75	75	150		150	150	300	147	147	294	
Avg.	.267	.279	.273	.244	.259	.252	109	.266	.279	.273	.254	.266	.260	105
AB	2487	2681	5168	2586	2505	5091	102	5047	5374	10421	5105	4936	10041	102
R	372	383	755	302	321	623	121	697	792	1489	654	681	1335	109
H	664	747	1411	632	649	1281	110	1342	1502	2844	1295	1312	2607	107
2B	165	148	313	114	127	241	128	318	319	637	238	266	504	122
3B	3	11	14	18	13	31	44	8	21	29	34	28	62	45
HR	83	103	186	79	57	136	135	159	201	360	166	133	299	116
BB	316	241	557	236	271	507	108	525	483	1008	451	506	957	101
SO	522	486	1008	588	430	1018	98	1021	936	1957	1156	852	2008	94
E	49	43	92	64	50	114	81	113	102	215	128	106	234	90
E-Infield	36	37	73	49	41	90	81	89	86	175	101	91	192	89
LHB-Avg.	.278	.283	.281	.262	.266	.264	106	.287	.282	.284	.275	.274	.274	104
LHB-HR	36	43	79	34	31	65	123	73	87	160	87	70	157	100
RHB-Avg.	.259	.276	.268	.230	.254	.242	111	.251	.278	.265	.237	.260	.249	107
RHB-HR	47	60	107	45	26	71	145	86	114	200	79	63	142	134

COLORADO

Home park: Coors Field   **Alt.:** 5,280 feet   **Surface:** Grass

| | 2002 Season | | | | | | | 2000-02 Seasons | | | | | | |
| | Home Games | | | Road Games | | | | Home Games | | | Road Games | | | |
Category	Col.	Opp.	Total	Col.	Opp.	Total	Index	Col.	Opp.	Total	Col.	Opp.	Total	Index
G	72	72	144	72	72	144		222	222	444	222	222	444	
Avg.	.310	.279	.294	.236	.270	.253	116	.326	.290	.308	.248	.260	.253	121
AB	2442	2543	4985	2447	2405	4852	103	7764	7930	15694	7639	7285	14924	105
R	435	419	854	259	361	620	138	1531	1398	2929	922	1031	1953	150
H	756	709	1465	577	649	1226	119	2534	2299	4833	1891	1892	3783	128
2B	141	142	283	108	121	229	120	489	475	964	361	413	774	118
3B	26	17	43	12	16	28	149	95	52	147	45	49	94	149
HR	83	120	203	51	80	131	151	303	367	670	182	243	425	150
BB	232	243	475	204	267	471	98	762	823	1585	708	783	1491	101
SO	403	424	827	541	381	922	87	1220	1389	2609	1522	1318	2840	87
E	49	51	100	42	40	82	122	142	197	339	129	147	276	123
E-Infield	41	38	79	36	32	68	116	111	153	264	110	132	242	109
LHB-Avg.	.332	.286	.309	.265	.284	.274	113	.341	.284	.316	.269	.267	.268	118
LHB-HR	41	48	89	27	30	57	147	164	142	306	110	93	203	142
RHB-Avg.	.295	.274	.284	.215	.262	.240	119	.313	.293	.302	.228	.255	.243	124
RHB-HR	42	72	114	24	50	74	153	139	225	364	72	150	222	157

FLORIDA Home park: Pro Player Stadium Alt.: 10 feet Surface: Grass

Category	2002 Season — Home Games			Road Games			Index	2000-02 Seasons — Home Games			Road Games			Index
	Fla.	Opp.	Total	Fla.	Opp.	Total		Fla.	Opp.	Total	Fla.	Opp.	Total	
G	72	72	144	72	72	144		215	215	430	217	217	434	
Avg.	.270	.255	.262	.252	.273	.262	100	.264	.251	.258	.256	.276	.266	97
AB	2398	2522	4920	2488	2402	4890	101	7137	7427	14564	7585	7228	14813	99
R	342	322	664	278	373	651	102	968	953	1921	928	1138	2066	94
H	647	644	1291	627	656	1283	101	1887	1865	3752	1939	1997	3936	96
2B	130	133	263	117	130	247	106	376	380	756	391	392	783	98
3B	22	20	42	8	16	24	174	54	66	120	26	53	79	154
HR	63	58	121	67	84	151	80	197	195	392	223	238	461	86
BB	294	291	585	226	277	503	116	771	851	1622	651	878	1529	108
SO	497	556	1053	517	437	954	110	1515	1631	3146	1605	1302	2907	110
E	43	47	90	49	56	105	86	132	143	275	165	157	322	86
E-Infield	31	39	70	43	51	94	74	109	116	225	137	134	271	84
LHB-Avg.	.261	.254	.257	.255	.301	.284	90	.279	.252	.262	.265	.288	.279	94
LHB-HR	11	20	31	12	36	48	61	47	64	111	49	98	147	74
RHB-Avg.	.273	.256	.265	.251	.253	.252	105	.259	.251	.255	.252	.268	.259	99
RHB-HR	52	38	90	55	48	103	89	150	131	281	174	140	314	93

HOUSTON Home park: Minute Maid Park Alt.: 22 feet Surface: Grass

Category	2002 Season — Home Games			Road Games			Index	2000-02 Seasons — Home Games			Road Games			Index
	Hou.	Opp.	Total	Hou.	Opp.	Total		Hou.	Opp.	Total	Hou.	Opp.	Total	
G	75	75	150	75	75	150		222	222	444	222	222	444	
Avg.	.284	.256	.270	.238	.259	.248	109	.281	.268	.274	.257	.264	.261	105
AB	2524	2596	5120	2558	2458	5016	102	7461	7837	15298	7696	7430	15126	101
R	380	312	692	318	314	632	109	1251	1140	2391	1072	1027	2099	114
H	717	665	1382	608	637	1245	111	2093	2099	4192	1981	1961	3942	106
2B	142	143	285	132	143	275	102	428	416	844	388	397	785	106
3B	18	10	28	13	22	35	78	61	50	111	33	49	82	134
HR	83	60	143	73	72	145	97	307	294	601	263	253	516	115
BB	289	218	507	251	275	526	94	866	710	1576	828	772	1600	97
SO	488	575	1063	549	539	1088	96	1475	1687	3162	1602	1513	3115	100
E	41	49	90	38	43	81	111	142	148	290	157	147	304	95
E-Infield	34	37	71	32	34	66	108	121	119	240	131	123	254	94
LHB-Avg.	.299	.272	.285	.262	.269	.266	107	.297	.291	.293	.273	.271	.272	108
LHB-HR	42	25	67	26	32	58	114	101	138	239	74	108	182	134
RHB-Avg.	.275	.246	.261	.225	.253	.238	110	.274	.252	.264	.251	.258	.254	104
RHB-HR	41	35	76	47	40	87	85	206	156	362	189	145	334	106

LOS ANGELES Home park: Dodger Stadium Alt.: 340 feet Surface: Grass

Category	2002 Season — Home Games			Road Games			Index	2000-02 Seasons — Home Games			Road Games			Index
	L.A.	Opp.	Total	L.A.	Opp.	Total		L.A.	Opp.	Total	L.A.	Opp.	Total	
G	72	72	144	72	72	144		219	219	438	219	219	438	
Avg.	.251	.233	.242	.279	.249	.265	91	.251	.235	.243	.269	.259	.264	92
AB	2372	2463	4835	2597	2365	4962	97	7170	7490	14660	7753	7245	14998	98
R	270	265	535	363	300	663	81	909	872	1781	1164	1010	2174	82
H	596	574	1170	725	588	1313	89	1797	1761	3558	2084	1879	3963	90
2B	103	98	201	154	127	281	73	318	315	633	421	396	817	79
3B	11	3	14	15	15	30	48	31	20	51	47	38	85	61
HR	60	75	135	77	66	143	97	247	229	476	276	240	516	94
BB	202	251	453	187	264	451	103	725	780	1505	737	729	1466	105
SO	400	530	930	448	488	936	102	1379	1653	3032	1411	1513	2924	106
E	45	57	102	32	56	88	116	166	155	321	144	172	316	102
E-Infield	40	50	90	27	41	68	132	139	125	264	124	140	264	100
LHB-Avg.	.238	.222	.230	.267	.252	.260	88	.242	.230	.236	.262	.261	.262	90
LHB-HR	16	21	37	28	23	51	78	83	100	183	98	102	200	94
RHB-Avg.	.258	.239	.249	.286	.246	.268	93	.256	.239	.247	.273	.258	.266	93
RHB-HR	44	54	98	49	43	92	106	164	129	293	178	138	316	95

MILWAUKEE

Home park: Miller Park   **Alt.:** 635 feet   **Surface:** Grass

| | 2002 Season | | | | | | | 2001-02 Seasons | | | | | | |
| | Home Games | | | Road Games | | | | Home Games | | | Road Games | | | |
Category	Mil.	Opp.	Total	Mil.	Opp.	Total	Index	Mil.	Opp.	Total	Mil.	Opp.	Total	Index
G	75	75	150	75	75	150		147	147	294	150	150	300	
Avg.	.249	.255	.252	.252	.277	.264	96	.253	.261	.257	.247	.270	.258	100
AB	2417	2579	4996	2580	2473	5053	99	4808	5074	9882	5164	4946	10110	100
R	277	354	631	305	388	693	91	618	711	1329	639	760	1399	97
H	603	658	1261	649	684	1333	95	1218	1324	2542	1277	1336	2613	99
2B	122	141	263	126	127	253	105	239	273	512	263	265	528	99
3B	12	14	26	14	13	27	97	25	28	53	30	34	64	85
HR	58	95	153	71	88	159	97	150	189	339	164	164	328	106
BB	242	284	526	238	340	578	92	455	591	1046	476	646	1122	95
SO	485	519	1004	550	431	981	104	1099	984	2083	1208	919	2127	100
E.	46	40	86	53	44	97	89	87	82	169	101	77	178	97
E-Infield	42	33	75	45	35	80	94	78	67	145	83	60	143	103
LHB-Avg.	.249	.267	.259	.248	.281	.264	98	.260	.273	.267	.252	.264	.258	103
LHB-HR	20	47	67	21	41	62	104	61	91	152	61	71	132	118
RHB-Avg.	.250	.247	.248	.254	.274	.263	94	.250	.253	.251	.245	.274	.259	97
RHB-HR	38	48	86	50	47	97	92	89	98	187	103	93	196	97

MONTREAL

Home park: Olympic Stadium   **Alt.:** 90 feet   **Surface:** Turf

| | 2002 Season | | | | | | | 2000-02 Seasons | | | | | | |
| | Home Games | | | Road Games | | | | Home Games | | | Road Games | | | |
Category	Mon.	Opp.	Total	Mon.	Opp.	Total	Index	Mon.	Opp.	Total	Mon.	Opp.	Total	Index
G	72	72	144	72	72	144		216	216	432	216	216	432	
Avg.	.271	.260	.265	.252	.273	.262	101	.266	.267	.267	.253	.277	.265	101
AB	2396	2520	4916	2492	2434	4926	100	7163	7597	14760	7434	7213	14647	101
R	341	309	650	315	341	656	99	982	1088	2070	919	1072	1991	104
H	649	656	1305	627	664	1291	101	1908	2032	3940	1883	1997	3880	102
2B	145	150	295	128	123	251	118	453	432	885	380	382	762	115
3B	15	15	30	16	16	32	94	37	41	78	51	50	101	77
HR	76	71	147	69	79	148	100	206	252	458	206	222	428	106
BB	266	201	467	253	256	509	92	681	662	1343	681	749	1430	93
SO	458	492	950	545	467	1012	94	1360	1491	2851	1522	1378	2900	98
E.	64	60	124	61	54	115	108	175	155	330	171	152	323	102
E-Infield	50	52	102	52	46	98	104	141	129	270	139	126	265	102
LHB-Avg.	.287	.266	.276	.245	.272	.258	107	.265	.288	.277	.245	.288	.266	104
LHB-HR	34	31	65	25	34	59	108	83	112	195	82	102	184	107
RHB-Avg.	.260	.256	.258	.256	.273	.265	97	.267	.253	.260	.260	.269	.264	98
RHB-HR	42	40	82	44	45	89	94	123	140	263	124	120	244	105

NEW YORK

Home park: Shea Stadium   **Alt.:** 20 feet   **Surface:** Grass

| | 2002 Season | | | | | | | 2000-02 Seasons | | | | | | |
| | Home Games | | | Road Games | | | | Home Games | | | Road Games | | | |
Category	N.Y.	Opp.	Total	N.Y.	Opp.	Total	Index	N.Y.	Opp.	Total	N.Y.	Opp.	Total	Index
G	72	72	144	71	71	142		215	215	430	214	214	428	
Avg.	.244	.254	.249	.267	.260	.264	94	.251	.248	.250	.261	.266	.263	95
AB	2392	2555	4947	2496	2352	4848	101	7091	7550	14641	7450	7143	14593	100
R	290	311	601	326	313	639	93	909	909	1818	985	1011	1996	91
H	583	648	1231	666	612	1278	95	1783	1871	3654	1945	1898	3843	95
2B	96	104	200	119	122	241	81	338	339	677	374	387	761	89
3B	11	13	24	8	17	25	94	23	39	62	27	48	75	82
HR	72	74	146	67	68	135	106	211	220	431	227	235	462	93
BB	222	230	452	222	244	466	95	754	652	1406	775	697	1472	95
SO	459	515	974	476	460	936	102	1367	1638	3005	1441	1410	2851	105
E.	68	46	114	63	52	115	98	175	158	333	153	162	315	105
E-Infield	57	42	99	53	44	97	101	144	131	275	127	136	263	104
LHB-Avg.	.254	.261	.257	.257	.246	.252	102	.246	.247	.246	.244	.259	.251	98
LHB-HR	39	30	69	23	20	43	162	70	75	145	60	78	138	109
RHB-Avg.	.235	.250	.243	.274	.269	.272	89	.254	.248	.251	.270	.270	.270	93
RHB-HR	33	44	77	44	48	92	80	141	145	286	167	157	324	86

PHILADELPHIA

Home park: Veterans Stadium   **Alt.:** 20 feet   **Surface:** Turf

Category	2002 Season Home Games			Road Games			Index	2000-02 Seasons Home Games			Road Games			Index
	Phi.	Opp.	Total	Phi.	Opp.	Total		Phi.	Opp.	Total	Phi.	Opp.	Total	
G	71	71	142	72	72	144		215	215	430	216	216	432	
Avg.	.251	.233	.242	.270	.274	.272	89	.254	.249	.251	.262	.272	.266	94
AB	2338	2402	4740	2571	2452	5023	96	7072	7386	14458	7556	7182	14738	99
R	295	287	582	347	365	712	83	933	972	1905	976	1057	2033	94
H	588	560	1148	695	673	1368	85	1796	1840	3636	1977	1950	3927	93
2B	134	110	244	160	147	307	84	408	449	857	404	406	810	108
3B	20	13	33	16	19	35	100	56	48	104	44	45	89	119
HR	73	67	140	77	73	150	99	202	224	426	212	238	450	97
BB	274	242	516	291	264	555	99	798	780	1578	795	753	1548	104
SO	487	524	1011	488	425	913	117	1492	1608	3100	1473	1321	2794	113
E	33	39	72	45	52	97	75	103	121	224	144	168	312	72
E-Infield	28	28	56	39	41	80	71	87	99	186	110	136	246	76
LHB-Avg.	.240	.237	.239	.282	.288	.285	84	.249	.245	.247	.271	.281	.276	90
LHB-HR	32	25	57	33	31	64	94	87	76	163	76	78	154	104
RHB-Avg.	.262	.231	.245	.259	.266	.263	93	.258	.252	.255	.254	.266	.261	98
RHB-HR	41	42	83	44	42	86	102	115	148	263	136	160	296	93

PITTSBURGH

Home park: PNC Park   **Alt.:** 730 feet   **Surface:** Grass

Category	2002 Season Home Games			Road Games			Index	2001-02 Seasons Home Games			Road Games			Index
	Pit.	Opp.	Total	Pit.	Opp.	Total		Pit.	Opp.	Total	Pit.	Opp.	Total	
G	74	74	148	75	75	150		149	149	298	147	147	294	
Avg.	.250	.272	.262	.236	.263	.249	105	.254	.269	.261	.235	.272	.253	103
AB	2389	2576	4965	2523	2430	4953	102	4878	5202	10080	4931	4793	9724	102
R	317	362	679	286	321	607	113	639	762	1401	549	712	1261	110
H	598	701	1299	595	639	1234	107	1237	1398	2635	1157	1302	2459	106
2B	122	145	267	121	126	247	108	255	294	549	224	265	489	108
3B	6	16	22	14	12	26	84	16	28	44	26	31	57	74
HR	57	81	138	78	71	149	92	127	154	281	154	150	304	89
BB	269	254	523	243	278	521	100	484	519	1003	451	522	973	99
SO	451	445	896	593	423	1016	88	918	877	1795	1143	822	1965	88
E	59	50	109	51	40	91	121	128	117	245	105	95	200	121
E-Infield	50	44	94	44	35	79	121	103	103	206	89	82	171	119
LHB-Avg.	.264	.278	.272	.253	.270	.263	103	.262	.278	.271	.243	.288	.267	102
LHB-HR	25	29	54	31	34	65	82	54	62	116	56	64	120	90
RHB-Avg.	.244	.269	.256	.229	.259	.242	106	.249	.263	.256	.230	.262	.245	104
RHB-HR	32	52	84	47	37	84	100	73	92	165	98	86	184	88

ST. LOUIS

Home park: Busch Stadium   **Alt.:** 535 feet   **Surface:** Grass

Category	2002 Season Home Games			Road Games			Index	2000-02 Seasons Home Games			Road Games			Index
	St.L.	Opp.	Total	St.L.	Opp.	Total		St.L.	Opp.	Total	St.L.	Opp.	Total	
G	75	75	150	75	75	150		223	223	446	221	221	442	
Avg.	.265	.242	.253	.268	.263	.266	95	.274	.247	.260	.265	.265	.265	98
AB	2495	2568	5063	2615	2442	5057	100	7347	7571	14918	7685	7260	14945	99
R	362	273	635	365	333	698	91	1173	924	2097	1115	998	2113	98
H	661	622	1283	702	643	1345	95	2010	1869	3879	2037	1923	3960	97
2B	126	134	260	136	117	253	103	362	395	757	398	389	787	96
3B	8	1	9	17	10	27	33	39	22	61	39	34	73	84
HR	80	63	143	81	68	149	96	289	248	537	271	244	515	104
BB	276	259	535	231	260	491	109	859	807	1666	754	744	1498	111
SO	439	500	939	440	443	883	106	1445	1577	3022	1571	1346	2917	104
E	43	53	96	49	52	101	95	144	169	313	150	154	304	102
E-Infield	34	49	83	38	46	84	99	114	131	245	112	135	247	98
LHB-Avg.	.275	.244	.260	.267	.255	.261	99	.284	.251	.268	.280	.262	.271	99
LHB-HR	37	22	59	30	29	59	101	138	97	235	115	103	218	112
RHB-Avg.	.258	.241	.249	.270	.268	.269	93	.267	.244	.255	.255	.267	.261	98
RHB-HR	43	41	84	51	39	90	93	151	151	302	156	141	297	99

SAN DIEGO **Home park:** Qualcomm Stadium **Alt.:** 20 feet **Surface:** Grass

| | 2002 Season | | | | | | | 2000-02 Seasons | | | | | | |
| | Home Games | | | Road Games | | | | Home Games | | | Road Games | | | |
Category	S.D.	Opp.	Total	S.D.	Opp.	Total	Index	S.D.	Opp.	Total	S.D.	Opp.	Total	Index
G	72	72	144	72	72	144		219	219	438	219	219	438	
Avg.	.270	.261	.265	.239	.290	.264	101	.250	.252	.251	.258	.283	.270	93
AB	2440	2531	4971	2479	2412	4891	102	7292	7703	14995	7650	7452	15102	99
R	307	312	619	277	419	696	89	913	995	1908	1083	1208	2291	83
H	658	661	1319	592	699	1291	102	1823	1942	3765	1972	2109	4081	92
2B	102	120	222	113	159	272	80	327	334	661	399	443	842	79
3B	16	17	33	10	19	29	112	42	38	80	41	50	91	89
HR	57	73	130	64	91	155	83	178	254	432	232	282	514	85
BB	249	227	476	227	283	510	92	811	708	1519	820	826	1646	93
SO	427	524	951	526	466	992	94	1543	1566	3109	1641	1373	3014	104
E..................	53	52	105	59	48	107	98	210	139	349	166	159	325	107
E-Infield	47	39	86	47	42	89	97	191	110	301	137	133	270	111
LHB-Avg.	.295	.275	.285	.239	.310	.271	105	.269	.257	.263	.266	.292	.279	94
LHB-HR	31	28	59	33	47	80	73	81	111	192	95	127	222	84
RHB-Avg.	.245	.251	.248	.239	.275	.258	96	.235	.248	.242	.252	.276	.264	92
RHB-HR	26	45	71	31	44	75	93	97	143	240	137	155	292	85

SAN FRANCISCO **Home park:** Pacific Bell Park **Alt.:** 0 feet **Surface:** Grass

| | 2002 Season | | | | | | | 2001-02 Seasons | | | | | | |
| | Home Games | | | Road Games | | | | Home Games | | | Road Games | | | |
Category	S.F.	Opp.	Total	S.F.	Opp.	Total	Index	S.F.	Opp.	Total	S.F.	Opp.	Total	Index
G	72	72	144	72	72	144		147	147	294	144	144	288	
Avg.	.258	.245	.251	.275	.255	.265	95	.257	.249	.253	.278	.262	.271	94
AB	2329	2443	4772	2545	2346	4891	98	4852	5085	9937	5145	4771	9916	98
R	320	249	569	388	300	688	83	650	585	1235	800	671	1471	82
H	601	599	1200	700	598	1298	92	1248	1268	2516	1432	1252	2684	92
2B	119	105	224	149	108	257	89	261	245	506	290	232	522	97
3B	22	17	39	11	10	21	190	45	41	86	26	28	54	159
HR	62	34	96	116	67	183	54	152	82	234	245	153	398	59
BB	277	216	493	284	253	537	94	578	476	1054	563	529	1092	96
SO	399	440	839	460	411	871	99	871	964	1835	987	879	1866	98
E..................	44	57	101	41	45	86	117	96	94	190	95	92	187	100
E-Infield	34	44	78	31	41	72	108	76	76	152	69	79	148	101
LHB-Avg.	.260	.248	.253	.297	.265	.278	91	.249	.254	.252	.299	.279	.288	87
LHB-HR	23	12	35	38	27	65	54	71	24	95	104	61	165	56
RHB-Avg.	.257	.243	.251	.266	.247	.258	97	.261	.246	.254	.269	.250	.261	97
RHB-HR	39	22	61	78	40	118	54	81	58	139	141	92	233	60

2000-2002 N.L. BALLPARK INDEX RANKINGS

RUNS PER GAME

Team	Home Games Games	Home Games Team	Home Games Opp.	Home Games Total	Road Games Games	Road Games Team	Road Games Opp.	Road Games Total	Index
Colorado	222	1531	1398	2929	222	922	1031	1953	150
Houston	222	1251	1140	2391	222	1072	1027	2099	114
Arizona.........	219	1193	1003	2196	219	1025	899	1924	114
Pittsburgh* ..	149	639	762	1401	147	549	712	1261	110
Cincinnati*	150	697	792	1489	147	654	681	1335	109
Montreal.......	216	982	1088	2070	216	919	1072	1991	104
Atlanta	216	988	860	1848	215	972	844	1816	101
St. Louis	223	1173	924	2097	221	1115	998	2113	98
Milwaukee* ..	147	618	711	1329	150	639	760	1399	97
Philadelphia ..	215	933	972	1905	216	976	1057	2033	94
Florida	215	968	953	1921	217	928	1138	2066	94
New York	215	909	909	1818	214	985	1011	1996	91
Chicago	221	987	994	1981	221	1037	1169	2206	90
San Diego	219	913	995	1908	219	1083	1208	2291	83
Los Angeles ..	219	909	872	1781	219	1164	1010	2174	82
San Fran.*	147	650	585	1235	144	800	671	1471	82

*Current dimensions began in 2001.

HOME RUNS PER AT-BAT

Team	Home Games Games	Home Games Team	Home Games Opp.	Home Games Total	Road Games Games	Road Games Team	Road Games Opp.	Road Games Total	Index
Colorado	222	303	367	670	222	182	243	425	150
Cincinnati*	150	159	201	360	147	166	133	299	116
Houston	222	307	294	601	222	263	253	516	115
Arizona.........	219	256	267	523	219	249	221	470	110
Montreal.......	216	206	252	458	216	206	222	428	106
Milwaukee* ..	147	150	189	339	150	164	164	328	106
St. Louis	223	289	248	537	221	271	244	515	104
Atlanta	216	228	198	426	215	228	198	426	101
Chicago	221	246	257	503	221	270	253	523	98
Philadelphia ..	215	202	224	426	216	212	238	450	97
Los Angeles ..	219	247	229	476	219	276	240	516	94
New York	215	211	220	431	214	227	235	462	93
Pittsburgh* ..	149	127	154	281	147	154	150	304	89
Florida	215	197	195	392	217	223	238	461	86
San Diego	219	178	254	432	219	232	282	514	85
San Fran.*	147	152	82	234	144	245	153	398	59

*Current dimensions began in 2001.

BATTING AVERAGE

Team	Home Games Games	Home Games Team	Home Games Opp.	Home Games Total	Road Games Games	Road Games Team	Road Games Opp.	Road Games Total	Index
Colorado	222	.326	.290	.308	222	.248	.260	.253	121
Arizona.........	219	.283	.257	.270	219	.250	.248	.249	108
Houston	222	.281	.268	.274	222	.257	.264	.261	105
Cincinnati*	150	.266	.279	.273	147	.254	.266	.260	105
Pittsburgh* ..	149	.254	.269	.261	147	.235	.272	.253	103
Atlanta	216	.267	.251	.259	215	.257	.249	.253	102
Montreal.......	216	.266	.267	.267	216	.253	.277	.265	101
Milwaukee* ..	147	.253	.261	.257	150	.247	.270	.258	100
St. Louis	223	.274	.247	.260	221	.265	.265	.265	98
Florida	215	.264	.251	.258	217	.256	.276	.266	97
Chicago	221	.255	.243	.249	221	.252	.272	.262	95
New York	215	.251	.248	.250	214	.261	.266	.263	95
Philadelphia ..	215	.254	.249	.251	216	.262	.272	.266	94
San Fran.*	147	.257	.249	.253	144	.278	.262	.271	94
San Diego	219	.250	.252	.251	219	.258	.283	.270	93
Los Angeles ..	219	.251	.235	.243	219	.269	.259	.264	92

*Current dimensions began in 2001.

2002 STATISTICAL LEADERS

2002 American League leaders

2002 National League leaders

2002 Active career leaders

2002 AMERICAN LEAGUE LEADERS

BATTING

Batting Average
(minimum 502 PA)

Player, Team	AB	H	Avg.
M. Ramirez, Bos.	436	152	.349
M. Sweeney, K.C.	471	160	.340
B. Williams, N.Y.	612	204	.333
I. Suzuki, Sea.	647	208	.321
M. Ordonez, Chi.	590	189	.320
J. Giambi, N.Y.	560	176	.314
A. Kennedy, Ana.	474	148	.312
N. Garciaparra, Bos.	635	197	.310
M. Tejada, Oak.	662	204	.308
G. Anderson, Ana.	638	195	.306

On-Base Percentage
(minimum 502 PA; *AB+BB+HBP+SF)

Player, Team	*PA	OB	OBP
M. Ramirez, Bos.	518	233	.450
J. Thome, Cle.	613	273	.445
J. Giambi, N.Y.	689	300	.435
M. Sweeney, K.C.	545	227	.417
B. Williams, N.Y.	699	290	.415
C. Delgado, Tor.	628	255	.406
J. Olerud, Sea.	668	269	.403
A. Rodriguez, Tex.	725	284	.392
R. Palmeiro, Tex.	663	259	.391
I. Suzuki, Sea.	725	281	.388

Slugging Percentage
(minimum 502 PA)

Player, Team	AB	TB	Slg.
J. Thome, Cle.	480	325	.677
M. Ramirez, Bos.	436	282	.647
A. Rodriguez, Tex.	624	389	.623
J. Giambi, N.Y.	560	335	.598
M. Ordonez, Chi.	590	352	.597
R. Palmeiro, Tex.	546	312	.571
M. Sweeney, K.C.	471	265	.563
C. Delgado, Tor.	505	277	.549
A. Soriano, N.Y.	696	381	.547
E. Burks, Cle.	518	280	.541

Games
C. Beltran, K.C.	162
T. Long, Oak.	162
A. Rodriguez, Tex.	162
M. Tejada, Oak.	162
T. Batista, Bal.	161

Plate Appearances
A. Soriano, N.Y.	741
D. Jeter, N.Y.	730
I. Suzuki, Sea.	728
A. Rodriguez, Tex.	725
C. Beltran, K.C.	722

At-Bats
A. Soriano, N.Y.	696
M. Tejada, Oak.	662
I. Suzuki, Sea.	647
D. Jeter, N.Y.	644
G. Anderson, Ana.	638

Hits
A. Soriano, N.Y.	209
I. Suzuki, Sea.	208
M. Tejada, Oak.	204
B. Williams, N.Y.	204
N. Garciaparra, Bos.	197

Singles
I. Suzuki, Sea.	165
D. Jeter, N.Y.	147
B. Williams, N.Y.	146
D. Eckstein, Ana.	142
M. Tejada, Oak.	140

Doubles
G. Anderson, Ana.	56
N. Garciaparra, Bos.	56
A. Soriano, N.Y.	51
M. Ordonez, Chi.	47
C. Beltran, K.C.	44

Triples
J. Damon, Bos.	11
R. Winn, T.B.	9
I. Suzuki, Sea.	8
M. Young, Tex.	8
C. Beltran, K.C.	7

Home Runs
A. Rodriguez, Tex.	57
J. Thome, Cle.	52
R. Palmeiro, Tex.	43
J. Giambi, N.Y.	41
A. Soriano, N.Y.	39

Total Bases
A. Rodriguez, Tex.	389
A. Soriano, N.Y.	381
M. Ordonez, Chi.	352
G. Anderson, Ana.	344
M. Tejada, Oak.	336

Runs Scored
A. Soriano, N.Y.	128
A. Rodriguez, Tex.	125
D. Jeter, N.Y.	124
J. Giambi, N.Y.	120
J. Damon, Bos.	118

Runs Batted In
A. Rodriguez, Tex.	142
M. Ordonez, Chi.	135
M. Tejada, Oak.	131
G. Anderson, Ana.	123
J. Giambi, N.Y.	122

GDP
J. Posada, N.Y.	23
M. Ordonez, Chi.	21
M. Tejada, Oak.	21
J. Olerud, Sea.	19
B. Williams, N.Y.	19

Sacrifice Hits
D. Eckstein, Ana.	14
J. Cirillo, Sea.	13
M. Young, Tex.	13
R. Durham, Chi.-Oak.	10
A. Rowand, Chi.	9

Sacrifice Flies
J. Olerud, Sea.	12
N. Garciaparra, Bos.	11
J. Randa, K.C.	11
4 tied with	10

Stolen Bases
A. Soriano, N.Y.	41
C. Beltran, K.C.	35
D. Jeter, N.Y.	32
3 tied with	31

Caught Stealing
I. Suzuki, Sea.	15
D. Eckstein, Ana.	13
C. Guzman, Min.	13
A. Soriano, N.Y.	13
C. Koskie, Min.	11

Walks
J. Thome, Cle.	122
J. Giambi, N.Y.	109
R. Palmeiro, Tex.	104
C. Delgado, Tor.	102
J. Olerud, Sea.	98

Intentional Walks
I. Suzuki, Sea.	27
C. Delgado, Tor.	18
J. Thome, Cle.	18
R. Palmeiro, Tex.	16
M. Ramirez, Bos.	14

Hit by Pitch
D. Eckstein, Ana.	27
M. Mora, Bal.	20
B. Fullmer, Ana.	15
J. Giambi, N.Y.	15
A. Soriano, N.Y.	14

Strikeouts
M. Cameron, Sea.	176
A. Soriano, N.Y.	157
T. Glaus, Ana.	144
J. Posada, N.Y.	143
2 tied with	139

2002 NATIONAL LEAGUE LEADERS

BATTING

Batting Average
(minimum 502 PA)

Player, Team	AB	H	Avg.
B. Bonds, S.F.	403	149	.370
L. Walker, Col.	477	161	.338
V. Guerrero, Mon.	614	206	.336
T. Helton, Col.	553	182	.329
C. Jones, Atl.	548	179	.327
J. Vidro, Mon.	604	190	.315
A. Pujols, St.L.	590	185	.314
J. Kent, S.F.	623	195	.313
J. Edmonds, St.L.	476	148	.311
E. Alfonzo, N.Y.	490	151	.308

On-Base Percentage
(minimum 502 PA; *AB+BB+HBP+SF)

Player, Team	*PA	OB	OBP
B. Bonds, S.F.	612	356	.582
B. Giles, Pit.	644	290	.450
C. Jones, Atl.	662	288	.435
T. Helton, Col.	667	286	.429
L. Walker, Col.	553	233	.421
J. Edmonds, St.L.	576	242	.420
V. Guerrero, Mon.	709	296	.417
B. Abreu, Phi.	685	283	.413
L. Berkman, Hou.	692	280	.405
G. Sheffield, Atl.	579	234	.404

Slugging Percentage
(minimum 502 PA)

Player, Team	AB	TB	Slg.
B. Bonds, S.F.	403	322	.799
B. Giles, Pit.	497	309	.622
L. Walker, Col.	477	287	.602
S. Sosa, Chi.	556	330	.594
V. Guerrero, Mon.	614	364	.593
L. Berkman, Hou.	578	334	.578
T. Helton, Col.	553	319	.577
J. Kent, S.F.	623	352	.565
A. Pujols, St.L.	590	331	.561
J. Edmonds, St.L.	476	267	.561

Games

A. Boone, Cin	162
D. Lee, Fla.	162
V. Guerrero, Mon.	161
M. Lowell, Fla.	160
A. Beltre, L.A.	159

Plate Appearances

V. Guerrero, Mon.	709
J. Rollins, Phi.	705
R. Furcal, Atl.	693
L. Berkman, Hou.	692
F. Vina, St.L.	692

At-Bats

J. Rollins, Phi.	637
R. Furcal, Atl.	636
J. Kent, S.F.	623
F. Vina, St.L.	622
V. Guerrero, Mon.	614

Hits

V. Guerrero, Mon.	206
J. Kent, S.F.	195
J. Vidro, Mon.	190
L. Castillo, Fla.	185
A. Pujols, St.L.	185

Singles

L. Castillo, Fla.	160
J. Pierre, Col.	144
F. Vina, St.L.	133
R. Furcal, Atl.	128
V. Guerrero, Mon.	128

Doubles

B. Abreu, Phi.	50
M. Lowell, Fla.	44
O. Cabrera, Mon.	43
J. Vidro, Mon.	43
2 tied with	42

Triples

J. Rollins, Phi.	10
R. Furcal, Atl.	8
Q. McCracken, Ari.	8
S. Rolen, Phi.-St.L.	8
B. Wilkerson, Mon.	8

Home Runs

S. Sosa, Chi.	49
B. Bonds, S.F.	46
L. Berkman, Hou.	42
S. Green, L.A.	42
V. Guerrero, Mon.	39

Total Bases

V. Guerrero, Mon.	364
J. Kent, S.F.	352
L. Berkman, Hou.	334
A. Pujols, St.L.	331
S. Sosa, Chi.	330

Runs Scored

S. Sosa, Chi.	122
A. Pujols, St.L.	118
B. Bonds, S.F.	117
S. Green, L.A.	110
T. Helton, Col.	107

Runs Batted In

L. Berkman, Hou.	128
A. Pujols, St.L.	127
P. Burrell, Phi.	116
S. Green, L.A.	114
V. Guerrero, Mon.	111

GDP

B. Ausmus, Hou.	30
T. Zeile, Col.	27
S. Green, L.A.	26
M. Piazza, N.Y.	26
2 tied with	22

Sacrifice Hits

J. Wilson, Pit.	17
G. Rusch, Mil.	14
5 tied with	13

Sacrifice Flies

M. Lowell, Fla.	11
A. Ramirez, Pit.	11
T. Helton, Col.	10
J. Bagwell, Hou.	9
10 tied with	7

Stolen Bases

L. Castillo, Fla.	48
J. Pierre, Col.	47
D. Roberts, L.A.	45
V. Guerrero, Mon.	40
A. Sanchez, Mil.	37

Caught Stealing

V. Guerrero, Mon.	20
L. Castillo, Fla.	15
R. Furcal, Atl.	15
A. Sanchez, Mil.	14
J. Rollins, Phi.	13

Walks

B. Bonds, S.F.	198
B. Giles, Pit.	135
A. Dunn, Cin.	128
L. Berkman, Hou.	107
C. Jones, Atl.	107

Intentional Walks

B. Bonds, S.F.	68
V. Guerrero, Mon.	32
B. Giles, Pit.	24
C. Jones, Atl.	23
S. Green, L.A.	22

Hit by Pitch

C. Wilson, Pit.	21
F. Vina, St.L.	18
C. Biggio, Hou.	17
J. Spivey, Ari.	16
M. Lieberthal, Phi.	14

Strikeouts

J. Hernandez, Mil.	188
A. Dunn, Cin.	170
D. Lee, Fla.	164
B. Wilkerson, Mon.	161
P. Burrell, Phi.	153

Earned Run Average
(minimum 162 IP)

Pitcher, Team	IP	ER	ERA
P. Martinez, Bos.	....199.1	50	2.26
D. Lowe, Bos.	........219.2	63	2.58
B. Zito, Oak.	............229.1	70	2.75
T. Wakefield, Bos.	..163.1	51	2.81
R. Halladay, Tor.	......239.1	78	2.93
T. Hudson, Oak.	......238.1	79	2.98
J. Washburn, Ana.	..206.0	72	3.15
J. Pineiro, Sea.	......194.1	70	3.24
J. Moyer, Sea.	........230.2	85	3.32
M. Mulder, Oak.	......207.1	80	3.47

Won-Lost Percentage
(minimum 15 decisions)

Pitcher, Team	W	L	Pct.
P. Martinez, Bos.	20	4	.833
B. Zito, Oak.	23	5	.821
J. Washburn, Ana.	18	6	.750
B. Koch, Oak.	11	4	.733
R. Halladay, Tor.	19	7	.731
M. Mulder, Oak.	19	7	.731
D. Wells, N.Y.	19	7	.731
D. Lowe, Bos.	21	8	.724
A. Pettitte, N.Y.	13	5	.722
T. Wakefield, Bos.	11	5	.688

Opponents' Batting Average
(minimum 162 IP)

Pitcher, Team	AB	H	Avg.
P. Martinez, Bos.	726	144	.198
T. Wakefield, Bos.	592	121	.204
D. Lowe, Bos.	787	166	.211
B. Zito, Oak.	836	182	.218
J. Moyer, Sea.	860	198	.230
R. Ortiz, Ana.	816	188	.230
M. Mulder, Oak.	786	182	.232
R. Lopez, Bal.	735	172	.234
J. Washburn, Ana.	779	183	.235
R. Halladay, Tor.	913	223	.244

Games

B. Koch, Oak.	84
J. Romero, Min.	81
M. Stanton, N.Y.	79
S. Karsay, N.Y.	78
K. Escobar, Tor.	76

Games Started

B. Zito, Oak.	35
5 tied with	34

Complete Games

P. Byrd, K.C.	7
M. Buehrle, Chi.	5
J. Kennedy, T.B.	5
5 tied with	4

Games Finished

B. Koch, Oak.	79
K. Escobar, Tor.	68
E. Guardado, Min.	62
J. Julio, Bal.	61
2 tied with	55

Wins

B. Zito, Oak.	23
D. Lowe, Bos.	21
P. Martinez, Bos.	20
4 tied with	19

Losses

T. Sturtze, T.B.	18
S. Sparks, Det.	16
J. Suppan, K.C.	16
3 tied with	15

Saves

E. Guardado, Min.	45
B. Koch, Oak.	44
T. Percival, Ana.	40
U. Urbina, Bos.	40
K. Escobar, Tor.	38

Shutouts

J. Weaver, Det.-N.Y.	3
7 tied with	2

Hits Allowed

T. Sturtze, T.B.	271
S. Sparks, Det.	238
T. Hudson, Oak.	237
M. Buehrle, Chi.	236
J. Suppan, K.C.	229

Doubles Allowed

T. Sturtze, T.B.	57
S. Sparks, Det.	55
M. Buehrle, Chi.	53
D. Wells, N.Y.	51
J. Washburn, Ana.	50

Triples Allowed

R. Drese, Cle.	8
M. Redman, Det.	8
R. Reed, Min.	8
C. Sabathia, Cle.	8
S. Sparks, Det.	8

Home Runs Allowed

R. Ortiz, Ana.	40
P. Byrd, K.C.	36
T. Sturtze, T.B.	33
3 tied with	32

Batters Faced

T. Sturtze, T.B.	1008
R. Halladay, Tor.	993
M. Buehrle, Chi.	984
T. Hudson, Oak.	983
F. Garcia, Sea.	955

Innings Pitched

R. Halladay, Tor.	..........239.1
M. Buehrle, Chi.	............239.0
T. Hudson, Oak.	............238.1
J. Moyer, Sea.	..............230.2
B. Zito, Oak.	................229.1

Runs Allowed

T. Sturtze, T.B.	141
S. Sparks, Det.	134
J. Suppan, K.C.	134
D. Wright, Chi.	124
J. Kennedy, T.B.	114

Strikeouts

P. Martinez, Bos.	239
R. Clemens, N.Y.	192
M. Mussina, N.Y.	182
B. Zito, Oak.	182
F. Garcia, Sea.	181

Walks Allowed

T. Sturtze, T.B.	89
C. Sabathia, Cle.	88
J. Garland, Chi.	83
D. Baez, Cle.	82
2 tied with	78

Hit Batsmen

C. Park, Tex.	17
J. Kennedy, T.B.	16
P. Martinez, Bos.	15
P. Wilson, T.B.	13
2 tied with	12

Wild Pitches

J. Santana, Min.	15
R. Clemens, N.Y.	14
R. Drese, Cle.	11
M. Redman, Det.	11
4 tied with	10

Balks

S. Kent, T.B.	3
R. Ortiz, Ana.	3
C. Sabathia, Cle.	3
10 tied with	2

Earned-Run Average
(minimum 162 IP)

Pitcher, Team	IP	ER	ERA
R. Johnson, Ari.	....260.0	67	2.32
G. Maddux, Atl.	.....199.1	58	2.62
T. Glavine, Atl.	.......224.2	74	2.96
O. Perez, L.A.	.........222.1	74	3.00
R. Oswalt, Hou.	.....233.0	78	3.01
E. Dessens, Cin.	....178.0	60	3.03
T. Ohka, Mon.	.......192.2	68	3.18
R. Wolf, Phi.	.........210.2	75	3.20
K. Rueter, S.F.	........203.2	73	3.23
C. Schilling, Ari.	......259.1	93	3.23

Won-Lost Percentage
(minimum 15 decisions)

Pitcher, Team	W	L	Pct.
R. Johnson, Ari.	24	5	.828
W. Miller, Hou.	15	4	.789
C. Schilling, Ari.	23	7	.767
D. Stark, Col.	11	4	.733
G. Maddux, Atl.	16	6	.727
H. Nomo, L.A.	16	6	.727
K. Millwood, Atl.	18	8	.692
J. Simontacchi, St.L.	..11	5	.688
R. Oswalt, Hou.	19	9	.679
2 tied with			.667

Opponents' Batting Average
(minimum 162 IP)

Pitcher, Team	AB	H	Avg.
R. Johnson, Ari.	945	197	.208
A. Burnett, Fla.	732	153	.209
M. Clement, Chi.	752	162	.215
J. Schmidt, S.F.	678	148	.218
D. Moss, Atl.	633	140	.221
K. Wood, Chi.	764	169	.221
R. Wolf, Phi.	772	172	.223
C. Schilling, Ari.	974	218	.224
O. Perez, L.A.	807	182	.226
K. Millwood, Atl.	809	186	.230

Games

P. Quantrill, L.A.	86
O. Dotel, Hou.	83
T. Worrell, S.F.	80
T. Jones, Col.	79
3 tied with	78

Games Started

T. Glavine, Atl.	36
R. Johnson, Ari.	35
C. Schilling, Ari.	35
8 tied with	34

Complete Games

R. Johnson, Ari.	8
A. Burnett, Fla.	7
L. Hernandez, S.F.	5
C. Schilling, Ari.	5
5 tied with	4

Games Finished

J. Jimenez, Col.	69
E. Gagne, L.A.	68
J. Smoltz, Atl.	68
B. Kim, Ari.	66
R. Nen, S.F.	66

Wins

R. Johnson, Ari.	24
C. Schilling, Ari.	23
R. Oswalt, Hou.	19
T. Glavine, Atl.	18
K. Millwood, Atl.	18

Losses

L. Hernandez, S.F.	16
G. Rusch, Mil.	16
B. Sheets, Mil.	16
M. Hampton, Col.	15
2 tied with	14

Saves

J. Smoltz, Atl.	55
E. Gagne, L.A.	52
M. Williams, Pit.	46
J. Mesa, Phi.	45
R. Nen, S.F.	43

Shutouts

A. Burnett, Fla.	5
R. Johnson, Ari.	4
L. Hernandez, S.F.	3
6 tied with	2

Hits Allowed

J. Vazquez, Mon.	243
B. Sheets, Mil.	237
L. Hernandez, S.F.	233
B. Lawrence, S.D.	230
2 tied with	228

Doubles Allowed

J. Vazquez, Mon.	56
B. Sheets, Mil.	55
J. Tavarez, Fla.	54
T. Glavine, Atl.	49
J. Thomson, Col.-N.Y.	49

Triples Allowed

R. Dempster, Fla.-Cin.	11
J. Fogg, Pit.	8
R. Oswalt, Hou.	8
C. Schilling, Ari.	8
5 tied with	7

Home Runs Allowed

P. Astacio, N.Y.	32
R. Helling, Ari.	31
B. Tomko, S.D.	31
G. Rusch, Mil.	30
C. Schilling, Ari.	29

Batters Faced

R. Johnson, Ari.	1035
C. Schilling, Ari.	1017
J. Vazquez, Mon.	971
R. Oswalt, Hou.	956
T. Glavine, Atl.	936

Innings Pitched

R. Johnson, Ari.	...........260.0
C. Schilling, Ari.	...........259.1
R. Oswalt, Hou.	............233.0
J. Vazquez, Mon.	.........230.1
T. Glavine, Atl.	.............224.2

Runs Allowed

M. Hampton, Col.	135
R. Dempster, Fla.-Cin.	127
G. Rusch, Mil.	118
J. Thomson, Col.-N.Y.	116
L. Hernandez, S.F.	113

Strikeouts

R. Johnson, Ari.	334
C. Schilling, Ari.	316
K. Wood, Chi.	217
M. Clement, Chi.	215
R. Oswalt, Hou.	208

Walks Allowed

K. Ishii, L.A.	106
H. Nomo, L.A.	101
K. Wood, Chi.	97
R. Ortiz, S.F.	94
R. Dempster, Fla.-Cin.	93

Hit Batsmen

P. Astacio, N.Y.	16
K. Wood, Chi.	16
V. Padilla, Phi.	15
J. Tavarez, Fla.	15
R. Johnson, Ari.	13

Wild Pitches

T. Armas Jr., Mon.	14
A. Burnett, Fla.	14
D. Moss, Atl.	13
J. Schmidt, S.F.	12
D. Coggin, Phi.	11

Balks

B. Anderson, Ari.	5
O. Perez, L.A.	3
14 tied with	2

2002 STATISTICAL LEADERS N.L.

Scoring-Position Average†
(minimum 100 PA)

Player, Team	AB	H	Avg.
M. Ramirez, Bos.	108	47	.435
M. Sweeney, K.C.	107	43	.402
M. Tejada, Oak.	176	66	.375
B. Williams, N.Y.	174	65	.374
E. Burks, Cle.	130	48	.369
A. Rodriguez, Tex.	153	56	.366
B. Higginson, Det.	93	34	.366
I. Suzuki, Sea.	119	43	.361
J. Jones, Min.	128	45	.352
J. Valentin, Chi.	94	33	.351

Leadoff OBP†
(minimum 150 PA; *AB+BB+HBP+SF)

Player, Team	*PA	OB	OBP
I. Suzuki, Sea.	703	269	.383
J. Giambi, Oak.	171	65	.380
S. Stewart, Tor.	578	219	.379
R. Winn, T.B.	331	124	.375
R. Henderson, Bos.	212	78	.368
F. Catalanotto, Tex.	227	83	.366
D. Eckstein, Ana.	686	250	.364
R. Durham, Chi.-Oak.	277	99	.357
K. Lofton, Chi.	393	137	.349
M. Ellis, Oak.	251	87	.347

Cleanup Slugging†
(minimum 150 PA)

Player, Team	AB	TB	Slg.
J. Thome, Cle.	447	316	.707
J. Giambi, N.Y.	236	151	.640
M. Ordonez, Chi.	497	312	.628
M. Ramirez, Bos.	406	252	.621
M. Sweeney, K.C.	261	157	.602
R. Palmeiro, Tex.	349	203	.582
P. Konerko, Chi.	138	80	.580
G. Anderson, Ana.	607	336	.554
C. Delgado, Tor.	505	277	.549
R. Ibanez, K.C.	217	115	.530

Avg. vs. LHP
(minimum 125 PA)

S. Spiezio, Ana.	.368
I. Suzuki, Sea.	.356
B. Williams, N.Y.	.354
R. Winn, T.B.	.347
J. Posada, N.Y.	.326

Avg. vs. RHP
(minimum 377 PA)

M. Sweeney, K.C.	.334
J. Jones, Min.	.333
J. Thome, Cle.	.333
M. Ramirez, Bos.	.331
M. Ordonez, Chi.	.329

Avg. at Home
(minimum 251 PA)

J. Thome, Cle.	.350
M. Ramirez, Bos.	.336
T. Hunter, Min.	.334
J. Giambi, N.Y.	.333
M. Sweeney, K.C.	.331

Avg. on Road
(minimum 251 PA)

M. Ramirez, Bos.	.360
B. Williams, N.Y.	.354
M. Sweeney, K.C.	.349
E. Burks, Cle.	.341
M. Tejada, Oak.	.336

OBP vs. LHP
(minimum 125 PA)

S. Spiezio, Ana.	.448
B. Williams, N.Y.	.430
J. Posada, N.Y.	.420
I. Suzuki, Sea.	.416
T. Salmon, Ana.	.411

OBP vs. RHP
(minimum 377 PA)

J. Thome, Cle.	.485
J. Giambi, N.Y.	.448
C. Delgado, Tor.	.444
M. Ramirez, Bos.	.433
R. Palmeiro, Tex.	.420

Late & Close Avg.†
(minimum 50 PA)

S. Spiezio, Ana.	.420
B. Williams, N.Y.	.393
G. Matthews Jr., Bal.	.383
M. Sweeney, K.C.	.382
S. Hillenbrand, Bos.	.375

Bases Loaded Avg.
(minimum 10 PA)

T. Glaus, Ana.	.600
J. Posada, N.Y.	.579
T. Hall, T.B.	.571
D. Relaford, Sea.	.571
2 tied with	.545

Slg. vs. LHP
(minimum 125 PA)

M. Ordonez, Chi.	.624
E. Burks, Cle.	.581
A. Soriano, N.Y.	.571
J. Posada, N.Y.	.556
R. Winn, T.B.	.549

Slg. vs. RHP
(minimum 377 PA)

J. Thome, Cle.	.766
A. Rodriguez, Tex.	.682
C. Delgado, Tor.	.646
J. Giambi, N.Y.	.626
R. Palmeiro, Tex.	.615

AB per Home Run
(minimum 502 PA)

J. Thome, Cle.	9.2
A. Rodriguez, Tex.	10.9
R. Palmeiro, Tex.	12.7
M. Ramirez, Bos.	13.2
J. Giambi, N.Y.	13.7

Times on Base*
(*H+BB+HBP)

J. Giambi, N.Y.	300
B. Williams, N.Y.	290
A. Rodriguez, Tex.	284
I. Suzuki, Sea.	281
J. Thome, Cle.	273

Pitches Seen

J. Giambi, N.Y.	2892
C. Beltran, K.C.	2854
A. Rodriguez, Tex.	2812
M. Tejada, Oak.	2756
J. Damon, Bos.	2727

Pitches per PA
(minimum 502 PA)

F. Thomas, Chi.	4.26
J. Giambi, N.Y.	4.20
S. Hatteberg, Oak.	4.15
J. Dye, Oak.	4.12
R. Durham, Chi.-Oak.	4.07

Pct. of Pitches Taken
(minimum 1500 pitches)

J. Olerud, Sea.	66.4
M. McLemore, Sea.	64.9
S. Hatteberg, Oak.	64.5
J. Giambi, N.Y.	62.7
F. Thomas, Chi.	62.7

Ground/Fly Ratio†
(minimum 502 PA)

I. Suzuki, Sea.	2.48
D. Jeter, N.Y.	2.23
B. Grieve, T.B.	2.08
C. Guzman, Min.	2.04
B. Williams, N.Y.	1.87

GDP/GDP Opp.†
(minimum 50 PA)

K. Lofton, Chi.	0.00
M. McLemore, Sea.	0.03
J. Damon, Bos.	0.04
J. Thome, Cle.	0.04
C. Lee, Chi.	0.05

SB Success Pct.
(minimum 20 SB attempts)

D. Jeter, N.Y.	91.4
C. Singleton, Bal.	90.9
D. Erstad, Ana.	88.5
C. Knoblauch, K.C.	86.4
J. Damon, Bos.	83.8

Steals of Third

A. Soriano, N.Y.	9
I. Suzuki, Sea.	9
C. Knoblauch, K.C.	8
C. Singleton, Bal.	8
R. Winn, T.B.	6

Pct. CS by Catchers
(minimum 50 SB attempts)

B. Molina, Ana.	42.7
G. Gil, Bal.	34.4
B. Mayne, K.C.	32.8
K. Huckaby, Tor.	32.7
D. Mirabelli, Bos.	32.7

†**Scoring-Position Average** denotes batting average when a runner is at second and/or third base. **Leadoff OBP** denotes OBP for a player batting in the first position of the batting order. **Cleanup Slugging** denotes slugging percentage for a player batting in the fourth position of the batting order. **Late & Close Avg.** refers to batting average when the game is in the seventh inning or later and the batting team is either leading by one run, tied, or has the potential tying run on base, at bat or on deck (a batting situation coming close to a pitcher's save situation). **Ground/Fly Ratio** denotes ground balls hit divided by fly balls hit. All batted balls except line drives and bunts are included. **GDP/GDP Opp.** denotes the ratio of times grounding into double plays per opportunities to do so (any situation with a runner on first and less than two out).

Scoring-Position Average†
(minimum 100 PA)

Player, Team	AB	H	Avg.
B. Bonds, S.F.	85	32	.376
J. Vidro, Mon.	137	51	.372
E. Renteria, St.L.	148	55	.372
G. Sheffield, Atl.	120	44	.367
C. Counsell, Ari.	110	40	.364
L. Berkman, Hou.	144	52	.361
L. Walker, Col.	114	41	.360
L. Gonzalez, Ari.	151	53	.351
A. Pujols, St.L.	156	53	.340
J. Pierre, Col.	113	38	.336

Leadoff OBP†
(minimum 150 PA; *AB+BB+HBP+SF)

Player, Team	*PA	OB	OBP
M. Kotsay, S.D.	169	67	.396
M. Bellhorn, Chi.	252	98	.389
B. Wilkerson, Mon.	327	122	.373
R. Alomar, N.Y.	299	111	.371
K. Lofton, S.F.	198	72	.364
L. Castillo, Fla.	661	240	.363
R. Vazquez, S.D.	308	109	.354
C. Counsell, Ari.	186	65	.349
A. Sanchez, Mil.	355	124	.349
J. Kendall, Pit.	232	81	.349

Cleanup Slugging†
(minimum 150 PA)

Player, Team	AB	TB	Slg.
B. Bonds, S.F.	178	130	.730
V. Guerrero, Mon.	139	85	.612
L. Berkman, Hou.	166	99	.596
A. Dunn, Cin.	185	110	.595
B. Giles, Pit.	122	71	.582
A. Pujols, St.L.	466	267	.573
C. Floyd, Fla.-Mon.	238	136	.571
C. Jones, Atl.	394	223	.566
S. Green, L.A.	153	85	.556
M. Piazza, N.Y.	164	91	.555

Avg. vs. LHP
(minimum 125 PA)

B. Bonds, S.F.	.384
G. Colbrunn, Ari.	.368
S. Sosa, Chi.	.366
J. Kent, S.F.	.366
E. Alfonzo, N.Y.	.364

Avg. vs. RHP
(minimum 377 PA)

B. Bonds, S.F.	.363
V. Guerrero, Mon.	.347
T. Helton, Col.	.331
J. Edmonds, St.L.	.329
C. Jones, Atl.	.328

Avg. at Home
(minimum 251 PA)

T. Helton, Col.	.378
L. Walker, Col.	.362
B. Bonds, S.F.	.351
V. Guerrero, Mon.	.348
C. Jones, Atl.	.346

Avg. on Road
(minimum 251 PA)

B. Bonds, S.F.	.386
A. Pujols, St.L.	.340
G. Sheffield, Atl.	.336
E. Alfonzo, N.Y.	.335
B. Abreu, Phi.	.327

OBP vs. LHP
(minimum 125 PA)

B. Bonds, S.F.	.556
S. Sosa, Chi.	.526
E. Alfonzo, N.Y.	.477
P. Burrell, Phi.	.469
J. Bagwell, Hou.	.459

OBP vs. RHP
(minimum 377 PA)

B. Bonds, S.F.	.592
B. Giles, Pit.	.485
J. Edmonds, St.L.	.443
C. Jones, Atl.	.442
T. Helton, Col.	.424

Late & Close Avg.†
(minimum 50 PA)

L. Walker, Col.	.468
L. Castillo, Fla.	.379
J. Vizcaino, Hou.	.377
A. Ramirez, Pit.	.377
E. Alfonzo, N.Y.	.364

Bases Loaded Avg.
(minimum 10 PA)

T. Perez, N.Y.	.625
A. Pujols, St.L.	.538
7 tied with	.500

Slg. vs. LHP
(minimum 125 PA)

B. Bonds, S.F.	.976
S. Sosa, Chi.	.733
J. Bagwell, Hou.	.685
M. Bellhorn, Chi.	.672
J. Kent, S.F.	.669

Slg. vs. RHP
(minimum 377 PA)

B. Bonds, S.F.	.719
B. Giles, Pit.	.681
L. Berkman, Hou.	.639
V. Guerrero, Mon.	.616
J. Edmonds, St.L.	.592

AB per Home Run
(minimum 502 PA)

B. Bonds, S.F.	8.8
S. Sosa, Chi.	11.3
B. Giles, Pit.	13.1
L. Berkman, Hou.	13.8
S. Green, L.A.	13.9

Times on Base*
(*H+BB+HBP)

B. Bonds, S.F.	356
V. Guerrero, Mon.	296
B. Giles, Pit.	290
C. Jones, Atl.	288
T. Helton, Col.	286

Pitches Seen

B. Abreu, Phi.	2923
D. Lee, Fla.	2896
A. Dunn, Cin.	2893
P. Burrell, Phi.	2800
J. Bagwell, Hou.	2745

Pitches per PA
(minimum 502 PA)

T. Zeile, Col.	4.31
A. Dunn, Cin.	4.28
B. Abreu, Phi.	4.27
B. Wilkerson, Mon.	4.27
J. Burnitz, N.Y.	4.21

Pct. of Pitches Taken
(minimum 1500 pitches)

T. Zeile, Col.	65.2
B. Giles, Pit.	65.1
B. Bonds, S.F.	65.0
B. Abreu, Phi.	64.2
C. Counsell, Ari.	62.9

Ground/Fly Ratio†
(minimum 502 PA)

L. Castillo, Fla.	3.39
J. Pierre, Col.	3.20
R. Cedeno, N.Y.	2.03
P. Polanco, St.L.-Phi.	1.86
T. Zeile, Col.	1.79

GDP/GDP Opp.†
(minimum 50 PA)

C. Floyd, Fla.-Mon.	0.00
R. Mackowiak, Pit.	0.00
E. Durazo, Ari.	0.02
B. Bonds, S.F.	0.04
Q. McCracken, Ari.	0.04

SB Success Pct.
(minimum 20 SB attempts)

D. Glanville, Phi.	90.5
R. Cedeno, N.Y.	86.2
C. Patterson, Chi.	85.7
D. Roberts, L.A.	81.8
A. Fox, Fla.	81.6

Steals of Third

A. Fox, Fla.	8
A. Boone, Cin.	7
J. Rollins, Phi.	7
V Guerrero, Mon.	6
4 tied with	5

Pct. CS by Catchers
(minimum 50 SB attempts)

J. LaRue, Cin.	42.4
M. Redmond, Fla.	39.4
C. Johnson, Fla.	36.2
D. Miller, Ari.	35.9
R. Machado, Chi.-Mil.	34.4

2002 STATISTICAL LEADERS *N.L.*

†**Scoring-Position Average** denotes batting average when a runner is at second and/or third base. **Leadoff OBP** denotes OBP for a player batting in the first position of the batting order. **Cleanup Slugging** denotes slugging percentage for a player batting in the fourth position of the batting order. **Late & Close Avg.** refers to batting average when the game is in the seventh inning or later and the batting team is either leading by one run, tied, or has the potential tying run on base, at bat or on deck (a batting situation coming close to a pitcher's save situation). **Ground/Fly Ratio** denotes ground balls hit divided by fly balls hit. All batted balls except line drives and bunts are included. **GDP/GDP Opp.** denotes the ratio of times grounding into double plays per opportunities to do so (any situation with a runner on first and less than two out).

Baserunners per 9 IP
(minimum 162 IP)

Pitcher, Team	IP	BR	BR/9
P. Martinez, Bos.	....199.1	199	8.98
D. Lowe, Bos.	......219.2	226	9.26
T. Wakefield, Bos.	..163.1	181	9.97
J. Moyer, Sea.	......230.2	257	10.03
B. Zito, Oak.	.........229.1	269	10.56
P. Byrd, K.C.	.......228.1	269	10.60
J. Washburn, Ana.	..206.0	245	10.70
R. Reed, Min.	........188.0	224	10.72
M. Mulder, Oak.	....207.1	248	10.77
R. Ortiz, Ana.	........217.1	261	10.81

Strikeouts per 9 IP
(minimum 162 IP)

Pitcher, Team	IP	SO	SO/9
P. Martinez, Bos.	....199.1	239	10.79
R. Clemens, N.Y.	...180.0	192	9.60
M. Mussina, N.Y.	..215.2	182	7.60
T. Wakefield, Bos.	..163.1	134	7.38
F. Garcia, Sea.	......223.2	181	7.28
B. Zito, Oak.	.........229.1	182	7.14
D. Baez, Cle.	........165.1	130	7.08
M. Mulder, Oak.	....207.1	159	6.90
R. Ortiz, Ana.	........217.1	162	6.71
J. Burkett, Bos.	.....173.0	124	6.45

Run Support per 9 IP†
(minimum 162 IP)

Pitcher, Team	IP	R	R/9
D. Wells, N.Y.	........206.1	171	7.46
D. Lowe, Bos.	......219.2	167	6.84
B. Zito, Oak.	.........229.1	173	6.79
R. Ortiz, Ana.	.........217.1	161	6.67
M. Buehrle, Chi.	.....239.0	174	6.55
J. Burkett, Bos.	.....173.0	124	6.45
M. Mussina, N.Y.	..215.2	151	6.30
P. Martinez, Bos.	...199.1	138	6.23
R. Lopez, Bal.	......196.2	136	6.22
R. Reed, Min.	........188.0	128	6.13

Opposition OBP
(minimum 162 IP)

P. Martinez, Bos.	.254
D. Lowe, Bos.	.266
T. Wakefield, Bos.	.276
J. Moyer, Sea.	.278
R. Reed, Min.	.288

Opposition SLG
(minimum 162 IP)

D. Lowe, Bos.	.302
P. Martinez, Bos.	.309
T. Wakefield, Bos.	.333
R. Halladay, Tor.	.333
B. Zito, Oak.	.340

Hits per 9 IP
(minimum 162 IP)

P. Martinez, Bos.	.6.50
T. Wakefield, Bos.	.6.67
D. Lowe, Bos.	.6.80
B. Zito, Oak.	.7.14
J. Moyer, Sea.	.7.73

Home Runs per 9 IP
(minimum 162 IP)

R. Halladay, Tor.	.0.38
D. Lowe, Bos.	.0.49
P. Martinez, Bos.	.0.59
M. Redman, Det.	.0.67
T. Hudson, Oak.	.0.72

Avg. vs. LHB
(minimum 125 BFP)

A. Rhodes, Sea.	.158
K. Rogers, Tex.	.193
T. Wakefield, Bos.	.195
J. Washburn, Ana.	.199
S. Schoeneweis, Ana.	..202

Avg. vs. RHB
(minimum 225 BFP)

P. Martinez, Bos.	.191
B. Zito, Oak.	.203
J. Moyer, Sea.	.206
T. Wakefield, Bos.	.213
K. Lohse, Min.	.213

Avg. Allowed Sc. Pos.†
(minimum 125 BFP)

B. Zito, Oak.	.185
J. Pineiro, Sea.	.193
P. Martinez, Bos.	.196
B. Koch, Oak.	.196
O. Hernandez, N.Y.	.208

OBP Leading off Inn.
(minimum 150 BFP)

M. Mulder, Oak.	.221
P. Martinez, Bos.	.236
E. Milton, Min.	.243
J. Moyer, Sea.	.253
D. Lowe, Bos.	.253

SO/BB Ratio
(minimum 162 IP)

P. Martinez, Bos.	.5.98
R. Reed, Min.	.4.65
E. Milton, Min.	.4.03
M. Mussina, N.Y.	.3.79
P. Byrd, K.C.	.3.39

Grd/Fly Ratio Off†
(minimum 162 IP)

D. Lowe, Bos.	.3.46
R. Halladay, Tor.	.2.75
T. Hudson, Oak.	.2.03
K. Rogers, Tex.	.2.02
M. Mulder, Oak.	.1.58

Pitches per Start
(minimum 30 games started)

T. Sturtze, T.B.	.108.4
F. Garcia, Sea.	.106.1
M. Redman, Det.	.105.5
B. Zito, Oak.	.105.4
J. Washburn, Ana.	.105.1

Pitches per Batter
(minimum 162 IP)

P. Byrd, K.C.	.3.45
M. Mulder, Oak.	.3.49
T. Hudson, Oak.	.3.49
R. Halladay, Tor.	.3.52
J. Burkett, Bos.	.3.53

Stolen Bases Allowed

F. Castillo, Bos.	.24
R. Clemens, N.Y.	.23
R. Halladay, Tor.	.21
T. Wakefield, Bos.	.21
3 tied with	.19

Caught Stealing Off

T. Sturtze, T.B.	.15
K. Appier, Ana.	.13
D. Baez, Cle.	.11
M. Buehrle, Chi.	.10
M. Mussina, N.Y.	.10

SB Pct. Allowed
(minimum 162 IP)

K. Rogers, Tex.	.0.0
J. Weaver, Det.-N.Y.	.20.0
M. Buehrle, Chi.	.28.6
M. Mussina, N.Y.	.37.5
T. Hudson, Oak.	.38.5

Pickoffs

M. Buehrle, Chi.	.8
J. Kennedy, T.B.	.8
M. Mulder, Oak.	.7
A. Pettitte, N.Y.	.6
B. Zito, Oak.	.5

PkOf Throw/Runner†
(minimum 162 IP)

R. Clemens, N.Y.	.0.88
P. Wilson, T.B.	.0.65
B. Zito, Oak.	.0.63
C. Lidle, Oak.	.0.61
J. Burkett, Bos.	.0.60

GDP Induced

T. Hudson, Oak.	.35
J. Garland, Chi.	.32
D. Lowe, Bos.	.28
K. Rogers, Tex.	.27
T. Sturtze, T.B.	.26

GDP per 9 IP
(minimum 162 IP)

J. Garland, Chi.	.1.5
T. Hudson, Oak.	.1.3
K. Rogers, Tex.	.1.2
D. Lowe, Bos.	.1.1
J. Pineiro, Sea.	.1.1

Quality Starts†

B. Zito, Oak.	.27
R. Halladay, Tor.	.26
T. Hudson, Oak.	.24
D. Lowe, Bos.	.24
2 tied with	.23

†**Run Support per 9 IP** denotes the number of runs scored by a pitcher's team while he was still in the game times nine divided by his innings pitched. **Avg. Allowed Sc. Pos.** denotes batting average allowed when a runner is at second and/or third base. **Grd/Fly Ratio Off** denotes ground balls allowed divided by fly balls allowed. All batted balls except line drives and bunts are included. **PkOf Throw/Runner** denotes the number of pickoff throws made by a pitcher divided by the number of runners on first base. **Quality Starts** denote the number of outings in which a starting pitcher works at least six innings and allows three or fewer earned runs.

Baserunners per 9 IP
(minimum 162 IP)

Pitcher, Team	IP	BR	BR/9
C. Schilling, Ari.	259.1	254	8.81
O. Perez, L.A.	222.1	224	9.07
R. Johnson, Ari.	260.0	281	9.73
R. Wolf, Phi.	210.2	242	10.34
K. Millwood, Atl.	217.0	259	10.74
J. Schmidt, S.F.	185.1	223	10.83
R. Oswalt, Hou.	233.0	282	10.89
G. Maddux, Atl.	199.1	243	10.97
A. Burnett, Fla.	204.1	252	11.10
M. Clement, Chi.	205.0	253	11.11

Strikeouts per 9 IP
(minimum 162 IP)

Pitcher, Team	IP	SO	SO/9
R. Johnson, Ari.	260.0	334	11.56
C. Schilling, Ari.	259.1	316	10.97
J. Schmidt, S.F.	185.1	196	9.52
M. Clement, Chi.	205.0	215	9.44
B. Duckworth, Phi.	163.0	167	9.22
K. Wood, Chi.	213.2	217	9.14
A. Burnett, Fla.	204.1	203	8.94
R. Oswalt, Hou.	233.0	208	8.03
H. Nomo, L.A.	220.1	193	7.88
W. Miller, Hou.	164.2	144	7.87

Run Support per 9 IP†
(minimum 162 IP)

Pitcher, Team	IP	R	R/9
R. Jensen, S.F.	171.2	125	6.55
J. Jennings, Col.	185.1	134	6.51
W. Miller, Hou.	164.2	112	6.12
R. Johnson, Ari.	260.0	173	5.99
C. Schilling, Ari.	259.1	171	5.93
K. Wood, Chi.	213.2	139	5.85
R. Helling, Ari.	175.2	111	5.69
R. Dempster, Fla.-Cin.	209.0	131	5.64
R. Oswalt, Hou.	233.0	143	5.52
M. Hampton, Col.	178.2	108	5.44

Opposition OBP
(minimum 162 IP)

C. Schilling, Ari.	.251
O. Perez, L.A.	.262
R. Johnson, Ari.	.273
R. Wolf, Phi.	.285
K. Millwood, Atl.	.292

Opposition SLG
(minimum 162 IP)

A. Burnett, Fla.	.309
J. Schmidt, S.F.	.329
K. Millwood, Atl.	.337
M. Clement, Chi.	.344
R. Johnson, Ari.	.346

Hits per 9 IP
(minimum 162 IP)

A. Burnett, Fla.	6.74
R. Johnson, Ari.	6.82
D. Moss, Atl.	7.04
M. Clement, Chi.	7.11
K. Wood, Chi.	7.12

Home Runs per 9 IP
(minimum 162 IP)

A. Burnett, Fla.	0.53
M. Batista, Ari.	0.58
R. Ortiz, S.F.	0.63
G. Maddux, Atl.	0.63
R. Oswalt, Hou.	0.66

Avg. vs. LHB
(minimum 125 BFP)

A. Benitez, N.Y.	.160
D. Moss, Atl.	.165
W. Williams, St.L.	.182
O. Dotel, Hou.	.190
D. Veres, St.L.	.190

Avg. vs. RHB
(minimum 225 BFP)

A. Burnett, Fla.	.177
J. Schmidt, S.F.	.180
O. Perez, S.D.	.191
T. Armas Jr., Mon.	.192
R. Johnson, Ari.	.206

Avg. Allowed Sc. Pos.†
(minimum 125 BFP)

R. Johnson, Ari.	.146
K. Wood, Chi.	.182
T. Glavine, Atl.	.193
D. Moss, Atl.	.204
R. Wolf, Phi.	.207

OBP Leading off Inn.
(minimum 150 BFP)

C. Schilling, Ari.	.223
B. Tomko, S.D.	.242
R. Wolf, Phi.	.243
K. Millwood, Atl.	.254
O. Daal, L.A.	.262

SO/BB Ratio
(minimum 162 IP)

C. Schilling, Ari.	9.58
R. Johnson, Ari.	4.70
O. Perez, L.A.	4.08
J. Vazquez, Mon.	3.65
R. Oswalt, Hou.	3.35

Grd/Fly Ratio Off†
(minimum 162 IP)

B. Lawrence, S.D.	2.51
G. Maddux, Atl.	2.23
K. Wells, Pit.	1.98
V. Padilla, Phi.	1.98
M. Batista, Ari.	1.74

Pitches per Start
(minimum 30 games started)

R. Johnson, Ari.	114.2
R. Ortiz, S.F.	108.4
G. Rusch, Mil.	106.5
C. Schilling, Ari.	105.9
L. Hernandez, S.F.	105.0

Pitches per Batter
(minimum 162 IP)

G. Maddux, Atl.	3.23
B. Lawrence, S.D.	3.45
O. Perez, L.A.	3.47
B. Tomko, S.D.	3.50
J. Fogg, Pit.	3.51

Stolen Bases Allowed

A. Leiter, N.Y.	29
H. Nomo, L.A.	28
B. Duckworth, Phi.	24
G. Maddux, Atl.	24
L. Hernandez, S.F.	22

Caught Stealing Off

T. Glavine, Atl.	16
R. Johnson, Ari.	15
R. Dempster, Fla.-Cin.	13
A. Leiter, N.Y.	12
B. Sheets, Mil.	12

SB Pct. Allowed
(minimum 162 IP)

G. Rusch, Mil.	14.3
K. Rueter, S.F.	28.6
R. Helling, Ari.	33.3
R. Dempster, Fla.-Cin.	35.0
D. Moss, Atl.	42.1

Pickoffs

D. Moss, Atl.	9
O. Perez, L.A.	9
B. Anderson, Ari.	8
J. Anderson, Pit.	8
2 tied with	5

PkOf Throw/Runner†
(minimum 162 IP)

S. Trachsel, N.Y.	1.00
G. Maddux, Atl.	0.80
B. Anderson, Ari.	0.78
L. Hernandez, S.F.	0.78
A. Leiter, N.Y.	0.74

GDP Induced

L. Hernandez, S.F.	29
B. Lawrence, S.D.	29
M. Hampton, Col.	28
G. Rusch, Mil.	27
3 tied with	26

GDP per 9 IP
(minimum 162 IP)

M. Hampton, Col.	1.4
B. Lawrence, S.D.	1.2
J. Jennings, Col.	1.2
L. Hernandez, S.F.	1.2
G. Rusch, Mil.	1.2

Quality Starts†

R. Johnson, Ari.	30
C. Schilling, Ari.	27
H. Nomo, L.A.	25
R. Ortiz, S.F.	24
R. Oswalt, Hou.	24

2002 STATISTICAL LEADERS *N.L.*

†**Run Support per 9 IP** denotes the number of runs scored by a pitcher's team while he was still in the game times nine divided by his innings pitched. **Avg. Allowed Sc. Pos.** denotes batting average allowed when a runner is at second and/or third base. **Grd/Fly Ratio Off** denotes ground balls allowed divided by fly balls allowed. All batted balls except line drives and bunts are included. **PkOf Throw/Runner** denotes the number of pickoff throws made by a pitcher divided by the number of runners on first base. **Quality Starts** denote the number of outings in which a starting pitcher works at least six innings and allows three or fewer earned runs.

Saves

Pitcher, Team	Saves
E. Guardado, Min.	45
B. Koch, Oak.	44
T. Percival, Ana.	40
U. Urbina, Bos.	40
K. Escobar, Tor.	38
K. Sasaki, Sea.	37
J. Acevedo, Det.	28
M. Rivera, N.Y.	28
R. Hernandez, K.C.	26
J. Julio, Bal.	25

Save Percentage
(minimum 20 save opportunities)

Pitcher, Team	Opp.	Sv.	Pct.
B. Wickman, Cle.	22	20	90.9
T. Percival, Ana.	44	40	90.9
E. Guardado, Min.	51	45	88.2
B. Koch, Oak.	50	44	88.0
M. Rivera, N.Y.	32	28	87.5
U. Urbina, Bos.	46	40	87.0
K. Escobar, Tor.	46	38	82.6
K. Sasaki, Sea.	45	37	82.2
J. Julio, Bal.	31	25	80.6
2 tied with			80.0

Relief ERA
(minimum 50 relief IP)

Pitcher, Team	IP	ER	ERA
B. Groom, Bal.	62.0	11	1.60
J. Romero, Min.	81.0	17	1.89
T. Percival, Ana.	56.1	12	1.92
J. Julio, Bal.	68.0	15	1.99
L. Hawkins, Min.	80.1	19	2.13
J. Halama, Sea.	50.2	13	2.31
A. Rhodes, Sea.	69.2	18	2.33
K. Sasaki, Sea.	60.2	17	2.52
B. Weber, Ana.	78.0	22	2.54
J. Acevedo, Det.	74.2	22	2.65

Relief Wins

B. Koch, Oak.	11
A. Rhodes, Sea.	10
T. Fiore, Min.	9
J. Romero, Min.	9
3 tied with	8

Relief Losses

E. Yan, T.B.	8
J. Colome, T.B.	7
K. Escobar, Tor.	7
J. Grimsley, K.C.	7
5 tied with	6

Holds†

J. Romero, Min.	33
A. Rhodes, Sea.	27
R. Rincon, Cle.-Oak.	27
C. Politte, Tor.	25
C. Bradford, Oak.	24

Blown Saves†

K. Escobar, Tor.	8
K. Sasaki, Sea.	8
E. Yan, T.B.	8
3 tied with	7

Relief Games

B. Koch, Oak.	84
J. Romero, Min.	81
M. Stanton, N.Y.	79
S. Karsay, N.Y.	78
K. Escobar, Tor.	76

Games Finished

B. Koch, Oak.	79
K. Escobar, Tor.	68
E. Guardado, Min.	62
J. Julio, Bal.	61
2 tied with	55

Relief Innings

B. Koch, Oak.	93.2
R. Mendoza, N.Y.	91.2
S. Karsay, N.Y.	88.1
J. Romero, Min.	81.0
T. Fiore, Min.	80.2

Pct. Inherited Scored†
(minimum 30 inherited runners)

R. Rodriguez, Tex.	13.2
B. Donnelly, Ana.	15.6
J. Mecir, Oak.	17.9
J. Romero, Min.	18.5
S. Eyre, Tor.	20.8

Opposition Avg.
(minimum 50 relief IP)

C. Politte, Tor.	.186
A. Rhodes, Sea.	.187
T. Percival, Ana.	.188
L. Pote, Ana.	.194
B. Groom, Bal.	.196

Opposition OBP
(minimum 50 relief IP)

A. Rhodes, Sea.	.227
B. Groom, Bal.	.243
L. Hawkins, Min.	.253
C. Politte, Tor.	.258
K. Foulke, Chi.	.263

Opposition SLG
(minimum 50 relief IP)

A. Rhodes, Sea.	.274
B. Groom, Bal.	.281
C. Politte, Tor.	.284
J. Romero, Min.	.289
D. Marte, Chi.	.296

First Batter Avg.
(minimum 40 first BFP)

B. Donnelly, Ana.	.095
B. Groom, Bal.	.127
C. Politte, Tor.	.128
T. Fiore, Min.	.140
M. Wohlers, Cle.	.148

Avg. vs. LHB
(minimum 50 relief IP)

D. Marte, Chi.	.149
A. Rhodes, Sea.	.158
B. Groom, Bal.	.181
B. Ryan, Bal.	.192
R. Rincon, Cle.-Oak.	.203

Avg. vs. RHB
(minimum 50 relief IP)

T. Percival, Ana.	.138
U. Urbina, Bos.	.143
C. Politte, Tor.	.154
L. Pote, Ana.	.172
T. Fiore, Min.	.184

Avg., Runners On†
(minimum 50 relief IP)

T. Percival, Ana.	.170
K. Sasaki, Sea.	.179
U. Urbina, Bos.	.184
J. Julio, Bal.	.195
M. Jackson, Min.	.196

Avg., Scoring Pos.†
(minimum 50 relief IP)

M. Jackson, Min.	.167
J. Romero, Min.	.170
T. Fiore, Min.	.171
K. Sasaki, Sea.	.174
2 tied with	.176

Easy Saves†

U. Urbina, Bos.	31
E. Guardado, Min.	29
B. Koch, Oak.	26
3 tied with	22

Regular Saves†

E. Guardado, Min.	16
B. Koch, Oak.	16
T. Percival, Ana.	16
K. Escobar, Tor.	14
K. Sasaki, Sea.	14

Tough Saves†

J. Acevedo, Det.	4
J. Julio, Bal.	3
6 tied with	2

Pitches per Batter
(minimum 50 relief IP)

J. Farnsworth, Det.	3.25
S. Karsay, N.Y.	3.41
M. Jackson, Min.	3.45
C. Bradford, Oak.	3.48
B. Weber, Ana.	3.48

†**Holds** denote the number of times a relief pitcher enters the game in a save situation, records at least one out and leaves the game never having relinquished the lead. A pitcher cannot finish the game and receive credit for a hold, nor can he earn a hold and a save in the same game. **Blown Saves** denote the number of times a relief pitcher enters a game in a save situation and allows the tying or go-ahead run to score. **Pct. Inherited Scored** denotes the percent of interited runners (those on base when a reliever enters the game) that score. **Avg., Runners On** denotes batting average allowed when runners are on base. **Avg., Scoring Pos.** denotes batting average allowed when a runner is at second and/or third base. **Easy Saves** denote saves in which the first batter faced doesn't represent the tying run and the reliever pitches one inning or less. **Regular Saves** denote those saves that are not Easy Saves or Tough Saves. **Tough Saves** denote saves which occur after the reliever enters with the tying run anywhere on base.

Saves

Pitcher, Team	Saves
J. Smoltz, Atl.	55
E. Gagne, L.A.	52
M. Williams, Pit.	46
J. Mesa, Phi.	45
R. Nen, S.F.	43
J. Jimenez, Col.	41
T. Hoffman, S.D.	38
B. Kim, Ari.	36
B. Wagner, Hou.	35
A. Benitez, N.Y.	33

Save Percentage
(minimum 20 save opportunities)

Pitcher, Team	Opp.	Sv.	Pct.
J. Smoltz, Atl.	59	55	93.2
E. Gagne, L.A.	56	52	92.9
T. Hoffman, S.D.	41	38	92.7
M. Williams, Pit.	50	46	92.0
M. DeJean, Mil.	30	27	90.0
A. Benitez, N.Y.	37	33	89.2
J. Jimenez, Col.	47	41	87.2
J. Isringhausen, St.L.	37	32	86.5
B. Kim, Ari.	42	36	85.7
B. Wagner, Hou.	41	35	85.4

Relief ERA
(minimum 50 relief IP)

Pitcher, Team	IP	ER	ERA
C. Hammond, Atl.	76.0	8	0.95
J. Eischen, Mon.	53.2	8	1.34
D. Holmes, Atl.	54.2	11	1.81
O. Dotel, Hou.	97.1	20	1.85
M. Crudale, St.L.	50.2	11	1.95
E. Gagne, L.A.	82.1	18	1.97
M. Remlinger, Atl.	68.0	15	1.99
S. Reed, S.D.-N.Y.	67.0	15	2.01
B. Kim, Ari.	84.0	19	2.04
R. Nen, S.F.	73.2	18	2.20

Relief Wins

Pitcher, Team	
J. Fassero, Chi.-St.L.	8
B. Kim, Ari.	8
F. Rodriguez, S.F.	8
T. Worrell, S.F.	8
2 tied with	7

Relief Losses

Pitcher, Team	
J. Jimenez, Col.	10
S. Strickland, Mon.-N.Y.	9
D. Veres, St.L.	8
J. Fikac, S.D.	7
R. White, Col.-St.L.	7

Holds†

Pitcher, Team	
P. Quantrill, L.A.	33
O. Dotel, Hou.	31
T. Jones, Col.	30
M. Remlinger, Atl.	30
2 tied with	28

Blown Saves†

Pitcher, Team	
A. Alfonseca, Chi.	9
J. Mesa, Phi.	9
M. Herges, Mon.	8
R. Nen, S.F.	8
V. Nunez, Fla.	8

Relief Games

Pitcher, Team	
P. Quantrill, L.A.	86
O. Dotel, Hou.	83
T. Worrell, S.F.	80
T. Jones, Col.	79
3 tied with	78

Games Finished

Pitcher, Team	
J. Jimenez, Col.	69
E. Gagne, L.A.	68
J. Smoltz, Atl.	68
B. Kim, Ari.	66
R. Nen, S.F.	66

Relief Innings

Pitcher, Team	
V. Nunez, Fla.	97.2
O. Dotel, Hou.	97.1
J. Borowski, Chi.	95.2
M. Timlin, St.L.-Phi.	92.1
B. Looper, Fla.	86.0

Pct. Inherited Scored†
(minimum 30 inherited runners)

Pitcher, Team	
J. Speier, Col.	5.7
J. Orosco, L.A.	12.8
S. Stewart, Mon.	14.7
L. Vizcaino, Mil.	15.0
M. Guthrie, N.Y.	16.2

Opposition Avg.
(minimum 50 relief IP)

Pitcher, Team	
O. Dotel, Hou.	.173
S. Williamson, Cin	.181
E. Gagne, L.A.	.189
A. Benitez, N.Y.	.190
L. Vizcaino, Mil.	.192

Opposition OBP
(minimum 50 relief IP)

Pitcher, Team	
E. Gagne, L.A.	.235
O. Dotel, Hou.	.239
M. Timlin, St.L.-Phi.	.246
J. Isringhausen, St.L.	.257
B. Wagner, Hou.	.261

Opposition SLG
(minimum 50 relief IP)

Pitcher, Team	
J. Isringhausen, St.L.	.242
C. Hammond, Atl.	.261
O. Dotel, Hou.	.275
B. Kim, Ari.	.276
M. Koplove, Ari.	.276

First Batter Avg.
(minimum 40 first BFP)

Pitcher, Team	
D. Plesac, Phi.	.132
B. Boehringer, Pit.	.143
K. Ligtenberg, Atl.	.143
B. Looper, Fla.	.145
J. Smoltz, Atl.	.149

Avg. vs. LHB
(minimum 50 relief IP)

Pitcher, Team	
S. Sauerbeck, Pit.	.147
T. Spooneybarger, Atl.	.150
S. Stewart, Mon.	.159
A. Benitez, N.Y.	.160
K. Gryboski, Atl.	.169

Avg. vs. RHB
(minimum 50 relief IP)

Pitcher, Team	
O. Dotel, Hou.	.159
E. Gagne, L.A.	.163
J. Isringhausen, St.L.	.164
S. Williamson, Cin	.170
L. Vizcaino, Mil.	.170

Avg., Runners On†
(minimum 50 relief IP)

Pitcher, Team	
D. Holmes, Atl.	.133
O. Dotel, Hou.	.144
A. Benitez, N.Y.	.149
E. Gagne, L.A.	.157
C. Hammond, Atl.	.175

Avg., Scoring Pos.†
(minimum 50 relief IP)

Pitcher, Team	
E. Gagne, L.A.	.120
D. Holmes, Atl.	.122
K. Ligtenberg, Atl.	.130
O. Dotel, Hou.	.147
J. Witasick, S.F.	.148

Easy Saves†

Pitcher, Team	
J. Smoltz, Atl.	36
J. Mesa, Phi.	33
T. Hoffman, S.D.	27
M. Williams, Pit.	27
2 tied with	26

Regular Saves†

Pitcher, Team	
E. Gagne, L.A.	21
M. Williams, Pit.	19
J. Jimenez, Col.	15
3 tied with	14

Tough Saves†

Pitcher, Team	
B. Kim, Ari.	6
E. Gagne, L.A.	5
J. Smoltz, Atl.	5
R. Nen, S.F.	4
S. Stewart, Mon.	4

Pitches per Batter
(minimum 50 relief IP)

Pitcher, Team	
D. Graves, Cin.	3.25
M. Timlin, St.L.-Phi.	3.26
C. Zerbe, S.F.	3.27
G. Lloyd, Mon.-Fla.	3.32
J. Jimenez, Col.	3.44

†**Holds** denote the number of times a relief pitcher enters the game in a save situation, records at least one out and leaves the game never having relinquished the lead. A pitcher cannot finish the game and receive credit for a hold, nor can he earn a hold and a save in the same game. **Blown Saves** denote the number of times a relief pitcher enters a game in a save situation and allows the tying or go-ahead run to score. **Pct. Inherited Scored** denotes the percent of interited runners (those on base when a reliever enters the game) that score. **Avg., Runners On** denotes batting average allowed when runners are on base. **Avg., Scoring Pos.** denotes batting average allowed when a runner is at second and/or third base. **Easy Saves** denote saves in which the first batter faced doesn't represent the tying run and the reliever pitches one inning or less. **Regular Saves** denote those saves that are not Easy Saves or Tough Saves. **Tough Saves** denote saves which occur after the reliever enters with the tying run anywhere on base.

2002 ACTIVE CAREER LEADERS

BATTING

Batting Average
(minimum 1000 PA)

Rk.	Player	AB	H	Avg.
1.	I. Suzuki	1339	450	.336
2.	T. Helton	2921	973	.333
3.	N. Garciaparra	3154	1033	.328
4.	V. Guerrero	3369	1085	.322
5.	A. Pujols	1180	379	.321
6.	M. Piazza	5116	1641	.321
7.	L. Walker	5880	1863	.317
8.	D. Jeter	4388	1390	.317
9.	E. Martinez	6230	1973	.317
10.	M. Ramirez	4435	1400	.316
11.	F. Thomas	6065	1902	.314
12.	Ja. Giambi	3958	1224	.309
13.	C. Jones	4589	1419	.309
14.	A. Rodriguez	4382	1354	.309
15.	M. Sweeney	2914	899	.309
16.	J. Pierre	1409	434	.308
17.	B. Williams	5958	1833	.308
18.	B. Abreu	2989	918	.307
19.	M. Ordonez	2999	916	.305
20.	R. Simon	986	301	.305
21.	J. Vidro	2564	782	.305
22.	M. Grace	7930	2418	.305
23.	I. Rodriguez	5656	1723	.305
24.	R. Greer	3829	1166	.305
25.	L. Berkman	1601	487	.304

On-Base Percentage
(minimum 1000 PA; *AB+BB+HBP+SF)

Rk.	Player	*PA	OB	OBP
1.	F. Thomas	7505	3241	.432
2.	B. Bonds	10413	4458	.428
3.	E. Martinez	7510	3186	.424
4.	T. Helton	3410	1428	.419
5.	B. Giles	3662	1523	.416
6.	Ja. Giambi	4770	1982	.416
7.	J. Thome	5722	2371	.414
8.	J. Bagwell	7924	3281	.414
9.	M. Ramirez	5231	2148	.411
10.	B. Abreu	3550	1453	.409
11.	L. Berkman	1903	772	.406
12.	C. Jones	5408	2187	.404
13.	J. Olerud	7728	3122	.404
14.	R. Henderson	13232	5316	.402
15.	G. Sheffield	7348	2934	.399
16.	A. Pujols	1350	538	.399
17.	L. Walker	6776	2698	.398
18.	B. Williams	6864	2691	.392
19.	T. Salmon	5968	2328	.390
20.	C. Delgado	4762	1857	.390
21.	D. Jeter	4950	1925	.389
22.	M. Piazza	5734	2225	.388
23.	R. Greer	4414	1707	.387
24.	V. Guerrero	3753	1447	.386
25.	T. Raines Sr.	10320	3977	.385

Slugging Percentage
(minimum 1000 PA)

Rk.	Player	AB	TB	SLG
1.	T. Helton	2921	1791	.613
2.	M. Ramirez	4435	2657	.599
3.	B. Bonds	8335	4961	.595
4.	V. Guerrero	3369	1980	.588
5.	A. Pujols	1180	691	.586
6.	A. Rodriguez	4382	2535	.579
7.	L. Berkman	1601	926	.578
8.	M. Piazza	5116	2945	.576
9.	L. Walker	5880	3378	.574
10.	B. Giles	3010	1717	.570
11.	F. Thomas	6065	3445	.568
12.	J. Thome	4640	2633	.567
13.	J. Gonzalez	6101	3433	.563
14.	K. Griffey Jr.	6913	3883	.562
15.	N. Garciaparra	3154	1771	.562
16.	C. Delgado	3980	2203	.554
17.	Ja. Giambi	3958	2186	.552
18.	J. Bagwell	6520	3592	.551
19.	S. Sosa	7026	3835	.546
20.	C. Jones	4589	2498	.544
21.	E. Martinez	6230	3288	.528
22.	R. Klesko	4003	2112	.528
23.	M. Vaughn	5453	2868	.526
24.	J. Edmonds	4145	2171	.524
25.	M. Ordonez	2999	1569	.523

Hits

1. Rickey Henderson..3040
2. Rafael Palmeiro ...2634
3. Tim Raines Sr. 2605
4. Roberto Alomar ...2546
5. Barry Bonds 2462
6. Mark Grace 2418
7. Fred McGriff 2403
8. Julio Franco 2300
9. Craig Biggio 2295
10. Andres Galarraga ..2248
11. Barry Larkin 2172
12. Ellis Burks 2049
13. B.J. Surhoff 2048
14. Ken Griffey Jr. 2039
15. Steve Finley 2018
16. Edgar Martinez 1973
17. Jeff Bagwell 1969
18. Sammy Sosa 1955
19. Ruben Sierra.........1950
20. Jay Bell 1942

Home Runs

1. Barry Bonds 613
2. Sammy Sosa 499
3. Rafael Palmeiro 490
4. Fred McGriff 478
5. Ken Griffey Jr. 468
6. Juan Gonzalez........405
7. Andres Galarraga 386
8. Jeff Bagwell 380
9. Frank Thomas........376
10. Matt Williams 374
11. Greg Vaughn............352
12. Mike Piazza 347
13. Ellis Burks..............345
14. Gary Sheffield 340
15. Larry Walker 335
16. Jim Thome 334
17. Mo Vaughn..............325
18. Ron Gant 320
19. Manny Ramirez........310
20. David Justice 305

Runs Batted In

1. Barry Bonds 1652
2. Rafael Palmeiro 1575
3. Fred McGriff 1503
4. Andres Galarraga ..1381
5. Ken Griffey Jr. 1358
6. Sammy Sosa 1347
7. Jeff Bagwell 1321
8. Juan Gonzalez.......1317
9. Frank Thomas 1285
10. Matt Williams 1202
11. Ruben Sierra 1181
12. Ellis Burks.............1177
13. Larry Walker 1133
14. Mark Grace 1130
15. Rickey Henderson..1110
16. Edgar Martinez 1100
    Gary Sheffield 1100
18. Robin Ventura........1099
19. Tino Martinez 1077
20. Mike Piazza 1073

Stolen Bases

1. Rickey Henderson..1403
2. Tim Raines Sr. 808
3. Kenny Lofton 508
4. Barry Bonds 493
5. Delino DeShields 463
6. Roberto Alomar 462
7. Marquis Grissom 414
8. Eric Young 408
9. Chuck Knoblauch 407
10. Craig Biggio 381
11. Barry Larkin 375
12. Tom Goodwin 345
13. Brady Anderson 315
14. Tony Womack..........296
15. Omar Vizquel 291
16. Steve Finley 281
17. Mark McLemore 267
18. Julio Franco 265
19. Brian L. Hunter 260
20. Ray Lankford 256

Seasons Played

Rickey Henderson	24
Jesse Orosco	23
Tim Raines Sr.	23
Mike Morgan	22
Roger Clemens	19
Julio Franco	18
Shawon Dunston	18
12 tied with	17

Games

Rickey Henderson	3051
Tim Raines Sr.	2502
Barry Bonds	2439
Rafael Palmeiro	2413
Fred McGriff	2347
Roberto Alomar	2183
Mark Grace	2179
Andres Galarraga	2140
Craig Biggio	2100
Julio Franco	2041

At-Bats

Rickey Henderson	10889
Rafael Palmeiro	8992
Tim Raines Sr.	8872
Fred McGriff	8388
Roberto Alomar	8386
Barry Bonds	8335
Craig Biggio	7960
Mark Grace	7930
Andres Galarraga	7814
Julio Franco	7672

Runs Scored

Rickey Henderson	2288
Barry Bonds	1830
Tim Raines Sr.	1571
Rafael Palmeiro	1456
Roberto Alomar	1414
Craig Biggio	1401
Fred McGriff	1310
Jeff Bagwell	1293
Ken Griffey Jr.	1237
Barry Larkin	1235

Doubles

Rafael Palmeiro	522
Barry Bonds	514
Rickey Henderson	509
Mark Grace	506
Craig Biggio	473
Roberto Alomar	470
Edgar Martinez	466
John Olerud	438
Tim Raines Sr.	430
Andres Galarraga	429

Triples

Tim Raines Sr.	113
Steve Finley	98
Kenny Lofton	78
Roberto Alomar	76
Delino DeShields	74
Barry Bonds	73
Barry Larkin	72
Jose Offerman	69
Brady Anderson	67
Jay Bell	67

AB per HR
(minimum 1000 AB)

Barry Bonds	13.6
Jim Thome	13.9
Sammy Sosa	14.1
Manny Ramirez	14.3
Alex Rodriguez	14.7
Mike Piazza	14.7
Ken Griffey Jr.	14.8
Juan Gonzalez	15.1
Carlos Delgado	15.2
Todd Helton	15.7

AB per RBI
(minimum 1000 AB)

Manny Ramirez	4.3
Albert Pujols	4.6
Juan Gonzalez	4.6
Todd Helton	4.7
Frank Thomas	4.7
Lance Berkman	4.8
Mike Piazza	4.8
Carlos Delgado	4.9
Jeff Bagwell	4.9
Jason Giambi	5.0

Total Bases

Barry Bonds	4961
Rafael Palmeiro	4698
Rickey Henderson	4566
Fred McGriff	4309
Andres Galarraga	3899
Ken Griffey Jr.	3883
Sammy Sosa	3835
Roberto Alomar	3771
Tim Raines Sr.	3771
Ellis Burks	3599

Walks

Rickey Henderson	2179
Barry Bonds	1922
Tim Raines Sr.	1330
Frank Thomas	1286
Fred McGriff	1265
Jeff Bagwell	1199
Rafael Palmeiro	1140
Edgar Martinez	1133
John Olerud	1114
Mark Grace	1059

Intentional Walks

Barry Bonds	423
Ken Griffey Jr.	199
Fred McGriff	165
Frank Thomas	155
Tim Raines Sr.	148
Jeff Bagwell	145
John Olerud	144
Rafael Palmeiro	144
Mo Vaughn	142
Sammy Sosa	135

Hit by Pitch

Craig Biggio	214
Andres Galarraga	175
Brady Anderson	154
Fernando Vina	141
Chuck Knoblauch	139
Jason Kendall	133
Jeff Bagwell	113
Larry Walker	110
Mo Vaughn	106
Damion Easley	103

Strikeouts

Andres Galarraga	1939
Sammy Sosa	1834
Fred McGriff	1797
Rickey Henderson	1678
Greg Vaughn	1500
Ray Lankford	1495
Mo Vaughn	1407
Jay Bell	1405
Ron Gant	1402
Jim Thome	1377

SO/BB Ratio
(minimum 1000 AB)

Mark Grace	.592
Eric Young	.684
Barry Bonds	.691
Gary Sheffield	.724
Tim Raines Sr.	.726
Brian Giles	.728
Orlando Palmeiro	.742
Frank Thomas	.748
Rickey Henderson	.770
John Olerud	.779

Sacrifice Hits

Tom Glavine	168
Omar Vizquel	160
Jay Bell	158
Greg Maddux	135
Roberto Alomar	133
Mark McLemore	103
Darren Lewis	101
Curt Schilling	98
Mike Bordick	97
2 tied with	95

Sacrifice Flies

Ruben Sierra	109
Frank Thomas	101
Rafael Palmeiro	98
B.J. Surhoff	97
Mark Grace	96
Jeff Bagwell	92
Roberto Alomar	88
John Olerud	85
Barry Bonds	82
Gary Sheffield	80

SB Success Pct.
(minimum 100 SB attempts)

Carlos Beltran	87.2
Tim Raines Sr.	84.7
Pokey Reese	84.6
Tony Womack	83.6
Barry Larkin	83.0
Doug Glanville	81.7
Brian L. Hunter	81.0
Roberto Alomar	80.8
Rickey Henderson	80.7
Jose Cruz	80.4

Caught Stealing

Rickey Henderson	335
Delino DeShields	147
Tim Raines Sr.	146
Barry Bonds	140
Eric Young	139
Kenny Lofton	133
Omar Vizquel	120
Chuck Knoblauch	117
Ray Lankford	115
Tom Goodwin	113

GDP

Julio Franco	271
Fred McGriff	218
Todd Zeile	204
Rafael Palmeiro	201
John Olerud	195
Ivan Rodriguez	187
Mark Grace	186
Roberto Alomar	185
Jeff Bagwell	182
2 tied with	181

AB per GDP
(minimum 1000 AB)

Greg Maddux	170.4
Joe McEwing	166.4
Ichiro Suzuki	121.7
Peter Bergeron	117.9
Tony Womack	111.0
Tom Glavine	102.4
Brady Anderson	100.0
Johnny Damon	98.3
Rafael Furcal	94.3
Juan Pierre	93.9

2002 STATISTICAL LEADERS *Active career*

Wins

Roger Clemens	293
Greg Maddux	273
Tom Glavine	242
Randy Johnson	224
Chuck Finley	200
David Wells	185
Kevin Brown	183
Mike Mussina	182
Jamie Moyer	164
John Smoltz	163

Losses

Mike Morgan	186
Chuck Finley	173
Greg Maddux	152
Roger Clemens	151
Tom Glavine	143
Andy Benes	139
Scott Erickson	128
Kevin Appier	127
John Burkett	127
Terry Mulholland	127

Winning Percentage
(minimum 100 decisions)

Pedro Martinez	.707
Randy Johnson	.679
Roger Clemens	.660
Andy Pettitte	.646
Greg Maddux	.642
Mike Mussina	.641
Bartolo Colon	.634
Tom Glavine	.629
Kevin Millwood	.620
Kirk Rueter	.616

ERA
(minimum 750 IP)

Pedro Martinez	2.62
Greg Maddux	2.83
Jesse Orosco	3.04
Randy Johnson	3.06
Roger Clemens	3.15
Matt Morris	3.18
Roberto Hernandez	3.22
Kevin Brown	3.22
Jose Rijo	3.24
John Smoltz	3.34

Games

Jesse Orosco	1187
Dan Plesac	1006
Mike Jackson	960
Mike Stanton	835
Jose Mesa	701
Mark Guthrie	700
Roberto Hernandez	696
Steve Reed	671
Dennis Cook	665
2 tied with	664

Games Started

Roger Clemens	573
Greg Maddux	535
Tom Glavine	505
Chuck Finley	467
Randy Johnson	426
Mike Morgan	411
Kevin Brown	409
John Burkett	393
Andy Benes	387
Jamie Moyer	387

Innings Pitched

Roger Clemens	4067.0
Greg Maddux	3750.1
Tom Glavine	3344.2
Chuck Finley	3197.1
Randy Johnson	3008.1
Kevin Brown	2840.0
Mike Morgan	2772.1
David Wells	2613.2
John Smoltz	2553.2
Jamie Moyer	2522.2

Batters Faced

Roger Clemens	16775
Greg Maddux	15216
Tom Glavine	14030
Chuck Finley	13638
Randy Johnson	12411
Mike Morgan	11872
Kevin Brown	11789
David Wells	10924
Jamie Moyer	10688
Andy Benes	10645

Complete Games

Roger Clemens	116
Greg Maddux	102
Randy Johnson	87
Curt Schilling	76
Kevin Brown	72
Chuck Finley	63
Tom Glavine	52
Scott Erickson	51
Mike Mussina	51
David Wells	48

Complete Game Pct.
(minimum 100 games started)

Curt Schilling	0.24
Randy Johnson	0.20
Roger Clemens	0.20
Greg Maddux	0.19
Kevin Brown	0.18
Greg Swindell	0.15
Pedro Martinez	0.15
Terry Mulholland	0.15
Scott Erickson	0.15
Mike Mussina	0.14

Shutouts

Roger Clemens	45
Randy Johnson	34
Greg Maddux	34
Tom Glavine	22
Mike Mussina	20
Kevin Brown	17
Scott Erickson	17
Curt Schilling	17
Chuck Finley	15
Pedro Martinez	15

Quality Start Pct. *
(minimum 100 games started)

Pedro Martinez	70.7
Randy Johnson	70.0
Greg Maddux	69.0
Curt Schilling	68.2
Matt Morris	68.1
Kevin Brown	67.0
Kerry Wood	66.4
Roger Clemens	65.1
Tim Hudson	64.8
Tom Glavine	64.4

Strikeouts

Roger Clemens	3909
Randy Johnson	3746
Greg Maddux	2641
Chuck Finley	2610
Curt Schilling	2348
John Smoltz	2240
Pedro Martinez	2220
Kevin Brown	2079
Tom Glavine	2054
Andy Benes	2000

Walks Allowed

Chuck Finley	1332
Roger Clemens	1321
Randy Johnson	1231
Tom Glavine	1140
Mike Morgan	938
Andy Benes	909
Kevin Appier	887
Al Leiter	874
Kenny Rogers	848
Tom Gordon	839

Strikeouts per 9 IP
(minimum 750 IP)

Randy Johnson	11.21
Pedro Martinez	10.56
Hideo Nomo	9.32
Arthur Rhodes	8.90
Curt Schilling	8.74
Dan Plesac	8.70
Roger Clemens	8.65
Roberto Hernandez	8.31
Chan Ho Park	8.25
Jesse Orosco	8.21

Walks per 9 IP
(minimum 750 IP)

Rick Reed	1.63
Brad Radke	1.83
Brian Anderson	1.85
Jon Lieber	1.85
Greg Maddux	1.93
Shane Reynolds	1.99
Greg Swindell	2.02
Mike Mussina	2.04
Jose Lima	2.07
David Wells	2.08

*Quality Starts denote the number of outings in which a starting pitcher works at least six innings and allows three or fewer earned runs.

2002 STATISTICAL LEADERS Active career

SO/BB Ratio
(minimum 750 IP)

Pedro Martinez	4.38
Curt Schilling	4.11
Shane Reynolds	3.66
Jon Lieber	3.60
Rick Reed	3.51
Mike Mussina	3.47
Greg Maddux	3.28
Greg Swindell	3.08
Javier Vazquez	3.05
Randy Johnson	3.04

Hits per 9 IP
(minimum 750 IP)

Pedro Martinez	6.69
Randy Johnson	6.91
Jesse Orosco	7.24
Mike Jackson	7.32
Roger Clemens	7.70
Hideo Nomo	7.75
John Smoltz	7.77
Arthur Rhodes	7.78
Chan Ho Park	7.82
Curt Schilling	7.97

Baserunners per 9 IP
(minimum 750 IP)

Pedro Martinez	9.53
Curt Schilling	10.23
Greg Maddux	10.33
Mike Mussina	10.61
John Smoltz	10.76
Roger Clemens	10.92
Randy Johnson	11.01
Rick Reed	11.11
Kevin Millwood	11.13
Mike Jackson	11.27

Home Runs per 9 IP
(minimum 750 IP)

Greg Maddux	0.50
Kevin Brown	0.56
Matt Morris	0.58
Hipolito Pichardo	0.63
Bob Wickman	0.64
Roger Clemens	0.66
Tom Glavine	0.66
Pedro Martinez	0.68
Shawn Estes	0.68
Andy Pettitte	0.69

Opposition Avg.
(minimum 750 IP)

Pedro Martinez	.205
Randy Johnson	.212
Jesse Orosco	.221
Mike Jackson	.223
Roger Clemens	.230
Hideo Nomo	.232
John Smoltz	.233
Arthur Rhodes	.234
Chan Ho Park	.235
Curt Schilling	.237

Opposition OBP
(minimum 750 IP)

Pedro Martinez	.267
Curt Schilling	.283
Greg Maddux	.287
Mike Mussina	.291
John Smoltz	.294
Roger Clemens	.296
Randy Johnson	.298
Kevin Millwood	.299
Rick Reed	.301
Mike Jackson	.304

Opposition Slg.
(minimum 750 IP)

Pedro Martinez	.315
Jesse Orosco	.332
Randy Johnson	.334
Greg Maddux	.335
Roger Clemens	.341
Roberto Hernandez	.343
Kevin Brown	.345
John Smoltz	.353
Mike Jackson	.354
Jose Rijo	.361

Home Runs Allowed

David Wells	306
Chuck Finley	304
Roger Clemens	297
Jamie Moyer	295
Andy Benes	289
Mike Morgan	270
Randy Johnson	267
Greg Swindell	262
Mike Mussina	257
Terry Mulholland	252

Hit Batsmen

Randy Johnson	138
Roger Clemens	136
Kevin Brown	124
Pedro Astacio	105
Greg Maddux	101
Tim Wakefield	97
Scott Erickson	96
Pedro Martinez	90
Chan Ho Park	87
Aaron Sele	86

Wild Pitches

Chuck Finley	130
Roger Clemens	120
John Smoltz	120
Mike Morgan	105
Kevin Appier	98
Tom Gordon	93
Kevin Brown	91
Randy Johnson	91
Hideo Nomo	91
David Wells	91

GDP Induced

Mike Morgan	331
Greg Maddux	318
Tom Glavine	313
Chuck Finley	306
Scott Erickson	297
Kevin Brown	286
Roger Clemens	273
Kenny Rogers	232
Terry Mulholland	227
Mike Hampton	216

GDP per 9 IP
(minimum 750 IP)

Jamey Wright	1.23
Shawn Estes	1.20
Julian Tavarez	1.19
Mike Hampton	1.18
Scott Erickson	1.18
Bob Wickman	1.15
Andy Pettitte	1.10
Hipolito Pichardo	1.10
Mike Morgan	1.07
Mike Timlin	1.01

Saves

Trevor Hoffman	352
Roberto Hernandez	320
Robb Nen	314
Troy Percival	250
Mariano Rivera	243
Jose Mesa	225
Todd Jones	184
Billy Wagner	181
Armando Benitez	176
Ugueth Urbina	174

Save Percentage
(minimum 50 save opportunities)

John Smoltz	92.9
Eric Gagne	92.9
Trevor Hoffman	88.9
Kazuhiro Sasaki	86.9
Armando Benitez	86.7
Mike Williams	86.6
Mariano Rivera	86.5
Kerry Ligtenberg	86.3
Billy Koch	86.2
Troy Percival	85.9

Games Finished

Roberto Hernandez	585
Robb Nen	549
Trevor Hoffman	520
Jesse Orosco	488
Jose Mesa	426
Dan Plesac	413
Mike Jackson	410
Todd Jones	387
Troy Percival	369
2 tied with	348

SB Pct. Allowed
(minimum 750 IP)

Kirk Rueter	34.5
Terry Mulholland	41.3
Kenny Rogers	41.4
Omar Daal	41.7
Chris Carpenter	42.7
Chan Ho Park	49.1
Jeff Weaver	49.1
Wilson Alvarez	50.3
Rick Helling	51.5
Chris Hammond	51.7

2002 STATISTICAL LEADERS *Active career*

HISTORY

All-time results

Award winners

Hall of Fame

ALL-TIME RESULTS

AMERICAN LEAGUE CHAMPIONS

Year	Team	Manager	Year	Team	Manager
1901	Chicago	Clark Griffith	1953	New York	Casey Stengel
1902	Philadelphia	Connie Mack	1954	Cleveland	Al Lopez
1903	Boston	Jimmy Collins	1955	New York	Casey Stengel
1904	Boston	Jimmy Collins	1956	New York	Casey Stengel
1905	Philadelphia	Connie Mack	1957	New York	Casey Stengel
1906	Chicago	Fielder Jones	1958	New York	Casey Stengel
1907	Detroit	Hugh Jennings	1959	Chicago	Al Lopez
1908	Detroit	Hugh Jennings	1960	New York	Casey Stengel
1909	Detroit	Hugh Jennings	1961	New York	Ralph Houk
1910	Philadelphia	Connie Mack	1962	New York	Ralph Houk
1911	Philadelphia	Connie Mack	1963	New York	Ralph Houk
1912	Boston	Jake Stahl	1964	New York	Yogi Berra
1913	Philadelphia	Connie Mack	1965	Minnesota	Sam Mele
1914	Philadelphia	Connie Mack	1966	Baltimore	Hank Bauer
1915	Boston	Bill Carrigan	1967	Boston	Dick Williams
1916	Boston	Bill Carrigan	1968	Detroit	Mayo Smith
1917	Chicago	Pants Rowland	1969	Baltimore (East Division)	Earl Weaver
1918	Boston	Ed Barrow	1970	Baltimore (East Division)	Earl Weaver
1919	Chicago	Kid Gleason	1971	Baltimore (East Division)	Earl Weaver
1920	Cleveland	Tris Speaker	1972	Oakland (West Division)	Dick Williams
1921	New York	Miller Huggins	1973	Oakland (West Division)	Dick Williams
1922	New York	Miller Huggins	1974	Oakland (West Division)	Al Dark
1923	New York	Miller Huggins	1975	Boston (East Division)	Darrell Johnson
1924	Washington	Bucky Harris	1976	New York (East Division)	Billy Martin
1925	Washington	Bucky Harris	1977	New York (East Division)	Billy Martin
1926	New York	Miller Huggins	1978	New York (East Division)	Billy Martin, Bob Lemon
1927	New York	Miller Huggins	1979	Baltimore (East Division)	Earl Weaver
1928	New York	Miller Huggins	1980	Kansas City (West Division)	Jim Frey
1929	Philadelphia	Connie Mack	1981	New York (East Division)	Gene Michael, Bob Lemon
1930	Philadelphia	Connie Mack	1982	Milwaukee (East Division)	Buck Rodgers, Harvey Kuenn
1931	Philadelphia	Connie Mack	1983	Baltimore (East Division)	Joe Altobelli
1932	New York	Joe McCarthy	1984	Detroit (East Division)	Sparky Anderson
1933	Washington	Joe Cronin	1985	Kansas City (West Division)	Dick Howser
1934	Detroit	Mickey Cochrane	1986	Boston (East Division)	John McNamara
1935	Detroit	Mickey Cochrane	1987	Minnesota (West Division)	Tom Kelly
1936	New York	Joe McCarthy	1988	Oakland (West Division)	Tony La Russa
1937	New York	Joe McCarthy	1989	Oakland (West Division)	Tony La Russa
1938	New York	Joe McCarthy	1990	Oakland (West Division)	Tony La Russa
1939	New York	Joe McCarthy	1991	Minnesota (West Division)	Tom Kelly
1940	Detroit	Del Baker	1992	Toronto (East Division)	Cito Gaston
1941	New York	Joe McCarthy	1993	Toronto (East Division)	Cito Gaston
1942	New York	Joe McCarthy	1994	None†	
1943	New York	Joe McCarthy	1995	Cleveland (Central Division)	Mike Hargrove
1944	St. Louis	Luke Sewell	1996	New York (East Division)	Joe Torre
1945	Detroit	Steve O'Neill	1997	Cleveland (Central Division)	Mike Hargrove
1946	Boston	Joe Cronin	1998	New York (East Division)	Joe Torre
1947	New York	Bucky Harris	1999	New York (East Division)	Joe Torre
1948	Cleveland*	Lou Boudreau	2000	New York (East Division)	Joe Torre
1949	New York	Casey Stengel	2001	New York (East Division)	Joe Torre
1950	New York	Casey Stengel	2002	Anaheim (West Division)	Mike Scioscia
1951	New York	Casey Stengel		*Defeated Boston in one-game playoff. †New York finished	
1952	New York	Casey Stengel		the strike-shortened season with the league's best record.	

NATIONAL LEAGUE CHAMPIONS

Year	Team	Manager	Year	Team	Manager
1876	Chicago	Albert Spalding	1888	New York	James Mutrie
1877	Boston	Harry Wright	1889	New York	James Mutrie
1878	Boston	Harry Wright	1890	Brooklyn	William McGunnigle
1879	Providence	George Wright	1891	Boston	Frank Selee
1880	Chicago	Cap Anson	1892	Boston	Frank Selee
1881	Chicago	Cap Anson	1893	Boston	Frank Selee
1882	Chicago	Cap Anson	1894	Baltimore	Ned Hanlon
1883	Boston	Jack Burdock, John Morrill	1895	Baltimore	Ned Hanlon
1884	Providence	Frank Bancroft	1896	Baltimore	Ned Hanlon
1885	Chicago	Cap Anson	1897	Boston	Frank Selee
1886	Chicago	Cap Anson	1898	Boston	Frank Selee
1887	Detroit	William Watkins	1899	Brooklyn	Ned Hanlon

Year	Team	Manager	Year	Team	Manager
1900—Brooklyn	Ned Hanlon		1956—Brooklyn	Walter Alston	
1901—Pittsburgh	Fred Clarke		1957—Milwaukee	Fred Haney	
1902—Pittsburgh	Fred Clarke		1958—Milwaukee‡	Fred Haney	
1903—Pittsburgh	Fred Clarke		1959—Los Angeles‡	Walter Alston	
1904—New York	John McGraw		1960—Pittsburgh	Danny Murtaugh	
1905—New York	John McGraw		1961—Cincinnati	Fred Hutchinson	
1906—Chicago	Frank Chance		1962—San Francisco§	Al Dark	
1907—Chicago	Frank Chance		1963—Los Angeles	Walter Alston	
1908—Chicago	Frank Chance		1964—St. Louis	Johnny Keane	
1909—Pittsburgh	Fred Clarke		1965—Los Angeles	Walter Alston	
1910—Chicago	Frank Chance		1966—Los Angeles	Walter Alston	
1911—New York	John McGraw		1967—St. Louis	Red Schoendienst	
1912—New York	John McGraw		1968—St. Louis	Red Schoendienst	
1913—New York	John McGraw		1969—New York (East Division)	Gil Hodges	
1914—Boston	George Stallings		1970—Cincinnati (West Division)	Sparky Anderson	
1915—Philadelphia	Pat Moran		1971—Pittsburgh (East Division)	Danny Murtaugh	
1916—Brooklyn	Wilbert Robinson		1972—Cincinnati (West Division)	Sparky Anderson	
1917—New York	John McGraw		1973—New York (East Division)	Yogi Berra	
1918—Chicago	Fred Mitchell		1974—Los Angeles (West Division)	Walter Alston	
1919—Cincinnati	Pat Moran		1975—Cincinnati (West Division)	Sparky Anderson	
1920—Brooklyn	Wilbert Robinson		1976—Cincinnati (West Division)	Sparky Anderson	
1921—New York	John McGraw		1977—Los Angeles (West Division)	Tommy Lasorda	
1922—New York	John McGraw		1978—Los Angeles (West Division)	Tommy Lasorda	
1923—New York	John McGraw		1979—Pittsburgh (East Division)	Chuck Tanner	
1924—New York	John McGraw		1980—Philadelphia (East Division)	Dallas Green	
1925—Pittsburgh	Bill McKechnie		1981—Los Angeles (West Division)	Tommy Lasorda	
1926—St. Louis	Rogers Hornsby		1982—St. Louis (East Division)	Whitey Herzog	
1927—Pittsburgh	Donie Bush		1983—Philadelphia (East Division)	Pat Corrales, Paul Owens	
1928—St. Louis	Bill McKechnie		1984—San Diego (West Division)	Dick Williams	
1929—Chicago	Joe McCarthy		1985—St. Louis (East Division)	Whitey Herzog	
1930—St. Louis	Gabby Street		1986—New York (East Division)	Dave Johnson	
1931—St. Louis	Gabby Street		1987—St. Louis (East Division)	Whitey Herzog	
1932—Chicago	Rogers Hornsby, Charlie Grimm		1988—Los Angeles (West Division)	Tommy Lasorda	
1933—New York	Bill Terry		1989—San Francisco (West Division)	Roger Craig	
1934—St. Louis	Frank Frisch		1990—Cincinnati (West Division)	Lou Piniella	
1935—Chicago	Charlie Grimm		1991—Atlanta (West Division)	Bobby Cox	
1936—New York	Bill Terry		1992—Atlanta (West Division)	Bobby Cox	
1937—New York	Bill Terry		1993—Philadelphia (East Division)	Jim Fregosi	
1938—Chicago	Charlie Grimm, Gabby Hartnett		1994—None∞		
1939—Cincinnati	Bill McKechnie		1995—Atlanta (East Division)	Bobby Cox	
1940—Cincinnati	Bill McKechnie		1996—Atlanta (East Division)	Bobby Cox	
1941—Brooklyn	Leo Durocher		1997—Florida (East Division)	Jim Leyland	
1942—St. Louis	Billy Southworth		1998—San Diego (West Division)	Bruce Bochy	
1943—St. Louis	Billy Southworth		1999—Atlanta (East Division)	Bobby Cox	
1944—St. Louis	Billy Southworth		2000—New York (East Division)	Bobby Valentine	
1945—Chicago	Charlie Grimm		2001—Arizona (West Division)	Bob Brenly	
1946—St. Louis*	Eddie Dyer		2002—San Francisco (West Division)	Dusty Baker	
1947—Brooklyn	Clyde Sukeforth, Burt Shotton				
1948—Boston	Billy Southworth				
1949—Brooklyn	Burt Shotton				
1950—Philadelphia	Eddie Sawyer				
1951—New York†	Leo Durocher				
1952—Brooklyn	Charlie Dressen				
1953—Brooklyn	Charlie Dressen				
1954—New York	Leo Durocher				
1955—Brooklyn	Walter Alston				

*Defeated Brooklyn, two games to none, in playoff for pennant.
†Defeated Brooklyn, two games to one, in playoff for pennant.
‡Defeated Milwaukee, two games to none, in playoff for pennant.
§Defeated Los Angeles, two games to one, in playoff for pennant.
∞Montreal finished the strike-shortened season with the league's best record.

WORLD SERIES

Year	Winner	Loser	Games	Year	Winner	Loser	Games
1903—Boston A.L.	Pittsburgh N.L.	5-3		1917—Chicago A.L.	New York N.L.	4-2	
1904—No Series				1918—Boston A.L.	Chicago N.L.	4-2	
1905—New York N.L.	Philadelphia A.L.	4-1		1919—Cincinnati N.L.	Chicago A.L.	5-3	
1906—Chicago A.L.	Chicago N.L.	4-2		1920—Cleveland A.L.	Brooklyn N.L.	5-2	
1907—Chicago N.L.	Detroit A.L.	*4-0		1921—New York N.L.	New York A.L.	5-3	
1908—Chicago N.L.	Detroit A.L.	4-1		1922—New York N.L.	New York A.L.	*4-0	
1909—Pittsburgh N.L.	Detroit A.L.	4-3		1923—New York A.L.	New York N.L.	4-2	
1910—Philadelphia A.L.	Chicago N.L.	4-1		1924—Washington A.L.	New York N.L.	4-3	
1911—Philadelphia A.L.	New York N.L.	4-2		1925—Pittsburgh N.L.	Washington A.L.	4-3	
1912—Boston A.L.	New York N.L.	*4-3		1926—St. Louis N.L.	New York A.L.	4-3	
1913—Philadelphia A.L.	New York N.L.	4-1		1927—New York A.L.	Pittsburgh, N.L.	4-0	
1914—Boston N.L.	Philadelphia A.L.	4-0		1928—New York A.L.	St. Louis N.L.	4-0	
1915—Boston A.L.	Philadelphia N.L.	4-1		1929—Philadelphia A.L.	Chicago N.L.	4-1	
1916—Boston A.L.	Brooklyn N.L.	4-1		1930—Philadelphia A.L.	St. Louis N.L.	4-2	

Year	Winner	Loser	Games	Year	Winner	Loser	Games
1931	St. Louis N.L.	Philadelphia A.L.	4-3	1968	Detroit A.L.	St. Louis N.L.	4-3
1932	New York A.L.	Chicago N.L.	4-0	1969	New York N.L.	Baltimore A.L.	4-1
1933	New York N.L.	Washington A.L.	4-1	1970	Baltimore A.L.	Cincinnati N.L.	4-1
1934	St. Louis N.L.	Detroit A.L.	4-3	1971	Pittsburgh N.L.	Baltimore A.L.	4-3
1935	Detroit A.L.	Chicago N.L.	4-2	1972	Oakland A.L.	Cincinnati N.L.	4-3
1936	New York A.L.	New York N.L.	4-2	1973	Oakland A.L.	New York N.L.	4-3
1937	New York A.L.	New York N.L.	4-1	1974	Oakland A.L.	Los Angeles N.L.	4-1
1938	New York A.L.	Chicago N.L.	4-0	1975	Cincinnati N.L.	Boston A.L.	4-3
1939	New York A.L.	Cincinnati N.L.	4-0	1976	Cincinnati N.L.	New York A.L.	4-0
1940	Cincinnati N.L.	Detroit A.L.	4-3	1977	New York A.L.	Los Angeles N.L.	4-2
1941	New York A.L.	Brooklyn N.L.	4-1	1978	New York A.L.	Los Angeles N.L.	4-2
1942	St. Louis N.L.	New York A.L.	4-1	1979	Pittsburgh N.L.	Baltimore A.L.	4-3
1943	New York A.L.	St. Louis N.L.	4-1	1980	Philadelphia N.L.	Kansas City A.L.	4-2
1944	St. Louis N.L.	St. Louis A.L.	4-2	1981	Los Angeles N.L.	New York A.L.	4-2
1945	Detroit A.L.	Chicago N.L.	4-3	1982	St. Louis N.L.	Milwaukee A.L.	4-3
1946	St. Louis N.L.	Boston A.L.	4-3	1983	Baltimore A.L.	Philadelphia N.L.	4-1
1947	New York A.L.	Brooklyn, N.L.	4-3	1984	Detroit A.L.	San Diego N.L.	4-1
1948	Cleveland A.L.	Boston N.L.	4-2	1985	Kansas City A.L.	St. Louis N.L.	4-3
1949	New York A.L.	Brooklyn N.L.	4-1	1986	New York N.L.	Boston A.L.	4-3
1950	New York A.L.	Philadelphia N.L.	4-0	1987	Minnesota A.L.	St. Louis N.L.	4-3
1951	New York A.L.	New York N.L.	4-2	1988	Los Angeles N.L.	Oakland A.L.	4-1
1952	New York A.L.	Brooklyn N.L.	4-3	1989	Oakland A.L.	San Francisco N.L.	4-0
1953	New York A.L.	Brooklyn N.L.	4-2	1990	Cincinnati N.L.	Oakland A.L.	4-0
1954	New York N.L.	Cleveland A.L.	4-0	1991	Minnesota A.L.	Atlanta N.L.	4-3
1955	Brooklyn N.L.	New York A.L.	4-3	1992	Toronto A.L.	Atlanta N.L.	4-2
1956	New York A.L.	Brooklyn N.L.	4-3	1993	Toronto A.L.	Philadelphia N.L.	4-2
1957	Milwaukee N.L.	New York A.L.	4-3	1994	No Series		
1958	New York A.L.	Milwaukee N.L.	4-3	1995	Atlanta N.L.	Cleveland A.L.	4-2
1959	Los Angeles N.L.	Chicago A.L.	4-2	1996	New York A.L.	Atlanta N.L.	4-2
1960	Pittsburgh N.L.	New York A.L.	4-3	1997	Florida N.L.	Cleveland A.L.	4-3
1961	New York A.L.	Cincinnati N.L.	4-1	1998	New York A.L.	San Diego N.L.	4-0
1962	New York A.L.	San Francisco N.L.	4-3	1999	New York A.L.	Atlanta N.L.	4-0
1963	Los Angeles N.L.	New York A.L.	4-0	2000	New York A.L.	New York N.L.	4-1
1964	St. Louis N.L.	New York A.L.	4-3	2001	Arizona N.L.	New York A.L.	4-3
1965	Los Angeles N.L.	Minnesota A.L.	4-3	2002	Anaheim A.L.	San Francisco N.L.	4-3
1966	Baltimore A.L.	Los Angeles N.L.	4-0	*Includes tie game.			
1967	St. Louis N.L.	Boston A.L.	4-3				

DIVISION SERIES

AMERICAN LEAGUE

Year	Winner (Division)	Loser (Division)	Games
1981	New York (East)	Milwaukee (East)	3-2
	Oakland (West)	Kansas City (West)	3-0
1995	Cleveland (Central)	Boston (East)	3-0
	Seattle (West)	New York* (East)	3-2
1996	New York (East)	Texas (West)	3-1
	Baltimore (East)*	Cleveland (Central)	3-1
1997	Baltimore (East)	Seattle (West)	3-1
	Cleveland (Central)	New York (East)*	3-2
1998	New York (East)	Texas (West)	3-0
	Cleveland (Central)	Boston (East)*	3-1
1999	New York (East)	Texas (West)	3-0
	Boston (East)*	Cleveland (Central)	3-2
2000	New York (East)	Oakland (West)	3-2
	Seattle (West)*	Chicago (Central)	3-0
2001	New York (East)	Oakland (West)*	3-2
	Seattle (West)	Cleveland (Central)	3-2
2002	Anaheim (West)*	New York (East)	3-1
	Minnesota (Central)	Oakland (West)	3-2

NATIONAL LEAGUE

Year	Winner (Division)	Loser (Division)	Games
1981	Montreal (East)	Philadelphia (East)	3-2
	Los Angeles (West)	Houston (West)	3-2
1995	Atlanta (East)	Colorado* (West)	3-1
	Cincinnati (Central)	Los Angeles (West)	3-0
1996	Atlanta (East)	Los Angeles (West)*	3-0
	St. Louis (Central)	San Diego (West)	3-0
1997	Atlanta (East)	Houston (Central)	3-0
	Florida (East)*	San Francisco (West)	3-0
1998	Atlanta (East)	Chicago (Central)*	3-0
	San Diego (West)	Houston (Central)	3-1
1999	Atlanta (East)	Houston (Central)	3-1
	New York (East)*	Arizona (West)	3-1
2000	St. Louis (Central)	Atlanta (East)	3-0
	New York (East)*	San Francisco (West)	3-1
2001	Arizona (West)	St. Louis (Central)*	3-2
	Atlanta (East)	Houston (Central)	3-0
2002	St. Louis (Central)	Arizona (West)	3-0
	San Francisco (West)*	Atlanta (East)	3-2

*Wild-card team.

CHAMPIONSHIP SERIES

AMERICAN LEAGUE

Year	Winner (Division)	Loser (Division)	Games
1969	Baltimore (East)	Minnesota (West)	3-0
1970	Baltimore (East)	Minnesota (West)	3-0
1971	Baltimore (East)	Oakland (West)	3-0
1972	Oakland (West)	Detroit (East)	3-2
1973	Oakland (West)	Baltimore (East)	3-2

Year	Winner (Division)	Loser (Division)	Games
1974	Oakland (West)	Baltimore (East)	3-1
1975	Boston (East)	Oakland (West)	3-0
1976	New York (East)	Kansas City (West)	3-2
1977	New York (East)	Kansas City (West)	3-2
1978	New York (East)	Kansas City (West)	3-1
1979	Baltimore (East)	California (West)	3-1
1980	Kansas City (West)	New York (East)	3-0

Year	Winner (Division)	Loser (Division)	Games
1981—New York (East)	Oakland (West)		3-0
1982—Milwaukee (East)	California (West)		3-2
1983—Baltimore (East)	Chicago (West)		3-1
1984—Detroit (East)	Kansas City (West)		3-0
1985—Kansas City (West)	Toronto (East)		4-3
1986—Boston (East)	California (West)		4-3
1987—Minnesota (West)	Detroit (East)		4-1
1988—Oakland (West)	Boston (East)		4-0
1989—Oakland (West)	Toronto (East)		4-1
1990—Oakland (West)	Boston (East)		4-0
1991—Minnesota (West)	Toronto (East)		4-1
1992—Toronto (East)	Oakland (West)		4-2
1993—Toronto (East)	Chicago (West)		4-2
1994—No series			
1995—Cleveland (Central)	Seattle (West)		4-2
1996—New York (East)	Baltimore (East)*		4-1
1997—Cleveland (Central)	Baltimore (East)		4-2
1998—New York (East)	Cleveland (Central)		4-2
1999—New York (East)	Boston (East)*		4-1
2000—New York (East)	Seattle (West)		4-2
2001—New York (East)	Seattle (West)		4-1
2002—Anaheim (West)*	Minnesota (Central)		4-1

NATIONAL LEAGUE

Year	Winner (Division)	Loser (Division)	Games
1969—New York (East)	Atlanta (West)		3-0
1970—Cincinnati (West)	Pittsburgh (East)		3-0
1971—Pittsburgh (East)	San Francisco (West)		3-1
1972—Cincinnati (West)	Pittsburgh (East)		3-2
1973—New York (East)	Cincinnati (West)		3-2

Year	Winner (Division)	Loser (Division)	Games
1974—Los Angeles (West)	Pittsburgh (East)		3-1
1975—Cincinnati (West)	Pittsburgh (East)		3-0
1976—Cincinnati (West)	Philadelphia (East)		3-0
1977—Los Angeles (West)	Philadelphia (East)		3-1
1978—Los Angeles (West)	Philadelphia (East)		3-1
1979—Pittsburgh (East)	Cincinnati (West)		3-0
1980—Philadelphia (East)	Houston (West)		3-2
1981—Los Angeles (West)	Montreal (East)		3-2
1982—St. Louis (East)	Atlanta (West)		3-0
1983—Philadelphia (East)	Los Angeles (West)		3-1
1984—San Diego (West)	Chicago (East)		3-2
1985—St. Louis (East)	Los Angeles (West)		4-2
1986—New York (East)	Houston (West)		4-2
1987—St. Louis (East)	San Francisco (West)		4-3
1988—Los Angeles (West)	New York (East)		4-3
1989—San Francisco (West)	Chicago (East)		4-1
1990—Cincinnati (West)	Pittsburgh (East)		4-2
1991—Atlanta (West)	Pittsburgh (East)		4-3
1992—Atlanta (West)	Pittsburgh (East)		4-3
1993—Philadelphia (East)	Atlanta (West)		4-2
1994—No series			
1995—Atlanta (East)	Cincinnati (Central)		4-0
1996—Atlanta (East)	St. Louis (Central)		4-3
1997—Florida (East)*	Atlanta (East)		4-2
1998—San Diego (West)	Atlanta (East)		4-2
1999—Atlanta (East)	New York (East)*		4-2
2000—New York (East)*	St. Louis (Central)		4-1
2001—Arizona (West)	Atlanta (East)		4-1
2002—San Francisco (West)*	St. Louis (Central)		4-1

*Wild-card team.

ALL-STAR GAME

Date	Site	Score (Winner)	Winning pitcher (Losing pitcher)	Winning manager (Losing manager)	Att.
7-6-33	Comiskey Park Chicago	4-2 (A.L.)	Lefty Gomez, Yankees (Bill Hallahan, Cardinals)	Connie Mack, Athletics (John McGraw, Giants)	47,595
7-10-34	Polo Grounds New York	9-7 (A.L.)	Mel Harder, Indians (Van Mungo, Dodgers)	Joe Cronin, Senators (Bill Terry, Giants)	48,363
7-8-35	Municipal Stadium Cleveland	4-1 (A.L.)	Lefty Gomez, Yankees (Bill Walker, Cardinals)	Mickey Cochrane, Tigers (Frankie Frisch, Cardinals)	69,831
7-7-36	Braves Field Boston	4-3 (N.L.)	Dizzy Dean, Cardinals (Lefty Grove, Red Sox)	Charlie Grimm, Cubs (Joe McCarthy, Yankees)	25,556
7-7-37	Griffith Stadium Washington	8-3 (A.L.)	Lefty Gomez, Yankees (Dizzy Dean, Cardinals)	Joe McCarthy, Yankees (Bill Terry, Giants)	31,391
7-6-38	Crosley Field Cincinnati	4-1 (N.L.)	Johnny Vander Meer, Reds (Lefty Gomez, Yankees)	Bill Terry, Giants (Joe McCarthy, Yankees)	27,067
7-11-39	Yankee Stadium New York	3-1 (A.L.)	Tommy Bridges, Tigers (Bill Lee, Cubs)	Joe McCarthy, Yankees (Gabby Hartnett, Cubs)	62,892
7-9-40	Sportsman's Park St. Louis	4-0 (N.L.)	Paul Derringer, Reds (Red Ruffing, Yankees)	Bill McKechnie, Reds (Joe Cronin, Red Sox)	32,373
7-8-41	Briggs Stadium Detroit	7-5 (A.L.)	Ed Smith, White Sox (Claude Passeau, Cubs)	Del Baker, Tigers (Bill McKechnie, Reds)	54,674
7-6-42	Polo Grounds New York	3-1 (A.L.)	Spud Chandler, Yankees (Mort Cooper, Cardinals)	Joe McCarthy, Yankees (Leo Durocher, Dodgers)	33,694
7-13-43	Shibe Park Philadelphia	5-3 (A.L.)	Dutch Leonard, Senators (Mort Cooper, Cardinals)	Joe McCarthy, Yankees (Billy Southworth, Cardinals)	31,938
7-11-44	Forbes Field Pittsburgh	7-1 (N.L.)	Ken Raffensberger, Phillies (Tex Hughson, Red Sox)	Billy Southworth, Cardinals (Joe McCarthy, Yankees)	29,589
1945	No game played.				
7-9-46	Fenway Park Boston	12-0 (A.L.)	Bob Feller, Indians (Claude Passeau, Cubs)	Steve O'Neill, Tigers (Charlie Grimm, Cubs)	34,906
7-8-47	Wrigley Field Chicago	2-1 (A.L.)	Frank Shea, Yankees (Johnny Sain, Braves)	Joe Cronin, Red Sox (Eddie Dyer, Cardinals)	41,123
7-13-48	Sportsman's Park St. Louis	5-2 (A.L.)	Vic Raschi, Yankees (Johnny Schmitz, Cubs)	Bucky Harris, Yankees (Leo Durocher, Dodgers)	34,009
7-12-49	Ebbets Field Brooklyn	11-7 (A.L.)	Virgil Trucks, Tigers (Don Newcombe, Dodgers)	Lou Boudreau, Indians (Billy Southworth, Braves)	32,577
7-11-50	Comiskey Park Chicago	4-3* (N.L.)	Ewell Blackwell, Reds (Ted Gray, Tigers)	Burt Shotton, Dodgers (Casey Stengel, Yankees)	46,127
7-10-51	Briggs Stadium Detroit	8-3 (N.L.)	Sal Maglie, Giants (Ed Lopat, Yankees)	Eddie Sawyer, Phillies (Casey Stengel, Yankees)	52,075

Date	Site	Score (Winner)	Winning pitcher (Losing pitcher)	Winning manager (Losing manager)	Att.
7-8-52	Shibe Park Philadelphia	3-2† (N.L.)	Bob Rush, Cubs (Bob Lemon, Indians)	Leo Durocher, Giants (Casey Stengel, Yankees)	32,785
7-14-53	Crosley Field Cincinnati	5-1 (N.L.)	Warren Spahn, Braves (Allie Reynolds, Yankees)	Chuck Dressen, Dodgers (Casey Stengel, Yankees)	30,846
7-13-54	Municipal Stadium Cleveland	11-9 (A.L.)	Dean Stone, Senators (Gene Conley, Braves)	Casey Stengel, Yankees (Walter Alston, Dodgers)	68,751
7-12-55	Milwaukee Co. Stadium Milwaukee	6-5‡ (N.L.)	Gene Conley, Braves (Frank Sullivan, Red Sox)	Leo Durocher, Giants (Al Lopez, Indians)	45,314
7-10-56	Griffith Stadium Washington	7-3 (N.L.)	Bob Friend, Pirates (Billy Pierce, White Sox)	Walter Alston, Dodgers (Casey Stengel, Yankees)	28,843
7-9-57	Busch Stadium St. Louis	6-5 (A.L.)	Jim Bunning, Tigers (Curt Simmons, Phillies)	Casey Stengel, Yankees (Walter Alston, Dodgers)	30,693
7-8-58	Memorial Stadium Baltimore	4-3 (A.L.)	Early Wynn, White Sox (Bob Friend, Pirates)	Casey Stengel, Yankees (Fred Haney, Braves)	48,829
7-7-59	Forbes Field Pittsburgh	5-4 (N.L.)	Johnny Antonelli, Giants (Whitey Ford, Yankees)	Fred Haney, Braves (Casey Stengel, Yankees)	35,277
8-3-59	Memorial Coliseum Los Angeles	5-3 (A.L.)	Jerry Walker, Orioles (Don Drysdale, Dodgers)	Casey Stengel, Yankees (Fred Haney, Braves)	55,105
7-11-60	Municipal Stadium Kansas City	5-3 (N.L.)	Bob Friend, Pirates (Bill Monbouquette, Red Sox)	Walter Alston, Dodgers (Al Lopez, White Sox)	30,619
7-13-60	Yankee Stadium New York	6-0 (N.L.)	Vernon Law, Pirates (Whitey Ford, Yankees)	Walter Alston, Dodgers (Al Lopez, White Sox)	38,362
7-11-61	Candlestick Park San Francisco	5-4§ (N.L.)	Stu Miller, Giants (Hoyt Wilhelm, Orioles)	Danny Murtaugh, Pirates (Paul Richards, Orioles)	44,115
7-31-61	Fenway Park Boston	1-1 (tie)		Paul Richards, Orioles (A.L.) Danny Murtaugh, Pirates (N.L.)	31,851
7-10-62	District of Col. Stad. Washington	3-1 (N.L.)	Juan Marichal, Giants (Camilo Pascual, Twins)	Fred Hutchinson, Reds (Ralph Houk, Yankees)	45,480
7-30-62	Wrigley Field Chicago	9-4 (A.L.)	Ray Herbert, White Sox (Art Mahaffey, Phillies)	Ralph Houk, Yankees (Fred Hutchinson, Reds)	38,359
7-9-63	Municipal Stadium Cleveland	5-3 (N.L.)	Larry Jackson, Cubs (Jim Bunning, Tigers)	Alvin Dark, Giants (Ralph Houk, Yankees)	44,160
7-7-64	Shea Stadium New York	7-4 (N.L.)	Juan Marichal, Giants (Dick Radatz, Red Sox)	Walter Alston, Dodgers (Al Lopez, White Sox)	50,850
7-13-65	Metropolitan Stadium Bloomington, Minn.	6-5 (N.L.)	Sandy Koufax, Dodgers (Sam McDowell, Indians)	Gene Mauch, Phillies (Al Lopez, White Sox)	46,706
7-12-66	Busch Stadium St. Louis	2-1§ (N.L.)	Gaylord Perry, Giants (Pete Richert, Senators)	Walter Alston, Dodgers (Sam Mele, Twins)	49,936
7-11-67	Anaheim Stadium Anaheim, Calif.	2-1∞ (N.L.)	Don Drysdale, Dodgers (Jim Hunter, Athletics)	Walter Alston, Dodgers (Hank Bauer, Orioles)	46,309
7-9-68	Astrodome Houston	1-0 (N.L.)	Don Drysdale, Dodgers (Luis Tiant, Indians)	Red Schoendienst, Cardinals (Dick Williams, Red Sox)	48,321
7-23-69	R.F.K. Stadium Washington	9-3 (N.L.)	Steve Carlton, Cardinals (Mel Stottlemyre, Yankees)	Red Schoendienst, Cardinals (Mayo Smith, Tigers)	45,259
7-14-70	Riverfront Stadium Cincinnati	5-4‡ (N.L.)	Claude Osteen, Dodgers (Clyde Wright, Angels)	Gil Hodges, Mets (Earl Weaver, Orioles)	51,838
7-13-71	Tiger Stadium Detroit	6-4 (A.L.)	Vida Blue, Athletics (Dock Ellis, Pirates)	Earl Weaver, Orioles (Sparky Anderson, Reds)	53,559
7-25-72	Atlanta Stadium Atlanta	4-3§ (N.L.)	Tug McGraw, Mets (Dave McNally, Orioles)	Danny Murtaugh, Pirates (Earl Weaver, Orioles)	53,107
7-24-73	Royals Stadium Kansas City	7-1 (N.L.)	Rick Wise, Cardinals (Bert Blyleven, Twins)	Sparky Anderson, Reds (Dick Williams, Athletics)	40,849
7-23-74	Three Rivers Stadium Pittsburgh	7-2 (N.L.)	Ken Brett, Pirates (Luis Tiant, Red Sox)	Yogi Berra, Mets (Dick Williams, Athletics)	50,706
7-15-75	Milwaukee Co. Stadium Milwaukee	6-3 (N.L.)	Jon Matlack, Mets (Jim Hunter, Yankees)	Walter Alston, Dodgers (Alvin Dark, Athletics)	51,480
7-13-76	Veterans Stadium Philadelphia	7-1 (N.L)	Randy Jones, Padres (Mark Fidrych, Tigers)	Sparky Anderson, Reds (Darrell Johnson, Red Sox)	63,974
7-19-77	Yankee Stadium New York	7-5 (N.L.)	Don Sutton, Dodgers (Jim Palmer, Orioles)	Sparky Anderson, Reds (Billy Martin, Yankees)	56,683
7-11-78	San Diego Stadium San Diego	7-3 (N.L.)	Bruce Sutter, Cubs (Rich Gossage, Yankees)	Tommy Lasorda, Dodgers (Billy Martin, Yankees)	51,549
7-17-79	Kingdome Seattle	7-6 (N.L.)	Bruce Sutter, Cubs (Jim Kern, Rangers)	Tommy Lasorda, Dodgers (Bob Lemon, Yankees)	58,905
7-8-80	Dodger Stadium Los Angeles	4-2 (N.L.)	Jerry Reuss, Dodgers (Tommy John, Yankees)	Chuck Tanner, Pirates (Earl Weaver, Orioles)	56,088
8-9-81	Municipal Stadium Cleveland	5-4 (N.L.)	Vida Blue, Giants (Rollie Fingers, Brewers)	Dallas Green, Phillies (Jim Frey, Royals)	72,086
7-13-82	Olympic Stadium Montreal	4-1 (N.L.)	Steve Rogers, Expos (Dennis Eckersley, Red Sox)	Tommy Lasorda, Dodgers (Billy Martin, Athletics)	59,057
7-6-83	Comiskey Park Chicago	13-3 (A.L.)	Dave Stieb, Blue Jays (Mario Soto, Reds)	Harvey Kuenn, Brewers (Whitey Herzog, Cardinals)	43,801

Date	Site	Score (Winner)	Winning pitcher (Losing pitcher)	Winning manager (Losing manager)	Att.
7-10-84	Candlestick Park San Francisco	3-1 (N.L.)	Charlie Lea, Expos (Dave Stieb, Blue Jays)	Paul Owens, Phillies (Joe Altobelli, Orioles)	57,756
7-16-85	Metrodome Minneapolis	6-1 (N.L.)	LaMarr Hoyt, Padres (Jack Morris, Tigers)	Dick Williams, Padres (Sparky Anderson, Tigers)	54,960
7-15-86	Astrodome Houston	3-2 (A.L.)	Roger Clemens, Red Sox (Dwight Gooden, Mets)	Dick Howser, Royals (Whitey Herzog, Cardinals)	45,774
7-14-87	Oak.-Alameda Co. Col. Oakland	2-0▲ (N.L.)	Lee Smith, Cubs (Jay Howell, Athletics)	Dave Johnson, Mets (John McNamara, Red Sox)	49,671
7-12-88	Riverfront Stadium Cincinnati	2-1 (A.L.)	Frank Viola, Twins (Dwight Gooden, Mets)	Tom Kelly, Twins (Whitey Herzog, Cardinals)	55,837
7-11-89	Anaheim Stadium Anaheim, Calif.	5-3 (A.L.)	Nolan Ryan, Rangers (John Smoltz, Braves)	Tony La Russa, Athletics (Tommy Lasorda, Dodgers)	64,036
7-10-90	Wrigley Field Chicago	2-0 (A.L.)	Bret Saberhagen, Royals (Jeff Brantley, Giants)	Tony La Russa, Athletics (Roger Craig, Giants)	39,071
7-9-91	SkyDome Toronto	4-2 (A.L.)	Jimmy Key, Blue Jays (Dennis Martinez, Expos)	Tony La Russa, Athletics (Lou Piniella, Reds)	52,383
7-14-92	Jack Murphy Stadium San Diego	13-6 (A.L.)	Kevin Brown, Rangers (Tom Glavine, Braves)	Tom Kelly, Twins (Bobby Cox, Braves)	59,372
7-13-93	Oriole Park at Camden Yards, Baltimore	9-3 (A.L.)	Jack McDowell, White Sox (John Burkett, Giants)	Cito Gaston, Blue Jays (Bobby Cox, Braves)	48,147
7-12-94	Three Rivers Stadium Pittsburgh	8-7§ (N.L.)	Doug Jones, Phillies (Jason Bere, White Sox)	Jim Fregosi, Phillies (Cito Gaston, Blue Jays)	59,568
7-11-95	Ballpark in Arlington Arlington, Texas	3-2 (N.L.)	Heathcliff Slocumb, Phillies (Steve Ontiveros, A's)	Felipe Alou, Expos (Buck Showalter, Yankees)	50,920
7-9-96	Veterans Stadium Philadelphia	6-0 (N.L.)	John Smoltz, Braves (Charles Nagy, Indians)	Bobby Cox, Braves (Mike Hargrove, Indians)	62,670
7-8-97	Jacobs Field Cleveland	3-1 (A.L.)	Jose Rosado, Royals (Shawn Estes, Giants)	Joe Torre, Yankees (Bobby Cox, Braves)	44,916
7-7-98	Coors Field Colorado	13-8 (A.L.)	Bartolo Colon, Indians (Ugueth Urbina, Expos)	Mike Hargrove, Indians (Jim Leyland, Marlins)	51,267
7-13-99	Fenway Park Boston	4-1 (A.L.)	Pedro Martinez, Red Sox (Curt Schilling, Phillies)	Joe Torre, Yankees (Bruce Bochy, Padres)	34,187
7-11-00	Turner Field Atlanta	6-3 (A.L.)	James Baldwin, White Sox (Al Leiter, Mets)	Joe Torre, Yankees (Bobby Cox, Braves)	51,323
7-10-01	Safeco Field Seattle	4-1 (A.L.)	Freddy Garcia, Mariners (Chan Ho Park, Dodgers)	Joe Torre, Yankees (Bobby Valentine, Mets)	47,364
7-9-02	Miller Park Milwaukee	7-7 (tie)		Joe Torre, Yankees (Bob Brenly, Diamondbacks)	41,871

*14 innings. †5 innings (rain). ‡12 innings. §10 innings. ∞15 innings. ▲13 innings.

AWARD WINNERS

AMERICAN LEAGUE

Year	Player	Team	Pos.	Points
1929—Al Simmons	Philadelphia	OF	40
1930—Joe Cronin	Washington	SS	52
1931—Lou Gehrig	New York	1B	40
1932—Jimmie Foxx	Philadelphia	1B	46
1933—Jimmie Foxx	Philadelphia	1B	49
1934—Lou Gehrig	New York	1B	51
1935—Hank Greenberg	Detroit	1B	64
1936—Lou Gehrig	New York	1B	55
1937—Charlie Gehringer	Detroit	2B	78
1938—Jimmie Foxx	Boston	1B	304
1939—Joe DiMaggio	New York	OF	280
1940—Hank Greenberg	Detroit	OF	292
1941—Joe DiMaggio	New York	OF	291
1942—Joe Gordon	New York	2B	270
1943—Spud Chandler	New York	P	246
1944—Bobby Doerr	Boston	2B	
1945—Eddie Mayo	Detroit	2B	

NATIONAL LEAGUE

Year	Player	Team	Pos.	Points
1929—No selection			
1930—Bill Terry	New York	1B	47
1931—Chuck Klein	Philadelphia	OF	40
1932—Chuck Klein	Philadelphia	OF	46
1933—Carl Hubbell	New York	P	64
1934—Dizzy Dean	St. Louis	P	57
1935—Arky Vaughan	Pittsburgh	SS	42
1936—Carl Hubbell	New York	P	61
1937—Joe Medwick	St. Louis	OF	70
1938—Ernie Lombardi	Cincinnati	C	229
1939—Bucky Walters	Cincinnati	P	303
1940—Frank McCormick	Cincinnati	1B	274
1941—Dolf Camilli	Brooklyn	1B	300
1942—Mort Cooper	St. Louis	P	263
1943—Stan Musial	St. Louis	OF	267
1944—Marty Marion	St. Louis	SS	
1945—Tommy Holmes	Boston	OF	

AMERICAN LEAGUE

Year	Player	Team	Pos.
1944—Bobby Doerr	Boston	2B
Hal Newhouser	Detroit	P
1945—Eddie Mayo	Detroit	2B
Hal Newhouser	Detroit	P
1946—No selections		
1947—No selections		
1948—Lou Boudreau	Cleveland	SS
Bob Lemon	Cleveland	P
1949—Ted Williams	Boston	OF
Ellis Kinder	Boston	P
1950—Phil Rizzuto	New York	SS
Bob Lemon	Cleveland	P
1951—Ferris Fain	Philadelphia	1B
Bob Feller	Cleveland	P
1952—Luke Easter	Cleveland	1B
Bobby Shantz	Philadelphia	P
1953—Al Rosen	Cleveland	3B
Bob Porterfield	Washington	P
1954—Bobby Avila	Cleveland	2B
Bob Lemon	Cleveland	P
1955—Al Kaline	Detroit	OF
Whitey Ford	New York	P
1956—Mickey Mantle	New York	OF
Billy Pierce	Chicago	P
1957—Ted Williams	Boston	OF
Billy Pierce	Chicago	P
1958—Jackie Jensen	Boston	OF
Bob Turley	New York	P
1959—Nellie Fox	Chicago	2B
Early Wynn	Chicago	P
1960—Roger Maris	New York	OF
Chuck Estrada	Baltimore	P
1961—Roger Maris	New York	OF
Whitey Ford	New York	P
1962—Mickey Mantle	New York	OF
Dick Donovan	Cleveland	P
1963—Al Kaline	Detroit	OF
Whitey Ford	New York	P
1964—Brooks Robinson	Baltimore	3B
Dean Chance	Los Angeles	P
1965—Tony Oliva	Minnesota	OF
Jim Grant	Minnesota	P
1966—Frank Robinson	Baltimore	OF
Jim Kaat	Minnesota	P

NATIONAL LEAGUE

Year	Player	Team	Pos.
1944—Marty Marion	St. Louis	SS
Bill Voiselle	New York	P
1945—Tommy Holmes	Boston	OF
Hank Borowy	Chicago	P
1946—No selections		
1947—No selections		
1948—Stan Musial	St. Louis	OF-1B
Johnny Sain	Boston	P
1949—Enos Slaughter	St. Louis	OF
Howard Pollet	St. Louis	P
1950—Ralph Kiner	Pittsburgh	OF
Jim Konstanty	Philadelphia	P
1951—Stan Musial	St. Louis	OF
Preacher Roe	Brooklyn	P
1952—Hank Sauer	Chicago	OF
Robin Roberts	Philadelphia	P
1953—Roy Campanella	Brooklyn	C
Warren Spahn	Milwaukee	P
1954—Willie Mays	New York	OF
Johnny Antonelli	New York	P
1955—Duke Snider	Brooklyn	OF
Robin Roberts	Philadelphia	P
1956—Hank Aaron	Milwaukee	OF
Don Newcombe	Brooklyn	P
1957—Stan Musial	St. Louis	1B
Warren Spahn	Milwaukee	P
1958—Ernie Banks	Chicago	SS
Warren Spahn	Milwaukee	P
1959—Ernie Banks	Chicago	SS
Sam Jones	San Francisco	P
1960—Dick Groat	Pittsburgh	SS
Vern Law	Pittsburgh	P
1961—Frank Robinson	Cincinnati	OF
Warren Spahn	Milwaukee	P
1962—Maury Wills	Los Angeles	SS
Don Drysdale	Los Angeles	P
1963—Hank Aaron	Milwaukee	OF
Sandy Koufax	Los Angeles	P
1964—Ken Boyer	St. Louis	3B
Sandy Koufax	Los Angeles	P
1965—Willie Mays	San Francisco	OF
Sandy Koufax	Los Angeles	P
1966—Roberto Clemente	Pittsburgh	OF
Sandy Koufax	Los Angeles	P

Year	Player	Team	Pos.	Year	Player	Team	Pos.
1967	Carl Yastrzemski	Boston	OF	1967	Orlando Cepeda	St. Louis	1B
	Jim Lonborg	Boston	P		Mike McCormick	San Francisco	P
1968	Ken Harrelson	Boston	OF	1968	Pete Rose	Cincinnati	OF
	Denny McLain	Detroit	P		Bob Gibson	St. Louis	P
1969	Harmon Killebrew	Minnesota	1B-3B	1969	Willie McCovey	San Francisco	1B
	Denny McLain	Detroit	P		Tom Seaver	New York	P
1970	Harmon Killebrew	Minnesota	3B	1970	Johnny Bench	Cincinnati	C
	Sam McDowell	Cleveland	P		Bob Gibson	St. Louis	P
1971	Tony Oliva	Minnesota	OF	1971	Joe Torre	St. Louis	3B
	Vida Blue	Oakland	P		Ferguson Jenkins	Chicago	P
1972	Dick Allen	Chicago	1B	1972	Billy Williams	Chicago	OF
	Wilbur Wood	Chicago	P		Steve Carlton	Philadelphia	P
1973	Reggie Jackson	Oakland	OF	1973	Bobby Bonds	San Francisco	OF
	Jim Palmer	Baltimore	P		Ron Bryant	San Francisco	P
1974	Jeff Burroughs	Texas	OF	1974	Lou Brock	St. Louis	OF
	Jim Hunter	Oakland	P		Mike Marshall	Los Angeles	P
1975	Fred Lynn	Boston	OF	1975	Joe Morgan	Cincinnati	2B
	Jim Palmer	Baltimore	P		Tom Seaver	New York	P
1976	Thurman Munson	New York	C	1976	George Foster	Cincinnati	OF
	Jim Palmer	Baltimore	P		Randy Jones	San Diego	P
1977	Rod Carew	Minnesota	1B	1977	George Foster	Cincinnati	OF
	Nolan Ryan	California	P		Steve Carlton	Philadelphia	P
1978	Jim Rice	Boston	OF	1978	Dave Parker	Pittsburgh	OF
	Ron Guidry	New York	P		Vida Blue	San Francisco	P
1979	Don Baylor	California	OF	1979	Keith Hernandez	St. Louis	1B
	Mike Flanagan	Baltimore	P		Joe Niekro	Houston	P
1980	George Brett	Kansas City	3B	1980	Mike Schmidt	Philadelphia	3B
	Steve Stone	Baltimore	P		Steve Carlton	Philadelphia	P
1981	Tony Armas	Oakland	OF	1981	Andre Dawson	Montreal	OF
	Jack Morris	Detroit	P		Fernando Valenzuela	Los Angeles	P
1982	Robin Yount	Milwaukee	SS	1982	Dale Murphy	Atlanta	OF
	Dave Stieb	Toronto	P		Steve Carlton	Philadelphia	P
1983	Cal Ripken Jr.	Baltimore	SS	1983	Dale Murphy	Atlanta	OF
	LaMarr Hoyt	Chicago	P		John Denny	Philadelphia	P
1984	Don Mattingly	New York	1B	1984	Ryne Sandberg	Chicago	2B
	Willie Hernandez	Detroit	P		Rick Sutcliffe	Chicago	P
1985	Don Mattingly	New York	1B	1985	Willie McGee	St. Louis	OF
	Bret Saberhagen	Kansas City	P		Dwight Gooden	New York	P
1986	Don Mattingly	New York	1B	1986	Mike Schmidt	Philadelphia	3B
	Roger Clemens	Boston	P		Mike Scott	Houston	P
1987	George Bell	Toronto	OF	1987	Andre Dawson	Chicago	OF
	Jimmy Key	Toronto	P		Rick Sutcliffe	Chicago	P
1988	Jose Canseco	Oakland	OF	1988	Andy Van Slyke	Pittsburgh	OF
	Frank Viola	Minnesota	P		Orel Hershiser	Los Angeles	P
1989	Ruben Sierra	Texas	OF	1989	Kevin Mitchell	San Francisco	OF
	Bret Saberhagen	Kansas City	P		Mark Davis	San Diego	P
1990	Cecil Fielder	Detroit	1B	1990	Barry Bonds	Pittsburgh	OF
	Bob Welch	Oakland	P		Doug Drabek	Pittsburgh	P
1991	Cal Ripken Jr.	Baltimore	SS	1991	Barry Bonds	Pittsburgh	OF
	Roger Clemens	Boston	P		Tom Glavine	Atlanta	P

PITCHER OF THE YEAR

AMERICAN LEAGUE

Year	Pitcher	Team
1992	Dennis Eckersley	Oakland
1993	Jack McDowell	Chicago
1994	Jimmy Key	New York
1995	Randy Johnson	Seattle
1996	Pat Hentgen	Toronto
1997	Roger Clemens	Toronto
1998	Roger Clemens	Toronto
1999	Pedro Martinez	Boston
2000	Pedro Martinez	Boston
2001	Roger Clemens	New York
2002	Barry Zito	Oakland

NATIONAL LEAGUE

Year	Pitcher	Team
1992	Greg Maddux	Chicago
1993	Greg Maddux	Atlanta
1994	Greg Maddux	Atlanta
1995	Greg Maddux	Atlanta
1996	John Smoltz	Atlanta
1997	Pedro Martinez	Montreal
1998	Kevin Brown	San Diego
1999	Mike Hampton	Houston
2000	Tom Glavine	Atlanta
2001	Curt Schilling	Arizona
2002	Curt Schilling	Arizona

HISTORY *Award winners*

ROOKIE OF THE YEAR

1946—Combined selection—Del Ennis, Philadelphia N.L., OF
1947—Combined selection—Jackie Robinson, Brooklyn N.L., 1B
1948—Combined selection—Richie Ashburn, Philadelphia N.L., OF

AMERICAN LEAGUE

Year	Player	Team	Pos.
1949	Roy Sievers	St. Louis	OF
1950	Whitey Ford	New York	P
1951	Minnie Minoso	Chicago	OF
1952	Clint Courtney	St. Louis	C
1953	Harvey Kuenn	Detroit	SS
1954	Bob Grim	New York	P
1955	Herb Score	Cleveland	P
1956	Luis Aparicio	Chicago	SS
1957	Tony Kubek	New York	IF-OF
	(No pitcher named)		
1958	Albie Pearson	Washington	OF
	Ryne Duren	New York	P
1959	Bob Allison	Washington	OF
1960	Ron Hansen	Baltimore	SS
1961	Dick Howser	Kansas City	SS
	Don Schwall	Boston	P
1962	Tom Tresh	New York	OF-SS
1963	Pete Ward	Chicago	3B
	Gary Peters	Chicago	P
1964	Tony Oliva	Minnesota	OF
	Wally Bunker	Baltimore	P
1965	Curt Blefary	Baltimore	OF
	Marcelino Lopez	California	P
1966	Tommie Agee	Chicago	OF
	Jim Nash	Kansas City	P
1967	Rod Carew	Minnesota	2B
	Tom Phoebus	Baltimore	P
1968	Del Unser	Washington	OF
	Stan Bahnsen	New York	P
1969	Carlos May	Chicago	OF
	Mike Nagy	Boston	P
1970	Roy Foster	Cleveland	OF
	Bert Blyleven	Minnesota	P
1971	Chris Chambliss	Cleveland	1B
	Bill Parsons	Milwaukee	P
1972	Carlton Fisk	Boston	C
	Dick Tidrow	Cleveland	P
1973	Al Bumbry	Baltimore	OF
	Steve Busby	Kansas City	P
1974	Mike Hargrove	Texas	1B
	Frank Tanana	California	P
1975	Fred Lynn	Boston	OF
	Dennis Eckersley	Cleveland	P
1976	Butch Wynegar	Minnesota	C
	Mark Fidrych	Detroit	P
1977	Mitchell Page	Oakland	OF
	Dave Rozema	Detroit	P
1978	Paul Molitor	Milwaukee	2B
	Rich Gale	Kansas City	P
1979	Pat Putnam	Texas	1B
	Mark Clear	California	P
1980	Joe Charboneau	Cleveland	OF
	Britt Burns	Chicago	P
1981	Rich Gedman	Boston	C
	Dave Righetti	New York	P
1982	Cal Ripken Jr.	Baltimore	SS-3B
	Ed Vande Berg	Seattle	P
1983	Ron Kittle	Chicago	OF
	Mike Boddicker	Baltimore	P
1984	Alvin Davis	Seattle	1B
	Mark Langston	Seattle	P
1985	Ozzie Guillen	Chicago	SS
	Teddy Higuera	Milwaukee	P
1986	Jose Canseco	Oakland	OF
	Mark Eichhorn	Toronto	P
1987	Mark McGwire	Oakland	1B
	Mike Henneman	Detroit	P
1988	Walt Weiss	Oakland	SS
	Bryan Harvey	California	P

NATIONAL LEAGUE

Year	Player	Team	Pos.
1949	Don Newcombe	Brooklyn	P
1950	Combined A.L.-N.L. selection		
1951	Willie Mays	New York	OF
1952	Joe Black	Brooklyn	P
1953	Jim Gilliam	Brooklyn	2B
1954	Wally Moon	St. Louis	OF
1955	Bill Virdon	St. Louis	OF
1956	Frank Robinson	Cincinnati	OF
1957	Ed Bouchee	Philadelphia	1B
	Jack Sanford	Philadelphia	P
1958	Orlando Cepeda	San Francisco	1B
	Carlton Willey	Milwaukee	P
1959	Willie McCovey	San Francisco	1B
1960	Frank Howard	Los Angeles	OF
1961	Billy Williams	Chicago	OF
	Ken Hunt	Cincinnati	P
1962	Ken Hubbs	Chicago	2B
1963	Pete Rose	Cincinnati	2B
	Ray Culp	Philadelphia	P
1964	Dick Allen	Philadelphia	3B
	Billy McCool	Cincinnati	P
1965	Joe Morgan	Houston	2B
	Frank Linzy	San Francisco	P
1966	Tommy Helms	Cincinnati	3B
	Don Sutton	Los Angeles	P
1967	Lee May	Cincinnati	1B
	Dick Hughes	St. Louis	P
1968	Johnny Bench	Cincinnati	C
	Jerry Koosman	New York	P
1969	Coco Laboy	Montreal	3B
	Tom Griffin	Houston	P
1970	Bernie Carbo	Cincinnati	OF
	Carl Morton	Montreal	P
1971	Earl Williams	Atlanta	C
	Reggie Cleveland	St. Louis	P
1972	Dave Rader	San Francisco	C
	Jon Matlack	New York	P
1973	Gary Matthews	San Francisco	OF
	Steve Rogers	Montreal	P
1974	Greg Gross	Houston	OF
	John D'Acquisto	San Francisco	P
1975	Gary Carter	Montreal	OF-C
	John Montefusco	San Francisco	P
1976	Larry Herndon	San Francisco	OF
	Butch Metzger	San Diego	P
1977	Andre Dawson	Montreal	OF
	Bob Owchinko	San Diego	P
1978	Bob Horner	Atlanta	3B
	Don Robinson	Pittsburgh	P
1979	Jeff Leonard	Houston	OF
	Rick Sutcliffe	Los Angeles	P
1980	Lonnie Smith	Philadelphia	OF
	Bill Gullickson	Montreal	P
1981	Tim Raines	Montreal	OF
	Fernando Valenzuela	Los Angeles	P
1982	Johnny Ray	Pittsburgh	2B
	Steve Bedrosian	Atlanta	P
1983	Darryl Strawberry	New York	OF
	Craig McMurtry	Atlanta	P
1984	Juan Samuel	Philadelphia	2B
	Dwight Gooden	New York	P
1985	Vince Coleman	St. Louis	OF
	Tom Browning	Cincinnati	P
1986	Robby Thompson	San Francisco	2B
	Todd Worrell	St. Louis	P
1987	Benito Santiago	San Diego	C
	Mike Dunne	Pittsburgh	P
1988	Mark Grace	Chicago	1B
	Tim Belcher	Los Angeles	P

Year	Player	Team	Pos.	Year	Player	Team	Pos.
1989—	Craig Worthington	Baltimore	3B	1989—	Jerome Walton	Chicago	OF
	Tom Gordon	Kansas City	P		Andy Benes	San Diego	P
1990—	Sandy Alomar Jr.	Cleveland	C	1990—	David Justice	Atlanta	OF
	Kevin Appier	Kansas City	P		Mike Harkey	Chicago	P
1991—	Chuck Knoblauch	Minnesota	2B	1991—	Jeff Bagwell	Houston	1B
	Juan Guzman	Toronto	P		Al Osuna	Houston	P
1992—	Pat Listach	Milwaukee	SS	1992—	Eric Karros	Los Angeles	1B
	Cal Eldred	Milwaukee	P		Tim Wakefield	Pittsburgh	P
1993—	Tim Salmon	California	OF	1993—	Mike Piazza	Los Angeles	C
	Aaron Sele	Boston	P		Kirk Rueter	Montreal	P
1994—	Bob Hamelin	Kansas City	DH	1994—	Raul Mondesi	Los Angeles	OF
	Brian Anderson	California	P		Steve Trachsel	Chicago	P
1995—	Garret Anderson	California	OF	1995—	Chipper Jones	Atlanta	3B
	Julian Tavarez	Cleveland	P		Hideo Nomo	Los Angeles	P
1996—	Derek Jeter	New York	SS	1996—	Jason Kendall	Pittsburgh	C
	James Baldwin	Chicago	P		Alan Benes	St. Louis	P
1997—	Nomar Garciaparra	Boston	SS	1997—	Scott Rolen	Philadelphia	3B
	Jason Dickson	Anaheim	P		Matt Morris	St. Louis	P
1998—	Ben Grieve	Oakland	OF	1998—	Todd Helton	Colorado	1B
	Rolando Arrojo	Tampa Bay	P		Kerry Wood	Chicago	P
1999—	Carlos Beltran	Kansas City	OF	1999—	Preston Wilson	Florida	OF
	Tim Hudson	Oakland	P		Scott Williamson	Cincinnati	P
2000—	Mark Quinn	Kansas City	OF-DH	2000—	Rafael Furcal	Atlanta	2B-SS
	Kazuhiro Sasaki	Seattle	P		Rick Ankiel	St. Louis	P
2001—	Ichiro Suzuki	Seattle	OF	2001—	Albert Pujols	St. Louis	O-3-1B
	C.C. Sabathia	Cleveland	P		Roy Oswalt	Houston	P
2002—	Eric Hinske	Toronto	3B	2002—	Brad Wilkerson	Montreal	OF-1B
	Rodrigo Lopez	Baltimore	P		Jason Jennings	Colorado	P

FIREMAN OF THE YEAR

AMERICAN LEAGUE

Year	Pitcher	Team
1960—	Mike Fornieles	Boston
1961—	Luis Arroyo	New York
1962—	Dick Radatz	Boston
1963—	Stu Miller	Baltimore
1964—	Dick Radatz	Boston
1965—	Eddie Fisher	Chicago
1966—	Jack Aker	Kansas City
1967—	Minnie Rojas	California
1968—	Wilbur Wood	Chicago
1969—	Ron Perranoski	Minnesota
1970—	Ron Perranoski	Minnesota
1971—	Ken Sanders	Milwaukee
1972—	Sparky Lyle	New York
1973—	John Hiller	Detroit
1974—	Terry Forster	Chicago
1975—	Rich Gossage	Chicago
1976—	Bill Campbell	Minnesota
1977—	Bill Campbell	Boston
1978—	Rich Gossage	New York
1979—	Mike Marshall	Minnesota
	Jim Kern	Texas
1980—	Dan Quisenberry	Kansas City
1981—	Rollie Fingers	Milwaukee
1982—	Dan Quisenberry	Kansas City
1983—	Dan Quisenberry	Kansas City
1984—	Dan Quisenberry	Kansas City
1985—	Dan Quisenberry	Kansas City
1986—	Dave Righetti	New York
1987—	Dave Righetti	New York
	Jeff Reardon	Minnesota
1988—	Dennis Eckersley	Oakland
1989—	Jeff Russell	Texas
1990—	Bobby Thigpen	Chicago
1991—	Dennis Eckersley	Oakland
	Bryan Harvey	California
1992—	Dennis Eckersley	Oakland
1993—	Jeff Montgomery	Kansas City
1994—	Lee Smith	Baltimore
1995—	Jose Mesa	Cleveland

NATIONAL LEAGUE

Year	Pitcher	Team
1960—	Lindy McDaniel	St. Louis
1961—	Stu Miller	San Francisco
1962—	Roy Face	Pittsburgh
1963—	Lindy McDaniel	Chicago
1964—	Al McBean	Pittsburgh
1965—	Ted Abernathy	Chicago
1966—	Phil Regan	Los Angeles
1967—	Ted Abernathy	Cincinnati
1968—	Phil Regan	L.A.-Chicago
1969—	Wayne Granger	Cincinnati
1970—	Wayne Granger	Cincinnati
1971—	Dave Giusti	Pittsburgh
1972—	Clay Carroll	Cincinnati
1973—	Mike Marshall	Montreal
1974—	Mike Marshall	Los Angeles
1975—	Al Hrabosky	St. Louis
1976—	Rawly Eastwick	Cincinnati
1977—	Rollie Fingers	San Diego
1978—	Rollie Fingers	San Diego
1979—	Bruce Sutter	Chicago
1980—	Rollie Fingers	San Diego
	Tom Hume	Cincinnati
1981—	Bruce Sutter	St. Louis
1982—	Bruce Sutter	St. Louis
1983—	Al Holland	Philadelphia
	Lee Smith	Chicago
1984—	Bruce Sutter	St. Louis
1985—	Jeff Reardon	Montreal
1986—	Todd Worrell	St. Louis
1987—	Steve Bedrosian	Philadelphia
1988—	John Franco	Cincinnati
1989—	Mark Davis	San Diego
1990—	John Franco	New York
1991—	Lee Smith	St. Louis
1992—	Doug Jones	Houston
	Lee Smith	St. Louis
1993—	Randy Myers	Chicago
1994—	John Franco	New York
1995—	Randy Myers	Chicago

AMERICAN LEAGUE			NATIONAL LEAGUE		
Year	**Pitcher**	**Team**	**Year**	**Pitcher**	**Team**
1996—John Wetteland		New York	1996—Trevor Hoffman		San Diego
1997—Mariano Rivera		New York	1997—Jeff Shaw		Cincinnati
1998—Tom Gordon		Boston	1998—Trevor Hoffman		San Diego
1999—Mariano Rivera		New York	1999—Ugueth Urbina		Montreal
2000—Todd Jones		Detroit	2000—Antonio Alfonseca		Florida
2001—Mariano Rivera		New York	2001—Armando Benitez		New York
				Robb Nen	San Francisco
2002—Billy Koch		Oakland	2002—John Smoltz		Atlanta

COMEBACK PLAYER OF THE YEAR

AMERICAN LEAGUE			NATIONAL LEAGUE		
Year	**Pitcher**	**Team**	**Year**	**Pitcher**	**Team**
1965—Norm Cash		Detroit	1965— Vernon Law		Pittsburgh
1966—Boog Powell		Baltimore	1966— Phil Regan		Los Angeles
1967—Dean Chance		Minnesota	1967— Mike McCormick		San Francisco
1968—Ken Harrelson		Boston	1968— Alex Johnson		Cincinnati
1969—Tony Conigliaro		Boston	1969— Tommie Agee		New York
1970—Clyde Wright		California	1970— Jim Hickman		Chicago
1971—Norm Cash		Detroit	1971— Al Downing		Los Angeles
1972—Luis Tiant		Boston	1972— Bobby Tolan		Cincinnati
1973—John Hiller		Detroit	1973— Dave Johnson		Atlanta
1974—Ferguson Jenkins		Texas	1974— Jim Wynn		Los Angeles
1975—Boog Powell		Cleveland	1975— Randy Jones		San Diego
1976—Dock Ellis		New York	1976— Tommy John		Los Angeles
1977—Eric Soderholm		Chicago	1977— Willie McCovey		San Francisco
1978—Mike Caldwell		Milwaukee	1978— Willie Stargell		Pittsburgh
1979—Willie Horton		Seattle	1979— Lou Brock		St. Louis
1980—Matt Keough		Oakland	1980— Jerry Reuss		Los Angeles
1981—Richie Zisk		Seattle	1981— Bob Knepper		Houston
1982—Andre Thornton		Cleveland	1982— Joe Morgan		San Francisco
1983—Alan Trammell		Detroit	1983— John Denny		Philadelphia
1984—Dave Kingman		Oakland	1984— Joaquin Andujar		St. Louis
1985—Gorman Thomas		Seattle	1985— Rick Reuschel		Pittsburgh
1986—John Candelaria		California	1986— Ray Knight		New York
1987—Bret Saberhagen		Kansas City	1987— Rick Sutcliffe		Chicago
1988—Storm Davis		Oakland	1988— Tim Leary		Los Angeles
1989—Bert Blyleven		California	1989— Lonnie Smith		Atlanta
1990—Dave Winfield		California	1990— John Tudor		St. Louis
1991—Jose Guzman		Texas	1991— Terry Pendleton		Atlanta
1992—Rick Sutcliffe		Baltimore	1992— Gary Sheffield		San Diego
1993—Bo Jackson		Chicago	1993— Andres Galarraga		Colorado
1994—Jose Canseco		Texas	1994— Tim Wallach		Los Angeles
1995—Tim Wakefield		Boston	1995— Ron Gant		Cincinnati
1996—Kevin Elster		Texas	1996— Eric Davis		Cincinnati
1997—David Justice		Cleveland	1997— Darren Daulton		Phi.-Fla.
1998—Bret Saberhagen		Boston	1998— Greg Vaughn		San Diego
1999—John Jaha		Oakland	1999— Rickey Henderson		New York
2000—Frank Thomas		Chicago	2000— Andres Galarraga		Atlanta
2001—Ruben Sierra		Texas	2001— Matt Morris		St. Louis
2002—Tim Salmon		Anaheim	2002— Mike Lieberthal		Philadelphia

MAJOR LEAGUE PLAYER OF THE YEAR

Year	**Player**	**Team**	**Year**	**Player**	**Team**	**Year**	**Player**	**Team**
1936—Carl Hubbell		New York N.L.	1954—Willie Mays		New York N.L.	1971—Joe Torre		St. Louis N.L.
1937—Johnny Allen		Cleveland A.L.	1955—Duke Snider		Brooklyn N.L.	1972—Billy Williams		Chicago N.L.
1938—Johnny Vander Meer		Cincinnati N.L.	1956—Mickey Mantle		New York A.L.	1973—Reggie Jackson		Oakland A.L.
1939—Joe DiMaggio		New York A.L.	1957—Ted Williams		Boston A.L.	1974—Lou Brock		St. Louis N.L.
1940—Bob Feller		Cleveland A.L.	1958—Bob Turley		New York A.L.	1975—Joe Morgan		Cincinnati N.L.
1941—Ted Williams		Boston A.L.	1959—Early Wynn		Chicago A.L.	1976—Joe Morgan		Cincinnati N.L.
1942—Ted Williams		Boston A.L.	1960—Bill Mazeroski		Pittsburgh N.L.	1977—Rod Carew		Minnesota A.L.
1943—Spud Chandler		New York A.L.	1961—Roger Maris		New York A.L.	1978—Ron Guidry		New York A.L.
1944—Marty Marion		St. Louis N.L.	1962—Maury Wills		Los Angeles N.L.	1979—Willie Stargell		Pittsburgh N.L.
1945—Hal Newhouser		Detroit A.L.	Don Drysdale		Los Angeles N.L.	1980—George Brett		Kansas City A.L.
1946—Stan Musial		St. Louis N.L.	1963—Sandy Koufax		Los Angeles N.L.	1981—Fernando Valenzuela		Los Angeles N.L.
1947—Ted Williams		Boston A.L.	1964—Ken Boyer		St. Louis N.L.	1982—Robin Yount		Milwaukee A.L.
1948—Lou Boudreau		Cleveland A.L.	1965—Sandy Koufax		Los Angeles N.L.	1983—Cal Ripken Jr.		Baltimore A.L.
1949—Ted Williams		Boston A.L.	1966—Frank Robinson		Baltimore A.L.	1984—Ryne Sandberg		Chicago N.L.
1950—Phil Rizzuto		New York A.L.	1967—Carl Yastrzemski		Boston A.L.	1985—Don Mattingly		New York A.L.
1951—Stan Musial		St. Louis N.L.	1968—Denny McLain		Detroit A.L.	1986—Roger Clemens		Boston A.L.
1952—Robin Roberts		Philadelphia N.L.	1969—Willie McCovey		San Francisco N.L.	1987—George Bell		Toronto A.L.
1953—Al Rosen		Cleveland A.L.	1970—Johnny Bench		Cincinnati N.L.	1988—Orel Hershiser		Los Angeles N.L.

Year	Player	Team	Year	Player	Team	Year	Player	Team
1989—Kevin Mitchell	San Francisco N.L.		1994—Jeff Bagwell	Houston N.L.		1999—Rafael Palmeiro	Texas A.L.	
1990—Barry Bonds	Pittsburgh N.L.		1995—Albert Belle	Cleveland A.L.		2000—Carlos Delgado	Toronto A.L.	
1991—Cal Ripken Jr.	Baltimore A.L.		1996—Alex Rodriguez	Seattle A.L.		2001—Barry Bonds	San Francisco N.L.	
1992—Gary Sheffield	San Diego N.L.		1997—Ken Griffey Jr.	Seattle A.L.		2002— Alex Rodriguez	Texas A.L.	
1993—Frank Thomas	Chicago A.L.		1998—Sammy Sosa	Chicago N.L.				

MAJOR LEAGUE MANAGER OF THE YEAR

Year	Manager	Team	Year	Manager	Team	Year	Manager	Team
1936—Joe McCarthy	New York A.L.		1965—Sam Mele	Minnesota A.L.			Don Zimmer	Chicago N.L.
1937—Bill McKechnie	Boston N.L.		1966—Hank Bauer	Baltimore A.L.		1990—Jeff Torborg	Chicago A.L.
1938—Joe McCarthy	New York A.L.		1967—Dick Williams	Boston A.L.			Jim Leyland	Pittsburgh N.L.
1939—Leo Durocher	Brooklyn N.L.		1968—Mayo Smith	Detroit A.L.		1991—Tom Kelly	Minnesota A.L.
1940—Bill McKechnie	Cincinnati N.L.		1969—Gil Hodges	New York N.L.			Bobby Cox	Atlanta N.L.
1941—Billy Southworth	St. Louis N.L.		1970—Danny Murtaugh	Pittsburgh N.L.		1992—Tony La Russa	Oakland A.L.
1942—Billy Southworth	St. Louis N.L.		1971—Charlie Fox	San Francisco N.L.			Jim Leyland	Pittsburgh N.L.
1943—Joe McCarthy	New York A.L.		1972—Chuck Tanner	Chicago A.L.		1993—Johnny Oates	Baltimore A.L.
1944—Luke Sewell	St. Louis A.L.		1973—Gene Mauch	Montreal N.L.			Bobby Cox	Atlanta N.L.
1945—Ossie Bluege	Washington A.L.		1974—Bill Virdon	New York A.L.		1994—Buck Showalter	New York A.L.
1946—Eddie Dyer	St. Louis N.L.		1975—Darrell Johnson	Boston A.L.			Felipe Alou	Montreal N.L.
1947—Bucky Harris	New York A.L.		1976—Danny Ozark	Philadelphia N.L.		1995—Mike Hargrove	Cleveland A.L.
1948—Bill Meyer	Pittsburgh N.L.		1977—Earl Weaver	Baltimore A.L.			Don Baylor	Colorado N.L.
1949—Casey Stengel	New York A.L.		1978—George Bamberger	Milwaukee A.L.		1996—Johnny Oates	Texas A.L.
1950—Red Rolfe	Detroit A.L.		1979—Earl Weaver	Baltimore A.L.			Bruce Bochy	San Diego N.L.
1951—Leo Durocher	New York N.L.		1980—Bill Virdon	Houston N.L.		1997—Dave Johnson	Baltimore A.L.
1952—Eddie Stanky	St. Louis N.L.		1981—Billy Martin	Oakland A.L.			Dusty Baker	San Fran. N.L.
1953—Casey Stengel	New York A.L.		1982—Whitey Herzog	St. Louis N.L.		1998—Joe Torre	New York A.L.
1954—Leo Durocher	New York N.L.		1983—Tony La Russa	Chicago A.L.			Bruce Bochy	San Diego N.L.
1955—Walter Alston	Brooklyn N.L.		1984—Jim Frey	Chicago N.L.		1999—Jimy Williams	Boston A.L.
1956—Birdie Tebbetts	Cincinnati N.L.		1985—Bobby Cox	Toronto A.L.			Bobby Cox	Atlanta N.L.
1957—Fred Hutchinson	St. Louis N.L.		1986—John McNamara	Boston A.L.		2000—Jerry Manuel	Chicago A.L.
1958—Casey Stengel	New York A.L.			Hal Lanier	Houston N.L.			Dusty Baker	San Fran. N.L.
1959—Walter Alston	Los Angeles N.L.		1987—Sparky Anderson	Detroit A.L.		2001—Lou Piniella	Seattle A.L.
1960—Danny Murtaugh	Pittsburgh N.L.			Buck Rodgers	Montreal N.L.			Larry Bowa	Philadelphia N.L.
1961—Ralph Houk	New York A.L.		1988—Tony La Russa	Oakland A.L.		2002—Mike Scioscia	Anaheim A.L.
1962—Bill Rigney	Los Angeles A.L.			Tommy Lasorda	L.A. N.L. (tie)			Bobby Cox	Atlanta N.L.
1963—Walter Alston	Los Angeles N.L.			Jim Leyland	Pit. N.L. (tie)				
1964—Johnny Keane	St. Louis N.L.		1989—Frank Robinson	Baltimore A.L.				

MAJOR LEAGUE EXECUTIVE OF THE YEAR

Year	Executive	Team	Year	Executive	Team	Year	Executive	Team
1936—Branch Rickey	St. Louis N.L.		1959—Buzzie Bavasi	Los Angeles N.L.		1982—Harry Dalton	Milwaukee A.L.
1937—Ed Barrow	New York A.L.		1960—George Weiss	New York A.L.		1983—Hank Peters	Baltimore A.L.
1938—Warren Giles	Cincinnati N.L.		1961—Dan Topping	New York A.L.		1984—Dallas Green	Chicago N.L.
1939—Larry MacPhail	Brooklyn N.L.		1962—Fred Haney	Los Angeles A.L.		1985—John Schuerholz	Kansas City A.L.
1940—Walter Briggs Sr.	Detroit A.L.		1963—Bing Devine	St. Louis N.L.		1986—Frank Cashen	New York N.L.
1941—Ed Barrow	New York A.L.		1964—Bing Devine	St. Louis N.L.		1987—Al Rosen	San Francisco N.L.
1942—Branch Rickey	St. Louis N.L.		1965—Cal Griffith	Minnesota A.L.		1988—Fred Claire	Los Angeles N.L.
1943—Clark Griffith	Washington A.L.		1966—Lee MacPhail	Commissioner's Off.		1989—Roland Hemond	Baltimore A.L.
1944—Billy DeWitt	St. Louis A.L.		1967—Dick O'Connell	Boston A.L.		1990—Bob Quinn	Cincinnati N.L.
1945—Phil Wrigley	Chicago N.L.		1968—Jim Campbell	Detroit A.L.		1991—Andy MacPhail	Minnesota A.L.
1946—Tom Yawkey	Boston A.L.		1969—John Murphy	New York N.L.		1992—Dan Duquette	Montreal N.L.
1947—Branch Rickey	Brooklyn N.L.		1970—Harry Dalton	Baltimore A.L.		1993—Lee Thomas	Philadelphia N.L.
1948—Bill Veeck	Cleveland A.L.		1971—Cedric Tallis	Kansas City A.L.		1994—John Hart	Cleveland A.L.
1949—Bob Carpenter	Philadelphia N.L.		1972—Roland Hemond	Chicago A.L.		1995—John Hart	Cleveland A.L.
1950—George Weiss	New York A.L.		1973—Bob Howsam	Cincinnati N.L.		1996—Doug Melvin	Texas A.L.
1951—George Weiss	New York A.L.		1974—Gabe Paul	New York A.L.		1997—Cam Bonifay	Pittsburgh N.L.
1952—George Weiss	New York A.L.		1975—Dick O'Connell	Boston A.L.		1998—Gerry Hunsicker	Houston N.L.
1953—Lou Perini	Milwaukee N.L.		1976—Joe Burke	Kansas City A.L.		1999—Billy Beane	Oakland A.L.
1954—Horace Stoneham	New York N.L.		1977—Bill Veeck	Chicago A.L.		2000—Walt Jocketty	St. Louis N.L.
1955—Walter O'Malley	Brooklyn N.L.		1978—Spec Richardson	San Francisco N.L.		2001—Pat Gillick	Seattle A.L.
1956—Gabe Paul	Cincinnati N.L.		1979—Hank Peters	Baltimore A.L.		2002—Terry Ryan	Minnesota A.L.
1957—Frank Lane	St. Louis N.L.		1980—Tal Smith	Houston N.L.				
1958—Joe Brown	Pittsburgh N.L.		1981—John McHale	Montreal N.L.				

1925

1B— Jim Bottomley, St. Louis N.L.
2B— Rogers Hornsby, St. Louis N.L.
SS— Glenn Wright, Pittsburgh N.L.
3B— Pie Traynor, Pittsburgh N.L.
OF— Kiki Cuyler, Pittsburgh N.L.
OF— Max Carey, Pittsburgh N.L.
OF— Goose Goslin, Washington A.L.
C— Mickey Cochrane, Phil. A.L.
P— Walter Johnson, Washington A.L.
P— Ed Rommel, Philadelphia A.L.
P— Dazzy Vance, Brooklyn N.L.

1926

1B— George Burns, Cleveland A.L.
2B— Rogers Hornsby, St. Louis N.L.
SS— Joe Sewell, Cleveland A.L.
3B— Pie Traynor, Pittsburgh N.L.
OF— Goose Goslin, Washington A.L.
OF— John Mostil, Chicago A.L.
OF— Babe Ruth, New York A.L.
C— Bob O'Farrell, St. Louis N.L.
P— Herb Pennock, New York A.L.
P— George Uhle, Cleveland A.L.
P— Grover Alexander, St. Louis N.L.

1927

1B— Lou Gehrig, New York A.L.
2B— Rogers Hornsby, New York N.L.
SS— Travis Jackson, New York N.L.
3B— Pie Traynor, Pittsburgh N.L.
OF— Babe Ruth, New York A.L.
OF— Al Simmons, Philadelphia A.L.
OF— Paul Waner, Pittsburgh N.L.
C— Gabby Hartnett, Chicago N.L.
P— Charley Root, Chicago N.L.
P— Ted Lyons, Chicago A.L.

1928

1B— Lou Gehrig, New York A.L.
2B— Rogers Hornsby, Boston N.L.
SS— Travis Jackson, New York N.L.
3B— Fred Lindstrom, New York N.L.
OF— Babe Ruth, New York A.L.
OF— Heinie Manush, St. Louis A.L.
OF— Paul Waner, Pittsburgh N.L.
C— Mickey Cochrane, Phil. A.L.
P— Lefty Grove, Philadelphia A.L.
P— Waite Hoyt, New York A.L.

1929

1B— Jimmie Foxx, Philadelphia A.L.
2B— Rogers Hornsby, Chicago N.L.
SS— Travis Jackson, New York N.L.
3B— Pie Traynor, Pittsburgh, N.L.
OF— Al Simmons, Philadelphia A.L.
OF— Hack Wilson, Chicago N.L.
OF— Babe Ruth, New York A.L.
C— Mickey Cochrane, Phil. A.L.
P— Lefty Grove, Philadelphia A.L.
P— Burleigh Grimes, Pittsburgh N.L.

1930

1B— Bill Terry, New York N.L.
2B— Frank Frisch, St. Louis N.L.
SS— Joe Cronin, Washington A.L.
3B— Fred Lindstrom, New York N.L.
OF— Al Simmons, Philadelphia A.L.
OF— Hack Wilson, Chicago N.L.
OF— Babe Ruth, New York A.L.
C— Mickey Cochrane, Phil. A.L.
P— Lefty Grove, Philadelphia A.L.
P— Wes Ferrell, Cleveland A.L.

1931

1B— Lou Gehrig, New York A.L.
2B— Frank Frisch, St. Louis N.L.
SS— Joe Cronin, Washington A.L.
3B— Pie Traynor, Pittsburgh N.L.
OF— Al Simmons, Philadelphia A.L.
OF— Earl Averill, Cleveland A.L.
OF— Babe Ruth, New York A.L.
C— Mickey Cochrane, Phil. A.L.
P— Lefty Grove, Philadelphia A.L.
P— George Earnshaw, Phil. A.L.

1932

1B— Jimmie Foxx, Philadelphia A.L.
2B— Tony Lazzeri, New York A.L.
SS— Joe Cronin, Washington A.L.
3B— Pie Traynor, Pittsburgh N.L.
OF— Lefty O'Doul, Brooklyn N.L.
OF— Earl Averill, Cleveland A.L.
OF— Chuck Klein, Philadelphia N.L.
C— Bill Dickey, New York A.L.
P— Lefty Grove, Philadelphia A.L.
P— Lon Warneke, Chicago N.L.

1933

1B— Jimmie Foxx, Philadelphia A.L.
2B— Charley Gehringer, Detroit A.L.
SS— Joe Cronin, Washington A.L.
3B— Pie Traynor, Pittsburgh N.L.
OF— Al Simmons, Chicago A.L.
OF— Wally Berger, Boston N.L.
OF— Chuck Klein, Philadelphia N.L.
C— Bill Dickey, New York A.L.
P— Alvin Crowder, Washington A.L.
P— Carl Hubbell, New York N.L.

1934

1B— Lou Gehrig, New York A.L.
2B— Charley Gehringer, Detroit A.L.
SS— Joe Cronin, Washington A.L.
3B— Mike Higgins, Philadelphia A.L.
OF— Al Simmons, Chicago A.L.
OF— Earl Averill, Cleveland A.L.
OF— Mel Ott, New York N.L.
C— Mickey Cochrane, Detroit A.L.
P— Lefty Gomez, New York A.L.
P— Schoolboy Rowe, Detroit A.L.
P— Dizzy Dean, St. Louis N.L.

1935

1B— Hank Greenberg, Detroit A.L.
2B— Charley Gehringer, Detroit A.L.
SS— Arky Vaughan, Pittsburgh N.L.
3B— Pepper Martin, St. Louis N.L.
OF— Joe Medwick, St. Louis N.L.
OF— Doc Cramer, Philadelphia A.L.
OF— Mel Ott, New York N.L.
C— Mickey Cochrane, Detroit A.L.
P— Carl Hubbell, New York N.L.
P— Dizzy Dean, St. Louis N.L.

1936

1B— Lou Gehrig, New York A.L.
2B— Charley Gehringer, Detroit A.L.
SS— Luke Appling, Chicago A.L.
3B— Mike Higgins, Philadelphia A.L.
OF— Joe Medwick, St. Louis N.L.
OF— Earl Averill, Cleveland A.L.
OF— Mel Ott, New York N.L.
C— Bill Dickey, New York A.L.
P— Carl Hubbell, New York N.L.
P— Dizzy Dean, St. Louis N.L.

1937

1B— Lou Gehrig, New York A.L.
2B— Charley Gehringer, Detroit A.L.
SS— Dick Bartell, New York N.L.
3B— Red Rolfe, New York A.L.
OF— Joe Medwick, St. Louis N.L.
OF— Joe DiMaggio, New York A.L.
OF— Paul Waner, Pittsburgh N.L.
C— Gabby Hartnett, Chicago N.L.
P— Carl Hubbell, New York N.L.
P— Red Ruffing, New York A.L.

1938

1B— Jimmie Foxx, Boston A.L.
2B— Charley Gehringer, Detroit A.L.
SS— Joe Cronin, Boston A.L.
3B— Red Rolfe, New York A.L.
OF— Joe Medwick, St. Louis N.L.
OF— Joe DiMaggio, New York A.L.
OF— Mel Ott, New York N.L.
C— Bill Dickey, New York A.L.
P— Red Ruffing, New York A.L.
P— Lefty Gomez, New York A.L.
P— Johnny Vander Meer, Cin. N.L.

1939

1B— Jimmie Foxx, Boston A.L.
2B— Joe Gordon, New York A.L.
SS— Joe Cronin, Boston A.L.
3B— Red Rolfe, New York A.L.
OF— Joe Medwick, St. Louis N.L.
OF— Joe DiMaggio, New York A.L.
OF— Ted Williams, Boston A.L.
C— Bill Dickey, New York A.L.
P— Red Ruffing, New York A.L.
P— Bob Feller, Cleveland A.L.
P— Bucky Walters, Cincinnati N.L.

1940

1B— Frank McCormick, Cincinnati N.L.
2B— Joe Gordon, New York A.L.
SS— Luke Appling, Chicago A.L.
3B— Stan Hack, Chicago N.L.
OF— Hank Greenberg, Detroit A.L.
OF— Joe DiMaggio, New York A.L.
OF— Ted Williams, Boston A.L.
C— Harry Danning, New York N.L.
P— Bob Feller, Cleveland A.L.
P— Bucky Walters, Cincinnati N.L.
P— Paul Derringer, Cincinnati N.L.

1941

1B— Dolf Camilli, Brooklyn N.L.
2B— Joe Gordon, New York A.L.
SS— Cecil Travis, Washington A.L.
3B— Stan Hack, Chicago N.L.
OF— Ted Williams, Boston A.L.
OF— Joe DiMaggio, New York A.L.
OF— Pete Reiser, Brooklyn N.L.
C— Bill Dickey, New York A.L.
P— Bob Feller, Cleveland A.L.
P— Whitlow Wyatt, Brooklyn N.L.
P— Thornton Lee, Chicago A.L.

1942

1B— Johnny Mize, New York N.L.
2B— Joe Gordon, New York A.L.
SS— Johnny Pesky, Boston A.L.
3B— Stan Hack, Chicago N.L.
OF— Ted Williams, Boston A.L.
OF— Joe DiMaggio, New York A.L.
OF— Enos Slaughter, St. Louis N.L.
C— Mickey Owen, Brooklyn N.L.
P— Mort Cooper, St. Louis N.L.
P— Tiny Bonham, New York A.L.
P— Tex Hughson, Boston A.L.

1943
1B— Rudy York, Detroit A.L.
2B— Billy Herman, Brooklyn N.L.
SS— Luke Appling, Chicago A.L.
3B— Billy Johnson, New York A.L.
OF— Dick Wakefield, Detroit A.L.
OF— Stan Musial, St. Louis N.L.
OF— Bill Nicholson, Chicago N.L.
C— Walker Cooper, St. Louis N.L.
P— Spud Chandler, New York A.L.
P— Mort Cooper, St. Louis N.L.
P— Rip Sewell, Pittsburgh N.L.

1944
1B— Ray Sanders, St. Louis N.L.
2B— Bobby Doerr, Boston A.L.
SS— Marty Marion, St. Louis N.L.
3B— Bob Elliott, Pittsburgh N.L.
OF— Stan Musial, St. Louis N.L.
OF— Dick Wakefield, Detroit A.L.
OF— Dixie Walker, Brooklyn, N.L.
C— Walker Cooper, St. Louis N.L.
P— Hal Newhouser, Detroit A.L.
P— Mort Cooper, St. Louis N.L.
P— Dizzy Trout, Detroit A.L.

1945
1B— Phil Cavarretta, Chicago N.L.
2B— George Stirnweiss, N.Y. A.L.
SS— Marty Marion, St. Louis N.L.
3B— Whitey Kurowski, St. Louis N.L.
OF— Tommy Holmes, Boston N.L.
OF— Andy Pafko, Chicago N.L.
OF— Goody Rosen, Brooklyn N.L.
C— Paul Richards, Detroit A.L.
P— Hal Newhouser, Detroit A.L.
P— Boo Ferriss, Boston A.L.
P— Hank Borowy, Chicago N.L.

1946
1B— Stan Musial, St. Louis N.L.
2B— Bobby Doerr, Boston A.L.
SS— Johnny Pesky, Boston A.L.
3B— George Kell, Detroit A.L.
OF— Ted Williams, Boston A.L.
OF— Dom DiMaggio, Boston A.L.
OF— Enos Slaughter, St. Louis N.L.
C— Aaron Robinson, New York A.L.
P— Hal Newhouser, Detroit A.L.
P— Bob Feller, Cleveland A.L.
P— Boo Ferriss, Boston A.L.

1947
1B— Johnny Mize, New York N.L.
2B— Joe Gordon, Cleveland A.L.
SS— Lou Boudreau, Cleveland A.L.
3B— George Kell, Detroit A.L.
OF— Ted Williams, Boston A.L.
OF— Joe DiMaggio, New York A.L.
OF— Ralph Kiner, Pittsburgh N.L.
C— Walker Cooper, New York N.L.
P— Ewell Blackwell, Cincinnati N.L.
P— Bob Feller, Cleveland A.L.
P— Ralph Branca, Brooklyn N.L.

1948
1B— Johnny Mize, New York N.L.
2B— Joe Gordon, Cleveland A.L.
SS— Lou Boudreau, Cleveland A.L.
3B— Bob Elliott, Boston N.L.
OF— Ted Williams, Boston A.L.
OF— Joe DiMaggio, New York A.L.
OF— Stan Musial, St. Louis N.L.
C— Birdie Tebbetts, Boston A.L.
P— Johnny Sain, Boston N.L.
P— Bob Lemon, Cleveland A.L.
P— Harry Brecheen, St. Louis N.L.

1949
1B— Tommy Henrich, New York A.L.
2B— Jackie Robinson, Brooklyn N.L.
SS— Phil Rizzuto, New York A.L.
3B— George Kell, Detroit A.L.
OF— Ted Williams, Boston A.L.
OF— Stan Musial, St. Louis N.L.
OF— Ralph Kiner, Pittsburgh N.L.
C— Roy Campanella, Brooklyn N.L.
P— Mel Parnell, Boston A.L.
P— Ellis Kinder, Boston A.L.
P— Joe Page, New York A.L.

1950
1B— Walt Dropo, Boston A.L.
2B— Jackie Robinson, Brooklyn N.L.
SS— Phil Rizzuto, New York A.L.
3B— George Kell, Detroit A.L.
OF— Stan Musial, St. Louis N.L.
OF— Ralph Kiner, Pittsburgh N.L.
OF— Larry Doby, Cleveland A.L.
C— Yogi Berra, New York A.L.
P— Vic Raschi, New York A.L.
P— Bob Lemon, Cleveland A.L.
P— Jim Konstanty, Phil. N.L.

1951
1B— Ferris Fain, Philadelphia A.L.
2B— Jackie Robinson, Brooklyn N.L.
SS— Phil Rizzuto, New York A.L.
3B— George Kell, Detroit A.L.
OF— Stan Musial, St. Louis N.L.
OF— Ted Williams, Boston A.L.
OF— Ralph Kiner, Pittsburgh N.L.
C— Roy Campanella, Brooklyn N.L.
P— Sal Maglie, New York N.L.
P— Preacher Roe, Brooklyn N.L.
P— Allie Reynolds, New York A.L.

1952
1B— Ferris Fain, Philadelphia A.L.
2B— Jackie Robinson, Brooklyn N.L.
SS— Phil Rizzuto, New York A.L.
3B— George Kell, Boston A.L.
OF— Stan Musial, St. Louis N.L.
OF— Hank Sauer, Chicago N.L.
OF— Mickey Mantle, New York A.L.
C— Yogi Berra, New York A.L.
P— Robin Roberts, Philadelphia N.L.
P— Bobby Shantz, Philadelphia A.L.
P— Allie Reynolds, New York A.L.

1953
1B— Mickey Vernon, Washington A.L.
2B— Red Schoendienst, St. Louis N.L.
SS— Pee Wee Reese, Brooklyn N.L.
3B— Al Rosen, Cleveland A.L.
OF— Stan Musial, St. Louis N.L.
OF— Duke Snider, Brooklyn N.L.
OF— Carl Furillo, Brooklyn N.L.
C— Roy Campanella, Brooklyn N.L.
P— Robin Roberts, Philadelphia N.L.
P— Warren Spahn, Milwaukee N.L.
P— Bob Porterfield, Washington A.L.

1954
1B— Ted Kluszewski, Cincinnati N.L.
2B— Bobby Avila, Cleveland A.L.
SS— Alvin Dark, New York N.L.
3B— Al Rosen, Cleveland A.L.
OF— Willie Mays, New York N.L.
OF— Stan Musial, St. Louis N.L.
OF— Duke Snider, Brooklyn N.L.
C— Yogi Berra, New York A.L.
P— Bob Lemon, Cleveland A.L.
P— Johnny Antonelli, New York N.L.
P— Robin Roberts, Philadelphia N.L.

1955
1B— Ted Kluszewski, Cincinnati N.L.
2B— Nellie Fox, Chicago A.L.
SS— Ernie Banks, Chicago N.L.
3B— Ed Mathews, Milwaukee N.L.
OF— Duke Snider, Brooklyn N.L.
OF— Ted Williams, Boston A.L.
OF— Al Kaline, Detroit A.L.
C— Roy Campanella, Brooklyn N.L.
P— Robin Roberts, Philadelphia N.L.
P— Don Newcombe, Brooklyn N.L.
P— Whitey Ford, New York A.L.

1956
1B— Ted Kluszewski, Cincinnati N.L.
2B— Nellie Fox, Chicago A.L.
SS— Harvey Kuenn, Detroit A.L.
3B— Ken Boyer, St. Louis N.L.
OF— Mickey Mantle, New York A.L.
OF— Hank Aaron, Milwaukee N.L.
OF— Ted Williams, Boston A.L.
C— Yogi Berra, New York A.L.
P— Don Newcombe, Brooklyn N.L.
P— Whitey Ford, New York A.L.
P— Billy Pierce, Chicago A.L.

1957
1B— Stan Musial, St. Louis N.L.
2B— Red Schoendienst, N.Y.-Mil. N.L.
SS— Gil McDougald, New York A.L.
3B— Ed Mathews, Milwaukee N.L.
OF— Mickey Mantle, New York A.L.
OF— Ted Williams, Boston A.L.
OF— Willie Mays, New York N.L.
C— Yogi Berra, New York A.L.
P— Warren Spahn, Milwaukee N.L.
P— Billy Pierce, Chicago N.L.
P— Jim Bunning, Detroit A.L.

1958
1B— Stan Musial, St. Louis N.L.
2B— Nellie Fox, Chicago A.L.
SS— Ernie Banks, Chicago N.L.
3B— Frank Thomas, Pittsburgh N.L.
OF— Ted Williams, Boston A.L.
OF— Willie Mays, San Francisco N.L.
OF— Hank Aaron, Milwaukee N.L.
C— Del Crandall, Milwaukee N.L.
P— Bob Turley, New York A.L.
P— Warren Spahn, Milwaukee N.L.
P— Bob Friend, Pittsburgh N.L.

1959
1B— Orlando Cepeda, S.F. N.L.
2B— Nellie Fox, Chicago A.L.
SS— Ernie Banks, Chicago N.L.
3B— Ed Mathews, Milwaukee N.L.
OF— Minnie Minoso, Cleveland A.L.
OF— Willie Mays, San Francisco N.L.
OF— Hank Aaron, Milwaukee N.L.
C— Sherm Lollar, Chicago A.L.
P— Early Wynn, Chicago A.L.
P— Sam Jones, San Francisco N.L.
P— Johnny Antonelli, S.F. N.L.

1960
1B— Bill Skowron, New York A.L.
2B— Bill Mazeroski, Pittsburgh N.L.
SS— Ernie Banks, Chicago N.L.
3B— Ed Mathews, Milwaukee N.L.
OF— Minnie Minoso, Chicago A.L.
OF— Willie Mays, San Francisco N.L.
OF— Roger Maris, New York A.L.
C— Del Crandall, Milwaukee N.L.
P— Vernon Law, Pittsburgh N.L.
P— Warren Spahn, Milwaukee N.L.
P— Ernie Broglio, St. Louis N.L.

1961

AMERICAN LEAGUE
1B— Norm Cash, Detroit
2B— Bobby Richardson, New York
SS— Tony Kubek, New York
3B— Brooks Robinson, Baltimore
OF— Mickey Mantle, New York
OF— Roger Maris, New York
OF— Rocky Colavito, Detroit
C— Elston Howard, New York
P— Whitey Ford, New York
P— Frank Lary, Detroit

NATIONAL LEAGUE
1B— Orlando Cepeda, San Francisco
2B— Frank Bolling, Milwaukee
SS— Maury Wills, Los Angeles
3B— Ken Boyer, St. Louis
OF— Willie Mays, San Francisco
OF— Frank Robinson, Cincinnati
OF— Roberto Clemente, Pittsburgh
C— Smoky Burgess, Pittsburgh
P— Joey Jay, Cincinnati
P— Warren Spahn, Milwaukee

1962

AMERICAN LEAGUE
1B— Norm Siebern, Kansas City
2B— Bobby Richardson, New York
SS— Tom Tresh, New York
3B— Brooks Robinson, Baltimore
OF— Leon Wagner, Los Angeles
OF— Mickey Mantle, New York
OF— Al Kaline, Detroit
C— Earl Battey, Minnesota
P— Ralph Terry, New York
P— Dick Donovan, Cleveland

NATIONAL LEAGUE
1B— Orlando Cepeda, San Francisco
2B— Bill Mazeroski, Pittsburgh
SS— Maury Wills, Los Angeles
3B— Ken Boyer, St. Louis
OF— Tommy Davis, Los Angeles
OF— Willie Mays, San Francisco
OF— Frank Robinson, Cincinnati
C— Del Crandall, Milwaukee
P— Don Drysdale, Los Angeles
P— Bob Purkey, Cincinnati

1963

AMERICAN LEAGUE
1B— Joe Pepitone, New York
2B— Bobby Richardson, New York
SS— Luis Aparicio, Baltimore
3B— Frank Malzone, Boston
OF— Carl Yastrzemski, Boston
OF— Albie Pearson, Los Angeles
OF— Al Kaline, Detroit
C— Elston Howard, New York
P— Whitey Ford, New York
P— Gary Peters, Chicago

NATIONAL LEAGUE
1B— Bill White, St. Louis
2B— Jim Gilliam, Los Angeles
SS— Dick Groat, St. Louis
3B— Ken Boyer, St. Louis
OF— Tommy Davis, Los Angeles
OF— Willie Mays, San Francisco
OF— Hank Aaron, Milwaukee
C— John Edwards, Cincinnati
P— Sandy Koufax, Los Angeles
P— Juan Marichal, San Francisco

1964

AMERICAN LEAGUE
1B— Dick Stuart, Boston
2B— Bobby Richardson, New York
SS— Jim Fregosi, Los Angeles
3B— Brooks Robinson, Baltimore
OF— Harmon Killebrew, Minnesota
OF— Mickey Mantle, New York
OF— Tony Oliva, Minnesota
C— Elston Howard, New York
P— Dean Chance, Los Angeles
P— Gary Peters, Chicago

NATIONAL LEAGUE
1B— Bill White, St. Louis
2B— Ron Hunt, New York
SS— Dick Groat, St. Louis
3B— Ken Boyer, St. Louis
OF— Billy Williams, Chicago
OF— Willie Mays, San Francisco
OF— Roberto Clemente, Pittsburgh
C— Joe Torre, Milwaukee
P— Sandy Koufax, Los Angeles
P— Jim Bunning, Philadelphia

1965

AMERICAN LEAGUE
1B— Fred Whitfield, Cleveland
2B— Bobby Richardson, New York
SS— Zoilo Versalles, Minnesota
3B— Brooks Robinson, Baltimore
OF— Carl Yastrzemski, Boston
OF— Jimmie Hall, Minnesota
OF— Tony Oliva, Minnesota
C— Earl Battey, Minnesota
P— Jim Grant, Minnesota
P— Mel Stottlemyre, New York

NATIONAL LEAGUE
1B— Willie McCovey, San Francisco
2B— Pete Rose, Cincinnati
SS— Maury Wills, Los Angeles
3B— Deron Johnson, Cincinnati
OF— Willie Stargell, Pittsburgh
OF— Willie Mays, San Francisco
OF— Hank Aaron, Milwaukee
C— Joe Torre, Milwaukee
P— Sandy Koufax, Los Angeles
P— Juan Marichal, San Francisco

1966

AMERICAN LEAGUE
1B— Boog Powell, Baltimore
2B— Bobby Richardson, New York
SS— Luis Aparicio, Baltimore
3B— Brooks Robinson, Baltimore
OF— Frank Robinson, Baltimore
OF— Al Kaline, Detroit
OF— Tony Oliva, Minnesota
C— Paul Casanova, Washington
P— Jim Kaat, Minnesota
P— Earl Wilson, Detroit

NATIONAL LEAGUE
1B— Felipe Alou, Atlanta
2B— Pete Rose, Cincinnati
SS— Gene Alley, Pittsburgh
3B— Ron Santo, Chicago
OF— Willie Stargell, Pittsburgh
OF— Willie Mays, San Francisco
OF— Roberto Clemente, Pittsburgh
C— Joe Torre, Atlanta
P— Sandy Koufax, Los Angeles
P— Juan Marichal, San Francisco

1967

AMERICAN LEAGUE
1B— Harmon Killebrew, Minnesota
2B— Rod Carew, Minnesota
SS— Jim Fregosi, California
3B— Brooks Robinson, Baltimore
OF— Carl Yastrzemski, Boston
OF— Al Kaline, Detroit
OF— Frank Robinson, Baltimore
C— Bill Freehan, Detroit
P— Jim Lonborg, Boston
P— Earl Wilson, Detroit

NATIONAL LEAGUE
1B— Orlando Cepeda, St. Louis
2B— Bill Mazeroski, Pittsburgh
SS— Gene Alley, Pittsburgh
3B— Ron Santo, Chicago
OF— Hank Aaron, Atlanta
OF— Jim Wynn, Houston
OF— Roberto Clemente, Pittsburgh
C— Tim McCarver, St. Louis
P— Mike McCormick, San Francisco
P— Ferguson Jenkins, Chicago

1968

AMERICAN LEAGUE
1B— Boog Powell, Baltimore
2B— Rod Carew, Minnesota
SS— Luis Aparicio, Chicago
3B— Brooks Robinson, Baltimore
OF— Ken Harrelson, Boston
OF— Willie Horton, Detroit
OF— Frank Howard, Washington
C— Bill Freehan, Detroit
P— Dave McNally, Baltimore
P— Denny McLain, Detroit

NATIONAL LEAGUE
1B— Willie McCovey, San Francisco
2B— Tommy Helms, Cincinnati
SS— Don Kessinger, Chicago
3B— Ron Santo, Chicago
OF— Billy Williams, Chicago
OF— Curt Flood, St. Louis
OF— Pete Rose, Cincinnati
C— Johnny Bench, Cincinnati
P— Bob Gibson, St. Louis
P— Juan Marichal, San Francisco

1969

AMERICAN LEAGUE
1B— Boog Powell, Baltimore
2B— Rod Carew, Minnesota
SS— Rico Petrocelli, Boston
3B— Harmon Killebrew, Minnesota
OF— Frank Howard, Washington
OF— Paul Blair, Baltimore
OF— Reggie Jackson, Oakland
C— Bill Freehan, Detroit
RHP— Denny McLain, Detroit
LHP— Mike Cuellar, Baltimore

NATIONAL LEAGUE
1B— Willie McCovey, San Francisco
2B— Glenn Beckert, Chicago
SS— Don Kessinger, Chicago
3B— Ron Santo, Chicago
OF— Cleon Jones, New York
OF— Matty Alou, Pittsburgh
OF— Hank Aaron, Atlanta
C— Johnny Bench, Cincinnati
RHP— Tom Seaver, New York
LHP— Steve Carlton, St. Louis

1970

AMERICAN LEAGUE
- 1B— Boog Powell, Baltimore
- 2B— Dave Johnson, Baltimore
- SS— Luis Aparicio, Chicago
- 3B— Harmon Killebrew, Minnesota
- OF— Frank Howard, Washington
- OF— Reggie Smith, Boston
- OF— Tony Oliva, Minnesota
- C— Ray Fosse, Cleveland
- RHP— Jim Perry, Minnesota
- LHP— Sam McDowell, Cleveland

NATIONAL LEAGUE
- 1B— Willie McCovey, San Francisco
- 2B— Glenn Beckert, Chicago
- SS— Don Kessinger, Chicago
- 3B— Tony Perez, Cincinnati
- OF— Billy Williams, Chicago
- OF— Bobby Tolan, Cincinnati
- OF— Hank Aaron, Atlanta
- C— Johnny Bench, Cincinnati
- RHP— Bob Gibson, St. Louis
- LHP— Jim Merritt, Cincinnati

1971

AMERICAN LEAGUE
- 1B— Norm Cash, Detroit
- 2B— Cookie Rojas, Kansas City
- SS— Leo Cardenas, Minnesota
- 3B— Brooks Robinson, Baltimore
- OF— Merv Rettenmund, Baltimore
- OF— Bobby Murcer, New York
- OF— Tony Oliva, Minnesota
- C— Bill Freehan, Detroit
- RHP— Jim Palmer, Baltimore
- LHP— Vida Blue, Oakland

NATIONAL LEAGUE
- 1B— Lee May, Cincinnati
- 2B— Glenn Beckett, Chicago
- SS— Bud Harrelson, New York
- 3B— Joe Torre, St. Louis
- OF— Willie Stargell, Pittsburgh
- OF— Willie Davis, Los Angeles
- OF— Hank Aaron, Atlanta
- C— Manny Sanguillen, Pittsburgh
- RHP— Ferguson Jenkins, Chicago
- LHP— Steve Carlton, St. Louis

1972

AMERICAN LEAGUE
- 1B— Dick Allen, Chicago
- 2B— Rod Carew, Minnesota
- SS— Luis Aparicio, Boston
- 3B— Brooks Robinson, Baltimore
- OF— Joe Rudi, Oakland
- OF— Bobby Murcer, New York
- OF— Richie Scheinblum, Kansas City
- C— Carlton Fisk, Boston
- RHP— Gaylord Perry, Cleveland
- LHP— Wilbur Wood, Chicago

NATIONAL LEAGUE
- 1B— Willie Stargell, Pittsburgh
- 2B— Joe Morgan, Cincinnati
- SS— Chris Speier, San Francisco
- 3B— Ron Santo, Chicago
- OF— Billy Williams, Chicago
- OF— Cesar Cedeno, Houston
- OF— Roberto Clemente, Pittsburgh
- C— Johnny Bench, Cincinnati
- RHP— Ferguson Jenkins, Chicago
- LHP— Steve Carlton, Philadelphia

1973

AMERICAN LEAGUE
- 1B— John Mayberry, Kansas City
- 2B— Rod Carew, Minnesota
- SS— Bert Campaneris, Oakland
- 3B— Sal Bando, Oakland
- OF— Reggie Jackson, Oakland
- OF— Amos Otis, Kansas City
- OF— Bobby Murcer, New York
- C— Thurman Munson, New York
- RHP— Jim Palmer, Baltimore
- LHP— Ken Holtzman, Oakland

NATIONAL LEAGUE
- 1B— Tony Perez, Cincinnati
- 2B— Dave Johnson, Atlanta
- SS— Bill Russell, Los Angeles
- 3B— Darrell Evans, Atlanta
- OF— Bobby Bonds, San Francisco
- OF— Cesar Cedeno, Houston
- OF— Pete Rose, Cincinnati
- C— Johnny Bench, Cincinnati
- RHP— Tom Seaver, New York
- LHP— Ron Bryant, San Francisco

1974

AMERICAN LEAGUE
- 1B— Dick Allen, Chicago
- 2B— Rod Carew, Minnesota
- SS— Bert Campaneris, Oakland
- 3B— Sal Bando, Oakland
- OF— Joe Rudi, Oakland
- OF— Paul Blair, Baltimore
- OF— Jeff Burroughs, Texas
- C— Thurman Munson, New York
- DH— Tommy Davis, Baltimore
- RHP— Jim Hunter, Oakland
- LHP— Mike Cuellar, Baltimore

NATIONAL LEAGUE
- 1B— Steve Garvey, Los Angeles
- 2B— Joe Morgan, Cincinnati
- SS— Dave Concepcion, Cincinnati
- 3B— Mike Schmidt, Philadelphia
- OF— Lou Brock, St. Louis
- OF— Jim Wynn, Los Angeles
- OF— Richie Zisk, Pittsburgh
- C— Johnny Bench, Cincinnati
- RHP— Andy Messersmith, Los Angeles
- LHP— Don Gullett, Cincinnati

1975

AMERICAN LEAGUE
- 1B— John Mayberry, Kansas City
- 2B— Rod Carew, Minnesota
- SS— Toby Harrah, Texas
- 3B— Graig Nettles, New York
- OF— Jim Rice, Boston
- OF— Fred Lynn, Boston
- OF— Reggie Jackson, Oakland
- C— Thurman Munson, New York
- DH— Willie Horton, Detroit
- RHP— Jim Palmer, Baltimore
- LHP— Jim Kaat, Chicago

NATIONAL LEAGUE
- 1B— Steve Garvey, Los Angeles
- 2B— Joe Morgan, Cincinnati
- SS— Larry Bowa, Philadelphia
- 3B— Bill Madlock, Chicago
- OF— Greg Luzinski, Philadelphia
- OF— Al Oliver, Pittsburgh
- OF— Dave Parker, Pittsburgh
- C— Johnny Bench, Cincinnati
- RHP— Tom Seaver, New York
- LHP— Randy Jones, San Diego

1976

AMERICAN LEAGUE
- 1B— Chris Chambliss, New York
- 2B— Bobby Grich, Baltimore
- 3B— George Brett, Kansas City
- SS— Mark Belanger, Baltimore
- OF— Joe Rudi, Oakland
- OF— Mickey Rivers, New York
- OF— Reggie Jackson, Baltimore
- C— Thurman Munson, New York
- DH— Hal McRae, Kansas City
- RHP— Jim Palmer, Baltimore
- LHP— Frank Tanana, California

NATIONAL LEAGUE
- 1B— Willie Montanez, S.F.-Atl.
- 2B— Joe Morgan, Cincinnati
- 3B— Mike Schmidt, Philadelphia
- SS— Dave Concepcion, Cincinnati
- OF— George Foster, Cincinnati
- OF— Cesar Cedeno, Houston
- OF— Ken Griffey, Cincinnati
- C— Bob Boone, Philadelphia
- RHP— Don Sutton, Los Angeles
- LHP— Randy Jones, San Diego

1977

AMERICAN LEAGUE
- 1B— Rod Carew, Minnesota
- 2B— Willie Randolph, New York
- 3B— Graig Nettles, New York
- SS— Rick Burleson, Boston
- OF— Jim Rice, Boston
- OF— Larry Hisle, Minnesota
- OF— Bobby Bonds, California
- C— Carlton Fisk, Boston
- DH— Hal McRae, Kansas City
- RHP— Nolan Ryan, California
- LHP— Frank Tanana, California

NATIONAL LEAGUE
- 1B— Steve Garvey, Los Angeles
- 2B— Joe Morgan, Cincinnati
- 3B— Mike Schmidt, Philadelphia
- SS— Garry Templeton, St. Louis
- OF— George Foster, Cincinnati
- OF— Dave Parker, Pittsburgh
- OF— Greg Luzinski, Philadelphia
- C— Ted Simmons, St. Louis
- RHP— Rick Reuschel, Chicago
- LHP— Steve Carlton, Philadelphia

1978

AMERICAN LEAGUE
- 1B— Rod Carew, Minnesota
- 2B— Frank White, Kansas City
- 3B— Graig Nettles, New York
- SS— Robin Yount, Milwaukee
- OF— Jim Rice, Boston
- OF— Larry Hisle, Milwaukee
- OF— Fred Lynn, Boston
- C— Jim Sundberg, Texas
- DH— Rusty Staub, Detroit
- RHP— Jim Palmer, Baltimore
- LHP— Ron Guidry, New York

NATIONAL LEAGUE
- 1B— Steve Garvey, Los Angeles
- 2B— Dave Lopes, Los Angeles
- 3B— Pete Rose, Cincinnati
- SS— Larry Bowa, Philadelphia
- OF— George Foster, Cincinnati
- OF— Dave Parker, Pittsburgh
- OF— Jack Clark, San Francisco
- C— Ted Simmons, St. Louis
- RHP— Gaylord Perry, San Diego
- LHP— Vida Blue, San Francisco

HISTORY *Award winners*

1979

AMERICAN LEAGUE
1B— Cecil Cooper, Milwaukee
2B— Bobby Grich, California
3B— George Brett, Kansas City
SS— Roy Smalley, Minnesota
OF— Jim Rice, Boston
OF— Fred Lynn, Boston
OF— Ken Singleton, Baltimore
C— Darrell Porter, Kansas City
DH— Don Baylor, California
RHP— Jim Kern, Texas
LHP— Mike Flanagan, Baltimore

NATIONAL LEAGUE
1B— Keith Hernandez, St. Louis
2B— Dave Lopes, Los Angeles
3B— Mike Schmidt, Philadelphia
SS— Garry Templeton, St. Louis
OF— Dave Kingman, Chicago
OF— Omar Moreno, Pittsburgh
OF— Dave Winfield, San Diego
C— Ted Simmons, St. Louis
RHP— Joe Niekro, Houston
LHP— Steve Carlton, Philadelphia

1980

AMERICAN LEAGUE
1B— Cecil Cooper, Milwaukee
2B— Willie Randolph, New York
3B— George Brett, Kansas City
SS— Robin Yount, Milwaukee
OF— Ben Oglivie, Milwaukee
OF— Al Bumbry, Baltimore
OF— Reggie Jackson, New York
DH— Reggie Jackson, New York
C— Rick Cerone, New York
RHP— Steve Stone, Baltimore
LHP— Tommy John, New York

NATIONAL LEAGUE
1B— Keith Hernandez, St. Louis
2B— Manny Trillo, Philadelphia
3B— Mike Schmidt, Philadelphia
SS— Garry Templeton, St. Louis
OF— Dusty Baker, Los Angeles
OF— Cesar Cedeno, Houston
OF— George Hendrick, St. Louis
C— Gary Carter, Montreal
RHP— Jim Bibby, Pittsburgh
LHP— Steve Carlton, Philadelphia

1981

AMERICAN LEAGUE
1B— Cecil Cooper, Milwaukee
2B— Bobby Grich, California
3B— Buddy Bell, Texas
SS— Rick Burleson, California
OF— Rickey Henderson, Oakland
OF— Dwayne Murphy, Oakland
OF— Tony Armas, Oakland
C— Jim Sundberg, Texas
DH— Richie Zisk, Seattle
RHP— Jack Morris, Detroit
LHP— Ron Guidry, New York

NATIONAL LEAGUE
1B— Pete Rose, Philadelphia
2B— Manny Trillo, Philadelphia
3B— Mike Schmidt, Philadelphia
SS— Dave Concepcion, Cincinnati
OF— George Foster, Cincinnati
OF— Andre Dawson, Montreal
OF— Pedro Guerrero, Los Angeles
C— Gary Carter, Montreal
RHP— Tom Seaver, Cincinnati
LHP— Fernando Valenzuela, Los Angeles

1982

AMERICAN LEAGUE
1B— Cecil Cooper, Milwaukee
2B— Damaso Garcia, Toronto
3B— Doug DeCinces, California
SS— Robin Yount, Milwaukee
OF— Dave Winfield, New York
OF— Gorman Thomas, Milwaukee
OF— Dwight Evans, Boston
C— Lance Parrish, Detroit
DH— Hal McRae, Kansas City
RHP— Dave Stieb, Toronto
LHP— Geoff Zahn, California

NATIONAL LEAGUE
1B— Al Oliver, Montreal
2B— Manny Trillo, Philadelphia
3B— Mike Schmidt, Philadelphia
SS— Ozzie Smith, St. Louis
OF— Lonnie Smith, St. Louis
OF— Dale Murphy, Atlanta
OF— Pedro Guerrero, Los Angeles
C— Gary Carter, Montreal
RHP— Steve Rogers, Montreal
LHP— Steve Carlton, Philadelphia

1983

AMERICAN LEAGUE
1B— Eddie Murray, Baltimore
2B— Lou Whitaker, Detroit
3B— Wade Boggs, Boston
SS— Cal Ripken, Baltimore
OF— Jim Rice, Boston
OF— Dave Winfield, New York
OF— Lloyd Moseby, Toronto
C— Carlton Fisk, Chicago
DH— Greg Luzinski, Chicago
RHP— LaMarr Hoyt, Chicago
LHP— Ron Guidry, New York

NATIONAL LEAGUE
1B— George Hendrick, St. Louis
2B— Glenn Hubbard, Atlanta
3B— Mike Schmidt, Philadelphia
SS— Dickie Thon, Houston
OF— Dale Murphy, Atlanta
OF— Andre Dawson, Montreal
OF— Tim Raines, Montreal
C— Tony Pena, Pittsburgh
RHP— John Denny, Philadelphia
LHP— Larry McWilliams, Pittsburgh

1984

AMERICAN LEAGUE
1B— Don Mattingly, New York
2B— Lou Whitaker, Detroit
3B— Buddy Bell, Texas
SS— Cal Ripken, Baltimore
OF— Tony Armas, Boston
OF— Dwight Evans, Boston
OF— Dave Winfield, New York
C— Lance Parrish, Detroit
DH— Dave Kingman, Oakland
RHP— Mike Boddicker, Baltimore
LHP— Willie Hernandez, Detroit

NATIONAL LEAGUE
1B— Keith Hernandez, New York
2B— Ryne Sandberg, Chicago
3B— Mike Schmidt, Philadelphia
SS— Ozzie Smith, St. Louis
OF— Dale Murphy, Atlanta
OF— Jose Cruz, Houston
OF— Tony Gwynn, San Diego
C— Gary Carter, Montreal
RHP— Rick Sutcliffe, Chicago
LHP— Mark Thurmond, San Diego

1985

AMERICAN LEAGUE
1B— Don Mattingly, New York
2B— Damaso Garcia, Toronto
3B— Wade Boggs, Boston
SS— Cal Ripken, Baltimore
OF— Rickey Henderson, New York
OF— Harold Baines, Chicago
OF— Phil Bradley, Seattle
C— Carlton Fisk, Chicago
DH— Don Baylor, Boston
RHP— Bret Saberhagen, Kansas City
LHP— Ron Guidry, New York

NATIONAL LEAGUE
1B— Keith Hernandez, New York
2B— Tom Herr, St. Louis
3B— Tim Wallach, Montreal
SS— Ozzie Smith, St. Louis
OF— Dave Parker, Cincinnati
OF— Willie McGee, St. Louis
OF— Dale Murphy, Atlanta
C— Gary Carter, New York
RHP— Dwight Gooden, New York
LHP— John Tudor, St. Louis

1986

AMERICAN LEAGUE
1B— Don Mattingly, New York
2B— Tony Bernazard, Cleveland
3B— Wade Boggs, Boston
SS— Tony Fernandez, Toronto
OF— Jim Rice, Boston
OF— George Bell, Toronto
OF— Kirby Puckett, Minnesota
C— Rich Gedman, Boston
DH— Don Baylor, Boston
RHP— Roger Clemens, Boston
LHP— Teddy Higuera, Milwaukee

NATIONAL LEAGUE
1B— Keith Hernandez, New York
2B— Steve Sax, Los Angeles
3B— Mike Schmidt, Philadelphia
SS— Ozzie Smith, St. Louis
OF— Tim Raines, Montreal
OF— Tony Gwynn, San Diego
OF— Dave Parker, Cincinnati
C— Gary Carter, New York
RHP— Mike Scott, Houston
LHP— Fernando Valenzuela, Los Angeles

1987

AMERICAN LEAGUE
1B— Don Mattingly, New York
2B— Willie Randolph, New York
3B— Wade Boggs, Boston
SS— Alan Trammell, Detroit
OF— George Bell, Toronto
OF— Kirby Puckett, Minnesota
OF— Dwight Evans, Boston
C— Matt Nokes, Detroit
DH— Paul Molitor, Milwaukee
RHP— Roger Clemens, Boston
LHP— Jimmy Key, Toronto

NATIONAL LEAGUE
1B— Jack Clark, St. Louis
2B— Juan Samuel, Philadelphia
3B— Tim Wallach, Montreal
SS— Ozzie Smith, St. Louis
OF— Andre Dawson, Chicago
OF— Tony Gwynn, San Diego
OF— Eric Davis, Cincinnati
C— Benito Santiago, San Diego
RHP— Rick Sutcliffe, Chicago
LHP— Zane Smith, Atlanta

1988

AMERICAN LEAGUE
1B— George Brett, Kansas City
2B— Johnny Ray, California
3B— Wade Boggs, Boston
SS— Alan Trammell, Detroit
OF— Kirby Puckett, Minnesota
OF— Mike Greenwell, Boston
OF— Jose Canseco, Oakland
C— Ernie Whitt, Toronto
DH— Harold Baines, Chicago
RHP— Dave Stewart, Oakland
LHP— Frank Viola, Minnesota

NATIONAL LEAGUE
1B— Will Clark, San Francisco
2B— Ryne Sandberg, Chicago
3B— Bobby Bonilla, Pittsburgh
SS— Barry Larkin, Cincinnati
OF— Darryl Strawberry, New York
OF— Andy Van Slyke, Pittsburgh
OF— Kevin McReynolds, New York
C— Mike LaValliere, Pittsburgh
RHP— Orel Hershiser, Los Angeles
LHP— Danny Jackson, Cincinnati

1989

AMERICAN LEAGUE
1B— Fred McGriff, Toronto
2B— Julio Franco, Texas
3B— Carney Lansford, Oakland
SS— Cal Ripken, Baltimore
OF— Ruben Sierra, Texas
OF— Kirby Puckett, Minnesota
OF— Robin Yount, Milwaukee
C— Mickey Tettleton, Baltimore
DH— Harold Baines, Chi.-Tex.
RHP— Bret Saberhagen, Kansas City
LHP— Chuck Finley, California

NATIONAL LEAGUE
1B— Will Clark, San Francisco
2B— Ryne Sandberg, Chicago
3B— Howard Johnson, New York
SS— Shawon Dunston, Chicago
OF— Tony Gwynn, San Diego
OF— Kevin Mitchell, San Francisco
OF— Eric Davis, Cincinnati
C— Benito Santiago, San Diego
RHP— Mike Scott, Houston
LHP— Mark Davis, San Diego

1990

AMERICAN LEAGUE
1B— Cecil Fielder, Detroit
2B— Julio Franco, Texas
3B— Kelly Gruber, Toronto
SS— Alan Trammell, Detroit
OF— Rickey Henderson, Oakland
OF— Jose Canseco, Oakland
OF— Ellis Burks, Boston
C— Carlton Fisk, Chicago
DH— Dave Parker, Milwaukee
RHP— Bob Welch, Oakland
LHP— Chuck Finley, California

NATIONAL LEAGUE
1B— Eddie Murray, Los Angeles
2B— Ryne Sandberg, Chicago
3B— Matt Williams, San Francisco
SS— Barry Larkin, Cincinnati
OF— Barry Bonds, Pittsburgh
OF— Bobby Bonilla, Pittsburgh
OF— Darryl Strawberry, New York
C— Mike Scioscia, Los Angeles
RHP— Doug Drabek, Pittsburgh
LHP— Frank Viola, New York

1991

AMERICAN LEAGUE
1B— Cecil Fielder, Detroit
2B— Julio Franco, Texas
3B— Wade Boggs, Boston
SS— Cal Ripken, Baltimore
OF— Jose Canseco, Oakland
OF— Joe Carter, Toronto
OF— Ken Griffey Jr., Seattle
C— Mickey Tettleton, Detroit
RHP— Roger Clemens, Boston
LHP— Jim Abbott, California

NATIONAL LEAGUE
1B— Will Clark, San Francisco
2B— Ryne Sandberg, Chicago
3B— Terry Pendleton, Atlanta
SS— Barry Larkin, Cincinnati
OF— Barry Bonds, Pittsburgh
OF— Bobby Bonilla, Pittsburgh
OF— Ron Gant, Atlanta
C— Benito Santiago, San Diego
RHP— Jose Rijo, Cincinnati
LHP— Tom Glavine, Atlanta

1992

AMERICAN LEAGUE
1B— Mark McGwire, Oakland
2B— Roberto Alomar, Toronto
3B— Edgar Martinez, Seattle
SS— Travis Fryman, Detroit
OF— Joe Carter, Toronto
OF— Mike Devereaux, Baltimore
OF— Kirby Puckett, Minnesota
C— Mickey Tettleton, Detroit
RHP— Jack McDowell, Chicago
LHP— Dave Fleming, Seattle

NATIONAL LEAGUE
1B— Fred McGriff, San Diego
2B— Ryne Sandberg, Chicago
3B— Gary Sheffield, San Diego
SS— Barry Larkin, Cincinnati
OF— Barry Bonds, Pittsburgh
OF— Andy Van Slyke, Pittsburgh
OF— Larry Walker, Montreal
C— Darren Daulton, Philadelphia
RHP— Greg Maddux, Chicago
LHP— Tom Glavine, Atlanta

1993

AMERICAN LEAGUE
1B— Frank Thomas, Chicago
2B— Carlos Baerga, Cleveland
3B— Travis Fryman, Detroit
SS— Cal Ripken Jr., Baltimore
OF— Albert Belle, Cleveland
OF— Juan Gonzalez, Texas
OF— Ken Griffey Jr., Seattle
C— Mike Stanley, New York
DH— Paul Molitor, Toronto
RHP— Jack McDowell, Chicago
LHP— Jimmy Key, New York

NATIONAL LEAGUE
1B— Fred McGriff, S.D.-Atl.
2B— Robby Thompson, San Francisco
3B— Matt Williams, San Francisco
SS— Jay Bell, Pittsburgh
OF— Barry Bonds, San Francisco
OF— Lenny Dykstra, Philadelphia
OF— David Justice, Atlanta
C— Mike Piazza, Los Angeles
RHP— Greg Maddux, Atlanta
LHP— Steve Avery, Atlanta

1994

AMERICAN LEAGUE
1B— Frank Thomas, Chicago
2B— Chuck Knoblauch, Minnesota
3B— Wade Boggs, New York
SS— Cal Ripken Jr., Baltimore
OF— Albert Belle, Cleveland
OF— Ken Griffey Jr., Seattle
OF— Kirby Puckett, Minnesota
C— Ivan Rodriguez, Texas
DH— Paul Molitor, Toronto
RHP— David Cone, Kansas City
LHP— Jimmy Key, New York

NATIONAL LEAGUE
1B— Jeff Bagwell, Houston
2B— Craig Biggio, Houston
3B— Matt Williams, San Francisco
SS— Barry Larkin, Cincinnati
OF— Moises Alou, Montreal
OF— Barry Bonds, San Francisco
OF— Tony Gwynn, San Diego
C— Mike Piazza, Los Angeles
RHP— Greg Maddux, Atlanta
LHP— Danny Jackson, Philadelphia

1995

AMERICAN LEAGUE
1B— Mo Vaughn, Boston
2B— Carlos Baerga, Cleveland
3B— Jim Thome, Cleveland
SS— Cal Ripken Jr., Baltimore
OF— Albert Belle, Cleveland
OF— Tim Salmon, California
OF— Jim Edmonds, California
Manny Ramirez, Cleveland
C— Ivan Rodriguez, Texas
DH— Edgar Martinez, Seattle
RHP— Mike Mussina, Baltimore
LHP— Randy Johnson, Seattle

NATIONAL LEAGUE
1B— Eric Karros, Los Angeles
2B— Craig Biggio, Houston
3B— Vinny Castilla, Colorado
SS— Barry Larkin, Cincinnati
OF— Reggie Sanders, Cincinnati
OF— Dante Bichette, Colorado
OF— Sammy Sosa, Chicago
C— Mike Piazza, Los Angeles
RHP— Greg Maddux, Atlanta
LHP— Pete Schourek, Cincinnati

1996

AMERICAN LEAGUE
1B— Mark McGwire, Oakland
2B— Roberto Alomar, Baltimore
3B— Jim Thome, Cleveland
SS— Alex Rodriguez, Seattle
OF— Albert Belle, Cleveland
OF— Juan Gonzalez, Texas
OF— Ken Griffey Jr., Seattle
C— Ivan Rodriguez, Texas
DH— Paul Molitor, Minnesota
RHP— Pat Hentgen, Toronto
LHP— Andy Pettitte, New York

NATIONAL LEAGUE
1B— Jeff Bagwell, Houston
2B— Eric Young, Colorado
3B— Ken Caminiti, San Diego
SS— Barry Larkin, Cincinnati
OF— Barry Bonds, San Francisco
OF— Ellis Burks, Colorado
OF— Gary Sheffield, Florida
C— Mike Piazza, Los Angeles
RHP— John Smoltz, Atlanta
LHP— Al Leiter, Florida

1997

AMERICAN LEAGUE
1B— Tino Martinez, New York
2B— Chuck Knoblauch, Minnesota
3B— Matt Williams, Cleveland
SS— Nomar Garciaparra, Boston
OF— Ken Griffey Jr., Seattle
OF— David Justice, Cleveland
OF— Tim Salmon, Anaheim
C— Ivan Rodriguez, Texas
DH— Edgar Martinez, Seattle
RHP— Roger Clemens, Toronto
LHP— Randy Johnson, Seattle

NATIONAL LEAGUE
1B— Jeff Bagwell, Houston
2B— Craig Biggio, Houston
3B— Vinny Castillo, Colorado
SS— Jeff Blauser, Atlanta
OF— Barry Bonds, San Francisco
OF— Tony Gwynn, San Diego
OF— Larry Walker, Colorado
C— Mike Piazza, Los Angeles
RHP— Pedro Martinez, Montreal
LHP— Denny Neagle, Atlanta

1998

AMERICAN LEAGUE
1B— Rafael Palmeiro, Baltimore
2B— Roberto Alomar, Baltimore
3B— Scott Brosius, New York
SS— Alex Rodriguez, Seattle
OF— Ken Griffey Jr., Seattle
OF— Juan Gonzalez, Texas
OF— Albert Belle, Chicago
C— Ivan Rodriguez, Texas
DH— Jose Canseco, Toronto
RHP— Pedro Martinez, Boston
LHP— David Wells, New York

NATIONAL LEAGUE
1B— Mark McGwire, St. Louis
2B— Craig Biggio, Houston
3B— Vinny Castillo, Colorado
SS— Barry Larkin, Cincinnati
OF— Sammy Sosa, Chicago
OF— Moises Alou, Houston
OF— Greg Vaughn, San Diego
C— Mike Piazza, L.A.-Fla.-N.Y.
RHP— Kevin Brown, San Diego
LHP— Tom Glavine, Atlanta

1999

AMERICAN LEAGUE
1B— Rafael Palmeiro, Texas
2B— Roberto Alomar, Cleveland
3B— Dean Palmer, Detroit
SS— Nomar Garciaparra, Boston
OF— Shawn Green, Toronto
OF— Ken Griffey Jr., Seattle
OF— Manny Ramirez, Cleveland
C— Ivan Rodriguez, Texas
RHP— Pedro Martinez, Boston
LHP— Jamie Moyer, Seattle

NATIONAL LEAGUE
1B— Jeff Bagwell, Houston
2B— Edgardo Alfonzo, New York
3B— Chipper Jones, Atlanta
SS— Barry Larkin, Cincinnati
OF— Sammy Sosa, Chicago
OF— Vladimir Guerrero, Montreal
OF— Larry Walker, Colorado
C— Mike Piazza, New York
RHP— Jose Lima, Houston
LHP— Mike Hampton, Houston

2000

AMERICAN LEAGUE
1B— Carlos Delgado, Toronto
2B— Roberto Alomar, Cleveland
3B— Travis Fryman, Cleveland
SS— Alex Rodriguez, Seattle
OF— Darin Erstad, Anaheim
OF— Magglio Ordonez, Chicago
OF— Bernie Williams, New York
C— Jorge Posada, New York
RHP— Pedro Martinez, Boston
LHP— David Wells, Toronto

NATIONAL LEAGUE
1B— Todd Helton, Colorado
2B— Jeff Kent, San Francisco
3B— Chipper Jones, Atlanta
SS— Edgar Renteria, St. Louis
OF— Barry Bonds, San Francisco
OF— Vladimir Guerrero, Montreal
OF— Sammy Sosa, Chicago
C— Mike Piazza, New York
RHP— Greg Maddux, Atlanta
LHP— Tom Glavine, Atlanta

2001

AMERICAN LEAGUE
1B— Jim Thome, Cleveland
2B— Bret Boone, Seattle
3B— Troy Glaus, Anaheim
SS— Alex Rodriguez, Texas
OF— Juan Gonzalez, Cleveland
OF— Manny Ramirez, Boston
OF— Ichiro Suzuki, Seattle
C— Jorge Posada, New York
RHP— Roger Clemens, New York
LHP— Mark Mulder, Oakland
DH— Edgar Martinez, Seattle

NATIONAL LEAGUE
1B— Todd Helton, Colorado
2B— Craig Biggio, Houston
3B— Chipper Jones, Atlanta
SS— Rich Aurilia, San Francisco
OF— Barry Bonds, San Francisco
OF— Luis Gonzalez, Arizona
OF— Sammy Sosa, Chicago
C— Mike Piazza, New York
RHP— Curt Schilling, Arizona
LHP— Randy Johnson, Arizona

2002

AMERICAN LEAGUE
1B— Jason Giambi, New York
2B— Alfonso Soriano, New York
3B— Eric Chavez, Oakland
SS— Alex Rodriguez, Texas
OF— Garret Anderson, Anaheim
OF— Torii Hunter, Minnesota
OF— Bernie Williams, New York
C— Jorge Posada, New York
RHP— Derek Lowe, Boston
LHP— Barry Zito, Oakland
DH— Manny Ramirez, Boston

NATIONAL LEAGUE
1B— Todd Helton, Colorado
2B— Jeff Kent, San Francisco
3B— Scott Rolen, Phil.-St.L.
SS— Edgar Renteria, St. Louis
OF— Barry Bonds, San Francisco
OF— Vladimir Guerrero, Montreal
OF— Sammy Sosa, Chicago
C— Mike Piazza, New York
RHP— Curt Schilling, Arizona
LHP— Randy Johnson, Arizona

MINOR LEAGUE PLAYER OF THE YEAR

Year	Player, Team, League
1936	John Vander Meer, Durham, Piedmont
1937	Charlie Keller, Newark, International
1938	Fred Hutchinson, Seattle, Pacific Coast
1939	Lou Novikoff, Tulsa, Texas; Los Angeles, Pacific Coast
1940	Phil Rizzuto, Kansas City, American Association
1941	John Lindell, Newark, International
1942	Dick Barrett, Seattle, Pacific Coast
1943	Chet Covington, Scranton, Eastern
1944	Rip Collins, Albany, Eastern
1945	Gil Coan, Chattanooga, Southern
1946	Sibby Sisti, Indianapolis, American Association
1947	Hank Sauer, Syracuse, International
1948	Gene Woodling, San Francisco, Pacific Coast
1949	Orie Arntzen, Albany, Eastern
1950	Frank Saucier, San Antonio, Texas
1951	Gene Conley, Hartford, Eastern
1952	Bill Skowron, Kansas City, American Association
1953	Gene Conley, Toledo, American Association
1954	Herb Score, Indianapolis, American Association
1955	John Murff, Dallas, Texas
1956	Steve Bilko, Los Angeles, Pacific Coast
1957	Norm Siebern, Denver, American Association
1958	Jim O'Toole, Nashville, Southern
1959	Frank Howard, Victoria-Spokane
1960	Willie Davis, Spokane, Pacific Coast
1961	Howie Koplitz, Birmingham, Southern
1962	Bob Bailey, Columbus, International
1963	Don Buford, Indianapolis, International
1964	Mel Stottlemyre, Richmond, International
1965	Joe Foy, Toronto, International
1966	Mike Epstein, Rochester, International
1967	Johnny Bench, Buffalo, International
1968	Merv Rettenmund, Rochester, International
1969	Danny Walton, Oklahoma City, American Association
1970	Don Baylor, Rochester, International
1971	Bobby Grich, Rochester, International
1972	Tom Paciorek, Albuquerque, Pacific Coast
1973	Steve Ontiveros, Phoenix, Pacific Coast
1974	Jim Rice, Pawtucket, International
1975	Hector Cruz, Tulsa, American Association

Year	Player, Team, League	Year	Player, Team, League
1976	Pat Putnam, Asheville, Western Carolina	1990	Jose Offerman, Albuquerque, Pacific Coast
1977	Ken Landreaux, S.L.C., Pacific Coast; El Paso, Texas	1991	Pedro Martinez, Albuquerque, Pacific Coast
1978	Champ Summers, Indianapolis, American Association	1992	Tim Salmon, Edmonton, Pacific Coast
1979	Mark Bomback, Vancouver, Pacific Coast	1993	Cliff Floyd, Harrisburg, Eastern
1980	Tim Raines, Denver, American Association	1994	Derek Jeter, Tampa, Florida State; Albany, Eastern;
1981	Mike Marshall, Albuquerque, Pacific Coast		Columbus, International
1982	Ron Kittle, Edmonton, Pacific Coast	1995	Karim Garcia, Albuquerque, Pacific Coast
1983	Kevin McReynolds, Las Vegas, Pacific Coast	1996	Vladimir Guerrero, West Palm Beach, Florida State;
1984	Alan Knicely, Wichita, American Association		Harrisburg, Eastern
1985	Jose Canseco, Hunt., Southern-Tac., Pacific Coast	1997	Ben Grieve, Huntsville, Southern; Edmonton, Pacific Coast
1986	Tim Pyznarski, Las Vegas, Pacific Coast	1998	Gabe Kapler, Jacksonville, Southern
1987	Randy Milligan, Tidewater, International	1999	Rick Ankiel, Arkansas, Texas; Memphis, Pacific Coast
1988	Sandy Alomar Jr., Las Vegas, Pacific Coast	2000	Jon Rauch, Win.-Salem, Carolina; Birmingham, Southern
	Gary Sheffield, Denver, American Association (tie)	2001	Josh Beckett, Brevard County, Fla. State; Portland, Eastern
1989	Sandy Alomar Jr., Las Vegas, Pacific Coast	2002	Jason Stokes, Kane County, Midwest

MINOR LEAGUE MANAGER OF THE YEAR

Year	Manager, Team, League	Year	Manager, Team, League
1936	Al Sothoron, Milwaukee, American Association	1970	Tommy Lasorda, Spokane, Pacific Coast
1937	Jake Flowers, Salisbury, Eastern Shore	1971	Del Rice, Salt Lake City, Pacific Coast
1938	Paul Richards, Atlanta, Southern	1972	Hank Bauer, Tidewater, International
1939	Bill Meyer, Kansas City, American Association	1973	Joe Morgan, Charleston, International
1940	Larry Gilbert, Nashville, Southern	1974	Joe Altobelli, Rochester, International
1941	Burt Shotton, Columbus, American Association	1975	Joe Frazier, Tidewater, International
1942	Eddie Dyer, Columbus, American Association	1976	Vern Rapp, Denver, American Association
1943	Nick Cullop, Columbus, American Association	1977	Tommy Thompson, Arkan., Texas
1944	Al Thomas, Baltimore, International	1978	Les Moss, Evansville, American Association
1945	Lefty O'Doul, San Francisco, Pacific Coast	1979	Vern Benson, Syracuse, International
1946	Clay Hopper, Montreal, International	1980	Hal Lanier, Springfield, American Association
1947	Nick Cullop, Milwaukee, American Association	1981	Del Crandall, Albuquerque, Pacific Coast
1948	Casey Stengel, Oakland, Pacific Coast	1982	George Scherger, Indianapolis, American Association
1949	Fred Haney, Hollywood, Pacific Coast	1983	Bill Dancy, Reading, Eastern
1950	Rollie Hemsley, Columbus, American Association	1984	Bob Rodgers, Indianapolis, American Association
1951	Charlie Grimm, Milwaukee, American Association	1985	Jim Fregosi, Louisville, American Association
1952	Luke Appling, Memphis, Southern	1986	Joe Sparks, Indianapolis, American Association
1953	Bobby Bragan, Hollywood, Pacific Coast	1987	Terry Collins, Albuquerque, Pacific Coast
1954	Kerby Farrell, Indianapolis, American Association	1988	Joe Sparks, Indianapolis, American Association
1955	Bill Rigney, Minneapolis, American Association	1989	Bob Bailor, Syracuse, International
1956	Kerby Farrell, Indianapolis, American Association	1990	Sal Rende, Omaha, American Association
1957	Ben Geraghty, Wichita, American Association	1991	Chris Chambliss, Greenville, Southern
1958	Cal Ermer, Birmingham, Southern	1992	Grady Little, Greenville, Southern
1959	Pete Reiser, Victoria, Texas	1993	Jim Tracy, Harrisburg, Eastern
1960	Mel McGaha, Toronto, International	1994	Mike Jirschele, Wilmington, Carolina
1961	Kerby Farrell, Buffalo, International	1995	Pete Mackanin, Ottawa, International
1962	Ben Geraghty, Jacksonville, International	1996	John Mizerock, Wilmington, Carolina
1963	Rollie Hemsley, Indianapolis, International	1997	Marv Foley, Rochester, International
1964	Harry Walker, Jacksonville, International	1998	Doug Davis, Columbia, South Atlantic
1965	Grady Hatton, Oklahoma City, Pacific Coast	1999	DeMarlo Hale, Trenton, Eastern
1966	Bob Lemon, Seattle, Pacific Coast	2000	Joel Skinner, Buffalo, International
1967	Bob Skinner, San Diego, Pacific Coast	2001	Tony Pena, New Orleans, Pacific Coast
1968	Jack Tighe, Toledo, International	2002	Eric Wedge, Buffalo, International
1969	Clyde McCullough, Tidewater, International		

MINOR LEAGUE EXECUTIVE OF THE YEAR (HIGHER CLASSIFICATIONS, 1936-1992)

(Restricted to Class AAA starting in 1963)

Year	Executive, Team, League	Year	Executive, Team, League
1936	Earl Mann, Atlanta, Southern	1951	Robert Howsam, Denver, West
1937	Robert LaMotte, Savannah, Sally	1952	Jack Cooke, Toronto, International
1938	Louis McKenna, St. Paul, American Association	1953	Richard Burnett, Dallas, Texas
1939	Bruce Dudley, Louisville, American Association	1954	Edward Stumpf, Indianapolis, American Association
1940	Roy Hamey, Kansas City, American Association	1955	Dewey Soriano, Seattle, Pacific Coast
1941	Emil Sick, Seattle, Pacific Coast	1956	Robert Howsam, Denver American Association
1942	Bill Veeck, Milwaukee, American Association	1957	John Stiglmeier, Buffalo, International
1943	Clarence Rowland, Los Angeles, Pacific Coast	1958	Edward Glennon, Birmingham, Southern
1944	William Mulligan, Seattle, Pacific Coast	1959	Edward Leishman, Salt Lake City, Pacific Coast
1945	Bruce Dudley, Louisville, American Association	1960	Ray Winder, Little Rock, Southern
1946	Earl Mann, Atlanta, Southern	1961	Elten Schiller, Omaha, American Association
1947	William Purnhage, Waterloo, I.I.I.	1962	George Sisler Jr., Rochester, International
1948	Edward Glennon, Birmingham, Southern	1963	Lewis Matlin, Hawaii, Pacific Coast
1949	Ted Sullivan, Indianapolis, American Association	1964	Edward Leishman, San Diego, Pacific Coast
1950	Clearnce (Brick) Laws, Oakland, Pacific Coast	1965	Harold Cooper, Columbus, International

Year	Executive, Team, League	Year	Executive, Team, League
1966—John Quinn Jr., Hawaii, Pacific Coast		1980—Jim Burris, Denver, American Association	
1967—Hillman Lyons, Richmond, International		1981—Pat McKernan, Albuquerque, Pacific Coast	
1968—Gabe Paul Jr., Tulsa, Pacific Coast		1982—A. Ray Smith, Louisville, American Association	
1969—Bill Gardner, Louisville, International		1983—A. Ray Smith, Louisville, American Association	
1970—Dick King, Wichita, American Association		1984—Mike Tamburro, Pawtucket, International	
1971—Carl Steinfeldt Jr., Rochester, International		1985—Patty Cox Hampton, Oklahoma City, American Association	
1972—Don Labbruzzo, Evansville, American Association		1986—Bob Goughan, Rochester, International	
1973—Merle Miller, Tucson, Pacific Coast		1987—Stu Kehoe, Vancouver, Pacific Coast	
1974—John Carbray, Sacramento, Pacific Coast		1988—Bob Rich, Buffalo, American Association	
1975—Stan Naccarato, Tacoma, Pacific Coast		1989—Larry Schmittou, Nashville, American Association	
1976—Art Teece, Salt Lake City, Pacific Coast		1990—Greg Corns, Phoenix, Pacific Coast	
1977—George Sisler Jr., Columbus, International		1991—Tom Maloney, Denver, American Association	
1978—Willie Sanchez, Albuquerque, Pacific Coast		1992—Lou Schwechheimer, Pawtucket, International	
1979—George Sisler Jr., Columbus, International			

MINOR LEAGUE EXECUTIVE OF THE YEAR (LOWER CLASSIFICATIONS, 1950-1990)

(Separate awards for Class AA and Class A started in 1963; for Short Class A in 1988)

Year	Executive, Team, League	Year	Executive, Team, League
1950—H. Cooper, Hutchinson, Western Association		1975—Jim Paul, El Paso, Texas	
1951—O. W. (Bill) Hayes, Triple, B.S.		Cordy Jensen, Eugene, Northwest	
1952—Hillman Lyons, Danville, MOV		1976—Woodrow Reid, Chattanooga, Southern	
1953—Carl Roth, Peoria, I.I.I.		Don Buchheister, Cedar Rapids, Midwest	
1954—James Meagham, Cedar Rapids, I.I.I.		1977—Jim Paul, El Paso, Texas	
1955—John Petrakis, Dubuque, MOV		Harry Pells, Quad Cities, Midwest	
1956—Marvin Milkes, Fresno, California		1978—Larry Schmittou, Nashville, Southern	
1957—Richard Wagner, Lincoln, West.		Dave Hersh, Appleton, Midwest	
1958—Gerald Waring, Macon, Sally		1979—Bill Rigney Jr., Midland, Texas	
1959—Clay Dennis, Des Moines, I.I.I.		Tom Romenesko, Greensboro, W.C.	
1960—Hubert Kittle, Yakima, Northwest		1980—Frances Crockett, Charlotte, Southern	
1961—David Steele, Fresno, California		Tom Romenesko, Greensboro, W.C.	
1962—John Quinn Jr., San Jose, California		1981—Allie Prescott, Memphis, Southern	
1963—Hugh Finnerty, Tulsa, Texas		Dan Overstreet, Hagerstown, Caro.	
Ben Jewell, M. Valley, Pioneer		1982—Art Clarkson, Birmingham, Southern	
1964—Glynn West, Birmingham, Southern		Bob Carruesco, Stockton, California	
James Bayens, Rock Hill, W. Carolina		1983—Edward Kenney, New Britain, Eastern	
1965—Dick Butler, Dallas-Ft. Worth, Texas		Terry Reynolds, Vero Beach, Florida State	
Ken. Blackman, Quad Cities, Midwest		1984—Bruce Baldwin, Greenville, Southern	
1966—Tom Fleming, Evansville, Southern		Dave Tarrolly, Beloit, Midwest	
Cappy Harada, Lodi, California		1985—Ben Bernard, Albany-Colonie, Eastern	
1967—Robert Quinn, Reading, Eastern		Pete Vonachen, Peoria, Midwest	
Pat Williams, Spar'burg, W.C.		1986—Bill Davidson, Midland, Texas	
1968—Phil Howser, Charlotte, Southern		Rob Dlugozima, Durham, Carolina	
Merle Miller, Burlington, Midwest		1987—Joe Preseren, Tulsa, Texas	
1969—Charlie Blaney, Albuquerque, Texas		Skip Weisman, Greensboro, South Atlantic	
Bill Gorman, Visalia, California		1988—Bill Valentine, Arkansas, Texas	
1970—Carl Sawatski, Arkansas, Texas		Dennis Bastien, Charleston (W.Va.), South Atlantic	
Bob Williams, Bakersfield, California		Bob Beban, Eugene, Northwest	
1971—Miles Wolff, Savannah, Dixie Association		1989—Chuck Domino, Reading, Eastern	
Ed Holtz, Appleton, Midwest		John Baxter, South Bend, Midwest	
1972—John Begzos, S. Antonio, Texas		Bill Pereira, Boise, Northwest	
Bob Piccinini, Modesto, California		1990—Joe Preseren, Tulsa, Texas	
1973—Dick Kravitz, Jacksonville, Southern		Dan Chapman, Stockton, California	
Fritz Colschen, Clinton, Midwest		Dave Baggott, Salt Lake City, Pioneer	
1974—Jim Paul, El Paso, Texas			
Bing Russell, Portland, Northwest			

MINOR LEAGUE EXECUTIVE OF THE YEAR

Year	Executive, Team, League	Year	Executive, Team, League
1993—Todd Vander Woude, Harrisburg, Eastern (AA)		1998—Chuck Domino, Reading, Eastern (AA)	
1994—Scott Lane, West Michigan, Midwest (A)		1999—Ben Mondor, Pawtucket, International (AAA)	
1995—Jack and Mary Cain, Portland, Northwest (A)		2000—Art Savage, Sacramento, Pacific Coast (AAA)	
1996—Wayne Hodes, Trenton, Eastern (AA)		2001—Jay Miller, Round Rock, Texas (AA)	
1997—Andy Milovich, Erie, New York-Pennsylvania (A)		2002—Gary Arthur, Sacramento, Pacific Coast (AAA)	

1957
MAJORS
P— Bobby Shantz, New York A.L.
C— Sherm Lollar, Chicago A.L.
1B— Gil Hodges, Brooklyn N.L.
2B— Nellie Fox, Chicago A.L.
3B— Frank Malzone, Boston A.L.
SS— Roy McMillan, Cincinnati N.L.
OF— Minnie Minoso, Chicago A.L.
OF— Willie Mays, New York N.L.
OF— Al Kaline, Detroit A.L.

1958
AMERICAN LEAGUE
P— Bobby Shantz, New York
C— Sherm Lollar, Chicago
1B— Vic Power, K.C.-Cle.
2B— Frank Bolling, Detroit
3B— Frank Malzone, Boston
SS— Luis Aparicio, Chicago
OF— Norm Siebern, New York
OF— Jimmy Piersall, Boston
OF— Al Kaline, Detroit

NATIONAL LEAGUE
P— Harvey Haddix, Cincinnati
C— Del Crandall, Milwaukee
1B— Gil Hodges, Los Angeles
2B— Bill Mazeroski, Pittsburgh
3B— Ken Boyer, St. Louis
SS— Roy McMillan, Cincinnati
OF— Frank Robinson, Cincinnati
OF— Willie Mays, San Francisco
OF— Hank Aaron, Milwaukee

1959
AMERICAN LEAGUE
P— Bobby Shantz, New York
C— Sherm Lollar, Chicago
1B— Vic Power, Cleveland
2B— Nellie Fox, Chicago
3B— Frank Malzone, Boston
SS— Luis Aparicio, Chicago
OF— Minnie Minoso, Cleveland
OF— Al Kaline, Detroit
OF— Jackie Jensen, Boston

NATIONAL LEAGUE
P— Harvey Haddix, Pittsburgh
C— Del Crandall, Milwaukee
1B— Gil Hodges, Los Angeles
2B— Charley Neal, Los Angeles
3B— Ken Boyer, St. Louis
SS— Roy McMillan, Cincinnati
OF— Jackie Brandt, San Francisco
OF— Willie Mays, San Francisco
OF— Hank Aaron, Milwaukee

1960
AMERICAN LEAGUE
P— Bobby Shantz, New York
C— Earl Battey, Washington
1B— Vic Power, Cleveland
2B— Nellie Fox, Chicago
3B— Brooks Robinson, Baltimore
SS— Luis Aparicio, Chicago
OF— Minnie Minoso, Chicago
OF— Jim Landis, Chicago
OF— Roger Maris, New York

NATIONAL LEAGUE
P— Harvey Haddix, Pittsburgh
C— Del Crandall, Milwaukee
1B— Bill White, St. Louis
2B— Bill Mazeroski, Pittsburgh

3B— Ken Boyer, St. Louis
SS— Ernie Banks, Chicago
OF— Wally Moon, Los Angeles
OF— Willie Mays, San Francisco
OF— Hank Aaron, Milwaukee

1961
AMERICAN LEAGUE
P— Frank Lary, Detroit
C— Earl Battey, Minnesota
1B— Vic Power, Cleveland
2B— Bobby Richardson, New York
3B— Brooks Robinson, Baltimore
SS— Luis Aparicio, Chicago
OF— Al Kaline, Detroit
OF— Jimmy Piersall, Cleveland
OF— Jim Landis, Chicago

NATIONAL LEAGUE
P— Bobby Shantz, Pittsburgh
C— John Roseboro, Los Angeles
1B— Bill White, St. Louis
2B— Bill Mazeroski, Pittsburgh
3B— Ken Boyer, St. Louis
SS— Maury Wills, Los Angeles
OF— Willie Mays, San Francisco
OF— Roberto Clemente, Pittsburgh
OF— Vada Pinson, Cincinnati

1962
AMERICAN LEAGUE
P— Jim Kaat, Minnesota
C— Earl Battey, Minnesota
1B— Vic Power, Minnesota
2B— Bobby Richardson, New York
3B— Brooks Robinson, Baltimore
SS— Luis Aparicio, Chicago
OF— Jim Landis, Chicago
OF— Mickey Mantle, New York
OF— Al Kaline, Detroit

NATIONAL LEAGUE
P— Bobby Shantz, Hou.-St.L.
C— Del Crandall, Milwaukee
1B— Bill White, St. Louis
2B— Ken Hubbs, Chicago
3B— Jim Davenport, San Francisco
SS— Maury Wills, Los Angeles
OF— Willie Mays, San Francisco
OF— Roberto Clemente, Pittsburgh
OF— Bill Virdon, Pittsburgh

1963
AMERICAN LEAGUE
P— Jim Kaat, Minnesota
C— Elston Howard, New York
1B— Vic Power, Minnesota
2B— Bobby Richardson, New York
3B— Brooks Robinson, Baltimore
SS— Zoilo Versalles, Minnesota
OF— Al Kaline, Detroit
OF— Carl Yastrzemski, Boston
OF— Jim Landis, Chicago

NATIONAL LEAGUE
P— Bobby Shantz, St. Louis
C— Johnny Edwards, Cincinnati
1B— Bill White, St. Louis
2B— Bill Mazeroski, Pittsburgh
3B— Ken Boyer, St. Louis
SS— Bobby Wine, Philadelphia
OF— Willie Mays, San Francisco
OF— Roberto Clemente, Pittsburgh
OF— Curt Flood, St. Louis

1964
AMERICAN LEAGUE
P— Jim Kaat, Minnesota
C— Elston Howard, New York
1B— Vic Power, Min.-L.A.
2B— Bobby Richardson, New York
3B— Brooks Robinson, Baltimore
SS— Luis Aparicio, Baltimore
OF— Al Kaline, Detroit
OF— Jim Landis, Chicago
OF— Vic Davalillo, Cleveland

NATIONAL LEAGUE
P— Bobby Shantz, St.L.-Chi.-Phi.
C— Johnny Edwards, Cincinnati
1B— Bill White, St. Louis
2B— Bill Mazeroski, Pittsburgh
3B— Ron Santo, Chicago
SS— Ruben Amaro, Philadelphia
OF— Willie Mays, San Francisco
OF— Roberto Clemente, Pittsburgh
OF— Curt Flood, St. Louis

1965
AMERICAN LEAGUE
P— Jim Kaat, Minnesota
C— Bill Freehan, Detroit
1B— Joe Pepitone, New York
2B— Bobby Richardson, New York
3B— Brooks Robinson, Baltimore
SS— Zoilo Versalles, Minnesota
OF— Al Kaline, Detroit
OF— Tom Tresh, New York
OF— Carl Yastrzemski, Boston

NATIONAL LEAGUE
P— Bob Gibson, St. Louis
C— Joe Torre, Milwaukee
1B— Bill White, St. Louis
2B— Bill Mazeroski, Pittsburgh
3B— Ron Santo, Chicago
SS— Leo Cardenas, Cincinnati
OF— Willie Mays, San Francisco
OF— Roberto Clemente, Pittsburgh
OF— Curt Flood, St. Louis

1966
AMERICAN LEAGUE
P— Jim Kaat, Minnesota
C— Bill Freehan, Detroit
1B— Joe Pepitone, New York
2B— Bobby Knoop, California
3B— Brooks Robinson, Baltimore
SS— Luis Aparicio, Baltimore
OF— Al Kaline, Detroit
OF— Tommie Agee, Chicago
OF— Tony Oliva, Minnesota

NATIONAL LEAGUE
P— Bob Gibson, St. Louis
C— John Roseboro, Los Angeles
1B— Bill White, Philadelphia
2B— Bill Mazeroski, Pittsburgh
3B— Ron Santo, Chicago
SS— Gene Alley, Pittsburgh
OF— Willie Mays, San Francisco
OF— Curt Flood, St. Louis
OF— Roberto Clemente, Pittsburgh

1967
AMERICAN LEAGUE
P— Jim Kaat, Minnesota
C— Bill Freehan, Detroit
1B— George Scott, Boston
2B— Bobby Knoop, California
3B— Brooks Robinson, Baltimore

HISTORY *Award winners*

SS— Jim Fregosi, California
OF— Carl Yastrzemski, Boston
OF— Paul Blair, Baltimore
OF— Al Kaline, Detroit

NATIONAL LEAGUE
P— Bob Gibson, St. Louis
C— Randy Hundley, Chicago
1B— Wes Parker, Los Angeles
2B— Bill Mazeroski, Pittsburgh
3B— Ron Santo, Chicago
SS— Gene Alley, Pittsburgh
OF— Roberto Clemente, Pittsburgh
OF— Curt Flood, St. Louis
OF— Willie Mays, San Francisco

1968
AMERICAN LEAGUE
P— Jim Kaat, Minnesota
C— Bill Freehan, Detroit
1B— George Scott, Boston
2B— Bobby Knoop, California
3B— Brooks Robinson, Baltimore
SS— Luis Aparicio, Chicago
OF— Mickey Stanley, Detroit
OF— Carl Yastrzemski, Boston
OF— Reggie Smith, Boston

NATIONAL LEAGUE
P— Bob Gibson, St. Louis
C— Johnny Bench, Cincinnati
1B— Wes Parker, Los Angeles
2B— Glenn Beckert, Chicago
3B— Ron Santo, Chicago
SS— Dal Maxvill, St. Louis
OF— Willie Mays, San Francisco
OF— Roberto Clemente, Pittsburgh
OF— Curt Flood, St. Louis

1969
AMERICAN LEAGUE
P— Jim Kaat, Minnesota
C— Bill Freehan, Detroit
1B— Joe Pepitone, New York
2B— Dave Johnson, Baltimore
3B— Brooks Robinson, Baltimore
SS— Mark Belanger, Baltimore
OF— Paul Blair, Baltimore
OF— Mickey Stanley, Detroit
OF— Carl Yastrzemski, Boston

NATIONAL LEAGUE
P— Bob Gibson, St. Louis
C— Johnny Bench, Cincinnati
1B— Wes Parker, Los Angeles
2B— Felix Millan, Atlanta
3B— Clete Boyer, Atlanta
SS— Don Kessinger, Chicago
OF— Roberto Clemente, Pittsburgh
OF— Curt Flood, St. Louis
OF— Pete Rose, Cincinnati

1970
AMERICAN LEAGUE
P— Jim Kaat, Minnesota
C— Ray Fosse, Cleveland
1B— Jim Spencer, California
2B— Dave Johnson, Baltimore
3B— Brooks Robinson, Baltimore
SS— Luis Aparicio, Chicago
OF— Mickey Stanley, Detroit
OF— Paul Blair, Baltimore
OF— Ken Berry, Chicago

NATIONAL LEAGUE
P— Bob Gibson, St. Louis
C— Johnny Bench, Cincinnati

1B— Wes Parker, Los Angeles
2B— Tommy Helms, Cincinnati
3B— Doug Rader, Houston
SS— Don Kessinger, Chicago
OF— Roberto Clemente, Pittsburgh
OF— Tommie Agee, New York
OF— Pete Rose, Cincinnati

1971
AMERICAN LEAGUE
P— Jim Kaat, Minnesota
C— Ray Fosse, Cleveland
1B— George Scott, Boston
2B— Dave Johnson, Baltimore
3B— Brooks Robinson, Baltimore
SS— Mark Belanger, Baltimore
OF— Paul Blair, Baltimore
OF— Amos Otis, Kansas City
OF— Carl Yastrzemski, Boston

NATIONAL LEAGUE
P— Bob Gibson, St. Louis
C— Johnny Bench, Cincinnati
1B— Wes Parker, Los Angeles
2B— Tommy Helms, Cincinnati
3B— Doug Rader, Houston
SS— Bud Harrelson, New York
OF— Roberto Clemente, Pittsburgh
OF— Bobby Bonds, San Francisco
OF— Willie Davis, Los Angeles

1972
AMERICAN LEAGUE
P— Jim Kaat, Minnesota
C— Carlton Fisk, Boston
1B— George Scott, Milwaukee
2B— Doug Griffin, Boston
3B— Brooks Robinson, Baltimore
SS— Ed Brinkman, Detroit
OF— Paul Blair, Baltimore
OF— Bobby Murcer, New York
OF— Ken Berry, California

NATIONAL LEAGUE
P— Bob Gibson, St. Louis
C— Johnny Bench, Cincinnati
1B— Wes Parker, Los Angeles
2B— Felix Millan, Atlanta
3B— Doug Rader, Houston
SS— Larry Bowa, Philadelphia
OF— Roberto Clemente, Pittsburgh
OF— Cesar Cedeno, Houston
OF— Willie Davis, Los Angeles

1973
AMERICAN LEAGUE
P— Jim Kaat, Chicago
C— Thurman Munson, New York
1B— George Scott, Milwaukee
2B— Bobby Grich, Baltimore
3B— Brooks Robinson, Baltimore
SS— Mark Belanger, Baltimore
OF— Paul Blair, Baltimore
OF— Amos Otis, Kansas City
OF— Mickey Stanley, Detroit

NATIONAL LEAGUE
P— Bob Gibson, St. Louis
C— Johnny Bench, Cincinnati
1B— Mike Jorgensen, Montreal
2B— Joe Morgan, Cincinnati
3B— Doug Rader, Houston
SS— Roger Metzger, Houston
OF— Bobby Bonds, San Francisco
OF— Cesar Cedeno, Houston
OF— Willie Davis, Los Angeles

1974
AMERICAN LEAGUE
P— Jim Kaat, Chicago
C— Thurman Munson, New York
1B— George Scott, Milwaukee
2B— Bobby Grich, Baltimore
3B— Brooks Robinson, Baltimore
SS— Mark Belanger, Baltimore
OF— Paul Blair, Baltimore
OF— Amos Otis, Kansas City
OF— Joe Rudi, Oakland

NATIONAL LEAGUE
P— Andy Messersmith, Los Angeles
C— Johnny Bench, Cincinnati
1B— Steve Garvey, Los Angeles
2B— Joe Morgan, Cincinnati
3B— Doug Rader, Houston
SS— Dave Concepcion, Cincinnati
OF— Cesar Cedeno, Houston
OF— Cesar Geronimo, Cincinnati
OF— Bobby Bonds, San Francisco

1975
AMERICAN LEAGUE
P— Jim Kaat, Chicago
C— Thurman Munson, New York
1B— George Scott, Milwaukee
2B— Bobby Grich, Baltimore
3B— Brooks Robinson, Baltimore
SS— Mark Belanger, Baltimore
OF— Paul Blair, Baltimore
OF— Joe Rudi, Oakland
OF— Fred Lynn, Boston

NATIONAL LEAGUE
P— Andy Messersmith, Los Angeles
C— Johnny Bench, Cincinnati
1B— Steve Garvey, Los Angeles
2B— Joe Morgan, Cincinnati
3B— Ken Reitz, St. Louis
SS— Dave Concepcion, Cincinnati
OF— Cesar Cedeno, Houston
OF— Cesar Geronimo, Cincinnati
OF— Garry Maddox, S.F.-Phi.

1976
AMERICAN LEAGUE
P— Jim Palmer, Baltimore
C— Jim Sundberg, Texas
1B— George Scott, Milwaukee
2B— Bobby Grich, Baltimore
3B— Aurelio Rodriguez, Detroit
SS— Mark Belanger, Baltimore
OF— Joe Rudi, Oakland
OF— Dwight Evans, Boston
OF— Rick Manning, Cleveland

NATIONAL LEAGUE
P— Jim Kaat, Philadelphia
C— Johnny Bench, Cincinnati
1B— Steve Garvey, Los Angeles
2B— Joe Morgan, Cincinnati
3B— Mike Schmidt, Philadelphia
SS— Dave Concepcion, Cincinnati
OF— Cesar Cedeno, Houston
OF— Cesar Geronimo, Cincinnati
OF— Garry Maddox, Philadelphia

1977
AMERICAN LEAGUE
P— Jim Palmer, Baltimore
C— Jim Sundberg, Texas
1B— Jim Spencer, Chicago
2B— Frank White, Kansas City
3B— Graig Nettles, New York
SS— Mark Belanger, Baltimore
OF— Juan Beniquez, Texas
OF— Carl Yastrzemski, Boston
OF— Al Cowens, Kansas City

NATIONAL LEAGUE
P— Jim Kaat, Philadelphia
C— Johnny Bench, Cincinnati
1B— Steve Garvey, Los Angeles
2B— Joe Morgan, Cincinnati
3B— Mike Schmidt, Philadelphia
SS— Dave Concepcion, Cincinnati
OF— Cesar Geronimo, Cincinnati
OF— Garry Maddox, Philadelphia
OF— Dave Parker, Pittsburgh

1978
AMERICAN LEAGUE
P— Jim Palmer, Baltimore
C— Jim Sundberg, Texas
1B— Chris Chambliss, New York
2B— Frank White, Kansas City
3B— Graig Nettles, New York
SS— Mark Belanger, Baltimore
OF— Fred Lynn, Boston
OF— Dwight Evans, Boston
OF— Rick Miller, California

NATIONAL LEAGUE
P— Phil Niekro, Atlanta
C— Bob Boone, Philadelphia
1B— Keith Hernandez, St. Louis
2B— Dave Lopes, Los Angeles
3B— Mike Schmidt, Philadelphia
SS— Larry Bowa, Philadelphia
OF— Garry Maddox, Philadelphia
OF— Dave Parker, Pittsburgh
OF— Ellis Valentine, Montreal

1979
AMERICAN LEAGUE
P— Jim Palmer, Baltimore
C— Jim Sundberg, Texas
1B— Cecil Cooper, Milwaukee
2B— Frank White, Kansas City
3B— Buddy Bell, Texas
SS— Rick Burleson, Boston
OF— Dwight Evans, Boston
OF— Sixto Lezcano, Milwaukee
OF— Fred Lynn, Boston

NATIONAL LEAGUE
P— Phil Niekro, Atlanta
C— Bob Boone, Philadelphia
1B— Keith Hernandez, St. Louis
2B— Manny Trillo, Philadelphia
3B— Mike Schmidt, Philadelphia
SS— Dave Concepcion, Cincinnati
OF— Garry Maddox, Philadelphia
OF— Dave Parker, Pittsburgh
OF— Dave Winfield, San Diego

1980
AMERICAN LEAGUE
P— Mike Norris, Oakland
C— Jim Sundberg, Texas
1B— Cecil Cooper, Milwaukee
2B— Frank White, Kansas City
3B— Buddy Bell, Texas
SS— Alan Trammell, Detroit
OF— Fred Lynn, Boston
OF— Dwayne Murphy, Oakland
OF— Willie Wilson, Kansas City

NATIONAL LEAGUE
P— Phil Niekro, Atlanta
C— Gary Carter, Montreal
1B— Keith Hernandez, St. Louis
2B— Doug Flynn, New York
3B— Mike Schmidt, Philadelphia
SS— Ozzie Smith, San Diego
OF— Andre Dawson, Montreal
OF— Garry Maddox, Philadelphia
OF— Dave Winfield, San Diego

1981
AMERICAN LEAGUE
P— Mike Norris, Oakland
C— Jim Sundberg, Texas
1B— Mike Squires, Chicago
2B— Frank White, Kansas City
3B— Buddy Bell, Texas
SS— Alan Trammell, Detroit
OF— Dwayne Murphy, Oakland
OF— Dwight Evans, Boston
OF— Rickey Henderson, Oakland

NATIONAL LEAGUE
P— Steve Carlton, Philadelphia
C— Gary Carter, Montreal
1B— Keith Hernandez, St. Louis
2B— Manny Trillo, Philadelphia
3B— Mike Schmidt, Philadelphia
SS— Ozzie Smith, San Diego
OF— Andre Dawson, Montreal
OF— Garry Maddox, Philadelphia
OF— Dusty Baker, Los Angeles

1982
AMERICAN LEAGUE
P— Ron Guidry, New York
C— Bob Boone, California
1B— Eddie Murray, Baltimore
2B— Frank White, Kansas City
3B— Buddy Bell, Texas
SS— Robin Yount, Milwaukee
OF— Dwight Evans, Boston
OF— Dave Winfield, New York
OF— Dwayne Murphy, Oakland

NATIONAL LEAGUE
P— Phil Niekro, Atlanta
C— Gary Carter, Montreal
1B— Keith Hernandez, St. Louis
2B— Manny Trillo, Philadelphia
3B— Mike Schmidt, Philadelphia
SS— Ozzie Smith, St. Louis
OF— Andre Dawson, Montreal
OF— Dale Murphy, Atlanta
OF— Garry Maddox, Philadelphia

1983
AMERICAN LEAGUE
P— Ron Guidry, New York
C— Lance Parrish, Detroit
1B— Eddie Murray, Baltimore
2B— Lou Whitaker, Detroit
3B— Buddy Bell, Texas
SS— Alan Trammell, Detroit
OF— Dwight Evans, Boston
OF— Dave Winfield, New York
OF— Dwayne Murphy, Oakland

NATIONAL LEAGUE
P— Phil Niekro, Atlanta
C— Tony Pena, Pittsburgh
1B— Keith Hernandez, St.L.-N.Y.
2B— Ryne Sandberg, Chicago
3B— Mike Schmidt, Philadelphia
SS— Ozzie Smith, St. Louis
OF— Andre Dawson, Montreal
OF— Dale Murphy, Atlanta
OF— Willie McGee, St. Louis

1984
AMERICAN LEAGUE
P— Ron Guidry, New York
C— Lance Parrish, Detroit
1B— Eddie Murray, Baltimore
2B— Lou Whitaker, Detroit
3B— Buddy Bell, Texas
SS— Alan Trammell, Detroit
OF— Dwight Evans, Boston
OF— Dave Winfield, New York
OF— Dwayne Murphy, Oakland

NATIONAL LEAGUE
P— Joaquin Andujar, St. Louis
C— Tony Pena, Pittsburgh
1B— Keith Hernandez, New York
2B— Ryne Sandberg, Chicago
3B— Mike Schmidt, Philadelphia
SS— Ozzie Smith, St. Louis
OF— Dale Murphy, Atlanta
OF— Bob Dernier, Chicago
OF— Andre Dawson, Montreal

1985
AMERICAN LEAGUE
P— Ron Guidry, New York
C— Lance Parrish, Detroit
1B— Don Mattingly, New York
2B— Lou Whitaker, Detroit
3B— George Brett, Kansas City
SS— Alfredo Griffin, Oakland
OF— Gary Pettis, California
OF— Dave Winfield, New York
OF— Dwight Evans, Boston (tie)
　　Dwayne Murphy, Oakland (tie)

NATIONAL LEAGUE
P— Rick Reuschel, Pittsburgh
C— Tony Pena, Pittsburgh
1B— Keith Hernandez, New York
2B— Ryne Sandberg, Chicago
3B— Tim Wallach, Montreal
SS— Ozzie Smith, St. Louis
OF— Willie McGee, St. Louis
OF— Dale Murphy, Atlanta
OF— Andre Dawson, Montreal

1986
AMERICAN LEAGUE
P— Ron Guidry, New York
C— Bob Boone, California
1B— Don Mattingly, New York
2B— Frank White, Kansas City
3B— Gary Gaetti, Minnesota
SS— Tony Fernandez, Toronto
OF— Gary Pettis, California
OF— Jesse Barfield, Toronto
OF— Kirby Puckett, Minnesota

NATIONAL LEAGUE
P— Fernando Valenzuela, Los Angeles
C— Jody Davis, Chicago
1B— Keith Hernandez, New York
2B— Ryne Sandberg, Chicago
3B— Mike Schmidt, Philadelphia
SS— Ozzie Smith, St. Louis
OF— Tony Gwynn, San Diego
OF— Dale Murphy, Atlanta
OF— Willie McGee, St. Louis

1987
AMERICAN LEAGUE
P— Mark Langston, Seattle
C— Bob Boone, California
1B— Don Mattingly, New York
2B— Frank White, Kansas City
3B— Gary Gaetti, Minnesota
SS— Tony Fernandez, Toronto
OF— Jesse Barfield, Toronto
OF— Kirby Puckett, Minnesota
OF— Dave Winfield, New York

NATIONAL LEAGUE
P— Rick Reuschel, Pit.-S.F.
C— Mike LaValliere, Pittsburgh
1B— Keith Hernandez, New York
2B— Ryne Sandberg, Chicago
3B— Terry Pendleton, St. Louis
SS— Ozzie Smith, St. Louis
OF— Eric Davis, Cincinnati
OF— Tony Gwynn, San Diego
OF— Andre Dawson, Chicago

1988
AMERICAN LEAGUE
P— Mark Langston, Seattle
C— Bob Boone, California
1B— Don Mattingly, New York
2B— Harold Reynolds, Seattle
3B— Gary Gaetti, Minnesota
SS— Tony Fernandez, Toronto
OF— Kirby Puckett, Minnesota
OF— Devon White, California
OF— Gary Pettis, Detroit

NATIONAL LEAGUE
P— Orel Hershiser, Los Angeles
C— Benito Santiago, San Diego
1B— Keith Hernandez, New York
2B— Ryne Sandberg, Chicago
3B— Tim Wallach, Montreal
SS— Ozzie Smith, St. Louis
OF— Andy Van Slyke, Pittsburgh
OF— Eric Davis, Cincinnati
OF— Andre Dawson, Chicago

1989
AMERICAN LEAGUE
P— Bret Saberhagen, Kansas City
C— Bob Boone, Kansas City
1B— Don Mattingly, New York
2B— Harold Reynolds, Seattle
3B— Gary Gaetti, Minnesota
SS— Tony Fernandez, Toronto
OF— Kirby Puckett, Minnesota
OF— Devon White, California
OF— Gary Pettis, Detroit

NATIONAL LEAGUE
P— Ron Darling, New York
C— Benito Santiago, San Diego
1B— Andres Galarraga, Montreal
2B— Ryne Sandberg, Chicago
3B— Terry Pendleton, St. Louis
SS— Ozzie Smith, St. Louis
OF— Andy Van Slyke, Pittsburgh
OF— Tony Gwynn, San Diego
OF— Eric Davis, Cincinnati

1990
AMERICAN LEAGUE
P— Mike Boddicker, Boston
C— Sandy Alomar Jr., Cleveland
1B— Mark McGwire, Oakland
2B— Harold Reynolds, Seattle
3B— Kelly Gruber, Toronto
SS— Ozzie Guillen, Chicago
OF— Ken Griffey Jr., Seattle
OF— Ellis Burks, Boston
OF— Gary Pettis, Texas

NATIONAL LEAGUE
P— Greg Maddux, Chicago
C— Benito Santiago, San Diego
1B— Andres Galarraga, Montreal
2B— Ryne Sandberg, Chicago
3B— Tim Wallach, Montreal
SS— Ozzie Smith, St. Louis
OF— Barry Bonds, Pittsburgh
OF— Andy Van Slyke, Pittsburgh
OF— Tony Gwynn, San Diego

1991
AMERICAN LEAGUE
P— Mark Langston, California
C— Tony Pena, Boston
1B— Don Mattingly, New York
2B— Roberto Alomar, Toronto
3B— Robin Ventura, Chicago
SS— Cal Ripken, Baltimore
OF— Ken Griffey Jr., Seattle

OF— Kirby Puckett, Minnesota
OF— Devon White, Toronto

NATIONAL LEAGUE
P— Greg Maddux, Chicago
C— Tom Pagnozzi, St. Louis
1B— Will Clark, San Francisco
2B— Ryne Sandberg, Chicago
3B— Matt Williams, San Francisco
SS— Ozzie Smith, St. Louis
OF— Barry Bonds, Pittsburgh
OF— Andy Van Slyke, Pittsburgh
OF— Tony Gwynn, San Diego

1992
AMERICAN LEAGUE
P— Mark Langston, California
C— Ivan Rodriguez, Texas
1B— Don Mattingly, New York
2B— Roberto Alomar, Toronto
3B— Robin Ventura, Chicago
SS— Cal Ripken, Baltimore
OF— Ken Griffey Jr., Seattle
OF— Kirby Puckett, Minnesota
OF— Devon White, Toronto

NATIONAL LEAGUE
P— Greg Maddux, Chicago
C— Tom Pagnozzi, St. Louis
1B— Mark Grace, Chicago
2B— Jose Lind, Pittsburgh
3B— Terry Pendleton, Atlanta
SS— Ozzie Smith, St. Louis
OF— Barry Bonds, Pittsburgh
OF— Andy Van Slyke, Pittsburgh
OF— Larry Walker, Montreal

1993
AMERICAN LEAGUE
P— Mark Langston, California
C— Ivan Rodriguez, Texas
1B— Don Mattingly, New York
2B— Roberto Alomar, Toronto
3B— Robin Ventura, Chicago
SS— Omar Vizquel, Seattle
OF— Ken Griffey Jr., Seattle
OF— Kenny Lofton, Cleveland
OF— Devon White, Toronto

NATIONAL LEAGUE
P— Greg Maddux, Atlanta
C— Kirt Manwaring, San Francisco
1B— Mark Grace, Chicago
2B— Robby Thompson, San Fran.
3B— Matt Williams, San Francisco
SS— Jay Bell, Pittsburgh
OF— Barry Bonds, San Francisco
OF— Marquis Grissom, Montreal
OF— Larry Walker, Montreal

1994
AMERICAN LEAGUE
P— Mark Langston, California
C— Ivan Rodriguez, Texas
1B— Don Mattingly, New York
2B— Roberto Alomar, Toronto
3B— Wade Boggs, New York
SS— Omar Vizquel, Cleveland
OF— Ken Griffey Jr., Seattle
OF— Kenny Lofton, Cleveland
OF— Devon White, Toronto

NATIONAL LEAGUE
P— Greg Maddux, Atlanta
C— Tom Pagnozzi, St. Louis
1B— Jeff Bagwell, Houston
2B— Craig Biggio, Houston
3B— Matt Williams, San Francisco

SS— Barry Larkin, Cincinnati
OF— Barry Bonds, San Francisco
OF— Marquis Grissom, Montreal
OF— Darren Lewis, San Francisco

1995
AMERICAN LEAGUE
P— Mark Langston, California
C— Ivan Rodriguez, Texas
1B— J.T. Snow, California
2B— Roberto Alomar, Toronto
3B— Wade Boggs, New York
SS— Omar Vizquel, Cleveland
OF— Ken Griffey Jr., Seattle
OF— Kenny Lofton, Cleveland
OF— Devon White, Toronto

NATIONAL LEAGUE
P— Greg Maddux, Atlanta
C— Charles Johnson, Florida
1B— Mark Grace, Chicago
2B— Craig Biggio, Houston
3B— Ken Caminiti, San Diego
SS— Barry Larkin, Cincinnati
OF— Raul Mondesi, Los Angeles
OF— Marquis Grissom, Atlanta
OF— Steve Finley, San Diego

1996
AMERICAN LEAGUE
P— Mike Mussina, Baltimore
C— Ivan Rodriguez, Texas
1B— J.T. Snow, California
2B— Roberto Alomar, Baltimore
3B— Robin Ventura, Chicago
SS— Omar Vizquel, Cleveland
OF— Jay Buhner, Seattle
OF— Ken Griffey Jr., Seattle
OF— Kenny Lofton, Cleveland

NATIONAL LEAGUE
P— Greg Maddux, Atlanta
C— Charles Johnson, Florida
1B— Mark Grace, Chicago
2B— Craig Biggio, Houston
3B— Ken Caminiti, San Diego
SS— Barry Larkin, Cincinnati
OF— Barry Bonds, San Francisco
OF— Marquis Grissom, Atlanta
OF— Steve Finley, San Diego

1997
AMERICAN LEAGUE
P— Mike Mussina, Baltimore
C— Ivan Rodriguez, Texas
1B— Rafael Palmeiro, Baltimore
2B— Chuck Knoblauch, Minnesota
3B— Matt Williams, Cleveland
SS— Omar Vizquel, Cleveland
OF— Jim Edmonds, Anaheim
OF— Ken Griffey Jr., Seattle
OF— Bernie Williams, New York

NATIONAL LEAGUE
P— Greg Maddux, Atlanta
C— Charles Johnson, Florida
1B— J.T. Snow, San Francisco
2B— Craig Biggio, Houston
3B— Ken Caminiti, San Diego
SS— Rey Ordonez, New York
OF— Barry Bonds, San Francisco
OF— Raul Mondesi, Los Angeles
OF— Larry Walker, Colorado

1998
AMERICAN LEAGUE
P— Mike Mussina, Baltimore
C— Ivan Rodriguez, Texas
1B— Rafael Palmeiro, Baltimore

2B— Roberto Alomar, Baltimore
3B— Robin Ventura, White Sox
SS— Omar Vizquel, Cleveland
OF— Jim Edmonds, Anaheim
OF— Ken Griffey Jr., Seattle
OF— Bernie Williams, New York

NATIONAL LEAGUE
P— Greg Maddux, Atlanta
C— Charles Johnson, Fla.-L.A.
1B— J.T. Snow, San Francisco
2B— Bret Boone, Cincinnati
3B— Scott Rolen, Philadelphia
SS— Rey Ordonez, New York
OF— Barry Bonds, San Francisco
OF— Andruw Jones, Atlanta
OF— Larry Walker, Colorado

1999
AMERICAN LEAGUE
P— Mike Mussina, Baltimore
C— Ivan Rodriguez, Texas
1B— Rafael Palmeiro, Texas
2B— Roberto Alomar, Cleveland
3B— Scott Brosius, New York
SS— Omar Vizquel, Cleveland
OF— Shawn Green, Toronto
OF— Ken Griffey Jr., Seattle
OF— Bernie Williams, New York

NATIONAL LEAGUE
P— Greg Maddux, Atlanta
C— Mike Lieberthal, Philadelphia
1B— J.T. Snow, San Francisco
2B— Pokey Reese, Cincinnati
3B— Robin Ventura, New York
SS— Rey Ordonez, New York

OF— Steve Finley, Arizona
OF— Andruw Jones, Atlanta
OF— Larry Walker, Colorado

2000
AMERICAN LEAGUE
P— Kenny Rogers, Texas
C— Ivan Rodriguez, Texas
1B— John Olerud, Seattle
2B— Roberto Alomar, Cleveland
3B— Travis Fryman, Cleveland
SS— Omar Vizquel, Cleveland
OF— Jermaine Dye, Kansas City
OF— Darin Erstad, Anaheim
OF— Bernie Williams, New York

NATIONAL LEAGUE
P— Greg Maddux, Atlanta
C— Mike Matheny, St. Louis
1B— J.T. Snow, San Francisco
2B— Pokey Reese, Cincinnati
3B— Scott Rolen, Philadelphia
SS— Neifi Perez, Colorado
OF— Jim Edmonds, St. Louis
OF— Steve Finley, Arizona
OF— Andruw Jones, Atlanta

2001
AMERICAN LEAGUE
P— Mike Mussina, New York
C— Ivan Rodriguez, Texas
1B— Doug Mientkiewicz, Minnesota
2B— Roberto Alomar, Cleveland
3B— Eric Chavez, Oakland
SS— Omar Vizquel, Cleveland
OF— Mike Cameron, Seattle

OF— Torii Hunter, Minnesota
OF— Ichiro Suzuki, Seattle

NATIONAL LEAGUE
P— Greg Maddux, Atlanta
C— Brad Ausmus, Houston
1B— Todd Helton, Colorado
2B— Fernando Vina, St. Louis
3B— Scott Rolen, Philadelphia
SS— Orlando Cabrera, Montreal
OF— Jim Edmonds, St. Louis
OF— Andruw Jones, Atlanta
OF— Larry Walker, Colorado

2002
AMERICAN LEAGUE
P— Kenny Rogers, Texas
C— Bengie Molina, Anaheim
1B— John Olerud, Seattle
2B— Bret Boone, Seattle
3B— Eric Chavez, Oakland
SS— Alex Rodriguez, Texas
OF— Darin Erstad, Anaheim
OF— Torii Hunter, Minnesota
OF— Ichiro Suzuki, Seattle

NATIONAL LEAGUE
P— Greg Maddux, Atlanta
C— Brad Ausmus, Houston
1B— Todd Helton, Colorado
2B— Fernando Vina, St. Louis
3B— Scott Rolen, Phil.-St.L.
SS— Edgar Renteria, St. Louis
OF— Jim Edmonds, St. Louis
OF— Andruw Jones, Atlanta
OF— Larry Walker, Colorado

HILLERICH & BRADSBY SILVER SLUGGER TEAMS

1980
AMERICAN LEAGUE
1B— Cecil Cooper, Milwaukee
2B— Willie Randolph, New York
3B— George Brett, Kansas City
SS— Robin Yount, Milwaukee
OF— Ben Oglivie, Milwaukee
OF— Al Oliver, Texas
OF— Willie Wilson, Kansas City
C— Lance Parrish, Detroit
DH— Reggie Jackson, New York

NATIONAL LEAGUE
1B— Keith Hernandez, St. Louis
2B— Manny Trillo, Philadelphia
3B— Mike Schmidt, Philadelphia
SS— Garry Templeton, St. Louis
OF— Dusty Baker, Los Angeles
OF— Andre Dawson, Montreal
OF— George Hendrick, St. Louis
C— Ted Simmons, St. Louis
P— Bob Forsch, St. Louis

1981
AMERICAN LEAGUE
1B— Cecil Cooper, Milwaukee
2B— Bobby Grich, California
3B— Carney Lansford, Boston
SS— Rick Burleson, California
OF— Rickey Henderson, Oakland
OF— Dwight Evans, Boston
OF— Dave Winfield, New York
C— Carlton Fisk, Chicago
DH— Al Oliver, Texas

NATIONAL LEAGUE
1B— Pete Rose, Philadelphia
2B— Manny Trillo, Philadelphia

3B— Mike Schmidt, Philadelphia
SS— Dave Concepcion, Cincinnati
OF— Andre Dawson, Montreal
OF— George Foster, Cincinnati
OF— Dusty Baker, Los Angeles
C— Gary Carter, Montreal
P— Fernando Valenzuela, Los Angeles

1982
AMERICAN LEAGUE
1B— Cecil Cooper, Milwaukee
2B— Damaso Garcia, Toronto
3B— Doug DeCinces, California
SS— Robin Yount, Milwaukee
OF— Dave Winfield, New York
OF— Willie Wilson, Kansas City
OF— Reggie Jackson, California
C— Lance Parrish, Detroit
DH— Hal McRae, Kansas City

NATIONAL LEAGUE
1B— Al Oliver, Montreal
2B— Joe Morgan, San Francisco
3B— Mike Schmidt, Philadelphia
SS— Dave Concepcion, Cincinnati
OF— Dale Murphy, Atlanta
OF— Pedro Guerrero, Los Angeles
OF— Leon Durham, Chicago
C— Gary Carter, Montreal
P— Don Robinson, Pittsburgh

1983
AMERICAN LEAGUE
1B— Eddie Murray, Baltimore
2B— Lou Whitaker, Detroit
3B— Wade Boggs, Boston
SS— Cal Ripken Jr., Baltimore
OF— Jim Rice, Boston

OF— Dave Winfield, New York
OF— Lloyd Moseby, Toronto
C— Lance Parrish, Detroit
DH— Don Baylor, New York

NATIONAL LEAGUE
1B— George Hendrick, St. Louis
2B— Johnny Ray, Pittsburgh
3B— Mike Schmidt, Philadelphia
SS— Dickie Thon, Houston
OF— Andre Dawson, Montreal
OF— Dale Murphy, Atlanta
OF— Jose Cruz, Houston
C— Terry Kennedy, San Diego
P— Fernando Valenzuela, Los Angeles

1984
AMERICAN LEAGUE
1B— Eddie Murray, Baltimore
2B— Lou Whitaker, Detroit
3B— Buddy Bell, Texas
SS— Cal Ripken Jr., Baltimore
OF— Tony Armas, Boston
OF— Jim Rice, Boston
OF— Dave Winfield, New York
C— Lance Parrish, Detroit
DH— Andre Thornton, Cleveland

NATIONAL LEAGUE
1B— Keith Hernandez, New York
2B— Ryne Sandberg, Chicago
3B— Mike Schmidt, Philadelphia
SS— Garry Templeton, San Diego
OF— Dale Murphy, Atlanta
OF— Jose Cruz, Houston
OF— Tony Gwynn, San Diego
C— Gary Carter, Montreal
P— Rick Rhoden, Pittsburgh

1985
AMERICAN LEAGUE
1B— Don Mattingly, New York
2B— Lou Whitaker, Detroit
3B— George Brett, Kansas City
SS— Cal Ripken Jr., Baltimore
OF— Rickey Henderson, New York
OF— Dave Winfield, New York
OF— George Bell, Toronto
C— Carlton Fisk, Chicago
DH— Don Baylor, New York

NATIONAL LEAGUE
1B— Jack Clark, St. Louis
2B— Ryne Sandberg, Chicago
3B— Tim Wallach, Montreal
SS— Hubie Brooks, Montreal
OF— Willie McGee, St. Louis
OF— Dale Murphy, Atlanta
OF— Dave Parker, Cincinnati
C— Gary Carter, New York
P— Rick Rhoden, Pittsburgh

1986
AMERICAN LEAGUE
1B— Don Mattingly, New York
2B— Frank White, Kansas City
3B— Wade Boggs, Boston
SS— Cal Ripken Jr., Baltimore
OF— George Bell, Toronto
OF— Kirby Puckett, Minnesota
OF— Jesse Barfield, Toronto
C— Lance Parrish, Detroit
DH— Don Baylor, Boston

NATIONAL LEAGUE
1B— Glenn Davis, Houston
2B— Steve Sax, Los Angeles
3B— Mike Schmidt, Philadelphia
SS— Hubie Brooks, Montreal
OF— Tony Gwynn, San Diego
OF— Tim Raines, Montreal
OF— Dave Parker, Cincinnati
C— Gary Carter, New York
P— Rick Rhoden, Pittsburgh

1987
AMERICAN LEAGUE
1B— Don Mattingly, New York
2B— Lou Whitaker, Detroit
3B— Wade Boggs, Boston
SS— Alan Trammell, Detroit
OF— George Bell, Toronto
OF— Dwight Evans, Boston
OF— Kirby Puckett, Minnesota
C— Matt Nokes, Detroit
DH— Paul Molitor, Milwaukee

NATIONAL LEAGUE
1B— Jack Clark, St. Louis
2B— Juan Samuel, Philadelphia
3B— Tim Wallach, Montreal
SS— Ozzie Smith, St. Louis
OF— Andre Dawson, Chicago
OF— Eric Davis, Cincinnati
OF— Tony Gwynn, San Diego
C— Benito Santiago, San Diego
P— Bob Forsch, St. Louis

1988
AMERICAN LEAGUE
1B— George Brett, Kansas City
2B— Julio Franco, Cleveland
3B— Wade Boggs, Boston
SS— Alan Trammell, Detroit
OF— Kirby Puckett, Minnesota
OF— Jose Canseco, Oakland
OF— Mike Greenwell, Boston
C— Carlton Fisk, Chicago
DH— Paul Molitor, Milwaukee

NATIONAL LEAGUE
1B— Andres Galarraga, Montreal
2B— Ryne Sandberg, Chicago
3B— Bobby Bonilla, Pittsburgh
SS— Barry Larkin, Cincinnati
OF— Darryl Strawberry, New York
OF— Andy Van Slyke, Pittsburgh
OF— Kirk Gibson, Los Angeles
C— Benito Santiago, San Diego
P— Tim Leary, Los Angeles

1989
AMERICAN LEAGUE
1B— Fred McGriff, Toronto
2B— Julio Franco, Texas
3B— Wade Boggs, Boston
SS— Cal Ripken Jr., Baltimore
OF— Kirby Puckett, Minnesota
OF— Ruben Sierra, Texas
OF— Robin Yount, Milwaukee
C— Mickey Tettleton, Baltimore
DH— Harold Baines, Chi.-Tex.

NATIONAL LEAGUE
1B— Will Clark, San Francisco
2B— Ryne Sandberg, Chicago
3B— Howard Johnson, New York
SS— Barry Larkin, Cincinnati
OF— Kevin Mitchell, San Francisco
OF— Tony Gwynn, San Diego
OF— Eric Davis, Cincinnati
C— Craig Biggio, Houston
P— Don Robinson, San Francisco

1990
AMERICAN LEAGUE
1B— Cecil Fielder, Detroit
2B— Julio Franco, Texas
3B— Kelly Gruber, Toronto
SS— Alan Trammell, Detroit
OF— Rickey Henderson, Oakland
OF— Jose Canseco, Oakland
OF— Ellis Burks, Boston
C— Lance Parrish, California
DH— Dave Parker, Milwaukee

NATIONAL LEAGUE
1B— Eddie Murray, Los Angeles
2B— Ryne Sandberg, Chicago
3B— Matt Williams, San Francisco
SS— Barry Larkin, Cincinnati
OF— Barry Bonds, Pittsburgh
OF— Bobby Bonilla, Pittsburgh
OF— Darryl Strawberry, New York
C— Benito Santiago, San Diego
P— Don Robinson, San Francisco

1991
AMERICAN LEAGUE
1B— Cecil Fielder, Detroit
2B— Julio Franco, Texas
3B— Wade Boggs, Boston
SS— Cal Ripken Jr., Baltimore
OF— Jose Canseco, Oakland
OF— Joe Carter, Toronto
OF— Ken Griffey Jr., Seattle
C— Mickey Tettleton, Detroit
DH— Frank Thomas, Chicago

NATIONAL LEAGUE
1B— Will Clark, San Francisco
2B— Ryne Sandberg, Chicago
3B— Howard Johnson, New York
SS— Barry Larkin, Cincinnati
OF— Barry Bonds, Pittsburgh
OF— Bobby Bonilla, Pittsburgh
OF— Ron Gant, Atlanta
C— Benito Santiago, San Diego
P— Tom Glavine, Atlanta

1992
AMERICAN LEAGUE
1B— Mark McGwire, Oakland
2B— Roberto Alomar, Toronto
3B— Edgar Martinez, Seattle
SS— Travis Fryman, Detroit
OF— Joe Carter, Toronto
OF— Juan Gonzalez, Texas
OF— Kirby Puckett, Minnesota
C— Mickey Tettleton, Detroit
DH— Dave Winfield, Toronto

NATIONAL LEAGUE
1B— Fred McGriff, San Diego
2B— Ryne Sandberg, Chicago
3B— Gary Sheffield, San Diego
SS— Barry Larkin, Cincinnati
OF— Barry Bonds, Pittsburgh
OF— Andy Van Slyke, Pittsburgh
OF— Larry Walker, Montreal
C— Darren Daulton, Philadelphia
P— Dwight Gooden, New York

1993
AMERICAN LEAGUE
1B— Frank Thomas, Chicago
2B— Carlos Baerga, Cleveland
3B— Wade Boggs, New York
SS— Cal Ripken Jr., Baltimore
OF— Albert Belle, Cleveland
OF— Juan Gonzalez, Texas
OF— Ken Griffey Jr., Seattle
C— Mike Stanley, New York
DH— Paul Molitor, Toronto

NATIONAL LEAGUE
1B— Fred McGriff, S.D.-Atl.
2B— Robby Thompson, San Fran.
3B— Matt Williams, San Francisco
SS— Jay Bell, Pittsburgh
OF— Barry Bonds, San Francisco
OF— Lenny Dykstra, Philadelphia
OF— David Justice, Atlanta
C— Mike Piazza, Los Angeles
P— Orel Hershiser, Los Angeles

1994
AMERICAN LEAGUE
1B— Frank Thomas, Chicago
2B— Carlos Baerga, Cleveland
3B— Wade Boggs, New York
SS— Cal Ripken Jr., Baltimore
OF— Albert Belle, Cleveland
OF— Ken Griffey Jr., Seattle
OF— Kirby Puckett, Minnesota
C— Ivan Rodriguez, Texas
DH— Julio Franco, Chicago

NATIONAL LEAGUE
1B— Jeff Bagwell, Houston
2B— Craig Biggio, Houston
3B— Matt Williams, San Francisco
SS— Wil Cordero, Montreal
OF— Moises Alou, Montreal
OF— Barry Bonds, San Francisco
OF— Tony Gwynn, San Diego
C— Mike Piazza, Los Angeles
P— Mark Portugal, San Francisco

1995
AMERICAN LEAGUE
1B— Mo Vaughn, Boston
2B— Chuck Knoblauch, Minnesota
3B— Gary Gaetti, Kansas City
SS— John Valentin, Boston
OF— Albert Belle, Cleveland
OF— Tim Salmon, California
OF— Manny Ramirez, Cleveland
C— Ivan Rodriguez, Texas
DH— Edgar Martinez, Seattle

NATIONAL LEAGUE
1B— Eric Karros, Los Angeles
2B— Craig Biggio, Houston
3B— Vinny Castilla, Colorado
SS— Barry Larkin, Cincinnati
OF— Dante Bichette, Colorado
OF— Tony Gwynn, San Diego
OF— Sammy Sosa, Chicago
C— Mike Piazza, Los Angeles
P— Tom Glavine, Atlanta

1996
AMERICAN LEAGUE
1B— Mark McGwire, Oakland
2B— Roberto Alomar, Baltimore
3B— Jim Thome, Cleveland
SS— Alex Rodriguez, Seattle
OF— Albert Belle, Cleveland
OF— Juan Gonzalez, Texas
OF— Ken Griffey Jr., Seattle
C— Ivan Rodriguez, Texas
DH— Paul Molitor, Minnesota

NATIONAL LEAGUE
1B— Andres Galarraga, Colorado
2B— Eric Young, Colorado
3B— Ken Caminiti, San Diego
SS— Barry Larkin, Cincinnati
OF— Barry Bonds, San Francisco
OF— Ellis Burks, Colorado
OF— Gary Sheffield, Florida
C— Mike Piazza, Los Angeles
P— Tom Glavine, Atlanta

1997
AMERICAN LEAGUE
1B— Tino Martinez, New York
2B— Chuck Knoblauch, Minnesota
3B— Matt Williams, Cleveland
SS— Nomar Garciaparra, Boston
OF— Juan Gonzalez, Texas
OF— Ken Griffey Jr., Seattle
OF— David Justice, Cleveland
C— Ivan Rodriguez, Texas
DH— Edgar Martinez, Seattle

NATIONAL LEAGUE
1B— Jeff Bagwell, Houston
2B— Craig Biggio, Houston
3B— Vinny Castilla, Colorado
SS— Jeff Blauser, Atlanta
OF— Barry Bonds, San Francisco
OF— Tony Gwynn, San Diego
OF— Larry Walker, Colorado
C— Mike Piazza, Los Angeles
P— John Smoltz, Atlanta

1998
AMERICAN LEAGUE
1B— Rafael Palmeiro, Baltimore
2B— Damion Easley, Detroit
3B— Dean Palmer, Kansas City
SS— Alex Rodriguez, Seattle
OF— Juan Gonzalez, Texas
OF— Ken Griffey Jr., Seattle
OF— Albert Belle, Chicago
C— Ivan Rodriguez, Texas
DH— Jose Canseco, Toronto

NATIONAL LEAGUE
1B— Mark McGwire, St. Louis
2B— Craig Biggio, Houston
3B— Vinny Castilla, Colorado
SS— Barry Larkin, Cincinnati
OF— Sammy Sosa, Chicago
OF— Moises Alou, Houston
OF— Greg Vaughn, San Diego
C— Mike Piazza, L.A.-Fla.-N.Y.
P— Tom Glavine, Atlanta

1999
AMERICAN LEAGUE
1B— Carlos Delgado, Toronto
2B— Roberto Alomar, Cleveland
3B— Dean Palmer, Detroit
SS— Alex Rodriguez, Seattle
OF— Shawn Green, Toronto
OF— Ken Griffey Jr., Seattle
OF— Manny Ramirez, Cleveland
C— Ivan Rodriguez, Texas
DH— Rafael Palmeiro, Texas

NATIONAL LEAGUE
1B— Jeff Bagwell, Houston
2B— Edgardo Alfonzo, New York
3B— Chipper Jones, Atlanta
SS— Barry Larkin, Cincinnati
OF— Sammy Sosa, Chicago
OF— Vladimir Guerrero, Montreal
OF— Larry Walker, Colorado
C— Mike Piazza, New York
P— Mike Hampton, Houston

2000
AMERICAN LEAGUE
1B— Carlos Delgado, Toronto
2B— Roberto Alomar, Cleveland
3B— Troy Glaus, Anaheim
SS— Alex Rodriguez, Seattle
OF— Darin Erstad, Anaheim
OF— Manny Ramirez, Cleveland
OF— Magglio Ordonez, Chicago
C— Jorge Posada, New York
DH— Frank Thomas, Chicago

NATIONAL LEAGUE
1B— Todd Helton, Colorado
2B— Jeff Kent, San Francisco
3B— Chipper Jones, Atlanta
SS— Edgar Renteria, St. Louis
OF— Sammy Sosa, Chicago
OF— Barry Bonds, San Francisco
OF— Vladimir Guerrero, Montreal
C— Mike Piazza, New York
P— Mike Hampton, New York

2001
AMERICAN LEAGUE
1B— Jason Giambi, Oakland
2B— Bret Boone, Seattle
3B— Troy Glaus, Anaheim
SS— Alex Rodriguez, Texas
OF— Juan Gonzalez, Cleveland
OF— Manny Ramirez, Boston
OF— Ichiro Suzuki, Seattle
C— Jorge Posada, New York
DH— Edgar Martinez, Seattle

NATIONAL LEAGUE
1B— Todd Helton, Colorado
2B— Jeff Kent, San Francisco
3B— Albert Pujols, St. Louis
SS— Rich Aurilia, San Francisco
OF— Barry Bonds, San Francisco
OF— Luis Gonzalez, Arizona
OF— Sammy Sosa, Chicago
C— Mike Piazza, New York
P— Mike Hampton, Colorado

2002
AMERICAN LEAGUE
1B— Jason Giambi, New York
2B— Alfonso Soriano, New York
3B— Eric Chavez, Oakland
SS— Alex Rodriguez, Texas
OF— Garret Anderson, Anaheim
OF— Magglio Ordonez, Chicago
OF— Bernie Williams, New York
C— Jorge Posada, New York
DH— Manny Ramirez, Boston

NATIONAL LEAGUE
1B— Todd Helton, Colorado
2B— Jeff Kent, San Francisco
3B— Scott Rolen, Phi.-St.L.
SS— Edgar Renteria, St. Louis
OF— Barry Bonds, San Francisco
OF— Vladimir Guerrero, Montreal
OF— Sammy Sosa, Chicago
C— Mike Piazza, New York
P— Mike Hampton, Colorado

BASEBALL WRITERS' ASSOCIATION OF AMERICA
MOST VALUABLE PLAYER

AMERICAN LEAGUE

Year	Player	Team	Pos.	Points
1931—Lefty Grove	Philadelphia	P	78
1932—Jimmie Foxx	Philadelphia	1B	75
1933—Jimmie Foxx	Philadelphia	1B	74
1934—Mickey Cochrane	Detroit	C	67
1935—Hank Greenberg	Detroit	1B	*80
1936—Lou Gehrig	New York	1B	73
1937—Charley Gehringer	Detroit	2B	78
1938—Jimmie Foxx	Boston	1B	305
1939—Joe DiMaggio	New York	OF	280
1940—Hank Greenberg	Detroit	OF	292
1941—Joe DiMaggio	New York	OF	291
1942—Joe Gordon	New York	2B	270
1943—Spud Chandler	New York	P	246
1944—Hal Newhouser	Detroit	P	236

NATIONAL LEAGUE

Year	Player	Team	Pos.	Points
1931—Frank Frisch	St. Louis	2B	65
1932—Chuck Klein	Philadelphia	OF	78
1933—Carl Hubbell	New York	P	77
1934—Dizzy Dean	St. Louis	P	78
1935—Gabby Hartnett	Chicago	C	75
1936—Carl Hubbell	New York	P	60
1937—Joe Medwick	St. Louis	OF	70
1938—Ernie Lombardi	Cincinnati	C	229
1939—Bucky Walters	Cincinnati	P	303
1940—Frank McCormick	Cincinnati	1B	274
1941—Dolf Camilli	Brooklyn	1B	300
1942—Mort Cooper	St. Louis	P	263
1943—Stan Musial	St. Louis	OF	267
1944—Marty Marion	St. Louis	SS	190

AMERICAN LEAGUE

Year	Player	Team	Pos.	Points
1945—Hal Newhouser	Detroit	P	236
1946—Ted Williams	Boston	OF	224
1947—Joe DiMaggio	New York	OF	202
1948—Lou Boudreau	Cleveland	SS	324
1949—Ted Williams	Boston	OF	272
1950—Phil Rizzuto	New York	SS	284
1951—Yogi Berra	New York	C	184
1952—Bobby Shantz	Philadelphia	P	280
1953—Al Rosen	Cleveland	3B	*336
1954—Yogi Berra	New York	C	230
1955—Yogi Berra	New York	C	218
1956—Mickey Mantle	New York	OF	*336
1957—Mickey Mantle	New York	OF	233
1958—Jackie Jensen	Boston	OF	233
1959—Nellie Fox	Chicago	2B	295
1960—Roger Maris	New York	OF	225
1961—Roger Maris	New York	OF	202
1962—Mickey Mantle	New York	OF	234
1963—Elston Howard	New York	C	248
1964—Brooks Robinson	Baltimore	3B	269
1965—Zoilo Versalles	Minnesota	SS	275
1966—Frank Robinson	Baltimore	OF	*280
1967—Carl Yastrzemski	Boston	OF	275
1968—Denny McLain	Detroit	P	*280
1969—Harmon Killebrew	Minnesota	1B-3B	294
1970—Boog Powell	Baltimore	1B	234
1971—Vida Blue	Oakland	P	268
1972—Dick Allen	Chicago	1B	321
1973—Reggie Jackson	Oakland	OF	*336
1974—Jeff Burroughs	Texas	OF	248
1975—Fred Lynn	Boston	OF	326
1976—Thurman Munson	New York	C	304
1977—Rod Carew	Minnesota	1B	273
1978—Jim Rice	Boston	OF	352
1979—Don Baylor	California	OF	347
1980—George Brett	Kansas City	3B	335
1981—Rollie Fingers	Milwaukee	P	319
1982—Robin Yount	Milwaukee	SS	385
1983—Cal Ripken Jr.	Baltimore	SS	322
1984—Willie Hernandez	Detroit	P	306
1985—Don Mattingly	New York	1B	367
1986—Roger Clemens	Boston	P	339
1987—George Bell	Toronto	OF	332
1988—Jose Canseco	Oakland	OF	*392
1989—Robin Yount	Milwaukee	OF	256
1990—Rickey Henderson	Oakland	OF	317
1991—Cal Ripken Jr.	Baltimore	SS	318
1992—Dennis Eckersley	Oakland	P	306
1993—Frank Thomas	Chicago	1B	*392
1994—Frank Thomas	Chicago	1B	372
1995—Mo Vaughn	Boston	1B	308
1996—Juan Gonzalez	Texas	OF	290
1997—Ken Griffey Jr.	Seattle	OF	*392
1998—Juan Gonzalez	Texas	OF	357
1999—Ivan Rodriguez	Texas	C	252
2000—Jason Giambi	Oakland	1B	317
2001—Ichiro Suzuki	Seattle	OF	289
2002—Miguel Tejada	Oakland	SS	356

NATIONAL LEAGUE

Year	Player	Team	Pos.	Points
1945—Phil Cavarretta	Chicago	1B	279
1946—Stan Musial	St. Louis	1B	319
1947—Bob Elliott	Boston	3B	205
1948—Stan Musial	St. Louis	OF	303
1949—Jackie Robinson	Brooklyn	2B	264
1950—Jim Konstanty	Philadelphia	P	286
1951—Roy Campanella	Brooklyn	C	243
1952—Hank Sauer	Chicago	OF	226
1953—Roy Campanella	Brooklyn	C	297
1954—Willie Mays	New York	OF	283
1955—Roy Campanella	Brooklyn	C	226
1956—Don Newcombe	Brooklyn	P	223
1957—Hank Aaron	Milwaukee	OF	239
1958—Ernie Banks	Chicago	SS	283
1959—Ernie Banks	Chicago	SS	232 1/2
1960—Dick Groat	Pittsburgh	SS	276
1961—Frank Robinson	Cincinnati	OF	219
1962—Maury Wills	Los Angeles	SS	209
1963—Sandy Koufax	Los Angeles	P	237
1964—Ken Boyer	St. Louis	3B	243
1965—Willie Mays	San Francisco	OF	224
1966—Roberto Clemente	Pittsburgh	OF	218
1967—Orlando Cepeda	St. Louis	1B	*280
1968—Bob Gibson	St. Louis	P	242
1969—Willie McCovey	San Francisco	1B	265
1970—Johnny Bench	Cincinnati	C	326
1971—Joe Torre	St. Louis	3B	318
1972—Johnny Bench	Cincinnati	C	263
1973—Pete Rose	Cincinnati	OF	274
1974—Steve Garvey	Los Angeles	1B	270
1975—Joe Morgan	Cincinnati	2B	321 1/2
1976—Joe Morgan	Cincinnati	2B	311
1977—George Foster	Cincinnati	OF	291
1978—Dave Parker	Pittsburgh	OF	320
1979—Willie Stargell	Pittsburgh	1B	216
Keith Hernandez	St. Louis	1B	216
1980—Mike Schmidt	Philadelphia	3B	*336
1981—Mike Schmidt	Philadelphia	3B	321
1982—Dale Murphy	Atlanta	OF	283
1983—Dale Murphy	Atlanta	OF	318
1984—Ryne Sandberg	Chicago	2B	326
1985—Willie McGee	St. Louis	OF	280
1986—Mike Schmidt	Philadelphia	3B	287
1987—Andre Dawson	Chicago	OF	269
1988—Kirk Gibson	Los Angeles	OF	272
1989—Kevin Mitchell	San Francisco	OF	314
1990—Barry Bonds	Pittsburgh	OF	331
1991—Terry Pendleton	Atlanta	3B	274
1992—Barry Bonds	Pittsburgh	OF	304
1993—Barry Bonds	San Francisco	OF	372
1994—Jeff Bagwell	Houston	1B	*392
1995—Barry Larkin	Cincinnati	SS	281
1996—Ken Caminiti	San Diego	3B	*392
1997—Larry Walker	Colorado	OF	359
1998—Sammy Sosa	Chicago	OF	438
1999—Chipper Jones	Atlanta	3B	432
2000—Jeff Kent	San Francisco	2B	392
2001—Barry Bonds	San Francisco	OF	438
2002—Barry Bonds	San Francisco	OF	*448

*Unanimous selection.

CY YOUNG MEMORIAL AWARD

Year	Pitcher	Team	Votes
1956—Don Newcombe	Brooklyn	10
1957—Warren Spahn	Milwaukee	15
1958—Bob Turley	New York A.L.	5
1959—Early Wynn	Chicago A.L.	13
1960—Vernon Law	Pittsburgh	8
1961—Whitey Ford	New York A.L.	9
1962—Don Drysdale	Los Angeles N.L.	14
1963—Sandy Koufax	Los Angeles N.L.	*20
1964—Dean Chance	Los Angeles A.L.	17
1965—Sandy Koufax	Los Angeles N.L.	*20
1966—Sandy Koufax	Los Angeles N.L.	*20

Year	Pitcher	Team	Votes
1967—A.L.—Jim Lonborg	Boston	18
N.L.—Mike McCormick	San Francisco	18
1968—A.L.—Denny McLain	Detroit	*20
N.L.—Bob Gibson	St. Louis	*20
1969—A.L.—Denny McLain	Detroit	10
Mike Cuellar	Baltimore	10
N.L.—Tom Seaver	New York	23
1970—A.L.—Jim Perry	Minnesota	55
N.L.—Bob Gibson	St. Louis	118
1971—A.L.—Vida Blue	Oakland	98
N.L.—Fergie Jenkins	Chicago	97

Year	Pitcher	Team	Votes
1972—A.L.—Gaylord Perry	Cleveland	64
N.L.—Steve Carlton	Philadelphia	*120
1973—A.L.—Jim Palmer	Baltimore	88
N.L.—Tom Seaver	New York	71
1974—A.L.—Jim Hunter	Oakland	90
N.L.—Mike Marshall	Los Angeles	96
1975—A.L.—Jim Palmer	Baltimore	98
N.L.—Tom Seaver	New York	98
1976—A.L.—Jim Palmer	Baltimore	108
N.L.—Randy Jones	San Diego	96
1977—A.L.—Sparky Lyle	New York	56½
N.L.—Steve Carlton	Philadelphia	104
1978—A.L.—Ron Guidry	New York	*140
N.L.—Gaylord Perry	San Diego	116
1979—A.L.—Mike Flanagan	Baltimore	136
N.L.—Bruce Sutter	Chicago	72
1980—A.L.—Steve Stone	Baltimore	100
N.L.—Steve Carlton	Philadelphia	118
1981—A.L.—Rollie Fingers	Milwaukee	126
N.L.—Fernando Valenzuela	Los Angeles	70
1982—A.L.—Pete Vuckovich	Milwaukee	87
N.L.—Steve Carlton	Philadelphia	112
1983—A.L.—LaMarr Hoyt	Chicago	116
N.L.—John Denny	Philadelphia	103
1984—A.L.—Willie Hernandez	Detroit	88
N.L.—Rick Sutcliffe	Chicago	*120
1985—A.L.—Bret Saberhagen	Kansas City	127
N.L.—Dwight Gooden	New York	*120
1986—A.L.—Roger Clemens	Boston	*140
N.L.—Mike Scott	Houston	98
1987—A.L.—Roger Clemens	Boston	124
N.L.—Steve Bedrosian	Philadelphia	57
1988—A.L.—Frank Viola	Minnesota	138
N.L.—Orel Hershiser	Los Angeles	*120
1989—A.L.—Bret Saberhagen	Kansas City	138
N.L.—Mark Davis	San Diego	107
1990—A.L.—Bob Welch	Oakland	107
N.L.—Doug Drabek	Pittsburgh	118
1991—A.L.—Roger Clemens	Boston	119
N.L.—Tom Glavine	Atlanta	110
1992—A.L.—Dennis Eckersley	Oakland	107
N.L.—Greg Maddux	Chicago	112
1993—A.L.—Jack McDowell	Chicago	124
N.L.—Greg Maddux	Atlanta	119
1994—A.L.—David Cone	Kansas City	108
N.L.—Greg Maddux	Atlanta	*140
1995—A.L.—Randy Johnson	Seattle	136
N.L.—Greg Maddux	Atlanta	*140
1996—A.L.—Pat Hentgen	Toronto	110
N.L.—John Smoltz	Atlanta	136
1997—A.L.—Roger Clemens	Toronto	134
N.L.—Pedro Martinez	Montreal	134
1998—A.L.—Roger Clemens	Toronto	*140
N.L.—Tom Glavine	Atlanta	99
1999—A.L.—Pedro Martinez	Boston	*140
N.L.—Randy Johnson	Arizona	134
2000—A.L.—Pedro Martinez	Boston	*140
N.L.—Randy Johnson	Arizona	133
2001—A.L.—Roger Clemens	New York	122
N.L.—Randy Johnson	Arizona	156
2002—A.L.—Barry Zito	Oakland	114
N.L.—Randy Johnson	Arizona	*160

*Unanimous selection.

ROOKIE OF THE YEAR

1947—Combined selection—Jackie Robinson, Brooklyn N.L., 1B
1948—Combined selection—Alvin Dark, Boston N.L., SS

AMERICAN LEAGUE

Year	Player	Team	Pos.	Votes
1949—Roy Sievers	St. Louis	OF	10
1950—Walt Dropo	Boston	1B	15
1951—Gil McDougald	New York	3B	13
1952—Harry Byrd	Philadelphia	P	9
1953—Harvey Kuenn	Detroit	SS	23
1954—Bob Grim	New York	P	15
1955—Herb Score	Cleveland	P	18
1956—Luis Aparicio	Chicago	SS	22
1957—Tony Kubek	New York	IF-OF	23
1958—Albie Pearson	Washington	OF	14
1959—Bob Allison	Washington	OF	18
1960—Ron Hansen	Baltimore	SS	22
1961—Don Schwall	Boston	P	7
1962—Tom Tresh	New York	OF-SS	13
1963—Gary Peters	Chicago	P	10
1964—Tony Oliva	Minnesota	OF	19
1965—Curt Blefary	Baltimore	OF	12
1966—Tommie Agee	Chicago	OF	16
1967—Rod Carew	Minnesota	2B	19
1968—Stan Bahnsen	New York	P	17
1969—Lou Piniella	Kansas City	OF	9
1970—Thurman Munson	New York	C	23
1971—Chris Chambliss	Cleveland	1B	11
1972—Carlton Fisk	Boston	C	*24
1973—Al Bumbry	Baltimore	OF	13½
1974—Mike Hargrove	Texas	1B	16½
1975—Fred Lynn	Boston	OF	23½
1976—Mark Fidrych	Detroit	P	22
1977—Eddie Murray	Baltimore	DH-1B	12½
1978—Lou Whitaker	Detroit	2B	21
1979—John Castino	Minnesota	3B	7
Alfredo Griffin	Toronto	SS	7
1980—Joe Charboneau	Cleveland	OF	102
1981—Dave Righetti	New York	P	127

NATIONAL LEAGUE

Year	Player	Team	Pos.	Votes
1949—Don Newcombe	Brooklyn	P	21
1950—Sam Jethroe	Boston	OF	11
1951—Willie Mays	New York	OF	18
1952—Joe Black	Brooklyn	P	19
1953—Jim Gilliam	Brooklyn	2B	11
1954—Wally Moon	St. Louis	OF	17
1955—Bill Virdon	St. Louis	OF	15
1956—Frank Robinson	Cincinnati	OF	*24
1957—Jack Sanford	Philadelphia	P	16
1958—Orlando Cepeda	San Francisco	1B	*†21
1959—Willie McCovey	San Francisco	1B	*24
1960—Frank Howard	Los Angeles	OF	12
1961—Billy Williams	Chicago	OF	10
1962—Ken Hubbs	Chicago	2B	19
1963—Pete Rose	Cincinnati	2B	17
1964—Dick Allen	Philadelphia	3B	18
1965—Jim Lefebvre	Los Angeles	2B	13
1966—Tommy Helms	Cincinnati	3B	12
1967—Tom Seaver	New York	P	11
1968—Johnny Bench	Cincinnati	C	10½
1969—Ted Sizemore	Los Angeles	2B	14
1970—Carl Morton	Montreal	P	11
1971—Earl Williams	Atlanta	C	18
1972—Jon Matlack	New York	P	19
1973—Gary Matthews	San Francisco	OF	11
1974—Bake McBride	St. Louis	OF	16
1975—John Montefusco	San Francisco	P	12
1976—Butch Metzger	San Diego	P	11
Pat Zachry	Cincinnati	P	11
1977—Andre Dawson	Montreal	OF	10
1978—Bob Horner	Atlanta	3B	12½
1979—Rick Sutcliffe	Los Angeles	P	20
1980—Steve Howe	Los Angeles	P	80
1981—Fernando Valenzuela	Los Angeles	P	107

AMERICAN LEAGUE

Year	Player	Team	Pos.	Votes
1982—Cal Ripken	Baltimore	SS-3B	132
1983—Ron Kittle	Chicago	OF	104
1984—Alvin Davis	Seattle	1B	134
1985—Ozzie Guillen	Chicago	SS	101
1986—Jose Canseco	Oakland	OF	110
1987—Mark McGwire	Oakland	1B	*140
1988—Walt Weiss	Oakland	SS	103
1989—Gregg Olson	Baltimore	P	136
1990—Sandy Alomar Jr.	Cleveland	C	*140
1991—Chuck Knoblauch	Minnesota	2B	136
1992—Pat Listach	Milwaukee	SS	122
1993—Tim Salmon	California	OF	*140
1994—Bob Hamelin	Kansas City	DH	134
1995—Marty Cordova	Minnesota	3B	105
1996—Derek Jeter	New York	SS	*140
1997—Nomar Garciaparra	Boston	SS	*140
1998—Ben Grieve	Oakland	OF	130
1999—Carlos Beltran	Kansas City	OF	133
2000—Kazuhiro Sasaki	Seattle	P	104
2001—Ichiro Suzuki	Seattle	OF	138
2002—Eric Hinske	Toronto	3B	122

*Unanimous selection. †Three writers did not vote.

NATIONAL LEAGUE

Year	Player	Team	Pos.	Votes
1982—Steve Sax	Los Angeles	2B	63
1983—Darryl Strawberry	New York	OF	106
1984—Dwight Gooden	New York	P	118
1985—Vince Coleman	St. Louis	OF	*120
1986—Todd Worrell	St. Louis	P	118
1987—Benito Santiago	San Diego	C	*120
1988—Chris Sabo	Cincinnati	3B	79
1989—Jerome Walton	Chicago	OF	116
1990—Dave Justice	Atlanta	OF	118
1991—Jeff Bagwell	Houston	1B	118
1992—Eric Karros	Los Angeles	1B	116
1993—Mike Piazza	Los Angeles	C	*140
1994—Raul Mondesi	Los Angeles	OF	*140
1995—Hideo Nomo	Los Angeles	P	118
1996—Todd Hollandsworth	Los Angeles	OF	105
1997—Scott Rolen	Philadelphia	3B	*140
1998—Kerry Wood	Chicago	P	128
1999—Scott Williamson	Cincinnati	P	118
2000—Rafael Furcal	Atlanta	SS-2B	144
2001—Albert Pujols	St. Louis	OF-3B-1B	*160
2002—Jason Jennings	Colorado	P	150

MANAGER OF THE YEAR

AMERICAN LEAGUE

Year	Manager	Team	Points
1983—Tony La Russa	Chicago	17
1984—Sparky Anderson	Detroit	96
1985—Bobby Cox	Toronto	104
1986—John McNamara	Boston	95
1987—Sparky Anderson	Detroit	90
1988—Tony La Russa	Oakland	103
1989—Frank Robinson	Baltimore	125
1990—Jeff Torborg	Chicago	128
1991—Tom Kelly	Minnesota	138
1992—Tony La Russa	Oakland	132
1993—Gene Lamont	Chicago	72
1994—Buck Showalter	New York	132
1995—Lou Piniella	Seattle	86
1996—Johnny Oates	Texas	89
Joe Torre	New York	89
1997—Dave Johnson	Baltimore	88
1998—Joe Torre	New York	128
1999—Jimy Williams	Boston	115
2000—Jerry Manuel	Chicago	134
2001—Lou Piniella	Seattle	128
2002—Mike Scioscia	Anaheim	116

NATIONAL LEAGUE

Year	Manager	Team	Points
1983—Tommy Lasorda	Los Angeles	10
1984—Jim Frey	Chicago	101
1985—Whitey Herzog	St. Louis	86
1986—Hal Lanier	Houston	108
1987—Buck Rodgers	Montreal	92
1988—Tommy Lasorda	Los Angeles	101
1989—Don Zimmer	Chicago	118
1990—Jim Leyland	Pittsburgh	99
1991—Bobby Cox	Atlanta	96
1992—Jim Leyland	Pittsburgh	109
1993—Dusty Baker	San Francisco	105
1994—Felipe Alou	Montreal	138
1995—Don Baylor	Colorado	122
1996—Bruce Bochy	San Diego	76
1997—Dusty Baker	San Francisco	110
1998—Larry Dierker	Houston	102
1999—Jack McKeon	Cincinnati	115
2000—Dusty Baker	San Francisco	154
2001—Larry Bowa	Philadelphia	113
2002—Tony La Russa	St. Louis	129

EARLY MOST VALUABLE PLAYER AWARDS

CHALMERS AWARD

AMERICAN LEAGUE

Year	Player	Team	Pos.	Points
1911—Ty Cobb	Detroit	OF	64
1912—Tris Speaker	Boston	OF	59
1913—Walter Johnson	Washington	P	54
1914—Eddie Collins	Philadelphia	2B	63

NATIONAL LEAGUE

Year	Player	Team	Pos.	Points
1911—Frank Schulte	Chicago	OF	29
1912—Larry Doyle	New York	2B	48
1913—Jake Daubert	Brooklyn	1B	50
1914—Johnny Evers	Boston	2B	50

LEAGUE AWARDS

AMERICAN LEAGUE

Year	Player	Team	Pos.	Points
1922—George Sisler	St. Louis	1B	59
1923—Babe Ruth	New York	OF	64
1924—Walter Johnson	Washington	P	55
1925—Roger Peckinpaugh	Washington	SS	45
1926—George Burns	Cleveland	1B	63
1927—Lou Gehrig	New York	1B	56
1928—Mickey Cochrane	Philadelphia	C	53
1929—No selection			

NATIONAL LEAGUE

Year	Player	Team	Pos.	Points
1922—No selection			
1923—No selection			
1924—Dazzy Vance	Brooklyn	P	74
1925—Rogers Hornsby	St. Louis	2B	73
1926—Bob O'Farrell	St. Louis	C	79
1927—Paul Waner	Pittsburgh	OF	72
1928—Jim Bottomley	St. Louis	1B	76
1929—Rogers Hornsby	Chicago	2B	60

HALL OF FAME

ROSTER OF MEMBERS

Name	Des.*	Elec. year	Votes rec.†	Votes cast‡	% of vote	Teams as player
Aaron, Hank	P	1982	406	415	97.8	Milwaukee NL, Atlanta NL, Milwaukee AL
Alexander, Grover C.	P	1938	212	262	80.9	Philadelphia NL, Chicago NL, St. Louis NL
Alston, Walter	M	1983	CV	—	—	St. Louis NL
Anderson, Sparky	M	2000	CV	—	—	Philadelphia NL
Anson, Cap	P	1939	C1	—	—	Chicago NL
Aparicio, Luis	P	1984	341	403	84.6	Chicago AL, Baltimore AL, Boston AL
Appling, Luke	P	1964	189	225	84.0	Chicago AL
Ashburn, Richie	P	1995	CV	—	—	Philadelphia NL, Chicago NL, New York NL
Averill, Earl	P	1975	CV	—	—	Cleveland AL, Detroit AL, Boston NL
Baker, Home Run	P	1955	CV	—	—	Philadelphia AL, New York AL
Bancroft, Dave	P	1971	CV	—	—	Philadelphia NL, New York NL, Boston NL, Brooklyn NL
Banks, Ernie	P	1977	321	383	83.8	Chicago NL
Barlick, Al	U	1989	CV	—	—	
Barrow, Ed	E	1953	CV	—	—	
Beckley, Jake	P	1971	CV	—	—	Pittsburgh NL, Pittsburgh PL, New York NL, Cincinnati NL, St. Louis NL
Bell, Cool Papa	P	1974	SCNL	—	—	Negro Leagues
Bench, Johnny	P	1989	431	447	96.4	Cincinnati NL
Bender, Chief	P	1953	CV	—	—	Philadelphia AL, Philadelphia NL, Chicago AL
Berra, Yogi	P	1972	339	396	85.6	New York AL, New York NL
Bottomley, Jim	P	1974	CV	—	—	St. Louis NL, Cincinnati NL, St. Louis AL
Boudreau, Lou	P	1970	232	300	77.3	Cleveland AL, Boston AL
Bresnahan, Roger	P	1945	C2	—	—	Washington NL, Chicago NL, Baltimore AL, New York NL, St. Louis NL
Brett, George	P	1999	488	497	98.2	Kansas City AL
Brock, Lou	P	1985	315	395	79.7	Chicago NL, St. Louis NL
Brouthers, Dan	P	1945	C2	—	—	Troy NL, Buffalo NL, Detroit NL, Boston NL, Boston PL, Boston AA, Brooklyn NL, Baltimore NL, Louisville NL, Philadelphia NL, New York NL
Brown, Three Finger	P	1949	C2	—	—	St. Louis NL, Chicago NL, Cincinnati NL
Bulkeley, Morgan	E	1937	CC	—	—	
Bunning, Jim	P	1996	CV	—	—	Detroit AL, Philadelphia NL, Pittsburgh NL, Los Angeles NL
Burkett, Jesse	P	1946	C2	—	—	New York NL, Cleveland NL, St. Louis NL, St. Louis AL, Boston AL
Campanella, Roy	P	1969	270	340	79.4	Brooklyn NL
Carew, Rod	P	1991	401	443	90.5	Minnesota AL, California AL
Carey, Max	P	1961	CV	—	—	Pittsburgh NL, Brooklyn NL
Carlton, Steve	P	1994	436	455	95.8	St. Louis NL, Philadelphia NL, San Francisco NL, Chicago AL, Cleveland AL, Minnesota AL
Carter, Gary	P	2003	387	496	78.0	Montreal NL, New York NL, San Francisco NL, Los Angeles NL
Cartwright, Alexander	O	1938	CC	—	—	
Cepeda, Orlando	P	1999	CV	—	—	San Francisco NL, St. Louis NL, Atlanta NL, Oakland AL, Boston AL, Kansas City AL
Chadwick, Henry	O	1938	CC	—	—	
Chance, Frank	P	1946	C2	—	—	Chicago NL, New York AL
Chandler, Happy	E	1982	CV	—	—	
Charleston, Oscar	P	1976	SCNL	—	—	Negro Leagues
Chesbro, Jack	P	1946	C2	—	—	Pittsburgh NL, New York AL, Boston AL
Chylak, Nestor	U	1999	CV	—	—	
Clarke, Fred	P	1945	C2	—	—	Louisville NL, Pittsburgh NL
Clarkson, John	P	1963	CV	—	—	Worcester NL, Chicago NL, Boston NL, Cleveland NL
Clemente, Roberto	P	1973	393	424	92.7	Pittsburgh NL
Cobb, Ty	P	1936	222	226	98.2	Detroit AL, Philadelphia AL
Cochrane, Mickey	P	1947	128	161	79.5	Philadelphia AL, Detroit AL
Collins, Eddie	P	1939	213	274	77.7	Philadelphia AL, Chicago AL
Collins, Jimmy	P	1945	C2	—	—	Boston NL, Louisville NL, Boston AL, Philadelphia AL
Combs, Earle	P	1970	CV	—	—	New York AL
Comiskey, Charley	F/P	1939	C1	—	—	St. Louis AA, Chicago PL, Cincinnati NL
Conlan, Jocko	U	1974	CV	—	—	Chicago AL
Connolly, Tommy	U	1953	CV	—	—	
Connor, Roger	P	1976	CV	—	—	Troy NL, New York NL, New York PL, Philadelphia NL, St. Louis NL
Coveleski, Stan	P	1969	CV	—	—	Philadelphia AL, Cleveland AL, Washington AL, New York AL
Crawford, Sam	P	1957	CV	—	—	Cincinnati NL, Detroit AL
Cronin, Joe	P	1956	152	193	78.8	Pittsburgh NL, Washington AL, Boston AL

Name	Des.*	Elec. year	Votes rec.†	Votes cast‡	% of vote	Teams as player
Cummings, Candy	P	1939	C1	—	—	Hartford NL, Cincinnati NL
Cuyler, Kiki	P	1968	CV	—	—	Pittsburgh NL, Chicago NL, Cincinnati NL, Brooklyn NL
Dandridge, Ray	P	1987	CV	—	—	Negro Leagues
Davis, George S.	P	1998	CV	—	—	Cleveland NL, New York NL, Chicago AL
Day, Leon	P	1995	CV	—	—	Negro Leagues
Dean, Dizzy	P	1953	209	264	79.2	St. Louis NL, Chicago NL, St. Louis AL
Delahanty, Ed	P	1945	C2	—	—	Philadelphia NL, Cleveland PL, Washington AL
Dickey, Bill	P	1954	202	252	80.2	New York AL
Dihigo, Martin	P	1977	SCNL	—	—	Negro Leagues
DiMaggio, Joe	P	1955	223	251	88.8	New York AL
Doby, Larry	P	1998	CV	—	—	Cleveland AL, Chicago AL, Detroit AL
Doerr, Bobby	P	1986	CV	—	—	Boston AL
Drysdale, Don	P	1984	316	403	78.4	Brooklyn NL, Los Angeles NL
Duffy, Hugh	P	1945	C2	—	—	Chicago NL, Chicago PL, Boston AA, Boston NL, Milwaukee AL, Philadelphia NL
Durocher, Leo	M	1994	CV	—	—	New York AL, Cincinnati NL, St. Louis NL, Brooklyn NL
Evans, Billy	U	1973	CV	—	—	
Evers, Johnny	P	1946	C2	—	—	Chicago NL, Boston NL, Philadelphia NL, Chicago AL
Ewing, Buck	P	1939	C1	—	—	Troy NL, New York NL, New York PL, Cleveland NL, Cincinnati NL
Faber, Red	P	1964	CV	—	—	Chicago AL
Feller, Bob	P	1962	150	160	93.8	Cleveland AL
Ferrell, Rick	P	1984	CV	—	—	St. Louis AL, Boston AL, Washington AL
Fingers, Rollie	P	1992	349	430	81.2	Oakland AL, San Diego NL, Milwaukee AL
Fisk, Carlton	P	2000	397	499	79.6	Boston AL, Chicago AL
Flick, Elmer	P	1963	CV	—	—	Philadelphia NL, Philadelphia AL, Cleveland AL
Ford, Whitey	P	1974	284	365	77.8	New York AL
Foster, Bill	P	1996	CV	—	—	Negro Leagues
Foster, Rube	P	1981	CV	—	—	Negro Leagues
Fox, Nellie	P	1997	CV	—	—	Philadelphia AL, Chicago AL, Houston NL
Foxx, Jimmie	P	1951	179	226	79.2	Philadelphia AL, Boston AL, Chicago NL, Philadelphia NL
Frick, Ford	E	1970	CV	—	—	
Frisch, Frankie	P	1947	136	161	84.5	New York NL, St. Louis NL
Galvin, Pud	P	1965	CV	—	—	Buffalo NL, Pittsburgh AA, Pittsburgh NL, Pittsburgh PL, St. Louis NL
Gehrig, Lou	P	1939	SE	—	—	New York AL
Gehringer, Charlie	P	1949	159	187	85.0	Detroit AL
Gibson, Bob	P	1981	337	401	84.0	St. Louis NL
Gibson, Josh	P	1972	SCNL	—	—	Negro Leagues
Giles, Warren	E	1979	CV	—	—	
Gomez, Lefty	P	1972	CV	—	—	New York AL, Washington AL
Goslin, Goose	P	1968	CV	—	—	Washington AL, St. Louis AL, Detroit AL
Greenberg, Hank	P	1956	164	193	85.0	Detroit AL, Pittsburgh NL
Griffith, Clark	E	1946	C2	—	—	St. Louis AA, Boston AA, Chicago NL, Chicago AL, New York AL, Cincinnati NL, Washington AL
Grimes, Burleigh	P	1964	CV	—	—	Pittsburgh NL, Brooklyn NL, New York NL, Boston NL, St. Louis NL, Chicago NL, New York AL
Grove, Lefty	P	1947	123	161	76.4	Philadelphia AL, Boston AL
Hafey, Chick	P	1971	CV	—	—	St. Louis NL, Cincinnati NL
Haines, Jesse	P	1970	CV	—	—	Cincinnati NL, St. Louis NL
Hamilton, Billy	P	1961	CV	—	—	Kansas City AA, Philadelphia NL, Boston NL
Hanlon, Ned	M	1996	CV	—	—	Cleveland NL, Detroit NL, Pittsburgh NL, Pittsburgh PL, Baltimore NL
Harridge, Will	E	1972	CV	—	—	
Harris, Bucky	M	1975	CV	—	—	Washington AL, Detroit AL
Hartnett, Gabby	P	1955	195	251	77.7	Chicago NL, New York NL
Heilmann, Harry	P	1952	203	234	86.8	Detroit AL, Cincinnati NL
Herman, Billy	P	1975	CV	—	—	Chicago NL, Brooklyn NL, Boston NL, Pittsburgh NL
Hooper, Harry	P	1971	CV	—	—	Boston AL, Chicago AL
Hornsby, Rogers	P	1942	182	233	78.1	St. Louis NL, New York NL, Boston NL, Chicago NL, St. Louis AL
Hoyt, Waite	P	1969	CV	—	—	New York NL, Boston AL, New York AL, Detroit AL, Philadelphia AL, Brooklyn NL, Pittsburgh NL
Hubbard, Cal	U	1976	CV	—	—	
Hubbell, Carl	P	1947	140	161	87.0	New York NL
Huggins, Miller	M	1964	CV	—	—	Cincinnati NL, St. Louis NL
Hulbert, William	F	1995	CV	—	—	
Hunter, Catfish	P	1987	315	413	76.3	Kansas City AL, Oakland AL, New York AL
Irvin, Monte	P	1973	SCNL	—	—	New York NL, Chicago NL, Negro Leagues
Jackson, Reggie	P	1993	396	423	93.6	Kansas City AL, Oakland AL, Baltimore AL, New York AL, California AL
Jackson, Travis	P	1982	CV	—	—	New York NL
Jenkins, Ferguson	P	1991	334	443	75.4	Philadelphia NL, Chicago NL, Texas AL, Boston AL

Name	Des.*	Elec. year	Votes rec.†	Votes cast‡	% of vote	Teams as player
Jennings, Hugh	P	1945	C2	—	—	Louisville AA, Louisville NL, Baltimore NL, Brooklyn NL, Philadelphia NL, Detroit AL
Johnson, Ban	E	1937	CC	—	—	
Johnson, Judy	P	1975	SCNL	—	—	Negro Leagues
Johnson, Walter	P	1936	189	226	83.6	Washington AL
Joss, Addie	P	1978	CV	—	—	Cleveland AL
Kaline, Al	P	1980	340	385	88.3	Detroit AL
Keefe, Tim	P	1964	CV	—	—	Troy NL, New York AA, New York NL, New York PL, Philadelphia NL
Keeler, Willie	P	1939	207	274	75.5	New York NL, Brooklyn NL, Baltimore NL, New York AL
Kell, George	P	1983	CV	—	—	Philadelphia AL, Detroit AL, Boston AL, Chicago AL, Baltimore AL
Kelley, Joe	P	1971	CV	—	—	Boston NL, Pittsburgh NL, Baltimore NL, Brooklyn NL, Baltimore AL, Cincinnati NL
Kelly, George	P	1973	CV	—	—	New York NL, Pittsburgh NL, Cincinnati NL, Chicago NL, Brooklyn NL
Kelly, King	P	1945	C2	—	—	Cincinnati NL, Chicago NL, Boston NL, Boston PL, Cincinnati AA, Boston AA, New York NL
Killebrew, Harmon	P	1984	335	403	83.1	Washington AL, Minnesota AL, Kansas City AL
Kiner, Ralph	P	1975	273	362	75.4	Pittsburgh NL, Chicago NL, Cleveland AL
Klein, Chuck	P	1980	CV	—	—	Philadelphia NL, Chicago NL, Pittsburgh NL
Klem, Bill	U	1953	CV	—	—	
Koufax, Sandy	P	1972	344	396	86.9	Brooklyn NL, Los Angeles NL
Lajoie, Nap	P	1937	168	201	83.6	Philadelphia NL, Philadelphia AL, Cleveland AL
Landis, Kenesaw M.	E	1944	C2	—	—	
Lasorda, Tommy	M	1997	CV	—	—	Brooklyn NL, Kansas City AL
Lazzeri, Tony	P	1991	CV	—	—	New York AL, Chicago NL, Brooklyn NL, New York NL
Lemon, Bob	P	1976	305	388	78.6	Cleveland AL
Leonard, Buck	P	1972	SCNL	—	—	Negro Leagues
Lindstrom, Fred	P	1976	CV	—	—	New York NL, Pittsburgh NL, Chicago NL, Brooklyn NL
Lloyd, John Henry	P	1977	SCNL	—	—	Negro Leagues
Lombardi, Ernie	P	1986	CV	—	—	Brooklyn NL, Cincinnati NL, Boston NL, New York NL
Lopez, Al	M	1977	CV	—	—	Brooklyn NL, Boston NL, Pittsburgh NL, Cleveland AL
Lyons, Ted	P	1955	217	251	86.5	Chicago AL
Mack, Connie	M	1937	CC	—	—	Washington NL, Buffalo PL, Pittsburgh NL
MacPhail, Larry	E	1978	CV	—	—	
MacPhail, Lee	E	1998	CV	—	—	
Mantle, Mickey	P	1974	322	365	88.2	New York AL
Manush, Heinie	P	1964	CV	—	—	Detroit AL, St. Louis AL, Washington AL, Boston AL, Brooklyn NL, Pittsburgh NL
Maranville, Rabbit	P	1954	209	252	82.9	Boston NL, Pittsburgh NL, Chicago NL, Brooklyn NL, St. Louis NL
Marichal, Juan	P	1983	313	374	83.7	San Francisco NL, Boston AL, Los Angeles NL
Marquard, Rube	P	1971	CV	—	—	New York NL, Brooklyn NL, Cincinnati NL, Boston NL
Mathews, Eddie	P	1978	301	379	79.4	Boston NL, Milwaukee NL, Atlanta NL, Houston NL, Detroit AL
Mathewson, Christy	P	1936	205	226	90.7	New York NL, Cincinnati NL
Mays, Willie	P	1979	409	432	94.7	New York (Giants) NL, San Francisco NL, New York (Mets) NL
Mazeroski, Bill	P	2001	CV	—	—	Pittsburgh NL
McCarthy, Joe	M	1957	CV	—	—	
McCarthy, Tommy	P	1946	C2	—	—	Boston UA, Boston NL, Philadelphia NL, St. Louis AA, Brooklyn NL
McCovey, Willie	P	1986	346	425	81.4	San Francisco NL, San Diego NL, Oakland AL
McGinnity, Joe	P	1946	C2	—	—	Baltimore NL, Brooklyn NL, Baltimore AL, New York NL
McGowan, Bill	U	1992	CV	—	—	
McGraw, John	M	1937	CC	—	—	Baltimore AA, Baltimore NL, St. Louis NL, Baltimore AL, New York NL
McKechnie, Bill	M	1962	CV	—	—	Pittsburgh NL, Boston NL, New York AL, New York NL, Cincinnati NL
McPhee, Bid	P	2000	CV	—	—	Cincinnati AA, Cincinnati NL
Medwick, Joe	P	1968	240	283	84.8	St. Louis NL, Brooklyn NL, New York NL, Boston NL
Mize, Johnny	P	1981	CV	—	—	St. Louis NL, New York NL, New York AL
Morgan, Joe	P	1990	363	444	81.8	Houston NL, Cincinnati NL, San Francisco NL, Philadelphia NL, Oakland AL
Murray, Eddie	P	2003	423	496	85.3	Baltimore AL, Los Angeles NL, New York NL, Cleveland AL, Anaheim AL
Musial, Stan	P	1969	317	340	93.2	St. Louis NL
Newhouser, Hal	P	1992	CV	—	—	Detroit AL, Cleveland AL
Nichols, Kid	P	1949	C2	—	—	Boston NL, St. Louis NL, Philadelphia NL
Niekro, Phil	P	1997	380	473	80.3	Milwaukee NL, Atlanta NL, New York AL, Cleveland AL, Toronto AL

Name	Elec. Des.*	Votes year	% of rec.†	cast‡	vote	Teams as player
O'Rourke, Jim	P	1945	C2	—	—	Boston NL, Providence NL, Buffalo NL, New York NL, New York PL, Washington NL
Ott, Mel	P	1951	197	226	87.2	New York NL
Paige, Satchel	P	1971	SCNL	—	—	Cleveland AL, St. Louis AL, Kansas City AL, Negro Leagues
Palmer, Jim	P	1990	411	444	92.6	Baltimore AL
Pennock, Herb	P	1948	94	121	77.7	Philadelphia AL, Boston AL, New York AL
Perez, Tony	P	2000	385	499	77.2	Cincinnati NL, Montreal NL, Boston AL, Philadelphia NL
Perry, Gaylord	P	1991	342	443	77.2	San Francisco NL, Cleveland AL, Texas AL, San Diego NL, New York AL, Atlanta NL, Seattle AL, Kansas City AL
Plank, Eddie	P	1946	C2	—	—	Philadelphia AL, St. Louis AL
Puckett, Kirby	P	2001	423	515	82.1	Minnesota AL
Radbourn, Old Hoss	P	1939	C1	—	—	Buffalo NL, Providence NL, Boston NL, Boston PL, Cincinnati NL
Reese, Pee Wee	P	1984	CV	—	—	Brooklyn NL, Los Angeles NL
Rice, Sam	P	1963	CV	—	—	Washington AL, Cleveland AL
Rickey, Branch	E	1967	CV	—	—	St. Louis AL, New York AL
Rixey, Eppa	P	1963	CV	—	—	Philadelphia NL, Cincinnati NL
Rizzuto, Phil	P	1994	CV	—	—	New York AL
Roberts, Robin	P	1976	337	388	86.9	Philadelphia NL, Baltimore AL, Houston NL, Chicago NL
Robinson, Brooks	P	1983	344	374	92.0	Baltimore AL
Robinson, Frank	P	1982	370	415	89.2	Cincinnati NL, Baltimore AL, Los Angeles NL, California AL, Cleveland AL
Robinson, Jackie	P	1962	124	160	77.5	Brooklyn NL
Robinson, Wilbert	M	1945	C2	—	—	Philadelphia AA, Baltimore AA, Baltimore NL, St. Louis NL, Baltimore AL
Rogan, Bullet Joe	P	1998	CV	—	—	Negro Leagues
Roush, Edd	P	1962	CV	—	—	Chicago AL, New York NL, Cincinnati NL
Ruffing, Red	P	1967	266	306	86.9	Boston AL, New York AL, Chicago AL
Rusie, Amos	P	1977	CV	—	—	Indianapolis NL, New York NL, Cincinnati NL
Ruth, Babe	P	1936	215	226	95.1	Boston AL, New York AL, Boston NL
Ryan, Nolan	P	1999	491	497	98.8	New York NL, California AL, Houston NL, Texas AL
Schalk, Ray	P	1955	CV	—	—	Chicago AL, New York NL
Schmidt, Mike	P	1995	444	460	96.5	Philadelphia NL
Schoendienst, Red	P	1989	CV	—	—	St. Louis NL, New York (Giants) NL, Milwaukee NL
Seaver, Tom	P	1992	425	430	98.8	New York NL, Cincinnati NL, Chicago AL, Boston AL
Selee, Frank	M	1999	CV	—	—	
Sewell, Joe	P	1977	CV	—	—	Cleveland AL, New York AL
Simmons, Al	P	1953	199	264	75.4	Philadelphia AL, Chicago AL, Detroit AL, Washington AL, Boston NL, Cincinnati NL, Boston AL
Sisler, George	P	1939	235	274	85.8	St. Louis AL, Washington AL, Boston NL
Slaughter, Enos	P	1985	CV	—	—	St. Louis NL, New York AL, Kansas City AL, Milwaukee NL
Smith, Hilton	P	2001	CV	—	—	Negro Leagues
Smith, Ozzie	P	2002	433	472	91.7	San Diego NL, St. Louis NL
Snider, Duke	P	1980	333	385	86.5	Brooklyn NL, Los Angeles NL, New York NL, San Francisco NL
Spahn, Warren	P	1973	316	380	83.2	Boston NL, Milwaukee NL, New York NL, San Francisco NL
Spalding, Al	P	1939	C1	—	—	Chicago NL
Speaker, Tris	P	1937	165	201	82.1	Boston AL, Cleveland AL, Washington AL, Philadelphia AL
Stargell, Willie	P	1988	352	427	82.4	Pittsburgh NL
Stearnes, Turkey	P	2000	CV	—	—	Negro Leagues
Stengel, Casey	M	1966	CV	—	—	Brooklyn NL, Pittsburgh NL, Philadelphia NL, New York NL, Boston NL
Sutton, Don	P	1998	386	473	81.6	Los Angeles NL, Houston NL, Milwaukee AL, Oakland AL, California AL
Terry, Bill	P	1954	195	252	77.4	New York NL
Thompson, Sam	P	1974	CV	—	—	Detroit NL, Philadelphia NL, Detroit AL
Tinker, Joe	P	1946	C2	—	—	Chicago NL, Cincinnati NL
Traynor, Pie	P	1948	93	121	76.9	Pittsburgh NL
Vance, Dazzy	P	1955	205	251	81.7	Pittsburgh NL, New York AL, Brooklyn NL, St. Louis NL, Cincinnati NL
Vaughan, Arky	P	1985	CV	—	—	Pittsburgh NL, Brooklyn NL
Veeck, Bill	E	1991	CV	—	—	
Waddell, Rube	P	1946	C2	—	—	Louisville NL, Pittsburgh NL, Chicago NL, Philadelphia AL, St. Louis AL
Wagner, Honus	P	1936	215	226	95.1	Louisville NL, Pittsburgh NL
Wallace, Bobby	P	1953	CV	—	—	Cleveland NL, St. Louis NL, St. Louis AL

Name	Des.*	Elec. year	Votes rec.†	Votes cast‡	% of vote	Teams as player
Walsh, Ed	P	1946	C2	—	—	Chicago AL, Boston NL
Waner, Lloyd	P	1967	CV	—	—	Pittsburgh NL, Boston NL, Cincinnati NL, Philadelphia NL, Brooklyn NL
Waner, Paul	P	1952	195	234	83.3	Pittsburgh NL, Brooklyn NL, Boston NL, New York AL
Ward, Monte	P	1964	CV	—	—	Providence NL, New York NL, Brooklyn PL, Brooklyn NL
Weaver, Earl	M	1996	CV	—	—	
Weiss, George	E	1971	CV	—	—	
Welch, Mickey	P	1973	CV	—	—	Troy NL, New York NL
Wells, Willie	P	1997	CV	—	—	Negro Leagues
Wheat, Zack	P	1959	CV	—	—	Brooklyn NL, Philadelphia AL
Wilhelm, Hoyt	P	1985	331	395	83.8	New York NL, St. Louis NL, Cleveland AL, Baltimore AL, Chicago AL, California AL, Atlanta NL, Chicago NL, Los Angeles NL
Williams, Billy	P	1987	354	413	85.7	Chicago NL, Oakland AL
Williams, Smokey Joe	P	1999	CV	—	—	Negro Leagues
Williams, Ted	P	1966	282	302	93.4	Boston AL
Willis, Vic	P	1995	CV	—	—	Boston NL, Pittsburgh NL, St. Louis NL
Wilson, Hack	P	1979	CV	—	—	New York NL, Chicago NL, Brooklyn NL, Philadelphia NL
Winfield, Dave	P	2001	435	515	84.5	San Diego NL, New York AL, California AL, Toronto AL, Minnesota AL, Cleveland AL
Wright, George	P	1937	CC	—	—	Boston NL, Providence NL
Wright, Harry	M	1953	CV	—	—	Boston NL
Wynn, Early	P	1972	301	396	76.0	Washington AL, Cleveland AL, Chicago AL
Yastrzemski, Carl	P	1989	423	447	94.6	Boston AL
Yawkey, Tom	E	1980	CV	—	—	
Young, Cy	P	1937	153	201	76.1	Cleveland NL, St. Louis NL, Boston AL, Cleveland AL, Boston NL
Youngs, Ross	P	1972	CV	—	—	New York NL
Yount, Robin	P	1999	385	497	77.5	Milwaukee AL

*Designation for which he was honored. Abbreviations: E—executive; F—founder; M—manager; O—organizer; P—player; U—umpire.

†Where an abbreviation is listed rather than a vote total, the enshrinee was selected by one of the following groups: Centennial Commission (CC), committee of old-time players and writers (C1), committee on old-timers (C2), Committee on Veterans (CV), special election by Baseball Writers' Association of America (SE) or Special Committee on Negro Leagues (SCNL).

‡Votes cast by eligible members of the Baseball Writers' Association of America.

League abbreviations: AA—American Association; AL—American League; NL—National League; PL—Players League; UA—Union Association.

MINOR LEAGUES

Farm systems

International League

Mexican League

Pacific Coast League

Eastern League

Southern League

Texas League

California League

Carolina League

Florida State League

Midwest League

New York-Pennsylvania League

Northwest League

South Atlantic League

Appalachian League

Arizona League

Gulf Coast League

Pioneer League

Minor league index

FARM SYSTEMS

AMERICAN LEAGUE

ANAHEIM (6): AAA—Salt Lake. AA—Arkansas. A—Cedar Rapids, Rancho Cucamonga. Rookie—Mesa Angels, Provo.
BALTIMORE (7): AAA—Ottawa. AA—Bowie. A—Aberdeen, Delmarva, Frederick. Rookie—Bluefield, Gulf Coast Orioles.
BOSTON (6): AAA—Pawtucket. AA—Portland (ME). A—Augusta, Lowell, Sarasota. Rookie—Gulf Coast Red Sox.
CHICAGO (6): AAA—Charlotte. AA—Birmingham. A—Kannapolis, Winston-Salem. Rookie—Bristol, Great Falls.
CLEVELAND (6): AAA—Buffalo. AA—Akron. A—Kinston, Lake County, Mahoning Valley. Rookie—Burlington.
DETROIT (6): AAA—Toledo. AA—Erie. A—Lakeland, Oneonta, West Michigan. Rookie—Gulf Coast Tigers.
KANSAS CITY (5): AAA—Omaha. AA—Wichita. A—Burlington, Wilmington. Rookie—Arizona Royals.
MINNESOTA (6): AAA—Rochester. AA—New Britain. A—Fort Myers, Quad City. Rookie—Elizabethton, Gulf Coast Twins.
NEW YORK (6): AAA—Columbus (OH). AA—Trenton. A—Battle Creek, Staten Island, Tampa. Rookie—Gulf Coast Yankees.
OAKLAND (6): AAA—Sacramento. AA—Midland. A—Kane County, Modesto, Vancouver. Rookie—Scottsdale A's.
SEATTLE (6): AAA—Tacoma. AA—San Antonio. A—Everett, San Bernardino, Wisconsin. Rookie—Peoria (AZ) Mariners.
TAMPA BAY (6): AAA—Durham. AA—Orlando. A—Bakersfield, Charleston (SC), Hudson Valley. Rookie—Princeton.
TEXAS (6): AAA—Oklahoma. AA—Frisco. A—Clinton, Spokane, Stockton. Rookie—Arizona Rangers.
TORONTO (6): AAA—Syracuse. AA—New Haven. A—Auburn, Charleston (WV), Dunedin. Rookie—Pulaski.

NATIONAL LEAGUE

ARIZONA (6): AAA—Tucson. AA—El Paso. A—Lancaster, South Bend, Yakima. Rookie—Missoula.
ATLANTA (6): AAA—Richmond. AA—Greenville. A—Myrtle Beach, Rome. Rookie—Danville, Gulf Coast Braves.
CHICAGO (6): AAA—Iowa. AA—West Tenn. A—Boise, Daytona, Lansing. Rookie—Mesa Cubs.
CINCINNATI (6): AAA—Louisville. AA—Chattanooga. A—Dayton, Potomac. Rookie—Billings, Gulf Coast Reds.
COLORADO (6): AAA—Colorado Springs. AA—Tulsa. A—Asheville, Tri-City (WA), Visalia. Rookie—Casper.
FLORIDA (6): AAA—Albuquerque. AA—Carolina. A—Greensboro, Jamestown, Jupiter. Rookie—Gulf Coast Marlins.
HOUSTON (6): AAA—New Orleans. AA—Round Rock. A—Lexington, Salem, Tri-City (NY). Rookie—Martinsville.
LOS ANGELES (6): AAA—Las Vegas. AA—Jacksonville. A—South Georgia, Vero Beach. Rookie—Gulf Coast Dodgers, Ogden.
MILWAUKEE (6): AAA—Indianapolis. AA—Huntsville. A—Beloit, High Desert. Rookie—Helena, Maryvale.
MONTREAL (6): AAA—Edmonton. AA—Harrisburg. A—Brevard County, Savannah, Vermont. Rookie—Gulf Coast Expos.
NEW YORK (6): AAA—Norfolk. AA—Binghamton. A—Brooklyn, Capital City, St. Lucie. Rookie—Kingsport.
PHILADELPHIA (6): AAA—Scranton/Wilkes-Barre. AA—Reading. A—Batavia, Clearwater, Lakewood. Rookie—Gulf Coast Phillies.
PITTSBURGH (6): AAA—Nashville. AA—Altoona. A—Hickory, Lynchburg, Williamsport. Rookie—Gulf Coast Pirates.
ST. LOUIS (6): AAA—Memphis. AA—Tennessee. A—New Jersey, Palm Beach, Peoria (IL). Rookie—Johnson City.
SAN DIEGO (6): AAA—Portland (OR). AA—Mobile. A—Eugene, Fort Wayne, Lake Elsinore. Rookie—Idaho Falls.
SAN FRANCISCO (6): AAA—Fresno. AA—Norwich. A—Hagerstown, Salem-Keizer, San Jose. Rookie—Arizona Giants.

INTERNATIONAL LEAGUE

LEAGUE OFFICE

President
Randy Mobley

Address
55 S. High St., Suite 202
Dublin, OH 43017

Phone
614-791-9300

TEAMS

BUFFALO BISONS

General manager
Mike Buczkowski
Manager
Marty Brown
Ballpark (capacity, surface)
Dunn Tire Park (To be announced, grass)
Affiliation
Indians
Address
P.O. Box 450
Buffalo, NY 14205
Phone
716-846-2000

CHARLOTTE KNIGHTS

General manager
Bill Blackwell
Manager
Nick Capra
Ballpark (capacity, surface)
Knights Stadium (10,000, grass)
Affiliation
White Sox
Address
2280 Deerfield Drive
Fort Mill, SC 29715
Phone
704-357-8071

COLUMBUS CLIPPERS

General manager
Ken Schnacke
Manager
Bucky Dent
Ballpark (capacity, surface)
Cooper Stadium (15,000, grass)
Affiliation
Yankees
Address
1155 W. Mound St.
Columbus, OH 43223
Phone
614-462-5250

DURHAM BULLS

General manager
Mike Birling
Manager
Bill Evers
Ballpark (capacity, surface)
Durham Bulls Athletic Park (10,000, grass)
Affiliation
Devil Rays
Address
P.O. Box 507
Durham, NC 27702
Phone
919-687-6500

INDIANAPOLIS INDIANS

General manager
Cal Burleson
Manager
Cecil Cooper
Ballpark (capacity, surface)
Victory Field (15,500, grass)
Affiliation
Brewers
Address
501 W. Maryland St.
Indianapolis, IN 46225
Phone
317-269-3542

LOUISVILLE BATS

President
Gary Ulmer
Manager
Dave Miley
Ballpark (capacity, surface)
Louisville Slugger Field (13,200, grass)
Affiliation
Reds
Address
401 E. Main Street
Louisville, KY 40202
Phone
502-212-2287

NORFOLK TIDES

General manager
Dave Rosenfield
Manager
Bobby Floyd
Ballpark (capacity, surface)
Harbor Park (12,067, grass)
Affiliation
Mets
Address
150 Park Ave.
Norfolk, VA 23510
Phone
757-622-2222

OTTAWA LYNX

General manager
Kyle Bostwick
Manager
To be announced
Ballpark (capacity, surface)
Lynx Stadium (10,332, grass)
Affiliation
Orioles
Address
300 Coventry Rd.
Ottawa, Ontario K1K 4P5
Phone
613-747-5969

PAWTUCKET RED SOX

President
Mike Tamburro
Manager
Buddy Bailey
Ballpark (capacity, surface)
McCoy Stadium (10,031, grass)
Affiliation
Red Sox
Address
P.O. Box 2365
Pawtucket, RI 02861
Phone
401-724-7303

RICHMOND BRAVES

General manager
Bruce Baldwin
Manager
Pat Kelly
Ballpark (capacity, surface)
The Diamond (12,134, grass)
Affiliation
Braves
Address
P.O. Box 6667
Richmond, VA 23230
Phone
804-359-4444

ROCHESTER RED WINGS

General manager
Dan Mason
Manager
Phil Roof
Ballpark (capacity, surface)
Frontier Field (10,868, grass)
Affiliation
Twins
Address
1 Morrie Silver Way
Rochester, NY 14608
Phone
585-454-1001

SCRANTON/WILKES-BARRE RED BARONS

General manager
Rick Muntean
Manager
Marc Bombard
Ballpark (capacity, surface)
Lackawanna County Multi-Purpose Stadium (10,982, artificial)
Affiliation
Phillies
Address
P.O. Box 3449
Scranton, PA 18505
Phone
570-969-2255

SYRACUSE SKYCHIEFS

General manager
John Simone
Manager
Omar Malave
Ballpark (capacity, surface)
P&C Stadium (11,071, artificial)
Affiliation
Blue Jays

Address
One Tex Simone Dr.
Syracuse, NY 13208
Phone
315-474-7833

TOLEDO MUD HENS

General manager
Joe Napoli
Manager
Larry Parrish

Ballpark (capacity, surface)
Fifth Third Field (8,943, grass)
Affiliation
Tigers
Address
406 Washington St.
Toledo, OH 43604
Phone
419-725-4367

2002 FINAL STANDINGS

NORTH DIVISION

Team	W	L	T	Pct.	GB
Scranton/Wilkes-Barre (Phillies)	91	53	0	.632	...
Buffalo (Indians)	87	57	0	.604	4.0
Ottawa (Expos)	80	61	0	.567	9.5
Syracuse (Blue Jays)	64	80	0	.444	27.0
Pawtucket (Red Sox)	60	84	0	.417	31.0
Rochester (Orioles)	55	89	0	.382	36.0

SOUTH DIVISION

Team	W	L	T	Pct.	GB
Durham (Devil Rays)	80	64	0	.556	...
Richmond (Braves)	75	67	0	.528	4.0
Norfolk (Mets)	70	73	0	.490	9.5
Charlotte (White Sox)	55	88	0	.385	24.5

WEST DIVISION

Team	W	L	T	Pct.	GB
Toledo (Tigers)	81	63	0	.563	...
Louisville (Reds)	79	65	0	.549	2.0
Indianapolis (Brewers)	67	76	0	.469	13.5
Columbus (Yankees)	59	83	0	.415	21.0

COMPOSITE

Team	SWB.	Buf.	Ott.	Tol.	Dur.	Lou.	Rich.	Nor.	Ind.	Syr.	Paw.	Col.	Char.	Roch.	W	L	T	Pct.	GB
Scranton/Wilkes-Barre (Phillies)	...	6	9	6	4	7	4	5	3	10	11	5	7	14	91	53	0	.632	...
Buffalo (Indians)	10	...	10	5	4	6	5	5	4	13	9	4	3	9	87	57	0	.604	4.0
Ottawa (Expos)	7	6	...	3	4	3	4	5	4	11	8	6	4	15	80	61	0	.567	9.5
Toledo (Tigers)	2	3	5	...	5	8	5	10	7	6	5	10	8	7	81	63	0	.563	10.0
Durham (Devil Rays)	4	4	4	7	...	6	8	12	6	4	3	8	11	3	80	64	0	.556	11.0
Louisville (Reds)	1	2	5	8	6	...	4	9	9	5	6	9	6	6	79	65	0	.549	12.0
Richmond (Braves)	4	3	4	7	8	8	...	6	5	4	4	8	8	6	75	67	0	.528	15.0
Norfolk (Mets)	3	3	3	2	4	3	9	...	10	4	7	8	9	5	70	73	0	.490	20.5
Indianapolis (Brewers)	5	4	3	9	6	7	7	2	...	0	5	8	9	2	67	76	0	.469	23.5
Syracuse (Blue Jays)	6	3	5	2	4	3	4	4	8	...	8	4	6	7	64	80	0	.444	27.0
Pawtucket (Red Sox)	5	7	8	3	5	2	4	1	3	8	...	5	5	4	60	84	0	.417	31.0
Columbus (Yankees)	3	4	0	6	4	7	4	4	8	4	3	...	6	6	59	83	0	.415	31.0
Charlotte (White Sox)	1	5	4	4	5	3	7	7	3	2	3	6	...	5	55	88	0	.385	35.5
Rochester (Orioles)	2	7	1	1	5	2	3	6	9	12	2	3	...	55	89	0	.382	36.0

Major league affiliations in parentheses.

PLAYOFFS: Buffalo defeated Scranton-Wilkes Barre, three games to none; Durham defeated Toledo, three games to none; Durham defeated Buffalo, three games to none, to win International League championship.

REGULAR-SEASON ATTENDANCE: Buffalo, 642,272; Charlotte, 303,321; Columbus, 490,390; Durham, 519,122; Indianapolis, 571,984; Louisville, 659,340; Norfolk, 500,192; Ottawa, 191,305; Pawtucket, 615,540; Richmond, 452,961; Rochester, 421,494; Scranton-Wilkes Barre, 466,342; Syracuse, 413,566; Toledo, 567,804. Total—6,815,633. Playoff attendance (nine games)—56,876. Triple-A All-Star Game at Oklahoma City—11,343.

MANAGERS: Buffalo, Eric Wedge; Charlotte, Nick Capra; Columbus, Brian Butterfield (through May 15; 12-25), Frank Howard (May 16 through May 22; 3-4) and Stump Merrill (May 23 through end of season; 44-54); Durham, Bill Evers; Indianapolis, Ed Romero; Louisville, Dave Miley; Norfolk, Bobby Floyd; Ottawa, Tim Leiper; Pawtucket, Buddy Bailey; Richmond, Fredi Gonzalez; Rochester, Andy Etchebarren; Scranton-Wilkes Barre, Marc Bombard; Syracuse, Omar Malave; Toledo, Bruce Fields.

ALL-STAR TEAM: 1B—Joe Vitiello, Ottawa; 2B—Marco Scutaro, Norfolk; 3B—Joe Crede, Charlotte; SS—Nick Punto, Scranton-Wilkes Barre; OF—Marlon Byrd, Scranton-Wilkes Barre; OF—Endy Chavez, Ottawa; OF—Raul Gonzalez, Louisville; C—Johnny Estrada, Scranton-Wilkes Barre; DH—Kevin Witt, Louisville; Utility—David Doster, Scranton-Wilkes Barre; Starting pitcher—Joe Roa, Scranton-Wilkes Barre; Relief pitcher—Lee Gardner, Durham; Most Valuable Player—Raul Gonzalez, Louisville; Most Valuable Pitcher—Joe Roa, Scranton-Wilkes Barre; Rookie of the Year—Carl Crawford, Durham; Manager of the Year—Marc Bombard, Scranton-Wilkes Barre.

2002 BATTING
TEAM

Team	G	TPA	AB	R	H	TB	2B	3B	HR	RBI	SH	SF	HP	BB	IBB	SO	SB	CS	GDP	LOB	ShO	Avg.	OBP	Slg.
Ottawa	141	5244	4697	620	1319	1916	266	38	85	578	66	36	42	403	22	759	112	64	124	1006	9	.281	.341	.408
Buffalo	144	5446	4902	684	1367	2055	295	36	107	639	47	30	73	394	17	777	78	36	122	1001	5	.279	.340	.419
Louisville	144	5604	4989	699	1387	2116	282	24	133	668	56	49	56	454	30	870	57	43	134	1057	6	.278	.342	.424
Toledo	144	5512	4888	665	1319	2059	279	52	119	638	45	46	44	489	21	962	94	58	109	1044	11	.270	.339	.421
Scran./W.-B.	144	5582	4934	705	1328	1940	277	34	89	652	48	55	74	471	23	858	109	33	101	1091	8	.269	.338	.393
Rochester	144	5458	4974	596	1336	1911	239	36	88	535	25	44	35	380	22	811	85	34	152	1006	12	.269	.322	.384
Durham	144	5461	4885	681	1298	1941	228	50	105	616	68	41	83	384	19	913	153	53	90	990	4	.266	.327	.397
Syracuse	144	5523	4914	697	1295	2091	287	25	153	654	34	37	60	478	20	1014	77	36	122	1013	8	.264	.334	.426
Richmond	142	5243	4719	613	1228	1887	247	17	126	574	33	46	53	392	17	954	81	42	120	920	10	.260	.321	.400

Team	G	TPA	AB	R	H	TB	2B	3B	HR	RBI	SH	SF	HP	BB	IBB	SO	SB	CS	GDP	LOB	ShO	Avg.	OBP	Slg.
Pawtucket	144	5387	4834	607	1253	1987	237	28	147	572	31	34	48	440	19	969	52	37	120	993	12	.259	.325	.411
Columbus......	142	5317	4819	649	1242	1984	273	32	135	605	34	37	39	388	9	835	51	47	98	898	9	.258	.316	.412
Norfolk.........	143	5298	4751	598	1223	1887	243	32	119	546	38	37	41	431	26	934	110	52	89	958	8	.257	.322	.397
Charlotte	143	5296	4774	572	1221	1898	256	14	131	529	54	49	46	373	8	1023	110	48	92	958	11	.256	.313	.398
Indianapolis...	143	5265	4709	526	1170	1744	241	27	93	493	46	31	50	429	18	871	92	55	122	965	12	.248	.316	.370

INDIVIDUAL

TOP QUALIFIERS FOR BATTING CHAMPIONSHIP

Minimum 389 plate appearances. *Lefthanded batter. †Switch-hitter.

Player, Team	G	TPA	AB	R	H	TB	2B	3B	HR	RBI	SH	SF	HP	BB	IBB	SO	SB	CS	GDP	Avg.	OBP	Slg.
Chavez, Endy, Ott.*	103	449	405	67	139	189	28	5	4	41	10	1	0	33	2	37	21	13	8	.343	.392	.467
Gonzalez, Raul, Lou.	114	504	432	91	144	214	27	2	13	69	1	6	4	61	4	59	9	8	15	.333	.416	.495
Vitiello, Joe, Ott.	119	482	431	57	142	224	34	0	16	82	0	5	7	39	5	58	1	0	16	.329	.390	.520
Monroe, Craig, Tol.	99	402	358	61	115	183	30	4	10	49	1	6	2	35	4	57	7	3	8	.321	.379	.511
Scutaro, Marcos, Nor.	97	394	354	48	113	168	22	6	7	28	7	1	2	30	3	61	7	8	7	.319	.375	.475
Coste, Chris, Buf.	124	528	478	59	152	210	32	1	8	67	0	3	13	34	2	54	0	0	14	.318	.377	.439
Sexton, Chris, Lou.	108	468	414	79	131	188	29	5	6	49	8	3	1	42	2	41	3	2	18	.316	.378	.454
Rushford, Jim, Lou.*	117	461	405	54	128	188	33	3	7	68	1	3	7	45	1	41	0	2	4	.316	.391	.464
Crede, Joe, Char.	95	399	359	57	112	205	21	0	24	65	0	7	4	26	1	48	0	1	8	.312	.359	.571
Clark, Howie, Roch.*	108	469	418	57	129	179	21	4	7	43	2	5	2	41	2	28	3	4	11	.309	.369	.428
Hudson, Orlando, Syr.†	100	458	417	63	127	190	27	3	10	37	1	1	4	35	0	54	8	5	14	.305	.363	.456
Bigbie, Larry, Roch.*	98	389	348	42	105	138	23	2	2	35	0	4	1	35	7	79	7	3	9	.302	.363	.397
McMillon, Billy, Col.*	115	511	442	72	133	195	32	3	8	46	1	3	6	59	2	71	2	5	6	.301	.388	.441
Garcia, Karim, Col.-Buf.	97	410	379	60	114	192	23	5	15	71	0	2	0	29	5	62	1	6	3	.301	.349	.507
Wigginton, Ty, Nor.	104	435	383	49	115	165	26	3	6	48	0	8	1	43	4	50	5	3	7	.300	.366	.431
Roberge, J.P., S./W.B.	123	464	420	56	126	178	29	1	7	52	2	2	6	34	2	66	6	1	6	.300	.359	.424

DEPARTMENTAL LEADERS: G—Doster, 143; AB—Doster, 579; R—Byrd, 103; H—Doster, 171; TB—Byrd, 256; 2B—Utley, 39; 3B—Sorensen, 12; HR—Alcantara, 27; RBI—Witt, 107; SH—Bridges, Sorensen, 15 each; SF—T. Wilson, 11; HP—LaRocca, 23; BB—Munson, 77; IBB—Bigbie, Estrada, 7 each; SO—Henson, 151; SB—Punto, Torres, 42 each; CS—Infante, 15; GIDP—Estrada, 19; Slg.—Crede, .571; OBP—R. Gonzalez, .416.

ALL PLAYERS

*Lefthanded batter. †Switch-hitter.

Player, Team	G	TPA	AB	R	H	TB	2B	3B	HR	RBI	SH	SF	HP	BB	IBB	SO	SB	CS	GDP	Avg.	OBP	Slg.
Abbott, Jeff, Paw..................	100	405	367	47	104	164	28	1	10	41	3	6	4	25	2	44	4	2	7	.283	.331	.447
Abbott, Kurt, Col.	3	12	11	2	3	4	1	0	0	1	0	0	0	1	0	1	0	0	0	.273	.333	.364
Acevas, Jon, Char.	1	1	1	0	0	0	0	0	0	0	0	0	0	0	0	1	0	0	0	.000	.000	.000
Acevedo, Jose, Lou.	23	20	14	0	2	2	0	0	0	0	5	0	0	1	0	5	0	0	0	.143	.200	.143
Ackerman, Scott, Ott.	12	32	31	4	8	15	1	0	2	7	0	1	0	0	0	8	0	0	1	.258	.250	.484
Agamennone, Brandon, Ott....	27	2	2	0	0	0	0	0	0	0	0	0	0	0	0	2	0	0	0	.000	.000	.000
Agbayani, Benny, Paw.	5	20	17	1	3	4	1	0	0	2	0	0	0	3	0	6	0	0	1	.176	.300	.235
Alcantara, Izzy, Ind.................	110	463	410	61	110	216	21	2	27	65	0	1	1	51	2	88	9	3	13	.268	.350	.527
Alexander, Chad, Tol..............	97	341	313	36	86	136	23	3	7	34	2	5	1	20	1	58	2	4	8	.275	.316	.435
Alexander, Manny, Rich..........	22	90	85	11	25	36	6	1	1	7	1	0	0	4	0	17	5	3	2	.294	.326	.424
Allen, Chad, Roch.-Buf..........	78	329	311	46	91	147	22	2	10	63	0	1	2	15	0	40	0	1	12	.293	.328	.473
Almonte, Ed, Char.	50	1	1	0	1	1	0	0	0	1	0	0	0	0	0	0	0	0	0	1.000	1.000	1.000
Almonte, Erick, Col.	66	240	221	25	52	91	10	1	9	28	2	2	0	15	0	60	2	1	2	.235	.282	.412
Alomar, Sandy, Char..............	3	8	8	0	1	1	0	0	0	0	0	0	0	0	0	0	0	0	1	.125	.125	.125
Andreopoulos, Alex, Ott.*	6	22	20	4	6	8	2	0	0	1	0	0	0	2	0	3	0	0	0	.300	.364	.400
Andrews, Shane, Paw.	116	448	390	61	100	187	19	1	22	63	0	3	3	52	1	123	1	1	9	.256	.346	.479
Arias, Alex, Roch.-Col............	77	289	263	34	63	84	18	0	1	25	2	1	2	21	0	26	3	2	7	.240	.300	.319
Atchley, Justin, Lou.*	7	1	1	0	0	0	0	0	0	0	0	0	0	0	0	0	0	0	0	.000	.000	.000
Aven, Bruce, Buf.-S./W.B.	94	387	324	43	84	139	16	0	13	58	0	2	11	50	3	56	4	1	11	.259	.375	.429
Bacsik, Mike, Nor.*	26	15	13	0	1	1	0	0	0	0	1	0	0	1	0	2	0	0	0	.077	.143	.077
Badeaux, Brooks, Dur.†	99	388	340	45	85	109	14	2	2	29	12	2	6	28	0	45	8	2	7	.250	.316	.321
Baldelli, Rocco, Dur.	23	98	96	13	28	45	6	1	3	7	2	0	0	0	0	23	2	5	1	.292	.292	.469
Bale, John, Nor.*	12	2	1	0	0	0	0	0	0	0	0	0	0	1	0	1	0	0	0	.000	.500	.000
Bard, Josh, Buf.†	94	370	344	36	102	150	26	2	6	53	3	3	0	20	0	45	0	0	13	.297	.332	.436
Barker, Glen, Paw.†	15	49	43	6	7	10	3	0	0	1	0	0	1	5	0	10	1	1	0	.163	.265	.233
Basak, Chris, Nor.	17	63	60	6	13	16	1	1	0	6	0	0	0	3	0	14	5	0	0	.217	.254	.267
Bates, Fletcher, Nor.†	58	182	167	20	42	70	8	1	6	21	0	2	1	12	2	25	2	3	1	.251	.302	.419
Battersby, Eric, Char.	55	205	183	14	46	60	8	0	2	17	4	1	0	17	0	30	1	1	4	.251	.313	.328
Battle, Howard, Ott.	56	204	193	20	46	69	11	0	4	18	1	0	0	10	1	28	0	1	7	.238	.276	.358
Baughman, Justin, Char.	124	477	420	57	96	126	12	0	6	37	2	4	10	31	0	75	31	9	3	.229	.295	.300
Beasley, Ray, Rich.	64	2	2	0	0	0	0	0	0	0	0	0	0	0	0	0	0	0	0	.000	.000	.000
Beinbrink, Andy, Dur.	2	8	8	1	3	4	1	0	0	1	0	0	0	0	0	2	0	0	0	.375	.375	.500
Bell, Heath, Nor.	22	4	3	0	0	0	0	0	0	0	0	0	0	0	0	1	0	0	0	.000	.000	.000
Bergeron, Pete, Ott.*	104	393	340	51	99	119	9	4	1	29	11	2	1	39	1	65	7	7	1	.291	.364	.350
Betemit, Wilson, Rich.†	93	383	343	43	84	127	17	1	8	34	2	3	1	34	0	82	8	5	7	.245	.312	.370
Betts, Todd, Paw.*	121	489	416	60	121	183	16	2	14	45	2	1	7	63	6	58	3	5	4	.291	.392	.440
Bierek, Kurt, Col.*	51	163	147	13	32	46	8	0	2	12	0	0	4	12	0	29	1	1	4	.218	.294	.313
Bigbie, Larry, Roch.*	98	389	348	42	105	138	23	2	2	35	0	4	1	35	7	79	7	3	9	.302	.363	.397
Billingsley, Brent, Ott.*	28	7	7	0	2	2	0	0	0	0	0	0	0	0	0	4	0	0	0	.286	.286	.286
Blank, Matt, Ott.*	31	15	12	0	1	1	0	0	0	1	1	0	1	0	0	2	0	0	1	.083	.143	.083
Bohanon, Brian, Lou.*	14	9	8	0	1	2	1	0	0	2	1	0	0	0	0	3	0	0	1	.125	.125	.250
Borchard, Joe, Char.†	117	493	438	62	119	218	35	2	20	59	0	2	4	49	2	139	2	4	11	.272	.349	.498
Boscan, Jean, Rich.	2	7	6	0	1	1	0	0	0	0	0	0	1	0	0	2	0	0	0	.167	.286	.167
Bradley, Milton, Buf.†	6	28	23	3	6	6	0	0	0	3	0	2	0	3	0	5	2	1	0	.261	.321	.261

Player, Team	G	TPA	AB	R	H	TB	2B	3B	HR	RBI	SH	SF	HP	BB	IBB	SO	SB	CS	GDP	Avg.	OBP	Slg.
Bragg, Darren, Rich.*	22	96	75	15	22	30	5	0	1	8	1	0	0	20	0	15	4	2	0	.293	.442	.400
Bridges, Kary, Col.*	134	569	502	72	132	172	8	4	8	39	15	4	2	46	0	26	7	7	14	.263	.325	.343
Brinkley, Darryl, Roch.	128	544	509	58	145	206	31	3	8	73	1	7	2	25	4	67	19	5	12	.285	.317	.405
Broussard, Ben, Lou.-Buf.*	99	412	340	61	88	160	22	1	16	51	1	4	12	55	4	80	4	1	5	.259	.377	.471
Brown, Emil, Dur.	116	472	422	58	120	186	24	3	12	58	0	6	10	34	1	81	10	2	7	.284	.347	.441
Brown, Kevin, Dur.-Paw.	76	267	246	33	58	97	13	1	8	25	1	0	0	20	0	66	0	0	5	.236	.293	.394
Brunette, Justin, Nor.*	48	13	12	1	5	6	1	0	0	3	0	0	0	1	0	2	0	0	0	.417	.462	.500
Buford, Damon, Paw.-Char.	51	191	169	25	39	57	9	0	3	12	3	1	2	16	0	27	7	1	6	.231	.303	.337
Burkhart, Lance, Ind.	27	81	69	3	10	15	2	0	1	2	1	0	1	10	0	23	0	0	0	.145	.263	.217
Burnham, Gary, Syr.*	134	611	537	70	151	238	34	1	17	88	2	2	17	53	1	69	1	2	19	.281	.363	.443
Byrd, Marlon, S./W.B.	136	602	538	103	160	256	37	7	15	63	2	5	11	46	2	98	15	1	5	.297	.362	.476
Cabrera, Jolbert, Buf.	23	104	91	16	26	31	5	0	0	7	2	1	1	9	0	10	4	2	3	.286	.353	.341
Caceres, Wilmy, Dur.†	108	386	347	42	90	108	6	6	0	20	11	2	2	24	0	47	16	8	7	.259	.309	.311
Calloway, Ron, Ott.*	128	506	447	72	118	191	21	5	14	60	4	5	6	44	3	89	16	12	18	.264	.335	.427
Campos, Francisco, Ind.	5	6	5	0	1	1	0	0	0	1	0	0	0	1	0	0	0	0	0	.200	.333	.200
Canseco, Jose, Char.	18	75	64	11	11	27	1	0	5	9	0	1	1	9	1	21	1	0	1	.172	.280	.422
Caradonna, Brett, Char.*	2	4	3	0	0	0	0	0	0	0	0	0	0	1	0	0	0	0	0	.000	.250	.000
Carroll, Jamey, Ott.	117	469	421	57	118	165	19	2	8	49	7	1	3	37	1	39	6	10	8	.280	.342	.392
Casanova, Raul, Ind.†	14	48	43	2	12	16	4	0	0	8	0	2	0	3	0	8	0	0	3	.279	.313	.372
Casey, Sean, Lou.*	2	9	8	2	4	7	0	0	1	3	0	0	0	1	0	0	0	0	0	.500	.556	.875
Cash, Kevin, Syr.	67	266	236	27	52	100	18	0	10	26	2	1	2	25	0	72	0	1	3	.220	.299	.424
Casillas, Uriel, S./W.B.	9	23	21	4	9	13	1	0	1	3	0	0	0	2	0	3	0	0	2	.429	.478	.619
Castillo, Alberto, Col.	30	104	91	7	25	32	7	0	0	8	1	1	2	9	0	8	1	0	3	.275	.350	.352
Castro, Juan, Lou.	5	19	17	2	3	3	0	0	0	2	1	0	0	1	0	3	0	0	0	.176	.222	.176
Castro, Ramon, Rich.	39	142	121	22	28	55	7	1	6	14	1	0	6	14	0	22	4	3	1	.231	.340	.455
Cerros, Juan, Nor.	25	3	3	1	0	0	0	0	0	0	0	0	0	0	0	2	0	0	0	.000	.000	.000
Cesar, Dionys, Ind.†	133	520	479	52	123	169	22	3	6	38	5	4	2	30	0	75	8	7	8	.257	.301	.353
Chantres, Carlos, Char.	15	2	1	0	0	0	0	0	0	0	1	0	0	0	0	1	0	0	0	.000	.000	.000
Chavez, Endy, Ott.*	103	449	405	67	139	189	28	5	4	41	10	1	0	33	2	37	21	13	8	.343	.392	.467
Chevalier, Virgil, Nor.	19	71	60	5	18	25	1	0	2	8	0	1	0	10	0	7	1	1	3	.300	.408	.417
Christensen, McKay, Nor.*	97	414	377	52	107	157	23	6	5	30	4	0	7	26	0	72	20	13	4	.284	.341	.416
Christenson, Ryan, Ind.	67	284	260	38	66	102	17	2	5	30	3	1	2	18	0	28	11	5	5	.254	.306	.392
Clark, Brady, Lou.	25	117	109	17	33	43	7	0	1	17	1	2	2	3	0	9	0	2	3	.303	.328	.394
Clark, Howie, Roch.*	108	469	418	57	129	179	21	4	7	43	2	5	2	41	2	28	3	4	11	.309	.369	.428
Clemente, Edgard, Paw.-Ind.	103	404	373	38	90	137	19	2	8	40	3	1	4	23	1	100	6	1	5	.241	.292	.367
Coleman, Michael, Paw.	65	236	204	27	48	84	7	1	9	22	1	1	1	29	0	56	0	0	6	.235	.332	.412
Collier, Lou, Ott.	89	356	307	48	97	153	26	6	6	52	1	5	6	37	1	69	5	2	9	.316	.394	.498
Coste, Chris, Buf.	124	528	478	59	152	210	32	1	8	67	0	3	13	34	2	54	0	0	14	.318	.377	.439
Crawford, Carl, Dur.*	85	385	353	59	105	161	17	9	7	52	4	4	2	20	5	69	26	8	5	.297	.335	.456
Crede, Joe, Char.	95	399	359	57	112	205	21	0	24	65	0	7	4	26	1	48	0	1	8	.312	.359	.571
Crisp, Covelli, Buf.†	4	21	21	3	5	6	1	0	0	2	0	0	0	2	1	0	2	0	2	.238	.238	.286
Crowell, Jim, S./W.B.	4	1	1	0	0	0	0	0	0	0	0	0	0	0	0	1	0	0	0	.000	.000	.000
Crumpton, Chuck, Ott.	19	1	1	0	0	0	0	0	0	0	0	0	0	0	0	0	0	0	0	.000	.000	.000
Cruz, Jacob, Tol.*	11	53	43	6	7	10	1	1	0	5	0	1	1	8	0	14	1	0	3	.163	.302	.233
Cubillan, Darwin, Ott.	29	1	1	0	0	0	0	0	0	0	0	0	0	0	0	1	0	0	0	.000	.000	.000
Cummings, Midre, Ind.*	11	41	39	7	12	23	2	0	3	8	0	0	0	2	0	4	1	1	2	.308	.341	.590
Curry, Mike, Nor.*	26	109	92	12	27	31	4	0	0	4	0	1	1	15	0	18	4	4	2	.293	.394	.337
Dalesandro, Mark, Char.	46	172	160	12	36	50	8	0	2	10	3	2	2	5	0	13	0	0	8	.225	.254	.313
D'Amico, Jeff, S./W.B.-Lou.	26	16	15	1	4	7	0	0	1	4	1	0	0	0	0	3	0	0	0	.267	.267	.467
Darnell, Paul, Lou.	12	1	1	0	0	0	0	0	0	0	0	0	0	0	0	0	0	0	0	.000	.000	.000
Darula, Bobby, Lou.*	23	59	49	6	12	13	1	0	0	5	2	1	0	7	0	4	0	0	0	.245	.333	.265
Davidson, Cleatus, Col.†	1	1	1	0	0	0	0	0	0	0	0	0	0	0	0	0	0	0	0	.000	.000	.000
Davis, Lance, Lou.	11	11	10	0	0	0	0	0	0	0	1	0	0	0	0	5	0	0	0	.000	.000	.000
Davis, Tommy, Buf.	36	151	147	9	37	55	9	0	3	17	0	1	2	1	0	37	0	1	7	.252	.265	.374
Dawkins, Gookie, Lou.	47	182	167	14	42	51	5	2	0	8	0	2	1	12	2	34	2	3	5	.251	.302	.305
Dawley, Joey, Rich.	24	14	13	0	2	2	0	0	0	0	1	0	0	0	0	2	0	0	0	.154	.154	.154
Day, Zach, Ott.	17	14	13	0	1	1	0	0	0	0	0	0	0	1	0	6	0	0	0	.077	.077	.077
De La Rosa, Tomas, Ott.	2	6	3	0	0	0	0	0	0	0	0	1	0	2	0	1	0	0	0	.000	.400	.000
Dellarova, Jason, Char.	28	84	82	10	20	38	6	0	4	10	1	1	0	0	0	27	0	0	1	.244	.241	.463
De Los Santos, Eddy, Syr.	22	72	61	7	11	12	1	0	0	1	4	1	0	6	0	13	1	1	5	.180	.250	.197
De Los Santos, Luis, Roch.	50	201	187	21	50	78	8	1	6	16	0	0	0	14	0	43	0	0	11	.267	.318	.417
Depastino, Joe, Nor.	70	264	248	24	74	110	15	3	5	27	1	0	3	12	1	47	4	0	10	.298	.338	.444
DeRosa, Mark, Rich.	16	62	55	9	14	17	3	0	0	6	0	0	2	5	0	2	0	4	4	.255	.339	.309
Diaz, Juan, Paw.	104	419	389	47	101	175	14	0	20	53	0	3	3	24	2	105	0	0	17	.260	.305	.450
Diaz, Maikell, Roch.	4	10	10	1	0	0	0	0	0	0	0	0	0	0	0	2	0	0	0	.000	.000	.000
DiSarcina, Gary, Paw.	35	160	144	23	35	53	11	2	1	9	2	2	4	8	1	15	0	1	6	.243	.297	.368
Doster, Dave, S./W.B.	143	635	579	91	171	250	29	10	10	91	3	8	6	39	2	87	10	3	15	.295	.342	.432
Drew, Tim, Ott.	13	8	8	0	2	2	0	0	0	0	0	0	0	0	0	2	0	0	0	.250	.250	.250
Dunwoody, Todd, Buf.*	102	386	363	57	97	157	31	4	7	29	7	0	4	12	1	62	8	3	9	.267	.298	.433
Easley, Damion, Tol.	8	32	26	5	3	4	1	0	0	0	0	0	1	5	0	0	0	2	1	.115	.281	.154
Ebert, Derrin, Ind.	51	8	7	0	0	0	0	0	0	0	0	0	0	1	0	1	0	0	0	.000	.125	.000
Edwards, Mike, Lou.	15	63	57	7	23	36	5	1	2	8	0	0	0	6	0	9	0	0	1	.404	.460	.632
Estrada, Johnny, S./W.B.†	118	472	434	49	121	181	27	0	11	67	0	7	5	26	7	53	1	0	19	.279	.322	.417
Etherton, Seth, Lou.	5	5	1	0	0	0	0	0	0	1	3	1	0	0	0	1	0	0	0	.000	.000	.000
Evans, Keith, Ott.	16	1	1	0	1	1	0	0	0	0	0	0	0	0	0	0	0	0	0	1.000	1.000	1.000
Evans, Lee, Char.†	72	262	243	27	59	93	18	2	4	22	1	0	2	16	0	74	4	1	1	.243	.295	.383
Fasano, Sal, Dur.-Ind.	65	229	198	16	46	82	15	0	7	20	0	1	15	15	0	53	0	1	3	.232	.332	.414
Feliciano, Pedro, Lou.*	20	2	2	0	1	2	1	0	0	1	0	0	0	0	0	1	0	0	0	.500	.500	1.000
Fernandez, Jared, Lou.	26	16	13	0	1	1	0	0	0	0	3	0	0	0	0	4	0	0	0	.077	.077	.077
Fernandez, Osvaldo, Ott.	19	7	6	0	1	1	0	0	0	1	1	0	0	0	0	3	0	0	0	.167	.167	.167
Figga, Mike, Dur.	10	33	32	1	7	11	1	0	1	3	0	0	0	1	0	10	0	0	0	.219	.242	.344

Player, Team	G	TPA	AB	R	H	TB	2B	3B	HR	RBI	SH	SF	HP	BB	IBB	SO	SB	CS	GDP	Avg.	OBP	Slg.
Figueroa, Franky, Roch.	57	217	207	27	55	77	8	1	4	31	0	0	0	10	1	45	0	0	12	.266	.300	.372
Figueroa, Luis, Nor.-Ott.†	29	96	86	6	12	18	1	1	1	9	6	0	1	3	0	15	0	2	2	.140	.178	.209
Figueroa, Nelson, Ind.†	6	3	2	1	1	2	1	0	0	1	1	0	0	0	0	0	0	0	0	.500	.500	1.000
Fitzgerald, Jason, Buf.*	4	13	13	2	5	7	2	0	0	2	0	0	0	0	0	6	1	1	0	.385	.385	.538
Fleming, Ryan, Syr.*	16	57	53	6	7	9	2	0	0	2	0	1	0	3	0	3	1	0	1	.132	.175	.170
Forbes, P.J., S./W.B.	91	388	355	45	97	120	18	1	1	42	4	5	1	22	1	47	4	1	9	.273	.313	.338
Foster, John, Rich.*	55	1	1	0	0	0	0	0	0	0	0	0	0	0	0	0	0	0	0	.000	.000	.000
Francia, Dave, S./W.B.*	48	127	117	13	25	37	7	1	1	10	1	2	2	5	2	19	4	2	1	.214	.254	.316
Franco, Matt, Rich.*	47	192	173	24	50	79	11	0	6	28	0	2	3	14	0	19	1	0	6	.289	.349	.457
Freel, Ryan, Dur.	119	513	448	65	117	176	27	4	8	48	10	1	14	38	0	51	37	10	10	.261	.337	.393
Frias, Hanley, Roch.†	25	102	96	9	19	26	1	0	2	4	0	0	0	6	0	16	3	0	2	.198	.245	.271
Frye, Jeff, Lou.	93	395	357	44	106	122	13	0	1	24	2	5	2	29	1	34	4	3	15	.297	.349	.342
Garabito, Eddy, Roch.†	110	474	434	52	112	152	20	4	4	32	8	4	4	24	1	48	11	8	11	.258	.300	.350
Garcia, Jesse, Rich.	58	251	230	29	69	101	12	1	6	17	2	1	2	16	0	32	9	5	5	.300	.349	.439
Garcia, Jose, Ind.	17	15	13	0	0	0	0	0	0	0	0	2	0	0	0	1	0	0	2	.000	.000	.000
Garcia, Karim, Col.-Buf.*	97	410	379	60	114	192	23	5	15	71	0	2	0	29	5	62	1	6	3	.301	.349	.507
Garcia, Luis, Roch.†	89	351	339	23	82	112	14	2	4	31	1	2	2	7	0	45	1	1	15	.242	.260	.330
Geary, Geoff, S./W.B.	38	9	8	0	0	0	0	0	0	0	1	0	0	0	0	0	0	0	0	.000	.000	.000
Gerut, Jody, Buf.*	55	207	183	31	59	73	7	2	1	21	0	0	1	23	0	20	3	5	6	.322	.401	.399
Gil, Dave, Lou.	9	3	2	0	0	0	0	0	0	0	0	1	0	0	0	0	0	0	1	.000	.000	.000
Giles, Marcus, Rich.	31	130	115	25	37	52	6	0	3	16	0	2	0	13	0	15	3	0	1	.322	.385	.452
Glynn, Ryan, Ind.	12	7	4	0	0	0	0	0	0	0	3	0	0	0	0	2	0	0	0	.000	.000	.000
Goelz, Jim, Buf.	4	15	13	0	4	6	0	1	0	4	1	0	1	0	0	1	0	0	0	.308	.357	.462
Gonzalez, Dicky, Ott.	23	11	7	0	0	0	0	0	0	1	2	0	1	1	0	3	0	0	0	.000	.222	.000
Gonzalez, Luis, Buf.	6	21	19	0	2	2	0	0	0	1	0	0	1	1	0	4	0	0	1	.105	.190	.105
Gonzalez, Raul, Lou.	114	504	432	91	144	214	27	2	13	69	1	6	4	61	4	59	9	8	15	.333	.416	.495
Gubanich, Creighton, Col.	37	107	97	10	18	30	3	0	3	5	0	1	9	0	27	2	0	2	.186	.262	.309
Guillen, Jose, Lou.	8	29	29	4	9	19	4	0	2	8	0	0	0	0	0	5	0	0	1	.310	.310	.655
Haad, Yamid, Dur.	20	74	70	6	12	13	1	0	0	5	0	2	0	2	0	13	0	0	3	.171	.189	.186
Hall, Bill, Ind.	134	500	465	35	106	140	20	1	4	31	4	2	4	25	0	105	17	10	12	.228	.272	.301
Hall, Toby, Dur.	22	102	92	13	32	42	4	0	2	20	0	3	4	3	0	10	0	0	3	.348	.382	.457
Hamilton, Joey, Lou.	3	4	4	1	2	5	0	0	1	1	0	0	0	0	0	0	0	0	0	.500	.500	1.250
Hammond, Joey, Roch.	35	126	109	13	27	34	2	1	1	8	1	1	1	14	0	14	1	1	3	.248	.336	.312
Harikkala, Tim, Ind.	31	26	24	1	3	3	0	0	0	0	2	0	0	0	0	12	0	0	0	.125	.125	.125
Harris, Willie, Char.*	89	404	360	54	102	143	16	5	5	33	7	2	2	33	0	61	32	14	4	.283	.345	.397
Hassey, Brad, Syr.	2	8	7	0	2	3	1	0	0	0	1	0	0	0	0	0	0	0	0	.286	.286	.429
Heilman, Aaron, Nor.	10	9	7	0	0	0	0	0	0	0	2	0	0	0	0	2	0	0	0	.000	.000	.000
Henson, Drew, Col.	128	521	471	68	113	205	30	4	18	65	2	5	6	37	0	151	2	1	11	.240	.301	.435
Hernandez, Alex, Lou.*	10	25	21	1	5	6	1	0	0	3	1	0	0	3	0	7	0	0	2	.238	.333	.286
Hernandez, Carlos, Nor.	58	181	173	19	56	65	9	0	0	16	0	0	3	5	0	30	7	0	3	.324	.354	.376
Hernandez, Michel, Col.	41	132	121	11	34	44	5	1	1	12	1	0	2	8	0	13	1	3	5	.281	.336	.364
Hessman, Mike, Rich.	134	532	484	67	127	235	28	1	26	77	0	4	10	34	2	107	1	5	13	.262	.321	.486
Hiles, Cary, S./W.B.	27	9	7	2	1	1	0	0	0	1	0	0	0	2	0	2	0	0	0	.143	.333	.143
Hodges, Trey, Rich.	28	26	21	2	1	1	0	0	0	1	3	0	0	2	0	11	0	0	0	.048	.130	.048
Hollins, Damon, Rich.	128	541	498	66	139	211	34	1	12	59	4	3	1	35	1	77	10	2	13	.279	.329	.424
Hollins, Dave, S./W.B.†	14	54	38	8	9	16	1	0	2	7	0	0	5	11	0	9	0	1	0	.237	.463	.421
Hoover, Paul, Dur.	69	254	227	27	50	83	12	3	5	20	5	1	3	18	0	67	3	3	2	.220	.285	.366
Hubbard, Mike, Roch.	60	235	211	26	59	82	11	0	4	30	1	3	1	19	0	24	1	2	4	.280	.338	.389
Huckaby, Ken, Syr.	21	84	81	7	22	24	2	0	0	9	0	1	0	2	1	15	0	2	6	.272	.286	.296
Hudson, Luke, Lou.	30	14	10	0	1	1	0	0	0	0	2	0	1	1	0	2	0	0	0	.100	.250	.100
Hudson, Orlando, Syr.†	100	458	417	63	127	190	27	3	10	37	1	1	4	35	0	54	8	5	14	.305	.363	.456
Huff, Aubrey, Dur.*	32	140	126	18	41	59	9	0	3	20	0	1	1	12	5	13	0	0	4	.325	.386	.468
Hummel, Tim, Char.	142	603	523	55	136	181	33	0	4	41	10	9	10	51	0	95	6	5	7	.260	.332	.346
Hunter, Brian, Dur.	28	114	101	8	20	36	5	1	3	17	1	1	1	10	0	22	0	0	4	.198	.274	.356
Infante, Omar, Tol.	120	474	436	49	117	161	16	8	4	51	5	5	0	28	0	49	19	15	5	.268	.309	.369
Inge, Brandon, Tol.	21	81	65	10	17	36	2	4	3	13	2	1	2	11	0	16	1	3	2	.262	.380	.554
Inglin, Jeff, Char.	39	164	152	18	42	64	4	0	6	22	0	4	0	8	0	22	2	2	5	.276	.305	.421
Ingram, Darron, Char.	16	66	59	5	9	20	2	0	3	6	0	1	0	6	0	22	0	1	1	.153	.227	.339
Jackson, Ryan, Lou.*	104	439	420	40	114	175	35	1	8	50	2	1	3	13	1	84	5	3	13	.271	.297	.417
Jennings, Robin, Lou.*	107	384	351	29	78	111	21	0	4	48	1	2	3	27	2	56	4	4	8	.222	.282	.316
Jensen, Marcus, Ind.†	70	224	183	24	42	61	7	0	4	25	2	4	2	33	1	39	0	0	5	.230	.347	.333
Jimenez, D'Angelo, Char.†	42	185	157	24	44	75	11	1	6	18	1	2	0	24	1	14	6	2	2	.280	.372	.478
Johnson, Mark, Nor.*	77	309	270	45	70	131	17	1	14	37	0	3	4	32	4	53	1	0	2	.259	.343	.485
Johnson, Nick, Col.*	3	12	11	1	1	1	0	0	0	0	0	0	1	0	4	0	0	1	.091	.167	.091
Johnson, Reed, Syr.	44	183	159	27	37	57	8	3	2	10	3	1	8	12	0	23	1	4	1	.233	.317	.358
Johnson, Russ, Dur.	10	37	33	9	9	17	0	1	2	5	0	0	0	4	0	5	1	0	0	.273	.351	.515
Jones, Bobby M., Nor.	13	2	0	0	0	0	0	0	0	0	0	0	0	2	0	0	0	0	0	.000	.000	.000
Jones, Chris, Ind.	78	304	273	34	77	109	13	5	3	30	0	3	2	25	2	50	5	6	8	.282	.343	.399
Jordan, Kevin, Lou.	25	96	82	14	18	22	4	0	0	8	0	2	2	10	2	11	0	0	3	.220	.313	.268
Junge, Eric, S./W.B.	29	25	21	0	1	1	0	0	0	0	3	0	0	1	0	8	0	0	0	.048	.091	.048
Kearns, Austin, Lou.	1	5	4	3	3	5	2	0	0	2	0	0	0	1	0	0	0	0	0	.750	.800	1.250
Kieschnick, Brooks, Char.*	69	206	189	32	52	102	11	0	13	40	0	3	0	14	1	46	0	0	4	.275	.320	.540
Kim, Sun-Woo, Ott.	7	3	3	0	0	0	0	0	0	0	0	0	0	0	0	0	0	0	0	.000	.000	.000
Klimek, Josh, Char.	118	482	424	50	111	165	28	1	8	59	7	5	2	40	3	69	1	2	9	.262	.325	.389
Knight, Brandon, Col.*	37	1	1	0	0	0	0	0	0	0	0	0	0	0	0	0	0	0	0	.000	.000	.000
Knorr, Randy, Ott.	100	374	338	31	87	137	24	1	8	38	0	3	1	32	1	53	0	0	11	.257	.321	.405
Knupfer, Jensen, S./W.B.	77	305	259	42	70	85	11	2	0	28	6	3	1	36	2	64	10	3	8	.270	.358	.328
Komiyama, Saturo, Nor.	17	4	4	0	0	0	0	0	0	0	0	0	0	0	0	3	0	0	0	.000	.000	.000
LaForest, Pete, Dur.*	17	69	66	7	17	29	3	0	3	15	0	0	3	0	0	28	0	1	1	.258	.290	.439
Laker, Tim, Buf.	62	241	216	23	49	71	10	0	4	28	0	1	3	21	0	52	1	0	9	.227	.303	.329
Langaigne, Selwyn, Syr.*	73	281	263	25	64	93	12	1	5	21	3	0	1	14	1	61	1	4	8	.243	.284	.354

Player, Team	G	TPA	AB	R	H	TB	2B	3B	HR	RBI	SH	SF	HP	BB	IBB	SO	SB	CS	GDP	Avg.	OBP	Slg.
Lansing, Mike, Buf.	24	101	94	9	23	37	4	2	2	8	0	0	1	6	1	7	2	1	4	.245	.297	.394
LaRocca, Greg, Buf.	107	457	382	70	112	165	28	2	7	41	2	2	23	48	0	48	17	4	4	.293	.402	.432
Larson, Brandon, Lou.	80	327	297	47	101	198	20	1	25	69	1	2	3	24	2	70	1	1	5	.340	.393	.667
Latham, Chris, Nor.†	117	474	405	60	94	146	22	6	6	43	0	3	4	62	2	103	26	9	6	.232	.338	.360
Lawrence, Joe, Syr.	29	122	108	13	18	30	4	1	2	12	0	0	0	14	0	23	3	0	1	.167	.262	.278
Leach, Jalal, Col.*	92	306	287	35	72	117	14	5	7	28	0	0	0	19	1	49	6	4	8	.251	.297	.408
Lennon, Pat, Dur.	20	82	69	7	13	20	1	0	2	15	0	1	2	10	0	20	1	0	2	.188	.305	.290
Leon, Donny, Lou.†	18	72	68	9	17	31	5	0	3	13	0	1	1	2	0	10	0	0	1	.250	.278	.456
Leon, Jose, Roch.	83	336	312	39	87	129	16	1	8	40	1	3	2	18	1	54	0	0	9	.279	.319	.413
Lesher, Brian, Syr.	66	274	248	34	65	101	13	1	7	28	1	4	1	20	0	55	6	1	4	.262	.315	.407
Levis, Jesse, Lou.*	84	295	254	24	72	94	11	1	3	25	2	3	5	31	3	19	1	1	6	.283	.369	.370
Lewis, Derrick, Rich.	18	19	15	2	1	1	0	0	0	0	2	0	0	2	0	5	0	0	0	.067	.176	.067
Lindsey, Rodney, Tol.	11	35	31	2	7	8	1	0	0	2	2	0	0	2	0	4	5	1	1	.226	.273	.258
Linton, Doug, Rich.	28	20	18	0	1	1	0	0	0	0	2	0	0	0	0	6	0	0	2	.056	.056	.056
Lira, Felipe, Nor.-Lou.	33	12	11	0	0	0	0	0	0	0	1	0	0	0	0	7	0	0	0	.000	.000	.000
Little, Mark, Nor.	2	11	10	1	5	5	0	0	0	2	0	0	0	1	0	3	0	0	0	.500	.545	.500
Lofton, James, Paw.†	81	314	299	32	75	97	6	2	4	27	0	0	2	13	0	54	9	3	8	.251	.287	.324
Lomasney, Steve, Paw.	12	33	30	1	2	3	1	0	0	1	0	0	1	2	0	15	0	0	0	.067	.152	.100
Lombard, George, Rich.*	11	45	39	10	12	21	4	1	1	5	0	0	1	5	1	12	2	0	0	.308	.400	.538
Lopez, Felipe, Syr.†	43	204	173	35	55	79	11	2	3	16	1	0	1	29	1	37	13	0	3	.318	.419	.457
Lopez, Luis, Ind.-Roch.†	23	98	90	14	27	42	6	0	3	8	3	0	2	3	0	15	0	0	1	.300	.337	.467
Lopez, Rafael, Rich.	7	24	23	4	8	9	1	0	0	1	0	0	0	1	0	4	0	1	1	.348	.375	.391
Lorraine, Andrew, Ind.*	25	23	18	3	2	2	0	0	0	2	1	0	0	4	0	6	0	0	0	.111	.273	.111
Luke, Matt, Dur.*	29	122	106	14	25	33	5	0	1	11	1	1	0	14	1	28	0	0	1	.236	.322	.311
Lunar, Fernando, Roch.	42	154	145	7	28	35	1	0	2	8	0	1	4	4	0	27	1	0	9	.193	.234	.241
Luuloa, Keith, Ind.	31	63	53	7	10	10	0	0	0	3	3	0	0	7	0	11	0	2	4	.189	.283	.189
Machado, Albenis, Ott.†	15	54	41	10	10	15	2	0	1	5	0	3	1	9	0	9	1	1	1	.244	.370	.366
MacRae, Scott, Lou.	49	3	3	0	1	1	0	0	0	0	0	0	0	0	0	1	0	0	0	.333	.333	.333
Magruder, Chris, Buf.†	54	224	191	28	51	80	10	2	5	16	4	0	3	26	2	34	3	2	2	.267	.364	.419
Malave, Jaime, Nor.	4	4	3	0	1	1	0	0	0	0	0	0	0	1	0	0	0	0	0	.333	.500	.333
Mallette, Brian, Ind.	45	3	2	0	0	0	0	0	0	0	0	0	0	1	0	2	0	0	0	.000	.333	.000
Malloy, Marty, Lou.	56	205	180	25	44	65	7	1	4	16	2	0	2	21	0	24	7	4	2	.244	.330	.361
Maness, Nick, Nor.	3	5	4	0	0	0	0	0	0	0	1	0	0	0	0	2	0	0	0	.000	.000	.000
Manon, Julio, Ott.*	28	6	5	0	1	1	0	0	0	0	0	0	1	0	0	0	0	0	0	.200	.200	.200
Marquez, Rob, Ind.	47	3	3	0	1	1	0	0	0	0	0	0	0	0	0	2	0	0	0	.333	.333	.333
Marquis, Jason, Rich.*	1	2	2	0	0	0	0	0	0	0	0	0	0	0	0	1	0	0	0	.000	.000	.000
Martinez, Lou, Rich.	6	8	8	1	1	1	0	0	0	0	0	0	0	0	0	0	0	0	0	.125	.125	.125
Martinez, Sandy, Ott.*	39	146	133	12	30	44	3	1	3	18	0	1	2	10	2	41	2	0	3	.226	.288	.331
Mateo, Henry, Ott.†	74	314	285	35	73	110	10	6	5	25	7	1	3	18	0	53	15	6	6	.256	.306	.386
Mateo, Ruben, Lou.	52	225	209	37	63	104	14	0	9	23	0	2	3	11	1	40	6	2	2	.301	.342	.498
Maxwell, Jason, Lou.	80	317	269	44	81	114	21	3	2	31	7	4	1	36	0	45	5	4	6	.301	.381	.424
McCarty, Dave, Dur.	29	128	114	25	37	70	7	1	8	22	0	0	0	14	1	33	0	1	1	.325	.398	.614
McConnell, Sam, S./W.B.*	7	3	3	0	0	0	0	0	0	0	0	0	0	0	0	1	0	0	0	.000	.000	.000
McDonald, Darnell, Roch.	91	369	332	43	96	147	21	6	6	35	1	2	2	32	0	78	11	3	8	.289	.353	.443
McGuire, Ryan, Roch.*	81	348	315	44	90	142	15	2	11	46	1	3	0	29	4	69	0	1	10	.286	.343	.451
McKee, Scott, Char.†	1	1	1	0	0	0	0	0	0	0	0	0	0	0	0	1	0	0	0	.000	.000	.000
McKinley, Dan, Ott.*	17	28	25	2	3	4	1	0	0	3	0	1	1	1	0	6	0	1	1	.120	.179	.160
McMillon, Billy, Col.*	115	511	442	72	133	195	32	3	8	46	1	3	6	59	2	71	2	5	6	.301	.388	.441
McNeal, Aaron, Nor.	25	93	86	7	16	27	2	0	3	8	0	1	0	6	1	23	0	0	9	.186	.237	.314
Medrano, Tony, Buf.-Ott.	127	497	438	48	105	135	18	3	2	43	12	1	8	38	1	47	12	1	14	.240	.311	.308
Meran, Jorge, Tol.	3	12	12	1	2	2	0	0	0	0	0	0	0	0	0	2	0	0	1	.167	.167	.167
Mercado, Hector, S./W.B.*	26	1	1	0	0	0	0	0	0	0	0	0	0	0	0	0	0	0	0	.000	.000	.000
Merloni, Lou, Paw.	8	28	25	1	5	7	2	0	0	2	0	1	1	1	0	3	0	0	2	.200	.250	.280
Michaels, Jason, S./W.B.	9	39	32	3	9	11	2	0	0	7	0	2	0	5	0	5	1	3	0	.281	.359	.344
Middlebrook, Jason, Nor.	5	3	3	0	0	0	0	0	0	0	0	0	0	0	0	1	0	0	0	.000	.000	.000
Miller, Corky, Lou.	43	159	134	14	31	54	5	0	6	21	3	0	6	16	2	21	1	2	6	.231	.340	.403
Miller, Trever, Lou.	66	3	3	0	0	0	0	0	0	0	0	0	0	0	0	0	0	0	1	.000	.000	.000
Mitchell, Derek, Lou.	23	66	55	6	9	9	0	0	0	6	1	1	0	9	0	19	0	0	0	.164	.277	.164
Molina, Izzy, Roch.	42	160	146	11	25	35	4	0	2	15	0	2	3	9	0	24	1	1	5	.171	.231	.240
Monroe, Craig, Tol.	99	402	358	61	115	183	30	4	10	49	1	6	2	35	4	57	7	3	8	.321	.379	.511
Moon, Brian, Ind.†	39	114	99	8	24	29	5	0	0	7	3	0	0	12	5	24	1	0	3	.242	.324	.293
Morgan, Scott, Char.	84	331	309	33	83	125	15	0	9	34	1	4	3	14	0	81	3	1	4	.269	.303	.405
Moriarty, Mike, Roch.	90	359	311	48	86	118	18	1	4	26	3	4	4	37	0	50	4	1	6	.277	.357	.379
Morris, Warren, Paw.*	43	182	164	21	50	74	11	2	3	21	0	4	3	11	0	22	2	1	6	.305	.352	.451
Mottola, Chad, Syr.	122	539	476	77	124	200	35	1	13	67	0	7	4	51	2	87	12	2	9	.261	.333	.420
Mouton, James, Ott.	29	83	70	10	19	25	3	0	1	7	1	0	0	12	0	17	3	0	0	.271	.378	.357
Munson, Eric, Tol.*	136	569	477	77	125	235	30	4	24	84	0	8	7	77	5	114	0	1	9	.262	.367	.493
Myers, Brett, S./W.B.	19	23	19	0	5	7	2	0	0	5	4	0	0	0	0	5	0	0	0	.263	.263	.368
Myers, Kenton, Buf.	1	1	1	0	0	0	0	0	0	0	0	0	0	0	0	1	0	0	0	.000	.000	.000
Nelson, Bryant, Paw.†	60	240	223	25	66	104	8	3	8	24	2	0	1	14	1	19	1	5	3	.296	.340	.466
Nettles, Jeff, Col.	24	71	62	4	15	22	5	1	0	5	2	1	0	6	0	16	1	2	1	.242	.304	.355
Neugebauer, Nick, Ind.	5	2	2	0	1	1	0	0	0	0	0	0	0	0	0	0	0	0	0	.500	.500	.500
Nicholson, Derek, Tol.*	89	349	292	46	84	130	22	3	6	58	0	6	1	50	1	71	1	0	5	.288	.387	.445
Nickle, Doug, S./W.B.	34	1	0	0	0	0	0	0	0	0	0	0	0	1	0	0	0	0	0	.000	.000	.000
Nomura, Takahito, Ind.*	31	1	0	0	0	0	0	0	0	0	1	0	0	0	0	0	0	0	0	.000	.000	.000
Norris, Dax, Rich.	79	281	262	29	68	94	14	0	4	25	0	3	1	15	0	28	1	1	13	.260	.299	.359
Nunez, Franklin, S./W.B.	4	1	0	0	0	0	0	0	0	0	0	0	0	0	0	0	0	0	0	.000	.000	.000
Nunez, Jorge, Ott.	91	302	282	42	82	99	9	4	0	20	4	2	2	12	0	43	27	7	8	.291	.322	.351
O'Leary, Troy, Ott.*	23	93	86	11	29	44	6	0	3	16	0	0	2	7	2	15	0	1	1	.337	.387	.512
Ortiz, Luis, Ott.	106	410	382	47	111	164	38	0	5	63	0	4	2	22	2	35	1	0	13	.291	.329	.429
Osting, Jimmy, Ind.	22	14	14	0	3	3	0	0	0	1	0	0	0	0	0	4	0	0	1	.214	.214	.214

Player, Team	G	TPA	AB	R	H	TB	2B	3B	HR	RBI	SH	SF	HP	BB	IBB	SO	SB	CS	GDP	Avg.	OBP	Slg.
Parque, Jim, Char.*	22	1	1	0	0	0	0	0	0	0	0	0	0	0	0	1	0	0	0	.000	.000	.000
Patchett, Gary, Lou.	7	7	7	0	2	4	2	0	0	3	0	0	0	0	0	2	0	0	0	.286	.286	.571
Patterson, Jarrod, Tol.*	117	502	447	66	132	217	34	6	13	70	2	3	4	46	4	71	3	1	8	.295	.364	.485
Paul, Josh, Char.	65	257	231	18	63	82	15	2	0	17	6	2	1	17	1	45	10	4	7	.273	.323	.355
Pavano, Carl, Ott.	3	3	3	1	3	4	1	0	0	3	0	0	0	0	0	0	0	0	0	1.000	1.000	1.333
Pena, Elvis, Ind.†	34	112	97	17	25	34	4	1	1	6	1	0	4	10	1	19	7	3	2	.258	.351	.351
Perez, Jerson, Syr.	58	223	203	28	49	70	7	1	4	15	5	0	1	14	1	50	2	2	4	.241	.294	.345
Perez, Rob, Ind.-Col.	127	481	460	54	117	193	28	3	14	62	2	4	0	15	2	56	9	7	11	.254	.276	.420
Perez, Timo, Nor.*	5	23	21	5	12	19	2	1	1	5	0	0	0	2	0	2	3	1	1	.571	.609	.905
Person, Robert, S./W.B.	2	2	1	0	0	0	0	0	0	0	1	0	0	0	0	1	0	0	0	.000	.000	.000
Petersen, Chris, Rich.	76	247	223	29	51	61	6	2	0	15	3	2	1	18	0	40	0	2	3	.229	.287	.274
Phelps, Josh, Syr.	70	295	257	50	75	169	20	1	24	64	0	1	5	32	6	83	0	0	6	.292	.380	.658
Phillips, Andy, Col.	51	217	205	32	54	94	11	1	9	36	1	1	0	10	0	46	0	1	8	.263	.296	.459
Phillips, Brandon, Ott.-Buf.	65	284	258	31	72	117	18	0	9	32	4	5	1	16	0	45	8	2	6	.279	.318	.453
Phillips, Jason, Nor.	88	358	323	35	91	154	22	1	13	65	0	9	2	24	3	29	1	0	10	.282	.327	.477
Pineda, Luis, Lou.	3	5	5	0	1	3	0	1	0	0	0	0	0	0	0	3	0	0	0	.200	.200	.600
Porter, Bo, Rich.	108	455	392	55	116	170	26	2	8	52	5	5	2	50	1	113	18	9	7	.296	.374	.434
Pratt, Andy, Rich.*	6	4	4	0	3	3	0	0	0	1	0	0	0	0	0	1	0	0	0	.750	.750	.750
Pratt, Scott, Buf.*	4	21	20	2	5	6	1	0	0	3	0	0	1	0	2	0	1	0	.250	.286	.300
Pressley, Josh, Dur.*	16	56	47	2	7	8	1	0	0	5	0	1	0	8	1	6	0	1	2	.149	.268	.170
Punto, Nick, S./W.B.†	115	530	443	74	120	145	12	5	1	29	6	3	2	76	0	84	42	8	5	.271	.378	.327
Quatraro, Matt, Dur.	35	110	101	12	20	26	4	1	0	7	1	1	2	5	0	26	0	0	4	.198	.248	.257
Quintero, Humberto, Char.	15	44	41	2	9	10	1	0	0	5	0	0	0	3	0	8	0	0	3	.220	.273	.244
Quiroz, Guillermo, Syr.	13	49	45	7	10	17	4	0	1	6	1	0	0	3	0	14	0	0	1	.222	.271	.378
Ramirez, Manny, Paw.	11	39	30	2	3	7	1	0	1	2	0	0	1	8	0	9	0	0	0	.100	.308	.233
Reames, Britt, Ott.	7	6	6	0	0	0	0	0	0	0	0	0	0	0	0	2	0	0	0	.000	.000	.000
Reith, Brian, Lou.	23	21	20	1	2	2	0	0	0	1	0	0	0	1	0	12	0	1	1	.100	.100	.100
Reyes, Guillermo, Char.†	4	13	13	1	4	4	0	0	0	0	0	0	0	0	0	1	2	0	1	.308	.308	.308
Richard, Chris, Roch.*	14	63	53	10	17	41	6	0	6	18	0	2	2	6	1	14	0	0	2	.321	.397	.774
Rios, Brian, Tol.	80	283	262	28	69	96	12	3	3	28	0	1	2	18	0	45	0	2	5	.263	.314	.366
Rivera, Juan, Col.	65	283	265	40	86	133	21	1	8	47	1	3	1	13	1	39	5	1	4	.325	.355	.502
Rivera, Mike, Tol.	74	305	265	43	66	139	11	1	20	53	0	2	3	35	3	64	0	1	6	.249	.341	.525
Roa, Joe, S./W.B.	17	21	17	0	4	4	0	0	0	3	3	0	0	1	0	5	0	0	0	.235	.235	.235
Roach, Jason, Nor.	23	17	14	1	4	7	3	0	0	3	3	0	0	0	0	6	0	0	0	.286	.286	.500
Roberge, J.P., S./W.B.	123	464	420	56	126	178	29	1	7	52	2	2	6	34	2	66	6	1	6	.300	.359	.424
Roberts, Brian, Roch.†	78	359	313	49	86	118	9	7	3	30	2	1	3	40	1	46	22	4	3	.275	.361	.377
Rodriguez, Luis, Paw.	82	274	259	24	59	102	12	5	7	31	1	1	1	12	0	62	0	3	10	.228	.264	.394
Rolls, Damian, Dur.	67	280	244	41	65	97	6	4	6	35	6	4	5	21	0	43	15	0	4	.266	.332	.398
Rushford, Jim, Ind.*	117	461	405	54	128	188	33	3	7	68	1	3	7	45	1	41	0	2	4	.316	.391	.464
Ryan, Rob, Paw.*	63	277	233	44	62	114	16	3	10	31	0	2	6	36	1	39	4	1	3	.266	.375	.489
Saenz, Jason, Nor.*	5	1	1	0	0	0	0	0	0	0	0	0	0	0	0	0	0	0	0	.000	.000	.000
St. Pierre, Maxim, Tol.	1	2	2	0	0	0	0	0	0	0	0	0	0	0	0	0	0	0	0	.000	.000	.000
Saipe, Mike, Rich.	42	6	5	0	0	0	0	0	0	0	1	0	0	0	0	3	0	0	1	.000	.000	.000
Salazar, Jeremy, S./W.B.	42	145	129	10	27	33	6	0	0	10	4	1	0	11	0	34	1	0	4	.209	.270	.256
Salazar, Oscar, Tol.	8	22	19	0	6	6	0	0	0	1	0	0	0	3	0	1	0	1	0	.316	.409	.316
Salinas, Trey, Roch.	12	30	27	1	2	5	0	0	1	2	0	0	1	2	0	10	0	0	3	.074	.167	.185
Salzano, Jerry, Paw.	2	8	8	1	2	5	0	0	1	1	0	0	0	0	0	3	0	0	0	.250	.250	.625
Sanchez, Freddy, Paw.	45	205	183	25	55	79	10	1	4	28	5	2	3	12	0	21	5	3	3	.301	.350	.432
Sandberg, Jared, Dur.	30	130	114	20	32	53	9	0	4	21	0	0	2	14	1	42	1	0	2	.281	.369	.465
Sanders, Anthony, Lou.-Char.	91	359	335	32	80	137	15	3	12	48	2	4	1	17	1	95	7	3	7	.239	.275	.409
Santangelo, F.P., Col.†	7	23	15	1	1	1	0	0	0	1	3	0	0	5	0	4	2	0	1	.067	.300	.067
Santiago, Ramon, Tol.†	9	33	28	8	12	19	1	0	2	6	0	0	2	3	0	4	0	2	0	.429	.515	.679
Santos, Angel, Paw.†	102	405	350	40	91	140	15	2	10	50	10	5	2	38	3	70	12	8	8	.260	.332	.400
Sasser, Rob, Ind.	72	207	185	19	42	60	9	3	1	18	1	0	2	19	0	30	7	0	8	.227	.306	.324
Saunders, Chris, Char.	81	305	285	23	62	93	16	0	5	33	2	0	1	17	0	70	0	0	5	.218	.264	.326
Scarborough, Steve, Ind.	39	132	116	9	25	40	7	1	2	12	3	0	3	10	1	30	2	1	3	.216	.295	.345
Schall, Gene, S./W.B.	28	106	89	15	18	30	6	0	2	12	0	2	2	13	0	23	0	1	0	.202	.311	.337
Schrenk, Steve, Char.	38	1	1	0	0	0	0	0	0	0	0	0	0	0	0	1	0	0	0	.000	.000	.000
Scutaro, Marcos, Nor.	97	394	354	48	113	168	22	6	7	28	7	1	2	30	3	61	7	8	7	.319	.375	.475
Seabol, Scott, Col.	121	470	428	56	111	187	29	1	15	68	1	7	5	29	0	89	3	3	6	.259	.309	.437
Selby, Bill, Buf.*	51	206	184	28	55	88	14	2	5	22	0	2	0	20	2	33	4	1	0	.299	.364	.478
Seo, Jae, Nor.	26	17	11	1	2	2	0	0	0	1	3	0	0	3	0	5	0	0	0	.182	.357	.182
Sergio, Tom, Paw.*	1	4	4	0	0	0	0	0	0	0	0	0	0	0	0	0	0	0	1	.000	.000	.000
Serrano, Elio, S./W.B.	43	1	1	0	0	0	0	0	0	0	0	0	0	0	0	0	0	0	0	.000	.000	.000
Serrano, Jim, Nor.	53	1	0	0	0	0	0	0	0	0	1	0	0	0	0	0	0	0	0	.000	.000	.000
Sexton, Chris, Lou.	108	468	414	79	131	188	29	5	6	49	8	3	1	42	2	41	3	2	18	.316	.378	.454
Sheets, Andy, Dur.	98	411	374	55	110	189	25	6	14	69	2	4	3	28	1	72	7	2	9	.294	.345	.505
Sledge, Terrmel, Ott.*	24	92	80	12	21	33	5	2	1	11	0	0	1	11	0	15	1	1	2	.263	.359	.413
Small, Aaron, Rich.	14	2	2	0	0	0	0	0	0	0	0	0	0	0	0	0	0	0	0	.000	.000	.000
Smith, Bobby, Ind.	80	325	293	26	70	112	21	0	7	31	2	1	4	25	0	57	11	2	8	.239	.307	.382
Smith, Dan, Ott.	14	12	10	0	1	1	0	0	0	1	0	0	0	0	0	6	0	0	0	.100	.100	.100
Smith, Jason, Dur.*	54	220	206	29	57	84	11	2	4	28	2	1	1	10	1	44	5	1	2	.277	.312	.408
Smothers, Stewart, Rich.	17	22	18	3	4	4	0	0	0	2	1	0	0	3	0	5	0	0	1	.222	.333	.222
Snyder, Earl, Buf.	110	453	400	69	105	193	29	1	19	66	1	3	6	43	2	96	0	2	6	.263	.341	.483
Soler, Ramon, Nor.†	7	12	10	0	1	1	0	0	0	0	0	0	0	2	0	0	0	0	0	.100	.250	.100
Sorensen, Zach, Buf.†	120	499	455	55	120	177	12	12	7	54	15	4	1	24	1	72	13	6	9	.264	.300	.389
Stefanski, Mike, Lou.	73	222	203	23	57	88	8	1	7	23	4	1	1	13	1	26	0	0	4	.281	.326	.433
Stenson, Dernell, Paw.*	107	409	368	44	92	141	20	1	9	36	1	1	2	37	2	96	4	3	6	.250	.321	.383
Stinnett, Kelly, Lou.	30	89	86	6	17	23	6	0	0	5	0	0	0	3	0	24	0	0	1	.198	.225	.267
Strange, Pat, Nor.	29	25	24	1	3	4	1	0	0	2	1	0	0	0	0	8	0	0	0	.125	.125	.167
Stratton, Rob, Nor.	73	282	256	44	63	131	8	0	20	46	0	3	5	18	1	84	6	3	4	.246	.305	.512

– 399 –

Player, Team	G	TPA	AB	R	H	TB	2B	3B	HR	RBI	SH	SF	HP	BB	IBB	SO	SB	CS	GDP	Avg.	OBP	Slg.
Stull, Everett, Ind.	24	19	18	0	1	1	0	0	0	1	0	1	0	0	0	9	0	0	0	.056	.053	.056
Swann, Pedro, Syr.*	97	417	368	52	102	169	17	4	14	62	1	3	8	37	2	77	1	3	14	.277	.353	.459
Takeoka, Kazuhiro, Rich.	23	3	3	0	0	0	0	0	0	0	0	0	0	0	0	0	0	0	0	.000	.000	.000
Tamargo, John, Nor.*	44	118	101	12	20	29	3	0	2	9	3	0	1	13	1	10	2	0	2	.198	.296	.287
Tarasco, Tony, Nor.*	42	164	153	21	43	55	7	1	1	18	0	1	1	9	0	15	5	3	0	.281	.323	.359
Tessmer, Jay, Col.	64	1	1	0	0	0	0	0	0	0	0	0	0	0	0	1	0	0	0	.000	.000	.000
Thames, Marcus, Col.	107	438	386	51	80	146	21	3	13	45	0	2	7	43	0	71	5	4	8	.207	.297	.378
Thomas, Evan, S./W.B.	22	10	8	0	1	1	0	0	0	0	1	0	0	1	0	3	0	0	0	.125	.222	.125
Thompson, Andy, Dur.	77	307	277	30	65	101	11	2	7	43	1	4	10	15	0	51	1	1	4	.235	.294	.365
Thompson, Ryan, Ind.	70	293	273	36	80	134	12	3	12	40	0	5	4	11	1	46	0	4	9	.293	.324	.491
Timmons, Ozzie, Rich.	131	545	496	55	128	198	23	1	15	76	1	8	1	39	0	90	6	1	10	.258	.309	.399
Toca, Jorge, Nor.	54	205	195	21	49	64	9	0	2	15	0	1	0	9	0	31	2	1	7	.251	.283	.328
Torrealba, Steve, Rich.	61	215	191	19	45	65	11	0	3	18	1	1	3	19	2	31	0	0	5	.236	.313	.340
Torres, Andres, Tol.†	115	538	462	80	123	168	17	8	4	42	14	4	5	53	0	116	42	12	3	.266	.345	.364
Tracy, Andy, Nor.*	125	491	432	61	86	164	16	1	20	61	0	0	3	56	2	123	4	1	4	.199	.295	.380
Truby, Chris, Tol.	3	14	12	2	4	11	0	2	1	1	0	0	0	2	0	1	0	0	1	.333	.429	.917
Tyner, Jason, Dur.*	88	402	351	59	102	122	12	4	0	27	10	1	6	34	2	27	20	7	3	.291	.362	.348
Umbria, Jose, Syr.	5	18	16	5	6	6	0	0	0	2	1	0	1	0	0	4	0	0	0	.375	.412	.375
Unroe, Tim, Rich.	94	302	264	33	64	109	13	1	10	40	1	1	8	28	4	86	1	2	6	.242	.332	.413
Utley, Chase, S./W.B.*	125	534	464	73	122	214	39	1	17	70	0	4	20	46	2	89	8	3	5	.263	.352	.461
Valent, Eric, S./W.B.*	140	602	546	69	137	202	34	2	9	84	1	5	1	49	1	94	0	2	13	.251	.311	.370
Valera, Yohanny, Col.	44	142	131	15	33	46	8	1	1	6	0	0	4	7	0	36	0	0	2	.252	.310	.351
Velandia, Jorge, Nor.	115	450	407	43	82	122	20	1	6	37	7	4	2	30	2	79	5	2	6	.201	.257	.300
Velazquez, Gil, Nor.	12	37	33	2	7	8	1	0	0	1	0	0	0	4	0	9	0	0	2	.212	.297	.242
Veras, Wilton, Paw.	57	215	200	13	51	63	10	1	0	28	1	2	1	11	0	11	0	0	10	.255	.294	.315
Vitiello, Joe, Ott.	119	482	431	57	142	224	34	0	16	82	0	5	7	39	5	58	1	0	16	.329	.390	.520
Wakeland, Chris, Tol.*	90	324	297	38	72	115	11	1	10	32	0	1	2	24	0	106	5	3	6	.242	.302	.387
Walbeck, Matt, Tol.†	21	81	75	4	16	22	3	0	1	6	1	1	0	4	0	10	0	0	6	.213	.250	.293
Walker, Tyler, Nor.	28	23	22	1	3	3	0	0	0	0	1	0	0	0	0	5	0	0	1	.136	.136	.136
Ware, Jeremy, Buf.	42	141	135	18	40	53	10	0	1	17	0	0	0	6	0	23	2	1	4	.296	.326	.393
Wedel, Jeremy, S./W.B.	43	1	0	0	0	0	0	0	0	0	1	0	0	0	0	0	0	0	0	.000	.000	.000
Werth, Jayson, Syr.	127	523	443	65	114	197	25	2	18	82	0	9	4	67	2	125	24	7	7	.257	.354	.445
Wheeler, Dan, Rich.	28	32	29	3	5	5	0	0	0	1	2	0	0	1	0	8	0	0	2	.172	.200	.172
Widger, Chris, Col.	61	238	217	26	53	99	14	1	10	39	1	2	1	17	0	31	0	0	3	.244	.300	.456
Wigginton, Ty, Nor.	104	435	383	49	115	165	26	3	6	48	0	8	1	43	4	50	5	3	7	.300	.366	.431
Williams, Gerald, Ind.	48	219	205	29	54	76	10	3	2	12	1	0	2	11	0	36	6	4	4	.263	.307	.371
Williams, Glenn, Syr.†	94	362	339	49	93	162	18	3	15	47	1	0	2	20	0	80	2	0	7	.274	.319	.478
Wilson, Craig, Tol.	119	479	415	48	109	140	21	2	2	46	14	1	4	45	2	39	2	2	16	.263	.340	.337
Wilson, Travis, Rich.	133	526	494	59	130	202	23	5	13	71	0	11	8	13	0	106	10	3	14	.263	.287	.409
Winchester, Scott, Ott.	21	2	1	0	0	0	0	0	0	0	0	1	0	0	0	1	0	0	0	.000	.000	.000
Winkelsas, Joe, Rich.	16	2	2	0	0	0	0	0	0	0	0	0	0	0	0	2	0	0	0	.000	.000	.000
Witt, Kevin, Lou.*	131	555	509	77	134	240	32	1	24	107	0	5	6	34	5	140	0	1	18	.263	.314	.472
Woods, Ken, S./W.B.	51	181	161	21	40	62	5	4	3	21	4	3	4	9	0	20	4	3	2	.248	.299	.385
Wright, Jamey, Ind.	3	2	2	0	0	0	0	0	0	0	0	0	0	0	0	1	0	0	0	.000	.000	.000
Zamora, Pete, S./W.B.*	55	4	3	0	1	1	0	0	0	0	1	0	0	0	0	0	0	0	0	.333	.250	.333
Zapp, A.J., Rich.*	34	105	92	9	17	32	3	0	4	7	0	0	3	10	2	27	1	0	4	.185	.286	.348
Zuber, Jon, Ind.*	130	461	385	54	92	117	13	3	2	25	4	1	2	68	3	50	5	2	10	.239	.355	.304
Zywica, Mike, Char.	39	156	140	17	31	52	6	0	5	16	0	2	4	10	0	39	1	0	2	.221	.288	.371

PLAYERS WITH TWO OR MORE TEAMS

Player, Team	G	TPA	AB	R	H	TB	2B	3B	HR	RBI	SH	SF	HP	BB	IBB	SO	SB	CS	GDP	Avg.	OBP	Slg.
Allen, Chad, Roch.	8	32	32	1	7	11	2	1	0	1	0	0	0	0	0	6	0	0	2	.219	.219	.344
Allen, Chad, Buf.	70	297	279	45	84	136	20	1	10	62	0	1	2	15	0	34	0	1	10	.301	.340	.487
Arias, Alex, Roch.	16	57	52	2	7	9	2	0	0	3	0	0	0	5	0	11	0	0	3	.135	.211	.173
Arias, Alex, Col.	61	232	211	32	56	75	16	0	1	22	2	1	2	16	0	15	3	2	4	.265	.322	.355
Aven, Bruce, Buf.	35	136	119	17	34	54	5	0	5	16	0	0	3	14	1	21	1	0	4	.286	.375	.454
Aven, Bruce, S./W.B.	59	251	205	26	50	85	11	0	8	42	0	2	8	36	2	35	3	1	7	.244	.375	.415
Broussard, Ben, Lou.*	57	230	187	31	51	100	14	1	11	30	0	3	9	31	2	50	4	1	4	.273	.396	.535
Broussard, Ben, Buf.*	42	182	153	30	37	60	8	0	5	21	1	1	3	24	2	30	0	0	1	.242	.354	.392
Brown, Kevin, Dur.	6	22	20	4	3	9	0	0	2	4	0	0	0	2	0	6	0	0	1	.150	.227	.450
Brown, Kevin, Paw.	70	245	226	29	55	88	13	1	6	21	1	0	0	18	0	60	0	0	4	.243	.299	.389
Buford, Damon, Paw.	10	35	31	5	5	9	1	0	1	2	0	0	0	4	0	5	1	0	2	.161	.257	.290
Buford, Damon, Char.	41	156	138	20	34	48	8	0	2	10	3	1	2	12	0	22	6	1	4	.246	.314	.348
Clemente, Edgard, Paw.	63	248	231	28	61	94	12	0	7	31	2	0	1	14	0	63	5	0	3	.264	.309	.407
Clemente, Edgard, Ind.	40	156	142	10	29	43	7	2	1	9	1	1	3	9	1	37	1	1	2	.204	.265	.303
D'Amico, Jeff, S./W.B.	15	13	12	1	4	7	0	0	1	4	1	0	0	0	0	2	0	0	1	.333	.333	.583
D'Amico, Jeff, Lou.	11	3	3	0	0	0	0	0	0	0	0	0	0	0	0	1	0	0	0	.000	.000	.000
Fasano, Sal, Ind.	31	122	101	11	26	50	6	0	6	9	0	0	9	12	0	29	0	1	1	.257	.385	.495
Fasano, Sal, Ind.	34	107	97	5	20	32	9	0	1	11	0	1	6	3	0	24	0	0	2	.206	.271	.330
Figueroa, Luis, Nor.†	2	4	4	0	0	0	0	0	0	0	0	0	0	0	0	1	0	0	0	.000	.000	.000
Figueroa, Luis, Ott.†	27	92	82	6	12	18	1	1	1	9	6	0	1	3	0	14	0	2	2	.146	.186	.220
Garcia, Karim, Col.*	74	310	288	44	78	136	16	3	12	49	0	2	0	20	3	48	1	5	2	.271	.316	.472
Garcia, Karim, Buf.*	23	100	91	16	36	56	7	2	3	22	0	0	0	9	2	14	0	1	1	.396	.450	.615
Lira, Felipe, Nor.	22	6	6	0	0	0	0	0	0	0	0	0	0	0	0	6	0	0	0	.000	.000	.000
Lira, Felipe, Lou.	11	6	5	0	0	0	0	0	0	0	1	0	0	0	0	3	0	0	0	.000	.000	.000
Lopez, Luis, Ind.†	6	23	22	2	5	5	0	0	0	0	0	0	1	0	0	4	0	0	0	.227	.261	.227
Lopez, Luis, Roch.†	17	75	68	12	22	37	6	0	3	8	3	0	1	3	0	11	0	0	1	.324	.361	.544
Medrano, Tony, Buf.	74	296	264	28	58	75	10	2	1	30	7	1	4	20	1	25	7	1	7	.220	.284	.284
Medrano, Tony, Ott.	53	201	174	20	47	60	8	1	1	13	5	0	4	18	0	22	5	0	7	.270	.352	.345
Perez, Rob, Ind.	43	126	122	7	24	39	6	0	3	13	1	1	0	2	0	21	2	3	6	.197	.208	.320
Perez, Rob, Col.	84	355	338	47	93	154	22	3	11	49	1	3	0	13	2	35	7	4	5	.275	.299	.456

Player, Team	G	TPA	AB	R	H	TB	2B	3B	HR	RBI	SH	SF	HP	BB	IBB	SO	SB	CS	GDP	Avg.	OBP	Slg.
Phillips, Brandon, Ott.	10	37	35	1	9	16	4	0	1	5	0	0	0	2	0	6	0	0	0	.257	.297	.457
Phillips, Brandon, Buf.	55	247	223	30	63	101	14	0	8	27	4	5	1	14	0	39	8	2	6	.283	.321	.453
Sanders, Anthony, Lou..........	33	135	124	12	31	57	6	1	6	24	0	3	1	7	0	31	4	1	2	.250	.289	.460
Sanders, Anthony, Char.	58	224	211	20	49	80	9	2	6	24	2	1	0	10	1	64	3	2	5	.232	.266	.379

GRAND SLAMS—Larson, 3; Tracy, 2; Bard, Betts, Brinkley, Doster, F. Figueroa, K. Garcia, Harris, Hessman, Hubbard, Hummel, Inge, Knorr, Mottola, Lennon, J. Leon, Snyder, Sorensen, Stenson, Swann, Timmons, Ware, Werth, T. Wilson, Witt, Zuber, 1 each.

AWARDED FIRST BASE ON CATCHER'S INTERFERENCE—Klimek 4 (Jensen, S. Martinez, Norris, Valera); Crede 3 (Castillo, Estrada, Stefanski); Crawford 2 (Knorr, J. Phillips); Freel 2 (L. Evans, Knorr); Bigbie (Coste); H. Clark (J. Phillips); Forbes (Rodriguez); Jimenez (Laker); C. Jones (Valera); Mottola (Norris); Porter (LaForest); Witt (Hubbard); Zuber (Haad).

2002 PITCHING
TEAM

Team	W	L	Pct.	ERA	G	CG	ShO	Sv.	IP	H	TBF	R	ER	HR	SH	SF	HB	BB	IBB	SO	WP	Bk.
Scranton/W.-B. .	91	53	.632	3.27	144	7	10	45	1279.1	1218	5344	535	465	87	52	26	49	395	25	878	37	5
Buffalo..............	87	57	.604	3.30	144	8	13	43	1269.1	1209	5314	537	465	98	47	38	60	387	14	924	48	5
Richmond	75	67	.528	3.50	142	4	12	35	1241.2	1229	5294	562	483	97	57	32	46	403	29	950	58	5
Ottawa..............	80	61	.567	3.54	141	6	11	41	1215.0	1134	5115	555	478	100	61	38	45	415	23	786	49	8
Toledo	81	63	.563	3.63	144	11	13	40	1278.1	1274	5385	587	515	90	37	38	53	374	14	884	62	8
Norfolk	70	73	.490	3.74	143	6	13	30	1248.2	1296	5338	585	519	97	50	42	46	382	27	940	19	6
Durham	80	64	.556	3.87	144	3	9	49	1274.0	1305	5434	626	548	128	31	42	63	425	12	982	68	8
Indianapolis........	67	76	.469	3.87	143	6	5	42	1254.1	1241	5368	615	540	115	67	45	45	415	22	869	29	9
Louisville...........	79	65	.549	4.26	144	2	10	35	1288.0	1342	5541	671	610	138	35	40	55	433	19	1005	54	5
Rochester..........	55	89	.382	4.35	144	6	9	22	1268.1	1370	5543	705	613	123	45	42	39	413	17	862	45	5
Syracuse	64	80	.444	4.50	144	5	3	24	1262.0	1319	5525	743	631	137	27	52	60	469	16	781	65	5
Pawtucket	60	84	.417	4.62	144	4	6	37	1249.1	1357	5534	732	641	150	40	38	75	464	9	837	55	10
Charlotte	55	88	.385	4.63	143	4	7	29	1241.0	1322	5360	700	638	163	33	48	47	450	20	875	44	5
Columbus.........	59	83	.415	4.69	142	3	4	28	1245.1	1370	5561	759	649	107	43	51	61	481	24	977	54	11

INDIVIDUAL

TOP QUALIFIERS FOR EARNED-RUN AVERAGE TITLE
Minimum 115 innings.*Lefthanded pitcher.

Pitcher, Team	W	L	Pct.	ERA	G	GS	CG	ShO	GF	Sv.	IP	H	TBF	R	ER	HR	SH	SF	HB	BB	IBB	SO	WP	Bk.
De Los Santos, Luis, Dur.	9	2	.818	2.42	24	16	1	1	2	0	115.1	105	453	38	31	8	4	2	5	21	0	68	2	0
Linton, Doug, Rich.	9	11	.450	2.53	28	28	1	1	0	0	174	167	709	63	49	14	4	3	7	26	0	160	9	1
Dawley, Joey, Rich.	9	7	.563	2.63	24	23	1	1	1	0	140.1	113	564	44	41	10	5	4	5	36	0	136	3	1
Carter, Lance, Dur................	12	2	.857	2.80	33	18	2	1	2	1	132	111	498	43	41	15	1	1	12	0	90	0	0
Stephens, John, Roch.	11	5	.688	3.03	21	21	1	0	0	0	142.2	126	571	51	48	10	4	3	8	23	0	118	1	0
Lorraine, Andrew, Ind.*	7	11	.389	3.05	25	24	2	0	1	0	165	157	677	65	56	14	10	3	1	42	7	86	1	1
Drew, Tim, Buf.-Ott.	14	7	.667	3.08	28	28	2	2	0	0	181	173	750	74	62	11	10	6	7	47	3	72	3	2
Standridge, Jason, Dur..........	10	9	.526	3.12	29	29	0	0	0	0	173	168	732	71	60	12	2	7	10	64	1	111	2	2
Hodges, Trey, Rich...............	15	9	.625	3.19	28	28	1	1	0	0	172.1	158	716	66	61	9	7	5	8	56	1	116	2	1
Acevedo, Jose, Lou.	12	7	.632	3.20	23	23	0	0	0	0	154.2	146	631	61	55	16	7	4	3	34	0	128	1	0
Blank, Matt, Ott.*	11	7	.611	3.24	31	25	1	1	1	0	147	134	625	67	53	12	3	5	8	55	2	92	5	1
Smith, Mike, Syr.	4	4	.667	3.48	20	20	1	1	0	0	121.2	106	505	51	47	10	0	2	6	43	0	76	3	0
Osting, Jimmy, Ind.*	5	7	.417	3.48	22	22	3	1	0	0	126.2	115	529	52	49	7	6	5	6	38	1	112	2	1
Harikkala, Tim, Ind...............	8	10	.444	3.50	31	20	1	0	3	1	162	172	676	76	63	8	9	6	3	23	1	90	1	1
Junge, Eric, S./W.B.............	12	6	.667	3.54	29	29	1	0	0	0	180.2	170	766	77	71	16	8	4	5	67	1	126	10	0

DEPARTMENTAL LEADERS: W—Hodges, 15; L—Spurgeon, 14; Pct.—Roa, 1.000; G—Tre. Miller, 65; GS—Junge, Standridge, 29 each; CG—Loux, 5; ShO—Loux, 3; GF—Bowles, 46; Sv.—Almonte, 26; IP—Drew, 181.0; H—Wengert, 218; TBF—Junge, 766; R—Spurgeon, 104; ER—Spurgeon, 92; HR—Wheeler, 23; SH—Drew, Lorraine, 10 each; SF—Coco, 10; HB—Hudson, 16; BB—Chantres, Junge, 67 each; IBB—J. Foster, 8; SO—Linton, 160; WP—Magrane, 13; BK—A. Hernandez, 5.

ALL PITCHERS
*Lefthanded pitcher.

Pitcher, Team	W	L	Pct.	ERA	G	GS	CG	ShO	GF	Sv.	IP	H	TBF	R	ER	HR	SH	SF	HB	BB	IBB	SO	WP	Bk.
Abbott, David, Syr.	0	0	.000	2.84	2	0	0	0	0	0	6.1	9	28	3	2	1	0	0	0	0	2	0	0
Acevedo, Jose, Lou.	12	7	.632	3.20	23	23	0	0	0	0	154.2	146	631	61	55	16	7	4	3	34	0	128	1	0
Adkins, Jon, Char.	4	2	.667	3.69	8	7	1	0	1	0	46.1	47	196	20	19	4	0	1	2	12	0	31	1	0
Adkins, Tim, Tol.*	2	2	.500	4.06	31	8	0	0	11	0	68.2	66	301	34	31	3	3	4	34	0	54	6	1
Agamennone, Brandon, Ott. ...	5	1	.833	3.69	27	1	0	0	10	1	53.2	58	234	22	22	7	2	0	2	21	2	38	1	1
Agosto, Stevenson, Dur.*	4	4	.500	4.41	15	15	0	0	0	0	81.2	94	369	52	40	10	1	5	4	33	0	69	3	0
Ahearne, Pat, Tol.	5	4	.556	3.16	12	12	1	1	0	0	82.2	78	328	32	29	3	1	1	8	13	0	46	1	0
Allen, Wyatt, Char.................	0	1	.000	9.00	1	1	0	0	0	0	5	6	26	5	5	2	0	0	0	6	2	3	1
Almanzar, Carlos, Lou.	1	0	1.000	2.74	21	0	0	0	18	11	23	21	91	7	7	0	0	0	1	5	0	19	0	0
Almonte, Ed, Char................	2	3	.400	2.24	50	0	0	0	44	26	60.1	52	238	16	15	6	3	1	2	12	2	56	0	0
Anderson, Jason, Col.	1	1	.833	3.15	26	0	0	0	25	7	34.1	26	138	13	12	3	2	1	1	10	0	28	0	1
Andrews, Shane, Paw............	1	0	1.000	4.50	1	0	0	0	1	0	2	4	10	1	1	0	0	0	1	0	0	0	0
Atchley, Justin, Lou.-Roch.* ...	2	0	1.000	4.50	8	0	0	0	4	0	18	30	87	18	16	6	0	0	5	0	12	0	0
Ayala, Luis, Ott.	0	0	.000	3.52	6	0	0	0	3	0	7.2	7	32	3	3	1	0	0	4	0	6	0	0
Bacsik, Mike, Nor.*	5	5	.500	3.74	25	14	1	1	3	0	108.1	134	467	48	45	13	4	4	25	0	75	1	0
Baker, Chris, Syr.	4	7	.364	4.33	18	15	2	0	2	0	89.1	94	388	58	43	13	1	3	29	0	42	7	0
Bale, John, Nor.*	2	2	.500	3.54	12	2	0	0	4	0	28	22	111	11	11	2	2	0	7	0	27	1	0
Banks, Willie, Paw...............	1	2	.333	4.50	6	4	0	0	1	1	26	20	103	14	13	2	0	0	9	0	15	1	0
Barcelo, Lorenzo, Char.	0	0	.000	6.75	2	0	0	0	0	0	5.1	5	23	4	4	1	0	0	2	0	1	0	0
Bauer, Rick, Roch................	0	0	.000	6.75	1	1	0	0	0	0	4	4	18	4	3	2	0	1	2	0	1	0	0

Pitcher, Team	W	L	Pct.	ERA	G	GS	CG	ShO	GF	Sv.	IP	H	TBF	R	ER	HR	SH	SF	HB	BB	IBB	SO	WP	Bk.
Beal, Andy, Col.*	2	4	.333	6.04	8	8	0	0	0	0	44.2	50	201	36	30	6	3	2	1	21	0	31	0	1
Beasley, Ray, Rich.*	6	5	.545	2.59	64	0	0	0	19	4	55.2	55	230	24	16	3	2	1	1	16	2	45	2	0
Bechler, Steve, Roch.	6	11	.353	4.09	24	24	2	1	0	0	149.2	154	648	78	68	15	6	6	2	52	1	77	5	0
Beech, Matt, Col.*	3	7	.300	5.15	16	16	0	0	0	0	85.2	99	401	55	49	5	4	4	8	44	1	66	6	0
Bell, Heath, Nor.	3	4	.429	4.26	22	0	0	0	14	5	31.2	38	142	15	15	2	5	1	1	9	1	28	1	0
Bernero, Adam, Tol.	2	2	.500	1.58	9	9	2	1	0	0	57	46	225	13	10	2	2	2	2	13	0	49	2	0
Beverlin, Jason, Buf.-Tol.	13	8	.619	3.60	27	23	1	1	2	0	137.1	124	574	60	55	11	6	8	4	45	1	119	9	0
Biddle, Rocky, Char.	0	0	.000	1.29	2	2	0	0	0	0	7	4	27	1	1	0	0	1	1	0	9	0	0	0
Bierek, Kurt, Col.	0	0	.000	4.50	1	0	0	0	0	0	2	2	9	1	1	0	0	0	0	1	0	3	0	0
Billingsley, Brent, Ott.*	4	5	.444	4.07	28	12	0	0	7	1	86.1	75	356	39	39	7	2	3	2	32	0	67	11	2
Blank, Matt, Ott.*	11	7	.611	3.24	31	25	1	1	1	0	147	134	625	67	53	12	3	5	8	55	2	92	5	1
Blevins, Jeremy, Col.	1	3	.250	4.50	17	0	0	0	5	0	24	27	114	17	12	4	1	3	2	14	0	17	0	0
Bohanon, Brian, Lou.*	3	0	1.000	4.87	14	7	0	0	0	0	44.1	52	199	25	24	7	2	0	4	20	0	24	4	0
Bowers, Cedrick, Dur.*	4	3	.571	3.12	47	0	0	0	12	0	69.1	75	326	36	24	9	3	2	3	43	1	79	11	1
Bowles, Brian, Syr.	4	7	.364	3.36	59	0	0	0	46	14	59	46	259	24	22	4	5	1	8	32	5	53	3	1
Boyd, Jason, Paw.	1	0	1.000	3.94	9	0	0	0	4	1	16	13	71	7	7	3	0	0	1	9	0	15	1	0
Bradley, Ryan, Col.	0	0	.000	18.00	1	0	0	0	0	0	1	4	8	2	2	0	0	0	1	0	0	1	0	0
Brazelton, Dewon, Dur.	1	0	1.000	0.00	1	1	0	0	0	0	5	5	20	0	0	0	0	0	0	1	0	6	0	0
Brea, Lesli, Roch.	3	7	.300	3.22	60	0	0	0	20	3	86.2	81	377	37	31	4	5	4	0	37	3	75	4	1
Brewington, Jamie, Paw.	5	6	.455	4.43	18	16	0	0	1	0	91.1	86	395	55	45	17	0	2	6	35	0	61	2	0
Bridges, Kary, Col.	0	0	.000	0.00	1	0	0	0	1	0	1	1	4	0	0	0	0	0	0	0	0	0	0	0
Brownson, Mark, Paw.	0	1	.000	4.50	3	1	0	0	0	0	6	4	26	3	3	0	0	2	0	4	0	2	1	0
Brunette, Justin, Nor.*	2	2	.500	4.09	45	0	0	0	16	2	77	77	324	40	35	4	4	3	4	20	5	42	5	0
Buddie, Mike, Ott.	4	4	.500	4.07	29	0	0	0	11	2	42	34	183	21	19	2	5	2	1	23	3	18	5	0
Burkett, John, Paw.	0	1	.000	11.57	1	1	0	0	0	0	2.1	4	11	3	3	0	0	0	0	1	0	2	0	0
Cammack, Eric, Nor.	0	2	.000	13.50	11	0	0	0	4	0	10	13	53	15	15	1	0	1	0	12	0	6	0	0
Campos, Francisco, Ind.	3	0	1.000	2.05	4	2	0	0	0	0	22	15	85	6	5	2	1	0	0	1	0	14	0	0
Caraccioli, Lance, Buf.*	4	0	1.000	3.05	8	6	0	0	1	1	44.1	45	190	16	15	2	2	1	3	19	2	33	0	0
Carpenter, Chris, Syr.	0	1	.000	4.50	1	1	0	0	0	0	6	8	28	3	3	1	1	0	0	2	0	6	1	0
Carter, Lance, Dur.	12	2	.857	2.80	33	18	2	1	2	1	132	111	498	43	41	15	1	1	1	12	0	90	0	0
Casey, Joe, Syr.	1	1	.500	5.73	18	0	0	0	3	1	22	25	101	14	14	3	1	0	2	14	1	8	1	0
Cassidy, Scott, Syr.	1	0	1.000	4.00	3	2	0	0	1	0	9	8	33	4	4	2	0	0	0	0	0	4	1	0
Castellanos, Hugo, Syr.	0	1	.000	6.35	5	0	0	0	2	0	5.2	3	23	4	4	1	0	0	3	2	0	2	0	0
Cedeno, Blas, S./W.B.	0	1	.000	10.80	3	0	0	0	1	0	3.1	6	16	4	4	0	0	0	0	1	0	1	0	0
Cerda, Jaime, Nor.*	0	0	.000	0.43	12	0	0	0	4	1	21	10	77	2	1	0	0	0	0	7	1	17	0	0
Cerros, Juan, Nor.	1	3	.250	3.35	25	3	0	0	6	2	37.2	40	167	21	14	2	1	2	0	11	0	23	1	1
Chantres, Carlos, Dur.-Char.	8	9	.471	4.53	25	23	0	0	0	0	139	153	620	78	70	16	8	4	11	67	1	74	7	2
Childers, Jason, Ind.	2	3	.400	4.61	28	2	0	0	9	1	52.2	57	240	31	27	6	1	1	1	30	1	29	2	0
Childers, Matt, Ind.	0	0	.000	0.00	3	0	0	0	1	0	5	1	18	0	0	0	0	0	0	2	0	4	0	0
Cho, Jin Ho, Paw.	3	6	.333	5.63	20	8	0	0	8	2	54.1	74	243	37	34	10	4	1	3	12	1	20	1	0
Choate, Randy, Col.*	3	2	.600	1.72	31	0	0	0	7	1	36.2	25	150	8	7	0	1	0	2	15	1	32	2	0
Chulk, Vinny, Syr.	0	1	.000	5.79	2	1	0	0	1	0	4.2	6	27	6	3	0	0	2	0	6	0	2	2	0
Claussen, Brandon, Col.*	2	8	.200	3.28	15	15	0	0	0	0	93.1	85	408	47	34	4	7	3	1	46	0	73	2	0
Coco, Pasqual, Syr.	4	9	.308	4.98	30	23	1	0	2	0	141	145	621	91	78	17	0	10	9	57	0	98	6	1
Cole, Joey, Nor.	0	1	.000	9.00	1	0	0	0	1	0	2	3	11	2	2	0	1	0	2	1	2	0	0	0
Colome, Jesus, Dur.	2	2	.500	2.17	18	0	0	0	5	1	29	18	116	8	7	1	1	0	0	13	0	30	4	0
Comolli, Mark, Syr.	0	0	.000	18.00	1	0	0	0	0	0	1	3	7	2	2	0	0	0	0	1	0	1	1	0
Cooper, Brian, Syr.	9	9	.500	5.09	27	25	1	0	1	0	155.2	176	671	98	88	19	0	9	7	46	1	71	5	0
Cordova, Jorge, Lou.	1	0	1.000	4.50	2	0	0	0	0	0	2	1	8	1	1	1	0	0	0	0	0	2	0	0
Corey, Mark, Nor.	3	1	.750	1.03	25	0	0	0	21	7	26.1	14	100	3	3	1	3	0	1	7	1	37	0	0
Cornejo, Nate, Tol.	9	8	.529	4.42	21	20	1	0	0	0	132.1	163	576	72	65	11	4	2	8	31	1	86	1	2
Coste, Chris, Buf.	1	1	.500	3.60	2	0	0	0	2	0	5	3	18	2	2	1	0	0	0	0	0	3	1	0
Crabtree, Robbie, Syr.	3	4	.429	4.91	32	0	0	0	10	2	51.1	43	214	30	28	4	1	2	1	22	0	41	5	0
Crawford, Paxton, Paw.	2	3	.400	5.55	9	9	0	0	0	0	47	61	215	33	29	9	2	1	1	19	0	22	0	0
Croushore, Rich, Dur.	5	4	.556	3.38	36	3	0	0	18	7	64	55	268	26	24	5	1	0	6	26	3	62	7	1
Crowell, Jim, S./W.B.*	2	0	1.000	2.52	4	4	0	0	0	0	25	20	102	7	7	2	2	0	1	11	0	19	1	0
Crumpton, Chuck, Ott.	0	2	.000	5.40	19	0	0	0	9	0	25	26	106	15	15	1	0	1	2	8	1	11	1	0
Cubillan, Darwin, Ott.	1	1	.500	3.50	29	0	0	0	14	6	36	28	154	16	14	4	1	3	1	21	0	35	1	0
Cumberland, Chris, Syr.*	4	0	1.000	3.22	28	0	0	0	4	0	36.1	34	159	11	13	0	3	1	1	19	3	20	3	0
D'Amico, Jeff, S./W.B.-Buf.-Lou.	6	10	.375	4.94	27	21	0	0	3	1	118.1	130	519	80	65	17	2	2	6	39	4	73	4	2
Darnell, Paul, Lou.*	0	3	.000	3.67	12	3	0	0	3	0	27	27	116	11	11	5	1	0	1	14	0	14	1	1
Davis, Kane, Nor.	0	0	.000	0.00	1	0	0	0	1	0	1	1	4	0	0	0	0	0	0	0	0	2	0	0
Davis, Lance, Lou.*	3	4	.429	4.50	11	11	0	0	0	0	62	78	267	32	31	9	1	2	1	17	0	27	1	0
Dawley, Joey, Rich.	9	7	.563	2.63	24	23	1	1	1	0	140.1	113	564	44	41	10	5	4	5	36	0	136	3	1
Day, Zach, Ott.	5	6	.455	3.50	17	16	1	0	0	0	90	77	373	38	35	5	3	1	4	32	0	68	7	0
Dellaero, Jason, Char.	0	0	.000	0.00	1	0	0	0	1	0	1	0	3	0	0	0	0	0	0	0	0	2	0	0
De Los Santos, Luis, Dur.	9	2	.818	2.42	24	16	1	1	2	0	115.1	105	453	38	31	8	4	2	5	21	0	68	0	0
De Los Santos, Valerio, Ind.*..	1	0	1.000	0.00	2	0	0	0	2	0	2	1	8	0	0	0	0	0	1	0	0	5	0	0
De Paula, Sean, Buf.	2	3	.400	3.95	34	0	0	0	18	9	57	55	241	26	25	6	0	3	2	18	2	53	4	0
Dickson, Jason, Dur.	3	4	.429	5.70	9	9	0	0	0	0	47.1	54	208	31	30	7	0	2	2	23	0	32	3	0
Dillinger, John, Col.	0	1	.000	7.89	9	2	0	0	1	0	21.2	24	100	22	19	4	1	2	12	10	2	24	0	0
Dingman, Craig, Lou.-Col.	2	1	.667	4.61	24	0	0	0	7	0	27.1	26	121	18	14	3	1	0	2	14	1	28	2	0
Donaldson, Bo, Col.	5	4	.556	3.56	29	9	0	0	4	0	78.1	76	335	35	31	6	2	5	5	27	2	64	2	0
Douglass, Sean, Roch.	4	6	.400	4.73	14	13	0	0	1	0	66.2	66	299	39	35	4	1	3	2	35	0	71	3	0
Downs, Scott, Ott.*	2	1	.667	5.79	17	0	0	0	1	0	23.1	31	106	21	15	6	2	2	2	3	0	15	0	1
Drese, Ryan, Buf.	1	0	1.000	1.64	3	3	0	0	0	0	22	16	86	4	4	1	1	1	0	4	0	16	0	0
Drew, Tim, Buf.-Ott.	14	7	.667	3.08	28	28	2	2	0	0	181	173	750	74	62	11	10	6	7	47	3	72	3	2
Driskill, Travis, Roch.	2	2	.500	1.64	4	4	1	0	0	0	22	17	86	8	4	1	1	0	1	0	0	15	0	0
Drumright, Mike, Paw.-Roch.	6	8	.429	4.01	30	24	0	0	2	0	150.1	156	659	92	67	10	2	3	5	50	0	109	11	3
Dubose, Eric, Roch.*	0	0	.000	27.00	1	0	0	0	0	0	0.1	1	5	2	1	0	0	0	0	2	0	0	0	0
Durocher, Jayson, Ind.	1	0	1.000	2.73	20	0	0	0	9	2	26.1	19	115	9	8	3	0	0	2	15	0	39	2	0

CLASS AAA International League

Pitcher, Team	W	L	Pct.	ERA	G	GS	CG	ShO	GF	Sv.	IP	H	TBF	R	ER	HR	SH	SF	HB	BB	IBB	SO	WP	Bk.
Eason, Clay, Char.	0	0	.000	4.43	11	0	0	0	3	0	20.1	22	91	11	10	3	1	1	0	9	0	14	1	0
Ebert, Derrin, Ind.*	6	4	.600	3.50	50	1	0	0	19	4	74.2	66	311	33	29	11	5	4	3	25	5	46	3	0
Eckenstahler, Eric, Tol.*	2	4	.333	4.43	52	0	0	0	17	0	67	57	287	37	33	8	4	1	3	35	1	69	1	0
Edwards, Mike, Lou.	0	1	.000	20.25	1	0	0	0	1	0	1.1	3	8	3	3	1	0	0	0	1	0	0	1	0
Eischen, Joey, Ott.*	1	0	1.000	0.00	11	0	0	0	9	4	14	8	55	4	0	0	1	0	3	3	0	15	0	0
Elder, Dave, Buf.	3	1	.750	2.65	22	1	0	0	15	5	34	32	145	11	10	1	1	1	0	14	0	42	2	0
Elmore, Chris, Paw.*	0	3	.000	6.37	7	7	0	0	0	0	29.2	43	144	25	21	3	0	2	2	12	0	30	1	0
Erdos, Todd, Paw.	4	4	.500	3.22	52	2	0	0	25	10	78.1	87	340	31	28	4	2	4	2	21	2	48	1	0
Espina, Rendy, Syr.-Roch.*	2	2	.500	6.75	45	0	0	0	9	0	53.1	65	253	43	40	12	2	2	2	31	2	38	3	0
Etherton, Seth, Lou.	0	1	.000	8.22	5	5	0	0	0	0	15.1	21	71	16	14	4	0	1	0	6	0	10	2	0
Evans, Keith, Ott.	0	5	.000	2.22	16	2	0	0	2	0	28.1	29	126	15	7	2	3	1	2	10	1	15	1	0
Farmer, Tom, Tol.	0	0	.000	6.00	1	1	0	0	0	0	6	7	26	4	4	0	0	0	0	2	0	3	1	0
Feliciano, Pedro, Lou.-Nor.*	1	1	.500	4.04	25	0	0	0	9	2	35.2	49	157	17	16	4	1	4	1	5	0	30	1	0
Fernandez, Jared, Lou.	12	5	.706	3.93	26	18	1	0	4	1	128.1	151	547	63	56	14	2	2	5	31	1	80	7	1
Fernandez, Osvaldo, Ott.	3	2	.600	4.26	18	5	0	0	4	0	44.1	46	193	27	21	3	8	0	0	16	2	28	1	0
Field, Nathan, Col.	2	1	.667	6.75	21	2	0	0	5	0	38.2	46	180	30	29	6	0	7	1	21	1	25	1	0
Figueroa, Nelson, Ind.	5	0	1.000	3.63	6	6	0	0	0	0	39.2	39	170	18	16	2	1	2	0	13	0	25	1	0
File, Bob, Syr.	0	0	.000	5.94	33	0	0	0	12	2	36.1	39	168	29	24	2	1	1	6	15	1	23	1	0
Fortunato, Bartolome, Dur.	1	0	1.000	4.15	2	0	0	0	0	0	4.1	6	21	3	2	1	0	1	0	2	0	0	0	0
Fossum, Casey, Paw.*	0	3	.000	3.96	5	3	1	0	1	0	25	34	111	15	11	1	0	1	3	6	0	28	2	0
Foster, John, Rich.*	8	4	.667	4.21	55	0	0	0	25	8	62	67	277	30	29	5	4	1	1	28	8	48	3	0
Foster, Kevin, Lou.	0	0	.000	2.08	3	0	0	0	2	0	4.1	3	20	1	1	0	0	0	0	4	0	4	1	0
Foster, Kris, Roch.	0	1	.000	7.71	14	0	0	0	6	1	18.2	22	88	16	16	3	2	2	1	10	0	14	3	0
Freeman, Kai, Char.	0	0	.000	18.00	1	0	0	0	0	0	1	3	6	2	2	0	0	0	0	0	0	0	0	0
Gandarillas, Gus, Ind.	0	0	.000	18.00	2	0	0	0	1	0	2	4	12	4	4	1	1	0	0	1	0	3	0	0
Garcia, Gerardo, Dur.	2	7	.222	6.50	15	15	0	0	0	0	63.2	79	292	48	46	5	3	4	2	30	0	50	4	0
Garcia, Jose, Ind.	2	7	.222	5.70	17	13	0	0	1	0	83.2	96	374	56	53	9	5	8	4	37	0	43	5	1
Garcia, Mike, Roch.	1	0	1.000	0.00	9	0	0	0	8	2	10	7	38	0	0	0	0	0	0	1	0	9	0	0
Gardner, Lee, Dur.	2	1	.667	2.36	45	0	0	0	35	25	49.2	50	207	14	13	1	1	0	0	15	3	52	0	0
Gassner, Dave, Syr.*	0	1	.000	5.40	1	1	0	0	0	0	5	7	23	3	3	0	0	0	0	2	0	1	0	0
Geary, Geoff, S./W.B.	4	2	.667	3.03	38	8	0	0	6	1	101	108	427	46	34	9	0	1	4	32	1	82	1	0
German, Frank, Tol.	1	1	.500	1.59	23	0	0	0	21	13	22.2	15	88	4	4	0	0	1	0	7	0	31	1	1
Gil, Dave, Lou.	2	3	.400	8.86	9	4	0	0	3	0	21.1	29	102	21	21	8	0	2	1	11	0	18	0	0
Ginter, Matt, Char.	1	0	1.000	3.94	13	0	0	0	7	0	16	20	74	8	7	3	0	0	0	10	1	9	1	0
Giron, Roberto, Ind.	0	0	.000	6.75	15	0	0	0	7	1	17.1	19	86	14	13	2	1	0	4	9	0	26	2	0
Glynn, Ryan, Ind.	3	6	.333	5.23	12	11	0	0	0	0	63.2	75	293	48	37	7	3	2	0	26	0	36	0	0
Gomes, Wayne, Paw.	5	2	.714	2.64	42	0	0	0	12	4	71.2	61	306	30	21	8	6	2	4	28	2	54	1	0
Gonzalez, Dicky, Nor.-Ott.	8	5	.615	3.75	23	23	0	0	0	0	124.2	143	544	61	52	11	3	5	4	35	2	79	3	1
Graman, Alex, Col.*	6	9	.400	4.65	20	20	1	0	0	0	124	141	545	74	64	11	5	3	3	37	3	98	10	2
Greisinger, Seth, Tol.	1	1	.500	4.11	3	3	0	0	0	0	15.1	15	63	8	7	0	0	0	2	7	0	11	1	0
Gryboski, Kevin, Rich.	1	0	1.000	1.29	7	0	0	0	6	3	7	7	29	1	1	0	0	0	0	1	0	5	1	0
Haines, Talley, Dur.	4	7	.364	4.52	48	0	0	0	19	0	75.2	84	326	43	38	9	3	0	3	24	1	62	3	0
Hamann, Rob, Syr.	0	0	.000	4.96	7	2	0	0	2	0	16.1	20	70	12	9	3	1	1	0	4	0	6	0	1
Hamilton, Joey, Lou.	1	0	1.000	2.57	3	3	0	0	0	0	14	10	57	4	4	2	0	0	0	6	0	10	0	0
Hancock, Josh, Paw.	4	2	.667	3.45	8	8	0	0	0	0	44.1	39	198	20	17	2	2	2	2	26	0	29	3	0
Haney, Chris, Paw.*	2	0	1.000	2.79	25	0	0	0	14	4	29	27	124	10	9	1	0	0	2	10	0	31	5	0
Harikkala, Tim, Ind.	8	10	.444	3.50	31	20	1	0	3	1	162	172	676	76	63	8	9	6	3	23	1	90	1	1
Harper, Travis, Dur.	1	2	.333	6.98	4	4	0	0	0	0	19.1	31	87	15	15	5	0	2	1	3	0	17	1	0
Hasselhoff, Derek, Paw.	0	4	.000	5.04	39	0	0	0	29	11	44.2	47	190	29	25	5	2	2	2	8	0	30	0	1
Hazlett, Andy, Paw.*	1	0	1.000	1.59	5	0	0	0	0	0	11.1	6	41	2	2	1	0	0	0	2	0	6	0	0
Heams, Shane, Paw.	1	0	1.000	5.52	11	0	0	0	4	0	14.2	14	71	9	9	3	1	0	1	12	0	8	1	0
Hebson, Bryan, Ott.	1	0	1.000	4.82	5	0	0	0	1	0	9.1	8	41	5	5	0	1	0	1	3	0	11	0	0
Heilman, Aaron, Nor.	2	3	.400	3.28	10	7	0	0	2	0	49.1	42	196	18	18	3	3	1	1	16	1	35	0	0
Hendrickson, Mark, Syr.*	7	5	.583	3.52	19	14	0	0	3	0	92	90	385	38	36	12	4	4	1	22	0	68	2	2
Henriquez, Oscar, Tol.	2	1	.667	3.31	33	0	0	0	30	17	32.2	30	141	13	12	4	2	1	1	14	0	39	6	0
Hermanson, Dustin, Paw.	0	1	.000	2.63	5	3	0	0	0	0	13.2	9	56	5	4	0	0	0	2	7	0	11	0	0
Hernandez, Adrian, Col.	6	7	.462	5.25	20	20	0	0	0	0	109.2	114	488	67	64	9	4	5	11	45	1	109	9	5
Hernandez, Orlando, Col.	1	0	1.000	1.59	1	1	0	0	0	0	5.2	7	27	2	1	0	0	0	1	1	0	5	0	0
Herrera, Alex, Buf.*	0	1	.000	11.57	5	0	0	0	1	0	7	10	39	9	9	0	1	0	1	8	0	5	2	0
Hiles, Cary, S./W.B.	4	3	.571	3.81	26	2	0	0	9	1	52	51	227	24	22	2	4	1	4	21	3	27	0	0
Hitchcock, Sterling, Col.*	0	0	.000	13.50	2	2	0	0	0	0	7.1	19	42	11	11	2	0	0	0	3	0	3	0	1
Hodges, Trey, Rich.	15	9	.625	3.19	28	28	1	1	0	0	172.1	158	716	66	61	9	7	5	8	56	1	116	2	1
Hudson, Luke, Lou.	5	9	.357	4.51	30	17	0	0	6	3	117.2	102	518	64	59	6	4	4	16	57	1	129	10	1
Jacquez, Tom, Char.*	0	7	.000	6.75	14	7	1	0	2	0	61.1	79	272	48	46	7	3	4	1	21	1	45	0	0
James, Delvin, Dur.	2	1	.667	3.93	7	7	0	0	0	0	34.1	41	146	15	15	4	0	1	2	4	0	26	5	0
Jean, Domingo, Col.	0	2	.000	5.45	19	0	0	0	6	0	33	29	146	23	20	4	0	1	2	17	0	31	2	0
Jennings, Robin, Lou.*	0	0	.000	0.00	1	0	0	0	0	0	2	3	11	1	0	0	1	0	0	1	0	2	0	0
Jimenez, Jason, Dur.*	2	2	.500	2.63	44	0	0	0	15	3	51.1	47	222	21	15	3	2	2	6	16	1	55	2	0
Jodie, Brett, Col.	1	1	.500	5.40	6	2	0	0	2	0	18.1	24	85	14	11	1	2	2	1	7	1	7	1	0
Johnson, Mark, Ind.-Tol.	4	1	.800	4.95	12	6	0	0	1	0	43.2	50	190	27	24	2	2	2	1	17	1	23	1	0
Jones, Bobby M., Nor.*	1	4	.200	4.02	13	6	0	0	1	0	40.1	42	187	25	18	4	1	1	5	15	0	35	1	0
Joseph, Jake, Nor.	0	1	.000	12.27	1	1	0	0	0	0	3.2	8	22	5	5	0	0	0	0	3	0	1	0	1
Junge, Eric, S./W.B.	12	6	.667	3.54	29	29	1	0	0	0	180.2	170	766	77	71	16	8	4	5	67	1	126	10	0
Kalita, Tim, Tol.*	1	9	.100	4.93	15	15	0	0	0	0	87.2	93	379	56	48	10	3	4	3	22	0	47	4	0
Kane, Kyle, Char.	0	0	.000	4.26	4	0	0	0	1	0	6.1	7	30	3	3	1	0	0	1	3	0	9	1	0
Keller, Kris, Tol.-Rich.	3	0	1.000	2.95	46	0	0	0	14	2	61	46	256	26	20	5	4	1	1	30	3	40	8	0
Kieschnick, Brooks, Char.	0	1	.000	2.59	25	0	0	0	14	0	31.1	30	132	9	9	1	1	2	0	10	1	30	1	0
Kim, Sun-Woo, Paw.-Ott.	7	2	.778	2.22	15	15	2	1	0	0	89	63	353	29	22	6	1	3	3	32	0	65	1	0
King, Ray, Ind.*	0	0	.000	0.00	1	1	0	0	0	0	1	1	4	0	0	0	0	0	0	1	0	1	0	0
Kingrey, Jarrod, Syr.	4	1	.800	4.79	26	0	0	0	4	1	41.1	32	174	23	22	6	1	0	3	20	0	28	4	0
Knight, Brandon, Col.	2	7	.222	3.90	36	7	1	0	25	12	80.2	67	342	40	35	6	0	0	0	37	1	81	6	0

Pitcher, Team	W	L	Pct.	ERA	G	GS	CG	ShO	GF	Sv.	IP	H	TBF	R	ER	HR	SH	SF	HB	BB	IBB	SO	WP	Bk.
Kohlmeier, Ryan, Char.	2	1	.667	4.96	38	1	0	0	16	0	65.1	65	282	42	36	12	2	7	2	20	1	58	0	0
Kolb, Brandon, Lou.	3	2	.600	5.06	41	0	0	0	12	1	48	54	222	33	27	3	3	3	1	28	3	39	2	0
Komiyama, Saturo, Nor.	3	1	.750	1.42	17	6	1	0	7	0	44.1	27	168	8	7	4	3	0	3	9	2	43	0	0
Krawczyk, Jack, Ind.	0	0	.000	6.75	2	0	0	0	0	0	2.2	3	15	4	2	1	2	1	0	3	1	3	0	0
Kusiewicz, Mike, Paw.*	2	5	.286	4.99	10	10	0	0	0	0	48.2	52	226	31	27	5	1	1	4	21	0	42	6	0
Lantigua, Delvis, Char.	1	5	.167	5.85	15	8	0	0	2	0	52.1	46	228	36	34	10	1	2	3	29	1	41	1	0
Larson, Ryan, Buf.	0	0	.000	10.80	1	0	0	0	0	0	1.2	3	9	2	2	1	0	0	0	1	0	1	0	0
Lee, Cliff, Buf.*	3	2	.600	3.77	8	8	0	0	0	0	43	36	180	18	18	7	0	0	1	22	0	30	1	1
Lee, Corey, Char.*	7	6	.538	3.89	38	12	1	0	7	0	111	130	481	54	48	12	3	4	3	37	0	92	1	2
Lee, Garrett, Rich.	0	0	.000	5.19	5	1	0	0	1	0	8.2	15	43	7	5	3	0	0	2	2	0	2	0	0
Leskanic, Curt, Ind.	0	0	.000	1.35	5	1	0	0	0	0	6.2	5	28	1	1	0	1	0	1	0	1	7	0	0
Lewis, Derrick, Rich.	3	5	.375	4.56	18	13	0	0	1	0	77	77	337	49	39	9	5	2	2	34	1	52	3	1
Linton, Doug, Rich.	9	11	.450	2.53	28	28	1	1	0	0	174	167	709	63	49	14	4	3	7	26	0	160	9	1
Lira, Felipe, Ott.-Lou.	4	6	.400	4.91	32	11	0	0	5	1	99	108	422	55	54	7	5	8	3	30	1	57	2	1
Loaiza, Esteban, Syr.	0	0	.000	2.08	1	1	0	0	0	0	4.1	4	18	1	1	0	0	0	0	0	0	4	0	0
Looney, Brian, Roch.*	1	1	.500	4.73	9	0	0	0	3	0	13.1	12	58	7	7	2	1	0	0	7	1	14	1	1
Lorraine, Andrew, Ind.*	7	11	.389	3.05	25	24	2	0	1	0	165	157	677	65	56	14	10	3	1	42	7	86	1	1
Loux, Shane, Tol.	11	10	.524	4.72	26	26	5	3	0	0	158.1	196	696	94	83	11	4	4	10	38	1	87	9	2
Lovingier, Kevin, Col.*	0	2	.000	6.37	21	1	0	0	8	1	29.2	41	162	30	21	1	1	7	3	28	1	19	2	0
Lyon, Brandon, Syr.	4	9	.308	5.11	14	14	0	0	0	0	75.2	99	344	54	43	4	2	6	3	19	0	35	1	0
MacRae, Scott, Lou.	4	2	.667	3.34	49	0	0	0	13	2	72.2	74	321	39	27	5	1	2	1	28	3	54	4	1
Magrane, Jim, Dur.	7	8	.467	5.99	20	19	0	0	0	0	112.2	136	508	81	75	19	2	7	7	47	1	53	13	0
Mallette, Brian, Ind.	3	2	.600	2.78	45	0	0	0	38	25	45.1	39	191	15	14	4	3	2	3	17	1	50	0	0
Maness, Nick, Nor.	2	0	1.000	3.50	3	3	0	0	0	0	18	16	78	10	7	1	2	0	1	8	0	11	1	0
Manon, Julio, Ott.	8	6	.571	3.50	28	13	2	1	9	2	105.1	83	436	42	41	8	5	2	45	0	81	3	0
Maroth, Mike, Tol.*	8	1	.889	2.82	11	11	1	0	0	0	73.1	53	289	25	23	7	1	2	0	22	0	51	2	0
Marquez, Rob, Ind.	4	7	.364	3.82	47	0	0	0	22	8	68.1	61	293	34	29	10	7	4	3	24	2	43	4	1
Marquis, Jason, Rich.	0	1	.000	3.60	1	1	0	0	0	0	5	5	21	2	2	0	1	0	0	1	0	6	1	0
Marshall, Lee, Roch.	4	6	.400	4.85	59	0	0	0	33	4	78	101	361	47	42	6	6	2	0	32	4	36	1	1
Martin, Tom, Dur.*	0	0	.000	0.00	4	0	0	0	3	2	3.1	3	14	0	0	0	0	0	1	0	0	6	0	0
Matheny, Brandon, Buf.*	1	0	1.000	9.00	1	0	0	0	0	0	4	7	20	4	4	0	0	0	1	0	0	1	0	0
Maurer, Dave, Buf.*	5	1	.833	2.90	36	3	0	0	12	5	68.1	50	274	27	22	6	2	0	3	24	0	73	2	0
McAvoy, Jeff, Syr.	1	0	1.000	1.80	1	1	0	0	0	0	5	5	20	1	1	0	0	0	1	0	2	0	0
McClellan, Matt, Syr.	3	2	.600	5.40	12	1	0	0	4	0	18.1	23	84	11	11	3	0	0	9	1	20	1	0
McConnell, Sam, S./W.B.*	0	3	.000	3.53	7	7	0	0	0	0	35.2	41	159	17	14	6	1	1	0	16	0	23	0	0
McDill, Allen, Roch.*	1	1	.500	7.90	15	0	0	0	4	0	13.2	17	66	12	12	2	1	1	2	7	1	6	0	0
McLeary, Marty, Paw.	1	1	.500	7.32	18	1	0	0	6	0	35.2	44	168	30	29	6	1	1	2	23	0	19	6	0
McNichol, Brian, Col.*	0	1	.000	6.57	13	0	0	0	4	0	12.1	17	61	13	9	2	1	1	1	5	2	10	0	0
McWhirter, Kris, Char.	0	1	.000	4.09	2	2	0	0	0	0	11	13	48	6	5	1	0	1	1	0	5	0	0
Mendoza, Geronimo, Char.	1	9	.100	8.15	11	10	0	0	0	0	53	68	250	52	48	10	1	4	2	25	2	36	9	0
Mercado, Hector, S./W.B.*	3	1	.750	1.62	26	0	0	0	12	3	33.1	22	131	6	6	2	0	0	1	12	1	43	2	0
Mercedes, Jose, Buf.	2	0	1.000	3.49	5	5	0	0	0	0	28.1	32	121	11	11	4	0	0	2	6	0	13	1	0
Meyer, Jake, Char.	0	0	.000	1.17	4	0	0	0	2	0	7.2	1	23	1	1	1	0	0	0	0	0	9	0	0
Michalak, Chris, Paw.*	5	9	.357	5.77	17	16	0	0	0	0	93.2	125	432	68	60	15	3	2	9	31	0	52	2	4
Middlebrook, Jason, Nor.	2	1	.667	2.66	5	5	0	0	0	0	23.2	19	84	7	7	1	0	1	1	1	0	22	0	0
Miller, Justin, Syr.	3	2	.600	1.61	8	8	0	0	0	0	44.2	34	183	11	8	0	1	2	0	16	0	29	1	0
Miller, Travis, Buf.*	1	1	.500	2.45	7	0	0	0	3	0	14.2	15	66	9	4	1	3	1	0	8	3	5	1	0
Miller, Trever, Lou.*	9	5	.643	3.18	65	1	0	0	16	0	82	76	345	30	29	6	0	4	3	23	4	80	5	0
Moehler, Brian, Tol.	2	1	.667	4.88	4	4	0	0	0	0	24	28	104	15	13	3	0	0	3	7	0	7	0	0
Mohler, Mike, Roch.*	1	2	.333	2.76	34	0	0	0	12	1	49	51	207	16	15	2	2	0	0	15	4	44	4	0
Moreno, Juan, Paw.*	0	0	.000	10.13	3	0	0	0	0	0	2.2	2	14	4	3	1	1	0	3	0	1	0	0
Munoz, Bobby, Nor.	0	0	.000	30.86	3	0	0	0	1	0	2.1	9	19	8	8	0	0	0	4	0	3	0	0
Murray, Heath, Buf.*	1	2	.333	3.03	21	2	0	0	8	5	29.2	23	114	10	10	2	2	0	2	6	0	32	1	0
Myers, Brett, S./W.B.	9	6	.600	3.59	19	19	4	1	0	0	128	121	509	54	51	9	3	3	3	20	0	97	1	0
Nagy, Charles, Buf.	1	2	.333	3.19	5	5	2	0	0	0	36.2	38	150	18	13	6	1	2	1	4	0	18	2	0
Nance, Shane, Ind.*	3	0	1.000	0.00	9	0	0	0	4	0	16.2	12	67	0	0	0	0	0	3	6	0	10	0	2
Neu, Mike, Lou.	2	3	.400	4.02	40	0	0	0	34	16	40.1	35	172	19	18	4	2	1	0	18	0	47	1	0
Neugebauer, Nick, Ind.	0	3	.000	5.12	5	5	0	0	0	0	19.1	20	90	13	11	4	1	1	0	12	0	18	1	0
Nickle, Doug, S./W.B.	3	5	.375	2.97	34	1	0	0	22	7	60.2	58	250	24	20	4	3	2	4	16	4	37	2	0
Nomura, Takahito, Ind.*	1	2	.333	5.73	31	0	0	0	12	0	33	38	146	24	21	4	1	0	2	11	1	23	0	0
Nunez, Franklin, S./W.B.	2	1	.667	3.18	4	4	0	0	0	0	17	9	69	6	6	2	0	0	0	12	0	16	1	0
Nussbeck, Mark, Roch.	1	2	.333	6.39	11	3	0	0	1	0	25.1	30	108	20	18	5	0	1	8	0	6	2	0
Olivares, Omar, Buf.	0	2	.000	4.66	2	2	0	0	0	0	9.2	18	51	10	5	0	1	0	0	3	0	8	0	0
Osting, Jimmy, Ind.*	5	7	.417	3.48	22	22	3	1	0	0	126.2	115	529	52	49	7	6	5	6	38	1	112	2	1
Pacheco, Alexander, Col.	0	1	.000	2.03	14	0	0	0	2	0	13.1	13	61	5	3	1	1	1	1	6	0	15	0	0
Paniagua, Jose, Tol.	2	0	1.000	1.15	12	0	0	0	2	1	15.2	10	59	2	2	1	0	1	1	4	1	13	1	0
Paronto, Chad, Buf.	0	0	.000	0.00	8	0	0	0	5	1	13	10	49	0	0	0	1	0	1	1	0	7	0	0
Parque, Jim, Char.*	7	9	.438	6.47	20	20	0	0	0	0	105.2	131	472	80	76	21	2	5	4	38	0	63	5	1
Parris, Steve, Syr.	1	1	.500	1.29	2	2	0	0	0	0	14	10	54	6	2	0	0	0	2	0	5	0	0
Parrish, Wade, Char.*	5	5	.500	4.67	15	14	0	0	0	0	88.2	105	380	49	46	12	3	3	0	26	0	28	2	0
Patterson, Danny, Tol.	0	0	.000	0.00	5	1	0	0	0	0	5	1	15	0	0	0	0	0	0	0	0	3	0	0
Pavano, Carl, Ott.	3	0	1.000	3.10	3	3	0	0	0	0	20.1	23	82	8	7	2	0	2	0	2	0	9	1	0
Payne, Jerrod, Syr.	0	0	.000	3.24	6	0	0	0	4	0	8.1	8	39	3	3	2	0	0	3	0	7	0	0
Pearson, Terry, Tol.	3	8	.273	4.79	40	0	0	0	11	2	47	52	210	29	25	1	5	0	3	18	4	30	4	0
Pena, Juan, Paw.	4	11	.267	5.33	17	16	1	0	0	0	82.2	84	361	51	49	20	0	4	3	36	1	59	1	2
Perez, Yorkis, Roch.*	1	1	.500	3.79	28	0	0	0	5	0	40.1	42	181	20	17	4	1	2	0	20	1	44	3	0
Perisho, Matt, Tol.*	4	4	.500	2.45	51	2	0	0	16	8	66	62	279	20	18	4	1	5	2	19	4	44	3	0
Person, Robert, S./W.B.	1	1	.500	4.32	2	2	0	0	0	0	8.1	8	32	4	4	2	1	0	0	1	0	7	1	0
Petersen, Chris, Rich.	0	0	.000	0.00	1	0	0	0	1	0	3	0	0	0	0	0	0	0	0	0	0	2	0	0
Phelps, Travis, Dur.	3	2	.600	4.35	27	0	0	0	17	8	31	29	134	15	15	2	1	2	0	14	1	34	2	0
Phillips, Jason, Buf.	7	4	.636	3.39	16	16	1	0	0	0	98.1	88	392	37	37	8	4	1	7	17	0	71	0	0

Pitcher, Team	W	L	Pct.	ERA	G	GS	CG	ShO	GF	Sv.	IP	H	TBF	R	ER	HR	SH	SF	HB	BB	IBB	SO	WP	Bk.
Pina, Rafael, Roch.	6	5	.545	3.49	50	9	0	0	32	10	111	117	478	53	43	9	6	6	6	31	0	74	5	0
Pineda, Luis, Lou.	0	1	.000	4.26	3	3	0	0	0	0	12.2	9	50	6	6	1	0	0	1	4	0	12	0	0
Porzio, Mike, Char.*	6	5	.545	4.52	14	13	0	0	0	0	75.2	83	332	43	38	9	1	5	6	29	0	59	1	0
Powell, Brian, Tol.	10	3	.769	3.92	20	20	0	0	0	0	119.1	127	503	54	52	8	0	4	3	26	0	82	6	0
Pratt, Andy, Rich.*	4	2	.667	3.10	6	6	1	1	0	0	40.2	35	163	15	14	2	2	1	0	9	0	36	3	0
Prokopec, Luke, Syr.	0	0	.000	0.00	2	0	0	0	0	0	2	0	6	0	0	0	0	0	0	0	0	2	0	0
Pulsipher, Bill, Col.*	0	0	.000	14.73	0	0	0	0	0	0	3.2	10	20	6	6	1	0	0	0	4	0	4	0	0
Pumphrey, Ken, S./W.B.	4	2	.667	4.01	8	8	1	0	0	0	51.2	54	219	25	23	2	2	1	2	12	0	34	2	0
Quevedo, Ruben, Ind.	0	0	.000	0.00	1	1	0	0	0	0	2	1	8	0	0	0	0	0	1	0	3	0	0	0
Ratliff, Jon, Syr.	2	3	.400	3.86	27	0	0	0	12	1	37.1	43	169	21	16	2	1	2	0	22	1	19	7	0
Rauch, Jon, Char.	7	8	.467	4.28	19	19	1	0	0	0	109.1	91	451	60	52	14	2	1	3	42	2	97	2	0
Reames, Britt, Ott.	3	2	.600	2.79	7	7	0	0	0	0	42	31	170	16	13	3	3	1	2	14	0	26	1	0
Reimers, Cameron, Syr.	2	3	.400	4.99	12	10	0	0	1	0	48.2	68	229	39	27	8	1	2	5	11	1	17	1	0
Reith, Brian, Lou.-S./W.B.	8	13	.381	5.02	27	26	0	0	0	0	150.2	163	668	94	84	16	4	5	10	57	3	112	3	0
Reitsma, Chris, Lou.	2	0	1.000	3.86	3	3	1	0	0	0	21	17	86	10	9	2	1	1	0	8	1	13	1	0
Ricketts, Chad, Syr.	1	1	.500	3.24	15	0	0	0	11	2	16.2	15	73	7	6	3	0	0	0	7	0	19	2	0
Riedling, John, Lou.	0	1	.000	4.66	7	0	0	0	4	0	9.2	10	43	6	5	0	0	0	0	4	0	10	1	0
Rigdon, Paul, Ind.	0	1	.000	5.06	3	3	0	0	0	0	10.2	11	44	6	6	1	0	0	0	2	0	6	0	1
Riggan, Jerrod, Buf.	4	1	.800	2.38	27	0	0	0	18	3	45.1	40	178	12	12	3	2	1	2	11	2	37	3	0
Riske, David, Buf.	0	1	.000	3.72	9	0	0	0	8	3	9.2	6	40	4	4	2	0	1	4	0	17	0	0	
Rivera, Homero, Tol.*	1	1	.500	6.10	12	0	0	0	6	0	20.2	26	94	17	14	4	1	1	0	8	0	10	0	0
Roa, Joe, S./W.B.	14	6	.700	1.86	17	17	1	0	0	0	111	83	422	24	23	4	4	1	4	16	2	74	0	2
Roach, Jason, Nor.	6	6	.500	2.79	19	17	0	0	1	0	106.1	117	456	41	33	9	1	0	3	31	2	64	0	1
Robbins, Jake, Rich.	1	4	.200	4.76	47	0	0	0	17	3	56.2	59	270	36	30	3	3	2	3	43	6	37	12	0
Rodney, Fernando, Tol.	1	1	.500	0.81	20	0	0	0	11	4	22.1	13	90	4	2	1	1	3	1	9	0	25	2	2
Rodriguez, Nerio, Buf.	4	2	.667	1.82	13	10	1	0	0	0	74.1	55	286	20	15	6	2	0	1	12	0	44	0	0
Rodriguez, Ricardo, Buf.	3	1	.750	3.60	4	4	0	0	0	0	25	26	106	10	10	1	1	0	2	7	0	14	0	0
Rogers, Brian, Col.	6	6	.500	5.68	14	13	0	0	0	0	71.1	80	319	49	45	9	2	2	4	27	1	51	1	0
Rosario, Juan, Roch.	0	0	.000	11.57	2	0	0	0	0	0	2.1	4	13	3	3	0	0	0	1	1	0	1	1	0
Rose, Ted, Buf.	2	1	.667	2.93	5	5	0	0	0	0	27.2	26	116	9	9	1	0	0	0	11	0	13	3	0
Ruffin, Johnny, Lou.	0	0	.000	3.86	3	0	0	0	1	0	2.1	1	8	1	1	0	0	0	0	1	0	3	1	0
Runyan, Sean, Roch.*	0	0	.000	9.00	3	0	0	0	0	0	3	3	14	3	3	0	0	1	1	1	0	5	0	0
Sabel, Erik, Tol.	1	0	1.000	6.55	14	0	0	0	3	0	11	15	52	8	8	0	1	0	0	4	0	7	0	0
Sadler, Carl, Buf.*	1	1	.500	1.93	12	0	0	0	8	1	18.2	19	81	7	4	1	2	0	0	8	1	13	0	0
Saenz, Jason, Nor.*	1	0	1.000	9.95	5	0	0	0	0	0	6.1	10	38	7	7	2	0	0	0	10	0	3	1	0
Saipe, Mike, Rich.	4	6	.400	3.83	42	12	0	0	11	1	94	107	414	49	40	5	4	5	3	26	3	63	3	0
Sandoval, Marcos, Syr.	0	0	.000	0.00	1	0	0	0	0	0	0.2	2	4	0	0	0	0	0	0	0	0	0	0	0
Santana, Julio, Tol.	0	1	.000	2.13	7	0	0	0	4	1	12.2	12	52	5	3	1	0	1	0	3	0	12	1	0
Santiago, Jose, S./W.B.	3	2	.600	1.29	22	0	0	0	20	7	28	28	117	6	4	0	3	0	1	7	1	21	1	0
Scanlan, Bob, Col.	1	0	1.000	4.86	34	0	0	0	13	1	46.1	66	219	34	25	0	2	2	4	14	1	25	2	0
Schrenk, Steve, Char.	2	7	.222	4.06	38	3	0	0	12	0	77.2	74	327	36	35	8	3	2	3	25	3	44	1	0
Seale, Dustin, Ott.*	0	0	.000	4.50	1	0	0	0	1	0	2	4	10	1	1	0	0	0	0	1	0	1	0	0
Seay, Bobby, Dur.*	0	0	.000	6.00	10	0	0	0	2	0	15	15	64	10	10	1	1	1	2	0	14	0	2	
Seo, Jae, Nor.	6	9	.400	3.99	26	24	1	0	0	0	128.2	145	548	66	57	14	6	6	3	22	1	87	0	0
Sequea, Jacobo, Roch.	1	4	.200	5.27	5	5	0	0	0	0	27.1	26	119	16	16	7	0	2	1	11	0	16	2	0
Serrano, Elio, S./W.B.	1	3	.250	2.92	43	0	0	0	12	5	71	64	287	28	23	6	2	1	1	17	0	45	4	0
Serrano, Jim, Nor.	8	6	.571	4.01	53	0	0	0	20	3	74	88	342	40	33	3	2	4	4	31	5	76	1	0
Shepard, David, Col.	0	1	.000	7.20	1	1	0	0	0	0	5	6	23	5	4	0	0	0	0	2	0	2	0	0
Shibilo, Andy, Paw.*	0	1	.000	5.19	6	0	0	0	2	0	8.2	9	41	7	5	0	1	1	3	2	0	9	0	0
Silva, Jose, Lou.	1	2	.333	2.27	20	3	0	0	4	1	35.2	41	151	15	9	1	2	1	0	4	0	28	3	0
Simas, Bill, Char.	1	3	.250	3.60	28	0	0	0	8	2	40	46	168	22	16	4	1	2	1	8	2	22	3	1
Small, Aaron, Rich.	3	0	.000	6.39	14	4	0	0	3	0	31	48	154	27	22	2	2	4	2	14	1	19	1	0
Smith, Bud, S./W.B.*	0	1	.000	4.15	3	3	0	0	0	0	17.1	21	74	8	8	0	0	0	1	6	0	11	0	0
Smith, Dan, Ott.	5	4	.556	3.24	14	14	1	1	0	0	83.1	71	335	30	30	10	4	2	4	18	1	61	0	0
Smith, Mike, Syr.	8	4	.667	3.48	20	20	1	1	0	0	121.2	106	505	51	47	10	0	2	6	43	0	76	3	0
Smith, Roy, Buf.	5	4	.556	3.84	36	3	0	0	12	1	70.1	65	305	37	30	2	2	4	6	29	0	65	3	0
Sobkowiak, Scott, Rich.	2	0	1.000	3.18	5	1	0	0	3	0	11.1	8	49	5	4	1	1	0	0	8	0	11	1	1
Spencer, Corey, Paw.*	0	0	.000	5.81	15	0	0	0	4	0	26.1	29	122	18	17	2	2	0	15	0	23	3	0	
Spencer, Sean, Ott.*	1	0	1.000	5.14	16	0	0	0	7	0	21	24	92	13	12	1	2	2	0	8	1	15	6	0
Spiegel, Mike, Buf.*	0	0	.000	9.00	1	1	0	0	0	0	5	9	27	5	5	1	0	1	0	4	0	1	0	0
Spooneybarger, Tim, Rich.	1	0	1.000	0.90	18	0	0	0	17	11	20	13	82	2	2	1	0	1	8	0	21	4	0	
Spurgeon, Jay, Roch.	4	14	.222	5.04	29	26	1	0	1	0	154	184	685	104	92	16	6	6	3	42	0	84	2	0
Standridge, Jason, Dur.	10	9	.526	3.12	29	29	0	0	0	0	173	168	732	71	60	12	2	7	10	64	1	111	2	2
Stanford, Jason, Buf.*	3	1	.750	2.78	6	5	0	0	0	0	35.2	33	149	12	11	5	1	1	1	11	0	23	0	0
Steenstra, Kennie, Roch.	1	2	.333	4.76	6	4	0	0	1	0	22.2	31	106	15	12	2	0	1	7	0	4	0	0	
Stefanski, Mike, Lou.	0	0	.000	9.00	1	0	0	0	0	0	1	1	4	1	1	1	0	0	0	0	0	0	0	0
Stephens, John, Roch.	11	5	.688	3.03	21	21	1	0	0	0	142.2	126	571	51	48	10	4	3	8	23	0	118	1	0
Strange, Pat, Nor.	10	10	.500	3.82	29	25	2	0	1	0	165	165	699	77	70	12	6	4	7	59	2	109	3	0
Strong, Joe, Ind.	0	0	.000	4.19	15	0	0	0	10	1	19.1	23	88	9	9	2	1	2	1	8	0	7	1	0
Stull, Everett, Ind.	11	11	.500	3.87	24	24	0	0	0	0	151	149	644	72	65	13	7	3	8	49	2	119	4	1
Sylvester, Billy, Rich.	0	0	.000	3.86	7	0	0	0	3	1	9.1	10	44	4	4	1	0	0	0	5	0	5	0	0
Takeoka, Kazuhiro, Rich.	1	0	1.000	2.32	23	0	0	0	9	0	31	31	133	12	8	0	1	1	3	12	1	16	0	0
Tallet, Brian, Buf.*	2	3	.400	3.07	8	7	0	0	1	0	44	47	189	17	15	1	3	2	1	16	0	25	4	0
Telemaco, Amaury, S./W.B.	1	0	1.000	1.80	1	1	0	0	0	0	5	2	20	3	1	1	0	0	0	1	0	5	0	0
Tessmer, Jay, Col.	5	4	.556	4.37	63	0	0	0	28	4	78.1	109	353	42	38	6	2	1	3	14	4	54	2	0
Thomas, Evan, S./W.B.	10	2	.833	3.90	22	20	0	0	0	0	113	106	478	53	49	6	4	5	37	0	75	1	0	
Thompson, Mark, Lou.	1	1	.500	4.64	9	0	0	0	3	0	21.1	27	97	11	11	3	1	1	2	9	1	17	0	0
Thompson, Travis, Lou.	1	0	1.000	6.06	8	5	0	0	2	0	32.2	39	139	23	22	1	0	3	1	4	0	23	0	0
Thoms, Hank, Buf.	0	1	.000	5.40	1	1	0	0	0	0	5	7	23	5	3	0	0	1	1	0	2	1	0	
Thurman, Mike, Col.	7	3	.700	3.52	12	12	0	0	0	0	76.2	83	327	34	30	8	3	0	3	14	0	51	1	0
Towers, Josh, Roch.	0	9	.000	7.57	15	13	1	0	1	0	69	109	329	65	58	16	1	3	2	14	0	43	1	0

CLASS AAA International League

Pitcher, Team	W	L	Pct.	ERA	G	GS	CG	ShO	GF	Sv.	IP	H	TBF	R	ER	HR	SH	SF	HB	BB	IBB	SO	WP	Bk.
Traber, Billy, Buf.*	4	3	.571	3.29	9	9	0	0	0	0	54.2	58	229	22	20	3	1	4	2	12	0	33	1	1
Valdez, Santo, Syr.	0	2	.000	8.66	5	4	0	0	0	0	17.2	29	88	20	17	3	0	1	0	7	0	12	1	0
Van Hekken, Andy, Tol.*	5	0	1.000	1.82	7	7	1	1	0	0	49.1	41	194	14	10	4	1	0	2	11	0	19	2	0
Vargas, Martin, Buf.	3	2	.600	2.31	22	0	0	0	19	8	35	36	152	15	9	2	2	1	5	11	1	18	1	0
Viera, Rolando, Paw.*	0	0	.000	2.70	3	0	0	0	1	0	6.2	6	31	2	2	1	0	0	1	4	0	6	0	0
Vining, Ken, Char.*	2	5	.286	2.87	44	0	0	0	17	1	47	37	198	15	15	4	1	2	2	25	3	35	6	0
Wagner, Denny, Char.	0	1	.000	3.00	2	0	0	0	2	0	3	2	11	1	1	1	0	0	0	1	0	1	0	0
Walker, Adam, Nor.*	0	1	.000	9.00	1	1	0	0	0	0	5	6	24	6	5	1	0	0	0	3	0	3	0	0
Walker, Jamie, Tol.*	0	1	.000	1.98	10	0	0	0	4	1	13.2	7	49	3	3	2	1	0	0	3	0	9	0	0
Walker, Pete, Nor.	0	0	.000	3.00	2	2	0	0	0	0	9	9	38	3	3	1	0	0	1	6	0	6	0	0
Walker, Tyler, Nor.	10	5	.667	3.99	28	25	1	1	3	1	142	152	603	65	63	13	3	5	4	38	3	109	2	3
Wallace, Jeff, Paw.*	0	1	.000	6.57	23	0	0	0	1	0	24.2	30	117	20	18	1	1	2	1	14	0	19	5	1
Walling, Dave, Col.	2	7	.222	4.54	11	11	0	0	0	0	67.1	73	281	38	34	8	0	0	1	11	0	46	5	1
Wedel, Jeremy, S./W.B.	7	1	.875	2.69	43	0	0	0	8	1	60.1	60	258	24	18	1	2	3	4	20	1	34	1	1
Wengert, Don, Paw.	8	12	.400	4.53	29	28	1	0	0	0	169	218	749	95	85	18	5	5	10	33	1	74	2	1
Westbrook, Jake, Buf.	1	0	1.000	6.00	1	1	0	0	0	0	6	8	26	4	4	1	0	1	1	0	0	2	0	0
Wheeler, Dan, Rich.	9	6	.600	4.65	27	25	0	0	0	0	155	163	669	87	80	23	7	2	8	42	0	110	6	0
White, Matt, Buf.*	0	0	.000	4.76	7	1	0	0	2	0	17	23	81	13	9	1	0	1	2	6	0	12	0	0
Wiggins, Scott, Syr.*	2	0	1.000	2.57	12	0	0	0	0	0	14	11	60	6	4	0	0	1	2	7	0	14	3	0
Wilkins, Marc, Dur.	2	0	1.000	6.23	23	0	0	0	5	1	30.1	36	142	25	21	1	0	1	7	9	0	22	4	0
Williams, Matt, Nor.*	0	0	.000	27.00	1	0	0	0	0	0	0.1	1	4	1	1	0	0	0	0	2	0	0	0	0
Williams, Todd, Ott.	3	5	.375	3.75	46	0	0	0	39	24	48	56	208	26	20	4	2	2	2	13	3	21	2	2
Winchester, Scott, Ott.-Syr.	2	4	.333	5.94	44	0	0	0	16	2	63.2	74	285	47	42	10	3	2	1	20	4	41	0	0
Winkelsas, Joe, Rich.	1	2	.333	2.10	16	0	0	0	6	2	25.2	25	107	6	6	0	0	0	9	3	13	1	0
Woodard, Steve, S./W.B.	3	1	.750	2.16	15	1	0	0	10	5	25	17	97	6	6	1	2	0	0	6	1	13	1	0
Wright, Jamey, Ind.	1	1	.500	4.11	3	3	0	0	0	0	15.1	16	64	7	7	3	0	0	0	5	0	13	0	0
Wright, Jaret, Buf.	5	3	.625	3.88	10	10	1	0	0	0	55.2	57	244	27	24	5	1	1	4	24	0	43	4	1
Wunsch, Kelly, Char.*	1	0	1.000	2.25	10	2	0	0	0	0	12	13	49	3	3	0	0	0	0	5	0	9	0	0
Wylie, Mitch, Char.	2	3	.400	4.76	6	6	0	0	0	0	34	43	148	22	18	6	0	2	1	5	0	23	0	0
Yankosky, L.J., Rich.	0	2	.000	4.97	23	0	0	0	5	0	29	40	140	17	16	2	2	0	1	14	1	27	1	0
Yates, Tyler, Nor.	2	2	.500	1.32	24	0	0	0	20	6	34	29	142	10	5	1	1	0	0	13	1	34	0	0
Young, Tim, Paw.*	3	5	.375	3.59	57	0	0	0	25	4	72.2	56	309	34	29	5	6	0	6	37	2	63	5	0
Zambrano, Victor, Dur.	0	1	.000	1.93	10	0	0	0	6	1	14	9	55	4	3	2	0	1	4	0	15	0	0
Zamora, Pete, S./W.B.*	5	2	.714	3.48	55	0	0	0	37	15	62	63	274	25	24	2	3	0	4	29	3	32	5	0

PITCHERS WITH TWO OR MORE TEAMS

Pitcher, Team	W	L	Pct.	ERA	G	GS	CG	ShO	GF	Sv.	IP	H	TBF	R	ER	HR	SH	SF	HB	BB	IBB	SO	WP	Bk.
Atchley, Justin, Lou.*	1	0	1.000	7.27	7	0	0	0	1	0	8.2	13	41	8	7	3	0	0	3	0	7	0	0
Atchley, Justin, Roch.*	1	0	1.000	8.68	10	0	0	0	6	1	9.1	17	46	10	9	3	0	0	2	0	5	0	0
Beverlin, Jason, Buf.	10	8	.556	3.87	23	20	1	1	2	0	118.2	107	497	55	51	11	6	7	4	39	1	106	8	0
Beverlin, Jason, Tol.	3	0	1.000	1.93	4	3	0	0	0	0	18.2	17	77	5	4	0	0	1	0	6	0	13	1	0
Chantres, Carlos, Dur.	4	3	.571	3.93	10	8	0	0	0	0	52.2	54	226	27	23	6	3	4	2	18	0	29	2	2
Chantres, Carlos, Char.	4	6	.400	4.90	15	15	0	0	0	0	86.1	99	394	51	47	10	5	0	9	49	1	45	5	0
D'Amico, Jeff, S./W.B.	4	6	.400	4.13	14	14	0	0	0	0	72	77	316	46	33	9	2	1	3	25	2	45	3	2
D'Amico, Jeff, Buf.	0	1	.000	4.15	2	1	0	0	1	1	8.2	10	38	6	4	0	0	1	0	2	0	2	0	0
D'Amico, Jeff, Lou.	2	3	.400	6.69	11	6	0	0	0	0	37.2	43	165	28	28	8	0	1	2	12	2	26	1	0
Dingman, Craig, Lou.	1	0	1.000	4.15	22	0	0	0	7	0	26	20	109	12	12	3	1	0	2	13	0	26	2	0
Dingman, Craig, Col.	0	0	.000	13.50	2	0	0	0	0	0	1.1	6	12	6	2	0	0	0	1	1	2	0	0
Drew, Tim, Buf.	8	4	.667	3.27	15	15	2	2	0	0	96.1	96	402	43	35	6	3	4	23	1	43	3	0
Drew, Tim, Ott.	6	3	.667	2.87	13	13	0	0	0	0	84.2	77	348	31	27	5	7	2	3	24	2	29	0	0
Drumright, Mike, Paw.	1	1	.500	6.75	7	3	0	0	1	0	25.1	35	123	25	19	3	0	1	1	8	0	20	4	1
Drumright, Mike, Roch.	5	7	.417	3.46	23	21	0	0	1	0	125	121	536	67	48	7	2	2	4	42	0	89	7	2
Espina, Rendy, Syr.*	1	0	1.000	8.69	27	0	0	0	5	0	29	38	147	31	28	9	1	1	0	21	1	27	3	0
Espina, Rendy, Roch.*	2	2	.333	4.44	18	0	0	0	4	0	24.1	27	106	12	12	3	1	1	2	10	1	11	0	0
Feliciano, Pedro, Lou.*	1	1	.500	3.04	20	0	0	0	6	0	26.2	35	116	10	9	3	1	3	1	4	0	19	0	0
Feliciano, Pedro, Nor.*	0	0	.000	7.00	5	0	0	0	3	2	9	14	41	7	7	1	0	1	0	1	0	11	1	0
Gonzalez, Dicky, Nor.	0	0	.000	3.60	1	1	0	0	0	0	5	6	23	2	2	1	0	0	2	0	7	0	0
Gonzalez, Dicky, Ott.	8	5	.615	3.76	22	22	0	0	0	0	119.2	137	521	59	50	10	3	5	4	33	2	72	3	1
Johnson, Mark, Ind.	1	1	.500	7.97	4	4	0	0	0	0	20.1	26	95	18	18	1	1	1	1	12	0	8	0	0
Johnson, Mark, Tol.	3	0	1.000	2.31	8	2	0	0	1	0	23.1	24	95	9	6	1	1	1	0	5	1	15	1	0
Keller, Kris, Tol.	2	0	1.000	2.08	17	0	0	0	4	0	26	20	113	10	6	1	1	0	0	17	1	20	6	0
Keller, Kris, Rich.	1	0	1.000	3.60	29	0	0	0	10	2	35	26	143	16	14	4	3	1	1	13	2	20	2	0
Kim, Sun-Woo, Paw.	4	2	.667	3.18	8	8	1	0	0	0	45.1	34	186	18	16	4	0	2	3	16	0	37	1	0
Kim, Sun-Woo, Ott.	3	0	1.000	1.24	7	7	1	0	0	0	43.2	29	167	11	6	2	1	1	0	16	0	28	0	0
Lira, Felipe, Ott.	1	4	.200	5.03	21	1	0	0	5	1	39.1	45	170	22	22	1	3	7	2	13	1	22	0	0
Lira, Felipe, Lou.	3	2	.600	4.83	11	10	0	0	0	0	59.2	63	252	33	32	6	2	1	1	17	0	35	2	1
Reith, Brian, Lou.	8	9	.471	4.75	23	22	0	0	0	0	132.2	137	574	76	70	15	3	4	8	46	3	99	3	0
Reith, Brian, S./W.B.	0	4	.000	7.00	4	4	0	0	0	0	18	26	94	18	14	1	1	1	2	11	0	13	0	0
Winchester, Scott, Ott.	2	2	.500	6.00	21	0	0	0	7	1	33	33	142	24	22	5	1	1	0	11	3	22	0	0
Winchester, Scott, Syr.	2	2	.000	5.58	23	0	0	0	9	1	30.2	41	143	23	20	5	2	1	1	9	1	19	0	0

COMBINATION SHUTOUTS: **Buffalo (10)**—Beverlin-R. Smith-Sadler-DePaula, Murray-Maurer-DePaula, Phillips-DePaula, Phillips-Murray, Phillips-R. Smith, N. Rodriguez-Riggan, R. Smith-White-Elder, Tallet-Caraccioli-Riske, Traber-DePaula, Jar. Wright-Riggan. **Charlotte (7)**—Rauch-Almonte 2, J. Adkins-Vining-Simas, Chantres-Almonte, Chantres-Kieschnick, Parque-Simas, Parrish-Simas-Almonte. **Columbus (4)**—Donaldson-Tessmer-Choate, Thurman-Choate-Anderson, Thurman-Pulsipher-Knight, Thurman-Scanlan. **Durham (7)**—Brazelton-Seay-Colome, Carter-Colome-Croushore, G. Garcia-Colome-Bowers-Gardner, Standridge-Carter-Martin, Standridge-Haines-Jimenez-Croushore, Standridge-Jimenez-Gardner, Standridge-Phelps-Jimenez-Gardner. **Indianapolis (4)**—Campos-Mallette, Lorraine-Harikkala, Lorraine-Mallette, Stull-Marquez-Ebert-Mallette. **Louisville (10)**—Acevedo-MacRae-Bohanon-Neu, Acevedo-Tre. Miller-Feliciano, Acevedo-Silva, Bohanon-Tre. Miller, Etherton-MacRae-Kolb-Tre. Miller-Neu, J. Fernandez-Kolb-Almanzar, Hudson-Kolb-Almanzar, Hudson-MacRae, Hudson-Tre. Miller, Reith-Reidling-Bohanon-Neu. **Norfolk (11)**—Bacsik-Bale-Yates, Heilman-Bell, Jones-Bale-Brunette, Komiyama-J. Serrano-Yates, Komiyama-Strange, Middlebrook-Seo-J. Serrano, Middlebrook-J. Serrano-Heilman, Seo-Brunette-Corey, Seo-Lira-Corey, Strange-Cerros, Strange-Cerros-Yates. **Ottawa (8)**—Agamennone-Buddie, Billingsley-Winchester-T. Williams, Blank-Winchester, Day-Blank-Cubillan, Day-Winchester-T. Williams, Kim-Buddie, Reames-Buddie-Downs-S. Spencer, D. Smith-Day-Eischen. **Pawtucket (6)**—Brewington-

Haney-Hasselhoff, Elmore-Gomes-Young-Erdos-Hasselhoff, Hancock-Young-Hasselhoff, Kim-Hermanson-Hasselhoff, Pena-Banks, Wengert-Haney-Hasselhoff. **Richmond (8)**—Dawley-Robbins-Beasley-Winkelsas, Dawley-Spooneybarger, Hodges-Beasley, Hodges-Winkelsas, Linton-Beasley-Keller, Linton-J. Foster-Saipe, Linton-G. Lee-Beasley, Small-Wheeler-J. Foster. **Rochester (7)**—Bechler-Marshall, Drumright-Perez-Pina, Sequea-Brea-M. Garcia, Steenstra-Marshall-Mohler-Pina, Stephens-Marshall-Mohler, Stephens-Pina, Stephens-Runyan-Marshall. **Scranton/Wilkes-Barre (9)**—Roa-Woodard 2, D'Amico-Geary-E. Serrano-Zamora, D'Amico-E. Serrano, Geary-Santiago, Roa-Mercado-E. Serrano, Roa-Wedel, Roa-Wedel-Woodard, Thomas-Geary. **Syracuse (2)**—Hendrickson-Bowles, M. Smith-Kingrey-Ricketts. **Toledo (7)**—T. Adkins-Johnson-Perisho-German, T. Adkins-Sabel-Perisho-Rodney, Ahearne-Perisho-Eckenstahler, Beverlin-Rodney-Perisho-German, Kalita-Perisho-Pearson-Henriquez, Powell-Eckenstahler, Powell-Perisho-German.

NO-HIT GAMES: None.

2002 FIELDING

TEAM

Team	G	PO	A	E	TC	DP	TP	PB	Pct.
Charlotte	143	3723	1432	103	5258	135	1	16	.980
Ottawa	141	3645	1557	104	5306	147	0	8	.980
Norfolk	143	3746	1441	105	5292	117	0	7	.980
Scranton/W.-B.	144	3838	1609	118	5565	162	0	4	.979
Louisville	144	3864	1519	117	5500	132	0	19	.979
Buffalo	144	3808	1496	124	5428	142	0	13	.977
Rochester	144	3805	1394	129	5328	99	0	3	.976
Richmond	142	3725	1462	130	5317	128	0	15	.976
Durham	144	3822	1512	136	5470	178	0	14	.975
Pawtucket	144	3748	1468	133	5349	115	0	18	.975
Toledo	144	3835	1648	140	5623	144	0	15	.975
Indianapolis	143	3763	1493	144	5400	132	0	9	.973
Syracuse	144	3786	1574	152	5512	141	0	25	.972
Columbus	142	3736	1384	160	5280	111	0	10	.970

INDIVIDUAL

FIRST BASEMEN

NOTE: All caps denotes fielding-percentage leader based on 72 games for catchers, 96 for all other non-pitchers and 115 innings for pitchers. *Throws lefthanded.

Player, Team	Pct.	G	PO	A	E	TC	DP
Abbott, Kurt, Col.	1.000	1	13	1	0	14	1
Alcantara, Izzy, Ind.	.989	19	165	12	2	179	8
Andrews, Shane, Paw.	1.000	14	113	9	0	122	9
Arias, Alex, Roch.	.923	2	12	0	1	13	0
Battersby, Eric, Char.*	.994	42	337	19	2	358	31
Battle, Howard, Ott.	1.000	6	16	1	0	17	0
Baughman, Justin, Char.	.990	15	90	14	1	105	8
Betts, Todd, Paw.	.991	86	714	65	7	786	55
Bierek, Kurt, Col.	.979	36	262	20	6	288	25
Bridges, Kary, Col.	1.000	11	83	7	0	90	12
Broussard, Ben, Lou.-Buf.*	.995	54	407	28	2	437	41
Brown, Kevin, Dur.	1.000	1	10	0	0	10	1
Burnham, Gary, Syr.*	.992	125	1131	91	10	1232	111
Cabrera, Jolbert, Buf.	1.000	2	20	0	0	20	3
Casillas, Uriel, S./W.B.	1.000	1	1	0	0	1	0
Chevalier, Virgil, Nor.	1.000	3	19	0	0	19	2
Clark, Howie, Roch.	.993	16	134	8	1	143	5
Collier, Lou, Ott.	1.000	3	11	1	0	12	3
Coste, Chris, Buf.	.988	65	543	43	7	593	69
Dalesandro, Mark, Char.	1.000	13	79	4	0	83	9
Davis, Tommy, Buf.	1.000	10	101	6	0	107	11
De Los Santos, Luis, Roch.	.993	32	255	21	2	278	16
Diaz, Juan, Paw.	.986	51	401	22	6	429	42
Edwards, Mike, Lou.	.955	2	19	2	1	22	1
Evans, Lee, Char.	1.000	28	215	17	0	232	23
Fasano, Sal, Ind.	1.000	1	10	3	0	13	0
Figga, Mike, Dur.	1.000	1	6	1	0	7	0
Figueroa, Franky, Roch.	.977	49	394	36	10	440	32
Franco, Matt, Rich.	.993	32	274	21	2	297	25
Garcia, Karim, Col.*	1.000	5	26	1	0	27	1
Hernandez, Alex, Lou.*	1.000	1	11	2	0	13	1
Hessman, Mike, Rich.	.991	14	99	8	1	108	11
Hollins, Dave, S./W.B.	.990	10	96	6	1	103	9
Hoover, Paul, Dur.	.980	8	47	3	1	51	3
Hubbard, Mike, Roch.	1.000	1	6	1	0	7	0
Huckaby, Ken, Syr.	1.000	2	14	3	0	17	2
Huff, Aubrey, Dur.	1.000	25	212	19	0	231	26
Hummel, Tim, Char.	1.000	5	34	1	0	35	3
Hunter, Brian, Dur.*	1.000	15	129	7	0	136	19
Jackson, Ryan, Tol.*	1.000	13	124	7	0	131	11
Jennings, Robin, Lou.*	1.000	15	112	5	0	117	10
Johnson, Mark, Nor.*	.997	41	368	28	1	397	28
Johnson, Nick, Col.*	1.000	3	21	4	0	25	3
Jordan, Kevin, Lou.	.978	4	41	3	1	45	4

Player, Team	Pct.	G	PO	A	E	TC	DP
Knupfer, Jason, S./W.B.	.971	7	33	1	1	35	0
Laker, Tim, Buf.	.994	20	147	14	1	162	15
Lansing, Mike, Buf.	.971	4	30	3	1	34	3
Lesher, Brian, Dur.*	.990	11	88	7	1	96	10
Luke, Matt, Dur.*	1.000	24	186	7	0	193	22
McCarty, Dave, Dur.*	.992	25	220	19	2	241	25
McGuire, Ryan, Roch.*	.990	50	358	42	4	404	37
McMillon, Billy, Col.*	1.000	1	7	0	0	7	1
McNeal, Aaron, Nor.	.987	19	144	10	2	156	13
Morgan, Scott, Char.	.980	10	90	10	2	102	12
Munson, Eric, Tol.	.990	129	1159	89	12	1260	118
Nettles, Jeff, Col.	.963	3	21	5	1	27	4
Nicholson, Derek, Tol.	.900	3	9	0	1	10	3
Ortiz, Luis, Ott.	.988	34	306	17	4	327	29
Paul, Josh, Char.	1.000	4	40	5	0	45	10
Perez, Rob, Col.	1.000	1	5	1	0	6	2
Phelps, Josh, Syr.	.984	6	60	1	1	62	6
Phillips, Andy, Col.	1.000	2	14	1	0	15	1
Pressley, Josh, Dur.	1.000	13	95	9	0	104	8
Quatraro, Matt, Dur.	.984	22	175	12	3	190	31
Roberge, J.P., S./W.B.	.995	106	953	73	5	1031	120
Sandberg, Jared, Dur.	.952	2	19	1	1	21	3
Saunders, Chris, Char.	.988	37	298	18	4	320	31
Schall, Gene, S./W.B.	1.000	7	54	3	0	57	5
Seabol, Scott, Col.	.984	89	695	58	12	765	51
Sheets, Andy, Dur.	1.000	15	116	14	0	130	19
Sledge, Terrmel, Ott.*	1.000	5	35	6	0	41	6
Smith, Bobby, Ind.	.977	17	116	12	3	131	8
Snyder, Earl, Buf.	.989	40	334	22	4	360	30
Stefanski, Mike, Lou.	.958	22	123	13	6	142	5
Tamargo, John, Nor.	1.000	1	1	0	0	1	0
Tarasco, Tony, Nor.	1.000	2	6	1	0	7	0
Timmons, Ozzie, Rich.	.933	2	13	1	1	15	5
Toca, Jorge, Nor.	.985	41	288	30	5	323	32
Tracy, Andy, Nor.	.991	44	315	22	3	340	28
Unroe, Tim, Rich.	.990	46	350	41	4	395	41
Valent, Eric, S./W.B.*	.977	23	197	11	5	213	22
VITIELLO, Joe, Ott.	.996	102	901	73	4	978	98
Walbeck, Matt, Tol.	.900	1	8	1	1	10	1
Wigginton, Ty, Nor.	1.000	8	41	3	0	44	5
Wilson, Travis, Rich.	.989	45	322	23	4	349	28
Witt, Kevin, Lou.	.986	69	518	49	8	575	60
Zapp, A.J., Rich.	.986	17	134	10	2	146	10
Zuber, Jon, Ind.*	.995	125	971	72	5	1048	102

TRIPLE PLAY: Baughman.

FIRST BASEMEN WITH TWO OR MORE TEAMS

Player, Team	Pct.	G	PO	A	E	TC	DP
Broussard, Ben, Lou.*	.995	45	364	26	2	392	38
Broussard, Ben, Buf.*	1.000	9	43	2	0	45	3

SECOND BASEMEN

Player, Team	Pct.	G	PO	A	E	TC	DP
Abbott, Kurt, Col.	1.000	2	3	8	0	11	0
Andrews, Shane, Paw.	1.000	1	0	1	0	1	0
Arias, Alex, Roch.-Col.	1.000	10	4	10	0	14	1
Badeaux, Brooks, Dur.	.976	62	115	171	7	293	48
Basak, Chris, Nor.	1.000	17	29	28	0	57	5
Baughman, Justin, Char.	.966	8	26	30	2	58	9
BRIDGES, Kary, Col.	.984	100	184	238	7	429	48
Cabrera, Jolbert, Buf.	1.000	1	1	3	0	4	0
Caceres, Wilmy, Dur.	.971	10	13	20	1	34	8
Carroll, Jamey, Ott.	.993	29	57	90	1	148	24
Casillas, Uriel, S./W.B.	1.000	3	4	10	0	14	2
Castro, Juan, Lou.	.933	2	7	7	1	15	3
Castro, Ramon, Rich.	.957	20	30	58	4	92	17
Cesar, Dionys, Ind.	.977	82	153	194	8	355	43
Clark, Howie, Roch.	.957	11	21	24	2	47	3

Player, Team	Pct.	G	PO	A	E	TC	DP
Collier, Lou, Ott.	.972	15	30	40	2	72	11
Dawkins, Gookie, Lou.	1.000	1	4	2	0	6	0
DeRosa, Mark, Rich.	.947	10	16	20	2	38	4
DiSarcina, Gary, Paw.	.981	30	72	79	3	154	18
Doster, Dave, S./W.B.	.987	81	189	284	6	479	80
Easley, Damion, Tol.	.949	8	13	24	2	39	3
Forbes, P.J., S./W.B.	.993	32	50	88	1	139	20
Freel, Ryan, Dur.	.974	59	115	146	7	268	45
Frye, Jeff, Lou.	.980	54	106	142	5	253	34
Garabito, Eddy, Roch.	.962	37	64	87	6	157	18
Garcia, Jesse, Rich.	.980	43	80	118	4	202	21
Giles, Marcus, Rich.	.968	15	26	34	2	62	9
Gonzalez, Luis, Buf.	.967	6	17	12	1	30	3
Hammond, Joey, Roch.	.981	11	19	33	1	53	7
Harris, Willie, Char.	.986	82	192	220	6	418	64
Hassey, Brad, Syr.	1.000	2	5	7	0	12	2
Hernandez, Carlos, Nor.	.973	27	44	66	3	113	10
Hudson, Orlando, Syr.	.982	98	225	312	10	547	69
Hummel, Tim, Char.	.981	54	112	141	5	258	37
Jordan, Kevin, Lou.	1.000	2	7	6	0	13	1
Knupfer, Jason, S./W.B.	.981	34	51	102	3	156	21
Lansing, Mike, Buf.	.953	8	22	19	2	43	6
LaRocca, Greg, Buf.	.993	29	61	78	1	140	26
Lawrence, Joe, Syr.	.944	28	45	91	8	144	23
Lopez, Luis, Ind.-Roch.	.989	17	35	55	1	91	11
Luuloa, Keith, Ind.	1.000	5	3	1	0	4	1
Machado, Albenis, Ott.	.983	12	25	33	1	59	8
Malloy, Marty, Lou.	.965	41	86	80	6	172	19
Mateo, Henry, Ott.	.980	53	119	175	6	300	43
Maxwell, Jason, Lou.	.961	24	41	57	4	102	12
Medrano, Tony, Buf.	.980	10	24	24	1	49	3
Mitchell, Derek, Lou.	.966	6	14	14	1	29	6
Moriarty, Mike, Roch.	1.000	2	5	6	0	11	2
Morris, Warren, Paw.	.989	24	38	53	1	92	19
Nelson, Bryant, Paw.	.937	19	34	40	5	79	9
Nettles, Jeff, Col.	1.000	5	2	8	0	10	1
Nunez, Jorge, Ott.	.976	42	82	124	5	211	30
Patterson, Jarrod, Tol.	.952	47	68	109	9	186	25
Pena, Elvis, Ind.	.951	26	48	50	5	103	13
Perez, Jerson, Syr.	.985	7	26	39	1	66	12
Petersen, Chris, Rich.	.995	41	70	121	1	192	20
Phillips, Andy, Col.	.984	41	74	105	3	182	28
Phillips, Brandon, Buf.	.961	11	37	37	3	77	10
Pratt, Scott, Buf.	1.000	1	2	2	0	4	1
Roberts, Brian, Rich.	.978	71	125	180	7	312	35
Salazar, Oscar, Tol.	1.000	3	7	6	0	13	4
Sanchez, Freddy, Paw.	.945	11	17	35	3	55	7
Santos, Angel, Paw.	.967	67	147	179	11	337	37
Sasser, Rob, Ind.	1.000	4	3	5	0	8	0
Scarborough, Steve, Ind.	1.000	27	53	58	0	111	16
Scutaro, Marcos, Nor.	.978	50	100	119	5	224	30
Seabol, Scott, Col.	1.000	3	2	5	0	7	1
Selby, Bill, Buf.	.972	17	25	44	2	71	10
Sexton, Chris, Lou.	.986	26	50	90	2	142	21
Sheets, Andy, Dur.	.982	22	51	56	2	109	20
Smith, Bobby, Ind.	1.000	16	27	34	0	61	9
Soler, Ramon, Nor.	1.000	5	7	3	0	10	1
Sorensen, Zach, Buf.	.984	62	126	190	5	321	45
Tamargo, John, Nor.	1.000	14	15	18	0	33	2
Tessmer, Jay, Col.	.000	1	0	0	0	0	0
Velandia, Jorge, Nor.	.962	9	18	33	2	53	9
Velazquez, Gil, Nor.	.902	7	13	24	4	41	3
Wigginton, Ty, Nor.	1.000	32	58	86	0	144	18
Williams, Glenn, Syr.	.980	12	20	28	1	49	4
Wilson, Craig, Tol.	.978	94	204	275	11	490	73
Wilson, Travis, Col.	.976	29	51	71	3	125	25

TRIPLE PLAY: Hummel.

SECOND BASEMEN WITH TWO OR MORE TEAMS

Player, Team	Pct.	G	PO	A	E	TC	DP
Arias, Alex, Roch.	1.000	3	10	4	0	14	1
Arias, Alex, Col.	.000	1	0	0	0	0	0
Lopez, Luis, Ind.	1.000	3	5	10	0	15	2
Lopez, Luis, Roch.	.987	14	30	45	1	76	9

THIRD BASEMEN

Player, Team	Pct.	G	PO	A	E	TC	DP
Alcantara, Izzy, Ind.	1.000	1	1	0	0	1	0
Alexander, Manny, Ind.	.952	17	12	28	2	42	1
Andrews, Shane, Paw.	.951	79	54	141	10	205	10
Arias, Alex, Roch.-Col.	.952	10	4	16	1	21	2
Badeaux, Brooks, Dur.	.936	37	26	62	6	94	7
Battle, Howard, Ott.	.950	47	24	90	6	120	5
Baughman, Justin, Char.	.903	16	4	24	3	31	4
Beinbrink, Andy, Dur.	1.000	2	0	6	0	6	0
Bierek, Kurt, Col.	1.000	1	0	1	0	1	0
Cabrera, Jolbert, Buf.	1.000	2	3	3	0	6	0
Caceres, Wilmy, Dur.	.850	7	6	11	3	20	0
Carroll, Jamey, Ott.	.976	83	58	181	6	245	26
Casillas, Uriel, S./W.B.	1.000	2	1	3	0	4	1
Cesar, Dionys, Ind.	.915	40	30	88	11	129	10
Chevalier, Virgil, Nor.	1.000	1	1	2	0	3	0
Clark, Brady, Lou.	.000	1	0	0	0	0	0
Clark, Howie, Roch.	.500	1	1	0	1	2	0
Collier, Lou, Ott.	.852	17	6	40	8	54	2
Coste, Chris, Buf.	.950	16	4	34	2	40	5
Crede, Joe, Char.	.944	94	67	185	15	267	21
Davis, Tommy, Buf.	1.000	5	3	7	0	10	1
De La Rosa, Tomas, Ott.	1.000	1	0	1	0	1	0
Dellaero, Jason, Char.	.927	16	15	36	4	55	4
Forbes, P.J., S./W.B.	1.000	1	0	4	0	4	0
Franco, Matt, Rich.	1.000	6	2	8	0	10	1
Frias, Hanley, Roch.	1.000	1	0	1	0	1	0
Garabito, Eddy, Roch.	.875	5	2	5	1	8	0
Garcia, Jesse, Rich.	1.000	2	0	8	0	8	0
Giles, Marcus, Rich.	.974	13	9	28	1	38	4
Goelz, Jim, Buf.	1.000	3	1	5	0	6	1
Gubanich, Creighton, Col.	.000	1	0	0	0	0	0
Hammond, Joey, Roch.	.981	23	23	30	1	54	3
Henson, Drew, Col.	.893	125	87	204	35	326	11
Hernandez, Carlos, Nor.	1.000	9	7	13	0	20	3
HESSMAN, Mike, Rich.	.941	116	72	200	17	289	12
Hoover, Paul, Dur.	1.000	8	1	20	0	21	2
Hummel, Tim, Char.	1.000	5	6	4	0	10	1
Johnson, Russ, Dur.	.903	10	7	21	3	31	4
Jordan, Kevin, Lou.	.900	12	10	26	4	40	3
Klimek, Josh, Syr.	.932	101	86	201	21	308	24
Knupfer, Jason, S./W.B.	.962	19	12	38	2	52	2
Lansing, Mike, Buf.	.500	1	0	1	1	2	0
LaRocca, Greg, Buf.	.958	51	31	82	5	118	11
Larson, Brandon, Lou.	.912	64	38	138	17	193	11
Leon, Donny, Lou.	1.000	10	9	19	0	28	2
Leon, Jose, Roch.	.957	79	66	157	10	233	14
Lopez, Luis, Ind.	1.000	1	0	3	0	3	0
Luuloa, Keith, Ind.	.839	13	4	22	5	31	2
Malloy, Marty, Lou.	1.000	1	2	0	0	2	0
Medrano, Tony, Ott.	.833	2	1	4	1	6	1
Merloni, Lou, Paw.	1.000	3	1	6	0	7	1
Mitchell, Derek, Lou.	1.000	4	2	5	0	7	0
Moon, Brian, Ind.	1.000	1	2	2	0	4	0
Moriarty, Mike, Roch.	.950	38	35	80	6	121	5
Nelson, Bryant, Paw.	.826	9	10	9	4	23	1
Nettles, Jeff, Col.	.833	4	0	5	1	6	0
Nicholson, Derek, Tol.	.000	1	0	0	0	0	0
Patterson, Jarrod, Tol.	.938	72	34	149	12	195	14
Petersen, Chris, Rich.	1.000	4	2	5	0	7	1
Quatraro, Matt, Dur.	1.000	1	0	1	0	1	0
Reyes, Guillermo, Char.	1.000	1	0	1	0	1	1
Rios, Brian, Tol.	.951	52	27	110	7	144	10
Rodriguez, Luis, Paw.	.000	1	0	0	0	0	0
Rolls, Damian, Dur.	.800	5	7	9	4	20	2
Sandberg, Jared, Dur.	.926	21	13	37	4	54	3
Santos, Angel, Paw.	1.000	5	2	12	0	14	2
Sasser, Rob, Ind.	.927	58	30	109	11	150	7
Saunders, Chris, Char.	.981	19	11	41	1	53	2
Scarborough, Steve, Ind.	1.000	4	3	11	0	14	0
Scutaro, Marcos, Nor.	1.000	7	4	3	0	7	0
Seabol, Scott, Col.	1.000	9	7	18	0	25	2
Selby, Bill, Buf.	.870	10	5	15	3	23	3
Sexton, Chris, Lou.	.964	44	33	74	4	111	4
Sheets, Andy, Dur.	.953	51	50	92	7	149	13
Smith, Bobby, Ind.	.897	29	19	59	9	87	6
Smith, Jason, Dur.	.895	7	4	13	2	19	0
Snyder, Earl, Buf.	.911	62	45	109	15	169	11
Tamargo, John, Nor.	.885	14	4	19	3	26	1
Tessmer, Jay, Col.	.000	1	0	0	0	0	0
Tracy, Andy, Nor.	.962	71	33	117	6	156	13
Truby, Chris, Tol.	.818	3	4	5	2	11	2
Utley, Chase, S./W.B.	.918	123	88	224	28	340	17
Velandia, Jorge, Nor.	1.000	8	3	15	0	18	0
Veras, Wilton, Paw.	.930	54	34	99	10	143	11

Player, Team	Pct.	G	PO	A	E	TC	DP
Wigginton, Ty, Nor.	.913	46	39	66	10	115	5
Williams, Glenn, Syr.	.910	43	23	88	11	122	6
Wilson, Craig, Tol.	.955	24	11	53	3	67	3
Wilson, Travis, Rich.	.833	5	2	8	2	12	0
Witt, Kevin, Lou.	1.000	12	5	24	0	29	1

TRIPLE PLAY: Dellaero.

THIRD BASEMEN WITH TWO OR MORE TEAMS

Player, Team	Pct.	G	PO	A	E	TC	DP
Arias, Alex, Roch.	1.000	3	1	4	0	5	0
Arias, Alex, Col.	.938	7	3	12	1	16	2

SHORTSTOPS

Player, Team	Pct.	G	PO	A	E	TC	DP
Alexander, Manny, Ind.	.917	4	1	10	1	12	0
Almonte, Erick, Col.	.937	63	99	167	18	284	29
Arias, Alex, Roch.-Col.	.992	58	83	150	2	235	31
Badeaux, Brooks, Dur.	.000	1	0	0	0	0	0
Basak, Chris, Nor.	1.000	1	0	1	0	1	0
Baughman, Justin, Char.	.980	13	21	29	1	51	7
Betemit, Wilson, Rich.	.946	92	139	227	21	387	51
Bridges, Kary, Col.	.977	9	15	28	1	44	9
Cabrera, Jolbert, Buf.	1.000	3	11	13	0	24	1
Caceres, Wilmy, Dur.	.957	87	141	277	19	437	66
Carroll, Jamey, Ott.	1.000	3	6	14	0	20	5
Castro, Juan, Lou.	1.000	3	4	7	0	11	0
Castro, Ramon, Rich.	.985	18	20	46	1	67	5
Cesar, Dionys, Ind.	1.000	3	4	7	0	11	2
Collier, Lou, Ott.	.778	6	5	9	4	18	1
Dawkins, Gookie, Lou.	.982	46	69	151	4	224	27
De La Rosa, Tomas, Ott.	1.000	1	0	4	0	4	1
Dellaero, Jason, Char.	.952	8	13	27	2	42	4
De Los Santos, Eddy, Syr.	.969	22	33	62	3	98	13
DeRosa, Mark, Rich.	.958	6	11	12	1	24	2
Diaz, Maikell, Roch.	.947	3	8	10	1	19	2
Doster, Dave, S./W.B.	.975	27	33	84	3	120	14
Figueroa, Luis, Nor.-Ott.	.976	28	43	78	3	124	25
Forbes, P.J., S./W.B.	1.000	5	7	17	0	24	3
Frias, Hanley, Roch.	.966	24	33	53	3	89	7
Frye, Jeff, Lou.	.889	3	2	14	2	18	0
Garabito, Eddy, Roch.	.955	65	93	163	12	268	28
Garcia, Jesse, Rich.	.907	11	21	28	5	54	10
Goelz, Jim, Buf.	1.000	1	2	6	0	8	1
Hall, Bill, Ind.	.934	129	207	376	41	624	77
Hernandez, Carlos, Nor.	.976	13	12	28	1	41	4
Hummel, Tim, Char.	.980	78	113	222	7	342	56
Infante, Omar, Tol.	.959	120	191	416	26	633	91
Jimenez, D'Angelo, Char.	.966	42	65	106	6	177	17
Lansing, Mike, Buf.	.833	2	5	5	2	12	3
LaRocca, Greg, Buf.	.909	4	3	7	1	11	1
Lofton, James, Paw.	.986	77	120	232	5	357	41
Lopez, Felipe, Syr.	.934	43	80	148	16	244	42
Lopez, Luis, Ind.-Roch.	1.000	3	4	12	0	16	3
Luuloa, Keith, Ind.	.933	5	4	10	1	15	0
Machado, Albenis, Ott.	1.000	2	3	7	0	10	1
Malloy, Marty, Lou.	1.000	3	7	9	0	16	3
Martinez, Lou, Rich.	1.000	5	3	7	0	10	3
Mateo, Henry, Ott.	.941	22	33	62	6	101	12
Maxwell, Jason, Lou.	.975	52	85	152	6	243	46
Medrano, Tony, Buf.-Ott.	.977	87	131	255	9	395	47
Merloni, Lou, Paw.	1.000	3	6	7	0	13	3
Mitchell, Derek, Lou.	1.000	10	12	24	0	36	6
Moriarty, Mike, Roch.	.958	51	64	139	9	212	22
Nelson, Bryant, Paw.	.935	6	12	17	2	31	3
Nettles, Jeff, Col.	.947	9	18	18	2	38	4
Nunez, Jorge, Ott.	.922	30	29	89	10	128	14
Patchett, Gary, Lou.	.000	1	0	0	0	0	0
Perez, Jerson, Syr.	.968	46	53	131	6	190	23
Petersen, Chris, Rich.	.958	20	33	59	4	96	15
Phillips, Brandon, Ott.-Buf.	.955	54	84	173	12	269	40
Polcovich, Kevin, Col.	.000	1	0	0	1	1	0
Punto, Nick, S./W.B.	.967	115	158	401	19	578	101
Reyes, Guillermo, Char.	1.000	3	7	9	0	16	2
Rios, Brian, Tol.	.971	16	18	49	2	69	12
Salazar, Oscar, Tol.	.933	4	5	9	1	15	3
Sanchez, Freddy, Paw.	.942	37	53	108	10	171	16
Santangelo, F.P., Col.	.933	3	5	9	1	15	1
Santiago, Ramon, Tol.	.956	9	14	29	2	45	4
Santos, Angel, Paw.	.952	29	43	97	7	147	17
Scarborough, Steve, Ind.	.946	10	9	26	2	37	8
Scutaro, Marcos, Nor.	.969	25	47	79	4	130	16
Seabol, Scott, Col.	.912	14	19	33	5	57	5
Sexton, Chris, Lou.	.981	36	56	99	3	158	21
Sheets, Andy, Dur.	.983	13	17	42	1	60	10
Smith, Jason, Dur.	.940	47	69	149	14	232	43
Sorensen, Zach, Buf.	.970	55	85	170	8	263	42
Tamargo, John, Nor.	1.000	8	8	18	0	26	3
VELANDIA, Jorge, Nor.	.983	100	134	325	8	467	49
Velazquez, Gil, Nor.	1.000	4	5	9	0	14	4
Williams, Glenn, Syr.	.944	38	40	111	9	160	22
Wilson, Craig, Tol.	.000	1	0	0	0	0	0

SHORTSTOPS WITH TWO OR MORE TEAMS

Player, Team	Pct.	G	PO	A	E	TC	DP
Arias, Alex, Roch.	.833	3	1	4	1	6	0
Arias, Alex, Col.	.996	55	82	146	1	229	31
Figueroa, Luis, Nor.	1.000	2	1	3	0	4	0
Figueroa, Luis, Ott.	.975	26	42	75	3	120	25
Lopez, Luis, Ind.	1.000	2	3	9	0	12	2
Lopez, Luis, Roch.	1.000	1	1	3	0	4	1
Medrano, Tony, Buf.	.976	37	45	116	4	165	12
Medrano, Tony, Ott.	.978	50	86	139	5	230	35
Phillips, Brandon, Ott.	1.000	10	12	20	0	32	6
Phillips, Brandon, Buf.	.949	44	72	153	12	237	34

OUTFIELDERS

Player, Team	Pct.	G	PO	A	E	TC	DP
Abbott, Jeff, Paw.*	.994	85	173	2	1	176	2
Agbayani, Benny, Paw.	1.000	4	7	0	0	7	0
Alcantara, Izzy, Ind.	.974	62	109	2	3	114	0
Alexander, Chad, Tol.	.993	78	140	11	1	152	4
Allen, Chad, Roch.-Buf.	1.000	48	97	3	0	100	1
Andrews, Shane, Paw.	1.000	8	15	0	0	15	0
Aven, Bruce, Buf.-S./W.B.	1.000	36	60	5	0	65	1
Badeaux, Brooks, Dur.	.000	1	0	0	0	0	0
Baldelli, Rocco, Dur.	1.000	21	43	0	0	43	0
Barker, Glen, Paw.	.970	15	32	0	1	33	0
Bates, Fletcher, Nor.	.931	43	67	0	5	72	0
Battersby, Eric, Char.*	.963	16	24	2	1	27	0
Baughman, Justin, Char.	1.000	77	166	7	0	173	0
Bergeron, Pete, Ott.	.984	100	170	9	3	182	0
Bierek, Kurt, Col.	.833	3	5	0	1	6	0
Bigbie, Larry, Roch.*	.990	69	184	5	2	191	0
Borchard, Joe, Char.	.990	116	290	12	3	305	2
Bradley, Milton, Buf.	1.000	5	10	1	0	11	0
Bragg, Darren, Rich.	1.000	21	46	3	0	49	0
Brinkley, Darryl, Roch.	.986	106	202	6	3	211	2
Broussard, Ben, Buf.*	.959	34	69	1	3	73	0
Brown, Emil, Dur.	.963	102	223	8	9	240	1
Buford, Damon, Paw.-Char.	.970	48	94	4	3	101	1
Byrd, Marlon, S./W.B.	.975	136	298	8	8	314	1
Cabrera, Jolbert, Buf.	1.000	14	31	1	0	32	0
Calloway, Ron, Ott.*	.988	123	243	10	3	256	5
Cesar, Dionys, Ind.	.875	4	7	0	1	8	0
Chavez, Endy, Ott.*	.985	101	253	9	4	266	1
Chevalier, Virgil, Nor.	1.000	3	4	1	0	5	0
Christensen, McKay, Nor.*	.995	84	193	4	1	198	0
Christensen, Ryan, Ind.	1.000	64	186	5	0	191	3
Clark, Brady, Lou.	.955	25	60	4	3	67	0
Clark, Howie, Roch.	.973	68	140	4	4	148	1
Clemente, Edgard, Paw.-Ind.	.987	99	211	9	3	223	0
Coleman, Michael, Paw.	.977	58	121	5	3	129	0
Collier, Lou, Ott.	1.000	26	49	1	0	50	0
Crawford, Carl, Dur.*	.994	85	170	7	1	178	0
Crisp, Covelli, Buf.	1.000	4	8	0	0	8	0
Cruz, Jacob, Tol.*	1.000	6	12	0	0	12	0
Cummings, Midre, Ind.	1.000	2	6	0	0	6	0
Curry, Mike, Nor.	1.000	22	50	3	0	53	1
Darula, Bobby, Lou.	1.000	14	22	1	0	23	0
Davis, Tommy, Buf.	1.000	6	12	0	0	12	0
Dellaero, Jason, Char.	1.000	1	2	0	0	2	0
Doster, Dave, S./W.B.	.976	38	77	5	2	84	0
Dunwoody, Todd, Dur.*	.983	83	175	2	3	180	0
Edwards, Mike, Lou.	1.000	9	19	1	0	20	0
Evans, Lee, Char.	.889	3	8	0	1	9	0
Fitzgerald, Jason, Buf.	.909	4	10	0	1	11	0
Fleming, Ryan, Syr.*	.976	13	40	0	1	41	0
Forbes, P.J., S./W.B.	.976	50	73	10	2	85	1
Francia, Dave, S./W.B.*	.984	29	57	3	1	61	1
Freel, Ryan, Dur.	1.000	52	89	8	0	97	0

Player, Team	Pct.	G	PO	A	E	TC	DP
Frye, Jeff, Lou.	1.000	31	46	3	0	49	0
Garabito, Eddy, Roch.	1.000	2	3	0	0	3	0
Garcia, Jesse, Rich.	1.000	2	3	0	0	3	0
Garcia, Karim, Col.-Buf.*	.988	69	160	3	2	165	2
Garcia, Luis, Roch.	.991	77	206	7	2	215	2
Gerut, Jody, Buf.*	.993	53	137	3	1	141	1
Gonzalez, Raul, Lou.	.970	109	250	10	8	268	1
Guillen, Jose, Lou.	1.000	8	15	1	0	16	0
Harris, Willie, Char.	1.000	7	18	0	0	18	0
Hernandez, Alex, Lou.*	.923	8	12	0	1	13	0
Hernandez, Carlos, Nor.	.000	1	0	0	0	0	0
Hollins, Damon, Rich.*	.988	125	308	8	4	320	0
Hoover, Paul, Dur.	1.000	5	9	1	0	10	0
Inglin, Jeff, Char.	.982	31	52	4	1	57	0
Ingram, Darron, Char.	1.000	5	11	1	0	12	1
Jackson, Ryan, Tol.*	.986	62	131	5	2	138	1
Jennings, Robin, Lou.*	.957	76	126	8	6	140	3
Johnson, Mark, Nor.*	1.000	35	64	1	0	65	0
Johnson, Reed, Lou.	.991	44	111	3	1	115	1
Jones, Chris, Ind.	.980	74	144	2	3	149	2
Kearns, Austin, Lou.	1.000	1	1	0	0	1	0
Kieschnick, Brooks, Char.	1.000	1	1	0	0	1	0
Knight, Brandon, Col.	.000	1	0	0	0	0	0
Knupfer, Jason, S./W.B.	1.000	9	17	2	0	19	1
Langaigne, Selwyn, Syr.*	.968	71	176	7	6	189	1
Lansing, Mike, Buf.	.917	8	11	0	1	12	0
LaRocca, Greg, Buf.	.880	13	21	1	3	25	0
Larson, Brandon, Lou.	1.000	6	11	1	0	12	0
Latham, Chris, Nor.	.974	107	249	10	7	266	1
Leach, Jalal, Col.*	.970	56	96	0	3	99	0
Lennon, Pat, Dur.	1.000	4	10	0	0	10	0
Leon, Donny, Lou.	1.000	4	7	1	0	8	0
Lesher, Brian, Syr.*	.955	34	62	2	3	67	0
Lindsey, Rodney, Tol.	1.000	10	13	0	0	13	0
Little, Mark, Nor.	1.000	1	4	0	0	4	0
Lofton, James, Paw.	1.000	4	10	0	0	10	0
Lombard, George, Rich.	1.000	10	17	0	0	17	0
Magruder, Chris, Buf.	.991	49	112	0	1	113	0
Mateo, Ruben, Lou.	.967	49	86	1	3	90	1
McCarty, Dave, Dur.*	1.000	3	5	0	0	5	0
McDonald, Darnell, Roch.	.983	90	277	6	5	288	1
McGuire, Ryan, Roch.*	1.000	23	48	0	0	48	0
McKinley, Dan, Ott.	1.000	7	9	0	0	9	0
McMillon, Billy, Col.*	.993	75	131	2	1	134	1
Medrano, Tony, Buf.-Ott.	1.000	28	65	5	0	70	1
Merloni, Lou, Paw.	1.000	1	2	0	0	2	0
Michaels, Jason, S./W.B.	1.000	9	15	1	0	16	0
Monroe, Craig, Tol.	.983	79	161	8	3	172	0
Morgan, Scott, Char.	.958	68	157	1	7	165	0
Morris, Warren, Paw.	1.000	11	17	0	0	17	0
Mottola, Chad, Syr.	.946	94	202	8	12	222	0
Mouton, James, Ott.	1.000	16	31	1	0	32	0
Nelson, Bryant, Paw.	.968	25	59	2	2	63	0
Nicholson, Derek, Tol.	.978	45	88	3	2	93	0
Nunez, Jorge, Ott.	1.000	2	2	0	0	2	0
O'Leary, Troy, Ott.*	.974	20	37	0	1	38	0
Ortiz, Luis, Ott.	1.000	25	38	0	0	38	0
Paul, Josh, Char.	1.000	1	1	0	0	1	0
Perez, Rob, Ind.-Col.	.969	112	215	6	7	228	0
Perez, Timo, Nor.*	1.000	5	6	0	0	6	0
Porter, Bo, Rich.	.972	107	235	7	7	249	1
Pratt, Scott, Buf.	1.000	3	7	0	0	7	0
Ramirez, Manny, Paw.	1.000	4	3	0	0	3	0
Rios, Brian, Tol.	1.000	3	6	0	0	6	0
Rivera, Juan, Col.	.955	64	113	14	6	133	2
Rodriguez, Luis, Paw.	1.000	4	1	0	0	1	0
Rolls, Damian, Dur.	.986	57	129	7	2	138	4
Rushford, Jim, Ind.*	.988	91	161	6	2	169	1
Ryan, Rob, Paw.*	1.000	62	145	1	0	146	0
Salzano, Jerry, Paw.	1.000	2	3	0	0	3	0
Sanders, Anthony, Lou.-Char.	.988	83	161	8	2	171	1
Scutaro, Marcos, Nor.	.957	11	21	1	1	23	0
Seabol, Scott, Col.	1.000	2	5	0	0	5	0
Selby, Bill, Buf.	1.000	18	37	1	0	38	0
Sergio, Tom, Paw.	1.000	1	2	0	0	2	0
Sexton, Chris, Lou.	1.000	1	1	0	0	1	0
Sledge, Terrmel, Ott.*	.935	16	29	0	2	31	0
Smith, Bobby, Ind.	.967	16	27	2	1	30	0
Smothers, Stewart, Rich.	1.000	6	5	0	0	5	0
Snyder, Earl, Buf.	1.000	5	9	0	0	9	0
Stenson, Dernell, Paw.*	.957	101	191	10	9	210	0

Player, Team	Pct.	G	PO	A	E	TC	DP
Stratton, Rob, Nor.	.988	70	155	4	2	161	0
Swann, Pedro, Syr.	.994	78	151	6	1	158	0
Tarasco, Tony, Nor.	1.000	36	62	3	0	65	1
Thames, Marcus, Col.	.983	104	290	7	5	302	1
Thompson, Andy, Dur.	.948	30	50	5	3	58	2
Thompson, Ryan, Ind.	.984	66	118	2	2	122	1
TIMMONS, Ozzie, Rich.	.995	109	185	5	1	191	3
Toca, Jorge, Nor.	1.000	11	21	1	0	22	0
Torres, Andres, Tol.	.967	115	289	3	10	302	0
Tyner, Jason, Dur.*	.994	85	154	10	1	165	4
Unroe, Tim, Rich.	1.000	3	3	0	0	3	0
Valent, Eric, S./W.B.*	.982	118	260	14	5	279	4
Wakeland, Chris, Tol.*	.964	48	99	7	4	110	1
Ware, Jeremy, Buf.	1.000	34	55	3	0	58	0
Werth, Jayson, Syr.	.981	102	207	4	4	215	0
Widger, Chris, Col.	1.000	1	1	0	0	1	0
Wigginton, Ty, Nor.	.963	20	26	0	1	27	0
Williams, Gerald, Lou.	.992	48	122	1	1	124	1
Wilson, Travis, Rich.	.991	57	110	1	1	112	0
Witt, Kevin, Lou.	.985	39	60	6	1	67	0
Woods, Ken, S./W.B.	.980	47	94	4	2	100	0
Zywica, Mike, Char.	.978	26	41	3	1	45	0

OUTFIELDERS WITH TWO OR MORE TEAMS

Player, Team	Pct.	G	PO	A	E	TC	DP
Allen, Chad, Roch.	1.000	3	5	0	0	5	0
Allen, Chad, Buf.	1.000	45	92	3	0	95	0
Aven, Bruce, Buf.	1.000	28	48	5	0	53	1
Aven, Bruce, S./W.B.	1.000	8	12	0	0	12	0
Buford, Damon, Paw.	.967	10	28	1	1	30	1
Buford, Damon, Char.	.972	38	66	3	2	71	0
Clemente, Edgard, Paw.	1.000	60	124	7	0	131	0
Clemente, Edgard, Ind.	.967	39	87	2	3	92	0
Garcia, Karim, Col.*	.984	51	122	3	2	127	2
Garcia, Karim, Buf.*	1.000	18	38	0	0	38	0
Medrano, Tony, Buf.	1.000	26	62	3	0	65	1
Medrano, Tony, Ott.	1.000	2	3	2	0	5	0
Perez, Rob, Ind.	.967	34	58	1	2	61	0
Perez, Rob, Col.	.970	78	157	5	5	167	0
Sanders, Anthony, Lou.	1.000	33	77	2	0	79	0
Sanders, Anthony, Char.	.978	50	84	6	2	92	1

CATCHERS

Player, Team	Pct.	G	PO	A	E	TC	DP	PB
Acevas, Jon, Char.	1.000	1	5	0	0	5	0	0
Ackerman, Scott, Ott.	1.000	12	53	5	0	58	0	0
Alomar, Sandy, Char.	1.000	3	15	0	0	15	0	0
Andreopoulos, Alex, Ott.	1.000	6	31	2	0	33	0	0
Bard, Josh, Buf.	.984	93	609	60	11	680	2	11
Boscan, Jean, Rich.	.955	2	21	0	1	22	0	0
Brown, Kevin, Dur.-Paw.	.991	70	413	37	4	454	1	1
Burkhart, Lance, Ind.	1.000	26	138	8	0	146	1	1
Casanova, Raul, Ind.	1.000	11	44	5	0	49	0	0
Cash, Kevin, Syr.	.989	57	315	37	4	356	6	6
Castillo, Alberto, Col.	.984	30	230	15	4	249	2	1
Chevalier, Virgil, Nor.	1.000	8	50	4	0	54	0	2
Coste, Chris, Buf.	.992	20	118	9	1	128	3	1
Dalesandro, Mark, Char.	.978	33	211	8	5	224	0	4
Davis, Tommy, Buf.	1.000	2	12	0	0	12	0	0
Depastino, Joe, Nor.	.988	57	376	32	5	413	4	3
ESTRADA, Johnny, S./W.B.	.995	112	745	46	4	795	5	3
Evans, Lee, Char.	.984	39	229	18	4	251	0	6
Fasano, Sal, Ind.-Dur.	.983	56	374	36	7	417	5	1
Figga, Mike, Dur.	.986	9	66	7	1	74	0	1
Gubanich, Creighton, Col.	.972	34	192	15	6	213	1	3
Haad, Yamid, Dur.	.982	19	149	14	3	166	4	2
Hall, Toby, Dur.	.993	18	130	7	1	138	0	3
Hernandez, Michel, Col.	.966	37	208	16	8	232	1	3
Hoover, Paul, Dur.	.989	52	313	39	4	356	4	3
Hubbard, Trenidad, Roch.	.989	57	349	25	4	378	1	1
Huckaby, Ken, Syr.	.979	19	134	6	3	143	2	3
Inge, Brandon, Tol.	.978	21	157	19	4	180	1	2
Jensen, Marcus, Ind.	.986	67	389	21	6	416	2	3
Knorr, Randy, Ott.	.983	97	504	28	9	541	4	5
LaForest, Pete, Dur.	.950	13	91	5	5	101	1	5
Laker, Tim, Buf.	.991	31	198	16	2	216	1	1
Levis, Jesse, Lou.	.998	59	395	29	1	425	2	4
Lomasney, Steve, Paw.	.966	12	57	0	2	59	0	3
Lopez, Rafael, Rich.	1.000	7	41	2	0	43	0	3
Lunar, Fernando, Roch.	.982	42	246	32	5	283	3	1

Player, Team	Pct.	G	PO	A	E	TC	DP	PB
Martinez, Sandy, Ott.	.996	34	219	14	1	234	1	3
Meran, Jorge, Tol.	.968	3	29	1	1	31	0	1
Miller, Corky, Lou.	.993	41	279	26	2	307	2	8
Molina, Izzy, Roch.	.978	40	243	19	6	268	0	0
Moon, Brian, Ind.	.995	37	185	23	1	209	3	4
Myers, Kenton, Buf.	1.000	1	3	0	0	3	0	0
Nettles, Jeff, Col.	1.000	1	2	0	0	2	0	0
Norris, Dax, Rich.	.987	76	498	45	7	550	4	5
Paul, Josh, Char.	.993	61	377	25	3	405	4	3
Phelps, Josh, Syr.	.986	34	197	8	3	208	1	7
Phillips, Jason, Nor.	.993	82	552	31	4	587	6	2
Quatraro, Matt, Dur.	.913	6	21	0	2	23	0	0
Quintero, Humberto, Char.	.964	15	66	15	3	84	1	3
Quiroz, Guillermo, Syr.	.956	9	43	0	2	45	0	2
Rivera, Mike, Tol.	.993	67	381	35	3	419	3	6
Rodriguez, Luis, Paw.	.987	77	408	38	6	452	4	14
St. Pierre, Maxim, Tol.	1.000	1	6	0	0	6	0	0
Salazar, Jeremy, S./W.B.	.979	35	179	9	4	192	2	1
Salinas, Trey, Roch.	.982	12	48	6	1	55	0	1
Stefanski, Mike, Lou.	.996	36	205	23	1	229	2	6
Stinnett, Kelly, Lou.	.988	23	160	11	2	173	1	1
Torrealba, Steve, Rich.	.979	61	393	33	9	435	0	7
Umbria, Jose, Syr.	1.000	5	19	0	0	19	0	1
Valera, Yohanny, Tol.	.988	43	218	24	3	245	2	5
Walbeck, Matt, Tol.	.986	20	134	6	2	142	2	1
Werth, Jayson, Syr.	.991	23	105	4	1	110	1	6
Widger, Chris, Col.	.990	55	367	19	4	390	1	3

TRIPLE PLAY: Dalesandro.

CATCHERS WITH TWO OR MORE TEAMS

Player, Team	Pct.	G	PO	A	E	TC	DP	PB
Brown, Kevin, Dur.	1.000	3	18	2	0	20	0	0
Brown, Kevin, Paw.	.991	67	395	35	4	434	1	1
Fasano, Sal, Ind.	.983	25	150	19	3	172	2	1
Fasano, Sal, Dur.	.984	31	224	17	4	245	3	0

PITCHERS

Player, Team	Pct.	G	PO	A	E	TC	DP
Abbott, David, Syr.	1.000	2	1	0	0	1	0
Acevedo, Jose, Lou.	1.000	23	5	14	0	19	1
Adkins, Jon, Char.	1.000	8	4	7	0	11	1
Adkins, Tim, Tol.*	1.000	31	3	5	0	8	0
Agamennone, Brandon, Ott.	1.000	27	2	9	0	11	1
Agosto, Stevenson, Dur.*	.923	15	1	11	1	13	3
Ahearne, Pat, Tol.	1.000	12	7	20	0	27	2
Allen, Wyatt, Char.	1.000	1	0	1	0	1	0
Almanzar, Carlos, Lou.	1.000	21	1	1	0	2	1
Almonte, Ed, Char.	1.000	50	4	7	0	11	0
Anderson, Jason, Col.	1.000	26	2	3	0	5	0
Andrews, Shane, Paw.	.000	1	0	0	0	0	0
Atchley, Justin, Lou.-Roch.*	1.000	17	1	5	0	6	0
Ayala, Luis, Ott.	1.000	6	1	5	0	6	0
Bacsik, Mike, Nor.*	.882	25	7	23	4	34	3
Baker, Chris, Syr.	.875	18	4	17	3	24	0
Bale, John, Nor.*	1.000	12	1	5	0	6	0
Banks, Willie, Paw.	1.000	6	1	3	0	4	0
Barcelo, Lorenzo, Char.	1.000	2	1	1	0	2	0
Bauer, Rick, Roch.	1.000	1	1	1	0	2	0
Beal, Andy, Col.*	1.000	8	1	9	0	10	0
Beasley, Ray, Rich.*	1.000	64	9	10	0	19	1
Bechler, Steve, Roch.	1.000	24	12	13	0	25	1
Beech, Matt, Col.*	.824	16	2	12	3	17	0
Bell, Heath, Nor.	1.000	22	1	4	0	5	0
Bernero, Adam, Tol.	1.000	9	1	8	0	9	0
Beverlin, Jason, Buf.-Tol.	.944	27	7	10	1	18	0
Biddle, Rocky, Char.	.000	2	0	0	0	0	0
Bierek, Kurt, Col.	1.000	1	0	2	0	2	0
Billingsley, Brent, Ott.*	.929	28	4	9	1	14	0
BLANK, Matt, Ott.*	1.000	31	5	30	0	35	0
Blevins, Jeremy, Col.	.500	17	0	2	2	4	0
Bohanon, Brian, Lou.*	1.000	14	3	9	0	12	1
Bowers, Cedrick, Dur.*	.778	47	3	4	2	9	0
Bowles, Brian, Syr.	1.000	59	4	7	0	11	1
Boyd, Jason, Paw.	1.000	9	1	4	0	5	0
Bradley, Ryan, Col.	.000	1	0	0	0	0	0
Brazelton, Dewon, Dur.	.000	1	0	0	0	0	0
Brea, Lesli, Roch.	.815	60	6	16	5	27	0
Brewington, Jamie, Paw.	1.000	18	6	9	0	15	1
Bridges, Kary, Col.	1.000	1	0	1	0	1	0
Brownson, Mark, Paw.	.000	3	0	0	1	1	0

Player, Team	Pct.	G	PO	A	E	TC	DP
Brunette, Justin, Nor.*	.947	45	6	12	1	19	2
Buddie, Mike, Ott.	1.000	29	2	4	0	6	0
Burkett, John, Paw.	.000	1	0	0	0	0	0
Cammack, Eric, Nor.	1.000	11	2	2	0	4	0
Campos, Francisco, Ind.	1.000	4	0	2	0	2	0
Caraccioli, Lance, Buf.*	.750	8	0	3	1	4	1
Carpenter, Chris, Syr.	.000	1	0	0	0	0	0
Carter, Lance, Dur.	.889	33	15	9	3	27	2
Casey, Joe, Syr.	1.000	18	5	3	0	8	0
Cassidy, Scott, Syr.	1.000	3	2	2	0	4	0
Castellanos, Hugo, Syr.	1.000	5	1	1	0	2	0
Cedeno, Blas, S./W.B.	.000	3	0	0	0	0	0
Cerda, Jaime, Nor.*	1.000	12	3	1	0	4	0
Cerros, Juan, Nor.	1.000	25	2	6	0	8	0
Chantres, Carlos, Dur.-Char.	.838	25	7	24	6	37	1
Childers, Jason, Ind.	.938	28	7	8	1	16	2
Childers, Matt, Ind.	1.000	3	0	1	0	1	0
Cho, Jin Ho, Nor.	.857	20	5	7	2	14	1
Choate, Randy, Col.*	.944	31	4	13	1	18	0
Chulk, Vinny, Syr.	.000	2	0	0	0	0	0
Claussen, Brandon, Col.*	.955	15	1	20	1	22	0
Coco, Pasqual, Syr.	.893	30	9	16	3	28	1
Cole, Joey, Nor.	.000	1	0	0	0	0	0
Colome, Jesus, Dur.	1.000	18	1	1	0	2	0
Comolli, Mark, Syr.	.000	1	0	0	0	0	0
Cooper, Brian, Syr.	.889	27	8	16	3	27	4
Cordova, Jorge, Lou.	.000	2	0	0	0	0	0
Corey, Mark, Nor.	1.000	25	0	2	0	2	0
Cornejo, Nate, Tol.	.947	21	9	27	2	38	1
Coste, Chris, Buf.	1.000	2	1	0	0	1	0
Crabtree, Robbie, Syr.	1.000	32	7	10	0	17	0
Crawford, Paxton, Paw.	1.000	9	6	6	0	12	0
Croushore, Rich, Dur.	1.000	36	3	7	0	10	1
Crowell, Jim, S./W.B.*	1.000	4	2	4	0	6	1
Crumpton, Chuck, Ott.	.857	19	1	5	1	7	0
Cubillan, Darwin, Ott.	1.000	29	3	5	0	8	1
Cumberland, Chris, Syr.*	1.000	28	1	6	0	7	0
D'Amico, Jeff, S./W.B.-Buf.-Lou.	.900	27	10	8	2	20	3
Darnell, Paul, Lou.*	1.000	12	0	1	0	1	0
Davis, Kane, Nor.	.000	1	0	0	0	0	0
Davis, Lance, Lou.*	.929	11	1	12	1	14	0
Dawley, Joey, Rich.	.971	24	14	20	1	35	0
Day, Zach, Ott.	1.000	17	4	13	0	17	0
Dellaero, Jason, Char.	.000	1	0	0	0	0	0
De Los Santos, Luis, Dur.	1.000	24	10	19	0	29	4
De Los Santos, Valerio, Ind.*	.000	2	0	0	0	0	0
De Paula, Sean, Buf.	1.000	34	2	8	0	10	0
Dickson, Jason, Dur.	1.000	9	1	3	0	4	1
Dillinger, John, Col.	.857	9	0	6	1	7	0
Dingman, Craig, Lou.-Col.	1.000	24	0	0	0	0	0
Donaldson, Bo, Col.	.846	29	5	6	2	13	0
Douglass, Sean, Roch.	.875	14	6	8	2	16	0
Downs, Scott, Ott.*	1.000	17	0	3	0	3	0
Drese, Ryan, Buf.	1.000	3	3	0	0	3	0
Drew, Tim, Buf.-Ott.	.978	28	18	27	1	46	3
Driskill, Travis, Roch.	1.000	4	2	1	0	3	0
Drumright, Mike, Paw.-Roch.	.933	30	10	18	2	30	0
Dubose, Eric, Roch.*	.000	1	0	0	0	0	0
Durocher, Jayson, Ind.	1.000	20	1	3	0	4	0
Eason, Clay, Char.	1.000	11	2	0	0	2	0
Ebert, Derrin, Ind.*	1.000	50	4	15	0	19	2
Eckenstahler, Eric, Ind.*	.929	52	6	7	1	14	0
Edwards, Mike, Lou.	.000	1	0	0	0	0	0
Eischen, Joey, Ott.*	1.000	11	1	2	0	3	0
Elder, Dave, Buf.	.800	22	3	1	1	5	0
Elmore, Chris, Paw.*	1.000	7	2	4	0	6	0
Erdos, Todd, Paw.	.875	52	8	6	2	16	1
Espina, Rendy, Syr.-Roch.*	1.000	45	3	4	0	7	1
Etherton, Seth, Lou.	.000	5	0	0	0	0	0
Evans, Keith, Ott.	.909	16	4	6	1	11	0
Farmer, Tom, Tol.	1.000	1	2	0	0	2	0
Feliciano, Pedro, Lou.-Nor.*	1.000	25	6	5	0	11	1
Fernandez, Jared, Lou.	.974	26	12	26	1	39	3
Fernandez, Osvaldo, Ott.	1.000	18	3	9	0	12	0
Field, Nathan, Col.	1.000	21	4	3	0	7	0
Figueroa, Nelson, Ind.	1.000	6	5	5	0	10	0
File, Bob, Syr.	1.000	33	3	6	0	9	1
Fortunato, Bartolome, Dur.	1.000	2	0	1	0	1	0
Fossum, Casey, Paw.*	.833	5	0	5	1	6	1
Foster, John, Rich.*	.933	55	1	13	1	15	0
Foster, Kevin, Lou.	1.000	3	0	1	0	1	0

Player, Team	Pct.	G	PO	A	E	TC	DP
Foster, Kris, Roch.	1.000	14	2	5	0	7	0
Freeman, Kai, Char.	.000	1	0	0	0	0	0
Gandarillas, Gus, Ind.	.000	2	0	0	1	1	0
Garcia, Gerardo, Dur.	.933	15	3	11	1	15	0
Garcia, Jose, Ind.	1.000	17	7	12	0	19	1
Garcia, Mike, Roch.	1.000	9	1	0	0	1	0
Gardner, Lee, Dur.	1.000	45	8	5	0	13	0
Gassner, Dave, Syr.*	1.000	1	1	0	0	1	0
Geary, Geoff, S./W.B.	1.000	38	6	9	0	15	0
German, Frank, Tol.	1.000	23	1	2	0	3	0
Gil, Dave, Lou.	1.000	9	0	1	0	1	0
Ginter, Matt, Char.	1.000	13	2	4	0	6	0
Giron, Roberto, Ind.	.000	15	0	0	1	1	0
Glynn, Ryan, Ind.	1.000	12	4	9	0	13	1
Gomes, Wayne, Paw.	.850	42	7	10	3	20	0
Gonzalez, Dicky, Nor.-Ott.	.930	23	18	22	3	43	1
Graman, Alex, Col.*	1.000	20	3	16	0	19	2
Greisinger, Seth, Tol.	1.000	3	2	4	0	6	0
Gryboski, Kevin, Rich.	1.000	7	0	2	0	2	0
Haines, Talley, Dur.	.952	48	6	14	1	21	0
Hamann, Rob, Syr.	1.000	7	1	0	0	1	0
Hamilton, Joey, Lou.	1.000	3	0	1	0	1	0
Hancock, Josh, Paw.	1.000	8	3	1	0	4	0
Haney, Chris, Paw.*	1.000	25	2	3	0	5	0
Harikkala, Tim, Ind.	1.000	31	6	28	0	34	2
Harper, Travis, Dur.	1.000	4	0	1	0	1	0
Hasselhoff, Derek, Paw.	1.000	39	5	6	0	11	0
Hazlett, Andy, Paw.*	1.000	5	2	1	0	3	0
Hearns, Shane, Paw.	.000	11	0	0	0	0	0
Hebson, Bryan, Ott.	1.000	5	1	1	0	2	0
Heilman, Aaron, Nor.	1.000	10	2	9	0	11	0
Hendrickson, Mark, Syr.*	1.000	19	0	18	0	18	1
Henriquez, Oscar, Tol.	1.000	33	2	1	0	3	0
Hermanson, Dustin, Paw.	1.000	5	1	2	0	3	0
Hernandez, Adrian, Col.	.913	20	8	13	2	23	1
Hernandez, Orlando, Col.	.000	1	0	0	0	0	0
Herrera, Alex, Buf.*	.000	5	0	0	0	0	0
Hiles, Cary, S./W.B.	1.000	26	3	6	0	9	0
Hitchcock, Sterling, Col.*	1.000	2	0	1	0	1	0
Hodges, Trey, Rich.	.947	28	14	22	2	38	1
Hudson, Luke, Lou.	.909	30	6	14	2	22	2
Jacquez, Tom, Char.*	1.000	14	2	10	0	12	1
James, Delvin, Dur.	1.000	7	0	1	0	1	1
Jean, Domingo, Lou.	1.000	19	3	4	0	7	0
Jennings, Robin, Lou.*	1.000	1	0	1	0	1	0
Jimenez, Jason, Dur.*	1.000	44	2	6	0	8	0
Jodie, Brett, Col.	1.000	6	0	5	0	5	0
Johnson, Mark, Ind.-Tol.	1.000	12	2	6	0	8	0
Jones, Bobby M., Nor.*	.500	13	1	2	3	6	0
Joseph, Jake, Nor.	.000	1	0	0	0	0	0
Junge, Eric, S./W.B.	.938	29	13	17	2	32	1
Kalita, Tim, Tol.*	.880	15	4	18	3	25	0
Kane, Kyle, Char.	1.000	4	0	1	0	1	0
Keller, Kris, Tol.-Rich.	.933	46	2	12	1	15	0
Kieschnick, Brooks, Char.	1.000	25	0	6	0	6	1
Kim, Sun-Woo, Paw.-Ott.	.909	15	1	9	1	11	1
King, Ray, Ind.*	1.000	1	0	2	0	2	0
Kingrey, Jarrod, Syr.	1.000	26	2	5	0	7	0
Knight, Brandon, Col.	1.000	36	9	12	0	21	3
Kohlmeier, Ryan, Char.	1.000	38	1	7	0	8	1
Kolb, Brandon, Lou.	.800	41	1	3	1	5	0
Komiyama, Saturo, Nor.	.875	17	3	4	1	8	1
Krawczyk, Jack, Ind.	.500	2	0	1	1	2	0
Kusiewicz, Mike, Paw.*	.714	10	1	4	2	7	0
Lantigua, Delvis, Char.	1.000	15	2	9	0	11	0
Larson, Ryan, Buf.	1.000	1	1	0	0	1	0
Lee, Cliff, Buf.*	1.000	8	1	3	0	4	0
Lee, Corey, Char.*	.967	38	8	21	1	30	1
Lee, Garrett, Rich.	1.000	5	0	2	0	2	0
Leskanic, Curt, Ind.	1.000	5	1	1	0	2	0
Lewis, Derrick, Rich.	.889	18	2	14	2	18	0
Linton, Doug, Rich.	.943	28	11	22	2	35	2
Lira, Felipe, Nor.-Lou.	1.000	32	7	9	0	16	1
Loaiza, Esteban, Dur.	1.000	1	0	1	0	1	0
Looney, Brian, Roch.*	1.000	9	2	3	0	5	0
Lorraine, Andrew, Ind.*	.970	25	7	25	1	33	0
Loux, Shane, Tol.	.927	26	11	27	3	41	3
Lovingier, Kevin, Col.*	1.000	21	1	1	0	2	0
Lyon, Brandon, Syr.	.900	14	6	12	2	20	0
MacRae, Scott, Lou.	.882	49	6	9	2	17	2
Magrane, Jim, Dur.	.967	20	10	19	1	30	5
Mallette, Brian, Ind.	.800	45	1	7	2	10	0
Maness, Nick, Nor.	1.000	3	2	1	0	3	0
Manon, Julio, Ott.	.950	28	9	10	1	20	0
Maroth, Mike, Tol.*	1.000	11	4	16	0	20	3
Marquez, Rob, Ind.	.933	47	4	10	1	15	1
Marquis, Jason, Rich.	1.000	1	0	2	0	2	0
Marshall, Lee, Roch.	.875	59	4	10	2	16	0
Martin, Tom, Dur.*	.000	4	0	0	0	0	0
Matheny, Brandon, Buf.*	1.000	1	1	0	0	1	0
Maurer, Dave, Buf.*	.941	36	5	11	1	17	0
McAvoy, Jeff, Ott.	1.000	1	1	1	0	2	1
McClellan, Matt, Syr.	1.000	12	1	3	0	4	1
McConnell, Sam, S./W.B.*	.800	7	1	7	2	10	0
McDill, Allen, Roch.*	1.000	15	0	2	0	2	0
McLeary, Marty, Paw.	1.000	18	1	4	0	5	0
McNichol, Brian, Col.*	.750	13	0	3	1	4	0
McWhirter, Kris, Char.	1.000	2	0	1	0	1	0
Mendoza, Geronimo, Char.	1.000	11	4	2	0	6	0
Mercado, Hector, S./W.B.*	1.000	26	1	1	0	2	0
Mercedes, Jose, Buf.	1.000	5	6	2	0	8	1
Meyer, Jake, Char.	1.000	4	0	1	0	1	0
Michalak, Chris, Paw.*	1.000	17	4	18	0	22	0
Middlebrook, Jason, Nor.	1.000	5	2	0	0	2	0
Miller, Justin, Syr.	1.000	8	4	6	0	10	0
Miller, Travis, Buf.*	1.000	7	0	4	0	4	0
Miller, Trever, Lou.*	.889	65	4	12	2	18	0
Moehler, Brian, Tol.	1.000	4	0	3	0	3	0
Mohler, Mike, Roch.*	1.000	34	3	10	0	13	2
Moreno, Juan, Paw.*	.000	3	0	0	1	1	0
Munoz, Bobby, Nor.	.000	3	0	0	0	0	0
Murray, Heath, Buf.*	1.000	21	0	9	0	9	1
Myers, Brett, S./W.B.	.952	19	5	15	1	21	2
Nagy, Charles, Buf.	.923	5	5	7	1	13	0
Nance, Shane, Ind.*	1.000	9	1	4	0	5	3
Neu, Mike, Lou.	1.000	40	3	1	0	4	0
Neugebauer, Nick, Ind.	1.000	5	2	0	0	2	0
Nickle, Doug, S./W.B.	.944	34	4	13	1	18	1
Nomura, Takahito, Ind.*	1.000	31	0	2	0	2	0
Nunez, Franklin, S./W.B.	1.000	4	2	3	0	5	0
Nussbeck, Mark, Roch.	1.000	11	2	2	0	4	0
Olivares, Omar, Buf.	1.000	2	2	1	0	3	0
Osting, Jimmy, Ind.*	1.000	22	6	21	0	27	1
Pacheco, Alexander, Col.	.750	14	2	1	1	4	1
Paniagua, Jose, Tol.	1.000	12	2	1	0	3	0
Paronto, Chad, Buf.	.857	8	3	3	1	7	0
Parque, Jim, Char.*	1.000	20	4	12	0	16	0
Parris, Steve, Syr.	1.000	2	3	0	0	3	0
Parrish, Wade, Char.*	.909	15	6	14	2	22	1
Patterson, Danny, Tol.	.000	5	0	0	0	0	0
Pavano, Carl, Ott.	1.000	3	2	1	0	3	1
Payne, Jerrod, Syr.	.000	6	0	0	0	0	0
Pearson, Terry, Tol.	.750	40	1	2	1	4	0
Pena, Juan, Paw.	1.000	17	7	6	0	13	0
Perez, Yorkis, Roch.*	.833	28	2	3	1	6	0
Perisho, Matt, Tol.*	.900	51	3	6	1	10	1
Person, Robert, S./W.B.	1.000	2	0	1	0	1	0
Petersen, Chris, Rich.	1.000	1	0	1	0	1	0
Phelps, Travis, Dur.	1.000	27	1	5	0	6	0
Phillips, Jason, Buf.	.944	16	4	13	1	18	0
Pina, Rafael, Roch.	.947	50	7	11	1	19	0
Pineda, Luis, Lou.	1.000	3	1	0	0	1	0
Porzio, Mike, Char.*	.833	14	2	8	2	12	1
Powell, Brian, Tol.	.963	20	9	17	1	27	0
Pratt, Andy, Rich.*	.800	6	1	3	1	5	0
Prokopec, Luke, Syr.	.000	2	0	0	0	0	0
Pulsipher, Bill, Col.*	1.000	6	0	1	0	1	0
Pumphrey, Ken, S./W.B.	.800	8	5	3	2	10	0
Quevedo, Ruben, Ind.	1.000	1	0	1	0	1	0
Ratliff, Jon, Syr.	1.000	27	1	3	0	4	0
Rauch, Jon, Char.	1.000	19	3	9	0	12	0
Reames, Britt, Ott.	1.000	7	3	10	0	13	0
Reimers, Cameron, Syr.	1.000	12	2	8	0	10	0
Reith, Brian, Lou.-S./W.B.	.952	27	10	10	1	21	1
Reitsma, Chris, Lou.	1.000	3	1	2	0	3	0
Ricketts, Chad, Syr.	1.000	15	4	1	0	5	0
Riedling, John, Lou.	.800	7	1	3	1	5	1
Rigdon, Paul, Ind.	1.000	3	2	2	0	4	1
Riggan, Jerrod, Buf.	.889	27	1	7	1	9	0
Riske, David, Buf.	1.000	9	0	2	0	2	0
Rivera, Homero, Tol.*	1.000	12	0	9	0	9	1
Roa, Joe, S./W.B.	.963	17	10	16	1	27	1

Player, Team	Pct.	G	PO	A	E	TC	DP
Roach, Jason, Nor.	.885	19	7	16	3	26	0
Robbins, Jake, Rich.	.882	47	5	10	2	17	0
Rodney, Fernando, Tol.	1.000	20	0	3	0	3	0
Rodriguez, Nerio, Buf.	.923	13	6	6	1	13	1
Rodriguez, Ricardo, Buf.	1.000	4	5	3	0	8	0
Rogers, Brian, Col.	.692	14	6	3	4	13	0
Rosario, Juan, Roch.	1.000	2	0	1	0	1	0
Rose, Ted, Buf.	1.000	5	0	5	0	5	1
Ruffin, Johnny, Lou.	1.000	3	0	1	0	1	0
Runyan, Sean, Roch.*	1.000	3	1	0	0	1	0
Sabel, Erik, Tol.	1.000	14	0	2	0	2	0
Sadler, Carl, Buf.*	.800	12	0	4	1	5	0
Saenz, Jason, Nor.*	1.000	5	0	1	0	1	0
Saipe, Mike, Rich.	.917	42	5	17	2	24	1
Sandoval, Marcos, Syr.	.000	1	0	0	0	0	0
Santana, Julio, Tol.	1.000	7	3	0	0	3	0
Santiago, Jose, S./W.B.	.833	22	0	5	1	6	0
Scanlan, Bob, Col.	.947	34	8	10	1	19	0
Schrenk, Steve, Char.	1.000	38	4	13	0	17	2
Seale, Dustin, Ott.*	1.000	1	1	0	0	1	0
Seay, Bobby, Dur.*	1.000	10	1	1	0	2	1
Seo, Jae, Nor.	.760	26	5	14	6	25	0
Sequea, Jacobo, Roch.	1.000	5	1	2	0	3	0
Serrano, Elio, S./W.B.	1.000	43	1	11	0	12	1
Serrano, Jim, Nor.	.895	53	8	9	2	19	0
Shepard, David, Col.	1.000	1	1	0	0	1	0
Shibilo, Andy, Paw.	.000	6	0	0	1	1	0
Silva, Jose, Lou.	.875	20	3	4	1	8	1
Simas, Bill, Char.	1.000	28	4	7	0	11	0
Small, Aaron, Rich.	1.000	14	1	7	0	8	0
Smith, Bud, S./W.B.*	1.000	3	1	2	0	3	0
Smith, Dan, Ott.	.917	14	3	8	1	12	3
Smith, Mike, Syr.	.973	20	19	17	1	37	1
Smith, Roy, Buf.	.952	36	3	17	1	21	1
Sobkowiak, Scott, Rich.	.500	5	0	1	1	2	0
Spencer, Corey, Paw.*	1.000	15	4	5	0	9	0
Spencer, Sean, Ott.*	1.000	16	1	3	0	4	0
Spiegel, Mike, Buf.*	.000	1	0	0	0	0	0
Spooneybarger, Tim, Rich.	1.000	18	1	3	0	4	0
Spurgeon, Jay, Roch.	.944	29	8	9	1	18	0
Standridge, Jason, Dur.	.929	29	9	17	2	28	2
Stanford, Jason, Buf.*	.889	6	1	7	1	9	0
Steenstra, Kennie, Roch.	.800	6	1	3	1	5	0
Stefanski, Mike, Lou.	1.000	1	1	0	1	0	0
Stephens, John, Roch.	.971	21	12	22	1	35	3
Strange, Pat, Nor.	.980	29	13	37	1	51	4
Strong, Joe, Ind.	1.000	15	3	4	0	7	1
Stull, Everett, Ind.	.885	24	6	17	3	26	1
Sylvester, Billy, Rich.	.500	7	1	0	1	2	0
Takeoka, Kazuhiro, Rich.	1.000	23	2	8	0	10	1
Tallet, Brian, Buf.*	1.000	8	2	5	0	7	1
Telemaco, Amaury, S./W.B.	1.000	1	0	1	0	1	1
Tessmer, Jay, Col.	.962	63	3	22	1	26	2
Thomas, Evan, S./W.B.	.917	22	11	11	2	24	0
Thompson, Mark, Lou.	1.000	9	2	3	0	5	0
Thompson, Travis, Lou.	1.000	8	1	3	0	4	0
Thoms, Hank, Buf.	1.000	1	0	1	0	1	0
Thurman, Mike, Col.	1.000	12	5	12	0	17	0
Towers, Josh, Roch.	.941	15	8	8	1	17	1
Traber, Billy, Buf.*	1.000	9	1	5	0	6	0
Valdez, Santo, Syr.	1.000	5	3	1	0	4	1
Van Hekken, Andy, Tol.*	.875	7	1	6	1	8	0
Vargas, Martin, Buf.	.900	22	2	7	1	10	0
Viera, Rolando, Paw.*	1.000	3	0	1	0	1	0
Vining, Ken, Char.*	1.000	44	3	8	0	11	1
Wagner, Denny, Char.	1.000	2	1	1	0	2	0

Player, Team	Pct.	G	PO	A	E	TC	DP
Walker, Adam, Nor.*	1.000	1	1	0	0	1	0
Walker, Jamie, Tol.*	1.000	10	1	3	0	4	0
Walker, Pete, Nor.	1.000	2	2	2	0	4	0
Walker, Tyler, Nor.	.968	28	10	20	1	31	2
Wallace, Jeff, Paw.*	.500	23	0	2	2	4	0
Walling, Dave, Col.	1.000	11	2	4	0	6	0
Wedel, Jeremy, S./W.B.	1.000	43	3	9	0	12	0
Wengert, Don, Paw.	.907	29	12	27	4	43	2
Westbrook, Jake, Buf.	.000	1	0	0	0	0	0
Wheeler, Dan, Rich.	.929	27	6	20	2	28	0
White, Matt, Buf.*	1.000	7	0	1	0	1	0
Wiggins, Scott, Syr.*	.750	12	0	3	1	4	0
Wilkins, Marc, Dur.	1.000	23	1	2	0	3	0
Williams, Matt, Nor.*	.000	1	0	0	0	0	0
Williams, Todd, Ott.	1.000	46	5	9	0	14	1
Winchester, Scott, Ott.-Syr.	1.000	44	4	6	0	10	0
Winkelsas, Joe, Rich.	.889	16	4	4	1	9	1
Woodard, Steve, S./W.B.	1.000	15	2	6	0	8	0
Wright, Jamey, Ind.	1.000	3	3	1	0	4	0
Wright, Jaret, Buf.	.800	10	4	4	2	10	2
Wunsch, Kelly, Char.*	1.000	10	2	0	0	2	0
Wylie, Mitch, Char.	1.000	6	0	1	0	1	0
Yankosky, L.J., Rich.	1.000	23	3	7	0	10	0
Yates, Tyler, Nor.	1.000	24	0	3	0	3	0
Young, Tim, Paw.*	.944	57	5	12	1	18	0
Zambrano, Victor, Dur.	1.000	10	1	2	0	3	1
Zamora, Pete, S./W.B.	.952	55	7	13	1	21	0

PITCHERS WITH TWO OR MORE TEAMS

Player, Team	Pct.	G	PO	A	E	TC	DP
Atchley, Justin, Lou.*	1.000	7	0	4	0	4	0
Atchley, Justin, Roch.*	1.000	10	1	1	0	2	0
Beverlin, Jason, Buf.	.938	23	6	9	1	16	0
Beverlin, Jason, Tol.	1.000	4	1	1	0	2	0
Chantres, Carlos, Dur.	.867	10	2	11	2	15	0
Chantres, Carlos, Char.	.818	15	5	13	4	22	1
D'Amico, Jeff, S./W.B.	.857	14	7	5	2	14	1
D'Amico, Jeff, Buf.	.000	2	0	0	0	0	0
D'Amico, Jeff, Lou.	1.000	11	3	3	0	6	2
Dingman, Craig, Lou.	.000	22	0	0	0	0	0
Dingman, Craig, Col.	.000	2	0	0	0	0	0
Drew, Tim, Buf.	.957	15	8	14	1	23	2
Drew, Tim, Ott.	1.000	13	10	13	0	23	1
Drumright, Mike, Paw.	1.000	7	0	3	0	3	0
Drumright, Mike, Roch.	.926	23	10	15	2	27	0
Espina, Rendy, Syr.*	1.000	27	2	2	0	4	0
Espina, Rendy, Roch.*	1.000	18	1	2	0	3	1
Feliciano, Pedro, Lou.*	1.000	20	5	5	0	10	1
Feliciano, Pedro, Nor.*	1.000	5	1	0	0	1	0
Gonzalez, Dicky, Nor.	.000	1	0	0	0	0	0
Gonzalez, Dicky, Ott.	.930	22	18	22	3	43	1
Johnson, Mark, Ind.	1.000	4	1	3	0	4	0
Johnson, Mark, Tol.	1.000	8	1	3	0	4	0
Keller, Kris, Tol.	.833	17	1	4	1	6	0
Keller, Kris, Rich.	1.000	29	1	8	0	9	0
Kim, Sun-Woo, Paw.	1.000	8	1	7	0	8	0
Kim, Sun-Woo, Ott.	.667	7	0	2	1	3	1
Lira, Felipe, Nor.	1.000	21	3	4	0	7	1
Lira, Felipe, Lou.	1.000	11	4	5	0	9	0
Reith, Brian, Lou.	1.000	23	10	10	0	20	1
Reith, Brian, S./W.B.	.000	4	0	0	1	1	0
Winchester, Scott, Ott.	1.000	21	3	1	0	4	0
Winchester, Scott, Syr.	1.000	23	1	5	0	6	0

The following players appeared only as designated hitter, pinch-hitter or pinch runner: Canseco, dh; Caradonna, dh, ph; S. Casey, dh; Davidson, dh, pr; Malave, ph; McKee, ph.

LEAGUE CHAMPIONS

Year	Team	Pct.	Year	Team	Pct.	Year	Team	Pct.
1884—	Trenton	.520		Binghamton*	.667	1902—	Toronto	.669
1885—	Syracuse	.584	1893—	Erie	.606	1903—	Jersey City	.742
1886—	Utica	.646	1894—	Providence	.696	1904—	Buffalo	.657
1887—	Toronto	.644	1895—	Springfield	.687	1905—	Providence	.638
1888—	Syracuse	.723	1896—	Providence	.602	1906—	Buffalo	.607
1889—	Detroit	.649	1897—	Syracuse	.632	1907—	Toronto	.619
1890—	Detroit	.617	1898—	Montreal	.586	1908—	Baltimore	.593
1891—	Buffalo (reg. season)	.727	1899—	Rochester	.624	1909—	Rochester	.596
	Buffalo (supplemental)	.680	1900—	Providence	.616	1910—	Rochester	.601
1892—	Providence	.615	1901—	Rochester	.642	1911—	Rochester	.645

Year	Team	Pct.
1912—	Toronto	.595
1913—	Newark	.625
1914—	Providence	.617
1915—	Buffalo	.632
1916—	Buffalo	.586
1917—	Toronto	.604
1918—	Toronto	.693
1919—	Baltimore	.671
1920—	Baltimore	.719
1921—	Baltimore	.717
1922—	Baltimore	.689
1923—	Baltimore	.677
1924—	Baltimore	.709
1925—	Baltimore	.633
1926—	Toronto	.657
1927—	Buffalo	.667
1928—	Rochester	.549
1929—	Rochester	.613
1930—	Rochester	.629
1931—	Rochester	.601
1932—	Newark	.649
1933—	Newark	.622
	Buffalo (4th)†	.494
1934—	Newark	.608
	Toronto (3rd)†	.559
1935—	Montreal	.597
	Syracuse (2nd)†	.565
1936—	Buffalo‡	.610
1937—	Newark‡	.717
1938—	Newark‡	.684
1939—	Jersey City	.582
	Rochester (2nd)†	.556
1940—	Rochester	.611
	Newark (2nd)†	.594
1941—	Newark	.649
	Montreal (2nd)†	.584
1942—	Newark	.601
	Syracuse (3rd)†	.513
1943—	Toronto	.625
	Syracuse (3rd)†	.536
1944—	Baltimore‡	.553
1945—	Montreal	.621
	Newark (2nd)†	.582
1946—	Montreal‡	.649
1947—	Jersey City	.610
	Syracuse (3rd)†	.575
1948—	Montreal‡	.614
1949—	Buffalo	.584
	Montreal (3rd)†	.545

Year	Team	Pct.
1950—	Rochester	.609
	Baltimore (3rd)†	.556
1951—	Montreal‡	.617
1952—	Montreal	.629
	Rochester (3rd)†	.619
1953—	Rochester	.630
	Montreal (2nd)†	.586
1954—	Toronto	.630
	Syracuse (4th)§	.510
1955—	Montreal	.617
	Rochester (4th)†	.497
1956—	Toronto	.566
	Rochester (2nd)†	.553
1957—	Toronto	.575
	Buffalo (2nd)†	.571
1958—	Montreal‡	.588
1959—	Buffalo	.582
	Havana (3rd)†	.523
1960—	Toronto‡	.649
1961—	Columbus	.597
	Buffalo (3rd)†	.559
1962—	Jacksonville	.610
	Atlanta (3rd)†	.539
1963—	Syracuse∞	.533
	Indianapolis‡	.562
1964—	Jacksonville	.589
	Rochester (4th)†	.532
1965—	Columbus	.582
	Toronto (3rd)†	.556
1966—	Rochester	.565
	Toronto (2nd-tied)†	.558
1967—	Richmond	.574
	Toledo (3rd)†	.525
1968—	Toledo	.565
	Jacksonville (4th)†	.514
1969—	Tidewater	.563
	Syracuse (3rd)†	.536
1970—	Syracuse‡	.600
1971—	Rochester‡	.614
1972—	Louisville	.563
	Tidewater (3rd)†	.545
1973—	Charleston	.586
	Pawtucket‡†	.534
1974—	Memphis	.613
	Rochester ∞‡	.611
1975—	Tidewater‡	.610
1976—	Rochester	.638
	Syracuse (2nd)†	.590
1977—	Pawtucket	.571

Year	Team	Pct.
	Charleston (2nd)‡	.557
1978—	Charleston	.607
	Richmond (4th)†	.511
1979—	Columbus‡	.612
1980—	Columbus‡	.593
1981—	Columbus‡	.633
1982—	Richmond	.590
	Tidewater (3rd)†	.540
1983—	Columbus	.593
	Tidewater (4th)†	.511
1984—	Columbus	.590
	Pawtucket (4th)†	.536
1985—	Syracuse	.564
	Tidewater (4th)†	.540
1986—	Richmond‡	.571
1987—	Tidewater	.579
	Columbus†	.550
1988—	Rochester◆	.546
	Tidewater	.546
1989—	Syracuse	.572
	Richmond◆	.555
1990—	Rochester◆	.614
	Columbus	.596
1991—	Columbus◆	.590
	Pawtucket	.552
1992—	Columbus◆	.660
	Scr. W.B.	.592
1993—	Charlotte◆	.610
	Rochester	.525
1994—	Richmond◆	.567
	Pawtucket	.549
1995—	Norfolk	.606
	Ottawa◆	.507
1996—	Columbus◆	.599
	Rochester	.511
1997—	Rochester◆	.589
	Columbus	.556
1998—	Buffalo■	.566
1999—	Columbus	.589
	Charlotte▲	.569
2000—	Buffalo	.593
	Indianapolis▲	.563
2001—	Buffalo	.641
	Louisville▼	.583
2002—	Scranton/Wilkes-Barre	.632
	Durham▲	.556

*Won split-season playoff. †Won four-team playoff. ‡Won championship and four-team playoff. §Defeated Havana in game to decide fourth place, then won four-team playoff. ∞League was divided into Northern, Southern divisions. ◆League divided into Eastern, Western divisions; won playoffs. ■League divided into Eastern, Northern and Southern divisions; won four-team playoff. ▲League divided into North, South and West divisions; won four-team playoff. ▼League divided into North, South and West divisions; was leading final series of four-team playoff and was declared champion when Professional Baseball declared a stoppage of play. (NOTE—Known as Eastern League in 1884, New York State League in 1885, International League in 1886-87, International Association in 1888, International League in 1889-90, Eastern Association in 1891 and Eastern League from 1892 until 1912.)

MEXICAN LEAGUE

2002 FINAL STANDINGS

FIRST HALF

NORTHERN DIVISION

Team	W	L	T	Pct.	GB
Mexico City Reds	39	17	0	.696	...
Monclova	34	22	0	.607	5.0
Saltillo	31	25	0	.554	8.0
Dos Laredos	30	26	0	.536	9.0
Monterrey	29	26	0	.527	9.5
Reynosa	23	33	0	.411	16.0
Puebla	21	34	0	.382	17.5
Torreon	21	35	0	.375	18.0

SOUTHERN DIVISION

Team	W	L	T	Pct.	GB
Oaxaca	34	22	0	.607	...
Veracruz	33	23	0	.589	1.0
Cancun	28	27	0	.509	5.5
Yucatan	27	28	0	.491	6.5
Tabasco	27	29	0	.482	7.0
Mexico City Tigers	26	30	0	.464	8.0
Campeche	25	31	0	.446	9.0
Cordoba	18	38	0	.321	16.0

SECOND HALF

NORTHERN DIVISION

Team	W	L	T	Pct.	GB
Saltillo	35	18	0	.660	...
Mexico City Reds	35	19	0	.648	0.5
Dos Laredos	32	22	0	.593	3.5
Monterrey	31	23	0	.574	4.5
Torreon	23	30	0	.434	12.0
Monclova	22	32	0	.407	13.5
Reynosa	20	34	0	.370	15.5
Puebla	17	36	0	.321	18.0

SOUTHERN DIVISION

Team	W	L	T	Pct.	GB
Yucatan	33	19	0	.635	...
Mexico City Tigers	31	19	0	.620	1.0
Oaxaca	28	23	1	.549	4.5
Campeche	27	24	0	.529	5.5
Cancun	25	27	0	.481	8.0
Veracruz	22	30	1	.423	11.0
Tabasco	21	32	0	.396	12.5
Cordoba	19	33	0	.365	14.0

COMPOSITE

Team	Reds	Sal.	Oax.	D.L.	Yuc.	Mont.	Tig.	Ver.	Monc.	Can.	Cam.	Tab.	Tor.	Rey.	Pue.	Cor.	W	L	T	Pct.	GB
Mexico City Reds	...	5	3	6	3	7	2	2	9	1	3	2	9	8	11	3	74	36	0	.673	...
Saltillo	7	...	2	8	3	6	2	1	6	2	0	3	8	9	7	2	66	43	0	.606	7.5
Oaxaca	0	1	...	2	4	3	8	8	1	8	6	9	2	2	1	7	62	45	1	.579	10.5
Dos Laredos	6	4	1	...	1	8	2	1	9	1	2	1	5	10	9	2	62	48	0	.564	12.0
Yucatan	0	0	8	2	...	1	6	6	0	9	6	11	1	1	2	7	60	47	0	.561	12.5
Monterrey	5	8	0	4	2	...	2	1	6	2	2	1	8	10	7	2	60	49	0	.550	13.5
Mexico City Tigers	1	1	6	1	5	1	...	9	1	5	6	5	2	3	1	10	57	49	0	.538	15.0
Veracruz	1	2	3	2	6	2	3	...	3	9	8	4	2	0	0	10	55	53	1	.509	18.0
Monclova	3	6	2	3	3	6	2	0	...	2	2	1	11	6	8	1	56	54	0	.509	18.0
Cancun	2	1	4	2	4	1	5	3	1	...	7	7	1	3	3	9	53	54	0	.495	19.5
Campeche	0	3	4	1	6	1	6	3	1	5	...	11	2	1	1	7	52	55	0	.486	20.5
Tabasco	1	0	3	2	1	2	6	8	2	5	3	...	3	2	2	8	48	61	0	.440	25.5
Torreon	3	4	1	7	2	4	1	1	3	2	1	0	...	7	8	0	44	65	0	.404	29.5
Reynosa	4	3	1	4	2	2	0	3	6	0	2	1	5	...	8	2	43	67	0	.391	31.0
Puebla	3	4	2	3	1	4	2	3	4	0	2	1	4	4	...	1	38	70	0	.352	35.0
Cordoba	0	1	5	1	4	1	2	4	2	3	5	4	2	1	2	...	37	71	0	.343	36.0

PLAYOFFS: Mexico City Reds defeated Monclova, four games to one; Oaxaca defeated Veracruz, four games to none; Dos Laredos defeated Saltillo, four games to two; Mexico City Tigers defeated Yucatan, four games to three; Mexico City Tigers defeated Oaxaca, four games to three; Mexico City Reds defeated Dos Laredos, four games to three, Mexico City Reds defeated Mexico City Tigers, four games to three, to win Mexican League championship.

MANAGERS: Campeche, Manuel Cazarin; Cancun, Enrique Reyes; Cordoba, Julian Yan; Dos Laredos, Juan Francisco Rodriguez; Mexico City Reds, Bernie Tatis; Monterrey, Dan Firova; Monclova, Gerardo Sanchez; Oaxaca, Alfonso Jimenez; Puebla, Marco Antonio Guzman; Reynosa, Raul Cano; Saltillo, Tim Johnson; Tabasco, Marco Antonio Vasquez; Mexico City Tigers, Lee Sigman; Torreon, Juan Jose Pacho; Veracruz, Luis Mere; Yucatan, Francisco Estrada.

ALL-STAR TEAM: 1B—Cornelio Garcia, Mexico City Reds; Marco Antonio Romero, Saltillo; 2B—Arnoldo Castro, Cancun; Carlos Valencia, Dos Laredos; 3B—Oscar Robles, Oaxaca; Roberto Vizcarra, Mexico City Tigers; SS—Carlos Gastelum, Puebla; Jose Luis Sandoval, Puebla; C—Noe Munoz, Saltillo; Miguel Ojeda, Mexico City Reds; Roberto Saucedo, Dos Laredos; Saul Soto, Oaxaca; OF—Luis Arredondo, Yucatan; Matias Carrillo, Mexico City Tigers; Pedro Iturbe, Mexico City Tigers-Puebla; Christian Alan Quintero, Oaxaca; Ricardo Saenz, Monclova; RHP—Francisco Campos, Campeche; Jose Jimenez, Oaxaca; Jose Juan Lopez, Reynosa; Alberto Manrique, Reynosa; Salvador Rodriguez, Yucatan; Alejandro Romero, Monclova; Miguel Rubio, Monterrey; David Sinohui, Veracruz; LHP—Jose Luis Garcia, Puebla; Eleazar Mora, Veracruz; Roberto Ramirez, Mexico City Reds; Most Valuable Player—Ricardo Saenz, Monclova.

2002 BATTING

TEAM

Team	G	TPA	AB	R	H	TB	2B	3B	HR	RBI	SH	SF	HP	BB	IBB	SO	SB	CS	GDP	LOB	ShO	Avg.	OBP	Slg.
Mexico	110	4433	3871	738	1221	1959	218	35	150	712	16	38	37	471	22	631	66	35	91	856	4	.315	.391	.506
Saltillo	109	4335	3750	660	1136	1755	202	15	129	624	28	30	54	473	41	630	93	30	106	872	6	.303	.386	.468
Oaxaca	108	4288	3712	625	1116	1652	241	23	83	588	50	45	68	413	22	534	72	32	93	847	10	.301	.377	.445
Dos Laredos	110	4256	3765	580	1110	1673	181	5	124	550	43	27	71	350	19	565	28	25	109	809	6	.295	.363	.444
Tigres	106	4044	3552	590	1030	1578	177	19	111	552	42	42	68	340	20	565	83	38	100	723	6	.290	.359	.444
Torreon	109	4255	3744	550	1082	1581	165	11	104	511	51	41	52	367	17	589	46	32	104	835	5	.289	.357	.422
Monclova	110	4245	3750	536	1075	1502	186	11	73	495	38	26	47	384	32	614	77	24	102	844	5	.287	.358	.401
Monterrey	109	4187	3653	556	1044	1521	154	7	103	531	74	36	43	381	31	632	93	35	94	787	5	.286	.357	.416
Yucatan	107	4195	3651	473	1013	1393	146	21	64	429	65	28	57	394	46	600	51	28	91	882	6	.277	.354	.382
Puebla	108	4102	3646	453	1010	1392	178	24	52	422	52	23	56	325	21	579	57	37	96	813	6	.277	.343	.382
Veracruz	109	4147	3714	490	1023	1479	161	11	91	451	40	28	63	302	23	617	66	29	87	781	3	.275	.338	.398
Reynosa	110	3993	3596	423	983	1375	184	17	58	397	72	27	37	261	19	608	44	40	98	736	13	.273	.327	.382

Team	G	TPA	AB	R	H	TB	2B	3B	HR	RBI	SH	SF	HP	BB	IBB	SO	SB	CS	GDP	LOB	ShO	Avg.	OBP	Slg.
Cancun	107	3968	3542	443	957	1357	140	10	80	418	54	29	34	309	21	527	37	42	81	750	9	.270	.332	.383
Campeche	107	3970	3533	463	954	1364	148	8	82	423	64	20	43	310	27	513	41	31	101	722	5	.270	.335	.386
Tabasco	109	4065	3661	423	985	1361	164	7	66	397	49	23	44	288	40	550	43	24	104	769	12	.269	.328	.372
Cordoba	108	4029	3619	423	922	1316	140	13	76	389	36	22	39	313	18	679	53	33	88	749	11	.255	.319	.364

INDIVIDUAL

TOP QUALIFIERS FOR BATTING CHAMPIONSHIP

Minimum 297 plate appearances. *Lefthanded batter. †Switch-hitter.

Player, Team	G	TPA	AB	R	H	TB	2B	3B	HR	RBI	SH	SF	HP	BB	IBB	SO	SB	CS	GDP	Avg.	OBP	Slg.
Romero, Willie, Sal.	95	411	367	85	142	219	29	3	14	77	0	4	5	35	1	52	18	4	8	.387	.443	.597
Jose, Felix, Mex.†	85	390	324	88	124	230	21	2	27	102	0	4	0	62	5	56	4	1	10	.383	.477	.710
Garcia, Cornelio, Mex.*	96	449	395	81	151	213	19	11	7	54	3	1	2	48	1	54	12	7	10	.382	.451	.539
Grijak, Kevin, Tor.*	83	351	308	61	113	196	21	1	20	69	0	2	4	37	6	38	4	4	10	.367	.439	.636
Sherman, Darrell, Monc.*	98	447	364	73	132	164	23	3	1	35	1	0	11	71	3	36	25	4	7	.363	.480	.451
Connell, Lino, Oax.	108	526	458	102	163	242	45	5	8	65	4	2	3	59	4	78	31	8	9	.356	.431	.528
Ojeda, Miguel, Mex.	98	412	341	79	120	201	22	1	19	80	1	3	1	66	2	49	8	5	7	.352	.455	.589
Carrillo, Matias, Tig.*	102	422	364	61	127	186	18	1	13	71	0	7	9	42	5	34	4	0	13	.349	.422	.511
Robles, Oscar, Oax.*	105	465	368	67	128	180	25	0	9	76	6	11	5	74	7	35	4	3	7	.348	.452	.489
Arredondo, Luis, Yuc.*	100	465	416	62	144	179	16	5	3	31	4	4	1	40	6	38	21	8	3	.346	.390	.430
Orantes, Ramon, Mont.	89	379	343	49	117	177	16	1	14	61	2	4	4	26	2	53	4	1	14	.341	.386	.516
Castro, Arnoldo, Can.	97	424	370	51	126	177	19	1	10	45	3	2	1	48	0	29	2	5	7	.341	.416	.478
Arano, Wilfrido, Lar.*	105	403	344	53	117	145	22	0	2	32	3	0	8	48	4	20	3	4	6	.340	.433	.422
Kelly, Roberto, Mex.	78	361	314	61	105	182	16	2	19	80	0	2	9	36	1	48	0	2	14	.334	.416	.580
Bojorquez, Victor, Mex.	87	318	302	52	100	148	13	7	7	45	0	2	2	12	1	49	3	6	6	.331	.358	.490

DEPARTMENTAL LEADERS: G—J. Zazueta, 110; AB—Connell, 458; R—Connell, 102; H—Connell, 163; TB—Connell, 242; 2B—Connell, 45; 3B—C. Garcia, 11; HR—Saucedo, 32; RBI—Jose, 102; SH—Morejon, 19; SF—O. Robles, 11; HP—Fentanes, 22; BB—Jimenez, 84; IBB—Jimenez, 14; SO—G. Garcia, 94; SB—D. Smith, 41; CS—D. Smith, 12; GIDP—Nunez, 19; Slg.—Jose, .710; OBP—Jimenez, .484.

ALL PLAYERS

*Lefthanded batter. †Switch-hitter.

Player, Team	G	TPA	AB	R	H	TB	2B	3B	HR	RBI	SH	SF	HP	BB	IBB	SO	SB	CS	GDP	Avg.	OBP	Slg.
Abrego, Jesus, Can.-Ver.*	48	99	90	8	19	27	2	0	2	13	1	0	1	7	0	17	0	1	1	.211	.276	.300
Acosta, Jose, Tab.	10	16	14	0	0	0	0	0	0	1	1	0	0	1	0	7	0	0	1	.000	.067	.000
Acuna, Jose, Can.†	49	58	51	3	6	6	0	0	0	4	3	1	0	3	0	10	0	1	0	.118	.164	.118
Adriana, Sharnol, Cam.-Cor.	94	399	356	52	113	184	15	1	18	68	0	5	7	31	2	60	9	9	16	.317	.378	.517
Aganza, Ruben, Monc.	106	435	377	45	107	153	19	0	9	68	4	5	5	44	5	43	5	1	14	.284	.362	.406
Aguilar, Antonio, Cam.-Yuc.†	29	75	57	13	12	14	2	0	0	4	2	1	3	12	2	14	0	1	0	.211	.370	.246
Aguilera, Armando, Sal.*	10	15	12	2	3	7	1	0	1	2	0	1	0	2	0	2	0	0	2	.250	.333	.583
Aguirre, Francisco, Tab.	3	13	10	1	5	5	0	0	0	0	1	0	0	2	1	2	1	0	0	.500	.583	.500
Alejos, Fernando, Yuc.	5	2	1	0	1	1	0	0	0	0	1	0	0	0	0	0	0	0	0	1.000	1.000	1.000
Alexander, Manny, Cor.	54	236	217	31	64	81	10	2	1	21	1	1	1	16	2	26	14	4	4	.295	.345	.373
Almeida, Shammar, Oax.*	94	341	269	44	85	151	18	3	14	51	1	2	10	59	5	60	0	1	2	.316	.453	.561
Alvarez, Hector, Oax.	85	351	315	38	81	105	14	2	2	40	7	3	3	23	1	51	3	3	8	.257	.311	.333
Amador, Alfonso, Ver.*	14	34	28	4	7	11	1	0	1	4	0	1	0	5	0	8	0	0	1	.250	.353	.393
Arano, Eloy, Ver.†	92	355	321	39	85	109	9	0	5	31	9	1	2	21	2	35	10	2	12	.265	.313	.340
Arano, Wilfrido, Lar.*	105	403	344	53	117	145	22	0	2	32	3	0	8	48	4	20	3	4	6	.340	.433	.422
Arauz, Escarcega, Monc.	30	71	65	7	17	23	3	0	1	9	1	0	0	5	0	13	0	0	1	.262	.314	.354
Arauz, Leobardo, Yuc.†	85	273	223	26	41	55	8	3	0	14	6	2	7	35	5	50	0	1	6	.184	.311	.247
Arias, Francisco, Sal.	63	93	83	15	23	30	4	0	1	12	1	1	0	8	0	9	2	0	1	.277	.337	.361
Armenta, Guillermo, Cam.†.	31	122	102	13	21	27	3	0	1	4	3	0	1	16	3	16	3	1	3	.206	.319	.265
Arredondo, Alan, Tab.†	68	159	146	21	27	33	2	2	0	4	5	0	0	8	0	29	4	3	0	.185	.227	.226
Arredondo, Eduardo, Ver.	44	49	44	9	8	8	0	0	0	5	0	0	0	5	0	7	0	1	0	.182	.265	.182
Arredondo, Hernando, Cor.	80	287	263	29	69	101	14	0	6	27	6	1	0	17	3	55	5	3	7	.262	.306	.384
Arredondo, Jesus, Pue.*	100	422	360	52	100	141	22	5	3	24	7	2	9	44	7	36	5	2	8	.278	.369	.392
Arredondo, Luis, Yuc.*	100	465	416	62	144	179	16	5	3	31	4	4	1	40	6	38	21	8	3	.346	.401	.430
Arvizu, Martin, Cor.	10	20	20	1	3	5	2	0	0	1	0	0	0	0	0	10	0	0	1	.150	.150	.250
Avila, Carlos, Tig.*	37	71	67	10	15	18	3	0	0	5	0	1	1	2	0	15	0	2	0	.224	.254	.269
Avila, Ignacio, Cor.	54	157	136	23	33	45	4	1	2	11	1	1	2	17	0	42	1	5	3	.243	.333	.331
Aviles, Alejandro, Ver.†	2	4	4	0	0	0	0	0	0	0	0	0	0	0	0	2	0	0	0	.000	.000	.000
Baez, Carlos, Tab.	8	18	17	1	4	4	0	0	0	1	0	0	0	1	0	6	0	0	1	.235	.278	.235
Barajas, Edison, Cor.*	54	141	131	9	34	43	6	0	1	15	0	1	0	9	1	24	0	1	5	.260	.305	.328
Barker, Glen, Rey.†	23	96	85	17	28	40	1	4	1	9	1	0	1	9	0	16	3	3	1	.329	.400	.471
Barrera, Jorge, Tor.*	45	95	82	10	21	23	2	0	0	6	1	1	4	7	1	19	0	0	4	.256	.340	.280
Barrera, Nelson, Mex.-Cam.	5	12	12	1	3	3	0	0	0	1	0	0	0	0	0	2	0	0	1	.250	.250	.250
Barron, Tony, Ver.-Pue.	64	253	221	28	62	96	10	0	8	32	0	3	4	25	5	54	0	1	7	.281	.360	.434
Barry, Jeff, Tig.†	5	21	18	1	3	4	1	0	0	2	0	0	0	3	0	1	0	1	1	.167	.286	.222
Beltran, Juan, Cam.	20	45	37	9	8	10	2	0	0	5	1	0	0	7	1	6	0	0	0	.216	.341	.270
Benitez, Yamil, Rey.-Cam.	42	164	157	14	38	57	8	1	3	17	0	0	1	6	0	32	0	0	5	.242	.274	.363
Bernal, Cosme, Monc.	9	18	16	0	2	2	0	0	0	1	0	0	1	1	0	5	0	0	0	.125	.176	.125
Bojorquez, Victor, Mex.	87	318	302	52	100	148	13	7	7	45	0	2	2	12	1	49	3	6	6	.331	.358	.490
Bolado, Carlos, Ver.*	13	29	25	1	3	3	0	0	0	2	1	0	1	2	0	5	0	0	1	.120	.214	.120
Borges, Luis, Can.*	98	298	267	38	77	98	14	2	1	22	10	0	1	20	0	32	2	6	7	.288	.340	.367
Brena, Jaime, Oax.	55	105	87	15	16	21	5	0	0	15	1	3	2	12	0	13	1	0	2	.184	.288	.241
Brown, Ray, Tab.*	38	168	149	16	42	58	4	0	4	20	0	0	1	18	1	31	1	0	5	.282	.363	.389
Buelna, Lorenzo, Pue.	97	360	317	35	92	119	10	7	1	33	5	0	5	33	0	44	5	8	6	.290	.366	.375
Bustamante, Omar, Sal.	18	29	26	4	7	7	0	0	0	2	1	0	2	0	0	9	1	0	1	.269	.321	.269
Bustillos, Luis, Rey.	90	275	250	27	63	81	16	1	0	21	10	0	1	14	0	58	1	2	9	.252	.294	.324

Player, Team	G	TPA	AB	R	H	TB	2B	3B	HR	RBI	SH	SF	HP	BB	IBB	SO	SB	CS	GDP	Avg.	OBP	Slg.
Canales, Joel, Mont.	33	97	74	7	13	19	0	0	2	11	8	0	1	14	0	15	1	0	5	.176	.315	.257
Candelaria, Ben, Ver.*	37	154	143	8	37	49	9	0	1	15	1	0	2	8	1	26	0	1	2	.259	.307	.343
Canizalez, Juan, Cam.†	77	290	261	32	79	113	16	0	6	37	2	1	1	25	4	37	2	1	7	.303	.365	.433
Cansino, Jorge, Ver.	1	2	2	0	0	0	0	0	0	0	0	0	0	0	0	1	0	0	0	.000	.000	.000
Carpenter, Bubba, Sal.	21	99	80	15	21	32	5	0	2	10	0	0	1	18	2	19	1	2	3	.263	.404	.400
Carrasco, Ernesto, Pue.†	87	319	287	25	85	107	14	1	2	37	5	1	5	21	4	25	0	3	11	.296	.354	.373
Carrillo, Matias, Tig.*	102	422	364	61	127	186	18	1	13	71	0	7	9	42	5	34	4	0	13	.349	.422	.511
Carter, Mike, Yuc.	11	45	42	4	11	13	2	0	0	3	1	0	0	2	0	7	1	1	1	.262	.295	.310
Castaneda, Hector, Yuc.*	104	422	343	43	95	129	13	0	7	47	3	0	7	69	8	72	1	1	15	.277	.408	.376
Castaneda, Rafael, Rey.	81	272	223	24	63	78	9	0	2	18	3	4	5	37	1	27	0	2	8	.283	.390	.350
Castellano, Pedro, Oax.	48	196	168	29	52	81	11	0	6	34	0	4	7	17	2	36	1	0	6	.310	.388	.482
Castro, Arnoldo, Can.	97	424	370	51	126	177	19	1	10	45	3	2	1	48	0	29	2	5	7	.341	.416	.478
Castro, Domingo, Monc.	81	263	235	30	58	78	5	0	5	22	8	0	2	18	0	38	6	2	8	.247	.306	.332
Cazarin, Manuel, Cam.	101	369	336	41	101	162	22	0	13	54	7	0	5	21	5	25	1	1	12	.301	.351	.482
Cervantes, Ivan, Mex.	46	174	157	18	47	58	5	0	2	23	3	1	2	11	0	24	0	0	4	.299	.351	.369
Cervantes, Refugio, Can.*	25	58	53	5	11	22	2	0	3	13	0	2	0	3	1	14	0	0	0	.208	.241	.415
Cervera, Francisco, Yuc.	86	318	267	38	70	111	13	2	8	33	5	1	9	36	2	60	0	1	12	.262	.367	.416
Chimelis, Joel, Lar.	106	468	392	77	119	183	19	0	15	66	6	6	18	46	1	46	3	2	9	.304	.396	.467
Cisneros, Ventura, Rey.	45	96	84	11	26	31	5	0	0	9	1	0	1	10	0	17	1	2	1	.310	.389	.369
Cobos, Rogelio, Ver.-Can.	44	91	81	6	19	26	1	0	2	13	3	2	1	4	0	27	0	1	3	.235	.273	.321
Colina, Roberto, Pue.*	104	452	392	55	129	192	18	0	15	54	7	0	6	47	3	42	3	1	9	.329	.409	.490
Connell, Lino, Oax.	108	526	458	102	163	242	45	5	8	65	4	2	3	59	4	78	31	8	9	.356	.431	.528
Contreras, Albino, Pue.*	102	425	374	43	100	148	21	3	7	41	2	3	9	37	3	71	24	9	9	.267	.345	.396
Cookson, Brent, Rey.	27	101	92	6	23	37	8	0	2	6	1	1	0	7	0	22	2	0	3	.250	.300	.402
Correa, Miguel, Tor.†	44	184	172	23	50	80	12	0	6	30	1	1	0	10	1	41	4	1	3	.291	.328	.465
Cruz, Fausto, Yuc.	101	439	381	63	113	185	15	0	19	69	1	3	7	47	2	75	5	2	5	.297	.381	.486
Cruz, Marco, Yuc.-Cam.	28	49	43	6	6	11	2	0	1	2	3	0	2	1	0	7	0	0	1	.140	.196	.256
De La Torre, Francisco, Oax.	4	9	9	0	1	1	0	0	0	0	0	0	0	0	0	4	0	0	1	.111	.111	.111
De Los Santos, Luis, Mex.-Oax.	55	241	215	30	66	94	13	0	5	30	0	3	2	21	0	39	0	0	8	.307	.369	.437
Diaz, Edwin, Ver.	103	446	405	72	122	196	25	2	15	52	3	3	12	23	2	73	10	7	6	.301	.354	.484
Diaz, Luis, Monc.*	68	149	129	15	28	42	8	0	2	14	0	0	2	18	1	27	0	0	2	.217	.322	.326
Diaz, Pedro, Pue.	81	284	260	31	74	104	16	1	4	34	3	4	5	12	1	54	2	1	4	.285	.324	.400
Diaz, Remigio, Mont.	104	419	376	42	100	123	11	3	2	48	11	3	2	27	0	35	11	6	13	.266	.316	.327
Duenas, Arnaldo, Yuc.	38	47	42	6	9	12	1	1	0	2	1	0	1	3	1	18	0	0	0	.214	.283	.286
Elvira, Abraham, Cor.*	34	1	1	0	0	0	0	0	0	0	0	0	0	0	0	1	0	0	0	.000	.000	.000
Espino, Daniel, Tor.	93	368	338	46	98	121	15	1	2	31	4	0	12	14	1	24	10	6	13	.290	.341	.358
Espinoza, Efren, Mex.	72	266	242	36	65	94	12	4	3	25	1	5	5	13	0	45	3	1	5	.269	.313	.388
Espinoza, Jose, Lar.†	43	140	121	18	38	39	1	0	0	14	3	2	4	10	0	15	3	3	7	.314	.380	.322
Espinoza, Ramon, Tor.	29	39	37	2	7	9	2	0	0	1	1	0	0	1	0	15	0	0	0	.189	.211	.243
Espinoza, Ramon, Rey.-Yuc.	103	447	422	64	133	181	19	4	7	39	3	3	3	16	4	37	11	8	16	.315	.342	.429
Esqueda, Jonathan, Sal.	5	4	3	1	1	1	0	0	0	1	0	1	0	0	0	0	0	0	0	.333	.250	.333
Esquer, Ramon, Oax.*	30	94	84	11	21	29	5	0	1	14	0	1	3	6	0	11	2	4	0	.250	.319	.345
Estrada, Hector, Tor.	107	434	379	57	104	160	15	1	13	50	3	6	4	42	1	52	5	1	9	.274	.348	.422
Estrella, Isaac, Lar.	37	43	38	10	6	10	1	0	1	1	0	0	1	4	1	17	1	0	0	.158	.256	.263
Facundo, Armando, Can.	1	1	1	1	1	1	0	0	0	0	0	0	0	0	0	0	0	0	0	1.000	1.000	1.000
Felix, Lorenzo, Tor.	39	71	66	5	12	13	1	0	0	2	2	1	0	2	0	17	3	0	0	.182	.203	.197
Feliz, Alejandro, Mex.†	4	3	3	1	0	0	0	0	0	0	0	0	0	0	0	0	0	0	0	.000	.000	.000
Fentanes, Oscar, Tab.-Ver.	105	416	368	46	94	136	12	0	10	50	1	3	22	22	2	41	3	1	10	.255	.333	.370
Fernandez, Dan, Mex.*	82	384	335	56	85	117	15	4	3	36	6	1	1	41	1	37	14	4	1	.254	.336	.349
Figga, Mike, Pue.	5	23	21	4	7	10	0	0	1	5	0	0	0	2	0	8	0	0	0	.333	.391	.476
Flores, Kevin, Tig.	11	11	11	1	2	2	0	0	0	0	0	0	0	0	0	4	0	0	0	.182	.182	.182
Flores, Miguel, Mont.	42	165	133	23	28	36	5	0	1	10	0	1	4	27	0	38	7	0	4	.211	.358	.271
Fornes, Daniel, Rey.*	103	397	354	42	84	123	16	1	7	41	6	8	3	26	2	32	4	5	8	.237	.289	.347
Franco, Iker, Tig.	26	73	68	12	24	36	5	2	1	17	0	0	0	5	0	10	1	3	0	.353	.397	.529
Gamez, Miguel V., Mont.	1	0	0	1	0	0	0	0	0	0	0	0	0	0	0	0	0	0	0	.000	.000	.000
Garcia, Amaury, Cam.	46	193	172	29	45	67	6	2	4	18	1	1	2	17	0	26	8	3	1	.262	.333	.390
Garcia, Cornelio, Mex.*	96	449	395	81	151	213	19	11	7	54	3	1	2	48	1	54	12	7	10	.382	.451	.539
Garcia, Guillermo, Cor.-Tig.	105	450	381	66	106	211	24	0	27	92	0	6	5	58	5	94	0	1	14	.278	.376	.554
Garcia, Hector, Tab.	90	368	349	39	102	125	13	2	2	29	7	1	1	10	1	28	5	2	15	.292	.313	.358
Garcia, Heriberto, Oax.	73	269	238	40	69	77	8	0	0	18	9	0	2	20	0	28	1	3	5	.290	.350	.324
Garcia, Omar, Ver.	105	440	392	59	119	204	24	2	19	80	0	5	1	41	5	69	1	1	10	.304	.367	.520
Garland, Tim, Rey.	14	62	56	5	20	23	3	0	0	3	3	0	0	3	0	11	2	2	1	.357	.390	.411
Garza, Gerardo, Mont.	57	153	137	18	30	39	3	0	2	7	9	0	0	7	0	23	1	0	3	.219	.257	.285
Garzon, Eliseo, Mont.	78	238	205	28	51	65	8	0	2	24	11	2	1	19	1	33	0	0	4	.249	.313	.317
Gastelum, Carlos, Pue.-Tig.	95	414	374	64	116	138	15	2	1	28	10	5	7	18	3	41	19	7	7	.310	.349	.369
Gastelum, Gato, Tig.	40	53	48	3	8	9	1	0	0	4	1	0	0	4	0	5	1	0	3	.167	.231	.188
Gastelum, Sergio, Tig.	58	233	199	39	53	82	9	1	6	22	2	3	7	22	0	27	4	0	9	.266	.355	.412
Gavia, Jesus, Yuc.	65	183	167	14	43	53	7	0	1	17	5	1	2	8	0	22	1	0	4	.257	.298	.317
Gerardo, Benjamin, Tor.	17	21	18	4	4	7	0	0	1	1	0	0	0	3	0	4	0	0	2	.222	.333	.389
Gil, Eric, Tor.	26	15	15	7	6	7	1	0	0	1	0	0	0	0	0	3	0	0	0	.400	.400	.467
Gomez, Heber, Tab.	89	372	322	48	90	123	18	0	5	40	5	6	6	32	2	30	1	5	9	.280	.350	.382
Gonzalez, Fernando, Rey.	75	197	187	12	48	55	7	0	0	12	3	0	2	5	0	38	1	0	8	.257	.284	.294
Gonzalez, Israel, Cam.	72	210	186	25	49	61	12	0	0	18	7	2	4	11	1	23	0	2	7	.263	.315	.328
Gonzalez, Jesus, Yuc.-Monc.	78	343	309	45	97	132	12	1	7	41	2	2	3	27	3	44	14	0	8	.314	.372	.427
Gonzalez, Roman, Cor.	91	282	264	20	50	64	5	3	1	21	5	3	2	8	0	58	4	1	4	.189	.217	.242
Goytia, Francisco, Tor.	17	40	39	4	4	4	0	0	0	0	0	0	0	1	0	13	0	1	0	.103	.125	.103
Grijak, Kevin, Tor.*	83	351	308	61	113	196	21	1	20	69	0	2	4	37	6	38	4	4	10	.367	.439	.636
Guerrero, Epifano, Tab.*	23	96	83	11	19	23	4	0	0	8	2	1	1	9	2	10	1	0	4	.229	.309	.277
Guerrero, Sergio, Cam.	81	284	243	34	57	83	8	0	6	28	11	3	7	20	0	14	0	2	9	.235	.308	.342
Guizar, Hector, Monc.	71	220	205	16	52	60	6	1	0	20	4	0	4	7	0	21	1	4	9	.254	.292	.293
Gutierrez, Andres, Pue.	12	36	36	1	7	11	4	0	0	5	0	0	0	0	0	8	0	0	0	.194	.194	.306
Gutierrez, Said, Yuc.	70	199	178	18	46	65	7	0	4	15	4	2	2	13	1	32	1	0	5	.258	.313	.365

Player, Team	G	TPA	AB	R	H	TB	2B	3B	HR	RBI	SH	SF	HP	BB	IBB	SO	SB	CS	GDP	Avg.	OBP	Slg.
Hartman, Kory, Yuc.*	1	1	1	0	0	0	0	0	0	0	0	0	0	0	0	0	0	0	0	.000	.000	.000
Hernandez, Julio, Lar.	108	477	405	63	122	149	18	0	3	37	8	3	7	54	0	46	2	2	8	.301	.390	.368
Hernandez, Santos, Tig.	52	1	1	0	0	0	0	0	0	0	0	0	0	0	0	1	0	0	0	.000	.000	.000
Hunter, Brian, Sal.	9	36	30	6	9	24	3	0	4	11	0	1	1	4	0	5	0	0	1	.300	.389	.800
Hurtado, Hector, Lar.†	99	346	320	23	77	104	9	0	6	36	8	2	5	11	0	70	0	0	10	.241	.275	.325
Ibarra, Juvenal, Tor.*	16	34	33	2	6	9	0	0	1	3	0	0	1	0	0	8	0	0	2	.182	.206	.273
Iturbe, Pedro, Tig.-Pue.*	77	301	274	39	84	139	25	3	8	36	0	1	4	22	3	34	2	4	11	.307	.365	.507
Jennings, Doug, Cor.-Tab.*	36	148	125	19	37	58	9	0	4	12	0	1	6	16	0	21	0	1	6	.296	.399	.464
Jimenez, Eduardo, Sal.*	89	376	280	67	90	191	14	0	29	86	0	4	8	84	14	73	0	0	12	.321	.484	.682
Jones, Chris, Yuc.	39	164	144	18	38	54	6	2	2	23	0	3	1	16	1	33	3	2	4	.264	.335	.375
Jose, Felix, Mex.†	85	390	324	88	124	230	21	2	27	102	0	4	0	62	5	56	4	1	10	.383	.477	.710
Kelly, Roberto, Mex.	78	361	314	61	105	182	16	2	19	80	0	2	9	36	1	48	0	2	14	.334	.416	.580
Lara, Idelfonso, Cor.	77	251	232	22	52	74	8	1	4	16	0	0	3	16	2	69	2	0	5	.224	.283	.319
Leyva, German, Tab.-Yuc.*	61	234	205	22	53	68	9	0	2	21	3	1	0	25	8	14	1	2	7	.259	.338	.332
Leyva, Octavio, Ver.*	29	52	44	5	8	11	1	1	0	3	0	0	1	7	0	12	1	0	2	.182	.308	.250
Lizarraga, Norberto, Cor.	15	27	22	1	2	2	0	0	0	1	0	0	1	4	0	8	0	0	1	.091	.259	.091
Lizarraga, Rodolfo, Rey.	11	12	11	1	4	4	0	0	0	0	0	0	0	1	0	2	0	0	0	.364	.417	.364
Lopez, Baltazar, Mont.	4	12	12	0	5	5	0	0	0	2	0	0	0	0	0	2	0	0	0	.417	.417	.417
Lopez, Fabian, Oax.-Can.*	70	194	172	19	35	45	4	0	2	16	1	4	3	14	3	20	1	1	3	.203	.269	.262
Lopez, Jose, Rey.	20	44	36	4	6	6	0	0	0	4	0	1	3	0	11	1	1	0	0	.167	.250	.167
Lopez, Raul, Monc.*	102	422	364	57	110	158	19	1	9	54	4	3	1	50	9	57	5	3	10	.302	.385	.434
Lucca, Lou, Cam.	13	48	46	5	15	22	4	0	1	4	0	0	0	2	0	10	0	1	1	.326	.354	.478
Lugo, Roberto, Mont.	15	24	21	2	8	8	0	0	0	4	1	0	0	2	0	4	0	0	1	.381	.435	.381
Luke, Matt, Cam.*	19	80	73	16	27	43	4	0	4	17	0	0	1	6	0	16	0	0	1	.370	.425	.589
Machiria, Pablo, Lar.	27	85	81	5	18	26	5	0	1	7	0	0	2	2	0	9	0	1	0	.222	.259	.321
Magallanes, Ever, Mont.*	57	222	194	24	61	75	8	0	2	33	5	4	1	18	2	16	2	0	5	.314	.369	.387
Malave, Jose, Rey.	79	319	284	40	85	116	16	3	3	36	1	3	4	27	2	52	1	3	7	.299	.365	.408
Marquez, Leonardo, Tig.	5	6	6	1	1	1	0	0	0	0	0	0	0	0	0	1	0	0	0	.167	.167	.167
Martin, Norberto, Cam.	31	128	117	17	33	53	3	1	5	21	3	1	0	7	1	13	3	1	5	.282	.320	.453
Martinez, Abel, Can.	76	232	217	24	62	87	8	1	5	18	5	1	3	6	0	31	6	0	8	.286	.313	.401
Martinez, Augusto, Yuc.	8	2	2	1	0	0	0	0	0	0	0	0	0	0	0	1	0	0	0	.000	.000	.000
Martinez, Enrique, Pue.	74	240	211	29	48	73	11	1	4	28	5	2	1	21	2	44	2	1	3	.227	.298	.346
Martinez, Grimaldo, Cor.	98	416	379	42	102	124	15	2	1	30	3	1	3	30	0	42	1	2	5	.269	.327	.327
Martinez, Luis, Sal.	91	310	286	36	78	108	12	3	4	39	9	3	0	12	0	36	4	6	7	.273	.299	.378
Martinez, Rafael, Pue.*	25	108	89	14	28	36	2	0	2	13	0	0	2	17	0	15	0	1	3	.315	.435	.404
Martinez, Ramon, Mex.	107	462	392	84	117	222	27	0	26	80	0	4	7	59	4	86	9	0	10	.298	.396	.566
Mata, Noe, Ver.	107	422	394	42	112	136	13	1	3	32	5	4	2	17	1	83	17	6	10	.284	.314	.345
Matos, Francisco, Tab.	6	23	22	2	2	2	0	0	0	1	0	0	1	1	0	4	1	0	0	.091	.130	.091
Medina, Jose, Sal.*	31	70	63	9	19	32	4	0	3	14	0	0	2	5	0	10	0	1	3	.302	.371	.508
Mendez, Francisco, Lar.*	69	171	149	19	37	56	10	0	3	19	3	1	1	17	0	21	2	0	6	.248	.327	.376
Mendez, Roberto, Mex.	90	348	290	58	89	145	18	1	12	53	0	3	3	52	3	41	7	5	6	.307	.414	.500
Mendoza, Omar, Tab.†	76	246	225	21	56	67	11	0	0	18	6	1	1	13	1	51	4	3	3	.249	.292	.298
Mendoza, Ramon, Cam.	7	31	29	5	5	5	0	0	0	0	0	0	2	0	0	5	1	0	4	.172	.226	.172
Mercedes, Henry, Cor.	46	162	126	26	35	70	8	0	9	22	5	0	1	30	1	38	0	1	4	.278	.420	.556
Mere, Pedro, Ver.	109	470	419	68	126	190	21	2	13	69	4	6	8	33	0	64	6	5	6	.301	.358	.453
Meulens, Hensley, Pue.	38	159	137	14	28	36	3	1	1	24	0	0	0	22	0	37	0	0	6	.204	.314	.263
Meza, Alfredo, Ver.-Tab.†	100	352	325	23	88	106	9	0	3	27	6	3	4	14	2	44	0	3	12	.271	.306	.326
Meza, Gonzalo, Tor.*	100	406	351	46	95	129	11	4	5	38	10	2	2	41	0	68	2	0	11	.271	.348	.368
Miller, Orlando, Tab.	49	195	177	31	58	105	11	0	12	29	0	1	2	15	2	35	5	0	3	.328	.385	.593
Minjarez, Francisco, Pue.	63	217	201	24	51	62	9	1	0	24	3	3	0	10	0	37	3	3	6	.254	.285	.308
Miranda, Luis, Tor.*	10	1	1	0	0	0	0	0	0	0	0	0	0	0	0	1	0	0	0	.000	.000	.000
Montano, Angel, Cam.*	2	3	3	0	0	0	0	0	0	0	0	0	0	0	0	2	0	0	0	.000	.000	.000
Montenegro, Jose, Mex.	27	47	41	2	8	9	1	0	0	3	0	0	0	6	0	7	0	0	1	.195	.298	.220
Morales, Luis, Ver.*	23	1	0	0	0	0	0	0	0	0	0	0	0	1	0	0	0	0	0	.000	1.000	.000
Morejon, Oswaldo, Yuc.	107	467	414	41	113	150	17	4	4	48	19	2	10	22	4	36	0	4	7	.273	.324	.362
Moreno, David, Cam.	27	24	21	6	5	5	0	0	0	2	1	0	0	2	0	6	0	0	1	.238	.304	.238
Mota, Roberto, Pue.*	1	1	1	0	0	0	0	0	0	0	0	0	0	0	0	0	0	0	0	.000	.000	.000
Munoz, Adan, Monc.*	43	158	138	14	36	39	1	0	0	15	0	4	4	12	0	24	3	3	3	.261	.329	.283
Munoz, Jose, Sal.*	71	298	244	39	59	73	5	0	3	37	1	1	2	50	5	47	7	6	1	.242	.374	.299
Munoz, Noe, Sal.	103	424	352	61	108	165	30	0	9	50	2	1	7	62	3	57	0	2	13	.307	.419	.469
Murray, Glenn, Cam.-Yuc.	48	198	173	25	40	71	7	0	8	19	0	0	4	21	1	52	1	1	3	.231	.328	.410
Nerei, Yuji, Pue.*	4	12	12	0	1	1	0	0	0	0	0	0	0	0	0	2	0	0	0	.083	.083	.083
Newson, Warren, Mont.*	39	161	128	24	31	55	6	0	6	17	0	1	0	32	5	33	3	1	2	.242	.391	.430
Nieves, Melvin, Tor.†	61	257	197	43	62	121	17	0	14	52	0	3	6	51	2	62	4	1	3	.315	.463	.614
Nunez, Reymond, Lar.	107	449	422	71	137	219	29	1	17	92	0	2	3	22	2	68	2	1	19	.325	.361	.519
Ojeda, Miguel, Mex.	98	412	341	79	120	201	22	1	19	80	1	3	1	66	2	49	8	5	7	.352	.455	.589
Olivares, Roberto, Ver.	7	8	7	0	1	1	0	0	0	0	0	0	1	0	0	2	0	0	0	.143	.250	.143
Orantes, Ramon, Mont.	89	379	343	49	117	177	16	1	14	61	2	4	4	26	2	53	4	1	14	.341	.390	.516
Orrantia, Carlos, Mont.	37	65	53	11	8	8	0	0	0	4	0	2	6	0	11	0	0	0	.151	.262	.151
Ortega, Antonio, Cam.	28	47	37	6	11	11	0	0	0	5	1	1	1	7	1	11	0	0	1	.297	.413	.297
Ortiz, Alex, Tor.	102	453	394	63	115	193	9	0	23	70	0	6	2	51	1	52	0	1	9	.292	.371	.490
O'Sullivan, Patrick, Rey.	60	244	224	30	60	117	13	1	14	54	0	1	1	18	1	67	2	2	9	.268	.324	.522
Otanez, Willis, Can.-Monc.	70	298	263	29	71	120	13	0	12	43	0	3	0	32	2	52	0	2	6	.270	.346	.456
Otero, Ricky, Can.†	104	464	393	67	100	144	13	5	7	42	4	3	7	57	6	41	7	9	7	.254	.357	.366
Pacho, Carlos, Yuc.	12	15	13	2	3	3	0	0	0	3	0	0	1	1	0	2	0	0	0	.231	.333	.231
Pacho, Juan, Yuc.	28	92	82	7	17	19	2	0	0	7	4	0	0	6	0	4	0	1	3	.207	.261	.232
Paez, Hector, Cam.*	91	296	275	23	63	83	8	0	4	33	8	3	7	0	26	1	0	10	.229	.253	.302
Paez, Raul, Ver.-Tab.†	70	238	204	21	50	66	10	0	2	19	0	1	2	31	6	35	0	1	2	.245	.349	.324
Palafox, Sergio, Sal.	92	365	332	51	91	136	15	3	8	32	7	0	2	24	1	46	8	2	11	.274	.327	.410
Payro, Edison, Cam.-Yuc.*	29	72	60	6	11	13	2	0	0	3	2	2	0	8	1	16	0	1	0	.183	.271	.217
Pearson, Eddie, Tab.-Can.†	94	373	337	40	87	129	12	0	10	42	1	3	1	31	10	56	0	0	11	.258	.320	.383
Pemberton, Rudy, Monc.	57	238	215	51	82	144	18	1	14	53	0	1	3	19	3	26	5	2	5	.381	.437	.670

Player, Team	G	TPA	AB	R	H	TB	2B	3B	HR	RBI	SH	SF	HP	BB	IBB	SO	SB	CS	GDP	Avg.	OBP	Slg.
Perez, Alfredo, Cam.	36	70	61	6	8	8	0	0	0	1	3	0	2	4	1	9	0	0	3	.131	.209	.131
Perez, Francisco, Rey.*	69	176	164	13	46	70	16	1	2	28	3	1	3	5	1	47	0	1	2	.280	.312	.427
Perez, Jorge, Pue.*	25	62	49	10	9	15	1	1	1	4	2	1	4	6	0	14	0	0	3	.184	.317	.306
Perez, Jose, Mont.-Rey.	66	208	186	22	55	68	6	2	1	13	3	2	5	12	1	26	3	4	2	.296	.351	.366
Perez, Luis, Tor.	46	102	95	7	29	43	5	0	3	16	1	2	0	4	1	26	0	0	5	.305	.327	.453
Peterson, Charles, Tab.-Cam.	61	259	236	31	69	102	12	0	7	40	0	0	1	22	2	62	3	1	7	.292	.355	.432
Phillips, J.R., Yuc.-Mont.*	49	212	197	29	52	86	13	0	7	22	0	2	0	13	3	64	2	0	4	.264	.307	.437
Phillips, Tony, Mex.	7	35	30	8	7	7	0	0	0	2	0	0	0	5	0	8	2	0	0	.233	.343	.233
Pinto, Placido, Lar.	28	51	50	4	8	15	1	0	2	4	0	0	0	1	0	14	0	0	1	.160	.176	.300
Polonia, Luis, Tig.*	11	53	48	8	17	20	1	1	0	4	0	1	0	4	1	6	3	4	1	.354	.396	.417
Presichi, Cristian, Sal.	72	261	230	53	78	134	15	1	13	43	0	0	0	31	2	44	15	2	6	.339	.418	.583
Prieto, Chris, Oax.*	63	300	252	58	73	126	18	7	7	51	6	1	9	30	0	32	18	0	5	.290	.384	.500
Pulido, Raymundo, Cam.	23	1	1	0	1	1	0	0	0	1	0	0	0	0	0	0	0	0	0	1.000	1.000	1.000
Quinones, Ruben, Monc.-Cor.	47	132	121	5	33	42	9	0	0	8	2	0	2	7	0	12	0	1	7	.273	.323	.347
Quintero, Christian, Oax.	105	427	394	53	124	172	21	3	7	53	4	2	1	26	0	50	9	7	10	.315	.357	.437
Quintero, Edgar, Mont.	88	307	265	38	70	121	12	0	13	41	2	3	2	35	7	79	2	6	3	.264	.351	.457
Quintero, Guillermo, Ver.	33	94	89	5	13	17	4	0	0	3	3	0	0	2	0	18	0	0	2	.146	.165	.191
Ramirez, Deyby, Mex.	2	1	1	0	0	0	0	0	0	0	0	0	0	0	0	0	0	0	0	.000	.000	.000
Ramirez, Enrique, Can.	50	116	101	10	31	32	1	0	0	10	6	1	0	8	0	8	2	2	4	.307	.355	.317
Ramirez, Jesus, Oax.	48	151	127	27	34	39	3	1	0	7	6	1	5	12	0	12	1	1	5	.268	.352	.307
Ramirez, Johnathan, Oax.	11	11	10	2	2	2	0	0	0	1	0	0	0	1	0	3	0	0	2	.200	.273	.200
Ramirez, Omar, Ver.	107	490	437	78	138	204	27	3	11	44	3	3	7	40	1	37	19	3	7	.316	.380	.467
Ramirez, Oscar, Cam.	80	314	276	49	87	115	14	1	4	31	3	0	4	31	2	47	3	5	5	.315	.392	.417
Resendez, Carlos, Monc.	62	206	188	21	44	63	10	0	3	25	2	0	6	10	1	59	1	2	3	.234	.294	.335
Reyes, Eleazar, Mex.*	5	2	2	2	0	0	0	0	0	0	0	0	0	0	0	1	0	0	0	.000	.000	.000
Reyes, Jesus, Tor.*	1	1	1	0	0	0	0	0	0	0	0	0	0	0	0	1	0	0	0	.000	.000	.000
Riggs, Adam, Sal.	63	269	242	42	80	122	19	1	7	37	0	3	1	23	1	50	10	0	3	.331	.387	.504
Rincon, Isaias, Mex.	41	46	41	12	9	11	0	1	0	1	1	0	1	3	0	11	1	0	0	.220	.289	.268
Rios, Eduardo, Can.	106	458	424	57	107	189	19	0	21	69	1	3	5	25	1	84	4	2	15	.252	.300	.446
Rivera, Francisco, Ver.-Cor.*	48	97	84	6	22	30	5	0	1	9	0	1	0	12	1	12	1	0	2	.262	.351	.357
Rivera, Jesus, Tab.*	37	68	63	7	18	23	2	0	1	2	2	0	0	3	0	8	0	0	2	.286	.318	.365
Robles, Javier, Tig.	98	393	348	55	96	143	20	3	7	44	1	7	8	29	3	41	13	3	14	.276	.339	.411
Robles, Juan, Rey.	62	164	148	13	43	52	3	0	2	19	8	0	2	6	0	21	0	0	2	.291	.327	.351
Robles, Oscar, Oax.*	105	465	368	67	128	180	25	0	9	76	6	11	5	74	7	35	4	3	7	.348	.452	.489
Robles, Trinidad, Tig.	84	321	267	52	72	116	9	1	11	35	3	0	8	43	0	61	12	4	4	.270	.387	.434
Rodarte, Raul, Cor.-Mont.	102	425	374	69	121	193	20	2	16	74	1	5	7	38	2	50	11	8	11	.324	.392	.516
Rodriguez, Armando, Can.	31	70	60	4	12	16	1	0	1	5	3	0	0	7	0	18	0	3	4	.200	.284	.267
Rodriguez, Carlos, Tor.†	109	508	433	69	140	160	20	0	0	37	7	4	9	55	1	29	9	10	4	.323	.407	.370
Rodriguez, Erick, Oax.	24	46	40	3	13	21	2	0	2	7	2	1	0	3	0	9	0	0	0	.325	.364	.525
Rodriguez, Fernando, Cam.	97	376	341	33	98	131	12	0	7	37	2	2	1	30	1	39	1	0	14	.287	.345	.384
Rodriguez, Jose, Tor.	103	413	359	48	98	145	11	3	10	50	12	7	2	33	0	55	3	5	13	.273	.332	.404
Rodriguez, Liu, Sal.-Tab.†	69	273	238	39	72	92	10	2	2	22	1	0	8	26	1	28	7	0	8	.303	.390	.387
Rodriguez, Serafin, Tig.	76	284	252	44	77	98	7	1	4	35	9	2	3	18	0	21	10	6	4	.306	.356	.389
Rohrmeier, Dan, Tab.	11	45	40	3	10	13	3	0	0	3	0	0	0	5	0	9	0	0	1	.250	.333	.325
Rojas, Homar, Oax.	101	446	400	57	116	188	35	2	11	78	4	6	9	27	0	42	2	1	13	.290	.344	.470
Romero, Flavio, Sal.*	71	267	229	47	67	93	13	2	3	22	1	1	7	29	4	37	19	4	5	.293	.387	.406
Romero, Marco, Sal.	95	375	319	54	99	166	10	0	19	73	0	5	8	43	5	53	3	1	8	.310	.400	.520
Romero, Oscar, Rey.	94	311	274	25	63	93	12	0	6	23	4	3	4	26	2	32	3	0	6	.230	.303	.339
Romero, Willie, Sal.	95	411	367	85	142	219	29	3	14	77	0	4	5	35	1	52	18	4	8	.387	.443	.597
Romero, Yamil, Ver.*	15	22	19	2	3	4	1	0	0	0	0	0	0	3	0	5	0	0	1	.158	.273	.211
Roque, Rafael, Tig.*	15	0	0	1	0	0	0	0	0	0	0	0	0	0	0	0	0	0	0	.000	.000	.000
Ruiz, Juan, Mex.	42	96	90	9	20	26	3	0	1	18	1	2	0	3	0	11	0	0	3	.222	.242	.289
Ruiz, Ricardo, Ver.	9	12	11	0	2	2	0	0	0	1	0	0	0	1	0	1	0	0	0	.182	.250	.182
Saenz, Ricardo, Monc.	102	435	361	60	104	168	23	1	13	57	0	8	3	62	7	82	3	0	5	.288	.389	.465
Salas, Heriberto, Cor.-Yuc.	76	271	239	32	57	64	4	0	1	21	4	3	1	24	3	23	7	3	4	.238	.307	.268
Salazar, Carlos, Yuc.	6	5	2	1	0	0	0	0	0	0	0	0	1	2	0	1	0	0	0	.000	.600	.000
Salcedo, Eder, Mont.	11	19	18	0	1	1	0	0	0	0	1	0	0	0	0	7	0	0	0	.056	.056	.056
Samuels, Scott, Mont.*	15	53	50	4	10	15	2	0	1	5	0	0	0	3	0	7	1	0	2	.200	.245	.300
Sanchez. Wilfredo, Cor.	53	138	133	10	20	22	2	0	0	4	1	0	1	3	0	24	1	0	1	.150	.175	.165
Sanchez, Hector, Tor.	26	1	1	0	0	0	0	0	0	0	0	0	0	0	0	0	0	0	0	.000	.000	.000
Sanchez, Jesus, Can.	106	434	403	51	119	170	19	1	10	54	6	2	5	15	0	70	9	4	3	.295	.327	.422
Sanchez, Jose, Lar.	28	29	28	4	6	6	0	0	0	0	0	0	0	1	0	4	1	0	0	.214	.241	.214
Sanchez, Orlando, Lar.	27	70	65	10	18	24	6	0	0	6	1	0	1	3	0	15	2	1	1	.277	.319	.369
Sanchez, Roque, Cam.-Cor.	88	293	272	22	73	101	13	0	5	26	12	0	0	9	1	23	0	1	7	.268	.292	.371
Sanchez, Victor, Tab.	11	44	41	4	9	14	2	0	1	4	0	0	0	3	0	8	0	0	0	.220	.273	.341
Sandoval, Jose, Mex.	97	388	336	57	100	170	24	2	14	72	0	9	2	41	4	59	3	1	7	.298	.369	.506
Sandoval, Octavio, Tig.	96	323	286	42	72	105	12	3	5	38	12	3	4	18	1	47	5	2	3	.252	.302	.367
Santana, Mario, Tab.	49	112	101	9	27	36	3	0	2	6	4	0	1	6	1	18	0	0	4	.267	.315	.356
Santos, Andres, Lar.	26	82	74	11	20	38	3	0	5	12	1	0	1	6	0	9	0	0	1	.270	.333	.514
Sauceda, Victor, Can.†	58	42	35	13	6	7	1	0	0	1	0	0	0	7	0	5	1	2	0	.171	.310	.200
Saucedo, Robert, Lar.	108	446	390	68	123	233	14	0	32	84	0	2	4	50	6	69	5	3	7	.315	.397	.597
Sherman, Darrell, Monc.*	98	447	364	73	132	164	23	3	1	35	1	0	11	71	3	36	25	4	7	.363	.480	.451
Sievers, Carlos, Tab.*	33	95	85	10	22	38	7	0	3	15	1	1	0	8	1	15	0	0	0	.259	.319	.447
Sisco, Steve, Sal.	14	62	55	9	9	16	1	0	2	5	0	0	0	7	1	16	0	0	3	.164	.258	.291
Smith, Charles, Mont.	106	458	401	77	129	235	25	0	27	86	1	1	9	46	9	71	2	0	11	.322	.403	.586
Smith, Demond, Mont.†	87	406	352	74	111	154	12	2	9	48	6	3	7	38	3	72	41	12	3	.315	.390	.438
Solis, Marco, Ver.	8	12	12	1	1	1	0	0	0	0	0	0	0	0	0	6	0	0	1	.083	.083	.083
Soriano, Ricardo, Cor.*	60	200	175	18	44	54	8	1	0	12	1	2	3	19	1	24	2	3	5	.251	.332	.309
Soto, Saul, Oax.	99	409	364	61	104	176	27	0	15	58	0	5	7	33	3	46	0	1	13	.286	.352	.484
Soto, Victor, Ver.	1	1	1	0	0	0	0	0	0	0	0	0	0	0	0	0	0	0	0	.000	.000	.000
Sotomayor, Gilberto, Monc.*	91	298	272	32	72	86	14	0	0	26	4	2	1	19	0	36	4	1	10	.265	.313	.316
Suarez, Luis, Tig.*	39	128	119	12	36	56	12	1	2	17	0	2	1	6	1	14	4	0	4	.303	.336	.471

CLASS AAA Mexican League

Player, Team	G	TPA	AB	R	H	TB	2B	3B	HR	RBI	SH	SF	HP	BB	IBB	SO	SB	CS	GDP	Avg.	OBP	Slg.
Tellez, Alonso, Rey.-Yuc.	96	375	352	34	100	149	16	0	11	59	0	0	0	23	7	55	1	0	13	.284	.328	.423
Tolentino, Juan, Tig.	10	47	41	3	7	7	0	0	0	3	0	0	1	5	0	10	0	1	0	.171	.277	.171
Torrero, Miguel, Pue.	18	30	26	6	11	14	1	1	0	2	0	0	1	3	0	0	0	1	1	.423	.500	.538
Tovar, Jose, Rey.†	20	22	20	3	3	6	3	0	0	2	1	0	0	1	0	4	0	1	0	.150	.190	.300
Trapaga, Julio, Tig.-Pue.	63	190	179	23	49	75	8	0	6	23	1	3	0	7	0	52	3	2	6	.274	.296	.419
Tress, Irving, Cor.	10	28	23	3	5	6	1	0	0	2	1	0	0	4	0	8	1	0	0	.217	.333	.261
Valdez, Emmanuel, Tig.	75	249	204	47	64	109	15	0	10	44	6	1	5	33	0	60	4	0	3	.314	.420	.534
Valdez, Francisco, Tab.-Ver.	93	328	287	20	75	99	9	0	5	30	5	1	12	23	4	26	0	2	11	.261	.341	.345
Valdez, Ramon, Cam.*	102	404	366	41	94	116	11	4	1	25	8	1	5	24	1	34	17	6	8	.257	.311	.317
Valdez, Uriel, Cor.*	17	23	20	6	4	7	0	0	1	1	0	0	1	2	0	5	2	0	0	.200	.304	.350
Valencia, Abraham, Lar.	54	123	115	9	36	48	3	0	3	16	0	0	3	5	0	23	0	0	5	.313	.358	.417
Valencia, Carlos, Lar.	102	454	424	72	128	188	18	3	12	49	7	5	2	16	2	45	3	8	15	.302	.327	.443
Valenzuela, Irving, Monc.	28	40	38	7	9	9	0	0	0	2	0	0	0	2	0	9	1	0	1	.237	.275	.237
Valle, Cosme, Mex.	47	144	139	20	39	70	13	0	6	27	0	1	1	3	0	28	0	3	3	.281	.299	.504
Valle, Jorge, Tor.	108	461	425	53	118	161	23	1	6	54	9	6	7	14	2	61	2	2	16	.278	.308	.379
Valle, Roberto, Rey.	46	48	39	17	10	14	1	0	1	3	3	0	1	5	1	7	0	1	1	.256	.356	.359
Vaz, Roberto, Cam.*	6	24	19	0	3	3	0	0	0	3	0	2	0	3	0	6	1	1	0	.158	.250	.158
Vazquez, Gregorio, Tab.	94	374	338	42	99	133	13	3	5	33	7	3	1	25	2	39	10	4	9	.293	.341	.393
Vazquez, Jorge Alberto, Tig.	67	201	189	29	52	92	10	0	10	35	3	2	3	4	0	50	0	0	4	.275	.298	.487
Vega, Edgar, Pue.	87	293	270	28	75	103	16	0	4	39	6	0	2	15	1	40	0	1	9	.278	.321	.381
Vega, Jesus, Pue.	44	103	95	9	19	29	4	0	2	8	0	0	0	8	0	23	0	0	2	.200	.262	.305
Velazquez, Guillermo, Sal.-Cam.*	92	367	326	43	91	146	10	0	15	65	0	4	0	36	4	63	0	1	11	.279	.347	.448
Velez, Manuel, Mont.	105	420	360	47	106	135	20	0	3	51	12	8	4	36	0	39	3	1	12	.294	.358	.375
Verdugo, Vincente, Sal.	60	237	219	17	63	71	8	0	0	27	5	2	1	10	0	23	0	0	7	.288	.319	.324
Villalobos, Carlos, Monc.-Tab.	99	410	373	57	108	170	21	1	13	64	3	3	6	25	3	81	6	2	8	.290	.342	.456
Villarreal, Alejandro, Lar.	49	120	105	9	27	41	8	0	2	17	3	1	2	9	2	13	0	0	6	.257	.325	.390
Villegas, Fernando, Can.	93	344	304	29	95	120	16	0	3	26	0	2	5	33	2	52	2	3	5	.313	.387	.395
Virgen, Constancio, Cor.	31	84	77	10	13	16	3	0	0	5	1	0	1	5	0	16	1	0	1	.169	.229	.208
Vizcarra, Roberto, Tig.	88	343	306	44	92	121	10	2	5	42	1	4	7	25	2	17	10	3	10	.301	.363	.395
Warner, Michael, Yuc.*	35	144	115	20	31	42	8	0	1	15	2	3	2	22	3	26	1	1	2	.270	.387	.365
Whiten, Mark, Ver.†	34	144	117	14	31	45	2	0	4	22	1	1	2	23	4	25	1	0	4	.265	.392	.385
Whitmore, Darrell, Tab.*	14	55	52	5	13	18	5	0	0	3	0	0	0	3	0	10	0	0	2	.250	.291	.346
Yan, Julian, Cor.	104	421	374	50	106	188	8	1	24	70	0	0	4	43	2	90	4	0	9	.283	.363	.503
Yuriar, Jesus, Can.	14	28	24	2	7	8	1	0	0	0	1	0	1	2	1	3	0	1	1	.292	.370	.333
Zambrano, Eduardo, Can.	13	53	45	5	8	11	0	0	1	8	0	0	0	8	0	16	0	0	1	.178	.302	.244
Zambrano, Roberto, Lar.	68	299	242	54	73	149	14	1	20	58	0	3	9	45	1	61	1	0	8	.302	.425	.616
Zazueta, Juan, Rey.†	110	469	414	48	123	154	21	2	2	45	17	5	2	31	2	48	15	8	11	.297	.345	.372
Zazueta, Mauricio, Monc.	104	452	414	63	117	164	17	3	8	45	8	2	4	21	4	66	11	1	13	.283	.327	.396

PLAYERS WITH TWO OR MORE TEAMS

Player, Team	G	TPA	AB	R	H	TB	2B	3B	HR	RBI	SH	SF	HP	BB	IBB	SO	SB	CS	GDP	Avg.	OBP	Slg.
Abrego, Jesus, Can.*	23	43	39	1	7	7	0	0	0	4	1	0	0	3	0	8	0	0	1	.179	.238	.179
Abrego, Jesus, Ver.*	25	56	51	7	12	20	2	0	2	9	0	0	1	4	0	9	0	1	0	.235	.304	.392
Adriana, Sharnol, Cam.	23	99	83	11	17	27	1	0	3	9	0	1	3	12	1	19	2	4	4	.205	.323	.325
Adriana, Sharnol, Cor.	71	300	273	41	96	157	14	1	15	59	0	4	4	19	1	41	7	5	10	.352	.397	.575
Aguilera, Antonio, Cam.†	7	13	9	2	2	2	0	0	0	1	1	1	0	2	1	4	0	0	0	.222	.333	.222
Aguilera, Antonio, Yuc.†	22	62	48	11	10	12	2	0	0	3	1	0	3	10	1	10	0	1	0	.208	.377	.250
Barrera, Nelson, Mex.	4	9	9	1	3	3	0	0	0	1	0	0	0	0	0	2	0	0	1	.333	.333	.333
Barrera, Nelson, Cam.	1	3	3	0	0	0	0	0	0	0	0	0	0	0	0	0	0	0	0	.000	.000	.000
Barron, Tony, Ver.	35	146	125	19	38	61	5	0	6	16	0	0	4	17	2	34	0	0	3	.304	.404	.488
Barron, Tony, Pue.	29	107	96	9	24	35	5	0	2	16	0	3	0	8	3	20	0	1	4	.250	.299	.365
Benitez, Yamil, Rey.	35	144	138	12	32	46	6	1	2	13	0	0	1	5	0	29	0	0	5	.232	.264	.333
Benitez, Yamil, Cam.	7	20	19	2	6	11	2	0	1	4	0	0	0	1	0	3	0	0	0	.316	.350	.579
Cobos, Rogelio, Ver.	23	51	46	3	9	12	0	0	1	4	1	1	0	3	0	21	0	0	3	.196	.260	.261
Cobos, Rogelio, Can.	21	40	35	3	10	14	1	0	1	9	2	2	0	1	0	6	0	1	0	.286	.289	.400
Cruz, Marco, Yuc.	5	11	10	1	0	0	0	0	0	0	0	0	0	1	0	2	0	0	0	.000	.091	.000
Cruz, Marco, Cam.	23	38	33	5	6	11	2	0	1	2	3	0	2	0	0	5	0	0	1	.182	.229	.333
De Los Santos, Luis, Mex.	23	98	87	13	32	53	9	0	4	10	0	0	1	10	0	15	0	0	3	.368	.439	.609
De Los Santos, Luis, Oax.	32	143	128	17	34	41	4	0	1	20	0	3	1	11	0	24	0	0	5	.266	.322	.320
Espinoza, Ramon, Rey.	59	243	233	37	73	108	15	1	6	25	1	1	3	5	1	24	6	6	6	.313	.335	.464
Espinoza, Ramon, Yuc.	44	204	189	27	60	73	4	3	1	14	2	2	0	11	3	13	5	2	10	.317	.351	.386
Fentanes, Oscar, Tab.	64	244	210	27	49	72	8	0	5	29	0	2	15	17	2	24	2	1	5	.233	.332	.343
Fentanes, Oscar, Ver.	41	172	158	19	45	64	4	0	5	21	1	1	7	5	0	17	1	0	5	.285	.333	.405
Garcia, Guillermo, Cor.	29	126	115	8	26	39	7	0	2	13	0	2	0	9	0	27	0	0	3	.226	.278	.339
Garcia, Guillermo, Tig.	76	324	266	58	80	172	17	0	25	79	0	4	5	49	5	67	0	1	11	.301	.414	.647
Gastelum, Carlos, Pue.	68	292	266	46	85	103	11	2	1	20	7	3	4	12	3	28	12	4	5	.320	.354	.387
Gastelum, Carlos, Tig.	27	122	108	18	31	35	4	0	0	8	3	2	3	6	0	13	7	3	2	.287	.336	.324
Gonzalez, Jesus, Yuc.	64	283	254	36	83	115	9	1	7	36	2	2	3	22	2	36	11	0	7	.327	.384	.453
Gonzalez, Jesus, Monc.	14	60	55	9	14	17	3	0	0	5	0	0	0	5	1	8	3	0	1	.255	.317	.309
Iturbe, Pedro, Tig.*	62	245	224	35	73	121	21	3	7	31	0	1	3	17	2	25	2	3	10	.326	.380	.540
Iturbe, Pedro, Pue.*	15	56	50	4	11	18	4	0	1	5	0	0	1	5	1	9	0	1	1	.220	.304	.360
Jennings, Doug, Cam.*	27	111	95	14	29	46	5	0	4	12	0	1	5	10	0	15	0	1	3	.305	.394	.484
Jennings, Doug, Tab.*	9	37	30	5	8	12	4	0	0	0	0	1	0	6	0	6	0	0	3	.267	.405	.400
Leyva, German, Tab.*	42	162	142	14	38	49	5	0	2	16	1	0	19	6	6	8	1	1	6	.268	.354	.345
Leyva, German, Yuc.*	19	72	63	8	15	19	4	0	0	5	2	1	0	6	2	6	0	0	1	.238	.300	.302
Lopez, Fabian, Oax.*	3	2	1	1	0	0	0	0	0	0	0	0	1	0	0	0	0	0	0	.000	.500	.000
Lopez, Fabian, Can.*	67	192	171	18	35	45	4	0	2	16	1	4	2	14	3	20	1	1	3	.205	.267	.263
Meza, Alfredo, Ver.†	61	224	203	19	50	65	6	0	3	21	5	2	3	11	1	31	0	2	6	.246	.292	.320
Meza, Alfredo, Tab.†	39	128	122	4	38	41	3	0	0	6	1	1	1	3	1	13	0	1	6	.311	.331	.336
Murray, Glenn, Cam.	43	176	155	23	36	67	7	0	8	19	0	0	4	17	1	48	0	1	3	.232	.324	.432
Murray, Glenn, Yuc.	5	22	18	2	4	4	0	0	0	0	0	0	4	0	0	4	1	0	0	.222	.364	.222
Otanez, Willis, Can.	44	188	158	20	42	78	9	0	9	30	0	2	0	28	2	33	0	2	3	.266	.372	.494

Player, Team	G	TPA	AB	R	H	TB	2B	3B	HR	RBI	SH	SF	HP	BB	IBB	SO	SB	CS	GDP	Avg.	OBP	Slg.
Otanez, Willis, Monc.	26	110	105	9	29	42	4	0	3	13	0	1	0	4	0	19	0	0	3	.276	.300	.400
Paez, Raul, Ver.†	32	119	99	12	25	34	6	0	1	12	0	1	1	18	1	19	0	0	1	.253	.370	.343
Paez, Raul, Tab.†	38	119	105	9	25	32	4	0	1	7	0	0	1	13	5	16	0	1	1	.238	.328	.305
Payro, Edison, Cam.*	22	58	49	5	10	12	2	0	0	3	0	2	0	7	1	14	0	0	0	.204	.293	.245
Payro, Edison, Yuc.*	7	14	11	1	1	1	0	0	0	0	2	0	0	1	0	2	0	1	0	.091	.167	.091
Pearson, Eddie, Tab.†	59	241	221	22	55	87	8	0	8	33	1	2	0	17	5	35	0	0	9	.249	.300	.394
Pearson, Eddie, Can.†	35	132	116	18	32	42	4	0	2	9	0	1	1	14	5	21	0	0	2	.276	.356	.362
Perez, Jose, Mont.	45	145	131	11	36	42	3	0	1	11	1	2	3	8	0	21	2	3	2	.275	.326	.321
Perez, Jose, Rey.	21	63	55	11	19	26	3	2	0	2	2	0	2	4	1	5	1	1	0	.345	.410	.473
Peterson, Charles, Tab.	39	172	159	19	47	66	10	0	3	27	0	0	1	12	2	41	3	0	5	.296	.349	.415
Peterson, Charles, Cam.	22	87	77	12	22	36	2	0	4	13	0	0	0	10	0	21	0	1	2	.286	.368	.468
Phillips, J.R., Yuc.*	22	95	88	11	22	37	6	0	3	14	0	2	0	5	3	31	0	0	3	.250	.284	.420
Phillips, J.R., Mont.*	27	117	109	18	30	49	7	0	4	8	0	0	0	8	0	33	2	0	1	.275	.325	.450
Quinones, Ruben, Monc.	21	55	51	0	13	17	4	0	0	3	1	0	0	3	0	6	0	0	1	.255	.296	.333
Quinones, Ruben, Cor.	26	77	70	5	20	25	5	0	0	5	1	0	2	4	0	6	0	1	6	.286	.342	.357
Rivera, Francisco, Ver.*	2	2	2	0	1	1	0	0	0	0	0	0	0	0	0	1	0	0	0	.500	.500	.500
Rivera, Francisco, Cor.*	46	95	82	6	21	29	5	0	1	9	0	1	0	12	1	11	1	0	2	.256	.347	.354
Rodarte, Raul, Cor.	23	98	83	11	22	34	4	1	2	10	1	1	4	9	0	10	0	3	2	.265	.361	.410
Rodarte, Raul, Mont.	79	327	291	58	99	159	16	1	14	64	0	4	3	29	2	40	11	5	9	.340	.401	.546
Rodriguez, Liu, Sal.†	47	208	186	33	57	75	8	2	2	19	1	0	7	14	0	23	5	0	7	.306	.377	.403
Rodriguez, Liu, Tab.†	22	65	52	6	15	17	2	0	0	3	0	0	1	12	1	5	2	0	1	.288	.431	.327
Salas, Heriberto, Cor.	65	259	229	29	53	57	4	0	0	17	4	3	1	22	3	21	7	2	4	.231	.298	.249
Salas, Heriberto, Yuc.	11	12	10	3	4	7	0	0	1	4	0	0	0	2	0	2	0	1	0	.400	.500	.700
Sanchez, Roque, Cam.	63	204	193	14	54	74	11	0	3	21	7	0	0	4	0	15	0	0	4	.280	.294	.383
Sanchez, Roque, Cor.	25	89	79	8	19	27	2	0	2	5	5	0	0	5	1	8	0	1	3	.241	.286	.342
Tellez, Alonso, Rey.	65	238	225	25	61	95	10	0	8	33	0	0	0	13	5	38	1	0	10	.271	.311	.422
Tellez, Alonso, Yuc.	31	137	127	9	39	54	6	0	3	26	0	0	0	10	2	17	0	0	3	.307	.358	.425
Trapaga, Julio, Tig.	45	120	112	14	28	45	2	0	5	17	1	2	0	5	0	35	3	2	4	.250	.277	.402
Trapaga, Julio, Pue.	18	70	67	9	21	30	6	0	1	6	0	1	0	2	0	17	0	0	2	.313	.329	.448
Valdez, Francisco, Tab.	56	190	171	16	48	68	8	0	4	25	2	1	5	11	1	20	0	2	7	.281	.340	.398
Valdez, Francisco, Ver.	37	138	116	4	27	31	1	0	1	5	3	0	7	12	3	6	0	0	4	.233	.341	.267
Velazquez, Guillermo, Sal.* ...	33	126	112	14	32	53	6	0	5	25	0	2	0	12	2	19	0	0	4	.286	.349	.473
Velazquez, Guillermo, Cam.*..	59	241	214	29	59	93	4	0	10	40	0	2	0	24	2	44	0	1	7	.276	.346	.435
Villalobos, Carlos, Monc.	40	169	158	27	49	73	7	1	5	29	0	0	1	10	1	39	4	1	6	.310	.355	.462
Villalobos, Carlos, Tab.	59	241	215	30	59	97	14	0	8	35	3	3	5	15	2	42	2	1	2	.274	.332	.451

GRAND SLAMS: G. Garcia, 3; S. Almeida, E. Jimenez, C. Quintero, Ma. Romero, 2 each; Abrego, Adriana, Aganza, T. Barron, H. Castaneda, Cazarin, Connell, E. Diaz, Espinoza, R. Esquer, O. Fentanes, Grijak, Ju. Hernandez, Jose, Kelly, R. Lopez, E. Martinez, L. Martinez, Ram. Martinez, Nieves, Ojeda, Prieto, O. Ramirez, Riggs, E. Rios, O. Robles, Rojas, O. Romero, W. Romero, Salas, S. Soto, Velazquez, Vizcarra, Yan, R. Zambrano, J. Zazueta, M. Zazueta, 1 each.

AWARDED FIRST BASE ON CATCHER'S INTERFERENCE: Je. Sanchez 3 (M. Cruz, Gavia, S. Gutierrez), Prieto 2 (Franco, Gavia), E. Arano (S. Gutierrez), O. Garcia (S. Gutierrez), H. Gomez (E. Vega), Robles (C. Gastelum), Saenz (S. Gutierrez), Velazquez (H. Paez).

2002 PITCHING

TEAM

Team	W	L	Pct.	ERA	G	CG	ShO	Sv.	IP	H	TBF	R	ER	HR	SH	SF	HB	BB	IBB	SO	WP	Bk.
Yucatan	60	47	.561	3.21	107	9	7	24	953.0	929	4078	376	340	58	46	24	56	331	19	674	59	5
Cancun	53	54	.495	3.58	107	16	12	24	925.2	896	3873	410	368	82	41	28	37	293	44	572	46	0
Tabasco	48	61	.440	3.73	109	7	7	25	954.2	1032	4128	469	396	64	62	31	41	316	38	528	27	1
Campeche	52	55	.486	3.95	107	8	6	25	928.0	921	3970	450	407	104	55	28	62	289	21	685	45	2
Oaxaca	62	45	.579	4.04	108	5	9	28	945.2	1051	4138	499	424	74	26	20	42	340	7	621	43	6
Monterrey	60	49	.550	4.09	109	5	11	35	956.1	974	4180	486	435	76	47	30	66	384	36	680	45	2
Mex. City Reds..	74	36	.673	4.34	110	7	4	37	963.1	1151	4221	537	465	82	45	24	44	289	21	590	44	3
Saltillo	66	43	.606	4.45	109	4	5	29	947.0	1074	4170	516	468	96	52	32	42	332	15	607	34	3
Reynosa	43	67	.391	4.57	110	9	6	27	930.2	996	4184	560	473	91	45	27	51	469	20	658	48	9
Monclova	56	54	.509	4.68	110	7	6	32	955.1	1083	4243	549	497	87	40	32	59	369	11	509	50	3
Dos Laredos	62	48	.564	4.81	110	5	7	25	961.2	1126	4299	580	514	94	39	38	40	369	22	607	54	4
Veracruz	55	53	.509	4.83	109	6	14	35	956.2	1078	4213	564	513	107	50	30	50	312	25	524	36	3
Mex. City Tigers.	57	49	.538	5.03	106	2	3	31	918.2	1031	4099	560	513	96	57	19	64	394	38	651	62	4
Puebla	38	70	.352	5.10	108	6	8	24	929.1	1118	4125	565	527	113	58	40	46	335	27	495	40	3
Cordoba	37	71	.343	5.60	108	6	3	20	936.1	1080	4232	617	583	104	58	51	71	391	54	444	43	5
Torreon.............	44	65	.404	5.87	109	3	4	21	945.0	1121	4370	688	616	118	53	31	42	468	28	588	62	3

INDIVIDUAL

TOP QUALIFIERS FOR EARNED-RUN AVERAGE TITLE

Minimum 88 innings. *Lefthanded pitcher.

Pitcher, Team	W	L	Pct.	ERA	G	GS	CG	ShO	GF	Sv.	IP	H	TBF	R	ER	HR	SH	SF	HB	BB	IBB	SO	WP	Bk.
Hurtado, Edwin, Can.	9	5	.643	1.38	16	14	7	3	1	1	117	78	447	21	18	4	2	1	3	27	1	113	10	0
Rodriguez, Salvador, Yuc.	11	5	.688	2.09	21	21	7	3	0	0	155	146	619	40	36	5	8	7	5	22	2	104	6	1
Lomeli, Israel, Can.	7	5	.583	2.45	17	15	1	1	0	0	92	61	363	32	25	12	2	0	2	38	2	83	3	0
Mora, Eleazar, Ver.*	15	6	.714	2.50	23	23	2	0	0	0	154.2	126	614	53	43	9	4	2	5	32	0	89	4	1
Romero, Alejandro, Monc.	11	6	.647	2.77	22	21	3	1	1	0	149.2	145	630	51	46	10	6	1	8	44	1	85	3	1
Quiroz, Aaron, Sal.	8	3	.727	2.78	17	15	2	1	0	0	90.2	84	366	30	28	8	5	0	2	19	1	62	2	1
Valdez, Efrain, Cor.-Tab.*	11	9	.550	2.83	26	23	5	3	3	0	156	145	633	53	49	9	9	3	6	45	2	94	4	0
Delahoya, Javier, Sal.	11	3	.786	2.84	20	20	0	0	0	0	133.1	120	556	57	42	9	9	6	4	48	0	97	4	0
Ramirez, Roberto, Mex.*	14	2	.875	2.84	20	20	0	0	0	0	111	132	477	57	35	9	3	3	4	25	0	55	2	0
Palafox, Juan, Yuc.	10	6	.625	3.05	22	20	1	0	0	0	138.2	143	590	51	47	11	7	3	12	33	1	73	3	0
Dominguez, David, Oax.	7	5	.583	3.23	23	21	0	0	0	0	128.1	143	546	59	46	12	4	1	7	39	0	82	3	0

Pitcher, Team	W	L	Pct.	ERA	G	GS	CG	ShO	GF	Sv.	IP	H	TBF	R	ER	HR	SH	SF	HB	BB	IBB	SO	WP	Bk.
Vega, Obed, Can.	9	8	.529	3.35	24	23	6	1	1	1	156	142	633	62	58	11	7	4	1	41	6	107	3	0
Manrique, Alberto, Rey.-Mont.	8	7	.533	3.36	18	17	4	1	1	1	109.2	114	467	52	41	10	5	0	9	34	1	72	2	0
Rios, Jesus, Yuc.-Tab.	9	4	.692	3.37	21	21	3	2	0	0	120.1	124	518	48	45	7	6	5	9	37	2	72	5	0
Elizalde, Carlos, Oax.	9	6	.600	3.38	21	18	0	0	0	0	114.2	114	495	49	43	9	5	2	4	44	0	64	5	0

DEPARTMENTAL LEADERS: W—E. Mora, 15; L—L. Cruz, 14; Pct.—R. Ramirez, .875; G—J. Villegas, 57; GS—A. Moreno, 24; CG—Hurtado, S. Rodriguez, 7 each; ShO—Hurtado, S. Rodriguez, E. Valdez, 3 each; GF—Rubio, 50; Sv.—Rubio, 32; IP—E. Valdez, Vega, 156.0 each; H—Jose Nunez (Dos Laredos), 181; TBF—Jose Nunez (Dos Laredos), 663; R—Jose Nunez (Dos Laredos), 85; ER—Jose Nunez (Dos Laredos), O. Rivera, 75 each; HR—O. Rivera, 21; SH—Romano, 13; SF—E. Perez, 8; HB—Mi. Gomez, 15; BB—Loya, 62; IBB—F. Rivera, 12; SO—Campos, 125; WP—Atondo, 15; BK—Gutierrez, A. Medina, 3.

ALL PITCHERS

*Lefthanded pitcher.

Pitcher, Team	W	L	Pct.	ERA	G	GS	CG	ShO	GF	Sv.	IP	H	TBF	R	ER	HR	SH	SF	HB	BB	IBB	SO	WP	Bk.
Aceves, Alfredo, Yuc.	1	2	.333	3.00	23	4	0	0	3	0	45	42	200	22	15	0	1	1	4	20	1	25	2	0
Acosta, Aaron, Cam.	0	5	.000	5.84	16	12	0	0	0	0	61.2	77	297	47	40	7	2	1	6	36	1	41	4	0
Acosta, David, Mex.*	0	0	.000	5.30	11	0	0	0	5	0	18.2	18	90	15	11	3	0	1	1	17	0	9	1	0
Acosta, Jasiel, Monc.*	9	5	.643	4.89	19	18	1	0	1	0	105	106	452	62	57	15	4	4	6	50	0	66	3	0
Aguilar, Hugo, Monc.*	3	5	.375	4.87	16	11	1	0	1	0	68.1	73	300	38	37	6	2	0	1	33	0	37	6	0
Aguilar, Miguel, Tor.*	0	0	.000	5.40	11	0	0	0	3	0	15	16	71	13	9	1	0	0	1	9	0	8	2	0
Aguirre, Gaudencio, Mont.	1	3	.250	3.36	43	1	0	0	6	0	59	63	270	24	22	3	5	5	9	26	6	34	3	0
Alberro, Jose, Monc.	4	2	.667	2.62	42	1	0	0	36	22	55	41	230	19	16	2	3	3	22	0	51	2	0
Aleman, Paulo, Cor.	0	0	.000	14.40	12	0	0	0	2	0	15	26	77	24	24	4	1	1	4	9	1	6	1	0
Almeida, Rowsell, Lar.	0	0	.000	5.74	18	0	0	0	7	1	31.1	41	151	23	20	4	0	2	1	17	1	14	1	0
Alvarez, Antonio, Monc.	4	5	.444	3.97	16	16	1	0	0	0	90.2	101	392	47	40	9	4	0	10	25	0	33	1	1
Alvarez, Juan, Tor.	7	6	.538	3.65	25	22	1	0	2	1	135.2	136	578	65	55	8	11	5	7	50	2	74	5	0
Alvarez, Octavio, Mex.	9	3	.750	3.75	22	14	1	0	3	0	96	90	397	42	40	9	6	0	5	24	1	59	7	0
Alvarez, Trevor, Tor.	5	5	.500	2.82	46	1	0	0	34	11	60.2	43	257	22	19	4	2	1	3	32	2	58	3	0
Amarillas, Asdrubal, Cor.	1	2	.333	5.18	19	8	0	0	2	0	64.1	73	294	40	37	4	0	2	2	32	3	19	7	0
Angulo, Victor, Tig.*	0	0	.000	6.75	2	0	0	0	1	0	1.1	3	8	4	1	1	0	0	1	0	0	1	0	0
Antuna, Victor, Mont.	0	0	.000	1.59	13	0	0	0	9	0	11.1	11	53	4	2	1	0	0	0	10	0	6	1	0
Arellano, Salvador, Yuc.	6	5	.545	3.56	15	13	0	0	0	0	68.1	64	301	30	27	4	2	1	8	39	0	54	8	1
Armas, Noel, Pue.	0	2	.000	5.21	7	2	0	0	2	0	19	20	78	11	11	1	1	0	1	6	1	5	0	1
Armenta, Alejandro, Tig.*	0	0	.000	5.63	5	0	0	0	1	0	8	10	35	6	5	1	0	0	2	0	0	7	1	0
Arredondo, Eduardo, Ver.	0	0	.000	9.00	1	0	0	0	0	0	1	1	5	1	1	0	0	0	0	1	0	0	0	0
Atondo, Sergio, Yuc.	5	8	.385	4.05	17	16	0	0	0	0	93.1	89	422	46	42	7	7	1	3	59	1	81	15	1
Avalos, Jose, Oax.	1	1	.500	2.75	39	0	0	0	10	3	36	38	155	13	11	2	2	1	0	16	2	21	1	0
Ayala, Luis, Sal.	3	5	.375	1.68	49	0	0	0	43	23	53.2	43	225	16	10	2	2	0	7	15	2	43	0	0
Baez, Sixto, Oax.	3	1	.750	3.57	44	0	0	0	32	15	40.1	41	163	18	16	1	1	1	4	1		29	2	2
Barradas, Roberto, Sal.	0	1	.000	6.30	2	2	0	0	0	0	10	13	43	7	7	1	0	1	2	1	0	3	0	0
Barrett, Sigfrido, Can.	0	0	.000	0.00	1	0	0	0	0	0	2	0	7	0	0	0	0	0	0	1	0	1	0	0
Barron, Abelino, Tor.	1	0	1.000	4.50	7	0	0	0	1	0	8	8	37	5	4	1	0	1	1	5	1	2	1	0
Bell, Richard, Lar.*	2	0	1.000	2.41	18	0	0	0	15	7	18.2	14	79	6	5	1	3	0	1	12	1	13	0	0
Beltran, Alonso, Tig.	4	6	.400	5.46	13	11	0	0	0	0	62.2	72	279	40	38	6	7	1	5	23	1	42	2	0
Bencomo, Juan Carlos, Ver.	0	0	.000	13.50	6	0	0	0	3	0	6	16	40	12	9	0	0	2	3	0	4	1	0
Bernal, Christian, Mex.-Can.	0	0	.000	10.80	2	0	0	0	1	0	1.2	0	7	2	2	0	0	0	3	0	3	0	0
Bernal, Manuel, Mex.	12	9	.571	4.55	22	22	3	2	0	0	142.1	176	613	79	72	14	7	1	11	21	3	76	3	0
Blancas, Rigoberto, Cor.	1	2	.333	7.09	30	1	0	0	10	1	26.2	30	121	21	21	9	2	2	3	10	1	10	0	0
Cabrales, Gabriel, Pue.	3	5	.375	4.14	30	7	1	0	6	2	82.2	105	357	42	38	12	6	2	2	15	2	43	1	0
Camara, Pedro, Yuc.-Tor.*	0	6	.000	8.12	14	9	0	0	1	0	37.2	55	191	39	34	8	3	2	3	29	0	26	5	0
Campillo, Jorge, Tig.	5	5	.500	5.53	25	15	0	0	3	0	94.1	111	426	62	58	14	3	2	4	37	2	64	9	1
Campos, Francisco, Cam.	8	9	.471	3.45	21	20	3	2	1	0	133	127	556	60	51	15	8	4	11	25	3	125	3	0
Cardenas, Faustino, Cam.	0	0	.000	4.50	1	0	0	0	0	0	2	4	10	1	1	0	0	0	0	0	0	0	0	0
Carrasco, Alejandro, Mex.	2	2	.500	4.23	31	0	0	0	9	2	55.1	70	247	28	26	8	3	4	3	17	3	30	1	0
Castaneda, Aurelio, Can.	0	0	.000	5.40	15	0	0	0	10	0	16.2	17	72	13	10	1	0	4	4	0	10	4	0
Castillo, Ismael, Cam.	0	0	.000	4.82	11	0	0	0	7	0	9.1	11	39	5	5	1	0	0	3	0	5	1	0
Castro, Carlos, Sal.	0	0	.000	6.48	8	0	0	0	2	0	8.1	13	43	6	6	0	0	1	0	6	0	9	2	0
Cazares, Juan, Cam.*	1	1	.500	1.88	31	0	0	0	8	0	14.1	8	55	5	3	1	3	1	2	3	1	5	2	0
Cazares, Rosario, Sal.	1	1	.500	3.13	23	0	0	0	12	5	23	23	93	8	8	1	1	0	3	4	0	18	1	0
Cazares, Tomas, Monc.-Sal.*	0	0	.000	5.91	20	0	0	0	2	0	10.2	14	51	8	7	1	1	1	3	0	4	0	0
Cecena, Jose, Monc.	1	0	1.000	10.45	10	0	0	0	1	0	10.1	16	52	12	12	4	0	0	0	5	0	6	1	0
Chapa, Javier, Tor.	4	2	.667	2.14	16	0	0	0	4	1	21	9	79	7	5	0	2	2	9	1	19	1	1
Chavarria, Hector, Yuc.-Tor.-Cor.	2	6	.250	7.17	15	11	0	0	1	0	54	55	258	45	43	7	3	2	8	34	1	21	4	0
Chavez, Carlos, Yuc.-Tor.	3	3	.500	4.83	23	4	0	0	17	5	41	42	194	26	22	2	2	3	31	2	36	4	0
Cordova, Francisco, Tig.	0	0	.000	8.78	22	0	0	0	11	0	26.2	42	137	26	26	2	0	1	3	17	0	19	8	0
Cortes, David, Lar.	3	1	.750	4.18	39	0	0	0	31	14	47.1	52	205	22	22	2	0	1	15	2	50	3	0
Couoh, Enrique, Can.	3	4	.429	5.07	14	14	0	0	0	0	76.1	90	338	46	43	12	1	2	0	23	1	36	3	0
Cruz, Javier, Mex.	6	1	.857	1.84	37	0	0	0	16	1	49	44	193	14	10	2	5	0	11	1	26	3	1
Cruz, Luis Manuel, Pue.	4	14	.222	6.07	23	21	1	1	1	0	109.2	149	511	80	74	18	4	7	8	36	0	42	4	0
Cuervo, Bernardo, Yuc.-Tor.	0	3	.000	7.17	11	6	0	0	2	0	37.2	54	171	31	30	7	1	1	0	13	1	17	2	0
Delahoya, Javier, Sal.	11	3	.786	2.84	20	20	0	0	0	0	133.1	120	556	57	42	9	6	4	8	48	0	97	4	0
Delfin, Adolfo, Lar.	0	4	.000	6.87	29	1	0	0	11	0	38	45	181	31	29	1	1	3	6	21	5	30	3	1
Diaz, Marco, Sal.	5	3	.625	3.45	23	7	0	0	1	0	60	59	247	26	23	4	2	3	1	14	1	45	2	0
Diaz, Ralph, Mont.	8	6	.571	4.00	19	19	3	1	0	0	117	97	489	55	52	9	5	3	14	44	1	78	2	0
Dominguez, Carlos, Sal.*	7	1	.875	5.57	25	15	0	0	2	0	76	96	351	48	47	13	1	3	2	46	0	32	3	1
Dominguez, David, Oax.	7	5	.583	3.23	23	21	0	0	0	0	128.1	143	546	59	46	12	4	1	7	39	0	82	3	0
Dorame, Randey, Mex.*	3	2	.600	4.74	22	2	1	0	2	0	43.2	70	220	30	23	5	3	1	0	29	3	22	2	0
Duarte, Miguel, Sal.	3	7	.300	4.05	43	0	0	0	12	0	46.2	51	209	22	21	4	3	1	0	19	1	31	1	0
Elizalde, Carlos, Oax.	9	6	.600	3.38	21	18	0	0	0	0	114.2	114	495	49	43	9	5	2	4	44	0	64	5	0
Elvira, Abraham, Cor.*	1	9	.100	8.37	33	10	0	0	4	0	57	73	283	54	53	8	7	5	5	41	2	45	3	0
Elvira, Narciso, Cam.*	5	2	.714	2.11	9	9	1	0	0	0	64	46	255	16	15	5	2	6	10	0	73	1	0
Enriquez, Martin, Rey.	2	2	.500	3.02	35	1	0	0	1	0	44.2	47	196	18	15	3	1	3	22	5	29	2	0
Esparza, Emerson, Monc.	6	8	.429	6.88	25	9	0	0	1	0	69.1	86	324	58	53	6	1	4	5	34	1	34	9	0

Pitcher, Team	W	L	Pct.	ERA	G	GS	CG	ShO	GF	Sv.	IP	H	TBF	R	ER	HR	SH	SF	HB	BB	IBB	SO	WP	Bk.
Espinosa, Omar, Pue.	1	2	.333	7.88	11	0	0	0	2	0	16	22	83	14	14	2	1	0	2	13	2	7	2	0
Esquer, Mercedes, Rey.*	2	9	.182	4.72	20	19	0	0	0	0	103	121	446	56	54	16	7	4	3	26	1	61	1	1
Evans, Dave, Mex.-Oax.	0	1	.000	4.38	16	0	0	0	11	8	12.1	12	58	8	6	1	1	0	3	9	0	11	2	0
Federico, Gustavo, Sal.	5	2	.714	5.57	40	0	0	0	7	0	53.1	61	237	36	33	6	6	3	1	17	7	27	2	0
Felix, Antonio, Tor.*	0	2	.000	10.69	11	0	0	0	4	0	16	19	83	20	19	5	1	3	0	15	1	10	2	0
Felix, Jesus, Can.	0	0	.000	13.50	2	0	0	0	2	0	2.2	8	15	4	4	1	0	0	0	0	0	2	1	0
Fentanes, Ernesto, Ver.	0	0	.000	14.29	6	0	0	0	4	0	5.2	9	30	9	9	2	0	2	1	3	0	5	0	0
Fernandez, Amador, Cam.*	0	0	.000	7.94	10	0	0	0	1	0	5.2	3	27	8	5	0	0	2	3	5	0	1	0	0
Flores, Ignacio, Yuc.	7	1	.875	2.01	42	1	0	0	10	1	62.2	50	246	16	14	3	4	0	4	7	2	57	2	1
Flores, Ignacio, Can.	1	3	.250	4.78	31	1	0	0	14	6	52.2	53	224	29	28	4	6	4	2	23	5	32	4	0
Flores, Jorge, Monc.*	1	1	.500	3.88	26	2	0	0	12	0	53.1	70	233	23	23	4	2	1	1	10	0	23	3	0
Flores, Wilfredo, Tab.	0	0	.000	0.00	1	0	0	0	1	0	0.1	0	1	0	0	0	0	0	0	0	0	0	0	0
Flynt, Will, Can.*	2	3	.400	5.86	5	5	1	0	0	0	27.2	39	124	20	18	1	5	3	0	6	0	15	4	0
Fregoso, Raul, Tor.-Ver.	0	2	.000	6.81	28	2	0	0	8	0	39.2	49	197	32	30	6	0	3	1	27	2	25	9	0
Galvez, Randy, Mex.	2	2	.500	5.35	26	7	0	0	5	2	70.2	106	336	48	42	5	1	3	32	0	29	2	1	
Garcia, Adolfo, Cam.	6	0	1.000	2.41	29	9	1	1	3	1	82	68	325	24	22	8	2	3	3	13	0	39	3	0
Garcia, Alfredo, Mex.	12	4	.750	4.90	22	22	2	1	0	0	132.1	160	577	78	72	8	5	4	6	36	1	67	2	1
Garcia, David, Cor.	0	0	.000	0.00	2	0	0	0	0	0	3	3	3	0	0	0	0	1	0	0	0	0	0	
Garcia, Humberto, Rey.*	2	5	.286	4.23	30	6	0	0	1	0	44.2	38	198	26	21	7	2	1	0	27	0	37	3	1
Garcia, Jose, Pue.	2	4	.333	4.01	22	3	1	1	14	8	49.1	52	209	25	22	5	4	2	1	14	4	30	0	0
Garcia, Jose, Pue.*	3	8	.273	4.57	20	16	1	0	4	3	112.1	139	485	60	57	11	10	2	3	28	3	78	2	0
Garcia, Mike, Yuc.	1	1	.500	0.96	30	0	0	0	25	17	37.1	24	140	4	4	0	2	2	0	3	1	52	0	0
Garcia, Ramon, Can.	4	4	.333	5.19	30	0	0	0	14	1	34.2	42	163	24	20	3	4	4	0	19	1	20	7	0
Garibaldi, Cecilio, Tig.	0	0	.000	45.00	4	0	0	0	1	0	1	0	9	5	5	0	0	0	1	5	0	0	0	0
Garibay, Salvador, Lar.	4	3	.571	3.82	40	0	0	0	14	1	61.1	70	264	30	26	4	2	0	1	23	5	47	2	0
Garza, Conrado, Mont.*	1	0	1.000	3.86	17	0	0	0	2	0	9.1	13	45	5	4	0	0	0	6	5	6	2	0	
Gomez, Alejandro, Tab.	0	0	.000	0.00	1	0	0	0	0	0	0.2	3	5	0	0	0	0	0	0	0	0	0	0	0
Gomez, Martin, Tor.*	7	5	.583	6.22	40	9	0	0	8	1	98.1	135	455	72	68	10	6	0	1	40	5	54	5	0
Gomez, Miguel, Tig.	11	4	.733	4.12	22	22	0	0	0	0	129	140	560	70	59	10	7	4	15	36	2	90	8	0
Gonzalez, Arturo, Mont.	1	4	.200	10.13	7	7	0	0	0	0	24	37	113	27	27	3	0	0	2	4	0	9	4	0
Gonzalez, Erubiel, Ver.	5	1	.833	2.60	27	0	0	0	5	0	45	41	197	16	13	2	4	3	4	10	2	21	1	0
Gonzalez, Gilberto, Mont.*	4	3	.571	5.14	18	13	1	1	1	0	68.1	71	306	41	39	10	3	1	1	39	1	59	5	0
Gonzalez, Leonardo, Lar.	1	0	1.000	5.97	15	1	0	0	1	0	37.2	44	166	28	25	5	0	2	2	12	1	31	2	2
Gonzalez, Miguel, Sal.	0	0	.000	7.59	5	2	0	0	1	0	10.2	20	53	9	9	2	0	1	0	2	0	6	1	0
Gonzalez, Victor, Tab.	1	0	1.000	10.24	9	0	0	0	2	0	9.2	22	55	13	11	1	0	0	1	5	1	6	0	0
Grajales, Norberto, Tab.	1	4	.200	5.60	9	8	0	0	0	0	27.1	44	131	22	17	2	2	0	1	7	3	12	2	0
Guerra, Pascual, Cor.	2	2	.500	6.02	20	2	0	0	5	0	40.1	54	183	29	27	9	2	0	2	13	2	11	1	0
Gutierrez, Pablo, Cor.	2	0	.000	6.33	8	6	0	0	0	0	27	36	120	19	19	2	0	2	5	1	12	0	3	
Guzman, Christian, Monc.	1	1	.500	6.14	10	4	0	0	0	0	29.1	32	131	20	20	3	1	0	5	15	1	12	6	0
Guzman, Jesus, Tig.*	0	2	.000	9.45	17	0	0	0	5	0	20	24	92	21	21	4	0	0	1	11	1	12	0	0
Hartmann, Pete, Tor.*	3	4	.429	6.37	11	11	0	0	0	0	59.1	73	280	44	42	5	3	1	2	34	0	45	7	0
Henthorne, Kevin, Pue.	2	3	.400	4.95	7	7	1	0	0	0	36.1	45	160	21	20	2	4	2	2	8	1	16	0	0
Hernandez, Jose, Ver.-Cor.	5	4	.556	5.43	19	19	0	0	0	0	104.1	130	460	65	63	12	8	3	4	20	0	49	1	0
Hernandez, Martin, Ver.-Can.	6	2	.750	4.34	17	14	0	0	1	0	74.2	97	333	38	36	7	4	4	5	25	5	21	1	0
Hernandez, Santos, Tig.	4	8	.333	5.59	52	0	0	0	46	27	58	65	261	38	36	4	7	3	4	26	7	64	5	0
Herrera, Enrique, Tab.	4	4	.500	4.80	41	0	0	0	33	20	45	54	198	26	24	4	3	0	3	10	4	24	0	1
Hidalgo, Romeo, Oax.	0	0	.000	11.17	8	0	0	0	3	0	9.2	16	54	12	12	1	1	0	0	8	0	3	5	2
Higuera, Marcos, Tig.	0	0	.000	9.00	1	0	0	0	1	0	2	2	10	2	2	0	0	0	0	2	0	0	0	0
Huerta, Edgar, Tig.*	7	4	.636	4.47	29	15	1	0	2	2	102.2	98	454	55	51	7	8	1	6	56	4	84	8	0
Huerta, Francisco, Pue.	0	1	.000	9.64	8	0	0	0	5	1	4.2	7	24	5	5	0	1	0	2	2	0	1	0	0
Huerta, Luis, Lar.	10	6	.625	4.23	21	21	0	0	0	0	112.2	130	492	61	53	13	6	4	5	37	3	54	2	0
Hurtado, Edwin, Can.	9	5	.643	1.38	16	14	7	3	1	1	117	78	447	21	18	4	2	1	3	27	1	113	10	0
Izabal, Luis, Ver.	0	0	.000	23.63	4	0	0	0	2	0	2.2	9	21	7	7	0	0	0	2	3	0	0	1	0
Jimenez, Isaac, Tab.*	2	7	.222	4.72	16	16	1	0	0	0	74.1	91	336	59	39	3	5	2	5	28	3	45	3	0
Jimenez, Jose, Oax.	4	3	.571	3.92	42	9	0	0	3	0	59.2	77	285	36	26	3	2	1	3	34	0	40	1	0
Jimenez, Julio, Tor.*	2	4	.333	5.66	27	11	0	0	1	0	62	87	311	46	39	7	8	1	2	47	4	48	2	0
Kubenka, Jeff, Rey.*	4	4	.500	3.11	13	12	1	0	0	0	63.2	51	268	29	22	5	3	2	2	28	1	73	2	1
Landeros, Lorenzo, Oax.	0	1	.000	10.47	9	1	0	0	6	0	16.1	28	85	21	19	5	1	0	0	10	0	10	0	1
Lara, Jorge, Sal.-Can.	2	3	.400	2.75	36	1	0	0	14	6	72	58	281	23	22	8	2	0	4	16	3	30	2	0
Leal, Gerardo, Can.-Rey.	0	1	.000	5.61	17	0	0	0	6	0	25.2	30	119	17	16	6	1	1	3	14	1	12	3	0
Lemon, Donald, Cam.	5	5	.500	4.19	13	13	1	0	0	0	73	79	309	41	34	10	4	5	3	21	0	47	3	1
Leon, Cupertino, Oax.	5	3	.625	2.60	40	0	0	0	0	0	52	48	222	29	15	2	1	1	6	22	0	37	1	0
Leon, Juan, Tig.	3	4	.429	2.05	38	5	0	0	9	2	74.2	61	308	19	17	2	7	2	9	25	7	68	2	0
Lewis, Richie, Cam.	2	2	.500	4.64	6	6	0	0	0	0	33	40	148	18	17	2	1	1	0	7	0	26	3	0
Leyva, Edgar, Mont.	8	4	.667	3.86	15	14	0	0	0	0	84	77	346	36	36	7	4	1	10	19	1	57	3	0
Loaiza, Sabino, Cam.-Sal.	0	4	.000	6.05	29	5	0	0	6	0	58	80	270	41	39	8	6	1	7	16	0	26	0	0
Lomeli, Israel, Cam.	7	5	.583	2.45	17	15	1	1	0	0	92	65	363	32	25	12	2	2	38	2	83	3	0	
Lontayo, Alejandro, Oax.*	2	2	.500	3.55	6	6	1	1	0	0	33	26	143	14	13	4	1	3	1	22	0	28	4	1
Lopez, Emigdio, Cor.	10	6	.625	3.80	23	22	2	0	0	0	147	149	617	69	62	17	11	5	7	36	6	73	0	1
Lopez, Gilberto, Tor.-Cor.	3	3	.500	8.24	33	0	0	0	8	1	31.2	58	175	32	29	1	4	2	6	23	2	15	3	0
Lopez, Jesus, Can.*	1	2	.333	2.45	25	0	0	0	4	0	14.2	15	60	4	4	3	0	0	1	4	0	7	0	0
Lopez, Johan, Sal.	1	1	.500	4.45	7	5	0	0	0	0	32.1	39	139	16	16	4	2	1	2	8	1	24	2	0
Lopez, Jose, Monc.	0	0	.000	10.13	7	0	0	0	2	0	5.1	9	28	6	6	2	0	0	4	0	2	1	0	
Lopez, Juan, Rey.	6	5	.545	3.86	49	0	0	0	43	25	63	68	266	32	27	3	0	0	17	1	36	0	0	
Lopez, Mariano, Oax.	1	1	.500	6.60	12	1	0	0	4	0	15	17	71	11	11	2	0	1	0	8	0	8	0	0
Lopez, Miguel, Tig.	0	0	.000	7.27	9	0	0	0	2	0	8.2	9	44	8	7	1	0	1	2	7	1	6	1	1
Loya, Rigoberto, Lar.	6	7	.462	3.75	21	18	0	0	1	0	103.1	120	474	60	43	6	2	6	3	62	1	58	10	0
Lugo, Aaron, Rey.*	0	0	.000	0.00	1	0	0	0	0	0	1	0	4	0	0	0	0	0	0	1	0	1	0	0
Macias, Luis, Monc.	5	3	.625	6.53	47	0	0	0	8	0	60.2	81	301	48	44	7	2	4	8	38	4	28	4	0
Madero, Francisco, Oax.	5	7	.417	5.27	16	16	1	0	0	0	85.1	104	387	59	50	8	0	1	7	31	0	63	3	0
Manrique, Alberto, Rey.-Mont.	8	7	.533	3.36	18	17	4	1	1	1	109.2	114	467	52	41	10	5	0	9	34	1	72	2	0

Pitcher, Team	W	L	Pct.	ERA	G	GS	CG	ShO	GF	Sv.	IP	H	TBF	R	ER	HR	SH	SF	HB	BB	IBB	SO	WP	Bk.
Manzano, Adrian, Tig.	2	4	.333	3.79	46	0	0	0	6	0	57	64	246	25	24	5	4	0	2	15	4	32	3	0
Manzano, Rafael, Can.	0	0	.000	18.00	3	0	0	0	2	2	1	3	8	2	2	0	0	0	0	2	0	0	1	0
Marquez, Isidro, Cam.	5	5	.500	4.12	38	0	0	0	34	21	43.2	45	194	20	20	2	3	0	9	17	7	41	1	0
Martinez, Aaron, Rey.*	0	0	.000	0.00	1	0	0	0	0	0	0.2	0	3	0	0	0	0	0	1	0	0	2	0	0
Martinez, Cesar, Ver.*	0	0	.000	12.86	7	0	0	0	1	0	7	10	41	12	10	4	0	0	2	8	1	3	0	0
Martinez, Juan, Cor.*	0	0	.000	3.18	5	0	0	0	2	0	5.2	7	25	2	2	1	0	2	0	5	0	5	0	0
Martinez, Pedro, Tig.*	0	1	.000	9.82	2	2	0	0	0	0	7.1	14	37	12	8	2	0	0	3	0	4	0	0	0
Martinez, Renan, Pue.-Tig.*	5	5	.500	4.86	29	13	0	0	5	1	76	85	351	45	41	5	6	2	4	53	0	42	7	1
Medina, Alonso, Rey.	0	1	.000	4.00	11	0	0	0	2	0	9	12	43	4	4	0	1	0	6	1	6	1	3
Medina, Osvaldo, Pue.	2	3	.400	3.86	38	0	0	0	8	0	51.1	52	216	24	22	6	5	2	2	23	4	16	1	0
Medina, Rafael, Tor.	0	2	.000	11.17	3	2	0	0	0	0	9.2	15	53	13	12	3	0	0	0	7	1	11	2	0
Melendez, Nestor, Rey.*	3	4	.429	5.76	38	6	0	0	6	0	59.1	75	282	45	38	4	2	3	2	39	2	40	6	0
Mendoza, Marco, Cam.-Cor.*	0	0	.000	2.31	16	0	0	0	6	1	11.2	12	56	8	3	0	2	1	9	1	5	1	0
Mendoza, Omar, Pue.	0	1	.000	4.57	18	3	0	0	4	0	43.1	51	191	23	22	5	2	3	16	0	14	3	0
Mere, Fernando, Tab.	1	0	1.000	0.00	5	0	0	0	1	0	9.1	6	38	0	0	0	1	0	6	0	2	0	0
Meza, Leobardo, Monc.	3	8	.273	7.01	14	13	0	0	0	0	52.2	74	251	46	41	2	2	1	4	24	0	26	5	1
Miranda, Luis, Ver.*	2	6	.250	6.90	9	9	1	0	0	0	45.2	57	216	38	35	4	3	0	2	23	1	26	2	0
Molina, Primitivo, Rey.	2	6	.250	6.23	23	7	0	0	7	0	47.2	72	233	45	33	8	2	3	2	24	1	29	1	1
Montane, Ivan, Can.	0	2	.000	11.25	3	0	0	0	2	1	4	9	22	5	5	1	2	0	1	0	6	1	0
Montemayor, Humberto, Mont.	10	6	.625	4.13	22	22	1	0	0	0	133	146	569	66	61	8	6	2	6	29	2	92	4	1
Montoya, Saul, Rey.	2	4	.333	4.35	15	10	1	0	0	0	60	54	277	36	29	2	4	0	8	40	2	49	5	1
Mora, Eleazar, Ver.*	15	6	.714	2.50	23	23	2	0	0	0	154.2	126	614	53	43	9	4	2	5	32	0	89	4	1
Mora, Sergio, Mont.	0	1	.000	1.59	8	0	0	0	5	0	17	11	66	3	3	1	0	0	6	1	17	1	0
Morales, Luis, Ver.*	4	9	.308	6.84	22	15	0	0	2	0	73.2	98	343	61	56	8	2	1	5	27	1	44	4	1
Moreno, Angel, Ver.*	9	9	.500	3.80	24	24	2	1	0	0	147	159	628	69	62	11	7	1	2	39	3	84	4	0
Moreno, Claudio, Mex.	5	3	.625	6.43	39	5	0	0	10	2	66	92	304	49	47	5	1	1	5	25	3	42	3	0
Moreno, Edgar, Oax.	1	1	.500	8.38	16	1	0	0	6	0	19.1	30	94	20	18	0	0	1	0	12	0	6	3	0
Moreno, Elbnit, Tor.	2	2	.500	10.13	16	0	0	0	7	0	21.1	31	107	25	24	5	2	1	2	12	0	12	2	0
Moreno, Leo, Sal.-Ver.*	1	1	.500	3.34	20	5	0	0	4	0	35	36	145	15	13	0	5	1	0	15	0	14	2	0
Munoz, Leonardo, Lar.*	4	0	1.000	1.83	42	1	1	1	8	1	34.1	25	136	7	7	1	1	0	13	1	27	2	0
Munoz, Miguel, Can.	5	5	.500	5.23	10	10	0	0	0	0	53.1	70	236	36	31	11	0	1	4	5	2	24	2	0
Munoz, Pablo R., Oax.*	1	0	1.000	6.32	33	0	0	0	8	0	15.2	22	77	11	11	3	0	1	9	2	14	2	0
Murillo, Meza, Monc.	2	1	.667	2.93	44	0	0	0	26	7	55.1	62	228	21	18	5	3	2	1	10	2	28	0	0
Navarro, Hector, Ver.	2	3	.400	3.14	36	1	0	0	12	3	86	79	367	33	30	9	4	5	3	39	6	61	1	0
Navarro, Joel, Oax.	6	3	.667	4.63	21	12	0	0	1	0	83.2	102	370	46	43	10	3	1	3	20	0	59	4	0
Navarro, Jose, Tig.	6	3	.667	3.69	40	3	0	0	8	1	75.2	75	324	35	31	10	4	5	26	5	46	7	0
Navarro, Luis, Yuc.	2	2	.500	1.63	38	0	0	0	8	0	49.2	39	199	11	9	4	1	4	12	2	31	3	0
Navarro, Rodolfo, Yuc.	0	0	.000	16.88	2	1	0	0	1	0	5.1	10	32	10	10	3	0	0	0	6	0	2	0	0
Neri, Braulio, Sal.-Can.*	0	0	.000	11.50	28	0	0	0	2	0	18	29	95	24	23	1	0	2	2	15	1	7	2	0
Neri, Eduardo, Oax.*	3	2	.600	2.16	55	0	0	0	11	2	33.1	21	134	10	8	3	1	0	1	15	0	30	1	0
Nieblas, Mauro, Mont.*	5	1	.833	4.02	45	10	0	0	1	0	78.1	72	346	42	35	3	5	2	5	44	1	61	5	0
Nieblas, Omar, Tab.*	2	1	.667	3.32	31	0	0	0	10	0	19	23	86	7	7	3	1	2	1	9	1	12	0	0
Nunez, Javier, Tab.	1	1	.500	2.66	14	0	0	0	5	0	20.1	16	80	7	6	1	1	0	0	11	1	7	0	0
Nunez, Jose, Lar.	9	9	.500	4.37	23	23	3	1	0	0	154.1	181	663	85	75	17	9	7	2	25	1	93	5	0
Nunez, Jose, Tab.	1	2	.333	3.07	32	1	0	0	11	0	44	41	184	16	15	2	0	0	0	17	1	33	1	0
Ojeda, Miguel, Mex.	0	0	.000	0.00	1	0	0	0	0	0	1	1	1	0	0	0	0	0	0	0	0	1	0	0
Olague, Jesus, Pue.-Tig.	11	8	.579	4.27	22	22	1	1	0	0	128.2	135	543	63	61	9	4	4	4	41	1	116	5	1
Orea, Flavio, Cor.	0	3	.000	4.88	38	0	0	0	24	10	55.1	56	237	30	30	8	2	5	3	18	4	28	1	0
Ortega, Pablo, Pue.-Tig.	3	7	.300	6.94	24	10	0	0	1	0	70	94	330	56	54	12	4	2	6	34	4	53	1	1
Ortega, Roberto, Pue.*	4	10	.286	8.56	19	16	0	0	0	0	61	90	306	62	58	5	0	3	2	44	1	37	9	1
Ortega, Wilbert, Yuc.*	2	1	.667	4.87	25	0	0	0	4	0	20.1	24	91	11	11	3	0	1	2	7	1	16	1	0
Osteen, Gavin, Tig.*	0	0	.000	9.00	2	0	0	0	1	0	2	4	9	3	2	0	1	0	0	0	0	1	0	0
Osuna, Adrian, Cor.	0	0	.000	0.00	2	0	0	0	1	0	3	2	14	0	0	0	0	0	4	0	2	0	0
Osuna, Ricardo, Tab.-Yuc.	7	8	.467	4.71	18	18	0	0	0	0	91.2	110	412	57	48	7	5	7	3	30	1	46	3	0
Pacheco, Alexander, Pue.	1	1	.500	1.83	17	0	0	0	17	8	19.2	12	78	8	4	1	1	7	1	13	0	0	
Palacios, Joaquin, Ver.	0	2	.000	5.01	24	0	0	0	8	0	50.1	49	227	31	28	10	0	2	2	31	2	29	5	0
Palacios, Vicente, Sal.-Cam.	5	1	.833	3.54	34	0	0	0	12	1	40.2	35	168	19	16	6	4	1	1	9	1	37	1	0
Palafox, Juan, Yuc.	10	6	.625	3.05	20	20	1	0	0	0	138.2	143	590	51	47	11	7	3	12	33	1	73	3	0
Parra, Julio, Mont.	1	7	.125	3.14	44	0	0	0	13	1	48.2	49	217	23	17	4	2	4	25	7	37	3	0
Pena, Joel, Ver.	3	6	.333	6.86	49	2	0	0	16	1	63	88	299	51	48	8	9	2	3	27	6	32	5	0
Pena, Luis, Ver.*	0	0	.000	9.17	30	0	0	0	6	0	17.2	29	91	19	18	6	1	0	9	0	9	1	0
Perez, Edgar, Cor.	2	12	.143	5.72	19	18	2	0	1	0	107	132	490	71	68	9	6	8	9	38	4	65	5	0
Perez, Leonardo, Cor.-Ver.	2	11	.154	6.09	22	20	1	0	0	0	99	128	454	72	67	15	4	4	4	36	4	26	3	0
Perez, Sergio, Rey.	0	0	.000	5.19	9	0	0	0	7	0	8.2	8	38	6	5	1	0	1	2	3	0	4	2	0
Pesqueira, Omar, Yuc.	1	1	.500	3.94	19	0	0	0	7	0	32	28	145	17	14	5	1	2	3	18	1	12	5	1
Pimentel, Roberto, Yuc.*	3	4	.429	4.34	22	10	0	0	0	0	58	68	265	28	28	2	4	2	2	26	1	31	0	0
Preston, George, Rey.	3	5	.375	2.60	8	8	2	0	0	0	62.1	35	266	21	18	4	3	0	3	50	1	72	4	0
Pulido, Carlos, Oax.*	13	7	.650	3.57	23	23	3	0	0	0	151.1	174	639	66	60	7	3	5	4	27	0	95	5	0
Pulido, Raymundo, Cam.	1	4	.200	5.20	22	7	1	0	4	0	64	68	285	39	37	11	5	1	1	29	0	34	6	1
Quimbar, Juan, Lar.-Pue.*	0	4	.000	10.61	13	0	0	0	4	0	9.1	13	47	11	11	3	1	0	0	9	0	5	2	0
Quinones, Enrique, Rey.	1	4	.200	6.00	15	9	0	0	1	0	45	62	217	34	30	5	2	0	2	29	0	13	2	0
Quiroz, Aaron, Sal.	8	3	.727	2.78	17	15	2	1	0	0	90.2	84	366	30	28	8	5	2	2	19	1	62	2	1
Ramirez, Jose, Monc.	3	0	.000	7.71	7	2	0	0	1	0	11.2	16	61	13	10	1	1	0	3	4	0	6	1	0
Ramirez, Roberto, Mex.*	14	2	.875	2.84	20	20	0	0	0	0	111	132	477	57	35	9	3	3	4	25	0	55	2	0
Ramirez, Silvio, Cam.	0	0	.000	0.00	2	0	0	0	0	0	2	1	7	0	0	0	0	0	0	1	0	0	0	0
Ramon, Jose, Tab.	0	0	.000	7.02	11	0	0	0	7	0	16.2	26	77	14	13	3	3	2	1	1	0	4	0	0
Renovato, Nestor, Mont.-Rey.	7	4	.636	3.33	33	5	0	0	5	0	73	72	306	32	27	4	2	5	20	1	39	5	0	
Revenig, Todd, Cam.	1	2	.333	4.50	7	0	0	0	2	0	8	6	30	4	4	3	0	1	0	1	0	6	0	0
Reyes, Flavio, Pue.*	1	1	.500	3.81	29	2	0	0	6	0	26	33	111	11	11	5	0	1	4	0	10	0	0	
Reyes, Nate, Sal.*	8	5	.615	5.89	19	17	0	0	0	0	88.2	125	406	59	58	12	0	2	1	23	1	53	4	1
Rios, Alejandro, Sal.-Monc.	1	1	.500	8.59	26	1	0	0	3	0	36.2	60	188	38	35	5	2	3	0	22	3	18	5	0

Pitcher, Team	W	L	Pct.	ERA	G	GS	CG	ShO	GF	Sv.	IP	H	TBF	R	ER	HR	SH	SF	HB	BB	IBB	SO	WP	Bk.
Rios, Jesus, Yuc.-Tab.	9	4	.692	3.37	21	21	3	2	0	0	120.1	124	518	48	45	7	6	5	9	37	2	72	5	0
Rivas, Jesus, Tig.-Pue.*	0	0	.000	4.09	32	0	0	0	6	1	22	21	94	11	10	1	1	0	0	14	2	15	2	0
Rivera, Ben, Mex.	1	1	.500	1.53	44	0	0	0	43	30	47	41	188	9	8	2	0	0	0	10	2	59	6	0
Rivera, Francisco, Cor.	7	4	.636	5.27	40	0	0	0	10	0	66.2	68	309	41	39	7	10	4	7	38	12	30	10	0
Rivera, Lino, Monc.	6	4	.600	4.32	13	12	1	0	1	0	75	91	342	44	36	6	4	5	4	31	0	44	2	0
Rivera, Oscar, Yuc.-Cam.*	7	12	.368	4.53	48	23	1	0	7	0	149	159	652	80	75	21	10	0	11	59	1	97	12	0
Rivera, Paul, Tab.*	0	3	.000	4.43	31	0	0	0	7	0	20.1	21	88	11	10	1	2	1	0	11	2	10	1	0
Robles, Jorge, Cor.	2	3	.400	5.48	21	3	0	0	7	0	44.1	45	188	27	27	6	1	2	4	12	2	13	1	0
Rodriguez, Frank, Mex.	5	3	.625	4.62	8	8	0	0	0	0	48.2	48	208	27	25	5	1	0	3	15	1	44	3	0
Rodriguez, Manuel, Cam.	2	3	.400	2.93	35	0	0	0	11	1	43	40	183	16	14	5	1	2	1	13	0	35	2	0
Rodriguez, Raul, Mont.*	5	2	.714	4.43	22	12	0	0	1	0	83.1	109	375	53	41	6	6	5	4	21	1	47	1	1
Rodriguez, Salvador, Yuc.	11	5	.688	2.09	21	21	7	3	0	0	155	146	619	40	36	5	8	7	5	22	2	104	6	1
Romano, Mike, Sal.	11	6	.647	4.66	22	21	2	0	1	0	135.1	149	612	76	70	12	13	4	8	59	0	99	4	0
Romero, Alejandro, Monc.	11	6	.647	2.77	22	21	3	1	1	0	149.2	145	630	51	46	10	6	1	8	44	1	85	3	1
Romo, Eduardo, Lar.	1	0	1.000	7.67	17	0	0	0	2	0	29.2	46	147	28	25	7	0	2	3	13	0	12	2	0
Romo, Ricardo, Lar.	0	0	.000	9.95	3	2	0	0	0	0	6.1	10	32	7	7	1	0	0	1	5	0	1	0	1
Roque, Jorge, Tor.	0	3	.000	8.55	8	4	0	0	1	0	20	30	101	19	19	3	0	2	0	9	1	12	3	0
Roque, Rafael, Tig.*	8	0	1.000	2.73	14	12	1	1	0	0	79	70	319	26	24	9	7	1	2	27	2	49	1	0
Rubio, Miguel, Mont.	4	2	.667	0.84	54	0	0	0	50	32	64.2	43	261	8	6	3	2	1	1	26	4	80	4	0
Ruelas, Heriberto, Cor.*	3	5	.375	7.33	29	8	0	0	4	0	50.1	67	249	46	41	3	4	5	4	35	4	24	6	1
Ruiz, Cecilio, Tab.*	6	8	.429	3.76	22	20	0	0	0	0	122	134	513	63	51	8	2	2	1	21	2	68	2	0
Ruiz, Juan, Tor.	1	0	1.000	7.76	17	0	0	0	9	0	26.2	33	127	24	23	7	0	1	2	15	2	19	1	0
Salazar, Francisco, Tor.	0	0	.000	1.35	5	0	0	0	2	0	6.2	10	32	5	1	0	1	0	3	0	2	1	0
Saldana, Jose, Pue.	4	2	.667	7.93	24	9	0	0	4	0	64.2	100	314	59	57	12	3	7	4	29	2	26	6	0
Salgado, Eduardo, Ver.	7	9	.438	5.71	28	19	2	1	2	1	116.2	145	530	76	74	14	7	5	10	32	2	51	1	1
Sanchez, Alejandro, Can.	2	3	.400	4.19	36	0	0	0	17	4	43	44	185	24	20	5	3	2	1	16	6	15	1	0
Sanchez, Claudio, Oax.	1	1	.500	3.48	40	0	0	0	10	0	41.1	42	170	18	16	1	1	0	2	11	2	22	2	0
Sanchez, Efrain, Cam.	7	2	.778	2.91	45	1	0	0	9	0	65	59	269	23	21	4	5	2	2	19	6	59	2	0
Sanchez, Hector, Tor.	0	0	.000	9.57	26	1	0	0	5	0	36.2	68	185	42	39	11	1	2	1	6	1	13	1	0
Sanchez, Sergio, Tab.	0	0	.000	4.73	8	0	0	0	4	0	13.1	17	59	7	7	3	1	1	6	1	2	0	0
Sandoval, Guillermo, Tab.	1	1	.500	4.91	27	0	0	0	7	1	29.1	41	145	17	16	2	2	0	0	21	1	11	3	0
Sandoval, Ricardo, Cor.*	0	0	.000	0.00	1	0	0	0	0	0	0.1	0	3	0	0	0	0	0	0	2	0	0	0	0
Sangeado, Juan, Can.	0	0	.000	1.83	12	1	0	0	3	0	19.2	19	84	4	4	1	1	3	1	9	3	8	0	0
Sano, Shigeki, Tig.	0	2	.000	6.89	5	3	0	0	0	0	15.2	19	77	13	12	4	0	0	2	10	4	13	1	0
Sierra, Abel, Can.	2	4	.333	5.40	17	7	1	0	4	0	45	60	208	32	27	2	2	2	5	15	3	12	2	0
Silva, Walter, Mont.	1	2	.333	4.99	21	1	0	0	2	0	39.2	36	179	25	22	7	2	2	1	24	0	32	3	0
Sinohui, David, Ver.	3	2	.600	2.61	43	0	0	0	39	30	51.2	38	201	16	15	4	3	0	2	9	1	44	2	0
Solis, Tomas, Tig.*	0	1	.000	4.60	29	0	0	0	8	0	15.2	22	81	9	8	1	1	0	2	13	1	12	0	0
Soto, Cruz, Lar.	3	4	.429	5.68	19	6	0	0	7	0	52.1	68	247	35	33	5	0	4	27	0	36	3	0
Soto, Jesus, Monc.	0	0	.000	7.56	5	1	0	0	0	0	8.1	6	38	7	7	2	0	1	2	4	1	3	1	0
Sulu, Mario, Cam.	0	0	.000	5.40	5	2	0	0	2	0	11.2	14	50	7	7	2	0	0	0	4	0	7	0	0
Tejeda, Felix, Cam.*	0	0	.000	1.69	39	0	0	0	3	1	16	17	64	4	3	0	2	1	0	3	1	6	0	0
Tijerina, Carlos, Rey.	0	0	.000	14.21	4	0	0	0	2	0	6.1	12	41	12	10	0	0	1	3	6	0	4	3	0
Torres, Jorge, Cam.*	0	0	.000	6.10	12	0	0	0	2	0	10.1	10	48	7	7	2	0	0	1	7	0	9	2	0
Trevino, Jesus, Mex.*	0	0	.000	7.15	25	0	0	0	10	0	22.2	26	103	19	18	3	1	0	2	9	3	19	1	0
Trujillo, Jorge, Ver.	1	0	1.000	20.25	7	0	0	0	3	0	6.2	22	48	18	15	2	1	1	3	4	0	4	0	0
Turuda, Miyoki, Cor.	0	0	.000	0.00	1	0	0	0	0	0	0.1	0	2	0	0	0	0	0	0	1	0	1	0	0
Valdez, Armando, Lar.	14	6	.700	4.77	22	22	1	0	0	0	122.2	130	533	69	65	17	3	3	7	36	0	88	5	0
Valdez, Efrain, Cor.-Tab.*	11	9	.550	2.83	26	23	5	3	3	0	156	145	633	53	49	9	9	3	6	45	2	94	4	0
Valdez, Israel, Cor.	0	0	.000	0.00	1	0	0	0	0	0	1.2	1	7	0	0	0	0	0	0	0	0	1	0	0
Valdez, Joel, Cor.	0	3	.000	4.23	27	0	0	0	17	7	27.2	27	123	14	13	1	4	2	2	13	5	16	2	0
Valencia, Alonso, Monc.	0	0	.000	18.00	1	0	0	0	0	0	2	4	11	4	4	0	0	0	1	0	0	2	0	0
Valenzuela, Jose, Tig.	1	0	1.000	7.71	10	0	0	0	2	0	7	14	38	6	6	1	1	1	2	2	0	2	2	0
Valenzuela, Saul, Lar.	3	4	.429	6.54	19	15	0	0	1	0	74.1	103	351	59	54	7	6	4	3	29	0	32	6	0
Valerio, Julio, Monc.*	1	0	1.000	3.15	53	0	0	0	11	3	40	46	167	16	14	3	3	1	0	5	0	15	1	0
Vargas, Joel, Tab.	7	10	.412	3.52	22	22	0	0	0	0	135.2	139	576	63	53	8	8	4	6	41	3	55	1	0
Vazquez, Adrian, Mont.	4	4	.500	5.95	29	6	0	0	5	1	59	73	281	40	39	6	6	4	5	36	5	38	5	0
Vega, Obed, Can.	9	8	.529	3.35	24	23	6	1	1	1	156	142	633	62	58	11	7	4	1	41	6	107	3	0
Velarde, Francisco, Ver.	0	0	.000	4.91	3	0	0	0	1	0	3.2	5	16	2	2	1	0	0	0	1	0	1	0	0
Verdugo, Hugo, Tor.	0	0	.000	4.91	8	3	0	0	0	0	22	19	101	14	12	1	3	0	3	17	0	18	0	2
Verdugo, Orlando, Rey.	3	2	.600	5.36	45	0	0	0	10	2	50.1	58	248	37	30	6	2	3	3	40	3	31	4	0
Verdugo, Oswaldo, Yuc.	1	5	.167	3.59	33	0	0	0	16	2	47.2	46	203	24	19	2	1	0	0	22	5	40	5	0
Verdugo, Roberto, Tab.	3	3	.500	3.96	34	1	0	0	11	2	63.2	54	273	29	28	9	8	2	2	30	5	40	3	0
Villarreal, Antonio, Tab.	0	0	.000	6.75	2	0	0	0	0	0	4	7	21	3	3	1	0	1	0	1	0	2	1	0
Villarreal, Salvador, Rey.	0	1	.000	6.83	22	0	0	0	11	0	27.2	37	142	25	21	3	0	1	2	24	0	19	5	0
Villavicencio, Ismeal, Tig.	0	0	.000	6.75	1	0	0	0	0	0	1.1	3	7	1	1	0	0	0	0	0	0	1	0	0
Villegas, Francisco, Can.	4	4	.500	2.93	37	4	0	0	16	3	61.1	47	263	21	20	1	4	4	5	35	5	51	3	0
Villegas, Ismael, Cam.	0	2	.000	8.38	3	3	0	0	0	0	9.2	20	54	9	9	3	0	0	1	6	0	7	1	0
Villegas, Jose, Pue.	1	2	.333	3.42	57	0	0	0	24	1	73.2	68	298	32	28	12	5	4	5	18	3	27	2	0
Vosberg, Ed, Mex.*	3	4	.429	5.31	12	10	0	0	0	0	57.2	73	253	38	34	4	6	1	1	15	0	50	7	0
Wallace, Kent, Tor.	1	1	.500	4.70	13	0	0	0	11	6	15.1	17	68	9	8	5	0	0	0	2	0	11	0	0
Ward, Bryan, Tor.*	5	4	.556	2.86	10	9	1	0	0	0	66	56	265	25	21	5	3	1	1	17	0	33	2	0
Zambrano, Baudel, Rey.	5	8	.385	6.53	26	14	1	0	5	0	92.1	108	426	74	67	10	6	4	3	47	2	61	1	1
Zamudio, Aurelio, Ver.	0	4	.000	9.39	4	0	0	0	3	0	7.2	8	34	8	8	4	0	1	0	3	0	5	0	0

PITCHERS WITH TWO OR MORE TEAMS

Pitcher, Team	W	L	Pct.	ERA	G	GS	CG	ShO	GF	Sv.	IP	H	TBF	R	ER	HR	SH	SF	HB	BB	IBB	SO	WP	Bk.
Bernal, Christian, Mex.	0	0	.000	27.00	1	0	0	0	0	0	0.2	0	4	2	2	0	0	0	0	2	0	2	0	0
Bernal, Christian, Mex.	0	0	.000	0.00	1	0	0	0	1	0	1	0	3	0	0	0	0	0	0	1	0	1	0	0
Camara, Pedro, Yuc.*	0	0	.000	9.00	4	0	0	0	1	0	1	3	8	1	1	0	0	0	1	2	0	0	1	0
Camara, Pedro, Tor.*	0	6	.000	8.10	10	9	0	0	0	0	36.2	52	183	38	33	8	3	2	2	27	0	26	4	0

Pitcher, Team	W	L	Pct.	ERA	G	GS	CG	ShO	GF	Sv.	IP	H	TBF	R	ER	HR	SH	SF	HB	BB	IBB	SO	WP	Bk.
Cazares, Tomas, Monc.*	0	0	.000	5.79	6	0	0	0	0	0	4.2	7	25	3	3	0	1	0	0	3	0	3	0	0
Cazares, Tomas, Sal.*	0	0	.000	6.00	14	0	0	0	2	0	6	7	26	5	4	1	0	1	1	0	0	1	0	0
Chavarria, Hector, Yuc.	0	0	.000	11.57	2	1	0	0	0	0	2.1	3	17	3	3	1	1	0	1	6	0	0	1	0
Chavarria, Hector, Tor.	2	3	.400	6.27	10	7	0	0	1	0	37.1	35	170	28	26	4	2	1	5	21	1	16	3	0
Chavarria, Hector, Cor.	0	3	.000	8.79	3	3	0	0	0	0	14.1	17	71	14	14	2	0	1	2	7	0	5	0	0
Chavez, Carlos, Yuc.	2	1	.667	3.77	15	0	0	0	14	4	14.1	16	70	6	6	0	1	0	1	10	0	18	1	0
Chavez, Carlos, Tor.	1	2	.333	5.40	8	4	0	0	3	1	26.2	26	124	20	16	2	1	2	2	21	2	18	3	0
Cuervo, Bernardo, Yuc.	0	0	.000	6.23	6	1	0	0	2	0	8.2	15	42	6	6	1	1	0	0	5	1	3	1	0
Cuervo, Bernardo, Tor.	0	3	.000	7.45	5	5	0	0	0	0	29	39	129	25	24	6	0	1	0	8	0	14	1	0
Evans, Dave, Mex.	0	0	.000	0.00	3	0	0	0	0	0	1.2	4	10	1	0	0	0	0	0	1	1	1	0	0
Evans, Dave, Oax.	0	1	.000	5.06	13	0	0	0	11	8	10.2	8	48	7	6	1	1	0	3	8	0	10	1	0
Fregoso, Raul, Tor.	0	2	.000	5.97	25	2	0	0	8	0	37.2	44	180	27	25	6	0	3	1	20	2	24	6	0
Fregoso, Raul, Ver.	0	0	.000	22.50	3	0	0	0	0	0	2	5	17	5	5	0	0	0	0	1	0	1	3	0
Hernandez, Jose, Ver.	4	1	.800	4.85	11	11	0	0	0	0	59.1	78	265	34	32	7	6	1	3	10	0	27	0	0
Hernandez, Jose, Tor.	1	3	.250	6.20	8	8	0	0	0	0	45	52	195	31	31	5	2	2	1	10	0	22	1	0
Hernandez, Martin, Ver.	0	0	.000	10.80	5	2	0	0	1	0	10	19	52	12	12	2	0	3	1	4	0	4	0	0
Hernandez, Martin, Can.	6	2	.750	3.34	12	12	0	0	0	0	64.2	78	281	26	24	5	4	1	4	21	5	17	1	0
Lara, Jorge, Sal.	0	0	.000	8.31	6	0	0	0	2	0	8.2	18	45	8	8	2	0	0	1	2	0	3	1	0
Lara, Jorge, Can.	2	3	.400	1.99	30	1	0	0	12	6	63.1	40	236	15	14	6	2	0	3	14	3	27	1	0
Leal, Gerardo, Can.	0	1	.000	8.53	4	0	0	0	1	0	6.1	12	35	7	6	1	0	0	0	4	1	4	1	0
Leal, Gerardo, Rey.	0	0	.000	4.66	13	0	0	0	5	0	19.1	18	84	10	10	5	1	3	1	10	0	8	2	0
Loaiza, Sabino, Cam.	0	1	.000	6.53	10	3	0	0	2	0	20.2	27	98	15	15	2	4	1	3	7	0	7	0	0
Loaiza, Sabino, Sal.	0	3	.000	5.79	19	2	0	0	4	0	37.1	53	172	26	24	6	2	0	4	9	0	19	0	0
Lopez, Gilberto, Tor.	1	2	.333	12.86	17	0	0	0	2	0	14	34	87	23	20	1	2	1	2	10	1	6	2	0
Lopez, Gilberto, Cor.	2	1	.667	4.58	16	0	0	0	6	1	17.2	24	88	9	9	0	2	1	4	13	1	9	1	0
Manrique, Alberto, Rey.	6	5	.545	2.75	13	13	4	1	0	0	88.1	88	368	36	27	8	4	0	7	22	0	63	2	0
Manrique, Alberto, Mont.	2	2	.500	5.91	5	4	0	0	1	1	21.1	26	99	16	14	2	1	0	2	12	1	9	0	0
Martinez, Renan, Pue.*	3	3	.500	3.38	19	7	0	0	3	0	48	49	216	21	18	2	4	2	2	30	1	27	4	0
Martinez, Renan, Tig.*	2	2	.500	7.39	10	6	0	0	2	1	28	36	135	24	23	3	2	0	2	23	0	15	3	1
Mendoza, Marco, Cam.*	0	0	.000	0.00	2	0	0	0	2	0	1.1	1	5	0	0	0	0	0	0	1	0	1	0	0
Mendoza, Marco, Cor.*	0	0	.000	2.61	14	0	0	0	4	1	10.1	11	51	8	3	0	0	2	1	9	1	4	1	0
Moreno, Leo, Sal.*	0	1	.000	2.57	14	2	0	0	4	0	21	19	85	7	6	0	4	1	0	10	0	8	0	0
Moreno, Leo, Ver.*	1	0	1.000	4.50	6	3	0	0	0	0	14	17	60	8	7	0	1	0	0	5	0	6	2	0
Neri, Braulio, Sal.*	0	0	.000	10.43	23	0	0	0	2	0	14.2	22	76	18	17	1	0	2	2	12	0	7	1	0
Neri, Braulio, Can.*	0	0	.000	16.20	5	0	0	0	0	0	3.1	7	19	6	6	0	0	0	0	3	1	0	1	0
Olague, Jesus, Pue.	5	7	.417	5.31	14	14	1	1	0	0	78	90	342	47	46	5	3	4	3	23	1	78	4	1
Olague, Jesus, Tig.	6	1	.857	2.66	8	8	0	0	0	0	50.2	45	201	16	15	4	1	0	1	18	0	38	1	0
Ortega, Pablo, Pue.	2	1	.667	5.59	11	1	0	0	1	0	19.1	22	83	12	12	5	0	0	2	8	1	17	0	0
Ortega, Pablo, Tig.	1	6	.143	7.46	13	9	0	0	0	0	50.2	72	247	44	42	7	4	2	4	26	3	36	1	1
Osuna, Ricardo, Tab.	4	6	.400	5.03	12	12	0	0	0	0	62.2	82	291	43	35	3	5	7	2	22	1	29	3	0
Osuna, Ricardo, Yuc.	3	2	.600	4.03	6	6	0	0	0	0	29	28	121	14	13	4	0	0	1	8	0	17	0	0
Palacios, Vicente, Sal.	2	0	1.000	5.79	11	0	0	0	3	0	9.1	13	45	9	6	3	1	0	1	2	0	8	1	0
Palacios, Vicente, Cam.	3	1	.750	2.87	23	0	0	0	7	0	31.1	22	123	10	10	3	3	1	0	7	1	29	0	0
Perez, Leonardo, Cor.	1	6	.143	6.43	11	11	1	0	0	0	56	72	256	42	40	5	2	3	4	22	3	17	1	0
Perez, Leonardo, Ver.	1	5	.167	5.65	11	9	0	0	0	0	43	56	198	30	27	10	2	1	0	14	1	9	2	0
Quimbar, Juan, Lar.*	0	0	.000	16.88	4	0	0	0	1	0	2.2	5	15	5	5	0	0	0	0	3	0	1	1	0
Quimbar, Juan, Pue.*	0	0	.000	8.10	9	0	0	0	0	0	6.2	8	32	6	6	3	1	0	0	4	0	4	1	0
Renovato, Nestor, Mont.	5	2	.714	3.52	27	0	0	0	8	0	38.1	40	165	18	15	3	0	2	2	13	1	18	3	0
Renovato, Nestor, Rey.	2	2	.500	3.12	6	5	0	0	0	0	34.2	32	141	14	12	1	2	0	3	7	0	21	2	0
Rios, Alejandro, Sal.	1	1	.500	8.04	17	1	0	0	2	0	28	46	141	27	25	5	1	2	0	16	2	12	3	0
Rios, Alejandro, Monc.	0	0	.000	10.38	9	0	0	0	0	0	8.2	14	47	11	10	0	1	0	0	6	1	6	2	0
Rios, Jesus, Yuc.	4	2	.667	4.15	12	12	1	1	0	0	60.2	64	264	28	28	4	1	3	3	20	0	41	3	0
Rios, Jesus, Tab.	5	2	.714	2.56	9	9	2	1	0	0	59.2	60	254	20	17	3	5	2	6	17	2	31	2	0
Rivas, Jesus, Tig.*	0	0	.000	5.02	17	0	0	0	4	0	14.1	17	63	9	8	0	0	0	0	9	1	11	1	0
Rivas, Jesus, Pue.*	0	0	.000	2.35	16	0	0	0	2	1	7.2	4	31	2	2	1	1	0	0	5	1	4	1	0
Rivera, Oscar, Yuc.*	1	1	.500	2.66	26	1	0	0	7	0	23.2	27	103	8	7	3	1	0	2	6	0	17	1	0
Rivera, Oscar, Cam.*	6	11	.353	4.88	22	22	1	0	0	0	125.1	132	549	72	68	18	9	0	9	53	1	80	11	0
Valdez, Efrain, Cor.*	4	5	.444	3.54	11	8	1	0	3	0	53.1	55	224	23	21	4	2	1	4	18	2	27	1	0
Valdez, Efrain, Tab.*	7	4	.636	2.45	15	15	4	3	0	0	102.2	90	409	30	28	5	7	2	2	27	0	67	3	0

COMBINATION SHUTOUTS: **Campeche (3)**—N. Elvira-Marquez, Lemon-Loaiza-Revenig-E. Sanchez-Marquez, I. Villegas-Tejeda-Ad. Garcia-J. Cazares-V. Palacios. **Cancun (7)**—Couoh-Je. Lopez-F. Villegas, Couoh-F. Villegas-A. Sanchez, M. Hernandez-Lara-Montane, Hurtado-F. Villegas, Hurtado-F. Villegas-Je. Lopez, M. Munoz-Lara. **Cordoba (3)**—Amarillas-Ruelas, G. Lopez-F. Rivera-Blancas, E. Valdez-E. Perez. **Dos Laredos (5)**—L. Huerta-Cortes 2, Loya-R. Garcia-Bell-Cortes, J.J. Nunez-Bell, A. Valdez-L. Munoz-Delfin. **Mexico City Reds (1)**—Vosberg-J. Cruz-B. Rivera. **Mexico City Tigers (2)**—Mi. Gomez-S. Hernandez, Mi. Gomez-Manzano-Rivas. **Monclova (5)**—J. Acosta-Macias-Alberro, J. Acosta-Macias-Cecena-Alberro, J. Acosta-Valerio-Murillo, A. Alvarez-Macias-Murillo-Valerio, C. Guzman-J. Flores-Jose Lopez. **Monterrey (9)**—Leyva-Parra-Rubio 2, R. Diaz-Rubio, G. Gonzalez-Silva-Rubio, Leyva-Rubio, Montemayor-Rubio, Montemayor-Vazquez-M. Nieblas-Parra-Rubio, M. Nieblas-Parra, R. Rodriguez-Rubio. **Oaxaca (8)**—D. Dominguez-E. Neri, D. Dominguez-E. Neri-Baez, D. Dominguez-E. Neri-Avalos-Baez, Elizalde-C. Sanchez-Avalos, C. Pulido-Avalos-Jo. Jimenez, C. Pulido-Baez, C. Pulido-Evans, C. Pulido-Jo. Jimenez-Avalos-Baez. **Puebla (5)**—L. Cruz-J. Villegas, R. Martinez-J. Villegas-J. Garcia, R. Ortega-Cabrales, R. Ortega-Cabrales-F. Huerta, F. Reyes-P. Ortega-J. Villegas-Rivas. **Reynosa (5)**—Esquer-Enriquez-H. Garcia-Or. Verdugo-Ju. Lopez, Esquer-Quinones-Melendez-Molina, Kubenka-Ju. Lopez, Kubenka-Or. Verdugo-Ju. Lopez, Renovato-Ju. Lopez. **Saltillo (4)**—Quiroz-Federico-Duarte-Ayala, N. Reyes-Federico-Duarte-Ayala, Romano-Ayala, Romano-V. Palacios-Ayala. **Tabasco (3)**—E. Valdez-J. Leon-Herrera, Vargas-J. Leon-G. Sandoval-Herrera, Vargas-G. Sandoval-P. Rivera-Herrera. **Torreon (4)**—J. Alvarez-T. Alvarez, Chavez-T. Alvarez, Hartmann-Ma. Gomez-T. Alvarez, Ward-Salazar-M. Aguilar. **Veracruz (12)**—E. Mora-Sinohui 2, A. Moreno-Jo. Pena-Sinohui 2, E. Mora-E. Gonzalez-Sinohui, E. Mora-Jo. Pena, E. Mora-Salgado-H. Navarro, Morales-Sinohui, A. Moreno-Morales-Jo. Pena-Sinohui, Salgado-E. Gonzalez-Sinohui, Salgado-Jo. Pena-Sinohui, Salgado-Sinohui. **Yucatan (3)**—Arellano-J.I. Flores-M. Garcia, Palafox-J.I. Flores-M. Garcia, Palafox-M. Garcia-Flores.

NO-HIT GAMES: Olague, Puebla, defeated Mexico City Tigers, 6-0, April 13; Vega, Cancun, defeated Campeche, 11-0, June 13, second game.

TEAM

Team	G	PO	A	E	TC	DP	TP	PB	Pct.
Monterrey	109	2869	1097	73	4039	99	0	4	.982
Puebla	108	2788	1360	79	4227	139	0	3	.981
Mex. City Reds	110	2890	1311	88	4289	144	0	6	.979
Dos Laredos	110	2885	1269	90	4244	122	0	14	.979
Monclova	110	2866	1234	90	4190	113	0	17	.979
Cancun	107	2777	1159	90	4026	108	0	5	.978
Veracruz	109	2870	1273	95	4238	86	0	9	.978
Yucatan	107	2859	1128	94	4081	100	0	15	.977
Mex. City Tigers	106	2756	1263	95	4114	129	0	8	.977
Saltillo	109	2841	1253	100	4194	125	0	3	.976
Campeche	107	2784	1116	99	3999	87	0	9	.975
Oaxaca	108	2837	1294	107	4238	122	0	8	.975
Cordoba	108	2809	1242	106	4157	114	0	22	.975
Torreon	109	2835	1245	107	4187	100	0	9	.974
Tabasco	109	2864	1297	121	4282	130	0	12	.972
Reynosa	110	2792	1134	134	4060	122	0	11	.967

INDIVIDUAL

FIRST BASEMEN

NOTE: All caps denotes fielding-percentage leader based on 55 games for catchers, 73 for all other non-pitchers and 88 innings for pitchers. *Throws lefthanded.

Player, Team	Pct.	G	PO	A	E	TC	DP
Adriana, Sharnol, Cam.-Cor.	.994	55	444	26	3	473	54
AGANZA, Ruben, Monc.	.999	88	757	54	1	812	81
Aguilera, Armando, Sal.	1.000	4	7	1	0	8	0
Aguirre, Francisco, Tab.	1.000	1	3	0	0	3	0
Almeida, Shammar, Oax.	.993	86	825	43	6	874	94
Amador, Alfonso, Ver.	1.000	1	13	3	0	16	2
Arauz, Escarcega, Monc.	.000	1	0	0	0	0	0
Arias, Francisco, Sal.	1.000	1	6	2	0	8	1
Aviles, Alejandro, Ver.	1.000	1	4	0	0	4	0
Baez, Carlos, Tab.	1.000	1	2	0	0	2	1
Barajas, Edison, Cor.*	1.000	2	7	1	0	8	0
Barrera, Jorge, Tor.	1.000	8	48	2	0	50	3
Barron, Tony, Ver.-Pue.	.993	16	143	8	1	152	15
Bojorquez, Victor, Mex.	1.000	2	3	1	0	4	0
Brown, Ray, Tab.	.986	26	255	26	4	285	38
Buelna, Lorenzo, Pue.	.000	1	0	0	0	0	0
Bustamante, Omar, Sal.	1.000	1	2	0	0	2	1
Carrillo, Matias, Tig.*	1.000	6	47	9	0	56	6
Castaneda, Hector, Yuc.	.996	88	803	38	3	844	76
Castaneda, Rafael, Rey.	.979	31	216	14	5	235	28
Castellano, Pedro, Oax.	.967	10	82	5	3	90	10
Cazarin, Manuel, Cam.	1.000	1	4	0	0	4	1
Cervantes, Refugio, Cam.	1.000	10	79	5	0	84	6
Cobos, Rogelio, Ver.-Can.	.973	10	64	7	2	73	6
Colina, Roberto, Pue.*	.989	63	580	55	7	642	74
Connell, Lino, Oax.	1.000	2	3	1	0	4	0
Cruz, Fausto, Yuc.	1.000	3	19	1	0	20	2
De Los Santos, Luis, Mex.-Oax.	.992	27	226	18	2	246	29
Diaz, Pedro, Pue.	.992	24	213	26	2	241	33
Duenas, Arnaldo, Yuc.	1.000	5	6	1	0	7	0
Espino, Daniel, Tor.	1.000	9	55	11	0	66	6
Espinoza, Ramon, Rey.	.981	15	100	5	2	107	11
Espinoza, Ramon, Tor.	1.000	1	1	0	0	1	0
Estrada, Hector, Tor.	1.000	1	3	0	0	3	0
Fornes, Daniel, Rey.*	.998	54	374	32	1	407	41
Garcia, Cornelio, Mex.*	.988	73	683	35	9	727	70
Garcia, Guillermo, Tig.	.993	57	504	42	4	550	62
Garcia, Omar, Ver.	.996	65	627	49	3	679	46
Gonzalez, Jesus, Yuc.	.994	17	145	14	1	160	8
Grijak, Kevin, Tor.	.993	72	627	48	5	680	63
Ibarra, Juvenal, Tor.	.964	14	67	13	3	83	7
Iturbe, Pedro, Tig.*	.973	8	67	4	2	73	6
Jennings, Doug, Tab.*	1.000	1	8	0	0	8	0
Leyva, German, Tab.-Yuc.	1.000	7	48	4	0	52	5
Lizarraga, Norberto, Cor.	.000	1	0	0	0	0	0
Lopez, Baltazar, Mont.	1.000	2	5	0	0	5	0
Lopez, Raul, Monc.	.996	23	224	13	1	238	24
Lucca, Lou, Cam.	.875	2	5	2	1	8	0
Luke, Matt, Cam.*	.900	1	9	0	1	10	0
Martinez, Abel, Can.	1.000	1	3	0	0	3	0
Martinez, Ramon, Mex.	1.000	6	51	3	0	54	8
Mendez, Francisco, Lar.	.988	43	309	27	4	340	28
Mendez, Roberto, Mex.*	.000	1	0	0	0	0	0
Mendoza, Omar, Tab.	1.000	1	2	0	0	2	0
Mercedes, Henry, Cor.	.973	9	63	10	2	75	8
Meulens, Hensley, Pue.	.931	3	24	3	2	29	3
Meza, Gonzalo, Tor.	1.000	1	1	1	0	2	0
Munoz, Jose, Sal.*	.600	1	3	0	2	5	1
Murray, Glenn, Cam.	.944	2	16	1	1	18	0
Ojeda, Miguel, Ver.	.988	15	76	8	1	85	15
Orantes, Ramon, Mont.	.994	19	158	13	1	172	17
Ortega, Antonio, Cam.	.958	7	21	2	1	24	0
O'Sullivan, Patrick, Rey.	.980	20	135	11	3	149	20
Otanez, Willis, Can.	1.000	4	32	4	0	36	4
Paez, Raul, Ver.-Tab.*	.991	66	510	49	5	564	56
Palafox, Sergio, Sal.	1.000	1	1	0	0	1	1
Payro, Edison, Cam.*	1.000	1	3	1	0	4	0
Pearson, Eddie, Tab.-Can.	.970	21	179	15	6	200	14
Perez, Francisco, Rey.*	.968	10	55	5	2	62	7
Perez, Luis, Tor.	.991	32	208	18	2	228	17
Peterson, Charles, Tab.	1.000	1	10	5	0	15	1
Phillips, J.R., Mont.*	1.000	8	56	1	0	57	7
Quintero, Edgar, Mont.	1.000	1	2	0	0	2	0
Riggs, Adam, Sal.	1.000	5	25	1	0	26	3
Rios, Eduardo, Can.	.994	89	764	56	5	825	83
Rivera, Francisco, Cor.	1.000	1	5	0	0	5	1
Rivera, Jesus, Tab.	1.000	8	39	3	0	42	1
Robles, Oscar, Oax.	1.000	1	2	1	0	3	0
Rodarte, Raul, Mont.	1.000	1	10	0	0	10	1
Rodriguez, Fernando, Cam.	.974	13	106	7	3	116	7
Rohrmeier, Dan, Tab.	1.000	5	45	2	0	47	4
Rojas, Homar, Oax.	.972	9	64	6	2	72	5
Romero, Marco, Sal.	.994	84	728	62	5	795	84
Salcedo, Eder, Mont.	.000	1	0	0	0	0	0
Sanchez, Roque, Cam.	.987	15	70	7	1	78	4
Santana, Mario, Tab.	1.000	3	8	1	0	9	2
Santos, Andres, Lar.	1.000	1	2	0	0	2	0
Sauceda, Victor, Can.	1.000	1	1	0	0	1	1
Saucedo, Robert, Lar.	.992	64	574	37	5	616	69
Sievers, Carlos, Tab.	1.000	10	75	11	0	86	7
Smith, Charles, Mont.	.984	82	642	52	11	705	65
Solis, Marco, Ver.	1.000	5	15	3	0	18	3
Suarez, Luis, Tig.*	1.000	2	3	0	0	3	0
Trapaga, Julio, Pue.	1.000	16	132	17	0	149	14
Valdez, Emmanuel, Tig.	.950	2	19	0	1	20	2
Valle, Cosme, Mex.	1.000	14	85	4	0	89	15
Vazquez, Jorge Alberto, Tig.	.959	10	63	8	3	74	13
Velazquez, Guillermo, Sal.-Cam.	.987	77	630	65	9	704	64
Verduzco, Vincente, Sal.	.987	9	70	7	1	78	10
Villalobos, Carlos, Tab.	.986	16	135	11	2	148	17
Villarreal, Alejandro, Lar.	1.000	19	149	19	0	168	14
Vizcarra, Roberto, Tig.	.990	31	278	29	3	310	34
Yan, Julian, Cor.	.984	70	682	52	12	746	70
Yuriar, Jesus, Can.	.750	1	3	0	1	4	0
Zambrano, Eduardo, Can.	1.000	1	11	1	0	12	0
Zambrano, Roberto, Can.	1.000	1	8	0	0	8	1

FIRST BASEMEN WITH TWO OR MORE TEAMS

Player, Team	Pct.	G	PO	A	E	TC	DP
Adriana, Sharnol, Cam.	.995	23	183	12	1	196	22
Adriana, Sharnol, Cor.	.993	32	261	14	2	277	32
Barron, Tony, Ver.	.989	11	88	4	1	93	7
Barron, Tony, Pue.	1.000	5	55	4	0	59	8
Cobos, Rogelio, Ver.	.979	5	42	4	1	47	2
Cobos, Rogelio, Can.	.962	5	22	3	1	26	4
De Los Santos, Luis, Mex.	.993	17	141	11	1	153	23
De Los Santos, Luis, Oax.	.989	10	85	7	1	93	6
Leyva, German, Tab.	1.000	5	32	3	0	35	3
Leyva, German, Yuc.	1.000	2	16	1	0	17	2
Paez, Raul, Ver.*	.997	32	271	22	1	294	24
Paez, Raul, Tab.*	.985	34	239	27	4	270	32
Pearson, Eddie, Tab.	.966	18	155	13	6	174	13
Pearson, Eddie, Can.	1.000	3	24	2	0	26	1
Velazquez, Guillermo, Sal.	.984	19	159	24	3	186	21
Velazquez, Guillermo, Cam.	.988	58	471	41	6	518	43

SECOND BASEMEN

Player, Team	Pct.	G	PO	A	E	TC	DP
Acosta, Jose, Tab.	.000	1	0	0	0	0	0
Adriana, Sharnol, Cor.	.963	5	14	12	1	27	2

CLASS AAA Mexican League

Player, Team	Pct.	G	PO	A	E	TC	DP
Alexander, Manny, Cor.	1.000	4	10	6	0	16	4
Arias, Francisco, Sal.	1.000	11	14	15	0	29	6
Armenta, Guillermo, Cam.	.977	10	12	31	1	44	3
Arredondo, Alan, Tab.	.960	42	78	65	6	149	15
Arredondo, Jesus, Pue.	.991	98	245	322	5	572	99
Bojorquez, Victor, Mex.	1.000	1	2	0	0	2	0
Brena, Jaime, Oax.	.982	33	47	64	2	113	18
Carrasco, Ernesto, Pue.	1.000	3	1	7	0	8	1
Castaneda, Rafael, Rey.	1.000	1	1	0	0	1	0
Castro, Arnoldo, Can.	.986	97	227	284	7	518	76
Castro, Domingo, Monc.	.929	6	8	5	1	14	0
Cervantes, Ivan, Mex.	.965	26	62	77	5	144	24
Connell, Lino, Oax.	.967	35	74	104	6	184	29
Duenas, Arnaldo, Yuc.	.000	1	0	0	0	0	0
Espinoza, Efren, Mex.	.974	65	142	194	9	345	60
Esquer, Ramon, Oax.	.990	25	39	60	1	100	15
Feliz, Alejandro, Mex.	1.000	2	2	0	0	2	1
Flores, Kevin, Tig.	1.000	5	1	4	0	5	0
Flores, Miguel, Mont.	.990	20	53	50	1	104	8
Garcia, Amaury, Cam.	1.000	24	43	49	0	92	6
Garcia, Heriberto, Oax.	1.000	1	1	1	0	2	0
Gastelum, Carlos, Pue.-Tig.	1.000	28	72	90	0	162	33
Gastelum, Sergio, Tig.	.975	33	70	87	4	161	21
Gil, Eric, Tor.	1.000	5	0	3	0	3	0
Gonzalez, Israel, Cam.	.952	7	3	17	1	21	1
Gonzalez, Roman, Cor.	.000	1	0	0	0	0	0
Guerrero, Epifano, Tab.	.971	21	49	52	3	104	18
Guerrero, Sergio, Cam.	.974	68	182	154	9	345	47
Leyva, Octavio, Ver.	1.000	5	5	3	0	8	1
Lizarraga, Norberto, Cor.	.000	1	0	0	0	0	0
Lizarraga, Rodolfo, Rey.	1.000	2	3	1	0	4	1
Lopez, Fabian, Can.	1.000	7	12	11	0	23	3
Magallanes, Ever, Mont.	.962	14	29	21	2	52	1
Martin, Norberto, Cam.	.846	3	5	6	2	13	1
Martinez, Abel, Can.	1.000	2	6	6	0	12	2
Martinez, Grimaldo, Cor.	.985	96	231	302	8	541	78
Medina, Jose, Sal.*	1.000	1	4	0	0	4	0
Mendoza, Omar, Tab.	.973	55	116	140	7	263	42
Mere, Pedro, Ver.	.987	109	251	340	8	599	62
Minjarez, Francisco, Pue.	1.000	8	14	17	0	31	6
Morejon, Oswaldo, Yuc.	.975	107	272	320	15	607	64
Nunez, Reymond, Lar.	1.000	1	0	2	0	2	0
Ojeda, Miguel, Mex.	1.000	2	0	3	0	3	1
Orrantia, Carlos, Mont.	1.000	16	24	26	0	50	4
Paez, Raul, Tab.*	1.000	1	1	2	0	3	1
Palafox, Sergio, Sal.	.966	42	96	133	8	237	30
Perez, Alfredo, Cam.	1.000	7	9	17	0	26	6
Perez, Francisco, Rey.*	.000	1	0	0	0	0	0
Perez, Jorge, Pue.	.000	1	0	0	0	0	0
Perez, Jose, Mont.-Rey.	.975	37	85	70	4	159	19
Phillips, Tony, Mex.	.978	7	18	27	1	46	9
Quintero, Guillermo, Ver.	1.000	1	0	2	0	2	0
Ramirez, Deyby, Mex.	.000	1	0	0	0	0	0
Ramirez, Enrique, Can.	.000	1	0	0	0	0	0
Ramirez, Johnathan, Oax.	1.000	4	4	5	0	9	2
Rivera, Jesus, Tab.	1.000	6	16	13	0	29	9
Robles, Oscar, Oax.	.982	45	91	131	4	226	30
Robles, Trinidad, Tig.	1.000	25	51	77	0	128	19
RODRIGUEZ, Carlos, Tor.	.995	108	283	317	3	603	81
Rodriguez, Jose, Tor.	1.000	3	0	6	0	6	0
Rodriguez, Liu, Sal.-Tab.	.975	65	154	195	9	358	54
Romero, Flavio, Sal.	1.000	4	5	11	0	16	2
Ruiz, Juan, Mex.	.952	34	55	64	6	125	21
Ruiz, Ricardo, Ver.	.500	1	1	0	1	2	0
Sanchez, Wilfredo, Cor.	.977	13	17	25	1	43	7
Sanchez, Jose, Lar.	1.000	3	0	3	0	3	0
Sanchez, Orlando, Lar.	.987	19	26	50	1	77	5
Sanchez, Roque, Cor.	1.000	1	1	2	0	3	1
Sandoval, Jose, Mex.	1.000	1	1	0	0	1	0
Sauceda, Victor, Can.	.975	14	19	20	1	40	3
Torrero, Miguel, Pue.	1.000	5	9	8	0	17	1
Tovar, Jose, Rey.	1.000	3	1	0	0	1	0
Trapaga, Julio, Tig.-Pue.	.978	42	80	100	4	184	36
Valencia, Carlos, Lar.	.987	99	225	324	7	556	83
Valenzuela, Irving, Monc.	.961	19	28	21	2	51	10
Valle, Jorge, Tor.	1.000	1	1	4	0	5	0
Valle, Roberto, Rey.	1.000	2	6	2	0	8	2
Velez, Manuel, Mont.	.990	46	98	107	2	207	32
Verdugo, Vincente, Sal.	.991	19	49	66	1	116	17
Villalobos, Carlos, Monc.	.000	1	0	0	0	0	0
Zazueta, Juan, Rey.	.971	110	264	268	16	548	86
Zazueta, Mauricio, Monc.	.990	104	276	292	6	574	72

SECOND BASEMEN WITH TWO OR MORE TEAMS

Player, Team	Pct.	G	PO	A	E	TC	DP
Gastelum, Carlos, Pue.	1.000	3	5	8	0	13	3
Gastelum, Carlos, Tig.	1.000	25	67	82	0	149	30
Perez, Jose, Mont.	.975	36	84	70	4	158	19
Perez, Jose, Rey.	1.000	1	1	0	0	1	0
Rodriguez, Liu, Sal.	.974	47	106	156	7	269	39
Rodriguez, Liu, Tab.	.978	18	48	39	2	89	15
Trapaga, Julio, Tig.	.978	40	77	97	4	178	34
Trapaga, Julio, Pue.	1.000	2	3	3	0	6	2

THIRD BASEMEN

Player, Team	Pct.	G	PO	A	E	TC	DP
Acosta, Jose, Tab.	.800	6	1	7	2	10	0
Adriana, Sharnol, Cor.	.966	30	30	55	3	88	6
Aguirre, Francisco, Tab.	.900	3	0	9	1	10	0
Alexander, Manny, Cor.	.936	17	11	33	3	47	6
Arano, Eloy, Ver.	.957	82	61	185	11	257	19
Arias, Francisco, Sal.	.977	40	11	31	1	43	6
Arredondo, Alan, Tab.	1.000	3	1	4	0	5	0
Arredondo, Hernando, Cor.	.000	1	0	0	0	0	0
Arvizu, Martin, Cor.	.714	7	0	10	4	14	1
Beltran, Juan, Cam.	1.000	1	0	1	0	1	0
Brena, Jaime, Oax.	1.000	1	0	1	0	1	0
Carrasco, Ernesto, Pue.	.956	77	49	166	10	225	20
Castaneda, Rafael, Rey.	.914	33	19	45	6	70	6
Castellano, Pedro, Oax.	1.000	25	13	50	0	63	5
Cervantes, Ivan, Mex.	.920	12	5	18	2	25	1
CERVERA, Francisco, Yuc.	.967	79	72	162	8	242	15
Connell, Lino, Oax.	.857	10	1	5	1	7	0
Cruz, Fausto, Yuc.	.912	12	10	21	3	34	3
De Los Santos, Luis, Mex.-Oax.	.892	25	11	47	7	65	5
Diaz, Edwin, Ver.	.896	27	12	57	8	77	5
Diaz, Pedro, Pue.	.965	34	20	62	3	85	4
Duenas, Arnaldo, Yuc.	.950	15	7	12	1	20	1
Esquer, Ramon, Oax.	.000	1	0	0	0	0	0
Fentanes, Oscar, Ver.	1.000	2	1	0	0	1	0
Flores, Kevin, Tig.	1.000	4	0	3	0	3	1
Gastelum, Gato, Tig.	1.000	1	1	2	0	3	1
Gastelum, Sergio, Tig.	.932	25	15	54	5	74	5
Gil, Eric, Tor.	.000	4	0	0	0	0	0
Gonzalez, Israel, Cam.	.988	41	24	61	1	86	4
Guerrero, Sergio, Cam.	1.000	3	4	5	0	9	1
Guizar, Hector, Monc.	.978	22	16	28	1	45	6
Hernandez, Julio, Lar.	1.000	2	0	2	0	2	0
Leyva, German, Tab.-Yuc.	.947	54	44	116	9	169	11
Leyva, Octavio, Ver.	1.000	1	0	2	0	2	0
Lizarraga, Norberto, Cor.	.941	8	3	13	1	17	1
Lizarraga, Rodolfo, Rey.	.857	4	2	10	2	14	0
Lopez, Fabian, Oax.-Can.	.900	43	19	53	8	80	1
Lopez, Raul, Monc.	.930	66	57	142	15	214	11
Lucca, Lou, Cam.	.933	7	6	8	1	15	1
Magallanes, Ever, Mont.	.935	34	25	61	6	92	5
Martin, Norberto, Cam.	.949	14	10	27	2	39	2
Martinez, Abel, Can.	.932	65	40	111	11	162	11
Martinez, Ramon, Mex.	.963	99	76	213	11	300	19
Matos, Francisco, Tab.	.905	6	4	15	2	21	0
Mendoza, Omar, Tab.	.925	20	11	26	3	40	4
Meulens, Hensley, Pue.	1.000	2	3	0	0	3	0
Miller, Orlando, Tab.	.951	36	27	71	5	103	10
Minjarez, Francisco, Pue.	1.000	7	5	17	0	22	1
Nunez, Reymond, Lar.	.948	106	84	187	15	286	15
Ojeda, Miguel, Mex.	.750	4	1	2	1	4	1
Orantes, Ramon, Mont.	.962	39	34	67	4	105	7
Otanez, Willis, Monc.	.837	14	15	21	7	43	1
Perez, Alfredo, Cam.	.846	6	4	7	2	13	0
Perez, Jose, Mont.-Rey.	.828	16	5	19	5	29	2
Perez, Luis, Tor.	.000	2	0	0	1	1	0
Quintero, Guillermo, Ver.	1.000	2	2	2	0	4	0
Ramirez, Enrique, Can.	1.000	1	0	0	0	0	0
Ramirez, Oscar, Cam.	1.000	6	6	21	0	27	2
Riggs, Adam, Sal.	.926	61	33	130	13	176	18
Rios, Eduardo, Can.	.962	18	11	40	2	53	4
Robles, Javier, Tig.	.000	1	0	0	0	0	0
Robles, Oscar, Oax.	.937	70	44	164	14	222	19
Robles, Trinidad, Tig.	.955	49	31	96	6	133	8
Rodarte, Raul, Cor.-Mont.	.971	30	24	76	3	103	7
Rodriguez, Carlos, Tor.	1.000	1	2	2	0	4	0
Rodriguez, Jose, Tor.	.750	2	0	3	1	4	0
Romero, Flavio, Sal.	.929	5	4	9	1	14	0
Romero, Oscar, Rey.	.914	75	53	128	17	198	12

Player, Team	Pct.	G	PO	A	E	TC	DP
Ruiz, Juan, Mex.	1.000	8	4	2	0	6	1
Ruiz, Ricardo, Ver.	1.000	4	0	3	0	3	1
Salas, Heriberto, Yuc.	1.000	3	1	3	0	4	0
Sanchez. Wilfredo, Cor.	.957	11	6	16	1	23	0
Sanchez, Hector, Tor.	1.000	1	0	2	0	2	0
Sanchez, Roque, Cam.-Cor.	.965	72	54	136	7	197	16
Santos, Andres, Lar.	1.000	2	1	0	0	1	0
Sauceda, Victor, Can.	1.000	7	0	5	0	5	1
Sievers, Carlos, Tab.	.000	1	0	0	0	0	0
Sisco, Steve, Sal.	.913	14	13	29	4	46	6
Trapaga, Julio, Tig.	1.000	2	0	1	0	1	0
Valencia, Carlos, Lar.	1.000	5	0	6	0	6	0
Valle, Cosme, Mex.	.933	3	3	11	1	15	2
Valle, Jose, Tor.	.966	107	90	281	13	384	25
Valle, Roberto, Rey.	.750	11	1	2	1	4	0
Vazquez, Jorge Alberto, Tig.	1.000	2	1	8	0	9	0
Velez, Manuel, Mont.	.969	37	30	65	3	98	4
Verdugo, Vincente, Sal.	.927	27	14	37	4	55	5
Villalobos, Carlos, Monc.-Tab.	.902	31	27	74	11	112	7
Villarreal, Alejandro, Lar.	1.000	7	3	11	0	14	1
Vizcarra, Roberto, Tig.	.937	50	40	109	10	159	8
Zazueta, Juan, Rey.	1.000	1	1	0	0	1	0

THIRD BASEMEN WITH TWO OR MORE TEAMS

Player, Team	Pct.	G	PO	A	E	TC	DP
De Los Santos, Luis, Mex.	1.000	3	1	3	0	4	0
De Los Santos, Luis, Oax.	.885	22	10	44	7	61	5
Leyva, German, Tab.	.940	37	33	92	8	133	10
Leyva, German, Yuc.	.972	17	11	24	1	36	1
Lopez, Fabian, Oax.	.000	1	0	0	0	0	0
Lopez, Fabian, Can.	.900	42	19	53	8	80	1
Perez, Jose, Mont.	1.000	3	1	5	0	6	0
Perez, Jose, Rey.	.783	13	4	14	5	23	2
Rodarte, Raul, Cor.	.975	22	19	59	2	80	7
Rodarte, Raul, Mont.	.957	8	5	17	1	23	0
Sanchez, Roque, Cam.	.966	48	40	100	5	145	15
Sanchez, Roque, Cor.	.962	24	14	36	2	52	1
Villalobos, Carlos, Monc.	.905	24	19	57	8	84	6
Villalobos, Carlos, Tab.	.893	7	8	17	3	28	1

SHORTSTOPS

Player, Team	Pct.	G	PO	A	E	TC	DP
Alexander, Manny, Cor.	.933	24	39	73	8	120	18
Arano, Eloy, Ver.	.000	1	0	0	0	0	0
Arias, Francisco, Sal.	1.000	11	7	10	0	17	3
Armenta, Guillermo, Cam.	.928	18	26	51	6	83	13
Arredondo, Alan, Tab.	.910	16	21	40	6	67	9
Arredondo, Jesus, Pue.	1.000	1	4	5	0	9	1
Beltran, Juan, Cam.	.932	13	12	29	3	44	3
Borges, Luis, Can.	.964	96	135	240	14	389	53
Brena, Jaime, Oax.	.951	19	10	29	2	41	6
Bustillos, Luis, Rey.	.962	90	134	266	16	416	64
Castaneda, Rafael, Rey.	.872	9	15	19	5	39	5
Castro, Domingo, Monc.	.956	76	99	225	15	339	46
Cervantes, Ivan, Mex.	1.000	14	18	33	0	51	8
Cervera, Francisco, Yuc.	1.000	2	1	3	0	4	1
Connell, Lino, Oax.	.941	35	53	106	10	169	21
Cruz, Fausto, Yuc.	.960	86	140	272	17	429	50
Diaz, Edwin, Ver.	.952	77	123	251	19	393	39
Diaz, Pedro, Pue.	.000	1	0	0	0	0	0
DIAZ, Remigio, Mont.	.984	104	169	314	8	491	69
Espinoza, Efren, Mex.	.902	11	12	25	4	41	7
Feliz, Alejandro, Mex.	.000	1	0	0	0	0	0
Flores, Kevin, Tig.	1.000	1	0	2	0	2	1
Garcia, Amaury, Cam.	.950	7	7	12	1	20	1
Garcia, Heriberto, Oax.	.966	72	126	249	13	388	52
Gastelum, Carlos, Pue.	.973	66	124	265	11	400	63
Gastelum, Gato, Tig.	.667	1	0	2	1	3	0
Gil, Eric, Tor.	.667	4	0	2	1	3	0
Gomez, Heber, Tab.	.975	89	161	313	12	486	70
Goytia, Francisco, Tor.	.915	12	12	31	4	47	5
Guerrero, Sergio, Cam.	.750	1	0	3	1	4	0
Guizar, Hector, Monc.	.969	53	78	142	7	227	25
Gutierrez, Andres, Pue.	1.000	1	2	5	0	7	2
Hernandez, Julio, Lar.	.961	106	198	342	22	562	89
Leyva, Octavio, Ver.	.978	14	11	33	1	45	6
Lizarraga, Norberto, Cor.	.000	1	0	0	0	0	0
Lizarraga, Rodolfo, Rey.	.000	1	0	0	0	0	0
Lopez, Fabian, Can.	1.000	1	0	1	0	1	0
Magallanes, Ever, Mont.	.900	2	2	7	1	10	0

Player, Team	Pct.	G	PO	A	E	TC	DP
Martinez, Abel, Can.	1.000	1	1	0	0	1	0
Martinez, Augusto, Yuc.	.750	2	0	3	1	4	1
Martinez, Grimaldo, Cor.	1.000	4	5	4	0	9	2
Martinez, Luis, Sal.	.962	87	134	274	16	424	61
Martinez, Ramon, Mex.	.909	2	3	7	1	11	4
Meza, Alfredo, Ver.	.000	1	0	0	0	0	0
Minjarez, Francisco, Pue.	.963	44	67	140	8	215	34
Ojeda, Miguel, Mex.	1.000	1	0	2	0	2	0
Orrantia, Carlos, Mont.	.962	9	6	19	1	26	4
Pacho, Juan, Yuc.	.967	24	32	55	3	90	9
Palafox, Sergio, Sal.	1.000	1	2	3	0	5	1
Perez, Alfredo, Cam.	1.000	9	6	9	0	15	0
Perez, Jose, Mont.-Rey.	.909	6	9	11	2	22	4
Quintero, Guillermo, Ver.	.917	27	41	69	10	120	10
Ramirez, Enrique, Can.	.956	42	47	105	7	159	26
Ramirez, Jesus, Oax.	.000	1	0	0	0	0	0
Ramirez, Oscar, Cam.	.942	70	119	205	20	344	33
Reyes, Jesus, Tor.	.000	1	0	0	1	1	0
Rivera, Jesus, Tab.	.939	10	16	30	3	49	9
Robles, Javier, Tig.	.971	98	158	307	14	479	78
Robles, Trinidad, Tig.	.919	13	15	19	3	37	7
Rodriguez, Jose, Tor.	.952	101	137	316	23	476	62
Romero, Flavio, Sal.	.949	29	28	66	5	99	11
Romero, Oscar, Rey.	.800	7	5	3	2	10	0
Ruiz, Ricardo, Ver.	1.000	3	3	1	0	4	0
Salas, Heriberto, Cor.-Yuc.	.957	70	109	226	15	350	48
Sanchez. Wilfredo, Cor.	.955	23	48	80	6	134	8
Sanchez, Jose, Lar.	.947	12	14	22	2	38	5
Sanchez, Orlando, Lar.	1.000	3	1	2	0	3	0
Sandoval, Jose, Mex.	.975	96	141	356	13	510	81
Sauceda, Victor, Can.	1.000	7	1	3	0	4	1
Tellez, Alonso, Rey.	1.000	1	0	1	0	1	1
Torrero, Miguel, Pue.	.944	7	6	11	1	18	2
Tovar, Jose, Rey.	.944	9	4	13	1	18	4
Valenzuela, Irving, Monc.	1.000	3	3	7	0	10	1
Valle, Roberto, Rey.	.954	25	20	42	3	65	10
Verdugo, Vincente, Sal.	.000	1	0	0	0	0	0
Yuriar, Jesus, Can.	1.000	1	0	1	0	1	1

SHORTSTOPS WITH TWO OR MORE TEAMS

Player, Team	Pct.	G	PO	A	E	TC	DP
Perez, Jose, Mont.	.000	1	0	0	0	0	0
Perez, Jose, Rey.	.909	5	9	11	2	22	4
Salas, Heriberto, Cor.	.959	65	108	220	14	342	47
Salas, Heriberto, Yuc.	.875	5	1	6	1	8	1

OUTFIELDERS

Player, Team	Pct.	G	PO	A	E	TC	DP
Abrego, Jesus, Can.-Ver.	1.000	5	4	1	0	5	0
Acosta, Jose, Tab.	.000	1	0	0	0	0	0
Acuna, Jose, Can.	1.000	44	33	2	0	35	0
Aguilera, Antonio, Cam.-Yuc.	.938	21	30	0	2	32	0
Alejos, Fernando, Yuc.	1.000	2	1	0	0	1	0
Alvarez, Hector, Oax.	.958	85	129	7	6	142	1
Amador, Alfonso, Ver.	.000	1	0	0	0	0	0
Arano, Eloy, Ver.	1.000	12	25	3	0	28	1
Arano, Wilfrido, Lar.	.985	104	191	10	3	204	0
Arauz, Leobardo, Yuc.	.982	63	103	8	2	113	1
Armenta, Guillermo, Cam.	1.000	1	0	0	0	0	0
Arredondo, Alan, Tab.	1.000	3	3	1	0	4	0
Arredondo, Eduardo, Ver.	.903	34	27	1	3	31	0
Arredondo, Hernando, Cor.	.966	76	136	7	5	148	0
Arredondo, Luis, Yuc.*	.970	98	158	3	5	166	1
Avila, Carlos, Tig.*	.889	30	13	3	2	18	0
Avila, Ignacio, Cor.	.977	49	84	2	2	88	0
Baez, Carlos, Tab.	1.000	4	7	1	0	8	0
Barajas, Edison, Cor.*	.964	41	80	1	3	84	0
Barker, Glen, Rey.	.968	22	55	5	2	62	0
Barrera, Jorge, Tor.	1.000	29	30	0	0	30	0
Barron, Tony, Ver.-Pue.	.980	31	46	2	1	49	0
Barry, Jeff, Tig.	.875	5	7	0	1	8	0
Benitez, Yamil, Rey.-Cam.	.966	41	75	10	3	88	1
Bernal, Cosme, Monc.	1.000	8	13	0	0	13	0
Bojorquez, Victor, Mex.	.988	81	152	10	2	164	4
Bolado, Carlos, Ver.	1.000	7	6	0	0	6	0
Brena, Jaime, Oax.	1.000	1	1	0	0	1	0
Brown, Ray, Tab.	1.000	1	1	0	0	1	0
Buelna, Lorenzo, Pue.	.989	92	170	3	2	175	0
Canales, Joel, Mont.	.976	26	40	1	1	42	1
Candelaria, Ben, Ver.	.989	37	86	7	1	94	0

Player, Team	Pct.	G	PO	A	E	TC	DP
Canizalez, Juan, Cam.	.978	59	87	2	2	91	1
Carpenter, Bubba, Sal.	.969	21	31	0	1	32	0
Carrasco, Ernesto, Pue.	.000	1	0	0	0	0	0
Carrillo, Matias, Tig.*	.986	87	137	2	2	141	1
Carter, Mike, Yuc.	.955	10	21	0	1	22	0
CHIMELIS, Joel, Lar.	1.000	106	181	3	0	184	1
Cisneros, Ventura, Rey.	.867	19	23	3	4	30	0
Cobos, Rogelio, Ver.	.000	1	0	0	0	0	0
Connell, Lino, Oax.	.970	43	61	3	2	66	0
Contreras, Albino, Pue.*	.992	102	237	10	2	249	0
Cookson, Brent, Rey.	.972	22	34	1	1	36	0
Correa, Miguel, Tor.	.950	43	94	1	5	100	0
Cruz, Fausto, Yuc.	1.000	4	5	0	0	5	0
De La Torre, Francisco, Oax.	1.000	3	6	0	0	6	0
Diaz, Luis, Monc.*	1.000	49	53	1	0	54	0
Diaz, Pedro, Pue.	.000	1	0	0	0	0	0
Elvira, Abraham, Cor.*	.000	1	0	0	0	0	0
Espino, Daniel, Tor.	.993	83	137	1	1	139	1
Espinoza, Jose, Lar.	.960	42	69	3	3	75	0
Espinoza, Ramon, Rey.-Yuc.	.980	88	191	4	4	199	1
Espinoza, Ramon, Tor.	1.000	1	2	0	0	2	0
Estrella, Isaac, Lar.	1.000	37	27	1	0	28	0
Felix, Lorenzo, Tor.	.919	36	34	0	3	37	0
Fentanes, Oscar, Tab.-Ver.	.951	93	148	6	8	162	1
Fernandez, Dan, Mex.*	.983	82	176	0	3	179	0
Figga, Mike, Pue.	1.000	3	4	0	0	4	0
Fornes, Daniel, Rey.*	.953	54	96	6	5	107	0
Franco, Iker, Tig.	1.000	2	3	0	0	3	0
Garcia, Amaury, Cam.	.960	14	23	1	1	25	1
Garcia, Cornelio, Mex.*	1.000	17	17	1	0	18	0
Garcia, Hector, Tab.	.970	90	188	5	6	199	1
Garland, Tim, Rey.	.969	14	30	1	1	32	1
Gastelum, Carlos, Tig.	1.000	2	3	0	0	3	0
Gastelum, Sergio, Tig.	1.000	4	1	0	0	1	0
Gerardo, Benjamin, Tor.	1.000	12	11	0	0	11	0
Gonzalez, Israel, Cam.	1.000	13	16	2	0	18	0
Gonzalez, Jesus, Monc.	.800	2	4	0	1	5	0
Gonzalez, Roman, Cor.	.985	88	182	13	3	198	3
Grijak, Kevin, Tor.	.900	11	9	0	1	10	0
Guerrero, Sergio, Cam.	1.000	6	2	1	0	3	0
Gutierrez, Andres, Pue.	.882	7	14	1	2	17	0
Hunter, Brian, Sal.*	1.000	9	16	1	0	17	0
Ibarra, Juvenal, Tor.	1.000	3	1	0	0	1	0
Iturbe, Pedro, Tig.-Pue.*	.973	70	104	5	3	112	1
Jennings, Doug, Cor.-Tab.*	1.000	28	45	0	0	45	0
Jones, Chris, Yuc.	.964	39	49	5	2	56	2
Jose, Felix, Mex.	.969	30	59	3	2	64	0
Kelly, Roberto, Mex.	.967	70	117	1	4	122	0
Lara, Idelfonso, Cor.	.967	30	59	0	2	61	0
Leyva, German, Yuc.	.000	1	0	0	0	0	0
Lopez, Jose, Rey.	.929	18	25	1	2	28	0
Lopez, Raul, Monc.	1.000	16	26	0	0	26	0
Lugo, Roberto, Mont.	1.000	1	1	0	0	1	0
Machiria, Pablo, Lar.	.966	23	27	1	1	29	0
Malave, Jose, Rey.	.969	79	122	3	4	129	1
Martin, Norberto, Cam.	1.000	16	21	2	0	23	0
Martinez, Abel, Cam.	1.000	3	5	0	0	5	0
Martinez, Enrique, Pue.	.963	66	124	6	5	135	2
Martinez, Grimaldo, Cor.	1.000	2	3	0	0	3	0
Martinez, Luis, Sal.	1.000	1	1	0	0	1	0
Martinez, Rafael, Pue.*	.969	19	31	0	1	32	0
Mata, Noe, Ver.	.965	73	134	4	5	143	1
Medina, Jose, Sal.*	1.000	16	16	0	0	16	0
Mendez, Francisco, Lar.	1.000	5	7	0	0	7	0
Mendez, Roberto, Mex.*	.988	63	82	1	1	84	0
Mendoza, Ramon, Cam.	.833	7	5	0	1	6	0
Meulens, Hensley, Pue.	.966	21	27	1	1	29	0
Meza, Alfredo, Ver.	.000	1	0	0	0	0	0
Meza, Gonzalo, Tor.	.964	99	209	7	8	224	0
Miranda, Luis, Tor.*	.000	1	0	0	0	0	0
Moreno, David, Cam.	1.000	19	16	1	0	17	0
Munoz, Adan, Monc.	1.000	3	3	0	0	3	0
Munoz, Jose, Sal.*	.986	65	131	5	2	138	0
Murray, Glenn, Cam.-Yuc.	.978	29	44	0	1	45	0
Nerei, Yuji, Pue.*	.000	2	0	0	0	0	0
Newson, Warren, Mont.*	.982	39	53	1	1	55	0
Nieves, Melvin, Tor.	.972	61	102	2	3	107	0
Ojeda, Miguel, Mex.	1.000	2	2	0	0	2	0
Orantes, Ramon, Mont.	.929	9	12	1	1	14	0
Ortega, Antonio, Cam.	1.000	1	1	0	0	1	0
O'Sullivan, Patrick, Rey.	.957	44	83	7	4	94	2
Otero, Ricky, Can.*	.974	104	259	6	7	272	1
Pacho, Carlos, Yuc.	1.000	3	1	0	0	1	0
Palafox, Sergio, Sal.	.986	50	68	2	1	71	0
Payro, Edison, Cam.-Yuc.*	1.000	23	33	1	0	34	0
Pemberton, Rudy, Monc.	.989	48	87	1	1	89	0
Perez, Alfredo, Cam.	1.000	6	5	0	0	5	0
Perez, Francisco, Rey.*	1.000	1	2	0	0	2	0
Perez, Jose, Mont.-Rey.	1.000	5	5	0	0	5	0
Perez, Luis, Tor.	.000	2	0	0	0	0	0
Peterson, Charles, Tab.-Cam.	.944	59	97	5	6	108	0
Phillips, J.R., Yuc.-Mont.*	.941	33	63	1	4	68	1
Presichi, Cristian, Sal.	.940	69	105	4	7	116	1
Prieto, Chris, Oax.*	.986	63	134	9	2	145	1
Quintero, Christian, Oax.	.995	105	175	9	1	185	1
Quintero, Edgar, Mont.	.969	73	151	3	5	159	0
Ramirez, Jesus, Oax.	.982	40	52	2	1	55	0
Ramirez, Omar, Ver.	.996	107	238	5	1	244	0
Ramirez, Oscar, Cam.	.000	3	0	0	0	0	0
Reyes, Eleazar, Mex.	1.000	3	1	0	0	1	0
Rincon, Isaias, Mex.	1.000	25	22	2	0	24	0
Rivera, Jesus, Tab.	.000	4	0	0	0	0	0
Robles, Trinidad, Tig.	1.000	5	2	0	0	2	0
Rodarte, Raul, Mont.	.988	69	150	8	2	160	1
Rodriguez, Fernando, Cam.	.973	53	69	3	2	74	0
Rodriguez, Serafin, Tig.	.973	67	104	4	3	111	0
Romero, Flavio, Sal.	.986	38	65	4	1	70	1
Romero, Willie, Sal.	.984	93	181	7	3	191	0
Romero, Yamil, Ver.*	1.000	4	1	0	0	1	0
Saenz, Ricardo, Monc.	.982	61	102	8	2	112	2
Salazar, Carlos, Yuc.	1.000	3	2	1	0	3	0
Salcedo, Eder, Mont.	1.000	8	11	1	0	12	0
Samuels, Scott, Mont.	1.000	3	7	0	0	7	0
Sanchez, Wilfredo, Cor.	.000	1	0	0	0	0	0
Sanchez, Jesus, Can.	.986	106	200	9	3	212	1
Sanchez, Victor, Tab.	1.000	11	19	2	0	21	0
Sandoval, Octavio, Tig.	.990	92	177	15	2	194	2
Santos, Andres, Lar.	1.000	22	25	2	0	27	0
Sauceda, Victor, Can.	.000	2	0	0	0	0	0
Sherman, Darrell, Monc.*	.992	97	256	6	2	264	3
Sievers, Carlos, Tab.	1.000	1	0	0	0	0	0
Smith, Charles, Mont.	1.000	3	5	0	0	5	0
Smith, Demond, Mont.	.984	80	180	4	3	187	0
Soriano, Ricardo, Cor.*	.990	54	99	5	1	105	0
Sotomayor, Gilberto, Monc.*	1.000	77	140	4	0	144	0
Suarez, Luis, Tig.*	1.000	3	2	0	0	2	0
Tolentino, Juan, Tig.	1.000	10	13	0	0	13	0
Torrero, Miguel, Pue.	1.000	1	1	0	0	1	0
Tress, Irving, Cor.	.950	9	19	0	1	20	0
Valdez, Ramon, Cam.*	.984	102	231	12	4	247	1
Valdez, Uriel, Cor.	1.000	8	9	0	0	9	0
Valencia, Abraham, Lar.	.952	50	60	0	3	63	0
Valle, Cosme, Mex.	1.000	2	4	0	0	4	0
Valle, Roberto, Rey.	.000	1	0	0	0	0	0
Vaz, Roberto, Cam.*	1.000	6	6	1	0	7	1
Vazquez, Gregorio, Tab.	.976	92	197	7	5	209	2
Velez, Manuel, Mont.	.979	31	47	0	1	48	0
Verdugo, Vincente, Sal.	.833	3	5	0	1	6	0
Villalobos, Carlos, Monc.-Tab.	.943	45	76	7	5	88	1
Villarreal, Alejandro, Lar.	1.000	10	10	0	0	10	0
Villegas, Fernando, Can.	.982	87	152	13	3	168	0
Warner, Michael, Yuc.*	.975	35	74	3	2	79	0
Whiten, Mark, Ver.	.962	28	45	6	2	53	0
Whitmore, Darrell, Tab.	.968	13	30	0	1	31	0
Yuriar, Jesus, Can.	1.000	11	10	0	0	10	0

OUTFIELDERS WITH TWO OR MORE TEAMS

Player, Team	Pct.	G	PO	A	E	TC	DP
Abrego, Jesus, Cam.	1.000	3	2	1	0	3	0
Abrego, Jesus, Ver.	1.000	2	2	0	0	2	0
Aguilera, Antonio, Cam.	.818	7	9	0	2	11	0
Aguilera, Antonio, Yuc.	1.000	14	21	0	0	21	0
Barron, Tony, Ver.	.971	20	31	2	1	34	0
Barron, Tony, Pue.	1.000	11	15	0	0	15	0
Benitez, Yamil, Rey.	.961	35	67	7	3	77	0
Benitez, Yamil, Cam.	1.000	6	8	3	0	11	1
Espinoza, Ramon, Rey.	.980	44	97	3	2	102	1
Espinoza, Ramon, Yuc.	.979	44	94	1	2	97	0
Fentanes, Oscar, Tab.	.929	54	74	4	6	84	0
Fentanes, Oscar, Ver.	.974	39	74	2	2	78	0
Iturbe, Pedro, Tig.*	.963	55	74	4	3	81	1
Iturbe, Pedro, Pue.*	1.000	15	30	1	0	31	0

Player, Team	Pct.	G	PO	A	E	TC	DP
Jennings, Doug, Cor.*	1.000	23	36	0	0	36	0
Jennings, Doug, Tab.*	1.000	5	9	0	0	9	0
Murray, Glenn, Cam.	.975	24	39	0	1	40	0
Murray, Glenn, Yuc.	1.000	5	5	0	0	5	0
Payro, Edison, Cam.*	1.000	20	31	1	0	32	0
Payro, Edison, Yuc.*	1.000	3	2	0	0	2	0
Perez, Jose, Mont.	1.000	1	1	0	0	1	0
Perez, Jose, Rey.	1.000	4	4	0	0	4	0
Peterson, Charles, Tab.	.934	38	66	5	5	76	0
Peterson, Charles, Cam.	.969	21	31	0	1	32	0
Phillips, J.R., Yuc.*	.950	22	38	0	2	40	0
Phillips, J.R., Mont.*	.929	11	25	1	2	28	1
Villalobos, Carlos, Monc.	.960	16	22	2	1	25	0
Villalobos, Carlos, Tab.	.937	29	54	5	4	63	1

CATCHERS

Player, Team	Pct.	G	PO	A	E	TC	DP	PB
Abrego, Jesus, Can.-Ver.	.974	18	36	1	1	38	0	2
Aguilera, Antonio, Yuc.	.000	1	0	0	0	0	0	0
Aguilera, Armando, Sal.	1.000	5	20	0	0	20	0	0
Arauz, Escarcega, Monc.	.957	18	43	2	2	47	0	1
Arredondo, Eduardo, Ver.	.000	1	0	0	0	0	0	0
Baez, Carlos, Tab.	.000	2	0	0	0	0	0	0
Barron, Tony, Pue.	.000	1	0	0	0	0	0	0
Bustamante, Omar, Sal.	.939	17	29	2	2	33	0	0
Castaneda, Rafael, Rey.	1.000	1	2	0	0	2	0	0
Cazarin, Manuel, Cam.	.996	99	623	64	3	690	9	8
Cisneros, Ventura, Rey.	1.000	9	8	1	0	9	0	0
Cobos, Rogelio, Ver.-Can.	1.000	25	69	4	0	73	1	1
Cruz, Marco, Yuc.-Cam.	.970	27	94	3	3	100	0	2
Espinoza, Ramon, Tor.	1.000	24	48	0	0	48	0	0
Esqueda, Jonathan, Sal.	1.000	2	5	0	0	5	0	0
Estrada, Hector, Tor.	.984	107	572	42	10	624	2	8
Flores, Miguel, Mont.	1.000	1	0	0	0	0	0	0
Franco, Iker, Tig.	.980	21	86	10	2	98	2	3
Garcia, Guillermo, Cor.-Tig.	.987	36	204	24	3	231	1	8
Garza, Gerardo, Mont.	.997	56	293	22	1	316	2	1
Garzon, Eliseo, Mont.	.989	73	402	32	5	439	3	2
Gastelum, Gato, Tig.	.965	39	124	13	5	142	1	1
Gavia, Jesus, Yuc.	.976	63	335	29	9	373	2	5
Gonzalez, Fernando, Rey.	.992	75	360	32	3	395	4	8
Gonzalez, Israel, Cam.	.000	1	0	0	0	0	0	0
Grijak, Kevin, Tor.	.750	3	4	2	2	8	0	1
Gutierrez, Said, Yuc.	.982	67	342	31	7	380	9	7
Hartman, Kory, Yuc.	.000	1	0	0	0	0	0	0
Hurtado, Hector, Lar.	.977	99	540	55	14	609	5	11
Leyva, Octavio, Ver.	.000	1	0	0	0	0	0	0
Lizarraga, Norberto, Cor.	1.000	2	4	0	0	4	0	0
Lugo, Roberto, Mont.	1.000	10	12	1	0	13	0	1
Marquez, Leonardo, Tig.	1.000	5	7	0	0	7	0	0
Mercedes, Henry, Cor.	.980	35	135	12	3	150	0	3
MEZA, Alfredo, Ver.-Tab.	.998	97	511	48	1	560	3	6
Montano, Angel, Cam.	1.000	1	1	0	0	1	0	0
Montenegro, Jose, Mex.	1.000	26	86	6	0	92	3	1
Munoz, Adan, Monc.	.979	35	167	17	4	188	3	3
Munoz, Noe, Sal.	.992	103	598	42	5	645	3	3
Ojeda, Miguel, Mex.	.994	89	440	49	3	492	5	2
Olivares, Roberto, Ver.	.000	4	0	0	0	0	0	0
Ortega, Antonio, Cam.	1.000	9	16	3	0	19	0	0
Pacho, Carlos, Yuc.	.938	6	14	1	1	16	0	1
Pacho, Juan, Yuc.	1.000	1	4	0	0	4	0	1
Paez, Hector, Can.	.978	88	437	48	11	496	4	2
Pinto, Placido, Lar.	.986	25	68	4	1	73	1	3
Quinones, Ruben, Monc.-Cor.	.994	44	152	14	1	167	3	6
Ramirez, Jesus, Oax.	.000	1	0	0	0	0	0	0
Resendez, Carlos, Monc.	.983	59	252	35	5	292	1	8
Rivera, Francisco, Ver.-Cor.	.960	21	66	6	3	75	0	6
Robles, Juan, Rey.	.986	60	318	35	5	358	7	3
Rodriguez, Armando, Can.	.986	29	133	11	2	146	1	3
Rodriguez, Erick, Oax.	.959	24	70	1	3	74	0	1
Rodriguez, Serafin, Tig.	1.000	2	1	0	0	1	0	0
Sanchez, Wilfredo, Cor.	.000	1	0	0	0	0	0	0
Sanchez, Victor, Tab.	.000	1	0	0	0	0	0	0
Santana, Mario, Tab.	.994	39	150	12	1	163	3	4
Sauceda, Victor, Can.	.000	1	0	0	0	0	0	0
Saucedo, Robert, Lar.	.963	13	24	2	1	27	0	0
Soto, Saul, Oax.	.990	98	592	32	6	630	1	7
Valdez, Emmanuel, Tig.	.990	68	351	36	4	391	1	4
Valdez, Francisco, Tab.-Ver.	.985	91	404	43	7	454	6	8
Valle, Cosme, Mex.	.970	27	89	9	3	101	0	3

Player, Team	Pct.	G	PO	A	E	TC	DP	PB
Vazquez, Jorge Alberto, Tig.	.000	1	0	0	0	0	0	0
Vega, Edgar, Pue.	.985	87	405	43	7	455	3	1
Vega, Jesus, Pue.	.970	43	119	9	4	132	0	2
Virgen, Constancio, Cor.	.983	29	101	12	2	115	0	4

CATCHERS WITH TWO OR MORE TEAMS

Player, Team	Pct.	G	PO	A	E	TC	DP	PB
Abrego, Jesus, Can.	1.000	8	9	0	0	9	0	0
Abrego, Jesus, Ver.	.966	10	27	1	1	29	0	2
Cobos, Rogelio, Ver.	1.000	14	39	1	0	40	1	1
Cobos, Rogelio, Can.	1.000	11	30	3	0	33	0	0
Cruz, Marco, Yuc.	.889	5	16	0	2	18	0	1
Cruz, Marco, Cam.	.988	22	78	3	1	82	0	1
Garcia, Guillermo, Cor.	.983	20	104	13	2	119	0	8
Garcia, Guillermo, Tig.	.991	16	100	11	1	112	1	0
Meza, Alfredo, Ver.	.997	60	338	28	1	367	0	0
Meza, Alfredo, Tab.	1.000	37	173	20	0	193	3	4
Quinones, Ruben, Monc.	.988	21	78	6	1	85	2	5
Quinones, Ruben, Cor.	1.000	23	74	8	0	82	1	1
Rivera, Francisco, Ver.	1.000	2	4	1	0	5	0	0
Rivera, Francisco, Cor.	.957	19	62	5	3	70	0	6
Valdez, Francisco, Tab.	.986	55	246	26	4	276	3	4
Valdez, Francisco, Ver.	.983	36	158	17	3	178	3	4

PITCHERS

Player, Team	Pct.	G	PO	A	E	TC	DP
Aceves, Alfredo, Yuc.	.667	23	3	3	3	9	1
Acosta, Aaron, Cam.	.941	16	6	10	1	17	0
Acosta, David, Mex.*	1.000	11	3	1	0	4	0
Acosta, Jasiel, Monc.*	.955	19	4	17	1	22	3
Aguilar, Hugo, Monc.*	1.000	16	0	11	0	11	0
Aguilar, Miguel, Tor.*	.667	11	0	2	1	3	0
Aguirre, Gaudencio, Mont.	.938	43	6	9	1	16	1
Alberro, Jose, Monc.	1.000	42	4	12	0	16	0
Aleman, Paulo, Cor.	1.000	12	0	1	0	1	1
Almeida, Rowsell, Lar.	1.000	18	4	6	0	10	1
Alvarez, Antonio, Monc.	1.000	16	7	15	0	22	1
Alvarez, Juan, Tor.	.938	25	7	23	2	32	1
Alvarez, Octavio, Mex.	.938	22	4	11	1	16	0
Alvarez, Trevor, Tor.	.923	46	4	8	1	13	0
Amarillas, Asdrubal, Cor.	.929	19	3	10	1	14	0
Angulo, Victor, Tig.*	.000	2	0	0	0	0	0
Antuna, Victor, Mont.	.000	13	0	0	0	0	0
Arellano, Salvador, Yuc.	1.000	15	1	8	0	9	1
Armas, Noel, Pue.	1.000	7	0	2	0	2	0
Armenta, Alejandro, Tig.*	.000	5	0	0	1	1	0
Arredondo, Eduardo, Ver.	.000	1	0	0	0	0	0
Atondo, Sergio, Yuc.	1.000	17	1	7	0	8	0
Avalos, Jose, Oax.	1.000	39	1	6	0	7	1
Ayala, Luis, Sal.	1.000	49	3	8	0	11	0
Baez, Sixto, Oax.	.900	44	2	7	1	10	1
Barradas, Roberto, Sal.	.000	2	0	0	0	0	0
Barrett, Sigfrido, Can.	.000	1	0	0	0	0	0
Barron, Abelino, Tor.	.000	7	0	0	0	0	0
Bell, Richard, Lar.*	1.000	18	1	2	0	3	0
Beltran, Alonso, Tig.	.882	13	4	11	2	17	0
Bencomo, Juan Carlos, Ver.	.000	6	0	0	0	0	0
Bernal, Christian, Mex.-Can.	1.000	2	0	0	0	0	0
Bernal, Manuel, Mex.	.966	22	11	17	1	29	4
Blancas, Rigoberto, Cor.	1.000	30	3	2	0	5	0
Cabrales, Gabriel, Pue.	1.000	30	6	15	0	21	1
Camara, Pedro, Yuc.-Tor.*	.857	14	1	5	1	7	0
Campillo, Jorge, Tig.	1.000	25	2	10	0	12	0
Campos, Francisco, Cam.	.909	21	12	18	3	33	1
Cardenas, Faustino, Cam.	.000	1	0	0	0	0	0
Carrasco, Alejandro, Mex.	1.000	31	1	13	0	14	5
Castaneda, Aurelio, Can.	1.000	15	0	1	0	1	0
Castillo, Ismael, Cam.	1.000	11	1	1	0	2	0
Castro, Carlos, Sal.	.000	8	0	0	0	0	0
Cazares, Juan, Cam.*	1.000	31	0	4	0	4	0
Cazares, Rosario, Sal.	1.000	23	1	2	0	3	0
Cazares, Tomas, Monc.-Sal.*	.500	20	0	1	1	2	0
Cecena, Jose, Monc.	1.000	10	0	2	0	2	0
Chapa, Javier, Tor.	1.000	16	2	2	0	4	0
Chavarria, Hector, Yuc.-Tor.-Cor.	.857	15	0	6	1	7	0
Chavez, Carlos, Yuc.-Tor.	1.000	23	1	6	0	7	0
Cordova, Francisco, Tig.	1.000	22	2	3	0	5	0
Cortes, David, Lar.	1.000	39	3	6	0	9	0
Couoh, Enrique, Can.	.917	14	4	7	1	12	0
Cruz, Javier, Mex.	1.000	37	3	11	0	14	1

Player, Team	Pct.	G	PO	A	E	TC	DP
Cruz, Luis Manuel, Pue.	.947	23	4	14	1	19	1
Cuervo, Bernardo, Yuc.-Tor.	1.000	11	3	2	0	5	0
Delahoya, Javier, Sal.	.955	20	5	16	1	22	1
Delfin, Adolpho, Lar.	1.000	29	0	8	0	8	0
Diaz, Marco, Sal.	.933	23	4	10	1	15	2
Diaz, Ralph, Mont.	.958	19	7	16	1	24	1
Dominguez, Carlos, Sal.*	1.000	25	1	9	0	10	1
Dominguez, David, Oax.	.880	23	4	18	3	25	3
Dorame, Randey, Mex.*	1.000	22	1	7	0	8	0
Duarte, Miguel, Sal.	.900	43	4	5	1	10	0
Elizalde, Carlos, Oax.	.935	21	5	24	2	31	1
Elvira, Abraham, Cor.*	.867	33	0	13	2	15	0
Elvira, Narciso, Cam.*	1.000	9	3	10	0	13	0
Enriquez, Martin, Rey.	1.000	35	2	8	0	10	0
Esparza, Emerson, Monc.	.900	25	2	7	1	10	2
Espinosa, Omar, Pue.	1.000	11	2	2	0	4	0
Esquer, Mercedes, Rey.*	.955	20	5	16	1	22	2
Evans, Dave, Mex.-Oax.	.667	16	0	2	1	3	0
Federico, Gustavo, Sal.	.929	40	5	8	1	14	0
Felix, Antonio, Tor.*	1.000	11	0	2	0	2	0
Felix, Jesus, Cam.	1.000	2	0	1	0	1	1
Fentanes, Ernesto, Ver.	1.000	6	0	1	0	1	0
Fernandez, Amador, Cam.*	.500	10	0	1	1	2	0
Flores, Ignacio, Yuc.	1.000	42	3	8	0	11	0
Flores, Ignacio, Can.	1.000	31	5	9	0	14	2
Flores, Jorge, Monc.*	.938	26	2	13	1	16	1
Flores, Wilfredo, Tab.	.000	1	0	0	0	0	0
Flynt, Will, Can.*	.750	5	0	3	1	4	0
Fregoso, Raul, Tor.-Ver.	.833	28	1	4	1	6	0
Galvez, Randy, Mex.	1.000	26	4	9	0	13	0
Garcia, Adolfo, Cam.	1.000	29	4	11	0	15	0
Garcia, Alfredo, Mex.	.968	22	12	18	1	31	0
Garcia, David, Cor.	.000	2	0	0	0	0	0
Garcia, Humberto, Rey.*	1.000	30	1	6	0	7	0
Garcia, Jose, Pue.	1.000	23	3	10	0	13	0
Garcia, Jose, Pue.*	1.000	20	4	21	0	25	0
Garcia, Mike, Yuc.	1.000	30	2	1	0	3	0
Garcia, Ramon, Lar.	1.000	30	5	7	0	12	0
Garibaldi, Cecilio, Tig.	.000	4	0	0	0	0	0
Garibay, Salvador, Lar.	.929	40	3	10	1	14	1
Garza, Conrado, Mont.*	1.000	17	0	1	0	1	0
Gomez, Alejandro, Tab.	.000	1	0	0	0	0	0
Gomez, Martin, Tor.	.875	40	3	11	2	16	0
Gomez, Miguel, Tig.	.976	22	14	26	1	41	4
Gonzalez, Arturo, Mont.	1.000	7	0	4	0	4	0
Gonzalez, Erubiel, Ver.	.917	27	3	8	1	12	0
Gonzalez, Gilberto, Mont.*	.889	18	2	6	1	9	1
Gonzalez, Leonardo, Lar.	1.000	15	1	5	0	6	0
Gonzalez, Miguel, Sal.	.000	5	0	0	0	0	0
Gonzalez, Victor, Tab.	.000	9	0	0	0	0	0
Grajales, Norberto, Tab.	.833	9	2	8	2	12	3
Guerra, Pascual, Cor.	1.000	20	3	11	0	14	1
Gutierrez, Pablo, Cor.	1.000	8	0	5	0	5	0
Guzman, Christian, Monc.	.857	10	2	4	1	7	1
Guzman, Jesus, Tig.*	.000	17	0	0	0	0	0
Hartmann, Pete, Tor.*	.882	11	5	10	2	17	1
Henthorne, Kevin, Pue.	1.000	7	4	7	0	11	0
Hernandez, Jose, Ver.-Cor.	.955	19	3	18	1	22	1
Hernandez, Martin, Ver.-Can.	.909	17	4	6	1	11	1
Hernandez, Santos, Tig.	.875	52	3	4	1	8	0
Herrera, Enrique, Tab.	.889	41	3	13	2	18	0
Hidalgo, Romeo, Oax.	1.000	8	0	1	0	1	0
Higuera, Marcos, Tig.	.000	1	0	0	0	0	0
Huerta, Francisco, Pue.	1.000	29	0	13	0	13	0
Huerta, Francisco, Pue.	1.000	8	1	1	0	2	0
Huerta, Luis, Lar.	1.000	21	10	18	0	28	3
Hurtado, Edwin, Can.	1.000	16	6	19	0	25	3
Izabal, Luis, Ver.	.000	4	0	0	0	0	0
Jimenez, Isaac, Tab.*	.947	16	4	14	1	19	0
Jimenez, Jose, Oax.	1.000	42	3	12	0	15	1
Jimenez, Julio, Tor.*	.786	27	1	10	3	14	0
Kubenka, Jeff, Rey.*	1.000	13	3	4	0	7	0
Landeros, Lorenzo, Oax.	.000	9	0	0	0	0	0
Lara, Jorge, Sal.-Can.	1.000	36	7	9	0	16	2
Leal, Gerardo, Can.-Rey.	.833	17	1	4	1	6	0
Lemon, Donald, Cam.	.923	13	5	7	1	13	1
Leon, Cupertino, Oax.	.941	40	2	14	1	17	0
Leon, Juan, Tab.	1.000	38	5	9	0	14	1
Lewis, Richie, Cam.	.833	6	2	3	1	6	0
Leyva, Edgar, Mont.	.941	15	5	11	1	17	0
Loaiza, Sabino, Cam.-Sal.	1.000	29	6	8	0	14	0
Lomeli, Israel, Can.	1.000	17	2	4	0	6	0
Lontayo, Alejandro, Oax.*	.833	6	0	5	1	6	0
LOPEZ, Emigdio, Cor.	1.000	23	10	26	0	36	2
Lopez, Gilberto, Tor.-Cor.	1.000	33	3	4	0	7	1
Lopez, Jesus, Can.*	1.000	25	0	4	0	4	0
Lopez, Johan, Sal.	1.000	7	2	6	0	8	0
Lopez, Jose, Monc.	1.000	7	1	1	0	2	0
Lopez, Juan, Rey.	.929	49	3	10	1	14	3
Lopez, Mariano, Oax.	1.000	12	1	2	0	3	0
Lopez, Miguel, Tig.	.000	9	0	0	0	0	0
Loya, Rigoberto, Lar.	.889	21	5	19	3	27	3
Lugo, Aaron, Rey.*	.000	1	0	0	0	0	0
Macias, Luis, Monc.	1.000	47	0	3	0	3	0
Madero, Francisco, Oax.	.882	16	7	8	2	17	2
Manrique, Alberto, Rey.-Mont.	.913	18	4	17	2	23	2
Manzano, Adrian, Tig.	1.000	46	2	4	0	6	0
Manzano, Rafael, Can.	.000	3	0	0	1	1	0
Marquez, Isidro, Cam.	1.000	38	6	4	0	10	0
Martinez, Aaron, Rey.*	.000	1	0	0	0	0	0
Martinez, Cesar, Ver.*	.000	7	0	0	0	0	0
Martinez, Juan, Cor.*	1.000	5	1	1	0	2	0
Martinez, Pedro, Tig.*	.500	2	0	1	1	2	0
Martinez, Renan, Pue.-Tig.*	.941	29	4	12	1	17	1
Medina, Alonso, Rey.	1.000	11	0	1	0	1	1
Medina, Osvaldo, Pue.	1.000	38	3	6	0	9	1
Medina, Rafael, Tor.	1.000	3	1	0	0	1	0
Melendez, Nestor, Rey.*	1.000	38	2	7	0	9	0
Mendoza, Marco, Cam.-Cor.*	.667	16	1	1	1	3	0
Mendoza, Omar, Pue.	1.000	18	2	5	0	7	0
Mere, Fernando, Tab.	1.000	5	0	1	0	1	0
Meza, Leobardo, Monc.	.929	14	4	9	1	14	1
Miranda, Luis, Tor.*	.947	9	8	10	1	19	1
Molina, Primitivo, Rey.	1.000	23	2	6	0	8	0
Montane, Ivan, Can.	1.000	3	0	2	0	2	0
Montemayor, Humberto, Mont.	1.000	22	6	14	0	20	2
Montoya, Saul, Rey.	.938	15	4	11	1	16	1
Mora, Eleazar, Ver.*	.935	23	11	32	3	46	3
Mora, Sergio, Mont.	1.000	8	1	3	0	4	0
Morales, Luis, Ver.*	.833	22	3	7	2	12	0
Moreno, Angel, Ver.*	.966	24	16	41	2	59	5
Moreno, Claudio, Mex.	1.000	39	3	10	0	13	2
Moreno, Edgar, Oax.	.857	16	4	2	1	7	1
Moreno, Elbnit, Tor.	1.000	16	1	2	0	3	0
Moreno, Leo, Sal.-Ver.*	1.000	20	1	7	0	8	2
Munoz, Leonardo, Lar.*	.875	42	1	6	1	8	0
Munoz, Miguel, Can.	1.000	10	2	8	0	10	0
Munoz, Pablo R., Oax.*	.800	33	0	4	1	5	0
Murillo, Meza, Monc.	1.000	44	2	11	0	13	2
Navarro, Hector, Ver.	.929	36	6	7	1	14	0
Navarro, Joel, Oax.	1.000	21	5	13	0	18	1
Navarro, Jose, Tig.	.955	40	7	14	1	22	1
Navarro, Luis, Tig.	1.000	38	3	7	0	10	1
Navarro, Rodolfo, Yuc.	1.000	2	1	1	0	2	0
Neri, Braulio, Sal.-Can.*	1.000	28	1	6	0	7	1
Neri, Eduardo, Oax.*	1.000	55	0	8	0	8	0
Nieblas, Mauro, Mont.*	1.000	45	5	17	0	22	0
Nieblas, Omar, Tab.*	1.000	31	0	2	0	2	0
Nunez, Javier, Tab.	1.000	14	0	6	0	6	1
Nunez, Jose, Lar.	.926	23	9	16	2	27	1
Nunez, Jose, Tab.	1.000	32	0	6	0	6	0
Ojeda, Miguel, Mex.	.000	1	0	0	0	0	0
Olague, Jesus, Pue.-Tig.	.941	22	1	15	1	17	2
Orea, Flavio, Cor.	1.000	38	4	7	0	11	0
Ortega, Pablo, Pue.-Tig.	1.000	24	3	8	0	11	1
Ortega, Roberto, Pue.*	.941	19	2	14	1	17	0
Ortega, Wilbert, Yuc.*	1.000	25	1	1	0	2	1
Osteen, Gavin, Tig.*	.667	2	0	2	1	3	0
Osuna, Adrian, Cor.	.000	2	0	0	0	0	0
Osuna, Ricardo, Tab.-Yuc.	1.000	18	4	20	0	24	2
Pacheco, Alexander, Pue.	1.000	17	3	2	0	5	0
Palacios, Joaquin, Ver.	1.000	24	4	0	0	4	0
Palacios, Vicente, Sal.-Cam.	1.000	34	1	9	0	10	0
Palafox, Juan, Yuc.	1.000	20	5	18	0	23	0
Parra, Julio, Mont.	1.000	44	1	5	0	6	1
Pena, Joel, Ver.	1.000	49	9	13	0	22	0
Pena, Luis, Tor.*	.857	30	2	4	1	7	0
Perez, Edgar, Cor.	.850	19	5	12	3	20	0
Perez, Leonardo, Cor.-Ver.	.929	22	2	11	1	14	0
Perez, Sergio, Rey.	.000	9	0	0	0	0	0
Pesqueira, Omar, Yuc.	1.000	19	3	3	0	6	0
Pimentel, Roberto, Yuc.*	1.000	22	5	10	0	15	1

Player, Team	Pct.	G	PO	A	E	TC	DP
Preston, George, Rey.	.923	8	1	11	1	13	0
Pulido, Carlos, Oax.*	1.000	23	6	25	0	31	3
Pulido, Raymundo, Cam.	.944	22	8	9	1	18	1
Quimbar, Juan, Lar.-Pue.*	1.000	13	1	1	0	2	0
Quinones, Enrique, Rey.	1.000	15	2	6	0	8	1
Quiroz, Aaron, Sal.	1.000	17	3	12	0	15	2
Ramirez, Jose, Monc.	1.000	7	1	2	0	3	0
Ramirez, Roberto, Mex.*	.952	20	8	12	1	21	1
Ramirez, Silvio, Cam.	.000	2	0	0	0	0	0
Ramon, Jose, Tab.	1.000	11	2	6	0	8	0
Renovato, Nestor, Mont.-Rey.	1.000	33	5	13	0	18	4
Revenig, Todd, Cam.	1.000	7	1	0	0	1	0
Reyes, Flavio, Pue.*	1.000	29	1	3	0	4	1
Reyes, Nate, Sal.*	1.000	19	3	10	0	13	0
Rios, Alejandro, Sal.-Monc.	1.000	26	5	1	0	6	0
Rios, Jesus, Yuc.-Tab.	.875	21	5	16	3	24	4
Rivas, Jesus, Tig.-Pue.*	1.000	32	0	5	0	5	1
Rivera, Ben, Mex.	1.000	44	1	6	0	7	1
Rivera, Francisco, Cor.	1.000	40	6	10	0	16	0
Rivera, Lino, Monc.	1.000	13	1	8	0	9	1
Rivera, Oscar, Yuc.-Cam.*	.889	48	7	17	3	27	1
Rivera, Paul, Tab.*	1.000	31	1	4	0	5	1
Robles, Jorge, Cor.	1.000	21	3	8	0	11	0
Rodriguez, Frank, Mex.	.889	8	3	5	1	9	1
Rodriguez, Manuel, Cam.	1.000	35	2	4	0	6	0
Rodriguez, Raul, Mont.*	.952	22	6	14	1	21	4
Rodriguez, Salvador, Yuc.	1.000	21	4	20	0	24	1
Romano, Mike, Sal.	.920	22	6	17	2	25	1
Romero, Alejandro, Monc.	.967	22	7	22	1	30	1
Romo, Eduardo, Lar.	1.000	17	1	0	0	1	0
Romo, Ricardo, Lar.	1.000	3	0	2	0	2	0
Roque, Jorge, Tor.	1.000	8	0	4	0	4	0
Roque, Rafael, Tig.*	.923	14	3	9	1	13	0
Rubio, Miguel, Mont.	1.000	54	0	3	0	3	0
Ruelas, Heriberto, Cor.*	1.000	29	1	10	0	11	0
Ruiz, Cecilio, Tab.*	1.000	22	6	17	0	23	1
Ruiz, Juan, Tor.	1.000	17	1	2	0	3	0
Salazar, Francisco, Tor.	.000	5	0	0	1	1	0
Saldana, Jose, Pue.	.818	24	2	7	2	11	0
Salgado, Eduardo, Ver.	1.000	28	8	20	0	28	0
Sanchez, Alejandro, Can.	1.000	36	2	3	0	5	0
Sanchez, Claudio, Oax.	.875	40	3	4	1	8	0
Sanchez, Efrain, Cam.	.941	45	3	13	1	17	3
Sanchez, Hector, Tor.	1.000	26	2	8	0	10	0
Sanchez, Sergio, Tab.	1.000	8	2	2	0	4	0
Sandoval, Guillermo, Tab.	1.000	27	4	8	0	12	1
Sandoval, Ricardo, Cor.*	.000	1	0	0	0	0	0
Sangeado, Juan, Can.	1.000	12	1	2	0	3	0
Sano, Shigeki, Tig.	1.000	5	2	3	0	5	0
Sierra, Abel, Can.	.875	17	2	5	1	8	0
Silva, Walter, Mont.	.833	21	0	5	1	6	0
Sinohui, David, Ver.	.900	43	0	9	1	10	0
Solis, Tomas, Tig.*	1.000	29	2	1	0	3	0
Soto, Cruz, Lar.	1.000	19	2	7	0	9	1
Soto, Jesus, Monc.	.000	5	0	0	0	0	0
Sulu, Mario, Cam.	1.000	5	2	3	0	5	1
Tejeda, Felix, Cam.*	1.000	39	0	5	0	5	0
Tijerina, Carlos, Rey.	1.000	4	1	1	0	2	0
Torres, Jorge, Cam.*	1.000	12	0	1	0	1	0
Trevino, Jesus, Mex.*	1.000	25	0	2	0	2	0
Trujillo, Jorge, Ver.	1.000	7	0	1	0	1	0
Turuda, Miyoki, Cor.	.000	1	0	0	0	0	0
Valdez, Armando, Lar.	.974	22	8	29	1	38	3
Valdez, Efrain, Cor.-Tab.*	1.000	26	5	25	0	30	5
Valdez, Israel, Cor.	.000	1	0	0	0	0	0
Valdez, Joel, Cor.	.800	27	2	2	1	5	0
Valencia, Alonso, Monc.	.000	3	0	0	0	0	0
Valenzuela, Jose, Tig.	1.000	10	0	1	0	1	0
Valenzuela, Saul, Lar.	1.000	19	8	13	0	21	0
Valerio, Julio, Monc.*	1.000	53	2	7	0	9	0
Vargas, Joel, Tab.	.909	22	6	24	3	33	1
Vazquez, Adrian, Mont.	1.000	29	4	10	0	14	0
VEGA, Obed, Ver.	1.000	24	10	26	0	36	0
Velarde, Francisco, Ver.	.000	3	0	0	0	0	0
Verdugo, Hugo, Tor.	1.000	8	1	3	0	4	0
Verdugo, Orlando, Rey.	1.000	45	0	11	0	11	1
Verdugo, Oswaldo, Yuc.	1.000	33	4	6	0	10	2
Verdugo, Roberto, Tab.	1.000	34	4	10	0	14	0
Villarreal, Antonio, Tab.	.000	2	0	0	0	0	0
Villarreal, Salvador, Rey.	1.000	22	3	3	0	6	0

Player, Team	Pct.	G	PO	A	E	TC	DP
Villavicencio, Ismeal, Tig.	.000	1	0	0	0	0	0
Villegas, Francisco, Can.	.923	37	6	6	1	13	0
Villegas, Ismael, Cam.	1.000	3	1	1	0	2	0
Villegas, Jose, Pue.	1.000	57	2	13	0	15	1
Vosberg, Ed, Mex.*	1.000	12	4	8	0	12	0
Wallace, Kent, Tor.	.000	13	0	0	0	0	0
Ward, Bryan, Tor.*	.917	10	1	10	1	12	0
Zambrano, Baudel, Rey.	.857	26	7	11	3	21	0
Zamudio, Aurelio, Ver.	1.000	1	0	1	0	1	0

PITCHERS WITH TWO OR MORE TEAMS

Player, Team	Pct.	G	PO	A	E	TC	DP
Bernal, Christian, Mex.	.000	1	0	0	0	0	0
Bernal, Christian, Can.	.000	1	0	0	0	0	0
Camara, Pedro, Yuc.*	.000	4	0	0	0	0	0
Camara, Pedro, Tor.*	.857	10	1	5	1	7	0
Cazares, Tomas, Monc.*	.500	6	0	1	1	2	0
Cazares, Tomas, Sal.*	.000	14	0	0	0	0	0
Chavarria, Hector, Yuc.	.000	2	0	0	1	1	0
Chavarria, Hector, Sal.	1.000	10	0	4	0	4	0
Chavarria, Hector, Cor.	1.000	3	0	2	0	2	0
Chavez, Carlos, Yuc.	1.000	15	0	3	0	3	0
Chavez, Carlos, Tor.	1.000	8	1	3	0	4	0
Cuervo, Bernardo, Yuc.	.000	6	0	0	0	0	0
Cuervo, Bernardo, Tor.	1.000	5	3	2	0	5	0
Evans, Dave, Mex.	.000	3	0	0	0	0	0
Evans, Dave, Oax.	.667	13	0	2	1	3	0
Fregoso, Raul, Tor.	.833	25	1	4	1	6	0
Fregoso, Raul, Ver.	.000	3	0	0	0	0	0
Hernandez, Jose, Ver.	.941	11	2	14	1	17	1
Hernandez, Jose, Cor.	1.000	8	1	4	0	5	0
Hernandez, Martin, Ver.	1.000	5	0	1	0	1	1
Hernandez, Martin, Can.	.900	12	4	5	1	10	0
Lara, Jorge, Sal.	1.000	6	1	1	0	2	0
Lara, Jorge, Can.	1.000	30	6	8	0	14	2
Leal, Gerardo, Can.	.000	4	0	0	1	1	0
Leal, Gerardo, Rey.	1.000	13	1	4	0	5	0
Loaiza, Sabino, Cam.	1.000	10	1	4	0	5	0
Loaiza, Sabino, Sal.	1.000	19	5	4	0	9	0
Lopez, Gilberto, Tor.	1.000	17	2	1	0	3	1
Lopez, Gilberto, Can.	1.000	16	1	3	0	4	0
Manrique, Alberto, Rey.	.895	13	3	14	2	19	1
Manrique, Alberto, Mont.	1.000	5	1	3	0	4	1
Martinez, Renan, Pue.*	.857	19	2	4	1	7	0
Martinez, Renan, Tig.*	1.000	10	2	8	0	10	1
Mendoza, Marco, Cam.*	1.000	2	0	1	0	1	0
Mendoza, Marco, Monc.*	.500	14	1	0	1	2	0
Moreno, Leo, Sal.*	1.000	14	1	4	0	5	1
Moreno, Leo, Ver.*	1.000	6	0	3	0	3	1
Neri, Braulio, Sal.*	1.000	23	1	4	0	5	1
Neri, Braulio, Can.*	1.000	5	0	2	0	2	0
Olague, Jesus, Pue.	1.000	14	1	10	0	11	0
Olague, Jesus, Tig.	.833	8	0	5	1	6	2
Ortega, Pablo, Pue.	1.000	11	3	3	0	6	1
Ortega, Pablo, Tig.	1.000	13	0	5	0	5	0
Osuna, Ricardo, Tab.	1.000	12	4	15	0	19	1
Osuna, Ricardo, Yuc.	1.000	6	0	5	0	5	1
Palacios, Vicente, Sal.	1.000	11	0	2	0	2	0
Palacios, Vicente, Cam.	1.000	23	1	7	0	8	0
Perez, Leonardo, Cor.	.875	11	1	6	1	8	0
Perez, Leonardo, Ver.	1.000	11	1	5	0	6	0
Quimbar, Juan, Lar.*	1.000	4	1	0	0	1	0
Quimbar, Juan, Pue.*	1.000	9	0	1	0	1	0
Renovato, Nestor, Mont.	1.000	27	2	6	0	8	1
Renovato, Nestor, Rey.	1.000	6	3	7	0	10	3
Rios, Alejandro, Sal.	1.000	17	4	1	0	5	0
Rios, Alejandro, Monc.	1.000	9	1	0	0	1	0
Rios, Jesus, Yuc.	.889	12	2	6	1	9	2
Rios, Jesus, Tab.	.867	9	3	10	2	15	2
Rivas, Jesus, Tig.*	1.000	17	0	3	0	3	0
Rivas, Jesus, Pue.*	1.000	15	0	2	0	2	1
Rivera, Oscar, Yuc.*	1.000	26	0	3	0	3	0
Rivera, Oscar, Cam.*	.875	22	7	14	3	24	1
Valdez, Efrain, Cor.*	1.000	11	3	8	0	11	3
Valdez, Efrain, Tab.*	1.000	15	2	17	0	19	2

The following players appeared only as designated hitter, pinch-hitter or pinch runner: N. Barrera, dh, ph; Cansino, dh, ph; Facundo, dh, pr; E. Jimenez, dh, ph; Mota, ph; Ortiz, dh; Polonia, dh; Soto, ph; Tellez, dh.

CLASS AAA *Mexican League*

Year	Team	Pct.	Year	Team	Pct.	Year	Team	Pct.
1955—	Mexico City Tigers*	.539	1975—	Tampico∞	.541	1989—	Nuevo Laredo♦	.621
1956—	Mexico City Reds	.692		Cordoba	.649		Yucatan	.539
1957—	Yucatan	.567	1976—	Mexico City Reds∞	.543	1990—	Nuevo Laredo	.618
	Mex. C. Reds (2nd)†	.550		Union Laguna	.547		Leon♦	.565
1958—	Nuevo Laredo	.625	1977—	Mexico City Reds	.623	1991—	Monterrey♦	.683
1959—	Poza Rica	.575		Nuevo Laredo∞	.507		Mexico City Reds	.627
	Mex. C. Reds (3rd)†	.507	1978—	Aguascalientes∞	.589	1992—	Mexico City Tigers♦	.594
1960—	Mexico City Tigers	.538		Union Laguna	.523		Nuevo Laredo	.538
1961—	Veracruz	.575	1979—	Saltillo	.704	1993—	Nuevo Laredo	.589
1962—	Monterrey	.592		Puebla∞	.628		Tabasco♦	.528
1963—	Puebla	.606	1980—	No champion▲		1994—	Mexico City Red Devils♦	.646
1964—	Mexico City Reds	.586	1981—	Mexico City Reds	.615		Monterrey Sultans	.608
1965—	Mexico City Tigers	.590		Reynosa	.492	1995—	Mexico City Red Devils	.708
1966—	Mexico City Tigers‡	.614	1982—	Ciudad Juarez∞	.570		Monterrey Sultans♦	.570
	Mexico City Reds	.571		Mexico City Tigers	.508	1996—	Monterrey Sultans	.713
1967—	Jalisco	.607	1983—	Campeche♦	.614		Mexico City Reds♦	.619
1968—	Mexico City Reds	.586		Ciudad Juarez	.535	1997—	Mexico City Red Devils	.686
1969—	Reynosa	.591	1984—	Yucatan♦	.560		Mexico City Tigers■	.658
1970—	Aguila§	.580		Ciudad Juarez	.509	1998—	Monterrey	.672
	Mexico City Reds	.607	1985—	Mexico City Reds♦	.606		Oaxaca■	.576
1971—	Jalisco§	.558		Nuevo Laredo	.5275	1999—	Mexico City Tigers	.664
	Saltillo	.593	1986—	Puebla♦	.682		Mexico City Reds■	.632
1972—	Saltillo	.636		Monclova	.598	2000—	Saltillo	.647
	Cordoba§	.541	1987—	Mexico City Reds♦	.605		Mexico City Tigers■	.627
1973—	Saltillo	.656		Monterrey	.536	2001—	Mexico City Tigers■	.632
	Mexico City Reds∞	.590	1988—	Mexico City Reds♦	.646		Mexico City Reds	.575
1974—	Jalisco	.627		Nuevo Laredo	.602	2002—	Mexico City Reds▼	.673
	Mexico City Reds∞	.551						

*Defeated Nuevo Laredo, two games to none, in playoff for pennant. †Won four-team playoff. ‡Won split-season playoff. §League divided into Northern, Southern divisions; won two-team playoff. ∞League divided into Northern, Southern zones; sub-divided into Eastern, Western divisions, won eight-team playoff. ▲ A players strike on July 1 forced the cancellation of the regular season and playoff schedule. ♦ League divided into Northern, Southern zones; four clubs from each zone qualified for postseason play. Won final series for league championship. ■ League divided into Northern, Central and Southern zones; played split season, with top eight teams qualifying for playoffs. Won final series for league championship. ▼ League divided into Northern and Southern divisions; played split season, with top eight teams qualifying for playoffs. Won final series for league championship.

PACIFIC COAST LEAGUE

LEAGUE OFFICE

President
Branch Rickey

Address
1631 Mesa Ave., Suite A
Colorado Springs, CO 80906-2917

Phone
719-636-3399

TEAMS

ALBUQUERQUE ISOTOPES
General manager
Mel Kowalchuk
Manager
Dean Treanor
Ballpark (capacity, surface)
To be announced (13,000, grass)
Affiliation
Marlins
Address
1601 Avenida Cesar Chavez SE
Albuquerque, NM 87106
Phone
505-924-2255

COLORADO SPRINGS SKY SOX
General manager/president
Robert Goughan
Manager
Rick Sofield
Ballpark (capacity, surface)
Sky Sox Stadium (9,000, grass)
Affiliation
Rockies
Address
4385 Tutt Blvd.
Colorado Springs, CO 80922
Phone
719-597-1449

EDMONTON TRAPPERS
President
Rick LeLacheur
Manager
Dave Huppert
Ballpark (capacity, surface)
Telus Field (10,000; artificial infield, grass outfield)
Affiliation
Expos
Address
10233 96th Ave.
Edmonton, Alberta T5K 0A5
Phone
780-414-4450

FRESNO GRIZZLIES
General manager
Bill Gorman
Manager
Fred Stanley
Ballpark (capacity, surface)
Grizzlies Stadium (12,500, grass)
Affiliation
Giants
Address
700 W. Van Ness Avenue
Fresno, CA 93721

Phone
559-442-1994

IOWA CUBS
General manager
Sam Bernabe
Manager
Mike Quade
Ballpark (capacity, surface)
Sec Taylor Stadium (10,500, grass)
Affiliation
Cubs
Address
350 SW First St.
Des Moines, IA 50309
Phone
515-243-6111

LAS VEGAS 51's
General manager/president
Don Logan
Manager
John Shoemaker
Ballpark (capacity, surface)
Cashman Field (9,370, grass)
Affiliation
Dodgers
Address
850 Las Vegas Blvd. N
Las Vegas, NV 89101
Phone
702-386-7200

MEMPHIS REDBIRDS
President/general manager
Dave Chase
Manager
Tom Spencer
Ballpark (capacity, surface)
AutoZone Park (14,200; grass)
Affiliation
Cardinals
Address
175 Toyota Plaza, Suite 300
Memphis, TN 38103
Phone
901-721-6050

NASHVILLE SOUNDS
General manager
Glenn Yaeger
Manager
Trent Jewett
Ballpark (capacity, surface)
Greer Stadium (11,500, grass)
Affiliation
Pirates
Address
534 Chestnut Street
Nashville, TN 37203

Phone
615-242-4371

NEW ORLEANS ZEPHYRS
Vice president/general manager
Dan Rajkowski
Manager
Chris Maloney
Ballpark (capacity, surface)
Zephyr Field (11,000, grass)
Affiliation
Astros
Address
6000 Airline Dr.
Metairie, LA 70003
Phone
504-734-5155

OKLAHOMA REDHAWKS
President/general manager
Tim O'Toole
Manager
Bobby Jones
Ballpark (capacity, surface)
SBC Bricktown Ballpark (13,066, grass)
Affiliation
Rangers
Address
2 South Mickey Mantle Dr.
Oklahoma City, OK 73104
Phone
405-218-1000

OMAHA ROYALS
Vice president/general manager
Doug Stewart
Manager
Mike Jirschele
Ballpark (capacity, surface)
Omaha's Rosenblatt Stadium (23,000, grass)
Affiliation
Royals
Address
1202 Bert Murphy Ave.
Omaha, NE 68107
Phone
402-734-2550

PORTLAND BEAVERS
President/general manager
Mark Schuster
Manager
Rick Sweet
Ballpark (capacity, surface)
PGE Park (20,000, artificial)
Affiliation
Padres
Address
920 SW Sixth Avenue, Mezzanine Level
Portland Ore. 97204

Phone
503-553-5400

SACRAMENTO RIVER CATS

General Manager
Gary Arthur
Manager
Tony DeFrancesco
Ballpark (capacity, surface)
Raley Field (10,500, grass)
Affiliation
Athletics
Address
400 Ballpark Drive
West Sacramento, CA 95691
Phone
916-376-4700

SALT LAKE STINGERS

Vice president/ asst. general manager
Dorsena Picknell

Manager
Mike Brumley
Ballpark (capacity, surface)
Franklin Covey Field (15,500, grass)
Affiliation
Angels
Address
P.O. Box 4108
Salt Lake City, UT 84110
Phone
801-485-3800

TACOMA RAINIERS

General manager
Dave Lewis
Manager
Dan Rohn
Ballpark (capacity, surface)
Cheney Stadium (10,106, grass)
Affiliation
Mariners

Address
P.O. Box 11087
Tacoma, WA 98411
Phone
253-752-7707

TUCSON SIDEWINDERS

General manager
Rick Parr
Manager
Al Pedrique
Ballpark (capacity, surface)
Tucson Electric Park (10,000, grass)
Affiliation
Diamondbacks
Address
P.O. Box 27045
Tucson, AZ 85726
Phone
520-434-1021

2002 FINAL STANDINGS

EASTERN DIVISION

Team	W	L	T	Pct.	GB
Oklahoma (Rangers)	75	69	0	.521	...
New Orleans (Astros)	75	69	0	.521	...
Nashville (Pirates)	72	71	0	.503	2.5
Memphis (Cardinals)	71	71	0	.500	3.0

CENTRAL DIVISION

Team	W	L	T	Pct.	GB
Salt Lake (Angels)	78	66	0	.542	...
Omaha (Royals)	76	68	0	.528	2.0
Iowa (Cubs)	71	73	0	.493	7.0
Colorado Springs (Rockies)	58	86	0	.403	20.0

NORTHERN DIVISION

Team	W	L	T	Pct.	GB
Edmonton (Twins)	81	59	0	.579	...
Portland (Padres)	72	71	0	.503	10.5
Calgary (Marlins)	67	71	0	.486	13.0
Tacoma (Mariners)	65	76	0	.461	16.5

SOUTHERN DIVISION

Team	W	L	T	Pct.	GB
Las Vegas (Dodgers)	85	59	0	.590	...
Tucson (Diamondbacks)	73	68	0	.518	10.5
Sacramento (Athletics)	66	78	0	.458	19.0
Fresno (Giants)	57	87	0	.396	28.0

COMPOSITE

Team	L.V.	Edm.	S.L.	Oma.	Okla.	N.O.	Tuc.	Por.	Nash.	Mem.	Iowa	Cal.	Tac.	Sac.	C.S.	Fres.	W	L	T	Pct.	GB
Las Vegas (Dodgers)	...	5	3	6	5	6	8	6	5	4	4	5	6	9	3	10	85	59	0	.590	...
Edmonton (Twins)	3	...	2	5	4	4	3	10	5	5	4	8	10	6	6	6	81	59	0	.579	2.0
Salt Lake (Angels)	5	6	...	7	5	2	4	4	5	2	7	5	5	5	10	6	78	66	0	.542	7.0
Omaha (Royals)	2	3	9	...	3	6	5	4	4	4	7	4	5	4	12	4	76	68	0	.528	9.0
Oklahoma (Rangers)	3	4	3	5	...	10	4	3	9	9	3	4	5	5	3	5	75	69	0	.521	10.0
New Orleans (Astros)	2	4	6	2	6	...	4	2	7	10	6	6	5	4	5	6	75	69	0	.521	10.0
Tucson (Diamondbacks)	8	2	4	5	4	4	...	6	5	3	3	4	5	9	1	12	73	68	0	.518	10.5
Portland (Padres)	2	6	4	4	5	6	2	...	4	2	5	11	9	3	5	4	72	71	0	.503	12.5
Nashville (Pirates)	3	3	3	4	7	9	3	3	...	11	5	5	3	6	4	7	72	71	0	.503	12.5
Memphis (Cardinals)	4	3	6	4	7	6	5	6	5	...	6	1	5	5	4	4	71	71	0	.500	13.0
Iowa (Cubs)	4	4	9	9	5	2	5	3	2	2	...	3	3	5	10	4	71	73	0	.493	14.0
Calgary (Marlins)	3	7	3	4	4	2	4	5	5	5	5	...	5	5	7	5	67	71	0	.486	15.0
Tacoma (Mariners)	2	6	3	3	3	3	3	7	5	5	8	...	4	5	5	65	76	0	.461	18.5
Sacramento (Athletics)	7	3	2	4	3	4	7	5	5	3	3	4	...	5	8	66	78	0	.458	19.0
Colo. Springs (Rockies)	5	2	6	4	5	3	7	3	2	4	6	1	3	3	...	4	58	86	0	.403	27.0
Fresno (Giants)	6	2	2	4	3	2	4	4	4	4	4	3	8	4	...	57	87	0	.396	28.0

Major league affiliations in parentheses.

PLAYOFFS: Salt Lake defeated Oklahoma, three games to none; Edmonton defeated Las Vegas, three games to one; Edmonton defeated Salt Lake, three games to one, to win Pacific Coast League championship.

REGULAR-SEASON ATTENDANCE: Calgary, 182,931; Colorado Springs, 267,028; Edmonton, 340,387; Fresno, 563,079; Iowa, 509,384; Las Vegas, 327,269; Memphis, 794,550; Nashville, 322,059; New Orleans, 410,183; Oklahoma, 432,887; Omaha, 344,718; Portland, 454,197; Sacramento, 817,317; Salt Lake, 460,839; Tacoma, 300,910; Tucson, 268,807. Total—6,796,545. Playoff attendance (11 games)—54,880. Triple-A All-Star Game at Oklahoma City—11,343.

MANAGERS: Calgary, Dean Treanor; Colorado Springs, Chris Crow; Edmonton, John Russell; Fresno, Lenn Sakata; Iowa, Bruce Kimm (through July 4; 44-45) and Pat Listach (July 5 through end of season; 27-28); Las Vegas, Brad Mills; Memphis, Gaylen Pitts; Nashville, Marty Brown; New Orleans, Chris Maloney; Oklahoma, Bobby Jones; Omaha, Bucky Dent; Portland, Rick Sweet; Sacramento, Bob Geren; Salt Lake, Mike Brumley; Tacoma, Dan Rohn; Tucson, Al Pedrique.

ALL-STAR TEAM: 1B—Lyle Overbay, Tucson; 2B—Joe Thurston, Las Vegas; 3B—Jason Wood, Calgary; SS—Aaron Holbert, Tacoma; OF—Robb Quinlan, Salt Lake; OF—Michael Restovich, Edmonton; OF—Michael Ryan, Edmonton; C—Javier Valentin, Edmonton; DH—Ivan Cruz, Memphis; RHP—Scott Randall, Edmonton; LHP—Jeriome Robertson, New Orleans; Relief pitcher—Jeff Williams, Las Vegas; Most Valuable Player—Robb Quinlan, Salt Lake; Rookie of the Year—Robb Quinlan, Salt Lake; Pitcher of the Year—Jeriome Robertson, New Orleans; Manager of the Year—Brad Mills, Las Vegas.

2002 BATTING
TEAM

Team	G	TPA	AB	R	H	TB	2B	3B	HR	RBI	SH	SF	HP	BB	IBB	SO	SB	CS	GDP	LOB	ShO	Avg.	OBP	Slg.
Salt Lake	144	5580	5075	797	1489	2375	284	88	142	747	25	60	61	359	21	972	127	65	94	977	7	.293	.344	.468
Las Vegas	144	5639	5018	820	1462	2323	284	47	161	774	57	44	70	450	11	1015	63	31	130	998	3	.291	.355	.463
Edmonton	140	5342	4766	820	1370	2338	278	42	202	772	20	47	51	458	18	1021	96	45	105	935	2	.287	.353	.491
Tucson	141	5420	4869	729	1385	2125	288	40	124	694	48	42	67	394	14	1011	77	50	100	999	7	.284	.344	.436
Calgary	138	5178	4609	681	1304	2028	313	27	119	632	40	34	57	438	10	845	113	52	100	988	7	.283	.350	.440
Col. Springs	144	5472	4893	725	1356	2160	308	35	142	686	35	49	48	447	11	1015	90	50	120	985	10	.277	.340	.441
Oklahoma	144	5743	5049	754	1387	2160	289	32	140	709	37	37	69	551	15	1032	84	31	136	1110	5	.275	.352	.428
Sacramento	144	5739	4941	764	1350	2009	282	19	113	699	26	43	64	665	11	886	99	47	133	1154	4	.273	.364	.407
Omaha	144	5447	4874	723	1316	2091	254	45	145	670	30	46	12	485	14	922	173	58	120	1041	7	.270	.335	.429
Iowa	144	5496	4812	793	1297	2135	286	30	166	756	54	40	62	528	18	993	94	51	97	984	4	.270	.347	.444
Tacoma	141	5159	4602	597	1215	1921	253	45	121	560	49	42	55	411	15	921	140	65	116	943	5	.264	.329	.417
Nashville	143	5382	4760	662	1246	1868	256	18	110	608	61	52	56	453	19	986	117	60	90	967	7	.262	.330	.392
Portland	143	5197	4719	590	1225	1903	265	34	115	562	37	37	53	351	13	945	81	39	104	923	5	.260	.316	.403
New Orleans	144	5460	4907	617	1268	1898	248	38	102	562	52	36	67	398	17	1058	111	50	89	1012	8	.258	.320	.387
Fresno	144	5235	4752	543	1222	1820	218	31	106	504	57	40	48	338	11	968	72	44	106	936	10	.257	.311	.383
Memphis	142	5242	4623	628	1143	1863	250	13	148	594	47	38	75	459	25	911	105	47	108	914	8	.247	.323	.403

INDIVIDUAL

TOP QUALIFIERS FOR BATTING CHAMPIONSHIP
Minimum 389 plate appearances. *Lefthanded batter. †Switch-hitter.

Player, Team	G	TPA	AB	R	H	TB	2B	3B	HR	RBI	SH	SF	HP	BB	IBB	SO	SB	CS	GDP	Avg.	OBP	Slg.
Short, Rick, S.L.	105	446	410	71	146	200	29	2	7	68	0	4	9	23	1	43	3	2	4	.356	.399	.488
Overbay, Lyle, Tuc.*	134	579	525	83	180	277	40	0	19	109	0	5	7	42	3	86	0	0	12	.343	.396	.528
Hafner, Travis, Okla.*	110	492	401	79	137	224	22	1	21	77	0	0	12	79	4	76	2	1	9	.342	.463	.559
Thurston, Joe, L.V.*	136	631	587	106	196	297	39	13	12	55	5	2	12	25	1	60	22	9	10	.334	.372	.506
Quinlan, Robb, S.L.	136	588	528	95	176	293	31	13	20	112	0	15	4	41	2	93	8	2	16	.333	.376	.555
Allen, Luke, L.V.*	137	564	501	85	165	235	28	3	12	78	0	5	2	56	3	77	4	6	12	.329	.395	.469
Mendez, Carlos, Sac.	103	420	404	58	131	195	26	1	12	74	0	1	3	12	1	52	3	1	11	.324	.348	.483
Wood, Jason, Cal.	121	504	457	78	144	230	37	2	15	70	1	4	4	38	0	92	3	0	13	.315	.370	.503
Gload, Ross, C.S.*	104	468	442	69	139	227	28	6	16	71	1	6	1	18	0	59	9	4	4	.314	.338	.514
Barnes, Larry, S.L.*	114	492	452	71	142	253	29	11	20	95	0	8	4	28	5	90	8	1	11	.314	.354	.560
Holbert, Aaron, Tac.	120	440	399	62	124	175	24	3	7	42	7	3	12	19	0	50	17	13	12	.311	.358	.439
Sears, Todd, Edm.*	129	552	484	88	150	254	36	4	20	100	0	4	5	59	4	142	2	1	6	.310	.388	.525
Banks, Brian, Cal.†	130	525	439	90	136	237	38	3	19	89	0	7	6	73	2	77	10	5	6	.310	.410	.540
Blake, Casey, Edm.	126	546	482	87	149	237	25	3	19	68	0	6	4	54	1	78	24	9	11	.309	.383	.492
Lamb, Dave, Edm.†	123	501	440	72	136	197	25	3	10	72	5	5	6	45	0	57	2	6	16	.309	.377	.448
Pelaez, Alex, Port.	112	434	411	47	127	193	31	1	11	64	0	3	0	20	3	40	0	1	15	.309	.339	.470

DEPARTMENTAL LEADERS: G—Dransfeldt, 140; AB—Thurston, 587; R—Thurston, 106; H—Thurston, 196; TB—Thurston, 297; 2B—Overbay, Sutton, 40 each; 3B—Figgins, 18; HR—I. Cruz, 35; RBI—Quinlan, 112; SH—Ransom, 12; SF—Quinlan, 15; HP—Meyers, 21; BB—Choi, 95; IBB—C. Porter, 8; SO—Chen, 160; SB—Meyers, 43; CS—J. Clark, 16; GIDP—Harvey, 22; Slg.—I. Cruz, .566; OBP—Hafner, .463.

ALL PLAYERS
*Lefthanded batter. †Switch-hitter.

Player, Team	G	TPA	AB	R	H	TB	2B	3B	HR	RBI	SH	SF	HP	BB	IBB	SO	SB	CS	GDP	Avg.	OBP	Slg.
Abad, Andy, Cal.*	111	415	352	50	106	171	28	2	11	70	0	2	4	57	1	44	0	3	7	.301	.402	.486
Agbayani, Benny, C.S.	43	179	147	28	40	83	8	1	11	32	0	2	2	28	0	32	1	0	3	.272	.391	.565
Agosto, Stevenson, Iowa*	4	4	3	0	0	0	0	0	0	0	1	0	0	0	0	2	0	0	0	.000	.000	.000
Ainsworth, Kurt, Fres.	20	25	21	1	2	3	1	0	0	0	2	0	0	2	0	5	0	0	1	.095	.174	.143
Aldred, Scott, L.V.*	42	1	1	0	0	0	0	0	0	0	0	0	0	0	0	0	0	0	0	.000	.000	.000
Allen, Luke, L.V.*	137	564	501	85	165	235	28	3	12	78	0	5	2	56	3	77	4	6	12	.329	.395	.469
Alvarez, Victor, L.V.*	34	26	23	5	6	6	0	0	0	2	0	0	1	0	0	10	0	0	0	.261	.292	.261
Alviso, Jerome, C.S.†	112	327	304	32	95	112	14	0	1	26	7	3	1	12	0	29	4	1	10	.313	.338	.368
Amezaga, Alfredo, S.L.†	128	583	518	77	130	187	25	7	6	51	6	6	8	45	0	100	23	14	15	.251	.317	.361
Amezcua, Adan, Port.	43	154	138	17	43	62	9	2	2	19	0	1	4	11	0	14	0	0	5	.312	.377	.449
Amrhein, Mike, Iowa	29	98	85	13	25	30	5	0	0	11	1	1	5	6	0	12	0	0	2	.294	.371	.353
Andreopoulos, Alex, Mem.*	26	93	78	10	22	31	6	0	1	8	1	1	4	9	0	9	0	0	3	.282	.380	.397
Ardoin, Danny, Oma.-Okla.	58	212	183	20	40	63	8	0	5	21	2	4	2	21	1	56	1	0	2	.219	.300	.344
Arnold, Jamie, Cal.	16	16	15	0	4	5	1	0	0	1	0	0	0	1	0	4	0	0	0	.267	.313	.333
Arroyo, Bronson, Nash.	23	32	28	1	4	5	1	0	0	1	3	0	0	1	0	10	0	0	0	.143	.172	.179
Arteaga, J.D., N.O.*	42	28	23	2	5	5	0	0	0	5	0	0	0	0	0	8	0	0	0	.217	.217	.217
Aybar, Manny, Fres.	45	1	1	0	0	0	0	0	0	0	0	0	0	0	0	0	0	0	0	.000	.000	.000
Bair, Rod, C.S.	89	288	258	33	69	103	18	2	4	37	1	1	9	19	0	49	14	5	10	.267	.338	.399
Balfe, Ryan, Mem.†	6	15	14	0	2	2	0	0	0	0	0	0	1	0	0	3	0	0	0	.143	.200	.143
Banks, Brian, Cal.†	130	525	439	90	136	237	38	3	19	89	0	7	6	73	2	77	10	5	6	.310	.410	.540
Barajas, Rod, Tuc.	5	17	16	2	7	11	1	0	1	1	0	0	0	1	0	2	0	0	0	.438	.471	.688
Barker, Kevin, Port.*	113	442	390	54	98	156	14	1	14	48	0	3	3	46	2	70	1	1	10	.251	.333	.400
Barnes, John, C.S.	67	292	269	46	77	119	20	2	6	30	1	0	4	18	0	16	5	4	8	.286	.340	.442
Barnes, Larry, S.L.*	114	492	452	71	142	253	29	11	20	95	0	8	4	28	5	90	8	1	11	.314	.354	.560
Bartee, Kimera, Iowa†	133	474	419	59	106	167	27	2	10	64	9	4	1	41	0	111	25	13	3	.253	.318	.399
Barthol, Blake, Tac.	56	213	178	28	44	77	16	4	3	17	4	3	4	24	0	44	0	2	1	.247	.344	.433
Bass, Jayson, Iowa*	124	477	419	78	120	203	14	3	21	79	0	4	2	52	4	90	13	7	14	.286	.365	.484
Bausher, Andy, Port.	8	1	1	0	0	0	0	0	0	0	0	0	0	0	0	1	0	0	0	.000	.000	.000
Beirne, Kevin, L.V.*	24	28	25	3	4	5	1	0	0	2	0	0	1	0	0	7	0	0	0	.160	.192	.200
Belitz, Todd, C.S.*	22	2	1	0	0	0	0	0	0	0	0	0	0	1	0	1	0	0	0	.000	.500	.000

– 437 –

Player, Team	G	TPA	AB	R	H	TB	2B	3B	HR	RBI	SH	SF	HP	BB	IBB	SO	SB	CS	GDP	Avg.	OBP	Slg.
Bell, Jay, Tuc.	7	26	22	4	5	8	3	0	0	2	0	0	0	4	0	1	0	0	1	.227	.346	.364
Bell, Mike, C.S.	64	265	240	33	68	100	19	2	3	35	0	3	6	16	0	42	4	4	4	.283	.340	.417
Bell, Rick, L.V.	122	475	448	60	121	194	26	4	13	77	4	6	1	16	1	75	0	1	19	.270	.293	.433
Bellinger, Clay, S.L.	89	340	324	45	83	149	17	5	13	41	1	0	2	13	0	87	4	2	8	.256	.289	.460
Benes, Alan, Iowa	28	18	16	1	3	4	1	0	0	1	2	0	0	0	0	8	0	0	0	.188	.188	.250
Benes, Andy, Mem.	4	5	3	0	0	0	0	0	0	0	1	0	0	1	0	1	0	0	0	.000	.250	.000
Benjamin, Al, Port.	56	176	169	18	31	48	9	1	2	12	0	0	3	4	0	37	1	1	8	.183	.216	.284
Benson, Kris, Nash.	4	3	3	0	0	0	0	0	0	0	0	0	0	0	0	2	0	0	0	.000	.000	.000
Berger, Brandon, Oma.	68	292	261	34	76	133	16	1	13	47	0	1	5	25	0	43	11	2	4	.291	.363	.510
Berroa, Angel, Oma.	77	329	297	37	64	107	11	4	8	35	4	2	11	15	0	84	6	4	5	.215	.277	.360
Bierek, Kurt, Okla.*	20	82	73	8	15	22	2	1	1	8	0	1	1	7	0	15	0	0	3	.205	.280	.301
Bitter, Jarrod, Port.	1	3	3	1	1	1	0	0	0	2	0	0	0	0	0	0	0	0	0	.333	.333	.333
Blake, Casey, Edm.	126	546	482	87	149	237	25	3	19	58	0	4	6	54	1	78	24	9	11	.309	.383	.492
Blakely, Darren, Port.†	4	16	15	3	2	8	0	0	2	3	0	0	0	1	0	3	0	0	0	.133	.188	.533
Blalock, Hank, Okla.*	95	425	387	63	119	177	32	1	8	62	1	2	1	34	1	61	2	1	9	.307	.363	.457
Bloomquist, Willie, Tac.	104	381	337	47	91	129	14	3	6	47	9	3	3	29	1	44	20	10	5	.270	.331	.383
Bogar, Tim, C.S.	13	44	43	2	7	8	1	0	0	1	0	0	0	1	0	6	0	2	0	.163	.182	.186
Borders, Pat, Tac.	92	331	317	42	84	138	16	1	12	27	2	1	0	11	0	47	3	2	6	.265	.289	.435
Borland, Toby, Cal.	56	4	4	0	1	1	0	0	0	0	0	0	0	0	0	2	0	0	0	.250	.250	.250
Borrego, Ramon, Edm.†	28	54	50	7	9	13	4	0	0	3	0	1	1	2	0	17	2	0	3	.180	.222	.260
Boyd, Jason, Port.	19	1	1	0	0	0	0	0	0	0	0	0	0	0	0	0	0	0	0	.000	.000	.000
Branson, Jeff, L.V.*	88	260	233	30	57	83	15	1	3	26	5	0	2	20	0	53	0	1	5	.245	.310	.356
Brito, Juan, Oma.	3	10	9	1	2	3	1	0	0	1	0	0	0	1	0	1	0	0	0	.222	.300	.333
Brittan, Corey, C.S.	35	15	14	0	0	0	0	0	0	0	1	0	0	0	0	7	0	0	1	.000	.000	.000
Brohawn, Troy, Fres.*	56	6	4	0	0	0	0	0	0	0	2	0	0	0	0	2	0	0	1	.000	.333	.000
Brown, Adrian, Nash.†	51	214	184	36	62	80	7	1	3	16	6	1	0	23	0	18	22	6	3	.337	.409	.435
Brown, Dee, Oma.*	121	512	458	66	126	202	23	1	17	75	0	4	6	44	2	111	10	4	12	.275	.344	.441
Brown, Kevin, L.V.	2	1	1	0	0	0	0	0	0	0	0	0	0	0	0	0	0	0	0	.000	.000	.000
Brumbaugh, Cliff, C.S.	136	567	505	85	148	236	36	2	16	81	1	4	0	57	0	107	6	2	15	.293	.362	.467
Bruntlett, Eric, N.O.	18	79	68	9	14	17	3	0	0	1	1	0	0	10	0	10	1	1	3	.206	.308	.250
Buchanan, Brian, Edm.	1	3	3	0	0	0	0	0	0	0	0	0	0	0	0	0	0	0	0	.000	.000	.000
Budzinski, Mark, Iowa*	12	35	32	6	9	13	2	1	0	4	0	0	0	3	1	5	1	0	0	.281	.343	.406
Bullinger, Kirk, N.O.	55	2	2	0	0	0	0	0	0	0	0	0	0	0	0	1	0	0	0	.000	.000	.000
Burke, Jamie, S.L.	88	343	316	47	96	140	12	4	8	44	0	3	4	20	1	37	1	3	9	.304	.350	.443
Burroughs, Sean, Port.*	50	205	179	29	54	80	16	2	2	23	0	2	3	21	0	16	1	0	5	.302	.380	.447
Butler, Brent, C.S.	24	112	105	20	35	52	9	1	2	17	0	0	1	6	1	12	0	0	3	.333	.375	.495
Byas, Mike, Fres.†	20	62	55	5	11	15	0	2	0	4	2	0	0	5	0	15	4	1	1	.200	.267	.273
Bynum, Mike, Port.*	7	10	9	0	2	3	1	0	0	3	1	0	0	0	0	3	0	0	0	.222	.222	.333
Byrnes, Eric, Sac.	31	126	119	16	31	50	7	0	4	16	0	0	0	7	0	15	5	1	2	.261	.302	.420
Cabrera, Jolbert, L.V.	27	120	102	22	35	51	8	1	2	11	0	3	1	14	2	18	2	3	3	.343	.417	.500
Cadiente, Brett, Okla.*	7	21	19	5	7	11	2	1	0	5	0	0	0	2	0	6	1	0	0	.368	.429	.579
Camp, Shawn, Nash.	39	2	2	0	0	0	0	0	0	0	0	0	0	0	0	1	0	0	1	.000	.000	.000
Canales, Josh, L.V.	1	1	1	0	0	0	0	0	0	0	0	0	0	0	0	0	0	0	0	.000	.000	.000
Candelaria, Ben, Cal.*	11	27	25	3	6	11	2	0	1	6	0	1	0	1	0	4	0	0	0	.240	.259	.440
Canizaro, Jay, Edm.	66	281	247	43	71	128	11	2	14	37	0	1	3	30	0	46	6	3	7	.287	.370	.518
Capuano, Chris, Tuc.*	6	11	9	1	2	5	0	0	1	3	2	0	0	0	0	4	0	0	0	.222	.222	.556
Caraccioli, Lance, L.V.*	10	12	11	0	2	2	0	0	0	3	0	0	1	0	0	8	0	0	0	.182	.250	.182
Cardona, Javier, Port.	20	67	63	7	18	26	1	2	1	6	0	1	1	2	0	12	0	0	1	.286	.313	.413
Caruso, Joe, Oma.	14	57	52	4	10	14	4	0	0	5	0	0	1	4	0	10	0	0	0	.192	.263	.269
Caruso, Mike, Oma.*	60	240	219	28	67	83	3	2	3	23	3	2	4	12	1	14	10	3	2	.306	.350	.379
Castro, Nelson, Fres.†	28	100	94	8	17	28	1	2	2	5	0	2	1	3	0	20	7	1	2	.181	.210	.298
Chacon, Shawn, C.S.	5	6	4	0	1	1	0	0	0	1	0	1	1	0	0	2	0	0	0	.250	.333	.250
Chamblee, Jim, Mem.	5	11	10	1	1	1	0	0	0	1	0	0	1	0	0	4	0	0	0	.100	.182	.100
Charles, Frank, N.O.	105	358	332	30	88	120	10	2	6	49	2	3	4	17	2	83	1	3	11	.265	.306	.361
Chavez, Anthony, Tuc.	21	4	4	0	0	0	0	0	0	0	0	0	0	0	0	4	0	0	0	.000	.000	.000
Chavez, Raul, N.O.	111	411	373	24	85	104	10	0	3	36	5	5	7	21	2	50	3	4	11	.228	.278	.279
Chen, Chin-Feng, L.V.	137	576	511	90	145	257	26	4	26	84	0	7	0	58	1	160	1	0	19	.284	.352	.503
Choi, Hee Seop, Iowa*	135	587	478	94	137	245	24	3	26	97	0	7	6	95	4	119	3	2	6	.287	.406	.513
Cintron, Alex, Tuc.†	85	375	351	53	113	153	22	3	4	26	10	1	2	10	0	33	9	5	8	.322	.345	.436
Clapinski, Chris, L.V.†	102	397	342	58	101	168	25	3	12	57	8	3	5	39	0	52	2	0	6	.295	.373	.491
Clapp, Stubby, Mem.*	100	412	359	49	87	116	19	2	2	20	0	2	5	46	4	70	2	7	9	.242	.335	.323
Clark, Doug, Fres.*	70	234	212	24	57	83	9	1	5	19	1	1	5	15	2	52	3	3	5	.269	.330	.392
Clark, Jermaine, Tac.-Okla.*	121	507	425	60	115	162	16	5	7	40	5	6	2	69	2	70	35	16	3	.271	.371	.381
Coffie, Ivanon, Iowa*	124	424	373	55	89	152	32	5	7	51	0	5	5	41	2	65	2	5	6	.239	.318	.408
Colangelo, Mike, Sac.	70	264	217	22	46	55	9	0	0	22	4	3	7	33	0	36	3	3	16	.212	.331	.253
Colbrunn, Greg, Tuc.	6	28	25	6	9	18	3	0	2	7	0	0	0	3	0	3	0	0	1	.360	.429	.720
Cole, Eric, Okla.	66	263	242	28	64	94	15	3	3	23	1	2	2	16	1	54	3	1	14	.264	.313	.388
Colina, Javier, C.S.	95	353	322	40	79	120	23	3	4	30	1	5	3	22	1	53	0	2	14	.245	.295	.373
Condrey, Clay, Port.	25	34	31	3	3	3	0	0	0	0	3	0	0	0	0	13	0	0	0	.097	.097	.097
Connors, Greg, Tac.	95	358	325	39	83	143	27	0	11	54	3	3	2	25	1	64	0	2	9	.255	.310	.440
Coogan, Patrick, Mem.	7	6	4	1	1	1	0	0	0	1	1	0	0	1	0	2	0	0	0	.250	.400	.250
Cook, Aaron, C.S.	11	10	9	0	2	2	0	0	0	0	0	0	1	0	0	1	0	0	0	.222	.300	.222
Coolbaugh, Mike, Mem.	116	475	411	62	100	209	20	1	29	75	1	3	9	51	2	126	9	3	4	.243	.338	.509
Coquillette, Trace, Nash.	40	123	110	13	23	34	5	0	2	14	1	0	5	7	1	31	1	1	2	.209	.287	.309
Corey, Bryan, L.V.	37	7	5	0	0	0	0	0	0	1	0	0	1	0	0	2	0	0	0	.000	.167	.000
Cota, Humberto, Nash.	118	448	404	51	108	164	27	1	9	54	0	8	5	31	1	106	5	8	11	.267	.321	.406
Crabtree, Robbie, Fres.	24	3	2	0	0	0	0	0	0	0	1	0	0	0	0	1	0	0	0	.000	.000	.000
Crespo, Cesar, Port.†	92	378	322	43	83	131	17	2	9	37	3	0	3	50	2	78	21	7	5	.258	.363	.407
Cresse, Brad, Tuc.	36	134	126	23	34	50	10	0	2	14	0	1	3	4	0	38	0	0	1	.270	.306	.397
Cromer, Tripp, N.O.	77	283	265	31	68	106	13	2	7	26	3	2	4	9	0	42	0	0	9	.257	.289	.400
Crosby, Bubba, L.V.*	73	304	279	26	73	114	12	1	9	36	3	1	2	19	1	47	3	1	3	.262	.312	.409
Cruz, Ivan, Mem.*	125	518	461	83	129	261	27	0	35	100	0	5	3	49	7	96	0	0	14	.280	.349	.566

Player, Team	G	TPA	AB	R	H	TB	2B	3B	HR	RBI	SH	SF	HP	BB	IBB	SO	SB	CS	GDP	Avg.	OBP	Slg.
Cruz, Nelson, N.O.	6	1	0	0	0	0	0	0	0	0	1	0	0	0	0	0	0	0	0	.000	.000	.000
Cuddyer, Michael, Edm.	86	372	330	70	102	196	16	9	20	53	0	3	3	36	1	79	12	7	9	.309	.379	.594
Cunnane, Will, Iowa	43	13	9	0	0	0	0	0	0	0	2	0	0	2	0	5	0	0	0	.000	.182	.000
Curry, Chris, Iowa	7	21	19	0	2	3	1	0	0	0	1	0	1	1	0	8	0	0	0	.105	.190	.158
Cust, Jack, C.S.*	105	450	359	74	95	188	24	0	23	55	0	3	5	83	4	121	6	3	5	.265	.407	.524
Dallimore, Brian, Tuc.	122	469	419	62	123	171	26	2	6	50	7	6	9	28	0	72	13	4	10	.294	.346	.408
DaVanon, Jeff, S.L.†	25	120	100	21	33	60	10	1	5	18	1	1	1	17	0	24	5	3	1	.330	.429	.600
Davey, Tom, Port.	22	2	1	0	0	0	0	0	0	0	1	0	0	0	0	1	0	0	0	.000	.000	.000
Davis, Tommy, Mem.-L.V.	43	149	142	17	39	68	6	1	7	33	0	1	1	5	0	33	0	0	2	.275	.302	.479
DeHaan, Kory, Port.*	120	488	442	64	125	190	31	14	2	39	2	4	9	31	2	96	23	9	2	.283	.340	.430
De La Rosa, Tomas, Nash.	105	386	348	38	78	108	17	2	3	33	6	4	4	24	1	52	9	5	4	.224	.279	.310
Delgado, Wilson, Mem.†	98	397	365	31	95	139	19	2	7	35	5	1	3	23	4	54	2	5	6	.260	.309	.381
Dellucci, David, Tuc.*	4	17	15	2	2	3	1	0	0	1	0	0	0	2	0	4	0	0	0	.133	.235	.200
Devey, Phil, L.V.*	26	11	8	1	2	2	0	0	0	0	2	0	0	1	0	4	0	0	1	.250	.333	.250
Devore, Doug, Tuc.*	125	471	436	58	114	188	20	6	14	59	1	2	5	27	2	103	9	6	7	.261	.311	.431
Dewey, Jason, C.S.	36	110	103	7	20	35	3	0	4	20	1	2	0	4	0	27	0	0	6	.194	.220	.340
Dewitt, Matt, Port.	2	3	2	0	0	0	0	0	0	0	0	0	0	1	0	2	0	0	0	.000	.333	.000
Diaz, Edwin, Okla.	13	58	54	11	18	26	5	0	1	7	1	1	1	1	0	11	2	0	1	.333	.351	.481
Dillon, Joe, Edm.	6	20	18	5	3	4	1	0	0	0	0	0	0	2	0	2	1	0	1	.167	.250	.222
Donnels, Chris, Tuc.*	4	14	10	3	3	4	1	0	0	0	0	0	2	2	0	3	0	0	0	.300	.500	.400
Dougherty, Jim, Nash.	33	3	2	0	0	0	0	0	0	0	1	0	0	0	0	1	0	0	0	.000	.000	.000
Dransfeldt, Kelly, Okla.	140	564	507	60	116	190	21	7	13	66	5	4	4	44	0	133	9	3	6	.229	.293	.375
Duncan, Courtney, Iowa*	55	2	1	0	0	0	0	0	0	0	0	0	0	1	0	0	0	0	0	.000	.500	.000
Durazo, Erubiel, Tuc.*	7	23	22	5	7	14	2	1	1	3	0	0	1	0	0	2	0	0	1	.318	.348	.636
Durrington, Trent, S.L.	19	73	68	6	14	28	3	1	3	10	0	2	3	0	0	15	2	1	4	.206	.260	.412
Dye, Jermaine, Sac.	4	18	16	3	3	5	2	0	0	1	0	0	0	2	0	2	0	0	1	.188	.278	.313
Eberwein, Kevin, Port.	90	358	320	33	67	120	17	0	12	36	0	3	3	32	1	101	0	1	5	.209	.285	.375
Echevarria, Angel, Iowa	63	238	217	40	64	121	12	3	13	45	0	0	4	17	2	48	0	0	4	.295	.357	.558
Ellis, Mark, Sac.	21	94	84	14	25	37	10	1	0	5	0	0	4	6	0	13	4	0	1	.298	.372	.440
Ellis, Robert, L.V.	29	39	37	1	4	4	0	0	0	3	2	0	0	0	0	11	0	0	1	.108	.108	.108
Ellison, Jason, Fres.	49	221	196	31	61	80	8	1	3	8	0	0	4	21	0	28	16	3	4	.311	.389	.408
Encarnacion, Mario, Iowa	61	222	200	24	56	86	9	0	7	28	0	2	3	17	0	61	0	2	7	.280	.342	.430
Ensberg, Morgan, N.O.	83	353	292	50	84	123	12	3	7	37	1	3	7	50	1	56	9	5	9	.288	.401	.421
Erickson, Matt, Cal.*	108	427	379	63	109	146	30	2	1	27	6	0	11	31	1	63	15	4	11	.288	.359	.385
Espada, Joe, Oma.	74	255	223	18	50	62	12	0	0	23	6	4	3	19	0	26	14	4	10	.224	.289	.278
Esslinger, Cam, C.S.	30	1	1	1	0	0	0	0	0	0	0	0	0	0	0	1	0	0	0	.000	.000	.000
Estalella, Bobby, C.S.	23	91	79	16	23	50	9	0	6	20	0	1	0	11	0	20	0	0	0	.291	.374	.633
Estrada, Horacio, Tuc.*	31	38	30	2	4	4	0	0	0	0	6	0	0	2	0	4	0	0	0	.133	.188	.133
Estrella, Leo, Iowa	8	2	1	0	0	0	0	0	0	0	0	0	0	1	0	1	0	0	0	.000	.500	.000
Estrella, Luis, Fres.	38	34	30	4	8	12	1	0	1	4	4	0	0	0	0	3	0	0	0	.267	.267	.400
Everett, Adam, N.O.	88	385	345	51	95	131	16	7	2	25	7	3	6	24	1	59	12	3	3	.275	.331	.380
Fasano, Sal, S.L.	22	86	76	13	21	39	3	0	5	10	0	1	2	7	0	24	1	0	0	.276	.349	.513
Febles, Carlos, Oma.	13	60	54	10	12	19	2	1	1	5	0	1	1	4	0	5	2	1	1	.222	.283	.352
Fernandez, Alex, Port.*	22	84	80	7	25	35	4	0	2	13	0	1	1	2	0	13	1	3	0	.313	.333	.438
Fernandez, Osvaldo, Fres.	10	13	12	1	0	0	0	0	0	0	0	0	1	0	0	4	0	0	0	.000	.077	.000
Figgins, Chone, S.L.†	125	580	511	100	156	238	25	18	7	62	6	10	0	53	1	83	39	8	0	.305	.364	.466
Fitzgerald, Brian, C.S.*	7	1	1	0	0	0	0	0	0	0	0	0	0	0	0	1	0	0	0	.000	.000	.000
Flores, Jose, Sac.	95	435	363	64	111	138	19	1	2	38	7	6	3	56	1	53	16	4	11	.306	.397	.380
Flores, Randy, C.S.*	7	7	5	0	0	0	0	0	0	0	2	0	0	0	0	2	0	0	0	.000	.000	.000
Foppert, Jesse, Fres.	14	14	12	2	4	6	2	0	0	1	2	0	0	0	0	3	0	0	0	.333	.333	.500
Ford, Ben, Iowa	32	27	20	1	3	4	1	0	0	0	6	0	0	1	0	6	0	0	0	.150	.190	.200
Ford, Lew, Edm.	47	214	193	40	64	94	11	2	5	24	1	1	6	13	0	21	11	1	2	.332	.390	.487
Frank, Mike, Mem.*	88	289	262	29	72	105	13	1	6	39	0	2	7	18	1	21	9	2	9	.275	.336	.401
Franklin, Micah, Tuc.†	89	371	311	63	89	159	19	0	17	60	0	2	11	47	3	73	5	3	4	.286	.396	.511
Franklin, Wayne, N.O.*	29	38	33	2	6	7	1	0	0	5	2	0	0	3	0	9	0	0	0	.182	.250	.212
Freire, Alejandro, Fres.	46	165	146	12	40	58	7	1	3	7	0	0	5	14	0	28	0	0	3	.274	.358	.397
Frias, Hanley, Tuc.†	90	359	331	53	89	130	18	7	3	33	1	0	0	27	1	45	4	2	4	.269	.324	.393
Frye, Jeff, N.O.	15	44	40	1	8	9	1	0	0	0	0	0	4	0	3	0	1	0	0	.200	.273	.225
Fultz, Aaron, Fres.*	17	3	3	0	0	0	0	0	0	0	0	0	0	0	0	2	0	0	0	.000	.000	.000
Gandolfo, Rob, Tac.*	6	17	16	2	4	9	0	1	1	3	0	0	0	1	1	1	0	0	1	.250	.294	.563
Garcia, Douglas, Okla.*	3	11	11	0	0	0	0	0	0	0	0	0	0	0	0	3	0	0	0	.000	.000	.000
Garcia, Luis, Nash.	69	203	188	16	40	59	11	1	2	19	5	0	1	9	1	33	2	0	11	.213	.253	.314
Garrick, Matt, Mem.	27	93	82	9	18	31	7	0	2	8	0	1	0	10	1	28	0	1	4	.220	.312	.378
German, Esteban, Sac.	121	551	458	72	126	156	16	4	2	43	7	0	8	78	1	66	26	14	7	.275	.390	.341
Gil, Benji, S.L.	6	25	24	4	10	23	5	1	2	6	0	0	1	0	4	0	2	0	.417	.440	.958
Gilbert, Shawn, Nash.	48	173	143	18	39	46	2	1	1	15	0	3	4	23	0	31	2	4	0	.273	.382	.322
Ginter, Keith, N.O.	121	505	435	70	115	181	28	1	12	54	0	2	12	56	0	97	3	4	7	.264	.362	.416
Gissell, Chris, Iowa	29	42	36	5	8	19	2	0	3	11	5	0	0	1	0	13	0	0	1	.222	.243	.528
Gload, Ross, C.S.*	104	468	442	69	139	227	28	6	16	71	1	6	1	18	0	59	9	4	4	.314	.338	.514
Glynn, Ryan, Cal.	15	15	15	1	5	7	2	0	0	2	0	0	0	0	0	5	0	0	0	.333	.333	.467
Gomez, Rich, Oma.	113	370	334	43	79	131	15	2	11	53	3	3	5	25	0	74	13	5	8	.237	.297	.392
Gonzalez, Alfredo, L.V.	14	1	1	0	0	0	0	0	0	0	0	0	0	0	0	1	0	0	0	.000	.000	.000
Goodwin, Tom, Fres.*	17	71	62	11	14	19	3	1	0	7	1	0	0	8	0	8	3	2	1	.226	.314	.306
Grabowski, Jason, Sac.*	73	305	265	50	78	142	22	3	12	52	0	0	1	39	2	56	6	4	8	.294	.387	.536
Gray, Mike, Tuc.*	6	0	0	0	0	0	0	0	0	0	1	0	0	0	0	0	0	0	0	.000	.000	.000
Green, Andy, Tuc.	27	109	99	13	22	33	8	0	1	13	0	0	1	9	0	17	2	1	2	.222	.294	.333
Green, Chad, Edm.†	75	243	220	33	48	82	11	1	7	32	5	4	1	13	0	61	11	0	2	.218	.261	.373
Greene, Charlie, Cal.	99	336	320	34	80	125	24	0	7	41	0	1	4	11	0	53	0	0	11	.250	.283	.391
Greene, Todd, L.V.-Okla.	71	300	277	48	90	162	21	0	17	70	1	6	4	12	0	48	2	0	7	.325	.355	.585
Gregorio, Tom, S.L.	15	55	51	7	13	20	4	0	1	3	0	0	2	2	0	14	0	1	1	.255	.309	.392
Grilli, Jason, Cal.	1	2	2	0	0	0	0	0	0	0	0	0	0	0	0	1	0	0	0	.000	.000	.000
Guerra, Mark, N.O.	29	41	34	3	4	8	2	1	0	2	6	0	0	1	0	10	0	0	2	.118	.143	.235

Player, Team	G	TPA	AB	R	H	TB	2B	3B	HR	RBI	SH	SF	HP	BB	IBB	SO	SB	CS	GDP	Avg.	OBP	Slg.
Guerrier, Matt, Nash.	28	33	27	1	5	7	2	0	0	1	4	0	0	2	0	5	0	0	0	.185	.241	.259
Guiel, Aaron, Oma.*	61	255	215	44	76	116	11	1	9	50	0	3	8	29	3	34	8	1	4	.353	.443	.540
Guiel, Jeff, S.L.*	95	376	316	51	80	146	22	4	12	45	0	5	7	43	7	72	6	3	3	.253	.350	.462
Guillen, Jose, C.S.	5	19	17	2	7	10	3	0	0	5	0	0	1	1	0	2	0	1	1	.412	.474	.588
Gulin, Lindsay, L.V.*	14	21	16	1	1	1	0	0	0	1	5	0	0	0	0	9	0	0	0	.063	.063	.063
Gutierrez, Franklin, L.V.	2	11	10	2	3	5	2	0	0	2	0	0	0	1	0	4	0	0	1	.300	.364	.500
Guzman, Edwards, Fres.*	112	414	390	45	116	153	22	0	5	55	6	2	0	16	1	26	1	3	16	.297	.324	.392
Haas, Chris, Okla.*	11	41	33	6	12	20	5	0	1	4	0	1	0	7	0	8	0	0	1	.364	.463	.606
Hafner, Travis, Okla.*	110	492	401	79	137	224	22	1	21	77	0	0	12	79	4	76	2	1	9	.342	.463	.559
Hansen, Jed, Oma.	102	402	339	63	89	158	18	3	15	49	3	4	3	53	0	85	17	5	8	.263	.363	.466
Hart, Corey, Oma.†	11	37	30	1	3	3	0	0	0	3	1	0	0	6	0	4	1	0	1	.100	.250	.100
Hart, Jason, Okla.	134	593	514	78	135	244	32	1	25	83	1	2	8	68	1	122	1	0	14	.263	.356	.475
Harvey, Ken, Oma.	128	541	488	75	135	227	30	1	20	75	0	3	8	42	1	87	8	3	22	.277	.342	.465
Hatcher, Chris, Oma.	12	49	44	3	8	12	1	0	1	5	0	1	1	3	1	9	1	0	2	.182	.245	.273
Haverbusch, Kevin, Nash.	37	104	94	8	26	39	5	1	2	11	2	1	4	3	0	18	3	1	3	.277	.324	.415
Haynes, Nathan, S.L.*	67	298	283	37	80	112	14	6	2	12	1	1	1	12	0	53	10	10	3	.283	.313	.396
Hazlett, Andy, Port.*	13	7	6	0	1	1	0	0	0	0	1	0	0	0	0	1	0	0	0	.167	.167	.167
Heiserman, Rick, Mem.	22	4	3	0	0	0	0	0	0	0	0	0	0	1	0	1	0	0	0	.000	.250	.000
Helling, Rick, Tuc.	1	3	3	0	0	0	0	0	0	0	0	0	0	0	0	1	0	0	0	.000	.000	.000
Hermansen, Chad, Nash.	16	66	56	11	11	25	2	0	4	9	0	0	2	8	0	23	1	0	0	.196	.318	.446
Hernandez, Carlos, Okla.	10	42	41	2	7	8	1	0	0	3	1	0	0	0	0	10	0	0	2	.171	.171	.195
Hernandez, Carlos, C.S.	48	179	159	22	51	64	7	3	0	13	6	2	2	10	0	25	8	6	2	.321	.364	.403
Herndon, Junior, Port.	28	26	22	2	6	10	1	0	1	1	4	0	0	0	0	14	0	0	0	.273	.273	.455
Hiatt, Phil, L.V.	95	403	355	70	108	195	14	2	23	82	0	5	1	42	0	88	1	2	12	.304	.375	.549
Hill, Bobby, Iowa†	92	419	354	80	99	152	23	3	8	39	3	2	11	49	0	66	29	5	7	.280	.382	.429
Holbert, Aaron, Tac.	120	440	399	62	124	175	24	3	7	42	7	3	12	19	0	50	17	13	12	.311	.358	.439
Holt, Chris, C.S.	13	12	10	0	2	2	0	0	0	1	1	0	0	1	0	3	0	0	0	.200	.273	.200
Holtz, Mike, Port.*	7	1	1	0	0	0	0	0	0	0	0	0	0	0	0	1	0	0	0	.000	.000	.000
Holzemer, Mark, Tuc.*	51	2	2	0	1	1	0	0	0	0	0	0	0	0	0	1	0	0	0	.500	.500	.500
Hooper, Kevin, Cal.	117	498	452	70	130	163	21	3	2	38	6	2	4	34	0	51	17	10	7	.288	.341	.361
Hopper, Shane, Port.	35	127	115	12	32	52	3	1	5	16	2	0	3	7	0	27	4	1	1	.278	.336	.452
Horgan, Joe, Fres.*	27	7	7	0	1	1	0	0	0	0	0	0	0	0	0	3	0	0	0	.143	.143	.143
Horner, Jim, Tac.	7	22	20	5	6	8	2	0	0	1	0	0	2	0	0	4	0	0	0	.300	.364	.400
Howard, Ben, Port.	11	5	5	0	1	1	0	0	0	0	0	0	0	0	0	1	0	0	0	.200	.200	.200
Hubbard, Trenidad, Port.	8	32	29	9	11	22	2	0	3	6	0	1	0	2	0	3	2	2	0	.379	.406	.759
Hundley, Todd, Iowa†	3	10	9	1	2	5	0	0	1	4	0	0	0	1	0	2	0	0	0	.222	.300	.556
Hunter, Brian L., N.O.	5	21	19	4	3	5	0	1	0	0	0	0	0	2	0	7	2	0	1	.158	.238	.263
Hunter, Johnny, Port.	12	3	3	0	0	0	0	0	0	0	0	0	0	0	0	1	0	0	0	.000	.000	.000
Hutchison, Wesley, Fres.	17	3	2	0	0	0	0	0	0	0	1	0	0	0	0	2	0	0	0	.000	.000	.000
Hyzdu, Adam, Nash.	65	277	243	33	59	106	17	0	10	50	0	5	0	29	0	59	1	2	4	.243	.318	.436
Incaviglia, Pete, Port.	15	45	41	2	5	6	1	0	0	1	0	0	0	4	0	16	0	0	2	.122	.200	.146
Ingram, Garey, L.V.	25	72	63	9	20	26	3	0	1	10	1	0	2	6	0	14	0	0	1	.317	.394	.413
Izquierdo, Hansel, Cal.	13	24	24	1	4	5	1	0	0	4	0	0	0	0	0	9	0	0	1	.167	.167	.208
Jacome, Jason, Mem.*	28	18	16	0	0	0	0	0	0	0	1	0	0	1	0	2	0	0	0	.000	.059	.000
James, Mike, C.S.	24	1	1	0	0	0	0	0	0	0	0	0	0	0	0	0	0	0	0	.000	.000	.000
Jarvis, Matt, Fres.	20	1	1	0	0	0	0	0	0	0	0	0	0	0	0	1	0	0	0	.000	.000	.000
Johnson, Gary, S.L.*	40	164	143	30	38	68	9	3	5	35	0	3	3	15	0	49	1	1	3	.266	.341	.476
Johnson, Jonathan, Tuc.-Port.	26	11	9	0	2	2	0	0	0	0	1	0	0	1	0	1	0	0	0	.222	.300	.222
Johnson, Keith, S.L.	98	387	367	55	103	176	22	3	15	56	2	1	6	11	3	65	6	3	7	.281	.312	.480
Johnson, Mike, L.V.*	8	11	10	0	0	0	0	0	0	0	1	0	0	0	0	6	0	0	0	.000	.000	.000
Johnson, Rontrez, Oma.	109	478	403	71	121	183	27	4	9	53	0	6	19	50	1	51	31	11	6	.300	.397	.454
Jordan, Kevin, Fres.	60	204	188	13	43	58	4	1	3	14	2	3	3	8	0	23	1	0	6	.229	.267	.309
Journell, Jimmy, Mem.	7	10	10	1	2	2	0	0	0	2	0	0	0	0	0	5	0	1	0	.200	.200	.200
Judd, Mike, Cal.	23	26	23	1	4	6	2	0	0	2	0	0	1	0	0	9	0	0	1	.174	.208	.261
Kapler, Gabe, Okla.	5	20	17	6	8	13	2	0	1	5	0	0	3	0	2	1	0	0	0	.471	.550	.765
Keck, Brian, C.S.	11	25	25	0	4	6	2	0	0	2	0	0	0	0	0	3	1	0	1	.160	.160	.240
Kellner, Ryan, L.V.	11	39	35	3	14	18	4	0	0	6	0	0	1	3	0	11	0	0	0	.400	.462	.514
Kelly, Kenny, Tac.	122	432	391	51	97	163	13	10	11	53	9	4	2	26	0	93	11	3	11	.248	.296	.417
Kershner, Jason, Port.*	31	15	13	0	2	2	0	0	0	0	1	0	0	1	0	6	0	0	0	.154	.214	.154
Kielty, Bobby, Edm.†	2	9	7	0	3	4	1	0	0	0	1	0	0	1	0	1	0	0	1	.429	.500	.571
King, Brad, Okla.	8	34	26	7	8	12	1	0	1	6	2	0	2	4	0	5	0	0	0	.308	.438	.462
Kingsale, Eugene, Tac.†	49	207	188	25	49	88	15	3	6	26	2	1	1	15	0	30	10	3	6	.261	.317	.468
Kinkade, Mike, L.V.	74	387	287	63	98	165	22	6	11	50	0	2	19	29	1	49	6	2	9	.341	.433	.575
Klassen, Danny, Tuc.	103	397	361	41	83	119	20	5	2	42	3	7	4	22	0	106	6	1	7	.230	.277	.330
Knott, Eric, Tuc.*	31	33	32	0	5	5	0	0	0	4	1	0	0	0	0	9	0	0	0	.156	.156	.156
Knotts, Gary, Cal.	42	1	1	0	0	0	0	0	0	0	0	0	0	0	0	0	0	0	0	.000	.000	.000
Kolb, Brandon, Iowa	13	1	0	0	0	0	0	0	0	0	0	0	0	1	0	0	0	0	0	.000	1.000	.000
Koplove, Mike, Tuc.	23	1	1	0	0	0	0	0	0	0	0	0	0	0	0	0	0	0	0	.000	.000	.000
Krause, Scott, Tac.	19	59	51	5	15	25	4	0	2	7	2	0	2	4	0	10	1	0	5	.294	.368	.490
Kuzmic, Craig, Tac.†	63	246	216	23	48	85	9	5	6	22	2	3	0	25	1	68	5	0	8	.222	.299	.394
Lail, Denny, Mem.	10	8	6	0	1	1	0	0	0	0	1	0	0	1	0	2	0	0	0	.167	.286	.167
Lamb, Dave, Edm.†	123	501	440	72	136	197	25	3	10	72	5	5	6	45	0	57	2	6	16	.309	.377	.448
Lamb, Mike, Okla.†	6	29	28	3	11	12	1	0	0	4	0	0	0	1	0	4	0	0	1	.393	.414	.429
Landaeta, Luis, Nash.*	2	6	5	1	1	1	0	0	0	1	0	0	0	1	0	0	0	0	0	.200	.167	.200
Landry, Jacques, Sac.	57	217	185	24	45	76	8	1	7	35	0	5	1	26	0	68	5	3	2	.243	.332	.411
Lane, Jason, N.O.	111	470	426	65	116	201	36	2	15	83	0	6	7	31	0	90	13	3	6	.272	.328	.472
LeCroy, Matthew, Edm.	46	199	174	36	61	106	7	1	12	50	0	4	4	17	0	34	2	0	1	.351	.412	.609
Lidge, Brad, N.O.	24	27	23	1	3	3	0	0	0	0	4	0	0	0	0	12	0	0	1	.130	.130	.130
Lincoln, Mike, Nash.	10	1	1	0	0	0	0	0	0	0	0	0	0	0	0	1	0	0	0	.000	.000	.000
Linden, Todd, Fres.†	29	121	100	18	25	38	2	1	3	10	0	0	1	20	0	35	2	0	2	.250	.380	.380
Little, Mark, Tuc.	13	56	54	6	17	28	3	1	2	8	0	2	0	0	0	11	2	1	2	.315	.304	.519
Logan, Kyle, N.O.*	94	370	335	54	100	162	20	3	12	46	0	3	8	24	1	48	22	8	0	.299	.357	.484

Player, Team	G	TPA	AB	R	H	TB	2B	3B	HR	RBI	SH	SF	HP	BB	IBB	SO	SB	CS	GDP	Avg.	OBP	Slg.
Looney, Brian, Nash.*	6	2	2	0	0	0	0	0	0	0	0	0	0	0	0	0	0	0	0	.000	.000	.000
Lopez, Luis, Sac.................	131	585	516	66	146	201	28	0	9	72	0	4	1	64	1	63	2	3	17	.283	.361	.390
Lopez, Mendy, Nash.............	101	430	385	60	97	156	26	0	11	72	0	9	2	34	3	99	4	1	10	.252	.309	.405
Lopez, Mickey, Iowa†.............	107	391	338	48	89	131	25	1	5	39	3	7	4	39	0	45	8	5	5	.263	.340	.388
Lopez, Rafael, L.V.-C.S...........	18	61	53	7	14	22	2	0	2	6	1	0	2	5	1	13	1	0	3	.264	.350	.415
Lowe, Sean, Nash................	5	5	5	0	1	1	0	0	0	0	0	0	0	0	0	1	0	0	0	.200	.200	.200
Loyd, Brian, Port................	24	88	83	10	14	22	2	0	2	9	0	0	0	5	0	14	0	0	2	.169	.216	.265
Ludwick, Ryan, Okla..............	78	352	305	62	87	167	27	4	15	52	1	3	5	38	1	76	2	2	6	.285	.370	.548
Lunsford, Trey, Fres..............	19	66	57	3	10	16	0	0	2	9	0	2	1	6	0	15	0	0	2	.175	.258	.281
Luther, Ryan, Fres...............	5	13	8	2	2	3	1	0	0	3	0	1	1	3	0	3	1	0	0	.250	.462	.375
Magnante, Mike, L.V.*	7	1	1	0	0	0	0	0	0	0	0	0	0	0	0	0	0	0	0	.000	.000	.000
Mahay, Ron, Iowa*..............	39	4	4	1	2	3	1	0	0	3	0	0	0	0	0	0	0	0	1	.500	.500	.750
Mahomes, Pat, Iowa	45	8	8	1	2	2	0	0	0	0	0	0	0	0	0	3	0	0	0	.250	.250	.250
Mahoney, Mike, Iowa	78	246	223	33	57	77	12	1	2	18	5	0	1	17	1	44	1	1	0	.256	.311	.345
Maldonado, Carlos, N.O.	12	30	29	1	5	5	0	0	0	2	0	0	0	1	0	7	0	0	0	.172	.200	.172
Marsters, Brandon, Edm..........	57	205	184	27	51	74	8	0	5	23	5	2	2	12	1	37	0	0	3	.277	.325	.402
Martin, Chandler, C.S.	8	6	6	1	1	1	0	0	0	0	0	0	0	0	0	1	0	0	0	.167	.167	.167
Martinez, Felix, L.V.†	24	91	82	13	16	26	4	0	2	9	1	1	2	5	0	19	0	0	4	.195	.256	.317
Martinez, Thomas, Port.........	1	1	1	0	0	0	0	0	0	0	0	0	0	0	0	0	0	0	0	.000	.000	.000
Mashore, Damon, Tuc...........	21	64	56	3	11	14	3	0	0	10	0	1	0	7	1	13	0	1	4	.196	.281	.250
Matos, Julius, Port..............	50	205	186	20	58	87	17	0	4	26	5	3	2	9	0	20	1	2	6	.312	.345	.468
Matranga, Dave, N.O.	101	341	300	47	82	124	15	3	7	40	5	3	6	27	0	79	7	2	4	.273	.342	.413
Mayo, Blake, Tuc................	8	8	5	0	1	1	0	0	0	0	1	0	0	2	0	2	0	0	0	.200	.429	.200
McCool, Lee, Tuc.	2	6	6	1	2	2	0	0	0	1	0	0	0	0	0	1	0	0	0	.333	.333	.333
McDonald, Donzell, Oma.†	112	515	452	63	118	184	15	15	7	35	1	2	4	56	0	102	30	6	5	.261	.346	.407
McDonald, Keith, Mem.	81	299	267	33	72	128	20	0	12	36	7	3	7	15	0	55	1	2	8	.270	.322	.479
McGowan, Sean, Fres.	57	196	187	12	46	68	15	2	1	17	1	1	2	5	0	42	1	1	10	.246	.272	.364
McKay, Cody, Sac.*	108	419	378	55	109	166	16	1	13	57	4	6	10	21	0	59	2	1	4	.288	.337	.439
McKeel, Walt, C.S.	49	147	130	10	32	45	7	0	2	11	0	1	0	16	0	27	0	0	2	.246	.327	.346
McKnight, Tony, Nash.*	30	38	33	3	7	9	2	0	0	2	2	0	0	3	0	8	0	0	0	.212	.278	.273
Meadows, Brian, Nash...........	23	33	28	3	4	4	0	0	0	3	2	0	0	3	0	9	0	0	0	.143	.226	.143
Melhuse, Adam, Iowa-C.S.†......	106	387	341	58	106	176	29	1	13	59	1	1	0	44	3	70	4	4	8	.311	.389	.516
Meliah, Dave, Okla.*	60	239	219	31	54	83	13	2	4	23	1	0	2	17	3	32	1	2	6	.247	.307	.379
Melo, Juan, Fres.†	135	522	479	67	132	212	28	2	16	63	1	5	4	33	0	93	6	7	7	.276	.324	.443
Mench, Kevin, Okla.	26	117	98	17	21	47	8	0	6	15	0	0	2	17	0	33	0	0	7	.214	.342	.480
Menchaca, Eriberto, Tac.........	6	18	17	2	2	2	0	0	0	2	0	0	0	1	0	1	0	0	0	.118	.167	.118
Mendez, Carlos, Sac.	103	420	404	58	131	195	26	1	12	74	0	1	3	12	1	52	3	1	11	.324	.348	.483
Mendez, Donaldo, Port.	64	239	217	32	47	76	9	1	6	18	1	1	6	14	0	63	11	4	0	.217	.282	.350
Menechino, Frank, Sac...........	84	371	314	50	78	108	12	0	6	50	0	3	8	46	0	58	10	3	10	.248	.356	.344
Merrill, Ronnie, C.S.†	19	69	63	9	12	19	2	1	1	2	2	0	0	4	0	12	0	0	1	.190	.239	.302
Metcalfe, Mike, Oma.†	44	163	149	27	37	47	7	0	1	15	0	2	1	11	0	11	10	2	5	.248	.301	.315
Meyers, Chad, Sac.-Mem........	118	502	412	67	107	155	19	1	9	37	3	3	21	63	2	64	43	9	7	.260	.383	.376
Middlebrook, Jason, Port.........	10	8	6	1	2	2	0	0	0	1	2	0	0	0	0	3	0	0	0	.333	.333	.333
Miller, Damian, Tuc..............	3	9	9	1	3	4	1	0	0	0	0	0	0	0	0	1	0	0	1	.333	.333	.444
Miller, Wade, N.O.	2	1	1	0	0	0	0	0	0	0	0	0	0	0	0	0	0	0	0	.000	.000	.000
Minor, Damon, Fres.*	9	34	29	8	15	23	6	1	0	5	0	0	0	5	0	5	0	0	0	.517	.588	.793
Minor, Ryan, Tuc...............	42	172	157	15	36	47	6	1	1	8	0	0	3	12	0	29	0	0	3	.229	.297	.299
Moeller, Chad, Tuc..............	60	249	211	37	67	109	8	2	10	48	2	4	3	29	1	46	1	0	4	.318	.401	.517
Molina, Gabe, Mem..............	56	2	2	0	0	0	0	0	0	0	0	0	0	0	0	0	0	0	0	.000	.000	.000
Molina, Jose, S.L.	79	315	290	30	89	119	14	2	4	43	7	2	4	12	1	60	0	3	4	.307	.341	.410
Morales, Willie, Tuc.	93	340	315	44	98	140	24	0	6	53	1	6	3	15	0	57	4	4	8	.311	.342	.444
Morgan, Scott, Port.	25	84	75	8	16	21	2	0	1	10	0	3	0	6	0	19	0	0	4	.213	.262	.280
Morris, Warren, Edm.-Mem.*	56	208	192	31	50	78	10	3	4	24	1	4	0	11	0	28	2	2	8	.260	.295	.406
Mosquera, Julio, Okla............	81	301	272	40	78	113	14	0	7	32	2	1	10	16	0	51	14	1	14	.287	.348	.415
Mota, Guillermo, L.V.	20	5	4	0	1	1	0	0	0	2	0	0	0	1	0	2	0	0	0	.250	.400	.250
Mota, Tony, Mem.†	44	153	136	21	30	46	7	0	3	13	0	1	1	15	2	28	3	2	5	.221	.301	.338
Mouton, James, Tuc.............	75	293	263	50	75	123	21	3	7	36	1	2	4	23	0	79	7	6	4	.285	.349	.468
Mueller, Bill, Iowa†	6	19	16	2	6	10	1	0	1	5	0	0	0	3	0	1	0	1	0	.375	.474	.625
Munoz, Bobby, C.S..............	15	7	7	1	1	1	0	0	0	0	0	0	0	0	0	1	0	0	0	.143	.143	.143
Munro, Pete, N.O.	19	21	18	1	2	3	1	0	0	0	3	0	0	0	0	6	0	0	0	.111	.111	.167
Murphy, Mike, N.O.	15	41	39	0	7	7	0	0	0	1	0	0	0	2	0	10	0	0	0	.179	.220	.179
Murphy, Nate, Tuc.*	84	286	245	41	68	121	13	5	10	32	1	0	5	35	1	60	8	4	3	.278	.379	.494
Murray, Calvin, Okla.	33	155	139	23	37	52	7	1	2	14	4	1	0	11	0	20	4	0	3	.266	.318	.374
Myers, Rodney, Port.	42	2	2	0	0	0	0	0	0	0	0	0	0	0	0	0	0	0	0	.000	.000	.000
Nady, Xavier, Port...............	85	340	315	46	89	133	12	1	10	43	0	2	3	20	0	60	0	1	11	.283	.329	.422
Nance, Shane, L.V.*	37	7	5	1	1	2	1	0	0	0	0	0	0	2	0	1	0	0	0	.200	.429	.400
Nathan, Joe, Fres.	34	37	29	7	5	8	0	0	1	2	6	0	1	1	0	8	0	0	0	.172	.226	.276
Newson, Warren, Mem.*	20	33	30	6	8	15	4	0	1	5	0	0	0	3	0	10	0	0	2	.267	.333	.500
Nicholson, Kevin, C.S.-Mem.†....	57	186	161	13	35	51	9	2	1	20	4	2	0	19	2	32	2	3	3	.217	.297	.317
Nichting, Chris, C.S.	23	2	2	0	0	0	0	0	0	0	0	0	0	0	0	2	0	0	0	.000	.000	.000
Niecula, Aaron, Fres.	11	24	23	2	2	2	0	0	0	0	1	0	0	0	0	9	1	0	1	.087	.125	.087
Nieves, Jose, S.L.	15	67	63	12	18	35	3	1	4	13	0	0	0	4	0	6	2	1	1	.286	.328	.556
Nieves, Wil, Port................	70	245	237	24	73	118	20	2	7	29	2	1	0	5	0	40	0	0	7	.308	.321	.498
Norton, Greg, C.S.†	3	15	12	2	1	1	0	0	0	0	0	0	3	0	0	5	0	0	0	.083	.267	.083
Nunez, Abe, Nash.†	5	20	18	3	4	4	0	0	0	0	0	0	0	2	0	7	4	1	0	.222	.300	.222
Nunez, Abraham, Cal.†	129	484	428	68	107	204	24	5	21	60	0	4	1	51	3	112	31	6	4	.250	.329	.477
Nunnally, Jon, Oma.-Mem.* ..	107	406	360	56	87	159	19	1	17	58	0	1	3	42	2	101	14	4	3	.242	.325	.442
Ohme, Kevin, Mem.*	56	8	8	0	0	0	0	0	0	0	0	0	0	0	0	0	0	0	0	.000	.000	.000
Ojeda, Augie, Iowa†	73	306	291	54	67	98	20	4	1	27	0	5	9	31	0	30	5	3	2	.230	.318	.337
Oliver, Darren, Mem..............	5	6	4	0	0	0	0	0	0	0	1	0	0	1	0	5	0	0	0	.000	.200	.000
Olsen, Kevin, Cal................	8	7	6	0	0	0	0	0	0	0	1	0	0	0	0	5	0	0	0	.000	.000	.000
Ordaz, Luis, Iowa-Oma.	96	358	330	47	95	133	21	4	3	33	6	2	2	18	1	37	9	3	8	.288	.327	.403

Player, Team	G	TPA	AB	R	H	TB	2B	3B	HR	RBI	SH	SF	HP	BB	IBB	SO	SB	CS	GDP	Avg.	OBP	Slg.
Orie, Kevin, Iowa..................	86	321	294	51	88	170	16	3	20	63	0	0	2	25	1	40	0	1	10	.299	.358	.578
Oropesa, Eddie, Tuc.*	29	1	1	0	0	0	0	0	0	0	0	0	0	0	0	1	0	0	0	.000	.000	.000
Ortega, Bill, Mem.	96	338	293	46	74	116	17	2	7	35	2	3	4	36	1	43	1	4	10	.253	.339	.396
Ortiz, Hector, Okla.-Oma.	60	213	181	13	42	52	7	0	1	12	7	1	2	22	0	31	1	1	5	.232	.320	.287
Ortiz, Jose, C.S.	26	116	111	23	37	68	9	2	6	18	0	1	0	4	0	13	1	1	3	.333	.353	.613
Overbay, Lyle, Tuc.*	134	579	525	83	180	277	40	0	19	109	0	5	7	42	3	86	0	0	12	.343	.396	.528
Owens, Jeremy, Port.	13	27	23	4	4	12	0	1	2	7	0	1	0	3	0	9	1	1	0	.174	.259	.522
Owens, Ryan, C.S.	70	256	227	24	59	92	11	2	6	41	1	3	1	24	0	74	8	3	6	.260	.329	.405
Ozuna, Pablo, Cal.	77	290	261	37	85	124	16	1	7	33	7	2	3	17	0	37	16	3	5	.326	.371	.475
Patterson, John, Tuc.	19	27	27	0	3	5	2	0	0	3	0	0	0	0	0	10	0	0	1	.111	.111	.185
Pearce, Josh, Mem.	4	2	2	1	1	1	0	0	0	0	0	0	0	0	0	1	0	0	0	.500	.500	.500
Pearsall, J.J., Cal.*	9	3	2	0	0	0	0	0	0	0	0	1	0	0	0	1	0	0	0	.000	.000	.000
Pearson, Jason, Port.*	23	2	0	0	0	0	0	0	0	0	0	0	0	0	0	0	0	0	0	.000	.000	.000
Peeples, Mike, Cal.	75	253	231	32	60	99	14	2	7	36	3	4	3	12	0	41	8	4	7	.260	.300	.429
Pelaez, Alex, Port.	112	434	411	47	127	193	31	1	11	64	0	3	0	20	3	40	0	1	15	.309	.339	.470
Pellow, Kit, Oma.	105	446	402	65	116	226	25	2	27	76	0	4	19	21	1	82	4	2	7	.289	.350	.562
Pena, Angel, Fres.	72	266	248	27	65	104	11	2	8	34	0	3	0	15	2	55	2	2	4	.262	.301	.419
Pena, Carlos, Sac.*	44	206	175	30	42	84	10	1	10	33	0	3	4	24	0	49	3	0	3	.240	.340	.480
Perez, Santiago, Okla.†	14	60	51	6	17	23	1	1	1	9	0	1	1	7	1	12	3	2	0	.333	.417	.451
Pernalete, Marco, Fres.†	92	280	260	29	69	90	4	1	5	25	4	3	0	13	0	58	1	1	2	.265	.297	.346
Petrick, Ben, C.S.	79	311	265	51	85	159	18	4	16	54	1	4	1	40	1	77	10	6	4	.321	.406	.600
Phelps, Tommy, Cal.*	51	5	4	0	1	1	0	0	0	0	1	0	0	0	0	2	0	0	0	.250	.250	.250
Piatt, Adam, Sac.	62	273	234	46	69	108	15	0	8	44	0	3	1	35	0	30	4	3	12	.295	.385	.462
Pickford, Kevin, Port.*	20	12	11	0	1	1	0	0	0	0	0	0	0	1	1	5	0	1	0	.091	.167	.091
Pickler, Jeff, Okla.*	96	456	394	62	118	137	19	0	0	32	5	2	1	54	0	44	17	8	8	.299	.384	.348
Podsednik, Scott, Tac.*	125	505	438	63	122	186	25	6	9	61	4	11	9	43	5	70	35	13	18	.279	.347	.425
Porter, Bo, C.S.	14	51	47	5	8	13	2	0	1	7	0	0	1	3	0	16	3	1	1	.170	.235	.277
Porter, Colin, N.O.*	134	510	461	59	122	180	30	5	6	38	2	1	0	46	8	127	28	7	5	.265	.331	.390
Pose, Scott, L.V.-Okla.*	44	184	158	16	32	39	5	1	0	14	1	0	1	24	0	12	5	5	2	.203	.311	.247
Post, Dave, Nash.	96	396	345	59	105	141	16	1	6	39	6	1	6	38	0	56	11	4	8	.304	.382	.409
Powell, Dante, Fres.	17	50	48	5	11	16	5	0	0	2	0	0	0	2	0	16	2	1	0	.229	.260	.333
Pride, Curtis, Nash.*	110	432	385	71	114	168	22	1	10	46	6	1	7	33	2	75	22	8	7	.296	.362	.436
Prieto, Alex, Edm.	80	298	276	38	73	110	14	1	7	29	0	1	2	19	1	47	4	4	5	.264	.315	.399
Prieto, Chris, N.O.*	21	95	86	10	17	19	2	0	0	1	0	0	1	8	1	11	0	1	0	.198	.274	.221
Prior, Mark, Iowa	3	7	7	3	3	11	0	1	2	5	0	0	0	0	0	3	0	0	0	.429	.429	1.571
Pritchett, Chris, Nash.*	118	450	397	53	116	162	15	2	9	60	1	3	3	46	2	95	3	0	3	.292	.367	.408
Quinlan, Robb, S.L.	136	588	528	95	176	293	31	13	20	112	0	15	4	41	2	93	8	2	16	.333	.376	.555
Quinn, Mark, Oma.	12	45	39	4	7	11	2	1	0	2	0	0	2	4	1	7	0	0	1	.179	.289	.282
Radinsky, Scott, Cal.*	18	1	1	0	0	0	0	0	0	0	0	0	0	0	0	1	0	0	0	.000	.000	.000
Radmanovich, Ryan, Nash.*..	93	308	271	35	61	98	16	0	7	27	2	1	4	30	3	58	2	4	7	.225	.310	.362
Ramirez, Dan, Tuc.	85	257	236	32	71	88	6	4	1	20	1	1	2	17	1	49	7	9	5	.301	.352	.373
Ramirez, Julio, S.L.	39	145	139	17	38	57	3	5	2	10	1	0	1	4	0	31	8	3	2	.273	.299	.410
Ramirez, Santiago, N.O.	18	1	1	0	1	1	0	0	0	0	0	0	0	0	0	0	0	0	0	.000	.000	.000
Ramsey, Brad, Iowa	2	4	4	1	0	0	0	0	0	1	0	0	0	0	0	0	0	0	1	1.000	1.000	1.000
Randolph, Steve, Tuc.*	33	50	45	5	15	19	4	0	0	4	0	1	0	4	0	13	0	0	1	.333	.380	.422
Ransom, Cody, Fres.	135	517	449	53	93	158	18	4	13	46	12	6	3	47	0	151	6	4	5	.207	.283	.352
Reboulet, Jeff, L.V.	18	72	63	10	16	21	2	0	1	3	2	1	0	6	0	9	2	0	1	.254	.314	.333
Redding, Tim, N.O.	11	5	4	2	2	3	1	0	0	0	0	0	0	1	0	1	0	0	0	.500	.600	.750
Redman, Tike, Nash.*	76	339	311	40	84	107	9	4	2	20	3	3	1	21	1	24	16	7	3	.270	.315	.344
Rekar, Bryan, C.S.	20	21	20	1	1	2	1	0	0	1	0	0	0	0	0	9	0	0	2	.050	.050	.100
Restovich, Michael, Edm.......	138	580	518	95	148	281	32	7	29	98	0	5	4	53	2	151	11	7	10	.286	.353	.542
Reyes, Al, Nash.	43	3	3	0	0	0	0	0	0	0	0	0	0	0	0	0	0	0	0	.000	.000	.000
Reynoso, Armando, Tuc.	6	6	4	0	0	0	0	0	0	2	0	0	0	2	0	2	0	0	0	.000	.333	.000
Riggs, Adam, Mem.	43	147	122	26	28	43	9	0	2	11	0	2	0	23	0	27	5	1	3	.230	.347	.352
Rios, Armando, Nash.*	15	59	52	6	13	15	2	0	0	6	0	1	1	5	0	10	1	2	1	.250	.322	.288
Rivera, Ruben, Okla.	27	112	98	19	27	58	2	4	7	23	0	0	1	13	1	23	2	0	2	.276	.366	.592
Robbins, Jake, C.S.	11	1	1	0	1	1	0	0	0	0	0	0	0	0	0	0	0	0	0	1.000	1.000	1.000
Robertson, Jeriome, N.O.* ...	28	40	36	4	8	9	1	0	0	4	4	1	0	2	0	5	0	0	2	.222	.256	.250
Rodgers, Bobby, Cal.	25	12	12	1	2	2	0	0	0	0	0	0	0	0	0	1	0	0	1	.167	.167	.167
Rodriguez, Guillermo, Fres. ...	32	128	115	9	27	38	5	0	2	8	1	1	5	6	0	23	0	1	4	.235	.299	.330
Rodriguez, Nerio, Mem.	8	17	16	1	2	5	0	0	1	1	1	0	0	0	0	5	0	0	0	.125	.125	.313
Rodriguez, Ricardo, L.V.	2	5	4	1	0	0	0	0	0	0	0	0	1	0	0	3	0	0	0	.000	.200	.000
Rolison, Nate, Cal.-Tac.*	117	448	411	55	106	179	20	1	17	53	0	1	36	2	140	1	0	13		.258	.319	.436
Romano, Jason, Okla.-C.S.	79	366	325	48	93	126	15	3	4	37	11	5	0	25	0	68	18	6	6	.286	.332	.388
Romero, Mandy, Nash.†	88	320	283	40	84	160	25	0	17	51	4	5	4	24	2	47	1	1	7	.297	.354	.565
Roneberg, Brett, Cal.*	3	7	5	1	2	2	0	0	0	0	0	0	0	2	0	0	0	0	1	.400	.571	.400
Rose, Mike, Oma.†	52	207	177	22	46	71	12	2	3	17	1	0	1	28	1	40	1	2	3	.260	.364	.401
Ross, David, L.V.	92	346	293	48	87	152	16	2	15	68	5	4	9	35	0	86	1	1	4	.297	.384	.519
Ruan, Wilkin, L.V.	40	157	153	18	50	63	7	3	0	29	0	2	0	2	0	17	12	0	1	.327	.335	.412
Rumfield, Toby, Cal.-Mem......	69	220	198	21	55	72	8	0	3	27	1	3	1	17	2	31	0	0	7	.278	.333	.364
Ryan, Mike, Edm.*	131	600	540	92	141	282	36	6	31	101	0	3	2	55	6	124	4	5	9	.261	.330	.522
Ryan, Rob, Sac.*	61	239	209	34	52	89	14	1	7	27	1	2	3	24	0	40	0	0	4	.249	.332	.426
Saarloos, Kirk, N.O.	4	5	5	0	1	1	0	0	0	0	0	0	0	0	0	0	0	0	0	.200	.200	.200
Saba, Donnie, Tuc.*	1	5	3	1	0	0	0	0	0	0	0	0	0	2	0	1	0	0	0	.000	.400	.000
Sabel, Erik, Tuc.	25	17	15	1	1	1	0	0	0	1	1	0	0	1	0	7	0	0	1	.067	.125	.067
Sadler, Donnie, Oma.-Okla. ...	17	74	64	13	17	22	3	1	0	4	0	0	2	8	0	10	2	3	0	.266	.365	.344
Salazar, Ruben, Edm.	7	27	26	3	5	5	0	0	0	2	0	0	0	1	0	2	0	0	0	.192	.222	.192
Sanchez, Duaner, Tuc.	4	1	1	0	0	0	0	0	0	0	0	0	0	0	0	0	0	0	0	.000	.000	.000
Sanchez, Jesus, Iowa*	27	31	27	3	6	7	1	0	0	2	4	0	0	0	0	8	0	0	1	.222	.222	.259
Santangelo, F.P., Sac.†	44	106	86	10	15	22	4	0	1	6	1	0	6	13	0	19	1	1	3	.174	.324	.256
Santora, Jack, Tuc.†	16	24	21	3	2	2	0	0	0	4	1	0	0	3	0	7	0	0	1	.095	.208	.095
Santos, Deivis, Fres.*	23	91	88	8	25	39	3	1	3	14	0	1	0	2	0	14	4	0	2	.284	.297	.443

Player, Team	G	TPA	AB	R	H	TB	2B	3B	HR	RBI	SH	SF	HP	BB	IBB	SO	SB	CS	GDP	Avg.	OBP	Slg.
Santos, Victor, C.S.	21	26	23	3	7	7	0	0	0	2	1	0	0	2	0	9	0	0	0	.304	.360	.304
Saturria, Luis, Mem.	29	84	74	6	12	15	3	0	0	5	1	1	1	7	0	22	3	1	1	.162	.241	.203
Saylor, Jamie, N.O.*	100	260	237	23	53	75	7	3	3	12	2	0	0	21	1	60	4	1	2	.224	.287	.316
Scanlan, Bob, C.S.	17	1	1	0	0	0	0	0	0	0	0	0	0	0	0	0	0	0	0	.000	.000	.000
Schmidt, Jason, Fres.	2	5	5	0	1	2	1	0	0	1	0	0	0	0	0	1	0	0	0	.200	.200	.400
Sears, Todd, Edm.*	129	552	484	88	150	254	36	4	20	100	0	4	5	59	4	142	2	1	6	.310	.388	.525
Secoda, Jason, Cal.	35	21	17	0	3	3	0	0	0	2	0	0	2	0	0	10	0	0	0	.176	.263	.176
Secrist, Reed, Nash.*	114	420	358	59	92	158	24	3	12	56	2	5	3	52	2	87	7	4	5	.257	.352	.441
Seifert, Ryan, C.S.	21	13	12	1	5	6	1	0	0	1	1	0	0	0	0	4	0	0	0	.417	.417	.500
Selmo, Martin, Port.	2	2	2	0	0	0	0	0	0	0	0	0	0	0	0	1	0	0	0	.000	.000	.000
Servais, Scott, Fres.-C.S.	43	154	136	22	39	54	12	0	1	26	1	5	5	7	0	22	0	0	8	.287	.333	.397
Shearn, Tom, N.O.	57	5	5	0	1	1	0	0	0	0	0	0	0	0	0	2	0	0	1	.200	.200	.200
Shiell, Jason, Port.	56	3	2	0	0	0	0	0	0	0	1	0	0	0	0	0	0	0	0	.000	.000	.000
Shinjo, Tsuyoshi, Fres.	2	8	7	0	0	0	0	0	0	0	0	0	0	1	0	1	0	0	0	.000	.125	.000
Short, Rick, S.L.	105	446	410	71	146	200	29	2	7	68	0	4	9	23	1	43	3	2	4	.356	.399	.488
Simmons, Brian, Fres.†	91	361	319	45	93	152	18	4	11	40	1	3	4	34	2	76	7	4	9	.292	.364	.476
Simon, Ben, L.V.	23	15	14	1	1	1	0	0	0	0	0	1	0	0	0	5	0	0	0	.071	.071	.071
Simontacchi, Jason, Mem.	6	8	7	1	2	2	0	0	0	2	0	0	0	1	0	0	0	0	0	.286	.375	.286
Sinclair, Steve, Iowa*	53	3	3	0	0	0	0	0	0	0	0	0	0	0	0	1	0	0	1	.000	.000	.000
Smith, Brian, Nash.	33	1	1	0	0	0	0	0	0	0	0	0	0	0	0	1	0	0	0	.000	.000	.000
Smith, Bud, Mem.*	6	9	9	1	2	4	2	0	0	1	0	0	0	0	0	0	0	0	0	.222	.222	.444
Smith, Chuck, C.S.	4	2	2	0	0	0	0	0	0	0	0	0	0	0	0	1	0	0	0	.000	.000	.000
Smith, Jeff, Edm.*	10	32	27	0	2	3	1	0	0	2	2	0	0	3	0	8	0	0	1	.074	.167	.111
Smith, Mark, Cal.	115	442	389	60	113	179	30	0	12	55	0	3	9	41	0	79	5	2	10	.290	.369	.460
Smith, Travis, Mem.	18	17	14	0	1	1	0	0	0	1	2	0	0	1	0	4	0	0	0	.071	.133	.071
Smyth, Steve, Iowa*	6	6	5	1	1	1	0	0	0	1	1	0	0	0	0	3	0	0	0	.200	.200	.200
Snopek, Chris, Mem.	33	105	92	15	24	39	6	0	3	13	0	1	1	11	0	13	4	1	5	.261	.343	.424
Snyder, John, Port.	26	28	24	2	1	1	0	0	0	1	0	0	0	4	0	8	0	0	0	.042	.179	.042
Socarras, Tony, L.V.*	1	4	3	1	1	1	0	0	0	2	0	0	1	0	0	1	0	0	0	.333	.500	.333
Sollecito, Gabe, Tuc.†	13	1	1	0	0	0	0	0	0	0	0	0	0	0	0	0	0	0	0	.000	.000	.000
Speier, Justin, C.S.	12	2	2	0	0	0	0	0	0	0	0	0	0	0	0	1	0	0	0	.000	.000	.000
Spencer, Stan, L.V.	3	2	1	1	1	1	0	0	0	0	0	0	0	1	0	0	0	0	0	1.000	1.000	1.000
Sprague, Ed, Okla.	106	459	400	51	107	165	26	1	10	65	0	7	12	40	1	92	0	1	17	.268	.346	.413
Springer, Dennis, L.V.	26	29	27	1	4	4	0	0	0	0	2	0	0	0	0	11	0	0	0	.148	.148	.148
Stark, Dennis, C.S.	7	10	10	0	3	4	1	0	0	0	0	0	0	0	0	5	0	0	0	.300	.300	.400
Steenstra, Kennie, Cal.-Tuc.	18	8	6	0	1	2	1	0	0	0	2	0	0	0	0	2	0	0	0	.167	.167	.333
Stemle, Steve, Mem.	20	15	13	0	3	3	0	0	0	1	0	0	0	2	0	4	0	0	0	.231	.333	.231
Stephenson, Garrett, Mem.....	3	4	3	0	0	0	0	0	0	0	0	0	0	1	0	3	0	0	0	.000	.250	.000
Stratton, Rob, C.S.	23	91	80	13	17	42	2	1	7	14	0	0	5	6	0	42	0	1	0	.213	.308	.525
Sutton, Larry, Sac.*	116	528	431	83	126	206	40	2	12	81	0	3	1	93	1	108	2	0	9	.292	.417	.478
Sweeney, Brian, Tac.	31	1	1	0	0	0	0	0	0	0	0	0	0	0	0	0	0	0	0	.000	.000	.000
Sweeney, Mark, Port.*	1	1	1	0	1	1	0	0	0	0	0	0	0	0	0	0	0	0	0	1.000	1.000	1.000
Sweeney, Mike, Oma.	3	14	12	2	3	7	1	0	1	4	0	1	0	1	1	2	0	0	1	.250	.286	.583
Taguchi, So, Mem.	91	336	304	37	75	107	17	0	5	36	11	3	5	13	0	44	6	3	5	.247	.286	.352
Tankersley, Dennis, Port........	9	20	18	3	4	4	0	0	0	3	1	1	0	0	0	6	0	0	0	.222	.211	.222
Teut, Nate, Cal.	27	19	14	1	2	3	1	0	0	0	3	0	0	2	0	4	0	0	0	.143	.250	.214
Theodorou, Nick, L.V.†	2	6	5	1	3	3	0	0	0	0	0	0	0	1	0	0	0	0	0	.600	.667	.600
Thomas, Gary, Sac.	4	11	9	0	1	1	0	0	0	2	1	1	0	0	0	2	0	1	0	.111	.100	.111
Thomas, Juan, Tac.	121	480	429	47	113	201	33	2	17	57	0	1	7	43	0	102	3	1	8	.263	.340	.469
Thompson, Mark, C.S.	8	4	4	1	0	0	0	0	0	0	0	0	0	0	0	1	0	0	0	.000	.000	.000
Thrower, Jake, Port.†	111	397	362	45	98	143	31	1	4	33	4	3	4	24	2	53	1	0	6	.271	.321	.395
Thurston, Joe, L.V.*	136	631	587	106	196	297	39	13	12	55	5	2	12	25	1	60	22	9	10	.334	.372	.506
Tolar, Kevin, Nash.	44	14	12	3	3	5	2	0	0	1	1	0	1	0	0	4	0	0	1	.250	.308	.417
Torcato, Tony, Fres.*	130	527	490	64	142	210	23	3	13	64	2	4	2	29	3	65	4	6	6	.290	.330	.429
Torres, Salomon, Nash..........	27	38	33	0	5	6	1	0	0	1	4	0	0	1	0	11	0	1	0	.152	.176	.182
Treanor, Matt, Cal.	36	112	95	10	27	38	8	0	1	18	0	0	5	12	0	13	1	1	4	.284	.393	.400
Tyler, Brad, L.V.*	66	191	148	34	36	57	9	3	2	13	0	1	1	41	0	37	0	2	3	.243	.408	.385
Ugueto, Luis, Tac.†	12	55	51	5	13	14	1	0	0	5	0	1	0	3	0	13	2	1	0	.255	.291	.275
Urban, Jeff, Fres.	35	21	20	1	2	4	2	0	0	1	0	0	0	0	0	16	0	0	0	.100	.100	.200
Urquhart, Derick, S.L.*	14	59	54	6	12	19	2	1	1	6	0	0	0	5	0	11	0	2	1	.222	.288	.352
Valdez, Mario, Sac.*	85	365	304	43	79	110	18	2	3	25	0	2	1	58	1	56	1	0	6	.260	.378	.362
Valentin, Javier, Edm.†	127	509	455	69	130	228	33	1	21	80	0	8	5	41	2	96	0	1	15	.286	.346	.501
Vargas, Claudio, Cal.	17	19	17	0	3	4	1	0	0	0	2	0	0	0	0	8	0	0	0	.176	.176	.235
Velarde, Randy, Sac.	4	19	17	3	8	14	3	0	1	4	0	0	1	1	1	3	1	0	0	.471	.526	.824
Verplancke, Jeff, Fres............	51	3	3	1	1	2	1	0	0	0	0	0	0	0	0	0	0	0	0	.333	.333	.667
Villafuerte, Brandon, Port.......	47	3	3	1	1	1	0	0	0	0	0	0	0	0	0	1	0	0	0	.333	.333	.333
Villarreal, Oscar, Tuc.*	10	13	10	0	0	0	0	0	0	0	3	0	0	0	0	3	0	0	0	.000	.000	.000
Wade, Travis, N.O.	27	2	2	0	0	0	0	0	0	0	0	0	0	0	0	0	0	0	0	.000	.000	.000
Waldron, Jeff, Tuc.*	1	5	5	0	2	2	0	0	0	0	0	0	0	0	0	1	0	0	0	.400	.400	.400
Wall, Donne, C.S.	14	1	1	0	0	0	0	0	0	0	0	0	0	0	0	0	0	0	0	.000	.000	.000
Walrond, Les, Mem.*	29	26	25	1	1	1	0	0	0	0	0	0	0	1	0	10	0	0	0	.040	.040	.040
Ward, Bryan, C.S.*	6	10	8	0	0	0	0	0	0	0	2	0	0	0	0	2	0	0	0	.000	.000	.000
Ward, Jeremy, Tuc.	54	2	2	0	0	0	0	0	0	0	0	0	0	0	0	0	0	0	0	.000	.000	.000
Warner, Michael, Sac.*	36	120	103	10	18	32	3	1	3	12	1	1	0	15	1	28	5	3	3	.175	.277	.311
Wathan, Derek, Cal.†	102	358	329	43	92	139	18	7	5	41	3	1	2	23	1	44	7	11	4	.280	.330	.422
Wathan, Dusty, Oma.	49	190	160	22	46	60	9	1	1	26	3	1	10	16	0	36	1	1	9	.288	.385	.375
Watson, Mark, Iowa	28	2	2	0	0	0	0	0	0	0	0	0	0	0	0	2	0	0	0	.000	.000	.000
Wayne, Justin, Cal.	2	3	3	0	0	0	0	0	0	0	0	0	0	0	0	0	0	0	0	.000	.000	.000
Webb, Brandon, Tuc...............	1	2	1	0	0	0	0	0	0	0	0	0	0	1	0	0	0	0	0	.000	.000	.000
Weber, Jake, Tac.*	20	66	59	7	14	15	1	0	0	3	0	0	0	7	0	8	3	0	4	.237	.318	.254
Weekly, Chris, Iowa*	7	14	12	2	3	4	1	0	0	1	0	0	0	2	0	3	0	0	1	.250	.357	.333
Weibl, Clint, Mem.	25	18	16	3	5	6	1	0	0	1	1	0	1	0	0	4	0	0	0	.313	.353	.375

Player, Team	G	TPA	AB	R	H	TB	2B	3B	HR	RBI	SH	SF	HP	BB	IBB	SO	SB	CS	GDP	Avg.	OBP	Slg.
Wesson, Barry, N.O..............	111	439	413	43	121	189	25	5	11	61	2	3	5	16	0	100	4	7	9	.293	.325	.458
Whiten, Mark, L.V.†	8	28	25	3	4	8	1	0	1	2	0	0	1	2	0	4	1	0	0	.160	.250	.320
Whiteside, Matt, C.S.	60	1	1	0	0	0	0	0	0	0	0	0	0	0	0	1	0	0	0	.000	.000	.000
Williams, Gerald, Mem..........	21	78	73	11	11	17	3	0	1	3	1	0	1	3	0	8	2	0	2	.151	.195	.233
Williams, Jeff, L.V.	56	2	1	0	0	0	0	0	0	0	0	1	0	0	0	0	0	0	0	.000	.000	.000
Williams, Jerome, Fres.	28	41	34	2	3	4	1	0	0	2	4	0	1	2	0	17	0	0	0	.088	.162	.118
Williams, Matt, Tuc.	5	15	15	1	3	6	0	0	1	3	0	0	0	0	0	5	0	0	2	.200	.200	.400
Williams, Woody, Mem.	1	2	2	0	0	0	0	0	0	0	0	0	0	0	0	2	0	0	0	.000	.000	.000
Wood, Jason, Cal.................	121	504	457	78	144	230	37	2	15	70	1	4	4	38	0	92	3	0	13	.315	.370	.503
Woodard, Steve, Mem.*	7	12	11	0	0	0	0	0	0	0	0	1	0	0	0	6	0	0	0	.000	.000	.000
Wooten, Shawn, S.L.	10	43	42	2	11	13	2	0	0	7	0	0	1	0	0	11	0	0	1	.262	.279	.310
Wright, Ron, Tac.	99	405	359	52	98	165	20	1	15	57	0	2	5	39	2	89	0	1	6	.273	.351	.460
Wrigley, Jase, C.S.	9	1	1	0	0	0	0	0	0	0	0	0	0	0	0	1	0	0	0	.000	.000	.000
Wuertz, Mike, Iowa	28	30	22	1	1	1	0	0	0	0	7	0	0	1	0	14	0	0	0	.045	.087	.045
Young, Ernie, Tuc..............	48	190	160	29	52	105	9	1	14	48	0	1	5	24	1	33	0	3	5	.325	.426	.656
Young, Jason, C.S.	13	21	19	2	4	4	0	0	0	2	0	0	0	2	0	6	0	0	0	.211	.286	.211
Zambrano, Carlos, Iowa†.......	3	1	1	0	0	0	0	0	0	0	0	0	0	0	0	0	0	0	0	.000	.000	.000
Zerbe, Chad, Fres.*	3	4	4	0	3	3	0	0	0	1	0	0	0	0	0	0	0	0	1	.750	.750	.750
Zinter, Alan, N.O.†..............	63	248	225	30	52	99	14	0	11	39	0	1	0	22	0	64	2	0	3	.231	.298	.440
Zuleta, Julio, Iowa...............	120	497	444	80	130	244	21	0	31	104	0	3	7	43	2	106	0	1	21	.293	.362	.550
Zuniga, Tony, Fres...............	90	328	304	22	73	109	16	1	6	33	1	2	3	18	1	38	0	4	10	.240	.287	.359

PLAYERS WITH TWO OR MORE TEAMS

Player, Team	G	TPA	AB	R	H	TB	2B	3B	HR	RBI	SH	SF	HP	BB	IBB	SO	SB	CS	GDP	Avg.	OBP	Slg.
Ardoin, Danny, Oma.	25	91	77	10	16	28	3	0	3	10	0	3	0	11	0	25	1	0	0	.208	.297	.364
Ardoin, Danny, Okla.	33	121	106	10	24	35	5	0	2	11	2	1	2	10	1	31	0	0	2	.226	.303	.330
Clark, Jermaine, Tac.*..........	108	443	368	47	98	138	14	4	6	36	5	6	2	62	2	59	29	14	3	.266	.370	.375
Clark, Jermaine, Okla.*	13	64	57	13	17	24	2	1	1	4	0	0	0	7	0	11	6	2	0	.298	.375	.421
Davis, Tommy, Mem.	28	96	90	9	25	41	4	0	4	20	0	1	0	5	0	19	0	0	2	.278	.313	.456
Davis, Tommy, L.V.	15	53	52	8	14	27	2	1	3	13	0	0	1	0	0	14	0	0	0	.269	.283	.519
Greene, Todd, L.V.	32	134	125	27	44	89	12	0	11	41	0	3	3	3	0	21	0	0	5	.352	.373	.712
Greene, Todd, Okla.............	39	166	152	21	46	73	9	0	6	29	1	3	1	9	0	27	2	0	2	.303	.339	.480
Johnson, Jonathan, Tuc.	14	8	6	0	2	2	0	0	0	0	1	0	0	1	0	1	0	0	0	.333	.429	.333
Johnson, Jonathan, Port.......	12	3	3	0	0	0	0	0	0	0	0	0	0	0	0	0	0	0	0	.000	.000	.000
Lopez, Rafael, L.V.	15	53	46	6	13	21	2	0	2	5	1	0	2	4	1	12	1	0	3	.283	.365	.457
Lopez, Rafael, C.S.	3	8	7	1	1	1	0	0	0	1	0	0	0	1	0	1	0	0	0	.143	.250	.143
Melhuse, Adam, Iowa†	72	255	226	33	66	106	19	0	7	39	1	0	0	28	0	47	2	3	3	.292	.370	.469
Melhuse, Adam, C.S.†..........	34	132	115	25	40	70	10	1	6	20	0	1	0	16	3	23	2	1	5	.348	.424	.609
Meyers, Chad, Sac.	18	67	54	11	11	14	0	0	1	2	0	0	1	12	1	10	0	0	3	.204	.358	.259
Meyers, Chad, Mem.	100	435	358	56	96	141	19	1	8	35	3	3	20	51	1	54	43	9	4	.268	.387	.394
Morris, Warren, Mem.*	29	111	100	16	26	38	4	1	2	14	0	3	0	8	0	12	0	1	5	.260	.306	.380
Morris, Warren, Edm.*	27	97	92	15	24	40	6	2	2	10	1	1	0	3	0	16	2	1	3	.261	.281	.435
Nicholson, Kevin, C.S.†.........	18	41	36	1	3	4	1	0	0	1	0	0	0	5	1	11	0	0	1	.083	.195	.111
Nicholson, Kevin, Mem.†.......	39	145	125	12	32	47	8	2	1	19	4	2	0	14	1	21	2	3	2	.256	.326	.376
Nunnally, Jon, Oma.*	20	67	58	12	14	28	5	0	3	12	0	0	1	8	1	19	1	3	0	.241	.343	.483
Nunnally, Jon, Mem.*	87	339	302	44	73	131	14	1	14	46	0	1	2	34	1	82	13	1	3	.242	.322	.434
Ordaz, Luis, Iowa	61	208	194	22	53	66	10	0	1	14	4	0	1	9	1	21	5	2	2	.273	.309	.340
Ordaz, Luis, Oma................	35	150	136	25	42	67	11	4	2	19	2	2	1	9	0	16	4	1	6	.309	.351	.493
Ortiz, Hector, Okla.............	25	95	82	3	17	19	2	0	0	7	1	1	0	11	0	16	0	1	3	.207	.298	.232
Ortiz, Hector, Oma.............	35	118	99	10	25	33	5	0	1	5	6	0	2	11	0	15	1	0	2	.253	.339	.333
Pose, Scott, L.V.*...............	23	90	74	11	15	18	3	0	0	6	1	0	1	14	0	6	5	3	1	.203	.337	.243
Pose, Scott, Okla.*	21	94	84	5	17	21	2	1	0	8	0	0	0	10	0	6	0	2	1	.202	.287	.250
Rolison, Nate, Cal.*	37	140	126	22	32	66	7	0	9	21	0	0	0	14	0	45	0	0	3	.254	.329	.524
Rolison, Nate, Tac.*	80	308	285	33	74	113	13	1	8	32	0	1	0	22	2	95	1	0	10	.260	.315	.396
Romano, Jason, Okla............	48	227	196	28	53	75	8	1	4	28	8	4	0	19	0	41	10	3	5	.270	.329	.383
Romano, Jason, C.S.	31	139	129	20	40	51	7	2	0	9	3	1	0	6	0	27	8	3	1	.310	.338	.395
Rumfield, Toby, Cal.............	56	177	157	15	45	55	7	0	1	20	1	3	1	15	2	25	0	2	5	.287	.347	.350
Rumfield, Toby, Mem.	13	43	41	6	10	17	1	0	2	7	0	0	0	2	0	6	0	0	2	.244	.279	.415
Sadler, Donnie, Oma.	5	24	21	6	7	7	0	0	0	0	0	0	1	2	0	3	0	2	0	.333	.417	.333
Sadler, Donnie, Okla............	12	50	43	7	10	15	3	1	0	4	0	0	1	6	0	7	2	1	0	.233	.340	.349
Servais, Scott, Fres.	4	11	8	1	3	3	0	0	0	1	0	0	1	1	0	0	0	0	1	.375	.500	.375
Servais, Scott, C.S.	39	143	128	21	36	51	12	0	1	26	0	5	4	6	0	22	0	0	7	.281	.322	.398
Steenstra, Kennie, Cal.	9	5	4	0	1	2	1	0	0	0	1	0	0	0	0	1	0	0	0	.250	.250	.500
Steenstra, Kennie, Tuc.	9	3	2	0	0	0	0	0	0	0	1	0	0	0	0	0	0	0	0	.000	.000	.000

GRAND SLAMS—Bartee, Coolbaugh, A. Guiel, Zuleta, 3 each; L. Barnes, R. Bell, Brumbaugh, G. Johnson, Lane, L. Lopez, 2 each; Allen, Bair, Barker, Berger, Blake, Blalock, Canizaro, Choi, Cintron, Connors, Cota, Crespo, Cruz, Cust, Davis, Estalella, Frias, Hafner, J. Hart, Landry, LeCroy, Matranga, McKay, Melhuse, Mench, Mouton, Pelaez, Pellow, A. Pena, Piatt, B. Porter, Pritchett, Restovich, Romero, Ross, Sutton, J. Thomas, Valentin, Wesson, E. Young, 1 each.

AWARDED FIRST BASE ON CATCHER'S INTERFERENCE—J. Guiel 5 (Mahoney, K. McDonald, McKay, H. Ortiz, Servais); Choi (H. Ortiz).

2002 PITCHING
TEAM

Team	W	L	Pct.	ERA	G	CG	ShO	Sv.	IP	H	TBF	R	ER	HR	SH	SF	HB	BB	IBB	SO	WP	Bk.
New Orleans......	75	69	.521	3.40	144	5	11	41	1285.0	1165	5327	546	485	116	47	25	84	385	24	968	39	4
Memphis...........	71	71	.500	3.95	142	3	8	38	1232.2	1274	5272	601	541	155	38	31	49	396	8	889	55	4
Nashville...........	72	71	.503	4.00	143	10	9	30	1248.0	1209	5257	608	555	120	46	31	59	356	25	1080	44	9
Portland............	72	71	.503	4.04	143	4	4	43	1228.0	1159	5257	625	551	137	41	35	60	430	9	874	49	8
Omaha..............	76	68	.528	4.17	144	4	5	38	1268.1	1289	5509	673	587	113	36	56	55	510	16	970	70	5
Fresno	57	87	.396	4.29	144	2	7	41	1240.2	1263	5391	649	592	131	62	41	57	482	14	1031	71	7
Tucson	73	68	.518	4.30	141	4	7	36	1232.0	1279	5318	648	589	121	46	50	54	415	19	956	49	6

Team	W	L	Pct.	ERA	G	CG	ShO	Sv.	IP	H	TBF	R	ER	HR	SH	SF	HB	BB	IBB	SO	WP	Bk.
Salt Lake	78	66	.542	4.33	144	6	5	31	1275.0	1357	5535	729	614	153	27	36	66	438	4	1066	68	11
Tacoma	65	76	.461	4.43	141	7	7	35	1201.2	1278	5190	665	592	125	41	47	52	371	7	908	62	10
Las Vegas	85	59	.590	4.60	144	2	5	47	1288.1	1497	5686	743	658	130	61	48	68	433	8	918	52	7
Oklahoma	75	69	.521	4.71	144	5	7	33	1297.0	1375	5701	764	679	119	32	50	72	494	19	1062	67	4
Iowa	71	73	.493	4.87	144	2	4	35	1242.1	1307	5517	756	672	153	51	47	62	550	25	1018	63	7
Edmonton	81	59	.579	4.95	140	8	3	41	1200.1	1326	5267	731	660	137	26	53	53	430	5	965	53	8
Sacramento	66	78	.458	5.10	144	0	5	31	1269.0	1448	5688	815	719	129	32	54	80	462	15	977	76	9
Calgary	67	71	.486	5.34	138	4	6	33	1155.2	1288	5186	754	686	150	46	32	62	488	21	812	60	9
Col. Springs	58	86	.403	5.85	144	5	1	36	1245.1	1521	5766	936	809	167	43	51	82	545	24	1007	85	10

INDIVIDUAL

TOP QUALIFIERS FOR EARNED-RUN AVERAGE TITLE

Minimum 115 innings. *Lefthanded pitcher.

Pitcher, Team	W	L	Pct.	ERA	G	GS	CG	ShO	GF	Sv.	IP	H	TBF	R	ER	HR	SH	SF	HB	BB	IBB	SO	WP	Bk.
Robertson, Jeriome, N.O.*	12	8	.600	2.55	27	27	2	1	0	0	180	160	734	59	51	13	4	4	9	45	0	114	4	0
Arroyo, Bronson, Nash.	8	6	.571	2.96	22	21	3	2	0	0	143	126	574	57	47	10	6	3	2	28	1	116	5	0
Franklin, Wayne, N.O.*	13	9	.591	3.12	29	27	1	0	1	0	179	153	733	68	62	14	5	8	11	59	2	141	2	1
Ainsworth, Kurt, Fres.	8	6	.571	3.41	20	19	1	0	0	0	116	101	477	49	44	7	4	2	3	43	0	119	5	1
Calero, Kiko, Oma.	7	7	.500	3.44	20	18	0	0	0	0	125.2	112	510	52	48	11	5	7	4	35	1	109	6	1
Randolph, Steve, Tuc.*	15	7	.682	3.47	28	27	1	1	1	0	163.1	151	704	70	63	15	6	7	6	81	2	129	6	0
Condrey, Clay, Port.	10	4	.714	3.50	25	23	0	0	0	0	133.2	128	552	55	52	12	6	3	5	40	1	73	2	3
Williams, Jerome, Fres.	6	11	.353	3.59	28	28	0	0	0	0	160.2	140	671	76	64	16	8	5	9	50	1	130	5	3
Sweeney, Brian, Tac.	9	5	.643	3.60	30	23	1	1	4	2	142	157	606	67	60	16	3	1	3	28	0	113	5	0
Torres, Salomon, Nash.	8	5	.615	3.83	26	24	2	1	0	0	162.1	169	686	78	69	12	6	4	11	39	2	136	3	0
Estrada, Horacio, Tuc.*	8	7	.533	3.90	29	25	2	0	1	1	163.2	167	682	75	71	21	4	6	9	40	0	107	3	0
Guerra, Mark, N.O.	6	11	.353	4.01	28	28	1	1	0	0	173	183	723	88	77	16	5	3	13	35	1	89	1	0
Kelley, Rich, S.L.*	6	5	.545	4.08	40	15	1	0	7	0	119	128	514	64	54	15	4	1	6	40	1	72	5	2
Dickey, R.A., Okla.	8	7	.533	4.09	37	19	1	0	8	0	154	176	664	81	70	8	7	4	7	45	1	109	5	0
Snyder, John, Port.	7	12	.368	4.12	26	25	1	1	1	0	144.1	156	635	78	66	12	3	6	8	50	0	93	8	1

DEPARTMENTAL LEADERS: W—Randolph, 15; L—McKnight, 14; Pct.—Randall, 1.000; G—Whiteside, 60; GS—Several pitchers tied with 28; CG—Arroyo, Cloude, Rincon, 3 each; ShO—Arroyo, Bell, Herndon, 2 each; GF—Whiteside, 49; Sv.—Jef. Williams, 28; IP—Robertson, 180.0; H—Rekar, Springer, 203 each; TBF—Ellis, 753; R—B. Thomas, 112; ER—Gissell, 105; HR—Herndon, 28; SH—Ellis, 12; SF—Laxton, 12; HB—B. Thomas, 17; BB—Randolph, 81; IBB—M. Miller, 8; SO—Franklin, 141; WP—Luebbers, 16; BK—A. Lopez, 4.

ALL PITCHERS

*Lefthanded pitcher.

Pitcher, Team	W	L	Pct.	ERA	G	GS	CG	ShO	GF	Sv.	IP	H	TBF	R	ER	HR	SH	SF	HB	BB	IBB	SO	WP	Bk.
Abad, Andy, Cal.*	0	0	.000	9.00	2	0	0	0	2	0	3	4	13	3	3	2	0	0	0	0	0	1	0	0
Abbott, Paul, Tac.	0	1	.000	6.23	2	2	0	0	0	0	8.2	13	41	10	6	3	0	0	3	0	8	0	0	
Adkins, Jon, Sac.	7	6	.538	6.03	20	20	0	0	0	0	97	139	457	74	65	9	3	4	6	33	0	76	2	0
Agosto, Stevenson, Iowa*	2	1	.667	6.41	4	4	0	0	0	0	19.2	28	98	16	14	2	1	0	3	9	0	16	2	1
Ainsworth, Kurt, Fres.	8	6	.571	3.41	20	19	1	0	0	0	116	101	477	49	44	7	4	2	3	43	0	119	5	1
Aldred, Scott, L.V.*	2	2	.500	4.43	42	0	0	0	13	2	44.2	50	203	22	22	2	3	2	3	19	2	48	0	0
Alvarez, Juan, Okla.*	0	0	.000	3.63	15	0	0	0	3	1	17.1	19	78	7	7	1	2	1	1	9	1	13	2	0
Alvarez, Victor, L.V.*	10	7	.588	4.70	34	15	0	0	8	3	122.2	132	526	69	64	11	5	4	3	39	1	106	4	1
Alviso, Jerome, C.S.	0	0	.000	6.75	4	0	0	0	4	0	5.1	9	26	4	4	2	0	0	1	0	6	0	0	
Arnold, Jamie, Cal.	3	8	.273	7.39	16	10	1	0	2	0	67	82	309	59	55	10	4	2	6	29	0	25	1	1
Arroyo, Bronson, Nash.	8	6	.571	2.96	22	21	3	2	0	0	143	126	574	57	47	10	6	3	2	28	1	116	5	0
Arteaga, J.D., N.O.*	9	10	.474	4.29	42	15	0	0	9	3	119.2	135	529	70	57	18	6	1	7	40	3	77	2	0
Atchison, Scott, Tac.	5	10	.333	4.63	27	21	1	1	3	2	124.1	123	528	68	64	13	3	5	9	31	0	112	1	0
Austin, Jeff, Oma.	4	0	1.000	3.27	39	0	0	0	13	2	52.1	54	226	24	19	2	0	4	2	15	2	44	11	1
Aybar, Manny, Fres.	1	4	.200	3.75	45	0	0	0	42	24	50.1	46	216	24	21	6	4	3	2	18	1	53	3	0
Baerlocher, Ryan, Oma.	5	2	.714	4.41	13	7	0	0	1	0	49	50	213	31	24	8	1	3	2	22	1	37	3	0
Bailey, Cory, Oma.	1	0	1.000	1.83	18	0	0	0	16	9	19.2	13	77	4	4	0	0	0	0	10	0	17	1	0
Balfour, Grant, Edm.	2	4	.333	4.16	58	0	0	0	25	8	71.1	60	296	34	33	3	3	3	0	30	1	88	2	1
Bausher, Andy, Port.*	1	0	1.000	3.48	8	0	0	0	2	0	10.1	9	41	4	4	1	0	0	0	2	0	8	1	0
Beirne, Kevin, L.V.	10	3	.769	4.15	22	22	0	0	0	0	125.2	129	538	64	58	12	4	4	9	41	0	88	4	0
Belitz, Todd, C.S.*	1	3	.250	5.11	22	5	0	0	7	2	44	53	207	33	25	6	2	2	4	20	1	29	4	0
Bell, Rob, Okla.	5	0	1.000	4.06	12	11	2	2	1	0	75.1	70	312	36	34	10	0	2	2	25	0	55	3	0
Benes, Alan, Iowa	10	9	.526	5.65	28	19	0	0	3	0	113	130	512	79	71	17	5	5	4	53	0	85	5	1
Benes, Andy, Mem.	1	1	.500	3.12	4	4	0	0	0	0	17.1	17	72	7	6	2	1	1	1	4	0	8	0	0
Benoit, Joaquin, Okla.	8	4	.667	3.56	16	16	0	0	0	0	98.2	74	412	42	39	8	1	4	7	37	0	103	6	0
Benson, Kris, Nash.	0	2	.000	1.53	4	4	0	0	0	0	17.2	8	69	4	3	1	0	1	0	8	0	25	0	0
Bere, Jason, Iowa	1	0	1.000	1.80	1	1	0	0	0	0	5	2	20	1	1	0	0	0	0	3	0	3	0	0
Bergman, Dusty, S.L.*	1	1	.500	6.44	21	0	0	0	7	0	29.1	34	129	25	21	7	0	1	2	9	0	26	1	0
Bevel, Bobby, Tac.*	5	2	.714	5.09	31	0	0	0	8	1	40.2	46	183	25	23	7	2	1	0	18	0	37	4	0
Bochtler, Doug, Edm.	7	4	.636	3.68	34	9	1	0	6	0	88	71	364	41	36	6	3	5	2	44	0	79	4	0
Bones, Ricky, L.V.	0	2	.000	3.86	30	0	0	0	24	9	30.1	34	141	19	13	3	1	1	4	12	1	15	1	0
Bootcheck, Chris, S.L.	4	3	.571	3.88	9	9	1	1	0	0	58	64	247	29	25	5	1	2	2	16	0	38	1	0
Borland, Toby, Cal.	5	2	.714	2.96	56	0	0	0	38	14	70	55	295	24	23	2	1	2	7	30	3	75	9	0
Borrego, Ramon, Edm.	0	0	.000	0.00	1	0	0	0	1	0	1	3	3	0	0	0	0	0	0	0	0	1	0	0
Bost, Heath, Sac.	1	5	.167	3.35	52	0	0	0	21	12	78	67	322	33	29	8	5	0	5	19	0	69	3	0
Bowie, Micah, Sac.*	3	2	.600	3.13	46	0	0	0	15	4	54.2	40	229	21	19	2	1	3	2	24	2	64	1	1
Boyd, Jason, Port.	0	1	1.000	1.04	19	0	0	0	6	4	26	19	105	4	3	2	2	0	1	7	0	22	2	0
Brittan, Corey, C.S.	3	6	.333	5.64	35	12	0	0	6	0	97.1	122	458	79	61	14	5	3	4	46	4	70	8	1
Brohawn, Troy, Fres.*	3	3	.500	3.65	56	0	0	0	14	1	69	71	300	31	28	7	3	1	4	21	2	55	5	1
Brown, Eric, Iowa	0	0	.000	0.00	1	0	0	0	0	0	3	0	3	0	0	0	0	0	0	0	0	3	0	0
Brown, Kevin, L.V.	1	0	1.000	1.86	2	2	0	0	0	0	9.2	6	36	2	2	0	0	0	0	3	0	7	1	0

CLASS AAA *Pacific Coast League*

Pitcher, Team	W	L	Pct.	ERA	G	GS	CG	ShO	GF	Sv.	IP	H	TBF	R	ER	HR	SH	SF	HB	BB	IBB	SO	WP	Bk.
Bukvich, Ryan, Oma.	1	0	1.000	0.00	12	0	0	0	11	8	13.2	4	50	0	0	0	0	0	0	7	0	17	0	0
Bullinger, Kirk, N.O.	4	1	.800	2.75	55	1	0	0	16	4	75.1	61	293	25	23	6	5	0	3	11	4	46	0	0
Burke, Jamie, S.L.	0	0	.000	0.00	1	0	0	0	1	0	1	0	5	0	0	0	0	0	0	2	0	1	0	0
Butler, John, Tac.	0	0	.000	18.00	1	0	0	0	1	0	1	4	7	2	2	0	0	0	0	0	0	2	0	0
Bynum, Mike, Port.*	3	2	.600	3.51	7	7	0	0	0	0	41	36	167	19	16	6	3	1	3	7	0	35	0	0
Calero, Kiko, Oma.	7	7	.500	3.44	20	18	0	0	0	0	125.2	112	510	52	48	11	5	7	4	35	1	109	6	1
Callaway, Mickey, S.L.	9	2	.818	1.68	17	14	1	0	0	0	91.1	79	370	26	17	7	1	1	1	22	0	75	5	2
Cameron, Ryan, C.S.	0	1	.000	108.00	1	1	0	0	0	0	0.2	4	10	8	8	0	0	1	0	3	0	1	1	0
Camp, Shawn, Nash.	4	1	.800	3.24	39	0	0	0	15	2	58.1	50	234	22	21	5	3	1	6	15	3	59	0	1
Cannon, Jon, Fres.*	1	0	1.000	0.00	3	0	0	0	0	0	3.2	3	19	0	0	1	0	0	0	5	0	0	0	0
Capuano, Chris, Tuc.*	4	1	.800	2.72	6	6	0	0	0	0	36.1	30	146	12	11	1	1	2	0	11	0	29	1	0
Caraccioli, Lance, L.V.*	4	3	.571	4.14	10	10	0	0	0	0	58.2	58	256	30	27	4	5	4	2	28	0	39	3	2
Carnes, Matt, Edm.	4	3	.571	6.61	21	12	0	0	4	0	80.1	104	372	62	59	7	2	9	4	29	0	42	5	2
Cedeno, Blas, Nash.	0	1	.000	6.35	6	0	0	0	1	0	5.2	8	26	5	4	0	0	2	1	0	0	4	0	0
Chacon, Shawn, C.S.	2	0	1.000	4.79	4	4	0	0	0	0	20.2	23	93	12	11	3	1	1	2	10	0	15	0	1
Chavez, Anthony, Tuc.	2	2	.500	6.67	21	0	0	0	4	1	29.2	42	149	24	22	3	1	2	2	17	3	24	2	1
Chiasson, Scott, Iowa	1	4	.200	7.94	27	0	0	0	17	7	28.1	34	132	26	25	9	1	3	3	13	1	26	2	1
Chouinard, Bobby, C.S.	1	0	1.000	4.35	9	0	0	0	0	0	10.1	13	48	5	5	2	1	0	0	5	2	5	1	0
Christman, Tim, Cal.*	2	1	.667	7.07	11	0	0	0	5	0	14	16	69	11	11	1	0	0	1	9	0	11	1	0
Cloude, Ken, Tac.	9	4	.692	2.33	15	15	3	0	0	0	92.2	73	360	24	24	9	2	2	2	20	0	52	1	0
Condrey, Clay, Port.	10	4	.714	3.50	25	23	0	0	0	0	133.2	128	552	55	52	12	6	3	5	40	1	73	2	3
Coogan, Patrick, Mem.	1	4	.200	7.53	7	6	0	0	0	0	28.2	36	133	26	24	11	0	0	0	14	0	29	1	0
Cook, Aaron, C.S.	4	4	.500	3.78	10	10	1	0	0	0	64.1	67	275	40	27	6	0	3	18	0	32	7	1
Coppinger, Rocky, Sac.	0	0	.000	6.75	2	2	0	0	0	0	8	3	39	7	6	0	0	0	0	13	0	5	2	0
Cordero, Francisco, Okla.	0	2	.000	5.84	11	1	0	0	8	2	12.1	15	62	14	8	2	0	0	1	7	1	21	2	0
Corey, Bryan, L.V.	5	4	.556	4.36	37	0	0	0	10	1	53.2	79	251	31	26	5	3	1	2	18	1	33	0	0
Cortes, David, Tuc.	0	0	.000	0.00	3	0	0	0	3	0	4	3	16	0	0	0	0	0	0	0	0	1	0	0
Crabtree, Robbie, Fres.	1	4	.200	7.91	24	0	0	0	9	0	33	38	157	31	29	3	7	2	6	14	3	22	1	0
Crowell, Kyle, Sac.	1	0	1.000	4.50	5	0	0	0	3	0	14	17	63	7	7	2	1	0	0	4	0	9	0	0
Crudale, Mike, Mem.	1	0	1.000	1.84	13	0	0	0	13	7	14.2	10	57	3	3	1	0	0	5	1	16	2	0
Cruz, Nelson, N.O.	0	1	.000	4.50	6	0	0	0	2	1	8	4	31	4	4	2	0	0	4	0	8	0	0
Cummings, Ryan, S.L.	3	2	.600	3.80	22	0	0	0	7	0	23.2	24	98	11	10	2	1	0	1	6	0	13	2	0
Cunnane, Will, Iowa	4	1	.800	2.20	43	0	0	0	7	2	73.2	67	301	23	18	3	1	1	2	23	3	69	1	0
Cyr, Eric, Port.*	0	0	.000	3.14	9	2	0	0	2	0	14.1	14	69	6	5	0	0	0	2	10	0	11	3	0
Davey, Tom, Port.	2	1	.667	1.69	22	0	0	0	10	4	32	16	125	12	6	1	1	1	4	12	2	23	1	0
Davis, Doug, Okla.*	4	3	.571	4.99	9	9	0	0	0	0	61.1	70	257	38	34	7	1	1	3	11	0	48	0	0
DeHart, Rick, Oma.*	1	0	1.000	3.90	49	0	0	0	13	1	57.2	55	250	25	25	4	1	1	4	21	2	46	1	1
Delgado, Oscar, Tac.*	1	1	.500	8.49	3	3	0	0	0	0	11.2	14	52	11	11	3	1	1	0	6	0	8	0	1
Deschenes, Marc, Iowa	0	1	.000	7.20	4	0	0	0	3	0	5	5	23	4	4	1	1	0	0	4	0	3	1	0
Devey, Phil, L.V.*	2	4	.333	5.83	26	10	0	0	2	0	75.2	115	355	54	49	8	2	1	4	29	0	34	3	0
Dewitt, Matt, Port.	1	0	1.000	1.00	2	2	0	0	0	0	9	5	34	1	1	1	1	0	1	2	0	7	0	0
Dickey, R.A., Okla.	8	7	.533	4.09	37	19	1	0	8	0	154	176	664	81	70	8	7	9	4	47	5	109	5	0
Dillinger, John, S.L.	3	0	1.000	6.64	8	6	0	0	0	0	42	56	189	33	31	8	0	4	5	7	0	26	2	1
Donnelly, Brendan, S.L.	4	0	1.000	3.48	25	0	0	0	17	6	33.2	27	142	13	13	5	1	1	2	11	0	42	2	1
Dougherty, Jim, Nash.	2	3	.400	4.63	33	0	0	0	16	4	44.2	40	188	23	23	5	2	2	1	17	2	36	1	1
Duchscherer, Justin, Sac.	2	4	.333	5.57	14	11	0	0	0	0	63	73	279	45	39	7	0	2	2	17	0	52	1	0
Duff, Matt, Mem.	0	0	.000	1.93	4	0	0	0	1	1	4.2	2	19	1	1	1	0	0	0	4	0	3	0	0
Duncan, Courtney, Iowa	3	5	.375	3.99	55	0	0	0	22	6	67.2	67	295	35	30	6	3	3	0	33	1	64	6	0
Durbin, Chad, Oma.	0	1	.000	10.80	1	1	0	0	0	0	1.2	4	9	2	2	0	0	0	0	2	0	2	0	0
Eaton, Adam, Port.	1	1	.500	2.92	2	2	0	0	0	0	12.1	9	50	9	4	3	0	1	1	3	0	6	0	0
Ellis, Robert, L.V.	9	7	.563	4.17	29	28	1	0	0	0	172.2	195	753	100	80	17	12	4	13	37	0	110	12	2
Emanuel, Brandon, S.L.	2	3	.400	7.25	7	7	0	0	0	0	36	59	173	29	29	1	3	1	1	10	0	27	1	0
Enochs, Chris, Sac.	2	1	.667	4.71	6	5	0	0	0	0	28.2	34	134	16	15	2	1	3	4	13	0	22	5	0
Espada, Joe, Oma.	0	0	.000	0.00	1	0	0	0	1	0	1	1	3	0	0	0	0	0	0	0	0	0	0	0
Esslinger, Cam, C.S.	0	0	.000	6.19	29	0	0	0	11	0	32	30	148	27	22	2	0	3	5	17	0	23	10	0
Estrada, Horacio, Tuc.*	8	7	.533	3.90	29	25	2	0	1	1	163.2	167	682	75	71	21	4	6	9	40	0	107	3	0
Estrella, Leo, Iowa	0	0	.000	5.91	8	0	0	0	4	1	10.2	10	51	8	7	0	0	1	1	7	0	9	1	0
Estrella, Luis, Fres.	7	13	.350	4.43	38	20	0	0	13	7	144.1	168	636	77	71	16	4	4	4	64	1	98	11	0
Falkenborg, Brian, Tac.	4	4	.500	2.74	9	9	0	0	0	0	49.1	51	207	22	15	3	0	2	1	13	0	42	0	0
Falteisek, Steve, L.V.	0	2	.000	10.69	13	0	0	0	4	0	16	21	77	20	19	4	0	1	1	7	0	12	1	0
Farnsworth, Kyle, Iowa	0	1	.000	6.00	2	2	0	0	0	0	3	3	11	2	2	1	0	0	0	0	0	2	0	0
Fernandez, Osvaldo, Fres.	4	4	.500	4.70	10	9	0	0	0	0	59.1	64	251	33	31	4	2	4	3	15	0	37	2	0
Field, Nathan, Oma.	0	1	.000	3.31	18	0	0	0	17	7	16.1	22	81	10	6	0	0	0	8	0	13	0	0
Fiore, Tony, Edm.	2	0	1.000	4.15	2	2	0	0	0	0	13	15	53	6	6	2	0	0	0	2	0	6	0	0
Fitzgerald, Brian, Tac.-C.S.*	3	4	.429	5.34	36	0	0	0	13	2	57.1	65	259	40	34	5	1	3	0	26	1	41	0	1
Flores, Randy, Okla.-C.S.*	3	4	.429	5.18	22	7	0	0	6	1	56	58	245	28	26	2	1	2	3	23	1	43	1	0
Florie, Bryce, Sac.	4	6	.400	5.08	18	16	0	0	2	0	83.1	90	381	55	47	11	0	2	8	38	0	69	9	1
Foppert, Jesse, Fres.	3	6	.333	3.99	14	14	0	0	0	0	79	71	337	37	35	12	3	5	3	35	0	109	7	1
Ford, Ben, Iowa	6	11	.353	4.88	32	23	0	0	1	0	142	157	650	95	77	13	5	5	15	73	1	84	12	0
Franklin, Wayne, N.O.*	13	9	.591	3.12	29	27	1	0	1	0	179	153	733	68	62	14	5	8	11	59	2	141	2	1
Frederick, Kevin, Edm.	3	6	.333	4.58	46	2	0	0	38	22	55	63	246	31	28	8	1	4	2	21	1	47	4	0
Fuentes, Brian, C.S.*	3	3	.500	3.70	41	0	0	0	5	1	48.2	44	224	25	20	0	4	5	4	32	1	61	3	2
Fultz, Aaron, Fres.*	1	3	.250	3.18	17	0	0	0	14	4	22.2	18	95	8	8	1	2	1	0	11	2	22	0	0
Fussell, Chris, Oma.	12	6	.667	4.43	28	27	0	0	1	0	164.2	165	711	97	81	22	1	4	8	71	0	103	3	0
Fyhrie, Mike, Sac.	7	2	.778	2.33	13	13	0	0	0	0	77.1	61	317	22	20	4	1	1	5	23	0	68	0	1
Garcia, Reynaldo, Okla.	2	2	.500	2.84	25	0	0	0	10	4	31.2	23	135	12	10	2	1	2	2	14	1	33	2	0
George, Chris, Oma.*	6	12	.333	5.87	22	21	0	0	0	0	127.1	145	580	86	83	15	3	2	3	65	0	94	7	0
Gilfillan, Jason, Oma.	2	2	.500	3.69	33	0	0	0	24	4	39	32	158	16	16	5	1	2	3	14	0	28	1	0
Gissell, Chris, Iowa	8	12	.400	6.12	28	27	2	0	0	0	154.1	177	699	108	105	19	6	6	15	61	3	133	1	1
Glynn, Ryan, Cal.	5	5	.500	6.00	14	14	0	0	0	0	78	102	360	58	52	7	1	2	3	27	0	48	1	0
Gomes, Wayne, Nash.	0	2	.000	15.43	6	1	0	0	0	0	9.1	21	57	16	16	1	1	1	0	12	1	7	5	0
Gonzalez, Alfredo, L.V.	2	3	.400	2.91	14	0	0	0	7	1	21.2	23	96	10	7	1	3	0	2	9	0	23	2	0

Pitcher, Team	W	L	Pct.	ERA	G	GS	CG	ShO	GF	Sv.	IP	H	TBF	R	ER	HR	SH	SF	HB	BB	IBB	SO	WP	Bk.
Gonzalez, Jeremi, Okla.	6	5	.545	3.33	46	5	0	0	31	14	92	86	400	40	34	8	4	3	8	39	5	93	1	2
Gordon, Tom, Iowa	0	0	.000	16.20	2	0	0	0	1	1	1.2	1	9	4	3	0	0	0	0	3	0	0	0	0
Graham, Tom, Okla	0	0	.000	0.00	2	0	0	0	2	0	1.1	0	4	0	0	0	0	0	0	0	0	3	0	0
Gray, Mike, Tuc.*	0	0	.000	8.44	6	0	0	0	1	0	10.2	19	54	11	10	1	1	1	0	3	0	8	0	0
Gregg, Kevin, Sac.	2	5	.286	7.52	16	8	0	0	2	0	58.2	82	280	56	49	7	0	4	6	23	0	45	3	1
Grilli, Jason, Cal.	0	1	.000	1.59	1	1	0	0	0	0	5.2	3	22	1	1	0	0	0	0	3	0	8	0	0
Guerra, Mark, N.O.	6	11	.353	4.01	28	28	1	1	0	0	173	183	723	88	77	16	5	3	13	35	1	89	1	0
Guerrier, Matt, Nash.	7	12	.368	4.59	27	26	2	1	0	0	157	154	676	88	80	20	7	4	10	47	3	130	7	0
Gulin, Lindsay, L.V.*	5	2	.714	4.98	14	14	0	0	0	0	68.2	80	307	42	38	9	4	1	3	26	1	70	2	0
Halama, John, Tac.*	0	1	.000	6.14	2	2	0	0	0	0	14.2	19	62	11	10	0	1	0	1	1	1	9	1	0
Harang, Aaron, Sac.	3	3	.500	3.26	8	8	0	0	0	0	38.2	41	165	17	14	1	0	2	9	0	39	2	0	0
Harville, Chad, Sac.	1	2	.333	5.40	24	0	0	0	15	5	30	32	133	19	18	5	0	2	1	13	1	26	2	0
Hazlett, Andy, Port.*	0	1	.000	7.12	13	4	0	0	2	0	30.1	36	141	29	24	8	1	2	5	11	0	24	1	0
Heams, Shane, C.S.	0	1	.000	18.90	9	1	0	0	1	0	10	14	67	23	21	3	1	0	2	23	0	7	4	0
Heiserman, Rick, Mem.	1	1	.500	4.93	22	0	0	0	6	1	38.1	42	166	21	21	12	1	0	3	10	0	15	0	0
Helling, Rick, Tuc.	1	0	1.000	1.29	1	1	0	0	0	0	7	4	25	1	1	0	0	0	0	1	0	7	0	0
Hensley, Matt, S.L.	7	5	.583	4.97	19	18	1	0	1	0	117.2	132	511	76	65	16	3	2	8	39	0	106	5	2
Herbert, John, Port.	0	0	.000	27.00	1	0	0	0	1	0	1	2	6	3	3	0	0	1	0	1	0	0	0	0
Hernandez, Carlos, N.O.*	0	0	.000	0.00	1	1	0	0	0	0	3	1	11	0	0	0	0	0	0	1	0	2	0	0
Hernandez, Roberto, Oma.	0	0	.000	0.00	2	0	0	0	1	0	2	0	10	1	0	0	0	0	0	3	0	3	1	0
Herndon, Junior, Port.	7	13	.350	5.26	28	27	2	2	0	0	159	172	693	98	93	28	4	4	10	52	2	59	9	0
Hiljus, Erik, Sac.	1	3	.250	7.65	9	6	0	0	0	0	37.2	54	177	32	32	3	1	2	1	15	0	30	2	0
Holt, Chris, C.S.	6	3	.667	3.71	12	11	2	0	1	1	70.1	68	299	34	29	9	3	3	7	16	0	53	2	1
Holtz, Mike, Port.*	0	0	.000	4.26	7	0	0	0	1	0	6.1	3	26	3	3	0	0	0	1	3	0	3	0	0
Holzemer, Mark, Tuc.*	2	3	.400	5.29	51	0	0	0	13	2	34	36	155	23	20	4	3	3	2	20	2	33	3	1
Horgan, Joe, Fres.*	2	2	.500	5.93	27	4	0	0	6	0	57.2	65	258	38	38	8	4	2	4	21	0	37	5	0
House, Craig, L.V.	0	0	.000	7.40	19	0	0	0	4	0	20.2	25	105	19	17	3	2	0	3	16	0	25	2	1
Howard, Ben, Port.	0	4	.000	6.20	11	7	0	0	2	0	45	47	195	34	31	10	1	0	2	15	0	25	3	0
Hundley, Jeff, S.L.*	0	1	.000	9.28	4	2	0	0	1	0	10.2	16	57	13	11	2	0	0	2	7	0	8	1	0
Hunter, Johnny, Port.	0	1	.000	7.27	12	3	0	0	5	1	26	26	121	22	21	4	1	2	2	16	0	17	3	0
Hurtado, Edwin, Oma.	4	4	.500	4.50	11	10	0	0	1	0	60	69	270	36	30	5	3	2	3	19	1	46	0	0
Hutchison, Wesley, Fres.	1	4	.200	7.08	17	4	0	0	6	0	34.1	43	162	28	27	8	2	1	3	11	2	27	3	0
Izquierdo, Hansel, Cal.	4	5	.444	5.32	13	13	0	0	0	0	71	90	323	55	42	11	3	4	2	23	0	36	2	1
Jacome, Jason, Mem.*	8	6	.571	4.09	28	12	0	0	2	1	105.2	114	443	55	48	14	1	2	2	23	0	69	3	1
James, Mike, C.S.	1	1	.500	8.13	24	0	0	0	7	1	31	38	146	31	28	5	2	0	2	16	0	25	3	0
Janzen, Marty, S.L.	2	2	.500	4.40	11	6	0	0	2	0	28.2	34	121	17	14	5	1	0	3	9	0	16	2	0
Jarvis, Matt, Tac.-Fres.*	5	4	.556	3.34	43	0	0	0	10	3	56.2	57	240	25	21	4	2	1	2	20	1	49	2	1
Jerzembeck, Mike, Edm.	1	2	.333	11.70	3	2	0	0	0	0	10	16	47	14	13	2	1	1	0	4	0	6	0	0
Johnson, Adam, Edm.	13	8	.619	5.47	27	27	1	1	0	0	151.1	182	676	96	92	25	3	9	11	55	0	112	5	2
Johnson, Jonathan, Tuc.-Port.	0	3	.000	7.04	26	5	0	0	6	1	55	62	238	46	43	8	2	4	1	16	0	44	2	0
Johnson, Keith, S.L.	0	0	.000	0.00	1	0	0	0	1	0	0.2	1	3	0	0	0	0	0	0	0	0	0	0	0
Johnson, Mike, L.V.	2	1	.667	4.09	8	8	0	0	0	0	44	54	201	24	20	6	2	5	3	18	0	35	4	0
Jones, Greg, S.L.	7	4	.636	4.31	39	0	0	0	9	2	62.2	68	274	35	30	5	0	2	1	22	0	55	3	0
Joseph, Kevin, Mem.	1	1	.500	1.77	31	0	0	0	9	2	35.2	27	150	10	7	2	0	2	1	11	0	14	2	0
Journell, Jimmy, Mem.	2	4	.333	3.68	7	7	0	0	0	0	36.2	38	166	16	15	3	1	1	2	18	0	32	3	0
Judd, Mike, Cal.	8	6	.571	5.24	23	23	0	0	0	0	125.1	137	559	80	73	11	9	4	8	51	1	100	3	0
Karnuth, Jason, Mem.	0	0	.000	0.00	1	0	0	0	1	0	1	1	4	0	0	0	0	0	0	0	0	0	0	0
Kaye, Justin, Tac.	3	7	.300	4.04	47	0	0	0	31	6	62.1	54	284	32	28	2	9	5	3	42	1	65	14	0
Kelley, Rich, S.L.*	6	5	.545	4.08	40	15	1	0	7	0	119	128	514	64	54	15	4	1	6	40	1	72	5	2
Kershner, Jason, Port.*	7	2	.778	3.03	31	12	0	0	3	0	86	65	339	30	29	8	3	0	1	26	0	83	2	0
Ketchner, Ryan, Tac.*	0	1	.000	4.76	1	1	0	0	0	0	5.2	9	26	3	3	0	0	1	0	0	0	6	0	0
Kinney, Matt, Edm.	2	1	.667	8.89	5	5	0	0	0	0	27.1	42	125	27	27	9	1	0	0	4	0	21	0	0
Knott, Eric, Tuc.*	8	10	.444	4.86	31	23	1	1	2	1	150	188	650	91	81	12	6	6	1	23	1	96	2	0
Knotts, Gary, Cal.	5	3	.625	4.25	42	0	0	0	14	3	53	53	236	29	25	4	2	0	5	32	2	44	7	0
Kolb, Brandon, Iowa	0	1	.000	6.75	13	0	0	0	2	0	17.1	20	81	17	13	1	1	0	1	10	1	14	2	0
Koplove, Mike, Tuc.	1	2	.333	1.17	23	0	0	0	14	3	30.2	21	115	5	4	1	0	2	2	4	0	31	3	0
Lackey, John, S.L.	8	2	.800	2.57	16	16	2	1	0	0	101.2	89	412	35	29	5	2	1	2	28	0	82	5	2
Lail, Denny, Mem.	1	3	.250	4.57	10	8	0	0	2	0	41.1	42	191	23	21	3	0	1	2	26	0	23	3	0
Lankford, Frank, Sac.	6	6	.500	4.59	46	0	0	0	10	0	80.1	91	348	43	41	9	6	2	4	22	2	56	7	1
Laxton, Brett, Oma.	9	13	.409	4.94	29	28	1	0	1	0	156.2	182	693	97	86	13	8	12	7	49	1	104	4	1
Lee, Dave, Edm.	9	1	.900	4.59	51	0	0	0	30	5	64.2	80	303	44	33	5	0	2	31	3	70	5	0
Levine, Alan, S.L.	0	0	.000	3.00	2	0	0	0	0	0	3	5	13	1	1	0	0	0	0	0	0	4	0	0
Levrault, Allen, Sac.	7	8	.467	6.39	24	23	0	0	0	0	111.1	145	526	91	79	15	0	11	9	45	0	81	4	3
Lewis, Colby, Okla.	5	6	.455	3.63	20	20	0	0	0	0	106.2	100	448	49	43	4	1	4	7	28	0	99	5	0
Lidge, Brad, N.O.	5	5	.500	3.39	24	19	0	0	1	0	111.2	83	459	47	42	9	1	2	7	47	0	110	5	1
Lidle, Cory, Sac.	0	0	.000	2.25	1	1	0	0	0	0	4	2	16	1	1	0	0	0	0	3	0	3	0	0
Lincoln, Mike, N.O.	0	0	.000	1.23	10	0	0	0	7	2	14.2	14	61	2	2	0	0	0	0	2	0	15	1	0
Linebrink, Scott, N.O.	1	1	.500	6.00	13	0	0	0	3	0	15	17	71	11	10	1	1	0	1	11	3	16	2	0
Looney, Brian, Nash.*	0	1	.000	6.14	6	3	0	0	0	0	14.2	15	65	10	10	3	0	0	2	7	1	5	0	0
Lopez, Aquilino, Tac.	4	4	.500	2.39	34	11	0	0	10	5	109.1	89	438	33	29	6	3	4	2	27	2	103	4	4
Lopez, Mickey, Iowa	0	0	.000	0.00	2	0	0	0	2	0	2	3	7	0	0	0	0	0	0	1	0	0	0	0
Lowe, Sean, Nash.	1	1	.500	5.73	5	5	0	0	0	0	22	29	96	14	14	0	0	2	0	3	0	21	0	0
Luebbers, Larry, Sac.	11	11	.500	4.91	28	28	0	0	0	0	168.2	201	745	108	92	17	1	6	8	55	0	80	16	0
Lukasiewicz, Mark, S.L.*	3	2	.600	3.98	35	0	0	0	9	0	43	46	193	26	19	6	3	2	5	17	0	48	2	0
Lundberg, Spike, Okla.	3	4	.429	5.86	13	7	0	0	4	0	58.1	75	262	41	38	9	0	3	0	18	1	34	4	1
Lundquist, Dave, Port.	1	4	.200	5.63	30	0	0	0	29	21	32	28	138	21	20	6	2	2	0	15	1	31	0	0
MacDougal, Mike, Oma.	3	5	.375	5.60	12	10	0	0	0	0	53	52	260	42	33	4	1	3	5	55	0	30	15	0
Magnante, Mike, L.V.*	1	0	1.000	3.00	7	0	0	0	1	0	6	5	27	3	2	1	0	1	0	2	0	4	0	0
Mahay, Ron, Iowa*	0	1	.000	1.93	39	1	0	0	13	2	46.2	32	186	11	10	3	2	0	0	15	1	50	4	0
Mahomes, Pat, Iowa	4	5	.444	3.48	44	5	0	0	34	14	72.1	57	291	30	28	11	3	2	0	20	1	70	1	1
Mairena, Ozwaldo, Cal.*	3	0	1.000	4.97	25	0	0	0	8	1	29	39	139	20	16	2	1	1	1	13	0	19	1	0
Mann, Jim, N.O.	0	3	.000	4.15	33	0	0	0	28	22	34.2	33	142	20	16	6	2	1	1	8	1	29	3	0

Pitcher, Team	W	L	Pct.	ERA	G	GS	CG	ShO	GF	Sv.	IP	H	TBF	R	ER	HR	SH	SF	HB	BB	IBB	SO	WP	Bk.
Mantei, Matt, Tuc.	1	0	1.000	0.00	9	1	0	0	2	0	10	8	44	1	0	0	1	0	1	4	0	9	1	0
Manzanillo, Josias, Nash.	1	0	1.000	2.66	15	1	0	0	4	1	20.1	18	79	6	6	3	0	0	0	2	1	14	1	1
Martin, Chandler, C.S.	1	4	.200	7.07	8	6	0	0	0	0	28	39	136	24	22	1	0	2	1	21	2	14	0	0
Martinez, Gustavo, Tac.	0	1	.000	5.40	1	1	0	0	0	0	5	8	25	4	3	0	0	1	3	0	3	1	1
Mateo, Julio, Tac.	4	2	.667	4.06	20	0	0	0	16	6	31	39	137	15	14	2	1	2	4	7	1	23	2	0
Mathews, T.J., N.O.-Mem.	0	0	.000	3.00	8	0	0	0	2	0	9	6	37	3	3	1	0	0	3	0	6	1	0
Matos, Josue, Tac.	4	7	.364	5.92	25	25	1	0	0	0	135.1	166	606	96	89	25	2	9	8	35	0	95	6	0
May, Darrell, Oma.*	1	0	1.000	0.75	2	2	0	0	0	0	12	8	41	1	1	0	0	1	0	0	0	9	0	0
Mayo, Blake, Tuc.	1	4	.200	6.89	8	8	0	0	0	0	32.2	44	165	27	25	3	4	3	2	20	0	21	2	0
McClaskey, Tim, Sac.	0	0	.000	5.87	2	0	0	0	2	0	7.2	9	34	5	5	1	0	0	0	2	0	4	0	0
McKay, Cody, Sac.	0	0	.000	0.00	3	0	0	0	3	0	2.2	4	12	0	0	0	0	0	0	0	0	2	0	0
McKnight, Tony, Nash.	11	14	.440	5.24	30	28	1	1	0	0	175.1	198	747	108	102	22	5	4	4	45	1	120	6	0
Meadows, Brian, Nash.	9	8	.529	4.27	23	22	1	1	0	0	126.1	132	530	69	60	15	3	2	5	26	1	98	2	0
Mendoza, Mario, S.L.	0	1	.000	10.29	3	0	0	0	2	1	7	13	38	11	8	2	0	1	0	4	0	7	1	0
Mercker, Kent, C.S.*	0	0	.000	21.60	2	0	0	0	0	0	1.2	3	10	4	4	2	0	1	0	2	0	0	0	0
Meyer, Jake, Tac.	0	1	.000	13.50	2	0	0	0	0	0	2.2	4	15	4	4	0	0	0	0	5	0	2	0	0
Miadich, Bart, S.L.	4	3	.571	3.68	59	0	0	0	42	14	80.2	60	370	43	33	5	1	2	3	64	2	92	12	0
Michalak, Chris, Okla.*	0	0	.000	0.00	1	0	0	0	0	0	1	0	3	0	0	0	0	0	0	0	0	1	0	0
Middlebrook, Jason, Port.	2	5	.286	5.65	10	7	0	0	1	0	36.2	42	166	27	23	6	2	0	0	13	0	32	0	0
Miller, Matt, Sac.	3	7	.300	4.31	54	0	0	0	39	6	71	81	322	42	34	5	4	2	5	28	8	63	3	0
Miller, Travis, Edm.-Iowa*	4	0	1.000	4.61	33	0	0	0	8	1	41	48	175	23	21	4	1	5	0	10	1	32	4	0
Miller, Wade, N.O.	0	0	.000	2.25	2	2	0	0	0	0	8	10	34	4	2	0	0	1	1	1	0	9	0	0
Mlicki, Dave, N.O.	0	0	.000	0.00	1	1	0	0	0	0	3	2	11	0	0	0	0	0	0	1	0	2	0	0
Molina, Gabe, Mem.	5	4	.556	2.15	56	0	0	0	31	12	71	59	293	21	17	7	1	1	3	24	1	54	1	0
Morgan, Mike, Tuc.	0	0	.000	0.00	2	0	0	0	0	0	3	3	12	1	0	0	1	0	0	0	0	2	0	0
Mota, Guillermo, L.V.	1	3	.250	2.95	20	0	0	0	6	1	36.2	34	145	13	12	1	3	1	2	8	1	38	3	1
Mounce, Tony, Okla.*	0	1	.000	9.00	2	1	0	0	0	0	5	10	23	5	5	1	0	0	0	1	0	2	0	0
Mullen, Scott, Oma.*	1	2	.333	2.61	19	1	0	0	6	0	31	32	130	12	9	0	3	1	0	9	3	21	0	0
Munoz, Bobby, C.S.	1	4	.200	8.46	15	6	0	0	2	0	44.2	69	223	48	42	7	1	6	5	25	0	42	2	0
Munro, Pete, N.O.	7	1	.875	2.39	19	13	1	1	3	0	94.1	68	367	30	25	3	2	1	9	15	1	73	2	0
Murray, Dan, Okla.	5	7	.417	6.24	39	12	0	0	7	2	109.2	132	514	96	76	14	4	4	10	51	0	53	15	0
Myers, Rodney, Port.	5	2	.714	3.70	42	0	0	0	17	4	48.2	48	203	23	20	2	2	1	2	13	1	35	1	1
Myette, Aaron, Okla.	7	4	.636	3.14	16	16	2	1	0	0	106	86	444	41	37	5	1	5	7	44	0	106	7	0
Nakamura, Micheal, Edm.	4	3	.571	4.74	46	4	0	0	7	3	87.1	85	368	51	46	7	0	5	6	22	0	80	7	1
Nance, Shane, L.V.*	11	3	.786	4.17	37	0	0	0	10	1	58.1	58	255	32	27	5	2	2	2	26	1	53	1	0
Nathan, Joe, Fres.	6	12	.333	5.60	31	25	1	0	0	0	146.1	167	697	91	91	20	2	4	3	74	0	117	9	0
Neal, Blaine, Cal.	3	1	.750	2.90	29	0	0	0	25	11	31	27	134	11	10	2	0	1	2	15	1	26	1	0
Nichting, Chris, C.S.	1	4	.200	10.19	23	0	0	0	7	1	32.2	53	171	40	37	7	2	2	1	22	1	23	3	0
Nickle, Doug, Mem.	3	1	.750	4.60	14	0	0	0	7	3	15.2	13	66	8	8	3	0	0	1	7	0	10	1	0
Nina, Elvin, S.L.	5	9	.357	4.64	26	15	0	0	1	0	108.2	115	484	75	56	15	2	4	8	50	1	68	4	0
Nitkowski, C.J., N.O.-Mem.*	2	4	.333	5.54	40	1	0	0	14	2	37.1	45	177	25	23	4	2	0	4	16	1	32	2	1
Nitkowski, C.J., Okla.*	1	1	.500	1.80	9	0	0	0	3	0	10	8	43	3	2	0	0	1	4	0	11	0	0
O'Connor, Brian, Nash.*	0	1	.000	5.40	4	0	0	0	1	0	5	7	28	3	3	0	0	0	6	1	4	0	0
Ohme, Kevin, Mem.*	4	3	.571	4.52	56	5	0	0	19	2	87.2	103	376	44	44	10	6	4	7	21	1	56	2	0
Oliver, Darren, Mem.*	2	0	1.000	7.88	5	5	0	0	0	0	16	17	78	16	14	1	3	1	0	17	0	9	2	0
Olsen, Kevin, Cal.	2	5	.286	3.86	8	8	1	1	0	0	49	45	201	22	21	6	1	1	1	14	0	25	0	0
Oropesa, Eddie, Tuc.*	1	0	1.000	3.86	29	0	0	0	5	0	25.2	23	111	11	11	2	2	0	1	13	2	26	1	0
Palki, Jeromy, Edm.	3	3	.500	4.15	26	0	0	0	6	5	43.1	51	193	21	20	4	2	1	0	16	0	48	2	0
Palma, Rick, Iowa*	0	0	.000	6.00	2	0	0	0	0	0	3	3	12	2	2	1	1	0	0	1	1	2	0	0
Park, Chan Ho, Okla.	0	1	.000	27.00	1	1	0	0	0	0	3	9	21	9	9	0	0	0	0	3	0	3	1	0
Parra, Jose, Tuc.	0	0	.000	0.00	7	0	0	0	3	1	9.1	3	36	0	0	0	2	2	0	10	0	9	0	0
Patterson, John, Tuc.	10	5	.667	4.23	19	18	0	0	0	0	112.2	117	496	59	53	14	3	3	4	45	1	104	6	0
Pearce, Josh, Mem.	0	4	.000	7.65	4	4	0	0	0	0	20	28	91	18	17	8	1	0	3	0	17	1	0
Pearsall, J.J., Cal.*	1	0	1.000	7.43	9	0	0	0	5	0	13.1	15	64	11	11	2	0	1	6	1	14	2	0
Pearson, Jason, Port.-Fres.*	3	0	1.000	2.73	57	0	0	0	13	0	66	60	280	25	20	8	2	1	4	25	1	46	3	0
Pelaez, Alex, Port.	0	0	.000	0.00	1	0	0	0	0	0	1	1	4	0	0	0	0	0	0	0	0	0	0	0
Pena, Jesus, Okla.*	1	6	.143	7.26	29	5	0	0	9	2	57	73	284	48	46	7	1	1	2	45	0	57	5	0
Pena, Juan, Sac.*	0	0	.000	6.10	3	1	0	0	2	0	10.1	11	49	7	7	2	0	1	0	9	0	7	2	0
Phelps, Tommy, Cal.*	4	2	.667	3.15	51	0	0	0	10	2	74.1	76	314	27	26	8	4	1	2	21	3	62	3	0
Pichardo, Hipolito, N.O.	0	0	.000	0.00	5	1	0	0	3	0	6.2	6	24	0	0	0	0	1	0	4	0	0	0
Pickford, Kevin, Port.*	4	7	.364	5.94	20	12	1	0	2	1	69.2	79	313	50	46	5	2	5	3	31	1	40	3	0
Pine, Chris, S.L.	1	6	.143	5.44	19	6	0	0	4	0	41.2	56	198	30	25	5	2	0	3	23	0	21	5	1
Pote, Lou, S.L.	2	1	.667	6.00	7	7	0	0	0	0	39	42	170	29	26	3	0	2	1	10	0	43	4	0
Powell, Jay, Okla.	2	0	1.000	12.38	8	0	0	0	0	0	8	14	43	11	11	2	0	0	1	3	1	8	0	0
Prinz, Bret, Tuc.	1	0	1.000	2.97	37	0	0	0	32	18	39.1	42	165	14	13	4	0	0	0	9	1	34	3	0
Prior, Mark, Iowa	1	1	.500	1.65	3	3	0	0	0	0	16.1	13	75	10	3	1	1	1	8	0	24	0	1
Puffer, Brandon, N.O.	2	1	.667	1.80	11	0	0	0	4	0	15	8	57	3	3	1	0	0	2	4	0	13	1	0
Putz, J.J., Tac.	2	4	.333	3.83	9	9	0	0	0	0	54	51	225	23	23	4	1	1	4	21	0	39	8	0
Radinsky, Scott, Cal.*	0	3	.000	6.86	18	0	0	0	9	1	21	27	105	18	16	6	2	1	0	13	3	13	0	2
Ramirez, Erasmo, Okla.*	4	1	.800	1.29	25	0	0	0	7	1	21	15	83	5	3	0	0	1	1	4	1	17	1	0
Ramirez, Santiago, N.O.	2	0	1.000	3.38	18	0	0	0	5	1	21.1	17	91	8	8	2	0	0	3	11	0	15	3	1
Ramos, Mario, Okla.*	3	8	.273	7.40	34	19	0	0	2	0	121.2	162	572	107	100	20	2	6	7	53	0	75	0	1
Randall, Scott, Edm.	12	0	1.000	3.25	19	15	2	0	1	0	105.1	110	444	47	38	6	2	5	1	24	0	54	10	0
Randolph, Steve, Tuc.*	15	7	.682	3.47	28	27	1	1	1	0	163.1	151	704	70	63	15	6	7	6	81	2	129	6	0
Ratliff, Jon, Cal.	0	1	.000	0.00	1	1	0	0	0	0	0	5	6	6	1	0	0	1	0	0	0	0
Redding, Tim, N.O.	3	3	.500	5.21	11	7	0	0	2	0	38	32	158	22	22	6	3	1	3	13	1	50	5	0
Regilio, Nick, Okla.	1	0	1.000	10.80	1	1	0	0	0	0	5	9	29	6	6	1	0	1	0	5	0	4	0	0
Reichert, Dan, Oma.	0	0	.000	5.40	5	0	0	0	1	0	5	6	24	3	3	0	0	2	1	4	1	3	0	0
Rekar, Bryan, Oma.-C.S.	7	10	.412	5.69	25	24	0	0	1	0	147	203	678	107	93	18	6	3	9	40	1	108	8	1
Reyes, Al, Nash.	3	7	.300	2.70	43	0	0	0	10	1	66.2	40	270	21	20	5	0	0	9	22	2	90	5	0
Reynoso, Armando, Tuc.	1	2	.333	5.20	6	6	0	0	0	0	27.2	29	119	16	16	2	1	2	9	0	16	1	0
Rincon, Juan, Edm.	7	4	.636	4.78	19	16	3	0	1	0	101.2	111	444	56	54	12	2	1	6	35	0	75	4	0

Pitcher, Team	W	L	Pct.	ERA	G	GS	CG	ShO	GF	Sv.	IP	H	TBF	R	ER	HR	SH	SF	HB	BB	IBB	SO	WP	Bk.
Robbins, Jake, C.S.	1	2	.333	12.00	11	0	0	0	3	0	12	17	70	18	16	3	2	1	2	13	0	15	4	0
Robertson, Jeriome, N.O.*	12	8	.600	2.55	27	27	2	1	0	0	180	160	734	59	51	13	4	4	9	45	0	114	4	0
Rocker, John, Okla.*	1	0	1.000	0.00	6	0	0	0	1	0	8.2	4	32	0	0	0	0	0	0	2	0	14	0	0
Rodgers, Bobby, Cal.	5	5	.500	5.72	25	17	0	0	4	1	94.1	105	433	62	60	17	4	2	7	54	1	67	6	2
Rodriguez, Francisco, S.L.	2	3	.400	2.57	27	0	0	0	23	6	42	30	164	13	12	1	1	0	3	13	0	59	2	0
Rodriguez, Jose, Mem.-Edm.*	2	1	.667	2.63	26	0	0	0	16	3	24	30	106	13	7	2	0	2	0	8	0	20	2	1
Rodriguez, Nerio, Mem.	3	1	.750	2.79	8	8	0	0	0	0	51.2	42	206	22	16	7	1	1	2	10	0	43	6	1
Rodriguez, Ricardo, L.V.	1	0	1.000	3.86	2	2	0	0	0	0	11.2	13	51	5	5	1	0	1	1	5	0	7	0	0
Rodriguez, Rich, Okla.*	0	0	.000	13.50	3	0	0	0	0	0	2.2	6	14	4	4	0	0	0	0	0	0	1	0	0
Saarloos, Kirk, N.O.	2	0	1.000	2.25	4	2	0	0	2	0	16	12	65	4	4	1	1	0	5	2	0	19	0	0
Sabel, Erik, Tuc.	4	5	.444	4.32	25	7	0	0	4	1	66.2	67	282	37	32	7	2	1	4	19	1	46	0	1
Saladin, Miguel, N.O.	0	0	.000	4.50	2	0	0	0	1	0	2	3	10	1	1	0	0	0	1	1	0	2	0	0
Sampson, Benj, Edm.*	1	3	.250	7.01	13	8	0	0	2	0	51.1	69	234	41	40	9	1	2	1	19	0	19	0	0
Sanchez, Duaner, Tuc.-Nash.	1	4	.200	5.14	24	0	0	0	21	7	28	29	124	16	16	3	2	2	1	12	2	29	2	0
Sanchez, Jesus, Iowa*	8	9	.471	5.90	26	24	0	0	0	0	125	144	570	90	82	27	3	6	6	65	3	94	7	0
Santana, Johan, Edm.*	5	2	.714	3.14	11	9	0	0	0	0	48.2	37	212	24	17	7	2	0	0	27	0	75	2	0
Santos, Victor, C.S.	4	9	.308	5.72	21	21	1	1	0	0	118	147	535	81	75	17	2	6	4	43	0	134	5	0
Scanlan, Bob, C.S.	2	2	.500	4.13	17	0	0	0	6	2	24	34	115	14	11	3	2	0	3	9	1	6	3	0
Scheffer, Aaron, Sac.	4	1	.800	4.82	35	1	0	0	13	1	52.1	54	236	32	28	1	3	5	5	24	1	35	5	1
Schmack, Brian, Okla.	0	4	.000	4.94	29	1	0	0	11	1	54.2	66	241	35	30	6	2	2	4	18	0	45	5	0
Schmidt, Jason, Fres.	2	0	1.000	3.00	2	2	0	0	0	0	12	11	46	4	4	0	2	0	0	2	0	12	2	0
Seanez, Rudy, Okla.	0	0	.000	4.50	4	0	0	0	1	0	4	4	15	2	2	0	0	0	0	0	0	3	0	0
Secoda, Jason, Cal.	6	3	.667	4.47	35	10	1	1	8	0	116.2	107	486	60	58	13	2	4	2	41	0	64	7	1
Sedlacek, Shawn, Oma.	3	5	.545	3.70	11	11	2	1	0	0	80.1	67	326	37	33	6	1	3	5	15	0	66	1	0
Seifert, Ryan, C.S.	1	5	.167	7.04	21	9	1	0	7	0	62.2	80	292	52	49	14	1	2	3	28	1	35	3	0
Serrano, Wascar, Tac.	1	3	.250	6.31	41	3	0	0	18	5	71.1	85	333	53	50	6	4	4	8	30	0	56	9	2
Service, Scott, Nash.	4	4	.500	3.36	47	0	0	0	24	6	61.2	47	259	25	23	8	7	1	2	24	3	70	4	0
Sessions, Doug, N.O.	0	1	.000	6.57	11	0	0	0	2	0	12.1	15	53	9	9	3	1	0	0	5	0	4	0	0
Shaffar, Ben, Nash.	1	0	1.000	3.60	1	1	0	0	0	0	5	7	25	4	2	1	0	0	0	3	0	4	0	0
Shearn, Tom, N.O.	4	6	.400	2.92	57	0	0	0	27	8	83.1	77	360	29	27	7	5	2	4	41	6	80	7	0
Sheredy, Kevin, Mem.	1	2	.333	4.75	35	0	0	0	10	2	41.2	42	192	25	22	3	1	1	5	22	0	35	2	0
Shields, Scot, S.L.	2	2	.500	3.06	28	1	0	0	5	1	47	39	185	18	16	5	0	1	3	6	0	50	3	0
Shiell, Jason, Port.	4	3	.571	2.78	56	0	0	0	22	6	74.1	62	315	26	23	6	0	1	2	29	0	74	2	1
Shouse, Brian, Oma.-N.O.*	1	0	1.000	4.24	24	0	0	0	6	0	23.1	24	99	13	11	2	0	2	1	4	0	22	0	1
Simon, Ben, L.V.	4	1	.000	5.70	23	10	0	0	2	1	72.2	84	320	49	46	12	3	4	2	28	0	47	1	0
Simontacchi, Jason, Mem.	5	1	.833	2.34	6	6	0	0	0	0	42.1	44	170	12	11	2	3	0	1	5	1	28	0	0
Sinclair, Steve, Iowa*	6	2	.750	3.91	52	1	0	0	13	1	73.2	71	321	33	32	5	3	3	4	33	2	59	3	1
Skrmetta, Matt, Oma.-L.V.	9	1	.900	3.29	47	0	0	0	7	1	68.1	62	299	30	25	6	1	6	1	36	1	64	6	0
Sloan, Brandon, Cal.	0	0	.000	12.00	2	0	0	0	1	0	3	6	15	4	4	1	0	0	0	1	0	2	0	0
Smith, Brian, Nash.	3	3	.500	3.82	33	0	0	0	25	7	37.2	37	159	18	16	2	1	0	4	11	1	24	0	0
Smith, Bud, Mem.*	3	0	1.000	2.13	6	6	0	0	0	0	38	33	158	10	9	1	0	1	2	13	0	34	0	0
Smith, Chuck, C.S.	1	0	1.000	1.02	4	4	0	0	0	0	17.2	16	75	2	2	0	0	2	9	1	18	1	2
Smith, Travis, Mem.	4	7	.364	2.31	16	13	1	0	0	0	85.2	76	341	24	22	7	4	3	1	14	1	62	2	0
Smyth, Steve, Iowa*	3	2	.600	5.81	6	6	0	0	0	0	31	35	135	21	20	4	1	2	0	10	0	25	0	0
Sneed, John, Edm.	0	0	.000	0.00	1	0	0	0	1	0	1	0	5	0	0	0	0	0	0	2	0	1	0	0
Snyder, John, Port.	7	12	.368	4.12	26	25	1	1	1	0	144.1	156	635	78	66	12	3	6	8	50	0	93	8	1
Sollecito, Gabe, Iowa-Tuc.	2	1	.667	2.95	20	0	0	0	8	0	21.1	16	91	9	7	3	1	1	2	8	0	16	0	0
Soto, Darwin, Port.	0	1	.000	0.00	2	0	0	0	2	0	1.1	0	5	0	0	0	0	0	1	0	0	1	1	0
Sparks, Steve, Mem.-Fres.	0	0	.000	11.05	5	0	0	0	3	0	7.1	6	38	9	9	1	2	0	0	9	0	5	2	0
Speier, Justin, L.V.	0	1	.000	3.86	12	0	0	0	5	2	14	20	64	7	6	2	0	0	1	3	1	14	1	0
Spencer, Stan, L.V.	1	0	1.000	.000	3	1	0	0	1	0	8.1	9	30	1	0	0	0	0	0	1	0	5	1	0
Springer, Benj, L.V.	7	8	.467	5.85	26	22	1	1	2	1	143	203	642	100	93	21	3	9	4	37	0	38	7	0
Stark, Dennis, C.S.	2	2	.333	3.82	7	7	0	0	0	0	37.2	35	163	20	16	4	1	2	4	14	0	38	0	0
Stechschulte, Gene, Mem.	1	0	1.000	1.80	10	0	0	0	10	5	10	8	43	2	2	1	0	2	2	0	7	1	0
Steenstra, Kennie, Cal.-Tuc.	2	3	.400	8.27	18	6	0	0	1	0	53.1	84	259	50	49	5	2	3	3	18	5	31	2	0
Stemle, Steve, Mem.	5	3	.636	3.65	20	11	0	0	1	0	93.2	97	396	41	38	8	3	1	4	23	1	55	5	1
Stephens, Jason, S.L.	0	4	.000	6.91	5	5	0	0	0	0	27.1	37	129	25	21	7	1	0	2	7	0	14	0	0
Stephenson, Garrett, Mem.	1	0	1.000	3.55	3	3	0	0	0	0	12.2	12	49	5	5	0	1	0	0	2	0	12	1	0
Stottlemyre, Todd, Tuc.	1	1	.500	3.45	11	0	0	0	5	1	15.2	13	66	6	6	0	0	4	1	12	0	7	1	0
Suzuki, Mac, Oma.	0	4	.000	4.53	29	1	0	0	10	0	53.2	63	237	30	27	6	4	1	1	21	2	46	4	0
Sweeney, Brian, Nash.	9	5	.643	3.80	30	23	1	1	4	2	142	157	606	67	60	16	3	1	3	28	0	113	5	0
Swindell, Greg, Tuc.*	0	0	.000	0.00	1	1	0	0	0	0	1	0	3	0	0	0	0	0	0	0	0	0	0	0
Tam, Jeff, Sac.	1	3	.250	5.59	20	0	0	0	6	2	29	31	125	20	18	2	3	2	3	5	0	26	1	0
Tankersley, Dennis, Port.	3	4	.429	3.88	9	9	0	0	0	0	51	43	223	29	22	6	2	2	1	30	0	51	2	1
Tavarez, David, Tac.	0	0	.000	9.00	1	0	0	0	1	0	1	1	4	1	1	1	0	0	0	0	0	1	0	0
Telford, Anthony, Okla.	8	2	.800	3.40	35	0	0	0	25	5	50.1	47	217	19	19	3	4	1	3	21	2	35	2	0
Teut, Nate, Cal.*	6	5	.455	5.28	27	19	0	0	3	0	116	132	530	81	68	19	5	4	8	52	2	82	12	1
Thomas, Brad, Edm.*	6	12	.333	5.74	28	27	1	0	1	0	152	175	682	112	97	20	2	8	17	54	0	97	1	2
Thomas, Juan, Tac.	0	0	.000	.000	1	0	0	0	1	0	1	0	3	0	0	0	0	0	0	0	0	0	0	0
Thompson, Eric, Sac.	0	1	.000	9.15	11	1	0	0	2	1	20.2	33	102	22	21	7	0	0	1	7	0	14	3	0
Thompson, Mark, C.S.	0	0	.000	11.00	8	1	0	0	2	1	18	33	89	27	22	7	1	0	1	3	0	12	0	0
Tolar, Kevin, Nash.*	6	1	.857	2.54	44	7	1	1	12	1	78	66	328	23	22	5	3	2	7	20	2	82	2	1
Torres, Salomon, Nash.	8	5	.615	3.83	26	24	2	1	0	0	162.1	169	686	78	69	12	6	4	11	39	2	136	3	0
Trombley, Mike, Edm.	0	1	.000	5.19	9	0	0	0	3	0	8.2	11	37	6	5	1	0	0	0	2	0	13	0	0
Trujillo, J.J., Port.	2	0	1.000	4.33	18	1	0	0	2	0	27	30	121	14	13	2	0	0	4	8	0	28	2	1
Ulloa, Enmanuel, Tac.	4	7	.364	5.96	38	2	0	0	21	2	77	91	346	61	51	13	3	3	2	29	0	41	3	0
Urban, Jeff, Fres.*	5	7	.417	3.41	35	14	0	0	7	0	103	114	446	46	39	9	5	3	2	36	0	72	2	0
Valverde, Jose, Tuc.	4	4	.333	5.85	49	0	0	0	24	5	47.2	45	214	33	31	8	3	3	5	23	1	65	4	2
Vargas, Claudio, Cal.	4	11	.267	6.72	17	16	1	0	0	0	76.1	88	349	63	57	18	6	2	4	35	0	61	3	1
Venafro, Mike, Sac.*	0	1	.000	6.97	8	0	0	0	2	0	10.1	12	46	8	8	2	1	1	2	1	0	14	0	0
Verplancke, Jeff, Fres.	3	5	.375	3.78	51	0	0	0	15	3	64.1	60	276	30	27	6	4	2	6	25	0	52	3	1
Villafuerte, Brandon, Port.	8	4	.667	2.02	47	0	0	0	19	1	58	43	234	17	13	2	3	1	0	22	1	54	2	0

Pitcher, Team	W	L	Pct.	ERA	G	GS	CG	ShO	GF	Sv.	IP	H	TBF	R	ER	HR	SH	SF	HB	BB	IBB	SO	WP	Bk.
Villano, Mike, Fres.	0	1	.000	12.00	4	0	0	0	3	1	3	3	17	4	4	0	0	1	1	4	0	2	0	0
Villarreal, Oscar, Tuc.	3	3	.500	4.36	10	10	0	0	0	0	64	68	272	33	31	8	0	1	4	22	0	40	5	2
Villegas, Ismael, Sac.	0	0	.000	8.46	10	0	0	0	6	0	22.1	32	114	28	21	7	1	1	0	15	1	12	2	0
Voyles, Brad, Oma.	3	4	.429	4.18	26	0	0	0	12	5	32.1	29	145	15	15	2	0	2	4	22	1	34	4	0
Wade, Travis, N.O.	3	6	.333	6.32	27	0	0	0	18	0	37	44	173	26	26	5	4	0	4	18	1	22	0	0
Walker, Kevin, Port.*	0	0	.000	3.00	3	0	0	0	0	0	3	1	10	1	1	0	0	0	0	0	0	4	0	0
Wall, Donne, S.L.-C.S.	1	3	.250	5.21	15	1	0	0	4	0	19	17	76	11	11	2	1	3	1	4	0	13	0	0
Walrond, Les, Mem.*	8	7	.533	4.98	28	18	0	0	2	0	123	127	538	75	68	20	3	1	1	63	2	111	8	0
Ward, Bryan, C.S.*	1	2	.333	4.97	6	6	0	0	0	0	38	37	163	22	21	4	2	0	3	15	1	26	6	0
Ward, Jeremy, Tuc.	4	6	.400	4.31	54	0	0	0	19	1	62.2	68	265	35	30	5	4	2	1	14	2	40	4	0
Watson, Mark, Iowa-Tac.*	6	0	1.000	3.42	34	0	0	0	8	3	50	45	212	24	19	3	3	1	2	22	3	33	0	0
Watson, Mark, C.S.*	0	0	.000	16.03	10	0	0	0	4	0	10.2	22	65	19	19	3	1	0	1	11	1	10	1	0
Wayne, Justin, Oma.	0	1	.000	6.35	2	2	0	0	0	0	11.1	8	48	8	8	3	0	0	1	6	0	10	0	0
Webb, Brandon, Tuc.	0	1	.000	3.86	1	1	0	0	0	0	7	5	31	3	3	0	1	0	1	4	0	5	0	0
Weibl, Clint, Mem.	5	8	.385	3.50	24	18	1	1	1	0	110.2	122	467	49	43	16	2	7	4	24	0	63	2	0
Weis, Brad, Sac.*	0	0	.000	3.86	2	0	0	0	1	0	9.1	9	37	4	4	0	0	0	2	0	6	1	0
Wells, Bob, Edm.	0	1	.000	6.75	4	2	0	0	2	1	4	5	20	3	3	1	1	0	1	2	0	1	1	0
White, Rick, C.S.-Mem.	0	1	.000	4.76	5	0	0	0	1	0	5.2	7	26	3	3	1	0	0	0	3	0	6	0	0
Whiteside, Matt, C.S.	4	7	.364	5.50	60	0	0	0	49	26	70.1	85	314	50	43	12	2	3	15	4	79	3	1
Wilkins, Marc, Iowa	0	0	.000	0.79	8	0	0	0	3	0	11.1	6	44	3	1	0	1	0	1	3	0	6	1	0
Williams, Jeff, L.V.*	6	4	.600	2.60	56	0	0	0	48	28	79.2	80	334	25	23	3	4	0	5	22	0	75	0	0
Williams, Jerome, Fres.	6	11	.353	3.59	28	28	0	0	0	0	160.2	140	671	76	64	16	8	5	9	50	1	130	5	3
Williams, Woody, Mem.	1	0	1.000	1.80	1	1	0	0	0	0	5	1	16	1	1	0	0	0	0	0	0	7	0	0
Wilson, Kris, Oma.	2	0	1.000	3.08	8	3	0	0	1	1	26.1	38	115	9	9	0	2	1	0	1	0	17	0	0
Wise, Matt, S.L.	3	4	.429	5.42	16	16	0	0	0	0	78	102	340	51	47	12	2	3	5	15	0	76	0	0
Witasick, Jay, Fres.	0	0	.000	4.50	2	2	0	0	0	0	2	1	8	1	1	0	0	0	0	1	0	2	1	0
Woodard, Steve, Mem.	2	3	.400	6.30	7	6	1	0	0	0	40	53	173	28	28	7	2	1	1	3	0	42	2	0
Woodards, Orlando, Cal.	1	0	1.000	0.00	1	0	0	0	0	0	1	2	5	0	0	0	0	0	1	1	0	0	0	0
Wooten, Greg, Tac.	4	6	.400	4.91	14	14	1	0	0	0	73.1	88	318	47	40	6	5	3	3	16	1	26	3	0
Wrigley, Jase, C.S.	0	1	.000	5.79	9	0	0	0	6	1	14	23	73	13	9	1	0	0	0	7	0	8	0	0
Wuertz, Mike, Iowa	9	5	.643	5.55	28	27	0	0	1	0	154	185	712	109	95	24	8	3	4	69	3	131	11	0
Young, Jason, C.S.	6	5	.545	4.97	13	13	0	0	0	0	79.2	87	362	52	44	10	1	0	3	38	0	74	3	0
Zambrano, Carlos, Iowa	0	0	.000	0.00	3	3	0	0	0	0	2	2	35	0	0	0	0	0	6	0	11	0	0
Zerbe, Chad, Fres.*	0	0	.000	0.00	3	3	0	0	0	0	10.1	8	42	0	0	0	1	0	1	3	0	5	0	0
Zimmerman, Jordan, Oma.*	0	0	.000	40.50	1	0	0	0	0	0	0.2	1	7	3	3	1	0	0	0	4	0	1	1	0

PITCHERS WITH TWO OR MORE TEAMS

Pitcher, Team	W	L	Pct.	ERA	G	GS	CG	ShO	GF	Sv.	IP	H	TBF	R	ER	HR	SH	SF	HB	BB	IBB	SO	WP	Bk.
Fitzgerald, Brian, Tac.*	2	3	.400	5.59	29	0	0	0	11	2	48.1	57	222	36	30	4	1	2	0	23	1	37	0	1
Fitzgerald, Brian, C.S.*	1	1	.500	4.00	7	0	0	0	2	0	9	8	37	4	4	1	0	0	0	3	0	4	0	0
Flores, Randy, Okla.*	1	1	.500	5.75	15	0	0	0	6	1	20.1	22	89	13	13	1	1	0	1	5	1	16	1	0
Flores, Randy, C.S.*	2	2	.500	3.28	7	7	0	0	0	0	35.2	36	156	15	13	1	0	2	2	18	0	27	0	0
Jarvis, Matt, Tac.*	2	2	.500	3.67	23	0	0	0	7	2	27	26	112	15	11	2	0	1	1	10	0	20	0	1
Jarvis, Matt, Fres.*	3	2	.600	3.03	20	0	0	0	3	1	29.2	31	128	10	10	2	2	0	1	10	1	29	2	0
Johnson, Jonathan, Tuc.	0	3	.000	9.41	14	5	0	0	2	0	36.1	48	167	41	38	6	0	2	1	14	0	27	1	0
Johnson, Jonathan, Port.	0	0	.000	2.41	12	0	0	0	4	1	18.2	14	71	5	5	2	2	2	0	2	0	17	1	0
Mathews, T.J., N.O.	0	0	.000	1.80	4	0	0	0	1	0	5	3	20	1	1	0	0	0	0	1	0	3	1	0
Mathews, T.J., Mem.	0	0	.000	4.50	4	0	0	0	1	0	4	3	17	2	2	1	0	0	0	2	0	3	0	0
Miller, Travis, Edm.*	0	1	.000	3.99	24	0	0	0	3	1	29.1	35	122	15	13	3	0	0	0	5	0	24	1	0
Miller, Travis, Iowa*	0	1	.000	6.17	19	0	0	0	5	0	11.2	13	53	8	8	1	1	5	0	5	1	8	3	0
Nitkowski, C.J., N.O.*	1	2	.333	2.78	24	0	0	0	7	2	22.2	21	95	7	7	1	2	0	0	7	1	20	1	1
Nitkowski, C.J., Mem.*	1	2	.333	9.82	16	1	0	0	7	0	14.2	24	82	18	16	3	0	0	4	9	0	12	1	0
Pearson, Jason, Port.*	3	0	1.000	1.50	23	0	0	0	5	0	30	25	125	5	5	3	0	0	2	9	0	18	0	0
Pearson, Jason, Fres.*	0	0	.000	3.75	34	0	0	0	8	0	36	35	155	20	15	5	2	2	1	16	1	28	3	0
Rekar, Bryan, Oma.	0	0	.000	4.50	5	4	0	0	1	0	24	30	105	16	12	4	1	0	1	5	0	20	1	0
Rekar, Bryan, C.S.	7	10	.412	5.93	20	20	0	0	0	0	123	173	573	91	81	14	5	3	8	35	1	88	7	1
Rodriguez, Jose, Mem.*	2	1	.667	3.44	22	0	0	0	14	2	18.1	26	85	13	7	2	0	2	0	7	0	14	2	1
Rodriguez, Jose, Edm.*	0	0	.000	0.00	4	0	0	0	2	1	5.2	4	21	0	0	0	0	1	0	6	0	3	1	0
Sanchez, Duaner, Tac.	1	1	.500	6.75	4	0	0	0	4	1	5.1	6	24	4	4	1	0	0	1	9	0	9	0	0
Sanchez, Duaner, Nash.	0	3	.000	4.76	20	0	0	0	17	6	22.2	23	100	12	12	2	2	1	11	2	20	2	0
Shouse, Brian, Oma.*	0	0	.000	11.57	5	0	0	0	2	0	2.1	7	16	3	3	0	0	1	1	0	2	0	1
Shouse, Brian, N.O.*	1	0	1.000	3.43	19	0	0	0	4	0	21	17	83	10	8	2	1	0	3	0	20	0	0
Skrmetta, Matt, Oma.	8	0	1.000	2.51	40	0	0	0	7	1	61	48	262	21	17	5	1	4	1	34	1	58	6	0
Skrmetta, Matt, L.V.	1	1	.500	9.82	7	0	0	0	0	0	7.1	14	37	9	8	1	0	2	0	2	0	6	0	0
Sollecito, Gabe, Iowa	1	1	.500	4.26	7	0	0	0	3	0	6.1	7	29	3	3	1	0	0	3	0	3	0	0
Sollecito, Gabe, Tuc.	1	0	1.000	2.40	13	0	0	0	5	0	15	9	62	6	4	2	1	1	2	5	0	13	0	0
Sparks, Steve, Mem.	0	0	.000	10.80	2	0	0	0	1	0	3.1	1	17	4	4	0	2	0	0	6	0	2	2	0
Sparks, Steve, Fres.	0	0	.000	11.25	3	0	0	0	2	0	4	5	21	5	5	1	0	0	0	3	0	3	0	0
Steenstra, Kennie, Cal.	1	2	.333	11.13	9	4	0	0	0	0	32.1	64	171	41	40	4	1	2	1	11	3	19	1	0
Steenstra, Kennie, Tuc.	1	1	.500	3.86	9	2	0	0	1	0	21	20	88	9	9	1	1	1	2	7	2	12	1	0
Wall, Donne, S.L.	0	1	.000	5.40	1	1	0	0	0	0	1.2	1	6	1	1	1	0	0	0	0	0	2	0	0
Wall, Donne, C.S.	1	2	.333	5.19	14	0	0	0	4	0	17.1	16	70	10	10	1	1	3	1	4	0	11	0	0
Watson, Mark, Iowa*	4	0	1.000	4.30	28	0	0	0	6	1	37.2	35	162	22	18	3	3	1	2	19	3	25	0	0
Watson, Mark, Tac.*	2	0	1.000	0.73	7	0	0	0	2	2	12.1	10	50	2	1	0	0	0	3	0	8	0	0
White, Rick, C.S.	0	0	.000	9.00	2	0	0	0	0	0	2	3	9	2	2	1	0	0	0	0	2	0	0
White, Rick, Mem.	0	0	.000	2.45	3	0	0	0	2	3	3.2	4	17	1	1	0	0	0	1	0	3	0	0

COMBINATION SHUTOUTS: **Calgary (4)**—Izquierdo-Arnold, Izquierdo-Neal, Judd-Secoda-Phelps-Neal, Steenstra-Pearsall. **Colorado Springs (0). Edmonton (2)**—Carnes-Balfour-Lee, B. Thomas-Balfour. **Fresno (7)**—Lu. Estrella-Verplancke, Hutchison-Brohawn, Aybar, Nathan-Verplancke-Aybar, Urban-Crabtree, Urban-Verplancke-Crabtree-Horgan, Jer. Williams-Verplancke, Jer. Williams-Verplancke-Aybar. **Iowa (4)**—Ford-Mahomes, Mahay-Mahomes-Duncan, Je. Sanchez-Cunnane-Mahomes, Smyth-Duncan-Mahomes. **Las Vegas (4)**—Bierne-Aldred-Bones, Bierne-House-Bones, Bierne-Nance-Mota-Aldred-Bones, Ellis-A. Gonzalez. **Memphis (7)**—Jacome-Sheredy, Lail-Sheredy-Molina-Stechschulte, Ohme-Heiserman, Ohme-Molina-Sheredy-Crudale, Walrond-Joseph-Molina, Weibl-Joseph-Ohme, Weibl-Ohme-Molina.

Nashville (2)—McKnight-Manzanillo-Camp-Tolar-Service, Torres-Tolar. **New Orleans (8)**—Franklin-Bullinger, Franklin-Lidge, Guerra-Shearn-Mann, C. Hernandez-Arteaga-Bullinger-Linebrink, Lidge-Bullinger-Shouse, Mlicki-Mathews-Saarloos, Munro-Lidge-Bullinger-Nitkowski-Mann-Arteaga, Redding-Munro-Puffer. **Oklahoma (4)**—Benoit-Je. Pena, Davis-Powell-Schmack, Lewis-G. Gonzalez-Telford, Je. Pena-Garcia-Telford-G. Gonzalez. **Omaha (4)**—Calero-Bailey-Gilfillan, Fussell-DeHart-Bailey, May-Austin-Suzuki, Suzuki-Skrmetta-Austin-Voyles. **Portland (6)**—Kershner-Boyd-Villafuerte, Kershner-Pearson-Shiell, Kershner-Shiell-Villafuerte, Middlebrook-Shiell-Pearson-Myers-Lundquist, Snyder-Shiell-Pearson-Lundquist, Tankersley-Hunter. **Sacramento (5)**—Adkins-Bost-M. Miller, Adkins-Bowie-Scheffer-Harville, Fyhrie-M. Miller-Bowie-Harville, Harang-Lankford-Bost, Levrault-Bowie-Harville. **Salt Lake (3)**—Callaway-Jones-Pine-Miadich, Janzen-Kelley-Shields-Miadich, Kelley-Donnelly-F. Rodriguez. **Tacoma (5)**—Cloude-Kaye-Jarvis, Falkenborg-A. Lopez-Jarvis, Falkenborg-Watson-Mateo, A. Lopez-Fitzgerald-Kaye, Matos-A. Lopez. **Tucson (5)**—Estrada-Koplove, Randolph-Valverde-J. Ward, Randolph-J. Ward-Holzemer-Valverde, Randolph-J. Ward-Prinz, Steenstra-Knott-Cortes-Prinz.

NO-HIT GAMES: Herndon, Portland, defeated Tacoma, 5-0, May 14, second game; Arnold, Calgary, defeated Iowa, 12-1, May 25.

2002 FIELDING

TEAM

Team	G	PO	A	E	TC	DP	TP	PB	Pct.
Nashville	143	3744	1387	106	5237	132	0	21	.980
Fresno	144	3722	1372	108	5202	116	1	22	.979
Portland	143	3684	1434	110	5228	119	0	13	.979
Tucson	141	3696	1390	110	5196	115	0	6	.979
Calgary	138	3467	1378	106	4951	122	0	13	.979
New Orleans	144	3855	1570	121	5546	149	0	10	.978
Edmonton	140	3601	1343	111	5055	126	0	12	.978
Memphis	142	3698	1456	119	5273	157	0	4	.977
Tacoma	141	3605	1184	111	4900	121	0	12	.977
Iowa	144	3727	1489	125	5341	131	0	12	.977
Oklahoma	144	3891	1494	132	5517	118	0	34	.976
Sacramento	144	3807	1419	135	5361	129	0	18	.975
Las Vegas	144	3865	1557	144	5566	135	0	14	.974
Salt Lake	144	3825	1562	144	5531	139	0	17	.974
Omaha	144	3805	1369	151	5325	159	0	9	.972
Col. Springs	144	3736	1534	169	5439	156	0	20	.969

INDIVIDUAL

FIRST BASEMEN

NOTE: All caps denotes fielding-percentage leader based on 72 games for catchers, 96 for all other non-pitchers and 115 innings for pitchers. *Throws lefthanded.

Player, Team	Pct.	G	PO	A	E	TC	DP
Abad, Andy, Cal.*	.984	23	177	13	3	193	14
Alviso, Jerome, C.S.	.989	13	79	7	1	87	11
Ardoin, Danny, Oma.	1.000	2	8	0	0	8	3
Balfe, Ryan, Mem.	1.000	1	9	1	0	10	1
Banks, Brian, Cal.	.989	67	563	43	7	613	62
Barajas, Rod, Tuc.	1.000	1	8	0	0	8	2
Barker, Kevin, Port.*	.996	109	895	74	4	973	84
Barnes, Larry, S.L.*	.991	80	693	56	7	756	78
Bell, Mike, C.S.	.987	12	72	5	1	78	10
Bell, Rick, L.V.	1.000	9	58	4	0	62	6
Bellinger, Clay, S.L.	.989	20	170	7	2	179	14
Berger, Brandon, Oma.	1.000	1	4	0	0	4	1
Bierek, Kurt, Okla.	1.000	1	3	0	0	3	0
Blake, Casey, Edm.	1.000	6	49	3	0	52	4
Borders, Pat, Tac.	1.000	2	7	0	0	7	1
Brumbaugh, Cliff, C.S.	.983	34	267	27	5	299	31
Burke, Jamie, S.L.	1.000	19	147	12	0	159	16
Castro, Nelson, Fres.	1.000	1	2	0	0	2	0
Chamblee, Jim, Mem.	1.000	1	5	0	0	5	0
Charles, Frank, N.O.	.985	47	372	16	6	394	36
Chen, Chin-Feng, L.V.	.987	97	799	68	11	878	78
Choi, Hee Seop, Iowa*	.990	128	1074	75	12	1161	105
Colbrunn, Greg, Tuc.	.958	3	23	0	1	24	3
Connors, Greg, Tac.	.970	9	30	2	1	33	3
Coolbaugh, Mike, Mem.	1.000	1	11	0	0	11	2
Cota, Humberto, Nash.	1.000	1	1	0	0	1	0
Cromer, Tripp, N.O.	.994	38	305	18	2	325	36
Cruz, Ivan, Mem.*	.995	122	1020	70	5	1095	129
Cuddyer, Michael, Edm.	1.000	6	43	4	0	47	6
Davis, Tommy, Mem.-L.V.	.983	8	55	1	1	57	7
Durazo, Erubiel, Tuc.*	.971	5	32	2	1	35	5
Eberwein, Kevin, Port.	.995	21	167	19	1	187	15
Echevarria, Angel, Iowa	1.000	4	21	1	0	22	3
Ensberg, Morgan, N.O.	.967	4	26	3	1	30	2
Erickson, Matt, Cal.	.000	1	0	0	0	0	0
Frank, Mike, Mem.*	.943	6	33	0	2	35	2
Franklin, Micah, Tuc.	.938	4	27	3	2	32	3

Player, Team	Pct.	G	PO	A	E	TC	DP
Freire, Alejandro, Fres.	.987	20	146	10	2	158	13
Gil, Benji, S.L.	.889	1	8	0	1	9	0
Gload, Ross, C.S.*	.987	88	738	69	11	818	81
Grabowski, Jason, Sac.	1.000	5	25	3	0	28	5
Greene, Todd, L.V.-Okla.	1.000	4	26	2	0	28	4
Guiel, Jeff, S.L.	1.000	2	13	0	0	13	1
Guzman, Edwards, Fres.	.985	19	125	9	2	136	9
Haas, Chris, Okla.	1.000	3	28	1	0	29	5
Hafner, Travis, Okla.	.993	65	558	28	4	590	43
Hansen, Jed, Oma.	.953	10	53	8	3	64	6
Hart, Jason, Okla.	.998	51	464	40	1	505	41
Harvey, Ken, Oma.	.984	110	851	78	15	944	124
Hatcher, Chris, Oma.	1.000	4	16	2	0	18	1
Hiatt, Phil, L.V.	.993	45	269	27	2	298	28
Hopper, Shane, Port.	.929	3	22	4	2	28	1
Hyzdu, Adam, Nash.	.953	5	39	2	2	43	6
Johnson, Keith, S.L.	1.000	1	9	3	0	12	1
Jordan, Kevin, Fres.	.986	10	68	3	1	72	5
Keck, Brian, C.S.	1.000	2	1	2	0	3	0
Kinkade, Mike, L.V.	.988	9	76	5	1	82	7
Lane, Jason, N.O.*	1.000	10	63	7	0	70	11
LeCroy, Matthew, Edm.	1.000	8	69	3	0	72	8
McGowan, Sean, N.O.	.979	42	303	28	7	338	22
McKay, Cody, Sac.	1.000	2	11	0	0	11	2
McKeel, Walt, C.S.	1.000	1	5	1	0	6	1
Melhuse, Adam, Iowa-C.S.	.963	8	50	2	2	54	3
Meliah, Dave, Okla.	1.000	2	10	0	0	10	2
Melo, Juan, Fres.	1.000	1	1	0	0	1	1
Mendez, Carlos, Sac.	.992	16	119	11	1	131	10
Minor, Damon, Fres.*	.972	9	64	6	2	72	5
Minor, Ryan, Tac.	1.000	3	15	2	0	17	2
Morales, Willie, Tuc.	.969	7	57	5	2	64	3
Nieves, Jose, S.L.	.900	1	9	0	1	10	2
Nieves, Wil, Port.	1.000	1	2	0	0	2	0
Norton, Greg, C.S.	1.000	2	19	2	0	21	4
Nunnally, Jon, Oma.	.000	1	0	0	0	0	0
Overbay, Lyle, Tuc.*	.991	127	997	87	10	1094	89
Owens, Ryan, C.S.	1.000	1	7	2	0	9	1
Pelaez, Alex, Port.	.991	16	108	7	1	116	7
Pellow, Kit, Oma.	.984	24	172	17	3	192	17
Pena, Angel, Fres.	1.000	11	83	7	0	90	8
Pena, Carlos, Sac.*	.992	40	326	33	3	362	40
Pernalete, Marco, Fres.	1.000	24	146	14	0	160	18
Petrick, Ben, C.S.	.933	1	12	2	1	15	1
Piatt, Adam, Sac.	1.000	3	19	0	0	19	1
Post, Dave, Nash.	.980	7	43	5	1	49	3
Pritchett, Chris, Nash.	.990	109	879	81	10	970	78
Quinlan, Robb, S.L.	1.000	7	66	4	0	70	6
Ramsey, Brad, Iowa.	.900	2	9	0	1	10	0
Riggs, Adam, Mem.	.958	3	20	3	1	24	2
Rolison, Nate, Cal.-Tac.	.990	76	548	39	6	593	52
Romero, Mandy, Nash.	.988	19	153	16	2	171	24
Rumfield, Toby, Cal.-Mem.	1.000	23	166	20	0	186	18
Santos, Deivis, Fres.*	.985	23	180	23	3	206	20
SEARS, Todd, Edm.	.997	121	931	52	3	986	93
Secrist, Reed, Nash.	1.000	11	64	2	0	66	7
Servais, Scott, C.S.	1.000	1	8	0	0	8	0
Short, Rick, S.L.	.993	17	130	17	1	148	11
Snopek, Chris, Mem.	1.000	2	12	0	0	12	3
Sprague, Ed, Okla.	.995	25	210	10	1	221	14
Sutton, Larry, Sac.*	.985	48	361	30	6	397	44
Sweeney, Mark, Port.*	.000	1	0	0	0	0	0
Sweeney, Mike, Oma.	1.000	1	7	1	0	8	1
Thomas, Juan, Tac.	.990	56	369	13	4	386	47

Player, Team	Pct.	G	PO	A	E	TC	DP
Treanor, Matt, Cal.	1.000	2	14	0	0	14	0
Valdez, Mario, Sac.	.994	39	342	17	2	361	19
Valentin, Javier, Edm.	1.000	1	8	0	0	8	0
Wood, Jason, Cal.	.857	3	6	0	1	7	0
Wooten, Shawn, S.L.	.973	5	35	1	1	37	2
Wright, Ron, Tac.	.989	45	324	26	4	354	23
Zinter, Alan, N.O.	.998	58	502	54	1	557	53
Zuleta, Julio, Iowa	1.000	10	84	5	0	89	6

FIRST BASEMEN WITH TWO OR MORE TEAMS

Player, Team	Pct.	G	PO	A	E	TC	DP
Davis, Tommy, Mem.	.975	6	38	1	1	40	5
Davis, Tommy, L.V.	1.000	2	17	0	0	17	2
Greene, Todd, L.V.	1.000	1	4	0	0	4	1
Greene, Todd, Okla.	1.000	3	22	2	0	24	3
Melhuse, Adam, Iowa	1.000	4	28	1	0	29	2
Melhuse, Adam, C.S.	.920	4	22	1	2	25	1
Rolison, Nate, Cal.	.993	35	273	14	2	289	24
Rolison, Nate, Mem.	.987	41	275	25	4	304	28
Rumfield, Toby, Cal.	1.000	17	117	15	0	132	14
Rumfield, Toby, Mem.	1.000	6	49	5	0	54	4

SECOND BASEMEN

Player, Team	Pct.	G	PO	A	E	TC	DP
Alviso, Jerome, C.S.	.977	35	57	72	3	132	21
Amezaga, Alfredo, S.L.	1.000	1	1	2	0	3	1
Bell, Mike, C.S.	.989	17	39	49	1	89	16
Blake, Casey, Edm.	1.000	7	6	19	0	25	2
Blalock, Hank, Okla.	.967	4	11	18	1	30	3
Bloomquist, Willie, Tac.	.982	30	54	58	2	114	13
Bogar, Tim, C.S.	1.000	2	4	7	0	11	3
Borrego, Ramon, Edm.	.977	14	21	21	1	43	6
Branson, Jeff, L.V.	.958	9	19	27	2	48	8
Bruntlett, Eric, N.O.	.900	2	4	5	1	10	3
Burroughs, Sean, Port.	.974	29	67	84	4	155	21
Butler, Brent, C.S.	1.000	8	11	18	0	29	3
Cabrera, Jolbert, L.V.	.000	1	0	0	0	0	0
Canales, Josh, L.V.	1.000	1	0	2	0	2	0
Canizaro, Jay, Edm.	.971	58	101	136	7	244	32
Caruso, Joe, Oma.	1.000	1	1	2	0	3	0
Caruso, Mike, Oma.	.966	12	17	40	2	59	7
Castro, Nelson, Fres.	1.000	1	1	0	0	1	0
Chamblee, Jim, Mem.	1.000	1	1	2	0	3	0
Cintron, Alex, Tuc.	.961	35	60	87	6	153	22
Clapinski, Chris, L.V.	.917	6	16	17	3	36	4
Clapp, Stubby, Mem.	.978	92	182	261	10	453	70
Clark, Jermaine, Tac.-Okla.	.983	110	206	252	8	466	62
Coffie, Ivanon, Iowa	.929	3	6	7	1	14	3
Colina, Javier, C.S.	.973	66	137	187	9	333	37
Connors, Greg, Tac.	1.000	3	1	2	0	3	1
Coquillette, Trace, Nash.	1.000	8	14	19	0	33	3
Crespo, Cesar, Port.	.978	34	84	97	4	185	24
Cromer, Tripp, N.O.	.973	22	39	71	3	113	17
Dallimore, Brian, Tuc.	.949	19	28	28	3	59	4
De La Rosa, Tomas, Nash.	.967	33	61	84	5	150	16
Diaz, Edwin, Okla.	1.000	7	15	14	0	29	5
Dransfeldt, Kelly, Okla.	1.000	1	0	1	0	1	0
Durrington, Trent, S.L.	1.000	4	3	12	0	15	3
Erickson, Matt, Cal.	.978	62	92	180	6	278	36
Espada, Joe, Oma.	.977	61	109	150	6	265	46
Febles, Carlos, Oma.	.982	13	20	35	1	56	10
Figgins, Chone, S.L.	.966	117	214	380	21	615	81
Flores, Jose, Sac.	1.000	3	10	6	0	16	2
Frias, Hanley, Tuc.	.983	68	111	175	5	291	35
Gandolfo, Rob, Tac.	1.000	6	8	13	0	21	3
Garcia, Luis, Nash.	.988	20	34	46	1	81	14
German, Esteban, Sac.	.986	117	236	309	8	553	67
Gil, Benji, S.L.	1.000	2	8	2	0	10	1
Gilbert, Shawn, Nash.	1.000	10	10	22	0	32	7
Ginter, Keith, N.O.	.965	61	126	151	10	287	36
Green, Andy, Tuc.	.980	26	37	61	2	100	12
Guzman, Edwards, Fres.	.955	13	24	18	2	44	3
Hansen, Jed, Oma.	.947	17	25	46	4	75	14
Hernandez, Carlos, C.S.	.968	9	14	16	1	31	7
Hill, Bobby, Iowa	.986	91	170	245	6	421	67

Player, Team	Pct.	G	PO	A	E	TC	DP
Holbert, Aaron, Tac.	.957	11	20	24	2	46	7
Hooper, Kevin, Cal.	.985	43	73	126	3	202	28
Johnson, Keith, S.L.	1.000	8	13	26	0	39	7
Jordan, Kevin, Fres.	.990	27	36	60	1	97	13
Klassen, Danny, Tuc.	.875	2	1	6	1	8	1
Kuzmic, Craig, Tac.	1.000	2	2	3	0	5	1
Lamb, Dave, Edm.	1.000	3	5	6	0	11	0
Landry, Jacques, Sac.	1.000	4	6	10	0	16	4
Lopez, Mendy, Nash.	1.000	6	13	9	0	22	3
Lopez, Mickey, Iowa	.978	46	84	137	5	226	29
Luther, Ryan, Fres.	.750	1	2	1	1	4	0
Matos, Julius, Port.	1.000	1	3	4	0	7	1
Matranga, Dave, N.O.	.981	64	107	156	5	268	40
McCool, Lee, Tuc.	1.000	2	6	3	0	9	2
Meliah, Dave, Okla.	.907	11	26	23	5	54	7
MELO, Juan, Fres.	.991	97	186	244	4	434	57
Menchaca, Eriberto, Tac.	1.000	1	1	1	0	2	0
Menechino, Frank, Sac.	.953	10	15	26	2	43	5
Metcalfe, Mike, Oma.	.991	22	44	62	1	107	21
Meyers, Chad, Sac.-Mem.	.984	27	45	74	2	121	22
Morris, Warren, Edm.-Mem.	.970	49	79	117	6	202	31
Nicholson, Kevin, C.S.	.929	10	15	24	3	42	8
Nieves, Jose, S.L.	.917	4	3	8	1	12	1
Nunez, Abe, Nash.	1.000	1	2	3	0	5	1
Ordaz, Luis, Iowa-Oma.	.988	32	70	92	2	164	23
Ortiz, Jose, C.S.	.967	5	8	21	1	30	3
Ozuna, Pablo, Cal.	.963	40	79	104	7	190	19
Pelaez, Alex, Port.	1.000	19	34	52	0	86	11
Pernalete, Marco, Fres.	.967	21	28	31	2	61	7
Pickler, Jeff, Okla.	.974	85	181	230	11	422	47
Post, Dave, Nash.	.968	80	144	220	12	376	62
Prieto, Alex, Edm.	.983	32	64	111	3	178	25
Reboulet, Jeff, L.V.	.959	11	18	29	2	49	6
Riggs, Adam, Mem.	1.000	5	3	8	0	11	2
Romano, Jason, Okla.-C.S.	.984	28	57	68	2	127	10
Sadler, Donnie, Oma.-Okla.	1.000	6	17	20	0	37	5
Salazar, Ruben, Edm.	.926	7	7	18	2	27	2
Santangelo, F.P., Sac.	.967	8	17	12	1	30	2
Santora, Jack, Tuc.	1.000	7	4	8	0	12	0
Saylor, Jamie, N.O.	.982	14	22	33	1	56	6
Short, Rick, S.L.	.950	9	18	20	2	40	5
Snopek, Chris, Mem.	.939	8	12	19	2	33	8
Sprague, Ed, Okla.	.844	9	16	22	7	45	5
Thrower, Jake, Port.	.970	71	120	174	9	303	27
Thurston, Joe, L.V.	.972	118	285	378	19	682	77
Velarde, Randy, Sac.	.000	1	0	0	0	0	0
Weekly, Chris, Iowa	.750	2	1	2	1	4	1

TRIPLE PLAY: Melo.

SECOND BASEMEN WITH TWO OR MORE TEAMS

Player, Team	Pct.	G	PO	A	E	TC	DP
Clark, Jermaine, Tac.	.981	101	191	228	8	427	58
Clark, Jermaine, Okla.	1.000	9	15	24	0	39	4
Meyers, Chad, Sac.	1.000	7	14	22	0	36	6
Meyers, Chad, Mem.	.976	20	31	52	2	85	16
Morris, Warren, Edm.	.948	25	37	55	5	97	14
Morris, Warren, Mem.	.990	24	42	62	1	105	17
Ordaz, Luis, Iowa	.970	6	15	17	1	33	3
Ordaz, Luis, Oma.	.992	26	55	75	1	131	20
Romano, Jason, Okla.	.987	18	34	44	1	79	5
Romano, Jason, C.S.	.979	10	23	24	1	48	5
Sadler, Donnie, Oma.	1.000	1	5	5	0	10	2
Sadler, Donnie, Okla.	1.000	5	12	15	0	27	3

THIRD BASEMEN

Player, Team	Pct.	G	PO	A	E	TC	DP
Alviso, Jerome, C.S.	.909	10	3	7	1	11	0
Banks, Brian, Cal.	1.000	1	1	1	0	2	0
Bell, Jay, Tuc.	.833	7	1	9	2	12	0
Bell, Mike, C.S.	.943	41	22	78	6	106	6
Bell, Rick, L.V.	.920	108	61	192	22	275	13
Bellinger, Clay, S.L.	.943	26	13	37	3	53	0
Blake, Casey, Edm.	.961	111	76	216	12	304	14
Blalock, Hank, Okla.	.934	91	46	168	15	229	17
Bloomquist, Willie, Tac.	.917	25	19	36	5	60	6

Player, Team	Pct.	G	PO	A	E	TC	DP
Borders, Pat, Tac.	1.000	3	0	7	0	7	1
Branson, Jeff, L.V.	.948	29	10	45	3	58	2
Brumbaugh, Cliff, C.S.	.938	22	14	46	4	64	6
Burke, Jamie, S.L.	.916	31	23	64	8	95	5
Burroughs, Sean, Port.	.946	16	10	25	2	37	1
Cabrera, Jolbert, L.V.	.800	3	3	1	1	5	0
Canizaro, Jay, Edm.	1.000	4	1	8	0	9	0
Caruso, Joe, Oma.	.900	11	14	22	4	40	5
Caruso, Mike, Oma.	.923	12	5	19	2	26	3
Charles, Frank, N.O.	1.000	1	0	1	0	1	0
Clapp, Stubby, Mem.	.857	6	3	9	2	14	0
Coffie, Ivanon, Iowa	.922	58	26	92	10	128	13
Colbrunn, Greg, Tuc.	1.000	1	0	1	0	1	0
Colina, Javier, C.S.	.898	22	8	45	6	59	5
Connors, Greg, Tac.	.915	20	17	26	4	47	2
COOLBAUGH, Mike, Mem.	.965	109	86	213	11	310	20
Coquillette, Trace, Nash.	.917	7	3	8	1	12	1
Crespo, Cesar, Port.	1.000	5	2	9	0	11	3
Cromer, Tripp, N.O.	1.000	1	1	0	0	1	0
Cuddyer, Michael, Edm.	1.000	2	1	5	0	6	0
Dallimore, Brian, Tuc.	.957	99	65	157	10	232	9
Davis, Tommy, Mem.	1.000	3	4	1	0	5	0
De La Rosa, Tomas, Nash.	.000	1	0	0	0	0	0
Diaz, Edwin, Okla.	.909	2	1	9	1	11	1
Dillon, Joe, Edm.	1.000	2	0	1	0	1	0
Donnels, Chris, Tuc.	1.000	4	1	3	0	4	0
Durrington, Trent, S.L.	1.000	4	0	6	0	6	1
Eberwein, Kevin, Port.	.906	40	23	64	9	96	4
Encarnacion, Mario, Iowa	.000	1	0	0	0	0	0
Ensberg, Morgan, N.O.	.920	79	45	163	18	226	12
Erickson, Matt, Cal.	.955	29	24	60	4	88	5
Espada, Joe, Oma.	1.000	2	1	0	0	1	0
Flores, Jose, Sac.	.500	2	0	1	1	2	0
Franklin, Micah, Tuc.	1.000	4	1	0	0	1	0
Frye, Jeff, N.O.	.875	4	2	5	1	8	0
Garcia, Luis, Nash.	.940	35	6	57	4	67	7
Gilbert, Shawn, Nash.	.919	14	7	27	3	37	3
Ginter, Keith, N.O.	.929	53	30	128	12	170	12
Grabowski, Jason, Sac.	.923	6	1	11	1	13	1
Guiel, Jeff, S.L.	.500	1	0	1	1	2	0
Guzman, Edwards, Fres.	.962	25	9	41	2	52	5
Haas, Chris, Okla.	.955	7	6	15	1	22	0
Hansen, Jed, Oma.	.920	46	25	55	7	87	5
Hernandez, Carlos, C.S.	1.000	2	2	1	0	3	0
Hiatt, Phil, L.V.	.857	5	1	5	1	7	1
Holbert, Aaron, Tac.	.667	1	0	2	1	3	0
Hopper, Shane, Port.	.900	11	6	12	2	20	0
Johnson, Keith, S.L.	.952	78	47	151	10	208	11
Keck, Brian, C.S.	1.000	2	1	4	0	5	0
Kinkade, Mike, L.V.	.964	11	7	20	1	28	0
Klassen, Danny, Tuc.	1.000	24	18	51	0	69	8
Kuzmic, Craig, Tac.	.913	59	33	82	11	126	5
Lamb, Mike, Okla.	.000	1	0	0	1	1	0
Lopez, Luis, Sac.	.957	131	87	227	14	328	21
Lopez, Mendy, Nash.	.953	40	25	76	5	106	7
Lopez, Mickey, Iowa	1.000	14	5	18	0	23	4
Matranga, Dave, N.O.	.000	1	0	0	0	0	0
McKay, Cody, Sac.	1.000	4	2	9	0	11	1
Melhuse, Adam, Iowa	.867	13	5	21	4	30	1
Meliah, Dave, Okla.	.889	7	6	10	2	18	2
Melo, Juan, Fres.	.947	27	18	36	3	57	4
Menechino, Frank, Sac.	.500	2	0	1	1	2	0
Meyers, Chad, Sac.-Mem.	.833	5	2	3	1	6	0
Minor, Ryan, Tac.	.931	40	24	71	7	102	5
Morales, Willie, Tuc.	.927	24	11	40	4	55	5
Morris, Warren, Edm.-Mem.	.778	6	3	11	4	18	2
Mosquera, Julio, Okla.	.000	1	0	0	0	0	0
Mueller, Bill, Iowa	.909	5	0	10	1	11	0
Nicholson, Kevin, C.S.	1.000	1	1	0	0	1	0
Nieves, Jose, S.L.	.917	6	1	10	1	12	1
Norton, Greg, C.S.	1.000	1	1	1	0	2	1
Ojeda, Augie, Iowa	1.000	5	1	4	0	5	0
Orie, Kevin, Iowa	.954	75	43	144	9	196	9
Ortiz, Hector, Okla.	.750	1	1	2	1	4	0
Ortiz, Jose, C.S.	.950	7	4	15	1	20	4

Player, Team	Pct.	G	PO	A	E	TC	DP
Owens, Ryan, C.S.	.893	58	28	80	13	121	6
Pelaez, Alex, Port.	.969	74	55	135	6	196	10
Pellow, Kit, Oma.	.914	80	44	127	16	187	16
Perez, Santiago, Okla.	1.000	6	5	16	0	21	0
Pernalete, Marco, Fres.	.922	23	16	31	4	51	2
Pickler, Jeff, Okla.	1.000	3	3	3	0	6	1
Post, Dave, Nash.	1.000	1	0	1	0	1	0
Prieto, Alex, Edm.	.917	15	9	24	3	36	3
Reboulet, Jeff, L.V.	1.000	3	0	2	0	2	0
Riggs, Adam, Mem.	.881	13	21	16	5	42	3
Sadler, Donnie, Oma.	1.000	2	3	2	0	5	0
Santora, Jack, Tuc.	1.000	2	0	1	0	1	0
Saylor, Jamie, N.O.	.957	11	10	12	1	23	1
Secrist, Reed, Nash.	.934	68	46	109	11	166	12
Short, Rick, S.L.	.909	5	3	7	1	11	0
Snopek, Chris, Mem.	.885	11	2	21	3	26	2
Sprague, Ed, Okla.	.878	29	12	53	9	74	2
Thrower, Jake, Port.	.955	14	6	15	1	22	2
Valentin, Javier, Edm.	.826	9	7	12	4	23	1
Wathan, Derek, Cal.	1.000	2	2	3	0	5	0
Weekly, Chris, Iowa	.500	3	0	1	1	2	0
Williams, Matt, Tuc.	.875	4	2	5	1	8	1
Wood, Jason, Cal.	.962	112	85	192	11	288	22
Wooten, Shawn, S.L.	1.000	1	1	1	0	2	0
Zuniga, Tony, Fres.	.952	78	40	120	8	168	11

THIRD BASEMEN WITH TWO OR MORE TEAMS

Player, Team	Pct.	G	PO	A	E	TC	DP
Meyers, Chad, Sac.	.750	3	1	2	1	4	0
Meyers, Chad, Mem.	1.000	2	1	1	0	2	0
Morris, Warren, Edm.	.833	2	1	4	1	6	1
Morris, Warren, Mem.	.750	4	2	7	3	12	1

SHORTSTOPS

Player, Team	Pct.	G	PO	A	E	TC	DP
Alviso, Jerome, C.S.	.920	46	61	122	16	199	26
Amezaga, Alfredo, S.L.	.962	126	207	397	24	628	90
Berroa, Angel, Oma.	.956	77	133	212	16	361	54
Bloomquist, Willie, Tac.	.956	19	24	41	3	68	9
Bogar, Tim, C.S.	.950	10	11	27	2	40	10
Branson, Jeff, L.V.	.958	26	33	81	5	119	14
Bruntlett, Eric, N.O.	.946	16	30	57	5	92	12
Butler, Brent, C.S.	.953	16	27	55	4	86	18
Cabrera, Jolbert, L.V.	1.000	2	4	6	0	10	1
Caruso, Mike, Oma.	.943	34	56	77	8	141	17
Castro, Nelson, Fres.	1.000	2	4	2	0	6	0
Cintron, Alex, Tuc.	.960	53	73	119	8	200	30
Clapinski, Chris, L.V.	.977	80	131	206	8	345	47
Clark, Jermaine, Tac.	1.000	8	10	17	0	27	2
Coffie, Ivanon, Iowa	.931	17	17	37	4	58	10
Coolbaugh, Mike, Mem.	.958	5	10	13	1	24	5
Crespo, Cesar, Port.	.934	21	28	71	7	106	13
Cromer, Tripp, N.O.	.960	7	11	13	1	25	4
Dallimore, Brian, Tuc.	1.000	2	5	5	0	10	2
De La Rosa, Tomas, Nash.	.963	68	103	182	11	296	47
Delgado, Wilson, Mem.	.977	97	142	285	10	437	69
Diaz, Edwin, Okla.	.917	4	2	9	1	12	1
DRANSFELDT, Kelly, Okla.	.978	139	210	421	14	645	74
Ellis, Mark, Sac.	.974	21	44	68	3	115	18
Erickson, Matt, Cal.	1.000	3	1	6	0	7	1
Espada, Joe, Oma.	.857	4	8	4	2	14	1
Everett, Adam, N.O.	.984	86	144	285	7	436	66
Figgins, Chone, S.L.	.933	6	8	20	2	30	3
Flores, Jose, Sac.	.958	55	99	149	11	259	27
Frias, Hanley, Tuc.	.978	15	17	27	1	45	5
Frye, Jeff, N.O.	.900	3	2	7	1	10	1
Gil, Benji, S.L.	1.000	2	3	10	0	13	1
Gilbert, Shawn, Nash.	.965	14	21	34	2	57	11
Hansen, Jed, Oma.	.941	7	4	12	1	17	6
Hart, Corey, Oma.	.977	11	18	24	1	43	8
Hernandez, Carlos, C.S.	.947	34	51	93	8	152	18
Holbert, Aaron, Tac.	.961	106	175	224	16	415	65
Hooper, Kevin, Cal.	.971	72	100	206	9	315	45
Johnson, Keith, S.L.	.917	8	11	22	3	36	11
Keck, Brian, C.S.	.900	3	7	11	2	20	2

Player, Team	Pct.	G	PO	A	E	TC	DP
Klassen, Danny, Tuc.	.971	79	125	214	10	349	43
Lamb, Dave, Edm.	.963	115	173	294	18	485	77
Lopez, Mendy, Nash.	.984	62	103	151	4	258	28
Lopez, Mickey, Iowa	.934	22	28	43	5	76	10
Martinez, Felix, L.V.	.938	22	43	78	8	129	21
Matos, Julius, Port.	.959	49	67	121	8	196	28
Matranga, Dave, N.O.	.986	17	26	45	1	72	9
Melhuse, Adam, Iowa	.000	1	0	0	0	0	0
Melo, Juan, Fres.	.976	13	13	28	1	42	6
Menchaca, Eriberto, Tac.	.903	5	17	11	3	31	5
Mendez, Donaldo, Port.	.969	62	84	162	8	254	27
Menechino, Frank, Sac.	.942	74	115	196	19	330	42
Merrill, Ronnie, C.S.	.967	17	31	56	3	90	15
Metcalfe, Mike, Oma.	.870	4	8	12	3	23	6
Meyers, Chad, Sac.-Mem.	.941	9	7	25	2	34	4
Morris, Warren, Edm.	1.000	1	0	1	0	1	1
Nicholson, Kevin, C.S.-Mem.	.931	40	58	103	12	173	22
Nieves, Jose, S.L.	.750	2	2	1	1	4	0
Nunez, Abe, Nash.	1.000	3	6	11	0	17	2
Ojeda, Augie, Iowa	.983	68	94	204	5	303	41
Ordaz, Luis, Iowa-Oma.	.946	63	93	135	13	241	36
Ortiz, Jose, C.S.	.975	14	26	53	2	81	14
Owens, Ryan, C.S.	.865	12	10	22	5	37	3
Perez, Santiago, Okla.	.667	1	1	1	1	3	0
Pernalete, Marco, Fres.	.000	1	0	0	0	0	0
Post, Dave, Nash.	1.000	1	0	3	0	3	1
Prieto, Alex, Edm.	.946	26	29	76	6	111	15
Ransom, Cody, Fres.	.973	135	204	347	15	566	69
Reboulet, Jeff, L.V.	1.000	2	3	4	0	7	1
Romano, Jason, Okla.-C.S.	.963	7	11	15	1	27	5
Sadler, Donnie, Oma.	1.000	2	4	9	0	13	2
Santangelo, F.P., Sac.	1.000	1	0	1	0	1	0
Santora, Jack, Tuc.	1.000	3	2	3	0	5	0
Saylor, Jamie, N.O.	.939	25	50	57	7	114	19
Snopek, Chris, Mem.	.857	2	1	5	1	7	0
Theodorou, Nick, L.V.	1.000	1	3	4	0	7	2
Thrower, Jake, Port.	.972	21	20	49	2	71	12
Thurston, Joe, L.V.	.976	17	35	46	2	83	11
Ugueto, Luis, Tac.	1.000	12	19	36	0	55	6
Wathan, Derek, Cal.	.977	68	83	174	6	263	36
Wood, Jason, Cal.	.882	4	4	11	2	17	2

TRIPLE PLAY: Ransom.

SHORTSTOPS WITH TWO OR MORE TEAMS

Player, Team	Pct.	G	PO	A	E	TC	DP
Meyers, Chad, Sac.	.857	2	2	4	1	7	1
Meyers, Chad, Mem.	.963	7	5	21	1	27	3
Nicholson, Kevin, C.S.	1.000	1	2	3	0	5	0
Nicholson, Kevin, Mem.	.929	39	56	100	12	168	22
Ordaz, Luis, Iowa	.944	52	73	112	11	196	24
Ordaz, Luis, Oma.	.956	11	20	23	2	45	12
Romano, Jason, Okla.	1.000	1	2	4	0	6	1
Romano, Jason, C.S.	.952	6	9	11	1	21	4

OUTFIELDERS

Player, Team	Pct.	G	PO	A	E	TC	DP
Abad, Andy, Cal.*	1.000	74	130	4	0	134	2
Agbayani, Benny, C.S.	1.000	27	45	1	0	46	0
Allen, Luke, L.V.	.969	132	257	23	9	289	7
Ardoin, Danny, Okla.	.000	1	0	0	0	0	0
Bair, Rod, C.S.	.973	69	105	5	3	113	2
Balfe, Ryan, Mem.	1.000	2	4	0	0	4	0
Banks, Brian, Cal.	.990	43	93	3	1	97	0
Barker, Kevin, Port.*	1.000	2	1	0	0	1	0
Barnes, John, C.S.	.985	60	126	3	2	131	1
Barnes, Larry, S.L.*	.973	22	36	0	1	37	0
Bartee, Kimera, Iowa	.992	121	252	9	2	263	3
Bass, Jayson, Iowa*	.971	117	218	15	7	240	2
Bellinger, Clay, S.L.	.985	36	59	5	1	65	0
Benjamin, Al, Port.	.961	46	71	2	3	76	1
Berger, Brandon, Oma.	.974	52	108	6	3	117	3
Bierek, Kurt, Okla.	1.000	20	43	1	0	44	0
Blake, Casey, Edm.	1.000	6	4	1	0	5	0
Blakely, Darren, Port.	1.000	4	11	0	0	11	0
Bloomquist, Willie, Tac.	.970	39	62	3	2	67	0

Player, Team	Pct.	G	PO	A	E	TC	DP
Brown, Adrian, Nash.	.975	49	77	1	2	80	0
Brown, Dee, Oma.	.968	80	149	4	5	158	0
Brumbaugh, Cliff, C.S.	.947	83	115	9	7	131	2
Buchanan, Brian, Edm.	1.000	1	1	0	0	1	0
Budzinski, Mark, Iowa*	1.000	11	9	0	0	9	0
Byas, Mike, Fres.	1.000	17	41	3	0	44	1
Byrnes, Eric, Sac.	.971	30	67	1	2	70	0
Cabrera, Jolbert, L.V.	.980	24	47	1	1	49	0
Cadiente, Brett, Okla.*	1.000	7	7	0	0	7	0
Candelaria, Ben, Cal.	1.000	8	9	0	0	9	0
Caruso, Joe, Oma.	1.000	2	1	0	0	1	0
Castro, Nelson, Fres.	1.000	20	29	3	0	32	1
Chamblee, Jim, Mem.	1.000	1	1	0	0	1	0
Chen, Chin-Feng, L.V.	1.000	1	2	0	0	2	0
Clapinski, Chris, L.V.	.000	1	0	0	0	0	0
Clapp, Stubby, Mem.	1.000	3	6	1	0	7	0
Clark, Doug, Fres.	.982	58	108	2	2	112	0
Clark, Jermaine, Okla.	.941	4	16	0	1	17	0
Coffie, Ivanon, Iowa	.989	39	84	4	1	89	1
Colangelo, Mike, Sac.	.986	68	145	1	2	148	0
Cole, Eric, Okla.	.967	62	82	5	3	90	3
Connors, Greg, Tac.	1.000	61	90	3	0	93	1
Coquillette, Trace, Nash.	.978	26	44	0	1	45	0
Crespo, Cesar, Port.	.982	27	53	3	1	57	1
Crosby, Bubba, L.V.*	.989	71	182	5	2	189	2
Cuddyer, Michael, Edm.	.960	74	160	10	7	177	2
Cust, Jack, C.S.	.961	89	143	6	6	155	0
Dallimore, Brian, Tuc.	1.000	8	10	1	0	11	0
DaVanon, Jeff, S.L.	.962	25	49	2	2	53	0
Davis, Tommy, Mem.	1.000	1	1	0	0	1	0
DeHaan, Kory, Port.	.990	117	297	6	3	306	2
Dellucci, David, Tuc.*	1.000	4	11	0	0	11	0
Devore, Doug, Tuc.*	.968	119	233	6	8	247	1
Durrington, Trent, S.L.	.960	10	21	3	1	25	0
Eberwein, Kevin, Port.	1.000	29	43	3	0	46	1
Echevarria, Angel, Iowa	1.000	54	90	6	0	96	0
Ellison, Jason, Fres.	.992	49	115	5	1	121	1
Encarnacion, Mario, Iowa	.969	57	93	2	3	98	1
Erickson, Matt, Cal.	1.000	4	1	0	0	1	0
Fernandez, Alex, Port.*	1.000	22	43	4	0	47	2
Flores, Jose, Sac.	.967	40	85	2	3	90	0
Ford, Lew, Edm.	.964	46	126	8	5	139	1
Frank, Mike, Mem.*	.971	51	96	6	3	105	2
Franklin, Micah, Tuc.	.966	71	107	5	4	116	0
Freire, Alejandro, Fres.	1.000	7	13	0	0	13	0
Frye, Jeff, N.O.	1.000	1	2	0	0	2	0
Garcia, Douglas, Okla.*	1.000	3	4	0	0	4	0
Gilbert, Shawn, Nash.	.875	6	6	1	1	8	0
Ginter, Keith, N.O.	1.000	1	1	0	0	1	0
Gload, Ross, C.S.*	1.000	19	25	1	0	26	0
Gomez, Rich, Port.	.960	93	183	8	8	199	0
Goodwin, Tom, Fres.	1.000	16	39	0	0	39	0
Grabowski, Jason, Sac.	.984	38	60	3	1	64	1
Green, Chad, Edm.	1.000	69	169	0	0	169	0
Greene, Todd, L.V.-Okla.	1.000	7	6	0	0	6	0
Guiel, Aaron, Oma.	.977	54	120	9	3	132	2
Guiel, Jeff, S.L.	.980	81	144	6	3	153	1
Guillen, Jose, C.S.	1.000	4	7	0	0	7	0
Gutierrez, Franklin, L.V.	1.000	2	9	0	0	9	0
Guzman, Edwards, Fres.	1.000	10	17	0	0	17	0
Hansen, Jed, Oma.	.977	22	39	3	1	43	0
Hart, Jason, Okla.	.940	71	106	3	7	116	0
Haverbusch, Kevin, Nash.	.941	23	31	1	2	34	0
Haynes, Nathan, S.L.*	.974	66	147	5	4	156	1
Hermansen, Chad, Nash.	1.000	14	26	2	0	28	1
Hiatt, Phil, L.V.	1.000	47	63	1	0	64	0
Hopper, Shane, Port.	.971	22	32	2	1	35	0
Hubbard, Trenidad, Port.	1.000	7	12	1	0	13	0
Hunter, Brian L., N.O.	1.000	4	11	0	0	11	0
Hyzdu, Adam, Nash.	.990	59	104	0	1	105	0
Incaviglia, Pete, Port.	1.000	6	9	0	0	9	0
Ingram, Garey, L.V.	.963	16	26	0	1	27	0
Johnson, Gary, S.L.*	1.000	37	67	0	0	67	0
Johnson, Keith, S.L.	.000	1	0	0	0	0	0
Johnson, Rontrez, Oma.	.979	104	274	7	6	287	5

Player, Team	Pct.	G	PO	A	E	TC	DP
Jordan, Kevin, Fres.	1.000	15	18	1	0	19	0
Kapler, Gabe, Okla.	1.000	4	6	3	0	9	0
Kelly, Kenny, Tac.	.972	121	270	11	8	289	2
Kielty, Bobby, Edm.	1.000	2	2	0	0	2	0
Kingsale, Eugene, Tac.	1.000	48	94	0	0	94	0
Kinkade, Mike, L.V.	.979	53	87	5	2	94	0
Krause, Scott, Tac.	1.000	15	34	1	0	35	0
Landaeta, Luis, Nash.*	1.000	2	2	0	0	2	0
Landry, Jacques, Sac.	.980	52	93	3	2	98	0
Lane, Jason, N.O.*	.991	103	230	2	2	234	0
Linden, Todd, Fres.	1.000	29	50	1	0	51	0
Little, Mark, Tuc.	.976	13	38	3	1	42	3
Logan, Kyle, N.O.	.980	76	146	3	3	152	0
Lopez, Mickey, Iowa	1.000	18	27	0	0	27	0
Ludwick, Ryan, Okla.*	.973	78	172	5	5	182	1
Luther, Ryan, Fres.	1.000	1	2	0	0	2	0
Mashore, Damon, Tuc.	.938	12	15	0	1	16	0
McDonald, Donzell, Oma.	.979	108	268	10	6	284	0
McKay, Cody, Sac.	.000	2	0	0	0	0	0
Melhuse, Adam, Iowa	1.000	4	1	0	0	1	0
Meliah, Dave, Okla.	.978	26	41	3	1	45	1
Mench, Kevin, Okla.	.965	25	52	3	2	57	1
Mendez, Carlos, Sac.	1.000	2	1	0	0	1	0
Metcalfe, Mike, Oma.	.900	4	9	0	1	10	0
Meyers, Chad, Sac.-Mem.	.976	64	116	7	3	126	0
Morales, Willie, Tuc.	1.000	8	11	0	0	11	0
Morgan, Scott, Port.	1.000	20	27	0	0	27	0
Mosquera, Julio, Okla.	1.000	4	5	1	0	6	0
Mota, Tony, Mem.	.986	35	66	2	1	69	1
Mouton, James, Tuc.	.989	53	90	0	1	91	0
Murphy, Mike, N.O.	1.000	12	30	0	0	30	0
Murphy, Nate, Tuc.*	.994	74	176	4	1	181	1
Murray, Calvin, Okla.	1.000	33	88	0	0	88	0
Nady, Xavier, Port.	.981	55	102	0	2	104	0
Nieves, Jose, S.L.	1.000	2	4	0	0	4	0
Nunez, Abe, Nash.	1.000	1	1	0	0	1	0
Nunez, Abraham, Cal.	.978	125	306	10	7	323	1
Nunnally, Jon, Oma.-Mem.	.984	82	176	7	3	186	4
Ortega, Bill, Mem.	.978	70	129	4	3	136	0
Owens, Jeremy, Port.	1.000	10	8	0	0	8	0
Ozuna, Pablo, Cal.	.952	23	40	0	2	42	0
Peeples, Mike, Cal.	.979	54	90	2	2	94	0
Perez, Santiago, Okla.	.929	8	12	1	1	14	0
Pernalete, Marco, Fres.	.000	1	0	0	0	0	0
Petrick, Ben, C.S.	.971	59	92	7	3	102	0
Piatt, Adam, Sac.	.976	55	81	1	2	84	0
Pickler, Jeff, Okla.	.938	9	14	1	1	16	0
Podsednik, Scott, Tac.*	.985	123	322	2	5	329	0
Porter, Bo, C.S.	.923	13	23	1	2	26	0
Porter, Colin, N.O.	.965	124	204	15	8	227	2
Pose, Scott, L.V.-Okla.	.990	40	91	3	1	95	1
Post, Dave, Nash.	1.000	4	2	0	0	2	0
Powell, Dante, Fres.	1.000	13	21	0	0	21	0
Pride, Curtis, Nash.	.968	93	177	5	6	188	0
Prieto, Chris, N.O.*	.939	19	29	2	2	33	0
Pritchett, Chris, Nash.	.000	1	0	0	0	0	0
Quinlan, Robb, S.L.	.984	108	177	7	3	187	0
Quinn, Mark, Oma.	1.000	7	9	0	0	9	0
Radmanovich, Ryan, Nash.	.991	72	108	5	1	114	1
Ramirez, Dan, Tuc.	.981	73	155	4	3	162	0
Ramirez, Julio, S.L.	.976	37	80	1	2	83	0
Redman, Tike, Nash.*	.982	75	157	4	3	164	3
Restovich, Michael, Edm.	.976	124	224	20	6	250	5
Riggs, Adam, Mem.	.955	14	21	0	1	22	0
Rios, Armando, Nash.*	.923	12	12	0	1	13	0
Rivera, Ruben, Okla.	.955	26	58	6	3	67	0
Rolison, Nate, Tac.	1.000	29	40	0	0	40	0
Romano, Jason, Okla.-C.S.	.963	48	124	5	5	134	0
Roneberg, Brett, Cal.*	1.000	2	5	0	0	5	0
Ruan, Wilkin, L.V.	1.000	39	97	3	0	100	0
Rumfield, Toby, Cal.	1.000	2	4	0	0	4	0
Ryan, Mike, Edm.	.987	111	218	9	3	230	0
Ryan, Rob, Sac.*	.941	49	75	5	5	85	2
Saba, Donnie, Tuc.	1.000	1	1	0	0	1	0
Sadler, Donnie, Okla.	.944	7	16	1	1	18	1
Santangelo, F.P., Sac.	1.000	30	43	0	0	43	0
Saturria, Luis, Mem.	.948	24	71	2	4	77	0
Saylor, Jamie, N.O.	1.000	7	5	1	0	6	0
Secrist, Reed, Nash.	1.000	25	31	0	0	31	0
Shinjo, Tsuyoshi, Fres.	1.000	2	5	0	0	5	0
Short, Rick, S.L.	.917	9	11	0	1	12	0
Simmons, Brian, Fres.	.980	88	189	4	4	197	2
Smith, Mark, Cal.	.980	88	145	3	3	151	0
Snopek, Chris, Mem.	.000	1	0	0	0	0	0
Stratton, Rob, C.S.	1.000	22	38	1	0	39	0
Sutton, Larry, Sac.*	.950	46	93	3	5	101	0
Sweeney, Brian, Tac.	.000	1	0	0	0	0	0
Taguchi, So, Mem.	.990	88	196	11	2	209	1
Theodorou, Nick, L.V.	1.000	1	1	0	0	1	0
Thomas, Gary, Sac.	1.000	4	11	0	0	11	0
Torcato, Tony, Fres.	.964	122	212	4	8	224	0
Tyler, Brad, L.V.	.968	49	84	7	3	94	0
Urquhart, Derick, S.L.*	1.000	14	23	0	0	23	0
Valdez, Mario, Sac.	.972	26	35	0	1	36	0
Warner, Michael, Sac.*	.964	33	79	1	3	83	0
Wathan, Derek, Cal.	.941	18	30	2	2	34	0
Weber, Jake, Tac.	.968	18	29	1	1	31	0
WESSON, Barry, N.O.	.996	109	217	10	1	228	2
Whiten, Mark, L.V.	1.000	5	12	0	0	12	0
Williams, Gerald, Mem.	1.000	18	33	1	0	34	0
Young, Ernie, Tuc.	.988	41	83	2	1	86	0
Zuleta, Julio, Iowa	.931	57	66	1	5	72	1

TRIPLE PLAY: Ellison.

OUTFIELDERS WITH TWO OR MORE TEAMS

Player, Team	Pct.	G	PO	A	E	TC	DP
Greene, Todd, L.V.	1.000	1	1	0	0	1	0
Greene, Todd, Okla.	1.000	6	5	0	0	5	0
Meyers, Chad, Sac.	1.000	2	2	0	0	2	0
Meyers, Chad, Mem.	.976	62	114	7	3	124	0
Nunnally, Jon, Oma.	1.000	8	9	0	0	9	0
Nunnally, Jon, Mem.	.983	74	167	7	3	177	4
Pose, Scott, L.V.	1.000	21	48	2	0	50	1
Pose, Scott, Okla.	.978	19	43	1	1	45	0
Romano, Jason, Okla.	.957	30	85	4	4	93	0
Romano, Jason, C.S.	.976	18	39	1	1	41	0

CATCHERS

Player, Team	Pct.	G	PO	A	E	TC	DP	PB
Amezcua, Adan, Port.	.976	37	227	15	6	248	3	2
Amrhein, Mike, Iowa	.984	26	168	16	3	187	1	2
Andreopoulos, Alex, Mem.	.988	24	149	9	2	160	0	2
Ardoin, Danny, Oma.-Okla.	.984	55	392	29	7	428	3	11
Banks, Brian, Cal.	.981	9	49	3	1	53	0	2
Barajas, Rod, Tuc.	1.000	3	26	2	0	28	0	0
Barthol, Blake, Tac.	.988	54	374	25	5	404	9	6
Bellinger, Clay, S.L.	1.000	3	14	1	0	15	0	1
Bitter, Jarrod, Port.	1.000	1	4	0	0	4	0	0
Borders, Pat, Tac.	.991	80	536	46	5	587	9	5
Brito, Juan, Oma.	1.000	3	14	3	0	17	0	0
Burke, Jamie, S.L.	.980	35	225	20	5	250	1	3
Cardona, Javier, Port.	1.000	19	110	8	0	118	2	1
Charles, Frank, N.O.	.974	37	211	11	6	228	1	5
Chavez, Raul, N.O.	.991	107	734	77	7	818	9	4
Connors, Greg, Tac.	1.000	3	23	0	0	23	0	1
Coolbaugh, Mike, Mem.	.000	1	0	0	0	0	0	0
Cota, Humberto, Nash.	.994	85	600	33	4	637	3	10
Cresse, Brad, Tuc.	.992	35	219	20	2	241	2	1
Curry, Chris, Iowa	1.000	6	27	1	0	28	0	0
Davis, Tommy, Mem.-L.V.	1.000	31	141	11	0	152	2	0
Dewey, Jason, C.S.	.966	35	181	18	7	206	1	6
Durrington, Trent, S.L.	1.000	2	16	0	0	16	0	2
Estalella, Bobby, C.S.	.995	20	182	10	1	193	3	1
Fasano, Sal, S.L.	.978	22	168	13	4	185	3	2
Garrick, Matt, Mem.	.980	24	143	7	3	153	1	0
Grabowski, Jason, Sac.	.942	18	91	7	6	104	0	2
Greene, Charlie, Cal.	.989	92	560	49	7	616	8	8
Greene, Todd, L.V.-Okla.	.989	48	334	24	4	362	5	10
Gregorio, Tom, S.L.	1.000	13	59	9	0	68	0	4
Guiel, Jeff, S.L.	.000	1	0	0	0	0	0	0

Player, Team	Pct.	G	PO	A	E	TC	DP	PB
Guzman, Edwards, Fres.	.990	36	264	30	3	297	4	5
Hernandez, Carlos, Okla.	1.000	10	73	7	0	80	1	3
Horner, Jim, Tac.	1.000	6	37	7	0	44	1	0
Hundley, Todd, Iowa	1.000	3	18	0	0	18	0	0
Kellner, Ryan, L.V.	.987	11	73	4	1	78	1	1
King, Brad, Okla.	1.000	8	64	1	0	65	0	0
Kinkade, Mike, L.V.	.857	2	6	0	1	7	0	1
Kuzmic, Craig, Tac.	.000	1	0	0	0	0	0	0
Lamb, Mike, Okla.	.926	4	23	2	2	27	0	0
LeCroy, Matthew, Edm.	.987	10	71	6	1	78	1	2
Lopez, Rafael, L.V.-C.S.	.989	17	78	12	1	91	0	0
Loyd, Brian, Port.	1.000	24	150	8	0	158	1	1
Lunsford, Trey, Fres.	.987	19	139	8	2	149	2	1
Luther, Ryan, Fres.	1.000	2	4	0	0	4	0	0
Mahoney, Mike, Iowa	.978	74	499	45	12	556	7	5
Maldonado, Carlos, N.O.	1.000	10	43	6	0	49	1	1
Marsters, Brandon, Edm.	.981	56	381	23	8	412	5	2
McDONALD, Keith, Mem.	.995	78	516	37	3	556	7	2
McKay, Cody, Sac.	.991	77	497	41	5	543	4	9
McKeel, Walt, C.S.	.988	40	235	19	3	257	1	4
Melhuse, Adam, Iowa-C.S.	.991	81	497	43	5	545	3	7
Mendez, Carlos, Sac.	.991	63	419	24	4	447	1	7
Miller, Damian, Tuc.	1.000	1	5	0	0	5	0	0
Moeller, Chad, Tuc.	.994	59	431	29	3	463	0	1
Molina, Jose, S.L.	.994	76	582	62	4	648	1	5
Morales, Willie, Tuc.	.994	50	297	28	2	327	3	4
Mosquera, Julio, Okla.	.992	51	342	40	3	385	4	7
Nieckula, Aaron, Fres.	1.000	6	21	4	0	25	0	1
Nieves, Wil, Port.	.993	67	410	40	3	453	2	9
Ortiz, Hector, Okla.-Oma.	.986	59	388	30	6	424	2	9
Pena, Angel, Fres.	.981	56	372	36	8	416	8	10
Petrick, Ben, C.S.	.977	8	39	3	1	43	0	6
Rodriguez, Guillermo, Fres.	.989	32	255	12	3	270	0	5
Romero, Mandy, Nash.	.998	51	417	28	1	446	3	8
Rose, Mike, Oma.	.981	42	298	12	6	316	1	4
Ross, David, L.V.	.989	90	589	59	7	655	5	10
Rumfield, Toby, Cal.-Mem.	.984	25	120	3	2	125	0	3
Secrist, Reed, Nash.	.987	12	72	5	1	78	1	3
Selmo, Martin, Port.	1.000	2	5	0	0	5	0	0
Servais, Scott, Fres.-C.S.	.996	32	212	16	1	229	2	1
Smith, Jeff, Edm.	.984	10	59	3	1	63	1	2
Socarras, Tony, L.V.	1.000	1	5	0	0	5	0	0
Treanor, Matt, Cal.	.983	30	159	14	3	176	1	0
Valentin, Javier, Edm.	.990	71	482	39	5	526	5	6
Waldron, Jeff, Tuc.	1.000	1	4	0	0	4	0	0
Wathan, Dusty, Oma.	.988	46	306	24	4	334	3	1
Wooten, Shawn, S.L.	1.000	1	3	0	0	3	0	0

CATCHERS WITH TWO OR MORE TEAMS

Player, Team	Pct.	G	PO	A	E	TC	DP	PB
Ardoin, Danny, Oma.	.983	24	167	10	3	180	2	3
Ardoin, Danny, Okla.	.984	31	225	19	4	248	1	8
Davis, Tommy, Mem.		19	81	4	0	85	2	0
Davis, Tommy, L.V.	1.000	12	60	7	0	67	0	0
Greene, Todd, L.V.	.988	25	160	11	2	173	3	2
Greene, Todd, Okla.	.989	23	174	13	2	189	2	8
Lopez, Rafael, L.V.	.987	15	68	10	1	79	0	0
Lopez, Rafael, C.S.	1.000	2	10	2	0	12	0	0
Melhuse, Adam, Iowa	.991	55	322	24	3	349	1	5
Melhuse, Adam, C.S.	.990	26	175	19	2	196	2	2
Ortiz, Hector, Okla.	.995	25	167	19	1	187	1	8
Ortiz, Hector, Oma.	.979	34	221	11	5	237	1	1
Rumfield, Toby, Cal.	.988	18	84	1	1	86	0	3
Rumfield, Toby, Mem.	.974	7	36	2	1	39	0	0
Servais, Scott, Fres.	1.000	3	11	1	0	12	0	0
Servais, Scott, C.S.	.995	29	201	15	1	217	2	1

PITCHERS

Player, Team	Pct.	G	PO	A	E	TC	DP
Abad, Andy, Cal.*	1.000	2	0	1	0	1	0
Abbott, Paul, Tac.	1.000	2	1	0	0	1	1
Adkins, Jon, Sac.	.950	20	8	11	1	20	0
Agosto, Stevenson, Iowa*	1.000	4	0	3	0	3	1
Ainsworth, Kurt, Fres.	1.000	20	8	16	0	24	1
Aldred, Scott, L.V.*	1.000	42	3	2	0	5	0
Alvarez, Juan, Okla.*	1.000	15	0	4	0	4	0
Alvarez, Victor, L.V.*	.947	34	8	10	1	19	2
Alviso, Jerome, C.S.	1.000	4	2	0	0	2	0
Arnold, Jamie, Cal.	1.000	16	5	19	0	24	1
Arroyo, Bronson, Nash.	1.000	22	22	12	0	34	0
Arteaga, J.D., N.O.*	.960	42	6	18	1	25	0
Atchison, Scott, Tac.	.905	27	5	14	2	21	0
Austin, Jeff, Oma.	.800	39	2	2	1	5	0
Aybar, Manny, Fres.	1.000	45	2	7	0	9	0
Baerlocher, Ryan, Oma.	1.000	13	1	9	0	10	1
Bailey, Cory, Oma.	1.000	18	7	3	0	10	0
Balfour, Grant, Edm.	.941	58	3	13	1	17	4
Bausher, Andy, Port.*	.000	8	0	0	0	0	0
Beirne, Kevin, L.V.	.909	22	9	11	2	22	0
Belitz, Todd, C.S.*	.778	22	4	3	2	9	0
Bell, Rob, Okla.	1.000	12	2	7	0	9	0
Benes, Alan, Iowa	.926	28	6	19	2	27	3
Benes, Andy, Mem.	1.000	4	1	3	0	4	1
Benoit, Joaquin, Okla.	1.000	16	6	8	0	14	0
Benson, Kris, Nash.	1.000	4	0	1	0	1	0
Bere, Jason, Iowa	.000	1	0	0	0	0	0
Bergman, Dusty, S.L.*	1.000	21	0	4	0	4	0
Bevel, Bobby, Tac.*	1.000	31	2	3	0	5	0
Bochtler, Doug, Edm.	1.000	34	2	9	0	11	1
Bones, Ricky, L.V.	1.000	30	2	6	0	8	0
Bootcheck, Chris, S.L.	.800	9	1	3	1	5	1
Borland, Toby, Cal.	.875	56	3	4	1	8	0
Borrego, Ramon, Edm.	1.000	1	0	1	0	1	1
Bost, Heath, Sac.	.882	52	2	13	2	17	0
Bowie, Micah, Sac.*	.800	46	3	5	2	10	1
Boyd, Jason, Port.	1.000	19	2	4	0	6	0
Brittan, Corey, C.S.	.938	35	7	8	1	16	1
Brohawn, Troy, Fres.*	.880	56	7	15	3	25	0
Brown, Eric, Iowa	.000	1	0	0	0	0	0
Brown, Kevin, L.V.	1.000	2	2	0	0	2	0
Bukvich, Ryan, Oma.	1.000	12	0	1	0	1	0
Bullinger, Kirk, N.O.	.955	55	6	15	1	22	2
Burke, Jamie, S.L.	.000	1	0	0	0	0	0
Butler, John, Tac.	.000	1	0	0	0	0	0
Bynum, Mike, Port.*	1.000	7	2	6	0	8	0
Calero, Kiko, Oma.	1.000	20	8	15	0	23	0
Callaway, Mickey, S.L.	1.000	17	9	11	0	20	0
Cameron, Ryan, C.S.	.000	1	0	0	0	0	0
Camp, Shawn, Nash.	.933	39	6	8	1	15	1
Cannon, Jon, Fres.*	1.000	3	0	1	0	1	0
Capuano, Chris, Tuc.*	1.000	6	0	6	0	6	0
Caraccioli, Lance, L.V.*	1.000	10	4	11	0	15	0
Carnes, Matt, Edm.	1.000	21	4	9	0	13	1
Cedeno, Blas, Nash.	1.000	6	0	1	0	1	1
Chacon, Shawn, C.S.	1.000	4	1	4	0	5	0
Chavez, Anthony, Tuc.	.667	21	0	4	2	6	0
Chiasson, Scott, Iowa	1.000	27	3	1	0	4	0
Chouinard, Bobby, C.S.	1.000	9	3	1	0	4	0
Christman, Tim, Cal.*	1.000	11	1	1	0	2	0
Cloude, Ken, Tac.	1.000	15	2	3	0	5	0
Condrey, Clay, Port.	1.000	25	17	27	0	44	6
Coogan, Patrick, Mem.	1.000	7	1	2	0	3	0
Cook, Aaron, C.S.	.947	10	11	7	1	19	1
Coppinger, Rocky, Sac.	1.000	2	0	2	0	2	0
Cordero, Francisco, Okla.	.000	11	0	0	0	0	0
Corey, Bryan, L.V.	.944	37	7	10	1	18	0
Cortes, David, Tuc.	.000	3	0	0	0	0	0
Crabtree, Robbie, Fres.	.923	24	3	9	1	13	0
Crowell, Kyle, Sac.	1.000	5	0	2	0	2	0
Crudale, Mike, Mem.	1.000	13	0	1	0	1	0
Cruz, Nelson, N.O.	1.000	6	1	0	0	1	0
Cummings, Ryan, S.L.	.000	22	0	0	1	1	0
Cunnane, Will, Iowa	1.000	43	4	12	0	16	0
Cyr, Eric, Port.*	1.000	9	0	2	0	2	0
Davey, Tom, Port.	1.000	22	2	5	0	7	0
Davis, Doug, Okla.*	1.000	9	3	7	0	10	0
DeHart, Rick, Oma.*	1.000	49	4	8	0	12	1
Delgado, Oscar, Tac.*	.000	3	0	0	0	0	0
Deschenes, Marc, Iowa	1.000	4	0	1	0	1	0
Devey, Phil, L.V.*	.947	26	5	13	1	19	0

Player, Team	Pct.	G	PO	A	E	TC	DP
Dewitt, Matt, Port.	1.000	2	1	0	0	1	1
Dickey, R.A., Okla.	1.000	37	5	30	0	35	0
Dillinger, John, S.L.	.857	8	2	4	1	7	0
Donnelly, Brendan, S.L.	1.000	25	2	1	0	3	0
Dougherty, Jim, Nash.	1.000	33	1	10	0	11	1
Duchscherer, Justin, Sac.	1.000	14	3	9	0	12	0
Duff, Matt, Mem.	1.000	4	0	1	0	1	1
Duncan, Courtney, Iowa	.947	55	6	12	1	19	1
Durbin, Chad, Oma.	.000	1	0	0	0	0	0
Eaton, Adam, Port.	1.000	2	0	2	0	2	1
Ellis, Robert, L.V.	.868	29	15	31	7	53	1
Emanuel, Brandon, S.L.	1.000	7	2	4	0	6	0
Enochs, Chris, Sac.	1.000	6	2	3	0	5	0
Espada, Joe, Oma.	.000	1	0	0	0	0	0
Esslinger, Cam, C.S.	.875	29	5	2	1	8	1
Estrada, Horacio, Tuc.*	.909	29	11	29	4	44	1
Estrella, Leo, Iowa	1.000	8	1	3	0	4	0
Estrella, Luis, Fres.	.947	38	12	42	3	57	7
Falkenborg, Brian, Tac.	.889	9	2	6	1	9	1
Falteisek, Steve, L.V.	1.000	13	0	3	0	3	0
Farnsworth, Kyle, Iowa	1.000	2	0	1	0	1	1
Fernandez, Osvaldo, Fres.	.938	10	4	11	1	16	2
Field, Nathan, Oma.	1.000	18	2	0	0	2	0
Fiore, Tony, Edm.	1.000	2	2	5	0	7	1
Fitzgerald, Brian, Tac.-C.S.*	.923	36	4	8	1	13	1
Flores, Randy, Okla.-C.S.*	.917	22	2	9	1	12	3
Florie, Bryce, Sac.	.947	18	5	13	1	19	2
Foppert, Jesse, Fres.	.905	14	11	8	2	21	0
Ford, Ben, Iowa	.932	32	16	25	3	44	2
Franklin, Wayne, N.O.*	.913	29	3	18	2	23	5
Frederick, Kevin, Edm.	1.000	46	4	7	0	11	0
Freire, Alejandro, Fres.	.000	1	0	0	0	0	0
Fuentes, Brian, C.S.*	1.000	41	4	4	0	8	1
Fultz, Aaron, Fres.*	1.000	17	2	4	0	6	0
Fussell, Chris, Oma.	.926	28	9	16	2	27	2
Fyhrie, Mike, Sac.	.941	13	6	10	1	17	2
Garcia, Reynaldo, Okla.	1.000	25	1	2	0	3	0
George, Chris, Oma.*	.941	22	4	12	1	17	1
Gilfillan, Jason, Oma.	1.000	33	1	8	0	9	2
Gissell, Chris, Iowa	.958	28	7	16	1	24	0
Glynn, Ryan, Cal.	1.000	14	6	11	0	17	2
Gomes, Wayne, Nash.	1.000	6	0	1	0	1	0
Gonzalez, Alfredo, L.V.	.800	14	0	4	1	5	0
Gonzalez, Jeremi, Okla.	.889	46	5	11	2	18	1
Gordon, Tom, Iowa	.000	2	0	0	0	0	0
Graham, Tom, Okla.	.000	2	0	0	0	0	0
Gray, Mike, Tuc.*	1.000	6	2	4	0	6	0
Gregg, Kevin, Sac.	1.000	16	1	6	0	7	0
Grilli, Jason, Cal.	1.000	1	0	2	0	2	0
Guerra, Mark, N.O.	1.000	28	18	16	0	34	3
GUERRIER, Matt, Nash.	1.000	27	16	30	0	46	2
Gulin, Lindsay, L.V.*	.889	14	5	11	2	18	0
Halama, John, Tac.*	1.000	2	0	3	0	3	0
Harang, Aaron, Tac.	1.000	8	1	3	0	4	1
Harville, Chad, Sac.	.750	24	0	3	1	4	1
Hazlett, Andy, Port.*	1.000	13	1	4	0	5	0
Heams, Shane, C.S.	.000	9	0	0	0	0	0
Heiserman, Rick, Mem.	1.000	22	2	2	0	4	0
Helling, Rick, Tuc.	.000	1	0	0	0	0	0
Hensley, Matt, S.L.	.909	19	12	8	2	22	1
Herbert, John, Port.	1.000	1	0	1	0	1	0
Hernandez, Carlos, N.O.*	.000	1	0	0	0	0	0
Hernandez, Roberto, Oma.	.000	2	0	0	0	0	0
Herndon, Junior, Port.	.955	28	12	30	2	44	1
Hiljus, Erik, Sac.	1.000	9	3	3	0	6	1
Holt, Chris, C.S.	.900	12	2	7	1	10	0
Holtz, Mike, Port.*	1.000	7	1	1	0	2	0
Holzemer, Mark, Tuc.*	1.000	51	3	5	0	8	1
Horgan, Joe, Fres.*	1.000	27	3	10	0	13	1
House, Craig, L.V.	1.000	19	0	3	0	3	0
Howard, Ben, Port.	.857	11	2	4	1	7	0
Hundley, Jeff, S.L.*	.667	4	2	0	1	3	0
Hunter, Johnny, Port.	1.000	12	1	4	0	5	0
Hurtado, Edwin, Oma.	.867	11	5	8	2	15	0
Hutchison, Wesley, Fres.	.875	17	2	5	1	8	0

Player, Team	Pct.	G	PO	A	E	TC	DP
Izquierdo, Hansel, Cal.	.824	13	7	7	3	17	0
Jacome, Jason, Mem.*	.938	28	5	10	1	16	0
James, Mike, C.S.	.875	24	2	5	1	8	1
Janzen, Marty, S.L.	1.000	11	1	2	0	3	1
Jarvis, Matt, Tac.-Fres.*	.929	43	2	11	1	14	1
Jerzembeck, Mike, Edm.	1.000	3	0	2	0	2	0
Johnson, Adam, Edm.	.944	27	5	12	1	18	1
Johnson, Jonathan, Tuc.-Port.	1.000	26	5	8	0	13	0
Johnson, Keith, L.V.	.000	1	0	0	0	0	0
Johnson, Mike, L.V.	.938	8	5	10	1	16	1
Jones, Greg, S.L.	1.000	39	1	6	0	7	0
Joseph, Kevin, Mem.	1.000	31	2	7	0	9	2
Journell, Jimmy, Mem.	.571	7	0	4	3	7	0
Judd, Mike, Cal.	.941	23	2	14	1	17	0
Karnuth, Jason, Mem.	.000	1	0	0	0	0	0
Kaye, Justin, Tac.	1.000	47	5	8	0	13	0
Kelley, Rich, S.L.*	.917	40	8	25	3	36	3
Kershner, Jason, Port.*	.750	31	3	3	2	8	0
Ketchner, Ryan, Tac.*	.000	1	0	0	0	0	0
Kinney, Matt, Edm.	1.000	5	5	4	0	9	1
Knott, Eric, Tuc.*	.923	31	9	27	3	39	1
Knotts, Gary, Cal.	1.000	42	1	7	0	8	1
Kolb, Brandon, Iowa	1.000	13	0	6	0	6	0
Koplove, Mike, Tuc.	1.000	23	0	7	0	7	0
Lackey, John, S.L.	.897	16	10	16	3	29	3
Lail, Denny, Mem.	1.000	10	2	3	0	5	1
Lankford, Frank, Sac.	.969	46	12	19	1	32	1
Laxton, Brett, Oma.	.946	29	14	21	2	37	1
Lee, Dave, Edm.	1.000	51	2	6	0	8	0
Levine, Alan, S.L.	1.000	2	1	0	0	1	0
Levrault, Allen, Sac.	.842	24	9	7	3	19	0
Lewis, Colby, Okla.	.800	20	5	11	4	20	0
Lidge, Brad, N.O.	.929	24	7	6	1	14	1
Lidle, Cory, Sac.	1.000	1	0	1	0	1	0
Lincoln, Mike, Nash.	1.000	10	1	3	0	4	0
Linebrink, Scott, N.O.	.000	13	0	0	0	0	0
Looney, Brian, Nash.*	1.000	6	2	3	0	5	0
Lopez, Aquilino, Tac.	.962	34	12	13	1	26	1
Lopez, Mickey, Iowa	1.000	2	0	2	0	2	1
Lowe, Sean, Nash.	1.000	5	1	1	0	2	0
Luebbers, Larry, Sac.	.897	28	10	25	4	39	0
Lukasiewicz, Mark, S.L.*	.600	35	1	2	2	5	0
Lundberg, Spike, Okla.	1.000	13	2	6	0	8	1
Lundquist, Dave, Port.	1.000	30	2	3	0	5	0
MacDougal, Mike, Oma.	.933	12	6	8	1	15	2
Magnante, Mike, L.V.*	.333	7	1	0	2	3	0
Mahay, Ron, Iowa*	1.000	39	3	6	0	9	1
Mahomes, Pat, Iowa	1.000	44	3	13	0	16	0
Mairena, Ozwaldo, Cal.*	1.000	25	1	4	0	5	0
Mann, Jim, N.O.	1.000	33	1	5	0	6	0
Mantei, Matt, Tuc.	1.000	9	2	2	0	4	0
Manzanillo, Josias, Nash.	1.000	15	1	1	0	2	0
Martin, Chandler, C.S.	1.000	8	0	6	0	6	1
Martinez, Gustavo, Tac.	1.000	1	2	1	0	3	0
Mateo, Julio, Tac.	.750	20	0	3	1	4	0
Mathews, T.J., N.O.-Mem.	1.000	8	0	0	0	0	0
Matos, Josue, Tac.	.913	25	6	15	2	23	0
May, Darrell, Oma.*	1.000	2	0	2	0	2	0
Mayo, Blake, Tuc.	.909	8	5	5	1	11	1
McClaskey, Tim, Sac.	1.000	2	1	0	0	1	0
McKay, Cody, Sac.	1.000	3	0	1	0	1	0
McKnight, Tony, Nash.	.964	30	12	15	1	28	1
Meadows, Brian, Nash.	.952	23	6	14	1	21	0
Mendoza, Mario, S.L.	1.000	3	0	1	0	1	0
Mercker, Kent, C.S.*	1.000	2	0	1	0	1	0
Meyer, Jake, Tac.	1.000	2	1	3	0	4	0
Miadich, Bart, S.L.	.857	59	4	8	2	14	1
Michalak, Chris, Okla.*	.000	1	0	0	0	0	0
Middlebrook, Jason, Port.	.875	10	1	6	1	8	0
Miller, Matt, Sac.	.960	54	3	21	1	25	2
Miller, Travis, Edm.-Iowa*	1.000	33	2	6	0	8	0
Miller, Wade, N.O.	1.000	2	0	1	0	1	0
Mlicki, Dave, N.O.	.000	1	0	0	0	0	0
Molina, Gabe, Mem.	.938	56	7	8	1	16	1
Morgan, Mike, Tuc.	.500	2	0	1	1	2	1

Player, Team	Pct.	G	PO	A	E	TC	DP
Mota, Guillermo, L.V.	1.000	20	1	4	0	5	1
Mounce, Tony, Okla.*	.000	2	0	0	0	0	0
Mullen, Scott, Oma.*	1.000	19	1	4	0	5	0
Munoz, Bobby, C.S.	1.000	15	2	9	0	11	2
Munro, Pete, N.O.	1.000	19	15	20	0	35	2
Murray, Dan, Okla.	.893	39	11	14	3	28	2
Myers, Rodney, Port.	.818	42	4	5	2	11	0
Myette, Aaron, Okla.	.938	16	4	11	1	16	0
Nakamura, Micheal, Edm.	.765	46	7	6	4	17	0
Nance, Shane, L.V.*	.789	37	5	10	4	19	0
Nathan, Joe, Fres.	.913	31	10	11	2	23	0
Neal, Blaine, Cal.	1.000	29	2	3	0	5	0
Nichting, Chris, C.S.	1.000	23	2	6	0	8	1
Nickle, Doug, Mem.	.875	14	2	5	1	8	0
Nina, Elvin, S.L.	.935	26	10	19	2	31	1
Nitkowski, C.J., N.O.-Mem.-Okla.*	.923	49	0	12	1	13	1
O'Connor, Brian, Nash.*	1.000	4	1	0	0	1	0
Ohme, Kevin, Mem.*	1.000	56	7	14	0	21	1
Oliver, Darren, Mem.*	.889	5	2	6	1	9	0
Olsen, Kevin, Cal.	1.000	8	7	4	0	11	0
Oropesa, Eddie, Tuc.*	1.000	29	1	1	0	2	0
Palki, Jeromy, Edm.	1.000	26	1	8	0	9	0
Palma, Rick, Iowa*	1.000	2	0	2	0	2	0
Park, Chan Ho, Okla.	1.000	1	0	1	0	1	0
Parra, Jose, Tuc.	.000	7	0	0	0	0	0
Patterson, John, Tuc.	1.000	19	0	12	0	12	1
Pearce, Josh, Mem.	1.000	4	0	4	0	4	0
Pearsall, J.J., Cal.*	1.000	9	0	2	0	2	0
Pearson, Jason, Port.-Fres.*	1.000	57	3	8	0	11	1
Pelaez, Alex, Port.	.000	1	0	0	0	0	0
Pena, Jesus, Okla.*	.833	29	4	6	2	12	0
Pena, Juan, Sac.*	1.000	3	0	3	0	3	1
Phelps, Tommy, Cal.*	.900	51	6	12	2	20	4
Pichardo, Hipolito, N.O.	1.000	5	0	1	0	1	0
Pickford, Kevin, Port.*	1.000	20	2	12	0	14	0
Pine, Chris, S.L.	.900	19	2	7	1	10	0
Pote, Lou, S.L.	.875	7	1	6	1	8	0
Powell, Jay, Okla.	1.000	8	1	0	0	1	0
Prinz, Bret, Tuc.	1.000	37	2	3	0	5	0
Prior, Mark, Iowa	1.000	3	0	1	0	1	0
Puffer, Brandon, N.O.	1.000	11	1	1	0	2	0
Putz, J.J., Tac.	1.000	9	2	5	0	7	1
Radinsky, Scott, Cal.*	.500	18	0	1	1	2	0
Ramirez, Erasmo, Okla.*	1.000	25	3	5	0	8	0
Ramirez, Santiago, N.O.	1.000	18	2	2	0	4	0
Ramos, Armando, Okla.*	.966	34	7	21	1	29	0
Randall, Scott, Edm.	.914	19	15	17	3	35	3
Randolph, Steve, Tuc.*	1.000	28	5	29	0	34	2
Ratliff, Jon, Cal.	.000	1	0	0	0	0	0
Redding, Tim, N.O.	1.000	11	2	5	0	7	0
Regilio, Nick, Okla.	.000	1	0	0	0	0	0
Reichert, Dan, Oma.	1.000	5	1	0	0	1	0
Rekar, Bryan, Oma.-C.S.	1.000	25	19	25	0	44	3
Reyes, Al, Nash.	.889	43	3	5	1	9	0
Reynoso, Armando, Tuc.	.889	6	1	7	1	9	0
Rincon, Juan, Edm.	1.000	19	8	14	0	22	2
Robbins, Jake, C.S.	1.000	11	3	1	0	4	0
Robertson, Jeriome, N.O.*	.935	27	5	24	2	31	3
Rocker, John, Okla.*	1.000	6	0	1	0	1	0
Rodgers, Bobby, Cal.	1.000	25	8	9	0	17	2
Rodriguez, Francisco, S.L.	.857	27	2	4	1	7	2
Rodriguez, Jose, Mem.-Edm.*	1.000	26	1	4	0	5	2
Rodriguez, Nerio, Mem.	.909	8	3	7	1	11	1
Rodriguez, Ricardo, L.V.	1.000	2	1	0	0	1	0
Rodriguez, Rich, Okla.*	.000	3	0	0	0	0	0
Saarloos, Kirk, N.O.	1.000	4	1	3	0	4	1
Sabel, Erik, Tuc.	1.000	25	9	8	0	17	1
Saladin, Miguel, N.O.	1.000	2	1	0	0	1	0
Sampson, Benj, Edm.*	1.000	13	2	8	0	10	2
Sanchez, Duaner, Tuc.-Nash.	1.000	24	1	3	0	4	1
Sanchez, Jesus, Iowa*	.968	26	4	26	1	31	0
Santana, Johan, Edm.*	.929	11	1	12	1	14	1
Santos, Victor, C.S.	.875	21	5	9	2	16	1
Scanlan, Bob, C.S.	1.000	17	4	3	0	7	0
Scheffer, Aaron, Sac.	.889	35	2	6	1	9	0
Schmack, Brian, Okla.	1.000	29	3	9	0	12	0
Schmidt, Jason, Fres.	1.000	2	1	2	0	3	0
Seanez, Rudy, Okla.	1.000	4	0	1	0	1	0
Secoda, Jason, Cal.	.941	35	7	9	1	17	0
Sedlacek, Shawn, Oma.	.957	11	10	12	1	23	2
Seifert, Ryan, C.S.	.900	21	4	5	1	10	1
Serrano, Wascar, Tac.	1.000	41	3	9	0	12	1
Service, Scott, Nash.	.900	47	3	6	1	10	0
Sessions, Doug, N.O.	1.000	11	1	3	0	4	0
Shaffar, Ben, Nash.	.000	1	0	0	0	0	0
Shearn, Tom, N.O.	1.000	57	3	9	0	12	1
Sheredy, Kevin, Mem.	1.000	35	1	4	0	5	0
Shields, Scot, S.L.	1.000	28	4	5	0	9	0
Shiell, Jason, Port.	1.000	56	4	7	0	11	0
Shouse, Brian, Oma.-N.O.*	.833	24	1	4	1	6	0
Simon, Ben, L.V.	1.000	23	6	6	0	12	1
Simontacchi, Jason, Mem.	1.000	6	0	13	0	13	0
Sinclair, Steve, Iowa*	1.000	52	6	6	0	12	0
Skrmetta, Matt, Oma.-L.V.	1.000	47	2	10	0	12	1
Sloan, Brandon, Cal.	.000	2	0	0	0	0	0
Smith, Brian, Nash.	.833	33	4	1	1	6	0
Smith, Bud, Mem.*	1.000	6	0	5	0	5	0
Smith, Chuck, C.S.	1.000	4	1	1	0	2	0
Smith, Travis, Mem.	.947	16	9	9	1	19	0
Smyth, Steve, Iowa*	1.000	6	0	2	0	2	0
Sneed, John, Edm.	.000	1	0	0	0	0	0
Snyder, John, Port.	.920	26	14	9	2	25	1
Sollecito, Gabe, Iowa-Tuc.	1.000	20	1	5	0	6	0
Soto, Darwin, Port.	.000	2	0	0	0	0	0
Sparks, Steve, Mem.-Fres.	1.000	5	2	0	0	2	0
Speier, Justin, C.S.	1.000	12	0	2	0	2	1
Spencer, Stan, L.V.	1.000	3	1	0	0	1	0
Springer, Dennis, L.V.	1.000	26	10	13	0	23	1
Stark, Dennis, C.S.	.714	7	1	4	2	7	0
Stechschulte, Gene, Mem.	1.000	10	1	2	0	3	1
Steenstra, Kennie, Cal.-Tuc.	1.000	18	6	10	0	16	0
Stemle, Steve, Mem.	1.000	20	6	14	0	20	0
Stephens, Jason, S.L.	1.000	5	2	9	0	11	0
Stephenson, Garrett, Mem.	1.000	3	0	2	0	2	1
Stottlemyre, Todd, Tuc.	1.000	11	0	1	0	1	0
Suzuki, Mac, Oma.	1.000	29	2	10	0	12	1
Sweeney, Brian, Tac.	1.000	30	4	15	0	19	0
Swindell, Greg, Tuc.*	.000	1	0	0	0	0	0
Tam, Jeff, Sac.	1.000	20	4	5	0	9	0
Tankersley, Dennis, Port.	.857	9	5	7	2	14	0
Tavarez, David, Tac.	.000	1	0	0	0	0	0
Telford, Anthony, Okla.	1.000	35	4	9	0	13	1
Teut, Nate, Cal.*	.808	27	4	17	5	26	2
Thomas, Brad, Edm.*	1.000	28	3	18	0	21	4
Thomas, Juan, Tac.	1.000	1	1	0	0	1	0
Thompson, Eric, Sac.	1.000	11	1	2	0	3	0
Thompson, Mark, C.S.	1.000	8	0	2	0	2	1
Tolar, Kevin, Nash.*	1.000	44	2	5	0	7	0
Torres, Salomon, Nash.	.943	26	18	15	2	35	2
Trombley, Mike, Edm.	.000	9	0	0	0	0	0
Trujillo, J.J., Port.	1.000	18	1	2	0	3	0
Ulloa, Enmanuel, Tac.	1.000	38	4	10	0	14	0
Urban, Jeff, Fres.*	.958	35	10	13	1	24	0
Valverde, Jose, Tuc.	1.000	49	5	2	0	7	1
Vargas, Claudio, Cal.	.867	17	6	7	2	15	1
Venafro, Mike, Sac.*	1.000	8	0	2	0	2	0
Verplancke, Jeff, Fres.	1.000	51	5	7	0	12	0
Villafuerte, Brandon, Port.	.917	47	5	6	1	12	1
Villano, Mike, Fres.	1.000	4	1	0	0	1	0
Villarreal, Oscar, Tuc.	.929	10	5	8	1	14	2
Villegas, Ismael, Sac.	.833	10	2	3	1	6	1
Voyles, Brad, Oma.	1.000	26	1	0	0	1	0
Wade, Travis, N.O.	1.000	27	1	5	0	6	0
Walker, Kevin, Port.*	1.000	3	0	1	0	1	0
Wall, Donne, S.L.-C.S.	1.000	15	3	4	0	7	0
Walrond, Les, Mem.*	.839	28	7	19	5	31	5
Ward, Bryan, C.S.*	1.000	6	2	6	0	8	1
Ward, Jeremy, Tuc.	.900	54	2	7	1	10	0
Watson, Mark, Iowa-Tac.-C.S.*	.824	44	3	11	3	17	0
Wayne, Justin, Cal.	.000	2	0	0	0	0	0

Player, Team	Pct.	G	PO	A	E	TC	DP
Webb, Brandon, Tuc.	1.000	1	1	2	0	3	0
Weibl, Clint, Mem.	.905	24	4	15	2	21	2
Weis, Brad, Sac.*	1.000	2	0	1	0	1	0
Wells, Bob, Edm.	1.000	4	1	0	0	1	0
White, Rick, C.S.-Mem.	1.000	5	1	0	0	1	1
Whiteside, Matt, C.S.	.933	60	7	7	1	15	0
Wilkins, Marc, Iowa	.500	8	1	0	1	2	0
Williams, Jeff, L.V.*	.938	56	3	12	1	16	1
Williams, Jerome, Fres.	.919	28	11	23	3	37	0
Williams, Woody, Mem.	1.000	1	1	1	0	2	0
Wilson, Kris, Oma.	1.000	8	1	3	0	4	0
Wise, Matt, S.L.	.909	16	4	6	1	11	0
Witasick, Jay, Fres.	1.000	2	0	1	0	1	0
Woodard, Steve, Mem.	1.000	7	1	7	0	8	0
Woodards, Orlando, Cal.	.000	1	0	0	0	0	0
Wooten, Greg, Tac.	.929	14	3	10	1	14	0
Wrigley, Jase, C.S.	.800	9	0	4	1	5	0
Wuertz, Mike, Iowa	1.000	28	6	18	0	24	1
Young, Jason, C.S.	1.000	13	4	7	0	11	1
Zambrano, Carlos, Iowa	.500	3	0	1	1	2	0
Zerbe, Chad, Fres.*	1.000	3	1	4	0	5	0
Zimmerman, Jordan, Oma.*	.000	1	0	0	0	0	0
Mathews, T.J., Mem.	.000	4	0	0	0	0	0
Miller, Travis, Edm.*	1.000	24	1	4	0	5	0
Miller, Travis, Iowa*	1.000	9	1	2	0	3	0
Nitkowski, C.J., N.O.*	.000	24	0	0	0	0	0
Nitkowski, C.J., Mem.*	.889	16	0	8	1	9	0
Nitkowski, C.J., Okla.*	1.000	9	0	4	0	4	1
Pearson, Jason, Port.*	1.000	23	1	4	0	5	0
Pearson, Jason, Fres.*	1.000	34	2	4	0	6	1
Rekar, Bryan, Oma.	1.000	5	2	1	0	3	0
Rekar, Bryan, C.S.	1.000	20	17	24	0	41	3
Rodriguez, Jose, Mem.*	1.000	22	1	4	0	5	2
Rodriguez, Jose, Edm.*	.000	4	0	0	0	0	0
Sanchez, Duaner, Tuc.	1.000	4	0	1	0	1	0
Sanchez, Duaner, Nash.	1.000	20	1	2	0	3	1
Shouse, Brian, Oma.*	.000	5	0	0	0	0	0
Shouse, Brian, N.O.*	.833	19	1	4	1	6	0
Skrmetta, Matt, Oma.	1.000	40	2	8	0	10	1
Skrmetta, Matt, L.V.	1.000	7	0	2	0	2	0
Sollecito, Gabe, Iowa	1.000	7	1	2	0	3	0
Sollecito, Gabe, Tuc.	1.000	13	0	3	0	3	0
Sparks, Steve, Mem.	1.000	2	1	0	0	1	0
Sparks, Steve, Fres.	1.000	3	1	0	0	1	0
Steenstra, Kennie, Cal.	1.000	9	2	5	0	7	0
Steenstra, Kennie, Tuc.	1.000	9	4	5	0	9	0
Wall, Donne, S.L.	.000	1	0	0	0	0	0
Wall, Donne, C.S.	1.000	14	3	4	0	7	0
Watson, Mark, Iowa*	.846	28	1	10	2	13	0
Watson, Mark, Tac.*	1.000	6	1	1	0	2	0
Watson, Mark, C.S.*	.500	10	1	0	1	2	0
White, Rick, C.S.	.000	2	0	0	0	0	0
White, Rick, Mem.	1.000	3	1	0	0	1	1

PITCHERS WITH TWO OR MORE TEAMS

Player, Team	Pct.	G	PO	A	E	TC	DP
Fitzgerald, Brian, Tac.*	.917	29	3	8	1	12	1
Fitzgerald, Brian, C.S.*	1.000	7	1	0	0	1	0
Flores, Randy, Okla.*	1.000	15	2	4	0	6	1
Flores, Randy, C.S.*	.833	7	0	5	1	6	2
Jarvis, Matt, Tac.*	.833	23	0	5	1	6	1
Jarvis, Matt, Fres.*	1.000	20	2	6	0	8	0
Johnson, Jonathan, Tac.	1.000	14	5	7	0	12	0
Johnson, Jonathan, Port.	1.000	12	0	1	0	1	0
Mathews, T.J., N.O.	.000	4	0	0	0	0	0

The following players appeared only as designated hitter, pinch-hitter or pinch runner: Dye, dh; T. Martinez, ph; Newson, dh, ph.

LEAGUE CHAMPIONS

Year	Team	Pct.	Year	Team	Pct.	Year	Team	Pct.
1903—	Los Angeles	.630	1932—	Portland	.587	1961—	Tacoma	.630
1904—	Tacoma	.589	1933—	Los Angeles	.610	1962—	San Diego	.604
	Tacoma§	.571	1934—	Los Angeles▼	.786	1963—	Spokane	.620
	Los Angeles§	.571		Los Angeles▼	.689		Oklahoma City•	.632
1905—	Tacoma	.583	1935—	Los Angeles	.648	1964—	Arkansas	.609
	Los Angeles*	.604		San Francisco*	.608		San Diego•	.576
1906—	Portland	.657	1936—	Portland‡	.549	1965—	Oklahoma City	.628
1907—	Los Angeles	.608	1937—	Sacramento	.573		Portland	.547
1908—	Los Angeles	.585		San Diego (3rd)†	.545	1966—	Seattle•	.561
1909—	San Francisco	.623	1938—	Los Angeles	.590		Tulsa	.578
1910—	Portland	.567		Sacramento (3rd)†	.537	1967—	San Diego•	.574
1911—	Portland	.589	1939—	Seattle	.589		Spokane	.541
1912—	Oakland	.591		Sacramento (4th)†	.500	1968—	Tulsa•	.642
1913—	Portland	.559	1940—	Seattle‡	.629		Spokane	.586
1914—	Portland	.574	1941—	Seattle‡	.598	1969—	Tacoma•	.589
1915—	San Francisco	.570	1942—	Sacramento	.590		Eugene	.603
1916—	Los Angeles	.601		Seattle (3rd)†	.539	1970—	Spokane•	.644
1917—	San Francisco	.561	1943—	Los Angeles	.710		Hawaii	.671
1918—	Vernon	.569		S. Francisco (2nd)†	.574	1971—	Salt Lake City	.534
	Los Angeles (2nd)◆	.548	1944—	Los Angeles	.586		Tacoma	.545
1919—	Vernon	.613		S. Francisco (3rd)†	.509	1972—	Albuquerque	.622
1920—	Vernon	.556	1945—	Portland	.622		Eugene	.534
1921—	Los Angeles	.574		S. Francisco (4th)†	.525	1973—	Tucson	.583
1922—	San Francisco	.638	1946—	San Francisco‡	.628		Spokane•	.563
1923—	San Francisco	.617	1947—	Los Angeles▲	.567	1974—	Spokane•	.549
1924—	Seattle	.545	1948—	Oakland‡	.606		Albuquerque	.535
1925—	San Francisco	.643	1949—	Hollywood‡	.583	1975—	Salt Lake City	.556
1926—	Los Angeles	.599	1950—	Oakland	.590		Hawaii•	.611
1927—	Oakland	.615	1951—	Seattle‡	.593	1976—	Salt Lake City	.625
1928—	San Francisco*	.630	1952—	Hollywood	.606		Hawaii•	.531
	Sacramento∞	.626	1953—	Hollywood	.589	1977—	Phoenix•	.579
	San Francisco∞	.626	1954—	San Diego■	.604		Hawaii	.541
1929—	Mission	.643	1955—	Seattle	.552	1978—	Tacoma††	.584
	Hollywood*	.592	1956—	Los Angeles	.637		Albuquerque††	.557
1930—	Los Angeles	.576	1957—	San Francisco	.601	1979—	Albuquerque	.581
	Hollywood*	.650	1958—	Phoenix	.578		Salt Lake City‡‡	.541
1931—	Hollywood	.626	1959—	Salt Lake City	.552	1980—	Albuquerque	.578
	San Francisco*	.608	1960—	Spokane	.601		Hawaii	.539

Year	Team	Pct.
1981—	Albuquerque*	.712
	Tacoma	.561
1982—	Albuquerque*	.594
	Spokane	.545
1983—	Albuquerque	.594
	Portland*	.528
1984—	Hawaii	.621
	Edmonton*	.486
1985—	Vancouver*	.522
	Phoenix	.563
1986—	Vancouver	.616
	Las Vegas*	.563
1987—	Calgary	.596
	Albuquerque*	.542
1988—	Vancouver	.599

Year	Team	Pct.
	Las Vegas*	.529
1989—	Albuquerque	.563
	Vancouver*	.514
1990—	Albuquerque*	.641
	Edmonton	.553
1991—	Albuquerque	.580
	Tucson*	.564
1992—	Colorado Springs*	.596
	Portland	.576
1993—	Portland	.608
	Tucson*	.580
1994—	Albuquerque*	.597
	Vancouver	.542
1995—	Salt Lake	.549
	Colorado Springs*	.538

Year	Team	Pct.
1996—	Edmonton*	.592
	Phoenix	.479
1997—	Phoenix	.615
	Edmonton*	.556
1998—	Iowa	.590
	New Orleans†	.535
1999—	Vancouver‡	.592
2000—	Salt Lake	.629
	Memphis‡	.576
2001—	Tacoma§§	.590
	New Orleans§§	.590
2002—	Las Vegas	.590
	Edmonton†	.579

*Won split-season playoff. †Won four-team playoff. ‡Won pennant and four-team playoff. §Tied for second-half title with Tacoma winning playoff. ∞Tied for second-half title, with Sacramento winning playoff. ▲Ended regular season in tie with San Francisco and won one-game playoff for pennant, then won four-club playoff. ◆Won playoff from first-place Vernon and awarded championship. ■Defeated Hollywood in one-game playoff for pennant. ▼Won both halves, no playoff. •League was divided into Northern, Southern divisions in 1963, 1969-70-71, and Eastern, Western divisions in 1964 through 1968 and 1972 through 1977, won two-team playoff. ††League divided into Eastern and Western divisions, Tacoma and Albuquerque declared co-champions following cancellation of four-team playoff due to continuing rain and wet grounds. ‡‡Won second-half title and defeated Hawaii in four-team playoff. §§Were entering finals of four-team playoff and were declared co-champions when Professional Baseball declared a stoppage of play.

EASTERN LEAGUE

LEAGUE OFFICE

President
Joe McEacharn

Address
P.O. Box 9711
Portland, ME 04104

Phone
207-761-2700

TEAMS

AKRON AEROS

General manager/vice president
Jeff Auman
Manager
Brad Komminsk
Ballpark (capacity, surface)
Canal Park (9,097, grass)
Affiliation
Indians
Address
300 S. Main St.
Akron, OH 44308
Phone
330-253-5151

ALTOONA CURVE

General manager
Todd Parnell
Manager
Dale Sveum
Ballpark (capacity, surface)
Blair County Ballpark (7,200, grass)
Affiliation
Pirates
Address
1000 Park Avenue
Altoona, PA 16602
Phone
814-943-5400

BINGHAMTON METS

General manager
Bill Terlecky
Manager
John Stearns
Ballpark (capacity, surface)
NYSEG Stadium (6,012, grass)
Affiliation
Mets
Address
211 Henry Street
Binghamton, NY 13901
Phone
607-723-6387

BOWIE BAYSOX

General manager
Jon Danos
Manager
To be announced
Ballpark (capacity, surface)
Prince George's Stadium
(10,000, grass)
Affiliation
Orioles
Address
4101 NE Crain Highway
Bowie, MD 20716
Phone
301-805-6000

ERIE SEAWOLVES

General manager
John Frey
Manager
Kevin Bradshaw
Ballpark (capacity, surface)
Jerry Uht Park (6,000, grass)
Affiliation
Tigers
Address
110 E. 10th Street
Erie, PA 16501
Phone
814-456-1300

HARRISBURG SENATORS

General manager
Todd Vander Woude
Manager
Dave Machemer
Ballpark (capacity, surface)
RiverSide Stadium (6,300, grass)
Affiliation
Expos
Address
RiverSide Stadium/City Island
Harrisburg, PA 17101
Phone
717-231-4444

NEW BRITAIN ROCK CATS

General manager
Bill Dowling
Manager
Stan Cliburn
Ballpark (capacity, surface)
New Britain Stadium (6,146, grass)
Affiliation
Twins
Address
230 John Karbonic Way
New Britain, CT 06051
Phone
860-224-8383

NEW HAVEN RAVENS

General manager
Adam Schierholz
Manager
Marty Pevey
Ballpark (capacity, surface)
Yale Field (6,200, grass)
Affiliation
Blue Jays
Address
252 Derby Ave.
West Haven, CT 06516
Phone
203-782-1666

NORWICH NAVIGATORS

General manager
Brian Mahoney
Manager
Shane Turner
Ballpark (capacity, surface)
Thomas J. Dodd Memorial Stadium
(6,270, grass)
Affiliation
Giants
Address
14 Stott Ave.
Norwich, CT 06360
Phone
860-887-7962

PORTLAND SEA DOGS

General manager
Charlie Eshbach
Manager
Ron Johnson
Ballpark (capacity, surface)
Hadlock Field (6,975, grass)
Affiliation
Red Sox
Address
271 Park Avenue
Portland, ME 04102
Phone
207-874-9300

READING PHILLIES

General manager
Chuck Domino
Manager
Greg Legg
Ballpark (capacity, surface)
First Energy Stadium (9,100, grass)
Affiliation
Phillies
Address
Route 61 South/1900 South Centre Ave.
Reading, PA 19605
Phone
610-375-8469

TRENTON THUNDER

General manager
Rick Brenner
Manager
Stump Merrill
Ballpark (capacity, surface)
Samuel J. Plumeri, Sr. Field at Mercer
County Waterfront Park (6,341, grass)
Affiliation
Yankees
Address
One Thunder Road
Trenton, NJ 08611
Phone
609-394-3300

2002 FINAL STANDINGS

NORTHERN DIVISION

Team	W	L	T	Pct.	GB
Norwich (Yankees)	76	64	0	.543	...
New Haven (Cardinals)	74	65	0	.532	1.5
Binghamton (Mets)	73	68	0	.518	3.5
New Britain (Twins)	67	72	0	.482	8.5
Trenton (Red Sox)	63	77	0	.450	13.0
Portland (Marlins)	63	77	0	.450	13.0

SOUTHERN DIVISION

Team	W	L	T	Pct.	GB
Akron (Indians)	93	48	0	.660	...
Harrisburg (Expos)	79	63	0	.556	14.5
Reading (Phillies)	76	66	0	.535	17.5
Altoona (Pirates)	72	69	0	.511	21.0
Bowie (Orioles)	55	85	0	.393	37.5
Erie (Tigers)	52	89	0	.369	41.0

COMPOSITE

Team	Akr.	Har.	Nor.	Read.	N.H.	Bing.	Alt.	N.B.	Tren.	Por.	Bow.	Erie	W	L	T	Pct.	GB
Akron (Indians)	...	14	4	10	4	6	14	2	7	5	13	14	93	48	0	.660	...
Harrisburg (Expos)	6	...	5	12	3	5	8	4	4	6	13	13	79	63	0	.556	14.5
Norwich (Yankees)	3	2	...	4	11	8	4	10	11	15	5	3	76	64	0	.543	16.5
Reading (Phillies)	10	8	3	...	1	4	14	4	5	3	13	11	76	66	0	.535	17.5
New Haven (Cardinals)	3	4	9	6	...	11	2	8	13	8	4	6	74	65	0	.532	18.0
Binghamton (Mets)	1	2	12	3	9	...	3	12	12	10	5	4	73	68	0	.518	20.0
Altoona (Pirates)	6	12	3	6	4	4	...	5	3	13	13	72	69	0	.511	21.0
New Britain (Twins)	5	3	10	3	11	8	2	...	7	10	3	5	67	72	0	.482	25.0
Trenton (Red Sox)	0	3	8	2	6	8	4	13	...	10	4	5	63	77	0	.450	29.5
Portland (Marlins)	2	1	5	4	12	9	4	9	10	...	3	4	63	77	0	.450	29.5
Bowie (Orioles)	6	7	2	7	3	2	7	3	3	4	...	11	55	85	0	.393	37.5
Erie (Tigers)	6	7	3	9	1	3	7	2	2	3	9	...	52	89	0	.369	41.0

Major league affiliations in parentheses.

PLAYOFFS: Harrisburg defeated Akron, three games to two; Norwich defeated New Haven, three games to none; Norwich defeated Harrisburg, three games to two to win Eastern League championship.

REGULAR-SEASON ATTENDANCE: Akron, 400,187; Altoona, 363,871; Binghamton, 214,289; Bowie, 341,322; Erie, 211,899; Harrisburg, 266,808; New Britain, 265,484; New Haven, 182,164; Norwich, 222,134; Portland, 382,738; Reading, 486,570; Trenton, 408,463. Total—3,745,929. Playoffs (13 games)—52,132. Class AA All-Star Game at Norwich—8,009.

MANAGERS: Akron, Brad Komminsk; Altoona, Dale Sveum; Binghamton, Howie Freiling; Bowie, Dave Cash (through July 7; 29-59), Dave Stockstill (July 8 through end of season; 26-26); Erie, Kevin Bradshaw; Harrisburg, Dave Huppert; New Britain, Stan Cliburn; New Haven, Mark DeJohn; Norwich, Stump Merrill (through May 22; 24-16), Luis Sojo (May 23 through end of season; 52-48); Portland, Eric Fox; Reading, Greg Legg; Trenton, Ron Johnson.

ALL-STAR TEAM: 1B—Carlos Rivera, Altoona; 2B—Jesus Medrano, Portland; 3B—Travis Chapman, Reading; SS—Jose Reyes, Binghamton; OF—Tony Alvarez, Altoona; OF—Lew Ford, New Britain; OF—Dee Haynes, New Haven; C—Victor Martinez, Akron; DH—John Gall, New Haven; Utility—Freddy Sanchez, Trenton; RHP—Ryan Madson, Reading; LHP—Billy Traber, Akron; Relief pitcher—Matt Duff, New Haven; Most Valuable Player—Victor Martinez, Akron; Pitcher of the Year—Ryan Madson, Reading; Rookie of the Year—Dee Haynes, New Haven; Manager of the Year—Brad Komminsk, Akron.

2002 BATTING

TEAM

Team	G	TPA	AB	R	H	TB	2B	3B	HR	RBI	SH	SF	HP	BB	IBB	SO	SB	CS	GDP	LOB	ShO	Avg.	OBP	Slg.
New Haven	139	5287	4754	671	1320	1998	281	29	113	629	32	31	61	409	16	837	80	43	128	983	7	.278	.341	.420
Akron	141	5435	4803	734	1305	2124	283	43	150	682	31	56	58	487	21	915	95	38	91	1046	9	.272	.342	.442
New Britain	139	5279	4662	651	1262	1884	264	23	104	596	69	46	56	446	15	774	96	38	97	1006	5	.271	.339	.404
Altoona	141	5243	4703	642	1261	1916	244	33	115	596	43	37	74	386	17	849	99	55	94	944	8	.268	.331	.407
Binghamton	141	5307	4642	647	1217	1823	239	35	99	586	65	45	70	485	22	968	215	93	84	982	13	.262	.338	.393
Trenton	140	5348	4688	692	1227	1840	262	30	97	627	28	48	79	505	15	933	128	79	115	981	4	.262	.340	.392
Erie	141	5262	4674	602	1220	1871	247	34	112	556	30	41	52	465	10	1052	124	36	105	1005	11	.261	.332	.400
Norwich	140	5117	4492	669	1156	1826	249	26	123	609	34	31	61	499	19	927	113	74	101	891	7	.257	.338	.407
Harrisburg	142	5437	4706	676	1211	1858	219	34	120	627	41	52	69	569	21	940	68	45	101	1038	11	.257	.343	.395
Bowie	142	5119	4622	565	1178	1683	222	23	79	502	39	29	57	372	9	808	149	68	110	901	10	.255	.316	.364
Reading	142	5373	4725	643	1201	1750	241	25	86	594	56	48	99	445	24	922	172	63	73	1008	4	.254	.328	.370
Portland	140	5081	4512	606	1138	1746	255	34	95	556	43	32	57	437	15	1068	143	67	86	894	10	.252	.324	.387

INDIVIDUAL

TOP QUALIFIERS FOR BATTING CHAMPIONSHIP

Minimum 383 plate appearances. *Lefthanded batter. †Switch-hitter.

Player, Team	G	TPA	AB	R	H	TB	2B	3B	HR	RBI	SH	SF	HP	BB	IBB	SO	SB	CS	GDP	Avg.	OBP	Slg.
Martinez, Victor, Akr.†	121	515	443	84	149	255	40	0	22	85	0	6	8	58	6	62	3	3	10	.336	.417	.576
Alvarez, Tony, Alt.	125	548	507	79	161	245	37	1	15	59	2	3	9	27	1	71	29	18	6	.318	.361	.483
Gall, John, N.H.	135	569	526	82	166	277	45	3	20	81	0	3	2	38	1	75	4	1	26	.316	.362	.527
Heintz, Chris, N.H.	105	397	373	40	117	169	29	1	7	45	2	1	2	19	3	61	1	0	13	.314	.349	.453
Haynes, Dee, N.H.	131	544	504	75	157	257	29	4	21	98	1	3	11	25	0	67	3	2	15	.312	.355	.510
Ford, Lew, N.B.	93	435	373	81	116	192	27	2	15	51	4	1	8	49	0	47	17	5	5	.311	.401	.515
Crisp, Covelli, N.H.-Akr.†	96	433	387	70	120	169	17	1	10	51	6	1	0	39	2	59	30	10	6	.310	.372	.437
Sefcik, Kevin, Alt.	126	525	467	69	144	186	32	2	2	51	3	4	7	44	3	42	12	8	9	.308	.374	.398
Perez, Jhonny, Erie	94	387	343	45	105	132	14	2	3	47	5	5	2	30	2	51	8	6	8	.306	.361	.385
Rivera, Carlos, Alt.*	128	533	494	67	149	247	28	2	22	84	0	4	8	27	3	75	1	1	18	.302	.345	.500
Chapman, Travis, Read.	136	561	478	64	144	226	35	1	15	76	2	8	19	54	9	77	3	1	11	.301	.388	.473
Sledge, Terrmel, Har.*	102	468	396	74	119	173	18	6	8	43	4	1	12	55	2	70	11	8	4	.301	.401	.437
McNeal, Aaron, Bing.	96	400	348	52	104	176	15	0	19	69	0	6	1	45	3	95	1	2	12	.299	.375	.506
Morneau, Justin, N.B.*	126	548	494	72	147	234	31	4	16	80	0	6	6	42	5	88	7	0	8	.298	.356	.474
Medrano, Jesus, Port.	116	502	414	77	123	171	27	6	3	32	3	3	3	79	1	82	39	18	5	.297	.411	.413

DEPARTMENTAL LEADERS: G—Espy, 141; AB—Bolivar, 547; R—V. Martinez, 84; H—Gall, 166; TB—Gall, 277; 2B—Gall, 45; 3B—T. Brown, 9; HR—Pascucci, 27; RBI—Haynes, 98; SH—L. Rodriguez, 32; SF—Peralta, 11; HP—Chapman, 19; BB—Pascucci, 93; IBB—Chapman, 9; SO—Lomasney, 133; SB—Snead, 66; CS—Alvarez, Medrano, Snead, 18 each; GIDP—Gall, 26; Slg.—V. Martinez, .576; OBP—V. Martinez, .417.

ALL PLAYERS

*Lefthanded batter. †Switch-hitter.

Player, Team	G	TPA	AB	R	H	TB	2B	3B	HR	RBI	SH	SF	HP	BB	IBB	SO	SB	CS	GDP	Avg.	OBP	Slg.
Ackerman, Scott, Har.	5	18	17	1	4	4	0	0	0	2	0	1	0	0	0	2	0	0	0	.235	.222	.235
Acuna, Ron, Bing.	10	28	24	3	5	11	2	2	0	3	0	2	0	2	0	5	1	1	1	.208	.250	.458
Adams, Brian, Tren.*	16	1	1	0	0	0	0	0	0	0	0	0	0	0	1	0	0	0	0	.000	.000	.000
Agamennone, Brandon, Har. ...	8	1	1	0	1	1	0	0	0	0	0	0	0	0	0	0	0	0	0	1.000	1.000	1.000
Aguila, Chris, Port.	130	488	429	62	126	180	28	4	6	46	5	2	4	48	0	101	14	8	8	.294	.369	.420
Ahumada, Alex, Tren.	66	208	185	31	45	58	4	3	1	19	3	1	3	16	0	42	10	3	4	.243	.312	.314
Airoso, Kurt, Erie	109	458	386	76	111	189	18	0	20	63	0	6	8	57	2	107	6	3	9	.288	.385	.490
Almonte, Erick, Nor.	53	222	187	28	45	76	7	0	8	33	3	2	0	30	2	59	10	2	6	.241	.342	.406
Almonte, Wady, N.H.	17	50	48	3	9	10	1	0	0	3	0	0	1	1	0	11	1	0	2	.188	.220	.208
Alvarez, Tony, Alt.	125	548	507	79	161	245	37	1	15	59	2	3	9	27	1	71	29	18	6	.318	.361	.483
Bailey, Jeff, Har.	99	386	309	45	87	145	17	1	13	52	1	3	10	63	4	78	3	3	3	.282	.416	.469
Bailie, Matt, Read.	12	1	1	0	1	3	0	1	0	0	0	0	0	0	0	0	0	0	0	1.000	1.000	3.000
Baisley, Brad, Read.	21	20	17	0	3	3	0	0	0	2	2	1	0	0	0	7	0	0	0	.176	.167	.176
Baron, Brian, N.B.*	117	416	390	46	115	140	22	0	1	34	3	0	3	20	2	47	3	1	9	.295	.334	.359
Basak, Chris, Bing.	109	427	377	54	96	132	18	3	4	34	6	4	2	38	3	94	19	14	0	.255	.323	.350
Bates, Fletcher, Bing.†	35	117	101	16	31	51	8	3	2	20	1	3	2	10	3	24	3	1	1	.307	.371	.505
Bautista, Rayner, Erie	89	330	302	35	80	116	20	2	4	33	1	2	3	22	0	72	5	2	7	.265	.319	.384
Bay, Jason, Bing.	34	128	107	17	31	51	4	2	4	19	0	3	3	15	0	23	13	3	2	.290	.383	.477
Bell, Heath, Bing.	24	1	1	0	0	0	0	0	0	0	0	0	0	0	0	1	0	0	0	.000	.000	.000
Benson, Kris, Alt.	1	3	2	0	0	0	0	0	0	0	1	0	0	0	0	2	0	0	0	.000	.000	.000
Billingsley, Brent, Har.*	6	4	4	0	0	0	0	0	0	0	0	0	0	0	0	2	0	0	0	.000	.000	.000
Bolivar, Papo, N.B.	137	608	547	78	152	230	35	2	13	87	2	10	2	47	1	98	18	5	10	.278	.332	.420
Borrego, Ramon, N.B.†	2	6	5	1	1	1	0	0	0	0	1	0	0	0	0	2	0	0	0	.200	.200	.200
Bowe, Brandon, Port.	45	2	2	0	0	0	0	0	0	0	0	0	0	0	0	0	0	0	0	.000	.000	.000
Bowers, Jason, N.H.	104	385	343	45	98	131	18	3	3	37	3	4	8	26	1	49	3	2	9	.286	.346	.382
Bradley, Milton, Akr.†	3	12	11	1	3	4	1	0	0	1	0	0	0	1	0	1	0	1	0	.273	.333	.364
Braswell, Bryan, Bing.*	24	2	2	0	0	0	0	0	0	0	1	0	0	0	0	1	0	0	0	.000	.000	.000
Brazell, Craig, Bing.*	35	137	130	14	40	66	8	0	6	19	0	0	6	1	0	28	0	2	2	.308	.343	.508
Bridges, Donnie, Har.-Port.	20	14	12	4	2	2	0	0	0	1	0	1	0	1	0	2	0	0	0	.167	.214	.167
Brooks, Frank, Read.*	17	1	1	0	1	1	0	0	0	0	0	0	0	0	0	0	0	0	0	1.000	1.000	1.000
Brown, Jason, Alt.-Har.	38	120	106	9	22	35	7	0	2	13	0	3	2	9	0	42	0	0	1	.208	.275	.330
Brown, Rich, N.Y.*	23	91	83	9	21	31	7	0	1	8	1	0	1	6	0	14	1	1	2	.253	.311	.373
Brown, Tonayne, Tren.	125	513	472	70	125	201	22	9	12	59	2	1	3	35	2	86	12	16	20	.265	.319	.426
Buchholz, Taylor, Read.	4	6	6	0	0	0	0	0	0	0	0	0	0	0	0	5	0	0	0	.000	.000	.000
Bump, Nate, Port.	20	24	22	3	6	7	1	0	0	1	1	0	0	1	0	5	0	0	0	.273	.304	.318
Burnett, Mark, N.H.*	16	44	39	4	12	13	1	0	0	8	0	0	0	5	0	9	0	0	1	.308	.386	.333
Burnside, Adrian, Alt.	33	24	21	2	5	7	0	1	0	3	3	0	0	0	0	7	0	0	0	.238	.238	.333
Cabrera, Ray, Bow.	61	253	243	26	67	100	21	0	4	29	0	0	3	7	1	29	6	5	7	.276	.304	.412
Calabrese, Tony, Nor.	8	15	14	2	5	6	1	0	0	1	0	0	0	1	0	1	0	0	0	.357	.400	.429
Calzado, Napolean, Bow.	130	527	482	71	133	168	20	3	3	42	3	1	7	34	1	50	42	11	12	.276	.332	.349
Cameron, Troy, Akr.†	71	260	230	26	51	77	12	1	4	24	1	2	5	22	0	71	0	1	0	.222	.301	.335
Camilo, Juan, Erie*	45	175	156	17	32	62	7	4	5	21	0	3	0	16	1	49	5	0	1	.205	.274	.397
Cammack, Eric, Bing.	36	2	2	0	0	0	0	0	0	0	0	0	0	0	0	0	0	0	0	.000	.000	.000
Candelaria, Ben, Port.*	29	110	103	9	30	39	9	0	0	13	0	0	7	1	0	19	2	2	1	.291	.336	.379
Capista, Aaron, Tren.†	56	190	174	22	43	63	10	2	2	10	0	0	1	15	0	26	5	2	3	.247	.311	.362
Carreno, Jose, Har.	14	45	42	5	8	11	0	0	1	4	0	1	0	2	0	7	0	0	1	.190	.222	.262
Carroll, Jamey, Har.	3	12	9	1	4	4	0	0	0	0	0	0	0	3	0	0	0	0	0	.444	.583	.444
Carter, Charley, Erie	135	550	492	61	138	235	32	1	21	92	0	4	3	51	2	91	1	0	17	.280	.349	.478
Caruso, Joe, Alt.	47	164	148	19	37	55	5	2	3	20	2	0	6	8	0	16	3	3	2	.250	.315	.372
Casadiego, Gerardo, Har.	9	3	3	0	0	0	0	0	0	0	0	0	0	0	0	3	0	0	0	.000	.000	.000
Casillas, Uriel, Read.	86	272	231	35	62	83	9	3	2	29	3	3	8	27	1	34	4	1	5	.268	.361	.359
Castillo, Carlos, Erie†	35	115	112	7	24	33	5	2	0	6	0	0	0	3	1	35	1	1	2	.214	.235	.295
Cates, Gary, Bow.	7	22	18	1	6	6	0	0	0	2	0	0	1	3	0	0	2	1	0	.333	.455	.333
Cepicky, Matt, Har.*	109	463	419	54	116	193	25	2	16	76	1	8	2	33	4	94	7	1	14	.277	.327	.461
Cerda, Jaime, Bing.*	14	5	5	0	0	0	0	0	0	0	0	0	0	0	0	2	0	0	0	.000	.000	.000
Cervenak, Mike, Nor.	134	535	492	74	136	235	34	1	21	91	1	2	10	30	3	78	5	2	12	.276	.330	.478
Chambliss, Jim, N.H.	122	494	434	77	119	208	32	3	17	72	1	3	8	48	1	92	8	2	5	.274	.355	.479
Chapman, Travis, Read.	136	561	478	64	144	226	35	1	15	76	2	8	19	54	9	77	3	1	11	.301	.388	.473
Chevalier, Virgil, Bing.	98	385	337	58	99	142	25	0	6	45	0	3	2	43	2	39	4	2	5	.294	.374	.421
Chiavacci, Ron, Har.	35	11	9	0	1	1	0	0	0	0	2	0	0	0	0	2	0	0	0	.111	.111	.111
Christman, Tim, Port.*	11	1	1	0	0	0	0	0	0	0	0	0	0	0	0	0	0	0	0	.000	.000	.000
Chrysler, Clint, Alt.*	51	3	3	0	2	2	0	0	0	0	0	0	0	0	0	0	0	0	0	.667	.667	.667
Church, Ryan, Akr.*	71	308	291	39	86	147	17	4	12	51	0	3	2	12	2	58	1	0	8	.296	.325	.505
Clark, Chris, Port.	10	1	1	0	0	0	0	0	0	0	0	0	0	0	0	1	0	0	0	.000	.000	.000
Cleveland, Russ, Erie	16	56	51	3	13	17	2	1	0	1	0	0	0	5	0	17	0	0	0	.255	.321	.333
Cole, Joey, Bing.*	10	5	5	0	1	1	0	0	0	0	0	0	0	0	0	1	0	0	0	.200	.200	.200
Collins, Pat, Har.	29	4	4	0	0	0	0	0	0	0	0	0	0	0	0	2	0	0	0	.000	.000	.000
Connacher, Kevin, N.B.	117	411	356	48	87	157	25	3	13	47	10	3	0	42	0	86	25	10	7	.244	.322	.441
Cook, Andy, Bing.	30	1	1	0	0	0	0	0	0	0	0	0	0	0	0	0	0	0	0	.000	.000	.000
Cook, B.R., N.H.	28	26	22	1	2	3	1	0	0	0	3	0	0	1	0	8	0	0	0	.091	.130	.136
Coquillette, Trace, Port.	43	178	144	24	30	53	7	2	4	20	1	4	7	22	0	45	1	3	2	.208	.333	.368
Correa, Cristobal, N.H.	26	22	19	2	4	4	0	0	0	0	2	0	1	0	1	0	0	0	1	.211	.250	.211
Crisp, Covelli, N.H.-Akr.†	96	433	387	70	120	169	17	1	10	51	6	1	0	39	2	59	30	10	6	.310	.372	.437
Cronin, Shane, Nor.	23	80	69	8	16	30	5	0	3	16	0	2	1	8	0	10	0	1	3	.232	.313	.435

Player, Team	G	TPA	AB	R	H	TB	2B	3B	HR	RBI	SH	SF	HP	BB	IBB	SO	SB	CS	GDP	Avg.	OBP	Slg.
Crozier, Eric, Akr.*	43	169	142	19	42	55	8	1	1	13	3	0	3	21	0	50	1	0	0	.296	.398	.387
Crumpton, Chuck, Har.	21	4	3	0	1	1	0	0	0	0	1	0	0	0	0	2	0	0	0	.333	.333	.333
Cruz, Edgar, Read.	1	4	4	0	2	2	0	0	0	0	0	0	0	0	0	1	0	0	0	.500	.500	.500
Cueto, Jose, Port.	9	6	5	1	1	2	1	0	0	0	1	0	0	0	0	4	0	0	0	.200	.200	.400
Cummings, Jeremy, N.H.	14	11	9	0	0	0	0	0	0	1	0	1	0	1	0	4	0	0	0	.000	.091	.000
Curry, Mike, Bing.*	31	112	99	16	27	38	4	2	1	8	0	0	0	13	1	24	3	1	2	.273	.357	.384
Davidson, Cleatus, N.H.-Nor.†	54	136	118	19	30	41	2	3	1	19	5	0	2	11	1	25	6	6	1	.254	.328	.347
Davis, Allen, Har.*	9	3	3	1	1	2	1	0	0	0	0	0	0	0	0	1	0	0	0	.333	.333	.667
Davis, Glenn, Nor.-Har.†	34	132	114	18	31	59	3	2	7	18	0	1	0	17	0	34	1	1	1	.272	.364	.518
Davis, J.J., Alt.	101	387	348	51	100	183	17	3	20	62	0	3	3	33	0	101	7	4	3	.287	.351	.526
Derosso, Tony, Alt.	72	216	182	22	35	72	5	4	8	33	3	3	1	27	1	48	2	0	5	.192	.296	.396
Diaz, Maikell, Bow.	48	150	143	12	25	34	3	3	0	11	0	0	1	6	0	29	2	1	9	.175	.213	.238
Dillon, Joe, N.B.	103	408	344	47	90	141	20	2	9	50	0	4	6	54	3	62	3	1	10	.262	.368	.410
Dina, Allen, Port.	51	193	182	34	47	82	15	1	6	20	2	1	0	8	0	32	5	3	4	.258	.288	.451
Dominique, Andy, Tren.	103	412	361	40	98	145	21	1	8	51	0	6	9	36	1	60	2	1	9	.271	.347	.402
Duff, Matt, N.H.	47	1	1	0	0	0	0	0	0	0	0	0	0	0	0	1	0	0	0	.000	.000	.000
Edmondson, Brian, Erie	39	1	1	0	0	0	0	0	0	0	0	0	0	0	0	0	0	0	0	.000	.000	.000
Elwood, Brad, Nor.	1	1	1	0	0	0	0	0	0	0	0	0	0	0	0	0	0	0	0	.000	.000	.000
Erickson, Corey, Akr.	99	386	345	49	80	167	21	3	20	64	1	1	5	34	0	101	3	3	0	.232	.309	.484
Espy, Nate, Read.	141	602	517	83	138	212	28	2	14	76	0	4	7	73	3	83	18	1	11	.267	.363	.410
Estrella, Leo, N.H.	15	6	5	2	2	2	0	0	0	1	0	0	0	1	0	2	0	0	0	.400	.500	.400
Farnsworth, Troy, N.H.	20	64	58	1	5	5	0	0	0	1	0	0	1	5	0	25	0	1	0	.086	.172	.086
Ferrari, Anthony, Har.*	44	3	3	0	0	0	0	0	0	0	0	0	0	0	0	1	0	0	0	.000	.000	.000
Fesh, Sean, Port.*	24	5	3	2	0	0	0	0	0	0	0	0	0	1	0	2	0	0	0	.000	.250	.000
Figueroa, Franky, Bow.	8	32	30	6	11	15	2	1	0	3	1	0	0	1	0	7	0	0	1	.367	.387	.500
Figueroa, Luis, Har.†	66	283	250	47	68	94	17	3	1	30	4	2	2	25	0	16	6	7	5	.272	.341	.376
Fischer, Mark, Tren.	43	144	131	17	19	33	5	0	3	9	0	1	0	12	0	44	2	1	3	.145	.215	.252
Fitzgerald, Jason, Akr.*	106	439	392	43	100	156	23	0	11	57	0	4	1	41	4	80	21	6	7	.255	.324	.398
Ford, Lew, N.B.	93	435	373	81	116	192	27	2	15	51	4	1	8	49	0	47	17	5	5	.311	.401	.515
Foster, Quincy, Port.-Har.*	80	293	264	41	75	106	9	5	4	32	4	3	3	19	0	43	26	12	3	.284	.336	.402
Fox, Jason, Har.†	7	18	16	2	2	4	0	1	0	3	2	0	0	0	0	4	1	0	0	.125	.125	.250
Franco, Martire, Read.	16	12	11	1	2	3	1	0	0	1	0	0	0	1	0	4	0	0	0	.182	.182	.273
Frank, Mike, N.H.*	16	72	62	8	19	30	1	2	2	9	0	0	1	8	0	5	1	1	2	.306	.394	.484
French, Anton, Tren.†	20	91	85	15	21	30	2	2	1	7	0	0	1	5	0	24	13	6	1	.247	.297	.353
Gall, John, N.H.	135	569	526	82	166	277	45	3	20	81	0	3	2	38	1	75	4	1	26	.316	.362	.527
Garcia, Luis, N.H.-Akr.	127	524	474	66	130	211	25	1	18	58	0	3	2	45	4	86	4	2	17	.274	.338	.445
Garland, Ross, Erie	1	6	6	0	2	2	0	0	0	0	0	0	0	0	0	2	0	0	0	.333	.333	.333
Garrett, Shawn, Alt.†	131	533	489	71	142	215	24	8	11	73	1	3	7	33	4	88	19	6	16	.290	.342	.440
Gerut, Jody, Akr.*	65	291	256	44	72	118	15	2	9	39	0	0	1	34	3	30	17	8	7	.281	.368	.461
Gibbs, Kevin, Nor.†	63	246	217	36	64	84	8	3	2	18	5	2	1	21	0	32	20	8	3	.295	.357	.387
Gibbs, Mark, Bow.	2	6	6	0	1	2	1	0	0	2	0	0	0	0	0	3	0	0	0	.167	.167	.333
Gingrich, Troy, Har.*	1	3	3	0	1	1	0	0	0	0	0	0	0	0	0	0	0	0	0	.333	.333	.333
Glaser, Eric, Tren.	33	2	2	0	0	0	0	0	0	0	0	0	0	0	0	0	0	0	0	.000	.000	.000
Goelz, Jim, Akr.	17	52	49	7	6	9	3	0	0	4	0	0	1	2	0	6	0	1	3	.122	.173	.184
Goetz, Geoff, Port.*	2	1	1	0	1	2	1	0	0	0	0	0	0	0	0	0	0	0	0	1.000	1.000	2.000
Gonzalez, Adrian, Port.*	138	574	508	70	135	222	34	1	17	96	0	3	8	54	6	112	6	3	13	.266	.344	.437
Gonzalez, Jimmy, Bing.	96	356	299	33	72	104	10	2	6	38	1	3	8	45	2	51	3	3	8	.241	.352	.348
Gonzalez, Luis, Alt.	73	291	263	42	70	104	10	3	6	24	5	6	5	12	0	37	4	0	6	.266	.304	.395
Gonzalez, Manny, Read.†	33	95	83	9	17	25	3	1	1	6	0	0	3	9	0	12	0	1	1	.205	.305	.301
Gonzalez, Mike, Alt.	16	15	14	1	5	5	0	0	0	1	1	0	0	0	0	4	0	0	0	.357	.357	.357
Grabow, John, Alt.*	28	21	15	2	2	4	0	1	0	1	4	0	0	2	0	4	0	0	0	.133	.235	.267
Gredvig, Doug, Bow.	129	516	465	48	128	194	22	1	14	80	0	1	4	46	2	94	2	3	12	.275	.345	.417
Green, Chad, N.B.†	20	82	76	12	25	41	3	2	3	13	0	1	0	5	0	11	4	3	1	.329	.366	.539
Griffin, John-ford, Nor.*	18	75	67	17	22	40	3	0	5	10	0	0	0	8	1	13	0	1	5	.328	.400	.597
Griffiths, Jeremy, Bing.	27	22	16	2	1	1	0	0	0	0	4	0	0	2	0	7	0	0	0	.063	.167	.063
Grindell, Nate, Akr.	119	485	435	73	123	196	24	8	11	60	2	9	6	33	2	61	4	3	9	.283	.335	.451
Guy, Brad, Alt.	26	4	4	0	0	0	0	0	0	0	0	0	0	0	0	2	0	0	0	.000	.000	.000
Hage, Tom, Tren.*	27	78	64	7	16	22	3	0	1	9	0	1	1	12	2	16	0	1	0	.250	.372	.344
Hamilton, Jimmy, Read.*	46	2	1	1	0	0	0	0	0	0	0	1	0	0	0	0	0	0	0	.000	.000	.000
Hamilton, Jon, Akr.*	43	167	148	24	34	65	7	3	6	22	0	2	1	16	0	33	5	1	0	.230	.305	.439
Hammond, Joey, Bow.	52	209	176	25	45	56	9	1	0	13	0	3	0	30	0	32	3	1	1	.256	.359	.318
Hamulack, Tim, Port.*	38	1	1	0	0	0	0	0	0	0	0	0	0	0	0	1	0	0	0	.000	.000	.000
Hannahan, Buzz, Read.	84	327	269	47	62	82	7	2	3	23	2	5	9	42	0	49	14	4	1	.230	.348	.305
Hannahan, Jack, Erie*	65	249	226	17	54	77	12	1	3	20	0	0	2	21	0	50	2	1	7	.239	.309	.341
Hart, Bo, N.H.	104	463	410	61	101	142	17	6	4	39	1	2	12	43	1	82	14	7	6	.249	.338	.351
Haverbusch, Kevin, Alt.	35	135	130	18	38	60	7	0	5	16	0	0	1	4	0	21	4	2	2	.292	.319	.462
Haynes, Dee, N.H.	131	544	504	75	157	257	29	4	21	98	1	3	11	25	0	67	3	2	15	.312	.355	.510
Headley, Justin, Tren.*	112	431	377	60	101	159	23	1	11	56	0	4	7	43	3	61	4	7	3	.268	.350	.422
Hebson, Bryan, Har.	38	11	10	1	1	4	0	0	1	0	1	0	0	0	1	3	0	0	0	.100	.182	.400
Heilman, Aaron, Bing.	17	21	14	1	4	5	1	0	0	1	4	0	0	3	0	6	0	0	0	.286	.412	.357
Heintz, Chris, N.H.	105	397	373	40	117	169	29	1	7	45	2	1	2	19	3	61	1	0	13	.314	.349	.453
Henkel, Rob, Port.	13	16	15	2	3	3	0	0	0	0	1	0	0	0	0	6	0	0	2	.200	.200	.200
Hernandez, Michel, Nor.	20	67	61	11	19	28	6	0	1	12	0	1	0	5	0	6	0	1	2	.311	.358	.459
Hiles, Chris, Read.	21	2	2	0	1	2	1	0	0	0	0	0	0	0	0	0	0	0	0	.500	.500	1.000
Hitchcox, Brian, Read.*	91	322	297	43	79	119	18	2	6	27	3	1	5	16	0	30	4	5	3	.266	.313	.401
Hodge, Kevin, N.B.	41	60	52	4	10	14	1	0	1	5	0	1	2	5	0	15	1	3	0	.192	.283	.269
Hodges, Scott, Har.*	135	596	526	79	143	209	35	2	9	68	1	3	3	63	3	102	2	2	9	.272	.351	.397
Hoffpauir, Josh, Bow.*	86	331	302	31	81	102	12	3	1	25	4	1	3	21	2	28	10	6	5	.268	.321	.338
Honeycutt, Heath, Port.	12	48	44	7	6	15	0	0	2	6	0	1	0	3	0	15	1	0	1	.136	.188	.341
Hooper, Clay, Nor.	77	264	236	32	55	69	6	1	2	16	2	1	4	21	0	34	0	6	8	.233	.305	.292
House, J.R., Alt.	30	106	91	9	24	36	6	0	2	11	0	2	0	13	0	21	0	0	4	.264	.349	.396

Player, Team	G	TPA	AB	R	H	TB	2B	3B	HR	RBI	SH	SF	HP	BB	IBB	SO	SB	CS	GDP	Avg.	OBP	Slg.
Hunter, Scott, Bing.-Bow.	108	426	386	49	88	133	24	0	7	43	6	5	5	24	0	73	10	5	6	.228	.279	.345
Iapoce, Anthony, Port.	75	318	280	42	80	105	15	2	2	30	1	1	8	28	0	46	20	3	2	.286	.366	.375
Izquierdo, Hansel, Port.	1	2	1	0	0	0	0	0	0	0	0	0	0	1	0	0	0	0	0	.000	.500	.000
Izturis, Maicer, Akr.†	67	281	253	34	70	96	12	7	0	32	5	3	3	17	0	28	8	4	10	.277	.326	.379
Jackson, Brandon, Nor.	24	74	65	8	11	16	2	0	1	8	1	3	0	5	0	15	0	2	2	.169	.219	.246
Jacobsen, Bucky, N.H.	34	114	102	13	30	53	11	0	4	21	0	1	2	9	0	25	0	0	0	.294	.360	.520
Jacobson, Russ, Read.	86	309	282	20	55	79	15	0	3	34	1	0	8	18	2	78	1	0	6	.195	.263	.280
Jamison, Ryan, Bing.	11	4	2	0	1	1	0	0	0	0	0	0	1	0	0	1	0	0	0	.500	.667	.500
Janke, Cheyenne, N.H.	28	17	16	1	2	2	0	0	0	1	0	0	0	0	0	4	0	0	0	.125	.125	.125
Johnson, Jason, Read.	113	444	411	40	117	133	16	0	0	45	6	3	8	16	1	76	19	10	8	.285	.322	.324
Jones, Mitch, Nor.	61	240	216	31	47	93	16	0	10	27	2	0	4	18	1	59	1	4	4	.218	.290	.431
Jorgensen, Ryan, Port.	41	157	144	15	32	42	4	0	2	14	0	0	1	12	0	33	3	1	3	.222	.287	.292
Joseph, Jake, Bing.	14	17	15	1	4	4	0	0	0	1	0	0	1	0	0	2	0	0	0	.267	.313	.267
Journell, Jimmy, N.H.	10	14	13	2	3	3	0	0	0	1	1	0	0	0	0	5	0	0	0	.231	.231	.231
Karnuth, Jason, N.H.	58	1	0	0	0	0	0	0	0	0	0	0	0	1	0	0	0	0	0	.000	1.000	.000
Karp, Josh, Har.	16	13	10	1	2	2	0	0	0	2	1	0	0	2	0	1	0	0	1	.200	.333	.200
Kelly, Heath, Port.	69	201	180	25	36	67	8	1	7	24	2	1	2	16	0	74	3	0	2	.200	.271	.372
Kinchen, Jason, Nor.*	41	139	123	14	29	57	5	1	7	19	0	1	0	15	2	27	1	1	5	.236	.317	.463
King, Brad, Alt.	45	164	129	28	34	47	4	0	3	12	2	1	2	30	0	24	1	1	3	.264	.407	.364
Knupfer, Jason, Read.	10	46	40	9	9	20	2	0	3	4	0	0	0	6	0	8	4	0	4	.225	.326	.500
Kropf, Andy, Erie†	23	81	74	6	20	29	6	0	1	9	0	0	0	7	0	15	0	0	1	.270	.333	.392
Kubes, Greg, Read.	28	29	24	1	2	2	0	0	0	1	5	0	0	0	0	14	0	0	0	.083	.083	.083
Lambert, Jeremy, N.H.	18	2	2	0	0	0	0	0	0	0	0	0	0	0	0	2	0	0	0	.000	.000	.000
Larned, Drew, Tren.	1	4	4	1	1	4	0	0	1	1	0	0	0	0	0	1	0	0	1	.250	.250	1.000
Lawton, Matt, Akr.*	3	13	10	1	0	0	0	0	0	0	0	0	3	0	1	0	0	0	0	.000	.231	.000
Leach, Nick, Nor.*	10	25	19	2	3	6	0	0	1	3	1	0	1	4	1	4	0	0	1	.158	.333	.316
Lee, Cliff, Har.*	15	12	12	1	1	1	0	0	0	0	0	0	0	0	0	3	0	0	0	.083	.083	.083
Lee, Seung, Read.	1	2	2	0	1	1	0	0	0	0	0	0	0	0	0	0	0	0	0	.500	.500	.500
Lemonis, Chris, Alt.*	6	19	17	1	0	0	0	0	0	0	0	0	0	2	0	1	1	0	0	.000	.105	.000
Leon, Carlos, Tren.†	81	312	265	44	74	92	11	2	1	20	9	5	6	27	0	31	15	9	7	.279	.353	.347
Lewis, Craig, Har.	17	2	2	0	0	0	0	0	0	0	0	0	0	0	0	0	0	0	0	.000	.000	.000
LeBron, Juan, N.H.	33	115	107	18	28	46	7	1	3	12	0	2	1	5	0	17	3	1	6	.262	.296	.430
Lidle, Kevin, Erie†	24	1	1	1	1	1	0	0	0	0	0	0	0	0	0	0	0	0	0	1.000	1.000	1.000
Lindsey, Rodney, Erie	99	411	371	45	97	129	14	6	2	20	6	1	5	28	0	94	27	9	4	.261	.321	.348
Lofton, James, Tren.†	35	143	127	15	30	39	9	0	0	11	3	0	1	12	0	28	1	2	2	.236	.307	.307
Loggins, Josh, Nor.	34	104	98	6	20	28	5	0	1	5	1	0	0	5	0	26	1	1	1	.204	.243	.286
Lomasney, Steve, Tren.	109	406	338	43	71	118	17	3	8	56	0	4	9	55	1	133	5	5	8	.210	.333	.349
Lopez, Angel, Port.	5	17	17	2	6	10	1	0	1	2	0	0	0	0	0	6	0	0	0	.353	.353	.588
Lopez, Jose, Alt.	11	5	4	1	1	1	0	0	0	0	1	0	0	0	0	1	0	0	0	.250	.250	.250
Lorenzo, Juan, N.B.†	78	234	215	33	58	72	6	1	2	19	7	1	3	8	0	22	1	2	5	.270	.304	.335
Luderer, Brian, Akr.	50	172	155	29	38	60	11	1	3	17	0	2	4	11	0	32	0	0	5	.245	.308	.387
Machado, Albenis, Har.†	75	298	240	29	58	79	9	3	2	28	4	3	5	46	1	38	6	4	7	.242	.371	.329
Machado, Andy, Read.†	126	547	450	71	113	179	24	3	12	77	18	5	2	72	4	118	40	11	5	.251	.353	.398
Madson, Ryan, Read.*	27	20	16	2	4	6	2	0	0	1	3	0	1	0	0	4	0	0	0	.250	.294	.375
Malave, Jaime, Bing.	13	38	36	2	8	11	0	0	1	5	0	0	0	2	0	10	0	0	2	.222	.263	.306
Maness, Nick, Bing.	25	21	18	1	5	8	3	0	0	0	1	0	0	2	0	6	0	0	0	.278	.350	.444
Mangum, Mark, Har.	18	12	10	3	2	2	0	0	0	1	0	0	0	2	0	1	0	0	0	.200	.333	.200
Manon, Julio, Har.*	6	5	2	0	0	0	0	0	0	0	3	0	0	0	0	1	0	0	0	.000	.000	.000
Marrero, Darwin, Har.	19	21	21	1	2	2	0	0	0	1	0	0	0	0	0	5	0	0	0	.095	.095	.095
Marsters, Brandon, N.B.	22	87	76	12	18	32	8	0	2	13	0	2	2	7	0	18	0	0	2	.237	.310	.421
Martinez, Eddy, N.H.	24	91	80	8	17	21	4	0	0	3	3	0	4	4	0	17	1	1	1	.213	.284	.263
Martinez, Octavio, Bow.	7	25	23	4	5	5	0	0	0	1	0	1	0	0	0	3	0	0	2	.217	.250	.217
Martinez, Victor, Akr.†	121	515	443	84	149	255	40	0	22	85	0	6	8	58	6	62	3	3	10	.336	.417	.576
Matos, Luis, Bow.	62	255	218	34	60	105	14	2	9	40	1	2	2	32	1	45	14	4	6	.275	.370	.482
McAvoy, Jeff, Har.	16	3	2	1	1	4	0	0	1	1	0	0	0	1	0	0	0	0	0	.500	.667	2.000
McConnell, Sam, Read.*	30	12	10	1	3	6	0	0	1	1	0	0	0	2	0	2	0	0	0	.300	.417	.600
McDade, Neal, Alt.	49	7	6	0	0	0	0	0	0	0	0	0	0	1	0	3	0	0	0	.000	.143	.000
McDonald, Darnell, Bow.	37	168	144	21	42	65	9	1	4	15	0	0	2	22	0	27	9	3	1	.292	.393	.451
McDougall, Marshall, Akr.	7	24	18	6	7	12	2	0	1	4	0	0	0	6	0	2	0	0	1	.389	.542	.667
McEwing, Joe, Bing.	1	5	5	0	0	0	0	0	0	0	0	0	0	0	0	1	0	0	0	.000	.000	.000
McGee, Tom, Bow.	15	43	39	1	6	7	1	0	0	4	2	1	0	1	0	5	0	0	0	.154	.171	.179
McKinley, Dan, Har.*	52	185	169	20	38	60	5	4	3	20	1	2	2	11	1	35	3	2	3	.225	.277	.355
McKinley, Josh, Har.†	103	372	325	40	76	114	17	0	7	33	1	3	1	42	1	81	2	4	8	.234	.321	.351
McNally, Sean, Har.	9	25	22	0	3	3	0	0	0	3	0	3	0	0	0	6	0	0	2	.136	.120	.136
McNaughton, Troy, Read.*	18	62	57	7	9	17	2	0	2	7	0	0	0	5	0	19	0	0	2	.158	.226	.298
McNeal, Aaron, Bing.	96	400	348	52	104	176	15	0	19	69	0	6	1	45	0	95	1	2	12	.299	.375	.506
Meadows, Randy, Alt.	48	123	111	16	14	22	2	0	2	8	2	1	3	6	1	29	2	1	0	.126	.190	.198
Medrano, Jesus, Port.	116	502	414	77	123	171	27	6	3	32	3	3	3	79	1	82	39	18	5	.297	.411	.413
Meier, Dan, Alt.*	78	265	237	27	58	90	10	2	6	33	0	3	2	23	0	66	2	3	3	.245	.313	.380
Meran, Jorge, Erie	56	203	184	18	46	72	5	3	5	17	0	1	2	16	0	55	1	0	2	.250	.315	.391
Millar, Kevin, Port.	3	13	12	1	1	4	0	0	1	3	0	1	0	0	0	5	0	0	0	.083	.077	.333
Molina, Izzy, Bow.	57	220	196	23	51	73	7	0	5	18	0	3	2	19	0	34	1	0	4	.260	.327	.372
Montgomery, Matt, Alt.	44	1	0	0	0	0	0	0	0	0	1	0	0	0	0	0	0	0	0	.000	.000	.000
Mooney, Dan, Tren.	23	67	62	4	7	8	1	0	0	4	4	0	1	0	0	21	0	0	3	.113	.127	.129
Morales, Andy, Tren.	16	46	39	2	9	11	2	0	0	2	0	0	0	7	1	7	2	1	2	.231	.348	.282
Morales, Steve, Port.‡	51	174	164	16	43	68	10	0	5	25	3	0	2	5	0	22	0	1	7	.262	.292	.415
Morneau, Justin, N.B.*	126	548	494	72	147	234	31	4	16	80	0	6	6	42	5	88	7	0	8	.298	.356	.474
Munoz, Billy, Akr.*	74	295	248	37	62	101	22	1	5	44	0	5	1	41	1	47	0	1	12	.250	.353	.407
Myrow, Brian, Nor.*	61	236	188	37	57	82	16	0	3	30	0	1	6	41	1	42	5	0	4	.303	.441	.436
Neill, Ryan, Erie.	11	42	37	4	7	12	2	0	1	3	0	0	1	4	0	13	1	1	2	.189	.286	.324
Nettles, Jeff, Nor.	44	122	106	10	29	43	5	0	3	17	1	0	1	14	0	25	0	0	3	.274	.364	.406

Player, Team	G	TPA	AB	R	H	TB	2B	3B	HR	RBI	SH	SF	HP	BB	IBB	SO	SB	CS	GDP	Avg.	OBP	Slg.
Nicholson, Derek, Erie*	10	41	34	9	10	23	5	1	2	7	0	0	1	6	0	11	0	1	0	.294	.415	.676
Nicholson, Kevin, N.H.†	58	261	231	40	69	103	16	3	4	36	3	5	1	21	0	31	3	6	9	.299	.353	.446
Nieves, Raul, Tren.†	13	38	34	2	9	11	2	0	0	3	0	0	0	4	0	6	0	1	0	.265	.342	.324
Niles, Drew, Port.†	86	283	259	27	58	84	10	8	0	16	4	3	3	14	1	69	3	2	7	.224	.269	.324
Nye, Rodney, Bing.	121	469	394	51	93	149	17	0	13	53	4	3	13	55	1	99	4	2	9	.236	.346	.378
Oakes, Matty, Erie	9	27	27	0	5	6	1	0	0	2	0	0	0	0	0	6	0	0	1	.185	.185	.222
Ochoa, Pablo, Bing.	8	1	1	0	0	0	0	0	0	0	0	0	0	0	0	0	0	0	0	.000	.000	.000
O'Connor, Brian, Alt.*	24	13	8	0	2	2	0	0	0	0	0	0	3	0	0	2	0	1	0	.250	.400	.250
Olivares, Teuris, Nor.	40	160	142	22	37	51	6	1	2	15	1	2	2	13	0	30	4	3	4	.261	.327	.359
Ortiz, Omar, Port.†	33	14	12	0	3	5	2	0	0	2	1	0	0	1	0	3	0	0	0	.250	.308	.417
Outlaw, Mark, Read.*	41	1	1	0	0	0	0	0	0	0	0	0	0	0	0	0	0	0	0	.000	.000	.000
Ozias, Todd, Read.	31	3	3	0	0	0	0	0	0	0	0	0	0	0	0	0	0	0	0	.000	.000	.000
Pachot, John, Alt.	94	336	321	31	84	122	29	0	3	44	0	6	3	6	0	31	1	0	3	.262	.277	.380
Padgett, Matt, Port.*	117	452	406	52	95	171	26	1	16	63	1	0	2	43	3	131	6	5	3	.234	.310	.421
Padilla, Jorge, Read.	127	545	484	71	124	179	30	2	7	65	2	8	11	40	1	77	32	11	5	.256	.322	.370
Parrish, Dave, Read.	106	387	341	38	81	112	17	1	4	42	2	1	4	39	1	63	13	6	13	.238	.322	.328
Parrott, Rhett, N.H.	9	14	11	2	3	4	1	0	0	0	0	0	0	3	0	4	0	0	0	.273	.429	.364
Pascucci, Val, Har.	137	572	459	73	108	205	14	1	27	82	0	7	13	93	3	115	2	0	13	.235	.374	.447
Pautz, Brad, Read.	44	4	3	0	0	0	0	0	0	0	1	0	0	0	0	2	0	0	0	.000	.000	.000
Pearsall, J.J., Port.*	12	1	1	0	0	0	0	0	0	0	0	0	0	0	0	1	0	0	0	.000	.000	.000
Peeples, Mike, Port.	24	96	83	11	17	27	5	1	1	8	0	3	0	10	0	21	1	2	2	.205	.281	.325
Peralta, John, Akr.	130	538	470	62	132	215	28	5	15	62	7	11	5	45	0	97	4	2	6	.281	.343	.457
Perez, Frank, Read.	40	9	8	1	1	1	0	0	0	2	0	0	0	1	0	4	0	0	0	.125	.222	.125
Perez, Jhonny, Erie	94	387	343	45	105	132	14	2	3	47	5	5	2	30	2	51	8	6	8	.306	.361	.385
Perez, Josue, Read.†	64	216	196	14	42	53	8	0	1	17	3	2	2	13	0	41	6	5	2	.214	.268	.270
Perez, Tomas, Read.†	2	9	9	2	4	4	0	0	0	1	0	0	0	0	0	1	0	0	0	.444	.444	.444
Phillips, Andy, Nor.	73	312	272	58	83	168	24	2	19	51	0	4	3	33	2	56	4	3	6	.305	.381	.618
Phillips, Brandon, Har.	60	267	245	40	80	124	13	2	9	35	1	0	5	16	2	33	6	3	7	.327	.380	.506
Pogue, Jamie, N.H.	68	244	208	21	40	61	12	0	3	26	1	0	2	33	2	38	1	1	6	.192	.309	.293
Prather, Scott, N.H.*	11	2	2	0	0	0	0	0	0	0	0	0	0	0	0	1	0	0	0	.000	.000	.000
Pratt, Scott, Akr.*	115	521	446	81	119	195	17	4	17	54	6	1	6	62	2	88	19	4	2	.267	.363	.437
Pumphrey, Ken, Read.	20	20	20	1	6	6	0	0	0	0	0	0	0	0	0	6	0	0	0	.300	.300	.300
Rabe, Josh, N.B.	46	196	183	21	43	56	10	0	1	18	1	0	2	10	0	30	4	1	5	.235	.282	.306
Rachels, Wes, Bow.	69	225	199	19	40	48	6	1	0	19	3	1	1	21	1	33	4	0	7	.201	.279	.241
Raines, Tim, Bow.†	123	539	491	66	128	168	17	4	5	25	10	2	2	34	0	101	33	15	8	.261	.310	.342
Ramos, Kelly, Tren.†	10	31	29	0	4	4	0	0	0	3	0	0	0	2	0	8	0	0	2	.138	.194	.138
Reding, Josh, Har.	15	44	39	3	7	7	0	0	0	3	1	0	2	2	0	8	0	0	1	.179	.256	.179
Redman, Prentice, Bing.	135	570	491	79	139	211	35	2	11	63	6	5	9	59	1	112	43	9	0	.283	.367	.430
Reed, Keith, Bow.	137	543	488	57	120	187	20	1	15	64	2	3	10	40	0	107	3	10	13	.246	.314	.383
Reese, Kevin, Nor.*	138	602	514	80	149	197	24	6	4	45	5	2	4	77	1	87	22	14	6	.290	.385	.383
Reid, Justin, Alt.	25	24	22	2	4	6	0	1	0	1	2	0	0	0	0	8	0	0	0	.182	.182	.273
Reyes, Jose, Bing.†	65	295	275	46	79	117	16	8	2	24	2	0	2	16	1	42	27	11	2	.287	.331	.425
Richard, Chris, Bow.*	2	8	6	0	2	3	1	0	0	1	0	1	0	1	0	2	0	0	0	.333	.375	.500
Richardson, Corey, Erie†	109	444	377	53	96	117	13	1	2	23	3	2	2	60	0	80	30	5	5	.255	.358	.310
Rifkin, Aaron, Nor.*	70	267	235	40	59	86	13	1	4	34	0	1	3	28	1	64	5	3	2	.251	.337	.366
Rigsby, Randy, Port.*	53	172	156	10	39	64	10	0	5	21	4	0	3	9	0	47	5	2	4	.250	.304	.410
Rios, Armando, Alt.*	1	3	2	0	0	0	0	0	0	0	0	0	0	1	0	0	0	0	0	.000	.333	.000
Rivera, Carlos, Alt.*	128	533	494	67	149	247	28	4	22	84	0	4	8	27	3	75	1	1	18	.302	.345	.500
Rivera, Saul, Bing.	30	2	2	1	2	2	0	0	0	1	0	0	0	0	0	0	0	0	0	1.000	1.000	1.000
Roach, Jason, Bing.	8	6	4	2	2	3	1	0	0	0	1	0	0	1	0	1	0	0	0	.500	.600	.750
Roberge, J.P., Read.	3	12	11	2	2	5	0	0	1	3	0	0	1	0	0	1	0	0	0	.182	.250	.455
Robertson, Nathan, Port.	27	26	24	2	5	6	1	0	0	1	2	0	0	0	0	8	0	0	0	.208	.208	.250
Rodgers, Bobby, Port.	3	2	2	0	0	0	0	0	0	0	0	0	0	0	0	1	0	0	0	.000	.000	.000
Rodriguez, John, Nor.*	103	405	354	51	76	145	18	3	15	63	1	4	11	35	2	94	13	3	4	.215	.302	.410
Rodriguez, Luis, N.B.†	129	557	455	60	117	163	18	2	8	40	32	4	5	61	1	44	3	2	8	.257	.349	.358
Rodriguez, Victor, Alt.	61	203	188	29	55	70	6	0	3	20	3	1	2	9	1	20	3	0	5	.293	.330	.372
Rogers, Ed, Bow.	112	459	422	59	110	173	26	2	11	57	5	6	10	16	1	70	14	4	9	.261	.300	.410
Roneberg, Brett, Har.*	63	248	214	36	63	94	15	2	4	36	2	3	2	27	0	38	2	1	0	.294	.374	.439
Rose, Mike, Tren.†	10	34	29	1	3	6	1	1	0	0	0	0	5	0	0	7	0	0	2	.103	.235	.207
Ross, Cody, Erie	105	454	400	73	112	203	28	3	19	72	2	5	3	44	1	86	16	2	11	.280	.352	.508
Saenz, Jason, Bing.*	36	2	2	0	0	0	0	0	0	0	0	0	0	0	0	0	0	0	0	.000	.000	.000
St. Pierre, Maxim, Erie	60	229	207	24	55	73	9	0	3	28	1	3	1	17	1	31	0	1	10	.266	.320	.353
Salazar, Oscar, Erie-Bing.	81	290	266	22	54	97	20	1	7	31	0	1	4	19	0	55	2	2	8	.203	.266	.365
Salazar, Ruben, N.B.	103	405	371	49	103	143	24	2	4	41	1	3	3	27	1	72	4	0	7	.278	.329	.385
Salinas, Trey, Bow.	8	30	26	2	4	5	1	0	0	3	0	0	1	3	0	4	0	0	0	.154	.267	.192
Salzano, Jerry, Tren.	121	506	437	70	110	170	27	0	11	66	0	8	8	53	0	74	19	5	11	.252	.338	.389
Sanchez, Freddy, Tren.	80	362	311	60	102	136	23	1	3	38	5	4	5	37	0	45	19	3	9	.328	.403	.437
Sandusky, Scott, Har.	107	406	354	38	73	97	16	1	2	35	8	8	5	31	0	66	0	2	12	.206	.274	.274
Sansom, Trevor, N.H.	47	2	2	0	1	1	0	0	0	0	0	0	0	0	0	1	0	0	0	.500	.500	.500
Santiago, Ramon, Erie†	22	84	75	9	21	28	0	2	1	7	2	1	3	3	0	12	6	0	2	.280	.329	.373
Santos, Jose, Port.	68	242	214	24	45	64	8	1	3	33	0	3	2	23	1	57	3	3	3	.210	.289	.299
Scanlon, Matt, N.B.*	68	224	197	24	38	57	6	2	3	25	2	3	6	16	0	39	4	1	4	.193	.270	.289
Schnabel, Nick, Har.	16	23	18	2	5	5	0	0	0	1	0	0	0	5	0	0	0	0	0	.278	.435	.278
Schurman, Ryan, N.H.	18	8	6	0	2	2	0	0	0	0	0	0	0	2	0	0	0	0	0	.333	.500	.333
Seale, Dustin, Har.*	29	5	5	0	0	0	0	0	0	0	0	0	0	0	0	3	0	0	0	.000	.000	.000
Seestedt, Mike, Bow.	1	4	3	0	0	0	0	0	0	0	0	0	0	0	0	1	0	0	0	.000	.000	.000
Sefcik, Kevin, Alt.	126	525	467	69	144	186	32	2	2	51	3	4	7	44	3	42	12	8	9	.308	.374	.398
Seibel, Phil, Bing.*	28	20	18	0	3	4	1	0	0	1	2	0	0	0	0	8	0	0	0	.167	.167	.222
Seo, Jae, Bing.	1	2	2	0	0	0	0	0	0	0	0	0	0	0	0	1	0	0	1	.000	.000	.000
Sequea, Jorge, Erie†	112	461	397	55	106	151	24	3	5	39	9	6	8	41	0	79	13	2	9	.267	.343	.380
Sergent, Joe, Port.*	20	8	6	1	0	0	0	0	0	0	1	0	1	0	0	4	0	0	0	.000	.143	.000

Player, Team	G	TPA	AB	R	H	TB	2B	3B	HR	RBI	SH	SF	HP	BB	IBB	SO	SB	CS	GDP	Avg.	OBP	Slg.
Sergio, Tom, Tren.*	123	547	482	77	131	207	28	3	14	75	2	6	11	46	1	82	6	6	8	.272	.345	.429
Shaffar, Ben, Alt.†	18	12	9	0	0	0	0	0	0	0	3	0	0	0	0	7	0	0	0	.000	.000	.000
Sherrod, Justin, Tren.	70	280	243	37	62	110	19	1	9	47	0	3	5	29	0	81	8	4	4	.255	.343	.453
Shipp, Brian, Bing.	119	417	375	51	85	142	27	3	8	49	8	4	8	22	1	95	7	8	14	.227	.281	.379
Sitzman, Jay, Read.*	108	434	385	59	97	157	21	6	9	57	3	4	14	28	1	82	18	10	6	.252	.323	.408
Skrehot, Shaun, Alt.	80	345	312	40	75	102	15	3	2	25	2	0	8	23	0	60	9	4	8	.240	.309	.327
Sledge, Terrmel, Har.*	102	468	396	74	119	173	18	6	8	43	4	1	12	55	2	70	11	8	4	.301	.401	.437
Sloan, Brandon, Port.†	43	7	7	0	0	0	0	0	0	0	0	0	0	0	0	4	0	0	0	.000	.000	.000
Smith, Jeff, N.B.*	90	332	297	40	88	136	15	0	11	48	4	5	5	21	0	47	1	2	8	.296	.348	.458
Smith, Nestor, N.B.†	5	9	9	2	0	0	0	0	0	1	0	0	0	0	0	5	1	0	1	.000	.000	.000
Smith, Will, Tren.	2	5	5	0	0	0	0	0	0	0	0	0	0	0	0	2	0	0	0	.000	.000	.000
Snare, Ryan, Port.*	11	6	4	1	0	0	0	0	0	0	2	0	0	0	0	0	0	0	0	.000	.000	.000
Snead, Esix, Bing.†	125	470	401	62	101	131	9	6	3	42	16	2	6	45	0	72	66	18	4	.252	.335	.327
Snusz, Chris, Nor.	15	45	41	3	6	11	2	0	1	3	1	0	1	2	0	13	0	0	1	.146	.205	.268
Soler, Ramon, Bing.†	8	38	31	4	7	7	0	0	0	1	3	0	0	4	0	5	3	2	0	.226	.314	.226
Sosa, Nick, N.B.	4	15	14	0	1	1	0	0	0	0	0	0	0	1	0	7	0	0	1	.071	.133	.071
Spurling, Chris, Alt.	52	4	4	0	1	2	1	0	0	0	0	0	0	0	0	3	0	0	0	.250	.250	.500
Sternle, Steve, N.H.	8	9	9	0	1	2	1	0	0	1	0	0	0	0	0	5	0	0	0	.111	.111	.222
Taguchi, So, N.H.	26	120	107	21	33	46	10	0	1	15	0	1	3	9	0	15	3	1	1	.308	.375	.430
Thompson, Andy, N.H.	2	8	5	1	0	0	0	0	0	1	0	1	0	2	0	4	0	0	0	.000	.250	.000
Torres, Gabby, N.B.	73	226	191	21	52	73	13	1	2	24	2	2	3	28	0	26	0	2	4	.272	.371	.382
Trachsel, Steve, Bing.	1	2	2	1	2	2	0	0	0	0	0	0	0	0	0	0	0	0	0	1.000	1.000	1.000
Treanor, Matt, Port.	50	192	156	24	39	73	5	1	9	28	1	0	7	28	1	33	3	0	5	.250	.387	.468
Tyson, Torre, Nor.†	15	42	35	6	6	6	0	0	0	3	1	0	1	5	0	8	1	2	0	.171	.293	.171
Ullery, Dave, Bow.*	38	121	106	12	20	28	5	0	1	6	0	0	0	15	0	32	0	0	3	.189	.289	.264
Ust, Brant, Erie	60	237	209	28	42	82	11	1	9	20	1	2	5	20	0	55	0	1	1	.201	.284	.392
Valdez, Wilson, Port.	114	401	375	51	98	130	19	5	1	30	3	4	4	15	1	47	18	6	12	.261	.294	.347
Valera, Yohanny, Erie	4	15	15	0	2	3	1	0	0	1	0	0	0	0	0	5	0	0	0	.133	.133	.200
Van Iten, Bobby, Read.*	95	338	314	41	73	101	12	2	4	32	0	2	1	21	2	78	5	2	3	.232	.281	.322
Vargas, Claudio, Har.	8	8	6	0	1	1	0	0	0	0	0	0	0	2	0	1	0	0	1	.167	.375	.167
Vega, Rene, Bing.*	26	3	3	0	0	0	0	0	0	0	0	0	0	0	0	2	0	0	0	.000	.000	.000
Velazquez, Gil, Bing.	27	81	72	6	14	16	2	0	0	5	1	0	1	7	0	15	0	3	3	.194	.275	.222
Vento, Mike, Nor.	64	257	227	29	54	86	16	2	4	26	2	2	1	25	1	49	3	3	6	.238	.314	.379
Veras, Wilton, Tren.	68	300	271	40	91	133	22	1	6	55	0	3	3	23	3	29	0	2	11	.336	.390	.491
Vogelsong, Ryan, Alt.	8	5	5	1	1	1	0	0	0	0	0	0	0	0	0	1	0	0	0	.200	.200	.200
Walrond, Les, N.H.*	4	3	3	0	1	2	1	0	0	0	0	0	0	0	0	0	0	0	0	.333	.333	.667
Ware, Jeremy, Har.	24	103	95	13	25	51	6	1	6	18	0	0	1	7	0	17	0	0	6	.263	.320	.537
Washington, Rico, Alt.*	112	435	359	53	80	121	11	3	8	34	3	1	12	60	3	66	3	4	7	.223	.342	.337
Watson, Brandon, Har.*	2	7	6	2	2	2	0	0	0	0	0	0	1	0	0	0	0	0	0	.333	.429	.333
Watson, Matt, Har.-Bing.*	128	490	441	56	123	183	26	2	10	67	2	5	3	39	4	52	12	8	14	.279	.338	.415
Wayne, Justin, Har.-Port.	24	21	20	1	1	1	0	0	0	0	1	0	0	0	0	10	0	0	0	.050	.050	.050
Weaver, Eric, Read.	37	1	1	0	0	0	0	0	0	0	0	0	0	0	0	1	0	0	0	.000	.000	.000
Weber, Jake, N.H.*	70	213	196	20	57	69	6	0	2	23	2	1	0	14	0	22	3	4	5	.291	.336	.352
Weekly, Chris, N.H.*	40	104	91	13	23	29	6	0	0	4	0	0	0	13	1	25	0	1	2	.253	.346	.319
Weichard, Paul, Alt.†	1	1	1	0	0	0	0	0	0	0	0	0	0	0	0	1	0	0	0	.000	.000	.000
Whiteside, Eli, Bow.	27	107	99	11	26	37	5	0	2	11	1	0	3	4	0	18	0	1	4	.263	.311	.374
Williams, Brady, N.B.	8	20	17	0	1	1	0	0	0	0	0	0	0	3	0	8	0	0	0	.059	.200	.059
Wilson, Desi, Har.*	18	59	54	3	7	7	0	0	0	3	0	0	0	5	0	12	0	0	2	.130	.203	.130
Wilson, John, Bing.	10	27	24	0	5	6	1	0	0	1	0	0	2	1	0	8	0	0	0	.208	.296	.250
Wilson, Josh, Port.	12	44	41	5	14	23	3	0	2	5	1	0	0	2	0	6	0	1	0	.341	.372	.561
Wimberly, Larry, Alt.*	26	7	6	0	0	0	0	0	0	0	0	0	0	4	0	0	0	0	0	.000	.000	.000
Woodards, Orlando, Port.	28	12	12	0	1	1	0	0	0	0	0	0	0	0	0	6	0	0	0	.083	.083	.083
Woods, Ken, Read.	19	84	80	18	27	40	7	0	2	8	0	0	2	2	0	9	3	1	0	.338	.345	.500
Youkilis, Kevin, Tren.	44	197	160	34	55	80	10	0	5	26	0	1	5	31	1	18	5	4	1	.344	.462	.500

PLAYERS WITH TWO OR MORE TEAMS

Player, Team	G	TPA	AB	R	H	TB	2B	3B	HR	RBI	SH	SF	HP	BB	IBB	SO	SB	CS	GDP	Avg.	OBP	Slg.
Bridges, Donnie, Har.	14	12	11	4	2	2	0	0	0	1	0	1	0	0	0	2	0	0	0	.182	.167	.182
Bridges, Donnie, Port.	6	2	1	0	0	0	0	0	0	0	0	0	0	1	0	0	0	0	0	.000	.500	.000
Brown, Jason, Alt.	18	54	47	3	8	13	5	0	0	5	0	2	0	5	0	21	0	0	0	.170	.241	.277
Brown, Jason, Har.	20	66	59	6	14	22	2	0	2	8	0	1	2	4	0	21	0	0	1	.237	.303	.373
Crisp, Covelli, N.H.†	89	397	355	61	107	152	16	1	9	47	5	1	0	36	1	56	26	10	6	.301	.365	.428
Crisp, Covelli, Akr.†	7	36	32	9	13	17	1	0	1	4	1	0	0	3	0	4	0	0	0	.406	.457	.531
Davidson, Cleatus, N.H.†	23	59	52	7	10	15	0	1	1	7	2	0	0	5	1	12	2	0	0	.192	.263	.288
Davidson, Cleatus, Nor.†	31	77	66	12	20	26	2	2	0	12	3	0	2	6	0	13	4	6	1	.303	.378	.394
Davis, Glenn, Nor.†	7	27	23	5	6	14	1	2	1	1	0	0	0	4	0	5	0	1	0	.261	.370	.609
Davis, Glenn, Har.†	27	105	91	13	25	45	2	0	6	17	0	1	0	13	0	29	1	0	1	.275	.362	.495
Foster, Quincy, Port.*	23	84	74	6	18	26	2	0	2	14	2	2	1	5	0	13	10	4	2	.243	.293	.351
Foster, Quincy, Har.*	57	209	190	35	57	80	7	5	2	18	2	1	2	14	0	30	16	8	1	.300	.353	.421
Garcia, Luis, N.H.	88	343	308	42	82	136	16	1	12	37	0	2	1	32	4	59	3	2	12	.266	.335	.442
Garcia, Luis, Akr.	39	181	166	24	48	75	9	0	6	21	0	1	1	13	0	27	1	0	5	.289	.343	.452
Hunter, Scott, Bing.	24	100	89	13	21	31	4	0	2	12	1	1	1	8	0	18	6	2	0	.236	.303	.348
Hunter, Scott, Bow.	84	326	297	36	67	102	20	0	5	31	5	4	4	16	0	55	4	3	6	.226	.271	.343
Salazar, Oscar, Erie	53	208	191	16	41	79	18	1	6	26	0	0	3	14	0	36	2	1	6	.215	.279	.414
Salazar, Oscar, Bing.	28	82	75	6	13	18	2	0	1	5	0	1	1	5	0	19	0	1	2	.173	.232	.240
Watson, Matt, Har.*	1	4	4	1	1	1	0	0	0	0	0	0	0	0	0	0	0	0	0	.250	.250	.250
Watson, Matt, Bing.*	127	486	437	55	122	182	26	2	10	67	2	5	3	39	4	52	12	8	14	.279	.339	.416
Wayne, Justin, Har.	17	15	14	1	1	1	0	0	0	0	1	0	0	0	0	6	0	0	0	.071	.071	.071
Wayne, Justin, Port.	7	6	6	0	0	0	0	0	0	0	0	0	0	0	0	4	0	0	0	.000	.000	.000

GRAND SLAMS—Derosso, An. Machado, J. Rodriguez, Ross, 2 each; Aguila, Bolivar, T. Brown, Camilo, Cervenak, Chamblee, Connacher, Crisp, Davidson, Ford, Garrett, J. Gonzalez, Gredvig, Grindell, Hamilton, Haynes, Hodges, Lomasney, Reese, Rigsby, L. Rodriguez, Salzano, Shipp, Treanor, Veras, M. Watson, 1 each.

AWARDED FIRST BASE ON CATCHER'S INTERFERENCE—Jo. Perez 2 (Lomasney, O. Martinez); Airoso (Whiteside); Bowers (V. Martinez); Espy (Snusz); Fitzgerald (Pachot); Frank (Parrish); A. Gonzalez (Pogue).

2002 PITCHING

TEAM

Team	W	L	Pct.	ERA	G	CG	ShO	Sv.	IP	H	TBF	R	ER	HR	SH	SF	HB	BB	IBB	SO	WP	Bk.
Akron	93	48	.660	3.09	141	4	20	38	1239.0	1097	5199	492	425	78	40	26	78	435	12	1020	47	7
Norwich	76	64	.543	3.58	140	14	9	32	1192.2	1143	5109	567	474	70	49	38	76	384	11	982	72	5
Reading	76	66	.535	3.80	142	7	13	36	1247.1	1211	5298	609	527	114	50	47	52	440	19	847	56	4
Harrisburg	79	63	.556	3.92	142	1	13	33	1247.1	1226	5363	624	543	118	44	53	66	438	9	944	72	9
New Haven	74	65	.532	3.97	139	8	6	32	1213.2	1196	5226	631	536	101	47	38	54	451	21	913	81	1
Binghamton	73	68	.518	4.08	141	4	7	39	1225.2	1176	5248	635	555	96	44	44	63	505	23	983	61	4
Altoona	72	69	.511	4.19	141	5	9	34	1221.0	1241	5248	618	568	116	43	29	62	416	19	894	63	9
Portland	63	77	.450	4.21	140	10	5	33	1192.2	1163	5175	661	558	106	34	42	71	499	17	879	62	10
New Britain	67	72	.482	4.30	139	5	4	41	1202.1	1199	5207	686	575	93	34	41	76	478	27	849	77	3
Bowie	55	85	.393	4.62	140	1	6	26	1205.2	1308	5385	729	619	112	43	35	52	70	487	14	901	83	8
Trenton	63	77	.450	4.72	140	6	5	32	1217.0	1302	5378	741	638	122	43	35	57	484	21	1008	95	8
Erie	52	89	.369	5.29	141	4	2	30	1202.0	1434	5460	805	706	167	48	51	68	488	11	773	72	10

INDIVIDUAL

TOP QUALIFIERS FOR EARNED-RUN AVERAGE TITLE

Minimum 114 innings.*Lefthanded pitcher.

Pitcher, Team	W	L	Pct.	ERA	G	GS	CG	ShO	GF	Sv.	IP	H	TBF	R	ER	HR	SH	SF	HB	BB	IBB	SO	WP	Bk.
Borrell, Danny, Nor.*	9	4	.692	2.31	21	20	1	1	1	0	128.1	116	539	44	33	5	4	3	7	39	4	91	6	0
Wayne, Justin, Har.-Port.	8	5	.615	3.12	24	24	1	1	0	0	141.1	117	585	67	49	10	8	13	11	45	0	77	7	2
Madson, Ryan, Read.	16	4	.800	3.20	26	26	2	0	0	0	171.1	150	699	68	61	11	9	6	12	53	0	132	5	0
Bump, Nate, Port.	7	6	.538	3.38	20	20	3	0	0	0	127.2	110	525	56	48	5	3	1	8	29	0	81	2	1
Robertson, Nathan, Port.*	10	9	.526	3.42	27	27	3	0	0	0	163	156	670	77	62	12	6	8	7	50	2	109	0	2
De Paula, Julio, Nor.	14	6	.700	3.45	27	26	1	1	0	0	175	141	710	74	67	11	7	6	5	52	0	152	6	3
Kubes, Greg, Read.*	13	7	.650	3.46	28	27	0	0	0	0	174.1	177	725	74	67	16	5	6	0	45	0	106	1	0
Janke, Cheyenne, N.H.	12	8	.600	3.48	28	23	1	1	0	0	150	142	629	71	58	13	1	5	4	41	3	112	14	0
Hoard, Brent, N.B.*	11	8	.579	3.69	31	26	2	0	1	0	161	163	672	80	66	11	3	7	5	52	3	126	7	0
Van Hekken, Andy, Erie*	4	7	.364	3.83	21	21	1	0	0	0	134	138	565	69	57	10	6	7	7	34	0	97	7	2
Griffiths, Jeremy, Bing.	8	6	.571	3.89	27	26	2	0	0	0	152.2	157	652	75	66	13	5	4	11	54	0	126	5	0
Seibel, Phil, Bing.*	10	8	.556	3.97	28	25	2	0	1	0	149.2	147	630	78	66	17	8	5	10	49	2	114	6	0
Baisley, Brad, Read.	7	9	.438	4.17	21	21	1	0	0	0	116.2	111	506	69	54	12	2	6	8	51	0	64	9	0
Pumphrey, Ken, Read.	9	7	.563	4.28	20	20	2	1	0	0	120	119	505	65	57	9	3	8	7	34	2	63	6	0
Reid, Justin, Alt.	11	8	.579	4.33	25	25	1	0	0	0	153.2	151	643	87	74	21	8	5	6	28	2	108	4	0

DEPARTMENTAL LEADERS: W—Madson, 16; L—B. Cook, Grabow, Paradis, Pineda, C. Smith, 13 each; Pct.—Duff, .917; G—Karnuth, Layfield, 58 each; GS—B. Cook, Pineda, 28 each; CG—DePaula, 6; ShO—Traber, 2; GF—Layfield, 52; Sv.—J. Padilla, 29; IP—DePaula, 175.0; H—Tekavec, 196; TBF—Kubes, 669; R—Tekavec, 123; ER—Tekavec, 111; HR—Tekavec, 33; SH—Viera, 12; SF—Wayne, 13; HB—Burnside, 15; BB—Martinez, 75; IBB—Padilla, 6; SO—DePaula, 152; WP—Hill, Rosario, 16 each; BK—Grabow, 5.

ALL PITCHERS

*Lefthanded pitcher.

Pitcher, Team	W	L	Pct.	ERA	G	GS	CG	ShO	GF	Sv.	IP	H	TBF	R	ER	HR	SH	SF	HB	BB	IBB	SO	WP	Bk.
Adams, Brian, Tren.*	1	0	1.000	2.90	16	1	0	0	8	1	31	29	138	15	10	1	0	0	2	18	2	17	3	0
Adams, Daniel, Read.	0	0	.000	4.15	2	0	0	0	0	0	4.1	3	18	3	2	1	0	0	0	4	0	4	0	0
Adkins, Tim, Erie*	0	1	.000	15.88	3	0	0	0	1	0	5.2	11	32	10	10	3	0	0	0	4	0	6	0	0
Agamennone, Brandon, Har.	2	0	1.000	2.57	8	0	0	0	6	1	14	11	53	4	4	1	0	1	1	0	0	12	0	0
Ambrose, John, Tren.	2	2	.500	7.08	10	3	0	0	1	0	20.1	26	108	18	16	3	0	1	3	17	1	25	3	0
Anderson, Jason, Nor.	1	1	.500	0.93	16	0	0	0	10	2	19.1	14	72	2	2	1	1	0	0	5	1	21	3	0
Andrade, Jancy, Bow.	0	1	.000	162.00	1	0	0	0	0	0	0.1	5	9	6	6	2	0	0	0	3	0	1	1	0
Arias, Pablo, Erie	5	8	.385	6.86	29	15	0	0	4	0	106.1	138	511	94	81	25	0	4	12	60	1	53	8	1
Arnold, Jason, Nor.	1	2	.333	4.15	3	3	0	0	0	0	17.1	17	80	14	8	1	1	3	4	5	0	18	3	0
Babula, Shaun, Bow.*	0	1	.000	4.32	7	0	0	0	1	0	8.1	12	38	4	4	2	0	0	1	0	0	12	0	0
Bailie, Matt, Read.	0	1	.000	2.91	12	3	0	0	1	0	21.2	18	89	8	7	2	1	0	0	9	0	15	0	1
Baisley, Brad, Read.	7	9	.438	4.17	21	21	1	0	0	0	116.2	111	506	69	54	12	2	6	8	51	0	64	9	0
Beal, Andy, Nor.*	4	5	.444	3.30	10	10	1	1	0	0	62.2	56	261	26	23	3	5	0	1	22	0	61	4	0
Bean, Colter, Nor.	0	2	.000	6.75	12	0	0	0	4	0	10.2	14	54	8	8	1	1	1	2	6	0	9	0	0
Bechler, Steve, Bow.	2	1	.667	3.42	4	4	0	0	0	0	23.2	28	100	11	9	2	1	0	1	6	0	13	3	0
Bedard, Erik, Bow.*	6	3	.667	1.97	13	12	0	0	1	0	68.2	43	282	18	15	0	2	3	3	30	0	66	6	0
Beech, Matt, Nor.*	3	1	.750	1.56	7	5	1	1	1	0	34.2	28	143	11	6	2	0	1	2	13	0	39	0	0
Bell, Heath, Bing.	1	0	1.000	1.18	14	0	0	0	16	6	38	22	139	6	5	0	1	1	0	6	0	49	3	0
Benson, Kris, Alt.	1	0	1.000	1.29	1	1	0	0	0	0	7	5	25	1	1	1	0	1	0	0	0	7	0	0
Bevis, P.J., Bing.	1	0	1.000	1.29	4	0	0	0	2	0	7	5	27	1	1	0	1	0	0	3	0	14	0	0
Billingsley, Brent, Har.*	0	4	.000	10.23	6	4	0	0	0	0	22	37	114	28	25	4	2	1	9	1	26	7	0	
Bland, Nate, Bing.*	4	2	.667	2.55	15	0	0	0	8	0	24.2	16	98	9	7	0	1	0	1	8	3	19	0	0
Blevins, Jeremy, Nor.	4	0	1.000	2.77	19	0	0	0	3	0	26	20	117	10	8	0	0	0	14	0	23	2	0	
Borkowski, Dave, Erie	0	2	.000	7.56	2	2	0	0	0	0	8.1	12	38	7	7	0	0	0	1	2	0	6	0	0
Borrell, Danny, Nor.*	9	4	.692	2.31	21	20	1	1	1	0	128.1	116	539	44	33	5	4	3	7	39	4	91	6	0
Bowe, Brandon, Port.	6	4	.600	3.72	45	3	0	0	24	4	75	89	339	37	31	6	2	2	2	23	3	52	2	0
Braswell, Bryan, Bing.*	3	1	.750	6.29	24	0	0	0	7	1	34.1	48	163	26	24	1	2	1	0	11	2	19	3	0
Bridges, Donnie, Har.-Port.	4	8	.333	7.55	20	16	0	0	0	0	78.2	92	392	74	66	8	6	7	7	60	0	55	8	1
Brock, Chris, Bow.	0	0	.000	3.60	1	1	0	0	0	0	5	6	21	2	2	0	1	0	0	2	0	0	0	
Brooks, Frank, Read.*	1	1	.500	3.10	17	1	0	0	9	2	29	29	122	11	10	1	0	0	12	0	23	0	0	

Pitcher, Team	W	L	Pct.	ERA	G	GS	CG	ShO	GF	Sv.	IP	H	TBF	R	ER	HR	SH	SF	HB	BB	IBB	SO	WP	Bk.
Brown, Derek, Bow.	3	6	.333	5.07	41	3	0	0	17	0	87	116	409	62	49	10	3	2	4	25	3	53	7	1
Brown, Jamie, Akr.	9	5	.643	2.78	18	17	0	0	0	0	103.2	98	422	41	32	5	2	2	8	17	0	72	1	1
Brownson, Mark, Bow.	0	0	.000	6.75	3	0	0	0	1	0	6.2	10	30	5	5	1	0	0	0	2	0	3	1	0
Brunette, Justin, Bing.*	1	0	1.000	0.00	3	0	0	0	1	0	4	3	15	0	0	0	0	0	1	0	3	0	0
Buchanan, Brian, Nor.*	0	0	.000	5.74	11	0	0	0	8	0	15.2	20	74	13	10	0	0	1	2	6	0	11	0	0
Buchholz, Taylor, Read.	0	2	.000	7.43	4	4	0	0	0	0	23	29	102	19	19	5	2	1	1	6	0	17	0	0
Bump, Nate, Port.	7	6	.538	3.38	20	20	3	0	0	0	127.2	110	525	56	48	5	3	1	8	29	0	81	2	1
Burba, Dave, Akr.	0	0	.000	0.00	1	1	0	0	0	0	4.2	2	16	0	0	0	0	0	1	0	1	0	0
Burnside, Adrian, Alt.*	6	9	.400	4.55	32	23	0	0	3	0	130.2	120	583	70	66	18	3	3	15	67	0	122	12	0
Byrdak, Tim, Akr.*	0	0	.000	6.23	9	0	0	0	3	1	13	16	66	12	9	0	1	1	1	11	0	8	3	0
Cabrera, Fernando, Akr.	1	2	.333	5.33	7	4	0	0	1	1	27	26	118	16	16	1	0	0	3	12	0	29	0	0
Cammack, Eric, Bing.	3	2	.600	3.98	36	0	0	0	13	5	54.1	44	242	28	24	4	1	3	3	43	2	64	2	0
Camp, Jared, Erie.	2	2	.000	10.13	6	0	0	0	3	0	8	12	45	11	9	4	0	0	3	5	0	4	3	0
Carnes, Matt, N.B.	7	3	.700	2.86	21	0	0	0	3	1	44	33	175	16	14	1	1	1	2	14	1	42	3	0
Casadiego, Gerardo, Har.	1	3	.250	6.88	9	7	0	0	0	0	35.1	46	161	35	27	7	4	1	0	15	0	25	2	1
Cerda, Jaime, Bing.*	5	1	.833	1.78	27	14	0	0	5	0	31.2	21	121	8	8	0	1	1	0	10	0	33	2	0
Cerros, Juan, Bing.	0	0	.000	0.00	3	0	0	0	1	0	3	0	9	0	0	0	0	0	0	0	0	3	0	0
Chavez, Chris, Port.	1	0	1.000	5.24	15	0	0	0	7	2	22.1	22	114	18	13	3	1	3	3	21	0	19	1	0
Chevalier, Virgil, Bing.	0	0	.000	0.00	2	0	0	0	2	0	1	1	5	0	0	0	0	0	0	0	0	0	0	0
Chiavacci, Ron, Har.	6	9	.400	4.27	35	10	0	0	10	0	111.2	105	504	70	53	6	4	10	5	65	1	98	6	1
Chipperfield, Calvin, Erie	0	1	.000	5.79	1	1	0	0	0	0	4.2	5	24	3	3	0	0	1	1	5	0	5	0	0
Christman, Tim, Port.*	1	1	.500	5.52	11	0	0	0	6	2	14.2	17	70	12	9	2	0	1	2	5	0	10	5	0
Chrysler, Clint, Alt.*	3	2	.600	3.97	51	0	0	0	20	3	56.2	55	245	29	25	7	2	3	3	21	1	26	2	0
Clark, Chris, Port.	0	2	.000	9.00	10	0	0	0	1	0	15	14	74	15	15	1	0	0	2	17	1	7	1	0
Clemens, Roger, Nor.	1	0	1.000	1.29	1	1	0	0	0	0	7	5	26	1	1	0	0	1	0	0	0	7	1	0
Cole, Joey, Bing.	2	3	.400	5.24	10	8	0	0	0	0	46.1	56	218	34	27	6	3	3	6	21	1	27	0	0
Collins, Pat, Har.	3	0	1.000	1.78	29	0	0	0	17	7	50.2	42	210	11	10	3	0	2	0	19	2	51	11	0
Colon, Jose, Akr.	5	4	.556	2.37	46	2	0	0	30	5	76	72	305	21	20	6	6	1	4	8	3	43	1	0
Cook, Andy, Bing.	6	3	.667	5.07	30	3	0	0	9	0	55	64	249	36	31	6	2	2	3	22	2	39	3	0
Cook, B.R., N.H.	7	13	.350	4.57	28	28	2	0	0	0	163.1	180	721	106	83	14	9	3	5	65	3	111	13	0
Corcoran, Tim, Bow.	0	5	.000	3.67	35	0	0	0	23	1	49	61	239	31	20	5	4	3	4	29	3	48	6	0
Correa, Cristobal, N.H.	6	9	.400	4.53	26	26	0	0	0	0	137	143	602	77	69	8	11	8	6	58	0	76	4	1
Crawford, Paxton, N.H.	1	0	1.000	0.00	1	1	0	0	0	0	6	3	24	1	0	0	0	1	1	0	6	0	0
Crumpton, Chuck, Har.	2	3	.400	3.64	21	3	0	0	13	3	59.1	69	267	26	24	3	2	1	3	20	0	32	3	0
Cueto, Jose, Port.	1	4	.200	3.92	9	9	0	0	0	0	43.2	34	180	21	19	5	0	1	2	21	0	47	2	0
Cummings, Jeremy, N.H.	4	3	.571	3.69	14	13	0	0	0	0	78	68	309	33	32	6	3	2	1	23	1	52	1	0
Davis, Allen, Har.*	1	4	.200	7.14	9	5	0	0	1	0	29	44	135	24	23	6	0	1	2	8	0	14	1	0
Davis, Jason, Akr.	6	2	.750	3.51	10	10	0	0	0	0	59	63	250	26	23	2	1	1	5	16	0	45	3	0
De La Rosa, Jorge, Tren.*	1	2	.333	5.50	4	4	0	0	0	0	18	17	82	12	11	0	0	2	9	0	15	3	0
Denney, Kyle, Akr.	3	1	.750	1.56	6	5	0	0	0	0	34.2	23	135	7	6	2	1	0	3	5	0	32	2	0
De Paula, Julio, Nor.	14	6	.700	3.45	27	26	6	1	0	0	175	141	710	74	67	11	7	6	5	52	0	152	6	3
Deschenes, Marc, Alt.	0	0	.000	3.00	3	0	0	0	3	3	3	3	11	1	1	0	0	0	0	0	0	4	1	0
Dickinson, Rodney, Tren.	1	0	1.000	7.20	4	0	0	0	3	0	5	7	27	5	4	1	0	0	4	1	4	0	0
Donaldson, Bo, Nor.	0	1	.000	4.55	17	0	0	0	2	0	27.2	21	115	14	14	2	1	3	5	5	0	30	2	0
Dougherty, Jim, Alt.	1	1	.500	5.06	7	0	0	0	3	0	10.2	13	49	6	6	1	1	0	0	7	2	5	0	0
Dubose, Eric, Bow.*	5	3	.625	2.51	41	0	0	0	13	3	64.2	46	263	21	18	2	4	2	3	21	0	66	3	0
Duff, Matt, N.H.	11	1	.917	1.38	47	0	0	0	22	4	65	38	255	12	10	3	4	2	1	21	2	91	5	0
Edmondson, Brian, Akr.-Erie	6	2	.714	3.46	43	0	0	0	24	6	52	54	220	28	20	5	2	3	2	13	2	42	2	1
Einertson, Darrell, Nor.	0	2	.000	16.20	4	0	0	0	1	0	3.1	7	22	9	6	0	1	0	3	0	2	0	0
Elder, Dave, Akr.	2	1	.667	2.00	23	1	0	0	18	9	36	19	142	8	8	1	1	0	0	18	2	42	1	0
Elmore, Chris, Tren.*	8	2	.800	2.34	14	13	2	0	0	0	84.2	76	340	27	22	1	1	0	2	22	0	57	3	0
Estrella, Leo, N.H.	2	2	.500	4.81	14	5	0	0	4	0	39.1	46	187	30	21	4	2	4	2	20	0	23	4	0
Etherton, Seth, Nor.	0	0	.000	0.00	1	1	0	0	0	0	2	1	9	1	0	0	1	0	1	0	2	0	0
Evans, Kyle, Akr.	1	0	1.000	4.09	2	2	0	0	0	0	11	9	48	5	5	0	0	1	0	6	0	9	1	0
Eyre, Willie, N.B.	6	4	.600	3.24	28	0	0	0	9	2	50	40	209	21	18	1	1	2	3	21	0	43	5	0
Farmer, Tom, Erie	6	8	.429	5.33	18	18	1	0	0	0	103	122	461	68	61	12	5	2	7	32	0	51	6	0
Ferrari, Anthony, Har.*	7	4	.636	4.06	44	0	0	0	29	6	75.1	79	339	35	34	2	1	3	8	34	1	53	5	0
Fesh, Sean, Port.*	1	1	.500	4.22	24	0	0	0	8	5	42.2	35	189	23	20	1	0	2	9	22	1	49	5	1
Figueroa, Juan, Bow.	1	6	.143	5.06	24	11	0	0	5	1	89	100	394	51	50	14	2	3	4	26	1	68	3	0
Fisher, Pete, N.B.	4	4	.000	8.06	6	4	0	0	0	0	22.1	38	120	25	20	0	3	0	4	12	1	15	4	1
Flohr, Adam, N.B.*	4	5	.444	2.40	43	7	0	0	15	0	82.1	83	340	35	22	4	3	2	3	19	3	47	3	1
Fontana, Tony, Tren.	0	2	.000	6.23	11	0	0	0	4	0	21.2	26	96	16	15	4	0	3	0	5	1	15	3	0
Francisco, Frank, Tren.	2	2	.500	5.63	9	0	0	0	1	0	16	10	77	13	10	0	1	0	2	16	1	18	3	0
Franco, Martire, Read.	4	8	.333	5.76	16	16	2	0	0	0	89	109	396	62	57	13	5	4	4	25	1	50	0	1
Garza, Alberto, Akr.	2	0	1.000	1.72	20	0	0	0	4	1	36.2	15	146	7	7	2	0	2	3	29	0	45	5	0
Giese, Dan, Tren.	1	2	.333	3.83	23	0	0	0	9	3	49.1	53	204	24	21	6	3	3	1	9	3	39	1	0
Glaser, Eric, Tren.	2	9	.182	5.70	33	12	0	0	5	1	113.2	145	510	80	72	15	5	4	2	32	0	80	3	0
Glick, David, Nor.*	3	1	.750	2.57	8	4	0	0	0	0	28	23	120	12	8	4	3	0	2	11	0	24	0	0
Goetz, Geoff, Port.*	0	1	.000	3.86	2	2	0	0	0	0	7	5	32	4	3	1	0	1	0	7	0	9	2	0
Gonzalez, Mike, Alt.*	8	4	.667	3.80	16	16	0	0	0	0	85.1	77	367	38	36	4	0	0	4	47	2	82	7	1
Grabow, John, Alt.*	8	13	.381	5.47	28	27	1	1	1	0	146.1	181	653	94	89	10	6	6	6	47	0	97	9	5
Graman, Alex, Nor.*	5	2	.714	2.88	8	8	2	1	0	0	50	46	208	19	16	2	2	3	0	13	0	31	4	0
Gravelle, Nick, Alt.*	0	0	.000	18.00	1	0	0	0	1	0	1	3	6	2	2	1	0	0	0	0	0	0	0	0
Graves, Bobby, Erie*	1	2	.333	7.62	11	0	0	0	3	0	13	18	72	13	11	2	1	2	1	17	0	14	1	0
Greisinger, Seth, Erie	2	0	1.000	1.29	4	4	0	0	0	0	21	12	86	4	3	1	0	1	1	9	0	21	0	0
Griffiths, Jeremy, Bing.	8	6	.571	3.89	27	26	0	0	0	0	152.2	157	652	75	66	12	5	4	11	54	0	126	5	0
Guillory, Dan, Akr.	3	3	.500	1.13	19	0	0	0	6	2	32.1	20	136	11	4	1	2	0	1	20	1	35	1	0
Guy, Brad, Alt.	2	2	.600	3.17	26	5	1	1	5	1	76.2	87	322	31	27	7	3	0	3	16	3	40	2	1
Hale, Beau, Bow.	2	0	1.000	0.84	2	2	0	0	0	0	10.2	11	47	2	1	0	0	1	3	0	6	0	0
Hamilton, Jimmy, Read.*	3	2	.600	2.79	46	1	0	0	23	4	71	55	301	26	22	6	4	3	1	38	2	56	5	0
Hamulack, Tim, Port.*	8	4	.667	2.88	38	1	0	0	23	6	78	73	324	32	25	6	4	1	0	29	5	53	3	0

Pitcher, Team	W	L	Pct.	ERA	G	GS	CG	ShO	GF	Sv.	IP	H	TBF	R	ER	HR	SH	SF	HB	BB	IBB	SO	WP	Bk.
Hancock, Josh, Tren.	3	4	.429	3.61	15	14	2	0	1	1	84.2	82	351	40	34	9	0	0	5	18	0	69	5	0
Heams, Shane, Tren.	1	2	.333	4.02	14	0	0	0	6	0	15.2	12	76	8	7	1	2	1	3	16	0	17	6	0
Hebson, Bryan, Har.	10	1	.909	1.72	38	3	0	0	24	7	94.1	60	364	20	18	5	4	2	5	24	2	75	1	1
Heilman, Aaron, Bing.	4	4	.500	3.82	17	17	0	0	0	0	96.2	85	397	43	41	7	2	2	6	28	2	97	5	0
Henkel, Rob, Port.*	5	4	.556	3.86	13	13	0	0	0	0	70	54	289	31	30	6	4	2	1	27	0	68	4	0
Hentgen, Pat, Bow.	0	0	.000	1.50	1	1	0	0	0	0	6	5	24	1	1	0	0	0	0	3	0	3	0	0
Herrera, Alex, Akr.*	0	2	.000	3.38	30	0	0	0	9	5	61.1	47	261	24	23	8	3	0	6	30	1	65	3	0
Hiles, Cary, Read.	1	5	.167	4.55	21	0	0	0	12	7	31.2	43	150	20	16	1	3	2	3	12	0	23	2	0
Hill, Terry, Tren.*	6	5	.545	5.96	45	0	0	0	20	3	83	108	396	62	55	10	5	6	4	36	1	86	16	0
Hoard, Brent, N.B.*	11	8	.579	3.69	31	26	2	0	1	0	161	153	672	80	66	11	3	7	5	52	3	126	7	0
Hodge, Kevin, N.B.	3	2	.600	2.97	24	0	0	0	16	6	30.1	22	117	11	10	3	1	2	3	8	1	28	0	0
Izquierdo, Hansel, Port.	0	1	.000	1.29	1	1	0	0	0	0	7	5	27	2	1	0	0	0	1	0	0	4	0	0
Jamison, Ryan, Bing.	0	4	.000	4.34	11	6	0	0	2	0	37.1	41	165	19	18	1	3	0	4	16	1	33	1	0
Janke, Cheyenne, N.H.	12	8	.600	3.48	28	23	1	1	0	0	150	142	629	71	58	13	1	5	4	41	3	112	14	0
Jean, Domingo, Nor.	0	4	.000	3.38	36	0	0	0	31	19	37.1	38	163	16	14	5	3	1	7	8	1	26	3	0
Jerzembeck, Mike, N.B.	1	0	1.000	2.25	3	2	0	0	0	0	8	4	29	2	2	0	0	0	0	2	0	7	0	0
Jodie, Brett, Nor.	0	0	.000	1.69	2	2	0	0	0	0	10.2	5	38	2	2	0	0	0	0	4	0	7	1	0
Johnson, James, Akr.*	0	0	.000	4.50	5	0	0	0	2	0	6	4	27	3	3	1	0	1	0	4	0	6	1	0
Johnson, Jason, Bow.	1	0	1.000	0.00	1	1	0	0	0	0	5	4	20	0	0	0	0	0	0	1	0	6	0	0
Johnson, Jeremy, Erie	6	1	.857	3.88	8	8	0	0	0	0	48.2	51	213	24	21	8	0	2	0	15	0	26	1	0
Johnson, Mark, Erie	0	1	.000	3.00	5	1	0	0	1	0	9	10	38	4	3	1	1	0	0	1	0	8	0	0
Joseph, Jake, Bing.	6	4	.600	2.91	14	14	0	0	0	0	86.2	79	348	37	28	4	4	1	0	24	1	42	4	1
Journell, Jimmy, N.H.	3	3	.500	2.70	10	10	2	0	0	0	66.2	50	269	22	20	3	2	0	6	18	0	66	2	0
Karnuth, Jason, N.H.	3	4	.429	3.60	58	0	0	0	20	4	70	74	308	34	28	7	3	1	2	23	2	46	3	0
Karp, Josh, Har.	7	5	.583	3.84	16	16	0	0	0	0	86.2	83	372	43	37	6	2	4	8	34	0	69	4	2
Keelin, Chris, Erie	0	0	.000	32.40	2	0	0	0	2	0	1.2	6	12	6	6	1	0	0	0	1	0	0	0	0
Kinney, Matt, N.B.	0	0	.000	6.75	1	1	0	0	0	0	4	4	18	4	3	1	0	1	0	1	0	3	0	0
Kirsten, Rick, Erie	1	0	1.000	4.50	3	1	0	0	0	0	8	11	38	7	4	1	0	0	0	4	0	8	0	0
Klepacki, Ed, Har.-Port.	2	1	.667	3.51	19	0	0	0	10	2	33.1	23	142	15	13	2	0	2	0	23	1	21	1	0
Kline, Steve, N.H.*	0	0	.000	0.00	1	1	0	0	0	0	2	0	8	0	0	0	0	0	0	1	0	2	1	0
Kubes, Greg, Read.*	13	7	.650	3.46	28	27	0	0	0	0	174.1	177	725	74	67	16	5	6	0	45	0	106	1	0
Kusiewicz, Mike, Tren.*	5	3	.625	3.29	13	11	0	0	0	0	65.2	58	273	28	24	4	1	2	3	12	0	44	3	0
Lambert, Jeremy, N.H.	1	1	.500	6.16	18	0	0	0	3	0	19	24	90	13	13	1	0	1	2	11	1	21	0	0
Langen, Brian, N.H.*	2	0	1.000	4.08	46	0	0	0	13	0	53	48	242	28	24	3	3	2	6	31	2	33	7	0
Larson, Ryan, Akr.	2	3	.400	1.78	32	0	0	0	28	6	35.1	37	149	10	7	3	1	1	6	2	0	30	1	0
Lavigne, Tim, Bing.	2	3	.400	2.86	23	0	0	0	17	9	34.2	29	141	11	11	1	1	1	1	15	2	25	1	0
Layfield, Scotty, N.H.	6	4	.600	2.35	58	0	0	0	52	24	65	54	268	22	17	5	2	2	2	24	3	63	6	0
Lee, Cliff, Har.-Akr.*	9	3	.750	3.58	18	18	0	0	0	0	103	72	408	42	41	13	1	1	2	33	0	123	3	0
Lee, Seung, Read.	0	1	.000	0.00	1	1	0	0	0	0	6	5	23	2	0	1	0	0	0	0	0	6	0	0
Lewis, Craig, Har.	1	2	.333	3.95	17	0	0	0	8	0	27.1	37	131	16	12	0	2	3	1	8	1	13	3	0
Lidle, Kevin, Erie	2	11	.154	5.84	23	13	1	0	3	0	91	121	412	63	59	11	6	5	3	29	1	45	5	1
Looney, Brian, Alt.*	0	0	.000	1.17	4	0	0	0	0	0	7.2	5	28	1	1	1	0	0	1	1	0	3	0	0
Lopez, Gustavo, Port.	0	0	.000	13.50	2	2	0	0	0	0	3.1	6	19	6	5	0	0	0	1	1	0	5	2	0
Lopez, Jose, Alt.	0	2	.000	6.75	10	4	0	0	1	0	21.1	30	102	20	16	2	3	0	0	7	0	8	0	0
Lovinger, Kevin, Nor.*	0	2	.000	1.96	19	0	0	0	6	0	18.1	21	82	5	4	0	0	0	7	1	12	0	0
Madson, Ryan, Read.	16	4	.800	3.20	26	26	2	0	0	0	171.1	150	699	68	61	11	9	6	12	53	0	132	5	0
Maness, Nick, Bing.	5	9	.357	4.52	25	23	0	0	1	1	131.1	120	571	74	66	15	2	4	6	72	0	109	7	2
Mangum, Mark, Har.	7	5	.583	4.16	18	11	0	0	4	2	80	85	335	41	37	12	2	1	2	25	0	40	1	0
Manning, Charlie, Nor.*	4	2	.667	3.57	11	11	1	1	0	0	63	55	263	27	25	1	0	1	2	26	0	61	3	0
Manning, David, N.B.	3	3	.500	4.62	11	10	0	0	0	0	62.1	69	275	37	32	3	8	2	5	27	0	38	6	0
Manon, Julio, Har.	5	1	.833	3.00	6	6	0	0	0	0	39	37	158	13	13	3	1	1	1	4	0	51	1	0
Marquetti, Agustin, Erie	0	2	.000	6.75	8	4	0	0	1	0	18.2	24	99	20	14	4	1	0	3	17	0	10	2	0
Marrero, Darwin, Har.	6	5	.545	4.02	19	19	1	1	0	0	105.1	119	452	54	47	16	2	2	5	21	0	54	5	0
Marsonek, Sam, Nor.	5	8	.385	5.01	19	13	1	0	3	0	100.2	111	454	68	56	6	4	1	12	34	1	75	6	1
Martinez, Anastacio, Tren.	5	12	.294	5.31	27	27	0	0	0	0	139	152	637	98	82	12	4	2	6	75	0	127	15	1
Massingale, Matt, Port.	1	0	1.000	9.00	6	0	0	0	3	0	10	9	49	10	10	1	0	0	0	9	0	6	0	0
Mays, Joe, N.B.	1	0	1.000	1.29	1	1	0	0	0	0	7	2	25	1	1	1	0	0	1	1	0	5	1	0
McAvoy, Jeff, Har.	2	3	.400	6.23	16	1	0	0	8	3	34.2	40	155	25	24	4	2	1	3	11	0	21	0	0
McConnell, Sam, Read.*	2	4	.333	3.65	29	7	0	0	8	3	69	78	293	31	28	7	1	2	2	19	3	43	1	0
McDade, Neal, Alt.	8	3	.727	3.91	49	0	0	0	23	3	78.1	85	336	36	34	11	5	4	3	16	4	51	3	0
McDonald, Jon, N.B.	3	8	.273	6.10	21	12	0	0	6	0	72.1	77	334	58	49	4	1	4	3	47	2	28	15	0
McLeary, Marty, Tren.	0	2	.000	4.86	11	0	0	0	7	0	16.2	20	76	12	9	0	1	2	1	8	2	10	2	0
Meadows, Randy, Alt.	0	0	.000	0.00	1	0	0	0	1	0	1.1	2	5	0	0	0	0	0	0	0	0	0	0	0
Mendoza, Marcos, Akr.*	2	5	.286	2.41	21	0	0	0	8	0	37.1	30	166	17	10	2	4	2	0	24	2	27	4	1
Mills, Ryan, N.B.*	3	11	.214	5.37	26	21	0	0	2	0	105.1	117	504	80	63	10	1	1	11	68	0	68	11	0
Montano, Ignacio, Akr.*	0	0	.000	8.10	2	0	0	0	1	0	3.1	3	15	3	3	0	0	1	0	2	0	6	0	0
Montgomery, Matt, Alt.	3	0	1.000	4.21	44	0	0	0	18	3	66.1	62	279	32	31	3	2	1	2	26	3	50	3	0
Nelson, Joe, Tren.	0	0	.000	14.54	4	0	0	0	1	0	4.1	9	25	8	7	1	0	0	1	2	0	3	2	0
Ochoa, Pablo, Bing.	0	2	.000	9.00	8	4	0	0	1	0	20	31	101	21	20	5	0	0	8	1	13	3	0
O'Connor, Brian, Alt.*	5	7	.417	5.06	24	14	1	1	3	0	85.1	86	378	50	48	6	1	1	0	50	0	53	7	0
Ortiz, Omar, Port.	4	8	.333	5.38	33	16	0	0	13	3	103.2	107	482	69	62	17	2	4	10	70	0	74	10	1
Outlaw, Mark, Read.*	6	2	.750	4.44	41	0	0	0	14	2	50.2	45	227	30	25	3	2	1	2	34	1	29	5	0
Ozias, Todd, Read.	2	1	.667	2.50	31	0	0	0	10	2	39.2	33	163	12	11	3	1	0	1	14	2	40	1	0
Padilla, Juan, Bing.	3	5	.375	3.31	54	0	0	0	48	29	65.1	69	283	30	24	2	1	2	4	18	6	52	2	0
Padilla, Roy, N.H.*	0	1	.000	7.71	3	0	0	0	0	0	2.1	3	17	2	2	0	0	3	5	0	2	3	0
Pageler, Mick, N.H.	0	0	.000	9.00	3	0	0	0	2	0	2	5	12	2	2	0	0	0	1	0	3	1	0
Palki, Jeromy, N.H.	3	3	.500	3.17	30	0	0	0	9	2	48.1	45	208	19	17	6	3	0	4	17	3	52	1	0
Palma, Rick, Alt.*	1	1	.500	1.80	10	0	0	0	4	0	10	12	43	2	2	0	2	0	0	3	0	10	0	0
Paradis, Mike, Bow.	8	13	.381	5.64	27	27	1	1	0	0	151.2	174	691	108	95	12	4	11	12	66	0	94	11	1
Paronto, Chad, Akr.	0	0	.000	27.00	1	1	0	0	0	0	0.1	1	3	1	1	0	0	0	0	1	0	0	0	0
Parrott, Rhett, N.H.	4	1	.800	2.86	9	9	3	1	0	0	66	53	255	24	21	3	1	1	2	13	0	38	0	0

Pitcher, Team	W	L	Pct.	ERA	G	GS	CG	ShO	GF	Sv	IP	H	TBF	R	ER	HR	SH	SF	HB	BB	IBB	SO	WP	Bk.
Pautz, Brad, Read.	4	6	.400	3.06	43	3	0	0	14	3	79.1	70	330	36	27	7	3	3	2	26	2	59	2	1
Pavlovich, Tony, Alt.	0	0	.000	13.50	1	0	0	0	0	0	1.1	4	7	2	2	0	0	0	0	0	0	0	0	0
Pearsall, J.J., Port.-Erie*	2	3	.400	3.06	36	0	0	0	10	1	50	44	214	20	17	4	3	2	0	23	2	51	3	0
Pearson, Terry, Erie	0	0	.000	3.68	15	0	0	0	13	4	14.2	25	70	7	6	1	0	0	1	2	0	11	4	0
Perez, Frank, Read.	3	2	.600	3.72	40	12	0	0	16	5	101.2	98	436	48	42	8	5	3	8	36	2	68	11	1
Perez, Frank, Erie	0	7	.000	5.35	31	7	0	0	11	1	72.1	76	332	48	43	9	5	3	2	36	0	53	1	1
Peters, Chris, Erie*	3	3	.500	4.73	43	0	0	0	10	0	59	70	264	36	31	4	5	2	2	25	1	56	7	0
Pettitte, Andy, Nor.*	0	0	.000	1.42	1	1	0	0	0	0	6.1	2	21	1	1	0	0	0	0	0	0	5	0	0
Pierson, Jason, Nor.*	0	0	.000	7.71	11	0	0	0	2	0	14	22	67	12	12	2	0	1	1	3	0	12	1	0
Pineda, Isauro, Tren.	9	13	.409	5.65	28	28	2	0	0	0	156	172	686	109	98	20	7	6	8	68	0	121	10	0
Ponce Deleon, Damon, N.H.	2	2	.000	22.50	4	0	0	0	0	0	4	13	26	10	10	1	1	2	1	1	0	2	0	0
Prather, Scott, N.H.*	2	3	.400	6.07	11	4	0	0	1	0	29.2	37	147	25	20	5	1	2	1	18	0	21	4	0
Pridie, Jon, N.B.	5	3	.625	5.07	16	15	1	0	0	0	94	95	414	53	53	6	3	0	8	46	0	70	4	0
Pumphrey, Ken, Read.	9	7	.563	4.28	20	20	2	1	0	0	120	119	505	65	57	9	3	8	7	34	2	63	6	0
Rakers, Aaron, Bow.	5	1	.833	2.06	36	0	0	0	29	10	48	39	189	12	11	3	5	3	1	12	2	45	1	0
Rakers, Jason, Akr.	0	0	.000	6.00	1	1	0	0	0	0	3	4	14	2	2	0	0	1	0	1	0	0	0	0
Ramirez, Jose, Erie*	3	0	.000	6.00	28	0	0	0	10	0	45	54	217	30	30	7	6	3	4	28	2	37	1	2
Randall, Scott, N.B.	2	0	1.000	3.48	5	5	0	0	0	0	31	25	123	13	12	3	0	0	3	4	0	19	0	0
Reid, Justin, Alt.	11	8	.579	4.33	25	25	1	0	0	0	153.2	151	643	87	74	21	8	5	6	28	2	108	4	0
Riley, Matt, Bow.*	4	10	.286	6.34	22	22	0	0	0	0	109.1	136	502	84	77	12	0	7	3	48	1	105	11	2
Riske, David, Akr.	0	0	.000	3.00	4	2	0	0	2	0	6	5	24	2	2	1	0	0	0	1	0	10	0	0
Rivera, Homero, Erie*	5	3	.625	2.05	40	0	0	0	24	8	61.1	48	247	17	14	2	2	3	4	16	2	35	3	0
Rivera, Saul, Bing.-Har.	2	5	.286	3.12	45	0	0	0	33	16	57.2	46	254	26	20	2	4	3	5	32	3	47	3	1
Roach, Jason, Bing.	3	4	.429	3.65	8	8	0	0	0	0	44.1	40	175	19	18	3	1	3	0	12	0	23	3	0
Roberts, Grant, Bing.	0	0	.000	0.00	1	1	0	0	0	0	1	0	3	0	0	0	0	0	0	0	0	1	0	0
Robertson, Nathan, Port.*	10	9	.526	3.42	27	27	3	0	0	0	163	156	670	77	62	12	6	8	7	50	2	109	0	2
Rodgers, Bobby, Port.	0	0	.000	0.90	3	0	0	0	1	1	10	6	37	1	1	1	0	0	0	3	0	15	0	0
Rodney, Fernando, Erie	1	0	1.000	1.33	21	0	0	0	19	11	20.1	14	77	4	3	0	0	0	5	8	0	18	3	0
Rodriguez, Eddy, Bow.	0	0	.000	5.63	6	0	0	0	4	1	8	6	38	6	5	1	0	0	1	7	0	7	1	0
Rogers, Brian, Nor.	7	2	.778	2.77	13	11	1	0	0	0	68.1	69	287	29	21	4	3	1	5	16	0	48	2	1
Roller, Adam, Nor.	2	1	.667	3.27	21	0	0	0	20	9	22	19	99	10	8	1	0	2	2	13	0	20	6	0
Rosario, Juan, Bow.	4	10	.286	5.01	25	20	0	0	0	0	127.2	144	581	88	71	11	3	5	10	54	0	88	16	0
Rose, Ted, Akr.	2	2	.500	4.60	6	6	0	0	0	0	29.1	29	124	17	15	5	0	1	1	6	0	18	0	0
Sadler, Carl, Akr.*	4	1	.800	2.33	21	0	0	0	7	2	46.1	39	185	12	12	0	0	1	2	12	1	37	2	0
Saenz, Jason, Bing.*	5	3	.625	5.10	36	1	0	0	14	2	72.1	69	334	48	41	4	5	5	7	55	0	47	8	1
Salazar, Richard, Bow.*	0	0	.000	4.32	8	0	0	0	2	0	16.2	15	82	8	8	0	1	3	15	10	0	19	1	0
Sampson, Benj, N.B.*	5	5	.500	3.41	16	16	2	0	0	0	97.2	91	386	44	37	8	2	8	3	18	1	43	1	0
Sansom, Trevor, N.H.	4	4	.500	4.07	47	1	0	0	10	0	79.2	78	337	39	36	11	0	4	29	3	51	4	0	
Schoening, Brent, N.B.	3	1	.750	5.17	8	0	0	3	0	62.2	60	271	44	36	12	0	1	7	23	1	57	2	0	
Schurman, Ryan, N.H.	3	0	.000	7.06	18	8	0	0	2	0	51	67	238	41	40	9	2	1	2	20	0	40	3	0
Seale, Dustin, Har.*	1	2	.333	3.51	29	3	0	0	9	0	66.2	63	273	27	26	11	1	0	2	16	0	51	4	1
Seibel, Phil, Bing.*	10	8	.556	3.97	28	25	2	0	1	0	149.2	147	630	78	66	17	8	5	10	49	2	114	6	0
Seo, Jae, Bing.	0	0	.000	5.40	1	0	0	0	0	0	5	5	21	3	3	1	0	0	1	0	6	0	0	
Sequea, Jacobo, Bow.	1	6	.143	5.40	15	14	0	0	0	0	73.1	69	317	53	44	11	2	3	3	35	0	37	1	1
Sergent, Joe, Port.*	3	6	.333	6.43	20	12	1	0	5	0	70	85	316	61	50	13	4	5	4	22	0	41	3	1
Sergio, Tom, Tren.	0	0	.000	0.00	1	0	0	0	1	0	1.1	1	5	0	0	0	0	0	0	0	0	0	0	0
Serrano, Willy, Bow.	4	4	.500	7.58	27	2	0	0	9	0	48.2	75	249	44	41	10	0	3	4	30	0	28	2	0
Shaffar, Ben, Alt.	8	7	.533	3.15	18	18	1	0	0	0	111.1	110	479	46	39	6	4	2	4	40	1	97	8	1
Shepard, David, Nor.	8	7	.533	4.43	42	7	0	0	10	1	87.1	87	379	47	43	8	4	3	4	24	1	66	3	0
Shibilo, Andy, Tren.	1	0	1.000	3.19	21	0	0	0	13	6	31	27	124	11	11	1	0	0	1	7	0	34	1	2
Shuey, Paul, Akr.*	0	0	.000	4.50	2	2	0	0	0	0	2	2	8	1	1	0	0	0	0	0	0	3	0	0
Sido, Wilson, Akr.	0	0	.000	4.50	1	1	0	0	0	0	4	5	21	3	2	0	0	1	1	2	0	1	0	0
Silva, Carlos, Read.	0	0	.000	0.00	2	0	0	0	1	1	3	0	10	0	0	0	0	0	0	0	0	1	0	0
Silva, Doug, N.B.	0	0	.000	6.75	4	2	0	0	0	0	9.1	13	47	7	7	0	0	0	0	8	1	5	0	0
Sims, Kenny, Bow.	5	11	.313	5.62	28	18	0	0	3	0	107.1	131	490	82	67	6	2	4	12	40	1	52	3	2
Skinner, John, Port.	0	0	.000	2.25	2	0	0	0	1	0	4	2	14	1	1	0	0	0	0	3	0	0	0	0
Sloan, Brandon, Port.	2	6	.250	4.08	43	0	0	0	20	8	70.2	76	319	38	32	7	0	4	4	32	3	45	4	1
Smith, Clint, Erie	5	13	.278	6.19	38	19	1	0	5	0	120.2	169	573	92	83	19	3	4	5	59	1	76	12	0
Smith, Matt, Nor.*	3	8	.273	5.44	17	17	0	0	0	0	89.1	112	419	63	54	8	3	3	9	37	0	70	11	0
Snare, Ryan, Port.*	4	2	.667	3.44	11	9	0	0	2	0	55	46	226	25	21	6	0	1	1	19	0	52	5	0
Sneed, John, N.B.	3	7	.300	5.04	39	9	0	0	4	1	91	96	404	57	51	12	1	3	5	43	3	80	5	0
Song, Seung, Bing.-Har.	7	7	.500	4.20	22	22	0	0	0	0	113.2	111	480	63	53	11	6	4	6	37	1	121	7	1
Spencer, Corey, Tren.*	2	4	.333	5.59	32	2	0	0	20	7	48.1	60	225	34	30	5	1	0	0	25	3	49	2	1
Spiegel, Mike, Akr.*	7	3	.700	3.08	25	17	0	0	2	0	90.2	63	391	37	31	7	3	4	8	51	0	87	6	0
Sprague, Kevin, N.H.*	0	0	.000	6.75	4	0	0	0	1	0	4	5	18	3	3	0	0	0	2	0	1	2	0	
Spurling, Chris, Alt.	4	3	.571	2.19	51	0	0	0	45	20	70	54	275	18	17	8	2	1	2	12	1	60	1	0
Stanford, Jason, Akr.*	7	6	.538	3.43	18	18	1	1	0	0	102.1	108	440	44	39	3	4	5	6	33	0	86	2	2
Stemle, Steve, N.H.	5	2	.714	4.36	8	7	0	0	0	0	43.1	45	183	24	21	3	2	2	3	15	1	26	0	0
Stevens, Josh, Nor.	1	1	.500	3.83	24	0	0	0	7	0	40	50	175	21	17	2	1	2	8	1	33	3	0	
Sturdy, Tim, N.B.	1	0	1.000	6.37	35	0	0	0	18	0	53.2	63	253	49	38	5	2	5	2	29	1	21	7	1
Tallet, Brian, Akr.*	10	1	.909	3.08	18	16	1	0	0	0	102.1	93	425	41	35	9	1	1	9	32	0	73	2	1
Tekavec, Nate, Erie	6	9	.400	7.09	27	27	0	0	0	0	141	196	660	123	111	33	4	7	9	53	1	56	4	1
Telemaco, Amaury, Read.	0	0	.000	9.00	1	1	0	0	0	0	1	4	11	1	1	0	0	1	0	0	1	0	0	
Traber, Billy, Bing.*	13	2	.867	2.76	18	17	2	2	0	0	107.2	99	436	38	33	8	1	0	7	20	0	82	2	0
Trachsel, Steve, Bing.	1	0	1.000	0.00	1	1	0	0	0	0	5.2	3	25	1	0	0	1	0	4	0	5	0	0	
Van Hekken, Andy, Erie*	4	7	.364	3.83	21	21	1	0	0	0	134	138	565	69	57	10	6	7	7	34	0	97	7	2
Vargas, Claudio, Har.	2	2	.500	4.64	8	8	0	0	0	0	33	38	146	17	17	2	1	0	3	9	0	34	3	0
Vargas, Jose, Akr.	4	1	.800	4.31	18	1	0	0	6	2	39.2	42	176	21	19	1	1	1	3	16	0	33	1	0
Vega, Rene, Bing.*	1	6	.143	7.15	26	3	0	0	13	2	45.1	61	216	39	36	7	1	4	4	18	2	34	4	0
Viera, Rolando, Tren.*	5	1	.833	4.89	45	3	0	0	26	10	77.1	87	352	50	42	15	12	1	2	34	5	44	3	3
Villegas, Felix, Tren.	1	2	.333	3.20	12	0	0	0	8	0	19.2	16	86	9	7	2	0	1	2	13	0	12	1	0

Pitcher, Team	W	L	Pct.	ERA	G	GS	CG	ShO	GF	Sv.	IP	H	TBF	R	ER	HR	SH	SF	HB	BB	IBB	SO	WP	Bk.
Vogelsong, Ryan, Alt.	1	5	.167	5.56	8	8	0	0	0	0	43.2	47	186	27	27	5	1	0	6	10	0	35	2	1
Walker, Adam, Bing.*	0	0	.000	1.93	1	1	0	0	0	0	4.2	4	18	1	1	0	0	0	0	1	0	5	0	0
Walrond, Les, N.H.*	2	1	.667	2.42	4	4	0	0	0	0	22.1	19	96	8	6	2	0	0	0	10	0	31	3	0
Watson, Greg, Erie	0	1	.000	6.23	7	0	0	0	2	0	8.2	13	39	6	6	1	0	1	0	2	0	8	0	1
Wayne, Justin, Har.-Port.	8	5	.615	3.12	24	24	1	1	0	0	141.1	117	585	67	49	10	8	13	11	45	0	77	7	2
Weaver, Eric, Read.	5	4	.556	4.20	37	0	0	0	27	7	45	38	199	24	21	7	3	2	0	26	4	47	8	0
Weekly, Chris, N.H.	0	0	.000	45.00	1	0	0	0	1	0	1	4	9	5	5	0	0	0	1	1	0	2	1	0
Westbrook, Jake, Akr.	0	1	.000	4.80	3	3	0	0	0	0	15	13	62	8	8	0	2	0	2	1	0	8	1	0
White, Matt, Akr.*	6	2	.750	3.93	27	11	0	0	5	1	89.1	97	392	42	39	9	6	0	0	39	0	63	3	0
Wiggins, Scott, Nor.*	2	1	.667	2.28	24	0	0	0	12	0	27.2	19	112	8	7	1	1	1	2	9	1	26	2	0
Wilson, Jeff, Bow.*	4	4	.500	2.18	50	2	0	0	31	10	91	72	370	29	22	5	3	2	0	31	3	79	6	1
Wimberly, Larry, Alt.*	1	2	.333	4.05	26	0	0	0	6	1	53.1	49	226	25	24	4	0	2	7	18	0	36	2	0
Woodards, Orlando, Port.	4	9	.308	3.52	28	15	2	0	5	1	102.1	106	434	52	40	7	2	1	6	35	0	61	5	2

PITCHERS WITH TWO OR MORE TEAMS

Pitcher, Team	W	L	Pct.	ERA	G	GS	CG	ShO	GF	Sv.	IP	H	TBF	R	ER	HR	SH	SF	HB	BB	IBB	SO	WP	Bk.
Bridges, Donnie, Har.	4	4	.500	6.14	14	13	0	0	0	0	63	63	298	48	43	7	4	7	3	42	0	49	6	0
Bridges, Donnie, Port.	0	4	.000	13.21	6	3	0	0	0	0	15.2	29	94	26	23	1	2	0	4	18	0	6	2	1
Edmondson, Brian, Akr.	2	0	1.000	0.00	5	0	0	0	5	1	7	2	24	1	0	0	0	0	1	0	0	6	0	0
Edmondson, Brian, Erie	3	2	.600	4.00	38	0	0	0	19	5	45	52	196	27	20	5	2	3	2	12	2	36	2	1
Klepacki, Ed, Har.	0	0	.000	4.09	6	0	0	0	3	1	11	7	49	5	5	1	0	2	0	9	0	4	0	0
Klepacki, Ed, Port.	2	1	.667	3.22	13	0	0	0	7	1	22.1	16	93	10	8	1	0	0	0	14	1	17	1	0
Lee, Cliff, Har.*	7	2	.778	3.23	15	15	0	0	0	0	86.1	61	336	31	31	12	1	1	1	23	0	105	2	0
Lee, Cliff, Akr.*	2	1	.667	5.40	3	3	0	0	0	0	16.2	11	72	11	10	1	0	1	0	10	0	18	1	0
Pearsall, J.J., Port.*	0	1	.000	3.18	12	0	0	0	4	0	17	18	75	8	6	1	2	1	0	8	1	18	1	0
Pearsall, J.J., Erie*	2	2	.500	3.00	24	0	0	0	6	1	33	26	139	12	11	3	1	1	0	15	1	33	2	0
Rivera, Saul, Bing.	2	3	.400	3.03	30	0	0	0	24	13	38.2	25	165	18	13	2	1	3	1	23	2	32	1	0
Rivera, Saul, Har.	0	2	.000	3.32	15	0	0	0	9	3	19	21	89	8	7	0	3	0	4	9	1	15	2	1
Song, Seung, Tren.	7	7	.500	4.39	21	21	0	0	0	0	108.2	106	460	61	53	11	0	3	6	37	1	116	7	1
Song, Seung, Har.	0	0	.000	0.00	1	1	0	0	0	0	5	5	21	2	0	0	1	0	0	5	0	5	0	0
Wayne, Justin, Har.	5	2	.714	2.37	17	17	0	0	0	0	98.2	74	401	41	26	7	6	9	6	32	0	47	5	2
Wayne, Justin, Port.	3	3	.500	4.85	7	7	1	1	0	0	42.2	43	184	26	23	3	2	4	5	13	0	30	2	0

COMBINATION SHUTOUTS: Akron (17)—J. Brown-Cabrera-Herrera-Larson, J. Brown-Herrera-Larson, J. Brown-Larson, Burba-White-Larson, Rose-Garza-Guillory, Spiegel-Garza-Elder, Stanford-Cabrera, Stanford-Guillory-Elder, Stanford-Sadler-Elder, Tallet-Garza, Tallet-Guillory-Colon, Tallet-Guillory-White, Tallet-Sadler-Colon, Tallet-White-Mendoza, White-Guillory-Elder, Trabor-Guillory-Edmondson, Trabor-Herrera-Guillory. **Altoona (6)**—Burnside-McDade-Spurling, Burnside-Wimberly, Gonzalez-Montgomery, O'Connor-Guy, O'Connor-Guy-Chrysler-Wimberly, Reid-Montgomery-McDade-Spurling. **Binghamton (7)**—Griffiths-Cammack, Griffiths-A. Cook-Jamison, Heilman-Ochoa-S. Rivera, Jamison-Saenz-Bland, Joseph-Lavigne, Maness-A. Cook, Maness-Vega-Cerda. **Bowie (5)**—Bedard-Figueroa, Bedard-A. Rakers-Wilson, Hale-Dubose-A. Rakers, Paradis-Dubose, Sims-D. Brown-Rodriguez. **Erie (2)**—Arias-Ramirez-C. Smith, Lidle-H. Rivera. **Harrisburg (12)**—Bridges-Ferrari, Casadiego-Hebson, Chiavacci-Hebson, Hebson-Agamennone-S. Rivera, Karp-Billingsley-Crumpton, C. Lee-Hebson-Klepacki, C. Lee-Lewis-Hebson, Mangum-McAvoy, Manon-Hebson, Manon-S. Rivera-Hebson, Marrero-Crumpton, Seale-Crumpton-S. Rivera-Collins. **New Haven (4)**—Cummings-Karnuth-Langen, Janke-Sansom-Duff, Schurman-Sansom-Duff-Layfield, Walrond-Duff-Layfield. **Norwich (3)**—Beal-Jean-Anderson, Borrell-Blevins, De Paula-Donaldson-Roller. **Portland (4)**—Bowe-Clark-Fesh, Henkel-Hamulack, Robertson-Bridges-Bowe, Robertson-Ortiz-Fesh. **Reading (12)**—Baisley-Ozias-Pautz, Baisley-C. Silva, Kubes-McConnell, Kubes-McConnell-Hiles, Kubes-McConnell-Ozias, Madson-Pautz, McConnell-Ozias-Outlaw-Hamilton, Pautz-Outlaw-Hiles, F.L. Perez-Hamilton-Outlaw-Brooks, Pumphrey-Ozias, Pumphrey-Ozias-Weaver, Pumphrey-F.L. Perez. **Trenton (5)**—Ambrose-Hill-Viera, Pineda-Spencer-Shibilo, Pineda-Glaser, Song-Giese, Song-Glaser.

NO-HIT GAMES: None.

2002 FIELDING

TEAM

Team	G	PO	A	E	TC	DP	TP	PB	Pct.
Altoona............	141	3663	1420	113	5196	128	0	4	.978
Harrisburg........	142	3742	1335	130	5207	118	0	16	.975
Binghamton.......	141	3677	1474	133	5284	130	0	12	.975
New Britain	139	3607	1539	134	5280	121	0	13	.975
Akron	141	3717	1394	136	5247	111	0	13	.974
Reading...........	142	3742	1584	143	5469	144	0	15	.974
New Haven	139	3641	1509	148	5298	118	0	22	.972
Erie	141	3606	1451	151	5208	136	0	17	.971
Bowie	140	3617	1379	153	5149	103	0	19	.970
Trenton	140	3651	1411	160	5222	122	1	17	.969
Portland	140	3578	1457	163	5198	128	0	10	.969
Norwich	140	3578	1271	159	5008	100	0	26	.968

INDIVIDUAL

FIRST BASEMEN

NOTE: All caps denotes fielding-percentage leader based on 71 games for catchers, 95 for all other non-pitchers and 114 innings for pitchers. *Throws lefthanded.

Player, Team	Pct.	G	PO	A	E	TC	DP
Bailey, Jeff, Har.	.995	73	596	40	3	593	51
Brazell, Craig, Bing.	.972	32	225	17	7	249	22
Brown, Jason, Har.	1.000	1	4	0	0	4	0
Capista, Aaron, Tren.	1.000	9	50	6	0	56	8
Carter, Charley, Erie	.989	128	1073	52	13	1138	113

Player, Team	Pct.	G	PO	A	E	TC	DP
Caruso, Joe, Alt.	1.000	1	14	2	0	16	2
Cervenak, Mike, Nor.	.990	63	458	28	5	491	33
Chambliss, Jim, N.H.	.991	22	195	15	2	212	14
Chapman, Travis, Read.	1.000	6	45	6	0	51	5
Chevalier, Virgil, Bing.	.990	18	93	8	1	102	8
Cronin, Shane, Nor.	1.000	1	8	0	0	8	1
Crozier, Eric, Akr.*	.997	38	326	19	1	346	27
Davis, Glenn, Nor.-Har.*	.989	31	238	24	3	265	19
Derosso, Tony, Alt.	.982	7	56	0	1	57	3
Dillon, Joe, N.B.	1.000	8	71	3	0	74	7
Dominique, Andy, Tren.	.990	81	604	59	7	670	54
Erickson, Corey, Akr.	.996	30	229	13	1	243	18
ESPY, Nate, Read.	.994	137	1214	80	8	1302	131
Farnsworth, Troy, N.H.	.980	7	48	2	1	51	4
Figueroa, Franky, Bow.	1.000	5	26	2	0	28	2
Gall, John, N.H.	.990	95	862	40	9	911	77
Garcia, Luis, N.H.-Akr.	.992	13	111	8	1	120	6
Gonzalez, Adrian, Port.*	.987	136	1127	89	16	1232	107
Gonzalez, Luis, Akr.	1.000	2	12	1	0	13	1
Gredvig, Doug, Bow.	.990	125	1014	85	11	1110	80
Grindell, Nate, Akr.	1.000	2	22	1	0	23	2
Hage, Tom, Tren.	.994	24	150	8	1	159	7
Hammond, Joey, Bow.	1.000	1	1	1	0	2	0
Headley, Justin, Har.*	.966	8	55	2	2	59	6
Heintz, Chris, N.H.	.000	1	0	0	0	0	0
Hodge, Kevin, N.B.	1.000	6	55	7	0	62	3
Hooper, Clay, Nor.	1.000	2	2	0	0	2	0
Jacobsen, Bucky, N.H.	.984	16	109	12	2	123	11

Player, Team	Pct.	G	PO	A	E	TC	DP
Kelly, Heath, Port.	1.000	8	27	3	0	30	4
Kinchen, Jason, Nor.	.957	6	44	0	2	46	6
King, Brad, Alt.	1.000	2	5	0	0	5	1
Kropf, Andy, Erie	.938	2	15	0	1	16	3
Leach, Nick, Nor.	1.000	9	49	3	0	52	2
Luderer, Brian, Akr.	1.000	1	3	0	0	3	1
McNally, Sean, Har.	1.000	1	4	0	0	4	0
McNeal, Aaron, Bing.	.991	94	810	70	8	888	87
Meier, Dan, Alt.*	1.000	10	94	0	0	94	7
Meran, Jorge, Erie	1.000	7	25	2	0	27	2
Morneau, Justin, N.B.	.989	125	1061	96	13	1170	98
Munoz, Billy, Akr.*	.982	70	556	41	11	608	50
Nettles, Jeff, Nor.	1.000	1	6	0	0	6	0
Nicholson, Derek, Erie	1.000	1	6	0	0	6	0
Nye, Rodney, Bing.	.983	11	53	5	1	59	5
Oakes, Matty, Erie	.800	2	4	0	1	5	0
Pachot, John, Alt.	.980	12	87	12	2	101	7
Pascucci, Val, Har.	.987	19	140	8	2	150	7
Peeples, Mike, Port.	1.000	1	2	0	0	2	0
Perez, Jhonny, Erie	1.000	10	66	5	0	71	5
Rachels, Wes, Bow.	.971	15	93	7	3	103	7
Rifkin, Aaron, Nor.*	.992	63	467	22	4	493	48
Rivera, Carlos, Alt.*	.993	119	974	56	7	1037	88
Roneberg, Brett, Har.*	.995	25	180	9	1	190	24
Salazar, Oscar, Erie	1.000	1	6	0	0	6	1
Salzano, Jerry, Tren.	1.000	37	264	20	0	284	31
Santos, Jose, Port.	1.000	1	7	0	0	7	2
Sergio, Tom, Tren.	1.000	1	9	1	0	10	1
Sledge, Terrmel, Har.*	1.000	1	3	2	0	5	0
Van Iten, Bobby, Read.	1.000	1	2	0	0	2	1
Williams, Brady, N.B.	1.000	3	12	0	0	12	0
Wilson, Desi, Har.*	1.000	8	62	4	0	66	2

FIRST BASEMEN WITH TWO OR MORE TEAMS

Player, Team	Pct.	G	PO	A	E	TC	DP
Davis, Glenn, Nor.*	.981	6	50	3	1	54	3
Davis, Glenn, Har.*	.991	25	188	21	2	211	16
Garcia, Luis, N.H.	1.000	6	52	5	0	57	3
Garcia, Luis, Akr.	.984	7	59	3	1	63	3

SECOND BASEMEN

Player, Team	Pct.	G	PO	A	E	TC	DP
Ahumada, Alex, Tren.	.956	21	36	51	4	91	11
Basak, Chris, Bing.	1.000	17	23	46	0	69	8
Bowers, Jason, N.H.	1.000	7	15	9	0	24	3
Burnett, Mark, N.H.	.982	14	13	43	1	57	6
Calabrese, Tony, Nor.	1.000	2	3	5	0	8	0
Capista, Aaron, Tren.	.957	37	65	70	6	141	17
Carroll, Jamey, Har.	1.000	3	5	9	0	14	2
Casillas, Uriel, Read.	.969	14	23	39	2	64	5
Castillo, Carlos, Erie	.966	7	10	18	1	29	4
Cates, Gary, Bow.	1.000	5	10	8	0	18	1
Cervenak, Mike, Nor.	1.000	1	2	1	0	3	0
Chamblee, Jim, N.H.	.875	3	3	4	1	8	0
Connacher, Kevin, N.B.	.977	83	167	209	9	385	46
Davidson, Cleatus, N.H.-Nor.	.955	21	40	45	4	89	4
Diaz, Maikell, Bow.	.971	17	29	37	2	68	9
Erickson, Corey, Akr.	1.000	5	11	6	0	17	1
Gibbs, Kevin, Nor.	1.000	1	2	0	0	2	0
Gibbs, Mark, Bow.	.909	2	4	6	1	11	0
Goelz, Jim, Akr.	1.000	6	8	11	0	19	1
Gonzalez, Luis, Akr.	.972	31	59	81	4	144	23
Hammond, Joey, Bow.	.986	27	61	76	2	139	13
Hannahan, Buzz, Read.	.970	59	122	174	9	305	45
HART, Bo, N.H.	.985	102	188	270	7	465	61
Haverbusch, Kevin, Alt.	.969	6	11	20	1	32	7
Hitchcox, Brian, Read.	.983	83	172	235	7	414	58
Hodge, Kevin, N.B.	1.000	1	1	2	0	3	0
Hoffpauir, Josh, Bow.	.963	78	146	194	13	353	34
Hooper, Clay, Nor.	1.000	4	5	4	0	9	0
Izturis, Maicer, Akr.	.961	65	118	155	11	284	41
Jackson, Brandon, Nor.	1.000	6	9	10	0	19	4
Kelly, Heath, Port.	.826	5	9	10	4	23	1
Knupfer, Jason, Read.	1.000	1	4	3	0	7	1
Kropf, Andy, Erie	1.000	1	0	1	0	1	0
Lemonis, Chris, Alt.	1.000	4	11	12	0	23	2

Player, Team	Pct.	G	PO	A	E	TC	DP
Leon, Carlos, Tren.	.964	69	129	168	11	308	54
Lorenzo, Juan, N.B.	1.000	6	5	7	0	12	3
Machado, Albenis, Har.	.990	48	107	98	2	207	41
Martinez, Eddy, N.H.	.000	1	0	0	0	0	0
McEwing, Joe, Bing.	.000	1	0	0	0	0	0
McKinley, Josh, Har.	.950	90	166	197	19	382	36
Meadows, Randy, Alt.	1.000	8	14	11	0	25	6
Medrano, Jesus, Port.	.973	114	220	282	14	516	72
Myrow, Brian, Nor.	1.000	4	12	3	0	15	2
Nettles, Jeff, Nor.	.941	4	6	10	1	17	2
Nicholson, Kevin, N.H.	.967	13	17	41	2	60	8
Nieves, Raul, Tren.	.976	12	12	28	1	41	4
Niles, Drew, Port.	.979	24	53	41	2	96	13
Nye, Rodney, Bing.	1.000	3	3	2	0	5	1
Olivares, Teuris, Nor.	.959	22	47	47	4	98	15
Perez, Jhonny, Erie	.970	26	48	83	4	135	16
Perez, Tomas, Read.	1.000	1	5	2	0	7	2
Phillips, Andy, Nor.	.979	72	138	181	7	326	36
Pratt, Scott, Akr.	.970	39	70	89	5	164	17
Rachels, Wes, Bow.	.953	19	41	40	4	85	8
Reding, Josh, Har.	.918	10	19	26	4	49	0
Rodriguez, Luis, N.B.	.938	8	17	28	3	48	6
Rodriguez, Victor, Alt.	.989	40	80	108	2	190	20
Salazar, Oscar, Erie-Bing.	.983	36	88	80	3	171	28
Salazar, Ruben, N.B.	.970	50	111	112	7	230	30
Salzano, Jerry, Tren.	1.000	1	1	1	0	2	0
Sanchez, Freddy, Tren.	.963	11	25	27	2	54	7
Schnabel, Nick, Har.	.909	4	4	6	1	11	1
Sefcik, Kevin, Alt.	.979	86	171	207	8	386	40
Sequea, Jorge, Erie	.982	95	179	247	8	434	58
Shipp, Brian, Bing.	.962	100	180	228	16	424	65
Soler, Ramon, Bing.	.969	8	17	14	1	32	4
Tyson, Torre, Nor.	.964	12	28	25	2	55	9
Velazquez, Gil, Bing.	.978	12	16	28	1	45	4
Washington, Rico, Alt.	1.000	13	13	14	0	27	2
Weekly, Chris, N.H.	1.000	10	14	17	0	31	4

TRIPLE PLAY: Leon.

SECOND BASEMEN WITH TWO OR MORE TEAMS

Player, Team	Pct.	G	PO	A	E	TC	DP
Davidson, Cleatus, N.H.	.923	2	6	6	1	13	1
Davidson, Cleatus, Nor.	.961	19	34	39	3	76	3
Salazar, Oscar, Erie	.990	20	56	48	1	105	21
Salazar, Oscar, Bing.	.970	16	32	32	2	66	7

THIRD BASEMEN

Player, Team	Pct.	G	PO	A	E	TC	DP
Ahumada, Alex, Tren.	1.000	2	2	4	0	6	1
Almonte, Erick, Nor.	.000	2	0	0	0	0	0
Basak, Chris, Bing.	.962	16	8	42	2	52	3
Bautista, Rayner, Erie	1.000	3	4	3	0	7	0
Borrego, Ramon, N.B.	.778	2	2	5	2	9	0
Bowers, Jason, N.H.	.964	9	7	20	1	28	0
Calabrese, Tony, Nor.	.750	1	0	3	1	4	0
Calzado, Napolean, Bow.	.938	127	133	227	24	384	15
Cameron, Troy, Akr.	.906	61	35	109	15	159	5
Capista, Aaron, Tren.	1.000	5	2	10	0	12	1
Caruso, Joe, Alt.	.929	35	32	85	9	126	9
Casillas, Uriel, Read.	.867	33	23	75	15	113	6
Castillo, Carlos, Erie	.000	1	0	0	0	0	0
Cervenak, Mike, Nor.	.913	16	10	32	4	46	1
Chamblee, Jim, N.H.	.925	85	70	175	20	265	17
Chapman, Travis, Read.	.944	111	91	227	19	337	27
Chevalier, Virgil, Bing.	1.000	17	10	29	0	39	0
Coquillette, Trace, Port.	.903	34	22	71	10	103	5
Cronin, Shane, Nor.	1.000	1	1	1	0	2	0
Davidson, Cleatus, Nor.	.500	1	0	1	1	2	0
Derosso, Tony, Alt.	.960	29	21	51	3	75	7
Diaz, Maikell, Bow.	.933	7	2	12	1	15	1
Dillon, Joe, N.B.	.929	76	63	184	19	266	15
Erickson, Corey, Akr.	.941	59	33	111	9	153	12
Farnsworth, Troy, N.H.	.900	8	1	17	2	20	1
Gall, John, N.H.	.870	18	15	32	7	54	2
Goelz, Jim, Akr.	1.000	3	0	3	0	3	0
Gonzalez, Luis, Akr.	.882	11	5	25	4	34	1
Grindell, Nate, Akr.	.000	1	0	0	0	0	0

Player, Team	Pct.	G	PO	A	E	TC	DP
Hammond, Joey, Bow.	.778	5	3	4	2	9	0
Hannahan, Buzz, Read.	.833	8	5	5	2	12	0
Hannahan, Jack, Erie	.958	64	42	163	9	214	13
Heintz, Chris, N.H.	.000	1	0	0	0	0	0
Hodge, Kevin, N.B.	.944	6	3	14	1	18	1
Hodges, Scott, Har.	.931	130	81	256	25	362	24
Hoffpauir, Josh, Bow.	.800	4	2	6	2	10	0
Honeycutt, Heath, Port.	.976	11	11	29	1	41	3
Hooper, Clay, Nor.	.909	17	11	19	3	33	1
Jackson, Brandon, Nor.	1.000	3	1	6	0	7	1
Jones, Mitch, Nor.	.872	50	35	81	17	133	3
Kelly, Heath, Port.	.919	27	13	66	7	86	6
Lorenzo, Juan, N.B.	.853	32	26	61	15	102	3
Machado, Albenis, Har.	1.000	9	5	10	0	15	1
Martinez, Eddy, N.H.	.875	4	2	5	1	8	0
McDougall, Marshall, Akr.	.917	7	1	10	1	12	0
McEwing, Joe, Bing.	1.000	1	0	1	0	1	0
McNally, Sean, Har.	1.000	3	3	3	0	6	0
Morales, Andy, Tren.	.833	15	7	23	6	36	5
Myrow, Brian, Nor.	.912	50	26	78	10	114	7
Nettles, Jeff, Nor.	.708	10	7	10	7	24	0
Nicholson, Derek, Erie	.818	3	2	7	2	11	0
Nicholson, Kevin, N.H.	.891	16	12	29	5	46	5
Niles, Drew, Port.	.940	34	23	71	6	100	6
NYE, Rodney, Bing.	.965	104	74	198	10	282	21
Pachot, John, Alt.	1.000	1	0	1	0	1	0
Pascucci, Val, Har.	.667	2	0	2	1	3	0
Peeples, Mike, Port.	.667	2	1	1	1	3	0
Perez, Jhonny, Erie	.949	15	14	23	2	39	1
Pratt, Scott, Akr.	.912	10	7	24	3	34	2
Rodriguez, Victor, Alt.	1.000	2	0	1	0	1	0
Salazar, Oscar, Bing.	.900	7	3	6	1	10	0
Salzano, Jerry, Tren.	.957	10	6	16	1	23	0
Santos, Jose, Port.	.887	42	29	97	16	142	6
Scanlon, Matt, N.B.	.882	22	15	60	10	85	5
Schnabel, Nick, Har.	1.000	4	1	4	0	5	0
Sefcik, Kevin, Alt.	1.000	2	1	3	0	4	1
Shipp, Brian, Bing.	.846	9	4	18	4	26	2
Ust, Brant, Erie	.944	58	44	140	11	195	23
Velazquez, Gil, Bing.	.900	4	2	7	1	10	0
Veras, Wilton, Tren.	.957	67	43	157	9	209	10
Washington, Rico, Alt.	.944	49	68	166	14	248	17
Weekly, Chris, N.H.	.926	13	5	20	2	27	3
Williams, Brady, N.B.	.947	5	5	13	1	19	0
Youkilis, Kevin, Tren.	.916	44	34	86	11	131	7

TRIPLE PLAY: Veras.

SHORTSTOPS

Player, Team	Pct.	G	PO	A	E	TC	DP
Ahumada, Alex, Tren.	.933	28	41	70	8	119	11
Almonte, Erick, Nor.	.963	51	64	145	8	217	28
Basak, Chris, Bing.	.971	70	126	204	10	340	49
Bautista, Rayner, Erie.	.934	78	119	205	23	347	54
Bowers, Jason, N.H.	.953	86	153	230	19	402	55
Calabrese, Tony, Nor.	1.000	3	2	2	0	4	0
Capista, Aaron, Tren.	.750	3	3	6	3	12	3
Caruso, Joe, Alt.	.971	8	18	15	1	34	1
Casillas, Uriel, Read.	.912	9	8	23	3	34	4
Castillo, Carlos, Erie	.882	26	44	61	14	119	11
Cates, Gary, Bow.	.667	2	1	1	1	3	0
Davidson, Cleatus, N.H.-Nor.	.977	10	12	30	1	43	4
Diaz, Maikell, Bow.	.989	22	23	65	1	89	15
Figueroa, Luis, Har.	.981	66	114	192	6	312	49
Goelz, Jim, Akr.	.964	7	10	17	1	28	4
Gonzalez, Luis, Akr.	1.000	4	2	10	0	12	0
Hammond, Joey, Bow.	1.000	1	4	1	0	5	0
Hannahan, Buzz, Read.	1.000	5	6	10	0	16	4
Hart, Bo, N.H.	1.000	1	0	1	0	1	1
Hodges, Scott, Har.	1.000	2	4	6	0	10	1
Hoffpauir, Josh, Bow.	.846	6	8	14	4	26	4
Hooper, Clay, Nor.	.929	51	73	123	15	211	19
Jackson, Brandon, Nor.	.947	13	16	38	3	57	5
Knupfer, Jason, Read.	.935	9	16	27	3	46	2
Lemonis, Chris, Alt.	.714	2	2	3	2	7	0
Leon, Carlos, Tren.	.860	9	14	23	6	43	4
Lofton, James, Tren.	.961	35	54	92	6	152	19

Player, Team	Pct.	G	PO	A	E	TC	DP
Lorenzo, Juan, N.B.	.989	35	34	56	1	91	10
Machado, Albenis, Har.	.928	19	30	47	6	83	9
Machado, Andy, Read.	.954	124	195	391	28	614	79
Martinez, Eddy, N.H.	.926	19	26	49	6	81	10
Meadows, Randy, Alt.	.963	36	48	83	5	136	22
Nettles, Jeff, Nor.	.864	12	13	25	6	44	9
Nicholson, Kevin, N.H.	.944	32	43	91	8	142	12
Niles, Drew, Port.	.979	24	33	60	2	95	11
Olivares, Teuris, Nor.	.974	18	25	50	2	77	7
Peralta, John, Akr.	.965	130	201	374	21	596	73
Perez, Jhonny, Erie	.846	8	7	15	4	26	1
Perez, Tomas, Read.	1.000	1	1	3	0	4	0
Phillips, Brandon, Har.	.936	59	77	127	14	218	15
Pratt, Scott, Akr.	1.000	5	8	12	0	20	0
Reding, Josh, Har.	.889	3	2	6	1	9	1
Reyes, Jose, Bing.	.940	65	92	176	17	285	37
RODRIGUEZ, Luis, N.B.	.973	119	203	375	16	594	74
Rogers, Ed, Bow.	.958	111	153	301	20	474	47
Salazar, Oscar, Bing.	1.000	15	16	24	0	40	6
Sanchez, Freddy, Tren.	.953	69	121	165	14	300	38
Santiago, Ramon, Erie	.966	21	26	58	3	87	7
Sefcik, Kevin, Alt.	.953	28	39	63	5	107	12
Skrehot, Shaun, Alt.	.956	80	126	198	15	339	36
Valdez, Wilson, Port.	.944	113	171	304	28	503	67
Velazquez, Gil, Bing.	.943	8	12	21	2	35	4
Wilson, Josh, Port.	.967	12	25	33	2	60	14

SHORTSTOPS WITH TWO OR MORE TEAMS

Player, Team	Pct.	G	PO	A	E	TC	DP
Davidson, Cleatus, N.H.	.976	9	11	29	1	41	3
Davidson, Cleatus, Nor.	1.000	1	1	1	0	2	1

OUTFIELDERS

Player, Team	Pct.	G	PO	A	E	TC	DP
Acuna, Ron, Bing.	.875	7	6	1	1	8	0
Aguila, Chris, Port.	.988	122	233	15	3	251	0
Ahumada, Alex, Tren.	.947	12	17	1	1	19	0
Airoso, Kurt, Erie	.983	51	111	4	2	117	1
Almonte, Wady, N.H.	1.000	9	15	0	0	15	0
Alvarez, Tony, Alt.	.978	124	253	11	6	270	1
Arias, Pablo, Erie	.000	1	0	0	0	0	0
Baron, Brian, N.B.	.986	109	200	6	3	209	1
Basak, Chris, Bing.	1.000	3	6	0	0	6	0
Bates, Fletcher, Bing.	1.000	21	23	1	0	24	0
Bay, Jason, Bing.	.956	27	39	4	2	45	0
Bolivar, Papo, N.B.	.985	114	186	10	3	199	0
Bradley, Milton, Akr.	1.000	2	3	1	0	4	0
Brown, Rich, Nor.*	.962	15	25	0	1	26	0
Brown, Tonayne, Nor.*	.985	124	261	3	4	268	1
Cabrera, Ray, Bow.	.980	52	93	5	2	100	2
Camilo, Juan, Erie	.966	37	55	2	2	59	1
Candelaria, Ben, Port.	.970	21	32	0	1	33	0
Casillas, Uriel, Read.	.000	1	0	0	0	0	0
Cepicky, Matt, Har.	.988	84	153	5	2	160	1
Chamblee, Jim, N.H.	1.000	7	8	0	0	8	0
Chevalier, Virgil, Bing.	.944	16	16	1	1	18	0
Church, Ryan, Akr.*	.993	67	139	12	1	152	3
Connacher, Kevin, N.B.	.909	27	19	1	2	22	0
Coquillette, Trace, Port.	1.000	11	17	1	0	18	0
Crisp, Covelli, Akr.-N.H.	.985	86	192	9	3	204	1
Crozier, Eric, Akr.*	1.000	3	4	0	0	4	0
Curry, Mike, Bing.	1.000	21	27	1	0	28	0
Davidson, Cleatus, Nor.	1.000	4	5	0	0	5	0
Davis, J.J., Alt.	.971	100	194	6	6	206	2
Derosso, Tony, Alt.	1.000	10	9	1	0	10	0
Dina, Allen, Port.	.978	43	85	4	2	91	0
Edmondson, Brian, Erie	.000	1	0	0	0	0	0
Erickson, Corey, Akr.	1.000	2	3	0	0	3	0
Fischer, Mark, Tren.	.942	39	47	2	3	52	1
Fitzgerald, Jason, Akr.*	.994	83	169	3	1	173	0
Ford, Lew, N.B.	.986	93	202	6	3	211	3
Foster, Quincy, Port.-Har.	.969	67	155	3	5	163	2
Fox, Jacob, Har.	1.000	6	14	0	0	14	0
Frank, Mike, N.H.*	.975	16	38	1	1	40	0
French, Anton, Tren.	.944	20	51	0	3	54	0
Gall, John, N.H.	1.000	8	10	0	0	10	0

Player, Team	Pct.	G	PO	A	E	TC	DP
Garcia, Luis, N.H.-Akr.	.973	102	173	9	5	187	0
Garrett, Shawn, Alt.	.979	128	220	8	5	233	1
Gerut, Jody, Akr.*	.979	64	142	1	3	146	0
Gibbs, Kevin, Nor.	.974	59	149	1	4	154	0
Gingrich, Troy, Har.*	.500	1	1	0	1	2	0
Goelz, Jim, Akr.	1.000	1	5	0	0	5	0
Gonzalez, Luis, Akr.	1.000	3	6	0	0	6	0
Gonzalez, Manny, Read.	.970	19	29	3	1	33	0
Green, Chad, N.B.	.976	20	38	3	1	42	0
Griffin, John-ford, Nor.*	.935	18	27	2	2	31	1
Grindell, Nate, Akr.	.974	96	141	6	4	151	1
Hamilton, Jon, Akr.*	.975	38	72	5	2	79	0
Hannahan, Buzz, Read.	.950	9	16	3	1	20	0
Haverbusch, Kevin, Alt.	1.000	17	34	3	0	37	1
Haynes, Dee, N.H.	.946	122	213	14	13	240	0
HEADLEY, Justin, Tren.*	1.000	99	188	4	0	192	0
Hodge, Kevin, N.B.	1.000	1	2	0	0	2	0
Hooper, Clay, Nor.	1.000	2	2	0	0	2	0
Hunter, Scott, Bing.-Bow.	.972	89	132	5	4	141	0
Iapoce, Anthony, Port.*	.989	73	170	6	2	178	0
Jacobsen, Bucky, N.H.	1.000	4	4	0	0	4	0
Johnson, Jason, Read.	.976	112	194	11	5	210	0
Jones, Mitch, Nor.	1.000	7	9	0	0	9	0
Kelly, Heath, Port.	1.000	2	4	0	0	4	0
Lawton, Matt, Akr.	1.000	3	9	0	0	9	0
LeBron, Juan, N.H.	.980	31	47	2	1	50	0
Lindsey, Rodney, Erie	.978	97	214	10	5	229	2
Loggins, Josh, Nor.	.961	30	71	3	3	77	1
Lomasney, Steve, Tren.	1.000	1	1	0	0	1	0
Lorenzo, Juan, N.B.	.000	2	0	0	0	0	0
Luderer, Brian, Akr.	.000	1	0	0	0	0	0
Matos, Luis, Bow.	.992	57	121	4	1	126	1
McDonald, Darnell, Bow.	.984	24	58	2	1	61	0
McKinley, Dan, Har.	.979	41	92	1	2	95	0
McNaughton, Troy, Read.*	.947	11	18	0	1	19	0
Meier, Dan, Alt.*	.963	50	75	3	3	81	0
Meran, Jorge, Erie	1.000	1	2	1	0	3	0
Millar, Kevin, Port.	1.000	3	2	0	0	2	0
Mooney, Dan, Tren.	1.000	2	5	0	0	5	0
Myrow, Brian, Nor.	1.000	2	1	0	0	1	0
Neill, Ryan, Erie	1.000	6	10	1	0	11	0
Padgett, Matt, Port.*	.961	81	145	4	6	155	1
Padilla, Jorge, Read.	.971	122	257	12	8	277	2
Pascucci, Val, Har.	.972	107	200	11	6	217	1
Peeples, Mike, Port.	.957	15	22	0	1	23	0
Perez, Jhonny, Erie	.946	21	33	2	2	37	1
Perez, Josue, Read.	.971	54	95	4	3	102	2
Pratt, Scott, Akr.	.978	43	89	1	2	92	0
Rabe, Josh, N.B.	1.000	46	97	5	0	102	1
Rachels, Wes, Bow.	.905	12	17	2	2	21	0
Raines, Tim, Bow.	.978	114	254	8	6	268	1
Reding, Josh, Har.	1.000	1	1	0	0	1	0
Redman, Prentice, Bing.	.979	118	226	5	5	236	1
Reed, Keith, Bow.	.976	97	193	14	5	212	5
Reese, Kevin, Nor.*	.980	137	296	5	6	307	0
Richardson, Corey, Erie	.993	106	272	14	2	288	3
Rigsby, Randy, Port.*	.949	41	73	2	4	79	0
Rios, Armando, Alt.*	1.000	1	2	0	0	2	0
Roberge, J.P., Read.	1.000	2	4	0	0	4	0
Rodriguez, John, Nor.*	.985	102	195	3	3	201	1
Roneberg, Brett, Har.*	.972	35	68	2	2	72	1
Ross, Cody, Erie*	.975	102	216	16	6	238	2
Salazar, Oscar, Erie	.920	15	21	2	2	25	0
Salzano, Jerry, Tren.	.978	57	89	2	2	93	0
Scanlon, Matt, N.B.	1.000	24	28	1	0	29	1
Sefcik, Kevin, Alt.	.958	17	23	0	1	24	0
Sergio, Tom, Tren.	1.000	22	33	1	0	34	1
Sherrod, Justin, Tren.	.939	69	128	10	9	147	1
Sitzman, Jay, Read.*	.986	96	204	8	3	215	0
Sledge, Terrmel, Har.*	.996	93	231	8	1	240	4
Smith, Will, Tren.	.000	2	0	0	0	0	0
Snead, Esix, Bing.	.985	119	259	11	4	274	1
Taguchi, So, N.H.	.970	26	64	1	2	67	0
Thompson, Andy, N.H.	1.000	2	5	0	0	5	0
Vento, Mike, Nor.	.977	61	123	3	3	129	2
Ware, Jeremy, Har.	.948	24	53	2	3	58	0
Watson, Brandon, Har.	1.000	2	4	0	0	4	0
Watson, Matt, Har.-Bing.	.979	105	178	11	4	193	1

Player, Team	Pct.	G	PO	A	E	TC	DP
Weber, Jake, N.H.	1.000	49	65	1	0	66	0
Weekly, Chris, N.H.	1.000	6	7	1	0	8	0
Weichard, Paul, Alt.*	.000	1	0	0	0	0	0
Wilson, Desi, Har.*	1.000	2	3	0	0	3	0
Woods, Ken, Read.	.978	18	42	3	1	46	1

OUTFIELDERS WITH TWO OR MORE TEAMS

Player, Team	Pct.	G	PO	A	E	TC	DP
Crisp, Covelli, Akr.	1.000	6	9	0	0	9	0
Crisp, Covelli, N.H.	.985	80	183	9	3	195	1
Foster, Quincy, Port.	.979	20	45	1	1	47	0
Foster, Quincy, Har.	.966	47	110	2	4	116	2
Garcia, Luis, N.H.	.972	80	132	6	4	142	0
Garcia, Luis, Akr.	.978	22	41	3	1	45	0
Hunter, Scott, Bing.	.968	20	29	1	1	31	0
Hunter, Scott, Bow.	.973	69	103	4	3	110	0
Watson, Matt, Har.	1.000	1	1	0	0	1	0
Watson, Matt, Bing.	.979	104	177	11	4	192	1

CATCHERS

Player, Team	Pct.	G	PO	A	E	TC	DP	PB
Ackerman, Scott, Har.	1.000	4	18	1	0	19	0	1
Bailey, Jeff, Har.	.979	12	88	5	2	95	0	2
Brown, Jason, Alt.-Har.	1.000	26	165	8	0	173	0	0
Carreno, Jose, Har.	1.000	13	85	8	0	93	2	3
Chevalier, Virgil, Bing.	.986	37	263	20	4	287	2	8
Cleveland, Russ, Erie	.979	16	84	9	2	95	1	3
Cronin, Shane, Nor.	1.000	19	99	8	0	107	1	3
Cruz, Edgar, Read.	1.000	1	6	1	0	7	0	0
Dominique, Andy, Tren.	1.000	14	83	9	0	92	0	1
Elwood, Brad, Nor.	.000	1	0	0	0	0	0	0
Garland, Ross, Erie	.952	1	17	3	1	21	2	2
Gonzalez, Jimmy, Bing.	.987	92	636	70	9	715	5	4
Heintz, Chris, N.H.	.986	82	504	65	8	577	4	17
Hernandez, Michel, Nor.	.981	14	93	13	2	108	0	3
House, J.R., Alt.	.994	20	147	11	1	159	1	1
Jacobson, Russ, Read.	.992	75	451	41	4	496	3	11
Jorgensen, Ryan, Port.	.983	41	256	41	5	302	4	3
King, Brad, Alt.	.996	40	263	21	1	285	3	1
Kropf, Andy, Erie	.952	17	68	11	4	83	1	0
Larned, Drew, Tren.	1.000	1	9	1	0	10	0	0
Lomasney, Steve, Tren.	.983	100	675	66	13	754	7	12
Lopez, Angel, Port.	1.000	5	28	3	0	31	0	0
Luderer, Brian, Akr.	.981	44	290	20	6	316	2	5
Malave, Jaime, Bing.	.985	11	60	4	1	65	0	0
Marsters, Brandon, N.B.	1.000	22	151	16	0	167	1	1
Martinez, Octavio, Bow.	.986	7	68	3	1	72	2	0
Martinez, Victor, Akr.	.988	101	770	66	10	846	4	8
McGee, Tom, Bow.	.953	15	75	7	4	86	1	2
Meran, Jorge, Erie	.984	48	285	32	5	322	4	5
Molina, Izzy, Bow.	.988	56	362	39	5	406	3	7
Mooney, Dan, Tren.	.983	20	96	19	2	117	1	3
Morales, Steve, Port.	.982	49	285	36	6	327	4	5
Oakes, Matty, Erie	.971	6	32	1	1	34	0	0
Pachot, John, Alt.	.994	70	412	62	3	477	11	2
Parrish, Dave, Nor.	.981	100	700	75	15	790	6	19
Pogue, Jamie, N.H.	.985	64	397	53	7	457	0	6
Ramos, Kelly, Tren.	.953	10	80	2	4	86	0	1
Rose, Mike, Tren.	1.000	10	71	14	0	85	2	0
St. Pierre, Maxim, Erie	.991	58	299	35	3	337	2	7
Salinas, Trey, Bow.	1.000	5	26	4	0	30	1	2
SANDUSKY, Scott, Har.	.997	107	728	68	2	798	10	10
Seestedt, Mike, Bow.	1.000	1	6	1	0	7	0	1
Smith, Jeff, N.B.	.986	80	493	58	8	559	4	3
Snusz, Chris, Nor.	.980	15	91	5	2	98	0	1
Torres, Gabby, N.B.	.986	48	242	30	4	276	3	9
Treanor, Matt, Port.	.977	48	339	39	9	387	5	2
Ullery, Dave, Bow.	.988	38	240	17	3	260	3	5
Valera, Yohanny, Erie	1.000	4	25	3	0	28	0	0
Van Iten, Bobby, Read.	.987	77	425	45	6	476	2	4
Whiteside, Eli, Bow.	.972	25	160	14	5	179	0	2
Wilson, John, Bing.	1.000	8	45	7	0	52	0	0

CATCHERS WITH TWO OR MORE TEAMS

Player, Team	Pct.	G	PO	A	E	TC	DP	PB
Brown, Jason, Alt.	1.000	17	103	6	0	109	0	0
Brown, Jason, Har.	1.000	9	62	2	0	64	0	0

PITCHERS

Player, Team	Pct.	G	PO	A	E	TC	DP
Adams, Brian, Tren.*	1.000	16	1	4	0	5	0
Adams, Daniel, Read.	1.000	2	2	0	0	2	0
Adkins, Tim, Erie*	.000	3	0	0	0	0	0
Agamennone, Brandon, Har.	1.000	8	1	3	0	4	0
Ambrose, John, Tren.	1.000	10	1	2	0	3	0
Anderson, Jason, Nor.	1.000	16	0	3	0	3	0
Andrade, Jancy, Bow.	.000	1	0	0	0	0	0
Arias, Pablo, Erie	.952	29	8	12	1	21	0
Arnold, Jason, Nor.	.600	3	0	3	2	5	0
Babula, Shaun, Bow.*	1.000	7	4	1	0	5	0
Bailie, Matt, Read.	1.000	12	1	3	0	4	0
Baisley, Brad, Read.	.967	21	7	22	1	30	1
Beal, Andy, Nor.*	1.000	10	1	11	0	12	1
Bean, Colter, Nor.	1.000	12	2	2	0	4	0
Bechler, Steve, Bow.	.857	4	4	2	1	7	0
Bedard, Erik, Bow.*	1.000	13	3	5	0	8	0
Beech, Matt, Nor.*	1.000	7	1	6	0	7	0
Bell, Heath, Bing.	1.000	24	4	6	0	10	1
Benson, Kris, Alt.	.000	1	0	0	0	0	0
Bevis, P.J., Bing.	.000	4	0	0	0	0	0
Billingsley, Brent, Har.*	1.000	6	2	1	0	3	0
Bland, Nate, Bing.*	1.000	15	3	2	0	5	0
Blevins, Jeremy, Nor.	.833	19	2	3	1	6	1
Borkowski, Dave, Erie	1.000	2	1	0	0	1	0
Borrell, Danny, Nor.*	.920	21	5	18	2	25	1
Bowe, Brandon, Port.	.950	45	8	11	1	20	0
Braswell, Bryan, Bing.*	.909	24	2	8	1	11	0
Bridges, Donnie, Har.-Port.	.929	20	5	8	1	14	0
Brock, Chris, Bow.	1.000	1	0	1	0	1	0
Brooks, Frank, Read.*	1.000	17	0	4	0	4	0
Brown, Derek, Bow.	.792	41	4	15	5	24	2
Brown, Jamie, Akr.	.938	18	4	11	1	16	1
Brownson, Mark, Bow.	1.000	3	1	0	0	1	1
Brunette, Justin, Bing.*	1.000	3	1	0	0	1	0
Buchanan, Brian, Nor.*	.000	11	0	0	0	0	0
Buchholz, Taylor, Read.	1.000	4	1	1	0	2	0
Bump, Nate, Port.	.920	20	9	14	2	25	1
Burba, Dave, Akr.	1.000	1	0	1	0	1	1
Burnside, Adrian, Alt.*	.917	32	2	9	1	12	0
Byrdak, Tim, Akr.*	1.000	9	0	1	0	1	0
Cabrera, Fernando, Akr.	.667	7	1	1	1	3	0
Cammack, Eric, Bing.	.900	36	5	4	1	10	1
Camp, Jared, Erie	1.000	6	2	2	0	4	0
Carnes, Matt, N.B.	1.000	21	2	8	0	10	0
Casadiego, Gerardo, Har.	.571	9	0	4	3	7	0
Cerda, Jaime, Bing.*	1.000	14	2	4	0	6	0
Cerros, Juan, Bing.	.000	3	0	0	0	0	0
Chavez, Chris, Port.	1.000	15	1	5	0	6	0
Chevalier, Virgil, Bing.	.000	2	0	0	0	0	0
Chiavacci, Ron, Har.	.944	35	6	11	1	18	0
Chipperfield, Calvin, Erie	.000	1	0	0	0	0	0
Christman, Tim, Port.*	1.000	11	0	1	0	1	0
Chrysler, Clint, Alt.*	1.000	51	3	8	0	11	1
Clark, Chris, Port.	1.000	10	0	2	0	2	0
Clemens, Roger, Nor.	.000	1	0	0	0	0	0
Cole, Joey, Bing.	.818	10	2	7	2	11	1
Collins, Pat, Har.	1.000	29	2	6	0	8	0
Colon, Jose, Akr.	1.000	46	5	9	0	14	0
Cook, Andy, Bing.	1.000	30	6	1	0	7	0
Cook, B.R., N.H.	.956	28	15	28	2	45	4
Corcoran, Tim, Bow.	.818	35	1	8	2	11	0
Correa, Cristobal, N.H.	1.000	26	7	21	0	28	0
Crawford, Paxton, Tren.	.000	1	0	0	0	0	0
Crumpton, Chuck, Har.	1.000	21	4	10	0	14	0
Cueto, Jose, Port.	1.000	9	2	3	0	5	0
Cummings, Jeremy, N.H.	.958	14	6	17	1	24	0
Davis, Allen, Har.*	1.000	9	1	5	0	6	0
Davis, Jason, Akr.	.818	10	3	6	2	11	1
De La Rosa, Jorge, Tren.*	.667	4	0	2	1	3	0
Denney, Kyle, Akr.	1.000	6	2	3	0	5	0
De Paula, Julio, Nor.	.900	27	3	15	2	20	0
Deschenes, Marc, Alt.	.000	3	0	0	0	0	0
Dickinson, Rodney, Tren.	1.000	4	0	1	0	1	0
Donaldson, Bo, Nor.	.000	17	0	1	1	1	0
Dougherty, Jim, Alt.	1.000	7	2	3	0	5	0

Player, Team	Pct.	G	PO	A	E	TC	DP
Dubose, Eric, Bow.*	1.000	41	5	14	0	19	0
Duff, Matt, N.H.	.833	47	1	9	2	12	1
Edmondson, Brian, Akr.-Erie	.818	43	1	8	2	11	0
Einertson, Darrell, Nor.	1.000	4	0	1	0	1	0
Elder, Dave, Akr.	.875	23	2	5	1	8	0
Elmore, Chris, Tren.*	1.000	14	5	18	0	23	1
Estrella, Leo, N.H.	1.000	14	5	10	0	15	0
Etherton, Seth, Nor.	1.000	1	0	1	0	1	0
Evans, Kyle, Akr.	1.000	2	1	1	0	2	1
Eyre, Willie, N.B.	.933	28	8	6	1	15	1
Farmer, Tom, Erie	1.000	18	3	13	0	16	0
Ferrari, Anthony, Har.*	.913	44	8	13	2	23	2
Fesh, Sean, Port.*	1.000	24	4	2	0	6	0
Figueroa, Juan, Bow.	.900	24	4	5	1	10	2
Fisher, Pete, N.B.	.750	6	2	1	1	4	0
FLOHR, Adam, N.B.*	1.000	43	7	24	0	31	3
Fontana, Tony, Tren.	1.000	11	5	3	0	8	0
Francisco, Frank, Tren.	.667	9	1	1	1	3	0
Franco, Martire, Read.	.938	16	7	8	1	16	0
Garza, Alberto, Akr.	1.000	20	1	3	0	4	1
Giese, Dan, Tren.	.909	23	4	6	1	11	2
Glaser, Eric, Tren.	.917	33	9	13	2	24	0
Glick, David, Nor.*	.917	8	3	8	1	12	0
Goetz, Geoff, Port.*	1.000	2	0	2	0	2	0
Gonzalez, Mike, Alt.*	.882	16	1	14	2	17	0
Grabow, John, Alt.*	.933	28	5	23	2	30	1
Graman, Alex, Nor.*	1.000	8	1	3	0	4	0
Gravelle, Nick, Alt.*	.000	1	0	0	0	0	0
Graves, Bobby, Erie*	1.000	11	1	6	0	7	0
Greisinger, Seth, Erie	.857	4	1	5	1	7	0
Griffiths, Jeremy, Bing.	.927	27	14	24	3	41	3
Guillory, Dan, Akr.	.909	19	2	8	1	11	0
Guy, Brad, Alt.	1.000	26	4	15	0	19	3
Hale, Beau, Bow.	.000	2	0	0	1	1	0
Hamilton, Jimmy, Read.*	1.000	46	2	13	0	15	1
Hamulack, Tim, Port.*	1.000	38	3	15	0	18	0
Hancock, Josh, Tren.	1.000	15	6	8	0	14	0
Heams, Shane, Tren.	1.000	14	0	5	0	5	1
Hebson, Bryan, Har.	.842	38	6	10	3	19	2
Heilman, Aaron, Bing.	.950	17	4	15	1	20	1
Henkel, Rob, Port.*	.889	13	1	7	1	9	0
Hentgen, Pat, Bow.	1.000	1	1	1	0	2	0
Herrera, Alex, Akr.*	.750	30	0	6	2	8	1
Hiles, Cary, Read.	.778	21	1	6	2	9	0
Hill, Terry, Tren.*	.905	45	4	15	2	21	1
Hoard, Brent, N.B.*	.968	31	13	17	1	31	0
Hodge, Kevin, N.B.	1.000	24	1	4	0	5	0
Izquierdo, Hansel, Port.	.667	1	0	2	1	3	0
Jamison, Ryan, Bing.	1.000	11	2	5	0	7	0
JANKE, Cheyenne, N.H.	1.000	28	9	22	0	31	1
Jean, Domingo, Nor.	1.000	36	0	8	0	8	0
Jerzembeck, Mike, N.B.	.000	3	0	0	0	0	0
Jodie, Brett, Nor.	.000	2	0	0	0	0	0
Johnson, James, Akr.*	1.000	5	0	2	0	2	0
Johnson, Jason, Bow.	.000	1	0	0	1	1	0
Johnson, Jeremy, Erie	1.000	8	0	2	0	2	0
Johnson, Mark, Erie	1.000	5	1	3	0	4	1
Joseph, Jake, Bing.	.909	14	1	9	1	11	0
Journell, Jimmy, N.H.	.895	10	6	11	2	19	1
Karnuth, Jason, N.H.	.950	58	2	17	1	20	1
Karp, Josh, Har.	.889	16	7	9	2	18	0
Keelin, Chris, Erie	.000	2	0	0	0	0	0
Kinney, Matt, N.B.	.000	1	0	0	0	0	0
Kirsten, Rick, Erie	1.000	3	1	0	0	1	0
Klepacki, Ed, Har.-Port.	1.000	19	1	2	0	3	0
Kline, Steve, N.H.*	1.000	1	1	0	0	1	0
Kubes, Greg, Read.*	.913	28	7	14	2	23	0
Kusiewicz, Mike, Tren.*	.923	13	2	10	1	13	0
Lambert, Jeremy, N.H.	1.000	18	1	1	0	2	0
Langen, Brian, N.H.*	.952	46	7	13	1	21	0
Larson, Ryan, Akr.	1.000	32	1	5	0	6	0
Lavigne, Tim, Bing.	1.000	23	4	6	0	10	0
Layfield, Scotty, N.H.	1.000	58	2	9	0	11	0
Lee, Cliff, Har.-Akr.*	1.000	18	2	10	0	12	0
Lee, Seung, Read.	1.000	1	1	1	0	2	0
Lewis, Craig, Har.	1.000	17	0	4	0	4	0
Lidle, Kevin, Erie	.917	23	4	18	2	24	0

Player, Team	Pct.	G	PO	A	E	TC	DP
Looney, Brian, Alt.*	1.000	4	1	1	0	2	1
Lopez, Gustavo, Port.	1.000	2	0	1	0	1	0
Lopez, Jose, Alt.	.875	10	3	4	1	8	0
Lovingier, Kevin, Nor.*	.000	19	0	0	0	0	0
Madson, Ryan, Read.	.943	26	13	20	2	35	1
Maness, Nick, Bing.	.946	25	7	28	2	37	2
Mangum, Mark, Har.	1.000	18	5	13	0	18	2
Manning, Charlie, Nor.*	.909	11	1	9	1	11	0
Manning, David, N.B.	.933	11	5	9	1	15	0
Manon, Julio, Har.	.857	6	3	3	1	7	0
Marquetti, Agustin, Erie	.667	8	1	1	1	3	0
Marrero, Darwin, Har.	.941	19	7	9	1	17	0
Marsonek, Sam, Nor.	.955	19	6	15	1	22	4
Martinez, Anastacio, Tren.	.833	27	13	17	6	36	2
Massingale, Matt, Port.	1.000	6	3	0	0	3	0
Mays, Joe, N.B.	1.000	1	1	1	0	2	0
McAvoy, Jeff, Har.	1.000	16	1	4	0	5	0
McConnell, Sam, Read.*	.947	29	9	9	1	19	0
McDade, Neal, Alt.	.958	49	5	18	1	24	1
McDonald, Jon, N.B.	.828	21	12	12	5	29	1
McLeary, Marty, Tren.	.000	11	0	0	2	2	0
Meadows, Randy, Alt.	.000	1	0	0	0	0	0
Mendoza, Marcos, Akr.*	1.000	21	1	5	0	6	1
Mills, Ryan, N.B.*	1.000	26	5	22	0	27	0
Montano, Ignacio, Akr.*	.000	2	0	0	0	0	0
Montgomery, Matt, Alt.	.909	44	2	8	1	11	1
Nelson, Joe, Tren.	.333	4	1	0	2	3	0
Ochoa, Pablo, Bing.	1.000	8	1	3	0	4	0
O'Connor, Brian, Alt.*	1.000	24	0	16	0	16	0
Ortiz, Omar, Port.	.938	33	7	8	1	16	0
Outlaw, Mark, Read.*	.875	41	2	5	1	8	2
Ozias, Todd, Read.	1.000	31	0	2	0	2	0
Padilla, Juan, N.B.	1.000	54	9	6	0	15	0
Padilla, Roy, N.H.*	1.000	3	1	0	0	1	0
Pageler, Mick, N.H.	.000	3	0	0	0	0	0
Palki, Jeromy, N.B.	1.000	30	4	3	0	7	0
Palma, Rick, Alt.*	1.000	10	0	1	0	1	0
Paradis, Mike, Bow.	.972	27	19	16	1	36	0
Paronto, Chad, Akr.	.000	1	0	0	0	0	0
Parrott, Rhett, N.H.	.923	9	5	7	1	13	1
Pautz, Brad, Read.	.929	43	3	10	1	14	1
Pavlovich, Tony, Alt.	.000	1	0	0	0	0	0
Pearsall, J.J., Port.-Erie*	1.000	36	2	8	0	10	1
Pearson, Terry, Erie	1.000	15	1	1	0	2	0
Perez, Frank, Erie	.857	31	3	9	2	14	0
Perez, Frank, Read.	1.000	40	7	12	0	19	0
Peters, Chris, Erie*	1.000	43	3	7	0	10	1
Pettitte, Andy, Nor.*	1.000	1	0	2	0	2	0
Pierson, Jason, Nor.*	1.000	11	1	2	0	3	0
Pineda, Isauro, Tren.	.964	28	20	33	2	55	4
Ponce Deleon, Damon, N.H.	.000	4	0	0	0	0	0
Prather, Scott, N.H.*	1.000	11	1	4	0	5	0
Pridie, Jon, N.B.	.950	16	9	10	1	20	2
Pumphrey, Ken, Read.	.889	20	4	20	3	27	2
Rakers, Aaron, Bow.	.833	36	0	5	1	6	0
Rakers, Jason, Akr.	.000	1	0	0	0	0	0
Ramirez, Jose, Erie*	.857	28	1	5	1	7	0
Randall, Scott, N.B.	1.000	5	3	10	0	13	2
Reid, Justin, Alt.	1.000	25	9	14	0	23	2
Riley, Matt, Bow.*	.844	22	7	20	5	32	3
Riske, David, Akr.	1.000	4	0	1	0	1	0
Rivera, Homero, Erie*	.867	40	2	11	2	15	2
Rivera, Saul, Bing.-Har.	.909	45	4	6	1	11	0
Roach, Jason, Bing.	.947	8	4	14	1	19	2
Roberts, Grant, Bing.	.000	1	0	0	0	0	0
Robertson, Nathan, Port.*	.824	27	4	24	6	34	2
Rodgers, Bobby, Erie*	1.000	3	0	1	0	1	0
Rodney, Fernando, Erie	1.000	21	3	1	0	4	0
Rodriguez, Eddy, Bow.	.000	2	0	0	0	0	0
Rogers, Brian, Nor.	1.000	13	3	10	0	13	0
Roller, Adam, Nor.	1.000	21	1	2	0	3	0
Rosario, Juan, Bow.	.968	25	10	20	1	31	3
Rose, Ted, Alt.	.875	6	2	5	1	8	0
Sadler, Carl, Akr.*	.929	21	3	10	1	14	0
Saenz, Jason, Bing.*	1.000	36	6	14	0	20	0
Salazar, Richard, Bow.*	1.000	8	2	2	0	4	0
Sampson, Benj, N.B.*	.950	16	3	16	1	20	0
Sansom, Trevor, N.H.	1.000	47	7	11	0	18	0
Schoening, Brent, N.B.	1.000	21	6	7	0	13	1
Schurman, Ryan, N.H.	.875	18	3	4	1	8	0
Seale, Dustin, Har.*	1.000	29	3	9	0	12	0
Seibel, Phil, Bing.*	.970	28	8	24	1	33	2
Seo, Jae, Bing.	.000	1	0	0	0	0	0
Sequea, Jacobo, Bow.	1.000	15	6	16	0	22	0
Sergent, Joe, Port.*	1.000	20	2	9	0	11	0
Sergio, Tom, Tren.	1.000	1	0	1	0	1	0
Serrano, Willy, Bow.	.909	27	5	5	1	11	2
Shaffar, Ben, Alt.	.862	18	3	22	4	29	2
Shepard, David, Nor.	.917	42	2	9	1	12	0
Shibilo, Andy, Tren.	1.000	21	3	7	0	10	0
Shuey, Paul, Akr.	.000	2	0	0	0	0	0
Sido, Wilson, Akr.	.000	1	0	0	0	0	0
Silva, Carlos, Read.	.000	2	0	0	0	0	0
Silva, Doug, N.B.	1.000	4	1	0	0	1	0
Sims, Kenny, Bow.	.889	28	5	19	3	27	1
Skinner, John, Port.	.000	2	0	0	0	0	0
Sloan, Brandon, Port.	.833	43	1	4	1	6	0
Smith, Clint, Erie	.667	38	4	4	4	12	0
Smith, Matt, Nor.*	1.000	17	2	15	0	17	1
Snare, Ryan, Port.*	1.000	11	7	8	0	15	0
Sneed, John, N.B.	.857	39	4	8	2	14	1
Song, Seung, Tren.-Har.	1.000	22	8	15	0	23	1
Spencer, Corey, Tren.*	.900	32	1	8	1	10	0
Spiegel, Mike, Akr.*	.800	25	2	10	3	15	0
Sprague, Kevin, N.H.*	1.000	6	1	0	0	1	0
Spurling, Chris, Alt.	1.000	51	2	8	0	10	2
Stanford, Jason, Akr.*	.905	18	8	11	2	21	0
Stemle, Steve, N.H.	1.000	8	1	9	0	10	0
Stevens, Josh, Nor.	1.000	24	0	8	0	8	1
Sturdy, Tim, N.B.	1.000	35	3	8	0	11	0
Tallet, Brian, Akr.*	.944	18	2	15	1	18	1
Tekavec, Nate, Erie	1.000	27	5	14	0	19	0
Telemaco, Amaury, Read.	.000	1	0	0	0	0	0
Traber, Billy, Akr.*	1.000	18	1	22	0	23	3
Trachsel, Steve, Bing.	.000	1	0	0	1	1	0
Van Hekken, Andy, Erie*	.941	21	10	22	2	34	2
Vargas, Claudio, Har.	.750	8	3	3	2	8	1
Vargas, Jose, Akr.	1.000	18	1	2	0	3	0
Vega, Rene, Bing.*	.833	26	3	7	2	12	0
Viera, Rolando, Tren.*	1.000	45	5	15	0	20	0
Villegas, Felix, Tren.	1.000	12	2	1	0	3	0
Vogelsong, Ryan, Alt.	1.000	8	1	6	0	7	0
Walker, Adam, Bing.*	1.000	1	1	1	0	2	0
Walrond, Les, N.H.*	1.000	4	1	1	0	2	0
Watson, Greg, Erie	1.000	7	0	2	0	2	0
Wayne, Justin, Har.-Port.	.941	24	14	18	2	34	0
Weaver, Eric, Read.	1.000	37	2	3	0	5	0
Weekly, Chris, N.H.	.000	1	0	0	0	0	0
Westbrook, Jake, Akr.	1.000	3	3	2	0	5	0
White, Matt, Akr.*	.952	27	5	15	1	21	3
Wiggins, Scott, Nor.*	1.000	24	3	3	0	6	0
Wilson, Jeff, Bow.*	.950	50	6	13	1	20	0
Wimberly, Larry, Alt.*	1.000	26	0	7	0	7	0
Woodards, Orlando, Port.	.963	28	12	14	1	27	2

PITCHERS WITH TWO OR MORE TEAMS

Player, Team	Pct.	G	PO	A	E	TC	DP
Bridges, Donnie, Har.	.889	14	4	4	1	9	0
Bridges, Donnie, Port.	1.000	6	1	4	0	5	0
Edmondson, Brian, Akr.	.500	5	0	1	1	2	0
Edmondson, Brian, Erie	.889	38	1	7	1	9	0
Klepacki, Ed, Har.	.000	6	0	0	0	0	0
Klepacki, Ed, Port.	1.000	13	1	2	0	3	0
Lee, Cliff, Har.*	1.000	15	2	10	0	12	0
Lee, Cliff, Akr.*	.000	3	0	0	0	0	0
Pearsall, J.J., Port.*	1.000	12	2	3	0	5	0
Pearsall, J.J., Erie*	1.000	24	0	5	0	5	1
Rivera, Saul, Bing.	.833	30	2	3	1	6	0
Rivera, Saul, Har.	1.000	15	2	3	0	5	0
Song, Seung, Tren.	1.000	21	7	14	0	21	1
Song, Seung, Har.	1.000	1	1	1	0	2	0
Wayne, Justin, Har.	.926	17	13	12	2	27	0
Wayne, Justin, Port.	1.000	7	1	6	0	7	0

The following players appeared only as designated hitter, pinch-hitter or pinch runner: Richard, dh; N. Smith, dh, ph, pr; Sosa, dh.

CLASS AA *Eastern League*

Year	Team	Pct.	Year	Team	Pct.	Year	Team	Pct.
1923—	Williamsport	.661		Binghamton (2nd)‡	.636		Waterbury	.540
1924—	Williamsport	.654	1954—	Wilkes-Barre	.576	1981—	Glens Falls	.615
1925—	York§	.583		Albany (3rd)‡	.540		Bristol*	.577
	Williamsport§	.583	1955—	Reading	.613	1982—	West Haven*	.614
1926—	Scranton	.627		Allentown (2nd)‡	.565		Lynn	.590
1927—	Harrisburg	.630	1956—	Schenectady†	.609	1983—	Lynn	.554
1928—	Harrisburg	.603	1957—	Binghamton	.607		New Britain‡	.518
1929—	Binghamton	.597		Reading (3rd)‡	.529	1984—	Waterbury	.543
1930—	Wilkes-Barre	.572	1958—	Lancaster∞	.568		Vermont‡	.536
1931—	Harrisburg	.597		Binghamton (6th)‡	.493	1985—	Albany	.540
1932—	Wilkes-Barre	.561	1959—	Springfield†	.607		Vermont‡	.514
1933—	Binghamton	.690	1960—	Williamsport▲	.551	1986—	Reading	.566
1934—	Binghamton	.694		Springfield (3rd)▲	.496		Vermont‡	.554
	Williamsport*	.603	1961—	Springfield	.612	1987—	Pittsfield	.630
1935—	Scranton	.657	1962—	Williamsport	.593		Harrisburg‡	.550
	Binghamton*	.580		Elmira (2nd)‡	.514	1988—	Glens Falls	.584
1936—	Scranton*	.609	1963—	Charleston	.593		Albany‡	.522
	Elmira	.629	1964—	Elmira	.586	1989—	Albany‡	.657
1937—	Elmira†	.622	1965—	Pittsfield	.607		Harrisburg	.522
1938—	Binghamton	.622	1966—	Elmira	.633	1990—	Albany	.568
	Elmira (3rd)‡	.522	1967—	Binghamton♦	.586		London‡	.547
1939—	Scranton†	.571		Elmira	.532	1991—	Harrisburg	.621
1940—	Scranton	.568	1968—	Pittsfield	.604		Albany‡	.543
	Binghamton (2nd)‡	.554		Reading (2nd)‡	.579	1992—	Canton/Akron	.580
1941—	Wilkes-Barre	.630	1969—	York	.640		Binghamton‡	.572
	Elmira (3rd)‡	.514	1970—	Waterbury■	.560	1993—	Harrisburg‡	.681
1942—	Albany	.600		Reading■	.553		Canton/Akron	.543
	Scranton (2nd)‡	.593	1971—	Three Rivers	.569	1994—	Harrisburg	.633
1943—	Scranton	.630		Elmira▼	.561		Binghamton‡	.582
	Elmira (2nd)‡	.568	1972—	West Haven▼	.600	1995—	New Haven	.556
1944—	Hartford	.723		Three Rivers	.559		Reading‡	.514
	Binghamton (4th)‡	.474	1973—	Reading▼	.551	1996—	Portland	.589
1945—	Utica	.615		Pittsfield	.551		Harrisburg‡	.521
	Albany (3rd)‡	.564	1974—	Thetford Miners (2nd)•	.536	1997—	Harrisburg‡	.606
1946—	Scranton†	.691		Pittsfield (2nd)	.496		Portland	.556
1947—	Utica†	.652	1975—	Reading	.613	1998—	New Britain	.585
1948—	Scranton†	.636		Bristol*	.587		Harrisburg‡	.514
1949—	Albany	.664	1976—	Three Rivers	.601	1999—	Trenton	.648
	Binghamton (4th)‡	.500		West Haven††	.576		Harrisburg‡	.535
1950—	Wilkes-Barre‡	.652	1977—	West Haven‡‡	.623	2000—	Reading	.599
1951—	Wilkes-Barre‡	.612		Three Rivers	.551		New Haven‡	.577
	Scranton (2nd)†	.562	1978—	Reading	.642	2001—	New Britain∞∞∞	.613
1952—	Albany	.603		Bristol*	.580		Reading∞∞∞	.542
	Binghamton (2nd)‡	.562	1979—	West Haven§§	.597	2002—	Akron	.660
1953—	Reading	.682	1980—	Holyoke*	.561		Norwich‡	.543

*Won split-season playoff. †Won championship and four-team playoff. ‡Won four-team playoff. §Tied for pennant, York winning playoff. ∞League was divided into Northern, Southern divisions and played a split season; Lancaster was overall season leader. ▲Playoff finals canceled after one game because of rain with Williamsport and Springfield declared playoff co-champions. ♦League was divided into Eastern, Western divisions; Binghamton won playoff. ■Tied for pennant, Waterbury winning playoff. ▼League was divided into American, National divisions; won playoff. •League was divided into American and National divisions; won four-team playoff. ††League was divided into Northern, Southern divisions, won playoff. ‡‡League was divided into New England and Canadian-American divisions; won playoff. §§Won both halves of split season (no playoffs). ∞∞∞Were entering finals of four-team playoff and were declared co-champions when Professional Baseball declared a stoppage of play. (NOTE—Known as New York-Pennsylvania League prior to 1938.)

SOUTHERN LEAGUE

LEAGUE OFFICE

President
Don Mincher
Director of administration
Lori Webb

Director of media relations
Brian Benvie
Address
2551 Roswell Road, Suite 330
Marietta, GA 30062

Phone
770-321-0400

TEAMS

BIRMINGHAM BARONS
General manager
Tony Ensor
Manager
Wally Backman
Ballpark (capacity, surface)
Hoover Metropolitan Stadium
(10,800, grass)
Affiliation
White Sox
Address
P.O. Box 360007
Birmingham, AL 35236
Phone
205-988-3200

CAROLINA MUDCATS
General manager
Joe Kremer
Manager
Tracy Woodson
Ballpark (capacity, surface)
Five County Stadium (6,500, grass)
Affiliation
Marlins
Address
P.O. Drawer 1218
Zebulon, NC 27597
Phone
919-269-2287

CHATTANOOGA LOOKOUTS
President/general manager
J. Frank Burke
Manager
Phil Wellman
Ballpark (capacity, surface)
BellSouth Park (6,100, grass)
Affiliation
Reds
Address
201 Power Alley
Chattanooga, TN 37402
Phone
423-267-2208

GREENVILLE BRAVES
General manager
Steve DeSalvo
Manager
Brian Snitker

Ballpark (capacity, surface)
Greenville Municipal Stadium (7,027,
grass)
Affiliation
Braves
Address
P.O. Box 16683
Greenville, SC 29606
Phone
864-299-3456

HUNTSVILLE STARS
President/general manager
Bryan Dingo
Manager
Frank Kremblas
Ballpark (capacity, surface)
Joe W. Davis Stadium (10,400, grass)
Affiliation
Brewers
Address
3125 Leeman Ferry Road
Huntsville, AL 35801
Phone
256-882-2562

JACKSONVILLE SUNS
Vice president/general manager
Peter Bragan Jr.
Manager
Dino Ebel
Ballpark (capacity, surface)
Jacksonville Ballpark (10,000, grass)
Affiliation
Dodgers
Address
To be announced
Phone
904-358-2846

MOBILE BAYBEARS
Vice president/general manager
Bill Shanahan
Manager
Craig Colbert
Ballpark (capacity, surface)
Hank Aaron Stadium (6,000, grass)
Affiliation
Padres
Address
755 Bolling Brothers Blvd.
Mobile, AL 36606

Phone
251-479-2327

ORLANDO RAYS
General manager
Mitch Lukevics
Manager
To be announced
Ballpark (capacity, surface)
Disney's Wide World of Sports
Complex (9,500, grass)
Affiliation
Devil Rays
Address
P.O. Box 10000
Lake Buena Vista, FL 32830
Phone
407-939-4263

TENNESSEE SMOKIES
General manager
Brian Cox
Manager
Mark DeJohn
Ballpark (capacity, surface)
Smokies Park (6,000, grass)
Affiliation
Cardinals
Address
3540 Line Drive
Kodak, TN 37764
Phone
865-637-9494

WEST TENN DIAMOND JAXX
General manager
Jeff Parker
Manager
Bobby Dickerson
Ballpark (capacity, surface)
Pringles Park (6,000, grass)
Affiliation
Cubs
Address
4 Fun Place
Jackson, TN 38305
Phone
901-664-2020

2002 FINAL STANDINGS

FIRST HALF

EAST DIVISION

Team	W	L	T	Pct.	GB
Carolina (Rockies)	40	30	0	.571	...
Jacksonville (Dodgers)	36	33	0	.522	3.5
Tennessee (Blue Jays)	36	34	0	.514	4.0
Orlando (Devil Rays)	29	39	0	.426	10.0
Greenville (Braves)	28	41	0	.406	11.5

WEST DIVISION

Team	W	L	T	Pct.	GB
Birmingham (White Sox)	41	29	0	.586	...
Mobile (Padres)	37	32	0	.536	3.5
Chattanooga (Reds)	37	33	0	.529	4.0
West Tenn (Cubs)	32	38	0	.457	9.0
Huntsville (Brewers)	31	38	0	.449	9.5

SECOND HALF

EAST DIVISION

Team	W	L	T	Pct.	GB
Jacksonville (Dodgers)	41	29	0	.586	...
Greenville (Braves)	37	28	0	.569	1.5
Tennessee (Blue Jays)	33	37	0	.471	8.0
Orlando (Devil Rays)	29	40	0	.420	11.5
Carolina (Rockies)	25	41	0	.379	14.0

WEST DIVISION

Team	W	L	T	Pct.	GB
West Tenn (Cubs)	41	29	0	.586	...
Mobile (Padres)	39	31	0	.557	2.0
Huntsville (Brewers)	39	31	0	.557	2.0
Birmingham (White Sox)	38	32	0	.543	3.0
Chattanooga (Reds)	23	47	0	.329	18.0

COMPOSITE

Team	Birm.	Jax.	Mob.	W.T.	Hunt.	Tenn.	Gre.	Car.	Chat.	Orl.	W	L	T	Pct.	GB
Birmingham (White Sox)	...	7	10	14	14	3	6	7	14	4	79	61	0	.564	...
Jacksonville (Dodgers)	4	...	6	3	4	17	11	10	2	20	77	62	0	.554	1.5
Mobile (Padres)	14	1	...	12	13	2	5	4	16	9	76	63	0	.547	2.5
West Tenn (Cubs)	8	5	12	...	9	9	5	5	16	4	73	67	0	.521	6.0
Huntsville (Brewers)	9	4	10	15	...	8	2	5	11	6	70	69	0	.504	8.5
Tennessee (Blue Jays)	5	7	5	7	4	...	13	14	6	8	69	71	0	.493	10.0
Greenville (Braves)	6	12	2	3	5	10	...	10	6	11	65	69	0	.485	11.0
Carolina (Rockies)	1	13	4	3	6	10	9	...	7	12	65	71	0	.478	12.0
Chattanooga (Reds)	10	6	8	6	12	2	6	5	...	5	60	80	0	.429	19.0
Orlando (Devil Rays)	4	7	6	4	2	10	12	11	2	...	58	79	0	.423	19.5

Carolina's home games played in Zebulon, N.C.; Tennessee's home games played in Knoxville, Tenn.; West Tenn's home games played in Jackson, Tenn.

Major league affiliations in parentheses.

PLAYOFFS: Birmingham defeated West Tenn, three games to two; Jacksonville defeated Carolina, three games to two; Birmingham defeated Jacksonville, three games to none to win Southern League championship.

REGULAR-SEASON ATTENDANCE: Birmingham, 276,016; Carolina, 205,182; Chattanooga, 280,692; Greenville, 214,220; Huntsville, 206,068; Jacksonville, 230,156; Mobile, 216,597; Orlando, 139,489; Tennessee, 268,033; West Tenn, 224,698. Total—2,261,781. Playoffs (13 games)—35,373. All-Star Game at Tennessee—5,287. Class AA All-Star Game at Norwich, Conn.—8,009.

MANAGERS: Birmingham, Wally Backman; Carolina, P.J. Carey; Chattanooga, Phillip Wellman; Greenville, Brian Snitker; Huntsville, Frank Kremblas; Jacksonville, Dino Ebel; Mobile, Craig Colbert; Orlando, Mako Oliveras; Tennessee, Rocket Wheeler; West Tenn, Bobby Dickerson.

ALL-STAR TEAM: 1B—Dave Kelton, West Tenn; 2B—Aaron Miles, Birmingham; 3B—Donny Leon, Chattanooga; SS—Clint Barmes, Carolina; OF—Bobby Darula, Chattanooga; OF—Mike Edwards, Chattanooga; OF—Choo Freeman, Carolina; OF—Dewayne Wise, Tennessee; C—Miguel Olivo, Birmingham; DH—Tom Nevers, Chattanooga; Utility—Ben Risinger, Mobile; RHP—Vinnie Chulk, Tennessee; LHP—Josh Stewart, Birmingham; Relief pitcher—Joe Valentine, Birmingham; Most Valuable Player—Aaron Miles, Birmingham; Most Outstanding Pitcher—Vinnie Chulk, Tennessee; Hustler of the Year—Bernabel Castro, Mobile; Manager of the Year—Wally Backman, Birmingham.

2002 BATTING

TEAM

Team	G	TPA	AB	R	H	TB	2B	3B	HR	RBI	SH	SF	HP	BB	IBB	SO	SB	CS	GDP	LOB	ShO	Avg.	OBP	Slg.
Birmingham ..	140	5185	4564	610	1228	1740	238	26	74	549	74	55	40	452	19	866	220	127	82	931	9	.269	.337	.381
Carolina........	136	5344	4691	666	1242	1908	268	28	114	618	38	35	61	519	28	975	111	74	116	1008	6	.265	.343	.407
Orlando........	137	5073	4492	585	1187	1644	225	14	68	522	46	47	53	435	20	859	131	83	100	895	8	.264	.333	.366
Chattanooga..	140	5362	4711	594	1235	1824	243	23	100	539	73	32	61	485	23	1038	111	70	104	1062	12	.262	.337	.387
West Tenn	140	5443	4707	596	1203	1777	233	37	89	544	50	40	73	473	25	1022	131	70	89	1023	8	.256	.330	.378
Tennessee	140	5514	4737	739	1210	1797	223	26	104	667	55	40	65	617	14	956	146	65	88	1061	6	.255	.347	.379
Jacksonville...	139	5314	4556	586	1149	1585	211	21	61	532	82	42	49	585	24	776	129	61	102	1045	15	.252	.341	.348
Greenville	134	5172	4450	583	1110	1654	225	23	91	529	70	40	73	539	27	884	93	47	108	1025	5	.249	.338	.372
Mobile	139	5274	4614	580	1129	1658	226	30	81	523	36	38	75	511	25	1006	124	65	93	1020	13	.245	.327	.359
Huntsville	139	5183	4537	598	1097	1649	210	27	96	539	46	39	65	496	19	1075	157	87	86	896	9	.242	.323	.363

INDIVIDUAL

TOP QUALIFIERS FOR BATTING CHAMPIONSHIP

Minimum 378 plate appearances. *Lefthanded batter. †Switch-hitter.

Player, Team	G	TPA	AB	R	H	TB	2B	3B	HR	RBI	SH	SF	HP	BB	IBB	SO	SB	CS	GDP	Avg.	OBP	Slg.
Darula, Bobby, Chat.*	96	378	323	48	105	142	17	4	4	36	5	1	6	43	2	27	10	3	5	.325	.413	.440
Miles, Aaron, Birm.†	138	589	531	67	171	239	39	1	9	68	11	5	2	40	4	45	25	16	4	.322	.369	.450
Nevers, Tom, Chat.	126	489	444	58	139	208	26	2	13	77	1	3	4	37	2	77	9	6	17	.313	.369	.468
Collins, Mike, Jack.	117	437	384	40	120	136	14	1	0	45	6	2	1	44	1	36	7	1	14	.313	.383	.354
Edwards, Mike, Chat.	119	486	424	57	130	186	19	2	11	60	6	5	10	41	1	57	9	11	19	.307	.377	.439
Olivo, Miguel, Birm.	106	411	359	51	110	172	24	10	6	49	4	3	5	40	5	66	29	13	11	.306	.381	.479
Pressley, Josh, Orl.*	93	387	342	47	104	135	19	0	4	45	0	2	1	42	2	47	5	6	10	.304	.380	.395

Player, Team	G	TPA	AB	R	H	TB	2B	3B	HR	RBI	SH	SF	HP	BB	IBB	SO	SB	CS	GDP	Avg.	OBP	Slg.
Budzinski, Mark, W.T.*	114	486	427	68	127	170	19	6	4	36	1	2	5	51	3	85	21	7	4	.297	.377	.398
Wise, Dewayne, Ten.*	86	380	340	59	101	160	21	4	10	49	6	4	1	29	5	49	15	8	4	.297	.350	.471
Reyes, Rene, Car.†	123	495	455	64	133	216	33	4	14	54	2	4	5	29	4	69	10	11	10	.292	.339	.475
Freeman, Choo, Car.	124	514	430	81	125	191	18	6	12	64	4	1	15	64	1	101	15	13	15	.291	.400	.444
Fernandez, Alex, Birm.-Mob.* .	103	430	409	42	118	161	19	0	8	60	4	6	0	11	2	68	26	8	8	.289	.303	.394
Risinger, Ben, Mob.	128	526	466	43	134	169	26	0	3	44	5	3	12	40	2	62	1	2	17	.288	.357	.363
Abreu, Dennis, W.T.	122	436	402	45	115	161	17	4	7	51	3	4	3	24	3	102	18	14	10	.286	.328	.400
Leon, Donny, Chat.†	111	465	408	61	116	204	29	1	19	67	0	4	6	46	5	97	14	8	9	.284	.362	.500

DEPARTMENTAL LEADERS: G—Miles, 138; AB—R. Thompson, 554; R—R. Thompson, 109; H—Miles, 171; TB—Miles, 239; 2B—Miles, 39; 3B—Olivo, 10; HR—Kelton, LaForest, 20 each; RBI—Kelton, 79; SH—Victorino, 16; SF—Hankins, 9; HP—R. Thompson, 20; BB—Fagan, 102; IBB—Hill, 11; SO—Ingram, 140; SB—B. Castro, 53; CS—Sandoval, 24; GIDP—Edwards, 19; Slg.—Leon, .500; OBP—Darula, .413.

ALL PLAYERS

*Lefthanded batter. †Switch-hitter.

Player, Team	G	TPA	AB	R	H	TB	2B	3B	HR	RBI	SH	SF	HP	BB	IBB	SO	SB	CS	GDP	Avg.	OBP	Slg.
Abercrombie, Reggie, Jack. ...	1	4	4	1	1	1	0	0	0	0	0	0	0	0	0	1	1	0	0	.250	.250	.250
Abreu, Dennis, W.T.	122	436	402	45	115	161	17	4	7	51	3	4	3	24	3	102	18	14	10	.286	.328	.400
Acevas, Jon, Birm.	60	192	164	26	38	57	8	1	3	16	2	3	2	21	1	35	0	1	3	.232	.321	.348
Achilles, Matt, W.T.	41	24	21	3	5	9	1	0	1	2	3	0	0	0	0	5	0	0	0	.238	.238	.429
Adams, Mike, Hun.	13	1	1	0	0	0	0	0	0	0	0	0	0	0	0	0	0	0	0	.000	.000	.000
Alfonzo, Eliezer, Hun.	69	258	244	23	63	101	15	1	7	38	1	1	3	9	0	55	2	3	8	.258	.292	.414
Allen, Rodney, Hun.	16	4	3	0	0	0	0	0	0	0	0	0	0	1	0	3	0	0	0	.000	.250	.000
Allensworth, Jermaine, Gre. ...	77	330	270	46	76	103	18	3	1	36	4	7	1	48	2	48	8	2	9	.281	.383	.381
Altman, Gene, Hun.	24	7	6	1	1	2	1	0	0	2	1	0	0	0	0	3	0	0	1	.167	.167	.333
Alvarado, Joel, Hun.	15	36	32	4	8	8	0	0	0	1	1	0	1	2	0	2	1	1	1	.250	.314	.250
Alvarez, Gabe, Hun.	29	113	94	17	19	25	3	0	1	12	0	0	1	18	0	24	0	0	1	.202	.336	.266
Alvarez, Jimmy, Ten.†	133	603	497	83	138	200	32	3	8	69	13	5	9	79	2	121	20	11	6	.278	.383	.402
Amezcua, Adan, Mob.	25	98	91	6	25	36	2	0	3	12	0	1	3	3	0	19	0	0	3	.275	.316	.396
Amrhein, Mike, W.T.	63	260	232	26	70	102	13	2	5	30	0	1	7	20	1	24	4	3	7	.302	.373	.440
Andrews, Clayton, Chat.	4	4	2	0	0	0	0	0	0	0	0	2	0	0	0	0	0	0	0	.000	.000	.000
Aramboles, Ricardo, Chat.	4	5	5	0	0	0	0	0	0	0	0	0	0	0	0	1	0	0	0	.000	.000	.000
Atkins, Garrett, Car.	128	577	510	71	138	207	27	3	12	61	0	6	2	59	2	77	6	6	12	.271	.345	.406
Averette, Robert, Car.	11	12	10	1	0	0	0	0	0	0	0	1	0	1	0	6	0	0	0	.000	.091	.000
Baker, Brad, Mob.	12	15	13	1	1	1	0	0	0	0	0	0	0	2	0	7	1	0	0	.077	.200	.077
Baldelli, Rocco, Orl.	17	80	70	10	26	37	3	1	2	13	0	3	2	5	0	11	3	2	1	.371	.413	.529
Balfe, Ryan, W.T.†	23	90	85	5	17	23	3	0	1	7	0	0	1	4	1	15	0	0	5	.200	.244	.271
Barmes, Clint, Car.	103	485	438	62	119	191	23	2	15	60	2	5	9	31	3	72	15	11	3	.272	.329	.436
Bartosh, Cliff, Mob.*	62	6	6	0	0	0	0	0	0	0	0	0	0	0	0	5	0	0	0	.000	.000	.000
Battersby, Eric, Birm.	63	224	202	23	47	72	9	2	4	19	1	3	2	16	1	38	3	3	4	.233	.291	.356
Bauer, Greg, Jack.	38	5	4	0	1	1	0	0	0	0	0	1	0	0	0	3	0	0	0	.250	.250	.250
Bausher, Andy, Mob.	34	16	13	0	2	2	0	0	0	0	1	0	0	2	0	7	0	0	0	.154	.267	.154
Bay, Jason, Mob.	23	95	81	16	25	46	5	2	4	12	0	0	1	13	1	22	4	2	0	.309	.411	.568
Beattie, Andrew, Chat.†	43	187	166	23	41	70	9	1	6	19	2	1	0	18	2	30	2	2	5	.247	.319	.422
Beinbrink, Andy, Orl.	119	485	418	56	118	155	23	1	4	57	5	4	3	55	3	81	21	10	8	.282	.367	.371
Belisle, Matt, Gre.†	26	30	22	2	4	4	0	0	0	1	4	1	0	3	0	7	0	0	0	.182	.269	.182
Benjamin, Al, Birm.	16	54	52	4	15	24	3	0	2	5	0	0	0	2	2	13	0	1	2	.288	.315	.462
Bikowski, Scott, Birm.*	125	469	395	46	101	133	16	2	4	35	7	4	5	58	0	68	17	11	5	.256	.355	.337
Bitter, Jarrod, Mob.	8	27	25	1	5	7	2	0	0	0	0	0	0	2	0	7	0	0	2	.200	.259	.280
Blakely, Darren, Mob.†	123	511	424	63	92	146	22	4	8	57	0	6	11	70	8	132	10	4	5	.217	.339	.344
Bledsoe, Hunter, Jack.	110	415	348	39	97	131	18	2	4	38	0	6	7	54	2	42	3	4	12	.279	.381	.376
Bong, Jung, Gre.*	29	35	33	2	4	4	0	0	0	3	1	0	0	1	0	5	0	0	0	.121	.147	.121
Boscan, Jean, Gre.	10	31	27	2	7	11	1	0	1	3	0	0	0	4	0	10	0	0	0	.259	.355	.407
Bozied, Tagg, Mob.	60	254	234	35	50	91	14	0	9	32	0	2	2	16	1	43	1	0	8	.214	.268	.389
Bradley, Ryan, Car.	5	1	1	0	0	0	0	0	0	0	0	0	0	0	0	1	0	0	0	.000	.000	.000
Brantley, Brian, Car.	17	1	1	0	0	0	0	0	0	0	0	0	0	0	0	1	0	0	0	.000	.000	.000
Bravo, Danny, Birm.†	46	163	138	17	33	44	8	0	1	15	8	1	1	15	0	20	7	5	1	.239	.316	.319
Brewer, Jace, Orl.	39	169	153	13	33	41	5	0	1	16	5	4	3	4	0	27	2	0	6	.216	.244	.268
Brock, Tarrik, Jack.*	111	405	325	59	86	133	16	2	9	47	1	3	4	72	2	93	8	8	3	.265	.401	.409
Bruback, Matt, W.T.	28	37	37	2	5	5	0	0	0	0	0	0	0	0	0	15	0	0	0	.135	.135	.135
Brueggemann, Dean, Car.*	34	2	2	0	0	0	0	0	0	0	0	0	0	0	0	0	0	0	0	.000	.000	.000
Budzinski, Mark, W.T.*	114	486	427	68	127	170	19	6	4	36	1	2	5	51	3	85	21	7	4	.297	.377	.398
Burford, Kevin, Car.*	77	322	266	44	75	109	23	1	3	33	2	2	4	48	3	51	2	6	5	.282	.397	.410
Burkhart, Lance, Hun.	28	111	85	16	21	39	9	0	3	15	0	1	3	22	2	33	2	3	1	.247	.414	.459
Burrows, Angelo, Gre.*	14	52	47	3	10	15	3	1	0	1	3	0	0	2	0	6	5	2	0	.213	.245	.319
Bynum, Mike, Mob.*	6	5	5	2	3	6	0	0	1	1	0	0	0	0	0	1	0	0	0	.600	.600	1.200
Cameron, Ryan, Car.	37	28	26	0	5	5	0	0	0	4	1	0	0	1	0	14	0	0	0	.192	.222	.192
Cameron, Troy, Car.†	28	103	95	11	22	42	3	1	5	17	0	1	0	7	1	24	0	0	4	.232	.282	.442
Cantu, Jorge, Orl.	131	545	512	50	124	166	31	1	3	43	1	5	4	23	2	74	2	6	13	.242	.278	.324
Caraccioli, Lance, Jack.*	10	9	6	1	1	2	1	0	0	2	1	1	1	0	0	3	0	0	0	.167	.250	.333
Caruso, Mike, Chat.†	3	16	14	4	5	8	0	0	1	4	1	0	0	1	0	1	0	0	0	.357	.400	.571
Cash, Kevin, Ten.	55	252	213	38	59	100	15	1	8	44	0	2	1	36	2	44	5	2	4	.277	.381	.469
Castro, Bernabel, Mob.†	109	477	419	61	109	128	13	3	0	32	2	1	3	52	1	67	53	20	1	.260	.345	.305
Castro, Ramon, Gre.	56	261	210	47	68	104	17	2	5	22	1	2	9	39	2	44	14	8	3	.324	.446	.495
Cercy, Rick, Car.	47	3	2	0	0	0	0	0	0	1	0	1	0	0	0	2	0	0	0	.000	.000	.000
Chavez, Wilton, W.T.	18	26	23	2	2	2	0	0	0	1	0	0	0	1	0	10	0	0	2	.087	.125	.087
Chiaffredo, Paul, Ten.	83	286	258	38	50	94	7	2	11	38	4	2	8	13	0	81	4	0	5	.194	.253	.364
Childers, Jason, Hun.	11	1	1	0	0	0	0	0	0	0	0	0	0	0	0	1	0	0	0	.000	.000	.000
Childers, Matt, Hun.	35	13	11	1	4	5	1	0	0	1	1	0	0	1	0	6	0	0	0	.364	.417	.455
Chouinard, Bobby, Car.	5	2	2	0	0	0	0	0	0	0	0	0	0	0	0	1	0	0	0	.000	.000	.000
Christensen, Ben, W.T.	12	18	10	0	0	0	0	0	0	0	6	0	0	2	0	3	0	0	0	.000	.167	.000
Closser, J.D., Car.†	95	360	315	43	89	157	21	1	13	62	0	1	0	44	4	69	9	3	7	.283	.369	.498

Player, Team	G	TPA	AB	R	H	TB	2B	3B	HR	RBI	SH	SF	HP	BB	IBB	SO	SB	CS	GDP	Avg.	OBP	Slg.
Colina, Javier, Car.	35	147	136	17	37	48	6	1	1	17	2	1	1	7	0	21	4	3	3	.272	.310	.353
Collazo, William, Jack.*	51	6	5	1	2	2	0	0	0	1	1	0	0	0	0	0	0	0	0	.400	.400	.400
Collins, Mike, Jack.	117	437	384	40	120	136	14	1	0	45	6	2	1	44	1	36	7	1	14	.313	.383	.354
Colyer, Steve, Jack.*	59	2	2	0	1	1	0	0	0	0	0	0	0	0	0	0	0	0	0	.500	.500	.500
Cook, Aaron, Car.	14	27	25	1	4	4	0	0	0	2	1	1	0	0	0	4	0	0	0	.160	.154	.160
Crosby, Bubba, Jack.*	38	165	150	14	39	55	6	2	2	20	1	1	2	11	0	23	7	3	2	.260	.317	.367
Crowder, Chuck, Car.*	11	3	1	0	1	1	0	0	0	1	2	0	0	0	0	0	0	0	0	1.000	1.000	1.000
Curry, Chris, W.T.	12	39	35	4	6	8	2	0	0	2	2	0	1	1	0	10	0	0	0	.171	.216	.229
Curry, Mike, Chat.*	26	90	72	12	14	14	0	0	0	3	3	0	0	15	0	18	5	1	1	.194	.333	.194
Curtis, Daniel, Gre.	10	11	9	0	0	0	0	0	0	0	2	0	0	0	0	4	0	0	0	.000	.000	.000
Cyr, Eric, Mob.	14	22	19	0	1	1	0	0	0	0	2	0	0	1	0	4	0	0	0	.053	.100	.053
Darnell, Paul, Chat.	27	3	3	0	0	0	0	0	0	0	0	0	0	0	0	2	0	0	0	.000	.000	.000
Darula, Bobby, Chat.*	96	378	323	48	105	142	17	4	4	36	5	1	6	43	2	27	10	3	5	.325	.413	.440
Davis, Lance, Chat.	12	14	9	0	1	1	0	0	0	0	3	0	0	2	0	7	0	0	0	.111	.273	.111
Dawkins, Gookie, Chat.	40	182	155	21	42	57	10	1	1	12	2	0	0	25	0	28	5	5	8	.271	.372	.368
Deardorff, Jeff, Hun.	131	497	425	69	108	190	23	1	19	61	1	4	7	60	5	131	13	6	4	.254	.353	.447
De Hart, Blair, Mob.	7	5	5	0	0	0	0	0	0	0	0	0	0	0	0	2	0	0	0	.000	.000	.000
DeHart, Casey, Chat.*	21	3	3	0	0	0	0	0	0	0	0	0	0	0	0	1	0	0	0	.000	.000	.000
Dellaero, Jason, Birm.	63	200	182	20	38	62	7	1	5	20	4	2	1	11	1	53	6	4	2	.209	.255	.341
Denorfia, Christopher, Chat....	3	9	7	0	3	7	2	1	0	0	0	0	0	2	0	1	0	0	0	.429	.556	1.000
Dent, Doug, Hun.	12	7	7	0	2	3	1	0	0	1	0	0	0	0	0	1	0	0	0	.286	.286	.429
De Renne, Keoni, Gre.	107	378	320	51	88	128	25	3	3	47	12	4	1	41	0	39	2	4	4	.275	.355	.400
Deschaine, Jim, Ten.	118	469	405	59	91	152	13	0	16	66	3	6	4	51	1	85	3	3	14	.225	.313	.375
Detienne, Dave, Jack.	2	8	8	0	0	0	0	0	0	0	0	0	0	0	0	0	0	0	0	.000	.000	.000
Devey, Phil, Jack.*	8	7	4	1	0	0	0	0	0	0	0	0	0	0	0	2	0	0	0	.000	.000	.000
Dewey, Jason, Car.	73	284	255	42	66	115	22	0	9	44	1	3	1	24	1	75	5	4	6	.259	.322	.451
Diaz, Alejandro, Chat.	52	166	150	13	34	50	7	3	1	18	2	2	0	12	0	32	6	2	1	.227	.280	.333
Diaz, Matt, Orl.	122	499	449	71	123	183	28	1	10	50	3	3	10	34	1	72	31	9	11	.274	.337	.408
Diaz, Victor, Jack.	42	163	152	22	32	51	7	0	4	24	0	1	3	7	0	42	7	5	3	.211	.258	.336
Diggins, Ben, Hun.	8	9	9	0	2	2	0	0	0	0	0	0	0	0	0	4	0	0	0	.222	.222	.222
Donovan, Todd, Mob.	33	134	114	17	25	40	5	2	2	9	1	2	2	15	0	31	6	3	2	.219	.316	.351
Duarte, Justin, Mob.	7	28	22	2	3	3	0	0	0	0	0	0	0	6	0	3	0	0	1	.136	.321	.136
Dunn, Scott, Chat.	39	20	16	2	5	9	1	0	1	2	3	0	0	1	0	4	0	0	0	.313	.353	.563
Duplissea, Bill, Jack.	8	18	14	2	4	5	1	0	0	2	0	0	0	4	0	7	0	0	0	.286	.444	.357
Durham, Chad, Birm.	119	422	366	62	101	116	11	2	0	35	12	5	3	36	0	72	39	18	5	.276	.341	.317
Dzurilla, Mike, W.T.	6	18	16	3	4	5	1	0	0	2	1	0	0	1	0	3	0	0	1	.250	.294	.313
Edwards, Mike, Chat.	119	486	424	57	130	186	19	2	11	60	6	5	10	41	1	57	9	11	19	.307	.377	.439
Emiliano, Jamie, Gre.	42	1	0	0	0	0	0	0	0	0	0	0	0	1	0	0	0	0	0	.000	.000	.000
Ennis, John, Gre.	26	32	30	2	6	6	0	0	0	1	1	0	0	1	0	12	0	0	0	.200	.226	.200
Espino, Damaso, Chat.†	6	13	12	0	4	4	0	0	0	1	1	0	0	0	0	1	0	0	0	.333	.333	.333
Estrella, Leo, W.T.	10	4	4	1	0	0	0	0	0	0	0	0	0	0	0	0	0	1	0	.000	.000	.000
Etherton, Seth, Chat.	3	2	1	0	0	0	0	0	0	0	1	0	0	0	0	1	0	0	0	.000	.000	.000
Evans, Lee, Birm.†	22	70	65	13	18	35	3	1	4	7	0	0	0	5	0	19	0	0	3	.277	.329	.538
Evert, Brett, Gre.*	16	22	18	2	4	4	0	0	0	1	2	0	0	2	0	5	0	0	0	.222	.300	.222
Fagan, Shawn, Ten.	127	530	421	71	113	173	24	0	12	69	2	3	2	102	0	87	6	3	10	.268	.411	.411
Faison, Vince, Mob.*	100	410	359	40	91	145	23	5	7	44	0	3	9	39	2	103	5	7	4	.253	.339	.404
Farmer, Tom, Jack.	6	8	4	1	1	1	0	0	0	0	4	0	0	0	0	2	0	0	0	.250	.250	.250
Feliciano, Jesus, Jack.*	100	267	245	32	58	65	5	1	0	13	4	2	3	13	0	28	10	10	2	.237	.281	.265
Feliciano, Pedro, Chat.*	28	1	1	0	0	0	0	0	0	0	0	0	0	0	0	0	0	0	0	.000	.000	.000
Fernandez, Alex, Birm.-Mob.*	103	430	409	42	118	161	19	0	8	60	4	6	0	11	2	68	26	8	8	.289	.303	.394
Figga, Mike, Orl.	10	40	33	6	11	17	3	0	1	9	3	1	0	3	1	7	0	0	3	.333	.378	.515
Fiore, Curtis, Gre.	99	367	319	41	88	138	21	1	9	40	1	0	8	39	2	48	3	0	13	.276	.369	.433
Fleming, Ryan, Ten.*	62	275	245	36	72	98	14	0	4	37	1	1	1	27	2	26	3	5	9	.294	.365	.400
Foster, Brian, Hun.	11	34	33	2	8	11	3	0	0	6	0	0	1	0	0	16	1	2	0	.242	.265	.333
Fox, Chad, Hun.	3	1	1	0	0	0	0	0	0	0	0	0	0	0	0	0	0	0	0	.000	.000	.000
Fox, Jason, Hun.†	41	141	131	9	25	35	6	2	0	13	1	0	3	6	0	32	2	1	4	.191	.243	.267
Freed, Mark, W.T.*	30	34	30	2	8	12	1	0	1	4	3	0	0	1	0	10	0	0	0	.267	.290	.400
Freeman, Ashley, Car.	2	8	6	2	4	5	1	0	0	1	0	0	1	1	0	1	2	0	0	.667	.750	.833
Freeman, Choo, Car.	124	514	430	81	125	191	18	6	12	64	4	1	15	64	1	101	15	13	15	.291	.400	.444
Frese, Nate, W.T.	70	258	230	24	52	70	10	1	2	18	2	1	2	23	0	59	4	3	4	.226	.301	.304
Gaal, Bryan, Mob.	32	4	3	0	0	0	0	0	0	0	1	0	0	0	0	3	0	0	0	.000	.000	.000
Gandarillas, Gus, Hun.	1	1	1	0	0	0	0	0	0	0	0	0	0	0	0	0	0	0	0	.000	.000	.000
Garcia, Ariel, Mob.	7	1	1	0	0	0	0	0	0	0	0	0	0	0	0	1	0	0	0	.000	.000	.000
Garcia, Jose, Hun.	11	16	14	1	2	2	0	0	0	1	1	0	0	1	0	3	0	0	0	.143	.200	.143
German, Amado, Orl.†	106	391	344	55	92	117	11	4	2	34	3	3	2	39	3	95	15	15	5	.267	.343	.340
German, Rafael, Chat.	1	1	1	0	0	0	0	0	0	0	0	0	0	0	0	1	0	0	0	.000	.000	.000
Gibralter, Dave, W.T.	55	181	166	22	39	53	8	0	2	18	0	1	2	12	2	28	1	1	4	.235	.293	.319
Giese, Dan, Mob.	32	4	4	0	0	0	0	0	0	0	0	0	0	0	0	2	0	0	0	.000	.000	.000
Gil, Dave, Chat.	18	30	26	1	3	3	0	0	0	5	1	0	0	3	0	10	0	0	0	.115	.207	.115
Giron, Roberto, Hun.	36	5	4	0	1	1	0	0	0	0	1	0	0	0	0	3	0	0	0	.250	.250	.250
Gonzalez, Alfredo, Jack.	13	3	3	0	0	0	0	0	0	0	0	0	0	0	0	2	0	0	0	.000	.000	.000
Gooch, Arnie, Chat.	7	12	10	1	1	1	0	0	0	1	0	0	0	2	0	4	0	0	0	.100	.250	.100
Gray, Brett, Chat.	48	13	12	1	1	1	0	0	0	0	0	0	0	1	0	1	0	0	0	.083	.154	.083
Green, Nick, Gre.	94	402	355	49	85	150	16	2	15	50	0	8	3	36	3	92	2	5	9	.239	.321	.423
Gripp, Ryan, W.T.	116	438	380	51	88	146	24	2	10	49	2	5	5	46	2	85	4	2	9	.232	.319	.384
Gross, Gabe, Ten.*	112	465	403	57	96	153	17	5	10	54	2	5	5	53	4	71	8	2	4	.238	.333	.380
Gross, Rafael, W.T.	1	1	1	0	0	0	0	0	0	0	0	0	0	0	0	0	0	0	0	.000	.000	.000
Grummitt, Dan, Orl.	103	413	363	54	91	139	22	1	8	46	2	2	11	35	0	94	5	3	7	.251	.333	.383
Guerrero, Cristian, Hun.	111	427	394	47	88	131	17	1	8	48	0	4	3	26	3	101	21	9	17	.223	.274	.332
Gulin, Lindsay, Jack.*	19	10	9	1	1	1	0	0	0	1	1	0	0	0	0	3	0	0	0	.111	.111	.111
Gutierrez, Vic, Gre.	13	36	33	4	7	10	1	1	0	1	2	0	0	1	0	2	1	0	0	.212	.235	.303

Player, Team	G	TPA	AB	R	H	TB	2B	3B	HR	RBI	SH	SF	HP	BB	IBB	SO	SB	CS	GDP	Avg.	OBP	Slg.
Haad, Yamid, Orl.-Mob..........	47	178	161	18	35	50	3	0	4	28	1	5	0	11	1	31	3	1	4	.217	.260	.311
Haas, Chris, Gre.*..............	31	93	76	6	9	18	4	1	1	5	1	0	0	16	0	31	0	0	0	.118	.272	.237
Hall, Josh, Chat.................	22	36	34	2	8	8	0	0	0	0	2	0	0	0	0	14	0	0	0	.235	.235	.235
Hall, Noah, Chat.................	11	47	42	8	7	8	1	0	0	3	0	2	1	2	1	5	2	0	0	.167	.213	.190
Haltiwanger, Garrick, Ten.	44	159	133	21	29	48	8	1	3	19	1	4	2	18	2	39	8	2	1	.218	.312	.361
Hamilton, Jon, W.T.*	66	257	238	35	66	101	13	5	4	32	0	0	0	19	2	47	4	3	2	.277	.331	.424
Hampton, Matt, Mob..............	57	5	3	1	1	1	0	0	0	0	1	0	0	1	0	1	0	0	0	.333	.500	.333
Hankins, Ryan, Birm.	115	481	422	51	118	169	28	1	7	72	0	9	5	45	2	74	8	6	7	.280	.349	.400
Hanrahan, Joel, Jack.............	3	1	1	0	0	0	0	0	0	0	0	0	0	0	0	0	0	0	0	.000	.000	.000
Hardy, J.J., Hun.	38	160	145	14	33	43	7	0	1	13	4	2	0	9	0	19	1	2	4	.228	.269	.297
Harris, Blair, Birm..............	2	5	5	0	0	0	0	0	0	0	0	0	0	0	0	1	0	0	0	.000	.000	.000
Harris, Brendan, W.T.	13	55	53	8	17	29	4	1	2	11	0	0	0	2	0	5	1	1	1	.321	.345	.547
Hart, Corey, Hun.	28	106	94	16	25	34	3	0	2	15	0	1	4	7	0	16	3	2	1	.266	.340	.362
Harvey, Ian, Mob................	12	8	7	1	1	1	0	0	0	0	1	0	0	0	0	1	0	0	0	.143	.143	.143
Hendrickson, Ben, Hun.	13	12	11	0	1	1	0	0	0	0	0	0	0	1	0	4	0	1	0	.091	.167	.091
Hernandez, Alex, Chat.*.........	89	324	285	38	73	109	19	1	5	31	2	2	1	33	2	79	6	0	4	.255	.332	.381
Hernandez, Buddy, Gre.	40	3	3	0	0	0	0	0	0	0	0	0	0	0	0	0	0	0	0	.000	.000	.000
High, Andy, Hun.*	16	8	8	0	0	0	0	0	0	0	0	0	0	0	0	7	0	0	0	.000	.000	.000
Hill, Koyie, Jack.†..............	130	552	468	67	127	187	25	1	11	64	1	7	0	76	11	88	5	3	14	.271	.368	.400
Holliday, Matt, Car..............	130	539	463	79	128	181	19	2	10	64	1	1	7	67	2	102	16	2	14	.276	.375	.391
Hooten, Dave, W.T...............	65	3	2	0	0	0	0	0	0	0	1	0	0	0	0	1	0	0	0	.000	.000	.000
Hopper, Shane, Mob.	19	64	58	5	14	23	5	2	0	9	0	0	1	5	0	19	1	0	3	.241	.313	.397
Howard, Ben, Mob...............	6	12	10	0	1	1	0	0	0	0	2	0	0	0	0	5	0	0	1	.100	.100	.100
Howington, Ty, Chat.†	15	16	16	1	2	2	0	0	0	0	0	0	0	0	0	11	0	0	0	.125	.125	.125
Huisman, Justin, Car.	18	4	3	0	0	0	0	0	0	0	1	0	0	0	0	2	0	0	0	.000	.000	.000
Hunter, Johnny, Mob............	22	24	21	3	2	3	1	0	0	0	0	0	1	0	1	7	0	0	0	.095	.136	.143
Ingram, Darron, Birm............	107	431	375	50	90	165	20	2	17	64	0	4	4	48	1	140	9	6	8	.240	.329	.440
Iorg, Isaac, Ten.	27	90	80	12	16	23	2	1	1	10	0	1	0	9	0	19	2	1	5	.200	.289	.288
Jackson, Nic, W.T.*	32	140	131	18	38	58	9	1	3	20	0	1	2	6	0	23	8	2	1	.290	.329	.443
Jacobsen, Bucky, Hun.	61	227	198	31	50	96	9	2	11	39	1	2	4	22	1	41	2	2	6	.253	.336	.485
James, Kenny, Ten.†	13	43	34	7	8	8	0	0	0	2	2	0	1	6	0	7	2	0	0	.235	.366	.235
Johnson, Ben, Mob..............	131	528	456	58	110	171	23	4	10	55	0	4	3	65	1	127	11	9	9	.241	.337	.375
Johnson, Gary, W.T.............	121	463	389	48	100	137	15	2	6	45	2	8	14	50	2	77	13	8	7	.257	.356	.352
Johnson, Russ, Orl.	12	51	43	10	12	17	5	0	0	3	0	0	0	8	0	7	1	0	4	.279	.392	.395
Johnstone, Ben, W.T.	6	5	4	1	3	4	1	0	0	2	0	0	0	1	0	3	0	0	0	.750	.800	1.000
Jones, Damien, Gre.*............	66	236	211	21	46	59	8	1	1	12	2	0	0	23	2	55	9	5	2	.218	.295	.280
Jones, Ryan, Mob...............	89	307	266	39	56	109	10	2	13	53	1	6	4	30	2	56	2	1	9	.211	.294	.410
Jongejan, Ferenc, W.T.*	62	5	5	0	0	0	0	0	0	0	0	0	0	0	0	3	0	0	0	.000	.000	.000
Kaup, Nathan, Orl.	85	308	272	23	66	85	13	0	2	27	2	2	6	26	0	46	1	4	4	.243	.320	.313
Kearns, Austin, Chat.	12	53	41	10	11	28	2	0	5	13	0	0	3	9	0	9	1	0	0	.268	.434	.683
Keck, Brian, Car.................	24	74	62	6	8	11	3	0	0	3	2	0	1	9	0	8	4	0	1	.129	.250	.177
Kellner, Ryan, Jack.............	16	42	37	1	6	7	1	0	0	3	1	0	1	3	0	12	0	0	3	.162	.244	.189
Kelton, Dave, W.T.	129	555	498	68	130	230	28	6	20	79	0	3	2	52	2	129	12	6	10	.261	.332	.462
Kent, Nathan, Gre...............	1	1	1	0	0	0	0	0	0	0	0	0	0	0	0	1	0	0	0	.000	.000	.000
Kibler, Ryan, Gre.	25	30	25	2	7	8	1	0	0	4	2	1	0	2	0	7	0	0	0	.280	.321	.320
King, Brennan, Jack.	127	500	435	62	118	162	19	2	7	63	1	2	4	58	2	48	1	1	16	.271	.361	.372
King, Cesar, Chat................	12	38	34	4	7	13	1	1	1	3	0	0	1	3	0	10	0	0	1	.206	.289	.382
Knox, Ryan, Hun.	66	251	217	26	46	56	8	1	0	9	4	1	5	24	0	44	17	7	3	.212	.304	.258
Kopitzke, Casey, W.T.	76	272	244	16	54	60	6	0	0	20	5	5	5	13	2	34	2	3	6	.221	.270	.246
Koronka, John, Chat.*	16	26	19	1	3	3	0	0	0	0	2	0	0	5	0	8	1	0	0	.158	.333	.158
Krawczyk, Jack, Hun.	44	4	4	0	1	1	0	0	0	0	0	0	0	0	0	2	0	0	0	.250	.250	.250
Krynzel, Dave, Hun.*............	31	134	129	13	31	45	2	3	2	13	0	0	1	4	0	30	13	5	0	.240	.269	.349
LaForest, Pete, Orl.*	106	425	359	57	97	177	18	1	20	64	0	4	2	60	3	94	9	6	4	.270	.374	.493
Lambert, Casey, Car.	3	12	10	1	2	3	1	0	0	3	0	0	0	2	0	3	0	0	0	.200	.333	.300
Langaigne, Selwyn, Ten.*	6	18	14	1	2	2	0	0	0	2	1	0	0	3	1	5	0	0	0	.143	.294	.143
Langerhans, Ryan, Gre.*	109	474	391	57	98	152	23	2	9	62	4	5	6	68	3	83	10	5	9	.251	.366	.389
Langill, Eric, Gre...............	8	21	20	1	3	3	0	0	0	1	0	0	1	0	0	9	0	0	0	.150	.190	.150
Langone, Steve, Jack.	14	7	5	0	1	2	1	0	0	1	2	0	0	0	0	3	0	0	0	.200	.200	.400
Lantigua, Delvis, Birm..........	16	2	2	0	0	0	0	0	0	0	0	0	0	0	0	2	0	0	0	.000	.000	.000
LaRoche, Adam, Gre.*	45	193	173	17	50	71	9	0	4	19	0	0	1	19	2	38	1	1	6	.289	.363	.410
Lebron, Francisco, Birm.........	4	13	12	1	2	2	0	0	0	1	0	0	0	1	0	4	0	0	2	.167	.231	.167
Lee, Derek, Hun.*	34	30	25	2	6	6	0	0	0	2	4	0	0	1	0	11	0	0	0	.240	.269	.240
Lee, Garrett, Gre.	19	8	5	1	0	0	0	0	0	0	0	0	0	0	0	0	0	0	0	.000	.286	.000
Leek, Randy, Jack.*	15	19	13	0	3	3	0	0	0	1	5	0	0	1	0	3	0	0	0	.231	.286	.231
Leicester, Jon, W.T.............	5	8	8	0	0	0	0	0	0	0	0	0	0	0	0	3	0	0	0	.000	.000	.000
Leon, Donny, Chat.†............	111	465	408	61	116	204	29	1	19	67	0	4	6	46	5	97	14	8	9	.284	.362	.500
Logan, Matt, Ten.*	104	389	345	45	84	119	26	0	3	49	1	5	2	35	1	63	8	1	5	.243	.313	.345
Lombard, George, Gre.*	8	32	25	4	7	16	0	0	3	5	1	0	1	5	0	6	2	0	0	.280	.419	.640
Lopez, Albie, Gre...............	1	1	1	0	0	0	0	0	0	0	0	0	0	0	0	1	0	0	0	.000	.000	.000
Lopez, Mickey, W.T.†...........	17	71	62	11	17	19	2	0	0	7	0	3	1	5	0	9	5	2	0	.274	.324	.306
Lopez, Rafael, Jack.	20	62	51	4	7	10	0	0	1	9	4	0	0	7	0	6	0	0	3	.137	.241	.196
Lorenzana, Luis, Mob.	95	340	288	32	70	88	8	2	2	20	2	3	6	41	1	42	0	1	5	.243	.346	.306
Lowe, Benny, Chat.*	9	2	2	0	0	0	0	0	0	0	0	0	0	0	0	0	0	0	0	.000	.000	.000
Loyd, Brian, Mob...............	53	185	174	19	48	65	8	0	3	22	0	0	2	9	1	26	0	1	5	.276	.319	.374
Lugo, Ruddy, Jack.	11	4	3	0	1	1	0	0	0	0	1	0	0	0	0	1	0	0	0	.333	.333	.333
Luuloa, Keith, Hun.	80	347	287	52	73	120	12	4	9	39	0	5	2	52	2	42	5	1	7	.254	.367	.418
Marconi, Alex, Orl.	31	102	95	5	18	22	4	0	0	12	2	3	1	1	0	17	1	2	0	.189	.200	.232
Martin, Chandler, Car.	19	26	23	1	3	4	1	0	0	1	1	0	0	2	0	4	0	0	0	.130	.200	.174
Martinez, Casey, Ten.	2	7	6	3	3	7	1	0	1	4	0	0	1	0	0	0	0	0	0	.500	.571	1.167
Martinez, Greg, Orl.†...........	28	111	101	8	22	26	2	1	0	9	3	1	0	6	0	15	6	2	3	.218	.259	.257
Martinez, Javier, Chat...........	18	1	1	0	1	1	0	0	0	0	0	0	0	0	0	0	0	0	0	1.000	1.000	1.000

Player, Team	G	TPA	AB	R	H	TB	2B	3B	HR	RBI	SH	SF	HP	BB	IBB	SO	SB	CS	GDP	Avg.	OBP	Slg.
Martinez, Luis, Hun.*	29	26	22	1	0	0	0	0	0	0	2	0	0	2	0	14	0	0	1	.000	.083	.000
Martinez, Willie, Chat.	4	2	2	0	0	0	0	0	0	0	0	0	0	0	0	0	0	0	0	.000	.000	.000
Mathis, Jared, Hun.	82	217	203	23	47	68	6	3	3	18	2	1	2	9	0	26	5	5	2	.232	.270	.335
Matthews, Lamont, Jack.*	112	389	317	41	61	107	17	1	9	33	2	1	2	67	4	98	3	3	5	.192	.336	.338
McCrotty, Will, Jack.	43	2	0	0	0	0	0	0	0	0	2	0	0	0	0	0	0	0	0	.000	.000	.000
McKnight, Lukas, W.T.*	2	8	7	1	1	1	0	0	0	0	0	0	0	1	0	1	0	1	0	.143	.250	.143
McNamara, Rusty, Gre.	126	508	448	54	121	162	19	2	6	52	3	8	15	34	4	47	7	1	12	.270	.337	.362
Melian, Jackson, Hun.-W.T.	127	493	418	59	113	168	23	1	10	50	0	6	17	52	3	125	20	9	6	.270	.369	.402
Mendez, Donaldo, Mob.	56	250	224	36	49	77	16	0	4	18	1	0	6	19	1	53	15	5	2	.219	.297	.344
Miles, Aaron, Birm.†	138	589	531	67	171	239	39	1	9	68	11	5	2	40	4	45	25	16	4	.322	.369	.450
Miller, David, Chat.*	3	4	2	0	1	1	0	0	0	0	0	0	0	2	0	0	0	0	0	.500	.750	.500
Mitchell, Derek, Chat.	64	154	129	19	27	42	6	0	3	19	0	1	2	22	1	35	5	3	3	.209	.331	.326
Montero, Agustin, Jack.	31	1	0	0	0	0	0	0	0	0	0	0	0	1	0	0	0	0	0	.000	1.000	.000
Moon, Brian, Hun.†	36	143	122	14	23	30	4	0	1	11	2	1	2	16	0	30	3	1	1	.189	.291	.246
Moore, Frank, Orl.*	96	371	331	41	93	116	17	0	2	34	5	2	2	30	2	62	9	7	8	.281	.342	.350
Moseley, Dustin, Chat.	13	16	13	2	3	7	1	0	1	2	3	0	0	0	0	6	0	0	0	.231	.231	.538
Munoz, Adan, Gre.*	16	58	53	4	14	24	4	0	2	6	0	0	1	4	0	12	0	0	4	.264	.328	.453
Munoz, Arnaldo, Birm.*	51	1	1	0	0	0	0	0	0	0	0	0	0	0	0	0	0	0	0	.000	.000	.000
Neu, Mike, Chat.†	21	2	2	0	0	0	0	0	0	0	0	0	0	0	0	0	0	0	0	.000	.000	.000
Neuberger, Scott, Orl.	118	400	348	42	98	129	12	2	5	33	4	4	6	38	2	58	4	4	5	.282	.359	.371
Nevers, Tom, Chat.	126	489	444	58	139	208	26	2	13	77	1	3	4	37	2	77	9	6	17	.313	.369	.468
Noyce, Dave, W.T.*	53	6	6	0	0	0	0	0	0	0	0	0	0	0	0	3	0	0	0	.000	.000	.000
Olivo, Miguel, Birm.	106	411	359	51	110	172	24	10	6	49	4	3	5	40	5	66	29	13	11	.306	.381	.479
Olmedo, Rainer, Chat.†	132	552	478	62	118	150	21	1	3	30	14	0	7	53	2	86	15	16	4	.247	.331	.314
Orr, Pete, Gre.*	89	338	305	36	76	96	10	2	2	36	7	2	3	21	2	47	23	4	8	.249	.302	.315
Owens, Ryan, Car.	39	135	110	18	28	51	11	0	4	14	0	0	4	21	0	35	0	1	8	.255	.393	.464
Oxspring, Chris, Mob.*	6	1	1	0	0	0	0	0	0	0	0	0	0	0	0	1	0	0	0	.000	.000	.000
Ozias, Todd, Chat.	15	1	1	0	0	0	0	0	0	0	0	0	0	0	0	0	0	0	0	.000	.000	.000
Palma, Rick, W.T.*	43	5	5	1	1	1	0	0	0	0	0	0	0	0	0	4	0	0	0	.200	.200	.200
Parker, Matt, Hun.	40	11	10	0	1	1	0	0	0	0	0	1	0	0	0	4	0	0	0	.100	.100	.100
Peavy, Jake, Mob.	14	23	21	3	5	7	2	0	0	1	1	0	0	1	0	4	0	0	0	.238	.273	.333
Pember, David, Hun.	28	41	36	4	9	14	3	1	0	4	3	0	0	2	0	13	1	0	1	.250	.289	.389
Pena, Elvis, Hun.†	89	350	300	42	83	104	10	4	1	24	4	3	5	38	0	58	25	10	9	.277	.364	.347
Pena, Wily Mo, Chat.	105	436	388	47	99	157	23	1	11	47	0	3	9	36	2	126	8	0	9	.255	.330	.405
Penney, Mike, Hun.	37	7	6	0	1	1	0	0	0	0	0	0	1	0	0	2	0	0	0	.167	.286	.167
Perez, Oliver, Mob.*	4	6	5	0	0	0	0	0	0	0	1	0	0	0	0	1	0	0	0	.000	.000	.000
Peterson, Brian, Chat.	9	31	28	6	8	14	1	1	1	3	0	0	0	3	1	5	0	1	0	.286	.355	.500
Phillips, Dan, Car.	86	310	287	27	63	89	10	5	2	24	2	1	7	13	0	70	9	7	14	.220	.269	.310
Piedra, Jorge, W.T.*	23	65	60	5	10	15	3	1	0	4	1	0	1	3	0	11	2	0	1	.167	.219	.250
Piniella, Juan, Birm.	55	179	153	22	47	59	9	0	1	12	3	2	3	18	0	34	12	7	0	.307	.386	.386
Porter, Bo, Gre.	2	10	8	2	4	10	1	1	1	7	0	0	0	2	1	0	0	1	0	.500	.600	1.250
Powers, John, W.T.*	68	235	198	33	59	90	9	2	6	23	3	1	2	30	3	30	8	2	4	.298	.394	.455
Pratt, Andy, Gre.*	20	22	17	1	2	2	0	0	0	1	3	0	0	2	0	4	0	0	0	.118	.211	.118
Pressley, Josh, Orl.*	93	387	342	47	104	135	19	0	4	45	0	2	1	42	2	47	5	6	10	.304	.380	.395
Prior, Mark, W.T.	6	12	12	1	2	5	0	0	1	1	0	0	0	0	0	5	0	0	1	.167	.167	.417
Proctor, Scott, Jack.	26	26	22	2	9	11	2	0	0	3	2	0	0	2	0	8	0	0	0	.409	.458	.500
Quintero, Humberto, Birm.-Mob.	41	148	137	12	36	47	8	0	1	17	2	0	4	5	0	13	1	3	3	.263	.308	.343
Ramirez, Horacio, Gre.*	16	17	14	2	0	0	0	0	0	0	1	0	0	2	0	4	0	0	0	.000	.125	.000
Randolph, Jaisen, Hun.†	13	57	51	7	16	20	2	1	0	3	0	0	1	5	0	7	4	3	0	.314	.386	.392
Reinking, Kevin, Mob.	1	4	2	0	0	0	0	0	0	0	0	0	0	2	0	1	0	0	0	.000	.500	.000
Reyes, Jose, W.T.†	1	5	5	0	2	2	0	0	0	0	0	0	0	0	0	3	0	0	0	.400	.400	.400
Reyes, Rene, Car.†	123	495	455	64	133	216	33	4	14	54	2	4	5	29	4	69	10	11	10	.292	.339	.475
Rich, Dominic, Ten.*	38	153	132	14	36	45	4	1	1	14	2	0	1	18	0	23	2	4	7	.273	.364	.341
Riedling, John, Chat.	6	1	1	0	1	2	1	0	0	0	0	0	0	0	0	0	0	0	0	1.000	1.000	2.000
Riggs, Eric, Jack.†	128	539	455	69	113	174	36	2	7	69	8	8	6	62	1	74	4	4	9	.248	.341	.382
Rijo, Fernando, Jack.	27	31	27	0	3	4	1	0	0	0	3	0	1	0	0	6	0	0	0	.111	.143	.148
Risinger, Ben, Mob.	128	526	466	43	134	169	26	0	3	44	5	3	12	40	2	62	1	2	17	.288	.357	.363
Roberts, Rick, Jack.*	51	3	3	0	0	0	0	0	0	0	0	0	0	0	0	2	0	0	0	.000	.000	.000
Rodriguez, Ricardo, Jack.	11	13	13	0	2	2	0	0	0	0	0	0	0	0	0	9	0	0	0	.154	.154	.154
Rojas, Chris, Mob.	25	33	29	5	7	10	0	0	1	3	3	0	1	0	0	11	0	0	0	.241	.267	.345
Rojas, Jose, Jack.	10	10	9	0	1	1	0	0	0	0	1	0	0	0	0	6	0	0	0	.111	.111	.111
Rolls, Damian, Orl.	2	8	7	1	3	5	0	1	0	0	0	0	0	1	0	0	0	1	0	.429	.500	.714
Roney, Matt, Car.	13	6	6	0	1	2	1	0	0	0	0	0	0	0	0	3	0	0	0	.167	.167	.333
Rose, Pete, Chat.*	9	36	31	1	7	7	0	0	0	3	0	0	0	5	2	5	0	0	1	.226	.333	.226
Rouse, Michael, Ten.*	71	270	231	35	60	98	11	0	9	43	4	4	2	29	1	47	7	6	3	.260	.342	.424
Ruan, Wilkin, Jack.	78	356	324	44	82	119	16	6	3	34	5	1	8	17	0	33	23	3	4	.253	.306	.367
Rushford, Jim, Hun.*	8	21	19	2	4	5	1	0	0	1	0	0	0	2	0	5	1	0	0	.211	.286	.263
Sadler, Ray, W.T.	10	38	30	4	2	3	1	0	0	1	0	0	3	5	0	5	2	0	3	.067	.263	.100
Sanchez, Tino, Car.†	89	321	272	32	77	104	16	1	3	27	4	2	0	43	3	28	11	4	7	.283	.379	.382
Sandoval, Danny, Birm.	135	567	504	86	133	182	30	2	5	45	10	3	5	45	1	56	39	24	12	.264	.329	.361
Santana, Pedro, Chat.	121	388	350	39	98	139	17	3	6	29	10	2	1	25	0	79	12	9	7	.280	.328	.397
Sapp, Damian, Chat.	45	170	137	19	32	51	10	0	3	12	0	1	8	24	0	45	0	1	2	.234	.376	.372
Sardinha, Dane, Chat.	106	420	394	34	81	113	20	0	4	40	5	5	2	14	0	114	0	2	6	.206	.234	.287
Saunders, Chris, Birm.	19	74	67	9	16	18	2	0	0	10	0	1	0	6	0	10	0	1	3	.239	.297	.269
Scales, Bobby, Mob.†	97	282	250	40	69	100	13	3	4	27	1	0	4	27	1	56	6	3	3	.276	.356	.400
Scarborough, Steve, Hun.	88	387	322	50	91	143	29	1	7	40	4	6	6	48	2	66	8	8	3	.283	.380	.444
Scheschuk, John, Mob.*	51	191	153	17	41	56	10	1	1	27	0	3	2	33	1	19	1	2	2	.268	.398	.366
Schrager, Tony, W.T.	117	442	350	57	80	141	23	4	10	48	5	2	7	78	0	93	9	3	2	.229	.378	.403
Scott, Bill, Hun.	80	266	249	16	59	77	9	0	3	27	0	1	1	15	2	62	4	2	5	.237	.282	.309
Serrano, Ray, Gre.	20	74	65	7	16	25	3	0	2	7	1	1	2	5	0	9	1	0	0	.246	.315	.385
Shaffer, Josh, Birm.*	78	253	210	25	48	57	7	1	0	17	7	3	0	33	1	59	1	5	5	.229	.329	.271

Player, Team	G	TPA	AB	R	H	TB	2B	3B	HR	RBI	SH	SF	HP	BB	IBB	SO	SB	CS	GDP	Avg.	OBP	Slg.
Shibilo, Andy, Mob..............	29	5	5	1	1	1	0	0	0	0	0	0	0	0	0	1	0	0	0	.200	.200	.200
Shiyuk, Todd, Mob.*..........	10	2	2	0	0	0	0	0	0	0	0	0	0	0	0	1	0	0	0	.000	.000	.000
Simon, Ben, Jack..............	15	9	9	1	3	4	1	0	0	0	0	0	0	0	0	2	0	0	0	.333	.333	.444
Singleton, Justin, Ten.*.......	25	83	77	7	17	23	1	1	1	10	0	0	0	6	0	27	0	0	2	.221	.277	.299
Smothers, Stewart, Gre.........	29	107	87	7	13	20	1	0	2	7	0	1	5	14	1	31	0	3	3	.149	.299	.230
Smyth, Steve, W.T.*............	11	16	11	0	0	0	0	0	0	0	0	5	0	0	0	2	0	0	1	.000	.000	.000
Sobkowiak, Scott, Gre........	12	3	2	0	1	1	0	0	0	0	1	0	0	0	0	0	0	0	1	.500	.500	.500
Solano, Danny, Ten.	90	301	249	39	59	88	11	3	4	37	2	2	2	46	2	51	7	3	6	.237	.358	.353
Soler, Ramon, Orl.†............	38	171	144	24	36	46	7	0	1	12	7	1	0	19	0	29	14	5	3	.250	.335	.319
Stewart, Paul, Hun..............	28	36	27	3	7	8	1	0	0	3	2	0	0	7	0	16	1	0	0	.259	.412	.296
Sullivan, Kevin, Car.	5	12	11	0	2	2	0	0	0	2	0	0	0	1	0	2	0	0	1	.182	.250	.182
Taglienti, Jeff, Chat.............	24	1	0	0	0	0	0	0	0	0	0	1	0	0	0	0	0	0	0	.000	.000	.000
Takeoka, Kazuhiro, Gre........	21	1	1	0	0	0	0	0	0	0	0	0	0	0	0	0	0	0	0	.000	.000	.000
Tankersley, Dennis, Mob.	10	14	9	3	4	9	2	0	1	3	4	0	0	1	0	1	0	0	0	.444	.500	1.000
Taveras, Luis, Gre.	45	177	156	11	40	67	10	1	5	25	2	0	1	18	1	25	1	1	5	.256	.337	.429
Taylor, Seth, Car................	49	176	161	19	42	65	14	0	3	27	0	0	1	14	1	33	1	1	5	.261	.324	.404
Tejada, Mike, Car.†.............	2	8	8	1	2	2	0	0	0	0	0	0	0	0	0	2	0	0	0	.250	.250	.250
Tena, Hector, Car.	2	8	8	0	1	1	0	0	0	0	0	0	0	0	0	3	0	0	0	.125	.125	.125
Terveen, Bryce, Gre.*.........	55	208	172	23	37	54	8	0	3	13	4	0	4	28	1	42	0	2	6	.215	.338	.314
Theodorou, Nick, Jack.†	75	243	193	20	43	52	9	0	0	25	5	5	2	38	1	29	5	0	6	.223	.349	.269
Thomas, Chuck, Gre.*	71	267	229	40	53	67	8	0	2	18	3	3	4	28	1	43	5	3	5	.231	.322	.293
Thompson, Doug, Car.	51	5	4	0	0	0	0	0	0	0	1	0	0	0	0	4	0	0	0	.000	.000	.000
Thompson, Mark, Chat.........	3	5	5	0	2	2	0	0	0	0	0	0	0	0	0	1	0	0	0	.400	.400	.400
Thompson, Mike, Mob..........	1	2	2	0	1	1	0	0	0	0	0	0	0	0	0	1	0	0	0	.500	.500	.500
Thompson, Rich, Ten.*	135	631	554	109	155	182	13	4	2	44	7	0	20	50	1	86	45	13	1	.280	.361	.329
Thompson, Travis, Chat.	16	12	11	0	2	2	0	0	0	0	1	0	0	0	0	5	0	0	0	.182	.182	.182
Totten, Heath, Jack..............	9	9	8	0	0	0	0	0	0	0	1	0	0	0	0	3	0	0	0	.000	.000	.000
Trujillo, J.J., Mob..............	31	6	6	1	1	1	0	0	0	1	0	0	0	0	0	2	0	0	0	.167	.167	.167
Ulacia, Dennis, Birm.*	28	2	2	0	0	0	0	0	0	0	0	0	0	0	0	0	0	0	0	.000	.000	.000
Umbria, Jose, Ten.	37	113	100	5	21	24	3	0	0	7	4	0	2	7	0	25	1	1	2	.210	.275	.240
Vance, Cory, Car.*..............	27	36	31	6	9	13	1	0	1	1	1	0	0	4	0	10	0	0	2	.290	.371	.419
Veronie, Shanin, Gre...........	29	10	9	1	3	3	0	0	0	1	1	0	0	0	0	1	0	0	0	.333	.333	.333
Victorino, Shane, Jack.	122	550	481	61	124	153	15	1	4	34	16	2	4	47	0	49	45	16	6	.258	.328	.318
Warren, Chris, Car..............	65	239	205	31	44	73	6	1	7	23	5	3	3	23	3	60	2	2	1	.215	.299	.356
Wathan, Dusty, Hun.............	9	29	25	2	4	6	2	0	0	2	0	0	2	2	0	4	0	0	4	.160	.276	.240
Watkins, Steve, Mob.	37	24	22	0	4	4	0	0	0	1	2	0	0	0	0	8	0	0	0	.182	.182	.182
Webb, John, W.T................	12	15	13	0	3	3	0	0	0	1	2	0	0	0	0	4	0	0	0	.231	.231	.231
Weekly, Chris, W.T.*..........	18	41	36	4	7	10	3	0	0	4	0	0	0	5	0	12	0	2	0	.194	.293	.278
Wellemeyer, Todd, W.T.	8	8	7	2	1	1	0	0	0	0	1	0	0	0	0	5	0	0	0	.143	.143	.143
West, Brian, Birm.	28	5	5	0	1	2	1	0	0	1	0	0	0	0	0	1	0	0	0	.200	.200	.400
West, Todd, Hun.	46	133	120	13	26	31	5	0	0	8	5	0	0	8	0	24	6	3	2	.217	.266	.258
Wise, Dewayne, Ten.*	86	380	340	59	101	160	21	4	10	49	6	4	1	29	5	49	15	8	4	.297	.350	.471
Wrigley, Jase, Car..............	44	3	2	1	0	0	0	0	0	0	0	0	0	1	0	2	0	0	0	.000	.333	.000
Young, Colin, Car.*	15	1	1	1	1	1	0	0	0	0	0	0	0	0	0	0	0	0	0	1.000	1.000	1.000
Young, Jason, Car.†	14	25	23	2	6	7	1	0	0	3	1	0	0	1	0	8	0	0	0	.261	.292	.304
Zapp, A.J., Gre.*...............	85	347	300	37	71	128	15	0	14	46	0	3	3	31	0	81	0	0	9	.237	.312	.427
Zoccolillo, Peter, Hun.*	75	271	227	43	67	117	12	1	12	45	0	3	1	40	1	50	6	7	7	.295	.399	.515
Zywica, Mike, Birm.	18	60	49	6	10	14	1	0	1	8	1	3	1	6	0	8	4	0	2	.204	.288	.286

PLAYERS WITH TWO OR MORE TEAMS

Player, Team	G	TPA	AB	R	H	TB	2B	3B	HR	RBI	SH	SF	HP	BB	IBB	SO	SB	CS	GDP	Avg.	OBP	Slg.
Fernandez, Alex, Birm.*	87	358	343	34	100	136	15	0	7	52	3	4	0	8	2	60	20	7	8	.292	.304	.397
Fernandez, Alex, Mob.*	16	72	66	8	18	25	4	0	1	8	1	2	0	3	0	8	6	1	0	.273	.296	.379
Haad, Yamid, Orl................	29	118	108	12	20	31	2	0	3	15	1	3	0	6	1	23	2	1	3	.185	.222	.287
Haad, Yamid, Mob..............	18	60	53	6	15	19	1	0	1	13	0	2	0	5	0	8	1	0	1	.283	.333	.358
Melian, Jackson, Hun...........	56	229	184	34	41	67	6	1	6	24	0	3	7	35	1	63	10	3	2	.223	.362	.364
Melian, Jackson, W.T.	71	264	234	25	72	101	17	0	4	26	0	3	10	17	2	62	10	6	4	.308	.375	.432
Quintero, Humberto, Birm......	4	14	12	1	6	6	0	0	0	3	1	0	1	0	0	1	1	0	0	.500	.538	.500
Quintero, Humberto, Mob......	37	134	125	11	30	41	8	0	1	14	1	0	3	5	0	12	0	3	3	.240	.286	.328

GRAND SLAMS—Barmes, Fagan, 2 each; Atkins, Cantu, Cash, Deardorff, Deschaine, A. Diaz, M. Diaz, Gross, Haad, Ingram, R. Jones, Kelton, LaForest, Langerhans, Leon, R. Lopez, C. Martinez, Mathis, Nevers, W. Pena, Porter, Pressley, Reyes, Rouse, Schrager, Solano, Zoccolillo, 1 each.

AWARDED FIRST BASE ON CATCHER'S INTERFERENCE—Chiaffredo (Quintero); Haltiwanger (Hill); Leon (Loyd); Logan (Hill); Luuloa (Umbria); Moore (Taveras); Powers (Acevas); Ruan (LaForest); Scarborough (Olivo).

2002 PITCHING
TEAM

Team	W	L	Pct.	ERA	G	CG	ShO	Sv.	IP	H	TBF	R	ER	HR	SH	SF	HB	BB	IBB	SO	WP	Bk.
Jacksonville......	77	62	.554	3.09	139	6	14	38	1235.2	1072	5213	492	424	88	50	32	60	533	40	960	67	6
Mobile	76	63	.547	3.37	139	2	13	49	1230.2	1168	5247	552	461	77	53	35	52	491	28	1074	45	11
Huntsville	70	69	.504	3.45	139	4	14	36	1229.2	1171	5296	568	471	72	69	34	60	529	10	1005	73	8
West Tenn	73	67	.521	3.64	140	1	5	41	1244.2	1139	5262	577	503	81	72	53	70	458	9	1040	58	12
Birmingham	79	61	.564	3.75	140	1	11	52	1223.1	1129	5271	605	510	80	33	47	60	552	31	928	58	8
Greenville	65	69	.485	3.77	134	4	7	41	1188.1	1107	5066	597	498	92	54	44	56	475	15	953	57	6
Chattanooga	60	80	.429	4.13	140	5	4	27	1225.0	1267	5329	672	562	91	67	42	52	496	23	993	55	3
Orlando	58	79	.423	4.13	137	8	8	30	1191.2	1208	5293	658	547	97	45	44	57	553	25	834	94	10
Carolina...........	65	71	.478	4.22	136	6	7	29	1217.1	1190	5336	701	571	73	79	36	70	543	42	914	89	7
Tennessee	69	71	.493	4.48	140	9	8	30	1237.0	1339	5460	715	616	127	48	41	78	482	10	756	50	3

CLASS AA *Southern League*

TOP QUALIFIERS FOR EARNED-RUN AVERAGE TITLE

Minimum 112 innings.*Lefthanded pitcher.

Pitcher, Team	W	L	Pct.	ERA	G	GS	CG	ShO	GF	Sv.	IP	H	TBF	R	ER	HR	SH	SF	HB	BB	IBB	SO	WP	Bk.
Chulk, Vinny, Ten.	13	5	.722	2.96	25	24	0	0	1	1	152	133	626	55	50	12	3	2	5	53	0	108	6	0
Lee, Derek, Hun.*	5	10	.333	3.04	34	16	0	0	5	0	127.1	138	558	59	43	6	9	5	4	45	1	104	6	0
Bruback, Matt, W.T.	9	7	.563	3.16	28	28	0	0	0	0	174	157	718	70	61	9	7	8	48	2	158	7	0
Pember, David, Hun.	10	6	.625	3.17	27	27	2	0	0	0	156	157	669	69	55	13	9	2	6	53	1	111	13	1
Martin, Chandler, Car.	7	4	.636	3.18	19	19	1	0	0	0	113.1	109	472	48	40	8	9	3	7	34	0	82	7	0
Bong, Jung, Gre.*	7	8	.467	3.25	27	17	0	0	4	2	122	136	533	59	44	6	5	3	45	1	107	8	1
Cameron, Ryan, Car.	5	7	.417	3.26	37	15	0	0	6	0	118.2	84	492	55	43	9	9	2	6	55	3	139	9	0
Stewart, Paul, Hun.	12	9	.571	3.28	27	27	2	1	0	0	161.2	147	661	69	59	12	4	3	13	42	0	124	7	1
Brazelton, Dewon, Orl.	5	9	.357	3.33	26	26	1	0	0	0	146	129	620	69	54	7	5	3	10	67	1	109	10	2
Proctor, Scott, Jack.	7	9	.438	3.51	26	25	0	0	0	0	133.1	111	592	63	52	10	6	5	7	85	1	131	9	1
Stewart, Josh, Birm.*	11	7	.611	3.53	26	26	1	1	0	0	150.1	145	630	65	59	11	2	0	2	56	1	92	7	0
Rijo, Fernando, Jack.	8	8	.500	3.74	27	27	1	1	0	0	142	130	616	62	59	13	4	3	8	72	2	106	12	1
Hall, Josh, Chat.	7	8	.467	3.75	22	22	1	0	0	0	132	140	575	75	55	7	6	5	6	50	0	116	9	0
Vance, Cory, Car.*	10	8	.556	3.77	25	25	1	0	0	0	150.1	142	646	73	63	8	9	5	2	76	1	114	5	1
Watkins, Steve, Mob.	4	8	.333	3.78	37	15	1	0	5	0	116.2	124	505	65	49	8	4	6	3	49	3	88	2	1

DEPARTMENTAL LEADERS: W—Chulk, Markwell, 13 each; L—Ulacia, 14; Pct.—Roberts, .800; G—Hooten, 65; GS—P. Bauer, Bruback, 28 each; CG—Backe, P. Bauer, 3 each; ShO—Cook, 2; GF—Valentine, 48; Sv.—Valentine, 36; IP—P. Bauer, 177.0; H—P. Bauer, 208; TBF—P. Bauer, 773; R—Spille, 105; ER—Spille, 92; HR—Markwell, 23; SH—Ennis, Freed, 11 each; SF—Belisle, West, 9 each; HB—Kibler, 15; BB—Malone, 89; IBB—McCrotty, Sanders, 7 each; SO—Bruback, 158; WP—Kibler, 18; BK—Hampton, Jongejan, 3 each.

ALL PITCHERS

*Lefthanded pitcher.

Pitcher, Team	W	L	Pct.	ERA	G	GS	CG	ShO	GF	Sv.	IP	H	TBF	R	ER	HR	SH	SF	HB	BB	IBB	SO	WP	Bk.
Abreu, Winston, W.T.	1	0	1.000	7.20	11	0	0	0	3	0	15	9	75	12	12	2	2	0	0	20	0	20	2	1
Achilles, Matt, W.T.	8	7	.533	3.90	41	11	0	0	7	1	115.1	125	487	58	50	6	4	6	4	38	1	70	3	0
Adams, Mike, Hun.	1	0	1.000	3.38	13	0	0	0	7	1	18.2	14	81	11	7	3	1	0	1	12	0	17	1	0
Agosto, Stevenson, Orl.*	3	1	.750	2.58	7	6	0	0	1	0	38.1	43	169	19	11	4	2	1	0	13	0	28	3	0
Allen, Rodney, Hun.	0	0	.000	3.10	15	0	0	0	2	0	20.1	17	92	9	7	1	1	0	0	17	0	15	1	0
Altman, Gene, Hun.	0	3	.000	8.37	24	0	0	0	7	1	33.1	31	168	31	31	3	2	4	1	42	3	23	9	1
Alvarez, Wilson, Orl.*	1	0	1.000	1.13	2	2	0	0	0	0	8	6	29	1	1	0	0	0	0	2	0	7	0	0
Andrews, Clayton, Chat.*	0	3	.000	7.23	4	4	0	0	0	0	18.2	33	95	20	15	2	2	1	0	8	0	8	0	0
Aramboles, Ricardo, Chat.	1	0	1.000	3.13	4	4	0	0	0	0	23	22	92	8	8	0	2	0	0	8	0	22	0	0
Atchley, Justin, Chat.*	0	1	.000	19.29	2	0	0	0	1	0	2.1	5	14	5	5	1	0	0	1	2	0	1	0	0
Averette, Robert, Car.	1	6	.143	7.15	11	11	1	0	0	0	61.2	90	288	58	49	6	4	2	1	22	2	33	1	0
Backe, Brandon, Orl.	4	6	.400	4.68	20	14	3	1	4	2	92.1	91	400	58	48	9	2	1	5	37	1	45	9	0
Baker, Brad, Mob.	4	4	.500	4.48	12	12	1	0	0	0	64.1	47	277	33	32	5	3	1	2	45	0	57	4	0
Baker, Ryan, Gre.	1	0	1.000	5.06	5	0	0	0	5	0	5.1	4	22	3	3	0	0	0	0	4	0	2	0	0
Bartosh, Cliff, Mob.*	2	4	.333	3.18	62	0	0	0	42	25	70.2	54	298	28	25	4	4	4	2	32	5	70	5	0
Battersby, Eric, Birm.*	0	0	.000	0.00	1	0	0	0	1	0	1	1	4	0	0	0	0	0	0	0	0	1	0	0
Bauer, Greg, Jack.	2	4	.333	2.83	38	3	0	0	5	1	70	62	301	35	22	5	3	2	1	30	4	38	1	0
Bauer, Peter, Ten.	6	13	.316	4.42	28	28	3	1	0	0	177	208	773	103	87	14	1	4	12	53	0	93	7	0
Bausher, Andy, Mob.*	4	1	.800	3.11	34	1	0	0	9	0	63.2	70	269	27	22	6	2	3	3	17	2	40	3	1
Belisle, Matt, Gre.	5	9	.357	4.35	26	26	1	0	0	0	159.1	162	682	91	77	18	3	9	10	39	1	123	6	2
Beltran, Frank, W.T.	2	2	.500	2.59	39	0	0	0	35	23	41.2	28	171	14	12	2	3	1	2	19	2	43	3	2
Bohannan, Brad, Birm.	0	1	.000	7.71	8	0	0	0	5	0	11.2	18	58	14	10	2	2	2	0	7	1	0	0	0
Bong, Jung, Gre.*	7	8	.467	3.25	27	17	0	0	4	2	122	136	533	59	44	6	5	3	45	1	107	8	1
Bradley, Ryan, Car.	1	2	.333	12.38	5	0	0	0	1	0	8	13	45	14	11	2	1	0	1	6	1	7	2	1
Brantley, Brian, Car.	2	3	.400	4.56	17	0	0	0	2	0	23.2	25	107	12	12	1	1	0	0	12	2	11	3	1
Brazelton, Dewon, Orl.	5	9	.357	3.33	26	26	1	0	0	0	146	129	620	69	54	7	5	3	10	67	1	109	10	2
Brown, Eric, W.T.	1	0	1.000	0.00	4	0	0	0	0	0	3.1	1	11	0	0	0	0	0	0	0	0	3	0	0
Bruback, Matt, W.T.	9	7	.563	3.16	28	28	0	0	0	0	174	157	718	70	61	9	7	8	48	2	158	7	0
Brueggemann, Dean, Car.*	0	3	.000	6.97	34	0	0	0	7	0	51.2	61	250	49	40	4	5	4	4	33	4	36	6	0
Bullard, Jim, Birm.*	0	3	.000	4.50	3	3	0	0	0	0	20	21	83	10	10	1	0	1	4	2	12	3	0
Bynum, Mike, Mob.*	4	0	1.000	0.82	6	5	0	0	0	0	33	17	123	5	3	0	0	3	7	0	29	2	0
Cameron, Ryan, Car.	5	7	.417	3.26	37	15	0	0	6	0	118.2	84	492	55	43	9	9	2	6	55	3	139	9	0
Caraccioli, Lance, Jack.*	4	2	.667	3.06	10	10	1	1	0	0	61.2	53	254	21	21	2	2	1	1	25	0	48	2	2
Carpenter, Chris, Ten.	0	1	.000	8.20	5	0	0	0	0	0	18.2	26	88	18	17	5	2	1	0	8	0	9	2	0
Casey, Joe, Ten.	0	0	.000	6.75	11	0	0	0	5	0	13.1	17	72	15	10	2	0	0	3	14	0	4	0	0
Castellanos, Hugo, Ten.	3	4	.429	5.23	47	0	0	0	32	18	51.2	46	232	30	30	5	5	1	7	28	3	34	3	0
Castillo, Marcos, Jack.	0	0	.000	7.71	2	0	0	0	0	0	2.1	3	10	2	2	1	0	0	1	0	1	0	0
Cercy, Rick, Car.	3	4	.429	5.12	47	0	0	0	12	1	65	70	322	55	37	5	7	4	10	47	5	75	14	0
Chacin, Gustavo, Ten.*	6	5	.545	4.66	35	13	1	0	8	1	119.2	131	542	73	62	12	6	5	8	59	0	68	4	1
Chantres, Carlos, Orl.	1	1	.500	3.12	3	0	0	0	0	0	8.2	8	35	3	3	1	0	0	3	0	5	0	1
Chavez, Wilton, W.T.	8	5	.615	3.76	18	18	0	0	0	0	103	97	437	48	43	7	6	7	6	39	0	86	8	1
Chiasson, Scott, W.T.	0	0	.000	3.00	3	0	0	0	0	0	3	5	17	2	1	0	0	0	1	0	5	0	0
Childers, Jason, Hun.	1	1	.500	2.10	11	1	0	0	3	0	25.2	22	105	6	6	1	1	1	1	12	0	22	2	0
Childers, Matt, Hun.	2	5	.286	4.50	35	10	0	0	24	12	82	103	374	47	41	6	6	2	5	27	0	57	2	0
Chouinard, Bobby, Car.*	0	0	.000	0.00	5	0	0	0	3	1	7	4	29	3	0	0	0	0	3	2	10	0	0
Christensen, Ben, W.T.	2	6	.250	6.33	12	12	0	0	0	0	64	73	298	49	45	8	2	5	7	35	0	36	3	0
Chulk, Vinny, Ten.	13	5	.722	2.96	25	24	0	0	1	1	152	133	626	55	50	12	3	2	5	53	0	108	6	0
Collazo, William, Gre.*	4	2	.667	3.47	51	0	0	0	26	4	72.2	70	309	34	28	7	2	1	2	27	2	74	4	1
Colyer, Steve, Jack.*	5	4	.556	3.45	59	0	0	0	46	21	62.2	50	284	29	24	6	4	3	2	40	3	68	4	0
Cook, Aaron, Car.	7	2	.778	1.42	14	14	2	0	0	0	95	73	370	24	15	4	3	1	5	19	0	58	5	0
Cordova, Jorge, Chat.	4	2	.667	3.99	35	0	0	0	31	13	38.1	38	168	21	17	3	0	2	14	2	30	1	0
Coward, Chad, Orl.	9	4	.692	2.98	37	3	0	0	6	5	87.2	82	375	38	29	6	5	4	2	33	2	60	4	0

Pitcher, Team	W	L	Pct.	ERA	G	GS	CG	ShO	GF	Sv.	IP	H	TBF	R	ER	HR	SH	SF	HB	BB	IBB	SO	WP	Bk.
Crowder, Chuck, Car.*	2	0	1.000	12.27	11	0	0	0	3	1	14.2	18	77	22	20	2	0	1	1	16	1	9	0	0
Cumberland, Chris, Ten.*	0	1	.000	7.71	9	0	0	0	3	1	9.1	17	48	8	8	1	0	0	4	5	0	5	0	0
Curtis, Daniel, Gre.	4	2	.667	4.80	10	10	1	0	0	0	54.1	61	227	29	29	7	4	1	3	18	0	29	3	0
Cyr, Eric, Mob.*	4	6	.400	3.24	14	14	0	0	0	0	72.1	62	311	37	26	6	2	3	6	34	0	65	0	2
Darnell, Paul, Chat.*	3	1	.750	3.27	27	0	0	0	10	0	41.1	33	174	20	15	4	1	1	0	18	1	47	2	0
Davis, Lance, Chat.*	1	6	.143	3.58	12	11	1	0	0	0	65.1	72	279	38	26	5	6	3	1	17	0	51	3	1
De Hart, Blair, Mob.	2	3	.400	4.45	7	7	0	0	0	0	32.1	44	145	21	16	2	1	0	1	9	0	29	1	0
DeHart, Casey, Chat.*	1	3	.250	6.53	21	0	0	0	8	1	30.1	32	135	23	22	4	3	2	2	15	3	24	1	0
De La Cruz, Fernando, Car.	2	5	.286	5.45	31	0	0	0	26	6	33	39	158	25	20	1	6	1	2	15	3	15	6	1
Dellaero, Jason, Birm.	2	3	.400	9.00	13	0	0	0	6	0	16	23	81	16	16	2	2	1	1	10	2	16	2	0
Dent, Doug, Hun.	3	1	.750	3.81	12	2	0	0	1	0	28.1	27	120	13	12	1	0	1	3	9	0	23	0	1
Devey, Phil, Jack.*	3	1	.750	1.91	8	7	0	0	0	0	47	44	186	12	10	1	1	1	2	12	0	20	1	1
Diaz, Felix, Birm.	4	0	1.000	3.48	7	6	0	0	0	0	31	25	129	14	12	4	0	0	0	8	0	30	0	0
Diggins, Ben, Hun.	2	1	.667	1.91	7	7	0	0	0	0	37.2	26	151	13	8	0	6	2	3	15	0	34	2	1
Dunn, Scott, Chat.	5	7	.417	3.92	37	12	0	0	11	1	110.1	99	470	57	48	10	4	3	5	54	3	114	6	0
Dunning, Justin, Jack.	0	0	.000	4.82	8	0	0	0	3	0	9.1	5	44	7	5	0	0	2	0	11	0	8	3	0
Eason, Clay, Birm.	5	2	.714	2.00	29	3	0	0	8	4	67.2	48	270	16	15	3	2	2	7	26	4	60	5	0
Emiliano, Jamie, Gre.	3	3	.500	1.66	42	0	0	0	14	3	54.1	34	215	16	10	4	6	1	1	24	3	39	5	1
Ennis, John, Gre.	9	9	.500	4.18	26	26	0	0	0	0	148.2	131	625	79	69	7	11	5	7	62	0	103	6	0
Esslinger, Cam, Car.	0	1	.000	2.57	6	0	0	0	5	2	7	6	31	2	2	0	0	3	3	1	6	0	0		
Estrella, Leo, W.T.	2	2	.500	3.28	10	3	0	0	2	0	24.2	23	106	13	9	0	5	0	1	8	0	18	1	0
Etherton, Seth, Chat.	1	0	1.000	0.96	3	3	0	0	0	0	9.1	5	34	1	1	0	1	0	1	2	0	4	0	0
Evert, Brett, Gre.	5	8	.385	4.90	16	15	1	0	1	0	93.2	94	416	59	51	15	6	4	13	35	1	84	3	0
Falteisek, Steve, Jack.	0	0	.000	0.00	1	0	0	0	1	0	1	0	3	0	0	0	0	0	0	0	0	1	0	0
Farmer, Tom, Jack.	3	1	.750	3.19	6	6	0	0	0	0	36.2	36	149	13	13	3	0	1	2	9	0	26	2	0
Feliciano, Pedro, Chat.*	2	1	.667	2.56	28	0	0	0	14	4	38.2	33	160	14	11	1	4	1	3	11	1	26	0	0
Fikac, Jeremy, Mob.	1	0	1.000	3.00	3	0	0	0	3	1	3	5	11	1	1	0	0	0	0	0	0	3	0	0
Fortunato, Bartolome, Orl.	3	0	1.000	2.10	10	2	0	0	0	0	25.2	16	103	7	6	2	1	1	1	11	1	34	1	0
Fox, Chad, Hun.	0	1	.000	0.00	3	0	0	0	0	0	5.1	5	21	1	0	0	0	0	2	0	7	0	0	
Freed, Mark, W.T.*	9	11	.450	5.16	29	24	0	0	2	0	132.2	159	606	88	76	14	11	8	10	58	1	106	6	2
Frendling, Neal, Orl.	5	6	.455	4.50	22	21	0	0	0	0	112	107	505	67	56	14	3	6	5	65	0	69	11	2
Gaal, Bryan, Mob.	4	1	.800	2.95	32	0	0	0	15	3	36.2	40	156	14	12	1	2	0	0	11	3	32	1	0
Gandarillas, Gus, Hun.	0	0	.000	0.00	1	1	0	0	0	0	2.1	2	12	0	0	0	0	0	0	3	0	4	0	0
Garcia, Ariel, Mob.	1	0	1.000	7.15	7	0	0	0	2	0	11.1	20	59	16	9	2	0	1	0	4	1	9	1	0
Garcia, Gerardo, Orl.	2	1	.667	2.79	10	4	1	1	2	0	38.2	24	153	14	12	4	1	0	2	12	0	28	2	0
Garcia, Jose, Hun.	3	4	.429	2.37	11	11	0	0	0	0	60.2	47	257	19	16	0	4	0	3	31	0	37	4	0
Gassner, Dave, Ten.*	1	2	.333	2.49	4	4	0	0	0	0	25.1	22	103	8	7	1	0	0	1	7	1	14	1	1
Gawer, Matt, Gre.*	0	1	.000	7.00	6	0	0	0	3	0	9	6	41	8	7	1	1	1	1	5	0	8	1	0
German, Rafael, Chat.	0	0	.000	1.80	1	1	0	0	0	0	5	5	20	1	1	0	0	0	1	3	0	0		
Giese, Dan, Mob.	4	5	.444	2.91	32	0	0	0	8	0	52.2	56	222	24	17	3	2	3	0	13	6	51	1	0
Gil, Dave, Chat.	10	4	.714	3.66	18	18	2	0	0	0	110.2	102	466	49	45	16	5	2	8	36	0	103	5	0
Giron, Roberto, Hun.	2	4	.333	2.39	36	2	0	0	28	10	52.2	38	227	21	14	2	2	1	4	33	3	52	3	0
Gonzalez, Alfredo, Jack.	0	1	.000	1.35	13	0	0	0	5	3	20	13	71	4	3	0	1	0	0	2	0	18	1	0
Gooch, Arnie, Chat.	3	3	.500	6.21	7	7	0	0	0	0	37.2	45	178	30	26	2	2	2	1	16	0	27	1	0
Gooris, Dan, Mob.*	1	0	1.000	9.00	1	0	0	0	0	0	2	5	10	3	2	0	1	0	0	0	0	0	0	0
Gracesqui, Frank, Ten.*	4	2	.667	4.64	41	0	0	0	14	1	42.2	40	198	26	22	3	0	4	5	34	0	48	4	0
Gray, Brett, Chat.	6	6	.500	2.78	48	3	0	0	12	0	94	88	385	37	29	5	5	3	5	21	0	60	3	1
Gross, Rafael, W.T.	0	0	.000	6.00	1	1	0	0	0	0	3	4	16	2	2	0	0	0	3	0	1	0	0	
Gulin, Lindsay, Jack.*	5	2	.714	2.64	19	3	0	0	7	3	61.1	54	252	21	18	5	0	1	4	17	0	67	2	0
Hall, Josh, Chat.	7	8	.467	3.75	22	22	1	0	0	0	132	140	575	75	55	7	6	5	6	50	0	116	9	0
Hamann, Rob, Ten.	0	0	.000	2.41	12	0	0	0	6	1	18.2	21	85	8	5	0	1	0	4	7	0	7	1	0
Hamilton, Jon, W.T.*	0	1	.000	9.00	1	0	0	0	1	0	1	1	4	1	1	1	0	0	0	0	0	1	0	0
Hampton, Matt, Mob.*	6	5	.545	3.54	57	1	0	0	16	0	94	92	405	42	37	10	3	4	2	28	6	98	2	3
Hanrahan, Joel, Jack.	1	1	.500	10.64	3	3	0	0	0	0	11	15	55	14	13	2	0	2	0	7	0	10	0	0
Harrell, Tim, Jack.	3	1	.750	7.07	8	1	0	0	1	0	14	12	59	11	11	3	1	0	0	7	0	9	1	0
Harvey, Ian, Mob.	6	1	.857	1.89	12	9	0	0	1	0	57	54	229	14	12	2	0	1	1	15	0	44	0	0
Hazlett, Andy, W.T.*	0	0	.000	1.38	9	0	0	0	3	0	13	7	49	3	2	0	1	1	0	3	0	12	0	0
Hendrickson, Ben, Hun.	4	2	.667	2.97	13	13	0	0	0	0	69.2	57	295	31	23	2	8	2	3	35	0	50	2	1
Hernandez, Buddy, Gre.	4	0	1.000	1.22	40	0	0	0	11	1	59	36	234	13	8	0	0	3	3	23	0	81	0	0
High, Andy, Hun.*	1	1	.500	2.84	16	1	0	0	5	1	31.2	35	134	14	10	2	1	1	1	11	0	29	1	0
Hines, Carlos, Orl.	0	0	.000	16.20	3	0	0	0	1	0	3.1	8	27	9	6	0	0	0	2	5	0	3	2	0
Hooten, Dave, W.T.	5	1	.833	1.30	65	0	0	0	22	9	76	49	292	13	11	4	3	1	3	19	0	66	5	0
House, Craig, Jack.	0	0	.000	4.50	3	0	0	0	0	0	4	3	19	2	2	1	0	1	2	2	0	1	0	0
Howard, Ben, Mob.	3	1	.750	2.18	6	6	0	0	0	0	33	26	135	10	8	2	1	0	1	16	0	30	0	0
Howington, Ty, Chat.*	1	5	.167	5.12	15	15	1	0	0	0	65	65	288	39	37	5	2	1	3	33	0	51	5	0
Huisman, Justin, Car.	0	3	.000	6.66	18	0	0	0	10	2	24.1	30	116	22	18	4	0	0	1	12	3	10	2	0
Hunter, Johnny, Mob.	5	4	.556	3.40	21	14	0	0	3	0	87.1	92	390	38	33	6	7	1	3	27	0	43	2	1
James, Delvin, Orl.	2	3	.333	3.55	3	1	0	0	0	0	12.2	12	53	7	5	2	0	0	0	2	0	13	0	0
Jarvis, Kevin, Mob.	0	0	.000	0.00	1	1	0	0	0	0	3	2	11	0	0	0	0	0	0	0	0	3	0	0
Jongejan, Ferenc, W.T.*	3	4	.429	3.34	62	3	0	0	24	2	67.1	59	276	26	25	4	3	2	2	28	1	51	4	3
Kaup, Nathan, Orl.	0	0	.000	0.00	1	0	0	0	1	0	1	1	4	1	0	0	0	0	0	0	0	0	0	0
Kegley, Chuck, Ten.	1	3	.250	7.88	15	0	0	0	5	1	16	18	79	16	14	1	2	1	0	15	1	7	1	0
Kent, Nathan, Gre.	1	0	1.000	6.00	1	1	0	0	0	0	3	3	15	2	2	0	0	0	0	3	0	2	1	0
Kibler, Ryan, Car.	7	8	.467	4.91	25	25	0	0	0	0	143	158	656	98	78	6	8	5	15	64	5	59	18	0
Knoff, Justin, Chat.	0	0	.000	0.00	1	0	0	0	0	0	1	3	3	0	0	0	0	0	0	0	0	0	0	0
Kopitzke, Casey, W.T.	1	0	1.000	0.00	1	0	0	0	0	1	4	4	0	0	1	0	0	0	0	0	0	0	0	0
Koronka, John, Chat.*	2	8	.200	4.99	16	15	0	0	0	0	95.2	109	428	56	53	10	5	4	1	52	1	69	4	1
Krawczyk, Jack, Hun.	5	3	.625	2.71	44	0	0	0	18	5	66.1	54	273	22	20	3	1	0	3	15	0	69	3	0
Langone, Steve, Jack.*	2	2	.500	1.38	14	0	0	0	5	1	32.2	21	132	7	5	0	2	0	5	12	2	17	0	0
Lantigua, Delvis, Birm.	6	2	.750	3.48	16	15	0	0	0	0	85.1	67	350	36	33	6	2	0	5	35	1	66	1	0
Lee, Derek, Hun.*	5	10	.333	3.04	34	16	0	0	5	0	127.1	138	558	59	43	6	9	5	4	45	1	104	6	0
Lee, Garrett, Gre.	3	2	.600	3.52	19	2	0	0	4	0	46	47	189	21	18	3	2	0	2	10	1	26	0	0

Pitcher, Team	W	L	Pct.	ERA	G	GS	CG	ShO	GF	Sv.	IP	H	TBF	R	ER	HR	SH	SF	HB	BB	IBB	SO	WP	Bk.
Leek, Randy, Jack.*	7	5	.583	2.16	15	14	1	0	0	0	95.2	94	381	30	23	5	4	4	5	11	1	56	2	0
Leicester, Jon, W.T.	2	2	.500	4.61	5	4	0	0	0	0	27.1	24	123	16	14	1	2	1	3	13	0	18	4	0
Leskanic, Curt, Hun.	0	0	.000	3.00	3	0	0	0	1	0	3	4	14	2	1	0	0	0	0	2	0	2	0	0
Lewis, Derrick, Gre.	1	0	1.000	0.00	1	1	0	0	0	0	6	3	23	0	0	0	0	0	0	3	0	2	0	0
Loaiza, Esteban, Ten.	2	0	1.000	1.88	2	2	0	0	0	0	14.1	10	49	3	3	0	0	0	0	1	0	13	0	0
Lopez, Albie, Gre.	0	0	.000	4.50	1	1	0	0	0	0	4	2	18	2	2	0	0	0	0	4	0	4	0	0
Lowe, Benny, Chat.*	1	1	.500	5.93	9	0	0	0	1	0	13.2	13	63	11	9	4	0	2	0	8	0	12	1	0
Lugo, Ruddy, Jack.	3	1	.750	4.05	11	2	0	0	2	1	33.1	34	144	15	15	3	4	0	3	13	5	23	4	0
Magrane, Jim, Orl.	0	3	.000	3.09	9	6	1	0	1	0	43.2	35	181	17	15	1	3	2	0	22	1	25	2	0
Majewski, Gary, Birm.	5	3	.625	2.65	57	1	0	0	26	3	74.2	61	317	31	22	3	2	2	3	34	2	75	1	1
Malaska, Mark, Orl.*	4	5	.444	3.69	12	11	1	0	1	1	70.2	82	314	37	29	4	2	1	2	28	2	49	4	0
Malone, Corwin, Birm.*	10	7	.588	4.71	22	22	0	0	0	0	124.1	116	569	77	65	6	2	5	6	89	1	89	6	2
Markwell, Diegomar, Ten.*	13	9	.591	4.38	28	27	2	1	1	1	168.1	174	731	95	82	23	6	4	9	60	1	101	7	0
Martin, Chandler, Car.	7	4	.636	3.18	19	19	1	0	0	0	113.1	109	472	48	40	8	9	3	7	34	0	82	7	0
Martinez, Javier, Chat.	1	2	.333	4.94	18	0	0	0	7	0	23.2	21	107	13	13	0	3	0	1	18	1	17	6	0
Martinez, Luis, Hun.*	8	8	.500	5.20	29	18	0	0	2	1	109	114	489	70	63	6	5	1	6	65	0	106	10	2
Martinez, Willie, Chat.	1	0	1.000	3.38	4	1	0	0	0	0	13.1	12	53	5	5	0	1	2	0	4	0	6	1	0
Mathis, Jared, Hun.	0	1	.000	18.00	2	0	0	0	2	0	2	5	12	4	4	1	0	1	0	2	0	1	0	0
McClung, Seth, Chat.	5	7	.417	5.37	20	19	0	0	1	0	114	138	533	74	68	12	2	7	9	53	0	64	7	1
McCrotty, Will, Jack.	1	4	.200	2.39	43	0	0	0	26	6	52.2	37	219	16	14	3	3	2	1	30	7	57	1	1
Meyer, Jake, Birm.	2	0	1.000	3.38	23	0	0	0	5	0	40	35	168	15	15	4	0	3	2	20	0	31	2	0
Minix, Travis, Orl.	5	7	.417	3.04	38	1	0	0	15	0	68	70	300	31	23	3	5	2	2	29	3	49	1	0
Montero, Agustin, Jack.	1	3	.250	3.95	31	0	0	0	11	0	41	38	187	21	18	5	3	1	8	29	6	25	5	0
Moseley, Dustin, Chat.	5	6	.455	4.13	13	13	0	0	0	0	80.2	91	361	47	37	5	6	3	4	37	0	52	2	0
Munoz, Arnaldo, Birm.*	6	0	1.000	2.61	51	0	0	0	18	6	72.1	62	306	29	21	6	5	3	1	29	0	78	5	2
Neu, Mike, Chat.	1	0	1.000	1.33	21	0	0	0	12	7	27	22	113	4	4	0	1	1	1	9	1	38	3	0
Nevers, Tom, Chat.	1	0	1.000	3.60	1	0	0	0	1	0	5	3	20	2	2	1	0	0	0	3	0	3	0	0
Noyce, Dave, W.T.*	3	2	.600	2.72	53	0	0	0	12	0	76	64	321	25	23	7	7	4	6	36	1	55	3	1
Orloski, Joe, Ten.	6	5	.545	5.25	54	0	0	0	28	4	60	70	279	41	35	4	4	2	2	29	0	45	5	0
Oxspring, Chris, Mob.	0	0	.000	1.26	6	1	0	0	0	0	14.1	13	62	3	2	0	1	0	0	8	0	21	1	0
Ozias, Todd, Chat.	1	0	1.000	4.12	15	0	0	0	9	1	19.2	23	82	9	9	0	0	1	0	7	0	20	0	0
Ozuna, Francisco, Ten.*	2	2	.500	4.63	44	0	0	0	17	0	70	73	298	42	36	12	6	5	1	19	2	35	1	0
Palma, Rick, W.T.*	1	2	.333	1.71	43	0	0	0	9	0	58	52	233	14	11	2	2	1	0	17	0	56	1	0
Parker, Matt, Hun.	4	4	.500	3.84	40	3	0	0	9	2	77.1	73	338	39	33	5	4	2	4	34	1	80	4	0
Parris, Steve, Ten.	0	0	.000	3.00	1	1	0	0	0	0	6	7	28	2	2	0	0	0	0	2	0	5	0	0
Parrish, Wade, Birm.*	4	4	.500	3.38	13	13	0	0	0	0	72	75	313	31	27	2	3	8	2	31	1	43	2	0
Payne, Jerrod, Ten.	2	0	1.000	3.95	21	0	0	0	8	0	27.1	21	113	16	12	1	0	0	12	0	12	4	0
Peavy, Jake, Mob.	4	5	.444	2.80	14	14	0	0	0	0	80.1	65	335	26	25	4	3	1	5	30	0	89	1	1
Pember, David, Hun.	10	6	.625	3.17	27	27	2	0	0	0	156	157	669	69	55	13	9	2	6	53	1	111	13	1
Penney, Mike, Hun.	7	4	.636	2.34	37	0	0	0	20	3	57.2	53	239	15	15	4	4	3	1	22	1	37	3	0
Perez, Oliver, Mob.*	1	0	1.000	1.17	4	4	0	0	0	0	23	11	93	3	3	1	2	0	0	16	0	34	4	0
Pratt, Andy, Gre.*	4	9	.308	4.26	20	18	1	1	0	0	93	92	404	54	44	5	4	3	2	44	0	67	6	0
Prior, Mark, W.T.	4	1	.800	2.60	6	6	0	0	0	0	34.2	26	145	16	10	0	2	0	2	10	0	55	3	1
Proctor, Scott, Jack.	7	9	.438	3.51	26	25	0	0	0	0	133.1	111	592	63	52	10	6	5	7	85	1	131	9	1
Purvis, Rob, Birm.	1	1	.500	5.40	9	0	0	0	1	0	16.2	17	81	13	10	0	0	0	1	15	0	9	1	0
Ramirez, Horacio, Gre.*	9	5	.643	3.03	16	16	0	0	0	0	92	85	376	41	31	5	1	0	7	32	0	64	3	1
Reimers, Cameron, Ten.	3	6	.333	5.59	13	11	1	0	0	0	67.2	99	322	48	42	9	3	4	13	19	0	32	1	1
Riedling, John, Chat.	1	1	.500	11.05	6	0	0	0	0	0	7.1	13	42	11	9	0	1	2	0	5	2	5	0	0
Rijo, Fernando, Jack.	8	8	.500	3.74	27	27	1	1	0	0	142	130	616	62	59	13	4	3	8	72	2	106	12	1
Roberts, Rick, Jack.*	8	2	.800	3.18	51	0	0	0	17	2	87.2	66	365	34	31	5	6	0	1	42	5	85	7	0
Rodriguez, Ricardo, Jack.	5	4	.556	1.99	11	11	2	0	0	0	68	56	268	21	15	4	2	1	2	13	0	44	5	0
Rojas, Chris, Mob.	6	8	.429	5.19	25	24	0	0	1	0	126.2	125	569	81	73	10	8	3	12	74	0	80	10	0
Rojas, Jose, Jack.	3	4	.429	4.83	10	10	0	0	0	0	54	56	236	29	29	8	1	2	3	30	1	40	4	0
Roney, Matt, Car.	3	6	.333	6.11	13	13	0	0	0	0	70.2	73	312	52	48	6	1	1	2	33	0	61	2	1
Ruhl, Nathan, Orl.-Chat.	1	5	.167	4.88	44	0	0	0	39	19	48	47	230	32	26	4	1	3	1	34	3	40	11	0
Rust, Evan, Orl.	1	3	.250	3.70	26	0	0	0	21	8	24.1	30	117	10	10	0	0	0	1	14	2	25	2	0
Sanders, Dave, Birm.*	3	1	.750	1.84	47	0	0	0	10	0	63.2	56	272	17	13	3	1	1	3	28	7	61	4	0
Santos, Alex, Orl.	1	4	.200	8.24	7	5	0	0	1	0	31.2	49	155	30	29	4	1	3	3	9	0	14	1	1
Seay, Bobby, Orl.*	2	0	1.000	3.58	15	3	0	0	2	0	35.2	31	150	16	13	2	0	1	3	15	0	24	2	0
Severino, Ronni, Orl.*	0	4	.000	5.09	25	0	0	0	10	0	35.1	40	162	22	20	1	4	1	0	23	4	44	6	0
Shibilo, Andy, Mob.	4	3	.571	4.89	29	0	0	0	4	0	42.1	49	188	26	23	2	5	2	2	16	2	42	2	0
Shiyuk, Todd, Mob.*	0	0	.000	5.65	10	0	0	0	2	0	14.1	18	68	10	9	0	0	1	7	0	15	2	1
Simon, Ben, Jack.	3	0	1.000	0.83	15	6	1	0	3	0	43.1	31	180	7	4	1	1	0	2	18	2	31	0	0
Smith, Cam, Chat.	0	0	.000	27.00	6	0	0	0	1	0	4.1	5	35	14	13	0	1	0	4	13	0	5	1	0
Smith, Hans, Orl.*	2	4	.333	4.14	46	0	0	0	17	0	54.1	54	249	29	25	2	4	5	4	28	4	45	7	0
Smith, Matthew, Birm.	1	0	1.000	1.74	8	0	0	0	6	1	10.1	2	45	2	2	0	0	3	9	1	12	0	0
Smyth, Steve, W.T.*	4	4	.500	3.58	11	11	0	0	0	0	73	62	304	34	29	7	6	2	6	18	0	74	0	0
Snare, Ryan, Chat.*	0	0	.000	3.00	5	0	0	0	4	0	6	5	22	3	2	1	0	0	0	3	0	4	0	0
Sobkowiak, Scott, Gre.	1	2	.333	4.50	12	1	0	0	4	0	28	22	128	14	14	2	1	0	2	23	0	32	1	0
Sollecito, Gabe, W.T.	1	2	.333	3.60	30	0	0	0	19	6	30	28	127	15	12	2	2	1	2	5	1	24	0	0
Sosa, Jorge, Orl.	0	0	.000	0.00	2	2	0	0	0	0	7	4	25	2	0	1	0	0	0	1	0	3	0	0
Spille, Ryan, Ten.*	7	12	.368	5.19	27	25	2	1	2	0	159.2	188	712	105	92	22	7	6	7	53	1	97	3	0
Stewart, Josh, Birm.*	11	7	.611	3.53	26	26	1	1	0	0	150.1	145	630	65	59	11	2	2	2	56	1	92	7	0
Stewart, Paul, Hun.	12	9	.571	3.28	27	27	2	1	0	0	161.2	147	661	69	59	13	4	3	13	42	0	124	7	1
Stults, Eric, Jack.*	0	0	.000	0.00	1	0	0	0	0	0	1	0	3	0	0	0	0	0	0	0	0	0	0	0
Sylvester, Billy, Gre.	2	3	.400	3.47	51	0	0	0	44	25	49.1	31	213	20	19	6	4	2	4	32	1	48	3	0
Taglienti, Jeff, Chat.	2	0	1.000	3.52	24	0	0	0	8	0	30.2	37	133	14	12	1	0	0	2	18	0	0	0	0
Takeoka, Kazuhiro, Gre.	1	3	.250	5.82	21	0	0	0	9	4	34	33	156	25	22	1	2	2	19	3	26	1	0
Tankersley, Dennis, Mob.	3	3	.500	3.02	10	10	0	0	0	0	50.2	47	218	20	17	1	2	1	2	20	1	56	0	1
Thompson, Doug, Car.	6	2	.750	4.09	50	0	0	0	22	6	70.1	62	300	39	32	5	4	3	4	25	1	68	4	0
Thompson, Mark, Chat.	0	3	.000	1.42	3	3	0	0	0	0	19	21	77	6	3	0	0	0	3	0	11	0	0
Thompson, Mike, Mob.	1	0	1.000	3.60	1	1	0	0	0	0	5	5	19	2	2	1	0	0	0	0	0	0	0	0

Pitcher, Team	W	L	Pct.	ERA	G	GS	CG	ShO	GF	Sv.	IP	H	TBF	R	ER	HR	SH	SF	HB	BB	IBB	SO	WP	Bk.
Thompson, Travis, Chat.	0	7	.000	4.99	15	8	0	0	1	0	48.2	67	222	34	27	4	3	3	3	18	4	43	1	0
Totten, Heath, Jack.	3	3	.500	2.94	9	9	0	0	0	0	49	45	197	16	16	2	2	0	1	14	1	30	1	0
Trujillo, J.J., Mob.	3	0	1.000	0.66	31	0	0	0	26	20	41	25	159	3	3	1	1	0	3	12	0	49	1	0
Ulacia, Dennis, Birm.*	6	14	.300	4.82	28	25	0	0	3	1	145.2	173	651	95	78	15	5	8	8	51	4	88	4	0
Urdaneta, Lino, Jack.	0	0	.000	0.00	1	0	0	0	1	0	1	3	6	0	0	0	0	0	0	1	0	1	0	0
Valentine, Joe, Birm.	4	1	.800	1.97	55	0	0	0	48	36	59.1	36	245	16	13	1	3	3	1	30	3	63	6	0
Vance, Cory, Car.*	10	8	.556	3.77	25	25	1	0	0	0	150.1	142	646	73	63	8	9	5	2	76	1	114	5	1
Veronie, Shanin, Gre.	2	2	.500	3.93	29	0	0	0	8	0	52.2	54	231	27	23	5	2	0	0	22	3	32	6	0
Waechter, Doug, Orl.	1	3	.250	9.00	4	4	1	0	0	0	18	27	93	20	18	4	0	0	0	13	0	18	3	1
Wagner, Denny, Birm.	0	1	.000	12.75	9	0	0	0	2	1	12	19	61	17	17	2	1	0	3	4	2	4	0	1
Watkins, Steve, Mob.	4	8	.333	3.78	37	15	1	0	5	0	116.2	124	505	65	49	8	4	6	3	49	3	88	2	1
Webb, John, W.T.	4	5	.444	4.52	11	11	0	0	0	0	61.2	52	255	33	31	5	1	2	5	22	0	45	3	1
Wellemeyer, Todd, W.T.	3	3	.500	4.70	8	8	1	1	0	0	46	33	187	25	24	2	0	4	3	18	0	37	2	0
Wells, Mark, Chat.	0	0	.000	6.00	2	0	0	0	2	0	3	4	14	3	2	0	0	0	0	1	0	1	0	0
West, Brian, Birm.	9	11	.450	4.34	27	26	0	0	0	0	149.1	129	638	91	72	9	3	9	9	71	0	91	8	2
White, Matt, Orl.	1	2	.333	5.56	7	7	0	0	0	0	34	33	153	22	21	7	1	1	1	19	0	20	2	0
Wiggins, Scott, Ten.*	0	1	.000	0.93	16	0	0	0	6	1	19.1	18	82	3	2	0	2	2	1	5	1	19	0	0
Winkelsas, Joe, Gre.	0	0	.000	0.00	2	0	0	0	2	2	2	1	9	0	0	0	0	1	0	1	0	0	0	0
Wright, Chris, Orl.	1	3	.250	5.11	19	0	0	0	8	0	37	45	180	26	21	3	3	2	4	18	4	15	4	2
Wrigley, Jase, Car.	2	2	.500	2.18	44	0	0	0	28	10	57.2	48	240	15	14	1	10	2	2	28	6	31	4	0
Young, Colin, Car.*	0	1	.000	1.98	15	0	0	0	5	0	13.2	14	66	5	3	0	1	1	1	10	2	14	1	0
Young, Jason, Car.	7	4	.636	2.64	14	14	1	1	0	0	88.2	71	359	30	26	1	1	1	3	30	0	76	0	2
Zoccolillo, Peter, Hun.	0	1	.000	27.00	1	0	0	0	1	0	1	2	6	3	3	1	1	0	1	0	0	1	0	0

PITCHERS WITH TWO OR MORE TEAMS

Pitcher, Team	W	L	Pct.	ERA	G	GS	CG	ShO	GF	Sv.	IP	H	TBF	R	ER	HR	SH	SF	HB	BB	IBB	SO	WP	Bk.
Ruhl, Nathan, Orl.	1	4	.200	5.15	40	0	0	0	37	19	43.2	43	209	30	25	4	1	3	1	31	1	38	11	0
Ruhl, Nathan, Chat.	0	1	.000	2.08	4	0	0	0	2	0	4.1	4	21	2	1	0	0	0	3	2	2	0	0

COMBINATION SHUTOUTS: **Birmingham (10)**—Diaz-West-Sanders-Munoz-Majewski-M. Smith, Eason-Munoz, Lantigua-Munoz-Valentine, Malone-Majewski, Parrish-Eason, Parrish-Wagner-Valentine, J. Stewart-Eason, J. Stewart-Munoz-Eason-Valentine, Ulacia-Eason, Ulacia-Eason-Meyer. **Carolina (4)**—J. Young-D. Thompson 2, Roney-D. Thompson-Wrigley, J. Young-Crowder-Cameron. **Chattanooga (4)**—Gil-DeHart, Gooch-Gray, Hall-Ruhl-Cordova, Moseley-Cordova. **Greenville (6)**—Belisle-Collazo, Ennis-Collazo-Hernandez, Ennis-Sylvester, Evert-Takeoka, Lewis-Veronie-Emiliano-Sylvester, Ramirez-Hernandez-Collazo. **Huntsville (13)**—Gandarillas-L. Martinez-Penney, J. Garcia-M. Childers, J. Garcia-D. Lee, Hendrickson-D. Lee, Lee-Penney, Hendrickson-Parker-M. Childers, D. Lee-Penney-M. Childers, L. Martinez-Dent-M. Childers, Parker-Krawczyk-M. Childers, Pember-Penney-Giron, P. Stewart-Fox-Krawczyk, P. Stewart-High-Penney, P. Stewart-L. Martinez-High, P. Stewart-Parker. **Jacksonville (12)**—Caraccioli-House-Colyer, Leek-Gonzalez-Colyer, Lugo-G. Bauer, Proctor-Gulin, Proctor-Montero-Roberts, Proctor-Roberts-Gonzalez-Montero, Rijo-Gonzalez, Rijo-Gulin-Dunning-McCrotty, Rodriguez-Gulin, Rodriguez-Gulin-Colyer, Rodriguez-McCrotty-Colyer, J. Rojas-Harrell-Colyer. **Mobile (13)**—Howard-Hampton-Bartosh 2, B. Baker-Gaal, B. Baker-Gaal-Bartosh, Bynum-Bartosh, Cyr-Hampton-Bartosh-Trujillo, Harvey-Bartosh, Harvey-Giese-Gaal-Bartosh, Oxspring-Giese-Gaal, Perez-Shibilo-Bartosh-Trujillo, Perez-Shibilo-Trujillo, Tankersley-Watkins-Hampton-Bartosh, Watkins-Hampton-Bartosh-Gaal. **Orlando (13)**—Agosto-Ruhl, Brazelton-Frendling-Minix-Ruhl, Fortunato-H. Smith-Rust, Frendling-H. Smith-Backe, Malaska-H. Smith, McClung-Backe. **Tennessee (5)**—Gassner-Hamann, Loaiza-Chulk, Markwell-Castellanos, Markwell-Chacin, Reimers-Gracesqui-Castellanos. **West Tenn (4)**—Bruback-Hazlett-Jongejan-Hooten, Bruback-Jongejan-Hooten, Christensen-Palma-Jongejan-Beltran, Prior-Palma.

NO-HIT GAME: G. Garcia, Orlando, defeated Tennessee, 2-0, May 22.

2002 FIELDING

TEAM

Team	G	PO	A	E	TC	DP	TP	PB	Pct.
Jacksonville	139	3707	1452	115	5274	111	1	16	.978
Mobile	139	3692	1431	142	5265	104	2	11	.973
Greenville	134	3565	1447	139	5151	102	0	24	.973
West Tenn	140	3734	1410	144	5288	105	0	13	.973
Huntsville	139	3689	1560	157	5406	137	1	12	.971
Birmingham	140	3670	1482	156	5308	112	0	31	.971
Chattanooga	140	3675	1466	156	5297	140	0	9	.971
Tennessee	140	3711	1665	172	5548	145	0	19	.969
Orlando	137	3575	1420	173	5168	105	0	40	.967
Carolina	136	3652	1683	209	5544	143	0	15	.962

INDIVIDUAL

FIRST BASEMEN

NOTE: All caps denotes fielding-percentage leader based on 70 games for catchers, 93 for all other non-pitchers and 112 innings for pitchers. *Throws lefthanded.

Player, Team	Pct.	G	PO	A	E	TC	DP
Acevas, Jon, Birm.	.987	12	74	3	1	78	9
Alfonzo, Eliezer, Hun.	1.000	1	13	0	0	13	2
Alvarado, Joel, Hun.	1.000	1	2	0	0	2	0
Amrhein, Mike, W.T.	1.000	3	21	1	0	22	3
Atkins, Garrett, Car.	.985	7	62	2	1	65	7
Balfe, Ryan, W.T.	1.000	1	1	0	0	1	0
Battersby, Eric, Birm.*	.993	54	422	22	3	447	35
Beinbrink, Andy, Orl.	.800	2	4	0	1	5	1
Bledsoe, Hunter, Jack.	.999	79	669	72	1	742	50
Bozied, Tagg, Mob.	.988	57	456	27	6	489	43
Brock, Tarrik, Jack.*	.987	39	282	15	4	301	23
Burford, Kevin, Car.*	.984	72	728	57	13	798	68
Burkhart, Lance, Hun.	1.000	7	47	10	0	57	7
Chiaffredo, Paul, Ten.	1.000	6	47	4	0	51	2

Player, Team	Pct.	G	PO	A	E	TC	DP
Deardorff, Jeff, Hun.	.997	36	280	19	1	300	38
Deschaine, Jim, Ten.	.000	1	0	0	0	0	0
Diaz, Matt, Orl.	1.000	1	1	0	0	1	0
Diaz, Victor, Jack.	.991	28	220	12	2	234	25
Dzurilla, Mike, W.T.	1.000	3	22	1	0	23	1
Eason, Clay, Birm.	.000	1	0	0	0	0	0
Edwards, Mike, Chat.	1.000	46	353	15	0	368	35
Evans, Lee, Birm.	1.000	4	40	0	0	40	4
Fagan, Shawn, Hun.	.982	49	405	29	8	442	41
Fernandez, Alex, Mob.*	1.000	1	9	1	0	10	0
Fiore, Curtis, Gre.	.972	12	65	4	2	71	10
Foster, Brian, Hun.	1.000	1	10	0	0	10	0
Gibralter, Dave, W.T.	.965	8	52	3	2	57	2
Gripp, Ryan, W.T.	.942	9	59	6	4	69	10
Grummitt, Dan, Orl.	.984	76	637	48	11	696	57
Haas, Chris, Gre.	1.000	14	85	4	0	89	9
Hankins, Ryan, Birm.	.988	66	527	34	7	568	39
Hart, Corey, Hun.	.980	5	48	2	1	51	3
Hernandez, Alex, Chat.*	.991	25	210	20	2	232	23
Jacobsen, Bucky, Hun.	.988	46	381	27	5	413	34
Jones, Ryan, Mob.	.994	41	316	28	2	346	25
Kaup, Nathan, Orl.	.969	4	31	0	1	32	4
Keck, Brian, Car.	.993	17	138	13	1	152	9
KELTON, Dave, W.T.	.990	121	965	72	10	1047	78
King, Cesar, Chat.	1.000	4	17	1	0	18	2
LaForest, Pete, Orl.	1.000	1	6	1	0	7	1
LaRoche, Adam, Gre.*	.998	45	408	32	1	441	33
Lebron, Francisco, Birm.	.962	4	22	3	1	26	2
Logan, Matt, Ten.	.985	100	865	64	14	943	89
Luuloa, Keith, Hun.	1.000	6	28	2	0	30	2
Marconi, Alex, Orl.	1.000	1	8	1	0	9	0
Mathis, Jared, Hun.	.968	13	28	2	1	31	4
Mitchell, Derek, Chat.	.889	3	14	2	2	18	2
Moore, Frank, Orl.	1.000	2	17	1	0	18	4
Nevers, Tom, Chat.	.985	53	386	20	6	412	45
Pressley, Josh, Orl.	.978	54	455	29	11	495	28

Player, Team	Pct.	G	PO	A	E	TC	DP
Reyes, Rene, Car.	.985	41	372	30	6	408	40
Risinger, Ben, Mob.	1.000	1	9	0	0	9	1
Rose, Pete, Chat.	1.000	7	63	2	0	65	5
Sandoval, Danny, Birm.	1.000	4	29	6	0	35	3
Sapp, Damian, Chat.	.991	14	105	8	1	114	13
Scheschuk, John, Mob.*	.991	42	314	22	3	339	20
Scott, Bill, Hun.	.984	43	355	21	6	382	34
Taylor, Seth, Car.	1.000	9	66	4	0	70	4
Terveen, Bryce, Gre.	1.000	1	1	0	0	1	1
Umbria, Jose, Ten.	1.000	1	1	0	0	1	0
Zapp, A.J., Gre.	.982	77	611	51	12	674	41
Zoccolillo, Peter, Hun.	1.000	1	6	0	0	6	1
Zywica, Mike, Chat.	.984	9	58	5	1	64	7

TRIPLE PLAYS: Bozied, Brock, Deardorff, Scheschuk.

SECOND BASEMEN

Player, Team	Pct.	G	PO	A	E	TC	DP
Abreu, Dennis, W.T.	.977	36	76	91	4	171	20
Alvarez, Jimmy, Ten.	.968	112	243	333	19	595	76
Beattie, Andrew, Chat.	.950	6	10	9	1	20	3
Beinbrink, Andy, Orl.	.971	58	106	159	8	273	36
Bravo, Danny, Birm.	1.000	5	8	15	0	23	5
Cameron, Troy, Car.	.972	25	56	83	4	143	17
Cantu, Jorge, Orl.	.846	2	7	4	2	13	2
Caruso, Mike, Chat.	.909	2	5	5	1	11	1
Castro, Bernabel, Mob.	.980	105	250	287	11	548	56
Colina, Javier, Car.	.989	33	60	116	2	178	29
COLLINS, Mike, Jack.	.988	95	207	277	6	490	56
Darula, Bobby, Chat.	.000	1	0	0	0	0	0
Dawkins, Gookie, Chat.	.947	14	39	32	4	75	10
De Renne, Keoni, Gre.	.960	59	109	131	10	250	27
Deschaine, Jim, Ten.	.000	1	0	0	0	0	0
Detienne, Dave, Jack.	1.000	1	2	5	0	7	2
Diaz, Victor, Jack.	1.000	2	5	4	0	9	1
Espino, Damaso, Chat.	.941	3	7	9	1	17	3
Fiore, Curtis, Gre.	.875	2	2	5	1	8	0
Green, Nick, Gre.	.964	76	145	199	13	357	48
Harris, Brendan, W.T.	1.000	6	9	14	0	23	2
Iorg, Isaac, Ten.	.962	12	23	27	2	52	5
Johnson, Russ, Orl.	1.000	2	7	2	0	9	1
Lambert, Casey, Car.	1.000	1	0	6	0	6	0
Lopez, Mickey, W.T.	.889	2	3	5	1	9	2
Luuloa, Keith, Hun.	.938	15	48	43	6	97	15
Mathis, Jared, Hun.	.968	14	28	33	2	63	8
McNamara, Rusty, Gre.	.000	1	0	0	0	0	0
Miles, Aaron, Birm.	.955	129	243	314	26	583	56
Mitchell, Derek, Chat.	.973	20	32	41	2	75	11
Moore, Frank, Orl.	.929	45	85	112	15	212	18
Nevers, Tom, Chat.	.966	20	40	46	3	89	12
Olmedo, Rainer, Chat.	.965	21	50	59	4	113	18
Orr, Pete, Gre.	1.000	4	7	11	0	18	2
Owens, Ryan, Car.	.921	15	26	44	6	76	5
Pena, Elvis, Hun.	.974	82	173	209	10	392	48
Powers, John, W.T.	.982	49	91	123	4	218	24
Rich, Dominic, Ten.	.920	19	41	51	8	100	10
Riggs, Eric, Jack.	.955	7	9	12	1	22	1
Risinger, Ben, Mob.	.969	9	14	17	1	32	5
Sanchez, Tino, Car.	.968	4	15	15	1	31	5
Sandoval, Danny, Birm.	.978	11	21	23	1	45	6
Santana, Pedro, Chat.	.974	67	142	163	8	313	41
Scales, Bobby, Mob.	.969	29	54	72	4	130	10
Scarborough, Steve, Hun.	.904	15	31	44	8	83	11
Schrager, Tony, W.T.	.962	59	127	129	10	266	27
Shaffer, Josh, Birm.	.000	1	0	0	4	4	0
Solano, Danny, Ten.	.941	5	6	10	1	17	1
Soler, Ramon, Orl.	.967	34	82	94	6	182	15
Taylor, Seth, Car.	.968	26	49	72	4	125	18
Theodorou, Nick, Jack.	.961	45	54	94	6	154	18
Warren, Chris, Car.	.946	38	65	128	11	204	25
Weekly, Chris, W.T.	1.000	2	3	3	0	6	1
West, Todd, Hun.	.979	20	44	49	2	95	18

TRIPLE PLAYS: Castro, Scales.

THIRD BASEMEN

Player, Team	Pct.	G	PO	A	E	TC	DP
Abreu, Dennis, W.T.	.930	35	23	70	7	100	8
Alvarez, Gabe, Hun.	.806	27	13	45	14	72	6
Atkins, Garrett, Car.	.945	119	70	238	18	326	24
Balfe, Ryan, W.T.	.000	1	0	0	0	0	0
Beinbrink, Andy, Orl.	.943	59	39	111	9	159	3
Bozied, Tagg, Mob.	1.000	1	3	2	0	5	0

Player, Team	Pct.	G	PO	A	E	TC	DP
Bravo, Danny, Birm.	.946	34	19	68	5	92	2
Burkhart, Lance, Hun.	1.000	1	1	1	0	2	0
Cantu, Jorge, Orl.	.901	33	18	64	9	91	4
Cash, Kevin, Ten.	.833	1	4	1	1	6	0
Castro, Ramon, Gre.	.962	13	3	22	1	26	1
Collins, Mike, Jack.	1.000	5	2	3	0	5	1
Deardorff, Jeff, Hun.	.909	17	12	28	4	44	5
Deschaine, Jim, Ten.	.908	77	47	171	22	240	10
Diaz, Victor, Jack.	.947	9	5	13	1	19	2
Edwards, Mike, Chat.	.889	18	10	38	6	54	6
Evans, Lee, Birm.	.923	8	6	6	1	13	1
Fagan, Shawn, Ten.	.940	47	28	112	9	149	16
Fiore, Curtis, Gre.	.967	14	5	24	1	30	2
Freeman, Ashley, Car.	.833	2	1	4	1	6	0
Gripp, Ryan, W.T.	.944	87	52	151	12	215	12
Haas, Chris, Gre.	.964	9	8	19	1	28	2
Hankins, Ryan, Birm.	.926	13	4	21	2	27	0
Harris, Brendan, W.T.	1.000	7	3	11	0	14	0
Hart, Corey, Hun.	.836	21	9	37	9	55	5
Hopper, Shane, Mob.	.844	11	7	20	5	32	1
Iorg, Isaac, Ten.	.860	14	7	30	6	43	3
Johnson, Russ, Orl.	.818	5	2	7	2	11	1
Kaup, Nathan, Orl.	.905	40	15	71	9	95	4
Kelton, Dave, W.T.	.769	6	5	5	3	13	0
KING, Brennan, Jack.	.945	124	77	216	17	310	18
Leon, Donny, Chat.	.910	103	74	189	26	289	18
Logan, Matt, Ten.	1.000	2	0	1	0	1	0
Lopez, Rafael, Jack.	1.000	3	2	9	0	11	1
Lorenzana, Luis, Mob.	1.000	19	6	25	0	31	0
Luuloa, Keith, Hun.	.916	47	39	102	13	154	13
Marconi, Alex, Orl.	1.000	4	1	6	0	7	1
Mathis, Jared, Hun.	.988	35	24	60	1	85	2
McNamara, Rusty, Gre.	.927	104	84	220	24	328	12
Miles, Aaron, Birm.	1.000	1	1	1	0	2	0
Mitchell, Derek, Chat.	.926	9	9	16	2	27	3
Moore, Frank, Orl.	.857	4	4	8	2	14	0
Nevers, Tom, Chat.	.953	15	15	26	2	43	3
Orr, Pete, Gre.	1.000	2	1	1	0	2	0
Owens, Ryan, Car.	1.000	11	3	13	0	16	2
Pena, Elvis, Hun.	1.000	1	0	2	0	2	0
Risinger, Ben, Mob.	.940	97	71	148	14	233	17
Rose, Pete, Chat.	1.000	2	1	0	0	3	1
Sanchez, Tino, Car.	.500	1	0	1	1	2	0
Sandoval, Danny, Birm.	.885	35	24	53	10	87	4
Saunders, Chris, Birm.	.939	11	6	25	2	33	3
Scales, Bobby, Mob.	.841	19	5	32	7	44	4
Scarborough, Steve, Hun.	.889	4	3	5	1	9	1
Schrager, Tony, W.T.	.882	5	1	14	2	17	0
Shaffer, Josh, Birm.	.919	62	35	102	12	149	10
Solano, Danny, Ten.	.970	16	7	25	1	33	4
Taylor, Seth, Car.	.929	4	2	11	1	14	1
Theodorou, Nick, Jack.	1.000	4	1	7	0	8	1
Warren, Chris, Car.	.333	1	0	1	2	3	0
Weekly, Chris, W.T.	.938	8	6	9	1	16	1

SHORTSTOPS

Player, Team	Pct.	G	PO	A	E	TC	DP
Abreu, Dennis, W.T.	.938	35	42	79	8	129	15
Barmes, Clint, Car.	.940	102	162	359	33	554	76
Beinbrink, Andy, Orl.	1.000	4	8	12	0	20	1
Bravo, Danny, Birm.	.889	3	5	3	1	9	1
Brewer, Jace, Orl.	.961	37	52	94	6	152	26
Cantu, Jorge, Orl.	.939	95	165	293	30	488	53
Castro, Ramon, Gre.	.974	44	66	125	5	196	21
Collins, Mike, Jack.	.972	20	21	49	2	72	5
Dawkins, Gookie, Chat.	.982	26	39	70	2	111	17
Dellaero, Jason, Birm.	.972	55	105	174	8	287	35
De Renne, Keoni, Gre.	.917	12	9	24	3	36	4
Deschaine, Jim, Ten.	.936	23	45	72	8	125	15
Detienne, Dave, Jack.	1.000	1	1	2	0	3	2
Espino, Damaso, Chat.	1.000	1	0	3	0	3	0
Frese, Nate, W.T.	.973	65	89	162	7	258	35
Green, Nick, Gre.	.889	3	2	6	1	9	2
Gutierrez, Vic, Gre.	.917	9	9	24	3	36	2
Hardy, J.J., Hun.	.948	37	54	127	10	191	30
Lambert, Casey, Car.	1.000	1	1	7	0	8	1
Lopez, Mickey, W.T.	.849	12	21	24	8	53	7
Lorenzana, Luis, Mob.	.945	76	103	221	19	343	42
Luuloa, Keith, Hun.	1.000	16	26	45	0	71	10
Mendez, Donaldo, Mob.	.952	56	67	173	12	252	26
Mitchell, Derek, Chat.	.971	7	13	21	1	35	6
Nevers, Tom, Chat.	1.000	1	0	4	0	4	1

Player, Team	Pct.	G	PO	A	E	TC	DP
OLMEDO, Rainer, Chat.	.960	107	195	305	21	521	65
Orr, Pete, Gre.	.974	79	88	251	9	348	43
Owens, Ryan, Car.	.926	8	10	15	2	27	3
Pena, Elvis, Hun.	.818	2	2	7	2	11	1
Riggs, Eric, Jack.	.958	121	193	338	23	554	67
Risinger, Ben, Mob.	.952	11	13	27	2	42	4
Rouse, Michael, Ten.	.944	66	90	197	17	304	40
Sandoval, Danny, Birm.	.967	82	130	223	12	365	44
Scarborough, Steve, Hun.	.936	70	107	214	22	343	34
Schrager, Tony, W.T.	.933	43	60	93	11	164	15
Shaffer, Josh, Birm.	.828	12	15	33	10	58	3
Solano, Danny, Ten.	.972	62	103	214	9	326	43
Soler, Ramon, Orl.	.818	2	5	4	2	11	1
Taylor, Seth, Car.	.955	5	4	17	1	22	5
Tena, Hector, Car.	.889	2	2	6	1	9	1
Theodorou, Nick, Jack.	1.000	1	1	5	0	6	1
Warren, Chris, Car.	.913	22	40	75	11	126	14
West, Todd, Hun.	.961	19	23	51	3	77	10

TRIPLE PLAYS: Hardy, Lorenzana, Riggs.

OUTFIELDERS

Player, Team	Pct.	G	PO	A	E	TC	DP
Abercrombie, Reggie, Jack.	1.000	1	2	0	0	2	0
Abreu, Dennis, W.T.	1.000	4	7	0	0	7	0
Allensworth, Jermaine, Gre.	.963	74	127	2	5	134	0
Baldelli, Rocco, Orl.	.967	16	27	2	1	30	1
Balfe, Ryan, W.T.	1.000	17	13	3	0	16	0
Battersby, Eric, Birm.*	.950	9	18	1	1	20	0
Bay, Jason, Mob.	1.000	22	34	1	0	35	0
Beattie, Andrew, Chat.	.974	38	70	4	2	76	0
Benjamin, Al, Mob.	1.000	10	11	1	0	12	0
Bikowski, Scott, Birm.*	.977	119	235	15	6	256	1
Blakely, Darren, Mob.	.981	117	298	9	6	313	2
Bravo, Danny, Birm.	1.000	4	2	0	0	2	0
Brock, Tarrik, Jack.*	.989	41	81	5	1	87	2
Budzinski, Mark, W.T.*	.987	109	234	2	3	239	0
Burkhart, Lance, Hun.	.000	2	0	0	0	0	0
Burrows, Angelo, Gre.	.960	14	23	1	1	25	0
Caruso, Mike, Chat.	.833	1	4	1	1	6	1
Crosby, Bubba, Jack.*	1.000	34	68	2	0	70	1
Curry, Mike, Chat.	1.000	22	45	2	0	47	1
Darula, Bobby, Chat.	.977	85	126	2	3	131	0
Deardorff, Jeff, Hun.	.990	66	92	3	1	96	0
Denorfia, Christopher, Chat.	1.000	3	4	1	0	5	0
Deschaine, Jim, Ten.	1.000	3	3	0	0	3	0
Diaz, Alejandro, Chat.	.961	40	93	5	4	102	0
Diaz, Matt, Orl.	.987	113	212	11	3	226	0
Donovan, Todd, Mob.	.973	31	32	4	1	37	0
Durham, Chad, Birm.	.978	116	262	10	6	278	1
Edwards, Mike, Chat.	.965	56	103	6	4	113	0
Fagan, Shawn, Ten.	.800	3	4	0	1	5	0
Faison, Vince, Mob.	.968	98	168	11	6	185	0
Feliciano, Jesus, Jack.*	.991	61	106	7	1	114	0
Fernandez, Alex, Birm.-Mob.*	.979	99	169	14	4	187	2
Fiore, Curtis, Gre.	.966	58	81	3	3	87	2
Fleming, Ryan, Ten.*	.982	59	106	4	2	112	1
Fox, Jacob, Hun.	.989	38	82	4	1	87	1
Freeman, Choo, Car.	.977	117	244	9	6	259	3
German, Amado, Orl.	.975	104	264	6	7	277	2
Gibralter, Dave, W.T.	.952	27	37	3	2	42	0
Gross, Gabe, Ten.	.991	102	205	14	2	221	0
Grummitt, Dan, Orl.	.000	1	0	0	0	0	0
Guerrero, Cristian, Hun.	.970	102	190	6	6	202	2
Hall, Noah, Chat.	.957	11	21	1	1	23	0
Haltiwanger, Garrick, Ten.*	.943	19	33	0	2	35	0
Hamilton, Jon, W.T.*	.992	60	108	11	1	120	0
Hernandez, Alex, Chat.*	.974	50	108	6	3	117	1
Holliday, Matt, Car.	.961	117	166	6	7	179	0
Hopper, Shane, Mob.	1.000	3	3	0	0	3	0
Ingram, Darron, Birm.	1.000	48	91	1	0	92	0
Jackson, Nic, W.T.	.967	31	57	1	2	60	0
Jacobsen, Bucky, Hun.	.800	3	3	1	1	5	0
James, Kenny, Ten.	1.000	11	31	0	0	31	0
Johnson, Ben, Mob.	.965	124	244	6	9	259	2
Johnson, Gary, W.T.	.989	107	248	11	3	262	2
Johnson, Russ, Orl.	.833	2	5	0	1	6	0
Johnstone, Ben, W.T.	1.000	3	5	0	0	5	0
Jones, Damien, Gre.*	.960	57	92	4	4	100	1
Jones, Ryan, Mob.	1.000	12	13	1	0	14	0
Kaup, Nathan, Orl.	1.000	29	38	1	0	39	0
Kearns, Austin, Chat.	1.000	12	15	2	0	17	1

Player, Team	Pct.	G	PO	A	E	TC	DP
Keck, Brian, Car.	1.000	1	1	0	0	1	0
Kelton, Dave, W.T.	.000	1	0	0	0	0	0
Knox, Ryan, Hun.	1.000	61	103	6	0	109	1
Krynzel, Dave, Hun.*	.971	30	67	1	2	70	0
Langaigne, Selwyn, Ten.*	1.000	5	4	0	0	4	0
Langerhans, Ryan, Gre.*	.992	109	247	9	2	258	2
Lombard, George, Gre.	1.000	8	19	1	0	20	0
Lopez, Mickey, W.T.	1.000	4	6	0	0	6	0
Luuloa, Keith, Hun.	.000	1	0	0	0	0	0
Marconi, Alex, Orl.	.000	1	0	0	0	0	0
Martinez, Greg, Orl.	.981	28	51	2	1	54	0
Mathis, Jared, Hun.	.857	4	6	0	1	7	0
Matthews, Lamont, Jack.*	.977	88	156	12	4	172	1
Melian, Jackson, Hun.-W.T.	.973	110	206	12	6	224	4
Miller, David, Chat.*	1.000	3	1	0	0	1	0
Mitchell, Derek, Chat.	.000	1	0	0	0	0	0
Moore, Frank, Orl.	.950	26	34	4	2	40	1
Neuberger, Scott, Orl.	.988	117	245	11	3	259	1
Orr, Pete, Gre.	1.000	3	4	1	0	5	0
Pena, Wily Mo, Chat.	.979	100	171	14	4	189	2
Phillips, Dan, Car.	.941	77	121	7	8	136	1
Piedra, Jorge, W.T.*	.971	17	32	1	1	34	0
Piniella, Juan, Birm.	.989	53	90	3	1	94	0
Porter, Bo, Gre.	.833	2	5	0	1	6	0
Randolph, Jaisen, Hun.	.941	12	15	1	1	17	0
Reyes, Rene, Car.	.955	70	100	7	5	112	1
Risinger, Ben, Mob.	1.000	1	2	0	0	2	0
Rolls, Damian, Orl.	1.000	1	3	0	0	3	0
Ruan, Wilkin, Jack.	.979	77	182	4	4	190	2
Rushford, Jim, Hun.*	1.000	5	5	1	0	6	1
Sadler, Ray, W.T.	1.000	8	16	0	0	16	0
Sanchez, Tino, Car.	.970	41	59	5	2	66	0
Sandoval, Danny, Birm.	1.000	10	13	1	0	14	0
Santana, Pedro, Chat.	.977	21	42	1	1	44	0
Scales, Bobby, Mob.	1.000	4	1	0	0	1	0
Singleton, Justin, Ten.	1.000	24	57	4	0	61	1
Smothers, Stewart, Gre.	.964	28	50	3	2	55	1
Solano, Danny, Ten.	.500	2	1	0	1	2	0
Theodorou, Nick, Jack.	1.000	15	20	1	0	21	0
Thomas, Chuck, Gre.*	.987	70	153	3	2	158	0
THOMPSON, Rich, Ten.	.992	128	248	9	2	259	0
Victorino, Shane, Jack.	.986	120	259	14	4	277	2
West, Todd, Hun.	.000	1	0	0	0	0	0
Wise, Dewayne, Ten.*	.981	80	196	11	4	211	2
Zoccolillo, Peter, Hun.	.990	59	93	5	1	99	0
Zywica, Mike, Birm.	1.000	8	12	2	0	14	0

TRIPLE PLAYS: Blakely, Guerrero, Victorino.

OUTFIELDERS WITH TWO OR MORE TEAMS

Player, Team	Pct.	G	PO	A	E	TC	DP
Fernandez, Alex, Birm.*	.981	85	146	9	3	158	1
Fernandez, Alex, Mob.*	.966	14	23	5	1	29	1
Melian, Jackson, Hun.	.981	54	95	7	2	104	2
Melian, Jackson, W.T.	.967	56	111	5	4	120	2

CATCHERS

Player, Team	Pct.	G	PO	A	E	TC	DP	PB
Acevas, Jon, Birm.	.978	39	236	32	6	274	1	9
Alfonzo, Eliezer, Hun.	.987	62	476	62	7	545	3	4
Alvarado, Joel, Hun.	1.000	14	87	13	0	100	3	0
Amezcua, Adan, Mob.	.991	23	207	12	2	221	1	2
Amrhein, Mike, W.T.	.982	57	428	53	9	490	3	5
Bitter, Jarrod, Mob.	.964	7	47	7	2	56	0	0
Boscan, Jean, Gre.	.969	9	58	5	2	65	0	4
Burkhart, Lance, Hun.	.992	17	114	11	1	126	0	3
Cash, Kevin, Ten.	.987	42	196	31	3	230	2	7
Chiaffredo, Paul, Ten.	.984	72	386	37	7	430	5	9
Closser, J.D., Car.	.977	64	456	56	12	524	7	10
Curry, Chris, W.T.	.987	12	70	7	1	78	1	1
Dewey, Jason, Car.	.973	53	320	38	10	368	3	4
Duarte, Justin, Mob.	1.000	6	44	4	0	48	0	1
Duplissea, Bill, Jack.	1.000	5	42	2	0	44	1	2
Evans, Lee, Birm.	1.000	2	17	1	0	18	0	0
Fagan, Shawn, Ten.	1.000	1	5	2	0	7	0	0
Figga, Mike, Orl.	1.000	10	57	6	0	63	0	0
Foster, Brian, Hun.	.984	9	54	9	1	64	1	1
Haad, Yamid, Hun.-Mob.	.979	42	281	43	7	331	1	8
Hill, Koyie, Jack.	.981	117	815	81	17	913	7	11
Kellner, Ryan, Jack.	1.000	12	55	7	0	62	0	2
King, Cesar, Chat.	.946	7	27	8	2	37	1	2
KOPITZKE, Casey, W.T.	.994	73	545	68	4	617	3	7

Player, Team	Pct.	G	PO	A	E	TC	DP	PB
LaForest, Pete, Orl.	.976	79	492	45	13	550	6	26
Langill, Eric, Jack.	1.000	6	27	3	0	30	0	0
Lopez, Rafael, Jack.	.968	7	59	1	2	62	0	1
Loyd, Brian, Mob.	.987	48	357	29	5	391	3	3
Marconi, Alex, Orl.	.973	23	129	15	4	148	0	7
Martinez, Casey, Ten.	.875	1	7	0	1	8	0	0
McKnight, Lukas, W.T.	.938	2	14	1	1	16	0	0
Moon, Brian, Hun.	1.000	36	252	36	0	288	3	4
Munoz, Adan, Gre.	1.000	15	113	8	0	121	2	1
Olivo, Miguel, Birm.	.983	102	674	87	13	774	10	21
Peterson, Brian, Chat.	.985	8	52	15	1	68	1	1
Quintero, Humberto, Birm.-Mob. ..	.985	41	279	42	5	326	8	3
Reinking, Kevin, Mob.	1.000	1	9	1	0	10	0	0
Reyes, Jose, W.T.	1.000	1	10	0	0	10	0	0
Risinger, Ben, Mob.	.982	17	105	7	2	114	1	2
Sanchez, Tino, Car.	.976	24	149	17	4	170	1	1
Sapp, Damian, Chat.	.995	27	178	26	1	205	0	3
Sardinha, Dane, Chat.	.990	100	751	100	9	860	6	3
Serrano, Ray, Gre.	.993	20	143	9	1	153	1	1
Sullivan, Kevin, Car.	1.000	4	16	3	0	19	1	0
Taveras, Luis, Gre.	.975	45	320	24	9	353	1	15
Terveen, Bryce, Gre.	.992	54	337	47	3	387	4	3
Umbria, Jose, Ten.	.978	35	199	19	5	223	3	3
Wathan, Dusty, Hun.	.983	9	52	5	1	58	1	0

CATCHERS WITH TWO OR MORE TEAMS

Player, Team	Pct.	G	PO	A	E	TC	DP	PB
Haad, Yamid, Orl.	.991	25	183	29	2	214	0	7
Haad, Yamid, Mob.	.957	17	98	14	5	117	1	1
Quintero, Humberto, Birm.	1.000	4	32	0	0	32	0	1
Quintero, Humberto, Mob.	.983	37	247	42	5	294	8	2

PITCHERS

Player, Team	Pct.	G	PO	A	E	TC	DP
Abreu, Winston, W.T.	1.000	11	1	1	0	2	0
Achilles, Matt, W.T.	.966	41	8	20	1	29	0
Adams, Mike, Hun.	1.000	13	2	1	0	3	0
Agosto, Stevenson, Orl.*	1.000	7	1	5	0	6	0
Allen, Rodney, Hun.	1.000	15	3	2	0	5	0
Altman, Gene, Hun.	1.000	24	1	2	0	3	0
Alvarez, Wilson, Orl.*	1.000	2	1	0	0	1	0
Andrews, Clayton, Chat.*	1.000	4	0	1	0	1	0
Aramboles, Ricardo, Chat.	1.000	4	0	2	0	2	0
Atchley, Justin, Chat.*	.000	2	0	0	0	0	0
Averette, Robert, Car.	1.000	11	3	14	0	17	0
Backe, Brandon, Orl.	1.000	20	5	14	0	19	0
Baker, Brad, Mob.	.857	12	1	5	1	7	0
Baker, Ryan, Gre.	.000	5	0	0	0	0	0
Bartosh, Cliff, Mob.*	1.000	62	0	12	0	12	3
Battersby, Eric, Birm.*	.500	1	0	1	1	2	1
Bauer, Greg, Jack.	.938	38	5	10	1	16	0
Bauer, Peter, Ten.	1.000	28	13	24	0	37	7
Bausher, Andy, Mob.*	.875	34	0	7	1	8	0
Belisle, Matt, Gre.	.880	26	9	13	3	25	1
Beltran, Frank, W.T.	1.000	39	2	8	0	10	1
Bohannan, Brad, Birm.	1.000	8	1	1	0	2	0
Bong, Jung, Gre.*	.952	27	9	31	2	42	0
Bradley, Ryan, Car.	1.000	5	1	1	0	2	0
Brantley, Brian, Car.	1.000	17	1	3	0	4	0
Brazelton, Dewon, Orl.	.912	26	13	18	3	34	1
Brown, Eric, W.T.	.000	4	0	0	0	0	0
Bruback, Matt, W.T.	.875	28	7	14	3	24	0
Brueggemann, Dean, Car.*	.944	34	5	12	1	18	1
Bullard, Jim, Birm.*	1.000	3	0	3	0	3	0
Bynum, Mike, Mob.*	1.000	6	1	6	0	7	0
Cameron, Ryan, Car.	.857	37	3	15	3	21	0
Caraccioli, Lance, Jack.*	.929	10	5	8	1	14	1
Carpenter, Chris, Ten.	1.000	5	3	5	0	8	0
Casey, Joe, Ten.	.800	11	3	1	1	5	0
Castellanos, Hugo, Ten.	1.000	47	6	16	0	22	1
Castillo, Marcos, Jack.	1.000	2	0	2	0	2	0
Cercy, Rick, Car.	.786	47	4	7	3	14	0
Chacin, Gustavo, Ten.*	.935	35	6	23	2	31	0
Chantres, Carlos, Orl.	1.000	3	1	3	0	4	0
Chavez, Wilton, W.T.	.963	18	12	14	1	27	3
Chiasson, Scott, W.T.	1.000	3	1	1	0	2	0
Childers, Jason, Hun.	1.000	11	1	7	0	8	1
Childers, Matt, Hun.	1.000	35	12	22	0	34	0
Chouinard, Bobby, Car.	1.000	5	0	2	0	2	0
Christensen, Ben, W.T.	.833	12	2	3	1	6	0
Chulk, Vinny, Ten.	.871	25	8	19	4	31	1
Collazo, William, Gre.*	.941	51	1	15	1	17	0
Colyer, Steve, Jack.*	.769	59	2	8	3	13	0
Cook, Aaron, Car.	.944	14	9	25	2	36	3
Cordova, Jorge, Chat.	.750	35	2	7	3	12	1
Coward, Chad, Orl.	.850	37	4	13	3	20	0
Crowder, Chuck, Car.*	1.000	11	2	1	0	3	0
Cumberland, Chris, Ten.*	.000	9	0	0	0	0	0
Curtis, Daniel, Gre.	1.000	10	6	8	0	14	0
Cyr, Eric, Mob.*	.938	14	3	12	1	16	0
Darnell, Paul, Chat.*	.875	27	1	6	1	8	0
Davis, Lance, Chat.*	.667	12	0	10	5	15	0
De Hart, Blair, Mob.	1.000	7	1	4	0	5	0
De La Cruz, Fernando, Car.	.833	31	3	7	2	12	0
Dellaero, Jason, Birm.	1.000	13	1	2	0	3	0
Dent, Doug, Hun.	1.000	12	2	4	0	6	1
Devey, Phil, Jack.*	.950	8	6	13	1	20	0
DeHart, Casey, Chat.*	1.000	21	0	8	0	8	1
Diaz, Felix, Birm.	1.000	7	2	5	0	7	0
Diggins, Ben, Hun.	.750	7	4	5	3	12	0
Dunn, Scott, Chat.	.889	37	10	14	3	27	1
Dunning, Justin, Jack.	1.000	8	0	2	0	2	1
Eason, Clay, Birm.	1.000	29	3	7	0	10	1
Emiliano, Jamie, Gre.	.941	42	5	11	1	17	0
Ennis, John, Gre.	.975	26	17	22	1	40	0
Esslinger, Cam, Car.	1.000	6	0	1	0	1	1
Estrella, Leo, W.T.	.500	10	1	0	1	2	0
Etherton, Seth, Chat.	1.000	3	0	1	0	1	0
Evert, Brett, Gre.	.938	16	2	13	1	16	0
Falteisek, Steve, Jack.	.000	1	0	0	0	0	0
Farmer, Tom, Jack.	1.000	6	1	3	0	4	1
Feliciano, Pedro, Chat.*	.818	28	0	9	2	11	1
Fikac, Jeremy, Mob.	.000	3	0	0	0	0	0
Fortunato, Bartolome, Orl.	1.000	10	1	2	0	3	0
Fox, Chad, Hun.	.000	3	0	0	0	0	0
Freed, Mark, W.T.*	.871	29	2	25	4	31	0
Frendling, Neal, Orl.	1.000	22	6	10	0	16	1
Gaal, Bryan, Mob.	1.000	32	0	5	0	5	0
Gandarillas, Gus, Hun.	.000	1	0	0	0	0	0
Garcia, Ariel, Mob.	1.000	7	1	2	0	3	0
Garcia, Gerardo, Orl.	1.000	10	6	5	0	11	0
Garcia, Jose, Hun.	1.000	11	3	16	0	19	2
Gassner, Dave, Ten.*	1.000	4	1	5	0	6	0
Gawer, Matt, Gre.*	1.000	6	0	3	0	3	0
German, Rafael, Chat.	1.000	1	0	0	0	0	0
Giese, Dan, Mob.	.800	32	1	3	1	5	0
Gil, Dave, Chat.	.786	18	1	10	3	14	0
Giron, Roberto, Hun.	.750	36	0	6	2	8	0
Gonzalez, Alfredo, Jack.	1.000	13	2	3	0	5	0
Gooch, Arnie, Chat.	1.000	7	2	6	0	8	0
Gooris, Dan, Mob.*	1.000	1	0	0	1	1	0
Gracesqui, Frank, Ten.*	.818	41	1	8	2	11	0
Gray, Brett, Chat.	1.000	48	6	19	0	25	2
Gross, Rafael, W.T.	1.000	1	1	0	0	1	0
Gulin, Lindsay, Jack.*	.833	19	1	9	2	12	0
Hall, Josh, Chat.	.778	22	2	19	6	27	1
Hamann, Rob, Ten.	1.000	12	0	1	0	1	0
Hamilton, Jon, W.T.*	.000	1	0	0	0	0	0
Hampton, Matt, Mob.*	1.000	57	2	8	0	10	0
Hanrahan, Joel, Jack.	1.000	3	2	0	0	2	0
Harrell, Tim, Jack.	1.000	8	0	5	0	5	0
Harvey, Ian, Mob.	.875	12	4	3	1	8	0
Hazlett, Andy, W.T.*	1.000	9	2	7	0	9	0
Hendrickson, Ben, Hun.	1.000	13	5	16	0	21	2
Hernandez, Buddy, Gre.	1.000	40	3	4	0	7	0
High, Andy, Hun.*	1.000	16	0	5	0	5	2
Hines, Carlos, Orl.	1.000	3	0	1	0	1	0
Hooten, Dave, W.T.	1.000	65	5	12	0	17	0
House, Craig, Jack.	.000	3	0	0	0	0	0
Howard, Ben, Mob.	1.000	6	1	4	0	5	0
Howington, Ty, Chat.*	1.000	15	0	2	0	2	0
Huisman, Justin, Car.	1.000	18	2	6	0	8	0
Hunter, Johnny, Mob.	1.000	21	3	19	0	22	3
James, Delvin, Orl.	1.000	3	1	0	0	1	0
Jarvis, Kevin, Mob.	1.000	1	0	1	0	1	0
Jongejan, Ferenc, W.T.*	.810	62	2	15	4	21	2
Kaup, Nathan, Orl.	1.000	1	1	0	0	1	0
Kegley, Chuck, Ten.	1.000	15	2	1	0	3	0
Kent, Nathan, Gre.	1.000	1	1	0	0	1	0
Kibler, Ryan, Car.	.808	25	13	29	10	52	2
Knoff, Justin, Chat.	.000	1	0	0	0	0	0
Kopitzke, Casey, W.T.	1.000	1	0	1	0	1	0
Koronka, John, Chat.*	1.000	16	1	17	0	18	0

Player, Team	Pct.	G	PO	A	E	TC	DP
Krawczyk, Jack, Hun.	1.000	44	2	10	0	12	0
Langone, Steve, Jack.	1.000	14	2	5	0	7	0
Lantigua, Delvis, Birm.	.929	16	1	12	1	14	1
LEE, Derek, Hun.*	1.000	34	6	40	0	46	5
Lee, Garrett, Gre.	1.000	19	0	3	0	3	0
Leek, Randy, Jack.*	.974	15	9	29	1	39	2
Leicester, Jon, W.T.	1.000	5	2	5	0	7	0
Leskanic, Curt, Hun.	.000	3	0	0	0	0	0
Lewis, Derrick, Gre.	.000	1	0	0	1	1	0
Loaiza, Esteban, Ten.	1.000	2	2	3	0	5	1
Lopez, Albie, Gre.	1.000	1	1	0	0	1	0
Lowe, Benny, Chat.*	.000	9	0	0	0	0	0
Lugo, Ruddy, Jack.	1.000	11	1	7	0	8	0
Magrane, Jim, Orl.	1.000	9	6	8	0	14	2
Majewski, Gary, Birm.	.923	57	6	6	1	13	0
Malaska, Mark, Orl.*	1.000	12	4	16	0	20	1
Malone, Corwin, Birm.*	1.000	22	3	22	0	25	2
Markwell, Diegomar, Ten.*	.941	28	8	24	2	34	5
Martin, Chandler, Car.	1.000	19	9	28	0	37	3
Martinez, Javier, Chat.	1.000	18	0	2	0	2	0
Martinez, Luis, Hun.*	.846	29	2	9	2	13	0
Martinez, Willie, Chat.	1.000	4	1	0	0	1	0
Mathis, Jared, Hun.	.000	2	0	0	0	0	0
McClung, Seth, Orl.	.842	20	4	12	3	19	0
McCrotty, Will, Jack.	1.000	43	4	2	0	6	1
Meyer, Jake, Birm.	1.000	23	2	6	0	8	0
Minix, Travis, Orl.	.950	38	5	14	1	20	2
Montero, Agustin, Jack.	.800	31	2	2	1	5	0
Moseley, Dustin, Chat.	1.000	13	3	14	0	17	1
Munoz, Arnaldo, Birm.*	.773	51	1	16	5	22	0
Neu, Mike, Chat.	1.000	21	2	0	0	2	0
Nevers, Tom, Chat.	.000	1	0	0	0	0	0
Noyce, Dave, W.T.*	1.000	53	2	12	0	14	0
Orloski, Joe, Ten.	.929	54	2	11	1	14	1
Oxspring, Chris, Mob.	1.000	6	0	1	0	1	0
Ozias, Todd, Chat.	1.000	15	0	1	0	1	0
Ozuna, Francisco, Ten.*	.900	44	0	9	1	10	0
Palma, Rick, W.T.*	1.000	43	1	7	0	8	1
Parker, Matt, Hun.	1.000	40	5	11	0	16	2
Parris, Steve, Ten.	1.000	1	1	1	0	2	0
Parrish, Wade, Birm.*	.800	13	0	8	2	10	0
Payne, Jerrod, Ten.	1.000	21	2	7	0	9	0
Peavy, Jake, Mob.	1.000	14	6	13	0	19	0
Pember, David, Hun.	.926	27	6	19	2	27	1
Penney, Mike, Hun.	.923	37	6	6	1	13	1
Perez, Oliver, Mob.*	1.000	4	0	1	0	1	0
Pratt, Andy, Gre.*	.938	20	7	8	1	16	0
Prior, Mark, W.T.	.889	6	2	6	1	9	0
Proctor, Scott, Jack.	.850	26	8	9	3	20	1
Purvis, Rob, Birm.	1.000	9	1	3	0	4	0
Ramirez, Horacio, Gre.*	.893	16	6	19	3	28	0
Reimers, Cameron, Ten.	.882	13	6	9	2	17	3
Riedling, John, Chat.	1.000	6	0	2	0	2	0
Rijo, Fernando, Jack.	.875	27	10	18	4	32	1
Roberts, Rick, Jack.*	1.000	51	2	13	0	15	0
Rodriguez, Ricardo, Jack.	.923	11	8	4	1	13	0
Rojas, Chris, Mob.	.976	25	10	31	1	42	1
Rojas, Jose, Jack.	1.000	10	8	9	0	17	0
Roney, Matt, Car.	.882	13	5	10	2	17	0
Ruhl, Nathan, Orl.-Chat.	.889	44	3	5	1	9	0
Rust, Evan, Orl.	1.000	26	3	5	0	8	1
Sanders, Dave, Birm.*	1.000	47	2	15	0	17	2
Santos, Alex, Orl.	1.000	7	0	2	0	2	0
Seay, Bobby, Orl.*	1.000	15	1	2	0	3	0
Severino, Ronni, Orl.*	1.000	25	0	8	0	8	1
Shibilo, Andy, Mob.	.778	29	2	5	2	9	0
Shiyuk, Todd, Mob.*	1.000	10	0	4	0	4	0
Simon, Ben, Jack.	.923	15	3	9	1	13	1
Smith, Cam, Chat.	.667	6	1	1	1	3	0
Smith, Hans, Orl.*	.944	46	3	14	1	18	0
Smith, Matthew, Birm.	1.000	8	0	2	0	2	0
Smyth, Steve, W.T.*	.900	11	1	8	1	10	0
Snare, Ryan, Chat.*	.000	5	0	0	0	0	0
Sobkowiak, Scott, Gre.	1.000	12	4	9	0	13	0
Sollecito, Gabe, W.T.	1.000	30	3	9	0	12	0
Sosa, Jorge, Orl.	1.000	2	0	2	0	2	0
Spille, Ryan, Ten.*	.923	27	2	22	2	26	0
Stewart, Josh, Birm.*	1.000	26	5	18	0	23	3
Stewart, Paul, Hun.	1.000	27	8	23	0	31	0
Stults, Eric, Jack.*	1.000	1	1	0	0	1	0
Sylvester, Billy, Gre.	1.000	51	5	1	0	6	1
Taglienti, Jeff, Chat.	1.000	24	1	4	0	5	0
Takeoka, Kazuhiro, Gre.	.833	21	3	7	2	12	0
Tankersley, Dennis, Mob.	.923	10	5	7	1	13	0
Thompson, Doug, Car.	.727	50	9	7	6	22	1
Thompson, Mark, Chat.	.667	3	0	2	1	3	0
Thompson, Mike, Mob.	.000	1	0	0	0	0	0
Thompson, Travis, Chat.	1.000	15	0	7	0	7	0
Totten, Heath, Jack.	1.000	9	2	10	0	12	1
Trujillo, J.J., Mob.	.875	31	3	4	1	8	0
Ulacia, Dennis, Birm.*	1.000	28	7	26	0	33	1
Urdaneta, Lino, Jack.	.000	1	0	0	0	0	0
Valentine, Joe, Birm.	.800	55	2	6	2	10	1
Vance, Cory, Car.*	.917	25	5	28	3	36	1
Veronie, Shanin, Gre.	.923	29	5	7	1	13	0
Waechter, Doug, Orl.	1.000	4	1	2	0	3	1
Wagner, Denny, Birm.	1.000	9	0	2	0	2	0
Watkins, Steve, Mob.	.963	37	8	18	1	27	1
Webb, John, W.T.	.857	11	3	9	2	14	0
Wellemeyer, Todd, W.T.	1.000	8	2	1	0	3	0
Wells, Mark, Chat.	1.000	2	1	2	0	3	0
West, Brian, Birm.	.973	27	11	25	1	37	4
White, Matt, Orl.	1.000	7	4	1	0	5	1
Wiggins, Scott, Ten.*	1.000	16	2	4	0	6	0
Winkelsas, Joe, Gre.	1.000	2	1	0	0	1	0
Wright, Chris, Orl.	1.000	19	6	6	0	12	0
Wrigley, Jase, Car.	.882	44	7	8	2	17	1
Young, Colin, Car.*	1.000	15	1	2	0	3	0
Young, Jason, Car.	.947	14	6	12	1	19	0
Zoccolillo, Peter, Hun.	.000	1	0	0	0	0	0

PITCHERS WITH TWO OR MORE TEAMS

Player, Team	Pct.	G	PO	A	E	TC	DP
Ruhl, Nathan, Orl.	.875	40	3	4	1	8	0
Ruhl, Nathan, Chat.	1.000	4	0	1	0	1	0

The following players appeared only as designated hitter, pinch-hitter or pinch runner: Bl. Harris, dh, ph; Tejada, dh.

LEAGUE CHAMPIONS

Year	Team	Pct.	Year	Team	Pct.	Year	Team	Pct.
1904—	Macon	.598	1916—	Augusta*	.617	1930—	Greenville*	.620
1905—	Macon	.625		Columbia	.631		Macon	.643
1906—	Savannah	.637	1917—	Charleston	.741	1931-35—Did not operate.		
1907—	Charleston	.620		Columbia*	.667	1936—	Jacksonville	.652
1908—	Jacksonville	.694	1918—	Did not operate.			Columbus*	.650
1909—	Chattanooga*	.738	1919—	Columbia	.585	1937—	Columbus	.572
	Augusta	.702	1920—	Columbia	.633		Savannah (3rd)†	.565
1910—	Columbus	.588	1921—	Columbia	.642	1938—	Savannah	.574
1911—	Columbus*	.681	1922—	Charleston	.625		Macon (2nd)†	.570
	Columbia	.710	1923—	Charlotte*	.653	1939—	Columbus	.601
1912—	Jacksonville*	.679		Macon	.580		Augusta (2nd)†	.597
	Columbus	.632	1924—	Augusta	.612	1940—	Savannah	.627
1913—	Savannah	.754	1925—	Spartanburg	.620		Columbus (2nd)†	.583
	Savannah	.593	1926—	Greenville	.662	1941—	Macon	.643
1914—	Savannah*	.667	1927—	Greenville	.622		Columbia (2nd)†	.636
	Albany	.650	1928—	Asheville	.664	1942—	Charleston	.620
1915—	Macon	.588	1929—	Asheville	.605		Macon (2nd)†	.585
	Columbus*	.686		Knoxville*	.634	1943-45—Did not operate.		

Year	Team	Pct.	Year	Team	Pct.	Year	Team	Pct.
1946—	Columbus	.568	1967—	Birmingham	.604	1986—	Huntsville	.553
	Augusta (4th)†	.547	1968—	Asheville	.614		Columbus∞	.500
1947—	Columbus	.575	1969—	Charlotte	.579	1987—	Charlotte	.586
	Savannah (2nd)†	.563	1970—	Columbus	.569		Birmingham∞	.476
1948—	Charleston	.572	1971—	Did not operate as league—clubs were		1988—	Greenville	.604
	Greenville (3rd)†	.549		members of Dixie Association.			Chattanooga∞	.566
1949—	Macon‡	.623	1972—	Asheville	.583	1989—	Birmingham∞	.615
1950—	Macon‡	.588		Montgomery§	.561		Greenville	.504
1951—	Montgomery	.607	1973—	Montgomery§	.580	1990—	Orlando	.590
1952—	Columbia	.649		Jacksonville	.559		Memphis∞	.507
	Montgomery (3rd)†	.558	1974—	Jacksonville	.565	1991—	Greenville	.611
1953—	Jacksonville	.679		Knoxville§	.533		Orlando∞	.535
	Savannah (2nd)†	.571	1975—	Orlando	.587	1992—	Greenville	.699
1954—	Jacksonville	.593		Montgomery§	.545		Chattanooga	.629
	Savannah (2nd)†	.571	1976—	Montgomery∞	.591	1993—	Birmingham∞	.549
1955—	Columbia	.636		Orlando	.540		Knoxville	.500
	Augusta (3rd)†	.543	1977—	Montgomery∞	.628	1994—	Huntsville∞	.587
1956—	Jacksonville‡	.621		Jacksonville	.522		Carolina	.529
1957—	Augusta	.636	1978—	Knoxville∞	.611	1995—	Carolina∞	.618
	Charlotte (2nd)†	.562		Savannah	.500		Chattanooga	.580
1958—	Augusta	.550	1979—	Columbus	.587	1996—	Chattanooga	.579
	Macon (3rd)†	.500		Nashville∞	.576		Jacksonville∞	.543
1959—	Knoxville	.557	1980—	Memphis	.576	1997—	Huntsville	.554
	Gastonia (4th)†	.504		Charlotte∞	.500		Greenville∞	.529
1960—	Columbia	.597	1981—	Nashville	.566	1998—	Mobile∞	.614
	Savannah (3rd)†	.561		Orlando∞	.556		Jacksonville	.614
1961—	Asheville	.635	1982—	Jacksonville	.576	1999—	West Tenn.	.596
1962—	Savannah	.662		Nashville∞	.535		Orlando∞	.507
	Macon (3rd)†	.576	1983—	Birmingham∞	.628	2000—	West Tenn∞	.580
1963—	Augusta*	.661		Jacksonville	.531		Jacksonville	.493
	Lynchburg	.662	1984—	Charlotte∞	.510	2001—	Jacksonville▲	.597
1964—	Lynchburg	.579		Knoxville	.483		Huntsville▲	.543
1965—	Columbus	.572	1985—	Charlotte	.545	2002—	Birmingham∞	.564
1966—	Mobile	.629		Huntsville∞	.542			

*Won split season playoff. †Won four-club playoff. ‡Won championship and four-club playoff. §League was divided into Eastern and Western divisions; won playoff. ∞League was divided into Eastern and Western divisions and played split season; won playoff. ▲Were entering finals of four-team playoff and were declared co-champions when Professional Baseball declared a stoppage of play.

TEXAS LEAGUE

LEAGUE OFFICE

President/treasurer
Tom Kayser

Address
2442 Facet Oak
San Antonio, TX 78232

Phone
210-545-5297

TEAMS

ARKANSAS TRAVELERS
Vice president/general manager
Bill Valentine
Manager
Tyrone Boykin
Ballpark (capacity, surface)
Ray Winder Field (6,083, grass)
Affiliation
Angels
Address
P.O. Box 55066
Little Rock, AR 72215
Phone
501-664-1555

EL PASO DIABLOS
General manager
Andrew Wheeler
Manager
Scott Coolbaugh
Ballpark (capacity, surface)
Cohen Stadium (9,765, grass)
Affiliation
Diamondbacks
Address
9700 Gateway Blvd. N.
El Paso, TX 79924
Phone
915-755-2000

FRISCO ROUGHRIDERS
General manager
Mike McCall
Manager
Tim Ireland
Ballpark (capacity, surface)
To be announced (To be announced, grass)
Affiliation
Rangers

Address
To be announced
Phone
972-731-9200

MIDLAND ROCKHOUNDS
General manager
Monty Hoppel
Manager
Greg Sparks
Ballpark (capacity, surface)
First American Bank Ballpark (5,000, grass)
Affiliation
Athletics
Address
5514 Champions Dr.
Midland, TX 79706
Phone
915-520-2255

ROUND ROCK EXPRESS
General manager
Jay Miller
Manager
Jackie Moore
Ballpark (capacity, surface)
The Dell Diamond (7,500, grass)
Affiliation
Astros
Address
P.O. Box 5309
Round Rock, TX 78683
Phone
512-255-2255

SAN ANTONIO MISSIONS
President
Burl Yarbrough
Manager
Dave Brundage

Ballpark (capacity, surface)
Nelson Wolff Stadium (6,300, grass)
Affiliation
Mariners
Address
5757 Highway 90 West
San Antonio, TX 78227
Phone
210-675-7275

TULSA DRILLERS
Executive v.p./general manager
Chuck Lamson
Manager
Marv Foley
Ballpark (capacity, surface)
Drillers Stadium (10,842, grass)
Affiliation
Rockies
Address
4802 E. 15th St.
Tulsa, OK 74112
Phone
918-744-5998

WICHITA WRANGLERS
General manager
Steve Shaad
Manager
Keith Bodie
Ballpark (capacity, surface)
Lawrence-Dumont Stadium (6,111, artificial infield, grass outfield)
Affiliation
Royals
Address
P.O. Box 1420
Wichita, KS 67201
Phone
316-267-3372

2002 FINAL STANDINGS

FIRST HALF

EAST DIVISION

Team	W	L	T	Pct.	GB
Tulsa (Rangers)	39	30	0	.565	...
Wichita (Royals)	34	35	0	.493	5.0
Shreveport (Giants)	31	38	0	.449	8.0
Arkansas (Angels)	31	39	0	.443	8.5

WEST DIVISION

Team	W	L	T	Pct.	GB
Round Rock (Astros)	42	28	0	.600	...
El Paso (Diamondbacks)	40	28	0	.588	1.0
Midland (Athletics)	35	34	0	.507	6.5
San Antonio (Mariners)	25	45	0	.357	17.0

SECOND HALF

EAST DIVISION

Team	W	L	T	Pct.	GB
Wichita (Royals)	46	24	0	.657	...
Tulsa (Rangers)	33	37	0	.471	13.0
Shreveport (Giants)	29	41	0	.414	17.0
Arkansas (Angels)	20	50	0	.286	26.0

WEST DIVISION

Team	W	L	T	Pct.	GB
San Antonio (Mariners)	43	27	0	.614	...
Midland (Athletics)	40	30	0	.571	3.0
El Paso (Diamondbacks)	36	34	0	.514	7.0
Round Rock (Astros)	33	37	0	.471	10.0

COMPOSITE

Team	Wich.	E.P.	Mid.	R.R.	Tul.	S.A.	Shre.	Ark.	W	L	T	Pct.	GB
Wichita (Royals)	...	7	5	10	13	8	19	18	80	59	0	.576	...
El Paso (Diamondbacks)	8	...	9	14	9	18	7	11	76	62	0	.551	3.5
Midland (Athletics)	11	15	...	12	6	13	10	8	75	64	0	.540	5.0
Round Rock (Astros)	6	14	12	...	9	11	13	10	75	65	0	.536	5.5
Tulsa (Rangers)	11	7	9	7	...	8	14	16	72	67	0	.518	8.0
San Antonio (Mariners)	8	6	15	13	8	...	11	7	68	72	0	.486	12.5
Shreveport (Giants)	7	8	6	3	12	5	...	19	60	79	0	.432	20.0
Arkansas (Angels)	8	5	8	6	10	9	5	...	51	89	0	.364	29.5

Arkansas' home games played in Little Rock, Ark.

Major league affiliations in parentheses.

PLAYOFFS: Tulsa defeated Wichita, three games to none; San Antonio defeated Round Rock, three games to two; San Antonio defeated Tulsa, four games to three to win Texas League championship.

REGULAR-SEASON ATTENDANCE: Arkansas, 192,237; El Paso, 234,971; Midland, 276,380; Round Rock, 670,176; San Antonio, 316,983; Shreveport, 24,560; Tulsa, 306,705; Wichita, 142,265. Total—2,164,277. Playoffs (15 games)—44,467. Class AA All-Star Game at Norwich, Conn.—8,009.

MANAGERS: Arkansas, Doug Sisson; El Paso, Chip Hale; Midland, Tony DeFrancesco; Round Rock, Jackie Moore; San Antonio, Dave Brundage; Shreveport, Mario Mendoza; Tulsa, Tim Ireland; Wichita, Keith Bodie.

ALL-STAR TEAM: 1B—Royce Huffman, Round Rock; 2B—Matt Kata, El Paso; 3B—Chad Tracy, El Paso; SS—Brian Specht, Arkansas; OF—Alexis Gomez, Wichita; OF—Todd Linden, Shreveport; OF—Henri Stanley, Round Rock; C—John Buck, Round Rock; DH—Graham Koonce, Midland; Utility—Jason Alfaro, Round Rock; LHP—Craig Anderson, San Antonio; RHP—Andrew Good, El Paso; LHP—Mike Gosling, El Paso; RHP—Runelvys Hernandez, Wichita; RHP—Rodrigo Rosario, Round Rock; RHP—Miguel Saladin, Round Rock; RHP—Kirk Saarloos, Round Rock; Player of the Year—Chad Tracy, El Paso; Pitcher of the Year—Kirk Saarloos, Round Rock; Manager of the Year—Tim Ireland, Tulsa.

2002 BATTING

TEAM

Team	G	TPA	AB	R	H	TB	2B	3B	HR	RBI	SH	SF	HP	BB	IBB	SO	SB	CS	GDP	LOB	ShO	Avg.	OBP	Slg.
El Paso	139	5367	4787	693	1352	2028	278	49	100	640	37	50	73	420	33	972	66	72	105	1012	3	.282	.346	.424
Round Rock ..	140	5346	4722	685	1288	1941	256	41	105	625	34	50	69	471	23	895	129	83	107	988	9	.273	.344	.411
Wichita	139	5315	4653	689	1252	1800	227	36	83	628	42	55	77	488	19	757	151	93	101	983	6	.269	.345	.387
Shreveport	139	5075	4529	540	1186	1714	243	30	75	488	54	27	64	401	28	884	118	75	111	984	16	.262	.329	.378
Midland	141	5448	4714	670	1216	1859	251	31	110	614	43	33	70	588	32	1037	79	54	110	1078	9	.258	.347	.394
San Antonio ..	140	5316	4697	533	1188	1625	224	30	51	476	52	44	74	449	29	874	134	84	109	1017	8	.253	.325	.346
Tulsa	140	5233	4592	618	1141	1769	234	29	112	577	28	44	45	524	25	994	75	49	108	986	14	.248	.329	.385
Arkansas	140	5128	4605	566	1134	1698	226	37	88	503	35	38	68	382	15	870	161	72	88	913	15	.246	.311	.369

INDIVIDUAL

TOP QUALIFIERS FOR BATTING CHAMPIONSHIP

Minimum 378 plate appearances. *Lefthanded batter. †Switch-hitter.

Player, Team	G	TPA	AB	R	H	TB	2B	3B	HR	RBI	SH	SF	HP	BB	IBB	SO	SB	CS	GDP	Avg.	OBP	Slg.
Tracy, Chad, E.P.*	129	564	514	80	177	250	39	5	8	74	1	7	4	38	7	51	2	3	10	.344	.389	.486
Huffman, Royce, R.R.	132	587	522	79	168	246	36	3	12	91	1	9	14	41	0	70	13	6	14	.322	.381	.471
Perry, Chan, Wich.	105	435	399	59	126	192	20	2	14	73	0	6	1	29	3	44	6	5	11	.316	.359	.481
Alfaro, Jason, R.R.	124	519	455	71	143	231	36	2	16	74	0	3	11	50	6	75	11	9	13	.314	.393	.508
Linden, Todd, Shre.†	111	469	392	64	123	189	26	2	12	52	1	3	12	61	7	101	9	5	12	.314	.419	.482
Stanley, Henri, R.R.*	127	537	456	90	143	247	36	10	16	72	0	5	4	72	7	85	14	9	7	.314	.408	.542
Santos, Deivis, Shre.*	109	431	407	54	127	179	33	5	3	56	1	0	5	18	6	42	4	4	9	.312	.349	.440
Monahan, Shane, Wich.*	97	417	391	55	120	183	27	3	10	59	0	3	4	18	2	53	11	10	5	.307	.341	.468
Kata, Matt, E.P.†	136	629	578	95	172	256	33	9	11	57	4	5	4	37	4	79	12	7	6	.298	.341	.443
Jones, Jason, Tul.†	136	564	471	82	139	215	33	2	13	75	0	5	0	87	6	97	12	7	12	.295	.401	.456
Gomez, Alexis, Wich.*	114	515	461	72	136	215	21	8	14	75	2	4	3	45	5	84	36	24	9	.295	.359	.466
Hammock, Rob, E.P.	122	501	441	68	128	197	28	4	11	73	1	8	8	43	0	68	5	4	14	.290	.358	.447
Gordon, Brian, E.P.*	130	535	477	73	137	217	32	9	10	67	7	7	8	36	2	111	2	6	6	.287	.343	.455
Terrero, Luis, E.P.	104	395	360	49	103	159	20	6	8	54	3	1	8	23	1	89	18	22	9	.286	.342	.442
Paz, Rich, Wich.	137	582	479	83	136	178	27	0	5	74	2	11	9	81	0	80	5	6	13	.284	.390	.372

DEPARTMENTAL LEADERS: G—Koonce, 140; AB—Kata, 578; R—Kata, 95; H—Tracy, 177; TB—Kata, 256; 2B—Tracy, 39; 3B—Asche, Stanley, 10 each; HR—Koonce, 24; RBI—Koonce, 96; SH—Carvajal, 14; SF—Paz, 11; HP—Olson, 19; BB—Koonce, 133; IBB—Koonce, 12; SO—Asche, 132; SB—Strong, 46; CS—Gomez, 24; GIDP—Bruntlett, 17; Slg.—Stanley, .542; OBP—Koonce, .440.

ALL PLAYERS

*Lefthanded batter. †Switch-hitter.

Player, Team	G	TPA	AB	R	H	TB	2B	3B	HR	RBI	SH	SF	HP	BB	IBB	SO	SB	CS	GDP	Avg.	OBP	Slg.
Alcala, Juan, S.A.	3	13	13	1	4	4	0	0	0	1	0	0	0	0	0	1	1	0	0	.308	.308	.308
Alfaro, Jason, R.R.	124	519	455	71	143	231	36	2	16	74	0	3	11	50	6	75	11	9	13	.314	.393	.508
Anderson, Keith, Shre.	2	6	6	0	0	0	0	0	0	0	0	0	0	0	0	3	0	0	0	.000	.000	.000
Anderson, Luke, Shre.	26	2	2	0	0	0	0	0	0	0	0	0	0	0	0	1	0	0	0	.000	.000	.000
Ansman, Craig, E.P.	19	61	53	6	12	24	3	0	3	9	0	1	1	6	0	7	0	0	3	.226	.311	.453
Ardoin, Danny, Tul.	8	25	21	1	3	3	0	0	0	0	0	0	0	4	0	9	0	0	1	.143	.280	.143
Asche, Kirk, Mid.	115	424	376	50	91	160	13	10	12	56	1	5	2	40	2	132	9	6	8	.242	.314	.426
Barkett, Andy, S.A.*	115	484	421	55	105	159	23	2	9	60	0	4	4	55	10	75	9	9	9	.249	.339	.378
Bonser, Boof, Shre.	5	1	1	0	0	0	0	0	0	0	0	0	0	0	0	0	0	0	0	.000	.000	.000
Bowser, Matt, Mid.*	19	70	63	12	13	25	2	2	2	7	0	0	1	6	0	14	1	0	2	.206	.286	.397
Brito, Juan, Wich.	89	332	302	40	77	109	11	0	7	38	5	3	1	21	1	46	1	1	9	.255	.303	.361
Brown, Elliot, Shre.†	25	6	5	0	1	1	0	0	0	1	0	0	0	0	0	3	0	0	0	.200	.200	.200

Player, Team	G	TPA	AB	R	H	TB	2B	3B	HR	RBI	SH	SF	HP	BB	IBB	SO	SB	CS	GDP	Avg.	OBP	Slg.
Brown, Ray, S.A.*	26	96	89	4	20	27	4	0	1	6	0	0	0	7	0	15	0	0	3	.225	.281	.303
Bruntlett, Eric, R.R.	116	542	464	81	123	154	21	2	2	48	4	8	10	56	0	61	35	12	17	.265	.351	.332
Buck, John, R.R.	120	494	448	48	118	189	29	3	12	89	0	9	6	31	1	93	2	3	11	.263	.314	.422
Budde, Ryan, Ark.	3	10	9	1	1	4	0	0	1	1	0	0	0	1	0	2	0	0	0	.111	.200	.444
Burke, Chris, R.R.	136	538	481	66	127	171	19	8	3	37	5	3	10	39	3	61	16	15	8	.264	.330	.356
Burns, Kevan, E.P.*	58	210	187	36	61	89	9	5	3	26	0	0	1	22	1	25	2	5	3	.326	.400	.476
Burns, Kevin, Ark.*	56	208	169	20	30	55	11	1	4	21	0	2	3	34	2	49	1	0	2	.178	.322	.325
Cadiente, Brett, Tul.*	102	349	300	37	68	96	14	4	2	19	7	2	4	36	3	70	12	5	4	.227	.316	.320
Calderon, Henry, Wich.	18	54	49	3	7	7	0	0	0	4	1	0	1	3	0	8	0	1	0	.143	.208	.143
Camilli, Jason, Ark.	112	385	338	39	76	103	13	1	4	28	6	1	3	37	0	64	6	5	8	.225	.306	.305
Cancel, Robinson, Mid.	108	439	402	56	113	174	21	2	12	64	1	1	3	32	0	70	10	7	12	.281	.338	.433
Cannon, Jon, Shre.	38	2	2	0	0	0	0	0	0	0	0	0	0	0	0	1	0	0	0	.000	.000	.000
Carroll, Mark, S.A.	8	30	25	0	3	3	0	0	0	0	0	0	0	5	0	6	0	0	0	.120	.267	.120
Caruso, Joe, Wich.	46	171	154	19	43	62	7	3	2	22	4	1	1	11	0	25	1	1	4	.279	.329	.403
Carvajal, Jhonny, Shre.	113	477	419	58	117	170	28	5	5	34	14	2	5	37	2	67	11	4	16	.279	.343	.406
Cash, David, Shre.	34	9	9	0	0	0	0	0	0	0	0	0	0	0	0	5	0	0	0	.000	.000	.000
Castellano, John, S.A.	55	207	194	15	51	64	10	0	1	20	0	3	0	10	0	30	3	3	11	.263	.295	.330
Castillo, Ruben, S.A.	114	424	394	40	86	115	12	4	3	36	10	2	2	16	0	86	10	7	5	.218	.251	.292
Castro, Nelson, Shre.†	86	322	300	35	67	111	15	4	7	29	2	1	8	11	2	60	15	9	7	.223	.269	.370
Catalanotto, Frank, Tul.*	4	18	16	1	2	4	0	1	0	3	0	0	1	1	0	1	0	0	3	.125	.222	.250
Ceriani, Matt, E.P.	3	9	7	1	1	1	0	0	0	0	0	0	0	2	0	2	0	1	0	.143	.333	.143
Cervantes, Chris, E.P.*	33	11	7	1	3	4	1	0	0	1	4	0	0	0	0	1	0	0	0	.429	.429	.571
Christensen, Mike, Ark.	122	434	413	33	92	129	18	2	5	35	2	1	2	15	0	98	1	2	13	.223	.253	.312
Christianson, Ryan, S.A.	52	210	190	20	48	74	11	0	5	17	2	0	2	16	1	36	0	2	8	.253	.317	.389
Clark, Doug, Shre.*	44	160	138	13	36	50	6	1	2	13	2	1	0	19	4	35	5	7	4	.261	.348	.362
Clark, Jeff, Shre.	6	2	1	0	1	1	0	0	0	0	0	1	0	0	0	0	0	0	0	1.000	1.000	1.000
Cole, Eric, Tul.	47	168	155	10	30	46	7	0	3	18	0	1	1	11	0	41	0	2	3	.194	.250	.297
Connors, Greg, S.A.	14	49	41	6	7	10	3	0	0	5	0	1	1	6	0	10	3	1	3	.171	.286	.244
Cotto, Luis, Wich.	1	3	1	0	0	0	0	0	0	0	0	0	0	2	0	0	0	0	0	.000	.667	.000
Coughenour, Jory, R.R.	32	4	4	0	2	2	0	0	0	0	0	0	0	0	0	0	0	0	0	.500	.500	.500
Cox, Ryan, Shre.	27	11	10	0	1	1	0	0	0	0	0	1	0	0	0	5	0	0	0	.100	.100	.100
Cozier, Vance, Shre.	21	6	6	0	0	0	0	0	0	0	0	0	0	0	0	2	0	0	0	.000	.000	.000
Cresse, Brad, E.P.	66	262	240	25	55	79	15	0	3	24	0	3	3	16	0	74	1	0	4	.229	.282	.329
Crosby, Bobby, Mid.	59	251	228	31	64	101	16	0	7	31	3	1	0	19	1	41	9	2	9	.281	.335	.443
Cunningham, Marco, Wich.	77	271	215	39	40	59	7	0	4	29	5	2	12	37	1	39	13	8	2	.186	.335	.274
Daigle, Casey, E.P.	7	9	8	0	0	0	0	0	0	1	1	0	0	0	0	5	0	0	0	.000	.000	.000
DeCinces, Tim, Mid.*	26	89	82	10	23	40	8	0	3	20	0	0	0	7	0	10	0	0	3	.280	.337	.488
DeJesus, David, Wich.*	25	96	79	7	20	35	5	2	2	15	1	3	5	8	0	10	3	1	3	.253	.347	.443
Del Chiaro, Brent, Ark.	3	8	8	0	0	0	0	0	0	0	0	0	0	0	0	3	0	0	1	.000	.000	.000
Diaz, Felix, Shre.	12	3	3	1	3	3	0	0	0	1	0	0	0	0	0	0	0	0	0	1.000	1.000	1.000
Dobbs, Greg, S.A.*	27	108	96	13	35	52	2	0	5	15	2	0	1	9	2	17	1	3	2	.365	.425	.542
Duncan, Carlos, Ark.	60	238	215	31	59	90	11	1	6	23	0	2	10	11	1	44	15	5	4	.274	.336	.419
Durazo, Erubiel, E.P.*	5	18	14	5	7	16	3	0	2	7	0	0	4	0	1	0	1	0	1	.500	.611	1.143
Durrington, Trent, Ark.	107	441	382	59	94	147	18	4	9	47	2	7	11	39	2	71	25	14	3	.246	.328	.385
Fatheree, Danny, R.R.	10	30	29	3	5	6	1	0	0	3	0	0	1	0	0	8	0	0	0	.172	.200	.207
Figueroa, Luis, S.A.	48	206	180	25	61	77	13	0	1	25	0	1	1	24	0	14	2	1	6	.339	.417	.428
Flaherty, Tim, Shre.	76	282	247	23	54	86	10	2	6	34	0	5	2	28	2	81	0	1	4	.219	.298	.348
Foppert, Jesse, Shre.	11	9	7	0	2	3	1	0	0	0	2	0	0	0	0	2	0	0	0	.286	.286	.429
Freire, Alejandro, Shre.	55	201	177	24	50	89	9	0	10	32	0	1	4	19	1	38	0	2	4	.282	.363	.503
Furniss, Eddy, Tul.*	26	96	84	5	12	18	3	0	1	7	0	2	1	9	1	29	0	1	3	.143	.229	.214
Gajewski, Matt, Tul.†	14	34	30	1	5	7	2	0	0	2	1	1	0	2	0	6	2	0	2	.167	.212	.233
Gandolfo, Rob, S.A.*	75	204	185	16	36	42	4	1	0	13	2	1	1	15	4	25	1	3	4	.195	.257	.227
Gann, Jamie, E.P.	21	5	5	0	4	4	0	0	0	2	0	0	0	0	0	1	0	0	0	.800	.800	.800
Garcia, Douglas, Tul.*	45	148	142	10	43	55	9	0	1	18	0	0	3	3	0	32	0	0	3	.303	.331	.387
Gilfillan, Jason, Wich.	21	1	1	0	0	0	0	0	0	0	0	0	0	0	0	1	0	0	0	.000	.000	.000
Glendenning, Mike, Wich.	22	74	59	7	13	22	3	0	2	4	0	0	2	13	1	16	1	1	2	.220	.378	.373
Gomez, Alexis, Wich.*	114	515	461	72	136	215	21	8	14	75	2	4	3	45	5	84	36	24	9	.295	.359	.466
Good, Andrew, E.P.	28	22	19	1	4	4	0	0	0	2	0	0	1	0	0	7	0	1	0	.211	.250	.211
Gordon, Brian, E.P.*	130	535	477	73	137	217	32	9	10	67	7	7	8	36	2	111	2	6	6	.287	.343	.455
Gosling, Mike, E.P.*	27	18	15	2	0	0	0	0	0	0	0	0	3	0	0	10	0	0	0	.000	.167	.000
Gray, Mike, E.P.*	19	1	1	0	0	0	0	0	0	0	0	0	0	0	0	0	0	0	0	.000	.000	.000
Greer, Rusty, Tul.*	6	22	17	4	7	9	2	0	0	1	0	0	0	5	1	3	0	0	0	.412	.545	.529
Gregorio, Tom, Ark.	56	202	188	18	47	68	10	1	3	15	3	0	2	9	0	33	2	0	5	.250	.291	.362
Griffin, John-ford, Mid.*	2	8	7	0	1	1	0	0	0	0	1	0	0	0	0	3	0	0	0	.143	.250	.143
Guevara, Giomar, Mid.	103	417	363	49	91	117	17	3	1	19	8	0	7	37	1	88	8	6	3	.251	.332	.322
Guiel, Jeff, Ark.*	5	20	14	2	4	7	0	0	1	4	0	1	1	4	0	2	1	0	0	.286	.450	.500
Guzman, Elpidio, Ark.*	124	502	454	57	112	157	15	9	4	41	3	3	2	40	3	91	21	11	8	.247	.309	.346
Haas, Chris, Tul.*	60	200	180	23	40	78	8	0	10	27	0	1	0	19	0	63	0	0	5	.222	.295	.433
Hall, Victor, E.P.*	38	171	161	18	46	60	4	5	0	12	0	1	3	6	0	23	7	4	0	.286	.322	.373
Hallmark, Pat, Wich.	98	414	362	55	92	114	14	1	2	33	4	3	10	35	0	63	42	12	8	.254	.334	.315
Hammock, Rob, E.P.	122	501	441	68	128	197	28	4	11	73	1	8	8	43	0	68	5	4	14	.290	.358	.447
Harris, Brian, Wich.†	133	560	490	82	136	184	23	8	3	47	6	5	7	52	3	76	10	5	7	.278	.353	.376
Harris, Cedrick, E.P.	36	85	82	10	22	33	3	1	2	8	1	0	0	2	0	19	2	1	2	.268	.286	.402
Hart, Corey, Wich.†	79	298	252	32	60	80	13	2	1	33	1	4	0	41	0	49	4	5	2	.238	.340	.317
Henthorne, Kevin, E.P.†	5	4	4	0	0	0	0	0	0	0	0	0	0	0	0	1	0	0	0	.000	.000	.000
Hernandez, Carlos, R.R.†	2	1	1	0	0	0	0	0	0	0	0	0	0	0	0	0	0	0	0	.000	.000	.000
Hill, Jason, E.P.	118	464	431	41	117	160	21	2	6	54	3	7	8	14	0	63	2	4	14	.271	.302	.371
Hill, Mike, R.R.	135	573	527	75	149	233	30	6	14	61	0	2	5	39	0	105	14	8	13	.283	.337	.442
Hochgesang, Josh, Mid.	107	399	354	42	83	143	21	0	13	62	1	3	13	28	0	93	3	5	8	.234	.312	.404
Holt, Daylan, Mid.	57	221	201	18	56	78	10	4	1	25	1	3	1	15	1	50	1	4	4	.279	.327	.388
Horgan, Joe, Shre.*	10	6	6	1	2	2	0	0	0	0	0	0	0	0	0	1	0	0	0	.333	.333	.333
Horner, Jim, S.A.	63	237	209	29	62	94	18	1	4	30	0	2	7	19	1	48	1	1	4	.297	.371	.450

Player, Team	G	TPA	AB	R	H	TB	2B	3B	HR	RBI	SH	SF	HP	BB	IBB	SO	SB	CS	GDP	Avg.	OBP	Slg.
Howe, Matt, Mid.	57	216	187	20	48	77	15	1	4	19	0	0	4	25	0	50	4	3	2	.257	.356	.412
Huffman, Royce, R.R.	132	587	522	79	168	246	36	3	12	91	1	9	14	41	0	70	13	6	14	.322	.381	.471
Huisman, Jason, Ark.	77	289	263	41	64	96	15	1	5	36	2	1	9	13	2	33	11	6	6	.243	.301	.365
Hutchison, Wesley, Shre.	22	3	3	1	2	2	0	0	0	1	0	0	0	0	0	0	0	0	0	.667	.667	.667
James, Kenny, Ark.†	96	413	380	48	102	130	17	1	3	32	5	0	7	21	0	58	40	13	6	.268	.319	.342
Jamison, Ryan, R.R.	31	5	4	0	0	0	0	0	0	0	1	0	0	0	0	2	0	0	0	.000	.000	.000
Jester, Joe, Shre.	104	395	359	52	100	157	20	2	11	40	4	1	2	29	0	66	14	5	6	.279	.335	.437
Johnson, Brian, Wich.	37	123	109	15	27	35	5	0	1	13	2	1	5	6	0	16	3	0	4	.248	.314	.321
Jones, Chris, Shre.*	36	5	4	1	1	1	0	0	0	0	1	0	0	0	0	2	0	0	0	.250	.250	.250
Jones, Jason, Tul.†	136	564	471	82	139	215	33	2	13	75	0	5	3	87	6	97	12	7	12	.295	.401	.456
Jones, Jeremy, Tul.	55	158	132	17	29	39	4	0	2	8	5	2	3	16	0	21	1	1	5	.220	.314	.295
Kata, Matt, E.P.†	136	629	578	95	172	256	33	9	11	57	4	5	4	37	4	79	12	7	6	.298	.341	.443
Keith, Rusty, Mid.	95	397	358	52	95	114	16	0	1	22	9	1	3	26	1	44	7	4	11	.265	.320	.318
King, Brad, Tul.	15	53	43	3	8	8	0	0	0	1	0	0	1	9	1	5	0	0	0	.186	.340	.186
Klassen, Danny, E.P.	18	74	65	11	15	25	4	0	2	7	2	0	0	7	0	24	0	0	2	.231	.306	.385
Knoblauch, Chuck, Shre.	5	22	16	3	5	7	2	0	0	0	0	0	0	6	1	4	1	0	0	.313	.500	.438
Koonce, Graham, Mid.*	140	618	470	86	129	229	28	0	24	96	0	5	10	133	12	117	2	0	10	.274	.440	.487
Krause, Scott, S.A.	28	98	89	6	16	25	3	0	2	6	2	0	2	5	0	17	2	1	4	.180	.240	.281
Kremblas, Mike, Mid.	51	169	141	15	28	30	2	0	0	7	2	2	7	17	0	35	1	2	6	.199	.313	.213
Kuzmic, Craig, S.A.†	66	291	238	34	49	79	14	2	4	28	2	4	4	43	1	80	5	2	3	.206	.332	.332
Laird, Gerald, Tul.	123	503	442	70	122	184	21	4	11	67	1	10	5	45	1	95	8	6	14	.276	.343	.416
Landry, Jacques, Mid.	30	136	105	25	31	60	8	0	7	27	0	2	2	27	2	31	6	2	0	.295	.441	.571
LeBron, Juan, S.A.	56	234	204	26	46	70	12	0	4	21	0	3	7	20	1	55	3	3	3	.225	.312	.343
Lidge, Brad, R.R.	5	1	1	0	0	0	0	0	0	0	0	0	0	0	0	0	0	0	0	.000	.000	.000
Linden, Todd, Shre.†	111	469	392	64	123	189	26	2	12	52	1	3	12	61	7	101	9	5	12	.314	.419	.482
Lira, James, R.R.	28	1	1	0	0	0	0	0	0	0	0	0	0	0	0	0	0	0	0	.000	.000	.000
Lockwood, Mike, R.R.*	135	585	501	68	121	169	25	7	3	49	12	3	9	60	7	66	5	6	12	.242	.332	.337
Lopez, Javier, E.P.*	61	1	1	1	0	0	0	0	0	0	0	0	0	0	0	0	0	0	0	.000	.000	.000
Lunsford, Trey, Shre.	66	248	210	26	59	75	13	0	1	20	5	0	4	29	1	42	5	2	3	.281	.379	.357
Luther, Ryan, Shre.	32	123	108	10	30	41	5	0	2	14	0	2	2	11	0	25	4	0	1	.278	.350	.380
Maier, T.J., Tul.	20	73	57	14	13	19	3	0	1	5	1	0	0	15	0	12	1	0	1	.228	.389	.333
Maldonado, Carlos, R.R.	47	149	123	13	31	51	8	0	4	20	0	4	0	22	0	23	0	0	3	.252	.356	.415
Mann, Jim, R.R.	1	1	0	0	1	0	0	0	0	0	0	0	0	1	0	0	0	0	0	.000	1.000	.000
Martin, Billy, E.P.	83	302	264	34	57	94	16	0	7	38	0	4	2	32	1	92	0	0	5	.216	.301	.356
Martin, Tyler, Tul.†	4	14	13	1	1	4	0	0	1	4	0	0	0	1	0	3	0	0	0	.077	.143	.308
Martines, Jason, E.P.*	27	1	1	0	0	0	0	0	0	0	0	0	0	0	0	0	0	0	0	.000	.000	.000
Martinez, Felix, Wich.†	85	345	304	44	79	107	11	4	3	34	6	1	9	25	1	51	6	4	8	.260	.333	.352
Mashore, Damon, E.P.	4	17	16	4	6	9	0	0	1	4	0	0	0	1	0	3	0	0	1	.375	.412	.563
Maule, Jason, R.R.*	76	196	171	33	45	54	3	0	2	15	3	0	3	19	1	27	13	4	6	.263	.347	.316
Maynard, Scott, S.A.	29	101	92	7	15	20	5	0	0	6	3	1	0	5	0	21	0	0	3	.163	.204	.217
Mayne, Brent, Wich.*	2	5	4	0	2	2	0	0	0	1	0	0	0	1	0	0	0	0	1	.500	.500	.500
Mayo, Blake, E.P.	11	2	2	1	1	1	0	0	0	0	0	0	0	0	0	1	0	0	0	.500	.500	.500
McDougall, Marshall, Mid.	84	369	323	60	98	157	22	5	9	56	3	4	1	38	3	57	7	4	5	.303	.374	.486
McDowell, Arturo, Shre.*	59	243	221	18	40	45	3	1	0	11	3	0	4	15	1	46	10	5	3	.181	.246	.204
McGowan, Sean, Shre.	9	31	30	2	5	7	2	0	0	1	0	0	0	1	0	3	0	0	3	.167	.194	.233
McKinley, Dan, Ark.*	26	109	100	10	24	31	7	0	0	9	3	4	0	2	0	15	2	1	4	.240	.245	.310
McNally, Sean, Tul.	66	251	221	23	52	84	6	1	8	37	0	2	0	28	1	66	4	2	5	.235	.319	.380
Meadows, Tydus, Wich.	33	140	119	24	41	71	12	3	4	20	0	3	4	14	0	23	4	2	5	.345	.421	.597
Meliah, Dave, Tul.*	30	114	109	14	28	49	6	0	5	22	0	1	0	4	0	16	2	2	4	.257	.281	.450
Menchaca, Eriberto, S.A.	6	22	22	0	6	6	0	0	0	2	0	0	0	0	0	5	0	0	0	.273	.273	.273
Mendoza, Carlos, Shre.†	111	455	377	44	92	122	20	2	2	28	6	2	2	68	0	42	12	9	10	.244	.361	.324
Mensik, Todd, Mid.*	72	299	251	37	60	90	12	0	6	32	0	3	5	40	2	64	2	1	8	.239	.351	.359
Meyer, Drew, Tul.*	4	15	14	0	3	3	0	0	0	0	0	0	1	0	0	6	0	0	1	.214	.267	.214
Miller, Greg, R.R.*	14	3	3	0	0	0	0	0	0	0	0	0	0	0	0	1	0	0	1	.000	.000	.000
Micki, Dave, R.R.	2	2	0	1	0	0	0	0	0	0	0	0	0	1	0	0	0	0	0	.000	1.000	.000
Monahan, Shane, Wich.*	97	417	391	55	120	183	27	3	10	59	0	3	4	18	2	53	11	10	5	.307	.341	.468
Moore, Jason, Tul.†	116	475	417	54	101	169	21	4	13	69	0	4	6	48	2	94	3	4	10	.242	.326	.405
Moreta, Ramon, Shre.	88	300	273	34	71	98	12	3	3	37	2	3	2	20	1	52	17	16	10	.260	.312	.359
Morrissey, Adam, Mid.	90	343	302	39	71	94	15	1	2	22	2	0	1	38	0	71	4	2	7	.235	.323	.311
Mosquera, Julio, Tul.	2	6	6	1	2	2	0	0	0	0	0	0	0	0	0	1	0	0	0	.333	.333	.333
Myers, Adrian, S.A.	120	496	449	60	123	180	27	9	4	49	7	6	3	31	1	75	16	9	8	.274	.321	.401
Nannini, Mike, R.R.	30	19	16	2	5	5	0	0	0	1	2	0	0	1	0	5	0	0	0	.313	.353	.313
Ndungidi, Ntema, S.A.*	9	35	29	3	4	4	0	0	0	0	0	0	0	6	0	8	1	0	0	.138	.286	.138
Neal, Steve, E.P.*	122	482	407	57	115	192	29	0	16	75	0	5	6	63	11	106	3	1	12	.283	.383	.472
Nelson, Eric, Wich.†	12	27	22	2	5	6	1	0	0	1	1	0	0	4	0	2	1	1	0	.227	.346	.273
Nieckula, Aaron, Shre.	14	51	44	5	8	10	2	0	0	1	0	1	3	3	0	13	1	1	1	.182	.275	.227
Niekro, Lance, Shre.	79	310	297	33	92	126	20	1	4	34	1	3	2	7	0	32	0	2	11	.310	.327	.424
Obermueller, Wes, Wich.	17	3	3	0	0	0	0	0	0	0	0	0	0	0	0	1	0	0	0	.000	.000	.000
O'Keefe, Mike, Ark.*	132	537	468	72	131	242	34	7	21	78	0	3	4	62	4	73	10	3	9	.280	.367	.517
Oliver, Brian, Tul.	97	399	356	57	96	125	18	1	3	26	4	1	6	32	2	54	3	4	5	.270	.339	.351
Olson, Tim, E.P.	126	490	433	61	118	176	24	2	10	64	4	7	19	27	1	91	9	11	13	.273	.337	.406
Olszta, Eddie, S.A.	7	16	14	0	2	2	0	0	0	2	0	0	0	2	1	4	0	1	0	.143	.250	.143
Ottavinia, Paul, Tul.*	134	582	522	76	136	197	31	3	8	60	2	6	0	52	4	58	15	7	12	.261	.324	.377
Paz, Rich, Wich.	137	582	479	83	136	178	27	0	5	74	2	11	9	81	0	80	5	6	13	.284	.390	.372
Pecci, Jay, S.A.†	70	314	271	30	75	92	10	2	1	25	7	2	9	25	1	33	9	9	10	.277	.355	.339
Perez, Antonio, S.A.	72	274	240	30	62	80	8	2	2	24	8	5	10	11	0	64	15	9	3	.258	.312	.333
Perez, Beltran, E.P.	20	10	9	2	2	2	0	0	0	1	0	0	0	1	0	1	0	0	0	.222	.300	.222
Pernalete, Marco, Shre.†	15	59	54	5	12	19	4	0	1	5	2	0	2	1	0	8	1	1	0	.222	.263	.352
Perry, Chan, Tul.	105	435	399	59	126	192	20	2	14	73	0	6	1	29	3	44	6	5	11	.316	.359	.481
Pickler, Jeff, Tul.*	6	26	24	2	4	4	0	0	0	0	0	0	0	2	1	3	1	0	1	.167	.231	.167
Qualls, Chad, R.R.	29	19	15	1	4	5	1	0	0	3	0	0	0	1	0	4	0	0	0	.267	.313	.333
Quinn, Mark, Wich.	2	8	8	0	2	3	1	0	0	1	0	0	0	0	0	2	0	0	0	.250	.250	.375

Player, Team	G	TPA	AB	R	H	TB	2B	3B	HR	RBI	SH	SF	HP	BB	IBB	SO	SB	CS	GDP	Avg.	OBP	Slg.
Ramirez, Santiago, R.R.........	33	3	3	1	0	0	0	0	0	0	0	0	0	0	0	1	0	0	0	.000	.000	.000
Regilio, Nick, Tul.............	19	2	2	0	0	0	0	0	0	0	0	0	0	0	0	0	0	0	0	.000	.000	.000
Rivera, Ruben, Tul..............	59	237	205	38	64	119	17	4	10	43	0	4	5	23	2	46	4	3	5	.312	.388	.580
Roberts, Nick, R.R.............	29	21	18	3	3	5	2	0	0	1	3	0	0	0	0	5	0	0	0	.167	.167	.278
Robinson, Bo, S.A...............	116	477	420	39	103	132	20	0	3	41	2	4	6	45	2	51	1	3	12	.245	.324	.314
Rodriguez, Guillermo, Shre....	13	46	41	4	11	17	1	1	1	6	0	0	1	4	0	10	1	2	0	.268	.348	.415
Rogers, Brandon, Ark.	6	14	11	0	1	1	0	0	0	0	1	0	0	2	0	2	0	0	0	.091	.231	.091
Rosamond, Mike, R.R............	118	454	422	48	97	166	22	4	13	49	2	0	2	28	1	120	6	9	8	.230	.281	.393
Rosario, Rodrigo, R.R..........	26	13	9	2	0	0	0	0	0	0	3	0	0	1	0	3	0	0	0	.000	.100	.000
Rose, Mike, Wich.†..............	14	66	59	13	18	29	5	0	2	14	0	0	0	7	0	11	0	1	3	.305	.379	.492
Saarloos, Kirk, R.R............	15	13	10	2	3	3	0	0	0	3	0	0	0	0	0	3	0	0	0	.300	.300	.300
Saladin, Miguel, R.R...........	53	1	1	0	1	1	0	0	0	0	0	0	0	0	0	0	0	0	0	1.000	1.000	1.000
Sanchez, Duaner, E.P...........	31	1	1	1	1	4	0	0	1	1	0	0	0	0	0	0	0	0	0	1.000	1.000	4.000
Santora, Jack, E.P.†............	69	196	169	23	36	48	3	3	1	8	5	0	4	18	1	28	3	4	6	.213	.304	.284
Santos, Deivis, Shre.*.........	109	431	407	54	127	179	33	5	3	56	1	0	5	18	6	42	4	4	9	.312	.349	.440
Shabala, Adam, Shre.*..........	40	160	148	14	32	43	8	0	1	16	4	1	1	6	1	35	3	1	3	.216	.250	.291
Shackelford, Brian, Wich.*.....	86	276	244	29	53	81	10	0	6	31	2	4	3	23	0	42	3	4	3	.217	.288	.332
Silva, Jesus, E.P..............	21	1	1	0	0	0	0	0	0	0	0	0	0	0	0	1	0	0	0	.000	.000	.000
Silvestre, Juan, Tul...........	33	105	96	6	14	26	3	0	3	11	0	0	0	9	0	30	1	0	3	.146	.219	.271
Snelling, Chris, S.A.*	23	108	89	10	29	45	9	2	1	12	3	0	4	12	3	11	5	1	1	.326	.429	.506
Soto, T.J., R.R................	14	42	39	3	6	7	1	0	0	3	0	1	0	2	0	20	1	0	0	.154	.190	.179
Specht, Brian, Ark.†...........	126	534	476	64	118	189	24	4	13	60	1	4	4	49	1	129	18	4	6	.248	.321	.397
Stanley, Henri, R.R.*..........	127	537	456	90	143	247	36	10	16	72	0	5	4	72	7	85	14	9	7	.314	.408	.542
Strong, Jamal, S.A.............	127	582	503	63	140	169	16	5	1	31	2	5	10	62	1	87	46	16	7	.278	.366	.336
Teixeira, Mark, Tul.†..........	48	200	171	31	54	101	11	3	10	28	0	0	4	25	0	36	3	2	2	.316	.415	.591
Terrero, Luis, E.P.............	104	395	360	49	103	159	20	6	8	54	3	1	8	23	1	89	18	22	9	.286	.342	.442
Topolski, Jon, R.R.*...........	102	354	300	41	71	108	6	2	9	34	1	3	2	48	3	68	3	6	2	.237	.343	.360
Tracy, Chad, E.P.*.............	129	564	514	80	177	250	39	5	8	74	1	7	4	38	7	51	2	3	10	.344	.389	.486
Tremblay, Max, R.R.*...........	3	1	0	0	0	0	0	0	0	0	0	0	1	0	0	0	0	0	0	.000	1.000	.000
Tremie, Chris, R.R.............	50	149	134	16	31	40	3	0	2	19	0	2	0	13	1	18	0	1	3	.231	.295	.299
Urquhart, Derick, Ark.*	82	265	233	25	48	68	10	2	2	17	2	2	2	26	0	31	6	4	0	.206	.289	.292
Uzzell, Todd, Shre.............	5	1	1	0	0	0	0	0	0	0	0	0	0	0	0	1	0	0	0	.000	.000	.000
Valderrama, Carlos, Shre.	37	148	135	13	33	50	3	1	4	15	0	1	2	10	0	23	4	0	3	.244	.304	.370
Vaz, Roberto, Tul.*............	24	95	83	10	20	34	8	0	2	8	1	0	2	9	0	15	0	1	2	.241	.330	.410
Vent, Kevin, Shre.............	45	5	5	0	1	1	0	0	0	0	0	0	0	0	0	2	0	0	0	.200	.200	.200
Villano, Mike, Shre...........	5	1	1	0	0	0	0	0	0	0	0	0	0	0	0	0	0	0	0	.000	.000	.000
Villarreal, Oscar, E.P.*	14	12	10	0	3	3	0	0	0	0	1	0	1	0	0	4	0	0	0	.300	.364	.300
Waldron, Jeff, E.P.............	83	242	209	23	63	77	11	0	1	27	1	1	2	29	4	39	0	2	6	.301	.390	.368
Walk, Mitch, Shre.*...........	33	8	8	0	1	1	0	0	0	0	0	0	0	0	0	2	0	0	0	.125	.125	.125
Walker, Mark, Shre............	22	78	72	5	12	14	2	0	0	8	1	0	1	4	0	33	0	0	1	.167	.221	.194
Walter, Scott, Wich...........	22	78	71	6	14	19	2	0	1	7	0	1	0	6	1	12	0	1	2	.197	.256	.268
Warriax, Brandon, Tul.-Ark....	106	360	316	32	59	92	9	3	6	20	8	2	3	31	0	91	3	2	4	.187	.264	.291
Webb, Brandon, E.P............	26	18	17	2	2	2	0	0	0	0	0	0	1	0	0	9	0	0	1	.118	.167	.118
Whiteman, Tommy, R.R.	15	62	56	3	10	14	2	1	0	5	1	0	1	4	0	17	1	1	1	.179	.246	.250
Williams, Jason, E.P...........	7	10	9	3	1	2	1	0	0	0	0	0	0	1	0	1	0	0	0	.111	.200	.222
Wright, Gavin, R.R.............	2	12	9	2	3	3	0	0	0	2	1	1	1	0	0	2	0	0	0	.333	.364	.333

PLAYERS WITH TWO OR MORE TEAMS

Player, Team	G	TPA	AB	R	H	TB	2B	3B	HR	RBI	SH	SF	HP	BB	IBB	SO	SB	CS	GDP	Avg.	OBP	Slg.
Warriax, Brandon, Tul.	88	302	263	27	45	71	7	2	5	18	6	2	3	28	0	82	3	2	3	.171	.257	.270
Warriax, Brandon, Ark..........	18	58	53	5	14	21	2	1	1	2	2	0	0	3	0	9	0	0	1	.264	.304	.396

GRAND SLAMS—Cancel, Freire, Holt, Huffman, James, Koonce, Landry, B. Martin, Ottavinia, Perry, Shackelford, Stanley, Walter, 1 each.

AWARDED FIRST BASE ON CATCHER'S INTERFERENCE—Guevara 2 (Buck, Flaherty); Christensen (Lunsford); J. Hill (Buck); Huisman (Horner); J. Jones (Hammock); Kata (Christianson); Monahan (Durrington); Neal (Brito).

2002 PITCHING

TEAM

Team	W	L	Pct.	ERA	G	CG	ShO	Sv.	IP	H	TBF	R	ER	HR	SH	SF	HB	BB	IBB	SO	WP	Bk.
Wichita............	80	59	.576	3.27	139	6	10	34	1225.2	1102	5181	538	445	73	51	36	59	486	42	973	71	5
San Antonio	68	72	.486	3.43	140	4	18	33	1252.0	1134	5334	572	477	93	37	39	79	516	24	1022	48	3
El Paso	76	62	.551	3.75	139	9	10	38	1230.0	1241	5279	613	512	85	37	39	66	384	30	990	55	6
Round Rock	75	65	.536	3.87	140	4	9	37	1229.0	1187	5300	624	528	89	40	37	75	464	16	994	49	4
Midland............	75	64	.540	3.88	141	5	9	43	1239.0	1241	5372	636	534	86	43	54	62	504	33	1019	61	6
Tulsa.............	72	67	.518	3.88	140	4	10	34	1214.2	1260	5248	610	524	80	36	46	67	437	19	786	41	5
Shreveport	60	79	.432	4.27	139	6	7	28	1171.2	1258	5169	660	556	97	42	45	60	458	24	748	55	7
Arkansas	51	89	.364	4.74	140	14	7	22	1198.2	1334	5354	741	631	121	39	45	72	474	16	749	73	7

INDIVIDUAL

TOP QUALIFIERS FOR EARNED-RUN AVERAGE TITLE

Minimum 112 innings. *Lefthanded pitcher.

Pitcher, Team	W	L	Pct.	ERA	G	GS	CG	ShO	GF	Sv.	IP	H	TBF	R	ER	HR	SH	SF	HB	BB	IBB	SO	WP	Bk.
Walk, Mitch, Shre.*.................	6	5	.545	2.89	33	17	0	0	9	1	124.2	132	547	50	40	6	4	2	7	50	4	68	6	2
Rosario, Rodrigo, R.R..............	11	6	.647	3.11	26	23	0	0	1	0	130.1	106	561	56	45	5	2	4	19	59	1	94	2	0
Gosling, Mike, E.P.*	14	5	.737	3.13	27	27	2	2	0	0	166.2	149	705	66	58	7	8	6	4	62	4	115	9	1
Webb, Brandon, E.P...............	10	6	.625	3.14	26	25	1	1	1	0	152	141	647	66	53	4	2	3	13	59	1	122	12	1
Mears, Chris, S.A.	6	9	.400	3.14	30	20	1	0	4	0	143.1	138	597	57	50	16	1	2	9	38	2	103	2	1

Pitcher, Team	W	L	Pct.	ERA	G	GS	CG	ShO	GF	Sv.	IP	H	TBF	R	ER	HR	SH	SF	HB	BB	IBB	SO	WP	Bk.
Anderson, Craig, S.A.*	7	7	.500	3.20	27	27	1	1	0	0	152	143	641	61	54	12	2	7	4	64	1	94	2	2
Cervantes, Chris, E.P.*	6	4	.600	3.33	33	12	0	0	4	0	121.2	131	524	56	45	7	4	7	8	23	2	88	1	2
Rheinecker, John, Mid.*	7	7	.500	3.38	20	20	1	1	0	0	128	137	540	63	48	7	3	6	7	24	1	100	6	1
Hughes, Travis, Tul.	9	7	.563	3.52	26	26	1	1	0	0	143.1	139	637	68	56	11	1	2	7	82	0	137	3	0
Good, Andrew, E.P.	13	6	.684	3.54	28	27	2	1	0	0	178	170	730	89	70	21	5	6	7	26	0	127	3	0
Johnson, Rett, S.A.	10	4	.714	3.62	21	21	1	0	0	0	117	107	514	63	47	5	4	0	14	53	1	104	6	0
Stokley, Billy, Ark.	4	14	.222	4.33	38	19	4	0	9	1	131	158	564	77	63	11	5	3	9	34	2	41	1	0
Roberts, Nick, R.R.	12	7	.632	4.34	28	27	2	1	0	0	172	195	747	102	83	15	3	7	8	42	1	98	1	0
Qualls, Chad, R.R.	6	13	.316	4.36	29	29	0	0	0	0	163	174	722	92	79	9	3	6	9	67	3	142	3	4
Cox, Ryan, Shre.	7	9	.438	4.39	27	22	1	0	0	0	145.2	166	619	81	71	14	2	5	3	32	4	72	3	0

DEPARTMENTAL LEADERS: W—Gosling, 14; L—Stokley, 14; Pct.—Saarloos, .909; G—Galva, 62; GS—Qualls, 29; CG—Stokley, 4; ShO—Gosling, 2; GF—Runser, 53; Sv.—Runser, 25; IP—Good, 178.0; H—Roberts, 195; TBF—Roberts, 747; R—Roberts, 102; ER—Nannini, 91; HR—Good, 21; SH—Ro. Garcia, 10; SF—Stamler, 8; HB—Rosario, 19; BB—Hughes, 82; IBB—Lehr, 10; SO—Qualls, 142; WP—Webb, 12; BK—Qualls, 4.

ALL PITCHERS

*Lefthanded pitcher.

Pitcher, Team	W	L	Pct.	ERA	G	GS	CG	ShO	GF	Sv.	IP	H	TBF	R	ER	HR	SH	SF	HB	BB	IBB	SO	WP	Bk.
Abreu, Winston, Wich.	3	0	1.000	3.32	23	1	0	0	9	2	40.2	29	169	16	15	1	1	1	0	21	3	52	3	0
Affeldt, Jeremy, Wich.*	0	0	.000	1.50	3	3	0	0	0	0	6	1	21	1	1	0	0	0	1	3	0	3	2	0
Alvarez, Juan, Tul.*	0	0	.000	0.00	2	0	0	0	0	0	1.2	1	7	0	0	0	0	0	0	0	0	0	0	0
Anderson, Craig, S.A.*	7	7	.500	3.20	27	27	1	1	0	0	152	143	641	61	54	12	2	7	4	64	1	94	2	2
Anderson, Luke, Shre.	2	4	.333	2.81	26	0	0	0	21	11	32	31	141	10	10	1	3	0	1	13	3	47	4	0
Arnold, Jason, Mid.	5	1	.833	2.33	10	10	0	0	0	0	58	42	239	22	15	2	3	5	5	24	2	53	5	0
Baerlocher, Ryan, Wich.	3	2	.600	3.79	11	9	0	0	0	0	61.2	55	263	30	26	5	2	0	5	24	2	40	2	1
Barkett, Andy, S.A.*	0	0	.000	54.00	1	0	0	0	1	0	0.2	4	7	4	4	1	0	0	1	0	0	1	0	0
Bazzell, Shane, Mid.	5	7	.417	4.61	39	12	0	0	11	3	97.2	101	435	59	50	3	5	4	4	47	3	88	3	1
Belflower, Jay, E.P.	5	3	.625	4.04	36	0	0	0	9	2	55.2	67	246	29	25	5	5	2	4	14	7	53	3	0
Bell, Rob, Tul.	1	0	1.000	0.00	1	1	0	0	0	0	8	4	26	0	0	0	0	0	0	0	0	5	0	0
Bergman, Dusty, Ark.*	5	0	1.000	2.41	35	0	0	0	12	3	56	48	224	21	15	3	2	1	0	8	0	38	5	0
Bevel, Bobby, S.A.*	1	0	1.000	4.20	20	0	0	0	5	0	15	13	61	9	7	1	2	0	1	3	0	14	1	0
Bevis, P.J., E.P.	4	5	.444	2.83	49	0	0	0	28	11	63.2	50	263	22	20	3	2	3	2	29	5	62	5	0
Bonser, Boof, Shre.	1	2	.333	5.55	5	5	0	0	0	0	24.1	30	112	15	15	3	0	2	1	14	0	23	0	0
Bootcheck, Chris, Ark.	8	7	.533	4.81	19	19	3	0	0	0	116	130	517	68	62	11	4	2	6	35	0	90	4	0
Brink, Jim, Tul.	7	5	.583	4.94	42	6	0	0	14	0	85.2	102	372	51	47	12	2	5	5	21	2	41	1	0
Brown, Elliot, Shre.	8	4	.667	4.35	25	16	1	0	4	0	111.2	132	488	65	54	6	5	6	10	34	2	37	5	0
Bruney, Brian, E.P.	0	2	.000	2.92	10	0	0	0	4	0	12.1	11	47	5	4	1	0	1	1	4	1	14	1	0
Bukvich, Ryan, Wich.	1	1	.500	1.31	23	0	0	0	18	8	34.1	17	134	8	5	0	2	0	0	15	1	47	0	0
Burch, Matt, Wich.	1	1	.500	5.28	6	5	0	0	0	0	29	33	131	19	17	2	1	1	1	12	0	13	0	0
Calero, Kiko, Wich.	1	0	1.000	2.25	5	2	0	0	0	0	16	10	64	5	4	2	0	1	0	5	0	15	1	0
Camilli, Jason, Ark.	0	0	.000	6.75	2	0	0	0	2	0	1.1	2	8	2	1	1	0	0	0	0	0	1	0	0
Cannon, Jon, Shre.*	1	5	.167	4.20	38	0	0	0	20	4	63.1	57	289	40	30	6	1	1	5	40	2	57	1	2
Cash, David, Shre.	5	8	.385	3.05	34	12	0	0	17	5	109.1	94	456	41	37	9	4	4	4	39	1	88	9	0
Cervantes, Chris, E.P.*	6	4	.600	3.33	33	12	0	0	4	0	121.2	131	524	56	45	7	4	7	8	23	2	88	1	2
Clark, Jeff, Shre.	2	2	.500	5.05	6	6	1	1	0	0	35.2	45	153	21	20	5	1	3	1	2	0	20	2	0
Cogan, Tony, Wich.*	4	6	.400	3.47	17	16	0	0	1	0	90.2	92	390	48	35	4	4	3	8	26	0	62	2	0
Cotton, Joe, Mid.	2	1	.667	6.15	27	0	0	0	15	2	26.1	36	123	20	18	3	1	5	0	9	1	18	1	0
Coughenour, Jory, R.R.	3	2	.600	3.52	32	4	0	0	7	3	61.1	72	274	32	24	2	2	4	1	26	2	46	1	0
Cox, Ryan, Shre.	7	9	.438	4.39	27	22	1	0	0	0	145.2	166	619	81	71	14	2	5	3	32	4	72	3	0
Cozier, Vance, Shre.	3	7	.300	5.99	21	8	0	0	5	0	67.2	86	330	60	45	9	1	1	4	38	1	25	1	0
Cummings, Ryan, Ark.	4	3	.571	3.49	21	0	0	0	8	1	38.2	42	184	20	15	4	4	2	3	22	4	21	3	0
Daigle, Casey, E.P.	3	2	.600	3.25	7	7	0	0	0	0	44.1	46	182	19	16	5	2	1	3	9	0	29	2	0
Diaz, Felix, Shre.	3	5	.375	2.70	12	12	1	0	0	0	60	54	255	22	18	1	2	1	4	23	0	48	4	2
Dillinger, John, Ark.	2	1	.667	4.24	5	5	0	0	0	0	34	45	161	22	16	2	2	0	0	14	0	25	0	0
Dittfurth, Ryan, Tul.	1	3	.250	5.66	9	9	0	0	0	0	41.1	42	187	29	26	1	0	0	6	23	0	32	4	0
Durbin, Chad, Wich.	0	0	.000	5.06	3	1	0	0	0	0	5.1	5	26	4	3	1	1	0	0	4	0	6	0	0
Ellison, Jason, S.A.	1	6	.143	4.07	36	2	0	0	11	2	73	80	326	39	33	1	4	2	2	33	4	46	4	0
Emanuel, Brandon, Ark.	5	3	.625	2.81	14	14	1	0	0	0	83.1	76	335	32	26	9	2	0	2	18	0	47	0	1
Enochs, Chris, Mid.	5	12	.294	5.19	23	23	3	1	0	0	135.1	151	602	89	78	16	3	7	9	61	1	91	7	0
Esteves, Jake, Shre.	2	0	1.000	5.17	9	2	0	0	3	0	15.2	19	69	12	9	0	2	1	0	6	0	12	0	0
Ferguson, Ian, Wich.	6	2	.750	2.61	11	11	2	0	0	0	76	60	299	24	22	7	2	0	3	17	1	60	4	0
Figueroa, Carlos, Tul.*	0	2	.000	5.40	11	0	0	0	5	0	15	20	73	10	9	1	0	0	1	9	0	10	0	0
Fischer, Rich, Ark.	1	3	.250	4.23	7	7	0	0	0	0	44.2	40	185	22	21	8	1	0	2	10	0	36	0	1
Foppert, Jesse, Shre.	3	3	.500	2.79	11	11	1	0	0	0	61.1	44	249	22	19	3	3	1	3	21	0	74	3	0
Gajewski, Matt, Tul.	0	0	.000	0.00	1	0	0	0	1	0	1	0	3	0	0	0	0	0	0	0	0	0	0	0
Gallo, Mike, R.R.*	0	0	.000	6.75	1	0	0	0	0	0	1.1	1	5	1	1	0	0	0	0	0	0	0	0	0
Galva, Claudio, Mid.*	3	3	.500	3.74	62	0	0	0	17	4	65	64	288	36	27	8	3	3	0	33	3	54	2	1
Gandolfo, Rob, S.A.	0	2	.000	6.00	5	0	0	0	4	0	9	12	42	6	6	1	0	1	1	4	0	1	0	0
Gann, Jamie, E.P.	1	2	.333	6.14	19	2	0	0	6	1	29.1	41	148	25	20	4	0	0	4	15	0	22	2	1
Garcia, Reynaldo, Tul.	5	1	.833	3.69	18	9	0	0	1	0	68.1	63	294	36	28	11	3	2	3	30	1	54	4	1
Garcia, Rosman, Tul.	8	5	.615	3.01	53	0	0	0	28	6	74.2	75	326	34	25	1	10	3	3	32	9	38	3	2
Garcia, Sonny, Mid.	4	3	.571	3.94	21	7	0	0	6	1	59.1	68	259	27	26	5	3	2	2	19	3	38	3	0
German, Frank, Mid.	1	1	.500	3.05	37	0	0	0	28	16	41.1	28	174	14	14	0	0	3	0	27	2	59	7	0
Gilfillan, Jason, Wich.	2	2	.500	2.63	21	1	0	0	8	0	37.2	35	176	16	11	2	1	4	4	27	5	31	4	0
Glendenning, Mike, Wich.	0	0	.000	0.00	1	1	0	0	0	0	1.2	0	6	0	0	0	0	0	0	1	0	2	0	0
Gobble, Jimmy, Wich.*	5	7	.417	3.38	13	13	0	0	0	0	69.1	71	291	29	26	3	2	2	2	19	2	52	5	0
Good, Andrew, E.P.	13	6	.684	3.54	28	27	2	1	0	0	178	170	730	89	70	21	5	6	7	26	0	127	3	0
Gooding, Jason, Wich.*	2	1	.667	3.60	20	0	0	0	3	0	25	28	115	14	10	4	1	0	1	18	3	26	0	0
Gosling, Mike, E.P.*	14	5	.737	3.13	27	27	2	2	0	0	166.2	149	705	66	58	7	8	6	4	62	4	115	9	1
Graham, Tom, Tul.	1	2	.333	4.36	24	0	0	0	7	0	43.1	47	182	23	21	3	0	5	0	13	3	48	0	0
Gray, Mike, E.P.*	1	2	.333	3.46	19	1	0	0	2	0	26	39	134	15	10	1	1	2	2	12	2	20	0	0
Gregg, Kevin, Mid.	3	3	.500	4.30	11	4	0	0	0	0	37.2	31	162	20	18	3	0	1	3	18	0	45	3	0

Pitcher, Team	W	L	Pct.	ERA	G	GS	CG	ShO	GF	Sv	IP	H	TBF	R	ER	HR	SH	SF	HB	BB	IBB	SO	WP	Bk.
Grezlovski, Ben, Ark.	0	2	.000	5.13	38	2	0	0	16	1	59.2	70	284	41	34	3	2	2	6	34	5	29	6	0
Grimsley, Jason, Wich.	0	0	.000	9.00	1	1	0	0	0	0	1	1	5	1	1	0	0	0	0	1	0	0	0	0
Guerrero, Junior, Wich.	0	0	.000	3.38	11	0	0	0	3	0	18.2	17	77	10	7	0	0	0	2	3	0	9	1	0
Harang, Aaron, Mid.	2	0	1.000	1.08	3	3	0	0	0	0	16.2	12	66	3	2	0	1	0	3	7	0	21	1	0
Harden, Rich, Mid.	8	3	.727	2.95	16	16	1	0	0	0	85.1	67	365	33	28	2	1	0	3	52	1	102	1	1
Henthorne, Kevin, E.P.	1	1	.500	11.32	5	2	0	0	1	0	10.1	20	52	13	13	0	1	1	1	1	0	8	0	0
Hernandez, Carlos, R.R.*	0	0	.000	4.15	2	2	0	0	0	0	8.2	4	34	4	4	1	1	0	0	4	0	10	1	0
Hernandez, Runelvys, Wich.	8	3	.727	2.71	16	14	2	0	1	0	106.1	96	422	38	32	3	5	4	3	24	1	86	5	1
Hill, Jeremy, Wich.	4	7	.364	2.36	56	0	0	0	46	19	76.1	61	317	26	20	4	6	2	1	32	5	80	3	0
Horgan, Joe, Shre.*	4	3	.571	4.34	10	10	1	0	0	0	56	69	257	35	27	5	4	4	3	20	1	35	0	0
Huffaker, Mike, Tul.	0	0	.000	5.25	16	0	0	0	5	0	24	29	109	18	14	2	0	1	5	8	0	17	0	0
Hughes, Travis, Tul.	9	7	.563	3.52	26	26	1	1	0	0	143.1	139	637	68	56	11	1	2	7	82	0	137	3	0
Hundley, Jeff, Ark.*	1	4	.200	3.38	38	0	0	0	11	1	58.2	53	249	24	22	6	3	1	9	19	1	38	1	0
Hutchison, Wesley, Shre.	2	9	.182	5.81	22	7	0	0	11	3	66.2	80	316	50	43	4	2	5	5	33	2	35	6	1
Ireland, Eric, R.R.	1	0	1.000	1.00	4	0	0	0	2	0	9	6	33	1	1	0	0	0	0	1	0	6	1	0
Jackson, Dan, Ark.	1	0	1.000	9.00	8	0	0	0	4	0	12	25	65	15	12	1	0	1	0	6	0	8	3	0
Jamison, Ryan, R.R.	3	2	.600	3.77	31	1	0	0	7	1	57.1	63	257	31	24	4	2	2	4	23	1	57	5	0
Jenks, Bobby, Ark.	3	6	.333	4.66	10	10	1	0	0	0	58	49	260	34	30	2	2	3	2	44	0	58	2	1
Johnson, Jonathan, E.P.	0	1	.000	5.56	3	1	0	0	0	0	11.1	14	49	7	7	1	0	0	3	0	9	3	0
Johnson, Rett, S.A.	10	4	.714	3.62	21	21	1	0	0	0	117	107	514	63	47	5	4	0	14	53	1	104	6	0
Jones, Chris, Shre.*	1	7	.125	6.40	36	8	0	0	15	0	84.1	96	385	71	60	14	4	5	1	40	2	57	7	0
Jones, Marcus, Mid.	1	4	.200	5.40	7	7	0	0	0	0	31.2	37	146	29	19	3	1	1	2	17	0	24	1	1
Kolb, Dan, Tul.	0	1	.000	2.16	5	1	0	0	1	0	8.1	9	34	2	2	0	0	0	0	3	0	4	0	0
Kozlowski, Ben, Tul.*	4	2	.667	1.90	8	8	0	0	0	0	52	28	206	12	11	3	0	2	1	22	0	41	4	1
Lamber, Justin, S.A.*	2	4	.333	3.24	34	0	0	0	9	0	33.1	35	153	15	12	1	3	0	1	15	1	25	3	0
Lee, Garrett, Wich.	5	0	1.000	1.69	13	3	0	0	3	2	37.1	30	150	8	7	1	1	1	0	7	1	19	0	0
Lehr, Chuck, Mid.	8	3	.727	4.05	58	0	0	0	21	4	80	88	348	39	36	7	7	4	3	31	10	59	3	0
Lidge, Brad, R.R.	1	1	.500	2.45	5	0	0	0	1	0	11	9	44	4	3	0	0	0	0	3	0	18	0	0
Linebrink, Scott, R.R.	0	0	.000	0.00	2	2	0	0	0	0	2	2	9	0	0	0	0	0	0	2	0	1	0	0
Lira, James, Wich.*	3	4	.429	3.35	28	0	0	0	15	3	43	35	179	18	16	5	4	0	3	17	0	30	3	0
Looper, Aaron, S.A.	6	1	.857	2.28	57	0	0	0	9	0	90.2	76	377	33	23	4	6	1	9	30	6	73	4	0
Lopez, Javier, E.P.*	2	2	.500	2.72	61	0	0	0	25	6	46.1	34	186	16	14	3	2	1	0	16	1	47	1	0
Lundberg, Spike, Tul.	8	5	.615	3.41	16	16	1	0	0	0	105.2	113	440	43	40	6	3	4	4	23	0	60	0	0
MacDougal, Mike, Wich.	1	1	.500	3.06	4	4	1	0	0	0	17.2	11	85	12	6	1	1	1	2	24	0	14	7	0
Mangrum, Micah, Wich.	1	2	.333	3.55	23	0	0	0	17	1	38	46	159	18	15	2	2	1	1	9	2	19	1	0
Mann, Jim, R.R.	0	0	.000	4.50	1	0	0	0	1	0	2	1	7	1	1	0	0	0	0	0	0	2	0	0
Mantei, Matt, E.P.	0	1	.000	2.25	4	3	0	0	0	0	4	3	16	3	1	0	0	0	1	0	5	0	0	0
Martines, Jason, E.P.	2	1	.667	4.69	27	0	0	0	10	2	40.1	45	180	22	21	3	1	2	4	13	2	25	1	0
Martinez, Gustavo, S.A.	3	5	.375	3.24	21	14	0	0	5	0	97.1	89	419	42	35	7	5	2	8	43	1	76	3	0
Mateo, Julio, S.A.	1	0	1.000	0.52	12	0	0	0	4	0	17.1	7	61	3	1	2	0	0	0	3	0	18	0	0
Mathews, T.J., R.R.	0	0	.000	0.00	1	0	0	0	0	0	1	1	5	0	0	0	0	0	0	1	0	1	0	0
Matos, Josue, S.A.	1	0	1.000	4.91	3	3	0	0	0	0	14.2	15	62	8	8	2	0	0	6	0	14	0	0	0
May, Darrell, Wich.*	0	0	.000	2.08	1	1	0	0	0	0	4.1	4	18	1	1	0	0	0	0	1	0	5	0	0
Mayo, Blake, E.P.	0	1	.000	5.96	11	1	0	0	0	0	22.2	25	100	17	15	1	0	0	1	10	1	19	0	0
McClain, Kevin, Ark.	1	1	.500	4.63	8	0	0	0	4	1	11.2	11	52	8	6	3	0	0	1	3	0	8	2	0
McClaskey, Tim, Mid.	0	0	.000	10.20	13	0	0	0	8	0	15	28	78	19	17	2	0	1	0	6	0	13	2	0
McDill, Allen, Tul.*	1	2	.333	4.97	18	0	0	0	5	1	12.2	15	59	7	7	2	0	2	3	4	0	3	1	0
Mears, Chris, S.A.	6	9	.400	3.14	30	20	1	0	4	0	143.1	138	597	57	50	16	1	2	9	38	2	103	2	1
Meche, Gil, S.A.	4	6	.400	6.51	25	13	0	0	1	0	65	68	290	49	47	8	0	3	4	32	0	56	0	0
Mendoza, Hatuey, Mid.	3	10	.231	5.58	29	14	2	1	7	0	90.1	113	419	68	56	11	1	4	3	36	0	45	5	1
Mendoza, Mario, Ark.	0	4	.000	3.80	10	8	2	0	1	0	47.1	55	207	23	20	2	1	3	3	16	0	30	2	0
Miller, Greg, R.R.*	3	6	.333	5.00	14	12	0	0	1	0	68.1	77	307	44	38	6	2	2	2	20	0	51	6	0
Milo, Tony, Ark.*	2	4	.333	7.92	15	9	0	0	2	0	44.1	57	209	43	39	6	2	2	0	24	0	35	2	1
Milicki, Dave, R.R.	1	1	.500	3.00	2	2	0	0	0	0	9	8	37	3	3	0	1	0	0	2	0	7	0	0
Moreta, Ramon, Shre.	0	0	.000	9.00	1	0	0	0	1	0	1	1	4	1	1	0	0	0	0	0	0	0	0	0
Morrison, Robbie, Wich.	0	1	.000	4.50	12	0	0	0	7	0	18	20	81	12	9	1	1	2	1	7	1	11	1	0
Mounce, Tony, Tul.*	5	3	.625	3.90	11	11	0	0	0	0	57.2	59	238	28	25	7	3	0	2	15	0	47	2	0
Nannini, Mike, R.R.	7	10	.412	5.81	29	24	1	0	1	0	141	151	632	97	91	14	3	5	7	64	0	120	8	0
Natale, Mike, Wich.	4	3	.571	5.21	24	2	0	0	5	0	48.1	39	228	33	28	6	3	4	4	44	3	52	5	0
Navarro, Jason, S.A.*	0	0	.000	3.60	3	0	0	0	2	0	5	4	19	2	2	0	0	0	0	1	0	2	0	0
Nickoli, Mike, Ark.	3	10	.231	6.12	17	17	0	0	0	0	82.1	116	394	60	56	9	2	5	8	45	1	32	8	1
Obermueller, Wes, Wich.	9	5	.643	2.90	17	17	0	0	0	0	105.2	98	443	39	34	6	3	3	4	40	3	65	6	2
O'Brien, Matt, Mid.*	1	3	.250	2.98	54	0	0	0	9	2	63.1	47	256	29	21	7	4	4	3	20	2	49	2	0
O'Neal, Brandon, Ark.	0	0	.000	6.75	2	0	0	0	1	0	4	6	21	3	3	0	0	0	4	0	3	0	0
Peguero, Darwin, R.R.*	3	2	.600	4.48	54	0	0	0	12	1	60.1	66	276	42	30	6	3	2	5	28	1	41	6	0
Pena, Jesus, Tul.*	2	3	.400	3.27	17	0	0	0	7	0	22	24	93	9	8	2	1	1	1	5	0	15	0	0
Peralta, Joel, Ark.	2	0	.000	6.62	12	0	0	0	4	0	17.2	25	87	15	13	5	0	2	1	10	0	11	2	0
Perez, Beltran, E.P.	3	8	.273	5.47	20	19	1	0	0	0	97	114	434	70	59	10	4	1	4	33	2	77	4	1
Pine, Chris, Ark.	1	3	.250	6.39	17	4	1	0	9	1	38	38	166	29	27	5	2	2	3	15	2	16	6	0
Polanco, Elvis, S.A.	1	1	.500	3.48	4	1	0	0	1	0	8	9	43	4	3	1	0	1	1	12	1	5	0	0
Powell, Jay, Tul.	0	0	.000	0.00	2	0	0	0	0	0	2	0	7	0	0	0	0	0	0	1	0	0	0	0
Putz, J.J., S.A.	3	10	.231	3.64	15	15	1	1	0	0	84	84	354	41	34	7	0	3	5	28	0	60	5	0
Qualls, Chad, R.R.	6	13	.316	4.36	29	29	0	0	0	0	163	174	722	92	79	9	3	6	9	67	3	142	3	4
Ramirez, Erasmo, Tul.*	4	2	.667	3.00	34	0	0	0	3	2	54	51	215	23	18	1	2	0	4	8	0	34	1	0
Ramirez, Santiago, R.R.	5	2	.714	2.56	33	0	0	0	18	4	63.1	45	262	19	18	3	2	2	6	26	3	73	1	0
Regilio, Nick, Tul.	6	8	.429	3.44	19	19	2	1	0	0	104.2	97	452	46	40	8	3	3	3	47	2	59	4	0
Reichert, Dan, Wich.	0	1	.000	11.45	8	0	0	0	2	0	11	16	58	15	14	0	1	1	0	9	0	11	0	0
Rheinecker, John, Mid.*	7	7	.500	3.38	20	20	1	1	0	0	128	137	540	63	48	7	3	6	7	24	1	100	6	1
Roberts, Nick, R.R.	12	7	.632	4.34	28	27	2	1	0	0	172	195	747	102	83	15	3	7	8	42	1	98	1	0
Rocker, John, Tul.*	0	1	.000	13.50	3	0	0	0	0	0	2.2	3	12	4	4	0	0	0	0	2	0	5	1	0
Rodriguez, Francisco, Ark.	3	3	.500	1.96	23	0	0	0	16	9	41.1	32	170	13	9	2	0	0	0	15	0	61	7	1
Rodriguez, Rich, Tul.*	0	0	.000	6.75	3	0	0	0	0	0	2.2	4	14	2	2	0	0	0	0	2	0	3	1	0

Pitcher, Team	W	L	Pct.	ERA	G	GS	CG	ShO	GF	Sv.	IP	H	TBF	R	ER	HR	SH	SF	HB	BB	IBB	SO	WP	Bk.
Rosario, Rodrigo, R.R.	11	6	.647	3.11	26	23	0	0	1	0	130.1	106	561	56	45	5	2	4	19	59	1	94	2	0
Runser, Greg, Tul.	1	4	.200	3.84	61	0	0	0	53	25	61	74	286	34	26	3	3	4	3	29	1	26	2	0
Saarloos, Kirk, R.R.	10	1	.909	1.40	13	13	1	1	0	0	83.1	48	315	17	13	1	3	2	4	21	0	82	1	0
Saladin, Miguel, R.R.	4	5	.444	2.06	53	0	0	0	48	24	56.2	36	230	18	13	4	3	1	5	25	2	46	4	0
Sanches, Brian, Wich.	10	6	.625	4.40	33	15	0	0	7	0	116.2	111	498	60	57	8	5	3	6	43	5	101	7	1
Sanchez, Duaner, E.P.	4	3	.571	3.03	31	0	0	0	29	13	35.2	31	155	16	12	1	0	1	2	13	1	37	3	0
Schmack, Brian, Tul.	1	3	.250	5.79	12	7	0	0	0	0	37.1	45	162	26	24	1	1	2	3	7	0	20	2	0
Sedlacek, Shawn, Wich.	2	1	.667	1.47	3	3	0	0	0	0	18.1	14	78	6	3	0	1	2	2	4	0	16	0	0
Sessions, Doug, R.R.	2	1	.667	5.44	30	1	0	0	7	0	46.1	48	204	28	28	7	5	0	2	20	1	39	3	0
Shackelford, Brian, Wich.*	3	1	.750	3.51	22	0	0	0	7	0	25.2	23	120	12	10	1	2	0	3	26	2	15	6	0
Sikaras, Pete, E.P.	0	1	.000	6.75	4	0	0	0	3	0	4	7	21	3	3	1	0	0	1	2	0	4	0	0
Silva, Doug, Tul.	0	0	.000	19.89	5	0	0	0	4	0	6.1	14	39	14	14	0	0	2	0	7	0	5	1	0
Silva, Jesus, E.P.	1	3	.250	5.01	21	0	0	0	7	3	23.1	29	109	17	13	5	0	1	1	10	1	22	2	0
Simpson, Allan, S.A.	10	5	.667	3.06	56	0	0	0	28	7	82.1	53	346	33	28	4	4	4	6	50	5	99	5	0
Snow, Bert, Mid.	0	3	.000	4.98	24	0	0	0	14	8	21.2	21	97	12	12	1	0	1	1	11	2	29	2	0
Snyder, Kyle, Wich.	2	2	.500	4.21	6	6	0	0	0	0	25.2	21	101	12	12	4	0	1	1	7	1	18	3	0
Soriano, Rafael, S.A.	2	3	.400	2.31	10	8	0	0	0	0	46.2	32	185	13	12	6	0	1	1	15	0	52	0	0
Sparks, Steve, Shre.	0	0	.000	12.54	6	0	0	0	2	0	9.1	15	52	14	13	1	0	1	1	10	0	5	0	0
Stamler, Keith, Tul.	6	7	.462	4.56	30	21	0	0	1	0	134.1	163	591	80	68	5	2	8	12	28	1	57	6	1
Stein, Blake, Wich.	0	1	.000	3.48	6	3	0	0	0	0	10.1	11	46	4	4	1	0	0	0	7	0	7	2	0
Stephens, Jason, Ark.	1	4	.200	4.85	5	5	0	0	0	0	29.2	37	135	20	16	3	0	2	3	8	0	18	3	0
Stokley, Billy, Ark.	4	14	.222	4.33	38	19	4	0	9	1	131	156	564	77	63	11	5	3	9	34	2	41	1	0
Surkont, Keith, Mid.	2	3	.400	3.86	27	5	0	0	3	1	65.1	70	302	36	28	5	2	1	3	35	1	36	4	1
Suzuki, Mac, Wich.	0	0	.000	0.00	1	1	0	0	0	0	5	0	18	0	0	0	0	0	0	2	0	3	0	0
Taylor, Aaron, S.A.	4	3	.571	2.34	61	0	0	0	48	24	77	51	323	28	20	5	3	3	6	34	0	93	2	0
Thames, Charlie, Ark.	1	3	.250	5.03	38	0	0	0	19	4	53.2	45	246	34	30	4	4	7	8	35	1	42	3	0
Thompson, Eric, Mid.	6	4	.600	3.18	24	14	0	0	4	2	93.1	93	392	36	33	4	0	1	7	29	1	66	4	0
Thornton, Matt, S.A.*	1	5	.167	3.63	12	12	0	0	0	0	62	52	258	31	25	3	1	4	5	29	0	44	8	0
Topolski, Jon, R.R.	0	0	.000	0.00	1	0	0	0	1	0	1	1	5	0	0	0	0	0	0	1	0	0	0	0
Tremblay, Max, R.R.*	0	0	.000	1.59	3	0	0	0	2	0	5.2	7	23	1	1	1	0	0	0	0	0	5	0	0
Tremie, Chris, R.R.	0	0	.000	0.00	1	0	0	0	1	0	1	0	3	0	0	0	0	0	0	0	0	0	0	0
Urquhart, Derick, Ark.*	0	0	.000	33.75	1	0	0	0	1	0	1.1	5	12	6	5	0	0	0	0	3	0	1	0	0
Uzzell, Todd, Shre.	0	0	1.000	4.73	5	1	0	0	2	0	13.1	12	62	8	7	1	0	0	2	10	0	5	2	0
Van Dusen, Derrick, S.A.-Tul.*	2	3	.400	5.59	8	5	0	0	2	0	37	45	164	26	23	4	2	3	0	15	1	22	0	0
Vent, Kevin, Shre.	9	4	.692	3.43	45	2	0	0	21	3	81.1	83	345	35	31	6	3	3	5	29	2	32	2	0
Villano, Mike, Shre.	1	1	.500	7.56	5	0	0	0	2	1	8.1	12	40	7	7	2	1	0	0	4	0	8	0	0
Villarreal, Oscar, E.P.	6	3	.667	3.74	14	12	1	0	0	0	84.1	73	344	36	35	2	0	1	4	26	0	85	3	0
Wade, Travis, R.R.	0	2	.000	3.77	21	0	0	0	11	1	31	31	129	13	13	4	1	0	0	13	1	24	3	0
Waldron, Jeff, E.P.	0	0	.000	9.00	1	0	0	0	1	0	1	1	7	1	1	0	0	0	0	3	0	0	0	0
Walk, Mitch, Shre.*	6	5	.545	2.89	33	17	0	0	9	1	124.2	132	547	50	40	6	4	2	7	50	4	68	6	2
Warriax, Brandon, Ark.	0	0	.000	0.00	1	0	0	0	1	0	1	1	5	0	0	0	0	0	0	2	0	1	1	0
Webb, Brandon, E.P.	10	6	.625	3.14	26	25	1	1	1	0	152	141	647	66	53	4	2	3	13	59	1	122	12	1
Wilson, C.J., Tul.*	1	0	1.000	1.80	5	5	0	0	0	0	30	23	123	6	6	0	1	0	1	12	0	17	1	0
Wilson, Kris, Wich.	3	3	.500	1.88	13	7	1	0	1	0	48	47	192	17	10	4	3	0	4	4	1	33	1	0
Wilson, Phil, Ark.	2	4	.333	7.17	7	7	0	0	0	0	42.2	57	199	37	34	10	0	1	3	14	0	15	7	0
Wood, Mike, Mid.	11	3	.786	3.15	17	17	0	0	0	0	105.2	103	443	41	37	8	5	5	7	29	0	63	1	0
Wright, Chris, S.A.	5	1	.833	1.60	18	0	0	0	6	2	33.2	31	142	10	6	2	1	2	10	1	26	2	0
Ziegler, Mike, Mid.	1	0	1.000	5.11	3	3	0	0	0	0	12.1	17	57	9	7	0	1	2	0	5	0	11	3	0
Zimmerman, Jeff, Tul.	0	0	.000	0.00	3	0	0	0	0	0	3	2	11	0	0	0	0	0	0	1	0	3	0	0

PITCHERS WITH TWO OR MORE TEAMS

Pitcher, Team	W	L	Pct.	ERA	G	GS	CG	ShO	GF	Sv.	IP	H	TBF	R	ER	HR	SH	SF	HB	BB	IBB	SO	WP	Bk.
Van Dusen, Derrick, S.A.*	1	2	.333	7.20	5	4	0	0	1	0	25	31	114	21	20	4	1	3	0	12	1	17	0	0
Van Dusen, Derrick, Tul.*	1	1	.500	2.25	3	1	0	0	1	0	12	14	50	5	3	0	1	0	0	3	0	5	0	0

COMBINATION SHUTOUTS: **Arkansas (6)**—Emanuel-Thames-F. Rodriguez, Fischer-Pine, Jenks-Grevlovski-F. Rodriguez, H. Mendoza-F. Rodriguez, Milo-Bergman, Nickoli-Cummings-F. Rodriguez. **El Paso (6)**—Mantei-Good-Lopez-Sanchez, Villarreal-Gann-Lopez-Sanchez, Villarreal-Martinez-Bevis, Webb-Gann, Webb-Lopez-Belflower-Bevis, Webb-Lopez-Bevis-Sanchez. **Midland (7)**—Arnold-Bazzell, Bazzell-O'Brien-German, Harden-Bazzell, Harden-Surkont-O'Brien-German, Rheinecker-Snow, Thompson-Galva-German, Wood-O'Brien. **Round Rock (7)**—Nannini-Jamison-Lira, Qualls-Saladin, Roberts-Peguero-Saladin, Roberts-S. Ramirez, Rosario-Lira, Rosario-Sessions-Saladin, Saarloos-Peguero-Saladin. **San Antonio (16)**—C. Anderson-Simpson, E. Johnson-Simpson, Martinez-Lamber-Taylor, Martinez-Meche-Looper-Taylor, Martinez-Simpson, Mears-Lamber, Mears-Looper-Taylor, Mears-Meche-Bevel-Simpson, Mears-Wright-Lamber-Looper-Taylor, Meche-Looper-Taylor, Meche-Soriano-Lamber-Looper, Putz-Looper-Taylor-Bevel, Soriano-Mears-Taylor, Van Dusen-Looper-Taylor. **Shreveport (6)**—Brown-Vent, Cash-Brown-L. Anderson, Cash-Cox-Esteves, Diaz-L. Anderson, Diaz-Cash-C. Jones, Foppert-Vent. **Tulsa (8)**—Bell-Kolb, Brink-R. Rodriguez-Graham-E. Ramirez-Runser, Hughes-Re. Garcia, Hughes-E. Ramirez-Runser, Kozlowski-Brink, Lundberg-Brink, Regilio-Alvarez-Ro. Garcia-Runser. **Wichita (10)**—Affeldt-Sanches-Lee-Mangrum, Baerlocher-Lee-Hill, Baerlocher-Sanches-Bukvich, Gobble-Gooding-Shackelford-Hill, R. Hernandez-Shackelford, Lee-Bukvich-Hill, Obermueller-Hill, Sanches-Hill, Sedlacek-Bukvich, K. Wilson-Lee.

NO-HIT GAME: H. Mendoza, Arkansas, defeated Tulsa, 3-0, May 13.

2002 FIELDING

TEAM

Team	G	PO	A	E	TC	DP	TP	PB	Pct.
Round Rock	140	3687	1358	137	5182	116	0	20	.974
Shreveport	139	3515	1437	140	5092	126	0	14	.973
Tulsa	140	3644	1590	149	5383	116	0	13	.972
Wichita	139	3677	1480	148	5305	157	0	12	.972
El Paso	139	3690	1490	154	5334	118	0	14	.971
Midland	141	3717	1490	155	5362	120	0	23	.971
San Antonio	140	3756	1477	161	5394	148	0	15	.970
Arkansas	140	3596	1555	166	5317	137	0	23	.969

INDIVIDUAL

FIRST BASEMEN

NOTE: All caps denotes fielding-percentage leader based on 70 games for catchers, 93 for all other non-pitchers and 112 innings for pitchers. *Throws lefthanded.

Player, Team	Pct.	G	PO	A	E	TC	DP
Barkett, Andy, S.A.*	.984	75	613	54	11	678	64
Bowser, Matt, Mid.*	1.000	2	2	0	0	2	0
Brown, Ray, S.A.	1.000	5	31	4	0	35	2

Player, Team	Pct.	G	PO	A	E	TC	DP
Burns, Kevin, Ark.*	.988	36	302	25	4	331	30
Camilli, Jason, Ark.	1.000	1	1	0	0	1	1
Caruso, Joe, Wich.	1.000	6	37	6	0	43	3
Carvajal, Jhonny, Shre.	1.000	1	10	0	0	10	0
Castellano, John, S.A.	1.000	1	9	0	0	9	3
Castro, Nelson, Shre.	1.000	4	14	3	0	17	2
Catalanotto, Frank, Tul.	1.000	2	5	0	0	5	0
Christensen, Mike, Ark.	1.000	5	23	0	0	23	3
Christianson, Ryan, S.A.	1.000	2	9	0	0	9	1
Connors, Greg, S.A.	.977	4	39	3	1	43	4
Dobbs, Greg, S.A.	1.000	1	8	0	0	8	1
Durazo, Erubiel, E.P.*	1.000	4	35	4	0	39	4
Figueroa, Luis, S.A.	1.000	2	5	1	0	6	2
Flaherty, Tim, Shre.	.984	33	288	14	5	307	28
Freire, Alejandro, Tul.	.973	9	68	5	2	75	7
Furniss, Eddy, Tul.*	1.000	1	1	1	0	2	0
Glendenning, Mike, Wich.	.857	2	17	1	3	21	1
Haas, Chris, Tul.	.971	14	96	5	3	104	11
Hallmark, Pat, Wich.	.955	6	37	5	2	44	3
Hart, Corey, Wich.	.989	19	166	11	2	179	15
Hill, Jason, Ark.	.986	23	191	20	3	214	23
Howe, Matt, Mid.	1.000	7	40	4	0	44	4
Huffman, Royce, R.R.	.989	129	1067	63	13	1143	93
Huisman, Jason, Ark.	1.000	1	10	0	0	10	1
Jones, Jason, Tul.	.982	121	1145	72	22	1239	93
Jones, Jeremy, Tul.	1.000	3	8	0	0	8	0
Koonce, Graham, Mid.*	.987	119	1010	52	14	1076	89
Kremblas, Mike, Mid.	1.000	1	8	0	0	8	0
Lunsford, Trey, Shre.	1.000	3	22	4	0	26	2
Luther, Ryan, Shre.	1.000	3	25	1	0	26	4
Maldonado, Carlos, R.R.	1.000	3	17	3	0	20	0
Martin, Billy, E.P.	1.000	24	175	10	0	185	22
McDougall, Marshall, Mid.	.000	1	0	0	0	0	0
McGowan, Sean, Shre.	1.000	3	27	0	0	27	6
McNally, Sean, Tul.	1.000	3	7	1	0	8	0
Mensik, Todd, Mid.*	.984	18	169	10	3	182	10
Neal, Steve, E.P.*	.985	118	969	69	16	1054	75
Niekro, Lance, Shre.	1.000	50	418	21	0	439	39
O'Keefe, Mike, Ark.*	.991	89	714	65	7	786	70
Ottavinia, Paul, Tul.*	1.000	8	61	5	0	66	5
PERRY, Chan, Wich.	.998	100	885	56	2	943	98
Robinson, Bo, S.A.	.994	58	474	45	3	522	53
Santos, Deivis, Shre.*	.988	39	311	25	4	340	33
Shackelford, Brian, Wich.*	.981	12	90	14	2	106	18
Soto, T.J., R.R.	1.000	6	29	4	0	33	4
Tracy, Chad, E.P.	.980	6	46	3	1	50	7
Tremie, Chris, R.R.	1.000	6	43	4	0	47	7

SECOND BASEMEN

Player, Team	Pct.	G	PO	A	E	TC	DP
Alfaro, Jason, R.R.	1.000	1	2	0	0	2	0
Bruntlett, Eric, R.R.	.988	33	71	89	2	162	21
BURKE, Chris, R.R.	.976	94	173	280	11	464	62
Camilli, Jason, Ark.	.972	52	92	155	7	254	39
Carvajal, Jhonny, Shre.	.983	24	53	66	2	121	17
Catalanotto, Frank, Tul.	1.000	1	1	1	0	2	0
Duncan, Carlos, Ark.	.960	50	98	142	10	250	38
Durrington, Trent, Ark.	.964	30	60	74	5	139	11
Gandolfo, Rob, S.A.	.990	24	40	56	1	97	15
Guevara, Giomar, Mid.	.986	31	61	81	2	144	15
Haas, Chris, Tul.	1.000	6	6	10	0	16	3
Harris, Brian, Wich.	.976	129	256	393	16	665	104
Hart, Corey, Wich.	1.000	9	10	21	0	31	2
Howe, Matt, Mid.	.961	14	24	25	2	51	7
Huisman, Jason, Ark.	.971	20	27	40	2	69	8
Jester, Joe, Shre.	.952	88	163	251	21	435	54
Jones, Jeremy, Tul.	.000	1	0	0	0	0	0
Kata, Matt, E.P.	.974	127	235	361	16	612	66
Klassen, Danny, E.P.	1.000	1	3	1	0	4	0
Kuzmic, Craig, S.A.	.943	8	12	21	2	35	6
Luther, Ryan, Shre.	.750	2	1	2	1	4	0
Maier, T.J., Tul.	.978	18	42	45	2	89	17
Martinez, Felix, Wich.	.667	1	0	2	1	3	1
Maule, Jason, R.R.	.894	15	20	22	5	47	3
McDougall, Marshall, Mid.	.970	16	31	34	2	67	12
Meliah, Dave, Tul.	.959	11	22	49	3	74	9
Mendoza, Carlos, Shre.	.984	26	60	64	2	126	19
Moore, Jason, Tul.	.969	31	45	78	4	127	10
Morrissey, Adam, Mid.	.941	87	132	216	22	370	38
Nelson, Eric, Wich.	.950	5	9	10	1	20	5
Oliver, Brian, Tul.	.972	79	144	239	11	394	43
Olson, Tim, E.P.	.800	1	2	2	1	5	0

Player, Team	Pct.	G	PO	A	E	TC	DP
Pecci, Jay, S.A.	.980	53	85	162	5	252	36
Perez, Antonio, S.A.	.957	64	97	150	11	258	34
Pernalete, Marco, Shre.	.938	3	6	9	1	16	2
Pickler, Jeff, Tul.	.933	5	12	16	2	30	4
Santora, Jack, E.P.	.967	14	29	30	2	61	9
Warriax, Brandon, Ark.	1.000	2	0	1	0	1	0
Williams, Jason, E.P.	1.000	5	7	9	0	16	2

THIRD BASEMEN

Player, Team	Pct.	G	PO	A	E	TC	DP
ALFARO, Jason, R.R.	.963	113	87	196	11	294	18
Calderon, Henry, Wich.	.936	18	15	29	3	47	1
Camilli, Jason, Ark.	.878	17	8	28	5	41	1
Cancel, Robinson, Mid.	.000	1	0	0	0	0	0
Caruso, Joe, Wich.	.909	18	14	26	4	44	0
Carvajal, Jhonny, Shre.	.927	78	67	148	17	232	8
Castellano, John, S.A.	.667	3	0	2	1	3	0
Castro, Nelson, Shre.	.969	16	14	49	2	65	3
Christensen, Mike, Ark.	.941	117	74	263	21	358	24
Connors, Greg, S.A.	.000	1	0	0	0	0	0
Durrington, Trent, Ark.	.850	11	9	8	3	20	0
Figueroa, Luis, S.A.	.954	46	27	77	5	109	5
Gandolfo, Rob, S.A.	.917	10	11	11	2	24	3
Guevara, Giomar, Mid.	.935	11	6	23	2	31	1
Haas, Chris, Tul.	1.000	17	10	33	0	43	2
Hallmark, Pat, Wich.	1.000	4	3	10	0	13	2
Hammock, Rob, E.P.	.929	11	8	18	2	28	0
Harris, Brian, Wich.	.750	2	1	2	1	4	0
Hart, Corey, Wich.	.842	25	13	35	9	57	5
Hochgesang, Josh, Mid.	.907	87	52	144	20	216	10
Howe, Matt, Mid.	.878	17	8	28	5	41	2
Huisman, Jason, Ark.	1.000	1	0	1	0	1	0
Kata, Matt, E.P.	1.000	3	1	2	0	3	0
King, Brad, Tul.	1.000	6	4	6	0	10	0
Klassen, Danny, E.P.	.923	4	6	6	1	13	0
Krause, Scott, S.A.	.667	1	1	1	1	3	0
Kuzmic, Craig, S.A.	.916	56	36	106	13	155	11
Maier, T.J., Tul.	1.000	1	0	2	0	2	0
Martin, Tyler, Tul.	1.000	2	2	7	0	9	0
Maule, Jason, R.R.	.907	25	12	27	4	43	2
McDougall, Marshall, Mid.	.949	38	23	71	5	99	3
McNally, Sean, Tul.	.921	52	37	79	10	126	5
Meliah, Dave, Tul.	1.000	1	1	1	0	2	0
Menchaca, Eriberto, S.A.	.500	1	1	1	2	4	0
Mendoza, Carlos, Shre.	1.000	12	9	29	0	38	2
Moore, Jason, Tul.	.944	29	12	39	3	54	1
Nelson, Eric, Wich.	.778	5	1	6	2	9	0
Niekro, Lance, Shre.	.857	27	22	44	11	77	5
Oliver, Brian, Tul.	1.000	2	1	8	0	9	1
Olszta, Eddie, S.A.	1.000	2	0	1	0	1	0
Paz, Rich, Wich.	.912	77	57	129	18	204	16
Pecci, Jay, S.A.	1.000	3	4	3	0	7	0
Pernalete, Marco, Shre.	.917	10	10	12	2	24	1
Robinson, Bo, S.A.	.880	24	9	35	6	50	5
Santora, Jack, E.P.	.914	20	4	28	3	35	0
Soto, T.J., R.R.	1.000	1	0	1	0	1	0
Teixeira, Mark, Tul.	.925	47	46	103	12	161	11
Tracy, Chad, E.P.	.924	113	84	218	25	327	13
Tremie, Chris, R.R.	.941	12	2	14	1	17	0
Warriax, Brandon, Ark.	.818	4	3	6	2	11	1
Williams, Jason, E.P.	.000	1	0	0	0	0	0

SHORTSTOPS

Player, Team	Pct.	G	PO	A	E	TC	DP
Alfaro, Jason, R.R.	1.000	1	2	3	0	5	1
Bruntlett, Eric, R.R.	.957	83	147	230	17	394	55
Burke, Chris, R.R.	.938	43	72	108	12	192	17
Camilli, Jason, Ark.	.938	29	60	62	8	130	15
Carvajal, Jhonny, Shre.	.971	8	11	22	1	34	7
CASTILLO, Ruben, S.A.	.951	114	240	343	30	613	90
Castro, Nelson, Shre.	.958	63	100	176	12	288	36
Cotto, Luis, Wich.	.571	1	1	3	3	7	0
Crosby, Bobby, Mid.	.952	59	94	164	13	271	31
Duncan, Carlos, Ark.	.727	3	2	6	3	11	0
Durrington, Trent, Ark.	.842	4	5	11	3	19	3
Gandolfo, Rob, S.A.	.955	5	6	15	1	22	3
Guevara, Giomar, Mid.	.963	63	86	173	10	269	28
Harris, Brian, Wich.	1.000	1	2	4	0	6	1
Kata, Matt, E.P.	.941	9	13	19	2	34	7
Klassen, Danny, E.P.	.919	13	18	50	6	74	8
Maier, T.J., Tul.	1.000	2	2	1	0	3	0

Player, Team	Pct.	G	PO	A	E	TC	DP
Martinez, Felix, Wich.	.932	79	133	211	25	369	59
McDougall, Marshall, Mid.	.961	30	51	71	5	127	13
Meliah, Dave, Tul.	1.000	2	4	7	0	11	2
Menchaca, Eriberto, S.A.	.957	5	10	12	1	23	5
Mendoza, Carlos, Shre.	.949	72	99	215	17	331	47
Meyer, Drew, Tul.	.947	4	5	13	1	19	2
Moore, Jason, Tul.	.961	50	76	143	9	228	33
Morrissey, Adam, Mid.	1.000	1	0	1	0	1	0
Oliver, Brian, Tul.	1.000	6	10	16	0	26	3
Olson, Tim, E.P.	.943	107	158	301	28	487	62
Paz, Rich, Wich.	.962	62	99	183	11	293	48
Pecci, Jay, S.A.	.877	11	28	36	9	73	9
Perez, Antonio, S.A.	.929	10	7	19	2	28	7
Santora, Jack, E.P.	.950	25	39	57	5	101	9
Specht, Brian, Ark.	.932	95	179	301	35	515	61
Warriax, Brandon, Tul.-Ark.	.949	99	137	324	25	486	49
Whiteman, Tommy, R.R.	.875	15	25	31	8	64	11

SHORTSTOPS WITH TWO OR MORE TEAMS

Player, Team	Pct.	G	PO	A	E	TC	DP
Warriax, Brandon, Tul.	.948	87	124	281	22	427	43
Warriax, Brandon, Ark.	.949	12	13	43	3	59	6

OUTFIELDERS

Player, Team	Pct.	G	PO	A	E	TC	DP
Alfaro, Jason, R.R.	1.000	5	5	0	0	5	0
Asche, Kirk, Mid.	.984	106	235	5	4	244	3
Barkett, Andy, S.A.*	.962	13	24	1	1	26	0
Bowser, Matt, Mid.*	1.000	16	24	3	0	27	1
Burns, Kevan, E.P.*	1.000	48	64	1	0	65	0
Cadiente, Brett, Tul.*	.971	96	160	6	5	171	0
Camilli, Jason, Ark.	1.000	7	5	1	0	6	0
Caruso, Joe, Wich.	1.000	23	26	1	0	27	0
Carvajal, Jhonny, Shre.	.800	3	3	1	1	5	0
Castellano, John, S.A.	.943	28	31	2	2	35	1
Castro, Nelson, Shre.	1.000	3	12	1	0	13	1
Catalanotto, Frank, Tul.	.000	1	0	0	0	0	0
Clark, Doug, Shre.	.974	40	73	2	2	77	0
Cole, Eric, Tul.	.958	44	62	7	3	72	0
Connors, Greg, S.A.	1.000	2	4	0	0	4	0
Cunningham, Marco, Wich.	.993	75	133	8	1	142	2
DeJesus, David, Wich.*	.976	24	40	0	1	41	0
Dobbs, Greg, S.A.	.957	26	44	1	2	47	1
Duncan, Carlos, Ark.	1.000	8	15	0	0	15	0
Durrington, Trent, Ark.	1.000	16	27	1	0	28	1
Gajewski, Matt, Tul.	1.000	4	6	0	0	6	0
Gandolfo, Rob, S.A.	1.000	21	27	3	0	30	0
Gann, Jamie, E.P.	.000	1	0	0	0	0	0
Garcia, Douglas, Tul.*	.969	37	62	1	2	65	1
Gomez, Alexis, Wich.*	.967	112	228	6	8	242	0
Gordon, Brian, E.P.	.971	119	226	10	7	243	2
Greer, Rusty, Tul.*	1.000	3	2	0	0	2	0
Griffin, John-ford, Mid.*	1.000	2	2	0	0	2	0
Guevara, Giomar, Mid.	1.000	2	1	0	0	1	0
Guiel, Jeff, Ark.	1.000	5	11	0	0	11	0
Guzman, Elpidio, Ark.*	.970	121	247	15	8	270	4
Hall, Victor, E.P.*	.964	38	53	0	2	55	0
Hallmark, Pat, Wich.	.985	76	125	5	2	132	1
Hammock, Rob, E.P.	.989	55	80	7	1	88	3
Harris, Cedrick, E.P.	1.000	32	39	2	0	41	0
Hart, Corey, Wich.	.000	2	0	0	0	0	0
Hill, Mike, R.R.	.975	133	261	13	7	281	2
Holt, Daylan, Mid.	.964	52	99	9	4	112	2
Howe, Matt, Mid.	1.000	3	2	0	0	2	0
Huffman, Royce, R.R.	.000	1	0	0	0	0	0
Huisman, Jason, Ark.	.943	60	94	6	6	106	1
James, Kenny, Ark.	.982	90	217	2	4	223	1
Johnson, Brian, Wich.	1.000	1	0	1	0	1	0
Jones, Jason, Tul.	1.000	16	26	0	0	26	0
Keith, Rusty, Mid.	.981	89	143	10	3	156	4
King, Brad, Tul.	.000	2	0	0	0	0	0
Knoblauch, Chuck, Wich.	1.000	4	11	0	0	11	0
Krause, Scott, S.A.	.984	27	58	2	1	61	0
Kuzmic, Craig, S.A.	1.000	4	5	1	0	6	0
Laird, Gerald, Tul.	1.000	12	13	2	0	15	0
Landry, Jacques, Mid.	.966	30	52	4	2	58	1
LeBron, Juan, S.A.	.971	55	99	3	3	105	1
Linden, Todd, Shre.	.987	111	222	10	3	235	1
LOCKWOOD, Mike, Mid.*	.996	135	252	6	1	259	3
Luther, Ryan, Shre.	1.000	7	21	0	0	21	0
Martin, Billy, E.P.	.909	39	36	4	4	44	0
Mashore, Damon, E.P.	1.000	4	3	0	0	3	0

Player, Team	Pct.	G	PO	A	E	TC	DP
Maule, Jason, R.R.	1.000	1	1	0	0	1	0
McDowell, Arturo, Shre.*	.979	57	134	4	3	141	0
McGowan, Sean, Shre.	1.000	1	2	0	0	2	0
McKinley, Dan, Ark.	.979	23	43	4	1	48	1
Meadows, Tydus, Wich.	.968	17	30	0	1	31	0
Meliah, Dave, Tul.	1.000	12	15	1	0	16	0
Mensik, Todd, Mid.*	1.000	7	15	1	0	16	0
Monahan, Shane, Wich.	.993	87	141	2	1	144	0
Moreta, Ramon, Shre.	.988	76	150	11	2	163	1
Mosquera, Julio, Tul.	1.000	1	1	0	0	1	0
Myers, Adrian, S.A.	.973	112	176	6	5	187	1
Ndungidi, Ntema, S.A.	1.000	8	17	0	0	17	0
O'Keefe, Mike, Ark.*	.986	44	65	4	1	70	0
Oliver, Brian, Tul.	.000	1	0	0	0	0	0
Olson, Tim, E.P.	.951	21	37	2	2	41	0
Olszta, Eddie, S.A.	.000	1	0	0	0	0	0
Ottavinia, Paul, Tul.*	.983	127	272	12	5	289	2
Quinn, Mark, Wich.	.000	2	0	0	1	1	0
Rivera, Ruben, Tul.	.986	59	135	4	2	141	0
Rodriguez, Guillermo, Shre.	1.000	1	2	0	0	2	0
Rosamond, Mike, R.R.	.974	113	254	9	7	270	1
Rose, Mike, Wich.	.000	1	0	0	0	0	0
Santos, Deivis, Shre.*	.986	71	133	5	2	140	0
Shabala, Adam, Shre.	1.000	39	84	3	0	87	0
Shackelford, Brian, Wich.*	.974	20	37	1	1	39	0
Silvestre, Juan, Tul.	1.000	30	42	0	0	42	0
Snelling, Chris, S.A.*	1.000	23	48	2	0	50	0
Stanley, Henri, R.R.*	.984	98	177	6	3	186	1
Strong, Jamal, S.A.	.980	125	280	13	6	299	5
Terrero, Luis, E.P.	.973	100	243	11	7	261	3
Topolski, Jon, R.R.	.964	85	125	10	5	140	1
Urquhart, Derick, Ark.*	.992	72	123	3	1	127	1
Vaz, Roberto, Tul.*	.880	13	21	1	3	25	0
Walker, Mark, Shre.	.947	22	50	4	3	57	2
Wright, Gavin, R.R.	1.000	2	3	0	0	3	0

CATCHERS

Player, Team	Pct.	G	PO	A	E	TC	DP	PB
Alcala, Juan, S.A.	1.000	2	12	3	0	15	0	2
Anderson, Keith, Shre.	1.000	2	7	6	0	13	0	1
Ansman, Craig, E.P.	1.000	9	73	7	0	80	0	2
Ardoin, Danny, Tul.	1.000	6	40	8	0	48	0	0
Brito, Juan, Wich.	.992	85	583	72	5	660	5	3
Buck, John, R.R.	.990	104	727	64	8	799	4	14
Budde, Ryan, Ark.	1.000	2	15	2	0	17	0	0
CANCEL, Robinson, Mid.	.995	83	563	81	3	647	8	15
Carroll, Mark, S.A.	.970	8	59	6	2	67	1	1
Castellano, John, S.A.	1.000	4	25	1	0	26	0	0
Ceriani, Matt, E.P.	1.000	3	17	3	0	20	0	1
Christianson, Ryan, S.A.	.988	45	372	34	5	411	2	4
Connors, Greg, S.A.	1.000	3	17	2	0	19	0	0
Cresse, Brad, E.P.	.991	45	298	43	3	344	4	2
DeCinces, Tim, Mid.	.989	22	156	16	2	174	3	2
Del Chiaro, Brent, Ark.	1.000	2	13	0	0	13	0	2
Durrington, Trent, Ark.	.988	41	207	30	3	240	0	9
Fatheree, Danny, R.R.	1.000	9	58	4	0	62	0	1
Flaherty, Tim, Shre.	.976	37	227	13	6	246	2	6
Gajewski, Matt, Tul.	1.000	2	5	0	0	5	0	0
Gregorio, Tom, Ark.	.977	43	213	44	6	263	3	7
Hammock, Rob, E.P.	.989	56	397	36	5	438	2	3
Hill, Jason, Ark.	.994	58	310	38	2	350	2	5
Horner, Jim, S.A.	.985	55	377	26	6	409	2	3
Johnson, Brian, Wich.	.986	34	184	31	3	218	2	4
Jones, Jeremy, Tul.	.982	40	190	30	4	224	2	4
King, Brad, Tul.	.947	4	15	3	1	19	0	0
Kremblas, Mike, Mid.	.970	44	304	52	11	367	6	6
Kuzmic, Craig, S.A.	1.000	1	3	0	0	3	0	0
Laird, Gerald, Tul.	.988	101	565	72	8	645	2	9
Lunsford, Trey, Shre.	.986	63	313	45	5	363	2	1
Luther, Ryan, Shre.	.979	17	87	7	2	96	0	5
Maldonado, Carlos, R.R.	.976	18	116	7	3	126	0	5
Maynard, Scott, S.A.	.995	28	192	20	1	213	6	5
Mayne, Brent, Wich.	1.000	2	10	0	0	10	0	1
Mosquera, Julio, Tul.	.800	1	3	1	1	5	0	0
Nieckula, Aaron, Shre.	.991	14	97	12	1	110	0	1
Rodriguez, Guillermo, Shre.	1.000	7	39	4	0	43	1	0
Rogers, Brandon, Ark.	1.000	3	5	2	0	7	0	0
Rose, Mike, Wich.	.977	7	37	6	1	44	0	1
Tremie, Chris, R.R.	.993	20	125	10	1	136	2	0
Waldron, Jeff, E.P.	1.000	39	224	23	0	247	1	6
Walter, Scott, Wich.	1.000	22	166	13	0	179	3	3

Player, Team	Pct.	G	PO	A	E	TC	DP
Abreu, Winston, Wich.	1.000	23	6	4	0	10	0
Affeldt, Jeremy, Wich.*	.000	3	0	0	0	0	0
Alvarez, Juan, Tul.*	1.000	2	1	1	0	2	0
Anderson, Craig, S.A.*	.977	27	7	35	1	43	5
Anderson, Luke, Shre.	1.000	26	2	3	0	5	0
Arnold, Jason, Mid.	.889	10	7	9	2	18	1
Baerlocher, Ryan, Wich.	.944	11	4	13	1	18	1
Barkett, Andy, S.A.*	.000	1	0	0	0	0	0
Bazzell, Shane, Mid.	.960	39	5	19	1	25	0
Belflower, Jay, E.P.	1.000	36	4	1	0	5	0
Bell, Rob, Tul.	1.000	1	0	1	0	1	0
Bergman, Dusty, Ark.*	1.000	35	5	4	0	9	1
Bevel, Bobby, S.A.*	.750	20	1	2	1	4	0
Bevis, P.J., E.P.	.846	49	1	10	2	13	2
Bonser, Boof, Shre.	1.000	5	3	2	0	5	2
Bootcheck, Chris, Ark.	.950	19	11	8	1	20	1
Brink, Jim, Tul.	1.000	42	5	8	0	13	0
Brown, Elliot, Shre.	1.000	25	5	22	0	27	2
Bruney, Brian, E.P.	1.000	10	2	3	0	5	0
Bukvich, Ryan, Wich.	1.000	23	1	4	0	5	0
Burch, Matt, Wich.	.833	6	0	5	1	6	1
Calero, Kiko, Wich.	1.000	5	0	1	0	1	0
Camilli, Jason, Ark.	.000	2	0	0	0	0	0
Cannon, Jon, Shre.*	1.000	38	4	9	0	13	0
Cash, David, Shre.	.941	34	5	11	1	17	0
Cervantes, Chris, E.P.*	1.000	33	3	13	0	16	0
Clark, Jeff, Shre.	1.000	6	3	4	0	7	0
Cogan, Tony, Wich.*	.967	17	10	19	1	30	0
Cotton, Joe, Mid.	.833	27	0	5	1	6	1
Coughenour, Jory, R.R.	1.000	32	1	12	0	13	1
Cox, Ryan, Shre.	1.000	27	12	15	0	27	1
Cozier, Vance, Shre.	1.000	21	2	12	0	14	0
Cummings, Ryan, Ark.	.857	21	2	4	1	7	0
Daigle, Casey, E.P.	1.000	7	1	4	0	5	0
Diaz, Felix, Shre.	1.000	12	3	3	0	6	0
Dillinger, John, Ark.	.667	5	2	0	1	3	0
Dittfurth, Ryan, Tul.	.833	9	2	3	1	6	0
Durbin, Chad, Wich.	.000	3	0	0	0	0	0
Ellison, Jason, S.A.	.941	36	7	9	1	17	0
Emanuel, Brandon, Ark.	1.000	14	7	7	0	14	1
Enochs, Chris, Mid.	.967	23	6	23	1	30	1
Esteves, Jake, Shre.	.750	9	0	3	1	4	0
Ferguson, Ian, Wich.	1.000	11	5	12	0	17	0
Figueroa, Carlos, Tul.*	.000	11	0	0	0	0	0
Fischer, Rich, Ark.	.875	7	4	3	1	8	0
Foppert, Jesse, Shre.	1.000	11	1	5	0	6	0
Gajewski, Matt, Tul.	1.000	1	1	0	0	1	0
Gallo, Mike, R.R.*	.000	1	0	0	0	0	0
Galva, Claudio, Mid.*	1.000	62	2	14	0	16	0
Gandolfo, Rob, S.A.	1.000	5	1	0	0	1	0
Gann, Jamie, E.P.	1.000	19	2	2	0	4	0
Garcia, Reynaldo, Tul.	1.000	18	3	2	0	5	1
Garcia, Rosman, Tul.	.957	53	5	17	1	23	0
Garcia, Sonny, Mid.	.923	21	5	7	1	13	2
German, Frank, Mid.	.000	37	0	0	0	0	0
Gilfillan, Jason, Wich.	1.000	21	0	5	0	5	0
Glendenning, Mike, Wich.	.000	1	0	0	0	0	0
Gobble, Jimmy, Wich.*	.895	13	6	11	2	19	1
Good, Andrew, E.P.	.914	28	9	23	3	35	1
Gooding, Jason, Wich.*	1.000	20	0	3	0	3	1
Gosling, Mike, E.P.*	.960	27	2	22	1	25	0
Graham, Tom, Tul.	1.000	24	1	2	0	3	0
Gray, Mike, E.P.*	.500	19	2	1	3	6	0
Gregg, Kevin, Mid.	1.000	11	1	6	0	7	0
Grezlovski, Ben, Ark.	.895	38	4	13	2	19	3
Grimsley, Jason, Wich.	.000	1	0	0	0	0	0
Guerrero, Junior, Wich.	1.000	11	1	0	0	1	0
Harang, Aaron, Mid.	1.000	3	0	2	0	2	0
Harden, Rich, Mid.	.818	16	5	13	4	22	2
Henthorne, Kevin, E.P.	1.000	5	0	1	0	1	0
Hernandez, Carlos, R.R.*	1.000	2	0	2	0	2	0
Hernandez, Runelvys, Wich.	.923	16	9	15	2	26	1
Hill, Jeremy, Wich.	.923	56	4	8	1	13	0
Horgan, Joe, Shre.*	.750	10	2	4	2	8	0
Huffaker, Mike, Tul.	1.000	16	2	1	0	3	0
Hughes, Travis, Tul.	.889	26	4	12	2	18	1
Hundley, Jeff, Ark.*	.944	38	4	13	1	18	1
Hutchison, Wesley, Shre.	.846	22	4	7	2	13	0
Ireland, Eric, R.R.	1.000	4	3	2	0	5	0
Jackson, Dan, Ark.	1.000	8	2	4	0	6	0
Jamison, Ryan, R.R.	.875	31	2	5	1	8	1
Jenks, Bobby, Ark.	1.000	10	6	5	0	11	0
Johnson, Jonathan, E.P.	1.000	3	1	0	0	1	0
Johnson, Rett, S.A.	.957	21	7	15	1	23	0
Jones, Chris, Shre.*	.857	36	2	10	2	14	0
Jones, Marcus, Mid.	.867	7	4	9	2	15	0
Kolb, Dan, Tul.	1.000	5	0	2	0	2	1
Kozlowski, Ben, Tul.*	1.000	8	1	8	0	9	0
Lamber, Justin, S.A.*	.941	34	4	12	1	17	0
Lee, Garrett, Wich.	.857	13	2	4	1	7	0
Lehr, Chuck, Mid.	.949	58	8	29	2	39	3
Lidge, Brad, R.R.	.000	5	0	0	0	0	0
Linebrink, Scott, R.R.	1.000	2	0	1	0	1	0
Lira, James, R.R.	.833	28	2	8	2	12	0
Looper, Aaron, S.A.	.880	57	4	18	3	25	2
Lopez, Javier, E.P.*	1.000	61	4	12	0	16	2
Lundberg, Spike, Tul.	.926	16	9	16	2	27	4
MacDougal, Mike, Wich.	.833	4	2	3	1	6	0
Mangrum, Micah, Wich.	.933	23	6	8	1	15	3
Mann, Jim, R.R.	.000	1	0	0	0	0	0
Mantei, Matt, E.P.	.500	4	0	1	1	2	0
Martines, Jason, E.P.	1.000	27	3	5	0	8	1
Martinez, Gustavo, S.A.	1.000	21	10	21	0	31	2
Mateo, Julio, S.A.	1.000	12	3	1	0	4	0
Mathews, T.J., R.R.	1.000	1	0	0	0	0	0
Matos, Josue, S.A.	1.000	3	1	0	0	1	1
May, Darrell, Wich.*	.000	1	0	0	0	0	0
Mayo, Blake, E.P.	1.000	11	0	0	0	0	0
McClain, Kevin, Ark.	1.000	8	1	0	0	1	0
McClaskey, Tim, Mid.	1.000	13	1	0	0	1	0
McDill, Allen, Tul.*	1.000	18	0	1	0	1	0
Mears, Chris, S.A.	.971	30	15	18	1	34	1
Meche, Gil, S.A.	1.000	25	7	8	0	15	0
Mendoza, Hatuey, S.A.	1.000	29	13	14	0	27	0
Mendoza, Mario, Ark.	1.000	10	3	11	0	14	1
Miller, Greg, R.R.*	.909	14	3	7	1	11	1
Milo, Tony, Ark.*	1.000	15	2	5	0	7	0
Milicki, Dave, R.R.	1.000	2	0	2	0	2	0
Moreta, Ramon, Shre.	1.000	1	0	1	0	1	0
Morrison, Robbie, Wich.	1.000	12	1	0	0	1	0
Mounce, Tony, Tul.*	1.000	11	2	16	0	18	1
Nannini, Mike, R.R.	.947	29	8	10	1	19	1
Natale, Mike, Wich.	.778	24	3	4	2	9	1
Navarro, Jason, S.A.*	.000	3	0	0	0	0	0
Nickoli, Mike, Ark.	1.000	17	2	5	0	7	1
Obermueller, Wes, Wich.	1.000	17	6	13	0	19	2
O'Brien, Matt, Mid.*	1.000	54	7	7	0	14	0
O'Neal, Brandon, Ark.	1.000	2	0	1	0	1	0
Peguero, Darwin, R.R.*	.778	54	1	6	2	9	0
Pena, Jesus, Tul.*	1.000	17	3	4	0	7	0
Peralta, Joel, Ark.	1.000	12	3	4	0	7	0
Perez, Beltran, E.P.	.947	20	4	14	1	19	0
Pine, Chris, Ark.	1.000	17	5	6	0	11	0
Polanco, Elvis, S.A.	1.000	4	0	2	0	2	0
Powell, Jay, Tul.	.000	2	0	0	0	0	0
Putz, J.J., S.A.	.889	15	4	12	2	18	0
Qualls, Chad, R.R.	.806	29	4	25	7	36	1
Ramirez, Erasmo, Tul.*	1.000	34	7	22	0	29	1
Ramirez, Santiago, R.R.	1.000	33	5	10	0	15	0
Regilio, Nick, Tul.	.926	19	8	17	2	27	2
Reichert, Dan, Wich.	.800	8	0	4	1	5	0
Rheinecker, John, Mid.*	.909	20	6	14	2	22	1
ROBERTS, Nick, R.R.	1.000	28	11	23	0	34	1
Rocker, John, Tul.*	.000	3	0	0	0	0	0
Rodriguez, Francisco, Ark.	.889	23	5	3	1	9	1
Rodriguez, Rich, Tul.*	.000	2	0	0	0	0	0
Rosario, Rodrigo, R.R.	.920	26	9	14	2	25	2
Runser, Greg, Tul.	1.000	61	5	10	0	15	0
Saarloos, Kirk, R.R.	.917	13	13	20	3	36	0
Saladin, Miguel, R.R.	1.000	53	3	4	0	7	0
Sanches, Brian, Wich.	.900	33	4	14	2	20	1
Sanchez, Duaner, E.P.	1.000	31	4	8	0	12	1
Schmack, Brian, Tul.	.933	12	4	10	1	15	0
Sedlacek, Shawn, Wich.	1.000	3	1	2	0	3	0
Sessions, Doug, R.R.	1.000	30	1	3	0	4	0
Shackelford, Brian, Wich.*	1.000	22	4	9	0	13	0
Sikaras, Pete, E.P.	1.000	4	2	0	0	2	0
Silva, Doug, Tul.	1.000	5	0	1	0	1	0
Silva, Jesus, E.P.	1.000	21	1	2	0	3	0
Simpson, Allan, S.A.	.875	56	4	10	2	16	2
Snow, Bert, Mid.	1.000	24	0	1	0	1	0
Snyder, Kyle, Wich.	.667	6	0	2	1	3	0
Soriano, Rafael, S.A.	.800	10	2	2	1	5	1

Player, Team	Pct.	G	PO	A	E	TC	DP
Sparks, Steve, Shre.	1.000	6	1	1	0	2	0
Stamler, Keith, Tul.	.943	30	14	19	2	35	2
Stein, Blake, Wich.	1.000	6	2	1	0	3	1
Stephens, Jason, Ark.	1.000	5	5	3	0	8	0
Stokley, Billy, Ark.	.918	38	21	24	4	49	5
Surkont, Keith, Mid.	.929	27	5	8	1	14	0
Suzuki, Mac, Wich.	1.000	1	1	1	0	2	0
Taylor, Aaron, S.A.	.769	61	3	7	3	13	0
Thames, Charlie, Ark.	.929	38	4	9	1	14	2
Thompson, Eric, Mid.	.957	24	4	18	1	23	3
Thornton, Matt, S.A.*	.882	12	2	13	2	17	0
Topolski, Jon, R.R.	.000	1	0	0	0	0	0
Tremblay, Max, R.R.*	1.000	3	0	1	0	1	0
Tremie, Chris, R.R.	.000	1	0	0	0	0	0
Urquhart, Derick, Ark.*	.000	1	0	0	0	0	0
Uzzell, Todd, Shre.	.500	5	0	1	1	2	0
Van Dusen, Derrick, S.A.-Tul.*	.000	8	1	6	0	7	0
Vent, Kevin, Shre.	1.000	45	3	9	0	12	0
Villano, Mike, Shre.	1.000	5	2	4	0	6	1
Villarreal, Oscar, E.P.	.938	14	6	9	1	16	2
Wade, Travis, R.R.	1.000	21	0	5	0	5	0
Waldron, Jeff, E.P.	.000	1	0	0	0	0	0
Walk, Mitch, Shre.*	.968	33	7	23	1	31	5
Warriax, Brandon, Ark.	.000	1	0	0	0	0	0
Webb, Brandon, E.P.	.929	26	17	22	3	42	2
Wilson, C.J., Tul.*	1.000	5	2	7	0	9	1
Wilson, Kris, Wich.	1.000	13	2	13	0	15	0
Wilson, Phil, S.A.	1.000	7	4	6	0	10	0
Wood, Mike, Mid.	.926	17	6	19	2	27	1
Wright, Chris, S.A.	.833	18	2	3	1	6	0
Ziegler, Mike, Mid.	1.000	3	0	3	0	3	0
Zimmerman, Jeff, Tul.	.000	3	0	0	0	0	0

PITCHERS WITH TWO OR MORE TEAMS

Player, Team	Pct.	G	PO	A	E	TC	DP
Van Dusen, Derrick, S.A.*	1.000	5	0	5	0	5	0
Van Dusen, Derrick, Tul.*	1.000	3	1	1	0	2	0

The following player appeared only as designated hitter, pinch-hitter or pinch runner: Valderrama, dh, ph.

LEAGUE CHAMPIONS

Year	Team	Pct.	Year	Team	Pct.	Year	Team	Pct.
1888—	Dallas	.671	1929—	Dallas*	.588	1964—	San Antonio‡	.607
1889—	Houston	.551		Wichita Falls	.620	1965—	Tulsa	.574
1890—	Galveston	.705	1930—	Wichita Falls	.697		Albuquerque■	.550
1892—	Houston	.741		Fort Worth*	.632	1966—	Arkansas	.579
	Houston	.613	1931—	Houston♦	.625	1967—	Albuquerque	.557
1895—	Dallas	.754		Houston	.734	1968—	Arkansas	.586
	Fort Worth*	.750	1932—	Beaumont*	.640		El Paso■	.562
1896—	Fort Worth	.757		Dallas	.727	1969—	Amarillo	.593
	Houston*	.679	1933—	Houston	.623		Memphis■	.504
	Galveston	.548		San Antonio (4th)§	.523	1970—	Albuquerque♦	.615
1897—	San Antonio†	.657	1934—	Galveston‡	.579		Memphis	.507
	Galveston†	.717	1935—	Oklahoma City‡	.590	1971—	Did not operate as league—clubs	
1898—	League disbanded.		1936—	Dallas	.604		were members of Dixie Association.	
1899—	Galveston	.632		Tulsa (3rd)§	.519	1972—	Alexandria	.600
	Galveston	.762	1937—	Oklahoma City	.635		El Paso■	.557
1900-01—	Did not operate.			Fort Worth (3rd)§	.535	1973—	San Antonio	.590
1902—	Corsicana	.866	1938—	Beaumont	.635		Memphis■	.558
	Corsicana	.682	1939—	Houston	.606	1974—	Victoria■	.581
1903—	Paris-Waco	.615		Fort Worth (4th)§	.540		El Paso	.555
	Dallas*	.648	1940—	Houston‡	.652	1975—	Lafayette▼	.558
1904—	Corsicana*	.615	1941—	Houston	.673		Midland▼	.604
	Fort Worth	.800		Dallas (4th)§	.519	1976—	Amarillo■	.600
1905—	Fort Worth	.545	1942—	Beaumont	.605		Shreveport	.515
1906—	Fort Worth	.677		Shreveport (2nd)§	.576	1977—	El Paso	.600
	Cleburne∞	.609	1943-44-45—	Did not operate.			Arkansas•	.485
1907—	Austin	.629	1946—	Fort Worth	.656	1978—	El Paso•	.593
1908—	San Antonio	.664		Dallas (2nd)§	.591		Jackson	.567
1909—	Houston	.601	1947—	Houston‡	.623	1979—	Arkansas•	.571
1910—	Dallas†	.586	1948—	Fort Worth‡	.601		Midland	.563
	Houston†	.586	1949—	Fort Worth	.649	1980—	Arkansas•	.596
1911—	Austin	.575		Tulsa (2nd)§	.584		San Antonio	.544
1912—	Houston	.626	1950—	Beaumont	.595	1981—	San Antonio	.571
1913—	Houston	.620		San Antonio (4th)§	.513		Jackson•	.507
1914—	Houston†	.671	1951—	Houston‡	.619	1982—	El Paso•	.559
	Waco†	.671	1952—	Dallas	.571		Tulsa•	.515
1915—	Waco	.592		Shreveport (3rd)§	.522	1983—	Jackson	.507
1916—	Waco	.587	1953—	Dallas‡	.571		Beaumont•	.500
1917—	Dallas	.600	1954—	Shreveport	.559	1984—	Beaumont	.654
1918—	Dallas	.584		Houston (2nd)§	.553		Jackson•	.610
1919—	Shreveport*	.677	1955—	Dallas	.581	1985—	El Paso	.632
	Fort Worth	.651		Shreveport (3rd)§	.540		Jackson•	.537
1920—	Fort Worth	.703	1956—	Houston‡	.623	1986—	El Paso•	.630
	Fort Worth	.750	1957—	Dallas	.662		Jackson	.533
1921—	Fort Worth	.691		Houston (2nd)§	.630	1987—	Wichita•	.515
	Fort Worth	.662	1958—	Fort Worth	.582		Jackson	.515
1922—	Fort Worth	.694		Cor. Christi (3rd)§	.507	1988—	El Paso	.552
	Fort Worth	.711	1959—	Victoria	.589		Tulsa•	.522
1923—	Fort Worth	.632		Austin (2nd)§	.548	1989—	Arkansas•	.585
1924—	Fort Worth	.689	1960—	Rio Grande Valley	.590		Wichita	.537
	Fort Worth	.763		Tulsa (3rd)	.528	1990—	San Antonio	.582
1925—	Fort Worth	.711	1961—	Amarillo	.643		Shreveport•	.489
	Fort Worth▲	.653		San Antonio (3rd)§	.532	1991—	Shreveport•	.632
1926—	Dallas	.574	1962—	El Paso	.571		El Paso	.596
1927—	Wichita Falls	.654		Tulsa (2nd)§	.550	1992—	Shreveport	.566
1928—	Houston*	.679	1963—	San Antonio	.564		Wichita•	.515
	Wichita Falls	.731		Tulsa (3rd)§	.529	1993—	El Paso	.563

Year	Team	Pct.	Year	Team	Pct.	Year	Team	Pct.
	Jackson•	.541		Wichita	.500	2000—	Round Rock*	.593
1994—	El Paso•	.647	1997—	San Antonio•	.604	2001—	Round Rock	.614
	Jackson	.548		Shreveport	.551		Arkansas††	.485
1995—	Shreveport•	.652	1998—	Arkansas	.571	2002—	Wichita	.576
	Midland	.485		Tulsa•	.557		San Antonio§	.486
1996—	Jackson•	.547	1999—	Wichita•	.593			

*Won split-season playoff. †Won playoff for title. ‡Finished first and won four-club playoff. §Won four-club playoff. ∞Title to Cleburne by default. ▲Tied with Dallas in second half and won playoff for championship. ◆Tied with Beaumont at end of first half and won title in best-of-five series played as part of second-half schedule. ■League divided into Eastern, Western divisions; won two-team playoff. ▼League divided into Eastern, Western divisions; declared co-champions when playoffs were not completed. •League divided into Eastern and Western divisions and played split-season; won playoffs. NOTE—Championship awarded to winner of four-team playoff, 1933-51; first-place team and playoff winner co-champions, 1952-64. ††Was leading final round of split-season playoff, two games to none, and was declared champion when Professional Baseball declared a stoppage of play.

CLASS AA *Texas League*

CALIFORNIA LEAGUE

LEAGUE OFFICE

President
Joe Gagliardi
Address
2380 S. Bascom Ave., Suite 200
Campbell, CA 95008
Phone
408-369-8038

Teams (affiliation)
Bakersfield Blaze (Devil Rays)
High Desert Mavericks (Brewers)
Inland Empire 66ers of San Bernardino (Mariners)
Lake Elsinore Storm (Padres)
Lancaster Jethawks (Diamondbacks)

Modesto A's (A's)
Rancho Cucamonga Quakes (Angels)
San Jose Giants (Giants)
Stockton Ports (Rangers)
Visalia Oaks (Rockies)

CLASS A California League

2002 FINAL STANDINGS

FIRST HALF

NORTHERN DIVISION

Team	W	L	T	Pct.	GB
Stockton (Reds)	49	21	0	.700	...
Bakersfield (Devil Rays)	41	29	0	.586	8.0
San Jose (Giants)	37	33	0	.529	12.0
Visalia (Athletics)	34	36	0	.486	15.0
Modesto (Athletics)	34	36	0	.486	15.0

SOUTHERN DIVISION

Team	W	L	T	Pct.	GB
San Bernardino (Mariners)	37	33	0	.529	...
High Desert (Brewers)	34	36	0	.486	3.0
Lake Elsinore (Padres)	33	37	0	.471	4.0
Rancho Cucamonga (Angels)	28	42	0	.400	9.0
Lancaster (Diamondbacks)	23	47	0	.329	14.0

SECOND HALF

NORTHERN DIVISION

Team	W	L	T	Pct.	GB
Modesto (Athletics)	44	26	0	.629	...
Stockton (Reds)	40	30	0	.571	4.0
Visalia (Athletics)	36	35	0	.507	8.5
San Jose (Giants)	31	39	0	.443	13.0
Bakersfield (Devil Rays)	28	43	0	.394	16.5

SOUTHERN DIVISION

Team	W	L	T	Pct.	GB
Lake Elsinore (Padres)	42	28	0	.600	...
San Bernardino (Mariners)	40	30	0	.571	2.0
Lancaster (Diamondbacks)	40	30	0	.571	2.0
High Desert (Brewers)	26	44	0	.371	16.0
Rancho Cucamonga (Angels)	24	46	0	.343	18.0

COMPOSITE

Team	Sto.	Mod.	S.B.	L.E.	Vis.	Bak.	S.J.	Lan.	H.D.	R.C.	W	L	T	Pct.	GB
Stockton (Reds)	...	10	7	5	12	12	16	9	8	10	89	51	0	.636	...
Modesto (Athletics)	11	...	4	5	13	11	9	6	8	11	78	62	0	.557	11.0
San Bernardino (Mariners)	5	8	...	11	5	6	6	12	12	12	77	63	0	.550	12.0
Lake Elsinore (Padres)	3	7	10	...	9	8	7	10	11	10	75	65	0	.536	14.0
Visalia (Athletics)	9	8	3	3	...	12	11	8	8	8	70	71	0	.496	19.5
Bakersfield (Devil Rays)	9	10	6	4	10	...	10	9	4	7	69	72	0	.489	20.5
San Jose (Giants)	5	12	6	5	10	11	...	7	8	4	68	72	0	.486	21.0
Lancaster (Diamondbacks)	3	2	9	11	4	3	5	...	11	15	63	77	0	.450	26.0
High Desert (Brewers)	4	4	9	10	4	4	4	10	...	11	60	80	0	.429	29.0
Rancho Cucamonga (Angels)	2	1	9	11	4	5	4	6	10	...	52	88	0	.371	37.0

Major league affiliations in parentheses.

High Desert plays home games in Adelanto, Calif.

PLAYOFFS: Lake Elsinore defeated Lancaster, two games to none; Modesto defeated Visalia, two games to none; Stockton defeated Modesto, three games to none; Lake Elsinore defeated San Bernardino, three games to two. Stockton defeated Lake Elsinore, three games to one to win California League championship.

REGULAR-SEASON ATTENDANCE: Bakersfield, 101,377; High Desert, 139,348; Lake Elsinore, 230,957; Lancaster, 181,007; Modesto, 155,171; Rancho Cucamonga, 293,150; San Bernardino, 222,881; San Jose, 154,322; Stockton, 71,333; Visalia, 58,734. Total—1,608,280. Playoffs (16 games)—29,258. California-Carolina League All-Star Game at Wilmington, Del.—5,545.

MANAGERS: Bakersfield, Charlie Montoyo; High Desert, Mike Caldwell; Lake Elsinore, George Hendrick; Lancaster, Steve Scarsone (through May 15; 11-29), Bill Plummer (May 16 through end of season; 52-48); Modesto, Greg Sparks; Rancho Cucamonga, Bobby Meacham; San Bernardino, Daren Brown; San Jose, Bill Hayes; Stockton, Jayhawk Owens; Visalia, Webster Garrison.

ALL-STAR TEAM: 1B—Corey Hart, High Desert; 2B—Jake Gautreau, Lake Elsinore; 3B—Brian Barden, Lancaster; SS—Jose Lopez, San Bernardino; OF—Rocco Baldelli, Bakersfield; OF—Jonny Gomes, Bakersfield; OF—Stephen Smitherman, Stockton; C—Craig Ansman, Lancaster; DH—Mike Camp, Rancho Cucamonga; RHP—Jeff Clark, San Jose; RHP—Rich Fischer, Rancho Cucamonga; RHP— Evan Rust, Bakersfield; LHP—John Koronka, Stockton; Most Valuable Player—Rocco Baldelli, Bakersfield; Rookie of the Year—Jose Lopez, San Bernardino; Pitcher of the Year—Jeff Clark, San Jose; Manager of the Year—Bill Plummer, Lancaster.

2002 BATTING
TEAM

Team	G	TPA	AB	R	H	TB	2B	3B	HR	RBI	SH	SF	HP	BB	IBB	SO	SB	CS	GDP	LOB	ShO	Avg.	OBP	Slg.
Lancaster	140	5565	4945	741	1351	2002	257	44	102	671	54	44	67	455	6	1133	79	64	91	1055	5	.273	.340	.405
High Desert	140	5487	4866	818	1305	2135	255	55	155	752	38	48	65	470	12	1169	182	71	78	958	4	.268	.338	.439
S. Bernardino	140	5413	4783	710	1266	1935	267	54	98	637	36	30	78	486	18	1031	118	59	103	985	11	.265	.340	.405
Bakersfield	141	5417	4825	648	1276	1938	236	27	124	607	59	28	87	418	18	1211	107	39	100	1044	7	.264	.332	.402
Stockton	140	5396	4722	760	1245	1959	250	31	134	700	23	52	64	535	15	1179	134	64	89	977	1	.264	.343	.415
Modesto	140	5561	4845	690	1277	1872	263	34	88	638	56	42	51	567	15	1032	108	56	100	1148	7	.264	.344	.386
Visalia	141	5613	4804	750	1245	1945	249	32	129	694	49	41	77	642	19	1276	121	68	88	1125	6	.259	.353	.405
R. Cucamonga	140	5313	4777	662	1235	1860	265	36	96	600	27	41	101	467	10	1136	145	89	74	1017	6	.259	.322	.389
Lake Elsinore	140	5505	4835	702	1249	1857	250	44	90	617	25	49	44	532	18	1146	206	94	77	1034	7	.258	.337	.384
San Jose	140	5367	4808	663	1221	1804	233	37	92	587	53	39	70	397	15	1159	118	64	79	971	7	.254	.318	.375

TOP QUALIFIERS FOR BATTING CHAMPIONSHIP

Minimum 378 plate appearances. *Lefthanded batter. †Switch-hitter.

Player, Team	G	TPA	AB	R	H	TB	2B	3B	HR	RBI	SH	SF	HP	BB	IBB	SO	SB	CS	GDP	Avg.	OBP	Slg.
Knott, Jon, L.E.	93	420	367	55	125	198	33	8	8	73	0	4	3	46	2	68	5	4	7	.341	.414	.540
Lopez, Jose, S.B.	123	562	522	82	169	242	39	5	8	60	4	4	5	27	2	45	31	13	8	.324	.360	.464
Campo, Mike, R.C.*	126	569	450	86	141	215	35	6	9	53	2	2	40	75	4	127	18	10	6	.313	.451	.478
Smitherman, Stephen, Sto. ...	128	541	482	78	151	246	36	1	19	99	0	14	6	39	2	126	17	2	14	.313	.362	.510
Green, Andy, Lan.	102	477	401	74	124	186	36	4	6	50	6	5	5	60	0	59	15	10	7	.309	.401	.464
Bynum, Freddie, Vis.*	135	628	539	83	165	210	26	5	3	56	15	3	7	64	1	116	41	21	9	.306	.385	.390
Ansman, Craig, Lan.	100	426	374	67	114	203	21	7	18	55	0	2	16	34	1	113	3	3	6	.305	.385	.543
Brewer, Jace, Bak.	91	410	378	52	114	153	17	2	6	44	12	6	3	11	0	62	8	2	7	.302	.322	.405
Sellier, Brian, Mod.*	116	505	417	57	125	178	26	6	5	58	7	5	2	73	2	82	16	6	4	.300	.402	.427
Lindsey, John, S.B.	127	551	472	75	140	248	30	6	22	93	0	6	25	48	1	109	0	1	17	.297	.387	.525
Schneidmiller, Gary, Vis.	111	466	381	85	113	155	17	2	7	53	3	1	3	78	1	80	6	2	7	.297	.419	.407
Holst, Micah, S.J.	117	488	447	66	132	190	25	6	7	49	2	5	13	21	1	71	15	6	5	.295	.342	.425
Johnson, Dan, Mod.*	126	492	426	56	125	213	23	1	21	85	1	8	0	57	4	87	4	1	8	.293	.371	.500
Cosme, Caonabo, Mod.	131	602	529	90	154	232	33	6	11	68	14	5	7	46	1	113	19	14	10	.291	.353	.439
Bubela, Jaime, S.B.*	118	509	462	69	134	200	25	10	7	67	2	1	4	40	3	129	30	7	7	.290	.351	.433
Myers, Corey, Lan.	130	554	497	63	144	224	33	4	13	84	5	3	4	41	1	129	1	3	8	.290	.342	.451

DEPARTMENTAL LEADERS: G—Bynum, Cota, 135 each; AB—Cota, 540; R—Jon. Gomes, 102; H—Lopez, 169; TB—Jon. Gomes, 256; 2B—Lopez, 39; 3B—Krynzel, 12; HR—Soto, 31; RBI—Cota, 101; SH—Perez, 23; SF—Smitherman, 14; HP—Campo, 40; BB—Nettles, 101; IBB—Jon. Gomes, 6; SO—Soto, 195; SB—Nettles, 58; CS—Nettles, 26; GIDP—Cota, Lindsey, 17 each; Slg.—Jon. Gomes, .574; OBP—Campo, .451.

ALL PLAYERS

*Lefthanded batter. †Switch-hitter.

Player, Team	G	TPA	AB	R	H	TB	2B	3B	HR	RBI	SH	SF	HP	BB	IBB	SO	SB	CS	GDP	Avg.	OBP	Slg.
Abruzzo, Jared, R.C.†	101	423	385	53	94	169	27	0	16	53	0	5	3	30	0	124	1	1	2	.244	.300	.439
Adames, Epidaro, R.C.*	1	1	1	0	0	0	0	0	0	0	0	0	0	0	0	1	0	0	0	.000	.000	.000
Alcala, Juan, S.B.	28	100	92	8	17	21	1	0	1	6	3	1	2	2	0	23	1	0	1	.185	.216	.228
Alfonzo, Eliezer, H.D.	12	49	43	7	15	23	2	0	2	9	1	0	2	3	0	14	0	0	1	.349	.417	.535
Allegra, Matt, Vis..................	125	558	494	74	139	240	35	3	20	93	1	6	10	47	1	160	9	9	14	.281	.352	.486
Anderson, Bryan, Sto.	104	420	369	44	100	133	18	3	3	47	4	2	7	38	2	94	6	6	3	.271	.349	.360
Ansman, Craig, Lan.	100	426	374	67	114	203	21	7	18	55	0	2	16	34	1	113	3	3	6	.305	.385	.543
Arroyo, Abner, L.E.*	16	69	58	2	11	14	3	0	0	6	0	2	1	8	2	19	0	0	0	.190	.290	.241
Athas, Jamie, S.J.*	123	526	466	65	117	149	15	7	1	40	4	2	6	48	4	124	14	6	7	.251	.328	.320
Ayala, Elio, H.D.	16	37	35	3	3	4	1	0	0	2	0	0	0	0	0	7	0	0	0	.086	.086	.114
Baldelli, Rocco, Bak.	77	342	312	63	104	167	19	1	14	51	4	1	7	18	2	63	21	6	2	.333	.382	.535
Bannon, Jeff, Sto.	131	527	481	71	125	178	28	2	7	41	3	6	3	34	2	106	12	7	7	.260	.309	.370
Barden, Brian, Lan.	64	291	269	58	90	135	19	1	8	46	2	3	1	16	0	63	3	1	3	.335	.370	.502
Barfield, Josh, L.E.	6	26	23	2	2	2	0	0	0	4	1	1	0	1	0	4	0	0	1	.087	.120	.087
Barnwell, Chris, H.D.	35	145	132	19	32	42	7	0	1	14	2	1	2	8	0	14	1	1	2	.242	.294	.318
Bartlett, Jason, L.E..............	75	348	308	57	77	102	14	4	1	33	1	2	5	32	0	53	24	5	7	.250	.329	.331
Basil, Jason, Mod.-Vis.	112	466	403	48	99	149	13	2	11	65	2	3	7	51	0	93	0	0	11	.246	.338	.370
Beattie, Andrew, Sto.†	92	414	350	68	101	171	21	2	15	62	5	3	3	53	2	88	26	5	6	.289	.384	.489
Bell, Derek, S.J.†	12	45	38	6	6	7	1	0	0	3	1	0	0	6	0	6	0	0	0	.158	.273	.184
Bell, Jay, Lan.	7	24	20	4	4	8	1	0	1	7	0	0	0	4	0	6	0	0	1	.200	.333	.400
Benjamin, Al, L.E.................	34	145	136	15	40	65	17	1	2	23	0	3	1	5	0	30	3	0	3	.294	.317	.478
Berroa, Joandry, Lan.	85	276	251	27	58	70	7	1	1	17	10	0	3	12	0	49	4	5	2	.231	.274	.279
Bevins, Andy, Lan.	6	25	24	1	3	3	0	0	0	1	0	0	0	1	0	9	0	0	1	.125	.160	.125
Bone, Blake, S.B.*	89	346	286	52	67	145	18	6	16	50	2	0	3	55	1	63	0	3	3	.234	.363	.507
Bonilla, Clemente, Sto...........	19	77	62	13	17	25	5	0	1	4	0	0	0	15	0	11	0	2	1	.274	.416	.403
Bowser, Matt, Mod.*	84	354	305	34	71	98	13	1	4	36	3	3	5	38	4	54	0	1	5	.233	.325	.321
Boyd, Dan, H.D.	24	107	97	14	23	35	4	1	2	11	0	1	2	7	0	21	0	1	2	.237	.299	.361
Bozied, Tagg, L.E.................	71	324	282	45	84	154	23	1	15	60	0	4	3	35	4	60	3	4	1	.298	.377	.546
Bravo, Danny, L.E.†	77	330	268	43	77	109	15	4	3	33	0	5	4	53	1	30	8	6	3	.287	.406	.407
Brewer, Jace, Bak................	91	410	378	52	114	153	17	2	6	44	12	6	3	11	0	62	8	2	7	.302	.322	.405
Brooks, Jeff, L.E.	6	23	19	1	1	1	0	0	0	0	0	0	1	3	0	6	0	0	1	.053	.217	.053
Brown, Jeremy, Vis.	55	236	187	36	58	102	14	0	10	40	2	1	2	44	0	49	1	1	5	.310	.444	.545
Bubela, Jaime, S.B.*	118	509	462	69	134	200	25	10	7	67	2	1	4	40	3	129	30	7	7	.290	.351	.433
Budde, Ryan, R.C.	87	339	307	40	74	108	17	1	5	39	1	2	2	27	1	60	2	1	4	.241	.305	.352
Bynum, Freddie, Vis.*	135	628	539	83	165	210	26	5	3	56	15	3	7	64	1	116	41	21	9	.306	.385	.390
Calitri, Mike, Sto.	104	389	331	63	86	143	24	0	11	58	2	3	5	48	0	105	3	2	4	.260	.359	.432
Campo, Mike, R.C.*	126	569	450	86	141	215	35	6	9	53	2	2	40	75	4	127	18	10	6	.313	.451	.478
Candelaria, Scott, H.D.	60	238	225	37	67	92	8	4	3	27	1	1	2	9	0	39	9	4	1	.298	.329	.409
Candelario, Luis, Bak.	23	87	84	10	19	34	6	0	3	8	0	0	0	3	0	26	0	1	2	.226	.253	.405
Carroll, Mark, S.B.	72	281	233	34	62	82	8	0	4	28	3	2	4	39	0	60	0	0	6	.266	.378	.352
Castellano, John, S.B.	63	268	239	35	80	107	18	0	3	36	0	4	2	23	1	25	6	3	5	.335	.392	.448
Castro, Ismael, S.B.†	6	23	20	4	3	5	2	0	0	2	1	0	0	2	1	9	0	1	0	.150	.261	.250
Centeno, Irwin, Bak.	71	308	275	41	80	108	14	4	2	20	3	1	2	27	0	65	12	4	5	.291	.357	.393
Chavez, Angel, S.J.	130	520	471	61	121	175	20	5	8	62	8	7	6	28	1	83	21	7	12	.257	.303	.372
Choo, Shin-soo, S.B.*	11	51	39	14	12	22	5	1	1	9	1	0	2	9	1	9	3	0	0	.308	.460	.564
Christianson, Ryan, S.B.	21	78	71	12	20	30	5	1	1	9	0	0	3	4	0	17	1	0	1	.282	.346	.423
Christy, Jeff, Vis.*	111	439	384	54	104	144	29	4	1	39	7	2	0	46	1	79	12	7	5	.271	.347	.375
Clark, Aaron, Bak.*	125	504	446	59	112	190	26	2	16	77	0	3	13	42	1	149	11	1	3	.251	.331	.426
Clark, Daryl, H.D.*	93	411	340	57	83	162	18	2	19	78	2	8	3	58	0	117	4	5	4	.244	.352	.476
Contreras, Sergio, R.C.*	81	323	291	44	79	117	17	3	5	35	1	2	5	24	0	58	4	3	4	.271	.335	.402
Corbeil, Azarias, R.C.*	105	418	373	46	94	146	23	1	9	58	0	3	7	35	1	95	1	2	5	.252	.325	.391
Cordido, Julio, S.J.	61	250	226	32	54	69	6	0	3	23	5	1	1	17	1	31	3	1	4	.239	.294	.305
Cosme, Caonabo, Mod..........	131	602	529	90	154	232	33	6	11	68	14	5	7	46	1	113	19	14	10	.291	.353	.439
Cota, Jesus, Lan.*	135	588	540	73	151	238	33	3	16	101	0	7	2	38	2	121	0	1	17	.280	.325	.441
Coulie, Jason, R.C................	91	387	365	53	91	158	25	3	12	58	0	3	4	15	0	82	8	8	8	.249	.284	.433

CLASS A California League

CLASS A — California League

Player, Team	G	TPA	AB	R	H	TB	2B	3B	HR	RBI	SH	SF	HP	BB	IBB	SO	SB	CS	GDP	Avg.	OBP	Slg.
Craig, Beau, Mod.†	87	310	273	30	57	73	10	3	0	26	5	3	0	29	1	71	3	1	8	.209	.282	.267
Crosby, Bobby, Mod.	73	323	280	47	86	113	17	2	2	38	2	1	7	33	0	43	5	0	5	.307	.393	.404
Crowell, Kyle, Mod.	42	1	1	0	0	0	0	0	0	0	0	0	0	0	0	0	0	0	0	.000	.000	.000
Curry, Mike, Sto.*	28	126	106	24	35	51	7	3	1	13	2	2	0	16	0	16	5	4	1	.330	.411	.481
Davis, Mike, L.E.	28	100	90	10	11	19	5	0	1	8	0	1	0	9	0	27	4	0	5	.122	.200	.211
De Los Santos, Pedro, L.E.† .	21	89	81	13	21	27	3	0	1	6	0	0	0	8	0	12	14	4	1	.259	.326	.333
DeMent, Dan, Bak.	112	478	432	58	114	162	21	3	7	51	8	2	2	34	1	100	7	4	9	.264	.319	.375
Derosso, Tony, H.D.	28	123	103	28	38	74	11	2	7	34	0	1	3	16	0	20	2	0	1	.369	.463	.718
Donovan, Todd, L.E.	58	261	226	40	67	86	9	2	2	25	1	3	3	28	0	44	26	5	3	.296	.377	.381
Duarte, Justin, L.E.	32	116	101	4	13	15	2	0	0	12	0	4	3	8	0	21	0	1	2	.129	.207	.149
Duncan, Carlos, R.C.	70	313	274	45	72	144	19	4	15	68	0	4	5	30	2	80	20	5	3	.263	.342	.526
Dye, Jermaine, Mod.	2	8	8	1	4	7	3	0	0	2	0	0	0	0	0	0	0	0	0	.500	.500	.875
Eberwein, Kevin, L.E.	2	8	8	0	0	0	0	0	0	0	0	0	0	0	0	0	0	0	0	.000	.000	.000
Eddlemon, Kelly, Bak.	41	163	150	20	39	68	11	0	6	24	1	0	1	11	0	27	1	0	2	.260	.315	.453
Edge, Dwight, Lan.	131	504	451	56	126	145	15	2	0	44	6	2	10	35	0	103	10	8	7	.279	.343	.322
Ellison, Jason, S.J.	81	355	322	40	87	115	13	0	5	40	4	2	2	25	2	37	9	9	10	.270	.325	.357
Epke, Brian, Lan.	9	32	28	2	7	7	0	0	0	1	1	0	1	2	0	9	0	1	0	.250	.323	.250
Espinosa, David, Sto.†	95	433	367	71	90	138	13	7	7	44	1	1	2	62	1	104	26	17	5	.245	.356	.376
Falcon, Omar, L.E.	2	7	5	0	0	0	0	0	0	0	0	0	0	2	0	4	0	0	0	.000	.286	.000
Figga, Mike, Bak.	10	38	37	3	9	19	1	0	3	7	0	0	0	1	0	9	0	0	3	.243	.263	.514
Figueroa, Luis, S.B.	33	148	135	26	46	55	9	0	0	25	0	1	1	11	1	6	0	0	4	.341	.392	.407
Firlit, Dan, Lan.	23	84	74	13	19	25	4	1	0	13	3	0	2	5	0	18	0	1	3	.257	.321	.338
Florence, Branden, S.J.	5	22	21	5	8	12	1	0	1	5	1	0	0	0	0	3	0	0	1	.381	.381	.571
Foley, Steve, S.B.	21	66	49	10	11	17	1	1	1	5	1	1	1	14	1	12	1	2	1	.224	.400	.347
Foreman, JuJu, Lan.*	40	155	132	15	31	33	2	0	0	7	3	1	0	19	0	13	5	3	0	.235	.329	.250
Foster, Brian, H.D.	67	256	230	36	54	107	9	1	14	34	1	3	2	20	2	87	5	0	3	.235	.298	.465
Fox, Jason, H.D.†	59	165	151	25	37	50	4	3	1	15	2	1	0	11	0	29	9	2	3	.245	.294	.331
Freeman, Corey, S.B.	20	68	64	7	18	23	5	0	0	4	2	0	1	1	0	14	4	0	2	.281	.303	.359
Fulse, Sheldon, S.B.†	108	401	353	57	76	108	10	5	4	31	4	1	5	38	0	117	23	13	1	.215	.300	.306
Furmaniak, J.J., L.E.	106	423	381	50	98	147	16	6	7	43	5	5	6	26	1	100	11	9	8	.257	.311	.386
Gandolfo, Rob, S.B.*	13	34	30	3	9	12	1	1	0	4	0	0	1	3	0	4	1	0	0	.300	.382	.400
Garcia, Cip, S.B.	24	59	56	5	12	16	2	1	0	6	0	0	0	3	0	12	0	0	3	.214	.254	.286
Garcia, Isaac, Vis.-Mod.	74	218	197	36	47	63	7	0	3	26	1	3	1	16	0	48	2	3	7	.239	.295	.320
Garrido, Tomas, S.J.	16	43	39	2	0	0	0	0	0	1	2	0	0	2	1	7	0	0	2	.000	.049	.000
Garthwaite, Jay, Lan.	7	13	11	2	4	7	0	0	1	3	0	0	0	2	0	7	0	0	0	.364	.462	.636
Gautreau, Jake, L.E.*	93	419	371	43	106	158	20	1	10	62	0	4	2	42	2	86	2	3	6	.286	.358	.426
Gemoll, Brandon, H.D.*	46	195	175	29	49	73	12	3	2	27	0	2	2	16	0	33	2	1	7	.280	.344	.417
Gil, Jerry, Lan.	10	38	37	4	8	11	0	0	1	4	0	0	0	1	0	11	1	1	0	.216	.237	.297
Gomes, Joey, Bak.	5	22	22	1	5	8	0	0	1	4	0	0	0	0	0	4	0	0	0	.227	.227	.364
Gomes, Jonny, Bak.	134	569	446	102	124	256	24	9	30	72	0	1	31	91	6	173	15	3	4	.278	.432	.574
Gomez, Andre, L.E.	56	211	184	29	30	48	5	2	3	15	2	1	14	10	0	56	6	3	3	.163	.258	.261
Gonzalez, Wiki, L.E.	19	70	53	10	18	29	8	0	1	6	0	1	4	12	0	3	0	0	2	.340	.486	.547
Green, Andy, Lan.	102	477	401	74	124	186	36	4	6	50	6	5	5	60	0	59	15	10	7	.309	.401	.464
Greene, Khalil, L.E.	46	201	183	33	58	96	9	1	9	32	0	2	4	12	0	33	0	0	7	.317	.368	.525
Gregg, Mitch, Vis.*	63	237	197	33	27	54	4	1	7	24	0	3	3	34	2	87	0	1	2	.137	.270	.274
Groff, Matt, Vis.	45	139	121	20	28	44	7	0	3	10	1	0	1	16	2	24	2	2	4	.231	.326	.364
Hairston, Scott, Lan.	18	86	79	20	32	63	11	1	6	26	0	1	0	6	0	16	1	0	4	.405	.442	.797
Hall, Noah, Sto.	27	110	90	17	25	41	5	1	3	6	0	0	3	17	0	16	6	5	2	.278	.409	.456
Hall, Victor, Lan.*	91	413	352	72	98	133	10	8	3	32	6	1	7	47	0	72	26	15	2	.278	.373	.378
Hamilton, Josh, Bak.*	56	235	211	32	64	107	14	1	9	44	1	3	0	20	3	46	10	1	4	.303	.359	.507
Hammond, Derry, H.D.	92	381	353	49	79	147	18	1	16	54	1	1	2	24	1	112	3	1	4	.224	.276	.416
Hardy, J.J., H.D.	84	364	335	53	98	137	19	1	6	48	3	6	1	19	0	38	9	3	3	.293	.327	.409
Harris, Cedrick, H.D.	58	199	180	27	52	76	9	3	3	28	5	2	1	11	0	34	12	5	5	.289	.330	.422
Harrison, Vince, Bak.	32	128	116	5	29	37	2	0	2	11	2	1	0	9	0	28	0	1	2	.250	.302	.319
Hart, Corey, H.D.	100	437	393	76	113	225	26	10	22	84	1	1	5	37	2	101	24	11	3	.288	.356	.573
Haynes, Nathan, R.C.*	11	55	50	6	14	14	0	0	0	2	1	0	0	4	0	8	6	2	0	.280	.345	.280
Hernandez, Alexei, S.B.	79	310	283	29	68	101	17	2	4	32	1	2	2	22	1	57	0	4	11	.240	.298	.357
Hoffpauir, Josh, Mod.*	15	41	34	7	4	10	1	1	1	4	2	0	0	6	0	6	1	1	0	.118	.250	.294
Holst, Micah, S.J.	117	488	447	66	132	190	25	6	7	49	2	5	13	21	1	71	15	6	5	.295	.342	.425
Holt, Daylan, Vis.	77	346	309	48	90	166	26	1	16	63	0	4	4	29	3	75	3	5	2	.291	.355	.537
Howe, Matt, Mod.	71	317	277	42	71	123	17	1	11	53	2	2	5	31	1	66	8	1	1	.256	.340	.444
Hudson, Ben, S.B.	10	29	23	5	8	8	0	0	0	1	0	0	0	6	0	5	0	0	0	.348	.483	.348
Isenia, Chairon, Bak.	68	275	255	20	63	78	12	0	1	25	2	3	4	11	0	45	0	0	11	.247	.286	.306
Jackson, Steve, Mod.	99	356	314	35	79	127	21	0	9	42	2	3	5	32	0	92	0	0	6	.252	.328	.404
Jacobs, John, Bak.	17	54	51	3	10	14	4	0	0	1	1	0	0	2	0	25	0	1	1	.196	.226	.275
Johnson, Dan, Mod.*	126	492	426	56	125	213	23	1	21	85	1	8	0	57	4	87	4	1	8	.293	.371	.500
Johnson, Kade, H.D.	33	138	123	20	34	63	8	3	5	28	0	4	0	11	0	39	0	2	1	.276	.355	.512
Kaup, Nathan, Bak.	19	79	72	5	17	21	2	1	0	3	0	1	1	5	0	16	0	0	1	.236	.291	.292
Kelly, Tripp, Vis.	20	76	68	6	12	18	6	0	0	11	0	1	0	7	0	27	0	0	2	.176	.250	.265
Knott, Jon, L.E.	93	420	367	55	125	198	33	8	8	73	0	4	3	46	2	68	5	4	7	.341	.414	.540
Knox, Ryan, H.D.	25	104	93	21	33	57	7	1	5	15	0	0	3	8	0	12	15	3	0	.355	.423	.613
Kremblas, Mike, Vis.	20	81	57	11	14	18	4	0	0	5	1	1	13	9	0	10	1	2	1	.246	.450	.316
Kroeger, Josh, Lan.*	133	529	497	63	117	172	20	7	7	58	3	2	4	23	1	136	2	4	10	.235	.274	.346
Krynzel, Dave, H.D.*	97	445	365	76	98	168	13	12	11	45	1	3	11	64	3	100	29	17	2	.268	.391	.460
Kunich, Frank, S.B.	12	41	38	2	5	5	0	0	0	5	1	0	0	2	0	13	1	2	0	.132	.175	.132
Leone, Justin, S.B.	98	422	358	64	89	173	20	5	18	58	0	2	5	57	1	98	6	0	9	.249	.358	.483
Lindsey, John, S.B.	127	551	472	75	140	248	30	6	22	93	0	6	25	48	1	109	0	1	17	.297	.387	.525
Lopez, Jose, S.B.	123	562	522	82	169	242	39	5	8	60	4	4	5	27	2	45	31	13	8	.324	.360	.464
Lundquist, Ryan, Sto.	95	394	341	41	86	111	12	2	3	51	0	6	6	41	1	92	6	0	8	.252	.338	.326
Lunsford, Trey, S.J.	16	57	51	7	13	19	3	0	1	5	1	0	2	3	0	5	2	0	2	.255	.321	.373
Luster, Jeremy, S.J.†	49	204	187	23	41	61	9	1	3	23	0	2	3	12	0	40	3	1	3	.219	.275	.326
Luther, Ryan, S.J.	32	104	94	6	23	33	3	2	1	8	1	1	2	6	0	38	2	1	3	.245	.301	.351
Macha, Erick, Lan.	64	188	172	23	38	50	5	2	1	18	3	3	1	9	0	22	3	1	5	.221	.259	.291
Maher, Caleb, R.C.	3	11	9	0	4	5	1	0	0	0	0	0	0	2	0	2	0	0	0	.444	.545	.556
Maldonado, Edwin, S.J.	120	469	439	39	99	141	21	3	5	51	7	6	4	13	0	100	3	8	6	.226	.251	.321

– 510 –

Player, Team	G	TPA	AB	R	H	TB	2B	3B	HR	RBI	SH	SF	HP	BB	IBB	SO	SB	CS	GDP	Avg.	OBP	Slg.
Martin, Brian, Bak.	112	363	327	45	73	118	12	3	9	40	1	0	11	24	1	87	7	3	7	.223	.298	.361
Martinez, Candido, Sto.	53	187	179	36	47	82	9	4	6	24	0	1	1	6	0	46	19	4	3	.263	.289	.458
Martinez, Guillermo, S.B.†	60	225	207	13	43	52	6	0	1	16	3	2	2	11	0	39	1	2	7	.208	.252	.251
Mashore, Damon, Lan.	9	17	15	1	3	3	0	0	0	2	0	1	0	1	0	4	0	0	0	.200	.235	.200
Massiatte, Danny, Bak.	68	262	227	22	55	70	6	0	3	25	0	0	3	32	1	54	1	4	10	.242	.344	.308
Mathis, Jake, R.C.*	5	19	18	3	4	5	1	0	0	2	0	0	0	1	0	8	0	0	0	.222	.263	.278
McBeth, Marcus, Vis.	76	301	255	45	58	101	7	3	10	39	5	5	7	29	0	73	14	6	2	.227	.318	.396
McGee, Chris, H.D.	39	1	1	0	0	0	0	0	0	0	0	0	0	0	0	1	0	0	0	.000	.000	.000
McGowan, Sean, S.J.	55	234	212	22	64	88	12	0	4	31	0	1	6	15	0	34	0	1	4	.302	.363	.415
Melgarejo, Ransel, R.C.	4	17	15	0	3	3	0	0	0	3	0	1	0	1	0	0	0	0	1	.200	.235	.200
Menchaca, Eriberto, S.B.	11	43	38	5	11	12	1	0	0	9	2	0	1	2	0	10	1	0	1	.289	.341	.316
Mercado, Onix, Sto.	3	10	10	0	0	0	0	0	0	0	0	0	0	0	0	3	0	0	1	.000	.000	.000
Merritt, Graig, Bak.	14	51	45	5	10	17	4	0	1	8	1	0	1	4	0	15	0	0	0	.222	.300	.378
Merritt, Tim, S.B.	57	253	226	33	54	76	16	3	0	22	3	1	1	22	0	43	6	3	5	.239	.308	.336
Molina, Bengie, R.C.	1	4	2	0	1	1	0	0	0	0	0	0	1	1	0	0	0	0	0	.500	.750	.500
Morrissey, Adam, Mod.	36	164	141	23	41	59	7	1	3	26	2	0	1	20	0	28	4	3	3	.291	.383	.418
Murphy, Nate, Lan.*	10	43	37	6	9	15	3	0	1	5	0	1	1	4	0	10	0	1	0	.243	.326	.405
Myers, Casey, Mod.	60	251	219	23	54	82	16	0	4	30	1	3	4	24	0	33	1	2	13	.247	.328	.374
Myers, Corey, Lan.	130	554	497	63	144	224	33	4	13	84	5	8	3	41	1	129	1	3	8	.290	.342	.451
Nady, Xavier, L.E.	45	199	169	41	47	98	6	3	13	37	0	1	1	28	4	40	2	0	2	.278	.382	.580
Nagle, Austin, Mod.	64	246	216	26	47	70	13	2	2	25	1	2	0	27	0	58	3	2	2	.218	.302	.324
Nelson, Brad, H.D.*	26	114	102	24	26	46	11	0	3	17	0	0	0	12	1	28	0	0	4	.255	.333	.451
Nettles, Marcus, L.E.*	125	595	485	97	123	145	18	2	0	38	5	0	4	101	2	132	58	26	2	.254	.386	.299
Neufeld, Andy, Mod.*	39	130	111	22	29	39	5	1	1	8	0	0	0	19	0	26	3	2	1	.261	.369	.351
Nevin, Phil, L.E.	2	8	6	2	2	6	1	0	1	6	0	1	0	1	0	2	0	0	0	.333	.375	1.000
Nieckula, Aaron, S.J.	45	172	147	26	36	46	7	0	1	18	1	1	11	12	0	35	3	1	2	.245	.345	.313
Nunez, Felix, R.C.	5	18	14	3	2	2	0	0	0	0	0	0	0	4	0	5	0	0	1	.143	.333	.143
O'Donnell, Ryan, L.E.*	24	89	86	5	17	20	3	0	0	5	0	0	1	2	0	11	2	0	1	.198	.225	.233
Owens, Jeremy, L.E.	110	462	418	54	96	164	21	4	13	52	1	1	3	39	0	148	23	9	7	.230	.299	.392
Pagan, Andres, L.E.	71	272	258	16	56	67	9	1	0	18	2	3	1	8	0	74	1	3	2	.217	.241	.260
Patterson, Derek, H.D.	21	82	65	8	13	21	2	0	2	10	1	3	3	10	1	12	1	0	0	.200	.321	.323
Perez, Nestor, Bak.	120	440	381	40	96	117	15	0	2	34	23	3	0	33	1	52	8	6	12	.252	.309	.307
Peters, Samone, Sto.	73	279	257	32	51	110	8	0	17	52	0	3	6	13	0	106	0	0	4	.198	.251	.428
Peterson, Brian, Sto.	77	293	272	28	65	91	16	2	2	31	4	1	2	14	0	54	2	1	6	.239	.280	.335
Pichardo, Maximo, R.C.	51	179	168	15	42	53	6	1	1	14	2	2	1	6	0	27	7	5	3	.250	.277	.315
Pickens, Jordan, L.E.	3	11	10	0	0	0	0	0	0	0	0	0	0	1	0	6	0	0	0	.000	.091	.000
Raburn, Johnny, R.C.-H.D.†	131	608	514	79	145	183	23	6	1	39	4	3	3	84	2	101	40	20	5	.282	.384	.356
Ramirez, Manuel, H.D.	62	222	193	30	52	71	10	0	3	22	3	1	2	23	0	55	3	0	10	.269	.352	.368
Randolph, Jaisen, H.D.†	26	118	106	16	34	39	5	0	0	9	2	0	0	10	0	15	11	3	3	.321	.379	.368
Raymundo, G.J., Sto.	60	234	205	30	57	81	9	0	5	29	1	0	3	25	1	36	1	0	8	.278	.365	.395
Reding, Josh, S.B.	16	54	50	4	8	10	2	0	0	3	1	0	0	3	0	9	1	1	1	.160	.208	.200
Reece, Eric, Bak.*	21	65	56	3	9	16	2	1	1	8	0	0	2	7	0	18	0	0	2	.161	.277	.286
Riggins, Auntwan, L.E.†	73	279	259	35	69	87	10	4	0	20	7	1	0	12	0	77	14	12	3	.266	.298	.336
Rios, Fernando, Sto.	69	251	213	32	51	73	8	1	4	30	1	7	2	28	0	23	2	2	5	.239	.344	.343
Rodriguez, Guillermo, S.J.	42	164	152	24	55	75	15	1	1	20	1	0	1	10	0	26	2	1	4	.362	.405	.493
Rodriguez, Javy, R.C.	59	238	213	23	54	71	6	4	1	22	4	5	1	15	0	44	19	11	8	.254	.299	.333
Roper, Zach, R.C.	69	293	252	38	61	98	16	0	7	34	0	3	6	32	0	47	1	1	4	.242	.338	.389
Rowan, Chris, H.D.	87	306	282	52	76	146	16	3	16	52	4	2	6	12	0	95	16	3	7	.270	.311	.518
Ruiz, Randy, Sto.	28	115	100	16	26	44	9	0	3	17	0	0	2	13	0	29	0	3	4	.260	.357	.440
Ruiz, Willy, Sto.	5	9	9	1	1	1	0	0	0	0	0	0	0	0	0	1	0	1	0	.111	.111	.111
Salas, Juan, Bak.	66	272	260	32	84	109	13	0	4	25	0	1	2	9	1	59	6	3	7	.323	.349	.419
Santana, Manny, S.J.*	4	14	11	1	3	3	0	0	0	0	1	0	0	2	0	2	0	0	0	.273	.385	.273
Sapp, Damian, Sto.	45	188	160	34	38	84	5	1	13	35	0	0	5	23	0	64	1	0	3	.238	.351	.525
Schaub, Greg, H.D.	37	13	11	2	5	6	1	0	0	1	1	0	0	1	0	1	0	0	0	.455	.500	.545
Schmidt, J.P., Vis.*	65	250	217	32	59	89	9	6	3	23	5	0	0	28	1	50	13	3	4	.272	.355	.410
Schneidmiller, Gary, Vis.	111	466	381	85	113	155	17	2	7	53	3	1	3	78	1	80	6	2	7	.297	.419	.407
Schuda, Justin, Bak.*	76	272	242	27	46	69	11	0	4	25	0	2	4	24	1	88	0	0	6	.190	.272	.285
Sellier, Brian, Mod.*	116	505	417	95	125	178	26	6	5	58	7	5	2	73	2	82	16	6	4	.300	.402	.427
Selmo, Wilson, R.C.†	4	11	10	1	2	2	0	0	0	0	0	0	1	0	0	2	0	0	0	.200	.273	.200
Senjem, Guye, S.B.*	102	399	338	61	93	156	17	2	14	57	0	3	8	50	4	59	2	3	4	.275	.378	.462
Shabala, Adam, S.J.*	73	289	244	42	80	123	18	2	7	45	5	3	1	36	0	64	11	7	2	.328	.412	.504
Simpson, Bodie, Lan.	9	34	31	3	3	4	1	0	0	4	0	0	0	3	0	11	0	0	0	.097	.176	.129
Smith, Casey, R.C.	112	451	408	40	101	124	9	4	2	35	7	1	5	30	0	56	9	8	6	.248	.306	.304
Smitherman, Stephen, Sto.	128	541	482	78	151	246	36	1	19	99	0	14	6	39	2	126	17	2	14	.313	.362	.510
Snyder, Christopher, Lan.	60	250	217	31	56	99	16	0	9	44	1	4	3	25	0	54	0	0	7	.258	.337	.456
Soto, Jorge, Vis.	111	473	405	69	85	194	14	1	31	69	0	0	11	57	2	195	1	1	3	.210	.324	.480
Sprowl, Jon-Mark, Lan.*	76	283	230	39	64	96	12	1	6	27	3	1	6	43	1	42	2	4	6	.278	.404	.417
Stanley, Steve, Mod.*	63	309	262	48	75	91	11	1	1	17	5	1	2	39	1	46	4	6	10	.286	.382	.347
Stotts, J.T., Vis.	133	565	483	66	133	165	20	3	2	64	3	8	6	65	3	75	13	6	11	.275	.363	.342
Suomi, Richard, Vis.*	20	79	70	9	15	24	6	0	1	10	1	0	1	7	1	13	1	0	1	.214	.295	.343
Swenson, Sammy, R.C.	80	325	283	49	66	113	16	2	9	40	1	3	12	26	0	105	4	5	4	.233	.321	.399
Swisher, Nick, Vis.†	49	214	183	22	44	73	13	2	4	23	2	1	2	26	1	48	3	1	6	.240	.340	.399
Symonds, Grady, Lan.	6	11	10	1	2	2	0	0	0	0	0	0	0	1	0	4	0	0	0	.200	.273	.200
Teahen, Mark, Mod.*	59	257	234	25	56	70	9	1	1	26	0	0	2	21	1	53	1	2	4	.239	.307	.299
Thomas, Gary, Mod.	118	493	428	74	110	155	18	6	5	49	8	2	10	45	0	77	31	11	9	.257	.340	.362
Tritle, Chris, Mod.	51	193	178	20	35	56	9	0	4	23	2	1	0	11	0	55	3	1	1	.197	.242	.315
Trosper, Tanner, Mod.	26	0	0	1	0	0	0	0	0	0	0	0	0	0	0	0	0	0	0	.000	.000	.000
Trumble, Dan, S.J.	117	464	412	60	89	155	21	0	15	53	1	2	5	44	0	185	8	2	3	.216	.298	.376
Uggla, Dan, Lan.	54	211	184	21	42	62	7	2	3	16	2	2	2	21	0	51	3	2	3	.228	.311	.337
Urquhart, Derick, R.C.*	2	8	7	0	0	0	0	0	0	0	0	0	0	1	0	0	0	0	0	.000	.125	.000
Valderrama, Carlos, S.J.	74	333	299	65	94	170	19	6	15	45	0	0	0	34	4	60	14	5	5	.314	.384	.569
Valdez, Mario, Mod.*	2	9	8	2	2	3	1	0	0	1	0	0	0	1	0	0	0	0	0	.250	.333	.375
Villanueva, Florian, H.D.	28	120	111	14	23	34	4	2	1	14	0	2	1	6	0	20	2	1	3	.207	.250	.306
Voltz, Jude, H.D.*	49	180	166	18	38	55	9	1	2	17	0	2	2	10	0	52	1	0	0	.229	.278	.331
Walker, Mark, S.J.	21	81	66	4	8	8	0	0	0	3	1	1	2	11	0	42	0	1	0	.121	.263	.121

Player, Team	G	TPA	AB	R	H	TB	2B	3B	HR	RBI	SH	SF	HP	BB	IBB	SO	SB	CS	GDP	Avg.	OBP	Slg.
Warriax, Brandon, R.C.	18	61	56	4	9	15	3	0	1	5	1	0	0	4	0	19	0	0	1	.161	.217	.268
Wayment, Kory, Mod.	16	45	39	0	7	9	2	0	0	5	0	2	0	4	0	15	1	0	2	.179	.244	.231
Webb, Ryan, R.C.	82	269	241	23	60	75	11	2	0	26	4	1	2	21	0	63	10	7	7	.249	.313	.311
West, Todd, H.D.	64	270	229	38	61	74	8	1	1	19	5	3	4	29	1	36	17	6	5	.266	.355	.323
Wilfong, Nick, S.J.*	105	403	353	48	66	116	19	2	9	46	5	5	4	36	1	130	8	5	4	.187	.266	.329
Williams, Jonny, S.J.*	2	2	2	0	0	0	0	0	0	0	0	0	0	0	0	1	0	0	0	.000	.000	.000
Williams, Matt, Lan.	4	14	12	2	4	8	1	0	1	5	0	0	0	2	0	1	0	0	0	.333	.429	.667
Williamson, John, S.B.†	123	491	437	62	104	165	26	7	7	57	3	2	6	43	5	103	1	4	10	.238	.314	.378
Wooten, Shawn, R.C.	6	23	18	2	4	7	3	0	0	3	0	1	0	4	0	4	0	0	1	.222	.348	.389
Wright, Mike, S.J.	35	128	109	19	25	49	5	2	5	16	2	0	1	16	0	35	0	0	1	.229	.333	.450
Zamora, Junior, R.C.	30	123	119	17	32	51	10	0	3	14	0	0	3	1	0	31	0	1	1	.269	.293	.429
Zoccolillo, Peter, H.D.*	44	195	161	31	55	89	10	0	8	37	0	4	2	28	1	24	2	1	3	.342	.436	.553

PLAYERS WITH TWO OR MORE TEAMS

Player, Team	G	TPA	AB	R	H	TB	2B	3B	HR	RBI	SH	SF	HP	BB	IBB	SO	SB	CS	GDP	Avg.	OBP	Slg.
Basil, Jason, Mod.	17	56	52	6	12	20	3	1	1	5	0	0	0	4	0	9	0	0	4	.231	.286	.385
Basil, Jason, Vis.	95	410	351	42	87	129	10	1	10	60	2	3	7	47	0	84	0	0	7	.248	.346	.368
Garcia, Isaac, Vis.	34	116	104	15	14	19	2	0	1	12	1	2	0	9	0	31	1	1	3	.135	.200	.183
Garcia, Isaac, Mod.	40	102	93	21	33	44	5	0	2	14	0	1	1	7	0	17	1	2	4	.355	.402	.473
Raburn, Johnny, R.C.†	115	535	448	71	131	164	20	5	1	36	4	3	3	77	2	88	35	19	4	.292	.397	.366
Raburn, Johnny, H.D.†	16	73	66	8	14	19	3	1	0	3	0	0	0	7	0	13	5	1	1	.212	.288	.288

GRAND SLAMS: Duncan, 3; Allegra, Beattie, Sapp, Swenson, Trumble, Wright, 2 each; Alfonzo, Basil, J. Bell, Calitri, Chavez, A. Clark, D. Clark, Cota, Eddlemon, Gautreau, Lindsey, B. Martin, Co. Myers, Nady, Owens, Peters, Smitherman, Valderrama, M. Williams, 1 each.

AWARDED FIRST BASE ON CATCHER'S INTERFERENCE: Cosme (Isenia), Cota (Castellano), Krynzel (Pagan), Sellier (Nieckula), Tritle (Carroll).

2002 PITCHING

TEAM

Team	W	L	Pct.	ERA	G	CG	ShO	Sv.	IP	H	TBF	R	ER	HR	SH	SF	HB	BB	IBB	SO	WP	Bk.
Stockton	89	51	.636	3.20	140	5	12	36	1238.2	1108	5231	541	440	71	35	32	58	423	9	1137	57	14
Modesto	78	62	.557	3.74	140	3	3	36	1247.2	1203	5402	606	519	85	43	43	76	496	28	1269	83	22
San Bernardino	77	63	.550	3.83	140	4	9	37	1248.0	1145	5372	634	531	89	51	42	84	475	13	1266	85	10
Lake Elsinore	75	65	.536	3.96	140	0	5	43	1259.2	1210	5527	677	554	101	37	38	82	527	6	1227	73	10
Bakersfield	69	72	.489	3.99	141	3	8	47	1242.1	1345	5507	686	551	103	50	39	51	434	10	1281	86	14
Visalia	70	71	.496	4.14	141	4	2	25	1247.0	1336	5453	714	574	130	57	43	53	393	17	1111	84	19
San Jose	68	72	.486	4.22	140	1	7	32	1242.0	1246	5478	676	583	116	44	35	64	555	33	1007	74	17
R. Cucamonga	52	88	.371	4.94	140	9	9	23	1227.0	1287	5479	834	673	130	37	45	88	513	4	1131	104	10
Lancaster	63	77	.450	5.00	140	0	6	35	1248.0	1382	5566	797	693	128	37	43	76	495	11	1051	93	14
High Desert	60	80	.429	6.13	140	0	0	29	1227.2	1408	5727	979	836	155	29	54	92	658	15	992	137	17

INDIVIDUAL

TOP QUALIFIERS FOR EARNED-RUN AVERAGE TITLE

Minimum 112 innings. *Lefthanded pitcher.

Pitcher, Team	W	L	Pct.	ERA	G	GS	CG	ShO	GF	Sv.	IP	H	TBF	R	ER	HR	SH	SF	HB	BB	IBB	SO	WP	Bk.
Clark, Jeff, S.J.	12	3	.800	2.06	21	21	1	0	0	0	140	118	553	37	32	10	2	0	6	18	0	129	2	0
Bonser, Boof, S.J.	8	6	.571	2.88	23	23	0	0	0	0	128.1	89	537	44	41	9	1	2	7	70	0	139	7	1
Van Dusen, Derrick, S.B.*	7	6	.538	3.10	20	20	0	0	0	0	124.2	111	518	46	43	13	4	2	7	36	0	118	8	1
Stokes, Brian, Bak.	10	7	.588	3.26	28	28	1	1	0	0	165.2	156	704	79	60	13	4	6	8	57	1	152	10	0
McCall, Derell, Mod.	8	5	.615	3.32	25	23	1	0	1	0	132.2	140	581	54	49	4	4	4	10	50	3	82	13	4
Morgan, Russ, S.B.*	13	6	.684	3.36	36	11	0	0	4	0	123.1	112	515	58	46	10	7	1	8	36	0	107	2	2
Withers, Darvin, Mod.	7	3	.700	3.46	30	16	1	0	6	1	125	116	520	53	48	4	5	4	15	33	2	106	7	2
Blackley, Travis, S.B.*	5	9	.357	3.49	21	20	1	0	1	0	121.1	102	505	52	47	11	4	0	7	44	0	152	11	2
Mottl, Ryan, Sto.	13	6	.684	3.50	27	27	2	0	0	0	180	169	745	84	70	12	6	11	8	39	0	148	8	1
Fischer, Rich, R.C.	7	8	.467	3.50	19	19	5	4	0	0	131	118	533	61	51	14	1	3	7	29	0	138	4	2
Liriano, Pedro, R.C.	10	14	.417	3.60	28	28	1	1	0	0	167.1	129	699	86	67	14	6	1	10	74	1	176	5	0
Bonderman, Jeremy, Mod.	9	8	.529	3.61	25	25	1	0	0	0	144.2	129	627	77	58	15	6	7	5	55	1	160	9	3
Bott, Glenn, S.B.*	7	7	.500	3.88	30	23	2	1	1	0	150.2	141	658	70	65	13	5	6	9	64	0	142	6	0
McAdoo, Duncan, L.E.	8	4	.667	4.01	41	12	0	0	5	0	123.1	124	524	64	55	14	0	4	8	30	1	130	4	0
Cotts, Neal, Mod.*	12	6	.667	4.12	28	28	0	0	0	0	137.2	123	611	72	63	5	1	3	5	87	0	178	7	2

DEPARTMENTAL LEADERS: W—Morgan, Mottl, 13 each; L—Liriano, O'Neal, 14 each; Pct.—Koronka, 1.000; G—Nicolas, 65; GS—Nageotte, Smart, 29 each; CG—R. Fischer, 5; ShO—R. Fischer, 4; GF—Hoerman, 49; Sv.—Hoerman, 29; IP—Mottl, Smart, 180.0 each; H—Smart, 212; TBF—Smart, 796; R—Gordon, 128; ER—Gordon, 107; HR—Bruksch, 22; SH—Bruksch, Phillips, 10 each; SF—Mottl, 11; HB—O'Neal, 23; BB—Phillips, 94; IBB—Frick, 7; SO—Nageotte, 214; WP—Maysonet, G. Perez, 20 each; BK—McCall, 4.

ALL PITCHERS

*Lefthanded pitcher.

Pitcher, Team	W	L	Pct.	ERA	G	GS	CG	ShO	GF	Sv.	IP	H	TBF	R	ER	HR	SH	SF	HB	BB	IBB	SO	WP	Bk.
Abbott, Paul, S.B.	0	0	.000	0.00	1	1	0	0	0	0	5	3	19	0	0	1	0	0	2	0	0	5	0	0
Adams, Mike, H.D.	2	1	.667	2.57	10	0	0	0	7	5	14	9	59	6	4	2	0	0	0	7	0	23	2	0
Adkins, Jon, Mod.	0	1	.000	8.10	1	1	0	0	0	0	6.2	11	32	7	6	0	1	0	1	1	0	4	1	0
Aiello, Nick, Bak.*	1	1	.500	5.81	21	0	0	0	15	0	26.1	42	126	18	17	3	0	2	2	8	1	17	2	0
Alfano, Jeff, S.J.	1	1	.500	9.45	6	0	0	0	3	0	6.2	9	40	8	7	2	0	0	2	9	1	3	2	0
Altman, Gene, H.D.	0	1	.000	14.59	11	0	0	0	6	0	12.1	20	73	25	20	4	0	1	1	16	0	8	8	1
Alvarado, Carlo, H.D.	2	1	.667	3.00	17	0	0	0	4	0	27	22	122	12	9	3	1	1	3	16	2	31	4	1
Anderson, Jason, Vis.*	0	3	.000	6.35	19	0	0	0	5	0	22.2	20	109	17	16	1	0	0	3	18	1	26	2	0
Andujar, Jesse, R.C.	0	3	.000	6.64	32	1	0	0	17	1	59.2	68	276	48	44	8	0	4	10	24	0	53	7	1
Aquino, Greg, Lan.	4	1	.800	3.67	8	8	0	0	0	0	49	50	209	20	20	3	1	6	3	18	0	50	3	0
Arroyo, Luis, Sto.*	1	0	1.000	0.63	10	0	0	0	6	1	14.1	10	61	1	1	0	0	0	0	7	0	18	0	0

Pitcher, Team	W	L	Pct.	ERA	G	GS	CG	ShO	GF	Sv.	IP	H	TBF	R	ER	HR	SH	SF	HB	BB	IBB	SO	WP	Bk.
Balser, Jeff, R.C.	0	0	.000	8.22	4	0	0	0	2	0	7.2	16	47	8	7	2	0	1	6	0	6	1	0
Barber, Scott, Lan.	7	3	.700	4.25	32	9	0	0	5	0	110	118	467	57	52	11	4	3	5	24	1	81	5	0
Beck, David, Mod.*	0	1	.000	12.15	10	0	0	0	2	0	6.2	10	39	10	9	1	0	0	1	7	1	9	1	0
Belflower, Jay, Lan.	0	1	.000	3.86	16	0	0	0	8	1	18.2	17	77	8	8	0	0	0	0	3	0	14	0	0
Belson, Greg, Lan.	5	4	.556	6.88	40	2	0	0	9	0	70.2	88	323	56	54	6	3	3	6	25	1	59	3	0
Benedetti, John, Bak.	6	6	.500	3.87	54	0	0	0	28	13	76.2	74	320	33	33	4	4	3	0	21	2	74	4	1
Berry, Jon, Sto.	5	3	.625	4.59	19	0	0	0	10	0	33.1	27	143	23	17	5	0	2	2	16	2	33	3	0
Biggs, Billy, Lan.	1	0	1.000	3.48	8	0	0	0	1	1	10.1	12	44	6	4	0	1	1	1	1	0	9	0	0
Blackley, Travis, S.B.*	5	9	.357	3.49	21	20	1	0	1	0	121.1	102	505	52	47	11	4	0	7	44	0	152	11	2
Blanton, Joe, Mod.	0	1	.000	7.50	2	1	0	0	0	0	6	8	33	6	5	1	0	0	0	6	0	6	0	1
Blood, Justin, S.B.*	1	1	.500	3.91	20	0	0	0	4	0	25.1	18	118	13	11	2	1	1	1	24	0	34	4	0
Bludau, Frank, Sto.	3	3	.500	1.91	43	0	0	0	42	22	47	42	198	13	10	1	1	1	2	12	2	48	3	2
Bonderman, Jeremy, Mod.	9	8	.529	3.61	25	25	1	0	0	0	144.2	129	627	77	58	15	6	7	5	55	1	160	9	3
Bonser, Boof, S.J.	8	6	.571	2.88	23	23	0	0	0	0	128.1	89	537	44	41	9	1	2	7	70	0	139	7	1
Bott, Glenn, S.B.*	7	7	.500	3.88	30	23	2	1	1	0	150.2	141	658	70	65	13	5	6	9	64	0	142	6	0
Boutwell, Andy, Sto.	3	2	.600	3.83	7	7	0	0	0	0	42.1	35	180	18	18	3	0	0	1	24	0	39	3	0
Brannon, Nick, Sto.*	0	1	.000	3.68	22	0	0	0	8	0	36.2	39	166	18	15	2	1	0	1	18	0	52	2	1
Brous, Dave, S.J.*	2	1	.667	10.80	11	0	0	0	3	0	13.1	12	71	21	16	1	0	1	5	17	1	8	1	0
Brown, Elliot, S.J.	1	2	.333	4.91	6	6	0	0	0	0	29.1	30	128	19	16	0	0	1	1	11	0	13	1	0
Bruksch, Jeffrey, Vis.	8	11	.421	4.65	27	27	0	0	0	0	149	143	663	98	77	22	10	7	5	63	0	163	13	2
Brunet, Mike, R.C.	0	1	.000	3.57	39	0	0	0	36	16	40.1	39	167	16	16	5	0	1	0	11	0	50	5	0
Bukowski, Stan, R.C.	1	6	.143	5.89	14	12	1	0	1	0	73.1	92	328	54	48	9	2	3	4	22	0	53	1	0
Bulger, Jason, Lan.	1	1	.500	5.40	2	2	0	0	0	0	10	11	45	7	6	0	0	1	3	3	0	12	1	0
Bumstead, Mike, L.E.	10	10	.500	4.82	27	26	0	0	0	0	145.2	164	662	100	78	12	2	6	8	61	0	108	9	2
Burton, Timothy, S.B.	4	7	.364	4.11	40	0	0	0	15	0	65.2	65	283	48	30	5	5	4	4	15	1	46	8	0
Butler, John, S.B.	0	2	.000	4.50	15	0	0	0	3	0	30	26	128	16	15	2	2	2	2	12	0	24	3	0
Campbell, Jarrett, Bak.	7	6	.538	4.17	36	7	0	0	4	1	82	105	386	53	38	2	2	1	4	27	1	84	7	2
Candelaria, Scott, H.D.	0	0	.000	0.00	2	0	0	0	2	0	2	1	8	0	0	0	0	0	0	1	0	0	0	0
Carbajal, Alex, Bak.*	5	4	.556	3.20	43	1	0	0	9	2	76	77	319	30	27	5	3	3	3	19	1	92	3	2
Carter, Justin, Sto.*	2	3	.400	2.94	23	0	0	0	13	1	49	47	210	24	16	3	2	1	0	20	0	44	0	0
Cassel, Jack, L.E.	1	1	.500	2.43	23	0	0	0	4	1	37	33	154	15	10	0	1	0	3	11	0	25	0	1
Clark, Jeff, S.J.	12	3	.800	2.06	21	21	1	0	0	0	140	118	553	37	32	10	2	0	6	18	0	129	2	0
Coleman, Jeff, Vis.	5	1	.833	3.99	45	0	0	0	16	0	65.1	78	293	37	29	3	2	3	3	14	0	52	4	0
Cook, Dennis, R.C.*	0	1	.000	17.18	4	3	0	0	0	0	3.2	8	20	7	7	3	0	0	0	1	0	5	1	0
Coose, Austin, Bak.	1	4	.200	7.11	25	0	0	0	15	4	31.2	41	159	28	25	3	1	2	0	22	4	40	6	0
Coppinger, Rocky, Mod.	1	0	1.000	3.86	3	3	0	0	0	0	14	18	66	7	6	2	1	1	0	6	0	20	0	0
Cordero, Victor, H.D.	3	0	1.000	5.40	10	0	0	0	2	1	13.1	13	59	9	8	2	0	0	3	6	0	15	0	2
Cordova, Jorge, Sto.	4	0	1.000	0.40	14	0	0	0	4	0	22.1	11	81	2	1	0	0	0	0	5	0	27	3	0
Cotts, Neal, Mod.*	12	6	.667	4.12	28	28	0	0	0	0	137.2	123	611	72	63	5	1	3	5	87	0	178	7	2
Cozier, Vance, S.J.	3	3	.500	3.99	11	11	0	0	0	0	64.2	72	283	29	28	8	2	6	4	22	0	35	1	0
Cram, Josh, S.J.	0	0	.000	3.38	2	0	0	0	1	0	2.2	5	15	1	1	0	0	0	1	2	2	3	0	0
Cramblitt, Joey, Lan.	3	7	.300	3.92	48	4	0	0	18	2	82.2	98	370	46	36	8	2	5	6	28	0	74	4	0
Crider, J.R., Vis.	0	0	.000	8.44	12	0	0	0	7	0	10.2	12	56	10	10	1	1	0	2	13	1	11	3	1
Crowell, Kyle, Mod.	9	3	.750	2.99	42	0	0	0	18	3	72.1	64	294	24	24	5	3	1	3	20	2	89	2	1
Cullen, Ryan, Vis.*	3	4	.429	4.91	50	0	0	0	19	4	73.1	95	326	47	40	11	3	0	1	15	3	58	6	0
Culp, Brandon, Sto.	5	3	.625	2.50	35	8	0	0	14	3	100.2	73	420	34	28	7	1	0	5	47	0	104	3	1
Daigle, Casey, Lan.	4	10	.286	5.09	21	21	0	0	0	0	122	137	547	82	69	19	7	8	9	42	0	85	7	2
Davey, Tom, L.E.	0	1	.000	3.38	5	4	0	0	0	0	5.1	6	20	2	2	1	0	0	0	1	0	4	0	0
De Hart, Blair, L.E.	3	1	.750	2.70	5	5	0	0	0	0	30	29	124	10	9	2	0	1	2	5	0	32	0	0
DeHart, Casey, Sto.*	5	7	.417	3.66	16	16	0	0	0	0	96	87	407	44	39	7	4	2	5	38	1	57	8	1
Dennis, Jason, R.C.*	2	3	.400	3.75	28	0	0	0	12	0	36	29	151	15	15	2	2	4	2	17	0	22	3	0
Dent, Doug, H.D.	3	4	.571	4.01	13	12	0	0	0	0	67.1	64	297	35	30	4	0	3	4	36	0	62	2	1
Dickinson, Drew, Vis.*	1	1	.500	3.38	4	4	0	0	0	0	24	32	103	9	9	1	2	1	0	6	0	14	2	1
Eaton, Adam, L.E.	0	0	.000	2.70	3	3	0	0	0	0	13.1	10	54	7	4	0	0	0	0	3	0	19	0	0
Eusebio, Mike, Sto.	1	0	1.000	1.80	4	0	0	0	2	0	5	6	25	5	1	0	0	0	2	2	0	3	1	0
Fischer, Rich, R.C.	7	8	.467	3.50	19	19	5	4	0	0	131	118	533	61	51	14	1	3	7	29	0	138	4	2
Fischer, Steve, Vis.	7	4	.636	2.81	50	2	0	0	21	4	89.2	88	386	41	28	4	5	8	3	37	3	67	3	2
Flinn, Chris, Bak.	0	4	.000	8.64	7	7	0	0	0	0	33.1	52	166	36	32	9	1	2	1	17	0	22	1	1
Flores, Ron, Vis.*	8	6	.571	3.25	53	0	0	0	38	11	80.1	90	347	41	29	7	5	5	1	16	2	92	1	0
Fortunato, Bartolome, Bak.	2	4	.333	4.01	25	5	0	0	8	0	60.2	58	263	31	27	3	4	2	1	25	0	85	3	2
Frendling, Neal, Bak.	0	3	.000	5.32	4	4	0	0	0	0	23.2	28	112	15	14	2	1	0	1	15	0	21	4	0
Frick, Mike, Mod.	7	6	.538	2.89	50	0	0	0	46	23	62.1	54	270	26	20	5	7	4	6	21	7	66	2	1
Fritz, Ben, Vis.	1	0	1.000	3.71	3	3	0	0	0	0	17	15	72	7	7	1	2	0	2	6	0	16	1	0
Gaal, Bryan, L.E.	1	5	.167	2.60	32	0	0	0	27	15	34.2	28	145	15	10	3	0	0	3	9	1	45	2	1
Garcia, Sonny, Vis.	2	1	.667	1.09	6	6	0	0	0	0	33	32	136	4	4	1	0	0	2	8	0	34	1	2
Gavelek, Brad, S.J.*	3	3	.500	4.74	46	0	0	0	15	1	79.2	88	346	49	42	8	5	1	2	30	5	56	2	1
Germano, Justin, L.E.	2	0	1.000	0.95	3	3	0	0	0	0	19	12	75	3	2	1	0	0	1	5	0	18	1	0
Gilpatrick, T.Jay, Mod.	1	3	.250	6.91	16	0	0	0	7	1	28.2	39	136	24	22	9	0	0	0	12	0	25	0	1
Gold, J.M., H.D.	1	3	.250	7.63	7	7	0	0	0	0	30.2	33	143	29	26	4	3	3	2	22	0	33	4	2
Gomes, Tony, S.J.	2	3	.600	5.98	16	5	0	0	6	0	46.2	62	214	34	31	5	1	2	0	16	0	41	4	1
Gomez, Andre, L.E.	0	1	.000	9.00	1	0	0	0	1	0	1	2	6	1	1	0	0	0	0	2	0	1	0	0
Gonzalez, Christian, Vis.	5	7	.417	4.95	29	11	0	0	2	0	107.1	127	481	76	59	15	7	4	10	29	1	72	5	2
Gonzalez, Edgar, Lan.	3	0	1.000	0.78	4	4	0	0	0	0	23	24	97	7	2	1	0	1	2	3	0	21	0	0
Gonzalez, Enrique, Lan.	1	4	.200	12.27	5	5	0	0	0	0	18.1	34	100	27	25	3	1	1	1	14	0	11	4	0
Gooris, Dan, L.E.*	3	0	1.000	4.08	24	0	0	0	10	0	39.2	36	176	20	18	1	2	2	2	25	0	27	2	0
Gordon, Justin, H.D.*	4	9	.308	7.58	28	25	0	0	0	0	127	172	633	128	107	17	1	6	12	77	0	86	11	1
Gray, Mike, Lan.*	2	0	1.000	0.93	18	0	0	0	4	0	19.1	18	84	4	2	1	0	0	3	7	3	25	4	0
Gregg, James, S.J.	1	2	.333	2.16	5	0	0	0	0	0	8.1	9	43	7	2	1	0	0	0	7	1	1	0	0
Gregg, Kevin, Vis.	2	1	.667	2.08	3	3	0	0	0	0	17.1	8	69	5	4	0	2	0	0	9	0	11	2	0
Gross, Kyle, S.J.	0	0	.000	6.75	4	0	0	0	0	0	5.1	5	33	4	4	0	1	0	2	11	0	5	1	0
Grunwald, Erik, S.B.	2	2	.500	5.40	40	1	0	0	11	1	63.1	77	286	46	38	7	4	6	1	18	2	57	3	0
Gwyn, Marc, Mod.	1	3	.250	5.97	8	7	0	0	1	0	34.2	40	163	27	23	4	0	3	3	20	0	30	1	1
Hall, Josh, Sto.	4	0	1.000	2.27	7	7	1	0	0	0	43.2	31	176	13	11	1	0	2	2	13	0	51	5	0
Hannaman, Ryan, S.J.*	0	0	.000	3.00	1	1	0	0	0	0	6	3	23	2	2	1	0	1	0	3	0	7	0	0
Harden, Rich, Vis.	4	3	.571	2.93	12	12	1	0	0	0	67.2	49	271	27	22	4	0	2	1	24	0	85	3	1

Pitcher, Team	W	L	Pct.	ERA	G	GS	CG	ShO	GF	Sv.	IP	H	TBF	R	ER	HR	SH	SF	HB	BB	IBB	SO	WP	Bk.
Harriger, Mark, Vis.	2	4	.333	5.44	12	11	0	0	0	0	51.1	57	233	38	31	6	2	1	3	22	0	33	3	1
Harvey, Ian, L.E.	1	2	.333	3.48	34	0	0	0	14	2	51.2	49	219	24	20	6	0	2	3	9	0	52	1	0
Hendrickson, Ben, H.D.	5	5	.500	2.55	14	14	0	0	0	0	81.1	61	338	31	23	3	1	2	2	41	0	70	3	0
Henrie, Matthew, Lan.	0	1	.000	3.91	16	0	0	0	6	1	25.1	27	107	11	11	3	3	1	1	4	0	14	1	0
Hensley, Matt, R.C.	1	1	.500	5.40	12	2	0	0	3	0	31.2	42	145	21	19	3	0	1	1	11	0	27	3	1
Henthorne, Kevin, Lan.	0	1	.000	3.72	2	2	0	0	0	0	9.2	13	43	8	4	1	0	0	0	3	0	6	0	0
Herbert, John, L.E.	5	3	.625	5.21	42	0	0	0	15	1	65.2	69	306	46	38	8	4	2	4	33	0	54	6	1
Hernandez, Alexei, S.B.	0	0	.000	16.20	1	0	0	0	1	0	1.2	4	10	3	3	0	0	1	0	1	0	1	0	0
High, Andy, H.D.*	1	5	.167	4.11	12	6	0	0	4	0	50.1	60	211	24	23	7	3	1	2	9	1	39	2	0
Hoerman, Jared, S.B.	7	4	.636	2.77	54	4	0	0	49	29	74.2	54	319	31	23	0	6	2	11	32	6	97	8	0
Howington, Ty, Sto.*	1	1	.500	3.09	2	2	0	0	0	0	11.2	7	46	6	4	1	0	0	1	4	0	9	1	0
Jackson, Dan, R.C.	9	4	.692	4.22	31	9	0	0	6	4	98	96	427	58	46	8	1	2	4	34	1	111	5	1
Jarvis, Kevin, L.E.	1	0	1.000	0.00	1	1	0	0	0	0	5	2	17	0	0	0	1	0	0	1	0	1	0	0
Jenks, Bobby, R.C.	3	5	.375	4.82	11	10	1	1	0	0	65.1	50	295	42	35	4	4	5	4	46	0	64	11	2
Johnson, Rett, S.B.	3	1	.750	3.65	7	7	0	0	0	0	37	27	150	17	15	1	0	1	2	11	1	34	2	0
Kelly, Steve, Sto.	6	3	.667	4.09	19	19	0	0	0	0	105.2	119	472	63	48	6	6	3	6	32	0	80	4	0
Komine, Shane, Vis.	1	3	.250	5.96	18	0	0	0	2	0	25.2	23	120	20	17	2	3	0	1	20	3	22	3	0
Koronka, John, Sto.*	11	0	1.000	3.07	12	12	0	0	0	0	73.1	59	316	36	25	4	0	2	3	35	0	69	3	1
Kozol, Anthony, L.E.	0	0	.000	2.25	3	0	0	0	0	0	4	3	15	1	1	0	0	0	0	0	0	3	0	0
Krawczyk, Jack, H.D.	0	2	.000	6.52	6	0	0	0	4	2	9.2	13	45	10	7	3	1	1	0	3	0	12	0	0
Lamattina, Ryan, H.D.*	3	6	.333	6.12	42	1	0	0	14	3	60.1	77	289	49	41	4	1	7	6	32	5	30	10	0
Lamber, Justin, S.B.*	1	0	1.000	2.45	6	0	0	0	4	2	11	10	44	4	3	1	0	0	2	4	0	6	0	1
Lara, Nelson, S.J.	5	4	.556	3.29	20	13	0	0	1	0	82	64	355	37	30	7	6	0	3	45	3	72	4	3
Light, Scott, Sto.	0	1	.000	22.50	1	0	0	0	0	0	2	6	14	5	5	1	0	0	0	2	0	3	0	0
Liriano, Pedro, R.C.	10	14	.417	3.60	28	28	1	1	0	0	167.1	129	699	86	67	14	6	1	10	74	1	176	5	0
Lowry, Noah, S.J.*	6	5	.545	2.15	15	12	0	0	0	0	58.2	38	229	21	14	4	1	1	3	20	0	62	1	0
Luque, Roger, S.B.*	1	0	1.000	3.86	14	0	0	0	5	0	16.1	19	72	10	7	1	1	0	1	6	0	10	1	1
Mabeus, Chris, Mod.	3	1	.750	4.04	37	1	0	0	7	1	84.2	97	371	39	38	3	2	2	0	32	4	69	6	1
Malaska, Mark, Bak.*	7	4	.636	2.96	15	15	2	2	0	0	91.1	98	393	48	30	5	1	1	7	12	0	94	3	0
Markert, Jackson, S.J.	3	8	.273	5.61	41	0	0	0	35	12	59.1	73	268	40	37	4	5	1	1	23	2	41	3	1
Marquez, Jeff, R.C.	0	0	.000	3.00	2	0	0	0	2	0	3	4	14	1	1	1	0	0	0	0	0	1	0	0
Martin, Jeff, Sto.	4	5	.444	3.23	33	8	0	0	14	2	97.2	97	421	42	35	5	7	5	5	34	4	82	4	1
Martinez, Gustavo, S.B.	2	3	.400	3.79	16	0	0	0	12	2	19	15	87	11	8	1	1	0	2	11	1	14	1	0
Martinez, Javier, Sto.	0	1	.000	6.75	5	0	0	0	4	3	5.1	4	28	4	4	0	2	0	1	7	0	7	0	2
Matzenbacher, Brian, Lan.	2	0	1.000	4.56	38	1	0	0	14	1	79	89	354	43	40	12	2	0	2	32	3	65	9	0
Mayo, Blake, Lan.	0	1	.000	4.50	2	2	0	0	0	0	12	13	57	8	6	2	0	0	2	5	0	12	0	1
Maysonet, Roberto, H.D.	3	2	.600	9.48	35	5	0	0	12	0	81.2	97	427	93	86	14	2	3	12	80	0	61	20	0
McAdoo, Duncan, L.E.	8	4	.667	4.01	41	12	0	0	5	0	123.1	124	524	64	55	14	0	4	8	30	1	130	4	0
McCall, Derell, Mod.	8	5	.615	3.32	25	23	1	0	1	0	132.2	140	581	54	49	4	4	4	10	50	3	82	13	4
McClain, Kevin, R.C.	2	4	.333	6.00	40	0	0	0	20	1	54	60	238	37	36	8	2	5	4	18	0	52	7	0
McClaskey, Tim, Vis.	4	6	.400	4.31	19	17	2	0	1	0	102.1	131	454	59	49	15	4	3	4	21	0	64	4	1
McClung, Seth, Bak.	3	2	.600	2.92	7	7	0	0	0	0	37	35	158	16	12	1	1	0	2	11	0	48	0	1
McGee, Chris, H.D.	1	2	.333	7.54	39	0	0	0	18	4	51.1	62	252	49	43	10	2	2	4	30	2	48	4	1
McMachen, Clifford, Lan.*	0	1	.000	13.50	5	0	0	0	0	0	5.1	7	31	8	8	4	0	0	0	9	0	4	2	0
Medders, Brandon, Lan.	4	8	.333	5.38	43	12	0	0	25	15	98.2	111	442	73	59	9	2	3	8	36	1	104	10	3
Mendoza, Mario, R.C.	0	2	.000	4.79	21	0	0	0	10	0	41.1	51	191	27	22	7	2	2	4	14	2	33	1	1
Miller, Ryan, H.D.	6	5	.545	5.11	36	9	0	0	10	1	107.1	106	491	73	61	12	2	4	14	57	0	100	18	2
Milo, Tony, R.C.*	1	0	1.000	0.00	4	0	0	0	0	0	8	4	28	0	0	0	0	0	0	1	0	9	0	0
Minaya, Edwin, Vis.	1	5	.167	6.07	32	0	0	0	17	1	43	55	208	36	29	6	2	0	3	20	2	37	11	0
Montes, Albert, S.J.	2	0	1.000	2.37	24	0	0	0	20	5	30.1	26	123	9	8	0	1	0	1	10	3	18	2	0
Morgan, Russ, S.B.*	13	6	.684	3.36	36	11	0	0	4	0	123.1	112	515	58	46	10	7	1	8	36	0	107	2	2
Morris, Will, R.C.	1	0	1.000	5.79	4	0	0	0	2	0	9.1	10	40	7	6	1	0	0	0	7	0	5	0	0
Moseley, Dustin, Sto.	6	3	.667	2.74	14	14	2	2	0	0	88.2	60	350	28	27	3	2	0	8	21	0	80	2	3
Mottl, Ryan, Sto.	13	6	.684	3.50	27	27	2	0	0	0	180	169	745	84	70	12	6	11	8	39	0	148	8	1
Mozingo, Dan, R.C.*	2	3	.400	5.18	9	7	0	0	0	0	41.2	52	198	33	24	2	3	2	3	21	0	28	5	0
Munter, Scott, S.J.	0	0	.000	10.38	3	0	0	0	0	0	4.1	12	27	5	5	0	0	2	0	4	0	2	0	0
Nageotte, Clint, S.B.	9	6	.600	4.54	29	29	1	0	0	0	164.2	153	723	101	83	10	3	4	12	68	0	214	11	2
Nicolas, Mike, L.E.	3	2	.600	2.91	65	0	0	0	23	9	77.1	49	330	32	25	4	5	1	11	42	3	121	13	1
Nieckula, Aaron, S.J.	0	0	.000	27.00	1	0	0	0	1	0	0.1	2	4	1	1	0	0	0	0	1	0	0	0	0
Obenchain, Stephen, Vis.	2	0	1.000	3.00	4	4	0	0	0	0	24	23	95	8	8	2	1	1	0	3	0	10	1	0
O'Brien, Matt, Mod.*	1	2	.333	1.80	3	3	0	0	0	0	15	16	62	7	3	0	0	0	0	3	0	15	4	0
Olore, Kevin, S.B.	10	3	.769	2.73	25	18	0	0	4	1	105.1	89	440	37	32	4	3	5	6	41	1	128	9	1
O'Neal, Brandon, R.C.	5	14	.263	5.24	24	22	0	0	1	0	123.2	132	585	113	72	7	8	3	23	69	0	81	14	0
Oxspring, Chris, L.E.	0	1	.000	4.78	15	1	0	0	3	0	26.1	24	113	16	14	2	0	2	2	8	0	30	3	0
Parker, Josh, Bak.	0	2	.000	9.00	8	0	0	0	3	1	9	18	52	9	9	1	1	1	0	6	0	8	3	0
Parker, Matt, H.D.	0	1	.000	4.50	1	1	0	0	0	0	4	4	18	2	2	0	0	0	0	3	0	1	0	0
Patten, Lanny, S.B.	1	0	1.000	7.11	6	0	0	0	3	0	6.1	6	27	5	5	1	2	0	0	2	0	6	0	0
Peguero, Radhames, Bak.	3	7	.300	4.55	41	6	0	0	21	3	83	94	380	56	42	9	5	1	4	38	0	54	11	1
Pena, Juan, Mod.-Vis.*	1	5	.167	5.56	9	9	0	0	0	0	34	45	165	38	21	7	1	1	1	17	0	27	4	3
Perez, Beltran, Lan.	3	2	.600	2.51	5	5	0	0	0	0	32.1	31	127	11	9	1	2	2	2	3	0	30	1	0
Perez, Elvis, S.B.	1	1	.500	2.84	6	6	0	0	0	0	25.1	32	113	11	8	4	1	2	3	6	0	20	3	0
Perez, George, H.D.	5	12	.294	8.18	35	14	0	0	9	0	113.1	153	558	117	103	19	4	7	7	69	1	80	20	1
Perez, Oliver, L.E.*	3	3	.500	1.85	9	8	0	0	0	0	48.2	36	201	13	10	0	1	2	2	24	0	66	0	0
Phillips, Mark, L.E.*	10	8	.556	4.19	28	26	0	0	0	0	148.1	123	663	81	69	9	10	6	7	94	0	156	12	0
Poe, Ryan, H.D.	1	1	.500	3.95	3	3	0	0	0	0	13.2	18	62	8	6	0	0	1	3	3	0	6	0	0
Polanco, Elvis, S.B.	2	1	.667	2.54	25	0	0	0	6	2	39	33	171	16	11	1	1	1	3	22	0	21	1	0
Price, Brett, Mod.*	2	5	.286	3.09	35	2	0	0	18	2	46.2	42	214	22	16	4	2	2	3	28	1	61	6	0
Prinz, Bret, Lan.	1	0	1.000	0.00	5	0	0	0	1	0	7	2	25	0	0	0	0	0	0	1	0	6	0	0
Ramirez, Joslin, Lan.	0	0	.000	9.82	5	0	0	0	1	0	11	13	51	12	12	4	0	0	0	6	0	4	0	2
Ramos, Juan, Mod.	0	0	.000	6.00	4	0	0	0	3	0	3	5	18	4	2	0	0	0	2	2	0	6	0	0
Ransom, Troy, S.J.	0	4	.000	6.36	27	3	0	0	7	0	63.2	85	297	55	45	10	1	2	4	19	1	24	2	2
Renteria, Juan, Bak.	2	0	1.000	5.55	14	0	0	0	4	0	24.1	25	113	18	15	3	3	0	2	11	0	25	4	2
Reynolds, Josh, L.E.	3	2	.600	8.82	7	3	0	0	1	0	16.1	30	84	18	16	1	0	0	2	3	0	16	0	0
Rheinecker, John, Vis.*	3	0	1.000	2.31	9	9	0	0	0	0	50.2	41	203	16	13	2	0	0	3	10	0	62	1	0
Rigueiro, Rafael, S.J.	6	11	.353	4.22	25	25	0	0	0	0	130	133	577	66	61	14	2	4	3	66	3	87	16	2

Pitcher, Team	W	L	Pct.	ERA	G	GS	CG	ShO	GF	Sv.	IP	H	TBF	R	ER	HR	SH	SF	HB	BB	IBB	SO	WP	Bk.
Robertson, Luke, Mod............	6	5	.545	4.23	29	15	0	0	3	1	121.1	106	496	61	57	9	3	5	5	34	2	144	3	1
Robinson, Jeff, H.D.	0	0	.000	12.00	1	1	0	0	0	0	3	4	19	4	4	1	0	0	1	5	0	3	0	0
Rust, Evan, Bak.	0	1	.000	2.18	28	0	0	0	27	23	33	28	135	8	8	1	3	1	1	10	0	45	0	0
Sams, Aaron, H.D.*	3	3	.500	7.07	9	9	0	0	0	0	49.2	65	232	48	39	7	3	2	2	18	0	36	4	0
Santos, Alex, Bak.	6	4	.600	3.49	19	12	0	0	2	0	95.1	101	432	53	37	12	4	4	2	33	0	105	3	0
Schaub, Greg, H.D.	2	4	.333	6.60	34	0	0	0	21	10	43.2	41	204	37	32	7	0	2	1	30	4	59	3	0
Severino, Ronni, Bak.*	0	1	.000	3.97	13	1	0	0	2	0	22.2	14	99	13	10	0	0	2	1	17	0	28	6	0
Shabansky, Rob, Lan.*	0	0	.000	7.16	11	0	0	0	3	0	16.1	22	83	16	13	2	0	1	1	13	0	11	4	0
Shiyuk, Todd, Lan.*	4	3	.571	3.31	42	0	0	0	12	1	51.2	51	225	21	19	7	4	0	5	22	1	56	5	1
Shwam, Mike, H.D.	1	0	1.000	6.43	5	0	0	0	4	0	7	11	34	8	5	0	1	0	0	3	0	4	1	0
Silva, Jesus, Lan.	2	3	.400	2.08	34	0	0	0	29	12	43.1	30	162	12	10	1	1	2	0	5	1	51	2	0
Simmering, Bryan, Mod.	0	1	.000	4.18	17	4	0	0	4	1	47.1	48	203	23	22	3	2	0	6	17	1	41	4	0
Sismondo, Bobby, H.D.*	4	5	.444	6.57	38	4	0	0	17	3	75.1	89	347	62	55	12	0	3	34	0	69	8	2	
Slaten, Doug, Lan.*	1	6	.143	9.00	8	8	0	0	0	0	35	59	183	43	35	4	1	3	3	12	0	23	5	3
Smart, Pete, H.D.*	9	9	.500	5.10	29	29	0	0	0	0	180	212	796	119	102	20	4	5	10	59	0	116	13	3
Smith, Cliff, R.C.	3	8	.273	4.81	36	3	0	0	13	0	78.2	95	364	57	42	9	3	2	4	35	0	77	11	0
Snare, Ryan, Sto.*	8	2	.800	3.07	13	13	0	0	0	0	82	74	335	36	28	4	2	3	1	18	0	81	2	1
Snow, Bert, Vis.	0	0	.000	1.00	12	1	0	0	9	5	18	8	68	2	2	1	0	0	7	0	25	4	1	
Spiehs, R.D., S.J.	6	6	.500	3.66	47	0	0	0	19	11	83.2	86	364	36	34	13	5	2	3	32	2	80	3	1
Stanton, Kyle, Sto.	1	0	1.000	2.08	9	0	0	0	5	0	13	9	52	3	3	1	0	0	4	0	14	0	0
Stewart, Cory, L.E.*	5	3	.625	3.20	12	12	0	0	0	0	64.2	60	276	29	23	3	1	2	5	29	0	69	5	0
Stockman, Phil, Lan.	7	5	.583	4.40	20	20	0	0	0	0	108.1	91	463	58	53	10	4	1	7	58	0	108	7	0
Stokes, Brian, Bak.	10	7	.588	3.26	28	28	1	1	0	0	165.2	156	704	70	60	13	4	6	8	57	1	152	10	0
Switzer, Jon, Bak.*	7	5	.583	4.27	20	20	0	0	0	0	103.1	108	441	55	49	8	4	1	8	26	0	129	4	0
Taulli, Sam, Lan.*	5	4	.556	6.02	14	12	0	0	0	0	55.1	52	243	41	37	8	2	3	3	33	0	25	5	1
Therneau, Dave, Sto.	6	7	.462	3.44	29	7	0	0	13	4	89	96	385	39	34	5	0	2	5	24	0	88	2	0
Thomas, Adam, R.C.	0	3	.000	14.58	5	3	0	0	0	0	16.2	36	98	29	27	3	0	3	1	9	0	18	2	0
Thomas, J.T., S.J.*	1	5	.167	6.08	11	11	0	0	0	0	40	56	194	32	27	7	2	0	22	1	29	1	1	
Thompson, Mike, L.E.	5	7	.417	5.56	25	22	0	0	1	0	123	144	573	93	76	14	3	6	7	53	0	79	3	1
Threets, Erick, S.J.*	0	1	.000	6.67	26	0	0	0	4	0	28.1	23	136	24	21	2	2	1	3	28	1	43	6	1
Toledo, Jean, R.C.	0	1	.000	8.00	3	2	0	0	0	0	9	12	45	9	8	1	0	2	1	6	0	8	0	0
Trejo, Francisco, Lan.*	4	10	.286	6.91	28	14	0	0	7	0	86	107	422	75	66	8	1	1	2	68	0	78	11	1
Trosper, Tanner, Mod.	2	2	.500	2.60	25	0	0	0	14	1	45	40	198	21	13	2	1	3	2	22	2	39	9	1
Tucker, Rusty, L.E.*	3	2	.400	2.43	26	0	0	0	23	14	29.2	26	137	10	8	1	0	0	4	18	0	33	2	1
Turnbow, Derrick, R.C.	0	0	.000	5.25	13	0	0	0	4	0	12	16	59	11	7	1	0	0	0	9	0	14	2	1
Uzzell, Todd, S.J.	2	2	.500	5.33	7	5	0	0	1	0	25.1	29	120	17	15	0	1	1	1	12	0	15	4	2
Van Dusen, Derrick, S.B.*	7	6	.538	3.10	20	20	0	0	0	0	124.2	111	518	46	43	13	4	2	7	36	0	118	8	1
Velazquez, Elih, S.J.*	1	2	.333	6.47	35	4	0	0	11	1	65.1	81	323	55	47	9	2	7	5	43	6	61	6	1
Veras, Jose, Bak.	3	4	.429	5.34	11	11	0	0	0	0	59	77	283	44	35	10	1	5	3	30	0	57	2	2
Voltz, Jude, H.D.*	0	0	.000	0.00	3	0	0	0	2	0	2.1	1	10	1	0	0	0	0	0	1	0	0	4	0
Waechter, Doug, Bak.	6	3	.667	2.66	17	17	0	0	0	0	108.1	114	466	43	32	9	7	2	1	29	0	101	8	0
Walker, Kevin, L.E.*	0	0	.000	0.00	5	1	0	0	0	0	7	3	22	0	0	0	0	0	0	0	0	10	0	1
Wawrzyniak, Alan, R.C.	0	2	.000	7.67	10	5	0	0	2	1	29.1	35	149	32	25	5	1	1	1	20	0	29	5	1
Webb, Alan, Mod.*	0	1	.000	6.23	2	2	0	0	0	0	8.2	11	42	7	6	1	0	1	0	6	0	6	0	0
Webster, Jeremy, L.E.*	1	0	1.000	4.11	8	0	0	0	1	0	15.1	16	69	8	7	2	1	1	0	10	0	15	2	1
Weis, Brad, Mod.*	5	2	.714	2.24	32	0	0	0	7	2	52.1	40	214	16	13	3	2	0	5	23	2	51	2	2
Wells, Carlton, Lan.*	1	1	.750	3.99	37	3	0	0	9	2	70	77	308	35	31	3	0	1	6	23	1	54	4	0
White, Bill, Lan.*	0	3	.000	10.24	6	6	0	0	0	0	19.1	31	102	23	22	4	0	2	0	16	0	15	2	0
Wiedmeyer, Jason, L.E.*	4	5	.444	4.74	14	13	0	0	0	0	76	81	337	48	40	10	2	1	3	29	0	57	3	0
Wiles, Chad, S.B.	1	4	.200	8.92	29	0	0	0	13	0	38.1	48	186	39	38	2	0	4	3	20	1	30	4	0
Wilson, Phil, R.C.	5	5	.500	5.53	14	14	1	0	0	0	86.1	93	382	62	53	13	2	1	4	29	0	71	11	0
Withers, Darvin, Mod.	7	3	.700	3.46	30	16	1	0	6	1	125	116	520	53	48	4	5	4	15	33	2	106	7	2
Wood, Mike, Mod.	3	3	.500	3.48	7	7	0	0	0	0	41.1	41	170	17	16	4	3	3	6	0	50	4	1	
Yacco, Anthony, S.J.	3	1	.750	3.63	23	0	0	0	11	2	39.2	36	175	23	16	1	3	1	7	14	1	33	5	0
Ziegler, Mike, Vis.	11	6	.647	4.21	25	24	1	0	0	0	151.2	169	643	80	71	19	5	7	4	20	1	139	7	2

PITCHERS WITH TWO OR MORE TEAMS

Pitcher, Team	W	L	Pct.	ERA	G	GS	CG	ShO	GF	Sv.	IP	H	TBF	R	ER	HR	SH	SF	HB	BB	IBB	SO	WP	Bk.
Pena, Juan, Mod.*	1	0	1.000	0.82	2	2	0	0	0	0	11	5	42	2	1	1	0	0	0	5	0	9	0	0
Pena, Juan, Vis.*	0	5	.000	7.83	7	7	0	0	0	0	23	40	123	36	20	6	1	1	1	12	0	18	4	3

COMBINATION SHUTOUTS: **Bakersfield (5)**—Carbajal-Benedetti-Rust, McClung-Campbell-Rust, Santos-Coose, Stokes-Peguero-Rust, Waechter-Benedetti. **High Desert (0)**. **Lake Elsinore (5)**—Bumstead-Shiyuk-Gooris, O. Perez-McAdoo-Shiyuk-Gaal, Phillips-Gooris-Nicolas, Stewart-Thompson-Reynolds-Herbert-Nicolas, Thompson-Herbert-Nicolas-Tucker. **Lancaster (6)**—Aquino-McMachen-Matzenbacher, Belson-Cramblitt-Gray-Belflower, Stockman-Henrie-Medders, Stockman-Medders, Taulli-Silva, Trejo-Belflower. **Modesto (3)**—Bonderman-Weis-Frick, Cotts-Trosper-Price-Frick, McCall-Mabeus-Crowell-Price. **Rancho Cucamonga (3)**—Jackson-Dennis, Liriano-Brunet, Liriano-Dennis. **San Bernardino (8)**—Bott-Hoerman 2, Abbott-Blackley, Nageotte-Morgan-Wiles, Olore-Luque-Hoerman, Olore-Morgan-Grunwald, Van Dusen-Hoerman, Van Dusen-Polanco-Grunwald. **San Jose (7)**—Clark-Montes, Clark-Sebesta 2, Bonser-Spiehs, Clark-Gavelek, Clark-Gavelek-Markert, Clark-Spiehs, Rigueiro-Spiehs. **Stockton (10)**—Culp-Carter-Bludau 2, Boutwell-Martin, DeHart-Therneau, Hall-Martin-Cordova-J. Martinez, Kelly-Berry-Brannon-Bludau, Koronka-Culp, Koronka-Therneau, Moseley-Martin-Arroyo, Therneau-Brannon-Martin. **Visalia (2)**—Garcia-C. Gonzalez-Minaya-Anderson, Rheinecker-Gonzalez-Flores.

NO-HIT GAMES: None.

2002 FIELDING

TEAM

Team	G	PO	A	E	TC	DP	TP	PB	Pct.
Modesto	140	3743	1345	136	5224	104	0	36	.974
San Jose	140	3726	1487	142	5355	117	0	22	.973
San Bernardino	140	3744	1391	166	5301	111	0	41	.969
Lancaster	140	3744	1501	179	5424	110	0	20	.967
Lake Elsinore	140	3779	1400	180	5359	98	0	28	.966
Stockton	140	3716	1437	180	5333	86	0	28	.966
Visalia	141	3741	1524	199	5464	100	0	29	.964
Bakersfield	141	3727	1431	197	5355	106	0	31	.963
High Desert	140	3683	1483	205	5371	132	0	30	.962
R. Cucamonga	140	3681	1510	219	5410	124	0	23	.960

INDIVIDUAL

FIRST BASEMEN

NOTE: All caps denotes fielding-percentage leader based on 70 games for catchers, 93 for all other non-pitchers and 112 innings for pitchers. *Throws lefthanded.

Player, Team	Pct.	G	PO	A	E	TC	DP
Ansman, Craig, Lan.	1.000	4	33	2	0	35	1
Basil, Jason, Vis.	.982	51	396	36	8	440	29
Bell, Derek, S.J.	1.000	3	11	0	0	11	2
Bevins, Andy, Lan.	1.000	1	3	0	0	3	0
Bone, Blake, S.B.	.983	27	212	17	4	233	18
Bozied, Tagg, L.E.	.981	64	549	32	11	592	42
Bravo, Danny, L.E.	1.000	2	17	2	0	19	0
Calitri, Mike, Sto.	.994	73	591	46	4	641	43
Candelaria, Scott, H.D.	1.000	3	31	1	0	32	4
Castellano, John, S.B.	.995	28	198	16	1	215	20
Clark, Aaron, Bak.*	.985	85	604	38	10	652	52
Clark, Daryl, H.D.	1.000	12	89	3	0	92	8
Contreras, Sergio, R.C.*	.977	23	165	8	4	177	17
CORBEIL, Azarias, R.C.	.988	97	784	45	10	839	70
Cordido, Julio, S.J.	1.000	9	81	5	0	86	7
Cosme, Caonabo, Mod.	1.000	3	7	0	0	7	0
Cota, Jesus, Lan.	.989	72	601	54	7	662	50
Derosso, Tony, H.D.	1.000	1	7	2	0	9	0
Duarte, Justin, L.E.	1.000	7	52	4	0	56	3
Eddlemon, Kelly, Bak.	.988	10	79	5	1	85	5
Garcia, Cip, S.B.	1.000	3	15	1	0	16	2
Gemoll, Brandon, H.D.*	.990	24	178	14	2	194	19
Gomez, Andre, L.E.	1.000	4	18	1	0	19	0
Gregg, Mitch, Vis.	.975	59	469	36	13	518	40
Groff, Matt, Vis.	1.000	2	2	1	0	3	0
Hart, Corey, H.D.	.995	43	350	31	2	383	34
Howe, Matt, Mod.	1.000	1	2	0	0	2	0
Jackson, Steve, Mod.	.996	69	463	43	2	508	34
Johnson, Dan, Mod.	.990	89	603	62	7	672	53
Kaup, Nathan, Bak.	.985	15	125	10	2	137	9
Kelly, Tripp, Vis.	.992	15	121	5	1	127	3
Knott, Jon, L.E.	.987	46	366	19	5	390	25
Lindsey, John, S.B.	.991	91	712	48	7	767	56
Luster, Jeremy, S.J.	.992	42	351	24	3	378	21
Luther, Ryan, S.J.	.975	12	73	5	2	80	7
Martin, Brian, Bak.	1.000	1	1	0	0	1	0
McGowan, Sean, S.J.	.991	51	437	21	4	462	40
Myers, Casey, Mod.	1.000	1	5	0	0	5	0
Myers, Corey, Lan.	.988	67	545	38	7	590	49
Nelson, Brad, H.D.	.987	26	204	26	3	233	30
O'Donnell, Ryan, L.E.	.897	3	25	1	3	29	2
Pagan, Andres, L.E.	1.000	1	14	1	0	15	0
Perez, Nestor, Bak.	1.000	1	1	0	0	1	0
Peters, Samone, Sto.	.979	54	449	22	10	481	27
Ramirez, Manuel, H.D.	.967	8	51	7	2	60	8
Reece, Eric, Bak.	.969	4	30	1	1	32	0
Riggins, Auntwan, L.E.	.983	18	150	19	3	172	18
Roper, Zach, R.C.	.983	24	215	12	4	231	16
Rowan, Chris, H.D.	1.000	2	2	1	0	3	0
Ruiz, Randy, Sto.	.944	17	143	8	9	160	8
Sapp, Damian, Sto.	1.000	1	10	0	0	10	0
Schuda, Justin, Bak.	.980	51	354	35	8	397	27
Soto, Jorge, Vis.	.985	29	254	12	4	270	20
Sprowl, Jon-Mark, Lan.	.971	6	33	0	1	34	2
Trumble, Dan, S.J.	.976	31	264	26	7	297	27
Valdez, Mario, Mod.	1.000	1	5	0	0	5	0
Voltz, Jude, H.D.*	.992	32	220	16	2	238	17
Wooten, Shawn, R.C.	1.000	3	29	2	0	31	2
Zamora, Junior, R.C.	.966	7	51	5	2	58	4

SECOND BASEMEN

Player, Team	Pct.	G	PO	A	E	TC	DP
Anderson, Bryan, Sto.	.976	28	53	70	3	126	13
Ayala, Elio, H.D.	.963	6	14	12	1	27	3
Barfield, Josh, L.E.	.955	5	11	10	1	22	1
Beattie, Andrew, Sto.	1.000	6	12	14	0	26	2
Bonilla, Clemente, Sto.	.970	16	29	36	2	67	5
Bravo, Danny, L.E.	.960	24	50	70	5	125	16
Bynum, Freddie, Vis.	.948	134	288	364	36	688	73
Candelaria, Scott, H.D.	.937	43	93	99	13	205	29
Castro, Ismael, S.B.	1.000	6	8	22	0	30	5
Centeno, Irwin, Bak.	.942	16	31	34	4	69	5
Chavez, Angel, S.J.	.000	1	0	0	0	0	0
Clark, Daryl, H.D.	1.000	2	0	2	0	2	0
Cordido, Julio, S.J.	.963	23	55	49	4	108	12
Cosme, Caonabo, Mod.	.968	68	136	139	9	284	35

Player, Team	Pct.	G	PO	A	E	TC	DP
Davis, Mike, L.E.	1.000	2	6	4	0	10	2
De Los Santos, Pedro, L.E.	.926	5	10	15	2	27	1
DeMent, Dan, Bak.	.916	52	79	118	18	215	22
Eddlemon, Kelly, Bak.	.984	16	27	35	1	63	9
Espinosa, David, Sto.	.942	95	159	263	26	448	40
Figueroa, Luis, S.B.	1.000	4	4	11	0	15	2
Freeman, Corey, S.B.	.971	11	18	16	1	35	4
Furmaniak, J.J., L.E.	1.000	14	28	42	0	70	8
Gandolfo, Rob, S.B.	.938	5	8	7	1	16	2
Garcia, Isaac, Vis.-Mod.	.973	26	30	41	2	73	8
Garrido, Tomas, S.J.	1.000	8	5	22	0	27	1
Gautreau, Jake, L.E.	.957	87	181	238	19	438	38
Green, Andy, Lan.	.979	95	206	253	10	469	61
Greene, Khalil, L.E.	.900	3	4	14	2	20	4
Hairston, Scott, Lan.	.970	9	11	21	1	33	3
Hoffpauir, Josh, Mod.	.973	6	18	18	1	37	3
Lopez, Jose, S.B.	1.000	3	7	10	0	17	2
Macha, Erick, Lan.	.946	11	18	17	2	37	2
MALDONADO, Edwin, S.J.	.980	118	209	319	11	539	70
Martinez, Guillermo, S.B.	.960	52	91	125	9	225	31
Menchaca, Eriberto, S.B.	1.000	8	18	15	0	33	4
Merritt, Tim, S.B.	.966	49	78	121	7	206	27
Morrissey, Adam, Mod.	.941	29	49	62	7	118	12
Neufeld, Andy, Mod.	.955	28	40	44	4	88	10
Perez, Nestor, Bak.	.981	67	94	167	5	266	33
Pichardo, Maximo, R.C.	.983	24	51	62	2	115	19
Raburn, Johnny, R.C.-H.D.	.973	59	132	153	8	293	36
Reding, Josh, S.B.	.970	8	17	15	1	33	3
Rodriguez, Javy, R.C.	.967	9	10	19	1	30	2
Rowan, Chris, H.D.	.966	23	57	56	4	117	18
Schmidt, J.P., Vis.	1.000	5	6	9	0	15	0
Smith, Casey, R.C.	.955	66	114	182	14	310	34
Uggla, Dan, Lan.	.950	34	59	73	7	139	13
Wayment, Kory, Mod.	.833	4	5	5	2	12	0
West, Todd, H.D.	.975	60	118	160	7	285	38

SECOND BASEMEN WITH TWO OR MORE TEAMS

Player, Team	Pct.	G	PO	A	E	TC	DP
Garcia, Isaac, Vis.	.957	8	9	13	1	23	2
Garcia, Isaac, Mod.	.980	18	21	28	1	50	6
Raburn, Johnny, R.C.	.978	45	99	121	5	225	27
Raburn, Johnny, H.D.	.956	14	33	32	3	68	9

THIRD BASEMEN

Player, Team	Pct.	G	PO	A	E	TC	DP
Anderson, Bryan, Sto.	.925	56	34	89	10	133	9
Ayala, Elio, H.D.	1.000	6	1	2	0	3	0
Barden, Brian, Lan.	.946	57	37	121	9	167	16
Basil, Jason, Vis.	.837	20	12	29	8	49	0
Beattie, Andrew, Sto.	.815	9	8	14	5	27	1
Bell, Derek, S.J.	1.000	2	1	5	0	6	0
Bone, Blake, S.B.	.818	13	5	13	4	22	0
Bozied, Tagg, L.E.	.750	3	1	2	1	4	1
Bravo, Danny, L.E.	.935	44	26	74	7	107	3
Calitri, Mike, Sto.	.874	31	17	59	11	87	2
Castellano, John, S.B.	.714	4	2	3	2	7	0
CHAVEZ, Angel, S.J.	.928	113	94	242	26	362	25
Clark, Daryl, H.D.	.855	55	40	78	20	138	2
Cordido, Julio, S.J.	.949	29	17	76	5	98	6
Davis, Mike, L.E.	.902	19	8	29	4	41	1
De Los Santos, Pedro, L.E.	.778	3	2	5	2	9	3
DeMent, Dan, Bak.	.813	34	19	42	14	75	1
Derosso, Tony, H.D.	.927	26	15	61	6	82	7
Duncan, Carlos, R.C.	.868	50	35	110	22	167	9
Eberwein, Kevin, L.E.	.900	2	4	5	1	10	0
Eddlemon, Kelly, Bak.	.923	13	10	14	2	26	3
Epke, Brian, Lan.	.000	1	0	0	0	0	0
Figueroa, Luis, S.B.	.866	25	12	46	9	67	2
Foley, Steve, S.B.	.000	1	0	0	0	0	0
Furmaniak, J.J., L.E.	.927	69	48	143	15	206	15
Gandolfo, Rob, S.B.	1.000	8	3	10	0	13	2
Garcia, Isaac, Vis.-Mod.	.833	23	9	46	11	66	5
Garrido, Tomas, S.J.	1.000	2	3	2	0	5	0
Greene, Khalil, L.E.	1.000	3	3	5	0	8	2
Groff, Matt, Vis.	.000	1	0	0	0	0	0
Hairston, Scott, Lan.	.889	4	4	4	1	9	1
Harrison, Vince, Bak.	.930	32	22	85	8	115	11
Hart, Corey, H.D.	.866	47	31	98	20	149	8
Hoffpauir, Josh, Mod.	1.000	3	0	4	0	4	1
Howe, Matt, Mod.	.918	70	38	108	13	159	7
Jackson, Steve, Mod.	1.000	3	0	2	0	2	0
Knott, Jon, L.E.	.500	1	0	1	1	2	0
Kunich, Frank, S.B.	.500	1	0	2	2	4	0

Player, Team	Pct.	G	PO	A	E	TC	DP
Leone, Justin, S.B.	.923	96	59	206	22	287	23
Luther, Ryan, S.J.	1.000	1	1	0	0	1	0
Macha, Erick, Lan.	.889	7	3	5	1	9	0
Martinez, Guillermo, S.B.	1.000	5	0	6	0	6	0
Mathis, Jake, R.C.	.905	5	5	14	2	21	2
Myers, Corey, Lan.	.906	58	31	133	17	181	7
Neufeld, Andy, Mod.	1.000	4	2	10	0	12	0
Nevin, Phil, L.E.	.000	2	0	0	2	2	0
Pichardo, Maximo, R.C.	.857	17	8	28	6	42	4
Raburn, Johnny, R.C.-H.D.	.933	11	9	19	2	30	2
Raymundo, G.J., Sto.	.954	52	31	113	7	151	7
Rodriguez, Javy, R.C.	.000	1	0	0	0	0	0
Roper, Zach, R.C.	.964	12	3	24	1	28	1
Rowan, Chris, H.D.	.943	14	9	24	2	35	5
Ruiz, Willy, Sto.	.000	1	0	0	0	0	0
Salas, Juan, Bak.	.862	65	37	125	26	188	8
Schmidt, J.P., Vis.	1.000	3	3	4	0	7	0
Schneidmiller, Gary, Vis.	.916	104	69	214	26	309	20
Smith, Casey, R.C.	.976	34	23	60	2	85	2
Sprowl, Jon-Mark, Lan.	.833	3	2	3	1	6	0
Teahen, Mark, Mod.	.971	58	37	98	4	139	14
Uggla, Dan, Lan.	.870	16	15	25	6	46	3
Villanueva, Florian, H.D.	.500	1	0	2	2	4	1
Wayment, Kory, Mod.	.818	6	2	7	2	11	0
Williams, Matt, Lan.	.889	4	3	5	1	9	0
Zamora, Junior, R.C.	.918	21	10	46	5	61	2

THIRD BASEMEN WITH TWO OR MORE TEAMS

Player, Team	Pct.	G	PO	A	E	TC	DP
Garcia, Isaac, Vis.	.825	21	9	38	10	57	5
Garcia, Isaac, Mod.	.889	2	0	8	1	9	0
Raburn, Johnny, R.C.	.929	10	9	17	2	28	2
Raburn, Johnny, H.D.	1.000	1	0	2	0	2	0

SHORTSTOPS

Player, Team	Pct.	G	PO	A	E	TC	DP
Anderson, Bryan, Sto.	.909	13	18	32	5	55	8
ATHAS, Jamie, S.J.	.946	120	153	353	29	535	55
Bannon, Jeff, Sto.	.928	130	183	355	42	580	51
Barnwell, Chris, H.D.	.962	35	56	97	6	159	27
Bartlett, Jason, L.E.	.929	75	90	197	22	309	33
Bell, Jay, Lan.	1.000	7	8	17	0	25	3
Berroa, Joandry, Lan.	.925	85	113	208	26	347	37
Bravo, Danny, L.E.	1.000	7	8	23	0	31	3
Brewer, Jace, Bak.	.938	89	104	273	25	402	50
Candelaria, Scott, H.D.	1.000	1	1	0	0	1	0
Chavez, Angel, Vis.	.989	19	39	53	1	93	9
Cordido, Julio, S.J.	1.000	1	1	3	0	4	0
Cosme, Caonabo, Mod.	.953	64	100	163	13	276	27
Crosby, Bobby, Mod.	.938	70	79	208	19	306	32
Eddlemon, Kelly, Bak.	.800	2	3	5	2	10	0
Firlit, Dan, Lan.	.989	23	31	62	1	94	11
Freeman, Corey, S.B.	1.000	5	4	8	0	12	2
Furmaniak, J.J., L.E.	.920	21	25	56	7	88	5
Garcia, Isaac, Vis.-Mod.	.926	10	9	16	2	27	4
Garrido, Tomas, S.J.	.913	6	8	13	2	23	2
Gil, Jerry, Lan.	.917	10	19	36	5	60	6
Greene, Khalil, L.E.	.950	39	33	101	7	141	14
Hardy, J.J., H.D.	.973	82	122	268	11	401	57
Leone, Justin, S.B.	.750	1	1	5	2	8	0
Lopez, Jose, S.B.	.936	119	164	293	31	488	56
Macha, Erick, Lan.	.878	41	54	90	20	164	15
Menchaca, Eriberto, S.B.	.800	2	3	1	1	5	0
Merritt, Tim, S.B.	.935	9	12	31	3	46	7
Perez, Nestor, Bak.	.962	53	64	138	8	210	21
Pichardo, Maximo, R.C.	.875	6	12	23	5	40	6
Raburn, Johnny, R.C.	.910	57	94	160	25	279	34
Reding, Josh, S.B.	.929	9	8	31	3	42	3
Rodriguez, Javy, R.C.	.939	51	58	141	13	212	27
Rowan, Chris, H.D.	.915	26	36	72	10	118	10
Schmidt, J.P., Vis.	.848	8	8	20	5	33	5
Selmo, Wilson, R.C.	.923	4	4	8	1	13	1
Smith, Casey, R.C.	.889	13	18	30	6	54	5
Stotts, J.T., Vis.	.943	133	150	398	33	581	55
Warriax, Brandon, R.C.	.917	17	25	52	7	84	7
Wayment, Kory, Mod.	.917	4	1	10	1	12	2
West, Todd, H.D.	.960	6	6	18	1	25	3

SHORTSTOPS WITH TWO OR MORE TEAMS

Player, Team	Pct.	G	PO	A	E	TC	DP
Garcia, Isaac, Vis.	.857	4	2	4	1	7	1
Garcia, Isaac, Mod.	.950	6	7	12	1	20	3

OUTFIELDERS

Player, Team	Pct.	G	PO	A	E	TC	DP
Allegra, Matt, Vis.	.967	123	227	11	8	246	2
Anderson, Bryan, Sto.	1.000	10	18	0	0	18	0
Arroyo, Abner, L.E.*	1.000	6	8	0	0	8	0
Baldelli, Rocco, Bak.	.975	71	114	5	3	122	3
Basil, Jason, Vis.	1.000	5	4	0	0	4	0
Beattie, Andrew, Sto.	.982	78	156	5	3	164	0
Bell, Derek, S.J.	1.000	5	10	0	0	10	0
Benjamin, Al, L.E.	.909	8	8	2	1	11	1
Bevins, Andy, Lan.	1.000	1	3	0	0	3	0
Bone, Blake, S.B.	.963	23	25	1	1	27	0
Bowser, Matt, Mod.*	.984	67	124	1	2	127	0
Boyd, Dan, H.D.	.923	23	22	2	2	26	0
Bozied, Tagg, L.E.	1.000	2	1	0	0	1	0
Bubela, Jaime, S.B.	.981	109	202	6	4	212	1
Campo, Mike, R.C.	.952	96	115	4	6	125	1
Candelaria, Scott, H.D.	1.000	1	3	0	0	3	0
Candelario, Luis, Bak.	1.000	11	11	1	0	12	1
Centeno, Irwin, Bak.	.929	54	91	1	7	99	1
Choo, Shin-soo, S.B.*	1.000	6	8	0	0	8	0
Christy, Jeff, Vis.	.970	89	124	6	4	134	0
Clark, Aaron, Bak.*	.968	57	89	3	3	95	1
Clark, Daryl, H.D.	.931	23	25	2	2	29	0
Contreras, Sergio, R.C.*	.959	53	91	3	4	98	0
Cordido, Julio, S.J.	.800	3	4	0	1	5	0
Cota, Jesus, Lan.	.962	56	74	2	3	79	0
Coulie, Jason, R.C.	.963	90	146	8	6	160	3
Curry, Mike, Sto.	.971	27	67	0	2	69	0
De Los Santos, Pedro, L.E.	.813	12	13	0	3	16	0
DeMent, Dan, Bak.	.895	13	17	0	2	19	0
Derosso, Tony, H.D.	.500	1	1	0	1	2	0
Donovan, Todd, L.E.	.959	52	112	5	5	122	0
Duarte, Justin, L.E.	1.000	5	5	0	0	5	0
Duncan, Carlos, R.C.	.913	14	20	1	2	23	0
Dye, Jermaine, Mod.	1.000	2	3	1	0	4	0
Edge, Dwight, Lan.	.968	126	231	10	8	249	2
Ellison, Jason, S.J.	.980	79	197	4	4	205	3
Florence, Branden, S.J.	1.000	5	12	1	0	13	0
Foley, Steve, S.B.	.885	16	22	1	3	26	0
Foreman, JuJu, Lan.	1.000	25	27	5	0	32	1
Foster, Brian, H.D.	1.000	1	3	0	0	3	0
Fox, Jason, H.D.	.973	48	103	4	3	110	1
Freeman, Corey, S.B.	.833	5	5	0	1	6	0
Fulse, Sheldon, S.B.	.982	106	212	4	4	220	2
Garthwaite, Jay, Lan.	1.000	7	5	0	0	5	0
Gemoll, Brandon, H.D.*	.893	19	25	0	3	28	0
Gomes, Jonny, Bak.	.961	131	166	8	7	181	1
Gomez, Andre, L.E.	1.000	7	6	2	0	8	0
Groff, Matt, Vis.	.978	29	39	5	1	45	2
Hall, Noah, Sto.	.980	25	47	1	1	49	0
Hall, Victor, Lan.*	.975	84	188	6	5	199	0
Hamilton, Josh, Bak.*	1.000	8	13	2	0	15	1
Hammond, Derry, H.D.	.956	56	103	5	5	113	0
Harris, Cedrick, H.D.	.976	55	116	5	3	124	0
Haynes, Nathan, R.C.*	.955	11	21	0	1	22	0
Hernandez, Alexei, S.B.	.882	50	59	1	8	68	0
Hoffpauir, Josh, Mod.	1.000	1	1	0	0	1	0
HOLST, Micah, S.J.	1.000	110	224	8	0	232	2
Holt, Daylan, Vis.	.985	71	123	8	2	133	0
Jackson, Steve, Mod.	1.000	2	1	0	0	1	0
Jacobs, John, Bak.	1.000	16	25	0	0	25	0
Johnson, Kade, H.D.	.921	24	33	2	3	38	1
Knott, Jon, L.E.	.963	41	71	8	3	82	0
Knox, Ryan, H.D.	.947	24	30	6	2	38	0
Kroeger, Josh, Lan.*	.978	118	213	9	5	227	0
Krynzel, Dave, H.D.*	.971	96	223	11	7	241	1
Kunich, Frank, S.B.	1.000	5	6	1	0	7	0
Leone, Justin, S.B.	1.000	1	1	0	0	1	0
Lundquist, Ryan, Sto.	.981	82	148	9	3	160	1
Luther, Ryan, S.J.	1.000	4	6	1	0	7	0
Macha, Erick, Lan.	.000	2	0	0	0	0	0
Maher, Caleb, R.C.	1.000	2	3	0	0	3	0
Martin, Brian, Bak.	.981	102	145	12	3	160	2
Martinez, Candido, Sto.	.957	18	20	2	1	23	0
Mashore, Damon, Lan.	1.000	5	7	0	0	7	0
McBeth, Marcus, Vis.	.971	50	96	6	3	105	0
Melgarejo, Ransel, R.C.	1.000	4	9	0	0	9	0
Morrissey, Adam, Mod.	1.000	3	6	0	0	6	0
Murphy, Nate, Lan.*	1.000	8	8	0	0	8	0
Nady, Xavier, L.E.	1.000	1	1	0	0	1	0
Nagle, Austin, Mod.	.920	51	68	1	6	75	0
Nettles, Marcus, L.E.*	.966	122	193	4	7	204	0
Nunez, Felix, R.C.	1.000	5	14	0	0	14	0
O'Donnell, Ryan, L.E.	.946	21	30	5	2	37	0

Player, Team	Pct.	G	PO	A	E	TC	DP
Owens, Jeremy, L.E.	.969	105	241	13	8	262	2
Patterson, Derek, H.D.	1.000	1	1	0	0	1	0
Raburn, Johnny, R.C.	1.000	3	10	0	0	10	0
Randolph, Jaisen, R.C.	.955	26	60	3	3	66	1
Raymundo, G.J., Sto.	.000	1	0	0	0	0	0
Riggins, Auntwan, L.E.	.968	45	87	3	3	93	1
Rios, Fernando, Sto.	.949	63	106	6	6	118	0
Rowan, Chris, H.D.	.842	16	16	0	3	19	0
Ruiz, Randy, Sto.	1.000	1	1	0	0	1	0
Schaub, Greg, H.D.	.000	1	0	0	0	0	0
Schmidt, J.P., Vis.	.986	37	69	4	1	74	0
Sellier, Brian, Mod.	.985	86	127	3	2	132	0
Senjem, Guye, Sto.	1.000	9	16	1	0	17	0
Shabala, Adam, S.J.	.991	70	115	0	1	116	0
Simpson, Bodie, Lan.	1.000	9	16	0	0	16	0
Smitherman, Stephen, Sto.	.975	125	187	11	5	203	1
Sprowl, Jon-Mark, Lan.	1.000	18	18	3	0	21	0
Stanley, Steve, Mod.*	.988	63	158	2	2	162	1
Swenson, Sammy, R.C.	.975	77	113	6	3	122	1
Swisher, Nick, Vis.*	.953	40	81	1	4	86	0
Thomas, Gary, Mod.	.966	114	192	9	7	208	4
Tritle, Chris, Mod.	.976	46	78	2	2	82	0
Trumble, Dan, S.J.	.986	47	71	0	1	72	0
Urquhart, Derick, R.C.*	1.000	2	3	0	0	3	0
Villanueva, Florian, H.D.	.800	4	8	0	2	10	0
Walker, Mark, S.J.	1.000	21	53	1	0	54	0
Webb, Ryan, R.C.	.957	76	152	3	7	162	0
Wilfong, Nick, S.J.	.988	100	153	7	2	162	3
Williamson, John, S.B.	.973	120	207	8	6	221	3
Zoccolillo, Peter, H.D.	.986	37	71	0	1	72	0

CATCHERS

Player, Team	Pct.	G	PO	A	E	TC	DP	PB
Abruzzo, Jared, R.C.	.976	59	438	53	12	503	3	17
Alcala, Juan, S.B.	.995	26	199	20	1	220	2	12
Alfonzo, Eliezer, H.D.	.976	12	72	11	2	85	1	2
Ansman, Craig, Lan.	.991	70	517	54	5	576	0	7
Basil, Jason, Mod.	.986	8	64	8	1	73	0	4
Brown, Jeremy, Vis.	.985	52	350	43	6	399	1	8
Budde, Ryan, R.C.	.985	77	615	84	11	710	7	6
Carroll, Mark, S.B.	.992	69	657	60	6	723	4	14
Castellano, John, S.B.	.984	28	226	19	4	249	2	9
Christianson, Ryan, S.B.	1.000	18	150	13	0	163	2	3
Corbeil, Azarias, R.C.	.982	9	45	9	1	55	0	0
CRAIG, Beau, Mod.	.991	87	729	77	7	813	11	17
Duarte, Justin, L.E.	.989	19	160	14	2	176	1	3
Epke, Brian, Lan.	1.000	5	32	4	0	36	1	2
Falcon, Omar, L.E.	1.000	2	14	2	0	16	0	0
Figga, Mike, Bak.	.986	7	65	6	1	72	0	0
Foster, Brian, H.D.	.969	64	419	47	15	481	3	13
Garcia, Cip, S.B.	.969	6	25	6	1	32	0	2
Gomez, Andre, L.E.	.997	46	337	30	1	368	2	10
Gonzalez, Wiki, L.E.	.983	14	110	5	2	117	2	1
Hudson, Ben, S.B.	1.000	4	16	0	0	16	0	1
Isenia, Chairon, Bak.	.981	58	498	32	10	540	4	14
Jackson, Steve, Mod.	.983	20	154	17	3	174	1	12
Kremblas, Mike, Vis.	.988	17	153	18	2	173	1	2
Lunsford, Trey, S.J.	.991	16	104	10	1	115	0	3
Luther, Ryan, S.J.	1.000	12	70	4	0	74	0	2
Massiatte, Danny, Bak.	.989	64	585	55	7	647	1	10
Mercado, Onix, Sto.	.972	3	31	4	1	36	0	0
Merritt, Graig, Bak.	1.000	13	120	9	0	129	1	6
Molina, Bengie, R.C.	1.000	1	8	1	0	9	0	0
Myers, Casey, Mod.	1.000	35	317	23	0	340	3	3
Myers, Corey, Vis.	1.000	1	3	0	0	3	0	0
Nieckula, Aaron, S.J.	.977	43	309	24	8	341	4	5
Pagan, Andres, L.E.	.983	70	600	47	11	658	2	14
Patterson, Derek, H.D.	.993	20	126	8	1	135	1	3
Peterson, Brian, Sto.	.985	76	590	74	10	674	4	11
Ramirez, Manuel, H.D.	.978	32	201	23	5	229	3	9
Reece, Eric, Bak.	1.000	4	18	1	0	19	0	1
Rodriguez, Guillermo, S.J.	.982	41	299	29	6	334	1	7
Santana, Manny, S.J.	.950	2	18	1	1	20	0	0
Sapp, Damian, Sto.	.990	43	359	37	4	400	1	7
Senjem, Guye, Sto.	.994	22	164	7	1	172	1	10
Snyder, Christopher, Lan.	.992	43	355	32	3	390	1	6
Soto, Jorge, Vis.	.986	62	462	40	7	509	4	14
Sprowl, Jon-Mark, Lan.	1.000	28	140	13	0	153	0	5
Suomi, Richard, Vis.	.987	17	137	12	2	151	0	5
Symonds, Grady, Lan.	.889	3	8	0	1	9	0	0
Villanueva, Florian, H.D.	.995	22	185	15	1	201	1	3
Williams, Jonny, S.J.	.000	1	0	0	0	0	0	0
Wright, Mike, S.J.	.992	33	209	28	2	239	1	5

PITCHERS

Player, Team	Pct.	G	PO	A	E	TC	DP
Abbott, Paul, S.B.	1.000	1	0	1	0	1	0
Adams, Mike, H.D.	1.000	10	1	1	0	2	0
Adkins, Jon, Mod.	.000	1	0	0	0	0	0
Aiello, Nick, Bak.*	1.000	21	1	4	0	5	0
Alfano, Jeff, S.J.	.000	6	0	0	0	0	0
Altman, Gene, H.D.	.800	11	3	1	1	5	1
Alvarado, Carlo, H.D.	.500	17	2	0	2	4	0
Anderson, Jason, Vis.*	1.000	19	0	4	0	4	0
Andujar, Jesse, R.C.	.857	32	1	5	1	7	0
Aquino, Greg, Lan.	.923	8	0	12	1	13	0
Arroyo, Luis, Sto.*	.000	10	0	0	0	0	0
Balser, Jeff, R.C.	.000	4	0	0	0	0	0
Barber, Scott, Lan.	1.000	32	8	14	0	22	0
Beck, David, Mod.*	.000	10	0	0	0	0	0
Belflower, Jay, Lan.	1.000	16	1	2	0	3	0
Belson, Greg, Lan.	1.000	40	2	8	0	10	1
Benedetti, John, Bak.	.967	54	8	21	1	30	3
Berry, Jon, Sto.	.750	19	0	3	1	4	0
Biggs, Billy, Lan.	1.000	8	3	3	0	6	1
Blackley, Travis, S.B.*	.909	21	2	18	2	22	0
Blanton, Joe, Mod.	1.000	2	0	1	0	1	0
Blood, Justin, S.B.*	1.000	20	0	2	0	2	0
Bludau, Nick, S.B.*	.923	43	3	9	1	13	1
Bonderman, Jeremy, Mod.	.826	25	6	13	4	23	0
Bonser, Boof, S.J.	.947	23	10	8	1	19	0
Bott, Glenn, S.B.*	.893	30	7	18	3	28	2
Boutwell, Andy, Sto.	.889	7	3	5	1	9	0
Brannon, Nick, Sto.*	.917	22	2	9	1	12	0
Brous, Dave, S.J.*	1.000	11	0	2	0	2	0
Brown, Elliot, S.J.	.667	6	2	0	1	3	0
Bruksch, Jeffrey, Vis.	.818	27	10	17	6	33	1
Brunet, Mike, R.C.	1.000	39	2	5	0	7	1
Bukowski, Stan, R.C.	.950	14	6	13	1	20	1
Bulger, Jason, Lan.	.667	2	0	2	1	3	0
Bumstead, Mike, L.E.	.952	27	9	11	1	21	0
Burton, Timothy, S.B.	.941	40	8	8	1	17	0
Butler, John, S.B.	.857	15	3	3	1	7	0
Campbell, Jarrett, Bak.	1.000	36	4	11	0	15	0
Candelaria, Scott, H.D.	.000	2	0	0	0	0	0
Carbajal, Alex, Bak.*	1.000	43	3	9	0	12	1
Carter, Justin, Sto.*	1.000	23	2	14	0	16	1
Cassel, Jack, L.E.	.875	23	1	6	1	8	1
Clark, Jeff, S.J.	.962	21	10	15	1	26	0
Coleman, Jeff, Vis.	.947	45	9	9	1	19	0
Cook, Dennis, R.C.*	1.000	4	0	1	0	1	0
Coose, Austin, Bak.	1.000	25	1	2	0	3	0
Coppinger, Rocky, Mod.	1.000	3	0	2	0	2	0
Cordero, Victor, H.D.	.500	10	1	0	1	2	0
Cordova, Jorge, Sto.	1.000	14	2	2	0	4	0
Cotts, Neal, Mod.*	.973	28	14	22	1	37	1
Cozier, Vance, S.J.	.889	11	3	5	1	9	0
Cram, Josh, S.J.	.000	2	0	0	0	0	0
Cramblitt, Joey, Lan.	.786	48	5	6	3	14	0
Crider, J.R., Vis.	1.000	12	0	2	0	2	0
Crowell, Kyle, Mod.	1.000	42	6	6	0	12	0
Cullen, Ryan, Vis.*	1.000	50	4	17	0	21	0
Culp, Brandon, Sto.	1.000	35	7	6	0	13	0
Daigle, Casey, Lan.	.848	21	6	22	5	33	0
Davey, Tom, L.E.	1.000	5	0	1	0	1	0
De Hart, Blair, L.E.	1.000	5	3	2	0	5	1
DeHart, Casey, Sto.*	.941	16	3	13	1	17	1
Dennis, Jason, R.C.*	.889	28	2	6	1	9	1
Dent, Doug, H.D.	.875	13	7	7	2	16	0
Dickinson, Drew, Vis.*	1.000	4	3	4	0	7	1
Eaton, Adam, L.E.	1.000	3	0	1	0	1	0
Eusebio, Mike, Sto.	.500	4	1	0	1	2	0
Fischer, Rich, R.C.	.971	19	8	26	1	35	2
Fischer, Steve, Vis.	1.000	50	6	14	0	20	0
Flinn, Chris, Bak.	.917	7	4	7	1	12	0
Flores, Ron, Vis.*	1.000	53	3	11	0	14	0
Fortunato, Bartolome, Bak.	.846	25	4	7	2	13	0
Frendling, Neal, Bak.	1.000	4	1	2	0	3	0
Frick, Mike, Mod.	.941	50	3	13	1	17	0
Fritz, Ben, Vis.	1.000	3	0	5	0	5	1
Gaal, Bryan, L.E.	1.000	32	4	3	0	7	0
Garcia, Sonny, Vis.	1.000	6	2	8	0	10	0
Gavelek, Brad, S.J.*	1.000	46	8	15	0	23	1
Germano, Justin, L.E.	1.000	3	2	3	0	5	0
Gilpatrick, T.Jay, Mod.	1.000	16	5	0	0	5	0
Gold, J.M., H.D.	1.000	7	2	4	0	6	0
Gomes, Tony, S.J.	1.000	16	2	3	0	5	1
Gomez, Andre, L.E.	.000	1	0	0	0	0	0
Gonzalez, Christian, Vis.	.938	29	7	23	2	32	2

Player, Team	Pct.	G	PO	A	E	TC	DP
Gonzalez, Edgar, Lan.	.857	4	3	3	1	7	0
Gonzalez, Enrique, Lan.	.750	5	2	1	1	4	0
Gooris, Dan, L.E.*	1.000	24	0	2	0	2	0
Gordon, Justin, H.D.*	.850	28	10	7	3	20	0
Gray, Mike, Lan.*	.667	18	0	2	1	3	0
Gregg, James, S.J.	1.000	5	0	1	0	1	1
Gregg, Kevin, Vis.	1.000	3	3	1	0	4	0
Gross, Kyle, S.J.	.000	4	0	0	1	1	0
Grunwald, Erik, S.B.	1.000	40	3	7	0	10	0
Gwyn, Marc, Mod.	.909	8	4	6	1	11	1
Hall, Josh, Sto.	1.000	7	3	6	0	9	0
Hannaman, Ryan, S.J.*	.000	1	0	0	0	0	0
Harden, Rich, Vis.	.833	12	5	5	2	12	1
Harriger, Mark, Vis.	.917	12	5	6	1	12	2
Harvey, Ian, L.E.	.933	34	5	9	1	15	1
Hendrickson, Ben, H.D.	1.000	14	4	16	0	20	2
Henrie, Matthew, Lan.	1.000	16	1	10	0	11	0
Hensley, Matt, R.C.	.857	12	2	4	1	7	2
Henthorne, Kevin, Lan.	1.000	2	2	2	0	4	0
Herbert, John, L.E.	.875	42	2	5	1	8	0
Hernandez, Alexei, S.B.	.000	1	0	0	0	0	0
High, Andy, H.D.*	.933	12	3	11	1	15	1
Hoerman, Jared, S.B.	.800	54	3	9	3	15	0
Howington, Ty, Sto.*	.000	2	0	0	0	0	0
Jackson, Dan, R.C.	1.000	31	6	10	0	16	0
Jarvis, Kevin, L.E.	1.000	1	0	2	0	2	0
Jenks, Bobby, R.C.	.917	11	4	7	1	12	0
Johnson, Rett, S.B.	.917	7	4	7	1	12	1
Kelly, Steve, Sto.	1.000	19	4	9	0	13	0
Komine, Shane, Vis.	.667	18	0	2	1	3	0
Koronka, John, Sto.*	.900	12	1	8	1	10	0
Kozol, Anthony, L.E.	1.000	3	0	1	0	1	0
Krawczyk, Jack, H.D.	1.000	6	1	0	0	1	0
Lamattina, Ryan, H.D.*	1.000	42	3	8	0	11	1
Lamber, Justin, S.B.*	.667	6	0	2	1	3	0
Lara, Nelson, S.J.	.800	19	3	9	3	15	0
Light, Scott, Sto.	1.000	1	0	1	0	1	0
Liriano, Pedro, R.C.	.867	28	6	20	4	30	0
Lowry, Noah, S.J.*	1.000	15	4	11	0	15	0
Luque, Roger, S.B.*	1.000	14	1	2	0	3	1
Mabeus, Chris, Mod.	.923	37	3	9	1	13	1
Malaska, Mark, Bak.*	.900	15	4	14	2	20	1
Markert, Jackson, S.J.	1.000	41	4	8	0	12	0
Marquez, Jeff, R.C.	1.000	2	0	1	0	1	0
Martin, Jeff, Sto.	1.000	33	6	21	0	27	2
Martinez, Gustavo, S.B.	1.000	16	0	2	0	2	0
Martinez, Javier, Sto.	1.000	5	0	1	0	1	0
Matzenbacher, Brian, Lan.	.947	38	6	12	1	19	1
Mayo, Blake, Lan.	1.000	2	1	2	0	3	0
Maysonet, Roberto, H.D.	1.000	35	2	4	0	6	0
McAdoo, Duncan, L.E.	1.000	41	11	8	0	19	0
McCALL, Derell, Mod.	1.000	25	18	20	0	38	2
McClain, Kevin, R.C.	.714	40	2	3	2	7	0
McClaskey, Tim, Vis.	1.000	19	13	14	0	27	1
McClung, Seth, Bak.	.833	7	1	4	1	6	0
McGee, Chris, H.D.	1.000	39	3	3	0	6	0
McMachen, Clifford, Lan.*	.500	5	0	1	1	2	0
Medders, Brandon, Lan.	.929	43	6	7	1	14	1
Mendoza, Mario, R.C.	.889	21	1	7	1	9	1
Miller, Ryan, H.D.	.846	36	8	14	4	26	2
Milo, Tony, R.C.*	1.000	4	0	3	0	3	0
Minaya, Edwin, Vis.	1.000	32	2	5	0	7	0
Montes, Albert, S.J.	1.000	24	1	14	0	15	1
Morgan, Russ, S.B.*	1.000	36	6	29	0	35	0
Morris, Will, R.C.	.000	4	0	0	0	0	0
Moseley, Dustin, Sto.	1.000	14	7	16	0	23	0
Mottl, Ryan, Sto.	.969	27	13	18	1	32	1
Mozingo, Dan, R.C.*	1.000	9	0	8	0	8	0
Munter, Scott, S.J.	.000	3	0	0	0	0	0
Nageotte, Clint, S.B.	.882	29	12	18	4	34	2
Nicolas, Mike, L.E.	.875	65	1	6	1	8	0
Nieckula, Aaron, S.J.	.000	1	0	0	0	0	0
Obenchain, Stephen, Vis.	.000	4	0	0	0	0	0
O'Brien, Matt, Mod.*	1.000	3	1	1	0	2	1
Olore, Kevin, S.B.	.955	25	7	14	1	22	0
O'Neal, Brandon, R.C.	.860	24	6	31	6	43	2
Oxspring, Chris, L.E.	1.000	15	0	5	0	5	0
Parker, Josh, Bak.	1.000	8	0	1	0	1	0
Parker, Matt, H.D.	1.000	1	0	1	0	1	0
Patten, Lanny, S.B.	1.000	6	0	1	0	1	0
Peguero, Radhames, Bak.	.920	41	5	18	2	25	0
Pena, Juan, Mod.-Vis.*	1.000	9	0	5	0	5	0
Perez, Beltran, Lan.	.727	5	2	6	3	11	1
Perez, Elvis, S.B.	1.000	6	0	7	0	7	0
Perez, George, H.D.	.826	35	7	12	4	23	1
Perez, Oliver, L.E.*	.750	9	2	10	4	16	0
Phillips, Mark, L.E.*	.929	28	4	22	2	28	1
Poe, Ryan, H.D.	1.000	3	0	1	0	1	0
Polanco, Elvis, S.B.	1.000	25	5	6	0	11	0
Price, Brett, Mod.*	1.000	35	5	4	0	9	0
Prinz, Bret, Lan.	1.000	5	1	0	0	1	0
Ramirez, Joslin, Lan.	1.000	5	1	2	0	3	0
Ramos, Juan, Mod.	.000	4	0	0	0	0	0
Ransom, Troy, S.J.	.955	27	10	11	1	22	1
Renteria, Juan, Bak.	1.000	14	3	2	0	5	0
Reynolds, Josh, L.E.	.833	7	0	5	1	6	0
Rheinecker, John, Vis.*	1.000	9	2	12	0	14	0
Rigueiro, Rafael, S.J.	.737	25	4	10	5	19	0
Robertson, Luke, Mod.	.893	29	6	19	3	28	2
Robinson, Jeff, H.D.	.000	1	0	0	0	0	0
Rust, Evan, Bak.	1.000	28	4	3	0	7	0
Sams, Aaron, H.D.*	1.000	9	2	12	0	14	0
Santos, Alex, Bak.	.882	19	7	8	2	17	0
Schaub, Greg, H.D.	1.000	34	1	3	0	4	0
Severino, Ronni, Bak.*	1.000	13	0	1	0	1	0
Shabansky, Rob, Lan.*	1.000	11	0	2	0	2	0
Shiyuk, Todd, L.E.*	1.000	42	1	6	0	7	0
Shwam, Mike, H.D.	1.000	5	0	2	0	2	0
Silva, Jesus, Lan.	1.000	34	2	6	0	8	0
Simmering, Bryan, Mod.	1.000	17	5	8	0	13	0
Sismondo, Bobby, H.D.*	1.000	38	2	12	0	14	3
Slaten, Doug, Lan.*	.700	8	1	6	3	10	0
Smart, Pete, H.D.*	.887	29	11	36	6	53	1
Smith, Cliff, R.C.	.667	36	1	7	4	12	1
Snare, Ryan, Sto.*	1.000	13	3	8	0	11	0
Snow, Bert, Vis.	1.000	12	0	1	0	1	0
Spiehs, R.D., S.J.	1.000	47	2	9	0	11	0
Stanton, Kyle, Sto.	1.000	9	2	1	0	3	0
Stewart, Cory, L.E.*	1.000	12	0	7	0	7	0
Stockman, Phil, Lan.	.964	20	5	22	1	28	0
Stokes, Brian, Bak.	.914	28	11	21	3	35	3
Switzer, Jon, Bak.*	.970	20	14	18	1	33	5
Taulli, Sam, Lan.*	.833	14	4	11	3	18	0
Therneau, Dave, Sto.	.941	29	7	9	1	17	1
Thomas, Adam, R.C.	.667	5	2	0	1	3	0
Thomas, J.T., S.J.*	.875	11	0	7	1	8	1
Thompson, Mike, L.E.	1.000	25	4	20	0	24	0
Threets, Erick, S.J.*	.714	26	0	5	2	7	1
Toledo, Jean, R.C.	1.000	3	1	0	0	1	0
Trejo, Francisco, Lan.*	1.000	28	6	22	0	28	1
Trosper, Tanner, Mod.	.889	25	8	8	2	18	0
Tucker, Rusty, L.E.*	1.000	26	1	2	0	3	0
Turnbow, Derrick, R.C.	.000	13	0	0	1	1	0
Uzzell, Todd, S.J.	.857	7	1	5	1	7	0
Van Dusen, Derrick, S.B.*	1.000	20	3	15	0	18	0
Velazquez, Elih, S.J.*	.833	35	4	6	2	12	0
Veras, Jose, Bak.	.867	11	4	9	2	15	0
Voltz, Jude, H.D.*	.000	3	0	0	0	0	0
Waechter, Doug, Bak.	.889	17	7	9	2	18	0
Walker, Kevin, L.E.*	.000	5	0	0	0	0	0
Wawrzyniak, Alan, R.C.	1.000	10	0	1	0	1	0
Webb, Alan, Mod.*	.750	2	0	3	1	4	0
Webster, Jeremy, L.E.*	1.000	8	0	1	0	1	0
Weis, Brad, Mod.*	1.000	32	8	15	0	23	0
Wells, Carlton, Lan.*	1.000	37	2	10	0	12	1
White, Bill, Lan.*	.000	6	0	0	0	0	0
Wiedmeyer, Jason, L.E.*	1.000	14	2	10	0	12	1
Wiles, Chad, S.B.	1.000	29	1	3	0	4	0
Wilson, Phil, R.C.	.895	14	6	11	2	19	0
Withers, Darvin, Mod.	.900	30	6	12	2	20	2
Wood, Mike, Mod.	.909	7	3	7	1	11	0
Yacco, Anthony, S.J.	.889	23	1	7	1	9	1
Ziegler, Mike, Vis.	1.000	25	4	23	0	27	2

PITCHERS WITH TWO OR MORE TEAMS

Player, Team	Pct.	G	PO	A	E	TC	DP
Pena, Juan, Mod.*	1.000	2	0	1	0	1	0
Pena, Juan, Vis.*	1.000	7	0	4	0	4	0

The following players appeared only as designated hitter, pinch-hitter or pinch runner: Adames, ph; Brooks, dh; Joey Gomes, dh; Pickens, dh; Valderrama, dh, ph.

LEAGUE CHAMPIONS

Year	Team	Pct.	Year	Team	Pct.	Year	Team	Pct.
1914—	Fresno	.571	1965—	San Jose	.586	1984—	Modesto§	.597
1915—	Modesto	.857		Stockton§	.614		Bakersfield	.486
1916-40—	Did not operate.		1966—	Modesto	.577	1985—	Fresno§	.575
1941—	Fresno	.643		Modesto	.671		Stockton	.566
	Santa Barbara (2nd)*	.597	1967—	San Jose§	.676	1986—	Palm Springs	.613
1942—	Santa Barbara†	.642		Modesto	.586		Stockton§	.585
1943-44-45—	Did not operate.		1968—	San Jose	.629	1987—	Fresno§	.559
1946—	Stockton‡	.600		Fresno§	.623		Reno	.535
1947—	Stockton‡	.679	1969—	Stockton§	.600	1988—	Stockton	.657
1948—	Fresno	.607		Visalia	.614		Riverside§	.599
	Santa Barbara (3rd)*	.529	1970—	Bakersfield	.667	1989—	Stockton	.627
1949—	Bakersfield	.612		Bakersfield	.671		Bakersfield§	.577
	San Jose (4th)*	.543	1971—	Visalia§	.583	1990—	Visalia	.638
1950—	Ventura	.607		Fresno	.500		Stockton§	.582
	Modesto (2nd)*	.586	1972—	Modesto§	.547	1991—	San Jose	.676
1951—	Santa Barbara‡	.599		Bakersfield	.629		High Desert§	.537
1952—	Fresno‡	.629	1973—	Lodi§	.657	1992—	Stockton§	.610
1953—	San Jose‡	.664		Bakersfield	.571		Visalia	.551
1954—	Modesto‡	.623	1974—	Fresno§	.607	1993—	High Desert§	.620
1955—	Stockton	.733		San Jose	.579		Modesto	.529
	Fresno§	.718	1975—	Reno	.614	1994—	Modesto	.706
1956—	Fresno§	.650		Reno	.614		Rancho Cucamonga§	.566
1957—	Visalia∞	.622	1976—	Salinas	.650	1995—	San Bernardino§	.612
	Salinas (4th)*	.504		Reno§	.547		San Jose	.550
1958—	Fresno*	.639	1977—	Salinas	.564	1996—	San Jose	.636
	Bakersfield	.672		Lodi§	.579		Lake Elsinore‡	.550
1959—	Bakersfield	.592	1978—	Visalia§	.698	1997—	High Desert▲	.593
	Modesto§	.643		Lodi	.607		San Bernardino	.486
1960—	Reno	.614	1979—	San Jose§	.636	1998—	San Jose▲	.593
	Reno	.657		Reno	.525		Rancho Cucamonga	.550
1961—	Reno	.743	1980—	Stockton§	.638	1999—	Modesto	.629
	Reno	.643		Visalia	.507		San Bernardino▲	.567
1962—	San Jose§	.686	1981—	Visalia	.621	2000—	Lancaster	.636
	Reno	.587		Lodi§	.521		San Bernardino▲	.550
1963—	Modesto	.589	1982—	Modesto§	.671	2001—	Lake Elsinore◆	.650
	Stockton§	.687		Visalia	.586		San Jose◆	.550
1964—	Fresno	.638	1983—	Visalia	.621	2002—	Stockton▲	.636
	Fresno	.600		Redwood§	.529			

*Won four-club playoff. †League disbanded June 28. ‡Won championship and four-club playoff. §Won split-season playoff. ∞Won both halves of split season. ▲Played split season and won six-club playoff. ◆Played split season and were in midst of six-club playoff and declared co-champions when Professional Baseball declared a stoppage of play.

CAROLINA LEAGUE

LEAGUE OFFICE

President/treasurer
John Hopkins
Address
P.O. Box 9503
Greensboro, NC 27429
Phone
336-691-9030

Teams (affiliation)
Frederick Keys (Orioles)
Kinston Indians (Indians)
Lynchburg Hillcats (Pirates)
Myrtle Beach Pelicans (Braves)
Potomac Cannons (Reds)
Salem Avalanche (Astros)

Wilmington (Del.) Blue Rocks (Royals)
Winston-Salem Warthogs (White Sox)

2002 FINAL STANDINGS

FIRST HALF

NORTHERN DIVISION

Team	W	L	T	Pct.	GB
Wilmington (Royals)	47	23	0	.671	...
Lynchburg (Pirates)	47	23	0	.671	...
Potomac (Cardinals)	24	46	0	.343	23.0
Frederick (Orioles)	18	51	0	.261	28.5

SOUTHERN DIVISION

Team	W	L	T	Pct.	GB
Myrtle Beach (Braves)	43	27	0	.614	...
Salem (Rockies)	39	31	0	.557	4.0
Kinston (Indians)	34	35	0	.493	8.5
Winston-Salem (White Sox)	27	43	0	.386	16.0

SECOND HALF

NORTHERN DIVISION

Team	W	L	T	Pct.	GB
Wilmington (Royals)	42	28	0	.600	...
Lynchburg (Pirates)	40	30	0	.571	2.0
Potomac (Cardinals)	35	35	0	.500	7.0
Frederick (Orioles)	29	41	0	.414	13.0

SOUTHERN DIVISION

Team	W	L	T	Pct.	GB
Kinston (Indians)	40	30	0	.571	...
Myrtle Beach (Braves)	36	34	0	.514	4.0
Salem (Rockies)	35	35	0	.500	5.0
Winston-Salem (White Sox)	23	47	0	.329	17.0

COMPOSITE

Team	Wil.	Lyn.	M.B.	Kin.	Sal.	Pot.	W.S.	Fred.	W	L	T	Pct.	GB
Wilmington (Royals)	...	14	10	10	13	15	14	13	89	51	0	.636	...
Lynchburg (Pirates)	6	...	7	17	13	11	17	16	87	53	0	.621	2.0
Myrtle Beach (Braves)	10	13	...	7	8	11	14	16	79	61	0	.564	10.0
Kinston (Indians)	10	3	13	...	13	12	12	11	74	65	0	.532	14.5
Salem (Rockies)	7	7	12	7	...	13	16	12	74	66	0	.529	15.0
Potomac (Cardinals)	5	9	9	8	7	...	9	12	59	81	0	.421	30.0
Winston-Salem (White Sox)	6	3	6	8	4	11	...	12	50	90	0	.357	39.0
Frederick (Orioles)	7	4	4	8	8	8	8	...	47	92	0	.338	41.5

Major league affiliations in parentheses.

PLAYOFFS: Kinston defeated Myrtle Beach, two games to none; Lynchburg defeated Wilmington, two games to one; Lynchburg defeated Kinston, three games to one to win Carolina League championship.

REGULAR-SEASON ATTENDANCE: Frederick, 305,950; Lynchburg, 127,916; Myrtle Beach, 200,463; Potomac, 182,059; Salem, 196,347; Wilmington, 331,545; Winston-Salem, 136,302. Total—1,587,054. Playoffs (9 games)—12,592. Carolina-California All-Star Game at Wilmington, Del.—5,545.

MANAGERS: Frederick, Jack Voigt; Kinston, Ted Kubiak; Lynchburg, Pete Mackanin; Myrtle Beach, Randy Ingle; Potomac, Joe Cunningham; Salem, Stu Cole; Wilmington, Jeff Garber; Winston-Salem, Razor Shines.

ALL-STAR TEAM: 1B—Brad Hawpe, Salem; 2B—Josh Bonifay, Lynchburg; 3B—Justin Gemoll, Wilmington; SS—Joe Castillo, Lynchburg; Utility INF—Alejandro Machado, Wilmington; OF—Chris Duffy, Lynchburg; OF—Bill McCarthy, Myrtle Beach; OF—Skip Schumaker, Potomac; Utility OF—Byron Gettis, Wilmington; C—Ronny Paulino, Lynchburg; DH—Ray Navarrete, Lynchburg; SP—Sean Burnett, Lynchburg; RP—D.J. Carrasco, Lynchburg; Most Valuable Player—Brad Hawpe, Salem; Pitcher of the Year—Sean Burnett, Lynchburg; Manager of the Year—Jeff Garber, Wilmington.

2002 BATTING

TEAM

Team	G	TPA	AB	R	H	TB	2B	3B	HR	RBI	SH	SF	HP	BB	IBB	SO	SB	CS	GDP	LOB	ShO	Avg.	OBP	Slg.
Lynchburg	140	5367	4776	700	1317	2053	293	25	131	633	37	47	88	419	25	849	110	53	109	1001	7	.276	.342	.430
Wilmington	140	5320	4674	691	1281	1745	238	26	58	603	98	50	4	494	20	904	108	51	111	1095	5	.274	.341	.373
Salem	140	5359	4774	656	1262	1913	295	34	96	594	44	50	83	408	36	929	65	35	116	997	10	.264	.330	.401
Myrtle Beach	140	5129	4561	555	1161	1641	218	32	66	501	39	39	71	419	14	860	136	76	95	962	13	.255	.324	.360
Kinston	139	5272	4645	598	1168	1739	198	38	99	554	49	36	60	482	23	1101	184	75	77	996	12	.251	.327	.374
Frederick	139	5230	4662	562	1169	1559	193	19	53	503	64	33	61	410	13	900	65	46	115	951	11	.251	.317	.334
Potomac	140	5243	4646	555	1150	1597	204	24	65	501	53	36	58	450	26	935	143	76	106	988	14	.248	.319	.344
Win.-Salem	140	5203	4607	552	1120	1591	193	19	80	493	67	36	37	420	17	1002	210	76	86	935	11	.243	.314	.345

INDIVIDUAL

TOP QUALIFIERS FOR BATTING CHAMPIONSHIP

Minimum 378 plate appearances. *Lefthanded batter. †Switch-hitter.

Player, Team	G	TPA	AB	R	H	TB	2B	3B	HR	RBI	SH	SF	HP	BB	IBB	SO	SB	CS	GDP	Avg.	OBP	Slg.
Hawpe, Brad, Sal.*	122	535	450	87	156	264	38	2	22	97	0	2	2	81	23	84	1	1	7	.347	.447	.587
Navarrete, Ray, Lyn.	134	593	532	75	169	232	41	2	6	69	6	5	12	38	3	48	8	3	18	.318	.373	.436

Player, Team	G	TPA	AB	R	H	TB	2B	3B	HR	RBI	SH	SF	HP	BB	IBB	SO	SB	CS	GDP	Avg.	OBP	Slg.
Machado, Alejandro, Wil.	101	382	325	53	102	119	9	1	2	29	12	6	12	27	1	43	20	6	2	.314	.381	.366
Gemoll, Justin, Wil.	93	389	335	56	104	131	20	2	1	49	4	2	8	40	0	55	0	3	7	.310	.395	.391
Bonifay, Josh, Lyn.	126	539	463	83	142	258	36	1	26	102	1	8	4	63	2	97	3	3	4	.307	.388	.557
McCarthy, Bill, M.B.	128	508	442	52	135	202	26	4	11	65	0	5	23	38	3	88	6	5	11	.305	.388	.557
Piedra, Jorge, Sal.*	104	448	392	64	118	218	37	12	13	64	3	8	8	37	3	55	10	2	4	.301	.366	.556
Duffy, Chris, Lyn.†	132	597	539	85	162	229	27	5	10	52	10	3	12	33	1	101	22	7	1	.301	.353	.425
Tucker, Mamon, Fred.	127	520	473	62	142	178	16	4	4	55	6	4	4	33	1	75	9	8	19	.300	.348	.376
Castillo, Jose, Lyn.	134	572	503	82	151	228	25	2	16	81	1	8	11	49	1	95	27	14	18	.300	.370	.453
DeJesus, David, Wil.*	87	410	334	69	99	145	22	6	4	41	10	5	13	48	2	42	15	6	8	.296	.400	.434
Meadows, Tydus, Wil.	94	406	339	63	100	160	19	4	11	55	1	3	9	54	2	83	13	3	11	.295	.402	.472
Sullivan, Cory, Sal.*	138	622	560	90	161	251	42	6	12	67	7	7	12	36	3	70	26	5	3	.288	.340	.448
Schumaker, Skip, Pot.*	136	606	551	71	158	194	22	4	2	44	6	2	2	45	3	84	26	16	10	.287	.342	.352
Hernandez, Johnny, Pot.†	139	580	498	54	141	178	24	5	1	62	0	9	6	67	5	111	16	14	10	.283	.369	.357
Gettis, Byron, Wil.	120	526	449	76	127	188	33	2	8	70	10	6	13	48	3	103	10	5	8	.283	.364	.419

DEPARTMENTAL LEADERS: G—J. Hernandez, 139; AB—C. Sullivan, 560; R—C. Sullivan, 90; H—Navarrete, 169; TB—Hawpe, 264; 2B—C. Sullivan, 42; 3B—Piedra, 12; HR—Bonifay, 26; RBI—Bonifay, 102; SH—Hopper, 22; SF—J. Hernandez, 9; HP—McCarthy, 23; BB—Hawpe, 81; IBB—Hawpe, 23; SO—Welsh, 159; SB—Yan, 88; CS—Morris, Requena, Yan, 19 each; GIDP—Wilken, 19; Slg.—Hawpe, .587; OBP—Hawpe, .447.

ALL PLAYERS

*Lefthanded batter. †Switch-hitter.

Player, Team	G	TPA	AB	R	H	TB	2B	3B	HR	RBI	SH	SF	HP	BB	IBB	SO	SB	CS	GDP	Avg.	OBP	Slg.
Anderson, Travis, M.B.	40	141	120	19	32	45	4	0	3	12	0	1	6	14	0	26	0	4	2	.267	.369	.375
Araujo, Ramon, Pot.†	59	187	173	22	37	43	6	0	0	11	7	1	0	6	0	34	7	3	1	.214	.239	.249
Arnerich, Tony, Wil.	73	303	278	28	76	93	11	0	2	43	2	3	2	17	1	44	2	2	12	.273	.317	.335
Aspito, Jason, W.S.*	102	358	316	40	80	116	14	2	6	36	4	3	2	34	1	83	2	2	12	.253	.325	.367
Asprilla, Avelino, Lyn.	7	14	12	4	2	2	0	0	0	0	0	0	1	1	0	2	0	0	0	.167	.286	.167
Barns, B.J., Lyn.*	135	555	489	59	131	203	30	3	12	69	3	4	17	42	5	76	14	9	10	.268	.344	.415
Bastardo, Angel, Kin.	16	63	54	10	12	19	4	0	1	11	3	1	3	2	0	8	1	0	1	.222	.283	.352
Berroa, Cristian, Sal.†	91	351	326	40	89	115	21	1	1	29	3	2	8	12	2	48	6	0	16	.273	.313	.353
Blanco, Andres, Wil.†	5	16	13	2	4	5	1	0	0	0	2	0	0	1	0	4	0	0	0	.308	.357	.385
Bonifay, Josh, Lyn.	126	539	463	83	142	258	36	1	26	102	1	8	4	63	2	97	3	3	4	.307	.388	.557
Borchard, Joe, W.S.†	2	9	3	1	0	0	0	0	0	0	0	0	0	6	0	0	0	0	0	.000	.667	.000
Boscan, Jean, M.B.	86	313	276	21	60	85	19	0	2	27	4	2	3	28	1	71	3	1	6	.217	.294	.308
Brisson, Dustin, Pot.*	62	228	214	15	45	67	7	0	5	21	3	0	2	8	0	49	1	2	2	.210	.246	.313
Brown, Jason, Lyn.	7	21	19	1	4	5	1	0	0	0	0	0	0	2	0	8	0	0	1	.211	.286	.263
Brown, Kevin, M.B.	48	151	133	11	22	30	5	0	1	11	1	1	3	13	0	36	0	0	0	.165	.253	.226
Buford, Damon, W.S.	7	32	28	2	8	10	2	0	0	2	0	0	0	4	0	4	1	1	1	.286	.375	.357
Burnett, Mark, Pot.*	73	305	275	33	73	105	14	6	2	40	2	5	5	18	0	38	10	1	2	.265	.317	.382
Canelliz, Chris, Pot.	15	34	27	2	7	7	0	0	0	3	1	0	0	6	0	7	0	0	1	.259	.394	.259
Caradonna, Brett, W.S.*	110	425	390	42	105	144	16	1	7	55	4	4	2	25	1	47	10	4	9	.269	.314	.369
Castillo, Jose, Lyn.	134	572	503	82	151	228	25	2	16	81	1	8	11	49	1	95	27	14	18	.300	.370	.453
Catalanotte, Greg, Sal.†	37	141	119	18	30	51	6	3	3	21	1	2	1	18	0	33	0	1	2	.252	.350	.429
Cates, Gary, Fred.	32	138	126	12	25	31	6	0	0	7	4	1	0	7	0	18	2	2	3	.198	.239	.246
Church, Ryan, Kin.*	53	217	181	30	59	103	12	1	10	30	0	1	4	31	6	51	4	4	3	.326	.433	.569
Ciraco, Darren, W.S.	17	57	53	4	8	12	1	0	1	3	0	0	0	4	0	18	1	1	0	.151	.211	.226
Cockrell, Michael, Lyn.	9	9	7	0	0	0	0	0	0	0	0	0	0	2	0	0	0	0	0	.000	.222	.000
Coleman, Alph, M.B.	120	440	407	40	85	102	9	1	2	29	3	4	3	23	0	68	15	13	13	.209	.254	.251
Colmenter, Jesus, Kin.†	2	3	2	0	0	0	0	0	0	0	0	0	0	1	0	2	0	0	0	.000	.333	.000
Conway, Dan, Sal.	41	154	135	19	31	56	10	0	5	14	0	1	3	15	0	33	0	2	2	.230	.318	.415
Cordova, Ricardo, Pot.†	34	103	95	9	16	27	2	0	3	9	1	0	0	7	0	25	0	0	2	.168	.223	.284
Cotten, Jeremy, Lyn.	40	133	126	11	28	49	9	0	4	11	0	1	1	5	0	34	1	0	2	.222	.256	.389
Cotto, Luis, Wil.	14	39	36	3	6	6	0	0	0	0	0	0	0	3	0	11	0	0	0	.167	.231	.167
Cowan, Justin, Wil.	92	377	323	53	97	138	24	1	5	43	7	7	12	28	1	58	4	0	8	.300	.370	.427
Cox, George, Fred.	6	21	21	3	5	9	1	0	1	5	0	0	0	0	0	4	0	0	1	.238	.238	.429
Crozier, Eric, Kin.*	72	307	258	40	84	131	16	2	9	55	0	3	4	42	2	57	4	3	4	.326	.428	.508
Cruz, Alex, Lyn.	3	1	1	0	0	0	0	0	0	0	0	0	0	0	0	0	0	0	0	.000	.000	.000
Cunningham, Marco, Wil.	29	128	103	15	33	49	9	0	4	17	1	0	6	18	0	21	5	2	6	.320	.449	.476
Davidson, Seth, Pot.†	42	128	120	15	23	30	7	0	0	9	1	2	1	6	0	21	5	2	6	.192	.240	.250
De Caster, Yurendell, Lyn.	125	477	432	54	109	185	25	4	5	62	2	5	8	30	2	102	1	1	2	.252	.309	.428
DeJesus, David, Wil.*	87	410	334	69	99	145	22	6	4	41	10	5	13	48	2	42	15	6	8	.296	.400	.434
Del Rosario, Manny, Fred.†	8	20	20	2	3	4	1	0	0	0	0	0	0	0	0	5	0	0	0	.150	.150	.200
Dempsey, Nick, Kin.	9	32	31	2	4	4	0	0	0	1	0	0	0	1	0	3	0	0	0	.129	.156	.129
Depippo, Jeff, Kin.	48	170	149	11	36	52	4	0	1	15	4	2	5	10	0	35	1	2	1	.242	.307	.349
DeRosa, Mark, M.B.	2	8	7	0	0	0	0	0	0	0	0	0	0	1	0	0	0	0	0	.000	.125	.000
Duffy, Chris, Lyn.†	132	597	539	85	162	229	27	5	10	52	10	3	12	33	1	101	22	7	1	.301	.353	.425
Fenster, Darren, Wil.	74	294	245	25	60	68	5	0	1	28	8	5	3	33	2	32	1	3	4	.245	.336	.278
Fera, Aaron, Pot.	70	281	252	34	65	118	15	1	12	36	0	3	4	22	4	61	4	1	7	.258	.324	.468
Figueroa, Franky, Fred.	48	207	191	16	49	67	9	0	3	29	0	1	1	14	2	49	0	0	8	.257	.309	.351
Fontenot, Mike, Fred.*	122	547	481	61	127	175	16	4	8	53	9	5	10	42	1	117	13	9	3	.264	.333	.364
Forbes, Mike, M.B.*	34	115	98	14	20	31	5	0	2	6	0	0	0	17	0	32	4	2	0	.204	.322	.316
Ford, Tom, Fred.*	46	1	1	0	0	0	0	0	0	0	0	0	0	0	0	0	0	0	0	.000	.000	.000
Fox, Mike, Pot.	8	18	17	0	1	1	0	0	0	0	0	0	0	1	0	6	0	0	0	.059	.111	.059
Garcia, Nick, Fred.	58	213	198	13	50	59	6	0	1	21	8	1	1	5	0	18	1	1	4	.253	.271	.298
Garrick, Matt, Pot.	11	42	39	3	13	19	3	0	1	6	0	0	0	3	0	18	1	0	4	.333	.381	.487
Gemoll, Justin, Wil.	93	389	335	56	104	131	20	2	1	49	4	2	8	40	0	55	0	3	7	.310	.395	.391
Gettis, Byron, Wil.	120	526	449	76	127	188	33	2	8	70	10	6	13	48	3	103	10	5	8	.283	.364	.419
Gillikin, Joe, W.S.	2	5	4	1	2	3	1	0	0	1	0	0	0	1	0	0	0	0	0	.500	.600	.750
Gordon, Alex, Fred.*	49	171	158	19	32	52	5	0	5	16	1	1	1	10	0	67	1	1	4	.203	.253	.329
Hamill, Ryan, Pot.	96	372	338	38	74	118	15	1	9	32	6	1	4	23	0	60	1	1	10	.219	.276	.349
Harris, Blair, W.S.	2	5	5	1	1	2	1	0	0	0	0	0	0	0	0	1	0	0	0	.200	.200	.400
Hawpe, Brad, Sal.*	122	535	450	87	156	264	38	2	22	97	0	2	2	81	23	84	1	1	7	.347	.447	.587

Player, Team	G	TPA	AB	R	H	TB	2B	3B	HR	RBI	SH	SF	HP	BB	IBB	SO	SB	CS	GDP	Avg.	OBP	Slg.
Hernandez, Johnny, Pot.†	139	580	498	54	141	178	24	5	1	62	0	9	6	67	5	111	16	14	10	.283	.369	.357
Hickman, Brian, W.S.	28	84	64	9	6	6	0	0	0	2	2	0	8	10	1	21	1	2	1	.094	.293	.094
Hill, Willy, Lyn.*	20	58	54	2	10	10	0	0	0	1	1	0	0	3	0	14	3	0	1	.185	.228	.185
Hopper, Norris, Wil.	125	577	514	78	140	161	12	3	1	46	22	2	8	31	1	55	22	9	15	.272	.323	.313
Hudnall, Joshua, Lyn.	52	120	110	23	19	25	3	0	1	7	0	0	1	9	0	26	5	1	1	.173	.242	.227
Inglett, Joe, Kin.*	66	271	238	24	67	79	12	0	0	29	0	2	2	29	3	38	5	2	3	.282	.362	.332
Izturis, Maicer, Kin.†	58	262	233	28	61	79	13	1	1	30	3	1	1	24	0	26	24	6	2	.262	.332	.339
Janowicz, Nate, Kin.*	44	176	151	12	40	52	7	1	1	20	2	4	2	17	0	28	1	0	3	.265	.339	.344
Jaramillo, Milko, Pot.	109	413	374	43	90	115	17	1	2	30	4	2	5	28	2	63	5	2	9	.241	.301	.307
Jeffcoat, Bryon, M.B.	67	248	225	24	51	81	15	0	5	30	0	5	4	14	0	48	5	1	1	.227	.278	.360
Johnson, Kelly, M.B.*	126	540	482	62	123	190	21	5	12	49	2	4	1	51	0	105	12	15	5	.255	.325	.394
Jones, Damien, M.B.*	23	67	61	8	16	20	2	1	0	1	0	0	0	6	0	22	3	0	2	.262	.328	.328
Jurries, James, M.B.	48	193	176	23	51	81	9	3	5	30	0	0	0	17	1	26	2	2	6	.290	.352	.460
Kent, Mailon, M.B.	105	391	337	34	83	101	14	2	0	20	3	1	3	47	0	50	8	8	15	.246	.343	.300
Keppinger, Billy, Wil.*	5	14	11	1	2	2	0	0	0	1	0	0	0	3	0	4	0	0	0	.182	.357	.182
Kessick, Jon, Fred.	10	38	32	6	7	10	1	1	0	4	0	0	0	6	0	17	0	0	0	.219	.342	.313
Keylor, Cory, Fred.*	132	566	497	70	128	171	26	1	5	47	0	6	6	57	2	109	14	3	6	.258	.337	.344
Kohl, Doug, Pot.	17	4	4	0	1	1	0	0	0	0	0	0	0	0	0	0	0	0	0	.250	.250	.250
Koslowski, Kasey, W.S.	5	13	9	1	1	1	0	0	0	0	0	0	1	3	0	2	0	1	0	.111	.385	.111
Lambert, Casey, Sal.	69	285	240	34	56	66	10	0	0	24	6	4	10	25	0	36	1	1	7	.233	.326	.275
Landaeta, Luis, Lyn.*	65	238	220	26	58	99	16	2	7	31	0	2	2	14	4	29	2	3	6	.264	.311	.450
LaRoche, Adam, M.B.*	69	285	250	30	84	128	17	0	9	53	2	2	4	27	4	37	0	2	3	.336	.406	.512
Leach, Nick, Pot.*	16	66	60	4	13	18	2	0	1	8	0	1	2	3	2	15	0	0	1	.217	.273	.300
Lebron, Francisco, W.S.	56	219	203	22	54	93	15	0	8	27	0	0	1	15	2	54	3	0	3	.266	.320	.458
Leon, Alfredo, Fred.	74	259	235	24	62	69	7	0	0	28	3	1	5	15	0	23	2	2	10	.264	.320	.294
Lewis, Richard, M.B.	130	556	484	82	135	172	23	4	2	51	4	5	8	55	0	80	31	10	8	.279	.359	.355
Lewis, Russell, Pot.*	20	71	67	3	10	12	2	0	0	1	1	0	0	3	0	13	1	1	1	.149	.186	.179
Lincoln, Justin, Sal.	126	469	429	53	97	158	19	0	14	52	2	1	5	32	1	145	1	1	8	.226	.287	.368
Lisk, Charles, W.S.	18	58	54	5	10	16	3	0	1	9	0	0	1	3	0	19	2	0	1	.185	.241	.296
Littleton, Brandon, Fred.†	45	173	152	21	26	35	3	3	0	8	8	0	1	12	1	33	5	2	1	.171	.236	.230
Lopez-Cao, Mike, Lyn.*	70	241	212	33	64	106	16	1	8	20	2	0	3	18	1	35	0	0	4	.302	.365	.500
Lora, Tom, Wil.†	97	366	328	47	87	112	18	2	1	32	6	2	3	27	0	62	8	6	7	.265	.325	.341
Luna, Hector, Kin.	128	518	468	67	129	189	15	6	11	51	6	2	3	39	0	79	32	11	7	.276	.334	.404
Luster, Jeremy, Pot.†	53	211	192	22	39	61	8	1	4	25	0	1	1	16	2	23	3	5	10	.203	.267	.318
Machado, Alejandro, Wil.	101	382	325	53	102	119	9	1	2	29	12	6	12	27	1	43	20	6	2	.314	.381	.366
Mack, Tony, Fred.†	82	264	236	31	60	73	13	0	0	14	8	0	2	18	0	50	7	4	7	.254	.313	.309
Manning, Pat, M.B.	29	111	97	13	19	40	9	0	4	8	0	0	3	11	1	18	1	1	2	.196	.297	.412
Martel, Normand, W.S.*	81	287	254	33	59	87	15	2	3	29	3	0	1	29	1	58	12	2	6	.232	.313	.343
Martinez, Lou, M.B.	72	274	252	21	63	76	10	0	1	30	7	4	0	11	0	19	0	3	12	.250	.277	.302
Matos, Luis, Fred.	3	14	12	2	4	5	1	0	0	1	0	0	0	2	0	3	0	0	0	.333	.429	.417
McCarthy, Bill, M.B.	128	508	442	52	135	202	26	4	11	65	0	5	23	38	3	88	6	5	11	.305	.386	.457
McLouth, Nathan, Lyn.*	114	453	393	58	96	154	23	4	9	46	6	5	8	41	3	48	20	7	12	.244	.324	.392
Meadows, Randy, Lyn.	23	87	80	13	18	28	7	0	1	5	2	0	4	1	0	15	0	2	1	.225	.271	.350
Meadows, Tydus, Wil.	94	406	339	63	100	160	19	4	11	55	1	3	9	54	2	83	13	3	11	.295	.402	.472
Meath, Matt, Lyn.†	5	20	10	5	5	5	0	0	0	2	1	0	1	8	0	2	0	0	0	.500	.737	.500
Meier, Dan, Lyn.*	22	94	79	15	22	37	6	0	3	13	0	1	1	13	1	18	1	1	2	.278	.383	.468
Mejia, Manuel, Lyn.	2	2	2	1	1	4	0	0	1	1	0	0	0	0	0	0	0	0	0	.500	.500	2.000
Merrill, Ronnie, Sal.†	76	326	280	48	79	120	13	5	6	27	1	1	3	41	0	36	2	3	8	.282	.378	.429
Minges, Tyler, Lyn.	113	446	394	65	91	169	20	5	16	58	8	7	5	32	1	71	8	10	10	.231	.292	.429
Moore, Chris, Sal.*	61	251	214	20	48	66	10	1	2	29	0	7	3	27	0	39	1	1	7	.224	.311	.308
Moreno, Jorge, Kin.	82	304	267	31	55	82	8	5	3	20	7	1	5	24	1	75	2	1	8	.206	.283	.307
Morris, Chris, Pot.†	114	500	422	68	105	126	17	2	0	38	14	0	6	58	2	92	55	19	2	.249	.348	.299
Morton, Rickie, Kin.	95	378	339	45	81	141	13	4	13	39	4	3	2	30	2	100	1	1	10	.239	.302	.416
Moylan, Dan, Pot.*	66	267	215	34	61	73	3	0	3	33	2	1	3	46	1	35	3	1	7	.284	.415	.340
Munoz, Billy, Pot.*	47	197	166	22	42	71	9	1	6	27	0	0	1	30	5	51	4	2	2	.253	.371	.428
Muro, Robert, W.S.	34	123	101	12	21	28	4	0	1	10	0	1	3	18	1	21	2	0	1	.208	.341	.277
Muth, Edmund, Sal.*	72	289	262	29	59	88	16	2	3	28	0	1	3	21	1	87	1	2	6	.225	.289	.336
Navarrete, Ray, Lyn.	134	593	532	75	169	232	41	2	6	69	6	5	12	38	3	48	8	3	18	.318	.373	.436
Ndungidi, Ntema, Fred.*	55	222	189	29	42	65	7	2	4	17	1	0	3	29	2	40	6	5	2	.222	.335	.344
Nelson, Eric, Wil.†	80	288	255	28	53	74	11	2	2	32	4	1	2	26	0	76	2	3	2	.208	.285	.290
Netwall, Chris, Pot.	14	38	36	0	9	10	1	0	0	4	1	0	0	1	0	6	0	0	1	.250	.270	.278
Nicholson, Tommy, W.S.*	122	479	428	41	105	133	25	0	1	34	9	0	1	41	2	82	8	5	9	.245	.313	.311
Oborn, Spencer, W.S.	94	311	273	34	62	83	11	2	2	29	5	4	4	24	2	59	5	4	6	.227	.294	.304
Oropeza, Asdrubal, Fred.	91	357	315	33	64	98	13	0	7	43	2	2	5	33	0	58	1	1	6	.203	.287	.311
Orr, Pete, M.B.*	17	56	51	8	20	24	0	2	0	8	1	0	1	3	0	6	3	0	0	.392	.436	.471
Ortega, Sixto, Sal.	2	4	4	0	1	1	0	0	0	0	0	0	0	0	0	0	0	0	1	.250	.250	.250
Paulino, Ronny, Lyn.	119	488	442	60	116	182	26	2	12	55	2	4	1	39	2	87	2	1	15	.262	.321	.412
Peck, Bryan, Sal.	62	263	235	34	59	81	10	0	4	30	2	2	5	19	0	30	2	1	15	.251	.318	.345
Peguero, Miguel, Kin.†·	7	20	20	2	3	3	0	0	0	0	0	0	0	0	0	3	0	0	1	.150	.150	.150
Pena, Brayan, M.B.†	6	22	19	3	4	5	1	0	0	1	0	0	0	3	0	4	0	0	0	.211	.318	.263
Phillips, Dan, Sal.	12	50	47	4	16	23	1	0	2	7	0	0	3	0	0	11	3	1	0	.340	.380	.489
Pichardo, Henry, Kin.	74	263	248	23	53	76	10	2	3	37	2	4	1	8	0	64	4	3	7	.214	.238	.306
Piedra, Jorge, Sal.*	104	448	392	64	118	218	37	12	13	64	3	8	8	37	3	55	10	2	4	.301	.366	.556
Piniella, Juan, W.S.	55	213	187	13	46	59	5	1	2	12	2	0	2	22	0	47	8	2	5	.246	.332	.316
Quintero, Humberto, W.S.	52	181	160	15	31	34	1	1	0	12	7	2	4	8	0	23	2	1	3	.194	.247	.213
Requena, Alex, Kin.†	128	577	532	66	118	145	13	4	2	21	4	0	4	57	1	132	72	19	4	.230	.312	.283
Reyes, Ambiorix, Sal.†	19	62	58	7	12	13	1	0	0	5	3	0	1	0	0	6	1	0	1	.207	.220	.224
Reyes, Guillermo, W.S.†	122	519	455	51	127	161	20	1	4	49	16	6	6	35	2	71	30	15	11	.279	.335	.354
Rodgers, Albert, Pot.	104	409	354	46	89	139	21	1	9	45	4	7	11	33	0	98	1	5	13	.251	.328	.393
Rodriguez , Ricardo, M.B.	5	15	15	1	3	3	0	0	0	0	0	0	0	0	0	4	1	0	1	.200	.200	.200

Player, Team	G	TPA	AB	R	H	TB	2B	3B	HR	RBI	SH	SF	HP	BB	IBB	SO	SB	CS	GDP	Avg.	OBP	Slg.
Rogowski, Casey, W.S.*	55	219	184	27	47	61	5	0	3	23	1	3	3	28	1	46	16	3	3	.255	.358	.332
Rosa, Wally, W.S.	33	119	107	8	26	33	4	0	1	8	1	0	2	9	0	21	2	1	1	.243	.314	.308
Rosario, Melvin, Sal.*	79	237	216	26	46	63	10	2	1	17	7	0	2	12	2	69	3	4	2	.213	.261	.292
Ross, Don, Wil.*	38	157	125	19	25	45	7	2	3	21	1	4	4	23	1	39	1	2	6	.200	.333	.360
Ruiz, Willy, Wil.	15	65	60	8	17	21	2	1	0	5	0	0	0	5	0	4	4	1	0	.283	.338	.350
Salvo, Andrew, W.S.*	31	103	89	8	29	36	5	1	0	7	0	0	0	14	0	16	3	4	0	.326	.417	.404
Santos, Chad, Wil.*	110	439	379	46	91	139	21	0	9	54	6	2	6	46	3	122	0	0	9	.240	.330	.367
Schumaker, Skip, Pot.*	136	606	551	71	158	194	22	4	2	44	6	2	2	45	3	84	26	16	10	.287	.342	.352
Scott, Luke, Kin.*	48	186	163	22	39	72	7	1	8	30	2	0	5	16	0	47	2	1	2	.239	.326	.442
Seestedt, Mike, Fred.	53	176	141	16	29	33	4	0	0	11	4	1	2	28	0	16	1	2	4	.206	.343	.234
Serrano, Ray, M.B.	37	127	114	11	23	33	4	0	2	18	2	4	1	6	1	21	0	1	1	.202	.240	.289
Shanks, Eric, Fred.	57	224	186	22	50	59	9	0	0	26	5	2	9	21	0	23	2	2	7	.269	.367	.317
Shier, Peter, Fred.	35	121	97	21	33	43	5	1	1	9	1	0	1	22	0	24	0	4	1	.340	.467	.443
Sienko, Ryan, W.S.	34	132	114	18	24	47	8	0	5	17	0	1	8	9	0	40	1	1	0	.211	.311	.412
Sizemore, Grady, Kin.*	47	207	172	31	59	83	9	3	3	20	1	0	1	33	2	30	14	7	1	.343	.451	.483
Smith, Corey, Kin.	134	577	505	71	129	201	29	2	13	67	0	4	9	59	5	141	1	2	4	.255	.341	.398
Stern, Adam, M.B.*	119	503	462	65	117	168	22	10	3	47	10	1	3	27	2	89	40	8	3	.253	.298	.364
Sullivan, Cory, Sal.*	138	622	560	90	161	251	42	6	12	67	7	7	12	36	3	70	26	5	8	.288	.340	.448
Sullivan, Kevin, Sal.	77	302	280	29	74	109	24	1	3	37	3	5	3	11	0	49	3	0	9	.264	.294	.389
Terveen, Bryce, M.B.*	16	57	45	13	13	22	3	0	2	5	0	0	5	7	1	6	2	0	1	.289	.439	.489
Thomas, Chuck, M.B.*	2	7	7	0	2	2	0	0	0	0	0	0	0	0	0	2	0	0	0	.286	.286	.286
Tucker, Mamon, Fred.	127	520	473	62	142	178	16	4	4	55	6	4	4	33	1	75	9	8	19	.300	.348	.376
Vilorio, Miguel, Sal.	48	185	170	18	42	50	6	1	0	10	2	1	5	7	0	25	2	8	3	.247	.295	.294
Wainwright, Adam, M.B.	29	1	1	0	0	0	0	0	0	0	0	0	0	0	0	1	0	0	0	.000	.000	.000
Walter, Scott, Wil.	60	245	222	21	58	89	19	0	4	35	2	2	3	16	3	46	1	0	6	.261	.317	.401
Webster, Kevin, Fred.	22	91	82	7	19	20	1	0	0	6	0	1	4	4	0	12	0	0	2	.232	.297	.244
Weichard, Paul, Lyn.†	21	61	51	7	10	12	2	0	0	5	0	1	0	9	0	13	1	0	1	.196	.311	.235
Welsh, Eric, W.S.*	126	513	464	61	108	202	25	0	23	71	2	5	6	36	2	159	9	2	5	.233	.294	.435
Whiteside, Eli, Fred.	80	335	313	34	81	124	19	0	8	42	0	4	4	14	0	57	0	0	8	.259	.296	.396
Wilken, Kris, Fred.†	131	553	506	58	131	179	24	3	6	61	2	4	2	39	4	84	1	1	19	.259	.312	.354
Williams, Matt, Pot.	47	185	157	17	38	64	9	1	5	17	1	0	5	22	0	45	2	0	3	.242	.353	.408
Wilson, Heath, Kin.	80	295	260	18	48	59	6	1	1	18	3	1	3	28	0	106	2	1	4	.185	.271	.227
Winchester, Jeff, Sal.	97	387	357	36	88	120	21	1	3	36	4	6	5	15	1	59	2	2	11	.246	.282	.336
Yan, Edwin, W.S.†	132	550	490	78	124	156	6	7	4	35	11	5	2	42	1	57	88	19	8	.253	.312	.318
Zywica, Mike, W.S.	48	190	172	25	35	65	7	1	7	18	0	0	9	1	4	53	4	1	3	.203	.279	.378

GRAND SLAMS: Crozier, Hawpe, 2 each; Barns, Bastardo, Bonifay, Brisson, DeCaster, Fera, F. Figueroa, LaRoche, Moore, Navarrete, Piedra, Scott, C. Smith, Wilken, 1 each.

AWARDED FIRST BASE ON CATCHER'S INTERFERENCE: Lopez-Cao 6 (Bastardo 2, Anderson, Arnerich, Walter, Whiteside), Muth 2 (Lisk, Paulino), Arnerich (Paulino), Brisson (Paulino), Luster (Winchester), G. Reyes (Paulino), Shanks (Rosa).

2002 PITCHING

TEAM

Team	W	L	Pct.	ERA	G	CG	ShO	Sv.	IP	H	TBF	R	ER	HR	SH	SF	HB	BB	IBB	SO	WP	Bk.
Lynchburg	87	53	.621	2.96	140	3	13	46	1242.1	1117	5190	520	409	58	53	41	71	383	8	1054	54	6
Wilmington	89	51	.636	3.20	140	0	13	39	1233.0	1155	5141	519	438	75	60	37	37	363	6	960	61	5
Myrtle Beach	79	61	.564	3.20	140	8	18	37	1212.2	1098	5086	504	431	65	48	34	66	392	15	1010	53	7
Kinston	74	65	.532	3.61	139	1	11	41	1229.1	1173	5323	587	493	73	64	43	78	498	25	923	70	7
Potomac	59	81	.421	3.90	140	8	7	29	1219.2	1248	5324	646	529	82	69	44	75	431	33	888	78	5
Salem	74	66	.529	3.94	140	5	8	39	1241.0	1260	5400	647	543	87	49	35	94	467	23	847	79	12
Winston-Salem	50	90	.357	4.38	140	6	7	22	1217.0	1267	5343	686	592	95	56	38	81	512	50	810	61	11
Frederick	47	92	.338	4.75	139	4	6	27	1219.0	1310	5429	760	644	113	52	55	96	456	14	988	62	7

INDIVIDUAL

TOP QUALIFIERS FOR EARNED-RUN AVERAGE TITLE

Minimum 112 innings.*Lefthanded pitcher.

Pitcher, Team	W	L	Pct.	ERA	G	GS	CG	ShO	GF	Sv.	IP	H	TBF	R	ER	HR	SH	SF	HB	BB	IBB	SO	WP	Bk.
Nelson, Kenny, M.B.	11	5	.688	1.72	23	23	0	0	0	0	135.2	98	547	37	26	4	7	0	10	44	0	105	10	0
Burnett, Sean, Lyn.*	13	4	.765	1.80	26	26	2	0	0	0	155.1	118	605	46	31	4	5	5	1	33	0	96	3	1
Curtis, Daniel, M.B.	7	7	.500	2.53	17	17	3	3	0	0	117.1	106	468	37	33	10	3	3	5	18	0	99	3	0
Parrott, Rhett, Pot.	8	5	.615	2.71	19	19	2	1	0	0	113	91	467	42	34	6	3	2	9	41	0	82	6	1
Waters, Chris, M.B.*	13	7	.650	2.76	28	28	2	1	0	0	182.2	154	752	63	56	12	7	7	24	43	0	103	12	0
Tamayo, Danny, Wil.	14	4	.778	2.77	23	20	0	0	1	0	123.1	121	510	48	38	13	8	0	3	32	0	108	3	1
Jacobsen, Landon, Lyn.	12	10	.545	2.89	27	27	1	0	0	0	161.2	145	665	71	52	9	8	6	10	41	1	123	9	2
Connolly, Mike, Lyn.*	10	3	.769	2.94	29	19	0	0	1	0	122.1	111	507	46	40	5	8	1	9	46	1	100	7	3
Mejia, Juan, Pot.	6	7	.462	3.09	23	16	3	1	1	0	119.1	121	512	50	41	4	12	5	7	41	4	49	4	0
Buglovsky, Chris, Sal.	9	9	.500	3.12	27	27	1	1	0	0	164.2	161	706	68	57	12	2	4	20	58	2	126	3	1
Douglass, Ryan, Wil.	11	6	.647	3.22	27	19	0	0	2	1	145.1	144	603	60	52	13	10	3	5	35	0	98	9	1
Wainwright, Adam, M.B.	9	6	.600	3.31	28	28	1	0	0	0	163.1	149	700	67	60	7	1	2	10	66	0	167	11	3
Bullard, Jim, W.S.*	9	8	.529	3.32	23	23	0	0	0	0	143.2	147	614	64	53	8	4	10	46	4	89	3	0
Bouknight, Kip, Sal.*	14	7	.667	3.35	27	27	2	1	0	0	166.2	156	688	74	62	13	4	1	9	48	0	120	4	0
Phillips, Mike, W.S.*	6	16	.273	3.52	28	28	5	3	0	0	179	184	748	82	70	17	4	3	3	50	5	112	6	2

DEPARTMENTAL LEADERS: W—Bouknight, Tamayo, 14 each; L—Phillips, 16; Pct.—Ferguson, .923; G—Carrasco, 55; GS—Several pitchers tied with 28; CG—Phillips, 5; ShO—Curtis, Phillips, 3 each; GF—Carrasco, 44; Sv.—Carrasco, 29; IP—Waters, 182.2; H—Schwager, 185; TBF—Waters, 752; R—Schwager, 124; ER—Schwager, 100; HR—Dohmann, 22; SH—J. Mejia, 12; SF—Schwager, 10; HB—Waters, 24; BB—Allen, 80; IBB—Green, 8; SO—Wainright, 167; WP—Price, 16; BK—Webb, 4.

ALL PITCHERS

*Lefthanded pitcher.

Pitcher, Team	W	L	Pct.	ERA	G	GS	CG	ShO	GF	Sv.	IP	H	TBF	R	ER	HR	SH	SF	HB	BB	IBB	SO	WP	Bk.
Aguilar, Ray, M.B.*	8	1	.889	1.60	35	6	0	0	8	2	106.2	82	427	25	19	1	3	2	1	28	2	114	2	0
Alcala, Jason, Lyn.	2	5	.286	2.68	54	0	0	0	24	8	77.1	63	311	29	23	3	4	1	2	18	1	71	3	0
Allen, Wyatt, W.S.	8	9	.471	4.45	28	28	1	1	0	0	161.2	163	720	91	80	15	4	4	12	80	4	110	11	0
An, Byeong, W.S.*	2	0	1.000	3.80	11	1	0	0	3	0	21.1	29	96	10	9	2	1	1	0	7	1	11	2	0
Andrade, Jancy, Fred.	5	11	.313	3.84	30	22	1	0	1	0	145.1	133	612	73	62	13	8	5	9	52	1	151	4	1
Axelson, Josh, Pot.	6	7	.462	4.09	32	20	2	0	5	0	136.1	135	581	72	62	12	7	6	7	40	4	82	11	0
Baker, Ryan, M.B.	3	4	.429	3.72	36	0	0	0	28	6	38.2	40	174	17	16	3	1	3	1	20	2	44	2	0
Barry, Kevin, M.B.	4	2	.667	2.52	47	0	0	0	43	26	50	37	197	14	14	2	3	4	1	17	1	67	0	0
Bartlett, Richard, Fred.	6	10	.375	5.35	18	18	1	0	0	0	99.1	116	448	72	59	12	5	9	9	29	0	57	3	1
Benes, Andy, Pot.	0	0	.000	9.00	1	1	0	0	0	0	7	8	34	7	7	2	2	0	0	6	0	3	0	0
Bennett, Jeff, Lyn.	10	6	.625	3.62	24	20	0	0	1	0	124.1	137	535	64	50	7	2	5	8	30	0	90	2	0
Borner, Brady, Lyn.*	9	4	.692	2.00	37	9	0	0	6	1	94.2	84	383	32	21	8	4	3	4	12	1	81	3	0
Bouknight, Kip, Sal.	14	7	.667	3.35	27	27	2	1	0	0	166.2	156	688	74	62	13	4	1	9	48	0	120	4	0
Brantley, Brian, Sal.	0	0	.000	5.23	6	0	0	0	0	0	10.1	19	60	14	6	0	0	0	0	10	0	9	3	1
Buglovsky, Chris, Sal.	9	9	.500	3.12	27	27	1	1	0	0	164.2	161	706	68	57	12	2	4	20	58	2	126	3	1
Bullard, Jim, W.S.*	9	8	.529	3.32	23	23	0	0	0	0	143.2	147	614	64	53	8	4	6	10	46	4	89	3	0
Bumatay, Mike, Lyn.*	5	2	.714	3.24	52	0	0	0	14	2	66.2	50	280	27	24	2	4	3	2	31	0	79	1	0
Burgess, Richie, Pot.	0	1	.000	3.00	9	0	0	0	5	0	9	14	46	4	3	0	1	1	0	6	2	6	0	0
Burnett, Sean, Lyn.*	13	4	.765	1.80	26	26	2	0	0	0	155.1	118	605	46	31	4	5	5	1	33	0	96	3	1
Byrdak, Tim, Kin.*	1	0	1.000	4.50	2	0	0	0	0	0	4	3	18	2	2	0	0	0	4	0	3	0	0
Cabrera, Fernando, Kin.	6	8	.429	3.52	21	21	0	0	0	0	110	83	450	48	43	7	3	3	2	40	2	107	3	1
Cali, Carmen, Pot.*	2	2	.500	4.11	29	0	0	0	6	0	35	31	154	18	16	1	2	0	6	21	2	24	2	0
Carrasco, Dan, Lyn.	4	4	.500	1.61	55	0	0	0	44	29	72.2	52	286	18	13	1	4	4	6	18	1	83	2	0
Cedeno, Blas, Lyn.	0	0	.000	2.08	9	0	0	0	3	0	13	11	53	3	3	0	0	0	7	0	11	1	0
Cierlik, Jason, Fred.*	0	0	.000	3.00	4	0	0	0	2	0	6	3	24	2	2	0	2	1	1	2	0	1	0	0
Colon, Ramon, M.B.	9	8	.529	3.53	26	26	1	0	0	0	163	170	683	81	64	8	4	8	2	38	1	94	2	2
Connolly, Mike, Lyn.*	10	3	.769	2.94	29	19	0	0	1	0	122.1	111	507	46	40	5	8	1	9	46	1	100	7	3
Cook, Jeremy, Pot.	5	9	.357	4.76	47	5	0	0	23	6	87	95	380	51	46	4	4	2	4	24	5	70	4	2
Cooper, Chris, Kin.*	0	1	.000	1.93	8	0	0	0	4	1	14	9	57	4	3	0	3	0	0	7	0	9	0	1
Crowder, Chuck, Sal.*	1	2	.333	5.13	23	1	0	0	8	1	40.1	49	199	27	23	1	2	2	5	24	1	36	7	1
Cruceta, Alberto, Kin.	2	0	1.000	2.50	7	7	0	0	0	0	39.2	31	169	13	11	2	0	1	0	25	1	37	1	1
Cummings, Jeremy, Pot.	5	5	.500	3.75	14	14	0	0	0	0	81.2	83	346	40	34	6	2	3	4	21	0	86	1	0
Curreri, Joe, W.S.	0	0	.000	12.71	5	0	0	0	2	0	5.2	14	30	8	8	0	0	0	0	3	0	3	0	0
Curtis, Daniel, M.B.	7	7	.500	2.53	17	17	3	3	0	0	117.1	106	468	37	33	10	3	3	5	18	0	99	3	0
David, Brad, M.B.*	0	1	.000	14.29	5	0	0	0	1	0	5.2	10	32	9	9	1	1	0	0	6	1	7	0	0
Davis, Jason, Kin.	3	6	.333	4.15	17	17	1	1	0	0	99.2	107	442	64	46	7	7	3	8	31	2	68	6	0
De La Cruz, Carlos, Kin.	2	2	.500	5.59	6	6	0	0	0	0	29	33	132	23	18	3	2	2	2	11	0	23	3	0
Denney, Kyle, Kin.	7	6	.538	3.60	15	14	0	0	1	0	85	76	363	37	34	5	2	4	2	41	2	68	3	1
DePaula, Freddy, Wil.*	0	0	.000	5.17	33	0	0	0	8	2	55.2	57	266	35	32	0	1	4	3	46	0	55	4	0
Difelice, Mark, Sal.	3	0	1.000	2.80	6	6	0	0	0	0	35.1	40	146	12	11	3	1	0	2	5	0	21	0	0
Dohmann, Scott, Sal.	13	5	.722	4.23	28	28	0	0	0	0	170.1	149	720	85	80	22	6	6	15	53	0	131	8	0
Dotel, Melido, Sal.	2	3	.400	5.70	37	0	0	0	11	0	53.2	63	252	41	34	3	3	2	8	28	1	28	3	2
Douglass, Ryan, Wil.	11	6	.647	3.22	27	19	0	0	2	1	145.1	144	603	60	52	13	10	3	5	35	0	98	9	1
Duff, Matt, Pot.	0	0	.000	0.00	4	0	0	0	4	4	4.1	4	18	0	0	0	0	1	0	7	0	7	0	0
Dukeman, Greg, Lyn.	2	1	.667	3.53	25	0	0	0	11	0	35.2	32	151	17	14	3	3	2	1	13	1	21	2	0
Eppeneder, Jamie, Wil.*	1	1	.500	5.00	16	0	0	0	6	1	18	18	76	11	10	0	1	1	0	9	1	9	0	0
Evans, Kyle, Kin.	4	4	.500	3.36	11	11	0	0	0	0	69.2	66	294	30	26	5	2	3	5	26	1	42	2	0
Evert, Brett, M.B.	3	5	.375	3.75	10	10	1	0	0	0	57.2	53	246	30	24	3	3	0	2	21	0	51	0	0
Ewasko, Tod, Pot.	1	0	1.000	5.19	5	0	0	0	4	0	8.2	12	38	5	5	2	0	0	0	4	0	4	0	0
Ferguson, Ian, Wil.	12	1	.923	2.39	17	17	0	0	0	0	109.1	100	439	36	29	2	9	3	2	20	0	81	3	0
Fernley, Jason, Kin.	3	1	.750	1.17	15	0	0	0	9	3	23	19	93	3	3	0	1	1	4	6	0	15	2	1
Ferrand, Dario, W.S.	2	13	.133	4.36	27	20	0	0	1	1	121.2	116	515	67	59	12	9	5	12	43	2	60	4	1
Field, Luke, Kin.	1	0	1.000	5.79	6	0	0	0	4	1	9.1	13	45	6	6	1	0	1	0	4	0	8	4	0
Fields, Josh, W.S.	2	2	.500	2.96	36	0	0	0	18	4	45.2	45	200	23	15	1	3	1	2	19	6	50	6	0
Figueroa, Juan, Fred.	4	1	.800	2.28	9	9	1	0	0	0	59.1	47	232	16	15	8	2	2	7	0	53	1	0
Fitch, Steve, Kin.	0	4	.000	6.39	15	1	0	0	6	0	31	50	146	31	22	6	2	1	0	6	0	19	2	0
Ford, Tom, Fred.*	2	3	.400	4.85	46	0	0	0	14	0	65	75	303	38	35	3	4	3	7	32	3	55	5	1
Forystek, Brian, Fred.*	1	4	.200	4.50	43	1	0	0	6	3	70	71	323	47	35	4	5	3	6	36	2	79	5	0
Francisco, Frank, W.S.	0	4	.000	8.06	6	6	0	0	0	0	25.2	31	120	23	23	3	1	0	1	18	0	25	4	2
Freeman, Kai, W.S.	0	0	.000	18.00	1	0	0	0	1	0	1	3	7	2	2	1	0	0	1	0	1	0	0
Gallagher, Buddy, Sal.*	4	4	.500	3.76	15	12	0	0	1	0	64.2	66	293	42	27	5	1	3	7	30	0	37	5	1
Garza, Rolando, W.S.	0	1	.000	8.04	14	0	0	0	4	1	15.2	14	75	15	14	1	2	0	0	18	2	9	2	0
Gomez, Diogenes, Sal.	0	0	.000	9.00	6	0	0	0	2	1	6	10	28	6	6	0	1	1	0	1	1	4	0	1
Gooding, Jason, Wil.*	3	2	.600	3.30	17	0	0	0	6	0	30	21	116	12	12	6	2	1	0	7	0	15	1	0
Graves, Don, Pot.	2	7	.222	3.81	14	13	0	0	0	0	80.1	87	356	42	34	3	7	3	3	33	1	50	2	0
Green, Sean, Sal.	2	5	.286	3.90	52	0	0	0	17	2	67	92	319	41	29	5	6	4	1	31	8	26	8	0
Greinke, Zack, Wil.	0	0	.000	0.00	1	0	0	0	0	0	2	1	6	0	0	0	0	0	0	0	0	3	0	0
Griffin, Colt, Wil.	0	0	.000	3.86	3	0	0	0	1	0	4.2	3	21	2	2	0	1	0	1	5	0	3	2	0
Guerrero, Junior, Wil.	6	8	.429	4.55	36	1	0	0	25	4	65.1	74	283	42	33	4	3	6	0	17	2	45	4	0
Guzman, Juan, Fred.	0	4	.000	7.85	5	0	0	0	0	0	18.1	23	91	20	16	2	3	1	1	12	0	11	1	1
Guzman, Wilson, Lyn.*	1	2	.333	3.42	22	2	0	0	3	0	47.1	47	211	22	18	4	3	1	2	23	0	34	1	0

Pitcher, Team	W	L	Pct.	ERA	G	GS	CG	ShO	GF	Sv.	IP	H	TBF	R	ER	HR	SH	SF	HB	BB	IBB	SO	WP	Bk.
Hale, Beau, Fred.	8	8	.500	5.02	22	22	0	0	0	0	131	157	569	83	73	8	5	0	8	27	0	79	4	1
Haren, Danny, Pot.	3	6	.333	3.62	14	14	1	0	0	0	92	90	383	43	37	8	3	1	3	19	2	82	2	1
Hentgen, Pat, Fred.	1	0	1.000	2.57	1	1	1	0	0	0	7	5	26	2	2	0	0	0	0	2	0	5	0	0
Hernandez, Runelvys, Wil.	1	1	.500	3.75	2	2	0	0	0	0	12	12	46	6	5	0	1	0	0	1	0	9	0	0
Higgins, Joshua, Lyn.	4	2	.667	1.90	53	0	0	0	29	6	71	62	302	23	15	2	3	2	3	23	2	88	5	0
Honel, Kris, W.S.	0	0	.000	1.69	1	1	0	0	0	0	5.1	3	23	2	1	0	0	0	0	3	0	8	0	0
Huisman, Justin, Sal.	3	4	.429	1.57	41	0	0	0	37	20	51.2	47	212	11	9	0	5	1	4	14	3	24	1	0
Jackson, Brian, Kin.-Lyn.	4	1	.800	8.10	16	0	0	0	10	3	16.2	14	84	15	15	0	2	0	1	20	2	10	1	0
Jacobsen, Landon, Lyn.	12	10	.545	2.89	27	27	1	0	0	0	161.2	145	665	71	52	9	8	6	10	41	1	123	9	2
Johnston, Mike, Lyn.*	4	2	.667	3.63	15	10	0	0	1	0	57	50	253	29	23	2	1	2	7	26	0	50	8	0
Jones, Sean, Fred.	4	5	.444	3.44	32	1	0	0	15	3	55	62	247	27	21	3	1	1	5	17	2	35	3	0
Keppinger, Billy, Wil.*	0	0	.000	18.00	1	0	0	0	1	0	1	2	6	2	2	1	0	0	1	0	0	1	0	0
Kinney, Josh, Pot.	1	3	.250	2.29	44	0	0	0	28	7	55	52	239	21	14	2	2	1	3	23	1	42	6	0
Kirkland, Aaron, W.S.	3	5	.375	3.68	34	0	0	0	17	2	44	41	196	24	18	0	1	2	7	23	4	34	2	0
Kohl, Doug, Pot.	0	2	.000	3.42	16	1	0	0	7	0	23.2	26	108	14	9	0	1	0	2	10	0	16	1	0
Kozlowski, Ben, M.B.*	0	1	.000	4.50	1	1	0	0	0	0	4	4	21	5	2	0	1	0	0	3	0	3	0	1
Lantz, Doug, Kin.	4	2	.667	5.40	11	0	0	0	1	0	23.1	25	108	15	14	1	3	2	2	9	1	19	3	0
Larson, Ryan, Kin.	1	3	.250	3.05	23	0	0	0	14	8	38.1	35	163	14	13	3	5	0	1	15	3	33	2	0
Lavery, Tim, Lyn.*	1	1	.500	7.00	6	2	0	0	0	0	18	24	84	16	14	1	1	0	2	7	0	6	1	0
MacDougal, Mike, Wil.	0	1	.000	1.08	5	0	0	0	4	2	8.1	3	33	4	1	1	0	0	0	5	0	10	3	0
Madril, Steve, W.S.*	2	2	.500	5.82	36	0	0	0	11	2	38.2	50	181	27	25	3	6	0	1	16	5	27	2	1
Mangrum, Micah, Wil.	1	0	1.000	2.39	16	0	0	0	13	6	26.1	21	100	7	7	2	1	0	1	2	0	24	2	0
Martinez, Miguel, Pot.	4	3	.571	6.55	8	8	0	0	0	0	34.1	44	149	27	25	3	2	1	1	8	0	18	1	0
Matheny, Brandon, Kin.*	4	3	.571	3.35	30	12	0	0	9	4	75.1	69	338	28	28	1	6	4	8	42	3	41	4	1
McClellan, Zach, Wil.	7	9	.438	4.03	28	27	0	0	0	0	145.1	162	629	76	65	8	7	8	6	43	0	75	4	1
McClendon, Matt, M.B.	2	4	.333	8.66	17	1	0	0	4	0	17.2	10	94	20	17	0	1	1	3	28	0	12	5	0
McWhirter, Kris, W.S.	2	14	.125	5.46	24	22	0	0	1	0	125.1	147	559	84	76	10	3	6	10	55	2	76	3	2
Medlock, Chet, Pot.	1	1	.500	6.30	7	2	0	0	2	0	10	12	50	9	7	1	0	1	0	8	0	4	2	0
Mejia, Francisco, Fred.*	0	0	.000	0.00	1	0	0	0	0	0	3	2	13	0	0	0	0	0	0	3	0	0	0	0
Mejia, Juan, Pot.	6	7	.462	3.09	23	16	3	1	1	0	119.1	121	512	50	41	4	12	5	7	41	4	49	4	0
Mendoza, Marcos, Kin.*	4	0	1.000	0.97	22	0	0	0	8	4	46.1	37	190	7	5	0	1	3	18	0	36	3	0
Merrigan, Josh, Pot.*	0	0	.000	3.94	11	1	0	0	1	0	16	19	79	12	7	2	0	1	4	8	0	9	0	0
Meyer, Mike, Pot.	0	1	.000	7.71	13	0	0	0	2	0	21	34	98	22	18	3	1	1	2	4	1	9	0	0
Miller, Matt, M.B.*	2	2	.500	4.84	36	0	0	0	11	1	44.2	54	205	29	24	4	4	2	3	17	5	35	2	0
Montilla, Elvis, Fred.	0	3	.000	12.74	10	3	0	0	3	1	17.2	40	100	30	25	4	0	2	3	6	0	10	4	0
Moran, Nick, Kin.	2	3	.400	4.73	9	9	0	0	0	0	51.1	51	228	33	27	5	1	3	8	17	1	46	3	0
Morris, Cory, Fred.	1	10	.091	6.32	16	16	0	0	0	0	72.2	84	341	58	51	12	2	4	7	47	1	59	4	0
Morrison, Robbie, Wil.	3	4	.400	2.42	32	0	0	0	22	9	48.1	34	195	15	13	4	0	0	0	19	0	53	3	0
Murray, Brad, W.S.*	4	2	.667	3.82	53	0	0	0	20	1	66	62	275	31	28	9	5	2	2	23	2	42	2	0
Muth, Edmund, Sal.*	0	0	.000	0.00	1	0	0	0	1	0	1	0	4	0	0	0	1	0	1	0	1	0	0	0
Natale, Mike, Wil.	2	2	.500	2.48	13	2	0	0	8	4	29	20	117	10	8	2	1	0	1	9	0	41	2	0
Neil, Dan, Kin.*	1	1	.500	4.19	7	0	0	0	2	0	19.1	20	88	10	9	1	3	1	1	9	0	18	0	0
Nelson, Kenny, M.B.	11	5	.688	1.72	23	23	0	0	0	0	135.2	98	547	37	26	4	7	0	10	44	0	105	10	0
Novinsky, John, Pot.	7	6	.538	4.27	30	7	0	0	18	11	59	66	262	42	28	6	2	2	2	20	3	55	7	0
Obermueller, Wes, Wil.	5	0	1.000	2.76	8	4	0	0	1	0	45.2	38	182	14	14	1	0	1	0	14	0	44	4	0
Olivo, Rigal, Wil.	1	3	.250	5.54	15	1	0	0	6	0	26	27	119	18	16	2	0	0	4	9	1	20	1	0
Ormond, Rodney, Fred.	2	2	.333	2.25	46	0	0	0	24	6	72	62	297	24	18	3	1	1	5	20	0	61	1	0
Pacheco, Enemencio, Sal.-W.S.	3	3	.500	3.67	49	4	0	0	20	6	76	83	344	39	31	2	2	0	6	34	2	55	3	0
Parrott, Rhett, Pot.	8	5	.615	2.71	19	19	2	1	0	0	113	91	467	42	34	6	3	2	9	41	0	82	6	1
Pena, Ed, W.S.*	1	0	1.000	2.16	11	0	0	0	3	1	16.2	15	73	6	4	1	0	1	2	5	2	10	1	0
Phillips, Mike, W.S.*	6	16	.273	3.52	28	28	5	3	0	0	179	184	748	82	70	17	4	3	3	50	5	112	6	2
Pinales, Jesus, Kin.	3	4	.429	2.67	48	0	0	0	40	14	60.2	48	252	23	18	4	3	2	3	20	2	63	4	1
Ponce Deleon, Damon, Pot.	2	3	.400	6.42	27	0	0	0	8	0	40.2	54	191	33	29	5	5	4	3	11	2	35	3	1
Powalski, Rick, Kin.*	0	0	.000	7.94	3	0	0	0	0	0	5.2	7	29	5	5	1	0	0	1	5	0	6	1	0
Prahm, Ryan, Kin.	2	2	.500	5.40	4	4	0	0	0	0	20	22	88	12	12	3	0	0	9	6	0	16	2	0
Price, Ryan, Sal.	0	4	.000	11.30	21	2	0	0	9	0	28.2	30	165	40	36	2	2	2	11	43	0	19	16	0
Ramirez, Enrique, Fred.	3	4	.429	4.04	32	0	0	0	10	1	62.1	50	277	32	28	4	2	8	7	37	0	47	10	0
Rawson, Anthony, Pot.*	1	4	.200	3.63	48	0	0	0	10	0	52	46	237	28	21	4	9	1	5	31	4	47	5	0
Reilly, Christopher, Fred.	1	1	.500	9.45	14	0	0	0	11	0	13.1	24	75	14	14	2	0	2	8	1	0	11	1	0
Reinike, Chris, Kin.	0	0	.000	0.00	1	0	0	0	0	0	2	0	6	0	0	0	0	0	0	0	0	2	0	0
Ring, Royce, W.S.*	2	0	1.000	3.91	21	0	0	0	13	5	23	20	96	11	10	2	2	2	0	11	2	22	1	0
Rodriguez, Eddy, Fred.	3	0	.000	2.23	38	0	0	0	30	11	48.1	28	196	14	12	3	4	2	4	20	3	58	2	0
Roque, Darryl, Fred.	3	10	.231	5.45	32	12	0	0	6	1	102.1	116	460	69	62	9	2	3	11	35	1	87	6	0
Rupp, Mike, W.S.	2	3	.333	4.50	11	0	0	0	4	0	14	12	60	11	7	1	4	0	6	1	0	14	1	1
Schwager, Matt, Fred.	7	13	.350	6.04	28	28	0	0	0	0	149	185	690	124	100	17	6	10	10	53	0	108	7	2
Seestedt, Mike, Fred.	0	0	.000	0.00	1	0	0	0	1	0	1	3	3	0	0	0	0	0	0	1	0	1	0	0
Sharber, Jason, Lyn.	7	6	.538	3.71	22	21	0	0	0	0	104.1	109	461	52	43	7	3	5	12	37	0	96	5	0
Simpson, Gerrit, Sal.	3	0	.000	7.16	5	2	0	0	0	0	16.1	16	77	15	13	2	0	0	12	1	0	12	3	0
Smith, Jared, Pot.	0	0	.000	11.57	6	0	0	0	2	0	7	5	38	9	9	0	0	0	2	10	0	9	2	0
Smith, Matthew, W.S.	3	3	.500	4.30	10	0	0	0	22	4	69	65	312	35	33	5	2	5	7	36	5	50	7	0
Snyder, Kyle, Wil.	2	0	.000	2.98	15	15	0	0	0	0	48.1	49	207	19	16	1	1	2	5	11	0	48	2	0
Sobkowiak, Scott, M.B.	5	1	.833	2.83	16	0	0	0	9	0	28.2	25	114	9	9	2	1	0	2	7	1	32	0	0
Speier, Ryan, Sal.	2	2	.500	3.94	24	0	0	0	14	4	32	35	142	21	14	0	6	0	2	11	2	33	2	0
Sperring, Jayme, Fred.	0	0	.000	6.43	18	0	0	0	12	1	21	27	102	15	15	6	1	0	0	11	0	21	1	0
Sprague, Kevin, Pot.*	2	5	.286	2.89	28	9	0	0	6	1	65.1	65	294	30	21	2	7	3	4	25	2	46	15	0
Stepka, Tom, Sal.	5	4	.556	2.97	45	3	0	0	16	5	100	96	409	35	33	5	3	3	5	23	1	54	2	0
Stiles, Brad, Wil.*	4	0	1.000	3.40	38	0	0	0	13	4	50.1	44	214	21	19	3	4	1	2	21	1	49	3	1
Stocks, Nick, Pot.	0	2	.000	5.74	3	3	0	0	0	0	15.2	18	73	13	10	3	0	1	1	6	0	11	2	0
Sturkie, Scott, Kin.	3	1	.750	3.41	30	0	0	0	8	2	63.1	68	260	26	24	4	4	1	1	15	1	30	2	0
Tamayo, Danny, Wil.	14	4	.778	2.77	23	20	0	0	1	0	123.1	121	510	48	38	13	8	0	3	32	0	108	3	1

Pitcher, Team	W	L	Pct.	ERA	G	GS	CG	ShO	GF	Sv.	IP	H	TBF	R	ER	HR	SH	SF	HB	BB	IBB	SO	WP	Bk.
Thompson, Derek, Kin.*	2	3	.400	3.87	13	13	0	0	0	0	74.1	72	325	36	32	1	2	2	11	32	1	41	8	0
Thoms, Hank, Kin.	5	2	.714	2.43	17	7	0	0	3	0	63	57	257	25	17	6	3	1	5	15	0	50	1	0
Tillery, Josh, M.B.	2	3	.400	4.11	37	0	0	0	13	0	57	53	237	26	26	6	3	1	0	18	2	41	1	1
Tsao, Chin-hui, Sal.	4	2	.667	2.09	9	9	0	0	0	0	47.1	34	180	13	11	3	1	0	0	12	0	45	2	1
Vargas, Jose, Kin.	4	0	1.000	0.61	19	0	0	0	6	0	44	35	178	9	3	1	1	0	2	11	1	50	0	0
Vasquez, Jorge, Wil.	0	0	.000	4.91	10	0	0	0	5	0	11	12	50	6	6	1	0	0	0	3	0	17	1	0
Veronie, Shanin, M.B.	0	1	.000	7.36	5	0	0	0	1	1	11	16	48	9	9	0	1	0	0	1	0	12	0	0
Villacis, Eduardo, Wil.	2	1	.667	2.25	17	0	0	0	5	1	28	19	113	8	7	2	3	0	0	10	1	15	3	0
Villalon, Julio, Pot.	3	2	.600	2.33	7	7	0	0	0	0	46.1	36	191	12	12	3	1	0	3	14	0	42	2	0
Vogelsong, Ryan, Lyn.	1	1	.500	8.04	4	4	0	0	0	0	15.2	19	73	14	14	0	0	1	1	7	0	20	0	0
Wade, Matt, Kin.	3	0	1.000	5.51	20	1	0	0	13	1	32.2	34	152	24	20	2	1	4	4	13	1	15	4	0
Wagner, Denny, W.S.	1	5	.167	5.82	21	6	0	0	7	1	43.1	48	207	35	28	1	5	0	3	35	1	13	2	2
Wainwright, Adam, M.B.	9	6	.600	3.31	28	28	1	0	0	0	163.1	149	700	67	60	7	1	2	10	66	0	167	11	3
Wallace, Shane, Kin.*	3	4	.429	4.21	9	9	0	0	0	0	51.1	54	230	28	24	1	4	1	3	28	1	24	2	0
Warden, Jim Ed, Kin.	2	4	.333	6.61	7	7	0	0	0	0	32.2	38	168	27	24	3	3	2	2	30	0	29	5	0
Waters, Chris, M.B.*	13	7	.650	2.76	28	28	2	1	0	0	182.2	154	752	63	56	12	7	7	24	43	0	103	12	0
Watkins, Dave, M.B.	1	0	1.000	0.00	4	0	0	0	1	0	4	2	16	0	0	0	1	0	0	4	0	3	1	0
Webb, Nicholas, Sal.*	10	10	.500	5.05	26	23	2	1	0	0	133.2	145	573	80	75	10	4	5	4	37	2	90	10	4
Wilkerson, Wes, Wil.	9	5	.643	3.14	20	20	0	0	0	0	111.2	98	461	49	39	6	3	4	5	34	0	65	6	0
Wilson, Kris, Wil.	0	0	.000	0.00	4	3	0	0	0	0	8	3	29	0	0	0	0	0	0	1	0	10	0	0
Wrightsman, Dusty, Wil.	9	4	.692	2.38	39	10	0	0	19	5	106	99	439	36	28	5	2	3	3	18	1	85	2	1
Yankosky, L.J., M.B.	0	0	.000	0.00	1	0	0	0	1	0	1	2	4	1	0	0	0	0	0	0	0	0	0	0
Zumwalt, Alec, M.B.	0	3	.000	8.63	21	0	0	0	12	1	24	33	121	25	23	2	1	2	13	0	21	2	0

PITCHERS WITH TWO OR MORE TEAMS

Pitcher, Team	W	L	Pct.	ERA	G	GS	CG	ShO	GF	Sv.	IP	H	TBF	R	ER	HR	SH	SF	HB	BB	IBB	SO	WP	Bk.
Jackson, Brian, Kin.	2	1	.667	3.18	11	0	0	0	10	3	11.1	11	54	4	4	0	2	0	0	9	2	5	0	0
Jackson, Brian, Lyn.	2	0	1.000	18.56	5	0	0	0	0	0	5.1	3	30	11	11	0	0	0	1	11	0	5	1	0
Pacheco, Enemencio, Sal.	2	2	.500	3.16	41	0	0	0	19	6	51.1	52	227	22	18	1	2	0	1	26	1	31	2	0
Pacheco, Enemencio, W.S.	1	1	.500	4.74	8	4	0	0	1	0	24.2	31	117	17	13	1	0	0	5	8	1	24	1	0

COMBINATION SHUTOUTS: Frederick (5)—Figueroa-Ormond, Jones-Ormond, F. Mejia-Roque-Ormond, Morris-Andrade-Ford-Rodriguez, Schwager-Rodriguez. **Kinston (10)**—Cruceta-Cooper-Pinales, Davis-Mendoza, De La Cruz-Field, Denney-Mendoza, Matheny-Mendoza-Larson, Matheny-Sturkie-Mendoza, Moran-Larson-Pinales, Moran-Mendoza, Prahm-Mendoza, Thoms-Matheny. **Lynchburg (13)**—Bennett-Borner-Higgins, Burnett-Alcala, Burnett-Carrasco, Burnett-Carrasco-Alcala, Burnett-Higgins, Burnett-Higgins-Dukeman, Connolly-Alcala, Connolly-Bumatay-Alcala, Jacobsen-Carrasco, Jacobsen-Johnston-Alcala-Higgins, Johnston-Dukeman, Sharber-Alcala-Higgins, Sharber-Bumatay-Carrasco. **Myrtle Beach (14)**—Nelson-Barry 3, Aguilar-McClendon-Barry, Aguilar-Sobkowiak-Barry, Colon-Miller-Tillery, Curtis-Tillery-Miller, Evert-Aguilar, Evert-Miller-Zumwalt, Nelson-Aguilar, Wainwright-Barry, Wainwright-Tillery-Baker, Waters-Barry, Waters-Tillery-Barry. **Potomac (5)**—Axelson-Ponce Deleon, Cummings-Burgess-Cook, Parrott-Cali-Kinney, Parrott-Rawson-Kinney, Villalon-Novinsky. **Salem (5)**—Bouknight-Huisman, Difelice-Speier, Dohmann-Pacheco, Tsao-Price, Webb-Pacheco-Huisman. **Wilmington (13)**—Douglass-Stiles-Morrison, Ferguson-Gooding, Ferguson-Gooding-Wrightsman, Ferguson-Stiles-Morrison, McClellan-Wrightsman-Morrison, Obermueller-Guerrero-Wrightsman, Snyder-Douglass-Villacis-Morrison, Snyder-Wilson-Douglass, Tamayo-Mangrum-Morrison, Tamayo-Vasquez-Stiles, Wilkerson-Guerrero-Natale, Wilkerson-Morrison, Wilson-McClellan-Mangrum. **Winston-Salem (3)**—Bullard-Kirkland-Olivo, Bullard-Ring, Bullard-M. Smith-Murray.

NO-HIT GAMES: Bouknight, Salem defeated Frederick, 5-0, August 7.

2002 FIELDING

TEAM

Team	G	PO	A	E	TC	DP	TP	PB	Pct.
Myrtle Beach	140	3638	1330	121	5089	109	0	25	.976
Salem	140	3723	1582	140	5445	128	0	20	.974
Wilmington	140	3699	1475	145	5319	118	0	20	.973
Winston-Salem	140	3651	1595	149	5395	140	0	23	.972
Kinston	139	3688	1499	158	5345	111	0	25	.970
Lynchburg	140	3727	1466	177	5370	130	0	24	.967
Potomac	140	3659	1496	177	5332	131	1	20	.967
Frederick	139	3657	1392	189	5238	96	0	30	.964

INDIVIDUAL

FIRST BASEMEN

NOTE: All caps denotes fielding-percentage leader based on 70 games for catchers, 93 for all other non-pitchers and 112 innings for pitchers. *Throws lefthanded.

Player, Team	Pct.	G	PO	A	E	TC	DP
Brisson, Dustin, Pot.	.985	29	186	16	3	205	19
Brown, Jason, Lyn.	.818	3	8	1	2	11	1
Brown, Kevin, M.B.	.986	38	269	21	4	294	28
Canelliz, Chris, Pot.	1.000	1	0	0	0	1	0
Cotten, Jeremy, Lyn.	.975	26	175	17	5	197	18
Cowan, Justin, Wil.	.994	21	171	7	1	179	15
Crozier, Eric, Kin.*	.995	49	400	35	2	437	33
Dempsey, Nick, Kin.	.984	6	60	2	1	63	9
Figueroa, Franky, Fred.	.987	35	280	24	4	308	21
Forbes, Mike, M.B.	1.000	8	58	3	0	61	0
Gemoll, Justin, Wil.	1.000	5	34	3	0	37	1
Gordon, Alex, Fred.*	1.000	6	39	0	0	39	2
Hamill, Ryan, Pot.	.889	2	8	0	1	9	1
HAWPE, Brad, Sal.*	.994	120	1136	116	8	1260	103

Player, Team	Pct.	G	PO	A	E	TC	DP
Jeffcoat, Bryon, M.B.	.964	4	26	1	1	28	3
Jurries, James, M.B.	.988	30	225	17	3	245	27
Kohl, Doug, Pot.	1.000	1	6	0	0	6	1
LaRoche, Adam, M.B.*	.991	64	518	38	5	561	45
Leach, Nick, Pot.	.974	11	104	9	3	116	8
Lebron, Francisco, W.S.	.984	32	285	23	5	313	33
Leon, Alfredo, Fred.	.985	41	309	16	5	330	22
Lincoln, Justin, Sal.	.974	4	35	2	1	38	3
Lopez-Cao, Mike, Lyn.	1.000	3	10	3	0	13	3
Luster, Jeremy, Pot.	.980	24	179	17	4	200	25
Martinez, Lou, M.B.	1.000	3	20	0	0	20	1
Meier, Dan, Lyn.*	.995	22	192	14	1	207	21
Moore, Chris, Sal.	.988	16	152	10	2	164	12
Morton, Rickie, Wil.	.999	79	710	61	1	772	54
Moylan, Dan, Pot.	1.000	2	21	1	0	22	0
Munoz, Billy, Pot.*	.989	43	331	39	4	374	33
Navarrete, Ray, Lyn.	.988	99	801	52	10	863	81
Oborn, Spencer, W.S.	1.000	1	1	0	0	1	1
Oropeza, Asdrubal, Fred.	.000	1	0	0	0	0	0
Paulino, Ronny, Lyn.	1.000	2	20	1	0	21	1
Pichardo, Henry, Kin.	1.000	6	50	2	0	52	4
Rodgers, Albert, Pot.	.985	33	244	22	4	270	21
Rogowski, Casey, W.S.*	.991	42	411	19	4	434	38
Ross, Don, Wil.	.982	16	102	10	2	114	10
Santos, Chad, Wil.*	.989	106	914	65	11	990	76
Scott, Luke, Kin.	1.000	4	21	2	0	23	1
Seestedt, Mike, Fred.	1.000	1	11	0	0	11	1
Welsh, Eric, W.S.*	.992	66	625	29	5	659	58
Wilken, Kris, Fred.	.989	66	503	39	6	548	43
Williams, Matt, Pot.	.975	13	112	6	3	121	11
Wilson, Heath, Kin.	.000	1	0	0	0	0	0

TRIPLE PLAY: Brisson.

SECOND BASEMEN

Player, Team	Pct.	G	PO	A	E	TC	DP
Araujo, Ramon, Pot.	.980	45	115	126	5	246	27
Asprilla, Avelino, Lyn.	.900	4	11	7	2	20	1
Berroa, Cristian, Sal.	.961	40	68	105	7	180	22
Bonifay, Josh, Lyn.	.941	75	114	190	19	323	55
Burnett, Mark, Pot.	.959	65	131	176	13	320	41
Canelliz, Chris, Pot.	1.000	11	15	14	0	29	3
Cates, Gary, Fred.	.947	9	14	22	2	38	5
Cockrell, Michael, Lyn.	.889	7	2	6	1	9	1
Colmenter, Jesus, Kin.	1.000	1	1	3	0	4	1
Cordova, Ricardo, Pot.	.909	10	26	24	5	55	8
Cruz, Alex, Lyn.	1.000	2	0	1	0	1	0
Davidson, Seth, Pot.	.957	18	28	38	3	69	3
Del Rosario, Manny, Fred.	1.000	2	3	5	0	8	0
DeRosa, Mark, M.B.	.889	2	5	3	1	9	1
Fenster, Darren, Wil.	.982	12	17	37	1	55	7
Fontenot, Mike, Fred.	.955	116	199	327	25	551	59
Hudnall, Joshua, Lyn.	.978	24	35	55	2	92	10
Inglett, Joe, Kin.	.970	54	86	174	8	268	31
Izturis, Maicer, Kin.	.967	57	96	142	8	246	22
Jeffcoat, Bryon, M.B.	.944	6	3	14	1	18	3
Lambert, Casey, Sal.	.971	40	54	112	5	171	18
LEWIS, Richard, M.B.	.985	124	207	314	8	529	78
Lewis, Russell, Pot.	1.000	4	8	8	0	16	3
Lora, Tom, Wil.	.974	77	159	261	11	431	51
Machado, Alejandro, Wil.	1.000	3	4	11	0	15	0
Martinez, Lou, M.B.	1.000	8	6	18	0	24	3
Meadows, Randy, Lyn.	.976	12	18	22	1	41	3
Merrill, Ronnie, Sal.	.000	1	0	0	0	0	0
Moore, Chris, Sal.	.967	15	21	37	2	60	7
Navarrete, Ray, Lyn.	.945	34	42	62	6	110	15
Nelson, Eric, Wil.	.964	61	106	162	10	278	33
Nicholson, Tommy, W.S.	.981	14	25	27	1	53	8
Orr, Pete, M.B.	1.000	1	3	1	0	4	0
Peguero, Miguel, Kin.	.960	6	8	16	1	25	2
Pichardo, Henry, Kin.	.985	26	57	72	2	131	18
Reyes, Ambiorix, Sal.	.949	13	22	34	3	59	6
Reyes, Guillermo, W.S.	1.000	1	2	2	0	4	0
Rodriguez , Ricardo, M.B.	.933	2	3	11	1	15	3
Ruiz, Willy, Wil.	1.000	1	1	5	0	6	1
Salvo, Andrew, W.S.	1.000	4	6	9	0	15	3
Shanks, Eric, Fred.	1.000	5	7	12	0	19	0
Vilorio, Miguel, Sal.	.969	45	81	141	7	229	31
Wilken, Kris, Fred.	.969	14	27	35	2	64	10
Yan, Edwin, W.S.	.957	130	270	381	29	680	88

TRIPLE PLAY: Cordova.

THIRD BASEMEN

Player, Team	Pct.	G	PO	A	E	TC	DP
Araujo, Ramon, Pot.	.923	11	3	9	1	13	0
Berroa, Cristian, Sal.	1.000	8	6	14	0	20	3
Brisson, Dustin, Sal.	.933	8	7	21	2	30	2
Canelliz, Chris, Pot.	1.000	2	1	5	0	6	0
Cates, Gary, Fred.	.906	12	4	25	3	32	2
Cockrell, Michael, Lyn.	1.000	1	1	0	0	1	0
Cordova, Ricardo, Pot.	1.000	2	0	4	0	4	0
Cotto, Luis, Wil.	.500	1	0	1	1	2	1
Davidson, Seth, Pot.	.909	6	5	5	1	11	0
De Caster, Yurendell, Lyn.	.896	125	78	199	32	309	12
Fenster, Darren, Wil.	.901	48	20	71	10	101	7
Forbes, Mike, M.B.	.871	14	7	20	4	31	0
Fox, Mike, Pot.	.941	7	3	13	1	17	1
Gemoll, Justin, Wil.	.919	78	67	115	16	198	10
Hudnall, Joshua, Lyn.	.938	9	3	12	1	16	1
Jeffcoat, Bryon, M.B.	.877	35	20	44	9	73	7
Johnson, Kelly, M.B.	1.000	4	5	2	0	7	0
Jurries, James, M.B.	.625	6	2	3	3	8	1
Koslowski, Kasey, W.S.	.750	1	1	2	1	4	0
Lambert, Casey, Sal.	1.000	11	9	20	0	29	3
Leon, Alfredo, Fred.	.850	7	4	13	3	20	1
Lewis, Russell, Pot.	.967	12	6	23	1	30	2
Lincoln, Justin, Sal.	.949	117	73	208	15	296	18
Lopez-Cao, Mike, Lyn.	.800	3	0	4	1	5	0
Luster, Jeremy, Pot.	.889	14	6	34	5	45	1
Manning, Pat, M.B.	.938	28	19	42	4	65	1
Martinez, Lou, M.B.	.964	51	40	93	5	138	11
Meadows, Randy, Lyn.	1.000	5	2	3	0	5	0
Moore, Chris, Sal.	1.000	3	1	6	0	7	0
Morton, Rickie, Kin.	1.000	2	1	1	0	2	0

Player, Team	Pct.	G	PO	A	E	TC	DP
Muro, Robert, W.S.	.897	28	23	47	8	78	4
Navarrete, Ray, Lyn.	.909	5	1	9	1	11	1
Nelson, Eric, Wil.	.818	7	6	3	2	11	2
NICHOLSON, Tommy, W.S.	.959	104	77	248	14	339	30
Oborn, Spencer, W.S.	.963	7	6	20	1	27	3
Oropeza, Asdrubal, Fred.	.922	88	82	153	20	255	14
Orr, Pete, M.B.	.929	6	3	10	1	14	1
Peck, Bryan, Sal.	.893	10	12	13	3	28	1
Pichardo, Henry, Kin.	.905	12	5	14	2	21	0
Rodgers, Albert, Pot.	.943	70	54	128	11	193	12
Rodriguez , Ricardo, M.B.	1.000	3	1	4	0	5	0
Ruiz, Willy, Wil.	.839	14	6	20	5	31	0
Salvo, Andrew, W.S.	.810	9	4	13	4	21	2
Shanks, Eric, Fred.	.500	4	1	0	1	2	0
Smith, Corey, Kin.	.911	130	111	235	34	380	13
Wilken, Kris, Fred.	.950	37	26	50	4	80	0
Williams, Matt, Pot.	.849	24	21	41	11	73	3
Wilson, Heath, Kin.	.000	1	0	0	0	0	0
Yan, Edwin, W.S.	.000	1	0	0	0	0	0

TRIPLE PLAY: Rodgers.

SHORTSTOPS

Player, Team	Pct.	G	PO	A	E	TC	DP
Araujo, Ramon, Pot.	1.000	1	0	2	0	2	0
Asprilla, Avelino, Lyn.	1.000	1	1	3	0	4	0
Berroa, Cristian, Sal.	.924	42	59	112	14	185	21
Blanco, Andres, Wil.	.926	5	13	12	2	27	5
Canelliz, Chris, Pot.	.000	1	0	0	0	0	0
Castillo, Jose, Lyn.	.951	132	245	402	33	680	92
Cates, Gary, Fred.	.878	7	14	22	5	41	2
Cockrell, Michael, Lyn.	1.000	1	0	1	0	1	0
Colmenter, Jesus, Kin.	1.000	1	0	1	0	1	0
Cordova, Ricardo, Pot.	.907	20	30	38	7	75	9
Cotto, Luis, Wil.	.909	11	7	23	3	33	4
Cruz, Alex, Lyn.	.000	1	0	0	0	0	0
Davidson, Seth, Pot.	.963	16	29	50	3	82	17
Del Rosario, Manny, Fred.	.875	4	4	3	1	8	0
Fenster, Darren, Wil.	.971	17	26	42	2	70	8
Garcia, Nick, Fred.	.931	57	97	146	18	261	33
Hudnall, Joshua, Lyn.	1.000	10	6	15	0	21	5
Jaramillo, Milko, Fred.	.948	109	175	302	26	503	65
Jeffcoat, Bryon, M.B.	.972	12	19	16	1	36	5
Johnson, Kelly, M.B.	.952	118	168	313	24	505	72
Lambert, Casey, Sal.	.966	21	32	53	3	88	11
Lincoln, Justin, Sal.	1.000	6	10	13	0	23	2
Lora, Tom, Wil.	.967	22	30	57	3	90	20
Luna, Hector, Kin.	.947	126	226	348	32	606	74
Machado, Alejandro, Wil.	.954	98	130	243	18	391	46
Martinez, Lou, M.B.	.889	5	8	16	3	27	2
Meadows, Randy, Lyn.	.941	6	13	19	2	34	5
Merrill, Ronnie, Sal.	.959	76	133	220	15	368	49
Nicholson, Tommy, W.S.	.889	6	6	18	3	27	2
Orr, Pete, M.B.	.964	7	12	15	1	28	4
Peguero, Miguel, Kin.	1.000	1	2	3	0	5	0
Pichardo, Henry, Kin.	.962	19	29	46	3	78	8
Reyes, Ambiorix, Sal.	1.000	4	6	10	0	16	1
REYES, Guillermo, W.S.	.957	121	189	367	25	581	85
Salvo, Andrew, W.S.	.984	16	23	40	1	64	6
Shanks, Eric, Fred.	.912	44	66	99	16	181	18
Shier, Peter, Fred.	.969	34	57	68	4	129	12
Smith, Corey, Kin.	1.000	2	1	0	0	1	0
Wilken, Kris, Fred.	1.000	2	3	2	0	5	0

OUTFIELDERS

Player, Team	Pct.	G	PO	A	E	TC	DP
Aspito, Jason, W.S.	.970	93	158	4	5	167	0
Barns, B.J., Lyn.*	.976	131	269	12	7	288	3
Bonifay, Josh, Lyn.	1.000	21	31	1	0	32	0
Borchard, Joe, W.S.	1.000	2	3	0	0	3	0
Buford, Damon, W.S.	1.000	7	16	2	0	18	0
Burnett, Mark, Pot.	.929	10	13	0	1	14	0
Caradonna, Brett, W.S.	.991	73	103	10	1	114	1
Catalanotte, Greg, Sal.	.945	28	49	3	3	55	0
Church, Ryan, Kin.*	.965	48	79	3	3	85	1
Ciraco, Steven, Kin.	1.000	17	22	1	0	23	0
Coleman, Alph, M.B.	.991	115	216	7	2	225	0
Cowan, Justin, Wil.	1.000	13	14	0	0	14	0
Crozier, Eric, Kin.*	1.000	3	9	0	0	9	0
Cunningham, Marco, Wil.	1.000	29	66	3	0	69	1

Player, Team	Pct.	G	PO	A	E	TC	DP
DeJesus, David, Wil.*	.994	75	162	5	1	168	2
Duffy, Chris, Lyn.*	.989	130	274	6	3	283	0
Fera, Aaron, Pot.	.978	26	43	2	1	46	0
Forbes, Mike, M.B.	1.000	1	2	0	0	2	0
Gettis, Byron, Wil.	.981	110	196	8	4	208	1
Gordon, Alex, Fred.*	.929	16	23	3	2	28	0
Hernandez, Johnny, Pot.*	.982	139	266	9	5	280	2
Hickman, Brian, W.S.	.000	1	0	0	0	0	0
Hill, Willy, Lyn.	.882	11	15	0	2	17	0
Hopper, Norris, Wil.	.985	122	245	15	4	264	3
Hudnall, Joshua, Lyn.	1.000	3	0	1	0	1	0
Janowicz, Nate, Kin.*	.970	15	32	0	1	33	0
Jeffcoat, Bryon, M.B.	1.000	1	1	0	0	1	0
Jones, Damien, M.B.*	1.000	11	12	0	0	12	0
Kent, Mailon, M.B.	.984	95	172	7	3	182	1
Keppinger, Billy, Wil.*	.889	4	7	1	1	9	0
Keylor, Cory, Fred.	.956	127	229	9	11	249	1
Lambert, Casey, Sal.	1.000	1	0	1	0	1	0
Landaeta, Luis, Lyn.*	.971	20	34	0	1	35	0
Lewis, Russell, Pot.	1.000	2	7	0	0	7	0
Littleton, Brandon, Fred.*	.979	43	88	4	2	94	1
Lopez-Cao, Mike, Lyn.	1.000	2	1	0	0	1	0
Lora, Tom, Wil.	.750	4	6	0	2	8	0
Mack, Tony, Fred.	.974	72	177	7	5	189	2
Martel, Normand, W.S.	.980	78	141	5	3	149	0
Matos, Luis, Fred.	1.000	3	8	0	0	8	0
McCARTHY, Bill, M.B.	.994	94	173	4	1	178	0
McLouth, Nathan, Lyn.	.968	101	149	4	5	158	2
Meadows, Tydus, Wil.	.969	68	123	4	4	131	1
Meath, Matt, Lyn.	.875	5	6	1	1	8	0
Minges, Tyler, Kin.	.977	104	205	6	5	216	0
Moreno, Jorge, Kin.	.969	65	119	5	4	128	3
Morris, Chris, Pot.	.986	113	284	5	4	293	2
Munoz, Billy, Pot.*	.000	1	0	0	2	2	0
Muth, Edmund, Sal.*	.970	42	62	2	2	66	0
Navarrete, Ray, Lyn.	1.000	4	4	0	0	4	0
Ndungidi, Ntema, Fred.	.964	51	104	2	4	110	0
Oborn, Spencer, W.S.	.982	84	165	2	3	170	0
Orr, Pete, M.B.	1.000	1	4	0	0	4	0
Peck, Bryan, Sal.	.939	26	43	3	3	49	0
Phillips, Dan, Sal.	1.000	6	10	1	0	11	1
Pichardo, Henry, Kin.	1.000	5	3	0	0	3	0
Piedra, Jorge, Sal.*	.975	100	183	11	5	199	1
Piniella, Juan, W.S.	.985	54	126	5	2	133	3
Requena, Alex, Kin.	.981	123	246	11	5	262	1
Rodgers, Albert, Pot.	1.000	5	6	0	0	6	0
Rosa, Wally, W.S.	1.000	1	1	0	0	1	0
Rosario, Melvin, Sal.*	.987	73	143	4	2	149	0
Ross, Don, Wil.	.000	1	0	0	0	0	0
Schumaker, Skip, Pot.	.988	136	230	8	3	241	2
Scott, Luke, Kin.	.961	29	48	1	2	51	0
Sienko, Ryan, W.S.	.000	1	0	0	0	0	0
Sizemore, Grady, Kin.*	.949	42	73	1	4	78	0
Stern, Adam, M.B.	.990	117	280	3	3	286	0
Sullivan, Cory, Sal.*	.987	137	278	16	4	298	4
Sullivan, Kevin, Sal.	.983	32	56	1	1	58	0
Thomas, Chuck, M.B.*	1.000	2	4	1	0	5	0
Tucker, Mamon, Fred.	.960	121	188	6	8	202	0
Weichard, Paul, Lyn.*	.833	10	10	0	2	12	0
Welsh, Eric, W.S.*	.917	10	10	1	1	12	0
Wilken, Kris, Fred.	1.000	1	2	0	0	2	0
Zywica, Mike, W.S.	.939	40	58	4	4	66	0

Player, Team	Pct.	G	PO	A	E	TC	DP	PB
Lopez-Cao, Mike, Lyn.	.978	33	200	20	5	225	1	6
Mejia, Manuel, Lyn.	1.000	1	1	0	0	1	0	
Moylan, Dan, Pot.	.987	57	333	40	5	378	2	8
Netwall, Chris, Pot.	.989	13	74	14	1	89	0	
Ortega, Sixto, Sal.	1.000	1	2	0	0	2	0	
Paulino, Ronny, Lyn.	.981	111	854	88	18	960	5	17
Peck, Bryan, Sal.	.983	8	55	2	1	58	0	2
Pena, Brayan, M.B.	1.000	6	35	5	0	40	0	2
Quintero, Humberto, W.S.	.990	52	310	67	4	381	2	4
Rosa, Wally, W.S.	.986	31	184	31	3	218	0	4
Seestedt, Mike, Fred.	.985	51	360	36	6	402	1	5
Serrano, Ray, M.B.	1.000	19	117	12	0	129	2	0
Sienko, Ryan, W.S.	.985	22	119	12	2	133	3	2
Sullivan, Kevin, Sal.	.993	22	128	15	1	144	1	1
Terveen, Bryce, M.B.	.989	12	74	16	1	91	0	3
Walter, Scott, Wil.	.979	55	406	23	9	438	1	6
Webster, Kevin, Fred.	.985	19	113	16	2	131	1	7
Whiteside, Eli, Fred.	.975	70	516	58	15	589	3	17
Wilson, Heath, Kin.	.989	80	542	72	7	621	4	18
Winchester, Jeff, Sal.	.980	82	523	61	12	596	3	13

TRIPLE PLAY: Hamill.

CATCHERS

Player, Team	Pct.	G	PO	A	E	TC	DP	PB
Anderson, Travis, M.B.	.971	25	151	15	5	171	0	5
Arnerich, Tony, Wil.	.984	66	442	48	8	498	8	11
Bastardo, Angel, Kin.	.967	16	108	8	4	120	0	1
BOSCAN, Jean, M.B.	.992	83	666	56	6	728	3	15
Brown, Jason, Lyn.	1.000	1	5	1	0	6	0	0
Conway, Dan, Sal.	.985	32	174	20	3	197	2	4
Cowan, Justin, Wil.	.975	25	140	14	4	158	1	3
Cox, George, Fred.	1.000	6	36	1	0	37	0	1
Depippo, Jeff, Kin.	.982	48	290	34	6	330	1	6
Garrick, Matt, Pot.	.986	9	66	3	1	70	0	5
Hamill, Ryan, Pot.	.980	66	411	70	10	491	5	7
Harris, Blair, W.S.	1.000	1	5	1	0	6	0	0
Hickman, Brian, W.S.	.993	26	117	16	1	134	0	5
Koslowski, Kasey, W.S.	.909	3	10	0	1	11	0	1
Lisk, Charles, W.S.	.991	18	98	12	1	111	1	7

PITCHERS

Player, Team	Pct.	G	PO	A	E	TC	DP
Aguilar, Ray, M.B.*	.960	35	5	19	1	25	0
Alcala, Jason, Lyn.	.920	54	10	13	2	25	1
Allen, Wyatt, W.S.	.919	28	8	26	3	37	0
An, Byeong, W.S.*	.833	11	1	4	1	6	0
Andrade, Jancy, Fred.	.941	30	4	12	1	17	0
Axelson, Josh, Pot.	.964	32	13	14	1	28	1
Baker, Ryan, M.B.	1.000	36	2	3	0	5	0
Barry, Kevin, M.B.	1.000	47	2	11	0	13	1
Bartlett, Richard, Fred.	.875	18	9	19	4	32	0
Benes, Andy, Pot.	.000	1	0	0	0	0	0
Bennett, Jeff, Lyn.	.963	24	6	20	1	27	2
Borner, Brady, Lyn.*	1.000	37	10	16	0	26	2
Bouknight, Kip, Sal.	.979	27	19	27	1	47	3
Brantley, Brian, Sal.	.000	6	0	0	1	1	0
Buglovsky, Chris, Sal.	.930	27	15	25	3	43	5
Bullard, Jim, W.S.*	.926	23	3	22	2	27	1
Bumatay, Mike, Lyn.*	.929	52	3	10	1	14	1
Burgess, Richie, Pot.	.500	9	1	0	1	2	0
Burnett, Sean, Lyn.*	.977	26	4	39	1	44	4
Byrdak, Tim, Kin.*	1.000	2	0	2	0	2	0
Cabrera, Fernando, Kin.	.900	21	11	7	2	20	0
Cali, Carmen, Pot.*	.875	29	2	5	1	8	2
Carrasco, Dan, Lyn.	1.000	55	11	13	0	24	0
Cedeno, Blas, Lyn.	1.000	9	1	7	0	8	2
Cierlik, Jason, Fred.*	1.000	4	1	0	0	1	0
Colon, Roman, M.B.	.903	26	6	23	3	31	0
Connolly, Mike, Lyn.*	1.000	29	5	35	0	40	3
Cook, Jeremy, Pot.	.938	47	3	12	1	16	0
Cooper, Chris, Kin.*	1.000	8	0	3	0	3	0
Crowder, Chuck, Sal.*	1.000	23	5	9	0	14	0
Cruceta, Alberto, Kin.	.750	7	1	5	2	8	0
Cummings, Jeremy, Pot.	.909	14	6	14	2	22	3
Curreri, Joe, W.S.	1.000	5	0	1	0	1	0
Curtis, Daniel, M.B.	.975	17	13	26	1	40	1
David, Brad, M.B.*	1.000	5	0	1	0	1	0
Davis, Jason, Kin.	.816	17	7	24	7	38	2
De La Cruz, Carlos, Kin.	.857	6	4	2	1	7	0
Denney, Kyle, Kin.	.889	15	5	11	2	18	0
DePaula, Freddy, Wil.*	1.000	33	2	6	0	8	1
Difelice, Mark, Sal.	1.000	6	3	3	0	6	0
Dohmann, Scott, Sal.	.929	28	9	17	2	28	1
Dotel, Melido, Sal.	.867	37	6	7	2	15	2
DOUGLASS, Ryan, Wil.	1.000	27	16	40	0	56	1
Duff, Matt, Pot.	.000	4	0	0	0	0	0
Dukeman, Greg, Lyn.	1.000	25	1	6	0	7	0
Eppenender, Jamie, Wil.*	1.000	16	1	0	0	1	0
Evans, Kyle, Kin.	.950	11	7	12	1	20	0
Evert, Brett, M.B.	.667	10	1	1	1	3	0
Ewasko, Tod, Pot.	1.000	5	0	2	0	2	0
Ferguson, Ian, Wil.	.958	17	6	17	1	24	3
Fernley, Nathan, Pot.	1.000	15	0	9	0	9	0
Ferrand, Dario, W.S.	.870	27	7	13	3	23	1
Field, Luke, Kin.	1.000	6	0	3	0	3	0
Fields, Josh, W.S.	1.000	36	3	6	0	9	0
Figueroa, Juan, Fred.	.923	9	4	8	1	13	1

Player, Team	Pct.	G	PO	A	E	TC	DP
Fitch, Steve, Kin.	.875	15	4	3	1	8	0
Ford, Tom, Fred.*	.944	46	3	14	1	18	1
Forystek, Brian, Fred.*	1.000	43	7	11	0	18	0
Francisco, Frank, W.S.	1.000	6	0	1	0	1	0
Freeman, Kai, W.S.	.000	1	0	0	0	0	0
Gallagher, Buddy, Sal.*	.938	15	3	12	1	16	0
Garza, Rolando, W.S.	1.000	14	2	3	0	5	0
Gomez, Diogenes, Sal.	1.000	6	0	2	0	2	1
Gooding, Jason, Wil.*	1.000	17	6	5	0	11	0
Graves, Don, Pot.	.900	14	2	16	2	20	2
Green, Sean, Sal.	.906	52	6	23	3	32	0
Greinke, Zack, Wil.	.000	1	0	0	0	0	0
Griffin, Colt, Wil.	.000	3	0	0	0	0	0
Guerrero, Junior, Wil.	.833	36	2	3	1	6	1
Guzman, Juan, Fred.	1.000	5	0	10	0	10	1
Guzman, Wilson, Lyn.*	.929	22	3	10	1	14	0
Hale, Beau, Fred.	.923	22	7	17	2	26	0
Haren, Danny, Pot.	1.000	14	8	13	0	21	1
Hentgen, Pat, Fred.	.667	1	1	1	1	3	0
Hernandez, Runelvys, Wil.	1.000	2	0	3	0	3	0
Higgins, Joshua, Lyn.	.944	53	9	8	1	18	1
Honel, Kris, W.S.	1.000	1	1	0	0	1	0
Huisman, Justin, Sal.	1.000	41	5	17	0	22	2
Jackson, Brian, Kin.-Lyn.	.909	16	0	0	0	0	0
Jacobsen, Landon, Lyn.	.929	27	17	22	3	42	1
Johnston, Mike, Lyn.*	.913	15	6	15	2	23	0
Jones, Sean, Fred.	1.000	32	3	5	0	8	0
Keppinger, Billy, Wil.*	.000	1	0	0	0	0	0
Kinney, Josh, Pot.	.769	44	5	5	3	13	2
Kirkland, Aaron, W.S.	.917	34	3	8	1	12	2
Kohl, Doug, Pot.	1.000	16	2	6	0	8	0
Kozlowski, Ben, M.B.*	.333	1	1	0	2	3	0
Lantz, Doug, Kin.	1.000	11	2	8	0	10	0
Larson, Ryan, Kin.	.923	23	2	10	1	13	1
Lavery, Tim, Lyn.*	1.000	6	2	3	0	5	0
MacDougal, Mike, Wil.	1.000	5	1	1	0	2	0
Madril, Steve, W.S.*	1.000	36	3	10	0	13	0
Mangrum, Micah, Wil.	1.000	16	3	6	0	9	0
Martinez, Miguel, Pot.	.833	8	1	4	1	6	0
Matheny, Brandon, Kin.*	.895	30	3	14	2	19	0
McClellan, Zach, Wil.	1.000	28	11	35	0	46	2
McClendon, Matt, M.B.	1.000	17	0	2	0	2	0
McWhirter, Kris, W.S.	.952	24	3	17	1	21	1
Medlock, Chet, Pot.	1.000	7	1	1	0	2	0
Mejia, Francisco, Fred.*	1.000	1	0	1	0	1	0
Mejia, Juan, Pot.	.846	23	6	16	4	26	1
Mendoza, Marcos, Kin.*	.909	22	3	7	1	11	1
Merrigan, Josh, Pot.*	.667	11	0	2	1	3	0
Meyer, Mike, Pot.	1.000	13	3	1	0	4	0
Miller, Matt, M.B.*	.875	36	2	5	1	8	0
Montilla, Elvis, Fred.	.833	10	1	4	1	6	0
Moran, Nick, Kin.	.833	9	0	5	1	6	0
Morris, Cory, Fred.	.950	16	8	11	1	20	0
Morrison, Robbie, Wil.	.917	32	3	8	1	12	0
Murray, Brad, W.S.*	.933	53	5	9	1	15	1
Muth, Edmund, Sal.*	.000	1	0	0	0	0	0
Natale, Mike, Wil.	1.000	13	0	2	0	2	0
Neil, Dan, Kin.*	1.000	7	0	3	0	3	0
Nelson, Kenny, M.B.	.939	23	12	34	3	49	1
Novinsky, John, Pot.	.846	30	1	10	2	13	0
Obermueller, Wes, Wil.	1.000	8	4	9	0	13	0
Olivo, Rigal, W.S.	1.000	15	0	2	0	2	0
Ormond, Rodney, Fred.	.947	46	3	15	1	19	3
Pacheco, Enemencio, Sal.-W-S	.909	49	9	11	2	22	2

Player, Team	Pct.	G	PO	A	E	TC	DP
Parrott, Rhett, Pot.	.952	19	3	17	1	21	5
Pena, Ed, W.S.*	1.000	11	1	3	0	4	0
Phillips, Mike, W.S.*	.867	28	1	25	4	30	2
Pinales, Aquiles, Kin.	.929	48	4	9	1	14	0
Ponce Deleon, Damon, Pot.	.636	27	1	6	4	11	0
Powalski, Rick, Kin.*	1.000	3	0	2	0	2	0
Prahm, Ryan, Kin.	1.000	4	2	3	0	5	0
Price, Ryan, Sal.	.909	21	3	7	1	11	0
Ramirez, Enrique, Fred.	1.000	32	4	7	0	11	0
Rawson, Anthony, Pot.*	1.000	48	7	13	0	20	0
Reilly, Christopher, Fred.	1.000	14	0	2	0	2	0
Reinike, Chris, Kin.	.000	1	0	0	0	0	0
Ring, Royce, W.S.*	1.000	21	0	7	0	7	0
Rodriguez, Eddy, Fred.	.900	38	1	8	1	10	0
Roque, Darryl, Fred.	.950	32	3	16	1	20	0
Rupp, Mike, W.S.	1.000	11	0	5	0	5	0
Schwager, Matt, Fred.	1.000	28	3	23	0	26	1
Seestedt, Mike, Fred.	.000	1	0	0	0	0	0
Sharber, Jason, Lyn.	.926	22	8	17	2	27	0
Simpson, Gerrit, Sal.	.833	5	3	2	1	6	1
Smith, Jared, Pot.	1.000	6	0	1	0	1	0
Smith, Matthew, W.S.	.917	47	6	5	1	12	0
Snyder, Kyle, Wil.	.900	15	3	6	1	10	1
Sobkowiak, Scott, M.B.	1.000	16	4	2	0	6	0
Speier, Ryan, Sal.	.929	24	4	9	1	14	0
Sperring, Jayme, Fred.	1.000	18	1	5	0	6	0
Sprague, Kevin, Pot.*	.875	28	3	11	2	16	0
Stepka, Tom, Sal.	1.000	45	7	22	0	29	3
Stiles, Brad, Wil.*	.909	38	2	8	1	11	0
Stocks, Nick, Pot.	.500	3	0	1	1	2	0
Sturkie, Scott, Kin.	1.000	30	5	11	0	16	2
Tamayo, Danny, Wil.	.920	23	3	20	2	25	0
Thompson, Derek, Kin.*	1.000	13	5	12	0	17	3
Thoms, Hank, Kin.	.933	17	2	12	1	15	1
Tillery, Josh, M.B.	.900	37	7	2	1	10	0
Tsao, Chin-hui, Sal.	1.000	9	5	4	0	9	0
Vargas, Jose, Kin.	1.000	19	0	3	0	3	0
Vasquez, Jorge, Wil.	1.000	10	0	1	0	1	0
Veronie, Shanin, M.B.	1.000	5	0	2	0	2	0
Villacis, Eduardo, Wil.	1.000	17	8	4	0	12	0
Villalon, Julio, Pot.	1.000	7	3	4	0	7	0
Vogelsong, Ryan, Lyn.	.000	4	0	0	0	0	0
Wade, Matt, Kin.	1.000	20	1	8	0	9	0
Wagner, Denny, W.S.	1.000	21	1	8	0	9	1
Wainwright, Adam, M.B.	.889	28	6	18	3	27	0
Wallace, Mark, Kin.*	1.000	9	1	10	0	11	0
Warden, Jim Ed, Kin.	1.000	7	1	3	0	4	0
Waters, Chris, M.B.*	.914	28	20	33	5	58	0
Watkins, Dave, M.B.	1.000	4	1	1	0	2	0
Webb, Nicholas, Sal.*	1.000	26	8	21	0	29	0
Wilkerson, Wes, Wil.	1.000	20	2	21	0	23	2
Wilson, Kris, Wil.	1.000	4	0	2	0	2	0
Wrightsman, Dusty, Wil.	.833	39	6	9	3	18	0
Yankosky, L.J., M.B.	.000	1	0	0	0	0	0
Zumwalt, Alec, M.B.	1.000	21	2	3	0	5	0

PITCHERS WITH TWO OR MORE TEAMS

Player, Team	Pct.	G	PO	A	E	TC	DP
Jackson, Brian, Kin.	.000	11	0	0	0	0	0
Jackson, Brian, Lyn.	.000	5	0	0	0	0	0
Pacheco, Enemencio, Sal.	.882	41	6	9	2	17	1
Pacheco, Enemencio, W.S.	1.000	8	3	2	0	5	1

The following players appeared only as designated hitter, pinch-hitter or pinch runner: Gillikin, dh, ph; Kessick, dh, ph.

LEAGUE CHAMPIONS

Year	Team	Pct.	Year	Team	Pct.	Year	Team	Pct.
1945—	Danville	.681	1952—	Raleigh	.581		Burlington (4th)†	.511
1946—	Greensboro	.599		Reidsville (4th)†	.536	1959—	Raleigh	.600
	Raleigh (2nd)†	.563	1953—	Raleigh	.593		Wilson (2nd)†	.550
1947—	Burlington	.613		Danville (2nd)†	.572	1960—	Greensboro‡	.636
	Raleigh (3rd)†	.574	1954—	Fayetteville*	.628		Burlington	.586
1948—	Raleigh	.592	1955—	HP-Thomasville	.580	1961—	Wilson	.594
	Martinsville (2nd)†	.570		Danville (2nd)†	.533	1962—	Durham	.636
1949—	Danville	.601	1956—	HP-Thomasville	.591		Wilson	.600
	Burlington (4th)†	.500		Fayetteville (4th)§	.523		Kinston (2nd)†	.593
1950—	Winston-Salem*	.693	1957—	Durham	.632	1963—	Kinston§	.538
1951—	Durham	.600		HP-Thomasville	.622		Greensboro§	.590
	Winston-Salem (2nd)†	.583	1958—	Danville	.576		Wilson (2nd)†	.535

Year	Team	Pct.	Year	Team	Pct.	Year	Team	Pct.
1964—	Kinston§	.572	1976—	Winston-Salem	.618		Frederick‡	.544
	Winston-Salem§†	.590		Winston-Salem	.551	1991—	Kinston‡	.645
1965—	Peninsula§	.597	1977—	Lynchburg	.591		Lynchburg	.482
	Durham§	.580		Peninsula‡	.556	1992—	Lynchburg	.570
	Tidewater†	.528	1978—	Peninsula	.696		Peninsula‡	.536
1966—	Kinston§	.547		Lynchburg‡	.614	1993—	Wilmington	.532
	Winston-Salem§	.586	1979—	Winston-Salem■	.607		Winston-Salem‡	.514
	Rocky Mount†	.533	1980—	Peninsula‡	.714	1994—	Wilmington‡	.681
1967—	Durham∞(West.)	.536		Durham	.600		Winston-Salem	.555
	Raleigh (East.)	.542	1981—	Peninsula	.522	1995—	Wilmington	.601
1968—	Salem (West.)	.607		Hagerstown‡	.507		Kinston‡	.591
	Ral-Dur (East.)	.597	1982—	Alexandria‡	.597	1996—	Wilmington▼	.571
	HP-Thom.▲(W.)	.493		Durham	.588		Kinston	.551
1969—	Rocky M (East.)	.569	1983—	Lynchburg‡	.691	1997—	Kinston	.621
	Salem (West.)	.542		Winston-Salem	.529		Lynchburg†	.586
	Ral-Dur◆(East.)	.560	1984—	Lynchburg‡	.645	1998—	Wilmington▼	.614
1970—	Winston-Salem‡	.586		Durham	.486		Winston-Salem	.568
	Burlington	.597	1985—	Lynchburg	.679	1999—	Kinston	.577
1971—	Peninsula‡	.647		Winston-Salem‡	.417		Myrtle Beach•	.568
	Kinston	.623	1986—	Hagerstown	.655		Wilmington•	.568
1972—	Salem‡	.657		Winston-Salem‡	.594	2000—	Myrtle Beach▼	.629
	Burlington	.632	1987—	Salem‡	.576	2001—	Kinston	.636
1973—	Lynchburg	.588		Kinston	.536		Salem▼	.507
	Winston-Salem‡	.557	1988—	Kinston§	.629	2002—	Wilmington	.636
1974—	Salem	.671		Lynchburg	.486		Lynchburg▼	.621
	Salem	.582	1989—	Durham	.609			
1975—	Rocky Mount	.667		Prince William‡	.522			
	Rocky Mount	.614	1990—	Kinston	.652			

CLASS A *Carolina League*

*Won championship and four-club playoff. †Won four-club playoff. ‡Won split-season playoff. §League was divided into Eastern, Western divisions. ∞Won eight-club, two-division playoff. ▲Won eight-club, two-division playoff against Raleigh-Durham. ◆Won eight-club, two-division playoff against Burlington. ■Won both halves of split season (no playoffs). ▼League divided into Northern and Southern divisions and played a split-season, won playoffs. •Declared co-champions after final series cancelled due to hurricane.

FLORIDA STATE LEAGUE

LEAGUE OFFICE

President
Chuck Murphy
Address
P.O. Box 349
Daytona Beach, FL 32115
Phone
386-252-7479

Teams (affiliation)
Brevard County Manatees (Expos)
Clearwater Phillies (Phillies)
Daytona Cubs (Cubs)
Dunedin Blue Jays (Blue Jays)
Fort Myers Miracle (Twins)
Jupiter Hammerheads (Marlins)

Lakeland Tigers (Tigers)
Palm Beach Cardinals (Cardinals)
St. Lucie Mets (Mets)
Sarasota Red Sox (Red Sox)
Tampa Yankees (Yankees)
Vero Beach Dodgers (Dodgers)

2002 FINAL STANDINGS

FIRST HALF

EAST DIVISION

Team	W	L	T	Pct.	GB
St. Lucie (Mets)	40	32	0	.556	...
Lakeland (Tigers)	40	32	0	.556	...
Jupiter (Marlins)	39	32	0	.549	0.5
Vero Beach (Dodgers)	37	33	0	.529	2.0
Daytona (Cubs)	31	41	0	.431	9.0
Brevard County (Expos)	27	45	0	.375	13.0

WEST DIVISION

Team	W	L	T	Pct.	GB
Tampa (Yankees)	42	28	0	.600	...
Fort Myers (Twins)	40	32	0	.556	3.0
Sarasota (Red Sox)	39	33	0	.542	4.0
Charlotte (Rangers)	39	33	0	.542	4.0
Dunedin (Blue Jays)	33	38	0	.465	9.5
Clearwater (Phillies)	22	50	0	.306	21.0

SECOND HALF

EAST DIVISION

Team	W	L	T	Pct.	GB
Jupiter (Marlins)	42	25	0	.627	...
Vero Beach (Dodgers)	35	30	0	.538	6.0
Daytona (Cubs)	33	32	0	.508	8.0
St. Lucie (Mets)	31	37	0	.456	11.5
Lakeland (Tigers)	29	38	0	.433	13.0
Brevard County (Expos)	24	40	0	.375	16.5

WEST DIVISION

Team	W	L	T	Pct.	GB
Charlotte (Rangers)	45	23	0	.662	...
Fort Myers (Twins)	37	30	0	.552	7.5
Clearwater (Phillies)	35	29	0	.547	8.0
Dunedin (Blue Jays)	30	34	0	.469	13.0
Tampa (Yankees)	29	34	0	.460	13.5
Sarasota (Red Sox)	23	41	0	.359	20.0

COMPOSITE

Team	Char.	Jup	F.M.	Tam.	V.B.	St.L.	Lak.	Day.	Dun.	Sar.	Cle.	B.C.	W	L	T	Pct.	GB
Charlotte (Rangers)	...	4	15	9	5	5	3	3	12	11	12	5	84	56	0	.600	...
Jupiter (Marlins)	4	...	4	5	8	14	8	9	3	5	8	13	81	57	0	.587	2.0
Fort Myers (Twins)	9	4	...	7	5	8	4	5	8	10	10	7	77	62	0	.554	6.5
Tampa (Yankees)	9	2	11	...	3	4	8	4	8	6	11	5	71	62	0	.534	9.5
Vero Beach (Dodgers)	3	8	3	3	...	7	11	10	6	4	3	14	72	63	0	.533	9.5
St. Lucie (Mets)	3	10	0	4	13	...	7	8	5	7	6	8	71	69	0	.507	13.0
Lakeland (Tigers)	5	8	4	4	4	9	...	7	4	6	10	8	69	70	0	.496	14.5
Daytona (Cubs)	5	7	3	5	6	8	11	...	6	5	1	7	64	73	0	.467	18.5
Dunedin (Blue Jays)	4	4	8	8	2	3	4	4	...	10	11	5	63	72	0	.467	18.5
Sarasota (Red Sox)	7	3	7	11	4	1	2	7	7	...	6	7	62	74	0	.456	20.0
Clearwater (Phillies)	4	0	6	5	4	2	4	7	10	9	...	6	57	79	0	.419	25.0
Brevard County (Expos)	3	7	1	1	9	8	8	9	3	1	1	...	51	85	0	.375	31.0

Brevard County played home games in Melbourne, Fla.; Charlotte played home games in Port Charlotte, Fla.

Major league affiliations in parentheses.

PLAYOFFS: Charlotte defeated Tampa, two games to none; Lakeland defeated Jupiter, two games to none. Charlotte defeated Lakeland, three games to two to win Florida State League championship.

REGULAR-SEASON ATTENDANCE: Brevard County, 89,480; Charlotte, 23,988; Clearwater, 78,459; Daytona, 72,655; Dunedin, 47,717; Fort Myers, 109,293; Jupiter, 103,640; Lakeland, 21,503; St. Lucie, 78,564; Sarasota, 57,365; Tampa, 75,061; Vero Beach, 53,098. Total—810,823. Playoff (9 games)—5,596. Florida State League All-Star Game at Dunedin—2,483.

MANAGERS: Brevard County, Bob Didier (through May 6; 12-19) and Tony Torchia (May 7 through end of season; 39-66); Charlotte, Darryl Kennedy; Clearwater, John Morris (through June 16; 22-50), Roly Dearmas (June 17 through end of season; 35-29); Daytona, Dave Trembley; Dunedin, Marty Pevey; Fort Myers, Jose Marzan; Jupiter, Luis Dorante; Lakeland, Gary Green; St. Lucie, Ken Oberkfell; Sarasota, Billy Gardner; Tampa, Mitch Seoane; Vero Beach, Juan Bustabad.

ALL-STAR TEAM: 1B—Leo Daigle, Lakeland; 2B—Dominic Rich, Dunedin; 3B—Brendan Harris, Daytona; SS—Jose Reyes, St. Lucie; Utility INF—Ramon Martinez, Charlotte; LF—William Smith, Jupiter; CF—Laynce Nix, Charlotte; RF—Alexi Rios, Dunedin; Utility OF—Josh Rabe, Fort Myers; C (tie)—Guillermo Quiroz, Fort Myers and Kelly Shoppach, Sarasota; DH—Simon Pond, Dunedin; RHP—Taylor Buchholz, Clearwater; RHP—Preston Larrison, Lakeland; RHP—Josh Reynolds, St. Lucie; RHP—Beau Kemp, Fort Myers; RHP—Lino Urdaneta, Vero Beach; LHP—C.J. Wilson, Charlotte; Most Valuable Player—Laynce Nix, Charlotte; Most Valuable Pitcher—Taylor Buchholz, Clearwater; Manager of the Year—Darryl Kennedy, Charlotte. Coach of the Year (tie)—Luis Dorante, Jupiter and Jose Marzan, Fort Myers.

2002 BATTING

TEAM

Team	G	TPA	AB	R	H	TB	2B	3B	HR	RBI	SH	SF	HP	BB	IBB	SO	SB	CS	GDP	LOB	ShO	Avg.	OBP	Slg.
St. Lucie	140	5340	4702	693	1266	1857	236	41	91	635	40	55	90	453	20	885	227	80	102	987	4	.269	.341	.395
Dunedin	135	5302	4698	632	1251	1765	239	40	65	571	37	36	63	468	36	842	72	48	111	1052	12	.266	.338	.376
Daytona	137	5277	4644	682	1221	1852	250	30	107	606	32	48	77	476	17	841	154	76	99	980	7	.263	.338	.399

Team	G	TPA	AB	R	H	TB	2B	3B	HR	RBI	SH	SF	HP	BB	IBB	SO	SB	CS	GDP	LOB	ShO	Avg.	OBP	Slg.
Charlotte	140	5354	4646	709	1193	1820	227	50	100	645	46	47	61	554	22	952	131	45	94	1004	7	.257	.341	.392
Jupiter..........	138	5335	4689	691	1201	1838	244	45	101	616	26	41	84	495	12	914	109	42	101	993	12	.256	.335	.392
Fort Myers.....	139	5114	4476	619	1141	1630	210	27	75	554	38	58	78	464	14	842	101	55	112	943	12	.255	.332	.364
Lakeland	139	5168	4558	619	1110	1667	200	33	97	546	34	31	69	476	9	1069	175	70	94	936	13	.244	.322	.366
Tampa	133	5005	4334	581	1055	1539	208	27	74	531	24	49	73	525	12	919	64	35	105	996	11	.243	.332	.355
Vero Beach....	135	4912	4398	564	1066	1579	198	36	81	504	41	28	74	371	8	985	151	78	77	857	10	.242	.310	.359
Sarasota	136	5069	4443	530	1071	1480	197	22	56	470	25	37	81	483	14	912	88	46	111	1001	17	.241	.324	.333
Brev. County..	136	4952	4423	498	1064	1441	181	26	48	443	52	38	42	397	21	914	99	71	101	883	15	.241	.307	.326
Clearwater	136	5008	4498	502	1064	1601	216	36	83	459	29	31	59	391	15	864	58	47	102	915	11	.237	.304	.356

INDIVIDUAL

TOP QUALIFIERS FOR BATTING CHAMPIONSHIP

Minimum 378 plate appearances. *Lefthanded batter. †Switch-hitter.

Player, Team	G	TPA	AB	R	H	TB	2B	3B	HR	RBI	SH	SF	HP	BB	IBB	SO	SB	CS	GDP	Avg.	OBP	Slg.
Rich, Dominic, Dun.*	95	448	377	72	130	178	14	5	8	50	4	3	7	57	9	49	8	6	5	.345	.437	.472
Harris, Brendan, Day.	110	475	425	82	140	226	35	6	13	54	1	2	4	43	4	57	16	4	7	.329	.395	.532
Dubois, Jason, Day.	99	431	361	64	116	203	25	1	20	85	0	4	9	57	0	95	6	2	7	.321	.422	.562
Martinez, Ramon, Char.†	114	521	472	98	144	190	21	8	3	41	5	6	6	32	4	44	39	15	15	.305	.353	.403
Rios, Alexis, Dun.	111	492	456	60	139	186	22	8	3	61	1	5	3	27	0	55	14	8	19	.305	.344	.408
Smith, Will, Jup.*	133	591	549	84	164	260	30	12	14	73	0	6	3	31	4	75	8	3	13	.299	.336	.474
Acuna, Ron, S.L.	115	499	443	67	132	166	18	5	2	54	1	5	12	38	1	74	36	12	13	.298	.365	.375
Magness, Pat, Jup.*	111	481	390	73	114	190	26	1	16	73	1	6	5	79	4	86	2	1	7	.292	.413	.487
Cruz, Enrique, S.L.	124	509	467	69	136	179	21	2	6	45	3	5	2	32	2	76	33	16	15	.291	.336	.383
Sadler, Ray, Day.	112	499	462	81	132	198	31	1	11	47	3	1	6	27	2	91	30	12	7	.286	.333	.429
Nix, Laynce, Char.*	137	599	512	86	146	242	27	3	21	110	0	9	6	72	8	105	17	1	9	.285	.374	.473
Pond, Simon, Dun.*	103	457	401	58	114	192	25	7	13	88	1	6	3	46	11	73	2	3	9	.284	.357	.479
Tiffee, Terry, F.M.†	126	509	473	47	133	188	31	0	8	64	3	6	2	25	3	49	0	3	12	.281	.316	.397
Van Buizen, Rodney, V.B.	131	540	497	74	139	195	24	4	8	51	4	1	16	22	2	59	17	8	10	.280	.330	.392
Bozanich, Sam, Tam.	102	415	365	44	102	152	26	3	6	47	0	4	4	41	0	58	4	6	11	.279	.355	.416

DEPARTMENTAL LEADERS: G—Nix, 137; AB—W. Smith, 549; R—R. Martinez, 98; H—W. Smith, 164; TB—W. Smith, 260; 2B—Cabrera, 43; 3B—Abercrombie, 13; HR—Daigle, 23; RBI—Nix, 110; SH—Da. Garcia, 14; SF—Brazell, 10; HP—Daigle, 17; BB—Magness, 79; IBB—Pond, 11; SO—Abercrombie, 158; SB—Logan, 55; CS—Abercrombie, 17; GIDP—Miller, 21; Slg.—Dubois, .562; OBP—Rich, .437.

ALL PLAYERS

*Lefthanded batter. †Switch-hitter.

Player, Team	G	TPA	AB	R	H	TB	2B	3B	HR	RBI	SH	SF	HP	BB	IBB	SO	SB	CS	GDP	Avg.	OBP	Slg.
Abercrombie, Reggie, V.B.	132	569	526	80	145	224	23	13	10	56	6	1	9	27	0	158	41	17	3	.276	.321	.426
Acevedo, Carlos, Cle.	32	124	115	8	25	31	6	0	0	6	1	0	2	6	1	19	0	2	1	.217	.268	.270
Acevedo, Inocencio, Char......	59	200	185	28	44	57	5	1	2	13	2	2	2	9	0	36	11	3	1	.238	.278	.308
Ackerman, Scott, B.C............	61	236	217	24	64	100	11	2	7	35	1	3	1	14	1	39	1	0	3	.295	.336	.461
Acuna, Ron, S.L.	115	499	443	67	132	166	18	5	2	54	1	5	12	38	1	74	36	12	13	.298	.365	.375
Adams, Russ, Dun.*	37	169	147	23	34	45	4	2	1	12	1	1	2	18	0	17	5	2	1	.231	.321	.306
Ahumada, Alex, Sar.	24	87	73	11	18	22	1	0	1	9	0	1	4	9	1	18	3	2	2	.247	.356	.301
Allec, Jason, Lak.	1	3	3	0	2	4	2	0	0	0	0	0	0	0	0	1	0	0	0	.667	.667	1.333
Alou, Moises, Day.	2	9	8	0	5	6	1	0	0	2	0	0	0	1	0	1	0	0	0	.625	.667	.750
Alvarez, Nick, V.B.	55	218	195	22	44	60	4	0	4	23	2	1	7	13	1	34	7	2	5	.226	.296	.308
Ambres, Chip, Jup.	123	578	509	88	120	186	25	7	9	37	2	1	9	57	0	98	23	8	6	.236	.323	.365
Anderson, Dennis, Jup.†	42	159	126	13	39	50	6	1	1	16	1	2	7	23	1	23	1	0	1	.310	.437	.397
Angell, Rick, Char.	98	312	272	42	63	83	12	1	2	29	6	4	1	29	0	69	10	5	3	.232	.304	.305
Aracena, Sandy, V.B.	70	253	224	19	44	50	3	0	1	15	3	4	2	20	0	50	2	0	8	.196	.264	.223
Arteaga, Joshua, Day.	29	85	79	8	15	18	1	1	0	4	2	0	1	3	0	19	0	2	1	.190	.229	.228
Avila, Rob, Cle.	74	269	238	26	52	78	11	0	5	26	0	1	5	24	0	41	4	2	5	.218	.302	.328
Aybar, Willy, V.B.†	108	450	372	56	80	135	18	2	11	65	2	4	3	69	4	54	15	4	9	.215	.339	.363
Bailie, Stefan, Sar.	43	182	159	16	41	59	8	2	2	26	0	4	3	16	0	33	1	0	7	.258	.330	.371
Barbier, Blair, Day.	95	391	351	43	82	134	19	0	11	49	0	4	4	32	2	66	7	5	11	.234	.302	.382
Bartlett, Jason, F.M.	39	168	145	24	38	51	7	0	2	9	1	3	2	17	0	24	11	2	1	.262	.341	.352
Bautista, Rayner, Lak.	9	43	39	8	9	12	1	1	0	2	0	0	0	4	0	10	1	0	3	.231	.302	.308
Bay, Jason, S.L.	69	305	261	48	71	114	12	2	9	54	2	3	5	34	3	54	22	2	4	.272	.363	.437
Bennett, Kris, Cle.	30	123	110	13	24	27	3	0	0	10	1	0	2	10	0	11	5	1	6	.218	.295	.245
Bernhardt, Joe, Dun.	99	392	357	38	84	139	20	1	11	47	0	4	4	27	3	88	0	3	13	.235	.293	.389
Blanco, Tony, Sar.	65	256	244	22	54	89	13	2	6	32	0	2	4	6	0	70	2	0	3	.221	.250	.365
Blasi, Blake, Day.-Sar.†	40	170	150	11	36	43	4	0	1	10	1	0	2	17	1	33	6	0	3	.240	.325	.287
Blum, Greg, B.C.	94	326	285	30	68	101	12	0	7	40	0	5	8	28	2	69	0	1	6	.239	.319	.354
Boitel, Rafael, F.M.†	81	277	254	28	61	80	10	3	1	28	2	4	2	15	1	48	11	3	2	.240	.284	.315
Boone, Doug, Tam.	14	41	32	6	7	11	4	0	0	4	0	0	0	9	0	13	0	0	0	.219	.390	.344
Boone, Matt, Lak.	51	209	195	24	48	64	5	1	3	19	1	0	2	11	0	51	3	3	3	.246	.293	.328
Botts, Jason, Char.†	116	493	401	67	102	161	22	5	9	54	0	3	14	75	3	99	7	2	4	.254	.387	.401
Bourgeois, Jason, Char.†	9	30	27	5	5	6	1	0	0	4	0	1	0	2	0	4	1	1	0	.185	.233	.222
Bowen, Rob, F.M.†	100	392	342	52	63	107	12	1	10	49	2	5	5	38	0	69	1	0	12	.184	.272	.313
Bowman, Addison, Sar.........	6	26	23	1	3	4	1	0	0	2	1	0	0	2	0	6	0	0	0	.130	.200	.174
Boyd, Patrick, Char.†	4	13	12	0	3	4	1	0	0	3	0	0	0	1	0	3	0	1	0	.250	.308	.333
Boyer, Brett, B.C.†	56	177	164	13	30	39	1	1	2	13	3	2	2	6	0	41	5	2	3	.183	.218	.238
Bozanich, Sam, Tam.	102	415	365	44	102	152	26	3	6	47	0	4	4	41	0	58	4	6	11	.279	.355	.416
Brazell, Craig, S.L.*	100	431	402	38	107	186	25	3	16	82	0	10	6	13	3	78	2	1	7	.266	.292	.463
Brisson, Dustin, Sar.*	34	135	119	15	34	60	9	1	5	19	0	0	0	16	0	20	0	0	4	.286	.370	.504
Brosseau, Richard, Dun.*	36	80	64	13	12	14	2	0	0	5	1	0	1	15	0	12	0	0	1	.188	.350	.219
Brown, Andy, Tam.*	121	499	438	59	94	159	15	4	14	59	1	6	3	51	2	151	12	4	5	.215	.297	.363
Brown, Matthew, B.C.†	3	6	6	0	1	1	0	0	0	0	0	0	0	0	0	0	0	0	0	.167	.167	.167
Bryan, Jason, Char.	2	3	3	0	0	0	0	0	0	0	0	0	0	0	0	3	0	0	0	.000	.000	.000
Buchanan, Brian, Tam.*	27	1	1	0	0	0	0	0	0	0	0	0	0	0	0	1	0	0	0	.000	.000	.000

Player, Team	G	TPA	AB	R	H	TB	2B	3B	HR	RBI	SH	SF	HP	BB	IBB	SO	SB	CS	GDP	Avg.	OBP	Slg.
Bush, Brian, Cle.	51	207	192	20	50	71	10	1	3	21	2	2	0	11	0	23	3	6	1	.260	.298	.370
Butler, Keith, Day.	27	102	90	15	19	25	3	0	1	9	2	0	3	7	0	11	6	1	2	.211	.290	.278
Cabrera, Miguel, Jup.	124	545	489	77	134	206	43	1	9	75	1	8	9	38	2	85	10	1	19	.274	.333	.421
Calabrese, Tony, Tam.	28	108	100	8	23	40	4	2	3	15	0	1	0	7	0	24	1	1	0	.230	.278	.400
Cameron, Antoine, Day.*	41	151	132	11	22	29	5	1	0	12	0	1	3	15	2	35	0	0	0	.167	.265	.220
Camilo, Juan, Lak.*	81	333	283	48	83	141	24	5	8	53	0	2	3	45	2	73	25	8	8	.293	.393	.498
Canales, Josh, V.B.	71	200	185	23	35	45	6	2	0	16	2	0	3	10	0	38	5	9	8	.189	.242	.243
Cannizaro, Andy, Tam.	112	427	366	52	91	114	18	1	1	46	5	4	14	38	0	31	3	4	14	.249	.339	.311
Carreno, Jose, B.C.	36	110	102	9	23	36	5	1	2	8	0	0	2	6	1	10	0	0	1	.225	.282	.353
Carroll, Wes, Cle.	12	45	43	5	9	11	2	0	0	1	0	0	0	2	0	9	0	0	1	.209	.244	.256
Carter, Shannon, Dun.*	123	468	424	66	118	153	18	1	5	35	7	1	7	29	0	68	18	9	4	.278	.334	.361
Castillo, Carlos, Lak.†	5	21	21	0	4	4	0	0	0	0	0	0	0	0	0	3	0	0	2	.190	.190	.190
Catalanotte, Greg, Sar.†	30	102	92	9	16	25	3	0	2	4	0	0	1	9	1	34	1	0	3	.174	.255	.272
Cerminaro, Michael, Day.	16	51	43	6	9	9	0	0	0	1	2	0	0	6	0	12	3	0	2	.209	.306	.209
Cleveland, Russ, Lak.	25	91	86	7	19	38	7	0	4	13	0	0	2	3	0	18	1	1	2	.221	.264	.442
Coleman, Michael, Sar.	1	3	3	0	1	1	0	0	0	0	0	0	0	0	0	0	0	0	1	.333	.333	.333
Corporan, Elvis, Tam.†	108	432	378	46	99	145	19	3	7	45	0	3	3	48	2	74	10	3	6	.262	.347	.384
Crespo, Manny, Sar.	51	178	158	12	38	54	7	0	3	18	1	2	0	17	0	30	0	0	5	.241	.311	.342
Cronin, Shane, Tam.	18	54	44	7	6	7	1	0	0	1	0	0	2	8	0	10	0	0	3	.136	.296	.159
Cruz, Edgar, Cle.	73	264	243	26	52	84	11	0	7	17	2	0	1	18	0	58	0	0	5	.214	.271	.346
Cruz, Enrique, S.L.	124	509	467	69	136	179	21	2	6	45	3	5	2	32	2	76	33	16	15	.291	.336	.383
Curry, Chris, Day.	44	171	155	16	38	50	12	0	0	13	0	1	0	15	1	43	2	0	4	.245	.310	.323
Dacey, Ryan, V.B.	28	89	76	6	13	16	3	0	0	2	0	0	4	9	0	17	0	0	2	.171	.292	.211
Daigle, Leo, Lak.	129	537	466	75	120	212	23	0	23	85	0	5	17	49	3	99	3	1	14	.258	.346	.455
Davenport, Ron, Dun.*	79	286	264	26	60	87	15	3	2	21	2	0	2	18	3	42	5	4	2	.227	.282	.330
Davis, Glenn, B.C.†	11	44	43	2	11	19	5	0	1	5	0	0	0	1	0	12	0	0	1	.256	.273	.442
Delgado, Mario, Cle.*	51	197	187	16	38	59	9	0	4	14	0	1	2	7	0	47	0	0	8	.203	.239	.316
De Los Santos, Eddy, Dun.	3	12	10	2	3	3	0	0	0	4	1	0	0	1	0	2	0	0	0	.300	.364	.300
Demarco, Matt, Jup.*	109	406	368	41	98	117	13	3	0	46	7	5	5	21	1	36	5	2	8	.266	.311	.318
Dempsey, Nick, B.C.	51	175	163	10	41	50	9	0	0	30	0	2	1	9	1	45	1	3	6	.252	.291	.307
Deschenes, Pat, S.L.*	75	284	248	33	74	94	15	1	1	28	0	4	2	30	0	34	0	2	2	.298	.373	.379
Desena, Francis, B.C.	8	9	9	0	1	1	0	0	0	0	0	0	0	0	0	4	0	0	0	.111	.111	.111
Detienne, Dave, V.B.	103	376	342	34	85	122	20	1	5	40	1	5	5	23	0	96	10	4	8	.249	.301	.357
Devarez, Noel, S.L.	34	135	122	18	32	53	9	0	4	21	0	1	3	9	0	41	2	0	3	.262	.326	.434
Diaz, Frank, B.C.	10	37	31	3	7	9	2	0	0	1	0	0	0	6	0	4	3	0	2	.226	.351	.290
Diaz, Jose, V.B.	3	12	10	3	2	5	0	0	1	3	0	0	1	1	0	3	0	0	0	.200	.333	.500
Diaz, Robinzon, Dun.	10	28	25	3	3	3	0	0	0	1	1	1	0	1	0	4	0	0	0	.120	.148	.120
Diggins, Ben, V.B.	21	1	1	0	0	0	0	0	0	0	0	0	0	0	0	0	0	0	0	.000	.000	.000
Dill, Jason, Char.*	83	298	271	32	72	101	17	3	2	38	1	1	1	24	1	49	2	1	8	.266	.327	.373
Dominique, Andy, Cle.	8	36	34	5	14	19	5	0	0	2	0	0	1	1	0	4	0	0	0	.412	.444	.559
Dorta, Melvin, Sar.	99	443	378	46	97	107	8	1	0	31	7	6	3	49	0	54	9	10	7	.257	.342	.283
Downing, Phil, B.C.*	59	188	170	22	41	65	11	2	3	14	0	0	1	17	1	65	0	5	4	.241	.314	.382
Dubois, Jason, Day.	99	431	361	64	116	203	25	1	20	85	0	4	9	57	0	95	6	2	7	.321	.422	.562
Duncan, Jeff, S.L.*	29	128	102	20	35	46	5	0	2	10	1	0	1	24	1	15	10	1	4	.343	.472	.451
Duplissea, Bill, V.B.	25	87	70	10	13	14	1	0	0	7	2	0	1	14	0	20	0	0	1	.186	.329	.200
Durazo, William, Sar.†	7	20	19	0	1	1	0	0	0	0	0	0	0	1	0	3	0	0	1	.053	.100	.053
Dzurilla, Mike, Day.	104	413	363	51	94	152	21	5	9	48	1	7	5	37	2	44	12	6	7	.259	.330	.419
Easterday, Matt, Jup.	81	302	254	42	58	80	9	5	1	30	1	3	6	38	0	41	13	4	4	.228	.339	.315
Elwood, Brad, Tam.	64	229	204	23	39	50	5	0	2	12	2	0	3	20	0	55	1	0	4	.191	.273	.245
Esposito, Brian, Sar.	31	107	99	8	16	27	5	0	2	7	1	1	1	5	0	20	0	0	1	.162	.208	.273
Everett, Carl, Char.†	1	4	4	1	2	4	0	1	0	1	0	0	0	0	0	1	0	0	0	.500	.500	1.000
Farnsworth, Troy, Cle.	97	399	358	35	83	141	18	2	12	50	1	6	6	28	1	85	1	0	7	.232	.294	.394
Ferrand, Frank, Jup.*	31	109	99	8	12	12	0	0	0	7	3	1	1	5	0	19	2	0	4	.121	.170	.121
Figueroa, Luis, B.C.†	15	67	61	8	16	19	1	1	0	8	0	0	1	5	0	2	2	4	3	.262	.328	.311
Flamont, Sam, Lak.*	16	52	45	3	7	8	1	0	0	7	1	1	0	5	0	14	0	1	1	.156	.235	.178
Fowler, David, Tam.	67	208	173	24	34	42	4	2	0	14	7	4	3	21	0	61	3	3	2	.197	.289	.243
Frazier, Charles, Jup.	8	33	29	8	8	9	1	0	0	3	0	0	0	4	0	8	0	1	0	.276	.364	.310
Fuentes, Omar, Tam.	61	237	210	29	56	85	8	0	7	32	0	4	6	17	1	32	0	0	5	.267	.333	.405
Gajewski, Matt, Char.†	9	36	28	3	5	7	0	1	0	1	0	0	1	7	0	10	0	0	2	.179	.361	.250
Garbe, B.J., F.M.	115	476	427	46	102	134	13	2	5	45	1	5	7	36	0	89	18	6	10	.239	.305	.314
Garcia, Daniel, S.L.	122	518	432	69	118	174	34	5	4	52	14	4	15	53	0	77	13	6	9	.273	.369	.403
Garcia, Douglas, Char.*	50	201	189	25	55	88	12	3	5	33	0	0	2	10	1	31	4	1	5	.291	.333	.466
Garcia, Juan-Carlos, Jup.†	10	31	30	2	1	1	0	0	0	0	0	0	0	1	0	14	0	0	0	.033	.065	.033
Garcia, Nick, Sar.	7	16	14	1	2	2	0	0	0	0	0	0	0	2	0	0	1	0	0	.143	.250	.143
Garcia, Tony, Day.	97	340	292	36	73	99	15	1	3	37	4	6	10	28	0	38	16	8	6	.250	.330	.339
Garland, Ross, Lak.	31	98	87	11	18	24	3	0	1	10	0	0	4	7	0	19	0	0	2	.207	.296	.276
Gibbs, Kevin, Tam.†	2	8	5	2	1	1	0	0	0	0	0	0	0	3	0	2	0	1	0	.200	.500	.200
Gingrich, Troy, B.C.*	111	391	334	46	79	101	10	3	2	29	4	1	4	48	1	69	12	8	5	.237	.339	.302
Giron, Alejandro, Cle.	41	156	142	11	32	43	1	2	2	15	1	2	1	10	0	24	2	1	2	.225	.277	.303
Goldbach, Jeff, Day.	76	311	272	40	71	121	17	0	11	47	2	3	4	30	1	43	0	0	2	.261	.340	.445
Gomez, Ramon, Cle.	22	77	68	6	10	15	3	1	0	2	2	0	0	7	0	26	3	2	1	.147	.227	.221
Gonzalez, Manny, Cle.†	76	309	280	20	64	86	15	2	1	24	3	2	3	21	4	48	1	5	3	.229	.288	.307
Greenberg, Adam, Day.*	21	90	73	20	28	42	5	3	1	9	0	0	3	14	1	18	15	2	0	.384	.500	.575
Griffin, John-ford, Tam.*	65	291	255	32	68	95	16	1	3	31	0	4	3	29	0	45	1	0	9	.267	.344	.373
Grove, Jason, Tam.*	75	315	273	37	75	114	18	6	3	35	1	1	4	36	3	62	3	2	10	.275	.366	.418
Gulledge, Kelley, F.M.	76	278	242	29	65	92	9	0	6	34	1	2	11	20	1	60	0	2	4	.269	.349	.380
Hannahan, Jack, Lak.*	66	289	246	28	67	98	11	1	6	42	0	4	1	36	2	44	9	3	2	.272	.362	.398
Harris, Brendan, Day.	110	475	425	82	140	226	35	6	13	54	1	2	4	43	4	57	16	4	7	.329	.395	.532
Harris, Cory, S.L.	26	96	83	10	23	30	4	0	1	15	1	1	4	7	0	8	4	2	0	.277	.358	.361
Hattig, John, Sar.†	24	93	85	6	21	27	6	0	0	6	0	1	0	7	0	16	0	0	2	.247	.301	.318
Heath, Demetrius, Lak.	37	136	128	15	33	45	5	2	1	13	0	1	1	6	0	22	8	3	5	.258	.294	.352
Helps, Jason, Jup.†	25	63	56	8	13	18	3	1	0	7	0	0	2	5	0	13	2	0	0	.232	.317	.321
Hensley, Anthony, Cle.†	119	460	384	56	91	131	18	8	2	24	2	5	3	66	1	81	13	7	9	.237	.349	.341
Hernandez, Anderson, Lak.†	123	458	410	52	106	139	13	7	2	42	10	5	0	33	0	102	16	14	2	.259	.310	.339

Player, Team	G	TPA	AB	R	H	TB	2B	3B	HR	RBI	SH	SF	HP	BB	IBB	SO	SB	CS	GDP	Avg.	OBP	Slg.
Hernandez, Vladimir, B.C.	36	123	108	12	30	32	2	0	0	10	5	3	0	7	0	15	6	3	1	.278	.314	.296
Herrera, Christian, V.B.	27	95	81	10	14	15	1	0	0	5	2	1	1	10	0	23	1	0	0	.173	.269	.185
Hitchcox, Brian, Cle.*	32	136	121	17	30	37	4	0	1	12	0	1	2	12	0	17	4	3	2	.248	.324	.306
Hooper, Clay, Tam.	16	64	54	9	15	18	3	0	0	0	0	0	1	9	0	9	0	3	3	.278	.391	.333
Howarth, Jason, F.M.	8	24	22	1	3	3	0	0	0	2	0	0	0	2	0	7	0	0	0	.136	.208	.136
Huber, Justin, S.L.	28	119	100	15	27	40	2	1	3	15	0	2	6	11	0	18	0	0	3	.270	.370	.400
Iorg, Isaac, Dun.	23	86	80	8	20	25	5	0	0	7	0	0	1	5	0	20	0	0	1	.250	.302	.313
Jackson, Brandon, Tam.	43	167	139	16	25	27	2	0	0	8	1	1	5	21	0	31	3	0	3	.180	.307	.194
Jacobs, Mike, S.L.*	118	501	467	62	117	178	26	1	11	64	0	5	4	25	5	95	2	3	11	.251	.291	.381
Jaile, Chris, Char.	76	274	238	19	42	50	4	2	0	16	8	1	0	27	1	50	0	0	6	.176	.259	.210
Jenkins, Neil, Lak.	56	239	228	27	55	98	9	2	10	34	0	0	2	9	0	87	3	0	4	.241	.276	.430
Jimenez, Rich, Dun.†	4	16	12	1	2	2	0	0	0	2	2	0	1	1	1	3	0	0	1	.167	.286	.167
Johnson, Charles, Jup.	5	18	16	5	7	16	0	0	3	9	0	0	0	2	0	4	0	0	0	.438	.500	1.000
Johnson, Forrest, Lak.	12	52	47	4	9	13	1	0	1	2	0	0	3	2	0	8	0	1	2	.191	.269	.277
Johnson, Jeremy, Dun.*	12	38	33	4	10	13	3	0	0	4	1	0	1	3	0	9	0	0	0	.303	.378	.394
Johnson, Reed, Dun.	8	38	33	7	9	12	3	0	0	6	0	0	2	3	0	3	0	1	0	.273	.368	.364
Johnstone, Ben, Day.	81	267	240	32	56	62	6	0	0	22	7	3	3	13	0	34	18	13	6	.233	.278	.258
Jones, Jeremy, Char.	1	4	4	0	1	1	0	0	0	1	0	0	0	0	0	1	0	0	0	.250	.250	.250
Jones, Mitch, Tam.	61	255	229	36	61	119	19	0	13	49	0	3	3	20	1	71	0	0	8	.266	.329	.520
Jorgensen, Ryan, Jup.	60	251	223	26	58	83	16	0	3	35	3	0	1	24	0	38	4	1	4	.260	.335	.372
Kavourias, Jim, Jup.	97	386	337	42	72	114	17	2	7	35	0	0	8	41	0	90	7	4	10	.214	.313	.338
Kay, Brett, S.L.	64	264	221	37	49	73	6	0	6	20	3	0	11	29	1	37	6	1	6	.222	.341	.330
Keene, Kurt, Dun.	108	424	379	46	99	121	17	1	1	37	3	2	1	39	2	39	6	2	12	.261	.330	.319
Kellner, Ryan, V.B.	25	100	89	9	18	22	1	0	1	7	2	0	4	5	0	14	0	1	4	.202	.276	.247
Kelly, Heath, Jup.	1	4	4	0	0	0	0	0	0	0	0	0	0	0	0	1	0	0	0	.000	.000	.000
Kinchen, Jason, Tam.*	7	27	25	1	5	5	0	0	0	3	0	0	1	1	0	4	0	0	0	.200	.259	.200
Kropf, Andy, Lak.†	5	21	19	2	9	10	1	0	0	3	0	0	1	1	0	2	0	0	1	.474	.524	.526
Kweon, Yoon-Min, Day.	88	335	300	32	66	92	11	0	5	36	3	3	6	23	1	34	1	4	10	.220	.286	.307
Lane, Rich, B.C.*	121	495	454	54	123	166	27	2	4	50	2	3	2	34	5	97	7	1	17	.271	.323	.366
Langs, Ronte, V.B.	50	209	190	21	39	52	3	2	2	17	2	2	1	14	0	50	7	5	3	.205	.261	.274
Lepine, Olivier, Jup.	1	1	0	1	0	0	0	0	0	0	0	0	0	1	0	0	0	0	0	.000	1.000	.000
Liniak, Cole, Char.	33	131	116	13	32	41	3	0	2	19	1	2	3	9	0	15	4	1	6	.276	.338	.353
Logan, Nook, Lak.†	124	554	506	75	136	170	14	7	2	26	6	2	0	40	0	111	55	16	2	.269	.321	.336
Loney, James, V.B.*	17	74	67	6	20	26	6	0	0	5	1	0	0	6	0	10	0	0	2	.299	.356	.388
Lopez, Angel, Jup.	45	158	142	20	32	65	7	1	8	21	1	1	1	13	0	42	1	0	1	.225	.293	.458
Lopez, Gustavo, Jup.	19	3	3	0	0	0	0	0	0	0	0	0	0	0	0	2	0	0	0	.000	.000	.000
Lynam, Guy, Jup.	4	11	11	0	0	0	0	0	0	0	0	0	0	0	0	7	0	0	1	.000	.000	.000
Machado, Albenis, B.C.†	5	22	18	3	5	6	1	0	0	0	1	0	0	3	0	1	0	0	1	.278	.381	.333
Magness, Pat, Jup.*	111	481	390	73	114	190	26	1	16	73	1	6	5	79	4	86	2	1	7	.292	.413	.487
Martin, Tyler, Char.†	115	463	375	61	102	178	20	4	16	60	4	5	9	70	1	70	7	4	3	.272	.394	.475
Martinez, Candido, V.B.	24	101	88	11	17	27	2	1	2	14	1	1	2	9	0	27	6	3	2	.193	.280	.307
Martinez, Casey, Dun.	7	15	12	1	1	1	0	0	0	0	0	0	1	2	0	3	0	0	1	.083	.267	.083
Martinez, Ramon, Char.†	114	521	472	98	144	190	21	8	3	41	5	6	6	32	4	44	39	15	15	.305	.353	.403
Marx, Tommy, Lak.	30	3	2	0	0	0	0	0	0	0	1	0	0	0	0	1	0	0	0	.000	.000	.000
Maza, Luis, F.M.	105	391	344	44	83	116	15	3	4	38	10	5	13	19	0	53	4	6	6	.241	.302	.337
McEachran, Aaron, Dun.*	90	319	283	27	72	91	17	1	0	31	1	2	3	30	3	58	2	0	10	.254	.330	.322
McKnight, Lukas, Day.*	1	2	2	1	1	1	0	0	0	1	0	0	0	0	0	1	0	0	0	.500	.500	.500
McMillan, Drew, B.C.	48	178	158	14	27	49	1	0	7	18	1	1	6	12	0	50	0	0	4	.171	.254	.310
McNaughton, Troy, Cle.*	87	372	324	50	110	181	20	6	13	45	1	2	6	39	3	74	2	1	5	.340	.418	.559
McRoberts, Mark, Cle.	1	2	2	0	0	0	0	0	0	0	0	0	0	0	0	1	0	0	0	.000	.000	.000
Mendez, Deivi, Tam.	2	6	6	2	2	5	0	0	1	1	0	0	0	0	0	1	0	0	0	.333	.333	.833
Michaelis, Derek, V.B.*	122	474	426	59	113	202	30	4	17	58	0	3	1	44	0	114	0	0	5	.265	.333	.474
Miller, Eric, B.C.	129	515	472	49	121	149	19	3	1	38	11	2	2	28	0	62	8	8	21	.256	.300	.316
Money, Freddie, Sar.	120	446	397	56	93	101	6	1	0	34	0	4	8	35	0	74	22	9	12	.234	.306	.254
Montague, Ed, V.B.*	28	100	89	5	19	29	4	0	2	14	0	0	1	10	0	18	1	3	1	.213	.300	.326
Montanez, Luis, Day.	124	547	487	69	129	172	21	5	4	59	0	7	9	44	0	89	14	8	16	.265	.333	.353
Montas, Ricardo, Cle.	16	54	47	6	9	13	1	0	1	5	0	0	0	7	0	5	2	0	2	.191	.296	.277
Mooney, Dan, Sar.	20	71	67	3	13	16	3	0	0	7	0	1	3	0	0	16	0	0	1	.194	.225	.239
Moore, Jason, Char.†	5	21	20	2	3	5	2	0	0	1	0	0	0	1	0	2	0	0	0	.150	.190	.250
Morban, Jose, Char.	126	547	485	75	126	201	27	12	8	66	10	3	3	46	1	111	21	9	2	.260	.326	.414
Myrow, Brian, Tam.*	61	279	225	29	63	92	12	1	5	40	0	3	9	42	2	45	0	0	4	.280	.409	.409
Navarro, Dioner, Tam.†	1	2	2	1	1	1	0	0	0	0	0	0	0	0	0	0	0	0	0	.500	.500	.500
Navarro, Mandy, Day.†	11	40	23	7	3	4	1	0	0	3	3	0	0	14	0	7	2	1	1	.130	.459	.174
Neill, Ryan, Lak.	43	166	143	24	28	43	6	0	3	13	0	1	2	20	0	43	8	1	4	.196	.301	.301
Nicolas, Jose, B.C.	4	9	9	0	0	0	0	0	0	1	0	0	0	0	0	3	0	0	1	.000	.000	.000
Nieves, Raul, Sar.†	93	330	299	36	76	87	11	0	0	19	4	2	2	23	1	36	5	4	4	.254	.310	.291
Nix, Laynce, Char.*	137	599	512	86	146	242	27	3	21	110	0	9	6	72	8	105	17	1	9	.285	.374	.473
Nunez, Alexis, Cle.*	10	31	25	3	4	6	2	0	0	1	1	0	1	4	0	6	0	2	0	.160	.300	.240
Ochoa, Javier, S.L.	2	7	7	0	2	2	0	0	0	1	0	0	0	0	0	2	0	0	0	.286	.286	.286
Olivari, Reinaldo, Char.	4	12	8	1	0	0	0	0	0	0	0	0	1	3	0	0	0	0	0	.000	.333	.000
O'Sullivan, Patrick, S.L.	10	30	24	3	6	13	1	0	2	7	0	1	3	2	0	8	0	1	1	.250	.367	.542
Pack, Branden, Char.†	13	39	37	4	8	14	3	0	1	9	0	1	0	1	0	9	0	0	1	.216	.231	.378
Pagan, Angel, S.L.†	16	75	67	12	23	30	2	1	1	7	1	0	0	7	1	9	10	2	5	.343	.405	.448
Perez, Kenny, Sar.†	121	506	447	53	112	138	12	4	2	28	2	3	3	51	0	58	16	5	15	.251	.329	.309
Perry, Jason, Dun.*	13	54	45	7	13	19	3	0	1	5	0	1	3	5	0	11	0	0	0	.289	.389	.422
Perry, Rod, Cle.	7	26	24	3	3	3	0	0	0	1	1	0	0	1	0	4	0	0	1	.125	.160	.125
Petersen, Ryan, Sar.	1	1	0	0	0	0	0	0	0	0	1	0	0	0	0	0	0	0	0	.000	.000	.000
Piercy, Mike, B.C.*	9	17	13	4	2	2	0	0	0	0	0	0	0	4	0	1	1	0	0	.154	.353	.154
Pineda, Jairo, Lak.	33	1	1	1	1	4	0	0	1	1	0	0	0	0	0	0	0	0	0	1.000	1.000	4.000
Pittman, Sean, S.L.†	44	147	129	11	33	47	9	1	1	16	0	2	0	16	0	36	2	1	5	.256	.333	.364
Pond, Simon, Dun.*	103	457	401	58	114	192	25	7	13	88	1	6	3	46	11	73	2	3	9	.284	.357	.479
Price, Jared, V.B.	12	42	35	0	7	8	1	0	0	1	0	0	1	6	0	16	0	0	0	.200	.333	.229
Quattlebaum, Hugh, Lak.	20	69	58	8	9	11	2	0	0	1	1	0	0	10	0	16	0	1	1	.155	.279	.190
Quiroz, Guillermo, Dun.	111	460	411	50	107	173	28	1	12	68	2	3	9	35	2	91	1	0	18	.260	.330	.421

Player, Team	G	TPA	AB	R	H	TB	2B	3B	HR	RBI	SH	SF	HP	BB	IBB	SO	SB	CS	GDP	Avg.	OBP	Slg.
Rabe, Josh, F.M.	85	349	297	60	101	143	23	2	5	40	2	3	3	44	2	36	16	4	10	.340	.427	.481
Radwan, Jason, V.B.	11	40	37	4	8	12	1	0	1	4	0	0	0	3	0	7	0	0	1	.216	.275	.324
Renick, Josh, F.M.	107	426	368	61	100	119	14	1	1	26	5	2	7	44	0	68	10	10	13	.272	.359	.323
Repko, Jason, V.B.	120	513	470	73	128	194	29	5	9	53	8	2	8	25	1	92	29	13	3	.272	.319	.413
Reyes, Ambiorix, Cle.	47	141	131	11	21	24	3	0	0	4	4	1	0	5	0	21	3	2	2	.160	.190	.183
Reyes, Deurys, F.M.*	90	283	229	48	55	95	9	8	5	32	4	4	3	43	1	59	8	7	2	.240	.362	.415
Reyes, Jose, S.L.†	69	327	288	58	83	133	10	11	6	38	4	4	1	30	1	35	31	13	5	.288	.353	.462
Rich, Dominic, Dun.*	95	448	377	72	130	178	14	5	8	50	4	3	7	57	9	49	8	6	5	.345	.437	.472
Richardson, Juan, Cle.	122	516	456	52	117	196	21	2	18	83	0	2	14	44	1	122	0	6	17	.257	.339	.430
Rifkin, Aaron, Tam.*	66	276	252	33	70	99	11	0	6	44	0	3	1	20	1	52	1	3	7	.278	.330	.393
Rigsby, Randy, Jup.*	27	111	103	11	28	37	4	1	1	15	1	1	1	5	0	25	3	1	3	.272	.309	.359
Rios, Alexis, Dun.	111	492	456	60	139	186	22	8	3	61	1	5	3	27	0	55	14	8	19	.305	.344	.408
Rivas, Luis, F.M.	6	24	22	1	2	4	0	1	0	3	0	0	0	2	0	2	1	0	0	.091	.167	.182
Rivera, Eric, Cle.	4	17	16	1	2	3	1	0	0	1	0	0	0	1	0	2	0	0	0	.125	.176	.188
Rodriguez, Carlos, Sar.	127	510	472	59	104	176	27	3	13	59	0	2	10	26	6	129	6	5	14	.220	.275	.373
Rodriguez, Edgar, S.L.	8	31	29	3	6	17	1	2	2	8	0	0	0	2	0	9	0	1	0	.207	.258	.586
Rodriguez, Ivan, Char.	3	9	9	1	3	3	0	0	0	0	0	0	0	0	0	3	0	0	0	.333	.333	.333
Rombley, Danny, B.C.	54	210	191	26	56	71	6	3	1	16	2	2	2	13	1	36	15	7	4	.293	.341	.372
Roneberg, Brett, Jup.*	15	64	57	4	12	15	1	1	0	7	0	0	0	7	0	11	1	1	1	.211	.297	.263
Rooi, Vince, B.C.	118	432	367	38	71	96	11	1	4	38	8	3	2	52	4	86	7	5	3	.193	.295	.262
Roper, Zach, Char.	6	27	24	1	6	6	0	0	0	2	0	0	1	2	0	7	0	0	1	.250	.333	.250
Ruiz, Carlos, Cle.	92	369	342	35	73	112	18	3	5	32	2	1	6	18	1	30	3	1	16	.213	.264	.327
Rundles, Rich, B.C.*	12	3	3	0	0	0	0	0	0	0	0	0	0	0	0	1	0	0	1	.000	.000	.000
Sadler, Ray, Day.	112	499	462	81	132	198	31	1	11	47	3	1	6	27	2	91	30	12	7	.286	.333	.429
St. Pierre, Maxim, Lak.	55	216	195	20	50	74	12	0	4	27	0	1	7	13	0	30	2	4	4	.256	.324	.379
Sanchez, Danilo, Lak.	34	115	96	10	17	28	2	0	3	12	3	0	3	13	0	18	0	0	4	.177	.295	.292
Sandberg, Eric, F.M.*	19	72	65	5	15	20	5	0	0	8	0	0	1	6	0	13	0	0	1	.231	.306	.308
Santoro, Pat, Sar.	27	108	95	15	21	40	7	0	4	17	0	0	2	11	0	34	1	2	1	.221	.315	.421
Santos, Jose, Jup.	29	112	98	14	23	36	5	4	0	5	1	1	3	9	0	33	2	0	5	.235	.315	.367
Scanlon, Matt, F.M.*	47	186	164	28	53	83	8	2	6	37	0	1	2	19	0	11	1	1	5	.323	.398	.506
Schnabel, Nick, B.C.	17	64	56	3	11	11	0	0	0	0	1	0	0	7	0	11	0	0	0	.196	.286	.196
Seale, Marvin, S.L.†	127	552	477	72	118	169	19	4	8	57	4	6	11	54	2	109	38	13	3	.247	.334	.354
Segar, Jeff, Tam.	5	21	19	1	4	5	1	0	0	4	0	1	0	1	0	4	0	0	2	.211	.238	.263
Shoppach, Kelly, Sar.	116	480	414	54	112	179	35	1	10	66	0	1	6	59	2	112	2	1	11	.271	.369	.432
Silvestre, Juan, Char.	1	5	4	1	0	0	0	0	0	1	0	0	0	1	0	1	0	0	0	.000	.200	.000
Sing, Brandon, Day.	125	516	440	65	109	191	18	5	18	64	1	5	6	64	1	96	5	7	10	.248	.348	.434
Singleton, Justin, Dun.*	101	407	354	54	96	136	17	7	3	38	4	4	3	42	0	91	9	5	4	.271	.350	.384
Sisk, Aaron, Dun.	78	280	239	32	53	87	13	3	5	23	2	1	2	36	1	57	0	3	7	.222	.327	.364
Sizemore, Grady, B.C.*	75	296	256	37	66	89	15	4	0	26	0	2	2	36	3	41	9	9	6	.258	.351	.348
Slavik, Corey, Day.*	10	41	35	1	9	14	3	1	0	3	1	1	1	3	0	5	0	1	0	.257	.325	.400
Smith, Will, Sar.	80	357	277	51	71	99	12	5	2	23	6	0	11	63	0	55	14	5	6	.256	.413	.357
Smith, Will, Jup.*	133	591	549	84	164	260	30	12	14	73	0	6	3	31	4	75	8	3	13	.299	.336	.474
Socarras, Tony, B.C.-V.B.*	67	202	175	21	35	70	11	0	8	30	0	4	3	20	0	56	0	0	0	.200	.287	.400
Soler, Ramon, S.L.†	21	76	64	11	13	17	4	0	0	4	4	0	1	7	0	13	10	2	1	.203	.292	.266
Sosa, Juan, Cle.	54	227	210	17	55	68	9	2	0	16	3	1	2	11	0	28	9	2	3	.262	.304	.324
Sosa, Nick, F.M.	25	108	90	10	25	37	9	0	1	14	0	1	2	15	0	27	1	0	5	.278	.389	.411
Soules, Ryan, Char.*	52	215	174	26	39	65	9	1	5	30	1	3	2	35	0	42	2	1	4	.224	.355	.374
Tarbett, Brent, Sar.	3	12	11	1	1	2	1	0	0	0	0	0	0	1	0	3	0	0	1	.091	.167	.182
Tatis, Fernando, B.C.	6	23	17	2	4	5	1	0	0	2	0	1	2	3	1	4	0	0	1	.235	.391	.294
Teixeira, Mark, Char.†	38	175	150	32	48	89	10	2	9	41	0	1	3	21	2	24	2	0	4	.320	.411	.593
Tempesta, Nick, Dun.	18	68	59	7	11	15	4	0	0	3	2	1	3	3	0	10	0	0	0	.186	.258	.254
Thomas, Charles, V.B.	80	295	266	31	65	94	13	2	4	37	3	2	2	22	0	69	10	5	4	.244	.305	.353
Thompson, Kevin, Tam.	25	106	87	10	16	21	5	0	0	7	2	2	2	13	0	15	11	1	3	.184	.298	.241
Tiffee, Terry, F.M.†	126	509	473	47	133	188	31	0	8	64	3	6	2	25	3	49	0	3	12	.281	.316	.397
Torres, Digno, F.M.*	48	159	138	9	24	27	3	0	0	11	0	2	2	17	1	36	0	2	4	.174	.270	.196
Torres, Frederick, Char.	58	197	183	23	44	70	11	0	5	22	2	1	0	11	0	43	0	0	4	.240	.282	.383
Tousa, Scott, Lak.*	117	479	395	55	85	108	14	0	3	33	7	3	6	68	1	75	14	4	6	.215	.337	.273
Turner, Jason, Tam.*	36	150	135	16	31	36	5	0	0	8	0	1	0	13	0	24	1	0	4	.230	.295	.267
Tyson, Torre, Tam.†	85	380	309	58	67	96	12	4	3	26	5	4	6	56	0	42	10	4	2	.217	.344	.311
Umbria, Jose, Dun.	17	59	49	3	19	20	1	0	0	8	1	0	0	9	0	8	0	1	0	.388	.483	.408
Ust, Brant, Lak.	61	243	216	26	51	82	12	2	5	29	1	2	3	21	0	47	9	0	6	.236	.310	.380
Valencia, Vic, Char.	80	304	256	37	62	101	13	1	8	33	1	3	2	42	0	68	0	0	11	.242	.350	.395
Van Buizen, Rodney, V.B.	131	540	497	74	139	195	24	4	8	51	4	1	16	22	2	59	17	8	10	.280	.330	.392
Vasquez, Wuillians, Tam.†	2	9	8	0	0	0	0	0	0	0	0	0	0	1	0	2	0	0	0	.000	.111	.000
Vaz, Roberto, Char.*	2	5	4	1	1	2	1	0	0	1	0	0	0	1	0	0	0	0	0	.250	.400	.500
Velazquez, Gil, S.L.	33	125	118	13	25	31	6	0	0	16	1	0	0	6	0	30	2	0	1	.212	.250	.263
Walker, Matt, Lak.	112	448	409	66	100	162	23	0	13	53	3	2	5	29	1	94	10	1	11	.244	.301	.396
Warren, Chris, Sar.	13	49	41	1	6	9	1	1	0	4	1	0	2	5	0	13	0	0	1	.146	.271	.220
Watkins, Tommy, F.M.	94	310	269	38	63	79	10	0	2	24	7	2	3	29	0	46	10	5	5	.234	.314	.294
Watson, Brandon, B.C.*	111	467	424	57	113	133	16	2	0	24	11	2	3	27	0	53	22	13	5	.267	.314	.314
West, Kevin, F.M.	129	510	444	62	122	191	25	4	12	64	0	9	11	46	4	96	7	4	16	.275	.351	.430
Williams, Brady, F.M.†	50	174	141	26	33	61	7	0	7	26	0	4	2	27	1	49	2	0	4	.234	.356	.433
Williams, Jason, B.C.	68	204	179	19	36	53	9	1	2	18	2	3	0	20	0	53	0	2	2	.201	.277	.296
Willingham, Josh, Jup.	107	454	376	72	103	183	21	4	17	69	0	2	13	63	0	88	18	5	7	.274	.394	.487
Wilson, John, S.L.	46	181	151	24	36	65	7	2	6	21	1	2	3	24	0	27	4	1	4	.238	.350	.430
Wilson, Josh, Jup.	111	443	398	51	102	154	17	1	11	50	3	4	10	28	0	67	7	10	6	.256	.318	.387
Woods, Michael, Lak.	33	143	111	20	25	45	6	4	2	11	0	2	2	28	0	25	7	5	2	.225	.385	.405
Woodward, Chris, Dun.	2	7	6	1	2	2	0	0	0	0	0	0	1	0	0	0	0	0	0	.333	.429	.333
Wright, Corey, Char.-Sar.*	70	271	233	25	44	63	7	3	2	18	5	1	5	27	0	62	4	1	6	.189	.286	.270
Youkilis, Kevin, Sar.	76	339	268	45	79	104	16	0	3	48	0	7	15	49	2	37	0	2	5	.295	.422	.388
Youngbauer, Scott, Cle.†	106	452	406	60	96	162	25	7	9	47	2	4	2	38	3	78	3	4	5	.236	.302	.399
Yount, Andy, Lak.	39	151	123	10	19	30	3	1	2	15	0	0	5	23	0	56	1	3	3	.154	.311	.244
Zapey, Winton, Jup.	6	23	22	1	3	6	0	0	1	3	1	0	0	0	0	8	0	0	1	.136	.136	.273
Zieour, Neesan, Dun.	57	199	178	23	40	48	8	0	0	15	1	1	3	16	1	29	2	1	3	.225	.298	.270

Player, Team	G	TPA	AB	R	H	TB	2B	3B	HR	RBI	SH	SF	HP	BB	IBB	SO	SB	CS	GDP	Avg.	OBP	Slg.
Blasi, Blake, Day.†	3	11	11	2	4	4	0	0	0	1	0	0	0	0	0	2	1	0	0	.364	.364	.364
Blasi, Blake, Sar.†	37	159	139	9	32	39	4	0	1	9	1	0	2	17	1	31	5	0	3	.230	.323	.281
Socarras, Tony, B.C.*	46	128	113	13	17	38	6	0	5	19	0	3	1	11	0	40	0	0	0	.150	.227	.336
Socarras, Tony, V.B.*	21	74	62	8	18	32	5	0	3	11	0	1	2	9	0	16	0	0	0	.290	.392	.516
Wright, Corey, Char.*	56	216	183	25	35	51	6	2	2	16	5	1	4	23	0	52	4	0	5	.191	.294	.279
Wright, Corey, Sar.*	14	55	50	0	9	12	1	1	0	2	0	1	0	4	0	10	0	1	1	.180	.255	.240

GRAND SLAMS: Barbier 3, Blum, A. Brown, Camilo, Nix, Richardson, 2 each; R. Adams, Aybar, Botts, Brazzell, Brisson, Cabrera, Cannizaro, Cleveland, Corporan, Daigle, Detienne, Jacobs, Jenkins, C. Johnson, M. Jones, Magness, Morban, Rios, Sacarras, Sadler, Shoppach, Tiffee, Youngbauer, Yount, 1 each.

AWARDED FIRST BASE ON CATCHER'S INTERFERENCE: Gulledge 2 (Jacobs, Kay), Hannahan 2 (Aracena 2), Money 2 (McEachran 2), W. Smith (Aracena, Kay), Avila (Gulledge), Bozanich (An. Lopez), Johnstone (Kay), Turner (Sanchez).

2002 PITCHING
TEAM

Team	W	L	Pct.	ERA	G	CG	ShO	Sv.	IP	H	TBF	R	ER	HR	SH	SF	HB	BB	IBB	SO	WP	Bk.
Charlotte	84	56	.600	3.40	140	0	16	47	1224.0	1025	5159	554	462	66	25	29	69	471	15	922	87	8
Jupiter	81	57	.587	3.41	138	1	11	38	1228.1	1159	5154	550	465	64	29	40	54	374	8	944	66	14
Tampa	71	62	.534	3.56	133	2	13	30	1149.1	1081	4948	560	454	62	29	47	61	434	12	954	69	20
Fort Myers	77	62	.554	3.67	139	4	13	43	1193.1	1178	5164	591	486	80	38	31	74	463	26	927	66	12
Vero Beach	72	63	.533	3.87	135	6	13	38	1166.0	1089	4990	574	502	86	36	43	81	434	12	1009	90	9
Brevard County	51	85	.375	3.88	136	2	5	24	1174.0	1142	5054	613	506	94	40	34	58	449	18	814	63	3
Clearwater	57	79	.419	3.93	136	12	11	30	1188.1	1157	5150	605	519	78	42	47	75	464	16	833	65	7
Sarasota	62	74	.456	3.97	136	2	11	32	1174.0	1144	5067	617	518	76	50	51	51	442	25	836	71	2
St. Lucie	71	69	.507	3.99	140	6	11	32	1224.0	1176	5348	660	542	73	31	41	99	483	2	943	102	7
Lakeland	69	70	.496	4.13	139	9	10	32	1206.0	1125	5206	643	553	113	38	47	79	529	9	867	67	18
Dunedin	63	72	.467	4.25	135	3	10	34	1202.0	1204	5290	671	568	108	29	43	65	527	25	893	83	9
Daytona	64	73	.467	4.31	137	3	7	26	1198.0	1223	5318	682	574	78	37	46	85	483	32	997	99	11

INDIVIDUAL

TOP QUALIFIERS FOR EARNED-RUN AVERAGE TITLE

Minimum 112 innings. *Lefthanded pitcher.

Pitcher, Team	W	L	Pct.	ERA	G	GS	CG	ShO	GF	Sv.	IP	H	TBF	R	ER	HR	SH	SF	HB	BB	IBB	SO	WP	Bk.
Ford, Matt, Dun.*	9	5	.643	2.37	21	18	0	0	1	0	114	100	466	43	30	7	3	2	2	42	0	85	2	1
Larrison, Preston, Lak.	10	5	.667	2.39	21	19	3	1	0	0	120.1	86	489	39	32	6	5	2	6	45	1	92	13	4
Grace, Bryan, Tam.	8	6	.571	2.86	23	21	0	0	1	0	119.2	101	507	46	38	3	2	6	1	61	0	70	12	4
Foote, Joe, F.M.	12	7	.632	3.11	26	23	2	1	1	0	144.2	141	604	64	50	9	4	3	10	35	0	92	4	0
Reynolds, Josh, S.L.	11	5	.688	3.13	22	20	1	0	1	0	126.1	123	528	51	44	10	5	4	9	26	0	70	0	0
McNutt, Mike, Jup.	12	8	.600	3.17	27	23	0	0	2	2	144.2	138	602	66	51	8	1	8	8	33	0	102	7	1
Chipperfield, Calvin, Lak.	9	10	.474	3.29	27	20	3	1	2	0	126	97	542	57	46	4	4	3	11	74	0	114	5	1
Buchholz, Taylor, Cle.	10	6	.625	3.29	23	23	4	2	0	0	158.2	140	666	66	58	11	3	3	7	51	1	129	7	0
Lockwood, Luke, B.C.*	10	7	.588	3.37	26	26	0	0	0	0	147	155	616	69	55	13	2	5	6	38	0	86	3	0
Gassner, Dave, Dun.*	11	6	.647	3.44	23	21	2	1	0	0	146.2	143	600	64	56	17	5	4	4	26	1	104	4	1
Frasor, Jason, Lak.	5	6	.455	3.54	24	24	0	0	0	0	117	112	494	54	46	10	2	2	8	46	1	87	2	2
Hernandez, Yoel, Cle.	7	16	.304	3.54	28	28	3	0	0	0	170.1	176	731	76	67	6	10	6	12	54	3	116	10	1
Diggins, Ben, V.B.	10	10	.375	3.63	20	19	0	0	0	0	114	103	487	54	46	8	3	1	10	41	1	101	10	0
De La Rosa, Jorge, Sar.*	7	7	.500	3.65	23	23	1	1	0	0	120.2	105	515	53	49	10	1	2	6	52	1	95	5	1
Dequin, Benji, B.C.*	6	9	.400	3.89	27	27	0	0	0	0	143.1	145	622	70	62	7	3	3	6	58	1	111	6	1

DEPARTMENTAL LEADERS: W—Foote, McNutt, 12 each; L—Hernandez, 16; Pct.—C. Wilson, .833; G—Kemp, 59; GS—Hernandez, Krawiec, 28 each; CG—Buchholz, 4; ShO—Buchholz, 2; GF—Flannery, 52; Sv.—Urdaneta, 32; IP—Hernandez, 170.1; H—Messenger, 178; TBF—Hernandez, 731; R—Bucktrot, 101; ER—Bucktrot, 87; HR—Gassner, Wolfe, 17 each; SH—Hernandez, 10; SF—Marx, 11; HB—Bucktrot, 19; BB—Marx, 83; IBB—Contreras, Dean, Fontana, 6 each; SO—Hanrahan, 139; WP—Viole, 21; BK—Flannery, 5.

ALL PITCHERS

*Lefthanded pitcher.

Pitcher, Team	W	L	Pct.	ERA	G	GS	CG	ShO	GF	Sv.	IP	H	TBF	R	ER	HR	SH	SF	HB	BB	IBB	SO	WP	Bk.
Abbott, David, Dun.	6	5	.545	4.13	17	16	1	0	0	0	104.2	114	452	54	48	9	2	5	6	32	0	49	5	0
Adams, Brian, Sar.*	0	2	.000	1.58	21	0	0	0	4	1	45.2	27	181	8	1	3	1	4	25	1	28	0	0
Adams, Daniel, Cle.	3	6	.333	4.31	35	1	0	0	20	4	62.2	55	260	31	30	6	2	5	2	19	1	29	2	0
Albright, Eric, Day.	0	0	.000	7.94	12	0	0	0	3	2	17	27	88	17	15	3	1	1	0	10	0	14	3	0
Almanza, Armando, Jup.*	0	0	.000	0.00	6	5	0	0	0	0	6.2	1	23	0	0	0	0	0	3	0	6	0	0
Alvarez, Gabriel, V.B.	0	0	.000	11.81	3	0	0	0	1	0	5.1	12	33	7	7	1	0	1	1	4	0	4	0	0
Alvarez, Larry, Day.	1	0	1.000	0.00	1	0	0	0	1	0	2	1	8	0	0	0	0	1	1	0	0	0	0
An, Byeong, Sar.*	4	7	.364	5.33	25	12	0	0	8	0	98	102	424	64	58	8	5	3	2	33	1	58	3	0
Anderson, Jason, Tam.	4	2	.667	4.07	12	3	0	0	3	1	24.1	27	102	13	11	2	1	2	0	3	0	22	2	1
Andrew, Jason, Char.	0	0	.000	2.25	1	1	0	0	0	0	4	3	15	1	1	0	0	0	0	3	0	0
Andrews, Aron, V.B.	1	5	.167	4.70	25	0	0	0	10	0	38.1	44	165	21	20	3	1	2	1	7	1	31	1	0
Arnold, Jason, Tam.	7	1	.875	2.48	13	13	0	0	0	0	80	64	330	27	22	2	2	9	22	0	83	8	3
Arrojo, Rolando, Sar.	0	0	.000	0.00	1	0	0	0	0	0	2	2	7	0	0	0	0	0	0	0	2	0	0
Arthurs, Shane, B.C.	0	10	.000	5.13	23	10	0	0	4	0	72	87	342	55	41	1	4	2	7	40	2	42	12	0
Artiles, Carlos, Tam.*	2	0	1.000	7.91	17	0	0	0	3	0	19.1	20	96	22	17	3	0	1	1	20	0	12	4	1
Baker, Brad, Sar.	7	1	.875	2.79	12	12	1	0	0	0	61.1	53	256	22	19	4	2	1	1	25	1	65	6	0
Barnett, John, Char.	3	0	1.000	1.44	9	7	0	0	0	0	43.2	21	159	7	7	3	0	0	1	8	0	28	2	0
Bauer, Greg, V.B.	2	0	1.000	2.08	9	0	0	0	2	1	26	16	100	9	6	1	0	0	3	0	27	2	0
Bautista, Denny, Jup.	4	6	.400	4.99	19	15	0	0	1	0	88.1	80	379	52	49	6	3	2	4	40	0	79	15	3
Beal, Andy, Tam.*	6	0	1.000	2.65	10	10	0	0	0	0	54.1	59	233	19	16	0	1	2	1	13	0	37	2	0
Bean, Colter, Tam.	2	2	.500	1.98	46	0	0	0	25	9	54.2	34	226	17	12	2	3	2	5	21	2	78	1	0

Pitcher, Team	W	L	Pct.	ERA	G	GS	CG	ShO	GF	Sv.	IP	H	TBF	R	ER	HR	SH	SF	HB	BB	IBB	SO	WP	Bk.
Beckett, Josh, Jup.	1	0	1.000	0.00	1	1	0	0	0	0	6	4	24	0	0	0	0	0	0	1	0	12	0	0
Beirne, Kevin, V.B.	0	0	.000	0.00	1	0	0	0	0	0	2	1	7	0	0	0	0	0	0	0	0	2	0	0
Benik, Brett, Day.	2	2	.500	7.99	5	5	0	0	0	0	23.2	37	112	23	21	3	1	2	4	3	1	14	0	0
Benitez, Fabricio, Sar.	1	0	1.000	4.94	10	0	0	0	5	1	23.2	32	102	14	13	3	0	1	0	4	1	10	0	0
Bennett, Steve, S.L.	5	5	.500	1.97	41	0	0	0	28	7	68.2	43	294	19	15	4	2	9	37	2	73	6	0	
Benoit, Joaquin, Char.	0	0	.000	0.00	1	1	0	0	0	0	5	1	20	0	0	0	0	0	0	3	0	8	0	0
Bentz, Chad, B.C.*	0	1	.000	3.64	23	0	0	0	16	5	29.2	30	136	14	12	1	3	1	2	14	2	34	2	0
Berry, Jon, V.B.	2	4	.333	5.84	13	11	0	0	2	0	49.1	56	237	35	32	5	1	2	6	33	0	32	8	1
Blalock, Casey, Jup.	0	1	.000	1.50	4	0	0	0	1	0	6	7	27	1	1	0	1	0	2	1	6	0	0	
Blaney, Matthew, Sar.	0	0	.000	9.00	1	0	0	0	1	0	1	1	5	2	1	0	0	0	1	0	1	1	0	
Blankenship, John, Tam.*	4	5	.444	4.07	13	12	1	1	0	0	66.1	64	281	34	30	5	1	2	3	20	2	48	0	0
Blanton, Jason, Day.	2	2	.500	2.29	20	0	0	0	7	2	39.1	25	153	14	10	1	0	3	0	11	3	32	5	0
Bonderman, Jeremy, Lak.	0	1	.000	6.00	2	2	1	0	0	0	12	11	49	8	8	1	0	1	2	4	0	10	1	0
Bonilla, Henry, F.M.	3	1	.750	5.04	19	0	0	0	8	1	30.1	39	135	19	17	4	1	0	1	7	0	18	1	0
Borrell, Danny, Tam.*	4	1	.800	2.33	7	6	0	0	1	0	38.2	33	154	11	10	0	2	3	1	10	0	44	0	0
Bradley, Ryan, Tam.	0	2	.000	5.68	5	0	0	0	1	0	6.1	2	27	4	4	0	1	1	3	0	7	4	0	
Brantley, Brian, S.L.	1	2	.333	4.81	12	4	0	0	3	1	39.1	48	173	25	21	3	0	1	3	7	0	34	6	0
Brito, Eude, Cle.*	3	3	.500	5.71	20	0	0	0	11	0	34.2	40	154	22	22	5	2	1	0	14	1	27	7	0
Brooks, Frank, Cle.*	3	5	.375	3.46	35	0	0	0	24	7	39	34	178	18	15	2	2	2	1	27	3	33	2	1
Brown, Andrew, V.B.	10	10	.500	4.11	25	24	1	1	0	0	127	97	530	63	58	13	3	6	8	62	0	129	9	3
Brown, Eric, Day.	1	0	1.000	0.93	25	0	0	0	22	9	29	16	112	7	3	2	1	0	1	4	0	39	0	0
Buchanan, Brian, Tam.*	0	3	.000	2.87	27	2	0	0	10	0	47	36	193	15	15	5	2	1	1	17	1	32	1	3
Buchholz, Taylor, Cle.	10	6	.625	3.29	23	23	4	2	0	0	158.2	140	666	66	58	11	3	3	7	51	1	129	7	0
Bucktrot, Keith, Cle.	8	9	.471	4.88	27	24	2	1	1	0	160.1	167	717	101	87	10	7	8	19	78	1	84	7	2
Burke, Erick, Char.*	7	5	.583	3.35	46	1	0	0	21	3	83.1	79	349	33	31	7	0	3	2	28	1	42	6	0
Bush, David, Dun.	0	1	.000	2.03	7	0	0	0	1	0	13.1	10	49	3	3	1	1	0	1	2	0	9	1	1
Bye, Chris, B.C.	2	5	.286	4.50	38	0	0	0	22	2	68	58	299	43	34	8	4	3	4	32	2	45	11	0
Byron, Terry, Jup.-Sar.	4	3	.571	5.14	39	0	0	0	17	0	61.1	64	274	37	35	7	7	2	3	30	3	49	7	0
Campos, David, Jup.*	0	1	.000	5.19	24	0	0	0	4	0	34.2	38	167	26	20	3	0	2	3	22	0	27	3	1
Caputo, Rob, B.C.	0	1	.000	10.80	2	0	0	0	1	0	1.2	3	11	2	2	0	0	0	3	1	1	0	0	
Carter, Mark, Day.*	3	5	.375	5.52	24	2	0	0	9	1	44	42	192	28	27	5	0	5	1	17	3	40	2	0
Carter, Ryan, Cle.*	9	9	.500	4.34	25	24	1	0	0	0	134.2	129	591	74	65	9	2	5	5	68	0	101	7	0
Casadiego, Gerardo, B.C.	3	4	.429	3.01	16	8	0	0	4	1	71.2	57	304	27	24	4	1	1	3	36	0	41	2	0
Castillo, Marcos, V.B.	0	1	.000	3.07	17	1	0	0	2	0	29.1	25	122	13	10	3	3	0	2	8	1	27	1	0
Cavazos, Andy, Char.	6	5	.545	3.92	33	10	0	0	13	1	82.2	66	345	40	36	7	2	1	2	33	4	63	6	1
Cedeno, Blas, Cle.	0	0	.000	0.00	3	0	0	0	2	0	3.2	2	13	0	0	0	1	1	0	3	0	0	
Cento, Tony, F.M.*	2	3	.400	3.74	15	2	0	0	5	1	33.2	32	146	14	14	1	2	0	2	14	1	23	1	0
Chavez, Carlos, V.B.	0	1	.000	6.66	11	2	0	0	2	0	24.1	29	110	20	18	3	1	4	2	5	0	16	5	0
Chavez, Chris, Jup.	0	0	.000	2.91	12	0	0	0	4	1	21.2	24	99	14	7	3	0	1	7	0	24	0	0	
Chavez, Wilton, Day.	0	3	.000	4.74	8	6	0	0	1	0	24.2	30	118	18	13	2	1	1	4	12	1	25	1	0
Chenard, Ken, S.L.	2	4	.333	3.72	13	13	0	0	0	0	55.2	42	234	27	23	5	0	4	2	25	0	39	8	0
Chipperfield, Calvin, Lak.	9	10	.474	3.29	27	20	3	1	2	0	126	97	542	57	46	4	4	3	11	74	0	114	5	1
Clark, Ryan, Tam.*	0	0	.000	4.26	5	0	0	0	1	0	6.1	5	27	3	3	1	0	1	0	4	0	4	0	0
Clark, Wade, Lak.	0	2	.000	8.14	5	5	0	0	0	0	21	33	105	22	19	3	1	3	1	14	0	9	0	0
Clemens, Roger, Tam.	1	0	1.000	5.40	1	1	0	0	0	0	5	5	21	3	3	1	0	0	0	2	0	6	0	0
Cole, Joey, S.L.	8	2	.800	3.20	18	18	1	0	0	0	107	93	442	46	38	7	1	6	9	25	0	74	4	2
Collins, Pat, B.C.	1	5	.167	2.70	17	0	0	0	11	2	26.2	15	113	14	8	1	1	2	1	14	0	31	1	0
Colson, Jason, Dun.	2	8	.200	5.44	20	14	0	0	3	0	82.2	83	380	64	50	9	2	3	2	53	1	55	10	0
Contreras, Jean, F.M.*	2	2	.500	3.63	31	0	0	0	6	1	44.2	38	198	21	18	3	4	1	3	26	6	43	3	2
Corbin, John, Day.	0	2	.000	7.31	5	2	0	0	1	0	16	25	80	14	13	2	1	1	1	8	1	14	2	0
Cordero, Jesus, Cle.	0	3	.000	6.43	8	2	0	0	3	0	21	29	104	16	15	2	0	3	2	12	1	16	0	0
Corey, Mark, S.L.	0	0	.000	0.00	1	0	0	0	1	0	2	0	6	0	0	0	0	0	0	0	0	3	0	0
Corona, Ronnie, F.M.	4	4	.500	2.25	23	5	0	0	6	2	60	46	252	22	15	1	2	0	1	26	4	75	4	4
Corrado, Matthew, Lak.	4	2	.667	4.87	37	4	0	0	16	3	94.1	102	413	52	51	13	3	5	6	36	1	58	9	3
Costello, Ryan, Dun.*	3	5	.375	6.44	26	10	0	0	4	1	79.2	98	378	63	57	9	0	5	3	51	1	63	3	0
Cox, Mike, S.L.*	0	0	.000	14.29	4	0	0	0	2	0	5.2	7	37	9	9	1	0	1	2	11	0	11	1	0
Crabtree, Tim, V.B.	1	0	1.000	8.53	4	1	0	0	0	0	6.1	10	31	6	6	1	0	0	0	4	0	6	0	0
Crawford, Paxton, Sar.	1	0	1.000	0.00	1	1	0	0	0	0	6	1	19	0	0	0	0	0	1	0	5	1	0	
Cressend, Jack, F.M.	1	0	1.000	3.60	3	1	0	0	1	0	5	4	21	2	2	0	0	0	0	2	0	5	0	0
Dagley, Corey, Cle.	0	2	.000	6.60	15	2	0	0	3	0	30	46	143	33	22	0	2	2	4	1	7	2	0	
Daws, Josh, F.M.	2	0	1.000	2.08	21	0	0	0	10	2	21.2	17	88	7	5	0	0	0	2	6	2	13	1	0
Dean, Aaron, Dun.	3	7	.300	5.42	28	15	0	0	3	1	99.2	118	463	63	60	8	2	7	5	44	6	82	16	1
De La Rosa, Jorge, Sar.*	7	7	.500	3.65	23	23	1	1	0	0	120.2	105	515	53	49	10	1	2	6	52	1	95	5	1
Dequin, Benji, B.C.*	6	9	.400	3.89	27	27	0	0	0	0	143.1	145	622	70	62	7	3	3	6	58	1	111	6	1
Detillion, Jamie, Lak.*	4	0	1.000	1.50	7	0	0	0	4	0	12	8	48	2	2	0	1	1	0	5	2	5	2	0
Diaz, Eddie, B.C.	0	0	.000	1.59	4	0	0	0	2	0	5.2	3	22	1	1	1	0	0	1	2	0	9	0	0
Diaz, Eddy, Day.	2	4	.333	7.93	25	2	0	0	10	1	36.1	47	185	37	32	0	0	1	6	21	1	30	4	0
Diggins, Ben, V.B.	6	10	.375	3.63	20	19	0	0	0	0	114	103	487	54	46	8	3	1	10	41	1	101	10	0
Dittfurth, Ryan, Char.	3	2	.600	2.45	6	3	0	0	1	0	25.2	11	95	7	7	2	1	0	2	7	0	21	0	0
Downs, Scott, Dun.*	0	0	.000	3.00	7	0	0	0	2	1	9	7	36	3	3	0	0	0	0	2	0	7	0	0
Dumatrait, Phillip, Sar.*	0	2	.000	3.86	4	4	0	0	0	0	14	10	68	9	6	0	0	1	0	15	0	16	2	0
Dunning, Justin, V.B.	4	5	.444	5.14	26	9	0	0	5	1	70	68	318	48	40	7	1	2	11	46	0	46	15	0
Echols, Britt, B.C.	0	0	.000	5.40	1	1	0	0	0	0	5	6	24	3	3	1	0	0	0	3	0	3	0	0
Echols, Justin, Char.	7	5	.583	3.93	46	11	0	0	11	4	112.1	94	485	57	49	6	4	2	7	54	0	117	10	1
Elliott, Chad, S.L.*	5	6	.455	2.94	28	13	1	1	4	0	110.1	99	462	49	36	4	3	6	4	37	0	61	6	0
Ellis, Steve, Day.	0	2	.000	8.40	10	0	0	0	6	0	15	17	75	14	14	2	0	1	1	14	1	19	3	1
Elskamp, Andy, Cle.	3	0	1.000	4.47	26	0	0	0	10	0	44.1	44	200	26	22	5	0	2	1	21	0	35	2	1
Engels, Jackson, Char.*	1	2	.333	4.36	10	4	0	0	1	0	33	33	145	19	16	3	0	2	1	13	1	24	2	0
Esquivia, Manuel, Jup.	0	2	.000	11.25	3	3	0	0	0	0	8	5	41	12	10	0	0	0	2	12	0	8	1	0
Eyre, Willie, F.M.	4	1	.800	2.41	19	0	0	0	6	2	33.2	28	136	9	9	0	1	1	1	13	1	25	1	0
Figueroa, Carlos, Char.*	3	1	.750	3.13	15	0	0	0	5	0	23	20	103	12	8	2	1	2	12	0	16	2	1	
File, Bob, Dun.	0	2	.000	11.12	4	3	0	0	0	0	5.2	13	33	9	7	0	1	0	0	3	0	1	0	1
Fisher, Marc, Day.	1	1	.500	1.23	6	0	0	0	1	0	14.2	12	61	5	2	1	0	0	1	4	0	9	0	0
Fisher, Pete, F.M.	1	0	1.000	3.38	4	0	0	0	1	0	5.1	5	20	2	2	0	0	0	0	2	0	2	0	0

Pitcher, Team	W	L	Pct.	ERA	G	GS	CG	ShO	GF	Sv.	IP	H	TBF	R	ER	HR	SH	SF	HB	BB	IBB	SO	WP	Bk.
Flannery, Mike, Jup.	2	5	.286	2.21	58	0	0	0	52	26	61	58	250	20	15	4	3	2	3	10	1	44	3	5
Fontana, Tony, Sar.	4	2	.667	2.70	31	4	0	0	9	2	73.1	79	317	34	22	3	6	4	2	17	6	68	3	0
Foote, Joe, F.M.	12	7	.632	3.11	26	23	2	1	1	0	144.2	141	604	64	50	9	4	3	10	35	0	92	4	0
Ford, Matt, Dun.*	9	5	.643	2.37	21	18	0	0	1	0	114	100	466	43	30	7	3	2	2	42	0	85	2	1
Francisco, Frank, Sar.	1	5	.167	2.55	16	10	0	0	2	0	53	33	217	19	15	1	3	5	4	27	0	58	4	0
Frasor, Jason, Lak.	5	6	.455	3.54	24	24	0	0	0	0	117	112	494	54	46	10	2	2	8	46	1	87	2	2
Fries, Scott, Day.*	3	1	.750	4.43	13	0	0	0	3	0	20.1	29	102	10	10	2	3	1	2	13	5	12	2	0
Gahan, Matt, S.L.	2	1	.667	5.95	9	0	0	0	1	1	19.2	18	85	15	13	3	0	1	6	0	16	3	0
Gardner, Hayden, Char.	6	7	.462	3.10	45	5	0	0	29	18	93	78	380	39	32	2	3	5	7	19	1	71	8	0
Gassner, Dave, Dun.*	11	6	.647	3.44	23	21	2	1	0	0	146.2	143	600	64	56	17	5	4	4	26	1	104	4	1
Gerk, Jordan, Lak.*	0	1	.000	4.96	8	0	0	0	4	0	16.1	20	73	10	9	1	0	1	2	3	1	14	1	0
Gilbert, Rich, Char.*	9	6	.600	5.20	34	16	0	0	3	1	109	110	479	66	63	10	4	3	4	54	2	62	9	0
Glen, William, Dun.	8	5	.615	4.21	41	5	0	0	17	4	94	85	415	47	44	7	1	1	6	51	2	85	5	1
Gonzalez, Alfredo, V.B.	2	1	.667	1.57	17	0	0	0	10	5	34.1	20	135	6	6	3	3	1	3	11	1	47	3	0
Gordon, Tom, Day.	0	0	.000	3.38	2	2	0	0	0	0	2.2	1	12	1	1	0	0	0	0	3	1	0	
Grace, Bryan, Tam.	8	6	.571	2.86	23	21	0	0	1	0	119.2	101	507	46	38	3	2	6	1	61	0	70	12	4
Gracesqui, Frank, Dun.*	2	1	.667	2.49	10	0	0	0	3	1	21.2	15	91	8	6	1	1	1	0	11	0	25	1	0
Graham, Tom, Char.	4	3	.571	2.87	25	0	0	0	22	13	31.1	24	130	15	10	0	2	0	0	7	3	32	1	0
Guzman, Angel, Day.	6	2	.750	2.39	16	15	1	0	0	0	94	99	412	34	25	2	2	4	4	33	1	74	9	2
Hamann, Rob, Dun.	4	5	.444	4.23	23	7	0	0	8	0	72.1	78	319	44	34	6	1	3	5	24	2	37	5	0
Hamman, Corey, Lak.*	1	0	1.000	0.49	16	0	0	0	11	4	18.1	11	70	1	1	0	0	0	1	3	0	18	0	0
Hanrahan, Joel, V.B.	10	6	.625	4.20	25	25	2	1	0	0	143.2	129	608	74	67	11	4	7	11	51	1	139	7	1
Harber, Ryan, Jup.*	0	0	.000	4.12	15	0	0	0	5	1	19.2	24	82	9	9	2	1	0	0	4	0	7	1	0
Hawkins, Chad, Char.	0	4	.000	7.48	9	5	0	0	1	1	27.2	35	142	28	23	4	1	1	1	22	0	12	1	1
Heams, Shane, Sar.	0	0	.000	6.75	2	0	0	0	0	0	2.2	2	15	2	2	0	0	0	1	4	0	1	3	0
Hecker, Steven, Dun.	5	0	1.000	5.45	19	0	0	0	6	0	34.2	40	167	25	21	4	1	2	5	18	0	21	2	0
Hee, Aaron, S.L.*	5	5	.500	4.66	34	4	0	0	14	4	67.2	69	316	44	35	3	3	1	7	38	0	69	9	0
Henkel, Rob, Jup.*	8	3	.727	2.51	14	12	0	0	0	0	75.1	55	293	22	21	4	1	2	1	22	0	82	5	0
Hernandez, Yoel, Cle.	7	16	.304	3.54	28	28	3	0	0	0	170.1	176	731	76	67	6	10	6	12	54	3	116	10	1
Hitchcock, Sterling, Tam.*	0	0	.000	1.50	1	1	0	0	0	0	6	3	22	1	1	0	1	0	1	0	0	3	0	0
Hodge, Kevin, F.M.	3	0	1.000	0.61	10	0	0	0	7	3	14.2	10	55	1	1	0	0	0	0	3	2	18	0	0
Holubec, Ken, F.M.*	5	6	.455	3.22	26	24	1	1	1	0	111.2	93	467	46	40	8	0	2	13	44	0	125	3	0
Howell, Michael, Lak.	0	2	.000	5.46	6	6	0	0	0	0	29.2	32	127	21	18	5	2	2	1	10	0	28	1	0
Hubbel, Travis, Dun.	0	3	.000	9.47	13	2	0	0	5	0	19	13	100	24	20	3	1	1	3	29	0	14	11	0
Huffaker, Mike, Char.	1	0	1.000	0.00	2	0	0	0	0	0	2.1	3	9	0	0	0	0	0	0	0	0	2	1	0
Hutchison, Ryan, Cle.	1	2	.333	3.51	29	0	0	0	13	0	51.1	56	230	26	20	0	3	2	7	20	2	37	4	0
Johansen, Ryan, Cle.	1	3	.250	5.04	16	0	0	0	9	0	25	30	116	21	14	1	0	1	2	9	0	21	2	0
Johnson, Jeremy, Lak.	7	1	.875	3.10	15	7	0	0	3	1	58	50	239	20	20	4	1	0	1	21	0	42	3	1
Joseph, Jake, S.L.	3	3	.500	3.59	13	13	0	0	0	0	72.2	75	304	33	29	1	0	5	13	0	47	2	1
Karp, Josh, B.C.	4	1	.800	1.59	7	7	0	0	0	0	45.1	31	175	9	8	1	0	1	11	0	43	3	0
Keelin, Chris, Lak.	1	2	.333	2.92	19	0	0	0	15	8	24.2	18	110	9	8	1	2	1	1	20	2	30	0	3
Keirstead, Michael, V.B.	0	1	.000	7.71	2	0	0	0	1	0	2.1	4	13	3	2	1	1	0	0	2	0	1	0	0
Kemp, Beau, F.M.	3	2	.600	0.66	59	0	0	0	51	29	68.1	49	268	14	5	0	5	1	2	18	1	49	4	0
Kennard, Jeff, Tam.	0	2	.000	3.92	12	0	0	0	4	0	20.2	18	94	9	9	2	0	1	14	0	14	3	0
Keppel, Bob, S.L.	9	7	.563	4.32	27	26	0	0	0	0	152	162	646	83	73	13	5	7	16	43	0	109	12	1
Key, Chris, Jup.*	6	2	.750	1.63	47	0	0	0	14	4	94	84	361	20	17	5	3	1	1	7	1	54	1	0
Kinney, Matt, F.M.	0	0	.000	0.00	1	1	0	0	0	0	5	4	22	2	0	0	0	1	3	0	5	0	0	
Klepacki, Ed, B.C.-Jup.	0	0	.000	7.53	8	1	0	0	1	0	14.1	15	69	15	12	1	1	0	0	8	0	7	1	0
Knowles, Mike, Tam.	3	4	.429	4.20	50	0	0	0	38	19	49.1	45	229	29	23	2	1	2	1	35	1	43	2	2
Koenig, Ross, Lak.	2	0	1.000	9.69	8	0	0	0	3	0	13	12	63	17	14	2	4	1	3	10	0	9	1	0
Kolb, Dan, Char.	1	0	1.000	1.50	4	0	0	0	0	0	6	5	26	1	1	0	0	0	4	0	2	0	0	
Kozlowski, Ben, Char.*	4	4	.500	2.05	21	12	0	0	2	0	79	63	323	31	18	2	2	5	3	25	0	76	6	1
Krawiec, Aaron, Day.*	7	10	.412	4.09	28	28	0	0	0	0	169.1	159	706	89	77	8	7	1	13	48	2	128	7	2
Kremer, John, Tam.	2	2	.500	4.83	25	0	0	0	9	1	41	52	192	28	22	3	2	0	5	17	1	27	3	0
Kumagai, Ryo, Sar.	2	1	.667	4.50	21	0	0	0	20	5	32	29	147	18	16	1	1	1	5	17	2	27	5	0
Kuo, Hong-chih, V.B.*	0	1	.000	6.75	4	4	0	0	0	0	8	11	39	6	6	0	0	3	2	8	1	0	
Lamber, Justin, F.M.*	0	0	.000	3.86	5	0	0	0	0	0	7	13	38	7	3	0	0	1	6	0	5	0	0
Lara, Mauricio, Sar.*	4	2	.667	4.35	23	4	0	0	0	0	62	74	277	36	30	3	6	1	5	27	0	43	2	0
Larrison, Preston, Lak.	10	5	.667	2.39	21	19	3	1	0	0	120.1	86	489	39	32	6	5	2	6	45	1	92	13	4
Lavery, Tim, Day.*	5	6	.455	2.98	29	8	1	0	8	1	90.2	99	382	37	30	4	2	3	14	2	56	1	2
Lavigne, Tim, S.L.	0	2	.000	3.76	22	0	0	0	20	7	26.1	21	108	11	11	3	0	0	1	9	0	25	1	0
Lee, Seung, Cle.	2	0	1.000	0.00	3	3	1	1	0	0	19	6	65	1	0	0	0	0	2	0	16	0	1
Leicester, Jon, Day.	2	3	.400	3.97	20	14	0	0	0	0	81.2	77	371	43	36	2	2	2	8	48	1	57	8	1
Leuenberger, Jeff, Lak.	0	0	.000	5.40	3	0	0	0	1	0	5	6	25	3	3	1	0	1	0	4	0	3	0	0
Lewis, Craig, B.C.	1	2	.333	4.05	12	0	0	0	5	0	20	24	89	14	9	1	2	1	0	3	1	11	0	0
Lidle, Kevin, Lak.	1	3	.250	2.79	9	6	0	0	1	1	48.1	37	185	17	15	5	1	0	3	6	0	31	0	0
Lincoln, Jeff, F.M.	9	9	.500	4.66	24	22	0	0	1	0	116	138	514	68	60	6	2	6	4	46	2	78	9	1
Lizarraga, Edgar, V.B.	4	0	1.000	1.04	12	0	0	0	3	0	17.1	12	69	3	2	1	1	1	2	2	0	19	0	0
Loaiza, Esteban, Dun.	0	0	.000	0.00	2	2	0	0	0	0	5	2	18	0	0	0	0	0	0	2	0	2	0	0
Lockwood, Luke, B.C.*	10	7	.588	3.37	26	26	0	0	0	0	147	155	616	69	55	13	2	5	6	38	0	86	3	0
Lohrman, Dave, S.L.	1	0	1.000	2.35	8	0	0	0	4	0	15.1	8	67	5	4	0	0	3	13	0	22	5	1
Lombardi, Justin, Tam.*	0	1	.000	27.00	2	0	0	0	1	0	1.1	3	11	4	4	0	0	0	4	0	1	1	0
Lopez, Arturo, V.B.*	0	0	.000	54.00	1	0	0	0	0	0	0.1	2	7	4	2	0	0	0	3	0	0	0	0
Lopez, Gustavo, Jup.	8	3	.727	2.33	18	17	0	0	0	0	88.2	70	352	23	23	2	4	2	3	24	0	73	9	1
Lugo, Ruddy, V.B.	8	2	.800	3.54	22	9	1	1	6	1	87	68	347	28	23	5	1	3	3	26	0	77	7	0
Luna, Brandon, Char.	0	0	.000	6.14	7	0	0	0	4	0	7.1	9	35	5	5	0	0	1	0	6	0	2	0	0
Maberry, Mark, S.L.	0	1	.000	2.25	10	0	0	0	3	0	16	10	65	6	4	0	0	7	0	9	1	0
Manning, Charlie, Tam.*	6	4	.600	3.24	17	16	0	0	0	0	100	82	419	48	36	4	3	4	10	31	0	85	5	3
Marrero, Darwin, B.C.	3	2	.600	3.46	9	9	0	0	0	0	54.2	57	223	21	21	4	0	3	8	0	41	0	0
Martin, Greg, B.C.*	1	1	.500	9.00	4	0	0	0	0	0	6	13	36	8	6	1	1	0	1	4	0	7	0	0
Martin, Luke, F.M.*	0	0	.000	12.71	3	0	0	0	0	0	5.2	8	30	8	8	2	0	0	5	0	7	0	0
Martin, Nick, Day.*	1	1	.500	3.20	4	4	0	0	0	0	19.2	18	88	15	7	2	0	1	3	6	0	16	3	0
Martinez, Oscar, Tam.	1	3	.250	7.54	25	0	0	0	9	0	37	45	179	38	31	2	1	4	3	17	1	33	3	0
Marx, Tommy, Lak.*	6	8	.429	5.04	30	19	2	1	6	0	123.1	115	560	84	69	16	2	11	12	83	0	64	10	3

Pitcher, Team	W	L	Pct.	ERA	G	GS	CG	ShO	GF	Sv.	IP	H	TBF	R	ER	HR	SH	SF	HB	BB	IBB	SO	WP	Bk.
Massingale, Matt, Jup.	0	0	.000	3.86	4	0	0	0	3	1	7	8	30	3	3	1	0	0	0	1	0	6	0	0
Mata, Gustavo, B.C.	3	4	.429	2.55	11	11	0	0	0	0	67	50	261	21	19	6	2	0	2	19	0	27	0	0
Matthews, Barry, Lak.*	1	2	.333	7.46	12	5	0	0	2	0	35	42	159	29	29	4	2	1	1	14	0	32	0	0
Mattioni, Nick, S.L.	4	3	.571	4.78	41	0	0	0	24	3	79	71	353	52	42	5	4	3	6	42	0	68	9	0
Mattox, David, S.L.	4	4	.500	2.82	9	9	2	1	0	0	51	46	220	21	16	2	2	1	5	24	0	34	0	0
Maust, David, B.C.*	1	1	.500	5.32	14	0	0	0	7	4	22	20	93	14	13	5	1	0	0	8	0	15	0	0
Mayfield, Brandon, Cle.	0	0	.000	3.07	7	0	0	0	2	1	14.2	14	61	9	5	1	0	0	1	1	0	12	3	0
Mays, Joe, F.M.	0	1	.000	2.08	3	3	0	0	0	0	8.2	9	36	2	2	0	0	0	0	3	0	7	0	0
McAvoy, Jeff, B.C.	3	3	.500	5.40	12	6	1	0	3	0	46.2	55	202	28	28	6	3	0	3	8	2	22	1	1
McDonald, Jon, F.M.	1	0	1.000	4.66	2	2	0	0	0	0	9.2	13	45	7	5	0	0	0	3	0	5	1	0
McGinley, Blake, S.L.*	1	1	.500	5.97	18	0	0	0	9	4	31.2	40	148	22	21	2	0	1	13	0	22	3	0
McMullen, Jeremy, Day.	0	0	.000	8.22	3	1	0	0	0	0	7.2	11	42	7	7	3	1	1	3	6	0	8	2	0
McNutt, Mike, F.M.	12	8	.600	3.17	27	23	0	0	2	2	144.2	138	602	66	51	8	1	8	8	33	0	102	7	1
Mendoza, Cristian, Tam.	0	0	.000	6.75	1	1	0	0	0	0	2.2	1	11	2	2	1	0	0	1	2	0	2	0	0
Messenger, Randall, Jup.	11	8	.579	4.37	28	27	1	0	0	0	156.2	178	700	94	76	4	5	4	7	58	0	96	4	2
Meyer, Todd, B.C.	0	1	.000	7.45	4	2	0	0	2	0	9.2	9	45	8	8	1	2	0	1	7	0	7	2	0
Miller, Josh, Cle.	3	2	.600	2.42	49	0	0	0	32	17	70.2	78	302	26	19	3	5	1	4	11	1	39	5	0
Miniel, Rene, Sar.	7	10	.412	4.51	26	26	0	0	0	0	127.2	125	540	72	64	11	4	7	4	39	1	78	12	0
Moehler, Brian, Lak.	1	1	.500	2.92	2	2	0	0	0	0	12.1	10	51	9	4	2	1	0	1	1	0	7	2	0
Montero, Agustin, V.B.	1	0	1.000	3.46	7	0	0	0	0	0	13	10	53	5	5	1	1	0	1	4	0	14	2	3
Montero, Oscar, Day.	5	7	.417	4.39	51	0	0	0	39	9	69.2	64	311	41	34	5	5	3	2	40	3	79	8	0
Moore, Darin, Char.	3	4	.429	5.64	45	2	0	0	12	0	52.2	46	274	48	33	0	0	1	16	53	1	37	12	0
Moreno, Edwin, Char.	3	0	1.000	0.59	6	6	0	0	0	0	30.2	20	116	2	2	0	0	0	2	3	0	23	0	0
Moseley, Marcus, F.M.	2	2	.500	5.16	35	2	0	0	10	1	61	64	301	39	35	6	1	1	12	51	1	47	13	0
Moser, Todd, Jup.*	7	4	.636	3.59	17	12	0	0	1	0	77.2	73	315	33	31	7	0	3	5	12	0	70	2	0
Mounce, Tony, Char.*	3	0	1.000	2.06	11	5	0	0	2	0	39.1	32	153	12	9	1	1	2	0	11	0	31	1	0
Mowday, Chris, Dun.	1	1	.500	4.32	10	0	0	0	5	0	16.2	17	76	9	8	4	1	1	1	10	1	17	3	0
Murphy, Matt, Day.*	7	5	.583	4.13	48	0	0	0	14	0	69.2	76	318	37	32	2	2	0	5	26	4	69	10	0
Murray, Arlington, Char.*	3	3	.500	3.02	19	14	0	0	3	2	83.1	77	339	31	28	4	1	1	0	20	0	68	3	1
Murray, Steve, F.M.*	2	1	.667	3.12	8	0	0	0	4	0	8.2	11	39	3	3	0	0	0	3	2	0	8	0	0
Musser, Neal, S.L.*	2	0	1.000	1.42	4	4	0	0	0	0	19	20	80	4	3	1	0	1	1	5	0	12	1	0
Nall, T.J., V.B.	2	1	.667	4.17	17	2	0	0	8	1	36.2	42	157	19	17	0	1	0	13	0	30	4	0
Newman, Eric, V.B.	1	1	.500	3.86	7	0	0	0	0	0	14	12	59	6	6	2	1	0	8	1	13	1	0
Norderum, Jason, B.C.*	1	0	1.000	13.50	2	0	0	0	1	0	2	3	12	3	3	1	0	0	0	3	2	0	0
Nunley, Derrek, Dun.	0	3	.000	4.81	39	0	0	0	23	0	58	51	269	37	31	6	1	0	8	38	5	51	7	0
Ochoa, Pablo, S.L.	1	0	1.000	8.56	4	1	0	0	1	0	13.2	19	68	13	13	1	1	1	0	10	0	10	1	0
Ogiltree, John, Dun.	5	4	.556	4.01	45	0	0	0	42	26	51.2	50	231	27	23	4	4	2	3	31	5	37	1	0
Olson, Jason, V.B.	1	0	1.000	2.66	10	0	0	0	4	0	20.1	21	94	7	6	1	2	1	1	8	0	16	3	0
Ortiz, Javier, Tam.	4	3	.571	2.52	9	9	1	1	0	0	50	47	208	20	14	1	1	3	3	13	0	35	1	1
Ortiz, Julio, B.C.*	0	0	.000	0.00	2	0	0	0	1	0	0.2	1	5	0	0	0	0	0	2	0	1	0	0
Osoria, Franquelis, V.B.	0	1	.000	2.45	3	0	0	0	1	0	7.1	4	29	2	2	0	0	0	2	0	10	0	0
Ostlund, Ian, Lak.*	2	3	.400	2.89	29	0	0	0	17	3	37.1	30	150	13	12	3	2	1	0	8	1	30	3	0
Parris, Steve, Dun.	0	1	.000	4.41	3	3	0	0	0	0	16.1	19	68	10	8	1	0	1	1	0	8	0	0
Peeples, Ross, S.L.*	2	3	.400	5.59	6	6	0	0	0	0	29	33	131	24	18	2	1	0	13	0	26	1	1
Penny, Brad, Jup.	0	0	.000	0.00	2	2	0	0	0	0	7.2	5	28	0	0	0	0	0	0	0	0	9	0	0
Perez, Frank, Lak.	2	2	.500	5.71	8	0	0	0	3	0	17.1	13	71	11	11	3	0	0	5	0	24	1	0
Perez, Juan, Sar.*	0	6	.000	3.78	16	14	0	0	0	0	66.2	71	286	34	28	4	2	4	2	19	0	39	4	0
Perez, Julio, Tam.	1	1	.500	3.00	6	0	0	0	2	0	9	5	43	3	3	1	0	2	1	7	4	0
Perez, Michelandy, Sar.	0	1	.000	6.00	2	0	0	0	0	0	3	2	14	2	2	0	1	3	0	1	0	0
Persby, Andy, F.M.	3	2	.600	8.24	25	0	0	0	5	0	43.2	54	225	46	40	2	3	2	6	33	1	33	4	1
Peterson, Matt, S.L.*	1	0	1.000	1.50	1	1	0	0	0	0	6	5	27	2	1	0	0	1	2	0	5	0	0
Pettitte, Andy, Tam.*	0	0	.000	0.00	2	2	0	0	0	0	5	3	18	0	0	0	0	0	0	0	4	0	0
Pierson, Jason, Tam.*	0	2	.000	5.11	11	0	0	0	5	0	12.1	16	58	7	7	2	1	0	6	1	9	0	0
Pike, Matthew, Tam.	0	0	.000	5.91	6	1	0	0	3	0	10.2	11	48	10	7	1	0	0	2	4	0	10	0	0
Pilkington, Brian, V.B.	2	1	.667	2.37	3	3	0	0	0	0	19	16	74	7	5	2	1	2	0	3	1	10	0	0
Pineda, Jairo, Lak.	2	5	.286	3.32	33	0	0	0	17	5	57	59	249	26	21	2	2	2	1	26	0	30	0	1
Pinto, Renyel, Day.*	3	3	.500	5.51	7	7	0	0	0	0	32.2	45	149	23	20	5	1	1	3	11	0	24	3	2
Portobanco, Luz, S.L.	0	2	.000	8.18	2	2	1	0	0	0	11	12	53	10	10	0	1	1	2	9	0	6	1	0
Pridie, Jon, F.M.	4	4	.500	3.27	12	12	0	0	0	0	66	62	284	29	24	2	3	0	2	30	0	40	3	0
Quick, Ben, Dun.	1	6	.143	4.91	32	7	0	0	9	1	95.1	114	433	63	52	7	1	4	6	31	1	79	5	0
Radke, Brad, F.M.	0	1	.000	3.12	2	2	0	0	0	0	8.2	11	39	6	3	1	0	1	0	0	6	1	0
Ramirez, Jose, Lak.*	0	1	.000	5.48	13	0	0	0	4	0	23	26	104	18	14	5	0	3	6	0	20	1	0
Ratliff, Jon, Jup.	0	0	.000	3.38	2	2	0	0	0	0	5.1	4	20	2	2	0	1	0	4	0	0
Reina, Dimas, V.B.	0	0	.000	23.63	3	0	0	0	1	0	2.2	4	18	7	7	0	0	1	5	0	1	0	0
Rengifo, Nohemar, B.C.	0	0	.000	7.71	1	0	0	0	0	0	2.1	1	14	3	2	0	1	0	5	0	1	0	0
Reyes, Luis, Day.	0	1	.000	4.15	2	0	0	0	0	0	4.1	6	22	2	2	1	0	0	2	0	2	0	0
Reynolds, Josh, S.L.	11	5	.688	3.13	22	20	1	0	1	0	126.1	123	528	51	44	10	5	4	9	26	0	70	0	0
Rivard, Reggie, Char.	3	0	1.000	2.17	15	9	0	0	3	1	54	38	213	14	13	0	1	0	1	14	0	36	6	1
Rodney, Lee, Lak.	6	4	.600	3.74	22	13	0	0	4	0	84.1	79	368	40	35	7	2	4	7	40	0	60	4	0
Rodriguez, Cristobal, B.C.	2	3	.400	1.62	11	0	0	0	8	2	16.2	11	63	4	3	2	2	0	0	4	0	21	1	0
Rodriguez, Orlando, V.B.*	0	0	.000	0.00	7	0	0	0	3	1	7	6	30	0	0	0	2	0	3	1	10	0	0
Romero, Josmir, F.M.	6	3	.667	4.20	18	13	1	1	1	0	79.1	78	340	43	37	16	3	5	3	25	2	52	5	0
Rosario, Francisco, Dun.	3	3	.500	1.29	13	12	0	0	0	0	63	33	248	10	9	3	1	1	3	25	0	65	1	2
Rundles, Rich, B.C.*	2	7	.222	4.08	12	11	0	0	0	0	57.1	66	243	34	26	5	1	1	2	16	1	31	2	0
Russell, Eddie, Jup.	0	0	.000	9.00	4	0	0	0	1	0	6	5	34	6	6	0	0	1	10	1	7	0	0
Russo, Scott, B.C.*	0	0	.000	4.67	11	0	0	0	3	0	17.1	19	71	9	9	3	1	1	6	0	11	1	0
Sadowski, Chad, Cle.	0	0	.000	0.00	2	0	0	0	0	0	2	1	7	0	0	0	0	0	0	0	1	0	0
Sandberg, Eric, F.M.*	0	0	.000	0.00	1	0	0	0	1	0	1	0	3	0	0	0	0	0	0	1	0	0
Sandoval, Marcos, Dun.	0	1	.000	4.50	3	0	0	0	2	0	8	8	34	4	4	2	0	0	1	3	0	4	1	1
Santiago, Victor, V.B.	0	1	.000	6.75	4	1	0	0	1	0	8	15	41	6	6	0	0	1	3	0	5	0	1
Sauer, Marc, Jup.	4	1	.800	2.26	30	0	0	0	12	0	51.2	32	192	14	13	3	0	0	1	7	0	31	1	0
Sawyer, Steve, Jup.	6	4	.600	4.38	46	0	0	0	12	1	76	77	345	43	37	1	2	5	7	39	0	77	10	1
Schmitt, Eric, Tam.	6	6	.500	2.36	19	19	0	0	0	0	91.1	75	377	30	24	4	2	0	2	32	1	97	4	0
Schoening, Brent, F.M.	0	2	.000	7.30	4	3	0	0	0	0	12.1	14	59	12	10	0	1	1	10	1	10	0	0

Pitcher, Team	W	L	Pct.	ERA	G	GS	CG	ShO	GF	Sv.	IP	H	TBF	R	ER	HR	SH	SF	HB	BB	IBB	SO	WP	Bk.
Schroder, Chris, B.C.	2	2	.500	1.52	23	0	0	0	21	6	29.2	13	118	6	5	2	0	1	0	19	1	36	2	0
Seale, Dustin, B.C.*	1	0	1.000	0.00	8	0	0	0	3	0	16.2	6	64	1	0	1	0	0	6	1	0	14	1	0
Sergent, Joe, Jup.*	4	3	.571	2.15	12	10	0	0	1	0	62.2	61	258	26	15	1	0	3	4	13	0	34	1	0
Silva, Doug, F.M.	1	2	.333	1.74	17	1	0	0	6	1	31	19	117	6	6	1	1	2	0	7	0	26	0	0
Simpson, Andre, V.B.	0	0	.000	16.20	4	0	0	0	3	0	3.1	7	20	6	6	1	0	0	0	4	0	2	0	0
Skinner, John, Jup.	1	1	.500	4.50	11	0	0	0	5	0	14	18	63	7	7	0	1	0	0	6	1	10	0	0
Sloan, Brandon, Jup.	1	0	1.000	1.17	6	0	0	0	6	2	7.2	9	30	1	1	1	0	0	1	0	3	0	0
Smith, Dan, Lak.	0	0	.000	1.29	9	0	0	0	1	0	14	10	56	3	2	1	0	2	0	5	0	13	1	0
Smith, Matt, Tam.*	0	4	.000	6.59	8	6	0	0	1	0	27.1	37	133	23	20	1	0	4	0	17	0	20	2	0
Solano, Alex, Sar.	9	3	.750	5.33	45	1	0	0	28	4	79.1	83	356	55	47	7	3	4	3	35	5	52	1	0
Spencer, Sean, B.C.*	0	0	.000	0.00	3	0	0	0	1	0	3.2	1	16	0	0	0	0	0	0	5	0	3	0	0
Stefani, Jason, V.B.*	0	0	.000	1.93	8	0	0	0	4	0	14	14	61	5	3	0	0	2	1	4	0	8	2	0
Steffek, Brian, V.B.	0	0	.000	2.45	2	0	0	0	1	0	7.1	8	28	2	2	0	0	0	0	1	0	5	0	0
Stevens, Josh, Tam.	2	0	1.000	2.89	21	1	0	0	4	0	37.1	34	155	12	12	1	0	2	2	8	1	41	2	0
Strelitz, Brian, Tam.	2	1	.667	4.43	27	0	0	0	7	0	44.2	54	206	29	22	4	0	1	4	22	0	20	2	0
Stults, Eric, V.B.*	3	1	.750	3.00	13	6	0	0	1	0	42	39	185	19	14	3	2	2	1	20	0	40	2	0
Szuminski, Jason, Day.	5	2	.714	5.12	39	7	0	0	7	1	91.1	95	419	61	52	7	2	6	6	41	0	53	12	0
Tejeda, Rob, Cle.	4	8	.333	3.97	17	17	1	0	0	0	99.2	73	416	48	44	14	2	4	5	48	0	87	3	1
Telemaco, Amaury, Cle.	1	0	1.000	1.50	3	3	0	0	0	0	12	15	54	5	2	0	0	1	0	3	0	10	0	0
Thompson, Matt, Sar.	6	14	.300	4.21	25	24	0	0	0	0	119.2	131	533	70	56	10	5	7	3	44	1	64	3	0
Torres, Luis, B.C.	4	8	.333	4.97	16	15	1	0	1	0	87	99	380	56	48	11	2	6	4	28	0	46	5	0
Totten, Heath, V.B.	9	5	.643	3.63	18	18	2	1	0	0	109	115	457	47	44	6	2	3	7	20	1	83	1	0
Trombley, Mike, F.M.	0	0	.000	0.00	1	0	0	0	0	0	2	2	8	1	0	0	0	0	0	0	0	3	0	0
Tucker, Julien, B.C.	1	5	.167	3.12	25	0	0	0	8	1	43.1	35	199	24	15	2	2	2	5	29	3	43	4	0
Ungs, Nick, Jup.	1	3	.250	4.34	4	4	0	0	0	0	18.2	20	79	9	9	0	1	1	4	6	0	14	0	0
Urdaneta, Lino, V.B.	2	2	.500	2.41	52	0	0	0	50	32	52.1	39	210	15	14	3	2	1	2	17	3	30	3	0
Urena, Sixto, Char.	0	0	.000	5.40	2	0	0	0	1	0	3.1	4	16	2	2	0	0	0	2	1	0	1	0	0
Valdez, Domingo, Char.	4	3	.571	3.42	26	13	0	0	3	2	84.1	67	352	36	32	8	1	1	12	31	0	67	4	1
Valle, Yoiset, Sar.*	7	4	.636	4.37	37	0	0	0	13	2	80.1	98	367	53	39	5	2	3	5	24	1	34	10	0
Vega, Rene, S.L.*	1	3	.250	4.91	5	5	0	0	0	0	29.1	33	135	20	16	3	0	0	1	14	0	31	1	1
Villegas, Felix, Sar.	1	1	.500	2.52	29	0	0	0	21	7	39.1	24	155	11	11	2	1	2	2	13	1	30	0	0
Viole, Paul, S.L.	3	9	.250	5.99	40	0	0	0	19	5	67.2	76	346	67	45	0	1	0	10	54	0	64	21	0
Walker, Adam, S.L.*	0	1	.000	9.00	1	1	0	0	0	0	2	3	10	2	2	0	0	1	1	0	0	3	0	0
Wallace, Jeff, Sar.*	0	1	.000	9.00	1	1	0	0	0	0	2	1	8	2	2	1	0	0	1	0	1	0	0	0
Washburn, Ben, B.C.	0	3	.000	7.41	19	2	0	0	7	0	37.2	52	178	41	31	5	1	3	5	13	1	25	1	1
Watkins, Tommy, F.M.	0	0	.000	0.00	1	0	0	0	1	0	0.1	0	1	0	0	0	0	0	0	0	0	0	0	0
Watson, Greg, Lak.	3	1	.750	4.87	16	0	0	0	13	5	20.1	25	96	16	11	2	0	2	8	15	1	0	0	0
Weatherby III, Charles, Sar.	0	3	.000	4.57	17	0	0	0	13	9	21.2	23	93	15	11	1	0	1	5	2	17	0	1	1
Webb, John, Day.	5	3	.625	3.43	10	10	1	1	0	0	57.2	43	240	23	22	3	1	5	3	23	0	65	4	1
Weis, Brad, F.M.*	1	0	1.000	1.66	13	0	0	0	4	0	21.2	16	89	7	4	1	0	1	2	8	0	22	1	1
Wellemeyer, Todd, Day.	2	4	.333	3.79	14	14	0	0	0	0	73.2	63	301	33	31	7	1	3	4	19	1	87	3	0
Willis, Dontrelle, Jup.*	2	0	1.000	1.80	5	5	0	0	0	0	30	24	115	7	6	2	0	0	3	0	27	0	0
Wilson, C.J., Char.*	10	2	.833	3.06	26	15	0	0	2	1	106	86	449	48	36	4	2	0	6	41	1	76	7	0
Wilson, Mike, Cle.	1	7	.125	4.28	12	8	0	0	3	1	54.2	51	243	27	26	2	4	3	4	29	1	44	4	0
Witte, Lou, Tam.	6	7	.462	4.11	22	8	0	0	4	0	76.2	79	319	46	35	8	2	3	1	12	0	53	1	2
Wolf, Randy, Cle.*	0	0	.000	0.00	1	1	0	0	0	0	5	1	15	0	0	0	0	0	0	1	0	8	0	0
Wolfe, Brian, F.M.	6	9	.400	4.64	25	23	0	0	0	0	132	160	584	84	68	17	5	4	7	34	0	85	5	3
Wood, Bobby, Tam.	0	0	.000	10.80	1	1	0	0	0	0	5	11	29	7	6	2	0	2	0	2	0	7	2	0
Woodyard, Mark, Lak.	2	8	.200	7.64	17	7	0	0	3	2	66	81	310	62	56	10	4	6	32	0	22	6	0
Wynegar, Adam, Day.*	1	4	.200	6.66	13	10	0	0	1	0	51.1	59	259	49	38	4	3	2	4	46	2	28	6	0
Yennaco, Jay, Sar.	0	1	.000	11.25	4	0	0	0	2	1	8	12	39	10	10	1	0	0	0	3	0	10	0	0
Yoo, Byung Mok, Sar.	0	0	.000	5.87	5	0	0	0	2	0	7.2	10	37	7	5	0	0	1	3	0	2	2	0
Zimmerman, Jeff, Char.	0	0	.000	0.00	2	0	0	0	2	0	2	0	7	0	0	0	0	0	1	0	2	0	0
Zink, Charlie, Sar.	0	0	.000	0.00	4	0	0	0	1	0	9	2	33	1	0	0	1	1	0	3	1	11	0	0

PITCHERS WITH TWO OR MORE TEAMS

Pitcher, Team	W	L	Pct.	ERA	G	GS	CG	ShO	GF	Sv.	IP	H	TBF	R	ER	HR	SH	SF	HB	BB	IBB	SO	WP	Bk.
Byron, Terry, Jup.	3	2	.600	5.94	31	0	0	0	13	0	47	52	218	33	31	7	3	1	3	28	3	29	3	0
Byron, Terry, Sar.	1	1	.500	2.51	8	0	0	0	4	0	14.1	12	56	4	4	0	4	1	0	2	0	20	4	0
Klepacki, Ed, B.C.	0	0	.000	7.27	3	1	0	0	1	0	8.2	10	42	8	7	1	1	0	0	4	0	4	1	0
Klepacki, Ed, Jup.	0	0	.000	7.94	5	0	0	0	3	0	5.2	7	5	0	0	0	4	0	0	0	0	0	0	0

COMBINATION SHUTOUTS: **Brevard County (5)**—Casadiego-Washburn-Collins, Karp-Casadiego, Maya-Bye, Mata-Maust-Schroder, Rundles-McAvoy-Shroder. **Charlotte (16)**—Barnett-Figueroa-Moore, Cavazos-Valdez-Gardner, Cavazos-C. Wilson, Engels-Cavazos-Gardner, Kozlowski-Gardner-Graham, Moreno-Burke, Moreno-J. Echols, Moreno-J. Echols-Moore, A. Murray-Figueroa-J. Echols-Gardner, A. Murray-Gardner, A. Murray-Moore, Rivard-Moore-Gilbert-Burke, Valdez-Gilbert, Valdez-Gilbert-Burke-Figueroa, Valdez-C. Wilson, C. Wilson-Valdez. **Clearwater (7)**—Buchholz-Brooks, Buchholz-Miller, R. Carter-Bucktrot-Miller, R. Carter-Hutchinson-Miller, Hernandez-D. Adams-M. Wilson, Hernandez-Brito-Miller, Hernandez-Brooks. **Daytona (6)**—Benik-E. Brown, M. Carter-O. Montero, Guzman-Leicester-Ellis, Krawiec-Albright, Krawiec-E. Brown, Krawiec-M. Fisher-Fries-O. Montero. **Dunedin (9)**—Abbott-Hamann, Dean-Costello-Nunley, Ford-Bush-Nunley, Ford-Glen-Gracesqui-Ogiltree, Ford-Hamann-Ogiltree, Gassner-Dean, Gassner-Ogiltree, Glen-Nunley-Ogiltree, Rosario-Glen. **Fort Myers (10)**—Corona-S. Murray-Silva-Daws, Foote-Cressend-Contreras-Kemp, Foote-Daws-Kemp, Foote-Kemp, Foote-Romero-S. Murray-Kemp, Holubec-Cento-Weis, Mays-Daws-Foote, Moseley-Silva-Contreras-Daws-Kemp, Pridie-Cento-Bonilla. **Jupiter (12)**—Almanza-Henkel-Byron, Almanza-Messenger-Flannery, Bautista-Byron-Harber-Flannery, Bautista-Campos-Flannery, Beckett-McNutt, G. Lopez-Key-Flannery, McNutt-Campos-Byron, McNutt-Campos-Key, McNutt-Ch. Chavez-Sawyer-Massingale, Sergent-Sauer-Skinner, Willis-Flannery. **Lakeland (7)**—Chipperfield-Corrado, Frasor-Ramirez-Corrado-Hamman, Larrison-Pineda, Marx-Lidle, Matthews-Corrado, Rodney-Pineda-Hamman, Rodney-D. Smith-Keelin. **St. Lucie (9)**—Chenard-Elliott, Chenard-Mattioni, Chenard-Viole-Bennett, Cole-Elliott-Lavigne, Elliott-Viole-Bennett, Joseph-Maberry-Lavigne, Keppel-Bennett-Lavigne, Musser-Gahan-Lavigne, Reynolds-Hee. **Sarasota (10)**—Baker-B. Adams, De La Rosa-Ville, Francisco-An, Lara-Villegas, Miniel-D. Adams-Yennaco, Miniel-An, Miniel-Valle, Thompson-Fontana-Weatherby, Thompson-Heams-Kumagai, Thompson-Lara-Solano. **Tampa (11)**—Beal-Borrell, Blankenship-Kremer-Knowles-Bean, Borrell-Anderson-Martinez, Borrell-Buchanan, Grace-Buchanan-Stevens-Knowles, Grace-Manning-Buchanan-Strelitz, Manning-Stevens-Bean, Ja. Ortiz-Knowles-Bean, Schmitt-Bean-Knowles, Schmitt-Martinez-Knowles, Schmitt-Pierson-Bean-Knowles. **Vero Beach (9)**—Diggins-Gonzalez, Diggins-Gonzalez-Urdaneta, Dunning-A. Brown-Beirne-Urdaneta, Kuo-Nall, Lugo-Andrews-Urdaneta, Lugo-O. Rodriguez-Urdaneta, Lugo-Urdaneta, Stults-Urdaneta, Totten-Dunning-Urdaneta.

NO-HIT GAMES: Hanrahan, Vero Beach defeated Jupiter, 5-0, April 21; Hanrahan, Vero Beach defeated Brevard County, 5-1, July 6, six innings.

2002 FIELDING

TEAM

Team	G	PO	A	E	TC	DP	TP	PB	Pct.
Tampa	133	3448	1395	131	4974	100	0	35	.974
Jupiter	138	3685	1403	141	5229	132	0	16	.973
Charlotte	140	3672	1480	151	5303	118	0	28	.972
Vero Beach	135	3498	1331	142	4971	102	0	29	.971
Brevard County	136	3522	1404	147	5073	130	1	23	.971
Clearwater	136	3565	1399	152	5116	118	0	14	.970
Fort Myers	136	3580	1446	156	5182	153	0	20	.970
Dunedin	135	3606	1402	158	5166	128	0	26	.969
Lakeland	139	3618	1452	162	5232	149	2	28	.969
St. Lucie	140	3672	1511	172	5355	120	0	18	.968
Sarasota	136	3522	1378	168	5068	112	0	28	.967
Daytona	137	3594	1399	177	5170	121	0	29	.966

INDIVIDUAL

FIRST BASEMEN

NOTE: All caps denotes fielding-percentage leader based on 70 games for catchers, 93 for all other non-pitchers and 112 innings for pitchers. *Throws lefthanded.

Player, Team	Pct.	G	PO	A	E	TC	DP
Alvarez, Nick, V.B.	1.000	10	69	7	0	76	7
Anderson, Dennis, Jup.	1.000	1	1	0	0	1	0
Avila, Rob, Cle.	.994	21	155	15	1	171	14
Bailie, Stefan, Sar.	.978	39	318	33	8	359	32
Barbier, Blair, Day.	.980	29	227	12	5	244	21
Bernhardt, Joe, Dun.	.981	84	639	50	13	702	72
Blum, Greg, B.C.	.983	22	159	11	3	173	16
Botts, Jason, Char.	.971	9	64	4	2	70	6
Bowen, Rob, F.M.	1.000	1	1	0	0	1	0
Bowman, Addison, Sar.	.963	3	24	2	1	27	1
Brazell, Craig, S.L.	.987	100	945	45	13	1003	77
Brisson, Dustin, Sar.	.993	33	259	16	2	277	24
Calabrese, Tony, Tam.	1.000	1	1	1	0	2	1
Carreno, Jose, B.C.	1.000	2	6	0	0	6	1
Crespo, Manny, Sar.	1.000	9	56	3	0	59	6
Cronin, Shane, Tam.	1.000	4	36	3	0	39	1
Curry, Chris, Day.	1.000	2	5	0	0	5	0
Dacey, Ryan, V.B.	.989	10	87	6	1	94	4
Daigle, Leo, Lak.	.987	126	1046	74	15	1135	115
Davis, Glenn, B.C.*	1.000	9	78	10	0	88	13
Delgado, Mario, Cle.*	.986	45	397	22	6	425	41
Demarco, Matt, Jup.	1.000	3	3	1	0	4	0
Dempsey, Nick, B.C.	.973	28	205	11	6	222	13
Deschenes, Pat, S.L.	.990	35	294	16	3	313	22
Detienne, Dave, V.B.	1.000	9	24	1	0	25	3
Dill, Jason, Char.*	.989	30	255	20	3	278	23
Dominique, Andy, Cle.	1.000	5	34	2	0	36	4
Durazo, William, Sar.	.923	1	11	1	1	13	1
DZURILLA, Mike, Day.	.994	94	747	60	5	812	76
Esposito, Brian, Sar.	.966	9	52	4	2	58	6
Farnsworth, Troy, Cle.	.994	70	579	42	4	625	43
Gajewski, Matt, Char.	.968	9	81	10	3	94	3
Garcia, Juan-Carlos, Jup.	1.000	3	25	2	0	27	2
Goldbach, Jeff, Day.	1.000	5	27	1	0	28	2
Hattig, John, Sar.	.985	9	62	3	1	66	8
Jacobs, Mike, S.L.	.965	9	79	3	3	85	10
Jaile, Chris, Char.	.971	10	97	3	3	103	8
Johnson, Forrest, Lak.	.938	3	29	1	2	32	4
Jones, Mitch, Tam.	.992	27	225	14	2	241	21
Kinchen, Jason, Tam.	.973	4	36	0	1	37	3
Lane, Rich, B.C.*	.986	92	716	43	11	770	73
Loney, James, V.B.*	1.000	13	100	6	0	106	16
Magness, Pat, Jup.	.985	96	823	33	13	869	81
Martin, Tyler, Char.	1.000	42	354	16	0	370	31
McEachran, Aaron, Dun.	.974	29	212	9	6	227	23
Michaelis, Derek, V.B.*	.987	101	740	64	11	815	57
Neill, Ryan, Lak.	1.000	5	44	3	0	47	5
Pack, Branden, Char.	1.000	4	16	1	0	17	2
Perry, Jason, Dun.	1.000	6	42	4	0	46	2
Pond, Simon, Dun.	.996	27	229	17	1	247	23
Quattlebaum, Hugh, Lak.	1.000	2	8	0	0	8	0
Radwan, Jason, V.B.	1.000	3	23	1	0	24	1
Rifkin, Aaron, Tam.*	.991	66	593	39	6	638	47
Rigsby, Randy, Jup.*	.750	3	3	0	1	4	0
Roneberg, Brett, Jup.*	1.000	11	90	9	0	99	9
Sandberg, Eric, F.M.*	.979	14	128	10	3	141	11
Scanlon, Matt, Tam.	1.000	2	1	0	0	1	0
Segar, Jeff, Tam.	1.000	2	22	0	0	22	0
Sing, Brandon, Day.	.984	16	112	8	2	122	8
Sisk, Aaron, Dun.	1.000	2	2	0	0	2	0

Player, Team	Pct.	G	PO	A	E	TC	DP
Socarras, Tony, V.B.	.976	5	39	2	1	42	5
Sosa, Nick, F.M.	.978	11	85	5	2	92	9
Soules, Ryan, Char.	.992	42	347	22	3	372	30
Tiffee, Terry, F.M.	.991	77	641	58	6	705	70
Torres, Digno, F.M.*	.992	46	322	38	3	363	41
Torres, Frederick, Char.	.962	5	45	5	2	52	7
Turner, Jason, Tam.*	.990	35	285	24	3	312	20
Ust, Brant, Lak.	.974	5	33	4	1	38	5
Valencia, Vic, Char.	.952	4	20	0	1	21	2
Walker, Matt, Lak.	1.000	1	13	2	0	15	0
Williams, Brady, F.M.	1.000	1	3	0	0	3	1
Willingham, Josh, Jup.	.989	32	254	18	3	275	30
Youkilis, Kevin, Sar.	.984	40	334	27	6	367	22

SECOND BASEMEN

Player, Team	Pct.	G	PO	A	E	TC	DP
Acevedo, Inocencio, Char.	.952	13	27	33	3	63	6
Ahumada, Alex, Sar.	.833	2	3	2	1	6	0
Arteaga, Joshua, Day.	.927	13	15	23	3	41	5
Bartlett, Jason, F.M.	.000	1	0	0	0	0	0
Bennett, Kris, Cle.	.955	4	6	15	1	22	1
Blasi, Blake, Day.-Sar.	.979	31	62	78	3	143	19
Bourgeois, Jason, Char.	.907	8	20	19	4	43	8
Boyer, Brett, B.C.	.936	52	98	136	16	250	30
Bozanich, Sam, Tam.	.955	86	129	250	18	397	50
Brosseau, Richard, Dun.	1.000	4	10	9	0	19	1
Calabrese, Tony, Tam.	.971	7	9	25	1	35	7
Canales, Josh, V.B.	.990	21	34	61	1	96	13
Cannizaro, Andy, Tam.	.985	13	28	36	1	65	6
Carroll, Wes, Cle.	.889	11	15	25	5	45	6
Cerminaro, Matt, Jup.	.931	15	30	37	5	72	10
Demarco, Matt, Jup.	.984	81	151	207	6	364	60
Desena, Francis, B.C.	1.000	3	2	4	0	6	1
Dorta, Melvin, Sar.	.969	99	228	273	16	517	57
Dzurilla, Mike, Day.	1.000	5	13	6	0	19	1
Easterday, Matt, Jup.	.966	62	116	165	10	291	33
Flamont, Sam, Lak.	.000	1	0	0	0	0	0
Garcia, Daniel, S.L.	.972	105	184	300	14	498	57
Garcia, Tono, Day.	.961	32	72	77	6	155	18
Harris, Brendan, Day.	.972	54	119	163	8	290	37
Heath, Demetrius, Lak.	.951	25	46	51	5	102	16
Helps, Jason, Jup.	.960	7	8	16	1	25	5
Hernandez, Vladimir, B.C.	.976	10	16	24	1	41	2
Hitchcox, Brian, Cle.	.969	29	58	97	5	160	23
Iorg, Isaac, Dun.	.971	9	13	20	1	34	5
Jackson, Brandon, Tam.	.961	28	35	88	5	128	15
Keene, Kurt, Dun.	.986	29	70	70	2	142	9
Machado, Albenis, B.C.	1.000	1	1	3	0	4	0
Martin, Tyler, Char.	1.000	28	35	56	0	91	15
MARTINEZ, Ramon, Char.	.984	100	190	317	8	515	62
Maza, Luis, F.M.	.950	24	34	62	5	101	7
Miller, Eric, B.C.	.963	39	83	101	7	191	23
Montanez, Luis, Day.	.945	22	41	62	6	109	16
Montas, Ricardo, Cle.	.962	11	20	30	2	52	5
Navarro, Mandy, Day.	.960	8	10	14	1	25	4
Nieves, Raul, Sar.	.980	11	24	25	1	50	10
Nunez, Alexis, Cle.	.941	9	19	13	2	34	6
Pittman, Sean, S.L.	.956	18	18	47	3	68	6
Renick, Josh, F.M.	.976	98	193	258	11	462	76
Reyes, Ambiorix, Cle.	.965	15	30	52	3	85	8
Rich, Dominic, Dun.	.977	93	241	277	12	530	73
Rivas, Luis, F.M.	.900	6	6	12	2	20	1
Scanlon, Matt, F.M.	1.000	1	2	3	0	5	2
Schnabel, Nick, B.C.	1.000	5	12	17	0	29	3
Sisk, Aaron, Dun.	.950	4	10	9	1	20	3
Socarras, Tony, B.C.	1.000	1	1	0	0	1	0
Soler, Ramon, S.L.	.947	20	40	50	5	95	11
Soules, Ryan, Char.	1.000	3	5	4	0	9	1
Tempesta, Nick, Dun.	1.000	4	4	4	0	8	1
Tousa, Scott, Lak.	.983	90	169	241	7	417	68
Tyson, Torre, Tam.	1.000	1	1	0	0	1	0
Van Buizen, Rodney, V.B.	.976	118	217	322	13	552	61
Vasquez, Wuillians, Tam.	.917	2	3	8	1	12	1
Velazquez, Gil, S.L.	1.000	1	2	1	0	3	1
Watkins, Tommy, F.M.	.984	19	22	40	1	63	11
Williams, Brady, F.M.	1.000	1	1	2	0	3	1
Williams, Jason, B.C.	.957	37	58	77	6	141	19
Wilson, Josh, Jup.	1.000	3	4	6	0	10	0
Woods, Michael, Lak.	.962	31	51	75	5	131	14
Youngbauer, Scott, Cle.	.953	61	109	196	15	320	34

TRIPLE PLAYS: Heath, Tousa.

SECOND BASEMEN WITH TWO OR MORE TEAMS

Player, Team	Pct.	G	PO	A	E	TC	DP
Blasi, Blake, Day.	1.000	3	6	9	0	15	0
Blasi, Blake, Sar.	.977	28	56	69	3	128	19

THIRD BASEMEN

Player, Team	Pct.	G	PO	A	E	TC	DP
Acevedo, Inocencio, Char.	.900	24	8	46	6	60	9
Ahumada, Alex, Sar.	.917	12	7	26	3	36	1
Angell, Rick, Char.	.800	4	4	4	2	10	2
Arteaga, Joshua, Day.	1.000	1	0	1	0	1	0
AYBAR, Willy, V.B.	.943	107	71	178	15	264	20
Barbier, Blair, Day.	.926	44	19	68	7	94	8
Bartlett, Jason, F.M.	1.000	2	1	3	0	4	0
Bennett, Kris, Cle.	.952	16	11	29	2	42	1
Bernhardt, Joe, Dun.	1.000	1	0	1	0	1	0
Blanco, Tony, Sar.	.828	61	32	112	30	174	9
Blasi, Blake, Sar.	.000	1	0	0	1	1	0
Brosseau, Richard, Dun.	.906	14	10	19	3	32	2
Brown, Matthew, B.C.	.500	1	2	1	3	6	0
Cabrera, Miguel, Jup.	.936	88	58	177	16	251	16
Calabrese, Tony, Tam.	1.000	1	2	2	0	4	0
Canales, Josh, V.B.	1.000	2	1	0	0	1	0
Cannizaro, Andy, Tam.	1.000	2	1	5	0	6	0
Corporan, Elvis, Tam.	.932	106	72	188	19	279	15
Crespo, Manny, Sar.	.000	1	0	0	0	0	0
Cruz, Enrique, S.L.	.920	103	63	223	25	311	19
Dacey, Ryan, V.B.	1.000	2	1	2	0	3	0
Demarco, Matt, Jup.	.933	9	3	11	1	15	1
Deschenes, Pat, S.L.	.968	21	18	43	2	63	1
Detienne, Dave, V.B.	.912	16	10	21	3	34	1
Easterday, Matt, Jup.	1.000	1	1	2	0	3	0
Farnsworth, Troy, Cle.	.979	17	18	28	1	47	7
Garcia, Juan-Carlos, Jup.	.929	7	5	8	1	14	2
Garcia, Tony, Day.	.926	36	16	59	6	81	6
Hannahan, Jack, Lak.	.942	66	44	150	12	206	21
Harris, Brendan, Day.	.951	59	43	112	8	163	19
Hattig, John, Sar.	1.000	5	0	14	0	14	2
Helps, Jason, Jup.	1.000	1	0	1	0	1	0
Iorg, Isaac, Dun.	.933	7	1	13	1	15	3
Jackson, Brandon, Tam.	.909	6	3	7	1	11	1
Keene, Kurt, Dun.	.867	3	5	8	2	15	2
Kelly, Heath, Jup.	1.000	1	1	1	0	2	0
Liniak, Cole, Char.	.957	33	33	56	4	93	4
Machado, Albenis, B.C.	1.000	1	1	1	0	2	0
Martin, Tyler, Char.	.921	34	15	55	6	76	1
Miller, Eric, B.C.	.913	8	12	9	2	23	0
Montas, Ricardo, Cle.	1.000	1	0	1	0	1	0
Moore, Jason, Char.	.941	5	1	15	1	17	0
Myrow, Brian, Tam.	.960	20	8	40	2	50	4
Neill, Ryan, Lak.	.500	1	0	1	1	2	0
Nieves, Raul, Sar.	.886	31	10	52	8	70	4
Olivari, Reinaldo, Char.	.800	4	2	2	1	5	0
Pittman, Sean, S.L.	1.000	3	0	5	0	5	2
Pond, Simon, Dun.	.941	67	49	128	11	188	12
Quattlebaum, Hugh, Lak.	.667	1	1	1	1	3	0
Reyes, Ambiorix, Cle.	.000	3	0	0	0	0	0
Richardson, Juan, Cle.	.924	103	74	182	21	277	25
Rooi, Vince, B.C.	.922	118	77	230	26	333	24
Roper, Zach, Char.	.889	5	2	6	1	9	1
Santos, Jose, Jup.	.885	20	16	30	6	52	2
Scanlon, Matt, F.M.	.919	40	22	69	8	99	6
Schnabel, Nick, B.C.	1.000	1	1	7	0	8	0
Sisk, Aaron, Dun.	.886	45	33	68	13	114	7
Slavik, Corey, Day.	.913	10	9	12	2	23	1
Socarras, Tony, B.C.	1.000	1	0	1	0	1	0
Soules, Ryan, Char.	1.000	1	0	2	0	2	0
Tatis, Fernando, B.C.	.929	5	1	12	1	14	2
Teixeira, Mark, Char.	.902	38	26	57	9	92	5
Tempesta, Nick, Dun.	.964	14	7	20	1	28	0
Tiffee, Terry, F.M.	.912	39	19	64	8	91	5
Tousa, Scott, Lak.	.910	18	17	44	6	67	4
Ust, Brant, Lak.	.933	57	45	135	13	193	13
Van Buizen, Rodney, V.B.	.969	13	3	28	1	32	1
Velazquez, Gil, S.L.	.976	15	7	33	1	41	3
Watkins, Tommy, F.M.	.907	33	20	48	7	75	9
Williams, Brady, F.M.	.900	43	25	65	10	100	6
Williams, Jason, B.C.	.938	7	2	13	1	16	1
Willingham, Josh, Jup.	.931	20	15	39	4	58	2
Wilson, Josh, Jup.	.000	1	0	0	0	0	0
Youkilis, Kevin, Sar.	.936	33	19	69	6	94	6

TRIPLE PLAYS: Hannahan, Tousa.

SHORTSTOPS

Player, Team	Pct.	G	PO	A	E	TC	DP
Acevedo, Inocencio, Char.	.967	10	8	21	1	30	3
Adams, Russ, Dun.	.947	37	55	106	9	170	16
Alvarez, Nick, V.B.	.667	1	1	1	1	3	0
Arteaga, Joshua, Day.	.891	12	18	39	7	64	6
Bartlett, Jason, F.M.	.948	29	52	75	7	134	22
Bautista, Rayner, Lak.	.947	9	12	24	2	38	3
Bennett, Kris, Cle.	.930	10	15	25	3	43	5
Blasi, Blake, Sar.	.900	2	6	3	1	10	2
Bourgeois, Jason, Char.	1.000	1	3	2	0	5	0
Brosseau, Richard, Dun.	.957	8	8	14	1	23	4
Cabrera, Miguel, Jup.	.972	9	10	25	1	36	9
Calabrese, Tony, Tam.	.957	13	14	30	2	46	5
Canales, Josh, V.B.	.930	38	39	67	8	114	14
Cannizaro, Andy, Tam.	.952	98	131	290	21	442	56
Carroll, Wes, Cle.	1.000	1	1	1	0	2	0
Castillo, Carlos, Lak.	1.000	4	2	12	0	14	1
Cerminaro, Michael, Day.	.500	1	0	1	1	2	0
Cruz, Enrique, S.L.	.918	21	28	61	8	97	10
De Los Santos, Eddy, Dun.	1.000	3	6	10	0	16	2
Demarco, Matt, Jup.	.949	17	28	46	4	78	10
Desena, Francis, B.C.	.875	4	4	3	1	8	0
Detienne, Dave, V.B.	.948	78	121	205	18	344	43
Easterday, Matt, Jup.	.000	1	0	0	0	0	0
Figueroa, Luis, B.C.	.918	15	29	38	6	73	9
Garcia, Daniel, S.L.	.907	18	23	45	7	75	9
Garcia, Nick, Sar.	.905	6	7	12	2	21	3
Garcia, Tony, Day.	.888	26	29	66	12	107	12
Helps, Jason, Jup.	.951	11	19	39	3	61	7
Hernandez, Anderson, Lak.	.953	121	209	334	27	570	88
Hernandez, Vladimir, B.C.	.965	26	41	68	4	113	15
Herrera, Christian, V.B.	.925	26	36	75	9	120	7
Hitchcox, Brian, Cle.	.714	2	4	1	2	7	0
Hooper, Clay, Tam.	.988	16	24	60	1	85	8
Howarth, Jason, F.M.	.923	7	8	16	2	26	2
Jackson, Brandon, Tam.	1.000	7	11	17	0	28	2
Keene, Kurt, Dun.	.953	76	109	235	17	361	57
Machado, Albenis, B.C.	.950	3	7	12	1	20	8
Martinez, Ramon, Char.	.971	13	26	40	2	68	7
Maza, Luis, F.M.	.915	74	97	192	27	316	47
Mendez, Deivi, Tam.	.889	2	3	5	1	9	2
Miller, Eric, B.C.	.974	85	115	263	10	388	45
Montanez, Luis, Day.	.928	101	162	250	32	444	52
Montas, Ricardo, Cle.	.833	2	1	4	1	6	1
Morban, Jose, Char.	.943	123	170	389	34	593	63
Navarro, Mandy, Day.	1.000	3	5	10	0	15	2
Nieves, Raul, Sar.	.964	33	51	109	6	166	19
Perez, Kenny, Sar.	.948	101	157	277	24	458	48
Pittman, Sean, S.L.	.890	18	29	44	9	82	7
Reyes, Ambiorix, Cle.	.936	27	49	68	8	125	18
Reyes, Jose, S.L.	.967	69	115	236	12	363	43
Rooi, Vince, B.C.	.000	1	0	0	0	0	0
Schnabel, Nick, B.C.	1.000	7	13	28	0	41	9
Sisk, Aaron, Dun.	.964	18	31	49	3	83	10
Sosa, Juan, Cle.	.963	54	96	163	10	269	25
Tousa, Scott, Lak.	1.000	9	10	22	0	32	6
Van Buizen, Rodney, V.B.	.000	1	0	0	0	0	0
Velazquez, Gil, S.L.	.943	16	27	55	5	87	9
Watkins, Tommy, F.M.	.935	41	75	111	13	199	28
Williams, Jason, B.C.	.857	3	3	3	1	7	1
WILSON, Josh, Jup.	.963	107	168	305	18	491	68
Woodward, Chris, Dun.	1.000	2	1	7	0	8	1
Youngbauer, Scott, Cle.	.901	44	64	118	20	202	23

TRIPLE PLAYS: Figueroa, A. Hernandez.

OUTFIELDERS

Player, Team	Pct.	G	PO	A	E	TC	DP
Abercrombie, Reggie, V.B.	.957	125	229	15	11	255	5
Acevedo, Carlos, Cle.	.969	29	58	4	2	64	1
Acuna, Ron, S.L.	.988	114	226	16	3	245	4
Alou, Moises, Day.	1.000	1	1	0	0	1	0
Alvarez, Nick, V.B.	.982	26	52	4	1	57	1
Ambres, Chip, Jup.	.987	122	292	8	4	304	3
Angell, Rick, Char.	.976	81	160	4	4	168	0
Avila, Rob, Cle.	.978	20	41	3	1	45	2
Bailie, Stefan, Sar.	.000	1	0	0	0	0	0
Barbier, Blair, Day.	.750	3	3	0	1	4	0
Bay, Jason, S.L.	.950	68	106	9	6	121	2
Blasi, Blake, Sar.	1.000	1	2	0	0	2	0
Boitel, Rafael, F.M. *	.987	73	147	3	2	152	0
Boone, Matt, Lak.	.964	36	51	2	2	55	1
Botts, Jason, Char.	.988	86	159	5	2	166	1

Player, Team	Pct.	G	PO	A	E	TC	DP
Bowman, Addison, Sar.	1.000	3	7	0	0	7	0
Boyd, Patrick, Char.	1.000	4	3	0	0	3	0
Brosseau, Richard, Dun.	.000	1	0	0	0	0	0
Brown, Andy, Tam.*	.960	111	182	9	8	199	0
Brown, Matthew, B.C.	1.000	1	2	0	0	2	0
Bryan, Jason, Char.	1.000	2	2	0	0	2	0
Bush, Brian, Cle.	.975	49	115	3	3	121	1
Butler, Keith, Day.	.921	20	34	1	3	38	1
Calabrese, Tony, Tam.	1.000	1	4	0	0	4	0
Cameron, Antoine, Day.*	1.000	29	32	3	0	35	2
Camilo, Juan, Lak.	.986	74	132	7	2	141	0
Canales, Josh, V.B.	1.000	1	2	0	0	2	0
Carter, Shannon, Dun.*	.964	115	209	7	8	224	0
Catalanotte, Greg, Sar.	1.000	29	51	2	0	53	0
Crespo, Manny, Sar.	.909	5	10	0	1	11	0
Dacey, Ryan, V.B.	1.000	2	1	0	0	1	0
Daigle, Leo, Lak.	1.000	1	2	0	0	2	0
Davenport, Ron, Dun.	.969	54	91	2	3	96	0
Demarco, Matt, Jup.	1.000	1	2	0	0	2	0
Devarez, Noel, S.L.	1.000	34	50	3	0	53	2
Diaz, Frank, B.C.	.941	10	14	2	1	17	0
Dill, Jason, Char.*	.956	53	87	0	4	91	0
Dominique, Andy, Cle.	.000	1	0	0	0	0	0
Downing, Phil, B.C.*	.946	49	84	3	5	92	0
Dubois, Jason, Day.	.975	88	151	6	4	161	1
Duncan, Jeff, S.L.*	.967	29	57	2	2	61	1
Easterday, Matt, Jup.	1.000	11	26	0	0	26	0
Everett, Carl, Char.	1.000	1	3	0	0	3	0
Ferrand, Frank, Jup.*	.917	31	43	1	4	48	0
Flamont, Sam, Lak.	1.000	6	3	3	0	6	1
Fowler, David, Tam.	.979	60	133	6	3	142	0
Frazier, Charles, Jup.	1.000	7	14	0	0	14	0
Garbe, B.J., F.M.	.987	104	225	10	3	238	3
Garcia, Daniel, S.L.	.000	1	0	0	0	0	0
Garcia, Douglas, Char.*	.938	35	45	0	3	48	0
Garcia, Tony, Day.	1.000	3	1	0	0	1	0
Gibbs, Kevin, Tam.	1.000	2	5	0	0	5	0
Gingrich, Troy, B.C.*	.975	98	187	11	5	203	3
Giron, Alejandro, Cle.	1.000	33	52	2	0	54	0
Gomez, Ramon, Cle.	.938	15	29	1	2	32	0
Gonzalez, Manny, Cle.	.964	62	129	5	5	139	1
Greenberg, Adam, Day.*	.943	21	45	5	3	53	1
Griffin, John-ford, Tam.*	.959	50	70	0	3	73	0
Grove, Jason, Tam.*	.970	56	96	1	3	100	0
Harris, Cory, S.L.	.962	25	47	3	2	52	0
HENSLEY, Anthony, Cle.	.992	116	255	7	2	264	1
Jenkins, Neil, Lak.	.969	55	118	5	4	127	2
Jimenez, Rich, Dun.	1.000	2	3	2	0	5	1
Johnson, Reed, Dun.	1.000	8	16	3	0	19	0
Johnstone, Ben, Day.	.986	80	142	3	2	147	0
Jones, Mitch, Tam.	.959	23	45	2	2	49	1
Kavourias, Jim, Jup.	.970	89	191	6	6	203	1
Lane, Rich, B.C.*	.984	33	60	3	1	64	1
Langs, Ronte, V.B.	.989	42	83	4	1	88	0
Logan, Nook, Lak.	.970	122	316	7	10	333	1
Martin, Tyler, Char.	1.000	4	1	1	0	2	0
Martinez, Candido, V.B.	1.000	16	34	1	0	35	0
McNaughton, Troy, Cle.*	.978	82	169	6	4	179	3
Michaelis, Derek, V.B.*	.500	5	1	0	1	2	0
Money, Freddie, Sar.	.984	117	294	6	5	305	1
Montague, Ed, V.B.	.957	26	41	3	2	46	0
Myrow, Brian, Tam.	1.000	12	20	0	0	20	0
Neill, Ryan, Lak.	.946	13	35	0	2	37	0
Nicolas, Jose, B.C.	1.000	4	3	0	0	3	0
Nieves, Raul, Sar.	.972	16	34	1	1	36	1
Nix, Laynce, Char.*	.988	124	251	1	3	255	0
O'Sullivan, Patrick, S.L.	1.000	3	4	0	0	4	0
Pagan, Angel, S.L.	1.000	16	28	1	0	29	0
Perry, Jason, Dun.	1.000	3	7	0	0	7	0
Perry, Rod, Cle.	1.000	7	8	0	0	8	0
Piercy, Mike, B.C.*	1.000	4	3	0	0	3	0
Rabe, Josh, F.M.	.983	73	112	5	2	119	0
Repko, Jason, V.B.	.973	120	245	10	7	262	3
Reyes, Deurys, F.M.*	.983	75	106	7	2	115	4
Rigsby, Randy, Jup.*	1.000	25	51	1	0	52	0
Rios, Alexis, Dun.	.967	110	233	2	8	243	1
Rivera, Eric, Cle.	1.000	2	3	0	0	3	0
Rodriguez, Carlos, Sar.	.968	123	252	18	9	279	4
Rodriguez, Edgar, S.L.	1.000	8	10	0	0	10	0
Rombley, Danny, B.C.	.983	54	108	7	2	117	3
Roneberg, Brett, Jup.*	1.000	5	10	1	0	11	0
Rooi, Vince, B.C.	1.000	1	1	0	0	1	0
Sadler, Ray, Day.	.971	110	236	2	7	245	0
Santoro, Pat, Sar.	1.000	24	39	1	0	40	0

Player, Team	Pct.	G	PO	A	E	TC	DP
Scanlon, Matt, F.M.	1.000	1	3	0	0	3	0
Seale, Marvin, S.L.	.980	127	246	3	5	254	0
Segar, Jeff, Tam.	1.000	2	3	2	0	5	0
Sing, Brandon, Day.	.965	91	132	4	5	141	0
Singleton, Justin, Dun.	.986	101	212	4	3	219	0
Sisk, Aaron, Dun.	.947	11	16	2	1	19	0
Sizemore, Grady, B.C.*	.977	71	126	4	3	133	1
Smith, Will, Sar.	1.000	77	156	5	0	161	1
Smith, Will, Jup.	.967	126	221	10	8	239	2
Tarbett, Brent, Sar.	1.000	1	1	0	0	1	0
Tempesta, Nick, Dun.	1.000	1	1	0	0	1	0
Thomas, Charles, V.B.	.978	47	84	3	2	89	0
Thompson, Kevin, Tam.	.960	24	47	1	2	50	0
Tyson, Torre, Tam.	.986	69	139	5	2	146	1
Vaz, Roberto, Char.*	1.000	1	3	0	0	3	0
Walker, Matt, Lak.	.979	90	187	2	4	193	0
Warren, Chris, Sar.	.944	10	17	0	1	18	0
Watkins, Tommy, Tam.*	1.000	3	7	0	0	7	0
Watson, Brandon, B.C.	.983	111	268	14	5	287	6
West, Kevin, F.M.	.970	117	178	13	6	197	4
Williams, Jason, B.C.	.923	10	9	3	1	13	0
Willingham, Josh, Jup.	.935	10	27	2	2	31	1
Wright, Corey, Char.-Sar.*	.975	69	157	1	4	162	0
Yount, Andy, Lak.	.917	26	40	4	4	48	1
Zieour, Neesan, Dun.	.965	38	55	0	2	57	0

TRIPLE PLAYS: Gingrich, Jenkins, Walker.

OUTFIELDERS WITH TWO OR MORE TEAMS

Player, Team	Pct.	G	PO	A	E	TC	DP
Wright, Corey, Char.*	.971	55	132	1	4	137	0
Wright, Corey, Sar.*	1.000	14	25	0	0	25	0

CATCHERS

Player, Team	Pct.	G	PO	A	E	TC	DP	PB
Ackerman, Scott, B.C.	.996	39	233	23	1	257	3	4
Allec, Jason, Lak.	1.000	1	8	0	0	8	0	0
Anderson, Dennis, Jup.	.992	38	234	22	2	258	2	5
Aracena, Sandy, V.B.	.982	66	495	56	10	561	3	11
Avila, Rob, Cle.	1.000	18	118	9	0	127	1	4
Blum, Greg, B.C.	.985	43	254	15	4	273	3	11
Boone, Doug, Tam.	.976	14	68	13	2	83	1	4
Bowen, Rob, F.M.	.981	88	554	68	12	634	8	12
Carreno, Jose, B.C.	.977	13	77	7	2	86	1	3
Cleveland, Russ, Lak.	.986	24	127	9	2	138	1	6
Crespo, Manny, Sar.	1.000	1	11	1	0	12	0	2
Cronin, Shane, Tam.	1.000	9	32	2	0	34	0	0
Cruz, Edgar, Cle.	.987	61	396	43	6	445	3	4
Curry, Chris, Day.	.989	37	250	30	3	283	3	11
Diaz, Joe, V.B.	1.000	3	25	1	0	26	0	3
Diaz, Robinzon, Dun.	.981	7	46	6	1	53	0	2
Duplissea, Bill, V.B.	.989	25	162	22	2	186	3	5
Durazo, William, Sar.	.947	6	36	0	2	38	0	2
Dzurilla, Mike, Day.	1.000	4	14	0	0	14	0	3
Elwood, Brad, Tam.	.992	64	459	37	4	500	2	23
Esposito, Brian, Sar.	.969	21	111	14	4	129	2	5
Fuentes, Omar, Tam.	.991	60	391	31	4	426	2	8
Garland, Ross, Lak.	.978	31	167	11	4	182	1	7
Goldbach, Jeff, Day.	.976	35	225	20	6	251	1	6
Gulledge, Kelley, F.M.	.993	58	389	25	3	417	7	8
Huber, Justin, S.L.	.983	23	159	17	3	179	2	2
Jacobs, Mike, S.L.	.988	56	397	29	5	431	2	7
Jaile, Chris, Char.	.986	65	388	46	6	440	3	11
Johnson, Charles, Jup.	1.000	5	30	3	0	33	1	0
Jones, Jeremy, Char.	1.000	1	7	0	0	7	0	0
Jorgensen, Ryan, Jup.	.990	59	367	40	4	411	2	4
Kay, Brett, S.L.	.970	37	232	25	8	265	3	5
Kellner, Ryan, V.B.	.996	25	221	15	1	237	0	6
Kropf, Andy, Lak.	1.000	4	20	1	0	21	0	0
Kweon, Yoon-Min, Day.	.995	69	528	47	3	578	3	9
Lepine, Olivier, Jup.	.750	1	3	0	1	4	0	0
Lopez, Angel, Jup.	.987	40	275	25	4	304	2	5
Lynam, Guy, Jup.	1.000	3	8	1	0	9	0	0
Martinez, Casey, Dun.	1.000	6	24	6	0	30	0	1
McEachran, Aaron, Dun.	.968	25	145	8	5	158	0	7
McKnight, Lukas, Day.	1.000	1	1	0	0	1	0	0
McMillan, Drew, B.C.	1.000	37	190	32	0	222	7	1
McRoberts, Mark, Cle.	1.000	1	0	1	0	1	0	0
Mooney, Dan, Sar.	.992	20	116	10	1	127	1	4
Navarro, Dioner, Tam.	1.000	1	3	0	0	3	0	0
Ochoa, Javier, Lak.	1.000	2	17	2	0	19	0	0
Price, Jared, V.B.	1.000	12	80	4	0	84	0	3
Quiroz, Guillermo, Dun.	.984	93	607	54	11	672	2	15
Rodriguez, Ivan, Char.	1.000	3	22	2	0	24	0	0

Player, Team	Pct.	G	PO	A	E	TC	DP	PB
Ruiz, Carlos, Cle.	.988	60	363	39	5	407	6	6
St. Pierre, Maxim, Lak.	.988	55	366	54	5	425	8	10
Sanchez, Danilo, Lak.	.966	34	196	29	8	233	3	5
SHOPPACH, Kelly, Sar.	.986	92	573	62	9	644	6	15
Socarras, Tony, B.C.-V.B.	.981	26	140	13	3	156	0	5
Tempesta, Nick, Dun.	.000	1	0	0	0	0	0	0
Torres, Frederick, Char.	.990	34	185	23	2	210	1	8
Umbria, Jose, Dun.	1.000	13	88	12	0	100	0	1
Valencia, Vic, Char.	.994	48	303	26	2	331	2	9
Wilson, John, S.L.	.962	24	159	16	7	182	3	4
Zapey, Winton, Jup.	.969	4	30	1	1	32	0	2

CATCHERS WITH TWO OR MORE TEAMS

Player, Team	Pct.	G	PO	A	E	TC	DP	PB
Socarras, Tony, B.C.	.980	19	90	8	2	100	0	4
Socarras, Tony, V.B.	.982	7	50	5	1	56	0	1

TRIPLE PLAY: Garland.

PITCHERS

Player, Team	Pct.	G	PO	A	E	TC	DP
Abbott, David, Dun.	.818	17	6	3	2	11	0
Adams, Brian, Sar.*	1.000	21	3	8	0	11	0
Adams, Daniel, Cle.	1.000	35	7	8	0	15	0
Albright, Eric, Day.	1.000	12	1	3	0	4	0
Almanza, Armando, Jup.*	1.000	6	0	1	0	1	0
Alvarez, Gabriel, V.B.	1.000	3	1	0	0	1	0
Alvarez, Larry, Day.	.000	1	0	0	0	0	0
An, Byeong, Sar.*	.941	25	2	14	1	17	1
Anderson, Jason, Tam.	1.000	12	1	4	0	5	0
Andrew, Jason, Char.	.000	1	0	0	0	0	0
Andrews, Aron, V.B.	1.000	25	4	10	0	14	0
Arnold, Jason, Tam.	1.000	13	5	7	0	12	0
Arrojo, Rolando, Sar.	.000	1	0	0	0	0	0
Arthurs, Shane, B.C.	1.000	23	5	5	0	10	0
Artiles, Carlos, Tam.*	1.000	17	0	1	0	1	0
Baker, Brad, Sar.	1.000	12	1	4	0	5	0
Barnett, John, Char.	1.000	9	5	3	0	8	0
Bauer, Greg, V.B.	.667	9	2	0	1	3	0
Bautista, Denny, Jup.	.952	19	5	15	1	21	0
Beal, Andy, Tam.*	1.000	10	2	8	0	10	0
Bean, Colter, Tam.	.750	46	6	3	3	12	0
Beckett, Josh, Jup.	1.000	1	1	0	0	1	0
Beirne, Kevin, V.B.	1.000	1	0	1	0	1	0
Benik, Brett, Day.	1.000	5	1	3	0	4	0
Benitez, Fabricio, Sar.	.857	10	3	3	1	7	0
Bennett, Steve, S.L.	1.000	41	2	9	0	11	1
Benoit, Joaquin, Char.	.000	1	0	0	0	0	0
Bentz, Chad, B.C.*	1.000	23	2	4	0	6	0
Berry, Jon, V.B.	1.000	13	2	5	0	7	0
Blalock, Casey, Jup.	1.000	4	1	1	0	2	0
Blaney, Matthew, Sar.	.000	1	0	0	0	0	0
Blankenship, John, Tam.*	.938	13	6	9	1	16	1
Blanton, Jason, Day.	.700	20	1	6	3	10	0
Bonderman, Jeremy, Lak.	1.000	2	1	1	0	2	0
Bonilla, Henry, F.M.	.909	19	2	8	1	11	2
Borrell, Danny, Tam.*	.909	7	1	9	1	11	1
Bradley, Ryan, Tam.	1.000	5	0	1	0	1	0
Brantley, Brian, S.L.	.833	12	1	4	1	6	0
Brito, Eude, Cle.*	1.000	20	1	7	0	8	0
Brooks, Frank, Cle.*	.857	35	3	3	1	7	0
Brown, Andrew, V.B.	.824	25	5	9	3	17	1
Brown, Eric, Day.	.500	25	0	1	1	2	0
Buchanan, Brian, Tam.*	1.000	27	3	6	0	9	0
Buchholz, Taylor, Cle.	1.000	23	12	16	0	28	2
Bucktrot, Keith, Cle.	.964	27	9	18	1	28	0
Burke, Erick, Char.*	1.000	46	5	10	0	15	1
Bush, David, Dun.	1.000	7	0	3	0	3	1
Bye, Chris, B.C.	.875	38	4	10	2	16	0
Byron, Terry, Jup.-Sar.	1.000	39	2	12	0	14	0
Campos, David, Jup.*	1.000	24	3	3	0	6	0
Caputo, Rob, B.C.	.000	2	0	0	1	1	0
Carter, Mark, Day.*	1.000	24	0	1	0	1	0
Carter, Ryan, Cle.*	.941	25	4	12	1	17	0
Casadiego, Gerardo, B.C.	1.000	16	7	8	0	15	1
Castillo, Marcos, V.B.	.857	17	0	6	1	7	0
Cavazos, Andy, Char.	.938	33	4	11	1	16	0
Cedeno, Blas, Cle.	1.000	3	0	1	0	1	1
Cento, Tony, F.M.*	1.000	15	1	6	0	7	0
Chavez, Carlos, V.B.	1.000	11	1	3	0	4	0
Chavez, Chris, Jup.	.600	12	0	3	2	5	0
Chavez, Wilton, Day.	1.000	8	2	3	0	5	0
Chenard, Ken, S.L.	1.000	13	3	9	0	12	1
Chipperfield, Calvin, Lak.	.926	27	8	17	2	27	2

Player, Team	Pct.	G	PO	A	E	TC	DP
Clark, Ryan, Tam.*	.000	5	0	0	0	0	0
Clark, Wade, Lak.	.750	5	1	2	1	4	1
Clemens, Roger, Tam.	.000	1	0	0	0	0	0
Cole, Joey, S.L.	1.000	18	3	11	0	14	0
Collins, Pat, B.C.	.714	17	1	4	2	7	0
Colson, Jason, Dun.	.955	20	9	12	1	22	2
Contreras, Jean, F.M.*	.933	31	6	8	1	15	1
Corbin, John, Day.	1.000	5	3	3	0	6	1
Cordero, Jesus, Cle.	1.000	8	0	1	0	1	0
Corey, Mark, S.L.	.000	1	0	0	0	0	0
Corona, Ronnie, F.M.	.923	23	4	8	1	13	0
Corrado, Matthew, Lak.	1.000	37	7	14	0	21	2
Costello, Ryan, Dun.*	.800	26	0	4	1	5	0
Cox, Mike, S.L.*	1.000	4	0	1	0	1	0
Crabtree, Tim, V.B.	.000	4	0	0	0	0	0
Crawford, Paxton, Sar.	1.000	1	0	0	0	0	0
Cressend, Jack, F.M.	.000	3	0	0	0	0	0
Dagley, Corey, Cle.	1.000	15	1	5	0	6	0
Daws, Josh, F.M.	1.000	21	1	2	0	3	0
Dean, Aaron, Dun.	1.000	28	6	6	0	12	1
De La Rosa, Jorge, Sar.*	1.000	23	7	10	0	17	0
Dequin, Benji, B.C.*	1.000	27	6	10	0	16	0
Detillion, Jamie, Lak.*	1.000	7	1	4	0	5	0
Diaz, Eddie, B.C.	1.000	4	0	1	0	1	0
Diaz, Eddy, Day.	.875	25	2	5	1	8	1
Diggins, Ben, V.B.	.875	20	11	10	3	24	0
Dittfurth, Ryan, Char.	.750	6	2	4	2	8	0
Downs, Scott, B.C.*	1.000	7	0	1	0	1	0
Dumatrait, Phillip, Sar.*	1.000	4	1	1	0	2	0
Dunning, Justin, V.B.	.909	26	7	3	1	11	0
Echols, Britt, B.C.	.000	1	0	0	0	0	0
Echols, Justin, Char.	.842	46	6	10	3	19	1
Elliott, Chad, S.L.*	1.000	28	6	14	0	20	1
Ellis, Steve, Day.	1.000	10	1	2	0	3	0
Elskamp, Andy, Cle.	1.000	26	1	2	0	3	0
Engels, Jackson, Char.*	1.000	10	1	5	0	6	0
Esquivia, Manuel, Jup.	.000	3	0	0	0	0	0
Eyre, Willie, F.M.	1.000	19	4	4	0	8	0
Figueroa, Carlos, Char.*	1.000	15	1	4	0	5	0
File, Bob, Dun.	.000	4	0	0	1	1	0
Fisher, Marc, Day.	1.000	6	1	2	0	3	1
Fisher, Pete, F.M.	1.000	4	0	1	0	1	0
Flannery, Mike, Jup.	1.000	58	4	4	0	8	1
Fontana, Tony, Sar.	1.000	31	7	11	0	18	0
Foote, Joe, F.M.	.977	26	17	25	1	43	3
Ford, Matt, Dun.*	1.000	21	10	18	0	28	2
Francisco, Frank, Sar.	.818	16	5	4	2	11	0
Frasor, Jason, Lak.	.846	24	9	13	4	26	3
Fries, Scott, Day.*	.818	13	3	6	2	11	1
Gahan, Matt, S.L.	1.000	9	1	3	0	4	1
Gardner, Hayden, Char.	.900	45	4	14	2	20	0
Gassner, Dave, Dun.*	.933	23	8	34	3	45	2
Gerk, Jordan, Lak.*	1.000	8	1	3	0	4	0
Gilbert, Rich, Char.*	.964	34	4	23	1	28	1
Glen, William, Dun.	1.000	41	2	3	0	5	0
Gonzalez, Alfredo, V.B.	1.000	17	2	5	0	7	0
Gordon, Tom, Day.	1.000	2	0	1	0	1	0
Grace, Bryan, Tam.	.943	23	10	23	2	35	1
Gracesqui, Frank, Dun.*	.500	10	1	0	1	2	0
Graham, Tom, Char.	.667	25	0	2	1	3	0
Guzman, Angel, Day.	1.000	16	9	14	0	23	2
Hamann, Rob, Dun.	.857	23	1	11	2	14	2
Hamman, Corey, Lak.*	1.000	16	0	2	0	2	0
Hanrahan, Joel, V.B.	.786	25	8	14	6	28	0
Harber, Ryan, Jup.*	1.000	15	1	4	0	5	1
Hawkins, Chad, Char.	1.000	9	2	4	0	6	0
Heams, Shane, Sar.	.000	2	0	0	0	0	0
Hecker, Steven, Dun.	.750	19	1	2	1	4	0
Hee, Aaron, S.L.*	.688	34	2	9	5	16	0
Henkel, Rob, Jup.*	1.000	14	3	8	0	11	0
Hernandez, Yoel, Cle.	1.000	28	9	25	0	34	0
Hitchcock, Sterling, Tam.*	.000	1	0	0	0	0	0
Hodge, Kevin, F.M.	1.000	10	1	1	0	2	0
Holubec, Ken, F.M.*	.964	26	7	20	1	28	5
Howell, Michael, Lak.	1.000	6	2	3	0	5	1
Hubbel, Travis, Dun.	.667	13	0	2	1	3	0
Huffaker, Mike, Char.	.000	2	0	0	0	0	0
Hutchison, Ryan, Cle.	1.000	29	8	15	0	23	0
Johansen, Ryan, V.B.	.714	16	1	4	2	7	0
Johnson, Jeremy, Lak.	1.000	15	3	1	0	4	0
Joseph, Jake, S.L.	1.000	13	5	13	0	18	0
Karp, Josh, B.C.	1.000	7	4	5	0	9	0
Keelin, Chris, Lak.	1.000	19	0	2	0	2	0
Keirstead, Michael, V.B.	.000	2	0	0	0	0	0

Player, Team	Pct.	G	PO	A	E	TC	DP
Kemp, Beau, F.M.	1.000	59	15	14	0	29	0
Kennard, Jeff, Tam.	1.000	12	0	2	0	2	0
Keppel, Bob, S.L.	.850	27	11	23	6	40	3
Key, Chris, Jup.*	1.000	47	6	21	0	27	1
Kinney, Matt, F.M.	.000	1	0	0	1	1	0
Klepacki, Ed, B.C.-Jup.	.500	8	0	1	1	2	0
Knowles, Mike, Tam.	.818	50	3	6	2	11	0
Koenig, Ross, Lak.	1.000	8	1	3	0	4	0
Kolb, Dan, Char.	1.000	4	1	0	0	1	0
Kozlowski, Ben, Char.*	.632	21	1	11	7	19	3
Krawiec, Aaron, Day.*	.933	28	9	33	3	45	1
Kremer, John, Tam.	1.000	25	2	4	0	6	0
Kumagai, Ryo, Sar.	1.000	21	4	2	0	6	0
Kuo, Hong-chih, V.B.*	1.000	4	0	1	0	1	0
Lamber, Justin, F.M.*	.000	5	0	0	1	1	0
Lara, Mauricio, Sar.*	1.000	23	2	13	0	15	0
Larrison, Preston, Lak.	.969	21	9	22	1	32	2
Lavery, Tim, Day.*	.952	29	5	15	1	21	0
Lavigne, Tim, S.L.	1.000	22	0	6	0	6	0
Lee, Seung, Cle.	.000	3	0	0	0	0	0
Leicester, Jon, Day.	.944	20	6	11	1	18	0
Leuenberger, Jeff, Lak.	.000	3	0	0	0	0	0
Lewis, Craig, B.C.	1.000	12	4	4	0	8	0
Lidle, Kevin, Lak.	1.000	9	2	8	0	10	1
Lincoln, Jeff, F.M.	1.000	24	5	20	0	25	1
Lizarraga, Edgar, V.B.	1.000	12	1	0	0	1	0
Loaiza, Esteban, Dun.	1.000	2	1	2	0	3	1
Lockwood, Luke, B.C.*	.917	26	4	18	2	24	1
Lohrman, Dave, S.L.	.500	8	0	1	1	2	0
Lombardi, Justin, Tam.*	.000	2	0	0	0	0	0
Lopez, Arturo, V.B.*	.000	1	0	0	0	0	0
Lopez, Gustavo, Jup.	1.000	18	2	7	0	9	0
Lugo, Ruddy, V.B.	.926	22	16	9	2	27	1
Luna, Brandon, Char.	1.000	7	3	0	0	3	0
Maberry, Mark, S.L.	.857	10	2	4	1	7	1
Manning, Charlie, Tam.*	.917	17	3	19	2	24	0
Marrero, Darwin, B.C.	1.000	9	3	6	0	9	0
Martin, Greg, B.C.*	1.000	4	1	1	0	2	0
Martin, Luke, F.M.*	1.000	3	1	0	0	1	0
Martin, Nick, Day.*	1.000	4	1	3	0	4	0
Martinez, Oscar, Tam.	1.000	25	2	6	0	8	0
Marx, Tommy, Lak.*	.958	30	10	13	1	24	3
Massingale, Matt, Jup.	.500	4	0	1	1	2	0
Mata, Gustavo, B.C.	1.000	11	7	10	0	17	0
Matthews, Barry, Lak.*	.875	12	2	5	1	8	0
Mattioni, Nick, S.L.	.818	41	1	8	2	11	1
Mattox, David, S.L.	1.000	9	2	8	0	10	0
Maust, David, B.C.*	1.000	14	4	5	0	9	0
Mayfield, Brandon, Cle.	1.000	7	1	1	0	2	0
Mays, Joe, F.M.	.000	3	0	0	0	0	0
McAvoy, Jeff, B.C.	1.000	12	1	6	0	7	0
McDonald, Jon, F.M.*	1.000	2	1	1	0	2	1
McGinley, Blake, S.L.*	1.000	18	0	3	0	3	0
McMullen, Jeremy, Day.	1.000	3	0	4	0	4	1
McNutt, Mike, Jup.	.625	27	3	7	6	16	1
Mendoza, Cristian, Tam.	.000	1	0	0	0	0	0
Messenger, Randall, Jup.	.946	28	12	23	2	37	0
Meyer, Todd, B.C.	1.000	4	0	3	0	3	0
Miller, Josh, Cle.	.862	49	7	18	4	29	0
Miniel, Rene, Sar.	.941	26	7	9	1	17	0
Moehler, Brian, Lak.	.714	2	4	1	2	7	0
Montero, Agustin, V.B.	1.000	7	1	1	0	2	0
Montero, Oscar, Day.	.917	51	2	9	1	12	1
Moore, Darin, Char.	1.000	45	6	8	0	14	1
Moreno, Edwin, Char.	1.000	6	1	3	0	4	0
Moseley, Marcus, F.M.	1.000	35	4	5	0	9	2
Moser, Todd, Jup.*	.875	17	3	4	1	8	0
Mounce, Tony, Char.*	1.000	11	2	4	0	6	0
Mowday, Chris, Dun.	.000	10	0	0	0	0	0
Murphy, Matt, Day.*	.947	48	4	14	1	19	0
Murray, Arlington, Char.*	1.000	19	2	13	0	15	0
Murray, Steve, F.M.*	1.000	8	0	1	0	1	0
Musser, Neal, S.L.*	1.000	4	1	5	0	6	0
Nall, T.J., V.B.	1.000	17	0	4	0	4	1
Newman, Eric, V.B.	1.000	7	1	3	0	4	0
Norderum, Jason, B.C.*	.000	2	0	0	0	0	0
Nunley, Derrek, Dun.	1.000	39	5	5	0	10	2
Ochoa, Pablo, S.L.	1.000	4	1	2	0	3	0
Ogiltree, John, Dun.	.933	45	5	9	1	15	2
Olson, Jason, V.B.	.875	10	1	6	1	8	0
Ortiz, Javier, Tam.	.941	9	9	7	1	17	0
Ortiz, Julio, B.C.*	.000	2	0	0	0	0	0
Osoria, Franquelis, V.B.	1.000	3	0	2	0	2	0
Ostlund, Ian, Lak.*	1.000	29	0	3	0	3	0
Parris, Steve, Dun.	1.000	3	0	8	0	8	0
Peeples, Ross, S.L.*	1.000	6	2	3	0	5	1
Penny, Brad, Jup.	.000	2	0	0	0	0	0
Perez, Frank, Lak.	1.000	8	1	0	0	1	0
Perez, Juan, Sar.*	1.000	16	3	11	0	14	0
Perez, Julio, Tam.	1.000	6	1	1	0	2	0
Perez, Michelandy, Sar.	.000	2	0	0	0	0	0
Persby, Andy, F.M.	.857	25	2	4	1	7	0
Peterson, Matt, S.L.	1.000	1	0	1	0	1	0
Pettitte, Andy, Tam.*	1.000	2	1	0	0	1	0
Pierson, Jason, Tam.*	1.000	11	2	3	0	5	0
Pike, Matthew, Tam.	1.000	6	1	1	0	2	0
Pilkington, Brian, V.B.	1.000	3	1	2	0	3	0
Pineda, Jairo, Lak.	.769	33	3	7	3	13	2
Pinto, Renyel, Day.*	1.000	7	2	5	0	7	0
Portobanco, Luz, S.L.	1.000	2	2	1	0	3	0
Pridie, Jon, F.M.	1.000	12	5	9	0	14	1
Quick, Ben, Dun.	.852	32	6	17	4	27	3
Radke, Brad, F.M.	1.000	2	2	1	0	3	0
Ramirez, Jose, Lak.*	1.000	13	0	1	0	1	0
Ratliff, Jon, Jup.	1.000	2	1	1	0	2	0
Reina, Dimas, V.B.	1.000	3	1	0	0	1	0
Rengifo, Nohemar, B.C.	.000	1	0	0	0	0	0
Reyes, Luis, Day.	.667	2	0	2	1	3	0
REYNOLDS, Josh, S.L.	1.000	22	11	28	0	39	6
Rivard, Reggie, Char.	.960	15	9	15	1	25	2
Rodney, Lee, Lak.	.923	22	4	8	1	13	0
Rodriguez, Cristobal, B.C.	1.000	11	0	2	0	2	0
Rodriguez, Orlando, V.B.*	1.000	7	0	2	0	2	0
Romero, Josmir, F.M.	.931	18	8	19	2	29	3
Rosario, Francisco, Dun.	.929	13	5	8	1	14	0
Rundles, Rich, B.C.*	1.000	12	5	11	0	16	0
Russell, Eddie, Jup.	.000	4	0	0	0	0	0
Russo, Scott, B.C.*	1.000	11	1	3	0	4	0
Sadowski, Chad, Cle.	.000	2	0	0	0	0	0
Sandberg, Eric, F.M.*	.000	1	0	0	0	0	0
Sandoval, Marcos, Dun.	.000	3	0	0	0	0	0
Santiago, Victor, V.B.	1.000	4	0	1	0	1	0
Sauer, Marc, Jup.	1.000	30	6	3	0	9	0
Sawyer, Steve, Jup.	.667	46	1	1	1	3	1
Schmitt, Eric, Tam.	1.000	19	5	5	0	10	0
Schoening, Brent, F.M.	1.000	4	2	1	0	3	1
Schroder, Chris, B.C.	1.000	23	3	3	0	6	1
Seale, Dustin, B.C.*	1.000	8	0	3	0	3	0
Sergent, Joe, Jup.*	.909	12	1	9	1	11	1
Silva, Doug, F.M.	1.000	17	8	2	0	10	0
Simpson, Andre, V.B.	1.000	4	0	2	0	2	0
Skinner, John, Jup.	1.000	11	0	4	0	4	1
Sloan, Brandon, Jup.	1.000	6	0	1	0	1	0
Smith, Dan, Lak.	1.000	9	0	1	0	1	0
Smith, Matt, Tam.*	1.000	8	0	3	0	3	0
Solano, Alex, Sar.	1.000	45	7	5	0	12	0
Spencer, Sean, B.C.*	1.000	3	0	1	0	1	0
Stefani, Jason, V.B.*	1.000	8	0	3	0	3	0
Steffek, Brian, V.B.	1.000	2	0	1	0	1	0
Stevens, Josh, Tam.	1.000	21	3	8	0	11	0
Strelitz, Brian, Tam.	1.000	27	7	4	0	11	0
Stults, Eric, V.B.*	.875	13	1	6	1	8	1
Szuminski, Jason, Day.	.966	39	4	24	1	29	2
Tejeda, Rob, Cle.	.800	17	4	8	3	15	1
Telemaco, Amaury, Cle.	1.000	3	4	0	0	4	1
Thompson, Matt, Sar.	.846	25	8	14	4	26	2
Torres, Luis, B.C.	.909	16	6	14	2	22	2
Totten, Heath, V.B.	.968	18	10	20	1	31	0
Trombley, Mike, F.M.	.000	1	0	0	0	0	0
Tucker, Julien, B.C.	1.000	25	1	1	0	2	0
Ungs, Nick, Jup.	.889	4	2	6	1	9	0
Urdaneta, Lino, V.B.	1.000	52	0	9	0	9	0
Urena, Sixto, Char.	1.000	2	0	2	0	2	0
Valdez, Domingo, Char.	1.000	26	0	7	0	7	1
Valle, Yoiset, Sar.*	.875	37	6	8	2	16	1
Vega, Rene, S.L.*	.625	5	1	4	3	8	0
Villegas, Felix, Sar.	.750	29	2	1	1	4	0
Viole, Paul, S.L.	.867	40	5	8	2	15	0
Walker, Adam, S.L.*	.000	1	0	0	0	0	0
Wallace, Jeff, Sar.*	.000	1	0	0	0	0	0
Washburn, Ben, B.C.	1.000	19	1	6	0	7	0
Watkins, Tommy, F.M.	1.000	1	0	0	0	0	0
Watson, Greg, Lak.	1.000	16	1	2	0	3	0
Weatherby Iii, Charles, Sar.	1.000	17	0	2	0	2	0
Webb, John, Day.	.786	10	6	5	3	14	1
Weis, Brad, F.M.*	1.000	13	1	2	0	3	0
Wellemeyer, Todd, Day.	.857	14	5	7	2	14	2
Willis, Dontrelle, Jup.*	1.000	5	3	5	0	8	0

Player, Team	Pct.	G	PO	A	E	TC	DP
Wilson, C.J., Char.*	.840	26	8	13	4	25	2
Wilson, Mike, Cle.	1.000	12	2	7	0	9	0
Witte, Lou, Tam.	.944	22	6	11	1	18	1
Wolf, Randy, Cle.*	1.000	1	1	0	0	1	0
Wolfe, Brian, F.M.	.963	25	4	22	1	27	1
Wood, Bobby, Tam.	1.000	1	0	3	0	3	0
Woodyard, Mark, Lak.	.818	17	1	8	2	11	2
Wynegar, Adam, Day.*	.800	13	6	6	3	15	0
Yennaco, Jay, Sar.	1.000	4	1	0	0	1	0
Yoo, Byung Mok, Sar.	1.000	5	0	1	0	1	1
Zimmerman, Jeff, Char.	.000	2	0	0	0	0	0
Zink, Charlie, Sar.	1.000	4	1	2	0	3	0

TRIPLE PLAY: Matthews.

PITCHERS WITH TWO OR MORE TEAMS

Player, Team	Pct.	G	PO	A	E	TC	DP
Byron, Terry, Jup.	1.000	31	1	9	0	10	0
Byron, Terry, Sar.	1.000	8	1	3	0	4	0
Klepacki, Ed, B.C.	1.000	3	0	1	0	1	0
Klepacki, Ed, Jup.	.000	5	0	0	1	1	0

The following players appeared only as designated hitter, pinch-hitter or pinch runner: Abreu, pr; Coleman, dh; J. Johnson, dh, ph, pr; Petersen, ph; Silvestre, dh.

LEAGUE CHAMPIONS

Year	Team	Pct.
1919—	Sanford*	.605
	Orlando*	.703
1920—	Tampa	.654
	Tampa	.722
1921—	Orlando	.635
1922—	St. Petersburg	.503
	St. Petersburg	.618
1923—	Orlando	.667
	Orlando	.678
1924—	Lakeland	.695
	Lakeland	.683
1925—	St. Petersburg	.667
	Tampa†	.696
1926—	Sanford	.647
	Sanford	.623
1927—	Orlando†	.600
	Miami	.661
1928-35—	Did not operate.	
1936—	Gainesville	.542
	St. Augustine (4th)†	.492
1937—	Gainesville§	.616
1938—	Leesburg	.626
	Gainesville (2nd)‡	.615
1939—	Sanford§	.787
1940—	Daytona Beach	.619
	Orlando (4th)‡	.507
1941—	St. Augustine	.659
	Leesburg (4th)‡	.488
1942-45—	Did not operate.	
1946—	Orlando§	.681
1947—	St. Augustine	.625
	Gainesville (2nd)‡	.584
1948—	Orlando	.643
	Daytona Beach (2nd)‡	.616
1949—	Gainesville	.635
	St. Augustine (3rd)‡	.556
1950—	Orlando	.629
	DeLand (3rd)‡	.590
1951—	DeLand§	.643
1952—	DeLand∞	.704
	Palatka (3rd)‡	.569
1953—	Daytona Beach†	.657
	DeLand	.703
1954—	Jacksonville Beach	.629
	Lakeland†	.594
1955—	Orlando	.671
	Orlando	.643

Year	Team	Pct.
1956—	Cocoa	.614
	Cocoa	.671
1957—	Palatka	.629
	Tampa†	.681
1958—	St. Petersburg	.732
	St. Petersburg	.681
1959—	Tampa	.591
	St. Petersburg†	.612
1960—	Lakeland	.731
	Palatka†	.614
1961—	Tampa†	.710
	Sarasota	.696
1962—	Sarasota	.689
	Fort Lauderdale†	.623
1963—	Sarasota	.645
	Sarasota	.667
1964—	Fort Lauderdale†	.629
	St. Petersburg	.594
1965—	Fort Lauderdale	.627
	Fort Lauderdale	.634
1966—	Leesburg†	.781
	St. Petersburg	.700
1967—	St. Petersburg▲	.691
	Orlando	.638
1968—	Miami	.613
	Orlando♦	.579
1969—	Miami■	.606
	Orlando	.606
1970—	Miami▼	.662
	St. Petersburg	.600
1971—	Miami▼	.667
	Daytona Beach	.586
1972—	Miami•	.562
	Daytona Beach	.606
1973—	St. Petersburg††	.575
	West Palm Beach	.580
1974—	West Palm Beach††	.598
	Fort Lauderdale	.626
1975—	St. Petersburg††	.652
	Miami	.581
1976—	Tampa	.559
	Lakeland††	.536
1977—	Lakeland††	.616
	West Palm Beach	.583
1978—	Lakeland	.565
	Miami§	.539
1979—	Fort Lauderdale	.643

Year	Team	Pct.
	Winter Haven‡‡	.577
1980—	Daytona Beach	.628
	Fort Lauderdale††	.606
1981—	Fort Myers	.554
	Daytona Beach§§	.504
1982—	Fort Lauderdale§§	.621
	Tampa	.546
1983—	Daytona Beach	.634
	Vero Beach§§	.515
1984—	Tampa	.532
	Fort Lauderdale§§	.521
1985—	Fort Myers∞∞∞	.590
	Fort Lauderdale	.550
1986—	St. Petersburg∞∞∞	.647
	West Palm Beach	.593
1987—	Fort Lauderdale∞∞∞	.616
	Osceola	.576
1988—	Osceola	.606
	St. Lucie▲▲	.532
1989—	Port Charlotte▲▲	.540
	St. Petersburg	.540
1990—	West Palm Beach	.697
	Vero Beach▲▲	.585
1991—	Clearwater	.623
	West Palm Beach▲▲	.550
1992—	Sarasota	.639
	Lakeland♦♦	.530
1993—	St. Lucie	.600
	Clearwater§§	.556
1994—	Tampa§§	.606
	Brevard County	.561
1995—	Daytona§§	.644
	Fort Myers	.577
1996—	Tampa	.627
	St. Lucie§§	.534
1997—	St. Petersburg■ ■.	.591
	Vero Beach	.511
1998—	Charlotte	.594
	St. Lucie■ ■.	.515
1999—	Dunedin	.628
	Kissimmee■ ■.	.578
2000—	Dunedin	.609
	Daytona■ ■.	.547
2001—	Brevard County▼▼	.593
	Tampa▼▼	.554
2002—	Charlotte■■.	.600

*Split-season playoff abandoned after each team won three games. †Won split-season playoff. ‡Won four-club playoff. §Won championship and four-club playoff. ∞Won both halves of split season. ▲League divided into Eastern and Western divisions with split season. St. Petersburg and Orlando won both halves of split season; St. Petersburg won playoff. ♦League divided into Eastern and Western divisions. Miami won regular-season pennant on basis of highest won-lost percentage. Orlando won four-club playoff involving first two teams in each division. ■ League divided into Southern and Central divisions. Miami won playoff between division leaders. (NOTE—Pennant awarded to playoff winner in 1936.) ▼League divided into Eastern and Western divisions. Miami won regular-season pennant on basis of highest won-loss percentage, and also won four-club playoff involving first two teams in each division. •League divided into Eastern and Western divisions. Won four-club playoff involving first two teams in each division. ††League divided into Northern and Southern divisions. Won four-club playoff involving first two teams in each division. ‡‡League divided into Northern and Southern divisions. Same two clubs won both halves; won playoffs. §§Won split-season playoff. ∞∞∞League divided into Western, Central and Southern divisions. Won four-club playoff. ▲▲League divided into Eastern, Western and Central divisions; played split-season. Won six-club playoff. ♦♦League divided into Eastern, Western and Central divisions; played split-season. Won eight-club playoff. ■ ■ League divided into East and West divisions and played split season; won four-club playoff. ▼▼League divided into East and West divisions and played split season; teams were about to start final round of playoffs, but were declared co-champions when Professional Baseball declared a stoppage of play.

MIDWEST LEAGUE

LEAGUE OFFICE

President
George H. Spelius
Address
P.O. Box 936
Beloit, WI 53512
Phone
608-364-1188

Teams (affiliation)
Battle Creek Yankees (Yankees)
Beloit Snappers (Brewers)
Burlington Bees (Royals)
Cedar Rapids Kernels (Angels)
Clinton Lumber Kings (Rangers)
Dayton Dragons (Reds)
Fort Wayne Wizards (Padres)

Kane County Cougars (A's)
Lansing Lugnuts (Cubs)
Peoria Chiefs (Cardinals)
Quad City River Bandits (Twins)
South Bend Silver Hawks
 (Diamondbacks)
West Michigan Whitecaps (Tigers)
Wisconsin Timber Rattlers (Mariners)

2002 FINAL STANDINGS

FIRST HALF

EASTERN DIVISION

Team	W	L	T	Pct.	GB
Michigan (Astros)	42	28	0	.600	...
West Michigan (Tigers)	41	29	0	.586	1.0
Fort Wayne (Padres)	39	28	0	.582	1.5
Lansing (Cubs)	37	32	0	.536	4.5
Dayton (Reds)	32	38	0	.457	10.0
South Bend (Diamondbacks)	29	40	0	.420	12.5

WESTERN DIVISION

Team	W	L	T	Pct.	GB
Peoria (Cardinals)	42	26	0	.618	...
Cedar Rapids (Angels)	37	32	0	.536	5.5
Burlington (Royals)	33	36	0	.478	9.5
Quad City (Twins)	31	35	0	.470	10.0
Wisconsin (Mariners)	30	39	0	.435	12.5
Beloit (Brewers)	30	39	0	.435	12.5
Clinton (Expos)	28	38	0	.424	13.0
Kane County (Marlins)	29	40	0	.420	13.5

SECOND HALF

EASTERN DIVISION

Team	W	L	T	Pct.	GB
West Michigan (Tigers)	42	28	0	.600	...
Dayton (Reds)	41	29	0	.586	1.0
Michigan (Astros)	37	33	0	.529	5.0
Lansing (Cubs)	37	33	0	.529	5.0
Fort Wayne (Padres)	30	40	0	.429	12.0
South Bend (Diamondbacks)	23	47	0	.329	19.0

WESTERN DIVISION

Team	W	L	T	Pct.	GB
Cedar Rapids (Angels)	44	26	0	.629	...
Peoria (Cardinals)	43	27	0	.614	1.0
Quad City (Twins)	40	30	0	.571	4.0
Kane County (Marlins)	35	35	0	.500	9.0
Burlington (Royals)	35	35	0	.500	9.0
Clinton (Expos)	33	37	0	.471	11.0
Beloit (Brewers)	27	43	0	.386	17.0
Wisconsin (Mariners)	23	47	0	.329	21.0

COMPOSITE

Team	Peo.	W.M.	C.R.	Mich.	Lan.	Q.C.	Day.	F.W.	Burl.	K.C.	Clin.	Bel.	Wis.	S.B.	W	L	T	Pct.	GB
Peoria (Cardinals)	...	4	7	6	5	7	5	4	8	9	6	7	10	7	85	53	0	.616	...
West Michigan (Tigers)	4	...	5	7	8	3	11	9	6	4	5	4	6	11	83	57	0	.593	3.0
Cedar Rapids (Angels)	5	3	...	5	5	7	5	3	7	8	7	11	9	6	81	58	0	.583	4.5
Michigan (Astros)	2	5	3	...	8	6	7	8	7	4	6	6	6	11	79	61	0	.564	7.0
Lansing (Cubs)	3	8	3	8	...	5	8	7	5	4	7	4	3	9	74	65	0	.532	11.5
Quad City (Twins)	7	5	4	2	3	...	4	3	8	7	5	8	8	7	71	65	0	.522	13.0
Dayton (Reds)	3	5	3	9	8	4	...	7	4	3	5	8	4	10	73	67	0	.521	13.0
Fort Wayne (Padres)	4	7	5	8	6	5	7	...	4	4	2	4	6	7	69	68	0	.504	15.5
Burlington (Royals)	4	2	7	1	3	5	4	4	...	10	9	7	5	7	68	71	0	.489	17.5
Kane County (Marlins)	5	3	4	4	4	6	5	4	4	...	7	4	11	3	64	75	0	.460	21.5
Clinton (Expos)	5	3	7	2	1	7	3	4	5	5	...	8	9	2	61	75	0	.449	23.0
Beloit (Brewers)	4	5	5	2	4	6	0	4	5	8	6	...	4	4	57	82	0	.410	28.5
Wisconsin (Mariners)	6	2	3	2	5	3	4	2	7	3	5	8	...	3	53	86	0	.381	32.5
South Bend (Diamondbacks)	1	5	2	5	5	1	4	9	1	6	5	3	5	...	52	87	0	.374	33.5

Quad City's home games played in Davenport, Iowa; Kane County's home games played in Geneva, Ill.; Michgan's home games played in Battle Creek, Mich.; West Michigan's home games played in Comstock Park, Mich.

Major league affiliations in parentheses.

PLAYOFFS: Cedar Rapids defeated Quad City, two games to none; Peoria defeated Burlington, two games to none; West Michigan defeated Dayton, two games to none; Lansing defeated Michigan, two games to one; Peoria defeated Cedar Rapids, two games to none; Lansing defeated West Michigan, two games to one. Peoria defeated Lansing, three games to one to win Midwest League championship.

REGULAR-SEASON ATTENDANCE: Beloit, 74,096; Burlington, 58,511; Cedar Rapids, 196,066; Clinton, 78,550; Dayton, 571,094; Fort Wayne, 260,166; Kane County, 510,390; Lansing, 380,820; Michigan, 84,723; Peoria, 254,407; Quad City, 117,559; South Bend, 181,021; West Michigan, 400,166; Wisconsin, 199,210. Total—3,366,779. Playoff (18 games)—50,827. Midwest League All-Star Game at Lansing—10,334.

MANAGERS: Beloit, Don Money; Burlington, Joe Szekely; Cedar Rapids, Todd Claus; Clinton, Dave Machemer; Dayton, Donnie Scott; Fort Wayne, Tracy Woodson; Kane County, Steve Phillips; Lansing, Julio Garcia; Michigan, John Massarelli; Peoria, Danny Sheaffer; Quad City, Jeff Carter; South Bend, Dick Schofield; West Michigan, Phil Regan; Wisconsin, Gary Thurman.

ALL-STAR TEAM: 1B—Jason Stokes, Kane County; 2B—Scott Hairston, South Bend; 3B—Edwin Encarnacion, Dayton; SS—John Nelson, Peoria; OF—Gary Varner, Dayton-West Michigan; OF—Shin-Soo Choo, Wisconsin; OF—Jason Kubel, Quad City; C—Joe Mauer, Quad City; DH—Steve Checksfield, Michigan; RHP—Donald Levinski, Clinton; LHP—Dontrelle Willis, Kane County; RH Relief pitcher—Nate Cotton, Dayton; LH Relief pitcher—Rusty Tucker, Fort Wayne; Most Valuable Player—Jason Stokes, Kane County; Prospect of the Year—Joe Mauer, Quad City; Manager of the Year—Todd Claus, Cedar Rapids.

TEAM

Team	G	TPA	AB	R	H	TB	2B	3B	HR	RBI	SH	SF	HP	BB	IBB	SO	SB	CS	GDP	LOB	ShO	Avg.	OBP	Slg.
Dayton..........	140	5293	4719	663	1233	1859	252	37	100	593	36	41	76	421	10	990	151	61	112	945	4	.261	.329	.394
Peoria...........	138	5283	4688	671	1224	1916	256	35	122	620	34	40	57	464	23	1075	117	60	97	980	2	.261	.332	.409
Cedar Rapids.	139	5398	4679	698	1212	1764	248	35	78	619	43	47	67	562	10	1069	146	75	83	1042	5	.259	.344	.377
Burlington	139	5394	4653	654	1205	1695	244	42	54	567	70	51	74	546	8	1005	79	59	110	1096	8	.259	.343	.364
Quad City	136	5051	4548	592	1164	1662	223	19	79	527	42	34	3	424	15	824	71	41	119	992	12	.256	.318	.365
Fort Wayne....	137	5113	4615	567	1181	1699	234	28	76	516	27	39	59	373	15	989	133	56	96	953	6	.256	.317	.368
Beloit	139	5241	4687	606	1195	1671	223	26	67	543	63	39	63	389	11	883	90	44	80	982	13	.255	.318	.357
Michigan	140	5264	4598	703	1172	1712	239	44	71	620	40	53	61	512	11	944	175	70	85	947	6	.255	.334	.372
W. Michigan..	140	5393	4677	634	1165	1627	216	51	48	573	66	45	64	541	24	1067	148	54	99	1045	9	.249	.332	.348
Clinton..........	136	5069	4498	588	1117	1671	226	29	90	528	34	52	58	427	13	1059	83	64	101	910	6	.248	.318	.371
Wisconsin	139	5107	4569	531	1113	1546	194	28	61	468	32	27	80	399	17	934	124	82	101	934	17	.244	.314	.338
Lansing	139	5159	4612	572	1114	1622	237	35	67	508	34	30	75	408	18	855	103	66	82	916	14	.242	.312	.352
Kane County..	139	5215	4547	559	1086	1528	190	27	66	500	65	35	62	506	22	1090	147	70	88	987	6	.239	.321	.336
South Bend ...	139	5201	4593	526	1044	1514	223	29	63	470	52	36	65	455	13	1182	90	51	81	967	10	.227	.304	.330

INDIVIDUAL

TOP QUALIFIERS FOR BATTING CHAMPIONSHIP

Minimum 378 plate appearances. *Lefthanded batter. †Switch-hitter.

Player, Team	G	TPA	AB	R	H	TB	2B	3B	HR	RBI	SH	SF	HP	BB	IBB	SO	SB	CS	GDP	Avg.	OBP	Slg.
Stokes, Jason, K.C.	97	407	349	73	119	225	25	0	27	75	0	5	5	47	15	96	1	1	5	.341	.421	.645
Hairston, Scott, S.B.	109	468	394	79	131	222	35	4	16	72	1	5	10	58	3	74	9	3	11	.332	.426	.563
Kubel, Jason, Q.C.*	115	471	424	60	136	221	26	4	17	69	2	3	1	41	2	48	3	5	11	.321	.380	.521
Boyd, Shaun, Peo.	129	588	520	91	163	245	36	5	12	60	5	5	4	54	1	78	32	7	10	.313	.379	.471
Self, Todd, Mich.*	136	575	491	81	152	234	36	5	12	94	2	8	9	65	4	104	10	1	8	.310	.394	.477
Barfield, Josh, F.W.	129	574	536	73	164	216	22	3	8	57	3	5	4	26	0	105	26	8	13	.306	.340	.403
Varner, Noochie, Day.-W.M. ..	133	574	534	83	163	247	28	13	10	70	1	2	5	32	0	121	37	4	16	.305	.349	.463
Choo, Shin-soo, Wis.*	119	507	420	69	127	185	24	8	6	48	3	1	13	70	5	98	34	21	2	.302	.417	.440
Mauer, Joe, Q.C.*	110	476	411	58	124	161	23	1	4	62	0	2	2	61	4	42	0	0	16	.302	.393	.392
Tejeda, Juan, W.M.	137	596	524	68	157	236	34	6	11	106	0	7	5	60	8	89	5	1	7	.300	.372	.450
Nelson, Brad, Bel.*	106	459	417	70	124	217	38	2	17	99	0	4	4	34	4	86	4	1	9	.297	.353	.520
Ayala, Odannys, Burl.	114	479	401	68	119	173	22	7	6	61	6	5	6	61	0	70	5	3	13	.297	.393	.431
Shanks, James, Burl.	126	589	515	81	152	204	26	4	6	53	12	5	6	51	2	94	26	11	4	.295	.362	.396
Fallon, Chris, Burl.*	125	543	463	58	136	193	33	3	6	77	5	6	2	67	4	91	0	4	14	.294	.381	.417
Gorneault, Nicholas, C.R.	103	383	346	60	100	161	17	7	10	53	2	3	2	30	0	106	12	5	3	.289	.346	.465

DEPARTMENTAL LEADERS: G—Asadoorian, Tejeda, 137 each; AB—Barfield, 536; R—Conrad, Francia, M. Rodriguez, 94 each; H—Barfield, 164; TB—Varner, 247; 2B—Gotay, 42; 3B—Conrad, 14; HR—Stokes, 27; RBI—Tejeda, 106; SH—Francia, 20; SF—Labandeira, 12; HP—Sandoval, 18; BB—McPherson, 78; IBB—Stokes, 15; SO—Lemon, 165; SB—Francia, 53; CS—Choo, 21; GIDP—Rabelo, 21; Slg.—Stokes, .645; OBP—Hairston, .426.

ALL PLAYERS

*Lefthanded batter. †Switch-hitter.

Player, Team	G	TPA	AB	R	H	TB	2B	3B	HR	RBI	SH	SF	HP	BB	IBB	SO	SB	CS	GDP	Avg.	OBP	Slg.
Abram, Matt, Q.C.	80	268	242	23	54	81	9	0	6	32	0	2	5	19	1	51	1	3	8	.223	.291	.335
Acors, Bo, Wis.	14	1	1	0	0	0	0	0	0	0	0	0	0	0	0	1	0	0	0	.000	.000	.000
Agar, Cory, Q.C.	15	59	53	4	8	9	1	0	0	2	1	0	2	3	0	14	0	0	4	.151	.224	.170
Allec, Jason, W.M.	3	8	7	0	0	0	0	0	0	0	1	0	0	0	0	3	0	0	0	.000	.000	.000
Alleva, J.D., Burl.*	58	212	187	15	42	48	6	0	0	18	1	2	2	20	0	24	0	0	6	.225	.303	.257
Amador, Jerry, Wis.	20	80	76	7	11	12	1	0	0	1	0	1	0	3	0	15	0	0	2	.145	.188	.158
Ambrosini, Anthony, Clin.	70	229	199	21	43	52	7	1	0	20	4	5	2	19	0	31	0	0	8	.216	.284	.261
Ambrosini, Dominick, Clin.* ..	121	477	441	53	123	175	29	4	5	50	3	1	1	31	1	113	7	5	10	.279	.327	.397
Anderson, Dennis, K.C.†	47	191	166	17	41	66	7	3	4	19	1	1	5	18	1	23	4	2	4	.247	.337	.398
Anderson, Keto, F.W.*	88	326	310	32	87	117	11	8	1	28	2	3	1	10	0	34	11	9	3	.281	.302	.377
Anderson, Sam, W.M.	16	46	43	1	7	7	0	0	0	5	1	0	0	2	0	12	0	0	1	.163	.200	.163
Aquino, Jackson, F.W.†	101	361	320	33	66	83	12	1	1	25	6	3	4	28	0	70	12	10	5	.206	.276	.259
Arnerich, Tony, Burl.	11	44	39	5	9	10	1	0	0	3	0	1	0	4	0	9	0	0	0	.231	.295	.256
Arnott, George, K.C.	89	346	308	29	64	104	16	0	8	36	2	4	6	26	0	96	4	2	9	.208	.279	.338
Arroyo, Abner, F.W.*	8	35	34	1	4	7	0	0	1	3	0	0	1	0	0	14	0	0	2	.118	.143	.206
Arroyo, William, K.C.*..........	72	284	223	30	53	62	5	2	0	22	7	3	3	48	1	38	11	10	7	.238	.375	.278
Arteaga, Joshua, Lan.	45	161	143	16	36	50	9	1	1	12	2	1	1	14	2	15	1	2	3	.252	.321	.350
Asadoorian, Rick, Peo..........	137	500	445	70	118	176	12	11	8	55	3	1	7	44	1	96	14	8	7	.265	.340	.396
Ayala, Elio, Bel.	58	217	196	23	51	60	5	2	0	18	2	0	2	17	0	29	4	1	1	.260	.326	.306
Ayala, Odannys, Burl.	114	479	401	68	119	173	22	7	6	61	6	5	6	61	0	70	5	3	13	.297	.393	.431
Ball, Jarred, S.B.†	87	375	321	48	77	104	13	4	2	23	5	1	6	42	1	85	12	1	7	.240	.338	.324
Barfield, Josh, F.W.	129	574	536	73	164	216	22	3	8	57	3	5	4	26	0	105	26	8	13	.306	.340	.403
Barnwell, Chris, Bel.	91	386	344	37	78	97	12	2	1	40	5	3	7	27	0	47	13	5	4	.227	.294	.282
Barrett, Rich, S.B.	54	196	178	17	40	55	10	1	1	14	1	1	5	11	0	60	12	2	2	.225	.287	.309
Bassett, Mike, Day.*	12	46	44	5	11	12	1	0	0	2	0	0	2	0	7	0	0	0	.250	.283	.273
Bastida-Martinez, Evel, Wis.*.	11	46	40	8	14	17	1	1	0	3	0	0	0	6	2	5	4	4	0	.350	.435	.425
Belcher, Jason, Bel.*	98	399	348	44	91	128	19	0	6	38	0	3	3	45	1	42	3	1	10	.261	.348	.368
Bell, Paul, Bel.	19	68	59	3	11	17	3	0	1	4	2	0	0	7	0	23	0	0	0	.186	.273	.288
Benick, Jon, F.W.†	133	563	490	59	133	210	30	1	15	73	0	8	2	61	7	106	5	3	8	.271	.349	.429
Bergolla, William, Day.	68	297	274	38	68	92	13	1	3	23	5	1	1	16	0	36	13	2	6	.248	.291	.336
Biernbaum, L.J., F.W.*	42	160	132	20	34	44	7	0	1	17	2	1	1	24	0	24	5	2	0	.258	.373	.333
Blackburn, Franco, K.C.*........	17	60	52	4	8	9	1	0	0	3	2	0	0	6	0	8	1	0	1	.154	.241	.173

Player, Team	G	TPA	AB	R	H	TB	2B	3B	HR	RBI	SH	SF	HP	BB	IBB	SO	SB	CS	GDP	Avg.	OBP	Slg.
Boone, Matt, Day.	33	135	121	13	23	38	6	0	3	19	0	1	4	9	0	37	1	1	2	.190	.267	.314
Bouras, Brad, Lan.	127	521	457	54	124	204	30	1	16	71	1	2	7	54	3	72	1	2	8	.271	.356	.446
Bowen, Rob, Q.C.†	5	23	21	1	4	5	1	0	0	0	0	0	0	2	0	4	0	0	0	.190	.261	.238
Boyd, Dan, Bel.	95	435	381	62	109	149	22	3	4	54	1	5	11	37	0	54	2	0	6	.286	.362	.391
Boyd, Shaun, Peo.	129	588	524	90	163	245	36	5	12	60	5	5	4	54	1	78	32	7	10	.313	.379	.471
Boyer, Brett, Clin.	60	259	221	31	53	78	11	1	4	23	4	3	1	30	0	70	6	7	1	.240	.329	.353
Brand, Kevin, S.B.†	28	102	92	7	23	24	1	0	0	4	1	1	0	8	0	18	3	1	2	.250	.307	.261
Brewer, Anthony, K.C.	119	473	405	52	80	113	14	5	3	32	7	2	7	52	0	112	22	12	6	.198	.298	.279
Brooks, Doc, F.W.	73	270	237	30	55	75	11	0	3	17	0	2	9	22	0	54	5	2	6	.232	.319	.316
Brostrom, Jeremy, W.M.*	42	140	125	9	32	44	10	1	0	13	1	1	0	13	3	24	1	0	2	.256	.324	.352
Brown, Hunter, Wis.	44	189	152	20	36	58	7	0	5	21	0	2	3	32	1	33	3	1	1	.237	.376	.382
Brown, Matthew, Clin.†	102	384	342	39	78	130	20	1	10	41	0	5	5	32	1	89	3	2	12	.228	.299	.380
Cadena, Alex, Wis.	40	159	140	14	37	47	7	0	1	19	1	2	4	12	0	11	0	0	5	.264	.335	.336
Cahill, Jonathan, C.R.	72	257	221	26	46	59	8	1	1	28	6	2	1	27	0	42	4	3	8	.208	.295	.267
Callahan, Dan, S.B.*	50	193	181	21	53	61	4	2	0	11	3	1	0	8	0	36	2	1	5	.293	.321	.337
Cameron, Antoine, Lan.*	34	146	128	22	35	64	14	0	5	22	0	0	1	17	0	39	2	2	2	.273	.363	.500
Campana, Wandel, Day.	115	464	432	68	121	166	21	3	6	44	4	5	3	20	1	40	15	13	9	.280	.313	.384
Candelaria, Scott, Bel.	34	140	126	23	41	52	7	2	0	17	5	3	0	6	1	20	2	1	0	.325	.348	.413
Carrow, Tom, Bel.	75	296	270	30	71	103	11	0	7	35	3	2	6	15	0	51	2	2	1	.263	.314	.381
Carter, Josh, F.W.	77	286	272	28	73	91	10	1	2	21	0	0	3	11	0	33	5	2	9	.268	.304	.335
Cedeno, Ronny, Lan.	98	417	376	44	80	111	17	4	2	31	8	3	8	22	0	74	14	10	6	.213	.269	.295
Chauncey, Clinton, Peo.	20	49	43	6	10	13	3	0	0	3	0	0	1	5	1	11	1	1	2	.233	.327	.302
Chavez, Ozzie, Bel.†	128	531	463	55	118	146	13	6	1	36	14	5	3	46	0	86	10	6	8	.255	.323	.315
Checksfield, Steven, Mich.	122	495	440	59	96	173	21	4	16	87	1	11	3	40	1	113	4	5	9	.218	.281	.393
Choo, Shin-soo, Wis.*	119	507	420	69	127	185	24	8	6	48	3	1	13	70	5	98	34	21	2	.302	.417	.440
Cleveland, Matt, Burl.	55	184	160	19	29	39	4	0	2	14	5	1	4	14	0	45	2	2	5	.181	.263	.244
Clute, Kris, K.C.	91	382	328	49	79	103	20	2	0	24	9	2	5	38	0	73	22	8	6	.241	.327	.314
Coats, Buck, Lan.*	133	544	501	65	129	170	21	4	4	47	2	6	4	31	4	67	14	3	5	.257	.303	.339
Cole, John, Wis.	31	129	117	14	30	39	2	2	1	7	1	0	0	11	0	20	4	1	5	.256	.320	.333
Collins, Chris, Wis.	101	411	374	34	97	136	24	0	5	44	4	2	4	27	0	52	0	0	11	.259	.314	.364
Conrad, Brooks, Mich.†	133	577	499	94	143	238	25	14	14	94	1	8	7	62	0	102	18	8	2	.287	.368	.477
Cordova, Ben, Burl.*	70	267	229	26	59	81	8	1	4	27	0	3	2	33	0	36	1	0	6	.258	.352	.354
Cordova, Ricardo, Peo.†	24	37	37	11	12	19	2	1	1	6	0	0	0	0	0	8	2	0	0	.324	.324	.514
Cordova, Roman, Wis.†	44	176	165	20	33	42	6	0	1	8	1	0	4	6	0	26	5	7	5	.200	.246	.255
Creighton, Matt, Lan.	2	8	6	0	1	1	0	0	0	1	0	0	1	1	0	1	0	0	0	.167	.375	.167
Davidson, Seth, Q.C.†	56	234	209	22	48	62	8	0	2	24	2	0	4	19	1	14	4	4	4	.230	.306	.297
Davis, Justin, Day.*	114	413	354	45	98	140	25	4	3	36	0	4	1	54	1	56	5	6	4	.277	.370	.395
Dean, Erik, Burl.*	21	77	70	11	17	24	5	1	0	8	1	1	2	3	0	9	1	0	2	.243	.289	.343
Del Chiaro, Brent, C.R.	37	108	94	12	20	21	1	0	0	9	2	1	1	10	0	38	0	0	2	.213	.292	.223
De Los Santos, Pedro, F.W.†.	47	210	190	35	53	70	7	5	0	18	2	0	0	18	0	37	39	7	3	.279	.341	.368
Denorfia, Christopher, Day.	3	10	10	2	0	0	0	0	0	0	0	0	0	0	0	3	0	1	0	.000	.000	.000
Diaz, Felix, Clin.†	52	216	191	34	48	99	7	4	12	30	0	3	3	19	2	63	1	1	1	.251	.324	.518
Dibetta, John, F.W.	17	63	50	7	10	10	0	0	0	5	3	1	1	8	1	5	2	0	0	.200	.317	.200
DiRosa, Michael, S.B.	67	258	205	23	45	69	12	0	4	21	5	0	4	44	1	81	1	4	4	.220	.368	.337
Dobbs, Greg, Wis.*	86	355	320	43	88	138	16	2	10	48	0	3	1	31	4	50	13	3	6	.275	.338	.431
Draper, John, Burl.	94	354	317	45	88	111	12	4	1	23	10	4	6	17	0	38	2	2	7	.278	.323	.350
Duncan, Chris, Peo.*	129	544	487	58	132	213	25	4	16	75	1	5	7	44	4	118	5	5	8	.271	.337	.437
Durham, Miles, W.M.*	4	18	18	1	4	6	2	0	0	0	0	0	0	0	0	8	2	0	0	.222	.222	.333
Eickhorst, Chris, Peo.	16	38	36	3	7	11	4	0	0	0	1	0	1	0	0	13	0	0	1	.194	.216	.306
Ellena, Jeff, Wis.	48	192	174	18	46	61	7	1	2	23	4	0	7	7	0	48	7	4	3	.264	.319	.351
Emmerick, Josh, Clin.	8	26	22	1	1	1	0	0	0	1	0	0	1	3	0	3	0	0	2	.045	.192	.045
Encarnacion, Edwin, Day.	136	571	518	80	146	237	32	4	17	73	0	6	7	40	2	108	25	7	15	.282	.338	.458
Encarnacion, Henry, Clin.†	36	61	53	8	6	7	1	0	0	3	2	0	0	6	0	20	1	2	0	.113	.203	.132
Ervin, Josh, F.W.	4	15	14	1	1	4	0	0	1	2	0	0	0	1	0	8	0	0	1	.071	.133	.286
Esparragoza, Pedro, Bel.	57	214	180	18	35	43	3	1	1	18	8	1	4	21	0	36	5	3	1	.194	.291	.239
Esterlin, Yban, Lan.*	53	171	154	23	35	51	3	2	3	22	1	1	0	15	0	30	3	5	3	.227	.294	.331
Eylward, Mike, C.R.	98	394	350	55	92	146	22	4	8	43	0	2	11	31	0	55	2	3	7	.263	.340	.417
Fallon, Chris, Burl.*	125	543	463	58	136	193	33	3	6	77	5	6	2	67	4	91	0	4	14	.294	.381	.417
Ferrand, Frank, K.C.*	17	68	62	5	19	28	2	2	1	9	0	0	0	6	1	0	1	0	2	.306	.368	.452
Fielder, Prince, Bel.*	32	125	112	15	27	43	7	0	3	11	0	0	3	10	0	27	0	0	1	.241	.320	.384
Figuereo, Anibal, Burl.	68	277	258	22	57	81	11	2	3	24	3	1	5	10	0	77	2	1	5	.221	.263	.314
Figueroa, Eduardo, Wis.	26	81	70	11	12	18	1	1	1	8	0	1	0	10	0	22	3	3	0	.171	.272	.257
Floyd, Dan, Wis.	111	456	427	41	113	137	13	1	3	43	6	3	5	15	1	64	6	11	6	.265	.296	.321
Foreman, JuJu, S.B.*	9	35	31	0	4	5	1	0	0	2	2	0	1	1	0	8	1	0	1	.129	.182	.161
Francia, Juan, W.M.†	128	586	503	94	136	165	13	5	2	41	20	3	7	53	0	94	53	14	5	.270	.346	.328
Francisco, Alfredo, Lan.	2	7	7	0	0	0	0	0	0	0	0	0	0	0	0	1	0	0	0	.000	.000	.000
Frazier, Charles, K.C.	114	510	440	63	110	138	18	2	2	38	4	2	5	59	0	111	48	16	5	.250	.344	.314
Freeman, Corey, Wis.	77	273	253	29	63	88	16	0	3	19	1	0	7	12	0	61	5	4	2	.249	.301	.348
Garcia, Cip, Wis.	45	167	140	19	30	44	5	0	3	18	1	2	8	16	0	30	0	0	3	.214	.325	.314
Garcia, Hector, Bel.	107	379	359	38	83	110	15	0	4	38	5	3	4	8	0	88	8	3	6	.231	.254	.306
Garcia, Juan-Carlos, K.C.†	5	17	11	0	2	4	2	0	0	0	2	0	0	4	0	4	0	0	0	.182	.400	.364
Garcia, Lino, S.B.	67	259	232	28	43	64	9	0	4	18	3	1	6	17	0	69	4	4	0	.185	.258	.276
Garthwaite, Jay, S.B.	46	176	162	21	40	60	10	2	2	18	0	1	2	11	0	62	2	2	1	.247	.301	.370
Gates, David, C.R.	29	103	82	13	18	27	1	1	2	9	0	4	17	0	0	21	2	0	2	.220	.379	.329
Gemoll, Brandon, Bel.*	47	199	173	31	49	69	8	0	4	23	0	2	2	20	0	42	2	2	1	.283	.367	.399
Gomez, Galinda, Bel.	95	374	326	42	77	118	18	1	7	43	1	2	8	37	0	75	1	4	11	.236	.327	.362
Gonzalez, Juan, W.M.†	120	529	444	71	112	160	17	8	5	50	11	3	7	64	0	104	21	11	13	.252	.353	.360
Gorneault, Nicholas, C.R.	103	383	346	60	100	161	17	7	10	53	2	3	2	30	0	106	12	5	3	.289	.346	.465
Gotay, Ruben, Burl.†	133	603	509	87	145	232	42	9	9	83	4	9	8	73	1	110	6	4	5	.285	.377	.456
Greenberg, Adam, Lan.*	35	140	116	20	26	40	7	2	1	11	4	1	4	15	2	22	2	1	0	.224	.331	.345
Groves, Brett, Burl.†	112	491	413	64	105	130	21	0	1	38	8	1	7	62	0	86	15	18	9	.254	.360	.315

Player, Team	G	TPA	AB	R	H	TB	2B	3B	HR	RBI	SH	SF	HP	BB	IBB	SO	SB	CS	GDP	Avg.	OBP	Slg.
Guerrero, Pedro, Clin.	38	112	102	15	23	30	4	0	1	7	0	0	0	10	0	29	1	1	2	.225	.295	.294
Gutierrez, Jesse, Day.	123	500	458	51	125	194	28	1	13	66	0	5	5	32	1	78	2	2	10	.273	.324	.424
Guzman, Angel, Lan.	9	1	1	0	1	1	0	0	0	0	0	0	0	0	0	0	0	0	0	1.000	1.000	1.000
Guzman, Jonathan, Burl.	123	495	423	56	93	151	18	5	10	57	6	3	8	55	1	159	17	7	16	.220	.319	.357
Hairston, Scott, S.B.	109	468	394	79	131	222	35	4	16	72	1	5	10	58	3	74	9	3	11	.332	.426	.563
Hanigan, Ryan, Day.	6	12	11	1	3	4	1	0	0	0	0	0	0	1	0	2	0	0	0	.273	.333	.364
Hanna, Warren, Lan.	57	197	182	16	34	53	11	1	2	17	2	0	1	12	0	36	1	1	3	.187	.241	.291
Hartig, Philip, K.C.	12	53	48	5	9	14	5	0	0	2	0	1	1	3	1	8	0	1	0	.188	.245	.292
Hastings, Joseph, F.W.*	118	505	451	51	118	189	38	0	11	69	4	4	4	42	3	124	3	1	12	.262	.327	.419
Hawes, B.J., Day.	55	209	191	17	49	64	11	2	0	27	1	4	4	9	0	32	10	7	3	.257	.298	.335
Haydel, Rick, S.B.	124	468	413	45	80	107	10	1	5	40	7	6	7	35	1	119	14	9	6	.194	.265	.259
Hellman, Matthew, F.W.	8	29	26	2	5	8	1	1	0	5	0	0	0	3	0	6	0	1	0	.192	.276	.308
Helps, Jason, K.C.†	21	75	61	12	11	16	2	0	1	4	0	0	4	10	0	22	0	0	0	.180	.333	.262
Hernandez, Vladimir, Clin.	4	10	9	0	0	0	0	0	0	0	0	0	0	1	0	0	0	0	0	.000	.100	.000
Hicks, Scott, K.C.*	124	516	452	44	103	123	11	3	1	58	2	5	4	53	3	107	5	6	7	.228	.311	.272
Hilinski, Scott, S.B.	43	142	125	10	17	19	2	0	0	6	1	4	0	12	0	52	0	3	0	.136	.206	.152
Hinton, Travis, Bel.*	76	301	269	28	68	91	14	0	3	23	1	1	4	26	3	61	2	0	1	.253	.327	.338
Hodges, Kerry, Mich.	84	271	243	35	61	83	13	3	1	17	1	2	5	20	0	74	11	7	5	.251	.319	.342
Honeycutt, Heath, S.B.	22	94	82	9	20	27	2	1	1	7	0	1	2	9	0	22	3	1	2	.244	.330	.329
Huff, Ken, Q.C.*	32	106	102	8	16	22	6	0	0	1	0	1	0	3	0	36	1	1	1	.157	.179	.216
Huguet, J.C., Day.	20	51	36	4	5	5	0	0	0	2	2	0	2	11	0	12	1	0	1	.139	.367	.139
Humphries, Jared, Day.*	32	77	70	14	21	23	2	0	0	8	0	0	0	7	1	10	1	0	0	.300	.364	.329
Hurtado, Omar, Day.	56	200	187	15	42	61	8	1	3	17	1	0	1	11	0	45	5	2	3	.225	.271	.326
Hutchinson, Burnell, S.B.*	38	134	117	11	28	44	5	1	3	13	3	0	0	14	0	17	0	3	1	.239	.321	.376
Jacobo, Kervin, S.B.†	29	114	98	9	16	23	4	0	1	7	2	0	0	14	1	42	3	2	2	.163	.268	.235
Janz, Jeramy, S.B.*	31	123	113	11	24	33	6	0	1	8	0	0	1	9	0	23	0	1	3	.212	.276	.292
Johnson, Gabe, Peo.	134	578	516	76	128	238	32	0	26	93	0	3	2	57	3	153	6	6	10	.248	.324	.461
Johnson, J.J., Lan.	112	470	420	58	101	136	25	2	2	56	2	5	5	38	1	89	7	12	7	.240	.308	.324
Jones, Garrett, Q.C.*	63	238	223	21	45	83	8	0	10	32	3	1	0	11	1	82	3	1	5	.202	.238	.372
Jones, Kennard, F.W.*	20	89	77	15	22	26	4	0	0	5	0	0	1	11	0	21	3	4	2	.286	.382	.338
Keim, Adam, Burl.	7	31	27	3	4	7	3	0	0	5	0	1	0	3	0	8	0	0	2	.148	.226	.259
Kelly, Donald, W.M.*	128	524	455	72	130	164	21	5	1	59	2	5	3	59	1	40	9	6	11	.286	.368	.360
Kelly, Heath, K.C.	24	94	76	9	17	23	1	1	1	7	4	2	2	10	0	28	1	1	1	.224	.322	.303
Kennedy, Bryan, Q.C.*	69	263	215	28	60	85	12	2	3	27	4	4	11	29	0	35	0	1	6	.279	.386	.395
Kennedy, Jason, W.M.	41	160	131	15	33	43	8	1	0	16	0	0	10	19	0	36	0	1	4	.252	.388	.328
Kerner, Craig, Clin.*	40	133	117	15	31	47	6	2	2	12	5	2	1	8	1	18	8	4	0	.265	.313	.402
Kimpton, Nick, C.R.*	93	355	302	51	79	99	12	4	0	26	6	1	4	42	0	61	20	12	2	.262	.358	.328
Knoedler, Jason, W.M.†	135	497	417	63	87	128	14	6	5	33	6	2	4	68	1	145	18	8	5	.209	.324	.307
Knott, Jon, F.W.	37	146	126	19	42	69	12	3	3	18	0	2	1	17	1	33	2	1	1	.333	.411	.548
Kolodzey, Chris, W.M.	66	170	151	16	34	51	10	2	1	18	2	1	4	12	1	41	2	0	3	.225	.298	.338
Kotchman, Casey, C.R.*	81	347	288	42	81	128	30	1	5	50	1	4	6	48	2	37	2	1	7	.281	.390	.444
Kubel, Jason, Q.C.*	115	477	424	60	136	221	26	4	17	69	2	3	1	41	2	48	3	5	11	.321	.380	.521
Kuhaulua, Kaulana, Q.C.	73	289	264	33	61	88	10	1	5	23	1	0	11	13	0	64	9	5	4	.231	.295	.333
Labandeira, John, Clin.	129	563	493	60	141	198	27	3	8	67	3	12	10	45	1	73	15	12	16	.286	.350	.402
Lafferty, Will, Peo.	17	42	36	1	4	4	0	0	0	4	0	2	1	3	0	9	0	1	1	.111	.190	.111
Lemon, Tim, Peo.	133	568	500	67	118	193	36	3	11	78	0	7	8	53	4	165	17	6	6	.236	.315	.386
Lentini, Fehlandt, Mich.	71	277	246	41	71	92	12	3	1	35	1	1	0	29	0	35	25	5	6	.289	.362	.374
Lewis, Domonique, Day.	62	180	151	23	37	53	5	4	1	12	5	4	1	18	0	36	10	4	5	.245	.320	.351
Likely, Cameron, Mich.	100	384	315	56	86	106	10	5	0	28	3	5	11	50	0	49	26	7	7	.273	.386	.337
Loeb, Bryan, S.B.	98	400	362	44	83	122	23	2	4	46	3	3	8	24	0	71	4	4	7	.229	.290	.337
Lopez, Michael, S.B.	29	116	105	10	18	25	7	0	0	5	3	1	0	7	0	19	4	0	3	.171	.221	.238
Louisa, Lorvin, Clin.	41	137	124	16	22	32	4	0	2	8	0	1	3	9	0	55	1	0	1	.177	.248	.258
Lucas, Matt, Mich.	65	201	189	19	36	50	11	0	1	13	2	2	5	3	0	39	3	0	7	.190	.221	.265
Luellwitz, Sean, S.B.	48	191	162	15	35	51	9	2	1	21	2	1	4	22	0	35	0	1	3	.216	.323	.315
Lugo, Alfredo, W.M.	89	267	235	25	68	84	14	1	0	31	4	2	1	25	0	50	1	2	4	.289	.357	.357
Lutz, David, Clin.*	58	198	176	16	34	51	6	1	3	17	0	3	2	17	2	36	1	2	3	.193	.268	.290
Lydic, Joe, Mich.	70	249	234	36	51	84	16	1	5	27	0	2	1	12	1	57	3	0	7	.218	.257	.359
Lynam, Guy, K.C.	6	21	20	1	4	6	2	0	0	1	0	0	0	1	0	5	0	1	0	.200	.238	.300
Mace, Clark, S.B.*	8	23	21	1	2	3	1	0	0	1	0	0	0	0	0	5	1	0	1	.095	.095	.143
Mallory, Mike, Lan.	131	533	495	60	131	223	34	5	16	65	0	2	12	24	1	119	6	6	11	.265	.313	.451
Manning, Ricky, Q.C.*	24	69	61	8	11	12	1	0	0	2	2	1	1	4	0	15	3	0	2	.180	.239	.197
Mansfield, Monte, Mich.	20	2	2	0	0	0	0	0	0	0	0	0	0	0	0	0	0	0	0	.000	.000	.000
Marmol, Carlos, Lan.	15	48	47	2	7	9	0	1	0	4	0	0	0	1	0	7	0	2	2	.149	.167	.191
Martinez, Guillermo, Wis.†	38	139	124	18	28	31	3	0	0	12	2	1	2	10	0	17	2	0	4	.226	.292	.250
Mathis, Jeff, C.R.	128	549	491	75	141	218	41	3	10	73	2	8	8	40	3	75	7	4	6	.287	.346	.444
Mattle, David, W.M.*	136	577	511	62	139	206	26	10	7	68	8	6	6	46	7	110	9	4	11	.272	.336	.403
Mauer, Jake, Q.C.	84	302	252	37	57	66	9	0	0	20	6	2	16	26	0	25	2	0	7	.226	.334	.262
Mauer, Joe, Q.C.*	110	476	411	58	124	161	23	1	4	62	0	2	2	61	4	42	0	0	16	.302	.393	.392
Mayo, Terry, Bel.	50	187	170	12	19	37	3	0	5	10	4	0	3	10	0	69	1	2	5	.112	.175	.218
McClanahan, Jonah, Bel.	14	49	45	3	10	11	1	0	0	2	2	0	0	2	0	9	0	0	0	.222	.255	.244
McCool, Lee, F.W.-S.B.	54	216	196	26	40	59	7	3	2	13	2	2	3	12	0	47	2	2	6	.204	.258	.301
McKnight, Lukas, Lan.*	53	197	173	20	51	68	8	0	3	22	3	1	2	18	0	27	3	1	6	.295	.366	.393
McMillan, Drew, Clin.	37	143	133	16	23	34	6	1	1	11	1	1	1	7	0	34	3	1	4	.173	.218	.256
McPherson, Dallas, C.R.*	132	586	499	71	138	213	24	3	15	88	0	2	7	78	3	128	30	6	9	.277	.381	.427
Mejia, Gilberto, W.M.†	19	84	69	17	17	31	4	2	2	15	2	0	11	0	23	4	2	1	.246	.341	.449
Melgarejo, Ransel, C.R.	118	506	427	63	101	131	14	5	2	37	8	6	12	53	1	71	19	12	6	.237	.333	.307
Menchaca, Eriberto, Wis.	50	216	199	21	41	49	4	2	0	19	1	2	1	13	0	29	2	2	9	.206	.256	.246
Mercado, Onix, Day.	19	58	55	5	12	20	2	0	2	7	1	0	0	2	0	18	0	0	3	.218	.246	.364
Merchan, Jesus, Q.C.	92	342	308	47	86	115	18	1	3	31	3	3	6	22	1	35	8	0	8	.279	.336	.373
Merritt, Tim, Wis.	15	57	48	3	9	13	1	0	1	6	0	2	2	5	0	14	3	0	2	.188	.281	.271
Miliano, Hector, Lan.	31	110	105	10	23	29	4	1	0	4	0	0	1	4	0	26	1	4	3	.219	.255	.276

Player, Team	G	TPA	AB	R	H	TB	2B	3B	HR	RBI	SH	SF	HP	BB	IBB	SO	SB	CS	GDP	Avg.	OBP	Slg.
Miller, Chris, Lan.	5	19	14	0	2	2	0	0	0	1	0	0	2	3	0	1	0	0	0	.143	.368	.143
Molina, Angel, K.C.	35	138	122	16	31	54	3	1	6	25	2	1	2	11	0	41	0	0	2	.254	.324	.443
Molina, Yadier, Peo.	112	430	393	39	110	151	20	0	7	50	4	2	10	21	0	36	2	7	14	.280	.331	.384
Monahan, Joey, Lan.	25	98	89	9	20	26	3	0	1	6	0	1	4	4	0	21	4	0	0	.225	.286	.292
Monte, Harvey, Wis.*	24	82	65	5	8	8	0	0	0	5	1	0	0	16	0	30	3	5	2	.123	.296	.123
Montilla, Samuel, S.B.	5	16	15	0	2	3	1	0	0	3	0	1	0	0	0	2	0	0	0	.133	.125	.200
Moore, Bryan, Peo.*	12	37	33	2	4	5	1	0	0	2	1	0	1	2	0	15	1	0	0	.121	.194	.152
Morris, Chris, Bel.*	4	16	14	3	5	7	2	0	0	1	1	0	0	1	0	3	1	0	0	.357	.400	.500
Mote, Trevor, Mich.†	130	535	480	66	133	187	25	1	9	70	4	4	4	43	3	89	7	9	9	.277	.339	.390
Murphy, Donald, Burl.	33	141	120	12	27	39	6	3	0	15	1	5	4	11	0	31	0	2	1	.225	.300	.325
Murphy, Tommy, C.R.	128	538	485	72	131	164	20	2	3	48	7	5	1	40	0	115	31	11	8	.270	.324	.338
Napoli, Michael, C.R.	106	434	362	57	91	142	19	1	10	50	0	6	4	62	1	104	6	5	9	.251	.362	.392
Neill, Ryan, W.M.	62	231	204	25	46	68	8	1	4	20	1	3	2	21	1	61	15	1	5	.225	.300	.333
Nelson, Brad, Bel.*	106	459	417	70	124	217	38	2	17	99	0	4	4	34	4	86	4	1	9	.297	.353	.520
Nelson, John, Peo.	132	547	481	85	132	218	28	5	16	63	5	4	3	54	3	123	16	3	8	.274	.349	.453
Netwall, Chris, Peo.	2	5	4	1	1	1	0	0	0	0	0	0	0	1	0	0	0	0	0	.250	.400	.250
Nevins, Ryan, C.R.*	19	59	50	5	10	12	2	0	0	4	0	1	1	7	0	12	0	0	0	.200	.305	.240
Nichols, Kyle, S.B.	122	514	453	44	111	182	35	0	12	72	0	4	1	56	4	101	0	1	10	.245	.327	.402
Nina, Amaurys, Day.	29	100	92	12	21	29	5	0	1	10	1	0	2	5	0	24	7	1	3	.228	.283	.315
Norris, Shawn, Clin.*	9	33	26	2	7	8	1	0	0	3	0	1	0	6	0	8	1	0	2	.269	.394	.308
Obradovich, Mark, Mich.†	108	416	356	43	80	106	15	1	3	36	2	1	2	55	2	96	8	7	9	.225	.331	.298
Oeltjen, Trent, Q.C.*	10	29	25	4	6	7	1	0	0	1	1	0	0	3	0	2	1	0	1	.240	.321	.280
Oliveros, Luis, Wis.	82	300	280	16	64	75	11	0	0	20	3	2	7	8	0	32	1	4	8	.229	.266	.268
Ortiz, Daniel, K.C.	14	61	52	6	8	10	2	0	0	4	0	1	2	6	0	23	0	1	2	.154	.262	.192
O'Sullivan, Mark, C.R.	42	2	2	0	1	1	0	0	0	0	0	0	0	0	0	0	0	0	0	.500	.500	.500
O'Toole, Paul, Lan.*	25	77	67	9	14	19	5	0	0	4	0	0	2	8	0	10	2	0	3	.209	.312	.284
Paredes, Jeison, S.B.	40	180	172	17	40	57	6	4	1	14	1	0	1	6	2	47	9	3	2	.233	.263	.331
Patchett, Gary, Day.	94	318	278	42	63	90	15	0	4	30	6	1	13	20	0	73	5	3	7	.227	.308	.324
Peguero, Miguel, W.M.†	14	31	29	1	2	2	0	0	0	2	0	1	1	0	0	9	0	0	1	.069	.097	.069
Peless, Sean, Wis.*	108	399	370	32	81	140	15	4	12	38	1	0	4	24	2	111	1	3	10	.219	.274	.378
Pereyra, Joel, Burl.	7	12	12	0	0	0	0	0	0	0	0	0	0	0	0	7	0	0	0	.000	.000	.000
Pines, Greg, Mich.	13	17	15	1	2	2	0	0	0	0	0	0	0	2	0	4	0	0	0	.133	.235	.133
Porter, Greg, C.R.*	77	301	266	29	61	80	14	1	1	38	1	3	3	28	0	69	2	4	8	.229	.307	.301
Prince, Bryan, Day.	83	285	239	31	48	72	12	0	4	22	5	1	8	32	0	43	2	0	7	.201	.314	.301
Puccinelli, John, F.W.	5	16	14	0	0	0	0	0	0	1	1	0	0	1	0	6	0	0	0	.000	.067	.000
Quickstad, Barry, Q.C.*	42	132	107	12	15	16	1	0	0	3	2	0	3	20	0	47	5	2	0	.140	.292	.150
Rabelo, Mike, W.M.†	123	467	410	42	80	101	13	1	2	41	5	2	8	42	0	91	3	1	21	.195	.281	.246
Raburn, Ryan, W.M.	40	173	150	27	33	63	10	1	6	28	0	3	4	16	1	46	0	2	2	.220	.306	.420
Rainey, Jason, Wis.*	34	100	87	18	18	28	3	2	1	9	0	0	2	11	1	31	3	1	1	.207	.310	.322
Reed, Eric, K.C.*	12	55	50	11	18	19	1	0	0	2	2	0	0	3	0	11	7	1	1	.360	.396	.380
Reinking, Kevin, F.W.	43	156	145	8	35	44	6	0	1	15	0	0	4	7	1	34	0	0	8	.241	.295	.303
Robison, Jordan, Peo.	103	309	279	40	65	103	11	3	7	26	6	2	6	16	0	74	4	5	10	.233	.287	.369
Rodaway, Brian, Mich.*	23	1	0	0	0	0	0	0	0	0	0	1	0	0	0	0	0	0	0	.000	.000	.000
Rodriguez, Alex, Burl.†	21	69	58	8	13	13	0	0	0	4	4	0	2	5	0	13	0	0	1	.224	.308	.224
Rodriguez, Mike, Mich.*	133	587	499	94	126	169	23	4	4	46	12	5	2	65	0	85	35	11	5	.253	.338	.339
Rojas, Randy, C.R.	71	210	181	33	38	51	7	0	2	29	0	3	3	23	0	22	19	7	3	.210	.305	.282
Roman, Jesse, Peo.*	127	541	472	77	132	200	22	2	14	65	3	4	2	60	4	79	7	2	9	.280	.361	.424
Rombley, Danny, Clin.	72	307	279	49	76	104	14	4	2	23	1	0	6	21	0	62	13	7	2	.272	.337	.373
Rosado, Hector, Burl.*	31	1	1	0	0	0	0	0	0	0	0	0	0	0	0	1	0	0	0	.000	.000	.000
Rosario, Victor, Burl.*	36	151	125	32	33	41	5	0	1	14	3	1	2	20	0	22	3	1	3	.264	.372	.328
Ruiz, Junior, Day.*	23	81	63	11	14	18	4	0	0	4	1	1	2	14	1	7	1	0	1	.222	.375	.286
Ruiz, Randy, Day.	78	333	285	47	86	135	17	4	8	49	0	4	8	36	1	88	9	3	8	.302	.390	.474
Rundgren, Rex, K.C.	122	467	426	33	98	119	11	2	2	40	12	3	2	24	0	84	6	3	7	.230	.273	.279
Sain, Greg, F.W.	105	439	387	54	95	163	29	0	13	57	0	5	12	35	1	77	2	0	4	.245	.323	.421
Salas, Francisco, Lan.	12	43	37	5	10	17	4	0	1	9	0	1	2	3	0	3	0	1	0	.270	.349	.459
Sandoval, Michael, Q.C.	119	499	438	64	114	168	23	2	9	60	1	3	18	39	4	62	2	2	20	.260	.343	.384
Santana, Ralph, Bel.*	107	439	387	58	101	123	10	6	0	29	10	2	3	37	1	58	31	14	7	.261	.329	.318
Santor, John, Peo.†	1	4	4	0	0	0	0	0	0	0	0	0	0	0	0	1	0	0	0	.000	.000	.000
Schnabel, Nick, Clin.	39	152	124	17	41	52	9	1	0	20	4	3	2	19	0	13	1	4	1	.331	.419	.419
Schneider, Michael, Clin.	11	33	30	3	7	9	2	0	0	2	0	0	0	3	0	10	0	0	1	.233	.303	.300
Scott, Mike, W.M.*	45	131	113	15	25	32	4	0	1	11	2	0	1	15	1	21	4	1	0	.221	.318	.283
Self, Todd, Mich.*	136	575	491	81	152	234	36	5	12	94	2	8	9	65	4	104	10	1	8	.310	.394	.477
Serrano, Eddie, F.W.	74	236	218	24	48	70	10	0	4	28	0	3	1	14	0	50	1	2	7	.220	.267	.321
Shanks, James, Burl.	126	589	515	81	152	204	26	4	6	53	12	5	6	51	2	94	26	11	4	.295	.362	.396
Silver, Travis, Lan.	23	78	69	5	14	25	1	2	2	9	3	0	2	4	1	17	0	0	2	.203	.267	.362
Simoneaux, Neil, Peo.	19	61	56	4	9	12	0	0	1	4	0	0	1	4	0	16	2	1	3	.161	.230	.214
Slavik, Corey, Lan.*	90	350	308	33	67	101	14	4	4	34	2	2	4	34	1	49	4	6	3	.218	.302	.328
Sosa, Jovanny, Clin.	59	212	177	24	46	75	9	1	6	26	0	0	3	32	0	64	0	3	4	.260	.382	.424
Stegall, Ryan, Mich.	122	470	408	45	97	137	25	3	3	44	10	1	9	42	0	75	6	3	8	.238	.322	.336
Stockton, Rick, F.W.*	17	56	51	6	12	15	1	1	0	5	2	0	1	2	0	16	1	0	0	.235	.278	.294
Stokes, Jason, K.C.	97	407	349	73	119	225	25	0	27	75	0	5	5	47	15	96	1	1	5	.341	.425	.645
Stringham, Jed, W.M.	13	44	36	5	6	11	2	0	1	6	0	2	0	6	0	13	0	0	1	.167	.273	.306
Swope, Matt, Clin.	45	160	135	19	29	40	5	0	2	8	1	2	1	21	1	23	2	1	5	.215	.321	.296
Tamburrino, Brett, Q.C.†	87	369	320	40	85	124	21	3	4	33	6	2	3	38	0	78	9	3	3	.266	.347	.388
Tejeda, Juan, W.M.	137	596	524	68	157	236	34	6	11	106	0	7	5	60	8	89	5	1	7	.300	.372	.450
Thede, Matthew, Clin.	45	162	156	15	38	57	8	1	3	17	0	0	1	4	0	40	0	1	6	.244	.267	.365
Theriot, Ryan, Lan.	130	558	489	75	123	153	19	4	1	37	3	3	4	59	1	77	32	8	3	.252	.335	.313
Thissen, Greg, Clin.	129	549	486	69	124	192	27	1	13	68	5	4	6	48	1	101	13	6	15	.255	.327	.395
Thornton-Murray, Jandin, Lan.†..	8	20	16	2	1	1	0	0	0	0	0	0	1	3	0	3	0	0	1	.063	.250	.063
Tomlin, James, Q.C.	105	476	427	62	116	144	17	1	3	27	7	0	8	34	1	58	18	13	8	.272	.337	.337
Tope, Stephen, Q.C.	72	300	260	42	67	115	16	1	10	47	0	7	11	22	0	76	2	0	6	.258	.333	.442

Player, Team	G	TPA	AB	R	H	TB	2B	3B	HR	RBI	SH	SF	HP	BB	IBB	SO	SB	CS	GDP	Avg.	OBP	Slg.
Torres, Digno, Q.C.*	52	206	186	18	51	78	12	3	3	31	1	3	1	15	0	36	0	1	5	.274	.327	.419
Tremblay, Max, Mich.*	42	1	0	0	0	0	0	0	0	0	0	0	0	1	0	0	0	0	0	.000	1.000	.000
Trezza, Alex, W.M.*	18	41	38	2	8	12	4	0	0	5	0	0	0	3	0	11	0	0	0	.211	.268	.316
Trzesniak, Nick, F.W.	110	444	409	53	97	149	18	2	10	38	1	1	6	27	1	97	10	3	6	.237	.293	.364
Tucker, Michael, K.C.	121	495	435	53	106	150	20	3	6	61	2	1	3	53	1	100	6	2	10	.244	.329	.345
Turner, Justin, C.R.*	111	438	379	63	97	157	23	2	11	61	7	3	2	47	0	118	7	8	6	.256	.339	.414
Uggla, Dan, S.B.	53	199	171	16	34	47	5	1	2	10	3	2	0	23	0	34	0	2	2	.199	.291	.275
Urueta, Luis, S.B.†	9	34	33	1	4	5	1	0	0	0	1	0	0	0	0	11	0	0	1	.121	.121	.152
Van Meetren, Jason, Wis.	80	315	276	37	78	114	12	3	6	30	0	3	5	31	1	59	16	8	8	.283	.362	.413
Varner, Noochie, Day.-W.M.	133	574	534	83	163	247	28	13	10	70	1	2	5	32	0	121	37	4	16	.305	.349	.463
Villanueva, Florian, Bel.	95	401	374	53	104	168	30	2	10	51	0	5	4	18	1	60	2	2	11	.278	.314	.449
Villilo, Miguel, Wis.†	77	277	251	34	49	66	15	1	0	19	2	1	0	23	0	76	7	2	8	.195	.262	.263
Voshell, Chase, Peo.	110	406	346	40	79	114	24	1	3	36	5	5	4	45	2	80	8	8	8	.228	.320	.329
Vugteveen, Dustin, S.B.	84	313	285	29	61	82	9	3	2	31	3	1	7	17	0	77	5	5	3	.214	.274	.288
Welch, Ed, C.R.*	18	38	35	4	5	5	0	0	0	2	1	0	0	2	0	17	2	1	0	.143	.189	.143
Welsch, Travis, Lan.	40	133	116	14	24	31	4	0	1	9	1	1	4	11	0	25	1	3	4	.207	.295	.267
Weston, Aron, Lan.*	28	112	96	10	25	37	4	1	2	14	0	0	3	13	2	23	5	2	1	.260	.366	.385
Williams, Clyde, Clin.*	127	514	462	65	123	200	23	3	16	71	1	6	10	35	3	104	6	5	5	.266	.327	.433
Williamson, Chris, Day.*	99	396	333	57	80	165	17	1	22	73	0	3	10	50	2	118	2	6	6	.240	.354	.495
Wyant, Hunter, K.C.	56	228	209	25	44	57	8	1	1	17	1	2	1	15	0	39	7	0	7	.211	.264	.273
Yount, Andy, W.M.	18	56	47	2	6	7	1	0	0	4	0	2	1	6	0	32	1	0	2	.128	.232	.149
Zapey, Winton, K.C.	67	276	252	22	62	85	14	0	3	21	6	0	4	14	0	55	1	1	3	.246	.296	.337

PLAYERS WITH TWO OR MORE TEAMS

Player, Team	G	TPA	AB	R	H	TB	2B	3B	HR	RBI	SH	SF	HP	BB	IBB	SO	SB	CS	GDP	Avg.	OBP	Slg.
McCool, Lee, F.W.	36	137	126	16	27	39	5	2	1	9	1	1	3	5	0	35	1	1	4	.214	.259	.310
McCool, Lee, S.B.	18	79	70	10	13	20	2	1	1	4	1	1	0	7	0	12	1	1	2	.186	.256	.286
Varner, Noochie, Day.	129	557	517	82	160	241	27	12	10	69	1	2	5	32	0	117	37	4	16	.309	.354	.466
Varner, Noochie, W.M.	4	17	17	1	3	6	1	1	0	1	0	0	0	0	0	4	0	0	0	.176	.176	.353

GRAND SLAMS: Benick, Hairston, Williams, Williamson, 2 each; Asadoorian, Ball, Barfield, Boone, Cedeno, Checksfield, Collins, R. Cordova, Davidson, Dobbs, Ellena, E. Encarnacion, Gomez, Gorneault, Gotay, G. Johnson, J.J. Johnson, Lemon, Merritt, Patchett, Salas, Silver, Stokes, Tamburrino, Turner, Villanueva, 1 each.

AWARDED FIRST BASE ON CATCHER'S INTERFERENCE: M. Rodriguez 4 (Collins 2, Mathis, Zapey), Benick 2 (Zapey 2), Mace (Lucas), McCool (Marmol), Stokes (Cadena), Thede (Collins), M. Tucker (Trzesniak), Voshell (Collins).

2002 PITCHING

TEAM

Team	W	L	Pct.	ERA	G	CG	ShO	Sv.	IP	H	TBF	R	ER	HR	SH	SF	HB	BB	IBB	SO	WP	Bk.
Peoria	85	53	.616	2.78	138	6	19	36	1226.2	1075	5041	486	379	73	34	33	39	350	11	1100	76	22
Lansing	74	65	.532	3.16	139	5	10	36	1226.2	1077	5110	524	431	65	44	35	60	438	11	997	92	9
Cedar Rapids	81	58	.583	3.40	139	2	12	40	1230.0	1090	5211	563	465	92	40	36	71	474	19	1080	95	8
West Michigan	83	57	.593	3.43	140	5	8	39	1248.0	1172	5416	571	475	56	48	40	72	547	21	1010	107	19
Michigan	79	61	.564	3.44	140	4	10	43	1217.2	1117	5139	550	465	75	40	26	65	387	5	967	72	8
Quad City	71	65	.522	3.47	136	3	6	39	1190.1	1076	5069	540	459	90	45	38	75	474	11	1090	77	9
Fort Wayne	69	68	.504	3.49	137	3	5	40	1201.2	1188	5126	582	466	73	49	43	56	318	14	951	56	9
South Bend	52	87	.374	3.73	139	9	6	25	1220.1	1269	5287	650	506	64	41	50	56	385	19	928	95	11
Dayton	73	67	.521	3.74	140	8	10	45	1233.2	1155	5313	627	512	81	55	36	71	476	38	1103	89	20
Wisconsin	53	86	.381	4.01	139	7	6	29	1199.2	1157	5300	672	535	78	55	41	85	537	16	997	75	24
Kane County	64	75	.460	4.03	139	5	9	31	1219.2	1168	5279	653	546	74	51	43	82	445	6	952	99	24
Clinton	61	75	.449	4.17	136	3	6	32	1179.1	1186	5239	667	546	56	52	48	73	522	21	949	121	19
Burlington	68	71	.489	4.44	139	4	5	29	1209.2	1233	5357	734	597	87	41	50	77	484	5	822	130	7
Beloit	57	82	.410	4.56	139	2	6	37	1207.2	1262	5406	745	612	78	43	50	82	590	13	1020	114	26

INDIVIDUAL

TOP QUALIFIERS FOR EARNED-RUN AVERAGE TITLE

Minimum 112 innings.*Lefthanded pitcher.

Pitcher, Team	W	L	Pct.	ERA	G	GS	CG	ShO	GF	Sv.	IP	H	TBF	R	ER	HR	SH	SF	HB	BB	IBB	SO	WP	Bk.
Willis, Dontrelle, K.C.*	10	2	.833	1.83	19	19	3	2	0	0	127.2	91	491	29	26	3	5	2	8	21	0	101	9	3
Johnson, Tyler, Peo.*	15	3	.833	2.00	22	18	0	0	1	0	121.1	96	491	35	27	7	4	0	4	42	1	132	8	4
Yeatman, Matt, Bel.	11	7	.611	2.48	25	25	1	0	0	0	127	101	531	51	35	4	4	5	4	77	0	127	12	0
Burns, Mike, Mich.	14	9	.609	2.49	28	28	3	2	0	0	181	146	714	59	50	12	5	3	7	29	1	126	8	2
McDowell, Kevin, W.M.*	11	6	.647	2.60	27	27	0	0	0	0	166.1	156	706	63	48	5	8	4	8	64	0	123	7	6
Mitre, Sergio, Lan.	8	10	.444	2.83	27	27	2	0	0	0	168.2	166	685	72	53	7	6	6	10	27	1	96	10	0
Gonzalez, Edgar, S.B.	11	8	.579	2.91	23	23	4	2	0	0	151.1	141	625	66	49	4	4	7	3	34	0	110	10	1
Levinski, Donald, Clin.	12	6	.667	3.02	21	21	1	1	0	0	119.1	92	501	48	40	6	3	3	6	53	1	125	16	0
Woods, Jake, C.R.*	10	5	.667	3.05	27	27	1	0	0	0	153.1	128	633	66	52	12	4	3	11	54	0	121	5	0
Jones, Mike, Bel.	7	7	.500	3.12	27	27	0	0	0	0	138.2	135	601	63	48	3	2	2	7	62	0	132	5	1
Houlton, Dennis, Mich.	14	5	.737	3.14	35	16	0	0	7	2	140.2	120	577	57	49	12	2	4	3	30	0	138	4	0
Pignatiello, Carmen, Lan.*	9	11	.450	3.17	27	27	1	0	0	0	167.1	152	702	76	59	10	7	5	6	51	0	139	4	1
Germano, Justin, F.W.	12	5	.706	3.18	24	24	1	0	0	0	155.2	166	645	63	55	14	2	3	4	19	2	119	4	2
Durbin, J.D., Q.C.	13	4	.765	3.19	27	27	0	0	0	0	161	144	666	66	57	14	3	4	5	51	1	163	6	1
Petty, Chad, W.M.*	15	10	.600	3.24	28	28	3	2	0	0	161.1	155	701	73	58	4	3	4	9	77	0	119	13	0

DEPARTMENTAL LEADERS: W—T. Johnson, Petty, 15 each; L—Akens, 15; Pct.—T. Johnson, Willis, .833 each; G—Birtwell, 58; GS—Burns, Coenen, Holsten, Petty, Pluta, 28 each; CG—Basham, Ed. Gonzalez, 4 each; ShO—Basham, 3; GF—Kobow, 50; Sv.—Cotton, 34; IP—Burns, 181.0; H—Akens, Holsten, 180 each; TBF—Holsten, 732; R—Stodolka, 109; ER—Pluta, 94; HR—Pluta, 18; SH—Steward, 11; SF—Oakes, 13; HB—Belizario, 21; BB—Oakes, 84; IBB—Coffey, Cotton, 5 each; SO—Durbin, 163; WP—Steitz, 29; BK—Julianel, Moates, Steitz, 7 each.

ALL PITCHERS

*Lefthanded pitcher.

Pitcher, Team	W	L	Pct.	ERA	G	GS	CG	ShO	GF	Sv.	IP	H	TBF	R	ER	HR	SH	SF	HB	BB	IBB	SO	WP	Bk.
Abbott, Jim, Q.C.	4	8	.333	3.90	29	21	0	0	0	0	131.2	129	566	64	57	9	6	4	8	43	1	106	3	0
Ackerman, Eric, Burl.*	0	1	.000	11.72	7	2	0	0	2	1	17.2	24	87	23	23	5	0	1	0	10	0	10	2	0
Acors, Bo, Wis.	0	1	.000	2.38	13	0	0	0	6	3	22.2	26	100	6	6	0	2	1	3	8	0	23	1	0
Adams, Mike, Bel.	0	0	.000	2.93	11	0	0	0	8	5	15.1	13	60	6	5	1	1	0	0	2	0	21	0	0
Akens, Phil, K.C.	6	15	.286	4.89	28	26	1	0	1	0	160	180	705	101	87	14	9	5	8	47	1	109	7	1
Alvarez, Larry, Lan.	1	0	1.000	5.14	9	0	0	0	1	0	14	16	61	8	8	1	0	0	0	4	0	12	0	0
Andrade, Stephen, C.R.	1	1	.500	1.16	46	0	0	0	21	11	54.1	30	204	7	7	1	0	1	2	16	1	93	12	0
Armitage, Barry, Burl.	5	2	.714	2.04	38	3	0	0	24	10	75	51	314	23	17	1	3	1	2	38	0	79	9	0
Artman, Dane, Bel.*	2	9	.182	5.91	20	13	1	0	0	0	74.2	90	349	57	49	6	2	4	4	41	1	44	6	1
Asahina, Jonathan, K.C.	8	7	.533	4.02	27	16	0	0	4	0	112	102	492	65	50	5	2	2	8	50	0	87	10	1
Atlee, Rick, Lan.	0	0	.000	4.91	3	0	0	0	1	0	3.2	5	19	3	2	0	1	0	0	2	0	1	0	0
Badgley, Daniel, W.M.	0	1	.000	3.09	21	0	0	0	5	0	32	32	148	18	11	1	2	2	2	23	3	19	5	0
Banks, Tyler, K.C.	1	1	.500	7.78	13	0	0	0	5	0	19.2	27	96	20	17	2	0	0	1	9	0	21	1	0
Barlow, Chris, Clin.	2	5	.286	3.76	9	9	1	1	0	0	52.2	64	229	27	22	1	5	2	4	11	0	23	3	1
Barnes, Pat, Wis.*	1	1	.500	4.91	3	3	0	0	0	0	14.2	15	67	8	8	0	0	1	4	7	0	16	3	0
Barreto, Joel, Peo.	2	3	.400	2.42	42	0	0	0	23	10	44.2	34	190	19	12	3	2	3	0	22	3	67	6	0
Basham, Bobby, Day.	6	4	.600	1.64	13	13	4	3	0	0	87.2	64	342	25	16	4	0	2	3	9	1	97	6	1
Bass, Brian, Burl.	5	7	.417	3.83	20	20	1	0	0	0	110.1	103	456	57	47	8	1	3	2	31	0	60	9	0
Batista, Gorky, Day.	0	3	.000	7.86	11	3	0	0	3	1	26.1	37	132	27	23	3	1	1	0	15	2	23	2	0
Baxter, Allen, K.C.	0	2	.000	3.06	4	4	0	0	0	0	17.2	19	78	9	6	0	1	2	1	8	0	15	3	0
Belizario, Ronald, K.C.	6	5	.545	3.46	23	22	0	0	0	0	140.1	131	619	67	54	4	5	5	21	56	0	98	13	4
Benik, Brett, Lan.	6	2	.750	1.34	27	8	1	1	5	1	100.2	67	377	18	15	2	1	2	6	17	1	69	5	1
Birtwell, John, W.M.	7	2	.778	1.59	58	0	0	0	21	0	79.1	48	304	19	14	3	4	5	4	18	4	101	1	2
Blasdell, Jared, Peo.	6	2	.750	1.37	53	0	0	0	42	23	65.2	34	243	11	10	1	4	2	3	14	3	79	9	0
Boutwell, Andy, Day.	6	0	1.000	1.46	16	11	1	1	4	0	80	44	319	19	13	5	2	4	2	37	1	98	5	0
Bowyer, Travis, Q.C.	4	4	.500	2.16	39	9	0	0	12	3	91.2	74	390	28	22	2	7	3	3	46	0	90	11	0
Boyd, Dan, Bel.	0	0	.000	0.00	1	0	0	0	0	0	1	0	4	0	0	0	0	0	0	1	0	0	0	0
Brannon, Nick, Day.*	1	0	1.000	3.00	3	0	0	0	1	0	3	2	15	1	1	1	0	0	4	1	0	6	0	0
Brown, Eric, Lan.	3	1	.750	0.98	23	0	0	0	20	9	27.2	16	100	4	3	0	1	0	0	5	0	23	2	0
Bruney, Brian, S.B.	4	3	.571	1.68	37	0	0	0	28	10	48.1	32	203	15	9	1	5	3	2	17	4	54	2	1
Bulger, Jason, S.B.	4	9	.308	4.94	20	20	1	0	0	0	94.2	111	438	65	52	5	3	8	7	39	0	84	14	0
Burgess, Richie, Peo.	4	5	.444	2.69	19	6	0	0	2	0	67	55	276	28	20	2	3	0	2	10	0	51	5	0
Burns, Mike, Mich.	14	9	.609	2.49	28	28	3	2	0	0	181	146	714	59	50	12	5	3	7	29	1	126	8	2
Bye, Chris, Clin.	0	2	.000	10.38	5	0	0	0	2	1	4.1	8	23	6	5	0	1	0	0	2	0	2	1	0
Cahill, Jonathan, C.R.	0	0	.000	0.00	2	0	0	0	0	0	2.1	2	9	0	0	0	0	0	0	0	0	0	0	0
Cali, Carmen, Peo.*	1	1	.500	1.78	24	0	0	0	5	2	35.1	36	156	17	7	0	2	1	0	14	0	27	1	0
Campos, Juan, Mich.	3	2	.600	2.01	36	0	0	0	22	9	58.1	50	238	19	13	1	4	0	4	8	2	63	0	2
Candelaria, Scott, Bel.	0	0	.000	18.00	2	0	0	0	2	0	2	5	14	4	4	0	0	0	3	0	4	1	0
Caple, Chance, Peo.	1	1	.500	4.00	5	5	0	0	0	0	18	16	82	8	8	3	0	0	2	14	0	9	1	0
Caputo, Rob, Clin.	3	0	1.000	2.63	21	6	0	0	5	1	48	32	215	15	14	1	1	3	36	0	69	8	1
Carlsen, Jeff, Lan.	1	0	1.000	12.00	2	0	0	0	0	0	3	3	14	4	4	2	0	0	0	2	0	3	0	0
Carter, Justin, Day.*	0	1	.000	2.70	8	3	0	0	2	0	20	19	86	11	6	1	0	3	2	0	7	0	16	3	0
Carter, Mark, Lan.*	1	0	1.000	3.38	13	0	0	0	7	2	16	14	71	7	6	1	0	0	1	10	0	18	1	0
Cassel, Jack, F.W.	4	1	.800	3.02	27	0	0	0	9	0	50.2	58	222	22	17	0	0	0	2	11	3	34	4	1
Castellanos, Jonathan, S.B.	4	10	.286	4.36	28	20	1	1	2	0	130	134	551	73	63	10	1	6	5	42	0	84	11	0
Cave, Kevin, K.C.	3	7	.300	4.58	41	0	0	0	31	10	55	53	234	32	28	3	4	3	1	21	1	60	5	0
Charron, Eric, Clin.	0	0	.000	5.26	32	0	0	0	15	0	63.1	73	289	49	37	2	4	4	6	22	1	36	2	1
Childress, Daylan, Day.	9	10	.474	3.51	28	27	1	0	0	0	169	147	723	82	66	7	5	4	16	68	1	152	6	1
Clute, Kris, K.C.	0	0	.000	9.00	1	0	0	0	1	0	1	4	7	1	1	0	0	0	0	0	0	1	0	0
Coenen, Matt, W.M.*	14	8	.636	3.38	28	28	2	0	0	0	165.1	148	698	69	62	6	5	5	6	65	2	141	12	2
Coffey, Todd, Day.	6	4	.600	3.59	38	5	0	0	11	2	80.1	78	336	34	32	8	4	5	2	25	5	62	9	4
Contreras, Jean, Q.C.*	0	0	.000	1.62	11	0	0	0	1	0	16.2	14	70	4	3	0	1	0	2	3	0	21	0	2
Corcoran, John, Wis.	1	0	1.000	3.60	15	3	0	0	7	1	40	38	160	20	16	0	2	1	1	8	1	19	2	0
Corcoran, Roy, Clin.	3	4	.429	4.16	48	1	0	0	31	11	80	82	356	51	37	5	5	1	2	24	1	106	9	2
Cormier, Lance, S.B.	3	0	1.000	2.93	11	3	0	0	4	1	27.2	29	116	9	9	1	1	1	0	2	0	17	2	2
Cortez, Renee, Wis.	5	8	.385	4.12	17	17	0	0	0	0	98.1	102	438	62	45	12	6	5	9	32	0	67	6	3
Cotton, Nathan, Day.	2	5	.286	1.96	53	0	0	0	48	34	64.1	49	252	17	14	2	3	1	0	18	5	65	0	1
Coughenour, Jory, Mich.	1	0	1.000	1.46	5	0	0	0	4	3	12.1	10	47	2	2	0	1	0	0	6	0	8	0	0
Crain, Jesse, Q.C.	1	1	.500	1.50	9	0	0	0	6	1	12	6	45	3	2	0	1	0	1	4	0	11	0	0
Craker, Justin, F.W.	4	5	.444	3.51	54	0	0	0	20	1	59	66	259	28	23	4	3	3	2	29	2	51	3	0
Cullen, Phil, Wis.	4	7	.364	3.45	17	17	0	0	0	0	91.1	84	405	40	35	5	2	2	2	58	0	95	5	0
Daws, Josh, Q.C.	1	3	.250	2.43	26	0	0	0	23	17	29.2	26	129	14	8	3	3	0	1	13	3	36	1	0
De Hart, Blair, F.W.	0	0	.000	1.99	5	3	0	0	0	0	22.2	16	87	6	5	0	0	0	2	0	30	0	0
Dejesus, Elvis, K.C.	3	3	.500	4.01	29	0	0	0	18	3	42.2	38	184	19	19	1	2	0	2	20	0	40	5	0
Del Chiaro, Brent, C.R.	0	0	.000	0.00	1	0	0	0	1	0	1	0	3	0	0	0	0	0	0	0	0	0	0	0
Delgado, Oscar, Wis.*	1	5	.167	5.32	8	8	2	0	0	0	45.2	51	211	30	27	5	1	1	2	27	0	29	0	3
Dennis, Jason, C.R.*	2	0	1.000	2.92	8	0	0	0	4	0	12.1	10	53	4	4	2	0	0	2	3	0	14	0	0
Detillion, Jamie, Day.*	0	0	.000	5.63	6	0	0	0	2	0	8	10	38	5	5	0	1	0	0	5	1	8	5	1
Diaz, Eddie, Clin.	2	0	1.000	3.55	6	0	0	0	2	0	12.2	9	61	6	5	1	2	0	0	13	0	15	2	0
Diaz, Eddy, Lan.	1	0	1.000	2.25	6	0	0	0	1	0	12	5	50	4	3	0	1	0	9	1	9	2	0
Diaz, Luis, W.M.	2	1	.667	10.13	7	2	0	0	0	0	18.2	30	91	23	21	7	1	1	0	8	1	19	3	0
Dishman, Richard, Bel.	0	1	.000	6.75	6	2	0	0	0	0	14.2	17	65	14	11	2	1	0	1	6	0	13	1	0
Done, Juan, Wis.	9	13	.409	3.94	27	26	3	0	0	0	164.1	130	698	96	72	13	4	3	10	75	1	141	11	0
Dorn, Grant, Mich.	0	4	.000	3.57	39	0	0	0	22	3	68	62	243	26	23	7	2	1	1	11	0	57	3	0
Douglass, Ryan, Burl.	0	0	.000	3.48	4	0	0	0	1	0	10.1	10	39	4	4	1	0	0	0	3	1	7	1	0
Doyne, Cory, Mich.	9	8	.529	4.26	27	26	0	0	0	0	141.2	131	610	76	67	8	2	3	3	63	0	101	11	4
Dulkowski, Marc, F.W.	1	0	1.000	2.78	23	0	0	0	10	3	22.2	17	91	7	7	1	1	1	6	1	25	3	0
Dunn, Gerald, W.M.	1	5	.167	4.89	9	9	0	0	0	0	46	51	212	33	25	5	1	2	3	20	0	32	3	0

Pitcher, Team	W	L	Pct.	ERA	G	GS	CG	ShO	GF	Sv.	IP	H	TBF	R	ER	HR	SH	SF	HB	BB	IBB	SO	WP	Bk.
Durbin, J.D., Q.C.	13	4	.765	3.19	27	27	0	0	0	0	161	144	666	66	57	14	3	4	5	51	1	163	6	1
Earey, Ryan, F.W.	3	4	.429	2.94	47	0	0	0	10	1	67.1	71	291	30	22	3	7	5	3	16	2	41	2	0
Echols, Britt, Clin.	1	0	1.000	1.80	1	1	0	0	0	0	5	6	23	3	1	0	0	0	0	1	0	6	1	0
Ellis, Steve, Lan.	5	3	.625	1.90	37	0	0	0	29	16	47.1	31	203	13	10	1	4	1	2	29	1	70	3	1
Eppeneder, Jamie, Burl.*	1	1	.500	1.06	8	0	0	0	5	3	17	7	61	2	2	0	0	0	0	2	0	15	1	0
Esquivia, Manuel, K.C.	2	0	1.000	2.77	13	1	0	0	6	2	26	12	108	10	8	0	0	0	0	18	0	31	8	0
Etherton, Seth, Day.	0	0	.000	0.00	1	1	0	0	0	0	1	1	4	0	0	0	0	0	0	0	0	2	0	0
Eusebio, Mike, Day.	2	0	1.000	5.50	13	0	0	0	3	0	18	18	92	18	11	0	1	0	3	19	0	13	3	2
Evans, Louis, K.C.*	0	1	.000	27.00	4	0	0	0	2	0	3	8	23	11	9	1	0	2	0	5	0	2	1	0
Fallon, Chris, Burl.	0	0	.000	0.00	2	0	0	0	2	0	2	1	8	0	0	0	0	0	1	0	0	1	0	0
Farizo, Brad, K.C.	0	1	.000	6.00	2	2	0	0	0	0	9	12	42	6	6	1	0	3	0	4	0	7	2	0
Ferns, Robert, S.B.	1	0	1.000	0.00	1	0	0	0	1	0	2.2	0	9	0	0	0	0	0	0	1	0	2	0	0
Ferreras, Yorklin, Lan.*	3	6	.333	2.78	51	0	0	0	24	1	64.2	50	285	24	20	3	6	3	0	45	3	67	5	1
Foli, Daniel, Lan.	3	3	.500	3.16	32	2	0	0	13	1	57	51	241	21	20	2	2	4	5	25	4	44	5	0
Fox, Ben, F.W.*	4	4	.500	3.91	39	3	0	0	7	0	78.1	79	347	47	34	5	5	3	4	29	0	48	5	1
Freeman, Corey, Wis.	0	0	.000	0.00	1	0	0	0	1	0	1.2	0	5	0	0	0	0	0	0	0	0	2	0	0
Fruto, Emiliano, Wis.	6	6	.500	3.55	33	13	0	0	9	1	111.2	101	500	57	44	6	4	5	11	55	1	99	11	4
Fuell, Jerrod, W.M.	5	4	.556	2.34	51	0	0	0	14	2	77	68	315	25	20	3	6	2	2	20	2	63	6	0
Fulchino, Jeff, K.C.	5	5	.500	3.87	24	22	0	0	0	0	132.2	114	565	67	57	7	5	5	10	51	0	94	9	1
Garber, Mike, S.B.*	0	1	.000	2.93	15	0	0	0	3	0	30.2	41	136	15	10	0	1	0	0	10	1	20	2	0
Garcia, Carlos, F.W.	0	0	.000	1.29	2	2	0	0	0	0	7	3	25	2	1	0	1	0	0	0	0	1	0	0
Garcia, Hector, Bel.	0	0	.000	0.00	1	0	0	0	1	0	1	0	4	0	0	0	0	0	1	0	1	0	0	0
Gates, Brian, Q.C.	0	1	.000	5.30	11	0	0	0	5	1	18.2	28	87	14	11	2	1	3	0	5	0	11	1	0
Gemmell, Don, Day.	0	0	.000	0.00	1	0	0	0	0	0	4	6	5	5	0	0	0	2	0	0	0	0	0	0
Gerk, Jordan, W.M.*	0	0	.000	7.30	8	0	0	0	2	0	12.1	19	60	10	10	2	1	2	1	6	0	8	1	0
Germano, Justin, F.W.	12	5	.706	3.18	24	24	1	0	0	0	155.2	166	645	63	55	14	2	3	4	19	2	119	4	2
Gillman, Justin, Day.	1	3	.250	3.49	7	7	0	0	0	0	38.2	29	160	17	15	3	2	0	2	17	1	30	0	1
Girdley, Josh, Clin.*	3	0	.000	6.85	7	5	0	0	1	1	23.2	33	112	19	18	2	0	2	0	13	0	14	5	0
Gonzales, Jim, W.M.	2	3	.400	6.92	21	2	0	0	5	1	39	45	190	35	30	4	4	0	4	22	0	30	7	1
Gonzalez, Edgar, S.B.	11	8	.579	2.91	23	23	4	2	0	0	151.1	141	625	66	49	4	4	7	7	34	0	110	10	1
Gonzalez, Enrique, S.B.	1	2	.333	3.74	4	4	0	0	0	0	21.2	23	95	16	9	1	0	1	0	9	0	20	0	0
Gooris, Dan, F.W.*	4	3	.571	2.60	22	0	0	0	9	0	27.2	25	116	10	8	1	0	0	0	8	1	20	0	0
Granado, Jan, Day.*	0	0	.000	1.80	3	0	0	0	0	0	5	3	20	1	1	0	0	0	1	2	0	7	0	0
Griffin, Colt, Burl.	6	6	.500	5.36	19	19	0	0	0	0	90.2	75	431	60	54	1	2	10	15	82	0	66	27	1
Griffith, Dustin, C.R.	5	4	.556	3.91	45	0	0	0	12	2	73.2	68	314	36	32	12	3	5	1	25	2	52	6	0
Gruler, Chris, Day.	0	1	.000	5.60	7	7	0	0	0	0	27.1	23	120	19	17	2	1	1	1	16	0	31	6	0
Gutierrez, Jannio, Q.C.	6	4	.600	1.85	31	0	0	0	18	7	43.2	23	178	14	9	4	4	1	2	22	2	59	2	1
Guzman, Angel, Lan.	5	2	.714	1.89	9	9	1	0	0	0	62	42	244	18	13	3	0	1	16	0	49	5	1
Hall, Dan, Bel.	12	8	.600	2.92	41	5	0	0	13	0	98.2	86	401	38	32	6	2	3	3	35	1	87	10	1
Hamilton, Mark, Mich.*	2	0	1.000	2.63	11	2	0	0	0	0	24	22	98	11	7	1	0	1	2	5	0	14	3	0
Haren, Danny, Peo.	7	3	.700	1.95	14	14	1	0	0	0	101.2	89	399	32	22	6	0	4	2	12	0	89	4	2
Head, Daniel, Wis.	6	6	.500	4.68	35	9	1	0	11	3	109.2	123	487	73	57	7	4	3	13	36	1	81	9	0
Heiberger, Heath, S.B.*	0	4	.000	4.39	36	0	0	0	10	2	55.1	62	250	30	27	4	1	1	2	27	1	46	5	1
Hemus, Jared, Q.C.*	0	1	.000	7.06	14	0	0	0	5	1	21.2	25	110	18	17	1	0	3	2	24	0	10	11	0
Henderson, Eric, Bel.*	1	3	.250	6.75	6	6	0	0	0	0	28	35	129	24	21	2	1	1	4	12	0	17	3	4
Hill, Josh, Q.C.	0	0	.000	0.00	2	0	0	0	0	0	3	2	10	0	0	0	0	0	0	0	0	3	1	0
Hill, Shawn, Clin.	12	7	.632	3.44	25	25	0	0	0	0	146.2	149	626	75	56	7	3	6	11	35	2	99	11	1
Hines, Matthew, Lan.	2	0	1.000	5.79	11	0	0	0	0	0	18.2	21	81	13	12	2	0	0	2	7	0	15	3	0
Holdzkom, Lincoln, K.C.	1	5	.167	2.53	30	0	0	0	26	11	32	21	149	11	9	0	1	1	1	29	3	42	6	3
Holsten, Ryan, S.B.	6	13	.316	3.30	28	28	1	0	0	0	174.1	180	732	83	64	8	3	8	4	42	2	83	5	0
Houlton, Dennis, Mich.	14	5	.737	3.14	35	16	0	0	7	2	140.2	120	577	57	49	12	2	4	3	30	0	138	4	0
Huber, Jon, F.W.	8	12	.400	5.12	28	26	2	0	0	0	146	168	659	99	83	7	6	11	7	59	0	86	11	3
Johnson, Jeremy, W.M.	1	0	1.000	4.26	6	0	0	0	3	0	12.2	14	55	6	6	0	1	0	1	2	1	11	1	0
Johnson, Kelly, Peo.	0	1	.000	4.30	16	0	0	0	7	0	23	27	109	17	11	1	2	1	2	10	0	15	5	0
Johnson, Tyler, Peo.*	15	3	.833	2.00	22	18	0	0	1	0	121.1	96	491	35	27	7	4	0	4	42	1	132	8	4
Johnston, Dave, K.C.	0	1	.000	7.71	10	0	0	0	5	1	14	20	74	19	12	2	0	1	2	11	0	13	1	0
Jones, Geoffrey, F.W.*	1	5	.167	3.60	18	9	0	0	4	1	65	59	274	29	26	5	3	1	8	17	1	63	5	0
Jones, Mike, Bel.	7	7	.500	3.12	27	27	0	0	0	0	138.2	135	601	63	48	3	2	2	7	62	0	132	5	1
Julianel, Ben, Peo.*	8	3	.727	3.38	38	8	0	0	12	1	100.1	106	431	49	39	9	3	1	3	32	0	96	8	7
Kaanoi, Jason, Burl.	1	9	.100	5.07	29	15	0	0	3	0	120.2	151	557	89	68	9	5	7	11	38	1	76	9	0
Keelin, Chris, Day.	3	2	.600	2.76	22	0	0	0	8	3	32.2	24	136	12	10	2	1	0	1	15	1	48	3	2
Kelly, Steve, Day.	4	1	.800	3.15	7	7	1	0	0	0	45.2	42	184	16	16	1	2	1	1	7	1	35	0	1
Keppinger, Billy, Burl.*	0	0	.000	0.00	1	0	0	0	0	0	1	0	3	0	0	0	0	0	0	0	0	2	0	0
Kesten, Michael, Wis.*	1	6	.143	2.25	38	0	0	0	20	6	44	44	208	23	11	1	4	0	4	28	1	39	5	1
Ketchner, Ryan, Wis.*	3	6	.333	2.59	31	12	0	0	9	1	111	75	449	39	32	3	6	5	3	39	3	118	3	3
King, O.J., Day.	2	2	.500	3.70	8	6	0	0	0	0	41.1	44	179	23	17	2	1	3	2	14	1	37	6	1
Kline, Steve, Peo.*	0	0	.000	0.00	2	1	0	0	0	0	2.1	1	10	0	0	0	0	0	1	0	0	5	0	0
Kobow, Mike, W.M.	2	2	.500	1.99	55	0	0	0	50	31	58.2	41	240	13	13	2	2	1	3	23	4	50	7	0
Kolb, Dan, Bel.	8	9	.471	4.00	32	15	0	0	10	0	119.1	125	519	67	53	6	4	4	8	38	2	114	1	2
Kozol, Anthony, F.W.	1	3	.250	3.21	41	0	0	0	31	21	42	43	178	18	15	2	3	0	1	5	1	43	2	0
Leclair, Aric, Burl.*	1	0	1.000	6.52	12	0	0	0	7	3	17.1	16	82	15	13	1	0	0	1	6	0	25	1	0
Leu, Trevor, W.M.*	2	0	1.000	4.53	37	0	0	0	8	0	57.2	53	282	31	29	1	3	0	7	49	0	79	13	0
Levinski, Donald, Clin.	12	6	.667	3.02	21	21	1	1	0	0	119.1	92	501	48	40	6	3	3	6	55	1	125	16	0
Lewis, Jeremy, W.M.*	2	3	.400	5.27	6	6	0	0	0	0	27.1	31	127	21	16	2	1	1	2	11	0	15	1	0
Lipari, Thomas, Clin.*	1	1	.500	1.90	4	4	0	0	0	0	23.2	16	91	9	5	1	4	1	0	3	1	27	0	0
Lohse, Eric, Q.C.	2	3	.400	3.67	11	1	0	0	4	1	27	29	120	17	11	4	0	0	2	7	0	26	3	0
Mancha, Tony, Day.	0	1	.000	5.03	14	0	0	0	6	1	19.2	20	89	13	11	2	1	1	3	11	0	15	0	0
Mansfield, Monte, Mich.	4	4	.500	5.30	20	13	0	0	2	0	71.1	64	340	53	42	3	5	1	8	56	0	65	13	0
Marceau, Pierre-Luc, Clin.*	3	1	.250	6.52	12	4	0	0	4	0	29	31	139	21	21	3	1	1	3	28	0	13	5	3
Martin, Nick, Lan.*	2	7	.222	3.92	19	14	0	0	1	0	85	79	360	46	37	7	3	4	3	34	0	55	6	2
Martinez, Dionnar, Lan.	2	0	1.000	4.58	13	0	0	0	3	0	17.2	14	77	9	9	1	0	0	3	11	0	10	6	0

Pitcher, Team	W	L	Pct.	ERA	G	GS	CG	ShO	GF	Sv.	IP	H	TBF	R	ER	HR	SH	SF	HB	BB	IBB	SO	WP	Bk.
Martinez, Javier, F.W.	6	4	.600	3.38	12	12	0	0	0	0	69.1	55	289	28	26	5	2	1	6	19	0	69	1	0
Martinez, Miguel, Peo.	3	0	1.000	0.79	5	5	0	0	0	0	22.2	16	83	2	2	0	1	1	1	5	0	10	0	0
Mata, Gustavo, Clin.	1	3	.250	4.11	8	5	0	0	2	0	30.2	36	133	19	14	0	0	2	1	9	1	15	0	2
Maust, David, Clin.*	1	1	.500	1.87	35	0	0	0	17	5	57.2	45	227	13	12	1	3	0	5	10	0	57	3	0
McCrotty, Wes, K.C.*	4	1	.800	6.44	19	0	0	0	7	0	36.1	53	177	32	26	6	2	3	6	10	1	31	4	1
McDowell, Kevin, W.M.*	11	6	.647	2.60	27	27	0	0	0	0	166.1	156	706	63	48	5	8	4	8	64	0	123	7	6
McMachen, Clifford, S.B.*	5	3	.625	2.63	37	2	1	0	7	0	68.1	52	285	32	20	2	5	2	4	27	3	64	4	3
McMullen, Jeremy, Lan.	0	0	.000	0.00	1	0	0	0	1	0	1	0	3	0	0	0	0	0	0	0	0	1	0	0
McMurray, Heath, Day.	5	5	.500	4.04	14	13	0	0	1	0	75.2	75	335	42	34	8	7	4	3	33	4	57	8	3
Medlin, Corbey, S.B.	2	7	.222	5.03	45	0	0	0	34	6	59	60	274	41	33	3	5	3	6	33	4	54	7	0
Melnyk, Brian, Burl.*	1	1	.500	2.93	10	0	0	0	5	0	15.1	15	65	7	5	0	1	0	4	0	18	0	0
Merrigan, Josh, Peo.*	4	3	.571	2.27	30	0	0	0	11	0	43.2	35	179	13	11	3	2	1	1	16	3	35	2	1
Michaels, Carl, Bel.	0	3	.000	3.57	19	0	0	0	11	5	40.1	39	166	17	16	3	0	1	1	9	1	37	3	1
Middleton, Kyle, Burl.	14	5	.737	3.74	29	17	0	0	8	1	125	124	535	67	52	6	0	6	10	31	0	64	18	1
Miller, Colby, Q.C.	10	11	.476	3.78	27	27	1	1	0	0	154.2	143	659	71	65	11	3	4	11	67	0	139	6	3
Miller, Jason, Q.C.*	2	2	.500	2.34	23	8	0	0	6	0	65.1	55	270	23	17	7	0	0	2	22	0	71	2	0
Mitchell, Tom, Clin.	2	8	.200	6.11	22	15	1	0	1	0	95.2	120	455	73	65	10	6	5	5	59	3	42	11	0
Mitre, Sergio, Lan.	8	10	.444	2.83	27	27	2	0	0	0	168.2	166	685	72	53	7	6	6	10	27	1	96	10	0
Moak, Curtis, Day.*	3	4	.429	3.65	43	0	0	0	10	1	49.1	46	214	24	20	4	4	1	1	23	1	33	5	1
Moates, Jason, W.M.	11	5	.688	3.82	28	25	0	0	1	0	148.1	140	645	70	63	5	3	8	12	68	1	103	9	7
Mozingo, Dan, C.R.*	3	2	.600	4.24	22	3	0	0	7	1	46.2	44	204	28	22	6	1	0	2	22	0	41	3	0
Myers, Damien, W.M.*	0	0	.000	4.70	11	0	0	0	2	0	7.2	8	39	6	4	0	0	0	1	5	0	9	0	0
Narveson, Chris, Peo.*	2	1	.667	4.46	9	9	0	0	0	0	42.1	49	184	24	21	5	0	3	0	8	0	36	3	0
Nickoli, Mike, C.R.	0	1	.000	5.19	2	2	0	0	0	0	8.2	10	41	5	5	0	0	0	3	3	0	6	1	0
Nielsen, Brian, Bel.*	0	2	.000	7.36	9	2	0	0	2	0	25.2	34	121	28	21	5	3	2	1	10	0	25	3	1
Nolasco, Dave, Bel.	2	2	.500	5.65	32	3	0	0	11	1	73.1	88	338	55	46	8	3	3	4	29	2	44	7	0
Norderum, Jason, Clin.*	0	6	.000	8.74	9	4	0	0	1	0	34	45	180	34	33	1	3	1	5	32	0	26	10	1
Oakes, Gerard, Bel.	5	14	.263	7.17	27	20	0	0	2	0	113	136	546	99	90	12	3	13	13	84	1	53	16	0
Olivero, Pedro, Lan.	3	3	.500	3.54	48	0	0	0	23	3	56	52	248	28	22	1	1	0	3	34	0	54	17	1
O'Sullivan, Mark, C.R.	5	9	.357	5.47	42	3	0	0	16	1	75.2	94	360	53	46	8	3	4	2	46	1	80	13	1
Pace, Adam, Burl.*	3	2	.600	4.94	23	2	0	0	8	2	51	47	227	33	28	3	2	4	1	25	2	30	6	0
Palmer, Lucas, Burl.	0	1	.000	8.22	3	1	0	0	0	0	7.2	9	37	7	7	1	0	0	0	5	0	8	2	0
Patchett, Gary, Day.	0	0	.000	0.00	2	0	0	0	2	0	2	1	8	0	0	0	0	0	0	1	0	1	0	0
Patten, Lanny, Wis.	3	3	.500	3.97	39	0	0	0	32	8	47.2	45	217	24	21	3	2	4	2	29	4	57	5	0
Pawelczyk, Kyle, C.R.*	1	2	.333	4.62	7	6	0	0	0	0	25.1	20	121	13	13	1	0	1	1	27	0	28	7	0
Peralta, Joel, C.R.	5	0	1.000	0.95	41	0	0	0	39	21	47.1	28	184	7	5	2	0	0	2	11	3	53	6	1
Percosky, Mark, F.W.	1	5	.167	4.85	14	14	0	0	0	0	65	74	292	45	35	6	1	2	3	18	0	47	4	0
Perez, Jeffrey, Wis.	7	2	.778	3.89	38	3	0	0	20	4	71.2	69	317	35	31	3	5	2	3	31	2	62	7	1
Perkin, Greg, S.B.	2	6	.250	6.18	12	12	1	0	0	0	62.2	77	285	48	43	10	1	1	4	22	0	61	8	0
Petty, Chad, W.M.*	15	10	.600	3.24	28	28	3	2	0	0	161.1	155	701	73	58	4	3	4	9	77	0	119	13	0
Pignatiello, Carmen, Lan.*	9	11	.450	3.17	27	27	1	0	0	0	167.1	152	702	76	59	10	7	5	6	51	0	139	4	1
Pinto, Renyel, Lan.*	7	5	.583	3.31	17	16	0	0	0	0	98	79	400	39	36	9	0	6	8	28	0	92	3	0
Plancich, Nick, Peo.	1	5	.167	6.26	19	8	0	0	4	0	46	62	218	35	32	1	2	5	3	15	0	27	1	0
Pluta, Tony, Mich.	11	13	.458	5.92	28	28	1	1	0	0	143	155	668	100	94	18	6	3	16	83	0	120	15	2
Pope, Justin, Peo.	8	1	.889	1.38	12	12	2	0	0	0	78.1	48	290	15	12	3	0	0	2	12	0	72	3	1
Powell, Greg, Mich.	5	5	.500	2.78	48	1	0	0	26	7	81	75	327	28	25	0	3	1	6	13	0	41	2	0
Powers, Joe, Day.	1	5	.167	6.02	36	1	0	0	13	2	49.1	61	247	44	33	11	5	1	7	30	2	55	11	1
Puccinelli, John, F.W.	0	0	.000	0.00	1	0	0	0	1	0	1	1	4	0	0	0	0	0	0	0	0	0	0	0
Puello, Ignacio, Clin.	7	14	.333	4.77	27	26	0	0	0	0	139.2	155	644	95	74	5	1	9	10	66	2	91	12	2
Pylate, Chad, Q.C.	1	0	1.000	4.71	15	0	0	0	6	1	28.2	28	136	18	15	0	0	2	8	24	1	13	4	0
Ricciardi, Joe, S.B.	0	1	.000	6.10	8	0	0	0	2	0	10.1	16	57	11	7	0	0	1	1	7	1	7	1	0
Richards, John, F.W.*	0	1	.000	8.24	18	0	0	0	8	0	19.2	33	101	21	18	4	1	1	0	8	0	15	2	0
Richardson, Jason, Q.C.	11	9	.550	5.31	23	23	0	0	0	0	127	127	565	80	75	9	3	6	15	56	0	96	16	1
Richardson, Judd, Bel.	0	2	.000	7.13	5	5	0	0	0	0	17.2	25	93	23	14	2	0	0	0	14	0	15	5	2
Rodaway, Brian, Mich.*	2	2	.500	4.00	23	1	0	0	8	1	45	50	192	26	20	1	3	4	2	14	1	32	2	0
Rodriguez, Jose, Clin.	1	0	1.000	9.82	2	0	0	0	1	0	3.2	7	24	4	4	0	0	2	0	6	0	3	4	0
Rogers, Joe, Peo.*	0	0	.000	2.21	25	0	0	0	10	0	40.2	32	153	11	10	4	0	1	1	6	0	38	1	0
Rohlicek, Russ, Mich.-Lan.*	9	7	.563	3.29	27	27	0	0	0	0	164	160	679	68	60	13	3	3	6	42	0	106	5	0
Romero, Josmir, Q.C.	1	3	.250	2.68	9	6	1	0	0	0	37	31	151	12	11	3	0	2	2	9	0	36	1	0
Rosado, Hector, Burl.*	2	2	.500	7.50	31	0	0	0	10	0	54	77	272	49	45	10	4	0	4	34	0	28	5	0
Rouwenhorst, Jonathon, C.R.*	4	2	.667	1.26	44	3	0	0	9	1	85.2	54	332	15	12	1	4	0	3	29	2	78	5	0
Rowland-Smith, Ryan, Wis.*	1	2	.333	6.75	12	8	0	0	2	0	41.1	50	198	39	31	7	2	1	3	19	0	38	1	4
Royce, Ramon, Wis.	2	11	.154	4.47	34	8	0	0	7	2	86.2	109	393	57	43	7	4	3	6	25	1	52	3	0
Rueckel, Danny, Clin.	3	1	.750	4.15	14	0	0	0	5	0	26	23	111	12	12	1	1	1	0	11	1	25	4	1
Russelburg, Aaron, Peo.	8	8	.500	3.38	26	24	1	0	1	0	146.2	148	624	70	55	9	6	4	6	48	0	120	6	3
Russell, Eddie, K.C.	1	0	1.000	5.25	9	0	0	0	3	0	12	12	55	9	7	0	1	1	2	5	0	10	2	1
Ryu, Jae-kuk, Lan.	1	2	.333	7.11	5	4	0	0	0	0	19	26	91	16	15	1	3	0	2	8	0	21	5	0
Saenz, Chris, Bel.	3	5	.375	3.51	37	0	0	0	23	8	74.1	59	322	31	29	5	6	4	8	32	1	99	1	2
Salmon, Brad, Day.	12	9	.571	4.46	29	27	1	1	0	0	159.1	165	698	94	79	9	2	16	48	2	117	7	0
Sanchez, Felix, Lan.*	6	6	.500	4.15	26	21	0	0	4	2	119.1	130	514	67	55	7	7	3	6	44	0	101	5	1
Sanchez, Paul, Burl.	1	2	.333	8.82	28	0	0	0	18	1	33.2	41	180	38	33	5	2	1	9	31	0	26	8	0
Sandberg, Eric, Q.C.*	0	1	.000	13.50	2	0	0	0	1	0	1.1	3	7	3	2	0	1	0	0	1	0	0	0	0
Santana, Eddy, Clin.	0	0	.000	3.38	4	0	0	0	3	0	5.1	8	29	3	2	0	1	0	1	5	0	7	1	0
Santana, Johan, C.R.	14	8	.636	4.16	27	27	0	0	0	0	147	133	619	75	68	10	2	8	6	48	3	146	9	3
Saunders, Joe, C.R.*	3	1	.750	1.88	5	5	0	0	0	0	28.2	16	107	7	6	2	1	0	2	9	0	27	2	0
Schilling, Tim, K.C.*	1	4	.200	6.34	26	2	0	0	10	1	61	71	281	53	43	8	4	2	5	33	0	33	5	0
Schroder, Chris, Clin.	1	3	.250	1.65	22	0	0	0	20	10	27.1	15	113	7	5	1	0	2	14	1	42	1	0
Serafini, Vince, Q.C.*	0	3	.000	4.50	30	0	0	0	12	1	50	64	231	32	25	7	4	2	3	21	1	32	3	0
Severino, Cleris, Day.*	6	6	.500	4.43	16	9	0	0	0	0	63	81	284	37	31	3	3	4	25	2	37	2	1
Shell, Steven, C.R.	11	4	.733	3.72	22	21	1	0	0	0	121	119	506	59	50	12	1	3	9	26	0	86	3	2
Shouse, Dan, Peo.*	1	1	.500	2.19	17	0	0	0	4	0	24.2	20	99	10	6	0	0	1	2	7	0	16	2	0

– 556 –

Pitcher, Team	W	L	Pct.	ERA	G	GS	CG	ShO	GF	Sv.	IP	H	TBF	R	ER	HR	SH	SF	HB	BB	IBB	SO	WP	Bk.
Siemon, David, F.W.	0	1	.000	3.68	3	2	0	0	0	0	7.1	9	34	4	3	0	0	0	3	0	4	0	1
Sikaras, Pete, S.B.	2	4	.333	1.95	37	0	0	0	16	4	60	52	257	19	13	1	1	2	4	23	3	42	8	1
Skinner, John, K.C.	5	3	.625	2.11	22	0	0	0	11	2	47	28	180	11	11	2	1	0	2	10	0	49	6	4
Slaten, Doug, S.B.*	0	0	.000	4.40	7	0	0	0	2	0	14.1	18	63	8	7	0	1	0	0	4	0	5	1	0
Smart, Richard, Q.C.*	1	0	1.000	4.97	7	0	0	0	3	0	12.2	12	51	7	7	1	2	0	0	6	0	12	1	0
Smith, Dan, W.M.	0	0	.000	1.50	5	0	0	0	2	1	12	9	49	3	2	0	0	0	0	5	1	6	3	0
Smith, Jared, Peo.	2	2	.500	3.48	24	0	0	0	7	0	31	21	139	16	12	0	2	2	3	24	1	31	2	1
Soto, Darwin, F.W.	2	0	1.000	1.76	13	0	0	0	3	0	15.1	8	60	4	3	2	2	1	2	3	0	17	0	0
Stanton, Kyle, Day.	4	0	1.000	5.47	33	0	0	0	14	1	54.1	56	237	37	33	3	5	1	3	20	4	43	2	0
Stavros, Tony, Bel.	5	2	.714	1.68	42	0	0	0	34	17	69.2	50	276	16	13	4	4	1	4	25	2	72	2	1
Steitz, Jon, Bel.	0	11	.000	7.62	30	14	0	0	6	0	95.2	130	488	96	81	4	8	1	13	77	1	76	29	7
Stephenson, Garrett, Peo.	0	0	.000	0.00	2	2	0	0	0	0	8.2	0	26	0	0	0	0	0	0	0	0	11	0	0
Stevenson, Jason, Clin.*	3	4	.429	3.78	33	0	0	0	12	2	66.2	69	288	36	28	4	4	2	5	22	4	41	4	1
Steward, Jaime, C.R.*	6	6	.500	3.66	26	11	0	0	4	0	93.1	80	393	49	38	8	11	4	6	33	4	71	4	0
Stewart, Cory, F.W.*	6	3	.667	2.39	17	11	0	0	2	0	64	46	257	21	17	4	2	3	2	18	0	86	1	0
Stockman, Landon, W.M.	3	5	.375	3.97	43	0	0	0	22	4	56.2	55	252	29	25	4	3	2	1	27	1	53	9	1
Stocks, Nick, Peo.	1	0	1.000	2.25	1	1	0	0	0	0	8	6	29	2	2	0	1	1	0	3	0	3	0	0
Stodolka, Mike, Burl.*	8	14	.364	5.27	27	27	1	0	0	0	148.2	173	665	109	87	15	7	6	6	51	0	105	11	0
Tejada, Frailyn, K.C.*	1	5	.167	3.61	9	9	0	0	0	0	52.1	56	230	26	21	5	2	0	1	18	0	24	0	4
Tejada, Sandy, Q.C.	9	4	.692	2.76	14	14	1	0	0	0	91.1	70	361	32	28	9	3	1	1	23	0	78	2	1
Thomas, Adam, C.R.	0	4	.000	5.02	32	0	0	0	17	2	52	63	235	35	29	5	3	3	1	15	1	39	2	0
Tierney, Chris, Burl.*	9	14	.391	3.25	27	27	2	0	0	0	166	179	704	86	60	9	3	7	8	41	0	89	10	1
Torres, Joe, C.R.*	11	8	.579	3.52	25	25	0	0	0	0	133	125	584	73	52	7	5	1	13	66	0	87	10	0
Torres, Luis, Clin.	5	1	.833	3.73	7	7	0	0	0	0	41	29	169	17	17	2	3	1	2	14	0	41	2	3
Tremblay, Max, Mich.*	3	3	.500	1.26	41	0	0	0	27	14	57.1	39	233	14	8	0	2	0	3	20	1	61	3	0
Trytten, Ryan, Bel.	1	2	.333	5.50	31	2	0	0	13	0	68.2	82	318	50	42	5	1	5	7	29	0	35	8	1
Tucker, Rusty, F.W.*	5	1	.833	1.01	31	0	0	0	20	13	35.2	19	139	8	4	2	2	0	0	10	0	50	1	0
Ungs, Nick, K.C.	7	7	.500	3.73	24	16	0	0	4	1	118.1	116	489	55	49	10	7	6	3	19	0	84	2	1
Valera, Luis, Day.	0	1	.000	2.84	8	0	0	0	4	0	12.2	12	57	4	4	1	1	0	0	9	1	15	0	0
Vasquez, Jorge, Burl.	2	1	.667	1.57	22	0	0	0	14	6	46	22	176	8	8	3	1	1	0	15	0	55	4	3
Vorwald, Matt, Q.C.	5	3	.625	2.33	46	0	0	0	30	6	65.2	43	267	20	17	4	3	3	6	28	2	77	2	0
Walker, Jason, Clin.*	0	1	.000	7.04	12	1	0	0	2	0	15.1	15	88	17	12	1	1	0	0	25	1	11	3	0
Warren, Andy, W.M.	5	2	.714	2.45	13	13	0	0	0	0	69.2	69	302	24	19	2	1	1	6	35	1	29	6	0
Washburn, Ben, Clin.	3	9	.250	2.44	24	1	0	0	10	1	51.2	40	204	17	14	2	4	2	3	10	4	30	3	0
Watson, Tanner, Wis.	2	8	.200	5.36	28	12	1	0	8	0	92.1	89	420	61	55	6	7	4	9	54	1	54	2	3
Wear, Gregory, Wis.	1	1	.500	1.80	3	0	0	0	0	0	5	6	27	1	1	0	0	0	0	6	0	5	1	0
Wechsler, Justin, S.B.	7	12	.368	4.01	26	25	0	0	0	0	141.1	165	623	87	63	8	5	6	9	37	0	96	9	2
Wheeler, James, Bel.*	0	0	.000	2.00	4	0	0	0	1	0	9	12	41	6	2	0	0	1	0	3	1	4	1	2
Wilkerson, Wes, Burl.	2	3	.400	4.99	6	6	0	0	0	0	30.2	37	139	23	17	3	5	0	2	11	0	19	1	0
Wilkinson, Matthew, S.B.	0	4	.000	3.72	36	2	0	0	17	2	67.2	71	288	32	28	6	4	0	1	9	0	79	6	0
Willis, Dontrelle, K.C.*	10	2	.833	1.83	19	19	3	2	0	0	127.2	91	491	29	26	3	5	2	8	21	0	101	9	3
Wodnicki, Mike, Peo.	11	10	.524	3.49	26	25	1	1	0	0	154.2	144	630	72	60	16	1	3	1	37	0	131	9	3
Wolensky, Dave, C.R.	0	1	.000	3.15	30	6	0	0	8	1	68.2	66	309	31	24	3	2	5	41	2	58	7	1	
Wood, Brandon, Mich.	2	1	.667	2.55	34	0	0	0	17	4	53	45	227	21	15	2	2	4	19	0	46	4	0	
Woods, Jake, C.R.*	10	5	.667	3.05	27	27	1	0	0	0	153.1	128	633	66	52	12	4	3	11	54	0	121	5	0
Wynegar, Adam, Lan.*	5	2	.714	3.11	13	9	0	0	1	0	55	46	230	24	19	2	1	0	2	24	0	37	4	0
Yeatman, Matt, Bel.	11	7	.611	2.48	25	25	1	0	0	0	127	101	551	51	35	4	4	5	4	77	0	127	12	0
Yoshida, Nobuaki, F.W.*	6	10	.375	3.39	27	27	0	0	0	0	156.2	156	665	81	59	7	5	6	9	37	0	75	8	1
Zary, Richard, Burl.	4	0	1.000	5.94	20	0	0	0	8	1	33.1	44	156	30	22	4	1	2	3	6	0	25	4	1
Zurita, Tom, Burl.	3	0	1.000	4.46	26	0	0	0	20	1	36.1	37	167	20	18	3	2	1	2	19	1	15	2	0

PITCHERS WITH TWO OR MORE TEAMS

Pitcher, Team	W	L	Pct.	ERA	G	GS	CG	ShO	GF	Sv.	IP	H	TBF	R	ER	HR	SH	SF	HB	BB	IBB	SO	WP	Bk.
Rohlicek, Russ, Mich.*	9	5	.643	2.98	25	25	0	0	0	0	151	148	625	58	50	10	3	3	6	36	0	95	4	0
Rohlicek, Russ, Lan.*	0	2	.000	6.92	2	2	0	0	0	0	13	12	54	10	10	3	0	0	0	6	0	1	0	0

COMBINATION SHUTOUTS: **Beloit (6)**—Hall-Stanos-Stavros, M. Jones-Saenz-Hall, M. Jones-Stavros-Kolb, Kolb-Stavros, Yeatman-Stavros, Yeatman-Trytten-Stavros. **Burlington (5)**—Griffin-Armitage-Zurita, Middleton-Palmer-Leclair, Middleton-Rosado-Zurita, Stodolka-Vasquez, Tierney-Armitage. **Cedar Rapids (12)**—Rouwenhorst-O'Sullivan-Andrade, J. Santana-Andrade, J. Santana-Wolensky, Saunders-Andrade-Peralta, Shell-Griffith-O'Sullivan, Steward-Griffith, J. Torres-Andrade-O'Sullivan, J. Torres-Peralta, J. Torres-Thomas-Andrade, Woods-Andrade-Peralta, Woods-Griffith-O'Sullivan, Woods-Griffith-Wolensky. **Clinton (4)**—Levinski-Maust, Levinski-Washburn, Mata-Washburn-R. Corcoran, Puello-E. Santana. **Dayton (5)**—Salmon-Cotton 2, Boutwell-J. Carter-Cotton, Boutwell-Cotton, McMurray-Cotton. **Fort Wayne (5)**—Lipari-Earey, J. Martinez-Dulkowski, Stewart-Cassel-Craker, Stewart-Tucker, Yoshida-Earey-Tucker. **Kane County (7)**—Belizario-Esquivia, Belizario-Skinner, Fulchino-Cave-Dejesus, Fulchino-Skinner-Cave, Willis-Banks-Cave, Willis-Cave, Willis-Skinner. **Lansing (9)**—Benik-Olivero-Brown, Benik-Olivero-Ellis, Mitre-Foli, Pitnatiello-Olivero, Pinto-Hines-F. Sanchez, Pinto-F. Sanchez, F. Sanchez-Eddy Diaz-Ellis, F. Sanchez-Olivero-Ellis, Wynegar-Benik-Brown. **Michigan (7)**—Burns-Campos, Burns-Hamilton-Dorn-Rodaway, Burns-Tremblay, Houlton-Hamilton-Campos, Houlton-Hamilton-Dorn, Houlton-Powell-Tremblay, Mansfield-Powell. **Peoria (18)**—Burgess-Barreto 2, T. Johnson-Blasdell 2, Caple-Merrigan-K. Johnson, Haren-Shouse-Barreto, Haren-Shouse-Blasdell, T. Johnson-Barreto-Blasdell, T. Johnson-Burgess-Barreto, M. Martinez-Merrigan-Blasdell, M. Martinez-Merrigan-Rogers-Blasdell, Pope-Barreto, Pope-Rogers-Blasdell, Russelburg-Barreto, Russelburg-Shouse, Stephenson-K. Johnson, Stephenson-Russelburg, Wodnicki-Kline-Burgess-Blasdell. **Quad City (5)**—C. Miller-Abbott-Vorwald 2, Durbin-Vorwald, E. Tejada-Daws, Ja. Richardson-Gates. **South Bend (3)**—Wechsler-Bruney 2, Cormier-Ferns-Wilkinson. **West Michigan (6)**—McDowell-Birtwell-Kobow, McDowell-Fuell-Kobow, Moates-Stockman-Kobow, Moates-Stockman-Myers-Kobow, Petty-Fuell-Myers-Birtwell-Kobow, Petty-Fuell-Stockman. **Wisconsin (5)**—Fruto-Ketchner, Fruto-Royce-Perez, Ketchner-Perez, Perez-Acors, Watson-Perez.

NO-HIT GAMES: Ed. Gonzalez, South Bend defeated West Michigan, 5-0, April 14.

TEAM

Team	G	PO	A	E	TC	DP	TP	PB	Pct.
Michigan	140	3653	1490	140	5283	108	0	12	.973
Quad City	136	3571	1408	154	5133	117	0	14	.970
Kane County	139	3659	1496	160	5315	109	1	33	.970
Cedar Rapids	139	3690	1387	160	5237	130	0	15	.969
Lansing	139	3680	1586	179	5445	160	0	28	.967
Dayton	140	3701	1461	185	5347	100	0	14	.965
Peoria	138	3680	1441	185	5306	111	0	12	.965
South Bend	139	3661	1466	189	5316	119	0	22	.964
West Michigan	140	3744	1549	198	5491	134	0	23	.964
Fort Wayne	137	3605	1399	191	5195	100	0	15	.963
Beloit	139	3623	1485	198	5306	115	0	26	.963
Burlington	139	3629	1496	209	5334	125	0	17	.961
Wisconsin	139	3599	1426	210	5235	90	0	29	.960
Clinton	136	3538	1513	217	5268	126	0	20	.959

INDIVIDUAL

FIRST BASEMEN

NOTE: All caps denotes fielding-percentage leader based on 70 games for catchers, 93 for all other non-pitchers and 112 innings for pitchers. *Throws lefthanded.

Player, Team	Pct.	G	PO	A	E	TC	DP
Abram, Matt, Q.C.	.990	15	88	8	1	97	6
Agar, Cory, Q.C.	1.000	6	53	2	0	55	0
Ambrosini, Dominick, Clin.*	1.000	7	49	4	0	53	1
Anderson, Keto, F.W.	.667	1	2	0	1	3	0
Arnott, George, K.C.	1.000	1	2	0	0	2	0
Benick, Jon, F.W.	.989	61	490	34	6	530	37
BOURAS, Brad, Lan.	.989	111	992	43	11	1046	122
Cadena, Alex, Wis.	.984	20	160	21	3	184	12
Cahill, Jonathan, C.R.	1.000	1	1	0	0	1	0
Checksfield, Steven, Mich.	.988	54	463	34	6	503	38
Collins, Chris, Wis.	.882	2	14	1	2	17	2
Duncan, Chris, Peo.	.982	117	983	53	19	1055	80
Esterlin, Yban, Lan.*	.972	35	223	19	7	249	20
Eylward, Mike, C.R.	.983	59	488	32	9	529	53
Fallon, Chris, Burl.	.995	80	658	68	4	730	62
Fielder, Prince, Bel.	.973	32	243	14	7	264	20
Figuereo, Anibal, Burl.	.986	61	524	47	8	579	50
Garcia, Cip, Wis.	.955	10	77	7	4	88	6
Garcia, Hector, Bel.	1.000	5	35	2	0	37	3
Garcia, Juan-Carlos, K.C.	1.000	3	30	2	0	32	5
Gemoll, Brandon, Bel.*	1.000	2	13	0	0	13	2
Gomez, Galinda, Burl.	1.000	1	2	0	0	2	0
Gonzalez, Juan, W.M.	1.000	1	1	0	0	1	0
Gutierrez, Jesse, Day.	.991	70	580	49	6	635	36
Hartig, Philip, K.C.	.993	12	131	4	1	136	5
Hastings, Joseph, F.W.	.985	63	556	25	9	590	46
Hicks, Scott, K.C.	.997	35	317	11	1	329	32
Huff, Ken, Q.C.*	1.000	19	127	8	0	135	7
Johnson, Gabe, Peo.	1.000	1	1	1	0	2	0
Jones, Garrett, Q.C.*	.991	40	313	29	3	345	38
Kelly, Heath, K.C.	1.000	1	10	0	0	10	0
Knott, Jon, F.W.	1.000	2	14	1	0	15	1
Kotchman, Casey, C.R.*	.992	75	596	48	5	649	57
Loeb, Bryan, S.B.	.974	9	66	8	2	76	6
Lopez, Michael, S.B.	.974	5	35	2	1	38	4
Luellwitz, Sean, S.B.	.994	48	435	39	3	477	35
Lugo, Alfredo, W.M.	.967	6	27	2	1	30	2
Lutz, David, Clin.	1.000	2	17	2	0	19	2
Lydic, Joe, Mich.	.997	36	327	13	1	341	25
Mauer, Joe, Q.C.	.990	13	95	7	1	103	12
McKnight, Lukas, Lan.	1.000	4	10	0	0	10	1
Moore, Bryan, Peo.*	1.000	5	34	2	0	36	6
Mote, Trevor, Mich.	1.000	1	7	0	0	7	0
Napoli, Michael, C.R.	.955	9	60	4	3	67	9
Neill, Ryan, W.M.	1.000	6	22	1	0	23	1
Nelson, Brad, Bel.	.988	103	835	70	11	916	75
Nichols, Kyle, S.B.	.986	69	598	44	9	651	58
Obradovich, Mark, Mich.	1.000	1	9	1	0	10	1
Oliveros, Luis, Wis.	.984	15	110	13	2	125	9
Ortiz, Daniel, K.C.	1.000	3	29	1	0	30	3
O'Toole, Paul, Lan.	1.000	1	2	0	0	2	0
Patchett, Gary, Day.	1.000	1	5	1	0	6	1
Peless, Sean, Wis.*	.986	102	796	62	12	870	53

Player, Team	Pct.	G	PO	A	E	TC	DP
Roman, Jesse, Peo.*	.994	23	145	21	1	167	15
Ruiz, Junior, Day.	1.000	4	24	2	0	26	3
Ruiz, Randy, Day.	.982	45	374	14	7	395	30
Sain, Greg, F.W.	.986	16	130	6	2	138	9
Sandoval, Michael, Q.C.	1.000	6	27	4	0	31	4
Santor, John, Peo.	1.000	1	10	0	0	10	0
Self, Todd, Mich.	.994	57	472	30	3	505	41
Slavik, Corey, Lan.	.986	7	65	4	1	70	8
Sosa, Jovanny, Clin.	.964	5	26	1	1	28	0
Stokes, Jason, K.C.	.992	87	779	74	7	860	59
Tejeda, Juan, W.M.	.988	136	1187	84	16	1287	118
Thede, Matthew, Clin.	.957	8	85	3	4	92	8
Tope, Stephen, Q.C.	.977	31	239	17	6	262	24
Torres, Digno, Q.C.*	.978	26	159	17	4	180	15
Trzesniak, Nick, F.W.	1.000	1	2	0	0	2	0
Turner, Justin, C.R.	1.000	2	16	2	0	18	1
Urueta, Luis, S.B.	1.000	9	73	2	0	75	7
Voshell, Chase, Peo.	1.000	1	2	0	0	2	0
Williams, Clyde, Clin.*	.978	120	1098	74	26	1198	102
Williamson, Chris, Day.*	.979	29	209	20	5	234	20

TRIPLE PLAY: Stokes.

SECOND BASEMEN

Player, Team	Pct.	G	PO	A	E	TC	DP
Arroyo, William, K.C.	.942	43	73	122	12	207	21
Arteaga, Joshua, Lan.	1.000	10	13	24	0	37	7
Ayala, Elio, Bel.	1.000	11	28	30	0	58	4
Barfield, Josh, F.W.	.962	129	241	364	24	629	66
Barnwell, Chris, Bel.	.889	1	4	4	1	9	1
Bastida-Martinez, Evel, Wis.	1.000	10	18	23	0	41	5
Bell, Paul, Bel.	.833	5	3	12	3	18	3
Bergolla, William, Day.	.960	50	83	135	9	227	15
Boyd, Shaun, Peo.	.935	127	221	359	40	620	75
Boyer, Brett, Clin.	1.000	5	6	14	0	20	3
Brand, Kevin, S.B.	.882	4	5	10	2	17	3
Cahill, Jonathan, C.R.	.994	44	67	108	1	176	31
Campana, Wandel, Day.	.959	68	130	173	13	316	40
Candelaria, Scott, Bel.	.945	24	39	81	7	127	14
Cedeno, Ronny, Lan.	.968	32	63	90	5	158	20
Chauncey, Clinton, Peo.	.000	1	0	0	0	0	0
Cleveland, Matt, Burl.	.968	19	38	53	3	94	6
Clute, Kris, K.C.	.955	72	103	217	15	335	38
Conrad, Brooks, Mich.	.971	121	207	335	16	558	59
Cordova, Ricardo, Peo.	.700	7	3	4	3	10	1
Cordova, Roman, Wis.	.958	41	70	90	7	167	15
Creighton, Matt, Lan.	1.000	2	3	9	0	12	1
Davidson, Seth, Q.C.	1.000	1	1	4	0	5	2
Ellena, Jeff, Wis.	.948	43	93	124	12	229	24
Encarnacion, Henry, Clin.	.909	9	11	19	3	33	4
Floyd, Dan, Wis.	.932	22	35	47	6	88	4
Francia, Juan, W.M.	.947	125	312	351	37	700	91
Gonzalez, Juan, W.M.	.966	13	31	26	2	59	11
GOTAY, Ruben, Burl.	.973	115	266	338	17	621	88
Guerrero, Pedro, Clin.	.969	5	8	23	1	32	2
Hairston, Scott, S.B.	.949	95	171	277	24	472	56
Haydel, Rick, S.B.	.971	5	13	21	1	35	4
Helps, Jason, K.C.	1.000	2	1	2	0	3	0
Hernandez, Vladimir, Clin.	1.000	2	2	8	0	10	1
Hilinski, Scott, S.B.	.962	14	33	42	3	78	11
Jacobo, Kervin, S.B.	.958	6	9	14	1	24	5
Kelly, Heath, K.C.	.981	9	18	34	1	53	7
Kuhaulua, Kaulana, Q.C.	.989	15	40	49	1	90	11
Lewis, Domonique, Day.	.960	33	46	74	5	125	20
Martinez, Guillermo, Wis.	.986	18	29	42	1	72	7
Mauer, James, Q.C.	.993	66	126	162	2	290	45
McCool, Lee, F.W.-S.B.	.941	14	22	26	3	51	5
Mejia, Gilberto, W.M.	.968	6	15	15	1	31	5
Menchaca, Eriberto, Wis.	1.000	3	4	4	0	8	0
Merchan, Jesus, Q.C.	.967	32	56	62	4	122	9
Merritt, Tim, Wis.	.935	8	13	16	2	31	3
Monahan, Joey, Lan.	.960	16	26	46	3	75	10
Mote, Trevor, Mich.	1.000	2	5	5	0	10	2
Patchett, Gary, Day.	1.000	4	8	10	0	18	2
Peguero, Miguel, W.M.	1.000	2	5	3	0	8	3
Rodriguez, Alex, Burl.	.968	7	15	15	1	31	4
Rojas, Randy, Mich.	.980	21	38	59	2	99	11
Sain, Greg, F.W.	1.000	1	1	0	0	1	0
Salas, Francisco, Lan.	.962	5	8	17	1	26	6

Player, Team	Pct.	G	PO	A	E	TC	DP
Santana, Ralph, Bel.	.949	105	229	289	28	546	64
Schnabel, Nick, Clin.	1.000	4	7	9	0	16	1
Serrano, Eddie, F.W.	.921	7	16	19	3	38	3
Simoneaux, Neil, Peo.	1.000	9	15	19	0	34	2
Tamburrino, Brett, Q.C.	.971	35	64	106	5	175	16
Theriot, Ryan, Lan.	.959	66	146	202	15	363	57
Thissen, Greg, Clin.	.970	119	249	361	19	629	85
Thornton-Murray, Jandin, Lan.	1.000	1	2	2	0	4	2
Turner, Justin, C.R.	.952	107	184	248	22	454	60
Uggla, Dan, S.B.	.969	6	11	20	1	32	6
Welsch, Travis, Lan.	.966	12	30	27	2	59	6
Wyant, Hunter, K.C.	.941	18	28	52	5	85	7

TRIPLE PLAY: Clute.

SECOND BASEMEN WITH TWO OR MORE TEAMS

Player, Team	Pct.	G	PO	A	E	TC	DP
McCool, Lee, F.W.	.900	2	5	4	1	10	2
McCool, Lee, S.B.	.951	12	17	22	2	41	3

THIRD BASEMEN

Player, Team	Pct.	G	PO	A	E	TC	DP
Abram, Matt, Q.C.	.700	9	2	5	3	10	0
Ambrosini, Anthony, Clin.	.000	1	0	0	0	0	0
Arroyo, William, K.C.	.833	7	3	7	2	12	1
Arteaga, Joshua, Lan.	.951	26	15	62	4	81	12
Ayala, Elio, Bel.	.846	46	45	59	19	123	6
Barnwell, Chris, Bel.	.931	84	78	153	17	248	11
Bell, Paul, Bel.	.833	5	2	3	1	6	0
Benick, Jon, F.W.	.867	50	28	89	18	135	8
Boone, Matt, Day.	.935	19	9	34	3	46	3
Boyd, Dan, Bel.	.000	1	0	0	0	0	0
Boyer, Brett, Clin.	.500	2	0	3	3	6	0
Brand, Kevin, S.B.	.926	9	6	19	2	27	2
Brown, Hunter, Wis.	.952	43	36	83	6	125	3
Brown, Matthew, Clin.	.800	7	3	5	2	10	1
Cahill, Jonathan, C.R.	.909	12	8	12	2	22	4
Campana, Wandel, Day.	1.000	8	6	15	0	21	1
Candelaria, Scott, Bel.	1.000	4	4	9	0	13	0
Cleveland, Matt, Burl.	.786	6	3	8	3	14	0
Collins, Chris, Wis.	.667	2	1	1	1	3	0
Cordova, Ricardo, Peo.	1.000	1	0	1	0	1	0
Dean, Erik, Burl.	.750	4	0	6	2	8	0
Diaz, Felix, Clin.	.896	52	28	101	15	144	7
Dibetta, John, F.W.	.956	16	9	34	2	45	2
Dobbs, Greg, Wis.	.902	72	47	164	23	234	12
Encarnacion, Edwin, Day.	.901	116	89	211	33	333	15
Encarnacion, Henry, Clin.	.806	15	6	23	7	36	1
Eylward, Mike, C.R.	.931	14	6	21	2	29	4
Floyd, Dan, Wis.	.836	17	15	31	9	55	2
Francisco, Alfredo, Lan.	1.000	2	3	5	0	8	2
Garcia, Juan-Carlos, K.C.	.600	2	1	2	2	5	0
Gomez, Galinda, Burl.	.858	90	75	167	40	282	17
Gonzalez, Juan, W.M.	.910	77	49	153	20	222	18
Gotay, Ruben, Burl.	1.000	10	7	15	0	22	3
Groves, Brett, Burl.	.889	25	18	46	8	72	5
Guerrero, Pedro, Clin.	.909	7	1	9	1	11	1
Hairston, Scott, S.B.	.862	10	8	17	4	29	2
Helps, Jason, K.C.	1.000	7	4	21	0	25	2
Hernandez, Vladimir, Clin.	1.000	1	3	2	0	5	0
Hilinski, Scott, S.B.	.833	3	3	2	1	6	0
Honeycutt, Heath, S.B.	.934	22	20	37	4	61	5
Jacobo, Kervin, S.B.	.898	21	13	40	6	59	3
Johnson, Gabe, Peo.	.912	120	91	210	29	330	20
Keim, Adam, Burl.	.917	7	3	8	1	12	0
Kelly, Heath, K.C.	1.000	4	2	7	0	9	1
Kuhaulua, Kaulana, Q.C.	.000	1	0	0	0	0	0
Lopez, Michael, S.B.	.930	24	23	30	4	57	1
Lugo, Alfredo, W.M.	.936	61	29	102	9	140	12
Lutz, David, Clin.	1.000	4	4	9	0	13	0
Lydic, Joe, Mich.	.880	11	7	15	3	25	1
Martinez, Guillermo, Wis.	1.000	1	2	1	0	3	0
Mauer, Jake, Q.C.	.917	4	2	9	1	12	1
McCool, Lee, S.B.	.941	6	4	12	1	17	3
McPherson, Dallas, C.R.	.898	123	70	204	31	305	20
Menchaca, Eriberto, Wis.	1.000	3	3	8	0	11	0
Merchan, Jesus, Q.C.	.896	16	10	33	5	48	5
Mote, Trevor, Mich.	.913	121	69	257	31	357	18
Murphy, Tommy, C.R.	.000	1	0	0	0	0	0
Napoli, Michael, C.R.	1.000	1	1	1	0	2	0

Player, Team	Pct.	G	PO	A	E	TC	DP
Norris, Shawn, Clin.	1.000	9	4	5	0	9	0
Oliveros, Luis, Wis.	1.000	1	1	1	0	2	0
O'Toole, Paul, Lan.	.875	3	4	10	2	16	3
Peguero, Miguel, W.M.	.947	7	3	15	1	19	1
Pereyra, Joel, Burl.	.000	1	0	0	0	0	0
Puccinelli, John, F.W.	1.000	4	3	7	0	10	1
Raburn, Ryan, W.M.	.786	17	9	35	12	56	4
Sain, Greg, F.W.	.933	55	45	108	11	164	9
Salas, Francisco, Lan.	.762	7	5	11	5	21	0
Sandoval, Michael, Q.C.	.899	111	75	183	29	287	16
Schnabel, Nick, Clin.	.908	33	20	59	8	87	6
Serrano, Eddie, F.W.	.887	20	12	35	6	53	4
Slavik, Corey, Lan.	.922	82	65	182	21	268	22
Stegall, Ryan, Mich.	.917	18	7	26	3	36	1
Thede, Matthew, Clin.	.889	13	7	17	3	27	0
Thissen, Greg, Clin.	.714	6	1	9	4	14	1
Tope, Stephen, Q.C.	.818	3	2	7	2	11	0
TUCKER, Michael, K.C.	.921	116	64	216	24	304	13
Turner, Justin, C.R.	1.000	1	0	2	0	2	0
Uggla, Dan, S.B.	.923	46	37	94	11	142	9
Varner, Noochie, Day.	1.000	3	0	1	0	1	0
Villanueva, Florian, Bel.	.941	7	4	12	1	17	0
Voshell, Chase, Peo.	.778	19	12	23	10	45	2
Welsch, Travis, Lan.	.957	26	8	58	3	69	3
Wyant, Hunter, K.C.	.895	7	4	13	2	19	3

SHORTSTOPS

Player, Team	Pct.	G	PO	A	E	TC	DP
Aquino, Jackson, F.W.	.907	99	127	275	41	443	42
Arroyo, William, K.C.	.667	1	1	3	2	6	1
Barnwell, Chris, Bel.	.951	8	15	24	2	41	5
Bell, Paul, Bel.	1.000	5	7	13	0	20	2
Bergolla, William, Day.	.953	16	25	36	3	64	12
Brand, Kevin, S.B.	1.000	4	2	4	0	6	0
Cahill, Jonathan, C.R.	.972	18	30	39	2	71	11
Campana, Wandel, Day.	.926	38	48	65	9	122	10
Cedeno, Ronny, Lan.	.935	66	92	209	21	322	48
Chavez, Ozzie, Bel.	.950	128	202	351	29	582	70
Cleveland, Matt, Burl.	.800	6	10	18	7	35	3
Clute, Kris, K.C.	.909	3	2	8	1	11	1
Cordova, Ricardo, Peo.	.857	7	4	8	2	14	2
Cordova, Roman, Wis.	.857	5	6	6	2	14	1
Davidson, Seth, Q.C.	.961	50	86	158	10	254	36
Dean, Erik, Burl.	.897	6	8	18	3	29	1
Encarnacion, Edwin, Day.	.894	17	22	37	7	66	10
Encarnacion, Henry, Clin.	.875	7	7	7	2	16	2
Freeman, Corey, Wis.	.931	75	130	196	24	350	25
Gonzalez, Juan, W.M.	.966	33	38	103	5	146	15
Groves, Brett, Burl.	.923	83	146	235	32	413	53
Guerrero, Pedro, Clin.	.800	4	2	2	1	5	0
Haydel, Rick, S.B.	.934	119	163	357	37	557	71
Helps, Jason, K.C.	.977	8	15	28	1	44	8
Hilinski, Scott, S.B.	.933	23	29	68	7	104	13
Kelly, Donald, W.M.	.951	111	168	374	28	570	72
Kelly, Heath, K.C.	.857	2	2	4	1	7	0
Kuhaulua, Kaulana, Q.C.	.897	47	64	118	21	203	18
Labandeira, John, Clin.	.942	127	159	392	34	585	82
Lugo, Alfredo, W.M.	1.000	1	0	1	0	1	1
Martinez, Guillermo, Wis.	.816	13	9	22	7	38	3
Mauer, Jake, Q.C.	.967	7	16	13	1	30	4
Menchaca, Eriberto, Wis.	.979	44	71	116	4	191	25
Merchan, Jesus, Q.C.	.944	38	45	91	8	144	16
Merritt, Tim, Wis.	.939	8	15	16	2	33	1
Monahan, Joey, Lan.	.886	9	11	20	4	35	3
Murphy, Donald, Burl.	.934	33	41	101	10	152	17
Murphy, Tommy, C.R.	.942	126	203	329	33	565	74
Nelson, John, Peo.	.943	131	184	360	33	577	66
Patchett, Gary, Day.	.955	89	132	227	17	376	38
Rodriguez, Alex, Burl.	.891	14	27	30	7	64	7
Rojas, Randy, Mich.	.949	39	53	97	8	158	22
RUNDGREN, Rex, K.C.	.959	122	199	364	24	587	64
Schnabel, Nick, Clin.	1.000	2	2	2	0	4	1
Serrano, Eddie, F.W.	.901	47	58	105	18	181	17
Simoneaux, Neil, Peo.	.962	7	8	17	1	26	3
Stegall, Ryan, Mich.	.957	111	165	345	23	533	56
Theriot, Ryan, Lan.	.956	66	81	223	14	318	41
Thissen, Greg, Clin.	.917	2	2	9	1	12	1
Thornton-Murray, Jandin, Lan.	.000	1	0	0	0	0	0
Welsch, Travis, Lan.	1.000	3	0	4	0	4	0
Wyant, Hunter, K.C.	1.000	4	4	7	0	11	1

OUTFIELDERS

Player, Team	Pct.	G	PO	A	E	TC	DP
Abram, Matt, Q.C.	.966	42	54	2	2	58	0
Amador, Jerry, Wis.	.972	18	34	1	1	36	0
Ambrosini, Dominick, Clin.*	.925	112	169	17	15	201	2
Anderson, Keto, F.W.	.976	80	158	4	4	166	1
Arnott, George, K.C.	.967	73	112	5	4	121	1
Asadoorian, Rick, Peo.	.979	137	352	18	8	378	5
Ayala, Elio, Bel.	1.000	2	4	0	0	4	0
Ayala, Odannys, Burl.	.964	92	157	5	6	168	1
Ball, Jarred, S.B.	.981	83	158	1	3	162	0
Barfield, Josh, F.W.	1.000	1	1	0	0	1	0
Barrett, Rich, S.B.	.990	49	89	7	1	97	1
Bassett, Mike, Day.*	1.000	9	10	0	0	10	0
Belcher, Jason, Bel.	.965	33	52	3	2	57	0
Benick, Jon, F.W.	1.000	1	1	0	0	1	0
Biernbaum, L.J., F.W.*	.989	41	84	6	1	91	1
Blackburn, Franco, K.C.	.952	16	19	1	1	21	0
Boyd, Dan, Bel.	.970	85	121	7	4	132	2
Boyer, Brett, Clin.	.972	51	101	4	3	108	2
Brewer, Anthony, K.C.	.978	119	269	3	6	278	1
Brooks, Doc, F.W.	.964	66	100	6	4	110	0
Brostrom, Jeremy, W.M.*	.938	16	15	0	1	16	0
Brown, Matthew, Clin.	.979	63	91	3	2	96	0
Cahill, Jonathan, C.R.	1.000	1	1	0	0	1	0
Callahan, Dan, S.B.*	.963	43	76	1	3	80	0
Cameron, Antoine, Lan.*	1.000	19	26	1	0	27	0
Carrow, Tom, Bel.	.962	66	122	6	5	133	1
Carter, Josh, F.W.	.995	74	168	13	1	182	2
Checksfield, Steven, Mich.	.973	43	70	2	2	74	0
Choo, Shin-soo, Wis.*	.981	109	204	7	4	215	1
Coats, Buck, Lan.	.955	118	179	11	9	199	0
Cole, John, Wis.	.938	17	30	0	2	32	0
Cordova, Ben, Burl.*	.982	62	108	3	2	113	0
Davis, Justin, Day.*	.933	71	93	4	7	104	0
Del Chiaro, Brent, C.R.	.000	1	0	0	0	0	0
De Los Santos, Pedro, F.W.	.950	46	107	6	6	119	0
Denorfia, Christopher, Day.	1.000	3	6	0	0	6	0
Dibetta, John, F.W.	.000	1	0	0	0	0	0
Durham, Miles, W.M.	1.000	4	8	1	0	9	0
Esterlin, Yban, Lan.*	.909	9	9	1	1	11	0
Eylward, Mike, C.R.	.967	22	28	1	1	30	0
Ferrand, Frank, K.C.*	.950	8	19	0	1	20	0
Figueroa, Eduardo, Wis.	.919	23	33	1	3	37	0
Floyd, Dan, Wis.	.961	76	137	11	6	154	1
Foreman, JuJu, S.B.	.846	8	10	1	2	13	0
Frazier, Charles, K.C.	.970	113	218	6	7	231	3
Garcia, Cip, Wis.	.000	2	0	0	1	1	0
Garcia, Hector, Bel.	.964	102	175	11	7	193	2
Garcia, Lino, S.B.	.974	65	149	3	4	156	0
Garthwaite, Jay, S.B.	.980	45	98	0	2	100	0
Gates, David, C.R.	.958	27	45	1	2	48	0
Gemoll, Brandon, Bel.*	.966	20	27	1	1	29	0
Gorneault, Nicholas, C.R.	.979	101	183	4	4	191	0
Greenberg, Adam, Lan.*	1.000	22	36	1	0	37	0
Guerrero, Pedro, Clin.	.968	15	30	0	1	31	0
Guzman, Jonathan, Burl.	.939	122	218	11	15	244	4
Hastings, Joseph, F.W.	1.000	17	28	0	0	28	0
Hawes, B.J., Day.	.981	53	99	6	2	107	0
Hellman, Matthew, F.W.	1.000	8	12	1	0	13	0
Helps, Jason, K.C.	.000	1	0	0	0	0	0
Hernandez, Vladimir, Clin.	.000	1	0	0	0	0	0
Hicks, Scott, K.C.	.969	79	117	7	4	128	0
Hinton, Travis, Bel.*	.969	51	92	3	3	98	1
Hodges, Kerry, Mich.	.987	61	76	0	1	77	0
Humphries, Jared, Day.*	.929	23	24	2	2	28	0
Hurtado, Omar, Day.	.978	54	85	5	2	92	1
Hutchinson, Burnell, S.B.	1.000	26	41	1	0	42	0
Janz, Jeramy, S.B.	.939	22	43	3	3	49	0
Johnson, J.J., Lan.	.973	94	169	10	5	184	3
Jones, Garrett, Q.C.*	1.000	3	3	0	0	3	0
Jones, Kennard, F.W.*	1.000	19	40	0	0	40	0
Kennedy, Jason, W.M.	.955	38	41	1	2	44	0
Kerner, Craig, Clin.	.983	35	55	4	1	60	1
Kimpton, Nick, C.R.*	.990	92	186	4	2	192	1
Knoedler, Jason, W.M.	.977	134	299	5	7	311	2
Knott, Jon, F.W.	.948	35	51	4	3	58	2
Kolodzey, Chris, W.M.	.968	51	60	0	2	62	0
Kubel, Jason, Q.C.	.982	113	158	7	3	168	0
Kuhaulua, Kaulana, Q.C.	.000	1	0	0	0	0	0
Lemon, Tim, Peo.	.988	131	238	11	3	252	4
Lentini, Fehlandt, Mich.	.962	64	93	8	4	105	3

Player, Team	Pct.	G	PO	A	E	TC	DP
Lewis, Domonique, Day.	.952	21	19	1	1	21	0
Likely, Cameron, Mich.	.969	91	156	2	5	163	0
Loeb, Bryan, S.B.	1.000	6	9	1	0	10	0
Louisa, Lorvin, Clin.	.913	27	42	0	4	46	0
Lugo, Alfredo, W.M.	1.000	1	1	0	0	1	0
Mace, Clark, S.B.*	1.000	5	6	0	0	6	0
MALLORY, Mike, Lan.	.992	116	231	7	2	240	0
Manning, Ricky, Q.C.*	.935	22	29	0	2	31	0
Mattle, David, W.M.	.970	133	224	5	7	236	1
Mayo, Terry, Bel.	.973	50	98	9	3	110	1
McClanahan, Jonah, Bel.	.931	12	26	1	2	29	0
McCool, Lee, F.W.	.955	29	40	2	2	44	2
Melgarejo, Ransel, C.R.	.978	116	255	6	6	267	0
Merchan, Jesus, Q.C.	.000	1	0	0	0	0	0
Miliano, Hector, Lan.	.931	20	26	1	2	29	0
Monte, Harvey, Mich.*	1.000	23	47	3	0	50	2
Morris, Chris, Bel.	.857	4	5	1	1	7	0
Neill, Ryan, W.M.	.985	43	63	3	1	67	0
Nevins, Ryan, C.R.	1.000	13	15	1	0	16	0
Nina, Amaurys, Day.	.974	26	38	0	1	39	0
Oeltjen, Trent, Q.C.*	.938	10	15	0	1	16	0
O'Toole, Paul, Lan.	.875	3	7	0	1	8	0
Paredes, Jeison, S.B.	.988	33	79	4	1	84	0
Porter, Greg, C.R.	.982	72	105	3	2	110	0
Quickstad, Barry, Q.C.	.952	40	58	1	3	62	0
Rainey, Jason, Wis.*	.979	28	45	1	1	47	0
Reed, Eric, K.C.*	1.000	12	25	0	0	25	0
Robison, Jordan, Peo.	.959	100	132	7	6	145	0
Rodriguez, Mike, Mich.*	.984	124	237	5	4	246	1
Roman, Jesse, Peo.*	.956	84	105	3	5	113	0
Rombley, Danny, Clin.	.953	71	134	8	7	149	0
Rosario, Victor, Burl.	.982	24	53	3	1	57	0
Ruiz, Randy, Day.	.941	7	16	0	1	17	0
Scott, Mike, W.M.*	.946	32	49	4	3	56	0
Self, Todd, Mich.	.986	65	127	10	2	139	0
Serrano, Eddie, F.W.	.000	1	0	0	0	0	0
Shanks, James, Burl.	.978	126	316	2	7	325	0
Sosa, Jovanny, Clin.	.900	6	8	1	1	10	1
Stockton, Rick, F.W.*	1.000	10	14	0	0	14	0
Stringham, Jed, W.M.	1.000	1	1	0	0	1	0
Swope, Matt, Clin.	.964	43	78	2	3	83	1
Tamburrino, Brett, Q.C.	.986	55	67	5	1	73	1
Thede, Matthew, Clin.	1.000	5	5	0	0	5	0
Tomlin, James, Q.C.	.973	103	209	6	6	221	3
Tope, Stephen, Q.C.	1.000	30	37	3	0	40	0
Torres, Digno, Q.C.*	.957	22	43	2	2	47	0
Van Meetren, Jason, Wis.	.986	71	135	4	2	141	0
Varner, Noochie, Day.-W.M.	.986	129	274	11	4	289	2
Villanueva, Florian, Bel.	.857	16	15	3	3	21	0
Villilo, Miguel, Wis.	.902	67	82	10	10	102	2
Voshell, Chase, Peo.	1.000	3	3	0	0	3	0
Vugteveen, Dustin, S.B.	.963	48	98	7	4	109	4
Welch, Ed, C.R.	1.000	17	14	0	0	14	0
Weston, Aron, Lan.*	.930	24	39	1	3	43	0
Williamson, Chris, Day.*	.968	66	87	3	3	93	0
Wyant, Hunter, K.C.	1.000	6	9	0	0	9	0
Yount, Andy, W.M.	.857	9	10	2	2	14	0

OUTFIELDERS WITH TWO OR MORE TEAMS

Player, Team	Pct.	G	PO	A	E	TC	DP
Varner, Noochie, Day.	.986	125	261	11	4	276	2
Varner, Noochie, W.M.	1.000	4	13	0	0	13	0

CATCHERS

Player, Team	Pct.	G	PO	A	E	TC	DP	PB
Abram, Matt, Q.C.	1.000	2	1	0	0	1	0	0
Agar, Cory, Q.C.	1.000	2	17	2	0	19	0	0
Allec, Jason, W.M.	.917	3	21	1	2	24	0	1
Alleva, J.D., Burl.	.996	44	244	30	1	275	2	6
Ambrosini, Anthony, Clin.	.994	65	419	41	3	463	2	4
Anderson, Dennis, K.C.	.986	47	321	38	5	364	3	5
Anderson, Sam, W.M.	1.000	15	90	15	0	105	1	2
Arnerich, Tony, Burl.	1.000	5	33	8	0	41	0	0
Arnott, George, K.C.	1.000	2	13	1	0	14	0	0
Belcher, Jason, Bel.	.981	34	243	16	5	264	1	6
Bowen, Rob, Q.C.	1.000	4	24	2	0	26	0	0
Cadena, Alex, Wis.	.962	5	22	3	1	26	0	0
Cahill, Jonathan, C.R.	1.000	1	1	0	0	1	0	0
Chauncey, Clinton, Peo.	1.000	19	75	11	0	86	1	1
Collins, Chris, Wis.	.980	69	478	50	11	539	2	16
Davis, Justin, Day.*	.000	1	0	0	0	0	0	0

Player, Team	Pct.	G	PO	A	E	TC	DP	PB
Del Chiaro, Brent, C.R.	.986	35	194	16	3	213	2	1
DiRosa, Michael, S.B.	.995	59	390	40	2	432	0	12
Draper, John, Burl.	.989	91	549	58	7	614	7	11
Eickhorst, Chris, Peo.	.988	13	72	8	1	81	0	1
Emmerick, Josh, Clin.	.917	7	41	3	4	48	0	1
Esparragoza, Pedro, Bel.	.985	57	445	74	8	527	3	12
Garcia, Cip, Wis.	1.000	4	30	0	0	30	0	3
Gutierrez, Jesse, Day.	1.000	33	256	31	0	287	1	4
Hanigan, Ryan, Day.	.952	6	37	3	2	42	0	1
Hanna, Warren, Lan.	.991	57	389	37	4	430	2	10
Huguet, J.C., Day.	.963	20	114	16	5	135	2	0
Kennedy, Bryan, Q.C.	1.000	50	357	31	0	388	2	7
Lafferty, Will, Peo.	1.000	17	102	11	0	113	0	1
Loeb, Bryan, S.B.	.978	78	528	59	13	600	0	8
Lucas, Matt, Mich.	.993	62	411	27	3	441	1	2
Lutz, David, Clin.	.982	32	208	15	4	227	0	9
Lynam, Guy, K.C.	.930	6	51	2	4	57	0	1
Marmol, Carlos, Lan.	.961	14	88	10	4	102	1	3
MATHIS, Jeff, C.R.	.994	80	606	70	4	680	2	6
Mauer, Joe, Q.C.	.994	81	723	71	5	799	5	7
McKnight, Lukas, Lan.	.973	40	259	25	8	292	1	9
McMillan, Drew, Clin.	.982	31	200	23	4	227	1	5
Mercado, Onix, Day.	.984	19	105	19	2	126	1	4
Miller, Chris, Lan.	1.000	3	21	2	0	23	0	1
Molina, Angel, K.C.	.986	21	128	16	2	146	1	8
Molina, Yadier, Peo.	.985	112	809	140	14	963	9	8
Montilla, Samuel, S.B.	.968	5	26	4	1	31	1	2
Napoli, Michael, C.R.	.987	37	275	35	4	314	5	8
Netwall, Chris, Peo.	1.000	2	13	1	0	14	0	1
Obradovich, Mark, Mich.	.994	90	569	48	4	621	1	10
Oliveros, Luis, Wis.	.989	65	485	50	6	541	3	10
O'Toole, Paul, Lan.	.986	17	132	8	2	142	0	3
Pereyra, Joel, Burl.	1.000	3	3	0	0	3	0	0
Pines, Greg, Mich.	.889	6	8	0	1	9	0	0
Prince, Bryan, Day.	.986	82	587	70	9	666	1	5
Rabelo, Mike, W.M.	.984	122	813	102	15	930	5	16
Reinking, Kevin, F.W.	.988	40	324	15	4	343	1	7
Schneider, Michael, Clin.	.969	10	53	9	2	64	1	1
Silver, Travis, Lan.	.986	19	130	11	2	143	1	2
Thede, Matthew, Clin.	1.000	5	31	4	0	35	0	0
Trezza, Alex, W.M.	.977	15	81	4	2	87	1	4
Trzesniak, Nick, F.W.	.990	101	672	56	7	735	0	8
Villanueva, Florian, Bel.	.982	51	336	54	7	397	5	8
Zapey, Winton, K.C.	.984	64	458	32	8	498	2	19

PITCHERS

Player, Team	Pct.	G	PO	A	E	TC	DP
Abbott, Jim, Q.C.	.963	29	8	18	1	27	1
Ackerman, Eric, Burl.*	.000	7	0	0	0	0	0
Acors, Bo, Wis.	1.000	13	0	6	0	6	1
Adams, Mike, Bel.	1.000	11	1	1	0	2	0
Akens, Phil, K.C.	.946	28	13	22	2	37	3
Alvarez, Larry, Lan.	1.000	9	0	1	0	1	0
Andrade, Stephen, C.R.	.818	46	4	5	2	11	0
Armitage, Barry, Burl.*	.813	38	2	11	3	16	0
Artman, Dane, Bel.*	.917	20	3	8	1	12	0
Asahina, Jonathan, K.C.	.909	27	7	23	3	33	0
Atlee, Rick, Lan.	.000	3	0	0	0	0	0
Badgley, Daniel, W.M.	.875	21	3	4	1	8	0
Banks, Tyler, K.C.	.000	13	0	0	0	0	0
Barlow, Chris, Clin.	.889	9	4	12	2	18	1
Barnes, Pat, Wis.*	.600	3	1	2	2	5	0
Barreto, Joel, Peo.	1.000	42	3	4	0	7	0
Basham, Bobby, Day.	.875	13	8	6	2	16	0
Bass, Brian, Burl.	.978	20	20	25	1	46	0
Batista, Gorky, Day.	.857	11	4	2	1	7	0
Baxter, Allen, K.C.	1.000	4	1	3	0	4	0
Belizario, Ronald, K.C.	.882	23	8	22	4	34	2
Benik, Brett, Lan.	1.000	27	5	18	0	23	1
Birtwell, John, W.M.	.778	58	2	5	2	9	0
Blasdell, Jared, Peo.	1.000	53	1	9	0	10	0
Boutwell, Andy, Day.	.769	16	3	7	3	13	0
Bowyer, Travis, Q.C.	.962	39	14	11	1	26	3
Boyd, Dan, Bel.	1.000	1	0	1	0	1	0
Brannon, Nick, Day.*	1.000	3	0	1	0	1	0
Brown, Eric, Lan.	1.000	23	1	3	0	4	0
Bruney, Brian, S.B.	.875	37	2	5	1	8	1
Bulger, Jason, S.B.	.889	20	5	11	2	18	0
Burgess, Richie, Peo.	.875	19	2	5	1	8	0
Burns, Mike, Mich.	.892	28	12	21	4	37	0
Bye, Chris, Clin.	.000	5	0	0	0	0	0

Player, Team	Pct.	G	PO	A	E	TC	DP
Cahill, Jonathan, C.R.	.000	2	0	0	0	0	0
Cali, Carmen, Peo.*	.900	24	4	5	1	10	0
Campos, Juan, Mich.	.917	36	7	4	1	12	1
Candelaria, Scott, Bel.	.000	2	0	0	0	0	0
Caple, Chance, Peo.	1.000	5	1	2	0	3	0
Caputo, Rob, Clin.	1.000	21	1	3	0	4	0
Carlsen, Jeff, Lan.	.000	2	0	0	0	0	0
Carter, Justin, Day.*	.889	8	2	6	1	9	0
Carter, Mark, Lan.*	1.000	13	0	2	0	2	0
Cassel, Jack, F.W.	1.000	27	3	14	0	17	0
Castellanos, Jonathan, S.B.	1.000	28	11	13	0	24	0
Cave, Kevin, K.C.	.933	41	6	8	1	15	0
Charron, Eric, Clin.	.857	32	4	8	2	14	1
Childress, Daylan, Day.	.939	28	8	23	2	33	1
Clute, Kris, K.C.	.000	1	0	0	0	0	0
Coenen, Matt, W.M.*	1.000	28	8	20	0	28	3
Coffey, Todd, Day.	.909	38	0	10	1	11	1
Contreras, Jean, Q.C.*	1.000	11	0	5	0	5	0
Corcoran, John, Wis.	.875	15	2	12	2	16	0
Corcoran, Roy, Clin.	.850	48	5	12	3	20	0
Cormier, Lance, S.B.	1.000	11	3	5	0	8	0
Cortez, Renee, Wis.	.900	17	12	15	3	30	0
Cotton, Nathan, Day.	1.000	53	2	14	0	16	1
Coughenour, Jory, Mich.	1.000	5	1	1	0	2	0
Crain, Jesse, Q.C.	1.000	9	0	2	0	2	0
Craker, Justin, F.W.	.556	54	2	3	4	9	0
Cullen, Phil, Wis.	.800	17	3	9	3	15	1
Daws, Josh, Q.C.	1.000	26	1	6	0	7	0
De Hart, Blair, F.W.	1.000	5	1	4	0	5	0
Dejesus, Elvis, K.C.	1.000	29	1	3	0	4	1
Del Chiaro, Brent, C.R.	.000	1	0	0	0	0	0
Delgado, Oscar, Wis.*	.933	8	4	10	1	15	1
Dennis, Jason, C.R.*	1.000	8	1	2	0	3	0
Detillion, Jamie, Day.*	.000	6	0	0	1	1	0
Diaz, Eddie, Clin.	.750	6	1	2	1	4	0
Diaz, Eddy, Lan.	1.000	6	1	0	0	1	0
Diaz, Luis, W.M.	1.000	7	1	1	0	2	0
Dishman, Richard, Bel.	1.000	6	0	4	0	4	0
Done, Juan, Wis.	.939	27	10	36	3	49	0
Dorn, Grant, Mich.	1.000	39	3	3	0	6	0
Douglass, Ryan, Burl.	.833	4	1	4	1	6	1
Doyne, Cory, Mich.	.896	27	13	30	5	48	1
Dulkowski, Marc, F.W.	1.000	23	2	3	0	5	0
Dunn, Gerald, W.M.	.667	9	3	1	2	6	0
Durbin, J.D., Q.C.	.941	27	11	37	3	51	5
Earey, Ryan, F.W.	.909	47	6	14	2	22	0
Echols, Britt, Clin.	1.000	1	0	1	0	1	0
Ellis, Steve, Lan.	1.000	37	4	6	0	10	0
Eppeneder, Jamie, Burl.*	1.000	8	1	2	0	3	0
Esquivia, Manuel, K.C.	.667	13	1	1	1	3	0
Etherton, Seth, Day.	.000	1	0	0	0	0	0
Eusebio, Mike, Day.	1.000	13	4	3	0	7	0
Evans, Louis, K.C.*	.000	4	0	0	0	0	0
Fallon, Chris, Burl.	1.000	2	0	1	0	1	0
Farizo, Brad, K.C.	.000	2	0	0	0	0	0
Ferns, Robert, S.B.	.000	1	0	0	0	0	0
Ferreras, Yorkin, Lan.*	1.000	51	1	8	0	9	0
Foli, Daniel, Lan.	1.000	32	3	11	0	14	1
Fox, Ben, F.W.*	1.000	39	1	14	0	15	0
Freeman, Corey, Wis.	1.000	1	1	0	0	1	0
Fruto, Emiliano, Wis.	.939	33	11	20	2	33	4
Fuell, Jerrod, W.M.	.933	51	6	8	1	15	3
Fulchino, Jeff, K.C.	1.000	24	8	19	0	27	0
Garber, Mike, S.B.*	1.000	15	3	5	0	8	1
Garcia, Carlos, F.W.	1.000	2	2	1	0	3	0
Garcia, Hector, Bel.	.000	1	0	0	0	0	0
Gates, Brian, Q.C.	1.000	11	1	1	0	2	0
Gemmell, Don, Day.	.000	1	0	0	0	0	0
Gerk, Jordan, W.M.*	1.000	8	0	2	0	2	0
Germano, Justin, F.W.	1.000	24	12	18	0	30	3
Gillman, Justin, Day.	.917	7	1	10	1	12	0
Girdley, Josh, Clin.*	1.000	7	2	4	0	6	0
Gonzales, Jim, W.M.	1.000	21	2	8	0	10	1
Gonzalez, Edgar, S.B.	.935	23	18	25	3	46	2
Gonzalez, Enrique, S.B.	1.000	4	2	4	0	6	0
Gooris, Dan, F.W.*	1.000	22	1	2	0	3	0
Granado, Jan, Day.*	1.000	3	1	0	0	1	0
Griffin, Colt, Burl.	.967	19	13	16	1	30	1
Griffith, Dustin, C.R.	.917	45	2	9	1	12	0
Gruler, Chris, Day.	1.000	7	0	4	0	4	0
Gutierrez, Jannio, Q.C.	1.000	31	5	5	0	10	0

Player, Team	Pct.	G	PO	A	E	TC	DP
Guzman, Angel, Lan.	.964	9	7	20	1	28	1
Hall, Dan, Bel.	.957	41	5	17	1	23	0
Hamilton, Mark, Mich.*	1.000	11	0	6	0	6	0
Haren, Danny, Peo.	1.000	14	11	12	0	23	3
Head, Daniel, Wis.	.808	35	8	13	5	26	1
Heiberger, Heath, S.B.*	.923	36	1	11	1	13	0
Hemus, Jared, Q.C.*	.750	14	0	6	2	8	3
Henderson, Eric, Bel.*	1.000	6	2	12	0	14	0
Hill, Josh, Q.C.	1.000	2	1	0	0	1	0
Hill, Shawn, Clin.	.942	25	11	38	3	52	2
Hines, Matthew, Lan.	1.000	11	2	4	0	6	2
Holdzkom, Lincoln, K.C.	.750	30	0	6	2	8	0
Holsten, Ryan, S.B.	.971	28	8	26	1	35	3
Houlton, Dennis, Mich.	1.000	35	4	8	0	12	0
Huber, Jon, F.W.	.941	28	6	26	2	34	2
Johnson, Jeremy, W.M.	1.000	6	1	0	0	1	0
Johnson, Kelly, Peo.	1.000	16	0	3	0	3	0
Johnson, Tyler, Peo.*	.962	22	7	18	1	26	3
Johnston, Dave, K.C.	.500	10	1	0	1	2	0
Jones, Geoffrey, F.W.*	.875	18	2	12	2	16	0
Jones, Mike, Bel.	.833	27	11	19	6	36	0
Julianel, Ben, Peo.*	.895	38	4	13	2	19	0
Kaanoi, Jason, Burl.	.900	29	16	20	4	40	1
Keelin, Chris, Day.	.857	22	2	4	1	7	1
Kelly, Steve, Day.	.857	7	5	7	2	14	0
Keppinger, Billy, Burl.*	.000	1	0	0	0	0	0
Kesten, Michael, Wis.*	1.000	38	2	10	0	12	0
Ketchner, Ryan, Wis.*	.882	31	5	10	2	17	0
King, O.J., Day.	.750	8	1	5	2	8	0
Kline, Steve, Peo.*	.000	2	0	0	0	0	0
Kobow, Mike, W.M.	.923	55	5	7	1	13	0
Kolb, Dan, Bel.	1.000	32	11	10	0	21	0
Kozol, Anthony, F.W.	1.000	41	3	10	0	13	0
Leclair, Aric, Burl.*	1.000	10	1	1	0	2	0
Leu, Trevor, W.M.*	.929	37	4	9	1	14	1
Levinski, Donald, Clin.	.976	21	6	34	1	41	1
Lewis, Jeremy, W.M.*	1.000	6	0	3	0	3	0
Lipari, Thomas, F.W.*	1.000	4	1	2	0	3	0
Lohse, Eric, Q.C.	.667	11	2	0	1	3	0
Mancha, Tony, Day.	1.000	14	3	4	0	7	1
Mansfield, Monte, Mich.	.923	20	6	6	1	13	1
Marceau, Pierre-Luc, Clin.*	1.000	12	0	12	0	12	0
Martin, Nick, Lan.*	.929	19	2	11	1	14	0
Martinez, Dionnar, Lan.	1.000	13	3	3	0	6	2
Martinez, Javier, F.W.	1.000	12	3	10	0	13	1
Martinez, Miguel, Peo.	.833	5	1	4	1	6	1
Mata, Gustavo, Clin.	1.000	8	1	9	0	10	0
Maust, David, Clin.*	.933	35	6	8	1	15	0
McCrotty, Wes, K.C.*	1.000	19	1	1	0	2	0
McDowell, Kevin, W.M.*	.781	27	8	17	7	32	0
McMachen, Clifford, S.B.*	.700	37	2	5	3	10	0
McMullen, Jeremy, Lan.	.000	1	0	0	0	0	0
McMurray, Heath, Day.	.813	14	3	10	3	16	1
Medlin, Corbey, S.B.	1.000	45	3	10	0	13	1
Melnyk, Brian, Burl.*	.750	10	1	2	1	4	0
Merrigan, Josh, Peo.*	1.000	30	1	7	0	8	0
Michaels, Carl, Bel.	1.000	19	2	3	0	5	0
Middleton, Kyle, Burl.	.975	29	13	26	1	40	2
Miller, Colby, Q.C.	.925	27	10	27	3	40	1
Miller, Jason, Q.C.*	.833	23	4	6	2	12	0
Mitchell, Tom, Clin.	.786	22	1	10	3	14	1
Mitre, Sergio, Lan.	.909	27	15	35	5	55	4
Moak, Curtus, Day.*	.917	43	3	19	2	24	2
Moates, Jason, W.M.	.960	28	3	21	1	25	0
Mozingo, Dan, C.R.*	1.000	22	1	12	0	13	0
Myers, Damien, W.M.*	1.000	11	1	2	0	3	0
Narveson, Chris, Peo.*	.900	9	2	7	1	10	1
Nickoli, Mike, C.R.	1.000	2	1	3	0	4	0
Nielsen, Brian, Bel.*	.833	9	2	3	1	6	0
Nolasco, Dave, Bel.	.889	32	6	10	2	18	0
Norderum, Jason, Clin.*	1.000	9	1	7	0	8	0
Oakes, Gerard, Bel.	.905	27	5	14	2	21	1
Olivero, Pedro, Lan.	.900	48	5	4	1	10	0
O'Sullivan, Mark, C.R.	1.000	42	4	7	0	11	0
Pace, Adam, Burl.*	1.000	23	4	6	0	10	0
Palmer, Lucas, Burl.	.000	3	0	0	0	0	0
Patchett, Gary, Day.	.000	2	0	0	0	0	0
Patten, Lanny, Wis.	1.000	39	1	7	0	8	0
Pawelczyk, Kyle, C.R.*	.500	7	0	3	3	6	0
Peralta, Joel, C.R.	1.000	41	1	9	0	10	0
Percosky, Mark, F.W.	.857	14	7	5	2	14	0
Perez, Jeffrey, Wis.	.944	38	4	13	1	18	2
Perkin, Greg, S.B.	.667	12	5	7	6	18	0
Petty, Chad, W.M.*	.862	28	5	20	4	29	0
Pignatiello, Carmen, Lan.*	.944	27	6	28	2	36	3
Pinto, Renyel, Lan.*	1.000	17	3	8	0	11	2
Plancich, Nick, Peo.	1.000	19	1	3	0	4	0
Pluta, Tony, Mich.	.971	28	9	24	1	34	3
Pope, Justin, Peo.	1.000	12	3	14	0	17	1
Powell, Greg, Mich.	.917	48	7	15	2	24	2
Powers, Joe, Day.	1.000	36	6	5	0	11	0
Puccinelli, John, F.W.	.000	1	0	0	0	0	0
Puello, Ignacio, Clin.	.781	27	8	17	7	32	0
Pylate, Chad, Q.C.	1.000	15	1	3	0	4	1
Ricciardi, Joe, S.B.	1.000	8	2	0	0	2	0
Richards, John, F.W.*	1.000	18	2	2	0	4	0
Richardson, Jason, C.R.	1.000	23	11	17	0	28	0
Richardson, Judd, Bel.	1.000	5	1	6	0	7	0
Rodaway, Brian, Mich.*	.947	23	6	12	1	19	1
Rodriguez, Jose, Clin.	.000	2	0	0	0	0	0
Rogers, Joe, Peo.*	1.000	25	2	5	0	7	0
Rohlicek, Russ, Mich.-Lan.*	.951	27	7	32	2	41	2
Romero, Josmir, Q.C.	.857	9	3	3	1	7	0
Rosado, Hector, Burl.*	.917	31	4	7	1	12	3
Rouwenhorst, Jonathon, C.R.*	.962	44	6	19	1	26	1
Rowland-Smith, Ryan, Wis.*	.688	12	5	6	5	16	0
Royce, Ramon, Wis.	.944	34	5	12	1	18	0
Rueckel, Danny, Clin.	.833	14	2	3	1	6	0
Russelburg, Aaron, Peo.	.962	26	7	18	1	26	1
Russell, Eddie, K.C.	1.000	9	0	4	0	4	0
Ryu, Jae-kuk, Lan.	1.000	5	2	2	0	4	0
Saenz, Chris, Bel.	1.000	37	4	9	0	13	1
Salmon, Brad, Day.	.943	29	9	24	2	35	0
Sanchez, Felix, Lan.*	.862	26	7	18	4	29	1
Sanchez, Paul, Burl.	.833	28	2	3	1	6	0
Sandberg, Eric, Q.C.*	.000	2	0	0	0	0	0
Santana, Eddy, Clin.	.000	4	0	0	0	0	0
Santana, Johan, C.R.	.889	27	2	14	2	18	1
Saunders, Joe, C.R.*	1.000	5	0	5	0	5	0
Schilling, Tim, K.C.*	1.000	26	5	13	0	18	1
Schroder, Chris, Clin.	.750	22	0	3	1	4	0
Serafini, Vince, Q.C.*	.857	30	1	11	2	14	0
Severino, Cleris, Day.*	.952	16	5	15	1	21	1
Shell, Steven, C.R.	.931	22	7	20	2	29	2
Shouse, Dan, Peo.*	1.000	17	1	3	0	4	0
Siemon, David, F.W.	.000	3	0	0	1	1	0
Sikaras, Pete, S.B.	.769	37	5	5	3	13	0
Skinner, John, K.C.	.833	22	0	5	1	6	0
Slaten, Doug, S.B.*	1.000	7	2	0	0	2	0
Smart, Richard, Q.C.*	1.000	7	1	2	0	3	0
Smith, Dan, W.M.	.500	5	0	1	1	2	0
Smith, Jared, Peo.	1.000	24	3	2	0	5	1
Soto, Darwin, F.W.	1.000	13	0	3	0	3	0
Stanton, Kyle, Day.	.900	33	4	5	1	10	0
Stavros, Tony, Bel.	1.000	42	4	10	0	14	1
Steitz, Jon, Bel.	.885	30	4	19	3	26	0
Stephenson, Garrett, Peo.	.000	2	0	0	0	0	0
Stevenson, Jason, Clin.*	1.000	33	8	13	0	21	0
Steward, Jaime, C.R.*	.960	26	4	20	1	25	3
Stewart, Cory, F.W.*	1.000	17	1	4	0	5	0
Stockman, Landon, W.M.	1.000	43	1	5	0	6	0
Stocks, Nick, Peo.	.000	1	0	0	1	1	0
Stodolka, Mike, Burl.*	.875	27	11	24	5	40	1
Tejada, Frailyn, K.C.*	1.000	9	3	5	0	8	1
Tejada, Sandy, Q.C.	.913	14	7	14	2	23	2
Thomas, Adam, C.R.	.933	32	8	6	1	15	1
Tierney, Chris, Burl.*	.950	27	7	31	2	40	2
Torres, Joe, C.R.*	.829	25	4	25	6	35	3
Torres, Luis, Clin.	.833	7	0	5	1	6	0
Tremblay, Max, Mich.*	.750	41	1	5	2	8	0
Trytten, Ryan, Bel.	.909	31	10	10	2	22	1
Tucker, Rusty, F.W.*	1.000	31	0	3	0	3	0
Ungs, Nick, K.C.	.935	24	13	16	2	31	1
Valera, Luis, Day.	.667	8	0	2	1	3	0
Vasquez, Jorge, Burl.	1.000	22	5	8	0	13	1
Vorwald, Matt, Q.C.	.789	46	5	10	4	19	0
Walker, Jason, Clin.*	1.000	12	2	1	0	3	0
Warren, Andy, W.M.	.929	13	6	7	1	14	1
Washburn, Ben, Clin.	.800	24	3	5	2	10	0
Watson, Tanner, Wis.	.850	28	8	9	3	20	1
Wear, Gregory, Wis.	.000	3	0	0	2	2	0
Wechsler, Justin, S.B.	.929	26	12	14	2	28	0

Player, Team	Pct.	G	PO	A	E	TC	DP
Wheeler, James, Bel.*	1.000	4	1	0	0	1	0
Wilkerson, Wes, Burl.	.875	6	1	6	1	8	0
Wilkinson, Matthew, S.B.	.833	36	3	7	2	12	0
WILLIS, Dontrelle, K.C.*	1.000	19	10	35	0	45	2
Wodnicki, Mike, Peo.	.969	26	12	19	1	32	2
Wolensky, Dave, C.R.	1.000	30	1	12	0	13	0
Wood, Brandon, Mich.	1.000	34	1	8	0	9	0
Woods, Jake, C.R.*	.912	27	6	25	3	34	1
Wynegar, Adam, Lan.*	.857	13	5	7	2	14	2
Yeatman, Matt, Bel.	.857	25	4	14	3	21	1
Yoshida, Nobuaki, F.W.*	.911	27	11	30	4	45	3

Player, Team	Pct.	G	PO	A	E	TC	DP
Zary, Richard, Burl.	.800	20	0	4	1	5	1
Zurita, Tom, Burl.	.917	26	5	6	1	12	0

TRIPLE PLAY: Asahina.

PITCHERS WITH TWO OR MORE TEAMS

Player, Team	Pct.	G	PO	A	E	TC	DP
Rohlicek, Russ, Mich.*	.972	25	7	28	1	36	2
Rohlicek, Russ, Lan.*	.800	2	0	4	1	5	0

The following players appeared only as designated hitter, pinch-hitter or pinch runner: A. Arroyo.

LEAGUE CHAMPIONS

Year	Team	Pct.	Year	Team	Pct.	Year	Team	Pct.
1947—	Belleville	.667		Cedar Rapids	.762	1984—	Appleton•	.640
	Belleville	.672	1967—	Wisconsin Rapids	.685		Springfield	.504
1948—	West Frankfort*	.708		Appleton◆	.587	1985—	Kenosha▼	.568
1949—	Centralia	.627	1968—	Decatur	.656		Peoria	.536
	Paducah (4th)†	.454		Quad Cities◆	.648	1986—	Springfield	.621
1950—	Centralia‡	.675	1969—	Appleton	.648		Waterloo▼	.557
1951—	Paris§	.700		Appleton	.690	1987—	Springfield	.671
	Danville (4th)†	.432	1970—	Quincy◆	.691		Kenosha▼	.586
1952—	Danville∞	.685		Quad Cities	.581	1988—	Cedar Rapids■	.621
	Decatur (3rd)†	.584	1971—	Appleton	.642		Kenosha	.579
1953—	Decatur*	.576		Quad Cities■	.548	1989—	South Bend■	.644
1954—	Decatur	.587	1972—	Appleton	.598		Springfield	.541
	Danville (2nd)‡	.528		Danville	.584	1990—	Cedar Rapids	.657
1955—	Dubuque*	.587	1973—	Wisconsin Rapids■	.562		Quad City■	.579
1956—	Paris▲	.656		Danville	.537	1991—	Clinton■	.583
	Dubuque	.603	1974—	Appleton	.593		Madison	.558
1957—	Decatur▲	.683		Danville■	.517	1992—	Quad City	.664
	Clinton	.623	1975—	Waterloo■	.727		Cedar Rapids■	.594
1958—	Michigan City	.623		Quad Cities	.624	1993—	Clinton	.597
	Waterloo◆	.613	1976—	Waterloo■	.600		South Bend■	.566
1959—	Waterloo	.613		Cedar Rapids	.595	1994—	Rockford	.640
	Waterloo	.613	1977—	Waterloo	.580		Cedar Rapids■	.554
1960—	Waterloo	.629		Burlington■	.511	1995—	Beloit††	.633
	Waterloo	.677	1978—	Appleton■	.708		Michigan	.543
1961—	Waterloo	.613		Burlington	.500	1996—	Wisconsin	.570
	Quincy◆	.594	1979—	Waterloo	.600		West Michigan††	.558
1962—	Dubuque◆	.667		Quad Cities■	.579	1997—	Kane County	.507
	Waterloo	.625	1980—	Waterloo■	.610		Lansing**	.504
1963—	Clinton	.710		Quad Cities	.532	1998—	West Michigan††	.593
	Clinton	.629	1981—	Wausau■	.636	1999—	Kane County	.569
1964—	Clinton	.667		Quad Cities	.570		Burlington**	.511
	Fox Cities◆	.667	1982—	Madison	.626	2000—	West Michigan	.629
1965—	Burlington	.667		Appleton▼	.579		Michigan‡‡	.594
	Burlington	.677	1983—	Appleton•	.635	2001—	Kane County▲▲	.638
1966—	Fox Cities◆	.689		Springfield	.576	2002—	Peoria‡‡	.616

*Won championship and four-club playoff. †Won four-club playoff. ‡Playoff finals canceled because of bad weather. §Won both halves of split season. ∞Won first half of split season and tied Paris for second-half title. ▲Won first-half title and four-team playoff. ◆Won split season playoff. ■League divided into Northern and Southern divisions and played split season. Playoff winner. ▼League divided into Northern, Central and Southern divisions. Playoff winner. •League divided into Northern, Central and Southern divisions; regular season and playoff winner. ††League divided into Eastern, Central and Western divisions; regular season and playoff winner. **League divided into Eastern, Central and Western divisions, playoff winner. ‡‡League divided into Eastern and Western divisions and played split season. Playoff winner. (NOTE— Known as Illinois State League in 1947-48 and Mississippi-Ohio Valley League from 1949 through 1955.) ▲▲League divided into Eastern and Western divisions and played split season; was leading final series of four-team playoff and was declared champion when Professional Baseball declared a stoppage of play.

NEW YORK-PENN LEAGUE

LEAGUE OFFICE

President
Ben Hayes
Address
9410 International Court North
St. Petersburg, FL 33716
Phone
727-576-6300

Teams (affiliation)
Aberdeen IronBirds (Orioles)
Auburn Doubledays (Blue Jays)
Batavia Muckdogs (Phillies)
Brooklyn Cyclones (Mets)
Hudson Valley Renegades (Devil Rays)
Jamestown Jammers (Marlins)
Lowell Spinners (Red Sox)

Mahoning Valley Scrappers (Indians)
New Jersey Cardinals (Cardinals)
Oneonta Tigers (Tigers)
Staten Island Yankees (Yankees)
Tri-City ValleyCats (Astros)
Vermont Expos (Expos)
Williamsport Crosscutters (Pirates)

CLASS A New York-Pennsylvania League

2002 FINAL STANDINGS

McNAMARA DIVISION

Team	W	L	T	Pct.	GB
Staten Island (Yankees)	48	26	0	.649	...
Williamsport (Pirates)	46	28	0	.632	1.0
New Jersey (Cardinals)	39	37	0	.513	10.0
Brooklyn (Mets)	38	38	0	.500	11.0
Aberdeen (Orioles)	31	45	0	.408	18.0
Hudson Valley (Devil Rays)	26	49	0	.347	22.5

PINCKNEY DIVISION

Team	W	L	T	Pct.	GB
Auburn (Blue Jays)	47	29	0	.618	...
Mahoning Valley (Indians)	46	30	0	.605	1.0
Batavia (Phillies)	34	42	0	.447	13.0
Jamestown (Marlins)	32	42	0	.432	14.0

STEDLER DIVISION

Team	W	L	T	Pct.	GB
Oneonta (Tigers)	47	27	0	.635	...
Lowell (Red Sox)	34	41	0	.453	13.5
Vermont (Expos)	30	45	0	.400	17.5
Tri-City (Astros)	27	48	0	.360	20.5

COMPOSITE

Team	S.I.	One.	Wil.	Aub.	M.V.	N.J.	Bkn.	Low.	Bat.	Jam.	Aber.	Ver.	T.C.	H.V.	W	L	T	Pct.	GB
Staten Island (Yankees)	..	2	5	1	1	7	8	2	3	1	7	2	2	7	48	26	0	.649	...
Oneonta (Tigers)	1		2	2	2	2	1	8	2	1	0	11	13	2	47	27	0	.635	1.0
Williamsport (Pirates)	5	1	...	2	1	6	5	2	2	3	9	2	3	7	48	28	0	.632	1.0
Auburn (Blue Jays)	2	1	1	...	8	0	2	3	11	11	1	1	3	3	47	29	0	.618	2.0
Mahoning Valley (Indians)	2	1	2	7	...	3	2	2	10	9	3	0	3	2	46	30	0	.605	3.0
New Jersey (Cardinals)	3	1	4	3	0	...	6	0	2	0	6	2	2	10	39	37	0	.513	10.0
Brooklyn (Mets)	4	2	5	1	1	4	...	1	3	2	5	2	3	5	38	38	0	.500	11.0
Lowell (Red Sox)	1	6	1	0	1	3	2	...	0	2	2	8	7	1	34	41	0	.453	14.5
Batavia (Phillies)	0	1	1	5	5	1	0	3	...	9	3	3	2	1	34	42	0	.447	15.0
Jamestown (Marlins)	0	2	0	4	7	3	1	1	6	...	1	2	2	3	32	42	0	.432	16.0
Aberdeen (Orioles)	3	3	3	2	0	4	5	1	0	2	...	2	2	4	31	45	0	.408	18.0
Vermont (Expos)	1	4	1	2	3	1	1	8	0	1	1	...	5	2	30	45	0	.400	18.5
Tri-City (Astros)	1	3	0	0	0	1	0	8	1	1	1	9	...	2	27	48	0	.360	21.5
Hudson Valley (Devil Rays)	3	0	3	0	1	2	5	2	2	0	6	1	1	...	26	49	0	.347	22.5

Major league affiliations in parentheses.

PLAYOFFS: Staten Island defeated Williamsport, two games to none; Oneonta defeated Auburn, two games to one; Staten Island defeated Oneonta, two games to none to win New York-Pennsylvania League championship.

REGULAR-SEASON ATTENDANCE: Aberdeen, 231,935; Auburn, 62,419; Batavia, 43,494; Brooklyn, 317,124; Hudson Valley, 162,724; Jamestown, 56,545; Lowell, 185,500; Mahoning Valley, 158,500; New Jersey, 129,607; Oneonta, 56,602; Staten Island, 181,936; Tri-City, 108,454; Vermont, 108,081; Williamsport, 82,006. Total—1,884,927. Playoff (7 games)—12,048.

MANAGERS: Aberdeen, Joe Almaraz; Auburn, Dennis Holmberg; Batavia, Ronnie Ortegon; Brooklyn, Howard Johnson; Hudson Valley, David Howard; Jamestown, Johnny Rodriguez; Lowell, Mike Boulanger; Mahoning Valley, Chris Bando; New Jersey, Tommy Shields; Oneonta, Randy Ready; Staten Island, Derek Shelton; Tri-City, Ivan DeJesus; Vermont, Dave Barnett; Williamsport, Andy Stewart.

ALL-STAR TEAM: 1B—John Santor, New Jersey; 2B—William Rivera, Auburn; 3B—Travis Hanson, New Jersey; SS—Russ Adams, Auburn; Utility INF—Blake Whealy, Brooklyn; OF—Curtis Granderson, Oneonta; OF—Joey Gomes, Hudson Valley; OF—Jorge Cortes, Williamsport; C—Travis Chapman, Williamsport; DH—Bradley Eldred, Williamsport; RHP—Chien-Ming Wang, Staten Island; RHP—Ryan Bicondoa, Staten Island; LHP—Michael Hinckley, Vermont; LHP—Keith Ramsey, Mahoning Valley; Most Valuable Player—Curtis Granderson, Oneonta; Manager of the Year—Randy Ready, Oneonta.

2002 BATTING
TEAM

Team	G	TPA	AB	R	H	TB	2B	3B	HR	RBI	SH	SF	HP	BB	IBB	SO	SB	CS	GDP	LOB	ShO	Avg.	OBP	Slg.
Williamsport..	76	2930	2605	376	705	975	129	27	29	321	34	36	30	225	9	486	82	32	49	552	3	.271	.331	.374
Mahoning Val.	76	2893	2527	397	653	960	119	25	46	357	12	26	46	282	9	503	92	25	54	533	6	.258	.341	.380
Auburn	76	2995	2579	381	657	937	132	20	36	345	30	29	44	313	7	498	65	21	48	597	7	.255	.342	.363
Jamestown....	75	2894	2576	345	655	938	119	19	42	308	7	16	29	266	5	550	64	33	57	536	4	.254	.329	.364
Oneonta.......	74	2898	2537	389	645	923	117	34	31	343	18	22	48	273	7	536	65	30	37	550	5	.254	.335	.364
Staten Island.	75	2808	2490	322	619	867	118	17	32	285	19	20	38	241	8	584	61	32	52	525	2	.249	.322	.348
Brooklyn........	76	2877	2605	322	646	944	101	16	55	277	23	10	41	198	8	589	101	41	43	495	7	.248	.310	.362
Batavia	76	2921	2556	290	632	875	105	24	30	257	34	27	51	253	6	622	115	52	47	568	9	.247	.324	.342
Aberdeen.......	76	2837	2521	283	620	822	104	25	16	258	23	24	30	239	3	549	74	42	43	539	11	.246	.316	.326

Team	G	TPA	AB	R	H	TB	2B	3B	HR	RBI	SH	SF	HP	BB	IBB	SO	SB	CS	GDP	LOB	ShO	Avg.	OBP	Slg.
New Jersey	76	2764	2477	323	609	882	112	31	33	290	25	20	32	210	6	581	117	52	36	461	6	.246	.311	.356
Hudson Val.	75	2872	2568	310	630	942	113	20	53	278	15	22	58	209	3	591	38	22	46	538	10	.245	.314	.367
Lowell	75	2914	2539	337	614	846	112	15	30	298	24	27	58	266	3	590	68	38	49	554	6	.242	.325	.333
Tri-City	75	2801	2476	284	578	791	91	16	30	249	27	24	46	228	2	523	60	32	50	512	9	.233	.307	.319
Vermont	75	2825	2511	278	585	784	93	8	30	242	29	22	31	232	2	604	51	31	42	526	5	.233	.303	.312

INDIVIDUAL

TOP QUALIFIERS FOR BATTING CHAMPIONSHIP

Minimum 205 plate appearances. *Lefthanded batter. †Switch-hitter.

Player, Team	G	TPA	AB	R	H	TB	2B	3B	HR	RBI	SH	SF	HP	BB	IBB	SO	SB	CS	GDP	Avg.	OBP	Slg.
Francisco, Ben, M.V.	58	269	235	55	82	118	23	2	3	23	2	3	7	22	1	28	22	6	5	.349	.416	.502
Granderson, Curtis, One.*	52	240	212	45	73	105	15	4	3	34	0	1	7	20	0	35	9	2	1	.344	.417	.495
Cortes, Jorge, Wil.*	70	305	253	38	83	108	14	4	1	35	2	4	2	44	0	20	7	7	2	.328	.426	.427
Stephenson, Neal, Aber.*	70	273	255	30	79	117	17	6	3	40	1	1	3	13	0	50	4	4	3	.310	.349	.459
Reed, Eric, Jam.*	60	271	250	35	77	84	5	1	0	17	1	3	0	17	1	30	19	10	3	.308	.348	.336
Roughton, Jody, One.*	54	235	208	30	64	85	10	1	3	38	0	3	5	19	2	43	0	1	2	.308	.374	.409
Rohleder, Andy, Jam.	65	215	182	29	56	85	12	4	3	26	0	1	4	28	0	37	2	3	7	.308	.409	.467
Encarnacion, Henry, Ver.†	57	243	209	33	63	78	9	3	0	26	4	1	2	27	0	49	15	6	3	.301	.385	.373
Durazo, Ernie, Aub.*	62	225	200	22	59	83	14	2	2	31	1	2	1	21	1	37	0	0	4	.295	.362	.415
Siriveaw, Nom, Aub.†	56	212	180	26	53	82	8	6	3	30	4	1	3	24	1	53	8	3	4	.294	.385	.456
Hanson, Travis, N.J.*	75	291	272	31	80	119	17	5	4	40	0	4	3	12	0	55	1	1	4	.294	.326	.438
Owens, Justin, Aub.*	69	277	242	35	71	101	11	2	5	31	3	1	1	30	1	45	13	3	1	.293	.372	.417
Santor, John, N.J.†	68	276	239	44	70	135	24	1	13	62	0	2	3	32	2	62	4	2	5	.293	.380	.565
Lytle, Chaz, Wil.	46	208	192	22	56	58	2	0	0	12	3	5	1	7	1	16	14	6	3	.292	.312	.302
Rodriguez, Carlos, Bat.†	61	276	248	29	72	85	7	3	0	15	5	0	4	19	0	48	21	11	2	.290	.351	.343

DEPARTMENTAL LEADERS: G—Huggins, 76; AB—Riley, W. Rivera, 290 each; R—Francisco, Gorecki, 55 each; H—Cortes, 83; TB—Gomes, 145; 2B—Santor, 24; 3B—Gorecki, 13; HR—Gomes, 15; RBI—Santor, 62; SH—W. Rivera, 10; SF—Wright, 9; HP—Concepcion, 12; BB—Randel, 49; IBB—Eldred, W. Peavey, 4 each; SO—Gilhooly, 79; SB—Vandever, 31; CS—Gorecki, C. Rodriguez, 11 each; GIDP—Chop, 13; Slg.—Santor, .565; OBP—Cortes, .426.

ALL PLAYERS

*Lefthanded batter. †Switch-hitter.

Player, Team	G	TPA	AB	R	H	TB	2B	3B	HR	RBI	SH	SF	HP	BB	IBB	SO	SB	CS	GDP	Avg.	OBP	Slg.
Abreu, Angel, M.V.†	14	40	39	2	8	8	0	0	0	3	0	0	0	1	0	4	0	1	2	.205	.225	.205
Abreu, Nielsen, Bkn.	41	156	140	16	36	40	4	0	0	10	0	1	2	13	0	16	14	8	1	.257	.327	.286
Adams, Russ, Aub.*	30	141	113	25	40	53	7	3	0	16	1	2	1	24	0	11	13	1	1	.354	.464	.469
Alcala, Arian, Low.	51	201	178	16	35	45	5	1	1	18	2	2	5	14	0	41	0	0	4	.197	.271	.253
Aleman, Carlos, Low.	39	155	136	19	33	45	9	0	1	15	0	3	0	16	0	30	5	1	4	.243	.316	.331
Aliendo, Humberto, Wil.	40	162	151	19	36	52	5	1	3	17	0	0	0	11	0	31	2	1	3	.238	.290	.344
Allec, Jason, One.	7	27	24	2	8	9	1	0	0	5	0	0	1	2	0	6	0	0	0	.333	.407	.375
Anderson, Brian, Ver.	39	134	125	10	22	31	6	0	1	11	1	2	0	6	0	30	0	0	3	.176	.211	.248
Anderson, Jimmy, Bkn.	32	103	92	7	20	22	2	0	0	6	1	1	4	5	0	18	1	0	4	.217	.284	.239
Andino, Robert, Jam.	9	37	36	2	6	9	1	1	0	3	0	0	0	1	0	9	1	0	2	.167	.189	.250
Andujar, Elvin, Bkn.	16	64	59	7	9	22	1	0	4	10	0	0	0	5	0	22	1	2	1	.153	.219	.373
Apotheker, Joseph, Jam.*	55	195	181	19	51	68	9	1	2	20	0	0	5	9	0	22	2	2	8	.282	.333	.376
Arlis, Patrick, Jam.	47	175	148	17	40	58	9	0	3	25	0	3	2	22	0	40	0	1	4	.270	.366	.392
Arnold, Eric, Aub.	11	23	19	1	3	3	0	0	0	1	0	0	2	2	0	5	0	0	1	.158	.304	.158
Asprilla, Avelino, Wil.	24	94	85	14	19	33	1	2	3	6	2	2	0	5	1	18	0	2	1	.224	.261	.388
Ayala, Abraham, Bkn.	29	95	84	5	17	24	4	0	1	10	0	2	2	7	1	5	0	0	2	.202	.274	.286
Baldiris, Aaron, Bkn.	9	35	33	5	10	11	1	0	0	2	0	0	1	1	0	2	2	0	0	.303	.343	.333
Bankston, Wes, H.V.	8	34	33	2	10	11	1	0	0	1	0	1	0	0	0	6	1	0	0	.303	.294	.333
Barclay, Mike, Low.	7	18	16	1	4	8	1	0	1	3	0	0	1	1	0	6	0	0	0	.250	.333	.500
Barthelemy, Ryan, Bat.*	68	289	260	27	67	92	13	3	2	32	3	5	2	19	3	56	5	2	5	.258	.308	.354
Bass, Chris, Wil.	71	295	266	36	73	108	19	2	4	38	2	4	2	21	0	48	8	0	10	.274	.328	.406
Baxter, Andy, M.V.*	64	248	218	34	55	87	14	3	4	32	0	1	3	26	0	52	13	3	0	.252	.339	.399
Benson, Donald, Low.	44	166	142	16	24	29	5	0	0	9	1	0	2	21	0	43	0	2	1	.169	.285	.204
Beuerlein, Tyler, Bkn.†	4	11	9	1	2	2	0	0	0	0	0	0	1	1	0	3	0	0	0	.222	.364	.222
Blackburn, Alex, Aub.	22	64	55	7	10	12	2	0	0	3	2	0	0	7	0	9	0	0	1	.182	.274	.218
Blackburn, Franco, Jam.*	31	86	69	12	15	20	2	0	1	8	1	2	0	14	0	11	1	1	1	.217	.341	.290
Blase, Blake, S.I.*	21	50	44	5	7	12	2	0	1	6	1	0	0	5	0	25	1	0	0	.159	.245	.273
Blount, Pierre, H.V.	52	169	143	13	35	48	4	3	1	9	0	2	9	15	0	54	1	2	0	.245	.349	.336
Bocchino, Anthony, Wil.*	55	213	195	24	55	78	10	5	1	29	3	3	0	12	2	29	5	1	2	.282	.319	.400
Boran, Patrick, Low.†	53	228	191	39	50	70	9	1	3	22	6	2	3	23	0	36	8	6	3	.262	.347	.366
Bowden, Nathan, S.I.	17	57	50	6	10	13	3	0	0	3	1	0	0	6	0	18	1	1	1	.200	.286	.260
Bowman, Addison, S.I.	71	308	272	28	70	97	16	1	3	22	1	2	10	23	2	73	3	3	3	.257	.336	.357
Boyer, Kyle, N.J.	49	198	178	27	52	68	10	3	0	19	2	0	4	14	0	49	20	4	2	.292	.357	.382
Brackley, Carlos, Low.	4	16	15	1	3	6	0	0	0	1	0	0	0	1	0	4	0	0	0	.200	.250	.400
Bridges, Josh, N.J.	8	15	15	0	2	2	0	0	0	0	0	0	0	0	0	5	0	0	0	.133	.133	.133
Broadway, Larry, Ver.*	35	140	127	13	40	55	3	0	4	23	0	0	0	13	0	33	0	0	2	.315	.379	.433
Brown, Anthony, Ver.†	45	142	124	12	23	24	1	0	0	11	5	1	2	10	0	47	7	4	0	.185	.255	.194
Brown, Dustin, Low.	21	90	78	12	22	27	3	1	0	12	1	0	1	8	0	20	1	0	0	.282	.371	.346
Buckley, James, Low.	41	146	132	15	26	39	8	1	1	11	1	0	1	12	0	49	0	0	3	.197	.269	.295
Cafiero, Rob, Bat.	60	246	225	22	50	74	6	0	6	35	1	3	1	16	0	59	0	2	2	.222	.273	.329
Caligiuri, Jay, Bkn.	16	65	56	6	16	25	3	0	2	5	0	0	2	7	0	14	1	0	0	.286	.385	.446
Campos, Mario, Low.	59	248	229	21	48	83	15	1	6	29	1	3	2	13	0	71	2	3	9	.210	.255	.362
Candelario, Luis, H.V.	10	30	30	3	6	10	1	0	1	3	0	0	0	0	0	7	0	1	0	.200	.200	.333
Cano, Robinson, S.I.*	22	92	87	11	24	34	5	1	1	20	0	0	0	4	0	8	0	1	1	.276	.308	.391
Caravella, Drew, One.*	45	187	167	19	35	42	5	1	0	16	0	3	3	17	0	17	0	1	3	.210	.294	.251
Carlin, Luke, One.†	45	187	150	23	34	43	5	2	0	10	1	1	1	34	0	28	0	2	2	.227	.371	.287

Player, Team	G	TPA	AB	R	H	TB	2B	3B	HR	RBI	SH	SF	HP	BB	IBB	SO	SB	CS	GDP	Avg.	OBP	Slg.
Carson, Matt, S.I.	48	193	177	19	36	55	8	4	1	11	0	1	4	11	1	48	4	1	6	.203	.264	.311
Castillo, Osmar, Low.†	8	33	23	4	5	6	1	0	0	4	0	1	0	9	0	2	0	1	2	.217	.424	.261
Cespedes, Robinson, T.C.	69	297	274	25	73	96	12	4	1	23	1	2	7	13	0	34	10	3	1	.266	.314	.350
Chapman, Travis, Wil.	56	202	179	26	49	60	8	0	1	16	3	0	0	19	1	40	3	1	3	.274	.343	.335
Chauncey, Clinton, N.J.	50	175	152	21	36	45	7	1	0	11	3	1	2	17	0	27	7	3	2	.237	.320	.296
Chavez, Ender, Bkn.*	61	212	187	35	52	68	8	4	0	12	6	0	0	19	1	19	18	9	1	.278	.345	.364
Chop, Chad, Ver.*	70	303	272	31	69	102	18	0	5	37	1	6	5	19	0	50	3	2	13	.254	.308	.375
Christensen, Sam, Wil.*	38	139	125	15	27	31	4	0	0	13	1	2	6	5	0	9	0	4	6	.216	.275	.248
Clements, Zachary, Bkn.	6	21	21	1	1	1	0	0	0	0	0	0	0	0	0	4	0	0	0	.048	.048	.048
Cockrell, Michael, Wil.	8	41	38	11	16	27	4	2	1	8	0	2	0	1	0	5	5	1	3	.421	.415	.711
Collum, Mike, Wil.	57	227	196	27	51	61	8	1	0	35	3	4	3	21	0	66	4	3	2	.260	.335	.311
Combs, Will, Aber.*	30	104	93	10	23	28	5	0	0	14	0	2	1	8	0	21	2	1	0	.247	.308	.301
Concepcion, Alberto, Low.	56	258	209	29	47	75	8	4	4	39	3	2	12	31	0	51	3	1	4	.225	.354	.359
Conlisk, Jason, Ver.†	65	265	230	22	58	74	8	1	2	18	7	1	3	24	1	43	3	3	1	.252	.329	.322
Conroy, Mike, M.V.*	56	206	188	22	35	46	5	3	0	18	3	1	1	13	0	43	1	2	3	.186	.241	.245
Cordell, Brent, H.V.†	69	264	228	25	48	89	15	1	8	39	0	4	9	23	0	44	0	0	5	.211	.303	.390
Corr, Frank, Bkn.	33	130	123	15	26	45	7	0	4	15	1	2	2	2	0	20	1	1	2	.211	.233	.366
Cortes, Jorge, Wil.*	70	305	253	38	83	108	14	4	1	35	2	4	2	44	0	20	7	7	2	.328	.426	.427
Covarrubias, Nick, T.C.	57	222	200	13	42	54	10	1	0	21	2	1	7	12	1	36	7	1	10	.210	.277	.270
Cox, George, Aber.	11	27	23	2	3	3	0	0	0	0	1	0	1	2	0	8	0	0	0	.130	.231	.130
Cruz, Alex, Wil.	7	26	23	1	5	5	0	0	0	1	1	0	0	2	0	4	0	1	2	.217	.280	.217
Cuello, Domingo, Wil.	11	47	44	13	12	21	2	2	1	5	1	0	1	0	0	3	7	1	0	.273	.304	.477
Cuevas, Aneudi, T.C.	36	126	116	17	29	41	1	1	3	13	0	0	1	9	0	42	3	3	2	.250	.310	.353
Dancy, Cliff, Bat.	47	168	155	12	31	40	2	2	1	3	3	1	2	7	0	45	10	2	3	.200	.242	.258
Davies, Gregg, Aber.*	69	264	228	21	51	64	13	0	0	22	2	4	2	28	0	45	4	5	2	.224	.309	.281
Davis, Rajai, Wil.†	1	4	4	0	0	0	0	0	0	0	0	0	0	0	0	1	0	0	0	.000	.000	.000
Dean, Herman, One.	35	117	107	17	15	21	1	1	1	7	0	2	1	7	0	35	3	5	3	.140	.197	.196
Deck, Ronald, H.V.	7	18	18	0	2	2	0	0	0	1	0	0	0	0	0	4	0	0	2	.111	.111	.111
De Leon, Virgilio, One.	42	168	157	22	35	54	5	1	4	16	0	1	2	8	0	52	10	3	3	.223	.268	.344
Del Rosario, Manny, Aber.†	67	270	252	23	63	82	10	3	1	24	1	1	0	16	0	22	15	2	5	.250	.294	.325
Devarez, Noel, Bkn.	8	36	35	2	7	10	0	0	1	2	0	0	0	1	0	8	0	0	0	.200	.222	.286
Devine, Dean, Wil.	4	15	13	1	2	5	0	0	1	1	1	0	1	0	0	2	0	0	0	.154	.214	.385
Diaz, Einar, M.V.	3	14	13	2	5	7	2	0	0	5	0	0	1	0	0	1	0	0	1	.385	.429	.538
Dorsey, Ryan, H.V.	7	16	15	0	0	0	0	0	0	0	0	0	0	1	0	13	1	0	0	.000	.063	.000
Dragicevich, Scott, Aub.	3	13	12	1	2	2	0	0	0	0	0	0	0	1	0	1	0	0	1	.167	.231	.167
Drobiak, Jayson, S.I.*	31	111	103	17	32	50	8	2	2	16	2	0	1	5	0	22	1	0	0	.311	.349	.485
Duncan, Trae, H.V.	39	164	159	17	49	75	13	2	3	25	0	1	2	2	0	25	0	0	3	.308	.323	.472
Duran, Alexander, H.V.	14	32	28	3	7	7	0	0	0	1	1	0	0	3	0	5	0	1	1	.250	.323	.250
Durazo, Ernie, Aub.*	62	225	200	22	59	83	14	2	2	31	1	2	1	21	1	37	0	0	4	.295	.362	.415
Durham, Tyler, N.J.	57	222	196	19	44	52	5	0	1	20	6	1	6	13	0	51	10	5	2	.224	.292	.265
Eickhorst, Chris, N.J.	6	19	17	2	3	4	1	0	0	0	0	0	0	2	0	3	0	0	0	.176	.263	.235
Eldred, Brad, Wil.	72	302	276	43	78	136	22	3	10	48	0	2	6	18	4	74	10	1	4	.283	.338	.493
Ellerson, Brian, Ver.	15	49	47	4	9	16	1	0	2	3	0	0	1	1	0	11	0	0	0	.191	.224	.340
Emmerick, Josh, Ver.	33	120	108	10	22	26	4	0	0	7	1	1	2	8	0	32	0	1	1	.204	.269	.241
Encarnacion, Henry, Ver.†	57	243	209	33	63	78	9	3	0	26	4	1	2	27	0	49	15	6	3	.301	.385	.373
Estrada, Rafael, N.J.†	17	20	17	2	4	6	0	1	0	2	1	0	1	1	0	7	3	1	0	.235	.316	.353
Fahey, Brandon, Aber.*	63	280	253	31	71	93	10	6	0	15	4	2	1	20	1	34	5	8	4	.281	.333	.368
Falu, Melvin, N.J.†	49	157	145	12	32	46	9	1	1	12	1	1	3	7	1	22	1	5	3	.221	.269	.317
Fernando, Osvaldo, T.C.†	4	13	13	1	1	1	0	0	0	1	0	0	0	0	0	2	0	0	0	.077	.077	.077
Fitzpatrick, Reggie, Ver.*	71	304	270	34	64	80	10	0	2	16	4	1	2	27	0	59	15	10	1	.237	.310	.296
Francisco, Ben, M.V.	58	269	235	55	82	118	23	2	3	23	2	3	7	22	1	28	22	6	5	.349	.416	.502
Garcia, David, One.†	18	63	58	5	13	18	2	0	1	9	0	0	3	2	1	14	0	0	2	.224	.286	.310
German, Cesar, Aub.	44	165	139	21	27	37	7	0	1	19	3	2	5	16	0	36	7	0	5	.194	.296	.266
Gilhooly, Tim, Aber.	61	222	203	16	40	55	6	0	3	22	0	3	1	15	0	79	8	3	5	.197	.252	.271
Gomes, Joey, H.V.	68	308	276	45	78	145	14	4	15	48	0	4	7	21	1	50	4	3	7	.283	.344	.525
Gomez, Hose, M.V.†	37	73	62	10	9	14	2	0	1	3	1	0	2	8	0	14	3	0	3	.145	.264	.226
Gonce, Garris, N.J.	29	86	78	6	16	20	4	0	0	5	3	0	1	4	0	19	1	0	1	.205	.253	.256
Gonzalez, Patrick, Aber.	61	177	142	18	29	34	3	1	0	12	8	1	3	23	0	30	3	3	2	.204	.325	.239
Gorecki, Reid, N.J.	73	304	274	55	77	135	8	13	8	52	1	7	2	20	0	57	22	11	2	.281	.327	.493
Goss, Michael, Low.*	21	90	83	9	33	37	2	1	0	10	1	0	2	4	0	15	14	4	1	.398	.438	.446
Granderson, Curtis, One.*	52	240	212	45	73	105	15	4	3	34	0	1	7	20	0	35	9	2	1	.344	.417	.495
Green, Steve, N.J.*	7	25	23	2	5	5	0	0	0	1	0	0	0	3	0	0	0	1	0	.217	.280	.217
Grzecka, Casey, Jam.	18	57	46	8	14	20	4	1	0	2	0	0	2	9	0	9	1	1	0	.304	.439	.435
Guerrero, Jorge, Jam.	6	18	18	1	3	7	1	0	1	1	0	0	0	0	0	12	1	0	0	.167	.167	.389
Guglielmelli, Brad, M.V.	5	16	15	1	3	4	1	0	0	2	0	0	0	1	0	5	0	0	0	.200	.250	.267
Haase, Jeff, M.V.	48	174	148	29	41	70	3	1	8	29	0	2	6	18	0	26	6	1	6	.277	.374	.473
Hanson, Travis, N.J.*	75	291	272	31	80	119	17	5	4	40	0	4	3	12	0	55	1	1	4	.294	.326	.438
Harper, Brett, Bkn.*	53	199	183	21	51	60	6	0	1	20	1	0	1	14	2	37	2	2	3	.279	.333	.328
Harrington, Jesse, T.C.	30	84	67	8	14	15	1	0	0	7	4	1	3	9	0	12	4	0	1	.209	.325	.224
Harris, Mike, S.I.	5	7	4	1	1	1	0	0	0	2	2	1	0	0	0	0	1	0	0	.250	.250	.250
Harrison, Vince, H.V.	15	60	50	10	13	18	2	0	1	2	0	1	1	8	0	8	1	0	3	.260	.367	.360
Hartig, Philip, Jam.	52	213	196	29	51	74	5	0	6	35	0	0	1	16	1	39	8	1	7	.260	.319	.378
Hassey, Brad, Aub.	67	281	251	44	64	92	20	1	2	25	2	2	5	21	0	41	6	0	4	.255	.333	.367
Heath, Demetrius, One.	35	160	143	25	37	51	8	3	0	9	1	1	3	12	0	13	9	3	1	.259	.327	.357
Helps, Jason, Jam.†	9	21	19	0	3	4	1	0	0	0	1	0	0	1	0	8	0	0	0	.158	.200	.211
Hermida, Jeremy, Jam.*	13	54	47	8	15	19	2	1	0	7	0	0	0	7	0	10	1	3	0	.319	.407	.404
Hietpas, Joe, Bkn.	32	128	117	11	30	38	5	0	1	13	0	1	2	8	1	31	0	1	0	.256	.313	.325
Hileman, Jutt, N.J.	23	89	77	5	14	17	3	0	0	6	0	2	2	8	0	21	1	2	1	.182	.270	.221
Hoover, Clint, T.C.	8	26	24	2	6	7	1	0	0	3	0	1	0	1	0	10	0	0	0	.250	.269	.292
Hubele, Ryan, Aber.	50	177	155	11	32	43	3	1	2	12	3	2	1	16	0	35	2	3	2	.206	.282	.277
Hudson, William, Bkn.†	3	11	11	0	2	2	0	0	0	0	0	0	0	0	0	3	0	0	0	.182	.182	.182
Huggins, Mike, Aber.	76	307	271	32	71	93	15	2	1	27	1	2	2	31	1	55	9	4	7	.262	.340	.343

Player, Team	G	TPA	AB	R	H	TB	2B	3B	HR	RBI	SH	SF	HP	BB	IBB	SO	SB	CS	GDP	Avg.	OBP	Slg.
Isenhower, Jeremy, Bat.*	3	13	10	1	4	6	0	1	0	3	0	2	1	0	0	0	1	0	0	.400	.385	.600
Jiannetti, Joe, Bkn.	59	243	223	28	58	84	5	0	7	27	1	2	1	16	1	22	11	7	6	.260	.310	.377
Jimenez, Rich, Aub.†	37	98	89	11	22	30	6	1	0	13	1	1	2	5	0	19	4	2	0	.247	.299	.337
Johnson, Seth, Ver.	39	149	127	14	19	25	0	0	2	10	2	2	3	15	0	35	0	1	3	.150	.252	.197
Johnston, Clint, Aub.*	74	312	264	50	64	93	10	2	5	41	0	4	7	36	1	50	0	0	10	.242	.344	.352
Jones, Kendall, T.C.	21	71	57	12	17	19	2	0	0	4	1	1	0	11	0	11	1	3	1	.298	.406	.333
Jones, Terry, Bat.	43	176	157	13	35	54	8	4	1	16	1	1	5	12	0	40	5	1	1	.223	.297	.344
Jordan, Eddie, Aber.	37	108	93	14	22	25	3	0	0	7	0	0	4	11	0	27	3	1	2	.237	.343	.269
Kennedy, Jason, One.	13	56	40	10	9	14	1	2	0	7	0	0	1	15	0	11	1	1	0	.225	.446	.350
Kentner, Brandon, Bkn.	17	2	2	0	0	0	0	0	0	0	0	0	0	0	0	0	0	0	1	.000	.000	.000
Kessick, Jon, Aber.	17	63	56	9	11	15	4	0	0	7	0	0	3	4	0	23	0	1	1	.196	.286	.268
Kimberley, Glynn, Aub.	20	45	40	8	4	7	0	0	1	2	1	0	2	2	0	15	0	0	0	.100	.182	.175
Kingsbury, Bobby, Wil.*	39	147	131	17	35	54	10	3	1	12	5	1	1	8	0	20	6	1	0	.267	.312	.412
Knox, Matt, M.V.	14	48	47	4	15	21	2	2	0	6	0	0	0	1	0	7	1	1	0	.319	.333	.447
Koutnik, Jared, S.I.	14	54	45	2	6	8	2	0	0	3	1	2	1	5	0	14	0	0	2	.133	.226	.178
Laidlaw, Jacob, Jam.	64	222	205	28	42	66	13	1	3	27	1	1	3	12	0	51	0	1	2	.205	.258	.322
Lambin, Chase, Bkn.†	47	192	179	25	50	80	6	3	6	27	2	1	2	8	1	50	5	2	1	.279	.316	.447
Larkin, Shaun, M.V.*	71	281	235	35	53	92	8	2	9	38	0	2	2	42	0	40	5	3	2	.226	.345	.391
Larson, Ryan, T.C.	5	16	10	1	1	1	0	0	0	1	1	0	1	4	0	5	0	0	0	.100	.400	.100
Lee, Taber, Wil.†	40	164	135	23	33	43	7	0	1	16	2	3	3	21	0	31	2	0	3	.244	.352	.319
Lepine, Olivier, Jam.	35	119	108	16	37	52	10	1	1	21	0	0	1	10	1	13	0	0	2	.343	.403	.481
Loomis, Corey, One.*	32	125	110	18	24	34	4	3	0	17	0	1	1	13	0	39	2	1	0	.218	.304	.309
Lopez, Gabe, S.I.	46	191	164	28	35	45	8	1	0	18	3	2	8	14	0	15	7	2	5	.213	.303	.274
Louisa, Lorvin, Ver.	48	171	159	10	23	33	3	2	1	13	0	1	3	8	0	66	2	1	3	.145	.199	.208
Lytle, Chaz, Wil.	46	208	192	22	56	58	2	0	0	12	3	5	1	7	1	16	14	6	3	.292	.312	.302
Macchi, Brandon, T.C.†	68	291	255	30	71	99	8	1	6	31	1	3	1	31	1	53	3	2	5	.278	.355	.388
Mackor, Jeff, T.C.	32	105	90	13	18	26	5	0	1	9	0	0	4	11	0	19	3	0	2	.200	.314	.289
Majewski, Val, Aber.	31	125	110	22	33	51	7	4	1	15	0	1	1	13	0	14	8	4	3	.300	.376	.464
Malek, Bobby, Bkn.*	28	116	111	7	23	28	3	1	0	10	0	0	1	3	0	20	4	0	2	.207	.235	.252
Mamula, Matt, S.I.*	52	203	182	20	41	58	8	0	3	25	1	3	1	16	0	52	0	0	4	.225	.287	.319
Mancebo, Deni, Ver.†	7	23	19	3	4	5	1	0	0	1	0	0	0	4	0	1	1	1	0	.211	.348	.263
Manfred, Brian, Bat.	22	87	74	8	14	25	3	1	2	8	1	0	2	10	0	17	0	0	0	.189	.302	.338
Manfredonia, Sean, M.V.	8	22	21	0	5	5	0	0	0	2	0	0	1	0	0	7	0	0	1	.238	.273	.238
Mannix, Brendan, Bkn.†	3	8	7	1	1	2	1	0	0	1	0	0	1	0	0	2	0	0	0	.143	.250	.286
Maples, Chris, One.	31	131	115	17	23	39	6	2	2	16	1	4	1	10	1	23	1	0	3	.200	.262	.339
Marshall, Andre, Bat.†	46	174	143	13	32	38	4	1	0	12	5	2	0	24	0	42	6	2	4	.224	.331	.266
McClanahan, Scott, S.I.	45	178	162	16	36	49	7	0	2	17	1	0	1	14	0	35	4	3	3	.222	.288	.302
McDonald, Kevin, One.*	30	105	93	13	22	33	5	0	2	10	1	0	0	11	0	17	0	2	0	.237	.317	.355
McDougall, Marshall, M.V.	2	6	5	0	1	1	0	0	0	0	0	0	0	1	0	1	0	0	0	.200	.333	.200
McEwing, Joe, Bkn.	1	4	4	0	1	1	0	0	0	1	0	0	0	0	0	0	0	0	0	.250	.250	.250
McGarvey, Randy, T.C.*	41	129	108	13	28	32	4	0	0	7	2	1	4	14	0	27	1	0	2	.259	.362	.296
McRoberts, Mark, Bat.	46	195	166	27	49	77	12	2	4	17	2	2	4	21	1	40	6	1	3	.295	.383	.464
Meath, Matt, Wil.†	26	74	64	14	15	21	2	2	0	6	0	0	1	9	0	19	5	1	1	.234	.338	.328
Meihls, Mike, S.I.	18	46	39	5	9	10	1	0	0	4	0	1	0	6	0	11	0	1	1	.231	.326	.256
Mejia, Manuel, Wil.	12	38	31	7	11	18	4	0	1	3	0	0	1	6	0	7	1	0	0	.355	.474	.581
Mendez, Victor, One.†	59	270	241	36	68	98	11	5	3	31	4	3	2	20	0	50	16	5	2	.282	.338	.407
Menocal, Victor, Bat.	22	11	10	2	1	1	0	0	0	1	0	0	0	1	0	3	0	0	0	.100	.182	.100
Mercedes, Anselmo, H.V.	39	139	121	13	21	22	1	0	0	6	2	1	1	14	0	25	0	0	3	.174	.263	.182
Merkle, Tom, Jam.	12	47	45	7	10	21	2	0	3	4	0	0	0	2	1	14	1	0	0	.222	.255	.467
Molina, Angel, Jam.	3	10	9	1	2	6	1	0	1	2	0	0	0	1	0	5	0	0	0	.222	.300	.667
Monette, Daylon, N.J.†	17	57	53	2	8	11	3	0	0	3	0	0	0	4	0	13	2	2	2	.151	.211	.208
Mongeluzzo, Anthony, Ver.	16	53	45	6	8	10	2	0	0	3	1	0	2	5	0	17	0	0	0	.178	.288	.222
Moore, Bryan, N.J.*	7	22	20	0	1	1	0	0	0	1	0	0	0	2	0	4	0	0	0	.050	.136	.050
Myers, Kenton, M.V.	10	25	25	4	6	9	3	0	0	4	0	0	0	0	0	6	0	0	1	.240	.240	.360
Newman, Ryan, M.V.	37	120	106	14	21	22	1	0	0	10	5	2	1	6	0	26	3	1	1	.198	.243	.208
Nikolic, Adam, H.V.*	71	315	281	40	64	87	11	3	2	24	1	0	10	23	0	58	13	5	4	.228	.309	.310
Norris, Shawn, Ver.*	42	181	157	22	45	66	5	2	4	14	0	1	1	22	0	23	2	0	0	.287	.376	.420
Nunez, Alexis, Bat.*	15	61	47	9	12	18	3	0	1	6	0	1	2	11	0	8	3	0	2	.255	.410	.383
Nunez, Felix, H.V.	53	190	180	21	41	67	7	2	5	18	0	1	4	5	0	56	0	1	10	.228	.263	.372
O'Brien, Kevin, H.V.*	44	136	130	9	32	34	2	0	0	6	0	1	0	5	0	28	2	1	1	.246	.272	.262
Ohtsuka, Yoshiyuki, Wil.	2	6	4	0	0	0	0	0	0	0	0	0	0	2	0	1	0	0	0	.000	.333	.000
Ontiveros, Jeffrey, Low.	58	258	227	28	56	86	9	0	7	46	0	4	6	21	0	39	3	0	6	.247	.322	.379
Ordorica, Eric, Jam.	65	276	248	34	58	82	7	1	5	29	1	4	2	21	0	35	10	4	6	.234	.295	.331
Ortiz, Daniel, Jam.	18	54	48	7	9	13	1	0	1	4	0	0	0	6	0	25	0	0	0	.188	.278	.271
Osborn, Pat, M.V.	52	222	194	28	47	62	8	2	1	29	1	1	2	24	1	42	4	0	7	.242	.330	.320
Owens, Justin, Aub.*	69	277	242	35	71	101	11	2	5	31	3	1	1	30	1	45	13	3	1	.293	.372	.417
Parker, Tyler, N.J.	42	163	146	15	31	41	0	2	2	10	0	1	2	14	1	50	2	1	4	.212	.288	.281
Patterson, Ty, H.V.	12	27	27	2	6	6	0	0	0	0	0	0	0	0	0	7	0	0	0	.222	.222	.222
Peavey, Bill, M.V.*	71	286	247	33	69	101	14	0	6	41	0	2	6	31	4	37	1	0	4	.279	.371	.409
Peavey, Pat, T.C.	57	230	208	30	49	76	9	0	6	27	2	4	3	13	0	37	2	2	3	.236	.285	.365
Peguero, Miguel, M.V.†	25	77	65	7	13	15	2	0	0	4	2	1	2	7	0	16	6	2	2	.200	.293	.231
Perez, Jerson, Aub.	7	32	28	0	4	4	0	0	0	2	0	0	0	4	0	7	1	1	0	.143	.250	.143
Pitney, Jared, S.I.*	3	9	8	1	0	0	0	0	0	0	0	0	0	1	0	4	0	0	0	.000	.111	.000
Plancich, Nick, N.J.	8	3	3	0	0	0	0	0	0	0	0	0	0	0	0	1	0	0	0	.000	.000	.000
Porfirio, A.J., Aub.	47	147	122	17	27	38	8	0	1	20	1	4	2	18	0	28	3	0	3	.221	.322	.311
Porter, Thomas, H.V.	3	8	7	0	1	1	0	0	0	0	0	0	0	1	0	3	0	0	0	.143	.250	.143
Pratt, Trent, Bat.	39	144	118	10	28	35	7	0	0	12	2	3	2	19	0	33	0	1	4	.237	.352	.297
Pridie, Jason, H.V.*	8	35	32	4	11	17	1	1	1	10	0	0	3	1	6	0	0	0	0	.344	.400	.531
Puccinelli, John, Jam.	38	107	92	4	19	26	7	0	0	8	1	1	0	13	0	21	0	0	3	.207	.302	.283
Ragsdale, Corey, Bkn.	66	255	224	35	41	58	7	2	2	19	2	0	6	23	0	72	26	3	2	.183	.277	.259
Ramirez, Hanley, Low.†	22	105	97	17	36	52	9	2	1	19	0	2	2	4	0	14	4	3	2	.371	.400	.536
Ramistella, John, S.I.	49	161	137	19	32	51	6	2	3	14	0	1	5	18	0	51	7	2	2	.234	.342	.372

Player, Team	G	TPA	AB	R	H	TB	2B	3B	HR	RBI	SH	SF	HP	BB	IBB	SO	SB	CS	GDP	Avg.	OBP	Slg.
Ramos, Victor, Wil.*	31	94	88	10	26	32	6	0	0	9	0	2	1	3	0	13	0	0	3	.295	.319	.364
Randel, Kevin, Jam.*	69	307	253	49	70	112	11	5	7	27	0	0	5	49	1	56	13	3	1	.277	.404	.443
Recio, Bolivar, Aber.	10	34	31	2	8	8	0	0	0	3	1	1	0	1	0	5	1	1	1	.258	.273	.258
Reed, Eric, Jam.*	60	271	250	35	77	84	5	1	0	17	1	3	0	17	1	30	19	10	3	.308	.348	.336
Reuss, Jason, T.C.	31	105	93	11	18	32	3	1	3	9	0	1	2	9	0	41	1	1	2	.194	.276	.344
Reynolds, Wilton, One.	69	307	272	41	63	109	7	6	9	57	0	0	6	29	2	75	10	3	3	.232	.319	.401
Reynoso, Danilo, Bkn.	2	8	8	0	1	1	0	0	0	1	0	0	0	0	0	3	0	0	0	.125	.125	.125
Richard, Chris, Aber.*	1	5	5	2	3	7	1	0	1	3	0	0	0	0	0	1	0	0	0	.600	.600	1.400
Richmond, Paul, Aub.*	48	177	155	18	38	56	10	1	2	27	0	1	1	20	1	19	1	3	4	.245	.333	.361
Riggans, Shawn, H.V.	73	302	266	34	70	110	13	0	9	48	2	1	1	32	1	72	2	2	0	.263	.343	.414
Riley, Ryan, H.V.	75	341	290	40	80	105	17	1	2	21	6	0	10	34	0	47	8	2	3	.276	.371	.362
Rivera, Eric, Bat.	49	205	181	19	45	64	11	1	2	19	6	1	4	13	0	40	10	4	8	.249	.312	.354
Rivera, William, Aub.*	73	335	290	43	77	97	7	2	3	35	10	3	2	30	1	43	5	3	2	.266	.335	.334
Rivero, Luis, Bat.	34	109	100	10	16	24	1	2	1	12	1	0	0	8	0	29	3	2	4	.160	.222	.240
Roberson, Chris, Bat.	62	253	214	29	59	79	8	3	2	24	1	2	10	26	0	51	17	8	2	.276	.377	.369
Robertson, Cedric, H.V.	40	115	102	13	18	34	5	1	3	12	1	2	3	7	0	35	0	1	1	.176	.246	.333
Robinson-Pierce, Whitney, Aber.	15	49	47	1	7	9	2	0	0	0	0	0	0	2	0	12	0	0	0	.149	.184	.191
Rodriguez, Andres, Jam.	21	82	72	9	13	18	0	1	1	3	0	0	1	9	1	17	2	1	1	.181	.280	.250
Rodriguez, Carlos, Bat.†	61	276	248	29	72	85	7	3	0	15	5	0	4	19	0	48	21	11	2	.290	.351	.343
Rodriguez, Edgar, Bkn.	11	44	39	3	10	18	2	0	2	5	1	0	0	4	0	10	2	1	0	.256	.326	.462
Rodriguez, Raul, Aber.†	2	2	0	1	0	0	0	0	0	0	0	0	0	2	0	0	2	0	0	.000	1.000	.000
Rodriguez, Robert, Ver.	12	30	28	2	8	11	3	0	0	4	1	0	0	1	0	10	0	0	3	.286	.310	.393
Rohleder, Andy, Jam.	65	215	182	29	56	85	12	4	3	26	0	1	4	28	0	37	2	3	7	.308	.409	.467
Rojas, Ricardo, M.V.	6	24	22	4	7	9	0	1	0	5	0	0	1	0	0	5	5	0	0	.318	.375	.409
Rojas, Tommy, S.I.	43	167	140	17	45	54	6	0	1	18	1	1	5	20	1	27	2	5	2	.321	.422	.386
Romprey, Ed, One.	52	204	174	25	45	58	7	0	2	20	5	0	4	21	0	40	2	3	5	.259	.352	.333
Rosario, Olmo, H.V.	13	44	37	3	8	8	0	0	0	3	0	2	0	5	0	11	1	1	0	.216	.295	.216
Roughton, Jody, One.*	54	235	208	30	64	85	10	1	3	38	0	3	5	19	2	43	0	1	2	.308	.374	.409
Russell, Mike, Aber.	59	210	183	26	50	67	3	1	4	29	0	3	5	19	0	56	4	0	4	.273	.352	.366
St. Clair, Jason, H.V.	37	126	115	13	30	46	6	2	2	10	2	1	1	7	0	27	4	2	3	.261	.306	.400
Salmela, Andy, T.C.	68	256	221	23	42	62	6	1	4	26	6	3	3	23	0	57	2	3	3	.190	.272	.281
Sandoval, Jjallil, T.C.†	57	224	190	21	46	52	6	0	0	17	5	0	2	27	0	39	12	7	0	.242	.342	.274
Santor, John, N.J.†	68	239	44	70	135	24	1	13	62	0	2	3	32	2	62	4	2	5	.293	.380	.565
Santos, Omir, S.I.	61	251	232	22	67	98	10	0	7	44	0	3	4	12	0	32	2	1	6	.289	.331	.422
Sardinha, Bronson, S.I.*	36	150	124	25	40	60	8	0	4	16	0	1	1	24	2	36	4	1	3	.323	.433	.484
Sato, G.G., Bat.	20	85	72	16	22	36	5	0	3	8	1	2	2	8	1	25	2	1	1	.306	.381	.500
Scala, Mickey, Wil.*	5	9	6	1	2	2	0	0	0	1	0	0	0	3	0	1	0	0	0	.333	.556	.333
Schmitt, Billy, N.J.	52	174	164	19	40	54	8	0	2	9	1	0	0	9	1	35	1	0	4	.244	.283	.329
Schneider, John, Aub.	40	155	125	17	30	44	8	0	2	11	0	1	6	23	1	29	0	0	1	.240	.381	.352
Schneider, Michael, Ver.	8	31	27	3	10	14	1	0	1	6	0	1	0	3	0	6	0	0	4	.370	.419	.519
Schweitzer, Scott, N.J.*	23	1	1	0	0	0	0	0	0	0	0	0	0	0	0	0	0	0	0	.000	.000	.000
Seuss, Adam, T.C.*	69	271	243	29	53	79	10	2	4	28	1	2	3	22	0	32	3	3	5	.218	.289	.325
Sheaffer, Jon, S.I.	30	67	57	7	8	9	1	0	0	3	1	0	2	7	0	15	1	2	1	.140	.258	.158
Shier, Peter, Aber.	12	54	46	4	9	12	1	1	0	4	1	1	1	5	0	11	0	1	0	.196	.283	.261
Silvera, Andres, Bat.	31	131	113	13	26	46	6	1	4	12	2	1	3	12	1	40	10	5	3	.230	.318	.407
Simoneaux, Neil, N.J.-M.V.	38	115	109	17	26	34	4	2	0	15	0	1	0	5	0	27	3	3	3	.239	.270	.312
Siriveaw, Nom, Aub.†	56	212	180	26	53	82	8	6	3	30	4	1	3	24	1	53	8	3	4	.294	.385	.456
Slack, Jonathan, Bkn.*	47	173	147	16	36	49	8	1	1	11	3	1	2	20	0	47	5	5	0	.245	.341	.333
Soriano, Jairo, Aber.†	33	85	75	8	15	16	1	0	0	2	0	0	1	9	0	21	4	1	2	.200	.294	.213
Stephenson, Neal, Aber.*	70	273	255	30	79	117	17	6	3	40	1	1	3	13	0	50	4	4	3	.310	.349	.459
Stone, Greg, Low.*	71	305	267	45	65	72	5	1	0	22	4	3	2	29	0	42	14	5	3	.243	.319	.270
Sweeney, Tim, Ver.	45	155	140	12	26	28	2	0	0	7	1	2	1	11	0	26	1	1	4	.186	.247	.200
Swope, Matt, Ver.	7	21	18	3	4	4	0	0	0	1	0	0	2	0	1	0	0	0	2	.222	.286	.222
Tarbett, Brent, Low.	5	23	19	2	3	4	1	0	0	2	0	0	2	2	0	6	0	0	1	.158	.304	.211
Tejeda, Ferdin, S.I.	47	195	181	29	50	61	7	2	0	18	2	1	0	11	0	33	11	3	6	.276	.316	.337
Thede, Matthew, Ver.	9	37	34	8	12	29	5	0	4	9	1	1	0	1	0	6	0	0	0	.353	.361	.853
Thompson, Kevin, S.I.	36	158	139	25	42	63	5	2	4	14	1	1	0	17	1	24	6	3	1	.302	.376	.453
Tolotti, Jeff, N.J.*	25	79	75	8	19	31	6	0	2	10	1	0	0	3	0	23	1	1	1	.253	.282	.413
Toner, John, Bkn.	53	213	196	27	56	87	7	0	8	24	0	6	11	0	0	40	4	1	5	.286	.343	.444
Topham, Andrew, T.C.	47	196	181	22	42	58	8	1	2	16	0	4	4	7	0	45	5	2	10	.232	.270	.320
Torres, Eider, M.V.†	19	79	75	9	23	28	5	0	0	8	0	0	0	3	1	9	9	5	2	.307	.342	.373
Treadway, Jared, S.I.	15	20	18	5	5	5	0	0	0	1	0	0	0	1	0	5	0	0	0	.278	.350	.278
Trezza, Alex, One.*	12	40	34	3	12	14	2	0	0	4	1	1	0	4	0	6	0	0	0	.353	.410	.412
Turay, Haj, Bkn.	40	168	153	21	50	74	10	1	4	19	2	0	2	11	0	48	7	3	3	.327	.380	.484
Uegawachi, Bryce, M.V.†	42	98	88	13	23	28	5	0	0	10	2	0	0	8	0	13	0	0	2	.261	.323	.318
Urquhart, Adrian, Ver.	20	66	56	4	11	13	2	0	0	4	0	0	2	8	0	18	1	1	1	.196	.318	.232
Vandever, Joey, N.J.	71	250	207	38	48	54	4	1	0	9	5	0	2	36	1	51	31	9	1	.232	.351	.261
Van Every, Jon, M.V.*	42	164	140	31	36	73	7	6	6	26	1	2	1	20	0	45	6	0	3	.257	.350	.521
Vasquez, Wuillians, S.I.†	50	194	175	22	41	60	8	1	3	22	0	2	2	15	0	46	0	3	3	.234	.299	.343
Verbryke, Eric, S.I.*	30	129	114	8	25	33	6	1	0	9	1	0	0	14	1	31	3	0	3	.219	.305	.289
Wallace, Dave, M.V.	45	168	145	22	37	51	5	0	3	17	0	2	10	11	0	48	3	0	3	.255	.345	.352
Wardinsky, Ryan, Bat.†	26	95	84	8	22	27	2	0	1	7	0	0	3	8	0	24	2	2	0	.262	.347	.321
Watson, Rob, One.	62	276	232	38	65	96	22	3	1	37	4	4	7	29	1	32	2	0	5	.280	.371	.414
Watts, Derran, Bkn.	10	30	26	2	4	5	1	0	0	0	0	0	2	2	0	14	0	1	1	.154	.267	.192
Waugh, Jason, Bkn.	67	295	255	39	62	103	14	0	9	38	1	5	3	31	0	50	5	5	6	.243	.327	.404
Webster, Kevin, Aber.	1	1	0	0	0	0	0	0	0	0	0	0	0	1	0	0	0	0	0	.000	1.000	.000
Weese, Nathan, Ver.*	57	208	189	22	45	60	9	0	2	18	0	0	2	17	1	41	1	0	0	.238	.308	.317
West, Eric, Low.	64	270	225	35	54	65	6	1	1	14	3	3	5	34	0	48	11	9	3	.240	.348	.289
Whealy, Blake, Bkn.	59	230	204	32	59	109	14	3	10	34	3	0	2	21	0	58	9	2	4	.289	.361	.534
Whitesides, Jake, T.C.*	45	140	126	13	28	41	5	4	0	6	1	0	1	12	0	21	3	2	3	.222	.295	.325
Winegarden, Erik, Bat.*	10	47	39	6	11	14	3	0	0	5	0	1	1	6	0	6	0	0	2	.282	.383	.359
Woodrow, Justin, N.J.*	28	93	81	10	14	16	0	1	0	8	1	0	1	10	0	15	3	1	1	.173	.272	.198

Player, Team	G	TPA	AB	R	H	TB	2B	3B	HR	RBI	SH	SF	HP	BB	IBB	SO	SB	CS	GDP	Avg.	OBP	Slg.
Word, Robert, Jam.*	58	214	192	23	41	62	10	1	3	25	1	0	3	18	0	72	1	0	1	.214	.291	.323
Wright, Brian, M.V.*	67	283	235	40	67	97	9	3	5	47	0	9	1	38	2	35	7	0	5	.285	.375	.413
Wyant, Hunter, Jam.	53	196	184	16	36	50	6	1	2	17	0	1	1	10	0	31	3	4	6	.196	.240	.272
Zamora, Hector, S.I.*	33	125	108	12	27	38	9	1	0	6	0	0	2	15	2	32	0	3	2	.250	.352	.352

PLAYERS WITH TWO OR MORE TEAMS

Player, Team	G	TPA	AB	R	H	TB	2B	3B	HR	RBI	SH	SF	HP	BB	IBB	SO	SB	CS	GDP	Avg.	OBP	Slg.
Simoneaux, Neil, N.J.	12	45	44	5	13	20	3	2	0	10	0	1	0	0	0	8	3	2	1	.295	.289	.455
Simoneaux, Neil, M.V.	26	70	65	12	13	14	1	0	0	5	0	0	5	0	0	19	0	1	2	.200	.257	.215

GRAND SLAMS: Santor 2, Broadway, Gomes, C. Johnston, Kane, Laidlaw, Porfirio, T. Rojas, Seuss, Wright, 1 each.

AWARDED FIRST BASE ON CATCHER'S INTERFERENCE: Boran 3 (Ji. Anderson, Emmerick, Mackor), Chapman (Russell), Concepcion (Hubele), C. Johnston (Aleman), K. Jones (Emmerick), Kingsbury (Russell), Malek (Haase), Riley (Mejia).

2002 PITCHING
TEAM

Team	W	L	Pct.	ERA	G	CG	ShO	Sv.	IP	H	TBF	R	ER	HR	SH	SF	HB	BB	IBB	SO	WP	Bk.
Staten Island	48	26	.649	2.57	75	3	12	26	662.0	543	2699	240	189	20	27	16	26	185	5	638	26	8
Auburn	47	29	.618	3.05	76	0	11	28	681.1	560	2810	277	231	30	12	13	31	257	8	634	51	4
New Jersey	39	37	.513	3.05	76	3	10	18	663.0	556	2773	266	225	27	15	20	33	238	9	536	56	7
Oneonta	47	27	.635	3.10	74	0	7	28	665.1	597	2824	291	229	36	22	20	37	236	2	532	37	3
Brooklyn	38	38	.500	3.40	76	2	8	16	685.0	658	2919	314	259	29	23	27	46	233	9	614	52	9
Batavia	34	42	.447	3.44	76	1	5	12	686.0	628	2902	310	262	38	17	25	47	280	4	484	33	7
Williamsport	48	28	.632	3.45	76	1	8	21	678.1	621	2835	304	260	48	29	11	36	193	5	543	30	3
Mahoning Val.	46	30	.605	3.56	76	0	9	18	667.2	616	2890	310	264	30	25	22	48	266	3	589	54	5
Vermont	30	45	.400	3.67	75	0	4	18	665.0	571	2903	355	271	26	28	28	49	312	6	594	78	8
Aberdeen	31	45	.408	4.00	76	2	5	21	666.2	666	2881	360	296	40	23	40	38	226	7	537	34	7
Lowell	34	41	.453	4.19	75	0	3	16	670.2	670	2927	384	312	45	29	29	51	248	4	551	53	4
Hudson Valley	26	49	.347	4.29	75	2	0	16	663.2	723	2956	405	316	33	18	20	46	248	5	539	51	7
Tri-City	27	48	.360	4.35	75	0	6	16	658.2	650	2863	361	318	45	25	23	42	258	5	547	46	5
Jamestown	32	42	.432	5.36	75	3	3	8	665.1	789	3058	461	396	46	27	31	52	256	6	468	52	8

INDIVIDUAL

TOP QUALIFIERS FOR EARNED-RUN AVERAGE TITLE

Minimum 61 innings. *Lefthanded pitcher.

Pitcher, Team	W	L	Pct.	ERA	G	GS	CG	ShO	GF	Sv.	IP	H	TBF	R	ER	HR	SH	SF	HB	BB	IBB	SO	WP	Bk.
Hinckley, Michael, Ver.*	6	2	.750	1.37	16	16	0	0	0	0	91.2	60	357	19	14	4	3	1	4	30	0	66	6	3
Wang, Chien-ming, S.I.	6	1	.857	1.72	13	13	0	0	0	0	78.1	63	308	23	15	2	3	3	0	14	0	64	1	2
Hart, Alex, Wil.	7	0	1.000	1.85	15	10	0	0	3	2	68	52	275	15	14	1	5	0	3	20	0	73	0	0
Bicondoa, Ryan, S.I.	6	4	.600	1.90	14	14	3	0	0	0	85.1	64	332	25	18	3	1	6	7	0	94	1	3
Ramsey, Keith, M.V.*	6	3	.667	2.04	13	10	0	0	1	0	61.2	43	241	16	14	0	2	1	4	10	0	71	4	0
Davis, Stockton, Ver.	5	2	.286	2.15	19	2	0	0	11	7	71	51	295	23	17	2	6	0	7	22	1	81	8	0
Marceau, Pierre-Luc, Ver.*	5	4	.556	2.31	15	15	0	0	0	0	81.2	60	334	29	21	3	3	3	3	29	0	66	6	0
Pleiness, Chad, Aub.	8	3	.727	2.42	16	9	0	0	1	0	74.1	48	301	23	20	2	2	1	2	32	0	70	8	0
Warpinski, Ryan, Jam.	2	4	.333	2.48	15	15	0	0	0	0	76.1	70	335	31	21	3	3	4	8	29	0	61	1	1
Isaacson, Charlie, S.I.	5	3	.625	2.54	14	12	0	0	0	0	74.1	57	297	25	21	4	2	1	3	21	0	76	2	0
Davidson, Andy, N.J.*	5	3	.625	2.63	15	6	0	0	3	0	65	50	262	22	19	4	1	1	1	19	0	51	4	1
Arteaga, Erick, Bat.	3	1	.750	2.79	12	12	0	0	0	0	80.2	61	321	27	25	5	2	2	7	21	0	44	2	0
Read, Robby, Bat.	3	5	.375	2.82	13	11	1	0	0	0	67	58	281	26	21	4	0	4	5	32	0	43	3	0
Farren, Dave, Aber.	5	5	.500	2.86	14	14	1	0	0	0	85	74	348	31	27	7	4	6	2	28	0	58	2	0
Bergmann, Jason, Ver.	7	4	.636	2.89	14	14	0	0	0	0	71.2	48	297	27	23	4	5	2	9	33	0	57	2	1

DEPARTMENTAL LEADERS: W—Shortslef, 10; L—DeLeon, 10; Pct.—Hart, 1.000; G—Brumit, 33; GS—DeLeon, Hinckley, League, 16 each; CG—Bicondoa, 3; ShO—Ciprian, Kupper, Pinango, Scobie, 1 each; GF—Brumit, 31; Sv.—Brumit, 22; IP—Hinckley, 91.2; H—Connolly, 102; TBF—C. Cabrera, 388; R—Kupper, 54; ER—Kupper, 48; HR—Kupper, 10; SH—S. Davis, Grant, 6 each; SF—Cromer, Farren, Grant, H. Rodriguez, 6 each; HB—Anez, 10; BB—C. Cabrera, 46; IBB—D'Amato, Lyon, Makowsky, McNabb, 3 each; SO—Bicondoa, 94; WP—Walker, 18; BK—Bicondoa, Hinckley, 3 each.

ALL PITCHERS

*Lefthanded pitcher.

Pitcher, Team	W	L	Pct.	ERA	G	GS	CG	ShO	GF	Sv.	IP	H	TBF	R	ER	HR	SH	SF	HB	BB	IBB	SO	WP	Bk.
Acosta, Anthony, Bkn.	1	0	1.000	3.78	8	0	0	0	6	1	16.2	21	73	8	7	1	0	0	1	2	0	14	1	0
Acosta, Manuel, S.I.	2	1	.667	4.11	3	3	0	0	0	0	15.1	20	70	9	7	0	0	1	0	8	0	12	4	0
Allen, Blake, M.V.*	5	5	.500	4.82	15	15	0	0	0	0	80.1	94	358	50	43	4	3	1	6	17	0	62	4	0
Allen, Brian, H.V.	1	1	.500	2.55	14	0	0	0	4	0	24.2	25	112	12	7	1	0	1	3	9	0	20	3	0
Ally, Ben, T.C.	1	1	.500	3.72	9	3	0	0	1	0	29	31	125	12	12	0	0	1	2	5	0	23	0	0
Anderson, Julius, H.V.	3	3	.500	4.43	24	1	0	0	4	3	40.2	57	186	31	20	1	2	2	4	11	1	32	1	1
Anez, Omar, H.V.	4	4	.500	3.88	19	5	0	0	6	2	53.1	53	237	30	23	2	2	3	10	19	0	34	10	0
Arteaga, Erick, Bat.	3	1	.750	2.79	12	12	0	0	0	0	80.2	61	321	27	25	5	2	2	7	21	0	44	2	0
Autrey, Scott, H.V.	2	3	.400	3.57	11	11	0	0	0	0	58	55	238	24	23	3	0	0	3	14	0	36	4	0
Balan, Ryan, Low.	0	0	.000	1.35	4	0	0	0	2	0	6.2	4	27	1	1	0	0	0	4	0	10	0	0
Banks, Tyler, Jam.	2	1	.667	4.97	13	0	0	0	2	0	25.1	29	117	16	14	2	0	1	5	9	1	26	2	0
Barlow, Chris, Ver.	1	3	.250	2.35	5	5	0	0	0	0	23	18	95	10	6	1	0	2	1	0	11	0	1
Barrios, Rafael, One.	1	0	1.000	0.00	2	0	0	0	1	0	3	1	11	0	0	0	0	1	0	3	0	0
Basilio, Manuel, H.V.	1	1	.500	3.86	3	3	0	0	0	0	14	12	61	8	6	1	0	0	1	7	0	14	0	0
Batista, Roberto, N.J.	0	4	.000	2.91	27	1	0	0	25	13	34	33	144	18	11	0	2	0	2	8	1	19	1	1
Bayer, Russ, Wil.*	1	1	.500	5.52	17	0	0	0	5	0	31	32	135	19	19	5	0	1	1	12	1	21	0	0
Bayrer, Thomas, T.C.	0	0	.000	3.57	11	0	0	0	4	1	22.2	21	95	9	9	1	1	2	1	9	0	17	2	2

Pitcher, Team	W	L	Pct.	ERA	G	GS	CG	ShO	GF	Sv.	IP	H	TBF	R	ER	HR	SH	SF	HB	BB	IBB	SO	WP	Bk.
Bazardo, Yorman, Jam.	5	0	1.000	2.72	25	0	0	0	21	6	36.1	39	151	11	11	0	0	2	1	6	0	26	7	0
Beaven, John, H.V.	0	0	.000	6.62	17	0	0	0	4	0	17.2	15	94	18	13	1	0	1	4	24	0	17	6	0
Beck, Ken, Ver.	0	0	.000	5.29	14	0	0	0	8	1	17	28	89	17	10	1	0	3	1	7	0	14	1	1
Beigh, David, Wil.	1	4	.200	5.10	13	13	0	0	0	0	54.2	42	243	37	31	5	3	0	3	33	0	52	5	0
Bell, Gary, S.I.*	1	0	1.000	2.63	6	5	0	0	0	0	24	23	97	9	7	1	0	1	6	0	23	0	0
Bergmann, Jason, Ver.	7	4	.636	2.89	14	14	0	0	0	0	71.2	48	297	27	23	4	5	2	9	33	0	57	2	1
Berube, Martin, Aber.	2	4	.333	3.75	17	9	0	0	1	1	62.1	53	263	27	26	4	1	4	4	20	0	48	0	2
Bicondoa, Ryan, S.I.	6	4	.600	1.90	14	14	3	0	0	0	85.1	64	332	25	18	3	1	3	6	7	0	94	1	3
Blalock, Casey, Jam.	3	2	.600	1.64	23	0	0	0	18	2	33	17	127	10	6	3	3	1	3	9	1	30	3	0
Blethen, Matt, M.V.*	1	2	.333	5.23	16	0	0	0	6	0	31	32	146	22	18	1	1	1	1	19	0	19	1	0
Bomer, Alan, S.I.	0	0	.000	4.05	2	2	0	0	0	0	6.2	8	28	3	3	1	1	0	0	1	0	2	0	0
Bourgeois, Nick, Bat.*	0	3	.000	5.40	6	5	0	0	0	0	18.1	13	84	14	11	1	0	0	3	16	0	17	2	0
Bowen, Chad, Bkn.	2	4	.333	3.22	17	2	0	0	5	0	50.1	55	209	20	18	3	3	0	1	16	0	41	3	0
Brewer, Jeff, Bkn.	0	0	.000	9.00	2	0	0	0	1	0	2	3	11	2	2	0	0	0	0	2	0	1	1	0
Brewster, Derek, Bat.	0	0	.000	0.00	4	0	0	0	3	1	7	1	26	0	0	0	0	0	2	1	0	3	0	0
Brockman, Dave, N.J.	1	1	.500	5.52	12	2	0	0	5	0	14.2	12	66	10	9	1	1	1	1	7	0	9	2	0
Brumit, Matt, S.I.	1	2	.333	2.21	33	0	0	0	31	22	36.2	32	149	11	9	2	3	0	2	8	0	40	1	0
Bryant, Whit, Bat.*	1	5	.167	5.40	16	6	0	0	2	1	43.1	43	204	29	26	0	3	2	5	40	1	36	4	2
Bulger, Brian, H.V.	0	4	.000	5.53	12	8	0	0	1	0	42.1	44	190	28	26	1	0	2	2	25	0	38	6	1
Busbin, Brad, Bat.	2	2	.500	1.80	11	0	0	0	7	0	20	14	80	6	4	2	0	0	2	4	0	12	1	0
Bush, David, Aub.	1	1	.500	2.82	18	0	0	0	17	10	22.1	13	91	9	7	1	0	0	2	7	2	39	0	0
Bush, Jason, Jam.	1	1	.500	7.32	9	0	0	0	3	0	19.2	29	90	18	16	2	0	1	0	5	1	13	0	0
Bustillos, Oscar, H.V.	0	3	.000	4.79	22	0	0	0	11	1	35.2	33	154	22	19	3	1	0	1	16	0	38	0	0
Byers, Waylon, Jam.*	0	0	.000	7.71	4	0	0	0	2	0	4.2	5	23	4	4	1	0	0	0	4	0	7	2	0
Cabrera, Carlos, Bat.	9	2	.818	3.59	15	14	0	0	1	0	90.1	79	388	44	36	5	2	5	46	0	77	3	1
Cabrera, Yunior, Bkn.*	3	4	.429	2.89	8	8	0	0	0	0	37.1	31	160	18	12	2	2	0	1	15	0	39	2	0
Campbell, Dayle, One.	5	1	.833	3.35	20	1	0	0	4	0	37.2	33	172	16	14	1	2	1	2	28	0	28	1	0
Cardwell, Brian, Aub.	2	0	1.000	3.71	20	0	0	0	4	0	26.2	24	121	12	11	0	0	0	1	22	0	30	4	0
Carlson, Jesse, One.*	2	2	.500	1.66	19	0	0	0	4	0	38	19	143	8	7	1	2	0	1	10	0	47	1	1
Carmona, Fausto, M.V.	0	0	.000	0.00	3	0	0	0	2	0	4	2	13	0	0	0	1	0	1	0	0	0	0	0
Carney, Jake, H.V.	2	1	.667	5.48	13	0	0	0	2	0	23	33	112	16	14	1	1	1	1	9	0	19	2	0
Chenard, Ken, Bkn.	1	1	.500	3.21	3	3	0	0	0	0	14	14	58	5	5	0	0	1	0	4	0	7	0	0
Cierlik, Jason, Aber.*	0	0	.000	3.21	12	0	0	0	7	2	14	12	63	5	5	0	0	1	0	6	0	16	2	0
Ciprian, Wilson, N.J.	7	5	.583	3.32	15	15	2	1	0	0	89.1	78	369	43	33	5	3	2	4	22	1	71	6	1
Clark, Ray, S.I.	3	0	1.000	1.97	8	5	0	0	1	0	32	23	121	9	7	1	2	2	0	6	0	39	3	0
Coleman, Kevin, N.J.	1	0	1.000	2.04	14	0	0	0	6	0	18	12	73	4	4	1	0	0	2	7	1	13	3	0
Comolli, Mark, Aub.	0	1	.000	1.80	6	0	0	0	3	1	10	11	40	3	2	1	0	0	0	0	0	9	2	0
Connolly, Jon, One.*	5	3	.625	4.01	14	14	0	0	0	0	85.1	102	362	46	38	7	2	2	1	10	0	50	3	1
Cooney, Jim, Aber.*	3	1	.750	1.36	25	0	0	0	9	4	33	17	133	11	5	0	2	3	7	13	0	27	1	0
Crohan, Thomas, Jam.*	3	2	.600	5.64	7	5	0	0	1	0	30.1	38	136	20	19	1	1	2	2	11	0	15	3	1
Cromer, Jason, H.V.*	3	6	.333	3.81	15	14	1	0	1	0	75.2	87	327	45	32	4	2	6	2	15	0	53	5	0
Culp, Todd, M.V.	0	0	.000	5.23	18	0	0	0	9	0	20.2	20	109	14	12	2	0	0	2	27	0	27	5	0
Cummings, Eric, Bkn.	2	1	.667	2.61	5	0	0	0	2	0	10.1	12	44	3	3	1	0	0	3	1	0	5	0	0
D'Amato, Dan, N.J.*	1	1	.500	1.27	23	0	0	0	5	1	28.1	29	120	8	4	1	1	1	1	6	3	23	2	0
Danly, Ryan, Bkn.*	0	0	.000	0.00	2	0	0	0	1	0	3	4	14	4	0	1	1	0	0	0	0	2	0	0
Davidson, Andy, N.J.*	5	3	.625	2.63	15	6	0	0	3	0	65	50	262	22	19	4	1	1	1	19	0	51	4	1
Davila, Marcus, Wil.	0	2	.000	1.71	15	0	0	0	8	0	26.1	19	108	6	5	0	4	2	2	7	1	20	1	0
Davis, Lance, Jam.	2	3	.400	6.04	11	10	2	0	1	0	47.2	60	216	36	32	2	0	1	4	10	0	26	1	1
Davis, Stockton, Ver.	2	5	.286	2.15	19	2	0	0	11	7	71	51	295	23	17	2	6	0	7	22	1	81	8	0
Deaton, Kevin, Bkn.	7	1	.875	3.07	16	15	0	0	1	0	82	68	328	34	28	2	2	4	5	18	0	93	5	2
DeBarr, Nick, H.V.	1	2	.333	4.24	4	3	0	0	1	0	17	18	71	8	8	2	0	0	0	3	0	15	4	0
DeJong, Jordan, Aub.	1	0	1.000	0.00	2	0	0	0	1	0	4.1	0	13	0	0	0	0	0	1	0	0	3	0	0
Delacruz, Eulogio, One.	0	0	.000	23.14	2	0	0	0	1	0	2.1	7	20	8	6	0	0	1	1	4	0	4	0	0
Deleon, Joey, T.C.	4	10	.286	4.35	16	16	0	0	0	0	80.2	66	341	49	39	7	4	1	9	34	0	63	2	1
DeMaria, Chris, Wil.	1	1	.500	4.35	16	0	0	0	5	0	31	34	130	20	15	6	1	0	4	1	0	15	0	0
Demontel, Jimmy, Jam.	2	6	.250	7.69	15	7	0	0	1	0	48	72	248	50	41	5	1	1	5	27	1	35	4	0
Diaz, Eddie, Ver.	0	2	.000	6.43	3	3	0	0	0	0	7	3	37	6	5	0	0	1	1	12	0	9	2	0
Diaz, Luis, One.	4	1	.800	3.24	9	6	0	0	0	0	41.2	31	174	19	15	3	1	3	2	15	0	45	3	0
DiFranco, Joseph, S.I.	0	1	.000	2.84	6	1	0	0	1	0	6.1	5	28	2	2	0	0	0	0	4	0	9	0	0
Dischiavo, John, H.V.	0	0	.000	4.05	3	0	0	0	1	0	6.2	4	29	3	3	1	0	2	3	0	3	2	0
Dunn, Gerald, One.	4	0	1.000	0.67	5	5	0	0	0	0	27	17	100	4	2	1	0	0	1	5	0	14	0	0
Duran, J.P., T.C.	1	2	.333	4.65	20	0	0	0	9	2	31	24	138	17	16	2	2	2	2	21	0	30	7	0
Edwards, Brad, Aber.*	0	0	.000	4.98	17	1	0	0	7	0	21.2	20	93	14	12	1	2	1	1	9	0	24	1	0
Elliott, Adam, Bkn.	0	0	.000	1.50	3	0	0	0	1	0	6	3	23	2	1	0	0	0	1	0	0	6	0	0
Ellis, Rob, H.V.*	3	5	.375	5.73	15	7	0	0	3	0	44	49	205	40	28	1	2	2	1	21	0	39	2	0
Evans, Kyle, M.V.	1	0	1.000	1.59	3	3	0	0	0	0	17	16	71	3	3	0	3	0	1	7	0	18	1	0
Evans, Louis, Jam.*	1	0	1.000	2.70	5	0	0	0	0	0	13.1	15	61	5	4	0	0	1	1	5	0	13	2	0
Ewasko, Tod, N.J.	0	0	.000	0.76	18	0	0	0	5	2	23.2	8	86	2	2	0	1	1	0	6	0	17	2	0
Farren, Dave, Aber.	5	5	.500	2.86	14	14	1	0	0	0	85	74	348	31	27	7	4	6	2	28	0	58	2	0
Felfoldi, Jonathan, Ver.*	0	2	.000	3.38	3	3	0	0	0	0	8	10	35	6	3	0	0	0	3	2	0	6	1	0
Fiedler, Erik, Ver.	0	3	.000	4.68	10	0	0	0	2	0	25	30	115	19	13	2	3	2	1	9	1	19	0	0
Figueroa, Juan, One.	0	2	.000	3.81	28	0	0	0	25	21	28.1	23	121	14	12	1	1	1	1	13	0	34	6	0
Flores, Manuel, T.C.	3	2	.600	2.59	15	9	0	0	2	1	55.2	37	216	16	16	4	2	1	2	19	0	63	3	0
Flynn, Brian, N.J.	5	3	.625	2.96	18	4	1	0	3	1	51.2	47	214	19	17	3	1	3	12	2	41	4	0
Galvez, Willy, Low.	2	6	.250	6.42	15	12	0	0	1	0	54.2	68	265	49	39	8	1	1	5	30	0	41	8	0
George, Jahseam, M.V.*	0	0	.000	6.75	1	0	0	0	0	0	1.1	1	6	1	1	0	0	0	0	0	0	3	1	0
Gerk, Jordan, One.*	1	0	1.000	1.86	10	0	0	0	5	0	9.2	9	40	3	2	0	0	0	1	2	0	11	2	0
Gonzales, Jim, One.	1	0	1.000	5.30	7	1	0	0	0	0	18.2	18	84	12	11	0	0	2	10	0	10	1	0
Gonzalez, Jose, Low.	1	1	.500	3.70	12	1	0	0	2	0	24.1	16	112	10	10	1	0	6	21	0	13	6	0
Gothreaux, Jared, T.C.	2	3	.400	2.72	28	0	0	0	21	4	46.1	55	206	23	14	3	3	0	0	12	1	53	1	0
Graham, Jason, One.	1	1	.500	3.20	14	0	0	0	8	1	19.2	15	88	11	7	1	1	0	3	9	0	12	2	0
Grant, Michael, Low.	6	5	.545	3.81	22	3	0	0	5	0	56.2	51	246	29	24	2	6	6	7	26	1	59	0	0

Pitcher, Team	W	L	Pct.	ERA	G	GS	CG	ShO	GF	Sv.	IP	H	TBF	R	ER	HR	SH	SF	HB	BB	IBB	SO	WP	Bk.
Gravelle, Nick, Wil.*	7	4	.636	3.66	15	15	0	0	0	0	83.2	85	349	37	34	9	2	2	2	23	0	82	4	0
Greusel, Evan, Jam.	1	2	.333	5.06	8	7	0	0	0	0	32	29	144	18	18	2	1	1	3	15	0	38	4	1
Guerrero, Tomas, Ver.	0	1	.000	5.23	21	0	0	0	15	3	32.2	33	150	23	19	2	2	2	2	15	0	20	1	1
Gwaltney, Lee, Bat.	0	2	.000	3.60	7	7	0	0	0	0	25	26	103	12	10	2	0	2	3	6	0	18	0	0
Hall, Shane, Low.	1	1	.500	5.40	22	0	0	0	11	1	35	39	156	21	21	3	0	2	1	10	0	18	1	0
Halsey, Brad, S.I.*	6	1	.857	1.93	11	10	0	0	0	0	56	39	223	15	12	0	1	1	4	17	0	53	0	0
Hamilton, Mark, T.C.	6	4	.600	4.12	13	13	0	0	0	0	67.2	69	296	35	31	6	3	3	3	25	1	64	3	0
Hamman, Corey, One.	0	0	.000	0.00	3	0	0	0	1	1	6.2	2	21	0	0	0	0	0	0	0	0	8	1	0
Hammel, Jason, H.V.	1	5	.167	5.23	13	10	0	0	2	1	51.2	71	245	41	30	0	1	4	4	14	0	38	3	2
Hancock, Everett, One.*	0	1	.000	4.61	13	0	0	0	5	0	13.2	24	71	8	7	0	1	2	2	7	0	6	0	0
Hansack, Devorn, T.C.	3	4	.429	3.60	12	10	0	0	0	0	50	44	207	21	20	6	2	3	2	17	0	37	0	1
Hanson, D.J., Aub.	5	2	.714	1.68	9	9	0	0	0	0	48.1	35	186	11	9	4	1	0	2	11	0	51	3	0
Harrand, Rob, Bat.	1	5	.167	4.17	8	8	0	0	0	0	41	44	178	20	19	2	1	0	1	13	0	25	2	0
Hart, Alex, Wil.	7	0	1.000	1.85	15	10	0	0	3	2	68	52	275	15	14	1	5	0	3	20	0	73	0	0
Hawksworth, Blake, N.J.	1	0	1.000	0.00	2	0	0	0	1	0	9.2	6	37	0	0	0	0	0	0	2	0	8	0	0
Heagen, Doug, Low.*	1	0	1.000	4.32	4	0	0	0	1	0	8.1	10	35	4	4	1	0	0	1	2	0	6	1	0
Heitzman, Aaron, T.C.*	3	4	.429	3.05	23	3	0	0	6	0	59	58	250	25	20	3	2	1	3	22	1	34	2	0
Hentgen, Pat, Aber.	1	1	.500	3.09	2	2	0	0	0	0	11.2	16	51	8	4	1	0	0	0	0	0	10	0	0
Hernandez, Michael, M.V.*	3	1	.750	2.78	22	0	0	0	7	2	45.1	37	206	20	14	1	1	2	4	28	0	58	7	2
Hinckley, Michael, Ver.*	6	2	.750	1.37	16	16	0	0	0	0	91.2	60	357	19	14	4	3	1	4	30	0	66	6	3
Hines, Carlos, H.V.	2	2	.500	3.96	5	5	0	0	0	0	25	28	109	13	11	3	3	1	3	7	0	12	0	0
Holt, Chris, Wil.	2	2	.500	6.15	15	0	0	0	10	0	26.1	40	124	20	18	2	1	0	4	5	1	6	1	1
Houston, Ryan, Aub.	2	2	.500	4.06	7	7	0	0	0	0	31	32	139	15	14	1	0	1	3	15	0	19	2	0
Isaacson, Charlie, S.I.	5	3	.625	2.54	14	12	0	0	0	0	74.1	57	297	25	21	4	2	1	3	21	0	76	2	0
Jaillet, Wes, N.J.	3	2	.600	2.27	22	1	0	0	4	0	35.2	33	153	11	9	3	1	2	1	12	0	30	2	1
Johnson, Kelly, N.J.	1	1	.500	0.48	16	0	0	0	6	0	18.2	14	75	2	1	0	0	0	0	6	0	16	1	0
Johnson, Seth, Ver.	0	0	.000	5.40	1	0	0	0	1	0	1.2	1	7	1	1	0	0	0	0	1	0	0	0	0
Johnston, Dave, Jam.	2	3	.400	11.09	10	2	0	0	2	0	18.2	34	107	29	23	0	3	1	2	13	1	16	0	0
Johnston, Rikki, One.*	8	2	.800	3.17	15	12	0	0	0	0	82.1	79	352	37	29	9	5	2	2	29	0	60	2	1
Joyce, Michael, S.I.*	0	0	.000	3.00	4	0	0	0	2	0	6	9	28	3	2	0	0	1	0	0	0	4	0	0
Kazmir, Scott, Bkn.*	0	1	.000	0.50	5	5	0	0	0	0	18	5	65	2	1	0	0	0	2	7	0	34	0	0
Keefer, Ryan, Aber.	3	7	.300	3.91	13	13	0	0	0	0	69	77	300	38	30	4	2	3	2	18	0	64	0	0
Keinath, Tim, H.V.	1	0	1.000	3.86	4	0	0	0	0	0	7	10	34	4	3	2	0	0	0	4	0	5	0	0
Kentner, Brandon, Bkn.	3	1	.750	3.38	17	0	0	0	3	1	37.1	34	180	17	14	1	4	1	1	31	1	39	1	1
Kieninger, Billy, One.	1	2	.333	2.90	16	0	0	0	8	3	31	32	135	12	10	2	3	1	3	7	0	22	1	0
King, Bryan, Bkn.	0	1	.000	3.52	5	0	0	0	4	0	7.2	6	33	5	3	2	0	1	0	2	1	3	0	0
Kleine, Victor, M.V.*	9	3	.750	3.80	15	15	0	0	0	0	73.1	73	330	33	31	2	0	0	7	40	0	48	3	1
Koenig, Ross, One.	2	3	.400	1.67	18	0	0	0	7	0	32.1	18	132	9	6	1	1	0	2	16	2	33	6	0
Kopp, Nathan, S.I.*	2	2	.500	1.61	21	0	0	0	7	0	22.1	9	86	4	4	0	0	1	0	11	0	22	1	0
Korecky, Bobby, Bat.	2	2	.500	2.31	7	5	0	0	0	0	35	30	132	12	9	2	1	1	0	6	0	25	2	0
Kramer, Sean, T.C.	0	0	.000	4.58	21	0	0	0	9	2	37.1	35	168	22	19	0	0	2	3	16	1	31	1	0
Kupper, Dustin, Jam.	2	7	.222	5.68	16	14	1	1	0	0	76	84	334	54	48	10	4	3	9	21	0	39	4	0
League, Brandon, Aub.	7	2	.778	3.15	16	16	0	0	0	0	85.2	80	357	42	30	2	2	1	8	23	0	72	6	0
Lewis, Jeremy, One.*	4	3	.571	4.09	16	11	0	0	1	1	70.1	76	313	42	32	6	1	3	5	26	0	45	3	0
Lissir, Alexander, Wil.	1	2	.333	3.97	4	4	0	0	0	0	22.2	25	92	10	10	2	2	0	1	4	0	12	0	0
Lohrman, Dave, Bkn.	0	0	.000	3.44	12	0	0	0	7	2	18.1	16	83	10	7	0	0	4	0	10	0	19	3	0
Long, Nick, Ver.	1	3	.250	7.92	6	6	0	0	0	0	25	36	126	30	22	0	1	4	0	14	0	16	7	0
Lyon, Nick, H.V.	2	3	.400	2.16	20	0	0	0	11	3	33.1	26	136	9	8	0	2	2	1	9	3	33	0	0
MacLane, Thomas, Low.*	3	2	.600	1.54	19	0	0	0	5	1	41	36	178	15	7	2	2	1	3	19	1	38	2	0
Maine, John, Aber.	1	1	.500	1.74	4	2	0	0	1	0	10.1	6	42	2	2	0	0	0	3	0	0	21	2	0
Makowsky, Carl, Aber.	5	3	.625	3.45	23	0	0	0	6	1	31.1	26	137	13	12	2	4	0	1	20	3	32	5	1
Marceau, Pierre-Luc, Ver.*	5	4	.556	2.31	15	15	0	0	0	0	81.2	60	334	29	21	3	3	3	3	29	0	66	6	0
Martin, Kevin, M.V.	1	2	.333	4.08	26	0	0	0	11	5	46.1	43	196	23	21	4	4	2	1	13	1	37	4	1
Martinez, Wilmer, N.J.	2	5	.286	6.34	14	8	0	0	2	0	44	48	199	33	31	1	0	0	2	22	0	23	6	1
Mateo, Aneudis, Low.	2	0	1.000	1.45	3	3	0	0	0	0	18.2	8	66	3	3	1	0	0	4	2	0	13	1	0
Maureau, Justin, Aub.*	0	0	.000	1.44	22	0	0	0	11	5	43.2	24	166	10	7	1	1	0	1	12	0	51	2	0
McCurdy, Nick, Aber.	4	7	.364	3.55	13	12	1	0	1	1	71	67	291	29	28	1	1	3	5	16	0	45	2	0
McLemore, Mark, T.C.*	1	5	.167	14.09	9	6	0	0	1	0	23	42	124	37	36	2	0	0	0	17	0	16	3	0
McNabb, Tim, Bkn.	2	2	.500	3.44	17	0	0	0	6	2	34	33	149	16	13	2	1	4	8	12	3	30	4	1
Meccage, Justin, S.I.	2	2	.500	3.11	19	3	0	0	3	2	46.1	36	191	21	16	2	4	0	1	19	0	45	3	0
Menocal, Victor, Bat.	2	1	.667	3.45	19	0	0	0	16	2	31.1	36	138	13	12	0	2	0	5	13	0	16	1	0
Mieres, Alberto, S.I.	0	0	.000	5.91	6	1	0	0	4	0	10.2	9	51	8	7	0	0	1	7	0	7	4	0
Mildren, Paul, Jam.*	0	3	.000	5.54	3	3	0	0	0	0	13	16	62	10	8	1	1	1	0	9	0	6	1	1
Mims, Brandon, Low.*	0	2	.000	9.00	10	3	0	0	1	0	23	40	120	27	23	5	2	1	1	8	0	15	2	0
Mincey, T.W., Aber.*	1	2	.333	4.76	18	4	0	0	2	0	45.1	54	210	29	24	1	2	1	21	1	30	5	1
Minor, Zach, Bat.	2	2	.500	3.99	18	0	0	0	7	0	38.1	36	165	21	17	2	0	5	0	19	1	30	4	2
Montano, Ignacio, M.V.*	1	1	.500	2.70	12	0	0	0	9	3	16.2	13	65	5	5	1	1	0	0	2	0	17	0	0
Mora, Ramon, Aub.	2	1	.667	3.15	9	5	0	0	2	1	40	42	175	17	14	1	0	1	3	16	1	37	1	1
Moreno, Victor, Bat.	3	3	.500	3.71	17	0	0	0	13	5	26.2	19	121	14	11	3	2	0	2	21	0	34	2	1
Mosley, Eric, S.I.	0	0	.000	6.00	1	1	0	0	0	0	6	9	28	4	4	1	0	0	1	1	0	3	1	0
Musser, Neal, Bkn.*	0	0	.000	0.69	4	4	0	0	0	0	13	7	49	2	1	0	0	0	1	5	0	12	0	0
Myers, Damien, One.*	1	0	1.000	0.00	7	0	0	0	2	0	16.1	6	57	0	0	0	0	0	0	3	0	15	0	0
Naatjes, Darin, Bat.	0	0	.000	0.00	2	0	0	0	1	0	4	3	16	0	0	0	0	0	0	1	0	7	1	0
Naylor, Kody, Jam.	3	3	.500	4.60	25	0	0	0	10	0	47	52	216	28	24	4	3	2	3	24	0	33	3	0
Neitz, Josh, S.I.	4	3	.571	2.87	30	0	0	0	12	2	31.1	28	129	12	10	1	7	2	9	2	25	1	0
Neylan, Chris, Aub.*	0	0	.000	7.84	9	0	0	0	3	0	10.1	11	44	9	9	0	1	0	1	5	1	5	1	0
Nin, Sandy, Aub.	4	4	.500	2.92	17	11	0	0	3	2	74	61	285	29	24	3	1	2	0	11	0	61	6	2
Novoa, Roberto, Wil.	8	3	.727	3.65	12	12	0	0	0	0	66.2	62	277	32	27	4	3	1	8	0	56	5	0
O'Connor, Michael, Ver.*	2	3	.400	3.14	21	0	0	0	11	4	43	35	177	17	15	2	1	1	27	2	66	4	0
Ogle, Rylie, Bkn.*	1	2	.333	5.49	13	0	0	0	9	3	19.2	25	84	14	12	0	3	1	0	4	0	19	3	1
Olson, Ryan, Bkn.*	1	0	1.000	2.57	6	0	0	0	2	0	14	12	59	4	4	0	1	0	0	5	0	15	1	0
Ortiz, Julio, Ver.*	1	2	.333	3.82	15	1	0	0	4	0	33	28	148	18	14	2	2	3	2	16	1	28	1	0

Pitcher, Team	W	L	Pct.	ERA	G	GS	CG	ShO	GF	Sv.	IP	H	TBF	R	ER	HR	SH	SF	HB	BB	IBB	SO	WP	Bk.
Osberg, Tanner, Bkn.	1	1	.500	3.00	5	3	0	0	0	0	12	15	50	4	4	0	1	0	0	4	0	8	0	0
Ough, Wayne, Bkn.	1	4	.200	4.64	8	7	0	0	1	0	33	27	143	18	17	2	1	3	1	20	0	34	3	0
Owens, Henry, Wil.	0	3	.000	2.62	23	0	0	0	15	7	44.2	26	177	18	13	4	0	1	3	16	0	63	8	0
Paddock, Josh, Bat.	1	1	.500	3.27	13	0	0	0	2	0	22	28	97	14	8	0	0	2	1	3	0	12	1	0
Pahucki, David, Low.	1	2	.333	1.84	9	9	0	0	0	0	44	31	170	11	9	1	0	1	1	8	0	48	2	1
Parris, Matt, One.	1	1	.500	5.00	2	2	0	0	0	0	9	9	40	5	5	0	0	2	3	0	0	8	1	0
Paulk, Robert, Bkn.	3	0	1.000	4.82	9	0	0	0	4	1	18.2	27	85	10	10	2	1	0	0	5	0	17	2	1
Peguero, Jailen, T.C.	1	1	.500	3.44	25	3	0	0	14	6	49.2	49	208	20	19	3	1	2	0	17	1	42	6	0
Pender, Matthew, One.	2	2	.500	2.31	9	9	0	0	0	0	39	34	163	16	10	1	1	3	2	12	0	35	2	0
Pennington, Todd, M.V.	3	1	.750	0.59	8	0	0	0	6	2	15.1	6	57	1	1	0	1	1	1	6	1	23	0	1
Perez, Juan, Aub.	1	0	1.000	3.00	2	0	0	0	0	0	6	3	21	2	2	1	0	0	0	0	0	6	0	0
Perkins, Vince, Aub.	5	5	.500	3.34	15	15	0	0	0	0	72.2	51	306	32	27	3	1	2	2	44	0	85	5	0
Peterson, Adam, Aub.	2	0	1.000	2.30	18	0	0	0	10	5	31.1	29	130	10	8	2	2	0	1	9	1	19	1	0
Phillips, Chase, Aber.	2	1	.667	4.22	17	1	0	0	7	1	32	34	136	16	15	3	2	2	0	8	1	24	1	0
Pickford, Troy, One.	2	0	1.000	0.98	4	4	0	0	0	0	18.1	10	73	2	2	1	0	0	3	5	0	14	0	0
Pinango, Miguel, Bkn.	2	7	.222	3.59	16	15	1	1	1	0	80.1	85	337	39	32	2	0	3	4	14	1	64	6	1
Plancich, Nick, N.J.	3	2	.600	2.37	7	7	0	0	0	0	38	31	152	12	10	1	2	1	2	11	0	18	3	0
Pleiness, Chad, Aub.	8	3	.727	2.42	16	9	0	0	1	0	74.1	48	301	23	20	2	2	1	2	32	0	70	8	0
Portobanco, Luz, Bkn.	0	1	.000	6.00	2	2	0	0	0	0	12	12	53	8	8	2	0	1	3	2	0	3	1	1
Primus, Carl, Jam.	0	1	.000	7.71	24	1	0	0	6	0	49	69	238	47	42	1	3	1	1	27	1	27	4	2
Priola, John, Low.	3	0	1.000	2.54	27	0	0	0	22	13	46	36	175	15	13	4	5	2	4	5	0	33	1	1
Prochaska, Mike, H.V.*	3	6	.333	4.07	15	11	1	0	1	1	73	78	310	43	33	6	3	1	2	17	0	77	5	1
Puccinelli, John, Jam.	0	0	.000	9.00	1	0	0	0	1	0	1	1	4	1	1	0	0	0	0	1	0	0	1	0
Rada, Gerald, S.I.	1	1	.500	4.34	21	0	0	0	4	0	29	26	127	15	14	0	2	1	4	12	1	22	0	1
Ramirez, Ismael, Aub.	0	2	.000	7.15	3	3	0	0	0	0	11.1	17	51	10	9	2	0	1	0	2	0	7	0	0
Ramsey, Keith, M.V.*	6	3	.667	2.04	13	10	0	0	1	0	61.2	43	241	16	14	0	2	1	4	10	0	71	4	0
Rasner, Darrell, Ver.	2	5	.286	4.33	10	10	0	0	0	0	43.2	44	189	27	21	1	0	3	18	0	49	4	0
Read, Robby, Bat.	3	5	.375	2.82	13	13	1	0	0	0	67	58	281	26	21	4	0	4	5	32	0	43	3	0
Rengifo, Nohemar, Ver.	1	1	.500	5.40	12	0	0	0	2	0	20	19	99	15	12	0	0	1	1	20	0	13	1	0
Reyes, Maximo, Bat.	0	1	.000	4.70	4	0	0	0	3	0	7.2	11	34	4	4	1	0	1	0	0	0	5	0	0
Reynolds, Eric, S.I.*	6	0	1.000	1.22	14	1	0	0	2	0	37	23	145	8	5	1	0	0	0	10	1	43	1	1
Rice, Scott, Aber.*	1	7	.125	4.47	11	10	0	0	1	1	56.1	66	251	40	28	2	0	3	2	24	0	41	3	1
Rich, Dan, M.V.*	1	0	1.000	2.70	21	0	0	0	16	4	23.1	18	95	7	7	2	1	1	0	8	0	20	2	0
Richardson, Beau, Bat.*	5	4	.556	3.54	16	6	0	0	3	1	61	68	253	29	24	2	0	2	4	18	1	35	3	1
Rodriguez, Hector, Low.	2	6	.250	5.43	15	13	0	0	0	0	66.1	79	299	48	40	3	5	6	3	28	0	54	2	0
Rodriguez, Jose, Ver.	1	2	.333	5.97	17	0	0	0	5	0	31.2	29	155	28	21	0	1	1	1	27	0	40	12	1
Rodriguez, Juan, Wil.	2	2	.500	3.14	19	7	0	0	7	3	57.1	48	236	24	20	3	0	2	1	22	0	31	3	0
Rogelstad, Jeremy, Bat.	0	3	.000	3.77	24	0	0	0	14	2	45.1	39	190	19	19	5	3	3	2	15	1	30	1	0
Rogers, Brad, Aber.	0	1	1.000	5.17	17	0	0	0	9	2	31.1	32	138	24	18	5	0	2	2	11	0	21	2	0
Rogers, Michael, M.V.	8	4	.667	3.60	15	15	0	0	0	0	75	70	328	33	30	6	2	2	8	31	0	64	9	0
Rohr, Matthew, Aber.*	0	1	.000	12.64	14	0	0	0	6	0	15.2	30	90	24	22	4	2	1	1	10	0	12	4	1
Rueckel, Danny, Ver.	1	1	.500	1.53	10	0	0	0	9	3	17.2	12	70	8	3	0	0	1	2	3	1	23	4	0
Russ, Chris, S.I.	0	0	.000	4.70	4	0	0	0	1	0	7.2	7	31	4	4	1	0	0	2	0	6	0	0
Sanchez, Humberto, One.	2	2	.500	3.62	9	9	0	0	0	0	32.1	29	141	18	13	1	0	0	1	21	0	26	2	0
Sanders, Shane, H.V.	1	3	.250	3.23	24	0	0	0	18	7	30.2	34	138	16	11	2	3	0	1	17	1	21	3	2
Sandoval, Marcos, Aub.	2	3	.400	3.48	25	0	0	0	11	1	44	40	189	20	17	1	0	1	3	20	1	39	5	0
Santana, Eddy, Ver.	0	0	.000	3.00	4	0	0	0	3	0	6	5	26	2	2	0	0	0	3	0	1	0	0
Schneider, Jonathan, Wil.	0	0	.000	7.40	16	0	0	0	6	0	20.2	25	99	18	17	4	1	0	4	9	0	8	1	0
Schweitzer, Scott, N.J.*	2	1	.667	2.93	23	0	0	0	6	1	30.2	20	132	10	10	0	1	0	0	23	1	34	6	0
Scobie, Jason, Bkn.	2	2	.500	3.07	8	7	1	1	1	1	41	36	168	16	14	2	0	2	1	12	0	34	1	1
Selmo, Santo, Jam.	0	0	.000	5.87	8	0	0	0	2	0	15.1	21	73	11	10	1	0	1	1	5	0	10	5	0
Shafer, Kurt, Wil.	4	0	1.000	0.84	10	2	1	0	3	2	32.1	22	122	5	3	0	1	0	0	4	0	19	0	0
Sheffield, Christopher, Aub.	1	1	.500	9.00	6	0	0	0	2	0	6	3	33	7	6	1	0	0	0	12	0	6	3	0
Sherman, Chris, Bkn.	1	1	.500	3.35	19	0	0	0	9	2	37.2	32	157	15	14	2	2	1	3	13	1	28	3	0
Shortslef, Josh, Wil.*	10	4	.714	3.33	14	13	0	0	0	0	75.2	84	325	36	28	2	5	2	4	18	1	37	1	2
Simon, Billy, Low.	0	1	.000	1.64	3	3	0	0	0	0	11	10	51	6	2	0	0	3	6	0	12	1	0
Slocum, Brian, M.V.	5	2	.714	2.60	11	11	0	0	0	0	55.1	47	223	19	16	1	2	1	2	14	0	48	3	0
Smith, Brandon, Low.	0	3	.000	8.82	7	5	0	0	0	0	16.1	20	73	19	16	1	0	2	2	4	0	7	5	0
Smith, Chris, Low.	3	3	.500	4.13	14	14	0	0	0	0	56.2	54	237	29	26	3	1	0	2	14	0	50	5	0
Southerland, Chip, M.V.	0	0	.000	5.63	5	0	0	0	1	0	8	7	34	5	5	0	0	2	3	0	8	3	0
Spivey, Melvin, Aber.	0	0	.000	5.82	14	0	0	0	4	1	17	22	84	12	11	0	0	2	4	8	1	19	3	1
Steen, Adam, Bat.	0	0	.000	2.45	12	0	0	0	3	0	22	19	91	6	6	2	1	1	0	5	0	15	1	0
Steinborn, Chris, One.*	0	1	.000	3.38	2	0	0	0	0	0	2.2	3	11	1	1	0	0	1	0	0	0	2	0	0
Stocks, Nick, N.J.	0	2	.000	5.73	7	7	0	0	0	0	22	28	107	14	14	0	0	1	2	13	0	24	0	0
Sutton, Zach, Aber.	0	1	.000	2.08	14	0	0	0	13	7	17.1	12	64	4	4	0	1	2	0	4	1	15	0	0
Tate, Matt, Aber.	1	4	.200	5.64	6	6	0	0	0	0	30.1	34	135	27	19	3	0	4	5	4	0	22	1	0
Teekel, Josh, N.J.	4	4	.500	3.30	16	13	0	0	0	0	73.2	58	298	31	27	3	1	1	6	24	0	66	8	0
Teeter, Travis, Aber.	1	0	1.000	3.00	2	2	0	0	0	0	12	14	52	6	4	2	0	1	2	0	8	0	0
Templet, Eric, Bkn.	1	0	1.000	3.72	7	0	0	0	5	1	9.2	14	47	5	4	0	0	0	5	1	12	1	0
Thorp, Paul, S.I.	1	0	1.000	3.60	1	1	0	0	0	0	5	8	25	4	2	0	1	0	0	3	0	1	0	0
Tomaszewski, Eliot, T.C.	0	3	.000	4.85	17	2	0	0	5	0	42.2	47	202	26	23	2	0	1	7	23	0	31	8	1
Torres, Andy, Aub.	4	3	.571	3.43	17	1	0	0	8	0	39.1	36	162	16	15	4	2	2	3	15	2	25	2	1
Treanor, Bryan, Jam.	1	0	1.000	8.17	17	0	0	0	2	0	25.1	42	133	25	23	3	3	2	1	11	0	22	1	0
Tribe, Phillip, S.I.	2	1	.667	3.16	15	0	0	0	4	0	25.2	26	117	12	9	0	2	1	0	10	1	27	1	1
Valdez, Jose, S.I.	1	3	.250	5.40	4	4	0	0	0	0	20	19	88	14	12	0	2	1	9	0	21	2	0
Van Gorder, Joe, N.J.*	1	0	1.000	2.70	2	2	0	0	0	0	10	12	43	3	3	1	0	0	0	8	0	8	2	0
Vaquedano, Jose, Low.	1	3	.250	4.35	22	0	0	0	7	0	39.1	46	183	33	19	4	2	3	3	18	1	35	6	0
Vargas, Nelson, H.V.	0	0	.000	5.23	7	0	0	0	3	0	10.1	16	52	7	6	0	0	0	3	0	9	1	0
Veras, Jose, H.V.	0	0	.000	0.00	2	2	0	0	0	0	7	2	28	0	0	0	0	0	0	5	0	7	0	0
Villarreal, Luis, Low.*	4	3	.571	4.45	16	9	0	0	0	0	62.2	68	265	33	31	2	1	1	1	14	0	47	3	1
Volquez, Bolivar, H.V.	0	0	.000	5.66	13	0	0	0	3	0	20.2	24	100	15	13	0	0	0	5	12	0	8	4	0
Walker, Jason, Ver.*	0	2	.000	17.80	14	0	0	0	3	0	14.2	31	102	30	29	2	1	1	6	23	0	9	18	0

Pitcher, Team	W	L	Pct.	ERA	G	GS	CG	ShO	GF	Sv.	IP	H	TBF	R	ER	HR	SH	SF	HB	BB	IBB	SO	WP	Bk.
Wallace, Shane, M.V.*	2	2	.500	3.42	5	5	0	0	0	0	26.1	31	115	12	10	3	0	1	4	6	0	15	0	0
Wang, Chien-ming, S.I.	6	1	.857	1.72	13	13	0	0	0	0	78.1	63	308	23	15	2	3	3	0	14	0	64	1	2
Warpinski, Ryan, Jam.	2	4	.333	2.48	15	15	0	0	0	0	76.1	70	335	31	21	3	3	4	8	29	0	61	1	1
Weir, Jayson, Bkn.*	0	0	.000	4.91	2	0	0	0	0	0	3.2	8	20	3	2	0	0	0	0	2	0	1	1	0
Wells, Clint, Low.*	4	1	.800	2.78	16	0	0	0	0	6	35.2	27	155	17	11	3	3	2	1	13	0	23	1	0
Westhoff, Billy, T.C.	2	9	.182	6.19	18	10	0	0	0	3	64	72	287	49	44	6	5	4	8	21	0	43	8	0
White, Chris, M.V.*	0	2	.000	5.00	14	0	0	0	0	6	18	19	89	15	10	1	1	3	2	11	0	12	3	0
Williams, Blake, N.J.	0	2	.000	1.69	2	2	0	0	0	0	5.1	2	19	1	1	1	0	0	1	8	0	8	0	0
Williamson, Willie, N.J.*	2	1	.667	2.25	6	6	0	0	0	0	24	12	104	8	6	1	0	3	3	19	0	27	3	1
Withelder, Gregory, N.J.*	0	1	.000	4.73	21	0	0	0	0	3	26.2	23	121	15	14	1	0	3	3	17	0	30	1	1
Wolf, Ross, Jam.	2	4	.333	4.66	11	11	0	0	0	0	46.1	56	209	30	24	4	1	3	3	12	0	18	2	1
Wyrick, Patrick, Jam.	0	0	.000	9.00	4	0	0	0	0	0	7	11	34	7	7	1	0	2	0	3	0	7	2	0
Yarbrough, Joe, H.V.*	0	1	.000	3.18	6	0	0	0	0	3	5.2	2	25	2	2	0	0	0	2	4	0	5	0	0
Yoo, Byung Mok, Low.	0	2	.000	5.18	19	0	0	0	0	12	1	24.1	26	114	14	14	1	1	1	3	16	1	29	5	1
Youman, Shane, Wil.*	4	0	1.000	1.45	20	0	0	0	0	12	5	37.1	25	143	7	6	1	1	0	2	8	0	48	1	0
Young, Simon, M.V.*	0	2	.000	4.25	19	2	0	0	2	2	48.2	44	208	31	23	2	3	5	3	22	1	39	4	0

COMBINATION SHUTOUTS: **Aberdeen** (5)—Farren-Makowsky-Cierlik, Hentgen-McCurdy, Maine-Rohr-Phillips, McCurdy-Makowsky-Berube-Edwards, Tate-Berube-Sutton. **Auburn** (11)—Hanson-Peterson, Hanson-Peterson-D. Bush, Houston-Sandoval, Mora-Maureau, Nin-Comolli-Peterson, Perkins-De Jong-Peterson, Perkins-Sheffield-Maureau, Plieness-Cardwell-D. Bush, Plieness-Maureau, Plieness-Peterson, Torres-Maureau. **Batavia** (5)—C. Cabrera-Moreno-Cierlik, Arteaga-Richardson-Moreno, Bourgeois-Richardson, Harrand-Busbin-Bryant. **Brooklyn** (6)—Y. Cabrera-McNabb-Lohrman, Deaton-Bowen, Deaton-Kentner-Sherman-Oglen, Kazmir-Cummings-McNabb, Kazmir-McNabb-Ogle, Scobie-McNabb-Ogle. **Hudson Valley** (0). **Jamestown** (2)—Greusel-Banks-Naylor-Bazardo, Kupper-Bazardo. **Lowell** (3)—Mateo-Vaquedano, Pahucki-Priola, C. Smith-H. Rodriguez-Vaquedano-Bazardo. **Mahoning Valley** (9)—Bl. Allen-Hernandez-Pennington, Kleine-Montano-White, Kleine-Young-Montano, Ramsey-Martin, Ramsey-Martin-Fausto, M. Rogers-Hernandez, Slocum-Hernandez, Slocum-Rich-Martin, Wallace-Kulp-Pennington. **New Jersey** (8)—Ciprian-Martinez-Schweitzer-Batista, Jaillet-D'Amato-Coleman-Withelder, Martinez-Schweitzer-Ewasko-Batista, Plancich-D'Amato-K. Johnson-Batista, Teekel-Ewasko, Teekel-Jaillet-Ewasko-D'Amato-Batista, Williams-Flynn-Teekel-Ewasko-Coleman, Williamson-Flynn-Schweitzer-Ewasko. **Oneota** (7)—L. Diaz-Myers-Figueroa, Dunn-Campbell-Figueroa, Dunn-L. Diaz-Figueroa, Pender-Figueroa, Pickford-Carlson, Pickford-Koenig-Figueroa, Sanchez-Campbell-Carlson-Figueroa. **Staten Island** (12)—Bicondoa-Meccage-Neitz-Brumit, Bicondoa-Tribe, Bicondoa-Tribe-Neitz-Brumit, Clark-Neitz-Brumit, Halsey-Meccage, Halsey-Tribe-Neitz, Isaacson-Brumit, Isaacson-Difranco, Isaacson-Reynolds-Brumit, Valdez-Neitz-Brumit, Wang-Brumit, Wang-Rada-Neitz. **Tri-City** (6)—Deleon-Flores, Flores-Bayrer-Gothreaux, Flores-Gothreaux, Hamilton-Bayrer-Gothreaux, Heitzman-Flores-Kramer, Mclemore-Bayrer-Gothreaux. **Vermont** (4)—Hinckley-S. Davis, Hinckley-O'Conner-Guerrero, Marceau-O'Conner, Rasner-Fiedler-O'Conner. **Williamsport** (8)—Beigh-Davila-Schneider, Beigh-Holt-Youman, Gravelle-Demaria, Novoa-Hart, Novoa-Owens, Ju. Rodriguez-Owens, Shafer-Youman, Shortslef-Owens-Ju. Rodriguez.

NO-HIT GAMES: None.

2002 FIELDING

TEAM

Team	G	PO	A	E	TC	DP	TP	PB	Pct.
Tri-City	75	1976	757	80	2813	69	0	13	.972
Auburn	76	2044	816	88	2948	64	0	17	.970
Aberdeen	76	2000	795	87	2882	53	0	17	.970
Staten Island	75	1986	814	92	2892	50	0	17	.968
New Jersey	76	1989	853	95	2937	54	0	3	.968
Brooklyn	76	2055	911	100	3066	72	0	17	.967
Mahoning Val.	76	2003	779	95	2877	48	0	15	.967
Williamsport	76	2035	790	99	2924	51	0	6	.966
Batavia	76	2058	902	110	3070	75	0	12	.964
Lowell	75	2012	741	109	2862	56	0	14	.962
Jamestown	75	1996	741	111	2848	61	0	17	.961
Oneonta	74	1996	772	116	2884	70	0	13	.960
Hudson Valley	75	1991	783	118	2892	58	0	15	.959
Vermont	75	1995	814	129	2938	59	0	22	.956

INDIVIDUAL

FIRST BASEMEN

NOTE: All caps denotes fielding-percentage leader based on 38 games for catchers, 51 for all other non-pitchers and 61 innings for pitchers. *Throws lefthanded.

Player, Team	Pct.	G	PO	A	E	TC	DP
Baldiris, Aaron, Bkn.	1.000	5	29	1	0	30	4
Barthelemy, Ryan, Bat.	.990	36	286	20	3	309	28
Bass, Chris, Wil.	1.000	3	16	0	0	16	1
Baxter, Andy, M.V.	.990	44	399	14	4	417	29
Blase, Blake, S.I.	.950	12	52	5	3	60	1
Bowman, Addison, Low.	.977	15	118	9	3	130	9
Broadway, Larry, Ver.*	.984	33	279	26	5	310	17
Buckley, James, Low.	1.000	2	10	0	0	10	0
Cafiero, Rob, Bat.	.977	48	403	30	10	443	39
Caligiuri, Jay, Bkn.	.985	13	119	9	2	130	14
Caravella, Drew, One.*	.987	45	415	33	6	454	39
Chop, Chad, Ver.*	.956	7	79	8	4	91	7
Christensen, Sam, Wil.	.988	20	159	11	2	172	7
Combs, Will, Aber.*	1.000	2	24	2	0	26	0
Concepcion, Alberto, Low.	1.000	1	6	0	0	6	0
Corr, Frank, Bkn.	.981	11	98	5	2	105	8
Cox, George, Aber.	1.000	1	2	0	0	2	0
Davies, Gregg, Aber.*	1.000	3	21	1	0	22	2
Drobiak, Jayson, S.I.	.979	29	224	14	5	243	23
Duran, Alexander, H.V.	1.000	1	1	0	0	1	0

Player, Team	Pct.	G	PO	A	E	TC	DP
Durazo, Ernie, Aub.	.973	18	131	14	4	149	12
Eldred, Brad, Wil.	.982	60	489	46	10	545	38
Gomez, Hose, M.V.	.500	1	1	0	1	2	0
Harper, Brett, Bkn.	.991	35	293	24	3	320	23
Hartig, Philip, Jam.	.990	33	265	18	3	286	20
Hileman, Jutt, N.J.	1.000	1	1	1	0	2	0
Hoover, Clint, T.C.	.984	8	57	4	1	62	7
Huggins, Mike, Aber.	.991	72	601	53	6	660	49
Johnson, Seth, Ver.	.984	18	120	4	2	126	12
Johnston, Clint, Aub.*	.991	60	489	51	5	545	42
Knox, Matt, M.V.	1.000	1	1	1	0	2	0
Loomis, Corey, One.	.000	1	0	0	0	0	0
Mackor, Jeff, T.C.	1.000	1	6	0	0	6	2
Mamula, Matt, S.I.	.995	41	368	23	2	393	16
Manfredonia, Sean, M.V.	1.000	4	15	1	0	16	0
Meihls, Mike, S.I.	1.000	1	11	0	0	11	2
Moore, Bryan, N.J.*	1.000	3	27	2	0	29	3
Nunez, Felix, H.V.	.991	50	396	23	4	423	31
O'Brien, Kevin, H.V.*	.972	36	253	27	8	288	19
Ontiveros, Jeffrey, Low.	.987	57	473	51	7	531	40
Ortiz, Daniel, Jam.	.989	10	83	4	1	88	8
Parker, Tyler, N.J.	1.000	1	9	0	0	9	2
Peavey, Bill, M.V.*	.997	35	277	15	1	293	15
Pitney, Jared, S.I.*	1.000	3	16	1	0	17	1
Rivero, Luis, Bat.	.000	1	0	0	0	0	0
Rodriguez, Andres, Bkn.	.980	19	185	13	4	202	14
Rojas, Tommy, S.I.	1.000	1	6	1	0	7	1
Roughton, Jody, One.	.980	20	184	11	4	199	18
Salmela, Andy, T.C.	.992	68	574	41	5	620	53
SANTOR, John, N.J.	.996	55	500	26	2	528	32
Schmitt, Billy, N.J.	.990	22	187	11	2	200	11
Simoneaux, Neil, M.V.	1.000	1	2	0	0	2	0
Siriveaw, Nom, Aub.	1.000	2	12	2	0	14	3
Tarbett, Brent, Low.	1.000	2	13	0	0	13	2
Thede, Matthew, Ver.	.977	5	37	5	1	43	4
Trezza, Alex, One.	.990	12	90	6	1	97	6
Weese, Nathan, Ver.	.993	19	139	11	1	151	15
Winegarden, Erik, Bat.	.857	1	5	1	1	7	1
Word, Robert, Jam.*	.986	36	276	12	4	292	29

SECOND BASEMEN

Player, Team	Pct.	G	PO	A	E	TC	DP
Abreu, Angel, M.V.	1.000	4	8	6	0	14	1
Abreu, Nielsen, Bat.	.991	21	52	57	1	110	10
Arnold, Eric, Aub.	.867	3	6	7	2	15	2

Player, Team	Pct.	G	PO	A	E	TC	DP
Asprilla, Avelino, Wil.	1.000	2	3	3	0	6	0
Blackburn, Franco, Jam.	.857	3	5	7	2	14	3
Boran, Patrick, Low.	.962	12	21	29	2	52	2
Boyer, Kyle, N.J.	.909	3	4	6	1	11	0
Cano, Robinson, S.I.	.989	20	37	51	1	89	12
Castillo, Osmar, Low.	.976	8	14	27	1	42	7
Cockrell, Michael, Wil.	.923	4	4	8	1	13	1
Collum, Mike, Wil.	.945	39	67	105	10	182	18
Conlisk, Jason, Ver.	.969	63	119	165	9	293	36
Cruz, Alex, Wil.	1.000	5	14	11	0	25	1
Cuello, Domingo, Jam.	.930	9	15	25	3	43	7
DEL ROSARIO, Manny, Aber.	.974	64	104	154	7	265	28
Dorsey, Ryan, H.V.	1.000	6	11	17	0	28	4
Duran, Alexander, H.V.	1.000	2	1	1	0	2	1
Durham, Tyler, N.J.	.966	53	88	169	9	266	28
Encarnacion, Henry, Ver.	.963	7	14	12	1	27	3
Falu, Melvin, N.J.	.989	18	48	45	1	94	9
Gonzalez, Patrick, Aber.	.984	14	27	35	1	63	5
Guerrero, Jorge, Jam.	.864	3	7	12	3	22	6
Harrington, Jesse, T.C.	.924	26	45	52	8	105	12
Harris, Mike, S.I.	1.000	3	3	5	0	8	0
Heath, Demetrius, One.	.972	33	64	110	5	179	25
Helps, Jason, Jam.	.000	1	0	0	0	0	0
Isenhower, Jeremy, Bat.	1.000	3	7	6	0	13	2
Jiannetti, Joe, Bkn.	.965	49	104	144	9	257	31
Koutnik, Jared, S.I.	1.000	2	1	4	0	5	0
Lambin, Chase, Bkn.	.911	12	16	25	4	45	5
Larkin, Shaun, M.V.	.965	70	96	154	9	259	24
Loomis, Corey, One.	.908	19	31	38	7	76	10
Lopez, Gabe, S.I.	.986	44	78	136	3	217	17
Mancebo, Deni, Ver.	1.000	6	9	15	0	24	1
Newman, Ryan, Wil.	.942	24	32	49	5	86	4
Nunez, Alexis, Bat.	.913	14	30	33	6	69	16
Ordorica, Eric, Jam.	.960	23	42	53	4	99	10
Patterson, Ty, H.V.	.938	8	9	21	2	32	1
Perez, Jerson, Aub.	.867	2	4	9	2	15	3
Randel, Kevin, Jam.	.930	24	42	65	8	115	16
Riley, Ryan, H.V.	.958	55	112	136	11	259	26
Rivera, William, Aub.	.964	72	119	200	12	331	41
Robertson, Cedric, H.V.	.000	1	0	0	1	1	0
Rodriguez, Carlos, Bat.	.000	1	0	0	0	0	0
Rodriguez, Raul, Aber.	.667	1	1	1	1	3	0
St. Clair, Jason, H.V.	.935	13	30	28	4	62	4
Sandoval, Jlalil, T.C.	.958	55	81	149	10	240	34
Silvera, Andres, Bat.	.967	28	56	91	5	152	16
Simoneaux, Neil, N.J.-M.V.	.975	12	14	25	1	40	5
Soriano, Jairo, Aber.	.882	4	7	8	2	17	2
Stone, Greg, Low.	.971	35	72	98	5	175	20
Uegawachi, Bryce, M.V.	1.000	9	8	14	0	22	5
Vasquez, Wuillians, S.I.	.933	12	17	25	3	45	3
Wardinsky, Ryan, Bat.	1.000	14	25	43	0	68	5
Watson, Rob, One.	.970	22	34	63	3	100	11
West, Eric, Low.	.938	20	26	49	5	80	9
Whealy, Blake, Bkn.	.944	20	25	59	5	89	8
Wyant, Hunter, Jam.	.974	25	44	70	3	117	13
Duran, Alexander, H.V.	.750	8	4	8	4	16	0
Ellerson, Brian, Ver.	.882	12	6	24	4	34	1
Fahey, Brandon, Aber.	1.000	12	6	13	0	19	2
Falu, Melvin, N.J.	1.000	4	1	10	0	11	0
Garcia, David, One.	.933	6	3	11	1	15	1
German, Cesar, Aub.	.909	37	26	64	9	99	10
Gonzalez, Patrick, Aber.	.924	35	18	55	6	79	5
Guerrero, Jorge, Jam.	1.000	2	3	0	0	3	0
Guglielmelli, Brad, M.V.	1.000	5	3	5	0	8	0
Haase, Jeff, M.V.	.500	2	1	0	1	2	0
Hanson, Travis, N.J.	.925	63	27	145	14	186	11
Harper, Brett, Bkn.	.833	15	8	17	5	30	3
Harrison, Vince, H.V.	.911	15	12	29	4	45	6
Hassey, Brad, Aub.	.902	21	18	37	6	61	4
Helps, Jason, Jam.	1.000	1	0	1	0	1	0
Hubele, Ryan, Aber.	.846	9	3	8	2	13	0
Johnson, Seth, Ver.	.667	2	0	2	1	3	1
Jones, Terry, Bat.	.940	43	39	102	9	150	5
Knox, Matt, M.V.	.821	13	5	18	5	28	1
Koutnik, Jared, S.I.	.955	11	4	17	1	22	0
Lambin, Chase, Bkn.	.882	24	12	55	9	76	4
Larson, Jan, T.C.	1.000	3	7	4	0	11	0
Lepine, Olivier, Jam.	.000	2	0	0	0	0	0
Loomis, Corey, One.	.600	2	0	3	2	5	0
Mannix, Brendan, Bkn.	.875	3	3	4	1	8	0
Maples, Chris, One.	.870	31	22	45	10	77	3
McDougall, Marshall, M.V.	1.000	1	1	2	0	3	0
Meihls, Mike, S.I.	.923	10	5	7	1	13	0
Menocal, Victor, Bat.	.750	3	2	1	1	4	0
Merkle, Tom, Jam.	.931	12	8	19	2	29	2
Newman, Ryan, Wil.	1.000	7	1	11	0	12	0
Norris, Shawn, Ver.	.894	40	30	80	13	123	7
Ohtsuka, Yoshiyuki, Wil.	1.000	2	2	1	0	3	0
Ordorica, Eric, Jam.	.947	19	23	48	4	75	8
Ortiz, Daniel, Jam.	1.000	1	0	1	0	1	0
Osborn, Pat, Aub.	.919	52	31	106	12	149	4
Peavey, Pat, T.C.	.967	38	24	63	3	90	0
Peguero, Miguel, M.V.	1.000	9	1	13	0	14	1
Puccinelli, John, Jam.	.917	37	25	41	6	72	5
Recio, Bolivar, Aber.	.839	10	6	20	5	31	2
Riley, Ryan, H.V.	.800	6	3	9	3	15	0
Rodriguez, Edgar, Bkn.	.941	8	1	15	1	17	1
Rosario, Olmo, H.V.	.893	13	8	17	3	28	3
Roughton, Jody, One.	.920	8	6	17	2	25	1
Russell, Mike, Aber.	.846	7	3	8	2	13	1
Santor, John, N.J.	1.000	1	0	1	0	1	0
Schmitt, Billy, N.J.	.897	14	4	31	4	39	1
Simoneaux, Neil, M.V.	.833	5	1	4	1	6	0
Siriveaw, Nom, Aub.	.946	17	8	27	2	37	2
Soriano, Jairo, Aber.	.925	22	9	28	3	40	1
Sweeney, Tim, Ver.	.886	11	9	22	4	35	0
Vasquez, Wuillians, S.I.	.925	25	12	37	4	53	6
Wardinsky, Ryan, Bat.	.944	8	6	11	1	18	1
Watson, Rob, One.	.970	31	25	73	3	101	4
Weese, Nathan, Ver.	.853	14	7	22	5	34	1
Whealy, Blake, Bkn.	.922	28	17	54	6	77	5
Wyant, Hunter, Jam.	.886	20	10	29	5	44	2
Zamora, Hector, S.I.	.910	32	16	55	7	78	2

SECOND BASEMEN WITH TWO OR MORE TEAMS

Player, Team	Pct.	G	PO	A	E	TC	DP
Simoneaux, Neil, N.J.	1.000	6	10	16	0	26	2
Simoneaux, Neil, M.V.	.929	6	4	9	1	14	3

THIRD BASEMEN

Player, Team	Pct.	G	PO	A	E	TC	DP
Abreu, Angel, M.V.	1.000	1	0	1	0	1	0
Abreu, Nielsen, Bat.	1.000	3	0	1	0	1	0
Alcala, Arian, Low.	.921	30	18	64	7	89	3
Arnold, Eric, Aub.	.875	2	4	3	1	8	0
Asprilla, Avelino, Wil.	.929	4	7	6	1	14	2
Baldiris, Aaron, Bkn.	.852	6	4	19	4	27	2
Barthelemy, Ryan, Bat.	.931	26	27	54	6	87	10
BASS, Chris, Wil.	.932	67	55	110	12	177	8
Blackburn, Franco, Jam.	1.000	1	1	1	0	2	0
Boran, Patrick, Low.	.918	24	18	38	5	61	2
Bowman, Addison, Low.	.833	1	2	3	1	6	0
Collum, Mike, Wil.	.667	1	1	1	1	3	0
Concepcion, Alberto, Low.	.939	22	24	38	4	66	2
Covarrubias, Nick, T.C.	.899	36	33	56	10	99	7
Del Rosario, Manny, Aber.	.750	3	1	2	1	4	0
Dragicevich, Scott, Aub.	.714	3	2	3	2	7	0
Drobiak, Jayson, S.I.	.000	1	0	0	0	0	0
Duncan, Trae, H.V.	.896	39	29	66	11	106	6

SHORTSTOPS

Player, Team	Pct.	G	PO	A	E	TC	DP
Abreu, Angel, M.V.	.972	9	15	20	1	36	2
Abreu, Nielsen, Bat.	.978	12	12	33	1	46	4
Adams, Russ, Aub.	.963	30	48	81	5	134	18
Andino, Robert, Jam.	.976	9	11	30	1	42	2
Asprilla, Avelino, Wil.	.966	15	23	34	2	59	7
Blount, Pierre, H.V.	.000	1	0	0	0	0	0
Boran, Patrick, Low.	.933	8	12	16	2	30	3
Bowden, Nathan, S.I.	.849	15	18	44	11	73	4
Boyer, Kyle, N.J.	.925	43	58	103	13	174	18
Cano, Robinson, S.I.	.846	2	6	5	2	13	0
Cockrell, Michael, Wil.	1.000	5	9	12	0	21	0
Collum, Mike, Wil.	.940	17	25	38	4	67	8
Cuello, Domingo, Wil.	.778	1	1	6	2	9	2
Cuevas, Aneudi, T.C.	.983	36	74	95	3	172	24
Durham, Tyler, N.J.	.857	3	7	5	2	14	2
Encarnacion, Henry, Ver.	.897	50	76	151	26	253	24
Fahey, Brandon, Aber.	.961	55	88	132	9	229	20
Falu, Melvin, N.J.	.963	19	28	49	3	80	7
Fernando, Osvaldo, T.C.	.800	3	4	4	2	10	0
Garcia, David, One.	.841	12	12	25	7	44	5
Gonzalez, Patrick, Aber.	.976	16	15	26	1	42	7

Player, Team	Pct.	G	PO	A	E	TC	DP
Hanson, Travis, N.J.	.920	11	11	35	4	50	2
Harrington, Jesse, T.C.	1.000	1	1	3	0	4	1
Hassey, Brad, Aub.	.956	42	71	101	8	180	23
Helps, Jason, Jam.	.941	7	12	20	2	34	4
Hudson, William, Bkn.	1.000	3	2	8	0	10	1
Koutnik, Jared, S.I.	.857	1	4	2	1	7	1
Lambin, Chase, Bkn.	.943	8	10	23	2	35	3
Lee, Taber, Wil.	.948	40	64	100	9	173	15
Loomis, Corey, One.	.923	8	15	21	3	39	6
Menocal, Victor, Bat.	1.000	1	2	2	0	4	1
Mercedes, Anselmo, H.V.	.953	39	58	104	8	170	13
Newman, Ryan, Wil.	.923	4	4	8	1	13	1
Ordorica, Eric, Jam.	.913	22	35	60	9	104	15
Peguero, Miguel, M.V.	.938	19	28	47	5	80	6
Perez, Jerson, Aub.	.960	5	11	13	1	25	2
RAGSDALE, Corey, Bkn.	.966	65	116	199	11	326	45
Ramirez, Hanley, Low.	.935	22	47	53	7	107	9
Randel, Kevin, Jam.	.899	33	50	75	14	139	15
Riley, Ryan, H.V.	.888	19	25	46	9	80	8
Rodriguez, Carlos, Bat.	.944	61	122	182	18	322	41
Romprey, Ed, One.	.914	52	82	140	21	243	36
St. Clair, Jason, H.V.	.924	22	33	52	7	92	9
Sandoval, Jjalil, T.C.	.750	1	1	2	1	4	0
Shier, Peter, Aber.	.944	12	20	47	4	71	7
Simoneaux, Neil, N.J.-M.V.	.880	20	25	41	9	75	6
Soriano, Jairo, Aber.	.933	5	7	7	1	15	1
Stone, Greg, Low.	.875	3	3	4	1	8	3
Sweeney, Tim, Ver.	.934	28	34	80	8	122	18
Tejeda, Ferdin, S.I.	.969	47	53	136	6	195	18
Topham, Andrew, T.C.	.957	38	63	117	8	188	29
Torres, Eider, M.V.	.945	19	18	51	4	73	11
Uegawachi, Bryce, M.V.	.937	34	34	85	8	127	17
Vasquez, Wuilians, S.I.	.881	12	9	28	5	42	4
Wardinsky, Ryan, Bat.	.909	6	4	16	2	22	3
Watson, Rob, One.	.870	4	5	15	3	23	2
West, Eric, Low.	.938	44	81	101	12	194	18
Wyant, Hunter, Jam.	.821	9	6	26	7	39	2

SHORTSTOPS WITH TWO OR MORE TEAMS

Player, Team	Pct.	G	PO	A	E	TC	DP
Simoneaux, Neil, N.J.	.870	6	7	13	3	23	2
Simoneaux, Neil, M.V.	.885	14	18	28	6	52	4

OUTFIELDERS

Player, Team	Pct.	G	PO	A	E	TC	DP
Aleman, Carlos, Low.	1.000	1	2	0	0	2	0
Aliendo, Humberto, Wil.	.953	20	41	0	2	43	0
Andujar, Elvin, Bkn.	.950	16	19	0	1	20	0
Apotheker, Joseph, Jam.	.956	33	40	3	2	45	1
Bankston, Wes, H.V.	.947	8	15	3	1	19	0
Barclay, Mike, Low.	1.000	5	8	0	0	8	0
Benson, Donald, Low.	.971	38	64	4	2	70	0
Blackburn, Franco, Jam.	.952	24	37	3	2	42	0
Blount, Pierre, H.V.	.910	44	69	2	7	78	1
Bocchino, Anthony, Bkn.*	.988	48	76	4	1	81	0
Boran, Patrick, Low.	1.000	7	13	0	0	13	0
Bowman, Addison, Low.	.983	56	110	4	2	116	1
Brackley, Carlos, Low.	1.000	4	9	0	0	9	0
Brown, Anthony, Ver.	.928	42	74	3	6	83	1
Brown, Dustin, Low.	.929	15	26	0	2	28	0
Campos, Mario, Low.	.938	52	114	6	8	128	0
Candelario, Luis, H.V.	1.000	10	8	1	0	9	0
Carson, Matt, S.I.	.986	42	65	7	1	73	2
Cespedes, Robinson, T.C.	.967	69	142	5	5	152	2
Chavez, Ender, Bkn.*	.980	55	92	8	2	102	1
Chop, Chad, Ver.*	.951	63	95	2	5	102	0
Combs, Will, Aber.*	1.000	19	22	0	0	22	0
Conroy, Mike, M.V.*	.958	55	86	5	4	95	2
Corr, Frank, Bkn.	.969	18	27	4	1	32	1
Cortes, Jorge, Wil.*	.950	66	149	3	8	160	0
Covarrubias, Nick, T.C.	.957	14	22	0	1	23	0
Dancy, Cliff, Bat.	.949	42	70	4	4	78	1
Davies, Gregg, Aber.*	.989	53	77	9	1	87	0
Davis, Rajai, Wil.	1.000	1	4	0	0	4	0
Dean, Herman, One.	.918	27	45	0	4	49	0
De Leon, Virgilio, One.	.935	18	28	1	2	31	0
Devarez, Noel, Bkn.	.818	8	9	0	2	11	0
Durazo, Ernie, Aub.	.917	11	11	0	1	12	0
Eldred, Brad, Wil.	1.000	1	1	0	0	1	0
Estrada, Rafael, N.J.	1.000	13	7	0	0	7	0
Fitzpatrick, Reggie, Ver.*	.981	68	153	3	3	159	0
Francisco, Ben, M.V.	.978	57	131	3	3	137	0
Gilhooly, Tim, Aber.	.940	56	92	2	6	100	1
Gomes, Joey, H.V.	.956	68	108	1	5	114	0
Gomez, Hose, M.V.	1.000	22	27	0	0	27	0
Gonce, Garris, N.J.	1.000	24	39	2	0	41	1
Gorecki, Reid, N.J.	.982	70	150	13	3	166	4
Goss, Michael, Low.*	.977	21	41	1	1	43	0
Granderson, Curtis, One.	.989	51	84	3	1	88	2
Green, Steve, N.J.	.917	7	11	0	1	12	0
Guglielmelli, Brad, M.V.	1.000	1	1	0	0	1	0
Hermida, Jeremy, Jam.	.947	13	17	1	1	19	0
Hileman, Jutt, N.J.	.972	22	34	1	1	36	0
Hubele, Ryan, Aber.	1.000	3	2	0	0	2	0
Jimenez, Rich, Aub.	.978	33	44	1	1	46	0
Jordan, Eddie, Aber.	.982	34	52	2	1	55	0
Kennedy, Jason, One.	1.000	13	17	1	0	18	0
Kimberley, Glynn, Aub.	.947	14	15	3	1	19	0
Kingsbury, Bobby, Wil.*	.969	35	59	3	2	64	0
Laidlaw, Jacob, Jam.	.950	62	90	5	5	100	0
Louisa, Lorvin, Ver.	.956	43	59	6	3	68	0
Lytle, Chaz, Wil.	.969	45	91	2	3	96	1
Macchi, Brandon, T.C.*	1.000	38	68	1	0	69	0
Majewski, Val, Aber.*	.988	30	81	4	1	86	1
Marshall, Andre, Bat.	.927	46	95	6	8	109	1
McClanahan, Scott, S.I.	.988	45	77	2	1	80	1
McRoberts, Mark, Bat.	.818	13	17	1	4	22	0
Meath, Matt, Wil.	1.000	19	24	0	0	24	0
Mendez, Victor, One.	.973	59	145	1	4	150	1
Monette, Daylon, N.J.*	1.000	8	13	0	0	13	0
Mongeluzzo, Anthony, Ver.	1.000	3	1	0	0	1	0
Moore, Bryan, N.J.*	1.000	1	1	0	0	1	0
Nikolic, Adam, H.V.*	.976	71	162	4	4	170	0
Ortiz, Daniel, Jam.	.000	3	0	0	1	1	0
Owens, Justin, Aub.*	.983	63	109	9	2	120	1
Porfirio, A.J., Aub.	.969	39	55	8	2	65	1
Pridie, Jason, H.V.	.952	7	20	0	1	21	0
Ramistella, John, S.I.	.959	37	46	1	2	49	1
Ramos, Victor, Wil.	1.000	1	2	0	0	2	0
Reed, Eric, Jam.*	.985	60	189	3	3	195	0
Reuss, Jason, T.C.	.947	23	35	1	2	38	0
Reynolds, Wilton, One.	.975	61	112	4	3	119	0
Rivera, Eric, Bat.	.979	48	89	6	2	97	0
Rivero, Luis, Bat.	.918	28	41	4	4	49	1
Roberson, Chris, Bat.	.958	60	129	8	6	143	2
Robertson, Cedric, H.V.	.917	33	53	2	5	60	0
Rodriguez, Edgar, Bkn.	1.000	3	2	0	0	2	0
ROHLEDER, Andy, Jam.	.992	64	125	4	1	130	0
Rojas, Ricardo, M.V.	1.000	6	13	0	0	13	0
Santor, John, N.J.	.000	1	0	0	0	0	0
Sardinha, Bronson, S.I.	.902	31	54	1	6	61	0
Scala, Mickey, Wil.	1.000	3	3	1	0	4	0
Seuss, Adam, T.C.	.968	61	89	3	3	95	2
Sheaffer, Jon, S.I.	1.000	23	32	0	0	32	0
Simoneaux, Neil, M.V.	.000	1	0	0	0	0	0
Siriveaw, Nom, Aub.	1.000	32	55	1	0	56	0
Slack, Jonathan, Bkn.*	1.000	41	54	4	0	58	2
Stephenson, Neal, Aber.	.984	55	119	6	2	127	0
Stone, Greg, Low.	.974	32	70	4	2	76	0
Swope, Matt, Ver.	1.000	7	4	1	0	5	0
Thompson, Kevin, S.I.	.960	29	44	4	2	50	2
Tolotti, Jeff, N.J.*	1.000	17	29	0	0	29	0
Toner, John, Bkn.	.960	50	66	6	3	75	1
Treadway, Jared, S.I.	1.000	9	7	1	0	8	0
Turay, Haj, Bkn.	.947	38	54	0	3	57	0
Urquhart, Adrian, Ver.	.905	13	18	1	2	21	0
Vandever, Joey, N.J.	.931	68	90	4	7	101	0
Van Every, Jon, M.V.*	.963	38	77	2	3	82	1
Verbryke, Eric, S.I.*	.946	29	49	4	3	56	0
Watts, Derran, Bkn.	1.000	9	15	1	0	16	0
Waugh, Jason, Aub.	.976	66	116	7	3	126	0
Weese, Nathan, Ver.	1.000	2	3	0	0	3	0
Whealy, Blake, Bkn.	1.000	8	11	0	0	11	0
Whitesides, Jake, T.C.	.947	38	66	5	4	75	0
Woodrow, Justin, N.J.	.956	28	43	0	2	45	0
Word, Robert, Jam.*	.929	12	13	0	1	14	0
Wright, Brian, M.V.	.961	63	95	4	4	103	0

CATCHERS

Player, Team	Pct.	G	PO	A	E	TC	DP	PB
Aleman, Carlos, Low.	.981	32	224	28	5	257	3	9
Allec, Jason, One.	1.000	3	19	3	0	22	1	2
Anderson, Brian, Ver.	.993	35	250	36	2	288	1	11
Anderson, Jimmy, Bkn.	.989	27	158	26	2	186	3	7

Player, Team	Pct.	G	PO	A	E	TC	DP	PB
Arlis, Patrick, Jam.	.982	45	248	25	5	278	1	9
Ayala, Abraham, Bkn.	1.000	25	214	18	0	232	0	3
Blackburn, Alex, Aub.	.982	22	145	15	3	163	1	2
Bridges, Josh, N.J.	1.000	8	31	2	0	33	0	0
Brown, Dustin, Low.	1.000	1	6	0	0	6	0	0
Buckley, James, Low.	.947	21	131	12	8	151	0	3
Carlin, Luke, One.	.977	44	343	38	9	390	2	8
Chapman, Travis, Wil.	.989	52	342	34	4	380	1	5
CHAUNCEY, Clinton, N.J.	.997	46	299	39	1	339	2	1
Clements, Zachary, Bkn.	1.000	6	52	10	0	62	0	1
Concepcion, Alberto, Low.	.982	25	198	22	4	224	0	2
Cordell, Brent, H.V.	.989	69	447	79	6	532	7	13
Cox, George, Aber.	.968	9	53	7	2	62	2	1
Deck, Ronald, H.V.	.952	6	38	2	2	42	0	0
Devine, Dean, Wil.	.917	3	19	3	2	24	0	1
Diaz, M.V.	1.000	3	17	0	0	17	0	0
Eickhorst, Chris, N.J.	1.000	5	32	5	0	37	0	0
Emmerick, Josh, Ver.	.978	33	236	28	6	270	3	8
Grzecka, Casey, Jam.	.991	13	103	5	1	109	0	3
Haase, Jeff, M.V.	.982	31	200	24	4	228	0	1
Hietpas, Joe, Bkn.	.985	25	170	23	3	196	2	4
Hubele, Ryan, Aber.	.992	33	243	17	2	262	0	9
Jones, Kendall, T.C.	.979	19	133	8	3	144	1	5
Kessick, Jon, Aber.	.992	15	108	9	1	118	0	1
Lepine, Olivier, Jam.	.984	19	120	5	2	127	1	5
Mackor, Jeff, T.C.	.989	29	171	16	2	189	1	3
Manfred, Brian, Bat.	.972	18	120	18	4	142	0	2
McDonald, Kevin, One.	.985	30	170	23	3	196	1	3
McGarvey, Randy, T.C.	.993	39	244	22	2	268	0	5
McRoberts, Mark, Bat.	.987	22	140	16	2	158	2	5
Meihls, Mike, S.I.	1.000	5	19	2	0	21	0	0
Mejia, Manuel, Wil.	.971	8	28	6	1	35	0	0
Molina, Angel, Jam.	1.000	3	27	2	0	29	0	0
Myers, Kenton, M.V.	1.000	9	49	5	0	54	0	3
Parker, Tyler, N.J.	.959	24	163	23	8	194	1	2
Porter, Thomas, H.V.	.950	3	17	2	1	20	0	2
Pratt, Trent, Bat.	.991	34	184	32	2	218	0	3
Ramos, Victor, Wil.	.983	30	151	20	3	174	0	0
Reynoso, Danilo, Bkn.	.917	2	20	2	2	24	0	2
Richmond, Paul, Aub.	.983	33	256	29	5	290	1	7
Rickon, Jim, M.V.	.000	1	0	0	0	0	0	0
Riggans, Shawn, H.V.	.971	7	29	4	1	34	0	0
Robinson-Pierce, Whitney, Aber.	.980	14	87	12	2	101	0	3
Rodriguez, Robert, Ver.	.968	9	50	11	2	63	0	2
Rojas, Tommy, S.I.	.997	38	293	34	1	328	6	11
Russell, Mike, Aber.	.971	12	56	12	2	70	0	3
Santos, Omir, S.I.	.975	37	323	29	9	361	1	6
Schneider, John, Aub.	.992	34	226	32	2	260	2	8
Schneider, Michael, Ver.	1.000	6	52	5	0	57	0	1
Wallace, Dave, M.V.	.975	42	309	45	9	363	2	6
Winegarden, Erik, Bat.	1.000	7	47	10	0	57	0	2

PITCHERS

Player, Team	Pct.	G	PO	A	E	TC	DP
Acosta, Anthony, Bkn.	.750	8	1	2	1	4	1
Acosta, Manuel, S.I.	.500	3	0	2	2	4	0
Allen, Blake, M.V.*	.929	15	2	11	1	14	0
Allen, Brian, H.V.	1.000	14	2	5	0	7	0
Ally, Ben, T.C.	1.000	9	2	1	0	3	0
Anderson, Julius, H.V.	.778	24	2	5	2	9	1
Anez, Omar, Bkn.	.941	19	5	11	1	17	0
Arteaga, Erick, Bat.	1.000	12	8	12	0	20	0
Autrey, Scott, H.V.	1.000	11	1	7	0	8	0
Balan, Ryan, Low.	1.000	4	1	2	0	3	0
Banks, Tyler, Jam.	1.000	13	4	2	0	6	0
Barlow, Chris, Ver.	1.000	5	2	4	0	6	0
Barrios, Rafael, One.	.000	2	0	0	0	0	0
Basilio, Manuel, H.V.	1.000	3	1	0	0	1	0
Batista, Roberto, N.J.	.923	27	4	8	1	13	1
Bayer, Russ, Wil.*	1.000	17	1	5	0	6	0
Bayrer, Thomas, T.C.	1.000	11	1	9	0	10	1
Bazardo, Yorman, Jam.	1.000	25	1	4	0	5	0
Beaven, John, H.V.	.800	17	1	3	1	5	0
Beck, Ken, Ver.	1.000	14	3	1	0	4	0
Beigh, David, Wil.	.938	13	8	7	1	16	0
Bell, Gary, S.I.*	1.000	6	2	9	0	11	0
Bergmann, Jason, Ver.	.944	14	6	11	1	18	1
Berube, Martin, Aber.	.941	17	5	11	1	17	1
Bicondoa, Ryan, S.I.	.971	14	4	30	1	35	0
Blalock, Casey, Jam.	.909	23	4	6	1	11	0
Blethen, Matt, M.V.*	.667	16	0	2	1	3	0
Bomer, Alan, S.I.	1.000	2	0	1	0	1	0

Player, Team	Pct.	G	PO	A	E	TC	DP
Bourgeois, Nick, Bat.*	1.000	6	1	3	0	4	0
Bowen, Chad, Bkn.	1.000	17	5	12	0	17	0
Brewer, Jeff, Bkn.	.000	2	0	0	0	0	0
Brewster, Derek, Bat.	1.000	4	1	1	0	2	0
Brockman, Dave, N.J.	1.000	12	1	2	0	3	0
Brumit, Matt, S.I.	1.000	33	1	4	0	5	0
Bryant, Whit, Bat.*	1.000	16	3	12	0	15	0
Bulger, Brian, H.V.	1.000	12	7	5	0	12	1
Busbin, Brad, Jam.	.500	11	1	0	1	2	0
Bush, David, Aub.	1.000	18	3	0	0	3	0
Bush, Jason, Jam.	1.000	9	2	1	0	3	0
Bustillos, Oscar, H.V.	1.000	22	1	3	0	4	1
Byers, Waylon, Jam.*	.000	4	0	0	0	0	0
Cabrera, Carlos, Bat.	.950	15	6	13	1	20	1
Cabrera, Yunior, Bkn.*	1.000	8	0	10	0	10	0
Campbell, Dayle, One.	.900	20	2	7	1	10	0
Cardwell, Brian, Aub.	1.000	20	2	5	0	7	1
Carlson, Jesse, One.*	1.000	19	4	6	0	10	1
Carmona, Fausto, M.V.	.000	3	0	0	0	0	0
Carney, Jake, H.V.	1.000	13	0	1	0	1	0
Chenard, Ken, Bkn.	1.000	3	2	0	0	2	0
Cierlik, Jason, Aber.*	1.000	12	1	1	0	2	0
Ciprian, Wilson, N.J.	.857	15	5	13	3	21	0
Clark, Ray, S.I.	.625	8	0	5	3	8	0
Coleman, Kevin, N.J.	1.000	14	1	1	0	2	0
Comolli, Mark, Aub.	1.000	6	2	4	0	6	0
Connolly, Jon, One.*	.929	14	2	11	1	14	1
Cooney, Jim, Aber.*	1.000	25	3	7	0	10	0
Crohan, Thomas, Jam.*	1.000	7	0	4	0	4	0
CROMER, Jason, H.V.*	1.000	15	4	17	0	21	0
Culp, Todd, M.V.	.000	18	0	0	0	0	0
Cummings, Eric, Bkn.	1.000	5	1	1	0	2	0
D'Amato, Dan, N.J.*	.833	23	0	5	1	6	0
Danly, Ryan, Bkn.*	1.000	2	0	1	0	1	0
Davidson, Andy, N.J.*	.957	15	4	18	1	23	1
Davila, Marcus, Wil.	.900	15	3	6	1	10	0
Davis, Lance, Jam.	.800	11	0	4	1	5	0
Davis, Stockton, Ver.	1.000	19	5	10	0	15	0
Deaton, Kevin, Bkn.	.966	16	8	20	1	29	3
DeBarr, Nick, H.V.	1.000	4	2	4	0	6	1
DeJong, Jordan, Aub.	1.000	2	1	0	0	1	0
Delacruz, Eulogio, One.	.000	2	0	0	0	0	0
Deleon, Joey, T.C.	.960	16	3	21	1	25	2
DeMaria, Chris, Wil.	.929	16	5	8	1	14	0
Demontel, Jimmy, Jam.	.778	15	3	4	2	9	0
Diaz, Eddie, Ver.	.000	3	0	0	0	0	0
Diaz, Luis, One.	1.000	9	6	1	0	7	0
Dischiavo, John, H.V.	.000	3	0	0	0	0	0
DiFranco, Joseph, S.I.	1.000	6	2	0	0	2	0
Dunn, Gerald, One.	.889	5	2	6	1	9	1
Duran, J.P., T.C.	1.000	20	2	0	0	2	0
Edwards, Brad, Aber.*	.727	17	0	8	3	11	0
Elliott, Adam, Bkn.	.500	3	0	1	1	2	0
Ellis, Rob, H.V.*	.800	15	1	7	2	10	0
Evans, Kyle, M.V.	1.000	3	3	4	0	7	0
Evans, Louis, Jam.*	.333	5	1	0	2	3	0
Ewasko, Tod, N.J.	1.000	18	0	3	0	3	0
Farren, Dave, Aber.	.900	14	3	6	1	10	0
Felfoldi, Jonathan, Ver.*	1.000	3	1	2	0	3	0
Fiedler, Erik, Ver.	1.000	10	2	5	0	7	0
Figueroa, Juan, One.	1.000	28	1	5	0	6	0
Flores, Manuel, T.C.	1.000	15	1	7	0	8	0
Flynn, Brian, N.J.	.727	18	4	4	3	11	1
Galvez, Willy, Low.	.667	15	2	2	2	6	0
George, Jahseam, M.V.*	.000	1	0	0	0	0	0
Gerk, Jordan, One.*	.000	10	0	0	0	0	0
Gonzales, Jim, One.	1.000	7	1	1	0	2	0
Gonzalez, Jose, Low.	1.000	12	4	2	0	6	0
Gothreaux, Jared, T.C.	.786	28	3	8	3	14	1
Graham, Jason, One.	.750	14	2	1	1	4	0
Grant, Michael, Low.	1.000	22	2	7	0	9	0
Gravelle, Nick, Wil.*	.933	15	3	11	1	15	1
Greusel, Evan, Jam.	1.000	8	4	3	0	7	0
Guerrero, Tomas, Ver.	1.000	21	1	2	0	3	1
Gwaltney, Lee, Bat.	1.000	7	1	2	0	3	0
Hall, Shane, Low.	1.000	22	2	3	0	5	1
Halsey, Brad, S.I.*	.923	11	4	8	1	13	0
Hamilton, Mark, T.C.	.950	13	4	15	1	20	0
Hamman, Corey, One.	.000	3	0	0	0	0	0
Hammel, Jason, H.V.	1.000	13	1	5	0	6	1
Hancock, Everett, One.*	1.000	13	1	3	0	4	0
Hansack, Devorn, T.C.	1.000	12	2	4	0	6	0

Player, Team	Pct.	G	PO	A	E	TC	DP	Player, Team	Pct.	G	PO	A	E	TC	DP
Hanson, D.J., Aub.	1.000	9	2	9	0	11	1	Perkins, Vince, Aub.	.833	15	7	3	2	12	0
Harrand, Rob, Bat.	1.000	8	0	5	0	5	0	Peterson, Adam, Aub.	1.000	18	4	8	0	12	1
Hart, Alex, Wil.	.909	15	2	8	1	11	0	Phillips, Chase, Aber.	1.000	17	0	5	0	5	0
Hawksworth, Blake, N.J.	1.000	2	0	3	0	3	0	Pickford, Troy, One.	1.000	4	0	1	0	1	0
Heagen, Doug, Low.*	1.000	4	2	1	0	3	0	Pinango, Miguel, Bkn.	1.000	16	9	11	0	20	1
Heitzman, Aaron, T.C.*	.957	23	5	17	1	23	3	Plancich, Nick, N.J.	.857	7	1	5	1	7	0
Hentgen, Pat, Aber.	1.000	2	1	1	0	2	0	Pleiness, Chad, Aub.	.926	16	8	17	2	27	0
Hernandez, Michael, M.V.*	.909	22	3	7	1	11	0	Portobanco, Luz, Bkn.	1.000	2	0	1	0	1	0
Hinckley, Michael, Ver.*	.938	16	5	25	2	32	3	Primus, Carl, Jam.	1.000	24	3	8	0	11	1
Hines, Carlos, H.V.	1.000	5	5	6	0	11	0	Priola, John, Low.	1.000	27	1	9	0	10	0
Holt, Chris, Wil.	1.000	15	1	4	0	5	0	Prochaska, Mike, H.V.*	1.000	15	3	7	0	10	0
Houston, Ryan, Aub.	1.000	7	1	4	0	5	0	Puccinelli, John, Jam.	.000	1	0	0	0	0	0
Isaacson, Charlie, S.I.	1.000	14	6	10	0	16	1	Rada, Gerald, S.I.	1.000	21	1	5	0	6	0
Jaillet, Wes, N.J.	1.000	22	3	2	0	5	0	Ramirez, Ismael, Aub.	1.000	3	2	1	0	3	0
Johnson, Kelly, N.J.	1.000	16	2	5	0	7	0	Ramsey, Keith, M.V.*	.900	13	2	7	1	10	0
Johnson, Seth, Ver.	.000	1	0	0	0	0	0	Rasner, Darrell, Ver.	1.000	10	2	6	0	8	0
Johnston, Dave, Jam.	.750	10	3	3	2	8	0	Read, Robby, Bat.	.923	13	3	9	1	13	0
Johnston, Rikki, One.*	.857	15	7	17	4	28	1	Rengifo, Nohemar, Ver.	.667	12	1	1	1	3	0
Joyce, Michael, S.I.*	1.000	4	1	1	0	2	0	Reyes, Maximo, Bat.	.833	4	1	4	1	6	0
Kazmir, Scott, Bkn.*	1.000	5	0	2	0	2	0	Reynolds, Eric, S.I.*	.833	14	1	9	2	12	0
Keefer, Ryan, Aber.	.963	13	7	19	1	27	1	Rice, Scott, Aber.*	.882	11	5	10	2	17	0
Keinath, Tim, H.V.	1.000	4	3	0	0	3	0	Rich, Dan, M.V.*	1.000	22	2	3	0	5	0
Kentner, Brandon, Bkn.	.889	17	3	5	1	9	0	Richardson, Beau, Bat.*	.920	16	4	19	2	25	1
Kieninger, Billy, One.	.875	16	2	5	1	8	0	Rodriguez, Hector, Low.	.750	15	2	7	3	12	0
King, Bryan, Bkn.	1.000	5	0	1	0	1	0	Rodriguez, Jose, Ver.	.444	17	3	1	5	9	0
Kleine, Victor, M.V.*	.938	15	4	11	1	16	1	Rodriguez, Juan, Wil.	1.000	19	7	9	0	16	3
Koenig, Ross, One.	.833	18	2	3	1	6	0	Rogelstad, Jeremy, Bat.	1.000	24	4	6	0	10	0
Kopp, Nathan, S.I.*	1.000	21	3	2	0	5	0	Rogers, Brad, Aber.	1.000	17	1	3	0	4	0
Korecky, Bobby, Bat.	.818	7	2	7	2	11	1	Rogers, Michael, M.V.	1.000	15	4	9	0	13	1
Kramer, Sean, T.C.	1.000	21	2	3	0	5	1	Rohr, Matthew, Aber.*	.750	14	1	5	2	8	0
Kupper, Dustin, Jam.	.944	16	3	14	1	18	0	Rueckel, Danny, Ver.	.667	10	1	1	1	3	0
League, Brandon, Aub.	.923	16	7	17	2	26	2	Russ, Chris, S.I.	1.000	4	2	6	0	8	0
Lewis, Jeremy, One.*	1.000	16	6	13	0	19	0	Sanchez, Humberto, One.	1.000	9	1	2	0	3	0
Lissir, Alexander, Wil.	1.000	4	3	6	0	9	1	Sanders, Shane, H.V.	1.000	24	3	6	0	9	1
Lohrman, Dave, Bkn.	.667	12	1	1	1	3	0	Sandoval, Marcos, Aub.	1.000	25	4	5	0	9	0
Long, Nick, Ver.	.333	6	1	1	4	6	0	Santana, Eddy, Ver.	.000	4	0	0	0	0	0
Lyon, Nick, H.V.	1.000	20	2	9	0	11	0	Schneider, Jonathan, Wil.	1.000	16	5	2	0	7	1
MacLane, Thomas, Low.*	1.000	19	6	5	0	11	1	Schweitzer, Scott, N.J.*	.000	23	0	1	0	1	0
Maine, John, Aber.	1.000	4	0	1	0	1	0	Scobie, Jason, Bkn.	.900	8	2	16	2	20	1
Makowsky, Carl, Bkn.	.941	23	5	11	1	17	1	Selmo, Santo, Jam.	1.000	8	0	1	0	1	0
Marceau, Pierre-Luc, Ver.*	.909	15	3	7	1	11	0	Shafer, Kurt, Wil.	1.000	10	5	8	0	13	1
Martin, Kevin, M.V.	1.000	26	3	10	0	13	0	Sheffield, Christopher, Aub.	.000	6	0	0	0	0	0
Martinez, Wilmer, N.J.	.818	14	2	7	2	11	0	Sherman, Chris, Bkn.	1.000	19	5	6	0	11	1
Mateo, Aneudis, Low.	.800	3	1	3	1	5	0	Shortslef, Josh, Wil.*	.947	14	5	31	2	38	4
Maureau, Justin, Aub.*	1.000	22	4	7	0	11	0	Simon, Billy, Low.	.500	3	0	2	2	4	0
McCurdy, Nick, Aber.	.929	13	6	7	1	14	2	Slocum, Brian, M.V.	.933	11	3	11	1	15	1
McLemore, Mark, T.C.*	1.000	9	0	2	0	2	0	Smith, Brandon, Low.	1.000	7	2	2	0	4	1
McNabb, Tim, Bkn.	1.000	17	2	6	0	8	0	Smith, Chris, Low.	1.000	14	7	12	0	19	2
Meccage, Justin, S.I.	.857	19	0	6	1	7	0	Southerland, Chip, M.V.	1.000	5	0	1	0	1	0
Menocal, Victor, Bat.	1.000	19	5	9	0	14	1	Spivey, Melvin, Aber.	.750	14	0	3	1	4	1
Mieres, Alberto, S.I.	1.000	6	2	2	0	4	1	Steen, Adam, Bat.	.857	12	2	4	1	7	0
Mildren, Paul, Jam.*	1.000	3	0	4	0	4	0	Steinborn, Chris, One.*	.000	2	0	0	0	0	0
Mims, Brandon, Low.*	.000	10	0	0	1	1	0	Stocks, Nick, N.J.	1.000	7	2	3	0	5	0
Mincey, T.W., Aber.*	1.000	18	1	6	0	7	0	Sutton, Zach, Aber.	1.000	14	1	5	0	6	0
Minor, Zach, Bat.	1.000	18	2	2	0	4	0	Tate, Matt, Aber.	.625	6	1	4	3	8	1
Montano, Ignacio, M.V.*	1.000	12	0	4	0	4	0	Teekel, Josh, N.J.	1.000	16	1	10	0	11	0
Mora, Ramon, Aub.	1.000	9	1	0	0	1	0	Teeter, Travis, Aber.	1.000	2	4	2	0	6	0
Moreno, Victor, Bat.	.833	17	1	4	1	6	0	Templet, Eric, Bkn.	1.000	7	1	0	0	1	0
Mosley, Eric, S.I.	1.000	1	0	2	0	2	0	Thorp, Paul, S.I.	1.000	1	0	2	0	2	0
Musser, Neal, Bkn.*	.333	4	0	1	2	3	0	Tomaszewski, Eliot, T.C.	1.000	17	2	4	0	6	0
Myers, Damien, One.*	.800	7	1	3	1	5	0	Torres, Andy, Aub.	.941	17	5	11	1	17	2
Naatjes, Darin, Bat.	.000	2	0	0	0	0	0	Treanor, Bryan, Jam.	1.000	17	1	4	0	5	0
Naylor, Kody, Jam.	1.000	25	2	9	0	11	0	Tribe, Phillip, S.I.	1.000	15	0	2	0	2	0
Neitz, Josh, S.I.	1.000	30	1	7	0	8	1	Valdez, Jose, S.I.	.857	4	2	4	1	7	0
Neylan, Chris, Aub.*	1.000	9	0	3	0	3	0	Van Gorder, Joe, N.J.*	1.000	2	0	1	0	1	0
Nin, Sandy, Aub.	.867	17	9	4	2	15	0	Vaquedano, Jose, Low.	.714	22	1	4	2	7	0
Novoa, Roberto, Wil.	.850	12	3	14	3	20	2	Vargas, Nelson, H.V.	.000	7	0	0	0	0	0
O'Connor, Michael, Ver.*	1.000	21	1	8	0	9	0	Veras, Jose, H.V.	.750	2	1	2	1	4	0
Ogle, Rylie, Bkn.*	1.000	13	1	5	0	6	0	Villarreal, Luis, Low.*	.900	16	2	7	1	10	0
Olson, Ryan, Bkn.*	1.000	6	2	5	0	7	0	Volquez, Bolivar, H.V.	1.000	13	0	6	0	6	1
Ortiz, Julio, Ver.*	.900	15	4	5	1	10	0	Walker, Jason, Ver.*	1.000	14	1	1	0	2	0
Osberg, Tanner, Bkn.	1.000	5	0	2	0	2	0	Wallace, Shane, M.V.*	.857	5	2	4	1	7	1
Ough, Wayne, Bkn.	.833	8	2	8	2	12	0	Wang, Chien-ming, S.I.	.955	13	5	16	1	22	1
Owens, Henry, Wil.	1.000	23	2	1	0	3	0	Warpinski, Ryan, Jam.	1.000	15	5	14	0	19	0
Paddock, Josh, Bat.	1.000	13	3	2	0	5	0	Weir, Jayson, Bkn.*	.667	2	0	2	1	3	0
Pahucki, David, Low.	.875	9	2	5	1	8	0	Wells, Clint, Low.*	1.000	16	0	4	0	4	0
Parris, Matt, One.	1.000	2	3	0	0	3	0	Westhoff, Billy, T.C.	1.000	18	4	8	0	12	1
Paulk, Robert, Bkn.	1.000	9	0	5	0	5	0	White, Chris, M.V.*	1.000	14	2	3	0	5	0
Peguero, Jailen, T.C.	.909	25	5	5	1	11	0	Williams, Blake, N.J.	.000	2	0	0	1	1	0
Pender, Matthew, One.	.800	9	2	2	1	5	0	Williamson, Willie, N.J.*	1.000	6	0	3	0	3	0
Pennington, Todd, M.V.	1.000	8	0	1	0	1	0	Withelder, Gregory, N.J.*	1.000	21	0	3	0	3	0
Perez, Juan, Aub.	1.000	2	1	1	0	2	0	Wolf, Ross, Jam.	1.000	11	3	7	0	10	1

Player, Team	Pct.	G	PO	A	E	TC	DP
Wyrick, Patrick, Jam.	1.000	4	0	1	0	1	0
Yarbrough, Joe, H.V.*	1.000	6	0	1	0	1	0
Yoo, Byung Mok, Low.	1.000	19	1	3	0	4	1
Youman, Shane, Wil.*	1.000	20	1	9	0	10	0
Young, Simon, M.V.*	.833	19	1	9	2	12	0

The following players appeared only as designated hitter, pinch-hitter or pinch runner: Beuerlein, dh, ph; Malek, dh, pr; McEwing, dh; Richard, dh; Sato, dh; Webster, ph.

LEAGUE CHAMPIONS

Year	Team	Pct.
1939—	Olean*	.631
1940—	Olean*	.625
1941—	Jamestown	.618
	Bradford (2nd)†	.549
1942—	Jamestown*	.672
1943—	Lockport	.591
	Wellsville (3rd)†	.532
1944—	Lockport	.608
	Jamestown (2nd)†	.565
1945—	Batavia*	.677
1946—	Jamestown‡	.672
	Batavia‡	.672
1947—	Jamestown*	.690
1948—	Lockport*	.603
1949—	Bradford*	.635
1950—	Hornell	.653
	Olean (2nd)†	.568
1951—	Olean	.622
	Hornell (3rd)†	.568
1952—	Hamilton	.659
	Jamestown (2nd)†	.643
1953—	Jamestown*	.704
1954—	Corning*	.621
1955—	Hamilton*	.656
1956—	Wellsville*	.617
1957—	Wellsville	.632
	Erie (2nd)†	.598
1958—	Wellsville	.556
	Geneva (2nd)†	.548
1959—	Wellsville†	.635
1960—	Erie	.643
	Wellsville (2nd)†	.535
1961—	Geneva	.616
	Olean (4th)†	.512
1962—	Jamestown	.580
	Auburn (3rd)†	.521

Year	Team	Pct.
1963—	Auburn	.585
	Batavia (3rd)†	.485
1964—	Auburn§	.622
1965—	Binghamton	.677
	Binghamton	.607
1966—	Auburn∞	.620
	Binghamton	.646
1967—	Auburn	.667
1968—	Auburn	.645
	Oneonta (2nd)*	.558
1969—	Oneonta	.662
1970—	Oneonta	.623
1971—	Oneonta	.662
1972—	Niagara Falls	.686
1973—	Auburn	.667
1974—	Oneonta	.768
1975—	Newark	.688
	Newark	.714
1976—	Elmira	.727
	Elmira	.703
1977—	Oneonta▲	.671
	Batavia	.600
1978—	Oneonta	.729
	Geneva◆	.718
1979—	Geneva	.725
	Oneonta◆	.618
1980—	Oneonta▲	.662
	Geneva	.649
1981—	Oneonta▲	.658
	Jamestown	.649
1982—	Oneonta	.566
	Niagara Falls▲	.553
1983—	Utica▲	.649
	Newark	.649
1984—	Newark	.622
	Little Falls▲	.587

Year	Team	Pct.
1985—	Oneonta*	.705
	Auburn	.603
1986—	Oneonta	.766
	St. Catharines◆	.632
1987—	Geneva▲	.632
	Watertown	.579
1988—	Oneonta▲	.632
	Jamestown	.618
1989—	Pittsfield	.697
	Jamestown▲	.579
1990—	Oneonta■	.667
	Geneva	.662
1991—	Pittsfield	.662
	Jamestown■	.654
1992—	Hamilton	.737
	Geneva▼	.547
1993—	Niagara Falls▼	.603
	Pittsfield	.533
1994—	Auburn	.592
	New Jersey▼	.573
1995—	Vermont	.645
	Watertown▼	.630
1996—	Vermont▼	.649
	St. Catharines	.579
1997—	Batavia	.635
	Pittsfield▼	.568
1998—	Hudson Valley	.658
	Oneonta††	.592
	Auburn††	.573
1999—	Mahoning Valley	.566
	Hudson Valley‡‡	.553
2000—	Mahoning Valley	.632
	Staten Island§§	.622
2001—	Brooklyn∞∞∞	.684
	Williamsport∞∞∞	.649
2002—	Staten Island▲▲	.649

*Won championship and four-club playoff. †Won four-club playoff. ‡Jamestown and Batavia declared co-champions; Batavia defeated Jamestown in final of four-club playoff. §Won championship and two-club playoff. ∞Won split-season playoff. ▲League divided into Eastern and Western divisions; won playoff. League divided into Wrigley and Yawkey divisions; won playoff. ■League divided into Eastern, Western and Stedler divisions; won playoff. ▼League divided into McNamara, Pinckney and Stedler divisions; won playoff. ††Named co-champions due to final series being rained out. ‡‡League divided into McNamara and Pinckney divisions; won playoff. §§League divided into McNamara and Stedler divisions; won playoff. ∞∞∞League divided into McNamara and Stedler divisions; Brooklyn was leading final series of four-team playoff over Williamsport, but both teams were declared co-champions when Professional Baseball declared a stoppage of play. (NOTE—Known as Pennsylvania-Ontario-New York League from 1939 through 1956.) ▲▲League divided into McNamara, Pinckney and Stedler divisions; won playoff.

NORTHWEST LEAGUE

LEAGUE OFFICE

President/treasurer
Bob Richmond
Address
P.O. Box 1645
Boise, ID 83701
Phone
208-429-1511

Teams (affiliation)
Boise Hawks (Cubs)
Eugene Emeralds (Padres)
Everett AquaSox (Mariners)
Salem-Keizer Volcanoes (Giants)

Spokane Indians (Rangers)
Tri-City Dust Devils (Rockies)
Vancouver Canadians (A's)
Yakima Bears (Diamondbacks)

2002 FINAL STANDINGS

EAST DIVISION

Team	W	L	T	Pct.	GB
Boise (Cubs)	49	27	0	.645	...
Tri-City (Rockies)	40	36	0	.526	9.0
Spokane (Royals)	29	47	0	.382	20.0
Yakima (Diamondbacks)	23	53	0	.303	26.0

WEST DIVISION

Team	W	L	T	Pct.	GB
Everett (Mariners)	44	32	0	.579	...
Salem-Keizer (Giants)	41	35	0	.539	3.0
Eugene (Padres)	41	35	0	.539	3.0
Vancouver (Athletics)	37	39	0	.487	7.0

COMPOSITE

Team	Boi.	Ever.	S.K.	Eug.	T.C.	Van.	Spo.	Yak.	W	L	T	Pct.	GB
Boise (Cubs)	...	6	7	6	7	5	7	11	49	27	0	.645	...
Everett (Mariners)	4	...	4	8	5	7	8	8	44	32	0	.579	5.0
Salem-Keizer (Giants)	3	8	...	6	6	6	6	6	41	35	0	.539	8.0
Eugene (Padres)	4	4	6	...	2	8	7	10	41	35	0	.539	8.0
Tri-City (Rockies)	5	5	4	8	...	5	6	7	40	36	0	.526	9.0
Vancouver (Athletics)	5	5	6	4	5	...	8	4	37	39	0	.487	12.0
Spokane (Royals)	5	2	4	3	6	2	...	7	29	47	0	.382	20.0
Yakima (Diamondbacks)	1	2	4	0	5	4	5	...	23	53	0	.303	26.0

Major league affiliations in parentheses.

PLAYOFFS: Boise defeated Everett, three games to none to win the Northwest League championship.

REGULAR-SEASON ATTENDANCE: Boise, 109,646; Eugene, 123,389; Everett, 110,373; Salem-Keizer, 122,334; Spokane, 161,543; Tri-City, 69,824; Vancouver, 127,099; Yakima, 56,404. Total—880,612. Playoff (three games)—3,321.

MANAGERS: Boise, Steve McFarland; Eugene, Jeff Gardner; Everett, Omer Munoz (through Aug. 6; 29-19) and Roger Hansen (Aug. 7 through end of season; 15-13); Salem-Keizer, Fred Stanley; Spokane, Tom Poquette; Tri-City, Ron Gideon; Vancouver, Orv Franchuk; Yakima, Mike Aldrete.

ALL-STAR TEAM: 1B—Jon Nelson, Everett; 2B—Ismael Castro, Everett; 3B—Donnie Hood, Boise; SS—Oscar Materano, Tri-City; OF—Fred Lewis, Salem-Keizer; OF—Gary Harris, Everett; OF—Carlos Arroyo, Everett; C—Rene Rivera, Everett; DH—Micah Hoffpauir, Boise; RHP—Greg Bruso, Salem-Keizer; LHP (tie)—Jared Doyle, Yakima and Andrew Sisco, Boise; RH Relief pitcher—Gabe Rivas, Eugene; LH Relief pitcher (tie)—Billy Keppinger, Spokane and Isaac Pavlik, Tri-City; Most Valuable Player—Ismael Castro, Everett; Manager of the Year—Steve McFarland, Boise.

2002 BATTING

TEAM

Team	G	TPA	AB	R	H	TB	2B	3B	HR	RBI	SH	SF	HP	BB	IBB	SO	SB	CS	GDP	LOB	ShO	Avg.	OBP	Slg.
Salem-Keizer	76	3039	2632	368	694	952	110	20	36	321	43	30	40	294	6	511	43	31	36	645	4	.264	.343	.362
Boise	76	2924	2610	424	676	1094	149	19	77	383	23	32	47	212	4	630	102	44	31	482	1	.259	.322	.419
Everett	76	2989	2649	382	680	1016	145	16	53	339	25	19	52	244	9	603	55	25	36	566	7	.257	.329	.384
Vancouver	76	2918	2508	334	613	860	122	10	35	302	30	31	50	299	6	631	63	20	48	586	5	.244	.333	.343
Spokane	76	2969	2565	348	618	858	122	17	28	291	22	23	70	289	3	571	94	37	56	578	4	.241	.332	.335
Eugene	76	2885	2519	353	600	896	126	16	46	293	13	9	23	281	6	669	98	35	46	549	6	.238	.325	.356
Tri-City	76	2903	2497	288	560	788	104	11	34	260	48	15	41	302	1	583	60	36	48	566	8	.224	.316	.316
Yakima	76	2816	2496	268	546	721	90	20	15	227	28	22	43	227	3	596	113	36	62	498	6	.219	.293	.289

INDIVIDUAL

TOP QUALIFIERS FOR BATTING CHAMPIONSHIP

Minimum 205 plate appearances. *Lefthanded batter. †Switch-hitter.

Player, Team	G	TPA	AB	R	H	TB	2B	3B	HR	RBI	SH	SF	HP	BB	IBB	SO	SB	CS	GDP	Avg.	OBP	Slg.
Collins, Kevin, Boi.*	52	209	187	39	64	125	18	2	13	37	1	2	5	14	2	52	0	2	1	.342	.399	.668
Frend, Tim, Spo.	65	285	242	36	79	108	19	2	2	34	1	4	5	33	1	34	5	3	5	.326	.412	.446
Lewis, Fred, S.K.*	58	269	239	43	77	95	9	3	1	23	1	0	3	26	1	58	9	6	1	.322	.396	.397
Arroyo, Carlos, Ever.*	62	278	255	46	81	94	11	1	0	26	2	1	2	18	0	31	6	5	2	.318	.366	.369
Castro, Ismael, Ever.†	66	311	284	55	89	144	26	1	9	46	5	2	4	16	1	41	13	2	3	.313	.356	.507
Hoffpauir, Micah, Boi.*	60	228	216	35	65	111	10	3	10	41	1	1	3	7	1	35	2	6	1	.301	.330	.514
Ortmeier, Daniel, S.K.†	49	216	195	32	57	83	9	1	5	31	0	2	1	18	1	37	3	0	5	.292	.352	.426
Hagen, Matt, Ever.	63	249	204	40	59	92	10	1	7	30	2	0	6	35	0	47	3	1	1	.289	.408	.451
Walter, Paul, S.K.	69	283	258	26	74	111	11	4	6	40	2	1	2	20	0	59	6	3	6	.287	.342	.430
Harris, Gary, Ever.*	69	311	286	37	82	128	12	8	6	43	2	1	6	16	3	63	4	2	5	.287	.337	.448
Fransz, Jason, Boi.	59	253	221	44	63	108	19	1	8	40	0	6	5	21	0	52	2	1	5	.285	.352	.489
Gonzalez, Bernie, T.C.	66	285	265	34	75	104	14	3	3	36	0	2	3	15	0	67	7	3	5	.283	.326	.392
Sobieraj, Aaron, S.K.	67	270	237	28	67	100	19	4	2	27	2	2	1	28	0	30	2	2	3	.283	.358	.422

Player, Team	G	TPA	AB	R	H	TB	2B	3B	HR	RBI	SH	SF	HP	BB	IBB	SO	SB	CS	GDP	Avg.	OBP	Slg.
Stone, David, S.K.*	65	265	199	37	56	71	3	0	4	21	12	0	7	47	0	27	4	2	2	.281	.435	.357
Agosto, Rolando, Eug.	65	275	235	32	66	86	14	3	0	19	1	0	8	31	1	47	4	9	7	.281	.383	.366

DEPARTMENTAL LEADERS: G—Johnson, Richardson, Salazar, 72 each; AB—Harris, 286; R—Castro, 55; H—Castro, 89; TB—Castro, 144; 2B—Castro, 26; 3B—Harris, M. Williams, 8 each; HR—Nelson, 17; RBI—Nelson, 64; SH—Stone, 12; SF—Dryer, Fransz, Hood, 6 each; HP—Smith, Stocker, 11 each; BB—Bernier, 58; IBB—Harris, 3; SO—Nelson, 96; SB—M. Williams, 51; CS—Stocker, 12; GIDP—Stephens, 8; Slg.—Collins, .668; OBP—Stone, .435.

ALL PLAYERS

*Lefthanded batter. †Switch-hitter.

Player, Team	G	TPA	AB	R	H	TB	2B	3B	HR	RBI	SH	SF	HP	BB	IBB	SO	SB	CS	GDP	Avg.	OBP	Slg.
Agosto, Rolando, Eug.	65	275	235	32	66	86	14	3	0	19	1	0	8	31	1	47	4	9	7	.281	.383	.366
Alexander, Alexis, Spo.	48	145	124	14	32	41	6	0	1	11	2	2	7	10	0	34	6	2	2	.258	.343	.331
Arroyo, Carlos, Ever.*	62	278	255	46	81	94	11	1	0	26	2	1	2	18	0	31	6	5	2	.318	.366	.369
Bacon, Dwaine, Boi.†	64	254	218	46	49	76	8	2	5	20	3	2	4	27	0	67	31	6	1	.225	.319	.349
Baker, John, Van.*	39	144	115	15	27	35	5	0	1	13	0	0	7	22	0	37	2	0	3	.235	.389	.304
Baker, Steve, Eug.	62	253	232	30	56	107	12	3	11	41	0	1	4	16	1	88	12	3	5	.241	.300	.461
Banks, Gary, Boi.†	60	219	199	26	48	58	8	1	0	20	1	1	3	15	0	56	7	6	4	.241	.303	.291
Barden, Brian, Yak.	4	17	15	5	5	6	1	0	0	2	0	0	1	1	0	1	0	0	1	.333	.412	.400
Barker, Sean, T.C.	45	182	166	21	37	51	9	1	1	15	2	0	2	12	0	38	4	2	6	.223	.283	.307
Barrett, Rich, Yak.	56	205	172	22	34	44	5	1	1	11	6	1	8	18	0	44	14	4	1	.198	.302	.256
Bell, Derek, S.K.†	31	102	86	9	20	31	3	1	2	17	0	2	1	13	0	20	0	1	1	.233	.333	.360
Bernier, Doug, T.C.†	64	279	208	26	41	49	5	0	1	24	8	1	4	58	0	55	3	4	2	.197	.380	.236
Berroa, Joandry, Yak.	25	96	88	7	20	27	5	1	0	9	1	1	0	6	0	21	0	3	2	.227	.274	.307
Bibee, Hal, T.C.	33	129	106	8	21	28	4	0	1	8	4	2	2	15	0	25	0	2	2	.198	.304	.264
Biernbaum, L.J., Eug.*	12	41	34	1	2	4	0	1	0	3	0	0	0	7	0	10	0	1	0	.059	.220	.118
Blakeley, Eric, Ever.	9	16	15	3	3	6	0	0	1	2	0	0	0	0	0	5	1	0	0	.200	.250	.400
Bohn, T.J., Ever.	62	249	212	28	52	71	10	0	3	20	2	3	3	29	1	53	7	2	4	.245	.340	.335
Brooks, Jeff, Eug.	22	91	85	12	18	27	3	0	2	9	0	1	0	5	0	29	0	0	3	.212	.253	.318
Brown, Hunter, Ever.	15	57	49	5	9	17	2	0	2	5	0	0	0	7	0	13	1	0	0	.184	.286	.347
Brown, Jeremy, Van.	10	39	28	7	8	9	1	0	0	1	0	0	1	10	0	5	1	0	1	.286	.487	.321
Brown, Nebasett, Yak.*	63	197	173	20	32	41	9	0	0	13	2	3	1	18	0	38	5	1	3	.185	.262	.237
Buller, Dayton, S.K.	19	56	45	5	9	12	3	0	0	7	1	0	0	10	0	10	1	1	1	.200	.345	.267
Burgamy, Brian, Eug.†	70	303	261	44	70	116	17	1	9	43	1	2	1	38	0	64	14	4	2	.268	.361	.444
Bushey, Andrew, T.C.*	49	181	163	9	31	35	4	0	0	12	3	1	0	14	0	24	2	0	4	.190	.253	.215
Butler, Keith, Boi.	30	119	110	16	35	55	9	1	3	17	0	2	0	7	0	8	9	4	2	.318	.353	.500
Cabrera, Chi Chi, S.K.	44	130	120	18	29	39	5	1	1	8	1	0	1	8	1	22	1	3	0	.242	.295	.325
Cadena, Alex, Ever.	37	150	135	13	32	43	8	0	1	11	0	2	6	7	1	12	0	0	4	.237	.300	.319
Callahan, Dan, Yak.*	8	19	15	2	5	6	1	0	0	3	0	1	0	3	0	1	0	0	0	.333	.421	.400
Carter, Josh, Eug.	9	41	37	10	13	27	3	1	3	9	0	1	0	3	1	7	0	1	0	.351	.390	.730
Castro, Ismael, Ever.†	66	311	284	55	89	144	26	1	9	46	5	2	4	16	1	41	13	2	3	.313	.356	.507
Cedeno, Ronny, Boi.	29	122	110	17	24	33	5	2	0	6	2	1	0	9	0	25	8	2	1	.218	.275	.300
Chirinos, Robinson, Boi.	62	255	231	35	57	100	15	2	8	38	1	1	6	16	0	66	5	2	2	.247	.311	.433
Cleto, Carlos, S.K.*	4	12	6	4	3	7	1	0	1	3	0	1	0	5	0	2	0	1	0	.500	.667	1.167
Colamarino, Brant, Van.*	67	269	228	30	59	87	6	2	6	41	2	5	7	27	2	54	3	1	7	.259	.348	.382
Collins, Kevin, Boi.*	52	209	187	39	64	125	18	2	13	37	1	2	5	14	2	52	0	2	1	.342	.399	.668
Colton, Chris, Ever.	69	283	238	30	55	93	17	3	5	30	2	4	4	35	0	79	4	2	6	.231	.335	.391
Craig, Matt, Boi.†	37	156	140	19	27	44	2	0	5	20	1	3	0	12	1	28	0	0	4	.193	.252	.314
Cruz, Nelson, Van.	63	232	214	23	59	85	14	0	4	25	4	1	4	9	0	58	12	1	2	.276	.316	.397
Dean, Erik, Spo.*	12	39	31	5	9	11	2	0	0	2	0	0	1	7	0	5	0	0	0	.290	.436	.355
Delgado, Jorge, T.C.	4	16	12	2	2	2	0	0	0	1	0	0	2	2	0	4	0	0	0	.167	.375	.167
De Los Santos, Pedro, Eug.†	21	93	80	14	18	22	2	1	0	8	1	3	2	7	0	15	16	1	0	.225	.293	.275
Dibetta, John, Eug.	67	277	239	29	57	68	8	0	1	29	2	5	3	28	0	40	10	3	4	.238	.320	.285
Dryer, Matt, S.K.	41	173	146	21	37	57	3	1	5	21	0	6	7	14	0	41	4	0	0	.253	.335	.390
Dyson, Trey, Spo.*	48	187	174	15	41	68	9	0	6	36	1	1	3	8	1	30	2	1	7	.236	.280	.391
Ervin, Josh, Eug.	19	58	54	3	7	12	2	0	1	3	0	0	1	3	1	20	1	0	0	.130	.190	.222
Ferrara, Matt, Spo.	6	23	21	2	1	2	1	0	0	2	0	0	0	2	0	7	0	0	1	.048	.130	.095
Fransz, Jason, Boi.	59	253	221	44	63	108	19	1	8	40	0	6	5	21	0	52	2	1	5	.285	.352	.489
Frend, Tim, Spo.	65	285	242	36	79	108	19	2	2	34	1	4	5	33	1	34	5	3	5	.326	.412	.446
Garcia, Lino, Yak.	25	73	62	8	12	19	2	1	1	6	2	0	3	6	0	15	3	0	2	.194	.296	.306
Garciaparra, Michael, Ever.	9	36	31	3	5	7	2	0	0	3	1	0	0	4	0	15	0	1	1	.161	.257	.226
Garthwaite, Jay, Yak.	14	55	51	6	9	17	5	0	1	3	0	0	1	3	0	12	0	0	3	.176	.236	.333
Gates, Bookie, Yak.	61	240	223	20	52	62	4	3	0	23	3	1	3	9	0	42	12	6	6	.233	.271	.278
Gearlds, Aaron, T.C.	2	8	7	1	0	0	0	0	0	0	0	0	0	1	0	6	0	0	0	.000	.125	.000
Gibbons, Daniel, Van.*	20	58	50	7	6	7	1	0	0	3	0	1	0	7	0	9	0	0	2	.120	.224	.140
Gil, Jerry, Yak.	65	236	224	21	56	77	11	2	2	28	2	2	2	6	0	47	14	1	6	.250	.274	.344
Giorgis, David, Eug.†	37	142	133	9	33	52	9	2	2	24	0	1	0	8	0	46	1	1	5	.248	.289	.391
Glessner, Jeremiah, T.C.	2	9	8	0	0	0	0	0	0	0	0	0	0	1	0	3	0	0	0	.000	.111	.000
Gomez, Francis, Van.	21	77	68	15	18	29	8	0	1	9	0	1	0	8	0	10	1	0	4	.265	.338	.426
Gonzalez, Bernie, T.C.	66	285	265	34	75	104	14	3	3	36	0	2	3	15	0	67	7	3	5	.283	.326	.392
Gorman, Jason, Yak.	44	106	94	1	12	12	0	0	0	3	0	1	1	9	0	25	1	2	1	.128	.219	.128
Greene, Khalil, Eug.	10	45	37	5	10	11	1	0	0	6	0	0	3	5	1	6	0	0	0	.270	.400	.297
Guance, Walkill, T.C.	65	281	241	31	64	88	13	1	3	23	5	1	1	33	0	49	7	5	6	.266	.355	.365
Guzman, Jacob, Spo.	26	88	75	10	14	26	3	0	3	10	0	1	3	9	0	16	0	0	0	.187	.295	.347
Hagen, Matt, Ever.	63	249	204	40	59	92	10	1	7	30	2	0	6	35	0	47	3	1	1	.289	.408	.451
Haley, Adam, Yak.*	6	10	9	1	1	1	0	0	0	1	0	0	0	1	0	2	0	0	0	.111	.200	.111
Harriman, David, Van.	32	86	77	6	18	22	1	0	1	8	3	0	1	5	0	11	3	0	0	.234	.289	.286
Harrington, Corey, Ever.	49	184	165	23	34	48	11	0	1	17	3	1	2	13	0	35	3	2	1	.206	.271	.291
Harris, Gary, Ever.*	69	311	286	37	82	128	12	8	6	43	2	1	6	16	3	63	4	2	5	.287	.337	.448
Henriquez, Hector, Ever.†	17	52	51	3	8	9	1	0	0	0	0	0	0	1	0	9	0	1	0	.157	.173	.176
Hoffpauir, Micah, Boi.*	60	228	216	35	65	111	10	3	10	41	1	1	3	7	1	35	2	6	1	.301	.330	.514
Holm, Steve, S.K.	50	149	128	15	22	26	4	0	0	11	4	2	0	15	0	16	0	0	4	.172	.255	.203
Hood, Donnie, Boi.	49	200	172	36	48	99	13	1	12	42	3	6	8	11	0	42	0	2	0	.279	.340	.576
Hornostaj, Aaron, S.K.*	4	17	14	4	6	6	0	0	0	3	0	0	0	3	0	5	1	0	0	.429	.529	.429
Hudson, Ben, Ever.	8	20	18	1	1	1	0	0	0	2	0	0	0	2	0	6	1	1	0	.056	.150	.056
Huff, Ken, Yak.*	35	118	103	9	20	31	3	1	2	11	0	0	2	13	0	22	0	1	3	.194	.297	.301
Hutchinson, Burnell, Yak.*	7	19	15	0	2	3	1	0	0	3	1	0	1	0	0	3	0	0	0	.133	.167	.200
Ishikawa, Travis, S.K.*	23	96	88	14	27	34	2	1	1	17	1	1	1	5	0	22	1	1	2	.307	.347	.386
Jensen, David, Spo.*	70	312	267	41	69	92	10	2	3	34	5	3	7	30	0	63	8	1	2	.258	.345	.345
Jernigan, Karl, S.K.	34	106	94	14	27	36	6	0	1	10	3	2	1	6	1	17	3	1	3	.287	.330	.383
Johnson, Bryan, Yak.†	72	285	238	24	55	72	12	1	1	22	0	1	4	42	1	54	0	3	7	.231	.354	.303
Jones, Kennard, Eug.*	16	73	61	15	18	20	2	0	0	6	0	0	2	10	0	12	12	1	0	.295	.411	.328

Player, Team	G	TPA	AB	R	H	TB	2B	3B	HR	RBI	SH	SF	HP	BB	IBB	SO	SB	CS	GDP	Avg.	OBP	Slg.
Keim, Adam, Spo.	55	220	195	18	45	75	14	2	4	30	1	4	1	19	1	57	5	1	2	.231	.297	.385
Kelly, Kevin, S.K.	15	58	50	6	5	6	1	0	0	2	1	0	0	7	0	13	0	0	1	.100	.211	.120
Kelly, Tripp, Van.	35	115	100	6	19	24	3	1	0	11	0	1	1	13	1	34	3	0	3	.190	.287	.240
Kiger, Mark, Van.	66	296	246	44	60	89	12	1	5	27	7	3	0	40	1	58	7	4	3	.244	.346	.362
Kunich, Frank, Ever.	28	97	85	14	26	31	5	0	0	5	0	0	1	12	0	28	1	0	0	.306	.392	.365
Legendre, Curtis, Spo.	43	165	148	10	31	51	11	0	3	19	1	0	7	9	0	37	1	0	3	.209	.287	.345
Lewis, Fred, S.K.*	58	269	239	43	77	95	9	3	1	23	1	0	3	26	1	58	9	6	1	.322	.396	.397
Lonnquist, Eric, Spo.	55	240	202	33	41	49	6	1	0	14	2	0	3	33	0	50	11	2	3	.203	.324	.243
Luellwitz, Sean, Yak.	13	46	41	6	13	15	2	0	0	3	0	0	0	5	0	8	0	0	2	.317	.391	.366
Lytle, Derrik, Spo.*	31	101	88	7	22	25	3	0	0	8	1	0	3	9	0	25	2	2	3	.250	.340	.284
Madera, Sandy, Van.	2	9	9	2	2	2	0	0	0	0	0	0	0	0	0	1	0	0	1	.222	.222	.222
Maestrales, Pete, S.K.†	60	181	165	20	45	67	9	2	3	19	1	4	1	9	0	38	4	3	3	.273	.307	.406
Martinez, Thomas, Eug.	24	77	72	3	11	17	3	0	1	8	0	0	1	4	0	28	1	0	0	.153	.208	.236
Materano, Oscar, T.C.	68	294	270	38	70	111	14	0	9	40	7	3	3	11	0	61	7	5	6	.259	.293	.411
McCool, Lee, Yak.	15	52	44	4	9	13	2	1	0	5	1	0	2	5	0	8	1	0	4	.205	.314	.295
McCurdy, John, Van.	56	242	223	33	54	74	9	1	3	29	1	4	2	12	2	57	5	1	5	.242	.282	.332
Medlin, C.J., Boi.	42	149	134	10	29	40	8	0	1	14	2	1	3	9	0	34	0	0	1	.216	.279	.299
Menchaca, Eriberto, Ever.	6	26	22	3	4	4	0	0	0	3	1	0	0	3	0	3	1	0	1	.182	.280	.182
Meyer, Rusty, Van.	7	28	21	2	2	3	1	0	0	1	0	0	0	7	0	6	0	0	0	.095	.321	.143
Millan, Carlos, Eug.	24	71	64	9	14	22	5	0	1	7	0	1	0	6	0	20	4	3	3	.219	.282	.344
Miller, Chris, Boi.	29	116	104	16	26	48	7	0	5	23	0	1	5	6	0	20	0	0	1	.250	.319	.462
Monahan, Joey, Boi.	41	184	159	31	43	68	10	3	3	26	1	3	2	19	0	45	10	1	2	.270	.350	.428
Monte, Harvey, Ever.*	17	60	45	9	9	12	1	1	0	3	3	0	0	12	0	10	1	2	1	.200	.368	.267
Montilla, Samuel, Yak.	42	144	131	9	25	33	5	0	1	12	0	4	1	8	0	23	1	1	3	.191	.236	.252
Moore, Rusty, Eug.	5	13	11	0	1	1	0	0	0	0	0	0	0	2	0	4	0	0	0	.091	.231	.091
Mora, Ruben, Eug.†	27	98	92	16	19	24	2	0	1	3	0	0	1	5	0	31	7	1	1	.207	.255	.261
Morris, Jed, Van.*	31	110	87	6	23	33	7	0	1	16	1	2	7	13	0	20	1	1	2	.264	.394	.379
Murphy, Donald, Spo.	28	118	109	20	33	47	10	2	0	15	0	0	3	6	0	17	0	0	2	.303	.356	.431
Nagle, Austin, Van.	41	163	144	12	31	45	9	1	1	13	2	1	2	14	0	38	1	3	3	.215	.292	.313
Navarro, Mandy, Boi.†	15	44	35	3	3	3	0	0	0	2	0	0	0	9	0	14	0	2	0	.086	.273	.086
Nelson, Jon, Ever.	66	298	274	37	64	123	8	0	17	64	0	2	8	14	2	96	4	1	3	.234	.289	.449
Nordness, Kirk, Van.	12	51	44	8	10	14	4	0	0	5	0	1	1	5	0	7	0	0	1	.227	.314	.318
Nulton, Kevin, Eug.	47	174	153	22	36	44	3	1	1	13	2	3	1	15	0	28	5	2	4	.235	.302	.288
Ortmeier, Daniel, S.K.†	49	216	195	32	57	83	9	1	5	31	0	2	1	18	1	37	3	0	5	.292	.352	.426
O'Sullivan, Steve, Boi.	5	9	9	2	3	3	0	0	0	1	0	0	0	0	0	1	0	0	0	.333	.333	.333
O'Toole, Paul, Boi.*	2	8	7	0	0	0	0	0	0	1	0	1	0	0	0	1	0	0	0	.000	.000	.000
Paredes, Jeison, Yak.	37	115	110	12	23	31	5	0	1	9	1	0	2	2	0	25	4	1	5	.209	.237	.282
Peirce, Justin, Van.	1	1	1	0	0	0	0	0	0	0	0	0	0	0	0	0	0	0	0	.000	.000	.000
Pickens, Jordan, Eug.	35	147	119	23	32	53	9	0	4	20	0	2	7	19	0	39	4	1	2	.269	.395	.445
Pie, Felix, Boi.*	2	9	8	1	1	2	1	0	0	1	0	0	0	1	0	1	0	0	0	.125	.222	.250
Pinango, Ever. S.K.†	28	25	22	3	5	5	0	0	0	5	1	1	0	1	0	4	0	2	1	.227	.250	.227
Pinon, Alex, S.K.	46	140	117	20	31	40	6	0	1	11	5	2	2	14	0	20	2	1	1	.265	.348	.342
Richardson, Mike, Eug.	72	307	251	42	60	93	18	0	5	38	0	0	7	49	1	56	3	2	5	.239	.378	.371
Riley, Kenny, T.C.	9	25	23	0	1	1	0	0	0	0	1	0	1	0	0	4	0	0	1	.043	.083	.043
Rivera, Rene, Ever.	62	256	227	29	55	78	18	1	1	26	1	3	9	16	1	38	5	2	3	.242	.314	.344
Rodriguez, Alex, Spo.†	62	199	178	20	35	39	4	0	0	10	1	1	5	14	0	49	8	2	5	.197	.273	.219
Rooke, Brian, Van.	1	1	1	0	0	0	0	0	0	0	0	0	0	0	0	0	0	0	0	.000	.000	.000
Rosario, Victor, Spo.*	25	92	83	5	19	27	2	3	0	7	1	1	0	7	0	21	2	1	2	.229	.286	.325
Saba, Donnie, Yak.*	60	188	157	22	36	45	6	0	1	15	3	1	5	22	1	63	5	3	1	.229	.341	.287
Salazar, Jeff, T.C.*	72	328	265	38	63	88	5	4	4	21	9	2	2	47	0	43	10	6	2	.235	.351	.328
Santana, Manny, S.K.*	27	73	67	3	12	16	4	0	0	6	0	2	0	4	0	9	0	0	1	.179	.219	.239
Selmo, Martin, Eug.	9	33	31	1	3	3	0	0	0	1	0	0	0	2	0	5	2	0	0	.097	.152	.097
Servais, Eric, Boi.*	40	99	87	13	26	43	8	0	3	16	1	0	0	11	0	20	0	1	2	.299	.378	.494
Shorsher, Adam, Eug.	45	173	147	15	33	50	8	0	3	16	2	3	10	11	0	45	0	3	1	.224	.316	.340
Smith, Sam, T.C.	55	224	185	19	29	50	9	0	4	16	3	2	11	22	0	50	2	0	5	.157	.282	.270
Sobieraj, Aaron, S.K.	67	270	237	28	67	100	19	4	2	27	2	2	1	28	0	30	2	2	3	.283	.358	.422
Soto, Geovany, Boi.	1	5	5	1	2	2	0	0	0	0	0	0	0	0	0	1	0	0	0	.400	.400	.400
Spearman, Jemel, Boi.	3	12	11	1	3	3	0	0	0	0	0	0	0	1	0	1	1	0	0	.273	.333	.273
Spilborghs, Ryan, T.C.	71	295	261	34	60	85	11	1	4	34	1	1	3	29	1	61	11	7	5	.230	.313	.326
Stavisky, Brian, Van.*	32	125	102	12	30	45	10	1	1	15	2	1	5	15	0	30	5	0	1	.294	.407	.441
Stephens, Bernard, Spo.*	64	252	206	35	49	65	7	3	1	19	1	2	7	36	0	61	15	10	8	.238	.367	.316
Stocker, Mel, Spo.†	61	252	210	48	47	64	7	2	2	14	2	2	11	27	0	35	26	12	6	.224	.340	.305
Stone, David, S.K.*	65	255	199	37	56	71	3	0	4	21	12	0	7	47	0	27	4	2	2	.281	.435	.357
Street, Dan, T.C.	46	179	153	13	31	39	6	1	0	12	2	0	7	17	0	44	3	1	1	.203	.311	.255
Suomi, Richard, Van.*	41	156	142	20	36	58	7	0	5	24	1	1	1	11	0	36	0	0	0	.254	.310	.408
Sweeney, James, T.C.	19	66	54	5	6	11	2	0	1	5	1	0	0	11	0	22	2	1	1	.111	.262	.204
Swisher, Nick, Van.†	13	60	44	10	11	20	3	0	2	12	0	1	2	13	0	11	3	0	0	.250	.433	.455
Teahen, Mark, Van.*	13	63	57	10	23	30	5	1	0	6	0	1	0	5	0	9	4	1	0	.404	.444	.526
Tiesing, Tyler, Yak.	44	127	113	10	21	29	3	1	1	15	0	2	4	8	0	33	0	0	4	.186	.260	.257
Townsend, Rich, Eug.	29	100	91	18	23	37	5	3	1	11	0	0	2	7	0	29	2	0	2	.253	.320	.407
Tritle, Chris, Van.	56	210	190	22	42	58	10	1	2	13	0	2	2	15	0	60	3	2	4	.221	.282	.305
Tupman, Matt, Spo.*	51	201	170	26	46	59	7	0	2	23	3	2	4	22	0	22	3	0	4	.271	.364	.347
Turco, Anthony, S.K.*	15	43	38	2	5	5	0	0	0	2	1	0	1	3	0	8	0	0	0	.132	.214	.132
Turner, Lloyd, Van.	42	180	156	20	40	51	6	1	1	21	3	3	3	15	0	34	6	4	5	.256	.328	.327
Valles, Jake, Spo.	10	22	21	1	3	6	0	0	1	2	0	0	0	1	0	2	0	1	1	.143	.182	.286
Ventura, Juan, T.C.	4	18	14	0	4	4	0	0	0	2	2	0	0	2	0	4	2	0	0	.286	.375	.286
Wald, Jake, S.K.	64	264	228	30	55	72	7	2	2	24	7	1	5	23	1	43	2	3	6	.241	.323	.316
Walker, Chris, Boi.	60	257	231	33	57	69	7	1	1	18	6	1	2	17	0	52	25	11	2	.247	.303	.299
Walter, Paul, S.K.	69	283	258	26	74	111	11	4	6	40	2	1	2	20	0	59	6	3	6	.287	.342	.430
Wayment, Kory, Van.	60	232	182	26	37	43	1	1	1	10	4	2	4	40	0	52	3	2	0	.203	.355	.236
Wells, Randy, Boi.	9	17	16	0	3	4	1	0	0	0	0	0	0	0	0	9	0	0	0	.188	.235	.250
White, Carson, T.C.	27	105	93	9	25	42	8	0	3	11	0	0	0	12	0	23	0	0	2	.269	.352	.452
Wilkins, Joseph, Yak.†	49	158	138	13	35	39	4	0	0	14	3	1	1	15	0	23	2	3	3	.254	.329	.283
Williams, Jason, S.K.*	26	93	77	13	22	29	4	0	1	11	0	0	5	11	1	10	0	1	2	.286	.409	.377
Williams, Marland, Yak.	70	311	280	46	69	98	4	8	3	17	2	2	0	27	0	86	51	7	4	.246	.311	.350
Woody, Dominic, Ever.	18	59	53	3	12	15	3	0	0	3	1	0	2	3	0	19	0	2	0	.226	.293	.283
Zuniga, Tony, S.K.	4	19	13	1	3	4	1	0	0	2	0	1	1	4	0	0	0	0	0	.231	.421	.308

GRAND SLAMS: Suomi 2, S. Baker, Castro, Chirinos, Colamarino, Harris, Hoffpauir, Kiger, McCurdy, Jordan Pickens, Spilborghs, 1 each.

AWARDED FIRST BASE ON CATCHER'S INTERFERENCE: Hagen 2 (Bibee, Turco), H. Brown (Turco), Gates (Bibee), Maestrales (Guzman), Smith (Shorsher), Tritle (Turco).

CLASS A *Northwest League*

Team	W	L	Pct.	ERA	G	CG	ShO	Sv.	IP	H	TBF	R	ER	HR	SH	SF	HB	BB	IBB	SO	WP	Bk.
Boise	49	27	.645	3.10	76	0	3	21	682.2	569	2939	306	235	23	33	14	59	290	3	648	63	9
Salem-Keizer	41	35	.539	3.41	76	1	7	18	677.2	586	2879	313	257	29	27	26	45	270	11	627	45	6
Everett	44	32	.579	3.42	76	1	6	20	685.0	640	2958	328	260	41	35	20	44	254	3	645	57	11
Tri-City	40	36	.526	3.46	76	0	3	26	687.1	606	2932	315	264	43	33	33	47	239	3	606	63	6
Vancouver	37	39	.487	3.46	76	0	10	13	665.0	584	2843	310	256	27	26	23	47	243	5	606	53	11
Eugene	41	35	.539	3.83	76	0	4	21	664.2	636	2875	358	283	53	30	24	43	224	4	631	43	7
Yakima	23	53	.303	4.05	76	0	2	12	669.1	662	2997	396	301	40	23	24	54	331	7	582	65	12
Spokane	29	47	.382	4.79	76	0	6	22	673.1	704	3027	439	358	68	21	31	57	297	2	449	53	10

INDIVIDUAL

TOP QUALIFIERS FOR EARNED-RUN AVERAGE TITLE

Minimum 61 innings.*Lefthanded pitcher.

Pitcher, Team	W	L	Pct.	ERA	G	GS	CG	ShO	GF	Sv.	IP	H	TBF	R	ER	HR	SH	SF	HB	BB	IBB	SO	WP	Bk.
Bruso, Greg, S.K.	4	3	.571	1.99	14	13	0	0	1	0	81.1	58	319	23	18	5	2	4	7	17	0	78	1	0
Cate, Troy, Ever.*	6	1	.857	2.00	16	12	1	1	1	0	85.1	62	323	21	19	6	5	0	2	11	0	95	4	0
Young, Chris, T.C.	5	5	.500	2.34	17	6	0	0	1	0	61.2	45	255	20	16	1	3	2	5	23	0	47	6	1
Sisco, Andy, Boi.*	7	2	.778	2.43	14	14	0	0	0	0	77.2	51	319	23	21	3	3	0	6	39	0	101	6	0
Gonzalez, Enrique, Yak.	5	2	.714	2.45	11	11	0	0	0	0	66	53	278	27	18	2	1	5	7	23	0	57	7	0
Nolasco, Ricky, Boi.	7	2	.778	2.48	15	15	0	0	0	0	90.2	72	379	32	25	1	8	1	9	25	0	92	5	0
Hensley, Clay, S.K.	7	0	1.000	2.53	15	15	1	0	0	0	81.2	72	337	31	23	3	2	1	3	25	0	84	6	1
Davies, Michael, T.C.*	5	2	.714	2.75	16	9	0	1	0	0	68.2	55	271	25	21	3	2	3	1	18	0	72	1	1
Rowland-Smith, Ryan, Ever.*.	4	1	.800	2.77	18	6	0	0	5	2	61.2	58	267	22	19	2	3	2	4	22	0	58	4	3
Pauley, David, Eug.	6	1	.857	2.81	15	15	0	0	0	0	80	81	335	32	25	6	3	4	6	18	1	62	7	0
Bateman, Jamie, S.K.	4	3	.571	2.86	19	7	0	0	2	2	63	55	259	31	20	2	1	2	2	13	0	51	1	2
Doyle, Jared, Yak.*	4	4	.500	2.87	16	8	0	0	3	1	62.2	44	262	24	20	1	2	3	6	29	0	70	3	0
Whitaker, Brian, Eug.	5	8	.385	2.93	16	14	0	0	0	0	83	79	343	36	27	6	5	1	5	16	0	63	2	0
Woolard, Glenn, S.K.	3	2	.600	2.96	17	11	0	0	0	0	67	51	289	26	22	3	2	3	6	32	3	75	4	0
Livingston, Bobby, Ever.*	6	5	.545	3.02	15	14	0	0	1	0	80.1	80	338	33	27	2	1	2	7	13	0	76	4	2

DEPARTMENTAL LEADERS: W—Ribas, 8; L—Bayliss, Lizarraga, Whitaker, 8 each; Pct.—Hensley, L. Nelson, 1.000 each; G—Ribas, 32; GS—Several pitchers tied with 15; CG—Cate, Hensley, 1 each; ShO—Cate, 1; GF—Ribas, 29; Sv.—Beckstead, 19; IP—Lizarraga, 91.0; H—Lizarraga, 90; TBF—Lizarraga, Nolasco, 379 each; R—Dorman, 53; ER—Bayliss, 42; HR—Bayliss, 9; SH—Nolasco, 8; SF—D. Johnson, 6; HB—G. Atencio, Vasquez, 10 each; BB—Brown, 58; IBB—Habel, R. Medina, Mitchell, Woolard, 3 each; SO—Sisco, 101; WP—Dorman, 12; BK—Mercedes, 4.

ALL PITCHERS

*Lefthanded pitcher.

Pitcher, Team	W	L	Pct.	ERA	G	GS	CG	ShO	GF	Sv.	IP	H	TBF	R	ER	HR	SH	SF	HB	BB	IBB	SO	WP	Bk.
Ackerman, Eric, Spo.*	4	1	.800	3.10	8	8	0	0	0	0	40.2	33	162	14	14	5	0	1	2	13	0	36	1	0
Aquino, Greg, Yak.	1	1	.500	2.06	6	6	0	0	0	0	35	26	141	9	8	0	1	1	0	17	0	34	3	0
Atencio, Donald, Van.	0	0	.000	18.00	1	0	0	0	0	0	1	1	5	2	2	0	0	1	0	0	1	0	0	0
Atencio, Greg, Spo.	4	7	.364	6.07	14	12	0	0	0	0	59.1	70	268	45	40	8	2	4	10	16	0	35	8	1
Atlee, Rick, Boi.	1	2	.333	1.65	19	0	0	0	15	5	27.1	26	110	8	5	0	0	2	4	0	21	4	0	
Averette, Robert, T.C.	0	1	.000	1.29	3	3	0	0	0	0	14	11	52	2	2	0	0	0	0	0	13	0	0	
Baez, Federico, Boi.	0	0	.000	0.00	1	0	0	0	0	0	2	0	7	0	0	0	0	0	1	0	0	0	0	
Barnett, John, Spo.	0	0	.000	7.07	7	0	0	0	1	0	14	26	76	22	11	5	0	1	0	6	6	2	0	
Bartz, Jason, Spo.	0	2	.000	5.68	7	1	0	0	1	0	19	22	84	16	12	4	0	2	0	6	12	0	0	
Bateman, Jamie, S.K.	4	3	.571	2.86	19	7	0	0	2	2	63	55	259	31	20	2	1	2	2	13	0	51	1	2
Bayliss, Jonah, Spo.	4	8	.333	5.35	15	15	0	0	0	0	70.2	70	307	46	42	9	3	3	7	29	0	38	7	2
Beavers, Kevin, Eug.*	0	1	.000	1.88	4	4	0	0	0	0	24	23	94	7	5	1	2	0	0	4	0	16	0	1
Beck, David, Van.	0	0	.000	1.35	20	0	0	0	12	2	20	14	87	6	3	0	2	3	2	10	0	22	5	0
Beckstead, Jentry, T.C.	1	3	.250	1.21	29	0	0	0	25	19	29.2	12	119	6	4	0	0	1	1	18	1	37	8	0
Bernier, Doug, T.C.	0	0	.000	0.00	1	0	0	0	1	0	0.1	1	2	0	0	0	0	0	0	0	0	0	0	0
Biggs, Billy, Yak.	1	2	.333	2.42	20	0	0	0	17	8	26	18	101	9	7	1	2	0	0	8	1	19	1	0
Blanton, Joe, Van.	1	1	.500	3.14	4	2	0	0	0	0	14.1	11	53	5	5	0	0	0	2	0	15	0	0	
Blood, Justin, Ever.*	0	0	.000	0.00	2	0	0	0	1	1	4	1	13	0	0	0	0	0	0	1	0	8	0	0
Bochy, Greg, Eug.	0	0	.000	3.13	17	0	0	0	5	0	23	10	105	11	8	3	0	0	3	24	0	23	5	0
Bomar, Mike, Eug.*	0	1	.000	5.65	12	0	0	0	2	0	14.1	14	72	11	9	2	0	1	3	12	0	7	1	0
Bonnell, Jared, Yak.	1	1	.500	5.06	19	1	0	0	8	0	32	36	150	21	18	2	2	0	3	22	0	31	4	0
Brown, Ira, Spo.	2	5	.286	5.43	16	14	0	0	1	0	59.2	47	291	47	36	3	3	2	7	58	0	42	7	0
Bruso, Greg, S.K.	4	3	.571	1.99	14	13	0	0	1	0	81.1	58	319	23	18	5	2	4	7	17	0	78	1	0
Burnau, Ryan, Boi.	3	1	.750	2.95	25	0	0	0	0	0	42.2	39	184	15	14	2	3	1	2	19	0	46	5	0
Burton, Levi, Van.	0	4	.000	3.58	13	5	0	0	2	1	37.2	32	164	22	15	0	2	1	2	14	0	38	2	1
Carter, Ramsey, Spo.	0	0	.000	3.76	20	1	0	0	5	1	40.2	37	175	19	17	1	1	0	5	18	0	40	3	0
Cate, Troy, Ever.*	6	1	.857	2.00	16	12	1	1	1	0	85.1	62	323	21	19	6	5	0	2	11	0	95	4	0
Chamberlain, Steve, Spo.	0	2	.000	5.06	7	4	0	0	0	0	16	16	73	11	9	1	0	1	2	8	0	11	2	0
Christensen, Danny, Spo.*	2	0	1.000	1.10	9	0	0	0	6	4	32.2	24	139	6	4	3	1	0	3	14	0	23	0	1
Clanton, Matt, Boi.	1	0	1.000	9.00	1	0	0	0	0	0	2	1	9	2	2	0	0	1	1	1	0	1	0	1
Clarke, Darren, T.C.	4	3	.571	6.98	12	9	0	0	1	0	40	51	194	34	31	3	2	3	3	19	0	38	3	1
Collado, Jimmy, T.C.	0	1	.000	11.42	8	0	0	0	0	0	8.2	15	51	17	11	4	1	0	2	7	0	4	1	0
Coonrod, Aaron, Eug.	3	0	.500	5.54	15	12	0	0	1	0	65	75	297	48	40	2	2	2	8	24	1	45	2	0
Corley, Klent, Yak.	0	0	.000	7.55	19	5	0	0	1	0	39.1	57	209	44	33	2	1	1	4	32	0	19	2	1
Cormier, Lance, Van.	0	0	.000	27.00	1	1	0	0	0	0	1	4	8	4	3	0	0	0	0	0	0	3	0	0
Correia, Kevin, S.K.	2	2	.500	4.54	10	8	0	0	0	0	37.2	37	163	20	19	1	1	1	3	14	0	31	1	0
Cram, Josh, S.K.	0	1	.000	8.10	16	0	0	0	0	0	13.1	17	68	12	12	2	0	2	2	9	0	13	2	0
Crider, J.R., Van.	0	1	.000	9.00	2	0	0	0	0	0	2	5	14	6	2	1	0	0	1	2	0	1	1	1
Crockett, Ben, T.C.	0	1	.000	2.88	7	6	0	0	0	0	25	26	103	8	8	2	0	0	1	3	0	21	5	0
Crowder, Justin, Van.*	2	3	.400	2.25	17	3	0	0	3	2	40	31	153	12	10	2	0	1	0	3	0	50	0	0
Cruz, Jeff, T.C.*	1	0	1.000	4.57	15	0	0	0	8	1	21.2	26	100	14	11	2	0	1	1	12	0	19	1	0
Davies, Michael, T.C.*	5	2	.714	2.75	16	9	0	1	0	0	68.2	55	271	25	21	3	2	3	1	18	0	72	1	1
Davis, Mikael, Yak.	3	4	.429	4.38	22	1	0	0	7	0	51.1	46	224	31	25	4	2	2	2	26	0	46	5	2
Delgado, Oscar, Ever.*	2	2	.500	3.97	10	8	0	0	0	0	45.1	42	191	22	20	3	3	1	3	15	0	41	2	3
Dickinson, Drew, Van.*	4	0	1.000	2.06	11	10	0	0	0	0	48	37	184	11	11	1	0	1	0	12	0	40	4	0
Difelice, Mark, T.C.	0	0	.000	5.29	6	1	0	0	0	0	17	18	77	12	10	2	1	1	2	0	0	13	1	0

Pitcher, Team	W	L	Pct.	ERA	G	GS	CG	ShO	GF	Sv.	IP	H	TBF	R	ER	HR	SH	SF	HB	BB	IBB	SO	WP	Bk.
Dodson, Jeremy, Spo.	0	2	.000	16.50	8	0	0	0	2	0	6	9	40	14	11	1	0	2	2	10	0	3	2	0
Dooley, Jason, T.C.	3	3	.500	3.59	19	0	0	0	2	1	47.2	45	209	21	19	5	2	4	5	17	0	42	1	1
Dorman, Rich, Ever.	5	6	.455	4.30	15	15	0	0	0	0	75.1	85	347	53	36	2	4	5	3	33	0	68	12	0
Dossett, Dusty, Spo.	0	1	.000	2.49	15	0	0	0	5	0	25.1	21	109	8	7	1	2	1	3	10	0	11	1	0
Douglas, Mitch, Yak.*	0	0	.000	10.13	3	0	0	0	0	0	2.2	4	18	3	3	1	0	0	1	5	0	3	1	0
Doyle, Jared, Yak.*	4	4	.500	2.87	16	8	0	0	3	1	62.2	44	262	24	20	1	2	3	6	29	0	70	3	0
Dulkowski, Marc, Eug.	0	1	.000	2.25	4	0	0	0	4	1	4	4	18	1	1	0	0	1	0	2	0	4	1	0
Dunkle, Peter, T.C.	4	2	.667	2.91	20	0	0	0	6	1	43.1	22	177	17	14	2	6	1	3	19	1	27	4	0
Dunwell, Chris, Van.	1	5	.167	6.46	14	9	0	0	0	0	47.1	47	210	36	34	3	3	2	8	20	1	38	1	0
Encarnacion, Alexis, Spo.	0	0	.000	2.86	11	0	0	0	3	0	22	19	88	7	7	1	0	0	0	3	0	14	0	0
Endicott, Drew, Spo.	7	3	.700	3.06	19	6	0	0	1	0	67.2	62	282	28	23	4	2	0	0	25	0	44	2	0
Ervin, Josh, Eug.	0	0	.000	0.00	2	0	0	0	1	0	1.1	1	5	0	0	0	0	0	0	0	0	1	0	0
Flanagan, Jeremy, Boi.	1	0	1.000	3.16	22	0	0	0	12	1	31.1	28	140	18	11	0	0	1	3	11	0	25	3	1
Francis, Jeff, T.C.*	0	0	.000	0.00	4	3	0	0	0	0	10.2	5	40	0	0	0	0	0	1	4	0	16	0	0
Franklin, Ryan, Ever.	0	0	.000	0.00	1	1	0	0	0	0	2.2	2	12	1	0	0	0	0	2	0	0	1	0	0
Fritz, Ben, Van.	1	4	.200	2.95	9	9	0	0	0	0	39.2	29	165	16	13	1	2	0	3	14	0	33	3	0
Fulmer, T.A., Ever.	1	2	.333	3.24	12	4	0	0	1	0	33.1	35	145	16	12	2	1	1	2	9	0	34	2	0
Garber, Mike, Yak.*	1	6	.143	2.54	9	7	0	0	2	0	46	49	208	27	13	4	2	0	2	14	0	31	4	0
Garcia, Jairo, Van.	0	3	.000	7.30	3	3	0	0	0	0	12.1	15	59	11	10	1	0	1	1	7	0	16	1	1
Garcia, James, S.K.	1	3	.250	2.08	14	0	0	0	10	4	17.1	9	71	5	4	2	1	2	1	6	1	24	2	1
Gill, Chris, Van.	4	2	.667	4.13	20	0	0	0	5	0	28.1	30	132	15	13	1	1	1	1	17	0	24	3	0
Gonzalez, Enrique, Yak.	5	2	.714	2.45	11	11	0	0	0	0	66	53	278	27	18	2	1	5	7	23	0	57	7	0
Gorman, Jason, Yak.	0	0	.000	0.00	2	0	0	0	2	0	2	2	7	0	0	0	0	0	0	0	0	0	0	0
Greinke, Zack, Spo.	0	0	.000	7.71	2	2	0	0	0	0	4.2	9	23	4	4	0	0	0	0	0	0	5	1	0
Habel, Josh, S.K.*	2	2	.500	6.00	16	7	0	0	1	0	48	57	209	35	32	2	2	3	0	24	3	33	3	0
Hagerty, Luke, Boi.*	5	3	.625	1.13	10	10	0	0	0	0	48	32	188	15	6	2	2	0	2	15	0	50	1	0
Heflin, Theo, Ever.*	5	1	.833	2.43	20	0	0	0	4	1	33.1	25	145	12	9	1	1	0	4	21	1	25	7	0
Hensley, Clay, S.K.	7	0	1.000	2.53	15	15	1	0	0	0	81.2	72	337	31	23	3	2	1	3	25	0	84	6	1
Hill, Richard, Boi.*	0	2	.000	8.36	6	5	0	0	1	0	14	15	73	19	13	0	0	0	3	14	0	12	4	0
Hines, Matthew, Boi.	0	0	.000	0.00	3	0	0	0	1	0	5	2	20	1	0	0	0	0	0	2	0	2	1	0
Hixson, David, S.K.	0	0	.000	3.38	3	0	0	0	2	0	5.1	7	24	3	2	0	0	2	0	2	0	3	0	0
Hoffpauir, Micah, Boi.*	0	0	.000	0.00	1	0	0	0	1	0	1	0	3	0	0	0	0	0	0	0	0	0	0	0
Howay, Chris, Van.	1	0	1.000	2.37	11	0	0	0	4	0	19	14	74	5	5	1	0	0	1	1	0	12	3	2
Jefferson, Drew, S.K.*	2	2	.500	3.81	23	0	0	0	5	1	28.1	27	119	12	12	1	0	0	0	8	0	39	1	0
Jimenez, Cesar, Ever.*	2	1	.667	2.70	8	0	0	0	2	1	20	12	81	7	6	2	3	1	3	5	0	25	1	0
Johnson, Doug, T.C.	5	3	.625	3.47	15	15	0	0	0	0	70	63	299	33	27	5	2	6	7	24	0	43	8	0
Johnson, Thad, Van.	1	0	1.000	3.14	5	2	0	0	0	0	14.1	9	56	5	5	0	2	0	1	4	0	6	0	0
Jones, Geoffrey, Eug.*	0	0	.000	5.40	1	1	0	0	0	0	5	4	20	3	3	1	0	0	0	1	0	5	0	0
Jones, Justin, Boi.*	1	0	1.000	1.80	1	1	0	0	0	0	5	4	22	1	1	0	0	0	0	3	0	4	0	0
Keppinger, Billy, Spo.*	0	2	.000	1.29	28	0	0	0	24	16	42	29	164	9	6	2	2	1	1	10	0	39	1	1
Kohn, Shawn, Van.	3	2	.600	3.10	16	0	0	0	4	0	20.1	20	86	7	7	1	2	1	1	6	0	20	1	0
Korneev, Oleg, Ever.	0	3	.000	9.95	5	3	0	0	0	0	19	33	95	21	21	4	0	1	2	6	0	7	2	2
Landeros, Leonard, Van.*	6	1	.857	3.28	21	1	0	0	4	0	49.1	53	218	25	18	2	1	2	5	14	0	39	4	1
Laratta, E.J., Eug.	3	1	.750	1.33	12	0	0	0	2	0	20.1	16	85	8	3	1	1	0	0	10	0	13	2	0
Leon, Brigmer, Van.	3	1	.750	3.96	18	1	0	0	5	0	38.2	36	167	23	17	3	4	2	4	10	1	32	4	2
Lipari, Thomas, Eug.*	2	0	1.000	2.66	10	9	0	0	1	0	40.2	38	177	16	12	2	2	0	2	14	0	52	0	1
Livingston, Bobby, Ever.*	6	5	.545	3.02	15	14	0	0	1	0	80.1	80	338	33	27	2	1	2	7	14	0	76	4	2
Lizarraga, Sergio, Yak.	4	8	.333	4.05	16	13	0	0	2	0	91	90	379	48	41	6	5	4	7	19	0	86	4	0
Lopez, Nelson, S.K.	0	1	.000	6.23	5	0	0	0	1	0	4.1	3	26	5	3	0	0	0	3	6	0	1	3	0
Martin, Scott, Eug.*	1	2	.333	3.74	17	0	0	0	8	0	21.2	23	97	14	9	1	1	1	2	5	0	16	0	1
Martinez, Dionnar, Boi.	0	0	.000	0.00	2	0	0	0	2	0	2	0	8	0	0	0	0	0	0	1	0	2	0	0
Martinez, Javier, Eug.	0	0	.000	4.50	2	2	0	0	0	0	10	4	40	5	5	2	0	1	1	5	0	6	0	0
Martinez, Miguel, Ever.*	1	1	.500	3.38	11	0	0	0	9	2	16	8	62	6	6	2	0	0	1	7	1	24	1	0
Matos, Raymond, S.K.*	0	2	.000	4.05	18	0	0	0	5	0	26.2	23	119	15	12	1	3	0	2	11	0	18	1	0
McDonnell, Matt, Spo.	1	1	.500	4.29	21	0	0	0	6	2	35.2	30	148	17	17	2	3	1	3	16	0	17	3	1
Medina, Franklin, Yak.	0	3	.000	6.08	9	4	0	0	0	0	26.2	33	136	25	18	5	0	2	2	22	0	34	3	3
Medina, Roberto, Yak.*	1	2	.333	4.05	26	0	0	0	9	0	33.1	39	173	30	15	4	2	2	2	30	3	28	8	1
Mercedes, Gabriel, Yak.	0	5	.000	4.11	20	4	0	0	6	2	46	48	210	26	21	0	2	1	6	32	1	31	6	4
Mitchell, Ben, S.K.	2	4	.333	2.16	25	0	0	0	22	10	25	14	111	7	6	1	3	0	3	17	3	26	1	0
Modica, Greg, Eug.	0	2	.000	6.67	26	0	0	0	6	0	27	35	130	24	20	3	1	1	3	11	0	25	0	3
Montarbo, Adam, Eug.	0	2	.000	8.00	12	0	0	0	3	1	9	10	44	8	8	2	1	0	0	5	1	8	2	0
Morel, Eudy, Eug.	6	0	1.000	2.54	23	0	0	0	5	1	28.1	26	118	13	8	3	1	1	0	5	0	27	0	0
Morrow, David, Ever.	0	0	.000	4.00	17	0	0	0	10	0	18	19	89	13	8	1	0	0	1	19	0	14	5	1
Muessig, Jeff, Van.	2	0	1.000	1.78	24	0	0	0	18	5	30.1	16	125	8	6	1	1	0	3	16	0	47	2	0
Munter, Scott, S.K.	1	1	.500	6.98	10	4	0	0	1	0	29.2	33	141	24	23	0	1	3	2	20	0	20	3	1
Murphy, Bill, Van.*	1	4	.200	4.57	13	9	0	0	0	0	41.1	28	187	23	21	2	1	3	2	35	0	46	4	0
Nelson, Jeff, Ever.	0	1	.000	0.00	1	1	0	0	0	0	1.1	1	5	1	0	0	0	0	0	0	0	4	0	0
Nelson, Luke, S.K.	7	0	1.000	1.87	14	0	0	0	4	1	43.1	28	166	9	9	1	4	0	4	9	0	33	2	0
Nicholson, Scott, T.C.*	0	3	.000	4.91	9	4	0	0	2	0	29.1	36	132	20	16	1	1	2	1	8	0	20	0	0
Nolasco, Ricky, Boi.	7	2	.778	2.48	15	15	0	0	0	0	90.2	72	379	32	25	1	8	1	9	25	0	92	5	0
Nunez, Kelvin, Spo.	1	7	.125	9.19	10	7	0	0	0	0	32.1	57	165	37	33	6	0	4	4	15	0	17	4	2
Obenchain, Stephen, Van.	2	3	.400	2.85	11	10	0	0	1	0	41	35	172	18	13	1	1	2	4	10	1	29	2	1
O'Brien, Wes, Boi.	3	3	.500	2.89	23	1	0	0	11	2	43.2	34	195	15	14	1	3	0	6	25	1	51	1	2
O'Malley, Ryan, Boi.*	3	1	.750	2.52	23	0	0	0	5	1	39.1	32	162	16	11	3	3	3	0	15	1	26	2	1
Palmer, Matt, S.K.	3	2	.600	1.84	16	9	0	0	3	0	53.2	44	217	15	11	0	0	1	3	23	0	49	5	0
Pauley, David, Eug.	6	1	.857	2.81	15	15	0	0	0	0	80	81	335	32	25	6	3	4	6	18	1	62	7	0
Pavlik, Isaac, T.C.*	5	1	.833	1.13	27	0	0	0	13	1	32	26	131	6	4	0	6	3	0	10	1	32	5	0
Perez, Edwin, Yak.	0	0	.000	7.71	2	0	0	0	1	0	2.1	1	10	2	2	0	0	0	2	1	0	3	0	0
Perez, Elvis, Ever.	0	0	.000	0.00	1	1	0	0	0	0	1.2	1	8	0	0	0	0	0	0	2	0	1	0	0
Pickens, J.R., Van.	0	0	.000	0.00	1	0	0	0	1	1	2	0	7	0	0	0	0	0	0	1	0	2	0	0
Ponder, Steven, T.C.*	0	0	.000	18.00	1	0	0	0	1	0	3	5	18	7	6	3	0	0	2	3	0	5	1	0
Rapada, Clayton, Boi.*	0	0	.000	1.50	12	0	0	0	2	1	18	18	85	7	3	0	0	2	3	8	0	12	0	0
Reba, Steve, T.C.	1	1	.500	1.66	14	2	0	0	4	3	38	28	145	8	7	1	1	1	2	4	0	47	4	0
Reyes, Luis, Boi.	4	0	1.000	2.95	20	0	0	0	5	0	36.2	33	163	20	12	1	1	0	3	20	0	17	6	0
Ribas, Gabe, Eug.	8	1	.889	1.97	32	1	0	0	29	16	50.1	36	196	14	11	1	1	1	3	5	1	66	4	0
Richards, John, Eug.*	0	0	.000	0.00	3	0	0	0	1	0	3	1	10	0	0	0	1	0	0	1	0	4	0	0
Rivera, Jimmy, Ever.	2	2	.500	3.98	20	1	0	0	8	1	40.2	45	186	25	18	4	5	1	2	18	0	35	3	0
Rodriguez, Manuel, Van.	5	0	1.000	1.91	21	0	0	0	6	1	37.2	27	156	9	8	3	2	1	3	15	2	26	4	2
Rowland-Smith, Ryan, Ever.*	4	1	.800	2.77	18	6	0	0	5	2	61.2	58	267	22	19	2	3	2	4	22	0	58	4	3
Ryan, Kevin, Eug.	0	2	.000	13.50	14	0	0	0	2	0	14	26	85	26	21	0	1	1	1	17	0	16	8	0
Ryu, Jae-kuk, Boi.	6	1	.857	3.57	10	10	0	0	0	0	53	45	234	28	21	1	1	2	4	25	0	56	8	1

Pitcher, Team	W	L	Pct.	ERA	G	GS	CG	ShO	GF	Sv.	IP	H	TBF	R	ER	HR	SH	SF	HB	BB	IBB	SO	WP	Bk.
Schilsky, Stephen, Van.	0	0	.000	2.35	6	0	0	0	3	0	7.2	11	36	2	2	0	0	0	4	0	3	0	0
Schmidt, Jason, S.K.	1	1	.500	4.38	9	0	0	0	3	0	12.1	12	59	7	6	0	2	1	8	0	13	1	0
Serrato, Juan, S.K.	2	3	.400	7.04	9	0	0	0	2	0	15.1	17	76	18	12	3	3	1	10	0	19	5	1
Sevier, Nate, Ever.	3	4	.429	3.03	15	10	0	0	1	0	68.1	67	292	31	23	6	4	2	20	0	57	4	0
Shank, Chris, Van.	0	3	.000	3.43	19	5	0	0	8	1	44.2	41	185	19	17	3	1	1	9	0	43	5	0
Shartzer, Bryan, T.C.	0	1	.000	2.57	9	0	0	0	2	0	14	12	62	4	4	1	2	1	0	6	0	16	2	0
Sierra, Edwardo, Van.	2	2	.000	6.11	9	7	0	0	0	0	28	42	148	24	19	0	1	2	3	17	0	23	4	0
Silva, Erick, Yak.	1	0	1.000	5.40	6	0	0	0	2	0	11.2	11	53	7	7	0	0	1	9	1	12	6	0
Sisco, Andy, Boi.*	7	2	.778	2.43	14	14	0	0	0	0	77.2	51	319	23	21	3	3	0	6	39	0	101	6	0
Soto, Darwin, Eug.	1	0	1.000	2.00	7	0	0	0	3	0	9	6	34	2	2	0	0	0	2	0	17	0	0
Stefani, Jason, Spo.*	1	1	.500	6.14	12	0	0	0	7	0	14.2	16	68	11	10	1	0	2	1	6	0	11	1	1
Steidlmayer, Luke, Eug.	3	2	.600	3.07	15	11	0	0	1	0	70.1	58	289	31	24	6	2	5	3	20	0	80	6	0
Suarez, Victor, Spo.	1	0	1.000	10.57	7	0	0	0	1	0	7.2	14	48	16	9	1	1	1	0	8	0	3	2	0
Taulli, Sam, Yak.*	2	0	.000	3.91	5	5	0	0	0	0	23	22	101	14	10	1	0	0	3	8	0	19	2	0
Tavarez, David, Ever.	5	0	1.000	3.24	21	0	0	0	8	0	33.1	26	149	15	12	3	3	1	2	17	1	29	1	0
Taylor, Justin, Spo.	1	2	.333	6.69	18	0	0	0	5	0	35	50	166	34	26	7	1	3	2	7	0	28	0	0
Tetuan, John, T.C.	2	6	.250	5.58	15	15	0	0	0	0	59.2	61	274	40	37	6	1	2	7	27	0	39	6	1
Thomas, Jared, Ever.*	1	1	.500	2.21	19	0	0	0	16	11	20.1	8	82	6	5	0	1	2	1	13	0	25	0	0
Tsao, Chin-hui, T.C.	0	0	.000	0.00	3	3	0	0	0	0	11	6	42	2	0	0	0	0	2	0	16	2	1
Urrutia, Carlos, Boi.	1	3	.250	11.69	12	5	0	0	0	0	22.1	34	128	32	29	2	1	1	3	22	0	18	6	2
Vasquez, Carlos, Boi.*	5	6	.455	4.26	15	15	0	0	0	0	80.1	77	357	45	38	6	3	1	10	33	0	68	9	1
Viane, David, Ever.	1	1	.500	6.84	20	0	0	0	8	1	25	30	128	23	19	1	1	1	3	22	0	18	5	0
Villatoro, Wilmer, Eug.	3	7	.300	5.13	22	7	0	0	2	2	52.2	50	235	36	30	8	6	4	2	19	0	69	2	1
Waddell, Jason, S.K.*	0	2	.000	5.40	11	2	0	0	4	0	20	19	82	12	12	2	0	2	10	0	13	2	0
Waroff, Shane, Yak.	1	7	.125	4.31	24	8	0	0	11	1	62.2	69	283	36	30	5	1	3	6	24	1	45	5	0
Watson, Mike, T.C.	4	2	.667	3.43	18	0	0	0	3	0	42	37	179	19	16	2	3	2	3	15	0	39	4	0
Whitaker, Brian, Eug.	5	8	.385	2.93	16	14	0	0	0	0	83	79	343	36	27	6	5	1	5	16	0	63	2	0
White, Bill, Yak.*	0	1	.000	9.35	3	3	0	0	0	0	8.2	10	46	9	9	2	0	0	0	10	0	11	1	1
Woolard, Glenn, S.K.	3	2	.600	2.96	17	11	0	0	0	0	67	51	289	26	22	3	2	3	6	32	3	75	4	0
Wykoff, Zach, Eug.	0	1	.000	12.46	8	0	0	0	0	0	8.2	16	46	12	12	3	0	0	1	4	0	6	1	0
Wylie, Jason, Boi.	1	1	.500	1.99	24	0	0	0	14	11	40.2	26	153	9	9	1	4	1	2	7	1	44	2	0
Yacco, Anthony, S.K.	0	1	.000	0.00	2	0	0	0	0	0	4.1	3	24	3	0	0	0	0	6	1	4	1	0
Young, Chris, T.C.	5	5	.500	2.34	17	6	0	0	1	0	61.2	45	255	20	16	1	3	2	5	23	0	47	6	1
Zettler, Nate, Spo.	1	3	.250	7.16	22	0	0	0	15	2	27.2	43	151	28	22	3	0	4	3	19	2	14	6	1

COMBINATION SHUTOUTS: **Boise (3)**—Hagerty-Flanagan 2, Hill-Reyes-Rapada-Wylie. **Eugene (4)**—Lipari-Bomar-Modica-Martin-Dulkowski, Steidlmayer-Morel-Ribas, Steidlmayer-Ryan-Bochy, Whitaker-Martin-Modica-Riba. **Everett (5)**—Cate-Morrow, Fulmer-Heflin-Tavarez-Thomas, Livingston-Tavarez-Thomas, Rowland-Smith-Thomas, Rowland-Smith-Rivera-Heflin-Tavarez-Thomas. **Salem-Keizer (7)**—Bruso-L. Nelson-Mitchell 2, Bruso-Jefferson-Mitchell, Habel-Cram-Mitchell-Jefferson, Hensley-L. Nelson, Palmer-Woolard-Bateman-Mitchell, Woolard-Munter-Cram. **Spokane (6)**—Ackerman-Keppinger, G. Atencio-Endicott-Keppinger, G. Atencio-Taylor, Christensen-Endicott-McDonnell, Christensen-Keppinger, Endicott-Encarnacion-Keppinger. **Tri-City (3)**—Clarke-Cruz-Watson-Beckstead, Tsao-Davies-Collado, Young-Reba. **Vancouver (10)**—Blanton-Landeros, Crowder-Howay-Muessig, Dickinson-Kohn-Crowder-Shank, Dickinson-Kohn-Landeros-Muessig, Dickinson-Rodriguez-Crowder, Dunwell-Burton, Murphy-Howay-Muessig, Obenchain-Landeros-Muessig, Obenchain-Landeros-Shank-Beck-Muessig, Shank-Landeros-Beck-Muessig. **Yakima (2)**—Aquino-Doyle, Waroff-Bonnell-R. Medina.

NO-HIT GAMES: None.

2002 FIELDING

TEAM

Team	G	PO	A	E	TC	DP	TP	PB	Pct.
Tri-City	76	2062	810	105	2977	42	0	16	.965
Salem-Keizer	76	2033	805	104	2942	60	0	18	.965
Boise	76	2048	888	111	3047	67	0	19	.964
Vancouver	76	1995	723	104	2822	52	0	10	.963
Eugene	76	1994	708	110	2812	52	0	18	.961
Yakima	76	2008	805	119	2932	64	0	24	.959
Spokane	76	2020	841	125	2986	74	0	7	.958
Everett	76	2055	742	128	2925	53	0	13	.956

INDIVIDUAL

FIRST BASEMEN

NOTE: All caps denotes fielding-percentage leader based on 38 games for catchers, 51 for all other non-pitchers and 61 innings for pitchers. *Throws lefthanded.

Player, Team	Pct.	G	PO	A	E	TC	DP
Bell, Derek, S.K.	1.000	23	164	11	0	175	14
Bernier, Doug, T.C.	1.000	2	21	0	0	21	3
Brooks, Jeff, Eug.	.986	19	132	6	2	140	6
Cadena, Alex, Ever.	.979	14	87	5	2	94	3
Colamarino, Brant, Van.*	.988	63	470	30	6	506	29
Collins, Kevin, Van.	.975	26	226	11	6	243	22
Dibetta, John, Eug.	.992	47	366	19	3	388	27
Dryer, Matt, S.K.	1.000	5	46	2	0	48	4
Dyson, Trey, Spo.*	1.000	7	59	13	0	72	6
Guzman, Jacob, Spo.	.889	1	7	1	1	9	0
Hoffpauir, Micah, Boi.*	.986	58	539	17	8	564	44
Holm, Steve, S.K.	1.000	1	1	0	0	1	0
Huff, Ken, Yak.*	.989	13	82	8	1	91	9
Ishikawa, Travis, S.K.*	.980	22	182	12	4	198	13
Jensen, David, Spo.*	.989	66	590	40	7	637	59
JOHNSON, Bryan, Yak.	.994	57	477	33	3	513	44
Kelly, Tripp, Van.	.981	19	145	8	3	156	16
Kunich, Frank, Ever.	.955	2	20	1	1	22	2
Legendre, Curtis, Spo.	.969	4	30	1	1	32	3
Luellwitz, Sean, Yak.	1.000	6	57	2	0	59	3
Martinez, Thomas, Eug.	.969	14	85	8	3	96	9
Nelson, Jon, Ever.	.987	60	489	37	7	533	38

Player, Team	Pct.	G	PO	A	E	TC	DP
Santana, Manny, S.K.	.985	8	65	1	1	67	4
Smith, Sam, T.C.	.993	47	384	28	3	415	17
Stone, David, S.K.	.977	26	205	12	5	222	20
Street, Dan, T.C.	.988	26	239	13	3	255	16
Tiesing, Tyler, Yak.	1.000	6	26	2	0	28	2
Townsend, Rich, Eug.	1.000	2	14	1	0	15	2
Ventura, Juan, T.C.	1.000	3	33	1	0	34	0
Woody, Dominic, Ever.	.917	1	11	0	1	12	2

SECOND BASEMEN

Player, Team	Pct.	G	PO	A	E	TC	DP
Agosto, Rolando, Eug.	.000	1	0	0	0	0	0
Bernier, Doug, T.C.	.882	6	7	8	2	17	0
Berroa, Joandry, Yak.	.923	11	16	20	3	39	4
Brown, Nebasett, Yak.	.959	46	68	94	7	169	16
Burgamy, Brian, Eug.	.936	65	131	161	20	312	27
Cabrera, Chi Chi, S.K.	.986	16	39	31	1	71	6
Castro, Ismael, Ever.	.953	64	127	154	14	295	28
Cedeno, Ronny, Boi.	1.000	1	1	3	0	4	1
Chirinos, Robinson, Boi.	.963	61	129	185	12	326	40
Dean, Erik, Spo.	.929	11	14	25	3	42	5
Garciaparra, Michael, Ever.	.923	2	5	7	1	13	1
Gates, Bookie, Yak.	1.000	2	5	8	0	13	4
Gomez, Francis, Van.	1.000	1	1	0	0	1	0
Gorman, Jason, Yak.	.967	21	21	37	2	60	7
Guance, Walkill, T.C.	.957	61	101	166	12	279	25
Haley, Adam, Yak.	1.000	3	2	3	0	5	1
Henriquez, Hector, Ever.	1.000	2	1	3	0	4	1
Hood, Damien, Boi.	.955	6	3	18	1	22	1
Keim, Adam, Spo.	1.000	11	17	24	0	41	5
Kelly, Tripp, Van.	.000	1	0	0	0	0	0
KIGER, Mark, Van.	.969	52	101	119	7	227	20
Kunich, Frank, Ever.	.931	8	12	15	2	29	3
Lonnquist, Eric, Spo.	.967	53	101	134	8	243	28
McCool, Lee, Yak.	.962	13	24	26	2	52	3
Menchaca, Eriberto, Ever.	1.000	3	4	7	0	11	2
Monahan, Joey, Boi.	1.000	1	4	1	0	5	1
Navarro, Mandy, Boi.	.975	9	14	25	1	40	4
Nulton, Kevin, Eug.	.902	13	18	28	5	51	4
O'Sullivan, Steve, Boi.	1.000	4	5	9	0	14	2
Pinon, Alex, S.K.	.982	14	21	33	1	55	5

Player, Team	Pct.	G	PO	A	E	TC	DP
Richardson, Mike, Eug.	1.000	2	2	3	0	5	0
Rodriguez, Alex, Spo.	1.000	13	19	29	0	48	8
Sobieraj, Aaron, S.K.	.923	52	106	147	21	274	30
Spearman, Jemel, Boi.	1.000	1	1	2	0	3	1
Tiesing, Tyler, Yak.	.000	2	0	0	0	0	0
Turner, Lloyd, Van.	.966	13	23	34	2	59	7
Wayment, Kory, Van.	.981	13	18	34	1	53	8
White, Carson, T.C.	.935	14	27	31	4	62	4

THIRD BASEMEN

Player, Team	Pct.	G	PO	A	E	TC	DP
Agosto, Rolando, Eug.	.500	3	0	2	2	4	1
Barden, Brian, Yak.	.889	4	1	15	2	18	1
Bernier, Doug, T.C.	.951	48	33	102	7	142	7
Brooks, Jeff, Eug.	1.000	4	0	4	0	4	0
Brown, Hunter, Ever.	.824	8	4	10	3	17	0
Brown, Nebasett, Yak.	.909	12	3	17	2	22	1
Bushey, Andrew, T.C.	.833	10	4	16	4	24	1
Cabrera, Chi Chi, S.K.	1.000	2	0	5	0	5	1
Craig, Matt, Boi.	.921	30	18	52	6	76	1
Dean, Erik, Spo.	.000	1	0	0	0	0	0
Dibetta, John, Eug.	.911	21	14	37	5	56	4
Dryer, Matt, S.K.	.917	33	19	58	7	84	4
Ferrara, Matt, Spo.	.778	6	4	17	6	27	1
Gates, Bookie, Yak.	.857	56	43	83	21	147	5
Gil, Jerry, Yak.	1.000	1	0	1	0	1	0
Gomez, Francis, Van.	.889	12	11	21	4	36	0
Gorman, Jason, Yak.	.903	15	11	17	3	31	0
HAGEN, Matt, Ever.	.873	63	39	105	21	165	11
Harriman, David, Van.	.500	1	0	1	1	2	0
Henriquez, Hector, Ever.	.400	2	0	2	3	5	0
Hood, Donnie, Boi.	.892	40	16	83	12	111	9
Hornostaj, Aaron, S.K.	.500	1	0	1	1	2	0
Keim, Adam, Spo.	.927	42	19	70	7	96	6
Kelly, Kevin, S.K.	.927	15	7	31	3	41	4
Kunich, Frank, Ever.	.667	5	3	5	4	12	2
Legendre, Curtis, Spo.	.848	36	22	56	14	92	9
Lonnquist, Eric, Spo.	.667	2	0	2	1	3	0
Luellwitz, Sean, Yak.	.500	1	0	1	1	2	0
Maestrales, Pete, S.K.	.900	7	2	7	1	10	1
McCurdy, John, Van.	1.000	3	5	3	0	8	0
Menchaca, Eriberto, Ever.	1.000	1	2	2	0	4	1
Navarro, Mandy, Boi.	1.000	3	1	2	0	3	0
Nulton, Kevin, Eug.	.900	24	16	38	6	60	1
O'Sullivan, Steve, Boi.	.000	1	0	0	0	0	0
O'Toole, Paul, Boi.	.800	2	1	3	1	5	0
Pinon, Alex, S.K.	.860	24	13	36	8	57	4
Richardson, Mike, Eug.	.929	4	2	11	1	14	0
Servais, Eric, Boi.	.769	7	4	6	3	13	0
Street, Dan, T.C.	.849	22	13	32	8	53	0
Suomi, Richard, Van.	.000	1	0	0	0	0	0
Teahen, Mark, Van.	.882	13	4	26	4	34	2
Townsend, Rich, Eug.	.928	26	21	43	5	69	7
Turner, Lloyd, Van.	.909	15	7	23	3	33	2
Wayment, Kory, Van.	.916	37	30	68	9	107	6
Zuniga, Tony, S.K.	1.000	3	3	4	0	7	1

SHORTSTOPS

Player, Team	Pct.	G	PO	A	E	TC	DP
Agosto, Rolando, Eug.	.930	62	91	163	19	273	29
Bernier, Doug, T.C.	.960	10	14	34	2	50	2
Berroa, Joandry, Yak.	.927	17	32	44	6	82	6
Blakeley, Eric, Ever.	.727	1	5	3	3	11	1
Brown, Hunter, Ever.	.895	8	18	16	4	38	2
Burgamy, Brian, Eug.	1.000	1	0	2	0	2	0
Cabrera, Chi Chi, S.K.	.967	19	19	40	2	61	15
Castro, Ismael, Ever.	1.000	1	1	4	0	5	0
Cedeno, Ronny, Boi.	.941	28	32	96	8	136	18
Chirinos, Robinson, Boi.	.889	2	2	6	1	9	2
Craig, Matt, Boi.	1.000	1	2	3	0	5	0
Garciaparra, Michael, Ever.	.903	7	9	19	3	31	0
Gil, Jerry, Yak.	.918	60	86	170	23	279	36
Gomez, Francis, Van.	.944	9	12	22	2	36	6
Gorman, Jason, Yak.	1.000	7	7	17	0	24	3
Greene, Khalil, Eug.	.900	10	12	15	3	30	2
Haley, Adam, Eug.	1.000	3	5	2	0	7	1
Harrington, Corey, Ever.	.893	49	63	112	21	196	17
Henriquez, Hector, Ever.	.946	13	12	23	2	37	4
Hood, Donnie, Boi.	.895	3	5	12	2	19	2
Hornostaj, Aaron, S.K.	.750	2	3	6	3	12	4
Keim, Adam, Spo.	1.000	7	12	14	0	26	6
Kiger, Mark, Van.	.911	12	22	29	5	56	9
Lonnquist, Eric, Spo.	.958	6	9	14	1	24	2
Materano, Oscar, T.C.	.931	67	114	197	23	334	25
McCurdy, John, Van.	.908	51	70	127	20	217	18
Menchaca, Eriberto, Ever.	1.000	3	4	7	0	11	4
Monahan, Joey, Boi.	.910	40	54	139	19	212	22
Murphy, Donald, Spo.	.931	26	42	66	8	116	14
Navarro, Mandy, Boi.	.933	3	2	12	1	15	1
Nulton, Kevin, Eug.	.947	8	7	11	1	19	0

Player, Team	Pct.	G	PO	A	E	TC	DP
Pinon, Alex, S.K.	.750	1	1	2	1	4	0
Rodriguez, Alex, Spo.	.935	47	76	139	15	230	26
Spearman, Jemel, Boi.	1.000	2	0	6	0	6	0
WALD, Jake, S.K.	.944	62	94	177	16	287	21
Wayment, Kory, Van.	.878	9	16	20	5	41	3

OUTFIELDERS

Player, Team	Pct.	G	PO	A	E	TC	DP
Alexander, Alexis, Spo.	.984	40	55	5	1	61	3
Arroyo, Carlos, Ever.*	.972	36	67	3	2	72	2
Bacon, Dwaine, Boi.	1.000	61	90	0	0	90	0
Baker, Steve, Eug.	.964	59	99	9	4	112	2
Banks, Gary, Boi.	.983	59	109	4	2	115	0
Barker, Sean, T.C.	.966	35	49	7	2	58	0
Barrett, Rich, Yak.	.991	55	100	8	1	109	1
Biernbaum, L.J., Eug.*	1.000	8	21	3	0	24	1
Bohn, T.J., Ever.	.989	53	82	4	1	87	0
Cabrera, Chi Chi, S.K.	.667	2	4	0	2	6	0
Callahan, Dan, Yak.*	1.000	7	8	1	0	9	0
Carter, Josh, Eug.	.938	6	15	0	1	16	0
Cleto, Carlos, S.K.*	1.000	3	5	0	0	5	0
Colton, Chris, Ever.	.981	64	155	3	3	161	1
Cruz, Nelson, Van.	.961	62	96	3	4	103	0
De Los Santos, Pedro, Eug.	.921	20	34	1	3	38	0
Fransz, Jason, Boi.	.955	55	61	2	3	66	0
Frend, Tim, Spo.	.958	41	64	4	3	71	1
Garcia, Lino, Yak.	.975	24	35	4	1	40	0
Garthwaite, Jay, Yak.	1.000	14	20	1	0	21	0
Gates, Bookie, Yak.	.000	1	0	0	0	0	0
Gearlds, Aaron, T.C.	1.000	1	2	0	0	2	0
Gibbons, Daniel, Van.*	1.000	19	16	2	2	20	1
Giorgis, David, Eug.	.966	21	28	0	1	29	0
Gonzalez, Bernie, T.C.	.956	52	84	2	4	90	1
Gorman, Jason, Yak.	.000	1	0	0	0	0	0
Harris, Gary, Ever.	.984	64	114	8	2	124	1
Huff, Ken, Yak.*	1.000	9	12	1	0	13	0
Hutchinson, Burnell, Yak.	1.000	3	2	0	0	2	0
Jernigan, Karl, S.K.	1.000	32	39	2	0	41	0
Jones, Kennard, Eug.*	.932	16	41	0	3	44	0
Kunich, Frank, Ever.	.833	7	5	0	1	6	0
Lewis, Fred, S.K.	.955	53	82	2	4	88	0
Luellwitz, Sean, Yak.	.000	1	0	0	0	0	0
Lytle, Derrik, Spo.*	.900	27	42	3	5	50	0
Maestrales, Pete, S.K.	.964	27	23	4	1	28	0
Millan, Carlos, Eug.	1.000	19	18	0	0	18	0
Monte, Harvey, Ever.*	.962	12	25	0	1	26	0
Moore, Rusty, Eug.	1.000	4	5	0	0	5	0
Mora, Ruben, Eug.	.964	26	52	1	2	55	0
Morris, Jed, Van.	.000	1	0	0	0	0	0
Nagle, Austin, Van.	.986	40	72	1	1	74	0
Nordness, Kirk, Van.	1.000	12	22	3	0	25	0
Ortmeier, Daniel, S.K.*	.984	37	59	1	1	61	0
Paredes, Jeison, Yak.	.933	31	40	2	3	45	0
Peirce, Justin, Van.	.000	1	0	0	0	0	0
Pie, Felix, Boi.*	1.000	2	4	0	0	4	0
Pinango, Ever, S.K.	1.000	20	7	0	0	7	0
Richardson, Mike, Eug.	.990	60	94	4	1	99	0
Rooke, Brian, Van.	1.000	1	4	0	0	4	0
Rosario, Victor, Spo.	1.000	24	44	1	0	45	0
Saba, Donnie, Yak.	.969	43	58	4	2	64	0
SALAZAR, Jeff, T.C.*	1.000	71	151	6	0	157	3
Spilborghs, Ryan, T.C.	.977	64	123	6	3	132	0
Stavisky, Brian, Van.	.920	16	21	2	2	25	0
Stephens, Bernard, Spo.	.974	62	141	6	4	151	1
Stocker, Mel, Spo.	.977	58	124	3	3	130	0
Stone, David, S.K.	.951	33	38	1	2	41	0
Suomi, Richard, Van.	.929	15	13	0	1	14	0
Swisher, Nick, Van.*	1.000	13	26	0	0	26	0
Tritle, Chris, Van.	.961	56	123	0	5	128	0
Turner, Lloyd, Van.	1.000	14	22	0	0	22	0
Ventura, Juan, T.C.	1.000	1	3	0	0	3	0
Walker, Chris, Boi.	.976	58	73	7	2	82	0
Walter, Paul, S.K.	.985	64	128	3	2	133	0
Wayment, Kory, Van.	.000	1	0	0	0	0	0
White, Carson, T.C.	.900	4	9	0	1	10	0
Wilkins, Joseph, Yak.	1.000	2	2	0	0	2	0
Williams, Marland, Yak.	.930	67	129	3	10	142	0

CATCHERS

Player, Team	Pct.	G	PO	A	E	TC	DP	PB
Baker, John, Van.	.979	18	127	13	3	143	0	3
Bibee, Hal, T.C.	.978	25	202	16	5	223	0	3
Brown, Jeremy, Van.	.984	9	57	5	1	63	0	1
Buller, Dayton, S.K.	.981	19	138	18	3	159	0	2
Bushey, Andrew, T.C.	.983	36	265	23	5	293	0	6
Cadena, Alex, Ever.	1.000	1	1	0	0	1	0	0
Ervin, Josh, Eug.	1.000	17	126	10	0	136	1	4
Glessner, Jeremiah, T.C.	1.000	2	14	0	0	14	0	1
Guzman, Jacob, Spo.	.938	21	113	7	8	128	1	1
Harriman, David, Van.	.992	22	117	4	1	122	0	3

Player, Team	Pct.	G	PO	A	E	TC	DP	PB
HOLM, Steve, S.K.	.991	48	309	38	3	350	2	8
Hudson, Ben, Ever.	.941	8	29	3	2	34	1	1
Madera, Sandy, Van.	1.000	1	5	0	0	5	0	0
Martinez, Thomas, Eug.	.987	10	72	3	1	76	0	8
Medlin, C.J., Boi.	.983	42	325	32	6	363	0	4
Meyer, Rusty, Spo.	.946	6	41	12	3	56	1	1
Miller, Chris, Boi.	.985	29	234	21	4	259	1	11
Montilla, Samuel, Yak.	.986	35	247	30	4	281	2	13
Morris, Jed, Van.	1.000	17	123	18	0	141	3	2
Richardson, Mike, Eug.	1.000	2	5	0	0	5	0	0
Riley, Kenny, T.C.	1.000	8	45	4	0	49	0	4
Rivera, Rene, Ever.	.987	58	489	54	7	550	3	8
Santana, Manny, S.K.	1.000	14	75	8	0	83	0	3
Selmo, Martin, Eug.	1.000	8	71	11	0	82	0	1
Servais, Eric, Boi.	1.000	8	15	0	0	15	0	2
Shorsher, Adam, Eug.	.982	45	361	29	7	397	2	5
Soto, Geovany, Boi.	1.000	1	6	0	0	6	0	0
Suomi, Richard, Van.	.989	21	174	11	2	187	0	1
Sweeney, James, T.C.	.980	11	83	13	2	98	1	2
Tiesing, Tyler, Yak.	1.000	13	87	12	0	99	0	5
Tupman, Matt, Spo.	.991	50	293	52	3	348	1	5
Turco, Anthony, S.K.	.965	15	95	14	4	113	0	5
Valles, Jake, Spo.	.962	8	23	2	1	26	0	1
Wells, Randy, Boi.	.982	8	52	3	1	56	0	2
Wilkins, Joseph, Yak.	.983	37	247	40	5	292	5	6
Williams, Jonny, S.K.	.889	3	7	1	1	9	0	0
Woody, Dominic, Ever.	.986	17	131	11	2	144	0	4

PITCHERS

Player, Team	Pct.	G	PO	A	E	TC	DP
Ackerman, Eric, Spo.*	1.000	8	2	4	0	6	0
Aquino, Greg, Yak.	1.000	6	2	7	0	9	2
Atencio, Donald, Van.	.000	1	0	0	0	0	0
Atencio, Greg, Spo.	1.000	14	3	11	0	14	0
Atlee, Rick, Boi.	.800	19	3	1	1	5	0
Averette, Robert, T.C.	1.000	3	1	1	0	2	0
Baez, Federico, Boi.	1.000	1	0	1	0	1	0
Barnett, John, Spo.	1.000	7	0	2	0	2	0
Bartz, Jason, Spo.	.667	7	1	1	1	3	0
Bateman, Jamie, S.K.	1.000	19	1	12	0	13	1
Bayliss, Jonah, Spo.	.800	15	9	7	4	20	1
Beavers, Kevin, Eug.*	1.000	4	0	2	0	2	2
Beck, David, Van.*	1.000	20	1	5	0	6	0
Beckstead, Jentry, T.C.	1.000	29	3	0	0	3	0
Bernier, Doug, T.C.	1.000	1	1	0	0	1	0
Biggs, Billy, Yak.	1.000	20	0	7	0	7	0
Blanton, Joe, Van.	1.000	4	0	2	0	2	0
Blood, Justin, Ever.*	1.000	2	0	2	0	2	0
Bochy, Greg, Eug.	1.000	17	1	2	0	3	0
Bomar, Mike, Eug.*	1.000	12	1	0	0	1	0
Bonnell, Jared, Yak.	.875	19	0	7	1	8	0
Brown, Ira, Spo.	.692	16	6	12	8	26	0
Bruso, Greg, S.K.	1.000	14	6	6	0	12	0
Burnau, Ryan, Boi.	1.000	25	0	8	0	8	1
Burton, Levi, Van.	.909	13	3	7	1	11	0
Carter, Ramsey, Spo.	1.000	20	4	3	0	7	0
Cate, Troy, Ever.*	.773	16	2	15	5	22	0
Chamberlain, Steve, Spo.	.600	7	1	2	2	5	1
Christensen, Danny, Spo.*	1.000	6	1	4	0	5	0
Clanton, Matt, Boi.	.000	1	0	0	0	0	0
Clarke, Darren, T.C.	.818	12	4	5	2	11	0
Collado, Jerry, T.C.	1.000	8	0	3	0	3	0
Coonrod, Aaron, Eug.	1.000	15	2	6	0	8	0
Corley, Klent, Yak.	1.000	19	1	3	0	4	1
Cormier, Lance, Van.	.000	1	0	0	0	0	0
Correia, Kevin, S.K.	1.000	10	4	1	0	5	0
Cram, Josh, S.K.	1.000	16	0	2	0	2	0
Crider, J.R., Van.	.000	2	0	0	0	0	0
Crockett, Ben, T.C.	1.000	7	3	1	0	4	1
Crowder, Justin, Van.*	.909	17	8	2	1	11	1
Cruz, Jeff, T.C.*	.833	15	2	3	1	6	0
Davies, Michael, T.C.*	1.000	16	3	5	0	8	1
Davis, Mikael, Van.	.818	22	5	4	2	11	1
Delgado, Oscar, Ever.*	1.000	10	1	9	0	10	0
Dickinson, Drew, Van.*	1.000	11	4	9	0	13	0
Difelice, Mark, T.C.	.875	6	1	6	1	8	0
Dodson, Jeremy, Spo.	.000	8	0	0	0	0	0
Dooley, Jason, T.C.	.889	19	3	5	1	9	0
DORMAN, Rich, Ever.	1.000	15	9	8	0	17	0
Dossett, Dusty, Spo.	1.000	15	4	3	0	7	0
Douglas, Mitch, Yak.*	.000	3	0	0	0	0	0
Doyle, Jared, Yak.*	1.000	16	4	12	0	16	0
Dulkowski, Marc, Eug.	1.000	4	2	2	0	4	0
Dunkle, Peter, T.C.	.938	20	2	13	1	16	0
Dunwell, Chris, Van.	1.000	14	3	11	0	14	2
Encarnacion, Alexis, Spo.	.500	11	0	1	1	2	0
Endicott, Drew, Spo.	.923	19	8	16	2	26	1
Ervin, Josh, Eug.	.000	2	0	0	0	0	0
Flanagan, Jeremy, Boi.	1.000	22	2	5	0	7	1
Francis, Jeff, T.C.*	1.000	4	0	3	0	3	0
Franklin, Ryan, Ever.	1.000	1	1	0	0	1	0

Player, Team	Pct.	G	PO	A	E	TC	DP
Fritz, Ben, Van.	1.000	9	1	11	0	12	0
Fulmer, T.A., Ever.	1.000	12	3	4	0	7	0
Garber, Mike, Yak.*	.818	9	4	5	2	11	0
Garcia, Jairo, Van.	1.000	3	0	1	0	1	0
Garcia, James, S.K.	.667	14	0	2	1	3	0
Gill, Chris, Van.	.600	20	1	2	2	5	0
Gonzalez, Enrique, Yak.	.913	11	11	10	2	23	4
Gorman, Jason, Yak.	1.000	2	1	0	0	1	0
Greinke, Zack, Spo.	1.000	2	0	2	0	2	0
Habel, Josh, S.K.*	1.000	16	3	10	0	13	0
Hagerty, Luke, Boi.*	.923	10	2	10	1	13	0
Heflin, Theo, Ever.*	1.000	20	0	3	0	3	0
Hensley, Clay, S.K.	1.000	15	3	10	0	13	2
Hill, Richard, Boi.*	.800	6	0	4	1	5	0
Hines, Matthew, Boi.	1.000	3	1	2	0	3	0
Hixson, David, S.K.	1.000	3	1	1	0	2	0
Hoffpauir, Micah, Van.*	.000	1	0	0	0	0	0
Howay, Chris, Van.	1.000	11	3	0	0	3	0
Jefferson, Drew, S.K.*	1.000	23	0	1	0	1	0
Jimenez, Cesar, Ever.*	1.000	8	0	3	0	3	0
Johnson, Doug, T.C.	1.000	15	1	14	0	15	1
Johnson, Thad, Van.	1.000	5	1	5	0	6	0
Jones, Geoffrey, Eug.*	1.000	1	1	0	0	1	0
Jones, Justin, Boi.	1.000	1	0	1	0	1	0
Keppinger, Billy, Spo.*	1.000	28	2	11	0	13	1
Kohn, Shawn, Van.	1.000	16	1	5	0	6	1
Korneev, Oleg, Ever.	1.000	5	0	1	0	1	0
Landeros, Leonard, Van.*	1.000	21	4	4	0	8	0
Laratta, E.J., Eug.	.833	12	0	5	1	6	1
Leon, Brigmer, Van.	1.000	18	2	7	0	9	1
Lipari, Thomas, Eug.*	1.000	10	0	7	0	7	0
Livingston, Bobby, Ever.*	.923	15	7	17	2	26	1
Lizarraga, Sergio, Yak.	.897	16	12	14	3	29	1
Lopez, Nelson, S.K.	1.000	5	1	1	0	2	0
Martin, Scott, Eug.*	.857	17	3	3	1	7	0
Martinez, Dionnar, Boi.	.000	2	0	0	0	0	0
Martinez, Javier, Eug.	1.000	2	1	2	0	3	0
Martinez, Miguel, Ever.*	.800	11	0	4	1	5	0
Matos, Raymond, S.K.*	1.000	18	2	5	0	7	0
McDonnell, Matt, Spo.	1.000	21	5	8	0	13	0
Medina, Franklin, Yak.	.667	9	1	1	1	3	0
Medina, Roberto, Yak.*	.857	26	3	3	1	7	0
Mercedes, Gabriel, Yak.	.850	20	3	14	3	20	0
Mitchell, Ben, S.K.	1.000	25	0	3	0	3	0
Modica, Greg, Eug.	1.000	26	0	3	0	3	0
Montarbo, Adam, Eug.	1.000	12	1	1	0	2	0
Morel, Eudy, Eug.	.875	23	2	5	1	8	0
Morrow, David, Ever.	1.000	17	1	2	0	3	0
Muessig, Jeff, Van.	.667	24	0	2	1	3	0
Munter, Scott, S.K.	1.000	10	0	3	0	3	0
Murphy, Bill, Van.*	.889	13	2	6	1	9	0
Nelson, Jeff, Ever.	.000	1	0	0	0	0	0
Nelson, Luke, S.K.	.900	14	3	15	2	20	1
Nicholson, Scott, T.C.*	.500	9	0	2	2	4	0
Nolasco, Ricky, Boi.	.857	15	2	10	2	14	0
Nunez, Kelvin, Spo.	1.000	10	3	3	0	6	0
Obenchain, Stephen, Van.	.778	11	2	5	2	9	0
O'Brien, Wes, Boi.	.923	23	1	11	1	13	1
O'Malley, Ryan, Boi.*	1.000	23	2	12	0	14	1
Palmer, Matt, S.K.	1.000	16	4	7	0	11	0
Pauley, David, Eug.	1.000	15	8	6	0	14	2
Pavlik, Isaac, T.C.*	.867	27	1	12	2	15	0
Perez, Edwin, Yak.	.000	2	0	0	0	0	0
Perez, Elvis, Ever.	.000	1	0	0	0	0	0
Pickens, J.R., Van.	.000	1	0	0	0	0	0
Ponder, Steven, T.C.*	.000	1	0	0	1	1	0
Rapada, Clayton, Boi.*	1.000	12	0	1	0	1	0
Reba, Steve, T.C.	1.000	14	3	7	0	10	0
Reyes, Luis, Boi.	1.000	20	4	10	0	14	1
Ribas, Gabe, Eug.	.900	32	3	6	1	10	0
Richards, John, Eug.*	1.000	3	0	1	0	1	0
Rivera, Jimmy, Ever.	.882	20	3	12	2	17	0
Rodriguez, Manuel, Van.	1.000	21	2	2	0	4	0
Rowland-Smith, Ryan, Ever.*	.875	18	2	12	2	16	1
Ryan, Kevin, Eug.	.500	14	1	0	1	2	0
Ryu, Jae-kuk, Boi.	1.000	10	1	10	0	11	1
Schilsky, Stephen, Van.	1.000	6	1	1	0	2	1
Schmidt, Jason, S.K.	1.000	9	0	4	0	4	0
Serrato, Juan, S.K.	1.000	9	1	1	0	1	0
Sevier, Nate, Ever.	.870	15	7	13	3	23	2
Shank, Chris, Van.	.833	19	2	3	1	6	0
Shartzer, Bryan, T.C.	1.000	9	0	2	0	2	0
Sierra, Edwardo, Van.	.875	9	1	6	1	8	0
Silva, Erick, Yak.	1.000	6	2	1	0	3	0
Sisco, Andy, Boi.*	.929	14	0	13	1	14	1
Soto, Darwin, Eug.	1.000	7	0	2	0	2	0
Stefani, Jason, Eug.*	.667	12	0	2	1	3	0
Steidlmayer, Luke, Eug.	.917	15	4	7	1	12	0
Suarez, Victor, Spo.	1.000	7	2	1	0	3	0
Taulli, Sam, Yak.*	1.000	5	2	2	0	4	0
Tavarez, David, Ever.	1.000	21	2	5	0	7	0

Player, Team	Pct.	G	PO	A	E	TC	DP
Taylor, Justin, Spo.	1.000	18	3	8	0	11	0
Tetuan, John, T.C.	.846	15	4	7	2	13	0
Thomas, Jared, Ever.*	1.000	19	0	3	0	3	1
Tsao, Chin-hui, T.C.	1.000	3	2	2	0	4	0
Urrutia, Carlos, Boi.	.500	12	0	2	2	4	0
Vasquez, Carlos, Boi.*	.875	15	1	20	3	24	1
Viane, David, Ever.	1.000	20	3	6	0	9	0
Villatoro, Wilmer, Eug.	.667	22	4	6	5	15	0
Waddell, Jason, S.K.*	1.000	11	2	5	0	7	1
Waroff, Shane, Yak.	.857	24	4	8	2	14	0
Watson, Mike, T.C.	.778	18	2	5	2	9	0

Player, Team	Pct.	G	PO	A	E	TC	DP
Whitaker, Brian, Eug.	.958	16	7	16	1	24	4
White, Bill, Yak.*	1.000	3	0	1	0	1	0
Woolard, Glenn, S.K.	1.000	17	4	8	0	12	0
Wykoff, Zach, Eug.	1.000	8	0	3	0	3	0
Wylie, Jason, Boi.	1.000	24	1	7	0	8	0
Yacco, Anthony, S.K.	.000	2	0	0	3	3	0
Young, Chris, T.C.	1.000	17	6	9	0	15	0
Zettler, Nate, Spo.	.625	22	5	0	3	8	0

The following players appeared only as designated hitter, pinch-hitter or pinch runner: Butler, dh, pr; J. Delgado, dh; Jor. Pickens, dh.

LEAGUE CHAMPIONS

Year	Team	Pct.
1901—	Portland	.675
1902—	Butte	.608
1903—	Butte	.578
1904—	Boise	.625
1905—	Vancouver	.586
	Everett*	.667
1906—	Tacoma	.600
1907—	Aberdeen	.625
1908—	Vancouver	.578
1909—	Seattle	.653
1910—	Spokane	.596
1911—	Vancouver	.628
1912—	Seattle	.600
1913—	Vancouver	.600
1914—	Vancouver	.632
1915—	Seattle	.564
1916—	Spokane	.622
1917—	Great Falls	.592
1918—	Seattle	.588
1919—	Seattle	.590
1920—	Victoria	.600
1921—	Yakima	.710
	Yakima	.660
1922—	Calgary‡	.600
1923-36—	Did not operate.	
1937—	Wenatchee	.603
	Tacoma*	.627
1938—	Yakima	.583
	Bellingham (2nd)†	.511
1939—	Wenatchee	.601
	Tacoma (2nd)†	.533
1940—	Spokane	.587
	Tacoma (4th)†	.500
1941—	Spokane	.669
1942—	Vancouver	.594
1943-45—	Did not operate.	
1946—	Wenatchee	.622
1947—	Vancouver	.566
1948—	Spokane	.614
1949—	Yakima	.660
	Vancouver (2nd)†	.615
1950—	Yakima	.613
1951—	Spokane	.655
1952—	Victoria	.631
1953—	Salem	.635
	Spokane*	.590
1954—	Vancouver*	.636

Year	Team	Pct.
	Lewiston	.629
1955—	Salem	.646
	Eugene*	.639
1956—	Yakima	.691
	Yakima	.619
1957—	Eugene	.576
	Wenatchee*	.647
1958—	Lewiston	.621
	Yakima*	.594
1959—	Salem	.623
	Yakima*	.563
1960—	Yakima	.638
	Yakima	.562
1961—	Lewiston*	.621
	Yakima	.600
1962—	Wenatchee*	.574
	Tri-City	.580
1963—	Lewiston	.594
	Yakima*	.613
1964—	Eugene	.636
	Yakima*	.611
1965—	Lewiston	.667
	Tri-City*	.681
1966—	Tri-City	.679
1967—	Medford	.607
1968—	Tri-City	.600
1969—	Rogue Valley	.633
1970—	Lewiston§	.538
	Coos Bay-No. Bend	.563
1971—	Tri-City§	.625
	Bend	.538
1972—	Lewiston§	.675
	Walla Walla	.513
1973—	Walla Walla∞	.638
	Portland	.563
1974—	Bellingham	.619
	Eugene▲	.571
1975—	Portland	.545
	Eugene◆	.684
1976—	Portland	.556
	Walla Walla◆	.639
1977—	Bellingham■	.618
	Portland	.667
1978—	Grays Harbor▼	.671
	Eugene	.514
1979—	Central Oregon◆	.606
	Walla Walla	.571

Year	Team	Pct.
1980—	Bellingham•	.643
	Eugene•	.529
1981—	Medford◆	.600
	Bellingham	.557
1982—	Medford	.757
	Salem◆	.486
1983—	Medford††	.735
	Bellingham	.588
1984—	Tri-Cities††	.622
	Medford	.608
1985—	Everett††	.541
	Eugene	.541
1986—	Bellingham††	.608
	Eugene	.608
1987—	Spokane▲	.711
	Everett	.653
1988—	Southern Oregon	.605
	Spokane◆	.553
1989—	Southern Oregon	.600
	Spokane◆	.547
1990—	Boise	.697
	Spokane◆	.645
1991—	Boise◆	.658
	Yakima	.579
1992—	Bellingham◆	.566
	Bend	.566
1993—	Bellingham	.579
	Boise◆	.539
1994—	Yakima	.645
	Boise◆	.579
1995—	Boise◆	.640
	Bellingham	.566
1996—	Eugene	.645
	Yakima§	.526
1997—	Boise	.671
	Portland◆	.579
1998—	Spokane	.618
	Boise	.618
	Salem-Keizer◆	.566
1999—	Spokane◆	.579
	Boise	.539
2000—	Yakima◆	.539
	Boise	.693
2001—	Boise	.671
	Salem-Keizer◆	.671
2002—	Boise◆	.645

*Won split-season playoff. †Won four-club playoff. ‡League disbanded June 18. §League divided into Northern and Southern divisions, declared champion under league rules. ∞League divided into Eastern and Western divisions, declared champion under league rules. ▲League divided into Eastern and Western divisions; won two-team playoff. ◆League divided into North and South divisions; won two-team playoff. ■League divided into Affiliate and Independent divisions; won two-team playoff. ▼Declared league champion after winning one-game playoff. Balance of playoff canceled due to rain and wet grounds. •Declared co-champion after winning one game. Balance of playoff canceled due to rain and wet grounds. ††League divided into Washington and Oregon divisions; won two-team playoff. (NOTE—Known as Pacific Northwest League 1901-02, Pacific National League 1903-04, Northwestern League 1905-18, Pacific Coast International League 1919-22 and Western International League 1937-54.)

SOUTH ATLANTIC LEAGUE

LEAGUE OFFICE

President/secretary-treasurer
John Moss
Address
P.O. Box 38
504 Crescent Hill
Kings Mountain, NC 28086
Phone
704-739-3466

Teams (affiliation)
Asheville Tourists (Rockies)
Augusta GreenJackets (Red Sox)
Capital City Bombers (Mets)
Charleston (S.C.) RiverDogs (Devil Rays)
Charleston (W.Va.) Alley Cats (Blue Jays)
Delmarva Shorebirds (Orioles)
Greensboro Bats (Marlins)
Hagerstown Suns (Giants)

Hickory Crawdads (Pirates)
Kannapolis Intimidators (White Sox)
Lake County Captains (Indians)
Lakewood BlueClaws (Phillies)
Lexington Legends (Astros)
Rome Braves (Braves)
Savannah Sand Gnats (Expos)
South Georgia Waves (Dodgers)

2002 FINAL STANDINGS

FIRST HALF

NORTHERN DIVISION

Team	W	L	T	Pct.	GB
Hickory (Pirates)	44	26	0	.629	...
Lexington (Astros)	43	27	0	.614	1.0
Greensboro (Yankees)	37	33	0	.529	7.0
Kannapolis (White Sox)	36	34	0	.514	8.0
Hagerstown (Giants)	34	36	0	.486	10.0
Lakewood (Phillies)	33	36	0	.478	10.5
Delmarva (Orioles)	32	38	0	.457	12.0
Charleston, W.Va. (Blue Jays)	25	45	0	.357	19.0

SOUTHERN DIVISION

Team	W	L	T	Pct.	GB
South Georgia (Dodgers)	40	29	0	.580	...
Columbia (Mets)	40	29	0	.580	...
Asheville (Rockies)	38	31	0	.551	2.0
Columbus (Indians)	38	32	0	.543	2.5
Augusta (Red Sox)	34	35	0	.493	6.0
Charleston, S.C. (Devil Rays)	32	37	0	.464	8.0
Macon (Braves)	27	43	0	.386	13.5
Savannah (Rangers)	24	46	0	.343	16.5

SECOND HALF

NORTHERN DIVISION

Team	W	L	T	Pct.	GB
Delmarva (Orioles)	44	26	0	.629	...
Hickory (Pirates)	39	30	0	.565	4.5
Lexington (Astros)	38	32	0	.543	6.0
Greensboro (Yankees)	38	32	0	.543	6.0
Lakewood (Phillies)	36	34	0	.514	8.0
Charleston, W.Va. (Blue Jays)	36	34	0	.514	8.0
Kannapolis (White Sox)	30	40	0	.429	14.0
Hagerstown (Giants)	29	41	0	.414	15.0

SOUTHERN DIVISION

Team	W	L	T	Pct.	GB
Columbus (Indians)	41	28	0	.594	...
Macon (Braves)	39	31	0	.557	2.5
Augusta (Red Sox)	35	32	0	.522	5.0
South Georgia (Dodgers)	35	34	0	.507	6.0
Columbia (Mets)	35	35	0	.500	6.5
Charleston, S.C. (Devil Rays)	28	39	0	.418	12.0
Asheville (Rockies)	26	43	0	.377	15.0
Savannah (Rangers)	25	43	0	.368	15.5

COMPOSITE

Team	Hick.	Lex.	C'bus	S.G.	Del.	C'bia	Gbr.	Aug.	Lak.	Mac.	Kan.	Ash.	Hag.	CSC	CWV	Sav.	W	L	T	Pct.	GB
Hickory (Pirates)	...	8	1	3	10	3	9	3	8	2	7	3	14	1	7	4	83	56	0	.597	...
Lexington (Astros)	9	...	4	3	7	2	4	3	10	3	9	3	7	3	12	2	81	59	0	.579	2.5
Columbus (Indians)	3	0	...	5	3	7	2	7	3	5	3	15	2	11	3	10	79	60	0	.568	4.0
South Georgia (Dodgers)	1	1	10	...	3	6	4	5	0	6	4	12	2	7	2	12	75	63	0	.543	7.5
Delmarva (Orioles)	5	9	1	1	...	3	7	2	9	4	10	1	10	3	8	3	76	64	0	.543	7.5
Columbia (Mets)	1	2	9	8	1	...	2	10	1	15	2	5	2	7	1	9	75	64	0	.540	8.0
Greensboro (Yankees)	4	12	2	0	7	2	...	3	10	3	6	1	8	2	12	3	75	65	0	.536	8.5
Augusta (Red Sox)	1	1	7	9	2	8	1	...	1	10	2	9	3	5	2	8	69	67	0	.507	12.5
Lakewood (Phillies)	7	5	1	3	8	3	7	3	...	1	8	2	6	2	10	3	69	70	0	.496	14.0
Macon (Braves)	2	1	7	8	0	5	1	9	3	...	2	7	1	10	1	9	66	74	0	.471	17.5
Kannapolis (White Sox)	8	4	1	0	6	2	9	2	8	2	...	3	11	2	5	3	66	74	0	.471	17.5
Asheville (Rockies)	1	1	5	6	3	6	3	5	2	8	1	...	3	10	3	7	64	74	0	.464	18.5
Hagerstown (Giants)	5	7	2	2	4	2	7	1	7	3	8	1	...	3	8	3	63	77	0	.450	20.5
Charleston, S.C. (D. Rays)	2	1	6	6	1	7	2	8	2	4	2	4	1	...	2	12	60	76	0	.441	21.5
Charleston, W.Va. (B. Jays)	7	5	1	2	8	3	6	2	5	3	9	1	6	2	...	1	61	79	0	.436	22.5
Savannah (Rangers)	0	2	3	7	1	5	1	4	1	5	1	7	1	8	3	...	49	89	0	.355	33.5

Major league affiliations in parentheses.

PLAYOFFS: Hickory defeated Delmarva, two games to none; Columbus defeated Columbia, two games to one; Hickory defeated Columbus, three games to two to win South Atlantic League championship.

REGULAR-SEASON ATTENDANCE: Asheville, 145,065; Augusta, 127,314; Charleston, S.C., 242,143; Charleston, W.V., 95,187; Columbia, 111,349; Columbus, 52,103; Delmarva, 253,171; Greensboro, 179,393; Hagerstown, 103,188; Hickory, 182,800; Kannapolis, 105,873; Lakewood, 466,474; Lexington, 428,840; Macon, 84,001; Savannah, 119,223; South Georgia, 72,025. Total—2,768,149. Playoff (10 games)—12,237. All-Star Game at Lakewood—8,571.

MANAGERS: Asheville, Joe Mikulik; Augusta, Arnie Beyeler; Charleston, S.C., Buddy Biancalana; Charleston, W.V., Paul Elliott; Columbia, Tony Tijerina; Columbus, Torey Lovullo; Delmarva, Joe Ferguson; Greensboro, Bill Masse; Hagerstown, Mike Ramsey; Hickory, Tony Beasley; Kannapolis, John Orton; Lakewood, Jeff Manto; Lexington, J.J. Cannon; Macon, Lynn Jones; Savannah, Paul Carey; South Georgia, Scott Little.

ALL-STAR TEAM: 1B—Walter Young, Hickory; 2B—Jeff Keppinger, Hickory; 3B—Andy Marte, Macon; SS—Robinson Cano, Greensboro; Utility INF—Victor Diaz, South Georgia; OF—Wayne Lydon, Columbia; OF—Vic Butler, Hickory; OF—Jeremy Harts, Hickory; DH—Chris Shelton, Hickory; Utility OF—Willy Taveras, Columbus; C—Justin Huber, Columbia; RHP—Kris Honel, Kannapolis; LHP—Macay McBride, Macon; Manager—Tony Beasley, Hickory; Coach—Charley Taylor, Lexington; Most Valuable Player—Walter Young, Hickory; Most Valuable Pitcher—Macay McBride, Macon; Most Outstanding Major League Prospect—Walter Young, Hickory.

2002 BATTING

TEAM

Team	G	TPA	AB	R	H	TB	2B	3B	HR	RBI	SH	SF	HP	BB	IBB	SO	SB	CS	GDP	LOB	ShO	Avg.	OBP	Slg.
Hickory	139	5328	4645	747	1303	1921	233	26	111	676	74	42	92	475	16	954	142	76	79	994	7	.281	.356	.414
Ch'ton, W.Va.	140	5306	4751	621	1280	1734	231	35	51	558	33	41	55	426	22	797	108	58	116	1013	12	.269	.334	.365
S. Georgia	138	5209	4527	632	1216	1664	187	30	67	559	61	44	98	479	17	1036	182	78	76	998	10	.269	.348	.368
Columbia	139	5289	4640	691	1237	1692	219	25	62	615	32	46	86	485	17	1038	240	94	43	1011	7	.267	.344	.365
Lexington	140	5349	4749	687	1252	1904	270	26	110	618	33	43	53	471	15	1112	171	90	90	948	8	.264	.334	.401
Macon	140	5153	4609	587	1210	1772	213	41	89	533	43	35	74	392	13	896	118	73	100	955	12	.263	.328	.384
Hagerstown	140	5247	4651	587	1178	1703	220	19	89	525	38	34	76	448	9	961	106	51	94	1005	12	.253	.327	.366
Kannapolis	140	5258	4667	563	1181	1602	215	28	50	502	53	33	73	432	13	1013	170	83	106	989	9	.253	.324	.343
Greensboro	140	5265	4677	653	1168	1830	225	30	127	591	8	40	60	480	12	1080	119	42	91	943	7	.250	.325	.391
Asheville	138	5306	4694	639	1172	1761	240	17	105	591	18	31	82	481	18	1136	104	60	99	1024	8	.250	.328	.375
Delmarva	140	5209	4576	586	1126	1652	245	31	73	514	79	42	90	422	20	1022	121	44	85	951	8	.246	.319	.361
Lakewood	138	5148	4563	538	1116	1577	212	33	61	477	45	28	72	440	25	1026	142	94	87	952	12	.245	.319	.346
Columbus	139	5191	4483	625	1093	1620	188	33	91	544	45	46	93	524	14	1084	235	79	69	955	14	.244	.332	.361
Char'ton, S.C.	136	4919	4328	546	1051	1449	166	23	62	472	58	40	69	424	14	981	164	81	92	863	9	.243	.318	.335
Augusta	136	4871	4368	515	1019	1448	189	24	64	457	42	29	12	420	12	1002	74	50	86	946	14	.233	.300	.332
Savannah	138	5180	4538	529	1025	1486	203	30	66	470	68	30	1	543	17	1100	106	67	91	1039	8	.226	.307	.327

INDIVIDUAL

TOP QUALIFIERS FOR BATTING CHAMPIONSHIP

Minimum 378 plate appearances. *Lefthanded batter. †Switch-hitter.

Player, Team	G	TPA	AB	R	H	TB	2B	3B	HR	RBI	SH	SF	HP	BB	IBB	SO	SB	CS	GDP	Avg.	OBP	Slg.
Diaz, Victor, S.G.	91	391	349	64	122	182	26	2	10	58	0	5	10	27	6	69	20	6	4	.350	.407	.521
Shelton, Chris, Hick.	93	388	332	72	113	195	27	2	17	65	0	4	5	47	2	74	0	0	1	.340	.425	.587
Young, Walter, Hick.*	132	551	492	84	164	277	34	2	25	103	0	8	15	36	6	102	2	6	11	.333	.390	.563
Gretz, Nick, Ash.*	104	442	383	52	121	154	18	0	5	70	0	1	3	55	4	72	1	1	8	.316	.405	.402
Miller, Greg, Mac.	103	411	361	46	113	129	14	1	0	34	4	3	5	38	0	66	17	4	11	.313	.383	.357
Mann, Derek, S.G.*	101	430	350	55	108	125	13	2	0	36	7	4	5	64	2	64	17	11	4	.309	.418	.357
Whiteman, Tommy, Lex.	90	397	350	50	106	169	29	2	10	49	4	2	5	36	1	66	6	6	13	.303	.374	.483
Florence, Branden, Hag.	109	470	426	63	129	198	30	3	11	63	0	6	6	31	1	32	9	7	10	.303	.354	.465
Acevedo, Anthony, Lex.*	116	505	437	89	132	196	28	0	12	80	0	5	1	62	3	89	11	8	6	.302	.386	.449
Bautista, Jose, Hick.	129	520	438	72	132	206	26	3	14	57	5	2	8	67	3	104	3	2	12	.301	.402	.470
Wright, Gavin, Lex.	128	575	517	73	153	212	23	6	8	57	9	6	3	40	0	92	21	18	8	.296	.346	.410
Lydon, Wayne, C'bia†	127	541	473	93	139	158	9	5	0	46	5	5	4	54	0	104	87	13	1	.294	.368	.334
Thorman, Scott, Mac.*	127	534	470	57	138	230	38	3	16	82	0	6	7	51	5	83	2	2	16	.294	.367	.489
Cosby, Rob, C.W.Va.	109	453	419	52	123	164	20	3	5	59	0	6	0	28	2	55	2	2	10	.294	.333	.391
Spidale, Mike, Kan.	93	413	357	57	104	117	11	1	0	30	7	2	13	34	0	50	37	25	5	.291	.372	.328
Huber, Justin, C'bia	95	403	330	49	96	155	22	2	11	78	0	4	23	45	10	81	1	2	5	.291	.408	.470

DEPARTMENTAL LEADERS: G—N. Johnson, Snyder, 136 each; AB—C. Duran, 534; R—A. Miller, 109; H—Young, 164; TB—Young, 277; 2B—Thorman, 38; 3B—C. Duran, 10; HR—Young, 25; RBI—Marte, 105; SH—Buttler, 20; SF—Gillitzer, 9; HP—Huber, 23; BB—A. Miller, 88; IBB—Howard, 13; SO—Jimerson, 168; SB—Lydon, 87; CS—Spidale, 25; GIDP—D. Gonzalez, 20; Slg.—Shelton, .587; OBP—Shelton, .425.

ALL PLAYERS

*Lefthanded batter. †Switch-hitter.

Player, Team	G	TPA	AB	R	H	TB	2B	3B	HR	RBI	SH	SF	HP	BB	IBB	SO	SB	CS	GDP	Avg.	OBP	Slg.
Abreu, Nielsen, Lak.	2	1	1	1	0	0	0	0	0	0	0	0	0	0	0	0	0	0	0	.000	.000	.000
Acevedo, Anthony, Lex.*	116	505	437	89	132	196	28	0	12	80	0	5	1	62	3	89	11	8	6	.302	.386	.449
Albert, Luke, Mac.†	2	6	6	1	2	2	0	0	0	1	0	0	0	0	0	2	0	0	0	.333	.333	.333
Aleman, Carlos, Aug.	6	20	18	1	4	4	0	0	0	2	0	0	2	0	0	4	3	0	1	.222	.300	.222
Alexander, Kevin, Hag.	97	408	358	59	103	139	24	0	4	28	1	3	2	44	0	65	12	5	6	.288	.366	.388
Amador, Chris, Mac.	124	442	418	60	84	106	5	4	3	26	13	2	8	38	0	142	56	15	3	.201	.279	.254
Anderson, Keith, Hag.	47	169	153	20	44	65	12	0	3	20	0	1	0	15	1	34	0	1	2	.288	.349	.425
Andrew, Jason, Sav.	11	1	1	0	0	0	0	0	0	0	0	0	0	0	0	0	0	0	0	.000	.000	.000
Arko, Tommy, Del.	22	73	63	5	8	11	3	0	0	1	0	0	2	7	1	28	0	0	0	.127	.236	.175
Ascencion, Quincy, Del.	23	93	87	9	17	19	2	0	0	6	0	2	1	3	0	24	3	0	2	.195	.226	.218
Asprilla, Avelino, Sav.	54	195	176	27	44	59	4	1	3	21	5	0	2	12	0	47	7	2	5	.250	.305	.335
Bacani, David, C'bia	96	375	305	46	80	102	17	1	1	36	7	1	9	52	0	48	13	11	4	.262	.384	.334
Barnett, Dan, Kan.	18	52	45	8	11	17	2	2	0	8	0	2	1	4	0	12	0	0	0	.244	.308	.378
Barnowski, Bryan, Aug.	67	274	235	33	44	82	14	0	8	32	0	1	12	26	1	93	0	1	0	.187	.299	.349
Bass, Bryan, Del.†	130	519	457	60	101	153	20	7	6	59	9	5	13	40	0	146	15	2	7	.221	.299	.335
Bastardo, Angel, C'bus	23	76	72	7	12	18	4	1	0	7	0	0	0	4	0	26	1	1	0	.167	.211	.250
Bautista, Jose, Hick.	129	520	438	72	132	206	26	3	14	57	5	2	8	67	3	104	3	2	12	.301	.402	.470
Bellorin, Edwin, S.G.	92	351	318	28	89	104	13	1	0	38	7	1	6	19	2	39	4	2	8	.280	.331	.327
Benavidez, Julian, Hag.	125	522	465	58	123	192	32	2	11	72	0	3	5	49	3	148	5	5	2	.265	.339	.413
Bennett, Kris, Lak.	45	168	150	18	42	60	4	4	2	16	0	1	2	15	1	15	5	3	3	.280	.351	.400
Bernard, Miguel, Mac.	55	194	182	12	39	56	8	0	3	15	0	1	2	9	1	33	2	2	4	.214	.258	.308
Beuerlein, Tyler, C'bia†	22	72	66	7	12	18	0	0	2	4	1	0	0	5	0	24	1	0	5	.182	.239	.273
Bilezikjian, Charlie, Sav.	35	86	66	6	7	12	2	0	1	6	4	0	0	16	0	31	3	0	1	.106	.280	.182
Bird, T.J., Ash.*	94	358	327	36	80	132	16	3	10	42	0	1	6	23	4	99	1	0	6	.245	.305	.404
Blanco, Gregor, Mac.*	132	570	468	87	127	180	14	9	7	36	6	2	9	85	0	120	40	16	2	.271	.392	.385
Bonner, Adam, C.S.C.*	96	359	310	44	81	122	14	0	9	39	4	4	4	37	3	94	11	6	2	.261	.344	.394
Bourgeois, Jason, Sav.†	127	586	522	72	133	188	21	5	8	49	8	5	11	40	1	66	22	11	5	.255	.318	.360
Bowman, Addison, Aug.	3	10	8	1	4	9	2	0	1	2	0	0	0	1	0	0	1	0	0	.500	.600	1.125
Boyd, Patrick, Sav.†	69	285	257	25	62	96	15	2	5	30	1	0	3	24	4	68	8	4	6	.241	.313	.374
Brackley, Carlos, Aug.	12	37	33	1	2	3	1	0	0	0	1	0	0	3	0	11	0	0	0	.061	.139	.091

Player, Team	G	TPA	AB	R	H	TB	2B	3B	HR	RBI	SH	SF	HP	BB	IBB	SO	SB	CS	GDP	Avg.	OBP	Slg.
Brand, Kevin, Ash.†	30	111	95	6	18	23	3	1	0	8	1	0	1	13	0	22	2	1	2	.189	.294	.242
Brazoban, Yhency, Gre.	69	272	252	33	61	85	11	2	3	28	0	2	3	15	0	74	0	0	4	.242	.290	.337
Brown, Kevin, Mac.	37	143	117	17	26	53	7	1	6	17	0	1	4	21	1	39	0	1	2	.222	.357	.453
Brunner, Ryan, Aug.*	123	493	424	49	90	133	22	3	5	45	1	3	13	50	0	101	0	1	6	.212	.312	.314
Bryan, Jason, Sav.-Aug.	17	67	59	6	13	22	3	0	2	8	0	1	0	7	0	24	1	1	0	.220	.299	.373
Bunch, J.C., Sav.	5	11	11	0	2	4	2	0	0	5	0	0	0	0	0	6	0	0	0	.182	.182	.364
Burrows, Angelo, Mac.*	96	329	314	30	75	110	15	4	4	24	4	0	1	10	0	35	1	4	8	.239	.265	.350
Buttler, Vic, Hick.*	124	536	460	77	131	173	15	3	7	64	20	5	6	45	1	65	30	11	5	.285	.353	.376
Cabrera, Chi Chi, Hag.	37	130	117	13	19	20	1	0	0	5	3	1	2	7	0	15	4	1	4	.162	.220	.171
Cabrera, Ulises, Sav.	87	315	239	34	48	63	10	1	1	26	11	0	13	50	0	86	11	6	6	.201	.368	.264
Calabrese, Tony, Gre.	53	208	184	25	43	68	13	0	4	23	0	1	0	23	0	43	6	2	5	.234	.317	.370
Caligiuri, Jay, C'bia	62	249	221	25	52	80	13	0	5	38	0	3	3	22	0	40	0	4	1	.235	.309	.362
Camacaro, Armando, C'bus	91	336	303	27	66	80	8	0	2	33	2	1	10	20	0	56	11	6	8	.218	.287	.264
Camacho, Juan, Gre.†	124	514	478	51	115	182	16	0	17	59	0	5	3	28	6	85	0	0	15	.241	.284	.381
Cancio, Antonio, Lak.	57	208	187	19	33	47	8	0	2	15	3	0	2	16	0	63	2	0	5	.176	.249	.251
Candelario, Luis, C.S.C.	43	159	150	17	31	54	6	1	5	19	0	0	3	6	0	43	2	2	6	.207	.252	.360
Cano, Robinson, Gre.*	113	507	474	67	131	211	20	9	14	66	0	1	3	29	0	78	2	1	8	.276	.321	.445
Caraway, Brandon, Lex.†	89	376	332	62	101	149	25	1	7	30	2	4	6	32	0	53	22	10	5	.304	.372	.449
Carroll, Wes, Lak.	81	319	294	33	67	86	16	0	1	29	5	1	3	16	0	36	8	1	3	.228	.274	.293
Carter, Bryan, Hag.*	119	534	476	62	115	180	22	2	13	61	1	2	19	36	0	114	22	9	4	.242	.319	.378
Castillo, Osmar, Aug.†	37	145	117	22	24	25	1	0	0	7	3	2	1	22	0	28	4	3	3	.205	.331	.214
Cates, Gary, Del.	82	357	317	50	90	116	18	1	2	28	17	3	4	16	0	36	12	6	3	.284	.324	.366
Cavin, Jonathan, Kan.*	94	349	300	33	76	102	18	1	2	29	3	1	4	41	0	71	2	4	9	.253	.350	.340
Centeno, Irwin, C.S.C.	55	241	209	37	55	71	5	4	1	25	2	1	2	27	0	42	22	5	3	.263	.351	.340
Charles, Julin, Sav.	8	33	31	4	5	7	0	1	0	0	0	0	0	2	0	11	0	1	0	.161	.212	.226
Chaves, Brandon, Hick.†	105	396	335	56	83	117	18	2	4	44	10	4	7	40	0	89	10	7	7	.248	.337	.349
Choy Foo, Rodney, C'bus†	103	432	386	63	102	156	14	8	8	44	0	7	3	36	3	75	16	3	11	.264	.326	.404
Christensen, Jeff, Gre.*	78	277	237	36	56	85	9	4	4	30	0	4	2	34	0	76	8	4	6	.236	.332	.359
Christian, Josh, Sav.	26	99	93	5	18	29	6	1	1	12	0	0	3	3	0	29	0	0	3	.194	.242	.312
Ciraco, Darren, Kan.	44	176	159	15	30	34	4	0	0	11	0	1	0	16	0	39	3	1	4	.189	.261	.214
Cliffords, Woody, Del.*	87	386	314	50	83	109	21	1	1	20	4	4	11	53	4	57	15	5	6	.264	.385	.347
Coffey, Kris, Aug.	107	418	368	46	81	87	4	1	0	18	7	0	4	39	0	62	15	10	4	.220	.302	.236
Colina, Alvin, Ash.	59	239	212	22	50	79	8	0	7	36	2	1	4	20	0	57	1	0	3	.236	.312	.373
Colmenter, Jesus, C'bus†	33	115	103	10	23	30	4	0	1	8	3	2	0	7	0	17	2	1	2	.223	.268	.291
Cooper, Jason, C'bus*	17	62	55	9	14	31	5	0	4	17	0	0	1	6	1	17	0	0	1	.255	.339	.564
Cooper, Matt, Aug.	99	384	320	41	76	126	14	0	12	47	0	1	21	42	0	99	5	2	4	.238	.362	.394
Cordido, Julio, Hag.	55	220	196	24	51	72	7	1	4	18	5	0	1	18	0	30	6	3	6	.260	.326	.367
Corporan, Elvis, Gre.†	14	64	54	10	15	26	2	0	3	12	0	0	1	9	0	19	0	0	2	.278	.391	.481
Corr, Frank, C'bia	81	340	315	48	96	139	22	0	7	45	0	4	4	17	2	52	2	2	5	.305	.344	.441
Cortes, Jorge, Hick.*	17	69	59	13	15	23	3	1	1	11	2	0	1	7	0	11	1	1	2	.254	.343	.390
Cortez, Fernando, C.S.C.*	127	528	475	60	127	157	14	5	2	49	2	6	4	41	0	59	37	16	9	.267	.327	.331
Cosby, Rob, C.W.Va.	109	453	419	52	123	164	20	3	5	59	0	6	0	28	2	55	2	2	10	.294	.333	.391
Cruz, Luis, Aug.	58	214	202	16	38	56	7	1	3	15	1	2	0	9	0	30	0	2	6	.188	.221	.277
Cruz, Orlando, Sav.	32	112	100	7	23	28	2	0	1	10	2	0	3	7	0	24	3	3	2	.230	.300	.280
Cuevas, Aneudi, Lex.	8	34	31	4	11	15	2	1	0	5	0	0	0	3	0	7	1	1	0	.355	.412	.484
Dacey, Ryan, S.G.	32	134	113	14	31	43	6	3	0	19	0	1	3	17	0	25	1	3	3	.274	.381	.381
Davis, J.P., C.S.C.	80	317	259	41	67	105	8	0	10	41	0	1	10	47	2	46	4	4	5	.259	.391	.405
Davis, Rajai, Hick.†	6	22	14	4	6	6	0	0	0	3	1	0	1	6	0	2	2	0	0	.429	.619	.429
De La Cruz, Miguel, Hick.	56	164	151	15	32	52	9	1	3	14	0	0	2	11	0	40	0	0	5	.212	.274	.344
Delfino, Lee, C.W.Va.	113	441	367	59	82	119	24	2	3	46	4	4	4	62	0	76	9	1	4	.223	.339	.324
Delgado, Mario, Lak.*	37	135	128	16	30	44	6	1	2	13	0	0	0	7	0	35	0	0	4	.234	.274	.344
De Los Santos, Omar, S.G.	46	168	147	12	30	37	4	0	1	15	3	0	4	14	0	45	6	2	1	.204	.291	.252
Del Rosario, Manny, Del.†	36	128	107	11	23	24	1	0	0	6	10	2	2	7	0	16	5	1	4	.215	.271	.224
De Paula, Luis, C.S.C.	125	508	466	52	108	146	23	3	3	47	10	6	3	23	0	100	11	7	15	.232	.269	.313
Devarez, Noel, C'bia	17	66	62	8	15	22	5	1	0	7	0	0	1	3	0	17	4	1	2	.242	.288	.355
D'Jesus, Francisco, Hag.	17	57	51	7	6	9	3	0	0	9	1	1	2	2	0	17	0	0	2	.118	.179	.176
Diaz, Eduardo, Ash.	43	118	108	11	22	27	2	0	1	10	1	1	0	8	0	43	3	0	0	.204	.256	.250
Diaz, Victor, S.G.	91	391	349	64	122	182	26	2	10	58	0	5	10	27	6	69	20	6	4	.350	.407	.521
Dill, Jason, Sav.*	24	90	84	11	22	31	6	0	1	5	0	0	0	6	0	14	1	1	3	.262	.311	.369
Dion, Nate, C.S.C.	91	325	304	26	73	95	5	4	3	18	8	0	1	12	2	106	6	2	4	.240	.271	.313
Doumit, Ryan, Hick.†	68	291	258	46	83	117	14	1	6	47	2	5	8	18	0	40	3	5	6	.322	.377	.453
Downing, Lance, Lex.*	16	54	49	9	13	20	1	0	2	6	1	0	0	4	0	17	0	0	0	.265	.321	.408
Duncan, Jeff, C'bia*	40	172	150	33	59	90	13	3	4	17	1	0	3	18	1	34	15	3	1	.393	.468	.600
Duncan, Shelley, Gre.	101	419	356	58	95	164	23	2	14	56	0	1	3	59	1	88	15	3	4	.267	.375	.461
Duran, Alexander, C.S.C.	19	63	58	2	10	14	1	0	1	5	0	0	2	3	0	12	0	1	3	.172	.238	.241
Duran, Carlos, Mac.*	132	575	534	86	144	207	22	10	7	50	4	3	5	29	0	80	23	17	9	.270	.312	.388
Durazo, Ernie, C.W.Va.*	15	54	50	5	8	8	0	0	0	2	0	0	0	4	0	21	0	1	0	.160	.222	.160
Eddlemon, Kelly, C.S.C.	23	66	58	9	15	23	3	1	1	5	1	1	2	4	0	11	1	2	1	.259	.323	.397
Eldridge, Rashad, Sav.†	73	268	228	31	55	73	7	1	3	23	8	0	4	28	1	49	4	4	4	.241	.335	.320
Escalera, Jose, S.G.	60	200	193	18	52	66	6	1	2	15	1	0	3	3	0	25	3	1	4	.269	.291	.342
Esposito, Brian, Aug.	40	168	154	20	39	59	5	0	5	15	2	0	5	7	0	32	0	0	4	.253	.307	.383
Essian, James, S.G.†	27	95	72	13	13	14	1	0	0	8	0	0	5	18	1	25	9	4	0	.181	.379	.194
Ezi, Travis, S.G.†	70	261	227	31	53	67	0	4	2	23	7	1	2	24	0	75	19	7	2	.233	.311	.295
Fatheree, Danny, Lex.	39	130	109	12	23	33	7	0	1	11	1	1	2	17	0	17	0	3	3	.211	.326	.303
Fernandez, Alejandro, Gre.	51	177	160	17	38	69	10	0	7	27	0	1	3	13	0	56	1	0	3	.238	.305	.431
Figueroa, Daniel, Aug.*	107	422	377	33	89	144	20	7	7	51	0	2	10	33	4	122	2	1	3	.236	.313	.382
Florence, Branden, Hag.	109	470	426	63	129	198	30	3	11	63	0	6	6	31	1	32	9	7	10	.303	.354	.465
Floyd, Mike, Lak.	69	275	248	29	61	81	11	3	1	19	0	0	4	23	0	59	13	5	9	.246	.320	.327
Folsom, Mark, C'bus	91	344	311	38	61	99	10	2	8	26	0	1	1	31	1	120	6	2	7	.196	.270	.318
Foster, Gregg, Lak.	52	175	148	24	27	39	6	0	2	8	1	2	8	16	1	36	6	6	3	.182	.293	.264
Francisco, Ruben, Del.*	54	174	163	16	35	53	6	2	2	14	0	2	3	6	1	29	3	5	5	.215	.253	.325
Franco, Iker, C.S.C.	64	240	216	28	56	86	14	2	4	33	4	3	3	14	2	42	1	1	6	.259	.309	.398

Player, Team	G	TPA	AB	R	H	TB	2B	3B	HR	RBI	SH	SF	HP	BB	IBB	SO	SB	CS	GDP	Avg.	OBP	Slg.
Freeman, Ashley, Ash.	131	538	479	59	125	193	36	1	10	55	0	4	13	42	1	92	13	9	12	.261	.335	.403
Frome, Jason, Ash.*	37	155	142	22	36	51	10	1	1	13	2	0	0	11	1	45	6	3	3	.254	.307	.359
Gajewski, Matt, Sav.†	19	62	57	6	13	15	2	0	0	3	0	0	0	5	0	15	0	0	1	.228	.290	.263
Galante, Matt, C'bia	47	185	156	20	44	50	6	0	0	19	2	3	2	21	0	29	4	4	3	.282	.368	.321
Garcia, Jose, S.G.	128	518	468	59	122	169	24	7	3	59	2	6	5	37	0	110	25	5	9	.261	.318	.361
Garrido, Tomas, Hag.	48	156	141	18	39	46	3	2	0	13	3	1	0	11	1	18	2	2	5	.277	.327	.326
Gathright, Joey, C.S.C.*	59	244	208	30	55	56	1	0	0	14	5	0	10	21	1	36	22	7	1	.264	.360	.269
German, Ramon, Lex.†	86	373	328	46	79	129	15	1	11	49	1	1	0	43	4	77	15	4	11	.241	.328	.393
Gibbs, Mark, Del.	39	108	100	10	18	25	4	0	1	8	3	0	1	4	0	20	2	1	1	.180	.219	.250
Gillitzer, Scott, S.G.	123	526	474	47	136	170	20	4	2	70	2	9	5	36	1	51	15	7	17	.287	.338	.359
Gimenez, Hector, Lex.†	85	323	297	41	78	129	16	1	11	42	1	0	0	25	1	78	2	3	4	.263	.320	.434
Godwin, Tyrell, C.W.Va.*	48	209	185	31	52	70	8	5	0	16	0	0	4	20	3	23	10	2	2	.281	.364	.378
Gold, Nate, Sav.	37	155	142	12	27	49	7	0	5	14	0	0	2	11	1	38	0	2	4	.190	.258	.345
Gonzalez, Daniel, Lak.†	131	565	493	58	133	167	14	4	4	43	7	3	7	55	1	88	11	21	20	.270	.349	.339
Gonzalez, Edgar, C.S.C.	134	533	447	68	123	177	28	1	8	62	1	7	4	74	3	75	21	14	14	.275	.378	.396
Gonzalez, Jose, Sav.†	13	36	29	2	1	1	0	0	0	0	4	0	0	3	0	15	0	0	0	.034	.125	.034
Gordon, Alex, Del.*	60	223	206	32	48	100	11	1	13	33	0	0	3	14	0	76	1	0	3	.233	.291	.485
Gretz, Nick, Ash.*	104	442	383	52	121	154	18	0	5	70	0	1	3	55	4	72	1	1	8	.316	.405	.402
Gutierrez, Franklin, S.G.	92	408	361	61	102	164	18	4	12	45	4	6	6	31	1	88	13	4	5	.283	.344	.454
Guzman, Carlos, Mac.	7	24	20	4	2	2	0	0	0	0	1	0	0	3	0	10	0	0	0	.100	.217	.100
Hackett, Richard, Del.	64	184	172	11	32	37	3	1	0	5	1	0	1	10	0	48	4	1	6	.186	.235	.215
Harris, Blair, Kan.	15	56	52	4	13	20	4	0	1	6	0	0	0	4	0	12	0	0	3	.250	.304	.385
Harrison, Vince, C.S.C.	19	69	62	11	13	20	1	0	2	3	0	0	2	5	0	16	3	0	1	.210	.290	.323
Harts, Jeremy, Hick.†	76	293	257	55	83	129	14	1	10	49	1	2	3	30	2	79	7	5	2	.323	.397	.502
Hattig, John, Aug.†	93	403	347	46	98	139	20	0	7	56	0	2	2	52	4	73	1	2	13	.282	.377	.401
Heard, Scott, Sav.*	124	494	414	40	88	127	13	1	8	45	2	6	5	67	3	81	2	1	7	.213	.325	.307
Helquist, Jon, Lex.	105	400	346	47	88	126	15	4	5	38	4	4	9	37	1	87	17	4	4	.254	.338	.364
Henley, Bob, Hick.	1	4	3	0	0	0	0	0	0	0	0	0	0	1	0	1	0	0	0	.000	.250	.000
Hernandez, Jose, Hick.	59	225	202	16	57	85	14	1	4	36	2	2	10	9	0	48	2	0	3	.282	.341	.421
Herr, Aaron, Mac.	82	312	290	31	72	106	16	0	6	34	1	5	2	14	0	64	3	1	10	.248	.283	.366
Herrera, Christian, S.G.	75	268	218	35	54	63	6	0	1	19	9	1	5	35	0	57	7	4	1	.248	.363	.289
Hietpas, Joe, C'bia	33	120	105	9	26	37	8	0	1	16	1	0	0	14	0	23	0	2	1	.248	.336	.352
Hill, Willy, Hick.*	39	155	141	15	39	42	3	0	0	9	8	0	2	4	0	15	2	6	3	.277	.306	.298
Howard, Ryan, Lak.*	135	570	493	56	138	227	20	6	19	87	1	5	5	66	13	145	5	4	9	.280	.367	.460
Huber, Justin, C'bia	95	403	330	49	96	155	22	2	11	78	0	4	23	45	10	81	1	2	5	.291	.408	.470
Hudnall, Joshua, Hick.	30	94	86	5	16	17	1	0	0	6	2	0	4	2	0	30	2	3	0	.186	.239	.198
Huntingford, Matt, Hag.*	10	36	34	1	6	7	1	0	0	0	0	0	0	2	0	8	0	0	0	.176	.222	.206
Inglett, Joe, C'bus*	60	271	235	44	73	107	18	5	2	46	1	3	4	28	1	25	5	3	5	.311	.389	.455
Jeffcoat, Bryon, Mac.	48	185	159	24	41	64	6	1	5	13	3	1	3	18	0	35	8	2	1	.258	.343	.403
Jiannetti, Joe, C'bia	31	125	112	12	27	43	10	0	2	9	1	1	4	7	0	16	10	1	2	.241	.306	.384
Jimenez, Rich, C.W.Va.†	15	51	44	1	8	9	1	0	0	2	0	2	0	5	0	15	3	1	0	.182	.255	.205
Jimerson, Charlton, Lex.	125	486	439	65	100	172	22	4	14	57	2	2	7	36	0	168	34	9	7	.228	.295	.392
Johnson, Jeremy, C.W.Va.*	28	105	89	10	17	29	4	1	2	14	0	2	3	11	1	22	0	1	4	.191	.295	.326
Johnson, Tripper, Del.	136	571	493	73	128	205	32	6	11	71	4	4	8	62	6	88	19	6	6	.260	.349	.416
Jordan, Eddie, Del.	45	136	112	15	19	30	6	1	1	9	2	1	1	20	0	35	4	2	1	.170	.299	.268
Jova, Maikel, C.W.Va.	118	466	448	43	130	175	20	5	5	53	2	6	3	7	0	70	5	2	17	.290	.302	.391
Kay, Brett, C'bia	38	137	117	14	28	36	5	0	1	7	1	0	5	14	0	22	1	3	0	.239	.346	.308
Kent, Bryan, Aug.	91	355	318	35	76	102	18	1	2	27	7	4	9	17	0	57	4	2	10	.239	.293	.321
Keppinger, Jeff, Hick.	126	540	478	75	132	193	23	4	10	73	2	7	6	47	0	33	6	2	13	.276	.344	.404
Kirby, Brian, C'bus*	99	390	337	48	83	144	15	2	14	48	1	4	1	47	2	123	2	2	2	.246	.337	.427
Knoedler, Justin, Hag.	86	326	280	32	72	107	16	2	5	33	2	3	4	37	0	56	6	5	8	.257	.349	.382
Knox, Matt, C'bus	50	201	191	22	53	84	13	0	6	26	1	2	1	6	0	25	1	1	5	.277	.300	.440
Kochen, Ryan, Lex.	10	40	37	6	9	13	1	0	1	4	0	0	1	2	0	8	0	0	0	.243	.300	.351
Laker, Tim, C'bus	11	50	38	5	11	18	1	0	2	13	0	1	1	10	0	6	0	0	0	.289	.440	.474
Lambert, Casey, Ash.	19	60	53	7	11	14	3	0	0	3	0	0	1	6	0	11	2	1	2	.208	.300	.264
Landaeta, Luis, Hick.*	9	34	30	3	8	8	0	0	0	4	0	0	0	4	1	2	0	1	1	.267	.353	.267
Langill, Eric, S.G.	7	13	13	0	2	2	0	0	0	0	0	0	0	0	0	4	0	0	0	.154	.154	.154
Lawson, Forrest, C'bia	77	313	275	36	72	87	7	1	2	41	1	4	4	29	1	52	5	5	4	.262	.337	.316
Lee, Carlos, Kan.	10	36	35	2	10	12	2	0	0	6	0	0	0	1	0	6	0	0	0	.286	.306	.343
Lehr, Ryan, Del.	51	210	186	22	54	73	13	0	2	38	1	3	1	19	2	26	3	2	6	.290	.354	.392
Lewis, Russell, Aug.*	63	245	223	24	63	101	13	2	7	37	3	4	3	12	2	48	1	1	6	.283	.322	.453
Littleton, Brandon, Del.†	64	240	206	29	53	66	7	3	0	19	5	4	3	22	0	42	14	3	1	.257	.332	.320
Lockhart, Paul, Lex.†	87	338	296	30	66	117	20	2	9	29	2	2	3	32	3	64	5	3	5	.223	.303	.395
Lopez, Gabe, Gre.	17	72	61	11	17	20	1	1	0	7	1	1	0	9	0	4	5	1	1	.279	.366	.328
Lydon, Wayne, C'bia†	127	541	473	93	139	158	9	5	0	46	5	5	4	54	0	104	87	13	1	.294	.368	.334
Maduro, Jorge, C.S.C.	46	141	124	12	32	40	5	0	1	13	2	2	5	8	0	26	1	0	4	.258	.324	.323
Majewski, Val, Del.	7	19	17	2	2	5	0	0	1	3	0	1	0	1	0	1	0	0	1	.118	.158	.294
Malave, Dennis, C'bus*	90	358	301	35	74	100	8	3	4	27	13	2	7	35	1	56	32	11	4	.246	.336	.332
Manfred, Brian, Lak.	8	22	19	1	1	1	0	0	0	0	0	0	1	2	0	6	0	0	0	.053	.182	.053
Manley, Adam, Del.*	133	515	462	58	121	187	29	5	9	57	6	2	7	38	2	133	9	4	6	.262	.326	.405
Mann, Derek, S.G.*	101	430	350	55	108	125	13	2	0	36	7	4	5	64	2	64	17	11	4	.309	.418	.357
Margalski, Ben, Lak.*	79	296	266	25	56	80	11	2	3	27	2	1	4	23	0	65	6	4	5	.211	.282	.301
Marshall, Andre, Lak.†	56	214	186	30	42	53	8	0	1	10	3	0	2	23	0	72	13	5	3	.226	.318	.285
Marte, Andy, Mac.	126	542	488	69	137	240	32	4	21	105	0	7	6	41	3	114	2	1	6	.281	.339	.492
Martel, Normand, Kan.*	34	144	135	14	36	48	6	3	0	13	2	0	1	6	0	32	3	4	1	.267	.303	.356
Martin, Kyle, Del.	52	170	146	17	37	58	6	0	5	19	2	1	1	20	0	36	1	1	2	.253	.345	.397
Martinez, Casey, C.W.Va.	29	107	92	9	30	33	3	0	0	13	1	2	2	10	0	23	0	0	4	.326	.396	.359
Martinez, Edgar, Aug.	77	293	265	30	66	87	13	1	2	29	0	2	7	19	0	34	1	1	6	.249	.314	.328
Martinez, Octavio, Del.	20	87	81	9	23	26	3	0	0	11	1	0	2	3	0	5	3	2	3	.284	.326	.321
Mayorson, Manuel, C.W.Va.	133	555	508	72	139	160	19	1	0	45	10	4	2	31	1	29	28	15	18	.274	.316	.315
McDowell, Arturo, Hag.*	54	229	202	25	35	51	6	2	2	14	3	2	3	19	0	54	9	8	4	.173	.252	.252
McGee, Tom, Del.	68	219	193	16	48	74	8	0	6	18	6	1	2	17	0	45	0	1	6	.249	.315	.383

Player, Team	G	TPA	AB	R	H	TB	2B	3B	HR	RBI	SH	SF	HP	BB	IBB	SO	SB	CS	GDP	Avg.	OBP	Slg.
McIntyre, Robert, C'bia	98	376	345	46	87	124	16	3	5	50	1	7	6	16	0	102	10	6	2	.252	.291	.359
McKee, Mickey, Lex.	79	290	258	34	59	91	15	1	5	30	1	1	7	23	0	55	0	3	3	.229	.308	.353
McKee, Scott, Kan.†	119	488	439	47	119	178	26	0	11	65	0	2	2	45	7	81	0	2	11	.271	.340	.405
McMains, Derin, Hag.†	83	371	330	44	80	113	11	2	6	32	2	4	4	31	1	28	14	3	6	.242	.312	.342
Meath, Matt, Hick.†	15	50	40	8	5	5	0	0	0	2	2	0	0	8	0	13	2	0	0	.125	.271	.125
Medina, Rodney, C.W.Va.†	97	381	339	52	97	132	12	7	3	36	2	3	4	33	2	44	11	10	4	.286	.354	.389
Mercedes, Jose, Sav.	13	31	26	3	3	3	0	0	0	0	0	0	0	5	0	6	0	0	1	.115	.258	.115
Merritt, Graig, C.S.C.	63	208	184	10	35	39	4	0	0	11	5	1	3	15	0	32	4	0	3	.190	.261	.212
Meyer, Drew, Sav.*	54	237	214	15	52	68	5	4	1	24	11	2	0	10	0	53	7	6	2	.243	.274	.318
Meyer, Robert, Hag.	126	496	447	51	122	170	24	0	8	37	4	2	11	32	0	95	6	1	12	.273	.335	.380
Miller, Greg, Mac.	103	411	361	46	113	129	14	1	0	34	4	3	5	38	0	66	17	4	11	.313	.383	.357
Miller, Tony, Ash.	129	598	501	109	142	224	23	4	17	48	2	1	6	88	2	129	50	19	5	.283	.396	.447
Minami, Yasumichi, Aug.	4	11	10	1	0	0	0	0	0	0	0	0	0	1	0	5	0	0	0	.000	.091	.000
Miranda, Miguel, Hag.†	70	247	217	25	57	64	2	1	1	25	10	2	1	17	0	26	4	1	2	.263	.316	.295
Molina, Gustavo, Kan.	94	359	310	37	70	91	13	1	2	34	7	6	9	27	1	61	7	2	6	.226	.301	.294
Monegan, Anthony, Kan.*	23	79	77	8	10	10	0	0	0	3	1	0	0	1	0	17	5	1	0	.130	.141	.130
Mongeluzzo, Anthony, Sav.	95	402	352	51	76	129	24	1	9	43	1	1	9	38	2	79	10	6	10	.216	.308	.366
Morales, Michael, Mac.	10	31	26	3	6	9	3	0	0	5	0	0	4	1	0	4	0	0	2	.231	.355	.346
Morse, Michael, Kan.†	113	469	417	43	107	151	30	4	2	56	7	2	8	25	0	73	7	6	16	.257	.310	.362
Mosquera, Julio, Sav.	5	19	15	1	4	4	0	0	0	1	0	0	1	3	0	4	2	1	0	.267	.421	.267
Nathans, John, Aug.	20	64	55	9	10	13	3	0	0	6	1	0	1	7	0	13	3	0	2	.182	.286	.236
Navarro, Dioner, Gre.†	92	374	328	41	78	118	12	2	8	36	0	2	5	39	0	61	1	2	9	.238	.326	.360
Negron, Miguel, C.W.Va.*	118	462	420	56	107	141	15	2	5	41	4	2	1	35	1	77	20	7	8	.255	.312	.336
Nix, Jayson, Ash.	132	569	487	73	120	195	29	2	14	79	3	4	9	62	2	105	14	5	10	.246	.340	.400
Nunez, Alexis, Lak.*	6	16	15	0	3	3	0	0	0	0	1	0	0	0	0	5	0	0	0	.200	.200	.200
Nunez, Felix, C.S.C.	5	20	19	2	7	11	1	0	1	6	0	0	0	1	0	5	0	0	0	.368	.400	.579
Nunez, Manuel, S.G.	46	144	125	22	20	22	2	0	0	6	3	0	2	14	0	44	12	4	0	.160	.255	.176
Ochoa, Ivan, C'bus	125	466	391	54	85	100	9	3	0	28	9	3	9	54	0	87	47	10	4	.217	.324	.256
Ochoa, Javier, C'bia	32	99	85	13	20	27	1	0	2	10	0	0	3	11	0	15	0	0	2	.235	.343	.318
O'Connor, Brian, Gre.	9	23	21	0	2	2	0	0	0	1	0	0	0	2	0	13	0	1	0	.095	.174	.095
Oliva, Chad, Lak.	31	109	96	8	25	35	4	0	2	10	0	0	1	12	0	22	2	2	2	.260	.349	.365
Olivari, Reinaldo, Sav.	8	18	14	2	4	4	0	0	0	1	0	0	1	3	0	4	2	0	1	.286	.444	.286
O'Riordan, Chris, Sav.	9	41	33	6	9	12	3	0	0	2	1	0	0	7	1	5	1	1	2	.273	.400	.364
Ortega, Sixto, Ash.	17	55	54	1	7	7	0	0	0	2	0	0	0	1	0	12	0	0	1	.130	.145	.130
Pacheco, Julio, S.G.*	40	149	135	16	38	50	6	0	2	12	3	2	1	8	1	22	3	5	3	.281	.322	.370
Pagan, Angel, C'bia†	108	497	458	79	128	155	14	5	1	36	4	3	0	32	0	87	52	21	1	.279	.325	.338
Pagan, Felix, Sav.	30	115	104	13	25	40	6	3	1	9	1	1	2	7	1	25	3	2	2	.240	.298	.385
Patty, Jason, Sav.*	16	32	29	2	4	5	1	0	0	1	0	1	0	2	0	10	0	0	0	.138	.188	.172
Peck, Bryan, Ash.	55	232	212	32	77	122	14	2	9	49	0	2	1	17	0	32	1	2	5	.363	.409	.575
Pena, Brayan, Mac.†	81	300	271	26	62	81	10	0	3	25	3	2	2	22	1	37	0	3	5	.229	.290	.299
Pena, Tony, Mac.	118	434	405	42	101	126	9	5	2	36	8	2	5	14	0	68	11	15	6	.249	.282	.311
Perry, Rod, Lak.	108	463	408	57	98	128	20	2	2	30	7	5	4	39	2	61	25	18	5	.240	.309	.314
Peshke, Chad, C'bus	97	389	327	42	87	109	11	1	3	37	1	5	9	47	2	40	16	5	5	.266	.369	.333
Petersen, Ryan, Aug.	43	138	127	14	27	38	4	2	1	10	4	0	1	6	0	38	12	3	1	.213	.254	.299
Phelps, Jeff, Lak.	112	444	405	45	114	174	31	4	7	59	2	4	6	27	1	95	10	4	6	.281	.333	.430
Pierce, Sean, S.G.	88	346	291	57	77	109	10	2	6	38	3	3	5	44	0	67	18	5	5	.265	.367	.375
Pitney, Jared, Gre.*	36	131	112	12	24	33	3	0	2	10	1	1	1	16	0	40	0	0	1	.214	.315	.295
Pittman, Sean, C'bia†	14	53	46	6	11	13	0	1	0	4	0	1	1	5	0	18	1	0	0	.239	.321	.283
Porter, Thomas, C.S.C.	10	24	19	2	1	1	0	0	0	1	0	0	1	4	0	14	1	0	1	.053	.250	.053
Price, Jared, S.G.	69	266	210	31	45	86	12	1	9	34	8	0	13	35	2	83	5	4	2	.214	.360	.410
Quintana, Miguel, C'bus*	71	264	238	22	62	86	12	0	4	29	1	2	2	21	2	41	4	6	3	.261	.323	.361
Radwan, Jason, S.G.	22	82	70	12	10	24	2	0	4	8	0	1	4	7	0	34	1	1	0	.143	.256	.343
Ragsdale, Corey, C'bia	37	147	124	15	22	26	1	0	1	12	6	2	0	15	0	45	8	5	0	.177	.262	.210
Ravelo, Manny, Hick.	92	390	341	48	81	99	10	1	2	22	5	0	6	38	0	80	42	18	1	.238	.325	.290
Reece, Eric, C.S.C.*	65	223	192	21	37	50	5	1	2	23	6	4	1	20	0	46	4	3	2	.193	.267	.260
Reed, Jeremy, Kan.*	57	239	210	37	67	94	15	0	4	32	3	4	11	11	1	24	17	5	7	.319	.377	.448
Reyes, Ambiorix, Ash.†	27	100	99	7	18	19	1	0	0	5	1	0	0	0	0	14	1	2	5	.182	.182	.192
Reyes, Ivan, Gre.	71	206	177	22	21	30	3	0	2	17	2	3	6	18	1	74	2	1	1	.119	.221	.169
Reyes, Julio, Kan.*	55	204	195	25	56	95	14	2	7	24	0	0	3	6	2	35	2	1	7	.287	.319	.487
Reyes, Milver, Hick.	4	15	14	2	3	5	2	0	0	2	0	0	0	1	0	2	0	0	0	.214	.267	.357
Reynoso, Danilo, C'bia	3	8	6	0	1	1	0	0	0	1	0	0	1	1	0	1	0	0	0	.167	.375	.167
Rico, Matt, C.S.C.	106	372	332	42	73	109	16	1	6	37	3	1	4	32	0	90	9	6	11	.220	.295	.328
Riera, Zack, Hick.†	14	50	40	11	12	20	3	1	1	9	1	0	5	4	0	7	1	0	1	.300	.429	.500
Riley, Ryan, C.S.C.	17	57	45	11	9	10	1	0	0	3	0	0	2	10	0	9	1	2	0	.200	.368	.222
Ringe, Craig, Sav.	4	18	12	2	1	2	1	0	0	2	1	0	3	2	0	6	0	0	0	.083	.353	.167
Rivera, Eric, Lak.	62	245	218	24	45	57	6	0	2	27	2	3	5	17	1	57	3	7	4	.206	.276	.261
Rodriguez , Ricardo, Mac.	26	89	79	11	23	29	1	1	1	3	1	0	5	4	0	14	2	1	2	.291	.364	.367
Rodriguez, Andres, C'bia	60	226	207	21	41	56	10	1	1	23	0	2	1	16	1	57	2	0	0	.198	.257	.271
Rodriguez, Edgar, C'bia	23	78	72	7	15	21	3	0	1	7	0	2	1	3	0	25	2	3	1	.208	.244	.292
Rogers, Brandon, Hick.	22	72	65	5	10	13	3	0	0	5	3	0	1	3	0	16	0	0	1	.154	.203	.200
Rogers, Omar, Del.	78	339	297	47	82	114	21	1	3	27	4	3	9	26	0	53	3	1	7	.276	.349	.384
Rollins, Antwon, Sav.	54	170	148	23	30	52	10	3	2	17	2	2	6	12	0	48	3	2	3	.203	.286	.351
Rosa, Wally, Kan.	57	228	198	21	54	63	7	1	0	18	3	0	6	21	0	42	4	1	5	.273	.360	.318
Rosario, Carlos, Gre.	1	3	3	0	2	2	0	0	0	0	0	0	0	0	0	1	0	0	0	.667	.667	.667
Ruiz, Reinaldo, Lak.	29	113	96	15	18	24	6	0	0	14	1	3	1	12	0	16	1	3	2	.188	.277	.250
St. Clair, Jason, C.S.C.	6	19	18	1	5	6	1	0	0	1	0	0	0	0	0	5	0	0	0	.278	.278	.333
Salas, Jose, Mac.†	80	313	293	22	67	102	14	0	7	39	1	2	4	13	2	81	0	1	11	.229	.269	.348
Salazar, Juan, Aug.†	112	414	350	36	69	78	5	2	0	22	10	2	19	33	0	54	11	10	7	.197	.300	.223
Salinas, Trey, Del.	70	289	251	31	71	118	21	1	8	45	1	4	9	24	0	45	2	0	7	.283	.361	.470
Salvo, Andrew, Kan.*	57	240	202	24	51	68	7	2	2	23	1	2	2	33	0	29	10	6	2	.252	.360	.337
Sanchez, Jean, Sav.	50	144	134	13	27	41	5	0	3	18	1	2	1	6	0	24	2	1	6	.201	.238	.306
Santamarina, Juan, Kan.*	93	367	332	31	90	125	18	4	3	29	0	2	1	32	1	62	3	2	6	.271	.335	.377

Player, Team	G	TPA	AB	R	H	TB	2B	3B	HR	RBI	SH	SF	HP	BB	IBB	SO	SB	CS	GDP	Avg.	OBP	Slg.
Santos, Omir, Gre................	23	80	73	7	17	24	2	1	1	8	0	2	3	2	0	15	0	0	2	.233	.275	.329
Sardinha, Bronson, Gre.*........	93	389	342	49	90	139	13	0	12	44	0	7	6	34	2	78	15	6	6	.263	.334	.406
Scala, Mickey, Hick.*	4	7	7	0	0	0	0	0	0	0	0	0	0	0	0	5	0	0	0	.000	.000	.000
Schmitt, Brian, Lex.*............	121	433	386	46	99	144	24	3	5	61	3	4	8	32	2	113	6	4	10	.256	.323	.373
Schuerholz, Jon, Mac.	2	6	6	1	1	3	0	1	0	0	0	0	0	0	0	1	1	0	0	.167	.167	.500
Scott, Luke, C'bus*........	49	198	171	28	44	88	15	4	7	32	1	2	3	21	0	58	9	1	3	.257	.345	.515
Seestedt, Mike, Del.	9	26	22	2	3	5	2	0	0	2	1	0	0	3	0	2	0	0	1	.136	.240	.227
Segar, Jeff, Gre.	103	432	382	63	106	184	17	2	19	60	0	6	4	40	1	74	16	7	11	.277	.347	.482
Seiber, Antron, Aug.	76	335	309	46	92	121	15	4	2	22	2	3	3	18	0	68	10	9	3	.298	.339	.392
Shanks, Eric, Del.	14	48	39	3	8	12	4	0	0	4	2	0	4	3	0	9	1	1	1	.205	.326	.308
Shelley, Randall, Sav.	129	521	425	65	98	157	18	4	11	44	2	1	16	77	0	117	9	8	7	.231	.368	.369
Shelton, Chris, Hick.	93	388	332	72	113	195	27	2	17	65	0	4	5	47	2	74	0	0	1	.340	.425	.587
Sherrill, J.J., C'bus†	107	461	365	61	86	145	18	1	13	56	10	4	17	65	0	126	23	14	3	.236	.373	.397
Silvera, Andres, Lak.	21	60	55	5	11	21	2	1	2	8	0	0	0	5	0	11	0	1	0	.200	.267	.382
Smith, Dustin, Sav.	63	204	176	12	41	47	6	0	0	12	2	1	6	19	0	38	0	2	2	.233	.327	.267
Snyder, Mike, C.W.Va.*	136	600	518	67	148	225	21	4	16	87	0	3	3	76	10	107	5	2	9	.286	.378	.434
Soriano, Jairo, Del.†	15	51	47	5	11	18	2	1	1	5	4	0	0	0	0	16	1	0	0	.234	.234	.383
Soto, T.J., Lex.	66	222	197	24	48	81	9	0	8	33	0	4	0	21	0	75	11	3	2	.244	.311	.411
Soules, Ryan, Sav.*	30	130	106	14	34	55	10	1	3	22	0	1	2	21	0	25	0	0	2	.321	.438	.519
Spidale, Mike, Kan.	93	413	357	57	104	117	11	1	0	30	7	2	13	34	0	50	37	25	5	.291	.372	.328
Stockton, Brad, Sav.*	90	290	243	25	56	76	13	2	1	31	1	3	2	41	2	69	4	2	4	.230	.343	.313
Storey, Eric, Kan.	110	453	388	65	101	149	19	1	9	42	3	2	2	58	0	136	4	0	10	.260	.358	.384
Story-Harden, Thomari, S.G...	114	459	393	57	112	167	18	2	11	56	2	4	14	46	1	109	4	3	4	.285	.376	.425
Stringfellow, Christopher, Sav. .	69	274	229	27	56	67	8	0	1	15	5	4	8	28	1	53	9	3	7	.245	.342	.293
Summerville, Kaazim, Gre.	51	180	153	32	35	59	8	2	4	9	1	1	4	21	0	39	20	2	3	.229	.335	.386
Swedlow, Sean, C'bus*	76	318	285	32	66	95	9	1	6	36	0	4	4	25	0	89	5	1	3	.232	.299	.333
Tablado, Raul, C.W.Va.	103	389	361	38	80	109	23	0	2	29	4	1	2	21	0	98	2	1	13	.222	.268	.302
Taveras, Willy, C'bus	85	381	313	68	83	111	14	1	4	27	2	3	18	45	0	68	54	12	3	.265	.385	.355
Tejada, Mike, Ash.†	91	360	325	37	74	121	17	0	10	40	1	3	2	28	2	54	0	3	9	.228	.291	.372
Tempesta, Nick, C.W.Va.	57	219	200	29	56	76	15	1	1	27	2	0	5	12	0	28	1	4	3	.280	.336	.380
Tena, Hector, Ash.	131	487	435	55	83	122	16	1	7	39	4	4	15	29	0	129	0	5	12	.191	.263	.280
Testa, Chris, Ash.*	124	533	463	66	117	165	24	0	8	56	1	7	14	48	2	98	5	4	7	.253	.336	.356
Thompson, Kevin, Gre.	62	270	226	44	64	103	24	3	3	31	0	1	6	37	1	42	14	3	4	.283	.396	.456
Thorman, Scott, Mac.*	127	534	470	57	138	230	38	3	16	82	0	6	7	51	5	83	2	2	16	.294	.367	.489
Timmons, Wes, Mac.	40	156	120	17	34	43	4	1	1	14	7	0	10	19	0	10	6	3	1	.283	.423	.358
Toner, John, C'bia	35	129	114	19	34	53	7	0	4	16	0	0	6	9	0	32	2	2	2	.298	.380	.465
Tosca, Daniel, Lak.*	71	260	234	26	56	94	19	2	5	29	3	1	3	19	1	56	2	2	1	.239	.304	.402
Toven, John, Lex.	70	263	244	34	69	84	12	0	1	23	1	4	0	14	0	30	19	11	7	.283	.317	.344
Turco, Anthony, Hag.*	15	51	45	5	14	17	0	0	1	5	0	0	0	6	0	10	0	0	0	.311	.392	.378
Turner, Jason, Gre.	72	294	257	36	77	104	16	1	3	31	0	0	3	31	0	37	8	3	5	.300	.381	.405
Van Every, Jon, C'bus*	15	58	43	10	6	17	0	1	3	4	0	0	2	13	1	25	1	0	0	.140	.362	.395
Vasquez, Jose, Ash.*	93	358	319	44	71	113	20	2	6	36	0	2	7	30	0	122	4	5	9	.223	.302	.354
Verbryke, Eric, Gre.*	30	120	108	10	25	37	6	0	2	9	0	0	1	11	0	31	2	3	0	.231	.308	.343
Von Schell, Tyler, Hic.	130	550	483	54	116	176	16	1	14	69	0	3	10	54	2	126	3	0	9	.240	.327	.364
Vukovich, Vince, Lak.*	59	213	184	20	45	58	11	1	0	9	5	1	2	21	1	34	5	5	4	.245	.327	.315
Walker, Mark, Hag.	72	276	230	28	47	77	10	1	6	21	3	0	6	37	0	85	4	3	8	.204	.330	.335
Walsh, Sean, Lak.	90	321	274	34	71	85	9	1	1	28	3	1	12	31	3	58	26	4	3	.259	.358	.310
Webster, Kevin, Del.	13	44	38	3	11	14	0	0	1	7	0	0	2	4	0	6	1	0	0	.289	.386	.368
Weston, Aron, Hick.*	67	267	226	38	54	80	10	2	4	30	3	3	0	35	1	49	20	5	0	.239	.337	.354
Whiteman, Tommy, Lex.	90	397	350	50	106	169	29	2	10	49	4	2	5	36	1	66	6	6	13	.303	.374	.483
Whitney, Matthew, C'bus	6	21	18	0	2	2	0	0	0	0	0	0	0	3	0	4	0	0	1	.111	.238	.111
Whittaker, Tim, C.W.Va.	78	303	273	31	84	120	22	1	4	31	0	1	4	25	2	51	1	1	5	.308	.373	.440
Wigginton, Derek, Kan.*	110	437	398	32	92	122	14	2	4	47	3	5	2	29	1	89	10	8	11	.231	.283	.307
Winrow, Gary, Gre.*	73	256	239	29	56	85	12	1	5	27	3	1	3	10	0	52	4	3	1	.234	.273	.356
Wolotka, Brian, C.S.C.*	58	203	173	20	38	57	10	0	3	17	4	3	3	20	1	72	3	3	1	.220	.307	.329
Wright, David, C'bia	135	587	496	85	132	199	30	2	11	93	1	4	5	76	2	114	21	5	4	.266	.367	.401
Wright, Gavin, Lex.	128	575	517	73	153	212	23	6	8	57	9	6	3	40	0	92	21	18	8	.296	.346	.410
Yepez, Jose, C.W.Va.	76	294	263	34	66	92	11	0	5	37	0	1	6	24	0	31	4	2	12	.251	.327	.350
Youkilis, Kevin, Aug.	15	67	53	5	15	20	5	0	0	6	0	0	1	13	1	8	0	0	0	.283	.433	.377
Young, Walter, Hick.*	132	551	492	84	164	277	34	2	25	103	0	8	15	36	6	102	2	6	11	.333	.390	.563
Youngbauer, Scott, Lak.†	17	69	61	9	18	37	6	2	3	10	0	1	7	0	0	10	0	2	0	.295	.377	.607
Zieour, Neesan, C.W.Va.	48	217	175	32	53	72	13	3	0	20	4	4	12	22	0	27	7	6	3	.303	.408	.411

PLAYERS WITH TWO OR MORE TEAMS

Player, Team	G	TPA	AB	R	H	TB	2B	3B	HR	RBI	SH	SF	HP	BB	IBB	SO	SB	CS	GDP	Avg.	OBP	Slg.
Bryan, Jason, Sav.	1	4	4	0	1	1	0	0	0	0	0	0	0	0	0	1	0	0	0	.250	.250	.250
Bryan, Jason, Aug.	16	63	55	6	12	21	3	0	2	8	0	1	0	7	0	23	1	1	0	.218	.302	.382

GRAND SLAMS: Tejada 2; Barnowski, Benavidez, Bourgeois, Caligiuri, Carter, J. Cooper, M. Cooper, Doumit, Eldridge, D. Figueroa, Folsom, Franco, Gold, Harts, Hattig, Helquist, Huber, Kent, Laker, Lawson, Malave, Peck, Price, Segar, Tena, Tosca, Walker, D. Wright, 1 each.

AWARDED FIRST BASE ON CATCHER'S INTERFERENCE: D. Wright 5 (Bastardo, Bellorin, Kirby, Salas, D. Smith); Nix 4 (Bellorin, Camacaro, Franco, Huber); Amador 3 (Knoedler, J. Ochoa, Turco); Lockhart 3 (Rosa, Turco, Whittaker); Turner 3 (Bellorin, Riera, Yepez); Brunner 2 (K. Martin, D. Smith); Cabrerra 2 (Bellorin, B. Pena); Bacani (Heard); Brand (Brandon Rogers); Bird (E. Martinez); Florence (Molina); Galante (Hernandez); Huber (K. Anderson); Jeffcoat (D. Smith); McIntyre (D. Smith); Mongeluzzo (Bernard); Tejada (Maduro).

2002 PITCHING
TEAM

Team	W	L	Pct.	ERA	G	CG	ShO	Sv.	IP	H	TBF	R	ER	HR	SH	SF	HB	BB	IBB	SO	WP	Bk.
Lexington	81	59	.579	3.03	140	1	17	36	1252.1	1095	5221	517	422	91	47	30	76	415	14	1133	81	9
South Georgia ...	75	63	.543	3.40	138	5	11	30	1201.0	1120	5147	582	454	66	34	46	96	416	8	936	67	11

Team	W	L	Pct.	ERA	G	CG	ShO	Sv.	IP	H	TBF	R	ER	HR	SH	SF	HB	BB	IBB	SO	WP	Bk.
Lakewood	69	70	.496	3.42	139	20	12	28	1216.0	1139	5109	540	462	76	51	36	68	384	8	874	63	3
Columbus	79	60	.568	3.47	139	1	10	44	1210.2	1124	5185	585	467	70	45	30	80	460	15	1097	78	12
Delmarva	76	64	.543	3.49	140	5	12	46	1231.0	1197	5253	575	478	77	54	33	73	401	24	983	62	8
Hickory	83	56	.597	3.51	139	1	8	43	1206.0	1134	5128	567	470	97	32	30	60	404	17	1038	60	11
Charleston, S.C.	60	76	.441	3.58	136	2	6	32	1163.0	1170	5042	593	462	65	38	43	86	433	26	935	82	11
Columbia	75	64	.540	3.58	139	1	9	41	1206.1	1079	5234	593	480	60	59	35	16	552	12	1213	79	6
Kannapolis	66	74	.471	3.62	140	3	10	37	1232.0	1185	5320	630	496	74	50	47	72	488	23	1000	69	14
Augusta	69	67	.507	3.63	136	1	9	36	1168.1	1132	5011	578	471	73	42	29	62	471	14	1007	78	6
Macon	66	74	.471	3.68	140	4	13	25	1199.1	1086	5142	611	491	73	46	34	67	498	13	1041	105	8
Charleston, W.Va.	61	79	.436	3.76	140	4	9	26	1217.0	1141	5208	609	508	76	38	33	75	455	10	1055	86	10
Savannah	49	89	.355	3.98	138	0	10	22	1220.0	1179	5320	653	539	87	50	60	84	496	19	1010	107	9
Greensboro	75	65	.536	4.04	140	3	9	38	1228.2	1263	5428	670	552	83	48	39	80	547	24	917	118	13
Hagerstown	63	77	.450	4.35	140	3	4	38	1213.0	1258	5317	728	586	96	50	39	71	460	10	992	101	14
Asheville	64	74	.464	4.47	138	3	8	34	1211.1	1325	5395	715	602	114	46	40	20	462	17	1007	87	14

INDIVIDUAL

TOP QUALIFIERS FOR EARNED-RUN AVERAGE TITLE

Minimum 112 innings.*Lefthanded pitcher.

Pitcher, Team	W	L	Pct.	ERA	G	GS	CG	ShO	GF	Sv.	IP	H	TBF	R	ER	HR	SH	SF	HB	BB	IBB	SO	WP	Bk.
McBride, Macay, Mac.*	12	8	.600	2.12	25	25	2	1	0	0	157.1	119	624	49	37	6	2	3	1	48	1	138	13	1
Harper, Jesse, C.W.Va.	6	5	.545	2.16	21	14	0	0	3	1	112.2	98	453	38	27	4	2	4	6	25	0	97	4	1
Gaudin, Chad, C.S.C.	4	6	.400	2.26	26	17	0	0	5	1	119.1	106	491	43	30	3	5	5	11	37	0	106	4	3
Flinn, Chris, C.S.C.	8	6	.571	2.31	19	19	2	1	0	0	128.1	103	521	44	33	6	4	3	7	41	1	116	7	1
Roberson, Brandon, Lex.	8	5	.615	2.40	23	18	0	0	1	0	112.1	105	462	34	30	7	4	5	7	22	0	115	5	0
Peeples, Ross, C'bia*	7	7	.500	2.43	20	19	0	0	1	1	115	104	469	49	31	3	3	3	5	25	0	98	3	0
Oquendo, Ian, Hick.	11	6	.647	2.71	24	22	0	0	0	0	139.2	127	576	49	42	8	5	3	0	45	0	149	13	2
Dawson, Layne, Lak.	7	4	.636	2.76	27	8	3	2	11	5	117.1	103	472	41	36	5	6	2	5	21	0	89	5	0
Floyd, Gavin, Lak.	11	10	.524	2.77	27	27	3	0	0	0	166	119	671	59	51	13	4	1	8	64	0	140	14	0
Dumatrait, Phillip, Aug.*	8	5	.615	2.77	22	22	1	1	0	0	120.1	109	492	44	37	5	1	1	5	47	0	108	7	0
Lubisich, Nik, Kan.*	9	3	.750	2.79	34	13	2	1	7	0	122.2	123	505	45	38	3	6	6	3	26	2	81	2	0
Cruceta, Alberto, S.G.	8	5	.615	2.80	20	20	3	2	0	0	112.2	98	466	42	35	7	0	2	4	34	0	111	10	0
Van Benschoten, John, Hick.	11	4	.733	2.80	27	27	0	0	0	0	148	119	620	57	46	6	4	2	7	62	1	145	7	0
Hannaman, Ryan, Hag.*	7	6	.538	2.80	24	24	1	0	0	0	131.2	109	563	54	41	9	5	2	5	46	0	145	9	2
Barrett, Jimmy, Lex.	9	5	.643	2.81	27	22	0	0	3	1	134.1	112	549	53	42	13	5	4	12	40	0	131	8	0

DEPARTMENTAL LEADERS: W—Z. Parker, 16; L—Bittner, 13; Pct.—Gomez, Mattox, .800 each; G—Meaux, 54; GS—Bittner, 29; CG—Cable, Lee, 5 each; ShO—Cable, Cruceta, Dawson, Wood, 2 each; GF—Gronkiewicz, 48; Sv.—Gronkiewicz, 27; IP—Cable, 177.1; H—Cable, Z. Parker, 174 each; TBF—Cable, 735; R—Bittner, 98; ER—Bittner, 80; HR—Cable, 20; SH—G. Lopez, 14; SF—Van Buren, 10; HB—Hampson, 24; BB—Seddon, 68; IBB—Patten, 7; SO—McGowan, 163; WP—Gross, Mead, 17 each; BK—C. Merricks, 6.

ALL PITCHERS

*Lefthanded pitcher.

Pitcher, Team	W	L	Pct.	ERA	G	GS	CG	ShO	GF	Sv.	IP	H	TBF	R	ER	HR	SH	SF	HB	BB	IBB	SO	WP	Bk.
Abell, Joe, Ash.	0	0	.000	10.80	7	0	0	0	1	0	6.2	10	43	10	8	1	0	1	5	8	0	4	2	0
Abraham, Paul, Sav.	3	4	.429	3.52	52	0	0	0	28	7	69	68	310	32	27	8	3	6	7	35	2	55	7	1
Acosta, Manuel, Gre.	2	5	.286	6.40	13	10	0	0	0	0	52	65	257	47	37	4	3	3	1	44	0	35	5	0
Albertus, Roberto, Mac.*	2	3	.400	6.10	26	2	0	0	10	1	62	63	282	45	42	6	2	3	3	28	0	50	6	0
Allen, Brian, C.S.C.	0	0	.000	6.75	2	0	0	0	1	0	2.2	5	14	2	2	0	0	1	1	0	1	1	1	0
Alvarez, Juan, Mac.*	2	5	.286	6.79	12	11	0	0	1	0	51.2	71	245	43	39	7	2	3	5	27	0	45	7	2
Alvarez, Oscar, C'bus*	2	6	.250	3.45	33	5	0	0	7	2	78.1	88	351	42	30	7	3	2	4	34	2	61	2	2
Anderson, Travis, Lex.	4	5	.444	4.46	48	2	0	0	31	8	84.2	81	367	45	42	7	5	2	9	31	0	81	9	1
Andrew, Jason, Sav.	1	0	1.000	1.28	11	6	0	0	1	0	42.1	31	161	7	6	3	1	0	0	8	0	30	1	0
Arellan, Felix, S.G.*	4	5	.444	9.53	35	4	0	0	8	0	45.1	53	236	58	48	6	3	1	6	41	0	32	9	3
Arthurs, Shane, C'bus	1	1	.500	1.53	6	1	0	0	2	0	17.2	7	63	3	3	1	1	1	3	2	0	15	1	0
Artiles, Carlos, Gre.*	3	3	.500	2.38	34	0	0	0	26	12	45.1	37	208	17	12	0	5	2	2	34	4	46	8	1
Astacio, Andres, S.G.	5	5	.500	3.87	31	10	0	0	9	1	93	98	396	50	40	9	5	3	2	26	2	67	2	1
Astacio, Ezequiel, Lak.	10	7	.588	3.31	25	25	1	0	0	0	152.1	159	647	61	56	9	8	3	12	46	1	100	6	0
Barnett, John, Sav.	0	1	.000	5.00	3	1	0	0	0	0	9	12	39	5	5	0	2	1	0	2	1	8	0	0
Barrett, Jimmy, Lex.	9	5	.643	2.81	27	22	0	0	3	1	134.1	112	549	53	42	13	5	4	12	40	0	131	8	0
Barrios, Angel, Lex.	0	0	.000	0.00	1	0	0	0	1	0	2	0	6	0	0	0	0	0	0	0	0	3	0	0
Bartlett, Richard, Del.	6	0	1.000	2.63	9	8	0	0	0	0	48	45	204	16	14	1	2	0	1	16	1	33	1	1
Barzilla, Philip, Lex.*	6	9	.400	3.26	43	0	0	0	27	4	85.2	66	356	39	31	2	9	2	3	34	5	62	4	0
Bayrer, Thomas, Lex.	0	2	.000	4.13	12	0	0	0	6	0	24	24	105	12	11	2	0	3	0	12	0	21	2	0
Bengochea, Kiki, Sav.	3	4	.429	3.00	12	9	0	0	1	0	39	37	165	18	13	0	1	3	3	14	0	36	6	0
Benitez, Fabricio, Aug.	1	0	1.000	2.08	3	0	0	0	2	0	4.1	4	17	1	1	1	0	0	0	0	0	4	0	0
Benjamin, Petersen, Hag.	2	8	.200	5.83	13	13	0	0	0	0	58.2	90	284	55	38	6	2	3	5	15	0	32	4	0
Bernard, Jason, Lak.	1	0	1.000	4.87	11	0	0	0	7	0	20.1	21	95	17	11	3	0	0	3	13	0	13	1	0
Bierbrodt, Nick, C.S.C.*	0	0	.000	3.60	1	1	0	0	0	0	5	5	23	4	2	0	0	0	2	0	2	1	0	
Bilezikjian, Charlie, Sav.	0	0	.000	3.60	3	0	0	0	1	0	5	6	22	2	2	0	0	1	0	1	0	4	1	0
Birkins, Kurt, Del.*	9	7	.563	3.51	27	25	3	0	0	0	143.2	140	607	66	56	10	6	1	10	46	1	102	7	0
Bittner, Tim, Kan.*	5	13	.278	4.58	29	29	0	0	0	0	157.1	166	694	98	80	10	6	1	8	67	2	123	10	2
Blankenship, John, Gre.*	7	2	.778	3.05	12	12	1	1	0	0	76.2	73	330	30	26	3	5	1	5	23	1	89	8	0
Blethen, Matt, C'bus*	2	0	1.000	8.80	11	0	0	0	4	0	15.1	24	79	18	15	3	1	0	0	8	0	13	2	0
Bobbitt, Seth, Lex.	4	6	.636	3.08	14	14	0	0	0	0	84.2	79	347	31	29	6	1	0	2	21	0	63	4	0
Boughner, Anthony, Del.*	4	2	.667	4.32	18	8	0	0	0	2	50	57	218	29	24	2	4	1	2	14	0	37	2	0
Boyer, Blaine, Mac.	5	9	.357	3.07	43	0	0	0	22	1	70.1	52	305	30	24	0	6	3	5	39	3	73	8	2
Brian, Billy, Gre.	1	3	.250	4.75	7	7	0	0	0	0	36	37	154	21	19	3	0	1	2	13	0	14	6	0
Bright, Nathan, Sav.	2	6	.250	4.79	15	6	0	0	6	2	47	49	212	35	25	1	6	4	16	1	32	5	0	
Brito, Eude, Lak.*	1	1	.500	2.55	11	0	0	0	8	0	17.2	14	70	5	5	1	2	0	0	6	0	11	0	0

Pitcher, Team	W	L	Pct.	ERA	G	GS	CG	ShO	GF	Sv.	IP	H	TBF	R	ER	HR	SH	SF	HB	BB	IBB	SO	WP	Bk.
Burres, Brian, Hag.*	5	10	.333	4.75	32	16	0	0	4	1	119.1	114	522	78	63	15	4	4	9	53	0	119	8	1
Byard, David, C'bia	7	4	.636	3.57	45	0	0	0	24	5	68	55	296	32	27	0	7	2	5	43	4	48	2	0
Cable, Taft, Lak.	11	10	.524	3.76	27	27	5	2	0	0	177.1	174	735	84	74	20	2	8	11	24	2	115	5	0
Cabreja, Eny, Lex.*	11	4	.733	3.78	28	28	0	0	0	0	159.1	167	677	74	67	12	8	5	13	44	0	137	8	2
Cabrera, Yunior, C'bia*	1	0	1.000	0.82	3	1	0	0	2	0	11	11	47	4	1	0	0	1	2	2	0	8	1	0
Campos, Juan, Lex.	2	0	1.000	2.70	4	0	0	0	1	0	6.2	3	25	2	2	0	0	0	1	1	0	5	0	0
Caraballo, Angel, Gre.	2	1	.667	4.01	6	5	0	0	0	0	33.2	35	142	18	15	1	1	2	2	14	1	11	2	0
Carlson, Steve, Gre.*	6	1	.857	2.44	43	0	0	0	11	1	66.1	45	275	26	18	5	3	1	1	31	3	75	4	1
Carney, Jake, C.S.C.	0	1	.000	10.80	6	0	0	0	4	0	6.2	16	37	8	8	1	1	0	0	2	1	1	2	0
Castillo, Albenis, S.G.	0	0	.000	0.00	2	1	0	0	0	0	8	5	29	0	0	0	0	0	1	0	2	0	0	0
Castro, Julio, Kan.	5	2	.714	4.21	43	0	0	0	21	4	57.2	52	249	29	27	6	3	6	4	28	3	61	8	0
Cedeno, Blas, Hick.	0	0	.000	0.00	7	0	0	0	3	0	14	6	54	0	0	0	1	0	3	5	0	13	2	0
Chadwick, John, C.W.Va.	1	5	.167	5.54	19	2	0	0	6	1	52	47	238	35	32	4	3	1	5	41	1	38	3	0
Comolli, Mark, C.W.Va.	3	3	.500	4.86	15	1	0	0	8	2	37	43	164	25	20	5	2	0	3	9	1	36	4	0
Cooksey, Wes, Gre.	5	4	.556	1.95	51	0	0	0	30	16	78.1	65	338	28	17	2	2	2	5	35	0	62	5	2
Cooper, Chris, C'bus*	3	6	.333	3.36	38	0	0	0	24	5	61.2	51	256	33	23	3	2	0	1	21	1	69	3	0
Coose, Austin, C.S.C.	2	1	.667	0.32	20	0	0	0	18	9	28.1	15	111	3	1	0	2	0	0	9	1	39	0	0
Cordero, Jesus, Lak.	0	0	.000	3.00	6	0	0	0	3	0	6	5	26	2	2	0	0	0	1	3	0	1	0	0
Corrado, Rob, Sav.	2	3	.400	4.79	10	5	0	0	1	0	35.2	40	156	21	19	1	1	2	3	13	0	16	2	0
Cox, Adam, C'bus*	0	1	.000	5.40	4	0	0	0	1	0	5	5	23	3	3	0	1	0	0	5	0	5	0	0
Cox, Mike, C'bia*	4	1	.800	5.25	33	1	0	0	8	0	58.1	33	267	40	34	3	1	1	13	54	0	92	3	0
Cram, Josh, Hag.	1	0	1.000	6.20	17	0	0	0	7	0	24.2	36	121	17	17	2	1	0	2	11	0	9	4	0
Crawford, Chris, C.S.C.*	5	4	.556	4.57	42	0	0	0	14	1	65	70	291	39	33	6	2	5	7	28	3	49	5	0
Cristobal, Luis, Sav.	0	1	.000	5.06	5	0	0	0	3	0	5.1	5	23	3	3	0	1	2	0	3	0	4	1	0
Crockett, Ben, Ash.	2	3	.400	7.36	6	6	0	0	0	0	29.1	51	145	25	24	4	0	0	2	6	0	18	0	0
Cromer, Jason, C.S.C.*	1	1	.500	3.63	8	1	0	0	4	0	22.1	29	104	18	9	4	1	4	3	6	0	16	2	0
Cromer, Nathan, C.S.C.*	0	1	1.000	5.23	3	3	0	0	0	0	10.1	14	46	6	6	0	0	0	2	4	1	9	1	0
Crouthers, Dave, Del.	8	6	.571	3.34	25	25	1	1	0	0	129.1	117	562	66	48	4	5	2	15	58	1	108	9	2
Cruceta, Alberto, S.G.	8	5	.615	2.80	20	20	3	2	0	0	112.2	98	466	42	35	7	0	2	4	34	0	111	16	0
Cruz, Jeff, Ash.*	0	0	.000	2.89	6	0	0	0	2	0	9.1	11	45	6	3	0	0	0	1	6	0	4	1	0
Currier, Rik, Gre.	3	4	.429	3.92	24	2	0	0	9	2	39	41	174	19	17	2	1	2	1	24	0	41	4	0
Dagley, Corey, Lak.	0	1	.000	10.13	4	0	0	0	2	0	5.1	13	30	6	6	0	1	1	0	2	0	2	1	0
Dannemiller, Beau, Ash.	1	8	.111	4.65	19	10	0	0	3	1	60	76	275	40	31	5	3	4	3	23	0	40	4	0
Davies, Kyle, Mac.	0	1	.000	6.00	2	1	0	0	0	0	6	6	28	4	4	1	0	1	1	4	0	4	0	0
Davis, Tim, Lak.*	0	0	.000	1.88	11	0	0	0	5	2	14.1	7	57	5	3	0	0	0	0	7	0	8	2	0
Dawson, Layne, Lak.	7	4	.636	2.76	27	8	3	2	11	5	117.1	103	472	41	36	5	6	2	5	21	0	89	5	0
De La Cruz, Carlos, C'bus	5	2	.714	2.75	30	1	0	0	8	2	68.2	59	294	30	21	4	3	5	29	1	63	7	0
Delcarmen, Manny, Aug.*	7	8	.467	4.10	26	24	0	0	1	0	136	124	590	77	62	15	6	1	14	56	0	136	3	1
Delossantos, Carlos, Hick.	5	2	.714	2.52	37	1	0	0	13	4	75	57	324	31	21	5	1	4	5	43	4	77	4	3
Denham, Dan, C'bus	9	8	.529	4.76	28	28	0	0	0	0	124.2	123	550	76	66	7	5	5	11	65	0	109	14	1
Devenney, Nick, Sav.	2	0	.000	20.86	3	1	0	0	1	0	7.1	13	44	17	17	2	2	3	0	9	5	3	0	
Deza, Fredy, Del.	0	5	.000	4.38	12	12	0	0	0	0	49.1	50	211	26	24	4	1	1	2	15	0	38	2	0
DeChristofaro, Vinny, Lak.*	3	10	.231	4.92	22	22	1	0	0	0	130	155	579	88	71	4	6	8	4	37	0	62	8	0
DePriest, Derrick, Hick.	0	1	.000	5.14	5	0	0	0	4	0	7	9	30	5	4	0	0	1	2	0	3	1	0	
Diaz, Jose, S.G.	3	1	.750	4.21	19	0	0	0	9	1	25.2	14	122	12	12	1	1	2	8	25	0	33	4	0
Diaz, Jose, S.G.	1	1	.500	3.94	3	3	0	0	0	0	16	16	70	7	7	0	1	1	1	10	0	7	0	0
DiFranco, Joseph, Gre.	0	0	.000	5.59	11	0	0	0	5	0	19.1	27	102	14	12	2	0	1	4	13	0	18	3	0
Digby, Bryan, Mac.	1	2	.333	6.20	7	3	0	0	0	0	20.1	25	98	16	14	0	1	1	0	16	1	16	7	0
Dinardo, Lenny, C'bia*	5	5	.500	4.35	24	19	0	0	1	1	101.1	106	466	60	49	3	5	5	13	56	1	103	11	0
Dittler, Jake, C'bus	5	11	.313	4.28	25	25	0	0	0	0	128.1	127	560	77	61	4	0	6	9	51	0	108	13	3
Dobyns, Heath, Kan.	1	2	.333	4.12	23	0	0	0	12	0	43.2	50	198	30	20	5	1	0	6	13	1	23	1	0
Dominguez, Jose, Sav.	1	3	.250	2.16	16	9	0	0	6	1	66.2	50	270	23	16	4	2	2	6	21	1	70	5	2
Douglas, Shea, C'bus*	0	0	.000	0.00	1	0	0	0	0	0	2	2	8	1	0	0	0	0	0	0	0	2	0	0
Dukeman, Greg, Hick.	0	1	.000	3.13	11	0	0	0	5	1	23	22	98	11	8	2	1	0	2	7	1	17	2	0
Dumatrait, Phillip, Aug.*	8	5	.615	2.77	22	22	1	1	0	0	120.1	109	492	44	37	5	1	1	5	47	0	108	7	0
Eckert, Harold, C'bia	13	7	.650	3.88	27	22	0	0	2	1	139.1	121	597	66	60	7	3	4	20	51	1	149	5	1
Elliott, Adam, C'bia	0	1	.000	10.80	1	1	0	0	0	0	5	6	23	6	6	1	2	1	1	1	0	8	2	0
Engels, Jackson, Sav.*	2	1	.667	2.63	15	6	0	0	3	2	53.1	46	238	25	15	2	4	2	3	28	3	39	2	3
Esarey, Brad, C.W.Va.*	3	3	.500	5.14	40	0	0	0	14	2	49	58	225	31	28	5	2	1	2	20	0	39	4	1
Faigin, Jason, Gre.	0	0	.000	27.00	4	0	0	0	0	0	2	8	17	8	6	0	0	0	0	3	0	2	2	1
Farren, Dave, Del.	2	0	.600	3.15	21	0	0	0	7	0	40	32	167	17	14	3	0	4	5	8	1	43	1	0
Fernley, Nathan, C'bus	1	1	.500	1.61	15	0	0	0	5	1	28	17	114	10	5	1	1	0	6	8	0	25	4	0
Fields, Josh, Kan.	2	0	1.000	1.82	21	0	0	0	13	7	29.2	22	119	13	6	0	2	1	2	3	0	35	2	0
Figueroa, Jonathan, S.G.*	5	2	.714	1.42	8	8	0	0	0	0	44.1	22	171	10	7	1	0	1	1	20	0	57	0	1
Fitch, Steve, Hick.	2	2	.500	2.87	14	2	0	0	5	1	31.1	22	123	13	10	4	0	0	1	11	1	21	1	0
Flinn, Chris, C.S.C.	1	3	.571	2.31	19	19	2	1	0	0	128.1	103	521	44	33	6	4	3	7	41	1	116	7	1
Flores, Neomar, C.W.Va.*	8	10	.444	3.28	27	27	1	0	0	0	159	134	649	65	58	10	4	4	8	42	1	120	3	1
Floyd, Gavin, Lak.	11	10	.524	2.77	27	27	3	0	0	0	166	119	671	59	51	13	4	1	8	64	0	140	14	0
Foley, Travis, C'bus	13	4	.765	2.82	26	26	1	0	0	0	137.1	108	557	47	43	9	1	4	6	44	0	138	3	0
Francis, Jeff, Ash.*	0	0	.000	1.80	4	4	0	0	0	0	20	16	76	6	4	2	1	0	2	4	0	23	0	0
Friedberg, Drew, Hick.*	0	2	.000	3.80	37	0	0	0	21	0	45	43	201	24	19	2	2	0	3	18	2	34	1	0
Fryson, Andrew, Kan.	5	7	.417	5.03	17	16	0	0	0	0	82.1	100	376	62	46	11	4	3	9	41	1	54	3	0
Fuller, Brendan, C.W.Va.	3	5	.375	4.24	38	0	0	0	22	4	70	59	316	39	33	1	3	2	6	51	3	62	14	1
Gabbard, Kason, Aug.*	0	4	.000	1.89	7	7	0	0	0	0	38	31	150	14	8	0	1	0	2	7	0	31	9	0
Gajewski, Matt, Sav.	0	0	.000	0.00	1	0	0	0	1	0	0.1	0	1	0	0	0	0	0	0	1	0	0	0	0
Gallo, Mike, Lex.*	4	4	.500	1.83	42	2	0	0	25	8	88.1	69	359	29	18	6	3	2	1	26	4	93	2	0
Gamble, Jerome, Aug.	1	2	.333	1.82	14	14	0	0	0	0	49.1	34	204	12	10	2	0	3	2	22	0	42	5	1
Garcia, Carlos, S.G.	2	1	.000	4.26	1	1	0	0	0	0	6.1	6	27	3	3	0	0	1	1	2	0	4	0	0
Gaudin, Chad, C.S.C.	4	6	.400	2.26	26	17	0	0	5	1	119.1	106	491	43	30	5	3	5	11	37	0	106	4	3
Generelli, Daniel, Aug.	1	3	.250	4.30	39	1	0	0	15	5	73.1	86	340	43	35	6	4	1	3	32	3	65	9	0
Gibbs, Mark, Del.	0	0	.000	18.00	1	0	0	0	1	0	1	2	5	2	2	1	0	0	0	1	0	0	1	0
Gomez, Mariano, C'bus*	8	2	.800	2.75	34	13	0	0	6	1	111.1	106	480	44	34	3	4	1	5	40	1	98	10	3

Pitcher, Team	W	L	Pct.	ERA	G	GS	CG	ShO	GF	Sv.	IP	H	TBF	R	ER	HR	SH	SF	HB	BB	IBB	SO	WP	Bk.
Grace, Bryan, Gre.	1	1	.500	2.25	2	2	0	0	0	0	12	14	51	3	3	0	0	0	0	4	0	6	0	0
Gravelle, Nick, Hick.*	2	0	1.000	3.38	6	4	0	0	1	1	26.2	25	115	12	10	3	1	0	2	9	0	24	0	0
Gregg, James, Hag.	5	3	.625	5.77	24	0	0	0	11	1	34.1	47	157	24	22	4	1	0	2	9	1	19	2	0
Grinnell, Tyler, Gre.	1	0	1.000	6.19	11	0	0	0	6	0	16	19	77	11	11	4	0	1	1	15	0	5	4	0
Gronkiewicz, Lee, C'bus	4	2	.667	2.35	50	0	0	0	48	27	61.1	58	271	19	16	4	8	1	5	27	6	72	5	0
Gross, Kyle, Hag.	2	4	.333	8.22	18	7	0	0	4	0	38.1	35	205	48	35	1	3	2	9	54	0	27	17	0
Gryboski, Kevin, Mac.	0	0	.000	0.00	2	1	0	0	0	0	2	1	8	0	0	0	1	1	0	2	0	0	
Guerrero, Julio, Hick.	7	3	.700	3.66	31	1	0	0	8	2	71.1	72	299	39	29	8	1	0	3	12	0	49	0	1
Guzman, Leiby, Hag.	6	2	.750	4.35	44	0	0	0	11	2	80.2	95	359	47	39	6	1	3	1	27	2	66	5	0
Hackett, Richard, Del.	0	0	.000	13.50	1	0	0	0	0	0	1.1	2	8	2	2	0	0	0	1	1	0	1	0	0
Hall, Shane, Aug.	0	1	.000	13.50	6	0	0	0	3	0	10.2	17	55	16	16	1	0	1	1	9	0	3	1	0
Hampson, Justin, Ash.*	9	8	.529	3.83	27	27	1	0	0	0	164.1	162	710	87	70	12	5	2	24	58	1	123	7	1
Hampton, Royce, Sav.*	0	1	1.000	10.80	5	0	0	0	1	0	3.1	7	20	4	4	0	0	1	0	3	0	2	2	0
Hannaman, Ryan, Hag.*	7	6	.538	2.80	24	24	1	0	0	0	131.2	129	563	54	41	9	5	2	5	46	0	145	9	2
Harper, Jesse, C.W.Va.	6	5	.545	2.16	21	14	0	0	3	1	112.2	98	453	38	27	4	2	4	6	25	0	97	4	1
Hawk, David, C.S.C.*	4	7	.364	6.46	32	10	0	0	10	0	69.2	88	344	69	50	2	0	7	13	45	2	42	12	4
Hawley, Ross, S.G.	1	2	.333	5.61	18	1	0	0	4	0	25.2	28	131	20	16	1	2	1	8	17	0	17	0	0
Hecker, Steven, C.W.Va.	1	3	.250	3.12	19	0	0	0	10	2	40.1	38	164	17	14	1	0	0	3	12	0	28	4	1
Hentgen, Pat, Del.	0	1	.000	1.80	1	1	0	0	0	0	5	4	21	1	1	0	2	0	1	1	0	4	0	0
Herndon, Eric, Mac.	0	1	.000	6.00	5	0	0	0	1	0	6	12	31	6	4	0	2	0	1	0	6	5	0	
Herrera, Cesar, Sav.	0	4	.000	4.85	19	10	0	0	2	1	72.1	79	318	43	39	8	2	3	7	25	0	37	3	0
Hillaert, Victor, Sav.	2	6	.250	3.27	32	0	0	0	17	1	55	41	244	30	20	4	2	1	2	40	3	65	11	0
Hines, Carlos, C.S.C.	1	3	.250	5.21	24	7	0	0	7	2	48.1	54	205	29	28	1	0	1	1	15	0	26	5	0
Hixson, David, Hag.	0	2	.000	9.39	5	0	0	0	0	0	7.2	11	36	10	8	2	0	0	0	2	0	5	1	0
Honel, Kris, Kan.	9	8	.529	2.82	26	26	0	0	0	0	153.1	128	627	57	48	12	5	2	5	52	1	152	7	2
Hosford, Clint, S.G.	1	1	.500	3.60	6	6	0	0	0	0	25	24	98	13	10	3	1	1	2	3	0	23	2	0
Houston, Brian, C.W.Va.	1	2	.333	4.25	7	5	0	0	1	0	29.2	31	125	15	14	2	1	0	1	9	0	24	1	1
Howell, Jason, Aug.*	7	3	.700	2.11	40	0	0	0	31	16	76.2	73	321	30	18	3	3	1	2	16	2	47	1	0
Huang, Jun-chung, Aug.	6	2	.750	5.06	29	1	0	0	22	4	58.2	53	250	34	33	7	1	1	2	19	3	56	5	0
Hull, Eric, S.G.	1	0	1.000	2.05	13	0	0	0	5	1	22	22	89	6	5	1	1	0	6	0	13	0	0
Jackson, Brian, Hick.	1	0	1.000	14.09	7	0	0	0	4	1	7.2	13	45	12	12	2	1	1	0	11	1	3	0	0
Jackson, Edwin, S.G.	5	2	.714	1.98	19	19	0	0	0	0	104.2	79	428	34	23	2	2	2	6	33	0	85	3	1
Jimenez, Kelvin, Sav.	5	10	.333	3.20	29	16	0	0	8	0	121	122	524	63	43	9	7	1	7	37	2	116	4	0
Johansen, Ryan, S.G.	4	2	.667	2.88	27	0	0	0	23	6	34.1	27	148	14	11	1	3	1	6	16	1	31	2	1
Jones, D.J., Del.*	4	2	.667	3.42	26	5	0	0	7	1	50	53	221	24	19	3	3	2	2	18	4	32	1	1
Jordan, Eddie, Del.	0	0	.000	9.00	1	0	0	0	1	0	1	1	4	1	1	1	0	0	0	0	0	0	0	
Joyce, Michael, Gre.*	0	0	.000	5.84	11	0	0	0	4	1	12.1	17	59	9	8	2	0	0	1	4	1	10	0	0
Keefer, Ryan, Del.	2	3	.400	3.44	22	1	0	0	17	6	36.2	36	156	15	14	3	3	2	0	11	0	29	1	0
Keirstead, Michael, S.G.	4	5	.444	3.93	14	14	1	0	0	0	68.2	77	299	35	30	5	1	6	5	20	1	43	7	1
Keiter, Ben, Sav.	0	2	.000	5.06	4	2	0	0	1	0	16	17	72	11	9	1	1	0	2	5	0	8	2	0
Kennard, Jeff, Gre.	4	0	1.000	1.93	27	0	0	0	8	0	37.1	27	166	14	8	1	2	0	4	25	2	35	4	1
Kim, II, Lak.	2	1	.667	4.14	21	0	0	0	10	0	37	37	170	20	17	3	2	2	0	21	3	27	0	2
King, Jeremy, Gre.	7	7	.500	4.42	28	25	1	1	2	0	146.2	151	648	86	72	8	6	3	8	66	4	132	9	1
Knapp, Ben, Del.	8	11	.421	3.18	26	26	1	1	0	0	152.2	154	638	67	54	11	5	8	10	36	2	125	3	1
Korecky, Bobby, Lak.	2	2	.500	3.00	8	4	2	0	3	1	27	25	106	10	9	0	1	0	0	3	0	15	1	0
Kremer, John, Gre.	3	4	.429	2.86	20	0	0	0	9	2	34.2	41	156	12	11	2	2	1	2	10	1	35	5	1
Kumagai, Ryo, Aug.	1	1	.500	3.82	21	0	0	0	11	0	30.2	33	137	18	13	3	1	0	1	16	0	21	2	0
Lacorte, Vince, Del.	2	4	.333	4.32	20	5	0	0	7	1	41.2	46	177	23	20	5	2	0	0	8	1	23	1	0
Landaeta, Argenis, Gre.	0	2	.000	12.86	2	2	0	0	0	0	7	15	36	10	10	3	0	1	1	2	0	2	1	0
Langill, Eric, S.G.	0	0	.000	0.00	1	0	0	0	1	0	0.1	0	1	0	0	0	0	0	0	0	0	0	0	0
Lantz, Doug, C'bus	3	2	.600	2.93	26	0	0	0	10	4	58.1	53	247	23	19	2	1	0	4	12	0	51	1	0
Ledezma, Wil, Aug.*	2	2	.500	3.80	5	5	0	0	0	0	23.2	23	101	10	10	0	0	1	8	0	38	2	0
Lee, Seung, Lak.	7	10	.412	3.24	23	22	5	0	1	1	147.1	132	606	64	53	8	7	5	7	46	0	112	8	1
Leek, Randy, S.G.*	2	0	1.000	0.68	2	2	0	0	0	0	13.1	8	48	1	1	1	1	0	0	1	0	8	1	0
Lewis, Derrick, Mac.	0	0	.000	1.80	1	1	0	0	0	0	5	5	20	1	1	0	1	0	1	0	7	0	0	
Lewis, Rommie, Del.*	1	2	.333	2.15	53	0	0	0	36	25	71	50	282	19	17	1	4	1	4	20	1	77	5	0
Lira, James, Lex.	2	1	.667	0.00	15	0	0	0	14	6	18.2	7	66	2	0	1	0	0	0	3	0	27	5	0
Liriano, Francisco, Hag.*	3	6	.333	3.49	16	16	0	0	0	0	80	61	330	45	31	6	4	3	0	31	0	85	4	0
Lissir, Alexander, Hick.	0	2	.000	4.35	16	0	0	0	6	1	31	30	133	16	15	2	2	1	1	13	0	18	0	1
Lizarraga, Edgar, S.G.	5	3	.625	2.79	19	0	0	0	5	1	42	35	173	16	13	1	0	3	4	10	1	37	1	1
Lockwood, Brian, C.S.C.	4	7	.364	3.32	22	17	0	0	1	0	95	97	401	44	35	6	4	0	3	30	1	74	9	0
Lohrman, Dave, C'bia	1	0	1.000	2.79	7	0	0	0	4	2	9.2	9	43	3	3	0	0	0	7	1	10	1	0
Lombardi, Justin, Gre.*	0	0	.000	6.43	6	0	0	0	1	0	7	10	44	10	5	1	0	0	1	10	0	8	3	1
Lopez, Gonzalo, Mac.	7	10	.412	3.10	28	27	1	1	0	0	157	134	650	72	54	11	14	4	5	51	1	130	9	1
Lopez, Jose, Hick.	1	0	1.000	0.00	2	0	0	0	0	0	6	3	20	0	0	0	0	0	0	0	0	6	0	0
Lopez, Nelson, Hag.	0	0	.000	27.00	1	0	0	0	0	0	1	4	8	3	3	0	0	0	0	1	0	2	1	0
Lopez, Rafael, C'bia	1	3	.250	4.02	22	0	0	0	9	1	40.1	49	190	22	18	3	5	2	4	20	2	35	2	0
Lorenzo, Javier, Ash.	4	3	.571	5.98	39	0	0	0	10	0	61.2	64	297	43	41	6	2	1	5	50	3	75	15	0
Lubisich, Nik, Kan.*	9	3	.750	2.79	34	13	2	1	7	0	122.2	123	505	45	38	3	6	6	3	26	2	81	2	0
Luna, Brandon, Sav.	3	2	.600	4.89	32	0	0	0	16	1	42.1	44	189	27	23	6	2	1	0	21	0	36	1	0
Mabry, Barry, Mac.	0	1	.000	3.86	1	0	0	0	0	0	2.1	3	10	1	1	0	0	0	0	1	0	1	0	0
Maine, John, Del.	1	1	.500	1.36	6	5	0	0	0	0	33	21	128	8	5	0	3	1	2	4	0	39	2	1
Manzanillo, Josias, Hick.	0	0	.000	9.00	1	0	0	0	0	0	2	5	12	3	2	1	0	0	0	0	0	1	0	0
Marcano, Luis, Sav.	2	3	.400	2.93	28	0	0	0	14	4	40	36	162	15	13	3	2	3	0	12	0	32	2	0
Marchetti, Dan, Del.	5	4	.556	2.67	39	0	0	0	12	3	57.1	48	236	21	17	6	2	3	2	24	3	40	1	1
Martin, J.D., C'bus	14	5	.737	3.90	27	26	0	0	0	0	138.1	141	594	76	60	12	2	3	13	46	0	131	2	1
Masset, Nicholas, Sav.	5	8	.385	4.56	33	16	0	0	4	0	120.1	129	539	75	61	11	4	9	9	47	1	93	11	1
Matthews, Jarod, C.S.C.	7	9	.438	3.60	24	24	0	0	0	0	137.2	131	575	67	55	7	8	5	10	37	2	115	4	1
Mattox, David, C'bia	8	2	.800	3.55	17	17	0	0	0	0	91.1	78	385	42	36	3	1	3	6	42	0	92	3	3
Mayfield, Brandon, Lak.	4	1	.800	2.22	21	0	0	0	14	0	44.2	44	188	13	11	2	1	1	3	13	0	23	4	0
McBride, Macay, Mac.*	12	8	.600	2.12	25	25	1	0	0	0	157.1	119	624	49	37	6	2	3	1	48	1	138	13	1
McCracken, Vance, S.G.	2	4	.333	3.62	8	6	0	0	0	0	32.1	33	146	21	13	3	0	2	5	11	0	23	1	0

Pitcher, Team	W	L	Pct.	ERA	G	GS	CG	ShO	GF	Sv.	IP	H	TBF	R	ER	HR	SH	SF	HB	BB	IBB	SO	WP	Bk.
McGinley, Blake, C'bia*	1	1	.500	1.80	26	0	0	0	21	10	35	19	134	9	7	3	2	0	3	6	0	53	1	0
McGowan, Dustin, C.W.Va.	11	10	.524	4.19	28	28	1	0	0	0	148.1	143	643	77	69	10	6	3	5	59	0	163	12	0
McKee, Mickey, Lex.	0	0	.000	0.00	1	0	0	0	1	0	1	2	6	3	0	0	0	0	0	1	0	0	0	0
McNair, Pat, Lex.	1	2	.333	3.21	37	0	0	0	18	5	70	60	304	37	25	3	3	0	5	34	3	57	7	0
Mead, David, Sav.	1	10	.091	5.95	28	16	0	0	3	1	95.1	101	449	71	63	6	3	1	16	53	1	81	17	1
Meaux, Ryan, Hag.-Kan.*	4	5	.444	2.38	54	0	0	0	46	23	68	60	279	32	18	2	2	0	4	12	1	57	1	0
Mejia, Francisco, Del.*	5	2	.714	5.00	37	1	0	0	11	0	63	76	291	44	35	5	2	3	6	23	1	51	5	0
Mercedes, Jose, Sav.	1	0	1.000	9.00	1	0	0	0	1	0	1	1	7	1	1	1	0	0	0	3	0	0	0	0
Merricks, Charles, Ash.*	7	5	.583	6.70	29	10	0	0	6	0	83.1	109	405	73	62	13	2	5	7	48	0	42	9	6
Merricks, Matt, Mac.*	5	5	.500	5.12	19	14	0	0	2	0	82.2	82	378	54	47	6	1	0	6	51	0	60	8	0
Miller, Benji, Hag.	1	1	.500	4.87	12	0	0	0	6	1	20.1	25	93	11	11	2	0	2	2	8	0	17	2	0
Miller, Jeff, Hick.	13	5	.722	3.75	31	15	0	0	15	4	103.1	100	434	44	43	11	5	0	5	28	1	75	2	0
Miner, Zach, Mac.	8	9	.471	3.28	29	28	1	1	0	0	159	143	663	73	58	10	6	5	12	51	1	131	9	1
Minor, Zach, Lak.	0	1	.000	7.36	4	0	0	0	2	0	3.2	5	17	3	3	0	0	1	0	1	1	1	0	0
Mitchell, Andy, Del.	5	1	.833	2.36	27	0	0	0	3	0	42	34	176	16	11	0	3	0	1	17	2	20	3	0
Montano, Ignacio, C'bus*	0	0	.000	0.52	8	0	0	0	4	1	17.1	10	65	1	1	0	0	0	1	2	0	9	0	0
Montes, Albert, Hag.	3	2	.600	3.62	28	0	0	0	18	3	37.1	38	165	19	15	6	1	1	3	12	1	35	5	1
Montilla, Elvis, Del.	0	0	.000	18.00	1	0	0	0	0	0	1	4	7	2	2	0	0	0	0	0	0	0	2	0
Moore, Greg, Ash.	0	1	.000	9.64	7	0	0	0	2	0	14	26	75	15	15	4	0	1	3	6	1	12	0	0
Moreno, Victor, Lak.	1	0	1.000	0.00	7	0	0	0	5	1	10	5	38	0	0	0	1	0	1	4	0	13	1	0
Morris, Cory, Del.	3	1	.750	2.88	10	10	0	0	0	0	56.1	44	231	20	18	4	1	0	1	20	0	50	0	0
Mosley, Eric, Gre.	7	6	.538	3.76	19	19	0	0	0	0	107.2	116	474	60	45	5	4	8	5	47	2	47	9	1
Mounce, Tony, Sav.*	2	0	1.000	0.82	4	1	0	0	3	1	11	7	42	1	1	0	1	0	0	2	0	16	0	0
Mowday, Chris, C.W.Va.	2	1	.667	2.67	27	4	0	0	7	1	70.2	51	289	30	21	5	3	2	3	25	0	88	4	0
Murray, Arlington, Sav.*	5	3	.625	2.87	14	8	0	0	2	0	62.2	63	255	22	20	0	2	6	0	14	0	51	5	0
Nall, T.J., S.G.	3	1	.750	0.63	21	0	0	0	10	3	43	28	161	7	3	0	3	1	0	12	0	39	0	0
Navaroli, Michael, C.S.C.	2	4	.333	5.09	36	0	0	0	9	1	53	70	257	37	30	5	2	1	4	23	2	42	5	0
Nelson, Steve, S.G.	3	1	.750	5.27	18	1	0	0	5	0	41	41	180	27	24	2	1	3	5	9	1	32	5	1
Neuage, Leigh, S.G.	1	2	.333	3.07	8	8	0	0	0	0	41	35	170	17	14	1	2	1	3	13	0	35	4	0
Nieve, Fernando, Lex.	1	0	1.000	6.00	1	1	0	0	0	0	3	6	18	5	2	0	0	0	1	0	0	2	0	0
Novoa, Roberto, Hick.	1	5	.167	5.48	10	10	0	0	0	0	42.2	61	205	30	26	2	1	3	4	15	0	29	7	1
Nunez, Leo, Hick.	0	0	.000	0.00	1	1	0	0	0	0	4	5	18	0	0	0	0	0	0	3	0	1	0	0
O'Brien, Patrick, Hick.	12	7	.632	3.82	26	26	0	0	0	0	146	149	619	77	62	13	2	5	7	30	0	101	7	1
Ogle, Rylie, C'bia*	0	0	.000	0.56	9	0	0	0	4	0	16	17	62	2	1	0	0	1	3	0	0	15	1	1
Olivo, Rigal, Kan.	2	6	.250	4.55	30	2	0	0	11	2	57.1	53	244	31	29	5	3	2	5	18	3	45	4	1
Olson, Ryan, C'bia*	2	1	.667	3.57	23	1	0	0	2	1	45.1	49	209	24	18	3	6	1	4	19	0	55	5	0
Oquendo, Ian, Hick.	11	6	.647	2.71	24	22	0	0	0	0	139.2	127	576	49	42	8	5	3	0	45	0	149	13	2
Ortiz, Javier, Gre.	9	5	.643	4.11	18	18	3	1	0	0	127	128	534	66	58	8	3	15	25	0	63	10	3
Osberg, Tanner, C'bia	1	2	.667	0.47	3	3	0	0	0	0	19	8	73	3	1	0	1	0	3	3	0	18	0	0
Osoria, Franquelis, S.G.	2	2	.500	3.32	21	1	0	0	7	1	43.1	40	195	22	16	1	2	1	2	13	1	30	3	0
Ott, Thom, S.G.	3	4	.429	3.27	45	0	0	0	24	7	63.1	67	271	25	23	5	0	2	2	20	0	33	3	0
Ough, Wayne, C'bia	5	7	.417	3.61	19	10	0	0	5	2	77.1	69	335	36	31	5	5	2	2	42	1	58	5	0
Padgett, Daniel, Hag.*	0	1	.000	4.31	27	0	0	0	15	3	48	48	207	31	23	4	3	2	2	18	2	41	2	2
Padilla, Nick, Mac.	1	5	.167	3.74	16	1	0	0	8	1	33.2	38	148	21	14	5	2	1	6	12	1	15	5	0
Pahucki, David, Aug.	2	1	.667	4.15	4	4	0	0	0	0	21.2	24	91	10	10	0	0	0	7	0	15	0	1
Pannone, Anthony, Hag.	9	10	.474	3.11	28	28	2	1	0	0	168	157	712	73	58	7	7	3	6	61	0	116	12	1
Parker, Josh, C.S.C.	3	7	.300	2.85	45	0	0	0	36	15	60	75	282	29	19	3	4	2	3	64	10	0
Parker, Zach, Ash.*	16	7	.696	4.01	28	28	1	0	0	0	168.1	174	730	89	75	11	10	2	18	64	0	119	8	0
Patten, Scott, Kan.	4	4	.500	2.50	49	0	0	0	32	10	72	61	317	27	20	3	3	1	4	40	7	50	5	0
Patterson, Quenten, C'bia	1	1	.500	1.95	17	0	0	0	7	1	27.2	26	131	13	6	0	2	0	2	20	0	14	6	0
Pavon, Julio, Hag.	3	6	.333	3.26	43	8	0	0	21	10	116	112	472	54	42	5	7	3	2	21	3	90	5	2
Peeples, Ross, C'bia*	7	7	.500	2.43	20	19	0	0	1	1	115	104	469	49	31	3	3	3	5	25	0	98	3	0
Pena, Francisco, Lex.	7	6	.538	4.30	36	7	0	0	10	1	73.1	61	343	44	35	5	4	3	6	57	1	88	14	1
Pennington, Todd, C'bus	1	1	.500	1.75	16	0	0	0	10	2	25.2	15	102	5	5	2	1	1	0	12	1	32	1	1
Pereyra, Honeudis, C'bus	1	2	.333	9.00	8	0	0	0	5	0	11	10	53	12	11	2	1	0	2	10	0	9	1	1
Peshke, Chad, C'bus	1	0	1.000	.000	1	0	0	0	1	0	4	5	22	5	0	0	0	1	0	3	0
Peterson, Matt, C'bia	8	10	.444	3.86	26	26	1	0	0	0	137.2	109	569	67	59	13	3	3	8	61	0	153	9	0
Picco, John, Gre.*	0	1	.000	8.59	4	0	0	0	1	0	7.1	11	38	7	7	0	0	0	6	1	5	1	0
Pilkington, Brian, S.G.	8	4	.667	3.45	20	18	1	0	1	0	112.1	129	483	61	43	8	1	5	10	13	0	78	3	0
Portobanco, Luz, C'bia	4	5	.444	5.59	17	17	0	0	0	0	75.2	103	362	57	47	2	7	0	10	37	0	52	5	1
Quintana, Miguel, C'bus	0	0	.000	.000	1	0	0	0	1	0	0.1	0	2	0	0	0	0	0	1	0	0	0	0
Ramirez, Horacio, Mac.*	0	0	.000	6.00	2	1	0	0	0	0	6	11	35	10	4	0	1	0	1	2	0	5	0	0
Ramirez, Ismael, C.W.Va.	0	1	.000	4.86	6	1	0	0	3	0	16.2	20	76	10	9	2	0	0	0	7	0	14	0	0
Ramirez, Victor, Gre.	3	7	.300	4.65	13	13	0	0	0	0	81.1	71	353	45	42	9	3	4	7	36	2	94	5	1
Reynolds, Eric, Gre.*	0	0	.000	5.93	10	0	0	0	4	0	13.2	13	61	11	9	1	0	1	1	12	0	7	6	0
Reynoso, Paulino, Kan.*	6	8	.429	4.24	33	14	1	1	11	2	102	96	462	61	48	1	4	8	6	65	1	73	7	2
Rhodes, Shane, Aug.*	9	6	.600	3.09	31	20	0	0	4	0	134	117	556	57	46	6	5	3	7	62	1	97	11	1
Rice, Scott, Del.*	6	6	.000	5.40	18	3	0	0	5	3	40	45	182	26	24	2	1	1	3	21	0	22	6	1
Rleal, Sendy, Del.	1	0	1.000	6.10	28	1	0	0	7	1	41.1	53	188	28	28	4	4	1	1	15	0	34	7	0
Roberson, Brandon, Lex.	8	5	.615	2.40	23	18	0	0	1	0	112.1	105	462	34	30	7	4	5	7	22	0	115	5	0
Roberts, Ralph, Mac.	4	3	.571	2.30	49	0	0	0	46	19	54.2	37	217	16	14	2	1	1	1	14	2	58	0	0
Rodaway, Brian, Lex.*	6	3	.667	2.13	14	13	0	0	0	0	84.2	66	325	22	20	9	1	1	3	13	0	63	2	1
Rodriguez, Jose, Mac.	2	0	1.000	6.46	32	0	0	0	16	0	47.1	51	230	45	34	2	1	1	3	41	1	34	9	0
Rodriguez, Luis, Sav.	1	2	.667	4.09	9	3	0	0	3	0	22	15	89	10	10	0	0	1	0	11	1	17	3	0
Rodriguez, Orlando, S.G.*	3	0	1.000	0.00	20	0	0	0	9	5	28.1	12	103	0	0	0	1	0	3	10	0	42	0	0
Rogers, Brad, Del.	1	0	1.000	7.36	13	0	0	0	6	0	14.2	26	72	13	12	2	0	0	5	2	0	11	1	0
Roman, Orlando, C'bia	1	5	.167	2.77	45	1	0	0	32	12	78	59	337	31	24	6	5	5	8	39	0	100	11	0
Romero, Felix, C.W.Va.	0	7	.000	3.98	46	0	0	0	33	10	40.2	46	187	28	18	5	2	1	5	13	1	35	4	1
Roney, Matt, Ash.	4	6	.400	3.48	14	14	1	1	0	0	82.2	82	349	39	32	7	3	2	5	25	1	88	1	1
Rosario, Francisco, C.W.Va.	1	0	.857	2.57	13	13	1	0	0	0	66.2	50	265	22	19	5	2	2	4	14	0	78	2	0
Rowe, Steven, Sav.	1	2	.333	2.15	11	0	0	0	2	0	29.1	22	115	7	7	1	0	1	2	4	0	29	1	0
Rudrude, Brett, Aug.	6	7	.462	3.43	34	7	0	0	10	3	94.1	98	398	47	36	5	4	6	3	26	2	73	3	0

Pitcher, Team	W	L	Pct.	ERA	G	GS	CG	ShO	GF	Sv.	IP	H	TBF	R	ER	HR	SH	SF	HB	BB	IBB	SO	WP	Bk.
Russ, Chris, Gre.	1	4	.200	5.65	24	0	0	0	15	4	28.2	33	139	24	18	2	3	1	4	19	2	23	4	0
Sanchez, Rafael, Aug.	7	12	.368	5.15	29	22	0	0	2	1	129.1	152	580	85	74	11	4	6	4	63	0	109	7	1
Sanders, Shane, C.S.C.	0	0	.000	0.00	1	0	0	0	1	0	0.1	1	2	0	0	0	0	0	0	0	0	0	0	0
Santiago, Victor, S.G.	0	1	.000	7.56	5	0	0	0	0	0	8.1	14	47	12	7	1	0	0	2	6	0	2	1	0
Santillan, Manny, Lex.	5	5	.500	2.06	14	14	1	1	0	0	96	73	385	27	22	4	2	1	8	28	1	76	2	2
Schmitt, Brian, Lex. *	0	0	.000	0.00	1	0	0	0	0	0	1	2	5	0	0	0	0	0	1	0	0	0	0	0
Scobie, Jason, C'bia	2	2	.500	2.57	16	1	0	0	8	4	35	29	146	16	10	0	0	2	3	12	1	33	1	0
Scott, Josh, Lak. *	0	1	.000	7.71	3	0	0	0	1	0	4.2	7	26	5	4	0	1	1	1	5	0	2	0	0
Searles, Jon, Hick.	2	3	.400	5.81	31	4	0	0	7	1	79	86	360	59	51	10	1	6	10	34	0	53	3	1
Seddon, Chris, C.S.C. *	6	8	.429	3.62	26	0	0	0	2	1	117	93	507	63	47	7	2	3	6	68	0	88	10	0
Serrano, Alex, Ash.	5	5	.500	4.96	48	0	0	0	28	8	61.2	81	277	37	34	7	5	1	8	14	3	61	3	0
Sheffield, Christopher, C.W.Va.	0	0	.000	54.00	3	0	0	0	0	0	0.2	4	12	4	4	0	0	0	1	9	0	2	3	0
Shiery, Shaun, C.S.C. *	1	2	.333	3.72	22	0	0	0	7	0	36.1	43	165	19	15	1	0	2	5	14	2	31	0	0
Shouse, Dan, C'bus *	1	1	.500	8.53	11	0	0	0	2	0	19	28	93	19	18	1	2	1	1	11	3	8	2	0
Shumaker, Casey, Hick.	4	4	.500	3.07	47	0	0	0	43	22	58.2	53	255	28	20	7	3	1	2	22	5	83	7	0
Silverio, Carlos, Lak.	4	5	.444	3.26	21	3	0	0	13	1	60.2	49	253	23	22	5	5	1	5	28	0	62	3	0
Simpson, Andre, S.G.-Ash.	0	4	.000	4.46	28	2	0	0	13	1	36.1	40	166	20	18	5	3	2	0	19	2	26	3	1
Simpson, Gerrit, Ash.	3	12	.200	4.28	22	21	0	0	1	0	132.1	136	580	76	63	6	3	5	15	40	3	120	9	0
Sinclair, Ernnie, Lex.	9	3	.750	3.38	25	19	0	0	2	1	122.2	112	516	58	46	14	2	2	5	47	0	109	9	2
Smith, Dustin, Sav.	0	0	.000	0.00	1	0	0	0	1	0	1	1	4	0	0	0	0	0	0	0	0	0	0	0
Smith, Jason, Gre.	5	5	.500	3.47	17	16	1	1	0	0	96	94	395	44	37	5	4	3	8	21	0	46	2	0
Songster, Judson, Ash.	1	2	.333	2.81	47	0	0	0	28	12	64	65	270	27	20	5	5	4	0	21	1	57	7	0
Speier, Ryan, Ash.	3	1	.750	3.93	28	0	0	0	6	1	36.2	32	153	21	16	3	2	1	1	13	1	39	5	0
Sperring, Jayme, Del.	7	3	.700	1.73	33	0	0	0	15	6	52	47	218	15	10	2	1	2	2	15	4	55	2	0
Spillman, Jeromie, C.W.Va. *	1	0	1.000	4.24	8	0	0	0	6	0	17	17	80	10	8	1	1	2	1	12	0	10	3	0
Squires, Matt, Lak. *	5	6	.455	3.82	36	1	0	0	29	8	66	62	294	34	28	3	4	2	6	40	1	71	4	0
Stahl, Richard, Del. *	1	1	.500	5.59	2	2	0	0	0	0	9.2	10	43	8	6	3	0	0	2	5	0	9	0	0
Staveland, Toby, Mac.	2	1	.667	7.43	12	0	0	0	5	0	23	27	102	21	19	2	2	2	0	10	0	19	2	0
Stephenson, Eric, C.W.Va. *	6	12	.333	4.32	23	23	0	0	0	0	127	143	568	80	61	6	4	11	56	0	70	6	1
Strayhorn, Kole, S.G.	1	7	.125	4.24	31	13	0	0	12	4	93.1	99	419	61	44	4	2	5	10	38	1	50	6	1
Strelitz, Brian, Gre.	2	4	.333	14.40	8	1	0	0	3	0	10	21	52	16	16	3	0	0	1	4	1	1	3	0
Stumm, Jason, Kan.	0	1	.000	2.25	22	0	0	0	8	5	40	37	165	10	10	1	1	0	12	0	45	4	0
Sturkie, Scott, C'bus	3	0	1.000	0.99	10	0	0	0	3	0	27.1	17	102	5	3	2	1	0	1	4	0	29	2	0
Szado, Craig, Kan. *	5	9	.357	3.40	30	19	0	0	3	0	127	124	540	63	48	4	3	4	4	51	2	88	9	1
Templet, Eric, C'bia	2	1	.667	4.87	13	0	0	0	8	0	20.1	19	93	11	11	5	1	0	3	9	1	19	2	0
Thigpen, Joshua, Aug.	6	6	.500	3.92	25	9	0	0	2	2	82.2	76	364	45	36	5	3	5	10	45	0	87	7	0
Thompson, Derek, C'bus *	3	4	.429	3.42	14	14	0	0	0	0	73.2	71	316	39	28	3	1	2	3	27	0	50	2	0
Thorpe, Tracy, C.W.Va.	5	7	.417	4.18	20	19	1	0	0	0	103.1	96	437	55	48	6	1	3	6	31	0	70	8	0
Treadway, Brion, Hag.	5	4	.556	4.39	13	13	0	0	0	0	60.2	57	289	37	33	8	1	5	11	28	0	66	6	1
Truselo, Randy, Sav.	3	3	.500	4.30	18	9	0	0	3	0	62.2	58	265	33	29	6	2	3	5	27	1	25	6	0
Urena, Sixto, Sav.	0	2	.000	10.13	3	1	0	0	1	0	5.1	8	32	7	6	1	0	0	1	6	0	8	1	0
Uzzell, Todd, Hag.	4	7	.364	6.42	15	14	0	0	0	0	82.2	105	375	67	59	6	4	6	5	27	0	42	4	2
Valdez, Santo, C.W.Va.	5	2	.714	2.95	29	3	0	0	22	3	76.1	67	317	28	25	5	2	5	4	20	3	81	7	2
Van Benschoten, John, Hick.	11	4	.733	2.80	27	27	0	0	0	0	148	119	620	57	46	6	4	2	7	62	1	145	7	0
Van Buren, Jermaine, Ash.	6	9	.400	4.96	30	17	0	0	4	0	107	115	488	71	59	13	4	10	14	44	1	88	6	5
Vazquez, Will, Ash.	2	2	.500	4.21	48	0	0	0	27	11	62	73	277	34	29	10	0	2	4	16	0	65	6	0
Vianna, Marcel, Mac.	3	0	1.000	1.48	29	0	0	0	13	2	48.2	39	194	9	8	2	1	2	2	20	0	53	5	1
Vigue, John, C.S.C.	6	2	.750	3.49	38	0	0	0	16	2	67	68	282	28	26	4	2	2	3	20	5	45	1	0
Villacis, Eduardo, Ash.	1	0	1.000	1.89	11	1	0	0	5	0	19	12	72	4	4	2	0	0	1	2	0	8	1	0
Waddell, Jason, Hag. *	0	0	.000	6.75	4	0	0	0	2	0	6.2	6	30	5	5	1	1	0	1	1	0	4	0	0
Waechter, Doug, C.S.C.	3	3	.500	3.47	7	7	0	0	0	0	36.1	39	162	20	14	2	2	1	2	16	3	36	1	2
Watkins, Dave, Mac.	0	0	.000	0.00	7	0	0	0	7	1	12	3	49	2	0	0	0	0	6	0	14	1	0
Weatherby Iii, Charles, Aug.	4	0	1.000	2.92	17	0	0	0	16	4	24.2	20	100	8	8	2	1	0	5	1	23	0	1
White, Matt, C.S.C.	3	4	.429	3.15	10	10	0	0	0	0	54.1	48	222	21	19	5	1	4	15	0	38	2	0
Williams, Mike, Kan.	1	0	1.000	1.54	22	0	0	0	6	1	41	28	170	15	7	4	2	1	2	23	0	37	1	0
Wilson, Mike, Lak.	0	0	.000	0.00	5	0	0	0	4	3	8.1	3	29	0	0	0	0	1	0	1	0	7	0	0
Wing, Ryan, Kan. *	12	7	.632	3.78	25	21	0	0	1	0	123.2	111	544	64	52	6	5	4	12	60	0	109	5	3
Wood, Bobby, Gre.	7	5	.583	4.24	21	21	3	2	0	0	116.2	120	496	59	55	16	2	5	43	1	99	10	0
Wright, Matt, Mac.	10	8	.556	3.18	26	25	0	0	0	0	152.2	135	648	68	54	11	2	4	9	60	2	146	9	0
Yacco, Anthony, Hag.	3	2	.600	6.88	18	1	0	0	2	0	35.1	47	172	28	27	5	1	4	4	23	0	26	9	2
Yoo, Byung Mok, Aug.	0	2	.000	6.94	8	0	0	0	6	1	11.2	16	65	10	9	3	0	1	15	2	8	4	0
Young, Christopher, Hick.	11	9	.550	3.11	26	26	1	0	0	0	144.2	127	587	57	50	11	1	4	4	34	1	136	3	1
Young, Curtis, Kan.	0	2	.000	15.00	7	0	0	0	5	0	9	15	48	16	15	2	0	0	2	6	0	11	1	1
Zink, Charlie, Aug.	1	2	.333	1.68	26	0	0	0	10	0	48.1	42	200	17	9	1	2	3	4	16	0	48	2	0
Zumwalt, Alec, Mac.	2	1	.667	4.31	24	0	0	0	10	0	39.2	39	177	25	19	2	2	0	3	16	0	34	2	0

PITCHERS WITH TWO OR MORE TEAMS

Pitcher, Team	W	L	Pct.	ERA	G	GS	CG	ShO	GF	Sv.	IP	H	TBF	R	ER	HR	SH	SF	HB	BB	IBB	SO	WP	Bk.
Meaux, Ryan, Hag. *	4	3	.571	2.63	44	0	0	0	36	17	54.2	41	217	22	16	1	1	0	2	12	1	44	1	0
Meaux, Ryan, Lex. *	2	0	1.000	1.35	10	0	0	0	10	6	13.1	19	62	10	2	1	1	0	2	0	0	13	0	0
Simpson, Andre, S.G.	0	2	.000	7.36	4	2	0	0	1	0	7.1	10	38	8	6	2	1	0	0	5	0	5	0	0
Simpson, Andre, Ash.	0	2	.000	3.72	24	0	0	0	12	1	29	30	128	12	12	3	1	4	0	14	2	21	3	1

COMBINATION SHUTOUTS: **Asheville (7)**—Dannemiller-C. Merricks-Serrano-Vazquez, Hampson-Cruz, Hampson-Speier-Vazquez, Z. Parker-Lorenzo-Songster, Z. Parker-Songster, Roney-Songster, Roney-Vazquez. **Augusta (8)**—Dumatrait-Rudrude-Weatherby, Dumatrait-Zink-Howell, Gamble-Thigpen, Rhodes-Generelli, Rhodes-Kumagai-Huang, Rhodes-Rudrade, Rudrude-Delcarmen, Sanchez-Howell. **Charleston, S.C. (5)**—Gaudin-Crawford, Gaudin-J. Parker, Matthews-Crawford-Coose, Matthews-Navaroli-Crawford, Waechter-Navaroli. **Charleston, W.V. (9)**—Rosario-Fuller-Romero 2, Flores-Mowday, McGowan-Comolli-Esarey-Valdez, Stephenson-Comolli, Stephenson-Mowday-Houston, Stephenson-Romero, Thorpe-Valdez, Valdez-Fuller-Romero. **Columbia (9)**—Eckert-Ough 2, Mattox-Olson, Mattox-Roman, Mattox-Roman-McGinley, Osberg-McGinley-Roman, Ough-McGinley, Peeples-McGinley, Peeples-Roman. **Columbus (10)**—Foley-De la cruz 2, Denham-De la cruz-Pennington, Denham-Martin-Cooper-Pennington, Dittler-Pennington, Foley-Lantz-Fernley, Foley-Sturkie-Gronkiewicz, Martin-De la cruz-O. Alvarez, Martin-Montano, Thompson-Lantz-Cooper. **Delmarva (10)**—Bartlett-Marchetti, Birkins-Marchetti-R. Lewis, Boughner-Jones-Sperring-R. Lewis, Crouthers-R. Lewis, Jones-Mitchell-Lacorte, Keefer-R. Lewis, Knapp-Marchetti-R. Lewis, Maine-Mitchell-Lacorte-R. Lewis-Sperring, Morris-Mitchell-Lacorte, Morris-Sperring-R. Lewis. **Greensboro (3)**—Acosta-Kennard-Carlson, King-Carlson-Cooksey, Wood-Cooksey-Artiles. **Hagerstown (3)**—Hannaman-Guzman, Liriano-Meaux, Pavon-Gregg. **Hickory (8)**—J.

Miller-Cedeno, O'Brien-Delossantos, Oquendo-Cedeno, Oquendo-Fitch, Oquendo-Guerrero, Ch. Young-Guerrero, Ch. Young-J. Miller, Ch. Young-Shumaker-J. Miller. **Kannapolis (8)**—Bittner-Dobyns-Castro-Meaux, Fryson-Lubisich-Fields, Honel-Stumm, Honel-Williams, Lubisich-Reynoso, Lubisich-Stumm, Lubisich-Szado-Patten, Szado-Castro-Patten. **Lakewood (8)**—Floyd-Squires 2, E. Astacio-Mayfield-Kim, Cable-Brito, Cable-Cordero-Silverio, DeChristofaro-Bernard-Brito-Mayfield, Floyd-Squires, Silverio-Wilson. **Lexington (16)**—Barrett-Barzilla, Barrett-McNair-Barzilla, Cabreja-Pena-Barzilla, Cabreja-Pena-Gallo, Pena-McNair, Roberson-Barzilla 2, Rodaway-Gallo 2, Roberson-Anderson, Roberson-Anderson-Gallo, Roberson-Pena-Barzilla, Rodaway-McNair-Anderson, Rodaway-McNair-Bayrer, Santillan-Gallo-Anderson, Santillan-Gallo-Lira. **Macon (10)**—G. Lopez-Staveland-Boyer, McBride-Albertus-Roberts, McBride-Boyer, McBride-Boyer-Roberts-Albertus, McBride-Roberts, McBride-Zumwalt-Boyer, Miner-Boyer-Roberts, Miner-Herndon-Vianna, Miner-J. Rodriguez, Miner-Vianna. **Savannah (10)**—Bengochea-Corrado, Bengochea-Hillaert, Engels-V. Ramirez, Jimenez-Bengochea, Masset-Bright, Mounce-Murray-Abraham, Murray-Abraham-Mounce, Murray-Marcano-Hillaert, V. Ramirez-Abraham-Engels, L. Rodriguez-Masset-Luna. **South Georgia (9)**—Cruceta-Johansen, Cruceta-Osoria, Figueroa-J. Diaz-Ott, Figueroa-Strayhorn, Kierstead-Ott-Santiago-Hull, Leek-Johansen, McCracken-Lizarraga, McCracken-A. Simpson, A. Simpson-Nall-Arellan-Johansen.

NO-HIT GAMES: Cruceta, South Georgia defeated Delmarva, 6-0, April 29, game 1; Gavin Floyd, Lakewood defeated Lexington, 1-0, July 24.

2002 FIELDING

TEAM

Team	G	PO	A	E	TC	DP	TP	PB	Pct.
Lakewood	139	3648	1474	152	5274	119	0	23	.971
Delmarva	140	3693	1508	156	5357	97	0	26	.971
Char'ton, W.Va.	140	3651	1389	156	5196	104	0	22	.970
Lexington	140	3757	1596	172	5525	118	0	30	.969
Hickory	139	3618	1352	162	5132	107	0	25	.968
Augusta	136	3505	1386	164	5055	116	0	20	.968
Kannapolis	140	3696	1437	178	5311	102	0	26	.966
Savannah	138	3660	1475	183	5318	106	0	22	.966
Greensboro	140	3686	1570	188	5444	111	0	32	.965
Macon	140	3598	1380	179	5157	117	0	39	.965
Columbia	139	3619	1517	185	5321	83	0	36	.965
Hagerstown	140	3639	1544	191	5374	100	0	33	.964
Columbus	139	3632	1474	191	5297	110	0	23	.964
Asheville	138	3634	1534	218	5386	122	0	34	.960
Char'ton, S.C.	136	3489	1532	215	5236	100	0	38	.959
South Georgia	138	3603	1456	217	5276	112	0	23	.959

INDIVIDUAL

FIRST BASEMEN

NOTE: All caps denotes fielding-percentage leader based on 70 games for catchers, 93 for all other non-pitchers and 112 innings for pitchers. *Throws lefthanded.

Player, Team	Pct.	G	PO	A	E	TC	DP
Albert, Luke, Mac.	.857	1	6	0	1	7	1
Alexander, Kevin, Hag.	1.000	10	76	4	0	80	4
Barnowski, Bryan, Aug.	.975	9	74	4	2	80	8
Bastardo, Angel, C'bia	1.000	1	3	0	0	3	0
Beuerlein, Tyler, C'bia	.984	17	115	11	2	128	13
Bird, T.J., Ash.*	1.000	2	11	1	0	12	0
Brown, Kevin, Mac.	.990	12	93	9	1	103	6
Brunner, Ryan, Aug.*	.996	34	259	9	1	269	23
Bunch, J.C., Sav.	.923	2	11	1	1	13	0
Cabrerra, Ulises, Sav.	1.000	4	27	1	0	28	5
Calabrese, Tony, Gre.	1.000	4	22	2	0	24	3
Caligiuri, Jay, C'bia	.992	57	466	49	4	519	30
Cancio, Antonio, Lak.	1.000	14	109	4	0	113	8
Christian, Josh, Sav.	.977	23	192	21	5	218	12
Cooper, Matt, Aug.	.981	88	673	60	14	747	69
Cordido, Julio, Hag.	.978	10	80	7	2	89	4
Corr, Frank, C'bia	.983	17	158	11	3	172	7
Cosby, Rob, C.W.Va.	1.000	5	33	5	0	38	2
Dacey, Ryan, S.G.	1.000	5	33	2	0	35	4
Davis, J.P., C.S.C.	.982	66	553	58	11	622	44
De La Cruz, Miguel, Hick.	.982	17	106	5	2	113	8
Delgado, Mario, Lak.*	1.000	7	55	1	0	56	8
Diaz, Victor, S.G.	1.000	3	21	3	0	24	0
Dill, Jason, Sav.*	1.000	12	80	10	0	90	11
Duran, Alexander, C.S.C.	.500	1	1	0	1	2	0
Durazo, Ernie, C.W.Va.	.987	8	68	6	1	75	7
Eddlemon, Kelly, C.S.C.	1.000	3	16	1	0	17	4
Escalera, Jose, S.G.	1.000	5	26	3	0	29	4
Franco, Iker, C.S.C.	.990	26	195	12	2	209	20
Freeman, Ashley, Ash.	1.000	4	14	0	0	14	3
Gajewski, Matt, Sav.	1.000	2	7	1	0	8	1
German, Ramon, Lex.	1.000	1	2	0	0	2	0
Gibbs, Mark, Del.	1.000	19	139	9	0	148	6
Gillitzer, Scott, S.G.	.988	46	306	34	4	344	32
Gold, Nate, Sav.	.989	37	353	20	4	377	31
Gretz, Nick, Ash.	.989	99	844	73	10	927	88
Hattig, John, Aug.	.987	9	68	6	1	75	7
Howard, Ryan, Lak.*	.985	118	1064	64	17	1145	97
Jeffcoat, Bryon, Mac.	1.000	1	1	0	0	1	0
Kirby, Brian, C'bus	.996	31	206	19	1	226	18

Player, Team	Pct.	G	PO	A	E	TC	DP
Knox, Matt, C'bus	.989	40	335	32	4	371	28
Lee, Carlos, Kan.	.875	1	7	0	1	8	0
Lehr, Ryan, Del.	1.000	3	23	0	0	23	2
Maduro, Jorge, C.S.C.	.500	1	1	0	1	2	0
Manley, Adam, Del.*	.979	76	619	48	14	681	46
McGee, Tom, Del.	.938	2	14	1	1	16	1
McIntyre, Robert, C'bia	1.000	2	3	0	0	3	0
McKee, Mickey, Lex.	.981	15	93	8	2	103	10
McKee, Scott, Kan.	.983	100	785	49	14	848	57
Molina, Gustavo, Kan.	.982	19	150	10	3	163	13
Mongeluzzo, Anthony, Sav.	.981	26	186	20	4	210	14
Nunez, Felix, C.S.C.	.975	4	36	3	1	40	3
Ochoa, Javier, C'bia	1.000	1	1	0	0	1	0
Patty, Jason, Sav.	1.000	1	2	1	0	3	0
Peck, Bryan, Ash.	1.000	4	34	2	0	36	2
Peshke, Chad, C'bus	.944	2	16	1	1	18	3
Pitney, Jared, Gre.*	.997	35	315	25	1	341	28
Porter, Thomas, C.S.C.	.889	2	8	0	1	9	1
Radwan, Jason, S.G.	.976	9	80	2	2	84	6
Reece, Eric, C.S.C.	.983	49	373	36	7	416	20
Reyes, Julio, Kan.	1.000	7	44	0	0	44	3
Riley, Ryan, C.S.C.	1.000	1	1	1	0	2	1
Rodriguez, Andres, C'bia	.985	53	418	40	7	465	30
Rogers, Omar, Del.	.988	43	375	33	5	413	28
Salas, Jose, Mac.	.979	6	44	2	1	47	4
Salinas, Trey, Del.	1.000	10	78	8	0	86	11
Sanchez, Jean, Sav.	.990	34	186	20	2	208	12
Santamarina, Juan, Kan.	.944	4	32	2	2	36	4
Schmitt, Brian, Lex.*	.986	120	1028	80	16	1124	83
Segar, Jeff, Gre.	1.000	33	296	19	0	315	20
Shelton, Chris, Hick.	1.000	52	414	31	0	445	38
Smith, Dustin, Sav.	.955	3	19	2	1	22	1
Snyder, Mike, C.W.Va.	.989	127	1003	91	12	1106	82
Soto, T.J., Lex.	.986	23	201	12	3	216	19
Soules, Ryan, Sav.	.995	21	176	21	1	198	10
Storey, Eric, Kan.	.993	20	135	6	1	142	14
Story-Harden, Thomari, S.G.	.976	85	688	45	18	751	58
Swedlow, Sean, C'bus	.960	71	559	43	25	627	44
Tejada, Mike, Ash.	.935	6	40	3	3	46	1
Testa, Chris, Ash.*	.979	34	299	22	7	328	20
Thorman, Scott, Mac.	.986	122	976	44	14	1034	88
Turner, Jason, Gre.*	.993	72	655	62	5	722	56
VON SCHELL, Tyler, Hag.	.991	121	1081	78	10	1169	84
Walsh, Sean, Lak.	1.000	7	26	4	0	30	2
Wolotka, Brian, C.S.C.*	1.000	1	3	0	0	3	0
Young, Walter, Hick.	.977	77	584	58	15	657	54

SECOND BASEMEN

Player, Team	Pct.	G	PO	A	E	TC	DP
Abreu, Nielsen, Lak.	.000	2	0	0	0	0	0
Alexander, Kevin, Hag.	.970	43	79	113	6	198	24
Amador, Chris, Kan.	.960	115	239	288	22	549	54
Asprilla, Avelino, Hick.	.965	21	42	67	4	113	8
Bacani, David, C'bia	.976	66	121	208	8	337	30
Bennett, Kris, Lak.	.980	35	60	85	3	148	23
Bourgeois, Jason, Sav.	.973	20	41	67	3	111	8
Brand, Kevin, Ash.	.857	1	2	4	1	7	0
Cabrera, Chi Chi, Hag.	.949	8	15	22	2	39	2
Cabrerra, Ulises, Sav.	.966	56	98	127	8	233	26
Calabrese, Tony, Gre.	.968	36	63	116	6	185	20
Cano, Robinson, Gre.	.950	54	112	152	14	278	33
Carroll, Wes, Lak.	.976	74	130	201	8	339	37
Castillo, Osmar, Aug.	1.000	25	53	68	0	121	16
Cates, Gary, Del.	.963	77	167	196	14	377	32
Centeno, Irwin, C.S.C.	1.000	2	8	2	0	10	2
Choy Foo, Rodney, C'bus	.984	81	146	215	6	367	43
Colmenter, Jesus, C'bia	.933	7	5	9	1	15	2

Player, Team	Pct.	G	PO	A	E	TC	DP
Cordido, Julio, Hag.	.938	6	10	20	2	32	4
Cortez, Fernando, C.S.C.	.968	112	224	327	18	569	62
Delfino, Lee, C.W.Va.	.956	112	189	310	23	522	61
De Los Santos, Omar, S.G.	.964	31	53	108	6	167	24
Del Rosario, Manny, Del.	.938	33	49	71	8	128	12
De Paula, Luis, C.S.C.	.900	2	11	7	2	20	0
Diaz, Eduardo, Ash.	1.000	10	13	14	0	27	1
Diaz, Victor, S.G.	.981	15	21	31	1	53	7
Downing, Lance, Lex.	.984	15	25	36	1	62	4
Duran, Alexander, C.S.C.	.882	5	6	9	2	17	2
Eddlemon, Kelly, C.S.C.	.857	6	6	6	2	14	1
Galante, Matt, C'bia	.984	42	61	127	3	191	21
Garrido, Tomas, Hag.	1.000	5	5	10	0	15	3
Gibbs, Mark, Del.	.850	7	9	8	3	20	1
Gillitzer, Scott, S.G.	.946	35	71	104	10	185	19
Gonzalez, Edgar, C.S.C.	1.000	1	1	2	0	3	0
Gonzalez, Jose, Sav.	.907	11	16	23	4	43	4
Harrison, Vince, C.S.C.	1.000	4	4	13	0	17	1
Heard, Scott, Sav.	1.000	1	2	2	0	4	2
Helquist, Jon, Lex.	.964	102	160	290	17	467	61
Herr, Aaron, Mac.	.960	79	155	204	15	374	56
Herrera, Christian, S.G.	.000	1	0	0	0	0	0
Hudnall, Joshua, Hick.	1.000	9	13	23	0	36	4
Inglett, Joe, C'bus	.901	13	28	36	7	71	7
Jeffcoat, Bryon, Mac.	.943	29	49	84	8	141	10
Jiannetti, Joe, C'bia	.937	29	62	56	8	126	9
Kent, Bryan, Aug.	1.000	1	1	1	0	2	1
KEPPINGER, Jeff, Hick.	.981	113	201	306	10	517	69
Lambert, Casey, Ash.	1.000	3	9	5	0	14	1
Lewis, Russell, Aug.	.977	8	12	31	1	44	6
Lopez, Gabe, Gre.	1.000	16	34	37	0	71	11
Mann, Derek, S.G.	.949	59	115	147	14	276	34
Mayorson, Manuel, C.W.Va.	1.000	9	10	16	0	26	2
McIntyre, Robert, C'bia	1.000	5	8	9	0	17	2
McKee, Mickey, Lex.	1.000	2	4	2	0	6	1
McMains, Derin, Hag.	.981	81	153	258	8	419	44
Meyer, Drew, Sav.	.989	21	38	51	1	90	8
Minami, Yasumichi, Aug.	1.000	1	1	2	0	3	0
Mongeluzzo, Anthony, Sav.	1.000	1	2	5	0	7	1
Morales, Michael, Mac.	.909	10	15	15	3	33	5
Nix, Jayson, Ash.	.942	131	236	351	36	623	77
Nunez, Alexis, Lak.	.941	5	5	11	1	17	3
Nunez, Manuel, S.G.	.912	6	19	12	3	34	2
Olivari, Reinaldo, Sav.	.941	7	7	9	1	17	2
O'Riordan, Chris, Sav.	.981	9	27	26	1	54	9
Pagan, Felix, Sav.	1.000	21	31	60	0	91	10
Patty, Jason, Sav.	1.000	11	4	19	0	23	1
Peshke, Chad, C'bus	.750	2	2	1	1	4	1
Petersen, Ryan, Aug.	.991	22	45	62	1	108	8
Pittman, Sean, C'bia	1.000	3	4	4	0	8	0
Reyes, Ambiorix, Ash.	1.000	1	0	2	0	2	0
Reyes, Ivan, Gre.	.972	41	60	115	5	180	16
Riley, Ryan, C.S.C.	.933	6	10	18	2	30	1
Rodriguez , Ricardo, Mac.	.967	15	26	32	2	60	6
Rogers, Omar, Del.	.990	25	47	52	1	100	14
St. Clair, Jason, C.S.C.	.900	3	3	6	1	10	1
Salazar, Juan, Aug.	.976	84	166	233	10	409	56
Salvo, Andrew, Kan.	.965	23	51	58	4	113	23
Sardinha, Bronson, Gre.	1.000	1	1	0	0	1	0
Segar, Jeff, Gre.	1.000	2	1	1	0	2	0
Shanks, Eric, Del.	1.000	2	2	4	0	6	1
Sherrill, J.J., C'bus	.907	41	88	87	18	193	18
Silvera, Andres, Lak.	.975	21	31	46	2	79	15
Soriano, Jairo, Del.	.970	7	10	22	1	33	2
Soto, T.J., Lex.	1.000	8	19	22	0	41	5
Soules, Ryan, Sav.	1.000	4	6	5	0	11	2
Storey, Eric, Kan.	.938	9	10	20	2	32	2
Story-Harden, Thomari, S.G.	1.000	1	2	5	0	7	2
Tempesta, Nick, C.W.Va.	.963	27	43	61	4	108	7
Timmons, Wes, Mac.	1.000	9	13	24	0	37	5
Toven, John, Lex.	.979	24	37	55	2	94	10
Youngbauer, Scott, Lak.	.937	15	28	46	5	79	3

THIRD BASEMEN

Player, Team	Pct.	G	PO	A	E	TC	DP
Alexander, Kevin, Hag.	.720	8	9	9	7	25	1
Anderson, Keith, Hag.	1.000	1	0	1	0	1	0
Bacani, David, C'bia	.000	1	0	0	0	0	0
Bautista, Jose, Hick.	.916	124	74	187	24	285	12
Benavidez, Julian, Hag.	.885	118	78	253	43	374	23
Bennett, Kris, Lak.	1.000	3	1	0	0	1	0
Brand, Kevin, Ash.	.941	7	5	11	1	17	0

Player, Team	Pct.	G	PO	A	E	TC	DP
Cabrera, Ulises, Sav.	.929	17	11	15	2	28	0
Calabrese, Tony, Gre.	.500	1	1	0	1	2	0
Camacho, Juan, Gre.	.941	118	89	229	20	338	14
Carroll, Wes, Lak.	.000	1	0	0	1	1	0
Castillo, Osmar, Aug.	1.000	5	3	9	0	12	1
Cates, Gary, Del.	1.000	3	3	2	0	5	0
Chaves, Brandon, Hick.	1.000	1	0	1	0	1	0
Choy Foo, Rodney, C'bus	.909	9	5	15	2	22	1
Colmenter, Jesus, C'bus	1.000	7	0	11	0	11	1
Cordido, Julio, Hag.	1.000	9	8	23	0	31	1
Corporan, Elvis, Gre.	.925	12	5	32	3	40	2
Cortez, Fernando, C.S.C.	1.000	1	0	1	0	1	0
Cosby, Rob, C.W.Va.	.878	44	31	70	14	115	6
Dacey, Ryan, S.G.	.922	29	18	29	4	51	4
De La Cruz, Miguel, Hick.	.917	31	11	33	4	48	3
De Los Santos, Omar, S.G.	.889	15	9	23	4	36	3
Diaz, Eduardo, Ash.	.917	12	7	15	2	24	2
Diaz, Victor, S.G.	.863	67	31	108	22	161	13
Downing, Lance, Lex.	1.000	1	1	1	0	2	0
Duran, Alexander, C.S.C.	.667	2	1	3	2	6	0
Eddlemon, Kelly, C.S.C.	.857	2	0	6	1	7	0
Franco, Iker, C.S.C.	.000	1	0	0	0	0	0
Freeman, Ashley, Ash.	.891	98	74	156	28	258	9
Gajewski, Matt, Sav.	.500	2	0	1	1	2	0
Galante, Matt, C'bia	1.000	1	0	1	0	1	0
Garrido, Tomas, Hag.	1.000	5	1	6	0	7	0
German, Ramon, Lex.	.917	84	46	153	18	217	14
Gibbs, Mark, Del.	.895	8	0	17	2	19	1
Gillitzer, Scott, S.G.	.884	24	14	47	8	69	0
Gonzalez, Edgar, C.S.C.	.937	128	71	243	21	335	13
Gretz, Nick, Ash.	1.000	1	1	0	0	1	0
Harrison, Vince, C.S.C.	1.000	2	0	5	0	5	0
Hattig, John, Aug.	.929	83	44	153	15	212	17
Hudnall, Joshua, Hick.	1.000	1	1	0	0	1	0
Inglett, Joe, C'bus	.940	33	27	67	6	100	6
Jeffcoat, Bryon, Mac.	.885	10	4	19	3	26	3
JOHNSON, Tripper, Del.	.968	133	117	276	13	406	23
Kay, Brett, C'bia	.000	1	0	0	0	0	0
Kent, Bryan, Aug.	.910	30	20	41	6	67	2
Knox, Matt, C'bus	1.000	9	2	13	0	15	0
Lambert, Casey, Ash.	1.000	5	3	7	0	10	0
Lee, Carlos, Kan.	.909	5	4	6	1	11	0
Lehr, Ryan, Del.	.000	1	0	0	0	0	0
Lewis, Russell, Aug.	.857	5	4	8	2	14	0
Marte, Andy, Mac.	.917	121	93	207	27	327	25
McIntyre, Robert, C'bia	.959	17	11	36	2	49	3
McKee, Mickey, Lex.	.916	42	38	82	11	131	5
Minami, Yasumichi, Aug.	.500	1	0	1	1	2	0
Mongeluzzo, Anthony, Sav.	.000	1	0	0	0	0	0
Morse, Michael, Kan.	.937	23	10	49	4	63	3
Nunez, Manuel, S.G.	.920	17	11	35	4	50	3
Olivari, Reinaldo, Sav.	1.000	1	1	0	0	1	0
Patty, Jason, Sav.	.000	1	0	0	0	0	0
Peck, Bryan, Ash.	.938	6	6	9	1	16	1
Peshke, Chad, C'bus	.901	81	56	144	22	222	8
Petersen, Ryan, Aug.	1.000	1	0	1	0	1	0
Phelps, Jeff, Lak.	.923	93	60	192	21	273	11
Pittman, Sean, C'bia	1.000	3	0	3	0	3	0
Reyes, Ambiorix, Ash.	.916	26	26	50	7	83	2
Reyes, Ivan, Gre.	.929	11	5	21	2	28	2
Riley, Ryan, C.S.C.	.727	3	2	6	3	11	1
Santamarina, Juan, Kan.	.917	59	44	99	13	156	8
Shanks, Eric, Del.	1.000	1	1	3	0	4	0
Shelley, Randall, Sav.	.932	128	107	274	28	409	16
Soto, T.J., Lex.	.875	16	4	17	3	24	0
Storey, Eric, Kan.	.945	59	35	102	8	145	8
Tablado, Raul, C.W.Va.	.912	74	41	114	15	170	9
Tempesta, Nick, C.W.Va.	.949	30	22	52	4	78	6
Timmons, Wes, Mac.	.963	9	7	19	1	27	5
Toven, John, Lex.	.800	2	1	3	1	5	1
Walsh, Sean, Lak.	.922	49	31	88	10	129	5
Whitney, Matthew, C'bus	.818	6	1	8	2	11	0
Wright, David, C'bia	.942	123	81	228	19	328	14
Youkilis, Kevin, Aug.	.913	15	11	31	4	46	3

SHORTSTOPS

Player, Team	Pct.	G	PO	A	E	TC	DP
Alexander, Kevin, Hag.	.914	14	17	36	5	58	6
Amador, Chris, Kan.	.923	8	12	24	3	39	4
Asprilla, Avelino, Hick.	.962	31	45	82	5	132	20
Bacani, David, C'bia	.959	28	41	75	5	121	14
Bass, Bryan, Del.	.937	129	194	374	38	606	56

Player, Team	Pct.	G	PO	A	E	TC	DP
Bautista, Jose, Hick.	1.000	2	2	7	0	9	0
Bennett, Kris, Lak.	1.000	9	6	19	0	25	0
Bourgeois, Jason, Sav.	.920	99	145	268	36	449	45
Brand, Kevin, Ash.	.941	3	4	12	1	17	5
Cabrera, Chi Chi, Hag.	.975	30	42	77	3	122	13
Cabrera, Ulises, Sav.	.889	7	8	16	3	27	1
Calabrese, Tony, Gre.	.978	11	13	32	1	46	8
Cano, Robinson, Gre.	.922	57	102	170	23	295	35
Carroll, Wes, Lak.	.935	10	4	25	2	31	3
Castillo, Osmar, Aug.	.857	1	4	2	1	7	0
Cates, Gary, Del.	1.000	2	1	4	0	5	1
Chaves, Brandon, Hick.	.941	103	151	251	25	427	47
Choy Foo, Rodney, C'bus	1.000	3	7	5	0	12	3
Colmenter, Jesus, C'bus	.974	13	14	23	1	38	6
Cortez, Fernando, C.S.C.	.983	13	22	36	1	59	6
Cruz, Luis, Aug.	.934	58	103	150	18	271	34
Cuevas, Aneudi, Lex.	.946	8	9	26	2	37	7
De Paula, Luis, C.S.C.	.932	120	183	348	39	570	58
Diaz, Eduardo, Ash.	.000	1	0	0	0	0	0
Freeman, Ashley, Ash.	.000	2	0	0	0	0	0
Galante, Matt, C'bia	.818	1	4	5	2	11	0
Garrido, Tomas, Hag.	.935	37	48	82	9	139	11
Gillitzer, Scott, S.G.	.897	18	24	46	8	78	9
GONZALEZ, Daniel, Lak.	.962	128	213	387	24	624	88
Gonzalez, Jose, Sav.	.000	1	0	0	0	0	0
Harrison, Vince, C.S.C.	.000	1	0	0	0	0	0
Helquist, Jon, Lex.	.941	4	6	10	1	17	4
Herrera, Christian, S.G.	.951	74	119	212	17	348	39
Hudnall, Joshua, Hick.	.894	12	12	30	5	47	8
Jeffcoat, Bryon, Mac.	1.000	7	11	20	0	31	1
Kent, Bryan, Aug.	.964	56	95	120	8	223	25
Knox, Matt, C'bus	1.000	1	1	2	0	3	0
Kochen, Ryan, Lex.	.966	7	9	19	1	29	4
Lambert, Casey, Ash.	.964	8	10	17	1	28	0
Mann, Derek, S.G.	.907	39	68	78	15	161	16
Mayorson, Manuel, C.W.Va.	.954	125	212	303	25	540	62
McIntyre, Robert, C'bia	.916	75	108	197	28	333	25
McMains, Derin, Hag.	.000	1	0	0	0	0	0
Meyer, Drew, Sav.	.926	32	45	93	11	149	19
Minami, Yasumichi, Aug.	1.000	1	1	7	0	8	2
Miranda, Miguel, Hag.	.953	69	125	197	16	338	36
Morse, Michael, Kan.	.934	91	145	250	28	423	43
Nunez, Manuel, S.G.	.911	22	39	53	9	101	8
Ochoa, Ivan, C'bus	.959	125	218	394	26	638	69
Pena, Tony, Mac.	.940	117	186	311	32	529	58
Petersen, Ryan, Aug.	.800	1	2	2	1	5	1
Pittman, Sean, C'bia	.733	5	4	7	4	15	2
Ragsdale, Corey, C'bia	.932	37	56	121	13	190	17
Reyes, Ambiorix, Ash.	.929	3	5	8	1	14	1
Reyes, Ivan, Gre.	.886	10	14	17	4	35	2
Riley, Ryan, C.S.C.	.833	6	8	12	4	24	3
Ringe, Craig, Sav.	1.000	4	4	9	0	13	2
Rodriguez , Ricardo, Mac.	.880	6	8	14	3	25	2
St. Clair, Jason, C.S.C.	.857	2	5	7	2	14	2
Salazar, Juan, Aug.	.956	21	32	55	4	91	11
Salvo, Andrew, Kan.	.922	22	40	54	8	102	6
Sardinha, Bronson, Gre.	.889	64	93	170	33	296	30
Schuerholz, Jon, Mac.	.500	1	1	2	3	6	1
Shanks, Eric, Del.	.977	12	11	31	1	43	6
Soriano, Jairo, Del.	1.000	2	6	4	0	10	1
Storey, Eric, Kan.	.926	23	39	74	9	122	14
Tablado, Raul, C.W.Va.	.916	21	33	43	7	83	10
Tena, Hector, Ash.	.948	131	201	400	33	634	86
Timmons, Wes, Mac.	.981	10	16	35	1	52	7
Toven, John, Lex.	.952	41	70	110	9	189	22
Whiteman, Tommy, Lex.	.957	86	112	268	17	397	42

OUTFIELDERS

Player, Team	Pct.	G	PO	A	E	TC	DP
Abraham, Paul, Sav.	.000	1	0	0	0	0	0
Acevedo, Anthony, Lex.*	.969	84	91	4	3	98	0
Ascencion, Quincy, Del.	.960	21	23	1	1	25	0
Asprilla, Avelino, Hick.	1.000	3	6	0	0	6	0
Bilezikjian, Charlie, Sav.	1.000	29	34	4	0	38	0
Bird, T.J., Ash.*	.938	55	78	12	6	96	0
Blanco, Gregor, Mac.*	.946	123	219	7	13	239	0
Bonner, Adam, C.S.C.	.969	88	141	14	5	160	2
Boyd, Patrick, Sav.	.991	59	111	2	1	114	0
Brackley, Carlos, Aug.	.941	8	14	2	1	17	0
Brand, Kevin, Ash.	1.000	7	10	1	0	11	1
Brazoban, Yhency, Gre.	.948	54	100	10	6	116	1
Brunner, Ryan, Aug.*	.974	87	138	11	4	153	1

Player, Team	Pct.	G	PO	A	E	TC	DP
Bryan, Jason, Sav.-Aug.	.941	17	32	0	2	34	0
Burrows, Angelo, Mac.	.984	89	177	13	3	193	4
Buttler, Vic, Hick.*	.989	120	253	7	3	263	0
Cabrera, Ulises, Sav.	1.000	3	1	0	0	1	0
Candelario, Luis, C.S.C.	.885	35	48	6	7	61	1
Caraway, Brandon, Lex.	.982	64	101	6	2	109	1
Carter, Bryan, Hag.*	.971	117	199	5	6	210	0
Cavin, Jonathan, Kan.	.975	77	112	5	3	120	0
Centeno, Irwin, C.S.C.	.976	36	77	3	2	82	0
Charles, Julin, Sav.	.944	8	17	0	1	18	0
Chaves, Brandon, Hick.	.667	1	2	0	1	3	0
Christensen, Jeff, Gre.*	.974	44	74	0	2	76	0
Ciraco, Darren, Kan.	.976	42	81	0	2	83	0
Cliffords, Woody, Del.	.994	81	155	4	1	160	0
Coffey, Kris, Aug.	.969	104	181	4	6	191	1
Colmenter, Jesus, C'bus	1.000	1	2	0	0	2	0
Cordido, Julio, Hag.	1.000	2	2	0	0	2	0
Corr, Frank, C'bia	.922	46	55	4	5	64	0
Cortes, Jorge, Hick.*	.912	17	28	3	3	34	1
Cosby, Rob, C.W.Va.	.981	43	49	4	1	54	0
Cruz, Orlando, Sav.	.977	32	40	3	1	44	0
Davis, Rajai, Hick.	1.000	6	15	0	0	15	0
De La Cruz, Miguel, Hick.	1.000	1	1	0	0	1	0
Delgado, Mario, Lak.*	.000	1	0	0	0	0	0
Devarez, Noel, C'bia.	.926	15	25	0	2	27	0
Diaz, Eduardo, Ash.	.800	5	4	0	1	5	0
Dill, Jason, Sav.*	1.000	12	21	2	0	23	1
Dion, Nate, C.S.C.	.948	87	140	6	8	154	0
Duncan, Jeff, C'bia*	.882	28	26	4	4	34	0
Duncan, Shelley, Gre.	.953	69	113	10	6	129	0
Duran, Carlos, Mac.*	.964	125	264	7	10	281	1
Eddlemon, Kelly, C.S.C.	1.000	11	5	0	0	5	0
Eldridge, Rashad, Sav.	.986	71	140	5	2	147	1
Escalera, Jose, S.G.	1.000	16	11	2	0	13	0
Essian, James, S.G.	1.000	21	40	1	0	41	0
Ezi, Travis, S.G.*	.968	69	122	0	4	126	0
Figueroa, Daniel, Aug.*	.942	74	159	3	10	172	0
Florence, Branden, Hag.	.970	54	98	0	3	101	0
Floyd, Mike, Lak.	.954	69	159	7	8	174	1
Folsom, Mark, C'bus	.939	80	113	11	8	132	2
Foster, Gregg, Lak.	.975	42	76	2	2	80	0
Francisco, Ruben, Del.*	.955	51	79	6	4	89	1
Freeman, Ashley, Ash.	.957	32	38	6	2	46	0
Frome, Jason, Ash.*	.984	28	58	4	1	63	0
Gajewski, Matt, Sav.	1.000	6	7	1	0	8	0
Garcia, Jose, S.G.	.960	122	222	16	10	248	0
Gathright, Joey, C.S.C.	.992	56	120	7	1	128	2
Gillitzer, Scott, S.G.	.917	11	11	0	1	12	0
Godwin, Tyrell, C.W.Va.	.980	47	95	1	2	98	0
Gonzalez, Jose, Sav.	.000	1	0	0	0	0	0
Gordon, Alex, Del.*	.968	54	86	5	3	94	1
Gutierrez, Franklin, S.G.	.986	91	200	5	3	208	1
Guzman, Carlos, Mac.	1.000	7	6	1	0	7	0
Hackett, Richard, Del.	.984	51	62	1	1	64	0
Harrison, Vince, C.S.C.	.000	1	0	0	1	1	0
Harts, Jeremy, Hick.*	.931	75	142	7	11	160	0
Hill, Willy, Hick.	1.000	39	66	1	0	67	1
Hudnall, Joshua, Hick.	.929	7	13	0	1	14	0
Huntingford, Matt, Hag.*	1.000	7	13	0	0	13	0
Jimenez, Rich, C.W.Va.	.939	15	30	1	2	33	0
Jimerson, Charlton, Sav.	.970	122	250	5	8	263	1
Johnson, Jeremy, C.W.Va.*	.778	4	7	0	2	9	0
Jordan, Eddie, Del.	1.000	36	63	2	0	65	0
Jova, Maikel, C.W.Va.	.991	116	210	9	2	221	0
Kirby, Brian, C'bus	.977	20	40	3	1	44	0
Lambert, Casey, Ash.	1.000	4	8	0	0	8	0
Landaeta, Luis, Hick.*	1.000	9	11	0	0	11	0
Lawson, Forrest, C'bia	.963	74	95	8	4	107	1
Lehr, Ryan, Del.	.986	46	71	1	1	73	0
Lewis, Russell, Aug.	1.000	41	56	2	0	58	0
Littleton, Brandon, Del.*	.989	47	92	2	1	95	0
Lockhart, Paul, Lex.*	.960	37	46	2	2	50	0
Lydon, Wayne, C'bia	.967	117	166	8	6	180	2
Majewski, Val, Del.*	1.000	7	10	0	0	10	0
Malave, Dennis, C'bus*	.975	88	147	9	4	160	2
Manley, Adam, Del.*	.981	59	101	2	2	105	0
Marshall, Andre, Lak.	.993	55	133	4	1	138	0
Martel, Normand, Kan.	1.000	30	68	2	0	70	0
Martin, Kyle, Del.	1.000	4	3	1	0	4	0
McDowell, Arturo, Hag.*	.971	54	96	6	3	105	1
McIntyre, Robert, C'bia	1.000	5	5	2	0	7	0
Meath, Matt, Hick.	1.000	11	18	1	0	19	0

Player, Team	Pct.	G	PO	A	E	TC	DP
Medina, Rodney, C.W.Va.	.966	49	80	5	3	88	0
Meyer, Robert, Hag.	.971	121	189	12	6	207	0
Miller, Greg, Mac.	.993	83	133	8	1	142	1
Miller, Tony, Ash.	.952	129	246	13	13	272	3
Monegan, Anthony, Kan.	1.000	20	33	1	0	34	0
Mongeluzzo, Anthony, Sav.	.972	61	69	1	2	72	0
NEGRON, Miguel, C.W.Va.*	.991	118	212	19	2	233	4
Oliva, Chad, Lak.	.909	25	48	2	5	55	0
Pacheco, Julio, S.G.*	.952	38	75	4	4	83	0
Pagan, Angel, C'bia	.951	103	168	7	9	184	0
Pagan, Felix, Sav.	1.000	1	3	0	0	3	0
Patty, Jason, Sav.	1.000	2	1	0	0	1	0
Peck, Bryan, Ash.	.986	29	66	2	1	69	0
Perry, Rod, Lak.	.969	108	209	11	7	227	0
Petersen, Ryan, Aug.	1.000	16	21	4	0	25	0
Pierce, Sean, S.G.	.952	70	93	6	5	104	0
Quintana, Miguel, C'bus	1.000	56	96	9	0	105	2
Ravelo, Manny, Hick.	.960	87	162	5	7	174	0
Reece, Eric, C.S.C.	.000	1	0	0	0	0	0
Reed, Jeremy, Kan.*	1.000	55	119	5	0	124	0
Reyes, Julio, Kan.	1.000	20	19	2	0	21	0
Rico, Matt, C.S.C.	.958	90	130	8	6	144	0
Rivera, Eric, Lak.	.982	61	106	4	2	112	0
Rodriguez, Edgar, C'bia	.913	18	21	0	2	23	0
Rollins, Antwon, Sav.	.938	48	74	1	5	80	0
Rosa, Wally, Kan.	.000	1	0	0	0	0	0
Sanchez, Jean, Sav.	.000	1	0	0	0	0	0
Sardinha, Bronson, Gre.	1.000	17	14	3	0	17	1
Scala, Mickey, Hick.	1.000	4	4	0	0	4	0
Scott, Luke, C'bus	.971	32	32	2	1	35	0
Segar, Jeff, Gre.	.986	62	131	8	2	141	1
Seiber, Antron, Aug.	.982	76	163	5	3	171	1
Shelton, Chris, Hick.	.000	1	0	0	0	0	0
Sherrill, J.J., C'bus	.982	59	103	5	2	110	1
Soto, T.J., Lex.	1.000	1	1	0	0	1	0
Soules, Ryan, Sav.	.000	1	0	0	0	0	0
Spidale, Mike, Kan.	1.000	91	232	3	0	235	1
Stockton, Brad, Sav.	.975	55	78	1	2	81	0
Stringfellow, Christopher, Sav.	.981	68	101	5	2	108	2
Summerville, Kaazim, Gre.	.959	45	91	2	4	97	0
Tablado, Raul, C.W.Va.	1.000	1	2	3	0	5	0
Taveras, Willy, C'bus	.944	84	157	11	10	178	1
Testa, Chris, Ash.*	.963	91	122	8	5	135	1
Thompson, Kevin, Gre.	.951	61	129	8	7	144	0
Toner, John, C'bia	.913	25	20	1	2	23	0
Van Every, Jon, C'bus*	1.000	15	34	3	0	37	2
Vasquez, Jose, Ash.*	.952	52	75	5	4	84	1
Verbryke, Eric, Gre.*	.971	28	63	4	2	69	1
Vukovich, Vince, Lak.	.975	57	112	3	3	118	0
Walker, Mark, Hag.	.965	72	136	3	5	144	0
Walsh, Sean, Lak.	1.000	11	16	1	0	17	0
Weston, Aron, Hick.*	.975	61	110	7	3	120	0
Wigginton, Derek, Kan.*	.970	103	189	6	6	201	0
Winrow, Gary, Gre.*	.975	58	74	5	2	81	0
Wolotka, Brian, C.S.C.*	.917	31	42	2	4	48	0
Wright, Gavin, Lex.	.971	124	187	14	6	207	3
Zieour, Neesan, C.W.Va.	.978	47	87	3	2	92	0

OUTFIELDERS WITH TWO OR MORE TEAMS

Player, Team	Pct.	G	PO	A	E	TC	DP
Bryan, Jason, Sav.	1.000	1	3	0	0	3	0
Bryan, Jason, Aug.	.935	16	29	0	2	31	0

CATCHERS

Player, Team	Pct.	G	PO	A	E	TC	DP	PB
Aleman, Carlos, Aug.	1.000	5	28	2	0	30	0	0
Anderson, Keith, Hag.	.978	39	305	55	8	368	3	5
Arko, Tommy, Del.	.987	22	143	14	2	159	1	5
Barnett, Dan, Kan.	1.000	18	109	8	0	117	0	2
Barnowski, Bryan, Aug.	1.000	2	15	1	0	16	0	1
Bastardo, Angel, C'bus	.973	21	155	23	5	183	0	3
Bellorin, Edwin, S.G.	.978	79	539	50	13	602	1	12
Bernard, Miguel, Mac.	.981	47	302	50	7	359	2	14
Beuerlein, Tyler, C'bia	1.000	1	3	3	0	6	0	1
Bowman, Addison, Aug.	1.000	2	8	4	0	12	0	1
Bunch, J.C., Sav.	1.000	2	2	0	0	2	0	0
Camacaro, Armando, C'bus	.991	90	713	67	7	787	7	11
Colina, Alvin, Ash.	.980	54	395	55	9	459	3	11
D'Jesus, Francisco, Hag.	1.000	8	61	6	0	67	0	0
Doumit, Ryan, Hick.	.968	31	199	15	7	221	0	6
Esposito, Brian, Aug.	.980	39	307	41	7	355	4	3
Fatheree, Danny, Lex.	.993	38	250	24	2	276	2	8

Player, Team	Pct.	G	PO	A	E	TC	DP	PB
Fernandez, Alejandro, Gre.	.993	39	268	29	2	299	1	9
Franco, Iker, C.S.C.	.976	42	261	21	7	289	1	7
Freeman, Ashley, Ash.	.923	4	10	2	1	13	0	1
Gajewski, Matt, Sav.	1.000	1	4	0	0	4	0	0
GIMENEZ, Hector, Lex.	.993	85	665	67	5	737	6	19
Harris, Blair, Kan.	.933	4	27	1	2	30	0	1
Heard, Scott, Sav.	.989	81	564	51	7	622	3	11
Hernandez, Jose, Hick.	.987	57	393	46	6	445	3	6
Hietpas, Joe, C'bia	1.000	28	212	29	0	241	3	5
Huber, Justin, C'bia	.989	69	647	46	8	701	0	16
Kay, Brett, C'bia	.972	24	196	9	6	211	0	10
Kirby, Brian, C'bus	.986	25	191	13	3	207	1	8
Knoedler, Justin, Hag.	.977	83	559	70	15	644	2	20
Laker, Tim, C'bus	1.000	6	52	6	0	58	0	1
Langill, Eric, S.G.	1.000	5	23	5	0	28	0	3
Lee, Carlos, Kan.	1.000	1	1	0	0	1	0	2
Maduro, Jorge, C.S.C.	.959	38	213	21	10	244	0	11
Manfred, Brian, Lak.	.957	6	40	5	2	47	0	1
Margalski, Ben, Lak.	.988	72	444	58	6	508	2	15
Martin, Kyle, Del.	.987	15	72	6	1	79	0	1
Martinez, Casey, C.W.Va.	1.000	13	90	9	0	99	1	4
Martinez, Edgar, Aug.	.979	71	537	78	13	628	1	12
Martinez, Octavio, Del.	1.000	11	75	6	0	81	0	2
McGee, Tom, Del.	.991	61	386	38	4	428	0	9
McKee, Mickey, Lex.	1.000	1	2	0	0	2	0	0
Mercedes, Jose, Sav.	.966	5	25	3	1	29	0	2
Merritt, Graig, C.S.C.	.980	63	403	82	10	495	4	14
Molina, Gustavo, Kan.	.984	75	527	86	10	623	2	14
Mosquera, Julio, Sav.	1.000	2	7	2	0	9	0	1
Nathans, John, Aug.	.986	19	125	14	2	141	0	4
Navarro, Dioner, Gre.	.987	86	511	96	8	615	3	19
O'Connor, Brian, Gre.	1.000	6	19	2	0	21	0	0
Ochoa, Javier, C'bia	.977	25	154	16	4	174	1	3
Ortega, Sixto, Ash.	.992	17	104	13	1	118	0	5
Patty, Jason, Sav.	1.000	1	1	0	0	1	0	0
Peck, Bryan, Ash.	.970	12	88	10	3	101	2	5
Pena, Brayan, Mac.	.990	65	466	42	5	513	3	10
Porter, Thomas, C.S.C.	.976	5	37	4	1	42	0	5
Price, Jared, S.G.	.985	62	405	45	7	457	2	8
Radwan, Jason, S.G.	1.000	1	2	1	0	3	0	0
Reece, Eric, C.S.C.	.974	10	34	3	1	38	0	1
Reyes, Milver, Hick.	.971	4	29	4	1	34	0	1
Reynoso, Danilo, C'bia	.950	3	19	0	1	20	0	1
Riera, Zack, Hick.	.944	11	78	6	5	89	0	3
Rogers, Brandon, Hick.	.988	22	156	7	2	165	0	4
Rosa, Wally, Kan.	.985	50	349	42	6	397	4	7
Rosario, Carlos, Gre.	1.000	1	5	1	0	6	0	0
Ruiz, Reinaldo, Lex.	.976	29	223	21	6	250	1	3
Salas, Jose, Mac.	.988	40	276	44	4	324	7	15
Salinas, Trey, Del.	.983	32	199	27	4	230	0	5
Sanchez, Jean, Sav.	1.000	13	86	5	0	91	0	1
Santos, Omir, Gre.	.966	20	132	11	5	148	2	4
Seestedt, Mike, Del.	1.000	8	50	5	0	55	0	1
Shelton, Chris, Hick.	.995	25	189	7	1	197	1	5
Smith, Dustin, Sav.	.977	53	344	33	9	386	4	7
Tejada, Mike, Ash.	.981	59	426	36	9	471	3	12
Tosca, Daniel, Lak.	.983	65	418	37	8	463	2	7
Turco, Anthony, Hag.	.963	14	71	8	3	82	0	8
Walsh, Sean, Lak.	1.000	2	1	0	0	1	0	0
Webster, Kevin, Del.	.979	12	79	13	2	94	0	3
Whittaker, Tim, C.W.Va.	.988	60	475	35	6	516	3	4
Yepez, Jose, C.W.Va.	.986	73	540	40	8	588	3	14

PITCHERS

Player, Team	Pct.	G	PO	A	E	TC	DP
Abell, Joe, Ash.	.000	7	0	0	0	0	0
Abraham, Paul, Sav.	1.000	52	6	14	0	20	0
Acosta, Manuel, Gre.	1.000	13	6	9	0	15	1
Albertus, Roberto, Mac.*	1.000	26	3	10	0	13	0
Allen, Brian, C.S.C.	1.000	2	1	0	0	1	0
Alvarez, Juan, Mac.*	1.000	12	4	8	0	12	0
Alvarez, Oscar, C'bus*	1.000	33	4	16	0	20	0
Anderson, Travis, Lex.	.920	48	5	18	2	25	0
Andrew, Jason, Sav.	1.000	11	2	4	0	6	0
Arellan, Felix, S.G.*	1.000	35	5	13	0	18	2
Arthurs, Shane, C'bus	1.000	6	2	3	0	5	0
Artiles, Carlos, Gre.*	.833	34	1	14	3	18	1
Astacio, Andres, S.G.	.968	31	9	21	1	31	2
Astacio, Ezequiel, Lak.	.921	25	10	25	3	38	4
Barnett, John, Sav.	1.000	3	0	2	0	2	0
BARRETT, Jimmy, Lex.	1.000	27	9	32	0	41	1
Barrios, Angel, Lex.	.000	1	0	0	0	0	0

Player, Team	Pct.	G	PO	A	E	TC	DP
Bartlett, Richard, Del.	.750	9	7	5	4	16	0
Barzilla, Philip, Lex.*	.892	43	6	27	4	37	1
Bayrer, Thomas, Lex.	.500	12	0	1	1	2	0
Bengochea, Kiki, Sav.	.733	12	4	7	4	15	1
Benitez, Fabricio, Aug.	1.000	3	2	1	0	3	0
Benjamin, Petersen, Hag.	.667	13	2	6	4	12	0
Bernard, Jason, Lak.	1.000	11	0	4	0	4	0
Bierbrodt, Nick, C.S.C.*	.500	1	0	1	1	2	0
Bilezikjian, Charlie, Sav.	.000	3	0	0	0	0	0
Birkins, Kurt, Del.*	.900	27	5	31	4	40	1
Bittner, Tim, Kan.*	.978	29	9	35	1	45	0
Blankenship, John, Gre.*	1.000	12	1	8	0	9	0
Blethen, Matt, C'bus*	1.000	11	0	3	0	3	0
Bobbitt, Seth, Lex.	.950	14	4	15	1	20	2
Boughner, Anthony, Del.*	1.000	18	2	10	0	12	0
Boyer, Blaine, Mac.	1.000	43	3	11	0	14	0
Brian, Billy, Gre.	1.000	7	1	3	0	4	0
Bright, Nathan, Sav.	.941	15	10	6	1	17	0
Brito, Eude, Lak.*	1.000	11	1	2	0	3	0
Burres, Brian, Hag.*	.909	32	6	14	2	22	1
Byard, David, C'bia	.964	45	7	20	1	28	0
Cable, Taft, Lak.	.964	27	11	16	1	28	2
Cabreja, Eny, Lex.*	.973	28	4	32	1	37	2
Cabrera, Yunior, C'bia*	1.000	3	1	0	0	1	0
Campos, Juan, Lex.	.750	4	1	2	1	4	1
Caraballo, Angel, Gre.	.857	6	7	5	2	14	0
Carlson, Steve, Gre.*	.929	43	2	11	1	14	0
Carney, Jake, C.S.C.	1.000	6	2	1	0	3	0
Castillo, Albenis, S.G.	1.000	2	0	2	0	2	0
Castro, Julio, Kan.	1.000	43	4	1	0	5	0
Cedeno, Blas, Hick.	1.000	7	3	3	0	6	0
Chadwick, John, C.W.Va.	1.000	19	7	11	0	18	3
Comolli, Mark, C.W.Va.	.909	15	4	6	1	11	1
Cooksey, Wes, Gre.	1.000	51	4	11	0	15	0
Cooper, Chris, C'bus*	.923	38	1	11	1	13	0
Coose, Austin, C.S.C.	1.000	20	1	2	0	3	0
Cordero, Jesus, Lak.	1.000	6	0	1	0	1	0
Corrado, Rob, Sav.	.909	10	1	9	1	11	1
Cox, Adam, C'bus*	1.000	4	0	1	0	1	0
Cox, Mike, C'bia*	1.000	33	2	6	0	8	0
Cram, Josh, Hag.	1.000	17	1	4	0	5	0
Crawford, Chris, C.S.C.*	1.000	42	5	19	0	24	2
Cristobal, Luis, Sav.	.667	5	0	2	1	3	1
Crockett, Ben, Ash.	.909	6	3	7	1	11	0
Cromer, Jason, C.S.C.*	.333	8	0	1	2	3	0
Cromer, Nathan, C.S.C.*	1.000	3	0	4	0	4	0
Crouthers, Dave, Del.	.871	25	10	17	4	31	0
Cruceta, Alberto, S.G.	.931	20	8	19	2	29	3
Cruz, Jeff, Ash.*	.800	6	1	3	1	5	0
Currier, Rik, Gre.	.857	24	3	3	1	7	0
Dagley, Corey, Lak.	1.000	4	1	2	0	3	0
Dannemiller, Beau, Ash.	.818	19	2	7	2	11	1
Davies, Kyle, Mac.	1.000	2	1	1	0	2	0
Davis, Tim, Lak.*	1.000	11	0	1	0	1	0
Dawson, Layne, Lak.	.958	27	7	16	1	24	0
DeChristofaro, Vinny, Lak.*	.964	22	3	24	1	28	0
De La Cruz, Carlos, C'bia	.789	30	8	7	4	19	0
Delcarmen, Manny, Aug.	.800	26	3	21	6	30	2
Delossantos, Carlos, Hick.	1.000	37	2	5	0	7	0
Denham, Dan, C'bus	.826	28	1	18	4	23	2
DePriest, Derrick, Hick.	.500	5	0	1	1	2	1
Devenney, Nick, Sav.	1.000	3	1	2	0	3	0
Deza, Fredy, Del.	1.000	12	0	8	0	8	0
Diaz, Jose, S.G.	1.000	3	2	3	0	5	0
Diaz, Jose, S.G.	.800	19	0	4	1	5	0
DiFranco, Joseph, Gre.	1.000	11	1	2	0	3	0
Digby, Bryan, Mac.	.750	7	1	2	1	4	1
Dinardo, Lenny, C'bia*	.842	24	6	26	6	38	0
Dittler, Jake, C'bus	.885	25	12	11	3	26	0
Dobyns, Heath, Kan.	.714	23	1	4	2	7	0
Dominguez, Jose, Sav.	1.000	16	5	6	0	11	1
Douglas, Shea, C'bus*	.000	1	0	0	0	0	0
Dukeman, Greg, Hick.	.833	11	0	5	1	6	0
Dumatrait, Phillip, Aug.*	1.000	22	5	16	0	21	4
Eckert, Harold, C'bia	.885	27	10	13	3	26	0
Elliott, Adam, C'bia	1.000	1	0	1	0	1	0
Engels, Jackson, Sav.*	.947	15	7	11	1	19	1
Esarey, Brad, C.W.Va.*	.923	40	6	6	1	13	0
Faigin, Jason, Gre.	.250	4	0	1	3	4	0
Farren, Dave, Del.	.714	21	1	4	2	7	0
Fernley, Nathan, C'bus	.923	15	1	11	1	13	1
Fields, Josh, Kan.	.833	21	0	5	1	6	0
Figueroa, Jonathan, S.G.*	1.000	8	2	9	0	11	0
Fitch, Steve, Hick.	1.000	14	1	2	0	3	0
Flinn, Chris, C.S.C.	1.000	19	9	19	0	28	1
Flores, Neomar, C.W.Va.	.966	27	9	19	1	29	0
Floyd, Gavin, Lak.	.951	27	10	29	2	41	2
Foley, Travis, C'bus	.938	26	6	9	1	16	0
Francis, Jeff, Ash.*	1.000	4	2	7	0	9	0
Friedberg, Drew, Hick.*	.733	37	7	4	4	15	0
Fryson, Andrew, Kan.	.882	17	3	12	2	17	1
Fuller, Brendan, C.W.Va.	.864	38	11	8	3	22	0
Gabbard, Kason, Aug.*	.800	7	2	2	1	5	0
Gajewski, Matt, Sav.	.000	1	0	0	0	0	0
Gallo, Mike, Lex.*	1.000	42	3	17	0	20	1
Gamble, Jerome, Aug.	1.000	14	4	8	0	12	0
Garcia, Carlos, S.G.	1.000	1	0	1	0	1	0
Gaudin, Chad, C.S.C.	.783	26	8	10	5	23	0
Generelli, Daniel, Aug.	.842	39	6	10	3	19	0
Gibbs, Mark, Del.	.000	1	0	0	0	0	0
Gomez, Mariano, C'bus*	.900	34	4	23	3	30	2
Grace, Bryan, Gre.	1.000	2	1	2	0	3	0
Gravelle, Nick, Hick.*	1.000	6	0	2	0	2	1
Gregg, James, Hag.	1.000	24	3	3	0	6	0
Grinnell, Tyler, Gre.	1.000	11	1	1	0	2	0
Gronkiewicz, Lee, C'bus	1.000	50	5	8	0	13	1
Gross, Kyle, Hag.	.700	18	2	5	3	10	0
Gryboski, Kevin, Mac.	.000	2	0	0	0	0	0
Guerrero, Julio, Hick.	1.000	31	6	10	0	16	0
Guzman, Leiby, Hag.	.938	44	5	10	1	16	0
Hackett, Richard, Del.	.000	1	0	0	0	0	0
Hall, Shane, Aug.	1.000	6	1	2	0	3	0
Hampson, Justin, Ash.*	.919	27	7	27	3	37	0
Hampton, Royce, Sav.*	1.000	5	1	0	0	1	0
Hannaman, Ryan, Hag.*	.926	24	2	23	2	27	1
Harper, Jesse, C.W.Va.	1.000	21	5	17	0	22	0
Hawk, David, C.S.C.*	.677	32	2	19	10	31	0
Hawley, Ross, Hag.	.875	18	2	5	1	8	0
Hecker, Steven, C.W.Va.	.875	19	2	5	1	8	0
Hentgen, Pat, Del.	.000	1	0	0	0	0	0
Herndon, Eric, Mac.	1.000	5	1	0	0	1	0
Herrera, Cesar, Sav.	1.000	19	11	6	0	17	1
Hillaert, Victor, Sav.	.778	32	2	5	2	9	1
Hines, Carlos, C.S.C.	.875	24	4	3	1	8	2
Hixson, David, Hag.	1.000	5	1	1	0	2	0
Honel, Kris, Kan.	.806	26	6	19	6	31	0
Hosford, Clint, S.G.	1.000	6	1	5	0	6	0
Houston, Ryan, C.W.Va.	1.000	7	0	4	0	4	0
Howell, Jason, Aug.*	.850	40	2	15	3	20	0
Huang, Jun-chung, Aug.	.833	29	3	2	1	6	0
Hull, Eric, S.G.	.833	13	1	4	1	6	1
Jackson, Brian, Hick.	1.000	7	1	1	0	2	0
Jackson, Edwin, S.G.	.929	19	8	18	2	28	1
Jimenez, Kelvin, Sav.	.897	29	9	17	3	29	2
Johansen, Ryan, S.G.	1.000	27	1	4	0	5	0
Jones, D.J., Del.*	.909	26	4	16	2	22	2
Jordan, Eddie, Del.	.000	1	0	0	0	0	0
Joyce, Michael, Gre.*	.000	11	0	0	0	0	0
Keefer, Ryan, Del.	1.000	22	1	5	0	6	0
Keirstead, Michael, S.G.	.929	14	4	9	1	14	0
Keiter, Ben, Sav.	1.000	4	4	4	0	8	1
Kennard, Jeff, Gre.	.818	27	3	6	2	11	0
Kim, Il, Lak.	1.000	21	2	3	0	5	0
King, Jeremy, Gre.	.862	28	5	20	4	29	3
Knapp, Ben, Del.	.919	26	9	25	3	37	1
Korecky, Bobby, Lak.	1.000	8	2	3	0	5	0
Kremer, John, Gre.	1.000	20	0	4	0	4	0
Kumagai, Ryo, Aug.	1.000	21	1	4	0	5	0
Lacorte, Vince, Del.	1.000	20	4	6	0	10	0
Landaeta, Argenis, Gre.	.500	2	0	1	1	2	0
Langill, Eric, S.G.	.000	1	0	0	0	0	0
Lantz, Doug, C'bus	.955	26	10	11	1	22	1
Ledezma, Wil, Aug.*	.000	5	0	0	0	0	0
Lee, Seung, Lak.	.941	23	11	21	2	34	3
Leek, Randy, S.G.*	1.000	2	2	5	0	7	0
Lewis, Derrick, Mac.	.000	1	0	0	0	0	0
Lewis, Rommie, Del.*	.957	53	3	19	1	23	1
Lira, James, Lex.	1.000	15	2	4	0	6	0
Liriano, Francisco, Hag.*	1.000	16	2	8	0	10	1
Lissir, Alexander, Hick.	.750	16	2	4	2	8	1
Lizarraga, Edgar, S.G.	1.000	19	3	5	0	8	0
Lockwood, Brian, C.S.C.	.962	22	7	18	1	26	0
Lohrman, Dave, C'bia	1.000	7	0	1	0	1	0
Lombardi, Justin, Gre.*	.667	6	1	1	1	3	0

Player, Team	Pct.	G	PO	A	E	TC	DP
Lopez, Gonzalo, Mac.	.912	28	12	19	3	34	1
Lopez, Jose, Hick.	1.000	2	1	0	0	1	0
Lopez, Nelson, Hag.	.000	1	0	0	0	0	0
Lopez, Rafael, C'bia	.625	22	2	3	3	8	0
Lorenzo, Javier, Ash.	.900	39	1	8	1	10	1
Lubisich, Nik, Kan.*	.974	34	10	27	1	38	2
Luna, Brandon, Sav.	1.000	32	1	9	0	10	0
Mabry, Barry, Mac.	.000	1	0	0	0	0	0
Maine, John, Del.	1.000	6	1	2	0	3	0
Manzanillo, Josias, Hick.	.000	1	0	0	0	0	0
Marcano, Luis, Sav.	.833	28	1	4	1	6	0
Marchetti, Dan, Del.	.909	39	5	15	2	22	2
Martin, J.D., C'bus	.949	27	11	26	2	39	3
Masset, Nicholas, Sav.	.730	33	8	19	10	37	2
Matthews, Jarod, C.S.C.	1.000	24	10	23	0	33	2
Mattox, David, C'bia	1.000	17	4	13	0	17	1
Mayfield, Brandon, Lak.	1.000	21	1	8	0	9	0
McBride, Macay, Mac.*	.972	25	5	30	1	36	2
McCracken, Vance, S.G.	1.000	8	1	3	0	4	0
McGinley, Blake, C'bia*	.750	26	1	2	1	4	0
McGowan, Dustin, C.W.Va.	.960	28	7	17	1	25	0
McKee, Mickey, Lex.	.500	1	1	0	1	2	0
McNair, Pat, Lex.	.714	37	5	10	6	21	0
Mead, David, Sav.	.800	28	7	5	3	15	1
Meaux, Ryan, Hag.-Kan.*	1.000	54	4	10	0	14	1
Mejia, Francisco, Del.*	.923	37	5	7	1	13	0
Mercedes, Jose, Sav.	.000	1	0	0	0	0	0
Merricks, Charles, Ash.*	.917	29	4	18	2	24	3
Merricks, Matt, Mac.*	.714	19	1	9	4	14	1
Miller, Benji, Hag.	1.000	12	2	4	0	6	1
Miller, Jeff, Hick.	1.000	31	7	12	0	19	0
Miner, Zach, Mac.	.939	29	4	27	2	33	3
Minor, Zach, Lak.	.000	4	0	0	0	0	0
Mitchell, Andy, Del.	1.000	27	5	18	0	23	3
Montano, Ignacio, C'bus*	.750	8	2	1	1	4	0
Montes, Albert, Hag.	.923	28	3	9	1	13	0
Montilla, Elvis, Del.	.000	1	0	0	0	0	0
Moore, Greg, Ash.	.667	7	1	1	1	3	0
Moreno, Victor, Lak.	.000	7	0	0	0	0	0
Morris, Cory, Del.	1.000	10	6	4	0	10	0
Mosley, Eric, Gre.	.900	19	7	11	2	20	0
Mounce, Tony, Sav.*	.000	4	0	0	0	0	0
Mowday, Chris, C.W.Va.	.917	27	4	7	1	12	1
Murray, Arlington, Sav.*	.955	14	6	15	1	22	2
Nall, T.J., S.G.	1.000	21	1	7	0	8	1
Navaroli, Michael, C.S.C.	1.000	36	9	5	0	14	1
Nelson, Steve, Sav.	1.000	18	5	1	0	6	0
Neuage, Leigh, S.G.	.917	8	4	7	1	12	1
Nieve, Fernando, Lex.	1.000	1	1	1	0	2	0
Novoa, Roberto, Hick.	.750	10	1	2	1	4	0
Nunez, Leo, Hick.	.000	1	0	0	0	0	0
O'Brien, Patrick, Hick.	.970	26	10	22	1	33	1
Ogle, Rylie, C'bia*	1.000	9	1	5	0	6	0
Olivo, Rigal, Kan.	1.000	30	2	7	0	9	1
Olson, Ryan, C'bia*	1.000	23	2	13	0	15	0
Oquendo, Ian, Hick.	1.000	24	7	20	0	27	2
Ortiz, Javier, Gre.	.946	18	15	20	2	37	1
Osberg, Tanner, C'bia	1.000	3	1	2	0	3	0
Osoria, Franquelis, S.G.	.889	21	6	10	2	18	0
Ott, Thom, S.G.	.818	45	10	8	4	22	1
Ough, Wayne, C'bia	.964	19	9	18	1	28	0
Padgett, Daniel, Hag.*	1.000	27	6	5	0	11	0
Padilla, Nick, Mac.	.900	16	4	5	1	10	0
Pahucki, David, Aug.	1.000	4	0	2	0	2	0
Pannone, Anthony, Hag.	.911	28	15	36	5	56	3
Parker, Josh, C.S.C.	.857	45	4	8	2	14	0
Parker, Zach, Ash.*	.942	28	9	56	4	69	5
Patten, Scott, Kan.	.714	49	0	5	2	7	0
Patterson, Quenten, C'bia	1.000	17	3	4	0	7	0
Pavon, Julio, Hag.	.863	43	16	28	7	51	2
Peeples, Ross, C'bia*	.938	20	14	16	2	32	0
Pena, Francisco, Lex.	.742	36	5	18	8	31	0
Pennington, Todd, C'bus	.667	16	1	1	1	3	0
Pereyra, Honeudis, C'bia	1.000	8	0	1	0	1	0
Peshke, Chad, C'bia	.000	1	0	0	0	0	0
Peterson, Matt, C'bia	1.000	26	11	15	0	26	2
Picco, John, Gre.*	1.000	4	1	2	0	3	0
Pilkington, Brian, S.G.	.947	20	6	12	1	19	3
Portobanco, Luz, C'bia	.826	17	6	13	4	23	2
Quintana, Miguel, C'bus	.000	1	0	0	0	0	0
Ramirez, Horacio, Mac.*	.500	2	1	0	1	2	0
Ramirez, Ismael, C.W.Va.	.667	6	1	1	1	3	0
Ramirez, Victor, Sav.	.875	23	6	8	2	16	0
Reynolds, Eric, Gre.*	.750	10	2	1	1	4	0
Reynoso, Paulino, Kan.*	.875	33	2	12	2	16	1
Rhodes, Shane, Aug.*	.939	31	5	26	2	33	0
Rice, Scott, Del.*	.667	18	1	9	5	15	1
Rleal, Sendy, Del.	1.000	28	4	4	0	8	0
Roberson, Brandon, Lex.	.957	23	7	15	1	23	0
Roberts, Ralph, Mac.	1.000	49	1	3	0	4	0
Rodaway, Brian, Lex.*	.966	14	5	23	1	29	0
Rodriguez, Jose, Mac.	.833	32	1	9	2	12	0
Rodriguez, Luis, Sav.	1.000	9	0	2	0	2	0
Rodriguez, Orlando, S.G.*	1.000	20	2	2	0	4	0
Rogers, Brad, Del.	1.000	13	2	1	0	3	0
Roman, Orlando, C'bia	.846	45	3	8	2	13	0
Romero, Felix, C.W.Va.	1.000	37	7	3	0	10	1
Roney, Matt, Ash.	.833	14	3	7	2	12	0
Rosario, Francisco, C.W.Va.	.923	13	3	9	1	13	1
Rowe, Steven, Sav.	1.000	11	0	3	0	3	0
Rudrude, Brett, Aug.	1.000	34	6	13	0	19	1
Russ, Chris, Gre.	.875	24	1	6	1	8	1
Sanchez, Rafael, Aug.	.760	29	3	16	6	25	2
Sanders, Shane, C.S.C.	.000	1	0	0	0	0	0
Santiago, Victor, S.G.	1.000	5	2	0	0	2	0
Santillan, Manny, Lex.	.967	14	8	21	1	30	0
Schmitt, Brian, Lex.*	.000	1	0	0	0	0	0
Scobie, Jason, C'bia	.917	16	2	9	1	12	0
Scott, Josh, Lak.*	.000	3	0	0	1	1	0
Searles, Jon, Hick.	.941	31	6	10	1	17	1
Seddon, Chris, C.S.C.*	.950	26	7	12	1	20	1
Serrano, Alex, Ash.	1.000	48	3	15	0	18	0
Sheffield, Christopher, C.W.Va.	.000	3	0	0	0	0	0
Shiery, Shaun, C.S.C.*	1.000	22	1	8	0	9	0
Shouse, Dan, C'bus*	.600	11	2	4	4	10	0
Shumaker, Casey, Hick.	.875	47	4	10	2	16	0
Silverio, Carlos, Lak.	.769	21	2	8	3	13	0
Simpson, Andre, S.G.-Ash.	1.000	28	4	2	0	6	0
Simpson, Gerrit, Ash.	.833	22	12	18	6	36	0
Sinclair, Ernnie, Lex.	.846	25	10	23	6	39	1
Smith, Dustin, Sav.	1.000	1	0	1	0	1	0
Smith, Jason, Gre.	1.000	17	7	11	0	18	1
Songster, Judson, Ash.	.875	47	3	4	1	8	1
Speier, Ryan, Ash.	.625	28	0	5	3	8	0
Sperring, Jayme, Del.	1.000	33	2	3	0	5	0
Spillman, Jeromie, C.W.Va.*	1.000	8	0	4	0	4	0
Squires, Matt, Lak.*	1.000	36	2	3	0	5	0
Stahl, Richard, Del.*	1.000	2	2	2	0	4	1
Staveland, Toby, Mac.	1.000	12	0	2	0	2	0
Stephenson, Eric, C.W.Va.*	.852	23	7	45	9	61	2
Strayhorn, Kole, S.G.	.846	31	6	16	4	26	0
Strelitz, Brian, Gre.	1.000	8	0	4	0	4	0
Stumm, Jason, Kan.	.875	22	2	5	1	8	0
Sturkie, Scott, C'bus	.889	10	2	6	1	9	0
Szado, Craig, Kan.*	.870	30	1	19	3	23	0
Templet, Eric, C'bia	1.000	13	0	4	0	4	0
Thigpen, Joshua, Aug.	.786	25	5	6	3	14	0
Thompson, Derek, C'bus*	1.000	14	6	16	0	22	0
Thorpe, Tracy, C.W.Va.	1.000	20	8	17	0	25	0
Treadway, Brion, Hag.	.929	13	7	6	1	14	0
Truselo, Randy, Sav.	.750	18	3	6	3	12	0
Urena, Sixto, Sav.	1.000	3	0	1	0	1	0
Uzzell, Todd, Hag.	.769	15	4	6	3	13	0
Valdez, Santo, C.W.Va.	.947	29	8	10	1	19	3
Van Benschoten, John, Hick.	.974	27	14	23	1	38	2
Van Buren, Jermaine, Ash.	.882	30	3	12	2	17	1
Vazquez, Will, Ash.	1.000	48	1	7	0	8	0
Vianna, Marcel, Mac.	.714	29	1	4	2	7	0
Vigue, John, C.S.C.	.931	38	9	18	2	29	0
Villacis, Eduardo, Ash.	.857	11	4	2	1	7	1
Waddell, Jason, Hag.*	1.000	4	0	1	0	1	0
Waechter, Doug, C.S.C.	.818	7	2	7	2	11	0
Watkins, Dave, Mac.	.500	7	0	1	1	2	0
Weatherby Iii, Charles, Aug.	1.000	17	2	5	0	7	0
White, Matt, C.S.C.	.933	10	5	9	1	15	0
Williams, Mike, Kan.	.833	22	3	7	2	12	1
Wilson, Mike, Lak.	1.000	5	0	1	0	1	0
Wing, Ryan, Kan.*	.906	25	4	25	3	32	2
Wood, Bobby, Gre.	1.000	21	11	24	0	35	1
Wright, Matt, C.W.Va.	.939	26	6	25	2	33	1
Yacco, Anthony, Hag.	1.000	18	2	5	0	7	1
Yoo, Byung Woo, Aug.	.800	8	0	4	1	5	0
Young, Christopher, Hick.	.919	26	15	19	3	37	1
Young, Curtis, Kan.	1.000	7	1	1	0	2	0
Zink, Charlie, Aug.	1.000	26	3	6	0	9	0
Zumwalt, Alec, Mac.	.750	24	2	1	1	4	0

PITCHERS WITH TWO OR MORE TEAMS

The following players appeared only as designated hitter, pinch-hitter or pinch runner: J. Cooper, dh; Henley, dh.

Player, Team	Pct.	G	PO	A	E	TC	DP
Meaux, Ryan, Hag.*	1.000	44	4	9	0	13	1
Meaux, Ryan, Kan.*	1.000	10	0	1	0	1	0
Simpson, Andre, S.G.	1.000	4	1	1	0	2	0
Simpson, Andre, Ash.	1.000	24	3	1	0	4	0

LEAGUE CHAMPIONS

Year	Team	Pct.
1948—	Lincolnton*	.627
1949—	Newton-Conover	.667
	Rutherford Co. (2nd)†	.627
1950—	Newton-Conover	.627
	Lenoir (2nd)†	.626
1951—	Morganton	.645
	Shelby (2nd)†	.604
1952—	Lincolnton	.649
	Shelby (2nd)†	.645
1953-59—	League inactive.	
1960—	Lexington	.707
	Salisbury (2nd)†	.650
1961—	Salisbury	.627
	Shelby (4th)†	.481
1962—	Statesville	.563
	Statesville	.700
1963—	Greenville†	.576
	Salisbury	.631
1964—	Rock Hill	.672
	Salisbury‡	.631
1965—	Salisbury	.641
	Rock Hill‡	.603
1966—	Spartanburg	.682
	Spartanburg	.767
1967—	Spartanburg	.730
	Spartanburg	.567
1968—	Spartanburg	.597
	Greenwood‡	.597
1969—	Greenwood‡	.587
	Shelby	.565
1970—	Greenville	.576
	Greenville	.619

Year	Team	Pct.
1971—	Greenwood	.631
	Greenwood	.759
1972—	Spartanburg‡	.788
	Greenville	.652
1973—	Spartanburg‡	.646
	Gastonia	.619
1974—	Gastonia	.606
	Gastonia	.672
1975—	Spartanburg	.543
	Spartanburg	.614
1976—	Asheville	.544
	Greenwood‡	.600
1977—	Greenwood	.557
	Gastonia‡	.590
1978—	Greenwood	.614
	Greenwood	.565
1979—	Greenwood‡	.565
	Spartanburg	.525
1980—	Greensboro	.590
	Charleston	.561
1981—	Greensboro‡	.695
	Greenwood	.549
1982—	Greensboro‡	.681
	Florence	.546
1983—	Columbia	.620
	Gastonia‡	.587
1984—	Charleston	.549
	Asheville‡	.510
1985—	Florence‡	.599
	Greensboro	.540
1986—	Columbia‡	.682
	Asheville	.643

Year	Team	Pct.
1987—	Asheville	.655
	Myrtle Beach‡	.597
1988—	Charleston (S.C.)	.616
	Spartanburg‡	.500
1989—	Gastonia	.657
	Augusta‡	.535
1990—	Columbia	.580
	Charleston (W.Va.)‡	.538
1991—	Charleston (W.Va.)	.648
	Columbia‡	.614
1992—	Columbia	.572
	Myrtle Beach‡	.522
1993—	Savannah‡	.662
	Greensboro	.603
1994—	Columbus	.630
	Savannah‡	.599
1995—	Piedmont	.586
	Augusta‡	.551
1996—	Delmarva	.585
	Savannah†	.511
1997—	Delmarva§	.543
	Greensboro	.536
1998—	Columbia§	.638
	Hagerstown	.574
1999—	Hagerstown	.600
	Augusta§	.496
2000—	Piedmont	.657
	Delmarva∞	.544
2001—	Lexington††	.657
2002—	Hickory∞	.597

*Won championship and four-club playoff. †Won four-club playoff. ‡Won split-season playoff. §Won split season, eight-club playoff. ∞Won split season, four-club playoff. ††Was leading final series of split-season, four-club playoff and was declared champion when Professional Baseball declared a stoppage of play. (NOTE—Known as Western Carolina League from 1948 through 1962 and known as Western Carolinas League through 1979.)

APPALACHIAN LEAGUE

LEAGUE OFFICE

President
Lee Landers

Address
283 Deerchase Circle
Statesville, NC 28625

Phone
704-873-5300

Teams (affiliation)
Bluefield Orioles (Orioles)
Bristol White Sox (White Sox)
Burlington Indians (Indians)
Danville Braves (Braves)
Elizabethton Twins (Twins)
Johnson City Cardinals (Cardinals)

Kingsport Mets (Mets)
Martinsville Astros (Astros)
Princeton Devil Rays (Devil Rays)
Pulaski Blue Jays (Blue Jays)

2002 FINAL STANDINGS

EASTERN DIVISION

Team	W	L	T	Pct.	GB
Bluefield (Orioles)	45	23	0	.662	...
Martinsville (Astros)	41	26	0	.612	3.5
Danville (Braves)	37	31	0	.544	8.0
Burlington (Indians)	29	39	0	.426	16.0
Princeton (Devil Rays)	19	49	0	.279	26.0

WESTERN DIVISION

Team	W	L	T	Pct.	GB
Bristol (White Sox)	43	25	0	.632	...
Elizabethton (Twins)	37	30	0	.552	5.5
Pulaski (Rangers)	34	32	0	.515	8.0
Johnson City (Cardinals)	29	38	0	.433	13.5
Kingsport (Mets)	23	44	0	.343	19.5

COMPOSITE

Team	Blue.	Bris.	Mar.	Eliz.	Dan.	Pul.	J.C.	Burl.	King.	Prin.	W	L	T	Pct.	GB
Bluefield (Orioles)	...	4	6	2	4	7	3	5	3	11	45	23	0	.662	...
Bristol (White Sox)	2	...	2	5	3	5	7	5	9	5	43	25	0	.632	2.0
Martinsville (Astros)	1	4	...	3	7	4	5	9	4	4	41	26	0	.612	3.5
Elizabethton (Twins)	4	4	3	...	5	2	4	3	8	4	37	30	0	.552	7.5
Danville (Braves)	2	3	5	1	...	2	4	8	5	7	37	31	0	.544	8.0
Pulaski (Rangers)	5	2	1	5	4	...	3	4	4	6	34	32	0	.515	10.0
Johnson City (Cardinals)	3	5	2	4	2	3	...	2	4	4	29	38	0	.433	15.5
Burlington (Indians)	2	1	3	4	4	2	4	...	5	4	29	39	0	.426	16.0
Kingsport (Mets)	3	1	2	4	1	6	1	1	...	4	23	44	0	.343	21.5
Princeton (Devil Rays)	1	1	2	2	1	6	2	2	2	...	19	49	0	.279	26.0

Major league affiliations in parentheses.

PLAYOFFS: Bristol defeated Bluefield, two games to one to win the Appalachian League championship.

REGULAR-SEASON ATTENDANCE: Bluefield, 29,462; Bristol, 21,921; Burlington, 36,481; Danville, 32,981; Elizabethton, 24,959; Johnson City, 37,786; Kingsport, 21,911; Martinsville, 32,148; Princeton, 29,336; Pulaski, 25,492. Total—292,477. Playoff (three games)—4,420.

MANAGERS: Bluefield, Bien Figueroa; Bristol, Nick Leyva; Burlington, Rouglas Odor; Danville, Ralph Henriquez; Elizabethton, Ray Smith; Johnson City, Brian Rupp; Kingsport, Joey Cora; Martinsville, Jorge Orta; Princeton, Edwin Rodriguez; Pulaski, Pedro Lopez.

ALL-STAR TEAM: 1B—Dusty Gomon, Elizabethton; 2B—Chris O'Riordan, Pulaski; 3B—Aaron Baldiris, Kingsport; SS—Chris De La Cruz, Burlington; Utility INF—Mike McCoy, Johnson City; OF—Wes Bankston, Princeton; OF—Darren Ciraco, Bristol; OF—Jason Pridie, Princeton; Utility OF—Anthony Webster, Bristol; C—Tom Arko, Bluefield; DH—Luis Jimenez, Bluefield; RHP—Anthony Lerew, Danville; LHP—Ricky Barrett, Elizabethton; Relief pitcher—Fernando Tadefa, Danville; Player of the Year—Wes Bankston, Princeton; Pitchers of the Year (tie)—Ricky Barrett, Elizabethton and Anthony Lerew, Danville; Manager of the Year—Nick Leyva, Bristol.

2002 BATTING

TEAM

Team	G	TPA	AB	R	H	TB	2B	3B	HR	RBI	SH	SF	HP	BB	IBB	SO	SB	CS	GDP	LOB	ShO	Avg.	OBP	Slg.
Bristol	68	2755	2382	412	684	962	119	12	45	366	31	27	42	273	7	493	69	29	36	562	2	.287	.367	.404
Princeton	68	2626	2362	324	650	949	99	25	50	281	13	18	25	208	5	531	51	28	44	506	3	.275	.338	.402
Martinsville	67	2677	2264	419	618	834	107	11	29	347	35	29	43	306	5	493	100	33	48	515	1	.273	.366	.368
Bluefield	68	2693	2263	449	606	988	143	7	75	391	18	30	44	338	8	504	80	26	41	496	2	.268	.369	.437
Elizabethton	67	2545	2243	379	599	944	110	17	67	334	14	26	37	225	6	462	57	25	45	447	1	.267	.340	.421
Danville	68	2559	2250	341	587	860	110	17	43	304	18	16	37	238	1	527	78	27	38	481	6	.261	.339	.382
Kingsport	67	2550	2248	295	579	855	103	16	47	259	13	18	51	220	5	512	61	43	49	481	5	.258	.335	.380
Johnson City	67	2534	2220	345	567	907	131	25	53	297	14	14	37	249	2	575	53	36	33	464	3	.255	.338	.409
Burlington	68	2676	2367	304	604	863	93	23	40	251	25	23	25	236	3	580	92	30	52	534	2	.255	.326	.365
Pulaski	66	2540	2127	381	532	809	120	11	45	333	12	20	42	339	4	524	108	25	42	484	3	.250	.361	.380

INDIVIDUAL

TOP QUALIFIERS FOR BATTING CHAMPIONSHIP

Minimum 184 plate appearances. *Lefthanded batter. †Switch-hitter.

Player, Team	G	TPA	AB	R	H	TB	2B	3B	HR	RBI	SH	SF	HP	BB	IBB	SO	SB	CS	GDP	Avg.	OBP	Slg.
Jimenez, Luis, Blue.*	51	211	176	40	66	105	13	1	8	42	0	1	1	33	1	33	9	1	7	.375	.474	.597
O'Riordan, Chris, Pul.	48	221	173	37	64	91	16	1	3	24	1	2	8	37	0	20	14	3	3	.370	.495	.526
Pridie, Jason, Prin.*	67	308	285	60	105	156	12	9	7	33	1	1	2	19	1	35	13	9	2	.368	.410	.547
De La Cruz, Christopher, Burl.†	43	201	180	33	66	88	7	6	1	12	2	1	1	17	0	27	13	4	2	.367	.422	.489
Webster, Anthony, Bris.*	61	291	244	58	86	102	7	3	1	30	1	2	6	38	3	38	16	7	1	.352	.448	.418
Varela, Edgar, Bris.*	55	216	188	30	62	99	11	1	8	40	1	4	10	13	2	29	0	1	1	.330	.395	.527
Ciraco, Darren, Bris.	56	251	219	47	72	117	15	0	10	51	1	3	0	27	0	39	2	0	11	.329	.398	.534
Baldiris, Aaron, King.	58	241	217	31	71	91	9	1	3	24	0	1	9	14	0	24	9	5	7	.327	.390	.419
Deeds, Doug, Eliz.*	59	249	203	48	66	105	16	1	7	32	0	3	2	41	0	41	3	1	2	.325	.438	.517

Player, Team	G	TPA	AB	R	H	TB	2B	3B	HR	RBI	SH	SF	HP	BB	IBB	SO	SB	CS	GDP	Avg.	OBP	Slg.
Martinez, Gabriel, Prin.*	60	247	217	28	70	104	17	1	5	26	2	0	1	27	0	38	1	1	2	.323	.400	.479
Torres, Eider, Burl.†	45	218	194	26	62	70	6	1	0	13	8	0	1	15	0	22	28	3	4	.320	.371	.361
Lopez, Pedro, Bris.	63	298	260	42	83	94	11	0	0	35	17	0	1	20	0	27	22	8	3	.319	.370	.362
Done, Robert, Blue.†	58	256	193	46	61	93	12	1	6	39	0	3	6	54	2	37	6	3	1	.316	.473	.482
McCoy, Mike, J.C.	50	202	154	46	48	71	9	1	4	22	2	1	3	42	0	23	18	7	0	.312	.465	.461
Rijo, Carlos, Blue.	64	259	238	39	74	105	22	0	3	45	0	3	4	14	1	40	9	3	3	.311	.355	.441

DEPARTMENTAL LEADERS: G—Burrus, 68; AB—Pridie, 285; R—Ringe, 63; H—Pridie, 105; TB—Pridie, 156; 2B—Evans, Rijo, 22 each; 3B—Pridie, 9; HR—Bankston, 18; RBI—Bankston, 57; SH—Lopez, 17; SF—A. Gonzalez, 7; HP—Varela, 10; BB—Done, 54; IBB—Webster, 3; SO—Morris, 73; SB—Lemanczyk, 31; CS—Pridie, 9; GIDP—Ciraco, 11; Slg.—Jimenez, .597; OBP—O'Riordan, .495.

ALL PLAYERS

*Lefthanded batter. †Switch-hitter.

Player, Team	G	TPA	AB	R	H	TB	2B	3B	HR	RBI	SH	SF	HP	BB	IBB	SO	SB	CS	GDP	Avg.	OBP	Slg.
Abreu, Angel, Burl.†	30	121	106	14	30	34	1	0	1	9	3	2	0	10	0	22	4	3	1	.283	.339	.321
Acevedo, Freddy, Mar.	53	237	208	39	59	99	11	1	9	44	1	4	6	18	0	67	11	1	8	.284	.352	.476
Agar, Cory, Eliz.	27	102	92	9	26	38	3	0	3	13	0	2	4	4	0	11	0	0	3	.283	.333	.413
Albert, Luke, Dan.†	4	14	13	1	4	5	1	0	0	1	0	0	1	0	0	1	0	0	0	.308	.357	.385
Alvarez, Gera, Blue.	58	203	175	34	46	63	11	0	2	31	2	2	2	22	1	29	6	4	3	.263	.348	.360
Arhart, Josh, Prin.	55	218	200	25	60	87	15	0	4	31	0	3	2	13	1	28	0	1	7	.300	.344	.435
Arko, Tommy, Blue.	57	226	181	41	48	101	11	0	14	37	1	5	4	35	0	58	0	1	5	.265	.387	.558
Ascencion, Quincy, Blue.	54	221	199	28	47	64	11	0	2	30	0	3	6	13	1	29	7	2	6	.236	.299	.322
Babilonia, Edgar, Mar.	38	145	128	22	35	39	2	1	0	14	5	1	1	10	0	28	18	1	1	.273	.329	.305
Babilonia, Jose, Prin.	7	21	18	1	2	5	0	0	1	3	0	1	2	0	0	11	0	0	0	.111	.190	.278
Baez, Fleming, Pul.	16	54	43	6	7	9	2	0	0	5	0	1	0	10	0	15	1	1	3	.163	.315	.209
Baldiris, Aaron, King.	58	241	217	31	71	91	9	1	3	24	0	1	9	14	0	24	9	5	7	.327	.390	.419
Bankston, Wes, Prin.	62	270	246	48	74	140	10	1	18	57	0	4	1	18	1	46	2	1	3	.301	.346	.569
Batista, Ariel, Mar.	52	247	211	38	48	62	5	3	1	15	7	1	4	23	0	68	12	4	1	.227	.314	.294
Belz, Tim, J.C.	15	39	36	1	6	6	0	0	0	1	0	0	3	0	0	14	1	0	0	.167	.231	.167
Bera, Roberto, Blue.	28	79	72	7	14	25	5	0	2	8	3	3	0	1	0	20	1	1	1	.194	.197	.347
Bessa, Laumin, Dan.	39	118	111	15	32	45	6	2	1	24	0	1	1	5	0	27	4	2	3	.288	.322	.405
Betemit, Richard, Prin.†	45	163	142	18	30	34	0	2	0	10	4	0	1	16	0	36	5	4	1	.211	.296	.239
Beuerlein, Tyler, King.†	31	130	116	11	24	46	1	0	7	16	0	0	6	8	1	40	0	1	2	.207	.292	.397
Bilezikjian, Charlie, Pul.	12	57	44	9	10	12	2	0	0	9	1	1	0	11	0	10	2	1	0	.227	.375	.273
Bohlander, Michael, Bris.*	23	66	62	4	10	15	2	0	1	7	0	1	1	2	0	20	1	1	1	.161	.197	.242
Bounds, Brandon, Bris.*	55	233	193	34	55	100	14	2	9	38	1	1	2	36	0	48	0	0	0	.285	.401	.518
Brice, Thomas, Bris.*	29	115	98	11	32	38	4	1	0	20	1	3	3	10	0	11	1	0	2	.327	.395	.388
Bridges, Josh, J.C.	7	23	21	1	5	6	1	0	0	3	0	0	1	1	0	8	0	0	2	.238	.304	.286
Bryan, Jason, Pul.	14	57	43	13	13	23	1	0	3	12	0	0	2	12	1	14	3	0	1	.302	.474	.535
Bunch, J.C., Pul.	5	18	17	2	3	3	0	0	0	2	0	0	1	0	0	7	0	0	0	.176	.222	.176
Burrus, Josh, Dan.	68	311	263	34	62	77	13	1	0	23	2	3	7	35	0	60	16	7	5	.236	.338	.293
Buscher, Gregory, Pul.	52	212	182	34	49	75	11	0	5	26	0	0	2	28	0	63	1	1	0	.269	.373	.412
Camacho, Johan, King.†	30	110	101	10	22	33	5	0	2	9	1	1	2	5	0	24	0	0	4	.218	.266	.327
Capellan, Domingo, J.C.	33	104	100	13	28	42	8	0	2	9	0	0	3	1	0	20	5	1	1	.280	.308	.420
Carroll, Rich, Pul.	55	241	219	33	57	98	18	1	7	53	0	4	1	17	2	62	4	3	3	.260	.311	.447
Cates, Zach, J.C.*	53	204	170	28	35	68	8	2	7	22	2	3	4	27	0	36	3	2	2	.206	.322	.400
Charles, Julin, Pul.	62	268	241	40	61	101	12	2	8	44	0	2	5	20	0	61	18	3	7	.253	.321	.419
Ciraco, Darren, Bris.	56	251	219	47	72	117	15	0	10	51	1	3	0	27	0	39	2	0	11	.329	.398	.534
Clements, Zachary, King.	16	46	39	4	11	12	1	0	0	3	0	0	0	7	0	9	2	0	1	.282	.391	.308
Cruz, Jose, Burl.†	51	204	178	25	40	53	7	0	2	18	0	2	1	23	0	38	7	2	4	.225	.314	.298
Cruz, Orlando, Pul.	26	97	88	15	24	37	10	0	1	12	0	2	3	5	0	26	2	0	0	.273	.326	.420
Davidson, Aaron, Burl.	15	53	50	6	9	22	2	0	3	9	0	0	0	3	0	15	1	0	2	.180	.226	.440
Davidson, Kevin, Mar.	28	105	95	11	21	31	7	0	1	10	0	2	1	19	0	25	1	1	4	.221	.350	.326
Davie, Andrew, J.C.*	45	179	169	18	37	68	9	2	6	23	0	2	2	8	0	63	6	1	3	.219	.263	.402
Deck, Ronald, Prin.	11	38	31	1	6	8	2	0	0	3	1	1	0	5	0	8	0	0	3	.194	.297	.258
Deeds, Doug, Eliz.*	59	249	203	48	66	105	16	1	7	32	0	3	2	41	0	41	3	1	2	.325	.438	.517
De La Cruz, Christopher, Burl.†	43	201	180	33	66	88	7	6	1	12	2	1	1	17	0	27	13	4	2	.367	.422	.489
Done, Robert, Blue.†	58	256	193	46	61	93	12	1	6	39	0	3	6	54	2	37	6	3	1	.316	.473	.482
Duncan, Trae, Prin.	29	128	116	14	36	48	7	1	1	18	0	4	0	8	0	12	0	0	2	.310	.344	.414
Eldridge, Rashad, Pul.†	17	69	53	12	14	26	2	2	2	14	0	1	0	15	0	6	10	1	2	.264	.420	.491
Elliott, Justin, Eliz.	8	31	29	1	5	5	0	0	0	1	0	0	0	2	0	6	0	0	2	.172	.226	.172
Encarnacion, Teodoro, Burl.	39	166	148	18	35	53	4	4	2	13	0	1	1	17	0	51	5	0	4	.236	.319	.358
Esquivel, Matt, Dan.	61	255	227	38	63	95	13	2	5	41	0	3	4	21	0	67	2	0	4	.278	.345	.419
Estrada, Rafael, J.C.†	7	10	8	2	2	2	0	0	0	0	0	0	1	1	0	3	5	1	1	.250	.400	.250
Evans, Terry, J.C.	60	261	230	42	66	113	22	2	7	41	0	2	0	29	1	67	17	4	5	.287	.364	.491
Fagan, John, Mar.	26	118	86	29	25	41	7	0	3	26	0	4	4	24	0	21	1	2	2	.291	.449	.477
Fernando, Osvaldo, Mar.†	57	243	216	42	62	70	6	1	0	25	4	0	7	16	0	35	8	5	4	.287	.356	.324
Ford, Mark, Bris.	25	81	69	13	16	20	1	0	1	10	0	2	1	10	0	14	1	2	1	.232	.346	.290
Francoeur, Jeff, Dan.	38	167	147	31	48	86	12	1	8	31	0	2	3	15	0	34	8	5	2	.327	.395	.585
Frias, Fernando, Prin.	36	143	130	12	24	41	5	3	2	12	0	0	1	12	0	60	1	2	2	.185	.259	.315
Garcia, Williams, King.†	36	146	136	11	34	47	7	0	2	24	1	1	1	7	1	41	0	6	1	.250	.290	.346
Garcia, Yunir, King.	33	123	90	15	21	33	3	0	3	15	0	2	4	27	0	17	2	1	3	.233	.423	.367
German, Sandino, Prin.	11	23	21	0	2	2	0	0	0	1	0	1	0	1	0	2	0	1	0	.095	.130	.095
Gold, Nate, Pul.	30	132	113	19	36	62	9	1	5	30	1	1	0	17	0	20	2	0	3	.319	.405	.549
Gomon, Dusty, Eliz.	53	223	199	43	60	113	7	2	14	41	0	1	1	22	2	54	1	0	6	.302	.372	.568
Gonzalez, Andy, Eliz.	66	296	254	48	71	91	17	0	1	45	0	7	3	32	1	43	5	4	3	.280	.358	.358
Gonzalez, Jose, Pul.†	27	111	88	13	15	22	4	0	1	12	0	1	0	22	0	22	6	2	2	.170	.333	.250
Grasso, Mike, Dan.	61	196	169	22	34	36	2	0	0	11	1	1	4	21	0	42	22	4	1	.201	.303	.213
Gunn, Cody, J.C.*	29	100	86	8	21	33	6	0	2	11	1	0	4	9	1	22	2	1	3	.244	.343	.384
Guy, Jason, Pul.*	43	159	124	15	26	36	5	1	1	10	0	0	4	32	0	43	11	3	0	.210	.384	.290
Guzman, Carlos, Dan.	51	192	166	21	47	67	12	1	2	22	2	2	1	21	0	54	2	0	1	.283	.363	.404
Guzman, Garrett, Eliz.*	63	276	247	41	69	116	21	4	6	48	2	4	5	18	1	37	3	2	8	.279	.336	.470

Player, Team	G	TPA	AB	R	H	TB	2B	3B	HR	RBI	SH	SF	HP	BB	IBB	SO	SB	CS	GDP	Avg.	OBP	Slg.
Hamblen, Chris, Pul.†	46	190	156	27	27	51	5	2	5	20	2	2	2	28	0	33	1	3	3	.173	.303	.327
Hawkins, Dustin, Mar.*	31	138	118	26	34	46	7	1	1	22	2	0	0	18	0	17	9	1	2	.288	.382	.390
Hileman, Jutt, J.C.	26	102	91	14	17	26	3	0	2	9	0	0	3	8	0	27	1	0	1	.187	.275	.286
Hill, Jamar, King.	56	233	200	34	59	101	14	2	8	31	3	3	5	22	2	48	7	4	2	.295	.374	.505
Hiraldo, Sandy, Eliz.†	36	132	122	23	31	60	3	1	8	27	0	0	1	8	0	28	4	1	2	.254	.305	.492
Hodge, Luis, Burl.	60	255	234	31	63	79	9	2	1	19	0	3	6	12	1	52	1	3	2	.269	.318	.338
Housel, David, King.†	36	131	117	15	29	40	6	1	1	7	3	0	2	7	0	33	2	4	2	.248	.302	.342
Hudson, William, King.†	34	114	96	9	24	36	4	1	2	7	1	1	0	16	0	18	3	2	0	.250	.354	.375
Humphries, Justin, Mar.	51	208	185	30	49	75	11	0	5	28	2	3	3	15	0	49	0	2	4	.265	.325	.405
Huson, Tim, Bris.*	42	143	132	19	35	58	7	2	4	12	0	0	0	11	1	45	3	1	1	.265	.322	.439
Infante, Franklin, Dan.	23	56	51	7	8	14	3	0	1	6	0	1	2	2	0	23	0	0	2	.157	.214	.275
Irvin, Blair, Prin.*	11	39	36	5	6	9	1	1	0	1	1	0	1	1	0	17	2	1	0	.167	.211	.250
Ivy, Bjorn, Bris.	53	201	162	37	44	51	2	1	1	14	2	0	4	33	0	43	15	5	2	.272	.407	.315
Jaime, Willy, Prin.	30	110	101	19	31	51	4	2	4	13	0	0	1	8	0	35	4	0	4	.307	.364	.505
Jansen, Ardley, Dan.	62	224	207	33	61	105	8	3	10	44	1	1	2	13	0	44	9	2	6	.295	.341	.507
Jimenez, Luis, Blue.*	51	211	176	40	66	105	13	1	8	42	0	1	1	33	1	33	9	1	7	.375	.474	.597
Johnson, Elliot, Prin.†	42	172	152	21	40	55	10	1	1	13	1	0	1	18	0	48	14	2	2	.263	.345	.362
Joyce, Tom, Blue.*	44	173	141	35	39	67	11	4	3	15	1	0	1	30	1	34	4	2	1	.277	.407	.475
Jurries, James, Dan.	4	17	15	4	5	9	1	0	1	4	0	0	0	2	0	2	0	0	1	.333	.412	.600
Koslowski, Kasey, Bris.	5	19	15	2	1	1	0	0	0	1	1	0	0	2	1	3	0	0	0	.067	.222	.067
Larson, Ryan, Mar.	31	127	105	11	25	33	5	0	1	16	0	0	4	18	0	21	1	0	1	.238	.370	.314
Lebron, Edgardo, Eliz.†	61	235	219	31	44	66	10	4	4	29	1	5	0	10	1	66	3	1	3	.201	.233	.301
Lee, Carlos, Bris.	15	49	41	6	12	17	5	0	0	7	0	1	2	5	0	5	1	0	0	.293	.388	.415
Lemanczyk, Matt, J.C.	60	236	209	38	50	62	5	2	1	15	4	1	7	15	0	42	31	6	2	.239	.310	.297
Linares, Jesus, King.†	38	156	138	27	35	52	4	2	3	17	1	1	0	16	0	31	3	4	5	.254	.329	.377
Lisk, Charles, Bris.	28	111	104	9	21	34	4	0	3	16	1	2	1	3	0	32	0	0	5	.202	.227	.327
Lopez, Pedro, Bris.	63	298	260	42	83	94	11	0	0	35	17	0	1	20	0	27	22	8	3	.319	.370	.362
Lorsbach, Michael, Mar.*	43	180	142	26	39	54	7	1	2	28	3	4	0	31	1	32	2	0	1	.275	.395	.380
Mannix, Brendan, King.†	24	90	77	6	15	27	3	0	3	11	0	0	1	12	0	22	1	1	2	.195	.311	.351
Marin, Daniel, Eliz.	33	118	101	16	23	32	4	1	1	17	0	1	1	15	0	14	1	1	2	.228	.331	.317
Martinez, Gabriel, Prin.*	60	247	217	28	70	104	17	1	5	26	2	0	1	27	0	38	1	1	2	.323	.400	.479
Martinez, Luis, King.	11	39	34	1	7	9	2	0	0	2	0	1	0	4	0	8	1	2	2	.206	.308	.265
Martinez, Peter, Eliz.†	35	126	114	15	23	38	4	1	3	14	1	0	2	9	0	39	7	4	0	.202	.272	.333
Martinez, Raul, Blue.*	33	81	64	8	11	17	3	0	1	8	1	0	2	14	0	23	2	0	2	.172	.338	.266
Mather, Joe, J.C.	62	256	224	29	52	95	15	2	8	39	0	2	3	27	0	57	9	1	5	.232	.320	.424
Matienzo, Danny, Eliz.	33	133	112	15	34	56	7	0	5	27	1	4	3	13	0	18	1	0	5	.304	.379	.500
McCoy, Mike, J.C.	50	202	154	46	48	71	9	1	4	22	2	1	3	42	0	23	18	7	0	.312	.465	.461
McCullough, Clayton, Burl.*..	20	74	54	5	15	18	3	0	0	8	0	1	1	18	0	8	1	0	1	.278	.459	.333
Melendez, German, Mar.	38	165	141	23	41	50	6	0	1	21	2	4	1	17	0	27	7	5	4	.291	.362	.355
Mendez, Valentin, Mar.	52	235	199	26	61	78	14	0	1	38	5	1	3	27	1	24	8	6	7	.307	.396	.392
Mojica, Robinson, J.C.	27	67	61	10	16	24	3	1	1	5	1	0	1	4	0	20	2	1	0	.262	.318	.393
Molina, Felix, Eliz.†	50	199	175	31	46	68	9	2	3	21	2	1	3	18	1	21	6	1	5	.263	.340	.389
Monette, Daylon, J.C.†	16	65	57	10	21	31	7	0	1	11	0	2	0	6	0	11	4	0	0	.368	.415	.544
Montani, Jeff, Blue.	31	0	0	1	0	0	0	0	0	0	0	0	0	0	0	0	0	0	0	.000	.000	.000
Morales, Porfirio, Blue.	20	46	41	6	5	6	1	0	0	2	0	1	4	0	0	10	0	0	0	.122	.196	.146
Morris, Seth, Bris.	54	205	183	27	40	69	10	2	5	28	1	2	1	18	0	73	2	0	3	.219	.289	.377
Myers, Kenton, Burl.	4	11	7	0	3	4	1	0	0	0	0	0	1	3	0	3	1	0	0	.429	.636	.571
Nichols, Thomas, Prin.	5	17	13	1	4	4	0	0	0	0	0	0	0	4	0	3	1	0	2	.308	.471	.308
Nixon, Jason, Burl.	18	56	53	7	8	13	0	1	1	5	0	0	0	3	0	18	1	1	2	.151	.196	.245
Nolasco, Jose, J.C.†	52	197	188	25	51	86	11	3	6	32	2	1	1	5	0	36	13	4	4	.271	.292	.457
Noviskey, Josh, Burl.†	33	120	98	4	22	33	5	0	2	15	0	2	0	19	0	27	1	0	4	.224	.345	.337
Nunez, Yefresy, Prin.†	24	76	65	5	11	11	0	0	0	8	0	0	1	10	0	17	0	2	1	.169	.289	.169
Oeltjen, Trent, Eliz.*	54	243	215	36	64	84	7	2	3	18	3	2	7	16	0	34	7	5	0	.298	.363	.391
Olivari, Reinaldo, Pul.	4	14	10	4	2	2	0	0	0	1	1	0	0	3	0	2	0	1	0	.200	.385	.200
O'Riordan, Chris, Pul.	48	221	173	37	64	91	16	1	3	24	1	2	8	37	0	20	14	3	3	.370	.495	.526
Pacheco, Fernando, Burl.*	41	156	133	16	25	39	5	0	3	10	0	2	0	21	0	57	1	0	1	.188	.295	.293
Panther, Nathan, Burl.*	34	143	125	17	30	51	7	4	2	21	1	1	0	16	0	22	3	2	5	.240	.324	.408
Paredes, Salvador, Prin.	55	212	186	21	48	53	5	0	0	16	2	1	4	19	0	56	5	3	1	.258	.338	.285
Parra, Carlos, Burl.	26	104	95	11	24	44	6	1	4	18	2	0	2	5	0	26	0	1	2	.253	.304	.463
Peters, Yaron, Dan.	50	200	177	32	43	78	10	2	7	30	0	0	2	21	0	41	1	1	1	.243	.330	.441
Pridie, Jason, Prin.*	67	308	285	60	105	156	12	9	7	33	1	1	2	19	1	35	13	9	2	.368	.410	.547
Reid, Ivan, Prin.*	14	41	36	4	3	3	0	0	0	2	0	1	1	3	0	11	1	0	0	.083	.171	.083
Reyes, Eduardo, J.C.	29	102	94	20	29	49	4	2	4	12	1	0	1	6	0	26	6	1	2	.309	.356	.521
Reynoso, Danilo, King.	15	50	42	8	8	10	2	0	0	1	0	0	1	7	0	12	1	1	3	.190	.320	.238
Richardson, Kevin, Pul.	24	98	83	8	13	20	4	0	1	7	0	0	2	12	1	32	1	1	1	.157	.278	.241
Rijo, Carlos, Blue.	64	259	238	39	74	105	22	0	3	45	0	3	6	12	1	40	9	3	3	.311	.355	.441
Ringe, Craig, Pul.	64	297	236	63	60	72	9	0	1	23	3	2	5	51	0	55	10	1	6	.254	.395	.305
Rivas, Arturo, Blue.	55	241	213	45	58	95	11	1	8	34	4	1	4	19	0	47	11	4	3	.272	.342	.446
Roat, Kyle, Dan.	36	136	124	16	37	55	6	0	4	22	2	0	0	10	0	16	0	0	4	.298	.351	.444
Robinson-Pierce, Whitney, Blue..	18	39	38	3	8	9	1	0	0	2	0	0	1	0	0	8	0	0	1	.211	.231	.237
Robinson, Levi, Blue.	50	187	143	42	40	58	12	0	2	10	5	1	5	33	0	30	18	4	3	.280	.429	.406
Rodriguez, Marcos, J.C.*	18	61	56	7	12	19	3	2	0	9	1	0	1	3	0	20	0	1	0	.214	.267	.339
Rojas, Ricardo, Burl.	55	226	202	23	53	67	5	0	3	26	6	3	3	12	0	54	13	5	5	.262	.309	.332
Rosario, Olmo, Prin.	33	127	115	13	23	39	3	2	3	12	0	1	3	8	0	21	1	0	4	.200	.268	.339
Ruelas, Alonzo, Dan.	35	134	121	17	40	52	6	0	2	13	1	1	2	9	0	8	1	1	3	.331	.383	.430
Ruiz, Daniel, Dan.	49	159	135	19	31	42	8	0	1	6	1	0	3	20	1	30	1	0	2	.230	.342	.311
Sarabia, Hamilton, Mar.*	64	285	238	50	67	84	9	1	2	32	2	4	7	34	1	44	18	4	6	.282	.382	.353
Schilling, Micah, Burl.	33	145	126	13	26	34	6	1	0	10	0	1	3	15	0	39	5	2	4	.206	.303	.270
Schuerholz, Jon, Dan.	66	295	245	40	58	71	7	3	0	14	8	1	3	38	0	47	11	4	1	.237	.345	.290
Simmons, Coltyn, Prin.	31	119	113	12	41	49	4	2	0	8	0	0	1	5	2	13	1	1	6	.363	.395	.434
Sims, Justin, Eliz.*	37	128	109	18	27	39	4	1	2	13	1	0	2	16	1	21	1	2	2	.248	.354	.358
Skinner, Steve, Prin.	4	12	12	2	1	1	0	0	0	0	0	0	0	0	0	3	0	0	0	.083	.083	.083

Player, Team	G	TPA	AB	R	H	TB	2B	3B	HR	RBI	SH	SF	HP	BB	IBB	SO	SB	CS	GDP	Avg.	OBP	Slg.
Smallwood, Erik, Blue.*	53	224	186	36	40	80	10	0	10	37	0	1	0	37	0	62	4	1	3	.215	.344	.430
Solano, Roberto, King............	57	246	228	25	63	96	13	4	4	31	1	6	4	7	0	51	6	1	3	.276	.302	.421
Soto, Yllysh, King.†	33	136	122	18	34	45	3	1	2	12	0	0	2	12	0	17	2	3	0	.279	.353	.369
Stewart, Chris, Bris...............	42	181	158	25	44	56	9	0	1	12	4	1	4	14	0	23	0	0	2	.278	.350	.354
Sulbaran, Orlando, Pul..........	25	98	84	11	18	26	3	1	1	11	1	2	1	10	0	13	4	0	3	.214	.299	.310
Taylor, Sam, Eliz.†	48	174	146	25	33	41	5	0	1	10	1	2	3	22	0	22	8	5	2	.226	.335	.281
Threinen, Scott, Burl.............	7	29	22	5	6	11	2	0	1	1	1	0	2	4	0	2	0	0	2	.273	.429	.500
Tolotti, Jeff, J.C.*	31	125	114	14	33	50	5	6	0	10	0	1	0	10	0	37	1	0	2	.289	.344	.439
Torres, Eider, Burl.†	45	218	194	26	62	70	6	1	0	13	8	0	1	15	0	22	28	3	4	.320	.371	.361
Torres, Saul, Mar...................	54	233	192	46	52	72	10	2	2	28	2	1	2	36	2	35	4	1	3	.271	.390	.375
Varela, Edgar, Bris.*..............	55	216	188	30	62	99	11	1	8	40	1	4	10	13	2	29	0	1	1	.330	.395	.527
Vasquez, Domingo, Burl........	51	197	187	17	37	56	7	0	4	18	2	3	0	5	0	48	2	1	3	.198	.215	.299
Veloz, Gabe, J.C....................	49	201	152	19	38	56	12	0	2	23	0	2	3	44	0	43	2	3	2	.250	.423	.368
Volquez, Julio, Pul.†	41	148	130	20	33	43	7	0	1	18	0	1	9	8	0	20	18	1	3	.254	.338	.331
Watts, Derran, King...............	49	219	179	33	46	73	15	3	2	20	2	2	6	30	0	50	18	6	3	.257	.378	.408
Webster, Anthony, Bris.*........	61	291	244	58	86	102	7	3	1	30	1	2	6	38	3	38	16	7	1	.352	.448	.418
Wendt, Justin, King.*.............	41	157	140	22	33	44	3	1	2	15	0	0	6	11	1	21	3	0	4	.236	.318	.314
Whitney, Matthew, Burl.	45	198	175	33	50	94	12	1	10	33	0	2	3	18	2	49	5	1	4	.286	.359	.537
Whitrock, Scott, Eliz.............	48	178	160	27	48	83	10	2	7	23	2	1	3	11	0	50	12	2	3	.300	.354	.519
Wilson, Brandon, King............	35	147	139	11	35	48	7	0	2	12	0	0	0	8	0	35	0	2	5	.252	.293	.345
Wilson, Laron, King.	13	38	37	4	8	12	1	0	1	2	0	0	1	0	0	11	1	0	0	.216	.237	.324
Woodruff, Ernest, Prin...........	39	143	127	14	33	49	4	0	4	14	1	0	2	13	0	31	0	1	3	.260	.338	.386
Woods, Ahmad, Dan..............	31	86	79	11	14	23	2	2	1	12	0	0	2	5	0	31	1	1	2	.177	.244	.291
Yount, Dustin, Blue.*	61	248	203	38	49	100	9	0	14	51	1	6	2	35	1	44	3	0	2	.241	.350	.493

GRAND SLAMS: Bankston, 3; Acevedo, Bryan, Carroll, K. Davidson, J. Gonzalez, Hawkins, Ja. Hill, Hiraldo, Humphries, Jansen, Jimenez, Lebron, Lorsbach, Panther, Peters, Roat, Varela, 1 each.

AWARDED FIRST BASE ON CATCHER'S INTERFERENCE: Housel 2 (Melendez, Ruelas); Bankston (Melendez), Batista (Stewart), Burrus (Agar), Ciraco (Noviskey), Hiraldo (Lisk), Noviskey (Marin), Richardson (R. Martinez), Whitrock (Capellan), Yount (Agar).

2002 PITCHING
TEAM

Team	W	L	Pct.	ERA	G	CG	ShO	Sv.	IP	H	TBF	R	ER	HR	SH	SF	HB	BB	IBB	SO	WP	Bk.
Danville	37	31	.544	3.31	68	1	4	21	584.0	531	2498	284	215	31	27	21	33	209	1	584	28	1
Bristol	43	25	.632	3.60	68	0	6	17	602.0	544	2595	292	241	31	16	15	37	271	9	539	51	17
Burlington	29	39	.426	4.23	68	0	3	13	608.0	609	2731	366	286	52	33	26	44	304	1	521	66	9
Elizabethton	37	30	.552	4.24	67	0	5	21	577.2	537	2545	330	272	42	20	21	29	286	8	594	47	4
Martinsville	41	26	.612	4.32	67	0	4	15	587.0	573	2640	341	282	53	15	26	33	295	1	570	46	8
Bluefield	45	23	.662	4.47	68	1	1	20	592.1	608	2657	366	294	54	18	15	50	275	14	522	51	10
Johnson City	29	38	.433	5.04	67	0	1	15	573.1	646	2605	400	321	57	20	15	36	235	3	500	55	9
Kingsport	23	44	.343	5.21	67	0	1	7	580.0	648	2633	410	336	56	13	37	47	235	0	495	55	10
Pulaski	34	32	.515	5.31	66	0	2	16	559.0	638	2530	375	330	56	16	19	40	226	4	442	55	6
Princeton..........	19	49	.279	5.76	68	1	1	8	585.2	692	2732	485	375	62	15	26	34	296	5	434	66	18

INDIVIDUAL

TOP QUALIFIERS FOR EARNED-RUN AVERAGE TITLE

Minimum 54 innings.*Lefthanded pitcher.

Pitcher, Team	W	L	Pct.	ERA	G	GS	CG	ShO	GF	Sv.	IP	H	TBF	R	ER	HR	SH	SF	HB	BB	IBB	SO	WP	Bk.
Barrett, Ricky, Eliz.*	7	1	.875	1.27	12	11	0	0	0	0	63.2	49	256	15	9	2	3	2	0	25	0	79	4	1
Lerew, Anthony, Dan.	8	3	.727	1.73	14	14	0	0	0	0	83	60	327	23	16	2	3	2	5	25	0	75	0	0
Nieve, Fernando, Mar.	4	1	.800	2.39	13	13	0	0	0	0	67.2	46	280	23	18	5	1	2	2	27	0	60	1	0
Reed, Rylan, Bris.....................	3	0	1.000	2.44	12	12	0	0	0	0	55.1	38	236	23	15	2	3	3	7	37	0	44	6	1
Meyer, Dan, Dan.*..................	3	3	.500	2.74	13	13	1	0	0	0	65.2	47	262	22	20	4	2	0	5	18	0	77	4	0
Tyler, Scott, Eliz.....................	8	1	.889	2.93	14	13	0	0	0	0	67.2	37	278	23	22	5	0	1	1	46	0	92	5	0
Tracey, Sean, Bris..................	5	2	.714	3.02	13	12	0	0	0	0	65.2	57	261	27	22	4	1	0	4	19	0	50	1	0
Escobar, Rodrigo, Mar..........	6	2	.750	3.12	16	10	0	0	3	0	78	71	320	33	27	7	3	0	1	18	0	64	1	1
Hawksworth, Blake, J.C........	2	4	.333	3.14	12	12	0	0	0	0	66	58	275	31	23	8	1	1	4	18	0	61	4	0
Morales, Ruddy, Bris..............	6	0	1.000	3.15	13	13	0	0	0	0	65.2	62	273	26	23	4	1	4	4	21	0	45	4	4
Cabrera, Daniel, Blue.............	5	2	.714	3.28	12	12	0	0	0	0	60.1	52	253	25	22	0	1	1	4	25	0	69	2	2
Carmona, Fausto, Burl............	4	4	.333	3.30	11	11	0	0	2	1	76.1	89	326	34	28	4	4	4	6	10	0	42	1	3
Adamczyk, Tyler, J.C.	4	3	.571	3.41	13	11	0	0	1	0	63.1	56	281	31	24	3	1	1	3	35	0	54	9	2
Alvarez, Juan, Dan.*..............	3	5	.375	3.46	13	13	0	0	0	0	65	61	278	35	25	2	4	1	6	27	1	71	4	0
Davies, Kyle, Dan..................	5	3	.625	3.50	14	14	0	0	0	0	69.1	73	307	39	27	2	1	3	2	23	0	62	1	0

DEPARTMENTAL LEADERS: W—Freeman, 9; L—T. King, 9; Pct.—Freeman, .900; G—Montani, J. Morales, 30 each; GS—Davies, Lara, Lerew, 14 each; CG—J. Farrell, Meyer, Tiller, 1 each; ShO—Tiller, 1; GF—Montani, 26; Sv.—Tadeba, 16; IP—Lerew, 83.0; H—Carmona, 89; TBF—Lerew, 327; R—Peguero, 55; ER—Peguero, Sanchez, 45 each; HR—Narron, 10; SH—Adams, Kirsten, 5 each; SF—Prunty, 6; HB—Machen, 8; BB—Tyler, 46; IBB—Larson, 4; SO—Tyler, 92; WP—Haynes, 11; BK—B. Miller, 6.

ALL PITCHERS
*Lefthanded pitcher.

Pitcher, Team	W	L	Pct.	ERA	G	GS	CG	ShO	GF	Sv.	IP	H	TBF	R	ER	HR	SH	SF	HB	BB	IBB	SO	WP	Bk.
Abreu, Angel, Burl.	0	0	.000	0.00	1	0	0	0	1	0	0.2	3	5	2	0	0	0	1	0	0	0	0	1	0
Acosta, Anthony, King...........	4	1	.800	3.86	11	0	0	0	5	0	21	23	89	11	9	3	0	0	3	2	0	26	1	0
Acosta, Jasiel, Dan.*	2	2	.500	4.83	7	6	0	0	0	0	31.2	37	136	21	17	4	0	1	0	6	0	28	0	0
Acosta, Richal, Blue.	1	1	.500	6.39	3	3	0	0	0	0	12.2	19	58	10	9	3	0	1	0	2	0	12	0	0
Adamczyk, Tyler, J.C.	4	3	.571	3.41	13	11	0	0	1	0	63.1	56	281	31	24	3	1	1	3	35	0	54	9	2

Pitcher, Team	W	L	Pct.	ERA	G	GS	CG	ShO	GF	Sv.	IP	H	TBF	R	ER	HR	SH	SF	HB	BB	IBB	SO	WP	Bk.
Adams, Josh, Dan.*	1	5	.167	3.62	20	0	0	0	11	0	37.1	32	155	19	15	4	5	4	0	9	0	37	3	0
Aguero, Miguel, J.C.	3	3	.500	5.58	14	7	0	0	0	0	40.1	43	185	35	25	5	2	3	4	16	0	39	4	0
Aguilar, Ray, Dan.*	0	0	.000	0.00	1	0	0	0	1	0	2	1	9	1	0	0	0	0	0	2	0	0	0	0
Albers, Matthew, Mar.	2	3	.400	5.13	13	13	0	0	0	0	59.2	61	273	38	34	2	2	3	7	38	0	72	5	1
Alfonzo, Edgar, King.*	0	0	.000	1.13	6	0	0	0	2	0	8	9	35	2	1	0	1	0	1	3	0	5	2	1
Allen, Brian, Prin.*	0	0	.000	4.50	3	0	0	0	1	0	4	6	18	3	2	0	0	1	0	0	0	2	1	0
Ally, Ben, Mar.	4	3	.571	2.72	13	0	0	0	9	2	39.2	35	167	21	12	2	2	2	0	10	0	36	2	0
Almeida, Brian, Dan.	0	1	.000	3.91	13	1	0	0	2	0	23	22	109	13	10	0	2	1	0	15	0	17	2	0
Alvarado, Luis, Burl.*	4	1	.800	2.12	18	0	0	0	12	2	34	29	148	11	8	1	3	2	0	18	0	29	4	0
Alvarez, Juan, Dan.*	3	5	.375	3.46	13	13	0	0	0	0	65	61	278	35	25	2	4	1	6	27	1	71	4	0
Andrew, Jason, Pul.	0	0	.000	1.29	3	0	0	0	2	0	7	5	27	1	1	0	0	0	1	0	0	10	0	0
Arteaga, Francisco, Dan.	4	4	.500	3.48	21	0	0	0	8	2	33.2	36	158	19	13	3	1	1	6	10	0	43	2	1
Baez, Fleming, Pul.	0	0	.000	0.00	1	0	0	0	1	0	1	4	8	4	0	0	0	0	0	0	0	0	0	1
Barnett, John, Pul.	0	0	.000	0.00	1	1	0	0	0	0	3	0	9	0	0	0	0	0	0	0	0	1	0	0
Barrett, Ricky, Eliz.*	7	1	.875	1.27	12	11	0	0	0	0	63.2	49	256	15	9	2	3	2	0	25	0	79	4	1
Barrios, Angel, Mar.	1	0	1.000	1.40	7	0	0	0	2	0	19.1	13	79	3	3	0	1	0	1	7	0	26	0	0
Beltre, Juan, Mar.*	3	4	.429	3.89	24	0	0	0	19	6	41.2	41	182	20	18	5	1	3	1	16	0	52	1	2
Blackburn, Nick, Eliz.	3	3	.500	5.00	13	13	0	0	0	0	66.2	70	293	41	37	6	2	0	2	21	0	62	1	0
Brewer, Jeff, King.	1	1	.500	5.59	10	0	0	0	7	0	19.1	27	94	20	12	5	0	1	2	3	0	22	2	0
Britton, Chris, Blue.	3	0	1.000	4.54	9	8	0	0	1	0	35.2	30	145	21	18	5	1	2	0	10	0	27	0	0
Burton, T.J., Burl.	1	4	.200	7.36	12	12	0	0	0	0	44	56	213	39	36	8	3	2	4	24	0	29	8	0
Bush, Paul, Dan.	4	1	.800	2.35	20	2	0	0	4	0	46	39	192	19	12	2	3	1	1	14	0	48	0	0
Cabrera, Daniel, Blue.	5	2	.714	3.28	12	12	0	0	0	0	60.1	52	253	25	22	0	1	1	4	25	0	69	2	2
Carmona, Fausto, Burl.	2	4	.333	3.30	13	11	0	0	2	1	76.1	89	326	36	28	4	4	4	6	10	0	42	1	3
Casey, Reid, Burl.	2	4	.333	3.46	17	1	0	0	7	1	41.2	38	183	22	16	7	0	0	4	14	0	46	4	0
Castro, Rafael, King.	3	5	.375	4.80	13	12	0	0	0	0	54.1	61	239	32	29	7	0	3	1	22	0	40	7	0
Cevette, Dan, Burl.*	2	4	.333	4.67	13	13	0	0	0	0	52	52	230	32	27	3	3	3	1	31	0	36	6	1
Chafey, Hal, J.C.*	0	2	.000	6.10	17	0	0	0	7	1	20.2	22	105	17	14	1	3	0	3	19	1	20	2	0
Clements, Zachary, King.	0	1	.000	9.00	1	0	0	0	1	0	2	2	10	2	2	0	2	0	0	1	0	3	1	0
Coppinger, Joe, Blue.	5	2	.714	4.38	12	12	0	0	0	0	63.2	68	277	39	31	9	1	1	3	20	0	49	4	0
Corrado, Rob, Pul.	2	1	.667	3.86	8	4	0	0	2	0	30.1	32	133	15	13	2	0	0	3	9	0	20	1	1
Crain, Jesse, Eliz.	2	1	.667	0.57	9	0	0	0	6	2	15.2	4	61	2	1	0	2	1	1	7	3	18	0	0
Cristobal, Luis, Pul.	0	0	.000	5.19	3	1	0	0	2	1	8.2	10	41	5	5	0	0	1	2	4	0	4	2	0
Crump, Joel, Blue.*	1	0	1.000	2.49	15	0	0	0	3	0	21.2	23	101	13	6	0	1	0	2	10	1	25	2	2
Curreri, Joe, Bris.	2	0	1.000	2.00	9	0	0	0	3	2	18	11	73	6	4	1	0	0	0	5	0	18	1	1
Danly, Ryan, King.*	2	3	.400	5.03	13	8	0	0	1	0	53.2	61	238	34	30	2	1	3	3	17	0	27	1	0
David, Brad, Dan.*	3	1	.750	3.00	13	3	0	0	3	2	24	20	96	9	8	2	0	1	7	0	0	27	0	0
Davies, Kyle, Dan.	5	3	.625	3.50	14	14	0	0	0	0	69.1	73	307	39	27	2	1	3	2	23	0	62	1	0
Davis, Jeff, Burl.	0	0	.000	6.00	2	0	0	0	0	0	3	5	15	2	2	0	1	1	0	1	0	1	0	0
DeBarr, Nick, Prin.	3	1	.750	4.71	11	6	0	0	2	0	49.2	60	219	31	26	5	2	4	4	12	1	31	4	1
Deininger, Todd, Bris.	0	1	.000	1.38	19	0	0	0	1	1	39	26	161	9	6	1	1	1	1	20	0	41	3	0
DeLeon, Maikel, King.	0	2	.000	5.40	9	4	0	0	0	0	23.1	25	102	18	14	4	0	4	1	6	0	19	1	0
DePaula, Julio, Eliz.	0	2	.000	9.13	5	5	0	0	0	0	23.2	40	118	25	24	1	1	2	1	9	1	15	3	0
Devenney, Nick, Pul.	2	5	.286	8.33	21	0	0	0	4	0	40	50	205	38	37	2	2	2	3	35	0	39	5	0
Done, Robert, Blue.	1	0	1.000	0.00	1	0	0	0	1	0	1	3	3	0	0	0	0	0	0	0	0	2	0	0
Douglas, Shea, Burl.*	3	1	.750	1.36	12	0	0	0	6	1	33	26	141	13	5	1	2	0	1	10	0	49	4	0
Douglass, Chance, Mar.	2	1	.667	3.65	12	9	0	0	1	0	44.1	45	195	19	18	4	0	4	1	23	0	34	4	1
Dowdy, Justin, Bris.*	6	4	.600	3.72	13	11	0	0	0	0	58	61	251	29	24	4	1	0	2	21	0	47	1	0
Elliott, Adam, King.	2	2	.500	3.16	11	8	0	0	0	0	42.2	27	166	16	15	6	0	1	3	14	0	37	2	0
Escobar, Rodrigo, Mar.	6	2	.750	3.12	16	10	0	0	3	0	78	71	320	33	27	7	3	0	1	18	0	64	1	1
Estes, Jonathan, J.C.	4	1	.800	3.38	11	5	0	0	0	0	42.2	55	188	20	16	1	1	6	0	25	3	1	
Estrada, Paul, Mar.	2	2	.500	11.65	14	6	0	0	2	0	31.2	45	184	45	41	2	1	2	7	36	0	42	9	1
Farrell, Jarrod, Prin.	3	3	.500	3.59	12	8	1	0	0	0	57.2	46	237	34	23	5	2	0	2	24	0	34	2	1
Farrell, Sean, King.*	4	3	.571	6.98	20	0	0	0	12	0	29.2	39	148	24	23	2	2	2	2	22	0	26	3	0
Fischer, Sam, Mar.	3	2	.600	4.50	8	8	0	0	0	0	38	37	170	23	19	7	0	2	1	23	0	27	3	0
Freeman, Daniel, Mar.	9	1	.900	2.96	20	0	0	0	13	6	45.2	47	211	23	15	3	3	0	5	18	0	50	4	0
Freites, Julio, King.	1	4	.200	12.00	17	1	0	0	7	0	30	40	165	43	40	6	0	1	6	24	0	28	7	2
Frydendall, Craig, Pul.*	3	3	.500	4.40	16	7	0	0	6	1	43	46	194	23	21	4	1	2	3	23	1	35	3	0
Fryson, Andrew, Bris.	0	0	.000	4.50	3	1	0	0	0	0	4	5	17	2	2	0	0	0	0	2	0	0	0	0
Furnald, Donnie, Dan.	0	0	.000	8.31	4	0	0	0	1	0	4.1	1	21	4	4	0	0	1	3	7	0	1	3	0
Galbraith, Jason, J.C.*	1	2	.333	2.63	22	0	0	0	8	2	27.1	27	125	15	8	1	1	2	3	11	0	27	7	1
Garay, Kelvin, King.*	0	0	.000	6.48	6	0	0	0	1	0	8.1	8	38	6	6	1	0	1	1	5	0	7	3	0
Garcia, Benjamin, Pul.	2	1	.667	5.09	15	0	0	0	0	0	23	15	105	14	13	2	0	1	2	22	1	24	4	0
Garner, Isiah, Prin.*	0	0	.000	3.86	17	0	0	0	10	1	21	21	94	11	9	2	1	1	0	13	0	16	4	1
George, Jahseam, Burl.*	2	2	.500	4.86	15	0	0	0	4	1	33.1	40	154	23	18	5	3	2	1	16	0	29	2	0
George, Taylor, King.	0	3	.000	5.79	13	9	0	0	1	0	46.2	55	222	38	30	3	1	4	3	24	0	39	3	1
Guzman, Henry, Prin.*	0	0	.000	13.50	5	0	0	0	2	0	4	9	32	11	6	2	0	0	0	9	0	4	3	1
Hammel, Jason, Prin.	0	0	.000	0.00	2	0	0	0	1	1	5.1	7	22	0	0	0	0	0	0	5	0	5	0	0
Hawksworth, Blake, J.C.	2	4	.333	3.14	13	12	0	0	0	0	66	58	275	31	23	8	1	1	4	18	0	61	4	0
Haynes, Matthew, Mar.	3	3	.500	3.93	13	8	0	0	1	0	50.1	40	226	28	22	5	2	3	5	33	0	48	11	1
Hemus, Jared, Eliz.*	0	0	.000	2.70	4	0	0	0	1	1	10	11	46	7	3	0	0	1	2	0	1	13	0	0
Henkenjohann, Tim, Eliz.	2	3	.400	6.82	10	6	0	0	0	0	33	34	168	33	25	4	1	0	3	31	0	34	9	2
Henry, Paul, Blue.	2	1	.667	4.71	16	0	0	0	7	3	21	25	95	11	11	2	0	0	0	9	0	31	0	1
Herrera, Cesar, Pul.	3	3	.500	6.24	13	7	0	0	3	0	53.1	77	251	43	37	8	1	0	2	20	0	41	4	1
Hill, Josh, Eliz.	2	1	.667	2.18	10	0	0	0	3	0	20.2	12	85	6	5	0	0	0	0	13	1	23	1	0
Hogan, Gary, Pul.	1	2	.333	5.04	12	2	0	0	7	2	33	33	118	19	14	4	2	1	1	6	2	29	8	5
Hummel, Rick, Bris.*	1	1	.500	2.59	24	0	0	0	16	5	31.1	24	124	10	9	1	0	0	1	10	0	26	2	0
Humphries, Justin, Mar.	0	0	.000	10.80	1	0	0	0	1	0	1.2	1	9	2	2	0	2	0	3	0	1	0	0	
Johnson, James, Blue.	4	2	.667	4.37	11	9	0	0	0	0	55.2	52	231	36	27	5	2	2	3	16	2	36	1	1
Jones, Alvin, Blue.	0	0	.000	5.79	18	0	0	0	8	0	18.2	18	95	14	12	3	0	0	4	17	0	18	6	0
Keeling, Justin, Eliz.*	3	1	.750	6.16	22	0	0	0	11	0	30.2	37	142	26	21	3	2	2	0	16	1	34	8	0
Keinath, Tim, Prin.	2	1	.667	3.29	17	0	0	0	5	1	27.1	33	127	14	10	1	1	0	0	7	2	23	6	2

Pitcher, Team	W	L	Pct.	ERA	G	GS	CG	ShO	GF	Sv.	IP	H	TBF	R	ER	HR	SH	SF	HB	BB	IBB	SO	WP	Bk.
Killalea, John, J.C.*	3	1	.750	7.36	15	3	0	0	0	0	40.1	56	191	37	33	5	0	1	3	19	0	30	4	1
King, Bryan, King.	0	2	.000	3.23	14	0	0	0	8	3	30.2	24	131	13	11	1	1	3	7	13	0	34	3	0
King, Timothy, Prin.*	2	9	.182	6.20	14	11	0	0	0	0	45	59	220	41	31	4	0	2	1	27	0	30	4	1
Kirsten, Joel, Pul.*	2	1	.667	4.29	18	6	0	0	12	6	50.1	55	220	30	24	6	5	2	2	12	0	50	2	0
LaMura, B.J., Bris.	1	2	.333	4.50	11	0	0	0	2	0	18	21	85	11	9	1	2	0	1	7	1	20	4	0
Lara, Juan, Burl.*	2	6	.250	4.98	14	14	0	0	0	0	65	67	283	42	36	4	3	1	7	28	0	50	0	2
Larson, Adam, Bris.	2	1	.667	3.06	26	0	0	0	18	8	35.1	35	154	16	12	0	2	1	4	9	4	34	1	2
Lavergne, Jarrad, Prin.*	0	1	1.000	7.80	8	0	0	0	1	0	15	22	80	16	13	1	0	1	0	15	0	20	3	0
Ledbetter, Aaron, J.C.	2	4	.333	7.21	16	4	0	0	1	0	43.2	46	197	41	35	6	1	1	4	17	0	49	3	1
Lerew, Anthony, Dan.	8	3	.727	1.73	14	14	0	0	0	0	83	60	327	23	16	2	3	2	5	25	0	75	0	0
Lindstrom, Matthew, King.	0	6	.000	4.84	12	11	0	0	1	0	48.1	56	228	45	26	6	1	4	2	21	0	39	4	1
Loe, Kameron, Pul.	4	4	.500	4.47	14	11	0	0	2	1	58.1	64	263	34	29	3	3	1	6	17	0	55	6	1
Lohse, Eric, Eliz.	2	2	.500	5.35	8	7	0	0	0	0	37	39	162	23	22	7	1	3	1	14	0	20	1	1
Long, Brent, Mar.	1	3	.250	7.99	17	0	0	0	3	0	23.2	24	134	27	21	2	0	3	2	38	1	18	8	2
Lopez, Aleurys, Prin.	1	3	.250	7.48	15	0	0	0	11	2	21.2	31	102	21	18	4	1	1	0	9	1	19	4	4
Machen, Mike, Blue.	4	0	1.000	7.20	21	1	0	0	4	0	30	31	158	30	24	5	2	1	8	28	2	22	5	0
Maio, Mitch, J.C.	1	3	.250	2.67	24	0	0	0	6	0	33.2	29	138	12	10	2	1	0	2	7	0	35	1	0
Maldonado, Ivan, King.	0	0	.000	3.86	3	0	0	0	1	0	7	9	30	6	3	0	0	2	0	0	0	5	0	2
Mann, Brandon, Prin.*	1	2	.333	5.40	10	0	0	0	3	0	18.1	16	83	17	11	1	1	2	2	14	0	15	1	0
Martinez, Paul, Burl.*	1	2	.667	3.50	16	0	0	0	8	0	36	35	168	23	14	1	2	3	3	25	0	32	7	0
Mason, Robert, Dan.*	0	1	.000	3.24	3	1	0	0	1	0	8.1	11	40	4	3	0	1	2	1	2	0	3	0	0
McClellan, Kyle, J.C.	0	2	.000	11.25	7	3	0	0	1	0	12	17	60	17	15	3	0	1	7	0	8	3	0
McGary, Gerron, Bris.*	2	3	.400	5.90	20	0	0	0	9	0	29	29	138	25	19	2	2	1	24	0	34	5	0
McLemore, Mark, Mar.*	0	1	.000	1.80	4	2	0	0	0	0	10	9	44	3	2	0	0	1	0	5	0	11	0	0
Meisenheimer, Matt, Pul.	0	0	.000	20.00	8	0	0	0	4	0	9	13	59	22	20	4	0	0	14	0	4	9	0
Mendoza, Jorge, Pul.	0	0	.000	27.00	1	0	0	0	1	0	0.1	0	2	1	1	0	0	0	1	0	0	0	0
Meyer, Dan, Dan.*	3	3	.500	2.74	13	13	1	0	0	0	65.2	47	262	22	20	4	2	0	5	18	0	77	4	0
Miller, Brian, Bris.	7	3	.700	4.30	13	13	0	0	0	0	60.2	57	262	32	29	3	2	1	2	30	0	63	3	6
Miller, Eric, Prin.*	0	2	.000	7.23	8	5	0	0	1	0	23.2	29	110	21	19	5	1	0	2	13	0	18	1	0
Mondesir, James, J.C.	1	6	.143	8.26	14	9	0	0	1	0	40.1	60	198	46	37	9	2	1	2	21	0	27	4	0
Montani, Jeff, Blue.	3	3	.500	2.34	30	0	0	0	26	15	34.2	30	148	12	9	0	1	1	5	15	1	34	1	0
Morales, Juan, J.C.	2	0	.000	4.24	30	0	0	0	16	6	34	36	148	19	16	2	3	0	1	15	0	42	2	2
Morales, Ruddy, Bris.	6	0	1.000	3.15	13	13	0	0	0	0	65.2	62	273	26	23	4	1	4	4	21	0	45	4	4
Morban, Domingo, King.*	1	0	1.000	6.88	8	0	0	0	1	0	17	18	76	13	13	1	0	0	2	8	0	21	5	0
Moreno, Adam, Prin.	3	0	.000	4.33	14	8	0	0	3	0	62.1	68	275	39	30	4	1	5	4	22	0	40	2	1
Mueller, Mike, Dan.	3	2	.600	4.80	20	0	0	0	9	0	30	33	140	22	16	2	2	1	1	18	0	27	2	0
Narron, Sam, Pul.*	6	1	.857	3.88	14	9	0	0	5	3	69.2	78	279	34	30	10	1	3	0	8	0	50	3	0
Narveson, Chris, J.C.*	0	2	.000	4.91	6	6	0	0	0	0	18.1	23	83	12	10	2	0	1	1	6	0	16	0	0
Nash, Justin, Blue.	0	3	.000	5.18	16	7	0	0	2	1	48.2	58	224	35	28	6	1	0	3	16	0	39	6	0
Neshek, Pat, Eliz.	0	2	.000	0.99	23	0	0	0	22	15	27.1	13	102	6	3	0	1	0	2	6	0	41	1	0
Niedbalski, Nick, Eliz.*	2	4	.333	4.95	22	0	0	0	6	0	36.1	37	165	23	20	1	0	0	19	0	41	1	0
Nieve, Fernando, Mar.	4	1	.800	2.39	13	13	0	0	0	0	67.2	46	280	23	18	5	1	2	2	27	0	60	1	0
Nowlen, Jake, Bris.	1	0	.000	9.00	2	0	0	0	2	0	2	2	10	2	2	0	1	0	2	1	1	0	0
Osberg, Tanner, King.	1	1	.500	3.50	3	3	0	0	0	0	18	15	73	7	7	2	2	2	2	4	0	9	0	1
Parker, Aaron, Dan.	0	1	1.000	5.66	18	1	0	0	5	1	35	37	164	26	22	5	0	2	1	18	0	39	6	0
Patitucci, Mike, Blue.*	4	0	1.000	1.44	24	0	0	0	3	1	31.1	26	131	7	5	1	2	0	0	16	3	38	0	0
Paulk, Robert, King.	1	3	.250	7.91	10	1	0	0	7	1	21.2	26	95	13	7	2	1	3	0	8	0	19	0	0
Paustian, Michael, Pul.	1	2	.333	6.96	12	3	0	0	3	0	32.1	44	158	26	25	4	0	2	3	20	0	21	4	1
Payne, Matt, Bris.	0	2	.000	4.30	20	0	0	0	10	1	23	21	107	14	11	1	1	3	14	1	27	4	0
Peguero, Tony, Prin.	0	6	.000	7.45	13	11	0	0	1	0	54.1	80	254	55	45	8	1	1	6	13	0	28	6	1
Pereyra, Honeudis, Burl.	4	2	.667	2.73	10	0	0	0	6	1	26.1	9	112	10	8	0	3	1	2	22	1	46	3	0
Perez, Armando, Bris.*	5	1	.833	3.55	19	4	0	0	4	0	50.2	48	219	22	20	3	1	3	2	19	1	39	7	2
Prunty, Thomas, Eliz.	3	7	.300	4.45	13	10	0	0	0	0	62.2	77	271	38	31	9	4	6	5	9	0	42	1	0
Pylate, Chad, Eliz.	0	0	.000	8.44	4	0	0	0	1	0	5.1	4	24	5	5	0	0	0	5	0	2	0	0
Reed, Rylan, Bris.	3	0	1.000	2.44	12	12	0	0	0	0	55.1	38	236	23	15	2	0	2	3	37	0	44	6	1
Reedy, Shane, J.C.	0	0	.000	2.16	3	3	0	0	0	0	8.1	7	34	3	2	0	0	1	0	0	0	7	0	0
Rodriguez, Felix, Prin.	4	4	.500	5.14	15	8	0	0	1	0	49	50	231	40	28	5	0	2	3	30	0	35	4	2
Rondon, Celso, King.	2	1	.667	6.37	17	0	0	0	5	0	35.1	48	172	31	25	1	2	2	2	23	0	32	3	0
Rowe, Steven, Pul.	2	1	.667	3.00	5	0	0	0	2	1	9	7	34	4	3	0	0	0	0	1	0	12	1	0
Rupe, Joshua, Bris.	3	3	.500	5.26	17	2	0	0	2	0	37.2	38	173	23	22	4	1	0	4	22	1	40	6	1
Sager, Brian, Bris.	0	1	.000	12.46	6	0	0	0	1	0	8.2	9	51	15	12	0	0	0	5	11	0	8	3	0
Sala, Marino, Blue.	3	0	1.000	5.40	27	0	0	0	7	0	36.2	44	177	31	22	6	1	1	3	21	1	34	7	3
Salazar, Richard, Blue.*	1	0	1.000	0.82	7	0	0	0	1	0	11	3	43	1	1	0	1	1	2	5	1	15	1	0
Samuel, Dauwill, Prin.	1	3	.250	7.65	18	0	0	0	5	0	20	22	103	21	17	0	1	0	2	21	0	25	7	0
Sanchez, Juan, Prin.	1	5	.167	7.59	14	10	0	0	0	0	53.1	67	248	51	45	9	1	3	2	26	1	34	1	1
Santana, Hector, Burl.	1	0	.000	8.27	12	0	0	0	4	0	20.2	22	100	22	19	2	1	0	3	15	0	14	8	2
Scalamandre, Rich, J.C.	7	1	.875	4.67	25	0	0	0	15	6	27	34	128	19	14	2	4	1	0	15	2	20	2	0
Scheffel, Dustin, Pul.	4	4	.500	3.98	15	8	0	0	3	0	63.1	55	273	31	28	6	0	1	7	27	0	45	1	0
Schultz, Jimmy, Burl.	2	4	.333	6.51	13	0	0	0	1	0	27.2	34	141	28	20	7	0	1	4	23	0	16	6	0
Simon, Janewrys, Eliz.	0	0	.000	8.47	13	0	0	0	6	0	17	24	94	24	16	1	0	2	1	19	0	14	1	1
Smith, Chris, Blue.*	0	3	.000	11.45	5	5	0	0	0	0	11	12	67	14	14	1	0	1	5	21	0	4	6	0
Smith, Cole, Prin.	0	3	.000	6.48	10	1	0	0	4	1	16.2	13	82	17	12	0	0	1	1	18	0	15	7	1
Smith, Ryan, Eliz.	2	2	.500	2.45	23	2	0	0	9	3	40.1	26	174	13	11	1	3	2	5	24	2	52	4	0
Smith, Sean, Burl.	1	1	.500	3.24	10	9	0	0	0	0	33.1	29	139	14	12	1	2	1	12	0	29	1	0
Soler, Jose, Mar.	2	1	.667	5.29	18	6	0	0	5	0	47.2	49	215	32	28	5	1	2	4	23	0	43	5	0
Spaulding, Richard, Burl.*	0	1	.000	9.00	4	0	0	0	0	0	8	10	45	8	8	2	0	0	13	0	8	0	0
Spillers, Larry, Blue.*	4	1	.800	5.40	21	0	0	0	4	0	33.1	43	163	23	20	1	1	2	1	28	2	24	6	0
Stander, Mark, Mar.	2	2	.500	5.63	19	0	0	0	9	1	38.1	49	177	29	24	9	0	1	0	10	0	34	3	0
Streich, Isaac, Eliz.	1	0	1.000	8.05	14	0	0	0	1	0	19	22	101	22	17	2	0	6	19	0	14	4	0
Tadefa, Fernando, Dan.*	2	2	.500	2.45	23	0	0	0	22	16	25.2	21	107	8	7	1	1	1	1	8	0	29	1	0
Taylor, Blake, Burl.	0	2	.000	2.78	19	0	0	0	16	6	22.2	25	102	11	7	1	1	1	2	9	0	23	0	0
Taylor, Sam, Eliz.	0	0	.000	0.00	1	0	0	0	1	0	1	1	5	0	0	0	0	0	1	0	0	0	0

Pitcher, Team	W	L	Pct.	ERA	G	GS	CG	ShO	GF	Sv.	IP	H	TBF	R	ER	HR	SH	SF	HB	BB	IBB	SO	WP	Bk.
Thompson, Erik, Pul.	1	1	.500	3.18	3	3	0	0	0	0	17	19	69	6	6	0	0	2	1	2	0	16	0	0
Tiller, James, Blue.	4	5	.444	4.82	12	11	1	1	0	0	65.1	74	288	44	35	7	3	1	7	16	0	43	4	1
Tisdale, Andrew, Pul.	1	3	.250	11.93	7	4	0	0	2	1	14.1	25	72	20	19	1	1	1	0	5	0	7	4	0
Tracey, Sean, Bris.	5	2	.714	3.02	13	12	0	0	0	0	65.2	57	261	27	22	4	1	0	4	19	0	50	1	0
Tyler, Scott, Eliz.	8	1	.889	2.93	14	13	0	0	0	0	67.2	37	278	23	22	5	0	1	1	46	0	92	5	0
Urena, Sixto, Pul.	0	0	.000	36.00	1	0	0	0	0	0	1	6	10	5	4	0	0	0	1	0	0	1	0	0
Van Gorder, Joe, J.C.*	1	2	.333	7.36	6	4	0	0	0	0	18.1	25	86	16	15	2	0	0	2	5	0	17	4	0
Van Matre, Gary, J.C.*	0	0	.000	9.00	7	0	0	0	5	0	8	16	48	10	8	0	0	0	0	6	0	7	1	0
Van Ruiten, Danny, Prin.	1	0	1.000	8.31	14	0	0	0	3	0	17.1	21	88	19	16	3	1	1	2	11	0	12	3	0
Wehrfritz, Brad, J.C.	0	0	.000	4.97	21	0	0	0	6	0	29	36	135	19	16	5	1	1	2	12	0	16	2	1
Weintraub, Jason, King.	1	6	.143	5.91	10	10	0	0	0	0	45.2	61	214	32	30	4	1	1	6	14	0	37	5	2
Weir, Jayson, King.*	0	0	.000	1.56	10	0	0	0	7	3	17.1	14	68	4	3	0	0	0	1	0	0	20	2	0
Yarbrough, Joe, Prin.*	0	3	.000	7.20	17	0	0	0	13	2	20	32	107	23	16	3	1	1	3	12	0	28	3	1

COMBINATION SHUTOUTS: **Bluefield (0). Bristol (6)**—B. Miller-Curreri-Hummel, R. Morales-Curreri-Larson, Morales-Rupe, Perez-Payne, Reed-Dowdy-Deininger-Larson, Tracey-Larson. **Burlington (3)**—Cevette-Schultz-Casey, Haynes-Carmona, Lara-Douglas. **Danville (4)**—Alvarez-Arteaga, Davies-Bush-Tadefa, Lerew-Mueller-David, Larew-Tadefa. **Elizabethton (5)**—Tyler-R. Smith-Neshek 2, Barrett-Neshek, Barrett-Smith-Neshek, Tyler-Hill. **Johnson City (1)**—Estes-Chafey. **Kingsport (1)**—Deleon-Morban-A. Acosta. **Martinsville (4)**—Albers-Freeman, Douglass-Soler-Freeman, Escobar-Freeman, Estrada-Long-Beltre. **Princeton (1)**—T. King-Rodriguez. **Pulaski (3)**—Loe-Garcia-Frydendall, Loe-Hogan-Frydendall.

NO-HIT GAMES: None.

2002 FIELDING

TEAM

Team	G	PO	A	E	TC	DP	TP	PB	Pct.
Pulaski	66	1677	678	76	2431	41	0	15	.969
Bristol	68	1806	743	89	2638	58	0	12	.966
Kingsport	67	1740	673	102	2515	59	0	16	.959
Elizabethton	67	1733	668	102	2503	45	0	13	.959
Danville	68	1752	634	103	2489	44	0	8	.959
Burlington	68	1824	739	111	2674	64	1	28	.958
Bluefield	68	1777	767	111	2655	52	1	21	.958
Johnson City	67	1720	749	108	2577	54	0	17	.958
Martinsville	67	1761	631	105	2497	47	0	12	.958
Princeton	68	1757	756	148	2661	71	0	13	.944

INDIVIDUAL

FIRST BASEMEN

NOTE: All caps denotes fielding-percentage leader based on 34 games for catchers, 45 for all other non-pitchers and 54 innings for pitchers. *Throws lefthanded.

Player, Team	Pct.	G	PO	A	E	TC	DP
Agar, Cory, Eliz.	.989	11	85	5	1	91	5
Albert, Luke, Dan.	1.000	4	20	3	0	23	3
Arhart, Josh, Prin.	.987	13	74	2	1	77	7
Bessa, Laumin, Dan.	.964	4	26	1	1	28	2
Bohlander, Michael, Bris.	1.000	11	68	3	0	71	7
Bounds, Brandon, Bris.	.985	46	366	40	6	412	34
Bridges, Josh, J.C.	.667	1	2	0	1	3	0
Bunch, J.C., Pul.	.964	3	26	1	1	28	1
Camacho, Johan, King.	.969	28	229	17	8	254	21
Carroll, Rich, Pul.	.988	11	82	2	1	85	5
CATES, Zach, J.C.	.993	50	422	23	3	448	29
Cruz, Jose, Burl.	.917	2	11	0	1	12	2
Davie, Andrew, J.C.	.991	13	104	5	1	110	9
Fagan, John, Mar.	.990	26	194	11	2	207	14
Gold, Nate, Pul.	.996	27	235	23	1	259	12
Gomon, Dusty, Eliz.	.985	48	376	22	6	404	28
Humphries, Justin, Mar.	.980	39	274	15	6	295	26
Huson, Tim, Bris.	.967	18	137	9	5	151	11
Jimenez, Luis, Blue.*	.980	16	146	4	3	153	12
Jurries, James, Dan.	.952	4	38	2	2	42	3
Larson, Ryan, Mar.	1.000	3	17	4	0	21	1
Lebron, Edgardo, Eliz.	.987	11	74	3	1	78	8
Mannix, Brendan, King.	1.000	5	19	1	0	20	2
Martinez, Gabriel, Prin.	.986	56	469	32	7	508	50
Mather, Joe, J.C.	1.000	4	21	4	0	25	3
Nichols, Thomas, Prin.	.951	5	37	2	2	41	6
Noviskey, Josh, Burl.	1.000	2	7	0	0	7	0
Pacheco, Fernando, Burl.*	.985	39	321	18	5	344	32
Parra, Carlos, Burl.	1.000	1	1	0	0	1	0
Peters, Yaron, Dan.	.983	39	272	23	5	300	17
Reid, Ivan, Prin.*	.800	1	3	1	1	5	0
Richardson, Kevin, Pul.	.984	19	163	16	3	182	15
Rodriguez, Marcos, J.C.*	1.000	8	41	0	0	41	9
Ruiz, Daniel, Dan.	.988	26	163	8	2	173	15
Simmons, Coltyn, Prin.	1.000	3	25	1	0	26	2
Sulbaran, Orlando, Pul.	1.000	7	46	2	0	48	5
Torres, Saul, Mar.	.667	1	2	0	1	3	0

Player, Team	Pct.	G	PO	A	E	TC	DP
Vasquez, Domingo, Burl.	.974	31	251	11	7	269	25
Wendt, Justin, King.	.984	38	293	15	5	313	29
Wilson, Laron, King.	.950	3	17	2	1	20	2
Yount, Dustin, Blue.	.988	53	463	33	6	502	35

TRIPLE PLAYS: Vasquez, Yount.

SECOND BASEMEN

Player, Team	Pct.	G	PO	A	E	TC	DP
Abreu, Angel, Burl.	.947	8	16	20	2	38	5
Alvarez, Gera, Blue.	.912	19	15	37	5	57	4
Babilonia, Edgar, Mar.	.952	23	37	42	4	83	13
Betemit, Richard, Prin.	.940	35	72	99	11	182	28
Cruz, Jose, Burl.	.833	1	1	4	1	6	0
Davidson, Aaron, Burl.	.964	8	8	19	1	28	5
Done, Robert, Blue.	.966	45	97	130	8	235	27
Ford, Mark, Bris.	.928	16	32	32	5	69	8
German, Sandino, Prin.	1.000	1	1	1	0	2	1
Gonzalez, Jose, Pul.	.962	17	33	43	3	79	6
Grasso, Mike, Dan.	.966	59	99	129	8	236	28
Housel, David, King.	.919	35	66	92	14	172	24
Hudson, William, King.	.926	6	11	14	2	27	4
Huson, Tim, Bris.	1.000	3	6	9	0	15	1
Infante, Franklin, Dan.	1.000	18	17	22	0	39	3
Johnson, Elliot, Prin.	.952	34	57	81	7	145	21
Linares, Jesus, King.	.958	19	34	57	4	95	10
Lopez, Pedro, Bris.	.981	53	99	160	5	264	29
Martinez, Luis, King.	1.000	1	5	2	0	7	1
Martinez, Peter, Eliz.	.973	30	42	67	3	112	5
McCoy, Mike, J.C.	.954	25	38	66	5	109	14
Mendez, Valentin, Mar.	.932	46	73	105	13	191	13
Molina, Felix, Eliz.	.978	45	83	94	4	181	23
Olivari, Reinaldo, Pul.	.900	2	4	5	1	10	1
O'RIORDAN, Chris, Pul.	.983	48	97	138	4	239	25
Paredes, Salvador, Prin.	1.000	2	3	6	0	9	3
Reyes, Eduardo, J.C.	.968	22	40	50	3	93	13
Robinson, Levi, Blue.	.933	13	31	25	4	60	4
Ruiz, Daniel, Dan.	.952	8	10	10	1	21	3
Schilling, Micah, Burl.	.965	29	68	69	5	142	20
Soto, Yllysh, King.	.938	7	14	16	2	32	4
Torres, Eider, Burl.	.971	23	38	61	3	102	14
Vasquez, Domingo, Burl.	.900	2	5	4	1	10	0
Veloz, Gabe, J.C.	.899	29	52	72	14	138	12
Volquez, Julio, Pul.	1.000	1	1	2	0	3	0

THIRD BASEMEN

Player, Team	Pct.	G	PO	A	E	TC	DP
Abreu, Angel, Burl.	.857	11	8	22	5	35	4
Babilonia, Edgar, Mar.	.750	1	1	5	2	8	0
Baldris, Aaron, King.	.926	58	43	108	12	163	11
Betemit, Richard, Prin.	.000	2	0	0	1	1	0
Burrus, Josh, Dan.	.864	68	49	103	24	176	7
Buscher, Gregory, Pul.	.915	52	27	92	11	130	7
Done, Robert, Blue.	.895	9	3	14	2	19	0
Duncan, Trae, Prin.	.875	25	21	49	10	80	6
Ford, Mark, Bris.	.824	8	4	10	3	17	1
German, Sandino, Prin.	.810	8	6	11	4	21	2
Gonzalez, Jose, Pul.	1.000	8	4	18	0	22	0

Player, Team	Pct.	G	PO	A	E	TC	DP
Hiraldo, Sandy, Eliz.	.783	15	5	13	5	23	1
Huson, Tim, Bris.	.857	6	3	3	1	7	1
Infante, Franklin, Dan.	1.000	1	0	2	0	2	0
Koslowski, Kasey, Bris.	1.000	2	3	6	0	9	1
Larson, Ryan, Mar.	.875	18	12	30	6	48	1
Lebron, Edgardo, Eliz.	.900	51	32	94	14	140	4
Lee, Carlos, Bris.	.867	11	6	20	4	30	1
Linares, Jesus, King.	1.000	4	1	5	0	6	0
Mannix, Brendan, King.	1.000	9	7	14	0	21	2
Martinez, Gabriel, Prin.	.917	5	1	10	1	12	0
Martinez, Luis, King.	.857	2	1	5	1	7	0
Mather, Joe, J.C.	.886	57	35	121	20	176	6
Molina, Felix, Eliz.	1.000	6	3	8	0	11	0
Nolasco, Jose, J.C.	1.000	7	2	14	0	16	0
Olivari, Reinaldo, Pul.	1.000	1	0	3	0	3	0
Paredes, Salvador, Prin.	.889	4	2	6	1	9	1
Reyes, Eduardo, J.C.	.824	5	7	7	3	17	0
Rijo, Carlos, Blue.	.908	64	40	138	18	196	9
Rosario, Olmo, Prin.	.953	33	32	70	5	107	9
Threinen, Scott, Burl.	.500	7	1	5	6	12	0
Torres, Saul, Mar.	.859	48	29	87	19	135	8
VARELA, Edgar, Bris.	.930	53	36	97	10	143	10
Vasquez, Domingo, Burl.	.813	14	6	20	6	32	1
Volquez, Julio, Pul.	1.000	6	7	11	0	18	0
Whitney, Matthew, Burl.	.915	37	29	78	10	117	7
Yount, Dustin, Blue.	.000	1	0	0	0	0	0

TRIPLE PLAY: Rijo.

SHORTSTOPS

Player, Team	Pct.	G	PO	A	E	TC	DP
Abreu, Angel, Burl.	.893	9	19	31	6	56	6
Alvarez, Gera, Blue.	.970	37	53	108	5	166	17
Babilonia, Edgar, Mar.	.974	11	17	21	1	39	4
De La Cruz, Christopher, Burl.	.942	42	75	137	13	225	26
Fernando, Osvaldo, Mar.	.941	57	99	171	17	287	31
Gonzalez, Andy, Bris.	.942	62	105	154	16	275	27
Gonzalez, Jose, Pul.	1.000	1	0	3	0	3	0
Hiraldo, Sandy, Eliz.	.833	12	28	57	17	102	4
Hudson, William, King.	.942	24	38	59	6	103	18
Infante, Franklin, Dan.	1.000	2	2	6	0	4	2
Johnson, Elliot, Prin.	1.000	1	4	2	0	6	1
Lebron, Edgardo, Eliz.	.000	1	0	0	0	0	0
Linares, Jesus, King.	.945	16	18	51	4	73	9
Lopez, Pedro, Bris.	.974	8	14	24	1	39	9
Martinez, Luis, King.	.875	7	11	10	3	24	4
McCoy, Mike, J.C.	.916	27	32	77	10	119	15
Nolasco, Jose, J.C.	.950	45	66	141	11	218	25
Nunez, Yefresy, Prin.	.806	23	22	65	21	108	9
Paredes, Salvador, Prin.	.928	49	75	157	18	250	32
Rijo, Carlos, Blue.	1.000	1	0	1	0	1	0
RINGE, Craig, Pul.	.955	64	99	176	13	288	26
Robinson, Levi, Blue.	.943	35	52	113	10	175	15
Rojas, Ricardo, Burl.	1.000	2	0	3	0	3	0
Schuerholz, Jon, Dan.	.896	66	89	162	29	280	27
Skinner, Steve, Prin.	.778	1	4	3	2	9	0
Soto, Yllysh, King.	.923	24	27	69	8	104	9
Taylor, Sam, Eliz.	.948	47	65	137	11	213	24
Torres, Eider, Mar.	.952	17	21	59	4	84	14
Volquez, Julio, Pul.	1.000	2	1	2	0	3	0

TRIPLE PLAY: De La Cruz, Robinson.

OUTFIELDERS

Player, Team	Pct.	G	PO	A	E	TC	DP
Acevedo, Freddy, Mar.	.976	52	116	7	3	126	1
Ascencion, Quincy, Blue.	.905	43	53	4	6	63	0
Babilonia, Edgar, Mar.	.000	1	0	0	0	0	0
Babilonia, Jose, Prin.	.800	7	6	2	2	10	0
Bankston, Wes, Prin.	.949	58	106	6	6	118	3
Batista, Ariel, Mar.	.966	49	110	4	2	116	2
Bera, Roberto, Blue.	.931	24	27	0	2	29	0
Bessa, Laumin, Dan.	.900	27	18	0	2	20	0
Bilezikjian, Charlie, Pul.	1.000	12	14	0	0	14	0
Brice, Thomas, Bris.*	.882	12	15	0	2	17	0
Bryan, Jason, Pul.	1.000	14	22	1	0	23	0
Charles, Julin, Pul.	.927	62	106	8	9	123	2
Ciraco, Darren, Bris.	.949	50	65	10	4	79	1
Clements, Zachary, King.	.917	6	10	1	1	12	0
Cruz, Jose, Burl.	.976	41	79	3	2	84	1
Cruz, Orlando, Pul.	1.000	25	46	3	0	49	2
Davidson, Aaron, Burl.	1.000	3	6	0	0	6	0
Deeds, Doug, Eliz.*	1.000	35	53	3	0	56	1

Player, Team	Pct.	G	PO	A	E	TC	DP
Eldridge, Rashad, Pul.	.972	17	35	0	1	36	0
Encarnacion, Teodoro, Burl.	.930	33	61	5	5	71	1
Esquivel, Matt, Dan.	.930	58	76	4	6	86	1
Estrada, Rafael, J.C.	1.000	2	1	0	0	1	0
Evans, Terry, J.C.	.973	58	99	10	3	112	3
Francoeur, Jeff, Dan.	.990	36	90	7	1	98	2
Frias, Fernando, Prin.	.952	30	38	2	2	42	1
Garcia, Williams, King.	.951	32	57	1	3	61	0
Garcia, Yunir, King.	1.000	3	5	0	0	5	0
Guy, Jason, Pul.*	.959	43	93	1	4	98	0
Guzman, Carlos, Dan.	.976	34	40	0	1	41	0
Guzman, Garrett, Eliz.*	.971	45	62	5	2	69	0
Hawkins, Dustin, Mar.*	1.000	25	50	0	0	50	0
Hileman, Jutt, J.C.	.972	23	32	3	1	36	0
Hill, Jamar, King.	.978	55	83	4	2	89	0
Hodge, Luis, Burl.	.943	54	81	2	5	88	0
Huson, Tim, Bris.	.875	7	7	0	1	8	0
Irvin, Blair, Prin.	.571	8	4	0	3	7	0
IVY, Bjorn, Bris.	1.000	46	71	1	0	72	0
Jaime, Willy, Prin.	.938	20	29	1	2	32	1
Jansen, Ardley, Dan.	.962	59	97	3	4	104	0
Jimenez, Luis, Blue.*	.946	21	33	2	2	37	0
Joyce, Tom, Blue.*	.946	36	49	4	3	56	1
Larson, Ryan, Mar.	1.000	2	2	0	0	2	0
Lemanczyk, Matt, J.C.	.974	57	108	4	3	115	0
Lorsbach, Michael, Mar.	1.000	14	23	1	0	24	0
Mannix, Brendan, King.	1.000	7	15	1	0	16	0
Martinez, Gabriel, Prin.	1.000	1	1	0	0	1	0
Mojica, Robinson, J.C.	.962	19	24	1	1	26	0
Monette, Daylon, J.C.*	1.000	15	23	0	0	23	0
Morris, Seth, Bris.	.986	46	66	3	1	70	1
Nixon, Jason, Burl.	.867	11	13	0	2	15	0
Oeltjen, Trent, Eliz.*	.969	53	92	2	3	97	0
Panther, Nathan, Burl.*	1.000	22	33	1	0	34	0
Pridie, Jason, Prin.	.989	66	172	11	2	185	2
Reid, Ivan, Prin.*	.815	10	22	0	5	27	0
Rivas, Arturo, Blue.	.918	52	80	10	8	98	5
Robinson, Levi, Blue.	.000	2	0	0	0	0	0
Rodriguez, Marcos, J.C.*	1.000	7	7	1	0	8	0
Rojas, Ricardo, Burl.	.992	49	108	10	1	119	0
Sarabia, Hamilton, Mar.	.962	61	96	6	4	106	0
Simmons, Coltyn, Prin.	.833	14	11	4	3	18	0
Sims, Justin, Eliz.	.974	28	36	2	1	39	0
Smallwood, Erik, Blue.	.971	43	63	5	2	70	1
Solano, Roberto, King.	.970	57	127	4	4	135	0
Tolotti, Jeff, J.C.*	.932	29	39	2	3	44	0
Volquez, Julio, Pul.	.946	30	52	1	3	56	0
Watts, Derran, King.	.967	47	86	2	3	91	0
Webster, Anthony, Bris.	.983	58	114	4	2	120	0
Whitrock, Scott, Eliz.	.978	43	82	6	2	90	1
Wilson, Laron, King.	.000	1	0	0	0	0	0
Woods, Ahmad, Dan.	.800	16	16	0	4	20	0

CATCHERS

Player, Team	Pct.	G	PO	A	E	TC	DP	PB
Agar, Cory, Eliz.	.966	6	49	7	2	58	0	0
Arhart, Josh, Prin.	.980	23	129	21	3	153	1	0
Arko, Tommy, Blue.	.987	39	265	33	4	302	1	9
Baez, Fleming, Pul.	.983	15	106	12	2	120	0	2
Belz, Tim, J.C.	.987	11	72	4	1	77	0	2
Bridges, Josh, J.C.	.979	6	43	3	1	47	0	2
Bunch, J.C., Pul.	1.000	1	2	0	0	2	0	0
Capellan, Domingo, J.C.	.973	33	194	25	6	225	2	7
Clements, Zachary, King.	.962	8	70	6	3	79	0	3
Davidson, Kevin, Mar.	.988	28	223	26	3	252	2	3
Deck, Ronald, Prin.	1.000	11	51	4	0	55	0	2
Elliott, Justin, Eliz.	.963	8	72	5	3	80	0	1
Garcia, Yunir, King.	1.000	19	141	11	0	152	0	4
Gunn, Cody, J.C.	.995	29	191	14	1	206	0	6
Hamblen, Chris, Pul.	.990	42	256	29	3	288	1	13
Humphries, Justin, Mar.	1.000	1	9	1	0	10	0	0
Koslowski, Kasey, Bris.	1.000	2	17	0	0	17	0	1
Lee, Carlos, Bris.	1.000	1	2	1	0	3	0	0
Lisk, Charles, Bris.	.987	27	205	27	3	235	1	7
Marin, Daniel, Eliz.	.983	32	252	36	5	293	3	10
Martinez, Raul, Blue.	.981	28	141	10	3	154	2	3
Matienzo, Danny, Eliz.	.979	26	220	18	5	243	2	2
McCullough, Clayton, Burl.	.993	18	123	18	1	142	0	0
Melendez, German, Mar.	.990	38	340	37	4	381	1	9
Morales, Porfirio, Blue.	.981	13	96	6	2	104	0	7
Myers, Kenton, Burl.	1.000	3	19	0	0	19	0	0
Noviskey, Josh, Burl.	.974	30	205	21	6	232	0	19

Player, Team	Pct.	G	PO	A	E	TC	DP	PB
Parra, Carlos, Burl.	.995	24	188	19	1	208	3	9
Reynoso, Danilo, King.	.981	12	88	13	2	103	2	0
Roat, Kyle, Dan.	.984	36	270	36	5	311	1	6
Robinson-Pierce, Whitney, Blue.	.911	9	35	6	4	45	1	2
RUELAS, Alonzo, Dan.	.991	34	326	20	3	349	1	2
Simmons, Coltyn, Prin.	.957	8	36	8	2	46	2	5
Stewart, Chris, Bris.	.979	39	319	50	8	377	4	4
Sulbaran, Orlando, Pul.	.963	10	72	6	3	81	0	0
Volquez, Julio, Pul.	1.000	1	9	0	0	9	0	0
Wilson, Brandon, King.	.990	32	190	16	2	208	0	7
Woodruff, Ernest, Prin.	.968	35	217	27	8	252	0	6

TRIPLE PLAY: Martinez.

PITCHERS

Player, Team	Pct.	G	PO	A	E	TC	DP
Abreu, Angel, Burl.	.000	1	0	0	0	0	0
Acosta, Anthony, King.	1.000	11	0	4	0	4	1
Acosta, Jasiel, Dan.*	1.000	7	2	5	0	7	1
Acosta, Richal, Blue.	.500	3	0	1	1	2	0
Adamczyk, Tyler, J.C.	.700	13	5	9	6	20	0
Adams, Josh, Dan.*	1.000	20	2	4	0	6	0
Aguero, Miguel, J.C.	.833	14	1	4	1	6	0
Aguilar, Ray, Dan.*	1.000	1	1	2	0	3	0
Albers, Matthew, Mar.	1.000	13	1	4	0	5	0
Alfonzo, Edgar, King.*	1.000	6	0	2	0	2	0
Allen, Brian, Prin.	.000	3	0	0	0	0	0
Ally, Ben, Mar.	1.000	13	2	7	0	9	1
Almeida, Brian, Dan.	.833	13	3	2	1	6	0
Alvarado, Luis, Burl.*	1.000	18	1	5	0	6	0
Alvarez, Juan, Dan.*	1.000	13	5	13	0	18	0
Andrew, Jason, Pul.	1.000	3	2	3	0	5	0
Arteaga, Francisco, Dan.	.750	21	2	1	1	4	0
Baez, Fleming, Pul.	.000	1	0	0	0	0	0
Barnett, John, Pul.	1.000	1	1	1	0	2	0
Barrett, Ricky, Eliz.*	.889	12	1	7	1	9	0
Barrios, Angel, Mar.*	1.000	7	2	1	0	3	0
Beltre, Juan, Mar.*	.714	24	1	4	2	7	0
Blackburn, Nick, Eliz.	.929	13	2	11	1	14	0
Brewer, Jeff, King.	.000	13	0	0	1	1	0
Britton, Chris, Blue.	.909	9	3	7	1	11	0
Burton, T.J., Burl.	1.000	12	1	8	0	9	0
Bush, Paul, Dan.	.857	20	2	4	1	7	0
Cabrera, Daniel, Blue.	1.000	12	0	5	0	5	0
Carmona, Fausto, Burl.	.900	13	2	16	2	20	1
Casey, Reid, Burl.	1.000	17	4	6	0	10	0
Castro, Rafael, King.	1.000	13	2	2	0	4	0
Cevette, Dan, Burl.*	1.000	13	5	8	0	13	1
Chafey, Hal, J.C.*	1.000	17	0	3	0	3	0
Clements, Zachary, King.	.000	1	0	0	0	0	0
Coppinger, Joe, Blue.	.750	12	4	5	3	12	1
Corrado, Rob, Pul.	1.000	8	3	2	0	5	0
Crain, Jesse, Eliz.	.667	9	0	2	1	3	0
Cristobal, Luis, Pul.	1.000	3	1	0	0	1	0
Crump, Joel, Blue.*	1.000	15	0	5	0	5	0
Curreri, Joe, Bris.	1.000	9	2	0	0	2	0
Danly, Ryan, King.*	1.000	13	2	11	0	13	0
David, Brad, Dan.*	1.000	13	0	4	0	4	0
Davies, Kyle, Dan.	1.000	14	3	10	0	13	1
Davis, Jeff, Burl.	1.000	2	0	2	0	2	0
DeBarr, Nick, Prin.	.900	11	0	9	1	10	0
Deininger, Todd, Bris.	.900	19	4	5	1	10	0
DeLeon, Maikel, King.	1.000	9	1	4	0	5	0
DePaula, Julio, Eliz.	.889	5	2	6	1	9	0
Devenney, Nick, Pul.	.800	21	1	3	1	5	0
Done, Robert, Blue.	.000	1	0	0	0	0	0
Douglas, Shea, Burl.*	.800	12	0	4	1	5	0
Douglass, Chance, Mar.	.786	12	6	5	3	14	1
Dowdy, Justin, Bris.*	.952	13	5	15	1	21	1
Elliott, Adam, King.	.750	11	3	6	3	12	0
Escobar, Rodrigo, Mar.	.950	16	4	15	1	20	0
Estes, Jonathan, J.C.	.952	11	4	16	1	21	1
Estrada, Paul, Mar.	.667	14	3	1	2	6	0
Farrell, Jarrod, Prin.	.875	12	2	12	2	16	1
Farrell, Sean, King.*	1.000	20	1	2	0	3	0
Fischer, Sam, Mar.	1.000	8	3	4	0	7	0
Freeman, Daniel, Mar.	.667	20	2	4	3	9	0
Freites, Julio, King.	1.000	17	1	6	0	7	0
Frydendall, Craig, Pul.*	.818	16	1	8	2	11	0
Fryson, Andrew, Bris.	.000	3	0	0	0	0	0
Furnald, Donnie, Dan.	1.000	4	1	1	0	2	0
Galbraith, Jason, J.C.*	1.000	22	0	10	0	10	0
Garay, Kelvin, King.*	1.000	6	0	1	0	1	0
Garcia, Benjamin, Pul.	1.000	15	1	1	0	2	0
Garner, Isiah, Prin.*	.667	17	1	1	1	3	0
George, Jahseam, Burl.*	.667	15	0	4	2	6	0
George, Taylor, King.	1.000	13	5	7	0	12	0
Guzman, Henry, Prin.*	.000	5	0	0	1	1	0
Hammel, Jason, Prin.	1.000	2	0	1	0	1	0
Hawksworth, Blake, J.C.	.833	13	3	7	2	12	0
Haynes, Matthew, Burl.	.750	13	0	3	1	4	0
Hemus, Jared, Eliz.*	.800	4	2	2	1	5	0
Henkenjohann, Tim, Eliz.	.667	10	1	7	4	12	0
Henry, Paul, Blue.	1.000	16	1	2	0	3	0
Herrera, Cesar, Pul.	.941	13	10	6	1	17	1
Hill, Josh, Eliz.	1.000	10	0	4	0	4	1
Hogan, Gary, Pul.	.444	12	0	4	5	9	0
Hummel, Rick, Bris.	.909	24	3	7	1	11	0
Humphries, Justin, Mar.	.000	1	0	0	0	0	0
Johnson, James, Blue.	.938	11	6	9	1	16	0
Jones, Alvin, Blue.	1.000	18	2	1	0	3	0
Keeling, Justin, Eliz.*	.800	22	1	3	1	5	0
Keinath, Tim, Prin.	1.000	17	2	3	0	5	0
Killalea, John, J.C.*	.800	15	2	2	1	5	0
King, Bryan, King.	1.000	14	4	4	0	8	3
King, Timothy, Prin.*	.833	14	2	8	2	12	0
Kirsten, Joel, Pul.	1.000	18	3	9	0	12	0
Lara, Juan, Burl.*	1.000	14	1	16	0	17	2
Larson, Adam, Bris.	.875	26	5	2	1	8	0
Lavergne, Jarrad, Prin.*	1.000	8	0	3	0	3	0
LaMura, B.J., Bris.	.750	11	2	1	1	4	0
Ledbetter, Aaron, J.C.	1.000	16	0	6	0	6	0
Lerew, Anthony, Dan.	.933	14	8	20	2	30	1
Lindstrom, Matthew, King.	.833	12	5	10	3	18	0
Loe, Kameron, Pul.	.929	14	3	10	1	14	0
Lohse, Eric, Eliz.	1.000	8	1	3	0	4	0
Long, Brent, Mar.	1.000	17	2	2	0	4	0
Lopez, Aleurys, Prin.	1.000	15	0	1	0	1	0
Machen, Mike, Blue.	.750	21	1	2	1	4	0
Maio, Mitch, J.C.	1.000	24	1	6	0	7	0
Maldonado, Ivan, King.	.667	3	1	1	1	3	0
Mann, Brandon, Prin.*	1.000	10	0	3	0	3	0
Martinez, Paul, Burl.*	1.000	16	2	5	0	7	2
Mason, Robert, Dan.*	1.000	3	0	2	0	2	0
McClellan, Kyle, J.C.	1.000	7	1	2	0	3	0
McGary, Gerron, Bris.*	.250	20	0	1	3	4	0
McLemore, Mark, Mar.*	.667	4	1	1	1	3	0
Meisenheimer, Matt, Prin.*	1.000	8	0	1	0	1	0
Mendoza, Jorge, Pul.	1.000	1	1	0	0	1	0
Meyer, Dan, Dan.*	1.000	13	2	13	0	15	0
Miller, Brian, Bris.	.944	13	6	11	1	18	0
Miller, Eric, Prin.*	.750	8	2	1	1	4	1
Mondesir, James, J.C.	1.000	14	2	7	0	9	1
Montani, Jeff, Blue.	1.000	30	4	6	0	10	0
Morales, Juan, J.C.	.857	30	0	6	1	7	0
Morales, Ruddy, Bris.	1.000	13	3	8	0	11	1
Morban, Domingo, King.*	1.000	8	0	1	0	1	0
Moreno, Adam, Prin.	.909	14	7	3	1	11	0
Mueller, Mike, Dan.	1.000	20	0	7	0	7	0
NARRON, Sam, Pul.*	1.000	14	2	17	0	19	0
Narveson, Chris, J.C.*	1.000	6	1	4	0	5	0
Nash, Justin, Blue.	.882	16	4	11	2	17	0
Neshek, Pat, Eliz.	1.000	23	1	2	0	3	0
Niedbalski, Nick, Eliz.*	1.000	22	0	9	0	9	1
Nieve, Fernando, Mar.	.818	13	6	3	2	11	0
Nowlen, Jake, Bris.	1.000	2	0	1	0	1	0
Osberg, Tanner, King.	1.000	3	0	4	0	4	1
Parker, Aaron, Dan.	1.000	18	2	3	0	5	0
Patitucci, Mike, Blue.*	.833	24	2	8	2	12	0
Paulk, Robert, King.	1.000	10	2	1	0	3	0
Paustian, Michael, Pul.	.000	12	0	0	0	0	0
Payne, Matt, Bris.	.833	20	2	3	1	6	0
Peguero, Tony, Prin.	.824	13	7	7	3	17	0
Pereyra, Honeudis, Burl.	.875	10	1	6	1	8	0
Perez, Armando, Bris.*	1.000	19	3	7	0	10	0
Prunty, Thomas, Eliz.	.929	13	4	9	1	14	0
Pylate, Chad, Eliz.	1.000	4	1	2	0	3	0
Reed, Rylan, Bris.	1.000	12	1	6	0	7	0
Reedy, Shane, Bris.	1.000	3	0	1	0	1	0
Rodriguez, Felix, Prin.	.750	15	1	2	1	4	0
Rondon, Celso, King.	.750	17	3	3	2	8	0
Rowe, Steven, Pul.	1.000	5	1	1	0	2	0
Rupe, Joshua, Bris.	.923	17	7	5	1	13	1
Sager, Brian, Bris.	.500	6	0	1	1	2	0
Sala, Marino, Blue.	1.000	27	1	5	0	6	1
Salazar, Richard, Blue.*	1.000	7	0	2	0	2	0

Player, Team	Pct.	G	PO	A	E	TC	DP
Samuel, Dauwill, Prin.	1.000	18	0	3	0	3	0
Sanchez, Juan, Prin.	.727	14	1	7	3	11	0
Santana, Hector, Burl.	1.000	12	1	2	0	3	0
Scalamandre, Rich, J.C.	.889	25	1	7	1	9	1
Scheffel, Dustin, Pul.	.867	15	5	8	2	15	0
Schultz, Jimmy, Burl.	.875	13	2	5	1	8	0
Simon, Janewrys, Eliz.	.600	13	1	2	2	5	0
Smith, Chris, Blue.*	.667	5	0	2	1	3	0
Smith, Cole, Prin.	.750	10	1	2	1	4	0
Smith, Ryan, Eliz.	.800	23	3	9	3	15	1
Smith, Sean, Burl.	.667	10	1	5	3	9	0
Soler, Jose, Mar.	.600	18	2	1	2	5	0
Spaulding, Richard, Burl.*	.667	4	1	1	1	3	0
Spillers, Larry, Blue.*	1.000	21	4	6	0	10	0
Stander, Mark, Mar.	1.000	19	2	8	0	10	1
Streich, Isaac, Eliz.	1.000	14	0	2	0	2	0
Tadefa, Fernando, Dan.*	1.000	23	1	2	0	3	0
Taylor, Blake, Burl.	1.000	19	0	3	0	3	0

Player, Team	Pct.	G	PO	A	E	TC	DP
Taylor, Sam, Eliz.	.000	1	0	0	0	0	0
Thompson, Erik, Pul.	1.000	3	1	2	0	3	0
Tiller, James, Blue.	.833	12	3	7	2	12	0
Tisdale, Andrew, Pul.	.875	7	3	4	1	8	0
Tracey, Sean, Bris.	1.000	13	3	7	0	10	1
Tyler, Scott, Eliz.	.857	14	2	4	1	7	0
Urena, Sixto, Pul.	.000	1	0	0	0	0	0
Van Gorder, Joe, J.C.*	.909	6	2	8	1	11	0
Van Matre, Gary, J.C.*	1.000	7	0	2	0	2	0
Van Ruiten, Danny, Prin.	1.000	14	1	2	0	3	0
Wehrfritz, Brad, J.C.	.571	21	2	2	3	7	0
Weintraub, Jason, King.	.875	10	3	4	1	8	0
Weir, Jayson, King.*	.833	10	1	4	1	6	0
Yarbrough, Joe, Prin.*	.800	17	0	4	1	5	0

The following players appeared only as designated hitter, pinch-hitter or pinch runner: Beuerlein, dh, ph.

LEAGUE CHAMPIONS

Year	Team	Pct.
1921—	Greenville	.608
	Johnson City*	.627
1922—	Bristol	.557
1923—	Knoxville	.635
1924—	Knoxville*	.642
	Bristol	.607
1925—	Greenville	.667
1926-36—	Did not operate.	
1937—	Elizabethton	.559
	Pennington Gap*	.580
1938—	Elizabethton	.664
	Greenville (3rd)†	.571
1939—	Elizabethton‡	.597
1940—	Johnson City§	.726
	Elizabethton	.750
1941—	Johnson City	.614
	Elizabethton*	.661
1942—	Bristol	.667
	Bristol∞	.660
1943—	Bristol	.755
	Bristol▲	.617
1944—	Kingsport‡	.575
1945—	Kingsport‡	.670
1946—	New River‡	.675
1947—	Pulaski	.648
	New River (3rd)†	.516
1948—	Pulaski‡	.680
1949—	Bluefield‡	.721
1950—	Bluefield	.600
	Bluefield◆	.745
1951—	Kingsport‡	.659
1952—	Johnson City	.595
	Welch (3rd)†	.509
1953—	Welch*	.705
	Johnson City	.672
1954—	Bluefield‡	.619

Year	Team	Pct.
1955—	Salem■	.689
1956—	Did not operate.	
1957—	Bluefield	.701
1958—	Johnson City	.662
1959—	Morristown	.603
1960—	Wytheville	.614
1961—	Middlesboro	.591
1962—	Bluefield	.671
1963—	Bluefield	.652
1964—	Johnson City	.662
1965—	Salem	.614
1966—	Marion	.623
1967—	Marion	.627
1968—	Marion	.583
1969—	Pulaski▼	.576
	Johnson City	.544
1970—	Bluefield	.638
1971—	Bluefield▼	.609
	Kingsport	.559
1972—	Bristol▼	.588
	Covington	.586
1973—	Kingsport	.757
1974—	Bristol▼	.754
	Bluefield	.536
1975—	Marion	.515
	Johnson City▼	.603
1976—	Johnson City▼	.714
	Bluefield	.600
1977—	Kingsport	.623
1978—	Elizabethton	.594
1979—	Paintsville	.800
1980—	Paintsville	.657
1981—	Paintsville	.657
1982—	Bluefield▼	.681
	Johnson City	.478
1983—	Paintsville	.653

Year	Team	Pct.
1984—	Elizabethton•	.580
	Pulaski	.536
1985—	Bristol††	.638
1986—	Johnson City	.667
	Pulaski•	.621
1987—	Burlington•	.729
	Johnson City	.609
1988—	Kingsport•	.644
	Burlington	.529
1989—	Elizabethton•	.691
	Pulaski	.618
1990—	Elizabethton	.761
1991—	Pulaski•	.662
	Burlington	.597
1992—	Elizabethton	.742
	Bluefield•	.597
1993—	Burlington•	.647
	Elizabethton	.552
1994—	Princeton•	.621
	Johnson City	.618
1995—	Bluefield	.754
	Kingsport•	.727
1996—	Kingsport	.716
	Bluefield▼	.618
1997—	Pulaski	.632
	Bluefield	.580
1998—	Bristol•	.636
	Princeton	.559
1999—	Pulaski	.696
	Martinsville•	.586
2000—	Elizabethton•	.719
2001—	Elizabethton	.651
	Bluefield•	.500
2002—	Bluefield	.662
	Bristol•	.632

*Won split-season playoff. †Won four-team playoff. ‡Won championship and four-team playoff. §Johnson City, first-half winner, won playoff involving six clubs. ∞Won both halves and defeated second-place Elizabethton in playoff. ▲Won both halves, but Erwin won four-team playoff. ◆Won both halves, but Bristol won two-club playoff. ■Salem and Johnson City declared playoff co-champions when weather forced cancellation of final series. ▼League was divided into Northern, Southern divisions; declared league champion based on highest won-lost percentage. •League was divided into North and South divisions; won playoff. ††Bristol declared league champion based on regular-season record.

ARIZONA LEAGUE

LEAGUE OFFICE

President/treasurer
Bob Richmond

Address
P.O. Box 1645
Boise, ID 83701

Phone
208-429-1511

Teams*
Angels
Athletics
Brewers
Cubs
Giants

Mariners
Rangers
Royals

*Teams play their games in Maryvale, Mesa, Peoria, Phoenix, Scottsdale and Surprise, Ariz.

2002 FINAL STANDINGS

FIRST HALF

Team	W	L	T	Pct.	GB
Cubs	19	9	0	.679	...
Giants	17	11	0	.607	2.0
White Sox	14	14	0	.500	5.0
Athletics	13	15	0	.464	6.0
Angels	13	15	0	.464	6.0
Brewers	12	16	0	.429	7.0
Mariners	10	18	0	.357	9.0

SECOND HALF

Team	W	L	T	Pct.	GB
Giants	16	12	0	.571	...
Cubs	16	12	0	.571	...
Athletics	15	13	0	.536	1.0
Angels	15	13	0	.536	1.0
Brewers	14	14	0	.500	2.0
White Sox	13	15	0	.464	3.0
Mariners	9	19	0	.321	7.0

COMPOSITE

Team	Cubs	Gia.	Ath.	Ang.	W.S.	Brew.	Mar.	W	L	T	Pct.	GB
Cubs	...	6	7	7	5	6	4	35	21	0	.625	...
Giants	3	...	6	7	5	6	6	33	23	0	.589	2.0
Athletics	3	3	...	4	4	7	7	28	28	0	.500	7.0
Angels	3	3	5	...	4	7	5	28	28	0	.500	7.0
White Sox	4	4	6	4	...	3	6	27	29	0	.482	8.0
Brewers	3	4	2	4	6	...	7	26	30	0	.464	9.0
Mariners	5	3	2	2	4	3	...	19	37	0	.339	16.0

Club names are major league affiliations.

Games played in Mesa, Peoria, Phoenix and Tucson.

PLAYOFFS: Cubs defeated Giants, one game to none to win Arizona League championship.

REGULAR-SEASON ATTENDANCE: No total attendance figures reported.

MANAGERS: Angels, Brian Harper; Athletics, Ruben Escalera; Brewers, Carlos Lezcano; Cubs, Carmelo Martinez; Giants, Burt Hunter; Mariners, Darrin Garner; White Sox, Jerry Hairston.

ALL-STAR TEAM: 1B—Ruben Olguin, Mariners; 2B—Matt Creighton, Cubs; 3B—Micah Schnurstein, White Sox; SS—Jemel Spearman, Cubs; OF—Felix Pie, Cubs; OF—Carlos Sosa, Giants; OF (tie)—Joshua Ellison, Mariners and Nick Rogers, Athletics. C—Brian Munhall, Giants. DH—Luis Perez, Athletics; RHP—Carlos Portorreal, Giants; LHP—Daniel Haigwood, White Sox; RH Relief pitcher—Daniel Arias, Angels; LH Relief pitcher—Ambiorix Delgadillo, Angels; Most Valuable Player (tie)—Matt Creighton, Cubs and Felix Pie, Cubs; Manager of the Year—Carmelo Martinez, Cubs.

2002 BATTING

TEAM

Team	G	TPA	AB	R	H	TB	2B	3B	HR	RBI	SH	SF	HP	BB	IBB	SO	SB	CS	GDP	LOB	ShO	Avg.	OBP	Slg.
Cubs	56	2199	1943	316	543	788	94	35	27	263	17	26	53	160	8	406	79	38	22	397	2	.279	.346	.406
White Sox	56	2253	2011	332	548	823	130	33	23	282	17	22	31	172	3	418	75	37	26	407	2	.277	.340	.409
Brewers	56	2256	1975	339	538	715	90	21	15	293	9	22	35	215	3	439	62	20	41	430	1	.272	.351	.362
Giants	56	2240	1988	326	539	759	85	36	21	272	15	21	33	183	4	445	75	36	34	406	4	.257	.333	.343
Angels	56	2152	1903	255	490	652	100	22	6	217	6	19	39	185	7	494	75	34	45	404	4	.255	.345	.371
Athletics	56	2230	1931	249	492	717	76	28	31	267	9	16	49	225	6	491	75	29	28	409	2	.255	.340	.371
Mariners	56	2218	1918	286	483	691	88	27	22	236	20	15	55	210	2	470	68	32	30	424	1	.252	.340	.360

INDIVIDUAL

TOP QUALIFIERS FOR BATTING CHAMPIONSHIP

Minimum 151 plate appearances. *Lefthanded batter. †Switch-hitter.

Player, Team	G	TPA	AB	R	H	TB	2B	3B	HR	RBI	SH	SF	HP	BB	IBB	SO	SB	CS	GDP	Avg.	OBP	Slg.
Creighton, Matt, Cubs	50	223	169	43	61	101	14	1	8	39	0	2	19	31	2	27	12	7	1	.361	.502	.598
Perez, Luis, Ath.	42	190	168	33	57	85	8	4	4	32	1	1	4	16	1	18	8	7	3	.339	.407	.506
Rogers, Nick, Ath.	47	213	178	33	60	80	8	6	0	33	1	1	2	31	2	40	21	1	3	.337	.439	.449
Luna, Leonardo, W.S.	50	232	221	38	74	102	13	6	1	30	3	4	1	3	0	13	8	4	2	.335	.341	.462
Myers, Michael, W.S.	44	193	165	34	55	73	12	3	0	23	1	1	2	24	2	24	18	1	1	.333	.422	.442
Schnurstein, Micah, W.S.	50	226	205	28	68	105	26	1	3	48	1	4	4	12	1	34	1	2	4	.332	.373	.512
Ellison, Josh, Mar.	39	177	149	32	49	63	8	3	0	11	0	2	3	23	0	21	7	2	2	.329	.424	.423
Pie, Felix, Cubs*	55	248	218	42	70	124	16	13	4	37	1	4	4	21	1	47	17	8	1	.321	.385	.569
Kendrick, Howard, Ang.†	42	172	157	24	50	64	6	4	0	13	1	1	6	7	0	11	12	6	2	.318	.368	.408
Cleto, Carlos, Gia.*	54	237	209	42	66	104	11	6	5	33	1	2	4	21	1	52	10	6	3	.316	.386	.498
Acosta, Gilberto, Brew.†	50	218	184	38	58	71	9	2	0	25	1	1	6	26	1	29	4	4	5	.315	.415	.386
Spearman, Jemel, Cubs	54	242	208	46	65	85	7	5	1	21	0	3	3	28	0	22	29	1	4	.313	.397	.409

Player, Team	G	TPA	AB	R	H	TB	2B	3B	HR	RBI	SH	SF	HP	BB	IBB	SO	SB	CS	GDP	Avg.	OBP	Slg.
Olguin, Ruben, Mar.*	48	196	177	31	55	83	10	3	4	31	1	2	1	15	0	40	3	4	3	.311	.364	.469
Francois, Francisco, Ath.	40	187	165	30	50	64	5	3	1	22	1	1	6	14	0	44	7	4	1	.303	.376	.388
Maher, Caleb, Ang.	48	207	194	22	58	79	11	2	2	31	0	1	3	9	0	51	0	3	4	.299	.338	.407

DEPARTMENTAL LEADERS: G—Pie, C. Young, 55 each; AB—Luna, 221; R—Spearman, 46; H—Luna, 74; TB—Pie, 124; 2B—Schnurstein, 26; 3B—Pie, 13; HR—Creighton, 8; RBI—Schnurstein, 48; SH—Garciaparra, Olszta, 6 each; SF—Creighton, Luna, Peel, Pie, 4 each; HP—Creighton, 18; BB—W. Soto, 34; IBB—Several players tied with 2; SO—Walston, 67; SB—Spearman, 29; CS—W. Soto, 10; GIDP—Munhall, 8; Slg.—Creighton, .598; OBP—Creighton, .502.

ALL PLAYERS

*Lefthanded batter. †Switch-hitter.

Player, Team	G	TPA	AB	R	H	TB	2B	3B	HR	RBI	SH	SF	HP	BB	IBB	SO	SB	CS	GDP	Avg.	OBP	Slg.
Abad, Noel, Ang.	24	71	64	9	12	16	2	1	0	2	1	0	2	4	0	26	3	0	2	.188	.257	.250
Abreu, Johany, Gia.†	33	127	113	17	29	37	4	2	0	12	0	2	2	10	0	24	5	1	0	.257	.323	.327
Acosta, Gilberto, Brew.†	50	218	184	38	58	71	9	2	0	25	1	1	6	26	1	29	4	4	5	.315	.415	.386
Agustin, Pedro, Cubs	30	81	77	8	16	21	3	1	0	1	3	0	0	1	0	22	1	2	0	.208	.218	.273
Almanzar, Theiborh, Mar.	19	61	55	6	6	9	0	0	1	6	0	0	1	5	0	15	0	0	2	.109	.197	.164
Alvarado, Joel, Brew.	11	40	34	4	11	14	3	0	0	4	0	1	0	5	0	3	2	0	1	.324	.400	.412
Arias, Angel, W.S.	6	13	12	2	1	2	1	0	0	1	0	0	1	0	0	3	0	0	0	.083	.154	.167
Arias, Daniel, Ang.	27	5	5	0	1	1	0	0	0	0	0	0	0	0	0	3	0	0	0	.200	.200	.200
Avendano, Elvis, Ath.	14	0	0	0	0	0	0	0	0	0	0	0	0	0	0	0	1	0	0	.000	.000	.000
Barnett, Dan, W.S.	9	40	36	10	14	19	3	1	0	2	0	0	0	4	0	6	2	1	1	.389	.450	.528
Bates, Dallas, Brew.*	51	228	204	23	51	55	2	1	0	25	1	0	5	18	0	50	4	1	5	.250	.326	.270
Batista, Christian, Ang.	29	92	79	11	19	26	4	0	1	8	0	2	0	11	0	13	2	1	2	.241	.326	.329
Batista, Juan, Ang.†	48	161	143	23	34	42	2	3	0	5	1	0	3	14	0	50	7	4	2	.238	.319	.294
Blakeley, Eric, Mar.	16	69	62	8	15	20	3	1	0	7	1	1	1	4	1	12	3	1	1	.242	.294	.323
Bohlander, Michael, W.S.*	15	50	48	5	12	15	3	0	0	4	1	0	0	1	0	10	0	0	0	.250	.265	.313
Bravo, Arturo, Brew.	12	41	37	7	7	9	2	0	0	4	0	0	0	4	0	10	0	0	1	.189	.268	.243
Brown, Matthew, Ang.	28	115	97	16	35	48	7	0	2	22	0	2	1	15	0	14	3	1	2	.361	.443	.495
Bubalo, Ty, Ath.	32	140	115	16	25	37	6	0	2	14	0	3	7	15	0	37	0	2	4	.217	.336	.322
Buller, Dayton, Gia.	33	132	112	23	28	39	5	3	0	15	0	1	3	16	0	38	2	2	0	.250	.356	.348
Cabaniel, Tomas, Ath.	17	1	1	0	0	0	0	0	0	0	0	0	0	0	0	0	0	0	0	.000	.000	.000
Castillo, Cesar, W.S.	18	74	58	9	17	24	3	2	0	7	0	1	1	14	0	12	2	1	3	.293	.432	.414
Cavanaugh, Brian, Brew.*	12	41	33	3	7	8	1	0	0	2	0	0	1	7	0	9	0	0	0	.212	.366	.242
Christenson, Ryan, Brew.	4	11	10	1	4	6	2	0	0	2	0	1	0	0	0	2	0	0	0	.400	.364	.600
Ciesluk, Chris, Gia.	43	162	141	20	29	40	7	2	0	17	4	2	4	11	0	38	6	2	3	.206	.278	.284
Cleto, Carlos, Gia.*	54	237	209	42	66	104	11	6	5	33	1	2	4	21	1	52	10	6	3	.316	.386	.498
Cole, John, Mar.	5	21	17	0	3	4	1	0	0	2	1	0	0	3	1	3	0	1	0	.176	.300	.235
Collaro, Thomas, W.S.	39	146	127	22	27	58	4	3	7	29	2	2	1	14	0	45	3	0	1	.213	.292	.457
Collins, Mike, Ang.	43	173	153	23	42	54	10	1	0	22	0	1	5	14	0	31	7	3	2	.275	.353	.353
Columbus, Jason, Gia.	42	185	168	21	47	73	12	1	4	23	0	2	3	12	0	40	0	2	3	.280	.335	.435
Cordova, Roman, Mar.†	4	13	12	2	5	5	0	0	0	0	0	0	1	0	0	2	0	2	1	.417	.462	.417
Coulie, Jason, Gia.	4	14	13	0	6	7	1	0	0	4	0	1	0	0	0	3	1	0	1	.462	.429	.538
Creighton, Matt, Cubs	50	223	169	43	61	101	14	1	8	39	0	4	18	31	2	27	12	7	1	.361	.502	.598
Cruz, Elvis, Mar.	36	149	133	19	28	41	5	1	2	17	0	2	0	14	0	41	6	3	2	.211	.282	.308
DaVanon, Jeff, Ang.†	5	21	15	5	10	18	6	1	0	4	0	1	0	5	2	2	2	0	0	.667	.714	1.200
DeCinces, Tim, Ath.*	1	2	2	0	0	0	0	0	0	0	0	0	0	0	0	1	0	0	0	.000	.000	.000
De La Rosa, Isaias, Ath.	25	86	72	12	13	21	1	2	1	10	0	1	2	11	0	23	0	1	0	.181	.302	.292
De Vinney, Rick, Cubs	3	6	4	0	2	3	1	0	0	1	0	1	0	1	0	0	0	0	0	.500	.500	.750
Diaz, Randor, Gia.	48	197	185	24	54	71	3	4	2	22	0	1	1	10	1	23	6	2	6	.292	.330	.384
Dopirak, Brian, Cubs	21	85	79	10	20	24	4	0	0	6	0	0	0	6	0	23	0	0	0	.253	.306	.304
Dryer, Matt, Gia.	4	19	16	3	7	8	1	0	0	5	0	1	1	1	0	4	1	0	0	.438	.474	.500
Duenas, Tommy, Ang.	45	166	137	15	32	50	12	3	0	23	1	2	5	21	1	35	2	2	3	.234	.352	.365
Ellison, Josh, Mar.	39	177	149	32	49	63	8	3	0	11	0	2	3	23	0	21	7	2	2	.329	.424	.423
Figueroa, Luis, Mar.	3	13	13	2	6	10	1	0	1	5	0	0	0	0	0	0	0	0	0	.462	.462	.769
Francisco, Alfredo, Cubs	48	199	188	23	50	61	6	1	1	24	0	2	0	9	0	58	1	3	2	.266	.296	.324
Francois, Francisco, Ath.	40	187	165	30	50	64	5	3	1	22	1	1	6	14	0	44	7	4	1	.303	.376	.388
Franke, Michael, Brew.†	32	125	109	19	22	28	6	0	0	10	1	0	4	11	0	33	2	1	3	.202	.298	.257
Frost, Jeremy, Brew.	27	114	97	14	25	39	7	2	1	15	1	0	1	15	0	24	4	3	3	.258	.363	.402
Garcia, Eustaquio, Ath.	47	201	176	36	47	68	8	2	3	26	0	2	4	19	1	31	4	2	4	.267	.348	.386
Garcia, Jairo, Ath.	16	14	13	4	6	10	2	1	0	5	0	0	0	1	0	1	1	0	0	.462	.500	.769
Garciaparra, Michael, Mar.	46	194	160	27	44	62	8	5	0	20	6	0	8	20	0	42	13	4	5	.275	.383	.388
German, Carlos, Gia.	31	102	86	16	18	29	3	1	2	14	0	1	2	13	0	34	6	0	0	.209	.324	.337
Gomez, Andri, Brew.†	20	90	84	16	27	30	1	1	0	7	0	0	1	5	0	12	4	2	0	.321	.367	.357
Gomez, Francis, Ath.	6	27	23	6	6	11	0	1	1	4	0	0	0	4	0	4	2	0	0	.261	.370	.478
Guhring, Simon, Brew.	25	90	80	11	19	23	4	0	0	15	2	1	1	6	0	15	0	2	1	.238	.295	.288
Harris, Blair, W.S.	9	26	23	3	4	5	1	0	0	4	0	0	0	3	0	10	0	0	0	.174	.269	.217
Henriquez, Hector, Mar.†	9	30	29	1	3	4	1	0	0	1	0	0	0	0	0	8	2	0	0	.103	.133	.138
Herring, Matt, W.S.*	12	34	25	4	5	6	1	0	0	4	0	0	3	6	0	9	0	0	0	.200	.412	.240
Hodges, Jarrod, Mar.*	33	142	121	17	31	46	6	3	1	20	1	0	5	15	0	16	8	5	2	.256	.362	.380
Hornostaj, Aaron, Gia.*	53	235	199	33	58	76	11	2	1	27	4	2	2	28	0	43	12	3	2	.291	.381	.382
Hrynio, Mike, Mar.	39	156	134	17	33	48	8	2	1	15	1	1	7	13	0	40	2	1	0	.246	.342	.358
Hunt, Stephen, Brew.*	48	214	186	32	54	89	10	5	5	42	0	3	2	23	0	45	6	0	6	.290	.369	.478
Ido, Nobutoshi, W.S.	21	55	49	11	12	21	2	2	1	7	0	0	2	4	0	10	2	1	1	.245	.327	.429
Imperiali, Francesco, Mar.	51	214	186	27	53	62	7	1	0	26	1	0	1	26	0	33	6	0	5	.285	.376	.333
Ishikawa, Travis, Gia.*	19	77	68	10	19	30	4	2	1	10	0	0	2	7	1	20	7	0	1	.279	.364	.441
January, Javerro, Brew.	5	17	15	3	1	4	0	0	1	4	0	0	0	2	0	3	0	0	0	.067	.176	.267
Johnson, Kade, Brew.	3	9	7	1	0	0	0	0	0	0	0	0	0	2	0	4	0	0	2	.000	.222	.000
Jones, Joshua, Ang.	23	74	71	10	16	19	3	0	0	7	0	0	0	3	0	25	1	0	0	.225	.257	.268
Keefner, Eric, W.S.	36	139	127	15	29	45	8	1	2	16	0	1	1	10	0	41	2	1	1	.228	.288	.354
Kendrick, Howard, Ang.†	42	172	157	24	50	64	6	4	0	13	1	1	6	7	0	11	12	6	0	.318	.368	.408
Kenning, Ryan, Ang.*	6	26	22	4	7	11	4	0	0	4	0	0	0	4	1	8	0	0	0	.318	.423	.500
Klippenstein, Tyler, Ath.	51	225	205	25	42	60	7	1	3	30	0	1	3	16	0	54	6	3	2	.205	.272	.293
Knox, Brad, Ath.	10	0	0	0	0	0	0	0	0	0	0	0	0	0	0	0	3	0	0	.000	.000	.000
Kroski, Chris, Mar.*	32	102	82	14	20	36	5	1	3	19	1	0	3	16	0	19	1	2	0	.244	.386	.439
Lebron, Freddie, W.S.†	41	172	147	30	41	54	7	3	0	17	5	1	1	18	0	18	10	4	0	.279	.359	.367
Luna, Leonardo, W.S.	50	232	221	38	74	102	13	6	1	30	3	1	0	13	0	37	8	4	2	.335	.341	.462

Player, Team	G	TPA	AB	R	H	TB	2B	3B	HR	RBI	SH	SF	HP	BB	IBB	SO	SB	CS	GDP	Avg.	OBP	Slg.
Maher, Caleb, Ang.	48	207	194	22	58	79	11	2	2	31	0	1	3	9	0	51	0	3	4	.299	.338	.407
Marmol, Carlos, Cubs	47	195	186	22	48	63	6	3	1	16	3	2	1	3	0	35	10	4	3	.258	.271	.339
Martinez, Joan, Gia.	11	17	16	2	1	1	0	0	0	1	0	0	0	1	0	3	0	0	1	.063	.118	.063
Mateo, Aneudis, Mar.	12	42	39	3	7	10	3	0	0	4	0	1	0	2	0	7	0	0	1	.179	.214	.256
Maynard, Scott, Mar.	2	3	2	0	0	0	0	0	0	0	0	0	0	1	0	1	0	0	0	.000	.333	.000
Mazzanti, Giuseppe, Mar.	34	134	118	16	24	39	4	1	3	9	0	2	5	9	0	40	1	0	2	.203	.284	.331
McBeth, Marcus, Ath.	4	12	9	5	3	3	0	0	0	0	0	0	0	3	0	0	3	0	2	.333	.500	.333
McCormack, Taylor, Brew.	42	168	152	24	39	59	5	3	3	28	0	3	3	10	1	42	2	3	4	.257	.310	.388
Mejia, Jorge, Ath.	35	143	129	19	31	35	4	0	0	14	1	1	2	10	1	33	4	1	1	.240	.303	.271
Mejia, Lekis, Ath.	25	99	94	14	26	45	5	1	4	16	0	1	2	2	0	17	1	1	0	.277	.303	.479
Melo, Manuel, Brew.†	20	88	78	13	28	31	3	0	0	12	1	2	0	7	0	17	14	1	0	.359	.402	.397
Metzger, Gregory, Ath.	31	128	112	19	28	49	4	1	5	12	0	2	7	7	0	35	2	1	2	.250	.328	.438
Morban, Franklin, Ath.	17	57	50	2	8	12	2	1	0	4	1	1	1	4	0	15	1	0	1	.288	.380	.390
Morillo, Roberto, Gia.†	22	72	59	14	17	23	1	1	1	11	1	2	2	8	0	15	5	1	0	.288	.414	.434
Moss, Steve, Brew.	30	133	106	20	31	46	8	2	1	20	0	3	2	22	0	32	3	1	1	.292	.414	.434
Munhall, Brian, Gia.	46	193	175	25	52	65	9	2	0	23	0	3	3	11	1	25	5	1	8	.297	.344	.371
Myers, Michael, W.S.	44	193	165	34	55	73	12	3	0	23	1	1	2	24	2	24	18	1	1	.333	.422	.442
Nunez, Felix, Ang.	4	17	15	2	2	2	0	0	0	2	1	0	0	1	0	6	1	0	0	.133	.188	.133
Olguin, Ruben, Mar.*	48	196	177	31	55	83	10	3	4	31	1	2	1	15	0	40	3	4	3	.311	.364	.469
Olszta, Eddie, Mar.	32	98	80	11	15	19	2	1	0	9	6	1	3	8	0	38	2	2	0	.188	.283	.238
O'Toole, Paul, Cubs*	3	12	9	2	4	5	1	0	0	1	0	0	0	3	1	1	0	1	0	.444	.583	.556
Patterson, Derek, Brew.	19	71	60	13	17	27	5	1	1	8	0	2	1	8	0	11	0	0	2	.283	.366	.450
Paulino, Adalberto, Gia.	43	184	175	23	46	64	7	4	1	18	0	1	2	6	0	26	7	2	2	.263	.293	.366
Peel, Aaron, Ang.	43	161	147	13	37	49	10	1	0	15	1	4	0	9	1	35	4	2	2	.252	.288	.333
Perez, Antonio, Mar.	6	21	15	3	5	9	1	0	1	3	0	1	1	4	0	2	4	0	0	.333	.476	.600
Perez, Luis, Ath.	42	190	168	33	57	85	8	4	4	32	1	1	4	16	1	18	8	7	3	.339	.407	.506
Perez, Melvin, W.S.	44	147	135	18	33	46	7	3	0	13	0	3	0	9	0	36	0	4	5	.244	.286	.341
Pie, Felix, Cubs*	55	248	218	42	70	124	16	13	4	37	1	4	4	21	1	47	17	8	1	.321	.385	.569
Plasencia, Francisco, Brew.*.	17	75	66	15	23	30	2	1	1	14	0	0	1	8	0	13	4	1	1	.348	.427	.455
Ramirez, Juan, Ath.	16	60	48	6	11	13	2	0	0	5	2	0	2	8	0	15	3	1	0	.229	.362	.271
Randolph, Jaisen, Brew.†	2	6	5	0	1	1	0	0	0	1	0	0	0	1	1	0	0	0	0	.200	.333	.200
Renz, Jordan, Ang.†	42	172	145	16	31	38	5	1	0	10	0	0	7	20	2	51	1	1	5	.214	.337	.262
Reyes, Jose, Cubs†	19	58	50	4	9	11	0	1	0	7	0	1	0	6	0	13	3	1	1	.180	.276	.220
Rick, Alan, Cubs*	23	86	69	11	16	18	2	0	0	4	1	2	3	11	0	16	1	2	1	.232	.353	.261
Rivera, Jhonny, W.S.	46	172	153	26	41	59	10	4	0	21	1	1	5	12	0	31	7	4	2	.268	.339	.386
Rodriguez , William, Ath.*	38	158	120	22	26	39	6	2	1	12	0	1	7	30	0	46	3	1	2	.217	.399	.325
Rodriguez, Guilder, Brew.†.	47	203	186	38	48	55	3	2	0	20	2	3	1	11	0	23	6	1	0	.258	.299	.296
Rogers, Nick, Ath.	47	213	178	33	60	80	8	6	0	33	1	1	2	31	2	40	21	1	3	.337	.439	.449
Rogowski, Casey, W.S.*	8	33	31	4	15	27	6	0	2	8	0	1	0	1	0	5	2	1	1	.484	.485	.871
Saint Hilaire, Reynaldo, W.S. .	15	1	1	0	0	0	0	0	0	0	0	0	0	0	0	1	0	0	0	.000	.000	.000
Salas, Francisco, Cubs	34	143	122	33	38	59	2	2	5	24	5	0	7	9	0	14	4	1	2	.311	.391	.484
Sanchez, Ivan, Ath.	15	43	41	5	8	10	2	0	0	3	0	0	0	2	0	17	0	0	1	.195	.233	.244
Santana, Waner, Gia.†	47	208	182	36	46	64	3	3	3	29	4	1	1	20	0	39	3	5	3	.253	.328	.352
Schnurstein, Micah, W.S.	50	226	205	28	68	105	26	1	3	48	1	4	4	12	1	34	1	2	4	.332	.373	.512
Scoville, Shane, W.S.	32	119	108	16	30	41	8	0	1	13	0	1	2	8	0	19	1	1	1	.278	.336	.380
Seijas, Luis, Ang.†	16	32	31	5	10	13	3	0	0	6	0	0	0	0	0	6	1	0	1	.323	.313	.419
Serafini, Matt, Brew.	20	86	76	16	20	30	4	0	2	11	0	1	1	8	0	18	3	0	2	.263	.337	.395
Soto, Geovany, Cubs	44	175	156	24	42	65	10	2	3	24	1	2	3	13	1	35	0	2	2	.269	.333	.417
Soto, Maximo, Ang.	22	87	76	6	16	23	4	0	1	13	0	2	0	7	0	35	1	2	4	.211	.271	.303
Soto, Wilber, Ang.	52	228	189	35	41	53	4	4	0	15	0	1	4	34	0	36	28	10	5	.217	.346	.280
Spearman, Jemel, Cubs	54	242	208	46	65	85	7	5	1	21	0	3	3	28	0	22	29	1	4	.313	.397	.409
Summerall, Dennis, Cubs*	49	208	187	22	49	78	9	4	4	27	1	3	6	11	2	54	1	1	1	.262	.319	.417
Thornton-Murray, Jandin, Cubs†.	10	41	39	7	8	13	3	1	0	7	0	0	0	2	0	6	0	1	0	.205	.244	.333
Trinidad, Edgar, Ath.	26	117	102	18	25	30	3	1	0	10	1	1	0	13	0	20	2	2	3	.245	.328	.294
Turco, Anthony, Gia.*	5	16	11	3	4	7	1	1	0	4	0	0	1	4	0	2	0	1	0	.364	.563	.636
Valdez, Richard, Cubs	15	3	3	0	0	0	0	0	0	0	0	0	0	0	0	1	0	0	0	.000	.000	.000
Valdez, Tommy, Ath.	43	170	149	26	28	55	5	2	6	18	0	0	21	1	57	3	2	0	.188	.288	.369
Vazquez, Rafael, Cubs	36	147	138	13	39	50	9	1	0	20	0	3	4	2	0	16	0	4	4	.283	.306	.362
Viera, Orlando, Brew.*	5	9	7	0	1	1	0	0	0	1	0	0	0	1	0	3	1	0	0	.143	.250	.143
Walston, Chris, Ang.	41	160	150	16	31	39	6	1	0	10	0	0	2	8	0	67	0	1	4	.207	.256	.260
Ware, Matthew, Mar.	9	20	19	2	2	2	0	0	0	0	0	0	0	1	0	8	0	0	0	.105	.150	.105
Wear, Gregory, Mar.	17	7	7	0	2	2	0	0	0	0	0	0	0	0	0	4	0	0	0	.286	.286	.286
Wells, Randy, Cubs	14	49	41	6	6	7	1	0	0	4	2	1	2	3	1	16	0	0	1	.146	.234	.171
Williams, Jonny, Gia.*	10	35	32	9	10	18	1	2	1	5	1	0	0	2	0	0	1	1	0	.313	.353	.563
Willis, Lendon, Brew.	44	180	159	28	44	59	13	1	0	23	0	1	5	15	0	41	3	0	4	.277	.356	.371
Wilson, Michael, Mar.†	41	171	143	28	34	51	5	0	4	19	0	1	9	18	0	52	4	1	2	.238	.357	.357
Womack, Josh, Mar.*	43	179	160	20	43	66	10	5	1	12	1	1	4	13	0	25	8	1	4	.269	.337	.413
Woody, Dominic, Mar.	2	6	5	0	0	0	0	0	0	0	0	0	0	1	0	1	0	0	0	.000	.167	.000
Young, Chris, W.S.	55	210	184	26	40	70	13	1	5	17	2	0	5	19	0	54	7	8	1	.217	.308	.380
Young, Eddie, W.S.	45	171	156	31	40	51	3	2	1	22	1	2	2	10	0	37	10	4	2	.256	.306	.327

GRAND SLAMS: Hunt 2, Brown, January, W. Santana, 1 each.

AWARDED FIRST BASE ON CATCHER'S INTERFERENCE: Creighton 2 (Almanzar, J. Ramirez), M. Soto 2 (Morban 2), Munhall (Alvarado), Viera (Kroski).

2002 PITCHING
TEAM

Team	W	L	Pct.	ERA	G	CG	ShO	Sv.	IP	H	TBF	R	ER	HR	SH	SF	HB	BB	IBB	SO	WP	Bk.
Giants	33	23	.589	3.57	56	0	1	16	504.0	467	2157	264	200	22	8	26	39	178	2	457	42	13
White Sox	27	29	.482	3.62	56	1	3	12	505.0	501	2191	276	203	22	13	15	38	176	11	434	37	19
Cubs	35	21	.625	3.68	56	0	2	23	503.1	466	2210	264	206	14	14	16	53	194	6	505	43	21
Angels	28	28	.500	4.50	56	0	1	18	495.2	505	2210	326	248	14	13	24	30	225	8	505	46	15
Athletics	28	28	.500	4.61	56	0	3	14	498.1	563	2251	351	255	34	14	21	42	159	1	451	62	13
Mariners	19	37	.339	4.94	56	0	1	7	494.0	601	2265	341	271	19	12	16	35	165	0	409	55	19
Brewers	26	30	.464	5.23	56	0	2	12	493.2	540	2301	358	287	20	19	23	58	253	5	452	42	14

TOP QUALIFIERS FOR EARNED-RUN AVERAGE TITLE

Minimum 45 innings.*Lefthanded pitcher.

Pitcher, Team	W	L	Pct.	ERA	G	GS	CG	ShO	GF	Sv.	IP	H	TBF	R	ER	HR	SH	SF	HB	BB	IBB	SO	WP	Bk.
Jones, Justin, Cubs*	3	1	.750	1.80	11	11	0	0	0	0	50	31	198	12	10	0	2	1	6	18	2	63	4	2
Haigwood, Daniel, W.S.*	8	4	.667	2.28	14	14	0	0	0	0	75	69	319	31	19	2	2	3	5	26	1	74	6	2
Corchado, Jose, Ath.	3	1	.750	2.44	14	6	0	0	2	1	48	54	213	23	13	0	1	2	3	12	0	38	7	0
Garcia, Jairo, Ath.	2	1	.667	2.44	13	8	0	0	1	1	59	56	242	24	16	5	3	1	3	17	0	66	4	1
Burdette, Jason, Ath.	5	3	.625	2.52	15	8	0	0	2	1	60.2	59	252	26	17	2	2	2	5	17	0	59	2	0
English, Jesse, Gia.*	4	1	.800	2.68	12	12	0	0	0	0	47	33	195	17	14	2	0	0	7	18	0	68	2	1
McCarthy, Brandon, W.S.	4	4	.500	2.76	14	14	0	0	0	0	78.1	78	326	40	24	6	2	1	2	15	1	79	5	3
Portorreal, Carlos, Ang.	6	2	.750	3.00	14	14	0	0	0	0	72	60	295	31	24	1	1	5	8	22	0	64	6	4
Moreno, Abel, Ang.	2	3	.400	3.00	13	7	0	0	2	0	45	44	190	27	15	0	2	4	3	10	2	47	1	1
Espinal, Luis, Mar.	5	5	.500	3.46	11	9	0	0	1	0	65	66	275	28	25	1	2	2	4	13	0	33	6	1
Pena, Luismar, Brew.	4	1	.800	3.49	11	7	0	0	2	0	49	45	220	28	19	1	0	2	6	24	0	52	3	0
Tavarez, Carlos, Cubs	7	4	.636	3.64	14	13	0	0	0	0	71.2	65	304	39	29	5	0	3	6	16	0	71	0	2
Ramirez, Edward, Ang.	2	5	.286	3.69	13	7	0	0	1	0	46.1	47	197	22	19	1	0	1	4	13	0	45	1	0
Ramirez, Carlos, Brew.*	6	5	.545	3.70	15	14	0	0	0	0	75.1	84	332	41	31	2	4	1	4	25	0	60	2	2
Rodriguez, Ryan, W.S.*	5	2	.714	3.76	14	12	0	0	0	0	69.1	69	294	36	29	1	3	3	7	16	0	47	2	2

DEPARTMENTAL LEADERS: W—Haigwood, 8; L—Several pitchers tied with 5; Pct.—Portorreal, .750; G—Arias, 27; GS—Haigwood, McCarthy, Portorreal, C. Ramirez, 14 each; CG—Ortiz, 1; ShO—Ortiz, 1; GF—Arias, 26; Sv.—Arias, 15; IP—McCarthy, 78.1; H—Graterol, 86; TBF—C. Ramirez, 332; R—Mejia, 48; ER—Mejia, 36; HR—McCarthy, Reynoso, 6 each; SH—C. Ramirez, 4; SF—Jaquez, Portorreal, R. Ramirez, 5 each; HB—Mejia, 20; BB—A. Martinez, Ortiz, 32 each; IBB—Mitchell, 3; SO—McCarthy, 79; WP—C. Santana, 9; BK—R. Ramirez, 5.

ALL PITCHERS

*Lefthanded pitcher.

Pitcher, Team	W	L	Pct.	ERA	G	GS	CG	ShO	GF	Sv.	IP	H	TBF	R	ER	HR	SH	SF	HB	BB	IBB	SO	WP	Bk.
Acors, Bo, Mar.	3	1	.750	7.71	5	0	0	0	4	0	11.2	18	57	11	10	0	2	0	0	4	0	16	0	0
Albright, Eric, Cubs	0	0	.000	1.50	2	2	0	0	0	0	6	7	26	1	1	0	0	0	1	0	2	0	1
Alliston, Josh, Brew.	0	1	.000	2.45	4	0	0	0	3	0	7.1	6	30	4	2	0	2	0	0	2	1	8	1	0
Alvarez, Larry, Cubs	0	0	.000	5.06	5	3	0	0	1	0	10.2	11	44	6	6	0	0	0	2	0	12	1	0
Arias, Daniel, Ang.	1	2	.333	1.20	27	0	0	0	26	15	30	24	114	6	4	0	0	0	3	1	38	1	3
Arnold, Mitchell, Ang.	1	0	1.000	7.54	15	2	0	0	3	0	22.2	29	126	34	19	1	0	4	0	29	0	19	7	1
Avendano, Elvis, Ath.	1	5	.167	8.33	14	3	0	0	2	1	31.1	46	154	31	29	3	0	1	5	8	0	24	1	4
Baez, Federico, Cubs	0	0	.000	1.95	18	0	0	0	13	9	27.2	22	109	7	6	1	2	0	0	8	0	19	2	0
Baez, Hebel, Ath.	1	1	.500	9.00	5	1	0	0	1	0	10	17	52	11	10	1	1	0	3	0	8	1	1
Balser, Jeff, Ang.	1	0	1.000	4.35	8	0	0	0	3	0	10.1	12	48	8	5	1	1	0	6	1	11	0	0
Banks, Demetrius, W.S.*	0	0	.000	5.40	8	0	0	0	0	0	10	12	50	10	6	1	0	1	8	0	10	6	1
Barnett, Daniel, Ath.	0	2	.000	6.08	13	4	0	0	4	2	37	50	175	33	25	5	1	1	17	0	30	7	0
Barreras, Rene, Mar.*	0	0	.000	2.11	18	0	0	0	6	0	21.1	21	100	6	5	0	1	1	16	0	19	3	2
Benjamin, Petersen, Gia.	0	0	.000	0.00	1	0	0	0	0	0	2	0	7	0	0	0	0	0	0	0	2	0	0
Bergdall, Kendall, Mar.*	1	0	1.000	5.65	6	1	0	0	0	0	14.1	17	72	11	9	0	1	0	10	0	16	3	4
Bernat, David, Mar.	0	0	.000	9.53	5	1	0	0	2	0	5.2	5	34	7	6	0	0	3	7	0	6	4	1
Burdette, Jason, Ath.	5	3	.625	2.52	15	8	0	0	2	1	60.2	59	252	26	17	2	2	2	5	17	0	59	2	0
Cabaniel, Tomas, Ath.	3	4	.429	4.35	16	3	0	0	9	2	41.1	35	178	30	20	3	1	4	16	0	42	7	2
Cain, Matthew, Gia.	0	1	.000	3.72	8	7	0	0	0	0	19.1	13	83	10	8	1	0	2	11	0	20	3	0
Cervenka, Dennis, Mar.*	1	0	1.000	1.80	3	3	0	0	0	0	5	4	24	5	1	0	0	1	2	0	2	1	0
Corchado, Jose, Ath.	3	1	.750	2.44	14	6	0	0	2	1	48	54	213	23	13	0	1	2	3	12	0	38	7	0
Corcoran, John, Mar.	1	0	1.000	0.82	2	1	0	0	0	0	11	6	41	2	1	0	0	0	1	0	10	1	1
Cordero, Victor, Brew.	1	1	.500	6.10	6	0	0	0	3	0	10.1	7	47	8	7	0	0	0	2	7	0	10	2	0
Correa, Alexander, Brew.*	2	0	1.000	3.71	15	0	0	0	7	1	43.2	40	194	20	18	0	3	4	23	1	49	4	1
Cortez, Renee, Mar.	1	3	.250	3.56	7	5	0	0	0	0	43	47	185	22	17	0	1	1	2	6	0	54	5	0
Curreri, Joe, W.S.	0	0	.000	5.40	3	0	0	0	1	0	5	5	22	3	3	0	0	1	1	0	7	2	0
Delgadillo, Ambiroix, Ang.*	5	1	.833	3.86	21	1	0	0	4	1	35	19	144	16	15	1	1	2	24	0	44	5	0
De Vinney, Rick, Cubs	0	0	.000	5.40	1	0	0	0	0	0	1.2	4	10	1	1	0	0	0	1	0	0	0	0
Dominguez, Carlos, Cubs	1	0	1.000	2.76	7	0	0	0	3	1	16.1	11	69	7	5	0	1	1	6	0	16	3	0
English, Jesse, Gia.*	4	1	.800	2.68	12	12	0	0	0	0	47	33	195	17	14	2	0	0	7	18	0	68	2	1
Espinal, Luis, Mar.	5	5	.500	3.46	11	9	0	0	1	0	65	66	275	28	25	1	2	2	4	13	0	33	6	1
Fernando, Gilberto, Gia.*	0	0	.000	2.70	7	0	0	0	3	1	6.2	7	30	2	2	0	0	1	3	0	4	3	0
Figueroa, Eduardo, Mar.	0	2	.000	12.00	3	1	0	0	0	0	6	10	36	10	8	0	0	1	3	0	5	2	1
Figueroa, Luis, Mar.	0	0	.000	0.00	1	0	0	0	1	0	1	1	4	0	0	0	0	0	0	0	2	0	1
Forbes, Terry, Mar.	0	1	.000	4.50	5	2	0	0	1	0	14	21	64	17	7	0	3	0	4	0	11	3	1
Freeman, Kai, W.S.	0	0	.000	2.00	8	0	0	0	1	0	9	9	35	2	2	0	0	0	1	0	8	1	1
Frye, Randall, Mar.	1	4	.200	8.29	8	5	0	0	0	0	33.2	50	166	34	31	3	1	0	15	0	23	2	1
Fyvie, Dan, Ath.	3	1	.750	2.92	19	0	0	0	13	2	24.2	17	108	18	8	1	0	2	12	0	16	4	0
Garcia, Jairo, Ath.	2	1	.667	2.44	13	8	0	0	1	1	59	56	242	24	16	5	3	1	3	17	0	66	4	1
Garcia, James, Gia.	0	0	.000	0.75	9	0	0	0	7	3	12	4	42	1	1	0	0	0	4	0	18	0	0
Garcia, Miguel, Brew.	1	2	.333	10.38	10	0	0	0	4	0	26	48	139	34	30	1	4	7	12	0	7	3	4
Garcia, Ruddy, Gia.	1	2	.333	3.35	15	6	0	0	1	0	43	46	189	27	16	3	0	1	19	0	32	0	0
Gelatka, Todd, Brew.	0	1	.000	243.00	2	1	0	0	0	0	0.1	4	10	9	9	0	0	2	3	0	0	0	0
Gittings, Christopher, Brew.	0	0	.000	0.00	1	0	0	0	1	0	1	0	3	0	0	0	0	0	0	0	0	0	0
Gomez, Rafael, W.S.	1	1	.500	3.46	14	0	0	0	5	0	13	13	63	5	5	1	0	1	7	0	12	0	0
Graterol, Francisco, Mar.	1	4	.200	5.88	11	4	0	0	3	0	52	86	255	45	34	5	1	2	8	0	33	5	1
Gwyn, Marc, Ath.	1	3	.250	2.81	5	5	0	0	0	0	16	19	67	8	5	1	0	0	0	0	23	0	0
Haeger, Charles, W.S.*	1	4	.200	4.17	25	0	0	0	14	6	41	46	178	25	19	2	2	1	6	13	2	24	1	0
Haigwood, Daniel, W.S.*	8	4	.667	2.28	14	14	0	0	0	0	75	69	319	31	19	2	2	3	5	26	1	74	6	2
Hawkins, Al, Brew.	1	3	.250	5.95	6	6	0	0	0	0	19.2	30	94	20	13	4	1	3	1	5	0	12	1	0
Hernandez, Armando, Gia.	4	3	.571	4.18	18	0	0	0	5	0	28	34	130	20	13	2	1	3	1	6	0	29	2	0
Hines, Matthew, Cubs	0	0	.000	0.00	4	0	0	0	3	2	7	4	24	0	0	0	1	0	0	0	6	0	0
Hixson, David, Gia.	1	1	.500	4.26	5	0	0	0	0	0	6.1	8	27	3	3	0	0	0	4	0	4	0	0
Huchingson, Jamin, W.S.	0	0	.000	3.86	6	0	0	0	1	0	7	5	31	3	3	0	1	0	5	0	5	2	0
January, Javerro, Brew.	0	0	.000	0.00	1	0	0	0	1	0	1	1	4	0	0	0	0	0	0	0	0	0	0

SUMMER CLASS A Arizona League

Pitcher, Team	W	L	Pct.	ERA	G	GS	CG	ShO	GF	Sv.	IP	H	TBF	R	ER	HR	SH	SF	HB	BB	IBB	SO	WP	Bk.
Jaquez, Eddi, Gia.	4	2	.667	4.65	13	13	0	0	0	0	62	63	268	35	32	3	1	5	3	22	0	51	1	1
Jepsen, Kevin, Ang.	1	3	.250	6.84	8	5	0	0	1	0	26.1	29	125	22	20	2	0	2	5	12	0	19	1	0
Jimenez, Cesar, Mar.	0	0	.000	3.38	1	0	0	0	0	0	2.2	3	11	2	1	0	1	0	0	0	0	3	0	0
Jimenez, Julio, Brew.*	0	2	.000	4.98	16	0	0	0	6	3	34.1	34	161	23	19	1	1	1	4	24	0	22	2	0
Johnson, J.D., W.S.	1	1	.500	4.58	16	0	0	0	12	5	17.2	15	78	9	9	0	0	3	1	8	1	17	1	0
Jones, Justin, Cubs*	3	1	.750	1.80	11	11	0	0	0	0	50	31	198	12	10	0	2	1	6	18	2	63	4	2
Knox, Brad, Ath.	2	3	.400	4.17	10	7	0	0	1	0	41	44	181	28	19	2	0	2	5	9	0	42	2	2
Korneev, Oleg, Mar.	1	2	.333	4.50	3	1	0	0	0	0	12	19	56	9	6	1	0	0	4	0	0	12	2	0
Lara, Nelson, Gia.	0	0	.000	0.00	2	0	0	0	0	0	3.2	2	16	0	0	0	0	0	0	3	0	2	2	0
Lopez, Orionny, W.S.	1	4	.200	3.97	17	3	0	0	7	3	34	31	140	15	15	3	1	0	1	11	1	38	1	4
Magallanes , Fidel, Gia.	0	0	.000	22.09	4	0	0	0	2	0	3.2	2	22	9	9	0	0	0	1	8	0	5	1	0
Marmol, Carlos, Cubs	0	0	.000	0.00	1	0	0	0	1	0	1	1	5	0	0	0	0	0	0	1	0	1	0	1
Martinez Sosa, Alvaro, Brew. ..	0	5	.000	7.30	15	3	0	0	3	0	37	42	189	41	30	2	2	2	5	32	1	34	7	1
Martinez, Jose, Cubs*	1	0	1.000	2.84	3	0	0	0	0	0	6.1	4	23	2	2	0	0	0	0	1	0	4	1	2
Martinez, Miguel, Mar.*	0	0	.000	4.29	6	3	0	0	1	0	21	26	90	10	10	1	2	1	1	4	0	20	2	0
Martinez, Pedro, Ath.*	2	0	1.000	4.64	10	2	0	0	4	1	21.1	22	97	15	11	1	1	0	1	7	0	19	7	1
McCarthy, Brandon, W.S.	4	4	.500	2.76	14	14	0	0	0	0	78.1	78	326	40	24	6	2	1	2	15	1	79	5	3
McCormack, Taylor, Brew.	0	0	.000	7.71	3	0	0	0	2	0	2.1	4	11	2	2	0	0	0	2	0	0	1	0	0
McCurdy, Jason, W.S.*	2	0	1.000	3.38	17	0	0	0	2	0	21.1	17	83	8	8	1	1	0	1	7	0	15	0	1
McMullen, Jeremy, Cubs	1	1	.500	1.65	10	0	0	0	5	1	16.1	11	73	6	3	0	0	1	0	13	1	18	3	0
Mejia, Andy, Cubs	7	3	.700	6.04	15	10	0	0	2	1	53.2	60	264	48	36	2	1	3	20	24	0	28	6	1
Mena, Juan, Ang.	0	1	.000	7.71	5	0	0	0	2	0	4.2	5	25	5	4	0	0	0	4	0	0	5	1	0
Mendoza, Gabriel, Brew.*	2	1	.667	3.53	19	0	0	0	12	6	43.1	42	196	23	17	2	2	2	6	18	0	50	8	0
Mitchell, Nathan, Cubs	2	1	.667	2.53	14	0	0	0	11	5	21.1	25	90	6	6	3	0	1	7	3	0	22	1	0
Morban, Carlos, Ang.	2	0	1.000	5.19	17	0	0	0	4	1	26	26	121	19	15	0	0	3	2	15	2	35	7	0
Moreno, Abel, Ang.	2	3	.400	3.00	13	7	0	0	2	0	45	44	190	27	15	0	2	4	3	10	2	47	1	1
Moreno, Anthony, Gia.	1	1	.500	3.80	16	1	0	0	1	0	23.2	24	99	11	10	1	1	0	0	6	1	17	1	1
Nacar, Leslie, Gia.	2	1	.667	3.29	18	0	0	0	5	0	27.1	23	114	12	10	0	2	1	7	0	25	2	1
Nisbett, Marshall, Mar.	1	2	.333	4.30	16	0	0	0	13	5	23	26	101	13	11	0	0	1	9	0	28	2	0
Ortiz, Dario, W.S.	3	5	.375	4.87	14	12	1	1	0	0	61	55	277	46	33	3	1	1	4	32	0	49	5	3
Parra, Manuel, Brew.*	0	0	.000	4.50	1	1	0	0	0	0	2	1	7	1	1	0	0	0	0	0	0	4	0	0
Patterson, Derek, Brew.	0	1	.000	9.00	1	0	0	0	0	0	3	2	16	3	3	0	2	0	0	4	0	0	0	0
Pawelczyk, Kyle, Ang.*	0	0	.000	0.00	1	1	0	0	0	0	3	2	11	0	0	0	0	0	1	0	0	2	0	0
Pena, Luismar, Brew.	4	1	.800	3.49	11	7	0	0	2	0	49	45	220	28	19	1	2	6	24	0	52	3	0
Perez, Elvis, Mar.	0	0	.000	0.00	3	3	0	0	0	0	4	1	13	0	0	0	0	0	0	0	0	2	0	0
Perry, Brandon, Mar.*	3	2	.600	4.47	10	5	0	0	2	0	46.1	52	208	29	23	1	0	2	6	18	0	39	4	1
Petrick, Billy, Cubs	2	1	.667	1.71	6	6	0	0	0	0	31.2	21	120	8	6	0	0	3	6	0	35	0	0
Pierre, Adolfo, Brew.*	3	2	.600	7.84	17	0	0	0	11	2	31	39	161	31	27	0	3	5	24	2	26	0	2
Poe, Ryan, Brew.	1	0	1.000	1.80	3	3	0	0	0	0	10	8	41	3	2	0	0	2	0	13	0	0	0	0
Portorreal, Carlos, Gia.	6	2	.750	3.00	14	14	0	0	0	0	72	60	295	31	24	1	1	5	8	22	0	64	6	4
Pruett, Hubert, Brew.	4	1	.800	4.91	11	5	0	0	2	0	40.1	44	187	26	22	2	4	1	6	17	0	36	4	0
Ramirez, Carlos, Brew.*	6	5	.545	3.70	15	14	0	0	0	0	75.1	84	332	41	31	2	4	1	4	25	0	60	2	2
Ramirez, Edward, Ang.	2	5	.286	3.69	13	7	0	0	1	0	46.1	47	197	22	19	1	0	1	4	13	0	45	1	0
Ramirez, Luis, Mar.*	0	2	.000	14.94	12	4	0	0	1	0	15.2	30	97	30	26	0	1	2	22	0	17	6	3
Ramirez, Rafael, Gia.	2	5	.286	5.03	13	3	0	0	0	0	39.1	43	178	36	22	2	2	5	1	16	0	25	5	5
Ramos, Jonathan, Cubs*	3	0	1.000	0.95	4	2	0	0	0	0	19	10	75	2	2	0	0	1	0	6	0	25	2	2
Ray, Ronnie, Ang.	4	4	.500	4.91	16	7	0	0	3	0	58.2	59	257	34	32	2	1	1	4	22	1	65	4	0
Reyes, Julio, Ang.*	3	1	.750	7.58	16	0	0	0	3	0	19	35	98	21	16	1	1	0	1	4	0	14	3	3
Reynoso, Anibal, Ath.	1	0	1.000	12.54	10	2	0	0	3	0	18.2	38	110	32	26	6	1	0	2	9	1	9	3	1
Richardson, Judd, Brew.	0	3	.000	7.04	7	7	0	0	0	0	23	24	106	21	18	3	0	0	2	14	0	22	3	2
Ring, Royce, W.S.*	0	0	.000	0.00	3	0	0	0	2	0	5	2	17	0	0	0	0	0	0	0	0	9	0	0
Robinson, Jeff, Brew.	0	1	.000	10.80	3	3	0	0	0	0	8.1	13	40	10	10	2	0	0	0	3	0	9	1	0
Rodriguez , Rafael, Ang.	2	1	.667	3.99	8	8	0	0	0	0	38.1	37	172	19	17	4	2	0	5	20	0	50	3	0
Rodriguez, Pedro, Cubs	1	2	.333	6.38	16	1	0	0	6	1	36.2	53	176	34	26	1	0	2	4	16	0	27	5	0
Rodriguez, Ryan, W.S.*	5	2	.714	3.76	14	12	0	0	0	0	69.1	69	294	36	29	1	3	3	7	16	0	47	2	2
Rondon, Yosy, Gia.*	0	2	.000	5.74	16	0	0	0	5	0	15.2	10	75	12	10	0	2	2	2	16	0	25	2	0
Rupp, Mike, W.S.	1	1	.500	7.50	11	0	0	0	1	0	12	15	61	13	10	1	0	0	4	8	1	15	2	2
Sager, Brian, W.S.	0	0	.000	4.50	2	0	0	0	1	0	2	2	8	1	1	0	0	0	0	0	0	2	0	0
St. Amand, Reuben, Gia.	0	0	.000	3.86	6	0	0	0	1	0	7	8	34	5	3	0	0	1	2	1	0	4	2	0
Saint Hilaire, Reynaldo, W.S.	0	0	.000	2.42	15	1	0	0	3	1	22.1	28	98	16	6	1	0	0	9	2	9	1	0
Sanchez, Adiel, Ath.*	1	2	.333	5.76	16	1	0	0	3	0	29.2	35	136	25	19	1	1	3	2	9	0	22	4	0
Santana, Candido, Cubs*	2	3	.400	3.79	15	2	0	0	4	1	40.1	39	190	29	17	0	3	2	0	28	0	36	9	3
Santana, Roberto, Ath.*	1	0	1.000	9.45	11	0	0	0	6	0	13.1	18	72	21	14	1	0	2	1	10	0	11	7	1
Sarfate, Dennis, Brew.	0	0	.000	2.57	5	5	0	0	0	0	14	6	56	4	4	0	0	1	0	5	0	22	0	2
Schmidt, Jeremy, Gia.	1	0	1.000	0.00	12	0	0	0	9	7	13.1	12	51	0	0	0	0	1	0	11	1	0
Serafini, Matt, Brew.	0	0	.000	13.50	1	0	0	0	1	0	0.2	2	5	1	1	0	0	2	0	1	0	0	0
Shull, Johnathan, Ang.	0	0	.000	6.25	16	5	0	0	2	0	40.1	56	194	43	28	0	3	4	1	24	0	25	3	1
Sierra, Edwardo, Ath.	2	1	.667	4.64	6	6	0	0	0	0	33	29	142	19	17	2	2	2	7	10	0	35	2	0
Sisco, Kelly, Ang.*	1	0	.000	0.00	2	0	0	0	0	0	2.1	2	10	0	0	0	0	0	1	0	3	2	0
Solis, Hairo, Gia.	1	1	.500	4.68	16	0	0	0	3	0	25	36	119	21	13	1	0	3	7	0	10	7	0
Stewart, Scott, Ath.	0	1	.000	4.05	9	0	0	0	5	0	13.1	17	63	7	6	0	0	0	1	3	0	7	4	0
Stirm, Brian, Gia.	2	1	.667	4.32	14	0	0	0	5	2	16.2	15	70	9	8	3	0	0	1	6	1	18	2	0
Stitt, Brian, Mar.	0	1	.000	11.25	2	1	0	0	1	0	4	9	23	7	5	0	0	1	0	6	0	0	0
Tavarez, Carlos, Cubs	7	4	.636	3.64	14	13	0	0	0	0	71.2	65	304	39	29	5	0	3	6	16	0	71	0	2
Thompson, Richard, Ang.	2	0	1.000	2.70	15	0	0	0	2	1	23.1	14	96	12	7	0	1	1	9	0	29	1	1
Tisch, Timothy, W.S.*	0	3	.000	4.50	17	0	0	0	7	0	22	30	111	13	11	0	2	0	14	2	14	2	0
Toledo, Jean, Ang.	3	5	.375	4.47	11	10	0	0	0	0	56.1	60	248	33	28	0	1	3	26	1	42	3	4
Toribio, Auri, Cubs	3	3	.500	6.44	14	4	0	0	1	1	43.1	48	204	37	31	2	0	1	9	21	0	36	0	3
Turnbow, Derrick, Ang.	0	1	.000	4.50	3	3	0	0	0	0	8	5	34	4	4	0	0	0	4	0	3	0	1
Valdez, Richard, Cubs	2	2	.500	4.01	14	2	0	0	6	1	42.2	39	175	19	19	3	2	1	4	18	0	34	6	4
Vasquez, Rucki, Mar.*	1	1	.500	4.10	16	0	0	0	5	0	26.1	28	115	15	12	1	0	0	3	7	0	20	2	0
Villanueva, Carlos, Gia.	4	0	1.000	0.59	19	0	0	0	9	3	30.1	24	113	3	2	1	0	1	0	5	0	33	0	0
Walker, Edwin, Brew.*	1	0	1.000	1.69	4	1	0	0	0	0	10.2	14	52	5	2	0	0	0	1	5	0	14	1	0
Wang, Chao, Mar.	0	2	.000	5.14	13	4	0	0	4	0	21	29	100	19	12	4	0	0	3	5	0	7	1	1
Wear, Gregory, Mar.	0	2	.000	3.49	15	0	0	0	11	2	28.1	24	114	12	11	2	0	1	7	0	23	1	1
Wooten, Greg, Mar.	0	0	.000	0.00	3	3	0	0	0	0	6	2	21	0	0	0	0	0	0	0	2	0	0

COMBINATION SHUTOUTS: **Angels (1)**—R. Rodriguez-E. Ramirez. **Athletics (3)**—Corchado-Burdette, Gwyn-Jairo Garcia, Knox-Avendano. **Brewers (2)**—Pena-Mendoza, Sarfate-Correa. **Cubs (2)**—Alvarez-McMullen, Mejia-Baez. **Giants (1)**—Portorreal-An. Moreno-J. Garcia-Schmidt. **Mariners (1)**—Perez-Perry. **White Sox (2)**—Haigwood-Haeger, McCarthy-Banks-Gomez-McCurdy-Tisch.

NO-HIT GAMES: None.

2002 FIELDING

TEAM

Team	G	PO	A	E	TC	DP	TP	PB	Pct.
Giants	56	1512	564	87	2163	39	0	11	.960
Cubs	56	1510	555	90	2155	53	0	11	.958
Angels	56	1487	544	100	2131	36	0	18	.953
White Sox	56	1515	570	108	2193	50	0	12	.951
Brewers	56	1481	583	112	2176	44	0	27	.949
Mariners	56	1482	575	114	2171	41	0	11	.947
Athletics	56	1495	554	122	2171	36	0	22	.944

INDIVIDUAL

FIRST BASEMEN

NOTE: All caps denotes fielding-percentage leader based on 28 games for catchers, 37 for all other non-pitchers and 45 innings for pitchers. *Throws lefthanded.

Player, Team	Pct.	G	PO	A	E	TC	DP
Alvarado, Joel, Brew.	.950	3	18	1	1	20	2
Barnett, Dan, W.S.	.000	1	0	0	0	0	0
Batista, Christian, Ang.	.000	1	0	0	0	0	0
Bohlander, Michael, W.S.	.986	9	61	8	1	70	8
Bubalo, Ty, Ath.	.962	16	119	8	5	132	7
Cleto, Carlos, Ang.*	1.000	5	35	3	0	38	4
Collins, Mike, Ang.	.970	12	94	3	3	100	5
Columbus, Jason, Gia.	.993	32	291	12	2	305	23
Creighton, Matt, Cubs	.991	25	202	11	2	215	14
Diaz, Randor, Gia.	1.000	3	29	1	0	30	2
Dopirak, Brian, Cubs	1.000	10	71	2	0	73	8
Dryer, Matt, Gia.	.955	2	20	1	1	22	0
Franke, Michael, Brew.	.972	13	100	5	3	108	5
Frost, Jeremy, Brew.	.857	1	6	0	1	7	0
Harris, Blair, W.S.	.941	2	16	0	1	17	0
Herring, Matt, W.S.*	.953	10	57	4	3	64	4
Hrynio, Mike, Mar.	1.000	1	5	1	0	6	3
Ishikawa, Travis, Gia.*	.992	12	116	5	1	122	4
Keefner, Eric, W.S.	.947	22	184	12	11	207	18
Kenning, Ryan, Ang.*	1.000	2	18	4	0	22	0
KLIPPENSTEIN, Tyler, Ath.	.981	41	356	14	7	377	24
Maher, Caleb, Ang.	.000	1	0	0	0	0	0
Mazzanti, Giuseppe, Mar.	.964	13	95	11	4	110	6
McBeth, Marcus, Ath.	1.000	1	2	2	0	4	0
McCormack, Taylor, Brew.	.977	27	206	9	5	220	16
Olguin, Ruben, Mar.*	.973	47	378	26	11	415	26
Patterson, Derek, Ang.	1.000	5	35	1	0	36	3
Perez, Melvin, W.S.	.963	15	99	5	4	108	8
Rick, Alan, Cubs	1.000	2	16	1	0	17	1
Rogowski, Casey, W.S.*	1.000	8	54	1	0	55	6
Santana, Waner, Gia.	.964	4	27	0	1	28	3
Serafini, Matt, Brew.	.962	11	92	8	4	104	9
Soto, Geovany, Cubs	1.000	7	43	1	0	44	7
Soto, Maximo, Ang.	.972	15	129	8	4	141	9
Valdez, Richard, Cubs	.875	1	6	1	1	8	0
Valdez, Tommy, Ath.	.000	1	0	0	0	0	0
Vazquez, Rafael, Cubs	.987	17	144	6	2	152	16
Walston, Chris, Ang.	.983	28	216	11	4	231	16

SECOND BASEMEN

Player, Team	Pct.	G	PO	A	E	TC	DP
Abad, Noel, Ang.	1.000	1	1	0	0	1	0
Abreu, Johany, Gia.	.932	17	28	40	5	73	11
Batista, Christian, Ang.	1.000	1	0	1	0	1	0
Brown, Matthew, Ang.	.000	1	0	0	0	0	0
Cordova, Roman, Mar.	1.000	4	8	5	0	13	0
Creighton, Matt, Cubs	.986	26	57	80	2	139	22
Francisco, Francisco, Ath.	.938	11	33	28	4	65	7
Franke, Michael, Brew.	1.000	3	3	7	0	10	0
Garcia, Eustaquio, Ath.	1.000	1	5	3	0	8	1
Gomez, Andri, Brew.	.981	12	29	24	1	54	3
Henriquez, Hector, Mar.	1.000	1	0	1	0	1	0
Hornostaj, Aaron, Gia.	1.000	18	27	38	0	65	7
Hrynio, Mike, Mar.	.500	1	1	1	2	4	0
Imperiali, Francesco, Mar.	.953	50	86	115	10	211	24
Kendrick, Howard, Ang.	.953	34	61	81	7	149	12
Lebron, Freddie, W.S.	.945	13	18	34	3	55	10
LUNA, Leonardo, W.S.	.964	37	80	107	7	194	18
Mejia, Jorge, Ath.	.932	25	35	47	6	88	9

Player, Team	Pct.	G	PO	A	E	TC	DP
Morillo, Roberto, Gia.	.922	15	21	38	5	64	6
Perez, Antonio, Mar.	1.000	4	5	13	0	18	5
Perez, Luis, Ath.	.947	16	30	42	4	76	4
Perez, Melvin, W.S.	.978	12	21	24	1	46	6
Rodriguez, Guilder, Brew.	.939	42	101	115	14	230	30
Salas, Francisco, Cubs	1.000	26	43	71	0	114	17
Santana, Waner, Gia.	.950	13	29	28	3	60	8
Soto, Wilber, Ang.	.922	23	43	52	8	103	7
Spearman, Jemel, Cubs	.000	1	0	0	0	0	0
Thornton-Murray, Jandin, Cubs	.957	7	10	12	1	23	2
Trinidad, Edgar, Ath.	.958	5	7	16	1	24	5

THIRD BASEMEN

Player, Team	Pct.	G	PO	A	E	TC	DP
Abad, Noel, Ang.	.857	7	5	7	2	14	0
Batista, Christian, Ang.	.853	23	9	20	5	34	2
Brown, Matthew, Ang.	.985	23	23	44	1	68	5
Ciesluk, Chris, Gia.	.877	42	27	80	15	122	9
Collaro, Thomas, W.S.	1.000	1	2	0	0	2	0
Diaz, Randor, Gia.	.000	1	0	0	1	1	0
Dryer, Matt, Gia.	.500	1	0	1	1	2	0
Duenas, Tommy, Ang.	.800	1	2	2	1	5	0
Figueroa, Luis, Mar.	1.000	2	2	4	0	6	1
Francisco, Alfredo, Cubs	.857	46	26	76	17	119	5
Franke, Michael, Brew.	.833	6	5	10	3	18	0
Garcia, Eustaquio, Ath.	.912	21	19	33	5	57	1
Gomez, Andri, Brew.	1.000	1	0	1	0	1	1
Hornostaj, Aaron, Gia.	.750	2	0	3	1	4	0
Hrynio, Mike, Mar.	.881	35	29	75	14	118	10
Imperiali, Francesco, Mar.	.000	1	0	0	0	0	0
Klippenstein, Tyler, Ath.	.000	1	0	0	1	1	0
Lebron, Freddie, W.S.	.889	4	5	3	1	9	1
Mazzanti, Giuseppe, Mar.	.859	23	16	45	10	71	4
McCormack, Taylor, Brew.	.833	11	6	19	5	30	1
Mejia, Jorge, Ath.	.846	5	6	5	2	13	0
Mejia, Lekis, Ath.	.824	23	20	50	15	85	8
Myers, Michael, W.S.	.625	1	1	4	3	8	0
O'Toole, Paul, Cubs	1.000	1	0	3	0	3	0
Perez, Melvin, W.S.	.829	10	4	25	6	35	2
Salas, Francisco, Cubs	.800	3	0	4	1	5	0
Santana, Waner, Gia.	.902	14	8	29	4	41	1
SCHNURSTEIN, Micah, W.S.	.941	42	43	69	7	119	8
Soto, Wilber, Ang.	.914	14	8	24	3	35	1
Trinidad, Edgar, Ath.	.900	12	8	28	4	40	1
Vazquez, Rafael, Cubs	.833	8	11	9	4	24	2
Willis, Lendon, Brew.	.870	42	35	92	19	146	13

SHORTSTOPS

Player, Team	Pct.	G	PO	A	E	TC	DP
Abad, Noel, Ang.	.667	2	2	0	1	3	0
Abreu, Johany, Gia.	.917	13	20	46	6	72	8
Acosta, Gilberto, Brew.	.927	49	59	144	16	219	19
Batista, Juan, Ath.	.930	44	62	111	13	186	18
Brown, Matthew, Ang.	1.000	1	2	1	0	3	0
Cordova, Roman, Mar.	1.000	1	0	1	0	1	0
De La Rosa, Isaias, Ath.	.667	1	0	4	2	6	0
Francisco, Alfredo, Cubs	1.000	2	5	4	0	9	1
Francois, Francisco, Ath.	.931	25	44	64	8	116	6
Garcia, Eustaquio, Ath.	.892	23	30	44	9	83	9
Garciaparra, Michael, Mar.	.921	46	68	143	18	229	18
Gomez, Andri, Brew.	.972	6	21	14	1	36	4
Gomez, Francis, Ath.	.929	6	5	21	2	28	3
Henriquez, Hector, Mar.	1.000	8	9	26	0	35	6
Hornostaj, Aaron, Gia.	.945	31	42	79	7	128	11
Hrynio, Mike, Mar.	1.000	2	2	1	0	3	0
Imperiali, Francesco, Mar.	1.000	1	2	0	0	2	0
Lebron, Freddie, W.S.	.937	26	39	65	7	111	14
Luna, Leonardo, W.S.	.840	11	12	30	8	50	8
Mejia, Jorge, Ath.	.786	2	3	8	3	14	0
Morillo, Roberto, Gia.	.800	2	1	3	1	5	2
Myers, Michael, W.S.	.904	23	40	64	11	115	15
Perez, Antonio, Mar.	1.000	1	2	2	0	4	0
Rodriguez, Guilder, Brew.	.929	3	1	12	1	14	0
Salas, Francisco, Cubs	.889	3	8	8	2	18	2
Santana, Waner, Gia.	.900	15	24	39	7	70	3
Soto, Wilber, Ang.	.906	16	23	35	6	64	8
SPEARMAN, Jemel, Cubs	.933	52	83	152	17	252	39

Player, Team	Pct.	G	PO	A	E	TC	DP
Thornton-Murray, Jandin, Cubs......	.500	1	0	2	2	4	0
Willis, Lendon, Brew.	1.000	1	0	2	0	2	1

OUTFIELDERS

Player, Team	Pct.	G	PO	A	E	TC	DP
Abad, Noel, Ang.	.897	16	26	0	3	29	0
Agustin, Pedro, Cubs	.897	24	34	1	4	39	0
Arias, Daniel, Ang.	1.000	1	3	0	0	3	0
Bates, Dallas, Brew.*	.962	48	48	2	2	52	0
Bohlander, Michael, W.S.	.000	1	0	0	0	0	0
Cavanaugh, Brian, Brew.*	.909	10	9	1	1	11	0
Christenson, Ryan, Brew.	1.000	2	2	0	0	2	0
Cleto, Carlos, Gia.*	.970	48	94	3	3	100	1
Cole, John, Mar.	1.000	3	5	0	0	5	0
Collaro, Thomas, W.S.	1.000	25	38	2	0	40	0
Coulie, Jason, Ang.	1.000	2	2	0	0	2	0
Cruz, Elvis, Mar.	.860	30	39	4	7	50	0
DaVanon, Jeff, Ang.	1.000	3	4	1	0	5	0
De La Rosa, Isaias, Ath.	.932	21	39	2	3	44	1
Diaz, Randor, Gia.	.941	42	63	1	4	68	0
Dopirak, Brian, Cubs	1.000	4	4	0	0	4	0
Ellison, Josh, Mar.	.940	33	58	5	4	67	1
Frost, Jeremy, Brew.	1.000	1	2	0	0	2	0
Garcia, Eustaquio, Ath.	1.000	2	3	0	0	3	0
Garcia, Jairo, Ath.	1.000	3	5	0	0	5	0
German, Carlos, Gia.	.932	29	37	4	3	44	0
Hodges, Jarrod, Mar.*	.985	27	65	1	1	67	1
Hunt, Stephen, Brew.	.943	43	60	6	4	70	3
Ido, Nobutoshi, W.S.	1.000	16	19	1	0	20	1
Ishikawa, Travis, Gia.*	1.000	4	4	0	0	4	0
January, Javerro, Brew.	1.000	5	12	0	0	12	0
Johnson, Kade, Brew.	1.000	3	5	0	0	5	0
Jones, Joshua, Ang.	1.000	21	21	1	0	22	0
Kenning, Ryan, Ang.*	1.000	1	4	0	0	4	0
Maher, Caleb, Ang.	.935	43	41	2	3	46	0
Marmol, Carlos, Cubs	.916	46	75	1	7	83	1
Martinez, Joan, Gia.	.000	1	0	0	0	0	0
Mateo, Aneudis, Mar.	.955	10	20	1	1	22	0
McBeth, Marcus, Ath.	1.000	3	5	0	0	5	0
Melo, Manuel, Brew.	1.000	20	42	1	0	43	0
Moss, Steve, Brew.	.975	30	72	5	2	79	2
Munhall, Brian, Gia.	1.000	1	1	0	0	1	0
Nunez, Felix, Ang.	1.000	4	6	0	0	6	0
PAULINO, Adalberto, Gia.	.975	41	77	1	2	80	0
Peel, Aaron, Ang.	.964	42	77	3	3	83	0
Perez, Luis, Ath.	.929	20	25	1	2	28	0
Pie, Felix, Cubs*	.960	54	112	7	5	124	2
Plasencia, Francisco, Brew.*	.939	16	29	2	2	33	0
Randolph, Jaisen, Brew.	1.000	1	1	0	0	1	0
Renz, Jordan, Ang.	.937	40	57	2	4	63	0
Rivera, Jhonny, W.S.	.959	45	84	9	4	97	3
Rodriguez , William, Ath.*	.952	36	55	5	3	63	0
Rogers, Nick, Ath.	.929	45	76	2	6	84	0
Salas, Francisco, Cubs	1.000	2	8	0	0	8	0
Sanchez, Ivan, Gia.	.947	14	18	0	1	19	0
Soto, Wilber, Ang.	1.000	1	3	0	0	3	0
Summerall, Dennis, Cubs*	.950	47	75	1	4	80	0
Valdez, Tommy, Ath.	.938	41	76	0	5	81	0
Walston, Chris, Ang.	.923	11	11	1	1	13	1
Ware, Matthew, Mar.	.000	3	0	0	0	0	0
Wear, Gregory, Mar.	.000	1	0	0	0	0	0
Wilson, Michael, Mar.	.971	32	65	2	2	69	0
Womack, Josh, Mar.*	.900	39	62	1	7	70	0
Young, Chris, W.S.	.970	55	95	3	3	101	0
Young, Eddie, W.S.	.939	45	75	2	5	82	1

CATCHERS

Player, Team	Pct.	G	PO	A	E	TC	DP	PB
Almanzar, Theiborh, Mar.	.942	18	124	7	8	139	1	5
Alvarado, Joel, Brew.	.962	7	43	7	2	52	1	1
Arias, Angel, W.S.	.969	5	29	2	1	32	0	3
Barnett, Dan, W.S.	1.000	9	67	8	0	75	1	1
Bravo, Arturo, Brew.	1.000	7	43	2	0	45	0	0
Bubalo, Ty, Ath.	.939	5	28	3	2	33	0	5
Buller, Dayton, Gia.	.967	9	78	9	3	90	1	4
Castillo, Cesar, W.S.	.980	18	135	10	3	148	1	1
Collins, Mike, Ang.	.989	11	77	13	1	91	2	5
De Vinney, Rick, Cubs	1.000	2	18	3	0	21	0	1
Duenas, Tommy, Ang.	.977	44	388	38	10	436	4	6
Frost, Jeremy, Brew.	.960	17	153	17	7	177	0	8
Guhring, Simon, Brew.	.973	19	133	11	4	148	2	12
Harris, Blair, W.S.	.970	6	31	1	1	33	0	3
Kroski, Chris, Mar.	.969	23	141	15	5	161	2	1
Martinez, Joan, Gia.	1.000	6	25	6	0	31	1	2
Maynard, Scott, Mar.	1.000	2	3	1	0	4	0	0

Player, Team	Pct.	G	PO	A	E	TC	DP	PB
Metzger, Gregory, Ath.	.984	25	158	23	3	184	0	6
Morban, Franklin, Ath.	.969	16	137	18	5	160	2	4
MUNHALL, Brian, Gia.	.994	39	264	42	2	308	0	5
Olszta, Eddie, Mar.	.994	27	159	13	1	173	2	5
O'Toole, Paul, Cubs	1.000	1	10	1	0	11	0	0
Patterson, Derek, Brew.	.985	7	57	7	1	65	0	4
Ramirez, Juan, Ath.	.987	16	133	15	2	150	0	7
Reyes, Jose, Cubs	.967	19	106	13	4	123	0	4
Rick, Alan, Cubs	.993	19	133	16	1	150	0	4
Scoville, Shane, W.S.	.976	26	184	16	5	205	1	4
Seijas, Luis, Ang.	.947	13	48	6	3	57	0	7
Serafini, Matt, Brew.	1.000	5	34	5	0	39	0	2
Soto, Geovany, Cubs	.988	10	78	3	1	82	0	1
Turco, Anthony, Gia.	1.000	3	28	2	0	30	0	0
Wells, Randy, Cubs.	.984	14	105	18	2	125	1	1
Williams, Jonny, Gia.	.985	8	59	5	1	65	0	0
Woody, Dominic, Mar.	1.000	1	4	0	0	4	0	0

PITCHERS

Player, Team	Pct.	G	PO	A	E	TC	DP
Acors, Bo, Mar.	.667	5	0	2	1	3	0
Albright, Eric, Cubs	1.000	2	2	0	0	2	0
Alliston, Josh, Brew.	.667	4	0	2	1	3	0
Alvarez, Larry, Cubs.	.000	5	0	0	0	0	0
Arias, Daniel, Ang.	.750	27	1	2	1	4	0
Arnold, Mitchell, Ang.	.800	15	2	2	1	5	0
Avendano, Elvis, Ath.	.875	14	2	5	1	8	0
Baez, Federico, Cubs	1.000	18	0	3	0	3	0
Baez, Hebel, Ath.	1.000	6	3	3	0	6	0
Balser, Jeff, Ang.	1.000	8	0	3	0	3	0
Banks, Demetrius, W.S.*	.000	8	0	0	1	1	0
Barnett, Daniel, Ath.	.778	13	1	6	2	9	0
Barreras, Rene, Mar.*	1.000	18	1	2	0	3	0
Benjamin, Petersen, Gia.	.000	1	0	0	0	0	0
Bergdall, Kendall, Mar.*	.500	6	0	1	1	2	0
Bernat, David, Mar.	1.000	5	1	1	0	2	0
Burdette, Jason, Ath.	.941	15	6	10	1	17	1
Cabaniel, Tomas, Ath.	1.000	16	3	6	0	9	0
Cain, Matthew, Gia.	1.000	8	1	3	0	4	0
Cervenka, Dennis, Mar.*	.000	3	0	0	0	0	0
CORCHADO, Jose, Ath.	1.000	14	7	7	0	14	0
Corcoran, John, Mar.	1.000	2	1	0	0	1	0
Cordero, Victor, Brew.	1.000	6	0	2	0	2	0
Correa, Alexander, Brew.*	1.000	15	3	2	0	5	0
Cortez, Renee, Mar.	1.000	7	2	6	0	8	0
Curreri, Joe, W.S.	1.000	3	1	0	0	1	0
De Vinney, Rick, Cubs	.000	1	0	0	0	0	0
Delgadillo, Ambiroix, Ang.*	1.000	21	0	6	0	6	0
Dominguez, Carlos, Cubs	1.000	7	1	3	0	4	0
English, Jesse, Gia.*	1.000	12	2	1	0	3	0
Espinal, Luis, Mar.	1.000	11	2	7	0	9	0
Fernando, Gilberto, Gia.*	1.000	7	1	1	0	2	0
Figueroa, Eduardo, Mar.	.500	4	1	0	1	2	0
Forbes, Terry, Mar.	.000	5	0	0	0	0	0
Freeman, Kai, W.S.	.000	8	0	0	1	1	0
Frye, Randall, Mar.	.909	8	4	6	1	11	0
Fyvie, Dan, Brew.	1.000	19	2	2	0	4	1
Garcia, Jairo, Ath.	.786	13	3	8	3	14	2
Garcia, James, Gia.	1.000	10	0	2	0	2	1
Garcia, Miguel, Brew.	.833	10	3	2	1	6	0
Garcia, Ruddy, Gia.	1.000	15	2	3	0	5	1
Gelatka, Todd, Brew.	.000	2	0	0	0	0	0
Gittings, Christopher, Brew.	.000	1	0	0	0	0	0
Gomez, Rafael, W.S.	.000	14	0	0	0	0	0
Graterol, Francisco, Mar.	.929	11	6	7	1	14	0
Gwyn, Marc, Ath.	.750	5	0	3	1	4	0
Haeger, Charles, W.S.	.909	25	2	8	1	11	0
Haigwood, Daniel, W.S.*	.933	14	4	10	1	15	1
Hawkins, Al, Brew.	1.000	6	0	5	0	5	0
Hernandez, Armando, Gia.	1.000	18	0	3	0	3	0
Hines, Matthew, Cubs	1.000	4	2	0	0	2	0
Hixson, David, Gia.	1.000	5	0	2	0	2	0
Huchingson, Jamin, W.S.	1.000	6	1	2	0	3	0
January, Javerro, Brew.	1.000	1	1	0	0	1	0
Jaquez, Eddi, Gia.	1.000	13	3	7	0	10	0
Jepsen, Kevin, Ang.	.500	8	1	2	3	6	0
Jimenez, Cesar, Mar.*	1.000	1	0	1	0	1	0
Jimenez, Julio, W.S.*	.750	16	2	4	2	8	0
Johnson, J.D., W.S.	1.000	16	1	4	0	5	0
Jones, Justin, Cubs*	.857	11	2	4	1	7	0
Knox, Dennis, Mar.	.800	10	2	2	1	5	0
Korneev, Oleg, Mar.	.000	3	0	0	1	1	0
Lara, Nelson, Gia.	1.000	2	0	1	0	1	0
Lopez, Orionny, W.S.	.800	17	2	2	1	5	0
Magallanes , Fidel, Gia.	.000	4	0	0	0	0	0

Player, Team	Pct.	G	PO	A	E	TC	DP
Marmol, Carlos, Cubs	.000	1	0	0	0	0	0
Martinez Sosa, Alvaro, Brew.	.600	15	2	1	2	5	0
Martinez, Jose, Cubs*	.000	3	0	0	1	1	0
Martinez, Miguel, Mar.*	1.000	6	3	4	0	7	0
Martinez, Pedro, Ath.*	.833	10	1	4	1	6	0
McCarthy, Brandon, W.S.	1.000	14	3	9	0	12	1
McCormack, Taylor, Brew.	.000	3	0	0	0	0	0
McCurdy, Jason, W.S.*	1.000	17	0	4	0	4	0
McMullen, Jeremy, Cubs	1.000	10	1	2	0	3	0
Mejia, Andy, Cubs	.813	15	2	11	3	16	0
Mena, Juan, Ang.	.000	5	0	0	0	0	0
Mendoza, Gabriel, Brew.*	.833	19	0	5	1	6	0
Mitchell, Nathan, Cubs	1.000	14	3	2	0	5	0
Morban, Carlos, Ang.	1.000	17	1	1	0	2	0
Moreno, Abel, Ang.	.833	13	1	9	2	12	0
Moreno, Anthony, Gia.	.857	16	3	3	1	7	0
Nacar, Leslie, Gia.	1.000	18	1	4	0	5	0
Nisbett, Marshall, Mar.	.833	16	2	3	1	6	0
Ortiz, Dario, W.S.	.778	14	3	4	2	9	0
Parra, Manuel, Brew.*	1.000	1	0	1	0	1	0
Patterson, Derek, Brew.	1.000	1	0	1	0	1	0
Pawelczyk, Kyle, Ang.*	1.000	1	0	1	0	1	0
Pena, Luismar, Brew.	.778	11	0	7	2	9	0
Perez, Elvis, Mar.	.000	3	0	0	0	0	0
Perry, Brandon, Mar.*	1.000	10	0	5	0	5	0
Petrick, Billy, Cubs	.714	6	2	3	2	7	0
Pierre, Adolfo, Brew.*	.800	17	1	3	1	5	0
Poe, Ryan, Brew.	.000	3	0	0	1	1	0
Portorreal, Carlos, Gia.	.900	14	3	6	1	10	0
Pruett, Hubert, Brew.	1.000	11	2	0	0	2	0
Ramirez, Carlos, Brew.*	.944	15	3	14	1	18	1
Ramirez, Edward, Ang.	.900	13	4	5	1	10	1
Ramirez, Luis, Mar.*	1.000	12	0	1	0	1	0
Ramirez, Rafael, Gia.	.625	13	1	4	3	8	0
Ramos, Jonathan, Cubs*	1.000	4	1	0	0	1	0
Ray, Ronnie, Ang.	.917	16	1	10	1	12	1
Reyes, Julio, Ang.*	1.000	16	4	3	0	7	0
Reynoso, Anibal, Ath.	1.000	10	0	3	0	3	0
Richardson, Judd, Brew.	.500	7	1	0	1	2	0
Ring, Royce, W.S.*	.000	3	0	0	0	0	0
Robinson, Jeff, Brew.	.000	3	0	0	0	0	0
Rodriguez , Rafael, Ang.	1.000	8	2	2	0	4	0
Rodriguez, Pedro, Cubs	.000	16	0	0	1	1	0
Rodriguez, Ryan, W.S.*	.810	14	4	13	4	21	0
Rondon, Yosy, Gia.*	1.000	16	0	1	0	1	0
Rupp, Mike, W.S.	1.000	11	0	1	0	1	0
Sager, Brian, W.S.	.000	2	0	0	0	0	0
St. Amand, Reuben, Gia.	.500	6	0	1	1	2	0
Saint Hilaire, Reynaldo, W.S.	1.000	15	0	2	0	2	0
Sanchez, Adiel, Ath.*	1.000	16	1	5	0	6	0
Santana, Candido, Cubs*	.833	15	4	1	1	6	0
Santana, Roberto, Ath.*	.000	11	0	0	1	1	0
Sarfate, Dennis, Brew.	.000	5	0	0	0	0	0
Schmidt, Jeremy, Gia.	1.000	12	0	1	0	1	0
Serafini, Matt, Brew.	1.000	1	0	1	0	1	0
Shull, Johnathan, Ang.	.875	16	1	6	1	8	1
Sierra, Edwardo, Ath.	.714	6	2	3	2	7	0
Sisco, Kelly, Ang.*	1.000	2	1	0	0	1	0
Solis, Hairo, Gia.	.000	16	0	0	1	1	0
Stewart, Scott, Ath.	1.000	9	0	1	0	1	0
Stirm, Brian, Gia.	1.000	14	1	1	0	2	1
Stitt, Brian, Mar.	.000	2	0	0	0	0	0
Tavarez, Carlos, Gia.	.857	14	3	9	2	14	2
Thompson, Richard, Ang.	.800	15	1	3	1	5	0
Tisch, Timothy, W.S.*	.750	17	1	2	1	4	0
Toledo, Jean, Ang.	.850	11	1	16	3	20	0
Toribio, Auri, Cubs	1.000	14	0	6	0	6	0
Turnbow, Derrick, Ang.	1.000	3	0	2	0	2	0
Valdez, Richard, Cubs	1.000	14	4	4	0	8	0
Vasquez, Rucki, Mar.*	.667	16	1	1	1	3	0
Villanueva, Carlos, Gia.	1.000	19	1	1	0	2	0
Walker, Edwin, Brew.*	1.000	4	1	3	0	4	0
Wang, Chao, Mar.	.875	13	2	5	1	8	0
Wear, Gregory, Mar.	1.000	15	2	3	0	5	1
Wooten, Greg, Mar.	1.000	3	1	0	0	1	0

The following players appeared only as designated hitter, pinch-hitter or pinch runner: Blakeley, dh, ph; DeCinces, dh; Viera, dh, ph.

LEAGUE CHAMPIONS

Year	Team	Pct.	Year	Team	Pct.	Year	Team	Pct.
1988—	Peoria Brewers	.690	1993—	Scottsdale A's	.636	1998—	Rockies	.750
1989—	Peoria Brewers	.732	1994—	Chandler Cardinals	.607	1999—	Athletics	.696
1990—	Peoria Brewers	.679	1995—	Scottsdale A's	.661	2000—	Mariners	.709
1991—	Scottsdale A's	.650	1996—	Padres	.643	2001—	Athletics	.625
1992—	Scottsdale A's	.607	1997—	Cubs	.618	2002—	Cubs	.625

GULF COAST LEAGUE

LEAGUE OFFICE

President
Tom Saffell
Address
1503 Clower Creek Dr., H-262
Sarasota, FL 34231
Phone
941-966-6407

Teams*
Braves
Dodgers
Expos
Marlins
Orioles
Phillies
Pirates
Reds
Red Sox

Tigers
Twins
Yankees

*Teams play their games in Bradenton, Clearwater, Fort Myers, Jupiter, Kissimmee, Lakeland, Melbourne, Orlando, Sarasota, Tampa and Vero Beach.

2002 FINAL STANDINGS

EASTERN DIVISION

Team	W	L	T	Pct.	GB
Dodgers	33	27	0	.550	...
Marlins	31	29	0	.517	2.0
Expos	28	32	0	.467	5.0
Braves	28	32	0	.467	5.0

NORTHERN DIVISION

Team	W	L	T	Pct.	GB
Phillies	39	21	0	.650	...
Yankees	36	24	0	.600	3.0
Tigers	23	37	0	.383	16.0
Royals	22	38	0	.367	17.0

SOUTHERN DIVISION

Team	W	L	T	Pct.	GB
Pirates	37	23	0	.617	...
Twins	35	25	0	.583	2.0
Reds	30	30	0	.500	7.0
Rangers	28	32	0	.467	9.0
Red Sox	26	34	0	.433	11.0
Orioles	24	36	0	.400	13.0

COMPOSITE

Team	Phi.	Pir.	Yan.	Twi.	Dod.	Mar.	Reds	Rang.	Exp.	Brav.	R.S.	Ori.	Tig.	Roy.	W	L	T	Pct.	GB
Phillies	...	0	11	0	0	0	0	0	0	0	0	0	13	15	39	21	0	.650	...
Pirates	0	...	0	3	0	0	9	8	0	0	7	10	0	0	37	23	0	.617	2.0
Yankees	9	0	...	0	0	0	0	0	0	0	0	0	11	16	36	24	0	.600	3.0
Twins	0	9	0	...	0	0	6	6	0	0	7	7	0	0	35	25	0	.583	4.0
Dodgers	0	0	0	0	...	12	0	0	10	11	0	0	0	0	33	27	0	.550	6.0
Marlins	0	0	0	0	8	...	0	0	11	12	0	0	0	0	31	29	0	.517	8.0
Reds	0	3	0	6	0	0	...	8	0	0	6	7	0	0	30	30	0	.500	9.0
Rangers	0	4	0	6	0	0	4	...	0	0	8	6	0	0	28	32	0	.467	11.0
Expos	0	0	0	0	10	9	0	0	...	9	0	0	0	0	28	32	0	.467	11.0
Braves	0	0	0	0	9	8	0	0	11	...	0	0	0	0	28	32	0	.467	11.0
Red Sox	0	5	0	5	0	0	6	4	0	0	...	6	0	0	26	34	0	.433	13.0
Orioles	0	2	0	5	0	0	5	6	0	0	6	...	0	0	24	36	0	.400	15.0
Tigers	7	0	9	0	0	0	0	0	0	0	0	0	...	7	23	37	0	.383	16.0
Royals	5	0	4	0	0	0	0	0	0	0	0	0	13	...	22	38	0	.367	17.0

Games played in Bradenton, Dunedin, Fort Myers, Melbourne, Osceola, Port Charlotte, St. Lucie County, Sarasota, Tampa and West Palm Beach, Fla.

Club names are major league affiliations.

PLAYOFFS: Dodgers defeated Pirates, one game to none; Phillies defeated Dodgers, two games to one to win Gulf Coast League championship.

REGULAR-SEASON ATTENDANCE: No total attendance figures reported.

MANAGERS: Braves, Jim Saul; Dodgers, Luis Salazar; Expos, Andy Skeels; Marlins, Jesus Campos; Orioles, Jesus Alfaro; Phillies, Roly Dearmas; Pirates, Woody Huyke; Rangers, Carlos Subero; Red Sox, John Sanders; Reds, Edgar Caceres; Royals, Lloyd Simmons; Tigers, Howard Bushong; Twins, Rudy Hernandez; Yankees, Manny Crespo.

ALL-STAR TEAM: 1B—Travis Wong, Reds; 2B—Jose Morales, Twins; 3B—Damaso Espino, Reds; SS—Hanley Ramirez, Red Sox; OF—Alexander Romero, Twins; OF—Mike Arbinger, Pirates; OF—Rajai Davis, Pirates; C—Tim Gradoville, Phillies; SP—Elizardo Ramirez, Phillies; RP—Maximo Reyes, Phillies; Manager of the Year—Woody Huyke, Pirates.

2002 BATTING

TEAM

Team	G	TPA	AB	R	H	TB	2B	3B	HR	RBI	SH	SF	HP	BB	IBB	SO	SB	CS	GDP	LOB	ShO	Avg.	OBP	Slg.
Twins	60	2333	2038	330	581	746	84	21	13	275	16	28	44	207	5	320	97	41	45	444	5	.285	.359	.366
Pirates	60	2204	1903	302	528	752	93	28	25	257	22	28	35	216	9	308	71	33	36	422	4	.277	.357	.395
Reds	60	2173	1937	293	523	764	119	13	32	253	8	16	42	170	8	403	78	31	48	396	2	.270	.339	.394
Rangers	60	2143	1835	269	476	631	81	13	16	220	35	10	25	238	7	403	137	48	40	383	4	.259	.351	.344
Yankees	60	2165	1916	259	497	658	87	16	14	231	17	24	23	185	4	390	29	26	47	415	10	.259	.328	.343
Phillies	60	2172	1881	265	477	674	99	13	24	235	26	27	27	211	8	380	80	35	29	417	5	.254	.333	.358
Tigers	60	2157	1916	218	466	638	71	22	19	189	30	18	28	165	4	413	66	35	40	405	4	.243	.310	.333
Braves	60	2151	1897	235	451	636	77	18	24	195	18	15	41	180	0	397	65	28	39	395	7	.238	.315	.335
Dodgers	60	2128	1810	268	430	567	79	11	12	202	22	17	46	233	0	314	89	23	38	399	4	.238	.337	.313

Team	G	TPA	AB	R	H	TB	2B	3B	HR	RBI	SH	SF	HP	BB	IBB	SO	SB	CS	GDP	LOB	ShO	Avg.	OBP	Slg.
Expos	60	2120	1870	222	432	593	84	10	19	190	9	17	48	176	0	425	39	29	36	392	5	.231	.311	.317
Marlins	60	2089	1776	240	399	558	82	19	13	185	8	16	31	258	0	430	80	31	41	367	6	.225	.331	.314
Red Sox	60	2116	1842	246	409	597	84	18	23	199	10	17	31	216	4	461	59	34	33	366	3	.222	.311	.324
Orioles	60	2079	1811	206	398	514	66	13	8	159	15	15	45	193	5	406	47	15	54	396	7	.220	.308	.284
Royals	60	2174	1884	205	407	531	68	7	14	172	26	14	39	211	1	440	54	24	37	430	8	.216	.306	.282

INDIVIDUAL

TOP QUALIFIERS FOR BATTING CHAMPIONSHIP

Minimum 162 plate appearances. *Lefthanded batter. †Switch-hitter.

Player, Team	G	TPA	AB	R	H	TB	2B	3B	HR	RBI	SH	SF	HP	BB	IBB	SO	SB	CS	GDP	Avg.	OBP	Slg.
Davis, Rajai, Pir.†	58	250	224	38	86	124	16	5	4	35	0	3	3	20	0	25	24	6	3	.384	.436	.554
Ramirez, Hanley, R.S.†	45	184	164	29	56	91	11	3	6	26	0	2	2	16	1	15	8	6	5	.341	.402	.555
Denorfia, Christopher, Reds...	57	233	200	38	68	81	9	2	0	19	0	2	0	31	0	23	18	8	8	.340	.425	.405
Spataro, Ryan, Twi.*	53	222	189	36	63	70	3	2	0	19	3	1	1	28	1	34	12	6	3	.333	.420	.370
Romero, Alex, Twi.†	56	230	186	31	62	85	13	2	2	42	3	7	5	29	3	14	16	6	5	.333	.423	.457
Espino, Damaso, Reds†	58	246	223	35	74	96	22	0	0	32	2	2	3	16	1	30	8	1	7	.332	.381	.430
Arbinger, Mike, Pir.*	59	247	214	32	70	91	11	2	2	46	0	6	2	25	2	22	4	4	2	.327	.393	.425
Brown, Dustin, R.S.	45	183	159	28	51	70	12	2	1	20	0	1	0	23	1	24	11	4	1	.321	.404	.440
Wong, Travis, Reds	52	202	180	27	57	97	10	0	10	45	0	2	8	12	2	23	4	0	2	.317	.381	.539
Morales, Jose, Twi.†	53	192	175	25	54	65	7	2	0	28	2	3	5	7	0	28	3	1	5	.309	.347	.371
Nonemaker, Karl, Phi.*	59	247	221	32	68	87	14	1	1	28	3	2	1	20	0	20	13	5	3	.308	.365	.394
Grayson, Larry, Rang.	52	206	182	26	56	80	14	2	2	28	0	1	1	22	4	41	7	3	5	.308	.383	.440
Guzman, Javier, Pir.	50	222	199	42	61	94	6	6	5	20	6	3	2	12	1	25	13	6	1	.307	.347	.472
Bolivar, Luis, Reds†	50	206	186	39	57	88	17	1	4	24	0	1	11	8	0	37	13	6	0	.306	.369	.473
Guillen, Rudy, Yan.	59	240	219	38	67	87	7	2	3	35	1	3	3	14	0	39	7	2	5	.306	.351	.397
Saunches, Michael, Yan.*	48	171	157	13	48	66	12	0	2	29	0	3	0	11	1	44	0	1	2	.306	.345	.420
Kirkland, Kody, Pir.	46	177	157	22	48	62	10	2	0	18	0	2	4	14	2	39	2	1	2	.306	.373	.395
Hansen, Bryan, Phi.*	54	205	180	21	55	82	16	4	1	28	2	5	4	14	0	26	4	4	0	.306	.360	.456

DEPARTMENTAL LEADERS: G—Arbinger, Guillen, Nonemaker, 59 each; AB—R. Davis, 224; R—Ja. Guzman, 42; H—R. Davis, 86; TB—R. Davis, 124; 2B—Espino, 22; 3B—Aponte, 7; HR—Wong, 10; RBI—Arbinger, 46; SH—Blue, 10; SF—Romero, 7; HP—Bolivar, 11; BB—Coughlan, Fermin, Yepez, 35 each; IBB—Grayson, 4; SO—D. Williams, 68; SB—Coughlan, 34; CS—Several players tied with 8; GIDP—Huether, 11; Slg.—H. Ramirez, .555; OBP—R. Davis, .436.

ALL PLAYERS

*Lefthanded batter. †Switch-hitter.

Player, Team	G	TPA	AB	R	H	TB	2B	3B	HR	RBI	SH	SF	HP	BB	IBB	SO	SB	CS	GDP	Avg.	OBP	Slg.
Acosta, Johe, Pir.	12	42	35	6	8	16	2	3	0	6	0	0	2	5	0	10	4	1	1	.229	.357	.457
Agustin, Hugo, Rang.	41	158	122	29	39	69	11	2	5	22	2	2	3	29	1	40	21	8	4	.320	.455	.566
Aldridge, Cory, Brav.*	17	71	59	10	17	37	5	3	3	13	0	1	0	11	0	17	0	0	0	.288	.394	.627
Allec, Jason, Tig.	6	22	21	2	7	10	3	0	0	1	0	0	0	1	0	4	0	0	2	.333	.364	.476
Anderson, Rondon, Mar.*	45	152	120	20	25	37	1	1	3	14	0	1	1	30	0	35	4	2	0	.208	.368	.308
Andino, Robert, Mar.	9	33	27	2	7	7	0	0	0	2	0	1	0	5	0	6	3	0	1	.259	.364	.259
Andrus, Erold, Yan.†	55	230	204	30	60	83	13	2	2	27	2	4	6	14	0	23	1	4	4	.294	.351	.407
Andujar, Pedro, Dod.	38	134	119	10	26	33	7	0	0	19	0	3	3	9	0	13	5	1	2	.218	.284	.277
Apodaca, Luis, Exp.	12	46	39	4	9	10	1	0	0	2	0	0	0	7	0	7	1	0	0	.231	.348	.256
Aponte, Jose, Mar.*	53	194	165	35	47	76	3	7	4	18	0	4	1	24	0	31	10	1	0	.285	.371	.461
Araque, Tulio, Reds.	53	182	171	20	38	55	10	2	1	23	1	1	5	4	0	48	4	2	2	.222	.260	.322
Arbinger, Mike, Pir.*	59	247	214	32	70	91	11	2	2	46	0	6	2	25	2	22	4	4	2	.327	.393	.425
Arias, Garvi, Exp.	12	35	29	3	4	4	0	0	0	0	0	0	1	5	0	14	2	0	0	.138	.286	.138
Arias, Joaquin, Yan.	57	218	203	29	61	80	7	6	0	21	2	1	0	12	0	16	2	4	4	.300	.338	.394
Arneson, Justin, Twi.	37	143	125	37	43	59	7	3	1	17	1	0	2	15	0	22	16	3	2	.344	.423	.472
Arroyo, Xavier, Mar.†	27	101	76	8	12	16	4	0	0	6	1	0	1	23	0	22	5	3	5	.158	.360	.211
Assael, Samuel, Tig.	16	47	38	4	7	8	1	0	0	4	1	2	2	4	0	8	0	1	1	.184	.283	.211
Baez, Fleming, Rang.	4	8	8	0	0	0	0	0	0	0	0	0	0	0	0	2	0	0	0	.000	.000	.000
Baez, Lizahio, Rang.†	47	169	150	21	35	48	4	0	3	18	2	2	1	14	1	32	6	3	2	.233	.299	.320
Bailie, Stefan, R.S.	2	7	7	1	1	2	1	0	0	1	0	0	0	0	0	2	0	0	0	.143	.143	.286
Baker, Jordan, Mar.*	30	85	73	7	13	14	1	0	0	8	1	0	1	10	0	30	1	3	0	.178	.274	.192
Barthel, Cole, Brav.	52	209	177	24	49	72	6	1	5	15	1	1	7	23	0	27	11	1	6	.277	.380	.407
Bastardo, Frederick, Mar.	54	195	173	27	40	63	14	0	3	23	1	0	1	20	0	31	6	3	3	.231	.314	.364
Batista, Alexander, Roy.	50	202	181	15	38	50	7	1	1	25	2	0	3	16	1	36	9	6	6	.210	.285	.276
Benson, Cedric, Dod.	9	34	25	1	5	12	3	2	0	5	0	0	2	7	0	10	2	3	0	.200	.412	.480
Berkenbosch, Kenny, Mar.	4	11	9	1	3	4	1	0	0	1	0	0	0	1	0	2	0	1	0	.333	.455	.444
Bernadina, Rogearvino, Exp.*..	52	221	196	22	54	70	7	0	3	18	0	2	4	19	0	25	1	0	2	.276	.348	.357
Bernstine, David, Twi.	31	101	89	9	20	23	3	0	0	4	0	0	6	6	0	16	2	1	1	.225	.317	.258
Betemit, Wilson, Brav.†.	7	24	19	2	5	9	4	0	0	2	0	0	0	5	0	2	1	0	0	.263	.417	.474
Bianucci, Anthony, R.S.†.	38	94	79	16	7	10	1	1	0	1	0	0	2	13	0	37	6	1	3	.089	.234	.127
Blalock, Jake, Phi.	25	101	88	13	22	31	6	0	1	13	0	3	0	10	0	15	3	0	0	.250	.317	.352
Blanco, Andres, Roy.†	52	219	193	27	48	56	8	0	0	14	6	1	4	15	0	29	16	4	2	.249	.315	.290
Blanco, Luis, Exp.	45	165	148	17	34	55	12	0	3	17	0	1	9	7	0	55	0	0	3	.230	.303	.372
Blanton, Stephen, Ori.*	40	139	119	11	23	29	4	1	0	8	0	2	2	16	0	18	1	1	4	.193	.295	.244
Blasi, Blake, R.S.†	7	26	23	8	10	12	2	0	0	2	1	0	0	2	0	4	4	0	0	.435	.480	.522
Blue, Vincent, Tig.*	56	212	183	20	40	53	5	4	0	29	7	10	2	17	0	38	20	3	3	.219	.282	.290
Bolivar, Luis, Reds†	50	206	186	39	57	88	17	1	4	24	0	1	11	8	0	37	13	6	0	.306	.369	.473
Bonvechio, Brett, R.S.*	30	118	103	19	30	52	11	1	3	24	0	1	0	14	0	24	0	0	1	.291	.373	.505
Boone, Doug, Yan.	3	11	10	0	3	3	0	0	0	2	0	0	0	1	0	3	0	0	0	.300	.364	.300
Boone, Matt, Tig.	4	16	15	1	5	6	1	0	0	3	0	0	0	1	0	5	0	0	0	.333	.375	.400
Boullon, Luis, Yan.†	4	14	12	1	1	2	1	0	0	0	0	0	0	1	0	7	0	1	0	.083	.143	.167
Bramasco, Omar, Phi.	46	156	129	25	27	39	3	0	3	13	2	1	3	21	0	43	2	2	0	.209	.331	.302
Brito, Henry, Phi.	55	223	190	26	49	65	8	1	2	27	6	0	3	24	1	34	5	5	2	.258	.350	.342
Broadway, Larry, Exp.*	4	12	8	1	2	2	0	0	0	0	0	0	0	4	0	4	0	0	0	.250	.500	.250
Brown, Darrius, Ori.*	22	20	18	2	2	3	1	0	0	0	0	0	0	0	0	0	0	0	2	.111	.200	.167
Brown, Dustin, R.S.	45	183	159	28	51	70	12	2	1	20	0	1	0	23	1	24	11	4	1	.321	.404	.440

SUMMER CLASS A Gulf Coast League

Player, Team	G	TPA	AB	R	H	TB	2B	3B	HR	RBI	SH	SF	HP	BB	IBB	SO	SB	CS	GDP	Avg.	OBP	Slg.
Brown, Rich, Yan.*	7	25	22	4	6	7	1	0	0	4	0	0	0	3	0	5	0	0	0	.273	.360	.318
Brown, Tim, Pir.*	42	152	129	14	31	46	7	1	2	25	1	3	1	18	0	32	1	2	3	.240	.331	.357
Burgos, Jose, Twi.	50	206	188	30	52	65	10	0	1	29	0	1	4	13	0	42	6	5	5	.277	.335	.346
Cabrera, Ruben, Dod.	8	16	15	0	2	3	1	0	0	1	0	0	0	1	0	5	0	0	1	.133	.188	.200
Campos, Tiago, Reds	8	31	30	2	7	8	1	0	0	2	0	0	0	1	0	10	1	1	1	.233	.258	.267
Carbonara, William, Ori.	52	190	174	27	46	64	10	1	2	19	2	3	5	6	1	32	7	2	6	.264	.303	.368
Carofiles, Bladimir, Mar.	41	140	126	12	32	40	3	1	1	16	1	2	2	9	0	24	7	3	1	.254	.309	.317
Castillo, Carlos, Tig.†	6	20	19	3	5	10	2	0	1	2	0	0	1	0	0	4	0	2	0	.263	.300	.526
Castro, Ramon, Brav.	9	37	32	3	8	11	0	0	1	4	1	0	1	3	0	6	2	0	1	.250	.333	.344
Ciofrone, Peter, R.S.*	35	129	111	20	27	40	5	1	2	18	0	2	5	11	0	11	3	2	1	.243	.333	.360
Clanton, Ja'Mar, Exp.	56	214	190	23	30	36	6	0	0	10	2	0	1	21	0	30	7	4	9	.158	.245	.189
Clevien, Brent, Tig.	28	113	103	14	34	51	2	3	3	21	0	2	0	8	0	24	2	1	0	.330	.372	.495
Cobb, Maurice, Exp.	37	132	116	14	25	35	5	1	1	9	1	0	3	12	0	44	1	1	2	.216	.305	.302
Cockrell, Michael, Pir.	47	199	159	32	48	64	11	1	1	22	3	5	3	29	1	13	7	4	6	.302	.408	.403
Coffey, Josh, Mar.	19	57	50	3	8	8	0	0	0	2	0	0	1	6	0	10	0	0	0	.160	.263	.160
Colbert, Eddie, Ori.†	47	181	169	22	35	42	5	1	0	17	1	2	0	9	0	52	8	2	10	.207	.244	.249
Colina, Yinner, Reds	31	102	85	12	20	31	5	3	0	6	0	1	4	12	1	16	2	2	2	.235	.353	.365
Comfort, Geoffrey, Dod.	29	113	89	13	19	32	7	0	2	14	1	1	4	18	0	17	4	0	1	.213	.366	.360
Correll, Richard, Reds	5	18	18	1	2	2	0	0	0	0	0	0	0	0	0	3	1	0	3	.111	.111	.111
Cotto, Luis, Roy.	5	20	19	2	3	3	0	0	0	2	0	0	0	1	0	7	0	0	0	.158	.200	.158
Cotto, Pedro, Tig.*	13	45	45	4	9	11	2	0	0	1	0	0	0	0	0	4	3	0	2	.200	.200	.244
Coughlan, Cameron, Rang.†	50	221	182	36	53	58	5	0	0	15	4	0	35	0	38	34	7	3	.291	.406	.319
Crawford, Tristan, Twi.	21	1	1	0	0	0	0	0	0	0	0	0	0	0	0	0	0	0	0	.000	.000	.000
Cronkhite, Ian, R.S.*	52	186	171	11	33	45	8	2	0	13	0	1	0	14	1	53	3	5	3	.193	.253	.263
Cruz, Luis, R.S.	21	77	72	10	21	25	4	0	0	9	1	0	1	3	0	2	2	1	1	.292	.329	.347
Cruz, Ramon, Brav.	24	71	66	2	9	12	0	0	1	6	0	1	0	4	0	26	0	0	1	.136	.183	.182
Davenport, Juston, Yan.	23	56	51	4	7	8	1	0	0	2	0	0	0	5	0	12	1	0	1	.137	.214	.157
Davis, Rajai, Pir.†	58	250	224	38	86	124	16	5	4	35	0	3	3	20	0	25	24	6	3	.384	.436	.554
Davis, Zach, Ori.*	48	196	170	17	30	39	5	2	0	11	1	1	2	22	0	56	13	1	1	.176	.277	.229
De Aza, Alejandro, Dod.*	38	155	128	27	29	40	6	1	1	14	2	1	2	22	0	17	16	2	3	.227	.346	.313
De La Cruz, Carlos, R.S.†	42	159	143	20	24	31	2	1	1	9	1	2	0	13	0	31	3	3	2	.168	.234	.217
Delacruz, Jose, Reds	12	35	33	3	10	16	3	0	1	6	0	0	1	1	0	4	0	0	2	.303	.343	.485
Delos Santos, Esteban, Phi.†	50	191	167	24	37	64	6	3	5	29	2	2	5	15	0	50	6	6	5	.222	.302	.383
Denison, Brandon, Phi.*	12	1	1	1	1	1	0	0	0	0	0	0	0	0	0	0	0	0	0	1.000	1.000	1.000
Dennis, Billy, Reds*	1	1	1	0	0	0	0	0	0	0	0	0	0	0	0	0	0	0	0	.000	.000	.000
Denorfia, Christopher, Reds	57	233	200	38	68	81	9	2	0	19	0	2	0	31	0	23	18	8	8	.340	.425	.405
Desena, Francis, Dod.	29	106	99	10	23	30	5	1	0	13	1	1	0	5	0	18	3	0	2	.232	.267	.303
Devries, Jonathan, R.S.	43	155	119	13	22	28	3	0	1	11	0	1	5	30	0	31	3	0	1	.185	.368	.235
Diaz, Frank, Exp.	51	200	173	33	48	75	8	2	5	24	0	1	7	19	0	28	8	5	5	.277	.370	.434
Diaz, Jeury, Phi.†	21	72	61	12	20	25	5	0	0	5	2	0	0	9	0	11	4	0	2	.328	.414	.410
Diaz, Juan, Reds	27	101	98	11	23	33	5	1	1	11	0	0	2	1	0	19	2	1	4	.235	.257	.337
Donachie, Adam, Roy.	21	80	68	7	14	17	3	0	0	3	1	1	1	9	0	12	0	0	5	.206	.304	.250
Donato, Greg, Brav.	5	18	15	1	3	3	0	0	0	1	0	0	1	2	0	3	0	1	0	.200	.333	.200
Durazo, William, R.S.†	18	51	42	7	8	13	3	1	0	7	0	2	3	4	0	11	2	0	0	.190	.294	.310
Eazor, Kyle, Mar.*	16	0	0	0	0	0	0	0	0	0	0	0	0	0	0	0	0	0	0	.000	.000	.000
Ellerson, Brian, Exp.	8	24	20	3	3	5	0	1	0	0	0	0	1	3	0	2	0	1	0	.150	.292	.250
Elliott, Justin, Twi.	29	86	76	8	17	19	2	0	0	6	0	2	2	6	0	10	0	1	2	.224	.291	.250
Esparragoza, Eyoxy, Reds	18	58	53	6	10	17	4	0	1	5	0	0	5	0	0	22	1	4	1	.189	.259	.321
Espino, Damaso, Reds†	58	246	223	35	74	96	22	0	0	32	2	2	3	16	1	30	8	1	7	.332	.381	.430
Fermin, Angelo, Twi.†	57	233	193	39	55	73	4	4	2	29	1	2	2	35	1	25	19	5	3	.285	.397	.378
Ferrara, Matt, Roy.	45	165	140	15	26	40	5	0	3	14	0	2	0	23	0	44	2	0	3	.186	.297	.286
Ferrer, Simon, Dod.	37	124	103	18	18	26	5	0	1	13	1	0	4	16	0	23	3	0	1	.175	.309	.252
Figuereo, Anibal, Roy.	14	58	55	10	17	19	2	0	0	3	0	0	3	0	0	9	0	0	2	.309	.345	.345
Fisher, Kiel, Phi.*	35	123	105	9	24	39	4	1	3	20	2	1	2	13	0	34	1	2	0	.229	.322	.371
Flamont, Sam, Tig.*	40	157	130	26	43	52	4	1	1	17	1	1	1	24	0	12	5	5	3	.331	.436	.400
Flowers, Clarence, Tig.	26	105	97	18	27	33	4	1	0	7	2	0	3	3	0	24	8	1	2	.278	.320	.340
Foskey, Will, Brav.	18	51	40	1	7	9	2	0	0	6	0	0	2	9	0	14	0	2	1	.175	.353	.225
Fry, Ryan, Reds	8	24	24	3	4	6	2	0	0	0	0	0	0	0	0	8	0	0	1	.167	.167	.250
Fuentes, Omar, Yan.	4	13	11	0	2	2	0	0	0	2	0	0	0	2	0	3	0	0	0	.182	.308	.182
Galan, Jorman, Reds	35	63	50	14	8	16	0	1	2	6	1	0	1	11	0	12	2	1	2	.160	.323	.320
Garcia, Juan-Carlos, Mar.†	34	130	107	16	16	20	4	0	0	8	0	0	2	21	0	36	4	2	5	.150	.300	.187
Garcia, Nick, Ori.	7	26	23	2	5	6	1	0	0	3	0	0	2	1	0	4	1	0	3	.217	.308	.261
Garcia, Sergio, Dod.	47	193	157	29	43	54	8	0	1	9	5	2	6	23	0	18	12	3	4	.274	.383	.344
Garland, Ross, Tig.	6	16	15	0	2	2	0	0	0	2	1	0	0	0	0	1	0	0	0	.133	.133	.133
Gerlits, Gooby, Mar.	24	78	76	12	17	30	4	0	3	11	0	0	1	1	0	11	0	0	3	.224	.244	.395
Ghutzman, Phillip, Reds	3	9	6	2	1	1	0	0	0	0	0	0	0	3	0	1	0	0	0	.167	.444	.167
Gillies, Michael, Phi.	43	168	152	24	35	54	7	0	4	14	0	4	0	12	0	16	3	2	5	.230	.280	.355
Gonzalez, Alex, Mar.	5	13	12	0	2	3	1	0	0	1	0	1	0	0	0	5	0	0	1	.167	.154	.250
Gonzalez, Edwar, Yan.	19	53	51	7	14	21	2	1	1	8	0	1	0	1	0	11	0	0	1	.275	.283	.412
Gonzalez, Jose, Tig.†	45	163	139	22	33	44	3	4	0	8	4	1	0	19	0	28	7	2	1	.237	.327	.317
Gonzalez, Luis, Roy.	37	127	116	11	30	42	6	0	2	17	1	0	6	4	0	22	1	0	3	.259	.317	.362
Gradoville, Tim, Phi.	37	114	101	16	27	33	6	0	0	4	4	0	1	8	0	19	14	2	0	.267	.327	.327
Graham, Tyson, Mar.	6	22	20	2	7	10	3	0	0	0	0	0	0	2	0	3	0	0	2	.350	.409	.500
Grayson, Larry, Rang.	52	206	182	26	56	80	14	2	2	28	0	1	1	22	4	41	7	3	5	.308	.383	.440
Greene, Jason, Exp.*	16	51	45	4	11	16	1	2	0	6	0	1	2	3	0	13	0	1	1	.244	.314	.356
Grzecka, Casey, Mar.	9	33	30	1	7	8	1	0	0	5	0	1	0	2	0	5	0	0	2	.233	.273	.267
Guerra, Alex, Rang.†	55	211	178	26	39	49	5	1	1	17	3	0	3	27	0	38	26	6	3	.219	.332	.275
Guerrero, Henry, Ori.	35	111	93	16	27	41	8	0	2	9	2	0	2	14	2	15	0	0	3	.290	.394	.441
Guillen, Rudy, Yan.	59	240	219	38	67	87	7	2	3	35	1	3	3	14	0	39	7	2	5	.306	.351	.397
Guy, Jason, Rang.*	7	24	19	1	6	7	1	0	0	2	1	0	0	4	0	4	0	1	0	.316	.435	.368
Guzman, Heriberto, R.S.	47	167	143	11	26	32	3	0	1	9	0	2	5	17	1	53	5	4	6	.182	.287	.224
Guzman, Javier, Pir.	50	222	199	42	61	94	6	6	5	20	6	3	2	11	0	25	13	6	1	.307	.341	.472
Guzman, Joel, Dod.	10	38	33	4	7	9	2	0	0	2	0	0	5	0	0	8	1	0	0	.212	.316	.273
Hadad, Jorge, Ori.	39	146	127	10	38	51	6	2	1	16	3	1	0	15	2	25	0	2	7	.299	.371	.402
Hall, Noah, Reds	8	26	23	4	6	11	2	0	1	3	0	0	0	3	0	2	4	0	0	.261	.346	.478

Player, Team	G	TPA	AB	R	H	TB	2B	3B	HR	RBI	SH	SF	HP	BB	IBB	SO	SB	CS	GDP	Avg.	OBP	Slg.
Hansen, Bryan, Phi.*	54	205	180	21	55	82	16	4	1	28	2	5	4	14	0	26	3	3	0	.306	.360	.456
Harris, Mike, Yan.	1	1	1	1	0	0	0	0	0	0	0	0	0	0	0	0	0	0	0	.000	.000	.000
Hatton, Vern, Dod.	23	90	71	13	16	22	4	1	0	13	1	1	6	11	0	14	4	3	2	.225	.371	.310
Hawes, Don, Reds.	36	107	93	13	22	33	8	0	1	9	1	1	1	11	2	20	4	0	3	.237	.321	.355
Hermida, Jeremy, Mar.*	38	152	134	15	30	43	7	3	0	14	0	0	3	15	0	25	5	0	3	.224	.316	.321
Hernandez, Luis, Brav.†	53	225	201	34	51	67	8	4	0	20	1	0	4	19	0	29	11	6	1	.254	.330	.333
Hernandez, Miguel, Dod.	56	220	199	28	49	67	10	1	2	21	1	1	2	17	0	36	11	4	6	.246	.311	.337
Hicks, Joseph, Pir.	22	54	47	4	5	7	2	0	0	3	1	1	0	5	0	17	1	1	2	.106	.189	.149
Honeycutt, Shedrick, Exp.*	27	73	71	5	9	12	3	0	0	0	1	0	0	1	0	20	1	2	1	.127	.139	.169
House, J.R., Pir.	5	19	16	3	5	10	2	0	1	2	0	0	0	3	0	1	0	0	0	.313	.421	.625
Howarth, Jason, Twi.	3	7	6	3	2	2	0	0	0	0	0	0	0	1	0	1	0	0	0	.333	.429	.333
Howerton, Matthew, Ori.	40	151	122	21	25	29	2	1	0	9	0	1	4	24	0	35	6	2	4	.205	.351	.238
Huether, J.D., Twi.	47	184	164	21	39	51	9	0	1	24	0	6	2	12	0	12	2	2	11	.238	.288	.311
Isenhower, Jeremy, Phi.*	27	104	91	16	28	39	8	0	1	10	0	1	2	10	1	21	6	3	0	.308	.385	.429
James, Willie, Brav.†	39	141	126	20	29	34	5	0	0	5	3	0	2	10	0	21	5	3	2	.230	.297	.270
Jenkins, Darryl, Exp.*	1	1	1	0	0	0	0	0	0	0	0	0	0	0	0	0	0	0	0	.000	.000	.000
Jerzembeck, Mike, Twi.	3	1	1	0	0	0	0	0	0	0	0	0	0	0	0	0	0	0	0	.000	.000	.000
Jimenez, Franklyn, Exp.	43	149	129	16	39	44	5	0	0	12	1	2	3	14	0	22	5	3	4	.302	.378	.341
Johnson, Josh, Twi.	27	75	58	11	13	22	3	0	2	10	1	0	3	13	0	15	0	1	1	.224	.392	.379
Jordan, Mickey, Dod.*	33	114	99	9	18	18	0	0	0	6	3	0	1	11	0	25	2	2	2	.182	.270	.182
Kaaihue, Kila, Roy.*	43	168	139	15	36	53	8	0	3	21	0	1	2	26	0	35	0	0	4	.259	.381	.381
Kahr, Danny, Exp.†	39	142	126	12	22	29	7	0	0	13	2	1	5	8	0	50	1	1	2	.175	.250	.230
Kerner, Craig, Exp.*	8	32	25	3	6	9	1	1	0	4	0	1	1	5	0	4	2	0	0	.240	.375	.360
Khairy, Masjid, Rang.†	40	142	127	20	34	41	3	2	0	12	4	0	1	10	0	26	10	7	3	.268	.326	.323
Kirkland, Kody, Pir.	46	177	157	22	48	62	10	2	0	18	0	2	4	14	2	39	2	1	2	.306	.373	.395
Koutnik, Jared, Yan.	28	105	90	16	28	35	7	0	0	15	1	3	1	10	1	15	3	1	5	.311	.375	.389
Kreuzer, Josh, Rang.	51	195	165	25	48	66	13	1	1	28	1	2	9	18	0	24	2	1	2	.291	.387	.400
Leon, Alfredo, Ori.	8	27	23	2	2	2	0	0	0	2	0	0	2	2	0	3	0	1	0	.087	.222	.087
Lisson, Mario, Roy.	6	15	10	0	2	2	0	0	0	0	0	0	1	4	0	4	1	0	1	.200	.467	.200
Liz, Jose, Twi.	41	143	131	17	39	60	9	3	2	23	2	3	1	6	0	17	4	5	2	.298	.326	.458
Long, Robert, Tig.	3	2	2	0	0	0	0	0	0	0	0	0	0	0	0	2	0	0	0	.000	.000	.000
Lopez, Javier, Twi.	34	102	87	12	22	29	2	1	1	10	0	1	7	7	0	16	2	1	3	.253	.353	.333
Lynam, Guy, Mar.	11	37	30	2	6	8	2	0	0	6	0	0	1	6	0	6	1	0	1	.200	.351	.267
Lynch, Michael, Dod.	33	126	109	19	34	38	4	0	0	11	1	0	0	16	0	14	2	0	3	.312	.400	.349
Madrid, Mike, Pir.*	29	103	90	12	18	31	5	1	2	12	0	1	3	9	2	8	1	1	5	.200	.291	.344
Mancebo, Deni, Exp.†	35	143	126	16	29	35	1	1	1	11	0	1	5	11	0	24	6	3	1	.230	.315	.278
Mann, Jason, Rang.*	32	108	90	9	16	26	5	1	1	12	1	1	1	15	0	29	0	2	1	.178	.299	.289
Manriquez, Salomon, Exp.	41	151	131	21	37	59	10	0	4	26	0	5	3	12	0	29	0	3	3	.282	.344	.450
Maples, Chris, Tig.	4	18	17	6	7	13	3	0	1	4	0	0	1	0	0	1	0	0	0	.412	.444	.765
Mariot, Lino, Pir.	1	4	4	0	0	0	0	0	0	0	0	0	0	0	0	0	0	0	0	.000	.000	.000
Marmolejos, Hector, Ori.	2	8	7	2	1	1	0	0	0	1	0	0	1	0	0	1	1	0	0	.143	.250	.143
Martin, Russell, Dod.	41	155	126	22	36	45	3	3	0	10	2	0	4	23	0	18	7	1	4	.286	.412	.357
Martinez, Edwin, Brav.†	19	47	42	5	12	18	3	0	1	9	3	1	0	1	0	4	0	0	1	.286	.295	.429
Martinez, Octavio, Ori.	10	42	34	4	12	13	1	0	0	3	0	0	5	3	0	2	1	1	1	.353	.476	.382
Mateo, Dan, Reds†	9	28	25	6	6	7	1	0	0	1	0	0	1	2	0	2	3	1	0	.240	.321	.280
Maybin, Neal, Brav.	19	62	51	5	10	16	3	0	1	9	1	0	1	9	0	20	1	1	2	.196	.328	.314
McCann, Brian, Brav.*	29	112	100	9	22	33	5	0	2	11	0	1	1	10	0	22	0	0	2	.220	.295	.330
McCuistion, Mike, Pir.*	39	155	134	22	38	49	6	1	1	12	0	0	3	18	1	19	3	1	2	.284	.381	.366
McDonald, Chamar, Roy.	44	167	137	17	28	38	5	1	1	16	0	0	7	23	0	39	1	0	4	.204	.347	.277
McKinney, Garth, Tig.	11	33	29	3	8	9	1	0	0	3	0	0	0	4	0	10	2	2	0	.276	.364	.310
Mendez, Deivi, Yan.	31	102	90	9	21	33	6	0	2	11	0	0	2	10	0	16	1	1	1	.233	.324	.367
Mendez, Jose, Twi.	6	19	16	2	4	4	0	0	0	1	0	1	0	2	0	4	0	0	0	.250	.316	.250
Mendez, Rafael, Tig.	25	71	59	3	8	15	1	0	2	5	1	1	1	9	0	24	0	0	2	.136	.257	.254
Mercedes, Jose, Rang.	5	12	10	2	4	4	0	0	0	1	1	0	0	1	0	1	0	0	1	.400	.455	.400
Michelsen, Ross, Yan.*	29	104	90	9	23	27	2	1	0	12	0	0	1	11	0	27	0	0	2	.256	.343	.300
Milauskas, Adam, Pir.	18	46	38	6	6	11	0	1	1	4	1	1	2	4	0	7	0	2	2	.158	.267	.289
Milons, Jereme, Dod.	45	165	152	28	37	50	8	1	1	23	0	1	2	10	0	24	9	1	1	.243	.297	.329
Minami, Yasumichi, R.S.	8	26	25	3	7	11	1	0	1	5	0	0	0	1	0	4	1	1	0	.280	.308	.440
Moni-erigbali, Timi, Phi.	18	43	41	4	4	4	0	0	0	3	0	0	1	1	0	25	1	0	1	.098	.140	.098
Montague, Ed, Dod.*	10	39	34	3	5	7	0	1	0	3	1	1	0	3	0	7	3	0	0	.147	.211	.206
Moore, Scott, Tig.*	40	149	133	18	39	61	6	2	4	25	0	3	3	10	1	31	1	2	2	.293	.349	.459
Morales, Jose, Twi.†	53	192	175	25	54	65	7	2	0	28	2	3	5	7	0	28	3	1	5	.309	.347	.371
Morales, Porfirio, Ori.	3	10	10	0	2	2	0	0	0	2	0	0	0	0	0	4	0	0	0	.200	.200	.200
Moreta, Carlos, Brav.	39	140	126	9	24	44	5	0	5	19	1	1	6	6	0	38	0	0	4	.190	.259	.349
Mosby, Robert, Reds	39	134	118	11	25	33	5	0	1	14	0	1	0	15	1	36	0	1	3	.212	.299	.280
Moss, Brandon, R.S.*	42	130	113	10	23	33	6	2	0	6	1	1	2	13	0	40	1	2	2	.204	.295	.292
Mota, Miguel, Brav.	58	234	213	27	65	90	8	4	3	28	2	2	3	14	0	39	12	8	4	.305	.353	.423
Mujica, Jean, Exp.	2	6	5	0	3	4	1	0	0	1	0	0	0	1	0	0	0	0	0	.600	.600	.800
Nino, Denny, Pir.	11	35	26	3	5	6	1	0	0	3	1	0	1	7	0	5	0	0	0	.192	.382	.231
Nonemaker, Karl, Phi.*	59	247	221	32	68	87	14	1	1	28	3	2	1	20	0	20	13	5	3	.308	.365	.394
Norris, Shawn, Exp.*	9	37	34	1	7	8	1	0	0	3	0	0	0	3	0	3	0	0	0	.206	.270	.235
Nunez, Alexis, Phi.*	14	57	49	4	11	15	4	0	0	7	0	2	1	5	0	5	3	0	1	.224	.298	.306
Nunez, Andres, Yan.	33	121	111	12	25	29	2	1	0	9	1	1	1	7	0	24	0	1	4	.225	.275	.261
Oakes, Matty, Tig.	37	134	121	12	27	34	7	0	0	16	1	1	2	9	0	23	0	0	3	.223	.286	.281
Ohtsuka, Yoshiyuki, Pir.	10	42	37	6	10	13	0	0	1	5	2	1	0	2	0	8	0	1	1	.270	.300	.351
Oliva, Chad, Phi.	28	104	90	10	19	25	1	1	1	8	1	1	0	12	0	21	4	1	3	.211	.301	.278
Opel, Chad, Ori.	49	173	144	19	25	36	4	2	1	10	1	1	10	17	0	23	6	0	1	.174	.302	.250
Oriental, Rene, Roy.	44	161	140	19	30	43	7	3	0	16	1	4	2	14	0	43	2	5	0	.214	.288	.307
Orlandos, Nicholas, Yan.	27	79	73	8	15	15	0	0	0	3	0	1	1	4	0	12	0	1	3	.205	.253	.205
Ortega, Pedro, Brav.†	22	73	60	6	8	13	3	1	0	4	1	2	1	9	0	14	6	0	2	.133	.250	.217
Ortiz, Edgar, Tig.	34	128	113	10	28	42	8	0	2	10	1	0	6	8	1	23	2	2	3	.248	.331	.372
Partridge, Dominique, Brav.	58	212	185	27	50	61	5	3	0	8	0	1	5	21	0	40	2	4	3	.270	.358	.330
Patterson, Tarrence, Twi.	27	48	43	8	15	19	2	1	0	3	0	0	0	5	0	16	5	3	0	.349	.417	.442
Pena, Antonio, Rang.	41	126	107	17	20	24	2	1	0	10	2	0	5	12	0	26	5	3	3	.187	.298	.224
Pereyra, Joel, Roy.	7	22	19	1	2	2	0	0	0	1	0	1	1	0	0	3	0	0	1	.105	.190	.105

Player, Team	G	TPA	AB	R	H	TB	2B	3B	HR	RBI	SH	SF	HP	BB	IBB	SO	SB	CS	GDP	Avg.	OBP	Slg.
Perez, Jesus, Dod.	33	107	93	15	21	26	5	0	0	11	1	2	4	7	0	23	3	0	2	.226	.302	.280
Perez, Koby, R.S.	4	5	5	0	0	0	0	0	0	0	0	0	0	0	0	3	0	1	0	.000	.000	.000
Perez, Miguel, Reds	26	92	86	12	31	32	1	0	0	11	1	0	3	2	0	9	3	0	2	.360	.394	.372
Perodin, Ron, Twi.*	37	135	123	20	40	48	4	2	0	9	3	0	2	7	0	13	9	2	1	.325	.371	.390
Phillips, Kyle, Twi.*	35	116	101	10	20	29	4	1	1	12	0	1	0	14	0	18	0	0	0	.198	.293	.287
Piste, Carlos, Ori.†	47	150	133	15	25	34	2	2	1	8	0	0	4	13	0	37	1	0	2	.188	.280	.256
Pitney, Jared, Yan.*	10	44	35	8	8	13	5	0	0	9	0	1	1	7	1	6	0	0	1	.229	.364	.371
Raburn, Ryan, Tig.	8	33	30	4	9	17	3	1	1	5	0	0	0	3	0	7	0	0	2	.300	.364	.567
Radwan, Jason, Dod.	25	98	78	16	25	40	3	0	4	13	0	2	4	14	0	14	0	0	1	.321	.439	.513
Ramirez, Hanley, R.S.†	45	184	164	29	56	91	11	3	6	26	0	2	2	16	1	15	8	6	5	.341	.402	.555
Reames, Joe Don, Rang.	48	169	147	18	34	44	4	3	0	14	5	0	1	16	0	40	10	4	1	.231	.311	.299
Rengifo, Amado, Mar.	33	88	77	14	17	23	4	1	0	5	0	0	1	10	0	18	8	0	4	.221	.318	.299
Resop, Chris, Mar.	28	100	91	7	24	33	5	2	0	11	1	0	3	5	0	21	1	2	2	.264	.323	.363
Reyes, Angel, Tig.	37	109	100	8	20	28	5	0	1	6	3	0	1	5	0	34	0	0	0	.200	.245	.280
Reyes, Milver, Pir.	35	118	107	9	17	22	2	0	1	12	1	1	3	6	0	16	0	0	6	.159	.222	.206
Richard, Chris, Ori.*	1	2	1	1	1	1	0	0	0	0	0	0	0	1	0	0	0	0	0	1.000	1.000	1.000
Rivera, Juan, Yan.	4	16	13	1	4	6	2	0	0	4	0	0	1	2	0	3	0	0	1	.308	.438	.462
Rivero, Luis, Phi.	4	9	6	1	2	2	0	0	0	1	0	0	0	3	0	1	0	0	0	.333	.556	.333
Roa, Joel, Tig.	14	45	40	1	10	12	2	0	0	2	1	0	1	3	0	9	0	1	0	.250	.318	.300
Robles, Luis, Yan.	20	59	54	4	9	12	3	0	0	3	2	0	0	3	0	6	0	0	2	.167	.211	.222
Rodriguez, Reynaldo, Exp.	2	3	2	0	0	0	0	0	0	0	0	0	0	1	0	0	0	0	0	.000	.333	.000
Rodriguez, Robert, Exp.	18	58	49	4	10	14	4	0	0	4	0	0	2	7	0	10	0	2	1	.204	.328	.286
Rohan, James, Dod.	14	50	41	4	11	11	0	0	0	4	0	2	1	6	0	2	1	1	2	.268	.360	.268
Romero, Alex, Twi.†	56	230	186	31	62	85	13	2	2	42	3	7	5	29	3	14	16	6	5	.333	.423	.457
Rosario, Carlos, Yan.	39	119	103	9	24	41	9	1	2	15	3	2	2	9	0	33	0	2	0	.233	.302	.398
Roughton, Jody, Tig.*	9	31	25	5	10	17	1	0	2	4	0	0	0	6	0	2	1	0	0	.400	.516	.680
Rutgers, Paul, Twi.	31	89	86	11	21	23	2	0	0	9	0	0	2	1	0	18	0	0	1	.244	.270	.267
Salazar, Darwinson, Roy.	35	120	101	11	22	29	5	1	0	6	2	0	3	14	0	32	3	0	0	.218	.331	.287
Sanchez, Angel, Roy.	49	197	175	21	44	48	4	0	0	12	5	3	4	10	0	24	9	2	1	.251	.302	.274
Sanchez, Danilo, Tig.	11	29	27	2	3	8	0	1	1	3	0	0	0	2	0	5	0	0	1	.111	.172	.296
Sandoval, Abigail, Rang.	51	204	183	22	50	56	6	0	0	17	7	1	0	13	0	30	13	1	5	.273	.320	.306
Santa, Alexander, Yan.*	54	231	198	34	45	51	2	2	0	7	3	0	2	28	0	54	12	6	4	.227	.329	.258
Santana, Roberto, Brav.*	47	142	130	14	30	34	4	0	0	10	0	4	1	7	0	7	1	0	6	.231	.268	.262
Santoro, Pat, R.S.	8	26	25	1	6	7	1	0	0	3	0	0	1	0	0	6	0	0	0	.240	.269	.280
Sato, G.G., Phi.	17	67	60	5	16	22	4	1	0	1	0	0	7	0	0	10	4	1	1	.267	.343	.367
Saunches, Michael, Yan.*	48	171	157	13	48	66	12	0	2	29	0	3	0	11	1	44	0	2	3	.306	.345	.420
Schwab, Daniel, Yan.*	13	29	19	3	1	1	0	0	0	1	0	0	0	10	0	12	0	0	0	.053	.379	.053
Shields, Nick, Rang.	39	129	108	11	27	36	3	0	2	14	1	1	0	19	1	25	2	2	5	.250	.359	.333
Smith, John, Pir.*	35	151	127	22	29	45	7	3	1	14	4	1	1	18	0	19	2	3	0	.228	.327	.354
Smith, Justin, Rang.†	22	57	54	6	14	22	5	0	1	10	1	0	0	2	0	7	1	0	2	.259	.286	.407
Smith, Sean, Pir.	40	153	131	26	39	57	5	2	3	18	2	0	4	16	0	31	6	1	1	.298	.391	.435
Soto, Melvin, Reds†	26	73	59	5	7	8	1	0	0	3	2	0	1	11	0	33	1	1	1	.119	.268	.136
Sovie, Robbie, Tig.	24	82	80	9	15	16	1	0	0	7	0	0	0	2	0	24	3	2	0	.188	.207	.200
Spann, Chad, R.S.	57	219	203	20	45	77	8	3	6	28	1	1	2	12	0	37	1	2	5	.222	.271	.379
Spano, Robert, Mar.†	41	135	103	14	12	13	1	0	0	4	1	0	4	27	0	39	4	3	0	.117	.321	.126
Spataro, Ryan, Twi.*	53	222	189	36	63	70	3	2	0	19	3	1	1	28	1	34	12	6	3	.333	.420	.370
Springer, Kenard, Roy.	38	109	95	11	18	20	2	0	0	2	2	0	3	9	0	28	3	2	1	.189	.280	.211
Sucre, Antonio, Exp.	37	129	114	12	31	45	6	1	2	17	0	1	2	12	0	13	5	1	1	.272	.349	.395
Teeter, Travis, Ori.	17	1	1	0	0	0	0	0	0	0	0	0	0	0	0	1	0	0	0	.000	.000	.000
Tejeda, Ferdin, Yan.	16	71	60	13	18	21	3	0	0	2	0	1	0	10	1	9	3	1	3	.300	.394	.350
Thurman, Tim, Ori.	56	218	199	14	47	61	9	1	1	18	0	3	1	15	0	58	0	0	2	.236	.289	.307
Timmons, Wes, Brav.	2	9	4	1	2	3	1	0	0	1	1	0	1	3	0	0	0	0	0	.500	.750	.750
Tonis, Mike, Roy.	6	20	17	2	3	6	0	0	1	3	0	0	1	2	0	3	0	0	0	.176	.300	.353
Urquhart, Adrian, Exp.	9	25	23	1	0	0	0	0	0	0	0	0	0	2	0	9	0	0	0	.000	.080	.000
Valles, Jake, Roy.	10	34	34	0	5	6	1	0	0	1	0	0	0	0	0	9	0	1	1	.147	.147	.176
Vasquez, Wuillians, Yan.†	5	20	10	1	0	0	0	0	0	2	2	2	0	6	0	3	0	0	1	.000	.333	.000
Vaz, Roberto, Rang.*	1	4	3	0	1	1	0	0	0	0	0	0	0	1	0	0	0	0	0	.333	.500	.333
Votto, Joey, Reds*	50	202	175	29	47	93	13	3	9	33	0	5	1	21	1	45	7	2	3	.269	.342	.531
Wahl, Mark, Ori.*	33	115	96	5	23	25	2	0	0	9	1	1	3	14	0	14	0	0	5	.240	.351	.260
Wardinsky, Ryan, Phi.†	22	76	59	8	13	14	1	0	0	8	2	2	3	10	0	10	3	3	0	.220	.351	.237
Watkins, Cedric, Roy.	40	128	106	12	17	30	4	0	3	12	1	0	1	20	0	35	0	1	3	.160	.299	.283
Wayne, Brett, Dod.	43	157	139	9	29	34	3	1	0	13	3	0	1	14	0	26	4	2	3	.209	.286	.245
Weitz, Konrad, Roy.	16	27	25	1	4	4	0	0	0	0	0	0	0	2	0	10	0	0	1	.160	.222	.160
Wells, Dan, Mar.	28	99	85	13	19	25	3	0	1	8	0	2	5	7	0	29	2	0	2	.224	.313	.294
White, Dean, Brav.	51	182	168	23	31	46	5	2	2	17	2	0	3	9	0	48	10	1	3	.185	.239	.274
Willemburg, Brett, Roy.†	16	31	25	2	4	6	0	1	0	2	0	0	0	6	0	5	0	1	0	.160	.323	.240
Williams, Devoris, R.S.†	44	167	129	19	12	18	1	1	1	7	5	1	3	29	0	68	6	2	1	.093	.272	.140
Williams, Edwin, Tig.*	31	102	92	4	24	29	1	2	0	8	0	2	1	7	1	12	6	3	4	.261	.314	.315
Williams, John, R.S.	2	7	6	0	0	0	0	0	0	0	0	0	1	0	0	1	0	0	0	.000	.143	.000
Williams, Matt, Tig.†	55	180	160	15	29	36	3	2	0	10	4	1	4	11	0	37	3	8	7	.181	.250	.225
Williams, Mervin, Roy.*	38	104	89	6	16	17	1	0	0	3	4	2	0	9	0	26	6	2	0	.180	.250	.191
Wilson, Vontrez, Brav.†	24	91	83	12	19	24	5	0	0	7	1	0	2	5	0	20	3	1	2	.229	.289	.289
Winegarden, Erik, Phi.*	32	111	90	14	19	33	6	1	2	16	0	3	1	17	1	19	5	0	4	.211	.333	.367
Wise, Bradley, Tig.*	20	71	62	2	11	12	1	0	0	6	0	2	1	6	1	11	0	1	2	.177	.254	.194
Wong, Travis, Reds	52	202	180	27	57	97	10	0	10	45	0	2	8	12	2	23	4	0	2	.317	.381	.539
Woods, Michael, Tig.	7	24	21	2	6	9	1	1	0	2	0	0	0	3	0	6	3	0	0	.286	.375	.429
Yepez, Marcos, Mar.†	58	234	192	29	55	77	16	3	0	22	2	3	2	35	0	41	19	8	5	.286	.397	.401
Zamora, Hector, Yan.*	11	35	29	5	7	15	2	0	2	5	0	0	1	5	0	7	0	1	1	.241	.371	.517
Zapata, Jose, Ori.	52	173	148	16	29	35	6	0	0	12	4	0	2	19	0	28	1	4	2	.196	.296	.236

GRAND SLAMS: Agustin, Carbonara, Delos Santos, Fermin, Maybin, Shields, S. Smith, Sucre, Votto, 1 each.

AWARDED FIRST BASE ON CATCHER'S INTERFERENCE: Michelsen 2 (L. Gonzalez 2).

2002 PITCHING
TEAM

Team	W	L	Pct.	ERA	G	CG	ShO	Sv.	IP	H	TBF	R	ER	HR	SH	SF	HB	BB	IBB	SO	WP	Bk.
Phillies	39	21	.650	2.44	60	7	13	18	504.2	380	2027	173	137	9	22	18	26	139	4	405	19	4
Marlins	31	29	.517	2.88	60	3	8	12	497.2	405	2123	221	159	8	20	17	50	190	0	382	53	8
Dodgers	33	27	.550	2.90	60	0	5	13	490.0	406	2045	201	158	8	17	16	36	194	0	402	42	5
Twins	35	25	.583	3.25	60	3	1	15	526.1	452	2263	254	190	17	24	12	48	249	10	432	62	4
Pirates	37	23	.617	3.27	60	2	7	15	501.0	467	2107	230	182	26	23	15	42	165	2	339	25	5
Royals	22	38	.367	3.49	60	2	5	10	502.2	511	2205	253	196	20	20	27	28	183	3	356	44	7
Yankees	36	24	.600	3.53	60	1	4	14	502.2	441	2137	229	197	26	33	10	30	217	3	414	47	8
Rangers	28	32	.467	3.60	60	0	5	9	493.0	514	2139	253	197	24	14	18	36	163	2	337	38	4
Tigers	23	37	.383	3.68	60	1	5	9	506.0	515	2301	292	207	16	24	28	33	233	2	448	50	15
Expos	28	32	.467	3.73	60	0	6	15	499.1	484	2124	256	207	31	12	15	33	181	0	347	44	4
Orioles	24	36	.400	3.87	60	1	4	11	485.2	467	2138	286	209	18	18	16	27	244	19	449	43	15
Reds	30	30	.500	3.96	60	0	4	11	495.1	453	2159	293	218	19	18	30	36	220	3	381	53	5
Braves	28	32	.467	4.17	60	1	3	10	503.0	417	2196	287	233	21	8	17	47	282	0	435	76	7
Red Sox	26	34	.433	4.49	60	2	4	11	497.0	562	2242	330	248	13	9	23	33	199	2	363	36	6

INDIVIDUAL

TOP QUALIFIERS FOR EARNED-RUN AVERAGE TITLE
Minimum 48 innings.*Lefthanded pitcher.

Pitcher, Team	W	L	Pct.	ERA	G	GS	CG	ShO	GF	Sv.	IP	H	TBF	R	ER	HR	SH	SF	HB	BB	IBB	SO	WP	Bk.
Ramirez, Elizardo, Phi.	7	1	.875	1.10	11	11	2	1	0	0	73.1	44	275	18	9	3	3	1	3	2	0	73	3	1
Mateo, Aneudis, R.S.	4	3	.571	1.76	11	11	2	0	0	0	51	45	207	14	10	1	0	1	11	1	0	45	2	0
Peralta, Efigenio, Brav.	6	2	.750	1.78	14	5	0	0	3	0	55.2	32	214	13	11	1	1	2	0	18	0	44	3	1
Sanchez, Elby, Roy.	3	2	.600	1.80	15	5	0	0	7	2	50	49	210	18	10	0	1	3	3	7	1	36	8	0
Duke, Zach, Pir.*	8	1	.889	1.95	11	11	1	1	0	0	60	38	229	15	13	2	1	1	4	18	0	48	1	0
Figuereo, Victor, Rang.	5	2	.714	1.96	16	4	0	0	10	0	55	48	225	18	12	3	0	3	5	17	0	31	2	0
Mildren, Paul, Brav.*	3	4	.429	1.97	11	10	2	0	0	0	59.1	52	246	16	13	1	0	3	3	17	0	38	4	1
Mateo, Manuel, Brav.	7	3	.700	1.98	12	8	1	1	3	0	68.1	47	260	18	15	0	2	1	2	12	0	76	2	0
German, Rafael, Reds	6	2	.750	2.04	10	10	0	0	0	0	53	39	209	21	12	4	1	2	5	12	0	39	4	0
Garcia, Anderson, Yan.	4	1	.800	2.30	11	9	1	1	0	0	58.2	43	237	22	15	1	3	0	1	22	0	41	8	0
Butto, Francisco, Phi.	7	2	.778	2.31	12	9	3	2	2	1	62.1	37	236	18	16	1	1	1	4	20	0	52	0	2
Albaladejo, Jonathan, Pir.	3	2	.600	2.40	12	10	0	0	1	0	60	71	247	20	16	2	3	0	3	6	0	37	1	0
Smith, Julius, Rang.*	3	2	.600	2.44	13	7	0	0	4	1	48	43	203	18	13	4	0	1	2	17	0	44	1	1
Tussen, Denny, R.S.	2	2	.500	2.60	12	3	0	0	3	0	52	48	219	28	15	1	2	5	2	15	0	37	3	3
Medina, Dennis, Twi.	3	4	.429	2.63	11	8	2	0	0	0	61.2	60	253	24	18	0	5	2	1	11	1	40	3	1
Kiley, Jason, Pir.	4	2	.667	2.63	11	11	1	0	0	0	51.1	33	213	20	15	2	2	2	7	24	0	27	5	2

DEPARTMENTAL LEADERS: W—Duke, 8; L—Bolander, Morton, J. Nelson, 7 each; Pct.—Duke, .889; G—Williams, 25; GS—Granado, Meque, Sweeney, 12 each; CG—Butto, 3; ShO—Butto, 2; GF—Williams, 22; Sv.—Reyes, 12; IP—E. Ramirez, 73.1; H—C. Mendoza, 76; TBF—E. Ramirez, 275; R—Blaney, 49; ER—Blaney, 46; HR—Imotichey, 6; SH—Hader, S. Wright, 6 each; SF—J. Nelson, 6; HB—Blaney, Simpson, 10 each; BB—S. Wright, 39; IBB—Acosta, Perez, 3 each; SO—M. Mateo, 76; WP—S. Russell, 16; BK—Meque, 6.

ALL PITCHERS
*Lefthanded pitcher.

Pitcher, Team	W	L	Pct.	ERA	G	GS	CG	ShO	GF	Sv.	IP	H	TBF	R	ER	HR	SH	SF	HB	BB	IBB	SO	WP	Bk.
Acosta, Richal, Ori.	1	1	.500	1.93	10	9	0	0	0	0	46.2	44	189	13	10	1	2	0	0	12	3	30	3	2
Acuna, Jose, Exp.	1	2	.333	5.20	11	4	0	0	3	1	27.2	28	116	16	16	3	0	0	1	7	0	18	1	0
Aguilar, Rick, Brav.*	1	0	1.000	2.20	9	0	0	0	9	5	16.1	10	61	5	4	0	0	0	4	0	0	17	1	0
Ahumada, Edgar, Dod.*	1	0	1.000	2.08	9	2	0	0	3	2	26	22	109	8	6	0	1	0	1	12	0	13	2	0
Aichele, Shawn, Reds	0	4	.000	5.70	11	5	0	0	1	0	36.1	49	168	28	23	0	1	2	1	14	0	28	2	2
Albaladejo, Jonathan, Pir.	3	2	.600	2.40	12	10	0	0	1	0	60	71	247	20	16	2	3	0	3	6	0	37	1	0
Almonte, Henry, Pir.	0	0	.000	2.25	3	0	0	0	1	0	4	5	22	3	1	0	0	0	0	7	0	3	1	0
Alvarez, Gabriel, Dod.	2	1	.667	5.49	15	0	0	0	8	4	19.2	14	88	13	12	0	0	0	0	16	0	17	3	0
Alvarez, Melvin, Pir.*	0	3	.000	6.16	11	0	0	0	3	0	19	24	94	19	13	0	5	3	3	11	0	4	1	0
Anderson, Wes, Mar.	0	1	.000	3.00	4	4	0	0	0	0	15	15	63	6	5	0	1	0	3	3	0	7	1	0
Andrew, Jason, Rang.	1	0	1.000	2.08	2	1	0	0	0	0	8.2	7	35	2	2	0	1	0	2	3	0	10	0	0
Arias, Javier, Tig.	1	5	.167	7.92	15	4	0	0	4	0	30.2	46	157	34	27	1	3	2	2	17	1	33	3	1
Arias, Pedro, Pir.	5	1	.833	1.93	14	3	0	0	8	4	37.1	25	142	8	8	3	0	1	1	7	0	20	1	0
Arrojo, Rolando, R.S.	0	0	.000	0.00	1	1	0	0	0	0	3	3	11	0	0	0	0	0	0	0	0	1	0	0
Arteaga, Francisco, Brav.	0	0	.000	1.80	3	0	0	0	2	0	5	7	24	1	1	0	1	0	1	1	0	7	1	1
Astacio, Olivo, R.S.	0	2	.000	6.35	4	3	0	0	0	0	17	26	87	17	12	1	1	2	0	15	0	7	2	1
Baez, Benito, Mar.*	0	0	.000	3.86	5	3	0	0	0	0	4.2	3	22	2	2	0	1	0	2	0	5	1	0
Balan, Ryan, R.S.*	3	2	.600	3.38	13	0	0	0	1	0	21.1	23	98	12	8	0	2	0	17	0	10	5	0
Barrios, Rafael, Tig.	0	3	.000	5.40	20	0	0	0	13	4	20	28	106	15	12	1	3	1	3	13	0	13	2	1
Bartel, Richard, Reds	1	1	.500	3.14	7	0	0	0	3	0	14.1	19	66	8	5	1	0	1	2	1	4	9	0	0
Batista, Antonio, R.S.	3	3	.500	3.60	22	0	0	0	21	7	35	33	155	20	14	1	0	1	1	14	1	47	2	0
Bays, Leonard, Roy.	0	0	.000	11.57	2	0	0	0	0	0	2.1	2	12	3	3	0	0	0	0	2	0	6	1	2
Beck, Ken, Exp.	0	0	.000	6.75	5	0	0	0	4	2	8	8	35	6	6	0	0	2	1	3	0	6	2	0
Beckett, Josh, Mar.	0	0	.000	4.50	1	1	0	0	0	0	4	2	18	2	2	0	0	0	0	2	0	7	1	0
Bell, Chris, Reds	0	0	.000	10.80	3	0	0	0	2	0	5	6	25	6	6	0	1	0	1	0	1	3	1	0
Benitez, Fabricio, R.S.	1	1	.500	2.45	3	0	0	0	1	0	7.1	5	27	2	2	1	0	1	0	4	1	3	1	0
Birk, Ben, Mar.*	0	0	.000	0.00	1	1	0	0	0	0	4	0	12	0	0	0	0	0	0	1	0	4	0	0
Blaney, Matthew, R.S.	2	5	.500	15.15	21	1	0	0	9	0	27.1	54	163	49	46	0	0	4	10	19	0	14	6	0
Bohorquez, Carlos, Reds	0	0	.000	8.44	4	0	0	0	1	0	6.2	5	25	2	2	1	0	0	1	0	5	2	0
Bolander, Matt, Ori.	0	7	.000	8.16	9	8	0	0	0	0	28.2	40	155	39	26	1	1	4	28	2	12	2	0
Borkowski, Dave, Tig.	0	0	.000	8.44	3	2	0	0	0	0	5.1	9	26	5	5	2	0	1	0	1	0	6	0	0
Brazoban, Yhency, Yan.	0	0	.000	4.50	6	0	0	0	0	0	6	3	27	3	3	0	0	1	4	0	11	2	0
Bridwell, Jody, Pir.*	1	0	1.000	8.44	5	0	0	0	1	0	5.1	4	30	6	5	0	0	3	4	0	3	2	1
Brock, Tanner, Reds	0	0	.000	0.00	1	0	0	0	0	0	2.1	2	8	0	0	0	0	0	2	0	0
Brown, Darrius, Ori.*	1	1	.500	5.76	16	1	0	0	9	1	25	24	123	21	16	0	1	1	25	1	23	5	4

Pitcher, Team	W	L	Pct.	ERA	G	GS	CG	ShO	GF	Sv.	IP	H	TBF	R	ER	HR	SH	SF	HB	BB	IBB	SO	WP	Bk.
Brown, Jeremy, Twi.	0	0	.000	6.00	2	0	0	0	1	0	3	1	11	2	2	1	0	0	0	1	0	5	0	0
Brubaker, Douglas, Ori.	2	3	.400	2.51	11	10	0	0	0	0	43	29	179	17	12	0	0	0	8	17	2	38	4	1
Bryan, Robert, Roy.	0	2	.000	2.31	7	0	0	0	3	0	11.2	9	48	5	3	2	0	1	0	4	0	10	2	0
Burzynski, Cole, Pir.	0	0	.000	6.75	4	0	0	0	1	0	5.1	4	28	6	4	1	0	0	0	7	0	4	2	0
Bush, Jason, Mar.	0	0	.000	9.00	2	0	0	0	0	0	4	7	19	4	4	0	1	0	0	1	0	1	0	0
Butto, Francisco, Phi.	7	2	.778	2.31	12	9	3	2	2	1	62.1	37	236	18	16	1	1	1	4	20	0	52	0	2
Cahill, Casey, Ori.	0	3	.000	5.14	22	0	0	0	12	2	35	43	167	32	20	4	2	1	2	20	1	27	3	0
Cahill, John, Twi.	0	1	.000	6.35	14	0	0	0	4	0	17	13	77	14	12	1	0	0	3	17	0	9	5	0
Capps, Matt, Pir.	1	0	1.000	0.69	7	0	0	0	4	1	13	13	55	2	1	0	0	0	1	6	0	8	1	0
Carpenter, Miles, Reds	0	4	.000	7.71	9	4	0	0	0	0	23.1	35	118	23	20	0	2	0	16	0	12	8	1	
Carswell, Jeffery, Reds	0	4	.000	4.80	12	0	0	0	9	2	15	13	67	10	8	0	1	1	2	6	0	16	2	0
Carvajal, Marcos, Dod.	3	2	.600	1.71	13	5	0	0	3	0	42	30	169	12	8	0	0	1	4	15	0	35	1	0
Casadiego, Gerardo, Exp.	1	0	1.000	0.00	1	0	0	0	0	0	3	3	12	0	0	0	0	0	0	0	0	4	0	0
Caughey, Trevor, Ori.*	1	4	.200	4.87	10	9	0	0	0	0	40.2	50	180	27	22	0	2	0	13	1	45	6	0	
Cedeno, Blas, Pir.	0	0	.000	0.00	2	0	0	0	1	1	3	2	10	0	0	0	0	0	0	0	0	5	0	0
Cedeno, Jovanny, Rang.	0	0	.000	0.00	3	1	0	0	0	0	5	3	18	0	0	0	0	0	1	0	4	0	0	
Cedeno, Juan, R.S.*	2	5	.286	4.19	11	7	0	0	1	0	43	55	198	31	20	1	0	1	0	12	0	32	0	1
Cerrillo, Francisco, Dod.	0	1	.000	2.84	5	0	0	0	2	0	6.1	6	27	3	2	0	1	0	2	4	0	4	1	0
Chen, Jose, Roy.	0	2	.000	6.48	2	1	0	0	0	0	8.1	12	45	10	6	0	0	2	0	4	0	8	0	0
Chick, Travis, Mar.	3	2	.600	2.76	12	8	0	0	1	1	45.2	40	199	16	14	1	0	0	4	19	0	39	3	0
Christensen, Danny, Roy.*	1	3	.250	3.10	7	6	0	0	0	0	29	20	121	13	10	2	1	0	4	14	0	28	0	0
Cierlik, Jason, Ori.*	0	0	.000	6.00	3	0	0	0	1	0	3	4	18	4	2	0	0	0	0	5	0	2	0	0
Clark, Wade, Tig.	3	0	1.000	1.39	7	5	1	0	0	0	32.1	23	131	8	5	0	2	2	1	9	1	33	2	0
Colton, Kyle, Brav.	0	1	.000	3.38	4	2	0	0	0	0	8	5	31	3	3	0	0	0	5	0	7	0	1	
Contreras, Omar, Pir.	2	3	.400	4.35	11	0	0	0	8	2	20.2	27	97	16	10	1	3	0	4	5	1	13	0	0
Cooper, Dexter, Brav.	4	4	.500	3.12	11	7	0	0	1	0	57.2	43	233	24	20	3	0	2	5	22	0	36	9	1
Crawford, Tristan, Twi.	6	2	.750	4.28	20	1	0	0	6	2	27.1	24	124	22	13	1	3	2	5	18	1	18	8	0
Cressend, Jack, Twi.	0	0	.000	7.11	3	3	0	0	0	0	6.1	10	30	7	5	0	0	1	1	0	8	1	0	
Cuen, David, Dod.*	1	0	1.000	0.00	3	2	0	0	0	0	16	8	53	1	0	0	1	0	0	2	0	11	0	0
Delacruz, Eulogio, Tig.	1	1	.500	2.63	20	0	0	0	7	1	37.2	40	179	24	11	0	1	1	2	21	0	46	1	4
De la Cruz, Julio, Phi.	3	0	1.000	3.56	7	5	0	0	0	0	30.1	28	129	12	12	1	0	3	2	12	0	25	0	0
Delacruz, Maximo, Phi.	1	0	1.000	1.17	2	1	0	0	0	0	7.2	4	29	1	1	0	0	2	2	0	5	1	0	
Denison, Brandon, Phi.	0	2	.000	5.53	12	1	0	0	6	0	27.2	38	134	21	17	2	1	1	2	7	0	14	4	0
DePaula, Julio, Twi.	3	2	.600	1.82	7	6	1	0	1	0	39.2	39	164	16	8	0	2	0	4	5	0	21	2	0
Dewar, Andrew, Brav.*	0	0	.000	4.50	1	0	0	0	0	0	2	2	8	1	1	0	0	0	0	0	0	2	0	0
Diaz, Eddie, Exp.	0	3	.000	4.56	9	3	0	0	2	0	25.2	24	111	16	13	1	0	1	4	8	0	26	5	0
Diaz, Jose, Dod.	3	1	.750	1.95	10	6	0	0	2	0	32.1	19	128	11	7	0	2	1	4	12	0	26	1	1
Digby, Bryan, Brav.	0	0	.000	7.50	3	2	0	0	0	0	6	9	31	5	5	0	0	0	5	0	5	1	0	
Dodson, Jeremy, Roy.	1	2	.333	7.50	8	0	0	0	4	0	12	17	61	14	10	0	1	1	0	8	0	4	1	0
Dorsey, Brian, Phi.	3	2	.600	2.57	16	2	0	0	5	0	35	31	152	19	10	0	4	2	16	1	35	2	0	
Dossett, Dusty, Roy.	0	0	.000	9.00	1	0	0	0	0	0	2	5	11	2	2	0	0	0	0	0	0	0	0	0
Duke, Zach, Pir.*	8	1	.889	1.95	11	11	1	1	0	0	60	38	229	15	13	2	1	1	4	18	0	48	1	0
Dumesnil, Bryan, Dod.*	5	1	.833	2.87	8	0	0	0	7	0	31.1	28	144	15	10	0	2	1	3	24	0	30	8	0
Durbin, Chad, Roy.	0	0	.000	0.00	3	3	0	0	0	0	6	4	21	0	0	0	0	1	0	5	0	0		
Eazor, Kyle, Mar.*	2	0	1.000	3.72	16	0	0	0	8	3	29	27	128	17	12	0	0	3	15	0	24	0	0	
Echols, Britt, Exp.	4	2	.667	2.82	11	10	0	0	0	0	51	54	204	22	16	3	3	1	0	9	0	24	4	0
Elmore, Chris, R.S.*	0	1	.000	14.73	1	0	0	0	0	0	3.2	8	19	6	6	0	0	0	0	3	0	3	0	0
Encarnacion, Alexis, Roy.	1	0	1.000	3.60	6	0	0	0	2	1	15	15	63	6	6	0	0	1	4	0	13	0	0	
Escorcha, Orlando, Reds*	1	0	1.000	0.00	2	1	0	0	0	0	7	2	22	0	0	0	0	0	0	0	0	5	0	0
Espinal, Willy, Rang.	2	2	.500	3.12	11	2	0	0	6	2	34.2	37	152	18	12	1	2	2	4	13	0	21	4	0
Esquivia, Manuel, Mar.	1	0	1.000	1.00	2	1	0	0	0	0	9	3	33	1	1	0	1	0	3	0	11	0	0	
Eusebio, Mike, Reds	2	1	.667	4.08	9	0	0	0	3	0	17.2	15	81	13	8	0	3	1	1	14	1	19	6	0
Evans, Keith, Exp.	0	0	.000	1.13	3	2	0	0	0	0	8	7	32	2	1	0	0	0	1	0	9	0	0	
Ewin, Ryan, Brav.	1	1	.500	1.65	6	3	0	0	1	0	16.1	10	64	4	3	1	0	0	7	0	18	0	0	
Farfan, Alexander, Reds	3	4	.429	5.18	20	5	0	0	8	4	40	28	170	28	23	3	1	1	4	20	0	31	3	0
Farizo, Brad, Mar.	1	0	1.000	2.03	3	0	0	0	0	0	13.1	10	52	3	3	0	0	0	1	0	14	0	0	
Farley, Chris, R.S.	2	3	.400	4.40	12	6	0	0	0	0	43	34	195	28	21	1	1	4	5	29	0	38	3	0
Farr, Whitt, Brav.	3	0	1.000	4.50	7	0	0	0	5	2	16	18	67	8	8	1	0	1	0	3	0	17	0	2
Felfoldi, Jonathan, Exp.*	0	2	.000	7.36	4	3	0	0	0	0	11	12	49	9	9	0	1	1	0	6	0	11	1	0
Feliz, Welinton, Tig.	2	6	.250	2.76	20	3	0	0	12	4	49	50	211	18	15	1	2	4	2	17	0	36	3	4
Fernando, Juan, Rang.	1	1	.500	6.46	11	5	0	0	1	0	15.1	15	85	12	11	0	0	2	3	20	0	5	5	0
Figuereo, Victor, Rang.	5	2	.714	1.96	16	4	0	0	10	0	55	48	225	18	12	3	0	3	5	17	0	31	2	0
Figueroa, Williams, Exp.	0	0	.000	5.40	5	0	0	0	2	2	5	7	26	3	3	0	0	0	0	4	0	3	0	0
Fisher, Pete, Twi.	0	0	.000	2.95	7	3	0	0	1	0	21.1	16	87	10	7	2	0	1	7	0	13	1	0	
Frias, Junior, R.S.	2	3	.400	5.83	12	4	0	0	3	1	41.2	59	202	34	27	0	0	1	8	13	0	21	5	1
Gabriel, Chris, Mar.	2	2	.500	3.60	17	0	0	0	7	0	35	36	164	26	14	1	3	2	19	0	18	5	0	
Galan, Jorman, Reds	0	0	.000	0.00	6	0	0	0	3	0	6	6	28	5	4	1	0	0	4	0	5	0	0
Galarraga, Armando, Exp.	0	0	.000	2.45	2	2	0	0	0	0	3.2	1	12	1	1	0	2	0	0	1	0	0		
Garces, Rich, R.S.	0	0	.000	0.00	2	2	0	0	0	0	4	1	14	1	0	0	1	0	0	0	5	0	0	
Garcia, Anderson, Yan.	4	1	.800	2.30	11	9	1	1	0	0	58.2	43	237	22	15	1	3	0	1	22	0	41	8	0
Garcia, Angel, Twi.	4	4	.500	3.40	13	7	0	0	0	0	53	41	229	24	20	0	2	7	31	0	63	4	0	
Garcia, Benjamin, Rang.	1	0	1.000	9.00	2	1	0	0	0	0	2	4	10	3	2	0	0	0	1	0	1	0	0	
Garcia, Carlos, Dod.	1	1	.500	1.42	5	5	0	0	0	0	19	20	81	8	3	0	0	0	1	4	0	7	1	0
Garcia, Edwin, Twi.	0	0	.000	7.64	16	1	0	0	1	0	17.2	18	105	18	15	1	1	2	4	30	0	14	7	0
Garcia, Randy, Yan.*	2	0	1.000	3.27	13	1	0	0	7	0	22	18	92	10	8	2	0	1	1	10	0	24	5	0
Gault, Tim, Reds*	1	0	1.000	5.84	8	0	0	0	5	0	12.1	15	59	9	8	1	1	1	8	1	9	2	0	
George, Brad, Reds	1	2	.333	2.49	5	5	0	0	0	0	21.2	16	89	10	6	0	0	2	6	0	13	4	0
George, Jonathan, Reds	1	1	.500	5.14	10	8	0	0	1	1	35	31	158	28	20	2	0	3	2	16	0	27	4	0
German, Rafael, Reds	6	2	.750	2.04	10	10	0	0	0	0	53	39	209	21	12	4	1	2	5	12	0	39	4	0
Gomez, Warmar, Exp.	1	0	1.000	3.21	19	0	0	0	15	4	28	26	115	12	10	3	0	0	3	7	0	20	0	0
Gonzalez, Jose, Tig.	2	2	.500	4.08	17	1	0	0	8	0	35.1	31	164	24	16	0	4	0	29	0	28	2	1	
Gonzalez, Luis, Dod.*	1	1	.500	3.07	6	2	0	0	0	0	14.2	13	61	5	5	1	0	2	6	0	9	1	0
Gonzalez, Mike, Pir.*	2	0	1.000	0.00	2	2	0	0	0	0	13.1	5	47	1	0	0	0	0	3	0	14	0	0
Gore, Kirk, Roy.	0	0	.000	1.23	5	0	0	0	3	0	7.1	6	31	1	1	0	0	0	1	2	0	4	0	0
Gorman, Pat, Ori.	1	1	.500	4.91	4	0	0	0	0	0	7.1	8	34	4	4	1	0	0	2	3	0	7	0	0
Graham, Jason, Tig.	0	0	.000	3.00	2	0	0	0	1	0	3	2	14	1	1	0	2	1	0	3	0	0		
Granado, Jan, Reds*	4	2	.667	2.91	13	12	0	0	0	0	55.2	45	231	23	18	4	1	0	2	22	0	45	5	2

Pitcher, Team	W	L	Pct.	ERA	G	GS	CG	ShO	GF	Sv.	IP	H	TBF	R	ER	HR	SH	SF	HB	BB	IBB	SO	WP	Bk.
Greinke, Zack, Roy.	0	0	.000	1.93	3	3	0	0	0	0	4.2	3	19	1	1	0	0	0	0	3	0	4	1	0
Hacker, Eric, Yan.	0	0	.000	0.00	3	0	0	0	0	0	3.2	2	15	0	0	0	1	0	1	1	0	2	0	0
Hader, Ryan, Twi.*	2	1	.667	2.60	11	9	0	0	1	0	45	31	189	15	13	0	6	1	4	25	0	47	4	0
Hamilton, Jamaal, Dod.*	3	2	.600	4.50	10	3	0	0	0	0	28	33	123	15	14	1	1	1	2	7	0	21	0	0
Hammes, Zach, Dod.	2	2	.500	3.27	10	8	0	0	0	0	33	26	141	14	12	0	2	1	3	15	0	27	2	1
Hampton, Royce, Rang.*	0	3	.000	7.90	4	2	0	0	0	0	13.2	24	71	15	12	1	1	0	1	5	0	11	2	0
Harben, Adam, Twi.	4	1	.800	3.20	12	3	0	0	4	0	25.1	27	112	11	9	0	2	0	2	8	1	27	0	0
Harmsen, Brandon, Yan.	4	5	.444	3.59	12	10	0	0	0	0	57.2	51	237	29	23	2	4	1	3	17	0	46	7	0
Hentgen, Pat, Ori.	0	0	.000	0.00	1	1	0	0	0	0	3	2	11	0	0	0	0	0	0	0	0	3	0	0
Hermanson, Dustin, R.S.	0	0	.000	9.00	1	1	0	0	0	0	2	5	10	3	2	0	0	0	0	1	0	1	0	0
Hernandez, Marcos, Tig.*	0	4	.000	6.75	11	7	0	0	2	0	30.2	41	151	27	23	2	2	3	2	18	0	12	3	0
Herndon, Eric, Brav.	0	0	.000	0.00	3	1	0	0	0	0	4	2	15	0	0	0	0	1	0	0	0	5	0	0
Hill, Josh, Twi.	1	1	.500	3.54	14	0	0	0	3	2	20.1	17	88	8	8	0	0	2	0	11	2	21	2	1
Hitchcock, Sterling, Yan.*	0	0	.000	0.00	2	2	0	0	0	0	3	0	10	0	0	0	0	0	0	0	0	6	0	0
Hoelscher, Nate, Roy.*	2	2	.500	1.60	9	2	1	0	4	0	33.2	28	137	10	6	0	2	3	1	7	0	27	4	0
Holliday, Brian, Pir.*	1	1	.500	4.91	10	5	0	0	3	1	33	35	147	22	18	2	1	2	2	18	0	26	1	0
Hosford, Clint, Dod.	0	1	.000	4.50	2	2	0	0	0	0	4	4	16	2	2	0	1	0	0	0	0	3	0	0
Huguet, J.C., Reds	0	0	.000	4.76	6	0	0	0	2	1	11.1	16	54	7	6	0	1	1	0	5	0	10	1	0
Hummel, John, Pir.*	0	1	.000	3.49	11	1	0	0	5	0	28.1	34	121	16	11	2	0	1	0	10	0	16	1	1
Iehl, Jason, Mar.	2	3	.400	3.00	7	5	0	0	0	0	24	18	98	10	8	2	0	0	0	6	0	16	3	2
Imotichey, Tory, Exp.*	2	4	.333	6.35	13	8	0	0	3	1	39.2	43	182	33	28	6	3	0	4	26	0	25	5	1
Jackson, Kyle, R.S.	0	0	.000	0.00	1	1	0	0	0	0	2	0	6	0	0	0	0	0	0	0	0	1	0	0
Jerzembeck, Mike, Twi.	0	0	.000	1.93	2	0	0	0	0	0	4.2	4	19	2	1	1	0	0	0	2	0	8	0	0
Johnson, Blair, Pir.	0	1	.000	8.10	2	1	0	0	0	0	3.1	4	19	6	3	0	0	1	1	3	0	4	0	0
Johnson, Josh, Mar.	2	0	1.000	0.60	4	3	0	0	0	0	15	8	57	3	1	0	0	0	2	3	0	11	0	0
Jones, K.C., Twi.	0	0	.000	3.10	12	3	0	0	2	0	29	20	126	15	10	1	0	0	0	21	0	21	10	1
Jung, Sung, Brav.	0	0	.000	0.00	1	0	0	0	0	0	2	0	6	0	0	0	0	0	0	0	0	2	0	0
Kemlo, Christopher, Yan.	1	0	1.000	4.19	11	0	0	0	5	1	19.1	18	85	10	9	3	2	1	3	9	0	13	0	2
Kennedy, Dajuan, Dod.	0	2	.000	3.60	16	0	0	0	7	0	25	20	119	15	10	1	1	1	2	22	0	27	10	0
Kerschen, Joshua, Yan.	3	1	.750	4.00	17	0	0	0	14	6	18	20	76	8	8	1	2	1	1	1	0	14	0	0
Kiley, Jason, Pir.	4	2	.667	2.63	11	11	1	1	0	0	51.1	33	213	20	15	2	2	7	24	0	27	5	2
Kinney, Matt, Twi.	0	0	.000	3.00	2	2	0	0	0	0	6	2	24	2	2	1	0	0	0	4	0	7	0	0
Kirkman, Tyler, Exp.*	2	1	.667	5.14	7	3	0	0	0	0	21	23	88	14	12	2	1	0	5	6	0	6	1	0
Klahs, Dave, Yan.	3	1	.750	3.90	14	0	0	0	5	1	27.2	29	113	13	12	3	2	1	1	6	0	21	0	0
Knoff, Justin, Reds	4	1	.800	3.38	13	2	0	0	2	1	32	27	132	15	12	1	3	2	1	13	0	21	3	0
Kuo, Hong-chih, Dod.*	0	0	.000	4.50	3	3	0	0	0	0	6	4	23	3	3	0	0	1	1	0	0	9	0	0
Landaeta, Argenis, Yan.	2	1	.667	3.65	10	0	0	0	6	1	24.2	21	99	11	10	1	2	0	1	7	0	26	0	0
Lane, Josh, R.S.*	0	0	.000	9.95	13	0	0	0	8	0	12.2	17	74	16	14	1	1	1	0	21	0	9	0	0
Leach, B.J., R.S.	0	0	.000	4.76	5	0	0	0	3	1	5.2	5	23	3	3	0	0	0	2	0	3	0	0
Ledezma, Wil, R.S.*	0	0	.000	6.00	1	0	0	0	0	0	3	4	13	2	2	0	0	0	0	3	0	0	0	0
Lee, Garrett, Brav.	0	0	.000	0.00	1	0	0	0	0	0	3	2	11	0	0	0	0	0	0	1	0	3	0	0
Lester, Jonathan, R.S.*	0	1	.000	13.50	1	1	0	0	0	0	0.2	5	8	6	1	0	0	0	0	1	0	1	0	0
Locklear, Joseph, Reds*	2	1	.667	2.96	16	0	0	0	5	2	27.1	18	119	11	9	1	1	2	4	20	0	16	1	0
Long, Nick, Exp.	5	2	.714	1.67	8	6	0	0	1	0	37.2	34	159	15	7	3	0	1	1	12	0	37	5	0
Looney, Marshall, Dod.*	2	0	1.000	0.42	8	5	0	0	0	0	21.1	13	77	2	1	0	0	0	1	1	0	17	0	0
Lowery, Devon, Roy.	0	3	.000	3.86	15	0	0	0	12	4	25.2	25	114	13	11	1	3	1	1	11	1	26	2	2
Lyons, Thomas, Tig.	2	2	.500	2.97	7	6	0	0	0	0	30.1	29	132	10	10	1	1	1	1	11	0	36	3	1
Machi, Jean, Phi.	2	0	1.000	1.00	10	2	0	0	4	1	27	11	105	4	3	0	2	1	1	16	0	22	2	0
MacDougal, Mike, Roy.	0	0	.000	3.00	1	1	0	0	0	0	3	3	11	1	1	0	0	0	0	0	0	3	0	0
Mairena, Ozwaldo, Mar.*	0	0	.000	0.00	1	1	0	0	0	0	1.1	1	5	0	0	0	0	0	0	0	0	1	0	0
Marino, Nexcys, Exp.	3	1	.750	2.31	18	0	0	0	7	1	35	27	141	13	9	2	1	1	5	11	0	14	2	1
Marquetti, Agustin, Tig.	0	0	.000	0.00	1	1	0	0	0	0	2.2	3	14	1	0	0	1	0	1	1	0	1	1	0
Martin, Greg, Exp.*	2	3	.400	3.74	13	1	0	0	5	2	33.2	29	143	16	14	2	0	1	0	16	0	27	1	0
Martinez, Dave, Yan.*	1	3	.250	5.04	9	6	0	0	3	0	25	28	112	14	14	1	1	0	1	15	0	20	7	1
Mason, Robert, Brav.*	1	2	.333	3.71	4	2	0	0	0	0	17	20	71	8	7	2	0	1	0	3	0	12	1	0
Mateo, Aneudis, R.S.	4	3	.571	1.76	11	11	2	0	0	0	51	45	207	14	10	1	1	0	1	11	1	45	2	0
Mateo, Carlos, Rang.	2	5	.286	3.90	18	0	0	0	13	1	30	28	134	15	13	1	0	5	15	2	21	4	0
Mateo, Manuel, Brav.	7	3	.700	1.98	12	8	1	1	3	0	68.1	47	260	18	15	0	2	1	2	12	0	76	2	0
Mathieson, Scott, Phi.	0	2	.000	5.40	7	2	0	0	1	0	16.2	24	81	11	10	0	1	1	2	6	0	14	0	1
Mattison, Kieran, Roy.	1	1	.500	1.80	13	0	0	0	11	1	20	13	74	4	4	1	1	0	1	3	0	19	4	0
McAdam, Scott, Exp.	1	1	.500	3.29	19	0	0	0	13	2	27.1	32	117	13	10	0	0	3	6	0	11	2	2
McClendon, Matt, Brav.	0	0	.000	3.00	3	0	0	0	1	0	3	2	14	1	1	0	1	0	0	2	0	2	0	0
McDonald, Jon, Twi.	2	0	1.000	0.00	3	2	0	0	0	0	11	6	40	1	0	0	0	0	0	2	0	9	0	0
Mead, Dan, Brav.*	2	0	.000	7.03	15	0	0	0	3	1	32	30	163	28	25	0	0	1	5	33	0	23	6	0
Medina, Dennis, Twi.	3	4	.429	2.63	11	8	2	0	0	0	61.2	60	253	24	18	0	5	2	1	11	1	40	3	1
Megrew, Mike, Dod.*	1	1	.500	2.03	5	4	0	0	0	0	13.1	8	48	4	3	0	0	0	0	3	0	12	0	0
Melnyk, Brian, Roy.*	0	1	.000	4.66	7	1	0	0	2	1	9.2	10	45	5	5	0	1	0	1	7	1	8	1	0
Mena, Amarys, Tig.	0	2	.000	4.79	9	5	0	0	1	0	20.2	25	109	20	11	2	0	2	1	18	0	17	1	1
Mendez, Wimer, Ori.	3	1	.750	2.70	20	0	0	0	12	3	36.2	29	147	17	11	0	2	0	1	12	1	44	0	1
Mendoza, Cristian, Yan.	1	0	1.000	2.29	13	0	0	0	9	4	19.2	10	76	5	5	2	1	1	1	7	0	19	1	0
Mendoza, Jorge, Rang.	0	0	.000	0.00	1	1	0	0	0	0	2	2	8	0	0	0	0	0	0	0	0	1	0	0
Mendoza, Luis, R.S.	3	4	.429	4.21	13	10	0	0	2	1	57.2	76	245	36	27	3	2	1	3	8	0	21	4	0
Meque, Jacobo, Ori.*	2	4	.333	2.86	12	12	0	0	0	0	50.1	41	220	26	16	1	2	1	4	33	1	56	3	6
Merricks, Alexander, Twi.*	2	0	1.000	1.80	9	2	0	0	3	1	15	9	70	4	3	0	3	1	1	16	2	13	5	0
Meyer, Todd, Exp.	1	2	.333	2.23	9	4	0	0	1	0	40.1	33	161	14	10	2	1	1	2	9	0	30	1	0
Mieres, Alberto, Yan.	2	0	1.000	0.00	4	0	0	0	2	0	8	4	31	1	0	0	0	0	1	3	0	6	1	1
Mildren, Paul, Mar.*	3	4	.429	1.97	11	10	2	0	0	0	59.1	52	246	16	13	1	0	3	17	0	38	4	1
Morel, Jhosandy, Pir.*	1	1	.500	4.02	8	0	0	0	1	0	15.2	16	67	9	7	2	0	0	2	5	0	12	0	0
Moreno, Edwin, Rang.	2	2	.500	3.38	9	7	0	0	1	0	37.1	30	152	18	14	2	0	0	1	10	0	23	1	0
Moreno, Juan, R.S.*	0	1	.000	1.80	3	3	0	0	0	0	5	4	19	2	1	0	0	0	0	0	0	10	0	0
Moreno, Orber, Roy.	0	0	.000	0.00	2	2	0	0	0	0	7	0	19	0	0	0	0	0	0	3	0	4	0	0
Morton, Charles, Brav.	1	7	.125	4.54	11	5	0	0	1	0	39.2	37	186	34	20	1	1	1	2	30	0	32	5	0
Moye, Jeffrey, Rang.	1	1	.500	11.29	5	2	0	0	1	0	18.1	29	92	23	23	0	1	2	1	6	0	12	2	0
Mutch, Paul, Twi.	5	3	.625	2.95	12	8	0	0	1	1	58	49	241	28	19	4	0	1	6	20	0	39	5	0
Myers, Damien, Tig.*	0	1	.000	3.38	2	0	0	0	1	0	5.1	6	28	4	2	0	2	3	1	0	3	0	0
Nelson, David, Roy.*	6	2	.750	3.32	16	1	0	0	5	1	43.1	47	187	17	16	2	1	1	3	15	0	29	5	0
Nelson, Justin, Roy.*	1	7	.125	4.30	12	9	0	0	0	0	58.2	67	269	37	28	2	3	6	3	25	0	23	2	0

Pitcher, Team	W	L	Pct.	ERA	G	GS	CG	ShO	GF	Sv.	IP	H	TBF	R	ER	HR	SH	SF	HB	BB	IBB	SO	WP	Bk.
Nelson, Kenny, Brav.	0	0	.000	0.00	3	3	0	0	0	0	5	1	17	0	0	0	0	0	1	0	0	7	0	0
Neuage, Leigh, Dod.	0	2	.000	4.68	7	6	0	0	0	0	25	30	109	14	13	2	1	2	3	4	0	15	2	1
Nieves, Roberto, Brav.	0	3	.000	5.30	5	4	0	0	0	0	18.2	18	84	14	11	1	1	1	3	9	0	19	1	0
Norderum, Jason, Exp.*	0	1	.000	15.88	4	2	0	0	0	0	5.2	8	35	10	10	0	0	2	1	10	0	6	5	0
Nova, Juan, Mar.	1	2	.333	1.11	20	0	0	0	19	7	32.1	26	130	8	4	1	3	1	0	6	0	23	2	0
Nunez, Franklin, Phi.	0	0	.000	0.00	1	1	0	0	0	0	2	2	9	0	0	0	0	0	1	0	0	4	0	0
Nunez, Kelvin, Roy.	3	1	.750	1.32	5	5	0	0	0	0	27.1	20	114	6	4	0	1	0	2	15	0	15	4	1
Nunez, Leo, Pir.	4	2	.667	3.43	11	11	0	0	0	0	60.1	54	239	23	23	5	2	5	5	5	0	52	1	0
O'Connor, Shaun, Mar.	0	1	.000	7.36	3	0	0	0	1	0	3.2	1	17	3	3	0	2	0	2	3	0	1	2	0
O'Donnell, Tony, Reds*	0	0	.000	15.43	2	0	0	0	2	0	2.1	4	14	4	4	0	0	2	2	0	1	0	0	0
Olsen, Scott, Mar.*	2	3	.400	2.96	13	11	0	0	0	0	51.2	39	215	18	17	0	1	1	5	17	0	50	5	2
Paddock, Josh, Phi.	2	1	.667	2.16	6	2	0	0	2	0	25	16	94	7	6	0	2	2	1	5	1	13	2	0
Padilla, Nick, Brav.	0	0	.000	0.00	1	0	0	0	0	0	2	1	8	0	0	0	0	0	1	0	0	1	0	0
Palmer, Lucas, Roy.	2	4	.333	4.31	13	8	1	0	1	0	56.1	68	246	31	27	4	3	2	3	13	0	32	2	0
Parker, David, Dod.	2	2	.500	3.18	20	0	0	0	14	6	34	32	145	13	12	1	3	2	2	14	0	24	4	0
Parker, Justin, Brav.*	2	1	.667	1.32	8	0	0	0	0	0	13.2	12	59	3	2	1	0	0	1	8	0	17	2	1
Parris, Matt, Tig.	5	4	.556	3.34	11	10	0	0	0	0	62	70	269	35	23	0	2	2	3	11	0	45	6	1
Pearson, Anthony, Exp.	0	1	.000	8.22	4	2	0	0	0	0	7.2	11	42	8	7	1	1	0	1	6	0	4	1	0
Pena, Juan, R.S.	0	0	.000	0.00	1	1	0	0	0	0	3.2	4	16	0	0	0	0	0	2	0	0	4	0	0
Peralta, Efigenio, Brav.	6	2	.750	1.78	14	5	0	0	3	0	55.2	32	214	13	11	1	1	2	0	18	0	44	3	1
Perez, Carlos, Ori.*	2	2	.500	2.63	12	5	0	0	0	0	37.2	35	161	18	11	2	3	3	2	17	3	32	6	0
Pezely, Franco, Rang.*	0	1	.000	1.17	4	1	0	0	2	1	7.2	2	24	1	1	1	0	0	0	1	0	9	0	0
Picco, John, Yan.*	4	3	.571	5.58	11	8	0	0	1	0	50	53	230	33	31	5	5	0	5	27	0	39	2	2
Plank, Terry, Ori.	0	0	.000	9.00	7	0	0	0	1	1	8	9	39	8	8	1	0	1	0	6	0	4	1	0
Plummer, Jarod, Dod.	2	2	.500	2.94	16	2	0	0	3	0	33.2	28	138	17	11	0	1	1	2	7	0	41	2	1
Pole, Hank, Exp.	1	1	.500	3.65	6	0	0	0	2	0	12.1	13	50	5	5	0	1	0	2	0	6	0	0
Poles, Donnie, Roy.	0	0	.000	8.03	9	0	0	0	1	0	12.1	10	71	13	11	1	0	3	1	22	0	13	3	1
Potoczny, Robert, Dod.	3	3	.500	5.91	11	2	0	0	2	0	21.1	20	94	15	14	1	0	2	0	14	0	21	1	1
Potter, Joshua, Ori.	3	3	.500	2.98	19	1	0	0	5	0	42.1	48	187	20	14	1	2	2	1	17	0	22	2	0
Prieto, Victor, Mar.	4	2	.667	3.16	8	7	1	1	0	0	31.1	14	134	17	11	0	2	1	8	19	0	21	4	0
Radke, Brad, Twi.	0	0	.000	0.00	1	1	0	0	0	0	3	2	11	0	0	0	0	0	0	0	0	4	0	0
Ramirez, Elizardo, Phi.	7	1	.875	1.10	11	11	2	1	0	0	73.1	44	275	18	9	3	3	1	3	2	0	73	3	1
Ramirez, Luis, Ori.	2	1	.667	4.44	19	0	0	0	13	2	26.1	17	111	13	13	1	1	0	1	17	2	46	1	1
Randazzo, Jeffrey, Twi.*	0	0	.000	6.00	3	0	0	0	1	0	3	6	16	4	2	0	0	1	0	2	0	0	0	0
Reilly, Christopher, Ori.	1	1	.500	7.50	3	1	0	0	0	0	6	4	32	6	5	1	0	0	9	0	7	4	0
Reiss, Mike, Brav.	1	1	.500	14.67	13	0	0	0	6	1	15.1	16	106	34	25	3	1	1	6	35	0	9	7	0
Reiss, Steven, Brav.	0	2	.000	9.13	13	0	0	0	9	0	22.2	26	127	29	23	2	0	2	7	31	0	12	9	0
Reyes, Maximo, Phi.	2	0	1.000	0.35	22	0	0	0	20	12	25.2	12	93	2	1	0	1	0	3	0	29	0	0
Rivas, Gabriel, Tig.	1	1	.500	5.61	15	0	0	0	3	0	25.2	22	121	19	16	1	2	3	22	0	14	7	1
Rivera, Mariano, Yan.	0	0	.000	0.00	1	0	0	0	0	0	2	2	8	0	0	0	0	0	1	0	2	0	0
Rosa, Carlos, Roy.	0	4	.000	6.19	10	9	0	0	0	0	32	52	161	32	22	3	1	2	2	12	0	11	3	1
Rose, Brian, Roy.	1	0	1.000	9.00	2	2	0	0	0	0	3	6	14	3	3	1	0	0	1	0	1	0	0
Rowe, Steven, Rang.	1	1	.500	3.33	7	1	0	0	3	0	24.1	32	108	13	9	1	0	3	4	0	16	2	0
Runyon, Roy, Roy.	1	1	.500	2.03	11	2	0	0	0	0	31	22	119	9	7	1	1	1	3	28	1	0
Rupert, Christopher, Phi.*	1	3	.250	1.80	18	0	0	0	11	4	30	19	109	6	6	0	2	0	1	4	0	21	0	0
Russ, Chris, Yan.	1	0	1.000	5.40	5	0	0	0	1	0	8.1	4	37	5	5	0	0	0	6	0	6	1	0
Russell, Eddie, Mar.	2	0	1.000	0.00	3	0	0	0	2	0	3	0	9	0	0	0	0	0	0	0	7	0	0
Russell, Steve, Brav.	1	3	.250	5.68	11	6	0	0	1	0	44.1	43	197	30	28	3	0	4	29	0	42	16	1
Sanchez, Elby, Roy.	3	2	.600	1.80	15	5	0	0	7	2	50	49	210	18	10	0	1	3	3	7	1	36	8	0
Sanchez, Emilio, Phi.	2	0	1.000	2.63	3	2	0	0	0	0	13.2	10	54	4	4	0	0	1	0	3	0	15	0	0
Santana, Roberto, Brav.	0	0	.000	3.38	2	0	0	0	0	0	2.2	2	7	1	1	0	0	0	0	1	0	1	0	0
Santiago, Victor, Dod.	1	1	.500	1.35	10	0	0	0	7	1	13.1	7	50	3	2	0	1	2	4	0	12	1	0
Schara, Zackary, Rang.	2	2	.500	2.74	6	3	0	0	2	0	23	25	93	9	7	1	1	0	4	0	16	1	0
Segovia, Zachary, Phi.	3	2	.600	2.10	8	8	0	0	0	0	34.1	21	128	11	8	0	1	3	3	0	30	1	0
Selmo, Santo, Mar.	1	4	.200	1.50	14	1	0	0	5	1	30	19	123	16	5	0	2	2	3	6	0	18	2	0
Shafer, David, Reds	1	0	1.000	1.29	3	0	0	0	3	1	7	3	26	2	1	0	0	0	2	0	7	0	0
Shafer, Kurt, Pir.	3	2	.600	6.00	5	5	0	0	0	0	27	30	120	21	18	3	1	1	3	3	0	15	1	1
Silva, Efrain, Dod.	0	0	.000	3.86	5	0	0	0	2	0	9.1	8	40	4	4	1	0	1	6	0	6	2	0
Simon, Billy, R.S.	1	1	.500	1.64	5	0	0	0	0	0	22	12	82	6	4	0	0	0	5	0	24	3	0
Simpson, Brian, Brav.	0	0	.000	10.66	8	1	0	0	4	0	12.2	10	77	19	15	2	0	0	10	20	0	9	11	0
Small, Aaron, Brav.	0	0	.000	6.00	5	0	0	0	0	0	6	9	25	4	4	0	0	0	0	0	3	1	0
Smiley, Gerald, Rang.	0	2	.000	5.75	12	4	0	0	1	1	36	41	177	26	23	2	2	2	27	0	26	6	2
Smith, Dan, Tig.	0	0	.000	0.00	2	0	0	0	0	0	4	2	13	0	0	0	0	0	0	0	3	0	0
Smith, Julius, Rang.*	3	2	.600	2.44	13	7	0	0	4	1	48	42	203	18	13	4	0	1	2	17	0	44	1	1
Smith, Michael, Tig.*	3	2	.600	1.93	18	0	0	0	6	0	23.1	17	106	6	5	0	1	1	18	0	28	5	0
Soria, Joakim, Dod.	0	0	.000	3.60	4	0	0	0	0	0	5	6	21	2	2	0	0	0	3	0	4	0	0
Sosa, Alexis, Mar.*	1	0	1.000	5.14	3	0	0	0	1	0	7	9	37	5	4	1	0	1	0	7	0	8	2	0
Speir, Zach, Reds	0	0	.000	4.74	10	0	0	0	4	0	19	24	93	13	10	0	0	3	4	7	0	13	0	0
Steen, Adam, Phi.	1	1	.500	6.75	7	0	0	0	2	0	16	23	84	14	12	0	2	1	2	10	2	10	1	0
Steffek, Brian, Dod.	0	1	.000	2.84	3	3	0	0	0	0	6.1	4	26	2	2	0	0	0	2	2	0	6	0	0
Steinborn, Chris, Tig.*	1	3	.250	3.02	10	8	0	0	0	0	50.2	50	227	30	17	3	0	2	4	15	0	47	8	0
Sterrett, Adam, Mar.	0	0	.000	7.31	6	2	0	0	5	0	28.1	29	144	29	23	0	0	3	9	30	0	14	13	1
Suarez, Pedro, R.S.	0	0	.000	3.14	15	0	0	0	6	1	28.2	33	126	11	10	2	0	1	0	10	0	21	1	1
Sullivan, Mark, Rang.	1	1	.500	4.30	6	0	0	0	4	0	14.2	15	60	8	7	0	0	1	3	0	8	2	0
Sweeney, Matt, Phi.	4	5	.444	2.69	12	12	2	1	0	0	67	56	274	23	20	2	3	3	0	27	0	38	3	0
Taki, Yusuke, Mar.	0	2	.000	3.48	6	0	0	0	2	0	10.1	11	45	4	4	0	3	0	1	4	0	5	1	0
Targac, Matthew, Mar.*	0	1	.000	6.00	1	0	0	0	0	0	3	3	15	4	2	0	1	0	2	0	1	1	0
Teeter, Travis, Ori.	5	4	.556	3.72	16	3	1	1	6	2	46	40	185	21	19	4	2	1	10	2	51	3	0
Tejada, Frailyn, Mar.*	0	0	.000	4.50	1	0	0	0	0	0	2	1	8	1	1	0	0	1	0	0	4	0	0
Telemaco, Amaury, Phi.	1	0	1.000	1.64	2	2	0	0	0	0	11	4	41	2	2	0	0	0	3	0	8	0	0
Thompson, Erik, Rang.	2	2	.500	2.04	10	5	0	0	3	0	39.2	38	156	12	9	2	1	0	1	2	0	34	2	1
Thompson, Justin, Rang.*	0	0	.000	3.00	7	7	0	0	0	0	15	19	64	6	5	0	1	1	0	0	11	0	0
Thorne, David, Exp.	3	2	.600	1.50	9	9	0	0	0	0	42	33	179	12	7	1	1	5	19	0	45	3	0
Torrealba, Yoann, Pir.	2	1	.667	1.35	9	0	0	0	9	4	13.1	10	54	2	2	1	0	1	5	0	12	1	0
Torres, Luis, Exp.	0	0	.000	0.00	1	1	0	0	0	0	5	4	17	0	0	0	0	0	0	0	4	0	0
Tower, Scott, Pir.*	0	1	.000	3.72	6	0	0	0	2	0	9.2	10	46	5	4	0	1	0	8	0	8	3	0
Treanor, Bryan, Mar.	1	1	.500	0.00	3	1	0	0	1	0	11.2	11	45	1	0	0	1	0	0	0	14	0	1

Pitcher, Team	W	L	Pct.	ERA	G	GS	CG	ShO	GF	Sv.	IP	H	TBF	R	ER	HR	SH	SF	HB	BB	IBB	SO	WP	Bk.
Tussen, Denny, R.S.	2	2	.500	2.60	12	3	0	0	3	0	52	48	219	28	15	1	2	5	2	15	0	37	3	3
Urena, Sixto, Rang.	0	1	.000	0.84	3	2	0	0	1	0	10.2	9	41	2	1	0	0	0	1	2	0	7	0	0
Valdez, Jose, Yan.	1	4	.200	3.35	8	7	0	0	0	0	40.1	45	174	19	15	2	1	2	2	10	0	28	1	0
Wagnon, Dwayne, Reds	1	3	.250	2.78	10	8	0	0	1	0	35.2	28	161	23	11	1	3	2	4	24	0	39	4	0
Watts, Joldy, Rang.	5	3	.625	3.63	14	4	0	0	8	3	52	63	231	34	21	4	3	5	3	12	0	25	3	0
Weeden, Brandon, Yan.	2	1	.667	2.86	11	7	0	0	1	1	34.2	29	150	13	11	1	2	0	5	16	0	30	2	1
Wells, Clint, R.S.*	1	0	1.000	5.79	2	0	0	0	0	0	4.2	3	25	3	3	0	0	0	2	5	0	1	0	0
Wells, Mark, Reds	2	0	1.000	1.93	5	0	0	0	5	2	9.1	7	36	4	2	0	0	3	0	0	0	5	1	0
Wheeler, Adam, Yan.	0	0	.000	1.35	3	2	0	0	0	0	6.2	6	29	1	1	0	1	0	0	4	0	8	0	0
Wheldon, Rhys, Twi.	2	2	.500	3.00	15	1	0	0	6	0	30	23	124	12	10	1	0	0	4	15	1	24	4	1
White, Brian, Pir.	0	1	.000	5.00	11	0	0	0	5	1	18	18	80	10	10	1	3	2	0	12	0	8	2	0
White, Michael, Dod.*	0	0	.000	0.00	2	0	0	0	0	0	4	3	16	0	0	0	0	0	1	1	0	3	0	0
Williams, Aaron, Twi.	1	3	.250	4.03	25	0	0	0	22	9	29	34	123	15	13	3	0	1	4	4	2	19	1	0
Wiseman, Steven, Yan.	3	1	.750	3.91	14	0	0	0	6	0	25.1	23	105	13	11	2	0	1	1	12	2	29	0	0
Wright, Chase, Yan.*	2	3	.400	3.43	10	7	0	0	0	0	42	32	194	19	16	0	6	1	1	39	0	23	10	1
Wright, Isaiah, Exp.	1	2	.333	5.57	13	0	0	0	2	0	21	24	98	16	13	1	1	2	2	14	0	10	5	0
Wyrick, Patrick, Mar.	3	1	.750	2.70	10	0	0	0	5	0	20	17	88	9	6	1	0	2	4	5	0	22	3	1
Yankosky, L.J., Brav.	0	0	.000	0.00	6	6	0	0	0	0	8	3	30	0	0	0	0	0	1	3	0	7	0	0
Zumaya, Joel, Tig.	2	1	.667	1.93	9	8	0	0	0	0	37.1	21	143	9	8	2	0	2	1	11	0	46	3	0

COMBINATION SHUTOUTS: **Braves (2)**—Ewin-M. Mateo, Yankosky-Peralta-Aguilar. **Dodgers (5)**—Cuen-J. Diaz-White-Duesnil-D. Parker, J. Diaz-Carvajal-Dumesnil, C. Garcia-Soria-G. Alvarez, Megrew-Potoczny-Ahumada-Santiago, Neuage-Kennedy-J. Diaz. **Expos (2)**—Acuna-Long, Echols-Acuna-Gomez, Imotichey-I. Wright-Martin, Long-Beck, Long-Meyer-McAdam, Torres-McAdam-Gomez-Kirkman-Marino-Figueroa. **Marlins (4)**—Esquivia-Chick, Iehl-Selmo-Nova, Iehl-Wyrick, J. Johnson-Chick-Eazor, Mairena-Iehl-Selmo, Mildren-Nova, Olsen-Sterrett-Nova. **Orioles (3)**—Bolander-Plank-Potter-L. Ramirez-Teeter, Caughey-Potter-Mendez, Meque-Plank. **Phillies (9)**—E. Ramirez-Rupert-Reyes 2, Butto-Reyes, De La Cruz-Mathieson-Dorsey-Rupert, Em. Sanchez-Rupert-Reyes, Segovia-Denison, Segovia-Machi, Sweeney-Dorsey-Reyes, Telemaco-Butto. **Pirates (5)**—Duke-P. Arias, Duke-Hummel-Contreras, Holliday-Torrealba, Kiley-Torrealba, L. Nunez-P. Arias. **Rangers (5)**—Fernando-Espinal, J. Mendoza-E. Moreno, E. Moreno-Espinal, J. Smith-Pezely-C. Mateo, E. Thompson-Figuereo. **Reds (4)**—J. George-Farfan, German-Farfan, German-Knoff, Wagnon-D. Shafer. **Red Sox (4)**—Ju. Cedeno-Suarez, Frias-Mendoza, Mateo-Leach, Mendoza-Blaney-Batista. **Royals (5)**—Durbin-Sanchez, J. Nelson-Melnyk, K. Nunez-Encarnacion, Rosa-Hoelscher-Poles-Dodson, Runyon-D. Nelson. **Tigers (5)**—Clark-M. Smith-Barrios, Lyons-Hernandez-Rivas-Barrios, Parris-Feliz, Zumaya-DeLaCruz-J. Arias, Zumaya-Feliz-Barrios. **Twins (1)**—Wheldon-Williams. **Yankees (3)**—Harmsen-Klahs-Kerschen, Martinez-A. Garcia-Kemlo, Weeden-Mendoza-Wiseman.

NO-HIT GAMES: Butto, Phillies defeated Royals, 2-1, August 3, first game.

2002 FIELDING

TEAM

Team	G	PO	A	E	TC	DP	TP	PB	Pct.
Yankees	60	1508	646	61	2215	58	0	19	.972
Braves	60	1509	588	61	2158	47	0	23	.972
Phillies	60	1514	665	73	2252	45	0	9	.968
Rangers	60	1479	593	73	2145	55	0	15	.966
Dodgers	60	1470	643	75	2188	46	0	4	.966
Twins	60	1579	672	80	2331	65	0	18	.966
Pirates	60	1503	688	89	2280	57	0	8	.961
Expos	60	1498	587	86	2171	56	0	13	.960
Royals	60	1516	588	90	2194	55	1	16	.959
Marlins	60	1493	629	96	2218	49	0	20	.957
Reds	60	1486	628	100	2214	41	0	16	.955
Orioles	60	1457	595	102	2154	58	0	16	.953
Red Sox	60	1491	606	118	2215	58	0	16	.947
Tigers	60	1518	593	127	2238	43	0	12	.943

INDIVIDUAL

FIRST BASEMEN

NOTE: All caps denotes fielding-percentage leader based on 30 games for catchers, 40 for all other non-pitchers and 48 innings for pitchers. *Throws lefthanded.

Player, Team	Pct.	G	PO	A	E	TC	DP
Baker, Jordan, Mar.*	.989	11	84	4	1	89	5
Bastardo, Frederick, Mar.	1.000	6	39	1	0	40	1
Bernstine, David, Twi.	.986	22	134	12	2	148	13
Blanco, Luis, Exp.	.984	39	311	6	5	322	22
Blanton, Stephen, Ori.	.938	6	39	6	3	48	6
Bonvechio, Brett, R.S.	.996	29	223	12	1	236	27
Broadway, Larry, Exp.*	.964	4	24	3	1	28	3
Brown, Tim, Pir.*	.981	40	325	32	7	364	35
Burgos, Jose, Twi.	1.000	1	4	0	0	4	0
Carbonara, William, Ori.	1.000	4	16	0	0	16	0
Carofiles, Bladimir, Mar.	1.000	13	92	5	0	97	7
Coffey, Josh, Mar.	1.000	1	8	0	0	8	0
Colina, Yinner, Reds	1.000	7	59	2	0	61	2
Cotto, Pedro, Tig.*	.958	11	86	5	4	95	6
Davenport, Juston, Yan.	1.000	1	2	1	0	3	0
Durazo, William, R.S.	.989	12	83	7	1	91	8
Ferrara, Matt, Roy.	1.000	7	58	6	0	64	5
Figuereo, Anibal, Roy.	.957	12	105	7	5	117	10
Garcia, Juan-Carlos, Mar.	.987	23	206	16	3	225	21
Gillies, Michael, Phi.	.983	18	173	5	3	181	11
Gonzalez, Luis, Roy.	1.000	4	19	1	0	20	0
Guerra, Alex, Rang.	1.000	2	10	1	0	11	1
Guzman, Heriberto, R.S.	.967	23	191	14	7	212	17
Hadad, Jorge, Ori.	1.000	2	9	0	0	9	0
HANSEN, Bryan, Phi.*	.995	42	361	34	2	397	28
Hernandez, Miguel, Dod.	.986	45	398	27	6	431	30
House, J.R., Pir.	1.000	1	4	1	0	5	0
Huether, J.D., Twi.	.992	29	247	15	2	264	25
Jimenez, Franklyn, Exp.	1.000	4	23	1	0	24	3
Kaaihue, Kila, Roy.	.961	14	116	7	5	128	10
Koutnik, Jared, Yan.	.968	7	56	5	2	63	6
Kreuzer, Josh, Rang.	.986	50	415	10	6	431	40
Leon, Alfredo, Ori.	1.000	1	1	0	0	1	0
Lisson, Mario, Roy.	.962	4	21	4	1	26	5
Lopez, Javier, Twi.	.982	14	103	5	2	110	10
Lynch, Michael, Dod.	.966	5	26	2	1	29	3
Madrid, Mike, Pir.*	.995	23	178	17	1	196	19
Manriquez, Salomon, Exp.	.980	17	142	6	3	151	15
McDonald, Chamar, Roy.	.984	23	166	16	3	185	18
McKinney, Garth, Tig.	.833	1	5	0	1	6	1
Michelsen, Ross, Yan.*	.978	25	208	12	5	225	21
Moreta, Carlos, Brav.	.996	29	247	14	1	262	15
Mosby, Robert, Reds	1.000	14	107	6	0	113	7
Mujica, Jean, Exp.	1.000	1	6	0	0	6	1
Oakes, Matty, Tig.	1.000	5	42	3	0	45	2
Ortiz, Edgar, Tig.	.992	29	240	13	2	255	17
Patterson, Tarrence, Twi.	.000	1	0	0	0	0	0
Perez, Miguel, Reds	.917	2	8	3	1	12	0
Phillips, Kyle, Twi.	1.000	6	50	4	0	54	13
Pitney, Jared, Yan.*	1.000	10	116	4	0	120	9
Radwan, Jason, Dod.	.980	11	92	7	2	101	8
Romero, Alex, Twi.	.000	1	0	0	0	0	0
Sandoval, Abigail, Rang.	1.000	11	59	1	0	60	7
Santana, Roberto, Brav.	.989	38	264	9	3	276	29
Saunches, Michael, Yan.*	.974	19	170	14	5	189	17
Shields, Nick, Rang.	1.000	2	21	0	0	21	0
Spano, Robert, Mar.	.833	2	4	1	1	6	0
Thurman, Tim, Ori.	.988	52	397	21	5	423	40
Wahl, Mark, Ori.	.000	1	0	0	0	0	0
Wells, Dan, Mar.	.982	14	104	4	2	110	8
Williams, John, R.S.	.909	1	10	0	1	11	1
Winegarden, Erik, Phi.	.964	6	51	2	2	55	3
Wise, Bradley, Tig.	.959	18	129	10	6	145	7
Wong, Travis, Reds	.982	41	370	18	7	395	27

TRIPLE PLAY: McDonald.

SECOND BASEMEN

Player, Team	Pct.	G	PO	A	E	TC	DP
Anderson, Rondon, Mar.	.977	31	56	72	3	131	16
Arias, Joaquin, Yan.	.948	40	63	118	10	191	26
Arneson, Justin, Twi.	1.000	6	17	16	0	33	4
Bastardo, Frederick, Mar.	1.000	4	8	9	0	17	3
Batista, Alexander, Roy.	.956	20	42	44	4	90	10
Blasi, Blake, R.S.	1.000	7	11	13	0	24	5
Blue, Vincent, Tig.	1.000	1	3	0	0	3	0
Bolivar, Luis, Reds	.978	23	31	58	2	91	8
Bramasco, Omar, Phi.	.966	29	42	73	4	119	12

Player, Team	Pct.	G	PO	A	E	TC	DP
Burgos, Jose, Twi.	1.000	1	0	1	0	1	0
Carbonara, William, Ori.	1.000	1	1	1	0	2	0
Castillo, Carlos, Tig.	1.000	1	3	3	0	6	3
Castro, Ramon, Brav.	1.000	1	1	8	0	9	0
Ciofrone, Peter, R.S.	.933	15	12	30	3	45	3
Clanton, Ja'Mar, Exp.	.968	8	17	13	1	31	4
Cockrell, Michael, Pir.	.962	25	58	68	5	131	14
Coughlan, Cameron, Rang.	.951	32	52	83	7	142	16
Delos Santos, Esteban, Phi.	1.000	1	0	1	0	1	0
Diaz, Juan, Reds	.970	25	42	55	3	100	11
Espino, Damaso, Reds	.977	16	32	52	2	86	12
Fermin, Angelo, Twi.	1.000	2	1	2	0	3	1
Ferrer, Simon, Dod.	.967	25	40	76	4	120	9
Flamont, Sam, Tig.	.500	1	0	1	1	2	1
Garcia, Sergio, Dod.	.965	35	67	97	6	170	25
Gonzalez, Jose, Tig.	.919	45	57	113	15	185	20
Greene, Jason, Exp.	.938	8	10	20	2	32	7
Guerra, Alex, Rang.	.957	26	51	61	5	117	14
Hernandez, Luis, Brav.	.966	6	8	20	1	29	2
Isenhower, Jeremy, Phi.	.939	18	29	48	5	82	4
James, Willie, Brav.	.965	31	64	74	5	143	23
Jimenez, Franklyn, Exp.	.961	35	53	93	6	152	15
Kirkland, Kody, Pir.	1.000	1	2	3	0	5	1
Mancebo, Deni, Exp.	.943	10	19	14	2	35	6
Mateo, Dan, Reds	1.000	1	1	1	0	2	0
Maybin, Neal, Brav.	.000	1	0	0	0	0	0
Mendez, Deivi, Yan.	.000	1	0	0	0	0	0
Minami, Yasumichi, R.S.	.833	6	6	9	3	18	2
Morales, Jose, Twi.	.948	41	66	97	9	172	25
Moss, Brandon, R.S.	.983	31	43	73	2	118	21
Nunez, Alexis, Phi.	.948	11	19	36	3	58	4
OPEL, Chad, Ori.	.951	41	70	104	9	183	26
Orlandos, Nicholas, Yan.	.954	20	27	35	3	65	13
Ortega, Pedro, Brav.	.932	17	30	39	5	74	8
Piste, Carlos, Ori.	.940	19	26	37	4	67	12
Ramirez, Hanley, R.S.	1.000	5	5	18	0	23	6
Rodriguez, Robert, Exp.	1.000	4	8	12	0	20	3
Rutgers, Paul, Twi.	.960	25	44	52	4	100	13
Sanchez, Angel, Roy.	.967	39	70	105	6	181	21
Sandoval, Abigail, Rang.	.800	7	6	6	3	15	1
Smith, John, Pir.	.982	35	72	88	3	163	27
Spann, Chad, R.S.	1.000	1	0	1	0	1	0
Spano, Robert, Mar.	.974	17	41	35	2	78	8
Tejeda, Ferdin, Yan.	1.000	1	1	2	0	3	0
Timmons, Wes, Brav.	1.000	1	4	5	0	9	1
Vasquez, Wuillians, Yan.	1.000	4	4	15	0	19	3
Wardinsky, Ryan, Phi.	.962	8	5	20	1	26	4
Wayne, Brett, Dod.	.947	3	6	12	1	19	1
White, Dean, Brav.	.932	12	18	23	3	44	7
Willemburg, Brett, Roy.	.957	9	11	11	1	23	4
Williams, Devoris, R.S.	.944	7	11	6	1	18	2
Williams, Matt, Tig.	.900	12	16	20	4	40	2
Woods, Michael, Tig.	.975	7	17	22	1	40	4
Yepez, Marcos, Mar.	.972	18	31	39	2	72	8
Zapata, Jose, Ori.	.800	5	6	6	3	15	3

THIRD BASEMEN

Player, Team	Pct.	G	PO	A	E	TC	DP
Agustin, Hugo, Rang.	.967	24	19	40	2	61	7
Arias, Joaquin, Yan.	.000	1	0	0	0	0	0
Barthel, Cole, Brav.	.925	24	12	50	5	67	6
Bastardo, Frederick, Mar.	.856	38	25	64	15	104	4
Batista, Alexander, Roy.	.891	27	15	34	6	55	4
Blalock, Jake, Phi.	.875	8	1	13	2	16	0
Blanton, Stephen, Ori.	.000	1	0	0	0	0	0
Bonvechio, Brett, R.S.	1.000	1	0	3	0	3	0
Bramasco, Omar, Phi.	1.000	4	1	11	0	12	0
BURGOS, Jose, Twi.	.966	45	39	76	4	119	10
Carbonara, William, Ori.	.857	29	18	36	9	63	3
Castillo, Carlos, Tig.	1.000	3	0	6	0	6	1
Castro, Ramon, Brav.	.833	8	2	8	2	12	1
Ciofrone, Peter, R.S.	1.000	5	3	11	0	14	1
Clanton, Ja'Mar, Exp.	.750	3	2	4	2	8	0
Cockrell, Michael, Pir.	1.000	5	3	7	0	10	1
Correll, Richard, Reds	.857	4	4	2	1	7	0
Davenport, Juston, Yan.	1.000	1	1	0	0	1	0
Delos Santos, Esteban, Phi.	.500	1	0	1	1	2	0
Desena, Francis, Exp.	.941	15	12	20	2	34	2
Diaz, Juan, Reds	.000	1	0	0	0	0	0
Ellerson, Brian, Exp.	.833	8	6	14	4	24	1
Espino, Damaso, Reds	.898	37	11	68	9	88	3
Ferrara, Matt, Roy.	.900	36	23	49	8	80	3
Ferrer, Simon, Dod.	.906	10	10	19	3	32	4
Fisher, Kiel, Phi.	.907	33	17	51	7	75	3
Flamont, Sam, Tig.	.769	4	2	8	3	13	2
Flowers, Clarence, Tig.	.000	1	0	0	1	1	0
Garcia, Juan-Carlos, Mar.	.935	8	6	23	2	31	1
Gillies, Michael, Phi.	.821	11	4	19	5	28	0
Greene, Jason, Exp.	1.000	1	1	0	0	1	0
Guerra, Alex, Rang.	.872	21	15	26	6	47	2
Guzman, Heriberto, R.S.	.776	17	16	29	13	58	2
Guzman, Javier, Pir.	.000	1	0	0	0	0	0
Huether, J.D., Twi.	.939	16	13	33	3	49	7
Jimenez, Franklyn, Exp.	.000	1	0	0	0	0	0
Kirkland, Kody, Pir.	.907	45	36	91	13	140	15
Koutnik, Jared, Yan.	.917	21	11	33	4	48	1
Leon, Alfredo, Ori.	.889	7	8	8	2	18	1
Lopez, Javier, Twi.	.500	1	1	0	1	2	0
Mancebo, Deni, Exp.	.897	23	14	38	6	58	1
Mann, Jason, Rang.	1.000	1	0	2	0	2	0
Manriquez, Salomon, Exp.	.000	1	0	0	0	0	0
Maples, Chris, Tig.	.500	4	0	4	4	8	0
Martin, Russell, Dod.	.930	40	33	73	8	114	3
Mendez, Rafael, Tig.	.867	24	10	29	6	45	2
Minami, Yasumichi, R.S.	1.000	2	1	4	0	5	0
Morales, Jose, Twi.	.833	8	2	13	3	18	1
Moss, Brandon, R.S.	.000	1	0	0	0	0	0
Norris, Shawn, Exp.	.828	9	5	19	5	29	3
Nunez, Andres, Yan.	.968	33	12	48	2	62	7
Ohtsuka, Yoshiyuki, Pir.	.921	10	11	24	3	38	4
Opel, Chad, Ori.	.889	10	7	17	3	27	2
Orlandos, Nicholas, Yan.	.923	4	3	9	1	13	1
Pena, Antonio, Rang.	1.000	1	2	4	0	6	1
Perez, Miguel, Reds	.500	2	1	1	2	4	0
Raburn, Ryan, Tig.	.833	6	9	6	3	18	1
Ramirez, Hanley, R.S.	1.000	2	2	1	0	3	0
Reyes, Angel, Tig.	.821	18	5	27	7	39	0
Rodriguez, Reynaldo, Exp.	1.000	3	2	3	0	5	1
Rodriguez, Robert, Exp.	.769	6	0	10	3	13	0
Sanchez, Angel, Roy.	.000	1	0	0	0	0	0
Sandoval, Abigail, Rang.	.881	14	10	27	5	42	1
Santana, Roberto, Brav.	1.000	2	1	0	0	1	0
Smith, Justin, Rang.	.786	5	1	10	3	14	0
Soto, Melvin, Reds	.000	1	0	0	0	0	0
Spann, Chad, R.S.	.877	36	20	51	10	81	7
Spano, Robert, Mar.	.941	16	15	33	3	51	4
Springer, Kenard, Roy.	.750	3	1	2	1	4	0
Thurman, Tim, Ori.	.500	1	1	0	1	2	0
Vasquez, Wuillians, Yan.	1.000	1	1	0	0	1	0
Votto, Joey, Reds	.830	19	14	25	8	47	2
Wardinsky, Ryan, Phi.	1.000	10	4	15	0	19	2
Wayne, Brett, Dod.	1.000	11	10	21	0	31	5
White, Dean, Brav.	.934	30	20	51	5	76	3
Willemburg, Brett, Roy.	.000	2	0	0	0	0	0
Williams, Devoris, R.S.	.000	1	0	0	0	0	0
Williams, Matt, Tig.	.840	12	6	15	4	25	3
Wong, Travis, Reds	1.000	1	1	0	0	1	0
Zamora, Hector, Yan.	1.000	3	0	1	0	1	0
Zapata, Jose, Ori.	.979	20	14	32	1	47	3

SHORTSTOPS

Player, Team	Pct.	G	PO	A	E	TC	DP
Agustin, Hugo, Rang.	.901	14	16	48	7	71	7
Andino, Robert, Mar.	.974	9	11	27	1	39	7
Arias, Joaquin, Yan.	.875	18	25	45	10	80	10
Betemit, Wilson, Brav.	.867	6	2	11	2	15	1
Blanco, Andres, Roy.	.945	50	83	142	13	238	32
Bolivar, Luis, Reds	.949	30	40	91	7	138	11
Bramasco, Omar, Phi.	.983	15	17	40	1	58	10
Burgos, Jose, Twi.	1.000	6	12	14	0	26	8
Carofiles, Bladimir, Mar.	.940	8	8	39	3	50	6
Castillo, Carlos, Tig.	.889	2	5	3	1	9	1
Castro, Ramon, Brav.	1.000	1	2	1	0	3	1
Clanton, Ja'Mar, Exp.	.978	45	71	111	4	186	29
Cockrell, Michael, Pir.	.941	15	18	46	4	68	8
Cotto, Luis, Roy.	.955	5	7	14	1	22	2
Cruz, Luis, R.S.	.927	21	38	64	8	110	13
Delos Santos, Esteban, Phi.	.930	46	57	143	15	215	21
Desena, Francis, Exp.	.920	13	17	29	4	50	1
Diaz, Juan, Reds	.000	1	0	0	0	0	0
Espino, Damaso, Reds	.914	8	7	25	3	35	2
Fermin, Angelo, Twi.	.940	53	69	151	14	234	32
Ferrer, Simon, Dod.	1.000	1	1	1	0	2	1
Garcia, Nick, Ori.	.875	7	9	19	4	32	5
Garcia, Sergio, Dod.	1.000	11	6	34	0	40	3
Gonzalez, Alex, Mar.	.923	4	3	9	1	13	1
Greene, Jason, Exp.	.500	1	0	1	1	2	0
Guerra, Alex, Rang.	.967	8	13	16	1	30	4
Guzman, Javier, Pir.	.898	45	74	145	25	244	26
Guzman, Joel, Dod.	.921	10	8	27	3	38	3
Hadad, Jorge, Ori.	1.000	1	2	3	0	5	1
HERNANDEZ, Luis, Brav.	.990	47	54	137	2	193	23
Howarth, Jason, Twi.	1.000	2	4	3	0	7	1
James, Willie, Brav.	1.000	5	5	14	0	19	2

Player, Team	Pct.	G	PO	A	E	TC	DP
Koutnik, Jared, Yan.	.000	1	0	0	0	0	0
Leon, Alfredo, Ori.	.000	1	0	0	0	0	0
Mancebo, Deni, Exp.	1.000	4	4	9	0	13	1
Mariot, Lino, Pir.	.833	1	2	3	1	6	0
Martin, Russell, Dod.	.800	1	1	3	1	5	1
Mateo, Dan, Reds	.900	7	10	17	3	30	2
Mendez, Deivi, Yan.	.971	31	42	93	4	139	17
Moore, Scott, Tig.	.897	35	45	85	15	145	13
Morales, Jose, Twi.	1.000	4	4	11	0	15	2
Opel, Chad, Ori.	.500	1	2	0	2	4	0
Orlandos, Nicholas, Yan.	1.000	2	1	2	0	3	0
Pena, Antonio, Rang.	.963	18	30	47	3	80	8
Piste, Carlos, Ori.	.949	28	42	70	6	118	14
Ramirez, Hanley, R.S.	.905	40	72	118	20	210	25
Reyes, Angel, Tig.	.884	20	26	50	10	86	12
Rohan, James, Dod.	.974	11	12	26	1	39	2
Roughton, Jody, Tig.	1.000	1	1	1	0	2	0
Rutgers, Paul, Twi.	.600	2	2	1	2	5	0
Sanchez, Angel, Roy.	.688	8	6	5	5	16	1
Sandoval, Abigail, Rang.	.962	25	35	65	4	104	13
Soto, Melvin, Reds	.928	23	29	61	7	97	9
Spann, Chad, R.S.	1.000	3	3	7	0	10	1
Spano, Robert, Mar.	.867	5	6	7	2	15	1
Tejeda, Ferdin, Yan.	.989	16	34	55	1	90	16
Wardinsky, Ryan, Phi.	.923	5	10	14	2	26	2
Wayne, Brett, Dod.	.942	29	33	80	7	120	20
White, Dean, Brav.	1.000	6	2	13	0	15	1
Willemburg, Brett, Roy.	1.000	5	5	11	0	16	0
Williams, Devoris, R.S.	1.000	1	1	1	0	2	0
Williams, Matt, Tig.	.878	10	11	25	5	41	2
Yepez, Marcos, Mar.	.911	39	50	125	17	192	13
Zapata, Jose, Ori.	.910	28	41	70	11	122	19

TRIPLE PLAY: Blanco.

OUTFIELDERS

Player, Team	Pct.	G	PO	A	E	TC	DP
Acosta, Johe, Pir.	.941	11	15	1	1	17	1
Anderson, Rondon, Mar.	.000	1	0	0	0	0	0
Andrus, Erold, Yan.*	1.000	51	82	1	0	83	1
Aponte, Jose, Mar.	.980	50	93	4	2	99	0
Araque, Tulio, Reds	.953	51	79	3	4	86	1
Arbinger, Mike, Pir.	.964	42	52	1	2	55	0
Arias, Garvi, Pir.	.909	11	10	0	1	11	0
Arneson, Justin, Twi.	.971	21	29	4	1	34	0
Arroyo, Xavier, Mar.	.978	27	43	2	1	46	0
Baez, Fleming, Rang.	1.000	1	2	0	0	2	0
Baez, Lizaiho, Rang.	1.000	32	56	3	0	59	0
Baker, Jordan, Mar.*	.900	16	18	0	2	20	0
Barthel, Cole, Rang.	.958	27	41	5	2	48	0
Bastardo, Frederick, Mar.	1.000	5	5	0	0	5	0
Benson, Cedric, Dod.	1.000	7	14	0	0	14	0
Berkenbosch, Kenny, Mar.	.000	1	0	0	0	0	0
Bernadina, Rogearvin, Exp.*	.988	45	75	10	1	86	2
Bianucci, Anthony, R.S.	.954	33	58	4	3	65	1
Blalock, Jake, Phi.	.941	15	16	0	1	17	0
Blanton, Stephen, Ori.	.963	21	26	0	1	27	0
Blue, Vincent, Tig.	.983	55	116	3	2	121	0
Bramasco, Omar, Phi.	.000	1	0	0	0	0	0
Brito, Henry, Phi.	.990	55	99	5	1	105	1
Brown, Darrius, Ori.*	1.000	6	4	0	0	4	0
Brown, Dustin, R.S.	.945	28	48	4	3	55	2
Brown, Rich, Yan.*	1.000	2	1	0	0	1	0
Campos, Tiago, Reds	1.000	8	11	1	0	12	0
Carbonara, William, Ori.	.938	23	25	5	2	32	2
Carofiles, Bladimir, Mar.	.905	16	18	1	2	21	1
Clevlen, Brent, Tig.	.933	25	40	2	3	45	1
Cobb, Maurice, Exp.	.986	33	67	4	1	72	1
Colbert, Eddie, Ori.	.935	47	52	6	4	62	2
Colina, Yinner, Reds	1.000	17	12	1	0	13	0
Comfort, Geoffrey, Dod.	.960	16	20	4	1	25	0
Cotto, Pedro, Tig.*	1.000	1	2	0	0	2	0
Coughlan, Cameron, Rang.	1.000	20	37	3	0	40	1
Cronkhite, Ian, R.S.*	.951	49	95	3	5	103	0
Davenport, Juston, Yan.	1.000	10	11	1	0	12	0
Davis, Rajai, Pir.	.977	54	123	6	3	132	1
Davis, Zach, Ori.*	.989	48	81	6	1	88	2
De Aza, Alejandro, Dod.*	.908	37	56	3	6	65	2
De La Cruz, Carlos, R.S.*	.920	41	64	5	6	75	0
Dennis, Billy, Reds*	.000	1	0	0	0	0	0
Denorfia, Christopher, Reds	.966	57	107	5	4	116	2
Diaz, Frank, Exp.	.984	49	115	5	2	122	2
Donato, Greg, Brav.	1.000	4	5	1	0	6	0
Esparragoza, Eyoxy, Reds	.933	18	26	2	2	30	1
Flamont, Sam, Tig.	.983	33	54	5	1	60	0
Flowers, Clarence, Tig.	.967	23	26	3	1	30	0
Galan, Jorman, Reds	.968	28	30	0	1	31	0

Player, Team	Pct.	G	PO	A	E	TC	DP
Gillies, Michael, Phi.	1.000	7	5	0	0	5	0
Gonzalez, Edwar, Yan.	1.000	12	15	0	0	15	0
Gradoville, Tim, Phi.	.000	1	0	0	0	0	0
Graham, Tyson, Mar.	.889	5	7	1	1	9	0
Grayson, Larry, Rang.	.975	47	69	8	2	79	1
Greene, Jason, Exp.	1.000	1	1	0	0	1	0
Guerrero, Henry, Ori.	1.000	2	4	0	0	4	0
Guillen, Rudy, Yan.	.959	56	87	6	4	97	1
Guy, Jason, Rang.*	1.000	6	11	0	0	11	0
Hadad, Jorge, Ori.	1.000	5	3	0	0	3	0
Hall, Noah, Reds	1.000	8	16	2	0	18	0
Hatton, Vern, Dod.	1.000	23	41	5	0	46	1
Hawes, Don, Reds	1.000	3	3	0	0	3	0
Hermida, Jeremy, Mar.	.950	27	37	1	2	40	0
Hicks, Joseph, Pir.	.900	16	25	2	3	30	0
Honeycutt, Shedrick, Exp.*	.927	21	35	3	3	41	1
Howerton, Matthew, Ori.	.938	40	71	4	5	80	1
Isenhower, Jeremy, Phi.	.889	9	7	1	1	9	0
Jenkins, Darryl, Exp.	.000	1	0	0	0	0	0
Jimenez, Franklyn, Exp.	1.000	2	3	0	0	3	0
Jordan, Mickey, Dod.*	.974	22	37	0	1	38	0
Kerner, Craig, Exp.	.889	8	8	0	1	9	0
Khairy, Masjid, Rang.	.986	33	69	2	1	72	0
Liz, Jose, Twi.	.967	37	59	0	2	61	0
Lopez, Javier, Twi.	1.000	10	10	0	0	10	0
Marmolejos, Hector, Ori.	1.000	2	2	0	0	2	0
Maybin, Neal, Brav.	.867	8	13	0	2	15	0
McDonald, Chamar, Roy.	.941	19	29	3	2	34	1
McKinney, Garth, Tig.	.800	8	8	0	2	10	0
Milauskas, Adam, Pir.	1.000	16	22	0	0	22	0
Milons, Jereme, Dod.	.985	43	64	2	1	67	0
Moni-erigbali, Timi, Phi.	.923	16	12	0	1	13	0
Montague, Ed, Dod.	1.000	10	10	0	0	10	0
Mosby, Robert, Reds	1.000	10	10	0	2	12	0
Mota, Miguel, Brav.	.977	58	125	2	3	130	0
Mujica, Jean, Exp.	1.000	1	1	0	0	1	0
NONEMAKER, Karl, Phi.*	1.000	58	82	3	0	85	1
Nunez, Alexis, Phi.	1.000	2	2	0	0	2	0
Oliva, Chad, Phi.	.974	25	37	1	1	39	0
Oriental, Rene, Roy.	.987	44	75	3	1	79	0
Ortega, Pedro, Brav.	.667	1	2	0	1	3	0
Ortiz, Edgar, Tig.	.000	1	0	0	0	0	0
Partridge, Dominique, Brav.	.968	58	87	3	3	93	0
Patterson, Tarrence, Twi.	1.000	14	16	1	0	17	0
Perez, Jesus, Dod.	.976	28	39	2	1	42	0
Perez, Miguel, Reds	.000	1	0	0	0	0	0
Perodin, Ron, Twi.*	1.000	27	43	1	0	44	1
Reames, Joe Don, Rang.	.966	47	111	1	4	116	0
Rengifo, Amado, Mar.	.952	31	37	3	2	42	0
Resop, Chris, Mar.	1.000	19	25	3	0	28	1
Rivera, Juan, Yan.	1.000	3	6	0	0	6	0
Rivero, Luis, Phi.	1.000	4	3	0	0	3	0
Romero, Alex, Twi.	.971	51	96	4	3	103	1
Salazar, Darwinson, Roy.	.988	32	71	9	1	81	3
Santa, Alexander, Yan.*	.981	54	95	6	2	103	1
Santana, Roberto, Brav.	.800	4	4	0	1	5	0
Santoro, Pat, R.S.	1.000	8	11	1	0	12	0
Shields, Nick, Rang.	.000	1	0	0	0	0	0
Smith, Sean, Pir.	.988	39	78	7	1	86	2
Sovie, Robbie, Tig.	1.000	7	8	0	0	8	0
Spann, Chad, R.S.	1.000	1	2	0	0	2	0
Spataro, Ryan, Twi.	.986	47	64	4	1	69	1
Springer, Kenard, Roy.	.934	31	52	5	4	61	2
Sucre, Antonio, Exp.	.911	29	48	3	5	56	0
Teeter, Travis, Ori.	.000	1	0	0	0	0	0
Urquhart, Adrian, Exp.	1.000	7	4	0	0	4	0
Votto, Joey, Reds	.667	3	6	0	3	9	0
Watkins, Cedric, Roy.	.974	40	73	2	2	77	1
Weitz, Konrad, Roy.	1.000	2	5	0	0	5	0
White, Dean, Brav.	.000	1	0	0	0	0	0
Williams, Devoris, R.S.	.901	35	61	3	7	71	1
Williams, Edwin, Tig.*	.933	22	26	2	2	30	0
Williams, Matt, Tig.	.977	25	40	2	1	43	0
Williams, Mervin, Roy.	.946	35	70	0	4	74	0
Wilson, Vontrez, Brav.	1.000	22	26	4	0	30	0

CATCHERS

Player, Team	Pct.	G	PO	A	E	TC	DP	PB
Allec, Jason, Tig.	.984	6	55	6	1	62	1	0
Andujar, Pedro, Dod.	.975	33	203	34	6	243	2	7
Apodaca, Luis, Exp.	.983	9	50	7	1	58	2	0
Baez, Fleming, Rang.	1.000	1	2	0	0	2	0	0
Boone, Doug, Yan.	.950	3	17	2	1	20	0	0
Boullon, Luis, Yan.	1.000	4	27	2	0	29	1	1
Brown, Dustin, R.S.	.932	16	81	15	7	103	1	8
Cabrera, Ruben, Dod.	.959	7	37	10	2	49	0	1
Coffey, Josh, Mar.	.966	14	81	3	3	87	0	2

Player, Team	Pct.	G	PO	A	E	TC	DP	PB
Cruz, Ramon, Brav.	.987	21	137	13	2	152	0	11
Delacruz, Jose, Reds	1.000	6	25	5	0	30	0	2
Devries, Jonathan, R.S.	.983	39	256	27	5	288	0	8
Diaz, Jeury, Phi.	.988	20	150	11	2	163	2	2
Donachie, Adam, Roy.	1.000	19	115	11	0	126	0	2
Durazo, William, R.S.	.970	6	31	1	1	33	0	0
Elliott, Justin, Twi.	.950	29	147	23	9	179	2	7
Foskey, Will, Brav.	.990	15	85	10	1	96	0	5
Fry, Ryan, Reds	.974	7	33	5	1	39	0	3
Fuentes, Omar, Yan.	.913	4	19	2	2	23	0	1
Garland, Ross, Tig.	1.000	6	27	0	0	27	0	0
Gerlits, Gooby, Mar.	.994	24	147	14	1	162	1	4
Ghutzman, Phillip, Reds	.944	3	16	1	1	18	0	0
Gonzalez, Luis, Roy.	.983	30	141	30	3	174	2	10
Gradoville, Tim, Phi.	.991	33	204	27	2	233	1	4
Grzecka, Casey, Mar.	1.000	7	49	2	0	51	0	3
Guerrero, Henry, Ori.	.984	24	162	24	3	189	2	8
Hadad, Jorge, Ori.	.984	10	61	2	1	64	1	2
Hawes, Don, Reds	.976	28	145	16	4	165	1	1
House, J.R., Pir.	1.000	3	21	1	0	22	0	0
Huether, J.D., Twi.	.000	1	0	0	0	0	0	0
Johnson, Josh, Twi.	.986	25	126	15	2	143	0	5
Kahr, Danny, Exp.	.970	33	197	31	7	235	7	9
Lisson, Mario, Roy.	1.000	2	4	0	0	4	0	0
Long, Robert, Tig.	1.000	3	7	0	0	7	0	0
Lynam, Guy, Mar.	.967	11	54	4	2	60	0	3
Lynch, Michael, Dod.	.990	26	173	17	2	192	1	1
Mann, Jason, Rang.	.988	28	134	29	2	165	1	10
Manriquez, Salomon, Exp.	.957	16	95	16	5	116	1	3
Martinez, Edwin, Brav.	1.000	14	71	11	0	82	2	2
Martinez, Octavio, Ori.	1.000	6	50	8	0	58	3	1
McCann, Brian, Brav.	.993	17	134	11	1	146	0	4
McCuistion, Mike, Pir.	1.000	16	89	14	0	103	2	1
Mendez, Jose, Twi.	.980	6	45	5	1	51	0	2
Mercedes, Jose, Rang.	1.000	2	8	3	0	11	0	0
Morales, Jose, Twi.	1.000	1	1	0	0	1	0	0
Morales, Porfirio, Ori.	.957	2	19	3	1	23	0	0
Moreta, Carlos, Brav.	1.000	5	18	0	0	18	0	1
Nino, Denny, Pir.	.971	11	58	9	2	69	1	2
Oakes, Matty, Tig.	.988	33	217	26	3	246	0	7
Pereyra, Joel, Roy.	.953	7	34	7	2	43	0	1
Perez, Koby, R.S.	1.000	4	7	0	0	7	0	0
Perez, Miguel, Reds	.986	21	119	17	2	138	3	7
Phillips, Kyle, Twi.	.992	19	101	22	1	124	2	4
Reyes, Milver, Pir.	.982	35	188	29	4	221	1	5
Roa, Joel, Tig.	.992	14	98	20	1	119	2	3
Robles, Luis, Yan.	1.000	20	112	15	0	127	1	4
Rodriguez, Robert, Exp.	.970	6	30	2	1	33	0	1
ROSARIO, Carlos, Yan.	.992	39	226	32	2	260	2	13
Sanchez, Danilo, Tig.	.981	10	42	10	1	53	3	2
Shields, Nick, Rang.	.987	25	134	14	2	150	3	3
Smith, Justin, Rang.	.987	16	67	8	1	76	3	2
Valles, Jake, Roy.	1.000	5	32	1	0	33	0	1
Votto, Joey, Reds	.967	7	50	8	2	60	1	3
Wahl, Mark, Ori.	.984	24	168	17	3	188	1	5
Weitz, Konrad, Roy.	1.000	13	34	2	0	36	1	2
Wells, Dan, Mar.	.968	12	57	4	2	63	0	8
Winegarden, Erik, Phi.	.959	13	65	6	3	74	1	3

PITCHERS

Player, Team	Pct.	G	PO	A	E	TC	DP
Acosta, Richal, Ori.	.789	10	6	9	4	19	2
Acuna, Jose, Exp.	1.000	11	5	6	0	11	0
Aguilar, Rick, Brav.*	.667	9	0	2	1	3	0
Ahumada, Edgar, Dod.*	1.000	9	2	9	0	11	1
Aichele, Shawn, Reds	.875	11	5	2	1	8	0
Albaladejo, Jonathan, Pir.	.833	12	5	10	3	18	0
Almonte, Henry, Pir.	1.000	3	0	1	0	1	0
Alvarez, Gabriel, Dod.	1.000	15	1	4	0	5	1
Alvarez, Melvin, Pir.*	.667	11	0	2	1	3	0
Anderson, Wes, Mar.	1.000	4	3	2	0	5	1
Andrew, Jason, Rang.	1.000	2	0	3	0	3	0
Arias, Javier, Exp.	.846	15	3	8	2	13	1
Arias, Pedro, Pir.	.938	14	4	11	1	16	0
Arrojo, Rolando, R.S.	.000	1	0	0	0	0	0
Arteaga, Francisco, Brav.	.000	3	0	0	0	0	0
Astacio, Olivo, R.S.	1.000	6	1	1	0	2	0
Baez, Benito, Mar.*	1.000	5	0	1	0	1	0
Balan, Ryan, R.S.*	.750	13	1	2	1	4	1
Barrios, Rafael, Tig.	1.000	20	3	3	0	6	0
Bartel, Richard, Reds	1.000	7	1	1	0	2	0
Batista, Antonio, R.S.	1.000	22	1	1	0	2	0
Bays, Leonard, Roy.	1.000	2	1	0	0	1	0
Beck, Ken, Exp.	1.000	5	0	1	0	1	0
Beckett, Josh, Mar.	.000	1	0	0	0	0	0
Bell, Chris, Reds	1.000	3	0	3	0	3	0
Benitez, Fabricio, R.S.	1.000	3	0	4	0	4	0

Player, Team	Pct.	G	PO	A	E	TC	DP
Birk, Ben, Mar.*	1.000	1	1	1	0	2	0
Blaney, Matthew, R.S.	.750	21	1	2	1	4	0
Bohorquez, Carlos, Reds	.000	4	0	0	0	0	0
Bolander, Matt, Ori.	1.000	9	1	7	0	8	2
Borkowski, Dave, Tig.	1.000	3	0	2	0	2	0
Brazoban, Yhency, Yan.	1.000	6	0	1	0	1	0
Bridwell, Jody, Pir.*	.000	5	0	0	0	0	0
Brock, Tanner, Reds	.000	1	0	0	0	0	0
Brown, Darrius, Ori.*	.857	16	1	5	1	7	0
Brown, Jeremy, Twi.	.000	2	0	0	0	0	0
Brubaker, Douglas, Ori.	.667	11	1	7	4	12	0
Bryan, Robert, Roy.	.000	7	0	0	0	0	0
Burzynski, Cole, Pir.	.000	4	0	0	0	0	0
Bush, Jason, Mar.	1.000	2	1	0	0	1	0
Butto, Francisco, Phi.	1.000	12	5	6	0	11	2
Cahill, Casey, Ori.	1.000	22	0	8	0	8	0
Cahill, John, Twi.	1.000	14	0	1	0	1	0
Capps, Matt, Pir.	1.000	7	0	1	0	1	0
Carpenter, Miles, Reds	1.000	9	1	1	0	2	0
Carswell, Jeffery, Reds	.800	12	1	3	1	5	0
Carvajal, Marcos, Dod.	.800	13	2	2	1	5	0
Casadiego, Gerardo, Exp.	.000	1	0	0	1	1	0
Caughey, Trevor, Ori.*	.929	10	4	9	1	14	0
Cedeno, Blas, Pir.	.000	2	0	0	0	0	0
Cedeno, Jovanny, Rang.	.000	3	0	0	0	0	0
Cedeno, Juan, R.S.*	1.000	11	2	6	0	8	0
Cerrillo, Francisco, Dod.	1.000	5	1	2	0	3	0
Chen, Jose, Roy.	.000	2	0	0	0	0	0
Chick, Travis, Mar.	1.000	12	3	8	0	11	0
Christensen, Danny, Roy.*	1.000	7	0	4	0	4	0
Cierlik, Jason, Ori.*	1.000	3	1	0	0	1	0
Clark, Wade, Tig.	.800	7	1	3	1	5	0
Colton, Kyle, Brav.	.000	4	0	0	0	0	0
Contreras, Omar, Pir.	1.000	11	0	2	0	2	0
Cooper, Dexter, Brav.	1.000	11	4	10	0	14	0
Crawford, Tristan, Twi.	.750	20	1	5	2	8	0
Cressend, Jack, Twi.	1.000	3	2	0	0	2	0
Cuen, David, Dod.*	1.000	3	1	2	0	3	0
Delacruz, Eulogio, Tig.	.750	20	2	4	2	8	1
De la Cruz, Julio, Phi.	1.000	7	1	2	0	3	0
Delacruz, Maximo, Dod.	1.000	2	0	1	0	1	0
Denison, Brandon, Phi.	1.000	12	2	4	0	6	0
Dewar, Andrew, Brav.*	.000	1	0	0	0	0	0
DePaula, Julio, Twi.	.778	7	3	4	2	9	0
Diaz, Eddie, Exp.	1.000	9	2	0	0	2	1
Diaz, Jose, Dod.	.875	10	4	3	1	8	1
Digby, Bryan, Brav.	1.000	3	1	1	0	2	0
Dodson, Jeremy, Roy.	1.000	8	1	2	0	3	0
Dorsey, Brian, Phi.	.800	16	1	7	2	10	0
Dossett, Dusty, Roy.	.000	1	0	0	0	0	0
DUKE, Zach, Pir.*	1.000	11	6	22	0	28	0
Dumesnil, Bryan, Dod.*	.714	20	2	3	2	7	0
Durbin, Chad, Roy.	1.000	3	0	1	0	1	0
Eazor, Kyle, Mar.*	.875	16	2	5	1	8	1
Echols, Britt, Exp.	.933	11	2	12	1	15	1
Elmore, Chris, R.S.*	1.000	1	0	3	0	3	0
Encarnacion, Alexis, Roy.	1.000	6	2	0	0	2	0
Escorcha, Orlando, Reds*	.000	2	0	0	0	0	0
Espinal, Willy, Rang.	1.000	11	4	2	0	6	0
Esquivia, Manuel, Mar.	1.000	2	1	0	0	1	0
Eusebio, Mike, Reds	.857	9	1	5	1	7	1
Evans, Keith, Exp.	1.000	3	0	2	0	2	0
Ewin, Ryan, Brav.	.750	6	1	2	1	4	0
Farfan, Alexander, Reds	.889	20	2	6	1	9	1
Farizo, Brad, Mar.	1.000	3	0	1	0	1	0
Farley, Chris, R.S.	.900	12	2	7	1	10	1
Farr, Whitt, Brav.	1.000	7	1	0	0	1	0
Felfoldi, Jonathan, Exp.*	1.000	4	0	2	0	2	0
Feliz, Welinton, Tig.	1.000	20	6	9	0	15	2
Fernando, Juan, Rang.	1.000	11	0	2	0	2	0
Figuereo, Victor, Rang.	.833	16	4	6	2	12	1
Figueroa, Williams, Exp.	1.000	5	0	1	0	1	0
Fisher, Pete, Twi.	1.000	7	2	4	0	6	0
Frias, Junior, R.S.	.750	12	1	2	1	4	1
Gabriel, Chris, Mar.	1.000	17	3	6	0	9	2
Galan, Jorman, Reds	1.000	4	3	0	0	3	0
Galarraga, Armando, Exp.	1.000	2	1	1	0	2	0
Garces, Rich, R.S.	1.000	2	0	1	0	1	0
Garcia, Anderson, Yan.	.889	11	7	9	2	18	0
Garcia, Angel, Twi.	.889	13	1	7	1	9	2
Garcia, Benjamin, Rang.	.000	2	0	0	0	0	0
Garcia, Carlos, Dod.	1.000	5	3	0	0	3	1
Garcia, Edwin, Twi.	.750	16	0	3	1	4	0
Garcia, Randy, Yan.*	1.000	13	2	3	0	5	1
Gault, Tim, Reds*	1.000	8	0	1	0	1	0
George, Brad, Reds	1.000	5	0	3	0	3	0
George, Jonathan, Reds	.571	10	1	3	3	7	0

Player, Team	Pct.	G	PO	A	E	TC	DP
German, Rafael, Reds	.833	10	5	10	3	18	0
Gomez, Warmar, Exp.	1.000	19	1	6	0	7	0
Gonzalez, Jose, Tig.	.875	17	3	4	1	8	0
Gonzalez, Luis, Dod.*	1.000	6	1	2	0	3	0
Gonzalez, Mike, Pir.*	.778	2	1	6	2	9	1
Gore, Kirk, Roy.	1.000	5	1	0	0	1	0
Gorman, Pat, Ori.	1.000	4	0	1	0	1	0
Graham, Jason, Tig.	.000	2	0	0	0	0	0
Granado, Jan, Reds*	.952	13	4	16	1	21	2
Greinke, Zack, Roy.	1.000	3	1	3	0	4	1
Hacker, Eric, Yan.	1.000	3	1	2	0	3	0
Hader, Ryan, Twi.*	.846	11	4	7	2	13	0
Hamilton, Jamaal, Dod.*	.800	10	2	2	1	5	0
Hammes, Zach, Dod.	.600	10	1	5	4	10	0
Hampton, Royce, Rang.*	1.000	4	1	2	0	3	0
Harben, Adam, Twi.	1.000	12	2	9	0	11	0
Harmsen, Brandon, Yan.	1.000	12	2	11	0	13	1
Hentgen, Pat, Ori.	.000	1	0	0	0	0	0
Hermanson, Dustin, R.S.	.000	1	0	0	0	0	0
Hernandez, Marcos, Tig.*	.833	11	1	4	1	6	1
Herndon, Eric, Brav.	1.000	3	0	2	0	2	0
Hill, Josh, Twi.	.833	14	0	5	1	6	0
Hitchcock, Sterling, Yan.*	.000	2	0	0	0	0	0
Hoelscher, Nate, Roy.*	.875	9	4	3	1	8	0
Holliday, Brian, Pir.*	.857	10	1	5	1	7	0
Hosford, Clint, Dod.	1.000	2	0	1	0	1	0
Huguet, J.C., Reds	.500	6	1	0	1	2	0
Hummel, John, Pir.*	1.000	11	1	5	0	6	1
Iehl, Jason, Mar.	.667	7	2	2	2	6	0
Imotichey, Tory, Exp.*	1.000	13	1	6	0	7	0
Jackson, Kyle, R.S.	1.000	1	0	1	0	1	0
Jerzembeck, Mike, Twi.	1.000	2	1	1	0	2	1
Johnson, Blair, Pir.	.500	2	0	1	1	2	0
Johnson, Josh, Mar.	1.000	4	1	2	0	3	0
Jones, K.C., Twi.	1.000	12	2	5	0	7	1
Jung, Sung, Brav.	.000	1	0	0	0	0	0
Kemlo, Christopher, Yan.	.000	11	0	0	0	0	0
Kennedy, Dajuan, Dod.	.333	16	0	1	2	3	0
Kerschen, Joshua, Yan.	1.000	17	1	3	0	4	0
Kiley, Jason, Pir.	1.000	11	11	6	0	17	0
Kinney, Matt, Twi.	.000	2	0	0	1	1	0
Kirkman, Tyler, Exp.*	1.000	7	0	2	0	2	0
Klahs, Dave, Yan.	1.000	14	3	6	0	9	1
Knoff, Justin, Reds	.875	13	2	5	1	8	0
Kuo, Hong-chih, Dod.*	1.000	3	0	1	0	1	0
Landaeta, Argenis, Yan.	1.000	10	2	4	0	6	0
Lane, Josh, R.S.*	1.000	13	0	2	0	2	0
Leach, B.J., R.S.	1.000	5	0	2	0	2	0
Ledezma, Wil, R.S.*	.000	1	0	0	0	0	0
Lee, Garrett, Brav.	.000	1	0	0	0	0	0
Lester, Jonathan, R.S.*	.000	1	0	0	0	0	0
Locklear, Joseph, Reds*	.667	16	1	3	2	6	0
Long, Nick, Exp.	.750	8	0	6	2	8	0
Looney, Marshall, Dod.*	1.000	8	0	5	0	5	0
Lowery, Devon, Roy.	.750	15	1	2	1	4	0
Lyons, Thomas, Tig.	.857	7	1	5	1	7	0
Machi, Jean, Phi.	1.000	10	7	6	0	13	0
MacDougal, Mike, Roy.	1.000	1	0	1	0	1	0
Mairena, Ozwaldo, Mar.*	.000	1	0	0	0	0	0
Marino, Nexcys, Exp.	.875	18	1	6	1	8	0
Marquetti, Agustin, Tig.	.667	1	1	1	1	3	0
Martin, Greg, Exp.*	.833	13	2	3	1	6	0
Martinez, Dave, Yan.*	1.000	9	4	6	0	10	0
Mason, Robert, Brav.*	1.000	4	0	2	0	2	0
Mateo, Aneudis, R.S.	.909	11	3	7	1	11	0
Mateo, Carlos, Rang.	.500	18	0	1	1	2	0
Mateo, Manuel, Brav.	.929	12	5	8	1	14	0
Mathieson, Scott, Phi.	.667	7	0	4	2	6	0
Mattison, Kieran, Roy.	.750	13	4	2	2	8	0
McAdam, Scott, Exp.	1.000	19	5	5	0	10	0
McClendon, Matt, Brav.	.000	3	0	0	0	0	0
McDonald, Jon, Twi.	.857	3	0	6	1	7	0
Mead, Dan, Brav.*	1.000	15	0	3	0	3	0
Medina, Dennis, Twi.	.846	11	2	9	2	13	1
Megrew, Mike, Dod.*	1.000	5	0	3	0	3	0
Melnyk, Brian, Roy.*	.000	7	0	0	0	0	0
Mena, Amaurys, Tig.	.500	9	1	1	2	4	0
Mendez, Wimer, Ori.	.667	20	0	4	2	6	0
Mendoza, Cristian, Yan.	1.000	13	2	1	0	3	0
Mendoza, Jorge, Rang.	.000	1	0	0	0	0	0
Mendoza, Luis, R.S.	1.000	13	6	15	0	21	1
Meque, Jacobo, Ori.*	.750	12	0	12	4	16	0
Merricks, Alexander, Twi.*	1.000	9	0	4	0	4	0
Meyer, Todd, Exp.	1.000	9	0	6	0	6	0
Mieres, Alberto, Yan.	1.000	4	2	0	0	2	0
Mildren, Paul, Mar.*	.857	11	3	9	2	14	1
Morel, Jhosandy, Pir.*	.875	8	3	4	1	8	0
Moreno, Edwin, Rang.	.900	9	2	7	1	10	1
Moreno, Juan, R.S.*	.000	3	0	0	1	1	0
Moreno, Orber, Roy.	.000	2	0	0	0	0	0
Morton, Charles, Brav.	.778	11	3	4	2	9	1
Moye, Jeffrey, Rang.	1.000	5	1	2	0	3	0
Mutch, Paul, Twi.	.938	12	6	9	1	16	0
Myers, Damien, Tig.*	1.000	2	0	0	0	2	0
Nelson, David, Roy.*	.833	16	2	8	2	12	0
Nelson, Justin, Roy.*	.833	12	0	10	2	12	1
Nelson, Kenny, Brav.	.000	3	0	0	0	0	0
Neuage, Leigh, Dod.	1.000	7	1	2	0	3	0
Nieves, Roberto, Brav.	.500	5	1	0	1	2	0
Norderum, Jason, Exp.*	.000	4	0	0	0	0	0
Nova, Juan, Mar.	.500	22	0	2	2	4	0
Nunez, Franklin, Phi.	1.000	1	1	0	0	1	0
Nunez, Kelvin, Roy.	1.000	5	4	5	0	9	0
Nunez, Leo, Pir.	1.000	11	2	6	0	8	0
O'Connor, Shaun, Mar.	1.000	3	0	2	0	2	0
O'Donnell, Tony, Reds*	.000	2	0	0	0	0	0
Olsen, Scott, Mar.*	.714	13	0	5	2	7	0
Paddock, Josh, Phi.	1.000	6	3	8	0	11	0
Padilla, Nick, Brav.	.000	1	0	0	0	0	0
Palmer, Lucas, Roy.	.800	13	4	4	2	10	0
Parker, David, Dod.	1.000	20	3	2	0	5	0
Parker, Justin, Brav.*	1.000	8	1	2	0	3	0
Parris, Matt, Tig.	.867	11	7	6	2	15	0
Pearson, Anthony, Exp.	1.000	4	0	1	0	1	0
Pena, Juan, R.S.	1.000	1	1	1	0	2	0
Peralta, Efigenio, Brav.	.786	14	4	7	3	14	0
Perez, Carlos, Ori.*	.909	12	0	10	1	11	0
Pezely, Franco, Rang.*	1.000	4	0	2	0	2	1
Picco, John, Yan.*	1.000	11	2	12	0	14	0
Plank, Terry, Ori.	1.000	7	2	1	0	3	0
Plummer, Jarod, Dod.	1.000	16	1	3	0	4	0
Pole, Hank, Exp.	1.000	6	0	2	0	2	0
Poles, Donnie, Exp.	.000	9	0	0	1	1	0
Potoczny, Robert, Dod.	.800	11	2	2	1	5	0
Potter, Joshua, Ori.	1.000	19	0	7	0	7	0
Prieto, Victor, Mar.	.684	8	3	10	6	19	1
Radke, Brad, Twi.	.000	1	0	0	0	0	0
Ramirez, Elizardo, Phi.	1.000	11	6	14	0	20	0
Ramirez, Luis, Ori.	1.000	19	0	3	0	3	0
Randazzo, Jeffrey, Twi.*	.000	3	0	0	0	0	0
Reilly, Christopher, Ori.	.500	3	0	1	1	2	0
Reiss, Mike, Brav.	1.000	13	1	3	0	4	0
Reiss, Steven, Brav.	1.000	13	0	3	0	3	1
Reyes, Maximo, Phi.	.667	22	1	1	1	3	0
Rivas, Gabriel, Tig.	.778	15	1	6	2	9	0
Rivera, Mariano, Yan.	.000	1	0	0	0	0	0
Rosa, Carlos, Roy.	1.000	10	3	3	0	6	0
Rose, Brian, Roy.	.000	2	0	0	0	0	0
Rowe, Steven, Rang.	.727	7	2	6	3	11	0
Runyon, Roy, Roy.	.833	11	3	2	1	6	1
Rupert, Christopher, Phi.*	.867	18	2	11	2	15	0
Russ, Chris, Yan.	1.000	5	0	2	0	2	0
Russell, Eddie, Mar.	.000	2	0	0	0	0	0
Russell, Steve, Brav.	.500	11	1	1	2	4	0
Sanchez, Elby, Roy.	1.000	15	2	7	0	9	1
Sanchez, Emilio, Roy.	1.000	3	0	3	0	3	0
Santana, Roberto, Brav.	.000	2	0	0	0	0	0
Santiago, Victor, Dod.	1.000	10	2	1	0	3	1
Schara, Zackary, Rang.	1.000	6	0	6	0	6	1
Segovia, Zachary, Phi.	1.000	8	3	6	0	9	0
Selmo, Santo, Mar.	.778	14	2	5	2	9	0
Shafer, David, Reds	1.000	3	0	2	0	2	0
Shafer, Kurt, Pir.	1.000	5	1	3	0	4	0
Silva, Efrain, Dod.	1.000	5	2	3	0	5	0
Simon, Billy, R.S.	.700	6	1	6	3	10	0
Simpson, Brian, Brav.	1.000	8	0	1	0	1	0
Small, Aaron, Brav.	.000	5	0	0	0	0	0
Smiley, Gerald, Rang.	1.000	12	2	9	0	11	1
Smith, Dan, Tig.	.000	2	0	0	0	0	0
Smith, Julius, Rang.*	1.000	13	4	9	0	13	0
Smith, Michael, Tig.*	1.000	18	2	0	0	2	0
Soria, Joakim, Dod.	1.000	4	1	1	0	2	0
Sosa, Alexis, Mar.*	1.000	3	0	1	0	1	0
Speir, Zach, Reds.	1.000	10	3	5	0	8	0
Steen, Adam, Phi.	1.000	7	0	2	0	2	0
Steffek, Brian, Dod.	1.000	3	1	2	0	3	0
Steinborn, Chris, Tig.*	.750	10	0	3	1	4	0
Sterrett, Adam, Mar.	.833	15	0	5	1	6	0
Suarez, Pedro, R.S.	.500	15	0	2	2	4	0
Sullivan, Mark, Rang.	1.000	6	1	2	0	3	0
Sweeney, Matt, Phi.	.944	12	7	10	1	18	5
Taki, Yusuke, Mar.	1.000	6	0	1	0	1	0
Targac, Matthew, Mar.*	1.000	1	0	2	0	2	0
Teeter, Travis, Ori.	1.000	16	4	6	0	10	1
Tejada, Frailyn, Mar.*	.000	1	0	0	0	0	0
Telemaco, Amaury, Phi.	1.000	2	2	0	0	2	1

Player, Team	Pct.	G	PO	A	E	TC	DP
Thompson, Erik, Rang.	1.000	10	1	7	0	8	0
Thompson, Justin, Rang.*	.800	7	0	4	1	5	0
Thorne, David, Exp.	.889	9	1	7	1	9	0
Torrealba, Yoann, Pir.	1.000	9	2	2	0	4	0
Torres, Luis, Exp.	1.000	1	0	2	0	2	0
Tower, Scott, Pir.*	1.000	6	1	3	0	4	0
Treanor, Bryan, Mar.	1.000	3	0	3	0	3	0
Tussen, Denny, R.S.	1.000	12	6	6	0	12	0
Urena, Sixto, Rang.	.000	3	0	0	0	0	0
Valdez, Jose, Yan.	.909	8	2	8	1	11	0
Wagnon, Dwayne, Reds	.667	10	0	6	3	9	0
Watts, Joldy, Rang.	.875	14	2	5	1	8	0
Weeden, Brandon, Yan.	1.000	11	0	2	0	2	0
Wells, Clint, R.S.*	.000	2	0	0	0	0	0
Wells, Mark, Reds	.667	5	0	2	1	3	0
Wheeler, Adam, Yan.	1.000	3	0	2	0	2	0
Wheldon, Rhys, Twi.	1.000	15	0	1	0	1	0
White, Brian, Pir.	1.000	11	1	3	0	4	0
White, Michael, Dod.*	.000	2	0	0	0	0	0
Williams, Aaron, Twi.	1.000	25	4	7	0	11	0
Wiseman, Steven, Yan.	1.000	14	1	2	0	3	0
Wright, Chase, Yan.*	1.000	10	2	13	0	15	0
Wright, Isaiah, Exp.	.800	13	0	4	1	5	0
Wyrick, Patrick, Mar.	1.000	10	0	1	0	1	0
Yankosky, L.J., Brav.	1.000	6	2	0	0	2	0
Zumaya, Joel, Tig.	1.000	9	0	6	0	6	0

The following players appeared only as designated hitter, pinch-hitter or pinch runner: Aldridge, dh; Assael, dh, ph; Bailie, dh; M. Boone, dh; Harris, dh, pr; Richard, dh; Sato, dh, ph; Schwab, dh, ph; Tonis, dh; Vaz, dh.

LEAGUE CHAMPIONS

Year	Team	Pct.	Year	Team	Pct.	Year	Team	Pct.
1964—	Sarasota Braves	.610	1982—	New York AL	.667	1992—	Royals∞	.695
1965—	Bradenton Astros	.632	1983—	Texas	.645		Expos	.593
1966—	New York AL	.667		Los Angeles†	.617	1993—	Rangers▲	.667
1967—	Kansas City	.614	1984—	White Sox	.651		Astros	.593
1968—	Oakland	.650		Rangers†	.571	1994—	Royals♦	.797
1969—	Montreal	.585	1985—	Yankees§	.705		Astros	.695
1970—	Chicago AL	.600		Rangers	.532	1995—	Royals■	.649
1971—	Kansas City	.755	1986—	Reds	.548		Tigers	.579
1972—	Chicago NL*	.651		Dodgers†	.541	1996—	Yankees♦	.638
	Kansas City*	.651	1987—	Dodgers†	.683		Rangers	.617
1973—	Texas	.732		Royals	.635	1997—	Mets▼	.700
1974—	Chicago NL	.702	1988—	Yankees†	.714		Rangers	.567
1975—	Texas	.774		Royals	.619	1998—	Marlins	.633
1976—	Texas	.704	1989—	Yankees‡	.651		Rangers♦	.567
1977—	Chicago AL	.731		Dodgers	.635	1999—	Mets♦	.650
1978—	Texas	.600	1990—	Expos	.635	2000—	Rangers♦	.679
1979—	Houston	.635		Dodgers‡	.603	2001—	Dodgers	.683
1980—	Kansas City-Blue	.635	1991—	Orioles	.593		Yankees♦	.583
1981—	Kansas City-Gold	.688		Expos∞	.533	2002—	Phillies♦	.650

*Declared co-champions; no playoff. †League divided into Northern and Southern divisions; won one-game playoff for league championship. ‡League divided into Northern and Southern divisions; won best-of-three playoff for league championship. §Yankees declared champion based on winning percentage when one-game play-off against Rangers was rained out. ∞League divided into Northern, Southern and Central divisions; won best-of-three playoff for league championship. ▲League divided into Eastern, Central and Western divisions; won three-team playoff. ♦League divided into Eastern, Northern and Western divisions; won three-team playoff. ■League divided into Eastern, Northern, Northwest and Southwest divisions; won four-team playoff. ▼League divided into Eastern, Western and Northwest divisions; won four-club playoff. (Note—Known as Sarasota Rookie League in 1964 and Florida Rookie League in 1965.)

PIONEER LEAGUE
LEAGUE OFFICE

President
Jim McCurdy
Address
P.O. Box 2564
Spokane, WA 99220
Phone
509-456-7615

Teams (affiliation)
Billings Mustangs (Reds)
Casper Rockies (Rockies)
Great Falls White Sox (White Sox)
Helena Brewers (Brewers)
Idaho Falls Padres (Padres)

Missoula Osprey (Diamondbacks)
Ogden Raptors (Dodgers)
Provo Angels (Angels)

2002 FINAL STANDINGS

FIRST HALF

NORTHERN DIVISION

Team	W	L	T	Pct.	GB
Great Falls (Dodgers)	27	11	0	.711	...
Medicine Hat (Blue Jays)	18	20	0	.474	9.0
Billings (Reds)	15	22	0	.405	11.5
Missoula (Diamondbacks)	15	23	0	.395	12.0

SOUTHERN DIVISION

Team	W	L	T	Pct.	GB
Provo (Angels)	21	17	0	.553	...
Casper (Rockies)	20	18	0	.526	1.0
Ogden (Brewers)	18	19	0	.486	2.5
Idaho Falls (Padres)	17	21	0	.447	4.0

SECOND HALF

NORTHERN DIVISION

Team	W	L	T	Pct.	GB
Billings (Reds)	23	15	0	.605	...
Great Falls (Dodgers)	20	17	0	.541	2.5
Missoula (Diamondbacks)	20	18	0	.526	3.0
Medicine Hat (Blue Jays)	19	18	0	.514	3.5

SOUTHERN DIVISION

Team	W	L	T	Pct.	GB
Ogden (Brewers)	22	16	0	.579	...
Provo (Angels)	17	21	0	.447	5.0
Idaho Falls (Padres)	15	23	0	.395	7.0
Casper (Rockies)	15	23	0	.395	7.0

COMPOSITE

Team	G.F.	Og.	Bil.	Pro.	M.H.	Miss.	Cas.	I.F.	W	L	T	Pct.	GB
Great Falls (Dodgers)	...	4	13	5	7	12	3	3	47	28	0	.627	...
Ogden (Brewers)	3	...	4	7	3	5	9	9	40	35	0	.533	7.0
Billings (Reds)	3	3	...	4	11	8	4	5	38	37	0	.507	9.0
Provo (Angels)	2	9	3	...	1	3	10	10	38	38	0	.500	9.5
Medicine Hat (Blue Jays)	8	4	5	6	...	7	4	3	37	38	0	.493	10.0
Missoula (Diamondbacks)	4	1	8	4	9	...	5	4	35	41	0	.461	12.5
Casper (Rockies)	4	7	3	6	3	2	...	10	35	41	0	.461	12.5
Idaho Falls (Padres)	4	7	1	6	4	4	6	...	32	44	0	.421	15.5

Club names are major league affiliations.

PLAYOFFS: Great Falls defeated Billings, two games to none; Provo defeated Ogden, two games to one; Great Falls defeated Provo, two games to one to win Pioneer League championship.

REGULAR-SEASON ATTENDANCE: Billings, 98,345; Casper, 50,573; Great Falls, 90,079; Idaho Falls, 63,192; Medicine Hat, 26,285; Missoula, 55,268; Ogden, 126,700; Provo, 55,050. Total—565,492. Playoff (8 games)—9,532.

MANAGERS: Billings, Rick Burleson; Casper, Darren Cox; Great Falls, Dann Bilardello; Idaho Falls, Don Werner; Medicine Hat, Rolando Pino; Missoula, Jack Howell; Ogden, Tim Blackwell; Provo, Tom Kotchman.

ALL-STAR TEAM: 1B—Ryan Shealy, Casper; 2B—Alberto Callaspo, Provo; 3B—Scott Dragicevich, Medicine Hat; SS—Eric Aybar, Provo; OF—Mario Mendez, Ogden; OF—Travis Ezi, Great Falls; OF—Brian Barre, Casper; C—Alex Dvorsky, Provo; DH—Paul McAnulty, Idaho Falls; RHP—Santos Hernandez, Casper; LHP—Arturo Lopez, Great Falls; Relief pitcher—Jordan DeJong, Medicine Hat; Most Valuable Player—Ryan Shealy, Casper; Pitcher of the Year—Cleris Severino, Billings; Manager of the Year—Rick Burleson, Billings.

2002 BATTING
TEAM

Team	G	TPA	AB	R	H	TB	2B	3B	HR	RBI	SH	SF	HP	BB	IBB	SO	SB	CS	GDP	LOB	ShO	Avg.	OBP	Slg.
Provo	76	3060	2642	477	746	1067	136	40	35	405	20	22	56	320	10	539	78	35	50	620	1	.282	.369	.404
Great Falls	75	2979	2573	444	724	1050	134	21	50	384	26	15	74	291	6	652	69	38	52	590	1	.281	.369	.408
Casper	76	3025	2635	461	737	1104	131	37	54	394	18	33	53	286	10	576	72	22	79	571	1	.280	.358	.419
Billings	75	2968	2633	420	733	1070	125	16	60	372	21	19	49	246	8	622	88	30	45	574	1	.278	.349	.406
Ogden	75	2963	2593	446	699	1000	126	23	43	379	26	23	58	263	6	555	133	60	30	537	5	.270	.347	.386
Medicine Hat	75	2845	2537	355	676	981	112	17	53	319	11	22	43	232	10	532	57	32	68	544	5	.266	.336	.387
Idaho Falls	76	2983	2595	395	670	937	122	23	33	333	11	16	59	302	4	711	100	52	52	601	1	.258	.347	.361
Missoula	76	2982	2570	397	645	955	131	25	43	335	16	25	57	314	6	628	83	40	60	569	3	.251	.343	.372

SUMMER CLASS A *Pioneer League*

TOP QUALIFIERS FOR BATTING CHAMPIONSHIP

Minimum 205 plate appearances. *Lefthanded batter. †Switch-hitter.

Player, Team	G	TPA	AB	R	H	TB	2B	3B	HR	RBI	SH	SF	HP	BB	IBB	SO	SB	CS	GDP	Avg.	OBP	Slg.
McAnulty, Paul, I.F.*	67	291	235	56	89	142	29	0	8	51	0	3	4	49	2	43	7	2	5	.379	.488	.604
Shealy, Ryan, Cas.	69	308	231	55	85	165	21	1	19	70	0	9	18	50	7	52	0	0	7	.368	.497	.714
Bergolla, William, Bil.	53	242	210	35	74	94	9	1	3	29	2	6	0	24	1	26	16	5	2	.352	.408	.448
Callaspo, Alberto, Pro.	70	324	299	70	101	146	16	10	3	60	3	3	2	17	0	14	13	4	6	.338	.374	.488
Bagley, David, G.F.	51	209	175	39	59	81	7	0	5	31	1	0	12	21	0	37	2	2	5	.337	.442	.463
Crabbe, Callix, Og.†	67	287	250	55	82	118	16	4	4	38	2	1	5	29	0	34	22	9	2	.328	.407	.472
Ramos, Peeter, I.F.	56	230	202	26	66	81	10	1	1	25	0	0	5	23	1	36	12	8	4	.327	.409	.401
Aybar, Eric, Pro.†	67	308	273	64	89	128	15	6	4	29	2	1	11	21	1	43	15	10	4	.326	.395	.469
Dvorsky, Alex, Pro.	65	296	234	48	75	117	15	0	9	52	0	3	12	47	3	36	2	0	10	.321	.453	.500
Hendricks, K.J., Cas.†	64	304	258	51	81	97	11	1	1	32	3	4	3	36	0	24	21	3	6	.314	.399	.376
Nixon, Mike, G.F.	55	237	219	33	68	81	10	0	1	31	3	0	4	11	0	36	7	2	6	.311	.355	.370
Santana, Mayobanex, Miss. ..	53	218	202	24	62	86	11	2	3	35	0	1	2	13	1	32	3	3	13	.307	.353	.426
Vavao, Jason, Bil.	51	217	209	35	64	105	17	0	8	38	0	2	0	6	0	60	3	1	4	.306	.323	.502
Stanek, Jeff, Miss.*	71	304	232	41	71	116	16	1	9	51	0	4	0	68	4	66	2	0	8	.306	.457	.500
Ruiz, Junior, Bil.*	56	225	181	40	55	68	5	1	2	23	2	1	4	37	0	19	10	1	1	.304	.430	.376

DEPARTMENTAL LEADERS: G—Cosby, 76; AB—Callaspo, 299; R—Callaspo, 70; H—Callaspo, 101; TB—Shealy, 165; 2B—McAnulty, 29; 3B—Callaspo, 10; HR—Shealy, 19; RBI—Shealy, 70; SH—Several players tied with 5; SF—Shealy, 9; HP—Simon, 23; BB—Stanek, 68; IBB—Shealy, 7; SO—Falcon, 100; SB—Simon, 30; CS—Simon, 16; GIDP—Santana, 13; Slg.—Shealy, 714; OBP—Shealy, .497.

ALL PLAYERS

*Lefthanded batter. †Switch-hitter.

Player, Team	G	TPA	AB	R	H	TB	2B	3B	HR	RBI	SH	SF	HP	BB	IBB	SO	SB	CS	GDP	Avg.	OBP	Slg.
Almonte, Sandy, Cas.†	54	243	217	46	64	98	13	3	5	32	2	1	0	23	0	46	11	6	5	.295	.361	.452
Alvarado, Joel, Og.	17	73	67	8	15	17	2	0	0	5	1	0	1	4	0	3	1	1	0	.224	.278	.254
Andujar, Elvin, Bil.	40	161	140	23	40	62	3	2	5	20	2	1	6	12	1	49	2	1	1	.286	.365	.443
Antequera, Javier, I.F.	32	92	83	11	18	27	2	2	1	14	1	0	3	5	0	28	5	2	3	.217	.286	.325
Arnold, Eric, M.H.	17	65	56	11	15	19	2	1	0	1	1	0	1	7	0	13	2	2	3	.268	.359	.339
Ashford, Jon, M.H.*	1	3	3	0	0	0	0	0	0	0	0	0	0	0	0	3	0	0	0	.000	.000	.000
Avlas, Phil, Miss.	50	180	152	22	42	59	13	2	0	19	2	2	3	21	0	37	3	1	2	.276	.371	.388
Aybar, Eric, Pro.†	67	308	273	64	89	128	15	6	4	29	2	1	11	21	1	43	15	10	4	.326	.395	.469
Baez, Carlos, I.F.	49	212	199	24	55	60	5	0	0	19	1	0	5	7	0	43	9	7	7	.276	.318	.302
Bagley, David, G.F.	51	209	175	39	59	81	7	0	5	31	1	0	12	21	0	37	2	2	5	.337	.442	.463
Barre, Brian, Cas.*	62	274	227	60	68	117	12	5	9	35	2	1	4	40	2	55	11	0	4	.300	.412	.515
Bassett, Mike, Bil.*	50	212	183	35	55	91	12	0	8	44	0	2	5	22	3	38	2	2	9	.301	.387	.497
Bell, Paul, Og.	14	46	38	5	10	12	2	0	0	5	2	0	2	4	0	15	0	1	0	.263	.364	.316
Bello, Vladimir, Cas.	59	243	226	39	63	90	7	7	2	29	1	1	2	13	0	45	17	2	5	.279	.322	.398
Bergolla, William, Bil.	53	242	210	35	74	94	9	1	3	29	2	6	0	24	1	26	16	5	2	.352	.408	.448
Bibbs, Kennard, Og.*	64	292	235	53	57	66	3	3	0	18	5	2	5	44	1	31	22	11	2	.243	.371	.281
Bibee, Hal, Cas.	1	4	4	0	1	1	0	0	0	0	0	0	0	0	0	1	0	0	1	.250	.250	.250
Bohanan, Keith, Og.	54	200	170	27	33	39	2	2	0	14	1	1	8	20	0	39	2	3	5	.194	.307	.229
Bok, Matt, G.F.*	26	99	75	11	16	22	3	0	1	13	1	2	3	18	1	19	1	2	3	.213	.378	.293
Boll, Javier, Miss.	7	28	27	1	6	6	0	0	0	2	0	1	0	0	0	2	0	0	0	.222	.214	.222
Booth, Steve, Bil.	48	163	148	23	32	47	6	0	3	14	1	1	6	7	0	45	0	0	1	.216	.278	.318
Braun, Randy, M.H.*	20	68	61	6	12	17	2	0	1	7	1	0	0	6	0	14	0	1	1	.197	.269	.279
Brown, Matthew, Pro.	32	128	108	14	32	39	5	1	0	11	0	0	5	15	0	21	3	3	3	.296	.406	.361
Cairns, Troy, Bil.	39	156	145	19	47	54	7	0	0	9	0	1	1	9	0	13	8	1	1	.324	.365	.372
Callaspo, Alberto, Pro.	70	324	299	70	101	146	16	10	3	60	3	3	2	17	0	14	13	4	6	.338	.374	.488
Campos, Tiago, Bil.	18	65	56	9	20	28	5	0	1	14	0	0	3	6	0	11	6	1	1	.357	.446	.500
Cardona, David, G.F.	35	131	116	11	25	32	5	1	0	19	0	1	1	13	0	42	2	3	3	.216	.298	.276
Carter, Nic, Og.†	53	225	209	27	58	80	10	3	2	30	1	1	3	11	0	53	8	7	5	.278	.321	.383
Carter, Ryan, G.F.	18	66	55	11	13	24	3	1	2	8	5	0	1	5	0	14	1	0	2	.236	.311	.436
Chourio, Junior, M.H.	49	127	119	14	19	35	2	1	4	11	0	0	3	5	0	31	2	1	3	.160	.213	.294
Colina, Yinner, Bil.	6	18	17	0	1	1	0	0	0	0	1	0	0	0	0	4	0	0	0	.059	.059	.059
Correll, Richard, Bil.	56	242	224	34	64	96	11	3	5	41	0	0	1	17	0	41	2	2	8	.286	.339	.429
Corrente, David, M.H.	33	114	95	11	24	41	3	1	4	18	0	3	7	9	1	22	2	0	3	.253	.351	.432
Cosby, Quan, Pro.†	76	347	291	66	88	105	9	4	0	29	5	1	5	45	1	62	22	4	4	.302	.404	.361
Cota, Carlo, M.H.	58	235	207	21	56	74	14	2	0	21	1	2	2	23	0	45	4	0	4	.271	.346	.357
Crabbe, Callix, Og.†	67	287	250	55	82	118	16	4	4	38	2	1	5	29	0	34	22	9	2	.328	.407	.472
Dale, Lachlan, I.F.	38	149	133	12	31	40	4	1	1	14	0	0	3	13	0	36	0	1	1	.233	.315	.301
Davis, Morrin, M.H.	63	210	193	25	39	49	5	1	1	18	0	1	2	14	1	60	7	3	6	.202	.262	.254
De Los Santos, Omar, G.F. ...	33	138	123	29	32	48	5	4	1	14	0	1	2	12	0	41	3	4	0	.260	.333	.390
Diaz, Robinzon, M.H.	58	206	192	29	57	66	9	0	0	20	0	1	0	13	1	19	7	4	6	.297	.345	.344
Dragicevich, Scott, M.H.	57	242	211	30	64	99	13	2	6	37	0	4	4	23	1	35	7	4	2	.303	.376	.469
Duenas, Tommy, Pro.	1	1	1	0	1	1	0	0	0	1	0	0	0	0	0	0	0	0	0	1.000	1.000	1.000
Dvorsky, Alex, Pro.	65	296	234	48	75	117	15	0	9	52	0	3	12	47	3	36	2	0	10	.321	.453	.500
Eure, Jeffrey, Og.	70	302	265	50	66	113	18	1	9	44	0	6	8	23	1	90	14	2	3	.249	.321	.426
Ezi, Travis, G.F.†	54	255	219	36	62	77	6	3	1	16	2	2	5	26	1	70	12	6	2	.283	.369	.352
Falcon, Omar, I.F.	55	226	185	32	42	81	12	0	9	34	0	1	4	36	0	100	1	1	1	.227	.363	.438
Farmer, John, G.F.	17	53	39	12	17	19	2	0	0	7	1	0	6	7	0	13	3	1	0	.436	.577	.487
Fielder, Prince, Og.*	41	192	146	35	57	99	12	0	10	40	0	1	8	37	1	27	3	4	3	.390	.531	.678
Frazier, Alex, Miss.	65	266	235	32	61	102	11	3	8	35	0	2	12	17	1	51	1	2	4	.260	.338	.434
Frost, Jeremy, Og.	9	38	34	8	6	9	3	0	0	5	0	1	0	3	0	6	0	1	0	.176	.237	.265
Fry, Ryan, Bil.	21	89	82	11	16	33	5	0	4	17	0	0	0	7	0	32	0	0	3	.195	.258	.402
Fuller, Casey, Cas.*	50	205	187	22	42	63	8	5	1	27	1	1	1	15	0	50	0	0	3	.225	.284	.337
Gabriel, Justin, Og.*	13	1	0	0	0	0	0	0	0	0	0	0	0	0	0	1	0	0	3	.000	.000	.000
Galloway, Mike, M.H.	36	103	93	10	23	33	4	0	2	11	0	2	1	6	0	22	1	0	3	.247	.294	.355
Garcia, Angleidy, I.F.	26	106	91	14	28	34	3	0	1	11	0	0	3	12	0	21	1	2	1	.308	.406	.374
Garcia, Lino, Miss.	23	94	73	15	17	22	5	0	0	5	0	0	5	14	0	20	4	2	2	.233	.383	.301
Garcia, Luis, I.F.†	63	287	258	39	72	90	7	4	1	28	3	1	5	20	1	40	10	8	4	.279	.342	.349
Gates, David, Pro.	9	45	35	7	10	15	2	0	1	6	0	0	2	8	1	4	0	1	0	.286	.444	.429

Player, Team	G	TPA	AB	R	H	TB	2B	3B	HR	RBI	SH	SF	HP	BB	IBB	SO	SB	CS	GDP	Avg.	OBP	Slg.
George, Trey, Cas.	67	293	261	35	75	92	15	1	0	39	1	5	1	25	0	43	1	1	12	.287	.346	.352
Ghutzman, Phillip, Bil.	2	5	5	0	2	3	1	0	0	1	0	0	0	0	0	0	0	0	0	.400	.400	.600
Goelz, Bryan, G.F.*	42	167	133	27	37	47	6	2	0	20	1	0	2	31	0	22	8	4	3	.278	.422	.353
Gomez, Andri, Og.†	30	101	96	13	24	32	4	2	0	11	3	0	0	2	0	11	5	3	1	.250	.265	.333
Gonzalez, Juan, G.F.	47	144	131	27	32	36	4	0	0	12	3	1	1	8	0	23	2	0	2	.244	.291	.275
Gray, Josh, Pro.	51	197	183	22	34	42	8	0	0	21	1	1	4	8	0	43	0	0	7	.186	.235	.230
Guzman, Joel, G.F.	43	171	151	19	38	59	8	2	3	27	2	0	0	18	0	54	5	3	4	.252	.331	.391
Guzman, Junior, Pro.	57	229	215	22	55	88	13	4	4	28	0	2	2	10	1	45	0	1	2	.256	.293	.409
Hancock, Justin, Pro.	61	216	189	21	47	67	10	2	2	30	2	2	3	20	0	35	5	3	4	.249	.327	.354
Heath, Matt, Miss.†	25	84	71	9	12	15	3	0	0	3	1	1	0	11	0	30	2	1	1	.169	.277	.211
Hendricks, K.J., Cas.†	64	304	258	51	81	97	11	1	1	32	3	4	3	36	0	24	21	3	6	.314	.399	.376
Hoorelbeke, Jesse, G.F.	47	176	152	29	47	79	8	0	8	34	1	3	3	17	0	37	0	0	2	.309	.383	.520
Humphries, Jared, Bil.*	6	23	20	4	6	8	2	0	0	3	0	0	0	3	0	3	1	0	0	.300	.391	.400
Hunt, Stephen, Og.*	3	14	14	2	4	6	2	0	0	1	0	0	0	0	0	5	0	0	0	.286	.286	.429
Ison, Jeremy, Bil.	8	20	16	3	3	5	2	0	0	2	0	0	0	4	0	7	1	0	0	.188	.350	.313
Jacobo, Dioscar, G.F.	44	173	161	22	39	62	6	1	5	16	0	1	5	6	0	48	2	0	7	.242	.289	.385
Jacobo, Kervin, Miss.†	47	181	164	23	35	59	8	2	4	26	0	0	1	16	0	51	7	3	2	.213	.287	.360
Jenkins, Kevin, Pro.*	13	44	28	10	5	7	0	1	0	3	2	0	1	13	0	12	0	0	0	.179	.452	.250
Johanning, Ben, I.F.*	26	100	86	7	10	20	2	1	2	6	0	0	2	12	0	40	0	1	2	.116	.240	.233
Kenning, Ryan, Pro.*	33	122	87	20	18	34	8	1	2	10	0	1	1	33	2	42	0	0	2	.207	.426	.391
Kratz, Erik, M.H.	44	151	142	20	39	56	5	0	4	11	0	0	3	6	1	32	0	1	4	.275	.318	.394
Krimmel, Matt, Bil.*	21	87	69	14	24	37	5	1	2	16	0	0	5	13	0	19	0	1	0	.348	.483	.536
Langill, Eric, G.F.	4	16	15	5	6	8	2	0	0	6	0	1	0	0	0	0	1	0	0	.400	.375	.533
Lester, Anthony, I.F.	24	67	50	11	9	11	0	1	0	3	0	0	3	14	0	18	2	1	1	.180	.388	.220
Lewis, Domonique, Bil.	11	48	46	9	15	21	3	0	1	3	0	0	0	2	0	10	3	0	0	.326	.354	.457
Lima, Joseph, I.F.	63	280	258	39	66	108	16	1	8	41	0	3	4	15	0	67	6	4	4	.256	.304	.419
Loney, James, G.F.*	47	197	170	33	63	106	22	3	5	30	0	0	2	25	1	18	5	4	4	.371	.457	.624
Lopez, Luis, I.F.	12	34	29	2	6	7	1	0	0	4	0	0	2	3	0	14	1	1	1	.207	.324	.241
Mangioni, Jarad, M.H.	55	200	179	23	46	73	6	0	7	28	0	1	1	19	0	40	1	0	9	.257	.330	.408
Mateo, Dan, Bil.†	48	209	185	33	48	67	7	3	2	14	5	1	1	17	0	39	16	4	3	.259	.324	.362
Mathis, Jake, Pro.*	41	160	145	23	38	66	8	4	4	28	0	0	1	14	1	45	0	2	3	.262	.331	.455
McAnulty, Paul, I.F.*	67	291	235	56	89	142	29	0	8	51	0	3	4	49	2	43	7	2	5	.379	.488	.604
McClanahan, Jonah, Og.	23	88	83	12	22	28	6	0	0	8	1	0	2	2	0	10	5	0	1	.265	.299	.337
Melo, Manuel, Og.†	32	93	84	16	23	29	1	1	1	6	2	0	0	7	0	18	15	2	0	.274	.330	.345
Mendez, Mario, Og.	66	288	257	44	72	107	11	3	6	47	4	3	4	20	0	60	20	7	3	.280	.338	.416
Mercado, Onix, Bil.	8	30	29	6	9	14	2	0	1	5	0	0	1	0	0	6	0	0	0	.310	.333	.483
Mills, Rock, Cas.	48	215	196	24	49	87	13	2	7	41	0	1	6	12	0	49	0	1	6	.250	.312	.444
Montague, Ed, G.F.*	15	53	47	8	13	19	3	0	1	8	0	0	0	6	0	14	1	0	2	.277	.358	.404
Montero, Danilo, Miss.†	35	107	101	11	21	26	1	2	0	6	1	0	2	3	0	23	4	1	0	.208	.245	.257
Montero, Miguel, Miss.*	50	176	152	21	40	61	10	1	3	14	1	3	3	17	0	26	2	1	5	.263	.343	.401
Moore, Mewelde, I.F.	22	86	76	7	15	24	3	3	0	7	0	0	2	8	0	34	6	0	1	.197	.291	.316
Moore, Rusty, I.F.	43	163	127	20	20	22	2	0	0	13	2	5	4	25	0	37	15	1	1	.157	.304	.173
Mora, Ruben, I.F.†	31	133	114	22	27	35	5	0	1	13	3	0	1	15	0	28	4	4	4	.237	.331	.307
Morel, Robinson, Cas.	41	147	137	31	35	50	3	0	4	11	2	1	1	6	0	40	4	5	2	.255	.290	.365
Moreno, Juan J., Miss.*	40	117	103	17	22	29	3	2	0	8	0	1	0	13	0	34	5	0	4	.214	.299	.282
Morgan, Matt, Miss.	71	299	253	39	66	91	12	2	3	30	5	3	0	38	0	42	6	4	5	.261	.354	.360
Moss, Steve, Og.	5	13	8	3	4	8	2	1	0	3	0	2	2	1	0	1	0	1	0	.500	.538	1.000
Motooka, Rafael, Bil.	30	96	84	7	19	23	4	0	0	12	4	0	0	8	0	12	0	1	3	.226	.293	.274
Moye, Alan, Bil.	43	173	157	20	41	70	6	4	5	22	0	1	6	9	0	47	3	1	3	.261	.324	.446
Murray, Joshua, Og.	48	177	157	18	40	53	7	0	2	19	0	2	4	14	1	48	3	5	1	.255	.328	.338
Nixon, Mike, G.F.	55	237	219	33	68	81	10	0	1	31	3	0	4	11	0	36	7	2	6	.311	.355	.370
Nunez, Felix, Pro.	15	55	46	11	16	25	4	1	1	13	1	1	0	7	0	8	4	0	0	.348	.426	.543
Nunez, Florentino, Cas.†	52	222	193	32	57	88	15	5	2	23	4	2	4	19	0	41	2	1	4	.295	.367	.456
Olmstead, Walter, Bil.†	44	187	164	29	31	52	3	0	6	19	0	0	3	20	1	65	2	2	4	.189	.289	.317
Olson, David, I.F.	42	151	137	24	32	46	6	4	0	15	1	0	3	10	0	57	11	4	0	.234	.300	.336
Ortega, Sixto, Cas.	4	18	16	2	3	6	0	0	1	1	0	0	1	1	1	2	0	0	2	.188	.278	.375
Owen, Thomas, G.F.	23	88	64	9	9	16	2	1	1	7	1	0	8	15	0	24	5	0	0	.141	.368	.250
Pacheco, Julio, G.F.*	14	65	59	6	18	22	2	1	0	11	2	0	1	3	1	8	1	4	0	.305	.349	.373
Paula, Manuel, Bil.	38	141	127	14	29	36	4	0	1	9	3	1	4	6	1	39	9	4	0	.228	.283	.283
Peralta, Juan, M.H.†	71	322	283	45	77	107	12	3	4	30	3	4	2	30	2	38	16	8	5	.272	.342	.378
Perdomo, Mike, Pro.	56	244	204	33	55	89	16	3	4	39	0	2	3	35	0	71	4	1	2	.270	.381	.436
Perozo, Hector, G.F.	56	229	192	30	49	80	11	1	6	32	1	3	14	19	0	63	3	1	3	.255	.360	.417
Perry, Jason, M.H.*	30	124	106	25	45	85	6	2	10	36	0	0	6	12	2	19	0	2	3	.425	.508	.802
Petersen, Ryan, Bil.	5	17	15	3	4	9	2	0	1	1	0	0	0	2	0	2	0	0	0	.267	.353	.600
Plasencia, Francisco, Og.*	34	116	104	15	19	24	3	1	0	9	1	0	0	11	0	29	7	0	0	.183	.261	.231
Ramirez, Yordany, I.F.	23	86	78	8	14	15	1	0	0	5	0	1	4	3	0	24	0	2	3	.179	.244	.192
Ramos, Peeter, I.F.	56	230	202	26	66	81	10	1	1	25	0	0	5	23	1	36	12	8	4	.327	.409	.401
Raposo, Angel, Miss.	6	12	9	0	1	1	0	0	0	0	0	0	0	3	0	5	0	0	0	.111	.333	.111
Rico, Erik, M.H.*	60	182	163	27	52	77	14	1	3	29	1	0	2	15	1	31	3	1	6	.319	.383	.472
Robledo, Nelson, Cas.	38	156	134	13	31	35	2	1	0	13	0	2	4	16	0	27	0	1	10	.231	.327	.261
Ruiz, Junior, Bil.*	56	225	181	40	55	68	5	1	2	23	2	1	4	37	0	19	10	1	1	.304	.430	.376
Salas, Jose, M.H.†	37	93	76	15	19	22	1	1	0	6	2	1	3	11	0	20	3	1	1	.250	.363	.289
Sanchez, Braulio, Miss.*	21	50	45	6	9	12	3	0	0	5	0	0	0	5	0	12	0	0	1	.200	.280	.267
Santana, Mayobanex, Miss.	53	218	202	24	62	86	11	2	3	35	0	1	2	13	1	32	3	3	13	.307	.353	.426
Santiago, Ricardo, Miss.*	64	250	228	39	58	80	6	5	2	28	2	2	1	17	0	54	8	2	2	.254	.306	.351
Santos, Sergio, Miss.	54	237	202	38	55	105	19	2	9	37	0	3	3	29	0	49	6	3	5	.272	.367	.520
Sardinha, Duke, Cas.	41	162	137	21	34	47	8	1	1	16	1	0	5	19	0	49	2	1	5	.248	.360	.343
Schmidt, Jarrod, Bil.	35	142	121	14	34	46	4	1	2	16	1	2	3	15	1	35	4	3	0	.281	.369	.380
Selmo, Wilson, Pro.†	31	87	80	9	15	15	0	0	0	3	1	1	0	5	0	15	2	1	0	.188	.233	.188
Serafini, Matt, Og.	39	156	141	14	38	52	6	1	2	21	1	0	1	13	1	30	0	2	2	.270	.335	.369
Shealy, Ryan, Cas.	69	308	231	55	85	165	21	1	19	70	0	9	18	50	7	52	0	0	7	.368	.497	.714
Simon, Brandon, Miss.*	60	240	191	46	41	46	3	1	0	16	3	0	23	21	0	46	30	16	0	.215	.362	.241
Smith, David, M.H.	43	164	153	21	39	54	5	2	2	16	0	2	2	7	0	31	2	4	5	.255	.293	.353
Smith, Rashad, I.F.*	66	290	254	41	70	94	14	5	0	30	0	2	2	32	0	45	10	3	8	.276	.359	.370
Smith, Sam, Miss.	28	1	1	0	0	0	0	0	0	0	0	0	0	0	0	1	0	0	0	.000	.000	.000
Solis, Ricky, G.F.	13	42	37	5	9	10	1	0	0	1	2	0	0	3	0	9	1	0	2	.243	.300	.270
Soriano, Carlos, Og.	3	11	10	3	3	4	1	0	0	3	0	0	0	1	0	4	2	0	0	.300	.364	.400

Player, Team	G	TPA	AB	R	H	TB	2B	3B	HR	RBI	SH	SF	HP	BB	IBB	SO	SB	CS	GDP	Avg.	OBP	Slg.
Stanek, Jeff, Miss.*	71	304	232	41	71	116	16	1	9	51	0	4	0	68	4	66	2	0	8	.306	.457	.500
Steward, Jaime, Pro.*	4	0	0	0	0	0	0	0	0	0	0	0	0	0	0	0	1	0	0	.000	.000	.000
Sugden, Jason, Pro.†	65	257	224	37	67	83	7	3	1	42	3	4	4	22	0	43	7	4	3	.299	.366	.371
Symonds, Grady, Miss.	11	28	25	3	7	9	2	0	0	2	1	0	0	2	0	6	0	0	1	.280	.333	.360
Tejeda, Francisco, Cas.	25	79	77	12	17	22	1	2	0	8	1	0	0	1	0	22	3	1	3	.221	.231	.286
Urueta, Luis, Miss.†	41	110	102	10	18	29	5	0	2	9	0	0	2	5	0	41	0	1	5	.176	.229	.284
Vanden Berg, John, Og.	59	251	224	38	66	104	15	1	7	52	2	3	5	17	1	40	4	1	4	.295	.353	.464
Vavao, Jason, Bil.	51	217	209	35	64	105	17	0	8	38	0	2	0	6	0	60	3	1	4	.306	.323	.502
Whatley, Keith, Miss.*	23	3	2	0	1	1	0	0	0	0	0	0	1	0	0	0	0	0	0	.500	.667	.500

GRAND SLAMS: Bassett, 2; Corrente, Fielder, Fry, Jacobo, Mangioni, Mendez, Morgan, Rico, 1 each.

AWARDED FIRST BASE ON CATCHER'S INTERFERENCE: Simon 2 (R. Diaz 2); Bibbs (R. Diaz), Ezi (Vanden Berg), Rico (J. Guzman), Urueta (J. Guzman).

2002 PITCHING

TEAM

Team	W	L	Pct.	ERA	G	CG	ShO	Sv.	IP	H	TBF	R	ER	HR	SH	SF	HB	BB	IBB	SO	WP	Bk.
Billings	38	37	.507	3.72	75	1	2	21	662.1	652	2924	375	274	48	23	21	74	268	11	592	49	9
Great Falls	47	28	.627	3.72	75	0	4	23	655.0	638	2888	359	271	36	17	21	48	267	11	612	52	4
Missoula	35	41	.461	4.06	76	1	4	16	669.1	703	2984	404	302	33	12	17	54	246	4	615	72	5
Medicine Hat	37	38	.493	4.83	75	1	5	24	648.1	668	2889	426	348	68	15	12	54	269	5	659	92	10
Ogden	40	35	.533	4.87	75	0	0	11	661.1	759	3008	445	358	53	19	20	60	243	5	604	64	7
Idaho Falls	32	44	.421	4.92	76	0	2	22	657.0	712	3065	502	359	39	22	39	46	378	5	617	86	14
Casper	35	41	.461	4.93	76	0	0	12	660.2	730	3056	435	362	48	21	18	56	306	5	549	64	10
Provo	38	38	.500	5.10	76	0	1	18	656.0	768	2997	449	372	46	20	27	57	277	14	567	86	5

INDIVIDUAL

TOP QUALIFIERS FOR EARNED-RUN AVERAGE TITLE

Minimum 61 innings.*Lefthanded pitcher.

Pitcher, Team	W	L	Pct.	ERA	G	GS	CG	ShO	GF	Sv.	IP	H	TBF	R	ER	HR	SH	SF	HB	BB	IBB	SO	WP	Bk.
Severino, Cleris, Bil.*	7	1	.875	0.96	10	10	0	0	0	0	65.2	56	268	17	7	3	1	1	8	14	0	63	3	0
Juarez, William, Miss.	6	2	.750	2.43	16	11	1	0	1	0	81.1	85	330	30	22	2	3	2	1	12	0	56	1	0
Coffin, Ryan, Miss.	2	5	.286	2.61	22	8	0	0	9	3	62	55	265	25	18	0	2	2	9	12	0	54	3	0
Whatley, Keith, Miss.*	7	2	.778	2.85	22	9	0	0	2	0	66.1	56	267	25	21	3	2	1	1	14	1	75	2	0
Gomez, Jose, Bil.	2	3	.400	3.06	13	13	0	0	0	0	70.2	52	284	29	24	9	3	1	3	23	0	58	3	2
Hernandez, Santos, Cas.	8	1	.889	3.50	14	14	0	0	0	0	72	65	312	30	28	4	1	1	5	32	0	39	7	1
D'Amico, Leonardo, Pro.	3	0	1.000	3.57	14	14	0	0	0	0	63	58	263	27	25	6	0	1	7	14	0	54	2	1
Lopez, Arturo, G.F.*	7	3	.700	3.66	15	15	0	0	0	0	76.1	79	325	44	31	5	1	2	4	21	0	72	2	0
Hall, Bo, Og.	2	6	.250	3.82	16	9	0	0	1	0	66	53	270	29	28	4	2	1	2	21	0	58	3	0
Nelson, Steve, G.F.	6	5	.545	3.99	14	14	0	0	0	0	70	79	318	39	31	4	3	3	6	23	1	44	6	2
Talanoa, Charles, M.H.	4	3	.571	4.07	15	15	1	1	0	0	79.2	77	337	42	36	6	1	2	8	23	0	91	11	0
Beavers, Kevin, I.F.*	4	2	.667	4.13	11	11	0	0	0	0	61	71	265	32	28	5	2	6	1	14	0	49	0	1
Keller, Frankie, Bil.	1	4	.200	4.15	14	14	0	0	0	0	73.2	72	324	43	34	5	0	2	2	45	0	61	2	0
Carpenter, Calvin, Og.	4	2	.667	4.44	16	15	0	0	0	0	71	77	329	35	35	6	4	2	5	27	0	65	7	1
Astacio, Hector, Pro.	6	3	.667	4.72	17	6	0	0	4	0	61	77	276	38	32	4	3	3	7	17	0	56	11	2
Perez, Henry, I.F.	4	6	.400	4.72	15	15	0	0	0	0	74.1	73	327	52	39	4	4	3	6	36	1	70	1	1

DEPARTMENTAL LEADERS: W—Hernandez, 8; L—Reed, B. Williams, 7; Pct.—Hernandez, .889; G—DeJong, 33; GS—Mitchell, 16; CG—Juarez, King, Talanoa, 1 each; ShO—King, Talanoa, 1 each; GF—DeJong, 27; Sv.—DeJong, Krisch, 16 each; IP—Juarez, 81.1; H—K. Garcia, 86; TBF—Mitchell, 338; R—Thrasher, 59; ER—Jimenez, 45; HR—Neylan, 12; SH—Stewart, 5; SF—Beavers, 6; HB—George, 10; BB—Keller, 45; IBB—Reed, 4; SO—Talanoa, 91; WP—Thrasher, 18; BK—Several pitchers tied with 3.

ALL PITCHERS

*Lefthanded pitcher.

Pitcher, Team	W	L	Pct.	ERA	G	GS	CG	ShO	GF	Sv.	IP	H	TBF	R	ER	HR	SH	SF	HB	BB	IBB	SO	WP	Bk.
Allen, Blakely, Pro.	0	1	.000	15.43	1	0	0	0	0	0	2.1	5	14	4	4	2	0	0	0	3	0	1	0	0
Allender, John, Miss.	1	1	.500	8.49	21	0	0	0	2	0	35	43	179	39	33	3	0	1	1	34	0	21	12	1
Alliston, Josh, Og.	3	0	1.000	4.76	6	0	0	0	3	1	11.1	11	46	6	6	0	0	0	2	0	0	10	1	0
Aquino, Juan, G.F.	0	0	.000	5.40	2	0	0	0	0	0	1.2	2	10	1	1	0	0	0	3	0	1	2	0
Arias, Daniel, Pro.	0	1	.000	4.26	4	0	0	0	1	0	6.1	7	24	3	3	0	0	0	2	1	0	4	0	0
Astacio, Hector, Pro.	6	3	.667	4.72	17	6	0	0	4	0	61	77	276	38	32	4	3	3	7	17	0	56	11	2
Bailey, Ryan, Pro.	1	1	.500	21.00	4	0	0	0	2	0	3	4	18	8	7	0	0	1	5	1	4	1	0
Baker, Jason, Og.	4	3	.571	4.96	13	1	0	0	4	0	32.2	28	133	20	18	2	0	2	3	9	0	24	2	0
Ballouli, Khalid, Og.	4	0	1.000	4.37	15	12	0	0	0	0	59.2	78	263	31	29	6	0	4	4	11	1	65	5	2
Balser, Jeff, Pro.	0	0	.000	4.76	4	0	0	0	1	0	5.2	3	24	3	3	1	0	1	0	4	0	6	1	0
Barnett, Brian, Pro.	0	0	.000	0.00	1	0	0	0	1	0	1	0	3	0	0	0	0	0	0	0	0	1	0	0
Batista, Gorky, Bil.	2	0	1.000	4.91	2	2	0	0	0	0	11	14	46	6	6	2	1	0	0	8	0	0	0
Beavers, Kevin, I.F.*	4	2	.667	4.13	11	11	0	0	0	0	61	71	265	32	28	5	2	6	1	14	0	49	0	1
Bell, Chris, Bil.	0	2	.000	10.13	7	0	0	0	1	0	8	9	58	19	9	1	0	2	5	19	0	5	3	0
Bell, Paul, Og.	0	0	.000	27.00	1	0	0	0	1	0	1	2	6	3	3	1	0	0	1	1	0	0	0	0
Berroa, Yesson, M.H.	2	4	.333	6.84	20	0	0	0	5	0	26.1	32	130	20	20	5	1	0	5	16	0	23	4	0
Bilke, Austin, Pro.	2	2	.500	4.93	28	0	0	0	10	6	34.2	42	159	19	19	4	2	0	4	11	3	28	6	0
Bimeal, Matt, M.H.	2	1	.667	9.45	16	0	0	0	6	1	20	25	102	23	21	4	2	1	2	12	1	22	11	0
Bochy, Greg, I.F.	0	0	.000	0.00	1	0	0	0	0	0	1	1	4	0	0	0	0	1	0	0	0	0	0
Breslow, Craig, Og.*	6	2	.750	1.82	23	0	0	0	6	2	54.1	42	223	15	11	2	3	2	1	24	0	56	7	0
Broxton, Jonathan, G.F.	2	0	1.000	2.76	11	6	0	0	2	2	29.1	22	127	9	9	0	4	0	3	16	0	33	0	0
Burden, Randy, Pro.	0	1	.000	7.45	10	0	0	0	3	0	9.2	12	53	12	8	0	1	1	2	10	0	9	3	0
Buzachero, Bubbie, M.H.	1	0	1.000	3.83	26	0	0	0	11	2	40	34	185	20	17	2	0	0	9	25	1	42	10	0
Carpenter, Calvin, Og.	4	2	.667	4.44	16	15	0	0	0	0	71	77	329	48	35	6	4	2	5	27	0	65	7	1
Cartier, Richard, Cas.	5	3	.625	4.28	29	0	0	0	19	6	33.2	35	145	19	16	3	0	0	6	15	0	33	5	0
Chivilli, Pedro, Cas.	2	4	.333	5.66	14	13	0	0	0	0	70	84	313	50	44	5	1	2	2	20	0	72	11	0
Chourio, Junior, M.H.	0	0	.000	0.00	1	0	0	0	0	0	3	6	4	0	0	0	0	0	0	0	3	0	0

Pitcher, Team	W	L	Pct.	ERA	G	GS	CG	ShO	GF	Sv.	IP	H	TBF	R	ER	HR	SH	SF	HB	BB	IBB	SO	WP	Bk.
Cimorelli, Brett, Pro.	1	1	.500	3.52	10	0	0	0	2	0	15.1	13	66	7	6	0	0	0	1	12	0	4	4	0
Coffin, Ryan, Miss.	2	5	.286	2.61	22	8	0	0	9	3	62	55	265	25	18	0	2	2	9	12	0	54	3	0
Corpas, Manuel, Cas.	2	4	.333	5.73	29	0	0	0	20	2	33	37	159	24	21	4	4	0	2	18	3	42	3	1
Cuen, David, G.F.*	2	3	.400	4.07	10	9	0	0	0	0	42	48	185	23	19	0	0	2	1	13	2	42	4	0
Curran, Joe, Bil.*	2	2	.500	4.96	20	0	0	0	2	0	32.2	34	151	25	18	1	1	2	2	14	1	28	2	0
D'Amico, Leonardo, Pro.	3	0	1.000	3.57	14	14	0	0	0	0	63	58	263	27	25	6	0	1	7	14	0	54	2	1
Darby, James, I.F.	2	1	.667	6.75	24	0	0	0	5	1	28	24	140	25	21	1	2	2	5	29	0	35	7	0
DeJong, Jordan, M.H.	6	1	.857	1.43	33	0	0	0	27	16	44	23	170	10	7	1	1	0	5	10	2	62	11	1
Delgadillo, Ambiroix, Pro.*	0	0	.000	108.00	2	0	0	0	0	0	0.2	5	9	8	8	0	0	0	0	5	0	1	2	0
Desalme, Gene, Og.*	0	0	.000	5.68	14	1	0	0	9	0	25.1	25	115	17	16	0	1	0	4	12	0	28	3	0
Diaz, Jose, G.F.	1	1	.500	3.65	3	3	0	0	0	0	12.1	11	56	6	5	1	0	0	1	6	0	14	0	1
Diaz, Pedro, Cas.	1	2	.333	5.10	18	0	0	0	6	1	30	35	140	22	17	3	1	0	1	11	0	23	1	0
Escobedo, Edgar, G.F.	1	1	.500	4.62	18	0	0	0	3	0	37	39	175	20	19	2	1	2	5	22	1	28	4	1
Escorcha, Orlando, Bil.*	1	3	.250	6.07	11	2	0	0	0	0	29.2	35	141	25	20	2	3	2	5	17	0	24	4	1
Espinal, Jhovany, I.F.	3	2	.600	8.87	22	0	0	0	3	0	23.1	31	123	27	23	2	1	4	1	23	0	32	5	0
Eure, Jeffrey, Og.	0	0	.000	0.00	1	0	0	0	0	0	0	0	1	0	0	0	0	0	0	1	0	0	0	0
Fardella, Jason, Cas.	1	5	.167	5.68	21	3	0	0	3	0	58.2	78	277	44	37	3	1	1	9	17	0	47	7	0
Fernandez, Alfredo, I.F.	0	3	.000	4.91	6	6	0	0	0	0	22	27	106	23	12	1	1	0	3	8	0	10	1	1
Ferns, Robert, Miss.	0	2	.000	6.57	8	2	0	0	1	0	12.1	19	64	16	9	0	0	1	1	5	1	15	2	0
Figueroa, Jonathan, G.F.*	2	1	.667	1.42	7	7	0	0	0	0	31.2	16	130	7	5	0	0	0	2	19	0	48	4	0
Fuller, Justin, Pro.*	3	1	.750	4.22	26	0	0	0	3	1	42.2	32	171	22	20	7	0	0	1	12	0	58	4	0
Gabriel, Justin, Og.*	2	2	.500	3.93	12	1	0	0	6	1	18.1	18	81	11	8	1	0	0	1	8	1	12	0	0
Garcia, Kelvin, Miss.*	2	4	.333	4.96	18	11	0	0	5	1	65.1	86	302	46	36	6	0	3	5	16	0	56	8	0
Garcia, Rurik, Cas.*	0	0	.000	12.86	11	0	0	0	4	0	7	11	51	12	10	0	0	1	1	19	0	4	2	1
Gemmell, Don, Bil.	1	3	.250	3.14	25	0	0	0	23	12	28.2	27	118	15	10	1	0	2	3	4	1	41	2	0
George, Brad, Bil.	2	2	.500	5.36	9	9	0	0	0	0	47	62	213	34	28	2	0	1	10	11	0	33	6	0
Geraldo, Jose, I.F.	0	1	.000	8.79	14	0	0	0	4	0	14.1	27	79	19	14	2	0	0	2	10	0	5	2	2
Gilliam, Wes, Miss.*	1	0	1.000	6.43	8	0	0	0	4	1	7	6	38	8	5	1	0	0	1	7	0	8	3	0
Goas, Adrian, Pro.	1	3	.250	3.91	20	0	0	0	8	1	23	21	102	13	10	1	1	2	3	12	1	13	5	0
Gomez, Jose, Bil.	2	3	.400	3.06	13	13	0	0	0	0	70.2	52	284	29	24	9	3	1	3	23	0	58	3	2
Gonzalez, Luis, G.F.*	0	1	.000	7.71	4	3	0	0	0	0	11.2	18	59	12	10	1	0	1	1	5	0	15	2	0
Grant, Brian, M.H.	1	6	.143	4.59	14	10	0	0	0	0	51	70	237	33	26	4	1	0	5	14	0	29	2	3
Groeger, Jeff, Bil.	1	0	1.000	1.62	10	0	0	0	3	0	16.2	11	65	7	3	0	0	0	0	4	1	19	0	0
Gruler, Chris, Bil.	0	0	.000	1.08	4	4	0	0	0	0	16.2	11	69	3	2	1	0	0	3	6	0	11	0	1
Hall, Bo, Og.	2	6	.250	3.82	16	9	0	0	1	0	66	53	270	29	28	4	2	1	2	21	0	58	3	0
Hawley, Ross, G.F.	1	0	1.000	0.00	3	0	0	0	0	0	7.1	2	26	0	0	0	0	0	0	2	0	5	2	0
Hernandez, Santos, Cas.	8	1	.889	3.50	14	14	0	0	0	0	72	65	312	30	28	4	1	1	5	32	0	39	7	1
Hindman, Scott, Pro.*	0	1	.000	9.00	3	0	0	0	0	0	2	4	11	4	2	0	0	0	0	0	0	2	1	0
Holcomb, James, Pro.	2	1	.667	3.38	12	12	0	0	0	0	53.1	62	231	27	20	3	1	2	4	10	1	55	4	0
Hoorelbeke, Jesse, G.F.	0	0	.000	9.00	1	0	0	0	0	0	1	1	6	1	1	0	0	0	2	1	0	1	0	0
Housman, Jeff, Og.*	1	3	.250	8.07	16	5	0	0	4	0	32.1	55	163	38	29	5	0	1	2	12	0	23	1	0
Hull, Eric, G.F.	0	1	.000	0.00	11	0	0	0	9	5	11.2	4	41	1	0	0	0	0	0	4	0	17	0	0
Incinelli, Matt, Miss.	2	2	.500	2.98	27	0	0	0	7	0	42.1	46	182	19	14	2	1	1	4	11	1	38	0	0
Jimenez, Ubaldo, Cas.	3	5	.375	6.53	14	14	0	0	0	0	62	72	288	46	45	6	1	3	5	29	1	65	2	3
Juarez, William, Miss.	6	2	.750	2.43	16	11	1	0	1	0	81.1	85	330	30	22	2	3	2	1	12	0	56	1	0
Jumelles, Victor, Bil.	2	4	.333	3.45	22	0	0	0	16	2	31.1	23	140	14	12	2	0	1	7	20	2	29	3	0
Keller, Frankie, Bil.*	1	4	.200	4.15	14	14	0	0	0	0	73.2	72	324	43	34	5	0	2	2	45	0	61	2	0
King, O.J., Bil.	2	0	1.000	2.08	4	4	1	1	0	0	26	19	99	6	6	1	0	0	0	5	0	28	0	0
Kranawetter, Josh, Miss.	4	3	.571	2.42	30	0	0	0	12	3	44.2	41	190	26	12	2	1	1	3	14	1	41	2	0
Krisch, David, I.F.*	2	3	.400	4.31	32	0	0	0	26	16	31.1	34	144	18	15	1	1	2	0	19	0	32	5	0
Lane, Brian, Bil.	0	2	.000	4.07	13	2	0	0	4	0	24.1	27	120	18	11	4	3	0	3	14	0	23	0	1
Laratta, E.J., I.F.	2	0	1.000	5.68	9	2	0	0	1	0	19	25	89	15	12	3	1	0	0	9	0	9	1	0
LaSalle, Julio, G.F.	3	0	1.000	1.74	17	0	0	0	7	2	31	20	132	15	6	2	1	0	1	13	1	49	3	0
Light, Scott, Bil.	1	1	.500	5.09	4	4	0	0	0	0	23	26	106	16	13	3	3	0	6	6	0	14	0	1
Lo, Ching-Lung, Cas.	2	4	.333	3.20	14	9	0	0	1	0	45	44	207	22	16	3	1	1	4	22	0	21	4	1
Lopez, Arturo, G.F.*	7	3	.700	3.66	15	15	0	0	0	0	76.1	79	325	44	31	5	1	2	4	21	0	72	2	0
Lucas, Christopher, Bil.	2	0	1.000	1.93	10	3	0	0	1	0	18.2	27	88	11	4	0	1	2	0	5	0	17	1	0
Lugo, Osvaldo, Pro.	0	2	.000	4.28	17	0	0	0	4	0	27.1	41	130	23	13	2	1	2	0	13	2	23	2	0
Luther, Heath, Pro.*	0	2	.000	6.75	23	0	0	0	9	0	32	44	144	25	24	3	0	1	1	9	2	23	0	0
Mangioni, Jarad, M.H.	0	0	.000	0.00	1	0	0	0	1	0	1	0	2	0	0	0	0	0	0	0	0	0	0	0
Marquez, Jeff, Pro.	4	2	.667	4.22	14	10	0	0	0	0	59.2	69	281	36	28	4	3	3	5	34	0	43	7	1
Martinez, Hancen, I.F.	4	3	.571	3.72	14	9	0	0	1	0	58	54	258	32	24	2	3	3	6	27	0	61	6	3
McCarthy, Matt, Pro.*	0	1	.000	6.92	15	3	0	0	6	0	26	40	136	26	20	1	2	2	1	19	0	16	6	1
McWilliams, Matt, Bil.*	0	0	.000	6.35	3	0	0	0	0	0	5.2	7	29	5	4	2	0	1	3	3	0	6	1	0
Michaels, Carl, Og.	1	0	1.000	1.23	4	0	0	0	1	0	7.1	6	30	1	1	0	1	0	0	2	1	12	0	0
Miller, Greg, G.F.*	3	2	.600	2.37	11	7	0	0	0	0	38	27	152	14	10	1	0	1	2	13	0	37	2	0
Mitchell, Jay, Cas.	5	5	.500	4.95	16	16	0	0	0	0	72.2	85	338	50	40	5	2	3	6	34	0	46	6	0
Montarbo, Adam, I.F.	1	2	.333	2.04	14	0	0	0	1	0	17.2	16	85	10	4	0	1	0	4	10	2	12	2	0
Moore, Mewelde, I.F.	0	0	.000	0.00	1	0	0	0	1	0	0.2	0	3	0	0	0	0	0	0	0	0	1	0	0
Mora, Ramon, M.H.	2	3	.400	5.34	6	6	0	0	0	0	32	41	143	24	19	3	2	0	2	10	0	28	1	0
Moreira, Greg, Og.	1	3	.250	4.66	18	2	0	0	4	1	46.1	72	227	38	24	5	2	3	5	13	1	37	3	0
Morel, Eudy, I.F.	0	2	.000	3.24	8	0	0	0	6	1	8.1	9	38	9	3	2	1	0	0	2	1	10	0	0
Morel, Robinson, Cas.	0	0	.000	0.00	2	0	0	0	1	0	2	3	8	0	0	0	0	0	0	0	0	0	0	0
Moreno, Juan J., Miss.	0	0	.000	0.00	1	0	0	0	1	0	1	0	4	0	0	0	0	0	0	1	0	0	0	0
Nelson, Steve, G.F.	6	5	.545	3.99	14	14	0	0	0	0	70	79	318	39	31	4	3	3	6	23	1	44	6	2
Neylan, Chris, M.H.*	0	5	.000	9.63	12	6	0	0	2	0	38.1	50	186	48	41	12	1	3	4	21	0	15	7	1
Nippert, Dustin, Miss.	4	2	.667	1.65	17	11	0	0	2	0	54.2	42	212	12	10	2	0	0	1	9	0	77	4	0
Ortega, Sixto, Cas.	0	0	.000	0.00	1	0	0	0	0	0	0	0	0	0	0	0	0	0	0	0	0	0	0	0
Oyervidez, Jose, I.F.	0	4	.000	4.31	32	0	0	0	8	3	31.1	22	141	22	15	2	0	2	6	22	0	58	1	0
Parra, Manuel, Og.*	3	1	.750	3.21	11	10	0	0	0	0	47.2	59	213	30	17	3	0	1	4	10	0	51	5	0
Paulino, Johan, I.F.	0	0	.000	5.68	16	0	0	0	4	0	19	20	102	16	12	0	0	2	0	22	1	14	3	1
Pena, Luis, I.F.	1	2	.333	6.84	18	3	0	0	7	0	25	36	127	26	19	3	0	1	5	8	0	21	6	0
Perez, Edwin, Miss.	2	4	.333	4.41	8	7	0	0	1	0	32.2	33	149	23	16	2	0	1	2	18	0	25	0	1
Perez, Henry, I.F.	4	6	.400	4.72	15	15	0	0	0	0	74.1	73	327	52	39	4	4	4	3	36	1	70	1	1
Perez, Juan, M.H.	2	3	.400	6.16	13	11	0	0	1	0	49.2	59	233	41	34	5	0	3	3	24	0	42	6	0
Perez, Melvin, Og.	4	3	.571	3.55	26	0	0	0	14	2	33	25	150	14	13	4	1	0	1	21	0	34	4	1
Plummer, Jarod, G.F.	1	0	1.000	0.00	1	0	0	0	0	0	2	1	9	0	0	0	0	0	0	1	0	1	0	0

Pitcher, Team	W	L	Pct.	ERA	G	GS	CG	ShO	GF	Sv.	IP	H	TBF	R	ER	HR	SH	SF	HB	BB	IBB	SO	WP	Bk.
Ponce, William, I.F.	1	4	.200	8.47	14	7	0	0	0	0	34	188	43	32	3	1	3	2	33	0	31	9	1
Ponder, Steven, Cas.*	1	0	1.000	6.54	16	5	0	0	1	0	31.2	24	168	27	23	2	2	9	38	0	28	7	1
Price, Matt, Og.	0	0	.000	5.22	17	1	0	0	5	0	29.1	26	136	23	17	5	2	2	6	15	0	10	3	0
Quintero, Mayque, Bil.	2	1	.667	4.11	7	6	0	0	0	0	30.2	33	136	17	14	1	0	1	4	8	0	25	0	2
Ramirez, Edward, Pro.	1	0	1.000	9.31	2	1	0	0	0	0	9.2	14	47	10	10	0	2	3	4	0	4	2	0
Ramirez, Ismael, M.H.	4	2	.667	2.98	11	10	0	0	0	1	54.1	51	225	23	18	4	3	1	2	14	0	51	2	0
Reba, Steve, Cas.	0	0	.000	5.87	2	1	0	0	0	0	7.2	11	39	7	5	1	0	0	1	3	0	6	1	0
Reed, Anthony, Pro.	4	7	.364	5.83	29	0	0	0	23	10	29.1	40	148	27	19	1	2	2	3	19	4	24	5	0
Reina, Dimas, G.F.	5	1	.833	3.35	31	0	0	0	23	7	40.1	29	173	22	15	6	0	2	2	21	1	36	6	0
Rincon, Carlos, Bil.*	4	3	.571	4.45	23	0	0	0	8	1	30.1	29	143	17	15	1	3	1	7	21	2	30	9	0
Robinson, Jeff, Og.	0	2	.000	6.75	4	3	0	0	0	0	10.2	16	54	11	8	0	0	1	2	5	0	16	4	0
Rodriguez, Rafael, Pro.	1	1	.500	5.96	6	6	0	0	0	0	25.2	26	116	17	17	3	0	2	3	14	0	25	3	0
Rodriguez, Mike, G.F.	3	2	.600	4.17	18	4	0	0	3	1	41	35	180	21	19	3	0	1	3	25	0	52	3	0
Roga, Michael, M.H.	2	3	.400	5.08	24	3	0	0	2	1	51.1	53	229	39	29	5	0	1	2	24	0	62	9	1
Romero, Davis, M.H.*	3	2	.600	5.19	27	4	0	0	4	2	50.1	49	217	38	29	7	1	1	0	18	0	76	2	3
Rosario, Adriano, Miss.	1	2	.333	6.30	4	4	0	0	0	0	20	26	89	15	14	0	1	1	3	3	0	14	4	1
Rosen, Mark, Miss.*	1	1	.500	3.93	13	1	0	0	1	0	18.1	15	84	11	8	0	1	1	2	12	0	15	6	0
Salas, Pedro, Cas.	0	1	.000	4.11	13	0	0	0	3	0	15.1	18	65	7	7	2	0	1	1	2	0	8	3	1
Santiago, Tomas, Cas.	0	1	.000	4.50	19	0	0	0	1	0	34	41	161	24	17	1	2	2	2	20	0	24	3	0
Sarfate, Dennis, Og.	0	0	.000	9.00	1	0	0	0	0	0	1	2	6	1	1	0	0	0	0	1	0	2	0	0
Saunders, Joe, Pro.*	2	1	.667	3.62	8	8	0	0	0	0	32.1	40	146	19	13	1	2	1	1	11	0	21	3	0
Savickas, Russell, M.H.	4	4	.500	3.19	14	10	0	0	0	0	53.2	44	229	23	19	3	0	0	3	29	0	52	5	1
Seifert, Michael, M.H.*	1	1	.500	9.37	18	0	0	0	7	0	16.1	25	88	20	17	4	0	0	1	17	0	13	8	0
Severino, Cleris, Bil.*	7	1	.875	0.96	10	10	0	0	0	0	65.2	56	268	17	7	3	1	1	8	14	0	63	3	0
Shafer, David, Bil.	5	2	.714	1.72	19	0	0	0	11	4	31.1	30	138	14	6	0	1	2	11	3	30	1	0	
Shartzer, Bryan, Cas.	0	3	.000	5.29	12	1	0	0	8	1	17	17	75	10	10	1	0	0	0	5	0	20	2	0
Shepple, Tyler, Og.	3	4	.429	7.49	25	0	0	0	13	4	33.2	56	169	33	28	3	2	0	5	8	0	30	1	0
Sierra, Jairo, Miss.	0	3	.000	10.13	6	6	0	0	0	0	21.1	34	124	29	24	3	0	0	6	21	0	9	9	0
Silva, Erick, Miss.	0	3	.000	9.77	11	6	0	0	0	0	31.1	40	167	41	34	1	0	1	7	28	0	27	4	2
Sisco, Kelly, Pro.*	1	0	1.000	22.50	2	0	0	0	0	0	2	4	15	7	5	0	0	1	4	0	2	3	0	
Smith, Sam, Miss.	1	4	.200	2.59	27	0	0	0	23	8	41.2	41	179	18	12	4	1	1	8	18	0	45	4	0
Steward, Jaime, Pro.*	1	0	1.000	8.10	4	2	0	0	0	0	16.2	25	77	17	15	1	0	0	4	15	0	15	1	0
Stewart, James, G.F.	5	3	.625	3.78	19	6	0	0	3	0	50	47	209	30	21	5	5	0	2	9	1	33	0	1
Stone, Jeff, Og.*	0	0	.000	10.80	3	0	0	0	1	0	5	8	27	6	6	1	1	1	2	3	0	1	0	1
Stults, Eric, G.F.*	1	0	1.000	2.25	5	0	0	0	1	1	8	6	34	4	2	0	0	1	0	3	0	9	0	0
Talanoa, Charles, M.H.	4	3	.571	4.07	15	15	1	0	0	0	79.2	77	337	42	36	6	1	2	8	23	0	91	11	0
Thomas, Eric A., Og.	2	1	.667	5.36	15	9	0	0	1	0	45.1	50	210	31	27	0	0	1	9	21	1	38	7	1
Thomas, Eric M., Og.	0	3	.000	9.90	12	6	0	0	0	0	30	46	156	39	33	5	0	1	3	17	0	32	8	1
Thompson, Sean, I.F.*	4	3	.571	3.83	13	11	0	0	0	0	56.1	51	248	34	24	4	2	1	2	38	0	69	13	2
Thrasher, Jesse, I.F.	1	5	.167	5.34	21	8	0	0	2	0	57.1	69	279	59	34	2	1	4	4	37	0	38	18	0
Tibbs, Jeff, G.F.	3	1	.750	5.92	24	1	0	0	9	3	48.2	64	236	40	32	4	2	3	6	25	2	25	6	0
Torres, Andy, M.H.	0	0	.000	3.86	6	0	0	0	2	0	11.2	11	51	6	5	2	0	0	2	1	0	13	2	0
Torres, Steve, Pro.	0	0	.000	6.00	5	0	0	0	3	0	6	8	35	6	4	0	0	1	5	0	4	2	0	
Valcarcel, Jonathan, Cas.*	2	0	1.000	3.71	21	0	0	0	2	1	26.2	32	121	17	11	3	0	1	3	18	0	22	3	2
Valdes, Carlos, I.F.	0	1	.000	3.62	21	0	0	0	5	0	27.1	18	111	13	11	0	1	1	0	19	0	28	4	1
Valera, Luis, Bil.	0	1	.000	13.50	2	0	0	0	1	0	1.1	3	8	3	2	1	0	0	0	1	0	1	1	0
Vargas, Reynardo, Cas.	3	3	.500	3.61	26	0	0	0	7	1	42.1	38	189	24	17	2	2	1	2	22	1	45	0	0
Wachman, Corey, Bil.	1	1	.500	6.18	17	2	0	0	4	2	39.1	45	180	31	27	6	4	1	1	17	1	38	8	1
Wesley, John, M.H.	3	0	1.000	1.88	19	0	0	0	5	2	28.2	21	119	12	6	1	2	1	8	0	38	1	0	
Whatley, Keith, Miss.	7	2	.778	2.85	22	9	0	0	2	0	66.1	56	267	25	21	3	2	1	1	14	1	75	2	0
White, Michael, G.F.*	0	2	.000	5.93	20	0	0	0	8	0	27.1	46	141	29	18	2	0	1	6	10	2	22	3	0
Williams, Bryan, Pro.	5	7	.417	4.93	16	14	0	0	0	0	65.2	60	298	41	36	2	1	1	7	23	0	71	8	0
Williams, Ryan, G.F.	1	1	.500	4.66	18	0	0	0	7	2	36.2	42	164	21	19	0	3	4	11	0	28	3	0
Wilson, Brandon, I.F.	3	0	1.000	3.40	17	0	0	0	2	1	47.2	59	208	27	18	2	1	1	4	0	6	21	0	39	8	0
Yamaguchi, Tetsuya, Miss.*	1	1	.500	3.94	21	0	0	0	3	0	32	35	159	21	14	2	0	0	6	21	0	39	8	0

COMBINATION SHUTOUTS: **Billings (1)**—Severino-Wachman. **Casper (0)**. **Great Falls (4)**—Cuen-M. Rodriguez-Reina, Cuen-Tibbs, Figueroa-Stewart-LaSalle, Miller-Broxton. **Idaho Falls (2)**—Laratta-Thompson-Montarbo-Espinal-E. Morel. **Medicine Hat (4)**—Roga-Bimeal-Buzachero-Wesley-Berroa, Savickas-Roga-DeJong, Savickas-Romero-DeJong, Savickas-Wesley. **Missoula (4)**—Juarez-Allender, Nippert-Incinelli-Smith, Nippert-Yamaguchi-K. Garcia, Whatley-Incinelli-Rosen-K. Garcia. **Ogden (0)**. **Provo (1)**—Holcomb-Astacio-Fuller.

NO-HIT GAMES: None.

2002 FIELDING

TEAM

Team	G	PO	A	E	TC	DP	TP	PB	Pct.
Provo	76	1968	807	115	2890	72	0	14	.960
Casper	76	1982	806	121	2909	54	0	16	.958
Medicine Hat	75	1945	836	121	2902	69	0	15	.958
Great Falls	75	1965	750	119	2834	68	0	10	.958
Ogden	75	1984	739	135	2858	69	0	11	.953
Billings	75	1987	805	150	2942	74	0	9	.949
Missoula	76	2008	829	158	2995	64	0	12	.947
Idaho Falls	76	1971	830	191	2992	83	0	22	.936

INDIVIDUAL

FIRST BASEMEN

NOTE: All caps denotes fielding-percentage leader based on 38 games for catchers, 51 for all other non-pitchers and 61 innings for pitchers. *Throws lefthanded.

Player, Team	Pct.	G	PO	A	E	TC	DP
Avlas, Phil, Miss.	.667	1	2	0	1	3	0
Baez, Carlos, I.F.	1.000	1	3	0	0	3	0

Player, Team	Pct.	G	PO	A	E	TC	DP
Bell, Paul, Og.	.667	1	2	0	1	3	0
Bohanan, Keith, Og.	1.000	1	1	0	0	1	0
Bok, Matt, G.F.	.875	3	14	0	2	16	3
Colina, Yinner, Bil.	.971	4	32	2	1	35	6
Corrente, David, M.H.	1.000	3	19	0	0	19	3
Diaz, Robinzon, M.H.	1.000	1	3	0	0	3	0
Eure, Jeffrey, Og.	.987	29	208	13	3	224	22
Fielder, Prince, Og.	.974	35	275	19	8	302	28
Gray, Josh, Pro.	.983	39	318	20	6	344	34
Heath, Matt, Miss.	1.000	3	14	0	0	14	3
Hoorelbeke, Jesse, G.F.	.985	31	252	19	4	275	19
Johanning, Ben, I.F.*	1.000	15	94	8	0	102	12
Kenning, Ryan, Pro.*	.969	30	213	9	7	229	20
Loney, James, G.F.*	.987	42	351	15	5	371	39
Lopez, Luis, I.F.	1.000	1	13	0	0	13	2
Mangioni, Jarad, M.H.	.941	2	16	0	1	17	5
Mathis, Jake, Pro.	.983	16	106	7	2	115	14
McAnulty, Paul, I.F.	.979	55	476	37	11	524	55
Melo, Manuel, Og.	1.000	2	3	1	0	4	0
Mendez, Mario, Og.	1.000	1	3	0	0	3	0
Montero, Miguel, Miss.	1.000	1	1	0	0	1	0
Moore, Rusty, I.F.	1.000	9	71	2	0	73	6

Player, Team	Pct.	G	PO	A	E	TC	DP
Nixon, Mike, G.F.	1.000	2	2	2	0	4	1
Olmstead, Walter, Bil.	.978	22	205	13	5	223	22
Perry, Jason, M.H.	.979	18	180	7	4	191	17
Robledo, Nelson, Cas.	.988	10	80	5	1	86	6
Ruiz, Junior, Bil.	.988	10	76	5	1	82	4
Santana, Mayobanex, Miss.	.964	7	50	3	2	55	4
Sardinha, Duke, Cas.	.846	2	11	0	2	13	0
Serafini, Matt, Og.	.982	17	108	3	2	113	12
SHEALY, Ryan, Cas.	.991	65	621	36	6	663	47
Simon, Brandon, Miss.*	.000	1	0	0	0	0	0
Stanek, Jeff, Miss.	.988	46	552	47	7	606	49
Urueta, Luis, Miss.	1.000	11	41	1	0	42	3
Vavao, Jason, Bil.	.980	41	314	36	7	357	33
Young, Delwyn, G.F.	1.000	1	9	1	0	10	0
Zinsman, Zeph, M.H.*	.984	54	450	39	8	497	38

SECOND BASEMEN

Player, Team	Pct.	G	PO	A	E	TC	DP
Almonte, Sandy, Cas.	.893	13	24	43	8	75	6
Arnold, Eric, M.H.	.954	14	37	46	4	87	13
Baez, Carlos, I.F.	1.000	4	7	9	0	16	1
Bell, Paul, Og.	.958	5	9	14	1	24	1
Bergolla, William, Bil.	.934	50	109	131	17	257	31
Bohanan, Keith, Og.	1.000	9	5	12	0	17	0
Brown, Matthew, Pro.	1.000	6	3	6	0	9	0
Cairns, Troy, Bil.	1.000	9	15	24	0	39	8
CALLASPO, Alberto, Pro.	.972	68	134	207	10	351	53
Cota, Carlo, M.H.	.963	55	101	162	10	273	39
Crabbe, Callix, Og.	.930	63	111	170	21	302	43
De Los Santos, Omar, G.F.	.889	13	22	34	7	63	10
Eure, Jeffrey, Og.	1.000	1	0	1	0	1	0
Farmer, John, G.F.	.978	11	22	22	1	45	10
Gomez, Andri, Og.	1.000	4	8	4	0	12	3
Gonzalez, Juan, G.F.	.929	4	7	6	1	14	1
Hendricks, K.J., Cas.	.948	21	35	57	5	97	8
Hoorelbeke, Jesse, G.F.	1.000	1	2	5	0	7	0
Ison, Jeremy, Bil.	1.000	1	1	1	0	2	0
Jacobo, Kervin, Miss.	.938	29	54	81	9	144	19
Lewis, Domonique, Bil.	1.000	10	20	25	0	45	2
Lima, Joseph, I.F.	.875	24	41	57	14	112	15
Mateo, Dan, Bil.	.000	1	0	0	1	1	0
Morel, Robinson, Cas.	.981	32	60	99	3	162	18
Moreno, Juan J., Miss.	.944	16	27	41	4	72	12
Morgan, Matt, Miss.	.942	37	61	84	9	154	20
Ramos, Peeter, I.F.	.942	54	114	145	16	275	50
Ruiz, Junior, Bil.	.950	9	15	23	2	40	6
Salas, Jose, M.H.	.889	10	13	11	3	27	1
Santana, Mayobanex, Miss.	.875	4	5	9	2	16	2
Selmo, Wilson, Pro.	.935	9	15	14	2	31	2
Solis, Ricky, G.F.	.974	8	16	21	1	38	4
Tejeda, Francisco, Cas.	.939	12	19	27	3	49	4
Young, Delwyn, G.F.	.928	46	81	111	15	207	29

THIRD BASEMEN

Player, Team	Pct.	G	PO	A	E	TC	DP
Almonte, Sandy, Cas.	.973	16	7	29	1	37	3
Baez, Carlos, I.F.	.805	29	17	49	16	82	10
Bell, Paul, Og.	.714	4	2	8	4	14	1
Bohanan, Keith, Og.	.850	20	19	32	9	60	7
Brown, Matthew, Pro.	.900	30	23	40	7	70	7
Correll, Richard, Bil.	.880	34	22	66	12	100	4
Cota, Carlo, M.H.	.000	1	0	0	0	0	0
Dale, Lachlan, I.F.	.781	35	19	63	23	105	8
De Los Santos, Omar, G.F.	.977	16	12	30	1	43	0
Diaz, Robinzon, M.H.	.750	2	3	3	2	8	2
DRAGICEVICH, Scott, M.H.	.947	53	34	127	9	170	12
Eure, Jeffrey, Og.	.886	35	26	44	9	79	1
Farmer, John, G.F.	1.000	1	0	4	0	4	0
Fry, Ryan, Bil.	.886	20	11	28	5	44	0
Gomez, Andri, Og.	.889	23	10	46	7	63	3
Gonzalez, Juan, G.F.	.900	11	5	13	2	20	2
Hancock, Justin, Pro.	.846	32	16	39	10	65	4
Hendricks, K.J., Cas.	1.000	1	1	3	0	4	1
Ison, Jeremy, Bil.	.875	4	1	6	1	8	1
Jacobo, Kervin, Miss.	.800	9	2	14	4	20	0
Krimmel, Matt, Bil.	.831	18	11	38	10	59	1
Lima, Joseph, I.F.	.897	14	14	38	6	58	6
Mangioni, Jarad, M.H.	.889	12	6	18	3	27	1
Mathis, Jake, Pro.	.974	22	14	23	1	38	0
Montero, Miguel, Miss.	1.000	4	0	7	0	7	0
Moore, Rusty, I.F.	.000	1	0	0	2	2	0
Morel, Robinson, Cas.	.846	4	2	9	2	13	0
Moreno, Juan J., Miss.	.857	22	14	34	8	56	2
Morgan, Matt, Miss.	.920	10	3	20	2	25	1
Murray, Joshua, Og.	.000	1	0	0	0	0	0
Nunez, Florentino, Cas.	.857	28	12	48	10	70	7

Player, Team	Pct.	G	PO	A	E	TC	DP
Perozo, Hector, G.F.	.898	54	35	97	15	147	6
Ramos, Peeter, I.F.	.000	1	0	0	0	0	0
Raposo, Angel, Miss.	.500	5	1	3	4	8	0
Ruiz, Junior, Bil.	1.000	1	1	0	0	1	0
Salas, Jose, M.H.	.680	10	4	13	8	25	0
Santana, Mayobanex, Miss.	.867	42	20	91	17	128	10
Sardinha, Duke, Cas.	.878	23	17	62	11	90	4
Selmo, Wilson, Pro.	.929	6	2	11	1	14	1
Tejeda, Francisco, Cas.	.833	5	5	10	3	18	1
Urueta, Luis, Miss.	.000	1	0	0	0	0	0

SHORTSTOPS

Player, Team	Pct.	G	PO	A	E	TC	DP
Almonte, Sandy, Cas.	.947	20	36	54	5	95	9
AYBAR, Eric, Pro.	.950	67	107	197	16	320	40
Baez, Carlos, I.F.	.899	16	28	43	8	79	10
Bell, Paul, Og.	.857	3	0	6	1	7	1
Bergolla, William, Bil.	1.000	1	3	3	0	6	1
Bohanan, Keith, Og.	.922	28	44	74	10	128	15
Cairns, Troy, Bil.	.926	28	47	79	10	136	18
Callaspo, Alberto, Pro.	.800	1	2	2	1	5	1
Crabbe, Callix, Og.	1.000	2	1	2	0	3	0
De Los Santos, Omar, G.F.	.912	8	9	22	3	34	4
Eure, Jeffrey, Og.	1.000	1	0	1	0	1	0
Farmer, John, G.F.	.917	4	4	7	1	12	2
Garcia, Luis, I.F.	.890	62	85	175	32	292	36
Gomez, Andri, Og.	.875	4	2	5	1	8	1
Gonzalez, Juan, G.F.	.953	21	29	53	4	86	13
Guzman, Joel, G.F.	.918	43	59	120	16	195	23
Hendricks, K.J., Cas.	.949	40	54	131	10	195	19
Ison, Jeremy, Bil.	.800	3	2	2	1	5	0
Mateo, Dan, Bil.	.877	45	85	122	29	236	37
Moreno, Juan J., Miss.	.833	2	2	3	1	6	2
Morgan, Matt, Miss.	.923	24	41	67	9	117	13
Murray, Joshua, Og.	.886	48	57	114	22	193	26
Nunez, Florentino, Cas.	.915	13	16	38	5	59	7
Peralta, Juan, M.H.	.929	71	111	203	24	338	40
Ramos, Peeter, I.F.	.500	1	0	1	1	2	0
Salas, Jose, M.H.	.818	7	8	10	4	22	0
Santana, Mayobanex, Miss.	.667	1	2	0	1	3	0
Santos, Sergio, Miss.	.886	52	63	155	28	246	27
Selmo, Wilson, Pro.	.919	15	19	38	5	62	12
Solis, Ricky, G.F.	.917	6	9	13	2	24	3
Sugden, Jason, Pro.	1.000	1	0	1	0	1	0
Tejeda, Francisco, Cas.	.857	6	2	10	2	14	0

OUTFIELDERS

Player, Team	Pct.	G	PO	A	E	TC	DP
Almonte, Sandy, Cas.	1.000	3	1	0	0	1	0
Andujar, Elvin, Bil.	.889	39	54	2	7	63	1
Antequera, Javier, I.F.	.933	27	23	5	2	30	1
Barre, Brian, Cas.*	.992	62	128	0	1	129	0
Bassett, Mike, Bil.*	.967	42	55	4	2	61	0
Bello, Vladimir, Cas.	.950	58	109	4	6	119	0
BIBBS, Kennard, Og.*	1.000	59	114	5	0	119	1
Bok, Matt, G.F.	.975	19	36	3	1	40	1
Boll, Javier, Miss.	.750	7	6	0	2	8	0
Braun, Randy, M.H.*	.909	16	9	1	1	11	0
Campos, Tiago, Bil.	1.000	17	25	0	0	25	0
Cardona, David, G.F.	.962	34	49	1	2	52	1
Carter, Nic, Og.	.972	42	63	7	2	72	0
Carter, Ryan, G.F.	.917	16	22	0	2	24	0
Chourio, Junior, M.H.	.964	46	52	1	2	55	0
Correll, Richard, Bil.	.500	2	1	0	1	2	0
Cosby, Quan, Pro.	.974	76	148	2	4	154	0
Davis, Morrin, M.H.	.924	61	58	3	5	66	0
Eure, Jeffrey, Og.	1.000	5	7	0	0	7	0
Ezi, Travis, G.F.*	.954	54	101	2	5	108	1
Frazier, Alex, Miss.	.929	50	77	2	6	85	0
Fuller, Casey, Cas.*	.941	42	45	3	3	51	0
Galloway, Mike, M.H.	.833	19	9	1	2	12	0
Garcia, Lino, Miss.	.960	23	45	3	2	50	1
Gates, David, Pro.	1.000	8	13	0	0	13	0
George, Trey, Cas.	.954	65	100	3	5	108	0
Goelz, Bryan, G.F.*	1.000	42	68	0	0	68	0
Gonzalez, Juan, G.F.	.875	8	6	1	1	8	0
Hancock, Justin, Pro.	.977	30	40	3	1	44	0
Heath, Matt, Miss.	1.000	19	25	0	0	25	0
Hoorelbeke, Jesse, G.F.	.000	1	0	0	0	0	0
Humphries, Jared, Bil.*	1.000	5	7	0	0	7	0
Hunt, Stephen, Og.	1.000	2	3	0	0	3	0
Jacobo, Dioscar, G.F.	.925	41	60	2	5	67	0
Jenkins, Kevin, Pro.*	1.000	11	14	1	0	15	0
Johanning, Ben, I.F.*	1.000	2	2	0	0	2	0
Kenning, Ryan, Pro.*	1.000	1	2	0	0	2	0
Kratz, Erik, M.H.	.000	1	0	0	0	0	0

Player, Team	Pct.	G	PO	A	E	TC	DP
Lester, Anthony, I.F.	.900	6	8	1	1	10	0
Lima, Joseph, I.F.	.974	22	35	3	1	39	0
Mangioni, Jarad, M.H.	.946	31	33	2	2	37	0
McClanahan, Jonah, Og.	.977	22	40	2	1	43	1
Melo, Manuel, I.F.	.940	24	43	4	3	50	0
Mendez, Mario, Og.	.943	56	107	8	7	122	3
Montague, Ed, G.F.	.913	12	19	2	2	23	1
Montero, Danilo, Miss.	.911	30	48	3	5	56	1
Moore, Mewelde, I.F.	.931	17	27	0	2	29	0
Moore, Rusty, I.F.	.935	24	41	2	3	46	0
Mora, Ruben, I.F.	.970	31	60	4	2	66	1
Morel, Robinson, Cas.	1.000	1	1	0	0	1	0
Moss, Steve, Og.	1.000	5	4	0	0	4	0
Moye, Alan, Bil.	.970	41	64	1	2	67	0
Nixon, Mike, G.F.	1.000	4	5	0	0	5	0
Nunez, Felix, Pro.	.917	5	11	0	1	12	0
Olmstead, Walter, Bil.	1.000	4	4	0	0	4	0
Olson, David, I.F.	.983	39	55	3	1	59	0
Owen, Thomas, G.F.	1.000	1	2	0	0	2	0
Pacheco, Julio, G.F.*	1.000	14	21	0	0	21	0
Paula, Manuel, Bil.	.922	36	65	6	6	77	0
Perdomo, Mike, Pro.	.943	54	97	3	6	106	0
Petersen, Ryan, Bil.	1.000	3	7	0	0	7	0
Plasencia, Francisco, Og.*	.961	29	44	5	2	51	1
Ramirez, Yordany, I.F.	.947	23	33	3	2	38	0
Rico, Erik, M.H.*	.986	58	65	3	1	69	1
Ruiz, Junior, Bil.	.967	15	26	3	1	30	0
Salas, Jose, M.H.	.000	1	0	0	0	0	0
Sanchez, Braulio, Miss.*	1.000	7	9	0	0	9	0
Santiago, Ricardo, Miss.	.901	63	98	11	12	121	1
Schmidt, Jarrod, Bil.	.958	31	64	4	3	71	2
Simon, Brandon, Miss.*	.982	56	107	3	2	112	0
Smith, David, M.H.	.930	41	50	3	4	57	0
Smith, Rashad, I.F.	.925	50	71	3	6	80	0
Soriano, Carlos, Og.	1.000	1	1	0	0	1	0
Sugden, Jason, Pro.	.960	55	90	6	4	100	3
Urueta, Luis, Miss.	.000	2	0	0	0	0	0

CATCHERS

Player, Team	Pct.	G	PO	A	E	TC	DP	PB
Alvarado, Joel, Og.	.983	17	159	19	3	181	1	4
Avlas, Phil, Miss.	.988	40	288	36	4	328	1	5
Bok, Matt, G.F.	1.000	4	20	4	0	24	0	1
BOOTH, Steve, Bil.	.992	47	329	39	3	371	2	3
Corrente, David, M.H.	1.000	20	117	20	0	137	3	2
Diaz, Robinzon, M.H.	.976	31	250	35	7	292	2	5
Dvorsky, Alex, Pro.	.983	48	347	60	7	414	3	6
Eure, Jeffrey, Og.	1.000	3	8	0	0	8	0	0
Falcon, Omar, I.F.	.971	50	384	59	13	456	3	7
Frost, Jeremy, Og.	.961	9	69	5	3	77	1	1
Garcia, Angleidy, I.F.	.942	21	134	27	10	171	1	10
Ghutzman, Phillip, Bil.	1.000	2	8	0	0	8	0	0
Guzman, Junior, Pro.	.962	29	196	33	9	238	1	8
Kratz, Erik, M.H.	.990	33	278	29	3	310	0	8
Langill, Eric, G.F.	1.000	4	31	2	0	33	0	0
Lester, Anthony, I.F.	.966	9	24	4	1	29	0	3
Lopez, Luis, I.F.	.986	11	65	5	1	71	0	2
Mercado, Onix, Bil.	.982	7	51	3	1	55	0	0
Mills, Rock, Cas.	.983	21	163	12	3	178	0	6
Montero, Miguel, Miss.	.980	40	267	28	6	301	1	6
Motooka, Rafael, Bil.	.975	30	211	23	6	240	3	6
Nixon, Mike, G.F.	.986	51	405	30	6	441	2	7
Ortega, Sixto, Cas.	1.000	4	28	3	0	31	0	1
Owen, Thomas, G.F.	.976	21	148	17	4	169	0	2
Robledo, Nelson, Cas.	.990	25	179	25	2	206	0	5
Serafini, Matt, Og.	1.000	20	154	13	0	167	3	3
Symonds, Grady, Miss.	.960	9	46	2	2	50	0	1
Urueta, Luis, Miss.	1.000	1	1	0	0	1	0	0
Vanden Berg, John, Og.	.984	32	234	17	4	255	0	3
Wilson, Neil, Cas.	.975	28	186	12	5	203	0	4

PITCHERS

Player, Team	Pct.	G	PO	A	E	TC	DP
Allen, Blakely, Pro.	.000	1	0	0	0	0	0
Allender, John, Miss.	.800	21	2	6	2	10	0
Alliston, Josh, G.F.	1.000	6	1	2	0	3	0
Aquino, Juan, G.F.	.000	2	0	0	0	0	0
Arias, Daniel, Pro.	.000	4	0	0	0	0	0
Astacio, Hector, Pro.	.815	17	7	15	5	27	1
Bailey, Ryan, Pro.	1.000	4	1	0	0	1	0
Baker, Jason, Og.	.857	13	1	5	1	7	0
Ballouli, Khalid, Og.	1.000	15	6	12	0	18	1
Balser, Jeff, Pro.	1.000	4	1	1	0	2	0
Barnett, Brian, Pro.	.000	1	0	0	0	0	0
Batista, Gorky, Bil.	1.000	2	0	4	0	4	0
Beavers, Kevin, I.F.*	.846	11	3	8	2	13	0

Player, Team	Pct.	G	PO	A	E	TC	DP
Bell, Chris, Bil.	1.000	7	0	1	0	1	0
Bell, Paul, Og.	.000	1	0	0	0	0	0
Berroa, Yesson, M.H.	.875	20	1	6	1	8	1
Bilke, Austin, Pro.	.909	28	3	7	1	11	0
Bimeal, Matt, M.H.	.800	16	1	3	1	5	0
Bochy, Greg, I.F.	.000	1	0	0	0	0	0
Breslow, Craig, Og.*	1.000	23	1	5	0	6	0
Broxton, Jonathan, G.F.	.833	11	2	3	1	6	0
Burden, Randy, Pro.	1.000	10	1	1	0	2	0
Buzachero, Bubbie, M.H.	.923	26	6	6	1	13	2
Carpenter, Calvin, Og.	.833	16	5	15	4	24	0
Cartier, Richard, Cas.	.833	29	3	2	1	6	1
Chivilli, Pedro, Cas.	.929	14	4	9	1	14	0
Chourio, Junior, M.H.	.000	1	0	0	0	0	0
Cimorelli, Brett, Pro.	1.000	10	4	2	0	6	0
Coffin, Ryan, Miss.	.917	22	5	6	1	12	1
Corpas, Manuel, Cas.	.500	29	1	2	3	6	0
Cuen, David, G.F.*	1.000	10	4	10	0	14	0
Curran, Joe, Bil.*	.667	20	2	2	2	6	0
D'Amico, Leonardo, Pro.	.909	14	4	6	1	11	0
Darby, James, I.F.	.889	24	2	6	1	9	1
DeJong, Jordan, M.H.	.917	33	4	7	1	12	1
Delgadillo, Ambiroix, Pro.*	.000	2	0	0	0	0	0
Desalme, Gene, Og.*	.333	14	0	1	2	3	0
Diaz, Jose, I.F.	1.000	3	0	3	0	3	0
Diaz, Pedro, Cas.	.857	18	2	4	1	7	0
Escobedo, Edgar, G.F.	1.000	18	1	1	0	2	1
Escorcha, Orlando, Bil.*	1.000	11	1	6	0	7	1
Espinal, Jhovany, I.F.	.000	22	0	0	1	1	0
Eure, Jeffrey, Og.	.000	1	0	0	0	0	0
Fardella, Jason, Cas.	.769	21	6	4	3	13	0
Fernandez, Alfredo, I.F.	.857	6	3	3	1	7	0
Ferns, Robert, Miss.	.667	8	1	1	1	3	0
Figueroa, Jonathan, G.F.*	1.000	7	2	3	0	5	0
Fuller, Justin, Pro.*	1.000	26	1	3	0	4	0
Gabriel, Justin, Og.*	1.000	12	1	3	0	4	0
Garcia, Kelvin, Miss.*	.929	18	2	11	1	14	1
Garcia, Rurik, Miss.*	.500	11	0	2	2	4	0
Gemmell, Don, Bil.	1.000	9	6	3	0	9	0
George, Brad, M.H.	1.000	9	6	3	0	9	0
Geraldo, Jose, I.F.	.000	14	0	0	1	1	0
Gilliam, Wes, Miss.*	.000	8	0	0	0	0	0
Goas, Adrian, Pro.	.750	20	1	2	1	4	0
GOMEZ, Jose, Bil.	1.000	13	2	18	0	20	3
Gonzalez, Luis, G.F.*	.000	4	0	0	0	0	0
Grant, Brian, M.H.	1.000	14	3	7	0	10	0
Groeger, Jeff, Bil.	.857	10	0	6	1	7	0
Gruler, Chris, Bil.	1.000	4	1	3	0	4	0
Hall, Bo, Og.	1.000	16	5	7	0	12	0
Hawley, Ross, G.F.	.000	3	0	0	0	0	0
Hernandez, Santos, Cas.	1.000	14	4	12	0	16	1
Hindman, Scott, Pro.*	.000	3	0	0	0	0	0
Holcomb, James, Pro.	.923	12	7	5	1	13	0
Hoorelbeke, Jesse, G.F.	1.000	1	0	1	0	1	1
Housman, Jeff, Og.*	1.000	16	1	6	0	7	2
Hull, Eric, G.F.	1.000	11	0	3	0	3	1
Incinelli, Matt, Miss.	1.000	27	1	6	0	7	0
Jimenez, Ubaldo, Cas.	1.000	14	3	7	0	10	1
Juarez, William, Miss.	1.000	16	1	5	0	6	0
Jumelles, Victor, Bil.	.625	22	1	4	3	8	1
Keller, Frankie, Bil.*	.941	14	4	12	1	17	1
King, O.J., Bil.	1.000	4	2	2	0	4	1
Kranawetter, Josh, Miss.	.800	30	2	6	2	10	0
Krisch, David, I.F.*	1.000	32	0	3	0	3	1
Lane, Brian, Bil.	.857	13	2	4	1	7	0
Laratta, E.J., I.F.	1.000	9	1	4	0	5	0
LaSalle, Julio, G.F.	.600	17	1	2	2	5	0
Light, Scott, Bil.	.900	4	2	7	1	10	3
Lo, Ching-Lung, Cas.	.769	14	1	9	3	13	1
Lopez, Arturo, G.F.*	.938	15	2	13	1	16	1
Lucas, Christopher, Bil.	.857	10	3	3	1	7	0
Lugo, Osvaldo, Pro.	.600	17	1	2	2	5	0
Luther, Heath, Pro.*	1.000	23	0	6	0	6	0
Mangioni, Jarad, M.H.	.000	1	0	0	0	0	0
Marquez, Jeff, Pro.	1.000	14	1	10	0	11	0
Martinez, Hancen, I.F.	.875	14	3	4	1	8	0
McCarthy, Matt, Pro.*	.800	15	1	3	1	5	0
McWilliams, Matt, Bil.*	1.000	3	0	2	0	2	0
Michaels, Carl, Og.	1.000	4	1	1	0	2	0
Miller, Greg, G.F.*	.889	11	1	7	1	9	0
Mitchell, Jay, Cas.	1.000	16	7	11	0	18	2
Montarbo, Adam, I.F.	.714	14	0	5	2	7	0
Moore, Mewelde, I.F.	.000	1	0	0	0	0	0
Mora, Ramon, M.H.	.833	6	3	7	2	12	0
Moreira, Greg, Og.	1.000	18	1	7	0	8	1
Morel, Eudy, I.F.	1.000	8	0	1	0	1	0
Morel, Robinson, Cas.	.000	2	0	0	0	0	0

Player, Team	Pct.	G	PO	A	E	TC	DP
Moreno, Juan J., Miss.	.000	1	0	0	0	0	0
Nelson, Steve, G.F.	1.000	14	5	11	0	16	0
Neylan, Chris, M.H.*	1.000	12	1	10	0	11	0
Nippert, Dustin, Miss.	1.000	17	1	4	0	5	0
Oyervidez, Jose, I.F.	1.000	32	1	3	0	4	0
Parra, Manuel, Og.*	.909	11	4	6	1	11	0
Paulino, Johan, I.F.	1.000	16	1	2	0	3	0
Pena, Luis, I.F.	1.000	18	0	4	0	4	0
Perez, Edwin, Miss.	1.000	8	4	4	0	8	0
Perez, Henry, I.F.	.778	15	3	4	2	9	0
Perez, Juan, M.H.	.778	13	2	5	2	9	0
Perez, Melvin, Og.	1.000	26	5	0	0	5	0
Plummer, Jarod, G.F.	.500	1	1	0	1	2	0
Ponce, William, I.F.	.875	14	2	5	1	8	1
Ponder, Steven, Cas.*	.625	16	0	5	3	8	0
Price, Matt, Og.	1.000	17	2	3	0	5	0
Quintero, Mayque, Bil.	1.000	7	5	9	0	14	0
Ramirez, Edward, Pro.	1.000	2	1	1	0	2	0
Ramirez, Ismael, M.H.	.889	11	4	12	2	18	1
Reba, Steve, Cas.	1.000	2	2	1	0	3	0
Reed, Anthony, Pro.	.800	29	1	3	1	5	1
Reina, Dimas, G.F.	.889	31	4	4	1	9	1
Rincon, Carlos, Bil.*	.778	23	0	7	2	9	0
Robinson, Jeff, Og.	1.000	4	0	1	0	1	0
Rodriguez , Rafael, Pro.	1.000	6	0	1	0	1	0
Rodriguez, Mike, G.F.	.875	18	0	7	1	8	1
Roga, Michael, M.H.	.895	24	3	14	2	19	0
Romero, Davis, M.H.*	.778	27	0	7	2	9	0
Rosario, Adriano, Miss.	.833	4	2	3	1	6	1
Rosen, Mark, Miss.*	1.000	13	0	2	0	2	0
Salas, Pedro, Cas.	1.000	13	1	0	0	1	0
Santiago, Tomas, Cas.	.875	19	1	6	1	8	0
Sarfate, Dennis, Og.	.000	1	0	0	0	0	0
Saunders, Joe, Pro.*	1.000	8	2	7	0	9	0
Savickas, Russell, M.H.	1.000	14	4	6	0	10	1

Player, Team	Pct.	G	PO	A	E	TC	DP
Seifert, Michael, M.H.*	1.000	18	0	1	0	1	0
Severino, Cleris, Bil.*	.893	10	8	17	3	28	2
Shafer, David, Bil.	.750	19	1	2	1	4	1
Shartzer, Bryan, Cas.	1.000	12	3	3	0	6	0
Shepple, Tyler, Og.	.889	25	1	7	1	9	2
Sierra, Jairo, Miss.	1.000	6	4	2	0	6	0
Silva, Erick, Miss.	1.000	11	1	4	0	5	1
Sisco, Kelly, Pro.*	.000	2	0	0	1	1	0
Smith, Sam, Miss.	1.000	27	3	5	0	8	0
Steward, Jaime, Pro.*	1.000	4	0	3	0	3	0
Stewart, James, G.F.	.929	19	3	10	1	14	0
Stone, Jeff, Og.*	1.000	3	1	0	0	1	0
Stults, Eric, G.F.*	.000	5	0	0	0	0	0
Talanoa, Charles, M.H.	1.000	15	5	7	0	12	1
Thomas, Eric A., I.F.	1.000	15	4	4	0	8	0
Thomas, Eric M., Og.	.000	12	0	0	2	2	0
Thompson, Sean, I.F.*	.870	13	2	18	3	23	0
Thrasher, Jesse, I.F.	.846	21	4	7	2	13	0
Tibbs, Jeff, G.F.	.917	24	2	9	1	12	0
Torres, Andy, M.H.	1.000	6	1	0	0	1	0
Torres, Jose, Pro.	1.000	5	1	0	0	1	0
Valcarcel, Jonathan, Cas.*	1.000	21	0	2	0	2	1
Valdes, Carlos, I.F.	1.000	21	1	1	0	2	0
Valera, Luis, Bil.	1.000	2	2	0	0	2	0
Vargas, Reynardo, Cas.	.857	26	2	4	1	7	0
Wachman, Corey, Bil.	1.000	17	3	3	0	6	0
Wesley, John, M.H.	1.000	19	1	1	0	2	0
Whatley, Keith, Miss.*	.941	22	3	13	1	17	0
White, Michael, G.F.*	.750	20	2	1	1	4	1
Williams, Bryan, Pro.	.875	16	0	7	1	8	1
Williams, Ryan, G.F.	1.000	18	2	3	0	5	0
Wilson, Brandon, I.F.	1.000	17	1	6	0	7	2
Yamaguchi, Tetsuya, Miss.*	1.000	21	4	3	0	7	0

The following players appeared only as designated hitter, pinch-hitter or pinch runner: Ashford, dh; Bagley, dh, ph, pr; Bibee, dh; Duenas, dh.

LEAGUE CHAMPIONS

Year	Team	Pct.
1939—	Twin Falls*	.581
1940—	Salt Lake City	.608
	Ogden (4th)*	.492
1941—	Boise	.623
	Ogden (2nd)*	.598
1942—	Pocatello†	.690
	Boise	.683
1943-44-45—	Did not operate.	
1946—	Twin Falls‡	.585
	Salt Lake City†	.585
1947—	Salt Lake City	.618
	Twin Falls†	.600
1948—	Pocatello	.611
	Twin Falls (2nd)*	.595
1949—	Twin Falls	.624
	Pocatello (3rd)*	.595
1950—	Pocatello	.635
	Billings (3rd)*	.571
1951—	Salt Lake City	.618
	Great Falls (3rd)*	.559
1952—	Pocatello	.595
	Idaho Falls (2nd)*	.573
1953—	Ogden	.679
	Salt Lake City (4th)*	.527
1954—	Salt Lake City	.595
	Great Falls (4th)*	.530
1955—	Boise	.588
	Magic Valley (4th)*	.489
1956—	Boise	.561
1957—	Salt Lake City	.650
	Billings†	.582
1958—	Great Falls	.582
	Boise†	.615
1959—	Boise	.633
	Billings (2nd)*	.523

Year	Team	Pct.
1960—	Boise†	.686
	Idaho Falls	.650
1961—	Boise	.638
	Great Falls*	.571
1962—	Boise§	.565
	Billings†	.706
1963—	Idaho Falls	.702
	Magic Valley†	.643
1964—	Treasure Valley	.615
1965—	Treasure Valley	.530
1966—	Ogden	.591
1967—	Ogden	.621
1968—	Ogden	.609
1969—	Ogden	.620
1970—	Idaho Falls	.629
1971—	Great Falls	.643
1972—	Billings	.694
1973—	Billings	.629
1974—	Idaho Falls	.569
1975—	Great Falls	.577
1976—	Great Falls	.577
1977—	Lethbridge	.629
1978—	Billings∞	.735
1979—	Helena	.623
	Lethbridge▲	.559
1980—	Lethbridge▲	.743
	Billings	.629
1981—	Calgary	.657
	Butte▲	.557
1982—	Medicine Hat▲	.629
	Idaho Falls	.600
1983—	Billings▲	.614
	Calgary	.600
1984—	Helena	.691
	Helena▲	.647

Year	Team	Pct.
1985—	Great Falls	.771
	Salt Lake City▲	.657
1986—	Salt Lake City◆	.643
	Great Falls	.571
1987—	Salt Lake City◆	.700
	Helena	.657
1988—	Great Falls◆	.754
	Butte	.629
1989—	Great Falls◆	.791
	Butte	.621
1990—	Great Falls◆	.706
	Salt Lake.	.618
1991—	Salt Lake City◆	.700
	Great Falls	.657
1992—	Salt Lake.	.697
	Billings◆	.697
1993—	Billings◆	.653
	Helena	.589
1994—	Billings◆	.694
	Helena	.611
1995—	Billings.	.710
	Helena	.690
1996—	Helena■	.597
	Ogden	.583
1997—	Great Falls	.556
	Billings■	.549
1998—	Medicine Hat	.622
	Idaho Falls■	.618
1999—	Idaho Falls	.640
	Missoula■	.592
2000—	Idaho Falls■	.608
2001—	Provo	.697
	Billings■	.613
2002—	Great Falls■	.627

*Won four-club playoff. †Won split-season playoff. ‡Ended first half in tie with Salt Lake City and won one-game playoff. §Ended first half in tie with Billings and Great Falls and won playoff. ∞Billings (first place) defeated Idaho Falls (second place) in first place-second place playoff. ▲League divided into Northern and Southern divisions; won two-club playoff. ◆Won two-club playoff. ■League divided into Northern and Southern divisions; won four-club playoff.

MINOR LEAGUE INDEX

TEAMS AND CITIES

Aberdeen, Md.	564
Akron, Ohio	461
Albuquerque, N.M.	435
Altoona, Pa.	461
Appleton (see Wisconsin)	548
Arkansas	495
Asheville, N.C.	588
Auburn, N.Y.	564
Augusta, Ga.	588
Augusta, N.J. (see New Jersey)	564
Bakersfield, Calif.	508
Batavia, N.Y.	564
Battle Creek, Mich.	548
Beloit, Wis.	548
Billings, Mont.	639
Binghamton, N.Y.	461
Birmingham, Ala.	479
Bluefield, W.Va.	606
Boise, Idaho	579
Bowie, Md.	461
Bradenton, Fla. (Gulf Coast)	624
Brevard County, Fla.	532
Bristol, Va.	606
Brooklyn, N.Y.	564
Buffalo, N.Y.	393
Burlington, Iowa	548
Burlington, N.C.	606
Campeche, Mexico	415
Cancun, Mexico	415
Capital City	588
Carolina	479
Casper, Wyo.	639
Cedar Rapids, Iowa	548
Charleston, S.C.	588
Charleston, W.Va.	588
Charlotte, N.C.	393
Chattanooga, Tenn.	479
Clearwater, Fla. (Florida State)	532
Clearwater, Fla. (Gulf Coast)	624
Clinton, Iowa	548
Colorado Springs, Colo.	435
Columbus, Ohio	393
Comstock Park, Mich. (see West Michigan)	548
Cordoba, Mexico	415
Danville, Va.	606
Davenport, Iowa (see Quad City)	548
Dayton, Ohio	548
Daytona, Fla.	532
Delmarva, Md.	588
Des Moines, Iowa (see Iowa)	435
Dunedin, Fla.	532
Durham, N.C.	393
Edmonton, Alberta	435
Elizabethton, Tenn.	606
El Paso, Tex.	495
Erie, Pa.	461
Eugene, Ore.	579
Everett, Wash.	579
Fishkill, N.Y. (see Hudson Valley)	564
Fort Myers, Fla. (Florida State)	532
Fort Myers, Fla. (Gulf Coast)	624
Fort Wayne, Ind.	548
Frederick, Md.	521
Fresno, Calif.	435
Frisco, Tex.	495
Geneva, Ill. (see Kane County)	548
Great Falls, Mont.	639
Greensboro, N.C.	588

Greenville, S.C.	479
Hagerstown, Md.	588
Harrisburg, Pa.	461
Helena, Mont.	639
Hickory, N.C.	588
High Desert	508
Hudson Valley	564
Huntsville, Ala.	479
Idaho Falls, Idaho	639
Indianapolis, Ind.	393
Iowa	435
Jacksonville, Fla.	479
Jamestown, N.Y.	564
Johnson City, Tenn.	606
Jupiter, Fla. (Florida State)	532
Jupiter, Fla. (Gulf Coast)	624
Kane County	548
Kannapolis, N.C.	588
Kennewick, Wash. (see Tri-City)	579
Kingsport, Tenn.	606
Kinston, N.C.	521
Kissimmee, Fla.	624
Kodak, Tenn. (see Tennessee)	479
Lake Elsinore, Calif.	508
Lake County	588
Lakeland, Fla. (Florida State)	532
Lakeland, Fla. (Gulf Coast)	624
Lakewood, N.J.	588
Lancaster, Calif.	508
Lansing, Mich.	548
Las Vegas, Nev.	435
Lexington, Ky.	588
Little Rock, Ark. (see Arkansas)	495
Louisville, Ky.	393
Lowell, Mass.	564
Lynchburg, Va.	521
Mahoning Valley, Ohio	564
Martinsville, Va.	606
Maryvale, Ariz.	616
Melbourne, Fla. (Gulf Coast)	624
Memphis, Tenn.	435
Mesa, Ariz.	616
Mexico City, Reds	415
Mexico City, Tigers	415
Midland, Tex.	495
Missoula, Mont.	639
Mobile, Ala.	479
Modesto, Calif.	508
Monclova, Mexico	415
Monterrey, Mexico	415
Myrtle Beach, S.C.	521
Nashville, Tenn.	435
New Britain, Conn.	461
New Haven, Conn.	461
New Jersey	564
New Orleans	435
Norfolk, Va.	393
Norwich, Ct.	461
Nuevo Laredo, Mexico	415
Oaxaca, Mexico	415
Ogden, Utah	639
Oklahoma City, Okla.	435
Omaha, Neb.	435
Oneonta, N.Y.	564
Orlando, Fla. (Gulf Coast)	624
Orlando, Fla. (Southern)	479
Ottawa, Ont.	393
Palm Beach, Fla.	532
Pawtucket, R.I.	393

Peoria, Ariz.	616
Peoria, Ill.	548
Phoenix, Ariz.	616
Portland, Me.	461
Portland, Ore.	435
Potomac	521
Princeton, W.Va.	606
Provo, Utah	639
Puebla, Mexico	415
Pulaski, Va.	606
Quad City	548
Rancho Cucamonga, Calif.	508
Reading, Pa.	461
Reynosa, Mexico	415
Richmond, Va.	393
Rochester, N.Y.	393
Rome, Ga.	588
Round Rock, Tex.	495
Sacramento, Calif.	435
St. Lucie, Fla.	532
Salem, Va.	521
Salem-Keizer, Ore.	579
Saltillo, Mexico	415
Salt Lake, Utah	435
San Antonio, Tex.	495
San Bernardino, Calif.	508
San Jose, Calif.	508
Sarasota, Fla. (Florida State)	532
Sarasota, Fla. (Gulf Coast)	624
Savannah, Ga.	588
Scottsdale, Ariz.	616
Scranton/Wilkes-Barre, Pa.	393
South Bend, Ind.	548
South Georgia	588
Spokane, Wash.	579
Staten Island, N.Y.	564
Stockton, Calif.	508
Surprise, Ariz.	616
Syracuse, N.Y.	393
Tabasco, Mexico	415
Tacoma, Wash.	435
Tampa, Fla. (Florida State)	532
Tampa, Fla. (Gulf Coast)	624
Tennessee	479
Toledo, Ohio	393
Torreon, Mexico	415
Trenton, N.J.	461
Tri-City (Northwest)	579
Tri-City (New York-Pennsylvania)	564
Troy, N.Y. (see Tri-City)	564
Tucson, Ariz. (Pacific Coast)	435
Tulsa, Okla.	495
Vancouver, British Columbia	579
Veracruz, Mexico	415
Vermont	564
Vero Beach, Fla. (Florida State)	532
Vero Beach, Fla. (Gulf Coast)	624
Visalia, Calif.	508
West Michigan	548
West Tenn.	479
Wichita, Kan.	495
Williamsport, Pa.	564
Wilmington, Del.	521
Winooski, Vt. (see Vermont)	564
Winston-Salem, N.C.	521
Wisconsin	548
Yakima, Wash.	579
Yucatan, Mexico	415
Zebulon, N.C. (see Carolina)	479